C000108862

The HUTCHINSON ALMANAC 2001

'I shall certainly keep it close at hand'
Rt Hon Lord Callaghan of Cardiff

'the quotes are very useful, as are the obituaries'
Ned Sherrin

'really useful and incredibly interesting'
Sir Stirling Moss

'most impressive…extremely useful for checking the dozens of enquiries that crop up in this household every day'
Joan Aiken

'a wonderful work of reference…I've hardly been able to keep my nose out of it…if there is any fault it's only that at times it keeps me too much away from my work'
Alan Sillitoe

'I have had our bookshelf reinforced to carry the weight of this mighty, useful volume'
Rachael Heyhoe Flint

'a really useful reference work, and I am delighted to have it on my shelf'
Chris Bonington

The HUTCHINSON ALMANAC 2001

Helicon

Published annually since 1998
Second edition published 1999
This edition published 2000

Helicon Publishing Ltd
42 Hythe Bridge Street
Oxford
OX1 2EP

e-mail: admin@helicon.co.uk
Web sites: http://www.hutchinson-almanac.com
http://www.helicon.co.uk

Typesetting and Layout
Tradespools, Frome, UK

Printed and bound in Slovenia by
DELO-Tiskarna, d.d.
by arrangement with Korotan-Ljubljana

ISBN 1-85986-334-5

British Cataloguing in Publication Data

A catalogue record of this book is available from the British Library

Note: Every effort has been made to trace and acknowledge the copyright holders of proprietary information; however, the publishers are keen to hear of any omissions in this respect.

ACKNOWLEDGEMENTS

Feature Article Writers

Anthony Bailey, journalist, formerly on the staff of *Which? Magazine* and *Investors Chronicle*, contributor to a wide range of national newspapers, magazines, and books, writer of the *Express* 'Troubleshooter' column, editor of the annual *Which? Way to Save Tax*

Paul Bray, technology journalist who writes for *The Daily Telegraph*, *The Sunday Times*, and a number of computer magazines and Web sites

David Dalby, Director of the Linguasphere Observatory and Emeritus Reader at the London School of Oriental and African Studies

Dr Ian J Derbyshire, writer on history, politics, and government; co-author of *Political Systems of the World* and *Politics in Britain: from Callaghan to Thatcher*; and author and editor of the *Chambers Political Spotlights* series

Dr Denis J Derbyshire, author of *The Business of Government* and *An Introduction to Public Administration*; co-author of *Political Systems of the World* and *Politics in Britain: from Callaghan to Thatcher*

Jane DeVille-Almond, primary care editor at *Nursing Times*, also works as a practice nurse in a single-handed GP practice in the West Midlands

Dr Richard Dickens, Research Fellow at the Centre for Economic Performance, London School of Economics, and a Lecturer in the Department of Economics, Queen Mary and Westfield College

Anna Farkas, writer and researcher

Charlotte Hardman, writer on religion and theology

Tracey Kifford, writer, editor, and a Managing Partner of Dolphin Publishing

G P F Lane, Principal lecturer in Crop Production, The Royal Agricultural College, Cirencester

Maureen O'Connor, writer on education for *The Independent* and *The Times Educational Supplement*

Ben Ramos, sports writer

Linda Wain, business and industrial journalist

Dr Paul Wymer, science and education writer, was previously Director of the National Centre for Biotechnology Education and Head of Communication and Education at the Wellcome Trust, currently on the management committee of the European Initiative for Biotechnology Education

Editorial Advisors and Contributors

Andrew Colquhoun, legal researcher

Gerry Conaghan, consumer affairs writer and researcher

Stella Whyberd Pierce, travel and transport journalist

Tim Furniss, spaceflight correspondent for the UK aerospace magazine *Flight International*

Valerie MacGregor, legal journalist

William Gould, science writer

Dr Phill Watts, population geneticist

Researchers
Polly Clark
Susan Cuthbert
Mike Darton
Barry Fox
Nick Jones
Hester Kapur
Mike McGeorge
David Milsted
Rachel Richardson

Editorial Director
Hilary McGlynn

Managing Editor
Roger Tritton

Project Editor
Fran Alexander

Section Managing Editors
Clare Collinson
Susan Dickson
Shereen Karmali
Rachel Minay
Emma Pearse

Technical Project Editor
Stuart Brown

Editors
Stuart Allen
Peter Blair
Denise Dresner
Hugh Gazzard
Nicky Matthews
Sarah Mawditt
Stephen Pavlovich
Sue Purkis
Catherine Thompson

Indexer
Martin Hargreaves

Permissions Co-ordinator
Connie Hallam

Publishing Systems Manager
Graham Bennett

Database Managers
Tracey Auden
Claire Lishman
Louise Richmond

Production Manager
John Normansell

Production Assistant
Stacey Penny

Design Manager
Lenn Darroux

Cartography
Olive Pearson

Artwork
Lorraine Hodghton

Picture Research
Sophie Evans
Elizabeth Loving

CONTENTS

Feature Articles

Chronologies

Note to the Reader

This third edition of *The Hutchinson Almanac* has been completely revised and contains many new features. It continues to provide for the needs of information seekers by presenting thousands of facts, figures, and statistics about today's world in one accessible and clearly organized volume.

The book is divided into 20 themed sections covering all aspects of modern life. The sections are subdivided and the subdivisions are listed both in the contents and at the beginning of each section. Cross references in the text and a detailed index at the back of the book mean the reader can locate information easily. Within each section, the items have been carefully grouped, and lists are widely used for ease of reference. Throughout the *Almanac*, feature articles comment on and explain issues of contemporary interest. The Year in Review, a summary of relevant major developments and events of the past 12 months, introduces many of the sections. Useful Web site addresses are included at the end of most sections.

The sections of the *Almanac* each have their own icon; in addition, the following symbols are used throughout the book to denote recurring features:

Chronology

Directory

Detailed explanations of the data are given where necessary in the form of introductory notes and footnotes to the tables. The source of the information is given, with details of the copyright owner, where applicable. The term UK is used to refer to the entire United Kingdom. Britain is used when data for Northern Ireland are not available.

The information in the *Almanac* has been derived from the most accurate and up-to-date sources available at the time of compilation. Material in the book covers the period from July 1999 through to the end of June 2000, however, some later updates have been added up to August 2000. Every year all entries in the *Almanac* are checked and updated by a team of researchers and editors. Comments and suggestions from readers are welcome. Your feedback is invaluable for the continual improvement of the *Almanac*, which the editors hope you will enjoy now and for many years to come.

Quotations of the Year

We used an elephant to crush a gnat. The gnat is not dead and the elephant is limping.

ANONYMOUS US Senator.

Quoted by former Tory Defence Secretary Michael Portillo, on the NATO campaign in Kosovo. *Independent*, 3 July 1999

I really have to ask, 'What about Bloody Wednesday, Thursday, and Friday, and every day of the week? What about Bloody Omagh? What about Bloody Warrenpoint, Enniskillen, Hyde Park, Bloody Aldershot and Brighton? Bloody everything the IRA has ever touched?'

DEREK WILFORD Former Commander of the 1st Battalion of the Parachute Regiment.

On the new Bloody Sunday inquiry. The Army disassociated itself from his remarks. *Today*, BBC Radio 4, 6 July 1999

I have just heard the voice of Thomas. That man is how he would talk.

BRITT ALLCROFT Creator of the *Thomas the Tank Engine* TV series.

On John Bellis, fireman and part-time taxi driver from the Isle of Man, after he drove her to her hotel. He successfully auditioned for the Hollywood film part. *Daily Telegraph*, 16 July 1999

I am in my fifties and size 16 and I can only say your design team knows nothing about the shape of women. Your underwear's got boring too.

TERESA VANNECK-SURPLICE Marks & Spencer shareholder.

Berating the Board of Directors at their annual general meeting. Mark's and Spencer's sales figures for the first 15 weeks of the financial year had fallen by 9.6%. *Daily Telegraph*, 16 July 1999

We can all understand why rice costs less in China than Chingford, but why do trainers cost less in New York than Newcastle?

STEPHEN BYERS Trade and Industry Secretary.

Inviting consumers to strike back at 'rip-off Britain' by complaining more. *Daily Telegraph*, 23 July 1999

A team of Customs officers netted a £34 million haul of cocaine in an operation that cost £50 million. Why didn't they just buy it?

NICK ALLEN Oxford resident.

Letter to the *Independent*, 24 July 1999

He's all small talk. The smartest thing I've ever heard him say is 'Good morning'.

SPIKE MILLIGAN Author and entertainer.

On broadcaster Chris Evans. *Independent*, 24 July 1999

This is very much a personal decision at this late stage in his career.

BOB SHENNAN Head of BBC Sport.

On Des Lynam, then a sports presenter, who left to join ITV. *Daily Telegraph*, 3 August 1999

It would not be safe to try to drive and peer out of the window.

ANONYMOUS Spokesman for the Automobile Association.

Giving advice to drivers during the total solar eclipse. *Daily Telegraph*, 11 August 1999

From here on it's downhill all the way.

CHARLES KENNEDY Newly elected leader of the Liberal Democrats.

In his acceptance speech. *Independent on Sunday*, 15 August 1999

This talk of God's punishment is rubbish. It has to do with how we build our houses.

SIMAV BARGU Turkish geologist.

After a major earthquake struck the northwest of the country; three days later, the death toll was estimated at around 40,000. *Independent*, 19 August 1999

Eastern audiences tend to fall about at every mention of cheese. They just think it is ludicrously funny stuff to think of eating.

NICK PARK Creator of *Wallace and Gromit*.

Independent, 21 August 1999

I think that today's youth have a tendency to live in the present and work for the future – and to be totally ignorant of the past.

STEVEN SPIELBERG Film director.

Independent on Sunday, 22 August 1999

It is little, but in my view his head is not worth more.

MAULANA ABDUR RAHIM MUSLIMDOST Afghan religious scholar and Taliban supporter.

After offering a reward of 5 million afghanis (£72) to anybody who kills US president Bill Clinton. *Daily Telegraph*, 24 August 1999

A ceasefire is a ceasefire is a ceasefire. You are not on ceasefire when you are shooting people.

DAVID TRIMBLE Leader of the Ulster Unionists.

On Northern Ireland Secretary Mo Mowlam's ruling that the IRA ceasefire was still intact. *Daily Telegraph*, 27 August 1999

It has been a great honour, much more than I deserve.

FIDEL CASTRO President of Cuba.

On the unveiling of his waxwork at Madam Tussaud's. *Time*, 30 August 1999

Most towns only suffer loss of appeal when tasteless building work and over-population become rampant, but there are some places that have always been dreadful. Slough is one of them.

BILL MURPHY Author.

A Jaunt Around the Decaying Heart of England, September 1999

Wife is ghastly, / Marriage dead. / Debts enormous, / Children fled. / Home is awful, / Life's a pain. / Need your vote / To keep me sane.

ANONYMOUS Scottish peer.

Explaining, in no more than 75 words, why he should remain a member of the reformed House of Lords. *Daily Telegraph*, 1 September 1999

It is the school's responsibility, showing us videos of men and women naked. After all, we are just children.

ANONYMOUS 14-year-old boy who was 13 when his 12-year-old girlfriend became pregnant.

The boy also claimed to have had sex with 10 other girls, mostly when he was drunk. *Daily Telegraph*, 3 September 1999

I have heard cynics who say he's a very political old monk shuffling around in Gucci shoes.

RUPERT MURDOCH Chairman of News Corporation.

On the Dalai Lama, spiritual leader of Chinese-occupied Tibet. In an interview with *Vanity Fair* magazine, reported on BBC Radio 5 Live, 6 September 1999

We were ruining them. The TV, the electric light and running water. They were starting to like it here.

RUSSELL WEST Iowa jail administrator.

On his decision to release four Amish prisoners early. *Time*, 6 September 1999

I still do not think of myself as a spy. Other people will have to judge.

MELITA NORWOOD 87-year-old former KGB agent named 'Hola'.

After passing secrets about the British atomic programme to Moscow over a period of 40 years. *Independent on Sunday*, 12 September 1999

The contents of this exhibition may cause shock, vomiting, confusion, panic, euphoria, and anxiety.

NOTICE AT THE BROOKLYN MUSEUM GALLERY, NEW YORK

At the opening of 'Sensation: Young British Artists from the Saatchi Collection'. *Daily Telegraph*, 24 September 1999

This is so dumb. There seems to have developed across the whole space community a systematic problem of insufficient attention to detail.

JOHN LOGSDON Director of the Space Policy Unit, George Washington University.

On the loss of NASA's Mars probe as a result of a mix-up between metric and imperial measurements. *Daily Telegraph*, 2 October 1999

He remained a mystery to me, and worse still ... an apparent airhead.

EDMUND MORRIS Biographer of Ronald Reagan.

On the former US President. *Time*, 4 October 1999

In my lifetime all our problems have come from mainland Europe and all the solutions have come from the English-speaking nations.

MARGARET THATCHER Former Prime Minister.

Speaking to Scottish delegates at the Conservative Party conference. Radio 5 Live, 5 October 1999

The Swedes have done us proud.

KEVIN KEEGAN England football coach.

On Sweden's 2–0 win over Poland, which allowed England to qualify for the Euro 2000 Championship. *Sunday Telegraph*, 10 October 1999

They're like a couple of drunks walking out of the bar for the last time. When they get to the swinging door, they turn right around and say, 'I just can't quite get there'.

BILL CLINTON US President.

On the two sides of the Northern Ireland peace process. *Time* 18 October 1999

It is our view that some of these interruptive factors should have been avoided.

ZHU BANGZHAO Spokesman for China's President Jiang Zemin.

On the few human rights protestors who managed to evade the heavy policing of the President's visit to Britain. *Daily Telegraph*, 22 October 1999

The United States is good. We try to do our best everywhere.

MADELEINE ALBRIGHT US Secretary of State.

Addressing victims of the August 1998 bombing of the US Embassy in Nairobi. *Newsweek*, 25 October 1999

You can't look at a ... crop and know if it's been genetically modified. It doesn't glow and it doesn't have a different colour.

BRUCE FERGUSON President of the testing company Enviro Logix.

Explaining why he invented a dipstick test that identifies genetically modified foods. *Newsweek*, 25 October 1999

This is Darwin's natural selection at its very best. The highest bidder gets youth and beauty.

RON HARRIS Photographer.

On auctioning the eggs of fashion models over the Internet for as much as $150,000. *Newsweek*, 25 October 1999

It is not just the dead cows that have had their spines taken out.

WILLIAM HAGUE Leader of the Opposition.

On the Government's refusal to ban imports of French meat in retaliation for France's illegal ban on British beef, following reports of French cattle being fed on processed sewage. Radio 5 Live, 27 October 1999

He's got grey long hair, curly, with a grey beard, a grey-like dressy thing, and he does miracles.

NATASHA A seven-year-old Bristol girl.

Asked to describe the Prime Minister. *The World According To...* (BBC2), 27 October 1999

I remember being told how cable TV was going to change my life – well it did, in the sense that it provided a minor inconvenience while the road was dug up.

DESMOND SWAYNE Conservative MP.

Independent on Sunday, 31 October 1999

It's like being back at school; one is constantly looking for a suitable bike shed.

SOPHIE DAHL Model.

On being a smoker in New York. *Independent*, 6 November 1999

I don't think they would fit in today. I am not so sure that I fit in today.

GORDON MURRAY 78-year-old creator of the 60s and 70s children's TV series *Trumpton, Camberwick Green*, and *Chigley*.

Owning up to burning around 60 foam puppet characters in 1979; one soldier survived. *Daily Telegraph*, 10 November 1999

I've had a wonderful life with a great family and I suppose I see this as a chance to give something back.

RONALD JOHNSON Northamptonshire resident.

On the donation of one of his lungs in an effort to save the life of a 10-year-old Israeli girl, whom he had never met, who was dying of cystic fibrosis. *Daily Telegraph*, 16 November 1999

I was completely, totally, 100% stunned.

TONY BLAIR Prime Minister.

On learning that his wife Cherie was expecting their fourth child at the age of 45. Radio 5 Live, 19 November 1999

I have always hoped that my good points outweighed my bad.

JEFFREY ARCHER Conservative candidate for Mayor of London.

Withdraws after revelations that he persuaded a friend to commit perjury in his 1986 libel case, in which he was awarded £50,000 damages. Radio 5 Live, 20 November 1999

People keep saying, 'Are you still doing this or that?', implying it's bloody time I gave it up.

PHILIP Duke of Edinburgh.

On growing old. Interviewed by Douglas Keay in the *Daily Telegraph*, 24 November 1999

Of all the animals we consume, shellfish have the worst deal. No one is really bothered about the welfare of shellfish.

CHARLOTTE BUCKHAVEN Promotor of the 'Crustastun', a modified microwave oven designed to stun a lobster with 110 volts before it is cooked.

Daily Telegraph, 27 November 1999

I knew I wouldn't win. Visually, art is not my strong point, life is.

TRACEY EMIN BritArt practitioner.

On her *My Bed* – a double bed surrounded by detritus – which failed to win the £20,000 Turner Prize; it went to Steve McQueen, for three short video films. *Daily Telegraph*, 2 December 1999

Our elevators are Millennium-proof, but if you have any doubts, use the stairs.

OTIS Lift manufacturer.

Notice. *Independent on Sunday*, 5 December 1999

Involuntary euthanasia is not too strong a word for it.

ADRIAN TRELOAR Consultant and senior lecturer in geriatrics.

On the practice of 'inappropriately limiting care', as police announced they were investigating the deaths of 60 elderly patients, allegedly deprived of food and water in NHS hospitals. *Daily Telegraph*, 6 December 1999

There will be no talks. All those who do not leave will be destroyed. The countdown has started.

LEAFLETS Dropped by Russian planes over Grozny.

Threatening the destruction of the Chechen capital after 11 December 1999. *Daily Telegraph*, 7 December 1999

We all, to some extent, reinvent ourselves. Jeffrey has just gone to a bit more trouble.

BARRY HUMPHRIES Writer and performer, alias Dame Edna Everage.

On the propensity of Lord Archer to embroider his past. *Independent*, 8 December 1999

If we are isolated on that, and we are right, then that is the correct position.

TONY BLAIR Prime Minister.

On Britain's refusal to accept the EU's Withholding Tax of 20% on all savings. Speech in Helsinki, 10 December 1999, quoted in *Daily Telegraph*, 11 December 1999

I always thought I was a Tory until Blair got in. Now I can't see the difference.

CLIFF RICHARD Pop singer.

Independent, 11 December 1999

The cancellation of debt bondage will be as profound in its consequences as the abolition of slavery. Tony, go on... You are the man and now is the time.

BOB GELDOF Singer, fundraiser, and campaigner.

Calling on the Prime Minister to cancel all Third World debt. *Daily Telegraph*, 14 December 1999

I'm still the Tory the people of Witney elected.

SHAUN WOODWARD Politician.

On his defection from the Conservatives to New Labour. *Independent on Sunday*, 19 December 1999

Tonight mustn't be just another disappointment – it should be the biggest anti-climax of our entire lives.

MATT Cartoonist.

Caption to cartoon on Millennium Eve. *Daily Telegraph*, 31 December 1999

There will come a time when it will be impossible to disguise the inequality of the health service from the general population.

LORD WINSTON Gynaecologist and Labour Party supporter.

After consultations with the Prime Minister's press secretary, he issued a clarification stating that he was not accusing the government of deceit about their record on the health service. *New Statesman*, January 2000

I ask you to forgive me for not fulfilling some hopes of those who believed we could jump from the grey, totalitarian past into a bright, rich, and civilized future in one go.

Boris Yeltsin Retiring President of Russia.

Farewell address. *Daily Telegraph*, 1 January 2000

It was a bit of a laugh, really, some of those toffee-nosed people having to queue.

Frank Dobson Labour's preferred choice for the Mayoralty of London.

On the shambolic opening night of the Greenwich Millennium Dome. He later agreed that 'a lot other people who aren't snobby' had also been inconvenienced. *News Direct*, 7 January 2000

People say the Liberal Democrats don't make a difference, but through this we might just end up saving the world.

Lembit Opik Liberal Democrat MP.

On his campaign for a task force to examine the risk of the Earth being hit by asteroids. *Independent*, 8 January 2000

Since over the years, and indeed the centuries, homosexuals have served at every level in our Armed Forces with loyalty and distinction, we might as well accept the fact rather then pretend it did not exist.

Gerald Kaufman Labour MP.

On the ruling of the European Court of Human Rights that homosexual men and women should not be disbarred from the military. *Hansard*, 12 January 2000

We are only just scratching the surface in terms of the potential of electronic commerce.

John Pluthero Chief Executive of Internet Service Provider Freeserve (and former Corporate Development Director of Dixon's).

Daily Telegraph, 13 January 2000

I think it is great that the older you get, the more you can tell people to sod off.

Zoë Wannamaker Actress.

Independent, 15 January 2000

I haven't made any secret of being a child of Sixties, never have.

Mo Mowlam Cabinet minister in charge of anti-drugs policy.

Admitting to having smoked – and inhaled – marijuana as a student. *Daily Telegraph*, 17 January 2000

I am an animal.

Mike Tyson Heavyweight boxer.

Independent, 29 January 2000

People have described me as 'luminous' in the past... It's a beautiful word but when it's the only word used to describe a woman's acting technique or her abilities on-screen, it's just a kind of fobbing off. I find women's performances aren't analysed – there's this kind of laziness.

Cate Blanchett Australian actress.

Marie Claire, February 2000

I have little doubt each of your victims smiled and thanked you as she submitted to your fearful ministrations.

Justice Forbes Judge.

In the trial of Dr Harold Shipman, convicted of murdering 15 of his patients in Hythe, Greater Manchester, with lethal doses of diamorphine (heroin). Police suspect he may have murdered up to 150 more, over a 15 year period. *Daily Telegraph*, 1 February 2000

I am not a particularly brave person, but I am not afraid of chocolate eclairs.

Nick Brown Minister for Agriculture.

On being assaulted with a confection by protestor Birgit Cunningham. Radio 5 Live, 2 February 2000

It's an ocean of vulgarity and mediocrity ... a perfect advertisement for New Labour – philosophically vapid and cack-handed in execution.

Stephen Bayley Former creative director of the Greenwich Millennium Dome, who resigned in 1998.

Interviewed by Sandra Barwick in *Daily Telegraph*, 5 February 2000

If you feel too old for bungee jumping, it's the next best thing.

Lord Bill Deedes Journalist and Tory peer.

On the 'London Eye' Millennium Ferris wheel. *Independent*, 5 February 2000

I had Hamlet's disease of introspection. I was always looking for the integrity behind it.

Geri Halliwell Singer and former Spice Girl.

On the travails of stardom. *Independent*, 5 February 2000

I'll sit with my back to the wall, if you don't mind. In this place you want to see the knives coming.

Peter Kilfoyle Former defence minister.

After resigning in protest at the 'ideological vacuum at the heart of government'. *Daily Telegraph*, 5 February 2000

There's only one thing the public dislikes more than a leader in control of his party, and that's a leader not in control of his party.

Tony Blair UK Prime Minister.

Speaking at the Old Vic celebrations of the Labour Party's 100th birthday. *Daily Telegraph*, 28 February 2000

It's nice to meet a sensitive architect.

Charles Prince of Wales.

Speaking to Chris Stone, the young Jamaican architect helping to develop Trench Town, home of reggae singer Bob Marley. *Daily Telegraph*, 1 March 2000

These days we are not allowed to just hit them over the head with a shovel. They have to die with dignity.

Colin Chapman Chief rodent controller for Rentokil in London.

On killing rats. *Independent*, 4 March 2000

Everyone's trying to get on with life now, bar Fayed, who's never going to be happy until his version of events is taken as the truth. Which it won't be.

TREVOR REES JONES Former bodyguard of Dodi Fayed.

On the aftermath of the car crash that killed his employer and Diana, Princess of Wales. *The Bodyguard's Story*, serialized in the *Daily Telegraph*, 4 March 2000

I have concluded that defence of the principles of London's right to govern itself requires that I stand as an independent candidate for London Mayor.

KEN LIVINGSTONE Candidate for Mayor of London.

The newly-expelled Labour MP – controversially defeated in his former party's selection process – goes back on his previous pledge not to stand as an independent or oppose the official Labour candidate. Radio 5 Live, 6 March 2000

It has become a bit of a joke that it would be cheaper to make a video to post to our viewers.

ANONYMOUS Spokesman for BBC Wales.

After *The Point*, a weekly programme about events in the Welsh Assembly, attracted an audience of less that 2,500 – an official figure of zero. *Daily Telegraph*, 7 March 2000

I wish I'd died instead of Diana... If I could have done something... I go mad thinking about the if onlys.

TREVOR REES JONES Former bodyguard of Dodi Fayed.

On his survival of the crash that killed Princess Diana, Dodi Fayed, and driver Henri Paul. *Newsweek*, 13 March 2000

Let not one brick be thrown, not one bottle be thrown, not one evidence of violence by us. Those that believe in Amadou should not betray his memory by acting like those that killed him.

AL SHARPTON US reverend.

Speaking after the acquittal of the four officers that fired 41 shots in the killing of unarmed immigrant Amadou Diallo. *Newsweek*, 13 March 2000

You don't have cancer; it has you.

IAN DURY Singer and songwriter.

Interviewed shortly before his death from cancer. *Daily Telegraph*, 28 March 2000

I was back!

MICK JAGGER Singer with the Rolling Stones.

Graffiti scrawled on the wall of the Performing Arts Centre at his old school, Dartford Grammar School. *Daily Telegraph*, 31 March 2000

I don't like loud music.

BILL WYMAN Former Rolling Stone.

On not listening to the Stones' new records. *Independent*, 1 April 2000

Zimbabwe was created with blood.

CHANT Sung of ruling ZANU Party members.

As the Zimbabwean Parliament voted through a change to the Constitution allowing the seizure of all remaining white-owned farms; the proposal had previously been defeated in a national referendum. *Daily Telegraph*, 7 April 2000

The allegations are completely without substance.

HANSIE CRONJE South African cricket captain.

Denying that he had taken money from an Indian bookmaker; three days later he admitted taking money for 'match forecasting', and was sacked. *Daily Telegraph*, 8 April 2000

When I step before a camera, I am very grateful for every moment of my stupid little life.

KEVIN SPACEY Actor.

On winning the BAFTA Best Actor award for *American Beauty*; he also won the Best Actor Oscar. ITV, 9 April 2000

I'm not interested in money. It is all about reputation.

DAVID IRVING Historian.

On facing a bill for over £2 million after losing his libel action against Professor Deborah Lipstadt and Penguin Books, who had labelled him a 'dangerous Holocaust denier' and 'Hitler partisan'. Radio 5 Live, 11 April 2000

I'm a failed bookie, a failed journalist, a failed tipster. I'm a total failure. So I'm on the telly.

JOHN MCCRIRICK TV horseracing personality.

Independent, 22 April 2000

I have no signs saying 'Private property' or 'Trespassers will be prosecuted', but the mad glint in my eyes is meant to speak volumes.

GERMAINE GREER Feminist academic and author.

On being attacked and held captive in her home by a teenage girl stalker. *Daily Telegraph*, 27 April 2000

As I was saying before I was so rudely interrupted 14 years ago...

KEN LIVINGSTONE British expelled Labour MP and former leader of the abolished Greater London Council.

On winning the election for Mayor of London as an Independent candidate, with 58% of the vote; Steve Norris, the Tory candidate, was second with 42% and Labour's Frank Dobson third with just 12%. Radio 5 Live, 5 May 2000

The public must bring down these tyrants themselves. They must pick up rifles... Everyone here knows who I am talking about.

NELSON MANDELA Former South African President.

On corrupt and dictatorial leaders of southern African countries. *Sunday Telegraph*, 7 May 2000

Not a lot of people make drama any more. People need to continue to tell stories about real human feelings that don't necessarily tie up easily at the end.

UMA THURMAN Actress.

Daily Telegraph, 15 May 2000

I shall send him to bed without any supper for this.

JOHN BUTTON Father of British Formula 1 racing driver Jenson Butten (20).

After his son was caught driving at 143 mph in a diesel car' by French police. *Daily Telegraph*, 29 May 2000

Mr Blunkett regards it as an insult to him personally to suggest that a disabled person cannot be reliable, hardworking and enthusiastic.

ANONYMOUS Spokesperson for Education and Employment Secretary David Blunkett, who is blind.

After Mr Blunkett intervened personally when a Jobcentre in the Midlands banned an employer's job advertisement on the grounds that the words 'hardworking' and 'enthusiastic' were in breach of the 1999 Disability Discrimination Act. Radio 5 Live, 6 June 2000

There's been a lot of nonsense put about by PR companies. I don't like being exploited in this way but, as I get older, it's increasingly hard to prevent.

PRINCE WILLIAM Member of the British Royal Family.

On being linked with such showbusiness personalities as US pop singer Britney Spears. Interviewed by Peter Archer of the Press Association; quoted in the *Daily Telegraph*, 17 June 2000

Much of what passes for social life in England is actually a low-intensity riot. We are back in the era of Gin Lane, with consumerist knobs on.

THEODORE DALRYMPLE English physician and social commentator.

On the sort of behaviour exemplified by English 'football fans' in Belgium for the Euro 2000 Championships. The English team was eliminated at the group stage of the contest. *Sunday Telegraph*, 18 June 2000

The role of science is to inquire and discover and it is the role of society and government on behalf of society to make judgements on what we then do and how we respond. I don't ever want to see science limited in its inquiry.

TONY BLAIR UK prime minister.

On the publication of the first working (albeit incomplete) draft of the human genetic code. *Daily Telegraph*, 27 June 2000

The real world produced a greater response than we had anticipated.

TONY FITZPATRICK Engineer at Arup, builders of London's Millennium Bridge.

On the failure of computer models to forecast the degree of wobble when people walked over London's Millennium Bridge on its opening day. *Daily Telegraph*, 29 June 2000

I guess at least the mindless rot is delivered with a kind of wink. But when Tony Blair says this is not a day for soundbites and then delivers one, there's no wink involved. That's always been one of the great disappointments of Clinton: that a man that intelligent would have so little sense of irony.

JOE KLEIN US political writer.

The Guardian, 14 August 2000

Time and Calendars

Greenwich Mean Time

Greenwich Mean Time (GMT) is the local time on the zero line of longitude (the Greenwich or prime meridian) which passes through the Old Royal Observatory at Greenwich, London. It has been the basis of legal time in the UK since 1880. GMT has been replaced by International Atomic Time (TAI) for scientific purposes and the term GMT is now generally used to mean coordinated universal time, a time scale based on atomic time and the Earth's rotation. The Greenwich meridian, originally adopted at the International Meridian Conference in Washington, DC, in 1884, remains that from which all longitudes are measured and the world's standard time zones are calculated.

Summer Time

Summer time or daylight saving time is an adjustment of regional standard time that was first adopted by some countries to conserve fuel by reducing the need for artificial light in the evening hours. The practice was introduced in the UK in 1916 in an Act that ordained that legal time should be an hour in advance of Greenwich Mean Time (GMT). Since 1995 member states of the European Union have used a common date and time for the beginning and end of the summer time period.

World Time Zones

Since the adoption of the prime meridian (0° longitude) at Greenwich and Greenwich Mean Time (GMT) by international agreement in 1884, the surface of the Earth has been divided into 24 time zones within each of which most places share the same time, known as standard time. In a 24-hour period the Earth makes one complete rotation on its axis, so the direct rays of the Sun pass through 1° of longitude every 4 minutes (15° every hour). To mark longitudes at which different standard times would be set, meridians (lines of longitude) stretching from pole to pole, were established at intervals of 15° east and west of the prime meridian at Greenwich. Countries to the east of the prime meridian are ahead of GMT and countries to the west are behind. In practice, zone boundary lines are adjusted to accommodate political units and in many cases differ from the 15° intervals of longitude. In a few zones half-hour differences are in effect and some countries that lie in more than one time zone adopt a single standard time.

European Time Zones

Time zones	Hours ahead of GMT	Countries
GMT	0	Iceland, Republic of Ireland, Portugal, UK
Central European	1	Albania, Andorra, Austria, Belgium, Bosnia-Herzegovina, Croatia, Czech Republic, Denmark, France, Germany, Hungary, Italy, Liechtenstein, Luxembourg, Macedonia, Malta, Monaco, Netherlands, Norway, Poland, San Marino, Slovak Republic, Slovenia, Spain, Sweden, Switzerland, Vatican City State, Yugoslavia
East European	2	Belarus, Bulgaria, Cyprus, Estonia, Finland, Greece, Latvia, Lithuania, Moldova, Romania, Turkey, Ukraine

The Pips

The public broadcasting of GMT time signals, the 'pips', over the radio by the BBC was initiated by Frank Watson Dyson (1868–1939) in 1924. Six pips are broadcast at certain hours (five short, from second 55 to second 59, and one long, the start of which indicates the precise minute).

British Summer Time

British Summer Time (BST) is one hour in advance of Greenwich Mean Time (GMT). Time changes are implemented at 1 a.m. GMT.

Year	Period of summer time
2000	March 26–October 29
2001	March 25–October 28
2002	March 31–October 27

The International Date Line

The International Date Line (IDL) is an imaginary line that approximately follows the 180° meridian. The time zones 12 hours ahead and 12 hours behind GMT meet at this line, making a time difference of one day on either side of the line. When crossing the line going west the date is put forward a day and it is put back a day when going east. The IDL was adopted at the International Meridian Conference in 1884. The date line defining the day to which countries near the line adhere does not follow the 180° line of longitude exactly for geographical and political reasons.

Time Zones in the USA

Time zone	Hours behind GMT
Atlantic Standard Time	4
Eastern Standard Time	5
Central Standard Time	6
Mountain Standard Time	7
Pacific Standard Time	8
Alaska Standard Time	9
Hawaii/Aleutian Standard Time	10

Relative Times in Cities Throughout the World

The time indicated in the table below is fixed by law and is called standard time. At 12:00 noon, GMT, the standard time elsewhere around the world is as follows:

City	Time
Abu Dhabi, United Arab Emirates	16:00
Accra, Ghana	12:00
Addis Ababa, Ethiopia	15:00
Adelaide, Australia	21:30
Alexandria, Egypt	14:00
Algiers, Algeria	13:00
Al Manamah (also called Bahrain), Bahrain	15:00
Amman, Jordan	14:00
Amsterdam, Netherlands	13:00
Anchorage (AK), USA	03:00
Ankara, Turkey	14:00
Athens, Greece	14:00
Auckland, New Zealand	24:00
Baghdad, Iraq	15:00
Bahrain (also called Al Manamah), Bahrain	15:00
Bangkok, Thailand	19:00
Barcelona, Spain	13:00
Beijing, China	20:00
Beirut, Lebanon	14:00
Belgrade, Yugoslavia	13:00
Berlin, Germany	13:00
Bern, Switzerland	13:00
Bogotá, Colombia	07:00
Bombay, India	17:30
Bonn, Germany	13:00
Brazzaville, Republic of the Congo	13:00
Brisbane, Australia	22:00
Brussels, Belgium	13:00
Bucharest, Romania	14:00
Budapest, Hungary	13:00
Buenos Aires, Argentina	09:00
Cairo, Egypt	14:00
Calcutta, India	17:30
Canberra, Australia	22:00
Cape Town, South Africa	14:00
Caracas, Venezuela	08:00
Casablanca, Morocco	12:00
Chennai (formerly Madras), India	17:30
Chicago (IL), USA	06:00
Cologne, Germany	13:00
Colombo, Sri Lanka	18:00
Copenhagen, Denmark	13:00
Damascus, Syria	14:00
Dar es Salaam, Tanzania	15:00
Darwin, Australia	21:30

City	Time
Delhi, India	17:30
Denver (CO), USA	05:00
Dhaka, Bangladesh	18:00
Dubai, United Arab Emirates	16:00
Dublin, Republic of Ireland	12:00
Florence, Italy	13:00
Frankfurt am Main, Germany	13:00
Gdańsk, Poland	13:00
Geneva, Switzerland	13:00
Hague, The, Netherlands	13:00
Harare, Zimbabwe	14:00
Havana, Cuba	07:00
Helsinki, Finland	14:00
Hobart, Australia	22:00
Ho Chi Minh City, Vietnam	19:00
Hong Kong, China	20:00
Istanbul, Turkey	14:00
Jakarta, Indonesia	19:00
Jerusalem, Israel	14:00
Johannesburg, South Africa	14:00
Karachi, Pakistan	17:00
Kiev, Ukraine	14:00
Kuala Lumpur, Malaysia	20:00
Kuwait City, Kuwait	15:00
Kyoto, Japan	21:00
Lagos, Nigeria	13:00
Le Havre, France	13:00
Lima, Peru	07:00
Lisbon, Portugal	12:00
London, England	12:00
Luanda, Angola	13:00
Luxembourg, Luxembourg	13:00
Lyon, France	13:00
Madrid, Spain	13:00
Manila, Philippines	20:00
Marseille, France	13:00
Mecca, Saudi Arabia	15:00
Melbourne, Australia	22:00
Mexico City, Mexico	06:00
Milan, Italy	13:00
Minsk, Belarus	14:00
Monrovia, Liberia	12:00
Montevideo, Uruguay	09:00
Montreal, Canada	07:00
Moscow, Russian Federation	15:00
Munich, Germany	13:00
Nairobi, Kenya	15:00

City	Time
New Orleans (LA), USA	06:00
New York (NY), USA	07:00
Nicosia, Cyprus	14:00
Oslo, Norway	13:00
Ottawa, Canada	07:00
Panamá, Panama	07:00
Paris, France	13:00
Perth, Australia	20:00
Port Said, Egypt	14:00
Prague, Czech Republic	13:00
Rawalpindi, Pakistan	17:00
Reykjavík, Iceland	12:00
Rio de Janeiro, Brazil	09:00
Riyadh, Saudi Arabia	15:00
Rome, Italy	13:00
San Francisco (CA), USA	04:00
Santiago, Chile	08:00
Seoul, South Korea	21:00
Shanghai, China	20:00
Singapore City, Singapore	20:00
Sofia, Bulgaria	14:00
St Petersburg, Russian Federation	15:00
Stockholm, Sweden	13:00
Sydney, Australia	22:00
Taipei, Taiwan	20:00
Tashkent, Uzbekistan	17:00
Tehran, Iran	15:30
Tel Aviv-Yafo, Israel	14:00
Tenerife, Canary Islands	12:00
Tokyo, Japan	21:00
Toronto, Canada	07:00
Tripoli, Libya	13:00
Tunis, Tunisia	13:00
Valparaiso, Chile	08:00
Vancouver, Canada	04:00
Vatican City	13:00
Venice, Italy	13:00
Vienna, Austria	13:00
Vladivostok, Russian Federation	22:00
Volgograd, Russian Federation	16:00
Warsaw, Poland	13:00
Wellington, New Zealand	24:00
Yangon (formerly Rangoon), Myanmar	18:30
Yokohama, Japan	21:00
Zagreb, Croatia	13:00
Zürich, Switzerland	13:00

See also **Time zones map** *in colour section.*

Phases of the Moon 2001

The Moon is illuminated by sunlight and goes through a cycle of phases of shadow, waxing from new (dark) via first quarter (half Moon) to full, and a waning back again to new every 29.53 days (the synodic month, also known as a lunation).
Times are given in Greenwich Mean Time (GMT).

2001

New Moon

Month	Day	Time
January	24	13:07
February	23	08:21
March	25	01:21
April	23	15:26
May	23	02:46
June	21	11.58
July	20	19:44
August	19	02:55
September	17	10:27
October	16	19:23
November	15	06:40
December	14	20:47

First quarter

Month	Day	Time
January	2	22:31
February	1	14:02
March	3	02:03
April	1	10:49
April	30	17:08
May	29	22:09
June	28	03:20
July	27	10:08
August	25	19:55
September	24	09:31
October	24	02:58
November	22	23:21
December	22	20:56

Full Moon

Month	Day	Time
January	9	20:24
February	8	07:12
March	9	17:23
April	8	03:22
May	7	13:53
June	6	01:39
July	5	15:04
August	4	05:56
September	2	21:43
October	2	13:49
November	1	05:41
November	30	20:49
December	30	10:40

Last quarter

Month	Day	Time
January	16	12:35
February	15	03:23
March	16	20:45
April	15	15:31
May	15	10:11
June	14	03:28
July	13	18:45
August	12	07:53
September	10	18:59
October	10	04:20
November	8	12:21
December	7	19:52

The Calendar

The calendar is the division of the year into months, weeks, and days, and the method of ordering the years. The word 'calendar' comes from the Latin *kalendae* or *calendae*, the first day of the month on which, in ancient Rome, solemn proclamation was made of the appearance of the new Moon. All early calendars except the ancient Egyptian calendar were based on the lunar cycle, the Moon's motion around the Earth. Of the many different calendars in use throughout the world today, there are three main types: lunar calendars, based only on the phases of the Moon; solar calendars, based on the tropical or sidereal year; and luni-solar calendars, based on the motions of both the Sun and the Moon.

The tropical year and the sidereal year

The tropical (solar) year is based on the orbital period of the Earth around the Sun. It is defined as the time from the vernal equinox to the next vernal equinox – 365.2422 days – and it governs the occurrence of the seasons. The sidereal year is the time taken for the Earth to complete one orbit relative to the fixed stars, and lasts 365.2564 days (about 20 minutes longer than a tropical year).

The synodic or lunar month

A synodic (lunar) month is the time from one new or full Moon to the next – 29.53 days (called a lunation); the number of lunations in a year is 12.37. As the length of the tropical year is not an exact multiple of the length of the synodic month, calendar systems add extra days or months to reconcile the solar and lunar years.

Equinoxes

The vernal equinox is the time when the Sun passes the Earth's equator while moving from the southern to the northern hemisphere and day and night have approximately the same length. The autumnal equinox is the time in September when the Sun passes the equator moving from the northern to the southern hemisphere.

Solstices

The solstices are either of the days on which the Sun is farthest north or south of the Earth's equator each year. The summer solstice, when the longest day occurs in the northern hemisphere, is when the Sun reaches its northernmost latitude; the winter solstice, when the shortest day occurs in the northern hemisphere, is the time in December when the Sun reaches its southernmost latitude.

The Seasons

Times are for the northern hemisphere, in Greenwich Mean Time (GMT).

2001

Vernal equinox (spring begins)
20 March (13:31)
Summer solstice (summer begins)
21 June (07:38)
Autumnal equinox (autumn begins)
22 September (23:04)
Winter solstice (winter begins)
21 December (19:21)

2002

Vernal equinox (spring begins)
20 March (19:16)
Summer solstice (summer begins)
21 June (13:24)
Autumnal equinox (autumn begins)
23 September (04:56)
Winter solstice (winter begins)
22 December (01:15)

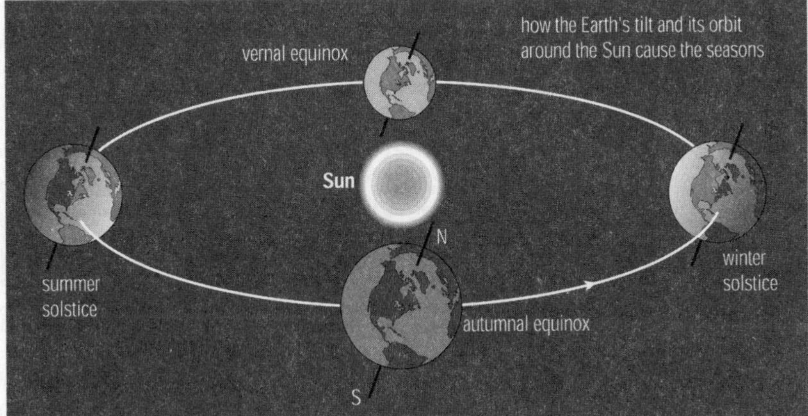

Seasons *As the Earth orbits the Sun, its axis of rotation always points in the same direction. This means that during the northern hemisphere summer solstice (21 June), the Sun is overhead in the northern hemisphere. At the northern hemisphere winter solstice (usually 22 December), the Sun is overhead in the southern hemisphere.*

Sunrise and Sunset Times for 2001

Times given are approximate for London, England.

Date	Rise	Set
1 January	08:06	16:02
1 February	07:38	16:50
1 March	06:45	17:40
1 April	06:35[1]	17:33[1]
1 May	05:32[1]	20:23[1]
1 June	04:49[1]	21:08[1]

Date	Rise	Set
1 July	04:47[1]	21:20[1]
1 August	05:24[1]	20:48[1]
1 September	06:13[1]	19:46[1]
1 October	07:01[1]	18:38[1]
1 November	06:54	16:33
1 December	07:43	15:55

[1] British Summer Time. For GMT subtract one hour.

See also **Astronomy**, pp 484–488.

The Western or Gregorian Calendar

The Western or Gregorian calendar derives from the Julian calendar instituted by Julius Caesar in 46 BC. The Julian calendar was adjusted in 1582 by Pope Gregory XIII, who eliminated error caused by the faulty calculation of the length of a year. The 'New Style' Gregorian calendar was only gradually adopted: Britain and its colonies, including America, adopted it in 1752, at which point the error was 11 days, so that 3 September 1752 became 14 September 1752, and at the same time the beginning of the year was put back from 25 March to 1 January. Russia did not adopt the Gregorian calendar until after the October Revolution of 1917, so the event (then 25 October) is currently celebrated on 7 November.

Leap years

From year one in the Western calendar, the assumed date of the birth of Jesus, dates are calculated backwards (BC 'before Christ' or BCE 'before the common era') and forwards (AD Latin Anno Domini, 'in the year of the Lord', or CE 'common era'). The lunar month (the period between one new Moon and the next) naturally averages 29.5 days, but the Western calendar uses for convenience a calendar month with a complete number of days, 30 or 31 (February has 28). Since this method leaves six extra hours per year, they are normally added to February as a 29th day every fourth year – a leap year. Leap year numbers are divisible by 4, with the exception of century years, which are leap years only if they are divisible by 400.

Millennia

A millennium is a period of 1,000 years. The question of which year is the first year of the millennium hinges on the date of the first year AD. The sequence of years going from BC to AD does not include the year 0. The sequence of years runs 3 BC, 2 BC, 1 BC, AD 1, AD 2, AD 3, and so on. This means that the first year of the first millennium was AD 1. The one thousandth year was AD 1000 and the first day of the second millennium was in AD 1001. It is thus clear that the start of the new millennium is 1 January 2001. Lavish celebrations took place in cities throughout the world to mark the dawning of the year 2000, but accurately speaking these celebrations were held at the beginning of the last year of the millennium, not the start of the new millennium.

Months of the Year

Month	Derivation of name	Number of days
January	Janus, Roman god of doorways and beginnings	31
February	Februa, Roman festival of purification	28 (29 in a leap year)
March	Mars, Roman god of war	31
April	Latin *aperire*, 'to open'	30
May	Maia, Roman goddess of spring	31
June	Juno, Roman goddess of marriage	30
July	Julius Caesar, Roman general and dictator	31
August	Augustus Caesar, Roman emperor	31
September	Latin *septem*, 'seven'; September was the seventh month of the earliest Roman calendar	30
October	Latin *octo*, 'eight'; October was the eighth month of the earliest Roman calendar	31
November	Latin *novem*, 'nine'; November was the ninth month of the earliest Roman calendar	30
December	Latin *decem*, 'ten'; December was the tenth month of the earliest Roman calendar	31

Days of the Week

The names of the days are based on the seven heavenly bodies used in traditional astrology: the Sun, the Moon, Mars, Mercury, Jupiter, Venus, and Saturn. These bodies were believed at the time (about 1100 to 1500) to revolve around the Earth and influence its events. The seven-day week became part of the Roman calendar in AD 321.

English	Latin	Saxon	German	French	Italian	Spanish
Sunday	Dies Solis	Sunnandaeg – Sun's Day	Sonntag	dimanche	domenica	domingo
Monday	Dies Lunae	Mōnandaeg – Moon's Day	Montag	lundi	lunedì	lunes
Tuesday	Dies Martis	Tīwesdaeg – Tiw's Day[1]	Dienstag	mardi	martedì	martes
Wednesday	Dies Mercurii	Wōdnesdaeg – Woden's Day[2]	Mittwoch	mercredi	mercoledì	miércoles
Thursday	Dies Jovis	Thunresdaeg – Thor's Day[3]	Donnerstag	jeudi	giovedì	jueves
Friday	Dies Veneris	Frigedaeg – Frigg's Day[4]	Freitag	vendredi	venerdì	viernes
Saturday	Dies Saturni	Saetern-daeg – Saturn's Day	Samstag	samedi	sabato	sábado

[1] Tiw: Anglo-Saxon name for Nordic Tyr, son of Odin and god of war, closest to Mars (Greek Ares), son of Roman god Jupiter (Greek Zeus).
[2] Woden: Anglo-Saxon name for Odin, Nordic dispenser of victory, closest to Mercury (Greek Hermes), Roman messenger of victory.
[3] Thor: Nordic god of thunder, eldest son of Odin, closest to Roman Jupiter (Greek Zeus).
[4] Frigg (or Freyja): wife of Odin, the Nordic goddess of love, equivalent to Roman Venus (Greek Aphrodite).

The Civil Calendar

Day	Date
Accession of Queen Elizabeth II	6 February
Duke of York's birthday	19 February
St David's Day	1 March
Earl of Wessex's birthday	10 March
Commonwealth Day (variable)	2001 – 12 March; 2002 – 11 March; 2003 – 10 March
St Patrick's Day	17 March
Birthday of Queen Elizabeth II	21 April
St George's Day	23 April
Coronation of Queen Elizabeth II	2 June
Duke of Edinburgh's birthday	10 June
Queen's official birthday (variable)	usually second Saturday in June
Queen Elizabeth the Queen Mother's birthday	4 August
Princess Royal's birthday	15 August
Princess Margaret's birthday	21 August
Lord Mayor's Day (variable)	2001 – 10 November; 2002 – 9 November; 2003 – 8 November
Remembrance Sunday (variable)	2001 – 11 November; 2002 – 10 November; 2003 – 9 November
Prince of Wales's birthday	14 November
Wedding day of Queen Elizabeth II	20 November
St Andrew's Day	30 November

Bank or Public Holidays in the UK

In the UK public holidays are either common law (adopted 'by habit or custom') or statutory (bank) holidays, and certain holidays are granted by royal proclamation. In England, Wales, and Northern Ireland Christmas Day and Good Friday are common law holidays. Statutory or bank holidays were instituted by the Bank Holiday Acts 1871 and 1875, which required the Bank of England and the clearing banks to close on specified days. The days that are to be public holidays in England, Wales, Scotland, and Northern Ireland are now stipulated by the provisions of the Banking and Financial Dealings Act 1971.

Dates of Easter 2001–2025

Easter, the spring feast of the Christian church, is a moveable feast falling on the first Sunday following the full Moon after the vernal equinox (21 March); that is, between 22 March and 25 April.

Year	Easter Day	Year	Easter Day
2001	15 April	2014	20 April
2002	31 March	2015	5 April
2003	20 April	2016	27 March
2004	11 April	2017	16 April
2005	27 March	2018	1 April
2006	16 April	2019	21 April
2007	8 April	2020	12 April
2008	23 March	2021	4 April
2009	12 April	2022	17 April
2010	4 April	2023	9 April
2011	24 April	2024	31 March
2012	8 April	2025	20 April
2013	31 March		

Chief Public or Legal Holidays in the UK

Public holidays[1]	England and Wales	Scotland	Northern Ireland
2001			
New Year's Day	1 January[2]	1, 2[2] January	1 January[2]
St Patrick's Day	–	–	17 March
Good Friday[3]	13 April	13 April	13 April
Easter Monday	16 April	–	16 April
First Monday in May (May Day)	7 May[2]	7 May	7 May[2]
Last Monday in May (Spring)	28 May	28 May[2]	28 May
Battle of the Boyne	–	–	12 July
Summer	27 August	6 August	27 August
Christmas[3]	25, 26 December	25, 26 December	25, 26 December
2002			
New Year's Day	1 January[2]	1, 2[2] January	1 January[2]
St Patrick's Day	–	–	18 March
Good Friday[3]	29 March	29 March	29 March
Easter Monday	1 April	–	1 April
First Monday in May (May Day)	1 May[2]	1 May	1 May[2]
Last Monday in May (Spring)	27 May	27 May[2]	27 May
Battle of the Boyne	–	–	12 July
Summer	26 August	5 August	26 August
Christmas[3]	25, 26 December	25, 26 December	25, 26 December

[1] In the Channel Islands, Liberation Day (9 May) is a bank and public holiday.
[2] Granted by royal proclamation.
[3] In England, Wales, and Northern Ireland, Christmas Day and Good Friday are common law holidays.

May Day
The celebration of May Day, the first day of May, has origins that date back to before Christian times and the day is still celebrated in parts of England as a pre-Christian magical rite, for example, with dancing around the maypole (an ancient fertility symbol). In many countries it is a national holiday in honour of labour; the idea of a holiday highlighting the achievements of workers was first adopted at the 1889 International Socialist Congress in Paris, where the date fixed on was 1 May. It has been celebrated as a public holiday on the first Monday in May in the UK since 1978.

Boxing Day
Boxing Day, the first weekday after Christmas Day, has been a bank holiday since 1871. In the Christian church calendar 26 December is the feast day of St Stephen; the day became known as Boxing Day in the early 19th century, originating from when boxes, or presents, were given to servants and tradesmen in acknowledgement of services rendered throughout the year.

New Year's Day
New Year's Day was first celebrated as a public holiday in 1974. It is a public holiday granted by royal proclamation in England, Wales, and Northern Ireland, and a bank holiday in Scotland.

The Jewish Calendar

The years of the Jewish calendar are counted from the Era of Creation (Era Mundi) taken as 7 October 3761 BC in the Gregorian calendar. The calendar is a complex combination of lunar and solar cycles, varied by considerations of religious observance. Each year consists of either 12 or 13 months, with a 13th month of 30 days being inserted in years 3, 6, 8, 11, 14, 17, and 19 of a 19-year cycle. The months of the Jewish calendar year have 29 or 30 days. The days of the week are reckoned from sunset to sunset and are traditionally designated by number. Only the seventh day, the Sabbath, has a specific name. The date of the Jewish new year varies, but usually falls in the second half of September (Gregorian calendar).

The Months of the Jewish Calendar

Jewish month	Number of days	Gregorian equivalent
Tishri	30	September–October
Heshvan	29 or 30	October–November
Kislev	29 or 30	November–December
Tebet	29	December–January
Shebat	30	January–February
Adar	29 or 30	February–March
Nisan	30	March–April
Iyar	29	April–May
Sivan	30	May–June
Tammuuz	29	June–July
Ab	30	July–August
Elul	29	August–September

Year Equivalents for the Jewish and Gregorian Calendars

The Jewish New Year (Rosh Hanshah) – 1 Tishri – falls between 5 September and 5 October in the Gregorian or Western calendar.

Jewish year	Gregorian equivalent
5761	30 September 2000–17 September 2001
5762	18 September 2001–6 September 2002
5763	7 September 2002–26 September 2003
5764	27 September 2003–15 September 2004
5765	16 September 2004–3 October 2005

The Islamic Calendar

The Islamic calendar is based on the lunar phase cycle. Each year consists of 12 months and is calculated from the Era of Hijra or Anno Hegirae (AH), which corresponds to AD 622, when the prophet Muhammad travelled from Mecca to Medina. For religious purposes, each month begins with the first sighting of the lunar crescent following the new Moon. In practice, owing to the Earth's axial rotation, the determination of first visibility varies from place to place. New Year's Day and the first days of all the months are, therefore, subject to variation. Some countries, including Iran, Turkey, Egypt, and Pakistan, have adopted a cyclic civil calendar of 30 years. In each 30-year cycle, 19 years are common and have 354 days and 11 are leap years of 355 days.

The Months of the Islamic Calendar

Month	Number of days
Muharram	30
Safar	29
Rabi I	30
Rabi II	29
Jumada I	30
Jumada II	29
Rajab	30
Sha'ban	29
Ramadan	30
Shawwal	29
Dhu al-Qadah	30
Dhu al-Hijjah	29 (30 in a leap year)

Year Equivalents for the Islamic and Gregorian Calendars

AH = Anno Hegirae, the first year of the Muslim calendar, when the prophet Muhammad travelled from Mecca to Medina.

Islamic year (AH)	Gregorian equivalent
1421	6 April 2000–24 March 2001
1422	26 March 2001–14 March 2002
1423	15 March 2002–3 March 2003

See also **Major Religious Festivals**, p 392.

The Hindu Calendar

The Gregorian calendar is used in India for administrative purposes and in 1957 the Calendar Reform Committee adopted a civil calendar, based on a year of 365 days (366 in leap years), 12 months of 30 or 31 days, and leap years coinciding with those of the Gregorian calendar. Hindu religious festivals are still determined according to the traditional Hindu calendar, a luni-solar calendar that consists of 12 months of 29 days 12 hours. Months are divided into a waxing phase, the Sukla, and a waning phase, the Drnsa. When the difference between the Hindu year of 360 lunar days (the equivalent of 354 days, 8 hours of solar time) and the solar year of 365 days, 6 hours, reaches the length of a Hindu month, a leap or 'intercalary' month is added (approximately every 32 lunar months). This leap month may be added at any point in the calendar and its name is taken from the month that immediately follows it.

The Months of the Traditional Hindu Calendar

Hindu month	Number of days	Gregorian equivalent
Chaitra	29 or 30	March–April
Vaisakha	29 or 30	April–May
Jyaistha	29 or 30	May–June
Asadha	29 or 30	June–July
Sravana	29 or 30	July–August
Bhadrapada	29 or 30	August–September
Asvina	29 or 30	September–October
Karttika	29 or 30	October–November
Margasirsa	29 or 30	November–December
Pausa	29 or 30	December–January
Magha	29 or 30	January–February
Phalguna	29 or 30	February–March

Year Equivalents for the Hindu and Gregorian Calendars

Years in the Hindu calendar are calculated from AD 78, the beginning of the Saka Era (SE).

Hindu year (SE)	Gregorian equivalent
1922	22 March 2000–21 March 2001
1923	22 March 2001–21 March 2002
1924	22 March 2002–21 March 2003

The Chinese Calendar

The Western or Gregorian calendar has been used in China for official and administrative purposes since 1911 (when the republic was established), but the traditional calendar is still important for determining festivals in China and southeast Asia, and it is used by Chinese communities throughout the world.

The Chinese calendar is luni-solar (based on astronomical observations of the Sun and the phases of the Moon). The year begins at the second new Moon after the winter solstice – between 21 January and 19 February in the Gregorian calendar. The normal year consists of 12 lunar months and has 353, 354, or 355 days. Leap years have 13 months and 383, 384, or 385 days. The lunar months have 29 or 30 days and are given numbers, 1–12, rather than names. The Chinese year is also divided into 24 periods of 15–16 days, according to the movement of the Sun.

Calendar cycles

The Chinese calendar is counted in 60-year cycles from 2637 BC, when the calendar was, according to legend, invented. The 78th cycle of the Chinese calendar started in 1984; the Chinese year 4699, the 18th year in the cycle, begins on 24 January 2001 (Gregorian calendar).

Each year in the major 60-year cycle is associated with an animal according to a 12-year cycle, 2001 being a year of the snake, and 2002 being a year of the horse. The animal associated with the year of a person's birth is said to have characteristics that influence the person's personality traits.

The Chinese Year

The Chinese year is traditionally divided into 12 lunar months (13 months in a leap year), beginning at the second new Moon after the winter solstice. The year is also divided into 24 periods of 15–16 days, according to the movement of the Sun. This calendar is sometimes referred to as the Chinese agricultural calendar or the farmer's calendar because it follows the tropical (solar) year and is closely related to changes in the seasons.

Chinese solar term	English translation	Gregorian date (approx)	Chinese solar term	English translation	Gregorian date (approx)
Li Chun	spring begins	4/5 February	Li Qiu	autumn begins	7/8 August
Yu Shui	rain water	19/20 February	Chu Shu	heat ends	23/24 August
Jing Zhe	insects waken	5/6 March	Bai Lu	white dew	7/8 September
Chun Fen	vernal equinox	20/21 March	Qui Fen	autumn equinox	23/24 September
Qing Ming	clear and bright	4/5 April	Han Lu	cold dew	8/9 October
Gu Yu	grain rains	20/21 April	Shuang Jiang	frost descends	23/24 October
Li Xia	summer begins	5/6 May	Li Dong	winter begins	7/8 November
Xiao Man	grain fills	20/21 May	Xiao Xue	little snow	22/23 November
Mang Zhong	grain in ear	5/6 June	Da Xue	heavy snow	7/8 December
Xia Zhi	summer solstice	21/22 June	Dong Zhi	winter solstice	22/23 December
Xiao Shu	slight heat	6/7 July	Xiao Han	little cold	5/6 January
Da Shu	great heat	22/23 July	Da Han	severe cold	20/21 January

The Chinese Zodiac

In the Chinese zodiac each successive year is named after one of 12 animals. The 12-year cycles are continuously repeated and combined with a sequence of the five elements (water, wood, fire, metal, earth) in a 60-year major cycle.

Dates	Animal
1900–10	
31 Jan 1900–18 Feb 1901	rat
19 Feb 1901–7 Feb 1902	ox
8 Feb 1902–28 Jan 1903	tiger
29 Jan 1903–15 Feb 1904	hare
16 Feb 1904–3 Feb 1905	dragon
4 Feb 1905–24 Jan 1906	snake
25 Jan 1906–12 Feb 1907	horse
13 Feb 1907–1 Feb 1908	goat
2 Feb 1908–21 Jan 1909	monkey
22 Jan 1909–9 Feb 1910	cockerel
1910–20	
10 Feb 1910–29 Jan 1911	dog
30 Jan 1911–17 Feb 1912	pig
18 Feb 1912–5 Feb 1913	rat
6 Feb 1913–15 Jan 1914	ox
16 Jan 1914–13 Feb 1915	tiger
14 Feb 1915–2 Feb 1916	hare
3 Feb 1916–22 Jan 1917	dragon
23 Jan 1917–10 Feb 1918	snake
11 Feb 1918–31 Jan 1919	horse
1 Feb 1919–19 Feb 1920	goat
1920–30	
20 Feb 1920–7 Feb 1921	monkey
8 Feb 1921–27 Jan 1922	cockerel
28 Jan 1922–15 Feb 1923	dog
16 Feb 1923–4 Feb 1924	pig
5 Feb 1924–24 Jan 1925	rat
25 Jan 1925–12 Feb 1926	ox
13 Feb 1926–1 Feb 1927	tiger
2 Feb 1927–22 Jan 1928	hare

Dates	Animal
23 Jan 1928–9 Feb 1929	dragon
10 Feb 1929–29 Jan 1930	snake
1930–40	
30 Jan 1930–16 Feb 1931	horse
17 Feb 1931–5 Feb 1932	goat
6 Feb 1932–25 Jan 1933	monkey
26 Jan 1933–13 Feb 1934	cockerel
14 Feb 1934–3 Feb 1935	dog
4 Feb 1935–23 Jan 1936	pig
24 Jan 1936–10 Feb 1937	rat
11 Feb 1937–30 Jan 1938	ox
31 Jan 1938–18 Feb 1939	tiger
19 Feb 1939–7 Feb 1940	hare
1940–50	
8 Feb 1940–26 Jan 1941	dragon
27 Jan 1941–14 Feb 1942	snake
15 Feb 1942–4 Feb 1943	horse
5 Feb 1943–24 Jan 1944	goat
25 Jan 1944–12 Feb 1945	monkey
13 Feb 1945–1 Feb 1946	cockerel
2 Feb 1946–21 Jan 1947	dog
22 Jan 1947–9 Feb 1948	pig
10 Feb 1948–28 Jan 1949	rat
29 Jan 1949–16 Feb 1950	ox
1950–60	
17 Feb 1950–5 Feb 1951	tiger
6 Feb 1951–26 Jan 1952	hare
27 Jan 1952–13 Feb 1953	dragon
14 Feb 1953–2 Feb 1954	snake
3 Feb 1954–23 Jan 1955	horse
24 Jan 1955–11 Feb 1956	goat

Dates	Animal
12 Feb 1956–30 Jan 1957	monkey
31 Jan 1957–17 Feb 1958	cockerel
18 Feb 1958–7 Feb 1959	dog
8 Feb 1959–27 Jan 1960	pig
1960–70	
28 Jan 1960–14 Feb 1961	rat
15 Feb 1961–4 Feb 1962	ox
5 Feb 1962–24 Jan 1963	tiger
25 Jan 1963–12 Feb 1964	hare
13 Feb 1964–1 Feb 1965	dragon
2 Feb 1965–20 Jan 1966	snake
21 Jan 1966–8 Feb 1967	horse
9 Feb 1967–29 Jan 1968	goat
30 Jan 1968–16 Feb 1969	monkey
17 Feb 1969–5 Feb 1970	cockerel
1970–80	
6 Feb 1970–26 Jan 1971	dog
27 Jan 1971–15 Jan 1972	pig
16 Jan 1972–2 Feb 1973	rat
3 Feb 1973–22 Jan 1974	ox
23 Jan 1974–10 Feb 1975	tiger
11 Feb 1975–30 Jan 1976	hare
31 Jan 1976–17 Feb 1977	dragon
18 Feb 1977–6 Feb 1978	snake
7 Feb 1978–27 Jan 1979	horse
28 Jan 1979–15 Feb 1980	goat
1980–90	
16 Feb 1980–4 Feb 1981	monkey
5 Feb 1981–24 Jan 1982	cockerel
25 Jan 1982–12 Feb 1983	dog

(continued)

The Chinese Zodiac (*continued*)

Dates	Animal
13 Feb 1983–1 Feb 1984	pig
2 Feb 1984–19 Feb 1985	rat
20 Feb 1985–8 Feb 1986	ox
9 Feb 1986–28 Jan 1987	tiger
29 Jan 1987–16 Feb 1988	hare
17 Feb 1988–5 Feb 1989	dragon
6 Feb 1989–26 Jan 1990	snake
1990–2000	
27 Jan 1990–14 Feb 1991	horse
15 Feb 1991–3 Feb 1992	goat
4 Feb 1992–22 Jan 1993	monkey
23 Jan 1993–9 Feb 1994	cockerel
10 Feb 1994–30 Jan 1995	dog
31 Jan 1995–18 Feb 1996	pig
19 Feb 1996–7 Feb 1997	rat
8 Feb 1997–27 Jan 1998	ox
28 Jan 1998–15 Feb 1999	tiger
16 Feb 1999–4 Feb 2000	hare
2000–10	
5 Feb 2000–23 Jan 2001	dragon
24 Jan 2001–11 Feb 2002	snake
12 Feb 2002–31 Jan 2003	horse
1 Feb 2003–21 Jan 2004	goat
22 Jan 2004–8 Feb 2005	monkey
9 Feb 2005–28 Jan 2006	cockerel
29 Jan 2006–17 Feb 2007	dog
18 Feb 2000–6 Feb 2008	pig
7 Feb 2008–25 Jan 2009	rat
26 Jan 2009–9 Feb 2010	ox

Signs of the Zodiac

Sign	Element	Symbol	Dates
Aries	Fire		21 March–20 April
Taurus	Earth		20 April–21 May
Gemini	Air		21 May–21 June
Cancer	Water		21 June–23 July
Leo	Fire		23 July–23 August
Virgo	Earth		23 August–23 September
Libra	Air		23 September–23 October
Scorpio	Water		23 October–22 November
Sagittarius	Fire		22 November–22 December
Capricorn	Earth		22 December–20 January
Aquarius	Air		20 January–19 February
Pisces	Water		19 February–21 March

Wedding Anniversaries

In many Western countries, wedding anniversaries have become associated with gifts of different materials. They differ from country to country; the following are traditional in the UK.

Anniversary	Material
1st	cotton
2nd	paper
3rd	leather
4th	fruit, flowers
5th	wood
6th	sugar, iron
7th	wool
8th	bronze, electrical appliances
9th	copper, pottery
10th	tin
11th	steel
12th	silk, fine linen
13th	lace
14th	ivory
15th	crystal
20th	china
25th	silver
30th	pearl
35th	coral
40th	ruby
45th	sapphire
50th	gold
55th	emerald
60th	diamond
70th	platinum

Birth Flowers

Month	Flower
January	carnation, snowdrop
February	primrose, violet
March	jonquil, violet
April	daisy, sweet pea
May	hawthorn, lily of the valley
June	honeysuckle, rose
July	larkspur, water lily
August	gladiolus, poppy
September	aster, morning glory
October	calendula, cosmos
November	chrysanthemum
December	holly, narcissus, poinsettia

Birthstones

Month	Stone	Quality
January	garnet	constancy
February	amethyst	sincerity
March	aquamarine, bloodstone	courage
April	diamond	innocence
May	emerald	love
June	alexandrite, pearl	health and purity
July	ruby	contentment
August	peridot, sardonyx	married happiness
September	sapphire	clear thinking
October	opal, tourmaline	hope
November	topaz	fidelity
December	turquoise, zircon	wealth

Web Sites

Calendar Zone

http://www.calendarzone.com/

The calendar zone site provides information on calendars of various types – religious, historical, cultural. It also provides links to many more.

Chinese Calendar

http://www.chinatown-online.co.uk/pages/culture/festivals.html

Information on the Chinese calendar and Chinese New Year from the Chinatown Online site.

Greenwich 2000

http://greenwich2000.co.uk/time/

Hundreds of information-packed pages about time, the millennium, history, as well as a section on watches and famous watchmakers.

Hindu Calendar

http://hindunet.org/hindu_calendar

Part of a larger Hindu resource centre, this is a thorough site that includes explanatory essays.

Islamic Calendar

http://www.assirat.org/Hcal

An easily navigable site that presents the Islamic calendar with Western equivalents.

National Physical Laboratory

http://www.npl.co.uk/

Official site of the National Physical Laboratory, home of the UK's atomic time scale and the focus for time and frequency measurements in the UK.

Royal Observatory

http://www.rog.nmm.ac.uk/

Official site of the Royal Observatory in Greenwich. Explains atomic time, universal time, meridians, standard time, Greenwich Mean Time, and has astronomical information on equinoxes, solstices, seasons, and eclipses.

The Worldwide Holiday and Festival Site

http://www.holidayfestival.com/

This site brings together information on national holidays and religious celebrations in countries throughout the world.

Time Zone Converter

http://www.timezoneconverter.com/

Here you can easily find out the time anywhere in the world.

US Naval Observatory

http://aa.usno.navy.mil/

Astronomical information on phases of the moon, equinoxes, solstices, sunset and sunrise times, as well as information on calendars.

World Time Server

http://www.worldtimeserver.com/

World Time Server provides the most accurate current local times of any world clock on the Internet.

WEIGHTS, MEASURES, AND NUMBERS

Weights and Measures

The Metric (SI) System

The metric system of weights and measures, a system based on units of ten, or decimals, was first developed in France in the 18th century. The system was refined in the 20th century and in 1960 the International System of Units (French 'Système International d'Unités'), or SI system, was proposed as the standard system of scientific units. The UK government agreed to the adoption of SI as the primary system of weights and measures in 1965 and the system is now used in the measurement of all physical quantities by scientists worldwide.

SI Units
The SI system is based on just seven basic units: the metre (m) for length, kilogram (kg) for mass, second (s) for time, ampere (A) for electrical current, kelvin (K) for temperature, mole (mol) for amount of substance, and candela (cd) for luminosity.

Two supplementary units are included in the SI system – the radian (rad) and steradian (sr) – used to measure plane and solid angles.

To measure other quantities, derived units are formed by multiplying or dividing any two or more of the base units, or powers of them. For example, velocity is measured in metres per second (metres and seconds being the base units) and acceleration is measured in metres per second per second. Many derived units have been given their own names; for example, force (mass times acceleration) is measured in newtons (1 newton is equal to that force which, applied to a mass of 1 kilogram, gives it an acceleration of 1 metre per second per second). Each unit name has been given an agreed symbol.

Some non-SI units, well established and internationally recognized, remain in use in conjunction with SI: minute, hour, and day in measuring time; multiples or submultiples of base or derived units which have long-established names, such as tonne for mass, the litre for volume; and specialist measures such as the metric carat for gemstones.

SI Units

Quantity	SI unit	Symbol
Base units		
length	metre	m
mass	kilogram	kg
time	second	s
electric current	ampere	A
temperature, thermodynamic	kelvin	K
amount of substance	mole	mol
luminous intensity	candela	cd
Derived units		
absorbed radiation dose	gray	Gy
electric capacitance	farad	F
electric charge	coulomb	C
electric conductance	siemens	S
energy or work	joule	J
force	newton	N
frequency	hertz	Hz
illuminance	lux	lx
inductance	henry	H
luminous flux	lumen	lm
magnetic flux	weber	Wb
magnetic flux density	tesla	T
plane angle	radian	rad
potential difference	volt	V
power	watt	W
pressure	pascal	Pa
radiation dose equivalent	sievert	Sv
radiation exposure	roentgen	R
radioactivity	becquerel	Bq
resistance	ohm	Ω
solid angle	steradian	sr
sound intensity	decibel	dB
temperature	degree Celsius	°C

SI Prefixes

To avoid the use of zeros in large or small numbers, prefixes are added to each of the SI units to indicate multiples and submultiples of ten.

Multiple	Prefix	Symbol	Example
1,000,000,000,000,000,000 (10^{18})	exa-	E	Eg (exagram)
1,000,000,000,000,000 (10^{15})	peta-	P	PJ (petajoule)
1,000,000,000,000 (10^{12})	tera-	T	TV (teravolt)
1,000,000,000 (10^{9})	giga-	G	GW (gigawatt)
1,000,000 (10^{6})	mega-	M	MHz (megahertz)
1,000 (10^{3})	kilo-	k	kg (kilogram)
100 (10^{2})	hecto-	h	hm (hectometre)
10 (10^{1})	deca-	da	daN (decanewton)
1/10 (10^{-1})	deci-	d	dC (decicoulomb)
1/100 (10^{-2})	centi-	c	cm (centimetre)
1/1,000 (10^{-3})	milli-	m	mm (millimetre)
1/1,000,000 (10^{-6})	micro-	μ	μF (microfarad)
1/1,000,000,000 (10^{-9})	nano-	n	nm (nanometre)
1/1,000,000,000,000 (10^{-12})	pico-	p	ps (picosecond)
1/1,000,000,000,000,000 (10^{-15})	femto-	f	frad (femtoradian)
1/1,000,000,000,000,000,000 (10^{-18})	atto-	a	aT (attotesla)

The Imperial System

The Imperial System is a traditional system of units based largely on the foot, pound, and second (fps) system. In the UK the system was formally established in 1824 and was the main system in use in the UK, British Commonwealth, and South Africa until the 1960s when the changeover to the metric system began.

Many imperial units have not been officially authorized for UK use since 1980: these include the square inch, square mile, cubic foot, grain, stone, hundredweight, ton, and horsepower. Other units, including the fathom for marine navigation and the therm for gas supply, have not been authorized for official use since 1 January 2000.

Units in the Metric System

Length		
1 centimetre	= 10 millimetres	
1 decimetre	= 10 centimetres	= 100 millimetres
1 metre	= 10 decimetres	= 1,000 millimetres
1 decametre	= 10 metres	
1 hectometre	= 10 decametres	= 100 metres
1 kilometre	= 10 hectometres	= 1,000 metres
Area		
1 square centimetre	= 100 square millimetres	
1 square metre	= 10,000 square centimetres	= 1,000,000 square millimetres
1 are	= 100 square metres	
1 hectare	= 100 ares	= 10,000 square metres
1 square kilometre	= 100 hectares	= 1,000,000 square metres
Mass (avoirdupois)		
1 centigram	= 10 milligrams	
1 decigram	= 10 centigrams	= 100 milligrams
1 gram	= 10 decigrams	= 1,000 milligrams
1 decagram	= 10 grams	
1 hectogram	= 10 decagrams	= 100 grams
1 kilogram	= 10 hectograms	= 1,000 grams
1 metric ton	= 1,000 kilograms	
Volume		
1 cubic centimetre	= 1,000 cubic millimetres	
1 cubic decimetre	= 1,000 cubic centimetres	= 1,000,000 cubic millimetres
1 cubic metre	= 1,000 cubic decimetres	= 1,000,000,000 cubic millimetres
Capacity		
1 centilitre	= 10 millilitres	
1 decilitre	= 10 centilitres	= 100 millilitres
1 litre	= 10 decilitres	= 1,000 millilitres
1 decalitre	= 10 litres	
1 hectolitre	= 10 decalitres	= 100 litres
1 kilolitre	= 10 hectolitres	= 1,000 litres

Units in the Imperial System

Length	
1 foot	= 12 inches
1 yard	= 3 feet
1 rod, pole, perch	= $5\frac{1}{2}$ yards (= $16\frac{1}{2}$ feet)
1 chain	= 4 rods (= 22 yards)
1 furlong	= 10 chains (= 220 yards)
1 mile	= 5,280 feet (= 1,760 yards/8 furlongs)
Nautical	
1 fathom	= 6 feet
1 cable length	= 100 fathoms (UK)/120 fathoms (USA)
1 nautical mile (UK)[1]	= 6,080 feet
1 nautical mile (international)	= 6,076 feet
Area	
1 square foot	= 144 square inches
1 square yard	= 9 square feet
1 square rod	= $30\frac{1}{4}$ square yards
1 rood	= 1,210 square yards
1 acre	= 4,840 square yards (= 4 roods)
1 square mile	= 640 acres
Volume	
1 cubic foot	= 1,728 cubic inches
1 cubic yard	= 27 cubic feet
Shipping	
1 register ton	= 100 cubic feet
Capacity	
1 fluid ounce	= 8 fluid drachms
1 gill	= 5 fluid ounces
1 pint	= 4 gills (= 20 fluid ounces)
1 quart	= 2 pints
1 gallon	= 4 quarts (= 8 pints)
1 peck	= 2 gallons
1 bushel	= 4 pecks (= 8 gallons)
1 quarter	= 8 bushels (= 64 gallons)
Weight (avoirdupois)	
1 ounce	= $437\frac{1}{2}$ grains
1 ounce	= 16 drams
1 pound	= 16 ounces
1 stone	= 14 pounds
1 quarter	= 2 stones (= 28 pounds)
1 hundredweight	= 4 quarters (= 112 pounds (UK)/100 pounds (USA))
1 ton (UK long ton)	= 20 hundredweights (= 2,240 pounds)
1 ton (US short ton)	= 20 hundredweights (= 2,000 pounds)

[1]Obsolete since 1970 when the international nautical mile was adopted in the UK by the Ministry of Defence.

Imperial Measures for Use in Trade

From 1 January 2000 retailers in the UK have been required by law to sell loose products such as fruit and vegetables in metric units and it has been unlawful to sell loose goods by the pound and ounce. In February 1999 a European directive announced that dual metric/imperial marking of labels would be permitted until the year 2009, but imperial equivalents on labels may be included only as supplementary, subordinate indicators. Shoppers are still able to use imperial measures to ask for what they want, but retailers are required to measure the goods out in the metric equivalent. Authorization for use has been given without time limit to the following imperial measures:

- pint for draught beer and cider, and milk sold in returnable containers
- troy ounce for transactions in precious metals
- inch, foot, yard, and mile for road signs
- acre for land registration

Apothecary Weights and Measures

Apothecary measures of liquid capacity and mass were formerly used in pharmacy and were officially discontinued in 1971. The minim in apothecary measures of liquid capacity is equal to 0.059 millilitres.

Apothecary measures of liquid capacity

1 fluid drachm	60 minims/3.54 millilitres
1 fluid ounce	8 drachms/28.32 millilitres
1 pint	20 fluid ounces/0.568 litres

Apothecary weights

1 scruple	20 grains/1.296 grams
1 drachm	3 scruples (= 60 grains)/3.888 grams
1 apothecary ounce	8 drachms (= 480 grains)/31.104 grams
1 apothecary pound	12 apothecary ounces (5,760 grains)/373.248 grams

Troy Weights

The troy system, used for weighing gold, silver, and gemstones, is thought to have derived its name from the town of Troyes, France, where the system was probably first used at the medieval fairs held in the town. The pound troy has been legally obsolete since 1878, but for transactions in precious metals the troy ounce is authorized for use without time limit.

Troy weight		Metric equivalent
1 pennyweight	= 24 grains	1.555 grams
1 ounce troy	= 20 pennyweights (= 480 grains)	31.103 grams
1 pound troy	= 12 ounces troy (= 5,760 grains)	373.242 grams

Cotton Yarn: Old Measures

1 thread	54 inches (= $1\frac{1}{2}$ yards/1.4 metres)
1 skein	80 threads (= 120 yards/110 metres)
1 hank	7 skeins (= 840 yards/768 metres)
1 spindle	18 hanks (= 15,120 yards/13,826 metres)

Champagne Bottle Sizes

Size	Number of standard champagne bottles
Magnum	2
Jeroboam	4
Rehoboam	6
Methuselah	8
Salmanazar	12
Balthazar	16
Nebuchadnezzar	20

Old Beer Measures

Measures are based on the 282 cubic inch beer and ale standard gallon.

1 firkin	9 gallons
1 kilderkin	2 firkins (= 18 gallons)
1 barrel	2 kilderkins (= 4 firkins/36 gallons)
1 hogshead	1.5 barrels (= 54 gallons)
1 puncheon	2 barrels (= 72 gallons)
1 butt or pipe	2 hogsheads (= 3 barrels/108 gallons)

The Avoirdupois System

The avoirdupois system of weights, the imperial system used for goods other than precious metals and pharmaceuticals, is based on the unit of a pound of 16 ounces (each of 16 drams). Avoirdupois in French means 'to have weight'.

The Fathom

The fathom, a nautical measurement of 6 feet (1.83 metres), is approximately the distance between an adult man's hands when the arms are outstretched to their fullest extent. The fathom was taken out of official use on 31 December 1999.

The Carat

The carat, a unit for measuring the mass of precious stones, is equal to 0.2 grams/0.00705 ounces. It is also the unit of purity in gold (US karat). Pure gold is 24-carat; 22-carat (the purest used in jewellery) is 22 parts gold and two parts alloy (to give greater strength).

The Grain

The grain, equal to 0.0648 grams, is the smallest unit of mass in three old systems of measurement: the avoirdupois, troy, and apothecaries' weights. There are 7,000 grains in the avoirdupois pound and 5,760 grains in the apothecary and troy pounds.

The Yard and the Cubit

It is said that Henry I of England (1068–1135) decreed that one yard was the length of his extended arm, measured from nose to fingertip.

The cubit, equalling approximately 45.7 centimetres/18 inches, is about the length of the arm from the elbow to the extended finger tips. It is said to have been devised in Egypt around 3000 BC as the standard unit of linear measure.

Paper Measures

Writing paper

1 quire	24 sheets (now often 25 sheets)
1 ream	20 quires (= 480 sheets; now often 500 sheets)
1 bundle	2 reams (= 960 sheets; now often 1,000 sheets)

Printing paper

1 printer's ream	516 sheets (now often 500 sheets)
1 bundle	2 reams (= 1032 sheets; now often 1,000 sheets)
1 bale	5 bundles (= 5160 sheets; now often 5,000 sheets)

Quick Conversions

- To convert Fahrenheit to Celsius, subtract 32, multiply the result by 5, then divide by 9
- To convert Celsius to Fahrenheit, multiply by 9, divide the result by 5, then add 32
- To convert miles to kilometres multiply by 8, then divide by 5
- To convert kilometres to miles, multiply by 5, then divide by 8
- To convert square metres to square yards, add one fifth
- To convert acres to hectares, multiply by 2, then divide by 5
- To convert hectares to acres, multiply by 5, then divide by 2

Imperial and Metric Conversion Factors

Imperial to metric

To convert from	Multiply by
Length	
inches to millimetres	25.4
feet to metres	0.3048
yards to metres	0.9144
furlongs to kilometres	0.201168
miles to kilometres	1.609344
Area	
square inches to square centimetres	6.4516
square feet to square metres	0.092903
square yards to square metres	0.836127
square miles to square kilometres	2.589988
acres to square metres	4,046.856422
acres to hectares	0.404685
Volume/capacity	
cubic inches to cubic centimetres	16.387064
cubic feet to cubic metres	0.028317
cubic yards to cubic metres	0.764555
cubic miles to cubic kilometres	4.1682
fluid ounces (imperial) to millilitres	28.413063
fluid ounces (US) to millilitres	29.5735
pints (imperial) to litres	0.568261
pints (US) to litres	0.473176
quarts (imperial) to litres	1.136523
quarts (US) to litres	0.946353
gallons (imperial) to litres	4.54609
gallons (US) to litres	3.785412
Mass/weight	
ounces to grams	28.349523
pounds to kilograms	0.453592
stones (14 lb) to kilograms	6.350293
tons (imperial) to kilograms	1,016.046909
tons (US) to kilograms	907.18474
tons (imperial) to metric tonnes	1.016047
tons (US) to metric tonnes	0.907185
Speed	
miles per hour to kilometres per hour	1.609344
feet per second to metres per second	0.3048
Force	
pounds-force to newtons	4.44822
kilograms-force to newtons	9.80665
Pressure	
pounds-force per square inch to kilopascals	6.89476
tons-force per square inch (imperial) to megapascals	15.4443
atmospheres to newtons per square centimetre	10.1325
atmospheres to pounds-force per square inch	14.695942
Energy	
calories to joules	4.1868
watt hours to joules	3,600
Power	
horsepower to kilowatts	0.7457
Fuel consumption	
miles per gallon (imperial) to kilometres per litre	0.3540
miles per gallon (US) to kilometres per litre	0.4251
gallons per mile (imperial) to litres per kilometre	2.824859
gallons per mile (US) to litres per kilometre	2.3521

Metric to imperial

To convert from	Multiply by
Length	
millimetres to inches	0.0393701
metres to feet	3.28084
metres to yards	1.09361
kilometres to furlongs	4.97097
kilometres to miles	0.621371
Area	
square centimetres to square inches	0.1550
square metres to square feet	10.7639
square metres to square yards	1.19599
square kilometres to square miles	0.386102
square metres to acres	0.000247
hectares to acres	2.471054
Volume/capacity	
cubic centimetres to cubic inches	0.061024
cubic metres to cubic feet	35.3147
cubic metres to cubic yards	1.30795
cubic kilometres to cubic miles	0.239912
millilitres to fluid ounces (imperial)	0.035195
millilitres to fluid ounces (US)	0.033814
litres to pints (imperial)	1.759754
litres to pints (US)	2.113377
litres to quarts (imperial)	0.879877
litres to quarts (US)	1.056688
litres to gallons (imperial)	0.219969
litres to gallons (US)	0.364172
Mass/weight	
grams to ounces	0.035274
kilograms to pounds	2.20462
kilograms to stones (14 lb)	0.157473
kilograms to tons (imperial)	0.000984
kilograms to tons (US)	0.001102
metric tonnes to tons (imperial)	0.984207
metric tonnes to tons (US)	1.10231
Speed	
kilometres per hour to miles per hour	0.621371
metres per second to feet per second	3.28084
Force	
newtons to pounds-force	0.224809
newtons to kilograms-force	0.101972
Pressure	
kilopascals to pounds-force per square inch	0.145038
megapascals to tons-force per square inch (imperial)	0.064779
newtons per square centimetre to atmospheres	0.098692
pounds-force per square inch to atmospheres	0.068948
Energy	
joules to calories	0.238846
joules to watt hours	0.000278
Power	
kilowatts to horsepower	1.34102
Fuel consumption	
kilometres per litre to miles per gallon (imperial)	2.824859
kilometres per litre to miles per gallon (US)	2.3521
litres per kilometre to gallons per mile (imperial)	0.3540
litres per kilometre to gallons per mile (US)	0.4251

Table of Equivalent Temperatures

Celsius and Fahrenheit temperatures can be interconverted as follows: C = (F − 32) × 100/180; F = (C × 180/100) + 32.

°C	°F	°C	°F	°C	°F	°C	°F	°C	°F	°C	°F	°C	°F	°C	°F
100	212.0	85	185.0	70	158.0	55	131.0	40	104.0	25	77.0	10	50.0	−5	23.0
99	210.2	84	183.2	69	156.2	54	129.2	39	102.2	24	75.2	9	48.2	−6	21.2
98	208.4	83	181.4	68	154.4	53	127.4	38	100.4	23	73.4	8	46.4	−7	19.4
97	206.6	82	179.6	67	152.6	52	125.6	37	98.6	22	71.6	7	44.6	−8	17.6
96	204.8	81	177.8	66	150.8	51	123.8	36	96.8	21	69.8	6	42.8	−9	15.8
95	203.0	80	176.0	65	149.0	50	122.0	35	95.0	20	68.0	5	41.0	−10	14.0
94	201.2	79	174.2	64	147.2	49	120.2	34	93.2	19	66.2	4	39.2	−11	12.2
93	199.4	78	172.4	63	145.4	48	118.4	33	91.4	18	64.4	3	37.4	−12	10.4
92	197.6	77	170.6	62	143.6	47	116.6	32	89.6	17	62.6	2	35.6	−13	8.6
91	195.8	76	168.8	61	141.8	46	114.8	31	87.8	16	60.8	1	33.8	−14	6.8
90	194.0	75	167.0	60	140.0	45	113.0	30	86.0	15	59.0	0	32.0	−15	5.0
89	192.2	74	165.2	59	138.2	44	111.2	29	84.2	14	57.2	−1	30.2	−16	3.2
88	190.4	73	163.4	58	136.4	43	109.4	28	82.4	13	55.4	−2	28.4	−17	1.4
87	188.6	72	161.6	57	134.6	42	107.6	27	80.6	12	53.6	−3	26.6	−18	−0.4
86	186.8	71	159.8	56	132.8	41	105.8	26	78.8	11	51.8	−4	24.8	−19	−2.2

Shoe Size Conversions

Size equivalents are approximate.

Men's shoes

UK	Europe	USA
3	35–36	3½
3½	36	4
4	37	4½
4½	37–38	5
5	38	5½
5½	39	6
6	39–40	6½
6½	40	7
7	41	7½
7½	41–42	8
8	42	8½
8½	42–43	9
9	43	9½
9½	44	10
10	44–45	10½
10½	45	11
11	46	11½
11½	46–47	12
12	47	12½
12½	47–48	13
13	48	13½

Women's shoes

UK	Europe	USA
3	35–36	4½
3½	36	5
4	37	5½
4½	37–38	6
5	38	6½
5½	39	7
6	39–40	7½
6½	40	8
7	41	8½
7½	41–42	9
8	42	9½
8½	42–43	10
9	43	10½

Children's shoes

UK	Europe	USA
1	16–17	1½
1½	17	2
2	18	2½
2½	18–19	3
3	19	3½
3½	20	4
4	20–21	4½
4½	21	5
5	22	5½
5½	22–23	6
6	23	6½
6½	24	7
7	24–25	7½
7½	25	8
8	26	8½
8½	26–27	9
9	27	9½
9½	27–28	10
10	28	10½
10½	28–29	11
11	29	11½
11½	30	12
12	30–31	12½
12½	31	13
13	31–32	13½
13½	32	1
1	33	1½
1½	33–34	2
2	34	2½
2½	35	3

Cooking Measurement Equivalents

Liquid measures

Imperial (UK/US)	Metric
⅙ fluid ounce/1 teaspoon	5 millilitres
½ fluid ounce/1 tablespoon	15 millilitres
1 fluid ounce/2 tablespoons	30 millilitres
8 fluid ounces/1 cup	240 millilitres
½ pint (10 fluid ounces)/1¼ cups	300 millilitres
16 fluid ounces/1 pint (2 cups)	470 millilitres
1 pint (20 fluid ounces)/2½ cups	600 millilitres
34 fluid ounces/4⅓ cups	1 litre
1¾ pints/4⅓ cups	1 litre

Dry measures

Imperial (UK and US)	Metric
1 ounce	28 grams
3½ ounces	100 grams
4 ounces	113 grams
8 ounces	225 grams
1 pound	450 grams
35 ounces (2.2 pounds)	1 kilogram

International Clothing Sizes

Size equivalents are approximate.

Women's suits/dresses

UK	Europe	USA
8	36	6
10	38	8
12	40	10
14	42	12
16	44	14
18	46	16
20	48	18
22	50	20
24	52	22

Men's suits

UK	Europe	USA
36	46	36
38	48	38
40	50	40
42	52	42
44	54	44
46	56	46

Men's shirts (collar sizes)

UK	Europe	USA
14	36	14
14½	37	14½
15	38	15
15½	39	15½
16	40	16
16½	41	16½
17	42	17
17½	43	17½

Oven Temperature

Gas mark	Electric °C	Electric °F	Rating
½	130	250	very cool
1	140	275	
2	150	300	cool
3	170	325	warm
4	180	350	moderate
5	190	375	fairly hot
6	200	400	
7	220	425	hot
8	230	450	very hot
9	240	475	

■ Weights and Measures

International Paper Sizes

Name	Dimensions	Classic series
large post	419 × 533 millimetres	$16\frac{1}{2}$ × 21 inches
demy	444 × 572 millimetres	$17\frac{1}{2}$ × $22\frac{1}{2}$ inches
medium	457 × 584 millimetres	18 × 23 inches
royal	508 × 635 millimetres	20 × 25 inches
double crown	508 × 762 millimetres	20 × 30 inches
A series (books, magazines, stationery)		
A0	841 × 1,189 millimetres	$33\frac{1}{8}$ × $46\frac{3}{4}$ inches
A1	594 × 841 millimetres	$23\frac{3}{8}$ × $33\frac{1}{8}$ inches
A2	420 × 594 millimetres	$16\frac{1}{2}$ × $23\frac{3}{8}$ inches
A3	297 × 420 millimetres	$11\frac{3}{4}$ × $16\frac{1}{2}$ inches
A4	210 × 297 millimetres	$8\frac{1}{4}$ × $11\frac{3}{4}$ inches
A5	148 × 210 millimetres	$5\frac{7}{8}$ × $8\frac{1}{4}$ inches

Name	Dimensions	Classic series
B series (posters, etc)		
B0	1,414 × 1,000 millimetres	$55\frac{5}{8}$ × $39\frac{3}{8}$ inches
B1	1,000 × 707 millimetres	$39\frac{3}{8}$ × $27\frac{7}{8}$ inches
B2	707 × 500 millimetres	$27\frac{7}{8}$ × $19\frac{5}{8}$ inches
B3	500 × 353 millimetres	$19\frac{5}{8}$ × $13\frac{7}{8}$ inches
B4	353 × 250 millimetres	$13\frac{7}{8}$ × $9\frac{7}{8}$ inches
B5	250 × 176 millimetres	$9\frac{7}{8}$ × 7 inches
C series (envelopes)		
C4	324 × 229 millimetres	$12\frac{3}{4}$ × 9 inches
C5	229 × 162 millimetres	9 × $6\frac{3}{8}$ inches
C6	162 × 114 millimetres	$6\frac{3}{8}$ × $4\frac{1}{2}$ inches
DL	220 × 110 millimetres	$8\frac{5}{8}$ × $4\frac{3}{8}$ inches

Physical Constants

Physical constants, or fundamental constants, are physical quantities that are constant in all circumstances thoughout the whole universe.

Constant	Symbol	Value in SI units
acceleration of free fall	g	$9.80665\ \mathrm{m\ s^{-2}}$
Avogadro's constant	N_A	$6.0221367 \times 10^{23}\ \mathrm{mol^{-1}}$
Boltzmann's constant	k	$1.380658 \times 10^{-23}\ \mathrm{J\ K^{-1}}$
elementary charge	e	$1.60217733 \times 10^{-19}\ \mathrm{C}$
electronic rest mass	m_e	$9.1093897 \times 10^{-31}\ \mathrm{kg}$
Faraday's constant	F	$9.6485309 \times 10^{4}\ \mathrm{C\ mol^{-1}}$
gas constant	R	$8.314510\ \mathrm{J\ K^{-1}\ mol^{-1}}$
gravitational constant	G	$6.672 \times 10^{-11}\ \mathrm{N\ m^{2}\ kg^{-2}}$
Loschmidt's number	N_L	$2.686763 \times 10^{25}\ \mathrm{m^{-3}}$
neutron rest mass	m_n	$1.6749286 \times 10^{-27}\ \mathrm{kg}$
Planck's constant	h	$6.6260755 \times 10^{-34}\ \mathrm{J\ s}$
proton rest mass	m_p	$1.6726231 \times 10^{-27}\ \mathrm{kg}$
speed of light in a vacuum	c	$2.99792458 \times 10^{8}\ \mathrm{m\ s^{-1}}$
standard atmosphere	atm	$1.01325 \times 10^{5}\ \mathrm{Pa}$
Stefan–Boltzmann constant	σ	$5.67051 \times 10^{-8}\ \mathrm{W\ m^{-2}\ K^{-4}}$

The Beaufort Scale

The Beaufort scale is a system of recording wind velocity (speed) devised in 1806 by Francis Beaufort (1774–1857). It is a numerical scale ranging from 0 to 12, calm being indicated by 0 and a hurricane by 12. The scale received international recognition in 1874. Measurements are made at 10 metres/33 feet above ground level.

Force	Description	Features	Air speed kph	Air speed mph
0	calm	smoke rises vertically; water smooth	0–2	0–1
1	light air	smoke shows wind direction; water ruffled	2–5	1–3
2	light breeze	leaves rustle; wind felt on face	6–11	4–7
3	gentle breeze	loose paper blows around	12–19	8–12
4	moderate breeze	branches sway	20–29	13–18
5	fresh breeze	small trees sway, leaves blown off	30–39	19–24
6	strong breeze	whistling in telephone wires; sea spray from waves	40–50	25–31
7	near gale	large trees sway	51–61	32–38
8	gale	twigs break from trees	62–74	39–46
9	strong gale	branches break from trees	75–87	47–54
10	storm	trees uprooted; weak buildings collapse	88–101	55–63
11	violent storm	widespread damage	102–117	64–73
12	hurricane	widespread structural damage	above 118	above 74

See also **Major Hurricanes, Typhoons, Cyclones, and Other Storms Since 1995,** p 627.

The Decibel Scale

The decibel (dB) scale is used primarily to measure relative sound intensities. It is used for audibility measurements because one decibel, representing an increase of about 25%, is about the smallest change the human ear can detect. An increase of 10 decibels is equivalent to a ten-fold increase in sound intensity or power. Decibels are also used to compare electric voltages or currents.

Decibels	Typical sound
0	threshold of human hearing
10	quiet whisper
20	average whisper
20–50	quiet conversation
40–45	light traffic
50–65	loud conversation
65–70	traffic on busy street
65–90	train
75–80	factory (light/medium work)
90	heavy traffic
90–100	thunder
110–140	jet aircraft at take-off
130	threshold of pain for humans
140–190	space rocket at take-off

The Richter Scale

The Richter scale is based on measurement of seismic waves, used to determine the magnitude of an earthquake at its epicentre. The magnitude of an earthquake differs from its intensity, measured by the Mercalli scale, which is subjective and varies from place to place for the same earthquake. The Richter scale was named after US seismologist Charles Richter (1900–1985). The relative amount of energy released indicates the ratio of energy between earthquakes of different magnitude.

Magnitude	Relative amount of energy released	Examples	Year
1	1		
2	31		
3	960		
4	30,000	Carlisle, England (4.7)	1979
5	920,000	Wrexham, Wales (5.1)	1990
6	29,000,000	San Fernando (CA), USA (6.5)	1971
		northern Armenia (6.8)	1988
7	890,000,000	Loma Prieta (CA), USA (7.1)	1989
		Kobe, Japan (7.2)	1995
		Izmit, Turkey (7.4)	1999
		Taichung and Nantou counties, Taiwan (7.6)	1999
		Rasht, Iran (7.7)	1990
		San Francisco (CA), USA (7.7–7.9)[1]	1906
8	28,000,000,000	Tangshan, China (8.0)	1976
		Gansu, China (8.6)	1920
		Lisbon, Portugal (8.7)	1755
9	850,000,000,000	Prince William Sound (AK), USA (9.2)	1964

[1] Richter's original estimate of a magnitude of 8.3 was revised by two studies carried out by the California Institute of Technology and the US Geological Survey.

See also **Major Earthquakes Since 1980**, p 628.

Mercalli Scale

The Mercalli scale is a measure of the intensity of an earthquake. It differs from the Richter scale, which measures magnitude. It is named after the Italian seismologist Giuseppe Mercalli (1850–1914). The scale shown here is the Modified Mercalli Intensity Scale, developed in 1931 by US seismologists Harry Wood and Frank Neumann.

Intensity value	Description
I	not felt except by a very few under especially favourable conditions
II	felt only by a few persons at rest, especially on upper floors of buildings
III	felt quite noticeably by persons indoors, especially on upper floors of buildings; many people do not recognize it as an earthquake; standing motor cars may rock slightly
IV	felt indoors by many, outdoors by a few persons during the day; at night, some awakened; dishes, windows, doors disturbed; walls make cracking sound; standing motor cars rock noticeably
V	felt by nearly everyone; many awakened; some dishes, windows broken; unstable objects overturned; pendulum clocks may stop
VI	felt by all; some heavy furniture moved; a few instances of fallen plaster; damage slight
VII	damage negligible in buildings of good design and construction; slight to moderate in well-built ordinary structures; considerable damage in poorly built or badly designed structures; some chimneys broken
VIII	damage slight in specially designed structures; considerable damage in ordinary substantial buildings with partial collapse; damage great in poorly built structures; fall of chimneys, factory stacks, columns, monuments, walls; heavy furniture overturned
IX	damage considerable in specially designed structures; damage great in substantial buildings, with partial collapse; buildings shifted off foundations
X	some well built wooden structures destroyed; most masonry and frame structures with foundations destroyed; rails bent
XI	few, if any (masonry) structures remain standing; bridges destroyed; rails bent greatly
XII	damage total; lines of sight and level are distorted; objects thrown into the air

Numbers

Large Numbers

Nomenclature for large numbers varies in different countries: in the UK and Germany numbers have traditionally advanced by increments of a million, whereas in the USA and France numbers advance by increments of a thousand. The US usage is becoming prevalent in the UK and is now universally used by economists and statisticians.

UK and Germany

million	1,000,000	1×10^{6}
billion	1,000,000,000,000	1×10^{12}
trillion	1,000,000,000,000,000,000	1×10^{18}
quadrillion	1,000,000,000,000,000,000,000,000	1×10^{24}

USA and France

billion	1,000,000,000	1×10^{9}
trillion	1,000,000,000,000	1×10^{12}
quadrillion	1,000,000,000,000,000	1×10^{15}

Higher numbers

Number	UK	USA
quintillion	1×10^{30}	1×10^{18}
sextillion	1×10^{36}	1×10^{21}
septillion	1×10^{42}	1×10^{24}
octillion	1×10^{48}	1×10^{27}
nonillion	1×10^{54}	1×10^{30}
decillion	1×10^{60}	1×10^{33}
vigintillion	1×10^{120}	1×10^{63}
centillion	1×10^{600}	1×10^{303}

Fractions as Decimals

Fraction	Decimal	Fraction	Decimal	Fraction	Decimal
$\frac{1}{2}$	0.5000	$\frac{8}{9}$	0.8889	$\frac{15}{16}$	0.9375
$\frac{1}{3}$	0.3333	$\frac{1}{10}$	0.1000	$\frac{1}{20}$	0.0500
$\frac{2}{3}$	0.6667	$\frac{3}{10}$	0.3000	$\frac{3}{20}$	0.1500
$\frac{1}{4}$	0.2500	$\frac{7}{10}$	0.7000	$\frac{7}{20}$	0.3500
$\frac{3}{4}$	0.7500	$\frac{9}{10}$	0.9000	$\frac{9}{20}$	0.4500
$\frac{1}{5}$	0.2000	$\frac{1}{11}$	0.0909	$\frac{11}{20}$	0.5500
$\frac{2}{5}$	0.4000	$\frac{2}{11}$	0.1818	$\frac{13}{20}$	0.6500
$\frac{3}{5}$	0.6000	$\frac{3}{11}$	0.2727	$\frac{17}{20}$	0.8500
$\frac{4}{5}$	0.8000	$\frac{4}{11}$	0.3636	$\frac{19}{20}$	0.9500
$\frac{1}{6}$	0.1667	$\frac{5}{11}$	0.4545	$\frac{1}{32}$	0.0312
$\frac{5}{6}$	0.8333	$\frac{6}{11}$	0.5455	$\frac{3}{32}$	0.9038
$\frac{1}{7}$	0.1429	$\frac{7}{11}$	0.6364	$\frac{5}{32}$	0.1562
$\frac{2}{7}$	0.2857	$\frac{8}{11}$	0.7273	$\frac{7}{32}$	0.2188
$\frac{3}{7}$	0.4286	$\frac{9}{11}$	0.8182	$\frac{9}{32}$	0.2812
$\frac{4}{7}$	0.5714	$\frac{10}{11}$	0.9091	$\frac{11}{32}$	0.3438
$\frac{5}{7}$	0.7143	$\frac{1}{12}$	0.0833	$\frac{13}{32}$	0.4062
$\frac{6}{7}$	0.8571	$\frac{5}{12}$	0.4167	$\frac{15}{32}$	0.4688
$\frac{1}{8}$	0.1250	$\frac{7}{12}$	0.5833	$\frac{17}{32}$	0.5312
$\frac{3}{8}$	0.3750	$\frac{11}{12}$	0.9167	$\frac{19}{32}$	0.5938
$\frac{5}{8}$	0.6250	$\frac{1}{16}$	0.0625	$\frac{21}{32}$	0.6562
$\frac{7}{8}$	0.8750	$\frac{3}{16}$	0.1875	$\frac{23}{32}$	0.7188
$\frac{1}{9}$	0.1111	$\frac{5}{16}$	0.3125	$\frac{25}{32}$	0.7812
$\frac{2}{9}$	0.2222	$\frac{7}{16}$	0.4375	$\frac{27}{32}$	0.8438
$\frac{4}{9}$	0.4444	$\frac{9}{16}$	0.5625	$\frac{29}{32}$	0.9062
$\frac{5}{9}$	0.5556	$\frac{11}{16}$	0.6875	$\frac{31}{32}$	0.9688
$\frac{7}{9}$	0.7778	$\frac{13}{16}$	0.8125		

Roman Numerals

Roman	Arabic	Roman	Arabic	Roman	Arabic
I	1	XI	11	CD	400
II	2	XIX	19	D	500
III	3	XX	20	CM	900
IV	4	XXX	30	M	1,000
V	5	XL	40	$\bar{V}$	5,000
VI	6	L	50	$\bar{X}$	10,000
VII	7	LX	60	$\bar{L}$	50,000
VIII	8	XC	90	$\bar{C}$	100,000
IX	9	C	100	$\bar{D}$	500,000
X	10	CC	200	$\bar{M}$	1,000,000

Prime Numbers

A prime number is a number that can be divided only by 1 and itself, that is, having no other factors. There is an infinite number of primes. Below are all the prime numbers between 1 and 1,000.

2	3	5	7	11	13	17	19	23	29
31	37	41	43	47	53	59	61	67	71
73	79	83	89	97	101	103	107	109	113
127	131	137	139	149	151	157	163	167	173
179	181	191	193	197	199	211	223	227	229
233	239	241	251	257	263	269	271	277	281
283	293	307	311	313	317	331	337	347	349
353	359	367	373	379	383	389	397	401	409
419	421	431	433	439	443	449	457	461	463
467	479	487	491	499	503	509	521	523	541
547	557	563	569	571	577	587	593	599	601
607	613	617	619	631	641	643	647	653	659
661	673	677	683	691	701	709	719	727	733
739	743	751	757	761	769	773	787	797	809
811	821	823	827	829	839	853	857	859	863
877	881	883	887	907	911	919	929	937	941
947	953	967	971	977	983	991	997		

Squares, Cubes, and Roots

Number	Square	Cube	Square root	Cube root
1	1	1	1.000	1.000
2	4	8	1.414	1.260
3	9	27	1.732	1.442
4	16	64	2.000	1.587
5	25	125	2.236	1.710
6	36	216	2.449	1.817
7	49	343	2.646	1.913
8	64	512	2.828	2.000
9	81	729	3.000	2.080
10	100	1,000	3.162	2.154
11	121	1,331	3.317	2.224
12	144	1,728	3.464	2.289
13	169	2,197	3.606	2.351
14	196	2,744	3.742	2.410
15	225	3,375	3.873	2.466
16	256	4,096	4.000	2.520
17	289	4,913	4.123	2.571
18	324	5,832	4.243	2.621
19	361	6,859	4.359	2.668
20	400	8,000	4.472	2.714
25	625	15,625	5.000	2.924
30	900	27,000	5.477	3.107
40	1,600	64,000	6.325	3.420
50	2,500	125,000	7.071	3.684

Multiplication Table

	2	3	4	5	6	7	8	9	10	11	12	13	14	15	16	17	18	19	20	21	22	23	24	25
2	4	6	8	10	12	14	16	18	20	22	24	26	28	30	32	34	36	38	40	42	44	46	48	50
3	6	9	12	15	18	21	24	27	30	33	36	39	42	45	48	51	54	57	60	63	66	69	72	75
4	8	12	16	20	24	28	32	36	40	44	48	52	56	60	64	68	72	76	80	84	88	92	96	100
5	10	15	20	25	30	35	40	45	50	55	60	65	70	75	80	85	90	95	100	105	110	115	120	125
6	12	18	24	30	36	42	48	54	60	66	72	78	84	90	96	102	108	114	120	126	132	138	144	150
7	14	21	28	35	42	49	56	63	70	77	84	91	98	105	112	119	126	133	140	147	154	161	168	175
8	16	24	32	40	48	56	64	72	80	88	96	104	112	120	128	136	144	152	160	168	176	184	192	200
9	18	27	36	45	54	63	72	81	90	99	108	117	126	135	144	153	162	171	180	189	198	207	216	225
10	20	30	40	50	60	70	80	90	100	110	120	130	140	150	160	170	180	190	200	210	220	230	240	250
11	22	33	44	55	66	77	88	99	110	121	132	143	154	165	176	187	198	209	220	231	241	253	264	275
12	24	36	48	60	72	84	96	108	120	132	144	156	168	180	192	204	216	228	240	252	264	276	288	300
13	26	39	52	65	78	91	104	117	130	143	156	169	182	195	208	221	234	247	260	273	286	299	312	325
14	28	42	56	70	84	98	112	126	140	154	168	182	196	210	224	238	252	266	280	294	308	322	336	350
15	30	45	60	75	90	105	120	135	150	165	180	195	210	225	240	255	270	285	300	315	330	345	360	375
16	32	48	64	80	96	112	128	144	160	176	192	208	224	240	256	272	288	304	320	336	352	368	384	400
17	34	51	68	85	102	119	136	153	170	187	204	221	238	255	272	289	306	323	340	357	374	391	408	425
18	36	54	72	90	108	126	144	162	180	198	216	234	252	270	288	306	324	342	360	378	396	414	432	450
19	38	57	76	95	114	133	152	171	190	209	228	247	266	285	304	323	342	361	380	399	418	437	456	475
20	40	60	80	100	120	140	160	180	200	220	240	260	280	300	320	340	360	380	400	420	440	460	480	500
21	42	63	84	105	126	147	168	189	210	231	252	273	294	315	336	357	378	399	420	441	462	483	504	525
22	44	66	88	110	132	154	176	198	220	242	264	286	308	330	352	374	396	418	440	462	484	506	528	550
23	46	69	92	115	138	161	184	207	230	253	276	299	322	345	368	391	414	437	460	483	506	529	552	575
24	48	72	96	120	144	168	192	216	240	264	288	312	336	360	384	408	432	456	480	504	528	552	576	600
25	50	75	100	125	150	175	200	225	250	275	300	325	350	375	400	425	450	475	500	525	550	575	600	625

Playing Cards and Dice Chances

Poker

Hand	Number possible	Odds against
Royal flush	4	649,739 to 1
Straight flush	36	72,192 to 1
Four of a kind	624	4,164 to 1
Full house	3,744	693 to 1
Flush	5,108	508 to 1
Straight	10,200	254 to 1
Three of a kind	54,912	46 to 1
Two pairs	123,552	20 to 1
One pair	1,098,240	1.37 to 1
High card	1,302,540	1 to 1
Total number of hands possible	2,598,960	

Bridge

Suit distribution in a hand	Odds against
4–4–3–2	4 to 1
5–4–2–2	8 to 1
6–4–2–1	20 to 1
7–4–1–1	254 to 1
8–4–1–0	2,211 to 1
13–0–0–0	158,753,389,899 to 1

Dice

(Chances with two dice and a single throw)

Total count	Odds against
2	35 to 1
3	17 to 1
4	11 to 1
5	8 to 1
6	31 to 5
7	5 to 1
8	31 to 5
9	8 to 1
10	11 to 1
11	17 to 1
12	35 to 1

See also **The National Lottery: The Odds,** p 335 and **The National Lottery: Thunderball Odds,** p 335.

Web Sites

A Dictionary of Units Requirements

`http://www.ex.ac.uk/cimt/dictunit/dictunit.htm`

Provides a summary of the units of measurement to be found in use around the world today (and a few of historical interest), together with conversion factors.

International Bureau of Weights and Measures

`http://www.bipm.fr/enus`

Official site of the body that was set up in Paris in 1875 and still coordinates world standards for mass, time, length, electric current, and other quantities.

National Weights and Measures Laboratory

`http://www.nwml.gov.uk/`

Official site of the body that was formed by the UK Weights and Measures Act of 1866 as the Standards Department of the Board of Trade.

Unit Converter

`http://www.webcom.com/legcysy/convert2/unitconvertIE.html`

Simple, but very effective, site that allows conversion from any of a wide variety of units to any other relevant unit.

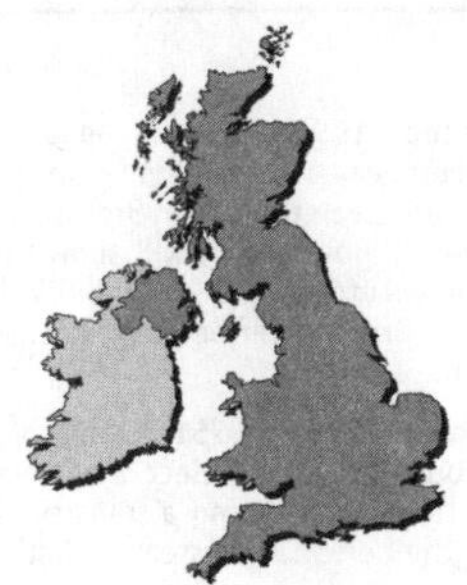

UNITED KINGDOM

The Year in Review

1 July 1999 Queen Elizabeth II formally opens the Scottish Parliament, the first Scottish legislature in nearly 200 years.

2 July 1999 Prime Minister Tony Blair and Irish prime minister Bertie Ahern announce a plan for the empowering of Northern Ireland's provincial government by 15 July, which would end the deadlock over the Good Friday Agreement of 1998.

4 July 1999 Members of the Orange Order, the largest Protestant organization in Northern Ireland, hold their annual parade in Drumcree, Portadown, Northern Ireland. The march ends peacefully, in contrast to many previous years when it has sparked off sectarian violence.

7 July 1999 The UK government resumes full diplomatic relations with Libya for the first time since the 1984 shooting of woman police constable Yvonne Fletcher outside the Libyan embassy in London.

14 July 1999 The European Commission votes to formally end its ban on beef exports from the UK after veterinary officials report that the epidemic of bovine spongiform encephalopathy (BSE) is under control.

14 July 1999 The Ulster Unionist Party rejects a peace plan proposed by Prime Minister Tony Blair and Irish prime minister Bertie Ahern, and refuses to attend the meeting scheduled for the following day to set up a new cabinet in Northern Ireland. The party's refusal to attend the meeting blocks the formation of the cabinet.

1 August 1999 The European Union (EU) lifts its ban on British beef, but subsequently the German health minister declares that the ban will remain in place in Germany.

9 August 1999 The Liberal Democrat party elects Charles Kennedy to succeed Paddy Ashdown as its new leader.

14 August 1999 Violence breaks out during Protestant parades through Catholic areas in Belfast, Lurgan, and Londonderry in Northern Ireland. Protesters attack riot police and burn vehicles.

15 August 1999 More than 10,000 people gather in Omagh, Northern Ireland, to commemorate the first anniversary of the bombing which killed 29 people in the town.

26 August 1999 The Metropolitan Police appoint John Stevens as Commissioner, to begin January 2000.

26 August 1999 Mo Mowlam, Northern Ireland secretary, declares that the IRA ceasefire is still intact despite continuing violent incidents.

28–29 August 1999 Five young men from county Tyrone leave Northern Ireland following death threats received from the IRA.

9 September 1999 Michael Portillo, prominent Conservative Party member, unexpectedly reveals in an interview that he had 'some homosexual experiences as a young person'.

11 September 1999 Melita Norwood, an Englishwoman from Bexleyheath, Kent, is revealed to have gathered intelligence for the USSR from the 1940s to the 1970s. The so-called 'granny spy' will not be prosecuted.

20–23 September 1999 The Liberal Democrat party holds its annual conference in Harrogate. The conference focuses on the party's commitment to remain separate and distinct from the ruling Labour Party and on developing stronger links with the EU.

October 1999 In a cabinet reshuffle, Peter Mandelson returns as minister for Northern Ireland.

1 October 1999 Lord Jeffrey Archer becomes the Conservative candidate for London mayor after winning the London members ballot.

4 October 1999 The Conservative Party conference opens in Blackpool. Party leader William Hague outlines five election pledges: more power for parents in schools, a guaranteed waiting time for National Health patients, a tax decrease, a guarantee that those who choose not to work would lose their unemployment benefit, and opposition to joining the European single currency.

6 October 1999 Former prime minister Lady Margaret Thatcher strongly expresses her support for former Chilean leader Augusto Pinochet, particularly in reference to his support for the UK in the 1982 war with Argentina over the Falkland Islands. She condemns efforts to extradite General Pinochet to Spain for trial on charges of torture and conspiracy.

12 October 1999 The Labour Party announces that its candidate for London mayor will be chosen by electoral college, and promotes Frank Dobson while attempting to block Ken Livingstone from standing.

12 October 1999 Peter Mandelson returns to the cabinet as minister for Northern Ireland ten months after his resignation over a mortgage scandal; Alan Milburn becomes secretary for health, replacing Frank Dobson; and Mo Mowlam, former Northern Ireland secretary, becomes cabinet enforcer and chancellor for the Duchy of Lancaster.

17 October 1999 The London Eye, a 151 m/435 ft ferris wheel erected in celebration of the millennium, is finally hauled into place after a series of setbacks, on the South Bank of the River Thames, opposite the Houses of Parliament in London.

25 October 1999 The House of Lords votes 221–81 to end the sitting and voting rights of hereditary peers. The measure includes a compromise that would allow 92 present hereditary peers to stay on during the interim period of reform.

November 1999 Main features of the Queen's Speech include announcements of a bill strengthening the 'right to roam' the countryside, a reintroduced bill lowering the age of consent for homosexuals to that of heterosexuals, and the freedom of information bill enabling public right of access to non-classified documents.

2 November 1999 Following negotiations at the European Commission in Brussels, agriculture secretary Nick Brown announces that the UK government will allow the French government to reopen an inquiry into the safety of British beef before it decides to lift the ban.

5 November 1999 The 751 hereditary peers in the House of Lords elect 75 members to retain their seats during a transitional phase before the hereditary system is abolished.

8 November 1999 In a final act of defiance before the majority of the hereditary peers in Parliament lose their voting privileges, the hereditary peers vote against a welfare reform bill, sending it back to the Commons.

16 November 1999 Ulster Unionist leader David Trimble and Sinn Fein president Gerry Adams offer conciliatory statements on the issue of IRA arms decommissioning in their talks with US ex-senator George Mitchell in Belfast, putting them a step closer to reaching a compromise on a power-sharing government in Northern Ireland.

18 November 1999 Leftwing politician Ken Livingstone makes the Labour Party shortlist for its candidate for mayor of London, despite lack of support from the party's leaders.

18 November 1999 Prime Minister Tony Blair announces that his wife Cherie, 45, is pregnant with their fourth child.

20 November 1999 Conservative candidate Jeffrey Archer leaves the mayoral race after admitting perjury. He is replaced as candidate by Steve Norris.

26 November 1999 Conservative politician Michael Portillo is elected Member of Parliament for Kensington and Chelsea.

27 November 1999 The Ulster Unionist Council in Northern Ireland votes 480–329 to support the creation of a power-sharing government in the province, including members representing Sinn Fein, the first such government for 25 years.

29 November 1999 Northern Ireland's main political parties select the area's first ever all-inclusive government, beginning with 12 ministers in a power-sharing executive. David Trimble is first minister and Seamus Mallon is deputy first minister. Former IRA chief of staff Martin McGuinness is minister for education.

30 November 1999 Agricultural minister Nick Brown announces an end to the ban on British beef on the bone.

December 1999 In announcing the largest public safety operation ever mounted in the UK, the Metropolitan Police says it plans to put 12,000 officers on duty in London, where a crowd of 3.5 million are expected on New Year's Eve.

2 December 1999 Northern Ireland's first all-inclusive power-sharing cabinet meets for the first time, in Belfast. Irish prime minister Bertie Ahern signs away articles two and three of the Irish constitution, giving up his country's territorial claim to Northern Ireland.

8 December 1999 Sinn Fein president Gerry Adams finds surveillance equipment hidden in the car he uses to meet IRA leaders and demands an explanation from Prime Minister Tony Blair. A government spokesman claims that the device was planted to protect Adams from dissident republicans as well as for tracking him.

17 December 1999 The two-year government ban on the sale of beef on the bone is lifted by Nick Brown, minister of agriculture, fisheries, and food.

30 December 1999 The London Eye millennium ferris wheel fails to open to the public as planned, due to a problem with a clutch device in one of its 32 capsules.

1 January 2000 The Millennium Dome in Greenwich, London, opens to the public, and is scheduled to remain open throughout 2000. Some 12,500 people visit it on the opening day.

January 2000 The Blair government comes under political fire as Labour peer Lord Winston criticizes the health system, the new freedom of information bill is considered too weak, and there is general outcry over plans to repeal Section 28, legislation banning the promotion of homosexuality by local authorities.

3 January 2000 The Millennium Commission launches an internal inquiry into why visitors to the Millennium Dome were forced to queue for hours on New Year's Eve and on subsequent days.

12 January 2000 The Neill Report from the Committee on Standards and Public Life attempts to encourage transparency in the financial affairs of political parties and the government. Its recommendations include making bribery of MPs a criminal offence and discouraging patronage and 'cronyism'.

20 January 2000 The Wakeham Royal Commission report on reform of the House of Lords is published, recommending that the chamber is composed mainly of appointed members, with a minority of elected members, gradually replacing life peers. No new name is proposed for the House.

1 February 2000 Conservative leader William Hague announces a surprise reshuffle of his top party leaders. He sacks John Redwood as shadow environment spokesman, replacing him with management consultant Archie Norman, and names Michael Portillo as shadow chancellor.

1 February 2000 The London Eye ferris wheel opens, delayed by a month owing to technical problems. The giant ferris wheel was designed by David Marks and cost £35 million to build.

6 February 2000 A bomb explodes outside a hotel in Irvinestown, County Fermanagh, Northern Ireland. A telephoned warning from the Continuity IRA, who claims responsibility, enables the area to be evacuated. No injuries are reported.

9 February 2000 First secretary of the Welsh Assembly, Alun Michael, is forced to resign as he faces a vote of no confidence in Wales. Cardiff West MP Rhodri Morgan replaces him.

11 February 2000 The UK government suspends Northern Ireland's new power-sharing government after the IRA fails to begin decommissioning weapons.

20 February 2000 The Labour Party nominates former health minister Frank Dobson as its candidate for forthcoming elections for mayor of London. The nomination is controversial because through the complex electoral representation system he was able to narrowly beat Ken Livingstone, the popular favourite.

March 2000 Controversy rages over political asylum and immigration issues, with Home Secretary Jack Straw calling for an overhaul of the 1951 United Nations Convention on the Status of Refugees, and announcing 'zero tolerance' for asylum seekers begging with children. Plans to disperse refugees around the country are postponed.

March 2000 Extradition proceedings against General Augusto Pinochet are abandoned by Home Secretary Jack Straw on the grounds that Pinochet is medically unfit to stand trial. Pinochet leaves after a costly 17-month stay in the UK, and his apparent sprightliness upon return to Chile causes outrage among human rights groups.

21 March 2000 Chancellor Gordon Brown releases the budget for 2000. He announces a £2 billion boost for the National Health Service (NHS) and an extra £1 billion for schools.

April 2000 Russian president Vladimir Putin meets Prime Minister Tony Blair in London, on his first official visit to the West since being elected in March.

3 April 2000 Labour MP Ken Livingstone is expelled from his party for standing as an independent against Labour's official candidate for London mayor, Frank Dobson.

19 April 2000 In a controversial verdict, English farmer Tony Martin is found guilty of murder for shooting 16-year-old Fred Barras, who was trying to burgle his isolated farmhouse.

27 April 2000 Conservative politician Michael Heseltine announces that he will stand down from the Commons at the next election, after 34 years as an MP.

May 2000 Anti-globalization protesters smash up a McDonald's restaurant in London and deface a statue of Winston Churchill and war memorial.

May 2000 The UK government admits that 30,000 acres of land have been accidentally planted with seed contaminated by a proportion of genetically modified seed from Canada.

4 May 2000 Ken Livingstone easily wins the election for London mayor as an independent candidate.

21 May 2000 Tony Blair and his wife Cherie celebrate the birth of Leo, their fourth child. The prime minister's intention to take time off to be with his family sparks a debate on paternity leave.

June 2000 Minister for the Cabinet Office Mo Mowlam provokes controversy and a rebuke from Buckingham Palace by her comments that the Royal family should move out of their palaces.

7 June 2000 Prime Minister Tony Blair is jeered and slow-handclapped by hundreds of women while addressing a 10,000-strong audience of the Women's Institute at their annual conference in Wembley Arena in London.

12 June 2000 The £18.2 million Millennium Bridge in London, which spans the Thames from St Paul's Cathedral to the Tate Modern, and is designed to appear as a 'blade of light', is closed for an indefinite period because of instability and swaying. Nearly 100,000 people, ten times more than anticipated, crossed the bridge on its opening day.

12 June 2000 The seven-month Burns inquiry into foxhunting concludes that hunting 'seriously compromises the welfare of the fox' but that up to 8,000 jobs could be lost if a ban was in place. Nevertheless, it is anticipated that most MPs will vote for a complete ban.

17 June 2000 Prince William, the heir to the throne, reaches the age of 18; appeals are made for the press to continue to respect his privacy, at least while he finishes his A-level exams.

18 June 2000 Jamie Andrew, a Scottish climber who lost both hands and both legs through frostbite after being trapped in a blizzard on the French Alps, successfully climbs Ben Nevis, the first quadruple amputee to do so.

19 June 2000 A group of 58 Chinese men and women attempting to enter the UK illegally are found dead at Dover docks in the sealed container of a Dutch lorry. Two survivors are treated for dehydration and trauma and questioned by police, and the driver is later charged with manslaughter.

23 June 2000 Prime Minister Tony Blair supports his millionaire friend and advisor Lord Levy who faces accusations of irregular financial affairs after it emerged that he paid only £5,000 in tax last year. Despite fighting to prevent the publication of his tax records, Lord Levy claims he has 'absolutely nothing to hide'.

25 June 2000 Home Secretary Jack Straw insists that most of the Kosovan refugees still in the UK no longer have any basis for asylum and must go back. The refugees cannot be forcibly repatriated until they have exhausted appeal processes, however.

27 June 2000 Transport minister John Prescott announces new initiatives for the UK's canal system, including creating a national grid for drinking water, laying fibre-optic cables under towpaths, and conveying waste to incinerators. Recognizing the potential of the canals, he says, will also help revitalize cities.

28 June 2000 Peter Mandelson reveals the prime minister's plans to change UK general elections to resemble the Australian system, so that voters list candidates for MP in order of preference. The new alternative vote (AV) system is likely to improve the standing of the Liberal Democrats at the expense of the Conservative Party.

28 June 2000 Trade and industry minister Helen Liddell says that the government will hold a referendum on the single currency after the next general election.

30 June 2000 A children's playground and six-mile walkway are opened in Kensington Gardens as a memorial to Diana, Princess of Wales. No member of the royal family attends the ceremony.

Geography

Countries of the UK

(– = not applicable.)

Country	Area sq km	Area sq mi	Population (1998 est)	Population density (persons per sq km)	Capital
England	130,410	50,351	49,495,000	380	London
Scotland	78,789	30,420	5,120,000	65	Edinburgh
Wales	20,758	8,015	2,933,000	141	Cardiff
Northern Ireland	14,160	5,467	1,689,000	119	Belfast
Total	244,101	94,248	59,237,000	243	–

Highest Points in the UK

Highest point	Region	Height m	Height ft
England			
Scafell Pike	Cumbria	977	3,206
Sca Fell	Cumbria	963	3,162
Helvellyn	Cumbria	955	3,113
Skiddaw	Cumbria	931	3,054
Bow Fell	Cumbria	902	2,960
Great Gable	Cumbria	898	2,949
Cross Fell	Cumbria	893	2,930
Pillar	Cumbria	892	2,927
Esk Pike	Cumbria	884	2,903
Fairfield	Cumbria	872	2,863
Wales			
Snowdon	Gwynedd	1,085	3,560
Carnedd Llewelyn	Gwynedd/Conwy	1,062	3,484
Carnedd Dafydd	Conwy	1,044	3,426
Glyder Fawr	Gwynedd/Conwy	999	3,279
Glyder Fach	Conwy	994	3,262
Y Garn	Gwynedd/Conwy	946	3,104
Foel-fras	Gwynedd/Conwy	942	3,091
Elidyr-fawr	Gwynedd	923	3,029
Tryfan	Conwy	917	3,010
Aran Fawddwy	Gwynedd	905	2,970
Scotland			
Ben Nevis[1]	Highland	1,344	4,409
Ben Macdhui	Aberdeenshire/Moray	1,309	4,296
Braeriach	Aberdeenshire/Highland	1,296	4,252
Cairn Toul	Aberdeenshire	1,292	4,241
Cairn Gorm	Moray	1,244	4,084
Aonach Beag	Highland	1,236	4,054
Carn Mor Dearg	Highland	1,222	4,012
Aonach Mor	Highland	1,218	3,999
Ben Lawers	Perth and Kinross	1,214	3,984
Beinn a'Bhuird	Aberdeenshire	1,196	3,924
Northern Ireland			
Slieve Donard	Down	852	2,796
Slieve Commedagh	Down	766	2,512
Slieve Bearnagh	Down	730	2,394
Slieve Meelbeg	Down	704	2,310
Slieve Lamagan	Down	703	2,306
Slieve Bingian	Down	685	2,249
Sawel Mountain	Tyrone	683	2,240
Slieve Meelmore	Down	682	2,237
Slieve Muck	Down	670	2,198
Shanlieve	Down	626	2,053

[1] Ben Nevis is the highest point in Scotland and the highest point in the UK.

Physical Features of the UK: Key Facts

Northernmost point on mainland Britain Dunnet Head in northeast Scotland

Southernmost point on mainland Britain Lizard Point in Cornwall, England

Highest point Ben Nevis in western Scotland, 7 km/4 mi southeast of Fort William; height 1,344 m/4,409 ft

Longest river River Severn, which rises in Ceredigion, west Wales, and flows east and then south, finally forming a long estuary leading into the Bristol Channel; length 354 km/220 mi

Largest lake Lough Neagh in Northern Ireland, 25 km/15 mi west of Belfast; area 396 sq km/153 sq mi

Deepest lake Loch Morar in the Highlands of Scotland; maximum depth 310 m/1,017 ft

Highest waterfall Eas Coul Aulin in northern Scotland; height 201 m/658 ft

Deepest cave Ogof Ffynnon Ddu Wales; maximum depth 308 m/1,010 ft

Closest point to mainland Europe Dover, southeast England, on the coast of the English Channel, 34 km/21 mi from Calais, France

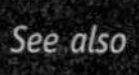
See also  **UK Climate and Weather**, pp 623–625;  **Areas of Outstanding Natural Beauty and National Scenic Areas in the UK**, p 640.

Largest Islands in the UK

Name	Location	Area sq km	Area sq mi
Lewis with Harris	Outer Hebrides	2,225	859
Skye	Inner Hebrides	1,666	643
Mainland, Shetland	Shetland Islands	967	373
Mull	Inner Hebrides	899	347
Anglesey	northwest coast of Wales	714	276
Islay	Inner Hebrides	614	237
Mainland, Orkney	Orkney Islands	536	207
Arran	Firth of Clyde	435	168
Wight, Isle of	south coast of England	380	147
Jura	Inner Hebrides	370	143
North Uist	Outer Hebrides	351	136
South Uist	Outer Hebrides	332	128
Yell	Shetland Islands	214	83
Hoy	Orkney Islands	137	53
Bute	Firth of Clyde	120	46
Unst	Shetland Islands	120	46
Rum	Inner Hebrides	110	42
Sheppey	north coast of Kent	94	36
Benbecula	Outer Hebrides	93	36
Barra	Outer Hebrides	90	35
Tiree	Inner Hebrides	75	29
Raasay	Inner Hebrides	60	24
Westray	Orkney Islands	48	19
South Ronaldsay	Orkney Islands	46	18
Sanday	Orkney Islands	40	15
Holy Island	northwest coast of Wales	39	15
Fetlar	Shetland Islands	36	14
Stronsay	Orkney Islands	35	14
Bressay	Shetland Islands	28	11
Hayling Island	coast of Hampshire	27	10
Shapinsay	Orkney Islands	26	10
Eigg	Orkney Islands	23	9

The United Kingdom of Great Britain and Northern Ireland
Shetland Islands
ATLANTIC OCEAN
Orkney Islands
Kirkwall
Thurso
Wick
North Sea
Outer Hebrides
Inner Hebrides
Inverness
Aberdeen
Dee
Mallaig
SCOTLAND
Tay
Dundee
Oban
Glasgow
Edinburgh
Clyde
UNITED KINGDOM
Tweed
Londonderry
NORTHERN IRELAND
Belfast
Dumfries
Carlisle
Newcastle upon Tyne
Middlesbrough
Isle of Man
Leeds
Aire
Kingston upon Hull
Irish Sea
Manchester
Liverpool
Sheffield
Holyhead
Dublin
REPUBLIC OF IRELAND
Caernarfon
Derby
Nottingham
Trent
Leicester
Gt Ouse
Norwich
Severn
Birmingham
Nene
Aberystwyth
Cambridge
WALES
Fishguard
Cork
ENGLAND
Oxford
Swansea
Thames
London
Cardiff
Bristol
Dover
Celtic Sea
Southampton
Brighton
Exeter
Plymouth
English Channel
Isles of Scilly
Channel Islands (UK)
FRANCE
0 50 mi
0 100 km

Longest Rivers in the UK

Name	Source	Outlet	Length km	Length mi
Severn	Ceredigion/Powys border	Bristol Channel	354	220
Thames	Gloucestershire	North Sea	346	215
Trent	Staffordshire/ Cheshire border	Humber estuary	297	185
Great Ouse	Northamptonshire	The Wash	230	143
Wye	Ceredigion	River Severn	215	135
Tay	Highland	Firth of Tay	188	117
Nene	Northamptonshire	The Wash	161	100
Clyde	South Lanarkshire	Firth of Clyde	158	98
Spey	Highland	Moray Firth	157	98
Tweed	Scottish Borders	North Sea	156	97
Dee (Scotland)	Aberdeenshire	North Sea	137	85
Usk	Carmarthenshire/ Powys border	Bristol Channel	137	85
Avon (Upper Avon or Warwickshire Avon)	Northamptonshire	River Severn	136	85
Don	Aberdeenshire	North Sea	133	83
Tees	Cumbria	North Sea	130	80
Witham	Leicestershire	The Wash	129	80
Bann	Co Down	Atlantic	122	76
Avon (Bristol Avon)	Gloucestershire	River Severn	121	75
Ribble	North Yorkshire	Irish Sea	120	75
Teifi	Ceredigion	Cardigan Bay	118	73
Dee (Wales)	Bala Lake, Gwynedd	Irish Sea	112	70
Mersey	Stockport, Greater Manchester	Irish Sea	112	70
Nith	East Ayrshire	Solway Firth	112	70
Towy (Welsh Tywi)	Ceredigion/Powys border	Carmarthen Bay	111	69
Welland	Leicestershire	The Wash	110	68
Aire	North Yorkshire	River Ouse	110	68
Wear	Durham	North Sea	107	67
Eden	Cumbria	Solway Firth	104	65
Deveron	Moray	North Sea	100	63
Tamar	Cornwall	Plymouth Sound	97	60
Swale	North Yorkshire	River Ure	97	60

See also  **Geography,** pp 126–131.

British Dependent Territories and Crown Dependencies

UK Crown Dependencies and British Dependent Territories: Introduction

Most of the one-time colonies of the old British Empire are now independent sovereign states and are members of the Commonwealth. Those parts of the old Empire which remain as British dependencies comprise tiny islands situated in Europe, the Caribbean, the South Atlantic, the Indian and Pacific Oceans, and the peninsula of Gibraltar. They enjoy varying degrees of autonomy, but all rely on the UK for defensive protection.

Crown dependencies

These comprise the Channel Islands and Isle of Man territories, which are in close proximity to, but do not form integral parts of, the UK. They are largely self-governing, with tax sovereignty and their own elected legislatures, but rely on the UK for their defence and international relations.

British dependent territories

These are territories situated overseas at a great distance from the UK and are remnants of the British Empire. Britain is responsible for the external affairs, defence, and internal security of each territory. To a varying extent, other matters are internal affairs and are the responsibility, typically, of a chief minister drawn from a largely elected assembly.

See also  **United Kingdom,** pp 257–258.

UK Crown Dependencies and British Dependent Territories

Name	Location	Date of first coming under British administration	Area (sq km/sq mi)	Population (1998 est)
UK crown dependencies				
Channel Islands[1]	Europe	1066	194/75	153,600
Isle of Man	Europe	1765	572/221	74,000
British dependent territories				
Anguilla	Caribbean	1650	96/37	11,100
Bermuda	Caribbean	1612	54/21	62,000
British Antarctic Territory	Antarctica	1908	1,810,000/700,000	uninhabited[2]
British Indian Ocean Territory	Indian Ocean	1965	60/23	uninhabited[2]
British Virgin Islands	Caribbean	1666	150/58	18,700
Cayman Islands	Caribbean	1670	260/100	37,700
Falkland Islands	South Atlantic	1765/1833	12,170/4,700	2,800
Gibraltar	Europe	1704	6/2	29,000
Montserrat	Caribbean	1632	100/39	4,000

(continued)

UK Crown Dependencies and British Dependent Territories *(continued)*

Name	Location	Date of first coming under British administration	Area (sq km/sq mi)	Population (1998 est)
Pitcairn Islands	Pacific	1790	36/14	50
St Helena and Dependencies	South Atlantic	1659	320/123	7,090
South Georgia and the South Sandwich Islands[3]	South Atlantic	1775	3,900/1,500	uninhabited[2]
Turks and Caicos Islands	Caribbean	1765	430/166	16,250

[1] Guernsey, Jersey, Alderney, and Sark.
[2] Except for scientific or military personnel.
[3] Dependencies of the Falkland Islands, 1908–85.

British Crown Dependencies and Dependent Territories: Tourist Offices

Anguilla Anguilla Tourist Board, 7 Westwood Road, London SW13 0LA; phone: (020) 8876 9025; fax: (020) 8876 2980

Bermuda Bermuda Tourism, 1 Battersea Church Road, London SW11 3LY, England; phone: (020) 7771 7001; fax: (020) 7771 7037; e-mail: bermudatourism@cibgroup.co.uk

British Virgin Islands British Virgin Islands Tourist Board, 54 Baker Street, London W1M 1DJ; phone: (020) 7240 4259; fax: (020) 7240 4270

Cayman Islands Cayman Islands Tourist Office, 6 Arlington Street, London SW1A 1RE; phone: (020) 7491 7771; fax: (020) 7409 7773; e-mail: info-uk@caymanislands.ky; Web site: www.caymanislands.ky

Falkland Islands Falkland House, 14 Broadway, London SW1H 0BH; phone: (020) 7222 2542; fax: (020) 7222 2375; e-mail: rep@figo.unet.com; Web site: www.falklands.gov.fk

Gibraltar Gibraltar Tourist Board, 179 Strand, London WC2R 1EH; phone: (020) 7836 0777; fax: (020) 7240 6612; e-mail: tourism@gibraltar.gi

Guernsey States Tourist Board, PO Box 23, Guernsey GY1 3AN, CI; phone: (01481) 723552; e-mail: enquiries@tourism.guernsey.net; Web site: www.guernseytourism.gov.gg

The Isle of Man Department of Tourism and Leisure Headquarters, Sea Terminal, Douglas, Isle of Man IM1 2RG; phone: (01624) 686801; fax: (01624 686800; e-mail: tourism@gov.im; Web site: www.gov.im/tourism

Jersey Jersey Tourism, Liberation Square, St Helier, Jersey JE1 1BB; phone: (01534) 500700; fax: (01534) 500899; e-mail: info@jtourism.com; Web site: www.jtourism.com

Montserrat Montserrat Tourist Board, PO Box 7, Plymouth, Montserrat, West Indies; phone: +1 (664) 491 2230/8730; fax: +1 (664) 491 7430; e-mail: mrattouristboard@candw.ag; Web site: http://innanen.com/montserrat/touristboard/index

Turks and Caicos Islands Turks and Caicos Tourist Board, 11645 Biscayne Boulevard, Suite 302, North Miami, FL 33181; phone: +1 (305) 891 4117; fax: +1 (305) 891 7096; Web site: www.turksandcaicostourism.com/main.htm

Pitcairn Islands Pitcairn Island Administration, PO Box 105, 696 Auckland, New Zealand; phone: +64 (9) 366 0186; fax: +64 (9) 366 0187; e-mail: pitcairn@iconz.co.nz

St Helena St Helena Tourist Office, Jamestown, St Helena; phone: +290 2158; fax: +290 2159; e-mail: StHelena.Tourism@atlantis.co.uk

The Commonwealth

Introduction

The Commonwealth is a free association of sovereign independent states that, almost universally, share a common heritage as former parts of the British Empire. The Commonwealth's 54 member countries, with a total population of 1.7 billion, comprise nearly a third of the world's population and include a mix of rich and poor, drawn from Europe, Africa, Asia, Oceania, and the Americas. Although 32 of its member states are republics, all accept Queen Elizabeth II as head of the Commonwealth.

Formation and principles

The Commonwealth has no formal constitution or charter. Its formation can be traced back to the 1931 Statute of Westminster, which linked together the self-governing 'white-settler' Dominions of Australia, Canada, Ireland, New Zealand, and South Africa with Britain. In the post-war period, the Commonwealth was transformed and expanded into a multiracial association and, under the Harare Commonwealth Declaration (1991), it has adopted the goals of advancing democracy, the rule of law, just and honest government, social justice, and the promotion of socio-economic development.

Membership

Only independent states may become members of the Commonwealth, but member states' dependencies, for example the British dependencies of Anguilla and the Cayman Islands, and the Australian dependencies of Christmas Island and Norfolk Island, participate in many Commonwealth activities and receive technical assistance. Some former British colonies, for example, Myanmar (Burma) and parts of the Middle East, chose not to join the Commonwealth members. However, Mozambique, which had never been a British colony, was allowed to enter, in 1995, as a special case as it is surrounded by Commonwealth states. The Republic of Ireland left the Commonwealth in 1949, as did South Africa (1961–94), Fiji (1987–97), and Pakistan (1972–89). Nigeria (1995–99), Pakistan (from October 1999), and Sierra Leone (1997–99) have had their membership suspended, following military coups.

Funding

Members pay subscriptions, which are assessed on a scale related to UN subscriptions. Tuvalu, as a particularly small and poor state, is a 'special member'. It pays a voluntary contribution and does not participate in the Heads of Government meeting.

Organization

The Commonwealth has a London-based permanent Secretariat (established in 1965), headed by the secretary general, E Chukwuemeka Anyaoku of Nigeria, with around 350 staff drawn from a wide range of (currently 25) member countries. However, unlike the United Nations (UN)

Introduction (*continued*)

for example, members are not bound by rigid contractual obligations. Commonwealth heads of government meet every two years to discuss international affairs and areas of cooperation, with decisions being reached by consensus and set out in a communique. Finance ministers meet annually. A Commonwealth Fund for Technical Cooperation was formed in 1971 to enable specialists from developing countries to assist the development of developing member nations. Additionally, professionals, interest groups, and sports people are linked by several hundred Commonwealth non-governmental organizations, and the most developed members (Australia, Britain, Canada, and New Zealand) channel around 30% of their overseas aid to assist other member states.

In 1999, a pamphlet produced by the Foreign Policy Centre, a think-tank with close links to Britain's Labour government, floated the ideas of: moving the Commonwealth's headquarters to Delhi, India, or Lagos, Nigeria; creating a revolving 'Commonwealth Presidency', to represent the organization at international summits; and imposing tough membership criteria based on democracy and human-rights records.

The Commonwealth: Key Facts

Date established 1931

Founding members Anguilla, Australia, Bermuda, British Antarctic Territory, British Virgin Islands, Canada, Cayman Islands, Channel Islands, Cook Islands, Falkland Islands, Falkland Islands Dependency, Gibraltar, Isle of Man, Montserrat, New Zealand, Niue, Norfolk Island, Pitcairn Islands, Tokelau, Turks and Caicos Islands, St Helena, UK

Address Commonwealth Secretariat, Marlborough House, Pall Mall, London SW1 5HX, UK; phone: (020) 7839 3411; fax: (020) 7930 0827; e-mail: info@commonwealth.int

Web site www.thecommonwealth.org

The Commonwealth

Country	Date joined
In Africa	
Botswana	1966
Cameroon	1995
Gambia	1965
Ghana	1957
Kenya	1963
Lesotho	1966
Malawi	1964
Mauritius	1968
Mozambique	1995
Namibia	1990
Nigeria	1960[1]
Seychelles	1976
Sierra Leone	1961[2]
South Africa	1910[3]
Swaziland	1968
Tanzania	1961
Uganda	1962
Zambia	1964
Zimbabwe	1980
In the Americas	
Antigua and Barbuda	1981
Bahamas	1973
Barbados	1966
Belize	1982
Canada	1931
Dominica	1978
Grenada	1974
Guyana	1966
Jamaica	1962
St Kitts and Nevis	1983
St Lucia	1979
St Vincent and the Grenadines	1979
Trinidad and Tobago	1962
In Asia	
Bangladesh	1972
Brunei	1984
India	1947
Malaysia	1957
Maldives	1982
Pakistan	1947[4]
Singapore	1965
Sri Lanka	1948
In Australasia and the Pacific	
Australia	1931
Fiji Islands	1970[5]
Kiribati	1979
Nauru	1968
New Zealand	1931
Papua New Guinea	1975
Samoa	1970
Solomon Islands	1978
Tonga	1970
Tuvalu	1978
Vanuatu	1980
In Europe	
Cyprus	1961
Malta	1964

[1] Suspended 1995–99. [2] Suspended 1997. [3] Withdrew from membership 1961 and readmitted 1994. [4] Left 1972 and rejoined 1989. Suspended in 1999. [5] Left 1987 and rejoined 1997.

Constitution and Important Legislation

The UK's Unwritten Constitution

The UK does not have a single basic written document that can be called its constitution. This makes it one of the few democracies to have an unwritten, or uncodified, constitution: Israel and New Zealand are two other such states. However, although the UK lacks a formal constitutional document, there are Acts of Parliament, along with an accumulation of customs, precedents, and accepted conventions, which form the basis of its constitution. The most notable is the 1689 Bill of Rights, which established the legislative supremacy of Parliament and from which the rest of the evolutionary constitution developed. In more recent years, the legislation restricting the powers of the Lords (the Parliament Acts of 1911 and 1949) and widening the franchise (a succession of Reform Acts) can be regarded as constitutional amendments. So can the 1997–99 acts that set up Welsh and Northern Ireland assemblies and the Scottish parliament, and abolished the hereditary elements in the House of Lords.

Cabinet government, which is at the heart of the political system, is founded on convention, as is the relationship between the monarch, as head of state, and the prime minister, as head of government. The UK's entry into the European Community in 1973, and subsequent European Union (EU) legislation, such as the Maastrict Treaty (1993) and Amsterdam Treaty (1997), and the incorporation of the European Convention of Human Rights, have resulted in a loss of a measure of UK parliamentary sovereignty. In certain circumstances, the legislation of the EU as a whole can override domestic legislation.

Magna Carta, 1215

A charter granted by King John at Runnymede on 15 June 1215 that placed certain limitations on royal power. It defined the barons' obligations to the monarch, confirmed the liberties of the English church, and opposed the arbitrary application of justice. It was originally proposed to the English barons in 1213 by the archbishop of Canterbury, Stephen Langton, as a reply to the king's demands for excessive feudal dues and attacks on the privileges of the church. The charter was reissued with changes in 1216, 1217, and 1225. As feudalism declined, the Magna Carta lost its significance, and under the Tudors was almost forgotten. During the 17th century it was rediscovered and reinterpreted by the Parliamentary party as a democratic document. Four original copies exist: one each in Salisbury and Lincoln cathedrals and two in the British Library in London.

Petition of Right, 1628

A petition drawn up by Edward Coke (former Lord Chief Justice of England) and accepted by Charles I in 1628, declaring illegal: taxation without parliamentary consent, imprisonment without trial, billeting of soldiers on private persons, and use of martial law. When Parliament challenged Charles over military funding in 1629, he dissolved Parliament, imprisoned its leaders, and ruled without Parliament until his execution in 1640.

Habeas Corpus, 1679

A law requiring that a prisoner be brought before a court to determine whether the detention is lawful. It was embodied in the English Habeas Corpus Act 1679 by Anthony Ashley Cooper, 1st Earl of Shaftesbury. The main principles were adopted in the US Constitution. The Scottish equivalent is the Wrongous Imprisonment Act 1701.

English Bill of Rights Act, 1689

The nearest approach to a written constitution that the UK possesses. It made illegal the suspension of laws by royal authority without Parliament's consent; the power to dispense with laws; the establishment of special courts of law; levying money by royal prerogative without Parliament's consent; and the maintenance of a standing army in peacetime without Parliament's consent. It also asserted a right to petition the sovereign, freedom of parliamentary elections, freedom of speech in parliamentary debates, and the necessity of frequent Parliaments.

Its provisions, where applicable, were incorporated in the US Constitution ratified in 1788.

Act of Settlement, 1701

A law passed during the reign of King William III to ensure a Protestant succession to the throne by allowing only descendants of Princess Sophia the Electress of Hanover (granddaughter of James I) to succeed. The act excluded the Roman Catholic descendants of James II. Elizabeth II still reigns under this act.

Triennial and Septennial Acts

Acts affecting the length of Parliament and the frequency of its meetings.

1641 Triennial Act required that Parliament should meet every three years, for at least 50 days.

1664 Triennial Act reinstated the act of 1641, which had fallen into abeyance.

1694 Triennial Act stipulated that Parliament should meet at least once every three years and not last more than three years.

1716 Septennial Act extended the term of a Parliament from three to seven years. It was superseded by the Parliament Act 1911 which reduced the term to five years.

Acts of Union

Several statutes that accomplished the joining of England with Wales (1536), England and Wales with Scotland (1707), and Great Britain with Ireland (1801).

Act of Union of 1536

Passed during the reign of King Henry VIII, this Act formally united England and Wales. By its terms, the Welsh Marches, estates held for centuries by semi-independent Marcher lords, became several new counties or were added to older counties. Counties and boroughs in Wales were granted representation in the English Parliament.

Act of Union of 1707

Passed by the parliaments of England and Scotland, this Act created the Kingdom of Great Britain. Although Scotland retained its judicial system and its Presbyterian church, its parliament was joined with that of England. The crowns of the two countries had been united in 1603 when James Stuart (James VI of Scotland) succeeded Elizabeth I as James I of England, but the kingdoms otherwise remained separate.

Act of Union of 1801

This Act joined the Kingdom of Great Britain and all of Ireland into the United Kingdom of Great Britain and Ireland. The act was revoked when the Irish Free State was constituted in 1922.

Scotland, Wales, and Northern Ireland Acts, 1998

The Scotland, Wales, and Northern Ireland Acts created a directly elected Scottish Parliament, with restricted tax-raising powers and devolved power to legislate on education, the environment, health, law enforcement, and the environment, and an elected Welsh Assembly, with some power to govern local affairs and influence distribution of the government budget for Wales. It also devolved a wide range of executive and legislative powers to an elected, power-sharing Northern Ireland Assembly.

Reform Acts

UK acts of Parliament that extended voting rights and redistributed parliamentary seats, also known as Representation of the People Acts.

1832 Reform Act abolished pocket and rotten boroughs (English parliamentary constituencies that returned members to Parliament in spite of having a small numbers of electors, thus leading to an unrepresentative House), redistributed seats on a more equitable basis in the counties, and formed some new boroughs. The franchise was extended to male householders in property worth £10 a year or more in the boroughs and to owners of freehold property worth £2 a year, £10 copyholders, or £50 leaseholders in the counties.

1867 (Second) Reform Act redistributed seats from corrupt and small boroughs to the counties and large urban areas. It also extended the franchise in boroughs to adult male heads of households, and in counties to males who owned, or held on long leases, land worth £5 a year, or who occupied land worth £12 on which they paid poor rates.

1884 (Third) Reform Act extended the franchise to male agricultural labourers.

1918 Representation of The People Act gave the vote to men over the age of 21 and women over the age of 30.

1928 Representation of The People Act extended the vote to women to over the age of 21.

1948 Representation of The People Act abolished the right, held by certain individuals, to have more than one vote.

1969 Representation of The People Act reduced the minimum age of voting to 18.

House of Lords Act, 1999

This act abolished the hereditary element in the House of Lords, with 92 hereditary peers, chosen by their fellow hereditaries, being allowed to remain as 're-tread' life peers.

Parliament Acts

The Parliament Act of 1911 A statute which prohibited the House of Lords from interfering with financial legislation passed by the House of Commons and abolished the power of the Lords to reject other types of legislation passed by the Commons, restricting them to delaying it for up to two years. The law also reduced the maximum life of a parliament from seven years to five. The act was introduced after the Lords rejected Lloyd George's radical People's Budget of 1909. It was fiercely resisted by the Lords and only received their assent when George V agreed that if necessary he would create sufficient Liberal peers to force it through.

The Parliament Act of 1949 This act further limited the period the Lords could delay legislation to one year.

Recent Important Legislation in the UK

Representation of the People Act
Enacted on 9 March 2000, this Act provides for replacement of annual registers with continuous or rolling electoral registration. This will enable voters to register at any time of the year, with the aim of cutting the maximum wait to get back on to a register, after for example moving home, from 18 months to about six weeks. It also seeks to make it easier for the homeless, remand prisoners, mental patients and service personnel to register as electors. It has provided for pilots of new electoral procedures, bringing them in line with changes in modern technology and people's lifestyles, with the aim of improving voter turnout. These included: electronic voting and counting; opening poll booths for longer hours and at weekends; freepost postal voting for all electors; allowing voting in supermarkets, railway stations and other public areas outside voters' immediate neighbourhood; and taking 'mobile poll booths' into homes for the elderly and hospitals. These pilot tests were carried out in the May 2000 local elections.

Human Rights Act
This Act meets the government's manifesto commitment to incorporate rights and freedoms guaranteed by the European Convention on Human Rights (ECHR) into United Kingdom domestic law. In force from 2 October 2000, people who believe their human rights have been violated by public authorities can now have their case judged in UK courts rather than having to take the case to the European Court in Strasbourg. All public authorities, including the courts, are under a statutory duty to act in a way compatible with Convention rights; and ministers, when introducing a government bill, are required to make a statement on compatibility of the bill's provisions. The Law Lords, within the House of Lords, now have a raised profile in issuing final judgement on controversial cases and in potentially overturning government decisions and regulations where they conflict with the ECHR. The UK ratified the ECHR in 1951 and since 1966 UK citizens have had a right of access to the Strasbourg Court.

Data Protection Act
Enacted in 1998, this Act came into force on 1 March 2000. It brings the requirements of the 1995 European Community Data Protection Directive into UK law, extending citizens' rights to include some manual records. Individuals' rights to claim compensation for breaches of the act have been enhanced and there is a specific right to prevent personal data being used for direct marketing purposes. The Data Protection Registrar has been renamed the Data Protection Commissioner, with wider powers of enforcement.

Freedom of Information Bill
Introduced to Parliament in November 1999, the Freedom of Information Bill is intended to give people a general statutory right of access to information held by a wide range of public authorities, subject to certain conditions and exemptions. It requires public authorities to consider disclosing information in the public interest even where the information is exempt, and adopt schemes for the publication of information. Bodies covered by the bill are central government, parliament, the police, schools and the National Health Service.

Political Parties, Elections, and Referendums Bill
Introduced to parliament in December 1999, this bill is a response to the recommendation, in October 1998, of the Committee on Standards in Public Life, chaired by Lord Neill, which had investigated concerns about the foreign and secretive funding of political parties that had led to accusations of 'political sleaze'. The bill proposes expenditure limits for a UK-wide referendum. Other key proposals include: the qualifying period for an overseas voter to be reduced from 20 years to 10 years; companies be required to obtain prior shareholder approval before making donations to political parties; parties be required to disclose, each quarter, the source and amount of national political donations above £5,000 and local constituency gifts above £1,000; parties' acceptance of donations made from outside the UK and from trust funds be prohibited; and national limits be set on election spending by political parties and third parties, including a maximum of £19.8 million for a party contesting all 659 parliamentary seats. (In the year preceding the 1997 general election, the Conservatives spent £28 million and Labour £26 million).

See also **Acts of Parliament and How a Bill Becomes Law**, p 44.

National Government

National Government in the UK: Introduction

The UK is a unitary state, with a parliamentary form of executive government, based on a prime minister and cabinet. In recent years, a range of powers, including some legislative, have been devolved by the UK Parliament to a Scottish parliament and Northern Ireland and Welsh assemblies.

A hereditary monarch is head of state but has a largely ceremonial function. The monarch's approval is necessary for the enactment of laws passed by Parliament, but, in practice, royal assent has never been withheld in modern times. The monarch also formally appoints the prime minister, but this is done on the basis of support in the House of Commons. Only where there is a 'hung parliament', with no single party or coalition enjoying majority, does the monarch have significant political power in deciding whom to invite to form a government, or whether to dissolve Parliament and call fresh elections to the Commons. Real executive power lies with the prime minister and the cabinet of 20 or so ministers, which he or she chooses and which work in conjunction with the professional civil service.

The Prime Minister

During the 19th century, the prime minister occupied the position of 'first among equals'. However, with the growth in the departmental responsibilities of ministers, and the personalization of election campaigns, the role of the prime minister as a broad policy-making and coordinating figure has been extended. In addition, successive prime ministers have built up an ever-growing staff of advisers, making the office increasingly presidential – particularly so under the current incumbent, Tony Blair. The prime minister also represents the nation internationally, for example at summit conferences. However, the prime minister, as leader of the party in power, is directly accountable to his or her fellow MPs and can be overthrown by them if he or she loses their confidence. This occurred with Margaret Thatcher in 1990.

Prime Ministers of Great Britain and the UK

Term	Name	Party
1721–42	Robert Walpole[1]	Whig
1742–43	Spencer Compton, Earl of Wilmington	Whig
1743–54	Henry Pelham	Whig
1754–56	Thomas Pelham-Holles, 1st Duke of Newcastle	Whig
1756–57	William Cavendish, 4th Duke of Devonshire	Whig
1757–62	Thomas Pelham-Holles, 1st Duke of Newcastle	Whig
1762–63	John Stuart, 3rd Earl of Bute	Tory
1763–65	George Grenville	Whig
1765–66	Charles Watson Wentworth, 2nd Marquess of Rockingham	Whig
1766–68	William Pitt, 1st Earl of Chatham	Tory
1768–70	Augustus Henry Fitzroy, 3rd Duke of Grafton	Whig
1770–82	Frederick North, Lord North[2]	Tory
1782	Charles Watson Wentworth, 2nd Marquess of Rockingham	Whig
1782–83	William Petty-Fitzmaurice, 2nd Earl of Shelburne[3]	Whig
1783	William Henry Cavendish-Bentinck, 3rd Duke of Portland	Whig
1783–1801	William Pitt, The Younger	Tory
1801–04	Henry Addington	Tory
1804–06	William Pitt, The Younger	Tory
1806–07	William Wyndham Grenville, 1st Baron Grenville	Whig
1807–09	William Henry Cavendish-Bentinck, 3rd Duke of Portland	Whig
1809–12	Spencer Perceval	Tory
1812–27	Robert Banks Jenkinson, 2nd Earl of Liverpool	Tory
1827	George Canning	Tory
1827–28	Frederick John Robinson, 1st Viscount Goderich	Tory
1828–30	Arthur Wellesley, 1st Duke of Wellington	Tory
1830–34	Charles Grey, 2nd Earl Grey	Whig
1834	William Lamb, 2nd Viscount Melbourne	Whig
1834	Arthur Wellesley, 1st Duke of Wellington	Tory
1834–35	Sir Robert Peel, 2nd Baronet	Tory
1835–41	William Lamb, 2nd Viscount Melbourne	Whig
1841–46	Sir Robert Peel, 2nd Baronet	Conservative
1846–52	John Russell, Lord Russell	Whig-Liberal
1852	Edward Geoffrey Stanley, 14th Earl of Derby	Conservative
1852–55	George Hamilton-Gordon, 4th Earl of Aberdeen	Peelite
1855–58	Henry John Temple, 3rd Viscount Palmerston	Liberal
1858–59	Edward Geoffrey Stanley, 14th Earl of Derby	Conservative
1859–65	Henry John Temple, 3rd Viscount Palmerston	Liberal
1865–66	John Russell, 1st Earl Russell	Liberal
1866–68	Edward Geoffrey Stanley, 14th Earl of Derby	Conservative
1868	Benjamin Disraeli	Conservative
1868–74	William Ewart Gladstone	Liberal
1874–80	Benjamin Disraeli[4]	Conservative
1880–85	William Ewart Gladstone	Liberal
1885–86	Robert Cecil, 3rd Marquess of Salisbury	Conservative
1886	William Ewart Gladstone	Liberal
1886–92	Robert Cecil, 3rd Marquess of Salisbury	Conservative
1892–94	William Ewart Gladstone	Liberal
1894–95	Archibald Philip Primrose, 5th Earl of Rosebery	Liberal
1895–1902	Robert Cecil, 3rd Marquess of Salisbury	Conservative
1902–05	Arthur James Balfour	Conservative
1905–08	Sir Henry Campbell-Bannerman	Liberal
1908–16	Herbert Henry Asquith	Liberal
1916–22	David Lloyd George	Liberal
1922–23	Bonar Law	Conservative
1923–24	Stanley Baldwin	Conservative
1924	Ramsay Macdonald	Labour
1924–29	Stanley Baldwin	Conservative
1929–35	Ramsay Macdonald	Labour
1935–37	Stanley Baldwin	Conservative
1937–40	Neville Chamberlain	Conservative
1940–45	Winston Churchill	Conservative
1945–51	Clement Attlee	Labour
1951–55	Winston Churchill[5]	Conservative
1955–57	Sir Anthony Eden	Conservative
1957–63	Harold Macmillan	Conservative
1963–64	Sir Alec Douglas-Home	Conservative
1964–70	Harold Wilson	Labour
1970–74	Edward Heath	Conservative
1974–76	Harold Wilson	Labour
1976–79	James Callaghan	Labour
1979–90	Margaret Thatcher	Conservative
1990–97	John Major	Conservative
1997–	Tony Blair	Labour

[1] From 1725, Sir Robert Walpole.
[2] From 1790, 2nd Earl of Guilford.
[3] From 1784, 1st Marquess of Lansdowne.
[4] From 1876, Earl of Beaconsfield.
[5] From 1953, Sir Winston Churchill.

UK Chancellors of the Exchequer

Date appointed	Name
July 1945	Hugh Dalton
November 1947	Sir Stafford Cripps
October 1950	Hugh Gaitskell
October 1951	'Rab' Butler
December 1955	Harold Macmillan
January 1957	Peter Thorneycroft
January 1958	Derick Heathcoat Amory
July 1960	Selwyn Lloyd
July 1962	Reginald Maudling
October 1964	James Callaghan
November 1967	Roy Jenkins
June 1970	Iain Macleod
July 1970	Anthony Barber
March 1974	Denis Healey
May 1979	Sir Geoffrey Howe
June 1983	Nigel Lawson
October 1989	John Major
November 1990	Norman Lamont
May 1993	Kenneth Clarke
May 1997	Gordon Brown

UK Secretaries of State for Foreign and Commonwealth Affairs

Known as Secretary of State for Foreign Affairs before 1968.

Date appointed	Name
July 1945	Ernest Bevin
March 1951	Herbert Morrison
October 1951	Sir Anthony Eden
December 1955	Selwyn Lloyd
July 1960	Earl of Home
October 1963	'Rab' Butler
October 1964	Patrick Gordon-Walker
January 1965	Michael Stewart
August 1966	George Brown
March 1968	Michael Stewart
June 1970	Sir Alec Douglas-Home
March 1974	James Callaghan
April 1976	Anthony Crosland
February 1977	David Owen
May 1979	Lord Carrington
April 1982	Francis Pym
June 1983	Sir Geoffrey Howe
June 1989	John Major
October 1989	Douglas Hurd
July 1995	Malcolm Rifkind
May 1997	Robin Cook

UK Secretaries of State for Home Affairs

Date appointed	Name
August 1945	Chuter Ede
October 1951	Sir David Maxwell Fyfe
October 1954	Gwilym Lloyd-George
January 1957	'Rab' Butler
July 1962	Henry Brooke
October 1964	Sir Frank Soskice
December 1965	Roy Jenkins
November 1967	James Callaghan
June 1970	Reginald Maudling
July 1972	Robert Carr
March 1974	Roy Jenkins
September 1976	Merlyn Rees
May 1979	William Whitelaw
June 1983	Leon Brittan
September 1985	Douglas Hurd
October 1989	David Waddington
November 1990	Kenneth Baker
April 1992	Kenneth Clarke
May 1993	Michael Howard
May 1997	Jack Straw

UK Secretaries of State for Defence

Known as Minister of Defence before 1964.

Date appointed	Name
July 1945	Clement Attlee
December 1946	Alan Alexander
February 1950	Emanuel Shinwell
October 1951	Winston Churchill
March 1952	Earl Alexander of Tunis
October 1954	Harold Macmillan
April 1955	Selwyn Lloyd
December 1955	Walter Monckton
October 1956	Anthony Head
January 1957	Duncan Sandys
October 1959	Harold Watkinson
July 1962	Peter Thorneycroft
October 1964	Denis Healey
June 1970	Lord Carrington
January 1974	Ian Gilmour
March 1974	Roy Mason
September 1976	Fred Mulley
May 1979	Francis Pym
January 1981	John Nott
January 1983	Michael Heseltine
January 1986	George Younger
July 1989	Tom King
April 1992	Malcolm Rifkind
July 1995	Michael Portillo
May 1997	George Robertson
October 1999	Geoff Hoon

The Cabinet: Introduction

The cabinet determines the government's policy and coordinates government business. Full cabinet meetings are held, in private, once or twice a week during parliamentary sittings and less often during recess. They are chaired by the prime minister. However, during recent decades the full cabinet has become something of a 'rubber stamping' body. Actual decisions are typically made earlier in the more than 30 smaller cabinet committees and sub-committees, which cover smaller subject areas, such as local government or drug misuse, and involve a smaller group of relevant ministers most closely concerned and affected by the issues being decided.

The cabinet is, by tradition, a collective body, with its members bound together by a convention of 'collective responsibility' for decisions taken. If a minister feels unable to support an agreed cabinet policy, he or she is expected to resign. However, members typically seek to promote the best interests of the department for which they are directly accountable to Parliament. This is most obviously seen when the department heads (secretaries of state) put in bids for their next year's expenditure during what is known as the 'annual spending round'. The Treasury (headed by the chancellor of the Exchequer), which controls public expenditure, determines, through its chief secretary, the final spending allocations. The prime minister's private office and the cabinet office also support the prime minister by promoting coordination and efficiency across government.

UK Cabinet Ministers

As of July 2000.

Position	Cabinet ministers
Prime Minister, First Lord of the Treasury, and Minister for the Civil Service	Tony Blair
Deputy Prime Minister and Secretary of State for the Environment, Transport, and the Regions	John Prescott
Chancellor of the Exchequer	Gordon Brown
Secretary of State for Foreign and Commonwealth Affairs	Robin Cook
Lord Chancellor	Lord Irvine of Lairg
Secretary of State for the Home Department	Jack Straw
Secretary of State for Education and Employment	David Blunkett
President of the Council and Leader of the House of Commons	Margaret Beckett
Minister for the Cabinet Office[1]	Mo (Marjorie) Mowlam
Secretary of State for Scotland	John Reid
Secretary of State for Defence	Geoff Hoon
Secretary of State for Health	Alan Milburn
Chief Whip and Parliamentary Secretary to the Treasury	Ann Taylor
Secretary of State for Culture, Media, and Sport	Chris Smith
Secretary of State for Northern Ireland	Peter Mandelson
Secretary of State for International Development	Clare Short
Secretary of State for Social Security	Alistair Darling
Secretary of State for Agriculture, Fisheries, and Food	Nick Brown
Leader of the House of Lords, and Minister for Women[2]	Baroness Jay of Paddington

(continued)

UK Cabinet Ministers (*continued*)

Secretary of State for Trade and Industry	Stephen Byers
Chief Secretary to the Treasury	Andrew Smith
Secretary of State for Wales	Paul Murphy
Minister of State (Transport)[3]	Lord Macdonald of Tradeston
Government Chief Whip, House of Lords[3]	Lord Carter

[1] The Minister is appointed as Chancellor of the Duchy of Lancaster.
[2] The Minister is appointed as Lord Privy Seal.
[3] Not members of the Cabinet, but will attend Cabinet metings.

See also **The Shadow Cabinet**, p 45.

UK Government Departments: Introduction

There are currently 18 government departments, each specializing in a different range of functions. Fourteen of these departments are headed by a secretary of state; one by the Lord Chancellor; one by the Attorney General; one, the cabinet office, by the chancellor of the Duchy of Lancaster; and one, the Treasury, by the prime minister.

UK Government Departments

(– = not applicable.) As of July 2000.

Department	Address	Responsibilities	Title	Ministers	Executive agencies
Agriculture, Fisheries, and Food (Ministry of)	3–8 Whitehall Place, London SW1A 2HH; phone: (020) 7270 3000; fax: (020) 7270 8125; Web site: www.maff.gov.uk	agriculture, horticulture, fisheries, and food; related environmental and rural issues	Minister Ministers of State	Nick Brown Joyce Quin; Baroness Hayman	Central Science Laboratory; Intervention Board; Centre for Environment, Fisheries, and Aquaculture Science; Farming and Rural Conservation Agency; Meat Hygiene Service; Pesticides Safety Directorate; Veterinary Laboratories Agency; Veterinary Medicines Directorate
Cabinet Office (Office of Public Service)	70 Whitehall, London SW1A 2AS; phone: (020) 7270 3000; fax: (020) 7270 0196; Web site: www.cabinet-office.gov.uk	key policy areas and issues include: Citizen's Charter; freedom of information; improving the effectiveness and efficiency of central government; machinery of government and standards; Her Majesty's Stationery Office; historical government records and official histories; public bodies and public appointments; quangos; MPs' and MEPs' pay; management of the civil service; Central Office of Information	Minister for the Cabinet Office and Chancellor of the Duchy of Lancaster Ministers of State Lord Privy Seal and Leader of the House of Lords	Marjorie (Mo) Mowlam Lord Falconer; Ian McCartney Baroness Jay of Paddington	The Buying Agency; Central Computer and Telecommunications Agency; Civil Service College; Government Car and Despatch Agency; Property Advisers to the Civil Estate; Security Facilities Executive; Recruitment and Assessment Services Executive
Culture, Media, and Sport	Trafalgar Place, 2–4 Cockspur Street, London SW1Y 5DH; phone: (020) 7211 6000; fax: (020) 7211 6210; e-mail: enquiries@culture.gov.uk; Web site: www.culture.gov.uk	the arts; public libraries; national museums; tourism; sport; film industry; press regulation; the National Lottery	Secretary of State Under Secretaries of State	Chris Smith Janet Anderson (Tourism, Film, and Broadcasting); Kate Hoey (Sport); Alan Howarth (Arts)	Historic Royal Palaces Agency; Royal Parks Agency

(continued)

UK Government Departments *(continued)*

Department	Address	Responsibilities	Title	Ministers	Executive agencies
Ministry of Defence	Main Building, Whitehall, London SW1A 2HB; phone: (020) 7218 9000; fax: (020) 7218 1562; e-mail: enquiries@mofd.fsnet.co.uk; Web site: www.mod.uk	defence policy; control and administration of the armed services	Secretary of State Minister for Defence Procurement Minister for Armed Forces Under Secretary of State	Geoffrey Hoon Baroness Symons of Vernham Dean John Spella Lewis Moonie	Armed Forces Personnel Administration Agency; Army Base Repair Organization; Army Base Storage and Distribution Agency; Army Individual Training Organization; Army Personnel Centre; Army Technical Support Agency; Army Training and Recruitment Agency; Defence Accounts Agency; Defence Analytical Services Agency; Defence Animal Centre; Defence Aviation Repair Agency; Defence Bills Agency; Defence Clothing and Textiles Agency; Defence Codification Agency; Defence Communication Services Agency; Defence Dental Agency; Defence Estate Organization; Defence Evaluation and Research Agency; Defence Intelligence and Security Centre; Defence Medical Training Organization; Defence Operational Analysis Centre; Defence Postal and Courier Services Agency; Defence Procurement Agency; Defence Secondary Care Agency; Defence Storage and Distribution Agency; Defence Transport and Movements Executive; Defence Vetting Agency; Disposal Sales Agency; Duke of York's Royal Military School; Flag Officer Naval Training/Reserves; Hydrographic Office; Joint Air Reconnaissance Intelligence Centre Agency; Logistic Information Systems Agency; Maintenance Group Defence Agency; Medical Supplies Agency; Meteorological Office; Military Survey; Ministry of Defence Police; Naval Aircraft Repair Organization; Naval Bases and Supply Agency; Naval Manning Agency; Naval Recruiting and Training Agency; Pay and Personnel Agency; Queen Victoria School; RAF Logistics Support Service; RAF Maintenance Group; RAF Personnel Management Agency; RAF Signals Engineering Establishment; RAF Training Group; Service Children's Education; Ships Support Agency; Specialist Procurement Services
Education and Employment	Sanctuary Buildings, Great Smith Street, London SW1P 3BT; phone: (020) 7925 5000; fax: (01928) 794 248; e-mail: info@dfee.gov.uk; Web site: www.dfee.gov.uk	school, college, and university education; the Careers Service, Employment Service; youth and adult training policy and programmes; equal opportunities in employment, social policy, and programmes in Europe	Secretary of State Minister for the New Deal Minister for School Standards Minister for Education and Employment Under Secretaries of State	David Blunkett Tessa Jowell Estelle Morris Baroness Blackstone Malcolm Wicks; Margaret Hodge; Jacqui Smith; Michael Wills	ACAS; Employment Service Agency; Teachers' Pensions Agency; Health and Safety Executive

(continued)

UK Government Departments *(continued)*

Department	Address	Responsibilities	Title	Ministers	Executive agencies
Environment, Transport, and the Regions	Eland House, Bressenden Place, London SW1E 5DU; phone: (020) 7890 3000; Web site: www.detr.gov.uk	land use planning; housing; construction industry; environmental protection; water industry; urban and rural regeneration; countryside and wildlife protection; local government finance and structure; land, sea, and air transport; domestic and international civil aviation; shipping and ports; marine pollution; regulation of the road haulage industry; motorways and trunk roads; London Transport; British Rail; Railtrack; Civil Aviation Authority	Deputy Prime Minister and Secretary of State	John Prescott	Coastguard Agency; Driver and Vehicle Licensing Agency; Driving Standards Agency; Highways Agency; Marine Safety Agency; Ordnance Survey; Planning Inspectorate; Queen Elizabeth II Conference Centre; Security Facilities Executive; Transport Research Laboratory; Vehicle Certification Agency; Vehicle Inspectorate
			Minister for the Environment	Michael Meacher	
			Minister for Local Government and Regions	Hilary Armstrong	
			Minister for Housing and Planning	Nick Raynsford	
			Minister for Transport	Lord Macdonald of Tradeston	
			Under Secretaries of State	Keith Hill; Lord Whitty; Chris Mullin; Beverley Hughes	
Foreign and Commonwealth Affairs Office	Whitehall, London SW1A 2AH; phone: (020) 7270 1500 fax: (020) 7839 2417; Web site: www.fco.gov.uk	Britain's overseas relations, including relations with overseas governments and international organizations, administration of British Dependent Territories, promoting British trade and exports, protecting British interests, and the welfare of Britons abroad	Secretary of State	Robin Cook	Wilton Park Conference Centre
			Ministers of State	Keith Vaz (Europe); Peter Hain; John Battle	
			Parliamentary Under Secretary of State	Baroness Scotland of Asthal	
Health	Richmond House, 79 Whitehall, London SW1A 2NS; phone: (020) 7210 3000; fax: (020) 7210 5523; e-mail: dhmail@doh.gsi.gov.uk; Web site: www.doh.gov.uk	National Health Service; local authority social services; public health issues, including the health consequences of environmental and food issues	Secretary of State	Alan Milburn	Medical Devices Agency; Medicines Control Agency; NHS Estates; NHS Pensions Agency
			Ministers of State	John Denham; John Hutton	
			Minister for Public Health	Yvette Cooper	
			Under Secretaries of State	Lord Hunt of Kings Heath; Gisela Stuart	
Home Office	50 Queen Anne's Gate, London SW1H 9AT; phone: (020) 7273 4000; fax: (020) 7273 2065; e-mail: gen.ho@gtnet.gov.uk; Web site: www.homeoffice.gov.uk	criminal law, probation and prison services; the police; crime prevention; licensing laws; passports, immigration, and nationality; race relations; administration of justice	Secretary of State	Jack Straw	Charity Commission; Fire Service College; Forensic Science Service; HM Prison Service; UK Passport Agency
			Ministers of State	Paul Boateng; Charles Clarke; Barbara Roche	
			Under Secretaries of State	Mike O'Brien; Lord Bassam of Brighton	
International Development	94 Victoria Street, London SW1E 5JL; phone: (020) 7917 7000; fax: (020) 7917 0016; e-mail: enquiry@dfid.gov.uk; Web site: www.dfid.gov.uk	Britain's overseas aid to developing countries; global environmental assistance; overseas superannuation	Secretary of State	Clare Short	Natural Resources Institute
			Under Secretary of State	George Foulkes	

(continued)

UK Government Departments *(continued)*

Department	Address	Responsibilities	Title	Ministers	Executive agencies
Law Officers' Department	Attorney General's Chambers, 9 Buckingham Gate, London SE1E 6JP; phone: (020) 7271 2450; fax: (020) 7210 8620; e-mail: general.queries @kdhq.gsi.uk	chief legal advisor to the government; all Crown litigation; Law Officers' departments (the Treasury Solicitor's Department, the Crown Prosecution Service, the Serious Fraud Office, and the Legal Secretariat to the Law Officers); aspects of civil and criminal law	Attorney-General Solicitor-General	Lord Williams of Mostyn Ross Cranston	Government Property Lawyers; Treasury Solicitor's Department
Lord Chancellor's Department	Selborne House, 54–60 Victoria Street, London SW1E 6QW; phone: (020) 7210 8500; fax: (020) 7210 8620; e-mail: general. enquiries@ lcdhq.gsi.uk; Web site: www. open.gov.uk/lcd	procedure of civil courts and administration of the Supreme Court, county courts, and tribunals under the Court Service executive agency; legal aid and promotion of general reforms in civil law (England and Wales); Northern Ireland Court Service	Lord Chancellor Under Secretaries of State	Lord Irvine of Lairg Jane Kennedy; David Lock	Court Service; Public Trust Office. Two further agencies, HM Land Registry and the Public Record Office, report to the Lord Chancellor but are departments in their own right and not part of the Lord Chancellor's Department
Northern Ireland Office	Stormont Castle, Belfast BT4 3ST; phone: (028) 9076 3011; fax: (028) 9052 8473; Whitehall, London SW1A 2AZ; phone: (020) 7210 3000; Web site: www.nio.gov.uk	constitutional developments; law and order; security and electoral issues	Secretary of State Minister of State Under Secretary of State	Peter Mandelson Adam Ingram George Howarth	The Compensation Agency; Forensic Science Agency of Northern Ireland; Northern Ireland Prison Service
Scotland Office	Dover House, Whitehall, London SW1A 2AU; phone: (020) 7270 3000; fax: (020) 7270 6812; Web site: www.scottish. secretary.gov.uk	foreign affairs, defence, taxation, social security, company regulation, economic management; most other areas of responsibility have devolved to the Scottish Parliament; includes the former Lord Advocate's Department	Secretary of State Minister of State Advocate General for Scotland	John Reid Brian Wilson Lynda Clarke	Fisheries Research Services; Historic Scotland; Pensions Agency; Scottish Agricultural Sciences Agency; Scottish Fisheries Protection Agency; Student Awards Agency for Scotland
Social Security	Richmond House, 79 Whitehall, London SW1A 2NS; phone: (020) 7238 0800; fax: (020) 7712 2386; Web site: www.dss.gov.uk	the British social security system	Secretary of State Minister of State Under Secretaries of State	Alistair Darling Jeff Rooker Hugh Bayley, Angela Eagle, Baroness Hollis of Heigham	Benefits Agency; Child Support Agency; Contributions Agency; Information Technology Services Agency; Resettlement Agency; War Pensions Agency
Trade and Industry	1 Victoria Street, London SW1H 0ET; phone: (020) 7215 5000; fax: (020) 7222 0612; Web site: www.dti.gov.uk	industrial and commercial affairs; innovation policy; regional industrial policy; international trade policy; competition policy; small businesses; business and education; industrial relations; employment legislation	Secretary of State Ministers of State Under Secretaries of State	Stephen Byers Helen Liddell; Richard Caborn; Patricia Hewitt Kim Howells; Alan Johnson; Lord Sainsbury of Turville	Accounts Services Agency; Companies House; Employment Tribunals Service; Insolvency Service; Laboratory of the Government Chemist; National Engineering Laboratory; National Weights and Measures Laboratory; Patent Office; Radiocommunications Agency

(continued)

National Government

UK Government Departments (*continued*)

Department	Address	Responsibilities	Title	Ministers	Executive agencies
HM Treasury	Treasury Chambers, Parliament Street, London SW1P 3AG; phone: (020) 7270 4558; Web site: www.hmtreasury.gov.uk	overseeing of Britain's tax and monetary policy; planning and control of public spending; international financial relations; Civil Service management	Prime Minister, First Lord of the Treasury, and Minister for the civil service	Tony Blair	National Savings; Office for National Statistics
			Chancellor of the Exchequer	Gordon Brown	
			Chief Secretary	Andrew Smith	
			Financial Secretary	Stephen Timms	
			Paymaster General	Dawn Primarolo	
			Economic Secretary	Melanie Johnson	
Wales Office	Gwydyr House, Whitehall, London SW1A 2ER; phone: (020) 7270 3000; Web site: www.ossw.wales.gov.uk	foreign affairs, defence, taxation, social security, broadcasting, overall economic policy; other areas of responsibility have devolved to the National Assembly for Wales)	Secretary of State and First Secretary to the National Assembly for Wales	Paul Murphy	Cadw (Welsh Historic Monuments)
			Under Secretary of State	David Hanson	

Modernizing Government

The *Modernizing Government* White Paper of April 1999 has led to major changes in the way government departments and agencies operate. It requires them to be consumer-focused, work more closely together to deliver shared goals ('joined-up government'), be 'forward looking in developing policies to deliver outcomes', and make full use of modern technologies (call centres and the Internet) to deliver services electronically. A target has been set for 25% of the public's dealings with government to be deliverable electronically by 2002 and 100% by 2008, with public services available 24 hours a day, seven days a week.

Government Agencies: Introduction

Today more than 270,000 people, or three-fifths of all staff in government departments and agencies, are employed in more than 100 executive agencies that carry out many of the day-to-day administrative, executive, and service functions of the government.

Executive agencies are semi-autonomous bodies, that have been set up, since 1988, under the 'Next Steps' programme aimed at increasing the efficiency and quality of government services. These agencies operate within an agreed framework determined by the responsible departmental minister, who also agrees forward plans and sets annual targets against which performance is monitored. The day-to-day operations of the agencies are the responsibilities of chief executives, who are typically recruited from outside the civil service. The chief executives work on fixed-term contracts and are accountable to the minister for their agency's performance and use of resources. The chief executive and agency staff are civil servants.

HM Customs and Excise, the Building Research Establishment, the Crown Prosecution Service, the Inland Revenue, and the Serious Fraud Office also operate on 'Next Steps' lines, and employ 85,000 staff. There also operate, within government departments, non-departmental public bodies (NDPBs). These have less autonomy than executive agencies. An example of an NDPD is the Police Information Technology Organization (PITO), within the Home Office.

UK Government Agencies

Agency	Address	Key responsibilities
Central Office of Information	Hercules House, 6 Hercules Road, London SE1 7DU; phone: (020) 7928 2345; fax: (020) 7928 5037; Web site: www.coi.gov.uk	offers consultancy and procurement services for publicity material to government departments and agencies and other public-sector bodies; a department in its own right, reporting to the Minister for the Cabinet Office
Crown Prosecution Service	50 Ludgate Hill, London EC4M 7EX; phone: (020) 7796 8000; Web site: www.cps.gov.uk	independently reviews and conducts criminal proceedings begun by the police in England and Wales, except for cases conducted by the Serious Fraud Office; headed by the Director of Public Prosecutions, who is accountable to the Attorney-General
ECGD (Export Credits Guarantee Department)	PO Box 2200, 2 Exchange Tower, Harbour Exchange Square, London E14 9GS; phone: (020) 7512 7000; fax: (020) 7512 7649; Web site: www.ecgd.gov.uk	supports the export of capital and project-related goods and services from the UK; provides insurance to British project and capital goods exporters against not being paid for goods and services; insures new British investment overseas; reports to the Secretary of State for Trade and Industry

(*continued*)

UK Government Agencies *(continued)*		
Government Offices for the Regions (Central Unit)	1/A3 Eland House, Bressenden Place, London SW1E 5DU; phone: (020) 7890 5157; fax: (020) 7890 5019	coordinates resources, personnel policy, promoting economic development, and administration for the Government Offices for the Regions (Eastern, East Midlands, London, Merseyside, North East, North West, South East, South West, West Midlands, Yorkshire and Humberside); reports to the Secretary of State for the Environment, Transport, and the Regions, the President of the Board of Trade, and the Secretary of State for Education and Employment
Her Majesty's Customs and Excise	New King's Beam House, 22 Upper Ground, London SE1 9PJ; phone: (020) 7620 1313; Web site: www.hmce.gov.uk	collects and accounts for Customs and Excise revenues; controls imports and exports, compiles trade statistics; polices prohibited goods; reports to the Chancellor of the Exchequer
Her Majesty's Land Registry	32 Lincoln's Inn Fields, London WC2A 3PH; phone: (020) 7917 8888; fax: (020) 7955 0110; Web site: www.landreg.gov.uk	registers title to land in England and Wales and records dealings once the property is registered, maintains register of landowners and guarantees their title; provides system for transfer and mortgage of land; executive agency responsible to the Lord Chancellor
Her Majesty's Procurator General and Treasury Solicitor	Queen Anne's Chambers, 28 Broadway, London SW1H 9JS; phone: (020) 7210 3000; fax: (020) 7210 3397; Web site: www.open.gov.uk/tsd/tsdhome.htm	provides legal services to many government departments, agencies, and public bodies, including litigation and general legal advice; instructs Parliamentary Counsel on drafting legislation; reports to the Attorney-General
Her Majesty's Stationery Office	St Clements House, 2–16 Colegate, Norwich NR3 1BQ; phone: (01603) 723000; e-mail: enquiries@hmso.gov.uk; Web site: www.hmso.gov.uk	body within the Office of Public Service with responsibilities for printing legislation and government publications; controls and administers Crown copyright and administers parliamentary copyright
Inland Revenue	Somerset House, London WC2R 1LB; phone: (020) 7438 6622; Web site: www.inlandrevenue.gov.uk	collection and administration of direct taxes in Britain; reports to the Chancellor of the Exchequer
Legal Secretariat to the Law Officers	Attorney General's Chambers, 9 Buckingham Gate, London SW1E 6JP; phone: (020) 7271 2400; fax: (020) 7271 2430	supports Law Officers of the Crown in their activities as the government's main legal advisers
National Savings	Charles House, 375 Kensington High Street, London W14 8QH; phone: (020) 7605 9300; fax: (020) 7605 9438; Web site: www.nationalsavings.gov.uk	administers and sells a range of investments to personal savers, with the aim of raising funds for the government; an executive agency of the Treasury, reporting to the Chancellor of the Exchequer
Office for National Statistics	Great George Street, London SW1P 3AQ; phone: (020) 7533 5888; e-mail: info@ons.gov.uk; Web site: www.ons.gov.uk	agency created by merger of the Central Statistical Office and the Office of Population, Censuses, and Surveys; responsibilities include collection and interpretation of key national economic and population statistics; administration of marriage laws; local registration of births, deaths, and marriages; accountable to the Chancellor of the Exchequer
Office of Fair Trading	Field House, 15–25 Bream Buildings, London EC4A 1PR; phone: (020) 7211 8000; fax: (020) 7211 8800; Web site: www.oft.gov.uk	a non-ministerial department headed by the Director-General of Fair Trading; reviews commercial activities in the UK with the aim of protecting consumers against unfair trading practices
Office of the Data Protection Registrar	Wycliffe House, Water Lane, Wilmslow, Cheshire SK9 5AF; phone: (01625) 545745; fax: (01625) 524510; Web site: www.dataprotection.gov.uk	reporting directly to parliament, maintains public register of data users and computer bureaux, enforces data protection legislation, and investigates complaints about breaches of the Data Protection Act; reports directly to parliament
Office of the Paymaster General	Sutherland House, Russell Way, Crawley, West Sussex RH10 1UH; phone: (01293) 560999; fax: (01293) 538979/604024	provides banking services for government departments and administers and pays public service pensions
Ordnance Survey	Romsey Road, Maybush, Southampton SO16 4GU; phone: (01703) 792000; fax: (01703) 792324/792921; Web site: www.ordsvy.gov.uk	provides official surveying, mapping, and related scientific work in Britain and some foreign countries; reports to the Secretary of State for the Environment
Parliamentary Counsel	36 Whitehall, London SW1A 2AY; phone: (020) 7210 6633; fax: (020) 7210 6632	drafts government Bills (except those that relate only to Scotland) and advises departments on parliamentary procedure in England, Wales, and Northern Ireland
Public Record Office	Ruskin Avenue, Kew, Richmond, Surrey TW9 4DU; phone: (020) 8876 3444; fax: (020) 8878 8905; Web site: www.pro.gov.uk	supervises the selection and maintenance of records of central government and courts of law, ensures their safety and preservation, and makes them available to the public; a department in its own right, reporting to the Lord Chancellor
Royal Mint	Llantrisant, Pontyclun, Mid Glamorgan CF72 8YT; phone: (01443) 222111; fax: (01443) 623190; e-mail: coinclub@royalmint.com	produces and issues coinage for Britain, including circulation coins and commemorative coins and medals
Serious Fraud Office	Elm House, 10–16 Elm Street, London WC1X 0BJ; phone: (020) 7239 7272; fax: (020) 7837 1689; Web site: www.sfo.gov.uk	investigates and prosecutes serious and complex fraud in England, Wales, and Northern Ireland; reports to the Attorney-General
Treasury Solicitor's Department	Queen Anne's Chambers, 28 Broadway, London SW1H 9JS; phone: (020) 7210 3000; fax: (020) 7210 3397; Web site: www.open.gov.uk/tsd/tsdhome.htm	provides legal and litigation services for most government departments, agencies, and public bodies; a department in its own right and an executive agency of the Treasury, reporting to the Attorney-General

National Government

UK Parliament

Introduction

Parliament is the supreme law-making authority in the UK. It comprises two chambers, or houses, the Commons and the Lords, and meets in the Palace of Westminster, London. All governments are subject to the laws that Parliament makes, as interpreted by the courts.

Origins

Parliament originated in the 11th century, in the Witans – councils of religious leaders and magnates, which were consulted by Saxon kings. By the 14th century, two Houses had begun to emerge, with shire and borough representatives forming the Commons, and religious leaders and magnates, the Lords. After the 'Glorious Revolution' of 1689, Parliament's powers were firmly established and its ascendancy over sovereign rule assured. The Scottish parliament amalgamated with that of England and Wales after the Act of Union of 1707.

The Commons and the Lords

The Commons, with directly elected members, has been the most powerful chamber since the 19th century. The dominant party or coalition within the Commons provides the prime minister and government, which decides on which major pieces of legislation to introduce. The Lords, which is currently in a transitional state, is made up of unelected members (peers). Its main purpose is to review and revise legislation drafted by the government and debated by the Commons. It has a particularly important role in relation to delegated legislation. The Lords may delay non-financial bills which have been approved by the Commons by a year, but it has no outright veto.

The duration of Parliament is five years, but it can be subject to earlier dissolution at the prime minister's request, with the sovereign's agreement. Fresh Commons' elections are held at the end of each Parliament. The life of Parliament is divided into year-long sessions, usually beginning or ending in October and November. The Queen, whose formal agreement is needed before an act passed by Parliament becomes law, opens each parliamentary session and reads out the government's programme of proposed legislation.

Parliament's powers

Parliament can legislate for the UK as a whole or for any part separately. It has chosen to 'devolve' certain powers to local government and to the Scottish Parliament and Northern Ireland and Welsh assemblies – but Parliament is sovereign, in that it is free to make and unmake any laws that it chooses. Consequently, this devolved authority could be revoked. However, since entry into the European Union (EU) in 1973 the supremacy of Parliament has come under increasing challenge from EU laws, including the European Convention of Human Rights (which was adopted by the 1997 Labour government). With the passage of the Human Rights Act in 2000, the Lords will be reconstituted to form within it a British version of a 'Supreme Court'.

UK Parliamentary Glossary

abstention refusal by an MP to vote for or against a motion

act of Parliament bill passed by the Houses of Parliament (Commons and Lords) and signed by the Queen

address formal message to the Crown, presented to the monarch by a Commons whip when the House of Commons wishes to make a point to the Monarch; the message is answered by the monarch and returned to the Commons by a whip or to the Lords by the Lord Chamberlain

adjournment of the House request by an MP in the House of Commons to terminate the day's proceedings

admonition reprimand to an MP who has done something wrong, made by the Speaker of the House of Commons

amendment alteration proposed in a motion or a bill; amendments can be voted on in order to change what is written in a bill

back bencher MP who does not hold office in the government, or any senior position on the leading opposition party

ballot paper on which an MP registers his/her vote in matters requiring the use of ballots to decide issues in Parliament

Bar of the House marked by a leather strip, the Bar of the House is the line at the entrance to the House of Commons which non-MPs must not cross

bill draft of an act of Parliament, presented to either the House of Commons or the House of Lords, to vote on. If successful, the bill is forwarded for Royal Assent; if granted, it becomes an Act

Black Rod officer of the Royal Household who looks after the doorkeepers and messengers of the House of Lords; Black Rod also issues the orders for entry into the Strangers' Gallery

budget annual financial statement of the chancellor of the Exchequer

by-election election to fill a vacancy in a constituency that arises during the course of a Parliament, usually as a result of the death or resignation of an MP

catching the Speaker's eye any MP who wishes to speak in the Houses of Commons must stand and wait for the Speaker to see him/her and give them permission to speak

clause subdivision of an act or bill

closure motion motion in the Commons that the question under discussion be put to a decision. To carry the closure, the motion needs the support of at least 100 MPs.

count if there are less that 40 MPs present in the House of Commons, the Speaker can close the House

crossing the floor changing allegiance from one political party to another is signified by 'crossing the floor' of the House and taking a seat with an opposing party

delegated legislation consequential rules or regulations made by ministers under the authority of an earlier 'enabling' act. Also known as 'secondary legislation', the most common example is a **statutory instrument**

dissolution bringing to an end the Parliament of the Houses of Commons and Lords by the monarch; it is followed by a general election

division method of voting by MPs on a question put by the chair. Those in favour of a motion, enter the ayes lobby, to the right of the Speaker, and those opposed, the noes, to the left. No division is valid unless a minimum of 40 members cast their votes

father of the House longest-serving MP in the House of Commons, currently Edward Heath

filibustering process of 'talking' out a bill through lengthy speeches or the tabling of voluminous amendments. The '**guillotine procedure**' is designed to counter this practice

front benches benches where members of the Government and senior opposition members sit in the House of Commons; nearest to the centre of the Table of the Commons

galleries areas in the House of Commons set aside for the public and press to attend sittings

general election election of a new government by all eligible voters in the country following the dissolution of Parliament

government bill bill introduced by a government minister

UK Parliamentary Glossary (*continued*)

'guillotine procedure' where time available for debate of a bill in the Commons is curtailed by the government in order to ensure that passage runs to a strict timetable

Hansard House of Commons' written reports

Houses of Parliament palace housing the House of Commons and the House of Lords

independent member elected MP who is not a member of any recognized political party. MPs can also leave or be expelled by a political party during a Parliament and sit as independents

maiden speech first speech in the House of Commons by a new member; traditionally, a new MP standing will be given preference over others by the Speaker

majority government government formed by the party with the majority of seats in the House of Commons

minority government government formed by a party that does not hold a majority of seats; it must maintain the confidence of the House in order to remain in government

oath of allegiance oath of loyalty to the sovereign that must be made by an MP before he/she can take his/her seat in the House of Commons

order paper daily timetable of events in the House of Commons and the House of Lords

pairs if an MP does not wish to vote in the Chamber, he/she has to come to an arrangement with an opposition MP who will not vote either. The overall vote is then reduced by one on each side

parliamentary procedure rules by which the House of Commons and the House of Lords conduct their business

passage of a bill process by which a bill obtains parliamentary approval and becomes law. Once parliamentary approval has been granted, the bill is forwarded to the monarch for royal assent

point of order a technical or procedural breach of order can be brought to the attention of the Speaker by an MP at any time during a debate or as House business is being conducted; the Speaker decides on the validity of the matter raised and his/her decision is final

portfolio responsibilities of a Cabinet minister

private bill bill which affects a single private interest only. Typically, such bills deal with local matters, such as boundary extensions, or give a public corporation the power to carry out specific works. They originate by petition. Special procedures apply to enable affected people to object

private members' bill public bill promoted by an MP or peer who is not a member of the government. In the Commons, there is ballot of backbench and opposition MPs early in each session. Those near the top may introduce their bills, with 13 Fridays each session being allocated for these bills. Contentious private members' bills can easily be 'filibustered'

Public Accounts Committee (PAC) Commons committee which examines the accounts of all government departments and public corporations. The National Audit Office produces reports on value for money achieved by government departments which the Committee receives, questioning the responsible senior civil servants

public bill bill affecting the public which is introduced by the government or a private member (MP or peer)

question time time when government ministers have to answer questions put by members of the House of Commons and the House of Lords. Prime Minister's questions are on Wednesdays; other days are rotated among other government departments

recess period between the end of one Parliament and the start of another

royal assent approval by the monarch of a bill passed by the House of Commons and the House of Lords, making it an act of Parliament; royal assent has never been withheld in modern times

select committee Commons' committee of not more than 17 members, in proportion to the parties in the House, which scrutinises the activities and policies of the government. The Committee may receive oral and written evidence, from ministers and civil servants, and demand the production of documents. There are also select committees in the Lords

Speaker presiding officer of the Commons, who is elected by MPs at the beginning of each Parliament or when the previous speaker retires or dies. Although originally aligned with a political party, once chosen, the Speaker is expected to be apolitical and is unopposed in his or her constituency at subsequent general elections. The Speaker maintains order during debates, but does not speak on the issues or vote in divisions, except when voting is equal

standing committee Commons' committee of between 16 and 50 members that is set up to examine in detail a proposed bill after it has received a second hearing: the 'committee stage'. Membership is in proportion to representation of the parties in the House and its chair operates in the same way as the Speaker. The committee may not receive written or oral evidence. Typically, around 10 standing committees are set up each session. Unlike a **select committee**, a Standing Committee exercises legislative power and is dissolved once the bill has been considered. There are no standing committees in the Lords, where the 'committee stage' of a bill is taken on the floor of the House

statutory instrument (SI) regulation made by a minister under the authority of an earlier 'enabling' act of Parliament. It is an example of delegated legislation. Each year there are around 2,000 SIs. The Commons and Lords have select committees which examine SIs to ensure that they are in accordance with their enabling act

teller appointed by the Speaker to count the number of ayes and noes in a vote

ten-minute rule MPs are given ten minutes in which to make their comments or statements on issues of particular concern to them. The Speaker keeps time and ends the session at the end of the ten minutes

whip member who makes sure that fellow party members vote according to party wishes; they are paid a higher salary than normal back-bench MPs

written questions questions asked of ministers by MPs to elicit facts about the operations of a department. They receive a written response included in *Hansard*

Acts of Parliament and How a Bill Becomes Law

Statutory law in Britain is provided by acts of Parliament. Before an act receives the royal assent it is known as a bill; bills are normally proposed by the government. Individual MPs may also propose bills (known as **private members bills**). The right to propose these is selected by ballot. Success rates for such bills are around 10%, whereas around 90% of government bills normally receive royal assent. In a typical parliamentary year around 80 bills are passed, of which around 15 may be private members' or private peers' bills. Government departments normally detail proposed legislation in a **Green Paper** which sets out various aspects of a matter on which legislation is contemplated, and invites public discussion and suggestions. This will be followed by a **White Paper** which is the introduction to a bill. In addition to acts of Parliament, there is also 'delegated legislation', which comprises rules and regulations laid down by the queen in council (Orders in Council) and by ministers, known as statutory instruments. There are also regulations made by local authorities and the European Community.

How a Bill Becomes an Act of Parliament

1. First reading of the bill The title is read out in the House of Commons and a minister names a day for the second reading.

2. The bill is officially printed.

3. Second reading A debate on the principles of the bill in the House of Commons followed by a vote on whether or not the bill should go on to the next stage.

4. Committee stage A standing committee of MPs considers the bill in detail, clause by clause, and makes amendments.

5. Report stage The bill is referred back to the House of Commons which may make further amendments.

6. Third reading The House of Commons votes whether the bill should be sent on to the House of Lords.

7. House of Lords The bill passes through much the same stages in the Lords as in the House of Commons. (Bills may be introduced in the Lords, in which case the House of Commons considers them at this stage.)

8. Last amendments The House of Commons considers any Lords' amendments, and may make further amendments which must usually be agreed by the Lords.

9. Royal assent The queen gives her formal assent.

10. The bill becomes an act of Parliament at royal assent. However, it may not come into force until a day appointed in the act.

See also **Recent Important Legislation in the UK**, p 34.

■ UK Parliament

The Shadow Cabinet

As of July 2000.

Position	Name
Conservative Party Leader and Leader of the Opposition	William Hague
Shadow Chancellor of the Exchequer	Michael Portillo
Party Chairman	Michael Ancram
Shadow Secretary of State for Home Affairs	Ann Widdecombe
Shadow Secretary of State for Foreign and Commonwealth Affairs	Francis Maude
Shadow Leader of the House of Commons and Spokesman on Constitutional Affairs	George Young
Shadow Secretary of State for the Environment, Transport, and the Regions	Archie Norman
Shadow Chief Secretary to the Treasury	David Heathcoat-Amory
Shadow Secretary of State for Defence	Iain Duncan Smith
Shadow Leader of the House of Lords	Lord Strathclyde
Shadow Secretary of State for Northern Ireland	Andrew Mackay
Shadow Secretary of State for Social Security	David Willetts
Shadow Secretary of State for Health	Liam Fox
Shadow Secretary of State for Culture, Media, and Sport	Peter Ainsworth
Shadow Secretary of State for International Development	Gary Streeter
Shadow Minister for Agriculture, Fisheries, and Food	Tim Yeo
Shadow Secretary of State for Trade and Industry	Angela Browning
Shadow Secretary of State for Education and Employment	Theresa May
Shadow Minister for the Cabinet Office and Policy Renewal	Andrew Lansley
Shadow Minister for Transport and Spokesman for London	Bernard Jenkin
Opposition Chief Whip (House of Commons)	James Arbuthnot
Opposition Chief Whip (House of Lords)	Lord Henley
Shadow Attorney General[1]	Edward Garnier

[1] Not a member of the Shadow Cabinet but attends all meetings.

See also **UK Cabinet Ministers**, p 36.

Political Parties Represented in the UK Parliament

This table includes parties represented in Parliament. Other political parties which stood in the general election of 1997 were: Albion Party; Alliance Party of Northern Ireland; British National Party; Green Party; Monster Raving Loony Party; National Democrats; Natural Law Party; New Communist Party; Prolife Alliance; Progressive Unionist Party; Referendum Party; Revolutionary Platform of the Socialist Labour Party; Socialist Party; Third Way; UK Independence Party; UK Virtual Party; Ulster Democratic Party.
As of July 4 2000.

Party	Headquarters	Leader	Chair	Brief history	Political position
Labour	Millbank Tower, Millbank, London SW1P 4GT; phone: (020) 7802 1000; fax: (020) 7802 1234; e-mail: join@labour.org.uk; Web site: www.labour.org.uk	Tony Blair	Margaret McDonagh (general secretary) Clive Soley (chair of Parliamentary Party)	Founded in 1900 as the Labour Representation Committee, the party simplified its name to the Labour Party in 1906. It first became the official opposition in 1922. The party's first government (minority) was in 1924, with its first elected majority government in 1945. It is traditionally associated with the Trade Union Movement, who provided much of its funding.	Traditionally a party of the left, its policies include: devolution of power to the regions, reform of the second chamber, and social and educational reform. The party has moved from an ethos of government control (nationalization of industry, strong employment legislation) towards a more free-market ideology, with a subsequent backing from the world of finance and the management of industry.
Conservative and Unionist Party	32 Smith Square, Westminster, London SW1P 3HH; phone: (020) 7222 9000; fax: (020) 7222 1135; e-mail: ccoffice@conservative-party.org.uk; Web site: www.tory.org.uk	William Hague	Michael Ancram	Historically one of the two great parties. Originally known as the Tory Party, the name Conservative was first used in 1830. The current name results from a merger with the Irish Liberal Unionist Party in 1912. The main party in British politics together with the Whigs (Liberal Democrats) until the 20th century, when the Labour party usurped the latter. Produced the first British woman prime minister, Margaret Thatcher.	Traditionally a party of the right, with commitment to maintaining the unity of the nation, low levels of taxation, and low inflation. The present Conservative Party espouses free-market capitalism and opposes the UK joining the European Monetary Union (EMU) for at least two Parliaments.

(continued)

Political Parties Represented in the UK Parliament *(continued)*

Party	Headquarters	Leader	Chair	Brief history	Political position
Liberal Democrats	4 Cowley Street, London SW1P 3NB; phone: (020) 7222 7999; fax: (020) 7799 2170; e-mail: libdems@cix.org.uk; Web site: www.libdems.org.uk	Charles Kennedy[1]	Baroness Diana Maddock (President) Malcolm Bruce (Chair of Parliamentary Party)	Historically one of the two great parties. Originally known as the Whigs, the modern Liberal Party began in 1859 and formed its first government in 1868. It last held power in 1919, although the party did forge a 'Lib-Lab' pact with the minority Labour government in 1977. It merged with the breakaway Labour party group, the Social Democratic Party (SDP), in 1988 to become the Social Liberal Democrats (SLD). Became Liberal Democrats in 1989.	Centrist, openly pro-European party, committed to electoral reform and the devolution of power. Advocates increase in taxation to raise money for health and education. Organized on a regional basis with separate headquarters for Welsh and Scottish parties.
Plaid Cymru	18 Park Grove, Cardiff CF10 3BN; phone: (029) 2064 6000; fax: (029) 2064 6001; e-mail: post@plaidcymru.org; Web site: www.plaidcymru.org	Ieuan Wyn Jones	Marc Phillips	Formed in 1925, and won its first parliamentary seat in 1966. Now the second party in Wales, with four members of Parliament.	Welsh nationalist party, committed to a separate socialist Welsh nation, including the promotion of the Welsh language and culture. Forms a joint parliamentary group with the Scottish National Party (SNP).
Scottish National Party (SNP)	6 North Charlotte Street, Edinburgh EH2 4JH; phone: (0131) 226 3661; fax: (0131) 225 9597; e-mail: snp.administration@snp.org.uk; Web site: www.snp.org.uk	Alex Salmond (national convener); Winnie Ewing (president)	Stewart Hosie (national secretary)	Formed in 1934 by the amalgamation of several early nationalist parties. Won its first parliamentary seat in 1945. SNP support was essential to the minority Labour government of 1977. It is the second party in Scotland, with six MPs.	Scottish nationalist party, advocating the separation of Scotland from the UK as an independent state within the European Union. Forms a joint parliamentary group with Plaid Cymru.
Ulster Unionist Party (UUP)	3 Glengall Street, Belfast BT12 5AE; phone: (028) 9032 4601; fax: (028) 9024 6738; e-mail: uup@uup.org; Web site: www.uup.org	David Trimble	Josias Cunningham (president of the Ulster Unionist Council)	Formed in 1905. Formally known as the Ulster Unionist Council, it governed the province between 1921 and 1972. Following the suspension of Home Rule in 1972, the party split in 1973, and other Unionist parties were formed. The Ulster Unionists rejected the Anglo-Irish Agreement of 1985, and joined forces with the Democratic Unionist Party (DUP) to campaign against it. All its MPs resigned their seats. The UUP is in favour of the 1998 Northern Ireland Peace Deal. Currently the largest political party in Northern Ireland, with ten MPs. Its leader David Trimble was elected first minister of the new Northern Ireland Assembly in June 1998. He was re-elected party leader in March 1999 after facing a challenge to his position.	Protestant party of Northern Ireland. Right-of-centre in orientation, it advocates equality for Northern Ireland within the UK, and opposes union with the Republic of Ireland. The party favours hardline policies on law and order and advocates the death penalty. Has traditionally voted with the Conservative Party in Parliament.
Democratic Unionist Party (DUP)	91 Dundela Avenue, Belfast BT4 3BU; phone: (028) 9047 1155; fax: (028) 9047 1797; e-mail: info@dup.org.uk; Web site: www.dup.org.uk	Ian R K Paisley	Maurice Morrow	Formed in 1973 as a breakaway group from the Ulster Unionist Council.	Protestant party, dedicated to maintaining the Constitution of Northern Ireland as an integral part of the UK. Usually supports the Conservative Party.

(continued)

Political Parties Represented in the UK Parliament *(continued)*

Party	Headquarters	Leader	Chair	Brief history	Political position
Social Democratic and Labour Party (SDLP)	121 Ormeau Road, Belfast BT7 1SH; phone: (028) 9024 7700; fax: (028) 9023 6699; e-mail: sdlip@indigo.ie; Web site: www.sdlp.ie	John Hume	Jim Lennon	Formed in 1970. It was responsible for setting up the New Ireland Forum in 1983. In 1993 it initiated talks with the leader of Sinn Fein, which prompted a joint UK–Irish peace initiative, and set in motion a Northern Ireland ceasefire (1994–96).	Largely Catholic, left-of-centre party. Aims ultimately at Irish unification, but has distanced itself from violent tactics, adopting a constitutional, conciliatory role. Has traditionally voted with the Labour Party.
Sinn Fein	Sinn Fein, 51/55 Falls Road, Belfast; phone: (028) 9062 4421; fax: (028) 9062 2112; e-mail: sinnfein@iol.ie; Web site: www.sinnfein.ie	Gerry Adams	Martin McGuinness	Irish party founded in 1905. The driving political force behind Irish nationalism between 1916 and 1921. It returned to prominence with the outbreak of 'the Troubles' in Northern Ireland in the late 1960s, when it split into Provisional and Official wings at the same time as the Irish Republican Army (IRA), with which it is closely associated. Currently has two MPs in the UK parliament, and one in the Irish parliament.	Nationalist party. Aims to create a united republican Ireland. The current members do not take their seats, and take no part in the parliamentary process.
UK Unionist Party (UKUP)	10 Hamilton Road, Bangor, Northern Ireland BT20 4LE; phone: (028) 9127 2994; fax: (028) 9146 5037; e-mail: contactus@ ukup.org; Web site: www.ukup.org	Robert McCartney		Formed in 1997 by Robert McCartney, UUP MP for the North Down constituency. He left the UUP and stood as an independent, and then formed his own party in order to take part in talks on the future of Northern Ireland.	Aims to preserve the constitutional position of Northern Ireland within the UK. Opposed to the Good Friday Agreement and to any involvement of the Irish Government in Northern Ireland affairs.

Liberal Democrats: Parliamentary Responsibilities

As of July 2000.

Position	Name
Party Leader	Charles Kennedy
Deputy Leader in the Commons	Alan Beith
Leader in the Lords	Lord Rodgers of Quarry Bank
Chief Whip in the Lords	Lord Harris of Greenwich
Deputy Whip in the Commons	Andrew Stunell
Party President	Baroness Maddock of Christchurch[1]
Chief Whip and Shadow Leader of the House	Paul Tyler
Agriculture, Fisheries, Food, and Rural Affairs	Colin Breed
Constitution, Culture and Sport	Robert Maclennan
Education and Employment	Phil Willis
Environment, Transport, the Regions and Social Justice	Don Foster
Foreign Affairs and Defence	Menzies Campbell
International Development	Jenny Tonge
Health	Nick Harvey
Home Affairs	Simon Hughes
Social Security	Steve Webb
Trade and Industry	Vincent Cable
Treasury	Matthew Taylor
Scotland	Jim Wallace
Wales	Richard Livsey
Additional responsibilities in the Commons	
Duchy of Lancaster	Robert Maclennan
Attorney General	John Burnett
Solicitor General	John Burnett
Lord Chancellor	John Burnett
Lord Advocate	Menzies Campbell

[1] Until September 2000; from then, Lord Navnit Dholakia.

The House of Commons

Introduction

The lower chamber of Parliament, the Commons, first emerged during the 14th century when it was formed by burgesses and knights of the shires. Since the 19th century, its members (MPs) have been elected as representatives of the people, with rights of voting (the franchise) being extended by successive Reform Acts. This has given it a legitimacy that has made it the most powerful of Parliament's two houses.

Today the Commons comprises 659 MPs directly elected for renewable terms of up to five years from single-member constituencies. Each constituency comprises an average of around 65,000 electors, and its MP is elected on a simple majority through the ('first past the post') electoral system. A candidate's nomination for election must be supported by the signatures of ten people registered in the constituency. Candidates are required to deposit £500 with the returning officer. This deposit is forfeit if the candidate does not receive more than 5% of the votes cast. When a sitting MP dies or retires between general elections, a by-election is held in the constituency.

The Commons' proceedings are presided over by the Speaker, an elected MP who becomes apolitical once in the post. The House operates on an adversarial principle, with benches to the right of the Speaker being occupied by the government and its supporters and those to the left by opposition parties. MPs holding ministerial office are known as frontbenchers since they occupy seats nearest to the Speaker. MPs receive a salary, plus office cost allowances, while ministers receive additional salaries, as does the leader of the opposition.

Parliamentary sessions

The Commons meets typically for around 160 days each year, with breaks (adjournments) at Christmas, Easter, Whitsun, and the summer: parliamentary sessions typically begin and end in October or November. Around a fifth of parliamentary time (29 days) is set aside for the opposition and another fifth for private members' business. The government controls the rest of the time. The House meets Monday to Thursday between 2.30 p.m. and 10.30 p.m., but its standing committees meet during mornings. On Friday, the Commons' hours are 11 a.m. to 4.30 p.m. There are questions to ministers, put by both backbenchers and the opposition, during the first 45–50 minutes of every sitting day, except Friday, while on Wednesdays there are 30 minutes of questions to the prime minister. Since February 2000 the adjacent Westminster Hall has been used as an alternative to the main Commons debating chamber.

MPs can be contacted in writing or in person, during regular 'surgeries' in their constituencies, and a growing number can be e-mailed, via the House of Commons' Web site (www.parliament.uk/commons). MPs will take up with government ministers matters raised by their constituents, regardless of party political persuasion.

The Functions of the House of Commons

The Commons' functions can be grouped into five elements:

Legislative: together with the House of Lords, it examines (using Standing Committees), approves, or rejects bills presented by the government, MPs, and peers. In practice, most bills originate within the Commons and are government bills.

Representative: its popularly elected members represent the will of the electorate and of individual geographical constituencies. They are able to raise and debate issues of general concern and ask oral and written questions of the government. The Commons' proceedings have been televised since 1989.

Financial: it approves all proposals for spending and raising public money. All fiscal bills must originate from the Commons and must be passed by the Lords within one month of their receipt.

Scrutiny: MPs examine and criticize the policies and activities of government, through debates and Select Committees.

Recruitment: it supplies the prime minister (able to command majority support within the House) and most of the members of the government and cabinet (the remainder are drawn from the Lords). It also provides the 'alternative government', Her Majesty's Opposition (the party with the second largest number of seats).

UK Leaders of the House of Commons

Date appointed	Name
July 1945	Herbert Morrison
March 1951	Chuter Ede
October 1951	Harry Crookshank
April 1955	'Rab' Butler
October 1961	Iain Macleod
October 1963	Selwyn Lloyd
October 1964	Herbert Bowden
August 1966	Richard Crossman
April 1968	Fred Peart
June 1970	William Whitelaw
April 1972	Robert Carr
November 1972	James Prior
March 1974	Edward Short
April 1976	Michael Foot
May 1979	Norman St John Stevas
January 1981	Francis Pym
April 1982	John Biffen
June 1987	John Wakeham
July 1989	Sir Geoffrey Howe
November 1990	John MacGregor
April 1992	Tony Newton
May 1997	Ann Taylor
July 1998	Margaret Beckett

Members of the House of Commons

Con = Conservative; DUP = Democratic Unionist Party; Ind = Independent; Lab = Labour; LD = Liberal Democrats; PC = Plaid Cymru; SDLP = Social Democratic and Labour Party; SF = Sinn Fein; SNP = Scottish National Party; SSP = Scottish Socialist Party; UKUP = UK Unionist Party; UUP = Ulster Unionist Party. Clifford Forsyth (UUP), elected MP for Antrim South with a majority of 16,611, died on 27 April 2000; the date of the by-election was still to be decided at the time of going to press.

As of July 2000.

Member	Party	Constituency	Majority at 1997 election
Abbott, Diane	Lab	Hackney North and Stoke Newington	15,627
Adams, Gerry[1]	SF	Belfast West	7,909
Adams, Irene	Lab	Paisley North	12,814
Ainger, Nick	Lab	Carmarthen West and Pembrokeshire South	9,621
Ainsworth, Robert	Lab	Coventry North East	22,569
Ainsworth, Peter	Con	Surrey East	15,093
Alexander, Douglas	Lab	Paisley South	2,731[2]
Allan, Richard	LD	Sheffield Hallam	8,271
Allen, Graham	Lab	Nottingham North	18,801
Amess, David	Con	Southend West	2,615
Ancram, Michael	Con	Devizes	9,782
Anderson, Donald	Lab	Swansea East	25,569
Anderson, Janet	Lab	Rossendale and Darwen	10,949
Arbuthnot, James	Con	Hampshire North East	14,398
Armstrong, Hilary	Lab	Durham North West	24,754
Ashdown, Paddy	LD	Yeovil	11,403
Ashton, Joe	Lab	Bassetlaw	17,348
Atherton, Candy	Lab	Falmouth and Cambourne	2,688
Atkins, Charlotte	Lab	Staffordshire Moorlands	10,049
Atkinson, David	Con	Bournemouth East	4,342
Atkinson, Peter	Con	Hexham	222
Austin, John	Lab	Erith and Thamesmead	17,424
Baker, Norman	LD	Lewes	1,300
Baldry, Tony	Con	Benbury	4,737
Ballard, Jackie	LD	Taunton	2,452
Banks, Tony	Lab	West Ham	19,494
Barnes, Harry	Lab	Derbyshire North East	18,321
Barron, Kevin	Lab	Rother Valley	23,485
Battle, John	Lab	Leeds West	19,771
Bayley, Hugh	Lab	York, City of	20,523
Beard, Nigel	Lab	Bexleyheath and Crayford	3,415
Beckett, Margaret	Lab	Derby South	16,106
Begg, Anne	Lab	Aberdeen South	3,365
Beggs, Roy	UUP	Antrim East	6,389
Beith, Alan	LD	Berwick-upon-Tweed	8,042
Bell, Martin	Ind	Tatton	11,077
Bell, Stuart	Lab	Middlesbrough	25,018
Benn, Hilary	Lab	Leeds Central	2,293[3]
Benn, Tony	Lab	Chesterfield	5,775
Bennett, Andrew	Lab	Denton and Reddish	20,311
Benton, Joe	Lab	Bootle	28,421
Bercow, John	Con	Buckingham	12,386
Beresford, Paul	Con	Mole Valley	10,221
Bermingham, Gerry	Lab	St Helens South	23,739
Berry, Roger	Lab	Kingswood	14,253
Best, Harold	Lab	Leeds North West	3,844
Betts, Clive	Lab	Sheffield Attercliffe	21,818
Blackman, Liz	Lab	Erewash	9,135
Blair, Tony	Lab	Sedgefield	25,143
Blears, Hazel	Lab	Salford	17,069
Blizzard, Bob	Lab	Waveney	12,093
Blunkett, David	Lab	Sheffield Brightside	19,954
Blunt, Crispin	Con	Reigate	7,741
Boateng, Paul	Lab	Brent South	19,691
Body, Richard	Con	Boston and Skegness	647
Boothroyd, Betty	Speaker	West Bromwich West	15,423
Borrow, David	Lab	Ribble South	5,084
Boswell, Tim	Con	Daventry	7,378
Bottomley, Peter	Con	Worthing West	7,713
Bottomley, Virginia	Con	Surrey South West	2,694
Bradley, Keith	Lab	Manchester Withington	18,581
Bradley, Peter	Lab	Wrekin, The	3,025
Bradshaw, Ben	Lab	Exeter	11,705
Brady, Graham	Con	Altrincham and Sale West	1,505
Brake, Thomas	LD	Carshalton and Wallington	2,267
Brand, Peter	LD	Isle of Wight	6,406
Brazier, Julian	Con	Canterbury	3,964
Breed, Colin	LD	Cornwall South East	6,480
Brinton, Helen	Lab	Peterborough	7,323
Brooke, Peter	Con	Cities of London and Westminster	4,881
Brown, Gordon	Lab	Dunfermline East	18,741
Brown, Nick	Lab	Newcastle upon Tyne East and Wallsend	23,811
Brown, Russell	Lab	Dumfries	9,643
Browne, Desmond	Lab	Kilmarnock and Loudoun	7,256
Browning, Angela	Con	Tiverton and Honiton	1,653
Bruce, Ian	Con	Dorset South	77
Bruce, Malcolm	LD	Gordon	6,997
Buck, Karen	Lab	Regent's Park and Kensington North	14,657
Burden, Richard	Lab	Birmingham Northfield	11,443
Burgon, Colin	Lab	Elmet	8,779
Burnett, John	LD	Devon West and Torridge	1,957
Burns, Simon	Con	Chelmsford West	6,691
Burstow, Paul	LD	Sutton and Cheam	2,097
Butler, Christine	Lab	Castle Point	1,116
Butterfill, John	Con	Bournemouth West	5,710
Byers, Stephen	Lab	Tyneside North	26,643
Cable, Vincent	LD	Twickenham	4,281
Caborn, Richard	Lab	Sheffield Central	16,906
Campbell, Alan	Lab	Tynemouth	11,273
Campbell, Anne	Lab	Cambridge	14,137
Campbell, Menzies	LD	Fife North East	10,356
Campbell, Ronnie	Lab	Blyth Valley	17,736
Campbell-Savours, Dale	Lab	Workington	19,656
Canavan, Dennis	Member for Falkirk West	Falkirk West	13,761
Cann, Jamie	Lab	Ipswich	10,439
Caplin, Ivor	Lab	Hove	3,959
Casale, Roger	Lab	Wimbledon	2,990
Cash, William	Con	Stone	3,818
Caton, Martin	Lab	Gower	13,007
Cawsey, Ian	Lab	Brigg and Goole	6,389
Chapman, Ben	Lab	Wirral South	7,004
Chapman, Sydney	Con	Chipping Barnet	1,035
Chaytor, David	Lab	Bury North	7,866
Chidgey, David	LD	Eastleigh	754
Chisholm, Malcolm	Lab	Edinburgh North and Leith	10,978
Chope, Christopher	Con	Christchurch	2,165
Church, Judith	Lab	Dagenham	17,054
Clapham, Michael	Lab	Barnsley West and Penistone	17,267
Clappison, James	Con	Hertsmere	3,075
Clark, David	Lab	South Shields	22,153
Clark, Lynda	Lab	Edinburgh Pentlands	4,862
Clark, Michael	Con	Rayleigh	10,684
Clark, Paul	Lab	Gillingham	1,980
Clarke, Charles	Lab	Norwich South	14,239
Clarke, Eric	Lab	Midlothian	9,870
Clarke, Kenneth	Con	Rushcliffe	5,055
Clarke, Tom	Lab	Coatbridge and Chryston	19,295
Clarke, Tony	Lab	Northampton South	744
Clelland, David	Lab	Tyne Bridge	22,906
Clifton-Brown, Geoffrey	Con	Cotswold	11,965
Clwyd, Ann	Lab	Cynon Valley	19,755
Coaker, Vernon	Lab	Gedling	3,802

(*continued*)

Members of the House of Commons *(continued)*

Member	Party	Constituency	Majority at 1997 election
Coffey, Ann	Lab	Stockport	18,912
Cohen, Harry	Lab	Leyton and Wanstead	15,186
Coleman, Iain	Lab	Hammersmith and Fulham	3,842
Collins, Tim	Con	Westmorland and Lonsdale	4,521
Coleman, Tony	Lab	Putney	2,976
Connarty, Michael	Lab	Falkirk East	13,385
Cook, Frank	Lab	Stockton North	21,365
Cook, Robin	Lab	Livingston	11,747
Cooper, Yvette	Lab	Pontefract and Castleford	25,725
Corbett, Robin	Lab	Birmingham Erdington	12,657
Corbyn, Jeremy	Lab	Islington North	19,955
Cormack, Patrick	Con	Staffordshire South	7,821
Corston, Jean	Lab	Bristol East	16,159
Cotter, Brian	LD	Weston-Super-Mare	1,274
Cousins, Jim	Lab	Newcastle upon Tyne Central	16,480
Cox, Tom	Lab	Tooting	15,011
Cran, James	Con	Beverley and Holderness	811
Cranston, Ross	Lab	Dudley North	9,457
Crausby, David	Lab	Bolton North East	12,669
Cryer, Ann	Lab	Keighley	7,132
Cryer, John	Lab	Hornchurch	5,680
Cummings, John	Lab	Easington	30,012
Cunliffe, Lawrence	Lab	Leigh	24,496
Cunningham, Jack	Lab	Copeland	11,944
Cunningham, Jim	Lab	Coventry South	10,953
Cunningham, Roseanna	SNP	Perth	3,141
Curry, David	Con	Skipton and Ripon	11,620
Curtis-Thomas, Clare	Lab	Crosby	7,182
Dalyell, Tam	Lab	Linlithgow	10,838
Darling, Alistair	Lab	Edinburgh Central	11,070
Darvill, Keith	Lab	Upminster	2,770
Davey, Edward	LD	Kingston and Surbiton	56
Davey, Valerie	Lab	Bristol West	1,493
Davidson, Ian	Lab	Glasgow Pollock	13,791
Davies, Denzil	Lab	Llanelli	16,039
Davies, Geraint	Lab	Croydon Central	3,897
Davies, Quentin	Con	Grantham and Stamford	2,692
Davies, Ron	Lab	Caerphilly	25,839
Davis, David	Con	Haltemprice and Howden	7,514
Davis, Terry	Lab	Birmingham Hodge Hill	14,200
Dawson, Hilton	Lab	Lancaster and Wyre	1,295
Day, Stephen	Con	Cheadle	3,189
Dean, Janet	Lab	Burton	6,330
Denham, John	Lab	Southampton Itchen	14,229
Dewar, Donald	Lab	Glasgow Anniesland	15,154
Dismore, Andrew	Lab	Hendon	6,155
Dobbin, Jim	Lab	Heywood and Middleton	17,542
Dobson, Frank	Lab	Holborn and St Pancras	17,903
Donaldson, Jeffrey	UUP	Lagan Valley	16,925
Donohoe, Brian	Lab	Cunninghame South	14,869
Doran, Frank	Lab	Aberdeen Central	10,801
Dorrell, Stephen	Con	Charnwood	5,900
Dowd, Jim	Lab	Lewisham West	14,317
Drew, David	Lab	Stroud	2,910
Drown, Julia	Lab	Swindon South	5,645
Duncan, Alan	Con	Rutland and Melton	8,836
Duncan Smith, Iain	Con	Chingford and Woodford Green	5,714
Dunwoody, Gwyneth	Lab	Crewe and Nantwich	15,798
Eagle, Angela	Lab	Wallasey	19,074
Eagle, Maria	Lab	Liverpool Garston	18,387
Edwards, Huw	Lab	Monmouth	4,178
Efford, Clive	Lab	Eltham	10,182
Ellman, Louise	Lab	Liverpool Riverside	21,799
Emery, Peter	Con	Devon East	7,489
Ennis, Jeff	Lab	Barnsley East and Mexborough	26,763
Etherington, William	Lab	Sunderland North	19,697
Evans, Nigel	Con	Ribble Valley	6,640
Ewing, Margaret	SNP	Moray	5,566
Faber, David	Con	Westbury	6,068
Fabricant, Michael	Con	Lichfield	238
Fallon, Michael	Con	Sevenoaks	10,461
Fearn, Ronnie	LD	Southport	6,170
Field, Frank	Lab	Birkenhead	21,845
Fisher, Mark	Lab	Stoke-on-Trent Central	19,924
Fitzpatrick, Jim	Lab	Poplar and Canning Town	18,915
Fitzsimons, Lorna	Lab	Rochdale	4,545
Flight, Howard	Con	Arundel and South Downs	14,035
Flint, Caroline	Lab	Don Valley	14,659
Flynn, Paul	Lab	Newport West	14,537
Follett, Barbara	Lab	Stevenage	11,582
Forth, Eric	Con	Bromley and Chislehurst	11,118
Foster, Derek	Lab	Bishop Auckland	21,064
Foster, Don	LD	Bath	9,319
Foster, Michael Jabez	Lab	Hastings and Rye	2,560
Foster, Michael S	Lab	Worcester	7,425
Foulkes, George	Lab	Carrick, Cumnock, and Doon Valley	21,062
Fowler, Norman	Con	Sutton Coldfield	14,885
Fox, Liam	Con	Woodspring	7,734
Fraser, Christopher	Con	Dorset Mid and Poole North	681
Fyfe, Maria	Lab	Glasgow Maryhill	14,264
Galbraith, Sam	Lab	Strathkelvin and Bearsden	16,292
Gale, Roger	Con	Thanet North	2,766
Galloway, George	Lab	Glasgow Kelvin	9,665
Gapes, Mike	Lab	Ilford South	14,200
Gardiner, Barry	Lab	Brent North	4,019
Garnier, Edward	Con	Harborough	6,524
George, Andrew	LD	St Ives	7,170
George, Bruce	Lab	Walsall-South	11,312
Gerrard, Neil	Lab	Walthamstow	17,149
Gibb, Nick	Con	Bognor Regis and Littlehampton	7,321
Gibson, Ian	Lab	Norwich North	9,470
Gidley, Sandra	LD	Romsey	3,311[4]
Gill, Christopher	Con	Ludlow	5,909
Gillan, Cheryl	Con	Chesham and Amersham	13,859
Gilroy, Linda	Lab	Plymouth Sutton	9,440
Godman, Norman	Lab	Greenock and Inverclyde	13,040
Godsiff, Roger	Lab	Birmingham Sparkbrook and Small Heath	19,526
Goggins, Paul	Lab	Wythenshawe and Sale East	15,019
Golding, Llin	Lab	Newcastle-under-Lyme	17,206
Gordon, Eileen	Lab	Romford	649
Gorman, Teresa	Con	Billericay	1,356
Gorrie, Donald	LD	Edinburgh West	7,253
Graham, Thomas	Scot Lab	Renfrewshire West	7,979
Gray, James	Con	Wiltshire North	3,475
Green, Damian	Con	Ashford	5,345
Greenway, John	Con	Ryedale	5,058
Grieve, Dominic	Con	Beaconsfield	13,987
Griffiths, Jane	Lab	Reading East	3,795
Griffiths, Nigel	Lab	Edinburgh South	11,452
Griffiths, Win	Lab	Bridgend	15,248
Grocott, Bruce	Lab	Telford	11,290
Grogan, John	Lab	Selby	3,836
Gummer, John	Con	Suffolk Coastal	3,254
Gunnell, John	Lab	Morley and Rothwell	14,750
Hague, William	Con	Richmond (Yorks)	10,051
Hain, Peter	Lab	Neath	26,741
Hall, Mike	Lab	Weaver Vale	13,448
Hall, Patrick	Lab	Bedford	8,300
Hamilton, Archie	Con	Epsom and Ewell	11,525

(continued)

Members of the House of Commons *(continued)*

Member	Party	Constituency	Majority at 1997 election
Hamilton, Fabian	Lab	Leeds North East	6,959
Hammond, Philip	Con	Runnymede and Weybridge	9,875
Hancock, Mike	LD	Portsmouth South	4,327
Hanson, David	Lab	Delyn	12,693
Harman, Harriet	Lab	Camberwell and Peckham	16,451
Harris, Evan	LD	Oxford West and Abingdon	6,285
Harvey, Nick	LD	Devon North	6,181
Haselhurst, Alan	Deputy Speaker	Saffron Walden	10,573
Hawkins, Nick	Con	Surrey Heath	16,287
Hayes, John	Con	South Holland and The Deepings	7,991
Heal, Sylvia	Lab	Halesowen and Rowley Regis	10,337
Heald, Oliver	Con	Hertfordshire North East	3,088
Healey, John	Lab	Wentworth	23,959
Heath, David	LD	Somerton and Frome	130
Heath, Edward	Con	Old Bexley and Sidcup	3,569
Heathcoat-Amory, David	Con	Wells	528
Henderson, Doug	Lab	Newcastle-upon-Tyne North	19,332
Henderson, Ivan	Lab	Harwich	1,216
Hepburn, Stephen	Lab	Jarrow	21,933
Heppell, John	Lab	Nottingham East	15,419
Heseltine, Michael	Con	Henley	11,167
Hesford, Stephen	Lab	Wirral West	2,738
Hewitt, Patricia	Lab	Leicester West	12,864
Hill, Keith	Lab	Streatham	18,423
Hinchliffe, David	Lab	Wakefield	14,604
Hodge, Margaret	Lab	Barking	15,896
Hoey, Kate	Lab	Vauxhall	18,660
Hogg, Douglas	Con	Sleaford and North Hykeham	5,123
Home Robertson, John	Lab	East Lothian	14,221
Hood, Jimmy	Lab	Clydesdale	13,809
Hoon, Geoff	Lab	Ashfield	22,728
Hope, Phil	Lab	Corby	11,860
Hopkins, Kelvin	Lab	Luton North	9,626
Horam, John	Con	Orpington	2,952
Howard, Michael	Con	Folkestone and Hythe	6,332
Howarth, Alan	Lab	Newport East	13,523
Howarth, George	Lab	Knowsley North and Sefton East	26,147
Howarth, Gerald	Con	Aldershot	6,621
Howells, Kim	Lab	Pontypridd	23,129
Hoyle, Lindsay	Lab	Chorley	9,870
Hughes, Beverley	Lab	Stretford and Urmston	13,640
Hughes, Kevin	Lab	Doncaster North	21,937
Hughes, Simon	LD	Southwark North and Bermondsey	3,387
Humble, Joan	Lab	Blackpool North and Fleetwood	8,946
Hume, John	SDLP	Foyle	13,664
Hunter, Andrew	Con	Basingstoke	2,397
Hurst, Alan	Lab	Braintree	1,451
Hutton, John	Lab	Barrow and Furness	14,497
Iddon, Brian	Lab	Bolton South East	21,311
Illsley, Eric	Lab	Barnsley Central	24,501
Ingram, Adam	Lab	East Kilbride	17,384
Jack, Michael	Con	Fylde	8,963
Jackson, Glenda	Lab	Hampstead and Highgate	13,289
Jackson, Helen	Lab	Sheffield Hillsborough	16,451
Jackson, Robert	Con	Wantage	6,089
Jamieson, David	Lab	Plymouth Devonport	19,127
Jenkin, Bernard	Con	Essex North	5,476
Jenkins, Brian	Lab	Tamworth	7,496
Johnson, Alan	Lab	Kingston upon Hull West and Hessle	15,525
Johnson, Melanie	Lab	Welwyn Hatfield	5,595
Johnson Smith, Geoffrey	Con	Wealden	14,204
Jones, Barry	Lab	Alyn and Deeside	16,403
Jones, Fiona	Lab	Newark	3,016
Jones, Helen	Lab	Warrington North	19,527
Jones, Ieuan Wyn	PC	Ynys Mon	2,481
Jones, Jenny	Lab	Wolverhampton South West	5,118
Jones, Jon Owen	Lab	Cardiff Central	7,923
Jones, Lynne	Lab	Birmingham Selly Oak	14,088
Jones, Martin	Lab	Clwyd South	13,810
Jones, Nigel	LD	Cheltenham	6,645
Jowell, Tessa	Lab	Dulwich and West Norwood	16,769
Kaufman, Gerald	Lab	Manchester Gorton	17,342
Keeble, Sally	Lab	Northampton North	10,000
Keen, Alan	Lab	Feltham and Heston	15,473
Keen, Ann	Lab	Brentford and Isleworth	14,424
Keetch, Paul	LD	Hereford	6,648
Kelly, Ruth	Lab	Bolton West	7,072
Kemp, Fraser	Lab	Houghton and Washington East	26,555
Kennedy, Charles	LD	Ross, Skye, and Inverness West	4,019
Kennedy, Jane	Lab	Liverpool Wavertree	19,701
Key, Robert	Con	Salisbury	6,276
Khabra, Piara	Lab	Ealing Southall	21,423
Kidney, David	Lab	Stafford	4,314
Kilfoyle, Peter	Lab	Liverpool Walton	27,038
King, Andrew	Lab	Rugby and Kenilworth	495
King, Oona	Lab	Bethnal Green and Bow	11,285
King, Tom	Con	Bridgwater	1,796
Kingham, Tess	Lab	Gloucester	8,259
Kirkbride, Julie	Con	Bromsgrove	4,895
Kirkwood, Archy	LD	Roxburgh and Berwickshire	7,906
Kumar, Ashok	Lab	Middlesbrough South and Cleveland East	10,607
Ladyman, Stephen	Lab	Thanet South	2,878
Laing, Eleanor	Con	Epping Forest	5,252
Lait, Jackie	Con	Beckenham	1,227[5]
Lammy, David	Lab	Tottenham	5,646[6]
Lansley, Andrew	Con	Cambridgeshire South	8,712
Lawrence, Jackie	Lab	Preseli Pembrokeshire	8,736
Laxton, Bob	Lab	Derby North	10,615
Leigh, Edward	Con	Gainsborough	6,826
Lepper, David	Lab	Brighton Pavilion	13,181
Leslie, Christopher	Lab	Shipley	2,996
Letwin, Oliver	Con	Dorset West	1,840
Levitt, Tom	Lab	High Peak	8,791
Lewis, Ivan	Lab	Bury South	12,387
Lewis, Julian	Con	New Forest East	5,215
Lewis, Terry	Lab	Worsley	17,741
Liddell, Helen	Lab	Airdrie and Shotts	15,412
Lidington, David	Con	Aylesbury	8,419
Lilley, Peter	Con	Hitchen and Harpenden	6,671
Linton, Martin	Lab	Battersea	5,360
Livingstone, Ken	Member for Brent East	Brent East	15,882
Livsey, Richard	LD	Brecon and Radnorshire	5,097
Lloyd, Peter	Con	Fareham	10,358
Lloyd, Tony	Lab	Manchester Central	19,682
Llywd, Elfyn	PC	Meirionnydd Nant Conwy	6,805
Lock, David	Lab	Wyre Forest	6,946
Lord, Michael	Deputy Speaker	Suffolk Central and Ipswich North	3,538
Loughton, Tim	Con	Worthing East and Shoreham	5,098
Love, Andrew	Lab	Edmonton	13,472
Luff, Peter	Con	Worcestershire Mid	9,412
Lyell, Nicholas	Con	Bedfordshire North East	5,883
McAllion, John	Lab	Dundee East	9,961
McAvoy, Thomas	Lab	Glasgow Rutherglen	15,007

(continued)

Members of the House of Commons *(continued)*

Member	Party	Constituency	Majority at 1997 election
McCabe, Steve	Lab	Birmingham Hall Green	8,420
McCafferty, Chris	Lab	Calder Valley	6,255
McCartney, Ian	Lab	Makerfield	26,177
McCartney, Robert	UKUP	North Down	1,449
McDonagh, Siobhain	Lab	Mitcham and Morden	13,741
MacDonald, Calum	Lab	Western Isles	3,576
McDonnell, John	Lab	Hayes and Harlington	14,289
McFall, John	Lab	Dumbarton	10,883
McGrady, Eddie	SDLP	South Down	9,933
MacGregor, John	Con	Norfolk South	7,378
McGuinness, Martin[1]	SF	Ulster Mid	1,883
McGuire, Anne	Lab	Stirling	6,411
McIntosh, Anne	Con	Vale of York	9,721
McIsaac, Shona	Lab	Cleethorpes	9,176
MacKay, Andrew	Con	Bracknell	10,387
McKenna, Rosemary	Lab	Cumbernauld and Kilsyth	11,128
Mackinlay, Andrew	Lab	Thurrock	17,256
MacLean, David	Con	Penrith and The Border	10,233
McLeish, Henry	Lab	Fife Central	13,713
MacLennan, Robert	LD	Caithness, Sutherland, and Easter Ross	2,259
McLoughlin, Patrick	Con	Derbyshire West	4,885
McNamara, Kevin	Lab	Kingston upon Hull North	19,705
McNulty, Tony	Lab	Harrow East	9,737
MacShane, Denis	Lab	Rotheram	21,469
MacTaggart, Fiona	Lab	Slough	13,071
McWalter, Tony	Lab	Hemel Hempstead	3,636
McWilliam, John	Lab	Blaydon	16,605
Madel, David	Con	Bedforshire South West	132
Maginnis, Ken	UUP	Fermanagh and South Tyrone	13,688
Mahon, Alice	Lab	Halifax	11,212
Major, John	Con	Huntingdon	18,140
Malins, Humfrey	Con	Woking	5,678
Mallaber, Judy	Lab	Amber Valley	11,613
Mallon, Seamus	SDLP	Newry and Armagh	4,889
Mandelson, Peter	Lab	Hartlepool	17,508
Maples, John	Con	Stratford-on-Avon	14,106
Marek, John	Lab	Wrexham	11,762
Marsden, Gordon	Lab	Blackpool South	11,616
Marsden, Paul	Lab	Shrewsbury and Atcham	1,670
Marshall, David	Lab	Glasgow Shettleston	15,868
Marshall, Jim	Lab	Leicester South	16,493
Marshall-Andrews, Robert	Lab	Medway	5,354
Martin, Michael	Deputy Speaker	Glasgow Springburn	17,326
Martlew, Eric	Lab	Carlisle	12,390
Mates, Michael	Con	Hampshire East	11,590
Maude, Francis	Con	Horsham	14,862
Mawhinney, Brian	Con	Cambridgeshire North West	7,754
Maxton, John	Lab	Glasgow Cathcart	12,965
May, Theresa	Con	Maidenhead	11,981
Meacher, Michael	Lab	Oldham West and Royton	16,201
Meale, Alan	Lab	Mansfield	20,518
Merron, Gillian	Lab	Lincoln	11,130
Michael, Alun	Lab	Cardiff South and Penarth	13,881
Michie, Bill	Lab	Sheffield Heeley	17,078
Michie, Ray	LD	Argyll and Bute	6,081
Milburn, Alan	Lab	Darlington	16,025
Miller, Andrew	Lab	Ellesmere Port and Neston	16,036
Mitchell, Austin	Lab	Great Grimsby	16,244
Moffatt, Laura	Lab	Crawley	11,707
Moonie, Lewis	Lab	Kirkcaldy	10,710
Moore, Michael	LD	Tweeddale, Ettrick, and Lauderdale	2,290
Moran, Margaret	Lab	Luton South	11,319
Morgan, Alasdair	SNP	Galloway and Upper Nithsdale	5,624
Morgan, Julie	Lab	Cardiff North	8,126
Morgan, Rhodri	Lab	Cardiff West	15,628
Morley, Elliott	Lab	Scunthorpe	14,173
Morris, Estelle	Lab	Birmingham Yardley	5,315
Morris, John	Lab	Aberavon	21,571
Moss, Malcolm	Con	Cambridgeshire North East	5,101
Mountford, Kali	Lab	Colne Valley	4,840
Mowlam, Marjorie	Lab	Redcar	21,664
Mudie, George	Lab	Leeds East	17,466
Mullin, Chris	Lab	Sunderland South	19,638
Murphy, Denis	Lab	Wansbeck	32,367
Murphy, Jim	Lab	Eastwood	3,236
Murphy, Paul	Lab	Torfaen	24,536
Naysmith, Douglas	Lab	Bristol North West	11,382
Nicholls, Patrick	Con	Teignbridge	281
Norman, Archie	Con	Tunbridge Wells	7,506
Norris, Dan	Lab	Wansdyke	4,799
O'Brien, Bill	Lab	Normanton	15,893
O'Brien, Mike	Lab	Warwickshire North	14,767
O'Brien, Stephen	Con	Eddisbury	1,606[7]
O'Hara, Eddie	Lab	Knowsley South	30,708
O'Neill, Martin	Lab	Ochil	4,652
Oaten, Mark	LD	Winchester	21,556[8]
Olner, Bill	Lab	Nuneaton	13,540
Opik, Lembit	LD	Montgomeryshire	6,303
Organ, Diana	Lab	Forest of Dean	6,343
Osborne, Sandra	Lab	Ayr	6,543
Ottaway, Richard	Con	Croydon South	11,930
Page, Richard	Con	Hertfordshire South West	10,021
Paice, James	Con	Cambridgeshire South East	9,349
Paisley, Ian	DUP	Antrim North	10,574
Palmer, Nick	Lab	Broxtowe	5,575
Paterson, Owen	Con	Shropshire North	2,195
Pearson, Ian	Lab	Dudley South	13,027
Pendry, Tom	Lab	Stalybridge and Hyde	14,806
Perham, Linda	Lab	Ilford North	3,224
Pickles, Eric	Con	Brentwood and Ongar	9,690
Pickthall, Colin	Lab	Lancashire West	17,119
Pike, Peter	Lab	Burnley	17,062
Plaskitt, James	Lab	Warwick and Leamington	3,398
Pollard, Kerry	Lab	St Albans	4,459
Pond, Chris	Lab	Gravesham	5,779
Pope, Greg	Lab	Hyndburn	11,448
Portillo, Michael	Con	Kensington and Chelsea	6,706[9]
Pound, Stephen	Lab	Ealing North	7,010
Powell, Raymond	Lab	Ogmore	24,447
Prentice, Bridget	Lab	Lewisham East	12,127
Prentice, Gordon	Lab	Pendle	10,824
Prescott, John	Lab	Kingston upon Hull East	23,318
Primarolo, Dawn	Lab	Bristol South	19,328
Prior, David	Con	Norfolk North	1,084
Prosser, Gwyn	Lab	Dover	11,739
Purchase, Ken	Lab	Wolverhampton North East	12,987
Quin, Joyce	Lab	Gateshead East and Washington West	24,950
Quinn, Lawrie	Lab	Scarborough and Whitby	5,124
Radice, Giles	Lab	Durham North	26,299
Rammell, Bill	Lab	Harlow	10,514
Randall, John	Con	Uxbridge	3,766[10]
Rapson, Syd	Lab	Portsmouth North	4,323
Raynsford, Nick	Lab	Greenwich and Woolwich	18,128
Redwood, John	Con	Wokingham	9,365
Reed, Andrew	Lab	Loughborough	5,712
Reid, John	Lab	Hamilton North and Bellshill	17,067
Rendel, David	LD	Newbury	8,617
Robathan, Andrew	Con	Blaby	6,474
Robertson, Lawrence	Con	Tewkesbury	9,234
Robinson, Geoffrey	Lab	Coventry North West	16,601
Robinson, Peter	DUP	Belfast East	6,754

(continued)

Members of the House of Commons *(continued)*

Member	Party	Constituency	Majority at 1997 election
Roche, Barbara	Lab	Hornsey and Wood Green	20,499
Roe, Marion	Con	Broxbourne	6,653
Rogers, Allan	Lab	Rhondda	24,931
Rooker, Jeff	Lab	Birmingham, Perry Barr	18,957
Rooney, Terry	Lab	Bradford North	12,770
Ross, Ernie	Lab	Dundee West	11,859
Ross, William	UUP	Londonderry East	3,794
Rowe, Andrew	Con	Faversham and Kent Mid	4,173
Rowlands, Ted	Lab	Merthyr Tydfil and Rhymney	27,086
Roy, Frank	Lab	Motherwell and Wishaw	12,791
Ruane, Chris	Lab	Vale of Clwyd	8,955
Ruddock, Joan	Lab	Lewisham Deptford	18,878
Ruffley, David	Con	Bury St Edmunds	368
Russell, Bob	LD	Colchester	1,551
Russell, Christine	Lab	Chester, City of	10,553
Ryan, Joan	Lab	Enfield North	6,812
St Aubyn, Nick	Con	Guildford	4,791
Salmond, Alex	SNP	Banff and Buchan	12,845
Salter, Martin	Lab	Reading West	2,997
Sanders, Adrian	LD	Torbay	12
Sarwar, Mohammad	Lab	Glasgow, Govan	2,914
Savidge, Malcolm	Lab	Aberdeen North	10,010
Sawford, Phil	Lab	Kettering	189
Sayeed, Jonathan	Con	Bedfordshire Mid	7,090
Sedgemore, Brian	Lab	Hackney South and Shoreditch	14,990
Shaw, Jonathon	Lab	Chatham and Aylesford	2,790
Sheerman, Barry	Lab	Huddersfield	15,848
Sheldon, Robert	Lab	Ashton-under-Lyne	22,965
Shephard, Gillian	Con	Norfolk South West	2,434
Shepherd, Richard	Con	Aldridge-Brownhills	2,526
Shipley, Debra	Lab	Stourbridge	5,645
Short, Clare	Lab	Birmingham Ladywood	23,082
Simpson, Alan	Lab	Nottingham South	13,364
Simpson, Keith	Con	Norfolk Mid	1,336
Singh, Marsha	Lab	Bradford West	3,877
Skinner, Dennis	Lab	Bolsover	27,149
Smith, Andrew	Lab	Oxford East	16,665
Smith, Angela	Lab	Basildon	13,280
Smith, Chris	Lab	Islington South and Finsbury	14,563
Smith, Geraldine	Lab	Morecambe and Lunesdale	5,965
Smith, Jacqui	Lab	Redditch	6,125
Smith, John	Lab	Vale of Glamorgan	10,532
Smith, Llew	Lab	Blaenau Gwent	28,032
Smith, Robert	LD	Aberdeenshire West and Kincardine	2,662
Smyth, Martin	UUP	Belfast South	4,600
Snape, Peter	Lab	West Bromwich East	13,584
Soames, Nicholas	Con	Sussex Mid	6,854
Soley, Clive	Lab	Ealing Acton and Shepherd's Bush	15,650
Southworth, Helen	Lab	Warrington South	10,807
Spellar, John	Lab	Warley	15,451
Spelman, Caroline	Con	Meriden	582
Spicer, Michael	Con	Worcestershire West	3,846
Spring, Richard	Con	Suffolk West	1,867
Squire, Rachel	Lab	Dunfermline West	12,354
Stanley, John	Con	Tonbridge and Malling	10,230
Starkey, Phyllis	Lab	Milton Keynes South West	10,092
Steen, Anthony	Con	Totnes	877
Steinberg, Gerry	Lab	Durham, City of	22,504
Stevenson, George	Lab	Stoke-on-Trent South	18,303
Stewart, David	Lab	Inverness East, Nairn, and Lochaber	2,339
Stewart, Ian	Lab	Eccles	21,916
Stinchcombe, Paul	Lab	Wellingborough	187
Stoate, Howard	Lab	Dartford	4,328
Strang, Gavin	Lab	Edinburgh East and Mussleburgh	14,530
Straw, Jack	Lab	Blackburn	14,445
Streeter, Gary	Con	Devon South West	7,433
Stringer, Graham	Lab	Manchester Blackley	19,588
Stuart, Gisela	Lab	Birmingham Edgbaston	4,842
Stunnell, Andrew	LD	Hazel Grove	11,814
Sutcliffe, Gerry	Lab	Bradford South	12,936
Swayne, Desmond	Con	New Forest West	11,332
Swinney, John	SNP	Tayside North	4,160
Syms, Robert	Con	Poole	5,298
Tapsell, Peter	Con	Louth and Horncastle	6,900
Taylor, Ann	Lab	Dewsbury	8,323
Taylor, Dari	Lab	Stockton South	11,585
Taylor, David	Lab	Leicestershire North West	13,219
Taylor, Ian	Con	Esher and Walton	14,528
Taylor, John D	UUP	Strangford	5,852
Taylor, John M	Con	Solihull	11,397
Taylor, Matthew	LD	Truro and St Austell	12,501
Taylor, Teddy	Con	Rochford and Southend East	4,225
Temple-Morris, Peter	Lab	Leominster	8,835
Thomas, Gareth	Lab	Clwyd West	1,848
Thomas, Gareth R	Lab	Harrow West	1,240
Thomas, Simon	PC	Ceredigion	4,948[11]
Thompson, William	UUP	Tyrone West	1,161
Timms, Stephen	Lab	East Ham	19,358
Tipping, Paddy	Lab	Sherwood	16,812
Todd, Mark	Lab	Derbyshire South	13,967
Tonge, Jenny	LD	Richmond Park	2,951
Touhig, Don	Lab	Islwyn	23,931
Townend, John	Con	Yorkshire East	3,337
Tredinnick, David	Con	Bosworth	1,027
Trend, Michael	Con	Windsor	9,917
Trickett, Jon	Lab	Hemsworth	23,992
Trimble, David	UUP	Upper Bann	9,252
Truswell, Paul	Lab	Pudsey	6,207
Turner, Dennis	Lab	Wolverhampton South East	15,182
Turner, Desmond	Lab	Brighton Kemptown	3,234
Turner, George	Lab	Norfolk North West	1,339
Turner, Neil	Lab	Wigan	6,729[12]
Twigg, Derek	Lab	Halton	23,650
Twigg, Stephen	Lab	Enfield Southgate	1,433
Tyler, Paul	LD	Cornwall North	13,847
Tynan, Bill	Lab	Hamilton South	556[13]
Tyrie, Andrew	Con	Chichester	9,734
Vaz, Keith	Lab	Leicester East	18,422
Viggers, Peter	Con	Gosport	6,258
Vis, Rudi	Lab	Finchley and Golders Green	3,189
Walker, Cecil	UUP	Belfast North	13,024
Wallace, Jim	LD	Orkney and Shetland	6,968
Walley, Joan	Lab	Stoke-on-Trent North	17,392
Walter, Robert	Con	Dorset North	2,746
Ward, Claire	Lab	Watford	5,792
Wardle, Charles	Con	Bexhill and Battle	11,100
Wareing, Robert	Lab	Liverpool West Derby	25,965
Waterson, Nigel	Con	Eastbourne	1,994
Watts, Dave	Lab	St Helens North	23,417
Webb, Steven	LD	Northavon	2,137
Wells, Bowen	Con	Hertford and Stortford	6,885
Welsh, Andrew	SNP	Angus	10,189
White, Brian	Lab	Milton Keynes North East	240
Whitehead, Alan	Lab	Southampton Test	13,684
Whitney, Raymond	Con	Wycombe	2,370
Whittingdale, John	Con	Maldon and Chelmsford East	10,039
Wicks, Malcolm	Lab	Croydon North	18,398
Widdecombe, Ann	Con	Maidstone and The Weald	9,603
Wigley, Dafydd	PC	Caernarfon	7,949
Wilkinson, John	Con	Ruislip Northwood	7,794
Willetts, David	Con	Havant	3,729
Williams, Alan, W	Lab	Swansea West	14,459

(continued)

Members of the House of Commons (*continued*)

Member	Party	Constituency	Majority at 1997 election
Williams, Alan W	Lab	Carmarthen East and Dinefwr	3,450
Williams, Betty	Lab	Conwy	1,596
Willis, Phil	LD	Harrogate and Knaresborough	6,236
Wills, Michael	Lab	Swindon North	7,688
Wilshire, David	Con	Spelthorne	3,473
Wilson, Brian	Lab	Cunninghame North	11,039
Winnick, David	Lab	Walsall North	12,588
Winterton, Ann	Con	Congleton	6,130
Winterton, Nicholas	Con	Macclesfield	8,654
Winterton, Rosie	Lab	Doncaster Central	17,856
Wise, Audrey	Lab	Preston	18,680
Wood, Mike	Lab	Batley and Spen	6,141
Woodward, Shaun	Lab	Witney	7,028
Woolas, Phil	Lab	Oldham East and Saddleworth	3,389
Worthington, Tony	Lab	Clydebank and Milngavie	13,320
Wray, James	Lab	Glasgow Bailliestown	14,840
Wright, Tony	Lab	Cannock Chase	14,478
Wright, Tony	Lab	Great Yarmouth	8,668
Wyatt, Derek	Lab	Sittingbourne and Sheppey	1,929
Yeo, Tim	Con	Suffolk South	4,175
Young, George	Con	Hampshire North West	11,551

[1] Do not take their seats.
[2] After a by-election on 6 November 1997 following the death of Gordon McMaster (Lab; majority at the 1997 general election 12,750) on 28 July 1997.
[3] After a by-election on 10 June 1999, following the death of Derek Fatchett (Lab; majority at the 1997 general election 20,689) on 9 May 1999.
[4] After a by-election on 4 May 2000 following the death of Michael Colvin (Con; majority at the 1997 general election 8,585) on 24 February 2000.
[5] After a by-election on 20 November 1997 following the resignation of Piers Merchant (Con; majority at the 1997 general election 4,953) on 21 October 1997.
[6] After a by-election on 22 June 2000 following the death of Bernie Grant (Lab; majority at the 1997 general election 20,200) on 8 April 2000.
[7] After a by-election on 22 July 1999 following the resignation of Alistair Goodlad (Con; majority at the 1997 general election 1,185) on 28 June 1999.
[8] After a by-election on 20 November 1997 following a successful election petition against the general election result where the majority over the Conservative candidate was 2.
[9] After a by-election on 25 November 1999 following the death of Alan Clark (Con; majority at the 1997 general election 9,519) on 5 September 1999.
[10] After a by-election on 31 July 1997 following the death of Michael Shersby (Con; majority at the 1997 general election 724) on 8 May 1997.
[11] After a by-election on 3 February 2000 following the resignation of Cynog Dafis (PC; majority at the 1997 general election 6,961) on 10 January 2000.
[12] After a by-election on 23 September 1999 following the death of Roger Stott (Lab; majority at the 1997 general election 22,643) on 8 August 1999.
[13] After a by-election on 23 September 1999 following the elevation to the peerage of George Robertson (Lab; majority at the 1997 general election 15,878) on 24 August 1999.

MP Nominations

MPs must be British subjects aged at least 21 years. They may not be: members of the House of Lords; persons medically certified as suffering from mental illness; judges; police officers; civil servants; members of the clergy; undischarged bankrupts; persons guilty of corrupt or illegal electoral practices; or convicted prisoners serving sentences of 12 months or more.

General Election Facts

Polling day It is the custom in the UK for general elections to be held on Thursdays, but the prime minister could choose a different day. The last time a general election was held on a day other than Thursday was 27 October 1931.

Constituencies The total number of constituencies in the UK is 659 (England 529; Scotland 72; Wales 40; Northern Ireland 18); the constituency with the largest electorate is the Isle of Wight (103,678 in 1997) and the constituency with the smallest electorate is the Western Isles (22,539 in 1997); the average size of constituency electorates in the UK is 67,077 (1997).

Majorities In the general election of 1997, the Liberal Democrat candidate for Winchester, Mike Oaten, won by two votes over the Conservative candidate Gerry Malone (the smallest majority since 1945). Following a successful election petition challenging the result, a by-election was held, and Mark Oaten was returned with a majority of over 21,000; in 1966 the Conservative candidate for Peterborough won by three votes, beating Labour candidate Michael Ward, and in 1974 Gwynoro Jones, the Labour candidate for Carmarthen, also won his seat by three votes, beating Gwynfor Evans, the Plaid Cymru candidate.

Parliamentary Elections in the UK

(– = not applicable)

Turnout (% of electorate)	25 Oct 1951	26 May 1955	8 Oct 1959	15 Oct 1964	31 Mar 1966	18 Jun 1970	28 Feb 1974	10 Oct 1974	3 May 1979	9 June 1983	11 June 1987	9 April 1992	1 May 1997[2]
England and Wales	82.8	77.0	79.1	77.1	76.1	71.2	78.1	72.5	75.2	71.8	74.8	77.5	71.5
Scotland	81.2	75.1	78.1	77.6	76.0	73.5	77.9	74.5	76.0	71.8	74.3	74.2	71.3
Great Britain	81.9	76.8	78.7	77.1	75.8	71.5	77.9	72.5	75.1	71.8	74.5	76.7	71.4
Northern Ireland	53.1	74.1	65.8	71.7	66.1	76.0	69.9	67.7	67.7	72.9	67.0	68.8	67.1
Number of members of Parliament elected													
Conservative	320	344	364	303	253	330	296	276	339	396	375	336	165
Labour	295	277	258	317	363	287	301	319	268	209	229	271	418
Liberal Democrat	6	6	6	9	12	6	14	13	11	17	17	20	46
Social Democratic Party	–	–	–	–	–	–	–	–	–	6	5	–	–
Scottish National Party	–	–	–	–	–	1	7	11	2	2	3	3	6
Plaid Cymru	–	–	–	–	–	–	2	3	2	2	3	4	4
Other[1]	4	3	2	1	2	6	15	13	13	18	18	17	20
Total	625	630	630	630	630	630	635	635	635	650	650	651	659

[1] Including the Speaker.
[2] Provisional.

Source: Annual Abstract of Statistics 2000,

■ UK Parliament

House of Commons Select Committees: Introduction

Parliamentary select committees were set up to restore parliamentary control of the executive, improve the quality of legislation, and scrutinize public spending and the work of government departments. Select committees usually consist of 10 to 15 members of all parties, and most are tied to government departments. Select committees represent a major 20th-century parliamentary reform and a possible means – through their all-party membership – of avoiding the repeal of one government's measures by its successor.

Smoking in the House of Commons

Smoking has been banned in the Chamber of the House of Commons and in House of Commons committees since 1693. However, at the doorkeeper's box at the entrance to the Chamber, snuff is still provided (until recently at public expense) for members and officers of the House.

House of Commons Select Committees

Con = Conservative; Lab = Labour; LD = Liberal Democrat.

As of July 2000.

Name	Number of members	Chair
Accommodation and Works Committee	9	Sydney Chapman (Con)
Administration Committee	9	Marion Roe (Con)
Agriculture Committee	11	David Curry (Con)
Broadcasting Committee	11	Eric Clarke (Lab)
Catering Committee	9	Dennis Turner (Lab)
Culture, Media, and Sport Committee	11	Gerald Kaufman (Lab)
Defence Committee	11	Bruce George (Lab)
Deregulation Committee	18	Peter L Pike (Lab)
Education and Employment Committee	17	
Education Sub-Committee	11	Barry Sheerman (Lab)
Employment Sub-Committee	8	Derek Foster (Lab)
Environment, Transport, and Regional Affairs Committee	17	
Environment Sub-Committee	11	Andrew F Bennett (Lab)
Transport Sub-Committee	11	Gwyneth Dunwoody (Lab)
Environmental Audit Committee	16	John Horam (Con)
European Scrutiny Committee	16	Jimmy Hood (Lab)
Foreign Affairs Committee	12	Donald Anderson (Lab)
Health Committee	11	David Hinchliffe (Lab)
Home Affairs Committee	11	Robin Corbett (Lab)
Information Committee	9	Richard Allan (LD)
International Development Committee	11	Bowen Wells (Con)
Liaison Committee	33	Robert Sheldon (Lab)
Modernization Committee	15	Margaret Beckett (Lab)
Northern Ireland Affairs Committee	13	Peter Brooke (Con)
Joint Committee on Parliamentary Privilege	12	Lord Nicholls of Birkenhead (nominated by the House of Lords)
Procedure Committee	14	Nicholas Winterton (Con)
Committee of Public Accounts	15	David Davis (Con)
Select Committee on Public Administration	11	Tony Wright (Lab)
Science and Technology Committee	11	Michael Clark (Con)
Scottish Affairs Committee	11	David Marshall (Lab)
Social Security Committee	11	Archy Kirkwood (LD)
Standards and Privileges Committee	11	Robert Sheldon (Lab)
Joint Committee on Statutory Instruments	14	David Tredinnick (Con)
Trade and Industry Committee	11	Martin O'Neill (Lab)
Treasury Committee	12	Giles Radice (Lab)
Welsh Affairs Committee	11	Martyn Jones (Lab)

Women MPs in the House of Commons

(– = not applicable.)

As of July 2000.

Political party	Number of members	Number of women members	(%) women members
Labour	416	101	24
Conservative	160	14	9
Liberal Democrats	47	4	8
Ulster Unionists	9	0	0
Scottish National Party	6	2	33
Plaid Cymru	4	0	0
Social Democratic and Labour Party	3	0	0
Ulster Democratic Unionist Party	2	0	0
Sinn Fein	2	0	0
United Kingdom Unionist	1	0	0
Independent	1	0	0
Member of Parliament for Falkirk West	1	0	0
Member of Parliament for Brent East	1	0	0
Scottish Labour	1	0	0
Vacant seat (South Antrim)	1	–	–
The Speaker and three Deputies (do not normally vote)	4	1	25
Total	659	122	19

UK Ministers' Pay

Full ministerial salary entitlement for Ministers in Commons (excluding Parliamentary salary). (In pounds.)

Year	Prime Minister	Cabinet Minister Commons	Cabinet Minister Lords	Minister of State Commons[1]	Minister of State Lords	Parliamentary Under Secretary Commons	Parliamentary Under Secretary Lords
1965	14,000	8,500	8,500	5,625	5,625	3,750	3,750
1972	20,000	13,000	13,000	7,500	7,500	5,500	5,500
1976	20,000	13,000	13,000	7,500	7,500	5,500	5,500
1977	20,000	13,000	13,000	7,500	7,500	5,500	6,020
1978	22,000	14,300	14,300	8,250	8,822	6,050	6,622
1979	33,000	19,650	19,650	12,625	12,911	9,525	9,811
1980	34,650	23,500	23,500	16,250	16,400	12,350	12,500
1981	36,725	27,825	27,825	19,775	23,275	15,100	18,600
1982	38,200	28,950	28,950	20,575	24,200	15,700	19,350
1983	38,987	29,367	30,110	20,867	25,350	15,917	20,390
1984	40,424	30,304	31,680	21,364	26,670	16,154	21,450
1985	41,891	31,271	33,260	21,881	28,000	16,411	22,520
1986	43,328	32,208	34,820	22,378	29,320	16,648	23,580
1987	44,775	33,145	36,390	22,875	30,640	16,885	24,640
1988	45,787	34,157	40,438	23,887	34,688	17,897	28,688
1989	46,109	34,479	41,997	24,209	37,047	18,219	30,647
1990	46,750	35,120	44,591	24,850	39,641	18,860	33,241
1991	50,724	38,105	48,381	26,962	43,010	20,463	36,066
1992	53,007	39,820	50,558	28,175	44,945	21,384	37,689
1994	54,438	40,895	52,260	28,936	46,333	21,961	38,894
1995	57,018	42,834	55,329	30,307	48,835	23,002	41,065
1996	58,557	43,991	57,161	31,125	50,328	23,623	42,361
1996	58,557	43,991	58,876	31,125	51,838	23,623	43,632
1997[2]	100,000	60,000	77,963	31,125	51,838	23,623	43,632
1998	102,750	61,650	80,107	31,981	53,264	24,273	44,832
1999	107,179	64,307	83,560	33,359	64,426	25,319	55,631
2000	110,287	66,172	85,983	34,326	66,294	26,053	57,244

[1] Until 1980 some Ministers of State received salaries higher than those shown here.
[2] In 1997, the prime minister and cabinet ministers decided to accept the pre-election salaries of £58,557 (prime minister), £43,991 (Cabinet Commons), and £58,876 (Cabinet Lords).

Source: House of Commons Information Office

Members of Parliament: Pay

Year	Salary (£)	Year	Salary (£)	Year	Salary (£)
1911	400	1978	6,897	1991	28,970
1931	360	1979	9,450	1992	30,854
1934	380	1980	11,750	1993	30,854
1935	400	1981	13,950	1994	31,687
1937	600	1982	14,510	1995	33,189
1946	1,000	1983	15,308	1996	34,085
1954[1]	1,250	1984	16,106	1996	43,000
1957	1,750	1985	16,904	1997	43,860
1964	3,250	1986	17,702	1998	45,066
1972	4,500	1987	18,500	1999	47,008
1975	5,750	1988	22,548	2000	48,371
1976	6,062	1989	24,107		
1977	6,270	1990	26,701		

[1] Includes sessional allowance.

Source: House of Commons Information Office

Members of Parliament: Office Cost Allowances

These allowances were first introduced in 1969. These figures represent the maximum that can be claimed.

Year	Allowance (£)	Year	Allowance (£)	Year	Allowance (£)
1969	500	1982	8,820	1993	40,380
1972	1,000	1983	11,364	1994	41,308
1974	1,750	1984	12,437	1995	42,754
1975	3,200	1985	13,211	1996 (paid at first)[1]	43,908
1976	3,512	1986	20,140	1996 (from July 1996)	46,364
1977	3,687	1987	21,302	1997	47,568
1978	4,200	1988	22,588	1998	49,232
1979	4,600	1989	24,903	1999	50,264
1980	6,750	1990	27,166	2000	51,572
1980	8,000	1991	28,986		
1981	8,480	1992	39,960		

[1] In July 1996 the House decided by resolution that allowances in any one quarter in the year should not exceed £11,591. Increases in subsequent years are to be linked to the Retail Prices Index for March and will apply from April.

Source: House of Commons Information Office

■ UK Parliament

Members of Parliament: Non-Office Cost Allowances

These allowances were first introduced in 1969. Amounts given are for 2000.

Allowance	Provisions	Amount
Supplementary London Allowance	members whose constituency is within Inner London can claim a London Supplement payment	£1,473
Additional Costs Allowance	members with constituencies outside Inner London can claim additional expenses incurred in staying overnight away from home while on parliamentary duties	annual maximum of £13,322
Motor mileage	for journeys made on parliamentary business between home, constituency, and Westminster	52.5 pence per mile up to 20,000 miles per annum; 24.2 pence per mile after 20,000 miles per annum
Bicycle allowance	for journeys undertaken by bicycle while on parliamentary duties in the UK	6.7 pence per mile
Travel warrants	members receive travel warrants which can be exchanged for tickets to travel by rail, sea, or air on parliamentary business; journeys cover home, constituency, and Westminster. For journeys outside this triangle, on parliamentary business, costs can be reimbursed if the Fees Office is notified at least three days in advance (three day rule can be waived in exceptional circumstances)	cost of journey
Parking	members can use the parliamentary car park	free
Travel for spouses and children	travel warrants are available for members' spouses and children under the age of 18, between London and the constituency and/or London and home by rail, sea, or air. Children and spouses can make 15 return journeys per calendar year	cost of journey
Travel to European Community institutions	members can reclaim their travel costs on parliamentary business between the UK and the European Community institutions in Brussels, Luxembourg, or Strasbourg. members are allowed one visit per calendar year	cost of a business class air fare from a London airport and a maximum of two days subsistence at the Civil Service Class A rate
Postage and telephone costs	members receive free stationery, and free inland telephone and postal services on parliamentary business	free
Winding-Up Allowance	up to a third of the annual Office Costs Allowance can be paid to reimburse the cost of any work done on parliamentary business undertaken on behalf of a retiring, defeated, or deceased member, after the date of cessation	annual limit £17,191
Resettlement Grant	to assist with the costs of adjusting to 'non-parliamentary life', members receive this grant if they lose their seat at a general election	amount varies between 50% and 100% of the member's annual salary at the time of the dissolution of Parliament, prior to the general election; amount is based on age

Source: House of Commons Information Office

House of Lords

Introduction

The upper chamber of Parliament, comprising 699 unelected peers. The Lords originated in the 11th century when it comprised religious leaders (Lords Spiritual), magnates (Lords Temporal) and court officials. It was the dominant chamber of Parliament until the direct election of Commons' members, from the 19th century, gave the lower chamber greater legitimacy. Except for some ecclesiastic members, peers were entirely hereditary from the 15th century. From 1876 non-hereditary lifetime 'Law Lord' peers were added, created by the sovereign to fulfil the chamber's judicial function, and from 1958 there was a new category of appointed 'life peers'. Peers are not paid salaries, but receive daily attendance allowances.

The hereditary element in the Lords was removed by the House of Lords Act (1999), but 92 of the 646 former hereditary peers were transformed into life peers, being selected by their fellow hereditaries of similar party political allegiance. The reforms of 1999 almost halved the size and substantially reduced the size of the Conservative party bloc.

The present Lords is a 'hung' chamber with no single party holding a majority and around a quarter of its members comprising independent 'cross benchers'. It includes 113 female peers and 209 peers appointed by the prime minister, Tony Blair. A fifth of peers were former MPs.

Composition of the House of Lords Before 1999 Reforms

Figures are percentages of the total membership of 1,213 members.

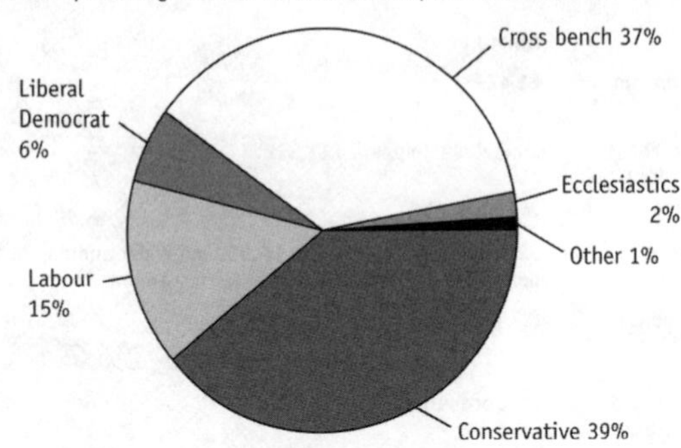

Composition of the House of Lords After 1999 Reforms

Figures are percentages of a total membership of 699. As of July 2000.

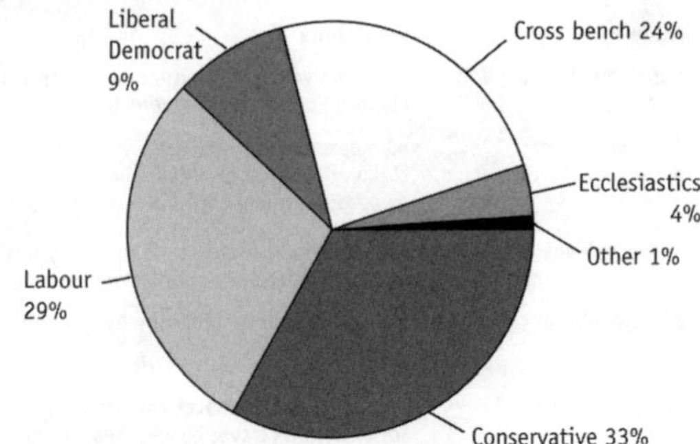

House of Lords: Key Facts

Oldest member: Lord Shawcross (born 4 February 1902)

Youngest member: Lord Freyberg (born 15 December 1970)

Longest serving active member: Earl Jellicoe (born 4 April 1918) who took his seat in 1939 and attended 94 times in the session 1998–99

Average age of members (in the year 2000): 68

Number of women members: 112

First female life peer: Baroness Wootton of Abinger (died 11 July 1988)

First female Leader of the House of Lords: Baroness Young (Conservative), Leader September 1981–May 1983

Average daily attendance per session: 446 (1998–99)

Length of average sitting day: 7 hours 36 minutes (1998–99)

Composition of the House of Lords by Party

Figures are based on those peers who are currently eligible to attend the House of Lords (ie, Peers without Writs of Summons or on leave of absence are excluded).
(– = not applicable.) As of July 2000.

Party	Life peers[1]	Hereditary peers			Bishops	Total
		Elected by party	Elected office holders	Appointed royal office holders[2]		
Conservative	181	42	9	1	–	474
Labour	195	2	2	–	–	176
Liberal Democrat	58	3	2	–	–	68
Cross bench	133	28	2	1	–	337
Archbishops	10	–	–	–	–	10
Other	10	–	–	–	26	108
Total	577	75	15	2	26	1,163

[1] Excludes four life peers on leave of absence.
[2] These are the Duke of Norfolk, The Earl Marshall (Conservative) and the Marquess of Cholmondeley, The Lord Great Chamberlain (Cross bench).

Source: House of Lords Journal Office, House of Lords, © Crown copyright 2000

The Power and the Role of the House of Lords

The Lords, since the Parliament Act of 1911, has been unable to veto legislation approved by the Commons. However, it can act as a check. Money bills approved by the Commons can be delayed by the Lords by only one month, while other bills can be delayed (since 1949) by one year in order to allow public opinion to be heard. Under the 'Salisbury Convention', developed in 1945, the House of Lords has agreed not to vote down legislation set out in a government's manifesto. In a typical year, a government is defeated around 13 times in the Lords, although the rate has increased to more than 20 for the Labour government of Tony Blair which came to power in 1997.

Despite its restricted powers, the Lords has an important role in examining and revising, or 'improving', Commons' legislation; scrutinizing delegated legislation (Statutory Instruments and European Union (EU) legislation) by means of special committees; debating matters of public interest; initiating non-controversial bills; and providing some government ministers. In addition, the Lords has a judicial role, acting as a final court of appeal. This function is carried out by the 'law lords': the Lord Chancellor, any former Lord Chancellors, the 11 lords of appeal, and any former lords of appeal. Appeals in both civil and criminal cases are heard by at least three law lords.

■ UK Parliament

The House of Lords: Further Reforms

The government plans to further reform the Lords, but there is a lack of consensus over whether a new Lords should be elected or partly elected and partly appointed, and, if elected, how so. The dilemma of Lords' reform is that, if all its members are directly elected, the upper chamber could challenge the legitimacy of the Commons, creating potential constitutional gridlock.

The government-appointed Royal Commission, chaired by Lord Wakeham, a Conservative, recommended, in its report of January 2000, that a majority of a reformed House of Lords should be appointed for renewable 15-year terms by an independent commission. This would remove patronage power from the prime minister. The commission would aim to ensure that a fifth of the House's membership had no party affiliation and that the Lords was representative of the country as a whole, including a significant minority of regional members and a mix of races and sexes. It suggested that up to around a fifth of members of an overall house of around 550 members be elected and that existing life peers should be allowed to remain for 15 years. The Wakeham report is being considered by a joint committee of the two Houses of Parliament.

Key Dates in the History of the House of Lords

11th century Origins of Parliament in the Witans, councils consulted by Saxon Kings and attended by religious leaders, magnates, and the king's own ministers.

13th century Attendance begins to include representatives of counties, cities, and boroughs.

14th century Two distinct houses emerge. One, composed of shire and borough representatives, becomes known as the Commons; the other, of religious leaders (Lords Spiritual) and magnates (Lords Temporal) becomes known as the Upper House.

15th century Membership of Lords Temporal is by now almost entirely hereditary and male; they are known as 'peers'.

16th century After the suppression of the monasteries in 1539, only bishops attend and the Lords Temporal form the majority for the first time. (Prior to 1539 Lords Spiritual consisted of bishops, abbots, and priors.)

1642 During the Civil War bishops are excluded from the House of Lords, but are returned by the Clergy Act 1661.

17 March 1649 The Rump Parliament officially abolishes the monarchy and two days later, as a result of the House of Lords' opposition to the trial of King Charles I, also abolishes the House of Lords. The House ceases to exist but resumes separate sittings in 1660.

13 February 1689 The Bill of Rights is drawn up by the Commons; it establishes the authority of Parliament over the King (enacted July).

1 May 1707 and 28 March 1800 The Acts of Union with Scotland and Ireland entitle Scottish and Irish peers to elect representatives to sit in the Lords.

8 October 1831 The Second Reform Bill to restructure the British parliamentary system is defeated in the House of Lords. Riots flare up in Nottingham and Derby in protest at the defeat of the bill.

1 November 1876 The Appellate Jurisdictions Act restores the jurisdiction of the House of Lords and of the Judicial Committee of the Privy Council, abolished in 1873. The act enables the sovereign to create Lords of Appeal in Ordinary (Law Lords) to fulfil the judicial function of the House of Lords. Unlike bishops, retired Law Lords can continue to sit and vote; they are, in effect, the first life peerages.

30 November 1909 The House of Lords rejects the 'People's Budget' by 350 votes to 75. The Liberal government then introduces a bill to end the Lords' power to reject legislation approved by the Commons.

10 August 1911 The Parliament Bill is passed by the House of Lords. Under the Parliament Act 1911 the power of the House of Lords to veto bills is converted into the power to suspend money bills for one month and other bills for a maximum period of two years. The maximum length of a Parliament is reduced from seven to five years (except in an emergency situation).

16 December 1949 The British Parliament Act, amending the original 1911 act, reduces from two years to one the period during which the House of Lords could delay the royal assent to a bill passed by the Commons.

1958 The Life Peerages Act permits the creation of baronies for life, with no limit on numbers. The first life peerages are created on 24 July. At about the same time allowances for peers' out-of-pocket expenses and the system of 'leave of absence' for peers who do not wish to or cannot attend the House for a long period are introduced.

1963 The Peerage Act allows members of the Lords to disclaim their titles (and thus be eligible for membership of the House of Commons); existing peers can disclaim within six months, new peers within one month of succession to a title.

1 November 1968 The Labour government introduces the Parliament (No. 2) Bill, which would create a two-tier House of Lords of created members who could speak and vote and others who could speak but not vote. The bill is abandoned on 17 April 1969.

23 January 1985 The proceedings of the House of Lords are televised for first time.

1997 Reform of the House of Lords is set out in Labour's election manifesto. The newly elected government is committed to abolish the rights of all 750 hereditary peers to sit and vote in the House of Lords.

Government Defeats in the House of Lords

Session	Number of defeats
Conservative	
1979–80	15
1980–81	18
1981–82	7
1982–83	5
1983–84	20
1984–85	17
1985–86	22
1986–87	3
1987–88	17
1988–89	12
1989–90	20
1990–91	17
1991–92	6
1992–93	19
1993–94	16
1994–95	7
1995–96	10
1996–97	10
Labour	
1997–98	39
1998–99	31
1999–2000	17[1]

[1] As of 30 June 2000.

October 1998 A MORI poll shows that 80% of the British public are in favour of the removal of hereditary peers.

24 November 1998 The government sets out its intention to bring forward proposals to reform the House of Lords in the Queen's speech. Labour MPs and peers break with tradition and interrupt the Queen's speech – normally listened to in complete silence – with murmurs of approval as she announces the government's plans.

2 December 1998 Conservative Party leader William Hague sacks Viscount Cranbourne, the Tory leader in the Lords, after it emerges that he helped to negotiate a deal with Labour over reform of the upper house without Hague's knowledge.

20 January 1999 The government sets out proposals to abolish the sitting and voting

Key Dates in the History of the House of Lords *(continued)*

rights of hereditary peers in the Lords. The House of Lords Bill, the first of the reform's two stages, outlines how the House of Lords will function during the transitional period; sets up an independent committee to appoint or oversee the appointment of new life peers; and establishes a Royal Commission. Hereditary peers and Conservative Lords react angrily to the proposals.

16 March 1999 The House of Lords Bill is passed by the House of Commons and is introduced in the House of Lords the next day.

23 March 1999 More than 130 MPs back cross-party calls for a fully elected chamber to replace the House of Lords.

11 May 1999 Peers overwhelmingly back the compromise Weatherhill amendment, which would retain 92 hereditary peers until lasting reform is completed, signalling first signs of consensus over the contentious legislation. The amendment, put forward by Lord Weatherhill, was the 'deal' that had caused the sacking of Viscount Cranbourne as the Opposition peers' leader in 1998.

12 May 1999 The Royal Commission on the Reform of the House of Lords starts the first of a series of hearings.

26 October 1999 The government's bill to expel hereditary peers is denounced as 'treason' by Lord Burford, who leaps on the Woolsack (seat of the Lord Chancellor).

November 1999 The House of Lords Act comes into force, removing all hereditary peers, with the exception of 92, chosen by their fellow hereditaries, who remain as special life peers.

20 January 2000 The Royal Commission on House of Lords Reform, chaired by the Conservative peer Lord Wakeham, issues its report. It recommends that the majority of a reformed House of Lords should be appointed, but, to give them greater independence, new members should be nominated by an independent commission and serve renewable 15-year terms. It recommends that at least a fifth of the Lords' membership should be without party affiliation and that it contain a significant minority of regional members and mix of sexes and races. Assuming an overall House of 550 members, the report suggests that between 65 and 195 be elected. The report is sent for consideration by a joint committee of the two houses of Parliament.

The Scottish Parliament

Introduction

The Scottish Parliament was created by the November 1998 Scotland Act, which was passed following the Scottish electorate's overwhelming approval of government proposals in a 11 September 1997 referendum on devolution.

The first elections to the parliament were held on 6 May 1999 and the parliament opened on 12 May 1999. It had last sat in 1707. The Labour Party fell nine short of an overall majority and on 13 May it concluded a pact with the Liberal Democrats to secure Scotland's first coalition government. Labour's leader, Donald Dewar, was elected the country's first minister.

Parliament consists of 129 members, who are elected for four-year terms through a 'semi-proportional' electoral system. The term of parliament is fixed. Seventy-three members are returned on a first-past-the-post basis from single-member constituencies, comprising Scotland's existing 72 Westminster constituencies, with an extra seat created through dividing the Orkney and Shetland constituency into two. An additional 56 members are selected on a proportional basis from party lists in the country's eight electoral regions. These regions are the same as the current European parliamentary boundaries and each elects seven members of the Scottish Parliament (MSPs) through the Additional Member System, a form of proportional representation.

Of the parliament's 129 MSPs, 48 were women, leaving only Sweden and Denmark with more women members of parliament.

The parliament has devolved law-making powers in all areas except defence, foreign affairs, immigration and nationality, employment, the constitution, social security, company regulation, economic management, and taxation. However, it has the authority to vary, upwards or downwards, the basic rate of income tax in Scotland by up to three pence in the pound, to supplement a block grant equivalent to the current Scottish Office budget of £14.8 billion (in 1998–99). A first minister (equivalent to a Scottish prime minister), with a main office in St Andrew's House, is drawn from the majority grouping within the parliament, and relevant ministers sit with their UK government counterparts at negotiating meetings in Brussels whenever Scottish interests are affected. Ministers are appointed by the first minister and, together with two Scottish law officers, form the Scottish Executive.

The new parliament has sought to be open and informal, adopt best practice from around the world, and use modern technology throughout its operation, including for voting. Much of the work is carried out by committees that meet in public. Each committee comprises between 5 and 15 MSPs, selected in accordance with party strength. Bills can be introduced by ministers, MSPs, and committees, and pass through three stages, including detailed examination by committee. One MSP is elected by fellow MSPs to act as the parliament's presiding officer, chairing its meetings. This position is occupied by David Steel.

The parliament's temporary base is the Church of Scotland General Assembly Hall (for debates) and City of Edinburgh Council buildings (for committee meetings), in the Lawnmarket and on George IV Bridge, in Edinburgh. A permanent home is being built at Holyrood by a design team led by the architect Enric Miralles of Barcelona, with completion planned for the autumn of 2001.

Key Dates in Scottish Devolution

31 October 1973 The Kilbrandon Commission on the British Constitution recommends a devolved parliament for Scotland.

27 November 1975 The British government White Paper, *Our Changing Democracy*, proposes devolution for Scotland and Wales.

18 January 1976 The Labour members of parliament Jim Sillars and John Robertson launch the Scottish Labour Party (SLP) to campaign for greater devolution for Scotland.

30 November 1976 The British government publishes a devolution bill for Scotland and Wales.

22 February 1977 The British government is defeated in a motion to stifle debate on the devolution bill; 22 Labour members vote 'no' and 20 others abstain.

25 January 1978 The British government passes an amendment to the Scottish and Welsh devolution bill, requiring the approval of 40% of the electorate in a referendum for devolution to take effect.

31 July 1978 Queen Elizabeth II of Britain gives the royal assent to the devolution bill for Scotland and Wales.

1 March 1979 Referenda are held in Britain on devolution. In Scotland, it is approved by 51.6% of the voters, but this falls short of the required 40% of the electorate. Devolution is not on the agenda of the centralizing conservative administrations that hold power for 18 years from May 1979 onwards.

11 September 1997 After gaining power, the Labour Party grants Scotland a devolution referendum, in which 74.3% of voters approve the creation of their own parliament, with 63.5% voting in favour of giving it tax-raising powers. One week later, Secretary of State for Scotland Donald Dewar announces plans to create a Scottish parliament in Edinburgh. The new parliament is to be granted the power to legislate on education, the environment, health, law enforcement, and transport.

6 May 1999 In the election for the new Scottish Parliament – the first election in Britain to contain an element of proportional representation – Labour is returned as the largest single party, winning 56 of the 129 seats (9 short of an overall majority). The Scottish National Party gains 35 seats, the Conservative Party 18, and the Liberal Democrats 17, while the remaining 3 seats are taken by independents and smaller fringe parties. Only 59% of the Scottish electorate exercises its right to vote. On 13 May, Scottish Labour leader Donald Dewar is elected as 'first minister', heading a Labour–Liberal Democrat coalition government.

1 July 1999 Official opening by Queen Elizabeth II in Edinburgh of the first Scottish parliament to sit for almost 300 years, since the Act of Union of 1707. Its temporary home is at the Church of Scotland Assembly Hall and City of Edinburgh Council buildings; a new building, to be constructed for the parliament in the Holyrood district of the city, is not due for completion until late 2001.

February 2000 An ICM poll in the *Scotsman* finds that 48% of Scots consider devolution to have been a good idea, but 41% consider that the Scottish parliament has made no difference.

16 March 2000 Conservatives win Labour-held seat of Ayr, after 16% swing in by-election.

The Scottish Parliament Executive

As of July 2000.

Position	Name
First Minister	Donald Dewar
Deputy First Minister and Minister for Justice	Jim Wallace
Deputy Minister for Justice	Angus Mackay
Minister for Finance	Jack McConnell
Minister for Health and Community Care	Susan Deacon
Deputy	Iain Gray
Minister for Communities (Local Government, Housing, and Social Inclusion)	Wendy Alexander
Deputies	Frank McAveety (Local Government)
	Jackie Baillie (Social Inclusion, Equality, and the Voluntary Sector)
Minister for Transport and the Environment	Sarah Boyack
Minister for Enterprise and Life-long Learning	Henry McLeish
Deputies	Nicol Stephen
	Alasdair Morrison (Highlands and Islands and Gaelic)
Minister for Rural Affairs	Ross Finnie
Deputy	John Home Robertson (Fisheries)
Minister for Children and Education	Sam Galbraith
Deputies	Rhona Brankin (Culture and Sport)
	Peter Peacock (Children and Education)
Minister for Parliament	Tom McCabe
Deputy Minister for Parliament	Iain Smith
Lord Advocate	Colin Boyd
Solicitor General for Scotland	Neil Davidson

Members of the Scottish Parliament

Con = Conservative; Ind = Independent; Lab = Labour; LD = Liberal Democrats; SNP = Scottish National Party; SSP = Scottish Socialist Party.
As of July 2000.

Member	Party	Constituency/region
Constituency MSPs		
Alexander, Wendy	Lab	Paisley North
Baillie, Jackie	Lab	Dumbarton
Barrie, Scott	Lab	Dunfermline West
Boyack, Sarah	Lab	Edinburgh Central
Brankin, Rhona	Lab	Midlothian
Canavan, Dennis	Ind	Falkirk West
Chilsholm, Malcolm	Lab	Edinburgh North and Leith
Craigie, Cathie	Lab	Cumbernauld and Kilsyth
Cunningham, Roseanna	SNP	Perth
Curran, Margaret	Lab	Glasgow Ballieston
Deacon, Susan	Lab	Edinburgh East and Musselburgh
Dewar, Donald	Lab	Glasgow Anniesland
Eadie, Helen	Lab	Dunfermline East
Ewing, Fergus	SNP	Inverness East, Nairn, and Lochaber
Ewing, Margaret	SNP	Moray
Ferguson, Patricia	Lab	Glasgow Maryhill
Galbraith, Sam	Lab	Strathkelvin and Bearsden
Gillon, Karen[1]	Lab	Clydesdale
Godman, Trish	Lab	West Renfrewshire
Gray, Iain	Lab	Edinburgh Pentlands
Henry, Hugh	Lab	Paisley South
Home Robertson, John	Lab	East Lothian

(continued)

Members of the Scottish Parliament *(continued)*

Member	Party	Constituency/region
Hughes, Janis	Lab	Glasgow Rutherglen
Jackson, Gordon	Lab	Glasgow Govan
Jackson, Sylvia	Lab	Stirling
Jamieson, Cathy	Lab	Carrick, Cumnock, and Doon Valley
Jamieson, Margaret	Lab	Kilmarnock and Loudoun
Jenkins, Ian	LD	Tweeddale, Ettrick, and Lauderdale
Kerr, Andy	Lab	East Kilbride
Lamont, Johann	Lab	Glasgow Pollok
Livingstone, Marilyn	Lab	Kirkaldy
Lyon, George	LD	Argyll and Bute
McAllion, John	Lab	Dundee East
McAveety, Frank	Lab	Glasgow Shettleston
McCabe, Tom	Lab	Hamilton South
McConnell, Jack	Lab	Motherwell and Wishaw
Macdonald, Lewis	Lab	Aberdeen Central
Macintosh, Kenneth	Lab	Eastwood
Mackay, Angus	Lab	Edinburgh South
MacLean, Kate	Lab	Dundee West
McLeish, Henry	Lab	Central Fife
McMahon, Michael	Lab	Hamilton North and Bellshill
McNeil, Duncan	Lab	Greenock and Inverclyde
McNeill, Pauline	Lab	Glasgow Kelvin
McNulty, Des	Lab	Clydebank and Milngavie
Martin, Paul	Lab	Glasgow Springburn
Morgan, Alasdair	SNP	Galloway and Upper Nithsdale
Morrison, Alasdair	Lab	Western Isles
Muldoon, Bristow	Lab	Livingston
Mulligan, Mary	Lab	Linlithgow
Munro, John	LD	Ross, Skye, and Inverness West
Murray, Elaine	Lab	Dumfries
Oldfather, Irene	Lab	Cunninghame South
Peattie, Cathy	Lab	Falkirk East
Radcliffe, Nora	LD	Gordon
Robson, Euan	LD	Roxburgh and Berwickshire
Rumbles, Mike	LD	West Aberdeenshire and Kincardine
Salmond, Alex	SNP	Banff and Buchan
Scott, John	Con	Ayr
Scott, Tavish	LD	Shetland
Simpson, Richard	Lab	Ochil
Smith, Elaine	Lab	Coatbridge and Chryston
Smith, Iain	LD	North East Fife
Smith, Margaret	LD	Edinburgh West
Stephen, Nicol	LD	Aberdeen South
Stone, Jamie	LD	Caithness, Sutherland, and Easter Ross
Swinney, John	SNP	North Tayside
Thomson, Elaine	Lab	Aberdeen North
Wallace, Jim	LD	Orkney
Watson, Mike	Lab	Glasgow Cathcart
Welsh, Andrew	SNP	Angus
Whitefield, Karen	Lab	Airdrie and Shotts
Wilson, Allan	Lab	Cunninghame North
Regional MSPs		
Adam, Brian	SNP	North East Scotland
Aitken, Bill	Con	Glasgow
Brown, Robert	LD	Glasgow
Campbell, Colin	SNP	West of Scotland
Crawford, Bruce	SNP	Mid Scotland and Fife
Davidson, David	Con	North East Scotland
Douglas-Hamilton, James	Con	Lothians
Elder, Dorothy Grace	SNP	Glasgow
Ewing, Winnie	SNP	Highlands and Islands
Fabiani, Linda	SNP	Central Scotland
Fergusson, Alex	Con	South of Scotland
Finnie, Ross	LD	West of Scotland
Gallie, Phil	Con	South of Scotland
Gibson, Kenneth	SNP	Glasgow
Goldie, Annabel	Con	West of Scotland
Gorrie, Donald	LD	Central Scotland
Graham, Christine[2]	SNP	South of Scotland
Grant, Rhoda	Lab	Highlands and Islands
Hamilton, Duncan	SNP	Highlands and Islands
Harding, Keith	Con	Mid Scotland and Fife
Harper, Robin	Green	Lothians
Hyslop, Fiona	SNP	Lothians
Ingram, Adam	SNP	South of Scotland
Johnston, Nick	Con	Mid Scotland and Fife
Johnstone, Alex	Con	North East Scotland
Lochhead, Richard	SNP	North East Scotland
MacAskill, Kenny	SNP	Lothians
MacDonald, Margo	SNP	Lothians
McGrigor, Jamie	Con	Highlands and Islands
McGugan, Irene	SNP	North East Scotland
McIntosh, Lindsay	Con	Central Scotland
McLeod, Fiona	SNP	West of Scotland
McLetchie, Davie	Con	Lothians
MacMillan, Maureen	Lab	Highlands and Islands
Marwick, Tricia	SNP	Mid Scotland and Fife
Matheson, Michael	SNP	Central Scotland
Monteith, Brian	Con	Mid Scotland and Fife
Mundell, David	Con	South of Scotland
Neil, Alex	SNP	Central Scotland
Paterson, Gil	SNP	Central Scotland
Peacock, Peter	Lab	Highlands and Islands
Quinan, Lloyd	SNP	West of Scotland
Raffan, Keith	LD	Mid Scotland and Fife
Reid, George	SNP	Mid Scotland and Fife
Robison, Shona	SNP	North East Scotland
Russell, Michael	SNP	South of Scotland
Scanlon, Mary	Con	Highlands and Islands
Sheridan, Tommy	SSP	Glasgow
Steel, David	LD	Lothians
Sturgeon, Nicola	SNP	Glasgow
Tosh, Murray	Con	South of Scotland
Ullrich, Kay	SNP	West of Scotland
Wallace, Ben	Con	North East Scotland
White, Sandra	SNP	Glasgow
Wilson, Andrew	SNP	Central Scotland
Young, John	Con	West of Scotland

[1] Elected as Karen Turnbull.
[2] Elected as Christine Creech.

The First Year of the Scottish Parliament

by Ian Derbyshire

In May 2000, at the close of the new Scottish Parliament's first year, commentators in Scotland were divided over its impact. For some, the Parliament had changed little and remained a sideshow to the 'main event' – Westminster. The former secretary of state, Donald Dewar, continued to dominate Scottish politics: now with the title of first minister. Five bills had been passed, but with the exception of the abolition of university tuition fees and their replacement with a graduate loan scheme for students, the measures were worthy but minor. For example, they included bills addressing the neglected rights of people incapacitated by illness, setting up national parks, and abolishing outdated feudal property ownership law. Much of the rest of the year had been occupied by media stories critical of the allowances and expenses enjoyed by Members of Scottish Parliament (MSPs); the spiralling projected cost of a new building for the Parliament (£190 million and rising); a minor lobbying scandal; and Dewar's enforced three-month medical sabbatical, from May 2000, following a heart valve operation.

The Scottish Parliament

THE FIRST YEAR OF THE SCOTTISH PARLIAMENT (*continued*)

For other commentators, the Scottish Parliament had brought symbolic and significant changes. Scotland now had a new political focus, a new cast of characters and a new body to represent the views of its people. Four-fifths of its MSPs were new to parliamentary life. However, they were quickly gaining experience and learning both how to hold the executive to account and how to make their own legislation. This made Scotland's Parliament very different from Westminster, where the executive dominated. It was a true legislature (in the traditional sense of members making laws) and a body closer to the Scandinavian model of a parliament than to Westminster.

Scotland was also pioneering other forms of politics new to the UK. Elected by proportional representation, no single party enjoyed an overall majority and a Labour-Liberal Democrat coalition government was formed. Labour held the upper hand, with eight cabinet seats to the Liberal Democrats' two, but when a dispute arose over student tuition fees, with Labour favouring their retention and the Liberal Democrats' their removal, the compromise solution was largely in the Liberal Democrats' favour. Furthermore, the Liberal Democrat Jim Wallace took over as acting first minister from May 2000, when Dewar started his medical leave.

At the end of year one, opinion polls showed Scottish voters still reserving judgement on the Parliament and devolution. However, changes in the political landscape were apparent. Support for Labour in Scotland had fallen significantly since the May 1997 general election and, although the Scottish National Party (SNP) was its main challenger, the SNP had moderated its stance on independence, which would now be subject to a referendum if the party won a Scottish election. Scottish Conservative support was reviving, highlighted by the party's capture, in the March 2000 parliamentary by-election, of Labour-held Ayr.

The National Assembly for Wales

Introduction

The National Assembly for Wales was created by the July 1998 Government of Wales Act, which was passed following the Welsh electorate's narrow approval of government proposals in an 18 September 1997 referendum on devolution.

The Assembly comprises 60 members, who are elected for fixed four-year terms through a 'semi-proportional' electoral system. Forty are returned on a first-past-the-post basis from single-member constituencies, comprising Wales's existing Westminster constituencies. An additional 20 members are selected on a proportional basis from party lists based on Wales's five European Parliament constituencies. The Assembly's first elections were held on 6 May 1999. Labour won 28 seats, three short of a majority in the 60-seat assembly; Plaid Cymru won 17; the Conservatives 9; and the Liberal Democrats 6. Labour's leader, Alun Michael, was elected first secretary.

The first secretary (prif ysgrifennydd y Cynulliad) is elected from within the Assembly, by majority vote, to act as the Assembly's political leader and to appoint a cabinet comprising assembly secretaries.

Work in the Assembly is mostly carried out through subject committees; the balance of membership of the committees reflects party strengths. The committees develop policies and examine what the Assembly does. There are also four regional committees, comprising members from the relevant regions; these convey issues of local concern to the full Assembly and subject committees.

The Assembly has taken over virtually all of the functions of the secretary of state for Wales, spending the Welsh Office's £7 billion budget. Foreign affairs, defence, taxation, social security, broadcasting, and overall economic policy remain with the government in London. The Assembly may pass secondary legislation, but, unlike the Scottish Parliament, does not have primary law-making powers, even in areas such as the Welsh language. It implements Westminster legislation and oversees quangos, making them more accountable. It funds and makes appointments to National Health Service bodies in Wales and administers European structural funds.

The English and Welsh languages are treated equally in the Assembly's work.

The Assembly's temporary base is the Cardiff University Council Chamber and then Crickhowell House on Cardiff Bay. A new building is planned for 2001.

The Cabinet of the National Assembly for Wales

As of July 2000

Position	Cabinet member
First Secretary	Rhodri Morgan
Business Secretary	Andrew Davies
Agriculture and Rural Development Secretary	Carwen Jones
Health and Social Services Secretary	Jane Hutt
Secretary for Education and Children	Rosemary Butler
Secretary for Education and Training	Tom Middlehurst
Finance Secretary	Edwina Hart
Local Government and Housing Secretary	Peter Law
Environment Secretary	Sue Essex

Members of the National Assembly for Wales

Con = Conservative; Lab = Labour; LD = Liberal Democrats; PC = Plaid Cymru.
As of July 2000.

Member	Party	Constituency
Constituency members		
Barrett, Lorraine	Lab	Cardiff South and Penarth
Bates, Mick	LD	Montgomeryshire
Butler, Rosemary	Lab	Newport West
Chapman, Christine	Lab	Cynon Valley
Davidson, Jane	Lab	Pontypridd
Davies, Andrew	Lab	Swansea West
Davies, David	Con	Monmouth
Davies, Geraint	PC	Rhondda
Davies, Ron	Lab	Caerphilly
Edwards, Richard	Lab	Preseli Pembrokeshire
Essex, Sue	Lab	Cardiff North
Feld, Val	Lab	Swansea East
Gibbons, Brian	Lab	Aberavon
Glyn Thomas, Rhodri	PC	Carmarthen East and Dinefwr
Gregory, Janice	Lab	Ogmore
Griffiths, John	Lab	Newport East
Gwyther, Christine	Lab	Carmarthen West and South Pembrokeshire
Halford, Alison	Lab	Delyn
Hancock, Brian	PC	Islwyn
Hart, Edwina	Lab	Gower
Hutt, Jane	Lab	Vale of Glamorgan
Jones, Ann	Lab	Vale of Clwyd
Jones, Gareth	PC	Conwy
Jones, Carwyn	Lab	Bridgend
Jones, Elin	PC	Ceredigion
Jones, Helen Mary	PC	Llanelli
Law, Peter	Lab	Blaenau Gwent
Lewis, Huw	Lab	Merthyr Tydfil and Rhymney
Marek, John	Lab	Wrexham
Middlehurst, Tom	Lab	Alyn and Deeside
Morgan, Rhodri	Lab	Cardiff West
Neagle, Lynne	Lab	Torfaen
Pugh, Alun	Lab	Clwyd West
Randerson, Jenny	LD	Cardiff Central
Sinclair, Karen	Lab	Clwyd South
Thomas, Dafydd Elis	PC	Meirionnydd Nant Conwy
Thomas, Gwenda	Lab	Neath
Wigley, Dafydd	PC	Caernarfon
Williams, Kirsty	LD	Brecon and Radnor
Wyn Jones, Ieuan	PC	Ynys Môn
Regional members		
Black, Peter	LD	South Wales West
Bourne, Nicholas	Con	Mid and West Wales
Cairns, Alun	Con	South Wales West
Dafis, Cynog	PC	Mid and West Wales
Davies, Glyn	Con	Mid and West Wales
Davies, Janet	PC	South Wales West
Davies, Jocelyn	PC	South Wales East
Evans, Delyth	Lab	Mid and West Wales
German, Michael	LD	South Wales East
Graham, William	Con	South Wales East
Humphreys, Christine	LD	North Wales
Jarman, Pauline	PC	South Wales Central
Lloyd, Dai	PC	South Wales West
Melding, David	Con	South Wales Central
Morgan, Jonathan	Con	South Wales Central
Richards, Rod	Con	North Wales
Rogers, Peter	Con	North Wales
Ryder, Janet	PC	North Wales
Thomas, Owen John	PC	South Wales Central
Williams, Phil	PC	South Wales East

Key Dates in Welsh Devolution

31 October 1973 The Kilbrandon Commission on the British Constitution recommends a devolved parliament for Wales.

1 March 1979 Referenda are held in Britain on devolution in Scotland and Wales. It is rejected in Wales by 79.7% of the voters, on a 58.8% turnout. Devolution is not on the agenda of the centralizing Conservative administrations that come to power for 18 years from May 1979 onwards.

1992 The Labour Party supports devolution for Wales in its election manifesto, but fails to oust the Conservatives at the polls.

22 July 1997 The new Labour government announces plans for partial home rule in Wales, whereby an elected assembly would have some power to govern local affairs and to influence distribution of the annual £7–8 billion government budget for Wales. This assembly is not granted the same tax-raising and legislative powers as its Scottish counterpart.

18 September 1997 Welsh voters narrowly approve the establishment of a representative assembly for Wales (with 50.3% in favour). Its Welsh title is Cynulliad Cenedlaethol Cymru.

March 1998 Welsh secretary Ron Davies announces construction of a new waterfront building for the National Assembly for Wales, designed by English architect Richard Rogers, on the Cardiff Bay redevelopment site. While the new assembly building is being completed, the Assembly will meet at nearby Crickhowell House.

October 1998–99 The architect of devolution, Ron Davies, resigns after a personal indiscretion. In the ensuing Welsh Labour leadership contest, Alun Michael, regarded by many as the prime minister's preferred choice, defeats the grass-roots populist candidate Rhodri Morgan.

6 May 1999 The Assembly elections, using the same Additional Member System of proportional representation as in Scotland, attract only 40% of Welsh voters. Labour emerges as the largest single party, but with no overall majority. The nationalist party Plaid Cymru scores unexpected successes, notably in the former Labour heartland of the South Wales valleys. The final results are: Labour 28 seats, Plaid Cymru 17 seats, Conservatives 9 seats, and the Liberal Democrats 6 seats. On 12 May, Alun Michael is elected 'first secretary' for Wales, heading a minority Labour government.

26 May 1999 Official opening of the National Assembly for Wales by Queen Elizabeth II.

1 July 1999 The National Assembly for Wales takes over full responsibility for the duties formerly attached to the secretary of state for Wales and the Welsh Office.

3 February 2000 Labour slip to fourth place in Ceredigion, a rural constituency held by Plaid Cymru, in a parliamentary by-election.

9 February 2000 Facing the prospect of defeat in a no-confidence motion brought by Plaid Cymru, Alun Michael resigns as first secretary. He is replaced by Rhodri Morgan of Labour.

■ The National Assembly for Wales

The Northern Ireland Assembly

Introduction

The Northern Ireland Assembly came into being as a result of the 10 April 1998 Good Friday peace agreement, which negotiated the devolution of a range of executive and legislative powers – in areas such as agriculture, economic development, education, the environment, finance, health, and social security – from the secretary of state for Northern Ireland to an elected Assembly. A referendum held on 22 May 1998 resulted in a majority voting in favour of the agreement. Elections were first held on 25 June 1998. The Assembly met for the first time on 1 July 1998, but did not become fully operational until late in 1999. The Assembly was suspended by the UK Parliament in February 2000, following lack of progress on decommissioning by the IRA, but power was transferred back to the Northern Ireland executive on 30 May 2000.

Based at the Castle Buildings, Stormont, Belfast, the Assembly comprises 108 members, 6 from each of the 18 Westminster constituencies in Northern Ireland. Its members are elected by proportional representation, using a system of single transferable votes.

The Assembly has legislative powers and is specifically charged with setting up interconnecting bodies between Northern Ireland and the Republic of Ireland. Important decisions of the Assembly are made by a weighted majority system, which is designed to ensure that minority interests in the Assembly can influence legislation.

The first minister of the Assembly is David Trimble of the Ulster Unionist Party (UUP). His deputy is Seamus Mallon of the Social Democratic and Labour Party (SDLP). The first minister and deputy first minister sit on an executive committee, that includes up to ten departmental ministers, with posts allocated on the basis of party support.

Members of the Northern Ireland Assembly

All = The Alliance Party; DUP = Democratic Unionist Party; IU = Independent Unionist; NIUP = Northern Ireland Unionist Party; NIWC = Northern Ireland Women's Coalition; PUP = Progressive Unionist Party; SDLP = Social Democratic and Labour Party; SF = Sinn Fein; UKUP = UK Unionist Party; UUAP = United Unionist Assembly Party; UUP = Ulster Unionist Party.
As of July 2000.

Member	Party	Constituency
Adams, Gerry	SF	West Belfast
Adamson, Ian	UUP	East Belfast
Agnew, Fraser[1]	UUAP	North Belfast
Lord Alderdice	Speaker	East Belfast
Armitage, Pauline	UUP	East Londonderry
Armstrong, Billy	UUP	Mid Ulster
Attwood, Alex	SDLP	West Belfast
Beggs Jr, Roy	UUP	East Antrim
Bell, Billy	UUP	Lagan Valley
Bell, Eileen	All	North Down
Benson, Tom	UUP	Strangford
Berry, Paul	DUP	Newry and Armagh
Birnie, Esmond	UUP	South Belfast
Boyd, Norman[2]	NIUP	South Antrim
Bradley, P J	SDLP	South Down
Byrne, Joe	SDLP	West Tyrone
Campbell, Gregory	DUP	East Londonderry
Carrick, Mervyn	DUP	Upper Bann
Carson, Joan	UUP	Fermanagh & South Tyrone
Close, Seamus	All	Lagan Valley
Clyde, Wilson	DUP	South Antrim
Cobain, Fred	UUP	North Belfast
Coulter, Robert	UUP	North Antrim
Dallat, John	SDLP	East Londonderry
Davis, Ivan	UUP	Lagan Valley
De Brun, Bairbre	SF	West Belfast
Dodds, Nigel	DUP	North Belfast
Doherty, Arthur	SDLP	East Londonderry
Doherty, Pat	SF	West Tyrone
Douglas, Boyd[1]	UUAP	East Londonderry
Durkan, Mark	SDLP	Foyle
Empey, Reg	UUP	East Belfast
Ervine, David	PUP	East Belfast
Farren, Sean	SDLP	North Antrim
Fee, John	SDLP	Newry and Armagh
Ford, David	All	South Antrim
Foster, Sam	UUP	Fermanagh & South Tyrone
Gallagher, Tommy	SDLP	Fermanagh & South Tyrone
Gibson, Oliver	DUP	West Tyrone
Gildernew, Michelle	SF	Fermanagh & South Tyrone
Gorman, John	UUP	North Down
Hanna, Carmel	SDLP	South Belfast
Haughey, Denis	SDLP	Mid Ulster
Hay, William	DUP	Foyle
Hendron, Joe	SDLP	West Belfast
Hilditch, David	DUP	East Antrim
Hume, John	SDLP	Foyle
Hussey, Derek	UUP	West Tyrone
Hutchinson, Billy	PUP	North Belfast
Hutchinson, Roger[2,3]	IU	East Antrim
Kane, Gardiner	DUP	North Antrim
Kelly, Gerry	SF	North Belfast
Kelly, John	SF	Mid Ulster
Kennedy, Danny	UUP	Newry and Armagh
Leslie, James	UUP	North Antrim
Lewsley, Patricia	SDLP	Lagan Valley
Maginness, Alban	SDLP	North Belfast
Mallon, Seamus	SDLP	Newry and Armagh
Maskey, Alex	SF	West Belfast
McCarthy, Kieran	All	Strangford
McCartney, Robert	UKUP	North Down
McClarty, David	UUP	East Londonderry
McCrea, William	DUP	Mid Ulster
McCleland, Donovan	SDLP	South Antrim
McDonnell, Alasdair	SDLP	South Belfast
McElduff, Barry	SF	West Tyrone
McFarland, Alan	UUP	North Down
McGimpsey, Michael	UUP	South Belfast
McGrady, Eddie	SDLP	South Down
McGuinness, Martin	SF	Mid Ulster
McHugh, Gerry	SF	Fermanagh & South Tyrone
McLaughlin, Mitchel	SF	Foyle
McMenamin, Eugene	SDLP	West Tyrone
McNamee, Pat	SF	Newry and Armagh
McWilliams, Monica	NIWC	South Belfast
Molloy, Francie	SF	Mid Ulster
Murphy, Conor	SF	Newry and Armagh
Murphy, Mick	SF	South Down
Morrice, Jane	NIWC	North Down
Morrow, Maurice	DUP	Fermanagh & South Tyrone
Neeson, Sean	All	East Antrim
Nelis, Mary	SF	Foyle
Nesbitt, Dermot	UUP	South Down
O'Connor, Danny	SDLP	East Antrim
O'Hagan, Dara	SF	Upper Bann
O'Neill, Eamon	SDLP	South Down
Paisley, Ian	DUP	North Antrim
Paisley Jr, Ian	DUP	North Antrim
Poots, Edwin	DUP	Lagan Valley
Ramsey, Sue	SF	West Belfast
Robinson, Iris	DUP	Strangford
Robinson, Ken	UUP	East Antrim
Robinson, Mark	DUP	South Belfast
Robinson, Peter	DUP	East Belfast
Roche, Patrick[2]	NIUP	Lagan Valley
Rodgers, Brid	SDLP	Upper Bann
Savage, George	UUP	Upper Bann
Shannon, Jim	DUP	Strangford
Shipley-Dalton, Duncan	UUP	South Antrim
Taylor, John	UUP	Strangford
Tierney, John	SDLP	Foyle
Trimble, David	UUP	Upper Bann
Watson, Denis[1]	UUAP	Upper Bann
Weir, Peter	UUP	North Down
Wells, Jim	DUP	South Down
Wilson, Cedric[2]	NIUP	Strangford
Wilson, Jim	UUP	South Antrim
Wilson, Sammy	DUP	East Belfast

[1] Elected as an Independent candidate and formed the United Unionist Assembly Party (UUAP) with effect from 21 September 1998. [2] Elected as a UK Unionist candidate and formed the Northern Ireland Unionist Party (NIUP) with effect from 15 January 1999. [3] Expelled from the NIUP with effect from 2 December 1999.

Political Composition of the Northern Ireland Assembly

As of July 2000.

Party	Seats
Ulster Unionist Party (UUP)	28
Social Democratic and Labour Party (SDLP)	24
Democratic Unionist Party (DUP)	20
Sinn Fein (SF)	18
The Alliance Party (All)	6
Northern Ireland Unionist Party (NIUP)[1]	3
United Unionist Assembly Party (UUAP)[2]	3
Northern Ireland Women's Coalition (NIWC)	2
Progressive Unionist Party (PUP)	2
UK Unionist Party (UKUP)	1
Independent Unionist (IU)	1

[1] Elected as UK Unionist Party, resigned, and formed the Northern Ireland Unionist Party with effect from 15 January 1999.
[2] Elected as independent candidates and formed the United Unionist Assembly Party with effect from 21 September 1998.

Key Dates in the Northern Ireland Peace Process Since 1993

15 December 1993 The prime ministers of the UK and the Republic of Ireland, John Major and Albert Reynolds, make the 'Downing Street Declaration', starting the basis for talks on peace in Northern Ireland; constitutional change will require the majority agreement of the population of Northern Ireland and the Republic of Ireland.

31 January 1994 Gerry Adams, the president of the Irish republican party Sinn Fein, is granted a visa to visit the USA.

31 August 1994 The Irish Republican Army (IRA) in Northern Ireland announces its complete cessation of violence (the British government lifts it broadcasting ban on representatives of Sinn Fein on 16 September).

22 February 1995 At a press conference in Belfast, the prime ministers of the Republic of Ireland and the UK, John Bruton and John Major, present a framework document for all-party peace negotiations over the future of Northern Ireland.

16 March 1995 The US president Bill Clinton meets Gerry Adams at the White House, Washington, DC, and permits him to raise funds in the USA.

10 May 1995 The British government minister Michael Ancram meets representatives of Sinn Fein, led by Martin McGuinness, in Belfast. It is the first meeting of a government minister and Sinn Fein since 1973.

24 May 1995 Patrick Mayhew, secretary of state for Northern Ireland, meets Gerry Adams in Washington, DC.

28 November 1995 On the eve of US president Bill Clinton's visit to the British Isles, the prime ministers of the UK and the Republic of Ireland, John Major and John Bruton, announce the establishment of a three-person commission to examine the decommissioning of terrorist arms and the aim of holding all-party talks on Northern Ireland by the end of February 1996.

30 November–1 December 1995 President Clinton visits Northern Ireland and Dublin.

9 February 1996 The bombing of South Quay, Canary Wharf, London, breaks the IRA's 17-month ceasefire.

10 June 1996 All-party talks on the future of Northern Ireland begin at Stormont Castle, Belfast; Sinn Fein is not admitted because of the IRA's ceasefire violations.

7–13 July 1996 The Royal Ulster Constabulary (RUC) bans a controversial loyalist Apprentice Boys' march in Londonderry; the decision is reversed on 11 July and the march takes place; violence continues until 13 July.

21 December 1996 Loyalist terrorists in Northern Ireland break their ceasefire, in force since August 1994, with a car-bomb attack in Belfast.

5 April 1997 The Grand National at Aintree is postponed less than an hour before it is due to start after a coded IRA bomb warning is received.

6 July 1997 Violence flares up at an Orange Order march in Drumcree; the Order subsequently agrees (11 July) to cancel or re-route marches in Londonderry, Belfast, Newry, and Armagh.

20 July 1997 The IRA restores its ceasefire (broken on 9 February 1996) in order to participate in talks on the future of Northern Ireland.

29 August 1997 Britain's Northern Ireland secretary Mo Mowlam invites Sinn Fein to all-party talks.

13 October 1997 Tony Blair meets Gerry Adams at Stormont Castle, Belfast, the first meeting between a British prime minister and a Sinn Fein leader since 1921.

27 December 1997 Billy Wright, a leading member of the Loyalist Volunteer Force (LVF), is shot and killed by two members of the Irish National Liberation Army (INLA) at the Maze Prison, near Belfast. The incident escalates concerns for the future of the Northern Ireland peace process.

9 January 1998 Mo Mowlam visits convicted loyalist terrorists in the Maze prison.

10 April 1998 Ireland, Britain, and the political parties in Northern Ireland reach a historic peace agreement over Northern Ireland (known as the Good Friday Agreement) involving the devolution of a wide range of executive and legislative powers to a Northern Ireland Assembly.

25 June 1998 Elections to the Northern Ireland Assembly take place.

13 July 1998 Orangemen throughout Northern Ireland march to celebrate the 308th anniversary of the Battle of the Boyne – despite pressure to abandon the march following the deaths of three Catholic brothers in an arson attack.

15 July 1998 The standoff between Orangemen and British and RUC forces at Drumcree, Northern Ireland, ends when security forces forcibly remove the remaining protestors in a dawn raid.

15 August 1998 A car bomb explodes in Omagh, County Tyrone, Northern Ireland, killing 28 people, including 15 women and 8 children, in Northern Ireland's worst terrorist act to date. The IRA militant splinter group, the Real IRA, later admit responsibility.

8 September 1998 The Real IRA announces a complete ceasefire.

8 September 1998 Sinn Fein president Gerry Adams and Ulster first minister David Trimble hold talks in Northern Ireland, the first meeting between a Sinn Fein leader and an Ulster Unionist leader since 1922.

16 October 1998 Northern Ireland first minister David Trimble, leader of the Ulster Unionists, and SDLP leader John Hume share the Nobel Peace Prize for their work in negotiating the Good Friday Agreement.

The Northern Ireland Assembly

Key Dates in the Northern Ireland Peace Process Since 1993 *(continued)*

1 November 1998 Renegade loyalist terrorists admit the murder of Brian Service, a Catholic they chose randomly and shot five times in the head on 31 October in Belfast, Northern Ireland.

11 December 1998 In a new obstacle to the peace process, the IRA rejects Unionist demands that they decommission their weapons as a prerequisite for Sinn Fein members to gain seats in the new executive in Northern Ireland.

4 February 1999 Both republican and loyalist paramilitary groups issue warnings of fresh violence, threatening Northern Ireland peace efforts and the Good Friday Agreement. The IRA also reveals that some of its weapons were stolen by republican extremists.

16 February 1999 Despite Protestant calls for the unconditional decommissioning of IRA weapons, the Northern Ireland Assembly approves a plan for the province's new government structure, which would give it control over local issues such as taxation and law enforcement.

17 February 1999 Representatives of the Ulster Unionist Party and Sinn Fein hold bilateral talks for the first time. They meet to resolve the dispute over the decommissioning of IRA weapons, but make no significant progress.

8 March 1999 British Northern Ireland secretary Mo Mowlam announces that the deadline for the creation of the Northern Ireland Executive as outlined in the 1998 peace accord is being pushed back from 10 March to 29 March in an effort to resolve the dispute over the decommissioning of IRA weapons.

15 March 1999 A car bomb in Lurgan, Northern Ireland, kills prominent Roman Catholic lawyer and human rights advocate Rosemary Nelson. The Red Hand Defenders, an extremist Protestant group that opposes the Northern Ireland peace process, claims responsibility.

17 March 1999 Frankie Currie, a prominent member of the extremist Protestant unionist group the Red Hand Defenders, is shot dead in Belfast, Northern Ireland. Police suspect members of a rival Protestant group of the shooting.

1 April 1999 British prime minister Tony Blair announces that Northern Ireland peace talks will be suspended until 13 April, thereby missing the deadline agreed in April 1998 for establishing the Northern Ireland Executive, the province's new cabinet. The participants in the talks are in a deadlock over the issue of the decommissioning of weapons by the IRA.

20 May 1999 Prime Minister Tony Blair sets a deadline of 30 June 1999 for the formation of the executive, stating that the executive will be suspended if agreement is not reached by that date.

29 June 1999 The Parades Commission in Northern Ireland ban the Orange Order's Drumcree Parade from going down the nationalist Garvachy Road in Portadown.

29 June 1999 As talks approach the 30 June deadline, the Ulster Unionists insist that they will not take part in a power sharing executive with Sinn Fein unless the IRA begins decommissioning.

30 June 1999 Marathon talks at Belfast pass the 30 June deadline without agreement being reached.

2 July 1999 The report of the international decommissioning body chaired by General John de Chastelain states that decommissioning is possible by 22 May 2000.

3 July 1999 Following talks at Stormont, Prime Minister Tony Blair and Taoiseach Bertie Ahern announce a plan to break the deadlock. The executive is to be set up on 15 July and a Devolution Order is to take effect on 18 July. Decommissioning is to begin within days and to be complete by May 2000.

12 July 1999 Drumcree Parade passes off peacefully amid tight security.

13 July 1999 Prime Minister Tony Blair publishes 'fail-safe' emergency legislation aimed at giving Ulster Unionists the guarantees they need to enter into a power sharing executive with Sinn Fein.

14 July 1999 Ulster Unionists reject the government's 'fail-safe' proposals.

15 July 1999 Ulster Unionists boycott the Northern Ireland Assembly meeting at which ministers for the power sharing executive were to be nominated. Seamus Mallon resigns as Deputy First Minister of Northern Ireland.

20 July 1999 Prime Minister Tony Blair and Taoiseach Bertie Ahern meet to plan the review of the Northern Ireland peace process.

October 1999 Mo Mowlam is replaced as Northern Ireland Secretary by Peter Mandelson.

15 November 1999 Former US senator George Mitchell concludes his four-month-long review of the stalled peace process with the brokering of an historic agreement to establish a cross-party power-sharing agreement to exercise devolved powers. The agreement is made possible by the Unionists' dropping their long-standing demand that IRA disarmament must precede Sinn Fein's entry into the government and by Britain dropping its claim, in the Government of Northern Ireland Act, to be the 'sovereign' power in Northern Ireland.

1 December 1999 The Northern Ireland Assembly and its power-sharing executive begin work. The former IRA commander, Martin McGuinness, of Republican Sinn Fein, becomes education minister, and the Ulster Unionist Party (UUP) leader, David Trimble, first minister. The new government includes members of Ian Paisley's Democratic Unionist Party, which has been a persistent critic of the Good Friday Agreement.

2 December 1999 A new British-Irish Accord is signed, in which the two sides pledge to facilitate change in the status of Northern Ireland only when a majority there wish it. An IRA 'interlocutor' on decommissioning is appointed.

13 December 1999 A North-South Council, comprising ministers from Belfast and Dublin, meets for the first time, with the goal of increasing cross-border cooperation.

January 2000 Richard Jameson, a leading figure in the Ulster Volunteer Force (UVF), is killed by the renegade Loyalist Volunteer Force.

30 January 2000 Prime Minister Tony Blair announces the establishment of a new two-year-long public inquiry to examine fresh evidence about the events of 'Bloody Sunday' (30 January 1972), when British soldiers shot and fatally injured 14 unarmed men and youths at an illegal civil rights march.

9 February 2000 The Northern Ireland Assembly and its power-sharing executive are suspended by the United Kingdom Parliament. This is the result of a failure by the IRA to begin to decommission its weapons and a consequent threat by David Trimble to resign as first minister.

February 2000 A poll conducted in the Irish Republic shows that 49% blame David Trimble or Peter Mandelson for the collapse of the power-sharing executive while 36% blame Sinn Fein or the IRA.

25 March 2000 David Trimble narrowly sees off, by 56% to 43% of the votes of the 860-member Ulster Unionist Council (UUC), a challenge to his leadership of the UUP by Rev Martin Smith, a 69-year-old former Orange Order leader and a hardliner who opposed the peace agreement. The UUC bars Trimble from engaging in new talks about power-sharing unless the British government agrees to retain the 'Royal Ulster' title for Northern Ireland's police after the Royal Ulster Constabulary is reformed.

6 May 2000 The IRA offers to allow its arms dumps to be inspected by Martti Ahtisaari, a former president of Finland, and Cyril Ramaphosa, a leading member of South Africa's African National Congress, as a way foward through the decommissioning impasse.

27 May 2000 The Ulster Unionist Council, the policy-making council of the Ulster Unionist Party (UUP), narrowly backs (by 459 votes to 403) UUP leader David Trimble's proposal to go back into the power-sharing government with Sinn Fein, the Social Democratic and Labour Party (SDLP), and the Democratic Unionist Party (DUP).

30 May 2000 Power is transferred back to the Belfast Northern Ireland Executive, led by First Minister David Trimble.

1 June 2000 Hammersmith Bridge, London, is damaged by a bomb explosion, claimed to be the work of the dissident republican group Continuity IRA.

4 July 2000 A water cannon is used by police on demonstrators at Dumcree in County Armagh, Northern Ireland. It is the first time that a water cannon has been used by police since the early days of the troubles in the 1970s.

10 July 2000 In support of their banned march along the mainly nationalist Garvaghy Road at Dumcree in County Armagh, Orange Order supporters erect blockades sporadically throughout Northern Ireland, thereby creating widespread disruption and leading to a night of violence in many parts of the province. The night's violence is set against a backdrop of escalating violence since the beginning of the month leading up to the 12 July celebrations.

The Northern Ireland Assembly

Key Players in the Northern Ireland Peace Process

Adams Gerry (1948–) Northern Ireland politician, president of Sinn Fein (the political wing of the Irish Republican Army, IRA) from 1978, and representative of Sinn Fein in the Northern Ireland Assembly since June 1998

Ahern Bertie (1951–) Irish politician, leader of the Fianna Fail (FF) from 1994, and Republic of Ireland prime minister from 1997

Blair Tony (1953–) British politician, leader of the Labour Party from 1994, and UK prime minister from 1997

Bruton John (1947–) Irish politician, leader of Fine Gael (United Ireland Party) from 1990, and Republic of Ireland prime minister 1994–97

de Chastelain General John (1937–) Canadian soldier and chairman of the international commission to oversee the decommissioning of weapons in Northern Ireland from 1997

Democratic Unionist Party (DUP) Northern Ireland political party, which is orientated towards the Protestant Unionist community, opposes union with the Republic of Ireland, and has been led by Ian Paisley since 1971

Hume John (1937–) Northern Ireland politician, leader of the Social Democratic and Labour Party (SDLP) from 1979

McGuinness Martin (1950–) Northern Ireland politician and chief negotiator for Sinn Fein in peace talks

Major John (1943–) British politician and leader of the Conservative Party and UK prime minister 1990–97

Mandelson Peter (1953–) British Labour politician, appointed secretary of state for Northern Ireland in 1999

Mitchell George (1933–) US politician, Senate majority leader 1989–95, and chairman of the international commission on weapons decommissioning in Northern Ireland 1995–96, and brought back in 1999 to revive process

Molyneaux Jim (1920–) Northern Ireland Unionist politician and leader of the Official Ulster Unionist Party (the largest Northern Ireland party) from 1979 until his resignation in 1995

Mowlam Mo (1949–) British Labour politician, secretary of state for Northern Ireland 1997–99

Paisley Ian (1926–) Northern Ireland politician, cleric, and leader of the Democratic Unionist Party (DUP) from 1971

Sinn Fein Irish political party founded in 1905 that aims at creating a united republican Ireland; Gerry Adams has been the party's president since 1978

Social Democratic Labour Party (SDLP) Northern Ireland left-of-centre political party formed in 1970 and led by John Hume; it aims ultimately at Irish unification

Trimble David (1944–) Northern Ireland politician, leader of the Ulster Unionist Party (UUP) from 1995, and Northern Ireland's first minister from 1998

Ulster Unionist Party (UUP) the largest political party in Northern Ireland; it is right-of-centre in orientation and has been led by David Trimble since 1995

UK Members of the European Parliament

Introduction

Elections

The UK's MEPs are directly elected, representing multi-member regional constituencies. Since 1999, elections in Britain have been held using a 'closed list system' of proportional representation. Electors vote for a party rather than a candidate, with each party putting forward a list of candidates in their own order of preference. Seats are then allocated in proportion to each party's share of the region's vote, and to candidates in order of their appearance on the party's list. If a sitting MEP resigns or dies, the vacant seat goes to the next eligible person from the relevant party's list. If there is no one remaining on the party's list, or if the MEP was an independent, a by-election is held.

The number of MEPs per European Union (EU) member state, which is laid down by treaty, is related to the populations of the member states, with the UK currently providing 87 of the total 626 MEPs. Scotland elects 8 MEPs, Wales 5, and the 9 regions of England 71: East Midlands, 6; Eastern, 8; London, 10; North East, 4; North West, 10; South East, 11; South West, 7; West Midlands, 8; and Yorkshire and Humber, 7. Northern Ireland, which elects three MEPs, uses a single transferable vote form of proportional representation.

In the UK, as in all other EU member states, MEPs are prohibited from holding certain other offices, such as judge, minister, or director of a public corporation. Candidates must be aged 21 or over. Elections are held every five years (the most recent being in June 1999).

Pay

MEPs currently receive the same parliamentary allowance as members of their national parliament, although proposals to standardize salaries between MEPs of different nationalities were announced in June 2000. According to the recommended new pay scale, all MEPs would receive the same flat pay of 8,420 euros a month (about £62,000 a year).

Each member state pays the parliamentary allowances of its MEPs. The European Parliament provides 'top-up' payments to cover costs incurred in performance of duties and recruitment of assistants. This allowance is cut if a member does not regularly participate in Parliament sittings.

The role of the MEPs

MEPs sit in the European Parliament, which meets in Strasbourg, France, for debates and votes, and in Brussels, Belgium, for its committees, with a secretariat being based in Luxembourg. MEPs exert influence in three areas:

- legislative
- the power of the purse
- supervision of the executive

Legislative MEPs cannot directly initiate legislation, but, under the Maastricht Treaty (1993), they have a co-decision-making role in approving legislation in many fields by the policy-making Council of Ministers. The fields include the free movement of workers, creation of the internal market, research and technological development, the environment, consumer protection, education, culture, and health. If after the Parliament's second reading of a proposal the Council and Parliament fail to agree, a conciliation committee of the two is set up. If this fails to reach a compromise solution, the Parliament can reject the legislation on an absolute majority vote. As a result many Parliament amendments find their way into Community laws.

Introduction (*continued*)

The Parliament also approves international agreements.

Financial control The European Parliament has the power to reject or amend the European Union budget, which is adopted for the following year each December.

Supervision of the executive MEPs scrutinize the work of the Commission and the Council by putting oral questions or questions on topical issues to members of the Commission and Council. The Parliament also votes to approve a new Commission, which it can dismiss at any time by a two-thirds majority.

See also  **The European Union,** p 280–287.

UK Members of the European Parliament

Con = Conservative; DUP = Democratic Unionist Party; Lab = Labour; LD = Liberal Democrats; Grn = Green; PC = Plaid Cymru; SDLP = Social Democratic and Labour Party; SNP = Scottish National Party; UKIP = UK Independence Party; UUP = Ulster Unionist Party.

Region	1999 election turnout (%)	Member	Party
Eastern	24.74	Beazley, Christopher	Con
		Duff, Andrew	LD
		Howitt, Richard	Lab
		Khanbhai, Bashir	Con
		McNally, Eryl	Lab
		Sturdy, Robert	Con
		Titford, Jeffrey	UKIP
		Van Orden, Geoffrey	Con
East Midlands	22.83	Clegg, Nicholas	LD
		Dunn, William Newton	Con
		Heaton-Harris, Christopher	Con
		Helmer, Roger	Con
		Read, Mel	Lab
		Whitehead, Phillip	Lab
London	23.10	Balfe, Richard	Lab
		Bethell, Nicholas	Con
		Bowis, John	Con
		Evans, Robert	Lab
		Green, Pauline	Lab
		Lambert, Jean	Grn
		Ludford, Sarah	LD
		Moraes, Claude	Lab
		Tannock, Charles	Con
		Villiers, Theresa	Con
North East	19.6	Callanan, Martin	Con
		Donnelly, Alan	Lab
		Hughes, Stephen	Lab
		O'Toole, Mo	Lab
North West	19.67	Atkins, Robert	Con
		Davies, Chris	LD
		Dover, Den	Con
		Foster, Jacqueline	Con
		Inglewood, William Richard	Con
		McCarthy, Arlene	Lab
		Simpson, Brian	Lab
		Sumberg, David	Con
		Titley, Gary	Lab
		Wynn, Terry	Lab
South East	24.95	Deva, Nirj	Con
		Elles, James	Con
		Farage, Nigel	UKIP
		Hannan, Daniel	Con
		Huhne, Christopher	LD
		Lucas, Caroline	Grn
		Nicholson of Winterbourne, Emma	LD
		Perry, Roy	Con
		Provan, James	Con
		Skinner, Peter	Lab
		Watts, Mark	Lab
South West	27.81	Chichester, Giles	Con
		Ford, James Glyn	Lab
		Holmes, Michael	UKIP
		Jackson, Caroline	Con
		Parish, Neil	Con
		Stockton, Alexander	Con
		Watson, Graham	LD
West Midlands	21.21	Bradbourn, Philip	Con
		Bushill-Matthews, Philip	Con
		Cashman, Michael	Lab
		Corrie, John	Con
		Gill, Neena	Lab
		Harbour, Malcolm	Con
		Lynne, Liz	LD
		Murphy, Simon	Lab
Yorkshire and the Humber	19.75	Bowe, David	Lab
		Corbett, Richard	Lab
		Goodwill, Robert	Con
		Kirkhope, Timothy	Con
		McAvan, Linda	Lab
		McMillan-Scott, Edward	Con
		Wallis, Diana	LD
Northern Ireland	48.67	Hume, John	SDLP
		Nicholson, Jim	UUP
		Paisley, Ian	DUP
Scotland	24.83	Attwooll, Elspeth	LD
		Hudghton, Ian	SNP
		MacCormick, Neil	SNP
		Martin, David	Lab
		Miller, William	Lab
		Purvis, John	Con
		Stevenson, Struan	Con
		Taylor, Catherine	Lab
Wales	26.7	Evans, Jillian	PC
		Evans, Jonathan	Con
		Kinnock, Glenys	Lab
		Morgan, Mair Eluned	Lab
		Wyn, Eurig	PC

European Parliament: UK Election Results 1994 and 1999

Party	Number of MEPs	
	1994	1999
Conservative	18	36
Labour	62	29
Liberal Democrats	2	10
UK Independence Party	0	3
Green	0	2
Scottish National Party	2	2
Plaid Cymru	0	2
Pro-Euro Conservative Party	0	0
Others[1]	3	3

[1] All other UK parties including those of Northern Ireland.

European Parliament: UK Apathy

British voters' apathy to the work of the 'remote' European Parliament and its MEPs has been reflected in consistently low turnouts in European Parliament elections. In June 1999 UK turnout fell to a level of 23% of the electorate (down from 36% in 1994). This compared to turnouts ranging from 30% (in Finland and the Netherlands) to 91% (in Belgium) in other EU states.

European Parliament: UK Election Results Breakdown

Party	Votes received in 1999 election		Number of MEPs
	Number	%	
Conservative Party	3,578,217	35.77	36
Labour Party	2,803,821	28.03	29
Liberal Democrats	1,266,549	12.66	10
UK Independence Party	696,057	6.96	3
Green Party	625,378	6.25	2
Scottish National Party	268,528	2.68	2
Plaid Cymru	185,235	1.85	2
Pro-Euro Conservative Party	138,097	1.38	0
British National Party	102,647	1.13	0
Liberal Party	93,051	1.93	0
Socialist Labour Party	86,749	0.87	0
Scottish Socialist Party	39,720	0.40	0
MEP Independent Labour Party	36,849	0.37	0
Alternative Labour List	26,963	0.27	0
Natural Law Party	20,329	0.20	0
Socialist Alliance	7,203	0.07	0
Architect, Human Rights Peace in Europe	4,851	0.05	0
EDP English Freedom Party	3,066	0.03	0
Independent Anti-Value Added Tax	2,596	0.03	0
The Humanist Party	2,586	0.03	0
The Hemp Coalition	2,358	0.02	0
Anit-Corruption Pro-Family Christian Alliance	2,251	0.02	0
Independent Open Democracy for Stability	1,857	0.02	0
Weekly Worker	1,724	0.02	0
Socialist Party (Great Britain)	1,510	0.02	0
Independent Making a Profit in Europe	1,400	0.01	0
English Independent Humanist Party	1,049	0.01	0
Accountant for Lower Scottish Taxes	1,632	0.02	0
Northern Ireland: First Preference Votes			
Democratic Unionist Party	192,762	28.40	1
Social Democratic and Labour Party	190,731	28.10	1
Ulster Unionist Party	119,507	17.61	1
Sinn Fein	117,643	17.33	0
Progressive Unionist Party	22,494	3.31	0
UK Unionist Party	20,283	2.99	0
Alliance	14,391	2.12	0
Natural Law Party	998	0.15	0

Local Government in the UK

The Structure of Local Government in the UK

The powers and structure of local government are determined by Parliament. Between 1995 and 1998 far-reaching changes were carried out. A two-tier structure, which had existed since the mid-1970s, was replaced in Scotland, Wales, and parts of England by a single-tier system, in which all-purpose councils have responsibility for all local authority functions. In Scotland, Wales, and in the parts of non-metropolitan England where changes have occurred, these bodies are termed unitary authorities. In the heavily urbanized areas of England they are known as metropolitan authorities, and include the Greater London Authority (established in July 2000, after elections in May 2000). In the remainder of non-metropolitan England the existing two-tier structure remains, in which responsibility for local authority functions is divided between an upper level of 'shire' county councils and a lower tier of district councils.

The mixed structures which exist in non-metropolitan England are the result of decisions taken by a Local Government Commission, set up under the Local Government Act 1992, which consulted

The Structure of Local Government in the UK *(continued)*

local opinion. Four former counties, Avon, Berkshire, Cleveland, and Humberside, were abolished between 1996 and 1998, and replaced (along with their district councils) by 18 new unitary authorities. A further 28 unitary authorities were created out of parts of 21 other English counties. In Wales, the Local Government (Wales) Act 1994 abolished the two-tier structure of 8 county and 37 district councils (in existence since 1974), and replaced it, from April 1996, with 22 unitary authorities. In Scotland, the Local Government (Scotland) Act 1994 created 29 mainland unitary authorities from the two-tier system which had operated in Scotland's nine regions since 1975.

Local Authority Structures in the UK

(– = not applicable.)

Area	Single-tier structures	Two-tier structures
England	46 unitary authorities in the non-metropolitan 'shires' 36 metropolitan district councils situated within 6 metropolitan areas: Greater Manchester (10), Merseyside (5), South Yorkshire (4), Tyne and Wear (5), West Midlands (7), and West Yorkshire (5)	238 district councils within 34 'shire' counties In London, 32 borough councils (which are similar to metropolitan district councils), within the all-London Greater London Authority (GLA)
Scotland	29 unitary authorities on the mainland 3 islands councils (Orkney, Shetland, and Western Isles)	–
Wales	22 unitary authorities	–
Northern Ireland	26 district councils	–

Local Administration: Parishes and Regions

Although local government in the United Kingdom is referred to as 'single-tier' or 'two-tier', in reality there exist two further levels of local administration in many areas: the parish or (in Scotland and Wales) the community council, at the lowest level; and the region at the highest.

Parishes are the most local form of government, originating in the subdivision containing a parish church. There are around 10,000 parishes in England, of which more than three-quarters are sufficiently large (including at least 200 electors) to have a parish council. These councils are elected every four years, at the same time as district councils. Their functions include commenting on planning applications, and responsibility for local allotments, community halls, cemeteries, and footpaths. They secure funds through the levy of a precept (which forms part of a citizen's Council Tax charge) on district councils, with which they share their powers. In every parish an annual election must be held, which every elector can attend – making them, arguably, the most truly democratic institution in the country. In Scotland and Wales there are, respectively, more than 735 and 1,000 community councils.

In England, there exist eight regions – the East of England, East Midlands, North East, North West, South East, South West, West Midlands, and Yorkshire and Humberside – and the Greater London Authority. Each region is the site of a government office, which acts as an arm of government, with responsibilities in housing, planning, and transport. There are also Regional Development Agencies (RDAs), which were set up in April 1999 (in July 2000 in London) to coordinate regional economic development and regeneration, reduce imbalances within and between regions, and formulate 'regional strategies'.

RDAs are accountable to ministers and Parliament, but are responsive to regional views through consultation with the newly formed appointed regional chambers. There are currently no elected regional assemblies, although the Labour government of Tony Blair has promised to create such assemblies 'where public demand exists'.

Glossary of Local Government Terms

best value: a new efficiency performance regime for local government (established by the Local Government Act of 1999) which applies from April 2000. It requires local authorities to be constantly looking at new ways to improve the efficiency, quality, and effectiveness of their service delivery.

borough: a district council in England and Wales, which has been granted borough status through a royal charter. Its chair is known as mayor. As a unit of local government, it dates back to the 8th century. In London, borough councils acted as single-tier authorities before the election of the Greater London Authority in 2000.

city: a district council in England and Wales, which has been granted city status through a royal charter. Its chair is known as Lord Mayor.

community council: the lowest level of local government in Scotland and Wales: the equivalent of a parish. Larger community councils may be termed a 'town council' and be headed by a mayor.

council tax: a tax for local government, which replaced the community charge (or poll tax) from April 1993. It is based on property values at April 1991, with properties placed in eight valuation bands, ranging from 'A' (for properties valued at £40,000 or lower) to 'H' (for properties valued over £ 320,000). There is a 25% reduction in the tax charge for single (adult) occupancy.

county: the upper level of local government in non-metropolitan parts of England. It was the name given by the Normans to Anglo-Saxon 'shires', and the boundaries of some counties date back to Saxon times. A Lord Lieutenant, an unpaid official who recommends magistrates for appointment, represents the Queen in each county.

district: in non-metropolitan parts of England, the second level of local government (beneath the county). In metropolitan areas, the metropolitan district is the equivalent of a unitary authority, and is responsible for all local services within its area.

Great London Authority: top tier body, first elected in May 2000, which is responsible for transport (including London Underground), economic development, strategic planning, culture, health improvement, the environment, the police, and fire and emergency planning in London. It covers the area of the 32 London boroughs and scrutinizes the activities of the directly elected London mayor.

Glossary of Local Government Terms *(continued)*

mayor: the chair of a borough, county borough or parish/community council 'town council' in England or Wales. The chair of a city council is called a Lord Mayor.

non domestic rate: a tax levied on businesses. It is based on a multiplier (poundage) of the ratable value of a business property and is collected by district councils or unitary authorities for the area where the property is located. The income collected is pooled together nationally and then re-distributed to local authorities on the basis of their adult populations.

parish: the lowest level of local government in England. Larger parishes may be termed 'town councils' and be headed by a mayor.

Regional Development Agency (RDA) : bodies formed from 1999 to coordinate regional economic development, working closely with Government Offices of the Regions and accountable to ministers and Parliament. RDAs comprise 13 board members, of whom four are drawn from local government, reflecting a balance between type and size of authority.

'shire': an administrative area formed for raising taxes in Anglo-Saxon times. Shire has been retained in the name of many counties, for example Derbyshire.

single tier: where local government services are the responsibility of only one major layer of government: a unitary authority or a metropolitan district authority.

two tier: where local government services are (as in parts of England) the responsibility of two major layers of government: a county council and a non-metropolitan district council.

unitary authority: an administrative unit, created in 1996, which is responsible for all local government services.

Local Government: Elected Members and their Role

Elections to local councils are held on the first Thursday in May. The electoral arrangements vary according to the type of body. Candidates must be nominated by electors registered in the area that they are contesting. A register of electors is prepared and published annually by local electoral registration officers.

Councillors are elected to represent the community and to decide the council's policies. Although some councillors are elected as independents, in practice most represent a political party and find themselves either in opposition or part of the governing majority. However, unlike in central government, where only members of the cabinet are directly involved in major policy decisions, all councillors have some influence, since the council as a whole is the final decision-making body within an authority. Questions of policy are settled by the full council, whilst administration of individual services is the responsibility of committees of councillors. Opposition councillors are proportionally represented on all standing committees.

The leader (or chair) of the council is elected by the other members and is drawn from the party which controls a majority of seats. The leader chairs meetings of the full council and acts as its public figurehead – for example, receiving foreign visitors and other dignitaries. The chair of an English city, town, or borough council is known as mayor or lord mayor, and is elected to the office by fellow councillors. In Scotland the chair is known as 'Convenor' or 'Provost' in 28 councils and as 'Lord Provost' in 4 cities. The government has plans to introduce directly elected mayors for major cities, on the model of London, and also to move to a cabinet form of executive government for local councils.

Day-to-day decisions are delegated to the council's officers or employees, who put into effect the councillors' policies. They are led by an appointed chief executive, who is responsible for the smooth running and coordination of the council and acts as its principal adviser. Like central government, local authorities operate through departments relating to a service function. Control and supervision, however, do not follow the model of central government. The departments are answerable not to ministers, but to committees of elected councillors, with a chair, which usually meet monthly, and later report to the full council. In 1999 the government urged councils to adopt a more executive style of control, suggesting that they consult voters about three options to replace the committee system:

- an elected mayor with executive powers able to choose a cabinet;
- a cabinet system with back-bench councillors scrutinizing cabinet decisions; and
- an elected mayor making overall strategy, to be implemented by a chief executive.

The great majority of councils have expressed a preference in favour of the second option.

Local Authority Electoral Arrangements

Body	Electoral arrangements
English county council	held every four years: next due in 2001; counties are divided into electoral divisions, with one county councillor per division
English district council and 'shire' unitaries	held either for all seats every four years, or for one third of seats each year for three years out of four; districts are divided into electoral wards
English metropolitan district council	one third of seats are up for election each year for three years out of four; metropolitan districts are divided into electoral wards, each represented by three councillors
Greater London Authority	assembly members are elected for four-year terms using the Additional Member System (AMS) and comprise 14 members drawn from specific voting areas and elected on a first-past-the-post basis, and 11 London-wide members distributed to parties on a basis that ensures overall proportional representation in seats won; the mayor is directly elected for four years using a Supplementary Vote system on a single London-wide voting area; first elections were on 4 May 2000
Northern Ireland district council	held every four years, using proportional representation
Scottish unitary authority	held every three years (currently); next elections are in 2002 (the 1999 McIntosh Commission recommended that future elections should be held every four years, using proportional representation)
Welsh unitary authority	held every four years, with a mixture of single- and multi-member wards; next elections are in 2003

■ Local Government in the UK

Responsibilities of Unitary Authorities and County and District Councils

Local authorities are empowered by acts of Parliament to carry out a wide range of functions in the areas for which they are responsible. The most important, in terms of level of expenditure, are:

- education
- social services
- housing benefit administration
- local environmental services
- road maintenance and
- library, culture, and leisure amenities.

Police services also account for a significant proportion of local expenditure, but outside Scotland (where they are directly under council control), accountability is to local police authorities (established in 1994), which contain a mixture of local councillors and appointed members.

In those parts of non-metropolitan England where there is a two-tier structure of local government, the upper (county) tier has control over the strategic and more costly services, including education, highways, transport, the fire service, libraries, social services, strategic planning, and waste disposal. It is the district council which provides the more local services, such as environmental health, housing, leisure and recreation, planning applications, and waste collection. Elsewhere, and in Scotland and Wales, the single-tier authority provides the full range of services, with the exception of fire services, which are accountable to 'joint boards' (which include appointed members).

Local Authority Services: Best Value – the 'Four Cs'

Since April 2000 local authorities have been required to secure 'Best Value' from the services for which they are responsible. They are required to draw up five-year plans for the fundamental review of each service, in which they must:

- consult with the users of the service
- compare their performance with that of other councils
- challenge the need for the service and its current method of delivery
- ensure that there is competition in service provision.

Local Government Finance

In England, about a half of local government expenditure (in 2000–01 budgets) is financed by central government in the form of grants: revenue support grant (35%), police grant (7%), and other specific and special grants (6%). As a result, central government exerts a measure of strategic control, setting broad performance targets and monitoring performance through agencies such as Ofsted (for education). A further 27% of local government expenditure is financed from national non-domestic (unified business) Rate, which is a charge to local business and is set by central government, and 25% from a locally raised council tax. In practice, part of this council tax is provided by central government in the form of council tax benefit, which ensures that those unemployed and on low incomes (receiving job seekers' allowance and income support) have their council tax bills reduced. A small proportion of local government spending is also financed through charges for local authority services. Financing arrangements are similar in Scotland and Wales, but in Northern Ireland a local property tax, based on a property's rateable value, applies instead of council tax.

Local Authority Net Revenue Expenditure in England, 1999–2000

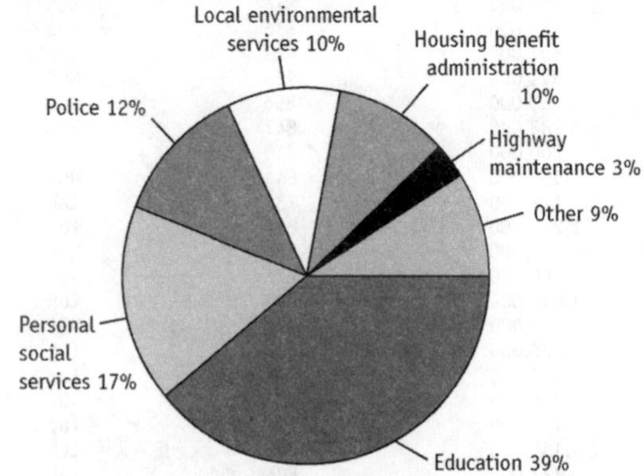

Contacting Your Local Council – Making Complaints

Anyone dissatisfied with a council service or decision should first write to, phone, or e-mail the council. Where the response is unsatisfactory, contact should be made with the local councillor, who will take the matter further, or, in England, Wales, and Scotland, with the Commissioners for Local Administration (or local Ombudsmen). There are three commissioners in England, and one each in Scotland and Wales, who are responsible for investigating complaints of local maladministration. The Northern Ireland Commissioner for Complaints performs a similar role there.

(*See also* **How to Complain**, p 301.)

Council Tax Bands in England, Scotland, and Wales

Council Tax assessment is performed in the following way: having taken into account its budgeted expenditure and precepts levelled by County Councils, the billing authority (that is, the District Council) then deducts whatever income it derives from the Business Rate, Rate Support Grant, and any other items of income; the amount then remaining is that raised by the Council Tax. This is divided among the number of houses in the District. The amount actually payable per house is adjusted according to the value of properties (at 1991 prices) within eight bands, A–H.

Band	England	Scotland	Wales
A	up to £40,000	up to£27,000	up to £30,000
B	£40,001–£52,000	£27,001–£35,000	£30,001–£39,000
C	£52,001–£68,000	£35,001–£45,000	£39,001–£51,000
D	£68,001–£88,000	£45,001–£58,000	£51,001–£66,000
E	£88,001–£120,000	£58,001–£80,000	£66,001–£90,000
F	£120,001–£160,000	£80,001–£106,000	£90,001–£120,000
G	£160,001–£320,000	£106,001–£212,000	£120,001–£240,000
H	£320,001 or over	£212,001or over	£240,001 or over

English Local Authorities

Local Authorities in England

Type: C = county; MC = metropolitan county; MET = metropolitan district (called metropolitan borough or city councils); UA = unitary authority.
Political control: Con = Conservative; Lab = Labour; LD = Liberal Democrat; NOC = no overall control.
Band D refers to property valued at between £68,000 and £88,000 at 1991 prices. For payments in other bands, multiply the Band D figure by the ratios 6/9 (for Band A), 7/9 (for Band B), 8/9 (for Band C), 11/9 (for Band E), 13/9 (for Band F), 15/9 (for Band G), and 18/9 (for Band H). Figures do not include police authority costs.
(– = not applicable.) As of May 2000.

Authority	Type	Area (sq km/sq mi)	Population (1997)	Band D council tax 2000–01 (£)[1]	Political control
Bath and North East Somerset	UA	351/136	166,000	871	NOC
Barnsley	MET	328/127	227,000	850	Lab
Bedfordshire	C	1,192/460	371,000	931	Con
Birmingham	MET	265/102	1,014,000	938	Lab
Blackburn with Darwen	UA	137/53	139,000	966	Lab
Blackpool	UA	35/14	151,000	725	Lab
Bolton	MET	140/54	266,000	928	Lab
Bournemouth	UA	46/18	162,000	764	NOC
Bracknell Forest	UA	109/42	111,000	736	Con
Bradford	MET	366/141	483,000	834	NOC
Brighton and Hove	UA	82/32	253,000	781	Lab
Bristol	UA	110/42	401,000	999	Lab
Buckinghamshire	C	1,568/605	477,000	821	Con
Bury	MET	99/38	182,000	851	Lab
Calderdale	MET	363/140	193,000	911	Con
Cambridgeshire	C	3,056/1,179	555,000	784	Con
Cheshire	C	2,081/803	670,000	920	NOC
Cornwall	C	3,559/1,374	488,000	820[2]	NOC
Coventry	MET	97/37	304,000	1,020	Lab
Cumbria	C	6,824/2,635	492,000	921	Lab
Darlington	UA	197/76	101,000	741	Lab
Derby	UA	78/30	235,000	827	Lab
Derbyshire	C	2,551/985	730,000	934	Lab
Devon	C	6,560/2,533	686,000	828	LD
Doncaster	MET	581/224	292,000	798	Lab
Dorset	C	2,542/981	385,000	874	NOC
Dudley	MET	98/38	311,000	836	Lab
Durham	C	2,232/862	507,000	928	Lab
East Riding of Yorkshire	UA	2,415/932	311,000	924	NOC
East Sussex	C	1,713/661	488,000	866	NOC
Essex	C	3,469/1,339	1,288,000	847	NOC
Gateshead	MET	143/55	200,000	1,010	Lab
Gloucestershire	C	2,653/1,024	559,000	841	NOC
Halton	UA	74/29	122,000	737	Lab
Hampshire	C	3,689/1,424	1,231,000	819	Con
Hartlepool	UA	94/36	92,000	1,022	NOC
Herefordshire	UA	2,162/835	166,000	775	NOC
Hertfordshire	C	1,639/633	1,025,000	809	Con
Isle of Wight	UA	380/147	126,000	823	NOC
Kent	C	3,543/1,368	1,326,000	825	Con
Kingston-upon-Hull	UA	71/27	264,000	794	Lab
Kirklees	MET	410/158	389,000	910	NOC
Knowsley	MET	97/37	154,000	1,008	Lab
Lancashire	C	2,898/1,119	1,135,000	965	Lab
Leeds	MET	562/217	727,000	805	Lab

(continued)

Local Authorities in England *(continued)*

Authority	Type	Area (sq km/sq mi)	Population (1997)	Band D council tax 2000–01 (£)[1]	Political control
Leicester	UA	73/28	294,000	873	Lab
Leicestershire	C	2,084/805	600,000	859	NOC
Lincolnshire	C	5,921/2,286	619,000	834	Con
Liverpool	MET	113/44	464,000	1,172	LD
Luton	UA	43/17	182,000	761	Lab
Manchester	MET	116/45	428,000	1,006	Lab
Manchester, Greater	MC	1,286/497	2,572,000	–	–
Medway Towns	UA	192/74	240,000	702	NOC
Merseyside	MC	655/253	1,413,000	–	–
Middlesbrough	UA	54/21	145,000	843	Lab
Milton Keynes	UA	309/119	200,000	786	NOC
Newcastle upon Tyne	MET	112/43	280,000	1,006	Lab
Norfolk	C	5,372/2,074	783,000	831	NOC
Northamptonshire	C	2,367/914	610,000	808	Lab
North East Lincolnshire	UA	192/74	158,000	917	Lab
North Lincolnshire	UA	833/322	152,000	1,027	Lab
North Somerset	UA	373/144	186,000	780	Con
North Tyneside	MET	84/32	193,000	967	Lab
Northumberland	C	5,026/1,941	309,000	954	Lab
North Yorkshire	C	8,038/3,103	561,000	801	Con
Nottingham	UA	75/29	287,000	922	Lab
Nottinghamshire	C	2,085/805	745,000	979	Lab
Oldham	MET	141/54	220,000	965	LD
Oxfordshire	C	2,606/1,006	611,000	833	NOC
Peterborough	UA	334/129	157,000	817	NOC
Plymouth	UA	80/31	255,000	764	Con
Poole	UA	65/25	141,000	790	NOC
Portsmouth	UA	40/15	190,000	703	NOC
Reading	UA	40/15	146,000	908	Lab
Redcar and Cleveland	UA	245/95	139,000	1,081	Lab
Rochdale	MET	160/62	207,000	909	Lab
Rotherham	MET	283/109	255,000	874	Lab
Rutland	UA	394/152	36,000	1,022	NOC
St Helens	MET	133/51	179,000	1,009	Lab
Salford	MET	97/37	228,000	1,033	Lab
Sandwell	MET	86/33	291,000	898	Lab
Sefton	MET	153/59	289,000	956	NOC
Sheffield	MET	367/142	530,000	938	LD
Shropshire	C	3,198/1,235	277,000	841	NOC
Slough	UA	27/10	111,000	719	Lab
Solihull	MET	179/69	205,000	786	Con
Somerset	C	3,452/1,333	487,000	823	LD
Southampton	UA	50/19	215,000	752	NOC
Southend-on-Sea	UA	42/16	175,000	735	Con
South Gloucestershire	UA	497/192	239,000	859	LD
South Tyneside	MET	64/25	155,000	930	Lab
South Yorkshire	MC	1,559/602	1,305,000	–	–
Staffordshire	C	2,623/1,013	807,000	805	Lab
Stockport	MET	126/49	292,000	953	NOC
Stockton-on-Tees	UA	204/79	180,000	904	Lab
Stoke-on-Trent	UA	93/36	253,000	787	Lab
Suffolk	C	3,798/1,466	667,600	815	NOC
Sunderland	MET	138/53	293,000	857	Lab
Surrey	C	1,677/647	1,057,000	804	Con
Swindon	UA	230/89	177,000	742	NOC
Tameside	MET	103/40	221,000	938	Lab
Telford and Wrekin	UA	290/112	147,000	798	Lab
Thurrock	UA	164/63	132,000	716	Lab
Torbay	UA	63/24	123,000	792	Con
Trafford	MET	106/41	219,000	723	Lab
Tyne and Wear	MC	540/208	1,121,000	–	–
Wakefield	MET	333/129	317,000	797	Lab
Walsall	MET	106/41	262,000	858	NOC
Warrington	UA	176/68	190,000	775	Lab
Warwickshire	C	1,979/764	504,000	880	NOC
West Berkshire	UA	704/272	144,000	881	LD
West Midlands	MC	899/347	2,631,000	–	–
West Sussex	C	1,988/768	747,000	804	Con
West Yorkshire	MC	2,034/785	2,110,000	–	–
Wigan	MET	199/77	310,000	887	Lab
Wiltshire	C	3,246/1,253	422,000	840	Con
Windsor and Maidenhead	UA	198/76	142,000	778	NOC
Wirral	MET	159/61	328,000	1,031	Lab
Wokingham	UA	179/69	144,000	889	NOC

(continued)

Local Authorities in England *(continued)*

Authority	Type	Area (sq km/sq mi)	Population (1997)	Band D council tax 2000–01 (£)[1]	Political control
Wolverhampton	MET	69/27	242,000	998	Lab
Worcestershire	C	1,761/680	536,000	808	NOC
York	UA	271/105	176,000	748	NOC

[1] Average Band D council tax rates are given for counties. Rates for districts within counties may differ from the figures given.
[2] Excluding the Scillies. Band D council tax for the Isles of Scilly is £566.

See also **The Greater London Authority and the London Borough Councils**, p 79–82.

English Counties: Directory

Bedfordshire County Hall, Cauldwell Street, Bedford MK42 9AP; phone: (01234) 363222; fax: (01234) 272982; e-mail: bedsonline@csd.bedfordshire.gov.uk; Web site: www.bedfordshire.gov.uk **Chief executive**: David Bell

Buckinghamshire County Hall, Walton Street, Aylesbury HP20 1UA; phone: (01296) 395000; fax: (01296) 382481; e-mail: webmaster@buckscc.gov.uk; Web site: www.buckscc.gov.uk **Chief executive**: Ian Crookhall

Cambridgeshire Shire Hall, Castle Hill, Cambridge CB3 0AP; phone: (01223) 717111; fax: (01223) 717201; e-mail: charterline@camcnty.gov.uk; Web site: www.camcnty.gov.uk **Chief executive**: Alan Barnish

Cheshire County Hall, Chester CH1 1SF; phone: (01244) 602424; fax: (01244) 602100; Web site: www.cheshire.gov.uk **Chief executive**: Colin Cheeseman (acting)

Cornwall New County Hall, Truro, Cornwall TR1 3AY; phone: (01872) 322000; fax: (01872) 270340; e-mail: enquiries@cornwall.gov.uk; Web site: www.cornwall.gov.uk **Chief executive**: Peter Davies

Cumbria The Courts, Carlisle CA3 8NA; phone: (01228) 606060; fax: (01228) 606302; e-mail: information@cumbriacc.gov.uk; Web site: www.cumbria.gov.uk **Chief executive**: Bill Swarbrick

Derbyshire County Hall, Matlock DE4 3AG; phone: (01629) 580000; fax: (01629) 585120; e-mail: sarah.colvin@derbyshire.gov.uk; Web site: www.derbyshire.gov.uk **Chief executive**: Nick Hodgson

Devon County Hall, Topsham Road, Exeter EX2 4QD; phone: (01392) 382000; fax: (01392) 382286; e-mail: issu@devon-cc.gov.uk; Web site: www.devon-cc.gov.uk Philip Jenkinson

Dorset County Hall, Colliton Park, Dorchester DT1 1XJ; phone: (01305) 251000; fax: (01305) 224839; e-mail: d.h.jenkins@dorset-cc.gov.uk; Web site: www.dorset-cc.gov.uk **Chief executive**: David Jenkins

Durham County Hall, Durham DH1 5UL; phone: (0191) 386 4411; fax: (0191) 383 3243; e-mail: help@durham.gov.uk; Web site: www.durham.gov.uk **Chief executive**: Kingsley Smith

East Sussex Pelham House, St Andrew's Lane, Lewes BN7 1UN; phone: (01273) 481000; fax: (01273) 483317; e-mail: transenv@eastsussexcc.gov.uk; Web site: www.eastsussex.gov.uk **Chief executive**: Cheryl Miller

Essex County Hall, Chelmsford CM1 1LX; phone: (01245) 492211; fax: (01245) 256731; Web site: www.essexcc.gov.uk **Chief executive**: Stuart Ashurst

Gloucestershire Shire Hall, Westgate Street, Gloucester GL1 2TG; phone: (01452) 425000; fax: (01452) 425876; Web site: www.gloscc.gov.uk **Chief executive**: Richard Cockcroft (County Director)

Hampshire The Castle, Winchester SO23 8UJ; phone: (01962) 841841; fax: (01962) 867273; e-mail: hantsinf@hants.gov.uk; Web site: www.hants.gov.uk **Chief executive**: Peter Robertson

Hertfordshire County Hall, Peggs Lane, Hertford SG13 8DE; phone: (01992) 555555; fax: (01992) 555644; e-mail: webadmin@hertscc.gov.uk; Web site: www.hertscc.gov.uk **Chief executive**: Bill Ogley

Kent Sessions House, County Hall, Maidstone, Kent ME14 1XQ; phone: (01622) 671411; fax: (01622) 694060; e-mail: mick.pitt@kent.gov.uk; Web site: www.kent.gov.uk **Chief executive**: Michael Pitt

Lancashire County Hall, PO Box 78, Preston PR1 8XS; phone: (01772) 254868; fax: (01772) 263506; e-mail: max.winterbottom@resdir.lancss.gov.uk; Web site: www.lancashire.com/sitemaf.htm **Chief executive**: Max Winterbottom

Leicestershire County Hall, Leicester Road, Glenfield, Leicester LE3 8RA; phone: (0116) 232 3232; fax: (0116) 265 6260; e-mail: information@leics.gov.uk; Web site: www.leics.gov.uk **Chief executive**: John Sinnott

Lincolnshire County Offices, Newland, Lincoln LN1 1YL; phone: (01522) 552000; fax: (01522) 552004; e-mail: public.relations@lincolnshire.gov.uk; Web site: www.lincolnshire.gov.uk **Chief executive**: David Bowles

Norfolk County Hall, Martineay Lane, Norwich NR1 2DH; phone: (01603) 222222; fax: (01603) 222959; e-mail: information@norfolk.gov.uk; Web site: www.norfolk.gov.uk **Chief executive**: Tim Byles

Northamptonshire PO Box 93, Northampton NN1 1AS; phone: (01604) 236236; fax: (01604) 236223; e-mail: genie@northamptonshire.gov.uk **Chief executive**: John Picking

Northumberland County Hall, Morpeth NE61 2EF; phone: (01670) 533000; fax: (01670) 533124; Web site: www.northumberland.gov.uk **Chief executive**: Alan Clarke

North Yorkshire County Hall, Race Course Lane, Northallerton DL7 8AD; phone: (01609) 780780; fax: (01609) 778199; Web site: www.northyorks.gov.uk **Chief executive**: Jeremy Walker

Nottinghamshire County Hall, West Bridgeford, Nottingham NG2 7QP; phone: (0115) 982 3823; fax: (0115) 977 2419; Web site: www.notscc.gov.uk Peter Housden

Oxfordshire County Hall, New Road, Oxford OX1 1ND; phone: (01865) 792422; fax: (01865) 726155; e-mail: online@oxfordshire.gov.uk; Web site: www.oxfordshire.gov.uk **Chief executive**: John Harwood

Shropshire The Shire Hall, Abbey Foregate, Shrewsbury SY2 6ND; phone: (01743) 251000; fax: (01743) 360315; e-mail: enquiries@shropshire-cc.gov.uk; Web site: www.shropshire-cc.gov.uk **Chief executive**: Nigel Pursey

Somerset County Hall, Taunton TA1 4DY; phone: (01823) 355455; fax: (01823) 355887; e-mail: info@somerset.gov.uk; Web site: www.somerset. gov.uk **Chief executive**: David Radford

Staffordshire Walton Building, PO Box 11, Martin Street, Stafford ST16 2LH; phone: (01785) 223121; fax: (01785) 215153; Web site: www.staffordshire.gov.uk **Chief executive**: Bernard Price (Clerk and Chief Executive)

Suffolk County Hall, St Helen Court, Ipswich IP4 2JS; phone: (01473) 583000; fax: (01473) 639002; e-mail: webmaster@uffolkcc.gov.uk; Web site: www.suffolkcc.gov.uk **Chief executive**: Lin Homer

Surrey County Hall, Penrhyn Road, Kingston-upon-Thames KT1 2DN; phone: (020) 8541 8800; fax: (020) 8541 8968; Web site: www.surreycc.gov.uk **Chief executive**: Paul Coen

Warwickshire PO Box 9, Shire Hall, Warwick CV34 4RR; phone: (01926) 410410; fax: (01926) 412326; e-mail: edcomms@warwickshire.gov.uk; Web site: www.warwickshire.gov.uk **Chief executive**: Ian Caulfield

West Sussex County Hall, West Street, Chichester PO19 1RO; phone: (01243) 777100; fax: (01243) 777952 **Chief executive**: Paul Rigg

Wiltshire County Hall, Bythesea Road, Trowbridge BA14 8JG; phone: (01225) 713000; fax: (01225) 713092; Web site: www.wiltshire.gov.uk **Chief executive**: Keith Robinson

Worcestershire County Hall, Spetchley Road, Worcester WR5 2NP; phone: (01905) 766333; fax: (01905) 766109; Web site: www.worcestershire.gov.uk **Chief executive**: Rob Sykes

Local Government in the UK

England – local government divisions

BA	BATH AND NE SOMERSET
BE	BEDFORDSHIRE
BR	BRACKNELL FOREST
BT	BRISTOL
BU	BUCKINGHAMSHIRE
DA	DARLINGTON
DC	DERBY CITY
GR	GREATER MANCHESTER
HA	HALTON
HE	HERTFORDSHIRE
LC	LEICESTER CITY
LE	LEICESTERSHIRE
LU	LUTON
MK	MILTON KEYNES
NH	NORTHAMPTONSHIRE
NL	NORTH LINCOLNSHIRE
NS	NORTH SOMERSET
NT	NOTTINGHAMSHIRE
PB	PETERBOROUGH
PT	PORTSMOUTH
R	READING
RU	RUTLAND
SG	SOUTH GLOUCESTERSHIRE
SO	SOUTHAMPTON
SS	STOCKTON-ON-TEES
ST	STOKE-ON-TRENT
TW	TELFORD AND WREKIN
WA	WARRINGTON
WK	WEST BERKSHIRE
WM	WEST MIDLANDS
WN	WINDSOR AND MAIDENHEAD
WO	WOKINGHAM
WR	WORCESTERSHIRE

SCOTLAND
NORTHERN IRELAND
REPUBLIC OF IRELAND
WALES
ENGLAND
Irish Sea
North Sea
English Channel
Isle of Man
Isles of Scilly
FRANCE
NORTHUMBERLAND
TYNE AND WEAR
DURHAM
HARTLEPOOL
REDCAR AND CLEVELAND
MIDDLESBROUGH
CUMBRIA
DA
SS
NORTH YORKSHIRE
YORK
THE EAST RIDING OF YORKSHIRE
KINGSTON UPON HULL
LANCASHIRE
BLACKPOOL
BLACKBURN AND DARWEN
WEST YORKSHIRE
NL
NORTH EAST LINCOLNSHIRE
MERSEYSIDE
GR
SOUTH YORKSHIRE
WA
HA
CHESHIRE
DERBYSHIRE
NT
LINCOLNSHIRE
ST
NOTTINGHAM CITY
DC
TW
STAFFORDSHIRE
LE
LC
RU
PB
NORFOLK
SHROPSHIRE
WM
CAMBRIDGESHIRE
SUFFOLK
WR
WARWICKSHIRE
NH
HEREFORDSHIRE
MK
BE
LU
GLOUCESTERSHIRE
BU
HE
ESSEX
OXFORDSHIRE
SOUTHEND
SLOUGH
GREATER LONDON
THURROCK
SG
SWINDON
R
WN
WK
WO
BR
BT
NS
BA
WILTSHIRE
MEDWAY TOWNS
SURREY
KENT
HAMPSHIRE
SOMERSET
SO
PT
WEST SUSSEX
EAST SUSSEX
POOLE
DEVON
DORSET
ISLE OF WIGHT
BRIGHTON AND HOVE
BOURNEMOUTH
CORNWALL
PLYMOUTH
TORBAY

○ unitary authority within another local government area

0 50 mi
0 100 km

English Unitary Authorities: Directory

Bath and North East Somerset Riverside, Temple Street, Keynsham, Bristol BS3 1LA; phone: (01225) 477793; fax: (01225) 394470; Web site: www.bathnes.gov.uk **Chief executive**: John Everitt

Blackburn with Darwen Town Hall, King William Street, Blackburn BB1 7DY; phone: (01254) 585585; fax: (01254) 697223; Web site: www.blackburn.gov.uk **Chief executive**: Philip Watson

Blackpool Municipal Buildings, Corporation Street, Blackpool FY1 1AD; phone: (01253) 477477; fax: (01253) 477101, Web site: www.blackpool.gov.uk **Chief executive**: G Essex-Crosby Web site: www.blackpool.gov.uk

Bournemouth Town Hall, Bourne Avenue, Bournemouth BH2 6DY; phone: (01202) 451451; fax: (01202) 451000; Web site: www.bournemouth.gov.uk **Chief executive**: David Newell

Bracknell Civic Offices, East Hampstead House, Town Square, Bracknell RG12 1AQ; phone: (01344) 424642; fax: (01344) 352810; Web site: www.bracknell-forest.gov.uk **Chief executive**: Gordon Mitchell

Brighton and Hove Kings House, Grand Avenue, Hove BN3 2LS; phone: (01273) 290000; fax: (01273) 291003; Web site: www.brighton-hove.gov.uk **Chief executive**: Glynn Jones

Bristol The Council House, College Green, Bristol BS1 5TR; phone: (0117) 922 2000; fax: (0117) 922 2024; Web site: www.bristol-city.gov.uk **Chief executive**: Lucy de Groot

Darlington Town Hall, Darlington DL1 5QT; phone: (01325) 380651; fax: (01325) 388018; Web site: www.darlington.org.uk/council **Chief executive**: Barry Keel

Derby The Council House, Corporation Street, Derby DE1 2FS; phone: (01332) 293111; fax: (01332) 256223 **Chief executive**: Ray Cowlishaw

East Riding of Yorkshire County Hall, Beverley, East Riding of Yorkshire HU17 9BA; phone: (01482) 887700; fax: (01482) 884732; Web site: www.east-riding-of-yorkshire.gov.uk **Chief executive**: Darryl Stephenson

Halton Municipal Building, Kingsway, Widnes WA8 7QF; phone: (0151) 424 2061; fax: (0151) 471 7301, Web Site: www.halton.gov.uk **Chief executive**: Mike Cuff

Hartlepool Civic Centre, Victoria Road, Hartlepool TS24 8AY; phone: (01429) 266522; fax: (01429) 523856; Web site: www.hartlepool.gov.uk **Chief executive**: Brian Dinsdale

Herefordshire Brockington, 35 Haford Road HR1 1SH; phone: (01432) 260000; fax: (01432) 340189; Web site: www.herefordshire.gov.uk **Chief executive**: Neil Pringle

Isle of Wight County Hall, High Street, Newport, Isle of Wight PO30 1UD; phone: (01983) 823000; fax: (01983) 823138; Web site: www.isleofwight.gov.uk **Chief executive**: Bernard Quoroll

Kingston-upon-Hull Guildhall, Alfred Gelder Street, Kingston-upon-Hull HU1 2AA; phone: (01482) 610610; fax: (01482) 615135; Web site: www.hullcc.gov.uk **Chief executive**: Ian Crookham

Leicester New Walk Centre, Welford Place, Leicester LE1 6ZG; phone: (0116) 254 9922; fax: (0116) 255 3809; Web site: www.leicester.gov.uk **Chief executive**: Rodney Green

Luton Town Hall, George Street, Luton LU1 2BQ; phone: (01582) 746000; fax: (01582) 546223; Web site: www.luton.gov.uk **Chief executive**: K Jones

Medway Towns Civic Centre, High Street, Strood, Rochester ME2 4AU; phone: (01634) 727777; fax: (01634) 732756; Web site: www.intranet.medway.gov.uk **Chief executive**: Judith Armitt

Middlesbrough PO Box 99A, Municipal Buildings, Russel Street, Middlesbrough TS1 2QQ; phone: (01642) 245432; fax: (01642) 263519; Web site: www.middlesbrough.gov.uk **Chief executive**: John Foster (Managing Director)

Milton Keynes Civic Office, 1 Saxon Gate East, Milton Keynes MK9 3EJ; phone: (01908) 691691; fax: (01908) 252769; Web site: www.miltonkeynes.gov.uk **Chief executive**: Howard Miller

West Berkshire Council Offices, Market Street, Newbury RG14 5LD; phone: (01635) 42400; fax: (01635) 519547; Web site: www.westberks.gov.uk **Chief executive**: Stella Manzie

North East Lincolnshire Municipal Offices, Town Hall Square, Grimsby DN31 1HU; phone: (01472) 313131; fax: (01472) 325902; Web site: www.nelincs.gov.uk **Chief executive**: Roy Benthan

North Lincolnshire Pittwood House, Ashby Road, Scunthorpe DN16 1AB; phone: (01724) 296296; fax: (01724) 271617; Web site: www.northlincs.gov.uk **Chief executive**: Michael Garnett

North Somerset Town Hall, Walliscote Grove Road, Weston-super-Mare, BS23 1UJ; phone: (01934) 888888; fax: (01934) 888822; Web site: www.n-somerset.gov.uk **Chief executive**: Paul May

Nottingham The Guildhall, South Sherwood Street, Nottingham NG1 4BT; phone: (0115) 915 5555; fax: (0115) 915 4635; Web site: www.nottinghamcity.gov.uk **Chief executive**: Edward Cantle

Peterborough Town Hall, Bridge Street, Peterborough PE1 1HQ; phone: (01733) 563141; fax: (01733) 452537; Web site: www.peterborough.gov.uk **Chief executive**: W E Samuels

Plymouth Civic Centre, Armada Way, Plymouth PL1 2EW; phone: (01752) 668000; fax: (01752) 304880; Web site: www.plymouth.gov.uk **Chief executive**: Alison Stone

Poole Municipal Buildings, Civic Centre, Poole BH15 2RU; phone: (01202) 633633; fax: (01202) 633899; Web site: www.poole.gov.uk **Chief executive**: Jim Brooks

Portsmouth Civic Offices, Floor 3, Guildhall Square, Portsmouth PO1 2BG; phone: (01705) 822251; fax: (01705) 834571; Web site: www.portsmouth.gov.uk **Chief executive**: Nick Gurney

Reading Civic Centre, Reading RG1 7TD; phone: (0118) 939 0900; fax: (0118) 939 0969; Web site: www.reading.gov.uk **Chief Executive**: Joyce Markham

Redcar and Cleveland Town Hall, Fabian Road, South Bank, Middlesbrough, Cleveland TS6 9AR; phone: (01642) 444000; fax: (01642) 444599; Web site: www.redcar-cleveland.gov.uk **Chief executive**: Andrew Kilburn

Rutland Council Offices, Catmose, Oakham, Rutland LE15 6HP; phone: (01572) 722577; fax: (01572) 758307 **Chief executive**: Janice Morphet

Slough Town Hall, Bath Road, Slough SL1 3UQ; phone: (01753) 552288; fax: (01753) 692499; Web site: www.slough.gov.uk **Chief executive**: Cheryl Coppell

Southampton Civic Centre, Southampton SO14 7LY; phone: (01703) 223855; fax: (01703) 833232; Web site: www.southampton.gov.uk **Chief executive**: John Cairns

Southend on Sea Civic Centre, Victoria Avenue, Southend on Sea SS2 6ER; phone: (01702) 215000; fax: (01702) 215110; Web site: www.southend.gov.uk **Chief executive**: George Krawiec

South Gloucestershire The Council Office, Castle Street, Thornbury BS35 1HF; phone: (01454) 868686; fax: (01454) 863855; Web site: www.southglos.gov.uk **Chief executive**: Mike Robinson

Stockton-on-Tees Municipal Buildings, Church Road, Stockton-on-Tees TS18 1LD; phone: (01642) 393939; fax: (01642) 393002; Web site: www.stockton-bc.gov.uk **Chief executive**: George Garlick

Stoke-on-Trent PO Box 636, Civic Centre, Glebe Street, Stoke on Trent ST4 1RN; phone: (01782) 234567; Web site: www.stoke.gov.uk **Chief executive**: Brian Smith

Swindon Civic Offices, Euclid Street, Swindon, Wilts SN1 2JH; phone: (01793) 463000; fax: (01793) 463930; Web site: www.swindon.gov.uk **Chief executive**: Paul Doherty

Telford and Wrekin Civic Office, Telford TF3 4LD; phone: (01952) 202100; fax: (01952) 291060; Web site: www.telford.gov.uk **Chief executive**: David Hutchison

Thurrock Civic Offices, New Road, Grays, Essex RM17 6SL; phone: (01375) 390000; fax: (01375) 652359; Web site: www.thurrock-community.org.uk **Chief executive**: Keith Barnes

Torbay Civic Offices, Castle Circus, Torquay TQ1 3DR; phone: (01803) 201201; fax: (01803) 207006; Web site: www.torbay.gov.uk **Chief executive**: Anthony Hodgkiss

Warrington Town Hall, Sankey Street, Warrington WA1 1UH; phone: (01925) 442140; fax: (01925) 442138; Web site: www.warrington.gov.uk **Chief executive**: Steven Broomhead

Windsor and Maidenhead Town Hall, St Ives Road, Maidenhead, Berks SL6 1RF; phone: (01628) 798888; fax: (01628) 796408; Web site: www.rbwn.gov.uk **Chief executive**: David Lunn

Wokingham Shute End, Wokingham RG40 1WQ; phone: (0118) 974 6000; fax: (0118) 978 9078; Web site: www.wokingham.gov.uk **Chief executive**: Gillian Norton

York The Guildhall, St Helen's Square, York YO1 9QN; phone: (01904) 613161; fax: (01904) 551998; Web site: www.york.gov.uk **Chief executive**: David Clark

Local Government in the UK

English Metropolitan Borough Councils: Directory

Greater Manchester Metropolitan County

Bolton 2nd Floor, Town Hall, Civic Centre, Bolton BL1 1RU; phone: (01204) 522311; fax (01204) 381942 **Chief executive**: Bernard Knight

Bury Town Hall, Knowsley Street, Bury BL9 0SW; phone: (0161) 253 5000; fax: (0161) 253 5108; e-mail: chiefexec@bury.gov.uk; Web site: www.bury.gov.uk **Chief executive**: Dennis Taylor

Manchester Town Hall, Manchester M60 2LA; phone: (0161) 234 5000; fax: (0161) 234 3098; Web site: www.manchester.gov.uk **Chief executive**: Howard Bernstein

Oldham PO Box 160, Civic Centre, West Street, Oldham OL1 1UG; phone: (0161) 911 3000; fax: (0161) 911 4684; Web site: www.oldham.gov.uk **Chief executive**: Colin Smith

Rochdale The Town Hall, The Esplanade, Rochdale OL16 1AB; phone: (01706) 647474; fax (01706) 864755/865450 **Chief executive**: Frances Done

Salford Salford Civic Centre, Chorley Road, Swinton, Salford M27 5FJ; phone: (0161) 794 4711; fax: (0161) 728 4290; Web site: www.salford.gov.uk **Chief executive**: John Willis

Stockport Town Hall, Edward Street, Stockport SK1 3XE; phone: (0161) 480 4949; fax: (0161) 480 6773; Web site: www.stockport.gov.uk **Chief executive**: John Schultz

Tameside Wellington Road, Ashton-under-Lyne, Lancashire OL6 6DL; phone: (0161) 342 8355; fax: (0161) 342 3543; e-mail: anne.drinkhill@chiefex.tameside.gov.uk **Chief executive**: Michael Greenwood

Trafford PO Box 10, Trafford Town Hall, Talbot Road, Stretford M32 0YT; phone: (0161) 912 1212; fax: (0161) 912 4184 **Chief executive**: Allan Lewis

Wigan New Town Hall, Library Street, Greater Manchester WN1 1YN; phone: (01942) 244991; fax: (01942) 827451; Web site: www.wiganmbc.gov.uk **Chief executive**: Stephen Jones

Merseyside Metropolitan County

Knowsley Municipal Buildings, Archway Road, Huyton L36 9UX; phone: (0151) 489 6000; fax: (0151) 443 3507; Web site: www.knowsley.gov.uk **Chief executive**: David Henshaw

Liverpool Municipal Buildings, Dale Street, Liverpool L69 2DH; phone: (0151) 227 3911; fax: (0151) 225 2017; Web site: www.liverpool.gov.uk **Chief executive**: Peter Bounds

St Helens Town Hall, Victoria Square, Corporation Street, St Helens WA10 1HP; phone: (01744) 456000; fax: (01744) 456889; Web site: www.merseyworld.com/sthelensmbc/ **Chief executive**: Carol Hudson

Sefton Town Hall, Lord Street, Southport PR8 1DA; phone: (01704) 533133; fax: (0151) 934 2268; Web site: www.sefton.gov.uk **Chief executive**: Graham Haywood

Wirral Town Hall, Brighton Street, Wallasey L44 8ED; phone: (0151) 638 7070; fax: (0151) 691 8583 **Chief executive**: Stephen Maddox

South Yorkshire Metropolitan County

Barnsley Town Hall, Church Street, Barnsley S70 2TA; phone: (01226) 770770; fax: (01226) 773305; Web site: www.barnsley.gov.uk **Chief executive**: John Edwards

Doncaster 2 Priory Place, Doncaster DN1 1BN; phone: (01302) 734000; fax: (01302) 734040; e-mail: john.leash@doncaster.gov.uk **Chief executive**: Alf Taylor

Rotherham Civic Building, Walker Place, Rotherham S65 1UF; phone: (01709) 382121; fax: (01709) 822406; Web site: www.rotherham.gov.uk **Chief executive**: Alan Carruthers

Sheffield Town Hall, Pinstone Street, Sheffield S1 2HH; phone: (0114) 272 6444; fax: (0114) 273 6844; Web site: www.sheffield.gov.uk **Chief executive**: Bob Kerslake

Tyne and Wear Metropolitan County

Gateshead Civic Centre, Regent Street, Gateshead NE8 1HH; phone: (0191) 477 1011; fax: (0191) 478 2755 **Chief executive**: Leslie Elton

Newcastle-upon-Tyne Civic Centre, Newcastle-upon-Tyne NE99 2BN; phone: (0191) 232 8520; fax (0191) 230 1107; e-mail: kevin.lavery@newcastle.gov.uk **Chief executive**: Kevin Lavery

North Tyneside Town Hall, High Street East, Wallsend NE28 7RR; phone: (0191) 200 6565; fax: (0191) 200 7272 **Chief executive**: Chief executive: J Doughty (acting)

South Tyneside Town Hall and Civic Offices, Westoe Road, South Shields NE33 2RL; phone: (0191) 427 1717; fax (0191) 454 5678; Web site: www.s-tyneside-nbc.gov.uk **Chief executive**: Peter Haigh (Director of Corporate Services)

Sunderland Civic Centre, Burdon Road, Sunderland SR2 7DN; phone: (0191) 553 1000; fax: (0191) 553 1188; e-mail: economic.team@sunderland.btinternet.com **Chief executive**: Colin Sinclair

West Midlands Metropolitan County

Birmingham The Council House, Victoria Square, Birmingham B1 1BB; phone: (0121) 303 2000; fax: (0121) 303 1309 **Chief executive**: Michael Lyons

Coventry Council House, Earl Street, Coventry CV1 5RR; phone: (01203) 833333; fax: (01203) 833680; Web site: www.coventry.gov.uk **Chief executive**: Ian Roxburgh

Dudley The Council House, Priory Road, Dudley DY1 1HF; phone: (01384) 818181; fax (01384) 815226; Web site: www.dudley.gov.uk **Chief executive**: A Sparke

Sandwell The Sandwell Council House, Oldbury, Warley B69 3DE; phone: (0121) 569 2200; fax: (0121) 569 3100; Web site: www.sandwell.gov.uk **Chief executive**: Nigel Summers

Solihull PO Box 18, Council House, Solihull B91 3QS; phone: (0121) 704 6000; fax: (0121) 704 6884; e-mail: info@solihull.gov.uk **Chief executive**: Norman Perry

Walsall Civic Centre, Darwall Street, Walsall WS1 1TP; phone: (01922) 650000; fax: (01922) 720885; Web site: www.walsall.gov.uk **Chief executive**: David Winchurch

Wolverhampton Civic Centre, St Peter's Square, Wolverhampton WV1 1SH; phone: (01902) 556556; fax: (01902) 554030; Web site: www.wolverhampton.gov.uk **Chief executive**: Derek Anderson

West Yorkshire Metropolitan County

Bradford City Hall, Channing Way, Bradford BD1 1HY; phone: (01274) 752111; fax: (01274) 392718; Web site: www.bradford.gov.uk **Chief executive**: Ian Stewart

Calderdale Town Hall, Crossley Street, Halifax HX1 1UJ; phone: (01422) 357257; fax: (01422) 393102 **Chief executive**: Paul Sheehan

Kirklees PO Box B24, Civic Centre, Huddersfield HD1 1WG; phone: (01484) 221801; fax: (01484) 221777; Web site: www.kirkleesmc.gov.uk **Chief executive**: Tony Elson

Leeds Civic Hall, Leeds LS1 1UR; phone: (0113) 234 8080; fax: (0113) 247 4870 **Chief executive**: Philip Smith

Wakefield Town Hall, Wood Street, Wakefield WF1 2HQ; phone: (01924) 306090; fax: (01924) 305113 **Chief executive**: Martin Pullham (Head of Paid Service)

The Greater London Authority and the London Borough Councils

The Greater London Authority (GLA): Introduction

The Greater London Authority (GLA) comprises a 25-member London assembly and mayor. The mayor is elected every four years by a supplementary vote system in which electors are asked to choose their preferred and second preference candidates. If no candidate wins 50% or more of the first preference vote, then the second preference votes of the candidates other than the leading two are distributed in a 'second count'.

The assembly is elected every four years by the additional member system, involving 14 members who are elected, by the first-past-the-post system, to individual constituencies, and 11 members from London-wide party lists. Electors have two votes, one for a constituency member and one for a party list, with the list seats being allocated to ensure that a party's overall number of assembly seats is proportional to its share of the London vote.

The Greater London Authority (GLA): Introduction *(continued)*

The mayor oversees a budget of £3.6 billion, and has no special new tax-raising powers (although some money may be raised through traffic charges in London). The mayor has a staff of around 250 and free use of offices in Romney House, Westminster, pending the opening of the GLA's new offices in 2002. The mayor is paid a salary of £75,136, but this is reduced to a third if he or she is an MP and chooses to remain so. Assembly members are paid £34,438 each and the deputy mayor £51,743. These salaries are similarly reduced if the postholder is an MP.

The GLA has responsibility for: economic development and regeneration; culture and tourism; public health; environment; transport; planning; fire and emergency planning; and London's police. The 32 London boroughs continue to provide day-to-day services. The mayor produces a strategic plan for London, develops an environmental strategy (that includes promoting biodiversity and sustainable development), and promotes London as a cultural capital. A new body, Transport for London, is to be appointed by the mayor to run the London Undergound and buses, as well as a London Development Agency, to promote economic development. For fire and emergency planning and policing two new bodies will be set up: a 17-member London Fire and Emergency Planning Authority, appointed by the mayor; and a 23-member Metropolitan Police Authority, of which the mayor will appoint 11 members from the assembly. The mayor will set their budgets.

The assembly scrutinizes the mayor's proposals and performance through monthly questioning and an annual state-of-London debate. It can block the mayor's budget by a two-third's majority, as long as it agrees on another budget. The mayor can select a number of assembly members to act as his advisers in specific areas. The GLA's running costs are split between central government (80%) and council tax (20%).

Greater London Authority Romney House, 43 Marsham street, London, SW1P 3PY; phone: (020) 7983 4000; Web site: www.london.gov.uk

See also **The Corporation of London**, p 96.

London Borough Councils

Con = Conservative; Lab = Labour; LD = Liberal Democrat; NOC = no overall control. Band D refers to property valued at between £68,000 and £88,000 at 1991 prices. For payments in other bands, multiply the Band D figure by the ratios 6/9 (for Band A), 7/9 (for Band B), 8/9 (for Band C), 11/9 (for Band E), 13/9 (for Band F), 15/9 (for B and G), and 18/9 (for Band H). Council tax figures do not include police authority costs. As of May 2000.

Borough	Area (sq km/sq mi)	Population (1997)	Band D council tax 2000–2001 (£)	Controlling party
Barking and Dagenham	34/13	154,000	784	Lab
Barnet	89/34	324,000	815	NOC
Bexley	61/24	217,000	802	Con
Brent	44/17	250,000	740	Lab
Bromley	152/59	298,000	736	NOC
Camden	22/9	190,000	906	Lab
Croydon	87/34	336,000	808	Lab
Ealing	55/21	299,000	756	Lab
Enfield	81/31	265,000	797	Lab
Greenwich	48/19	214,000	883	Lab
Hackney	20/8	192,000	842	NOC
Hammersmith and Fulham	16/6	157,000	878	Lab
Haringey	30/12	220,000	932	Lab
Harrow	51/20	211,000	853	Lab
Havering	118/46	230,000	853	NOC
Hillingdon	110/42	249,000	824	NOC
Hounslow	58/22	210,000	860	Lab
Islington	15/6	177,000	887	NOC
Kensington and Chelsea	12/5	164,000	623	Con
Kingston-upon-Thames	38/15	144,000	864	NOC
Lambeth	27/10	265,000	656	Lab
Lewisham	35/14	241,000	798	Lab
Merton	38/15	183,000	867	Lab
Newham	36/14	229,000	768	Lab
Redbridge	56/22	232,000	811	NOC
Richmond-upon-Thames	55/21	184,000	909	LD
Southwark	29/11	231,000	845	Lab
Sutton	43/17	176,000	796	LD
Tower Hamlets	20/8	180,000	727	Lab
Waltham Forest	40/15	219,000	878	Lab
Wandsworth	35/14	265,000	401	Con
Westminster	22/9	212,000	375	Con

■ Local Government in the UK

London Borough Councils: Directory

Barking and Dagenham Civic Centre, Dagenham RM10 7BN; phone: (020) 8227 2139; fax: (020) 8227 2806; Web site: www.barking-dagenham.gov.uk **Chief executive**: William Smith

Barnet The Town Hall, The Burroughs, Hendon, London NW4 4BG; phone: (020) 8359 2000; fax: (020) 8359 2480; Web site: www.barnet.gov.uk **Chief executive**: Max Caller

Bexley Bexley Civic Offices, Broadway, Bexleyheath, Kent DA6 7LB; phone: (020) 8303 7777; fax: (020) 8308 4873; e-mail: info@bexley.gov.uk; Web site: www.bexley.gov.uk **Chief executive**: Chris Duffield (**Chief Executive and Director of Finance**)

Brent Brent Town Hall, Forty Lane, Wembley HA9 9HD; phone: (020) 8937 1234; fax: (020) 8937 1003; Web site: www.brent.gov.uk **Chief executive**: Gareth Daniel

Bromley Bromley Civic Centre, Stockwell Close, Kentish Way, Bromley BR1 3UH; phone: (020) 8464 3333; fax: (020) 8313 4445; Web site: www.bromley.gov.uk **Chief executive**: David Vartlett

Camden Town Hall, Judd Street, London WC1H 9JE; phone: (020) 7278 4444; fax: (020) 7974 5998; Web site: www.camden.gov.uk **Chief executive**: Steve Bundred

Croydon Taberner House, Park Lane, Croydon CR9 1DH; phone: (020) 8686 4433; fax: (020) 8760 5463; Web site: www.croydon.gov.uk **Chief executive**: David Wechsler

Ealing Town Hall, New Broadway, London W5 2BY; phone: (020) 8579 2424; fax: (020) 8840 5574; Web site: www.ealing.gov.uk **Chief executive**: Gillian Guy

Enfield Civic Centre, Silver Street, Enfield, London EN1 3XA; phone: (020) 8366 6565; fax: (020) 8379 3819; Web site: www.enfield.gov.uk **Chief executive**: David Plank

Greenwich Town Hall, 29–37 Wellington Street, London SE18 6PS; phone: (020) 8854 8888; fax: (020) 8921 5943; Web site: www.greenwich.gov.uk **Chief executive**: David Brooks

Hackney Town Hall, Mare Street, London E8 1EA; phone: (020) 8356 5000; fax: (020) 8356 3314; Web site: www.hackney.gov.uk **Chief executive**: Sarah Ebanja (**interim Managing Director**)

Hammersmith and Fulham Town Hall, King Street, Hammersmith, London W6 9JU; phone: (020) 8748 3020; fax: (020) 8741 0307; Web site: www.lbhf.gov.uk **Chief executive**: Richard Harbord (**Managing Director**)

Haringey Civic Centre, PO Box 264, High Road, London N22 8LE; phone: (020) 8489 0000; fax: (020) 8489 2906; Web site: www.haringey.gov.uk **Chief executive**: Gurbux Singh

Harrow Civic Centre, PO Box 57, Station Road, Harrow HA1 2XF; phone: (020) 8863 5611; fax: (020) 8420 9683; Web site: www.harrowlb.demon.co.uk **Chief executive**: Tony Redmond (**Chief Executive and Director of Finance**)

Havering Havering Town Hall, Main Road, Romford RM1 3BD; phone: (01708) 772222; fax: (01708) 772068; Web site: www.havering.gov.uk **Chief executive**: Harold Tinworth

Hillingdon Civic Centre, High Street, Uxbridge UB8 1UW; phone: (01895) 250111; fax: (01895) 277047; Web site: www.hillingdon.gov.uk **Chief executive**: Dorian Leatham

Hounslow Civic Centre, Lampton Road, Hounslow, London TW3 4DN; phone: (020) 8583 2000; fax: (020) 8583 2013; Web site: www.hounslow.gov.uk **Chief executive**: Derek Myers

Islington Town Hall, Upper Street, London N1 2UD; phone: (020) 7527 2000; fax: (020) 7527 3063; Web site: www.islington.gov.uk **Chief executive**: Leisha Fullick

Kensington and Chelsea Town Hall, Hornton Street, London W8 7NX; phone: (020) 7937 5464; fax: (020) 7938 1445; Web site: www.rbkc.gov.uk **Chief executive**: Alan Taylor

Kingston-upon-Thames Guildhall, High St, Kingston-upon-Thames KT1 1EU; phone: (020) 8546 2121; fax: (020) 8547 5188; Web site: www.kingston.gov.uk **Chief executive**: Bruce McDonald (**acting Chief Executive**)

Lambeth Town Hall, Brixton Hill, London SW2 1RW; phone: (020) 7926 1000; fax: (020) 7926 2255; e-mail: hrabbatts@lambeth.gov.uk; Web site: www.lambeth.gov.uk **Chief executive**: Heather Du Quesnay

Lewisham Town Hall, Catford Road, Catford, London SE6 4IU; phone: (020) 8695 6000; fax: (020) 8314 3028; Web site: www.lewisham.gov.uk **Chief executive**: Barry Quirk

Merton Merton Civic Centre, London Road, Morden SM4 5DX; phone: (020) 8543 2222; fax: (020) 8545 0446 (press office); Web site: www.merton.gov.uk **Chief executive**: Roger Paine

Newham Town Hall, Barking Rd, East Ham, London E6 2RP; phone: (020) 8472 1430; fax: (020) 7557 8662; Web site: www.newham.gov.uk **Chief executive**: Dave Burbage

Redbridge Town Hall, 128–142 High Road, Ilford, Essex IG1 1DD; phone: (020) 8478 3020; fax: (020) 8478 2356; Web site: www.redbridge.gov.uk **Chief executive**: Michael Frater

Richmond-upon-Thames Civic Centre, 44 York Street, Twickenham TW1 3BZ; phone: (020) 8891 1411; fax: (020) 8891 7703; e-mail: press-prrichmond.gov.uk; Web site: www.richmond.gov.uk **Chief executive**: Gillian Norton

Southwark Town Hall, Peckham Road, London SE5 8UB; phone: (020) 7525 7171; fax: (020) 7525 7506; Web site: www.southwark.gov.uk **Chief executive**: Robert Coomber (**Chief Executive and Director of Finance**)

Sutton Civic Offices, St Nicholas Way, Sutton SM1 1EA; phone: (020) 8770 5000; fax: (020) 8770 5504; Web site: www.sutton.gov.uk **Chief executive**: Patricia Hughes

Tower Hamlets Mulberry Place, 5 Clove Crescent, London E14 2BG; phone: (020) 7364 5000; fax: (020) 7364 4911; Web site: www.towerhamlets.gov.uk **Chief executive**: Eleanor Kelly

Waltham Forest Town Hall, Forest Road, Walthamstow, London E17 4JF; phone: (020) 8527 5544; fax: (020) 8925 5245; Web site: www.lbwf.gov.uk **Chief executive**: Alan Tobias

Wandsworth Town Hall, Wandsworth High Street, London SW18 2PU; phone: (020) 8871 6000; fax: (020) 8871 8181; Web site: www.wandsworth.gov.uk **Chief executive**: Gerald Jones

Westminster City Hall, 64 Victoria Street, London SW1E 6QP; phone: (020) 7641 6000; fax: (020) 7641 3438; Web site: www.westminster.gov.uk **Chief executive**: William Roots

London's Elections: Key Dates on the Road to May 2000

1986 The government of Conservative prime minister Margaret Thatcher abolishes the Greater London Council (GLC), the tier of government above the 32 London boroughs. Since 1981 the GLC had been led by the Labour radical, Ken Livingstone.

May 1997 The Labour Party, led by Tony Blair, wins the general election. Its manifesto includes a commitment to hold a referendum to establish a new, directly elected strategic authority and mayor.

29 July 1997 The environment secretary, John Prescott, unveils a Green Paper setting out the government's proposals for a Greater London Authority (GLA) and mayor.

7 May 1998 In the referendum, 72% of London's voters approve the government's plans for the GLA; turnout is 34%.

3 August 1998 Ken Livingstone launches his manifesto, making the improvement of transport his top priority.

26 February 1999 The government selects a South Bank site as a new £150 million home for the future GLA. Situated opposite the Tower of London, it is set to open in 2002.

5 May 1999 The GLA bill is passed by the Commons.

23 July 1999 The Conservative Party announces a mayoral shortlist of eight, including Stephen Norris and Jeffrey Archer.

28 July 1999 Glenda Jackson resigns as minister for transport in London to contest the Labour mayoral nomination.

12 August 1999 Susan Kramer is chosen as the Liberal Democrats' mayoral candidate after a ballot of the party's 10,000 London members.

3 September 1999 The prime minister, Tony Blair, approves a ten-point loyalty test for Labour candidates.

1 October 1999 Jeffrey Archer wins a postal ballot of the Conservative Party's 39,000 London members and is made favourite to become mayor.

4 October 1999 Frank Dobson becomes a candidate for the Labour nomination and steps down as health secretary a week later. He receives the backing of the prime minister, Tony Blair, and former London minister Nick Raynsford and broadcaster Trevor Phillips pull out of the race (on 11 and 20 October, respectively) and back Frank Dobson.

12 October 1999 Labour announces an electoral college system to select its mayoral candidate, with shares of the vote given to trades unions, London Labour MPs, and party members.

15 October 1999 An opinion poll shows that Livingstone will easily be elected mayor even if he loses the Labour selection contest and stands as an independent.

28 November 1999 There are complaints that Frank Dobson's campaign had been given a centrally-held list of Labour's 68,000 London members, in possible contravention of data protection laws.

18 November 1999 The Labour party allows Ken Livingstone to join Dobson and Jackson in the electoral college vote.

20 November 1999 Jeffrey Archer resigns as the Conservative Party candidate following newspaper allegations that he had asked a friend to lie ahead of a libel case against the *Daily Star* that he won in 1986.

14 December 1999 Conservative leader William Hague exerts pressure to have Steven Norris re-instated on the Tory candidate shortlist, after he had been banned on 11 December following complaints from party officials about conduct in his private life.

17 January 2000 Steven Norris is selected as the Conservative Party's mayoral candidate.

20 February 2000 Backed by the party machine, Frank Dobson narrowly wins Labour's electoral college vote, by 51.5% to Ken Livingstone's 48.5%, after Glenda Jackson drops out. Livingstone, who won a clear majority of the members' and union vote, declares the result 'tainted'.

6 March 2000 Ken Livingstone announces he will run for mayor as an independent.

7 March 2000 A *Guardian*/ICM poll gives Ken Livingstone a 55 point lead over Frank Dobson.

15 March 2000 Ken Livingstone apologizes to the House of Commons for failing to declare £159,000 in earnings from speechmaking and newspaper articles.

21 March 2000 Virgin Radio DJ Chris Evans donates £200,000 to Ken Livingstone's campaign, after Frank Dobson makes jokes about red-heads.

3 April 2000 Ken Livingstone is expelled from the Labour Party.

17 April 2000 Ken Livingstone's manifesto opposes the government's plans for a partial sell-off of the London Underground. He pledges to fund tube modernization by bonds and to introduce a congestion charge for motorists.

5 May 2000 Ken Livingstone is elected mayor, with 776,000 votes, defeating Norris, with 564,000 votes, after the counting of second preferences. The GLA elections produce a 'hung' assembly, with Labour and Conservatives each winning nine seats in the 25-seat assembly. Turnout is 33%.

6 May 2000 Ken Livingstone announces the creation of an 'inclusive' cabinet, including Nicky Gavron (a Labour GLA member) as his deputy, and Darren Johnson (a Green Party GLA member) as environment adviser.

8 May 2000 Ken Livingstone is sworn in as London mayor.

Scottish Unitary Authorities

Scottish Unitary Authorities

Lab = Labour; Ind = Independent; NOC = no overall control; SNP = Scottish National Party. Band D refers to property valued at between £45,000 and £58,000 at 1991 prices. For payments in other bands, multiply the Band D figure by the ratios 6/9 (for Band A), 7/9 (for Band B), 8/9 (for Band C), 11/9 (for Band E), 13/9 (for Band F), 15/9 (for Band G), and 18/9 (for Band H). Council tax figures do not include police authority costs.
As of May 2000.

Authority	Area (sq km/sq mi)	Population (1997)	Band D council tax 2000–2001 (£)	Controlling party
Aberdeen	186/72	216,000	873	Lab
Aberdeenshire	6,318/2,439	226,000	777	NOC
Angus	2,181/842	110,000	771	SNP
Argyll and Bute	6,930/2,676	91,000	938	Ind
Clackmannanshire	157/61	49,000	913	SNP
Dumfries and Galloway	6,439/2,486	147,000	817	NOC
Dundee	65/25	149,000	1,056	NOC
East Ayrshire	1,252/483	122,000	878	Lab
East Dunbartonshire	172/66	111,000	830	NOC
East Lothian	678/262	89,000	858	Lab
East Renfrewshire	173/67	89,000	810	NOC
Edinburgh	262/101	450,000	915	Lab
Falkirk	299/115	143,000	757	NOC
Fife	1,323/511	348,000	849	Lab
Glasgow	175/68	612,000	1,094	Lab
Highland	25,784/9,955	209,000	839	Ind
Inverclyde	162/63	87,000	933	Lab
Midlothian	356/137	81,000	963	Lab

(continued)

Scottish Unitary Authorities *(continued)*

Authority	Area (sq km/sq mi)	Population (1997)	Band D council tax 2000–2001 (£)	Controlling party
Moray	2,238/864	86,000	786	Ind
North Ayrshire	884/341	140,000	827	Lab
North Lanarkshire	474/183	327,000	876	Lab
Orkney	992/383	20,000	690	Ind
Perth and Kinross	5,311/2,051	133,000	795	NOC
Renfrewshire	261/101	178,000	846	Lab
Scottish Borders	4,734/1,828	106,000	725	NOC
Shetland Islands	1,438/555	23,000	684	Ind
South Ayrshire	1,202/464	115,000	832	Lab
South Lanarkshire	1,771/684	307,000	901	Lab
Stirling	2,196/848	84,000	900	NOC
West Dunbartonshire	162/63	96,000	999	Lab
Western Isles	3,134/1,210	28,000	724	Ind
West Lothian	425/164	152,000	888	Lab

Scottish Unitary Authorities: Directory

Aberdeen City Town House, Broad Street, Aberdeen AB10 1FY; phone: (01224) 522000; fax: (01224) 644346 **Chief executive**: Douglas Paterson

Aberdeenshire c/o Woodhill House, Westburn Road, Aberdeen AB16 5GB; phone: (01224) 620981; fax: (01224) 697445; Web site: www.aberdeenshire.gov.uk **Chief executive**: Alan G Campbell

Angus Angus Council, 7 The Cross, Forfar, Angus DD8 1BX; phone: (01307) 461460; fax: (01307) 461874; e-mail: chiefexec@angus.gov.uk; Web site: www.angus.gov.uk **Chief executive**: Alexander Watson

Argyll and Bute Kilmory, Lochgilphead, Argyll PA31 8RT; phone: (01546) 602127; fax: (01546) 604349; Web site: www.argyll-bute.gov.uk **Chief executive**: James McLellan

Clackmannanshire Greenfield, Alloa, Clackmannanshire FK10 2AD; phone: (01259) 452000; fax: (01259) 452230 **Chief executive**: Keir Bloomer

Dumfries and Galloway Council Offices, English Street, Dumfries DG1 2DD; phone: (01387) 260000; fax: (01387) 260034; e-mail: CIS@dumgal.gov.uk; Web site: www.dumgal.gov.uk **Chief executive**: Philip Jones

Dundee City 21 City Square, Dundee DD1 3BY; phone: (01382) 434000; fax: (01382) 434996; Web site: www.dundeecity.gov.uk **Chief executive**: Alex Stephen

East Ayrshire Council Headquarters, London Road, Kilmarnock KA3 7BU; phone: (01563) 576000; fax: (01563) 576200; Web site: www.east-ayrshire.gov.uk **Chief executive**: David Montgomery

East Dunbartonshire Tom Johnston House, Civic Way, Kirkintilloch G66 4TJ; phone: (0141) 578 8000; fax: (0141) 578 8330 **Chief executive**: Vicki Nash

East Lothian Council Buildings, 25 Court Street, Haddington EH41 3HA; phone: (01620) 827200; fax: (01620) 827140 **Chief executive**: John Lindsay

East Renfrewshire Council Headquarters, Eastwood Park, Rouken Glen Road, Glasgow G46 6UG; phone: (0141) 577 3000; fax: (0141) 620 0844; Web site: www.eastrenfrewshire.gov.uk **Chief executive**: Peter Daniels

Edinburgh City Council Headquarters, Wellington Court, 10 Waterloo Place, Edinburgh EH1 3EG; phone: (0131) 200 2000; fax: (0131) 469 3002; Web site: www.edinburgh.gov.uk **Chief executive**: Tom Aitchison

Falkirk Municipal Buildings, West Bridge Street, Falkirk FK1 5RS; phone: (01324) 506070; fax: (01324) 506061; Web site: www.falkirk.electricscotland.com **Chief executive**: Mary Pitcaithly

Fife Fife House, North Street, Glenrothes KY7 5LT; phone: (01592) 414141; fax: (01592) 413990 **Chief executive**: Douglas Sinclair

Glasgow City City Chambers, George Square, Glasgow G2 1DU; phone: (0141) 287 2000; fax: (0141) 287 3627; Web site: www.glasgow.gov.uk **Chief executive**: James Andrews

Highland Regional Buildings, Glenurquhart Road, Inverness IV3 5NX; phone: (01463) 702837; fax: (01463) 702837 **Chief executive**: Arthur McCourt

Inverclyde Municipal Buildings, Greenock PA15 1LY; phone: (01475) 717171; fax: (01475) 712777 **Chief executive**: Robert Cleary

Midlothian Midlothian House, Buccleuch Street, Dalkeith EH22 1DJ; phone: (0131) 270 7500; fax: (0131) 271 3014; e-mail: info@midlothian.gov.uk; Web site: www.midlothian.gov.uk **Chief executive**: Trevor Muir

Moray Council Office, High Street, Elgin IV30 1BX; phone: (01343) 543451; fax: (01343) 548218; Web site: www.moray.org **Chief executive**: Alastair Keddle

North Ayrshire Cunninghame House, Irvine KA12 8EE; phone: (01294) 324100; fax: (01294) 324441 **Chief executive**: Chief executive: Chief executive: Bernard Devine

North Lanarkshire PO Box 14, Civic Centre, Motherwell ML1 1TW; phone: (01698) 302222; fax: (01698) 275125 **Chief executive**: (vacant as of April 2000)

Orkney Council Offices, School Place, Kirkwall, Orkney KW15 1NY; phone: (01856) 873535; fax: (01856) 874615 **Chief executive**: Alastair Buchan

Perth and Kinross Council Building, PO Box 2, High Street, Perth, PH1 5PH; phone: (01738) 475000; fax: (01738) 475710; e-mail: enquiries@pkc.gov.uk; Web site: www.pkc.gov.uk **Chief executive**: Harry Robertson

Renfrewshire North Building, Cotton Street, Paisley PA1 1WB; phone: (0141) 842 5000; fax: (0141) 840 3349 **Chief executive**: Thomas Scholes

Scottish Borders Council Headquarters, Newtown Street, Boswells, Melrose TD6 0SA; phone: (01835) 824000; fax: (01835) 825059 **Chief executive**: Alastair Croall

Shetland Town Hall, Hillhead, Lerwick, Shetland ZE1 0HB; phone: (01595) 693535; fax: (01595) 744509; e-mail: sic@shetland.gov.uk; Web site: www.shetland.gov.uk **Chief executive**: Morgan Goodlad

South Ayrshire County Buildings, Wellington Square, Ayr KA7 1DR; phone: (01292) 612000; fax: (01292) 612158; Web site: www.south-ayrshire.gov.uk **Chief executive**: George Thorley

South Lanarkshire Council Offices, Almada Street, Hamilton ML3 0AA; phone: (01698) 454444; fax: (01698) 454637 **Chief executive**: Michael Docherty

Stirling Council Headquarters, Viewforth, Stirling FK8 2ET; phone: (01786) 443322; fax: (01786) 443474; Web site: www.stirling.gov.uk **Chief executive**: Chief executive: Keith Yates

West Dunbartonshire Council Offices, Garshake Road, Dumbarton G82 3PU; phone: (01389) 737000; fax: (01389) 737780; e-mail: wdcmgr1@post.almac.co.uk; Web site: www.west-dunbarton.gov.uk **Chief executive**: Tim Huntingford

Western Isles Sandwick Road, Stornoway, Isle of Lewes HS1 2BW; phone: (01851) 703773; fax: (01851) 705349; Web site: www.w-isles.gov.uk **Chief executive**: Neil Galbrache

West Lothian West Lothian House, Almondvale Boulevard, Livingston EH54 6QG; phone: (01506) 777000; fax: (01506) 777102; Web site: www.wlonline.org **Chief executive**: Alex Linkston

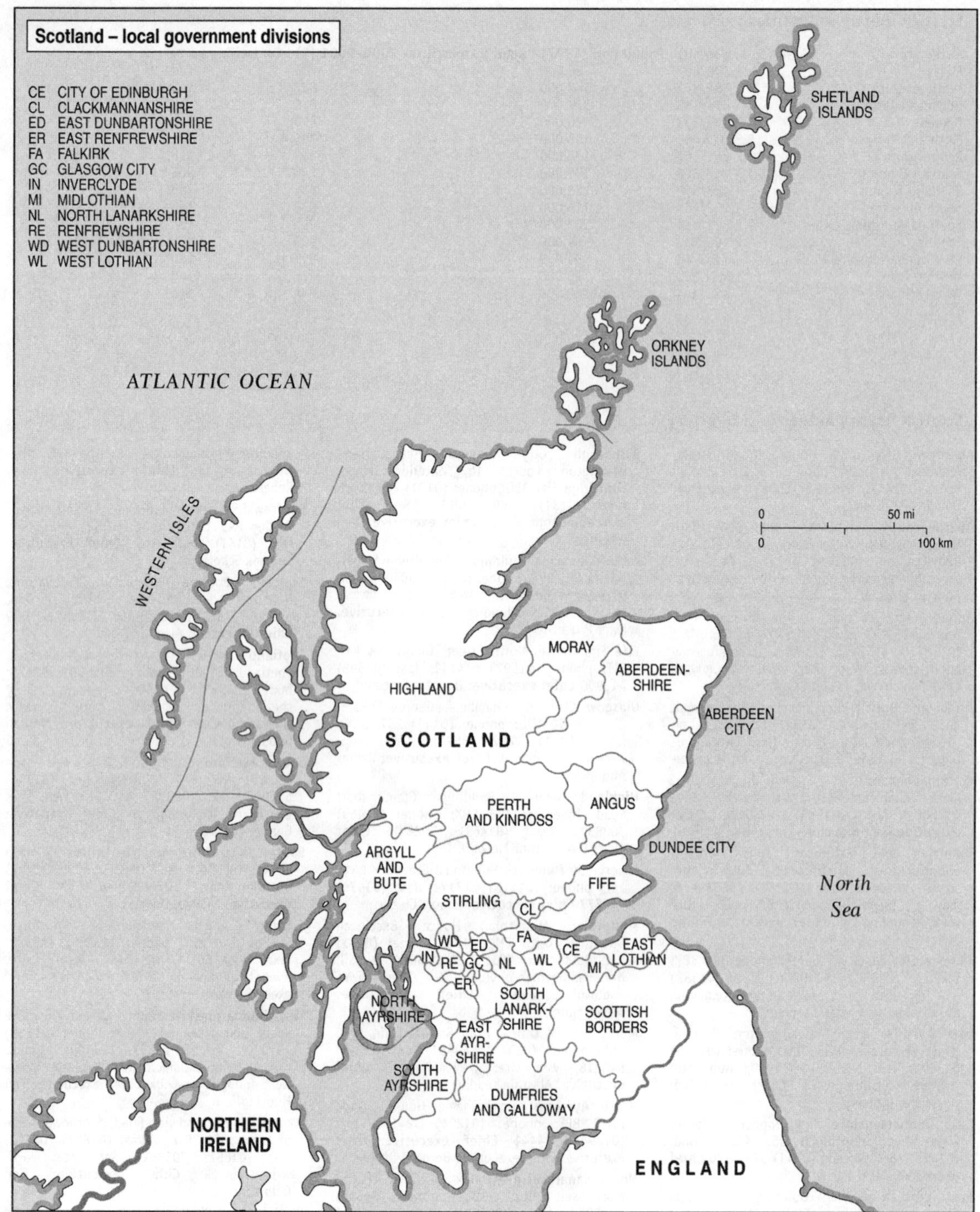
Scotland – local government divisions
CE CITY OF EDINBURGH
CL CLACKMANNANSHIRE
ED EAST DUNBARTONSHIRE
ER EAST RENFREWSHIRE
FA FALKIRK
GC GLASGOW CITY
IN INVERCLYDE
MI MIDLOTHIAN
NL NORTH LANARKSHIRE
RE RENFREWSHIRE
WD WEST DUNBARTONSHIRE
WL WEST LOTHIAN
SHETLAND ISLANDS
ORKNEY ISLANDS
ATLANTIC OCEAN
WESTERN ISLES
0 50 mi
0 100 km
MORAY
ABERDEEN-SHIRE
HIGHLAND
ABERDEEN CITY
SCOTLAND
PERTH AND KINROSS
ANGUS
DUNDEE CITY
ARGYLL AND BUTE
FIFE
North Sea
STIRLING
CL
WD
ED
FA
IN
RE
GC
NL
WL
CE
MI
EAST LOTHIAN
ER
NORTH AYRSHIRE
SOUTH LANARK-SHIRE
SCOTTISH BORDERS
EAST AYR-SHIRE
SOUTH AYRSHIRE
DUMFRIES AND GALLOWAY
NORTHERN IRELAND
ENGLAND

Welsh Unitary Authorities

Welsh Unitary Authorities

Lab = Labour; PC = Plaid Cymru; Ind = Independent; NOC = no overall control. Band D refers to property valued at between £51,000 and £66,000 at 1991 prices. For payments in other bands, multiply the Band D figure by the ratios 6/9 (for Band A), 7/9 (for Band B), 8/9 (for Band C), 11/9 (for Band E), 13/9 (for Band F), 15/9 (for Band G), and 18/9 (for Band H). Council tax figures do not include police authority costs.
As of May 2000.

Authority	Area (sq km/sq mi)	Population (1997)	Band D council tax 2000–2001 (£)	Controlling party
Anglesey	714/276	66,000	621	Ind
Blaenau Gwent	109/42	73,000	727	Lab
Bridgend	246/95	131,300	702	Lab
Caerphilly	278/107	169,000	670	PC
Cardiff	140/54	318,000	633	Lab
Carmarthenshire	2,395/925	169,000	724	NOC
Ceredigion	1,795/693	70,000	723	NOC
Conwy	1,130/436	111,000	551	NOC
Denbighshire	844/326	90,000	733	NOC
Flintshire	438/169	145,000	654	Lab
Gwynedd	2,548/984	118,000	594	PC
Merthyr Tydfil	111/43	57,000	799	NOC
Monmouthshire	850/328	87,000	597	NOC
Neath Port Talbot	442/171	139,000	837	Lab
Newport	190/73	137,000	567	Lab
Pembrokeshire	1,590/614	113,000	603	Ind
Powys	5,196/2,006	125,000	628	Ind
Rhondda Cynon Taff	424/164	241,000	772	PC
Swansea	378/146	230,000	681	Lab
Torfaen	126/49	90,000	624	Lab
Vale of Glamorgan	335/129	120,000	600	NOC
Wrexham	498/192	125,000	701	NOC

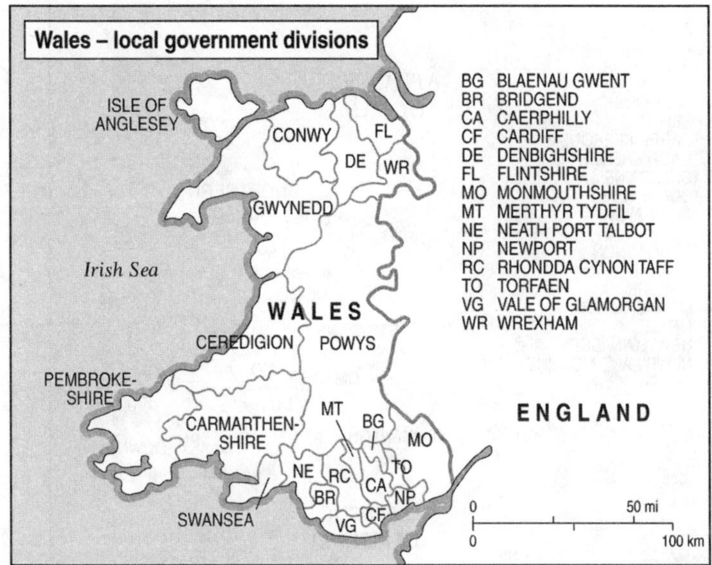

Welsh Unitary Authorities: Directory

Anglesey Council Offices, Llangefni, Anglesey LL77 7TW; phone: (01248) 752480; fax: (01248) 750839; Web site: www.anglesey.gov.uk **Chief executive:** Geraint Edwards

Blaenau Gwent Municipal Offices, Civic Centre, Ebbw Vale NP23 6XB; phone: (01495) 350555; fax: (01495) 356111 **Chief executive:** Roger Leadbeter

Bridgend Civic Offices, PO Box 4, Angel Street, Bridgend CF31 4WB; phone: (01656) 643643; fax: (01656) 767152; Web site: www.bridgend.gov.uk **Chief executive:** Kerry Lewis

Caerphilly Nelson Road, Tredomen, Ystrad Mynach, Hengoed CF82 7WF; phone: (01443) 815588; fax: (01443) 864202; Web site: www.caerphilly.gov.uk **Chief executive:** Malgwyn Davies

Cardiff County Hall, Atlantic Wharf, Cardiff CF10 4UW; phone: (029) 2087 2000; fax: (029) 2087 2422; Web site: www.cardiff.gov.uk **Chief executive:** Byron Davies

Carmarthenshire County Hall, Carmarthen SA31 1JP; phone: (01267) 234567; fax: (01267) 222097; Web site: www.carmarthenshire.gov.uk **Chief executive:** Bradley Roynon

Ceredigion Neuadd Cyngor Ceredigion, Penmorfa, Aberaeron SA46 0PA; phone: (01545) 572000; fax: (01545) 572009; Web site: www.ceredigion.gov.uk **Chief executive:** R Owen Watkin

Conwy Bodlondeb, Bangor Road, Conwy LL32 8DU; phone: (01492) 574000; fax: (01492) 576003; Web site: www.conwy.gov.uk **Chief executive:** Derek Barker

Northern Ireland Counties and Districts

Welsh Unitary Authorities: Directory *(continued)*

Denbighshire Council Offices, Wynnstay Road, Ruthin LL15 1YN; phone: (01824) 706000; fax: (01824) 707446; Web site: www.denbighshire.gov.uk **Chief executive:** Huw Vaughan Thomas

Flintshire County Hall, Mold CH7 6NB; phone: (01352) 702100; fax: (01352) 755910; Web site: www.flintshire.gov.uk **Chief executive:** Philip McGreevy

Gwynedd Shire Hall Street, Caernarfon, Gwynedd LL55 1SH; phone: (01286) 672255; fax: (01286) 679488; e-mail: enquiries@gwynedd.gov.uk; Web site: www.gwynedd.gov.uk **Chief executive:** Geraint Jones

Merthyr Tydfil Civic Centre, Castle Street, Merthyr Tydfil CF47 8AN; phone: (01685) 725000; fax: (01685) 722146; Web site: www.merthyr.gov.uk **Chief executive:** Gary Meredith

Monmouthshire County Hall, Cwmbran NP44 2XH; phone: (01633) 644644; fax: (01633) 644045; Web site: www.monmouthshire.gov.uk **Chief executive:** Joyce Redfearn

Neath and Port Talbot Civic Centre, Port Talbot SA13 1PJ; phone: (01639) 763333; fax: (01639) 763355; Web site: www.neathporttalbot.gov.uk **Chief executive:** Ken Sawyers

Newport Civic Centre, Newport NP9 4UR; phone: (01633) 244491; fax: (01633) 232001; Web site: www.newport.gov.uk **Chief executive:** Sandy Blair

Pembrokeshire County Hall, Haverfordwest, Pembrokeshire SA61 1TP; phone: (01437) 764551; fax: (01437) 775838; Web site: www.pembrokeshire.gov.uk **Chief executive:** Bryn Parry-Jones

Powys County Hall, Spa Road, Llandrindod Wells LD1 5LG; phone: (01597) 826368; fax: (01597) 826220; Web site: www.powys.gov.uk **Chief executive:** Jacky Tonge

Rhondda Cynon Taff The Pavilions, Cambrian Park, Clydach Vale CF40 2XX; phone: (01443) 424000; fax: (01443) 424027; Web site: www.rhondda-cynon-taff.gov.uk **Chief executive:** Kim Ryley

Swansea County Hall, Swansea SA1 3SN; phone: (01792) 636000; fax: (01792) 636704; Web site: ww.swansea.gov.uk **Chief executive:** Vivienne Sugar

Torfaen Civic Centre, Pontypool, Gwent NP4 6YB; phone: (01495) 762200; fax: (01495) 750797 **Chief executive:** Clive Grace

Vale of Glamorgan Civic Offices, Holton Road, Barry CF63 4RU; phone: (01446) 700111; fax: (01446) 421479; Web site: www.valeofglamorgan.gov.uk **Chief executive:** John Maitland-Evans

Wrexham County Borough Guildhall, Wrexham LL11 1WF; phone: (01978) 292000; fax: (01978) 292106 **Chief executive:** Derek Griffin

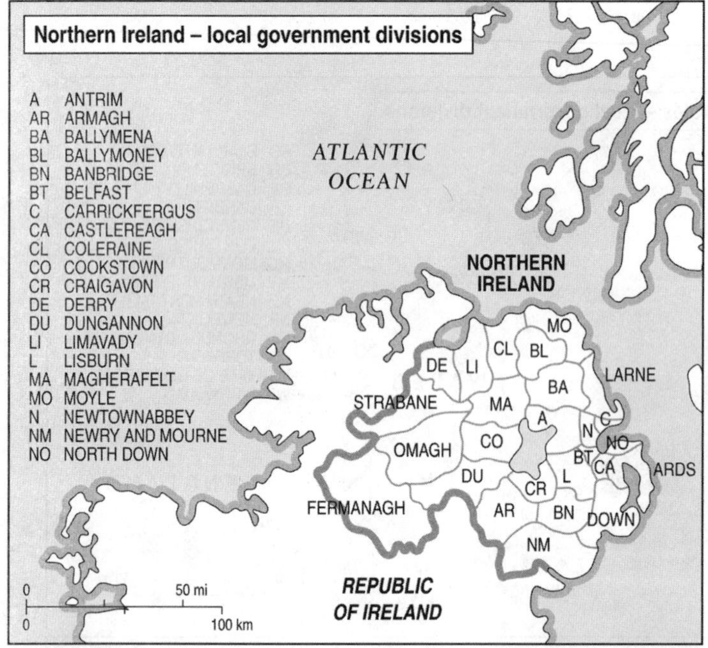

Local Government in Northern Ireland

Northern Ireland has a single-tier system of 26 district councils. Historically there are six counties (Antrim, Armagh, Down, Fermanagh, Londonderry (Derry), and Tyrone), but these perform no administrative function. Health and Social Services, and Education and Library Services are organized by regional boards.

Northern Ireland Councils, by Board

District council	Area (sq km/sq mi)	Population (1997)
Eastern		
Ards	380/147	70,000
Belfast	110/42	288,000
Castlereagh	85/33	67,000
Down	649/251	63,000
Lisburn	447/173	111,000
North Down	81/31	76,000
Northern		
Antrim	421/163	50,000
Ballymena	630/243	59,000
Ballymoney	416/161	25,000
Carrickfergus	81/31	37,000
Coleraine	486/188	56,000
Cookstown	514/198	32,000
Larne	337/130	31,000
Magherafelt	564/218	38,000
Moyle	494/191	16,000
Newtownabbey	151/58	80,000
Southern		
Armagh	671/259	54,000
Banbridge	451/174	38,000
Craigavon	282/109	78,000
Dungannon	773/298	48,000
Newry and Mourne	898/347	86,000
Western		
Derry	1,699/656	104,000
Fermanagh	381/147	57,000
Limavady	586/226	31,000
Omagh	1,130/436	48,000
Strabane	862/333	37,000

Northern Ireland Councils: Directory

Antrim Council Offices, The Steeple, Antrim BT41 1BJ; phone: (028) 9446 3113; e-mail: contact@antrim.gov.uk; Web site: antrim.gov.uk

Ards 2 Church Street, Newtownards, Co Down BT23 4AP; phone: (028) 9182 4000; fax: (028) 9181 9628; e-mail: ards@ards-council.gov.uk; Web site: www.ards-council.gov.uk **Chief executive:** David J Fallows

Armagh The Palace Demesne, Armagh BT60 4EL; phone: (028) 3752 9600; fax: (028) 3752 9601; e-mail: info@armagh.gov.uk; Web site: www.armagh.gov.uk **Chief executive:** Desmond R D Mitchell

Ballymena 'Ardeevin', 80 Galgorm Road, Ballymena, BT42 1AB; phone: (028) 2566 0300; fax: (028) 2566 0400; e-mail: townclerk@ballymena.gov.uk; Web site: www.ballymena.gov.uk **Chief executive:** Mervin G Rankin

Ballymoney Riada House, 14 Charles Street, Ballymoney BT53 6DZ; phone: (028) 2766 2280; fax: (028) 2766 5150 **Chief executive:** John Dempsey

Banbridge Civic Building, Downshire Road, Banbridge BT32 3JY; phone: (028) 4066 0600; fax: (028) 4066 0601 **Chief executive:** Robert Gilmore

Belfast City Hall, Belfast, BT1 5GS; phone: (028) 9032 0202; fax: (028) 9023 6116; e-mail: webmaster@belfastcity.gov.uk; Web site: www.belfastcity.gov.uk **Chief executive:** Brian Hanna

Carrickfergus Town Hall, Carrickfergus BT38 7DL; phone: (028) 9335 1604; fax: (028) 9336 6676; e-mail: info@carrickfergus.org; Web site: www.carrickfergus.org **Chief executive:** Raymond Boyd

Castlereagh Bradford Court, Upper Galwally, Castlereagh BT8 6RB; phone: (028) 9049 4500; fax: (028) 9049 4515; e-mail: chief@castlereagh.gov.uk; Web site: www.castlereagh.gov.uk **Chief executive:** Adrian Donaldson

Coleraine Cloonavin, 41 Portstewart Road, Coleraine BT52 1EY; phone: (028) 7035 2181; fax: (028) 7035 3489; e-mail: webmaster@colerainebc.gov.uk; Web site: www.colerainbc.gov.uk **Chief executive:** H Wavell T Moore

Cookstown Council Offices, Burn Road, Cookstown BT80 8DT; phone: (028) 8676 2205; fax: (028) 8676 4360; e-mail: info@cookstown.gov.uk; Web site: www.cookstown.gov.uk **Chief executive:** Michael McGuckin

Craigavon Civic Centre, PO Box 66, Lakeview Road, Craigavon, BT64 1AL; phone: (028) 3834 1199; fax: (028) 3834 5514; e-mail: info@craigavon.gov.uk; Web site: www.craigavon.gov.uk **Chief executive:** Trevor E Reaney

Derry Council Offices, 98 Strand Road, Londonderry BT48 7NN; phone: (028) 7136 5151; fax: (028) 7136 8536; e-mail: townclerk@derrycity.gov.uk; Web site: www.derrycity.gov.uk **Chief executive:** John Keanie

Down 24 Strangford Road, Downpatrick, County Down BT30 6SR; phone: (028) 4461 0800; fax: (028) 4461 0801; Web site: www.downdc.gov.uk **Chief executive:** Owen P O'Connor

Dungannon Council Offices, Circular Road, Dungannon BT71 6DT; phone: (028) 8772 0300; fax: (028) 8772 0368; e-mail: general@dungannon.gov.uk; Web site: www.dungannon.gov.uk **Chief executive:** William J Beattie

Fermanagh Townhall, Enniskillen BT74 7BA; phone: (028) 6632 5050; fax: (028) 6632 2024; e-mail: fdc@fermanagh.gov.uk Web site: www.fermanagh.gov.uk **Chief executive:** Aideen McGinley

Larne Smiley Buildings, Victoria Road, Larne BT40 1RU; phone: (028) 2827 2313; fax: (028) 2826 0660; e-mail: mail@larne-bc.com; Web site: www.larne.com/borough_council **Chief executive:** Colm McGarry

Limavady 7 Connell Street, Limavady, Co Londonderry BT49 0HA; phone: (028) 7772 2226; fax: (028) 7172 2010 **Chief executive:** John K Stevenson

Lisburn Borough Offices, The Square, Hillsborough BT26 6AH; phone: (028) 9268 2477; fax: (028) 9268 9016; e-mail: lisburnbc@compuserve.com; Web site: www.lisburn.gov.uk **Chief executive:** Norman Davidson

Magherafelt Council Offices, 50 Ballyronan Road, Magherafelt BT45 6EN; phone: (028) 7939 7979; (028) 7939 7980; email: mdc@magherafelt.demon.co.uk; Web site: www.magherafelt.demon.co.uk **Chief executive:** John A McLaughlin

Moyle Sheskburn House, 7 Mary Street, Ballycastle BT54 6QH; phone: (028) 2076 2225; fax: (028) 2076 2515; e-mail: info@moyle-council.org.uk; Web site: www.moyle-council.org **Chief executive:** Richard G Lewis

Newry and Mourne O'Hagan House, District Council Offices, Monaghan Row, Newry BT35 8DL; phone: (028) 3026 5411; fax: (028) 3025 7859 **Chief executive:** Kevin O'Neill

Newtownabbey Headquarters, 1 The Square, Ballyclare BT39 9BA; phone: (028) 9335 2861; fax: (028) 9334 0417; e-mail: info@newtonabbey.gov.uk; Web site: www.newtonabbey.gov.uk **Chief executive:** Norman Dunn

North Down Town Hall, The Castle, Bangor BT20 4BT; phone: (028) 9127 0371; fax: (028) 9127 1370; e-mail: edo@north-down.gov.uk; Web site: www.north-down.gov.uk **Chief executive:** Adrian McDowell

Omagh Council Offices, The Grange, Mountjoy Road, Omagh BT79 7BL; phone: (028) 8224 5321; fax: (028) 8224 3888; e-mail: info@omagh.gov.uk Web site: www.omagh.gov.uk **Chief executive:** John P McKinney

Strabane District Council Offices, 47 Derry Road, Strabane BT82 8DY; phone: (028) 7138 2204; fax: (028) 7138 2264; e-mail: strabanedc@nics.gov.uk; Web site: www.strabanedc.org.uk **Chief executive:** Victor Eakin

Cities and Major Towns

The 50 Most Populous Cities and Towns in England

Population figures are based on the 1991 census unless otherwise stated.

City/town	Population	City/town	Population	City/town	Population
London[1]	7,122,000	Southampton	210,100	Huddersfield	143,700
Birmingham	1,220,000[2]	Dudley	192,200	Bolton	139,000
Liverpool	481,800	Newcastle-upon-Tyne	189,500	Poole	138,500
Sheffield	431,600	Sunderland	183,300	Peterborough	134,800
Leeds	424,200	Northampton	179,600	Stockport	132,800
Bristol	408,000	Preston	177,700	Ipswich	130,600
Manchester	402,900	Walsall	174,700	Brighton	124,900
Leicester	318,500	Portsmouth	174,700	York	127,700
Kingston upon Hull	310,600	Luton	171,700	Rotherham	121,400
Coventry	303,000[2]	Norwich	171,300	Oxford	121,000[2]
Bradford	357,000[2]	Southend-on-Sea	158,500	Cambridge	117,000[2]
Nottingham	270,200	Bournemouth	155,500	Gloucester	114,000
Stoke-on-Trent	266,200	Middlesbrough	147,400	Slough	110,700
Wolverhampton	257,900	West Bromwich	146,400	St Helens	106,300
Plymouth	245,300	Blackpool	146,300	Sutton Coldfield	106,000
Derby	223,800	Oldbury/Smethwick	145,500	Blackburn	106,000
Reading	213,500	Swindon	145,200		

[1] 1997.
[2] 1994 est.

See also **Top 20 Most Visited Towns in the UK by Overseas Visitors**, p 604.

The 20 Most Populous Cities and Towns in Scotland

Population figures are based on the 1991 census.

City/town	Population	City/town	Population	City/town	Population
Glasgow	663,000	Dunfermline	55,100	Coatbridge	43,600
Edinburgh	401,900	Greenock	55,000	Livingston	41,600
Aberdeen	189,700	Hamilton	50,000	Perth	41,500
Dundee	159,000	Cumbernauld	48,800	Inverness	41,200
Paisley	75,500	Ayr	48,000	Glenrothes	38,650
East Kilbride	72,400	Kirkcaldy	47,200	Airdrie	37,000
Motherwell	60,500	Kilmarnock	44,300		

The 20 Most Populous Cities and Towns in Wales

Population figures are based on the 1991 census.

City/town	Population	City/town	Population	City/town	Population
Cardiff	272,100	Neath	46,000	Aberdare	29,000
Swansea	171,000	Merthyr Tydfil	39,500	Pontypridd	28,500
Newport	115,500	Wrexham	40,600	Caerphilly	28,500
Rhondda	59,900	Port Talbot	36,600	Rhyl	24,900
Barry	49,900	Bridgend	35,800	Shotton/Hawarden	23,300
Cwmbran	46,000	Pontypool	35,600	Mountain Ash/Abercynon	21,300
Llanelli	45,000	Colwyn Bay	29,900		

The 10 Most Populous Cities and Towns in Northern Ireland

Population figures are based on the 1991 census.

City/town	Population	City/town	Population	City/town	Population
Belfast	279,200	Coleraine	50,700	Carrickfergus	22,800
Londonderry	95,400	Lisburn	42,100	Lurgan	21,900
Newtownabbey	56,800	Ballymena	28,100		
Bangor	52,400	Newtownards	23,900		

Roman Names of English and Welsh Cities and Towns

City/town	Roman settlement	City/town	Roman settlement
England			
Ancaster	Causennae	Chester	Deva
Bath	Aquae Sulis	Chichester	Noviomagus Regnensium
Buxton	Aquae Arnemetiae	Cirencester	Corinium Dobunnorum
Canterbury	Durovernum Cantiacorum	Colchester	Camulodunum
Carlisle	Luguvalium	Dorchester	Durnovaria
Castleford	Lagentium	Dover	Dubris
Catterick	Cataractonium	Exeter	Isca Dumnoniorum
Chelmsford	Caesaromagus		

(continued)

Roman Names of English and Welsh Cities and Towns *(continued)*

City/town	Roman settlement
Gloucester	Glevum
Leicester	Ratae Coritanorum
Lincoln	Lindum
London	Londinium
Manchester	Mancunium
Newcastle-upon-Tyne	Pons Aelius
Rochester-upon-Medway	Durobrivae
Salisbury	Sorbiodonum
Shrewsbury	Viroconium
Tadcaster	Calcaria
Towcester	Lactodorum
Winchester	Venta Belgarum
York	Eboracum
Wales	
Abergavenny	Gobannium
Caerwent	Venta Silurum
Carmarthen	Maridunum

Major Cities in the UK

Aberdeen

City in northeast Scotland, situated in a low-lying coastal area on estuaries of the rivers Dee and Don; population (1996) 219,100. Formerly part of Aberdeenshire, it has been a unitary authority (as Aberdeen City) since 1996; area 185 sq km/71 sq mi. The third-largest city in Scotland, it is the main centre in Europe for offshore oil exploration, as well as an important fishing port, cultural centre, and university city.

Features
Dominating Old Aberdeen are the 15th-century cathedral of St Machar and King's College, Aberdeen's first university (1495). The Aberdeen Maritime Museum, housed in the oldest building in Aberdeen, focuses on the history of the city's fishing, shipbuilding, and oil industries. Other attractions include the Art Gallery, St Andrew's Cathedral, and Duthie Park, which includes the Winter Garden, Europe's largest indoor garden. Seaside attractions include Aberdeen Fun Beach, one of Scotland's main leisure complexes. The city hosts a variety of festivals. Marischal College united with King's College in the 19th century to form Aberdeen University.

Bath

Historic city and administrative headquarters of Bath and North East Somerset, southwest England, 171 km/106 mi west of London; population (1991) 78,700. Of Roman origins, Bath flourished in the 18th century as a fashionable spa. Today the city is a World Heritage Site and a major tourist destination. The city hosts a number of festivals, including the Bath International Music Festival, held in May–June.

Features
Bath has the only naturally occurring hot mineral springs in the UK. The Roman bathing complex preserves the open-air Great Bath as well as remains of smaller baths and the Roman heating system. The Roman Baths Museum, adjoining the complex, displays many Roman relics. Bath is known for its elegant 18th-century crescents, terraces, and squares, outstanding examples of which are Queen Square, the Circus, the Assembly Rooms, and the Royal Crescent. The present Abbey church, dating from 1499, is a fine example of Perpendicular Gothic architecture. 'Reviving Spa Culture' is a millennium project designed to create a new spa complex in the centre of Bath. The University of Bath was established in 1966.

Belfast (Gaelic Beal Feirste, 'the mouth of the Farset')

Capital city of Northern Ireland and industrial port in County Antrim and County Down, at the mouth of the River Lagan on Belfast Lough; population (1994 est) 290,000. Belfast was at the centre of the sectarian conflicts known as 'the Troubles' from 1968. In recent years, the city has undergone extensive urban renewal, with many new industrial, business, and leisure initiatives. Stormont, seat of the Northern Ireland Assembly from 1998, is nearby.

Features
The City Hall (1906) is one of the city's principal landmarks. Belfast Castle includes a Heritage Centre illustrating all aspects of the area's history. Waterfront Hall, a concert and conference venue, opened on the redeveloped waterfront in 1997; the Odyssey landmark millennium project includes a science centre, IMAX cinema, and indoor arena. The area of the city known as the Golden Mile includes the refurbished Grand Opera House as well as old 'gin palaces'. Other attractions include the Ulster Museum, St Anne's Cathedral (1899), the Botanic Gardens, and Belfast Zoo. The Queen's University was founded in 1849.

Birmingham

Second-largest city in the UK, administrative headquarters of West Midlands metropolitan county, 177 km/110 mi northwest of London; population (1994 est) 1,220,000, metropolitan area 2,632,000. It is Britain's largest manufacturing city, home to Britain's principal conference and exhibition venues, and, with its many cultural venues and three universities, a major centre of culture and learning. The city hosts a number of festivals, including the annual ArtsFest and an international jazz festival.

Features
The industrial heritage of the city is reflected in its museums, in its imposing 19th-century civic buildings, and in the extensive system of canals that runs through the city. Birmingham's museums include the Birmingham Museum and Art Gallery, the Gas Hall, the Barber Institute of Fine Arts, and the Museum of Science and Industry. Millennium Point is a major millennium project with a science, technology, and entertainment complex. The city is home to the City of Birmingham Symphony Orchestra and the Birmingham Royal Ballet (formerly Sadlers Wells Royal Ballet). The University of Birmingham was founded in 1900.

Bradford

Industrial city and metropolitan borough in West Yorkshire, England, 14 km/9 mi west of Leeds; population (1994 est) 357,000. Bradford was an important centre of the textile trade and the world's largest producer of worsted cloth in the 19th century.

Features
The city's imposing Victorian civic and public buildings include the Gothic-style town hall, Commerce House, St George's Hall (1853), and the refurbished Wool Exchange. Little Germany, the city's historic quarter, includes many 19th-century warehouses and houses. The city's museums include the Colour Museum, the Bradford Industrial Museum, and the National Museum of Photography, Film, and Television. The Alhambra Theatre is a major venue for ballet, opera, and plays. Saltaire, an industrial model village north of the city centre, houses a large collection of works by the artist David Hockney, who was born in Bradford. Bradford University was established in 1966.

Bristol

Industrial port in southwest England, at the confluence of the rivers Avon and Frome; population (1996) 374,300, urban area (1991) 516,500. Part of the former county of Avon until 1996, it is now a unitary authority; area 109 sq km/42 sq mi. Long-established as a leading port and commercial centre, Bristol flourished in the 17th and 18th centuries as Britain's principal port for transatlantic trade.

Features
The city centre is a diverse mixture of medieval, Georgian, Victorian, and contemporary architecture, with Brunel's Temple Meads railway station at its heart. The redeveloped city docks include the Bristol Industrial Museum and the Maritime Heritage Centre. The millennium landmark project '@Bristol' is a major new visitor attraction in the harbour area. Other attractions include the cathedral, the City Museum and Art Gallery, and the Theatre Royal, home to the Bristol Old Vic since 1946. One of Bristol's best known landmarks is Brunel's Clifton Suspension Bridge, spanning the Avon Gorge. The city hosts a varied programme of festivals and is the site of two universities.

Cambridge

Historic city and administrative headquarters of Cambridgeshire, eastern England, on the River Cam, 80 km/50 mi north of London; population (1994 est) 117,000. The seat of Cambridge University from the 13th century, the city is also a major tourist destination known for some of Britain's most outstanding architectural treasures. The city hosts a variety of annual festivals and events including Strawberry Fair, the Cambridge Folk Festival, and an international arts festival.

Features
The Backs, an ancient strip of land by the banks of the Cam overlooking the colleges, command the most famous views of the colleges, King's College Chapel, and the river, with its many bridges and punts. Historic buildings in the city centre include St Bene't's church, of Saxon origins, and the Holy Sepulchre (or Round Church), which dates from about 1130. Museums include the Fitzwilliam Museum, the Cambridge and County Folk Museum, the Museum of Archaeology and Anthropology, and the Sedgwick Museum. Kettle's Yard gallery houses a large collection of 20th-century art and sculpture, including works by Henry Moore and Barbara Hepworth. Cambridge's theatres and concert venues include the Arts Theatre, the ADC Theatre, and the restored Corn Exchange, a venue for opera, concerts, and musicals.

Canterbury

Historic cathedral city in Kent, southeast England, on the River Stour, 100 km/62 mi southeast of London; population (1991) 36,500. It is the seat of the archbishop of Canterbury. The city hosts a number of annual festivals including the international Canterbury Festival, the largest mixed arts festival in Kent.

Features
St Augustine first established Christ Church on the site of the cathedral in 603, but the foundations of the present cathedral were laid in Norman times; subsequent additions range from Norman to Perpendicular. The cathedral has fine medieval stained glass and the largest Norman crypt in Britain. Canterbury Cathedral, St Augustine's Abbey, and St Martin's Church are together a World Heritage site. The city retains a wealth of 17th- and 18th-century buildings as well as remains of a Norman castle and the medieval city walls. Among the city's main attractions are the Canterbury Heritage Museum and the Roman Museum. The University of Kent was established here in 1965.

Cardiff (Welsh Caerdydd)

Capital of Wales, seaport, and administrative centre of Cardiff unitary authority, situated at the mouth of the Taff, Rhymney, and Ely rivers; population (1994 est) 290,000. The city is an important political, administrative, and commercial centre which has undergone major redevelopment in recent years. Cardiff Bay is the site of the National Assembly for Wales and the city hosts a variety of festivals including an annual summer festival.

Features
The civic buildings of Cardiff, including the grand City Hall and Civic Centre, reflect the city's prosperity in the Victorian and Edwardian eras. The castle was originally built in the 11th century and was substantially altered over the succeeding centuries; the Norman keep survives and now includes two regimental museums. The National Museum of Wales illustrates the history of Wales and Cardiff and houses a large collection of Impressionist paintings. The Cardiff Bay Millennium Waterfront project has helped transform the docklands area and includes a large entertainment complex, an interactive science centre, and the Wales Millennium Centre (a showcase for opera, dance, and museum displays).

Carlisle

City and administrative headquarters of Cumbria, northwest England; population (1991) 72,400. The city developed rapidly in the 19th century as a railway hub and, lying on the main line from London to Glasgow, it remains a major railway and service centre. Carlisle is the northern end of the scenic Settle–Carlisle Railway.

Features
Surviving as impressive evidence of Carlisle's strategic importance, Carlisle Castle, dating from 1092, underwent many alterations during centuries of military use, but still has its large Norman keep. The Tullie House Museum illustrates the city's history from Roman times onwards. The cathedral, completed in 1123, was originally the church of an Augustinian priory and was rebuilt and embellished at various stages.

Chester

Historic city and administrative headquarters of Cheshire, England, on the River Dee 26 km/16 mi south of Liverpool; population (1991) 80,100. Chester is a popular tourist destination, known for its medieval centre, and hosts the Chester Mystery Plays, the oldest and most complete of the surviving mystery-play cycles performed in the UK. Chester Summer Music Festival is held here annually.

Features
Remains from Chester's Roman past include the amphitheatre – the largest stone-built arena discovered in Britain – and parts of the Roman walls; Roman artifacts are displayed in the Grosvenor Museum. Chester has the most complete city walls in England and is also famed for its half-timbered galleried shops known as the 'Rows'. The Roodee, once the site of the large Roman harbour, is now the venue for the Chester Races. Chester Cathedral dates originally from the late 11th century, but work of the 14th century is dominant, and restoration was carried out in the 19th century. Chester Zoo is the largest in area in the country, spreading over 324 ha/80 acres.

Coventry

Industrial city in the West Midlands, England, 29 km/18 mi southeast of Birmingham; population (1994 est) 303,000. Long established as one of Britain's principal engineering and manufacturing centres, Coventry has an industrial heritage dating back many centuries. It is the site of a modern cathedral and two universities.

Features

Postwar architecture dominates most of the city centre and few historic buildings survive. The impressive modern cathedral, built next to the ruins of the medieval cathedral, was consecrated in 1962. Every three years the city hosts one of the four surviving mystery-play cycles performed in England. Under a millennium initiative, Coventry is undergoing a programme of regeneration, with parts of the city centre being excavated prior to redevelopment.

Derby

Industrial city in north central England, 200 km/124 mi north of London; population (1996) 218,800. Part of the county of Derbyshire until 1997, it is now, as Derby City, a unitary authority; area 87 sq km/30 sq mi. A centre for the manufacture of porcelain from the 18th century, Derby was established as the headquarters of Rolls-Royce cars in 1908 and is still important for the manufacture of cars and aero engines.

Features

Originally built as All Saints' parish church in medieval times, the cathedral was rebuilt in the early 18th century. The City Museum and Art Gallery has a collection of Royal Crown Derby porcelain and paintings by Joseph Wright (born in Derby in 1734). Derby Industrial Museum, on the site of the first 18th-century silk mill, includes a collection of Rolls-Royce aero engines. The University of Derby was established in 1993.

Dundee City

Scotland's fourth-largest city, lying on the north side of the Firth of Tay in eastern Scotland; population (1996) 155,000. It is also a unitary authority; area 62 sq km/24 sq mi. The city developed around the jute industry in the 19th century.

Features

Discovery, the ship used by Robert Falcon Scott on his expedition to the Antarctic (1901–04) is moored on the Tay, to the west of the Tay Road Bridge. At nearby Broughty Ferry there is a 15th-century castle, with a museum of Dundee's 18th-century whaling industry. Other notable buildings include the Albert Institute (1867) and Caird Hall. The university (1967) developed from Queen's College (founded in 1881).

Durham

City and administrative headquarters of the county of Durham, northeast England, on the River Wear, 19 km/12 mi south of Newcastle-upon-Tyne; population (1991) 36,900. Durham was an important defensive site and the seat of a powerful bishopric in medieval times, as well as a place of pilgrimage. Its Norman cathedral and castle are situated on a bend in the River Wear, and are today a World Heritage site.

Features

The castle was built in 1072 by William I. It was the palace of the bishops of Durham until 1836. Durham University now occupies most of the castle buildings. St Oswald's Church dates from the 11th century; St Giles was built in 1112. The two main bridges, Framwellgate and Elvet, both date from the 12th century. The university (1832) is home to the Gulbenkian Museum of Oriental Art and Archaeology (1960), the UK's only museum wholly devoted to the subject.

Edinburgh

Capital of Scotland and, as the City of Edinburgh, a unitary authority, located near the southern shores of the Firth of Forth; population (1996) 477,600; area 263 sq km/122 sq mi. Historically the cultural and political centre of Scotland, Edinburgh is also the country's centre of finance, banking, tourism, and law, and home to the new Scottish Parliament. The Old Town and New Town are a World Heritage site. The city hosts the annual Edinburgh Festival, an international arts festival, and the Edinburgh Fringe Festival.

Features

Edinburgh Castle contains St Margaret's chapel (12th century), the oldest building in Edinburgh. The palace of Holyrood House (15th–16th centuries) is the British sovereign's official Scottish residence. Edinburgh's principal church, St Giles, became a cathedral in 1633. Other public buildings of note are the Royal Scottish Academy, the National Gallery of Scotland, the Royal Scottish Museum, and the Scottish National War Memorial. A Museum of Scotland was opened in 1998. 'Our Dynamic Earth' is a major millennium project that provides the world's first geological visitor centre. A permanent home for the new Scottish Parliament is being built on the Royal Mile, with completion planned for 2001. The city has three universities: the University of Edinburgh (1583), Heriot-Watt University, and Napier University.

Exeter

City and administrative headquarters of Devon, England, on the River Exe; population (1994 est) 107,000. Of Roman origins, Exeter later developed into a medieval cathedral town and today preserves fine examples of medieval, Georgian, and Regency architecture.

Features

A cathedral was first established at Exeter in 1050; the present building was begun around 1275. Its fine ceiling is the longest stretch of Gothic vaulting in the world. Cathedral Close has buildings dating from medieval to Georgian times, including the Elizabethan Mol's Coffee House. The Guildhall (1330) is one of the oldest surviving civic buildings in England. Sections of the Roman and medieval walls survive, and there are some remains of Rougemont Castle. Other features include part of the Benedictine Priory of St Nicholas, the Custom House (1681), and the Maritime Museum at the Quay. The Royal Albert Memorial Museum includes collections illustrating zoology and local archaeology. Exeter University (formerly University College, founded in 1922) was established in 1955.

Glasgow

Largest city in Scotland, lying on both sides of the River Clyde; as Glasgow City, also a unitary authority, formed in 1995 from part of Strathclyde region; population (1996) 618,400. Glasgow has seen much urban redevelopment in recent decades and today is an international centre of culture and tourism. It was the 1990 European City of Culture and the 1999 UK City of Architecture and Design.

Features
The present cathedral dates mainly from the 13th century. At the heart of the city are George Square and the redeveloped 18th-century Merchant City. Glasgow's many galleries include the Burrell Collection, Kelvingrove Art Gallery and Museum, and the Hunterian Art Gallery. The Glasgow School of Art (1897–1909) was designed by Charles Rennie Mackintosh. The city has many concert venues and theatres and is home to the Royal Scottish National Orchestra, Scottish Opera, and Scottish Ballet. It has over 70 parks and three football stadia, including Scotland's new National Stadium at Hampden Park, a millennium project. The Glasgow Science Centre is another major millennium project (opened in 1999). Glasgow is the site of three universities: the University of Glasgow, established in 1451, Strathclyde University (1964), and Glasgow Caledonian University.

Kingston upon Hull (or Hull)

City, port, and unitary authority created in 1996 from part of the former county of Humberside, situated where the River Hull flows into the north side of the Humber estuary, northeast England; area 71 sq km/27 sq mi; population (1996) 265,000. It is one of the UK's major seaports, with 11 km/7 mi of modern docks located on the Humber estuary. There are ferries from here to Rotterdam and Zeebrugge.

Features
The large parish church of Holy Trinity dates from the 13th century. The city is home to several museums and galleries, including the Maritime Museum, housed in the old Town Docks offices; Wilberforce House (birthplace of the reformer William Wilberforce); Streetlife, the Hull Museum of Transport, which includes among its exhibits rare trams; and the Ferens Art Gallery. The old Grammar School has also been converted into a museum, with collections dedicated to Victorian Britain and the history of Hull and its people. The town has two universities: the University of Hull (1954) and the University of Lincolnshire and Humberside, which has a campus here (1992, formerly Humberside Polytechnic).

Leeds

Industrial city and metropolitan borough in West Yorkshire, England, 40 km/25 mi southwest of York, on the River Aire; population (1991) 424,200 (city), 680,700 (district). It is the industrial capital of Yorkshire and a major transport hub for road, rail, and canals. An important wool-producing centre in the 16th century, the city still has a clothing industry.

Features
The city's museums include the City Museum, Leeds Industrial Museum, and a folk museum at Abbey House, Kirkstall. The Leeds City Art Gallery (1888), with the adjoining Henry Moore Institute (1993), is the largest gallery in Europe devoted solely to sculpture. Other notable buildings include the Town Hall (1858), the University of Leeds (1904), Temple Newsam House (early 16th century), and the Cistercian Abbey of Kirkstall (1147). Leeds has two main parks, Roundhay and Temple Newsam; Roundhay Park has natural woodlands and lakes, and was formerly a royal hunting ground. The opera company Opera North is based in Leeds, and the city hosts the Leeds Music Festival and the Leeds International Pianoforte Competition. The city has two universities, the University of Leeds and Leeds Metropolitan University.

Leicester

Industrial city in central England, on the River Soar; population (1996) 270,500. Formerly part of the county of Leicestershire, it became a unitary authority in 1997; area 73 sq km/ 28 sq mi.

Features
Places of note are the 14th-century Guildhall, St Martin's Cathedral, and the 15th-century Bradgate House, located in nearby Bradgate. The city's museums include the Leicestershire Museum and Art Gallery, with a large collection of German expressionist paintings and an Egyptian Gallery; the Jewry Wall and Archaeology Museum, illustrating the city's history to the Middle Ages; Newarke Houses Museum, which traces the industrial and social history of Leicestershire from the 16th century to the present; and the Museum of Technology. The National Space Science Centre is a major millennium project. There are two universities: the University of Leicester, established in 1957, and De Montfort University, formerly Leicester Polytechnic, established in 1992.

Lincoln

Industrial and cathedral city, administrative headquarters of Lincolnshire, England, situated on the River Witham, 210 km/130 mi north of London; population (1991) 80,300. It is the market centre for a large agricultural area.

Features
Lincoln Castle was built by William the Conqueror in 1068; it houses one of the four surviving copies of the Magna Carta. The 11th–15th-century cathedral has the earliest Gothic work in Britain. The 12th-century High Bridge, which spans the Witham, is the oldest in Britain still to have buildings on it (half-timbered houses dating to about 1540). Grey Friars (founded in 1090 as a friars' house) is today a museum, and preserves a 13th-century chapel. The three most interesting medieval parish churches, St Benedict, St Mary-le-Wigford, and St Peter-at-Gowts, are all south of the river. The Usher Art Gallery contains important permanent collections. In 1996 a campus was opened in Lincoln for the newly formed University of Lincolnshire and Humberside.

Liverpool

City, seaport, and metropolitan borough in Merseyside, northwest England; population (1991) 481,800. Liverpool is the UK's chief Atlantic port, with miles of specialized mechanized quays on the River Mersey, and 2,100 ha/5,187 acres of dockland. There are ferries to Ireland and the Isle of Man.

Features
Landmarks include the Bluecoat Chambers (1717); the Town Hall (1754); St George's Hall (1838–54); the Brown Library and Museum (1860); the Picton Library (1879); the Walker Art Gallery (1877); and the Anglican Cathedral (begun 1904, completed 1980). The historic waterfront is a major tourist attraction and the restored Albert Dock includes the Merseyside Maritime Museum as well as the Tate Gallery in the North. The members of the Beatles were born in Liverpool. The city is home to the Liverpool Philharmonic Orchestra (founded in 1840, the Royal LPO since 1957). The Grand National steeplechase (first instituted in 1839) takes place at nearby Aintree every year. There are two universities: the University of Liverpool (1903) and John Moores University.

London (see page 95)

Londonderry (also known as Derry)

Historic city and port on the River Foyle, 35 km/22 mi from Lough Foyle, county town of County Londonderry, Northern Ireland; population (1991) 95,400.

Features
The old city walls that still surround Londonderry include several gates and bastions. The waterside, the part of the city on the right bank of the Foyle, is connected to the old city by the Craigavon Bridge. Among the city's parks are Brooke Park, St Columba's Park, and Meenan Park. The Protestant Cathedral of St Columba dates from 1633, and the Roman Catholic Cathedral of St Eugene from 1833. The Guildhall (rebuilt in 1912) contains stained-glass windows presented by livery companies of the City of London. There are modern iron statues by Anthony Gormley on the city walls.

Manchester

Metropolitan district of Greater Manchester, and city in northwest England, on the River Irwell, 50 km/31 mi east of Liverpool; population (1991) 402,900. It was Britain's second city by the mid-19th century, and the first huge urban conurbation to develop after the industrial revolution. Manchester is linked to the River Mersey and the Irish Sea by the Manchester Ship Canal, opened in 1894.

Features
The cathedral dates from the 15th century. Of 18th-century Manchester there remain the church of St Ann and Georgian terraces on St John Street. Liverpool Road station is the world's oldest surviving passenger station. Other notable features include the Whitworth Art Gallery, the Cotton Exchange, the Central Library designed by Frank Lloyd Wright (1934, the world's largest municipal library), and the John Rylands Library (1900). The 'Manchester Millennium Quarter' is a major millennium regeneration project at the historical heart of the city. Manchester is the home of the Hallé Orchestra, the Royal Northern College of Music, four universities (the University of Manchester, UMIST, Manchester Metropolitan University, and the University of Salford), and Manchester United Football Club. Manchester will host the Commonwealth Games in 2002.

Newcastle upon Tyne

City and metropolitan borough in Tyne and Wear in northeast England on the north bank of the River Tyne opposite Gateshead, 17 km/10 mi from the North Sea; population (1991) 189,150, metropolitan district (1994) 274,000. It is the administrative centre of Tyne and Wear and regional centre for retail, commerce, communications, and the arts. Newcastle is connected with Gateshead by eight bridges and a tunnel.

Features
There are remains of the Norman castle wall and of the second castle built on the site in the 12th century. St Nicholas Cathedral (mainly 14th century) was formerly the parish church of Newcastle. Newcastle's museums include the Laing Art Gallery, the Newcastle Discovery Museum, and the Hancock Museum. The high-level bridge designed by Robert Stephenson (1849) was the largest bridge in the world at the time of its construction. The quayside with its historic buildings has been restored. The International Centre for Life is a major millennium project for the North East, combining a visitor centre with research facilities. The University of Newcastle was established in 1963 and the University of Northumbria in 1992.

Norwich

Historic cathedral city and administrative headquarters of Norfolk, eastern England, on the River Wensum, 160 km/100 mi northeast of London; population (1991) 172,600. Norwich has a fine Norman cathedral and castle and more than 30 medieval churches. It preserves the most complete medieval street pattern in England, including cobbled streets and many historic buildings within its large walled centre.

Features
The largely Norman cathedral was begun in 1096; the cathedral's cloisters, built in 1297, are the only two-storey monastic cloisters surviving in England. The imposing castle dates to the 12th century. Other features include Tombland, the marketplace of the original Anglo-Saxon settlement; the Stranger's Hall, a 14th-century merchant's house, now a folk museum; the Bridewell, built in 1370, now a museum of local industries; the Norwich Castle Museum; and the 13th-century Bishop's Bridge, one of the oldest bridges in England. The fine Georgian Assembly House was restored in 1950 as an arts centre. Norfolk and Norwich Millennium Project is a major millennium project which will create a new civic space in the historic centre. The University of East Anglia (1963) includes the Sainsbury Centre for Visual Arts (1978).

Nottingham

Industrial city in central England, on the River Trent, 200 km/124 mi northwest of London; population (1996) 285,000. It was the administrative headquarters of the county of Nottinghamshire until 1998, when, as Nottingham City, it became a unitary authority; area 74 sq km/29 sq mi.

Features
The original Norman castle on Castle Rock became a royal palace and fortress, but was dismantled in 1651; it was restored and opened as a museum in 1878 as England's first provincial museum and art gallery. The 'Trip to Jerusalem' Inn, below the castle, is said to be the oldest inn in England. Other features include the Roman Catholic cathedral of St Barnabas (designed by Augustus Pugin), the old Lace Market and Lace Hall museum, the Costume Museum, and the natural history museum at Wollaton Hall. The remnants of Sherwood Forest, formerly a royal forest and the legendary home of Robin Hood, are north of the city. There are two universities, the University of Nottingham (1881) and Nottingham Trent University (1992), formerly Trent Polytechnic.

Oxford

University city and administrative centre of Oxfordshire in south central England, at the confluence of the rivers Thames (called the Isis around Oxford) and Cherwell, 84 km/52 mi northwest of London; population (1994 est) 121,000. Oxford University, established in the 12th century, is Britain's oldest university. Known as 'the city of dreaming spires' because of its skyline of Gothic towers and steeples, the city is also an important centre of publishing and tourism.

Features
Oxford University has 36 colleges; its buildings date mostly from the 15th, 16th, and 17th centuries. Notable landmarks include Christ Church cathedral, the smallest, but one of the most beautiful of English cathedrals (12th century); the Sheldonian Theatre (designed by Christopher Wren); the Ashmolean museum (1845); the 17th-century Bodleian Library; and the Divinity School and Duke Humphrey's Library (1488). Other museums include the University Museum, the Pitt-Rivers Museum, and the Museum of Modern Art. The Botanic Gardens (laid out in 1621) are the oldest in Britain. Oxford's 'Bridge of Sighs' (1913–14) connects the two sections of Hertford College.

Plymouth

City, seaport, and resort in southwest England; population 257,000. Part of the county of Devon until 1998, it is now a unitary authority; area 79 sq km/31 sq mi. Lying at the head of the bay of Plymouth Sound, the city is a thriving commercial and regional centre and holiday resort, with a dockyard, naval base, and ferry links with France and Spain. Plymouth has a rich maritime history dating back to the 15th century, when it became an important naval garrison. The *Mayflower* Pilgrims sailed from here to North America in 1620.

Features
Dominating the city are the ramparts of the 17th-century citadel. The city's attractions include the Hoe, Plymouth Aquarium, Plymouth Dome (which illustrates Plymouth's past and present with high-tech displays), and the Mayflower Stone and Steps. While much of the city centre is modern, many historic buildings survive in the Barbican harbour area. Plymouth University, formerly South West Polytechnic, was established in 1992.

Portsmouth

City and naval port in southern England, 118 km/73 mi southwest of London; population (1996) 189,300. Part of the county of Hampshire until 1997, it is now a unitary authority; area 42 sq km/16 sq mi. Lying on the peninsula of Portsea Island, opposite the Isle of Wight, Portsmouth is the site of Britain's principal naval station and it has ferry links with France, the Isle of Wight, and the Channel Islands. It is also a major centre of tourism with a wealth of attractions reflecting its rich maritime heritage and long history as a naval dockyard.

Features
Some Georgian and Tudor buildings survive in Old Portsmouth around the harbour. The building where Charles Dickens was born now houses a museum. The Historic Ships complex in the Royal Naval Base is home to the Tudor warship *Mary Rose* and Nelson's flagship HMS *Victory*; the complex also houses the Royal Naval Museum. 'The Renaissance of Portsmouth Harbour' is a major millennium project to redevelop the historic waterfront. Portsmouth University, formerly Portsmouth Polytechnic, was established in 1992.

St Albans

City in Hertfordshire, England, 40 km/25 mi northwest of London; population (1991) 80,400. It is a major tourist centre with many historic attractions, including the ruins of the Roman city of Verulamium and a large cathedral dating from the 11th century.

Features
The ruins include the foundations of a Roman theatre and fragments of the city walls. The Verulamium Museum includes one of the largest collections of Roman archaeological finds in Britain, including some fine mosaics. The abbey church, which became a cathedral in 1877, was built in 1077 on the site of the original Saxon abbey. Other features include the Clock Tower in the High Street, dating from 1411, and Ye Olde Fighting Cocks, said to be one of the oldest inns in Britain.

Sheffield

Industrial city and metropolitan borough in South Yorkshire, England; population of metropolitan district (1991) 501,200. England's fourth largest city, Sheffield is a major centre for the manufacture of steel. Lying amid some of Britain's most attractive scenery close to the Peak District National Park, it is a touring centre for the southern Pennines.

Features
The city's cultural attractions include Graves Art Gallery, the Ruskin Gallery, the Mappin Art Gallery, and the City Museum. Reflecting the city's industrial heritage are the Kelham Island Industrial Museum and Abbeydale Industrial Hamlet, on the River Sheaf. The National Centre for Popular Music opened in 1999 and, as part of a major millennium project designed to contribute to the revitalization of the city centre, a new Millennium Gallery is planned. The city has two universities, the University of Sheffield, and Sheffield Hallam University.

Southampton

Industrial city and seaport in southern England, at the head of Southampton Water, 20 km/12 mi southwest of Winchester; population (1996) 207,100. It was part of the county of Hampshire to 1997, when it became a unitary authority; area 52 sq km/20 sq mi. It is a major passenger and container port, and has a ferry link to the Isle of Wight.

Features
Parts of the medieval town wall survive, including Bargate, the elaborate old north gateway to the city. Norman House and Canute's Palace are among the oldest examples of Norman domestic architecture in Britain. Tudor House Museum is situated in a 15th-century building, and the 14th-century Wool House now houses a maritime museum. The 15th-century God's House Tower houses a museum of archaeology. Southampton University was established in 1952. The headquarters of the Ordnance Survey are here.

Stoke-on-Trent

City in central England, on the River Trent, 23 km/14 mi north of Stafford; population (1996) 254,200. It was part of the county of Staffordshire until 1997 when it became a unitary authority; area 93 sq km/36 sq mi. Stoke is the heart of the Potteries, a major ceramics centre, and the largest clayware producer in the world.

Features
The ceramics factories of Minton, Wedgwood, Spode, and Royal Doulton are all based here. An industrial museum at Etruria houses a steam-powered potters' mill. The Gladstone Working Pottery Museum gives demonstrations and lets visitors throw pots.

Swansea (Welsh Abertawe)

Port and administrative centre of Swansea unitary authority, south Wales, at the mouth of the River Tawe 70 km/43 mi west of Cardiff; population (1994 est) 172,000. It is the second-largest city in Wales. Once the chief metal port of Britain, Swansea is now also a large oil port.

Features
Swansea's notable buildings include the old Guildhall or town hall, built in 1847 near the docks; the civic building, in Victoria Park; the Royal Institution of South Wales, with museum and library; the public library, which includes the corporation art gallery; the Glynn Vivian Art Gallery; and the Exchange Buildings or Chamber of Commerce. The residential and holiday area of The Mumbles is 8 km/5 mi to the southwest. The University College of Swansea, a constituent college of the University of Wales, was established here in 1920.

Winchester

Cathedral city and administrative headquarters of Hampshire, England, on the River Itchen, 19 km/12 mi northeast of Southampton; population (1991) 36,100. Originally a Roman town, Winchester was capital of the Anglo-Saxon kingdom of Wessex, and later of England.

Features
Winchester Cathedral (1079–93) is the longest medieval church in Europe; the Saxon kings of Wessex were crowned here, as were later kings of England, including William the Conqueror and Richard I. Of Winchester Castle, the only part remaining above ground is the 13th-century hall, with its medieval 'reconstruction' of King Arthur's Round Table. The Westgate, one of the two remaining gates of the city, is now a museum which houses the finest civic collection of old weights and measures in England. The parish church of St John's is of particular note for the medieval woodwork of its screens and pulpit. The old city mill, which for hundreds of years has spanned the Itchen above the City Bridge, has been preserved by the National Trust.

York

Cathedral and industrial city and administrative headquarters of York unitary authority in northern England, on the River Ouse; population (1991) 127,700. It was the administrative headquarters of the county of North Yorkshire until 1996. The Gothic York Minster is England's largest medieval cathedral, and the town retains many of its medieval streets and buildings and much of its 14th-century city wall. The York Cycle of Mystery Plays, originally played on wagons in the street in the 14th and 15th centuries, is performed every four years.

Features
The oldest surviving part of York Minster dates from about 1220, and the central tower was completed in about 1480. The restored medieval Guildhall was originally built in 1448. Clifford's Tower (13th century) is all that remains of York Castle. The network of narrow medieval streets in the centre of York includes Stonegate and the Shambles. The Yorkshire Museum contains fine archaeological, natural history, and geological collections. The Jorvik Viking Centre depicts life in York in the time of the Vikings. Other museums include the City Art Gallery, the Castle Museum, and the National Railway Museum. York University was established in 1963.

London

Capital of England and the United Kingdom, on the River Thames; Greater London, from 1965, comprises the City of London and 32 boroughs. London is the only major European capital without a strategic authority covering the whole area. In a referendum held on 7 May 1998, Londoners voted in favour of the instigation of office of elected mayor.

Area 1,580 sq km/610 sq mi (Greater London)
Population 7,122,000 (1997 est)
Universities University of London (Birkbeck College; Goldsmiths College; University College; King's College; Imperial College; Queen Mary & Westfield College; Royal Holloway & Bedford College); City University; Greenwich University; Kingston University; London Guildhall University; London School of Economics and Political Science; Middlesex University; University of East London; University of North London; South Bank University; Thames Valley University; Westminster University
Airports Gatwick; Heathrow; Stansted
Rail London has an extensive rail network which is linked to the London Underground (tube) at all mainline and several branch railway lines; the Eurostar service to the continent runs from Waterloo Station
Major railway stations Euston; Charing Cross; King's Cross; St Pancras; Paddington; Waterloo; Victoria
Main bus station Victoria Coach Station
Industries and products finance (major international centre); newspapers; broadcasting; film; recording; tourism; government; the world's largest office development project is at Canary Wharf
Places of interest the National Gallery; the National Portrait Gallery; the British Museum; the Science Museum; the Natural History Museum; the Tate Gallery; the Victoria and Albert Museum; Wallace Collection; Courtauld Institute; the South Bank Complex (Royal Festival Hall; Hayward Gallery; National Theatre; Barbican arts and conference centre); Royal Opera House with the Royal Ballet and Opera Companies; the Royal Albert Hall; many other theatres in the West End; Royal Philharmonic and London Symphony Orchestras; the Tower of London (houses the crown jewels and the royal armouries); Westminster Abbey; the Palace of Westminster (containing the houses of Parliament); Lambeth Palace; Southwark Cathedral; St James's Palace; Buckingham Palace; Horse Guards Parade; St Paul's Cathedral; Mansion House (residence of the lord mayor); Guildhall (15th century); Trafalgar Square; Nelson's Column; Criminal Court (Old Bailey) and the Inner and Middle Temples; the Royal Parks; the London Eye
Tourist information centre London Tourist Board and Convention Bureau, 6th Floor, Glen House, Stag Place, London SW1E 5LT; phone: (020) 7932 2000; fax: (020) 7932 0222; e-mail: enquiries@londontouristboard.co.uk; Web site: www.londontown.com
Chamber of Commerce London Chamber of Commerce & Industry (LCCI) 33 Queen Street, London EC4R 1AP; phone: (020) 7248 4444; fax: (020) 7489 0391; Web site: www.londonchamber.co.uk.

London Royal Parks

London's royal parks are official public open spaces belonging to the crown. They are managed by the Royal Parks Agency; address: Royal Parks Agency, The Police House, Hyde Park, London W2 2UH; phone: (020) 7298 2000; fax: (020) 7298 2005.

Name	Park office	Notes
Brompton Cemetery	The Chapel Office, Brompton Cemetery, Fulham Road, London SW10 9UG; phone: (020) 7352 1201	laid out in 1840 by Benjamin Baud; has a central avenue leading to an octagonal chapel with flanking colonnades; catacombs run under the colonnades and along the west wall; around 205,000 burials have been recorded with an estimated 35,000 headstones; burial record search (small fee includes map and location of grave)
Bushy Park and Longford River	Stockyard Education Centre, Bushy Park, Hampton Court Road, Hampton Hill, Middlesex TW12 2EJ; phone: (020) 8979 1586; fax: (020) 8941 8196	enclosed by Cardinal Wolsey and Henry VIII between 1500 and 1537; Longford River is an artificial waterway created by Charles I in 1639 and running from the River Colne, beyond Heathrow Airport, to the River Thames at Hampton
Greenwich Park	Park Manager, Blackheath Gate, Greenwich Park, London SE10 8QY; phone: (020) 8858 2608; fax: (020) 8293 3782	created in 1433, the first Royal Park to be enclosed; the Old Royal observatory; observatory planetarium (by appointment)

(continued)

London Royal Parks (*continued*)

Hyde Park	Park Manager, Rangers Lodge, Hyde Park, London W2 2UH; phone: (020) 7298 2100; fax: (020) 7402 3298	came into existence in 1536; has a tradition of events and public spectacles; gun salutes are fired from the Parade Ground of Knightsbridge barracks on its boundary
Kensington Gardens	Park Manager, Magazine Storeyard, Magazine Gate, Kensington Gardens, London W2 2UH; phone: (020) 7724 2826	formed from land taken from Hyde Park in 1689; Serpentine Gallery
Regent's Park and Primrose Hill	Park Manager, The Store Yard, Inner Circle, Regent's Park, London NW1 4NR; phone: (020) 7486 7905; fax: (020) 7224 1895	royal chase until 1646; the park started to evolve in 1811 with the plans of John Nash, crown architect; also contains the London Zoo; open air theatre
Richmond Park	Superintendent's Office, Holly Lodge, Bog Lodge Yard, Richmond Park, Surrey TW10 5HS; phone: (020) 8948 3209; fax: (020) 8332 2730	enclosed as a hunting park by Charles I in 1637; herds of fallow and red deer roam the park; in 1992 the park was notified as a Site of Special Scientific Interest by English Nature; Pen Ponds
St James's Park and Green Park	Park Manager, The Storeyard, St James's Park, Horse Guards Parade, London SW1A 2BJ; phone (020) 7930 1793; fax: (020) 7839 7639	these two parks lying to the east of Buckingham Palace were acquired by Henry VIII in 1536; provide the backdrop for British ceremonial life with The Mall, the processional route between the Palace and Whitehall and Horse Guards Parade, the venue for major ceremonial occasions

The Corporation of London

The Corporation of London is the local authority for the City of London, known as the square mile. Its responsibilities extend beyond the City boundaries, and it provides a number of additional facilities. The Corporation of London is unique in operating on a non-party political basis. It is currently engaged in a major review of its electoral arrangements. In response to the Government's Green Paper, *New Leadership for London*, the Corporation is examining ways in which it can improve the City's franchise and work alongside the proposed strategic authority for London. For more information, contact: Town Clerk, Corporation of London, PO Box 270, Guildhall, London EC2P 2EJ; phone: (020) 7606 3030; fax: (020) 7796 2621; Web site: www.cityoflondon.gov.uk.

Committees
Committees of elected Members set Corporation policy and oversee the work of departments. These committees are: Barbican Centre; Barbican Residential; Billingsgate and Leadenhall Markets; Board of Governors, City of London Freemen's School; Board of Governors, City of London School; Board of Governors, City of London School for Girls; Board of Governors of the Museum of London; Central Markets; City Lands and Bridge House Estates; City of London Police; Committee of Managers of West Ham Park; Education; Epping Forest and Open Spaces; Establishment; Finance; Hampstead Heath Management; Housing and Sports Development; Libraries, Guildhall Art Gallery, and Archives; Music and Drama; Planning and Transportation; Policy and Resources; Port and City of London Health and Social Services; Spitalfields Market.

Departments
Barbican Centre; Barbican Estate; Billingsgate Market; Chamberlain; City of London Freemen's School; City of London Police; City of London School; City of London School for Girls; City Surveyor; Cleansing; Comptroller and City Solicitor; Education; Environmental Services; Epping Forest; Guildhall School of Music and Drama; Hampstead Heath; Housing and Sports Development; Libraries and Guildhall Art Gallery; London Central Markets; Mansion House; Museum of London; Parks and Gardens; Planning; Remembrancer; Secondary; Social Services; Spitalfields Market; Technical Services; Town Clerk; West Wickham and Coulsdon Commons, Ashtead Common and Burnham Beeches.

The Wards
Within the geographical area covered by the Corporation of London there are 25 wards or voting districts. Each ward elects an alderman and between three and twelve Commoners to represent them in the Court of Common Council, the City of London's 'town council'. All members of the following wards can be contacted via the Corporation of London, PO Box 270, Guildhall, London EC2P 2EJ; phone: (020) 7606 3030; fax: (020) 7796 2621; Web site: www.cityoflondon.gov.uk.

Aldersgate Nicholas Anstee (Alderman), Clifford Green, Peter Leck, Jeremy Mayhew, Joyce Nash (Deputy), Barbara Newman

Aldgate Charles Bowman, Bruce Farthing, Peter Hardwick, John Holland (Deputy), The Rt Hon the Lord Mayor Clive Martin (Alderman), Patrick O'Ferrall

Bassishaw Kenneth Ayers, Nigel Branson, David Brewer (Alderman), John Brewster, Peter Martinelli (Deputy), Stuart Thompson

Billingsgate William Baverstock Brooks, John Hughesdon (Alderman), Douglas Mobsby (Deputy), Clive Thorp, John Trotter

Bishopsgate William Dove, Graham Forbes, Stanley Ginsburg, Anthony Graves, Michael Oliver (Alderman), Dorothy Robinson, Patrick Roney, Philip Willoughby

Bread Street Barry Davis, Rodney FitzGerald (Deputy), Tom Jackson, Michael Savory (Alderman), John Taylor

Bridge and Bridge Without John Bird, Daniel Caspi, Maurice Hart (Deputy), John Owen-Ward, Sir David Rowe-Ham (Alderman)

Broad Street Sir Christopher Collett (Alderman), Fergus Falk, Archibald Galloway, Brian Harris, John Scott, John Spanner

Candlewick Kevin Everett, Keith Knowles, Sir Richard Nichols (Alderman), Richard Saunders (Deputy), Richard Scriven

Castle Baynard Richard Agutter (Alderman), Derek Balls, Sir Colin Cole, Catherine McGuinness, Christopher Mitchell (Deputy)

Cheap Peter Bull (Alderman), Joseph Byllam-Barnes, Robin Eve, Ann Pembroke (Deputy)

Coleman Street Hugh Barnes-Yallowley, Michael Cassidy (Deputy), Robert Finch (Alderman), Stuart Fraser, Michael Henderson-Begg, Derek Kemp, Gordon Wixley

Cordwainer George Gillon, Sir Brian Jenkins (Alderman), Tony Sellon, Michael Snyder (Deputy), Tom Wilmot

Cornhill Wilfred Archibald (Deputy), John Haynes, David Howard (Alderman), Keith Sargant

Cripplegate Within Lionel Altman, Gavyn Arthur (Alderman), John Barker (Deputy), David Bradshaw, Christopher Punter, Francis Stevenson, Douglas Warner

Cripplegate Without Ernest Angell, Gavyn Arthur (Alderman), Stella Currie (Deputy), Roger Daily-Hunt, Vivienne Littlechild, Stephen Quilter

Dowgate Alison Gowman (Deputy), Sir Christopher Leaver (Alderman), Bryan Montgomery, Robin Sherlock

Farringdon Within North Side: Benson Catt, Henry Horlock, Peter Rigby (Deputy), David Shalit; South Side: Anthony Eskenzi (Deputy), Benjamin Hall, Richard Regan, Sir Christopher Walford (Alderman)

Farringdon Without North Side: Philip Andrade, Erasmus Darwin, Wendy Mead, John Platts-Mills, Edward Price, Simon Walsh; South Side: John Absalom, Jonathan Charkham, Michael Farrow, Gregory Lawrence, Ian Luder, Julian Malins (Deputy)

Langbourn Stephen Barter, Michael Bramwell, George Challis (Deputy), Janet Owen, Sir Alan Traill (Alderman)

Lime Street Michael Beale (Deputy), Christine Cohen, Dennis Cotgrove, Michael Everard (Alderman), Ian McNeil

■ Cities and Major Towns

The Corporation of London (*continued*)

Portsoken Roger Brighton, Alfred Dunitz, Geoffrey Lawson, Lord Levene of Portsoken (Alderman), Iris Samuel (Deputy)

Queenhithe Sir Alexander Graham (Alderman), Alistair King, Judith Mayhew, Brian Mooney, Ivy Sharp (Deputy)

Tower Roger Chadwick, Sir Roger Cork (Alderman), Maureen Kellett, Anthony Moss, Gerald Pulman (Deputy)

Vintry Sir John Chalstrey (Alderman), William Fraser, Elizabeth Holliday, Andrew Parmley, Peter Revell-Smith (Deputy)

Walbrook Martin Farr, Pauline Halliday (Sheriff), Patrick MacLellan (Deputy), Sir Paul Newall (Alderman)

The Lord Mayor
Clive Martin. Born: 20 March 1935; elected to the Court of Aldermen for Ward of Aldergate (1985); Sheriff of the City of London (1996–97).

The City Guilds (Livery Companies)

The City of London companies, collectively known as the Livery, are surviving members of medieval trade and craft associations, known as guilds. Each livery company is governed by an annually elected court, typically composed as follows: The Master (elected from the Wardens); Upper Warden; Middle Warden; Lower Warden (elected from the Court assistant); between 10 and 20 Court Assistants (elected from the Livery); a Clerk (to keep the records); a Beadle (to keep order).

After years of dispute, an order of precedence for livery companies was settled in 1515, starting with Mercers at number 1 and so on down to number 48. Merchant Taylors and Skinners, however, continued to switch between numbers 6 and 7 in alternate years, following a compromise reached some 30 years earlier. Numbers 1 to 12 inclusive are known as the Great Twelve. Through choice, the companies of Parish Clerks and Watermen and Lightermen remain City Guilds without grant of livery.

Livery companies in order of precedence
Mercers (general merchants); Grocers; Drapers; Fishmongers; Goldsmiths; Merchant Taylors (tailors); Skinners (fur trade); Haberdashers; Salters; Ironmongers; Vintners; Clothworkers; Dyers; Brewers; Leathersellers; Pewterers; Barbers (also surgeons and dentists); Cutlers; Bakers; Waxchandlers; Tallowchandlers; Armourers and Brasiers (armour-makers and workers in brass); Girdlers (girdles and belts as clothing); Butchers; Saddlers; Carpenters; Cordwainers (workers in fine leather); Painter Stainers; Curriers (dressers of tanned leather); Masons; Plumbers; Innholders; Founders; Poulters; Cooks; Coopers (barrel makers); Tylers and Bricklayers; Bowyers (longbow makers); Fletchers (arrow makers); Blacksmiths; Joiners; Weavers; Woolmen (winders and packers of wool); Scriveners (writers of court letters and legal documents); Fruiterers; Plaisterers (plasterers); Stationers and Newspaper Makers; Broderers (embroiderers); Upholders (upholsterers); Musicians; Turners; Basketmakers; Glaziers; Horners; Farriers (shoers of horses/veterinary surgeons); Paviors (paving, highways); Loriners (stirrups and other harness for horses); Apothecaries (medicine); Shipwrights; Spectaclemakers; Clockmakers; Glovers; Feltmakers (hats); Framework Knitters; Needlemakers; Gardeners; Tinplate Workers; Wheelwrights; Distillers; Pattenmakers (makers of wooden clog-style footwear); Glass Sellers; Coachmakers and Coach Harness Makers; Gunmakers; Gold and Silver Wyre Drawers (gold and silver braid for uniforms); Makers of Playing Cards; Fan Makers; Carmen; Master Mariners; Solicitors; Farmers; Air Pilots and Air Navigators; Tobacco Pipe Makers and Tobacco Blenders; Furniture Makers; Scientific Instrument Makers; Chartered Surveyors; Chartered Accountants; Chartered Secretaries and Administrators; Builders Merchants; Launderers; Marketors; Actuaries; Insurers; Arbitrators; Engineers; Fuellers; Lightmongers; Environmental Cleaners; Chartered Architects; Constructors; Information Technologists.

Millennium Projects in the UK

Major Millennium Commission Projects in the UK

The Millennium Commission was set up in 1994 as an independent body under the National Lottery Act 1993. It is one of the six good causes that share 28p of every pound spent on the National Lottery. The Commission uses this money to encourage projects throughout the UK that enjoy public support and make a lasting contribution to the public good.

The Commission operates a three-fold funding strategy, representing the largest single non-governmental investment ever made in social and community works throughout the UK: £1.25 billion for capital projects; £200 million for Millennium Awards; £100 million towards the Millennium Festival.

There are 28 major capital projects awarded a grant between £15 and £50 million each, and many smaller, community-based projects designed to enhance the local environment and provide a focal point for the community. Altogether more than 3,000 sites are involved. Listed below are the 28 major capital projects.

• East Anglia
Norfolk and Norwich Millennium Project (Norwich) This project links three primary facilities – a Millennium Library, a Business and Learning Centre, and a Heritage Attraction – around a new urban square, creating a major new civic meeting place within the historic city centre of Norwich. The complex will also include a learning shop, multimedia auditorium, and a range of cafés and restaurants. Opening date: June 2001. Phone: (01603) 610 524; Web site: www.norfolk.gov.uk/announce.ht

• East Midlands
National Space Science Centre (Leicester) This project will provide the UK with a unique education and leisure facility based on space science. The scheme comprises four key elements: the Exhibition Centre, the Space Theatre, the Challenger Learning Centre, and the Research Centre. The design of the building will make imaginative use of the existing site and will include a tower housing real rockets. Opening date: May 2001. Phone: (0116) 253 0811; Web site: www.nssc.co.uk

• Greater London
The British Museum Great Court The restoration and glazed covering of the Great Court at the heart of the British Museum. The project will open up the inner court for the first time in 150 years, creating a dramatic new public space where people can meet and gather, close to one of the world's greatest cultural resources. Opening date: July 2000. Phone: (020) 7323 8263; Web site: www.british-museum.ac.uk/court.htm

Tate Modern A project to establish a new national art gallery enabling the Tate's modern collection to be housed on a permanent basis, and, as a corollary, the British collection to be better displayed at Millbank. Opening date: May 2000. Phone: (020) 7887 8701; Web site: www.tate.org.uk (*see also* **Tate Modern,** p 420.)

• North
International Centre for Life (Newcastle) A landmark project for the North East – a science-based venture which combines a high-tech visitor centre with research facilities and commercial developments. It will enhance Newcastle's world reputation in the field of genetic research. Opening date: November 2000. Phone: (0191) 261 6006; Web site: www.centreforlife.co.uk

• North West
Manchester Millennium Quarter This regeneration project will create a cultural quarter in the centre of Manchester and consists of four new features – City Park, Exchange Square, Cathedral Visitors Centre, and Urbis, an attraction based on the development of modern cities. The project will create a new focus at the historical heart of the city and provide a new high-quality urban environment for the residents of Manchester and visitors to the city. Opening date: March 2002. Phone: (0161) 234 5217

The Lowry (Salford) A project to develop a waterfront complex in Salford, that includes two theatres, a gallery to display works by the artist L S Lowry, an Interactive Artwork Gallery and a Digital World Centre. The development also includes a new footbridge and public

Major Millennium Commission Projects in the UK *(continued)*

plaza. This is a joint lottery distributors' initiative with the Arts Council of England and the Heritage Lottery Fund. Opening date: April 2000. Phone: (0161) 876 2037; Web site: www.thelowry.org.uk (*see also* **The Lowry** p 420.)

• South East

The Renaissance of Portsmouth Harbour Project to create an international maritime attraction. It comprises numerous elements including promenade and boundaries, visitor attractions, and the 'Millennium Tower' as its centrepiece. Opening date: April 2002. Phone: (023) 9283 4178; Web site: www.millennium-city.co.uk

The Millennium Seed Bank (West Sussex) Project to collect 25,000 species of UK and worldwide flora and freeze them for conservation. The project will also provide a world-class building of high architectural quality, access for the public to view the scientific process, and the opportunity to train new scientists. Opening date: September 2000. Phone: (020) 8332 5113; Web site: www.rbgkew.org.uk/seedbank/ab

• South West

Bristol A landmark project for the South West. Major attractions 'Explore' and 'Wildscreen' will be surrounded by squares and city spaces. This project will regenerate a derelict site in Bristol. Opening date: June 2000. Phone: (0117) 909 2000; Web site: www.at-bristol.org.uk

The Eden Project (Cornwall) A world-class landmark project which will demonstrate and explore the relationship between plants and humans. In a worked out china clay pit near St Austell, Cornwall, huge biomes (controlled environments) will be built, capable of exhibiting plants from three climates: the rainforest, Mediterranean, and temperate. This will enable unprecedented scientific research of plants as whole populations rather than individual species. Opening date: December 2000. Phone: (01726) 222 900; Web site: www.edenproject.com/welcome

• West Midlands

Millennium Point (Birmingham) A world-class centre of technology and learning. There will be four elements: the Discovery Centre will integrate new multimedia technologies with historic and modern artefacts; the Technology Innovation Centre will become a centre of excellence for technology and innovation; the University of the First Age will provide a new learning experience for up to 90,000 young people in the West Midlands; the Hub will link the component parts and contain numerous facilities. Opening date: September 2001. Phone: (0121) 303 4271; Web site: www.millenniumpoint.org.uk

• Yorkshire and Humberside

The Deep (Hull) A visitor attraction dedicated to the development of our enjoyment, knowledge, and understanding of the world's seas and oceans, incorporating research laboratories and a learning centre. It will also include a business centre. Opening date: August 2001. Phone: (01482) 615 776

The Earth Centre (near Doncaster) Formerly the site of the Denaby Main and Conisbrough coal mines, the project is a major regeneration scheme comprising a visitor attraction promoting sustainability. The project includes viewing galleries, exhibits on sustainable living, extensive gardens, nature trails, a solar canopy, shop, and café. Opening date: April 1999. Phone: (01709) 512 000

Magna (Rotherham) Project to convert the existing but redundant Templeborough Steel Mill in Rotherham into a major visitor attraction. The visitor centre will focus on the four components of steel, marking Earth, Air, Fire, and Water. Space will be provided in this huge building for exhibitions and events. Opening date: April 2001. Phone: (01709) 720002

Sheffield – Remaking the Heart of the City An initiative to revitalize the city centre. The project comprises three remodelled public squares including the Peace Gardens with the new Goodwin Fountains. Phase 2 of the project is the building of the new Millennium Galleries that will display exhibits of decorative fine arts, both historic and modern. Phase 3 is the Winter Gardens, a temperate greenhouse connecting the Peace Gardens to the Millennium Galleries. Opening date: April 2002. Phone: (0114) 273 6604

• Northern Ireland

The Odyssey Project (Belfast) This project provides a mixture of education, entertainment, and sporting activities, and includes the Science Centre, IMAX film theatre, Indoor Arena, Pavilion, and public open space. It is the first major development on the east side of the River Lagan and is seen as a catalyst for future regeneration. Opening date: March 1999. Phone: (028) 9045 1055

• Scotland

The Glasgow Science Centre Located on a 5-acre site, the scheme comprises: Exploratorium, with a planetarium, interactive theatre, interlinked galleries for themed exhibitions, education, and demonstrations, and catering/retail facilities; Millennium Tower, housing exhibitions, broadband links to other science centres, lifts, and a viewing platform; IMAX cinema based on educational themes; and Civic Square works such as landscaping, outdoor events, and footbridge relocation. Opening date: March 1999. Phone: (0141) 204 4448

Hampden – Scotland's 'Field of Dreams' (Glasgow) Project to bring Scotland's National Stadium to international standards by building a new South Stand with facilities for players, officials, and supporters; an International Media Centre; and a Museum of Football. The West Stand will be refurbished and there will be provision for a Sports Medical Research and Rehabilitation Centre. Opening date: May 1999. Phone: (0141) 636 1390; Web site: www.scottishfa.co.uk

Our Dynamic Earth (Edinburgh) A project that provides the world's first geological visitor centre. Visitors can participate in the exhibition which uses state-of-the-art technology to present the creation of the planet, evolution, and natural disasters such as earthquakes, volcanoes, and meteorites. Opening date: July 1999. Phone: (01620) 890 202; Web site: www.dynamicearth.co.uk

University of the Highlands and Islands (multisite) Project to create a new university for the Highlands and Islands. It involves partnership with many sectors including the business community. It will link colleges and research institutions and create new forms of access to lifelong learning opportunities for many sectors of the community. Opening date: December 2001. Phone: (01463) 236 000; Web site: www.uhi.ac.uk

The Millennium Link Project to reopen to navigation the Forth and Clyde Canal and the Union Canal, thus linking not only Scotland's major east- and west-coast rivers but also the cities of Glasgow and Edinburgh. This will be achieved by removing obstacles such as in-filled sections and low-headroom bridges, refurbishing locks, and building a transfer mechanism – the Falkirk Wheel – to allow boats to pass between the two canals. Opening date: September 2001. Phone: (0141) 332 6936; Web site: www.millenniumlink.org.uk

• Wales

Millennium Stadium (Cardiff) A new 75,000-seat stadium at Cardiff Arms Park with a retractable roof and all-year-weather capacity. It serves as a venue for a wide range of sporting and non-sporting events in Wales and houses a fitness and medical centre, media facilities, and conference and hospitality suites. There is also 'The Rugby Experience' museum, a riverside walk, and a new public plaza opening up the city centre site. Opening date: November 1999. Phone: (029) 2023 2661; Web site: www.cardiff-stadium.co.uk

Wales Millennium Centre (Cardiff) A project that will provide a theatre with state-of-the-art acoustics and audience facilities, and rehearsal and performance space for the Welsh National Opera; residential and workshop space for a headquarters for the Welsh Academy of Writers, contemporary dance companies, and other residents, to provide a broad artistic mix; public spaces and commercial areas. Opening date: June 2002. Phone: (029) 2040 2000

National Botanic Garden of Wales (near Middleton, Dyfed) A project to create a National Botanic Garden for Wales of international significance. It will be dedicated to the sustainability and protection of threatened plant species. Opening date: June 2001. Phone: (01558) 668 768; Web site: www.gardenofwales.org.uk

• England and Wales

Changing Places Reclaiming wasteland to enhance local environments and benefit local people through community schemes in England and Wales. Opening date: March 2001. Phone: (0121) 236 8565; Web site: www.changingplaces.
org.uk

• UK-wide

National Cycle Network The National Cycle Network will provide a 5,000-mile network of traffic-free paths and traffic-calmed roads connecting towns and cities in the UK. Opening date: June 2000. Phone: (0117) 927 7555; Web site: www.sustrans.org.uk

Source: The Millennium Commission

See also **The Millennium Dome**, p 603.

Millennium Projects in the UK

Population, Demography, and Society

Population of the UK: Introduction

The UK is the world's 19th most populous state and the second ranking in the European Union. The population now exceeds 59 million. This represents an increase of an eighth since 1961. Growth has been fastest in Northern Ireland (up 18% since 1961), England (up 14%), and Wales (up 11%), whereas in Scotland the population actually contracted by 1%. The current net population growth rate is around 0.3% per annum, but the rate is expected to slow to 0.2% per annum by 2021. A half of the current annual growth is contributed by immigration. The other half is a result of 'natural increase' (more births than deaths).

Population Summary of the UK

Year	Female	Male	Total
Enumerated population: census figures			
1851	11,404,000	10,855,000	22,259,000
1901	19,745,000	18,492,000	38,237,000
1911	21,725,000	20,357,000	42,082,000
1921	22,994,000	21,033,000	44,027,000
1931	23,978,000	22,060,000	46,038,000
1951	26,107,000	24,118,000	50,225,000
1961	27,228,000	25,481,000	52,709,000
Resident population: mid-year estimates			
1971	28,761,000	27,167,000	55,928,000
1981	28,943,000	27,409,000	56,352,000
1991	29,562,000	28,246,000	57,808,000
1998	30,108,000	29,128,000	59,237,000
Resident population: projections (mid-year)[1]			
2001	30,241,000	29,377,000	59,618,000
2011	30,723,000	30,206,000	60,929,000
2021	31,328,000	30,916,000	62,244,000

[1] These projections are 1996-based.

Source: Annual Abstract of Statistics 2000, © *Crown copyright 2000*

Population Changes in the UK

Year	Population at start of period[1]	Average annual change: Overall annual change (increase)	Births	Deaths[2]	Excess of births over deaths	Net migration and other adjustments[3]
1901–11	38,237,000	385,000	1,091,000	624,000	467,000	– 82,000
1911–21	42,082,000	195,000	975,000	689,000	286,000	– 92,000
1921–31	44,027,000	201,000	824,000	555,000	268,000	– 67,000
1931–51	46,038,000	213,000	793,000	603,000	190,000	22,000
1951–61	50,225,000	258,000	839,000	593,000	246,000	12,000
1961–71	52,807,000	230,000	962,000	638,000	324,000	– 14,000
1971–81	55,928,000	42,000	736,000	666,000	69,000	– 27,000
1981–91	56,352,000	146,000	757,000	655,000	103,000	43,000
1991–98	57,808,000	204,000	748,000	637,000	112,000	93,000
1998–2001[4]	59,237,000	236,000	714,000	630,000	84,000	115,000
2001–11	59,954,000	178,000	701,000	614,000	87,000	95,000
2011–21	61,773,000	185,000	712,000	620,000	92,000	95,000

[1] Figures give census-enumerated population up to 1951, mid-year estimates of resident population from 1961 to 1998, and mid-1998-based projections of resident population thereafter. [2] Figures include deaths of non-civilians and merchant seamen who died outside the country. These deaths numbered 577,000 in 1911–21, and 240,000 in 1931–51 for England and Wales; 74,000 in 1911–21, and 34,000 in 1931–51 for Scotland; and 10,000 in 1911–26 for Northern Ireland. [3] Other adjustments include changes in census visitor balance, in Armed Forces, asylum seekers, etc. [4] Figures are 1998-based national population projections.

Source: Annual Abstract of Statistics 2000, © *Crown copyright 2000*

The UK's Ageing Population

In common with other developed states, the average age of the UK's population is increasing. Between 1971 and 1997, the number of people aged 65 and over increased by a quarter. Currently, 19% of the UK population falls into this age range. This is in line with the European Union (EU) average, and in eight EU states the proportion is even higher, exceeding 20% in Italy. Meanwhile, between 1961 and 1997, the proportion of the UK population who were under the age of 16 fell by a quarter to 20%.

Increasing life expectancy With improvements in diet, medicine, and social conditions, the most significant increases in life expectancy occurred during the first half of the 20th century: life expectancy at birth rising from around 50 years to around 70 years. Nevertheless, since 1971, life expectancy has risen each decade by around two years for males and one and half years for females, to reach the level of 79 for females and 74 for males. This is in line with the EU and North American average, but is significantly ahead of the world averages of 68 and 63 years respectively.

Rates of childbirth are decreasing Women born in each decade since 1937 have given birth to fewer children than those born in the preceding decade. An important reason is the increasing participation of women in employment: in 1997 three-quarters of women aged between 25 and 44 were either in work or seeking work, compared to only half in 1971. As a consequence of these changes, the annual number of births, which had averaged more than 750,000 during the 1980s and 1990s, is set to fall below 700,000 during the current decade.

If current trends continue, those aged 65 or over will amount to a fifth of the UK population by 2016 and will exceed those aged under 16 for the first time. By 2050 there will be two persons of working age for every pensioner: currently there are 3.5.

See also **A Silver World: The Ageing Population**, p 274.

Age Distribution in the UK

1998			
Age	**Male**	**Female**	**Total**
Under 1	366,000	349,000	715,000
1–4	1,516,000	1,440,000	2,956,000
5–9	2,005,000	1,909,000	3,914,000
10–14	1,948,000	1,848,000	3,795,000
15–19	1,884,000	1,785,000	3,670,000
20–29	4,055,000	3,855,000	7,910,000
30–44	6,763,000	6,583,000	13,347,000
45–59	5,387,000	5,433,000	10,820,000
60–64	1,380,000	1,438,000	2,818,000
65–74	2,290,000	2,674,000	4,965,000
75–84	1,237,000	1,968,000	3,205,000
85 and over	297,000	825,000	1,122,000
School ages (5–15)	4,328,000	4,111,000	8,439,000
Under 18	6,966,000	6,616,000	13,582,000
Pensionable age[1]	3,824,000	6,906,000	10,730,000
All ages	29,128,000	30,108,000	59,237,000

[1] The pensionable age population is that over state retirement age.

Source: Annual Abstract of Statistics 2000, © *Crown copyright 2000*

See also **Life Expectancy in the UK**, p 523.

Births in the UK

Dates are annual averages or for calendar years and figures have been rounded.
(N/A = not available.)

Year(s)	Live births			Sex ratio[1]	Rates		Total period fertility rate[4]	Stillbirths[5]	Stillbirth rate[5]
	Male	Female	Total		Crude birth rate[2]	General fertility rate[3]			
1900–02	558,000	537,000	1,095,000	1,037	28.6	115.1	N/A	N/A	N/A
1910–12	528,000	508,000	1,037,000	1,039	24.6	99.4	N/A	N/A	N/A
1920–22	522,000	496,000	1,018,000	1,052	23.1	93.0	N/A	N/A	N/A
1930–32	383,000	367,000	750,000	1,046	16.3	66.5	N/A	N/A	N/A
1940–42	372,000	351,000	723,000	1,062	15.0	N/A	1.89	26,000	N/A
1950–52	413,000	390,000	803,000	1,061	16.0	73.7	2.21	18,000	N/A
1960–62	487,000	459,000	946,000	1,063	17.9	90.3	2.80	18,000	N/A
1970–72	453,000	427,000	880,000	1,064	15.8	82.5	2.36	12,000	13
1980–82	377,000	358,000	735,000	1,053	13.0	62.5	1.83	5,000	7
1981	375,000	356,000	731,000	1,053	13.0	62.1	1.81	5,000	7
1982	369,000	350,000	719,000	1,054	12.8	60.6	1.78	5,000	6
1983	371,000	351,000	721,000	1,058	12.8	60.2	1.77	4,000	6
1984	373,000	356,000	730,000	1,049	12.9	60.3	1.77	4,000	6
1985	385,000	366,000	751,000	1,053	13.3	61.4	1.80	4,000	6
1986	387,000	368,000	755,000	1,053	13.3	61.1	1.78	4,000	5
1987	398,000	378,000	776,000	1,053	13.6	62.3	1.82	4,000	5
1988	403,000	384,000	788,000	1,049	13.8	63.2	1.84	4,000	5
1989	398,000	379,000	777,000	1,051	13.6	62.4	1.81	4,000	5
1990	409,000	390,000	799,000	1,049	13.9	64.2	1.84	4,000	5
1991	406,000	386,000	793,000	1,052	13.7	63.6	1.82	4,000	5
1992	400,000	380,000	781,000	1,052	13.5	63.4	1.80	3,000	4
1993	391,000	371,000	762,000	1,054	13.1	62.4	1.76	4,000	6
1994	385,000	365,000	751,000	1,054	12.9	61.6	1.74	4,000	6
1995	375,000	357,000	732,000	1,052	12.5	60.1	1.71	4,000	6
1996	376,000	357,000	733,000	1,055	12.5	60.1	1.72	4,000	6
1997	373,000	354,000	726,000	1,051	12.3	59.5	1.72	4,000	5
1998	366,000	351,000	717,000	1,042	12.1	58.7	1.70	4,000	5

[1] Sex ratio is the number of male births per 1,000 female births.
[2] Rate per 1,000 population (male and female).
[3] Rate per 1,000 women aged 15–44.
[4] Total period fertility rate is the average number of children which would be born per woman if women experienced the age-specific fertility rates of the period in question throughout their child-bearing life span. Figures for the years 1970–72 and earlier are estimates.
[5] Figures given are based on stillbirths of 28 or more completed weeks of gestation. On 1 October 1992, the legal definition of a stillbirth was altered to include babies born dead between 24 and 27 completed weeks' gestation. Between 1 October and 31 December 1992 in the UK, there were 258 babies born dead between 24 and 27 completed weeks' gestation (216 in England and Wales, 35 in Scotland, and 7 in Northern Ireland). If these babies were included in the stillbirth figures given, the UK stillbirth rates would be 5. Stillbirth rate = number of stillbirths ÷ by total births (stillbirths + total live births) × 1,000.

Source: Annual Abstract of Statistics 2000, © *Crown copyright 2000*

See also **Infant and Maternal Mortality in the UK**, p 526.

Death Rates per 1,000 Population in the UK

(N/A = not available.)

Year	0–4	5–9	10–14	15–19	20–24	25–34	35–44	45–54	55–64	65–74	75–84	85 and over	All ages
Men													
1900–02	57.0	4.1	2.4	3.7	5.0	6.6	11.0	18.6	35.0	69.9	143.6	289.6	18.4
1910–12	40.5	3.3	2.0	3.0	3.9	5.0	8.0	14.9	29.8	62.1	133.8	261.5	14.9
1920–22	33.4	2.9	1.8	2.9	3.9	4.5	6.9	11.9	25.3	57.8	131.8	259.1	13.5
1930–32	22.3	2.3	1.5	2.6	3.3	3.5	5.7	11.3	23.7	57.9	134.2	277.0	12.9
1940–42	N/A	N/A	N/A	N/A	N/A	N/A	N/A	N/A	N/A	N/A	N/A	N/A	N/A
1950–52	7.7	0.7	0.5	0.9	1.4	1.6	3.0	8.5	23.2	55.2	127.6	272.0	12.6
1960–62	6.4	0.5	0.4	0.9	1.1	1.1	2.5	7.4	22.2	54.4	123.4	251.0	12.5
1970–72	4.6	0.4	0.4	0.9	1.0	1.0	2.4	7.3	20.9	52.9	116.3	246.1	12.4
1980–82	3.2	0.3	0.3	0.8	0.9	0.9	1.9	6.3	18.2	46.7	107.1	224.9	12.1
1990–92	2.0	0.2	0.2	0.7	0.9	0.9	1.8	4.6	14.3	38.7	92.9	195.7	11.1
1998	1.5	0.1	0.2	0.6	0.9	1.0	1.6	4.1	11.7	33.1	82.0	188.1	10.3
Women													
1900–02	47.9	4.3	2.6	3.5	4.3	5.8	9.0	14.4	27.9	59.3	127.0	262.6	16.3
1910–12	34.0	3.3	2.1	2.9	3.4	4.4	6.7	11.5	23.1	50.7	113.7	234.0	13.3
1920–22	26.9	2.8	1.9	2.8	3.4	4.1	5.6	9.3	19.2	45.6	111.5	232.4	11.9
1930–32	17.7	2.1	1.5	2.4	2.9	3.3	4.6	8.3	17.6	43.7	110.1	246.3	11.5
1940–42	N/A	N/A	N/A	N/A	N/A	N/A	N/A	N/A	N/A	N/A	N/A	N/A	N/A
1950–52	6.0	0.5	0.4	0.7	1.0	1.4	2.3	5.3	12.9	35.5	98.4	228.8	11.2
1960–62	4.9	0.3	0.3	0.4	0.5	0.8	1.8	4.5	11.0	30.8	87.3	218.5	11.2
1970–72	3.6	0.3	0.2	0.4	0.4	0.6	1.6	4.5	10.5	27.5	76.7	196.1	11.3
1980–82	2.3	0.2	0.2	0.3	0.4	0.5	1.3	3.9	9.9	24.8	67.2	179.5	11.4
1990–92	1.6	0.1	0.2	0.3	0.3	0.4	1.1	2.9	8.4	22.2	58.5	154.6	11.1
1998	1.2	0.1	0.1	0.3	0.3	0.4	1.0	2.7	7.0	20.3	54.4	153.3	10.9

Source: Annual Abstract of Statistics 2000, © *Crown copyright 2000*

The UK's Increasingly Diverse Population

Over recent years the UK population has grown by around 150,000 per annum, with around half of this growth contributed by net immigration. This has largely been a result of settlement of children, wives, and husbands born overseas of spouses already settled in the UK, although there has also been a recent increase in the number of political asylum refugees from troubled parts of the Balkans and Africa. The current ethnic minority population in the UK amounts to 3.6 million, equivalent to 6% of the total population. Nearly half of this community has its origins in the Indian subcontinent. Some of the ethnic minority groups have much younger age structures than the broader population. For example, 45% of the UK Bangladeshi community are under the age of 16.

Ethnic Groups in Great Britain

Average over the period summer 1998 to spring 1999.

Ethnic group	Number
Black	
Caribbean	485,000
African	365,000
other (non-mixed)	108,000
mixed	192,000
Indian	942,000
Pakistani	591,000
Bangladeshi	257,000
Chinese	159,000
Other	
Asian (non-mixed)	191,000
other (non-mixed)	165,000
mixed	248,000
All ethnic minority groups	3,702,000
White	53,090,000
All ethnic groups[1]	56,807,000

[1] Figure includes ethnic groups not stated.

Source: Annual Abstract of Statistics 2000, © *Crown copyright 2000*

Migration into and out of the UK

Year	Inflow	Outflow	Balance
1986	250,000	213,000	37,000
1987	212,000	210,000	2,000
1988	216,000	237,000	– 21,000
1989	250,000	205,000	44,000
1990	267,000	231,000	36,000
1991	267,000	239,000	28,000
1992	216,000	227,000	– 11,000
1993	213,000	216,000	– 2,000
1994	253,000	191,000	62,000
1995	245,000	192,000	54,000
1996	272,000	216,000	56,000
1997	285,000	225,000	60,000

Source: Annual Abstract of Statistics 2000, © *Crown copyright 2000*

See also **Asylum Seekers in the UK**, p 103.

The Size of Households in the UK

The average size of UK households has almost halved since the beginning of the 20th century to 2.4 people per household in 1998. This has been a result of the declining birth rate, but also an increase in the number of single persons per household.

Between 1961 and 1998, the proportion of households which comprised only one person more than doubled to 28%. Half of these comprised lone pensioners, particularly female, who, with higher life expectancy, had outlived their spouses. A half of women aged 65 and over in 1998 were widows and in the age group of 75 years and above the ratio of women to men is 1.8:1. However, the growth in single person households below pensionable age has been even greater. This has been caused partly by an increasing tendency for marriages to end in divorce: the number of divorces in the UK more than doubled between 1970 and 1996, although the 1996 total was slightly lower than the peak year of 1993. However, those divorced frequently re-marry or co-habit with another partner after an interval alone: in 1996 two-fifths of all marriages were remarriages.

In 1998, out of the total population of around 59 million, around an eighth lived alone, a quarter as couples without children, a half as couples with children, and a tenth in lone parent families. Since 1961, the proportion of households consisting of a lone parent with dependent children has trebled. In 1998, lone parent families made up a quarter of all households with dependent children (defined as children under 15 years or of any age in full-time education): up from 8% in 1971.

Households by Type of Occupancy in Great Britain

A household is defined as a person or group of persons residing at the same address. Figures are expressed as percentages of the total. (N/A = not available.)

Household		1961	1971	1981	1991	1998–99
One person	under pensionable age	4	6	8	11	14
	over pensionable age	7	12	14	16	15
Two or more unrelated adults		5	4	5	3	2
Single family households[1]	couple, no children	26	27	26	28	30
	couple, one or two dependent children[2]	30	26	25	20	19
	couple, three or more dependent children[2]	8	9	6	5	4
	couple, non-dependent children only	10	8	8	8	6
	lone parent, dependent children[2]	2	3	5	6	7
	lone parent, non-dependent children only	4	4	4	4	3
	Multi-family households	3	1	1	1	1
	All households	16.3	18.6	20.2	22.4	N/A

[1] Other individuals who were not family members may be included.
[2] May also include non-dependent children.

Source: Social Trends 30,

See also  **Birth, Marriage, and Death,** pp 314–320.

Wealth Distribution in the UK: Introduction

In 1995, 10% of the population held a half of the country's wealth and a half of the population barely 8%. This pattern of wealth distribution has been broadly stable since the 1980s.

Across the UK, there are significant differences in levels of wealth, GDP per head, in 1996, being 52% higher in the richest region, London, than in the poorest, Northern Ireland. Although it can be overly simplistic to refer to a broad 'North-South divide', as there exist pockets of extreme wealth and poverty within many of the UK's regions, there are broad differences between London and the South East and Eastern regions of England and other parts of the UK. There are differences in wealth per head, earnings and house price level, and a range of social and economic indicators. Significantly, the three richest regions of the UK are also the closest to the European continent, which is now the focus of UK economic activity.

See also **Wealthiest Executives in the UK**, p 682.

The Richest and Poorest Regions of the UK

Data are for GDP per head at factor cost (excluding taxes on expenditure and subsidies). Figures are index numbers where UK = 100.

Region	1997
London	125
South East	118
Eastern	102
South West	98
East Midlands	96
West Midlands	93
North West and Merseyside	91
Yorkshire and the Humber	89
North East	83
England	102
Scotland	96
Wales	82
Northern Ireland	80
UK	100

Source: Social Trends 30,

Individual Distribution of Wealth in the UK

Marketable wealth owned by sectors of the population (adults aged 18 and over). Figures are expressed as percentages of the total marketable wealth.

Sector of population	Percentage of wealth owned				
	1976	1981	1986	1991	1996
Most wealthy 1%	21	18	18	17	19
Most wealthy 5%	38	36	36	35	39
Most wealthy 10%	50	50	50	47	52
Most wealthy 25%	71	73	73	71	74
Most wealthy 50%	92	92	90	92	93

Source: Social Trends 30, © *Crown copyright 2000*

Life in the UK – Yesterday and Today

(– = not applicable.)

	May 1979	May 1989	May 1999
Leaders and economy			
Government	Conservative	Conservative	Labour
Prime Minister	Margaret Thatcher	Margaret Thatcher	Tony Blair
Chancellor of the Exchequer	Geoffrey Howe	Nigel Lawson	Gordon Brown
Inflation rate	13.4%	7.8%	3.4%
Interest rate	12%	13.75%	5.5%
Unemployment	1.86 million 4.1%	1.81 million 6.1%	1.31 million 4.6%
Women in the workforce	44%	49%	51%
Average income	£5,000	£11,700	£19,000
Average manager's income	£9,000	£25,700	£36,400
What things cost			
Average house price in Britain	£19,800	£61,500	£68,300
Price of a loaf of bread	28p	48p	51p
Price of a Mars bar	14p	22p	25p
Price of a pint of beer	38p	91p	£1.73
What we liked			
Most popular car	Ford Cortina	Ford Fiesta	Ford Focus
Most popular wine	Hirondelle	Piat d'Or	Jacob's Creek
Popular TV programmes	*Blankety Blank, Top of the Pops, Little and Large Show*	*Coronation Street, Neighbours, EastEnders, The Bill*	*EastEnders, Coronation Street, Emmerdale, Stars in their Eyes*
Popular leisure activities	Gardening (59%), dancing (58%), eating out (42%)	Pubs/bars (55%), eating out (47%), DIY (44%)	Pubs/bars (74%), eating out (69%), gardening (52%)
Most popular holiday destination	Spain (visited by 1.9 million)	Spain (visited by 5.7 million)	Spain (visited by 7.7 million)
What we owned (% of individuals/households)			
Cars	60	68	70
Houses	52	66	68
Telephones	75	88	93
Colour televisions	74	95	98
Washing machines	74	87	91
Videos	–	60	82
Home computers	–	19	27
CD players	–	15	58

Source: The Independent

Asylum in the UK

Asylum Seekers in the UK

(N/A = not available.)

Applications and decisions	1996	1997	1998
Applications received (region of origin)			
Europe	6,470	5,210	17,740
Africa	11,290	5,470	12,380
Asia[1]	10,030	5,850	14,730
Other	1,840	790	1,170
Total	29,640	17,310	46,010
Cases considered under normal procedures			
Recognized as a refugee and granted asylum			
Europe	1,220	820	1,060
Africa	210	1,240	3,320
Asia	800	300	800
Other	10	20	180
Total	2,240	2,390	5,350

(continued)

Asylum Seekers in the UK *(continued)*

Not recognized as a refugee but granted exceptional leave			
Europe	370	230	170
Africa	3,900	920	1,290
Asia[1]	780	500	2,380
Other	10	20	70
Total	5,050	1,670	3,910
Refused asylum and exceptional leave			
Europe	4,910	3,380	7,260
Africa	15,950	4,590	5,470
Asia[1]	10,090	4,590	7,680
Other	720	1,030	1,910
Total	31,670	13,590	22,320
Total number of decisions	38,960	17,640	31,570

[1] Including Middle East.

Source: Home Office Statistical Bulletin, Issue 20/99, © *Crown copyright 1999*

See also **Numbers of Refugees Worldwide**, p 296; **Migration into and out of the UK**, p 101.

The Determination of Asylum Applications in the UK

Decisions = the number of cases considered each month that are resolved.

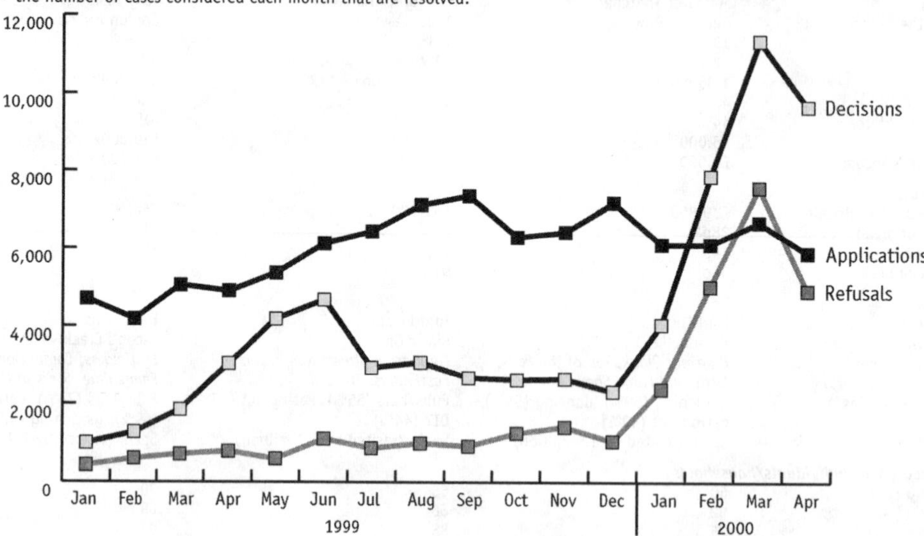

Asylum Seekers: Is the UK a Safe Haven?

by Denis Derbyshire and Ian Derbyshire

Introduction The right of asylum for people fleeing from oppression is a fundamental liberty. It is enshrined in the United Nations' Universal Declaration of Human Rights (1948) and 1951 Convention Relating to the Status of Refugees (and its 1967 Protocol), which prohibit the return of those persecuted on the grounds of race, religion, nationality, or membership of a political or social group. Article 3 of the European Convention on Human Rights (1953) and Article 3.1 of the UN Convention Against Torture (1984) prohibit the return of those facing torture and inhuman or degrading treatment.

Applications Rise Political turmoil, civil war, border conflicts, and intolerant leadership create refugee outflows. These events are abnormal: consequently, demand for asylum tends to ebb and flow. Between 1989 and 1991, with the collapse of the USSR, growing ethnic tensions in Yugoslavia, and war between Iraq and the UN, the number of asylum applications to the UK, which had previously averaged around 4,000 per annum, rose suddenly to 82,000. This was beyond the capacity of the asylum determination system. As a consequence, the backlog of undecided cases awaiting an initial decision grew from 12,000 to 72,000. Despite a reduced application level during the next few years, the backlog remained high and, with turmoil in the Balkans, it began to increase once again between 1997 and 1999 as the monthly number of asylum applications doubled to more than 6,000. The chief countries of origin of the most recent asylum applications have been Yugoslavia (including Kosovan refugees), Sri Lanka (where the civil war has entered its 17th year), Somalia, Afghanistan, Turkey, Iraq (including many Kurds), China, and Albania.

The Crisis in Asylum Management In December 1999 the backlog of applications outstanding passed 100,000 for the first time and tensions began to mount in the communities of the main entry ports, notably Dover, where large numbers of asylum

ASYLUM SEEKERS: IS THE UK A SAFE HAVEN? (*continued*)

seekers were being held. This prompted stinging criticism of the Labour government's asylum management by the Conservative party's leader, William Hague, and its home affairs spokesperson, Ann Widdecombe. With inordinate delays in processing applications and recent amnesties for around 30,000 applicants who had been waiting since 1996 for a final ruling, the government was charged with having made the UK a 'soft target' for 'bogus' asylum seekers, who were really economic migrants. Statistics did show that, typically, less than a fifth of applicants whose cases have been considered are eventually recognized as genuine refugees and granted asylum. A further eighth are granted exceptional leave on compassionate grounds. The remainder, amounting to more than two-thirds of asylum applicants, are refused asylum. Many of these escape deportation through 'disappearing' amongst the general population: at least 100,000 during the 1990s.

A New Approach In July 1998, in response to these criticisms, the government published a white paper, 'Fairer, Faster, and Firmer: a Modern Approach to Immigration and Asylum', that formed the basis for a new Immigration and Asylum Act (1999). The act was intended to deal with abuses of the asylum system and make the UK less attractive to 'economic migrants'. This it sought to achieve through:

- Moving from a three-tier asylum determination system – comprising initial decision, independent review, and second stage appeal – to a two-tier system. Initial decisions are made by a new National Asylum Support Services (NASS) within two months for families with children (against the prevailing average of 13 months), and appeals are resolved by the Immigration Appeal Tribunal (IAT) within a further four months.
- Replacing asylum seekers' entitlements to cash welfare benefits with food and clothing vouchers, and no longer offering them a choice of where to live.
- Removing such responsibility for destitute asylum seekers from individual local authorities to the NASS and dispersing those awaiting decisions from the southeast, particularly London where 80% of asylum seekers were based, to 'cluster areas' around the country.
- Imposing financial penalties of £2,000 for each person discovered on carriers of illegal entrants hidden in vehicles entering the UK.
- Experimenting with the detention of applicants with straightforward cases in special camps and making a decision within seven days

A new 'fast-track' processing centre was opened in March 2000 in Oakington. Cambridgeshire, with accommodation for 400 asylum seekers and the capacity to deal with 13,000 cases a year. It was expected to cost £11 million to run each year and to save £30 million on benefits and other spending for asylum seekers. Other centres were planned for Manston, Kent, and Thurleigh, Bedfordshire. In May 2000 Home Secretary Jack Straw also announced the establishment of a special squad of immigration officers, equipped with handcuffs and body armour, to track down the more than 20,000 asylum seekers who had 'gone missing' to escape deportation.

The Cost – Is the UK a 'Soft Target'? The Conservatives, who advocated more detention centres like Oakington, played the 'asylum card' in the May 2000 local elections and may have benefited electorally. However, by the early summer of 2000 the government was able to claim that their recent changes had brought progress. The number of decisions taken each month began to average around 10,000 from March 2000, while applications began to fall below 6,000 a month. This enabled the backlog in asylum applications to be brought down to around 90,000, although, at this rate it would still take several years for the backlog to be fully cleared. The direct and indirect cost to the UK of supporting asylum seekers soared to more than £900 million in 1999– 2000. However, measured by asylum applications per 100 of population, the UK ranked eighth out of the 15 EU countries, while financial support provided to asylum seekers was considerably more generous in the Republic of Ireland and Sweden – facts that belie Conservative rhetoric that the UK is a 'soft target' for 'bogus asylum seekers'.

Employment and Unemployment

Distribution of the Workforce in the UK

Figures are the number at mid-June of each year. (In thousands.)

Category	1992	1993	1994	1995	1996	1997	1998	1999
Claimant unemployed[1]	2,734	2,919	2,644	2,308	2,146	1,598	1,361	1,269
Workforce jobs[2]	25,973	25,629	25,776	26,063	26,728	27,239	27,508	27,747
HM Forces[3]	290	271	250	230	221	210	210	208
Self-employment jobs[4]	3,441	3,446	3,548	3,608	3,609	3,598	3,475	3,497
Employees jobs	21,902	21,586	21,661	21,985	22,702	23,257	23,699	23,929
Government-supported trainee[5]	340	326	317	240	195	173	124	112

[1] Claimant unemployment: those people who were claiming unemployment-related benefits (Unemployment Benefit, Income Support, or National Insurance Credits) at Employment Service local offices on the day of the monthly count. [2] Workforce jobs comprise employee jobs, self-employment jobs, HM Forces, and government-supported trainees. [3] HM Forces figures represent the total number of UK service personnel, male and female, in HM Regular Forces, wherever serving, and including those on release leave. [4] Estimates of self-employed jobs are based on the results of the Labour Force Survey. The Northern Ireland estimates are not seasonally adjusted. [5] Figures include all participants on government training and employment programmes who are receiving some work experience on their placement but do not have a contract of employment. The numbers are not subject to seasonal adjustment.

Source: Annual Abstract of Statistics 2000, © *Crown copyright 2000*

Labour Force by Gender and Age in the UK

(In millions.)

Year	16–24	25–44	45–54	55–59	60–64	65 and over	All aged 16 and over
Men							
1971	3.0	6.5	3.2	1.5	1.3	0.6	16.0
1981	3.2	7.1	3.0	1.4	1.0	0.3	16.0
1991	3.1	8.1	3.0	1.1	0.8	0.3	16.4
1997	2.4	8.1	3.4	1.1	0.7	0.3	16.0
2001[1]	2.4	8.2	3.4	1.3	0.7	0.3	16.3
2011[1]	2.8	7.3	3.9	1.3	0.9	0.3	16.5
Women							
1971	2.3	3.5	2.1	0.9	0.5	0.3	10.0
1981	2.7	4.6	2.1	0.9	0.4	0.2	10.9
1991	2.6	6.1	2.4	0.8	0.3	0.2	12.4
1997	2.0	6.4	2.9	0.8	0.4	0.2	12.7
2001[1]	2.1	6.4	3.0	0.9	0.4	0.2	13.1
2011[1]	2.3	6.2	3.6	1.0	0.7	0.2	14.1

[1] Data for 2001 and 2011 are based on the spring 1996 Labour Force Survey and mid-1996 based population projections.

Source: Social Trends 30, © *Crown copyright 2000*

See also Employment, pp 275–277.

Economic Activity of Women with Children in the UK

In percentages unless otherwise indicated. As of spring 1999.
(N/A = not available.)

Status	Age of youngest dependent child				No dependent children	All women[2]
	Under 5	5–10	11–15	16–18[1]		
Not married/cohabiting[3]						
working full time	11	19	32	48	47	40
working part time	20	30	32	25	20	22
unemployed[4]	7	11	6	N/A	5	6
economically inactive	62	39	31	21	28	32
Total (millions)	0.7	0.6	0.4	0.1	4.5	6.2
Married/cohabiting						
working full time	21	25	37	41	50	38
working part time	38	50	42	38	25	34
unemployed[4]	3	3	2	N/A	2	2
economically inactive	38	22	19	20	23	25
Total (millions)	2.3	1.7	1.2	0.5	5.2	10.9

[1] Those in full-time education. [2] All women aged 16 to 59. [3] Includes single, widowed, separated, or divorced. [4] Based on the International Labour Organization definition.

Source: Social Trends 30, © *Crown copyright 2000*

Average Gross Weekly Earnings by Region and Gender in the UK

As of April 1996. Data relate to full-time employees on adult rates whose pay for the survey pay-period was not affected by absence.
(In pounds.)

Region	Manual male employees	Non-manual male employees	All full-time male employees	Manual female employees	Non-manual female employees	All full-time female employees
England						
North East	319.1	442.6	377.5	206.8	290.2	273.6
North West	323.7	480.1	404.4	207.3	303.7	287.1
Yorkshire and the Humber	316.3	440.5	387.7	197.0	300.7	281.0
East Midlands	320.5	456.0	387.8	203.8	293.0	271.5
West Midlands	327.3	471.6	399.1	203.7	303.5	282.3
East	336.0	483.2	416.7	218.8	323.6	307.7
London	366.7	645.9	565.6	242.1	420.1	402.8
South East	337.4	525.2	453.9	223.2	340.8	323.5
South West	309.3	461.2	392.4	202.3	304.5	286.2
England average	329.1	513.1	432.8	212.0	334.4	314.2
Wales	327.0	431.9	376.4	210.3	301.9	282.8
Scotland	322.6	462.3	394.6	201.1	298.2	276.7
Northern Ireland	284.4	440.0	367.7	182.4	297.4	277.6
UK AVERAGE	327.2	504.5	425.6	209.9	329.1	308.7

Source: Regional Trends 34, © *Crown copyright 1999*

■ Employment and Unemployment

Average Weekly Earnings and Hours in the UK

Data relate to full-time employees on adult rates.

Year	Manufacturing industries				All industries and services			
	Weekly earnings (£)	Hours	Hourly earnings (£) Including overtime pay and overtime hours	Hourly earnings (£) Excluding overtime pay and overtime hours	Weekly earnings (£)[1]	Hours	Hourly earnings (£) Including overtime pay and overtime hours	Hourly earnings (£) Excluding overtime pay and overtime hours
Men								
1990	289.2	43.4	6.55	6.50	295.6	42.2	6.88	6.89
1991	308.1	42.1	7.20	7.15	318.9	41.5	7.55	7.57
1992	328.3	42.3	7.62	7.58	340.1	41.4	8.07	8.10
1993	342.7	42.1	7.99	7.95	353.5	41.3	8.44	8.47
1994	350.9	42.5	8.16	8.12	362.1	41.6	8.61	8.65
1995	364.0	43.0	8.44	8.41	374.6	41.9	8.91	8.97
1996	380.0	42.7	8.86	8.81	391.3	41.7	9.33	9.38
1997	392.7	42.8	9.17	9.12	408.7	41.8	9.74	9.82
1998	416.8	42.6	9.75	9.72	427.1	41.7	10.20	10.26
1999	424.6	42.0	10.10	10.06	442.4	41.1	10.68	10.75
Women								
1990	177.1	39.1	4.48	4.44	201.5	37.5	5.30	5.28
1991	192.9	38.8	4.94	4.91	222.4	37.4	5.91	5.89
1992	207.1	38.9	5.28	5.24	241.1	37.3	6.40	6.38
1993	220.0	38.9	5.61	5.57	252.6	37.4	6.70	6.68
1994	226.8	39.1	5.76	5.72	261.5	37.6	6.89	6.88
1995	236.7	39.4	6.01	5.96	269.8	37.6	7.15	7.14
1996	246.7	39.3	6.27	6.23	283.0	37.6	7.51	7.49
1997	258.8	39.2	6.60	6.56	297.2	37.6	7.88	7.88
1998	274.5	39.2	7.01	6.97	309.6	37.6	8.23	8.22
1999	292.1	39.0	7.49	7.46	326.5	37.5	8.71	8.70
Average								
1990	262.8	42.4	6.09	6.01	263.1	40.5	6.37	6.34
1991	280.7	41.3	6.69	6.62	284.7	40.0	7.00	6.98
1992	299.7	41.5	7.09	7.02	304.6	39.9	7.50	7.49
1993	313.7	41.3	7.45	7.39	316.9	39.8	7.84	7.83
1994	321.6	41.7	7.62	7.55	325.7	40.1	8.03	8.03
1995	334.3	42.2	7.92	7.85	336.3	40.3	8.31	8.32
1996	349.3	41.9	8.29	8.22	351.5	40.2	8.70	8.71
1997	361.7	42.0	8.61	8.53	367.6	40.3	9.10	9.13
1998	384.5	41.8	9.17	9.10	384.5	40.2	9.53	9.54
1999	395.3	41.4	9.55	9.49	400.1	40.0	10.01	10.03

[1] Excluding those whose pay was affected by absence.

Source: Annual Abstract of Statistics 2000

The Minimum Wage – Is it Working?

by Richard Dickens

Introduction On 1 April 1999 a national minimum wage was introduced in the UK. Workers aged over 22 years would receive minimum compensation of £3.60 per hour, while those aged 18 to 21 would receive at least £3 per hour. The government introduced the minimum wage in response to growing inequality of wages within the labour market. In June 1998 the first report of the Low Pay Commission found that the pay gap between high- and low-paid workers had increased sharply over the previous 20 years or so to levels not observed in over 100 years, with a resulting rise in 'inwork' poverty. The minimum wage was designed to redress this by raising the wages of the lowest-paid British workers.

Have Wages Risen? At present there is little evidence on what has actually happened to wages, but the available information suggests that there has been a significant increase in wages for workers covered. In February 2000, based on evidence prior to introduction, the Low Pay Commission's second report suggested that 1.5–1.7 million workers will have been affected by the minimum wage,with an average wage increase of about 30%. Two thirds of those affected are women and, of these, two thirds are part-time workers. Currently the best piece of evidence on the impact of introduction comes from a survey of residential care homes, one of the lowest-paying sectors, published by Rahman, Machn, and Manning of the Centre for Economic Performance, London School of Economics, in 2000. This shows a huge fall in the number of low-paid workers, as those paid below the minimum wage prior to enforcement experienced wage increases bringing them up to the minimum. Before introduction, about 5.5% of workers were paid the minimum wage; after introduction, this increased sharply to 25.5%. The introduction of the wage floor resulted in a sharp fall in pay inequalities within this sector.

THE MINIMUM WAGE – IS IT WORKING? *(continued)*

Have Jobs Been Lost? Much of the debate over the introduction of the minimum wage concerned its potential impact on jobs. The Low Pay Commission was keen to stress that it was acting cautiously in setting the rate and did not expect any significant impact on jobs. The projected increase of 0.5% in the overall wage bill was very small and earlier studies of the wages councils, which had previously set minimum rates in selected industries, had failed to find any evidence of job loss. Since introduction, employment growth has remained strong in all sectors of the economy, making it difficult to isolate any effects from the minimum wage. Evidence from the study of residential care homes shows that those homes forced to raise their wages the most to comply with the minimum wage were more likely to experience some fall in employment or hours worked. However, although the largest effects on employment would be expected in this sector, the impact is estimated to be small.

Where To From Here? The minimum wage is generally considered to have been successful in raising the wages of the low-paid without significantly hurting their employment prospects. Consequently, the government has legislated for an increase in the minimum to £3.70 per hour for adults from October 2000 and £3.20 per hour for young workers in June 2000. Furthermore, the secretary of state for trade and industry is discussing the possibility of linking future increases in the minimum wage to average earnings growth.

Average Weekly Earnings and Hours in Great Britain

Earnings and hours are calculated in April for each year. Data relate to full-time employees on adult rates.
(In pounds.)

Worker category	Average weekly earnings[1]		Average hours	
	1994	1999	1994	1999
Men				
Manual	280.7	335.0	44.7	44.4
Non-manual	428.2	525.5	38.9	39.0
All men	362.1	442.4	41.6	41.4
Women				
Manual	181.9	221.9	40.1	39.9
Non-manual	278.4	346.9	37.0	37.0
All women	261.5	326.5	37.6	37.5
TOTAL	325.7	400.1	40.1	40.0

[1] Figures exclude those whose pay was affected by absence.

Source: Annual Abstract of Statistics 2000, © *Crown copyright 2000*

Unemployment Rates by Gender and Age in the UK

At spring each year. Unemployment is based on the International Labour Organization definition as a percentage of all economically active persons.
(In percentages. N/A = not available.)

Age	1994	1995	1996	1997	1998	1999
Men						
16–17	18.8	18.9	21.2	19.3	18.0	21.6
18–24	19.2	17.7	17.1	14.8	13.0	12.5
25–44	10.2	9.0	8.7	7.0	5.8	5.6
45–54	8.6	7.4	6.4	6.1	4.8	4.9
55–59	11.6	10.2	9.9	8.0	6.7	6.4
60–64	11.6	9.9	8.9	7.6	7.0	6.4
65 and over	3.7	N/A	4.1	4.0	N/A	N/A
Average	11.4	10.1	9.7	8.1	6.8	6.8
Women						
16–17	17.0	15.6	15.1	16.0	15.2	14.0
18–24	11.8	11.5	10.2	9.7	9.3	9.3
25–44	7.0	6.7	6.3	5.4	5.2	4.8
45–54	5.0	4.5	4.1	3.8	3.1	3.2
55–59	6.5	4.7	4.2	4.8	3.5	3.6
60 and over	2.9	N/A	N/A	2.0	2.0	1.9
Average	7.3	6.8	6.3	5.8	5.3	5.1

Source: Social Trends 30, © *Crown copyright 2000*

Unemployment by Region of the UK

Figures are for the spring quarter of each year.
(In percentages.)

Region	1994	1995	1996	1997	1998
England					
North East	12.5	11.4	10.8	9.8	8.2
North West	10.3	9.0	8.4	6.9	6.6
Yorkshire and the Humber	9.9	8.7	8.1	8.1	7.0
East Midlands	8.3	7.5	7.4	6.3	4.9
West Midlands	10.0	9.0	9.2	6.8	6.3
East	8.2	7.5	6.2	5.9	5.0
London	13.1	11.5	11.3	9.1	8.1
South East	7.1	6.4	6.0	5.2	4.3
South West	7.5	7.8	6.3	5.2	4.5
Average England	9.5	8.6	8.1	6.9	6.0
Scotland	10.0	8.3	8.7	8.5	7.4
Wales	9.3	8.8	8.3	8.4	6.7
Northern Ireland	11.7	11.0	9.7	7.5	7.3
Average UK	9.6	8.6	8.2	7.1	6.1

Source: Regional Trends 34, © *Crown copyright 1999*

Trade Unions of the UK

The Largest Trade Unions in the UK

Rank	1990 Union	Membership	1998 Union	Membership
1	Transport and General Workers Union	1,224,000	UNISON – The Public Service Union	1,272,330
2	GMB	865,000	Transport and General Workers Union	881,625
3	National and Local Government Officers Association	744,000	Amalgamated Engineering and Electrical Union	727,977
4	Amalgamated Engineering Union	702,000	GMB	712,010
5	Manufacturing Science and Finance Union	653,000	Manufacturing Science and Finance Union	416,000
6	National Union of Public Employees	579,000	Royal College of Nursing of the UK	320,206
7	Electrical Electronic Telecommunication and Plumbing Union	367,000	Union of Shop Distributive and Allied Workers	303,060
8	Union of Shop Distributive and Allied Workers	362,000	Communication Workers Union	287,732
9	Royal College of Nursing of the UK	289,000	National Union of Teachers	286,503
10	National Union of Teachers	218,000	National Association of School Masters and Union of Women Teachers	250,783

Source: Annual Report of the Certification Officer for Trades Unions and Employers' Associations 1999–2000, © *Crown copyright 2000*

The Largest Trade Unions of the UK

The TUC membership now stands at 78 unions, representing 6.8 million people. For more information, contact: Trades Union Congress, Congress House, Great Russell Street, London WC1B 3LS; phone: (020) 7636 4030; fax: (020) 7636 0632; e-mail: info@tuc.org.uk; Web site: www.tuc.org.uk. (GS = General Secretary; NS = National Secretary)

Amalgamated Engineering and Electrical Union (AEEU) Hayes Court, West Common Road, Bromley, Kent BR2 7AU; phone: (020) 8462 7755; fax: (020) 8315 8234; e-mail: a.mayne@headoffice.aeeu.org.uk; Web site: www.aeeu.org.uk **Membership** m 678,135, f 47,161, total 720,296. **GS** Ken Jackson

Communication Workers Union (CWU) 150 The Broadway, Wimbledon, London 5W19 1RX; phone: (020) 8971 7200; fax: (020) 8971 7300; Web site: www.cwu.org **GS** Derek Hodgson

GMB 22/24 Worple Road, London SW19 4DD; phone: (020) 8 947 3131; fax: (020) 8944 6552; e-mail: john.edmonds@gmb.org.uk; Web site: www.gmbunion.org **GS and treasurer** John Edmonds

Manufacturing Science Finance (MSF) MSF Centre, 33–37 Moreland Street, London EC1V 8HA; phone: (020) 7505 3000/7939 7000; fax: (020) 7505 3030; Web site: www.msf.org.uk **GS** Roger Lyons

National Association of Schoolmasters and Union of Women Teachers (NASUWT) 5 Wendle Court, 131–137 Wandsworth Road, London SW8 2LH; phone: (020) 7920 5706; fax: (020) 7978 1860; Web site: www.teachersunion.org.uk **GS** Nigel de Gruchy

National Union of Teachers (NUT) Hamilton House, Mabledon Place, London WC1H 9BD; phone: (020) 7388 6191; fax: (020) 7387 8458; Web site: www.teachers.org.uk **GS** Doug McAvoy

Royal College of Nursing 194 Euston Road, London NW11 2DG (until autumn 2000); 20 Cavendish Square, London W1M OAB (from autumn 2000); phone: (020) 7409 3333; fax: (020) 7647 3435; Web site: www.rcn.org.uk **GS** Christine Hancock

Transport and General Workers Union (TGWU) Transport House, 128 Theobald Road, Holborn, London WC1X 8TA; phone: (020) 7611 2500; fax (020) 7611 2555; e-mail: tgwu@tgwu.org.uk; Web site: www.tgwu.org.uk **GS** Bill Morris

Union of Shop, Distributive, and Allied Workers (USDAW) Oakley, 188 Wilmslow Road, Fallowfield, Manchester M14 6LJ; phone: (0161) 224 2804; fax: (0161) 257 2566; e-mail: usdaw-co@mcr1.poptel.org.uk; Web site: www.poptel.org.uk/usdaw/ **GS** Bill Connor

UNISON 1 Mabledon Place, London WC1H 9AJ; phone: (020) 7388 2366; fax: (020) 7387 6692; e-mail: union-mable@unison.org.uk; Web site: www.unison.org.uk **GS** Rodney Bickerstaffe

Trade Union Membership by Type of Job and Length of Service in Great Britain

Figures include all employees, except for those in the armed forces.
(N = base too low to provide a reliable estimate.)

1998	All (%)	Full time (%)	Part time (%)
All employees	30	33	20
Length of service			
Less than 1 year	11	13	8
1 to 2 years	16	18	12
2 to 5 years	22	24	16
5 to 10 years	35	37	27
10 to 20 years	47	49	40
20 years or more	59	61	42
Occupational group			
Managers and administrators	19	19	17
Professional	49	50	45
Associate professional/technical	44	42	52
Clerical and secretarial	24	27	18
Craft and related	32	33	13
Personal and protective	27	37	17
Sales	11	11	11
Plant and machine operatives	38	40	18
Other occupations	27	37	16
Managerial status			
Manager	25	25	25
Foreman or supervisor	38	38	36
No managerial duties	29	35	18
Employment status			
Permanent	31	34	21
Temporary	19	20	18
Special working arrangements			
Flexitime	42	45	30
Job sharing	37	N	36
Term-time working	45	71	27
Annualized hours contract	46	49	32
9-day fortnight/4.5-day week	45	46	N

Source: Labour Market Trends, © *Crown copyright 1999*

Labour Disputes in the UK

These figures exclude details of stoppages involving fewer than ten workers or lasting less than one day except any in which the aggregate number of working days lost exceeded 100. There may be some under-recording of small or short stoppages. Some stoppages that affected more than one industry group have been counted under each of the industries but only once in the totals. The figures have been rounded and consequently the sum of the constituent items may not agree with the totals. Classifications by size are based on the full duration of stoppages where these continue into the following year. Working days lost per 1,000 employees are based on the latest available mid-year (June) estimates of employees in employment.
(N = nil or negligible. In thousands.)

		1994	1995	1996	1997	1998
Working days lost through all stoppages in progress						
Analysis by industry	mining, quarrying, electricity, gas, and water	1	1	2	2	N
	manufacturing	58	65	97	86	34
	construction	5	10	8	17	13
	transport, storage, and communication	110	120	884	36	139
	public administration and defence	11	95	158	29	28
	education	70	67	128	28	6
	health and social work	5	16	8	7	16
	other community, social, and personal services	11	23	3	5	30
	all other industries and services	8	16	15	25	15
	Total	278	415	1,303	235	282
Analysis by number of working days lost in each stoppage	under 250 days	11	11	14	12	8
	250–499 days	6	10	13	6	11
	500–999 days	24	19	13	17	11
	1,000–4,999 days	53	82	61	72	48
	5,000–24,999 days	68	195	123	101	118
	25,000–49,999 days	N	29	54	26	N
	50,000 days and over	117	68	1,025	N	86
Working days lost per 1,000 employees, all industries and services		13	19	58	10	12
Workers directly and indirectly involved						
Analysis by industry	mining, quarrying, electricity, gas, and water	N	2	1	N	1
	manufacturing	23	33	34	28	14
	construction	1	2	3	13	2
	transport, storage, and communication	37	54	146	24	39
	public administration and defence	8	28	32	20	4
	education	29	30	122	15	4

(continued)

Labour Disputes in the UK (*continued*)

		1994	1995	1996	1997	1998
	health and social work	2	4	5	5	2
	other community, social, and personal services	2	10	2	1	22
	all other industries and services	5	11	21	23	4
	Total	107	174	364	130	93
Analysis by duration of stoppage	not more than 5 days	75	142	208	108	57
	6–10 days	5	11	133	7	32
	11–20 days	1	2	4	14	1
	21–30 days	6	2	3	N	N
	31–50 days	N	10	16	1	1
	51 days and over	20	7	1	N	1

Source: Annual Abstract of Statistics 2000, © *Crown copyright 2000*

Government Spending and Social Protection

Government Expenditure on Welfare Services in the UK

(N = nil or negligible. Years ending 31 March. Does not include school meals and milk. In millions of pounds.)

Item	1988–89	1989–90	1990–91	1991–92	1992–93	1993–94	1994–95	1995–96	1996–97	1997–98	1998–99
Personal social services											
central government current expenditure	127	143	163	190	202	216	197	140	101	73	53
local authorities current expenditure: running expenses	3,971	4,395	5,022	5,725	6,122	7,113	8,400	9,716	10,947	11,105	11,439
capital expenditure	163	213	227	200	189	190	235	229	221	213	191
Total	4,346	4,877	5,626	4,732	6,513	7,519	8,832	10,085	11,269	11,391	11,683
Welfare foods service											
central government current expenditure on welfare foods (including administration)	105	108	120	142	171	182	185	228	264	306	355
less receipts from the public	N	N	–1	–1	–1	–1	–1	–1	–1	–1	–1
Total	105	108	119	141	170	181	184	227	263	305	354
Total government expenditure	4,451	4,985	5,745	4,873	6,683	7,700	9,016	10,127	10,581	11,075	12,037
Total government expenditure as % of GDP[1]	0.93	0.95	1.02	0.83	1.09	1.19	1.31	1.40	1.38	1.36	1.41

[1] GDP is adjusted to take account of change from rates of community charge.

Source: Annual Abstract of Statistics 2000, © *Crown copyright 2000*

Government Expenditure on Social Security Benefits in the UK

(– = not applicable. Years ending 31 March. In millions of pounds.)

Government current expenditure	1990–91	1991–92	1992–93	1993–94	1994–95	1995–96	1996–97	1997–98	1998–99
National insurance fund									
retirement pensions	22,725	25,691	27,076	28,481	28,925	30,162	32,174	33,640	35,714
lump sums to pensioners	114	114	115	122	123	124	129	118	120
widows' and guardians' allowances	893	884	1,014	1,041	1,034	1,018	974	992	973
unemployment benefit	892	1,627	1,761	1,623	1,277	1,099	588	–	–1
jobseeker's allowance[1]	–	–	–	–	–	–	351	590	475
sickness benefit	222	278	365	294	426	12	–	–	–
invalidity benefit	4,544	5,461	6,198	7,146	8,042	271	–	–	–
incapacity benefit[2]	–	–	–	–	–	7,615	7,668	7,471	7,295
maternity benefit	35	40	42	32	17	28	31	36	39
death grant	–	–	–	–	–	–	–	–	–
disablement benefit	526	–	–	–	–	–	–	–	–
industrial death benefit	62	–	–	–	–	–	–	–	–
statutory sick pay	966	725	688	688	24	24	24	28	28
statutory maternity pay	344	396	416	440	498	476	500	516	552
payments in lieu of benefits foregone	–	–	–	–	–	–	–	–	–
Total	31,323	35,216	37,675	39,867	40,366	40,829	42,440	43,391	45,195

(*continued*)

Government Expenditure on Social Security Benefits in the UK *(continued)*

Government current expenditure	1990–91	1991–92	1992–93	1993–94	1994–95	1995–96	1996–97	1997–98	1998–99
Maternity fund	–	–	–	–	–	–	–	–	–
Redundancy fund	130	276	321	110	208	128	108	88	116
Social fund	123	130	175	189	183	216	203	152	216
Non-contributory benefits									
war pensions	688	844	976	913	1,083	1,247	1,352	1,284	1,262
family benefits									
child benefit	4,840	5,433	5,950	6,347	6,294	6,332	6,645	7,095	7,328
one parent benefit	227	249	275	282	289	310	317	9	–
family credit	466	626	929	1,208	1,441	1,739	2,084	2,338	2,430
family income supplement	–	–	–	–	–	–	–	–	–
maternity grants	–	–	–	–	–	–	–	–	–
income support/supplementary benefits									
supplementary pensions	–	–	–	–	–	–	–	–	–
supplementary allowances	–	–	–	–	–	–	–	–	–
income support	9,106	12,325	15,578	16,997	16,387	16,650	14,438	11,998	11,793
other									
old persons' pensions	38	36	36	36	35	36	30	29	29
lump sums to pensioners	8	11	13	14	13	15	15	17	17
attendance allowance	1,698	1,706	1,553	1,795	1,963	2,194	2,393	2,640	2,682
invalid care allowance	229	285	345	442	526	617	736	745	783
mobility allowance	895	1,063	68	–	–	–	–	–	–
disability living allowance	–	–	1,973	2,772	3,125	3,802	4,498	5,018	5,367
disability working allowance	–	–	3	7	11	19	34	44	49
severe disablement allowance	407	596	640	703	776	820	906	1,007	984
industrial injury benefits	142	655	668	687	706	731	744	754	–
retail price index adjustment	–	–	–	–	–	–	–	–	–
housing benefit	4,735	6,053	7,670	9,163	10,345	10,773	11,276	11,328	11,208
Administration	3,206	3,617	3,998	4,273	4,190	4,076	3,998	4,170	4,349
Total government expenditure	58,261	69,121	78,846	85,805	87,941	90,534	92,217	92,107	93,808
Total government expenditure as % of GDP[3]	10.35	11.72	12.87	13.26	12.82	12.53	12.03	11.31	11.03

[1] Jobseeker's allowance was introduced in October 1996 to replace unemployment benefit and income support for the unemployed.
[2] Sickness benefit and invalidity benefit were replaced by a single incapacity benefit in 1995.
[3] GDP is adjusted to take account of the change from rates to community charge.

Source: Annual Abstract of Statistics 2000, © *Crown copyright 2000*

Government Expenditure as a Percentage of GDP in the UK

(– = not applicable.)

Category	1987–88	1989–90	1991–92	1992–93	1993–94	1994–95	1995–96	1996–97	1997–98 (est)
Defence[1]	4.4	4.0	3.9	3.8	3.6	3.3	3.0	2.8	2.7
International development assistance and other international services	0.5	0.5	0.5	0.6	0.5	0.5	0.5	0.4	0.4
Agriculture, fisheries, food, and forestry	0.6	0.4	0.5	0.5	0.6	0.5	0.6	0.8	0.7
Trade, industry, energy, employment, and training	1.6	1.6	1.7	1.7	1.7	1.5	1.4	1.2	1.1
Transport	1.3	1.3	1.6	1.8	1.6	1.5	1.2	1.2	1.1
Housing	1.0	1.0	1.0	1.0	0.8	0.8	0.7	0.5	0.4
Other environmental services	1.3	1.3	1.4	1.5	1.3	1.4	1.4	1.3	1.2
Law, order, and protective services	1.9	2.0	2.2	2.3	2.3	2.3	2.2	2.2	2.1
Education	4.8	4.8	5.0	5.2	5.2	5.2	5.0	4.9	4.6
Culture, media, and sport	0.4	0.4	0.4	0.4	0.4	0.4	0.4	0.4	0.3
Health and personal social services									
health	4.8	4.8	5.4	5.7	5.6	5.5	5.5	5.4	5.3
Total	5.7	5.7	6.4	6.7	6.7	6.8	6.8	6.7	6.7
Social security	11.4	10.2	12.1	13.1	13.6	13.1	13.1	12.9	12.4
Central administration and associated expenditure[2]	1.3	1.3	0.8	1.1	1.1	0.9	1.2	0.9	0.8
Total expenditure on services	36.1	34.5	37.7	39.7	39.5	38.2	37.5	36.2	34.6
General government net debt interest	2.8	2.3	1.9	2.1	2.3	2.6	2.8	2.9	3.0
Other accounting adjustments	1.5	1.5	1.4	1.6	1.6	1.9	2.0	1.9	1.9
Allowance for shortfall	–	–	–	–	–	–	–	– 0.1	– 0.2
General government interest and dividend receipts	1.4	1.4	1.0	0.9	0.8	0.8	0.8	0.7	0.6
National Lottery	–	–	–	–	–	–	–	–	0.1
Privatization proceeds	– 1.2	– 0.8	– 1.4	– 1.3	– 0.9	– 0.9	– 0.3	– 0.6	– 0.2
General government expenditure	40.6	38.9	40.6	42.9	43.2	42.5	42.7	41.1	39.8

[1] The items for defence for 1990–91 and 1991–92 are net of other governments' contributions to the cost of the Gulf conflict. Figures for 1996–97 and 1997–98 include receipts from the sale of Ministry of Defence married quarters.
[2] Includes contributions to the European Communities and activities required for the general maintenance of government such as tax collection and the registration of population.

Source: Public Expenditure: Statistical Analyses 1998–99, © *Crown copyright 1998*

Government Spending and Social Protection

Benefit Expenditure by Recipient Group in the UK

(In millions of pounds.)

Recipient		1984–85	1989–90	1994–95	1995–96	1996–97	1997–98	1998–99 (est)
Elderly		18,496	25,715	37,364	38,804	40,981	42,823	44,567
Sick and disabled	short-term sick	870	1,351	714	954	988	1,167	1,506
	long-term sick and disabled	4,662	8,422	19,661	21,082	22,550	23,234	23,918
	Total	5,532	9,773	20,375	22,036	23,537	24,401	25,423
Family	lone parents	2,034	3,961	8,853	9,579	10,133	9,988	10,440
	Total	6,836	8,874	16,088	17,207	18,163	18,666	17,859
Unemployed		6,220	4,516	9,152	8,651	7,568	6,149	5,347
Widows and others		1,140	1,296	1,872	2,055	2,019	2,074	2,650
Total contributory		20,863	27,702	39,825	40,702	42,159	43,169	45,026
Total non-contributory		17,361	22,472	45,025	48,052	50,109	50,944	50,821
TOTAL BENEFIT EXPENDITURE		38,224	50,174	84,850	88,754	92,268	94,113	95,847

Source: The Government's Expenditure Plans 1999/2000, © *Crown copyright 1999*

Number of Recipients of Social Security Benefits in the UK

(– = not applicable. N/A = not available.)

Benefit	1984	1989	1994	1995	1996	1997	1998
Income-related benefits							
Family credit[1 2]	–	286,000	536,000	602,000	676,000	739,000	767,000
Income support[3]	–	4,161,000	5,675,000	5,670,000	5,549,000	3,958,000	3,853,000
Rent rebate (LA tenants)[4 5]	3,745,000	2,970,000	3,009,000	2,922,000	2,849,000	2,733,000	2,635,000[6]
Rent allowance (private tenants)[4 5]	1,080,000	960,000	1,702,000	1,838,000	1,860,000	1,813,000	1,791,000[6]
Rent rebate	7,230,000	4,350,000	–	–	–	–	–
Community charge benefit[4]	–	875,000	–	–	–	–	–
Council tax benefit[5 7]	–	–	5,641,000	5,696,000	5,587,000	5,434,000	5,281,000[6]
Retirement pension	9,368,000	9,836,000	10,167,000	10,289,000	10,451,000	10,600,000	10,737,000
Unemployment benefit[8]	974,000	289,000	458,000	387,000	397,000	–	–
Jobseeker's allowance							
income-based[9]	–	–	–	–	–	1,224,000	1,027,000
contribution-based[10]	–	–	–	–	–	181,000	154,000
Sickness and invalidity benefits							
Sickness benefit	191,000	109,000	127,000	127,000	–	–	–
Invalidity benefit	797,000	1,126,000	1,681,000	1,767,000	–	–	–
Incapacity benefit	–	–	–	–	1,813,000	1,749,000	1,671,000
Severe disablement allowance[11]	–	275,000	329,000	348,000	344,000	364,000	369,000
Disability benefits							
Attendance allowance	470,000	763,000	962,000	1,046,000	1,108,000	1,166,000	1,211,000
Mobility allowance	353,000	599,000	–	–	–	–	–
Disability living allowance	–	–	1,038,000	1,491,000	1,688,000	1,853,000	1,980,000
Disability working allowance[2]	–	–	4,000	6,000	9,000	12,000	15,000
Invalid care allowance	9,000	121,000	274,000	316,000	357,000	374,000	373,000
War pensions	302,000	252,000	309,000	315,000	327,000	321,000	310,000
Industrial injuries							
disablement benefit	189,000	193,000	226,000	235,000	249,000	258,000	276,000[12]
reduced earnings allowance	148,000	155,000	154,000	152,000	155,000	155,000	157,000[12]
Industrial death benefit	30,000	28,000	21,000	20,000	19,000	17,000	16,000
Workmen's compensation	3,000	2,000	1,000	1,000	1,000	1,000	1,000
Pneumo byss and misc	1,000	1,000	–	–	–	–	–
Family benefits							
Child benefit	6,882,000	6,695,000	6,995,000	6,996,000	7,024,000	6,968,000	6,946,000
One parent benefit	523,000	722,000	941,000	994,000	1,027,000	1,057,000[13]	1,032,000
Widows benefit	400,000	371,000	324,000	314,000	301,000	284,000	270,000
Child's special allowance	800	300	100	100	–	–	–
Guardian's allowance	3,000	2,000	2,000	2,000	2,000	2,000	2,000
Maternity allowance	105,000	14,000	11,000	12,000	13,000	11,000	N/A

[1] Family income supplement before April 1988.
[2] Figures are for March of each year.
[3] Supplementary benefit before April 1988. Figures are for May of each year. Support for the unemployed was replaced by income-based jobseeker's allowance from October 1996.
[4] Estimated average caseloads.
[5] Source from 1994: HBMIS Quarterly 100% stock count enquiry taken at the end of November.
[6] Source from 1998: HBMIS Quarterly 100% stock count enquiries taken on the second Thursday in August.
[7] Council tax benefit recipients include second adult rebates.
[8] Source: Quarterly analysis of registered unemployed claimants as at November. (Figures for 1994 and before are based on a 100% count, figures for 1995 and 1996 and based on a 5% sample.)
[9] Income support for the unemployed prior to 7 October 1996. Figures are for May of each year.
[10] Unemployment benefit prior to 7 October 1996. Figures are for May of each year.
[11] Non-contributory invalidity pension and housewives non-contributory invalidity pension before 29 November 1984.
[12] Includes an allowance for late returns.
[13] From April 1997 the supplement for the eldest or only child where someone brings up children alone, formerly known as one parent benefit, is now known as child benefit (lone parent).

Source: Social Security Statistics 1999, © *Crown copyright 1999*

National Insurance Fund of the UK

The National Insurance Fund is a social-security scheme that provides child allowances, maternity benefits, and payments to the unemployed, sick, and retired, and also covers medical treatment. It is paid for by weekly or monthly contributions from employees and employers.
(N/A = not available. Years ending 31 March. In millions of pounds.)

	1990–91	1991–92	1992–93	1993–94	1994–95	1995–96	1996–97	1997–98
Receipts								
Opening balance	10,579.7	12,161.2	8,637.6	3,577.7	4,672.3	7,042.1	8,044.9	7,869.1
Contributions	31,480.9	33,156.7	34,331.7	N/A	38,712.2	40,874.6	42,806.4	46,754.7
Grant from consolidated fund	N/A	N/A	N/A	7,785.0	6,445.0	3,680.0	1,951.5	966.2
Compensation for statutory sick pay/ statutory maternity pay	N/A	1,089.8	1,124.5	1,158.3	563.4	474.7	541.8	600.5
Consolidated fund supplement	N/A	N/A	N/A	N/A	N/A	N/A	N/A	N/A
Reimbursement for industrial injury benefit payments	436.5	N/A	N/A	N/A	N/A	N/A	N/A	N/A
Transfers from Great Britain	225.0	125.0	40.0	40.0	145.0	125.0	75.0	150.0
Income from investments	1,022.5	1,160.0	970.9	488.5	365.1	459.2	488.7	474.3
Other receipts	944.7	19.4	24.8	42.0	60.6	76.5	85.1	97.2
Redundancy receipts[1]	2.0	19.1	27.0	25.7	25.3	23.9	26.2	24.7
Total receipts	44,691.3	47,731.2	45,156.4	48,990.0	50,989.0	52,756.0	54,019.7	56,936.7
Expenditure								
Unemployment	899.0	1,641.9	1,800.6	1,689.6	1,330.9	1,131.3	605.1	0.1
Sickness	227.0	286.5	378.1	378.4	350.7	14.7	N/A	N/A
Invalidity	4,613.0	5,701.2	6,452.7	7,341.2	8,009.3	599.8	N/A	N/A
Incapacity	N/A	N/A	N/A	N/A	N/A	7,622.9	7,992.7	7,739.5
Maternity	34.6	32.1	32.7	34.2	28.2	29.9	34.3	36.7
Widows' pensions	920.7	1,044.7	1,044.4	1,076.0	1,057.4	1,050.7	1,016.8	1,020.7
Guardians' allowances[2] and child's special allowance	1.6	1.6	2.1	1.1	1.1	1.8	1.6	1.6
Retirement pensions[3]	23,305.4	28,605.0	29,995.4	31,720.9	31,366.9	32,616.6	34,735.7	36,396.4
Disablement[4]	419.8	N/A	N/A	N/A	N/A	N/A	N/A	N/A
Death	47.9	N/A	N/A	N/A	N/A	N/A	N/A	N/A
Pensioners' lump sum payments	118.3	117.2	118.0	125.1	126.3	127.2	131.6	126.3
Other benefits	3.2	N/A	N/A	N/A	N/A	N/A	N/A	N/A
Total benefits	30,590.4	37,430.2	39,824.0	N/A	42,270.8	35,575.1	44,517.9	45,321.4
Other payments	9.6	9.7	10.5	35.0	8.9	14.2	17.4	19.0
Administration	1,056.8	1,243.5	1,379.2	1,604.5	1,323.6	1,218.8	1,065.3	1,073.4
Transfers to Northern Ireland	225.0	125.0	40.0	40.0	145.0	125.0	75.0	150.0
Redundancy payments	N/A	285.3	325.0	271.6	198.5	155.1	133.6	120.0
Total expenditure	31,881.8	39,093.6	41,578.7	44,317.7	43,946.9	37,088.1	45,809.2	46,683.8
Accumulated funds	12,530.6	8,637.6	3,577.7	4,672.3	7,042.1	8,044.9	7,869.1	9,763.3

[1] The assets of the redundancy fund became those of the National Insurance fund on 31 January 1991.
[2] Includes figures of child's special allowance for Northern Ireland.
[3] Includes figures for personal pensions.
[4] From 1 April 1990, industrial injury benefits are no longer paid for out of the National Insurance fund; this amount is reimbursement for expenditure incurred by the fund for the period 1 April 1990 to 31 December 1990.

Source: Annual Abstract of Statistics 2000, © *Crown copyright 2000*

Income Support: Average Weekly Amounts of Benefit in the UK

(Figures are for February of each year. In pounds per week.)

Recipient	**1995**	**1996**	**1997**	**1998**	**1999**
Aged 60 and over	40.70	40.34	41.11	41.64	42.28
Disabled	58.42	59.56	60.59	62.76	65.68
Lone parent	75.03	76.38	77.34	78.44	82.33
Other	64.94	62.01	62.36	63.42	66.36
All income support	55.31	55.70	56.60	57.61	59.91

Source: Social Security Statistics 1999, © *Crown copyright 1999*

Child Benefit in the UK

Number of families and children receiving allowances. Data are for 31 December of each year.
(N/A = not available.)

Type of family		**1983**	**1988**	**1992**	**1993**	**1994**	**1995**	**1996**	**1997**	**1998**
Families with	1 child	2,905,000	2,878,000	2,906,000	2,920,000	2,941,000	2,970,000	2,983,000	N/A	N/A
	2 children	2,904,000	2,714,000	2,752,000	2,772,000	2,781,000	2,783,000	2,794,000	N/A	N/A
	3 children	878,000	839,000	894,000	908,000	920,000	928,000	929,000	N/A	N/A
	4 children	205,000	205,000	226,000	231,000	228,000	231,000	236,000	N/A	N/A
	5 children	48,000	48,000	55,000	57,000	60,000	60,000	59,000	N/A	N/A
	6 or more children	19,000	21,000	24,000	24,000	24,000	24,000	23,000	N/A	N/A
Total		6,958,000	6,706,000	6,857,000	6,913,000	6,955,000	6,996,000	7,024,000	6,956,000[1]	6,976,000[2]
Children attracting benefit total		12,526,000	12,021,000	12,425,000	12,555,000	12,632,000	12,698,000	12,745,000	12,615,000[1]	12,621,000[2]

[1] As at 3 December 1997.
[2] As at 30 December 1998.

Source: Social Security Statistics 1999, © *Crown copyright 1999*

Awards of Family Credit in the UK

As of 28 February 1999.

Type of family		Average amount (£ per week)	Range of family credit award							
			All amounts	Under £30.00	£30.00 -39.99	£40.00 -49.99	£50.00 -59.99	£60.00 -69.99	£70.00 -79.99	£80.00 and over
All families	with 1 child	49,970	301,500	58,800	30,700	34,200	38,900	108,100	24,100	6,700
	with 2 children	61,190	281,500	42,500	22,200	24,200	25,900	29,600	67,100	69,900
	with 3 children	72,990	135,000	16,000	8,500	9,900	9,300	10,000	11,400	69,700
	with 4 or more children	93,860	70,200	5,400	2,700	3,600	3,500	4,100	4,100	46,700
	All children	61,830	788,100	122,800	64,200	72,000	77,600	151,800	106,700	193,100
Couples	with 1 child	45,910	97,100	28,700	11,000	9,700	9,600	23,200	11,000	3,900
	with 2 children	56,950	143,900	30,500	13,800	13,800	12,400	13,200	26,000	34,100
	with 3 children	68,610	89,800	14,200	7,200	7,600	6,900	6,600	6,700	40,600
	with 4 or more children	91,690	57,300	5,100	2,500	3,400	3,300	3,700	3,500	35,700
	All children	62,020	388,100	78,500	34,600	34,500	32,200	46,700	47,100	114,500
Lone parents	with 1 child	51,900	204,400	30,100	19,700	24,500	29,300	84,900	13,100	2,800
	with 2 children	65,620	137,600	12,000	8,400	10,400	13,500	16,400	41,100	35,800
	with 3 children	81,700	45,200	1,900	1,300	2,300	2,400	3,500	4,700	29,100
	with 4 or more children	103,530	12,900	300	200	300	200	400	600	10,900
	All children	61,640	400,100	44,300	29,600	37,500	45,400	105,200	59,600	78,600

Source: Social Security Statistics 1999,

Government and Other Public Sector Expenditure on Housing in the UK

(N = nil or negligible. Years ending 31 March. In millions of pounds.)

Type of expenditure	1989–90	1990–91	1991–92	1992–93	1993–94	1994–95	1995–96	1996–97	1997–98	1998–99
Government expenditure										
Current expenditure										
central government housing subsidies										
to local authorities	714	1,273	1,144	992	874	814	687	717	711	737
to public corporations	285	284	260	208	214	228	228	236	244	239
to housing associations	53	67	40	135	180	207	235	215	216	– 46
grants to housing associations	7	85	117	59	13	3	1	1	N	N
local authorities housing subsidies	487	3	N	1	N	N	3	1	1	1
administration	249	320	373	394	364	405	402	447	509	571
Total	1,794	2,032	1,934	1,789	1,645	1,657	1,556	1,617	1,681	1,502
Capital expenditure										
investment in housing by local authorities	1,387	1,322	822	913	780	842	1,009	937	– 52	64
capital grants to housing associations	552	1,495	2,045	2,583	2,136	1,774	1,329	1,393	1,102	1,021
improvement grants	885	863	1,152	1,240	1,287	1,105	846	980	1,157	950
net lending for house purchase	– 259	– 596	– 782	– 211	– 402	– 141	– 136	– 719	– 816	– 175
capital grants to public corporations	241	774	482	631	439	387	837	386	400	415
net lending to public corporations	672	176	– 104	39	34	10	7	– 1	– 57	– 10
Total	3,479	4,033	3,613	5,195	4,274	3,977	3,889	2,976	1,734	2,265
Total expenditure										
central government	2,547	3,835	3,697	4,595	3,839	3,409	3,313	2,362	1,962	2,356
local authorities	2,726	2,230	1,850	2,389	2,080	2,225	2,132	2,231	1,453	1,411
Total government expenditure	5,273	6,065	5,547	6,984	5,919	5,634	5,445	4,593	3,415	3,767
Public corporations' capital expenditure										
Investment in housing	451	519	673	549	568	560	580	574	450	364
Net lending to private sector	– 2	– 3	– 4	3	1	– 1	– 5	– 1	– 1	– 1
Total	449	516	669	552	569	559	575	569	449	363
Total public sector expenditure[1]	4,809	5,631	5,838	6,866	6,015	5,796	5,176	4,777	3,521	3,725
Total public sector expenditure as % of GDP[2]	0.92	1.00	0.99	1.12	0.93	0.85	0.72	0.62	0.43	0.44

[1] Total government expenditure less grants and loans to public corporations, plus public corporations' capital expenditure.
[2] GDP is adjusted to take account of change from rates to community charge.

Source: Annual Abstract of Statistics 2000,

See also **Taxation,** pp 331–333;

Government Spending on Education in the UK, p 353;

Government Spending on the National Health Service in the UK, p 521; and

UK Defence Expenditure, p 571.

The Royal Family and Peerage

Members of the Royal Family

Senior members of the Royal Family are all related to the three middle sons of King George V: King George VI (1895–1952); Henry, Duke of Gloucester (1900–1974); and George, Duke of Kent (1902–1942). The eldest son, the Duke of Windsor (1894–1972), who abdicated from the throne as King Edward VIII in 1936, died childless.
(- = not applicable.)

Name and titles	Married	Date of birth	Office	Official residence(s)	Issue
Family of George VI					
The Sovereign: Her Majesty Queen Elizabeth II, of the United Kingdom of Great Britain and Northern Ireland and of her other Realms and Territories, Queen, Head of the Commonwealth, Defender of the Faith	His Royal Highness the Duke of Edinburgh, 20 November 1947	21 April 1926	Buckingham Palace, London SW1A 1AA; phone: (020) 7930 4832; Web site for royal family: www.royal.gov.uk	Buckingham Palace, Windsor Castle, Palace of Holyrood House	Prince Charles, Princess Anne, Prince Andrew, Prince Edward
Husband of the Queen: His Royal Highness, the Prince Philip, Duke of Edinburgh, KG, KT, OM, GBE, AC, QSO, PC, Ranger of Windsor Great Park	Her Majesty the Queen, 20 November 1947	10 June 1921			
Mother of the Queen: Her Majesty Queen Elizabeth the Queen Mother, Lady of the Garter, Lady of the Thistle, CI, GCVO, GBE, Dame Grand Cross of the Order of St John, Royal Victorian Chain, Lord Warden and Admiral of the Cinque Ports, Constable of Dover Castle	Prince Albert, Duke of York (later King George VI; died 1952), 26 April 1923	4 August 1900	Clarence House, St James' Palace, London SW1A 1BA; phone: (020) 7930 3141	Clarence House; Royal Lodge, Windsor; Castle of Mey	Queen Elizabeth II, Princess Margaret
Children of the Queen					
His Royal Highness the Prince of Wales (Prince Charles), KG, KT, GCB and Great Master of the Order of the Bath, AK, QSO, PC, ADP (P)	Lady Diana Spencer (later Diana, Princess of Wales; died 1997), 29 July 1981, marriage dissolved 1996	14 November 1948	St James' Palace, London SW1A 1BS; phone: (020) 7930 4832	St James' Palace; Highgrove, Tetbury	His Royal Highness Prince William of Wales (born 21 June 1982), His Royal Highness Prince Henry of Wales (born 15 September 1984)
Her Royal Highness the Princess Royal (Princess Anne), KG, GCVO	Captain Mark Phillips, 14 November 1973, marriage dissolved 1992; Captain Timothy Laurence, 12 December 1992	15 August 1950	Buckingham Palace, London SW1A 1AA; phone: (020) 7930 4832	Gatcombe Park, Minchinhampton	Peter Phillips (born 15 November 1977), Zara Phillips (born 15 May 1981)
His Royal Highness the Duke of York (Prince Andrew), CVO, ADC(P)	Sarah Ferguson (now Sarah, Duchess of York), 23 July 1986, marriage dissolved 1996	19 February 1960		Buckingham Palace; Sunninghill Park, Ascot	Princess Beatrice (born 8 August 1988), Princess Eugenie (born 23 March 1990)
His Royal Highness the Prince Edward, CVO, Earl of Wessex	Sophie Rhys-Jones (now the Countess of Wessex), 19 June 1999	10 March 1964		Windsor Castle	none
Sister of the Queen					
Her Royal Highness the Princess Margaret, Countess of Snowdon, CI, GCVO, Royal Victorian Chain, Dame Grand Cross of the Order of St John of Jerusalem	Antony Armstrong-Jones (later Earl of Snowdon), 6 May 1960, marriage dissolved 1978	21 August 1930	Kensington Palace, London W8 4PU; phone: (020) 7930 3141	Kensington Palace	David, Viscount Linley (born 3 November 1961), Lady Sarah Chatto[1] (born 1 May 1964)
Family of Henry, Duke of Gloucester					
Aunt of The Queen					
Her Royal Highness Princess Alice, Duchess of Gloucester, GCB, CI, GCVO, GBE	Prince Henry, Duke of Gloucester (died 1974), 6 November 1935	25 December 1901	Kensington Palace, London W8 4PU; phone: (020) 7930 6374	Kensington Palace	Prince William (1941–72), Richard, Duke of Gloucester
Cousin of the Queen					
His Royal Highness the Duke of Gloucester (Prince Richard), KG, GCV, Grand Prior of the Order of St John of Jerusalem	Birgitte Eva van Deurs (now HRH The Duchess of Gloucester), 8 July 1972	26 August 1944	Kensington Palace, London W8 4PU; phone: (020) 7930 6374	Kensington Palace	Alexander, Earl of Ulster (born 24 October 1974), Lady Davina Windsor (born 19 November 1977), Lady Rose Windsor (born 1 March 1980)

(continued)

Members of the Royal Family (continued)

Name and titles	Married	Date of birth	Office	Official residence(s)	Issue
Family of George, Duke of Kent					
His Royal Highness the Duke of Kent (Prince Edward), KG, GCMG, GCVO, ADC (P)	Katherine Worsley (now HRH The Duchess of Kent), 8 June 1961	9 October 1935	York House, St James' Palace, London SW1A 1BQ; phone: (020) 7930 1223	Wren House, London	George, Earl of St Andrews[2] (born 26 June 1962), Lady Helen Taylor[3] (born 28 April 1964), Lord Nicholas Windsor (born 25 July 1970)
Her Royal Highness Princess Alexandra, the Honourable Lady Ogilvy, GCVO	The Right Honourable Sir Angus Ogilvy, 24 April 1963	25 December 1936	Buckingham Palace, London SW1A 1AA; phone: (020) 7930 1860	Thatched House Lodge, Richmond Park, Surrey	James Ogilvy[4] (born 29 February 1964), Marina Mowatt[5] (born 31 July 1966)
His Royal Highness Prince Michael of Kent, KCVO	Baroness Marie-Christine von Reibnitz (now HRH Princess Michael of Kent), 30 June 1978	4 July 1942	Kensington Palace, London W8 4PU; phone: (020) 7938 3519	Kensington Palace; Nether Lypiatt Manor, Stroud	Lord Frederick Windsor (born 6 April 1979), Lady Gabriella Windsor (born 23 April 1981)

[1] Has one son: Samuel Chatto (born 28 July 1996).
[2] Has three children: Lady Marina Windsor (born 30 September 1982), Edward, Baron Downpatrick (born 2 December 1988), Lady Amelia Windsor (born 24 August 1995).
[3] Has two children: Columbus Taylor (born 6 August 1994), Cassius Taylor (born 26 December 1996).
[4] Has two children: Flora Ogilvy (born 15 December 1994), Alexander Ogilvy (born 12 November 1996).
[5] Has two children: Zenouska Mowatt (born 26 May 1990), Christian Mowatt (born 4 June 1993).

The Succession to the Throne

The current succession was determined following the end of the Commonwealth in the 17th century, by the Bill of Rights of 1689. This was amended by the Act of Settlement in 1701 which laid down that only Protestant descendants of Princess Sophia – the Electress of Hanover, granddaughter of James I – can succeed. In February 1998 the government announced that The Queen has agreed that the law should be changed to give females equal rights to succeed to the throne.
The Bill which should result from this decision will negate the rule of male primogeniture written into the 1701 Act of Settlement on which royal succession is currently based.

Order of succession	Relationship
The Prince of Wales	eldest son of Her Majesty the Queen
Prince William of Wales	eldest son of the Prince of Wales
Prince Henry of Wales	second son of the Prince of Wales
The Duke of York	second son of Her Majesty the Queen
Princess Beatrice of York	eldest daughter of the Duke of York
Princess Eugenie of York	second daughter of the Duke of York
The Earl of Wessex	third son of Her Majesty the Queen
The Princess Royal	only daughter, second child of Her Majesty the Queen
Peter Phillips	only son, eldest child, of the Princess Royal
Zara Phillips	only daughter of the Princess Royal

The Royal Family: the Civil List

Under the Civil List acts, the Queen Mother and the Duke of Edinburgh receive annual parliamentary allowances to enable them to carry out their public duties. Since 1993, The Queen has repaid to the Treasury the annual parliamentary allowances received by other members of the Royal family. The Queen's income is taxable.

The annual amounts payable to members of the Royal Family are:
Parliamentary annuities (not repaid by the Queen)
Her Majesty Queen Elizabeth The Queen Mother £643,000
His Royal Highness The Duke of Edinburgh £359,000
Parliamentary annuities (repaid by the Queen)
His Royal Highness the Duke of York £249,000
His Royal Highness the Prince Edward £96,000
Her Royal Highness the Princess Royal £228,000
Her Royal Highness the Princess Margaret £219,000
Her Royal Highness Princess Alice, Duchess of Gloucester £87,000
Their Royal Highnesses the Duke and Duchess of Gloucester £175,000
Their Royal Highnesses the Duke and Duchess of Kent £236,000
Her Royal Highness Princess Alexandra, Hon Lady Ogilvy £225,000

The Royal Family: Sources of Income

The Queen
The Queen (or officials of the Royal Household acting on her behalf) has four sources of funding:

The Civil List
Set by Parliament as a fixed annual amount of £7.9 million for a period of up to ten years; it is not taxed.

Grants-in-Aid
Paid by the appropriate government departments for expenses incurred.

Property Paid annually by the Department of Culture, Media, and Sport and used for the upkeep of the palaces occupied by members of the Royal Family. These are Buckingham Palace, St James's Palace and Clarence House, Marlborough House Mews, parts of Kensington Palace, Windsor Castle and related buildings, and Hampton Court Mews and Paddocks. Accounts are published and presented to Parliament each year. In 1997–98 the Grant-in-Aid amounted to £16.4 million and it is planned to reduce to £15 million in 1999–2000.

Travel From April 1997, the Royal Household received a Grant-in-Aid from Parliament, through the Department of the Environment, Transport, and the Regions to pay for Royal travel. The Grant-in-Aid for the year to March 1998 amounted to £19.4 million, of which £14.441 million was spent on flying for official engagements by 32 (the Royal) Squadron. It is proposed that the two 32 Squadron Wessex helicopters should be replaced by one Sikorsky S76, with an expected saving of £1.3 million per year.

The Privy Purse
The Privy Purse Office manages the Sovereign's private income from the Duchy of Lancaster. This amounted to £5.7 million before tax for the year to 31 March 1998. The Duchy is a landed estate held in trust for the Sovereign since 1399. The Queen uses the larger part of the Privy Purse to meet official expenses incurred by other members of the Royal Family. Only the Queen Mother and the Duke of Edinburgh receive payments from Parliament which are not reimbursed by the Queen.

The Queen's personal wealth and income
The Queen's personal income, derived from her personal investment portfolio, is used to meet private expenditure. The Queen owns Balmoral and Sandringham, both inherited from her father. She also owns the stud at Sandringham (with a small amount of land in Hampshire), West Ilsley Stables, and Sunninghill Park, home of the Duke of York. Income derived from public access to Balmoral and Sandringham goes to charity and towards meeting the costs of managing the properties. The Queen owns no property outside the UK.

The Prince of Wales
The Prince of Wales does not receive any money from the state. Instead, he receives the annual net revenues of the Duchy of Cornwall and uses them to meet the costs of all aspects of his public and private commitments and those of his children.

The Duchy of Cornwall
For the year to 31 March 1998, the Duchy's net surplus was £5,955,000. The Duchy is tax exempt because it is a crown body. However, the Prince of Wales has volunteered to pay tax on this amount at the rate of 40%.

The Peerage

The peerage comprises holders, in descending order, of the titles of duke, marquess, earl, viscount, and baron. Most hereditary peerages pass on death to the nearest male relative, but some of these titles may be held by a woman in default of a male heir; no title can be passed on to the untitled husband of a woman peer. In the late 19th century, the peerage was augmented by the Lords of Appeal in Ordinary (the nonhereditary life peers) and, from 1958, by a number of specially created life peers of either sex (usually long-standing members of the House of Commons). Since 1963 peers have been able to disclaim their titles, usually to enable them to take a seat in the Commons (where peers are disqualified from membership).

Duke
The title originated in England in 1337, when Edward III created his son Edward, Duke of Cornwall; **Coronet:** eight strawberry leaves; **Title:** His Grace, The Duke of
Wife's title: Her Grace, The Duchess of; **Eldest son's title:** takes his father's second title (Marquess, Earl, or Viscount) as a courtesy title; **Younger sons' title:** 'Lord' before forename and family name; **Daughters' title:** 'Lady' before forename and family name.

Marquess
The first English marquess was created in 1385, but the lords of the Scottish and Welsh Marches were known as marchiones before this date; **Coronet:** four strawberry leaves alternating with four silver balls; **Title:** The Most Honourable, the Marquess of; **Wife's title:** The Most Honourable, The Marchioness of; **Eldest son's title:** takes his father's second title (Earl or Viscount) as a courtesy title; **Younger sons' title:** 'Lord' before forename and family name; **Daughters' title:** 'Lady' before forename and family name.

Earl
Earldoms first became hereditary during the Norman period, and the title of earl was the highest hereditary dignity until 1337; **Coronet:** eight silver balls on stalks alternating with eight gold strawberry leaves; **Title:** The Right Honourable, the Earl of; **Wife's title:** The Right Honourable, The Countess of; **Eldest son's title:** takes his father's second title as a courtesy title; **Younger sons' title:** 'The Honourable' before forename and family name; **Daughters' title:** 'Lady' before forename and family name.

Viscount
The title was first granted in England in 1440 to John, Lord Beaumont. Originally the title was given to the deputy sheriff, who acted on behalf of an earl within his estate; **Coronet:** sixteen silver balls; **Title:** The Right Honourable, the Viscount of; **Wife's title:** The Right Honourable, the Viscountess of; **Eldest son's title:** takes his father's second title as a courtesy title; **Younger sons' title:** 'The Honourable' before forename and family name; **Daughters' title:** 'The Honourable' before forename and family name.

Baron
Historically, a baron is any member of the higher nobility, a direct vassal (feudal servant) of the king, not bearing other titles such as duke or count. Life peers, created under the Act of 1958, are always of this rank; **Coronet:** six silver balls; **Title:** the Right Honourable, the Lord; **Wife's title:** the Right Honourable, the Lady; **Eldest son's title:** 'the Honourable' before forename and family name; **Younger sons' title:** 'The Honourable' before forename and family name; **Daughters' title:** 'The Honourable' before forename and family name.

Notes
For Royal Dukes, His Royal Highness and Her Royal Highness are used instead of His or Her Grace. In Scotland, Marquis is used for peers created before the Union with England. In Scotland, 'The Master of' followed by the Viscount's title can be used. The title Baron does not exist in Scotland.

See also **Forms of Address in the UK**, p 441.

Orders of Chivalry and the Honours List

Modern orders of chivalry are awarded as a mark of royal favour or as a reward for public services. Members of orders are normally created Knights or Dames, titled Sir or Dame; some orders are graded, with the lower grades not being knighted. Honours are awarded by the sovereign and published on New Year's Day, and on the official royal birthday in June. Suggestions for awards are provided by: (1) senior government officials; (2) personal nominations from the Queen; (3) the major political parties, through the Chief Whip; and (4) the prime minister, who can add to, or subtract from, all the above lists.

Order	Created	Ribbon	Motto	Initials	Other
Order of the Garter[1]	1348	blue	*honi soit qui mal y pense* (shame on him who thinks evil of it)	KG	founded by Edward III
Order of the Thistle[2]	1687[3]	green	*nemo me impune lacessit* (no one provokes me with impunity)	KT	ancient Scottish order
Order of the Bath	1725	crimson	*tria juncta in ino* (three joined in one)	GCB, KCB, DCB, CB[4]	founded by Henry IV; divided into civil and military divisions; women became eligible in 1971
Order of Merit[1 5]	1902	blue and crimson	none	OM	founded by Edward VII
Order of the Star of India	1861	light blue with white edges	Heaven's light our guide	GCSI, KCSI, CSI[6]	no new members created since 1947
Order of St Michael and St George	1818	blue with scarlet centre	*auspicium melioris aevi* (token of a better age)	GCMG, KCMG, DCMG, CMG[7]	
Order of the Indian Empire	1868	purple	*imperatricis auspiciis* (under the auspices of the Empress)	GCIE, KCIE, CIE[8]	no new members created since 1947
Imperial Order of the Crown of India[9]	1877	light blue with white edge	none	CI	no new members created since 1947
Royal Victorian Order	1896	blue with red and white edges	Victoria	GCVO, KCVO, DCVO, CVO, LVO, MVO[10]	
Order of the British Empire	1917	pink edged with grey; vertical grey stripe in centre for the military division	for God and the Empire	GBE, KBE, DBE, CBE, OBE, MBE[11]	divided into civil and military divisions in 1918
Companions of Honour[5 12]	1917	carmine with gold edges	none	CH	
Distinguished Service Order	1886	red with blue edges	none	DSO	awarded to members of the armed forces for services in action; a bar may be added for any additional act of service
Imperial Service Order[13]	1902	crimson with blue centre	none	ISO	awarded to members of the Civil Service; no new members created since 1993

[1] Only 24 people may hold this order at any one time. [2] Only 16 people may hold this order at any one time. [3] Revived in this year.
[4] GCB (Knight/Dame of the Grand Cross); KCB, DCB (Knight/Dame Commander); CB (Companion). [5] Members are not given a knighthood.
[6] GCSI (Knight Grand Commander); KCSI (Knight Commander); CSI (Companion).
[7] GCMG (Knight/Dame Grand Commander); KCMG, DCMG (Knight/Dame Commander); CMG (Companion).
[8] GCIE (Knight/Dame Grand Commander); KCIE (Knight/Dame Commander); CIE (Companion). [9] For women only.
[10] GCVO (Knight/Dame of The Grand Cross); KCVO, DCVO (Knight/Dame Commander); LVO (Lieutenant); MVO (Member).
[11] GBE/KBE (Knight/Dame Grand Cross); DBE (Knight/Dame Commander); CBE (Commander); OBE (Officer); MBE (Member).
[12] Only 65 people may hold this order at any one time. [13] Membership is limited to 1,900 people.

National Anthems and Patriotic Songs

The National Anthem: 'God Save The Queen'

The melody resembles a composition by John Bull and similar words are found from the 16th century. In its present form it was arranged by Dr Thomas Arne, under the title 'Song for Two Voices'. This version was first performed at Drury Lane Theatre in London on 28 September 1745, following the news of the defeat of the army of King George II by the 'Young Pretender' to the British Throne, Prince Charles Edward Stuart, at the battle of Prestonpans. The song immediately became popular as an anti-Jacobite Party song during the 1745 Jacobite Rebellion.

The words below are those sung in 1745, substituting 'Queen' for 'King' where appropriate. On official occasions, only the first verse is usually sung.

God save our gracious Queen, Long live our noble Queen
God save the Queen!
Send her victorious, Happy and Glorious
Long to reign over us
God save the Queen!

O Lord our God arise, Scatter her enemies
And make them fall
Confound their politics, Frustrate their knavish tricks
On Thee our hopes we fix
Oh, save us all!

Thy choicest gifts in store On her be pleased to pour
Long may she reign
May she defend our laws, And ever give us cause
To sing with heart and voice
God save the Queen!

Not in this land alone, But be God's mercies known
From shore to shore!
Lord make the nations see, That men should brothers be,
And form one family
The wide world over.

From every latent foe, From the assassins blow
God save the Queen!
O'er her thine arm extend, For Britain's sake defend
Our mother, prince, and friend
God save the Queen!

Rule Britannia

Words by James Thomson.

When Britain first, at heaven's command
Arose from out the azure main
This was the charter the charter of the land
And guardian Angels sung this strain:

Rule, Britannia, rule the waves
Britons never will be slaves.

The nations, not so blest as thee
Must, in their turns, to tyrants fall
While thou shalt flourish great and free
The dread and envy of them all.

Still more majestic shalt thou rise
More dreadful, from each foreign stroke
As the loud blast that tears the skies
Serves but to root thy native oak.

Thee haughty tyrants ne'er shall tame
All their attempts to bend thee down
Will but arouse thy generous flame
But work their woe, and thy renown.

To thee belongs the rural reign
Thy cities shall with commerce shine
All thine shall be the subject main
And every shore it circles thine.

The Muses, still with freedom found
Shall to thy happy coast repair
Blest isle! with matchless beauty crowned
And manly hearts to guard the fair.

Scotland The Brave

Hark where the night is falling
Hark hear the pipes a calling
Loudly and proudly calling down thru the glen
There where the hills are sleeping
Now feel the blood a leaping
High as the spirits of the old highland men.
Towering in gallant fame
Scotland my mountain hame
High may your proud standards gloriously wave
Land of my high endeavour
Land of the shining river
Land of my heart forever, Scotland the Brave.
High in the misty mountains
Out by the purple highlands
Brave are the hearts that beat beneath Scottish skies
Wild are the winds to meet you
Staunch are the friends that greet you
Kind as the love that shines from fair maidens' eyes.

The Scottish National Anthem: 'Flower of Scotland'

Although modern, this anthem commemorates the Battle of Bannockburn in 1314 when the Scottish Army under Robert I (the Bruce) King of Scots defeated Edward II, King of England.

O Flower of Scotland, When will we see Your like again
That fought and died for, Your wee bit Hill and Glen
And stood against him, Proud Edward's Army
And sent him homeward, Tae think again.

The Hills are bare now, and Autumn leaves lie thick and still
O'er land that is lost now, Which those so dearly held
That stood against him, Proud Edward's Army
And sent him homeward, Tae think again.

Those days are past now, And in the past they must remain
But we can still rise now, And be the nation again
That stood against him, Proud Edward's Army
And sent him homeward, Tae think again.

Flower of Scotland, When will we see Your like again
That fought and died for, Your wee bit Hill and Glen
And stood against him, Proud Edward's Army
And sent him homeward, Tae think again.

The Unofficial English National Anthem: 'Land of Hope and Glory'

Although this anthem can identify with the whole of the UK by references to the empire 'wider and still wider, shall thy bounds be set', it is also the unofficial national anthem of England, and is used for the English teams at the Commonwealth Games, although the English national football and rugby teams use 'God Save the Queen'.

Words by A C Benson, music by Sir Edward Elgar from 'Pomp & Circumstance March No. 1'.

Dear Land of Hope, thy hope is crowned.
God make thee mightier yet!
On Sov'ran brows, beloved, renowned, Once more thy crown is set.
Thine equal laws, by Freedom gained, Have ruled thee well and long
By Freedom gained, by Truth maintained, Thine Empire shall be strong.

Land of Hope and Glory, Mother of the Free
How shall we extol thee, who are born of thee?
Wider still and wider shall thy bounds be set
God, who made thee mighty, make thee mightier yet,
God, who made thee mighty, make thee mightier yet.

Thy fame is ancient as the days, As Ocean large and wide
A pride that dares, and heeds not praise, A stern and silent pride
Not that false joy that dreams content With what our sires have won
The blood a hero sire hath spent, Still nerves a hero son.

The Welsh National Anthem: 'Hen Wlad Fy Nhadau'/'Land Of My Fathers'

The words are given in Welsh and English.

Hen Wlad Fy Nhadau
Mae hen wlad fy nhadau yn annwyl i mi
Gwlad beirdd a chantorion, enwogion o fri
Ei gwrol ryfelwyr, gwladgarwyr tra mad
Tros ryddid collasant eu gwaed.

Gwlad, gwlad, pleidiol wyf i'm gwlad
Tra mor yn fur i'r bur hoffbau
O bydded i'r heniaith barhau.

Hen Gymru fynyddig, paradwys y bardd
Pob dyffryn, pob clogwyn i'm golwg sydd hardd
Trwy deimlad gwladgarol, mor swynol yw si
Ei nentydd, afonydd, i mi.

Os treisiodd y gelyn fy ngwlad tan ei droed
Mae hen iaith y Cymry mor fyw ag erioed
Ni luddiwyd yr awen gan erchyll law brad
Na thelyn berseiniol fy ngwlad.

Land of My Fathers
The land of my fathers is dear unto me
Old land where the minstrels are honoured and free
Its warring defenders so gallant and brave
For freedom their life's blood they gave.

Home, home, true am I to home
While seas secure the land so pure
O may the old language endure.

Old land of the mountains, the Eden of bards
Each gorge and each valley a loveliness guards
Through love of my country, charmed voices will be
Its streams, and its rivers, to me.

Though foemen have trampled my land 'neath their feet
The language of Cambria still knows no retreat
The muse is not vanquished by traitor's fell hand.

Web Sites

About the National Trust

http://www.nationaltrust.org.uk/aboutnt.htm

Information about the charity that is entrusted with the care of large parts of the British countryside and a large number of historic buildings. There is a brief history of the organization, an outline of its work, and an appeal for assistance.

British Monarchy

http://www.royal.gov.uk/

The official site of the British monarchy includes reviews of its history, its present role and character, and details on the formal order of accession, coronation, and succession that applies to each monarch.

Cabinet Office Home Page

http://www.cabinet-office.gov.uk/

Site of the UK cabinet, with the latest news from Whitehall, access to reports and papers from the various departments, and statistics and information about government policy, as well as a full explanation of the structure of government.

Countryside Commission

http://www.countryside.gov.uk/

Guide to the work of the Commission and to the attractions of the British countryside. The Web site provides information on all of the UK's national parks and the officially designated areas of outstanding beauty. It also details the Commission's work to preserve the countryside.

English Heritage

http://www.english-heritage.org.uk/

Site of the public body that is charged with protecting England's historic environment. Includes information on the role and structure of the organization, its publications and educational activities, and an interactive map where you can get details on specific historic properties.

Foreign and Commonwealth Office Online

http://www.fco.gov.uk/news/

Official statements of British foreign policy. Updated several times daily, this is an invaluable source of information on British policy on a wide range of issues concerning the international community.

Hansard – House of Commons Debates

http://www.parliament.the-stationery-office.co.uk/pa/cm/cmhansrd.htm

The complete proceedings of the House of Commons, posted each day at 12.30 p.m. You can also search archived proceedings going back to 1996.

House of Commons – Members, Ministers, and Committees

http://www.parliament.uk/commons/lib/lists.htm

Regularly updated list of members of the British lower house provided by the House of Commons. MPs can be easily located by name, constituency, or county.

Houses of Parliament Home Page

http://www.parliament.uk/

Site of the UK's House of Commons and House of Lords, with a guide to visiting and access to the many government publications and committees.

Millennium Commission

http://www.millennium.gov.uk/

The Commission's site includes information about its grants and funding as well as details on the hundreds of landmark projects and events it has sponsored throughout the UK to commemorate the millennium.

National Assembly for Wales

http://www.assembly.wales.gov.uk/index_e.html

Describes the structure and business of the Welsh Assembly, including press notices, 'Who's who' in the Assembly, and records of proceedings.

Northern Ireland Office Online

http://www.nio.gov.uk/index.htm

Comprehensive information on the administration of criminal justice, security, and the police in Northern Ireland. Frequently updated, this site charts the latest developments in the search for peace and also provides a good introduction to the economy and culture of Ulster.

Northern Ireland Assembly

http://www.ni-assembly.gov.uk/index.htm

Information about the Assembly, its publications and committees, and a 'Register of members' interests'.

Northern Ireland Public Service Web

http://www.nics.gov.uk/

Details of many government services, including the departments of agriculture, economic development, the environment, and health and social services for Northern Ireland.

Northern Ireland Tourist Board

http://www.ni-tourism.com/index.asp

First-stop site for anyone who is planning to visit Northern Ireland. The site features a virtual tour covering history, activities, food and drink, accommodation, events, and attractions.

Oultwood Local Government Web Site Index

http://www.oultwood.com/localgov/

Covering England, Scotland, Wales, Northern Ireland, and the Republic of Ireland, this site provides interactive maps that enable the user to locate with ease your local council Web site.

Parliamentary Glossary

http://www.ukpol.co.uk/hou.shtml

Useful page which explains the terminology used in the UK's Houses of Parliament, from 'Act of parliament' to 'Whip'.

Scottish Parliament

http://www.scottish.parliament.uk/

Information about the Scottish Parliament, its activities, and members.

Select Committees

http://www.parliament.uk/commons/selcom/cmsel.htm

Complete guide to the many select committees of the UK's House of Commons. The site provides regularly updated news of the sittings of each committee, transcripts of their deliberations, press releases, and details of their members.

10 Downing Street

http://www.number-10.gov.uk/

Official site of the UK prime minister's residence includes a virtual tour, biographies of recent prime ministers, press releases, and copies of speeches and interviews.

This Is Britain

http://www.thisisbritain.co.uk/

News site that groups UK news headlines from regional sites, so that you can easily find out what local news stories are. There is also a comprehensive directory of local news and sports sites.

UK Maps

http://www.multimap.com/uk/

This site allows you to search for maps of towns and cities in the UK, and view the area in a variety of scales, from 1:50,000 to 1:200,000.

Union Jack

http://www.crwflags.com/fotw/flags/gb.html

Detailed discussion pages with historical information about the UK flag, its design, and uses.

Visit Britain – British Tourist Authority

http://www.visitbritain.com/uk/home3.htm

Comprehensive information on tourism in the British Isles, provided by the official tourist promotion agency. An interactive map and a good search engine make this an extremely useful first-stop site for anyone contemplating a visit to Britain.

Welcome to CNT

http://www.cnt.org.uk/

Site of the UK Commission for New Towns, the body charged with the management of assets of the UK's new towns. The commission's role to promote relocation of enterprises is described, along with profiles of the infrastructure and workforce of each new town.

Work of the Audit Commission

http://www.audit-commission.gov.uk/

Explanation of the functions of the body charged with ensuring the financial accountability of the UK government. The site includes a history of the external checking of public finances in Britain, an executive summary of the commission reports, and a full description of services offered.

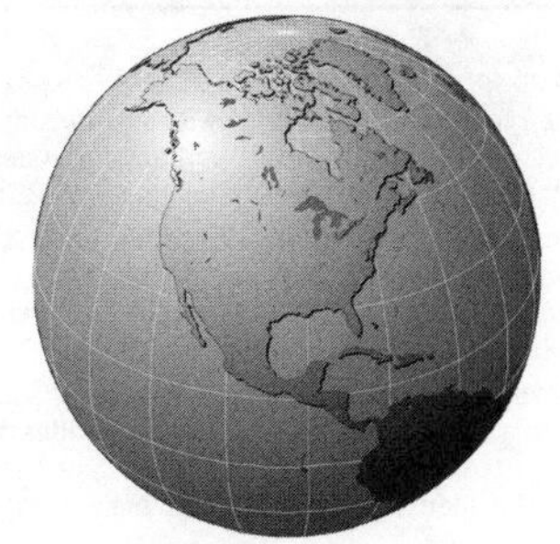

World

The Year in Review

July 1999 Student demonstrations for freedom of speech in Iran spread to 18 cities, leading to clashes between police and Islamic authorities and the death of at least one student. The protests stop on 17 July after denunciations by President Mohammed Khatami.

1 July 1999 UK foreign secretary Robin Cook announces that UK investigators have exhumed 20 bodies, including those of seven children, from mass graves in Bela Crvka, Yugoslavia, one of the massacre sites listed in the war crimes indictment against Yugoslav President Slobodan Milošević.

2 July 1999 Ethnic Albanian and Serbian representatives in Yugoslavia sign a joint statement calling for an end to the violence in the Serbian province of Kosovo.

2 July 1999 UN General Secretary Kofi Annan announces that he will appoint French health minister Bernard Kouchner as head of the UN mission in Kosovo. Kouchner is responsible for preparing the province for self-government.

5 July 1999 Around 15,000 Serbs gather in Leskovac, Serbia, to protest against President Milošević and his government.

6 July 1999 Ehud Barak, head of the One Israel alliance party, is sworn in as Prime Minister of Israel, succeeding Binjamin Netanyahu.

7 July 1999 UK foreign secretary Robin Cook announces that the UK is resuming diplomatic relations with Libya after the Libyan government agrees to cooperate with the investigation into the murder of English police officer Yvonne Fletcher, who was shot outside the Libyan embassy in London in 1984.

7 July 1999 A peace agreement is signed by Sierra Leone President Ahmad Tejan Kabbah and the leader of the Revolutionary United Front, Foday Sankoh, in Lomé, capital of Togo.

8–13 July 1999 Students protesting against press restrictions imposed by the hardline Islamic government clash with police and vigilante groups at Tehran University in Iran's worst civil unrest for 20 years.

8 July 1999 Christian Solidarity International, a Swiss humanitarian group which has rescued over 11,000 slaves in southern Sudan, says it has freed 2,035 in a single week, a record number.

9 July 1999 Former Italian Premier Romano Prodi, who became President of the European Commission in May, announces his 19 proposed appointments for the other members of the commission. Neil Kinnock, in charge of European Union reform, is one of only four members of the commission to be proposed for reappointment by Prodi. Former UK high commissioner to Hong Kong Chris Patten is proposed for the post of external relations.

10 July 1999 A cease-fire agreement is signed by the Democratic Republic of Congo and five countries involved in the civil war.

15 July 1999 Israeli Prime Minister Ehud Barak outlines a plan for peace in the Middle East, with a 15-month deadline, during talks with President Clinton in Washington, DC.

18 July 1999 The US Census Bureau reports that the world population has reached 6 billion.

20 July 1999 Cuba claims $181 billion in damages against the USA for alleged military crimes over the past 40 years.

21–23 July 1999 The Sudanese government drops 16 chemical bombs on the south of the country while fighting Christian and other rebel groups, according to the UK human rights group Christian Solidarity Worldwide (CSW), which condemns the brutality of President al-Bashir's regime.

28 July 1999 $2.1 billion, including $500 million from the USA, is pledged by a group of international organizations and governments for aid to Kosovo.

August 1999 Aid agencies warn of a hidden refugee crisis in the Balkans, with two-thirds of Kosovo's Serb population existing in temporary camps in Yugoslavia.

3 August 1999 Indonesian President B J Habibie formally ratifies the country's June election results, in which the opposition Indonesian Democratic Party of Struggle received 34% of the vote and his Golkar party received 22.4%. The results of the election have been delayed for nearly two months because of fraud charges and conflicts among election officials.

4 August 1999 Rebels against the government of Sierra Leone take more than 30 people hostage, including international observers, aid workers, journalists, and peacekeepers. Reportedly dissatisfied with a recent accord to help end the country's civil war, they demand supplies and a meeting with UN officials.

8–10 August 1999 Rebels against the government of Sierra Leone release the hostages they took on 4 August, without their demands being met.

9 August 1999 Russian President Boris Yeltsin dismisses Sergei Stepashin as premier less than three months after he took the position. Yeltsin names ally and supporter Vladimir Putin as Stepashin's successor.

19 August 1999 Tens of thousands of Serbs attend the largest rally since 1997 in Belgrade, Yugoslavia, to demand the resignation of President Milošević.

23 August 1999 German Chancellor Gerhard Schroeder formally inaugurates Berlin as the new capital of Germany. The German parliament held its final session in Bonn in July.

30 August 1999 A historic vote is held in East Timor to decide between remaining part of Indonesia or becoming an independent state. The UN estimates that more than 90% of the 450,000 people who registered turn out to vote.

September 1999 The United Nations High Commissioner for Refugees confirms that more than 90% of Kosovo's Serb population has now fled the province, and that the exodus is continuing.

13 September 1999 An explosion destroys a block of flats in a suburb of Moscow, Russia, killing at least 70 people. It is one of a series of bomb attacks blamed on Chechnya-based terrorists whose goal is to create an Islamic state in Dagestan.

3 October 1999 Austria's far-right Freedom Party increases its number of seats in parliamentary elections, becoming the second largest party in government in Austria. The party campaigned under an anti-immigration platform, and its leader, Jörg Haider, is reputedly a Nazi sympathizer.

3 October 1999 Violence marks the close of India's general election. At least 39 people are killed in bomb attacks and shoot-outs by rival gangs.

12 October 1999 In an apparently bloodless coup, the Pakistani army deposes Prime Minister Nawiz Sharif's government. General Pervez Musharraf, who had been sacked by Sharif a few hours before, imposes martial law, claiming that it will help prevent the country from becoming destabilized.

19 October 1999 Chinese President Jiang Zemin is the first Chinese leader to visit the UK, where he is entertained by the Queen. More than 200 human rights protesters gather outside Buckingham Palace, many of them campaigners for the charity Free Tibet.

20 October 1999 Violence flares in Jakarta, Indonesia, after Megawati Sukarnoputri, a popular choice for President, is narrowly beaten by Abdurrahman Wahid, leader of the country's largest Muslim organization. The violence subsides the following day when she is elected vice-President.

27 October 1999 Gunmen enter the parliament in Yerevan, Armenia, and shoot dead Vazgen Sarkisyan, the country's Prime Minister, as well as three top government officials.

6 November 1999 Australian voters reject a referendum by 55% to 45% that would make the country a republic with a President elected by the federal parliament. Queen Elizabeth II therefore remains head of state.

9 November 1999 Germans gather near the Brandenburg Gate in Berlin to celebrate the tenth anniversary of the fall of the Berlin Wall.

9 November 1999 The government of Saudi Arabia announces plans to issue identity cards to women. Currently women are listed on the identity cards of their male next of kin.

22 November 1999 UK foreign secretary Robin Cook announces that the Libyan government has finally paid compensation to the family of Yvonne Fletcher, an English policewoman who was shot outside the Libyan embassy in London in 1984. The move paves the way for a UK ambassador to be sent to Libya.

10 December 1999 The European Union summit opens in Helsinki, Finland. For the UK, the continued French ban on British beef overshadows key issues, such as taxation.

22 December 1999 Sri Lankan President Bandaranaike Kumaratunga is re-elected for another term, less than a week after surviving an attack by a suicide bomber.

24 December 1999 Five members of a Kashmiri separatist group take control of an Indian Airlines Airbus 300 flying from Kathmandu to Delhi, India, with 161 people on board. They force the plane to land in India, Pakistan, and Dubai, before landing in Afghanistan, where they threaten to blow up the plane unless the Indian government releases a Pakistani Muslim leader from prison.

28 December 1999 The hijackers of the Indian Airlines plane held for five days in Kandahar increase their demands to include a ransom of $200 million/£124 million and the release of 35 Kashmiri separatists in return for the 155 passengers aboard.

31 December 1999 The Portuguese territory of Macau is handed over to China after 442 years of colonial rule.

1 January 2000 The new millennium is celebrated across the world, with fireworks, street parties, ceremonies, and speeches. The computer 'millennium bug' does not appear to make a large impact, and despite fears of acts of extremism and terrorism, the global celebration passes peacefully.

3 January 2000 Leaders from Israel and Syria arrive in Shephardstown, West Virginia, for the first day of peace talks, presided over by President Clinton.

10 January 2000 Belgium and Luxembourg re-impose border controls to help prevent a feared influx of illegal immigrants. They are two of the nine EU countries that removed border restrictions under the Schengen Agreement of 1995.

15 January 2000 Masked assailants shoot dead Serbian war criminal Zeljko Raznatovic, known as Arkan, at the Hotel Intercontinental in Belgrade. He is alleged to have overseen the massacre of over 200 people at a hospital in Vukovar during the Croatian war, in 1991.

17 January 2000 Sectarian fighting in Indonesia spreads to the tourist island of Lombok, when Muslim rioters rampage through two towns, setting fire to buildings and churches.

31 January 2000 EU countries threaten to cut off all bilateral contacts with Austria if the far-right Freedom Party, led by Jörg Haider, joins its government.

February 2000 It is reported that Texas Governor George W Bush has raised and spent more on his campaign for US President than anyone in the history of US politics. The *Washington Post* newspaper reports that he is spending $400,000 daily on his campaign and has spent nearly all of the $71/£44 million he raised.

1 February 2000 US Republican Presidential candidate John McCain defeats Texas Governor George W Bush in the first primary election in New Hampshire.

4 February 2000 Austrian President Thomas Klestil swears in a new government, in which the majority of senior ministers are members of the far-right Freedom Party, led by Jörg Haider. The EU President, Portuguese Prime Minister Antonio Guterres, announces moves to isolate the country from the rest of the EU.

4 February 2000 Demonstrators against Austria's new right-wing coalition government clash with police, 25 of whom are injured, in Vienna. The EU, joined by the USA, begins to limit contact with the new government.

6 February 2000 Foreign Minister Tarja Halonen of the Social Democratic Party is elected Finland's first woman President.

6 February 2000 Mexican police officers raid the National Autonomous University of Mexico (UNAM) in Mexico City, and arrest more than 745 students who have occupied the buildings since April 1999. The students were on strike in response to increased tuition fees. The university officially reopens on 15 February 2000.

6 February 2000 US first lady Hillary Rodham Clinton formally announces that she is running for the Senate, as a representative for New York.

7 February 2000 A hijacked Afghan airline Boeing 727 lands at Stansted airport in England, with 165 passengers held hostage. The six hijackers demand the release of rebel Afghan leader Ismail Khan.

28 February 2000 Jörg Haider resigns as leader of Austria's Freedom Party, but retains his post as Governor of the region of Carinthia.

14 February 2000 Classes are resumed at Mexico's largest university one week after police arrested 150 students on strike over a controversial increase in tuition fees which put the university out of action for nine months.

March 2000 Israeli Prime Minister Ehud Barak and Palestinian leader Yassir Arafat resume peace talks, after Israel's commitment to withdraw from south Lebanon by July.

March 2000 In Mozambique, floods leave thousands dead and hundreds of thousands homeless in the country's worst floods in 40 years. An international rescue effort is mounted, but disaster relief agencies warn of famine and disease to come.

March 2000 Violence in Nigeria between Muslims and Christians in the north leaves 400 people dead. Troops eventually restore order, but the government announces that the Muslim states had suspended their plans to introduce Islamic law.

7 March 2000 George W Bush wins a major victory over John McCain in the Republican primaries to the November Presidential elections. At the same time Bill Bradley, one of the Democratic contenders, withdraws from the race after Al Gore's successes.

March 2000 A senior official of the Jiangxi province in China, Hu Changquing, is executed for accepting bribes of more than $650,000. This comes after an Amnesty International report in January condemning China's execution record.

8 March 2000 ETA, the guerilla group seeking separation of the Basque region from the rest of Spain, admits responsibility for two recent bombings in the area.

9 March 2000 Greek Prime Minister Costas Simitis submits an application for Greece to join the single European currency.

11 March 2000 An explosion in the Barakova mine in Sukhodolsk, Ukraine, kills 82 people in Europe's worst mining disaster for 20 years.

14 March 2000 Diplomatic ties are formally resumed between Egypt and Sudan. Contact had ceased after Egypt accused Sudan of attempting to assassinate Hosni Mubarak in 1995.

17 March 2000 Some 530 people die in the Restoration of the Ten Commandments of God church in Kanungu trading centre in Rukungiri, western Uganda. At first the deaths are treated as a mass suicide, but the discovery of mutilated and strangled corpses leads the authorities to consider the case as murder.

26 March 2000 Acting Russian President Vladimir Putin is elected President of Russia.

April 2000 According to a report issued by the UN, Angola is in the midst of a humanitarian crisis, after civil war has left thousands of people displaced and at risk of starvation. The report encourages the government to allow more aid workers into the country.

April 2000 Amnesty International reports the executions of over 1,800 people in 31 countries in 1999, over half of which have occurred in China. Although the overall figure has reduced from 1998, there have been increased numbers of people put to death in Saudi Arabia, Iran, and the USA.

April 2000 Veterans of Zimbabwe's civil war, supported by President Robert Mugabe's government, take over farms owned by whites.

5 April 2000 After Prime Minister Keizo Obuchi's collapse due to a stroke, Yoshiro Mori becomes Japan's interim Prime Minister before elections to be held in the autumn. He announces that he intends to continue Mr Obuchi's policies.

6 April 2000 Cuban Juan Miguel Gonzalez, father of six-year-old Elian who is at the centre of an international custody battle, arrives in Miami, Florida, to plead for the return of his son, who is staying there with relatives.

8 April 2000 A state of emergency is declared in Bolivia after protests over issues such as access to water, and the economic stagnation of the country. Six people are killed when troops attempt to control the demonstrations.

13 April 2000 The deadline arrives for Lazaro Gonzalez, the great-uncle of six-year-old Cuban boy Elian Gonzales, to hand over the boy to his father to return to Cuba. Gonzalez defies the justice department order and refuses to hand over the child.

13 April 2000 The high court in Harare, Zimbabwe, orders the police to evict the thousands of blacks who are occupying white farms around the country. The police show no signs of complying.

15 April 2000 A white farmer and two members of Zimbabwe's main opposition party are killed by supporters of President Mugabe, who continues to condone seizures of white farms by black war veterans.

16 April 2000 Anti-globalization protesters demonstrate against the World Bank and International Monetary Fund in Washington, DC. The protesters form a human barricade around the IMF headquarters, prompting a heavy show of force by the police, but fail to stop the IMF meetings.

18 April 2000 After a lengthy shootout, white Zimbabwean farmer Martin Olds is shot dead by black squatters intending to seize his farm, further plunging the country into turmoil.

22 April 2000 Heavily armed US federal agents seize six-year-old Cuban boy Elian Gonzalez in a pre-dawn raid at his relatives' home in Miami, Florida. He is later reunited with his father at an airbase near Washington, DC.

23 April 2000 Rebel Filipinos of the Abu Sayyaf, a Muslim militia fighting for independence from the majority Catholic Philippines, take 21 people hostage from a Malaysian diving resort and take them to the southern Philippine island of Jolo.

27 April 2000 Talks in London between officials from Zimbabwe and UK foreign secretary Robin Cook, aimed at restoring peace in Zimbabwe, end in deadlock after the Zimbabwean delegation refuse to make a commitment to end the violence.

11 May 2000 Vicente Fox, the main opposition candidate for Mexico's July elections, takes a lead in the polls for the first time. Analysts say the ruling party (Institutional Revolutionary Party) may lose for the first time in 70 years.

13 May 2000 At least 20 people are killed and 950 injured after an explosion at a fireworks factory in the Dutch town of Enschede, which left the surrounding area in ruins. An investigation is immediately launched.

23 May 2000 Israeli forces withdraw from southern Lebanon, ending their 22-year occupation. After the collapse of the Lebanese militia that had been supported by Israel, the retreat was hasty and chaotic.

June 2000 Ethiopia claims that its war with Eritrea has now ended, three weeks after making significant territorial gains.

10 June 2000 Maoist guerrillas attempting to overthrow Nepal's monarchy kill twelve policemen, five children and three other civilians. They are among the 1,200 victims of the 4-year conflict.

11 June 2000 In Yemen, Gudbrand Stuve, a Norwegian diplomat, dies in crossfire between Yemeni security forces and four men who were trying to kidnap him and his young son.

13 June 2000 A summit meeting between communist North and capitalist South Korea begins, raising hopes for a rapprochement between the countries divided since the 1950–53 Korean war.

25 June 2000 Japan's ruling party, the Liberal Democratic Party (LDP), clings onto power after a hastily called general election. They retain Yoshiro Mori as leader, despite his unpopular remarks regarding the military spirit of Japan which were seen as having encouraged lukewarm voters to stay at home.

29 June 2000 Up to 500 Christian refugees are feared dead after the sinking of their overloaded ferry in turbulent seas off the coast of Indonesia. The refugees were fleeing ethnic conflict in the Moluccan Islands, where thousands have already died in clashes between Muslims and Christians.

29 June 2000 Cuban refugee Elian Gonzalez returns to Cuba with his father at the conclusion of the bitter 7-month custody battle in the USA. One day prior to his departure from Washington, DC, Congress passed measures to relax the embargo on food and medicine to Cuba.

Robin Cook, UK foreign secretary, speaking at the Labour Party conference in Bournemouth, England, in September 1999. He emphasized Labour's commitment to a 'new internationalism' and to defending human rights, amidst calls for more progress on ethical foreign issues. *Syndication International*

Geography

Major Oceans and Seas of the World

Ocean/sea	Area[1]		Average depth	
	sq km	sq mi	m	ft
Pacific Ocean	166,242,000	64,186,000	3,939	12,925
Atlantic Ocean	86,557,000	33,420,000	3,575	11,730
Indian Ocean	73,429,000	28,351,000	3,840	12,598
Arctic Ocean	13,224,000	5,106,000	1,038	3,407
South China Sea	2,975,000	1,149,000	1,464	4,802
Caribbean Sea	2,754,000	1,063,000	2,575	8,448
Mediterranean Sea	2,510,000	969,000	1,501	4,926
Bering Sea	2,261,000	873,000	1,491	4,893
Sea of Okhotsk	1,580,000	610,000	973	3,192
Gulf of Mexico	1,544,000	596,000	1,614	5,297
Sea of Japan	1,013,000	391,000	1,667	5,468
Hudson Bay	730,000	282,000	93	305
East China Sea	665,000	257,000	189	620
Andaman Sea	565,000	218,000	1,118	3,667
Black Sea	461,000	178,000	1,190	3,906
Red Sea	453,000	175,000	538	1,764
North Sea	427,000	165,000	94	308
Baltic Sea	422,000	163,000	55	180
Yellow Sea	294,000	114,000	37	121
Persian Gulf	230,000	89,000	100	328
Gulf of California	153,000	59,000	724	2,375
English Channel	90,000	35,000	54	177
Irish Sea	89,000	34,000	60	197

[1] All figures are approximate as boundaries of oceans and seas cannot be exactly determined.

Largest Islands in the World

Island	Location	Area	
		sq km	sq mi
Greenland	northern Atlantic	2,175,600	840,000
New Guinea	southwestern Pacific	800,000	309,000
Borneo	southwestern Pacific	744,100	287,300
Madagascar	Indian Ocean	587,041	226,657
Baffin	Canadian Arctic	507,450	195,875
Sumatra	Indian Ocean	424,760	164,000
Honshu	northwestern Pacific	230,966	89,176
Great Britain	northern Atlantic	218,078	84,200
Victoria	Canadian Arctic	217,206	83,896
Ellesmere	Canadian Arctic	196,160	75,767
Sulawesi	Indian Ocean	189,216	73,057
South Island, New Zealand	southwestern Pacific	149,883	57,870
Java	Indian Ocean	126,602	48,900
North Island, New Zealand	southwestern Pacific	114,669	44,274
Cuba	Caribbean Sea	110,860	42,803
Newfoundland	northwestern Atlantic	108,860	42,030
Luzon	western Pacific	104,688	40,420
Iceland	northern Atlantic	103,000	39,768
Mindanao	western Pacific	94,630	36,537
Ireland (Northern Ireland and the Republic of Ireland)	northern Atlantic	84,406	32,590
Hokkaido	northwestern Pacific	83,515	32,245
Sakhalin	northwestern Pacific	76,400	29,500
Hispaniola (Dominican Republic and Haiti)	Caribbean Sea	76,192	29,418
Banks	Canadian Arctic	70,028	27,038
Tasmania	southwestern Pacific	67,800	26,171
Sri Lanka	Indian Ocean	65,610	25,332
Devon	Canadian Arctic	55,247	21,331

Longest Rivers in the World

River	Location	Approximate length	
		km	mi
Nile	Africa	6,695	4,160
Amazon	South America	6,570	4,083
Chang Jiang (Yangtze)	China	6,300	3,915
Mississippi–Missouri–Red Rock	USA	6,020	3,741
Huang He (Yellow River)	China	5,464	3,395
Ob–Irtysh	China/Kazakhstan/ Russian Federation	5,410	3,362
Amur–Shilka	Asia	4,416	2,744
Lena	Russian Federation	4,400	2,734
Congo	Africa	4,374	2,718
Mackenzie–Peace–Finlay	Canada	4,241	2,635
Mekong	Asia	4,180	2,597
Niger	Africa	4,100	2,548
Yenisei	Russian Federation	4,100	2,548
Paraná	Brazil	3,943	2,450
Mississippi	USA	3,779	2,348
Murray–Darling	Australia	3,751	2,331
Missouri	USA	3,726	2,315
Volga	Russian Federation	3,685	2,290
Madeira	Brazil	3,241	2,014
Purus	Brazil	3,211	1,995
São Francisco	Brazil	3,199	1,988
Yukon	USA/Canada	3,185	1,979
Rio Grande	USA/Mexico	3,058	1,900
Indus	Tibet/Pakistan	2,897	1,800
Danube	central and eastern Europe	2,858	1,776
Japura	Brazil	2,816	1,750
Salween	Myanmar/China	2,800	1,740
Brahmaputra	Asia	2,736	1,700
Euphrates	Iraq	2,736	1,700
Tocantins	Brazil	2,699	1,677
Zambezi	Africa	2,650	1,647
Orinoco	Venezuela	2,559	1,590
Paraguay	Paraguay	2,549	1,584
Amu Darya	Tajikistan/Turkmenistan/ Uzbekistan	2,540	1,578
Ural	Russian Federation/ Kazakhstan	2,535	1,575
Kolyma	Russian Federation	2,513	1,562
Ganges	India/Bangladesh	2,510	1,560
Arkansas	USA	2,344	1,459
Colorado	USA	2,333	1,450

(continued)

Longest Rivers in the World *(continued)*

River	Location	Approximate length	
		km	mi
Dnieper	Russian Federation/ Belarus/Ukraine	2,285	1,420
Syr Darya	Asia	2,205	1,370
Irrawaddy	Myanmar	2,152	1,337
Orange	South Africa	2,092	1,300

Largest Lakes in the World

Lake	Location	Area	
		sq km	sq mi
Caspian Sea	Azerbaijan/Russian Federation/Kazakhstan/ Turkmenistan/Iran	370,990	143,239
Superior	USA/Canada	82,071	31,688
Victoria	Tanzania/Kenya/Uganda	69,463	26,820
Aral Sea	Kazakhstan/Uzbekistan	64,500	24,903
Huron	USA/Canada	59,547	22,991
Michigan	USA	57,735	22,291
Tanganyika	Tanzania/Democratic Republic of Congo/Zambia/Burundi	32,880	12,695
Baikal	Russian Federation	31,499	12,162
Great Bear	Canada	31,316	12,091
Malawi (or Nyasa)	Malawi/Tanzania/Mozambique	28,867	11,146
Great Slave	Canada	28,560	11,027
Erie	USA/Canada	25,657	9,906
Winnipeg	Canada	25,380	9,799
Ontario	USA/Canada	19,010	7,340
Balkhash	Kazakhstan	18,421	7,112
Ladoga	Russian Federation	17,695	6,832
Chad	Chad/Cameroon/Nigeria	16,310	6,297
Maracaibo	Venezuela	13,507	5,215

Largest Deserts in the World

Desert	Location	Area[1]	
		sq km	sq mi
Sahara	northern Africa	9,065,000	3,500,000
Gobi	Mongolia/northeastern China	1,295,000	500,000
Patagonian	Argentina	673,000	260,000
Rub al-Khali	southern Arabian peninsula	647,500	250,000
Kalahari	southwestern Africa	582,800	225,000
Chihuahuan	Mexico/southwestern USA	362,600	140,000
Taklimakan	northern China	362,600	140,000
Great Sandy	northwestern Australia	338,500	130,000
Great Victoria	southwestern Australia	338,500	130,000
Kyzyl Kum	Uzbekistan/Kazakhstan	259,000	100,000
Thar	India/Pakistan	259,000	100,000
Sonoran	Mexico/southwestern USA	181,300	70,000
Simpson	Australia	103,600	40,000
Mojave	southwestern USA	65,000	25,000

[1] Desert areas are very approximate because clear physical boundaries may not occur.

Highest Waterfalls in the World

Waterfall	Location	Total drop	
		m	ft
Angel Falls	Venezuela	979	3,212
Yosemite Falls	USA	739	2,425
Mardalsfossen-South	Norway	655	2,149
Tugela Falls	South Africa	614	2,014
Cuquenan	Venezuela	610	2,000
Sutherland	New Zealand	580	1,903
Ribbon Fall, Yosemite	USA	491	1,612
Great Karamang River Falls	Guyana	488	1,600
Mardalsfossen-North	Norway	468	1,535
Della Falls	Canada	440	1,443
Gavarnie Falls	France	422	1,385
Skjeggedal	Norway	420	1,378
Glass Falls	Brazil	404	1,325
Krimml	Austria	400	1,312
Trummelbach Falls	Switzerland	400	1,312
Takkakaw Falls	Canada	366	1,200
Silver Strand Falls, Yosemite	USA	357	1,170
Wallaman Falls	Australia	346	1,137
Wollomombi	Australia	335	1,100
Cusiana River Falls	Colombia	300	984
Giessbach	Switzerland	300	984
Skykkjedalsfossen	Norway	300	984
Staubbach	Switzerland	300	984

Highest Elevations and Lowest Depressions in the World by Continent

Continent	Highest elevation	Height		Lowest depression	Depth below sea level	
		m	ft		m	ft
Africa	Kilimanjaro, Tanzania	5,895	19,337	Lake Assal, Djibouti	153	502
Antarctica	Vinson Massif	5,140	16,863	Lake Vostok[1]	4,000	13,123
Asia	Everest, China-Nepal	8,848	29,028	Dead Sea, Israel/Jordan	400	1,312
Europe	Elbrus, Russian Federation	5,642	18,510	Caspian Sea, Azerbaijan/ Russian Federation/ Kazakhstan/Turkmenistan/ Iran	28	92
North America	McKinley (AK), USA	6,194	20,321	Death Valley (CA), USA	86	282
Oceania	Jaya, New Guinea	5,030	16,502	Lake Eyre, South Australia	16	52
South America	Cerro Aconcagua, Argentina	6,960	22,834	Valdés Peninsula, Argentina	40	131

[1] Discovered by the British Antarctic Survey in 1996, the freshwater Lake Vostok lies beneath the ice sheets and covers an area of 14,000 sq km/5,400 sq mi.

Highest Mountains in the World by Region

Region/mountain	Location	Height	
		m	ft
Africa			
Kilimanjaro	Tanzania	5,895	19,337
Kenya (Batian)	Kenya	5,199	17,057
Ngaliema (formerly Mt Stanley and Margherita Peak)	Democratic Republic of Congo/Uganda	5,110	16,765

(continued)

Highest Mountains in the World by Region *(continued)*

Region/mountain	Location	Height m	Height ft
Duwoni (formerly Umberto Peak)	Uganda	4,896	16,063
Baker (Edward Peak)	Uganda	4,843	15,889
Alpine Europe			
Mont Blanc	France/Italy	4,807	15,771
Monte Rosa	Switzerland	4,634	15,203
Dom	Switzerland	4,545	14,911
Liskamm	Switzerland/Italy	4,527	14,852
Weisshorn	Switzerland	4,505	14,780
Antarctica			
Vinson Massif		5,140	16,863
Tyree		4,965	16,289
Shinn		4,800	15,748
Gardner		4,690	15,387
Epperley		4,511	14,800
Asia			
Everest	China/Nepal	8,848	29,028
K2	Kashmir/Jammu	8,611	28,251
Kangchenjunga	India/Nepal	8,598	28,208
Lhotse	China/Nepal	8,511	27,923
Yalung Kang	India/Nepal	8,502	27,893
Australia			
Kosciusko	Snowy Mountains, New South Wales	2,230	7,316
Carpathians			
Gerlachvka	Slovak Republic	2,655	8,711
Moldoveanu	Romania	2,544	8,346
Negoiu	Romania	2,535	8,317
Mindra	Romania	2,518	8,261
Peleaga	Romania	2,509	8,232
Caucasia			
Elbrus, West Peak	Russian Federation	5,642	18,510
Dykh Tau	Russian Federation/ Georgia	5,203	17,070
Shkhara	Russian Federation/ Georgia	5,201	17,063
Kashtan Tau	Russian Federation/ Georgia	5,144	16,876
Dzanghi Tau	Russian Federation	5,049	16,565
New Zealand			
Cook (called Aorangi in Maori)	west coast, South Island	3,754	12,316
North and Central America			
McKinley	Alaska, USA	6,194	20,321
Logan, Yukon	Canada	6,050	19,849
Citlaltépetl (Orizaba)	Mexico	5,610	18,405
St Elias	Alaska, USA/Yukon, Canada	5,489	18,008
Popocatépetl	Mexico	5,452	17,887
Oceania[1]			
Jaya	West Irian, Papua Guinea	5,030	16,502
Daam	West Irian, Papua New Guinea	4,922	16,148
Oost Carstensz (also known as Jayakusumu Timur)	West Irian, Papua New Guinea	4,840	15,879
Trikora	West Irian, Papua New Guinea	4,730	15,518
Enggea	West Irian, Papua New Guinea	4,717	15,476
Polynesia			
Mauna Kea	Hawaii, USA	4,205	13,796
Mauna Loa	Hawaii, USA	4,170	13,681
Pyrenees			
Pico de Aneto	Spain	3,404	11,168
Pico de Posets	Spain	3,371	11,060
Monte Perdido	Spain	3,348	10,984
Pico de la Maladeta	Spain	3,312	10,866
Pic de Vignemale	France/Spain	3,298	10,820
Scandinavia			
Glittertind	Norway	2,472	8,110
Galdhøpiggen	Norway	2,469	8,100
Skagastolstindane	Norway	2,405	7,890
Snohetta	Norway	2,286	7,500
South America			
Cerro Aconcagua	Argentina	6,960	22,834
Ojos del Salado	Argentina/Chile	6,908	22,664
Bonete	Argentina	6,872	22,546
Nevado de Pissis	Argentina/Chile	6,779	22,241
Huascarán Sur	Peru	6,768	22,204

[1] Including all of Papua New Guinea.

Highest Mountains in the World and First Ascents

Mountain	Location	Height m	Height ft	Year of first ascent	Expedition nationality (leader)
Everest	China/Nepal	8,848	29,028	1953	British/New Zealander (J Hunt)
K2	Kashmir/Jammu	8,611	28,251	1954	Italian (A Desio)
Kangchenjunga	India/Nepal	8,598	28,208	1955	British (C Evans; by the southwest face)
Lhotse	China/Nepal	8,511	27,923	1956	Swiss (E Reiss)
Yalung Kang (formerly Kangchenjunga West Peak)	India/Nepal	8,502	27,893	1973	Japanese (Y Ageta)
Kangchenjunga South Peak	India/Nepal	8,488	27,847	1978	Polish (W Wróż)
Makalu I	China/Nepal	8,481	27,824	1955	French (J Couzy)
Kangchenjunga Middle Peak	India/Nepal	8,475	27,805	1973	Polish (W Wróż)
Lhotse Shar	China/Nepal	8,383	27,503	1970	Austrian (S Mayerl)
Dhaulagiri	Nepal	8,172	26,811	1960	Swiss/Austrian (K Diemberger)
Manaslu	Nepal	8,156	26,759	1956	Japanese (T Imanishi)
Cho Oyu	China/Nepal	8,153	26,748	1954	Austrian (H Tichy)
Nanga Parbat	Kashmir/Jammu	8,126	26,660	1953	German (K M Herrligkoffer)
Annapurna I	Nepal	8,078	26,502	1950	French (M Herzog)
Gasherbrum I	Kashmir/Jammu	8,068	26,469	1958	US (P K Schoening; by the southwest ridge)
Broad Peak	Kashmir/Jammu	8,047	26,401	1957	Austrian (M Schmuck)
Gasherbrum II	Kashmir/Jammu	8,034	26,358	1956	Austrian (S Larch; by the southwest spur)
Gosainthan	China	8,012	26,286	1964	Chinese (195-strong team; accounts are inconclusive)
Broad Peak (Middle)	Kashmir/Jammu	8,000	26,246	1975	Polish (K Glazek)
Gasherbrum III	Kashmir/Jammu	7,952	26,089	1975	Polish (J Onyszkiewicz)

(continued)

Highest Mountains in the World and First Ascents *(continued)*

Mountain	Location	Height m	Height ft	Year of first ascent	Expedition nationality (leader)
Annapurna II	Nepal	7,937	26,040	1960	British (C Bonington)
Gasherbrum IV	Kashmir/Jammu	7,923	25,994	1958	Italian (W Bonatti, C Mouri)
Gyachung Kang	Nepal	7,921	25,987	1964	Japanese (Y Kato, K Sakaizqwa)
Disteghil Shar	Kashmir	7,884	25,866	1960	Austrian (G Stärker, D Marchart)
Himalchuli	Nepal	7,864	25,800	1960	Japanese (M Harada, H Tanabe)
Nuptse	Nepal	7,841	25,725	1961	British (D Davis, C Bonington, L Brown)
Manaslu II	Nepal	7,835	25,705	1970	Japanese (H Watanabe, Lhakpa Tsering)
Masherbrum East	Kashmir	7,821	25,659	1960	Pakistani/US (G Bell, W Unsoeld)
Nanda Devi	India	7,817	25,646	1936	British (H W Tilman)
Chomo Lonzo	Nepal	7,815	25,639	1954	French (J Couzy, L Terry)

Major Volcanoes Active in the 20th Century

As of 3 April 2000.

Volcano	Height m	Height ft	Location	Date of last eruption or activity
Africa				
Cameroon	4,096	13,353	isolated mountain, Cameroon	1999
Nyiragongo	3,470	11,385	Virunga, Democratic Republic of Congo	1994
Nyamuragira	3,056	10,028	Democratic Republic of Congo	2000
Ol Doinyo Lengai	2,886	9,469	Tanzania	1993
Lake Nyos	918	3,011	Cameroon	1986
Erta-Ale	503	1,650	Ethiopia	1995
Antarctica				
Erebus	4,023	13,200	Ross Island, McMurdo Sound	1995
Deception Island	576	1,890	South Shetland Island	1970
Asia				
Kerinci	3,800	12,467	Sumatra, Indonesia	1987
Rindjani	3,726	12,224	Lombok, Indonesia	1966
Semeru	3,676	12,060	Java, Indonesia	1995
Slamet	3,428	11,247	Java, Indonesia	1989
Raung	3,322	10,932	Java, Indonesia	1993
Agung	3,142	10,308	Bali, Indonesia	1964
On-Taka	3,063	10,049	Honshu, Japan	1991
Merapi	2,911	9,551	Java, Indonesia	1998
Marapi	2,891	9,485	Sumatra, Indonesia	1993
Asama	2,530	8,300	Honshu, Japan	1990
Nigata Yake-yama	2,475	8,111	Honshu, Japan	1989
Mayon	2,462	8,084	Luzon, Philippines	2000
Canlaon	2,459	8,070	Negros, Philippines	1993
Chokai	2,225	7,300	Honshu, Japan	1974
Galunggung	2,168	7,113	Java, Indonesia	1984
Azuma	2,042	6,700	Honshu, Japan	1977
Sangeang Api	1,935	6,351	Lesser Sunda Island, Indonesia	1988
Pinatubo	1,759	5,770	Luzon, Philippines	1995
Kelut	1,730	5,679	Java, Indonesia	1990
Unzen	1,360	4,462	Japan	1996
Krakatoa	818	2,685	Sumatra, Indonesia	1999
Taal	300	984	Philippines	1999
Atlantic Ocean				
Pico de Teide	3,716	12,192	Tenerife, Canary Islands, Spain	1909
Fogo	2,835	9,300	Cape Verde Islands	1995
Beerenberg	2,277	7,470	Jan Mayen Island, Norway	1985
Hekla	1,491	4,920	Iceland	2000
Krafla	654	2,145	Iceland	1984
Helgafell	215	706	Iceland	1973
Surtsey	174	570	Iceland	1967
Caribbean				
La Grande Soufrière	1,467	4,813	Basse-Terre, Guadeloupe	1977
Pelée	1,397	4,584	Martinique	1932
La Soufrière St Vincent	1,234	4,048	St Vincent and the Grenadines	1979
Soufrière Hills/ Chances Peak	968	3,176	Montserrat	2000
Central America				
Acatenango	3,960	12,992	Sierra Madre, Guatemala	1972
Fuego	3,835	12,582	Sierra Madre, Guatemala	1999
Tacana	3,780	12,400	Sierra Madre, Guatemala	1988
Santa Maria	3,768	12,362	Sierra Madre, Guatemala	1993
Irazú	3,452	11,325	Cordillera Central, Costa Rica	1992
Turrialba	3,246	10,650	Cordillera Central, Costa Rica	1992
Póas	2,721	8,930	Cordillera Central, Costa Rica	1994
Pacaya	2,543	8,346	Sierra Madre, Guatemala	2000
San Miguel	2,131	6,994	El Salvador	1986
Arenal	1,552	5,092	Costa Rica	1998
Europe				
Kliuchevskoi	4,750	15,584	Kamchatka Peninsula, Russia	1999
Koryakskaya	3,456	11,339	Kamchatka Peninsula, Russia	1957
Sheveluch	3,283	10,771	Kamchatka Peninsula, Russia	1997
Etna	3,236	10,625	Sicily, Italy	2000
Bezymianny	2,882	9,455	Kamchatka Peninsula, Russia	2000
Alaid	2,335	7,662	Kurile Islands, Russia	1986
Tiatia	1,833	6,013	Kurile Islands, Russia	1981
Sarychev Peak	1,512	4,960	Kurile Islands, Russia	1989
Vesuvius	1,289	4,203	Italy	1944
Stromboli	931	3,055	Lipari Islands, Italy	1998

(continued)

Major Volcanoes Active in the 20th Century *(continued)*

Volcano	Height m	Height ft	Location	Date of last eruption or activity
Santorini (Thera)	584	1,960	Cyclades, Greece	1950
Indian Ocean				
Karthala	2,440	8,000	Comoros	1991
Piton de la Fournaise (LeVolcan)	1,823	5,981	Réunion Island, France	2000
Mid-Pacific				
Mauna Loa	4,170	13,681	Hawaii, USA	1984
Kilauea	1,247	4,100	Hawaii, USA	2000
North America				
Popocatépetl	5,452	17,887	Altiplano de México, Mexico	2000
Colima	4,268	14,003	Altiplano de México, Mexico	1999
Spurr	3,374	11,070	Alaska Range (AK) USA	1953
Lassen Peak	3,186	10,453	California, USA	1921
Redoubt	3,108	10,197	Alaska Range (AK) USA	1991
Iliamna	3,052	10,016	Alaska Range (AK) USA	1978
Shishaldin	2,861	9,387	Aleutian Islands (AK) USA	2000
St Helens	2,549	8,364	Skamania County (WA), USA	1998
Pavlof	2,517	8,261	Alaska Range (AK) USA	1997
Veniaminof	2,507	8,225	Alaska Range (AK) USA	1995
Novarupta (Katmai)	2,298	7,540	Alaska Range (AK) USA	1931
El Chichon	2,225	7,300	Altiplano de México, Mexico	1982
Makushin	2,036	6,680	Aleutian Islands (AK) USA	1987
Oceania				
Ruapehu	2,796	9,175	New Zealand	1999
Ulawun	2,296	7,532	Papua New Guinea	1993
Ngauruhoe	2,290	7,515	New Zealand	1977
Bagana	1,998	6,558	Papua New Guinea	1993
Manam	1,829	6,000	Papua New Guinea	1998
Lamington	1,780	5,844	Papua New Guinea	1956
Karkar	1,499	4,920	Papua New Guinea	1979
Lopevi	1,450	4,755	Vanuatu	1982
Ambrym	1,340	4,376	Vanuatu	1991
Tarawera	1,149	3,770	New Zealand	1973
Langila	1,093	3,586	Papua New Guinea	1996
Rabaul	688	2,257	Papua New Guinea	1997
Pagan	570	1,870	Mariana Islands	1993
White Island	328	1,075	New Zealand	2000
South America				
San Pedro	6,199	20,325	Andes, Chile	1960
Guallatiri	6,060	19,882	Andes, Chile	1993
Lascar	5,990	19,652	Andes, Chile	1995
San José	5,919	19,405	Andes, Chile	1931
Cotopaxi	5,897	19,347	Andes, Ecuador	1975
Tutupaca	5,844	19,160	Andes, Ecuador	1902
Ubinas	5,710	18,720	Andes, Peru	1969
Tupungatito	5,640	18,504	Andes, Chile	1986
Islunga	5,566	18,250	Andes, Chile	1960
Nevado del Ruiz	5,435	17,820	Andes, Colombia	1992
Tolima	5,249	17,210	Andes, Colombia	1943
Sangay	5,230	17,179	Andes, Ecuador	1996

Latitude, Longitude, and Altitude of the World's Major Cities

City	Latitude °	Latitude '	Longitude °	Longitude '	Altitude m	Altitude ft
Adelaide, Australia	34	55 S	138	36 E	43	140
Algiers, Algeria	36	50 N	03	00 E	59	194
Almaty, Kazakhstan	43	16 N	76	53 E	775	2,543
Amsterdam, Netherlands	52	22 N	04	53 E	3	10
Ankara, Turkey	39	55 N	32	55 E	862	2,825
Asunción, Paraguay	25	15 S	57	40 W	139	456
Athens, Greece	37	58 N	23	43 E	92	300
Bangkok, Thailand	13	45 N	100	31 E	0	0
Barcelona, Spain	41	23 N	02	09 E	93	305
Beijing, China	39	56 N	116	24 E	183	600
Belfast, Northern Ireland	54	37 N	05	56 W	67	217
Belgrade, Yugoslavia	44	52 N	20	32 E	132	433
Berlin, Germany	52	31 N	13	25 E	34	110
Bogotá, Colombia	04	32 N	74	05 W	2,640	8,660
Brussels, Belgium	50	52 N	04	22 E	100	328
Bucharest, Romania	44	25 N	26	07 E	92	302
Budapest, Hungary	47	30 N	19	05 E	139	456
Buenos Aires, Argentina	34	36 S	58	28 W	0	0
Cairo, Egypt	30	03 N	31	15 E	116	381
Cape Town, South Africa	33	55 S	18	22 E	17	56
Caracas, Venezuela	10	28 N	67	02 W	1,042	3,418
Copenhagen, Denmark	55	40 N	12	34 E	9	33
Dakar, Senegal	14	40 N	17	28 W	40	131
Delhi, India	28	35 N	77	12 E	218	714
Detroit (MI), USA	42	19 N	83	02 W	178	585
Djibouti, Djibouti	11	30 N	43	03 E	7	23
Dublin, Republic of Ireland	53	20 N	06	15 W	47	154
Edinburgh, Scotland	55	55 N	03	10 W	134	440
Frankfurt, Germany	50	07 N	08	41 E	103	338
Guatemala City, Guatemala	14	37 N	90	31 W	1,480	4,855
Havana, Cuba	23	08 N	82	23 W	24	80
Helsinki, Finland	60	10 N	25	00 E	46	151
Hong Kong, China	22	18 N	114	10 E	33	109
Istanbul, Turkey	41	06 N	29	03 E	114	374
Jakarta, Indonesia	06	10 S	106	48 E	8	26
Jerusalem, Israel	31	46 N	35	14 E	762	2,500
Johannesburg, South Africa	26	12 S	28	05 E	1,750	5,740
Kabul, Afghanistan	34	30 N	69	13 E	1,827	5,955
Karachi, Pakistan	24	48 N	66	59 E	4	13
Katmandu, Nepal	27	43 S	85	19 E	1,372	4,500
Kiev, Ukraine	50	26 N	30	31 E	179	587
Kinshasa, Democratic Republic of Congo	04	18 S	15	17 E	322	1,066
Lagos, Nigeria	06	27 N	03	24 E	3	10
La Paz, Bolivia	16	27 S	68	22 W	3,658	12,001
Lhasa, Tibet	29	40 N	91	07 E	3,685	12,090
Lima, Peru	12	00 S	77	02 W	120	394
Lisbon, Portugal	38	44 N	09	09 W	77	253
London, England	51	32 N	00	05 W	75	245
Los Angeles (CA), USA	34	03 N	118	14 W	104	340
Madrid, Spain	40	26 N	03	42 W	660	2,165
Manila, Philippines	14	35 N	120	57 E	14	47
Mecca, Saudi Arabia	21	27 S	39	49 E	2,000	6,562
Melbourne, Australia	37	47 N	144	58 E	35	115
Mexico City, Mexico	19	24 N	99	09 W	2,239	7,347
Milan, Italy	45	27 S	09	10 E	121	397
Montevideo, Uruguay	34	53 N	56	10 W	22	72

(continued)

Latitude, Longitude, and Altitude of the World's Major Cities *(continued)*

City	Latitude °	Latitude '	Longitude °	Longitude '	Altitude m	Altitude ft
Moscow, Russian Federation	55	45 N	37	35 E	120	394
Mumbai, India	18	58 N	72	50 E	8	27
Nagasaki, Japan	32	48 S	129	57 E	133	436
Nairobi, Kenya	01	25 N	36	55 E	1,820	5,971
New Delhi, India	28	36 N	77	12 E	235	770
New York (NY), USA	40	45 N	73	59 W	17	55
Oslo, Norway	59	57 N	10	42 E	94	308
Ottawa, Canada	45	26 N	75	41 W	56	185
Panamá, Panama	08	58 N	79	32 W	0	0
Paris, France	48	52 N	02	20 E	92	300
Prague, Czech Republic	50	05 N	14	26 E	262	860
Quito, Ecuador	0	13 S	78	30 W	2,811	9,222
Reykjavik, Iceland	64	04 N	21	58 W	18	59
Rio de Janeiro, Brazil	22	43 S	43	13 W	9	30
Rome, Italy	41	53 N	12	30 E	29	95
St Petersburg, Russian Federation	59	56 N	30	18 E	4	13
Santiago, Chile	33	27 S	70	40 W	1,500	4,921
Seoul, South Korea	37	34 N	127	00 E	10	34
Shanghai, China	31	10 N	121	28 E	7	23
Singapore	01	14 N	103	55 E	10	33
Sofia, Bulgaria	42	40 N	23	20 E	550	1,805
Stockholm, Sweden	59	17 N	18	03 E	44	144
Sydney, Australia	33	53 S	151	12 E	8	25
Tehran, Iran	35	40 N	51	26 E	1,110	3,937
Tokyo, Japan	35	42 N	139	46 E	9	30
Toronto, Canada	43	39 N	79	23 W	91	300
Tripoli, Libya	32	54 N	13	11 E	0	0
Vancouver, Canada	49	18 N	123	04 W	43	141
Vienna, Austria	48	14 N	16	20 E	203	666
Warsaw, Poland	52	15 N	21	00 E	110	360
Washington, DC, USA	38	53 N	77	00 W	8	25
Wellington, New Zealand	41	18 S	174	47 E	0	0
Zürich, Switzerland	47	21 N	08	31 E	493	1,618

Countries of the World

Afghanistan Republic of

National name *Islamic Emirate of Afghanistan* **Area** 652,090 sq km/ 251,771 sq mi **Capital** Kabul **Major towns/cities** Kandahar, Herat, Mazar-i-Sharif, Jalalabad

Government

Head of state and government Muhammad Rabbani from 1996 **Political system** Islamic nationalist **Armed forces** approximately 429,000 (1997) **Conscription** compulsory for four years, with break of three years after second year (since 1992 conscription has been difficult to enforce and desertion is common) **Defence spend** (% GDP) 12.5 (1997) **Education spend** (% GNP) 2.0 (1992) **Health spend** (% GDP) 1.6 (1990) **Death penalty** retains and uses the death penalty for ordinary crimes

Population and society

Population 21,923,000 (1999 est) **Population growth rate** 2.9% (1995–2000) **Ethnic groups** Pathans, or Pushtuns, comprise the largest ethnic group, 54% of the population, followed by the Tajiks (concentrated in the north, 27%), the Uzbeks (8%), and Hazaras (7%) **Religion** Muslim (85% Sunni, 15% Shiite) **Life expectancy** 45 (men); 46 (women) (1995–2000) **Literacy rate** 44% (men); 14% (women) (1995 est) **Unemployment** 8% (1995 est)

Economy and resources

GDP (US$) 19.3 billion (1997 est) **GNP** (US$) N/A **GNP per capita (PPP)** (US$) 819 (1992) **Real GDP growth** (% change on previous year) N/A **Consumer price inflation** 240% (1996 est) **Foreign debt** (US$) 5.5 billion (1997) **Resources** natural gas, coal, iron ore, barytes, lapis lazuli, salt, talc, copper, chrome, gold, silver, asbestos, small petroleum reserves **Exports** fruit and nuts, carpets, wool, karakul skins, cotton, natural gas. Principal market: Kyrgyzstan 37.3% (1995) **Imports** basic manufactured goods and foodstuffs (notably wheat), petroleum products, textiles, fertilizers, vehicles and spare parts. Principal source: Japan 25.6% (1995)

■ Tourist information

Time difference GMT+4.5 **Currency** afgháni **Language** Pushtu, Dari (Persian), Uzbek, Turkoman, Kirgiz **Visa requirements** UK: visa required. USA: visa required **Embassy in the UK** 31 Prince's Gate, London SW7 1QQ. Tel: (020) 7589 8891; fax: (020) 7581 3452 **British embassy** Karte Parwan, Kabul. Tel: (93) 30511 (the embassy is closed at present) **Chamber of commerce** Afghan Chamber of Commerce and Industry, Mohd Jah Khan Wat, Kabul. Tel: (93) 26796; telex: 245 **Office hours** generally 0800–1200 and 1300–1630 Sat–Wed; 0830–1300 Thu **Banking hours** generally 0800–1200 and 1300–1630 Sat–Wed; 0800–1330 Thu **Airports** two international airports: Kabul (Khwaja Rawash) and Kandahar; 18 domestic airports; total passenger km: 276 million (1995) **Chief tourist attractions** Bamian (with its high statue of Buddha and thousands of painted caves); the Blue Mosque of Mazar; the suspended lakes of Bandi Amir; the Grand Mosque and minarets of Herat; the towns of Kandahar, Girishk, and Baekh (ancient Bactria); the high mountains of the Hindu Kush **Major holidays** 27 April, 1 May, 19 August; variable: Eid-ul-Adha, Arafa, Ashora, end of Ramadan, New Year (Hindu), Prophet's Birthday, first day of Ramadan

Chronology

6th century BC Part of Persian Empire under Cyrus II and Darius I. **329 BC** Conquered by Alexander the Great. **323 BC** Fell to the Seleucids, who ruled from Babylon. **304 BC** Ruled by Mauryan dynasty in south and independent Bactria in north. **135 BC** Central Asian tribes established Kusana dynasty. **3rd–7th centuries AD** Decline of Kusana dynasty. Emergence of Sassanids as ruling power with Hepthalites (central Asian nomads) and western Turks also fighting for control. **642–11th century** First Muslim invasion followed by a succession of Muslim dynasties, including Mahmud of Ghazni in 998. **1219–14th century** Mongol invasions led by Genghis Khan and Tamerlane. **16th–18th centuries** Much of Afghanistan came under the rule of the Mogul Empire under Babur (Zahir) and Nadir Shah. **1747** Afghanistan became an independent emirate under Dost Muhammad. **1838–42** First Afghan War, instigated by Britain to counter the threat to British India from expanding Russian influence in Afghanistan. **1878–80** Second Afghan War. **1919** Afghanistan recovered full independence following Third Afghan War. **1953** Lt-Gen Daud Khan became prime minister and introduced social and economic reform programme. **1963** Daud Khan forced to resign and constitutional monarchy established. **1973** Monarchy overthrown in coup by Daud Khan. **1978** Daud Khan assassinated in coup. Start of Muslim guerrilla (Mujahedin) resistance. **1979** USSR entered country to prop up government. **1986** Partial Soviet troop withdrawal. **1988** New non-Marxist constitution adopted. **1989** Withdrawal of Soviet troops; Mujahedin continued resistance to communist People's Democratic Party of Afghanistan (PDPA) regime and civil war intensified. **1991** US and Soviet military aid withdrawn. Mujahedin began talks with the Russians and Kabul government. **1992** Mujahedin leader Burhanuddin Rabbani was elected president. **1993–94** There was fighting around Kabul. **1996** The Talibaan controlled two-thirds of the country, including Kabul; the country was split between the Talibaan-controlled fundamentalist south and the more liberal north; strict Islamic law was imposed. **1997** The Talibaan was recognized as the legitimate government of Afghanistan by Pakistan and Saudi Arabia. **1998** Two earthquakes in the north killed over 8,000 people. The USA launched a missile attack on a suspected terrorist site in retaliation for bombings of US embassies in Nairobi and Dar es Salaam. Talibaan extended its control in the north, massacring 6,000 people at Mazar-I-Sharif. **1999** Fighting resumed in northern Afghanistan after a four-month lull. Intending to punish the Talibaan regime for failing to expel suspected terrorist Osama bin Laden, the United Nations (UN) imposed sanctions on Afghanistan in November, which provoked mobs to attack UN offices in the capital, Kabul.

Albania Republic of

National name *Republika e Shqipërisë* **Area** 28,748 sq km/ 11,099 sq mi **Capital** Tiranë (Tirana) **Major towns/cities** Durrës, Shkodër, Elbasan, Vlorë, Korçë

Government

Head of state Rexhep Mejdani from 1998 **Head of government** Ilir Meta from 1999 **Political system** emergent democracy **Armed forces** 54,000 (1997) **Conscription** compulsory for 15 months **Defence spend** (% GDP) 6.7 (1997) **Education spend** (% GDP) 3.1 (1996) **Health spend** (% GDP) 2.7 (1990–95) **Death penalty** retains the death penalty for ordinary crimes, but considered abolitionist in practice; committed in 1996 to put into place a moratorium on executions until total abolition

Population and society

Population 3,113,000 (1999 est) **Population growth rate** –0.4% (1995–2000) **Ethnic groups** 90% of Albanian, non-Slavic, descent; 8% ethnic Greek (concentrated in south) **Religion** Muslim, Orthodox, Roman Catholic **Life expectancy** 70 (men); 76 (women) (1995–2000) **Literacy rate** 85% (men); 85% (women) (1997) **Unemployment** 20% (1998 est)

Economy and resources

GDP (US$) 2.5 billion (1998) **GNP** (US$) (US$) 2.7 billion (1998) **GNP per capita (PPP)** (US$) 3,200 (1998 est) **Real GDP growth** (% change on previous year) 7 (1998) **Consumer price inflation** 20% (1998) **Foreign debt** (US$) 706 million (1997) **Resources** chromite (one of world's largest producers), copper, coal, nickel, petroleum and natural gas **Exports** chromium and chrome products, processed foodstuffs, textiles and footwear, base metals, machinery and equipment, bitumen, tobacco. Principal market: Italy 49.1% (1997) **Imports** machinery, fuels and minerals, plant and animal raw materials, chemical products. Principal source: Italy 46% (1997)

▪ Tourist information

Time difference GMT +1 **Currency** lek **Language** Albanian, Greek **Visa requirements** UK: visa not required. USA: visa not required **Embassy in the UK** 4th Floor, 38 Grosvenor Gardens, London SW1W 0EB. Tel: (020) 7730 5709; fax: (020) 7730 5747 **British embassy** Office of the British Chargé d'Affaires, c/o French Embassy, Rruga Skënderben 14, Tiranë. Tel: (42) 34250; telex: 2150 **Chamber of commerce** Chamber of Commerce of the Republic of Albania, Rruga Kavajes 6, Tiranë. Tel/fax: (42) 27997 **Office hours** 0700–1500 Mon–Fri **Banking hours** 0700–1500 Mon–Fri **Airports** international airport: Tiranë (Rinas); no regular domestic air service; total passenger km: 4 million (1995) **Major ports** Durrës **Chief tourist attractions** main tourist centres include Tiranë, Durrës, and Pogradec. The ancient towns of Apollonia and Butrint are important archaeological sites, and there are many other towns of historic interest **Major holidays** 1–2, 11 January, 8 March, 1 May, 28 November, 25 December; variable: end of Ramadan, Easter Monday, Good Friday, Eid-ul-Adha, Orthodox Easter

Chronology

2000 BC Albania was part of Illyria. **168 BC** Illyria was conquered by the Romans. **AD 395** Became part of Byzantine Empire. **6th–14th centuries** Byzantine decline exploited by Serbs, Normans, Slavs, Bulgarians, and Venetians. **1381** Ottoman invasion of Albania followed by years of resistance to Turkish rule. **1468** Resistance led by national hero Skanderbeg (George Kastrioti) largely collapsed, and Albania passed to Ottoman Empire. **15th–16th centuries** Thousands fled to southern Italy to escape Ottoman rule; over half of the rest of the population converted to Islam. **1878** Foundation of Albanian League promoted emergence of nationalism. **1912** Achieved independence from Turkey as a result of First Balkan War and end of Ottoman Empire in Europe. **1914–20** Occupied by Italy. **1925** Declared itself a republic. **1928–39** Monarchy of King Zog. **1939** Italian occupation led by Benito Mussolini. **1943–44** Under German rule following Italian surrender. **1946** Proclaimed Communist People's Republic of Albania, with Enver Hoxha as premier. **1949** Developed close links with Joseph Stalin in USSR and entered Comecon (Council for Mutual Economic Assistance). **1961** Broke with USSR in wake of Nikita Khrushchev's denunciation of Stalin, and withdrew from Comecon. In 1978 Albania also severed diplomatic links with China. **1987** Normal diplomatic relations restored with Canada, Greece, and West Germany. **1990–91** The one-party system was abandoned in the face of popular protest; the first opposition party was formed, and the first multiparty elections were held. **1992** Former communist officials were charged with corruption and abuse of power. Totalitarian and communist parties were banned. **1993** Conflict began between ethnic Greeks and Albanians, followed by a purge of ethnic Greeks from the civil service and army. **1997** Antigovernment riots; police killed demonstrators in the southern port of Vlorë. Southern Albania fell under rebel control. The government signed a World Bank and IMF rescue package to salvage the economy. **1998** A new constitution came into effect. **1999** Ilir Meta, a socialist, became prime minister.

Algeria Democratic and Popular Republic of

National name *al-Jumhuriya al-Jazairiya ad-Dimuqratiya ash-Shabiya* **Area** 2,381,741 sq km/919,590 sq mi **Capital** Algiers (al-Jaza'ir) **Major towns/cities** Oran, Annaba, Blida, Sétif, Constantine (Qacentina)

Government

Head of state Abdel Aziz Bouteflika from 1999 **Head of government** Ismail Hamdani from 1998 **Political system** military **Armed forces** 124,000 (1997) **Conscription** compulsory for 18 months **Defence spend** (% GDP) 4.6 (1997) **Education spend** (% GNP) 5.2 (1996) **Health spend** (% GDP) 3.3 (1990–95) **Death penalty** retained and used for ordinary crimes

Population and society

Population 30,774,000 (1999 est) **Population growth rate** 2.3% (1995–2000); 2% (2000–05) **Ethnic groups** 99% of Arab Berber origin, the remainder of European descent, mainly French **Religion** Sunni Muslim (state religion) **Life expectancy** 68 (men); 70 (women) (1995–2000) **Literacy rate** 73% (men); 48% (women) (1997 est) **Unemployment** 30% (1998)

Economy and resources

GDP (US$) 49.6 billion (1998) **GNP** (US$) 46.5 billion (1998) **GNP per capita (PPP)** (US$) 4,380 (1998 est) **Real GDP growth** (% change on previous year) 2.5 (1998) **Consumer price inflation** 12% (1998) **Foreign debt** (US$) 30.9 billion (1997) **Resources** natural gas and petroleum, iron ore, phosphates, lead, zinc, mercury, silver, salt, antimony, copper **Exports** crude oil, gas, vegetables, tobacco, hides, dates. Principal market: Italy 19.8% (1997) **Imports** machinery and transportation equipment, food and basic manufactures. Principal source: France 28.4% (1997)

▪ Tourist information

Time difference GMT +/– 0 **Currency** Algerian dinar **Language** Arabic (official); Berber, French **Visa requirements** UK: visa required. USA visa required **Embassy in the UK** 54 Holland Park, London W11 3RS. Tel: (020) 7221 7800; fax: (020) 7221 0448 **British embassy** BP 43, Résidence Cassiopée, Bâtiment B, 7 chemin des Glycines, 16000 Alger-Gare, Algiers. Tel: (2) 622 411; fax: (2) 692 410 **Chamber of commerce** Chambre Nationale de Commerce (CNC), BP100, Palais Consulaire, rue Amilcar Cabral, Algiers. Tel: (2) 575 555; fax: (2) 629 991 **Office hours** generally 0800–1200 and 1300–1700 Sat–Wed **Banking hours** 0900–1630 Sun–Thu **Airports** international airports: Algiers (Houari Boumédienne), Annaba (El Mellah), Oran (Es Senia), Constantine (Ain El Bey); ten domestic airports; total passenger km: 2,855 million (1995) **Major ports** Oran (Ouahran), Annaba (Bône) **Chief tourist attractions** include the Mediterranean coast, the Atlas Mountains, and the desert; the Hoggar massif and the Tassili N'Ajjer (Plateau of Chasms) – both important centres of Tuareg culture **Major holidays** 1 January, 1 May, 19 June, 5 July, 1 November; variable: Eid-ul-Adha, Ashora, end of Ramadan, New Year (Muslim), Prophet's Birthday

Chronology

9th century BC Part of Carthaginian Empire. **146 BC** Conquered by Romans, who called the area Numidia. **6th century** Part of the Byzantine Empire. **late 7th century** Conquered by Muslim Arabs, who spread Islam as the basis of a new Berberized Arab-Islamic civilization. **1516** Ottoman Turks expelled recent Christian Spanish invaders. **1816** Anglo-Dutch forces bombarded Algiers as a reprisal against the Barbary pirates' attacks on Mediterranean shipping. **1830–47** French occupation of Algiers, followed by extension of control to the north, overcoming fierce resistance from Amir Abd al-Qadir, a champion of Arab Algerian nationalism, and from Morocco. **1850–70** The mountainous inland region, inhabited by the Kabyles, was occupied by the French. **1871** There was a major rebellion against French rule as French settlers began to take over the best agricultural land. **1900–09** The Sahara region was subdued by France, who kept it under military rule. **1940** Following France's defeat by Nazi Germany, Algeria became allied to the pro-Nazi Vichy regime during World War II. **1945** 8,000 died following the ruthless suppression of an abortive uprising against French rule. **1954–62** Battle of Algiers: bitter war of independence fought between the National Liberation Front (FLN) and the French colonial army. **1958** French inability to resolve the civil war in Algeria, toppled the Fourth Republic and brought to power, in Paris, Gen Charles de Gaulle, who accepted the principle of national self-determination. **1962** Independence from France was achieved and a republic declared. Many French settlers fled. **1963** A one-party state was established. **1976** New Islamic-socialist constitution approved. **1988** Riots took place in protest at austerity policies; 170 people were killed. A reform programme was introduced. Diplomatic relations were restored with Morocco after a 12-year break. **1989** Constitutional changes introduced limited political pluralism. **1992** The military took control of the government and a state of emergency was declared. **1993** The civil strife worsened, with assassinations of politicians and other public figures. **1994** The fundamentalists' campaign of violence intensified. **1996** The constitution was amended to increase the president's powers and counter religious fundamentalism. Arabic was declared the official public language. **1998** The violence continued. Ismail Hamdani became prime minister. **1999** Abdel Aziz Bouteflika was elected president.

Andorra Principality of

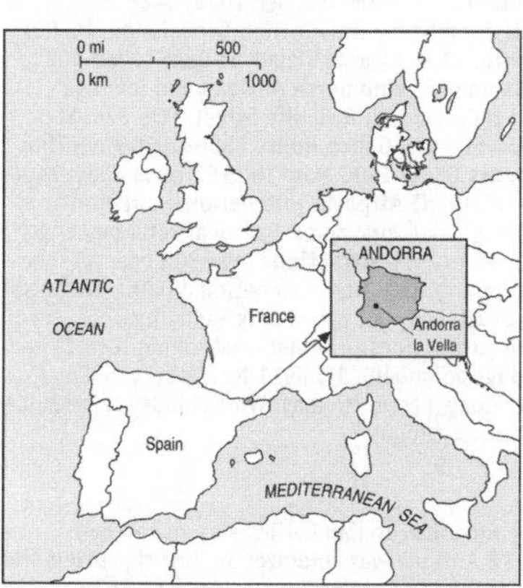

National name *Principat d'Andorra* **Area** 468 sq km/ 181 sq mi **Capital** Andorra-la-Vella **Major towns/cities** Les Escaldes, Escaldes-Engordany (suburb of capital)

Government

Heads of state Joan Marti i Alanis (bishop of Urgel, Spain) and Jacques Chirac (president of France) **Head of government** Marc Forne from 1994 **Political system** emergent democracy **Armed forces** no standing army **Death penalty** abolished in 1990 (last execution in 1943)

Population and society

Population 66,000 (1999 est) **Population growth rate** 3.9% (1995–2000) **Ethnic groups** 25% Andorrans, 75% immigrant Spanish workers **Religion** Roman Catholic **Life expectancy** 70 (men); 73 (women) (1994 est) **Literacy rate** 99% (men); 99% (women) (1995 est) **Unemployment** 0% (1997 est)

Economy and resources

GDP (US$) 960 million (1995) **GNP** (US$) 1 billion (1995 est) **GNP per capita (PPP)** (US$) 16,630 (1995 est) **Real GDP growth** (% change on previous year) 3 (1995) **Consumer price inflation** 0.8% (1998) **Resources** iron, lead, alum, hydro power **Exports** cigars and cigarettes, furniture, electricity. Principal market: Spain 47.5% (1997) **Imports** foodstuffs, electricity, mineral fuels. Principal source: Spain 39.8% (1997)

▪ Tourist information

Time difference GMT +1 **Currency** French franc and Spanish peseta **Language** Catalan (official); Spanish, French **Visa requirements** UK: visa not required. USA: visa not required **Embassy in the UK** none; Andorran Trade Delegation, 63 Westover Road, London SW18 2RF. Tel: (020) 8874 4806 **British embassy** British Consulate (Barcelona), 13th Floor, Edificio Torre de Barcelona, Avenida Diagonal 477, 08036 Barcelona. Tel: (3) 419 9044; fax: (3) 405 2411 **Chamber of commerce** Sindicat d'Initiativa de las Valls d'Andorra, Carrer Dr Vilanova, Andorra la Vella. Tel: 820 214; fax: 825 823 **Office hours** vary considerably **Banking hours** 0900–1300 and 1500–1700 Mon–Fri; 0900–1200 Sat **Airports** international airports: none; closest airport for Andorran traffic 20 km/12.5 mi from Andorra at Seo de Urgel, Spain **Chief tourist attractions** attractive mountain scenery, winter-sports facilities available at five skiing centres; duty-free shopping facilities; the spa town of Les Escaldes **Major holidays** 1, 6, January, 19 March, 1 May, 24 June, 15 August, 8 September, 1, 4, November, 8, 25–26 December; variable: Ascension Thursday, Carnival, Corpus Christi, Good Friday, Easter Monday, Whit Monday

Chronology

AD 803 Holy Roman Emperor Charlemagne liberated Andorra from Muslim control. **819** Louis I 'the Pious' the son of Charlemagne, granted control over the area to the Spanish bishop of Urgel. **1278** A treaty was signed making Spanish bishop and French count joint rulers of Andorra. Through marriage the king of France later inherited the count's right. **1806** After a temporary suspension during the French Revolution, from 1789 the feudal arrangement of dual allegiance to the French and Spanish rulers was re-established by the French emperor Napoleon Bonaparte. **1976** The first political organization, the Democratic Party of Andorra, was formed. **1981** The first prime minister was appointed by the General Council. **1991** Links with the European Community (EC) were formalized. **1993** A new constitution legalized political parties and introduced the first direct elections. Andorra became a member of the United Nations (UN). **1994** Andorra joined the Council of Europe. **1997** The Liberal Union (UL) won an assembly majority in a general election.

Angola People's Republic of

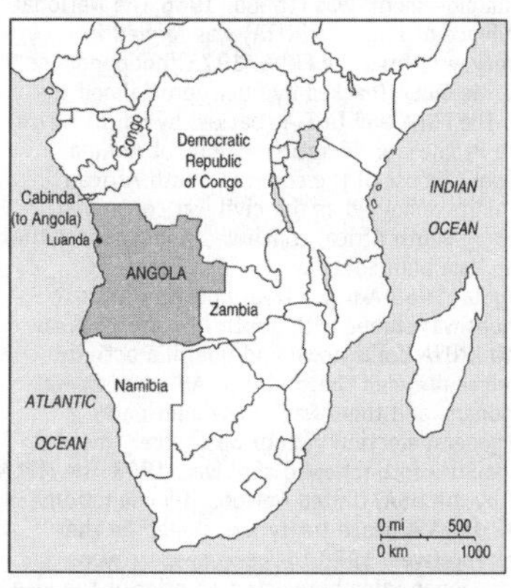

National name *República Popular de Angola* **Area** 1,246,700 sq km/481,350 sq mi **Capital** Luanda (and chief port) **Major towns/cities** Lobito, Benguela, Huambo, Lubango, Malange, Namibe (formerly Moçâmedes)

Government

Head of state José Eduardo dos Santos from 1979 **Head of government** Fernando Franca van Dunem from 1996 **Political system** emergent democracy **Armed forces** 110,500 (1997); plus a paramilitary force of approximately 15,000 **Conscription** military service is compulsory for two years **Defence spend** (% GDP) 8.8 (1997) **Education spend** (% GNP) 2.8 (1992) **Health spend** (% GDP) 4.0 (1990–95) **Death penalty** abolished in 1992

Population and society

Population 12,478,000 (1999 est) **Population growth rate** 3.2% (1995–2000); 3.1% (2000–05) **Ethnic groups** eight main ethnic groups (Bakonga, Mbunda, Ovimbundu, Lunda-Tchokwe, Nganguela, Nyaneka-Humbe, Hiriro, and Ambo), and about 100 subgroups. A major exodus of Europeans in the 1970s left around 30,000, mainly Portuguese **Religion** Roman Catholic 68%, Protestant 20%, animist 12% **Life expectancy** 45 (men); 48 (women) (1995–2000) **Literacy rate** 56%(men); 28% (women) (1995 est) **Unemployment** 21.5% (1995)

Economy and resources

GDP (US$) 6.6 billion (1998) **GNP** (US$) 4.1 billion (1998) **GNP per capita (PPP)** (US$) 840 (1998 est) **Real GDP growth** (% change on previous year) 1.0 (1998) **Consumer price inflation** 1,200% (1998) **Foreign debt** (US$) 10.2 billion (1997) **Resources** petroleum, diamonds, granite, iron ore, marble, salt, phosphates, manganese, copper **Exports** petroleum and petroleum products, diamonds, gas. Principal market: USA 65% (1997) **Imports** foodstuffs, transport equipment, base metals, electrical equipment. Principal source: Portugal 21.8% (1997)

▪ Tourist information

Time difference GMT +1 **Currency** kwanza **Language** Portuguese (official); Bantu dialects **Visa requirements** UK: visa required. USA: visa required **Embassy in the UK** 98 Park Lane, London W1Y 3TA. Tel: (020) 7495 1752; fax: (020) 7495 1635 **British embassy** CP 1244, Rua Diogo Cão 4, Luanda. Tel: (2) 392 991; fax: (2) 333 331 **Chamber of commerce** Angolan Chamber of Commerce and Industry, Largo do Kinaxixi 14, 1° andar, CP 92, Luanda. Tel: (2) 344 506 **Office hours** 0730–1230 and 1430–1830 Mon–Thu; 0730–1230 and 1430–1730 Fri **Banking hours** 0845–1600 Mon–Fri **Airports** international airports: Luanda (4 de Fevereio); domestic services to all major towns; total passenger km: 926 million (1997 est) **Major ports** Huambo, Lubango, Malange **Chief tourist attractions** travel within Angola remains unsafe due to the presence of undisciplined armed troops, unexploded landmines, hostile actions against aircraft, and widespread banditry (June 1996) **Major holidays** 1 January, 4 February, 27 March, 14 April, 1 May, 1 August, 17 September, 11 November, 1, 10, 25 December

Chronology

14th century The powerful Kongo kingdom controlled much of northern Angola. **early 16th century** The Kongo ruler King Afonso I adopted Christianity and sought relations with Portuguese traders. **1575 and 1617** Portugal secured control over the ports of Luanda and Benguela and began to penetrate inland, meeting resistance from Queen Nzinga, the Ndonga ruler. **17th–18th centuries** Inland, the Lunda peoples established powerful kingdoms that stretched into southern Congo. The Portuguese made Angola a key centre for the export of slaves; over 1 million were shipped to Brazil 1580–1680. **1836** The slave trade was officially abolished. **1885–1915** Military campaigns were waged by Portugal to conquer the interior. **1951** Angola became an overseas territory of Portugal. **1956** The People's Movement for the Liberation of Angola (MPLA), a socialist guerrilla independence movement based in the Congo, was formed. **1961** 50,000 people were massacred in rebellions on coffee plantations. Forced labour was abolished. There was an armed struggle for independence. **1962** The National Front for the Liberation of Angola (FNLA), a nationalist guerrilla movement, was formed. **1966** The National Union for the Total Independence of Angola (UNITA) was formed in southeastern Angola as a breakaway from the FNLA. **1975** Independence from Portugal was achieved. The MPLA (backed by Cuba) proclaimed the People's Republic of Angola. The FNLA and UNITA (backed by South Africa and the USA) proclaimed the People's Democratic Republic of Angola. **1976** The MPLA gained control of most of the country. South African troops withdrew, but Cuban units remained as the civil war continued. **1980** UNITA guerrillas, aided by South Africa, continued raids against the government and bases of the Namibian South West Africa People's Organization (SWAPO) in Angola. **1988** A peace treaty providing for the withdrawal of all foreign troops was signed with South Africa and Cuba. **1989** A ceasefire agreed with UNITA broke down and guerrilla activity resumed. **1991** A peace agreement ended the civil war. An amnesty was declared for all political prisoners, and there was a new multiparty constitution. **1992** A MPLA general election victory was fiercely disputed by UNITA, and plunged the country into renewed civil war. **1993** The MPLA government was recognized by the USA. United Nations (UN) sanctions were imposed against UNITA. **1994** A peace treaty was signed by the government and UNITA representatives. **1995** UN peacekeepers were drafted in. **1996** UNITA leader Jonas Savimbi rejected an offer of the vice presidency. President dos Santos appointed Fernando Franca van Dunem as his new prime minister. **1997** After some delay a national unity government was eventually sworn in but was boycotted by Savimbi. **1998** UNITA was demilitarized and transformed into a political party, but after UNITA was accused of massacres, UNITA ministers were suspended and the peace process threatened. **2000** Fighting between government forces and UNITA rebels continued along the Namibia–Angola border, and in southeastern Angola.

Antigua and Barbuda State of

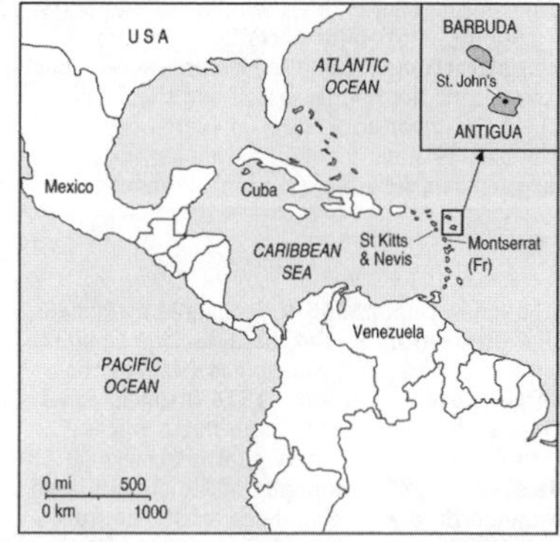

Area Antigua 280 sq km/108 sq mi, Barbuda 161 sq km/62 sq mi, plus Redonda 1 sq km/0.4 sq mi (440 sq km/169 sq mi altogether) **Capital** St John's (on Antigua) (and chief port) **Major towns/cities** Codrington (on Barbuda)

Government

Head of state Elizabeth II from 1981, represented by governor general James B Carlisle from 1993 **Head of government** Lester Bird from 1994 **Political system** liberal democracy **Armed forces** 200 (1997); US government leases two military bases on Antigua **Conscription** military service is voluntary **Defence spend** (% GDP) 0.5% (1997) **Education spend** (% GNP) 3.7% (1988); N/A (1990–95) **Health spend** (% GDP) 3.7% (1995) **Death penalty** retained and used for ordinary crimes

Population and society

Population 69,000 (1999 est) **Population growth rate** 0.5% (1995–2000) **Ethnic groups** population almost entirely of black African descent **Religion** Christian (mostly Anglican) **Life expectancy** 72 (men); 76 (women) (1998 est) **Literacy rate** 92% (men); 88% (women) (1992) **Unemployment** 7% (1997)

Economy and resources

GDP (US$) 502 million (1998) **GNP** (US$) 555 million (1998) **GNP per capita (PPP)** (US$) 9,440 (1998) **Real GDP growth** (% change on previous year) 1.5 (1998) **Consumer price inflation** 2% (1998) **Foreign debt** (US$) 280 million (1997) **Exports** petroleum products, food, manufactures, machinery and transport equipment. Principal market: USA (mainly re-exports) **Imports** petroleum, food and live animals, machinery and transport equipment, manufactures, chemicals. Principal source: USA 27% (1994 est)

▪ Tourist information

Time difference GMT –4 **Currency** East Caribbean dollar **Language** English **Visa requirements** UK: visa not required. USA: visa not required **Embassy in the UK** 15 Thayer Street, London W1M 5LD. Tel: (020) 7486 7073/4/5; fax: (020) 7486 9970 **British embassy** British High Commission, PO Box 483, Price Waterhouse Centre, 11 Old Parham Road, St John's. Tel: 462 0008/9; fax: 462 2806 **Chamber of commerce** Antigua and Barbuda Chamber of Commerce and Industry Ltd, Redcliffe Street, POB 774, St John's. Tel: 462 0743; fax: 462 4575 **Office hours** 0800–1630 Mon–Thu; 0800–1500 Fri **Banking hours** 0800–1400 Mon–Thu (Barclays 0800–1400 Mon, Tue, and Wed; 0800–1700 Fri) **Airports** international airports: St John's (V C Bird International); one airstrip on Barbuda; total passenger km: 252 million (1995) **Chief tourist attractions** over 300 beaches; the historic Nelson's Dockyard in English Harbour (a national park); cruise-ship facilities; Barbuda is less developed, but offers pink sandy beaches, scenic beauty, and wildlife; animal attractions; international sailing regatta and carnival week **Major holidays** 1 January, 1 July, 1 November, 25–26 December; variable: Good Friday, Easter Monday, Whit Monday, Labour Day (May), CARICOM (July), Carnival (August)

Chronology

1493 Antigua, peopled by American Indian Caribs, was visited by Christopher Columbus. **1632** Antigua was colonized by British settlers from St Kitts. **1667** The Treaty of Breda ceded Antigua to Britain. **1674** Christopher Codrington, a sugar planter from Barbados, established sugar plantations and acquired Barbuda island on lease from the British monarch in 1685; Africans were brought in as slaves. **1834** Antigua's slaves were freed. **1860** Barbuda was annexed. **1871–1956** Antigua and Barbuda were administered as part of the Leeward Islands federation. **1958–62** Antigua and Barbuda became part of the West Indies Federation. **1967** Antigua and Barbuda became an associated state within the Commonwealth. **1969** A separatist movement developed on Barbuda. **1981** Independence from Britain was achieved. **1983** Antigua and Barbuda assisted in the US invasion of Grenada. **1994** General elections were won by the ALP, with Lester Bird becoming prime minister.

Argentina Republic of

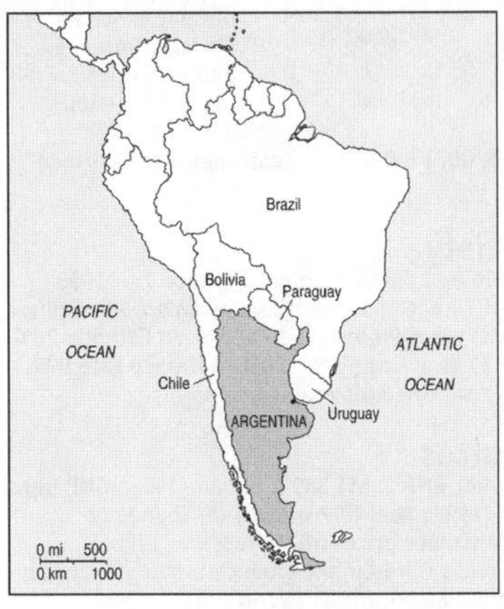

National name *República Argentina* **Area** 2,780,092 sq km/ 1,073,393 sq mi **Capital** Buenos Aires **Major towns/cities** Rosario, Córdoba, San Miguel de Tucumán, Mendoza, Santa Fé, La Plata **Territories** claims Falkland Islands (*Islas Malvinas*), South Georgia, the South Sandwich Islands, and part of Antarctica

Government

Head of state and government Fernando de la Rua from 1999 **Political system** liberal democracy **Armed forces** 73,000 plus paramilitary gendarmerie of 31,200 (1997) **Conscription** abolished in 1995 **Defence spend** (% GDP) 1.7 (1997) **Education spend** (% GNP) 3.5 (1996) **Health spend** (% GDP) 4.3 (1990–95) **Death penalty** abolished for ordinary crimes in 1984; laws provide for the death penalty for exceptional crimes only

Population and society

Population 36,577,000 (1999 est) **Population growth rate** 1.3% (1995–2000); 1.1% (2000–05) **Ethnic groups** 85% of European descent, mainly Spanish; 15% mestizo (offspring of Spanish-American and American Indian parents) **Religion** Roman Catholic (state-supported) **Life expectancy** 70 (men); 77 (women) (1995–2000) **Literacy rate** 97% (men); 97% (women) (1997) **Unemployment** 15.4% (1997)

Economy and resources

GDP (US$) 344.4 billion (1998) **GNP** (US$) 324.1 billion (1998) **GNP per capita (PPP)** (US$) 10,200 (1998) **Real GDP growth** (% change on previous year) 4.7 (1998) **Consumer price inflation** 1.9 (1998) **Foreign debt** (US$) 123.2 billion (1997) **Resources** coal, crude oil, natural gas, iron ore, lead ore, zinc ore, tin, gold, silver, uranium ore, marble, borates, granite **Exports** meat and meat products, prepared animal fodder, cereals, petroleum and petroleum products, soybeans, vegetable oils and fats. Principal market: Brazil 30.4% (1997) **Imports** machinery and transport equipment, chemicals and mineral products. Principal sources: Brazil 22.7% (1997)

▪ Tourist information

Time difference GMT –3 **Currency** peso = 10,000 australs (which it replaced in 1992) **Language** Spanish 95% (official); Italian 3% **Visa requirements** UK: visa not required for tourist visits; visa required for business purposes. USA: visa not required for tourist visits; visa required for business purposes **Embassy in the UK** 53 Hans Place, London SW1X 0LA. Tel: (020) 7584 6494; fax: (020) 7589 3106 **British embassy** Casilla de Correo 2050, Dr Luis Agote 2412/52, 1425 Buenos Aires. Tel: (1) 803 7070/1; fax: (1) 803 1731 **Chamber of commerce** Cámara Argentina de Comercio, Avda Leandro N Alem 36, 1003 Buenos Aires. Tel: (1) 331 8051; fax: (1) 331 8055 **Office hours** 0900–1900 Mon–Fri **Banking hours** 1000–1500 Mon–Fri **Airports** international airports: Buenos Aires, Aeroparque Jorge Newbery, Córdoba, Corrientes, El Plumerillo, Ezeiza, Jujuy, Resistencia, Río Gallegos, Salta, San Carlos de Bariloche; domestic services to all major towns; total passenger km: 13,957 million (1997 est) **Major ports** La Plata and Bahía Blanca **Chief tourist attractions** include the Andes Mountains; lake district centred on Bariloche; Atlantic beaches; Patagonia; Mar del Plata beaches; Iguaçu Falls; the Pampas; Tierra del Fuego **Major holidays** 1 January, 1, 25 May, 10, 20 June, 9 July, 17 August, 12 October, 8, 25, 31 December; variable: Good Friday, Holy Thursday

Chronology

1516 The Spanish navigator Juan Diaz de Solis discovered Río de La Plata. **1536** Buenos Aires was founded, but was soon abandoned because of attacks by American Indians. **1580** Buenos Aires was re-established as part of the Spanish province of Asunción. **1617** Buenos Aires became a separate province within the Spanish viceroyalty of Lima. **1776** The Spanish South American Empire was reorganized: Atlantic regions became viceroyalty of La Plata, with Buenos Aires as capital. **1810** After the French conquest of Spain, Buenos Aires junta took over government of viceroyalty. **1816** Independence was proclaimed, as the United Provinces of Río de La Plata, but Bolivia and Uruguay soon seceded; civil war followed between federalists and those who wanted a unitary state. **1835–52** Dictatorship of Gen Juan Manuel Rosas. **1853** Adoption of federal constitution based on US model; Buenos Aires refused to join confederation. **1861** Buenos Aires was incorporated into the Argentine confederation by force. **1865–70** Argentina took part in the War of Triple Alliance against Paraguay. **late 19th century** Large-scale European immigration and economic development. **1880** Buenos Aires became the national capital. **1880–1916** The government was dominated by an oligarchy of conservative landowners. **1916** The secret ballot was introduced and the Radical Party of Hipólito Irigoyen won elections, beginning a period of 14 years in government. **1930** A military coup ushered in a series of conservative governments sustained by violence and fraud. **1946** Col Juan Perón won presidential elections; he secured working-class support through welfare measures, trade unionism, and the popularity of his wife, Eva Perón (Evita). **1949** A new constitution abolished federalism and increased powers of president. **1952** Death of Evita. Support for Perón began to decline. **1955** Perón was overthrown; the constitution of 1853 was restored. **1966–70** Dictatorship of Gen Juan Carlos Ongania. **1973** Perónist Party won free elections; Perón returned from exile in Spain to become president. **1974** Perón died and was succeeded by his third wife, Isabel Perón. **1976** A coup resulted in rule by a military junta. **1976–83** The military regime conducted murderous campaign ('Dirty War') against left-wing elements. More than 8,000 people disappeared. **1982** Argentina invaded the Falkland Islands but was defeated by the UK. **1983** Return to civilian rule; an investigation into the 'Dirty War' was launched. **1989** Annual inflation reached 12,000%. **1990** Full diplomatic relations with the UK were restored. **1999** Fernando de la Rua won presidential elections.

Armenia Republic of

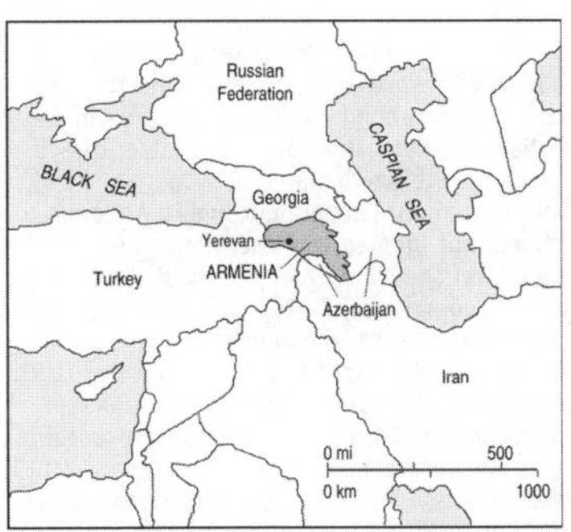

National name *Haikakan Hanrapetoutioun* **Area** 29,800 sq km/11,505 sq mi **Capital** Yerevan **Major towns/cities** Gyumri (formerly Leninakan), Vanadzor (formerly Kirovakan)

Government

Head of state Robert Kocharian from 1998 **Head of government** Amen Sarkisian from 1999 **Political system** authoritarian nationalist **Armed forces** 60,000 (1997) **Conscription** compulsory for 18 months **Defence spend** (% GDP) 8.9 (1997) **Education spend** (% GNP) 2 (1996) **Health spend** (% GDP) 3.1 (1990–95) **Death penalty** retained and used for ordinary crimes

Population and society

Population 3,525,000 (1999 est) **Population growth rate** –0.3% (1995–2000) **Ethnic groups** 91% of Armenian ethnic descent, 5% Azeri, 2% Russian, and 2% Kurdish **Religion** Armenian Christian **Life expectancy** 67 (men); 74 (women) (1995–2000) **Literacy rate** 99% (men); 99% (women) (1997) **Unemployment** 9.3% (1997)

Economy and resources

GDP (US$) 1.6 billion (1998 est) **GNP** (US$) 1.8 billion (1998) **GNP per capita (PPP)** (US$) 2,180 (1998 est) **Real GDP growth** (% change on previous year) 5 (1998) **Consumer price inflation** 8.5% (1998) **Foreign debt** (US$) 666 million (1997) **Resources** copper, zinc, molybdenum, iron, silver, marble, granite **Exports** machinery and metalworking products, chemical and petroleum products. Principal market: CIS 36.3% (1998) **Imports** light industrial products, petroleum and derivatives, industrial raw materials. Principal source: CIS 24.7% (1998)

▪ Tourist information

Time difference GMT +4 **Currency** dram (replaced Russian rouble in 1993) **Language** Armenian **Visa requirements** UK: visa required. USA: visa required **Embassy in the UK** 25A Cheniston Gardens, London W8 6TG. Tel: (020) 7938 5435; fax: (020) 7938 2595 **British embassy** Armenia Hotel, 1 Vramshapouh Arka Street, Yerevan 375010. Tel: (2) 151 807; fax: (2) 151 803 **Chamber of commerce** Chamber of Commerce and Industry of the Republic of Armenia, ulitsa Alevardyan 39, Yerevan. Tel: (2) 565 438; fax: (2) 565 071 **Airports** international airports Yerevan (Zvarnots); domestic services to most major towns **Chief tourist attractions** Armenian mountains in the Lesser Caucasus; Lake Sevan **Major holidays** 1, 6 January, 28–31 March, 24, 28 May, 21 September, 7 December; variable: Good Friday, Easter Monday

Chronology

6th century BC Armenian peoples moved into the area, which was then part of the Persian Empire. ***c.* 94–56 BC** Under King Tigranes II 'the Great', Armenia reached the height of its power, becoming the strongest state in the eastern Roman empire. ***c.* AD 300** Christianity became the state religion when the local ruler was converted by St Gregory the Illuminator. ***c.* AD 390** Armenia was divided between Byzantine Armenia, which became part of the Byzantine Empire, and Persarmenia, under Persian control. **886–1045** Became independent under the Bagratid monarchy. **13th century** After being overrun by the Mongols, a substantially independent Little Armenia survived until 1375. **early 16th century** Conquered by Muslim Ottoman Turks. **1813–28** Russia took control of eastern Armenia. **late 19th century** Revival in Armenian culture and national spirit, provoking Ottoman backlash in western Armenia and international concern at Armenian maltreatment: the 'Armenian Question'. **1894–96** Armenians were massacred by Turkish soldiers in an attempt to suppress unrest. **1915** Suspected of pro-Russian sympathies, two-thirds of Armenia's population of 2 million were deported to Syria and Palestine. Around 600,000–1 million died en route: the survivors contributed towards an Armenian diaspora in Europe and North America. **1916** Armenia was conquered by tsarist Russia and became part of a brief 'Transcaucasian Alliance' with Georgia and Azerbaijan. **1918** Armenia became an independent republic. **1920** Occupied by Red Army of Soviet Union (USSR), but western Armenia remained part of Turkey and northwest Iran. **1936** Became constituent republic of USSR; rapid industrial development. **late 1980s** Armenian 'national reawakening', encouraged by *glasnost* (openness) initiative of Soviet leader Mikhail Gorbachev. **1988** Around 20,000 people died in an earthquake. **1989** Strife-torn Nagorno-Karabakh was placed under direct rule from Moscow; civil war erupted with Azerbaijan over Nagorno-Karabakh and Nakhichevan, an Azerbaijani-peopled enclave in Armenia. **1990** Independence was declared, but ignored by Moscow and the international community. **1991** After the collapse of the USSR, Armenia joined the new Commonwealth of Independent States. Nagorno-Karabakh declared its independence. **1992** Armenia was recognized as an independent state by the USA and admitted into the United Nations (UN). **1993** Armenian forces gained control of more than a fifth of Azerbaijan, including much of Nagorno-Karabakh. **1994** A Nagorno-Karabakh ceasefire ended the conflict. **1997** There was border fighting with Azerbaijan. **1999** Prime Minister Vazgen Sarkisian was assassinated in October when gunmen burst into parliament and shot him and seven other officials. He was replaced by his brother, Amen Sarkisian.

Australia Commonwealth of

Area 7,682,300 sq km/2,966,136 sq mi **Capital** Canberra **Major towns/cities** Adelaide, Alice Springs, Brisbane, Darwin, Melbourne, Perth, Sydney, Hobart, Geelong, Newcastle, Townsville, Wollongong **Territories** Norfolk Island, Christmas Island, Cocos (Keeling) Islands, Ashmore and Cartier Islands, Coral Sea Islands, Heard Island and McDonald Islands, Australian Antarctic Territory

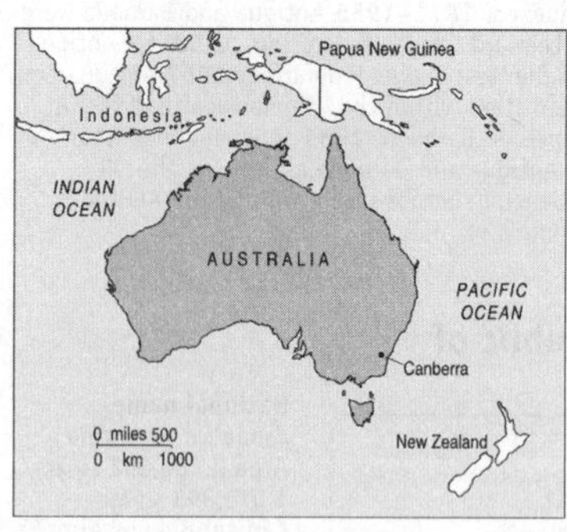

Government

Head of state Elizabeth II from 1952, represented by governor general Sir William Deane from 1996 **Head of government** John Howard from 1996 **Political system** liberal democracy **Armed forces** 57,400 (1997) **Conscription** military service is voluntary **Defence spend** (% GDP) 2.2 (1997) **Education spend** (% GNP) 5.6 (1996) **Health spend** (% GDP) 5.9 (1996) **Death penalty** abolished in 1985

Population and society

Population 18,705,000 (1999 est) **Population growth rate** 1% (1995–2000) **Ethnic groups** 99% of European descent; remaining 1% Aborigine or Asian **Religion** Anglican 26%, other Protestant 17%, Roman Catholic 26% **Life expectancy** 76 (men); 81 (women) (1995–2000) **Literacy rate** 99% (men); 99% (women) (1997 est) **Unemployment** 8% (1998)

Economy and resources

GDP (US$) 364.2 billion (1998) **GNP** (US$) 380.6 billion (1998) **GNP per capita (PPP)** (US$) 20,130 (1998) **Real GDP growth** (% change on previous year) 3.6 (1998) **Consumer price inflation** 1.8% (1998) **Resources** coal, iron ore (world's third-largest producer), bauxite, copper, zinc (world's second-largest producer), nickel (world's fifth-largest producer), uranium, gold, diamonds **Exports** major world producer of raw materials: iron ore, aluminium, coal, nickel, zinc, lead, gold, tin, tungsten, uranium, crude oil; wool, meat, cereals, fruit, sugar, wine. Principal markets: Japan 19.6% (1998) **Imports** processed industrial supplies, transport equipment and parts, road vehicles, petroleum and petroleum products, medicinal and pharmaceutical products, organic chemicals, consumer goods. Principal source: EU 23.9% (1998)

▪ Tourist information

Time difference GMT +8/10 **Currency** Australian dollar **Language** English, Aboriginal languages **Visa requirements** UK: visa required. USA: visa required **Embassy in the UK** High Commission, Australia House, The Strand, London WC2B 4LA. Tel: (020) 7379 4334; fax: (020) 7240 5333 **British embassy** British High Commission, Commonwealth Avenue, Yarralumla, Canberra, ACT 2600. Tel: (6) 270 6666; fax: (6)273 3236 **Chamber of commerce** International Chamber of Commerce, POB E118, Queen Victoria Terrace, Canberra, ACT 2600. Tel: (6) 295 1961; fax: (6) 295 0170. Australian Chamber of Commerce and Industry, POB E14, Queen Victoria Terrace, Canberra ACT 2600. Tel: (6) 273 2311; fax: (6) 273 3196 **Office hours** 0900–1730 Mon–Fri **Banking hours** 0930–1600 Mon–Thu; 1930–1700 Fri (hours vary throughout the country) **Airports** international airports: Sydney (NSW), Melbourne (Victoria), Canberra, Brisbane, Cairns (Queensland), Perth (Western Australia), Adelaide (South Australia), Hobart (Tasmania), Townsville (Quensland), Darwin (Northern Territory); domestic services to all major resorts and cities; total passenger km: 77,915 million (1997 est) **Chief tourist attractions** swimming and surfing on the Pacific beaches; skin-diving along the Great Barrier Reef; sailing from Sydney and other harbours; winter sports in the Australian Alps; summer sports in the Blue Mountains; Alice Springs and Ayers Rock in desert interior; unique wildlife **Major holidays** 1 January, 25 April, 25–26 December (except South Australia); variable: Good Friday, Easter Monday, Holy Saturday; additional days vary between states

Chronology

***c.* 40,000 BC** Aboriginal immigration from southern India, Sri Lanka, and Southeast Asia. **AD 1606** First recorded sightings of Australia by Europeans including discovery of Cape York by Dutch explorer Willem Jansz in *Duyfken*. **1770** Capt James Cook claimed New South Wales for Britain. **1788** Sydney founded as British penal colony. **late 18th–19th centuries** Great age of exploration. **1804** Castle Hill Rising by Irish convicts in New South Wales. **1813** Crossing of Blue Mountains removed major barrier to exploration of interior. **1825** Tasmania seceded from New South Wales. **1829** Western Australia colonized. **1836** South Australia colonized. **1840–68** End of convict transportation. **1850** British Act of Parliament permitted Australian colonies to draft their own constitutions and achieve

Australia: States and Territories

(– = not applicable.)

State	Capital	Area sq km	Area sq mi	Population (1998)
New South Wales	Sydney	801,600	309,500	6,341,600
Queensland	Brisbane	1,727,200	666,872	3,456,300
South Australia	Adelaide	984,377	380,070	1,487,300
Tasmania	Hobart	67,800	26,177	471,900
Victoria	Melbourne	227,620	87,884	4,660,900
Western Australia	Perth	2,525,500	975,095	1,831,400
Territory				
Australian Capital Territory	Canberra	2,400	926	308,400
Northern Territory	Darwin	1,346,200	519,767	190,000
External Territory				
Ashmore and Cartier Islands	–	5	2	uninhabited
Australian Antarctic Territory	–	6,044,000	2,333,590	uninhabited except for scientific stations
Christmas Island	–	135	52	2,500[1]
Cocos (Keeling) Islands	–	14	5.5	590[2]
Coral Sea Islands	–	[3]	[3]	uninhabited except for scientific stations
Heard Island and McDonald Islands	–	410	158	uninhabited
Norfolk Island	–	40	15.5	1,900[2]

[1] 1994 estimate.
[2] 1993 figure.
[3] Sea area of Coral Sea Islands is 780,000 sq km/301,158 sq mi; land area of the islands is approximately 2.6 sq km/1 sq mi.

virtual self-government. **1851–61** Gold rushes contributed to exploration and economic growth. **1851** Victoria seceded from New South Wales. **1855** Victoria achieved self-government. **1856** New South Wales, South Australia, and Tasmania achieved self-government. **1859** Queensland was formed from New South Wales and achieved self-government. **1890** Western Australia achieved self-government. **1891** Depression gave rise to the Australian Labor Party. **1901** The Commonwealth of Australia was created. **1919** Australia was given mandates over Papua New Guinea and the Solomon Islands. **1927** The seat of federal government moved to Canberra. **1931** Statute of Westminster confirmed Australian independence. **1933** Western Australia's vote to secede was overruled. **1948–75** Influx of around 2 million new immigrants, chiefly from continental Europe. **1967** A referendum gave Australian Aborigines full citizenship rights. **1970s** Japan became Australia's chief trading partner. **1974** 'White Australia' immigration restrictions were abolished. **1975** Papua New Guinea became independent. **1978** Northern Territory achieved self-government. **1986** The Australia Act was passed by British Parliament, eliminating the last vestiges of British legal authority in Australia. **1988** A Free Trade Agreement was signed with New Zealand. **1992** The Citizenship Act removed the oath of allegiance to the British crown. **1998** John Howard's Liberal–National coalition government was re-elected.

Austria Republic of

National name *Republik Österreich* **Area** 83,500 sq km/32,239 sq mi **Capital** Vienna **Major towns/cities** Graz, Linz, Salzburg, Innsbruck, Klagenfurt

Government

Head of state Thomas Klestil from 1992 **Head of government** Wolfgang Schüssel from 2000 **Political system** liberal democracy **Armed forces** 45,500 (1997) **Conscription** 6 months **Defence spend** (% GDP) 0.8 (1997) **Education spend** (% GNP) 5.7 (1996) **Health spend** (% GDP) 5.7 (1996) **Death penalty** abolished in 1968

Population and society

Population 8,177,000 (1999 est) **Population growth rate** 0.5% (1995–2000); 0.2% (2000–05) **Ethnic groups** 98% German, 0.7% Croatian, 0.3% Slovene **Religion** Roman Catholic 78%, Protestant 5% **Life expectancy** 74 (men); 80 (women) (1995–2000) **Literacy rate** 99% (men); 99% (women) (1997) **Unemployment** 4.4% (1998)

Economy and resources

GDP (US$) 212.1 billion (1998) **GNP** (US$) 217.2 billion (1998) **GNP per capita (PPP)** (US$) 22,740 (1998) **Real GDP growth** (% change on previous year) 2.8 (1998) **Consumer price inflation** 1.6% (1998) **Resources** lignite, iron, kaolin, gypsum, talcum, magnesite, lead, zinc, forests **Exports** dairy products, food products, wood and paper products, machinery and transport equipment, metal and metal products, chemical products. Principal market for exports: Germany 35.1% (1997) **Imports** petroleum and petroleum products, food and live animals, chemicals and related products, textiles, clothing. Principal source: Germany 41.7% (1997)

▪ Tourist information

Time difference GMT +1 **Currency** schilling **Language** German **Visa requirements** UK: visa not required. USA: visa not required **Embassy in the UK** 18 Belgrave Mews West, London SW1X 8HV. Tel: (020) 7235 3731; fax: (020) 7235 8025 **British embassy** Juarèsgasse 12, 1030 Vienna. Tel: (1) 713 1575; fax: (1) 714 7824 **Chamber of commerce** Wirtschaftskammer Österreich (Austrian Economic Chamber), Wiedner Haupstrasse 63, 1045 Vienna. Tel: (1) 50105; fax: (1) 50206 **Office hours** 0800–1600 Mon–Fri **Banking hours** 0800–1230 and 1330–1500 Mon, Tue, Wed, and Fri; 0800–1230 and 1330–1730 Thu (head offices do not close for the break) **Airports** international airports: Vienna (Wien-Schwechat), Graz (Thalerhof), Innsbruck (Kranebitten), Klagenfurt (Wörthersee), Linz (Hörsching), Salzburg (Maxglam); domestic services between the above; total passenger km: 10,047 million (1997 est) **Chief tourist attractions** mountain scenery, enjoyed by visitors in both summer and winter; arts festivals at cultural centres of Vienna and Salzburg **Major holidays** 1, 6 January, 1 May, 15 August, 26 October, 1 November, 8, 24–26 December; variable: Ascension Thursday, Corpus Christi, Easter Monday, Whit Monday

Chronology

14 BC Country south of River Danube conquered by Romans. **5th century AD** The region was occupied by Vandals, Huns, Goths, Lombards, and Avars. **791** Charlemagne conquered the Avars and established East Mark, the nucleus of the future Austrian Empire. **976** Holy Roman Emperor Otto II granted East Mark to House of Babenburg, which ruled until 1246. **1282** Holy Roman Emperor Rudolf of Habsburg seized Austria and invested his son as its duke; for over 500 years most rulers of Austria were elected Holy Roman Emperor. **1453** Austria became an archduchy. **1519–56** Emperor Charles V was both archduke of Austria and king of Spain; the Habsburgs were dominant in Europe. **1526** Bohemia came under Habsburg rule. **1529**

Austria: Federal States

Federal state	Capital	Area		Population (1997)
		sq km	sq mi	
Burgenland	Eisenstadt	3,965	1,531	276,000
Carinthia	Klagenfurt	9,533	3,681	564,000
Lower Austria	St Pölten	19,174	7,403	1,530,000
Salzburg	Salzburg	7,154	2,762	511,000
Styria	Graz	16,388	6,327	1,206,000
Tyrol	Innsbruck	12,648	4,883	662,000
Upper Austria	Linz	11,980	4,625	1,378,000
Vienna	Vienna	415	160	1,600,000
Vorarlberg	Bregenz	2,601	1,004	345,000

Vienna was besieged by the Ottoman Turks. **1618–48** Thirty Years' War: Habsburgs weakened by failure to secure control over Germany. **1683** Polish-Austrian force led by Jan Sobieski defeated the Turks at Vienna. **1699** Treaty of Karlowitz: Austrians expelled the Turks from Hungary, which came under Habsburg rule. **1713** By the Treaty of Utrecht, Austria obtained the Spanish Netherlands (Belgium) and political control over most of Italy. **1740–48** War of Austrian Succession: Prussia (supported by France and Spain) attacked Austria (supported by Holland and England) on the pretext of disputing rights of Maria Theresa; Austria lost Silesia to Prussia. **1772** Austria joined in partition of Poland, annexing Galicia. **1780–90** 'Enlightened despotism': Joseph II tried to impose radical reforms. **1792** Austria went to war with revolutionary France. **1804** Francis II took the title Emperor of Austria. **1806** The Holy Roman Empire was abolished. **1809–48** Austria took a leading role in resisting liberalism and nationalism throughout Europe. **1815** After the Napoleonic Wars, Austria lost its Netherlands but received Lombardy and Venetia. **1848** Outbreak of liberal-nationalist revolts throughout the Austrian Empire; Ferdinand I abdicated in favour of Franz Joseph; revolutions suppressed with difficulty. **1859** France and Sardinia expelled Austrians from Lombardy by force. **1866** Seven Weeks' War: Prussia defeated Austria, which ceded Venetia to Italy. **1867** Austria conceded equality to Hungary within the dual monarchy of Austria-Hungary. **1878** Treaty of Berlin: Austria-Hungary occupied Bosnia-Herzegovina; annexed in 1908. **1914** Archduke Franz Ferdinand, the heir to the throne, was assassinated by a Serbian nationalist; Austria-Hungary invaded Serbia, precipitating World War I. **1916** Death of Franz Joseph; succeeded by Karl I. **1918** Austria-Hungary collapsed in military defeat; empire dissolved; republic proclaimed. **1919** Treaty of St Germain reduced Austria to its present boundaries and prohibited union with Germany. **1934** Political instability culminated in brief civil war; right-wingers defeated socialists. **1938** The *Anschluss*: Nazi Germany incorporated Austria into the Third Reich. **1945** Following World War II, the victorious Allies divided Austria into four zones of occupation (US, British, French, and Soviet); the Second Republic was established under Karl Renner. **1955** Austrian State Treaty ended occupation; Austria regained independence on condition of neutrality. **1960–70s** Austria experienced rapid industrialization and prosperity. **1986** Kurt Waldheim was elected president, despite allegations of war crimes during World War II. This led to some diplomatic isolation until Waldheim's replacement by Thomas Klestil in 1992. **1995** Austria became a full member of the European Union (EU). **1998** NATO membership was ruled out. **2000** A new coalition government was elected, made up of the conservative People's Party and the far-right Freedom Party, led by Jörg Haider. Wolfgang Schüssel became prime minister, while Haider remained governor of the region of Carinthia, and a senior partner in the coalition. This marked the inclusion of the far right in a West European government for the first time since World War II, and was met with protests from across Europe. At the end of February, Haider resigned, but denied that this was a result of international pressure.

Azerbaijan Republic of

National name *Azarbaijchan Respublikasy* **Area** 86,600 sq km/33,436 sq mi **Capital** Baku **Major towns/cities** Gyandzha (formerly Kirovabad), Sumgait, Nakhichevan, Stepanakert

Government

Head of state Geidar Aliyev from 1993 **Head of government** Artur Rasizade from 1996 **Political system** authoritarian nationalist **Armed forces** 66,700 (1997) **Conscription** military service is for 17 months **Defence spend** (% GDP) 4.0 (1997) **Education spend** (% GNP) 3.3 (1996) **Health spend** (% GDP) 1.4 (1990–95) **Death penalty** abolished in 1998

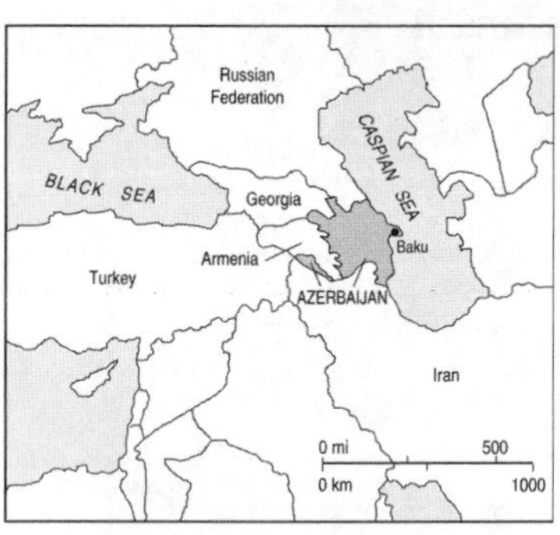

Population and society

Population 7,697,000 (1999 est) **Population growth rate** 0.5% (1995–2000) **Ethnic groups** 83% of Azeri descent, 6% Russian, 6% Armenian **Religion** Shiite Muslim 62%, Sunni Muslim 26%, Orthodox Christian 12% **Life expectancy** 66 (men); 74 (women) (1995–2000) **Literacy rate** 96% (men); 96% (women) (1997 est) **Unemployment** 1.1% (1997)

Economy and resources

GDP (US$) 4.13 billion (1998) **GNP** (US$) 3.9 billion (1998) **GNP per capita (PPP)** (US$) 1,820 (1998) **Real GDP growth** (% change on previous year) 5 (1998) **Consumer price inflation** 6% (1998) **Foreign debt** (US$) 504 million (1997) **Resources** petroleum, natural gas, iron ore, aluminium, copper, barytes, cobalt, precious metals, limestone, salt **Exports** refined petroleum products, machinery, food products, textiles. Principal market: Turkey 22.4% (1998) **Imports** industrial raw materials, processed food, machinery. Principal source: Turkey 20.4% (1998)

▪ Tourist information

Time difference GMT +4 **Currency** manat (left rouble zone in 1993) **Language** Azeri **Visa requirements** UK: visa required. USA: visa required **Embassy in the UK** 4 Kensington Court, London W8 5DL. Tel: (020) 7938 5482; fax: (020) 7937 1783 **British embassy** c/o Old Intourist Hotel, Room 214, Baku. Tel: (12) 924 813; fax: (12) (873) 144 6456 **Chamber of commerce** Chamber of Commerce and Industry, Istiglaliyat Street 31/33, 370001 Baku. Tel: (12) 928 912; fax: (12) 989 324 **Banking hours** 0930–1730 Mon–Fri (midday closing hours vary) **Airports** international airports: Baku; total passenger km: 1,650 million (1995) **Chief tourist attractions** resorts on Caspian Sea and on Apsheron peninsula, near Baku **Major holidays** 1 January, 8 March, 28 May, 9, 18 October, 17 November, 31 December

Chronology

4th century BC Established as an independent state for the first time by Atrophates, a vassal of Alexander III of Macedon. **7th century** Spread of Islam. **11th century** Immigration by Oghuz Seljuk peoples, from the steppes to the northeast. **13th–14th centuries** Incorporated within Mongol Empire; the Mongol ruler Tamerlane had his capital at Samarkand. **16th century** Baku besieged and incorporated within Ottoman Empire, before falling under Persian dominance. **1805** Khanates (chieftaincies), including Karabakh and Shirvan, which had won independence from Persia, gradually became Russian protectorates, being confirmed by the Treaty of Gulistan, which concluded the 1804–13 First Russo-Iranian War. **1828** Under the Treaty of Turkmenchai, which concluded the Second Russo-Iranian War begun in 1826, Persia was granted control over southern and Russia over northern Azerbaijan. **late 19th century** The petroleum industry developed, resulting in a large influx of Slav immigrants to Baku. **1917–18** Member of anti-Bolshevik Transcaucasian Federation. **1918** Became an independent republic. **1920** Occupied by Red Army and subsequently forcibly secularized. **1922–36** Became part of the Transcaucasian Federal Republic with Georgia and Armenia. **early 1930s** Peasant uprisings against agricultural collectivization and Stalinist purges of the local Communist Party. **1936** Became a constituent republic of the USSR. **late 1980s** Growth in nationalist sentiment, taking advantage of the *glasnost* initiative of the reformist Soviet leader Mikhail Gorbachev. **1988** Riots followed the request of Nagorno-Karabakh, an Armenian-peopled enclave within Azerbaijan, for transfer to Armenia. **1989** Nagorno-Karabakh was placed under direct rule from Moscow; civil war broke out with Armenia over Nagorno-Karabakh. **1990** Soviet troops were dispatched to Baku to restore order amid calls for secession from the USSR. **1991** Independence was declared after the collapse of an anti-Gorbachev coup in Moscow, which had been supported by Azeri communist leadership. Azerbaijan joined the new Commonwealth of Independent States (CIS); Nagorno-Karabakh declared independence. **1992** Azerbaijan was admitted into the United Nations (UN). **1993** Nagorno-Karabakh was overtaken by Armenian forces. **1995** An attempted coup was foiled. A market-centred economic reform programme was introduced. **1997** There was border

fighting with Armenia. **1998** A new pro-government grouping, Democratic Azerbaijan, was formed. Geidar Aliyev was re-elected president in a disputed poll. A Nagorno-Karabakh peace plan was rejected.

Bahamas Commonwealth of the

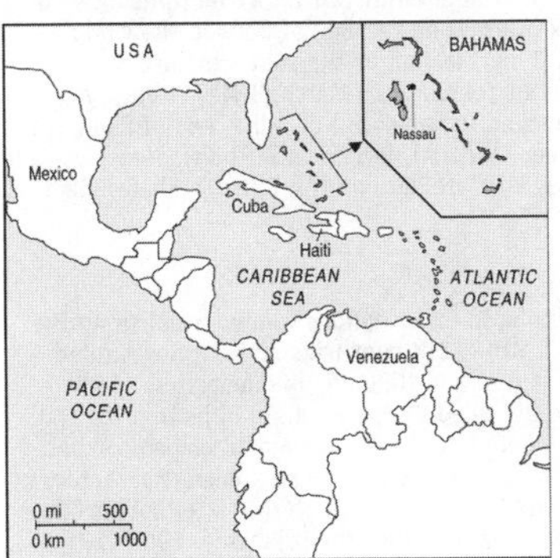

Area 13,864 sq km/ 5,352 sq mi **Capital** Nassau (on New Providence Island) **Major towns/cities** Freeport (on Grand Bahama) **Principal islands** Andros, Grand Bahama, Abaco, Eleuthera, New Providence, Berry Islands, Bimini Islands, Great Inagua, Acklins Island, Exuma Islands, Mayguana, Crooked Island, Long Island, Cat Islands, Rum Cay, Watling (San Salvador) Island, Inagua Islands

Government

Head of state Elizabeth II from 1973, represented by governor general Orville Turnquest from 1995 **Head of government** Hubert Ingraham from 1992 **Political system** liberal democracy **Armed forces** 900 (1997) and 2,300 paramilitary forces **Conscription** military service is voluntary **Defence spend** (% GDP) 0.6 (1997) **Education spend** (% GNP) 3.9 (1993–94) **Health spend** (% GDP) 2.5 (1995) **Death penalty** retained and used for ordinary crimes

Population and society

Population 301,000 (1999 est) **Population growth rate** 1.8% (1995–2000) **Ethnic groups** about 85% of the population is of African origin, remainder mainly British, American, and Canadian **Religion** Christian 94% (Roman Catholic 26%, Anglican 21%, other Protestant 48%) **Life expectancy** 71 (men); 77 (women) (1995–2000) **Literacy rate** 95% (men); 96% (women) (1997) **Unemployment** 9.8% (1997 est)

Economy and resources

GDP (US$) 3.74 billion (1998) **GNP** (US$) 3.3 billion (1998) **GNP per capita (PPP)** (US$) 10,460 (1998) **Real GDP growth** (% change on previous year) 4 (1998) **Consumer price inflation** 1.5% (1998) **Foreign debt** (US$) 1.8 billion (1997) **Resources** aragonite (extracted from seabed), chalk, salt **Exports** foodstuffs (fish), oil products and transhipments, chemicals, rum, salt. Principal market: USA 24.5% (1997) **Imports** machinery and transport equipment, basic manufactures, petroleum and products, chemicals. Principal source: USA 34.9% (1997)

▪ Tourist information

Time difference GMT –5 **Currency** Bahamian dollar **Language** English and some Creole **Visa requirements** UK: visa not required. USA: visa not required **Embassy in the UK** 10 Chesterfield St, London W1X 8AH. Tel: (020) 7408 4488; fax: (020) 7499 9937 **British embassy** British High Commission, PO Box N-7516, 3rd Floor, Bitco Building, East St, Nassau. Tel: 325 7471/2/3; fax: 323 3871 **Chamber of commerce** Bahamas Chamber of Commerce, Shirley St, POB N-665, Nassau. Tel: 322 2145; fax: 322 4649 **Office hours** 0900–1700 Mon–Fri **Banking hours** 0930–1500 Mon–Thu; 0930–1700 Fri **Airports** international airports: Nassau, Freeport, Moss Town; four domestic airports serve internal chartered flights; total passenger km: 220 million (1995) **Chief tourist attractions** mild climate and beautiful beaches **Major holidays** 1 January, 10 July, 25–26 December; variable: Good Friday, Easter Monday, Whit Monday, Labour Day (June), Emancipation (August), Discovery (October)

Chronology

8th–9th centuries AD Arawak Indians driven northwards to the islands by the Caribs. **1492** Visited by Christopher Columbus; Arawaks deported to provide cheap labour for the gold and silver mines of Cuba and Hispaniola (Haiti). **1629** King Charles I of England granted the islands to Robert Heath. **1666** The colonization of New Providence island began. **1783** Recovered after brief Spanish occupation and became a British colony, being settled during the American War of Independence by American loyalists, who brought with them black slaves. **1838** Slaves were emancipated. **from 1950s** Major development of the tourist trade. **1964** Became internally self-governing. **1967** First national assembly elections. **1973** Full independence was achieved within the British Commonwealth. **1992** A centre-left Free National Movement (FNM) led by Hubert Ingraham won an absolute majority in elections.

Bahrain State of

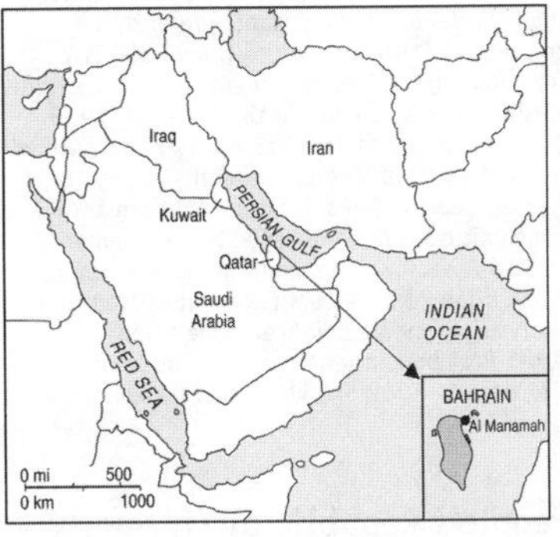

National name *Dawlat al Bahrayn* **Area** 688 sq km/266 sq mi **Capital** Al Manamah on the largest island (also called Bahrain) **Major towns/cities** Muharraq, Jiddhafs, Isa Town, Hidd, Rifa'a, Sitra

Government

Head of state Sheikh Hamad bin Isa al-Khalifa from 1999 **Head of government** Sheikh Khalifa bin Salman al-Khalifa from 1970 **Political system** absolutist **Armed forces** 11,000 (1997) **Conscription** military service is voluntary **Defence spend** (% GDP) 6.5 (1997) **Education spend** (% GNP) 4.8 (1995) **Health spend** (% GDP) 3.1 (1994) **Death penalty** retained and used for ordinary crimes

Population and society

Population 607,000 (1999 est) **Population growth rate** 2% (1990–95); 1.5% (1995–2025) **Ethnic groups** about 73% Arab and 9% Iranian; Pakistani and Indian minorities **Religion** 85% Muslim (Shiite 60%, Sunni 40%), Christian; Islam is the state religion **Life expectancy** 71 (men); 75 (women) (1995–2000) **Literacy rate** 90% (men); 81% (women) (1997 est) **Unemployment** 15% (1997 est)

Economy and resources

GDP (US$) 5.4 billion (1998) **GNP** (US$) 4.9 billion (1998) **GNP per capita (PPP)** (US$) 13,700 (1998 est) **Real GDP growth** (% change on previous year) 0.7 (1998) **Consumer price inflation** 0.8% (1998) **Foreign debt** (US$) 2.37 billion (1997) **Resources** petroleum and natural gas **Exports** petroleum and petroleum products, aluminium,chemicals (1996). Principal market: India 14% (1997) **Imports** crude petroleum, machinery and transport equipment, chemicals, basic manufactures. Principal source: Saudi Arabia 40.6% (1997)

▪ Tourist information

Time difference GMT +3 **Currency** Bahraini dinar **Language** Arabic (official); Farsi, English, Urdu **Visa requirements** UK: visa not required. USA: visa required **Embassy in the UK** 98 Gloucester Road, London SW7 4AV. Tel: (020) 7370 5132/3; fax: (020) 7370 7773 **British embassy** PO Box 114, 21 Government Avenue, Manama, 306. Tel: (973) 534 404; fax: (973) 531 273 **Chamber of commerce** Bahrain Chamber of Commerce and Industry, PO Box 248, Manama. Tel: (973) 233 913; fax: (973) 241 294 **Office hours** usually 0730–1200 and 1430–1800 Sat–Thu **Banking hours** 0800–1200 and usually 1600–1800 Sat–Wed; 0800–1100 Thu **Airports** international airports: Muharraq (Bahrain); total passenger km: 2,766 million (1995) **Major ports** Mina Sulman **Chief tourist attractions** Bahrain is the site of the ancient trading civilization of Dilmun, and there are several sites of archaeological importance **Major holidays** 1 January, 16 December; variable: Eid-ul-Adha, Ashora, end of Ramadan, New Year (Muslim), Prophet's Birthday

Chronology

4th century AD Became part of Persian (Iranian) Sassanian Empire. **7th century** Adopted Islam. **8th century** Came under Arab Abbasid control. **1521** Seized by Portugal and held for eight decades, despite local unrest. **1602** Fell under the control of a Persian Shiite dynasty. **1783** Persian rule was overthrown and Bahrain became a sheikdom under the Sunni Muslim al-Khalifa dynasty, which originated from the same tribal federation, the Anaza, as the al-Saud family who now rule Saudi Arabia. **1816–20** Friendship and peace treaties were signed with Britain, which sought to end piracy in the Gulf. **1861** Became British protectorate; government shared between the ruling sheikh (Arab leader) and a British adviser.

1923 British influence increased when Sheikh Isa al-Khalifa was deposed and Charles Belgrave was appointed as the dominating 'adviser' to the new ruler. **1928** Sovereignty was claimed by Persia (Iran). **1930s** Oil was discovered, providing the backbone for the country's wealth. **1953–56** Council for National Unity was formed by Arab nationalists, but was suppressed after large demonstrations against British participation in the Suez War. **1968** Britain announced its intention to withdraw its forces. Bahrain formed, with Qatar and the Trucial States of the United Arab Emirates, the Federation of Arab Emirates. **1970** Iran accepted a United Nations (UN) report showing that Bahrain's inhabitants preferred independence to Iranian control. **1971** Qatar and the Trucial States withdrew from the federation; Bahrain became an independent state under Sheikh Isa bin Sulman al-Khalifa, who assumed the title of emir. **1973** A new constitution was adopted. **1975** The national assembly was dissolved and political activists driven underground. The emir and his family assumed virtually absolute power. **early 1980s** Tensions between the Sunni and Shiite Muslim communities were heightened by the Iranian Shiite Revolution of 1979. **1986** A causeway opened linking the island with Saudi Arabia. **1991** Bahrain joined a UN coalition that ousted Iraq from its occupation of Kuwait, and signed a defence cooperation agreement with the USA. **1995** Prodemocracy demonstrations were violently suppressed, with 11 deaths. **1999** Sheikh Hamad became Emir and head of state.

Bangladesh People's Republic of (formerly East Pakistan)

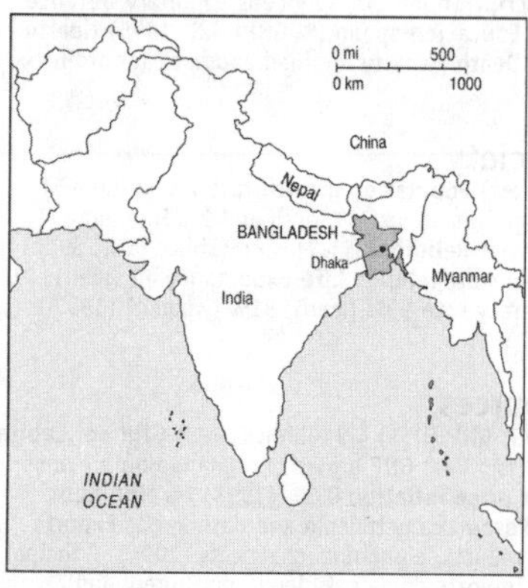

National name *Gana Prajatantri Bangladesh* **Area** 144,000 sq km/ 55,598 sq mi **Capital** Dhaka (formerly Dacca) **Major towns/cities** Rajshahi, Khulna, Chittagong, Comilla, Barisal, Sylhet

Government

Head of state Abdur Rahman Biswas from 1991 **Head of government** Sheikh Hasina Wazed from 1996 **Political system** emergent democracy **Armed forces** 121,000 (1997) **Conscription** military service is voluntary **Defence spend** (% GDP) 1.9 (1997) **Education spend** (% GNP) 2.9 (1996) **Health spend** (% GDP) 1.2 (1990–95) **Death penalty** retained and used for ordinary crimes

Population and society

Population 126,948,000 (1999 est) **Population growth rate** 1.7% (1995–2000) **Ethnic groups** 98% of Bengali descent, half a million Bihari, and around 1 million belonging to 'tribal' communities **Religion** Sunni Muslim 85%, Hindu 12%; Islam is the state religion **Life expectancy** 58 (men); 58 (women) (1995–2000) **Literacy rate** 57% (men); 22% (women) (1995 est) **Unemployment** 2.5% (1996)

Economy and resources

GDP (US$) 42.8 billion (1998) **GNP** (US$) 44 billion (1998) **GNP per capita (PPP)** (US$) 1,100 (1998) **Real GDP growth** (% change on previous year) 5.6 (1998) **Consumer price inflation** 8% (1998) **Foreign debt** (US$) 15.1 billion (1997) **Resources** natural gas, coal, limestone, china clay, glass sand **Exports** raw jute and jute goods, tea, clothing, leather and leather products, shrimps and frogs' legs. Principal market: USA 33.3% (1997) **Imports** wheat, crude petroleum and petroleum products, pharmaceuticals, cement, raw cotton, machinery and transport equipment. Principal source: India 11.6% (1997)

▪ Tourist information

Time difference GMT +6 **Currency** taka **Language** Bengali (official); English **Visa requirements** UK: visa required. USA: visa not required for a tourist visit of up to 15 days **Embassy in the UK** 28 Queen's Gate, London SW7 5JA. Tel: (020) 7584 0081; fax: (020) 7255 2130 **British embassy** British High Commission, PO Box 6079, United Nations Road, Baridhara, Dhaka 12. Tel: (2) 882 705; fax: (2) 883 437 **Chamber of commerce** Federation of Bangladesh Chambers of Commerce and Industry, Federation Bhaban, 60 Motijheel C/A, 4th Floor, POB 2079, Dhaka 1000. Tel: (2) 250 566 **Office hours** 0800–1430 Sat–Thu **Banking hours** 0900–1500 Sat–Wed; 0900–1300 Thu **Airports** international airports: Dhaka (Zia), Chittagong, Sylhet; seven domestic airports; total passenger km: 2,129 million (1997 est) **Major ports** Chittagong, Khulna **Chief tourist attractions** cities of Dhaka and Chittagong; Cox's Bazaar on the Bay of Bengal, the world's longest beach (120 km/74.5 mi); Tekhaf, at the southernmost point of Bangladesh **Major holidays** 21 February, 26 March, 1 May, 1 July, 7 November, 16, 25, 31 December; variable: Eid-ul-Adha, end of Ramadan, New Year (Bengali), New Year (Muslim), Prophet's Birthday, Jumat-ul-Wida (May), Shab-e-Barat (April), Buddah Purnima (April/May), Shab-I-Qadr (May), Durga-Puza (October)

Chronology

***c.* 1000 BC** Arrival of Bang tribe in lower Ganges valley, establishing the kingdom of Banga (Bengal). **8th–12th centuries AD** Bengal was ruled successively by the Buddhist Pala and Hindu Senha dynasties. **1199** Bengal was invaded and briefly ruled by the Muslim Khiljis from Central Asia. **1576** Bengal was conquered by the Muslim Mogul emperor Akbar. **1651** The British East India Company established a commercial factory in Bengal. **1757** Bengal came under de facto British rule after Robert Clive defeated the nawab (ruler) of Bengal at Battle of Plassey. **1905–12** Bengal was briefly partitioned by the British Raj into a Muslim-dominated east and Hindu-dominated west. **1906** The Muslim League (ML) was founded in Dhaka. **1947** Bengal was formed into an eastern province of Pakistan on the partition of British India, with the ML administration in power. **1954** The opposition United Front, dominated by the Awami League (AL) and campaigning for East Bengal's autonomy, trounced the ML in elections. **1955** East Bengal was renamed East Pakistan. **1966** Sheikh Mujibur Rahman of AL announced a Six-Point Programme of autonomy for East Pakistan. **1970** 500,000 people were killed in a cyclone. The pro-autonomy AL secured an electoral victory in East Pakistan. **1971** Bangladesh ('land of the Bangla speakers') emerged as an independent nation after a bloody civil war with Indian military intervention on the side of East Pakistan; 10 million refugees fled to India. **1974** Hundreds of thousands died in a famine; a state of emergency was declared. **1975** Martial law was imposed. **1978–79** Elections were held and civilian rule restored. **1982** Martial law was reimposed after a military coup. **1986** Elections were held but disputed. Martial law ended. **1987** A state of emergency was declared in response to demonstrations and violent strikes. **1988** Assembly elections were boycotted by the main opposition parties. The state of emergency was lifted. Islam was made the state religion. Monsoon floods left 30 million people homeless and thousands dead. **1991** A cyclone killed around 139,000 people and left up to 10 million homeless. Parliamentary government was restored. **1996** Power was handed to a neutral caretaker government. A general election was won by the AL, led by Sheikh Hasina Wazed. The BNP boycotted parliament. An agreement was made with India on the sharing of River Ganges water. **1998** The BNP ended its boycott of parliament. Two-thirds of Bangladesh was devastated by floods; 1,300 people were killed. Opposition-supported general strikes sought the removal of Sheikh Hasina's government.

Barbados

Area 430 sq km/166 sq mi **Capital** Bridgetown **Major towns/cities** Speightstown, Holetown, Oistins

Government

Head of state Elizabeth II from 1966, represented by Governor General Sir Clifford Straughn Husbands from 1996 **Head of government** Owen Arthur from 1994 **Political system** liberal democracy **Armed forces** 600 (1997) **Conscription** military service is voluntary **Defence spend** (% GDP) 0.6 (1997) **Education spend** (% GNP) 7.2 (1996) **Health spend** (% GDP) 4.4 (1995) **Death penalty** retained and used for ordinary crimes

Population and society

Population 269,000 (1999 est) **Population growth rate** 0.5% (1995–2000) **Ethnic groups** about 80% of African descent, about 16% mixed ethnicity, and 4% of European origin (mostly British) **Religion** 33% Anglican, 13% Pentecostalist, 6% Methodist, 4% Roman Catholic **Life expectancy** 74 (men); 79 (women) (1995–2000) **Literacy rate** 98% (men); 97% (women) (1997) **Unemployment** 13.2% (1998 est)

Economy and resources

GDP (US$) 1.8 billion (1998 est) **GNP** (US$) 2.1 billion (1998) **GNP per capita (PPP)** (US$) 12,260 (1998) **Real GDP growth** (% change on previous year) 3 (1998) **Consumer price inflation** 2.5% (1998) **Foreign debt** (US$) 459 million (1997) **Resources** petroleum and natural gas **Exports** sugar, molasses, syrup-rum, chemicals, electrical components. Principal market: USA 17.7% (1997) **Imports** machinery, foodstuffs, motor cars, construction materials, basic manufactures. Principal source: USA 41.6% (1997)

▪ Tourist information

Time difference GMT –4 **Currency** Barbados dollar **Language** English and Bajan (Barbadian English dialect) **Visa requirements** UK: visa not required (some visitors will require a business visa). USA: visa not required (some visitors will require a business visa) **Embassy in the UK** High Commission, 1 Great Russell Street, London WCN 22B 3JY. Tel: (020) 7631 4975; fax: (020) 7323 6872 **British embassy** British High Commission, PO Box 676, Lower Collymore Rock, St Michael. Tel: 436 6694; fax: 436 5398 **Chamber of commerce** Barbados Chamber of Commerce Inc, Nemwil House, 1st Floor, Lower Collymore Rock, PO Box 189, St Michael. Tel: 426 2056; fax: 429 2907 **Office hours** 0800/0830–1600/1630 Mon–Fri **Banking hours** generally 0800–1500 Mon–Thu; 0800–1300 and 1500–1700 Fri **Airports** international airports: Bridgetown (Grantley Adams) **Chief tourist attractions** good climate; coral beaches; swimming; outdoor sports **Major holidays** 1 January, 30 November, 25–26 December; variable: Good Friday, Easter Monday, Whit Monday, Kadooment (August), May Holiday, United Nations (October)

Chronology

1536 Visited by Portuguese explorer Pedro a Campos and the name Los Barbados ('The Bearded Ones') given in reference to its 'bearded' fig trees. Indigenous Arawak people were virtually wiped out, via epidemics, after contact with Europeans. **1627** British colony established; developed as a sugar-plantation economy, initially on basis of black slaves brought in from West Africa. **1639** The island's first parliament, the House of Assembly, was established. **1834** The island's slaves were freed. **1937** There was an outbreak of riots, followed by establishment of the Barbados Labour Party (BLP) by Grantley Adams, and moves towards a more independent political system. **1951** Universal adult suffrage was introduced. The BLP won a general election. **1954** Ministerial government was established, with BLP leader Adams as the first prime minister. **1955** A group broke away from the BLP and formed the Democratic Labour Party (DLP). **1961** Independence was achieved from Britain. **1966** Barbados achieved full independence within the Commonwealth. **1967** Barbados became a member of the United Nations (UN). **1972** Diplomatic relations with Cuba were established. **1983** Barbados supported the US invasion of Grenada. **1999** The BLP gained a landslide victory in general elections, securing 26 of the 28 House of Assembly seats.

Belarus Republic of

National name *Respublika Belarus* **Area** 207,600 sq km/ 80,154 sq mi **Capital** Minsk (Mensk) **Major towns/cities** Gomel, Vitebsk, Mogilev, Bobruisk, Hrodna, Brest

Government

Head of state Alexandr Lukashenko from 1994 **Head of government** Syargey Ling from 1996 **Political system** authoritarian nationalist **Armed forces** 81,800 (1997) **Conscription** compulsory for 18 months **Defence spend** (% GDP) 2.9 (1997) **Education spend** (% GNP) 2.9 (1997) **Health spend** (% GDP) 3.4 (1995) **Death penalty** retained and used for ordinary crimes

Population and society

Population 10,275,000 (1999 est) **Population growth rate** –0.3% (1995–2000) **Ethnic groups** 75% of Belorussian ('eastern Slav') descent, 13% ethnic Russian, 4% Polish, 3% Ukranian, 1% Jewish **Religion** Russian Orthodox, Roman Catholic; Baptist, Muslim, and Jewish minorities **Life expectancy** 62 (men); 74 (women) (1995–2000) **Literacy rate** 99% (men); 99% (women) (1997 est) **Unemployment** 2.3% (1998 est)

Economy and resources

GDP (US$) 22.6 billion (1998) **GNP** (US$) 22.5 billion (1998) **GNP per capita (PPP)** (US$) 4,100 (1998 est) **Real GDP growth** (% change on previous year) 7 (1998) **Consumer price inflation** 127% (1998) **Foreign debt** (US$) 1.16 billion (1997) **Resources** petroleum, natural gas, peat, salt, coal, lignite **Exports** machinery, chemicals and petrochemicals, iron and steel, light industrial goods. Principal market: Russia 65.5% (1998) **Imports** petroleum, natural gas, chemicals, machinery, processed foods. Principal source: Russia 53.8% (1998)

▪ Tourist information

Time difference GMT +2 **Currency** rouble and zaichik **Language** Belorussian (official); Russian, Polish **Visa requirements** UK: visa required. USA: visa required **Embassy in the UK** 6 Kensington Court, London W8 5DL. Tel: (020) 7937 3288; fax: (020) 73361 0005 **British embassy** Zakharova 26, 220034 Minsk. Tel: (172) 368 687; fax: (172) 144 7226 **Chamber of commerce** Chamber of Commerce and Industry, Masherava 14, 220600 Minsk. Tel: (172) 269 172; fax: (172) 269 860 **Office hours** 0900–1800 Mon–Fri **Banking hours** 0930–1730 Mon–Fri **Airports** international airports: Minsk; total passenger km: 910 million (1997) **Chief tourist attractions** forests; lakes; wildlife **Major holidays** 1, 7 January, 8 March, 1, 9 May, 3, 27 July, 2 November, 25 December; variable: Good Friday, Easter Monday

Chronology

5th–8th centuries Settled by East Slavic tribes, ancestors of present-day Belorussians. **11th century** Minsk was founded. **12th century** Part of Kievan Russia, to the south, with independent Belarus state developing around Polotsk, on River Dvina. **14th century** Incorporated within Slavonic Grand Duchy of Lithuania, to the west. **1569** Union with Poland. **late 18th century** Came under control of tsarist Russia as Belarussia ('White Russia'), following three partitions of Poland in 1772, 1793, and 1795. **1812** Minsk was destroyed by French emperor Napoleon Bonaparte during his campaign against Russia. **1839** The Belorussian Catholic Church was abolished. **1914–18** Belarus was the site of fierce fighting between Germany and Russia during World War I. **1918–19** Belarus was briefly independent from Russia. **1919–20** Wars between Poland and Soviet Russia over control of Belarus. **1921** West Belarus was ruled by Poland; East Belarus became a Soviet republic. **1930s** Agriculture was collectivized despite peasant resistance; over 100,000 people, chiefly writers and intellectuals, shot in mass executions ordered by the Soviet dictator Joseph Stalin. **1939** West Belarus was occupied by Soviet troops. **1941–44** The Nazi occupation resulted in the death of 1.3 million people, including many Jews; Minsk was destroyed. **1945** Belarus became a founding member of the United Nations (UN); much of West Belarus was incorporated into Soviet republic. **1950s–60s** Large-scale immigration of ethnic Russians and 'Russification'. **1986** Fallout from the nearby Chernobyl nuclear reactor in Ukraine rendered 20% of agricultural land unusable. **1989** The Belorussian Popular Front was established as national identity was revived under the *glasnost* initiative of Soviet leader Mikhail Gorbachev. **1990** Belorussian was established as the state language and republican sovereignty declared. **1991** Independence was recognized by the USA; the Commonwealth of Inndependent States (CIS) was formed in Minsk. **1996** An agreement on economic union was signed with Russia. Syargey Ling became prime minister. **1997** There were prodemocracy demonstrations. **1998** The Belarus rouble was devalued. A new left-wing and centrist political coalition was created. Food rationing was imposed as the economy deteriorated. Belarus signed a common policy with Russia on economic, foreign, and military matters.

Belau *see* Palau

Belgium Kingdom of

National name French *Royaume de Belgique*, Flemish *Koninkrijk België* **Area** 30,510 sq km/11,779 sq mi **Capital** Brussels **Major towns/cities** Antwerp, Ghent, Liège, Charleroi, Bruges, Mons, Namur, Leuven

Government

Head of state King Albert II from 1993 **Head of government** Guy Verhofstadt from 1999 **Political system** liberal democracy **Armed forces** 44,500 (1997) **Conscription** abolished in 1995 **Defence spend** (% GDP) 1.6 (1997) **Education spend** (% GNP) 3.2 (1996) **Health spend** (% GDP) 6.8 (1996) **Death penalty** abolished in 1996

Population and society

Population 10,152,000 (1999 est) **Population growth rate** 0.14% (1995–2000); 0.1% (2000–05) **Ethnic groups** mainly Flemings in north, Walloons in south **Religion** Roman Catholic 75%, various Protestant denominations **Life expectancy** 74 (men); 81 (women) (1995–2000) **Literacy rate** 99% (men); 99% (women) (1997) **Unemployment** 8.8% (1998)

Economy and resources

GDP (US$) 247 billion (1998) **GNP** (US$) 259 billion (1998) **GNP per capita (PPP)** (US$) 23,480 (1998) **Real GDP growth** (% change on previous year) 3.1 (1998) **Consumer price inflation** 2.1% (1998) **Resources** coal, coke, natural gas, iron **Exports** food, livestock and livestock products, gem diamonds, iron and steel manufacturers, machinery and transport equipment, chemicals and related products. Principal market: Germany 19% (1998) **Imports** food and live animals, machinery and transport equipment, precious metals and stones, mineral fuels and lubricants, chemicals and related products. Principal source: Germany 17.9% (1998)

▪ Tourist information

Time difference GMT +1 **Currency** Belgian franc **Language** in the north (Flanders) Flemish (a Dutch dialect, known as *Vlaams*) 55%; in the south (Wallonia) Walloon (a French dialect) 32%; bilingual 11%; German (eastern border) 0.6%. Dutch is official in the north, French in the south; Brussels is officially bilingual **Visa requirements** UK: visa not required. USA: visa not required **Embassy in the UK** 103–105 Eaton Square, London SW1W 9AB. Tel: (020) 7470 3700; fax: (020) 7259 6213 **British embassy** 85 rue d'Arlon, B-1040 Brussels. Tel: (2) 287 6211; fax: (2) 287 6355 **Chamber of commerce** Kamer van Koophandel en Nijverheid van Antwerpen, 12 Markgravestraat, B-2000 Antwerp. Tel: (3) 232 2219; fax: (3) 233 6442. Chambre de Commerce et d'Industrie de Bruxelles, 500 ave Louise, 1050 Brussels. Tel: (2) 648 5002; fax: (2) 640 9228 **Office hours** 0830–1730 Mon–Fri **Banking hours** 0900–1200 and 1400–1600 Mon–Fri; some banks open 0900–1200 Sat **Airports** international airports: Brussels (Zaventem), Antwerp (Deurne), Ostend, Liège, Charleroi; total passenger km: 11,277 million (1997 est) **Major ports** Antwerp, Ostend, Zeebrugge **Chief tourist attractions** towns of historic and cultural interest include Bruges, Ghent, Antwerp, Liège, Namur, Tournai, and Durbuy; seaside towns; forested Ardennes region **Major holidays** 1 January, 30 November, 25–26 December; variable: Ascension Thursday, Easter Monday, Whit Monday, May, August, and November holidays

Chronology

57 BC Romans conquered the Belgae (the indigenous Celtic people), and formed the province of Belgica. **3rd–4th centuries AD** The region was overrun by Franks and Saxons. **8th–9th centuries** Part of Frankish Empire; peace and order fostered growth of Ghent, Bruges, and Brussels. **843** Division of Holy Roman Empire; became part of Lotharingia, but frequent repartitioning followed. **10th–11th centuries** Seven feudal states emerged: Flanders, Hainaut, Namur, Brabant, Limburg, and Luxembourg, all nominally subject to French king or Holy Roman Emperor, but in practice independent. **12th century** The economy began to flourish. **15th century** One by one, the states came under rule of the dukes of Burgundy. **1477** Passed into Habsburg dominions through the marriage of Mary of Burgundy to Maximilian, archduke of Austria. **1555** Division of Habsburg dominions; Low Countries allotted to Spain. **1648** Independence of Dutch Republic recognized; south retained by Spain. **1713** Treaty of Utrecht transferred Spanish Netherlands to Austrian rule. **1792–97** Austrian Netherlands invaded by revolutionary France and finally annexed. **1815** The Congress of Vienna reunited north and south Netherlands as one kingdom under the House of Orange. **1830** The largely French-speaking people in south rebelled against union with Holland and declared Belgian independence. **1831** Leopold of Saxe-Coburg-Gotha became the first king of Belgium. **1839** The Treaty of London recognized the independence of Belgium and guaranteed its neutrality. **1914–18** Belgium was invaded and occupied by Germany. Belgian forces under King Albert I fought in conjunction with the Allies. **1919** Belgium acquired the Eupen-Malmédy region from Germany. **1940** Second invasion by Germany; King Leopold III ordered the Belgian army to capitulate. **1944–45** Belgium was liberated. **1948** Belgium formed the Benelux customs union with Luxembourg and the Netherlands. **1949** Belgium was a founding member of the North Atlantic Treaty Organization (NATO). Brussels became its headquarters in 1967. **1958** Belgium was a founding member of the European Economic Community (EEC), which made Brussels its headquarters. **1971** The constitution was amended to safeguard cultural rights of Flemish- (in Flanders in north) and French-speaking communities (Walloons in southeast). **1974** Separate regional councils and ministerial committees were established for Flemings and Walloons. **1980** There was violence over language divisions; regional assemblies for Flanders and Wallonia and a three-member executive for Brussels were created. **1999** In the general election, Guy Verhofstadt became liberal prime minister of a coalition government together with socialists and Greens.

Belize (formerly British Honduras)

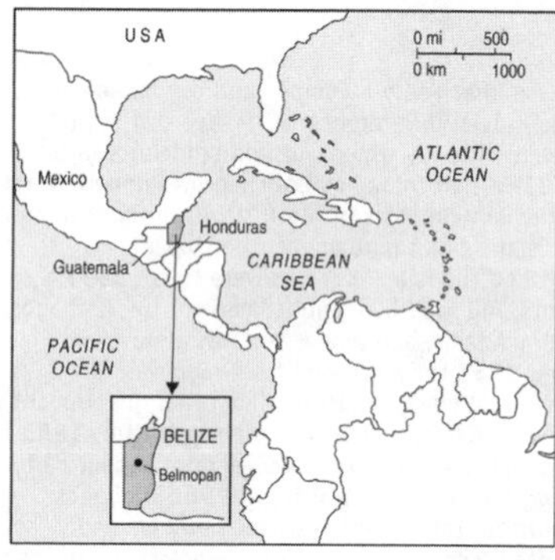

Area 22,963 sq km/8,866 sq mi **Capital** Belmopan **Major towns/cities** Belize City, Dangriga, Orange Walk, Corozal

Government

Head of state Elizabeth II from 1981, represented by governor general Dr Norbert Colville Young from 1993 **Head of government** Said Musa from 1998 **Political system** liberal democracy **Armed forces** 1,100 (1997); plus 700 militia reserves **Conscription** military service is voluntary **Defence spend** (% GDP) 2.6 (1997) **Education spend** (% GNP) 5.0 (1996) **Health spend** (% GDP) 5.7 (1995) **Death penalty** retained and used for ordinary crimes

Population and society

Population 235,000 (1999 est) **Population growth rate** 2.4% (1995–2000); 2.3% (2000–05) **Ethnic groups** Creoles, Mestizos, Caribs, East Indians, Mennonites, Canadians and Europeans, including Spanish and British **Religion** Roman Catholic 60%, Protestant 35% **Life expectancy** 73 (men); 76 (women) (1995–2000) **Literacy rate** 93% (men); 93% (women) (1994) **Unemployment** 12.7% (1998 est)

Economy and resources

GDP (US$) 649 million (1998 est) **GNP** (US$) 615 million (1998) **GNP per capita (PPP)** (US$) 3,940 (1998) **Real GDP growth** (% change on previous year) 2.5 (1998) **Consumer price inflation** 0.8% (1997) **Foreign debt** (US$) 366 million (1997) **Exports** sugar, clothes, citrus products, forestry and fish products, bananas. Principal market: UK 45.5% (1997) **Imports** foodstuffs, machinery and transport equipment, mineral fuels, chemicals, basic manufactures. Principal source: USA 51.5% (1997)

▪ Tourist information

Time difference GMT –6 **Currency** Belize dollar **Language** English (official); Spanish (widely spoken), Creole dialects

Visa requirements UK: visa not required. USA: visa not required **Embassy in the UK** 22 Harcourt House, 19 Cavendish Square, London W1M 9AD. Tel: (020) 7499 9728; fax: (020) 7491 4139 **British embassy** British High Commission, PO Box 91, Embassy Square, Belmopan. Tel: (8) 22146/7; fax: (8) 22761 **Chamber of commerce** Belize Chamber of Commerce and Industry, 63 Regent Street, POB 291, Belize City. Tel: (2) 75924; fax: (2) 74984 **Office hours** 0800–1200 and 1300–1700 Mon–Thu; 0800–1200 and 1300–1630 Fri **Banking hours** 0800–1300 Mon–Thu; 0800–1200 and 1500–1800 Fri **Airports** international airports: Belize City (Philip S W Goldson); domestic air services provide connections to major towns and offshore islands **Major ports** Belize City, Dangriga, Punta Gorda **Chief tourist attractions** beaches and barrier reef; hunting and fishing; Mayan remains; nine major wildlife reserves (including the only reserves for jaguar and red-footed booby) **Major holidays** 1 January, 9 March, 1, 24 May, 10, 24 September, 12 October, 19 November, 25–26 December; variable: Good Friday, Easter Monday, Holy Saturday

Chronology

325–925 AD Part of American Indian Maya civilization. **1600s** Colonized by British buccaneers and log-cutters **1862** Formally declared a British colony, known as British Honduras. **1893** Mexico renounced its longstanding claim to the territory. **1954** Constitution adopted, providing for limited internal self-government. **1964** Self-government was achieved. Universal adult suffrage and a two-chamber legislature were introduced. **1970** The capital was moved from Belize City to the new town of Belmopan. **1973** Name changed to Belize. **1975** British troops sent to defend the long-disputed frontier with Guatemala. **1980** The United Nations (UN) called for full independence. **1981** Full independence was achieved. **1991** Diplomatic relations were re-established with Guatemala, which finally recognized Belize's sovereignty. **1993** The UK announced its intention to withdraw troops following the resolution of the border dispute with Guatemala. **1998** The PUP won a sweeping victory in assembly elections, with Said Musa as prime minister.

Benin People's Republic of (formerly Dahomey)

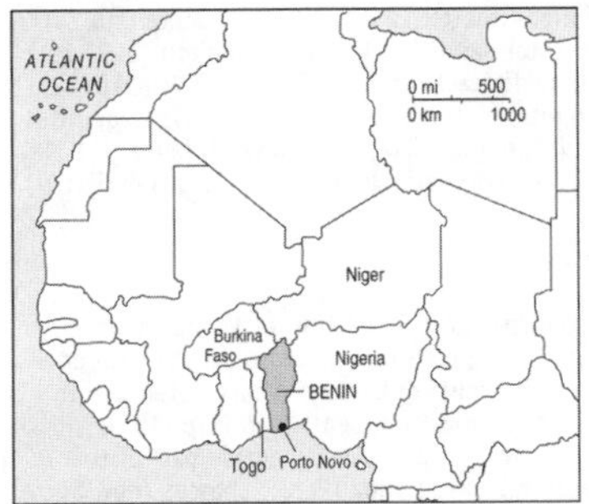

National name *République Populaire du Bénin* **Area** 112,622 sq km/43,483 sq mi **Capital** Porto-Novo (official), Cotonou (de facto) **Major towns/cities** Abomey, Natitingou, Parakou, Kandi, Ouidah, Djougou, Bohicou

Government

Head of state Mathieu Kerekou from 1996 **Head of government** vacant from 1998 **Political system** emergent democracy **Armed forces** 4,800 (1997) **Conscription** by selective conscription for 18 months **Defence spend** (% GDP) 1.3 (1997) **Education spend** (% GNP) 3.2 (1996) **Health spend** (% GDP) 1.7 (1990–95) **Death penalty** retained and used for ordinary crimes

Population and society

Population 5,937,000 (1999 est) **Population growth rate** 2.7% (1995–2000) **Ethnic groups** 98% indigenous African, distributed among 42 ethnic groups, the largest being the Fon, Adja, Yoruba, and Braiba; small European (mainly French) community **Religion** animist 60%, Muslim, Roman Catholic **Life expectancy** 52 (men); 55 (women) (1995–2000) **Literacy rate** 48% (men); 21% (women) (1997 est)

Economy and resources

GDP (US$) 2.32 billion (1998) **GNP** (US$) 2.3 billion (1998) **GNP per capita (PPP)** (US$) 1,250 (1998) **Real GDP growth** (% change on previous year) 3 (1998) **Consumer price inflation** 6% (1998) **Foreign debt** (US$) 1.6 billion (1997) **Resources** petroleum, limestone, marble **Exports** cotton, crude petroleum, palm oil and other palm products. Principal market: Brazil 18.2% (1997) **Imports** foodstuffs (particularly cereals), miscellaneous manufactured articles (notably cotton yarn and fabrics), fuels, machinery and transport equipment, chemicals, beverages, tobacco. Principal source: France 21.5% (1997)

▪ Tourist information

Time difference GMT +1 **Currency** franc CFA **Language** French (official); Fon 47% and Yoruba 9% in south; six major tribal languages in north **Visa requirements** UK: visa required. USA: visa required **Embassy in the UK** Dolphin House, 16 The Broadway, Stanmore, Middlesex HA7 4DW. Tel: (020) 8954 8800; fax: (020) 8954 8844 **British embassy** British Consulate, Lot 24, Patte d'oie, Cotonou. (All staff based in Nigeria.) Tel: 301120 **Chamber of commerce** Chambre de Commerce, d'Agriculture et d'Industrie de la République du Bénin, ave du Général de Gaulle, BP31, Cotonou. Tel: 313 299 **Office hours** 0830–1230 and 1500–1830 Mon–Fri **Banking hours** 0800–1100 and 1500–1700 Mon–Fri **Airports** international airports: Cotonou (Cootonou-Cadjehoun); four domestic airports; total passenger km: 223 million (1995) **Major ports** Cotonou **Chief tourist attractions** national parks; game reserves **Major holidays** 1, 16 January, 1 April, 1 May, 26 October, 30 November, 25, 31 December; variable: Eid-ul-Adha, end of Ramadan, Good Friday, Easter Monday, Whit Monday

Chronology

12th–13th centuries The area was settled by a Ewe-speaking people called the Aja, who mixed with local peoples and gradually formed the Fon ethnic group. **16th century** The Aja kingdom, called Great Ardha, was at its peak. **early 17th century** The Kingdom of Dahomey was established in the south by Fon peoples, who defeated the neighbouring Dan; following contact with European traders, the kingdom became an intermediary in the slave trade. **1800–50** King Dezo of Dahomey raised regiments of female soldiers to attack the Yoruba ('land of the big cities') kingdom of eastern Benin and southwest Nigeria in order to obtain slaves. **1857** A French base was established at Grand-Popo. **1892–94** War broke out between the French and Dahomey, after which the victorious French established a protectorate. **1899** Incorporated in federation of French West Africa as Dahomey. **1914** During World War I French troops from Dahomey participated in conquest of German-ruled Togoland to the west. **1940–44** During World War II, along with the rest of French West Africa, the country supported the 'Free French' anti-Nazi resistance cause. **1960** Independence achieved from France. **1960–77** Acute political instability, with frequent switches from civilian to military rule, and regional ethnic disputes. **1975** The name of the country was changed from Dahomey to Benin. **1989** The army was deployed against antigovernment strikers and protesters, inspired by Eastern European revolutions; Marxist-Leninism was dropped as the official ideology and a market-centred economic reform programme adopted. **1990** A referendum backed the establishment of multiparty politics. **1991** In multiparty elections, the leader of the new Benin Renaissance Party (PRB), Nicéphore Soglo, became president and formed a ten-party coalition government. **1996** Major Mathieu Kerekou became president. **1998** Prime Minister Adrien Houngbedji resigned; no immediate successor was appointed.

Bhutan Kingdom of

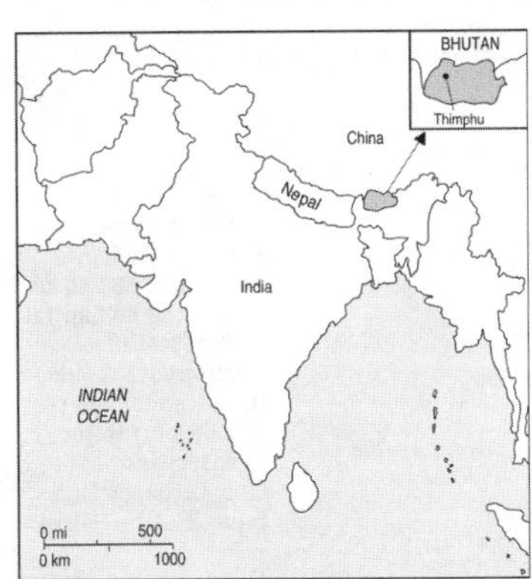

National name *Druk-yul* **Area** 46,500 sq km/17,953 sq mi **Capital** Thimphu (Thimbu) **Major towns/cities** Paro, Punakha, Mongar, P'sholing, W'phodrang, Bumthang

Government

Head of state Jigme Singye Wangchuk from 1972 **Head of government** Lyonpo Jigme Thimley from 1998 **Political system** absolutist **Armed forces** 6,000 (1996) **Conscription** military service is voluntary **Education spend** (% GNP) 4.2 (1995) **Health spend** (% GDP) 2.3 (1996) **Death penalty** retains the death penalty for ordinary crimes but can be considered abolitionist in practice (date of last known execution was 1964)

Population and society

Population 2,064,000 (1999 est) **Population growth rate** 2.8% (1995–2000); 2.3% (2000–05) **Ethnic groups** 54% Bhotia, living principally in

north and east; 32% of Tibetan descent; a substantial Nepali minority lives in the south – they are prohibited from moving into the Bhotia-dominated north **Religion** 70% Mahayana Buddhist (state religion), 25% Hindu **Life expectancy** 60 (men); 62 (women) (1995–2000) **Literacy rate** 58% (men); 30% (women) (1997 est)

Economy and resources

GDP (US$) 383 million (1998) **GNP** (US$) 296 million (1997) **GNP per capita (PPP)** (US$) 1,180 (1997 est) **Real GDP growth** (% change on previous year) 6.6 (1997) **Consumer price inflation** 5.7% (1997) **Foreign debt** (US$) 115 million (1997) **Resources** limestone, gypsum, coal, slate, dolomite, lead, talc, copper **Exports** cardamon, cement, timber, fruit, electricity (to India), precious stones, spices. Principal market: India 90.7% (1997) **Imports** aircraft, mineral fuels, machinery and transport equipment, rice. Principal source: India 65.3% (1997)

▪ Tourist information

Time difference GMT +6 **Currency** ngultrum; also Indian currency **Language** Dzongkha (official, a Tibetan dialect), Sharchop, Bumthap, Nepali, and English **Visa requirements** UK: visa required. USA: visa required **Embassy in the UK** no diplomatic representation **British embassy** no diplomatic representation **Chamber of commerce** Bhutan Chamber of Commerce and Industry, POB 147, Thimphu. Tel: (2) 23140; fax: (2) 23936 **Airports** international airports: Paro; total passenger km: 5 million (1995) **Chief tourist attractions** Bhutan is open only to 'controlled' tourism – many monasteries, mountains, and other holy places remain inaccessible to tourists; wildlife includes snow leopards and musk deer **Major holidays** 2 May, 2 June, 21 July, 11–13 November, 17 December

Chronology

to 8th century Under effective Indian control. **16th century** Came under Tibetan rule. **1616–51** Unified by Ngawang Namgyal, leader of the Drukpa Kagyu (Thunder Dragon) Tibetan Buddhist branch. **1720** Came under Chinese rule. **1774** Treaty signed with East India Company. **1865** Trade treaty with Britain signed after invasion. **1907** Ugyen Wangchuk, governor of Tongsa, became Bhutan's first hereditary monarch. **1910** Anglo-Bhutanese Treaty signed, placing foreign relations under the 'guidance' of the British government in India. **1949** Indo-Bhutan Treaty of Friendship signed, giving India continued influence over Bhutan's foreign relations, but returning territory annexed in 1865. **1953** The national assembly (Tshogdu) was established. **1958** Slavery was abolished. **1959** 4,000 Tibetan refugees were given asylum after Chinese annexation of Tibet. **1968** The first cabinet was established. **1973** Bhutan joined the nonaligned movement. **1979** Tibetan refugees were told to take Bhutanese citizenship or leave; most stayed. **1983** Bhutan became a founding member of the South Asian Regional Association for Cooperation. **1988** The Buddhist Dzongkha king imposed a 'code of conduct' suppressing the customs of the large Hindu-Nepali community in the south. **1990** Hundreds of people were allegedly killed during prodemocracy demonstrations. **1998** Political powers were ceded from the monarchy to the National Assembly. Lyonpo Jigme Thimley became prime minister.

Bolivia Republic of

National name *República de Bolivia* **Area** 1,098,581 sq km/ 424,162 sq mi **Capital** La Paz (seat of government), Sucre (legal capital and seat of judiciary) **Major towns/cities** Santa Cruz, Cochabamba, Oruro, El Alto, Potosí

Government

Head of state and government Hugo Banzer Suarez from 1997 **Political system** liberal democracy **Armed forces** 33,500 (1997) **Conscription** selective conscription for 12 months at the age of 18 **Defence spend** (% GDP) 2.0 (1997) **Education spend** (% GNP) 5.6 (1996) **Health spend** (% GDP) 2.7 (1990–95) **Death penalty** abolished for ordinary crimes in 1997; laws provide for the death penalty for exceptional crimes only (last execution in 1974)

Population and society

Population 8,142,000 (1999 est) **Population growth rate** 2.3% (1995–2000); 2.2% (2000–05) **Ethnic groups** 30% Quechua Indians, 25% Aymara Indians, 25–30% mixed, 5–15% of European descent **Religion** Roman Catholic 95% (state-recognized) **Life expectancy** 60 (men); 63 (women) (1995–2000) **Literacy rate** 91% (men); 77% (women) (1997 est) **Unemployment** 4.2% (1996)

Economy and resources

GDP (US$) 8.55 billion (1998) **GNP** (US$) 7.9 billion (1998) **GNP per capita (PPP)** (US$) 2,820 (1998) **Real GDP growth** (% change on previous year) 4.6 (1998) **Consumer price inflation** 6.5% (1998) **Foreign debt** (US$) 5.2 billion (1997) **Resources** petroleum, natural gas, tin (world's fifth-largest producer), zinc, silver, gold, lead, antimony, tungsten, copper **Exports** metallic minerals, natural gas, jewellery, soybeans, wood. Principal market: UK 16.1% (1998). Illegal trade in coca and its derivatives (mainly cocaine) was worth approximately $600 million in 1990 – almost equal to annual earnings from official exports. **Imports** industrial materials, machinery and transport equipment, consumer goods. Principal source: USA 31.6% (1998)

▪ Tourist information

Time difference GMT –4 **Currency** boliviano **Language** Spanish (official); Aymara, Quechua **Visa requirements** UK: visa not required for a stay of up to 90 days. USA: visa not required for a stay of up to 90 days **Embassy in the UK** Embassy and Consulate, 106 Eaton Square, London SW1W 9AD. Tel: (020) 7235 4248; fax: (020) 7235 1286 **British embassy** Avenida Arce 2732, Casilla 694, La Paz. Tel: (2) 357 424; fax: (2) 391 063 **Chamber of commerce** Cámara Nacional de Comercio, Edificio Cámara Nacional de Comercio, Avda Mariscal Santa Cruz 1392, 1°, Casilla 7, La Paz. Tel: (2) 350 042; fax: (2) 391 004 **Office hours** 0830–1200 and 1430–1830 Mon–Fri; 0900–1200 some Saturdays **Banking hours** 0830–1200 and 1430–1730 Mon–Fri **Airports** international airports: La Paz (El Alto), Santa Cruz (Viru-Viru); 28 domestic airports; total passenger km: 1,891 million (1997 est) **Chief tourist attractions** Lake Titicaca; pre-Inca ruins at Tiwanaku; Chacaltaga in the Andes Mountains; UNESCO World Cultural Heritage Sites of Potosí and Sucre; skiing in the Andes **Major holidays** 1 January, 1 May, 6 August, 1 November, 25 December; variable: Carnival, Corpus Christi, Good Friday

Chronology

c. AD 600 Development of sophisticated civilization at Tiahuanaco, south of Lake Titicaca. *c.* 1200 Tiahuanaco culture was succeeded by smaller Aymara-speaking kingdoms. **16th century** Became incorporated within westerly Quechua-speaking Inca civilization, centred in Peru. **1538** Conquered by Spanish and, known as 'Upper Peru', became part of the Viceroyalty of Peru, whose capital was at Lima (Peru); Charcas (now Sucre) became the local capital. **1545** Silver was discovered at Potosí in the southwest, which developed into chief silver-mining town and most important city in South America in the 17th and 18th centuries. **1776** Transferred to the Viceroyalty of La Plata, with its capital in Buenos Aires. **late 18th century** Increasing resistance of American Indians and Mestizos to Spanish rule; silver production slumped. **1825** Liberated from Spanish rule by the Venezuelan freedom fighter Simón Bolívar, after whom the country was named, and his general, Antonio José de Sucre; Sucre became Bolivia's first president. **1836–39** Bolivia became part of a federation with Peru, headed by Bolivian president Andres Santa Cruz, but it dissolved following defeat in war with Chile. **1879–84** Coastal territory in the Atacama, containing valuable minerals, was lost after defeat in war with Chile. **1903** Territory was lost to Brazil. **1932–35** Further territory was lost after defeat by Paraguay in the Chaco War, fought over control of the Chaco Boreal. **1952** After the military regime was overthrown in the Bolivian National Revolution, Dr Victor Paz Estenssoro of the centrist National Revolutionary Movement (MNR) became president and introduced social reforms. **1964** An army coup was led by Vice-President Gen René Barrientos. **1967** There was a peasant uprising, led by Ernesto 'Che' Guevara. The uprising was put down with US help, and Guevara was killed. **1969** Barrientos was killed in a plane crash, and replaced by Siles Salinas, who was soon deposed in an army coup. **1971** Col Hugo Banzer Suárez came to power after a military coup. **1974** An attempted coup prompted Banzer to postpone promised elections and ban political and trade-union activity. **1980** Inconclusive elections were followed by the country's 189th coup. Allegations of corruption and drug trafficking led to the cancellation of US and European Community (EC) aid. **1982** With the economy

worsening, the military junta handed power over to a civilian administration headed by Siles Zuazo. **1983** US and EC economic aid resumed as austerity measures were introduced. **1985** The inflation rate was 23,000%. **1993** Foreign investment was encouraged as inflation fell to single figures. **1997** Hugo Banzer was elected president.

Bosnia-Herzegovina Republic of

National name *Republika Bosna i Hercegovina* **Area** 51,129 sq km/19,740 sq mi **Capital** Sarajevo **Major towns/cities** Banja Luka, Mostar, Prijedor, Tuzla, Zenica

Government

Heads of state Rotating chairman of the collective presidency, Ante Jelavic from 1999 **Heads of government** Co-prime ministers Haris Silajdzic (from 1997) and Svetozar Mihajlovic (from 1998) **Political system** emergent democracy **Armed forces** 40,000 (1997) **Defence spend** (% GDP) 5.0 (1997) **Death penalty** abolished for ordinary crimes in 1997; laws provide for the death penalty for exceptional crimes only

Population and society

Population 3,838,000 (1999 est) **Population growth rate** 3% (1995–2000) **Ethnic groups** 44% ethnic Muslim, 31% Serb, 17% Croat, 6% 'Yugoslav'. Croats are most thickly settled in southwest Bosnia and western Herzegovina, Serbs in eastern and western Bosnia. Since the start of the civil war in 1992 many Croats and Muslims have fled as refugees to neighbouring states **Religion** Sunni Muslim, Serbian Orthodox, Roman Catholic **Life expectancy** 71 (men); 76 (women) (1995–2000) **Literacy rate** 90% (men); 90% (women) (1992) **Unemployment** 28% (1992 est)

Economy and resources

GDP (US$) 3.9 billion (1998 est) **GNP** (US$) 2.3 billion (1996) **GNP per capita (PPP)** (US$) 450 (1996 est) **Real GDP growth** (% change on previous year) 20 (1998) **Consumer price inflation** 40% (1998) **Foreign debt** (US$) 1.1 billion (1997) **Resources** copper, lead, zinc, iron ore, coal, bauxite, manganese **Exports** coal, domestic appliances (industrial production and mining remain low). Principal market: Croatia 34.3% (1997) **Imports** foodstuffs, basic manufactured goods, processed and semiprocessed goods. Principal source: Italy 25.3% (1997)

▪ Tourist information

Time difference GMT +1 **Currency** dinar **Language** Serbian variant of Serbo-Croatian **Visa requirements** UK: visa not required. USA: visa not required **Embassy in the UK** 40–41 Conduit Street, London W1R 9FB. Tel: (020) 7734 3758; fax: (020) 7734 3760 **British embassy** 8 Mustafe Golubica, 71000 Sarajevo. Tel: (71) 444 429; fax: (71) 444 429 **Chamber of commerce** Chamber of Economy of Bosnia and Herzegovina, Mis. Irbina 13, 71000 Sarajevo. Tel: (71) 211777 **Banking hours** normal banking services have broken down **Airports** international airport: Sarajevo; two smaller civil airports (civil aviation was severely disrupted by fighting in early 1990s; no air services to Sarajevo since 1992); **Major holidays** 1–2 January, 1 March, 1–2 May, 27 July, 25 November

Chronology

1st century AD Part of Roman province of Illyricum. **395** On division of Roman Empire, stayed in west, along with Croatia and Slovenia, while Serbia to the east became part of the Byzantine Empire. **7th century** Settled by Slav tribes. **12–15th centuries** Independent state. **1463 and 1482** Bosnia and Herzegovina, in south, successively conquered by Ottoman Turks; many Slavs were converted to Sunni Islam. **1878** Became an Austrian protectorate, following Bosnian revolt against Turkish rule in 1875–76. **1908** Annexed by Austrian Habsburgs in wake of Turkish Revolution. **1914** Archduke Franz Ferdinand, the Habsburg heir, was assassinated in Sarajevo by a Bosnian-Serb extremist, precipitating World War I. **1918** On the collapse of the Habsburg Empire, the region became part of the Serb-dominated 'Kingdom of Serbs, Croats, and Slovenes', known as Yugoslavia from 1929. **1941** The region was occupied by Nazi Germany and became 'Greater Croatia' fascist puppet state and the scene of fierce fighting. **1943–44** Bosnia was liberated by communist Partisans, led by Marshal Tito. **1945** The region became a republic within the Yugoslav Socialist Federation. **1980** There was an upsurge in Islamic nationalism. **1990** Ethnic violence erupted between Muslims and Serbs. Communists were defeated in multiparty elections; a coalition was formed by Serb, Muslim, and Croatian parties. **1991** The Serb–Croat civil war in Croatia spread unrest into Bosnia. Fears that Serbia planned to annex Serb-dominated parts of the republic led to a declaration of sovereignty by parliament. Serbs within Bosnia established autonomous enclaves. **1992** Bosnia was admitted into the United Nations (UN). Violent civil war broke out, as an independent 'Serbian Republic of Bosnia-Herzegovina', comprising parts of the east and the west, was proclaimed by Bosnian-Serb militia leader Radovan Karadzic, with Serbian backing. UN forces were drafted into Sarajevo to break the Serb siege of the city; Bosnian Serbs were accused of 'ethnic cleansing', particularly of Muslims. **1993** A UN-EC peace plan failed. The USA began airdrops of food and medical supplies. Six UN 'safe areas' were created, intended as havens for Muslim civilians. A Croat–Serb partition plan was rejected by Muslims. **1994** The Serb siege of Sarajevo was lifted after a UN–NATO ultimatum and Russian diplomatic intervention. A Croat–Muslim federation was formed. **1995** Hostilities resumed. A US-sponsored peace accord, providing for two sovereign states (a Muslim–Croat federation and a Bosnian Serb Republic, the Republika Srpska) as well as a central legislature (House of Representatives, House of Peoples, and three-person presidency), was agreed at Dayton, Ohio. A 60,000-strong NATO peacekeeping force was deployed. **1996** An International Criminal Tribunal for Former Yugoslavia began in the Hague and an arms-control accord was signed. Full diplomatic relations were established with Yugoslavia. The collective presidency was elected, consisting of Alija Izetbegovic (Muslim), Momcilo Krajisnik (Serb), and Kresimir Zubak (Croat); Izetbegovic was elected overall president. Biljana Plavsic was elected president of the Serb Republic and Gojko Klickovic its prime minister. Edhem Bicakcic became prime minister of the Muslim–Croat Federation. **1997** Haris Silajdzic (Muslim), and Boro Bosic (Serb), were appointed co-chairs of the central Council of Ministers (cabinet). The Serb part of Bosnia signed a customs agreement with Yugoslavia. Vladimir Soljic was elected president of the Muslim-Croat Federation. **1998** The first Muslims and Croats were convicted in The Hague for war crimes during 1992. Zivko Radisic became the first Bosnian Serb to hold power as rotating federal president. Edhem Bicakcic became prime minister of the Bosnian Muslim–Croat state, with Ejup Ganic (a Bosnian Muslim) as president. In January a moderate, pro-western government was formed in the Bosnian Serb republic, headed by Milorad Dodik; Nikola Poplasen became president. In December the moderate Brane Miljus took Dodik's place as prime minister. Haris Silajdzic (a Bosnian Muslim) and Svetozar Mihajlovic (a Bosnian Serb moderate) were nominated as co-chairs of the federation.

Botswana Republic of

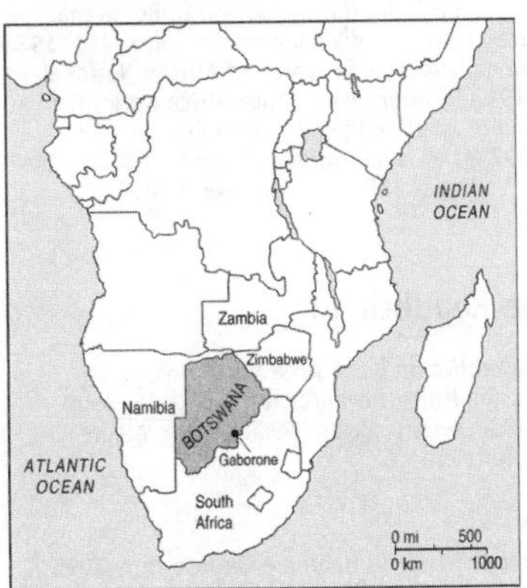

Area 582,000 sq km/224,710 sq mi **Capital** Gaborone **Major towns/cities** Mahalapye, Serowe, Tutume, Bobonong Francistown, Selebi-Phikwe, Lobatse, Molepolol, Kange

Government

Head of state and government Festus Mogae from 1998 **Political system** liberal democracy **Armed forces** 7,500 (1997) **Conscription** military service is voluntary **Defence spend** (% GDP) 6.5 (1997) **Education spend** (% GNP) 10.4 (1996) **Health spend** (% GDP) 2.2 (1995) **Death penalty** retained and used for ordinary crimes

Population and society

Population 1,597,000 (1999 est) **Population growth rate** 1.9% (1995–2000) **Ethnic groups** about 90% Tswana and 5% Kung and other hunter-gatherer groups; the remainder is European **Religion** Christian 50%, animist, Baha'i, Muslim, Hindu **Life expectancy** 46 (men); 48 (women) (1995–2000) **Literacy rate** 72% (men); 77% (women) (1997 est) **Unemployment** 21.5% (1997)

Economy and resources

GDP (US$) 5.69 billion (1998) **GNP** (US$) 5.6 billion (1998) **GNP per capita (PPP)** (US$) 8,310 (1998) **Real GDP growth** (% change on previous year) 3.1 (1998) **Consumer price inflation** 10% (1998) **Foreign debt** (US$) 562 million (1997) **Resources** diamonds (world's third-largest producer), copper-nickel ore, coal, soda ash, gold, cobalt, salt, plutonium, asbestos, chromite, iron, silver, manganese, talc, uranium
Exports diamonds, copper and nickel, beef. Principal market: EU 79.7% (1997) **Imports** machinery and transport equipment, food, beverages, tobacco, chemicals and rubber products, textiles and footwear, fuels, wood and paper products. Principal source: Southern African Customs Union (SACU) 72.5% (1997)

▪ Tourist information

Time difference GMT +2 **Currency** franc CFA **Language** English (official), Setswana (national) **Visa requirements** UK: visa not required. USA: visa not required **Embassy in the UK** High Commission, 6 Stratford Place, London W1N 9AE. Tel: (020) 7499 0031; fax: (020) 7495 8595 **British embassy** British High Commission, Private Bag 0023, Gaborone. Tel: 352 841/2/3; fax: (020) 7356 105 **Chamber of commerce** Botswana National Chamber of Commerce and Industry, PO Box 20344, Gaborone. Tel: 52677 **Office hours** 0800–1700 Mon–Fri, April–October; 0730–1630 Mon–Fri, October–April **Banking hours** 0900–1430 Mon, Tue, Thu, and Fri; 0815–1200 Wed; 0815–1045 Sat **Airports** international airports: Gaborone (Sir Seretse Khama), Kasane; six domestic airports; total passenger km: 53 million (1995) **Chief tourist attractions** Kalahari Desert; five game reserves and three national parks, including Chobe National Park, Moremi Wildlife Reserve, and Kalahari Gemsbok National Park **Major holidays** 1–2 January, 30 September, 25–26 December; variable: Ascension Thursday, Good Friday, Easter Monday, Holy Saturday, President's Day (July), July Holiday, October Holiday

Chronology

18th century Formerly inhabited by nomadic hunter-gatherer groups, including the Kung, the area was settled by the Tswana people, from whose eight branches the majority of the people are descended. **1872** Khama III the Great, a converted Christian, became chief of the Bamangwato, the largest Tswana group. He developed a strong army and greater unity among the Botswana peoples. **1885** Became the British protectorate of Bechuanaland at the request of Chief Khama, who feared invasion by Boers from the Transvaal (South Africa) following the discovery of gold. **1895** The southern part of the Bechuanaland Protectorate was annexed by Cape Colony (South Africa). **1960** A new constitution created a legislative council controlled (until 1963) by a British High Commissioner. **1965** The capital was transferred from Mafeking to Gaborone. Internal self-government was achieved. **1966** Independence was achieved from Britain. Name changed to Botswana. **mid-1970s** The economy grew rapidly as diamond mining expanded. **1985** South African raid on Gaborone, allegedly in search of African National Congress (ANC) guerrillas. **1993** Relations with South Africa were fully normalized following the end of apartheid and the establishment of a multiracial government. **1997** Major constitutional changes reduced the voting age to 18. **1998** Festus Mogae (BDP) became president.

Brazil Federative Republic of

National name *República Federativa do Brasil* **Area** 8,511,965 sq km/ 3,286,469 sq mi **Capital** Brasília **Major towns/cities** São Paulo, Belo Horizonte, Nova Iguaçu, Rio de Janeiro, Belém, Recife, Pôrto Alegre, Salvador, Curitiba, Manaus, Fortaleza

Government

Head of state and government Fernando Henrique Cardoso from 1995 **Political system** liberal democracy **Armed forces** 314,700; public security forces under army control 385,600 (1997) **Conscription** 12 months **Defence spend** (% GDP) 2.3 (1997) **Education spend** (% GNP) 5.2 (1996) **Health spend** (% GDP) 1.9 (1995) **Death penalty** for exceptional crimes only; last execution 1855

Population and society

Population 167,988,000 (1998 est) **Population growth rate** 1.3% (1995–2000) **Ethnic groups** wide range of ethnic groups, including 55% of European origin (mainly Portuguese, Italian, and German), 38% of mixed parentage, 6% of African origin, as well as American Indians and Japanese **Religion** Roman Catholic 89%; Indian faiths **Life expectancy** 63 (men); 71 (women) (1995–2000) **Literacy rate** 84% (men); 84% (women) (1997 est) **Unemployment** 7.6% (1998)

Economy and resources

GDP (US$) 778.3 billion (1998) **GNP** (US$) 758 billion (1998) **GNP per capita (PPP)** (US$) 6,160 (1998) **Real GDP growth** (% change on previous year) 0.8 (1998) **Consumer price inflation** 4.2% (1998) **Foreign debt** (US$) 193.6 billion (1997) **Resources** iron ore (world's second-largest producer), tin (world's fourth-largest producer), aluminium (world's fourth-largest producer), gold, phosphates, platinum, bauxite, uranium, manganese, coal, copper, petroleum, natural gas, hydroelectric power, forests **Exports** steel products, transport equipment, coffee, iron ore and concentrates, aluminium, iron, tin, soybeans, orange juice (85% of world's concentrates), tobacco, leather footwear, sugar, beef, textiles. Principal market: USA 17.8% (1998) **Imports** mineral fuels, machinery and mechanical appliances, chemical products, foodstuffs, coal, wheat, fertilizers, cast iron and steel. Principal source: USA 22.2% (1998)

▪ Tourist information

Time difference GMT -2/5 **Currency** real **Language** Portuguese (official); 120 Indian languages **Visa requirements** UK: visa not required for tourist visits. USA: visa required **Embassy in the UK** 32 Green Street, London W1Y 4AT. Tel: (020) 7499 0877; fax: (020) 7493 5105 **British embassy** Caixa Postal 07-0586, Setor de Embaixadas Sul, Quadra 801, Conjunto K, 70408-900 Brasília, Distrito Federal. Tel: (61) 225 2710; fax: (61) 225 1777 **Chamber of commerce** Confederaçao Nacional do Comércio, SCS, Edif. Presidente Dutra, 4° andar, Quadra 11, 70327 Brasília, Distrito Federal. Tel: (61) 223 0578 **Office hours** 0900–1800 Mon–Fri **Banking hours** 1000–1630 Mon–Fri **Airports** principal international airports: Rio de Janeiro (Brasília and Guarulhos), São Paulo (Guarulhos, Viracopos, and Congonhas), Manaus (Eduardo Gomes), Salvador (Dois de Julho); 27 domestic airports; total passenger km: 41,714 million (1997 est) **Major ports** Rio de Janeiro, Belém, Recife, Pôrto Alegre, Salvador **Chief tourist attractions** Rio de Janeiro and beaches; Iguaçu Falls; tropical forests of Amazon basin; wildlife of the Pantanal; Mato Grosso **Major holidays** 1 January, 21 April, 1 May, 7 September, 12 October, 2, 15 November, 25 December; variable: Carnival (2 days), Corpus Christi, Good Friday, Holy Saturday, Holy Thursday

Chronology

1500 Originally inhabited by South American Indians. Portuguese explorer Pedro Alvares Cabral sighted and claimed Brazil for Portugal. **1530** Start of Portuguese colonization; Portugal monopolized trade but colonial government was decentralized. **1580–1640** Brazil came under Spanish rule along with Portugal. **17th century** Sugar-cane plantations were established with slave labour in coastal regions, making Brazil the world's largest supplier of sugar; cattle ranching was developed inland. **1695** Gold was discovered in the central highlands. **1763** The colonial capital moved from Bahía to Rio de Janeiro. **1770** Brazil's first coffee plantations were established in Rio de Janeiro. **18th century** Population in 1798 totalled 3.3 million, of which around 1.9 million were slaves, mainly of African origin; significant growth of gold-mining industry. **1808** The Portuguese regent, Prince John, arrived in Brazil and established his court at Rio de Janeiro; Brazilian trade opened to foreign merchants. **1815** The United Kingdom of Portugal, Brazil, and Algarve made Brazil co-equal with

Portugal. **1821** Crown Prince Pedro took over the government of Brazil. **1822** Pedro defied orders to return to Portugal; he declared Brazil's independence to avoid reversion to colonial status. **1825** King John VI recognized his son as Emperor Pedro I of Brazil. **1831** Pedro I abdicated in favour of his infant son, Pedro II. **1847** The first prime minister was appointed, but the emperor retained many powers. **1865–70** Brazilian efforts to control Uruguay led to the War of the Triple Alliance with Paraguay. **1888** Slavery was abolished in Brazil. **1889** The monarch was overthrown by a liberal revolt; a federal republic was established, with a central government controlled by the coffee planters. **1902** Brazil produced 65% of the world's coffee. **1915–19** Lack of European imports during World War I led to rapid industrialization. **1930** A revolution against the coffee planter oligarchy placed Getúlio Vargas in power; he introduced social reforms. **1937** Vargas established an authoritarian corporate state. **1942** Brazil entered World War II as an ally of the USA. **1945–54** Vargas was ousted by a military coup. In 1951 he was elected president and continued to extend the state control of the economy. In 1954 he committed suicide. **1960** The capital moved to Brasília. **1964** A bloodless coup established a technocratic military regime; free political parties were abolished; intense concentration on industrial growth was aided by foreign investment and loans. **1970s** Economic recession and inflation undermined public support for the military regime. **1985** After gradual democratization from 1979, Tancredo Neves became the first civilian president in 21 years. **1988** A new constitution reduced the powers of the president. **1989** Fernando Collor was elected president. Brazil suspended its foreign debt payments. **1992** Collor was charged with corruption and replaced by Vice-President Itamar Franco. **1994** A new currency was introduced, the third in eight years. Fernando Henrique Cardoso won presidential elections. Collor was cleared of corruption charges. **1997** The constitution was amended to allow the president to seek a second term of office. **1998** President Cardoso was re-elected. An IMF rescue package was announced.

Brunei State of

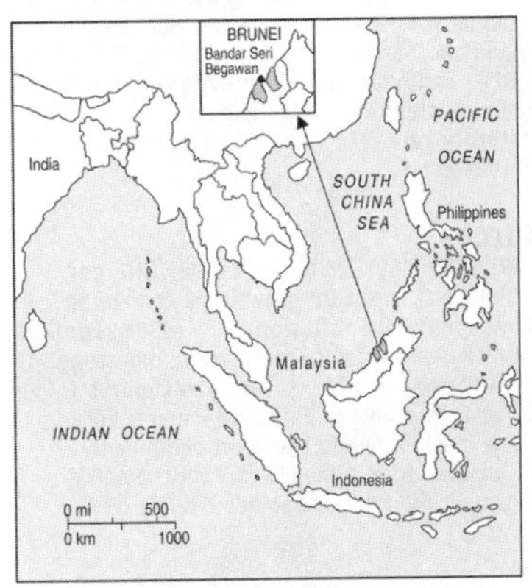

National name *Negara Brunei Darussalam* **Area** 5,765 sq km/2,225 sq mi **Capital** Bandar Seri Begawan **Major towns/cities** Seria, Kuala Belait, Bangar

Government

Head of state and government HM Muda Hassanal Bolkiah Mu'izzaddin Waddaulah, Sultan of Brunei, from 1967 **Political system** absolutist **Armed forces** 5,000 (1997); plus paramilitary forces of 4,100 **Conscription** military service is voluntary **Defence spend** (% GDP) 6.5 (1996) **Education spend** (% GNP) 3.1 (1996) **Health spend** (% GDP) 0.8 (1995) **Death penalty** retains the death penalty for ordinary crimes but can be considered abolitionist in practice (last execution 1957)

Population and society

Population 321,000 (1999 est) **Population growth rate** 2.2% (1995–2000) **Ethnic groups** 68% indigenous Malays, predominating in government service and agriculture; more than 20% Chinese, predominating in the commercial sphere **Religion** Muslim 66%, Buddhist 14%, Christian 10% **Life expectancy** 73 (men); 78 (women) (1995–2000) **Literacy rate** 94% (men); 86% (women) (1997 est) **Unemployment** 4.3% (1997)

Economy and resources

GDP (US$) 5.3 billion (1998) **GNP** (US$) 7 billion (1998 est) **GNP per capita (PPP)** (US$) 25,500 (1998 est) **Real GDP growth** (% change on previous year) 2.6 (1998) **Consumer price inflation** –0.5% (1998 est) **Foreign debt** (US$) 1.2 billion (1997) **Resources** petroleum, natural gas **Exports** crude petroleum, natural gas and refined products. Principal market: Japan 50.9% (1998) **Imports** machinery and transport equipment, basic manufactures, food and live animals, chemicals. Principal source: Singapore 32.3% (1998)

▪ Tourist information

Time difference GMT +8 **Currency** Brunei dollar (ringgit) **Language** Malay (official), Chinese (Hokkien), English **Visa requirements** UK: visa not required for visits of up to 30 days. USA: visa not required **Embassy in the UK** 19/20 Belgrave Square, London SW1X 8PG. Tel: (020) 7581 0521; fax: (020) 7235 9717 **British embassy** British High Commission, PO Box 2197, 3rd Floor, Hong Kong Bank Chambers, Jalan Pemancha, Bandar Seri Begawan 2085. Tel: (2) 222 231; fax: (2) 226 002 **Chamber of commerce** Brunei Darussalem International Chamber of Commerce and Industry, POB 2246, Bandar Seri Begawan 1922. Tel: (2) 236 601; fax: (2) 228 389 **Office hours** 0800–1200 and 1300–1700 Mon–Thu; 0900–1200 Sat **Banking hours** 0900–1200 and 1400–1500 Mon–Fri; 0900–110 Sat **Airports** international airports: Bandar Seri Begawan (Brunei International); total passenger km: 2,972 million (1997 est) **Chief tourist attractions** tropical rainforest **Major holidays** 1 January, 23 February, 31 May, 15 July, 25 December; variable: Eid-ul-Adha, end of Ramadan, Good Friday, New Year (Chinese), New Year (Muslim), Prophet's Birthday, first day of Ramadan, Meraj (March/April), Revelation of the Koran (May)

Chronology

15th century An Islamic monarchy was established, ruling Brunei and north Borneo, including the Sabah and Sarawak states of Malaysia. **1841** Control of Sarawak was lost. **1888** Brunei became a British protectorate. **1906** Brunei became a British dependency. **1929** Oil was discovered. **1941–45** Brunei was occupied by Japan. **1959** A written constitution made Britain responsible for defence and external affairs. **1962** The sultan began rule by decree after a plan to join the Federation of Malaysia was opposed by a rebellion organized by the Brunei People's Party (BPP). **1967** Hassanal Bolkiah became sultan. **1971** Brunei was given full internal self-government. **1975** A United Nations (UN) resolution called for independence for Brunei. **1984** Independence from Britain was achieved, with Britain maintaining a small force to protect the oil and gas fields. **1985** The Brunei National Democratic Party (BNDP) was legalized. **1986** The multiethnic Brunei National United Party (BNUP) was formed; nonroyals were given key cabinet posts for the first time. **1988** The BNDP and the BNUP were banned. **1991** Brunei joined the nonaligned movement. **1998** Prince Billah was proclaimed heir to the throne.

Bulgaria Republic of

National name *Republika Bulgaria* **Area** 110,912 sq km/42,823 sq mi **Capital** Sofia **Major towns/cities** Plovdiv, Varna, Ruse, Burgas, Stara Zagora

Government

Head of state Petar Stoyanov from 1997 **Head of government** Ivan Kostov from 1997 **Political system** emergent democracy **Armed forces** 101,500 (1997) **Conscription** compulsory for 12 months **Defence spend** (% GDP) 3.4 (1997) **Education spend** (% GNP) 3.3 (1996) **Health spend** (% GDP) 4.0 (1990–95) **Death penalty** abolished in 1998

Population and society

Population 8,280,000 (1999 est) **Population growth rate** –0.7% (1995–2000) **Ethnic groups** Southern Slavic Bulgarians constitute around 90% of the population; 9% are ethnic Turks, who during the later 1980s were subjected to government pressure to adopt Slavic names and to resettle elsewhere **Religion** Eastern Orthodox Christian, Muslim, Roman Catholic, Protestant **Life expectancy** 68 (men); 75 (women) (1995–2000) **Literacy rate** 99% (men); 98% (women) (1997 est) **Unemployment** 13.7% (1997)

Economy and resources

GDP (US$) 10.1 billion (1998) **GNP** (US$) 10.1 billion (1998) **GNP per capita (PPP)** (US$) 3,920 (1998 est) **Real GDP growth** (% change on previous year) 0.7 (1998) **Consumer price inflation** 32% (1998) **Foreign debt** (US$) 9.85 billion (1997) **Resources** coal, iron ore, manganese, lead, zinc, petroleum **Exports** base metals, chemical and rubber products, processed food, beverages, tobacco, chemicals, textiles, footwear. Principal market: Italy 12.7% (1998) **Imports** mineral products and fuels, chemical and rubber products, textiles, footwear, machinery and transport equipment, medicines. Principal source: Russia 25% (1998)

▪ Tourist information

Time difference GMT +2 **Currency** lev **Language** Bulgarian, Turkish **Visa requirements** UK: visa required. USA: visa not required for tourist visits of up to 30 days **Embassy in the UK** 186–188 Queen's Gate, London SW7 5HL. Tel: (020) 7584 9400; fax: (020) 7584 4948 **British embassy** Boulevard Vassil Levski 65–67, Sofia 1000. Tel: (2) 885 361/2; fax: (2) 656 022 **Chamber of commerce** Bulgarian Chamber of Commerce and Industry, 1040 Sofia, Suborna ST 11A. Tel: (2) 872 631; fax: (2) 873 209 **Office hours** 0800–1800 Mon–Fri **Banking hours** 0800–1130 and 1400–1800 Mon–Fri; 0830–1130 Sat **Airports** international airports: Sofia, Varna, Burgas; seven domestic airports; total passenger km: 1,796 million (1997 est) **Major ports** Black Sea ports Burgas and Varna **Chief tourist attractions** Black Sea coastal resorts; mountain scenery; historic towns; skiing resorts **Major holidays** 1 January, 3 March, 1, 24 May, 24–25 December; variable: Easter Monday

Chronology

***c.* 3500 BC onwards** Semi-nomadic pastoralists from the central Asian steppes settled in the area and formed the Thracian community. **mid-5th century BC** The Thracian state was formed; it was to extend over Bulgaria, northern Greece, and northern Turkey. **4th century BC** Phillip II and Alexander the Great of Macedonia waged largely unsuccessful campaigns against the Thracian Empire. **AD 50** The Thracians were subdued and incorporated within the Roman Empire as the province of Moesia Inferior. **3rd–6th centuries** The Thracian Empire was successively invaded and devastated by the Goths, Huns, Bulgars, and Avars. **681** The Bulgars, an originally Turkic group that had merged with earlier Slav settlers, revolted against the Avars and established, south of the River Danube, the first Bulgarian kingdom, with its capital at Pliska. **864** Orthodox Christianity was adopted by Boris I. **1018** Subjugated by the Byzantines, whose empire had its capital at Constantinople; led to Bulgarian Church breaking with Rome in 1054. **1185** Second independent Bulgarian Kingdom formed. **mid-13th century** Bulgarian state destroyed by Mongol incursions. **1396** Bulgaria became the first European state to be absorbed into the Turkish Ottoman Empire; the imposition of a harsh feudal system and the sacking of the monasteries followed. **1859** The Bulgarian Catholic Church re-established links with Rome. **1876** A Bulgarian nationalist revolt against Ottoman rule was crushed brutally by Ottomans, with 15,000 massacred at Plovdiv ('Bulgarian Atrocities'). **1878** At the Congress of Berlin, concluding a Russo-Turkish war in which Bulgarian volunteers had fought alongside the Russians, the area south of the Balkans, Eastern Rumelia, remained an Ottoman province, but the area to the north became the autonomous Principality of Bulgaria, with a liberal constitution and Alexander Battenberg as prince. **1885** Eastern Rumelia annexed by the Principality; Serbia defeated in war. **1908** Full independence proclaimed from Turkish rule, with Ferdinand I as tsar. **1913** Following defeat in the Second Balkan War, King Ferdinand I abdicated and was replaced by his son Boris III. **1919** Bulgarian Agrarian Union government, led by Alexander Stamboliiski, came to power and redistributed land to poor peasants. **1923** Agrarian government was overthrown in right-wing coup and Stamboliiski murdered. **1934** A semifascist dictatorship was established by King Boris III. **1944** Soviet invasion of German-occupied Bulgaria. **1946** The monarchy was abolished and a communist-dominated people's republic proclaimed following a plebiscite. **1947** Gained South Dobruja in the northeast, along the Black Sea, from Romania; Soviet-style constitution established a one-party state; industries and financial institutions were nationalized and cooperative farming introduced. **1954** Bulgaria became a loyal and cautious satellite of the USSR. **1968** Bulgaria participated in the Soviet-led invasion of Czechoslovakia. **1971** A new constitution was introduced. **1985–89** Haphazard administrative and economic reforms, known as *preustroistvo* ('restructuring'), were introduced under the stimulus of the reformist Soviet leader Mikhail Gorbachev. **1989** A programme of enforced 'Bulgarianization' resulted in a mass exodus of ethnic Turks to Turkey. Opposition parties were tolerated. **1991** A new liberal-democratic constitution was adopted. The first noncommunist government was formed. **1993** A voucher-based 'mass privatization' programme was launched. **1996** Radical economic and industrial reforms were imposed. There was mounting inflation and public protest at the state of the economy. **1997** There was a general strike. The UDF leader Ivan Kostov became prime minister. The Bulgarian currency was pegged to the Deutschmark in return for support from the International Monetary Fund. A new political group, the Real Reform Movement (DESIR), was formed. **1999** Bulgaria joined the Central European Free Trade Agreement (CEFTA).

Burkina Faso The People's Democratic Republic of (formerly Upper Volta)

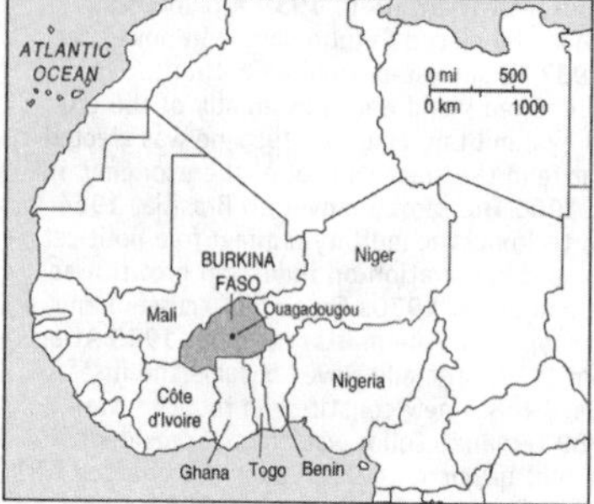

National name *République Démocratique Populaire de Burkina Faso* **Area** 274,122 sq km/105,838 sq mi **Capital** Ouagadougou **Major towns/cities** Bobo-Dioulasso, Koudougou

Government

Head of state Blaise Compaoré from 1987 **Head of government** Kadre Desire Ouedraogo from 1996 **Political system** emergent democracy **Armed forces** 5,800 (1997); includes gendarmerie of 4,200 **Conscription** military service is voluntary **Defence spend** (% GDP) 2.4 (1996) **Education spend** (% GNP) 1.5 (1996) **Health spend** (% GDP) 2.3 (1990–95) **Death penalty** retained and used for ordinary crimes

Population and society

Population 11,616,000 (1999 est) **Population growth rate** 2.7% (1995–2000) **Ethnic groups** over 50 ethnic groups, including the nomadic Mossi (48%), Fulani (10%), and Gourma (5%). Settled tribes include: in the north the Lobi-Dagari (7%) and the Mande (7%); in the SE the Bobo (7%); and in the SW the Senoufu (6%) and Gourounsi (5%) **Religion** animist 53%, Sunni Muslim 36%, Roman Catholic 11% **Life expectancy** 44 (men); 45 (women) (1995–2000) **Literacy rate** 30% (men); 11% (women) (1997 est) **Unemployment** 8.1% (1994 est)

Economy and resources

GDP (US$) 2.58 billion (1998) **GNP** (US$) 2.6 billion (1998) **GNP per capita (PPP)** (US$) 1,020 (1998 est) **Real GDP growth** (% change on previous year) 4.5 (1998) **Consumer price inflation** 3.0% (1998) **Foreign debt** (US$) 1.29 billion (1997) **Resources** manganese, zinc, limestone, phosphates, diamonds, gold, antimony, marble, silver, lead **Exports** cotton, gold, livestock and livestock products. Principal market: Côte d'Ivoire 12.7% (1997) **Imports** machinery and transport equipment, miscellaneous manufactured articles, food products (notably cereals), refined petroleum products, chemicals. Principal source: France 33% (1997)

▪ Tourist information

Time difference GMT+/− 0 **Currency** franc CFA **Language** French (official); about 50 Sudanic languages spoken by 90% of population **Visa requirements** UK: visa required. USA: visa required **Embassy in the UK** Honorary Consulate, 5 Cinnamon Row, Plantation Wharf, London SW11 3TW. Tel: (020) 7738 1800; fax: (020) 7738 2820 **British embassy** British Consulate, BP 1918 Ouagadougou. (All staff based in Abidjan, Côte d'Ivoire.) Tel: (226) 336 363 **Chamber of commerce** Chambre de Commerce, d'Industrie et d'Artisanat du Burkina, ave Nelson Mandela, 01 BP 502, Ouagadougou 01. Tel: (226) 306 114; fax: (226) 306 116 **Office hours** 0700–1230 and 1500–1730 Mon–Fri **Banking hours** 0730–1130 and 1500–1600 Mon–Thu; 0730–1130 and 1530–1700 Fri **Airports** international airports: Ouagadougou, Bobo-Dioulasso; total passenger km: 256 million (1995) **Chief tourist attractions** big-game hunting in east and southwest, and along banks of Mouhoun (Black Volta) River; wide variety of wildlife; biennial Ouagadougou film festival **Major holidays** 1, 3 January, 1 May, 4, 15 August, 1 November, 25 December; variable: Ascension Thursday, Eid-ul-Adha, Easter Monday, end of Ramadan, Prophet's Birthday, Whit Monday

Chronology

13th–14th centuries Formerly settled by Bobo, Lobi, and Gurunsi peoples, east and centre were conquered by Mossi and Gurma peoples, who established powerful warrior kingdoms, some of which survived until late

19th century. **1895–1903** France secured protectorates over the Mossi kingdom of Yatenga and the Gurma region, and annexed the Bobo and Lobi lands, meeting armed resistance. **1904** The French-controlled region, known as Upper Volta, was attached administratively to French Sudan; tribal chiefs were maintained in their traditional seats and the region was to serve as a labour reservoir for more developed colonies to the south. **1919** Made a separate French colony. **1932** Partitioned between French Sudan, the Côte d'Ivoire, and Niger. **1947** Became a French overseas territory. **1960** Independence was achieved, with Maurice Yaméogo as the first president. **1966** A military coup was led by Lt-Col Sangoulé Lamizana, and a supreme council of the armed forces established. **1977** The ban on political activities was removed. A referendum approved a new constitution based on civilian rule. **1978–80** Lamizana was elected president. In 1980 he was overthrown in a bloodless coup led by Col Saye Zerbo, as the economy deteriorated. **1982–83** Maj Jean-Baptiste Ouedraogo became president and Capt Thomas Sankara prime minister. In 1983 Sankara seized complete power. **1984** Upper Volta was renamed Burkina Faso ('land of upright men') to signify a break with the colonial past; literacy and afforestation campaigns were instigated by Sankara, who established links with Libya, Benin, and Ghana. **1987** Capt Blaise Compaoré became president. **1991** A new constitution was approved. **1992** Multiparty elections were won by the pro-Compaoré Popular Front (FP). **1996** Kadre Desire Ouedraogo was appointed prime minister. **1997** The CDP won assembly elections. Ouedraogo was reappointed prime minister. **1998** President Blaise Compaoré was re-elected with an overwhelming majority.

Burma *see* Myanmar

Burundi Republic of

National name *Republika y'Uburundi* **Area** 27,834 sq km/ 10,746 sq mi **Capital** Bujumbura **Major towns/cities** Kitega, Bururi, Ngozi, Muhinga, Muramuya

Government

Head of state Pierre Buyoya from 1996 **Head of government** Pascal-Firmin Ndimira from 1996 **Political system** military **Armed forces** 18,500 (1997); plus paramilitary forces of 3,500 **Conscription** military service is voluntary **Defence spend** (% GDP) 5.7 (1997) **Education spend** (% GNP) 3.2 (1996) **Health spend** (% GDP) 0.9 (1990–95) **Death penalty** retained and used for ordinary crimes

Population and society

Population 6,565,000 (1999 est) **Population growth rate** 1.7% (1995–2000) **Ethnic groups** two main groups: the agriculturalist Hutu, comprising about 85% of the population, and the predominantly pastoralist Tutsi, about 14%. There is a Pygmy minority, comprising about 1% of the population, and a few Europeans and Asians **Religion** Roman Catholic 62%, Pentecostalist 5%, Anglican 1%, Muslim 1%, animist **Life expectancy** 41 (men); 44 (women) (1995–2000) **Literacy rate** 54% (men); 36% (women) (1997 est) **Unemployment** 7.3% (1992)

Economy and resources

GDP (US$) 949 million (1998) **GNP** (US$) 922 million (1998) **GNP per capita (PPP)** (US$) 620 (1998 est) **Real GDP growth** (% change on previous year) 3 (1998) **Consumer price inflation** 10% (1998) **Foreign debt** (US$) 1.06 billion (1997) **Resources** nickel, gold, tungsten, phosphates, vanadium, uranium, peat, petroleum deposits have been detected **Exports** coffee, tea, glass products, hides and skins. Principal market: UK 29.1% (1997) **Imports** machinery and transport equipment, petroleum and petroleum products, cement, malt (and malt flour). Principal source: Belgium – Luxembourg 18.2% (1997)

▪ Tourist information

Time difference GMT +2 **Currency** Burundi franc **Language** Kirundi (a Bantu language) and French (both official), Kiswahili **Visa requirements** UK: visa required. USA: visa required **Embassy for the UK** Square Marie Louise 46, 1040 Brussels, Belgium. Tel: (2) 230 4535; fax: (2) 230 7883 **British embassy** British Consulate, 43 Avenue Bubanza, BP 1344, Bujumbura. (All staff based in Kampala, Uganda.) Tel: (2) 23711 **Chamber of commerce** Chambre de Commerce et de l'Industrie du Burundi, BP 313, Bujumbura. Tel: (2) 22280 **Office hours** 0730–1200 and 1400–1730 Mon–Fri **Banking hours** 0800–1130 Mon–Fri **Airports** international airports: Bujumbura; total passenger km: 2 million (1995) **Chief tourist attractions** tourism is relatively undeveloped **Major holidays** 1 January, 1 May, 1 July, 15 August, 18 September, 1 November, 25 December; variable: Ascension Thursday

Chronology

10th century Originally inhabited by the hunter-gatherer Twa Pygmies. Hutu peoples settled in the region and became peasant farmers. **13th century** Taken over by Banu Hutus. **15th–17th centuries** The majority Hutu community came under the dominance of the cattle-owning Tutsi peoples, immigrants from the east, who became a semi-aristocracy; the minority Tutsis developed a feudalistic political system, organized around a nominal king, with royal princes in control of local areas. **1890** Known as Urundi, the Tutsi kingdom, along with neighbouring Rwanda, came under nominal German control as Ruanda-Urundi. **1916** Occupied by Belgium during World War I. **1923** Belgium was granted a League of Nations mandate to administer Ruanda-Urundi; it was to rule 'indirectly' through the Tutsi chiefs. **1962** Burundi was separated from Ruanda-Urundi, and given independence as a monarchy under Tutsi King Mwambutsa IV. **1965** The king refused to appoint a Hutu prime minister after an election in which Hutu candidates were victorious; an attempted coup by Hutus was brutally suppressed. **1966** The king was deposed by his teenage son Charles, who became Ntare V; he was in turn was deposed by his Tutsi prime minister Col Michel Micombero, who declared Burundi a republic; the Tutsi-dominated Union for National Progress (UPRONA) was declared the only legal political party. **1972** Ntare V was killed, allegedly by Hutus, provoking a massacre of 150,000 Hutus by Tutsi soldiers; 100,000 Hutus fled to Tanzania. **1976** An army coup deposed Micombero and appointed the Tutsi Col Jean-Baptiste Bagaza as president. He launched a drive against corruption and a programme of land reforms and economic development. **1987** Bagaza was deposed in a coup by the Tutsi Maj Pierre Buyoya. **1988** About 24,000 Hutus were killed by Tutsis and 60,000 fled to Rwanda. **1992** A new multiparty constitution was adopted following a referendum. **1993** Melchior Ndadaye, a Hutu, was elected president in the first-ever democratic contest, but was killed in a coup by the Tutsi-dominated army; 100,000 people died in the massacres that followed. **1994** Cyprien Ntaryamira, a Hutu, became president but was later killed in an air crash along with the Rwandan president Juvenal Habyarimana. There was an eruption of ethnic violence; 750,000 Hutus fled to Rwanda. Hutu Sylvestre Ntibantunganya became head of state, serving with a Tutsi prime minister, as part of a four-year power-sharing agreement. **1995** Renewed ethnic violence erupted in the capital, Bujumbura, following a massacre of Hutu refugees. **1996** The former Tutsi president Pierre Buyoya seized power amid renewed ethnic violence; the coup provoked economic sanctions by other African countries. A 'government of national unity' was appointed, with Pascal-Firmin Ndimira as premier. Bujumbura was shelled by Hutu rebels. **1998** There was renewed fighting between Tutsi-led army and Hutu rebels. A ceasefire was agreed between the warring political factions.

Cambodia State of (formerly Khmer Republic, Democratic Kampuchea, People's Republic of Kampuchea)

National name *Roat Kampuchea* **Area** 181,035 sq km/69,897 sq mi **Capital** Phnom Penh **Major towns/cities** Battambang, Kompong Cham

Government

Head of state King Norodom Sihanouk from 1991 **Head of government** Hun Sen from 1998 **Political system** emergent democracy **Armed forces** 140,500 (1997) **Conscription** military service is compulsory for five years between ages 18 and 35 **Defence spend** (% GDP) 7.3 (1997) **Education spend** (% GNP) 2.9 (1996) **Health spend** (% GDP) 0.7 (1990–95) **Death penalty** abolished in 1989

Population and society

Population 10,946,000 (1999 est) **Population growth rate** 2.2% (1995–2000) **Ethnic groups** 91% Khmer, 4% Vietnamese, 3% Chinese **Religion** Theravāda Buddhist 95%, Muslim, Roman Catholic

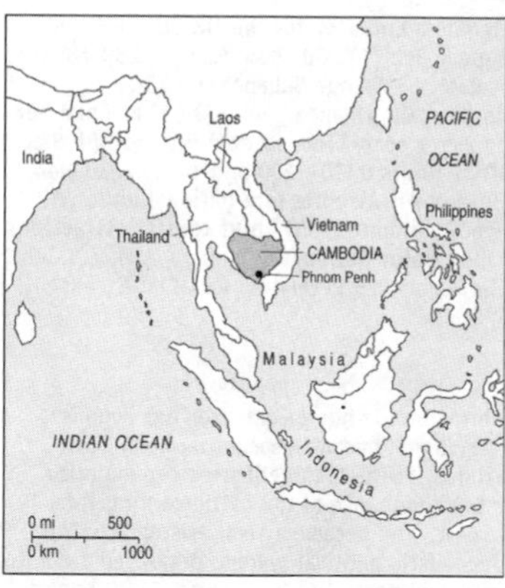

Life expectancy 52 (men); 55 (women) (1995–2000) **Literacy rate** 48% (men); 65% (women) (1995 est)

Economy and resources

GDP (US$) 3.09 billion (1998) **GNP** (US$) 3 billion (1998) **GNP per capita (PPP)** (US$) 1,240 (1998) **Real GDP growth** (% change on previous year) 2 (1998) **Consumer price inflation** 15% (1998) **Foreign debt** (US$) 2.13 billion (1997) **Resources** phosphates, iron ore, gemstones, bauxite, silicon, manganese **Exports** timber, rubber, fishery products, garments. Principal market: Vietnam 18% (1997) **Imports** cigarettes, construction materials, petroleum products, motor vehicles, alcoholic beverages, consumer electronics. Principal source: Thailand 15.9% (1997)

▪ Tourist information

Time difference GMT +7 **Currency** Cambodian riel **Language** Khmer (official), French **Visa requirements** UK: visa required. USA: visa required **Embassy in the UK** no diplomatic representation in the UK **British embassy** 29 Street 75, Phnom Penh. Tel: (855) 232 7124 **Chamber of commerce** Council for the Development of Cambodia, Government Palace, quai Sisowath, Wat Phnom, Phnom Penh. Tel: (23) 50428; fax: (23) 61616 **Office hours** 0700–1130 and 1400–1730 Mon–Fri **Banking hours** 0800–1500 Mon–Fri **Airports** international airports: Phnom Penh (Pochentong); five domestic airports **Major ports** Kompong Cham **Chief tourist attractions** ancient Khmer ruins and monuments, including great temples of Angkor Thom and Prasat Lingpoun; tropical vegetation and mangrove forests **Major holidays** 9 January, 17 April, 1, 20 May, 22 September; variable: New Year (April)

Chronology

1st century AD Part of the kingdom of Hindu-Buddhist Funan (Fou Nan), centred on Mekong delta region. **6th century** Conquered by the Chenla kingdom. **9th century** Establishment by Jayavarman II of extensive and sophisticated Khmer Empire, supported by an advanced irrigation system and architectural achievements. **14th century** Theravāda Buddhism replaced Hinduism. **15th century** Came under the control of Siam (Thailand), which made Phnom Penh the capital and, later, Champa (Vietnam). **1863** Became a French protectorate. **1887** Became part of French Indo-China Union, which included Laos and Vietnam. **1941** Prince Norodom Sihanouk was elected king. **1941–45** Occupied by Japan during World War II. **1946** Recaptured by France; parliamentary constitution adopted. **1949** Guerrilla war for independence secured semi-autonomy within the French Union. **1953** Independence was achieved from France as the Kingdom of Cambodia. **1955** Norodom Sihanouk abdicated as king and became prime minister, representing the Popular Socialist Community mass movement. His father, Norodom Suramarit, became king. **1960** On the death of his father, Norodom Sihanouk became head of state. **later 1960s** There was mounting guerrilla insurgency, led by the communist Khmer Rouge, and civil war in neighbouring Vietnam. **1970** Sihanouk was overthrown by US-backed Lt-Gen Lon Nol in a right-wing coup; the new name of Khmer Republic was adopted; Sihanouk, exiled in China, formed his own guerrilla movement. **1975** Lon Nol was overthrown by the Khmer Rouge, which was backed by North Vietnam and China; Sihanouk became head of state. **1976** The Khmer Republic was renamed Democratic Kampuchea. **1976–78** The Khmer Rouge, led by Pol Pot, introduced an extreme Maoist communist programme, forcing urban groups into rural areas and resulting in over 2.5 million deaths from famine, disease, and maltreatment; Sihanouk was removed from power. **1978–79** Vietnam invaded and installed a government headed by Heng Samrin, an anti-Pol Pot communist. **1979** Democratic Kampuchea was renamed the People's Republic of Kampuchea. **1980–82** Faced by guerrilla resistance from Pol Pot's Chinese-backed Khmer Rouge and Sihanouk's ASEAN and US-backed nationalists, more than 300,000 Cambodians fled to refugee camps in Thailand and thousands of soldiers were killed. **1985** The reformist Hun Sen was appointed prime minister and more moderate economic and cultural policies were pursued. **1987–89** Vietnamese troops were withdrawn. **1989** The People's Republic of Kampuchea was renamed the State of Cambodia and Buddhism was re-established as the state religion. **1991** There was a ceasefire, and a United Nations Transitional Authority in Cambodia (UNTAC) agreed to administer the country in conjunction with an all-party Supreme National Council; communism was abandoned. Sihanouk returned as head of state. **1992** Political prisoners were released, refugees resettled, and freedom of speech restored. However, the Khmer Rouge refused to disarm. **1993** FUNCINPEC won general elections (boycotted by the Khmer Rouge, who continued fighting); a new constitution was adopted. Sihanouk was reinstated as constitutional monarch; his son Prince Norodom Ranariddh, FUNCINPEC leader, was appointed prime minister, with CPP leader Hun Sen as deputy premier. **1994** An antigovernment coup was foiled. Seven thousand Khmer Rouge guerrillas surrendered in response to an amnesty. **1995** Prince Norodom Sirivudh, FUNCINPEC leader and half-brother of King Sihanouk, was exiled for allegedly plotting to assassinate Hun Sen and topple the government. **1996** There were heightened tensions between Hun Sen's CPP and the royalist FUNCINPEC. **1997** Pol Pot was sentenced to life imprisonment. FUNCINPEC troops were routed by the CPP, led by Hun Sen. Prime Minister Prince Norodom Ranariddh was deposed and replaced by Ung Huot. There was fighting between supporters of Hun Sen and Ranariddh. **1998** Ranariddh was found guilty of arms smuggling and colluding with the Khmer Rouge, but was pardoned by the king. Pol Pot died and thousands of Khmer Rouge guerrillas defected. The CPP won elections, and political unrest followed. A new CPP–FUNCINPEC coalition was formed, with Hun Sen as prime minister and Prince Norodom Ranariddh as president. Cambodia re-occupied its UN seat.

Cameroon Republic of

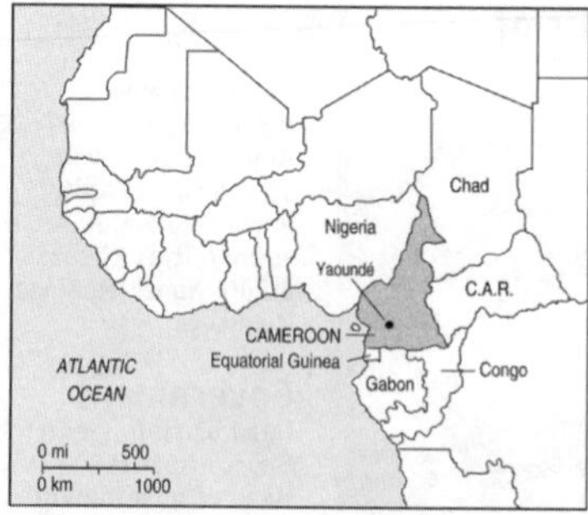

National name *République du Cameroun* **Area** 475,440 sq km/183,567 sq mi **Capital** Yaoundé **Major towns/cities** Garoua, Douala, Nkongsamba, Maroua, Bamenda, Bafoussam

Government

Head of state Paul Biya from 1982 **Head of government** Simon Achidi Achu from 1992 **Political system** emergent democracy **Armed forces** 13,100 (1997); plus 9,000 paramilitary forces **Conscription** military service is voluntary; paramilitary compulsory training programme in force **Defence spend** (% GDP) 2.9 (1997) **Education spend** (% GNP) 2.9 (1996) **Health spend** (% GDP) 1 (1990–95) **Death penalty** retained and used for ordinary crimes

Population and society

Population 14,710,000 (1999 est) **Population growth rate** 2.7% (1995–2000) **Ethnic groups** main groups include the Cameroon Highlanders (31%), Equatorial Bantu (19%), Kirdi (11%), Fulani (10%), Northwestern Bantu (8%), and Eastern Nigritic (7%) **Religion** Roman Catholic 35%, animist 25%, Muslim 22%, Protestant 18% **Life expectancy** 53 (men); 56 (women) (1995–2000) **Literacy rate** 79% (men); 65% (women) (1997 est) **Unemployment** N/A

Economy and resources

GDP (US$) 8.7 billion (1998) **GNP** (US$) 8.7 billion (1998) **GNP per capita (PPP)** (US$) 1,810 (1998) **Real GDP growth** (% change on previous year) 4.9 (1998) **Consumer price inflation** 3% (1998) **Foreign debt** (US$) 9.3 billion (1997) **Resources** petroleum, natural gas, tin ore, limestone, bauxite, iron ore, uranium, gold **Exports** crude petroleum and petroleum products, timber and timber products, coffee, aluminium, cotton, bananas. Principal market: Italy 25.4% (1997) **Imports** machinery and transport equipment, basic manufactures, chemicals, fuel. Principal source: France 25% (1997)

▪ Tourist information

Time difference GMT +1 **Currency** franc CFA **Language** French and English in pidgin variations (official); there has been some discontent with the emphasis on French – there are 163 indigenous peoples with their own

African languages (Sudanic languages in north, Bantu languages elsewhere) **Visa requirements** UK: visa not required. USA: visa not required **Embassy in the UK** 84 Holland Park, London W11 3SB. Tel: (020) 7727 0771/3; fax: (020) 7792 9353 **British embassy** BP 547, Avenue Winston Churchill, Yaoundé. Tel: (237) 220 545/796; fax: (237) 220 148 **Chamber of commerce** Chambre de Commerce, d'Industrie et des Mines du Cameroun, BP 4011, Place de Gouvernement, Douala. Tel: (237) 423 690; fax: (237) 425 596 **Banking hours** 1730–1130 and 1430–1630 Mon–Fri **Airports** international airports: Douala, Garoua, Yaoundé; eight domestic airports; total passenger km: 681 million (1997 est) **Major ports** Douala **Chief tourist attractions** national parks; game reserves; sandy beaches **Major holidays** 1 January, 11 February, 1, 20 May, 15 August, 25 December; variable: Ascension Thursday, Eid-ul-Adha, end of Ramadan, Good Friday

Chronology

1472 First visited by the Portuguese, who named it the Rio dos Camaroes ('River of Prawns') after the giant shrimps they found in the Wouri River estuary, and later introduced slave trading. **early 17th century** The Douala people migrated to the coastal region from the east and came to serve as intermediaries between Portuguese, Dutch, and English traders and interior tribes. **1809–48** The northern savannas were conquered by the Fulani, Muslim pastoral nomads from the southern Sahara. **1856** Douala chiefs signed a commercial treaty with Britain and invited British protection. **1884** A treaty was signed establishing German rule as the protectorate of Kamerun; cocoa, coffee, and banana plantations were developed. **1916** Captured by Allied forces in World War I. **1919** Divided under League of Nations' mandates between Britain, which administered the southwest and north (adjoining Nigeria), and France, which administered the east and south. **1946** The French Cameroon and British Cameroons were made UN trust territories. **1955** The French crushed a revolt by the Union of the Cameroon Peoples (UPC), southern-based radical nationalists. **1960** French Cameroon became the independent Republic of Cameroon, with the Muslim Ahmadou Ahidjo as president; a UPC rebellion in the southwest was crushed, and a state of emergency declared. **1961** Following a UN plebiscite, the northern part of the British Cameroons merged with Nigeria, and the southern part joined the Republic of Cameroon to become the Federal Republic of Cameroon. **1966** An autocratic one-party regime was introduced; government and opposition parties merged to form the Cameroon National Union (UNC). **1970s** Petroleum exports made successful investment in education and agriculture possible. **1972** A new constitution made Cameroon a unitary state. **1982** President Ahidjo resigned; he was succeeded by his prime minister Paul Biya, a Christian. **1983–84** Biya began to remove the northern Muslim political 'barons' close to Ahidjo, who went into exile in France. Biya defeated a plot by Muslim officers from the north to overthrow him. **1985** The UNC adopted the name RDPC. **1990** There was widespread public disorder as living standards declined; Biya granted an amnesty to political prisoners. **1992** The ruling RDPC won the first multiparty elections in 28 years, with Biya as president. **1995** Cameroon was admitted to the Commonwealth. **1997** RDPC won assembly elections; Biya was re-elected.

Canada

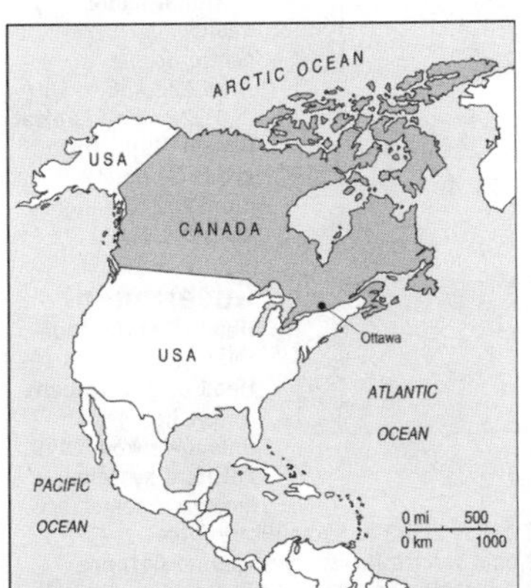

Area 9,970,610 sq km/ 3,849,652 sq mi **Capital** Ottawa **Major towns/cities** Toronto, Montréal, Vancouver, Edmonton, Calgary, Winnipeg, Québec, Hamilton, Saskatoon, Halifax, Regina, Windsor, Oshawa, London, Kitchener

Government

Head of state Elizabeth II from 1952, represented by governor general Roméo A LeBlanc from 1995 **Head of government** Jean Chrétien from 1993 **Political system** liberal democracy **Armed forces** 61,600 (1997) **Conscription** military service is voluntary **Defence spend** (% GDP) 1.3 (1997) **Education spend** (% GNP) 7 (1996) **Health spend** (% GDP) 6.4 (1996) **Death penalty** abolished 1998

Population and society

Population 30,857,000 (1999 est) **Population growth rate** 1% (1995–2000) **Ethnic groups** about 45% of British origin, 29% French, 23% of other European descent, and about 3% American Indians and Inuit **Religion** Roman Catholic, various Protestant denominations **Life expectancy** 76 (men); 82 (women) (1995–2000) **Literacy rate** 99% (men); 99% (women) (1997 est) **Unemployment** 8.3% (1998)

Economy and resources

GDP (US$) 598.8 billion (1998) **GNP** (US$) 612.2 billion (1998) **GNP per capita (PPP)** (US$) 24,050 (1998) **Real GDP growth** (% change on previous year) 2.8 (1998) **Consumer price inflation** 2.5% (1998) **Resources** petroleum, natural gas, coal, copper (world's third-largest producer), nickel (world's second-largest producer), lead (world's fifth-largest producer), zinc (world's largest producer), iron, gold, uranium, timber **Exports** motor vehicles and parts, lumber, wood pulp, paper and newsprint, crude petroleum, natural gas, aluminium and alloys, petroleum and coal products. Principal market: USA 83.7% (1998) **Imports** motor vehicle parts, passenger vehicles, computers, foodstuffs, telecommunications equipment. Principal source: USA 77% (1998)

■ Tourist information

Time difference GMT −3.5/9 **Currency** Canadian dollar **Language** English, French (both official; 60% English mother tongue, 24% French mother tongue); there are also American Indian languages and the Inuit Inuktitut **Visa requirements** UK: visa not required. USA: visa not required **Embassy in the UK** Macdonald House, 1 Grosvenor Square, London W1X 0AB. Tel: (020) 7258 6600; fax: (020) 7258 6333 **British embassy** British High Commission, 80 Elgin Street, Ottawa KIP 5K7. Tel: (613) 237 1530; fax: (613) 237 7980 **Chamber of commerce** Canadian Chamber of Commerce, 55 Metcalfe Street, Suite 1160, Ottawa ON KIP 6N4. Tel: (613) 238 400; fax: (613) 238 7643 **Office hours** 0900–1700 Mon–Fri **Banking hours** 1000–1500 Mon–Fri **Airports** international airports: Calgary, Edmonton, Gander, Halifax, Hamilton, Montréal (Dorval, Mirabel), Ottawa (Uplands), St John's, Saskatoon, Toronto (Lester B Pearson), Vancouver, Winnipeg; domestic services to all major cities/towns; total passenger km: 61,862 million (1997 est) **Chief tourist attractions** forests; lakes; rivers; Rockies of British Columbia; St Lawrence Seaway; Niagara Falls; fjords of Newfoundland and Labrador; historic cities of Montréal and Québec; museums and art galleries of Toronto, Vancouver, and Ottawa **Major holidays** 1 January, 1 July (except Newfoundland), 11 November, 25–26 December; variable: Good Friday, Easter Monday, Labour Day (September), Thanksgiving (October), Victoria (May), additional days vary between states

Canada: Provinces and Territories

Province	Capital	Area sq km	Area sq mi	Population (1996)
Alberta	Edmonton	661,190	255,285	2,696,800
British Columbia	Victoria	947,800	365,946	3,724,500
Manitoba	Winnipeg	649,950	250,946	1,113,900
New Brunswick	Fredericton	73,440	28,355	738,100
Newfoundland	St John's	405,720	156,648	551,800
Nova Scotia	Halifax	55,490	21,425	909,300
Ontario	Toronto	1,068,580	412,579	10,753,600
Prince Edward Island	Charlottetown	5,660	2,185	134,600
Québec	Québec	1,540,680	594,857	7,138,800
Saskatchewan	Regina	652,330	251,865	990,200
Territory				
Northwest Territories	Yellowknife	1,224,800	472,894	40,400
Yukon Territory	Whitehorse	483,450	186,660	30,800
Nunavut (Semi-autonomous region)		2,201,500	850,000	24,000[1]

[1] 1999

Chronology

35,000 BC First evidence of people reaching North America from Asia by way of Beringia. ***c.* 2000 BC** Inuit (Eskimos) began settling the Arctic coast from Siberia eastwards to Greenland. ***c.* 1000 AD** Vikings, including Leif Ericsson, established Vinland, a settlement in northeast America that did not survive. **1497** John Cabot, an Italian navigator in the service of English king Henry VII, landed on Cape Breton Island and claimed the area for England. **1534** French navigator Jacques Cartier reached the

Gulf of St Lawrence and claimed the region for France. **1608** Samuel de Champlain, a French explorer, founded Québec; French settlers developed fur trade and fisheries. **1663** French settlements in Canada formed the colony of New France, which expanded southwards. **1670** Hudson's Bay Company established trading posts north of New France, leading to Anglo-French rivalry. **1689–97** King William's War: Anglo-French conflict in North America arising from the 'Glorious Revolution' in Europe. **1702–13** Queen Anne's War: Anglo-French conflict in North America arising from the War of the Spanish Succession in Europe; Britain gained Newfoundland. **1744–48** King George's War: Anglo-French conflict in North America arising from the War of Austrian Succession in Europe. **1756–63** Seven Years' War: James Wolfe captured Québec in 1759; France ceded Canada to Britain by the Treaty of Paris. **1775–83** American Revolution caused an influx of 40,000 United Empire Loyalists, who formed New Brunswick in 1784. **1791** Canada was divided into Upper Canada (much of modern Ontario) and Lower Canada (much of modern Québec). **1793** British explorer Alexander Mackenzie crossed the Rocky Mountains to reach the Pacific coast. **1812–14** War of 1812 between Britain and USA; US invasions repelled by both provinces. **1820s** Start of large-scale immigration from British Isles caused resentment among French Canadians. **1837** Rebellions were led by Louis Joseph Papineau in Lower Canada and William Lyon Mackenzie in Upper Canada. **1841** Upper and Lower Canada united as Province of Canada; achieved internal self-government in 1848. **1867** British North America Act united Ontario, Québec, Nova Scotia, and New Brunswick in Dominion of Canada. **1869** Red River Rebellion of Métis (people of mixed French and American Indian descent), led by Louis Riel, against British settlers in Rupert's Land. **1870** Manitoba (part of Rupert's Land) formed the fifth province of Canada; British Columbia became the sixth in 1871, and Prince Edward Island became the seventh in 1873. **1885** The Northwest Rebellion was crushed and Riel hanged. The Canadian Pacific Railway was completed. **1905** Alberta and Saskatchewan were formed from the Northwest Territories and became provinces of Canada. **1914–18** Half a million Canadian troops fought for the British Empire on the western front in World War I. **1931** The Statute of Westminster affirmed equality of status between Britain and the Dominions. **1939–45** World War II: Canadian participation in all theatres. **1949** Newfoundland became the tenth province of Canada; Canada was a founding member of the North Atlantic Treaty Organization (NATO). **1960** The Québec Liberal Party of Jean Lesage launched a 'Quiet Revolution' to re-assert French-Canadian identity. **1970** Pierre Trudeau invoked the War Measures Act to suppress separatist terrorists of the Front de Libération du Québec. **1976** The Parti Québécois won control of the Québec provincial government; a referendum rejected independence in 1980. **1982** 'Patriation' of the constitution removed Britain's last legal control over Canada. **1987** Meech Lake Accord: a constitutional amendment was proposed to increase provincial powers (to satisfy Québec); failed to be ratified in 1990. **1992** A self-governing homeland for the Inuit was approved. **1994** Canada formed the North American Free Trade Area with USA and Mexico. **1995** A Québec referendum narrowly rejected a sovereignty proposal. **1997** The Liberals were re-elected by a narrow margin. **1999** Nunavut, the semi-autonomous Inuit bareland in Northern Territories was created after representatives of the Inuit population had negotiated hunting and fishing rights in the area.

Cape Verde Republic of

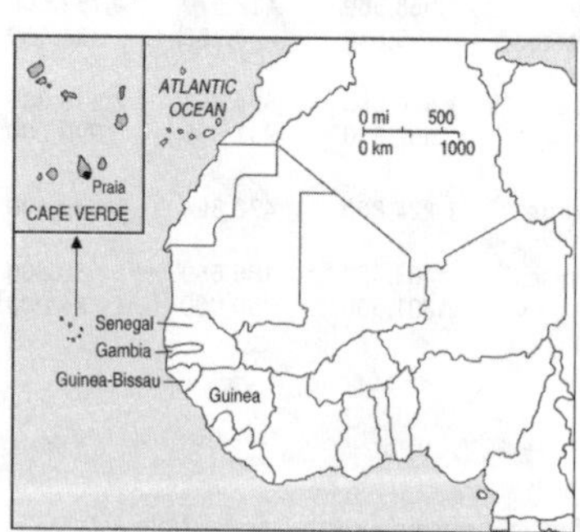

National name *República de Cabo Verde* **Area** 4,033 sq km/ 1,557 sq mi **Capital** Praia **Major towns/ cities** Mindelo

Government

Head of state Mascarenhas Monteiro from 1991 **Head of government** Carlos Viega from 1991 **Political system** emergent democracy **Armed forces** 1,100 (1997) **Conscription** selective conscription **Defence spend** (% GDP) 1.7 (1997) **Education spend** (% GNP) 4.4 (1993–94) **Health spend** (% GDP) 3.3 (1995) **Death penalty** abolished in 1981

Population and society

Population 418,000 (1999 est) **Population growth rate** 2.3% (1995–2000) **Ethnic groups** about 60% of mixed descent (Portuguese and African), known as *mestiços* or creoles; the remainder is mainly African. The European population is very small **Religion** Roman Catholic 93%, Protestant (Nazarene Church) **Life expectancy** 66 (men); 71 (women) (1995–2000) **Literacy rate** 82% (men); 63% (women) (1997 est) **Unemployment** N/A

Economy and resources

GDP (US$) 453 million (1998) **GNP** (US$) 437 million (1998) **GNP per capita (PPP)** (US$) 2,950 (1998) **Real GDP growth** (% change on previous year) 4.1 (1998) **Consumer price inflation** 4.3% (1998) **Foreign debt** (US$) 220 million (1997) **Resources** salt, pozzolana (volcanic rock), limestone, basalt, kaolin **Exports** fish, shellfish and fish products, salt, bananas. Principal market: Portugal 45% (1997) **Imports** food and live animals, machinery and electrical equipment, transport equipment, mineral products, metals. Principal source: Portugal 49.8% (1997)

▪ Tourist information

Time difference GMT –1 **Currency** Cape Verde escudo **Language** Portuguese (official), Creole **Visa requirements** UK: visa required. USA: visa required **Embassy for the UK** 44 Konninginnegracht, 2514 AD, The Hague, the Netherlands. Tel: (70) 346 9623; fax: (70) 346 7702 **British embassy** British Consulate, c/o Shell Cabo Verde, Sarl Ave, Amílcar Cabral CP4, Sarl Vincente. (All staff based in Dakar, Senegal.) Tel: (238) 314 470; fax: (238) 314 755 **Chamber of commerce** Associaçao Comercial, Industrial e Agricola de Barlavento, CP 62 Mindelo, São Vicente. Tel: (238) 313 281; fax: (238) 317 110 **Office hours** 0830–1230 and 1430–1800 Mon–Fri **Banking hours** 0800–1400 Mon–Fri **Airports** international airports: Sal Island (Amílcar Cabral), São Tiago; eight domestic airports; total passenger km: 181 million (1995) **Major ports** Mindelo **Chief tourist attractions** mountain scenery; extensive white sandy beaches on islands of São Tiago, Sal, Boa Vista, Maio **Major holidays** 1, 20 January, 8 March, 1 May, 1 June, 12 September, 24–25 December; variable: Good Friday

Chronology

1462 Originally uninhabited; settled by Portuguese, who brought in slave labour from West Africa. **later 19th century** There was a decline in prosperity as slave trade ended. **1950s** A liberation movement developed on the islands and the Portuguese African mainland colony of Guinea-Bissau. **1951** Cape Verde became an overseas territory of Portugal. **1975** Independence was achieved and a national people's assembly elected, with Aristides of the PAICV as the first executive president; a policy of nonalignment followed. **1981** The goal of union with Guinea-Bissau was abandoned; Cape Verde became a one-party state. **1988** There was rising unrest and demand for political reforms. **1991** In the first multiparty elections, the new MPD won a majority and Mascarenhas Monteiro became president; market-centred economic reforms were introduced.

Central African Republic

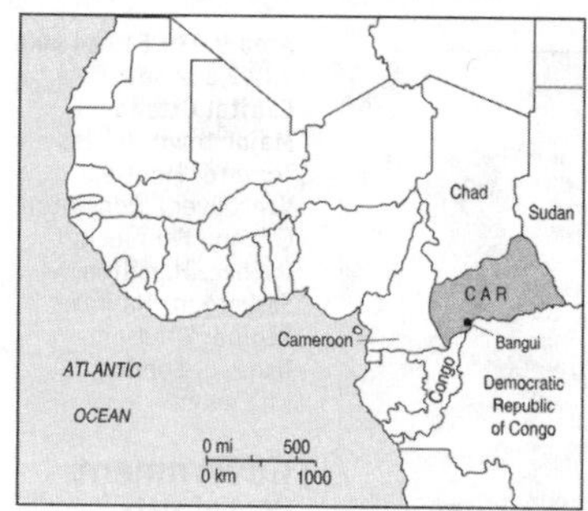

National name *République Centrafricaine* **Area** 622,436 sq km/ 240,322 sq mi **Capital** Bangui **Major towns/ cities** Berbérati, Bouar, Bambari, Bossangoa, Carnot

Government

Head of state Ange-Felix Patasse from 1993 **Head of government** Anicet Georges Dologuele from 1999 **Political system** emergent democracy **Armed forces** 2,700 (1997); plus 2,300 in paramilitary forces **Conscription** selective national service for two-year period **Defence spend** (% GDP) 4.0 (1997) **Education spend** (% GNP) 2.8 (1993–94) **Health spend** (% GDP) 1.9 (1990–95) **Death penalty** retains the death penalty for ordinary crimes but can be considered abolitionist in practice (last execution 1981)

Population and society

Population 3,594,000 (1999 est) **Population growth rate** 1.9% (1995–2000) **Ethnic groups** over 80 ethnic groups, but 66% of the population falls into one of three: the Banda (30%), the Baya-Mandjia (29%), and the Mbaka (7%). There are clearly defined ethnic zones; the forest region, inhabited by Bantu groups, the Mbaka, Lissongo, Mbimu, and Babinga; the river banks, populated by the Sango, Yakoma, Baniri, and Buraka; and the savanna region, where the Banda, Sande, Sara, Ndle, and Bizao live. Europeans number fewer than 7,000, the majority being French **Religion** Protestant, Roman Catholic, Muslim, animist **Life expectancy** 43 (men); 47 (women) (1995–2000) **Literacy rate** 56% (men); 30% (women) (1997 est) **Unemployment** 5.6% (1993)

Economy and resources

GDP (US$) 1.06 billion (1998) **GNP** (US$) 1.04 billion (1998) **GNP per capita (PPP)** (US$) 1,290 (1998 est) **Real GDP growth** (% change on previous year) 5.3 (1998) **Consumer price inflation** 2.6% (1998) **Foreign debt** (US$) 885 million (1997) **Resources** gem diamonds and industrial diamonds, gold, uranium, iron ore, manganese, copper **Exports** diamonds, coffee, timber, cotton. Principal market: Belgium – Luxembourg 36.2% (1997) **Imports** machinery, road vehicles and parts, basic manufactures, food and chemical products. Principal source: France 30.5% (1997)

▪ Tourist information

Time difference GMT +1 **Currency** franc CFA **Language** French (official), Sangho (national), Arabic, Hunsa, and Swahili **Visa requirements** UK: visa required. USA: visa required **Embassy for the UK** 30 rue des Perchamps, 75016, Paris, France. Tel: (1) 4224 4256; fax: (1) 4288 9895 **British embassy** British Consulate, PO Box 728, Bangui. (All staff based in Yaoundé, Cameroon.) Tel: (236) 610 300; fax: (236) 615 130 **Chamber of commerce** Chambre de Commerce, d'Industrie, des Mines et de l'Artisanat, BP 813, Bangui. Tel: (236) 614 255; telex: 5261 **Office hours** 0630–1330 Mon–Fri; 0700–1200 Sat **Banking hours** 0730–1130 Mon–Fri **Airports** international airports: Bangui-M'Poko; 37 small airports for international chartered services; total passenger km: 236 million (1995) **Chief tourist attractions** waterfalls; forests; wildlife; game reserves; hunting and fishing **Major holidays** 1 January, 29 March, 1 May, 1 June, 13, 15 August, 1 September, 1 November, 1, 25 December; variable: Ascension Thursday, Easter Monday, Whit Monday

Chronology

10th century Immigration by peoples from Sudan to the east and Cameroon to the west. **16th century** Part of the Gaoga Empire. **16th–18th centuries** Population reduced greatly by slave raids both by coastal traders and Arab empires in Sudan and Chad. **19th century** The Zande nation of the Bandia peoples became powerful in the east. Bantu speakers immigrated from Zaire and the Baya from northern Cameroon. **1889–1903** The French established control over the area, quelling insurrections; a French colony known as Oubangi-Chari was formed and partitioned among commercial concessionaries. **1920–30** A series of rebellions against forced labour on coffee and cotton plantations were savagely repressed by the French. **1946** Given a territorial assembly and representation in French parliament. **1958** Achieved self-government within French Equatorial Africa, with Barthélémy Boganda, founder of the pro-independence Movement for the Social Evolution of Black Africa (MESAN), as prime minister. **1960** Achieved independence as Central African Republic; David Dacko, the nephew of the late Boganda, was elected president. **1962** The republic became a one-party state, dominated by MESAN and loyal to the French interest. **1965** Dacko was ousted in a military coup led by Col Jean-Bedel Bokassa, as the economy deteriorated. **1972** Bokassa declared himself president for life. In 1977 he made himself emperor of the 'Central African Empire'. **1979** Bokassa was deposed by Dacko in a French-backed bloodless coup, following violent repressive measures including the massacre of 100 children. Bokassa went into exile. **1981** Dacko was deposed in a bloodless coup, led by Gen André Kolingba, and a military government was established. **1983** A clandestine opposition movement was formed. **1984** Amnesty for all political party leaders was announced. **1988** Bokassa, who had returned from exile, was found guilty of murder and embezzlement; he received a death sentence, later commuted to life imprisonment. **1991** Opposition parties were allowed to form. **1992** Multiparty elections were promised, but cancelled with Kolingba in last place. **1993** Kolingba released thousands of prisoners, including Bokassa. Ange-Félix Patasse of the leftist African People's Labour Party (MLPC) was elected president, ending 12 years of military dictatorship. **1996** There was an army revolt over pay; Patasse was forced into hiding. **1999** Anicet Georges Dologuele was appointed prime minister.

Chad Republic of

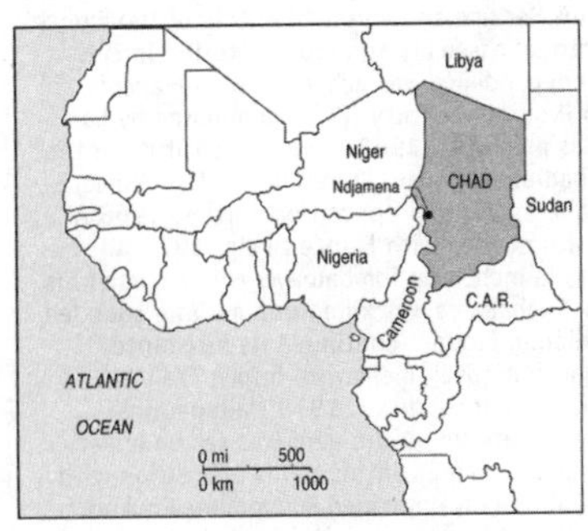

National name *République du Tchad* **Area** 1,284,000 sq km/ 495,752 sq mi **Capital** N'djaména (formerly Fort Lamy) **Major towns/cities** Sarh, Moundou, Abéché, Bongor, Doba

Government

Head of state Idriss Deby from 1990 **Head of government** Nassour Ouaidou Guelendouksia from 1997 **Political system** emergent democracy **Armed forces** 25,400 (1997); plus 9,500 in paramilitary forces **Conscription** conscription is for three years **Defence spend** (% GDP) 4.1 (1997) **Education spend** (% GNP) 2.9 (1995) **Health spend** (% GDP) 3.4 (1990–95) **Death penalty** retained and used for ordinary crimes

Population and society

Population 7,458,000 (1999 est) **Population growth rate** 2.6% (1995–2000) **Ethnic groups** mainly Arabs in the north, and Pagan, or Kirdi, groups in the south. There is no single dominant group in any region, the largest are the Sara, who comprise about a quarter of the total population. Europeans, mainly French, constitute a very small minority **Religion** Muslim, Christian, animist **Life expectancy** 46 (men); 49 (women) (1995–2000) **Literacy rate** 64% (men); 37% (women) (1997 est)

Economy and resources

GDP (US$) 1.6 billion (1998) **GNP** (US$) 1.7 billion (1998) **GNP per capita (PPP)** (US$) 1,020 (1998 est) **Real GDP growth** (% change on previous year) 6 (1998) **Consumer price inflation** 3.3% (1998) **Foreign debt** (US$) 1.03 billion (1997) **Resources** petroleum, tungsten, tin ore, bauxite, iron ore, gold, uranium, limestone, kaolin, titanium **Exports** cotton, live cattle, meat, hides and skins. Principal market: Portugal 29.8% (1997) **Imports** petroleum and petroleum products, cereals, pharmaceuticals, chemicals, machinery and transport equipment, electrical equipment. Principal source: France 41.3% (1997)

▪ Tourist information

Time difference GMT +1 **Currency** franc CFA **Language** French, Arabic (both official), over 100 African languages spoken **Visa requirements** UK: visa required. USA: visa required **Embassy for the UK** 65 rue des Belles Feuilles, 75116 Paris, France. Tel: (1) 4553 3675; fax: (1) 4553 1609 **British embassy** British Consulate, BP 877, avenue Charles de Gaulle, N'djaména. (All staff based in Abuja, Nigeria.) Tel: (235) 513 064; telex: 5234 **Chamber of commerce** Chambre de Commerce, Chambre Consulaire, BP 458, N'djaména. Tel: (235) 515 264 **Office hours** 0700–1400 Mon–Sat; 0700–1200 Fri **Banking hours** 0700–1100 Mon–Sat; 0700–1030 Fri **Airports** international airports: N'djaména; 12 small airports for domestic services; total passenger km: 231 million (1995) **Chief tourist attractions** varied scenery – desert in north, dense forest in south **Major holidays** 1 January, 1, 25 May, 7 June, 11 August, 1, 28 November, 25 December; variable: Eid-ul-Adha, Easter Monday, end of Ramadan, Prophet's Birthday

Chronology

7th–9th centuries Berber pastoral nomads, the Zaghawa, immigrated from the north and became a ruling aristocracy, dominating the Sao people, sedentary black farmers, and establishing the Kanem state. **9th–19th centuries** The Zaghawa's Saifi dynasty formed the kingdom of Bornu, which stretched to the west and south of Lake Chad, and converted to Islam in the 11th century. At its height between the 15th and 18th centuries, it raided the south for slaves, and faced rivalry from the 16th century from the Baguirmi and Ouadai Arab kingdoms. **1820s** Visited by British explorers. **1890s–1901** Conquered by France, who ended slave raiding by Arab kingdoms. **1910** Became a colony in French Equatorial Africa. Cotton production expanded in the south. **1944** The pro-Nazi Vichy government signed an agreement giving Libya rights to the Aouzou Strip in northern Chad. **1946** Became an overseas territory of the French Republic, with its own territorial assembly and representation in the French parliament. **1960** Independence was achieved, with François Tombalbaye of the Chadian Progressive Party (CPT), dominated by Sara Christians from the south, as president. **1963** Violent opposition in the Muslim north, led by the Chadian National Liberation Front (Frolinat), backed by Libya following the banning of opposition parties. **1968** A revolt of northern militias was quelled with France's help. **1973** An Africanization campaign was launched by Tombalbaye, who changed his first name to Ngarta. **1975** Tombalbaye was killed in a military coup led by southerner Gen Félix Malloum. Frolinat continued its resistance. **1978** Malloum formed a coalition government with former Frolinat leader Hissène Habré, but it soon broke down. **1979** Malloum was forced to leave the country; an interim government was set up under Gen Goukouni Oueddei (Frolinat). Habré continued his opposition with his Army of the North (FAN), and Libya provided support for Goukouni. **1981–82** Habré gained control of half the country. Goukouni fled and set up a 'government in exile'. **1983** Habré's regime was recognized by the Organization of African Unity (OAU) and France, but in the north, Goukouni's supporters, with Libya's help, fought on. Eventually a ceasefire was agreed, with latitude 16°north dividing the country. **1987** Chad, France, and Libya agreed on an OAU ceasefire to end the civil war between the Muslim Arab north and Christian and animist black African south. **1988** Libya relinquished its claims to the Aozou Strip. **1990** President Habré was ousted after the army was defeated by Libyan-backed Patriotic Salvation Movement (MPS) rebel troops based in the Sudan and led by Habré's former ally Idriss Deby. **1991–92** Several antigovernment coups were foiled. **1993** A transitional charter was adopted, as a prelude to full democracy at a later date. **1997** Nassour Ouaidou Guelendouksia was appointed prime minister. A reconciliation agreement was signed with rebel forces.

Chile Republic of

National name *República de Chile* **Area** 756,950 sq km/292,258 sq mi **Capital** Santiago **Major towns/cities** Concepción, Viña del Mar, Valparaiso, Talcahuano, San Bernardo, Puente Alto, Chillán, Rancagua, Talca, Temuco **Territories** Easter Island, Juan Fernández Islands, part of Tierra del Fuego, claim to part of Antarctica

Government

Head of state Ricardo Lagos from 2000 **Head of government** Dante Cordova from 1995 **Political system** emergent democracy **Armed forces** 94,300 (1997) **Conscription** one year (army) or two years (navy and air force) **Defence spend** (% GDP) 2.8 (1997) **Education spend** (% GNP) 3.1 (1996) **Health spend** (% GDP) 2.5 (1990–95) **Death penalty** retained and used for ordinary crimes

Population and society

Population 15,019,000 (1999 est) **Population growth rate** 1.4% (1995–2000); 1.2% (2000–05) **Ethnic groups** 65% mestizo (mixed American Indian and Spanish descent), 30% European, remainder mainly American Indian **Religion** Roman Catholic **Life expectancy** 72 (men); 78 (women) (1995–2000) **Literacy rate** 95% (men); 95% (women) (1997 est) **Unemployment** 7.2% (1998 est)

Economy and resources

GDP (US$) 78.02 billion (1998) **GNP** (US$) 71.3 billion (1998) **GNP per capita (PPP)** (US$) 12,890 (1998) **Real GDP growth** (% change on previous year) 4.7 (1998) **Consumer price inflation** 4.7% (1998) **Foreign debt** (US$) 31.4 billion (1997) **Resources** copper (world's largest producer), gold, silver, iron ore, molybdenum, cobalt, iodine, saltpetre, coal, natural gas, petroleum, hydroelectric power **Exports** copper, fruits, timber products, fishmeal, vegetables, manufactured foodstuffs and beverages. Principal market: USA 17.7% (1998) **Imports** machinery and transport equipment, wheat, chemical and mineral products, consumer goods, raw materials. Principal source: USA 23.3% (1998)

▪ Tourist information

Time difference GMT –4 **Currency** Chilean peso **Language** Spanish **Visa requirements** UK: visa not required. USA: visa not required **Embassy in the UK** 12 Devonshire Street, London W1N 2DS. Tel: (020) 7580 6392; fax: (020) 7436 5204 **British embassy** Avenida El Bosque Norte (Casilla 16552), Santiago 9. Tel: (2) 231 3737; fax: (2) 231 9771 **Chamber of commerce** Cámara de Comercio de Santiago de Chile, AG, Santa Lucía 302, 3°, Casilla 1297, Santiago. Tel: (2) 632 1232; fax: (2) 633 0962 **Office hours** 0900–1830 Mon–Fri **Banking hours** 0900–1400 Mon–Fri **Airports** international airports: Santiago (Arturo Merino Benítez), Arica (Chacalluta); domestic services to main towns; total passenger km: 8,597 million (1997 est) **Major ports** Valparaíso, Antofagasta, Arica, Iquique, Punta Arenas **Chief tourist attractions** beaches; Andean skiing resorts; lakes, rivers, desert scenery; Easter Island Neolithic sites **Major holidays** 1 January, 1, 21 May, 29 June, 15 August, 11, 18–19 September, 12 October, 1 November, 8, 25, 31, December; variable: Good Friday, Holy Saturday

Chronology

1535 The first Spanish invasion of Chile was abandoned in the face of fierce resistance from indigenous Araucanian Indians. **1541** Pedro de Valdivia began the Spanish conquest and founded Santiago. **1553** Valdivia was captured and killed by Araucanian Indians, led by Chief Lautaro. **17th century** The Spanish developed small agricultural settlements ruled by a government subordinate to the viceroy in Lima, Peru. **1778** The King of Spain appointed a captain-general to govern Chile. **1810** A Santiago junta proclaimed Chilean autonomy after Napoleon dethroned the king of Spain. **1814** The Spanish viceroy regained control of Chile. **1817** The Army of the Andes, led by José de San Martín and Bernardo O'Higgins, defeated the Spanish. **1818** Chile achieved independence from Spain with O'Higgins as supreme director. **1823–30** O'Higgins was forced to resign; a civil war between conservative centralists and liberal federalists ended with conservative victory. **1833** An autocratic republican constitution created a unitary Roman Catholic state with a strong president and limited franchise. **1851–61** President Manuel Montt bowed to pressure to liberalize the constitution and reduce privileges of landowners and the church. **1879–84** Chile defeated Peru and Bolivia in the War of the Pacific and increased its territory by a third. **late 19th century** Mining of nitrate and copper became a major industry; large-scale European immigration followed the 'pacification' of Araucanian Indians. **1891** A constitutional dispute between president and congress led to civil war; congressional victory reduced the president to figurehead status. **1925** A new constitution increased presidential powers, separated church and state, and made primary education compulsory. **1927** A military coup led to the dictatorship of Gen Carlos Ibánez del Campo. **1931** A sharp fall in price of copper and nitrate caused dramatic economic and political collapse. **1938** A Popular Front of Radicals, Socialists, and Communists took power under Pedro Aguirre Cedra, who introduced economic policies based on the US New Deal. **1948–58** The Communist Party was banned. **1970** Salvador Allende, leader of the Popular Unity coalition, became the world's first democratically elected Marxist president; he embarked on an extensive programme of nationalization and radical social reform. **1973** Allende was killed in a CIA-backed military coup; Gen Augusto Pinochet established a dictatorship combining severe political repression with free-market economics. **1981** Pinochet began an eight-year term as president under a new constitution described as a 'transition to democracy'. **1983** Economic recession provoked growing opposition to the governing regime. **1988** A referendum on whether Pinochet should serve a further term resulted in a clear 'No' vote. **1990** The military regime ended, with a Christian Democrat (Patricio Aylwin) as president, with Pinochet as commander in chief of the army. An investigation was launched into over 2,000 political executions

during the military regime. **1995** Dante Cordova was appointed prime minister. **1998** Pinochet retired from the army and was made life senator. Pinochet was placed under arrest in the UK; proceedings began to extradite him to Spain on murder charges. **1999** The ruling on the extradition of Pinochet to Spain was left to the British government. **2000** After Pinochet was found unfit for trial by a team of British doctors, British home secretary Jack Straw announced that he would allow Pinochet to return to Chile, and not extradite him to Spain. The Spanish judge who led the campaign for extradition demanded new medical tests by doctors appointed by the Spanish courts. Ricardo Lagos was elected president.

China People's Republic of

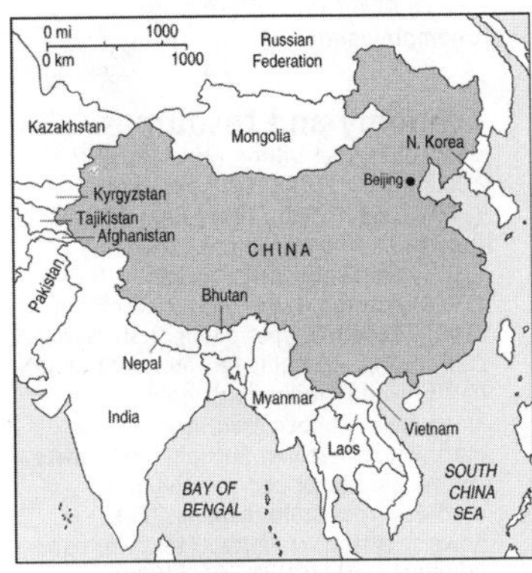

National name *Zhonghua Renmin Gonghe Guo* **Area** 9,572,900 sq km/ 3,696,000 sq mi **Capital** Beijing (Peking) **Major towns/ cities** Shanghai, Hong Kong, Chongqing (Chungking), Tianjin, Guangzhou (Canton), Shenyang (Mukden), Wuhan, Nanjing (Nanking), Harbin, Chengdu, Xi'an, Zibo

Government

Head of state Jiang Zemin from 1993 **Head of government** Zhu Rongji from 1998 **Political system** communist **Armed forces** 2,840,000; reserves approximately 1.2 million (1997) **Conscription** selective: 3 years (army and marines), 4 years (air force and navy) **Defence spend** (% GDP) 5.7 (1997) **Education spend** (% GNP) 2.3 (1996) **Health spend** (% GDP) 2.1 (1990–95) **Death penalty** retained and used for ordinary crimes

Population and society

Population 1,273,639,000 (1999 est) **Population growth rate** 0.9% (1995–2000) **Ethnic groups** 94% Han Chinese, the remainder being Zhuang, Uygur, Hui (Muslims), Yi, Tibetan, Miao, Manchu, Mongol, Buyi, or Korean; numerous lesser nationalities live mainly in border regions **Religion** Taoist, Confucianist, and Buddhist; Muslim 20 million; Catholic 3–6 million (divided between the 'patriotic' church established in 1958 and the 'loyal' church subject to Rome); Protestant 3 million **Life expectancy** 68 (men); 72 (women) (1995–2000) **Literacy rate** 91% (men); 75% (women) (1997 est) **Unemployment** 3.1% (1998)

Economy and resources

GDP (US$) 961 billion (1998) **GNP** (US$) 928.9 billion (1998) **GNP per capita (PPP)** (US$) 3,220 (1998) **Real GDP growth** (% change on previous year) 7.8 (1998) **Consumer price inflation** 7% (1998) **Foreign debt** (US$) 146.7 billion (1997) **Resources** coal, graphite, tungsten, molybdenum, antimony, tin (world's largest producer), lead (world's fifth-largest producer), mercury, bauxite, phosphate rock, iron ore (world's largest producer), diamonds, gold, manganese, zinc (world's third-largest producer), petroleum, natural gas, fish **Exports** basic manufactures, miscellaneous manufactured articles (particularly clothing and toys), crude petroleum, machinery and transport equipment, fishery products, cereals, canned food, tea, raw silk, cotton cloth. Principal market: Hong Kong 21.1% (1998) **Imports** machinery and transport equipment, basic manufactures, chemicals, wheat, rolled steel, fertilizers. Principal source: Japan 20.1% (1998)

▪ Tourist information

Time difference GMT +8 **Currency** yuan **Language** Chinese, including Mandarin (official), Cantonese, Wu, and other dialects **Visa requirements** UK: visa required. USA: visa required **Embassy in the UK** 49–51 Portland Place, London W1N 3AH. Tel: (020) 7636 9375/5726; fax: (020) 7636 2981 **British embassy** 11 Guang Hua Lu, Jian Guo Men Wai, Beijing 100600. Tel: (1) 532 1961/5; fax: (1) 532 1937 **Chamber of commerce** All-China Federation of Industry and Commerce, 93 Beiheyan Dajie, Beijing 100006. Tel: (1) 513 6677; fax: (1) 512 2631 **Office hours** 0800–1200 and 1400–1800 Mon–Sat **Banking hours** 0930–1200 and 1400–1700 Mon–Fri; 0900–1700 Sat **Airports** international airports: Beijing (Capital International Central), Guangzhou (Baiyun), Shanghai (Hongqiao), Hong Kong (Kai Tak); 59 domestic airports; total passenger km: 77,352 million (1997) **Major ports** Tianjin (Tientsin), Shanghai, Hong Kong, Qingdao (Tsingtao), Guangzhou (Canton) **Chief tourist attractions** scenery; historical sites such as the Great Wall, Temple of Heaven, Forbidden City (Beijing), Ming tombs, terracotta warriors (Xian); Buddhist monasteries and temples in Tibet (Xizang) **Major holidays** 1 January, 8 March, 1 May, 1 August, 9 September, 1–2 October; variable: Spring Festival (January/February, 4 days)

Chronology

***c.* 3000 BC** Yangshao culture reached its peak in the Huang He Valley; displaced by Longshan culture in eastern China. ***c.* 1766–*c.* 1122 BC** First major dynasty, the Shang, arose from Longshan culture; writing and calendar developed. ***c.* 1122–256 BC** Zhou people of western China overthrew Shang and set up new dynasty; development of money and written laws. ***c.* 500 BC** Confucius expounded the philosophy which guided Chinese government and society for the next 2,000 years. **403–221 BC** 'Warring States Period': Zhou Empire broke up into small kingdoms. **221–206 BC** Qin kingdom defeated all rivals and established first empire with strong central government; emperor Shi Huangdi built the Great Wall of China. **202 BC–AD 220** Han dynasty expanded empire into central Asia; first overland trade with Europe; art and literature flourished; Buddhism introduced from India. **AD 220–581** Large-scale rebellion destroyed the Han dynasty; the empire split into three competing kingdoms; several short-lived dynasties ruled parts of China. **581–618** Sui dynasty reunified China and repelled Tatar invaders. **618–907** Tang dynasty enlarged and strengthened the empire; great revival of culture; major rebellion 875–84. **907–60** 'Five Dynasties and Ten Kingdoms': disintegration of the empire amid war and economic decline; development of printing. **960–1279** Song dynasty reunified China and restored order; civil service examinations introduced; population reached 100 million; Manchurians occupied northern China in 1127. **1279** Mongols conquered all China, which became part of the vast empire of Kublai Khan, founder of the Yuan dynasty; the Venetian traveller Marco Polo visited China 1275–92. **1368** Rebellions drove out the Mongols; Ming dynasty expanded the empire; architecture flourished in the new capital of Beijing. **1516** Portuguese explorers reached Macau. Other European traders followed, with the first Chinese porcelain arriving in Europe in 1580. **1644** Manchurian invasion established the Qing (or Manchu) dynasty; Manchurians were assimilated and Chinese trade and culture continued to thrive. **1796–1804** Anti-Manchu revolt weakened the Qing dynasty; a population increase in excess of food supplies led to falling living standards and cultural decline. **1839–42** First Opium War; Britain forced China to cede Hong Kong and open five ports to European trade; Second Opium War extracted further trade concessions 1856–60. **1850–64** Millions died in the Taiping Rebellion; Taipings combined Christian and Chinese beliefs and demanded land reform. **1894–95** Sino-Japanese War: Chinese driven out of Korea. **1897–98** Germany, Russia, France, and Britain leased ports in China. **1898** Hong Kong was secured by Britain on a 99-year lease. **1900** Anti-Western Boxer Rebellion crushed by foreign intervention; jealousy between the Great Powers prevented partition. **1911** Revolution broke out; Republic of China proclaimed by Sun Zhong Shan (Sun Yat-sen) of Guomindang (National People's Party). **1912** Abdication of infant emperor Pu-i; Gen Yuan Shih-K'ai became dictator. **1916** The power of the central government collapsed on the death of Yuan Shih-K'ai; northern China dominated by local warlords. **1919** Beijing students formed the 4th May movement to protest at the transfer of German possessions in China to Japan. **1921** Sun Zhong Shan elected president of nominal national government; Chinese Communist Party founded; communists worked with Guomindang to reunite China from 1923. **1925** Death of Sun Zhong Shan; leadership of Guomindang gradually passed to military commander Jiang Jie Shi (Chiang Kai-shek). **1926–28** Revolutionary Army of Jiang Jie Shi reunified China; Guomindang broke with communists and tried to suppress them in civil war. **1932** Japan invaded Manchuria and established the puppet state of Manchukuo. **1934–35** Communists undertook Long March from Jiangxi and Fujian in south to Yan'an in north to escape encirclement by Guomindang. **1937–45** Japan renewed invasion of China; Jiang Jie Shi received help from USA and Britain from 1941. **1946** Civil war resumed between Guomindang and communists led by Mao Zedong. **1949** Victorious communists proclaimed People's Republic of China under Chairman Mao; Guomindang fled to Taiwan. **1950–53** China intervened heavily in Korean War. **1958** 'Great Leap Forward': extremist five-year plan to accelerate

China: Provinces

(– = not applicable.)

Province	Alternative transliteration/ English name	Capital	Area sq km	Area sq mi	Population (1997)
Anhui	Anhwei	Hefei	139,900	54,015	61,270,000
Fujian	Fukien	Fuzhou	123,100	47,528	32,820,000
Gansu	Kansu	Lanzhou	530,000	204,633	24,940,000
Guangdong	Kwantung	Guangzhou	231,400	89,343	70,510,000
Guizhou	Kweichow	Guiyang	174,000	67,181	36,060,000
Hainan	–	Haikou	34,000	13,127	7,430,000
Hebei	Hopei	Shijiazhuang	202,700	78,262	65,250,000
Heilongjiang	Heilungkiang	Harbin	463,600	178,996	37,510,000
Henan	Honan	Zhengzhou	167,000	64,479	92,430,000
Hubei	Hupei	Wuhan	187,500	72,394	58,730,000
Hunan	–	Changsha	210,500	81,274	64,650,000
Jiangsu	Kiangsu	Nanjing	102,200	39,459	71,480,000
Jiangxi	Kiangsi	Nanchang	164,800	63,629	41,500,000
Jilin	Kirin	Changchun	187,000	72,201	26,280,000
Liaoning	–	Shenyang	151,000	58,301	41,380,000
Qinghai	Tsinghai	Xining	721,000	278,378	4,960,000
Shaanxi	Shensi	Xian	195,800	75,598	35,700,000
Shandong	Shantung	Jinan	153,300	59,189	87,850,000
Shanxi	Shansi	Taiyuan	157,100	60,656	31,410,000
Sichuan	Szechwan	Chengdu	569,000	219,691	84,300,000
Yunnan	–	Kunming	436,200	168,417	40,940,000
Zhejiang	Chekiang	Hangzhou	101,800	39,305	44,350,000
Autonomous Region					
Guangxi Zhuang	Kwangsi Chuang	Nanning	220,400	85,096	46,330,000
Nei Mongol	Inner Mongolia	Hohhot	450,000	173,745	23,260,000
Ningxia Hui	Ninghsia-Hui	Yinchuan	170,000	65,637	5,300,000
Xinjiang Uygur	Sinkiang Uighur	Urumqi	1,646,800	635,829	17,180,000
Xizang	Tibet	Lhasa	1,221,600	471,660	2,480,000
Municipality					
Beijing	Peking	–	17,800	6,873	12,400,000
Chongqing	Chungking	–	23,000	8,900	30,420,000
Shanghai	–	–	5,800	2,239	14,570,000
Tianjin	Tientsin	–	4,000	1,544	9,530,000

output severely weakened the economy. **1960** Sino-Soviet split: China accused USSR of betraying communism. **1962** Economic recovery programme under Liu Shaoqi caused divisions between 'rightists' and 'leftists'; brief border war with India. **1966–69** 'Great Proletarian Cultural Revolution'; leftists overthrew Liu Shaoqi with support of Mao; Red Guards disrupted education, government, and daily life in attempt to enforce revolutionary principles. **1970** Mao supported the efforts of Prime Minister Zhou Enlai to restore order. **1971** People's Republic of China admitted to United Nations. **1976** Deaths of Zhou Enlai and Mao Zedong led to a power struggle between rightists and leftists; Hua Guofeng became leader. **1977–81** Rightist Deng Xiaoping emerged as supreme leader; pragmatic economic policies introduced market incentives and encouraged foreign trade. **1979** Full diplomatic relations with USA established **1987** Deng Xiaoping retired from Politburo but remained a dominant figure. **1989** Over 2,000 people were killed when the army crushed prodemocracy student demonstrations in Tiananmen Square, Beijing; international sanctions were imposed. **1991** China and the USSR reached an agreement on their disputed border. **1993** Jiang Zemin became head of state **1996** Reunification with Taiwan was declared a priority. **1997** A border agreement was signed with Russia. Hong Kong was returned to Chinese sovereignty. **1998** Zhu Rongji became prime minister. The Yangtze in Hubei province flooded, causing widespread devastation. Dissident Xu Wenli was jailed for trying to set up an opposition party. **1999** The USA and China announced a deal to allow for China's entry into the World Trade Organization (WTO), in exchange for opening China's markets to foreign firms. Macau was returned to China, with the promise that it would have an independent political system for 50 years.

Colombia Republic of

National name *República de Colombia* **Area** 1,141,748 sq km/440,828 sq mi **Capital** Bogotá **Major towns/cities** Medellín, Cali, Barranquilla, Cartagena, Bucaramanga, Buenaventura

Government

Head of state and government Andres Pastrana from 1998 **Political system** liberal democracy **Armed forces** 146,300 (1997); plus a paramilitary police force of 87,000 **Conscription** selective conscription for 1–2 years **Defence spend** (% GDP) 4.0 (1997) **Education spend** (% GNP) 4.4 (1996) **Health spend** (% GDP) 3.0 (1990–95) **Death penalty** abolished in 1910

Population and society

Population 41,564,000 (1999 est) **Population growth rate** 1.9% (1995–2000) **Ethnic groups** main ethnic groups are of mixed Spanish, American Indian, and African descent; Spanish customs and values predominate **Religion** Roman Catholic **Life expectancy** 67 (men); 74 (women) (1995–2000) **Literacy rate** 91% (men); 91% (women) (1997 est) **Unemployment** 13% (1998)

Economy and resources

GDP (US$) 91.1 billion (1998) **GNP** (US$) 106.1 billion (1998) **GNP per capita (PPP)** (US$) 7,500 (1998) **Real GDP growth** (% change on previous year) 2.3 (1998) **Consumer price inflation** 18.3% (1998) **Foreign debt** (US$) 31.8 billion (1997) **Resources** petroleum, natural gas, coal, nickel, emeralds (accounts for about half of world production), gold, manganese, copper, lead, mercury, platinum, limestone, phosphates **Exports** coffee, petroleum and petroleum products, coal, gold, bananas, cut flowers, cotton, chemicals, textiles, paper. Principal market: USA 36% (1998). Illegal trade in cocaine in 1995; it was estimated that approximately $3.5 billion (equivalent to about 4% of GDP) was entering Colombia as the proceeds of drug-trafficking **Imports** machinery and transport equipment, chemicals, minerals, food, metals. Principal source: USA 35.1% (1998)

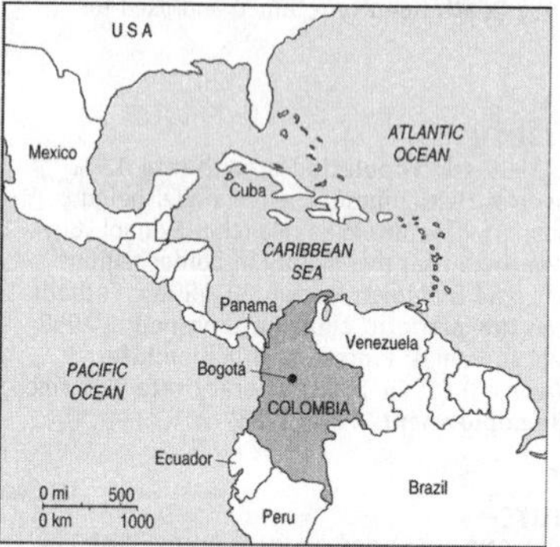

Tourist information

Time difference GMT –5 **Currency** Colombian peso **Language** Spanish **Visa requirements** UK: visa not required for a stay of up to 90 days. USA: visa not required for a stay of up to 90 days **Embassy in the UK** Flat 3A, 3 Hans Crescent, London SW1X 0LN. Tel: (020) 7589 9177; fax: (020) 7581 1829 **British embassy** Apartado Aéreo 4508, Torre Propaganda Sancho, Calle 98, No. 9–03, Piso 4, Santa Fe de Bogotá DC. Tel: (1) 218 5111; fax: (1) 218 2460 **Chamber of commerce** Instituto Colombiano de Comercio Exterior, Apartado Aéreo 240193, Calle 28, No. 13-A-15, 5° Santa Fe de Bogotá DC. Tel: (1) 283 3284; fax: (1) 281 2560, 283 1953 **Office hours** 0800–1200 and 1400–1700 Mon–Fri **Banking hours** 0900–1500 Mon–Fri **Airports** international airports: Santa Fe de Bogotá, DC (El Dorado International), Medellín, Cali, Barranquilla, Bucaramanga, Cartagena, Cúcuta, Leticia, Pereira, San Andrés, Santa Maria; over 80 smaller airports serving domestic flights; total passenger km: 6,733 million (1997 est) **Major ports** Barranquilla, Cartagena, Buenaventura **Chief tourist attractions** Caribbean coast; 16th-century walled city of Cartagena; Amazonian town of Leticia; Andes Mountains; forest and rainforest; pre-Columbian relics and colonial architecture **Major holidays** 1, 6 January, 29 June, 20 July, 7, 15 August, 12 October, 1, 15 November, 8, 25, 30–31 December; variable: Ascension Thursday, Corpus Christi, Good Friday, Holy Thursday, St Joseph (March), Sacred Heart (June)

Chronology

late 15th century Southern Colombia became part of Inca Empire, whose core lay in Peru. **1522** Spanish conquistador Pascual de Andagoya reached the San Juan River. **1536–38** Spanish conquest by Jimenez de Quesada overcame powerful Chibcha Indian chiefdom, which had its capital in the uplands at Bogotá and was renowned for its gold crafts; became part of Spanish Viceroyalty of Peru, which covered much of South America. **1717** Bogotá became capital of the new Spanish Viceroyalty of Nueva (New) Granada, which also ruled Ecuador and Venezuela. **1809** Struggle for independence from Spain began. **1819** Venezuelan freedom fighter Simón Bolívar, 'the Liberator', who had withdrawn to Colombia in 1814, raised a force of 5,000 British mercenaries and defeated the Spanish at the battle of Boyacá, establishing Colombia's independence; Gran Colombia formed, also comprising Ecuador, Panama, and Venezuela. **1830** Became a separate state, which included Panama, on the dissolution of the Republic of Gran Colombia. **1863** Became major coffee exporter. Federalizing, anti-clerical Liberals came to power, with the country divided into nine largely autonomous 'sovereign' states; the church was disestablished. **1885** Conservatives came to power, beginning 45 years of political dominance; power was recentralized and the church restored to influence. **1899–1903** Civil war between Liberals and Conservatives, ending with Panama's separation as an independent state. **1930** Liberals returned to power at the time of the economic depression; social legislation introduced and a labour movement encouraged. **1946** Conservatives returned to power. **1948** The left-wing mayor of Bogotá was assassinated to a widespread outcry. **1949–57** Civil war, 'La Violencia', during which over 250,000 people died. **1957** Hoping to halt violence, Conservatives and Liberals agreed to form National Front, sharing the presidency. **1970** National Popular Alliance (ANAPO) formed as left-wing opposition to National Front. **1974** National Front accord temporarily ended. **1975** Civil unrest due to disillusionment with government. **1978** Liberals, under Julio Turbay, revived the accord and began an intensive fight against drug dealers. **1982** The Liberals maintained their control of congress but lost the presidency. Conservative president Belisario Betancur granted guerrillas an amnesty and freed political prisoners. **1984** The minister of justice was assassinated by drug dealers; the campaign against them was stepped up. **1989** A drug cartel assassinated the leading presidential candidate and an antidrug war was declared by the president; a bombing campaign by drug traffickers killed hundreds; the police killed José Rodriguez Gacha, one of the most wanted cartel leaders. **1991** A new constitution prohibited the extradition of Colombians wanted for trial in other countries. Several leading drug traffickers were arrested. Many guerrillas abandoned the armed struggle, but the Colombian Revolutionary Armed Forces (FARC) and the National Liberation Army remained active. **1993** Medellín drug-cartel leader Pablo Escobar was shot while attempting to avoid arrest. **1995** President Samper came under pressure to resign over corruption allegations; a state of emergency was declared. Leaders of the Cali drug cartel were imprisoned. **1998** There were clashes between the army and left-wing guerrillas. The conservative Andres Pastrana won presidential elections. Peace talks were held with rebels. **1999** Formal peace talks began between the government and the leading rebel group. **2000** US president Clinton announced $1.3 billion in aid for Colombia, most of which was to go to the armed forces.

Comoros Federal Islamic Republic of

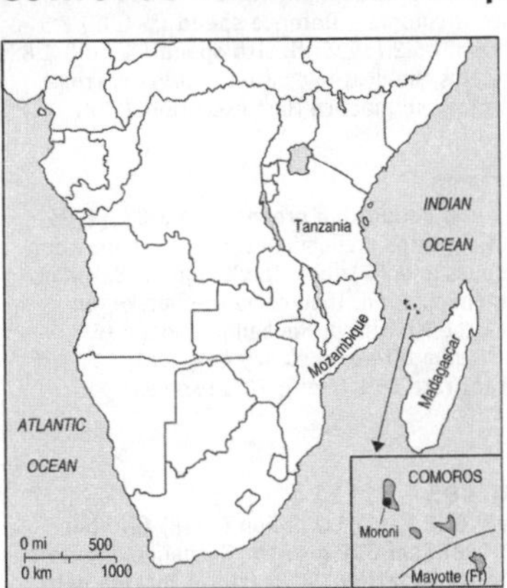

National name *Jumhurīyat al-Qumur al-Itthādīyah al-Islāmīyah* or *République Fédérale Islamique des Comoros* **Area** 1,862 sq km/718 sq mi **Capital** Moroni **Major towns/cities** Mutsamudu, Domoni, Fomboni, Dzaoudzi

Government

Head of state and government Azali Hassounani from 1999 **Political system** military **Armed forces** 800 (1995) **Conscription** military service is voluntary **Education spend** (% GNP) 3.9 (1995) **Health spend** (% GDP) 1.1 (1995) **Death penalty** retained and used for ordinary crimes

Population and society

Population 676,000 (1999 est) **Population growth rate** 2.7% (1995–2025) **Ethnic groups** population of mixed origin, with Africans, Arabs, and Malaysians predominating; the principal ethnic group is the Antalaotra **Religion** Muslim; Islam is the state religion **Life expectancy** 57 (men); 60 (women) (1995–2000) **Literacy rate** 63% (men); 48% (women) (1997 est) **Unemployment** 20% (1996 est)

Economy and resources

GDP (US$) 196 million (1998) **GNP** (US$) 196 million (1998) **GNP per capita (PPP)** (US$) 1,480 (1998) **Real GDP growth** (% change on previous year) 0.5 (1998) **Consumer price inflation** 2.5% (1997) **Foreign debt** (US$) 226 million (1997) **Exports** vanilla, cloves, ylang-ylang, essences, copra, coffee. Principal market: France 42.9% (1997) **Imports** rice, petroleum products, transport equipment, meat and dairy products, cement, iron and steel, clothing and footwear. Principal source: France 58.9% (1997)

▪ Tourist information

Time difference GMT +3 **Currency** Comorian franc **Language** Arabic (official), Comorian (Swahili and Arabic dialect), Makua, French **Visa requirements** UK: visa required. USA: visa required **Embassy for the UK** 20 rue Marbeau, 75016 Paris, France. Tel: (1) 4067 9054; fax: (1) 4067 7296 **British embassy** British Consulate, Henri Fraise et Fils 38, Co Océan Indien, PO Box 986, Moroni. Tel: (269) 733 182; fax: (269) 733 182. (All staff based in Madagascar.) **Chamber of commerce** Chambre de Commerce, d'Industrie et d'Agriculture, BP 763, Moroni. Tel: (269) 610 426 **Office hours** 0730–1430 Mon–Thu; 0730–1100 Fri **Banking hours** 0730–1300 Mon–Thu; 0730–1100 Fri **Airports** international airport: Moroni-Hahaya, on Njazídja; each of the three other islands has a small airfield; total passenger km: 3 million (1995) **Chief tourist attractions** rich marine life; beaches; underwater fishing; mountain scenery **Major holidays** 6 July, 27 November; variable: Eid-ul-Adha, Arafa, Ashora, first day of Ramadan, end of Ramadan, New Year (Muslim), Prophet's Birthday

Chronology

5th century AD First settled by Malay-Polynesian immigrants. **7th century** Converted to Islam by Arab seafarers and fell under the rule of local sultans. **late 16th century** First visited by European navigators. **1886** Moheli island in south became a French protectorate. **1904** Slave trade abolished, ending influx of Africans. **1912** Grande Comore and Anjouan, the main islands, joined Moheli to become a French colony, which was attached to Madagascar from 1914. **1947** Became a French Overseas Territory separate from Madagascar. **1961** Internal self-government achieved. **1975** Independence achieved from France, but island of Mayotte to the southeast voted to remain part of France. Joined the United Nations. **1976** President Ahmed Abdallah was overthrown in a coup by Ali Soilih; relations deteriorated with France as a Maoist-Islamic socialist programme was pursued. **1978** Soilih was killed by French mercenaries. A federal Islamic republic was proclaimed, with exiled Abdallah restored as president; diplomatic relations re-established with France. **1979** The Comoros became a one-party state; powers of the federal government increased. **1989** Abdallah killed by French mercenaries who, under French and South African pressure, turned authority over to French administration; Said Muhammad Djohar became president in a multiparty democracy. **1995** Djohar was overthrown in a coup led by Denard, who was persuaded to withdraw by French troops. **1997** Secessionist rebels took control of the island of Anjouan. **1999** The government was overthrown by an army coup, after granting greater autonomy to the islands of Anjouan and Moheli. The new president was Colonel Azali Hassoumani.

Congo Democratic Republic of (formerly Zaire)

National name *République Démocratique du Congo* **Area** 2,344,900 sq km/905,366 sq mi **Capital** Kinshasa **Major towns/cities** Lubumbashi, Kananga, Mbuji-Mayi, Kisangani, Bukavu, Kikwit, Matadi

Government

Head of state and government Laurent Kabila from 1997 **Political system** military **Armed forces** 40,000 (1997); plus paramilitary forces of 37,000 **Conscription** military service is compulsory **Defence spend** (% GDP) 5.3 (1997) **Education spend** (% GNP) 5.9 (1995) **Health spend** (% GDP) 0.2 (1990–95) **Death penalty** retained and used for ordinary crimes

Population and society

Population 50,336,000 (1999 est) **Population growth rate** 2.6% (1995–2000) **Ethnic groups** almost entirely of African descent, distributed among over 200 ethnic groups, the most numerous being the Kongo, Luba, Lunda, Mongo, and Zande **Religion** Roman Catholic, Protestant, Kimbanguist; also half a million Muslims **Life expectancy** 50 (men); 52 (women) (1995–2000) **Literacy rate** 84% (men); 61% (women) (1995 est) **Unemployment** N/A

Economy and resources

GDP (US$) 6.9 billion (1998) **GNP** (US$) 5.3 billion (1998) **GNP per capita (PPP)** (US$) 750 (1998 est) **Real GDP growth** (% change on previous year) -4.5 (1998) **Consumer price inflation** 65% (1998) **Foreign debt** (US$) 12.33 billion (1997) **Resources** petroleum, copper, cobalt (65% of world's reserves), manganese, zinc, tin, uranium, silver, gold, diamonds (one of the world's largest producers of industrial diamonds) **Exports** mineral products (mainly copper, cobalt, industrial diamonds, and petroleum), agricultural products (chiefly coffee). Principal market: Belgium and Luxembourg 42.7% (1997) **Imports** manufactured goods, food and live animals, machinery and transport equipment, chemicals, mineral fuels and lubricants. Principal source: South Africa 21.3% (1997)

▪ Tourist information

Time difference GMT +1/2 **Currency** congolese franc **Language** French (official); Swahili, Lingala, Kikongo, and Tshiluba are recognized as national languages; over 200 other languages **Visa requirements** UK: visa required. USA: visa required **Embassy in the UK** 26 Chesham Place, London SW1X 8HH. Tel: (020) 7235 6137; fax: (020) 7235 9048 **British embassy** BP 8049, avenue des Trois Z, Kinshasa-Gombe. Tel: (12) 34775/8 **Chamber of commerce** Chambre de Commerce, d'Industrie et d'Agriculture, BP 7247, 10 avenue des Aviateurs, Kinshasa. Tel: (12) 22286; telex: 21071 **Office hours** 0730–1500 Mon–Fri; 0730–1200 Sat **Banking hours** 0800–1130 Mon–Fri **Airports** international airports: Kinshasa (N'djili), Luano (near Lubumbashi), Bukava, Goma, Kisangani; over 40 domestic airports and 150 landing strips; total passenger km: 480 million (1994) **Major ports** Matadi, Kalemie **Chief tourist attractions** lake and mountain scenery; extensive tropical rainforests along Congo River **Major holidays** 1, 4 January, 1, 20 May, 24, 30 June, 1 August, 14, 27 October, 17, 24 November, 25 December

Chronology

13th century Rise of Kongo Empire, centred on banks of Zaïre/Congo River. **1483** First visited by the Portuguese, who named the area Zaire (from Zadi, 'big water') and converted local rulers to Christianity. **16th–17th centuries** Great development of slave trade by Portuguese, Dutch, British, and French merchants, initially supplied by Kongo intermediaries. **18th century** Rise of Luba state, in southern copper belt of north Katanga, and Lunda, in Kasai region in central south. **mid-19th century** Eastern Zaire invaded by Arab slave traders from East Africa. **1874–77** Welsh-born US explorer Henry Morton Stanley navigated Congo River to Atlantic Ocean. **1879–87** Stanley engaged by King Leopold II of Belgium to sign protection treaties with local chiefs and the 'Congo Free State' was awarded to Leopold by 1884–85 Berlin Conference; great expansion in rubber export, using forced labour. **1908** Leopold was forced to relinquish personal control of Congo Free State, after international condemnation of human-rights abuses. Became a colony of the Belgian Congo and important exporter of minerals. **1959** Riots in Kinshasa (Léopoldville) persuaded Belgium to decolonize rapidly. **1960** Independence achieved as Republic of the Congo. Civil war broke out between central government based in Kinshasa (Léopoldville) with Joseph Kasavubu as president, and rich mining province of Katanga. **1961** Former prime minister Patrice Lumumba was murdered in Katanga; fighting between mercenaries engaged by Katanga secessionist leader Moise Tshombe, and United Nations (UN) troops; Kasai and Kivu provinces also sought (briefly) to secede. **1963** Katanga secessionist war ended; Tshombe forced into exile. **1964** Tshombe returned from exile to become prime minister; pro-Marxist groups took control of eastern Zaire. **1965** Western-backed Col Sese Seko Mobutu seized power in coup, ousting Kasavubu and Tshombe. **1971** Country renamed Republic of Zaire, with Mobutu as president, as *authenticité* (Africanization) policy launched. **1972** Mobutu's Popular Movement of the Revolution (MPR) became the only legal political party. Katanga province was renamed Shaba. **1974** Foreign-owned businesses and plantations seized by Mobutu and given to his political allies. **1977** Zairean guerrillas invaded Shaba province from Angola, but were repulsed by Moroccan, French, and Belgian paratroopers. **1980s** The collapse in world copper prices increased foreign debts, and international creditors forced a series of austerity programmes. **1991** After antigovernment riots, Mobutu agreed to end the ban on multiparty politics and share power with the opposition. **1993** Rival pro- and anti-Mobutu governments were created. **1994** There was an influx of Rwandan refugees. **1995** There was secessionist activity in Shaba and Kasai provinces and interethnic warfare in Kivu, adjoining Rwanda in the east. **1996** Thousands of refugees were allowed to return to Rwanda. **1997** Mobutu was ousted by the rebel forces of Laurent Kabila, who declared himself president and renamed Zaire the Democratic Republic of the Congo. There was fighting between army factions. **1998** There was a rebellion by Tutsi-led forces, backed by Rwanda and Uganda, against President Kabila; government troops aided by Angola and Zimbabwe put down the rebellion. A constituent assembly was appointed prior to a general election. UN-urged peace talks and a ceasefire agreed by rebel forces failed. **1999** A peace deal, signed by both the government and rebel factions, was broken with fighting in the north of the country and a reported bombing by the government in an attempt to free 700 Zimbabwean troops besieged by rebels.

Congo Republic of

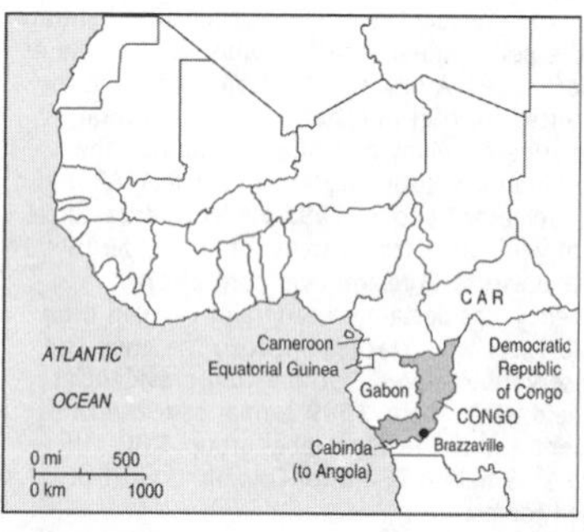

National name *République du Congo* **Area** 342,000 sq km/ 132,046 sq mi **Capital** Brazzaville **Major towns/cities** Pool, Pointe-Noire, Nkayi, Loubomo, Bouenza, Cuvette, Niari, Plateaux

Government

Head of state Denis Sassou-Nguessou from 1997 **Head of government** Charles David Ganao from 1996 **Political system** nationalistic socialist **Armed forces** 10,000 (1997); plus a paramilitary force of 5,000 **Conscription** national service is voluntary **Defence spend** (% GDP) 2.5 (1997) **Education spend** (% GNP) 6.2 (1996) **Health spend** (% GDP) 1.8 (1990–95) **Death penalty** retains the death penalty for ordinary crimes but can be considered abolitionist in practice (last execution 1982)

Population and society

Population 2,864,000 (1999 est) **Population growth rate** 2.8% (1995–2000); 2.6% (2000–05) **Ethnic groups** predominantly Bantu; population comprises 15 main ethnic groups and 75 tribes. The Kongo, or Bakongo, account for about 45% of the population, then come the Bateke, or Teke, at about 20%, and then the Mboshi, or Boubangui, about 16% **Religion** animist, Christian, Muslim **Life expectancy** 48 (men); 51 (women) (1995–2000) **Literacy rate** 85% (men); 70% (women) (1997 est)

Economy and resources

GDP (US$) 1.96 billion (1998) **GNP** (US$) 1.9 billion (1998) **GNP per capita (PPP)** (US$) 1,430 (1998) **Real GDP growth** (% change on previous year) 2.5 (1998) **Consumer price inflation** 19.1% (1997) **Foreign debt** (US$) 5.07 billion (1997) **Resources** petroleum, natural gas, lead, zinc, gold, copper, phosphate, iron ore, potash, bauxite **Exports** petroleum and petroleum products, saw logs and veneer logs, veneer sheets. Principal market: USA 36.9% (1997) **Imports** machinery, chemical products, iron and steel, transport equipment, foodstuffs. Principal source: France 21.5% (1997)

▪ Tourist information

Time difference GMT +1 **Currency** franc CFA **Language** French (official); Kongo languages; local patois Monokutuba and Lingala **Visa requirements** UK: visa required. USA: visa required **Embassy in the UK** Honorary Consulate of the Republic of the Congo, Alliance House, 12 Caxton Street, London SW1H 0QS. Tel: (020) 7222 7575; fax: (020) 7233 2087 **British embassy** British Consulate, Côte de l'Hotel Méridien, rue Lyantey 26, Brazzaville. Tel: (242) 838 527; fax: (242) 837 257 (The embassy closed on 26 July 1991; diplomatic accreditation has been transferred to the British embassy in Kinshasa on a nonresident basis.) **Chamber of commerce** Chambre Nationale de Commerce, BP 1438, Brazzaville. Tel: (242) 832 956 **Office hours** usually 0800–1200 and 1430–1800 Mon–Fri; 0800–1200 Sat **Banking hours** 0630–1300 Mon–Fri (counters close at 1130) **Airports** international airports: Brazzaville (Maya-Maya), Pointe-Noire; six domestic airports; total passenger km: 283 million (1995) **Major ports** Pointe-Noire **Major holidays** 1 January, 18 March, 1 May, 31 July, 13–15 August, 1 November, 25, 31 December; variable: Good Friday, Easter Monday

Chronology

late 15th century First visited by Portuguese explorers, at which time the Bakongo (a six-state confederation centred south of the Congo River in Angola) and Bateke, both Bantu groups, were the chief kingdoms. **16th century** The Portuguese, in collaboration with coastal peoples, exported slaves from the interior to plantations in Brazil and São Tomé; missionaries spread Roman Catholicism. **1880** French explorer Pierre Savorgnan de Brazza established French claims to coastal region, with the makoko (king) of the Bateke accepting French protection. **1905** There was international outrage at revelations of the brutalities of forced labour as ivory and rubber resources were ruthlessly exploited by private concessionaries. **1910** As Moyen-Congo became part of French Equatorial Africa, which also comprised Gabon and the Central African Republic, with the capital at Brazzaville. **1920s** More than 17,000 were killed as forced labour was used to build the Congo-Ocean railroad; first Bakongo political organization founded. **1940–44** Supported the 'Free French' anti-Nazi resistance cause during World War II, Brazzaville serving as capital for Gen Charles de Gaulle's forces. **1946** Became autonomous, with a territorial assembly and representation in French parliament. **1960** Achieved independence from France, with Abbé Fulbert Youlou, a moderate Catholic Bakongo priest, as the first president. **1963** Alphonse Massamba-Débat became president and a single-party state was established under the socialist National Revolutionary Movement (MNR). **1968** A military coup, led by Capt Marien Ngouabi, ousted Massamba-Débat. **1970** A Marxist People's Republic declared, with Ngouabi's PCT the only legal party. /ITEM> **1977** Ngouabi was assassinated in a plot by Massamba-Débat, who was executed. **early 1980s** Petroleum production increased fivefold. **1990** The PCT abandoned Marxist-Leninism and promised multiparty politics and market-centred reforms in an economy crippled by foreign debt. **1992** Multiparty elections gave the coalition dominated by the Pan-African Union for Social Democracy (UPADS) an assembly majority, with Pascal Lissouba elected president. **1995** A new broad-based government was formed, including opposition groups; market-centred economic reforms were instigated, including privatization. **1996** Charles David Ganao was appointed prime minister. **1997** Violence between factions continued despite the unity government. Sassou-Nguesso took over the presidency.

Costa Rica Republic of

National name *República de Costa Rica* **Area** 51,100 sq km/19,729 sq mi **Capital** San José **Major towns/cities** Alajuela, Cartago, Limón, Puntarenas

Government

Head of state and government Miguel Angel Rodriguez Echeverria, from 1998 **Political system** liberal democracy **Armed forces** army abolished in 1948; 4,300 civil guards and 3,200 rural guards **Defence spend** (% GDP) 0.7 (1997) **Education spend** (% GNP) 5.3 (1996) **Health spend** (% GDP) 6.3 (1990–95) **Death penalty** abolished in 1877

Population and society

Population 3,933,000 (1999 est) **Population growth rate** 2.5% (1995–2000) **Ethnic groups** about 97% of the population is of European descent, mostly Spanish, and about 2% is of African origin **Religion** Roman Catholic 90% **Life expectancy** 74 (men); 79 (women) (1995–2000) **Literacy rate** 95% (men); 95% (women) (1997 est) **Unemployment** 5.7% (1997)

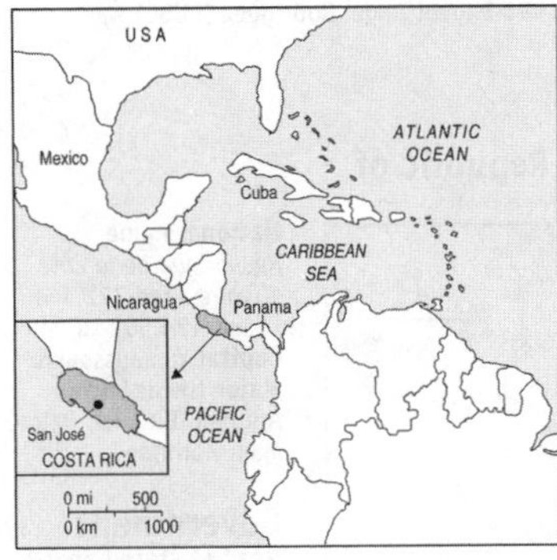

Economy and resources

GDP (US$) 10.25 billion (1998) **GNP** (US$) 9.8 billion (1998) **GNP per capita (PPP)** (US$) 6,620 (1997) **Real GDP growth** (% change on previous year) 4.6 (1997) **Consumer price inflation** 15% (1998) **Foreign debt** (US$) 3.54 billion (1997) **Resources** gold, salt, hydro power **Exports** bananas, coffee, sugar, cocoa, textiles, seafood, meat, tropical fruit. Principal market: USA 52.5% (1998) **Imports** raw materials for industry and agriculture, consumer goods, machinery and transport equipment, construction materials. Principal source: USA 42.1% (1998)

▪ Tourist information

Time difference GMT −6 **Currency** colón **Language** Spanish (official) **Visa requirements** UK: visa not required. USA: visa not required **Embassy in the UK** Embassy and Consulate, Flat 1, 14 Lancaster Gate, London W2 3LH. Tel: (020) 7706 8844; fax: (020) 7706 8655 **British embassy** Apartado 815, 11th Floor, Edificio Centro Colón, 1007 San José. Tel (506) 221 5566; fax: (506) 233 9938 **Chamber of commerce** Cámara de Comercio de Costa Rica, Apartado 1114, Urbanización Tournón, 1000 San José. Tel: (506) 221 0005; fax: (506) 233 7091 **Office hours** 0800–1200 and 1400–1600 Mon–Fri **Banking hours** 0900–1500 Mon–Fri **Airports** international airports: San José (Juan Santamaría), Liberia (Daniel Oduber Quirós); 11 domestic airports as well as charter services to provincial towns and villages); total passenger km: 1,920 million (1997 est) **Major ports** Limón, Puntarenas **Chief tourist attractions** nature reserves and national parks make up one-third of the country; Irazú and Poás volcanoes; Orosí valley; colonial ruins at Ujarras; railway through rainforest to Limón; San José (the capital); Pacific beaches; Caribbean beaches at Limón **Major holidays** 1 January, 19 March, 11 April, 1 May, 29 June, 25 July, 2, 15 August, 15 September, 12 October, 8, 25 December; variable: Corpus Christi, Good Friday, Holy Saturday, Holy Thursday

Chronology

1502 Visited by Christopher Columbus, who named the area Costa Rica (the rich coast), observing the gold decorations worn by the Guaymi American Indians. **1506** Colonized by Spain, but there was fierce guerrilla resistance by the indigenous population. Many later died from exposure to European diseases. **18th century** Settlements began to be established in the fertile central highlands, including San José and Alajuela. **1808** Coffee was introduced from Cuba and soon became the staple crop. **1821** Independence achieved from Spain, and was joined initially with Mexico. **1824** Became part of United Provinces (Federation) of Central America, also embracing El Salvador, Guatemala, Honduras, and Nicaragua. **1838** Became fully independent when it seceded from the Federation. **later 19th century** Immigration by Europeans to run and work small coffee farms. **1940–44** Liberal reforms, including recognition of workers' rights and minimum wages, were introduced by President Rafael Angel Calderón Guradia, founder of the United Christian Socialist Party (PUSC). **1948** Brief civil war following a disputed presidential election. **1949** New constitution adopted, giving women and blacks the vote. National army abolished and replaced by civil guard. José Figueres Ferrer, cofounder of the PLN, elected president; he embarked on an ambitious socialist programme, nationalizing the banks and introducing a social security system. **1958–73** Mainly conservative administrations. **1978** Sharp deterioration in the state of the economy. **1982** A harsh austerity programme was introduced. **1985** Following border clashes with Nicaraguan Sandinista forces, a US-trained antiguerrilla guard was formed. **1986** Oscar Arias Sanchez (PLN) won the presidency on a neutralist platform. **1987** Arias won the Nobel Prize for Peace for devising a Central American peace plan signed by the leaders of Nicaragua, El Salvador,

Guatemala, and Honduras. **1998** Miguel Angel Rodriguez (PUSC) was elected president.

Côte d'Ivoire Republic of

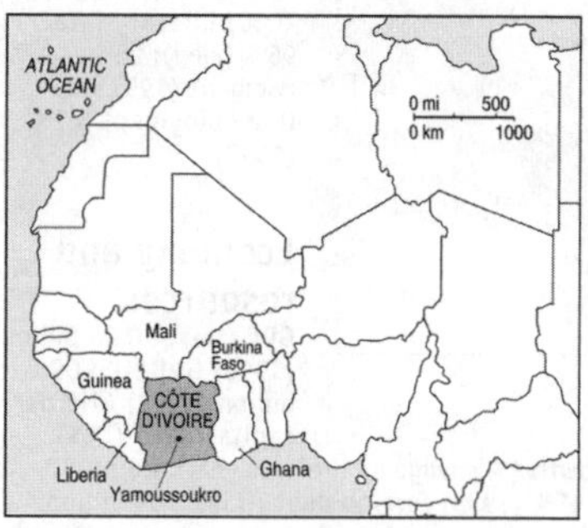

National name *République de la Côte d'Ivoire* **Area** 322,463 sq km/124,502 sq mi **Capital** Yamoussoukro **Major towns/cities** Abidjan, Bouaké, Daloa, Man, Korhogo

Government

Head of state General Robert Guei from 1999 **Head of government** Kablan Daniel Duncan from 1993 **Political system** emergent democracy **Armed forces** 8,400 (1997); plus paramilitary forces numbering 7,000 **Conscription** selective conscription for six months **Defence spend** (% GDP) 0.9 (1997) **Education spend** (% GNP) 5 (1996) **Health spend** (% GDP) 1.4 (1990–95) **Death penalty** retains the death penalty for ordinary crimes but can be considered abolitionist in practice

Population and society

Population 14,527,000 (1999 est) **Population growth rate** 1.8% (1995–2000) **Ethnic groups** no single dominant ethnic group; main groups include the Agni, Baoule, Krou, Senoufou, and Mandingo. There are about 2 million Africans who have settled from neighbouring countries, particularly Burkina Faso. Europeans number about 70,000 **Religion** animist, Muslim (mainly in north), Christian (mainly Roman Catholic in south) **Life expectancy** 46 (men); 47 (women) (1995–2000) **Literacy rate** 57% (men); 34% (women) (1997 est) **Unemployment** N/A

Economy and resources

GDP (US$) 11.04 billion (1998) **GNP** (US$) 10.1 billion (1998) **GNP per capita (PPP)** (US$) 1,730 (1998) **Real GDP growth** (% change on previous year) 5.5 (1998) **Consumer price inflation** 3.5% (1998) **Foreign debt** (US$) 15.6 billion (1997) **Resources** petroleum, natural gas, diamonds, gold, nickel, reserves of manganese, iron ore, bauxite **Exports** cocoa beans and products, petroleum products, timber, coffee, cotton, tinned tuna. Principal market: Netherlands 16.6% (1997) **Imports** crude petroleum, machinery and vehicles, pharmaceuticals, fresh fish, plastics, cereals. Principal source: France 28.5% (1997)

▪ Tourist information

Time difference GMT +/– 0 **Currency** franc CFA **Language** French (official); over 60 local languages **Visa requirements** UK: visa required. USA: visa not required for a stay of less than 90 days **Embassy in the UK** 2 Upper Belgrave Street, London SW1X 8BJ. Tel: (020) 7235 6991; fax: (020) 7259 5439 **British embassy** 3rd Floor, Immeuble 'Les Harmonies', Angle boulevard Carde et avenue Dr Jamot, Plateau, Abidjan. Tel: (225) 226850/1/2; fax: (225) 223 221 **Chamber of commerce** Chambre de Commerce et d'Industrie de Côte d'Ivoire, 01 BP 1399, 6 avenue Joseph Anoma, Abidjan 01. Tel: (225) 331 600; fax: (225) 323 946 **Office hours** 0730–1200 and 1430–1730 Mon–Fri; 0800–1200 Sat **Banking hours** 0800–1130 and 1430–1630 Mon–Fri **Airports** international airports: Abidjan (Port Bouet), Bouaké, Yamoussoukro (San Pedro); domestic services to all major towns; total passenger km: 302 million (1995) **Major ports** Abidjan, San Pedro **Chief tourist attractions** game reserves; lagoons; forests; Abidjan **Major holidays** 1 January, 1 May, 15 August, 1 November, 7, 24–25, 31 December; variable: Ascension Thursday, Eid-ul-Adha, Good Friday, Easter Monday, Whit Monday, end of Ramadan

Chronology

1460s Portuguese navigators arrived. **16th century** Ivory export trade developed by Europeans and slave trade, though to a lesser extent than neighbouring areas; Krou people migrated from Liberia to the west and Senoufo and Lubi from the north. **late 17th century** French coastal trading posts established at Assini and Grand Bassam. **18th–19th centuries** Akan peoples, including the Baoulé, immigrated from the east and Malinke from the northwest. **1840s** French began to conclude commercial treaties with local rulers. **1893** Colony of Côte d'Ivoire created by French, after war with Mandinkas; Baoulé resistance continued until 1917. **1904** Became part of French West Africa; cocoa production encouraged. **1940–42** Under pro-Nazi French Vichy regime. **1946** Became overseas territory in French Union, with own territorial assembly and representation in French parliament: Felix Houphouët-Boigny, a Western-educated Baoulé chief who had formed the Democratic Party (PDCI) to campaign for autonomy, was elected to the French assembly. **1947** A French-controlled area to the north, which had been added to Côte d'Ivoire in 1932, separated to create new state of Upper Volta (now Burkina Faso). **1950–54** Port of Abidjan constructed. **1958** Achieved internal self-government. **1960** Independence secured, with Houphouët-Boigny as president of a one-party state. **1960s–1980s** Political stability, close links maintained with France and economic expansion of 10% per annum, as the country became one of the world's largest coffee producers. **1986** The country's name was officially changed from Ivory Coast to Côte d'Ivoire. **1987–93** Per capita incomes fell by 25% owing to an austerity programme promoted by the International Monetary Fund. **1990** There were strikes and student unrest. Houphoüet-Boigny was re-electedas president as multiparty politics were re-established. **1993** Houphouët-Boigny died and was succeeded by parliamentary speaker and Baoulé Henri Konan Bedie. **1999** After a largely bloodless coup over Christmas 1999 Bedie was replaced by a new military leader, General Robert Guei.

Croatia Republic of

National name *Republika Hrvatska* **Area** 56,538 sq km/21,829 sq mi **Capital** Zagreb **Major towns/cities** Osijek, Split, Dubrovnik, Rijeka, Zadar, Pula

Government

Head of state Stipe Mesic from 2000 **Head of government** Zlatko Matesa from 1995 **Political system** emergent democracy **Armed forces** 58,000 (1997); plus 40,000 in paramilitary forces **Conscription** compulsory for ten months **Defence spend** (% GDP) 5.7 (1997) **Education spend** (% GDP) 5.3 (1996) **Health spend** (% GDP) 8.5 (1990–95) **Death penalty** abolished in 1990

Population and society

Population 4,477,000 (1999 est) **Population growth rate** –0.1% (1995–2000); –0.1% (2000–05) **Ethnic groups** in 1991, 77% of the population were ethnic Croats, 12% were ethnic Serbs, and 1% were Slovenes. The civil war that began in 1992 displaced more than 300,000 Croats from Serbian enclaves within the republic, and created some 500,000 refugees from Bosnia in the republic. Serbs are most thickly settled in areas bordering Bosnia-Herzegovina, and in Slavonia, although more than 150,000 fled from Krajina to Bosnia-Herzegovina and Serbia following the region's recapture by the Croatian army in August 1995. **Religion** Roman Catholic (Croats); Orthodox Christian (Serbs) **Life expectancy** 69 (men); 77 (women) (1995–2000) **Literacy rate** 99% (men); 97% (women) (1997 est) **Unemployment** 17.6% (1998)

Economy and resources

GDP (US$) 19.08 billion (1998 est) **GNP** (US$) 20.7 billion (1998) **GNP per capita (PPP)** (US$) 7,100 (1998 est) **Real GDP growth** (% change on previous year) 4 (1998) **Consumer price inflation** 4.3% (1998) **Foreign debt** (US$) 6.8 billion (1997) **Resources** petroleum, natural gas, coal, lignite, bauxite, iron ore, salt **Exports** machinery and transport equipment, chemicals, foodstuffs, miscellaneous manufactured items (mainly clothing). Principal market: Italy 17.7% (1998) **Imports** machinery and transport equipment, basic manufactures, mineral fuels, miscellaneous manufactured articles. Principal source: Germany 19.3% (1998)

▪ Tourist information

Time difference GMT +1 **Currency** kuna **Language** Croatian variant of Serbo-Croatian (official); Serbian variant of Serbo-Croatian also widely spoken, particularly in border areas in east **Visa requirements** UK: visa not required. USA: visa required **Embassy in the UK** 18–21 Jermyn Street, London SW1Y 6HP. Tel: (020) 7434 2946; fax: (020) 7434 2953 **British embassy** PO Box 454, 2nd Floor, Astra Tower, Tratinska, 4100 Zagreb. Tel: (1) 334 245; fax: (1) 338 893 **Chamber of commerce** Croatian Chamber of Commerce, Trg. Ruzveltov 1, 41000 Zagreb. Tel: (1) 453 422; fax: (1) 448 618 **Office hours** 0800–1600 Mon–Fri **Banking hours** 0700–1500 Mon–Fri; 0800–1400 Sat **Airports** international airports: Zagreb (Pleso), Dubrovnik; three domestic airports; total passenger km: 546 million (1997) **Major ports** chief port: Rijeka (Fiume); other ports: Zadar, Sibenik, Split, Dubrovnik **Chief tourist attractions** Adriatic coast with 1,185 islands. Owing to civil conflict which began in 1991, tourist activity has been greatly reduced; historic cities, notably Dubrovnik, have been severely damaged **Major holidays** 1, 6 January, 1, 30 May, 22 June, 15 August, 1 November, 25–26 December; variable: Good Friday, Easter Monday

Chronology

early centuries AD Part of Roman region of Pannonia. **AD 395** On division of Roman Empire, stayed in western half, along with Slovenia and Bosnia. **7th century** Settled by Carpathian Croats, from northeast; Christianity adopted. **924** Formed by Tomislav into independent kingdom, which incorporated Bosnia from 10th century. **12th–19th centuries** Autonomy under Hungarian crown, following dynastic union in 1102. **1526–1699** Slavonia, in east, held by Ottoman Turks, while Serbs were invited by Austria to settle along the border with Ottoman-ruled Bosnia, in Vojna Krajina (military frontier). **1797–1815** Dalmatia, in west, ruled by France. **19th century** Part of Austro-Hungarian Habsburg Empire. **1918** On dissolution of Habsburg Empire, joined Serbia, Slovenia, and Montenegro in 'Kingdom of Serbs, Croats, and Slovenes', under Serbian Karageorgevic dynasty. **1929** The Kingdom became Yugoslavia. Croatia continued its campaign for autonomy. **1930s** Ustasa, a Croat terrorist organization, began a campaign against dominance of Yugoslavia by the non-Catholic Serbs. **1941–44** Following German invasion, a 'Greater Croatia' Nazi puppet state, including most of Bosnia and western Serbia, formed under Ustasa leader, Ante Pavelic; more than half a million Serbs, Jews, and members of the Romany community were massacred in extermination camps. **1945** Became constituent republic of Yugoslavia Socialist Federation after communist partisans, led by Croat Marshal Tito, overthrew Pavelic. **1970s** Separatist demands resurfaced, provoking a crackdown. **late 1980s** Spiralling inflation and a deterioration in living standards sparked industrial unrest and a rise in nationalist sentiment, which affected the local communist party. **1989** The formation of opposition parties was permitted. **1990** The communists were defeated by the conservative nationalist CDU led by ex-Partisan Franjo Tudjman in the first free election since 1938. Sovereignty was declared. **1991** The Serb-dominated region of Krajina in the southwest announced its secession from Croatia. Croatia declared independence, leading to military conflict with Serbia, and civil war ensued. **1992** A United Nations (UN) peace accord was accepted; independence was recognized by the European Community (EC) and the USA; Croatia joined the UN. A UN peacekeeping force was stationed in Croatia. Tudjman was elected president. **1993** A government offensive was launched to retake parts of Serb-held Krajina, violating the 1992 UN peace accord. **1994** There was an accord with Muslims and ethnic Croats within Bosnia, to the east, to link the recently formed Muslim–Croat federation with Croatia. **1995** Serb-held western Slavonia and Krajina were captured by government forces; there was an exodus of Croatian Serbs. The offensive extended into Bosnia-Herzegovina to halt a Bosnian Serb assault on Bihac in western Bosnia. Serbia agreed to cede control of eastern Slavonia to Croatia over a two-year period. Zlatko Matesa was appointed prime minister **1996** Diplomatic relations between Croatia and Yugoslavia were restored. Croatia entered the Council of Europe. **1997** The opposition was successful in local elections. The constitution was amended to prevent the weakening of Croatia's national sovereignty. **1998** Croatia resumed control over East Slavonia. **2000** In parliamentary elections, the ruling Croatian Democratic Union (HDZ) lost heavily to a centre-left coalition. Stipe Mesic, an opponent of Tudjman, was elected to succeed him as president.

Cuba Republic of

National name *República de Cuba* **Area** 110,860 sq km/42,803 sq mi **Capital** Havana **Major towns/cities** Santiago de Cuba, Camagüey, Holguín, Guantánamo, Santa Clara, Bayamo, Cienfuegos

Government

Head of state and government Fidel Castro Ruz from 1959 **Political system** communist **Armed forces** 60,000 (1997) **Conscription** compulsory for two years **Defence spend** (% GDP) 5.2 (1997) **Education spend** (% GNP) 6.6 (1993–94) **Health spend** (% GDP) 7.9 (1990–95) **Death penalty** retained and used for ordinary crimes

Population and society

Population 11,160,000 (1999 est) **Population growth rate** 0.4% (1995–2000) **Ethnic groups** predominantly of mixed Spanish and African or Spanish and American Indian origin **Religion** Roman Catholic; also Episcopalians and Methodists **Life expectancy** 74 (men); 78 (women) (1995–2000) **Literacy rate** 96% (men); 96% (women) (1997 est) **Unemployment** 8% (1996 est)

Economy and resources

GDP (US$) 19.4 billion (1998 est) **GNP** (US$) 19.2 billion (1997 est) **GNP per capita (PPP)** (US$) 3,520 (1997 est) **Real GDP growth** (% change on previous year) 1 (1998) **Consumer price inflation** 3.3% (1998) **Foreign debt** (US$) 34.7 billion (1997) **Resources** iron ore, copper, chromite, gold, manganese, nickel, cobalt, silver, salt **Exports** sugar, minerals, tobacco, citrus fruits, fish products. Principal market: Russia 17.6% (1997) **Imports** mineral fuels, machinery and transport equipment, foodstuffs, beverages. Principal source: Spain 13.5% (1997)

▪ Tourist information

Time difference GMT –5 **Currency** Cuban peso **Language** Spanish **Visa requirements** UK: visa required. USA: visa required **Embassy in the UK** 167 High Holborn, London WC1V 6PA. Tel: (020) 7240 2488; fax: (020) 7836 2602 **British embassy** Calle 34, 708 Miramar, Havana. Tel: (7) 331 771; fax: (7) 338 104 **Chamber of commerce** Cámara de Comercio de la República de Cuba, Calle 21, No. 661/701, esq Calle A, Apartado 4237, Vedado, Havana. Tel: (7) 303 356; fax: (7) 333 042 **Office hours** 0830–1230 and 1330–1630 Mon–Fri; some offices also open 0800–1700 on alternate Saturdays **Banking hours** 0830–1200 and 1330–1500 Mon–Fri; 0830–1030 Sat **Airports** international airports: Havana, Santiago de Cuba, Holguín, Camagüey, Varadero; 11 domestic airports; total passenger km: 3,615 million (1997 est) **Chief tourist attractions** sandy beaches; Sierra Maestra Mountain range, which encircles the port of Santiago; mountain forest of pine and mahogany; Havana city centre, a United Nations (UN) World Heritage site, with colonial fortresses and castles; Santiago, the former capital, with Museum of Colonial Art and Festival de Carib (April) **Major holidays** 1 January, 1 May, 25–26 July, 10 October

Chronology

3rd century AD The Ciboney, Cuba's earliest known inhabitants, were dislodged by the immigration of Taino, Arawak Indians from Venezuela. **1492** Christopher Columbus landed in Cuba and claimed it for Spain. **1511** Spanish settlement established at Baracoa by Diego Velazquez. **1523** Decline of American Indian population and rise of sugar plantations led to import of slaves from Africa. **mid-19th century** Cuba produced one-third of the world's sugar. **1868–78** Unsuccessful first war for independence from Spain. **1886** Slavery was abolished. **1895–98** Further uprising against Spanish rule, led by José Martí, who died in combat; 200,000 soldiers deployed by Spain. **1898** USA defeated Spain in Spanish-American War; Spain gave up all claims to Cuba, which was ceded to the USA. **1901** Cuba achieved independence; Tomás Estrada Palma became first president of the Republic of Cuba. **1906–09** Brief period of US administration after Estrada resigned in the face of an armed rebellion by political opponents. **1924–33** Gerado Machado established a brutal dictatorship. **1925** Socialist Party founded, from which the Communist Party later developed. **1933** Army sergeant Fulgencio Batista seized power. **1934** USA abandoned its right to intervene in Cuba's internal affairs. **1944** Batista retired and was succeeded by the civilian Ramon Gray San Martin. **1952** Batista seized power again to begin an oppressive and corrupt regime. **1953** Fidel Castro Ruz led an unsuccessful coup against Batista. **1956** Second unsuccessful coup by Castro. **1959** Batista overthrown by Castro and his 9,000-strong guerrilla army. Constitution was replaced by a 'Fundamental Law', making Castro prime minister, his brother Raúl Castro his deputy, and Argentine-born Ernesto 'Che' Guevara third in command. **1960** All US businesses in Cuba appropriated without compensation; USA broke off diplomatic relations. **1961** USA sponsored an unsuccessful invasion by Cuban exiles at the Bay of Pigs. Castro announced that Cuba had become a communist state, with a Marxist-Leninist programme of economic development, and became allied with the USSR. **1962** Cuban missile crisis: Cuba was expelled from the Organization of American States. Castro responded by tightening relations with the USSR, which installed nuclear missiles in Cuba (subsequently removed at US insistence). US trade embargo imposed. **1965** Cuba's sole political party renamed Cuban Communist Party (PCC). With Soviet help, Cuba began to make considerable economic and social progress. **1972** Cuba became a full member of the Moscow-based Council for Mutual Economic Assistance (COMECON). **1976** New socialist constitution approved; Castro elected president. **1976–81** Castro became involved in extensive international commitments, sending troops as Soviet surrogates, particularly to Africa. **1982** Cuba joined other Latin American countries in giving moral support to Argentina in its dispute with Britain over the Falklands. **1984** Castro tried to improve US–Cuban relations by discussing exchange of US prisoners in Cuba for Cuban 'undesirables' in the USA. **1988** A peace accord with South Africa was signed, agreeing to the withdrawal of Cuban troops from Angola, as part of a reduction in Cuba's overseas military activities. **1991** Soviet troops were withdrawn with the collapse of the USSR. **1993** The US trade embargo was tightened; market-oriented reforms were introduced in the face of a deteriorating economy. **1994** There was a refugee exodus; US policy on Cuban asylum seekers was revised. **1998** Castro was confirmed as president for a further five-year term. **1999** In an immigration dispute with the US, which focused on one child, Cuba demanded the return of illegal immigrants, and condemned the use of the US justice system on such matters.

Cyprus Greek Republic of Cyprus in south, and Turkish Republic of Northern Cyprus in north

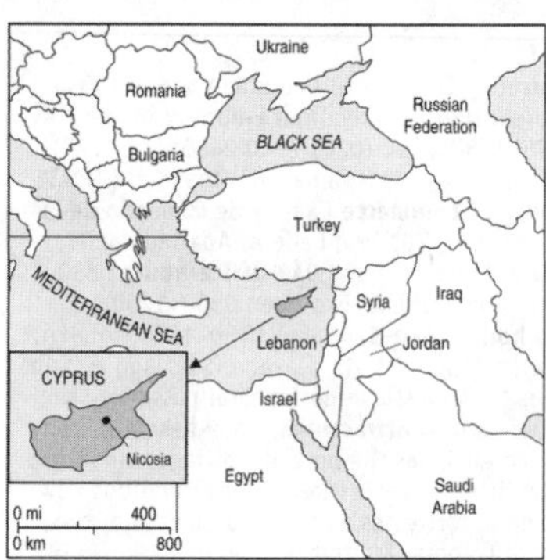

National name *Kypriakí Dimokratía* (south), and *Kibris Cumhuriyeti* (north) **Area** 9,251 sq km/3,571 sq mi (3,335 sq km/1,287 sq mi is Turkish-occupied) **Capital** Nicosia (divided between Greek and Turkish Cypriots) **Major towns/cities** Morphou, Limassol, Larnaca, Famagusta, Paphos

Government

Head of state and government Glafkos Clerides (Greek) from 1993, Rauf Denktaş (Turkish) from 1976 **Political system** liberal democracy **Armed forces** National Guard of 10,000 (1997); Turkish Republic of Northern Cyprus (TRNC) 4,000, plus 26,000 reserves (1995) **Conscription** is for 26 months **Defence spend** (% GDP) 5.2 (1996) **Education spend** (% GNP) 4.4 (1995) **Health spend** (% GDP) 2.1 (1994) **Death penalty** laws provide for the death penalty only for exceptional crimes such as under military law or crimes committed in exceptional circumstances such as wartime; last execution 1962

Population and society

Population 779,000 (1999 est) **Population growth rate** 1.1% (1995–2025) **Ethnic groups** about 80% of the population is of Greek origin, while about 18% are of Turkish descent, and live in the northern part of the island within the self-styled Turkish Republic of Northern Cyprus **Religion** Greek Orthodox, Sunni Muslim **Life expectancy** 76 (men); 80 (women) (1995–2000) **Literacy rate** 98% (men); 94% (women) (1997 est) **Unemployment** 3.4% (1998)

Economy and resources

GDP (US$) 9.0 billion (1998) **GNP** (US$) 10.8 billion (1997) **GNP per capita (PPP)** (US$) 14,090 (1997 est) **Real GDP growth** (% change on previous year) 5 (1998) **Consumer price inflation** 2.2% (1998) **Foreign debt** (US$) 7.9 billion (1997) **Resources** copper precipitates, beutonite, umber and other ochres **Exports** clothing, potatoes, pharmaceutical products, manufactured foods, minerals, citrus fruits, industrial products. Principal market: UK 15.5% (1998) **Imports** mineral fuels, textiles, vehicles, metals, tobacco, consumer goods, basic manufactures, machinery and transport equipment, food and live animals. Principal source: USA 11.8% (1998)

■ Tourist information

Time difference GMT +2 **Currency** Cyprus pound and Turkish lira **Language** Greek and Turkish (official), English **Visa requirements** UK: visa not required. USA: visa not required **Embassy in the UK** 93 Park Street, London W1Y 4ET. Tel: (020) 7499 8272; fax: (020) 7491 0691 **British embassy** British High Commission, PO Box 1978, Alexander Pallis Street, Nicosia. Tel: (2) 473 131/7; fax: (2) 367 198 **Chamber of commerce** Cyprus Chamber of Commerce and Industry, PO Box 1455, 38 Grivas Dhigenis Avenue, Nicosia. Tel: (2) 449 500; fax: (2) 449 048 **Office hours** all offices have half-day closing on Wed, otherwise 0800–1300 and 1600–1900 Mon–Fri (summer); 0800–1300 and 1500–1800 Mon–Fri (winter) **Banking hours** generally 0815–1230 Mon–Fri; in tourist areas also 1630–1830 (summer, except Tue) and 1530–1730 (winter) **Airports** international airports: Nicosia (Larnaca), Paphos; total passenger km: 2,657 million (1997 est) **Major ports** Limassol, Larnaca, and Paphos (Greek); Kyrenia and Famagusta (Turkish) **Chief tourist attractions** sandy beaches; forested mountains; winter skiing; archaeological and historic sites; the old city of Nicosia, with its Venetian walls and cathedral (International State Fair and Nicosia Art Festival in May); Limassol, with its 14th-century castle; Spring Carnival, arts festival (July), wine festival (September) **Major holidays** 1, 6 January, 25 March, 1 May, 28–29 October, 25–26 December; variable: Eid-ul-Adha, Good Friday, Easter Monday, end of Ramadan, Holy Saturday, Prophet's Birthday

Chronology

14th–11th centuries BC Colonized by Myceneans and Achaeans from Greece. **9th century BC** Phoenicans settled in Cyprus. **7th century BC** Several Cypriot kingdoms flourished under Assyrian influence. **414–374 BC** Under Evagoras of Salamis (in eastern Cyprus) the island's ten city kingdoms were united into one state and Greek culture, including the Greek alphabet, was promoted. **333–58 BC** Became part of the Greek Hellenistic and then, from 294 BC, the Egypt-based Ptolemaic empire. **58 BC** Cyprus was annexed by the Roman Empire. **AD** 45 Christianity introduced. **AD** 395 When the Roman Empire divided, Cyprus was allotted to the Byzantine Empire. **7th–10th centuries** Byzantines and Muslim Arabs fought for control of Cyprus. **1191** Richard the Lionheart of England conquered Cyprus as a base for Crusades; he later sold it to a French noble, Guy de Lusignan, who established a feudal monarchy which ruled for three centuries. **1498** The Venetian Republic took control of Cyprus. **1571** Conquered by Ottoman Turks, who introduced Turkish Muslim settlers, but permitted Christianity to continue in rural areas. **1821–33** Period of unrest, following execution of popular Greek Orthodox Archbishop Kyprianos. **1878** Anglo-Turkish Convention: Turkey ceded Cyprus to British administration in return for defensive alliance. **1914** Formally annexed by Britain after Turkey entered World War I as a Central Power. **1915** Greece rejected an offer of Cyprus in return for entry into World War I on Allied side. **1925** Cyprus became a crown colony. **1931** Greek Cypriots rioted in support of demand for union with Greece (*enosis*); legislative council suspended. **1948** Greek Cypriots rejected new constitution because it did not offer links with Greece. **1955** The National Organization of Cypriot Fighters (EOKA) began a terrorist campaign for *enosis*. **1958** Britain proposed autonomy for Greek and Turkish Cypriot communities under British sovereignty; plan accepted by Turks, rejected by Greeks; violence increased. **1959** Britain, Greece, and Turkey agreed to Cypriot independence, with partition and *enosis* both ruled out. **1960** Cyprus became an independent republic with Archbishop Makarios as president; Britain retained two military bases. **1963** Makarios proposed major constitutional reforms; Turkish Cypriots withdrew from government and formed separate enclaves; communal fighting broke out. **1964** United Nations (UN) peacekeeping force installed. **1968** Intercommunal talks made no progress; Turkish Cypriots demanded federalism; Greek Cypriots insisted on unitary state. **1974** Coup by Greek officers in Cypriot National Guard installed Nikos Sampson as president; Turkey, fearing *enosis*, invaded northern Cyprus; Greek Cypriot military regime collapsed; President Makarios restored. **1975** Northern Cyprus declared itself the Turkish Federated State of Cyprus, with Rauf Denktaş as president. **1977** Makarios died; succeeded by Spyros Kyprianou. **1983** Denktaş proclaimed independent Turkish Republic of Cyprus; recognized only by Turkey. **1985** Summit meeting between Kyprianou and Denktaş failed to reach agreement; further peace talks failed in 1989 and 1992. **1988** Kyprianou was succeeded as Greek Cypriot president by Georgios Vassiliou. **1993** Glafkos Clerides (DISY) replaced Vassiliou. **1994** The European Court of Justice declared trade with northern Cyprus illegal. **1996** Further peace talks were jeopardized by the boundary killing of a Turkish Cypriot soldier; there was mounting tension between north and south. **1997** The decision to purchase Russian anti-aircraft missiles created tension. UN-mediated peace talks between Clerides and Denktaş collapsed. **1998** President

Clerides was re-elected. Denktaş refused to meet a British envoy. US mediation failed. Full EU membership negotiations commenced. Greek Cyprus rejected Denktaş's confederation proposals.

Czech Republic

National name *Česká Republika* **Area** 78,864 sq km/30,449 sq mi **Capital** Prague **Major towns/cities** Brno, Ostrava, Olomouc, Liberec, Plzeň, Ustí nad Labem, Hradec Králové

Government

Head of state Václav Havel from 1993 **Head of government** Miloš Zeman from 1998 **Political system** liberal democracy **Armed forces** 61,700 (1997) **Conscription** compulsory for 12 months **Defence spend** (% GDP) 2.2 (1997) **Education spend** (% GNP) 5.4 (1996) **Health spend** (% GDP) 6.6 (1996) **Death penalty** abolished in 1990

Population and society

Population 10,263,000 (1999 est) **Population growth rate** –0.16% (1995–2000) **Ethnic groups** predominantly Western Slav Czechs; there is also a sizeable Slovak minority and small Polish, German, and Hungarian minorities **Religion** Roman Catholic, Hussite, Presbyterian Evangelical Church of Czech Brethren, Orthodox **Life expectancy** 70 (men); 77 (women) (1995–2000) **Literacy rate** 99% (men); 99% (women) (1997 est) **Unemployment** 6.3% (1998)

Economy and resources

GDP (US$) 52.03 billion (1998) **GNP** (US$) 51.8 billion (1998) **GNP per capita (PPP)** (US$) 11,640 (1998 est) **Real GDP growth** (% change on previous year) –1 (1998) **Consumer price inflation** 10.7% (1998) **Foreign debt** (US$) 21.4 billion (1997) **Resources** coal, lignite **Exports** basic manufactures, machinery and transport equipment, miscellaneous manufactured articles, chemicals, beer. Principal market: Germany 35.6% (1998) **Imports** machinery and transport equipment, basic manufactures, chemicals and chemical products, mineral fuels. Principal source: Germany 35% (1998)

▪ Tourist information

Time difference GMT +1 **Currency** koruna (based on Czechoslovak koruna) **Language** Czech (official) **Visa requirements** UK: visa not required. USA: visa not required **Embassy in the UK** 26–30 Kensington Palace Gardens, London W8 4QY. Tel: (020) 7243 1115; fax: (020) 7727 9654 **British embassy** Thunovská 14, 11 800 Prague 7. Tel: (2) 2451 0439; fax: (2) 539 927 **Chamber of commerce** Czech Chamber of Commerce and Industry, Argentinská 38, 170 05 Prague 7. Tel: (2) 6679 4880; fax: (2) 875 348 **Office hours** 0800–1600 Mon–Fri **Banking hours** generally 0800–1800 Mon–Fri **Airports** international airports: Prague (Ruzyně), Brno (Cernovice), Ostrava (International and Mosnov – domestic), Karlovy Vary; total passenger km: 2,442 million (1997 est) **Chief tourist attractions** scenery; winter-sports facilities; historic towns, including Prague, Karlovy Vary, Olomouc, and Ceský; castles and cathedrals; numerous resorts and spas **Major holidays** 1 January, 1 May, 5–6, July, 28 October, 24–26 December; variable: Easter Monday

Chronology

5th century Settled by West Slavs. **8th century** Part of Charlemagne's Holy Roman Empire. **9th century** Kingdom of Greater Moravia, centred around the eastern part of what is now the Czech Republic, founded by the Slavic prince Sviatopluk; Christianity adopted. **906** Moravia conquered by the Magyars (Hungarians). **995** Independent state of Bohemia in the northwest, centred around Prague, formed under the Premysl rulers, who had broken away from Moravia; became kingdom in 12th century. **1029** Moravia became a fief of Bohemia. **1355** King Charles IV of Bohemia became Holy Roman Emperor. **early 15th century** Nationalistic Hussite religion, opposed to German and papal influence, founded in Bohemia by John Huss. **1526** Bohemia came under the control of the Austrian Catholic Habsburgs. **1618** Hussite revolt precipitated the Thirty Years' War, which resulted in the Bohemians' defeat, more direct rule by the Habsburgs, and re-Catholicization. **1867** With creation of dual Austro-Hungarian monarchy, Bohemia was reduced to a province of Austria, leading to a growth in national consciousness. **1918** Austro-Hungarian Empire dismembered; Czechs joined Slovaks in forming Czechoslovakia as independent democratic nation, with Tomas Masaryk president. **1938** Under the Munich Agreement, Czechoslovakia was forced to surrender the Sudeten German districts in the north to Germany. **1939** The remainder of Czechoslovakia annexed by Germany, Bohemia-Moravia being administered as a 'protectorate'; President Eduard Beneš set up a government-in-exile in London; liquidation campaigns against intelligentsia. **1945** Liberated by Soviet and US troops; communist-dominated government of national unity formed under Beneš; 2 million Sudeten Germans expelled. **1948** Beneš ousted; communists assumed full control under a Soviet-style single-party constitution. **1950s** Political opponents purged; nationalization of industries. **1968** 'Prague Spring' political liberalization programme, instituted by Communist Party leader Alexander Dubček, crushed by invasion of Warsaw Pact forces to restore the 'orthodox line'. **1969** New federal constitution, creating a separate Czech Socialist Republic; Gustáv Husák became Communist Party leader. **1977** The formation of the 'Charter '77' human-rights group by intellectuals encouraged a crackdown against dissidents. **1987** Reformist Miloš Jakeš replaced Husák as communist leader, and introduced a *prestvaba* ('restructuring') reform programme on the Soviet leader Mikhail Gorbachev's *perestroika* model. **1989** Prodemocracy demonstrations in Prague; new political parties formed and legalized, including Czech-based Civic Forum under Havel; Communist Party stripped of powers. New 'grand coalition' government formed; Havel appointed state president. Amnesty granted to 22,000 prisoners. **1991** The Civic Forum split into the centre-right Civic Democratic Party (CDP) and the centre-left Civic Movement (CM), evidence of increasing Czech and Slovak separatism. **1992** Václav Klaus, leader of the Czech-based CDP, became prime minister; Havel resigned as president following nationalist Slovak gains in assembly elections. The creation of separate Czech and Slovak states and a customs union were agreed. A market-centred economic-reform programme was launched, including mass privatization. **1993** The Czech Republic became a sovereign state within the United Nations (UN), with Klaus as prime minister. Havel was elected president. **1994** The Czech Republic joined NATO's 'partnership for peace' programme. Strong economic growth was registered. **1996** The Czech Republic applied for European Union (EU) membership. **1997** The former communist leader Miloš Jakeš was charged with treason. The ruling coalition survived a currency crisis. The Czech Republic was invited to begin EU membership negotiations. Klaus resigned after allegations of misconduct. **1998** Havel was re-elected president. The centre-left Social Democrats won a general election and a minority government was formed by Miloš Zeman, including communist ministers and supported from outside by Vaclàv Klaus. Full EU membership negotiations commenced. **1999** The Czech Republic became a full member of NATO.

Denmark Kingdom of

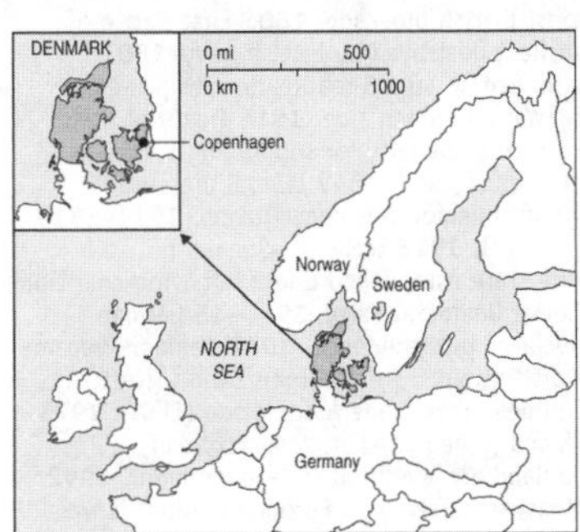

National name *Kongeriget Danmark* **Area** 43,075 sq km/16,631 sq mi **Capital** Copenhagen **Major towns/cities** Århus, Odense, Ålborg, Esbjerg, Randers **Territories** the dependencies of Faroe Islands and Greenland

Government

Head of state Queen Margrethe II from 1972 **Head of government** Poul Nyrup Rasmussen from 1993 **Political system** liberal democracy **Armed forces** 32,900; 70,400 reservists and volunteer Home Guard of 70,500 (1997) **Conscription** 9–12 months (27 months for some ranks) **Defence spend** (% GDP) 1.7 (1997) **Education spend** (% GNP) 8.2 (1996) **Health spend** (% GDP) 6.5 (1996) **Death penalty** abolished in 1978

Population and society

Population 5,283,000 (1999 est) **Population growth rate** 0.2% (1995–2000); 0% (2000–05) **Ethnic groups** all Danes are part of the Scandinavian ethnic group **Religion** Lutheran 97% **Life expectancy** 73 (men); 78 (women) (1995–2000) **Literacy rate** 99% (men); 99% (women) (1997 est) **Unemployment** 5.1% (1998)

Economy and resources

GDP (US$) 174.3 billion (1998) **GNP** (US$) 176.4 billion (1998) **GNP per capita (PPP)** (US$) 23,830 (1998) **Real GDP growth** (% change on previous year) 2.7 (1998) **Consumer price inflation** 2.4% (1998) **Resources** crude petroleum, natural gas, salt, limestone **Exports** pig meat and pork products, other food products, fish, industrial machinery, chemicals, transport equipment. Principal market: Germany 21.4% (1998) **Imports** food and live animals, machinery, transport equipment, iron, steel, electronics, petroleum, cereals, paper. Principal source: Germany 22.5% (1998)

■ Tourist information

Time difference GMT +1 **Currency** Danish krone **Language** Danish (official); there is a German-speaking minority **Visa requirements** UK: visa not required. USA: visa not required **Embassy in the UK** Royal Danish Embassy, 55 Sloane Street, London SW1X 9SR. Tel: (020) 7333 0200; fax: (020) 7333 0270 **British embassy** Kastelsvej 36–40, DK-2100 Copenhagen. Tel: (45) 3526 4600; fax: (45) 3332 1501 **Chamber of commerce** Det Danske Handelskammer, Børsen, DK-1217 Copenhagen K. Tel: (45) 3395 0500; fax: (45) 3332 5216 **Office hours** 0900–1700 Mon–Fri **Banking hours** 0930–1700 Mon, Tue, Wed, and Fri; 0930–1800 Thu **Airports** international airports: Copenhagen (Kastrup), Århus; ten major domestic airports; total passenger km: 5,262 million (1995) **Major ports** Århus, Odense, Ålborg, Esbjerg **Chief tourist attractions** landscape with woods, small lakes; volcanic Faeroe Islands with ancient culture and customs; Copenhagen, with its Tivoli Amusement Park (May–September), palaces, castle, cathedral, national museum, and Little Mermaid sculpture **Major holidays** 1 January, 5 June, 24–26 December; variable: Ascension Thursday, Good Friday, Easter Monday, Holy Thursday, Whit Monday, General Prayer (April/May)

Chronology

5th–6th centuries Danes migrated from Sweden. **8th–10th centuries** Viking raids throughout Europe. *c.* 940–85 Harald Bluetooth unified Kingdom of Denmark and established Christianity. **1014–35** King Canute I created an empire embracing Denmark, Norway, and England; the empire collapsed after his death. **12th century** Denmark re-emerged as dominant Baltic power. **1340–75** Valdemar IV restored order after a period of civil war and anarchy. **1397** Union of Kalmar: Denmark, Sweden, and Norway (with Iceland) united under a single monarch. **1449** Sweden broke away from union. **1536** Lutheranism established as official religion of Denmark. **1563–70** Unsuccessful war to recover Sweden. There were two further unsuccessful attempts to reclaim Sweden, 1643–45 and 1657–60. **1625–29** Denmark sided with Protestants in Thirty Years' War. **1665** Frederick III made himself absolute monarch. **1729** Greenland became a Danish province. **1780–81** Denmark, Russia, and Sweden formed 'Armed Neutrality' coalition to protect neutral shipping during the American revolution. **1788** Serfdom abolished. **1800** France persuaded Denmark to revive Armed Neutrality against British blockade. **1801** First Battle of Copenhagen: much of Danish fleet destroyed by British navy. **1807** Second Battle of Copenhagen: British seized rebuilt fleet to pre-empt Danish entry into Napoleonic War on French side. **1814** Treaty of Kiel: Denmark ceded Norway to Sweden as penalty for supporting France in Napoleonic War; Denmark retained Iceland. **1849** Liberal pressure compelled Frederick VII to grant a democratic constitution. **1914–1919** Denmark neutral during World War I. **1918** Iceland achieved full self-government. **1929–40** Welfare state established under left-wing coalition government dominated by Social Democrat Party. **1940–45** German occupation. **1944** Iceland declared independence. **1949** Denmark became a founding member of the North Atlantic Treaty Organization (NATO). **1960** Denmark joined the European Free Trade Association (EFTA). **1973** Denmark withdrew from EFTA and joined the European Economic Community (EEC). **1981** Greenland achieved full self-government. **1992** A referendum rejected the Maastricht Treaty on European union; it was approved in 1993 after the government negotiated a series of 'opt-out' clauses **1993** Conservative leader Poul Schlüter resigned as prime minister due to a legal scandal. **1994** Schlüter was succeeded as prime minister by Poul Rasmussen, who, leading a Social Democrat-led coalition, won the general election. **1998** The government won a slim majority in assembly elections. A referendum endorsed the Amsterdam European Union (EU) treaty.

Djibouti Republic of

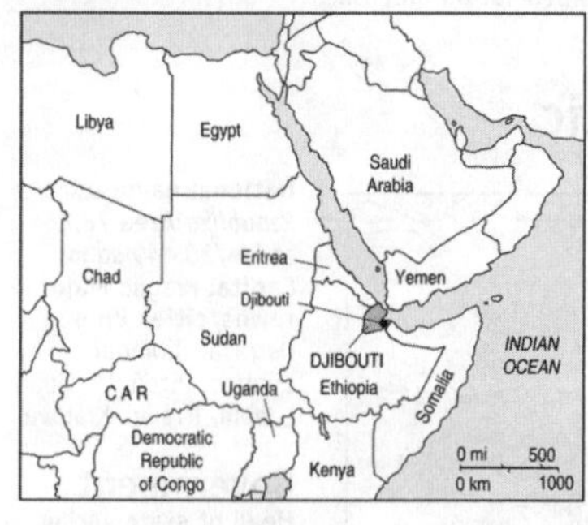

National name *Jumhouriyya Djibouti* **Area** 23,200 sq km/ 8,957 sq mi **Capital** Djibouti (and chief port) **Major towns/ cities** Tadjoura, Obock, Dikhil, Ali-Sabieh

Government

Head of state Hassan Gouled Aptidon from 1977 **Head of government** Barkat Gourad from 1981 **Political system** authoritarian nationalist **Armed forces** 9,600 (1997); plus 3,900 French troops **Conscription** military service is voluntary **Defence spend** (% GDP) 5.0 (1997) **Education spend** (% GNP) 3.8 (1993–94) **Health spend** (% GDP) 2.1 (1994) **Death penalty** retains the death penalty for ordinary crimes but can be considered abolitionist in practice (no executions since independence)

Population and society

Population 629,000 (1999 est) **Population growth rate** 1.2% (1995–2000) **Ethnic groups** population divided mainly into two Hamitic groups; the Issas (Somalis) in the south, and the minority Afars (or Danakil) in the north and west. There are also minorities of Europeans (mostly French), as well as Arabs, Sudanese, and Indians **Religion** Sunni Muslim **Life expectancy** 49 (men); 52 (women) (1995–2000) **Literacy rate** 62% (men); 35% (women) (1997 est) **Unemployment** 58% (1996 est)

Economy and resources

GDP (US$) 500 million (1998) **GNP** (US$) 515 million (1997 est) **GNP per capita (PPP)** (US$) 1,100 (1997 est) **Real GDP growth** (% change on previous year) N/A **Consumer price inflation** 3% (1997 est) **Foreign debt** (US$) 312 million (1997) **Exports** hides, cattle, coffee (exports are largely re-exports). Principal market: Somalia 41% (1997) **Imports** vegetable products, foodstuffs, beverages, vinegar, tobacco, machinery and transport equipment, mineral products. Principal source: France 15% (1997)

■ Tourist information

Time difference GMT +3 **Currency** Djibouti franc **Language** French (official), Somali, Afar, Arabic **Visa requirements** UK: visa required. USA: visa required **Embassy for the UK** 26 rue Emile Ménier, 75116 Paris, France. Tel: (1) 4727 4922; fax: (1) 4553 5053 **British embassy** British Consulate, BP 81 Gellatly Hankey et Cie, Djibouti. Tel: (253) 351 940; fax: (253) 353 294 **Chamber of commerce** Chambre Internationale de Commerce et d'Industrie, BP 84, Place de Lagarde, Djibouti. Tel: (253) 351 070; fax: (253) 350 096 **Office hours** 0620–1300 Sat–Thu **Banking hours** 0715–1145 Sat–Thu **Airports** international airport: Djibouti (Ambouli); six domestic airports; total passengers: 106,823 (1997) **Chief tourist attractions** desert scenery in interior; water-sports facilites on coast **Major holidays** 1 January, 1 May, 27 June (2 days), 25 December; variable: Eid-ul-Adha (2 days), end of Ramadan (2 days), New Year (Muslim), Prophet's Birthday, Al-Isra Wal-Mira'age (March–April)

Chronology

3rd century BC The north settled by Able immigrants from Arabia, whose descendants are the Afars (Danakil). **early Christian era** Somali Issas settled in coastal areas and south, ousting Afars. **825** Islam introduced by missionaries. **16th century** Portuguese arrived to challenge trading monopoly of Arabs. **1862** French acquired a port at Obock. **1888** Annexed by France as part of French Somaliland. **1900s** Railroad linked Djibouti port with the Ethiopian hinterland. **1946** Became overseas territory within French Union, with own assembly and representation in French parliament. **1958** Voted to become overseas territorial member of French Community. **1967** French Somaliland renamed the French Territory of the Afars and the Issas. **early 1970s** Issas (Somali) peoples campaigned for independence, but the minority Afars, of Ethiopian descent, and Europeans sought to remain French. **1977** Independence was achieved as Djibouti, with Hassan Gouled Aptidon, the leader of the independence movement, elected president. **1981** A new constitution made the People's Progress Assembly (RPP) the only legal party. Treaties of friendship were signed with

Ethiopia, Somalia, Kenya, and Sudan. **1984** The policy of neutrality was reaffirmed. The economy was undermined by severe drought. **1992** A new multiparty constitution was adopted; fighting erupted between government forces and Afar Front for Restoration of Unity and Democracy (FRUD) guerrilla movement in the northeast. **1993** Opposition parties were allowed to operate, but Gouled was re-elected president. **1994** A peace agreement was reached with Afar FRUD militants, ending the civil war.

Dominica Commonwealth of

Area 751 sq km/290 sq mi **Capital** Roseau, with a deepwater port **Major towns/cities** Portsmouth, Berekua, Marigot, Rosalie

Government

Head of state Vernon Shaw from 1998 **Head of government** Edison James from 1995 **Political system** liberal democracy **Armed forces** defence force disbanded in 1981; police force of approximately 300 **Education spend** (% GNP) 5.8 (1992); N/A (1990–95) **Health spend** (% GDP) 3.9 (1995) **Death penalty** retained and used for ordinary crimes

Population and society

Population 75,000 (1999 est) **Population growth rate** –0.06 (1995–2000) **Ethnic groups** majority descended from African slaves; a small number of the indigenous Arawaks remain **Religion** Roman Catholic 80% **Life expectancy** 75 (men); 81 (women) (1998 est) **Literacy rate** 94% (men); 94% (women) (1994 est) **Unemployment** 23% (1995 est)

Economy and resources

GDP (US$) 243 million (1998 est) **GNP** (US$) 222 million (1998) **GNP per capita (PPP)** (US$) 3,940 (1998) **Real GDP growth** (% change on previous year) 1 (1998) **Consumer price inflation** 0.7% (1998) **Foreign debt** (US$) 314 million (1997) **Resources** pumice, limestone, clay **Exports** bananas, soap, coconuts, grapefruit, galvanized sheets. Principal market: UK 32.8% (1997) **Imports** food and live animals, basic manufactures, machinery and transport equipment, mineral fuels. Principal source: USA 38.3% (1997)

▪ Tourist information

Time difference GMT –4 **Currency** East Caribbean dollar; pound sterling; French franc **Language** English (official), but the Dominican patois reflects earlier periods of French rule **Visa requirements** UK: visa not required for stays of up to six months. USA: visa not required for stays of up to six months **Embassy in the UK** High Commisssion, 1 Collingham Gardens, London SW5 0HW. Tel: (020) 7370 5194/5; fax: (020) 7373 8743 **British embassy** British High Commission, British Consulate, Office of the Honorary British Consul, PO Box 6, Roseau. (All staff based in Bridgetown, Barbados.) Tel: (809) 448 1000; fax: (809) 448 1110 **Chamber of commerce** Dominica Association of Industry and Commerce, PO Box 85, 111 Bath Road, Roseau. Tel: (809) 448 2874; fax: (809) 448 6868 **Office hours** 0800–1300 and 1400–1700 Mon; 0800–1300 and 1400–1600 Tue–Fri **Banking hours** 0800–1500 Mon–Thu; 0800–1700 Fri **Airports** international airports: Roseau (Canefield), Portsmouth/Marigot (Melville Hall); aircraft arrivals and departures: 18,672 (1997) **Major ports** Roseau, Portsmouth, Berekua, Marigot, Rosalie **Chief tourist attractions** scenery; nature reserves; marine reserves; rich birdlife, including rare and endangered species such as the imperial parrot **Major holidays** 1 January, 1 May, 3–4 November, 25–26 December; variable: Carnival (2 days), Good Friday, Easter Monday, Whit Monday, August Monday

Chronology

1493 Visited by the explorer Christopher Columbus, who named the island Dominica ('Sunday Island'). **1627** Presented by the English King Charles I to the Earl of Carlisle, but initial European attempts at colonization were fiercely resisted by the indigenous Carib community. **later 18th century** Succession of local British and French conflicts over control of the fertile island. **1763** British given possession of the island by the Treaty of Paris, but France continued to challenge this militarily until 1805, when there was formal cession in return for the sum of £12,000. **1834** Slaves, who had been brought in from Africa, were emancipated. **1870** Became part of the British Leeward Islands federation. **1940** Transferred to British Windward Islands federation. **1951** Universal adult suffrage established. **1958–62** Part of the West Indies Federation. **1960** Granted separate, semi-independent status, with a legislative council and chief minister. **1961** Edward le Blanc, leader of the newly formed DLP, became chief minister. **1978** Independence was achieved as a republic within the Commonwealth, with Patrick John (DLP) as prime minister. **1980** The DFP won a convincing victory in a general election, and Eugenia Charles became the Caribbean's first woman prime minister. **1983** A small force participated in the US-backed invasion of Grenada. **1985** The regrouping of left-of-centre parties resulted in the new Labour Party of Dominica (LPD). **1991** A Windward Islands confederation comprising St Lucia, St Vincent, Grenada, and Dominica was proposed. **1993** Charles resigned the DFP leadership, but continued as prime minister. **1995** DUWP won a general election; Edison James was appointed prime minister and Eugenia Charles retired from politics. **1998** Vernon Shaw elected president.

Dominican Republic

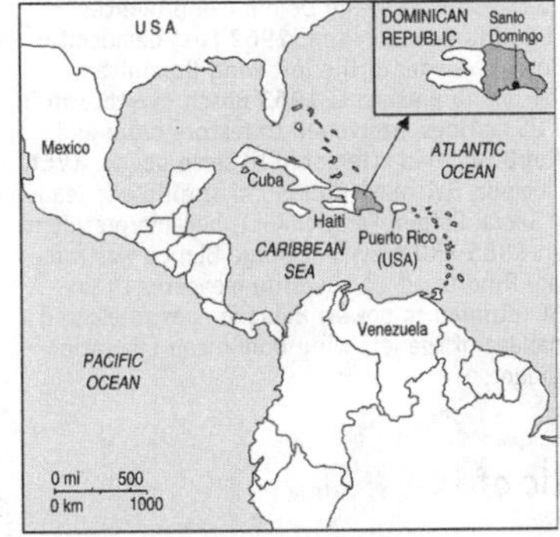

National name *República Dominicana* **Area** 48,442 sq km/ 18,703 sq mi **Capital** Santo Domingo **Major towns/cities** Santiago de los Caballeros, La Romana, San Pedro de Macoris, San Francisco de Macoris, Concepcion de la Vega, San Juan

Government

Head of state and government Hipolito Majia from 2000 **Political system** liberal democracy **Armed forces** 24,500 (1997); plus a paramilitary force of 15,000 **Conscription** military service is voluntary **Defence spend** (% GDP) 1.2 (1997) **Education spend** (% GNP) 2.0 (1996) **Health spend** (% GDP) 2.0 (1990–95) **Death penalty** abolished in 1966

Population and society

Population 8,365,000 (1999 est) **Population growth rate** 1.7% (1995–2000); 1.4% (2000–05) **Ethnic groups** about 73% of the population are mulattos, of mixed European and African descent; about 16% are European; 11% African **Religion** Roman Catholic **Life expectancy** 69 (men); 73 (women) (1995–2000) **Literacy rate** 83% (men); 82% (women) (1997 est) **Unemployment** 15.9% (1997)

Economy and resources

GDP (US$) 15.5 billion (1998) **GNP** (US$) 14.6 billion (1998) **GNP per capita (PPP)** (US$) 4,700 (1998) **Real GDP growth** (% change on previous year) 6.3 (1998) **Consumer price inflation** 8.1% (1998) **Foreign debt** (US$) 4.24 billion (1997) **Resources** ferro-nickel, gold, silver **Exports** raw sugar, molasses, coffee, cocoa, tobacco, ferro-nickel, gold, silver. Principal market: USA 44.7% (1997) **Imports** petroleum and petroleum products, coal, foodstuffs, wheat, machinery. Principal source: USA 44.1% (1997)

▪ Tourist information

Time difference GMT –4 **Currency** Dominican Republic peso **Language** Spanish (official) **Visa requirements** UK: visa not required for stays of up to 90 days. USA: visa not required for stays of up to 60 days **Embassy in the UK** Honorary Consulate of the Dominican Republic, 6 Queen's Mansions, Brook Green, London W6 7EB. Tel: (020) 7602 1885 **British embassy** Edificio Corominas Pepin, Ave 27 Febrero No. 233, Santo Domingo. Tel: (809) 472 7111; fax: (809) 472 7574 **Chamber of commerce** Cámara de Comercio y Produccíon del Distrito Nacional, Apartado Postal 815, Arz. Nouel 206, Santo Domingo. Tel: (809) 682 7206; fax: (809) 685 2228 **Office hours** 0830–1200 and 1400–1800 Mon–Fri **Banking hours** 0800–1600 Mon–Fri **Airports** international airports: Santo Domingo (Internacional de las Americas), Puerto Plata (La Union), Punta Cana, La Romana; most main cities have domestic airports; total passenger km: 234 million (1994) **Chief tourist attractions** beaches on north, east,

and southeast coasts; forested and mountainous landscape **Major holidays** 1, 6, 21, 26 January, 27 February, 1 May, 16 August, 24 September, 25 December; variable: Corpus Christi, Good Friday

Chronology

14th century Settled by Carib Indians, who followed an earlier wave of Arawak Indian immigration. **1492** Visited by Christopher Columbus, who named it Hispaniola ('Little Spain'). **1496** At Santo Domingo the Spanish established the first European settlement in the western hemisphere, which became capital of all Spanish colonies in America. **first half of 16th century** One-third of a million Arawaks and Caribs died, as a result of enslavement and exposure to European diseases; black African slaves were consequently brought in to work the island's gold and silver mines, which were swiftly exhausted. **1697** Divided between France, which held the western third (Haiti), and Spain, which held the east (Dominican Republic, or Santo Domingo). **1795** Santo Domingo was ceded to France. **1808** Following a revolt by Spanish Creoles, with British support, Santo Domingo was retaken by Spain. **1821** Became briefly independent after uprising against Spanish rule, and then fell under the control of Haiti. **1844** Separated from Haiti to form Dominican Republic. **1861–65** Under Spanish protection. **1904** The USA took over the near-bankrupt republic's debts. **1916–24** Temporarily occupied by US forces. **1930** Military coup established personal dictatorship of Gen Rafael Trujillo Molina. **1937** Army massacred 19,000–20,000 Haitians living in the Dominican provinces adjoining the frontier. **1961** Trujillo assassinated. **1962** First democratic elections resulted in Juan Bosch, founder of the left-wing Dominican Revolutionary Party (PRD), becoming president. **1963** Bosch overthrown in military coup. **1965** 30,000 US marines intervened to restore order and protect foreign nationals after Bosch had attempted to seize power. **1966** New constitution adopted. Joaquín Balaguer, protégé of Trujillo and leader of the centre-right Christian Social Reform Party (PRSC), became president. **1978** PRD returned to power. **1985** PRD president Jorge Blanco was forced by the International Monetary Fund to adopt austerity measures to save the economy. **1986** The PRSC returned to power; Balaguer was re-elected president. **1996** Leonel Fernandez of the left-wing Dominican Liberation Party (PLD) was elected president.

Ecuador Republic of

National name *República del Ecuador* **Area** 270,670 sq km/ 104,505 sq mi **Capital** Quito **Major towns/ cities** Guayaquil, Cuenca, Machala, Portoviejo, Manta, Ambeto, Esmeraldas

Government

Head of state and government Gustavo Noboa from 2000 **Political system** liberal democracy **Armed forces** 57,100 (1997) **Conscription** military service is selective for one year **Defence spend** (% GDP) 3.5 (1997) **Education spend** (% GNP) 3.5 (1996) **Health spend** (% GDP) 2 (1990–95) **Death penalty** abolished in 1906

Population and society

Population 12,411,000 (1999 est) **Population growth rate** 2.0% (1995–2000); 1.7% (2000–05) **Ethnic groups** about 55% mestizo (of Spanish-American and American Indian parentage), 25% American Indian, 10% Spanish, 10% African **Religion** Roman Catholic **Life expectancy** 67 (men); 73 (women) (1995–2000) **Literacy rate** 93% (men); 89% (women) (1997 est) **Unemployment** 11.5% (1998 est)

Economy and resources

GDP (US$) 19.76 billion (1998) **GNP** (US$) 18.6 billion (1998) **GNP per capita (PPP)** (US$) 4,630 (1998) **Real GDP growth** (% change on previous year) 0.7 (1998) **Consumer price inflation** 28.1% (1998) **Foreign debt** (US$) 14.9 billion (1997) **Resources** petroleum, natural gas, gold, silver, copper, zinc, antimony, iron, uranium, lead, coal **Exports** petroleum and petroleum products, bananas, shrimps (a major exporter), coffee, seafood products, cocoa beans and products, cut flowers. Principal market: USA 39.2% (1998) **Imports** machinery and transport equipment, basic manufactures, chemicals, consumer goods. Principal source: USA 29.7% (1998)

▪ Tourist information

Time difference GMT –5 **Currency** sucre **Language** Spanish (official), Quechua, Jivaro, and other indigenous languages **Visa requirements** UK: visa not required (except for business visits of three–six months). USA: visa not required (except for business visits of three–six months) **Embassy in the UK** Flat 3B, 3 Hans Crescent, London SW1X 0LS. Tel: (020) 7584 1367; fax: (020) 7823 9701 **British embassy** Casilla 314, Calle González Suárez 111, Quito. Tel: (2) 560 669; fax: (2) 560 730 **Chamber of commerce** Federación Nacional de Cámaras de Comercio del Ecuador, Avenida Olmedo 414, Casila y Boyacá, Guayaquil. Tel: (4) 323 130; fax: (4) 323 478 **Office hours** 0800–1230 and 1500–1900 Mon–Fri; 0930–1230 Sat **Banking hours** 0900–1330 and 1430–1830 Mon–Fri; some banks are also open 0930–1400 Sat **Airports** international airports: Quito (Mariscal Sucre), Guayaquil (Simón Bolívar); six domestic airports; total passenger km: 1,946 million (1997 est) **Major ports** Guayaquil **Chief tourist attractions** Andes Mountains; rainforests of upper Amazon basin; colonial churches and palaces of Guayaquil; Quito, the former Inca capital, with its cathedral, churches, and palaces – the old city is a designated UN World Heritage site; Galápagos Islands, with marine iguanas and giant tortoises **Major holidays** 1 January, 1, 24 May, 30 June, 24 July, 10 August, 9, 12 October, 2–3 November, 6, 25, 31 December; variable: Carnival (2 days), Good Friday, Holy Thursday

Chronology

1450s The Caras people, whose kingdom had its capital at Quito, conquered by Incas of Peru. **1531** Spanish conquistador Francisco Pizarro landed on Ecuadorean coast, en route to Peru, where Incas were defeated. **1534** Conquered by Spanish. Quito, which had been destroyed by American Indians, was refounded by Sebastian de Belalcazar; the area became part of the Spanish Viceroyalty of Peru, which covered much of South America, with its capital at Lima (Peru). **later 16th century** Spanish established large agrarian estates, owned by Europeans and worked by American Indian labourers. **1739** Became part of new Spanish Viceroyalty of Nueva Granada, which included Colombia and Venezuela, with its capital in Bogotá (Colombia). **1809** With the Spanish monarchy having been overthrown by Napoleon Bonaparte, the Creole middle class began to press for independence. **1822** Spanish Royalists defeated by Field Marshal Antonio José de Sucre, fighting for Simón Bolívar, 'The Liberator', at battle of Pichincha, near Quito; became part of independent Gran Colombia, which also comprised Colombia, Panama, and Venezuela. **1830** Became fully independent state, after leaving Gran Colombia. **1845–60** Political instability, with five presidents holding power, increasing tension between conservative Quito and liberal Guayaquil on the coast, and minor wars with Peru and Colombia. **1860–75** Power held by Gabriel García Moreno, an autocratic theocrat-Conservative who launched education and public-works programmes. **1895–1912** Dominated by Gen Eloy Alfaro, a radical, anticlerical Liberal from the coastal region, who reduced the power of the church. **1925–48** Great political instability; no president completed his term of office. **1941** Lost territory in Amazonia after defeat in war with Peru. **1948–55** Liberals in power. **1956** Camilo Ponce became first conservative president in 60 years. **1960** Liberals in power, with José María Velasco Ibarra as president. **1962** Military junta installed. **1968** Velasco returned as president. **1970s** Ecuador emerged as significant oil producer. **1972** Coup put military back in power. **1979** New democratic constitution; Liberals in power but opposed by right- and left-wing parties. **1981** Border dispute with Peru flared up again. **1982** The deteriorating economy and austerity measures provoked strikes, demonstrations, and a state of emergency. **1988** Unpopular austerity measures were introduced. **1992** PUR leader Sixto Duran Ballen was elected president; PSC became the largest party in congress. Ecuador withdrew from OPEC to enable it to increase its oil exports. **1994** There was mounting opposition to Duran's economic liberalization and privatization programme. **1998** Jamil Mahuad Witt was elected president. A 157-year border dispute was settled with Peru. **2000** After the currency lost 65% of its value in 1999, President Mahuad declared a state of emergency, froze all bank accounts valued at over £100, and said that he would introduce the dollar in favour of the sucre.

Egypt Arab Republic of

National name *Jumhuriyat Misr al-Arabiya* **Area** 1,001,450 sq km/386,659 sq mi **Capital** Cairo **Major towns/cities** El Gîza, Shubra Al Khayma, Alexandria, Port Said, El-Mahalla el-Koubra, Tauta, El-Mansoura

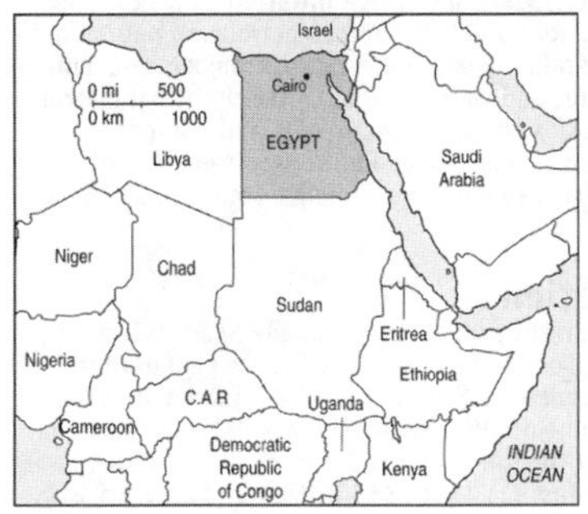

Government

Head of state Hosni Mubarak from 1981 **Head of government** Kamal Ahmed Ganzouri from 1996 **Political system** liberal democracy **Armed forces** 450,000 (1997) **Conscription** 3 years (selective) **Defence spend** (% GDP) 4.3 (1997) **Education spend** (% GNP) 5.6 (1995) **Health spend** (% GDP) 1.6 (1990–95) **Death penalty** retained and used for ordinary crimes

Population and society

Population 67,226,000 (1999 est) **Population growth rate** 1.9% (1995–2000) **Ethnic groups** 93% indigenous **Religion** Sunni Muslim 90%, Coptic Christian 7% **Life expectancy** 65 (men); 68 (women) (1995–2000) **Literacy rate** 65% (men); 41% (women) (1997 est) **Unemployment** 11.8% (1998)

Economy and resources

GDP (US$) 78.1 billion (1998) **GNP** (US$) 79.2 billion (1998) **GNP per capita (PPP)** (US$) 3,130 (1998) **Real GDP growth** (% change on previous year) 4.7 (1998) **Consumer price inflation** 6.2% (1998) **Foreign debt** (US$) 29.8 billion (1997) **Resources** petroleum, natural gas, phosphates, manganese, uranium, coal, iron ore, gold **Exports** petroleum and petroleum products, textiles, clothing, food, live animals. Principal market: EU 32% (1998) **Imports** wheat, maize, dairy products, machinery and transport equipment, wood and wood products, consumer goods. Principal source: EU 42% (1998)

▪ Tourist information

Time difference GMT +2 **Currency** Egyptian pound **Language** Arabic (official); ancient Egyptian survives to some extent in Coptic; English; French **Visa requirements** UK: visa required. USA: visa required **Embassy in the UK** 26 South Street, London W1Y 8EL. Tel: (020) 7499 2401; fax: (020) 7355 3568 **British embassy** 7 Sharia Ahmad Raghab, Garden City, Cairo. Tel: (2) 354 0850; fax: (2) 354 0859 **Chamber of commerce** Federation of Chambers of Commerce, 4 el-Falaki Square, Cairo. Tel: (2) 355 1164; telex: 92645 **Government office hours** 0900–1400 Sat–Thu **Banking hours** 0830–1400 Sat–Thu **Airports** international airports: Cairo (two), Alexandria (El Nouzha), Luxor; eight domestic airports; total passenger km: 9,018 million (1997 est) **Major ports** Alexandria, Port Said, Suez, Damietta, Shubra Al Khayma **Chief tourist attractions** beaches and coral reefs on coast south of Suez; Western Desert, containing the Qattara Depression, the world's largest and lowest depression; ancient pyramids and temples, including those at Saqqara, Gîza, and Karnak **Major holidays** 7 January, 25 April, 1 May, 18 June, 1, 23 July, 6 October; variable: Eid-ul-Adha (2 days), Arafa, end of Ramadan (2 days), New Year (Muslim), Prophet's Birthday, Palm Sunday and Easter Sunday (Eastern Orthodox), Sham-el-Nessim (April/May)

Chronology

1st century BC–7th century AD Conquered by Augustus in AD 30, Egypt passed under rule of Roman, and later Byzantine, governors. **AD 639–42** Arabs conquered Egypt, introducing Islam and Arabic; succession of Arab dynasties followed. **1250** Mamelukes seized power. **1517** Became part of Turkish Ottoman Empire. **1798–1801** Invasion by Napoleon followed by period of French occupation. **1801** Control regained by Turks. **1869** Opening of Suez Canal made Egypt strategically important. **1881–82** Nationalist revolt resulted in British occupation. **1914** Egypt became a British protectorate. **1922** Achieved nominal independence under King Fuad I. **1936** Full independence from Britain achieved. King Fuad succeeded by his son Farouk. **1946** Withdrawal of British troops except from Suez Canal zone. **1952** Farouk overthrown by army in bloodless coup. **1953** Egypt declared a republic, with Gen Neguib as president. **1956** Neguib replaced by Col Gamal Nasser. Nasser announced nationalization of Suez Canal; Egypt attacked by Britain, France, and Israel. Ceasefire agreed following US intervention. **1958** Short-lived merger of Egypt and Syria as United Arab Republic (UAR). **1967** Six-Day War with Israel ended in Egypt's defeat and Israeli occupation of Sinai and Gaza Strip. **1970** Nasser died suddenly; succeeded by Anwar Sadat. **1973** An attempt to regain territory lost to Israel led to the Yom Kippur War; ceasefire arranged by US secretary of state Henry Kissinger. **1978–79** Camp David talks in USA resulted in a peace treaty between Egypt and Israel. Egypt expelled from Arab League. **1981** Sadat was assassinated by Muslim fundamentalists and succeeded by Hosni Mubarak. **1983** Relations between Egypt and the Arab world improved; only Libya and Syria maintained a trade boycott. **1987** Egypt was readmitted to the Arab League. **1989** Relations with Libya improved; diplomatic relations with Syria were restored. **1991** Egypt participated in the Gulf War on the US-led side and was a major force in convening a Middle East peace conference in Spain. **1994** The government cracked down on Islamic militants. **1996** Kamal Ahmed Ganzouri was appointed prime minister. **1997** Islamic extremists killed and injured tourists at Luxor. **2000** At least 20 people were killed in clashes in southern Egypt in the worst violence in living memory to occur between Christians and Muslims in Egypt.

El Salvador Republic of

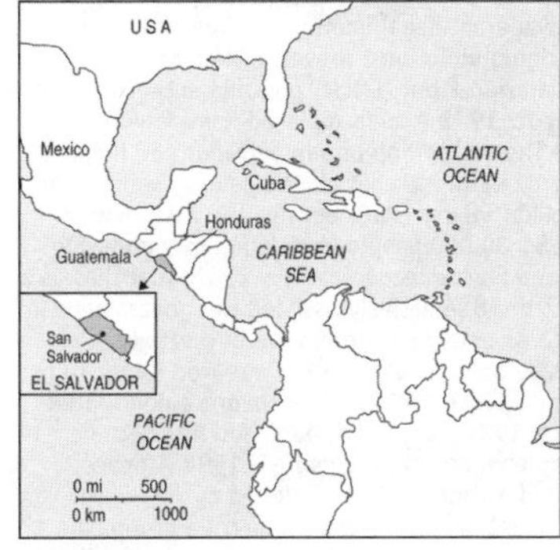

National name *República de El Salvador* **Area** 21,393 sq km/ 8,259 sq mi **Capital** San Salvador **Major towns/cities** Soyapango, Santa Ana, San Miguel, Nueva San Salvador, Mejicanos

Government

Head of state and government Francisco Guillermo Flores Pérez from 1999 **Political system** emergent democracy **Armed forces** 28,400 (1997); plus 12,000 in paramilitary forces **Conscription** selective conscription for two years **Defence spend** (% GDP) 1.9 (1997) **Education spend** (% GNP) 2.2 (1996) **Health spend** (% GDP) 1.2 (1990–95) **Death penalty** laws provide for the death penalty only for exceptional crimes such as crimes under military law or crimes committed in exceptional circumstances such as wartime (last known execution in 1973)

Population and society

Population 6,154,000 (1999 est) **Population growth rate** 2% (1995–2000) **Ethnic groups** about 92% of the population are mestizos, 6% Indians, and 2% of European origin **Religion** Roman Catholic, Protestant **Life expectancy** 67 (men); 73 (women) (1995–2000) **Literacy rate** 80% (men); 74% (women) (1997 est) **Unemployment** 8% (1997)

Economy and resources

GDP (US$) 12.1 billion (1998) **GNP** (US$) 11.2 billion (1998) **GNP per capita (PPP)** (US$) 2,850 (1998) **Real GDP growth** (% change on previous year) 3.7 (1998) **Consumer price inflation** 7.6% (1998) **Foreign debt** (US$) 3.28 billion (1997) **Resources** salt, limestone, gypsum **Exports** coffee, textiles and garments, sugar, shrimp, footwear, pharmaceuticals. Principal market: USA 59.4 % (1998) **Imports** petroleum and other minerals, cereals, chemicals, iron and steel, machinery and transport equipment, consumer goods. Principal source: USA 51.2% (1998)

▪ Tourist information

Time difference GMT −6 **Currency** Salvadorean colón **Language** Spanish, Nahuatl **Visa requirements** UK: visa not required for a stay of up to 90 days. USA: visa required (Tourist Card) **Embassy in the UK** Tennyson House, 159 Great Portland Street, London W1N 5FD. Tel: (020) 7436 8282; fax: (020) 7436 8181 **British embassy** PO Box 1591, Paeso General Escalón 4828, San Salvador. Tel: (503) 298 1768/9; fax: (503) 298 3328 **Chamber of commerce** Cámara de Comercio e Industria de El Salvador, Apartado 1640, 9a Avenida Norte y 5a Calle Poniente, San Salvador. Tel: (503) 771 2055; fax: (503) 771 4461 **Office hours** 0800–1200 and 1430–1730 Mon–Fri **Banking hours** 0900–1300 and 1345–1600 Mon–Fri **Airports** international airport: San Salvador (El Salvador International); three domestic airports; total passenger km: 2,290 million (1997 est) **Chief tourist attractions** Mayan temples and other remains; upland scenery with lakes and volcanoes; Pacific beaches **Major holidays** 1 January, 1 May, 29–30 June, 15 September, 12 October, 2, 5 November, 24–25, 30–31

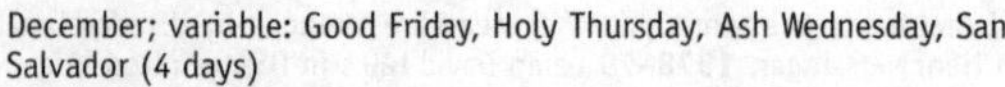

December; variable: Good Friday, Holy Thursday, Ash Wednesday, San Salvador (4 days)

Chronology

11th century Pipils, descendants of the Nahuatl-speaking Toltec and Aztec peoples of Mexico, settled in the country and came to dominate El Salvador until the Spanish conquest. **1524** Conquered by the Spanish adventurer Pedro de Alvarado and made a Spanish colony, with resistance being crushed by 1540. **1821** Independence achieved from Spain; briefly joined with Mexico. **1823** Became part of United Provinces (Federation) of Central America, also embracing Costa Rica, Guatemala, Honduras, and Nicaragua. **1833** Unsuccessful rebellion against Spanish control of land led by Anastasio Aquino. **1840** Became fully independent when the Federation was dissolved. **1859–63** Coffee growing introduced by President Gerardo Barrios. **1932** Peasant uprising, led by Augustín Farabundo Martí, suppressed by military at a cost of the lives of 30,000, virtually eliminating American Indian Salvadoreans. **1961** Following a coup, the right-wing National Conciliation Party (PCN) established and in power. **1969** Brief 'Football War' with Honduras, which El Salvador attacked, at the time of a football competition between the two states, following evictions of thousands of Salvadoran illegal immigrants from Honduras. **1977** Allegations of human-rights violations; growth of left-wing Farabundo Martí National Liberation Front (FMLN) guerrilla activities. Gen Carlos Romero elected president. **1979** A coup replaced Romero with a military-civilian junta. **1980** The archbishop of San Salvador and human-rights champion, Oscar Romero, was assassinated; the country was on the verge of civil war. José Napoleón Duarte (PDC) became the first civilian president since 1931. **1979–81** 30,000 people were killed by right-wing death squads. **1981** Mexico and France recognized the FMLN guerrillas as a legitimate political force, but the USA actively assisted the government in its battle against them. **1982** Assembly elections were boycotted by left-wing parties. Held amid considerable violence, they were won by far-right National Republican Alliance (ARENA). **1986** Duarte sought a negotiated settlement with the guerrillas. **1989** Alfredo Cristiani (ARENA) became president in rigged elections; rebel attacks intensified. **1991** A peace accord sponsored by the United Nations (UN) was signed by representatives of the government and the socialist guerrilla group, the FMLN, which became a political party. **1993** A UN-sponsored commission published a report on war atrocities; there was a government amnesty for those implicated; top military leaders officially retired. **1999** Francisco Guillermo Flores Pérez was elected president.

Equatorial Guinea Republic of

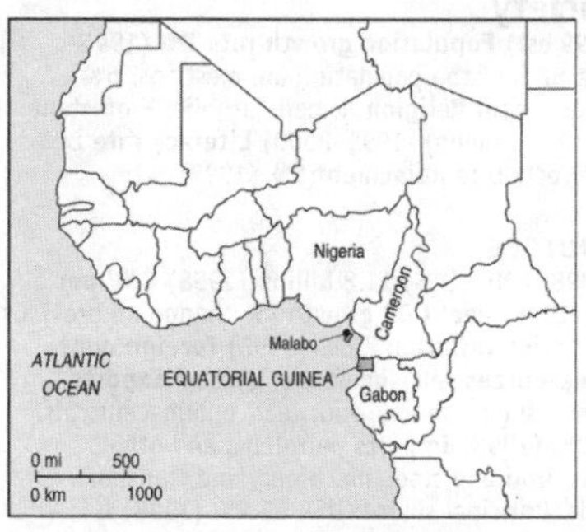

National name *República de Guinea Ecuatorial* **Area** 28,051 sq km/10,830 sq mi **Capital** Malabo **Major towns/cities** Bata, Evinayong, Ebebiyin, Mongomo

Government

Head of state Teodoro Obiang Nguema Mbasogo from 1979 **Head of government** Angel Serafin Seriche Dougan, from 1996 **Political system** authoritarian nationalist **Armed forces** 1,320 (1997) **Conscription** military service is voluntary **Defence spend** (% GDP) 1.3 (1997) **Education spend** (% GNP) 1.8 (1996) **Death penalty** retained and used for ordinary crimes

Population and society

Population 442,000 (1999 est) **Population growth rate** 2.5% (1995–2000); 2.4% (2000–05) **Ethnic groups** 80–90% of the Fang ethnic group, of Bantu origin; most other groups have been pushed to the coast by Fang expansion **Religion** Roman Catholic, Protestant, animist **Life expectancy** 48 (men); 52 (women) (1995–2000) **Literacy rate** 91% (men); 70% (women) (1997 est)

Economy and resources

GDP (US$) 486 million (1998 est) **GNP** (US$) 647 million (1998) **GNP per capita (PPP)** (US$) 4,400 (1998 est) **Real GDP growth** (% change on previous year) 14.7 (1998 est) **Consumer price inflation** 12% (1998) **Foreign debt** (US$) 250 million (1997) **Resources** petroleum, natural gas, gold, uranium, iron ore, tantalum, manganese **Exports** timber, re-exported ships and boats, textile fibres and waste, cocoa, coffee. Principal market: USA 66% (1997) **Imports** ships and boats, petroleum and related products, food and live animals, machinery and transport equipment, beverages and tobacco, basic manufactures. Principal source: USA 23% (1997)

▪ Tourist information

Time difference GMT +1 **Currency** franc CFA **Language** Spanish (official); pidgin English is widely spoken, and on Annobón (whose people were formerly slaves of the Portuguese) a Portuguese patois; Fang and other African patois spoken on Río Muni **Visa requirements** UK: visa required. USA: visa required **Embassy for the UK** 6 rue Alfred de Vigny, 75008 Paris, France. Tel: (1) 4766 4433; fax: (1) 4764 9452 **British embassy** British Consulate, Winston Churchill Avenue, BP 547, Yaoundé, Cameroon. Tel: (237) 220 545; fax: (237) 220 148 (All staff based in Yaoundé, Cameroon.) **Chamber of commerce** Cámara de Comercio Agrícola y Forestal de Malabo, Apartado 51, Malabo. Tel: (240) 151 **Office hours** 0800–1700 Mon–Fri **Banking hours** 0800–1200 Mon–Sat **Airports** international airports: Malabo, Bata; domestic services operate between major towns; total passenger km: 7 million (1995) **Chief tourist attractions** beaches around small offshore islands; tourism remains undeveloped **Major holidays** 1 January, 1 May, 5 June, 3 August, 12 October, 10, 25 December; variable: Corpus Christi, Good Friday, Constitution (August)

Chronology

1472 First visited by Portuguese explorers. **1778** Bioko (formerly known as Fernando Po) Island ceded to Spain, which established cocoa plantations there in the late 19th century, importing labour from West Africa. **1885** Mainland territory of Mbini (formerly Rio Muni) came under Spanish rule, the whole colony being known as Spanish Guinea, with the capital at Malabu on Bioko Island. **1920s** League of Nations special mission sent to investigate the forced, quasi-slave labour conditions on the Bioko cocoa plantations, then the largest in the world. **1959** Became a Spanish Overseas Province; African population finally granted full citizenship. **early 1960s** On the mainland, the Fang people spearheaded a nationalist movement directed against Spanish favouritism towards Bioko Island and its controlling Bubi tribe. **1963** Achieved internal autonomy. **1968** Independence achieved from Spain. Macias Nguema, a nationalist Fang, became first president, discriminating against the Bubi community. **1970s** The economy collapsed as Spanish settlers and other minorities fled in the face of intimidation by Nguema's brutal, dictatorial regime, which was marked by the murder, torture, and imprisonment of tens of thousands of political opponents and rivals. **1979** Nguema was overthrown, tried, and executed. He was replaced by his nephew, Teodoro Obiang Nguema Mbasogo, who established a military regime, but released political prisoners and imposed restrictions on the Catholic church. **1992** A new pluralist constitution was approved by referendum. **1993** Obiang's PDGE won the first multiparty elections on low turnout. **1996** Obiang was re-elected amid claims of fraud by opponents. Angel Serafin Seriche Dougan became prime minister, and was reappointed in 1998.

Eritrea State of

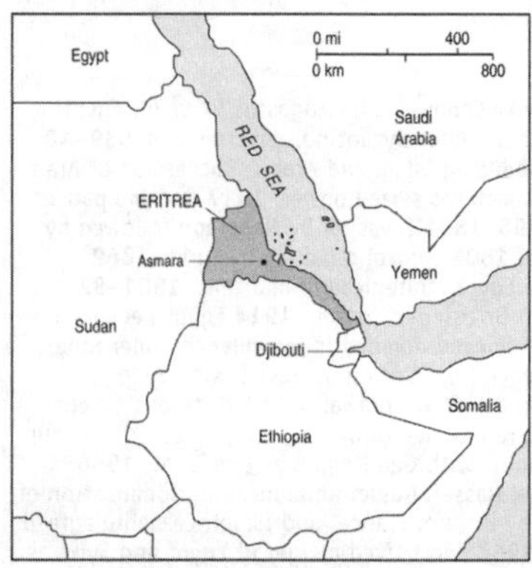

Area 125,000 sq km/48,262 sq mi **Capital** Asmara **Major towns/cities** Asab, Keren, Massawa

Government

Head of state and government Issaias Afwerki from 1993 **Political system** nationalistic socialist **Armed forces** 46,000 (1997) **Conscription** compulsory for 18 months **Defence spend** (% GDP) 8.3 (1997) **Education spend** (% GDP) 1.8 (1996) **Health spend** (% GDP) 1.1 (1990–95) **Death penalty** retained and used for ordinary crimes

Population and society

Population 3,720,000 (1999 est) **Population growth rate** 3.8% (1995–2000) **Ethnic groups** ethnic Tigrinya 50%, Tigre and Kunama 40%, Afar 4%, Saho 3% **Religion** Sunni Muslim, Coptic Christian **Life expectancy** 49 (men); 52 (women) (1995–2000) **Literacy rate** 20–25% (men); 5–10% (women) (1995 est) **Unemployment** 50% (1997 est)

Economy and resources

GDP (US$) 650 million (1998) **GNP** (US$) 776 million (1998) **GNP per capita (PPP)** (US$) 950 (1998) **Real GDP growth** (% change on previous year) -4 (1998) **Consumer price inflation** 9% (1997 est) **Foreign debt** (US$) 76 million (1997) **Resources** gold, silver, copper, zinc, sulphur, nickel, chrome, potash, basalt, limestone, marble, sand, silicates **Exports** textiles, leather and leather products, beverages, petroleum products, basic household goods. Principal market: Ethiopia 63.5% (1997) **Imports** machinery and transport equipment, petroleum, food and live animals, basic manufactures. Principal source: Saudi Arabia 15.7% (1997)

▪ Tourist information

Time difference GMT +3 **Currency** Ethiopian nakfa **Languages** Afar, Amharic, Arabic, Tigre, Kunama, Tigrinya **Visa requirements** UK: visa required. USA: visa required **Embassy in the UK** Eritrean Consulate, 96 White Lion Street, London N1 9PF. Tel: (020) 7713 0096; fax: (020) 7713 0161 **British embassy** British Consulate, PO Box 5584, c/o Mitchell Gotts Building, Emperor Yohannes Avenue 5, Asmara. Tel: (1) 120 145; fax: (1) 120 104 **Chamber of commerce** Asmara Chamber of Commerce, PO Box 856, Asmara. Tel: (1) 21388; fax: (1) 20138 **Office hours** 0800–1200 and 1400–1700 Mon–Fri; 0800–1200 Sat **Banking hours** 0800–1200 and 1400–1700 Mon–Fri; 0800–1200 Sat **Airports** international airport: Asmara (Yohannes IV); two domestic airports **Major ports** Asab, Massawa **Chief tourist attractions** tourism remains largely undeveloped; Dahlak Islands (a coral archipelago rich in marine life) near Massawa; unique ecosystem on escarpment that rises from coastal plain **Major holidays** 1, 6 January, 24 May, 20 June, 1 September, 25 December; variable: Eid-ul-Adha, Arafa, end of Ramadan

Chronology

4th–7th centuries AD Part of Ethiopian Aksum kingdom. **8th century** Islam introduced to coastal areas by Arabs. **12th–16th centuries** Under influence of Ethiopian Abyssinian kingdoms. **mid-16th century** Came under control of Turkish Ottoman Empire. **1882** Occupied by Italy. **1889** Italian colony of Eritrea created out of Ottoman areas and coastal districts of Ethiopia. **1920s** Massawa developed into the largest port in East Africa. **1935–36** Used as base for Italy's conquest of Ethiopia and became part of Italian East Africa. **1941** Became British protectorate after Italy removed from North Africa. **1952** Federation formed with Ethiopia by United Nations (UN). **1958** Eritrean People's Liberation Front (EPLF) was formed to fight for independence after a general strike was brutally suppressed by Ethiopian rulers. **1962** Annexed by Ethiopia, sparking a secessionist rebellion which was to last 30 years and claim 150,000 lives. **1974** Ethiopian emperor Haile Selassie was deposed by the military; the EPLF continued the struggle for independence. **1977–78** The EPLF cleared the territory of Ethiopian forces, but the position was soon reversed by the Soviet-backed Marxist Ethiopian government of Col Mengistu Haile Mariam. **mid-1980s** There was severe famine in Eritrea and a refugee crisis as the Ethiopian government sought forcible resettlement. **1990** The strategic port of Massawa was captured by Eritrean rebel forces. **1991** Ethiopian president Mengistu was overthrown. The EPLF secured the whole of Eritrea and a provisional government was formed under Issaias Afwerki. **1993** Independence was approved in a regional referendum and recognized by Ethiopia. A transitional government was established, with Afwerki elected president; 500,000 refugees outside Eritrea began to return. **1998** Border disputes with Ethiopia escalated, with bombing raids from both sides. **1999** The border dispute with Ethiopia erupted into war in February. Peace was agreed the following month, but fighting was renewed.

Estonia Republic of

National name *Eesti Vabariik* **Area** 45,000 sq km/17,374 sq mi **Capital** Tallinn **Major towns/cities** Tartu, Narva, Kohtla-Järve, Pärnu

Government

Head of state Lennart Meri from 1992 **Head of government** Mart Siimann from 1997 **Political system** emergent democracy **Armed forces** 3,500 (1997); plus 14,000 reservists and paramilitary border guard of 2,800 **Conscription** compulsory for 12 months (men and women) **Defence spend** (% GDP) 2.5 (1997) **Education spend** (% GNP) 7.3 (1996) **Health spend** (% GDP) 6.3% (1990–95) **Death penalty** abolished in 1998

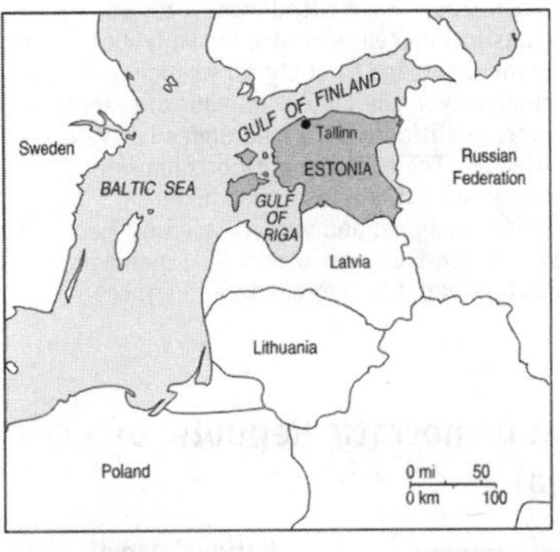

Population and society

Population 1,412,000 (1999 est) **Population growth rate** -1.2% (1995–2000) **Ethnic groups** 62% Finno-Ugric ethnic Estonians, 30% Russian, 3% Ukrainian, 2% Belarussian, 1% Finnish **Religion** Lutheran, Russian Orthodox **Life expectancy** 63 (men); 75 (women) (1995–2000) **Literacy rate** 99% (men); 99% (women) (1997 est) **Unemployment** 3.6% (1997)

Economy and resources

GDP (US$) 5.46 billion (1998) **GNP** (US$) 4.9 billion (1998) **GNP per capita (PPP)** (US$) 6,120 (1998 est) **Real GDP growth** (% change on previous year) 5.2 (1998) **Consumer price inflation** 9.6% (1998) **Foreign debt** (US$) 658 million (1997) **Resources** oilshale, peat, phosphorite ore, superphosphates **Exports** foodstuffs, animal products, textiles, timber products, base metals, mineral products, machinery. Principal market: Finland 22.1% (1998) **Imports** machinery and transport equipment, food products, textiles, mineral products. Principal source: Finland 37.2% (1998)

▪ Tourist information

Time difference GMT +2 **Currency** kroon **Language** Estonian (official), Russian **Visa requirements** UK: visa not required. USA: visa not required **Embassy in the UK** 16 Hyde Park Gate, London SW7 5DG. Tel: (020) 7589 3428; fax: (020) 7589 3430 **British embassy** Kentmanni 20, EE-0100 Tallinn. Tel: (2) 313 353; fax: (2) 313 354 **Chamber of commerce** Chamber of Commerce and Industry of the Republic of Estonia, Toom-Kooli Street 17, EE-0001 Tallinn. Tel: (2) 444 929; fax: (2) 443 656 **Office hours** 0830–1830 Mon–Fri **Banking hours** 0930–1630 Mon–Fri **Airports** international airports: Tallinn; three domestic airports; total passenger km: 209 million (1997) **Chief tourist attractions** historic towns of Tallinn and Tartu; nature reserves; coastal resorts **Major holidays** 1 January, 24 February, 1 May, 23–24 June, 25–26 December; variable: Good Friday

Chronology

1st century AD First independent state formed. **9th century** Invaded by Vikings. **13th century** Tallinn, in the Danish-controlled north, joined Hanseatic League, a northern European union of commercial towns; Livonia, comprising southern Estonia and Latvia, came under control of German Teutonic Knights and was converted to Christianity. **1561** Sweden took control of northern Estonia. **1629** Sweden took control of southern Estonia from Poland. **1721** Sweden ceded the country to tsarist Russia. **late 19th century** Estonian nationalist movement developed in opposition to Russian political and cultural repression and German economic control. **1914** Occupied by German troops. **1918–19** Estonian nationalists, led by Konstantin Pats, proclaimed and achieved independence, despite efforts by the Russian Red Army to regain control. **1920s** Land reforms and cultural advances under democratic regime. **1934** Pats overthrew parliamentary democracy in a quasi-fascist coup at a time of economic depression; Baltic Entente mutual defence pact signed with Latvia and Lithuania. **1940** Estonia incorporated into Soviet Union (USSR); 100,000 Estonians deported to Siberia or killed. **1941–44** German occupation during World War II. **1944** USSR regained control; 'Sovietization' followed, including agricultural collectivization and immigration of ethnic Russians. **late 1980s** Beginnings of nationalist dissent, encouraged by *glasnost* initiative of reformist Soviet leader Mikhail Gorbachev. **1988** Popular Front (EPF) established to campaign for democracy. Sovereignty declaration issued by state assembly rejected by USSR as unconstitutional. **1989** Estonian replaced Russian as the main language. **1990** The CPE monopoly of power was abolished; pro-independence candidates secured a majority after multiparty elections; a coalition government was formed with EPF leader Edgar Savisaar as prime minister; Arnold Rüütel became president. The prewar constitution was partially restored. **1991** Independence was achieved after an attempted anti-Gorbachev coup in Moscow; the CPE was outlawed. Estonia joined the United Nations (UN). **1992** Savisaar resigned over food and energy shortages; Isamaa leader Lennart Meri became president and free-marketer Mart Laar prime minister. **1993** Estonia joined the Council of Europe and signed a free-trade agreement with Latvia and

Lithuania. **1994** The last Russian troops were withdrawn. A radical economic reform programme was introduced; a controversial law on 'aliens' was passed, requiring non-ethnic Estonians to apply for residency. Laar resigned. **1995** Former communists won the largest number of seats in a general election; a left-of-centre coalition was formed under Tiit Vahi. **1996** President Meri was re-elected. The ruling coalition collapsed; Prime Minister Tiit Vahi continued with a minority government. **1997** Vahi, accused of corruption, resigned and was replaced by Mart Siimann. Estonia was invited to begin European Union (EU) membership negotiations. **1998** The legislature voted to ban electoral alliances in future elections.

Ethiopia Federal Democratic Republic of (formerly Abyssinia)

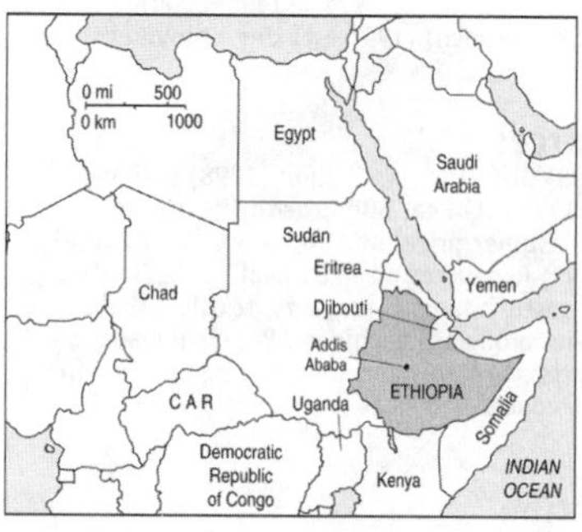

National name *Hebretesebawit Ityopia* **Area** 1,096,900 sq km/ 423,513 sq mi **Capital** Addis Ababa **Major towns/cities** Jimma, Dire Dawa, Harar, Nazret, Dessie, Gonder, Mek'elē

Government

Head of state Negasso Ghidada from 1995 **Head of government** Meles Zenawi from 1995 **Political system** emergent democracy **Armed forces** 120,000 (1997) **Conscription** mlitary service is voluntary **Defence spend** (% GDP) 2.1 (1997) **Education spend** (% GNP) 4 (1996) **Health spend** (% GDP) 1.7 (1990–95) **Death penalty** retained and used for ordinary crimes

Population and society

Population 61,095,000 (1999 est) **Population growth rate** 2.5% (1995–2000) **Ethnic groups** over 70 different ethnic groups; the two main ones are the Galla (mainly in the east and south of the central plateau), who comprise about 40% of the population, and the Amhara and Tigré (largely in the central plateau itself), who constitute about 35% **Religion** Sunni Muslim, Christian (Ethiopian Orthodox Church, which has had its own patriarch since 1976) 40%, animist **Life expectancy** 42 (men); 44 (women) (1995–2000) **Literacy rate** 42% (men); 29% (women) (1997 est) **Unemployment** N/A

Economy and resources

GDP (US$) 6.6 billion (1998) **GNP** (US$) 6.1 billion (1998) **GNP per capita (PPP)** (US$) 500 (1998) **Real GDP growth** (% change on previous year) 0.5 (1998) **Consumer price inflation** 3.9% (1998 est) **Foreign debt** (US$) 10.08 billion (1997) **Resources** gold, salt, platinum, copper, potash. Reserves of petroleum have not been exploited **Exports** coffee, hides and skins, petroleum products, fruit and vegetables. Principal market: Germany 22.4% (1997) **Imports** machinery, aircraft and other vehicles, petroleum and petroleum products, basic manufactures, chemicals and related products. Principal source: Italy 10.1% (1997)

▪ Tourist information

Time difference GMT +3 **Currency** Ethiopian birr **Language** Amharic (official), Tigrinya, Orominga, Arabic **Visa requirements** UK: visa required. USA: visa required **Embassy in the UK** 17 Prince's Gate, London SW7 1PZ. Tel: (020) 7589 7212; fax: (020) 7584 7054 **British embassy** PO Box 858, Fikre Mariam Abatechan Street, Addis Ababa. Tel: (1) 612 354; fax: (1) 610 588 **Chamber of commerce** Ethiopian Chamber of Commerce, PO Box 517, Mexico Square, Addis Ababa. Tel: (1) 518 240; telex: 21213 **Office hours** 0800–1200 and 1300–1700 Mon–Fri **Banking hours** 0800–1200 and 1300–1700 Mon–Thu; 0830–1130 and 1300–1700 Fri **Airports** international airports: Addis Ababa (Bole), Dire Dawa; over 40 small domestic airports or airfields; total passenger km: 1,915 million (1997) **Chief tourist attractions** early Christian churches and monuments; ancient capitals of Gonder and Aksum; Blue Nile Falls; national parks of Semien and Bale Mountains **Major holidays** 7, 19 January, 2 March, 6 April, 1 May, 12, 27 September; variable: Eid-ul-Adha, end of Ramadan, Ethiopian New Year (September), Prophet's Birthday, Ethiopian Good Friday and Easter

Chronology

1st–7th centuries AD Founded by Semitic immigrants from Saudi Arabia, the kingdom of Aksum and its capital, northwest of Ādwa, flourished. It reached its peak in the 4th century when Coptic Christianity was introduced from Egypt. **7th century onwards** Islam was spread by Arab conquerors. **11th century** Emergence of independent Ethiopian kingdom of Abyssinia, which was to remain dominant for nine centuries. **late 15th century** Abyssinia visited by Portuguese explorers. **1889** Abyssinia reunited by Menelik II. **1896** Invasion by Italy defeated by Menelik at Ādwa, who went on to annex Ogaden in the southeast and areas to the west. **1916** Haile Selassie became regent. **1930** Haile Selassie became emperor. **1936** Conquered by Italy and incorporated in Italian East Africa. **1941** Return of Emperor Selassie after liberation by the British. **1952** Ethiopia federated with Eritrea. **1962** Eritrea annexed by Selassie; Eritrean People's Liberation front (EPLF) resistance movement began, a rebellion that was to continue for 30 years. **1963** First conference of Selassie-promoted Organization of African Unity (OAU) held in Addis Ababa. **1973–74** Severe famine in northern Ethiopia; 200,000 died in Wallo province. **1974** Haile Selassie deposed and replaced by a military government. **1977** Col Mengistu Haile Mariam took over the government. Somali forces ejected from the Somali-peopled Ogaden in the southeast. **1977–79** 'Red Terror' period in which Mengistu's single-party Marxist regime killed thousands of people and promoted collective farming; Tigré People's Liberation Front guerrillas began fighting for regional autonomy in the northern highlands. **1984** The Workers' Party of Ethiopia (WPE) was declared the only legal political party. **1985** The worst famine in more than a decade; Western aid was sent and forcible internal resettlement programmes undertaken in Eritrea and Tigré in the north. **1987** Mengistu Mariam was elected president under a new constitution. There was another famine; food aid was hindered by guerrillas. **1989** Peace talks with Eritrean rebels were mediated by the former US president Jimmy Carter. **1991** Mengistu was overthrown; a transitional government was set up by the opposing Ethiopian People's Revolutionary Democratic Front (EPRDF), headed by Meles Zenawi. The EPLF took control of Eritrea. Famine again gripped the country. **1993** Eritrean independence was recognized after a referendum; private farming and market sector were encouraged by the EPRDF government. **1994** A new federal constitution was adopted. **1995** The ruling EPRDF won a majority in the first multiparty elections to an interim parliament. Negasso Ghidada was chosen as president; Zenawi was appointed premier. **1998** There was a border dispute with Eritrea. **1999** The border dispute with Eritrea erupted into war. Peace proposals were agreed by Eritrea but fighting continued.

Fiji Islands Republic of

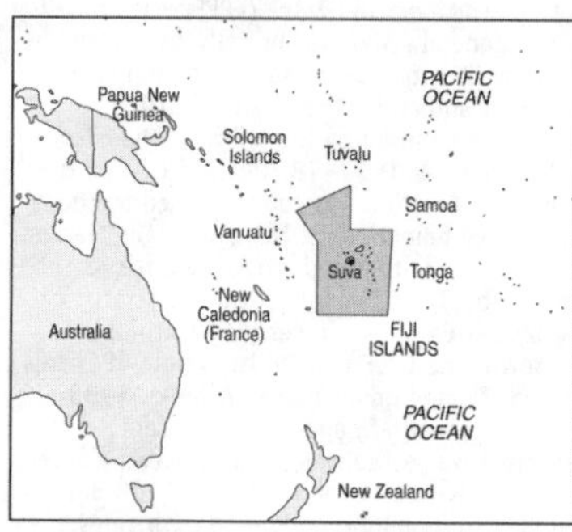

Area 18,333 sq km/ 7,078 sq mi **Capital** Suva **Major towns/ cities** Lautoka, Nadi, Ba, Labasa

Government

Head of state Commodore Frank Bainimarama from 2000 **Political system** military **Armed forces** 3,600 (1997) **Conscription** military service is voluntary **Defence spend** (% GDP) 2.6 (1997) **Education spend** (% GNP) 5.4 (1995) **Health spend** (% GDP) 1.3 (1994) **Death penalty** laws provide for the death penalty only for exceptional crimes such as crimes under military law or crimes committed in exceptional cricumstances such as wartime (last execution 1964)

Population and society

Population 806,000 (1999 est) **Population growth rate** 1.2% (1995–2000) **Ethnic groups** 48% Fijians (of Melanesian and Polynesian descent), 51% Asians **Religion** Methodist, Hindu, Muslim, Sikh **Life expectancy** 71 (men); 75 (women) (1995–2000) **Literacy rate** 94% (men); 89% (women) (1997 est) **Unemployment** 6% (1997 est)

Economy and resources

GDP (US$) 2.1 billion (1998 est) **GNP** (US$) 1.75 billion (1998) **GNP per capita (PPP)** (US$) 3,580 (1998) **Real GDP growth** (% change on previous

year) 1.0 (1998) **Consumer price inflation** 6% (1998) **Foreign debt** (US$) 205 million (1997) **Resources** gold, silver, copper **Exports** sugar, gold, fish and fish products, clothing, re-exported petroleum products, timber, ginger, molasses. Principal market: Australia 33.1% (1997) **Imports** basic manufactured goods, machinery and transport equipment, food, mineral fuels. Principal source: Australia 47.5% (1997)

▪ Tourist information

Time difference GMT +12 **Currency** Fiji dollar **Language** English (official), Fijian, Hindi **Visa requirements** UK: visa not required. USA: visa not required **Embassy in the UK** 34 Hyde Park Gate, London SW7 5DN. Tel: (020) 7839 2200; fax: (020) 7839 9050 **British embassy** PO Box 1355, Victoria House, 47 Gladstone Road, Suva. Tel: (679) 311 033; fax: (679) 301 406 **Chamber of commerce** Suva Chamber of Commerce, PO Box 337, 2nd Floor, GB Hari Building, 12 Pier Street, Suva. Tel: (679) 303 854; fax: (679) 300 475 **Office hours** 0800–1630 Mon–Fri (some businesses close 30 minutes earlier on Fri) **Banking hours** 0930–1500 Mon–Thu; 0930–1600 Fri **Airports** international airports: Nadi; 16 domestic airports and airfields; total passenger km: 1,979 million (1997 est) **Major ports** Lautoka and Levuka **Chief tourist attractions** climate; scenery; fishing; diving **Major holidays** 1 January, 12 October, 25–26 December; variable: Diwali, Good Friday, Easter Monday, Holy Saturday, Prophet's Birthday, August Bank Holiday, Queen's Birthday (June), Prince Charles's Birthday (November)

Chronology

c. 1500 BC Peopled by Polynesian and, later, by Melanesian settlers. **1643** The islands were visited for the first time by a European, the Dutch navigator Abel Tasman. **1830s** Arrival of Western Christian missionaries. **1840s–50s** Western Fiji came under dominance of a Christian convert prince, Cakobau, ruler of Bau islet, who proclaimed himself Tui Viti (King of Fiji), while the east was controlled by Ma'afu, a Christian prince from Tonga. **1857** British consul appointed, encouraging settlers from Australia and New Zealand to set up cotton farms in Fiji. **1874** Fiji became a British crown colony after a deed of cession was signed by King Cakobau. **1875–76** A third of the Fijian population were wiped out by a measles epidemic; a rebellion against the British was suppressed with the assitance of Fijian chiefs. **1877** Fiji became the headquarters of the British Western Pacific High Commission (WPHC), which controlled other British protectorates in the Pacific region. **1879–1916** Indian labourers brought in, on ten-year indentured contracts, to work sugar plantations. **1904** Legislative Council formed, with elected Europeans and nominated Fijians, to advise the British governor. **1963** Legislative Council enlarged; women and Fijians were enfranchised. The predominantly Fijian Alliance Party (AP) formed. **1970** Independence was achieved from Britain; Ratu Sir Kamisese Mara of the AP was elected as the first prime minister. **1973** Ratu Sir George Cakobau, the great-grandson of the chief who had sworn allegiance to the British in 1874, became governor general. **1985** The FLP was formed by Timoci Bavadra, with trade-union backing. **1987** After a general election had brought to power an Indian-dominated coalition led by Bavadra, Lt-Col Sitiveni Rabuka seized power in a military coup, and proclaimed a Fijian-dominated republic outside the Commonwealth. **1990** A new constitution, favouring indigenous (Melanese) Fijians, was introduced. Civilian rule was re-established, with resignations from the cabinet of military officers, but Rabuka remained as home affairs minister, with Mara as prime minister. **1992** A general election produced a coalition government with Rabuka of the FPP as prime minister. **1994** Ratu Sir Kamisese Mara became president. **1997** A nondiscriminatory constitution was introduced. Fiji was re-admitted to the Commonwealth. **1999** President Mara's term in office was renewed for an additional five years. Mahendra Chaudhry became Fiji's first female prime minister and first prime minister of Indian descent. **2000** A coup perpetrated by businessman George Speight brought an end to the presidency of Mara and led to rioting in the capital, Suva. The head of Fiji's armed forces, Commodore Frank Bainimarama, announced that he was taking power, proclaimed martial law, and revoked the 1997 nondiscriminatory constitution. Later, the members of the former cabinet, who had been held hostage by Speight's rebels, were released.

Finland Republic of

National name *Suomen Tasavalta* **Area** 338,145 sq km/130,557 sq mi **Capital** Helsinki (Helsingfors) **Major towns/cities** Tampere, Turku, Espoo, Vantaa

Government

Head of state Tarja Halonen from 2000 **Head of government** Paavo Lipponen from 1995 **Political system** liberal democracy **Armed forces** 31,000 (1997) **Conscription** up to 11 months, followed by refresher training of 40–100 days (before age 50) **Defence spend** (% GDP) 1.7 (1997) **Education spend** (% GNP) 7.6 (1996) **Health spend** (% GDP) 5.8 (1996) **Death penalty** abolished in 1972

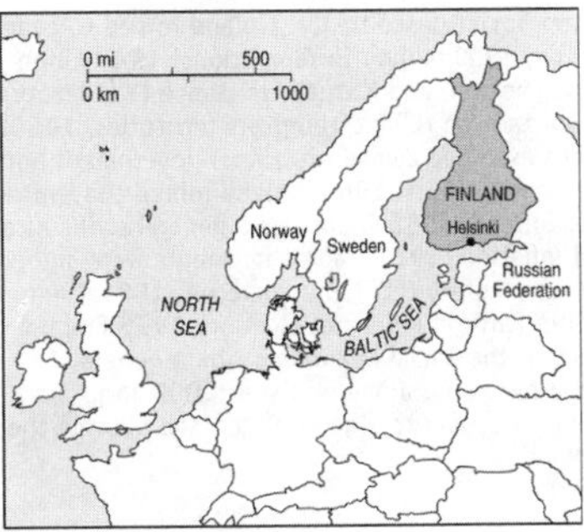

Population and society

Population 5,165,000 (1999 est) **Population growth rate** 0.3% (1995–2000); 0.3% (2000–05) **Ethnic groups** predominantly Finnish; significant Swedish minority; small minorities of native Saami and Russians **Religion** Lutheran 90%, Orthodox 1% **Life expectancy** 73 (men); 81 (women) (1995–2000) **Literacy rate** 99% (men); 99% (women) (1997 est) **Unemployment** 11.4% (1998)

Economy and resources

GDP (US$) 125.6 billion (1998) **GNP** (US$) 124.3 billion (1998) **GNP per capita (PPP)** (US$) 20,270 (1998) **Real GDP growth** (% change on previous year) 5 (1998) **Consumer price inflation** 1.5% (1998) **Resources** copper ore, lead ore, gold, zinc ore, silver, peat, hydro power, forests **Exports** metal and engineering products, gold, paper and paper products, machinery, ships, wood and pulp, clothing and footwear, chemicals. Principal market: Germany 11.8% (1998) **Imports** mineral fuels, machinery and transport equipment, food and live animals, chemical and related products, textiles, iron and steel. Principal source: Germany 15.2% (1998)

▪ Tourist information

Time difference GMT +2 **Currency** markka **Language** Finnish 93%, Swedish 6% (both official); small Saami- and Russian-speaking minorities **Visa requirements** UK: visa not required. USA: visa not required **Embassy in the UK** 38 Chesham Place, London SW1X 8HW. Tel: (020) 7235 9531; fax: (020) 7235 3680 **British embassy** Itäinen Puistotie 17, 00140 Helsinki. Tel: (0) 661 293; fax: (0) 661 342 **Chamber of commerce** Keskuskauppakamari (Central Chamber of Commerce of Finland), PO Box 1000, Fabianinkatu 14, 00101 Helsinki. Tel: (0) 650 133; fax: (0) 650 303 **Office hours** 0800–1615 Mon–Fri **Banking hours** 0915–1615 Mon–Fri **Airports** international airports: Helsinki (Vantaa); 20 domestic airports; total passenger km: 11,924 million (1997) **Major ports** Turku, Oulu **Chief tourist attractions** scenery: forests, lakes (Europe's largest inland water system) **Major holidays** 1 January, 1 May, 31 October, 1 November, 1, 24–26, 31 December; variable: Ascension Thursday, Good Friday, Easter Monday, Midsummer Eve and Day (June), Twelfthtide (January), Whitsuntide (May/June)

Chronology

1st century Occupied by Finnic nomads from Asia who drove out native Saami (Lapps) to the far north. **12th–13th centuries** A series of Swedish crusades conquered Finns and converted them to Christianity. **16th–17th centuries** Finland was a semi-autonomous Swedish duchy with Swedish landowners ruling Finnish peasants; Finland was allowed relative autonomy, becoming a grand duchy in 1581. **1634** Finland fully incorporated into Swedish kingdom. **1700–21** Great Northern War between Sweden and Russia; half of Finnish population died in famine and epidemics. **1741–43 and 1788–90** Further Russo-Swedish wars; much of the fighting took place in Finland. **1808** Russia invaded Sweden (with support of Napoleon). **1809** Finland ceded to Russia as grand duchy with Russian tsar as grand duke; Finns retained their own legal system and Lutheran religion and were exempt from Russian military service. **1812** Helsinki became capital of grand duchy. **19th century** Growing prosperity was followed by rise of national feeling among new Finnish middle class. **1904–05** Policies promoting Russification of Finland provoked a national uprising; Russians imposed military rule. **1917** Finland declared independence. **1918** Bitter civil war between Reds (supported by Russian Bolsheviks) and Whites (supported by Germany); Baron Carl Gustaf Mannerheim led the Whites to victory. **1919** Republican constitution adopted with Kaarlo Juho Ståhlberg as first president. **1927** Land reform broke up big estates and created many small peasant farms. **1939–40** Winter War: USSR invaded Finland after a demand for military bases was refused. **1940** Treaty of Moscow: Finland ceded territory to USSR. **1941** Finland joined the German attack on USSR in the hope of regaining lost territory. **1944** Finland agreed separate armistice with USSR; German troops withdrawn. **1947** Finno-Soviet peace treaty: Finland forced to cede 12% of its total area and to pay $300 million in reparations. **1948** Finno-Soviet Pact of Friendship, Cooperation, and Mutual Assistance (YYA treaty): Finland pledged to repel any attack on USSR through its territories. **1950s** Unstable centre-left coalitions excluded communists from government and adopted strict neutrality in foreign affairs. **1955** Finland joined the United Nations (UN) and the Nordic Council. **1956** There was a general strike as a result of unemployment and inflation. **1973** Trade agreements were signed with the European Economic Community (EEC) and Comecon. **1991** There was a swing towards the Centre Party in a general election. **1995** Finland joined the European Union (EU); the Social Democrats won a general election, with Paavo Lipponen becoming prime minister. **2000** Tarja Halonen was elected president. A former foreign minister, she became the first woman president of Finland.

France (French Republic)

National name *République Française* **Area** (including Corsica) 543,965 sq km/ 210,024 sq mi **Capital** Paris **Major towns/ cities** Lyon, Lille, Bordeaux, Toulouse, Nantes, Strasbourg, Montpellier, Saint-Etienne, Rennes, Reims, Grenoble **Territories** Guadeloupe, French Guiana, Martinique, Réunion, St Pierre and Miquelon, Southern and Antarctic Territories, New Caledonia, French Polynesia, Wallis and Futuna, Mayotte

Government

Head of state Jacques Chirac from 1995 **Head of government** Lionel Jospin from 1997 **Political system** liberal democracy **Armed forces** 380,800; paramilitary gendarmerie 92,300 (1997) **Conscription** military service is compulsory for 10 months **Defence spend** (% GDP) 3.0 (1997) **Education spend** (% GNP) 6.1 (1996) **Health spend** (% GDP) 7.3 (1996) **Death penalty** abolished in 1981

Population and society

Population 58,886,000 (1999 est) **Population growth rate** 0.4% (1995–2000); 0.2% (2000–05) **Ethnic groups** predominantly French ethnic, of Celtic and Latin descent; Basque minority in southwest; 7% of the population are immigrants – a third of these are from Algeria and Morocco and live mainly in the Marseille Midi region and in northern cities, 20% originate from Portugal, and 10% each from Italy and Spain **Religion** Roman Catholic; also Muslim, Protestant, and Jewish minorities **Life expectancy** 74 (men); 82 (women) (1995–2000) **Literacy rate** 99% (men); 99% (women) (1997 est) **Unemployment** 11.9% (1998)

Economy and resources

GDP (US$) 1,432.9 billion (1998) **GNP** (US$) 1,466.2 billion (1998) **GNP per capita (PPP)** (US$) 22,320 (1997) **Real GDP growth** (% change on previous year) 2.8 (1998) **Consumer price inflation** 1.6% (1998) **Resources** coal, petroleum, natural gas, iron ore, copper, zinc, bauxite **Exports** machinery and transport equipment, food and live animals, chemicals, beverages and tobacco, textile yarn, fabrics and other basic manufactures, clothing and accessories, perfumery and cosmetics. Principal market: Germany 15.9% (1998) **Imports** food and live animals, mineral fuels, machinery and transport equipment, chemicals and chemical products, basic manufactures. Principal source: Germany 17.2% (1998)

▪ Tourist information

Time difference GMT +1 **Currency** franc **Language** French (regional languages include Basque, Breton, Catalan, and Provençal) **Visa requirements** UK: visa not required. USA: visa not required **Embassy in the UK** 58 Knightsbridge, London SW1X 7JT. Tel: (020) 7201 1000; fax: (020) 7201 1004 **British embassy** 35 rue du Faubourg St Honoré, 75383 Paris. Tel: (1) 4266 9142; fax: (1) 4266 9590 **Chamber of commerce** Chambre de Commerce et d'Industrie de Paris, 27 avenue de Friedland, 75382 Paris. Tel: (1) 4289 7000; fax: (1) 4289 7286 **Office hours** generally 0900–1200 and 1400–1800 Mon–Fri **Banking hours** 0900–1200 and 1400–1600 Mon–Fri; some banks close on Mon. Banks close early (1200) on the day before a bank holiday; in rare cases, they may also close for all or part of the day after **Airports** international airports: Paris (Orly, Roissy-Charles de Gaulle, Le Bourget), Bordeaux (Merignac), Lille (Lesquin), Lyon, Marseille, Nice, Strasbourg, Toulouse (Blagnac); 45 domestic airports; total passenger km: 80,153 million (1997 est) **Major ports** Marseille, Nice, Le Havre **Chief tourist attractions** Paris, with its boulevards, historic buildings, art treasures, theatres, restaurants, and night clubs; resorts on Mediterranean and Atlantic coasts; many ancient towns; châteaux of the Loire valley; theme parks (Futuroscope and EuroDisney) **Major holidays** 1 January, 1, 8 May, 14 July, 14, 15 August, 31 October, 1, 11 November, 24–25, 31 December; variable: Ascension Eve, Ascension Thusday, Good Friday, Easter Monday, Holy Saturday, Whit Holiday Eve, Whit Monday, Law of 20 December 1906, Law of 23 December 1904

Chronology

5th century BC Celtic peoples invaded the region. **58–51 BC** Romans conquered Celts and formed province of Gaul. **5th century AD** Gaul overrun by Franks and other Germanic tribes. **481–511** Frankish chief Clovis accepted Christianity and formed a kingdom based at Paris; under his successors, the Merovingian dynasty, the kingdom disintegrated. **751–68** Pepin the Short usurped the Frankish throne, reunified the kingdom, and founded the Carolingian dynasty. **768–814** Charlemagne conquered much of western Europe and created the Holy Roman Empire. **843** Treaty of Verdun divided the Holy Roman Empire into three, with the western portion corresponding to modern France. **9th–10th centuries** Weak central government allowed the great nobles to become virtually independent. **987** Frankish crown passed to House of Capet; the Capets ruled the district around Paris, but were surrounded by vassals more powerful than themselves. **1180–1223** Philip II doubled the royal domain and tightened control over the nobles; the power of the Capets gradually extended with support of church and towns. **1328** When Charles IV died without an heir, Philip VI established the House of Valois. **1337** Start of the Hundred Years' War: Edward III of England disputed the Valois succession and claimed the throne. English won victories at Crécy in 1346 and Agincourt in 1415. **1429** Joan of Arc raised the siege of Orléans; Hundred Years' War ended with Charles VII expelling the English in 1453. **1483** France annexed Burgundy and Brittany after Louis XI had restored royal power. **16th–17th centuries** French kings fought the Habsburgs (of Holy Roman Empire and Spain) for supremacy in western Europe. **1562–98** Civil wars between nobles were fought under religious slogans, Catholic versus Protestant (or Huguenot). **1589–1610** Henry IV, first king of Bourbon dynasty, established peace, religious tolerance, and absolute monarchy. **1634–48** The ministers Richelieu and Mazarin, by intervening in the Thirty Years' War, secured Alsace and made France the leading power in Europe. **1701–14** War of the Spanish Succession: England, Austria, and allies checked expansionism of France under Louis XIV. **1756–63** Seven Years' War: France lost most of its colonies in India and Canada to Britain. **1789** French Revolution abolished absolute monarchy and feudalism; First Republic proclaimed and revolutionary wars began in 1792. **1799** Napoleon Bonaparte seized power in coup; crowned himself emperor in 1804; France conquered much of Europe. **1814** Defeat of France; restoration of Bourbon monarchy; comeback by Napoleon defeated at Waterloo in 1815. **1830** Liberal revolution deposed Charles X in favour of his cousin Louis Philippe, the 'Citizen King'. **1848** Revolution established Second Republic; conflict between liberals and socialists; Louis Napoleon, nephew of Napoleon I, elected president. **1852** Louis Napoleon proclaimed Second Empire, taking title Napoleon III. **1870–71** Franco-Prussian War: France lost Alsace-Lorraine; Second Empire abolished; Paris Commune crushed; Third Republic founded. **late 19th century** France colonized Indochina, much of North Africa, and South Pacific. **1914–18** France resisted German invasion in World War I; Alsace-Lorraine recovered in 1919. **1936–37** Left-wing 'Popular Front' government introduced many social reforms. **1939** France entered World War II. **1940** Germany invaded and occupied northern France; Marshal Pétain formed right-wing puppet regime at Vichy; resistance maintained by Maquis and Free French; Germans occupied all France in 1942. **1944** Allies liberated France; provisional government formed by Gen Charles de Gaulle, leader of Free French. **1946** Fourth Republic proclaimed. **1949** Became a member of NATO; withdrew from military command structure in 1966. **1954** French withdrew from Indochina after eight years of war; start of guerrilla war against French rule in Algeria. **1957** France was a founder member of the European Economic Community. **1958** Algerian crisis caused collapse of Fourth Republic; de Gaulle took power, becoming president of the Fifth Republic in 1959. **1962** Algeria achieved independence. **1968** Revolutionary students rioted in Paris; there was a general strike throughout France. **1981** François Mitterrand was elected the Fifth Republic's first socialist president. **1995** Jacques Chirac (RPR) was elected president. There was

France: Regions

Region	Capital	Area		Population (1996 est)
		sq km	sq mi	
Alsace	Strasbourg	8,280	3,197	1,701,000
Aquitaine	Bordeaux	41,308	15,949	2,880,000
Auvergne	Clermont-Ferrand	26,013	10,044	1,315,000
Basse-Normandie	Caen	17,589	6,791	1,416,000
Brittany (Bretagne)	Rennes	27,208	10,505	2,861,000
Burgundy (Bourgogne)	Dijon	31,582	12,194	1,625,000
Centre	Orléans	39,151	15,116	2,443,000
Champagne-Ardenne	Châlons-sur-Marne	25,606	9,886	1,353,000
Corsica (Corse)	Ajaccio	8,680	3,351	260,000
Franche-Comté	Besançon	16,202	6,256	1,116,000
Haute-Normandie	Rouen	12,317	4,756	1,782,000
Ile de France	Paris	12,012	4,638	11,027,000
Languedoc-Roussillon	Montpellier	27,376	10,570	2,243,000
Limousin	Limoges	16,942	6,541	718,000
Lorraine	Metz	23,547	9,091	2,312,000
Midi-Pyrénées	Toulouse	45,348	17,509	2,506,000
Nord-Pas-de-Calais	Lille	12,414	4,793	4,001,000
Pays de la Loire	Nantes	32,082	12,387	3,154,000
Picardie	Amiens	19,399	7,490	1,864,000
Poitou-Charentes	Poitiers	25,809	9,965	1,622,000
Provence-Alpes-Côte d'Azur	Marseille	31,400	12,123	4,448,000
Rhône-Alpes	Lyon	43,698	16,872	5,608,000

widespread condemnation of the government's decision to resume nuclear tests in the South Pacific, and this was stopped in 1996. **1996** Spending cuts were agreed to meet European Monetary Union entry criteria. Unemployment was at a post-war high. **1997** A general election was called by President Chirac, with victory for Socialists; Lionel Jospin (PS) was appointed prime minister. **1998** There were protests by the unemployed. **1999** Two-thirds of France was declared a disaster zone after powerful storms struck Europe and caused widespread damage.

Gabon (Gabonese Republic)

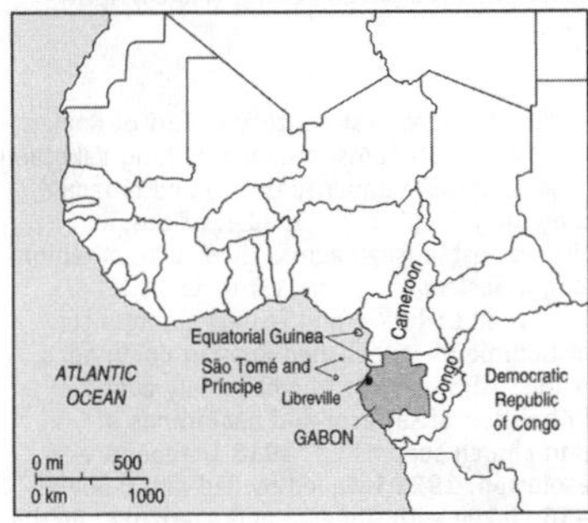

National name *République Gabonaise* **Area** 267,667 sq km/ 103,346 sq mi **Capital** Libreville **Major towns/ cities** Port-Gentil, Masuku (Franceville), Lambaréné, Mouanda

Government

Head of state Omar Bongo from 1967 **Head of government** Jean-François Ntoutoume-Emane from 1999 **Political system** emergent democracy **Armed forces** 4,700; plus a paramilitary force of 4,800 (1997) **Conscription** military service is voluntary **Defence spend** (% GDP) 1.9 (1997) **Education spend** (% GNP) 2.8 (1996) **Health spend** (% GDP) 0.6 (1990–95) **Death penalty** retained and used for ordinary crimes

Population and society

Population 1,197,000 (1999 est) **Population growth rate** 2.6% (1995–2000) **Ethnic groups** 40 Bantu peoples in four main groupings: the Fang, Eshira, Mbede, and Okande; there are also Pygmies and about 10% Europeans (mainly French) **Religion** Roman Catholic, also Muslim, animist **Life expectancy** 51 (men); 54 (women) (1995–2000) **Literacy rate** 76% (men); 57% (women) (1997 est) **Unemployment** 20% (1996 est)

Economy and resources

GDP (US$) 5.51 billion (1998) **GNP** (US$) 4.7 billion (1998) **GNP per capita (PPP)** (US$) 6,660 (1998) **Real GDP growth** (% change on previous year) 1.7 (1998) **Consumer price inflation** 3% (1998) **Foreign debt** (US$) 4.28 billion (1997) **Resources** petroleum, natural gas, manganese (one of world's foremost producers and exporters), iron ore, uranium, gold, niobium, talc, phosphates **Exports** petroleum and petroleum products, manganese, timber and wood products, uranium. Principal market: USA 67% (1997) **Imports** machinery and apparatus, transport equipment, food products, metals and metal products. Principal source: France 38% (1997)

▪ Tourist information

Time difference GMT +1 **Currency** franc CFA **Language** French (official), Bantu **Visa requirements** UK: visa required. USA: visa required **Embassy in the UK** 27 Elvaston Place, London SW7 5NL. Tel: (020) 7823 9986; fax: (020) 7584 0047 **British embassy** the British Embassy in Gabon closed in July 1991; all staff based in Yaoundé, Cameroon. The West African Department of the Foreign and Commonwealth Office is currently handling consular and commercial enquiries for Gabon; tel: (020) 7270 2516; fax: (020) 7270 3739 **Chamber of commerce** Chambre de Commerce, d'Agriculture, d'Industrie et de Mines du Gabon, BP 2234, Libreville. Tel: (241) 722 064; fax: (241) 746 477 **Office hours** 0730–1200 and 1430–1800 Mon–Fri **Banking hours** 0730–1130 and 1430–1630 Mon–Fri **Airports** international airports: Port-Gentil, Masuku, Libreville; 65 public domestic-services airfields; total passenger km: 764 million (1997 est) **Major ports** Port-Gentil and Owendo **Chief tourist attractions** national parks; tropical vegetation **Major holidays** 1 January, 12 March, 1 May, 17 August, 1 November, 25 December; variable: Eid-ul-Adha, Easter Monday, end of Ramadan, Whit Monday

Chronology

12th century Immigration of Bantu speakers into an area previously peopled by Pygmies. **1472** Gabon Estuary first visited by Portuguese navigators, who named it Gabao ('hooded cloak'), after the shape of the coastal area. **17th–18th centuries** Fang, from Cameroon in the north, and Omiene peoples colonized the area, attracted by the presence in coastal areas of European traders, who developed the ivory and slave trades, which lasted until the mid-19th century. **1839–42** Mpongwe coastal chiefs agreed to transfer sovereignty to France; Catholic and Protestant missionaries attracted to the area. **1849** Libreville ('Free Town') formed by slaves from a slave ship liberated by the French. **1889** Became part of French Congo, with Congo. **1910** Became part of French Equatorial Africa, which also comprised Congo, Chad, and Central African Republic. **1890s–1920s** Human and natural resources exploited by private concessionary companies. **1940–44** Supported the 'Free French' anti-Nazi cause during World War II. **1946** Became overseas territory within the French Community, with its own assembly. **1960** Independence achieved; Léon M'ba, a Fang of the pro-French Gabonese Democratic Block (BDG), became the first president. **1967** M'ba died and was succeeded by his protégé Albert Bernard Bongo, drawn from the Teke community. **1968** A one-party state established, with the BDG dissolved and replaced by Gabonese Democratic Party (PDG). **1973** Bongo converted to Islam and changed his first name to Omar, but continued to follow a pro-Western policy course and exploit rich mineral resources to increase prosperity. **1989** A coup attempt against Bongo was defeated; the economy deteriorated. **1990** The PDG won the first multiparty elections since 1964. French troops were sent in to maintain order following antigovernment riots. **1993** A national unity government was formed, including some opposition members. **1998** A new party, Rassemblement des Gaullois, was recognized. President Bongo was re-elected. **1999** Jean-François Ntoutoume-Emane was appointed prime minister.

Gambia, The Republic of

Area 10,402 sq km/4,016 sq mi **Capital** Banjul **Major towns/cities** Serekunda, Birkama, Bakau, Farafenni, Sukuta, Gunjur, Georgetown

Government

Head of state and government (interim) Yahya Jammeh from 1994 **Political system** transitional **Armed forces** 800 (1997) **Conscription** military service is mainly voluntary **Defence spend** (% GDP) 3.7 (1997) **Education spend** (% GNP) 5.5 (1995) **Health spend** (% GDP) 1.9 (1990–95) **Death penalty** retains the death penalty for ordinary crimes but can be considered abolitionist in practice (last execution 1981)

Population and society

Population 1,268,000 (1999 est) **Population growth rate** 3.2% (1995–2000) **Ethnic groups** wide mix of ethnic groups, the largest is the Mandingo (about 40%); other main groups are the Fula, Wolof, Jola, and Serahuli **Religion** Muslim 90%, with animist and Christian minorities

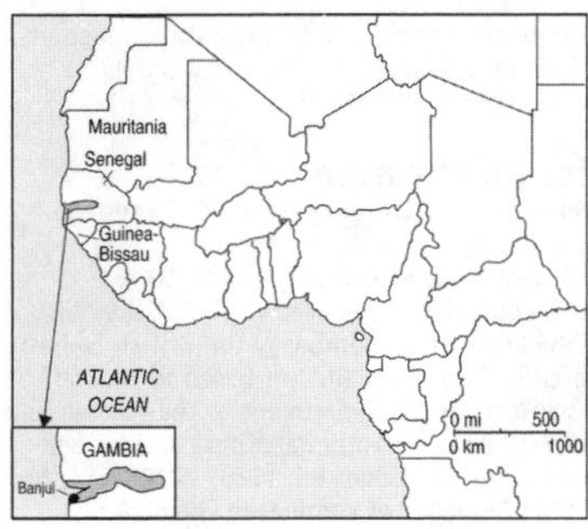

Life expectancy 45 (men); 49 (women) (1995–2000) **Literacy rate** 40% (men); 26% (women) (1997 est) **Unemployment** 26% (1995 est)

Economy and resources

GDP (US$) 424 million (1998) **GNP** (US$) 413 million (1998) **GNP per capita (PPP)** (US$) 1,430 (1998) **Real GDP growth** (% change on previous year) N/A **Consumer price inflation** 2.8% (1997) **Foreign debt** (US$) 430 million (1997) **Resources** ilmenite, zircon, rutile, petroleum (well discovered, but not exploited) **Exports** groundnuts and related products, cotton lint, fish and fish preparations, hides and skins. Principal market: Belgium-Luxembourg 78% (1997 est) **Imports** food and live animals, basic manufactures, machinery and transport equipment, mineral fuels and lubrications, miscellaneous manufactured articles, chemicals. Principal source: China (including Hong Kong) 25.1% (1997 est)

▪ Tourist information

Time difference GMT +/− 0 **Currency** dalasi **Language** English (official), Mandinka, Fula, and other indigenous tongues **Visa requirements** UK: visa not required for visits of up to 90 days. USA: visa required **Embassy in the UK** 57 Kensington Court, London W8 5DG. Tel: (020) 7937 6316/7/8; fax: (020) 7937 9095 **British embassy** British High Commission, PO Box 507, 48 Atlantic Road, Fajara, Banjul. Tel: (220) 495 133/4; fax: (220) 496 134 **Chamber of commerce** Gambia Chamber of Commerce and Industry, PO Box 33, 78 Wellington Street, Banjul. Tel: (220) 227 765 **Office hours** 0800–1600 Mon–Thu; 0800–1230 Fri and Sat **Banking hours** 0800–1330 Mon–Thu; 0800–1100 Fri **Airports** international airport: Banjul (Yundum); total passenger km: 50 million (1994) **Chief tourist attractions** beaches; coastal resorts; birdlife **Major holidays** 1 January, 1, 18 February, 1 May, 15 August, 25 December; variable: Eid-ul-Adha, Ashora, end of Ramadan (2 days), Good Friday, Prophet's Birthday

Chronology

13th century Wolof, Malinke (Mandingo), and Fulani tribes settled in the region from east and north. **14th century** Became part of the great Muslim Mali Empire, which, centred to northeast, also extended across Senegal, Mali, and southern Mauritania. **1455** The Gambia River was first sighted by the Portuguese. **1663 and 1681** The British and French established small settlements on the river at Fort James and Albreda. **1843** The Gambia became a British crown colony, administered with Sierra Leone until 1888. **1965** Independence was achieved as a constitutional monarchy within the Commonwealth, with Dawda K Jawara of the People's Progressive Party (PPP) as prime minister at the head of a multiparty democracy. **1970** The Gambia became a republic, with Jawara as president. **1982** The Gambia formed the Confederation of Senegambia with Senegal, which involved the integration of military forces, economic and monetary union, and coordinated foreign policy. **1994** Jawara was ousted in a military coup, and fled to Senegal; Yahya Jammeh was named acting head of state. **1996** A civilian constitution was adopted.

Georgia Republic of

Area 69,700 sq km/26,911 sq mi **Capital** Tbilisi **Major towns/cities** Kutaisi, Rustavi, Batumi, Sukhumi

Government

Head of state Eduard Shevardnadze from 1992 **Head of government** Otar Patsatsia from 1993 **Political system** emergent democracy **Armed forces** 33,200 (1997) **Conscription** compulsory for two years **Defence spend** (% GDP) 2.9 (1997) **Education spend** (% GDP) 5.2% (1995) **Health spend** (% GDP) 0.8 (1990–95) **Death penalty** abolished in 1997

Population and society

Population 5,005,000 (1999 est) **Population growth rate** −1.1% (1995–2000) **Ethnic groups** 70% ethnic Georgian, 8% Armenian, 7% ethnic Russian, 5% Azeri, 3% Ossetian, 2% Abkhazian, and 2% Greek **Religion** Georgian Orthodox, also Muslim **Life expectancy** 69 (men); 77 (women)

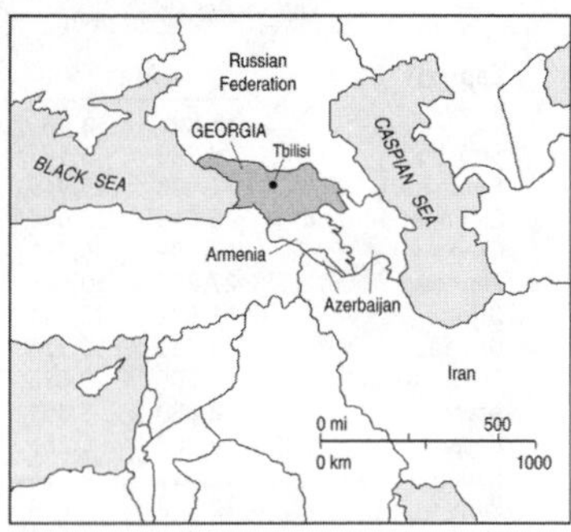

(1995–2000) **Literacy rate** 99% (men); 99% (women) (1995 est) **Unemployment** 2.8% (1996)

Economy and resources

GDP (US$) 5.24 billion (1998 est) **GNP** (US$) 5.1 billion (1998) **GNP per capita (PPP)** (US$) 2,620 (1998 est) **Real GDP growth** (% change on previous year) 2.9 (1998) **Consumer price inflation** 3.6% (1998) **Foreign debt** (US$) 1.44 billion (1997) **Resources** coal, manganese, barytes, clay, petroleum and natural gas deposits, iron and other ores, gold, agate, marble, alabaster, arsenic, tungsten, mercury **Exports** metal products, machinery, tea, beverages, food and tobacco products. Principal market: Russia 27.4% (1997) **Imports** mineral fuels, chemical and petroleum products, food products (mainly wheat and flour), light industrial products, beverages. Principal source: EU 22% (1997)

▪ Tourist information

Time difference GMT +3 **Currency** lari **Language** Georgian **Visa requirements** UK: visa required. USA: visa required **Embassy in the UK** 45 Avanmore Road, London W14. Tel/fax: (020) 7603 5325 **British embassy** Sosiiskaya Naberzehnaya, Moscow 72. Tel: (70095) 231 8511; fax: (70095) 233 3563 **Chamber of commerce** Chamber of Commerce and Industry of Georgia, Prospekt I, Chavchavadze 11, 380079 Tbilisi. Tel: (32) 230 045; fax: (32) 235 760 **Office hours** 0900–1300 and 1430–1700/1800 **Banking hours** 0930–1730 Mon–Fri **Airports** international airports: Tbilisi; total passenger km: 308 million (1995) **Chief tourist attractions** mountain scenery; health spas with mineral waters; waterfalls and caves **Major holidays** 1, 19 January, 3, 26 May, 28 August, 14 October, 23 November; variable: Orthodox Christmas (January), Orthodox Easter (March/April)

Chronology

4th century BC Georgian kingdom founded. **1st century BC** Part of Roman Empire. **AD 337** Christianity adopted. **458** Tbilisi founded by King Vakhtang Gorgasal. **mid-7th century** Tbilisi brought under Arab rule and renamed Tiflis. **1121** Tbilisi liberated by King David II the Builder, of the Gagrationi dynasty. An empire was established across the Caucasus region, remaining powerful until Mongol onslaughts in the 13th and 14th centuries. **1555** Western Georgia fell to Turkey and Eastern Georgia to Persia (Iran). **1783** Treaty of Georgievsk established Russian dominance over Georgia. **1804–13** First Russo-Iranian war fought largely over Georgia. **late 19th century** Abolition of serfdom and beginnings of industrialization, but Georgian church suppressed. **1918** Independence established after Russian Revolution. **1921** Invaded by Red Army; Soviet republic established. **1922–36** Linked with Armenia and Azerbaijan as the Transcaucasian Federation. **1930s** Rapid industrial development, but resistance to agricultural collectivization and violent political purges instituted by the Georgian Soviet dictator Joseph Stalin. **1936** Became separate republic within the USSR. **early 1940s** 200,000 Meskhetians deported from southern Georgia to Central Asia on Stalin's orders. **1972** Drive against endemic corruption launched by new Georgian Communist Party (GCP) leader Eduard Shevardnadze. **1978** Violent demonstrations by nationalists in Tbilisi. **1981–88** Increasing demands for autonomy were encouraged from 1986 by the *glasnost* initiative of the reformist Soviet leader Mikhail Gorbachev. **1989** The formation of the nationalist Georgian Popular Front led the minority Abkhazian and Ossetian communities in northwest and central-north Georgia to demand secession, provoking interethnic clashes. A state of emergency was imposed in Abkhazia; 20 pro-independence demonstrators were killed in Tbilisi by Soviet troops; Georgian sovereignty was declared by parliament. **1990** A nationalist coalition triumphed in elections and Gamsakhurdia became president. The GCP seceded from the Communist Party of the USSR. **1991** Independence was declared. The GCP was outlawed and all relations with the USSR severed. Demonstrations were held against the increasingly dictatorial Gamsakhurdia; a state of emergency was declared. **1992** Gamsakhurdia fled to Armenia; Shevardnadze, with military backing, was appointed interim president. Georgia was admitted into the United Nations (UN). Clashes continued in South Ossetia and Abkhazia, where independence had been declared. **1993** The conflict with Abkhazi separatists intensified, forcing

Shevardnadze to seek Russian military help. Otar Patsatsia was appointed prime minister. **1994** Georgia joined the Commonwealth of Independent States (CIS). A military cooperation pact was signed with Russia. A ceasefire was agreed with the Abkhazi separatists; 2,500 Russian peacekeeping troops were deployed in the region and paramilitary groups disarmed. Inflation exceeded 5,000% per annum. **1996** A cooperation pact with the European Union (EU) was signed as economic growth resumed. Elections to the secessionist Abkhazi parliament were declared illegal by the Georgian government. **1997** A new opposition party, Front for the Reinstatement of Legitimate Power in Georgia, was formed. There were talks between the government and the breakaway Abkhazi government. **1998** There was another outbreak of fighting in Abkhazia. **2000** President Shevardnadze won a second term in elections.

Germany Federal Republic of

National name *Bundesrepublik Deutschland* **Area** 357,041 sq km/137,853 sq mi **Capital** Berlin (government offices moving in phases from Bonn back to Berlin) **Major towns/cities** Cologne, Hamburg, Munich, Essen, Frankfurt am Main, Dortmund, Stuttgart, Düsseldorf, Leipzig, Dresden, Bremen, Duisburg, Hannover

Government

Head of state Johannes Rau from 1999 **Head of government** Gerhard Schroeder from 1998 **Political system** liberal democracy **Armed forces** 347,100 (1997) **Conscription** 10 months **Defence spend** (% GDP) 1.6 (1997) **Education spend** (% GNP) 4.8 (1996) **Health spend** (% GDP) 8.2 (1996) **Death penalty** abolished in the Federal Republic of Germany in 1949 and in the German Democratic Republic in 1987

Population and society

Population 82,177,000 (1999 est) **Population growth rate** 0.14% (1995–2000) **Ethnic groups** predominantly Germanic; notable Danish and Slavonic ethnic minorities in the north; significant population of foreigners, including 1.9 million officially recognized *Gastarbeiter* ('guest workers'), predominantly Turks, Greeks, Italians, and Yugoslavs; by 1993 Germany had received more than 200,000 refugees fleeing the Yugoslav civil war **Religion** Protestant (mainly Lutheran) 43%, Roman Catholic 36% **Life expectancy** 74 (men); 80 (women) (1995–2000) **Literacy rate** 99% (men); 99% (women) (1997 est) **Unemployment** 9.4% (1998)

Germany: States

State	Capital	Area		Population (1997 est)
		sq km	sq mi	
Baden-Württemberg	Stuttgart	35,752	13,804	10,393,000
Bavaria	Munich	70,551	27,240	12,057,000
Berlin	Berlin	889	343	3,447,000
Brandenburg	Potsdam	29,479	11,382	2,562,000
Bremen	Bremen	404	156	676,000
Hamburg	Hamburg	755	292	1,707,000
Hessen	Wiesbaden	21,114	8,152	6,031,000
Lower Saxony	Hannover	47,606	18,381	7,832,000
Mecklenburg-West Pomerania	Schwerin	23,170	8,946	1,816,000
North Rhine-Westphalia	Düsseldorf	34,077	13,157	17,962,000
Rhineland-Palatinate	Mainz	19,852	7,665	4,010,000
Saarland	Saarbrücken	2,570	992	1,083,000
Saxony	Dresden	18,412	7,109	4,538,000
Saxony-Anhalt	Magdeburg	20,446	7,894	2,715,000
Schleswig-Holstein	Kiel	15,770	6,089	2,750,000
Thuringia	Erfurt	16,171	6,244	2,485,000

Economy and resources

GDP (US$) 2,142 billion (1998) **GNP** (US$) 2,122.7 billion (1998) **GNP per capita (PPP)** (US$) 20,810 (1998) **Real GDP growth** (% change on previous year) 2.3 (1998) **Consumer price inflation** 1.9% (1998) **Resources** lignite, hard coal, potash salts, crude oil, natural gas, iron ore, copper, timber, nickel, uranium **Exports** road vehicles, electrical machinery, metals and metal products, textiles, chemicals. Principal market: France 11.7% (1998) **Imports** road vehicles, electrical machinery, food and live animals, clothing and accessories, crude petroleum and petroleum products. Principal source: France 11% (1998)

▪ Tourist information

Time difference GMT +1 **Currency** Deutschmark **Language** German **Visa requirements** UK: visa not required. USA: visa not required **Embassy in the UK** 23 Belgrave Square, London SW1X 8PZ. Tel: (020) 7824 1300; fax: (020) 7824 1435 **British embassy** Friedrich-Ebert-Allée 77, 53113 Bonn. Tel: (228) 91670; fax: (228) 9167 331 **Chamber of commerce** Deutscher Industrie- und Handelstag (Association of German Chambers of Industry and Commerce), Adenauerallée 148, 53113 Bonn. Tel: (228) 1040; fax: (228) 104 158 **Office hours** 0800–1600 Mon–Fri **Banking hours** generally 0830–1300 and 1400/1430–1600 Mon–Fri; Thu until 1730 in main cities. Main branches do not close for lunch **Airports** international airports: Berlin-Tegel (Otto Lilienthal), Berlin-Schönefeld, Berlin-Tempelhof, Leipzig/Halle, Dresden (Klotsche), Bremen (Neuenland), Cologne, Düsseldorf (Lohausen), Frankfurt, Hamburg, Hannover (Langenhagen), Munich (Franz Joseph Strauss), Münster-Osnabrück, Nuremberg, Saarbrucken (Ensheim), Stuttgart (Echterdingen); several domestic airports; total passenger km: 87,983 million (1997 est) **Major ports** Hamburg, Kiel, Bremerhaven, Rostock **Chief tourist attractions** spas; summer and winter resorts; medieval towns and castles; Black Forest; Rhine Valley; North and Baltic Sea coasts; mountains of Thuringia and Bavaria and the Erzgebirge **Major holidays** 1, 6 January, 1 May, 3 October, 1 November, 25–26 December; variable: Good Friday, Easter Monday, Ascension Thursday, Whit Monday, Corpus Christi, Assumption

Chronology

c. **1000 BC** Germanic tribes from Scandinavia began to settle the region between the rivers Rhine, Elbe, and Danube. **AD 9** Romans tried and failed to conquer Germanic tribes. **5th century** Germanic tribes plundered Rome, overran western Europe, and divided it into tribal kingdoms. **496** Clovis, King of the Franks, conquered the Alemanni tribe of western Germany. **772–804** After series of fierce wars, Charlemagne extended Frankish authority over Germany, subjugated Saxons, imposed Christianity, and took title of Holy Roman Emperor. **843** Treaty of Verdun divided the Holy Roman Empire into three, with eastern portion corresponding to modern Germany; local princes became virtually independent. **919** Henry the Fowler restored central authority and founded Saxon dynasty. **962** Otto the Great enlarged the kingdom and revived title of Holy Roman Emperor. **1024–1254** Emperors of Salian and Hohenstaufen dynasties came into conflict with popes; frequent civil wars allowed German princes to regain independence. **12th century** German expansion eastwards into lands between rivers Elbe and Oder. **13th–14th centuries** Hanseatic League of Allied German cities became a great commercial and naval power. **1438** Title of Holy Roman Emperor became virtually hereditary in the Habsburg family of Austria. **1517** Martin Luther began the Reformation; Emperor Charles V tried to suppress Protestantism; civil war ensued. **1555** Peace of Augsburg: Charles V forced to accept that each German prince could choose the religion of his own lands. **1618–48** Thirty Years' War: bitter conflict, partly religious, between certain German princes and emperor, with foreign intervention; the war wrecked the German economy and reduced the Holy Roman Empire to a name. **1701** Frederick I, Elector of Brandenburg, promoted to King of Prussia. **1740** Frederick the Great of Prussia seized Silesia from Austria and retained it through war of Austrian Succession (1740–48) and Seven Years' War (1756–63). **1772–95** Prussia joined Russia and Austria in the partition of Poland. **1792** Start of French Revolutionary Wars, involving many German states, with much fighting on German soil. **1806** Holy Roman Empire abolished; France formed puppet Confederation of the Rhine in western Germany and defeated Prussia at Battle of Jena. **1813–15** National revival enabled Prussia to take part in the defeat of Napoleon at Battles of Leipzig and Waterloo. **1814–15** Congress of Vienna rewarded Prussia with Rhineland, Westphalia, and much of Saxony; loose German Confederation formed by 39 independent states. **1848–49** Liberal revolutions in many German states; Frankfurt Assembly sought German unity; revolutions suppressed. **1862** Otto von Bismarck became prime minister of Prussia. **1866** Seven Weeks' War: Prussia defeated Austria, dissolved German Confederation, and established

North German Confederation under Prussian leadership. **1870–71** Franco-Prussian War; southern German states agreed to German unification; German Empire proclaimed, with King of Prussia as emperor and Bismarck as chancellor. **1890** Wilhelm II dismissed Bismarck and sought to make Germany a leading power in world politics. **1914** Germany encouraged the Austrian attack on Serbia that started World War I; Germany invaded Belgium and France. **1918** Germany defeated; a revolution overthrew the monarchy. **1919** Treaty of Versailles: Germany lost land to France, Denmark, and Poland; demilitarization and reparations imposed; Weimar Republic proclaimed. **1922–23** Hyperinflation: in 1922, one dollar was worth 50 marks; in 1923, one dollar was worth 2.5 trillion marks. **1929** Start of economic slump caused mass unemployment and brought Germany close to revolution. **1933** Adolf Hitler, leader of Nazi Party, became chancellor. **1934** Hitler took title of Führer (leader), murdered rivals, and created one-party state with militaristic and racist ideology; rearmament reduced unemployment. **1938** Germany annexed Austria and Sudeten; occupied remainder of Czechoslovakia in 1939. **1939** German invasion of Poland started World War II; Germany defeated France in 1940, attacked USSR in 1941, and pursued extermination of Jews. **1945** Germany defeated and deprived of its conquests; eastern lands transferred to Poland; USA, USSR, UK, and France established zones of occupation. **1948–49** Disputes between Western allies and USSR led to Soviet blockade of West Berlin. **1949** Partition of Germany: US, French, and British zones in West Germany became Federal Republic of Germany with Konrad Adenauer as chancellor; Soviet zone in East Germany became communist German Democratic Republic led by Walter Ulbricht. **1953** Uprising in East Berlin suppressed by Soviet troops. **1955** West Germany became a member of NATO; East Germany joined the Warsaw Pact. **1957** West Germany was a founder member of the European Economic Community. **1960s** West Germany achieved rapid growth and great prosperity. **1961** East Germany constructed Berlin Wall to prevent emigration to West Berlin (part of West Germany). **1969** Willy Brandt, Social Democratic Party chancellor of West Germany, sought better relations with USSR and East Germany. **1971** Erich Honecker succeeded Ulbricht as Communist Party leader, and became head of state in 1976. **1972** The Basic Treaty established relations between West Germany and East Germany as between foreign states. **1982** Helmut Kohl (Christian Democratic Union) became the West German chancellor. **1989** There was a mass exodus of East Germans to West Germany via Hungary; East Germany opened its frontiers, including the Berlin Wall. **1990** The communist regime in East Germany collapsed; Germany was reunified with Kohl as chancellor. **1991** Germany took the lead in pressing for closer European integration in the Maastricht Treaty. **1995** Unemployment reached 3.8 million. **1996** There was a public-sector labour dispute over welfare reform plans and the worsening economy. Spending cuts were agreed to meet European Monetary Union entry criteria. **1998** Unemployment reached a post-war high of 12.6%. The CDU-CSU-FDP coalition was defeated in a general election and a 'Red-Green' coalition government was formed by the SPD and the Greens, with Gerhard Schroeder as chancellor. Kohl was replaced as CDU leader by Wolfgang Schäuble. **1999** A delay was announced in the planned phasing out of nuclear power. Social Democrat Johannes Rau was elected president. **2000** Former chancellor Helmut Kohl admitted financial irregularities within his party, and a criminal investigation was launched as he resigned his honorary leadership of the CDU. Leader Wolfgang Schäuble was also forced to resign, and was replaced by Angela Merkel.

Ghana Republic of (formerly the Gold Coast)

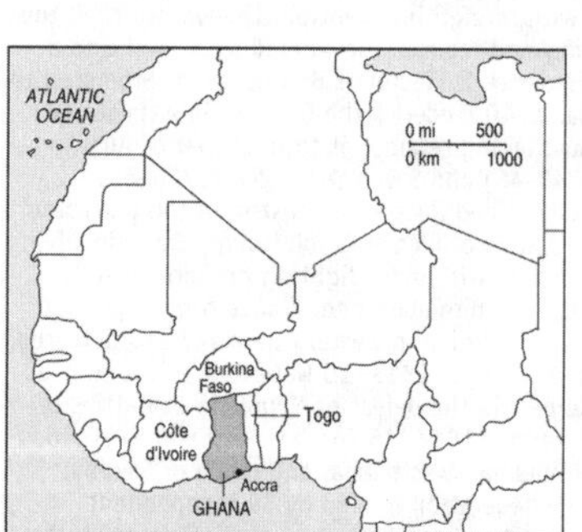

Area 238,305 sq km/ 92,009 sq mi **Capital** Accra **Major towns/ cities** Kumasi, Tamale, Tema, Sekondi-Takoradi, Cape Coast, Sunyani, Koforidua, Ho, Yendi, Tarkwa, Wa, Bolgatanga

Government

Head of state and government Jerry Rawlings from 1981 **Political system** emergent democracy **Armed forces** 7,000; plus a paramilitary force of 7,500 (1997) **Conscription** military service is voluntary **Defence spend** (% GDP) 1.5 (1997) **Education spend** (% GNP) 3.1 (1993–94) **Health spend** (% GDP) 1.3 (1990–95) **Death penalty** retained and used for ordinary crimes

Population and society

Population 19,678,000 (1999 est) **Population growth rate** 2.7% (1995–2000) **Ethnic groups** over 75 ethnic groups; most significant are the Akan in the south and west (44%), the Mole-Dagbani in the north, the Ewe in the south, the Ga in the region of the capital city, and the Fanti in the coastal area **Religion** Christian 62%, Muslim 16%, animist **Life expectancy** 58 (men); 62 (women) (1995–2000) **Literacy rate** 77% (men); 57% (women) (1997 est) **Unemployment** 20% (1997 est)

Economy and resources

GDP (US$) 7.5 billion (1998) **GNP** (US$) 7.2 billion (1998) **GNP per capita (PPP)** (US$) 1,610 (1998 est) **Real GDP growth** (% change on previous year) 1.2 (1998) **Consumer price inflation** 25% (1998) **Foreign debt** (US$) 5.98 billion (1997) **Resources** diamonds, gold, manganese, bauxite **Exports** gold, cocoa and related products, timber. Principal market: Togo 13% (1997) **Imports** raw materials, machinery and transport equipment, petroleum, food, basic manufactures. Principal source: UK 15% (1997)

▪ Tourist information

Time difference GMT +/– 0 **Currency** cedi **Language** English (official) and African languages **Visa requirements** UK: visa required. USA: visa required **Embassy in the UK** (education and visas) 104 Highgate Hill, London N6 5HE. Tel: (020) 8342 8686; fax: (020) 8342 8566; (tourist information) 102 Park Street, London W1Y 3RJ. Tel: (020) 7493 4901; fax: (020) 7629 1730 **British embassy** British High Commission, PO Box 296, Osu Link, off Gamel Abdul Nasser Avenue, Accra. Tel: (21) 221 665; fax: (21) 664 652 **Chamber of commerce** Ghana National Chamber of Commerce, PO Box 2325, Accra. Tel: (21) 662 427; fax: (21) 662 210 **Office hours** 0800–1200 and 1400–1700 Mon–Fri **Banking hours** 0830–1400 Mon–Thu and 0830–1500 Fri. A few city branches are open 0830–1200 Sat **Airports** international airport: Accra (Koteka); four domestic airports; total passenger km: 611 million (1995) **Major ports** Sekondi, Tema **Chief tourist attractions** game reserves; beaches; traditional festivals; old castles and trading posts **Major holidays** 1 January, 6 March, 1 May, 4 June, 1 July, 25–26, 31 December; variable: Good Friday, Easter Monday, Holy Saturday

Chronology

5th–12th century Ghana Empire (from which present-day country's name derives) flourished, with its centre 500 mi/800 km to the northwest, in Mali. **13th century** In coastal and forest areas Akan peoples founded the first states. **15th century** Gold-seeking Mande traders entered northern Ghana from the northeast, founding Dagomba and Mamprussi states; Portuguese navigators visited coastal region, naming it the 'Gold Coast', building a fort at Elmina, and slave trading began. **17th century** Gonja kingdom founded in north by Mande speakers; Ga and Ewe states founded in southeast by immigrants from Nigeria; in central Ghana, controlling gold reserves around Kumasi, the Ashanti, a branch of the Akans, founded what became the most powerful state in precolonial Ghana. **1618** British trading settlement established on Gold Coast. **18th–19th centuries** Centralized Ashanti kingdom at its height, dominating between Komoe River in the west and Togo Mountains in the east and active in slave trade; Fante state powerful along coast in the south. **1874** Britain, after ousting the Danes and Dutch and defeating the Ashanti, made the Gold Coast (the southern provinces) a crown colony. **1898–1901** After three further military campaigns, Britain finally subdued and established protectorates over Ashanti and the northern territories. **early 20th century** The colony developed into a major cocoa-exporting region. **1917** West Togoland, formerly German-ruled, was administered with the Gold Coast as British Togoland. **1949** Campaign for independence launched by Kwame Nkrumah, who formed the Convention People's Party (CPP) and became prime minister in 1952. **1957** Independence achieved, within the Commonwealth, as Ghana, which included British Togoland; Nkrumah became prime minister. Policy of 'African socialism' and nonalignment pursued. **1960** Became a republic, with Nkrumah as president. **1964** Ghana became a one-party state, dominated by the CCP, and developed links with communist bloc. **1972** A coup placed Col Ignatius Acheampong at the head of a military government as the economy deteriorated. **1978** Acheampong was deposed in a bloodless coup. Flight-Lt Jerry Rawlings, a populist soldier who launched a drive against corruption, came to power. **1979** There was a return to civilian rule. **1981** Rawlings seized power again. All political parties were banned. **1992** A pluralist constitution was approved in a referendum, lifting the ban on political parties. Rawlings won presidential elections. **1996** The New Democratic Congress (NDC) won an assembly majority.

Greece (Hellenic Republic)

National name *Elliniki Dimokratia* **Area** 131,957 sq km/50,948 sq mi **Capital** Athens **Major towns/cities** Thessaloníki, Piraeus, Patras, Irákleion, Larissa, Volos

Government

Head of state Costis Stephanopoulos from 1995 **Head of government** Costas Simitis from 1996 **Political system** liberal democracy **Armed forces** 162,300 (1997) **Conscription** 19–24 months **Defence spend** (% GDP) 4.6 (1997) **Education spend** (% GNP) 3 (1996) **Health spend** (% GDP) 5.2 (1996) **Death penalty** abolished in 1993

Population and society

Population 10,626,000 (1999 est) **Population growth rate** 0.3% (1995–2000); 0% (2000–05) **Ethnic groups** predominantly Greek; main minorities are Turks, Slavs, and Albanians **Religion** Greek Orthodox; also Roman Catholic **Life expectancy** 76 (men); 81 (women) (1995–2000) **Literacy rate** 98% (men); 95% (women) (1997 est) **Unemployment** 10% (1998 est)

Economy and resources

GDP (US$) 120.3 billion (1998) **GNP** (US$) 122.9 billion (1998) **GNP per capita (PPP)** (US$) 13,010 (1998) **Real GDP growth** (% change on previous year) 3.4 (1998) **Consumer price inflation** 4% (1998) **Resources** bauxite, nickel, iron pyrites, magnetite, asbestos, marble, salt, chromite, lignite **Exports** fruit and vegetables, clothing, mineral fuels and lubricants, textiles, iron and steel, aluminium and aluminium alloys. Principal market: Germany 25.2% (1997) **Imports** petroleum and petroleum products, machinery and transport equipment, food and live animals, chemicals and chemical products. Principal source: Italy 15.6% (1997)

▪ Tourist information

Time difference GMT +2 **Currency** drachma **Language** Greek (official), Macedonian (100,000–200,000 est) **Visa requirements** UK: visa not required. USA: visa not required **Embassy in the UK** Embassy of the Hellenic Republic, 1A Holland Park, London W11 3TP. Tel: (020) 7221 6467; fax: (020) 7243 3202 **British embassy** Odos Ploutarchon 1, 106 75 Athens. Tel: (1) 723 6211/9; fax: (1) 724 1872 **Chamber of commerce** Athens Chamber of Commerce, Odos Akademias 7, 106 71 Athens. Tel: (1) 360 2411; fax: (1) 360 7897 **Office hours** 0800–1430 and 1730–1730 Mon–Fri **Banking hours** 0800–1400 Mon–Fri. Many banks on larger islands stay open in the afternoon and some during the evening to offer currency-exchange facilities during the tourist season **Airports** international airports: Athens (Athinai), Iráklion/Crete, Thessaloníki (Micra), Corfu (Kerkira), Rhodes (Paradisi); 25 domestic airports, of which 14 are also international; total passenger km: 9,261 million (1997 est) **Major ports** Piraeus, Thessaloníki, Patras, Irákleion **Chief tourist attractions** Aegean islands; historical and archaeological remains – palace of Knossos on Crete, Delphi, the Acropolis in Athens; climate **Major holidays** 1, 6 January, 25 March, 1 May, 15 August, 28 October, 25–26 December; variable: Monday in Lent, Good Friday, Easter Monday, Whit Monday

Chronology

***c.* 2000–1200 BC** Mycenaean civilization flourished. ***c.* 1500–1100 BC** Central Greece and Peloponnese invaded by tribes of Achaeans, Aeolians, Ionians, and Dorians. ***c.* 1000–500 BC** Rise of the Greek city states; Greek colonies established around the shores of the Mediterranean. ***c.* 490–404 BC** Ancient Greek culture reached its zenith in the democratic city state of Athens. **357–338 BC** Philip II of Macedon won supremacy over Greece; cities fought to regain and preserve independence. **146 BC** Roman Empire defeated Macedon and annexed Greece. **476 AD** Western Roman Empire ended; Eastern Empire continued as Byzantine Empire, based at Constantinople, with essentially Greek culture. **1204** Crusaders partitioned Byzantine Empire; Athens, Achaea, and Thessaloniki came under Frankish rulers. **late 14th century–1461** Ottoman Turks conquered mainland Greece and captured Constantinople in 1453; Greek language and culture preserved by Orthodox Church. **1685** Venetians captured Peloponnese; regained by Turks in 1715. **late 18th century** Beginnings of Greek nationalism among émigrés and merchant class. **1814** *Philike Hetairia* ('Friendly Society') formed by revolutionary Greek nationalists in Odessa. **1821** *Philike Hetairia* raised Peloponnese brigands in revolt against Turks; War of Independence ensued. **1827** Battle of Navarino: Britain, France, and Russia intervened to destroy Turkish fleet; Count Ioannis Kapodistrias elected president of Greece. **1829** Treaty of Adrianople: under Russian pressure, Turkey recognized independence of small Greek state. **1832** Great Powers elected Otto of Bavaria as king of Greece. **1843** Coup forced King Otto to grant a constitution. **1862** Mutiny and rebellion led King Otto to abdicate. **1863** George of Denmark became king of the Hellenes. **1864** Britain transferred Ionian islands to Greece. **1881** Following Treaty of Berlin in 1878, Greece was allowed to annex Thessaly and part of Epirus. **late 19th century** Politics dominated by Kharilaos Trikoupis, who emphasized economic development, and Theodoros Deliyiannis, who emphasized territorial expansion. **1897** Greco-Turkish War ended in Greek defeat. **1908** Cretan Assembly led by Eleutherios Venizelos proclaimed union with Greece. **1910** Venizelos became prime minister and introduced financial, military, and constitutional reforms. **1912–13** Balkan Wars: Greece annexed a large area of Epirus and Macedonia. **1916** 'National Schism': Venizelos formed rebel pro-Allied government while royalists remained neutral. **1917–18** Greek forces fought on Allied side in World War I. **1919–22** Greek invasion of Asia Minor; after Turkish victory, a million refugees came to Greece. **1924** Republic declared amid great political instability. **1935** Greek monarchy restored with George II. **1936** Gen Ioannia Metaxas established right-wing dictatorship. **1940** Greece successfully repelled Italian invasion. **1941–44** German occupation of Greece; rival monarchist and communist resistance groups operated from 1942. **1946–49** Civil war: communists defeated by monarchists with military aid from Britain and USA. **1952** Became a member of NATO. **1967** 'Greek Colonels' seized power under George Papadopoulos; political activity banned; King Constantine II exiled. **1973** Republic proclaimed with Papadopoulos as president. **1974** Cyprus crisis caused downfall of military regime; Constantinos Karamanlis returned from exile to form Government of National Salvation and restore democracy. **1981** Andreas Papandreou was elected Greece's first socialist prime minister; Greece entered the European Community. **1989–93** The election defeat of Panhellenic Socialist Movement (PASOK) was followed by unstable coalition governments. **1993** PASOK returned to power. **1996** Costas Simitis succeeded Papandreou as prime minister. **1997** Direct talks with Turkey resulted in an agreement to settle all future disputes peacefully. **2000** Costas Simitis was re-elected as prime minister.

Grenada

Area (including the southern Grenadine Islands, notably Carriacou and Petit Martinique) 344 sq km/133 sq mi **Capital** St George's **Major towns/cities** Grenville, Sauteurs, Victoria, Hillsborough (Carriacou)

Government

Head of state Elizabeth II from 1974, represented by governor general Daniel Williams from 1996 **Head of government** Keith Mitchell from 1995 **Political system** liberal democracy **Armed forces** no standing army; 730-strong regional security unit (1997) **Health spend** (% GDP) 2.7 (1995) **Death penalty** retained and used for ordinary crimes but can be considered abolitionist in practice (last execution in 1978)

Population and society

Population 97,000 (1999 est) **Population growth rate** 0.3% (1995–2025) **Ethnic groups** majority is of black African descent **Religion** Roman Catholic 53%, Anglican, Seventh Day Adventist, Pentecostal **Life expectancy** 69 (men); 74 (women) (1998 est) **Literacy rate** 90% (1997 est) **Unemployment** 14% (1997)

Economy and resources

GDP (US$) 295 million (1998 est) **GNP** (US$) 305 million (1998) **GNP per capita (PPP)** (US$) 4,720 (1998) **Real GDP growth** (% change on previous year) 5 (1998) **Consumer price inflation** 1.2% (1998) **Foreign debt** (US$) 103 million (1997) **Exports** cocoa, bananas, cocoa, mace, fresh fruit. Principal market: UK, USA, France 18.5% each (1995) **Imports** foodstuffs, mineral fuels, machinery and transport equipment, basic manufactures, beverages, tobacco. Principal source: USA 30% (1995)

▪ Tourist information

Time difference GMT –4 **Currency** Eastern Caribbean dollar **Language** English (official); some French-African patois spoken **Visa requirements** UK: visa not required. USA: visa not required **Embassy in the UK** 1 Collingham Gardens, London SW5 0HW. Tel: (020) 7373 7809; fax: (020) 7370 7040 **British embassy** British High Commission, 14 Church Street, St George's. Tel: 440 3222; fax: 440 4939 **Chamber of commerce** Grenada Chamber of Industry and Commerce, PO Box 129, Decaul Building, Mount Gay, St George's. Tel: 440 2937; fax: 440 6627 **Office hours** 0800–1200 and 1300–1600 Mon–Fri **Banking hours** 0800–1400 Mon–Thu; 0800–1300 and 1400–1700 Fri **Airports** international airports: St George's (Point Salines); total aircraft arrivals: 11,310 (1995) **Chief tourist attractions** white sandy beaches; mountainous interior; rainforest **Major holidays** 1–2 January, 7 February, 1 May, 3–4 August, 25 October, 25–26 December; variable: Corpus Christi, Good Friday, Easter Monday, Whit Monday

Chronology

1498 Sighted by the explorer Christopher Columbus; Spanish named it Grenada since its hills were reminiscent of the Andalusian city. **1650** Colonized by French settlers from Martinique, who faced resistance from the local Carib Indian community armed with poison arrows, before the defeated Caribs performed a mass suicide. **1783** Ceded to Britain as a colony by the Treaty of Versailles; black African slaves imported to work cotton, sugar, and tobacco plantations. **1795** Abortive rebellion against British rule led by Julien Fedon, a black planter. **1834** Slavery abolished. **1950** Left-wing Grenada United Labour Party (GULP) founded by trade union leader Eric Gairy. **1951** Universal adult suffrage granted and GULP elected to power in a nonautonomous local assembly. **1958–62** Part of the Federation of the West Indies. **1967** Internal self-government achieved. **1974** Independence achieved within the Commonwealth, with Gairy as prime minister. **1979** Autocratic Gairy was removed in a bloodless coup led by left-wing Maurice Bishop of the New Jewel Movement. The constitution was suspended and a People's Revolutionary Government established. **1982** Relations with the USA and Britain deteriorated as ties with Cuba and the USSR strengthened. **1983** After attempts to improve relations with the USA, Bishop was overthrown by left-wing opponents, precipitating a military coup by Gen Hudson Austin. The USA invaded; there were 250 fatalities. Austin was arrested and the 1974 constitution was reinstated. **1984** Newly formed centre-left New National Party (NNP) won a general election and its leader became prime minister. **1991** Integration of the Windward Islands was proposed. **1995** A general election was won by the NNP, led by Keith Mitchell. A plague of pink mealy bugs caused damage to crops estimated at $60 million. **1999** The ruling NNP gained a sweeping general election victory.

Guatemala Republic of

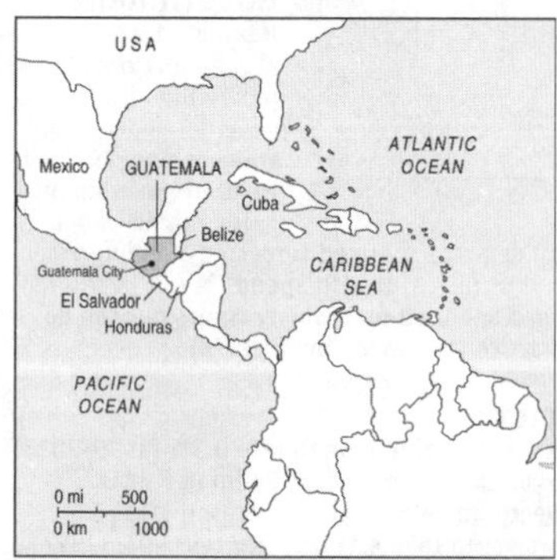

National name *República de Guatemala* **Area** 108,889 sq km/ 42,042 sq mi **Capital** Guatemala City **Major towns/cities** Quezaltenango, Escuintla, Puerto Barrios (naval base), Retalhuleu, Chiquimula

Government

Head of state and government Alfonso Portillo from 1999 **Political system** liberal democracy **Armed forces** 40,700; plus paramilitary forces of 9,800 (1997) **Conscription** selective conscription for 30 months **Defence spend** (% GDP) 1.5 (1997) **Education spend** (% GNP) 1.7 (1996) **Health spend** (% GDP) 0.9 (1990–95) **Death penalty** retained and used for ordinary crimes

Population and society

Population 11,090,000 (1999 est) **Population growth rate** 2.6% (1995–2000) **Ethnic groups** two main ethnic groups: American Indians and ladinos (others, including Europeans, black Africans, and mestizos). American Indians are descended from the highland Mayas **Religion** Roman Catholic 70%, Protestant 30% **Life expectancy** 61 (men); 67 (women) (1995–2000) **Literacy rate** 74% (men); 59% (women) (1997 est) **Unemployment** 5.2% (1997 est)

Economy and resources

GDP (US$) 19.28 billion (1998) **GNP** (US$) 17.7 billion (1998) **GNP per capita (PPP)** (US$) 4,070 (1998) **Real GDP growth** (% change on previous year) 4.5 (1998) **Consumer price inflation** 13% (1998) **Foreign debt** (US$) 4.08 billion (1997) **Resources** petroleum, antimony, gold, silver, nickel, lead, iron, tungsten **Exports** coffee, bananas, sugar, cardamoms, shellfish, tobacco. Principal market: USA 35.8% (1997) **Imports** raw materials and intermediate goods for industry, consumer goods, mineral fuels and lubricants. Principal source: USA 41.2% (1997)

▪ Tourist information

Time difference GMT –6 **Currency** quetzal **Language** Spanish (official); 45% speak Mayan languages **Visa requirements** UK: visa required for business visits and tourist visits of over 90 days. USA: visa not required for a stay of up to 90 days **Embassy in the UK** 13 Fawcett Street, London SW10 9HN. Tel: (020) 7351 3042; fax: (020) 7376 5708 **British embassy** British Embassy, 7th Floor, Edificio Centro Financiero, Tower Two, 7a Avenida 5–10, Zona 4, Guatemala City. Tel: (2) 321 601/2/4; fax: (2) 341 904 **Chamber of commerce** Cámara de Comercio de Guatemala, 10a Calle 3–80, Zona 1, Guatemala City. Tel: (2) 82681; fax: (2) 514 197 **Office hours** 0800–1800 Mon–Fri; 0800–1200 Sat **Banking hours** 1000–1500 Mon–Thu; 1000–1800 Fri **Airports** international airport: Guatemala City (La Aurora); over 380 airstrips serving internal travel; total passenger km: 500 million (1995) **Chief tourist attractions** mountainous and densely forested landscape; Mayan temples and ruins at Tikal, Palenque, and Kamihal Juyú; Guatemala City, with its archaeological and historical museums **Major holidays** 1 January, 1 May, 30 June, 1 July, 15 September, 12, 20 October, 1 November, 24–25, 31 December; variable: Good Friday, Holy Thursday, Holy Saturday

Chronology

c. AD 250–900 Part of culturally advanced Maya civilization. **1524** Conquered by the Spanish adventurer Pedro de Alvarado and became a Spanish colony. **1821** Independence achieved from Spain, joining Mexico initially. **1823** Became part of United Provinces (Federation) of Central America, also embracing Costa Rica, El Salvador, Honduras, and Nicaragua. **1839** Achieved full independence. **1844–65** Rafael Carrera held power as president. **1873–85** The country was modernized on liberal lines by President Justo Rufino Barrios, the army was built up, and coffee growing introduced. **1944** Juan José Arevalo became president, ending a period of rule by dictators. Socialist programme of reform instituted by Arevalo, including establishing a social security system and redistributing land expropriated from large estates to landless peasants. **1954** Col Carlos Castillo Armas became president in a US-backed coup, after United Fruit Company plantations had been nationalized. Land reform halted. **1966** Civilian rule was restored. **1970s** More than 50,000 died in a spate of political violence as the military regime sought to liquidate left-wing dissidents. **1970** The military were back in power. **1976** An earthquake killed 27,000 and left more than 1 million homeless. **1981** Growth of an antigovernment guerrilla movement. Death squads and soldiers killed an estimated 11,000 civilians during the year. **1985** A new constitution was adopted; PDCG won the congressional elections. **1989** Over 100,000 people were killed, and 40,000 reported missing, since 1980. **1991** Diplomatic relations established with Belize, which Guatemala had long claimed. **1994** Peace talks were held with Guatemalan Revolutionary National Unity (URNG) rebels. Right-wing parties secured a majority in congress after elections. **1995** The government was criticized by USA and United Nations for widespread human-rights abuses. There was a ceasefire by rebels, the first in 30 years. **1996** A peace agreement was signed which ended the 36-year war. **1999** Alfonso Portillo, a right-wing candidate, was elected president.

Guinea Republic of

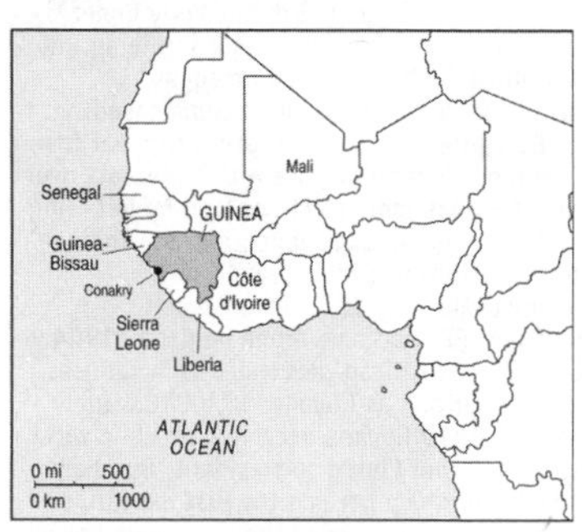

National name *République de Guinée* **Area** 245,857 sq km/ 94,925 sq mi **Capital** Conakry **Major towns/ cities** Labé, Nzérékoré, Kankan, Kindia

Government

Head of state Lansana Conté from 1984 **Head of government** Lamine Sidime from 1999 **Political system** emergent democracy **Armed forces** 9,700; plus paramilitary forces of 9,600 (1997) **Conscription** military service is compulsory for two years **Defence spend** (% GDP) 1.6 (1997) **Education spend** (% GNP) 2.2 (1993) **Health spend** (% GDP) 1.2 (1990–95) **Death penalty** retained and used for ordinary crimes

Population and society

Population 7,359,000 (1999 est) **Population growth rate** 0.8% (1995–2000) **Ethnic groups** 24 ethnic groups, including the Malinke, Peul, and Soussou **Religion** Muslim 95%, Christian **Life expectancy** 46 (men); 47 (women) (1995–2000) **Literacy rate** 52% (men); 24% (women) (1997 est)

Economy and resources

GDP (US$) 3.8 billion (1998) **GNP** (US$) 3.6 billion (1998) **GNP per capita (PPP)** (US$) 1,760 (1998) **Real GDP growth** (% change on previous year) 4.9 (1998) **Consumer price inflation** 2% (1998) **Foreign debt** (US$) 3.52 billion (1997) **Resources** bauxite (world's top exporter of bauxite and second-largest producer of bauxite ore), alumina, diamonds, gold, granite, iron ore, uranium, nickel, cobalt, platinum **Exports** bauxite, alumina, diamonds, coffee. Principal market: Russia 16.7% (1997) **Imports** foodstuffs, mineral fuels, semi-manufactured goods, consumer goods, textiles and clothing, machinery and transport equipment. Principal source: France 22.4% (1997)

■ Tourist information

Time difference GMT +/– 0 **Currency** Guinean franc **Language** French (official), African languages (of which eight are official) **Visa requirements** UK: visa required. USA: visa required **Embassy for the UK** 51 rue de la Faisanderie, 75016 Paris, France. Tel: (1) 4704 8148; fax: (1) 4704 5765 **British embassy** British Consulate, BP 834, Conakry. (All staff based in Dakar, Senegal.) Tel: (224) 442 959; fax: (224) 414 215 **Chamber of commerce** Chambre de Commerce, d'Industrie et d'Agriculture de Guinée, BP 545, Conakry. Tel: (224) 444 495; telex: 609 **Office hours** 0800–1630 Mon–Thu; 0800–1300 Fri **Banking hours** 0830–1230 and 1430–1630 Mon–Fri **Airports** international airport: Conakry; eight domestic airports; total passenger km: 52 million (1995) **Major holidays** 1 January, 3 April, 1 May, 15 August, 2 October, 1 November, 25 December; variable: Eid-ul-Adha, Easter Monday, end of Ramadan, Prophet's Birthday

Chronology

c. AD 900 The Susi people, a community related to the Malinke, immigrated from the northeast, pushing the indigenous Baga towards the Atlantic coast. **13th century** Susi kingdoms established, extending their influence to the coast; northeast Guinea was part of Muslim Mali Empire, centred to northeast. **mid-15th century** Portuguese traders visited the coast and later developed trade in slaves and ivory. **1849** French protectorate established over coastal region around Nunez River, which was administered with Senegal. **1890** Separate Rivières du Sud colony formed. **1895** Renamed French Guinea, the colony became part of French West Africa. **1946** French Guinea became an overseas territory of France. **1958** Full independence from France achieved as Guinea after referendum rejected remaining within French Community; Sékou Touré of the Democratic Party of Guinea (PDG) elected president. **1960s and 1970s** Touré established socialist one-party state, leading to deterioration in economy as 200,000 fled abroad. **1979** Strong opposition to Touré's rigid Marxist policies forced him to accept a return to mixed economy and legalize private enterprise. **1984** Touré died. A bloodless military coup brought Col Lansana Conté to power; the PDG was outlawed and political prisoners released; and there were market-centred economic reforms. **1991** Antigovernment general strike and mass protests. **1992** The constitution was amended to allow for multiparty politics. **1993** Conté was narrowly re-elected in the first direct presidential election. **1998–99** President Conté was re-elected, and named his prime minister as Lamine Sidime.

Guinea-Bissau Republic of (formerly Portuguese Guinea)

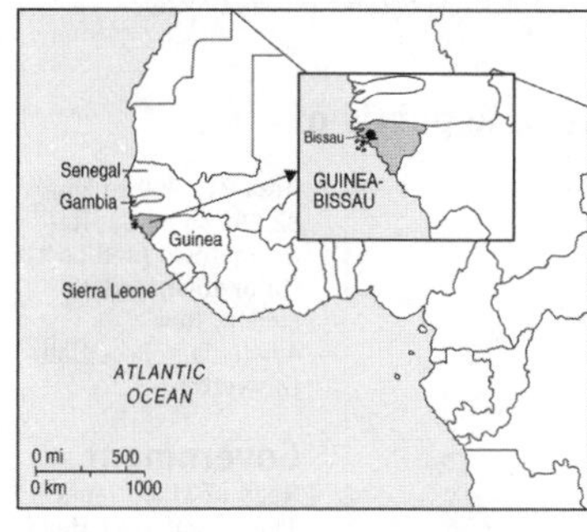

National name *República da Guiné-Bissau* **Area** 36,125 sq km/13,947 sq mi **Capital** Bissau (main port) **Major towns/ cities** Mansôa, São Domingos, Bolama/ Bijagós, Catio, Buba, Butata, Farim, Cacine

Government

Head of state Kumba Ialá from 2000 **Head of government** Caetano N'Tchama from 2000 **Political system** military **Armed forces** 7,300; plus paramilitary gendarmerie of 2,000 (1997) **Conscription** selective conscription **Defence spend** (% GDP) 2.6 (1997) **Education spend** (% GNP) 2.8 (1990) **Health spend** (% GDP) 1.1 (1990–95) **Death penalty** abolished in 1993

Population and society

Population 1,187,000 (1999 est) **Population growth rate** 2.2% (1995–2000) **Ethnic groups** majority originated in Africa, and comprises five main ethnic groups: the Balante in the central region, the Fulani in the north, the Malinke in the northern central area, and the Mandyako and Pepel near the coast **Religion** animist 65%, Muslim 38%, Christian 5% (mainly Roman Catholic) **Life expectancy** 44 (men); 47 (women) (1995–2000) **Literacy rate** 50% (men); 18% (women) (1997 est) **Unemployment** N/A

Economy and resources

GDP (US$) 206 million (1998) **GNP** (US$) 186 million (1998) **GNP per capita (PPP)** (US$) 750 (1998) **Real GDP growth** (% change on previous year) 5.2 (1997) **Consumer price inflation** 49.1% (1997) **Foreign debt** (US$) 921 million (1997) **Resources** bauxite, phosphate, petroleum (largely unexploited) **Exports** cashew nuts, palm kernels, groundnuts, fish and shrimp, timber. Principal market: India 59.1% (1997) **Imports** foodstuffs, machinery and transport equipment, fuels, construction materials. Principal source: Portugal 26.1% (1997)

■ Tourist information

Time difference GMT +/– 0 **Currency** Guinean peso **Language** Portuguese (official); Crioulo (Cape Verdean dialect of Portuguese), African languages **Visa requirements** UK: visa required. USA: visa required **Embassy in the UK** Consulate General of the Republic of Guinea-Bissau, 8 Palace Gate, London W8 4RP. Tel: (020) 7589 5253; fax: (020) 7589 9590 **British embassy** British Consulate, Maregro Int., CP 100, Bissau. (All staff reside at Dakar, Senegal.) Tel: (245) 201 224; fax: (245) 201 265 **Chamber of commerce** Associacão Comercial e Industrial e Agricola da Guiné-Bissau, Bissau. Tel/fax: (245) 201 602 **Banking hours** 0730–1430 Mon–Fri **Airports** international airport: Bissau (Bissalanca); ten domestic airports; total passenger km: 10 million (1995) **Major holidays** 1, 20 January, 8 February, 8 March, 1 May, 3 August, 12, 24 September, 14 November, 25 December

Chronology

10th century Known as Gabu, became a tributary kingdom of the Mali Empire to northeast. **1446** Portuguese arrived, establishing nominal control over coastal areas and capturing slaves to send to Cape Verde. **1546** Gabu kingdom became independent of Mali and survived until 1867. **1879** Portugal, which had formerly administered the area with Cape Verde islands, created the separate colony of Portuguese Guinea. **by 1915** The interior had been subjugated by the Portuguese. **1956** African Party for the Independence of Portuguese Guinea and Cape Verde (PAIGC) formed to campaign for independence from Portugal. **1961** The PAIGC began to wage a guerrilla campaign against Portuguese rule. **1973** Independence was declared in the two-thirds of the country that had fallen under the control of the PAIGC; heavy losses were sustained by Portuguese troops who tried to put down the uprising. **1974** Independence separately from Cape Verde accepted by Portugal, with Luiz Cabral (PAIGC) president. **1981** PAIGC was confirmed as the only legal party, with João Vieira as its secretary general; Cape Verde decided not to form a union. **1984** A new constitution made Vieira head of both government and state. **1991** Other parties were legalized in response to public pressure. **1994** PAIGC secured a clear assembly majority and Vieira narrowly won the first multiparty presidential elections. **1999** President Vieira ousted by the army. **2000** Kumba Ialá became president, and Caetano N'Tchama became prime minister.

Guyana Cooperative Republic of

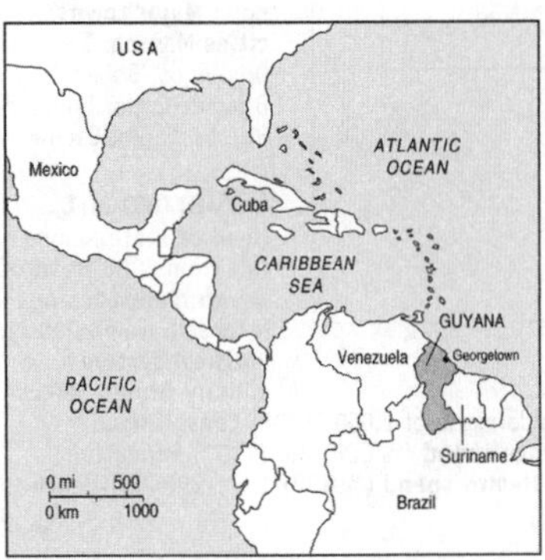

Area 214,969 sq km/ 82,999 sq mi **Capital** Georgetown (and port) **Major towns/cities** Linden, New Amsterdam, Rose Hall, Corriverton

Government

Head of state Janet Jagan from 1997 **Head of government** Samuel Hinds from 1992 **Political system** liberal democracy **Armed forces** 1,600; plus a paramilitary force of 1,500 (1997) **Conscription** military service is voluntary **Defence spend** (% GDP) 1 (1997) **Education spend** (% GNP) 4.9 (1996) **Health spend** (% GDP) 4.3 (1995) **Death penalty** retained and used for ordinary crimes

Population and society

Population 855,000 (1999 est) **Population growth rate** 0.7% (1995–2000) **Ethnic groups** about 51% descended from settlers from the subcontinent of India; about 43% Afro-Indian; small minorities of American Indians, Chinese, and Europeans **Religion** Hindu 54%, Christian 27%, Sunni Muslim 15% **Life expectancy** 61 (men); 68 (women) (1995–2000) **Literacy rate** 99% (men); 98% (women) (1997 est) **Unemployment** 12% (1992 est)

Economy and resources

GDP (US$) 782 million (1998) **GNP** (US$) 660 million (1998) **GNP per capita (PPP)** (US$) 2,680 (1998) **Real GDP growth** (% change on previous year) –1 (1998) **Consumer price inflation** 4% (1998) **Foreign debt** (US$) 1.48 billion (1997) **Resources** gold, diamonds, bauxite, copper, tungsten, iron, nickel, quartz, molybdenum **Exports** sugar, bauxite, alumina, rice, gold, rum, timber, molasses, shrimp. Principal market: Canada 24.2% (1997) **Imports** mineral fuels and lubricants, machinery, capital goods, consumer goods. Principal source: USA 28.2% (1997)

▪ Tourist information

Time difference GMT –3 **Currency** Guyana dollar **Language** English (official), Hindi, American Indian languages **Visa requirements** UK: visa not required. USA: visa not required **Embassy in the UK** 3 Palace Court, Bayswater Road, London W2 4LP. Tel: (020) 7229 7684; fax: (020) 7727 9809 **British embassy** British High Commission, PO Box 10849, 44 Main Street, Georgetown. Tel: (2) 65881–4; fax: (2) 53555 **Chamber of commerce** Georgetown Chamber of Commerce and Industry, PO Box 10110, 156 Waterloo Street, Cumminsburg, Georgetown. Tel: (2) 63519 **Office hours** 0800–1200 and 1300–1630 Mon–Fri **Banking hours** 0800–1200 Mon–Thu; 0800–1200 and 1530–1700 Fri **Airports** international airport: Georgetown (Timehri); the larger settlements in the interior have airstrips serving domestic flights; total passenger km: 235 million (1995) **Major ports** New Amsterdam **Chief tourist attractions** scenery – Kaietur Falls along Potaro River **Major holidays** 1 January, 23 February, 1 May, 1 August, 25–26 December; variable: Eid-ul-Adha, Diwali, Good Friday, Easter Monday, Prophet's Birthday, Phagwah (March), Caribbean (July)

Chronology

1498 The explorer Christopher Columbus sighted Guyana, whose name, 'land of many waters', was derived from a local American Indian word. **c. 1620** Settled by Dutch West India Company, who established armed bases and brought in slaves from Africa. **1814** After a period of French rule, Britain occupied Guyana during the Napoleonic Wars and purchased Demerara, Berbice, and Essequibo. **1831** Became British colony under name of British Guiana. **1834** Slavery was abolished, resulting in an influx of indentured labourers from India and China to work on sugar plantations. **1860** Settlement of the Rupununi Savanna commenced. **1860s** Gold was discovered. **1899** International arbitration tribunal found in favour of British Guiana in a long-running dispute with Venezuela over lands west of Essequibo River. **1953** Assembly elections won by left-wing People's Progressive Party (PPP), drawing most support from the Indian community; Britain suspended constitution and installed interim administration, fearing communist takeover. **1961** Internal self-government granted; Cheddi Jagan (PPP) became prime minister. **1964** Racial violence between the Asian- and African-descended communities. **1966** Independence achieved from Britain as Guyana, with PNC leader Forbes Burnham as prime minister. **1970** Guyana became a republic within the Commonwealth, with Raymond Arthur Chung as president; Burnham remained as prime minister. **1980** Burnham became the first executive president under the new constitution, which ended the three-year boycott of parliament by the PPP. **1992** PPP had a decisive victory in the first completely free assembly elections for 20 years; a privatization programme was launched. **1997** Cheddi Jagan died. His wife, Janet Jagan, was elected president. **1998** Violent antigovernment protests. Government and opposition agreed to an independent audit of elections. **1999** A constitutional reform commission was appointed.

Haiti Republic of

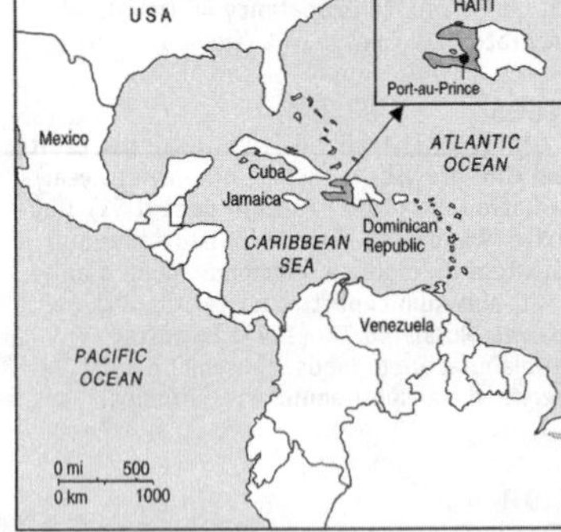

National name *République d'Haïti* **Area** 27,750 sq km/10,714 sq mi **Capital** Port-au-Prince **Major towns/cities** Cap-Haïtien, Gonaïves, Les Cayes, Port-de-Paix, Jérémie, Jacmée, St Marc

Government

Head of state René Préval from 1996 **Head of government** Jacques Edouard Alexis from 1998 **Political system** transitional **Armed forces** 7,300 (1994); armed forces effectively dissolved in 1995 following restoration of civilian rule in 1994; 5,500 in paramilitary forces (1997) **Conscription** military service is voluntary **Defence spend** (% GDP) 5.2 (1997) **Education spend** (% GNP) 1.4 (1993–94) **Health spend** (% GDP) 1.3 (1990–95) **Death penalty** abolished in 1987

Population and society

Population 8,087,000 (1999 est) **Population growth rate** 1.7% (1995–2000) **Ethnic groups** about 95% black African descent, the remainder are mulattos or Europeans **Religion** Christian 95% (of which 80% are Roman Catholic), voodoo 4% **Life expectancy** 51 (men); 56 (women) (1995–2000) **Literacy rate** 48% (men); 43% (women) (1997 est) **Unemployment** 68% (1997 est)

Economy and resources

GDP (US$) 2.8 billion (1998) **GNP** (US$) 13.1 billion (1998) **GNP per capita (PPP)** (US$) 1,250 (1998 est) **Real GDP growth** (% change on previous year) 3 (1998) **Consumer price inflation** 14% (1998) **Foreign debt** (US$) 1.05 billion (1997) **Resources** marble, limestone, calcareous clay, unexploited copper and gold deposits **Exports** manufactured articles, coffee, essential oils, sisal. Principal market: USA 81.4% (1997) **Imports** food and live animals, mineral fuels and lubricants, textiles, machinery, chemicals, pharmaceuticals, raw materials, vehicles. Principal source: USA 59.4% (1997)

▪ Tourist information

Time difference GMT –5 **Currency** gourde **Language** French (official, spoken by literate 10% minority), Creole (official) **Visa requirements** UK: visa not required. USA: visa not required **Embassy for the UK** BP 25, 160A avenue Louise, B-1050 Brussels, Belgium. Tel: (2) 649 7381; fax: (2) 640 6080 **British embassy** British Consulate, PO Box 1302, Hotel Montana, rue F Cardoza, Bourchon, Port-au-Prince. (All staff reside at Kingston, Jamaica.) Tel: (509) 573 969; fax: (509) 574 048 **Chamber of commerce**

Chambre de Commerce et de l'Industrie de Haiti, BP 982, Harry Truman Boulevard, Port-au-Prince. Tel: (509) 222 475; fax: (509) 220 281 **Office hours** 0700–1600 Mon–Fri **Banking hours** 0900–1300 Mon–Fri **Airports** international airport: Port-au-Prince (Mais Gaté); one domestic airport (Cap-Haïtien) and four smaller airfields **Chief tourist attractions** beaches; subtropical vegetation **Major holidays** 1–2 January, 14 April, 1 May, 15 August, 17, 24 October, 1–2, 18 November, 5, 25 December; variable: Ascension Thursday, Carnival, Corpus Christi, Good Friday

Chronology

14th century Settled by Carib Indians, who followed an earlier wave of Arawak Indian immigration. **1492** The first landing place of the explorer Christopher Columbus in the New World, who named the island Hispaniola ('Little Spain'). **1496** At Santo Domingo, now in the Dominican Republic to the east, the Spanish established the first European settlement in the Western hemisphere, which became capital of all Spanish colonies in America. **first half of 16th century** A third of a million Arawaks and Caribs died, as a result of enslavement and exposure to European diseases; black African slaves were consequently brought in to work the island's gold and silver mines, which were swiftly exhausted. **1697** Spain ceded western third of Hispaniola to France, which became known as Haiti, but kept the east, which was known as Santo Domingo (the Dominican Republic). **1804** Independence achieved after uprising against French colonial rule led by the former slave Toussaint l'Ouverture, who had died in prison in 1803, and Jean-Jacques Dessalines. **1818–43** Ruled by Jean-Pierre Boyer, who excluded the blacks from power. **1821** Santo Domingo fell under the control of Haiti until 1844. **1847–59** Blacks reasserted themselves under President Faustin Soulouque. **1915** Haiti invaded by USA as a result of political instability caused by black-mulatto friction; remained under US control until 1934. **1956** Dr François Duvalier (Papa Doc), a voodoo physician, seized power in military coup and was elected president one year later. **1964** Duvalier pronounced himself president for life, establishing a dictatorship based around a personal militia, the Tonton Macoutes. **1971** Duvalier died, succeeded by his son Jean-Claude (Baby Doc); thousands murdered during Duvalier era. **1988** A military coup installed Brig-Gen Prosper Avril as president, with a civilian government under military control. **1990** Left-wing Catholic priest Jean-Bertrand Aristide was elected president. **1991** Aristide was overthrown in a military coup led by Brig-Gen Raoul Cedras. Sanctions were imposed by the Organization of American States (OAS) and the USA. **1993** United Nations (UN) embargo was imposed. Aristide's return was blocked by the military. **1994** The threat of a US invasion led to the regime recognizing Aristide as president. **1995** UN peacekeepers were drafted in to replace US troops. Assembly elections were won by Aristide's supporters. René Préval was elected to replace Aristide as president. **1998** Jacques Edouard Alexis was nominated prime minister and endorsed by the assembly.

Honduras Republic of

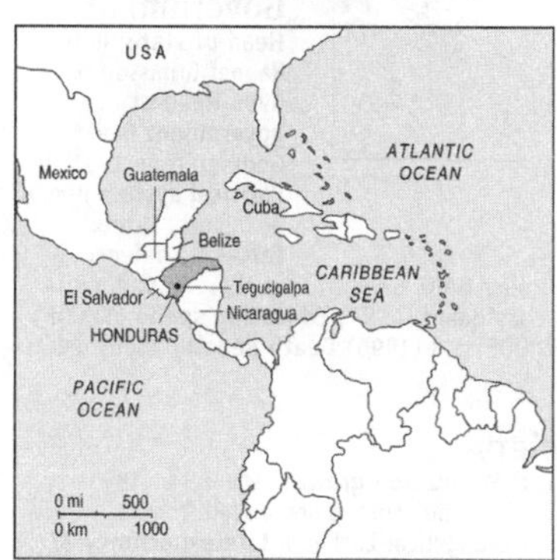

National name *República de Honduras* **Area** 112,100 sq km/ 43,281 sq mi **Capital** Tegucigalpa **Major towns/cities** San Pedro Sula, La Ceiba, El Progreso, Choluteca, Juticalpa, Danlí

Government

Head of state and government Carlos Flores from 1998 **Political system** liberal democracy **Armed forces** 18,800; plus paramilitary forces numbering 5,500 (1997) **Conscription** military service is voluntary (conscription abolished in 1995) **Defence spend** (% GDP) 2.1 (1997) **Education spend** (% GNP) 3.6 (1996) **Health spend** (% GDP) 2.8 (1990–95) **Death penalty** abolished in 1956

Population and society

Population 6,315,000 (1999 est) **Population growth rate** 2.8% (1995–2000); 2.5% (2000–05) **Ethnic groups** about 90% of mixed American Indian and Spanish descent (known as ladinos or mestizos); there are also Salvadorean, Guatemalan, American, and European minorities **Religion** Roman Catholic **Life expectancy** 68 (men); 72 (women) (1995–2000) **Literacy rate** 71% (men); 70% (women) (1997 est) **Unemployment** 3.2% (1997)

Economy and resources

GDP (US$) 4.7 billion (1998) **GNP** (US$) 4.5 billion (1998) **GNP per capita (PPP)** (US$) 2,140 (1998) **Real GDP growth** (% change on previous year) 3.7 (1998) **Consumer price inflation** 19.3% (1998) **Foreign debt** (US$) 4.69 billion (1997) **Resources** lead, zinc, silver, gold, tin, iron, copper, antimony **Exports** bananas, lobsters and prawns, zinc, meat. Principal market: USA 73.2% (1998) **Imports** machinery, appliances and electrical equipment, mineral fuels and lubricants, chemical products, consumer goods. Principal source: USA 60% (1998)

▪ Tourist information

Time difference GMT –6 **Currency** lempira **Language** Spanish (official); English, American Indian languages **Visa requirements** UK: visa not required with full British passport. USA: visa not required **Embassy in the UK** 115 Gloucester Place, London W1H 3PJ. Tel: (020) 7486 4880; fax: (020) 7486 4550 **British embassy** Apartado Postal 290, Edificio Palmira, 3° Piso, Colonia Palmira, Tegucigalpa. Tel: (504) 325 429; fax: (504) 325 480 **Chamber of commerce** Federación de Cámaras de Comercio e Industrias de Honduras, Apartado Postal 3393, Edificio Castañito 2° Nivel, 6a Avenida, Colonia Los Castaños, Tegucigalpa. Tel: (504) 326 083; fax: (504) 321 870 **Office hours** 0800–1200 and 1400–1700 Mon–Fri; 0800–1100 Sat **Banking hours** 0900–1500 Mon–Fri; some branches 0900–1100 Sat **Airports** international airports: Tegucigalpa (Toncontín), San Pedro Sula, Roatún, La Ceiba; over 30 smaller airports serving domestic flights; total passenger km: 341 million (1995) **Major ports** La Ceiba, Puerto Cortés **Chief tourist attractions** Mayan ruins at Copán; beaches on north coast; fishing and boating in Trujillo Bay and Lake Yojoa, near San Pedro **Major holidays** 1 January, 14 April, 1 May, 15 September, 3, 12, 21 October, 25, 31 December; variable: Good Friday, Holy Thursday

Chronology

c. AD 250–900 Part of culturally advanced Maya civilization. **1502** Visited by Christopher Columbus, who named the country Honduras ('depths') after the deep waters off the north coast. **1525** Colonized by Spain, who founded the town of Trujillo, but met with fierce resistance from the American Indian population. **17th century onwards** The northern 'Mosquito Coast' fell under the control of British buccaneers, as the Spanish concentrated on the inland area, with a British protectorate being established over the coast until 1860. **1821** Achieved independence from Spain and became part of Mexico. **1823** Became part of United Provinces (Federation) of Central America, also embracing Costa Rica, El Salvador, Guatemala, and Nicaragua, with the Honduran liberal Gen Francisco Morazan, president of the Federation from 1830. **1838** Achieved full independence when federation dissolved. **1880** Capital transferred from Comayagua to Tegucigalpa. **later 19th–early 20th centuries** The USA's economic involvement significant, with banana production, which provided two-thirds of exports in 1913, being controlled by the United Fruit Company; political instability, with frequent changes of constitution and military coups. **1925** Brief civil war. **1932–49** Under a right-wing National Party (PNH) dictatorship, led by Gen Tiburcio Carias Andino. **1963–74** Following a series of military coups, Gen Oswaldo López Arelano held power, before resigning after allegedly accepting bribes from a US company. **1969** Brief 'Football War' with El Salvador, which attacked Honduras at the time of a football competition between the two states, following evictions of thousands of Salvadoran illegal immigrants from Honduras. **1980** The first civilian government in more than a century was elected, with Roberto Suazo of the centrist Liberal Party (PLH) as president, but the commander in chief of the army, Gen Gustavo Alvárez, retained considerable power. **1983** There was close involvement with the USA in providing naval and air bases and allowing Nicaraguan counter-revolutionaries ('Contras') to operate from Honduras. **1989** The government and opposition declared support for a Central American peace plan to demobilize Nicaraguan Contras (thought to number 55,000 with their dependents) based in Honduras. **1992** A border dispute with El Salvador dating from 1861 was finally resolved. **1997** Carlos Flores (PLH) won the presidential elections, beginning his term of office in January 1998.

Hungary Republic of

National name *Magyar Köztársaság* **Area** 93,032 sq km/35,919 sq mi **Capital** Budapest **Major towns/cities** Miskolc, Debrecen, Szeged, Pécs, Gyor, Nyiregyháza, Székesfehérvár, Kecskemét

Government

Head of state Arpád Göncz from 1990 **Head of government** Viktor Orban from 1998 **Political system** liberal democracy **Armed forces** 49,100 (1997) **Conscription** 12 months (men aged 18–23) **Defence spend** (% GDP) 1.4 (1997) **Education spend** (% GNP) 4.7 (1996) **Health spend** (% GDP) 4.7 (1996) **Death penalty** abolished in 1990

Population and society

Population 10,075,000 (1999 est) **Population growth rate** –0.4% (1995–2000) **Ethnic groups** 93% indigenous, or Magyar; there is a large Romany community of around 600,000; other ethnic minorities include Germans, Croats, Romanians, Slovaks, Serbs, and Slovenes **Religion** Roman Catholic 67%, Calvinist 20%, other Christian denominations, Jewish **Life expectancy** 67 (men); 75 (women) (1995–2000) **Literacy rate** 99% (men); 99% (women) (1997 est) **Unemployment** 9.6% (1998)

Economy and resources

GDP (US$) 45.7 billion (1998) **GNP** (US$) 45.6 billion (1998) **GNP per capita (PPP)** (US$) 7,320 (1998 est) **Real GDP growth** (% change on previous year) 4.7 (1998) **Consumer price inflation** 16% (1998) **Foreign debt** (US$) 24.4 billion (1997) **Resources** lignite, brown coal, natural gas, petroleum, bauxite, hard coal **Exports** raw materials, semi-finished products, industrial consumer goods, food and agricultural products, transport equipment. Principal market: Germany 36.6% (1998) **Imports** mineral fuels, raw materials, semi-finished products, transport equipment, food products, consumer goods. Principal source: Germany 28.2% (1998)

▪ Tourist information

Time difference GMT +1 **Currency** forint **Language** Hungarian (or Magyar), one of the few languages of Europe with non-Indo-European origins; it is grouped with Finnish, Estonian, and others in the Finno-Ugric family **Visa requirements** UK: visa not required. USA: visa not required **Embassy in the UK** 35 Eaton Place, London SW1X 8BY. Tel: (020) 7235 4048; fax: (020) 7823 1348 **British embassy** Harmincad Utca 6, 1051 Budapest. Tel: (1) 266 2888; fax: (1) 266 0907 **Chamber of commerce** Magyar Kereskedelmi és Iparkamara (Hungarian Chamber of Commerce and Industry), PO Box 106, H-1389 Budapest. Tel: (1) 153 3333; fax: (1) 153 1285 **Office hours** 0800–1630 Mon–Fri **Banking hours** 0900–1400 Mon–Fri **Airports** international airport: Budapest (Ferihegy); six domestic airports; total passenger km: 3,049 million (1997) **Chief tourist attractions** boating and fishing on Lake Balaton; Budapest and other historical cities; Budapest has thermal springs feeding swimming pools equipped with modern physiotherapy facilities **Major holidays** 1 January, 15 March, 1 May, 20 August, 23 October, 25–26 December; variable: Easter Monday

Chronology

1st century AD Region formed part of Roman Empire. **4th century** Germanic tribes overran central Europe. **c. 445** Attila the Hun established a short-lived empire, including Hungarian nomads living far to the east. **c. 680** Hungarians settled between the Don and Dniepr rivers under Khazar rule. **9th century** Hungarians invaded central Europe; ten tribes united under Árpád, chief of the Magyar tribe, who conquered the area corresponding to modern Hungary 896. **10th century** Hungarians colonized Transylvania and raided their neighbours for plunder and slaves. **955** Battle of Lech: Germans led by Otto the Great defeated the Hungarians. **1001** St Stephen founded the Hungarian kingdom to replace tribal organization and converted the Hungarians to Christianity. **12th century** Hungary became a major power when King Béla III won temporary supremacy over the Balkans. **1308–86** Angevin dynasty ruled after the Arpádian line died out. **1456** Battle of Belgrade: János Hunyadi defeated Ottoman Turks and saved Hungary from invasion. **1458–90** Under Mátyás I Corvinus, Hungary enjoyed military success and cultural renaissance. **1526** Battle of Mohács: Turks under Suleiman the Magnificent decisively defeated the Hungarians. **16th century** Partition of Hungary between Turkey, Austria, and the semi-autonomous Transylvania. **1699** Treaty of Karlowitz: Austrians expelled the Turks from Hungary, which was reunified under Habsburg rule. **1707** Prince Ferenc Rákóczi II led an uprising against the Austrians. **1780–90** Joseph II's attempts to impose uniform administration throughout Austrian Empire provoked nationalist reaction among Hungarian nobility. **early 19th century** 'National Revival' movement led by Count Stephen Széchenyi and Lajos Kossuth. **1848** Hungarian Revolution: nationalists proclaimed self-government; Croat minority resisted Hungarian rule. **1849** Austrians crushed revolution with Russian support. **1867** Austria conceded equality to Hungary within the dual monarchy of Austria-Hungary. **1918** Austria-Hungary collapsed in military defeat; Count Mihály Károlyi proclaimed Hungarian Republic. **1920** Treaty of Trianon: Hungary lost 72% of its territory to Czechoslovakia, Romania, and Yugoslavia; Admiral Miklós Horthy restored the Kingdom of Hungary with himself as regent. **1938–41** Diplomatic collaboration with Germany allowed Hungary to regain territories lost in 1920; Hungary declared war on USSR in alliance with Germany in 1941. **1944** Germany occupied Hungary and installed a Nazi regime. **1945** USSR 'liberated' Hungary. **1947** Peace treaty restored 1920 frontiers. **1949** Hungary became a Soviet-style dictatorship; communist leader Mátyás Rákosi pursued Stalinist policies. **1956** Hungarian uprising: anti-Soviet demonstrations led the USSR to invade, crush dissent, and install János Kádár as communist leader. **1961** Kádár began to introduce limited liberal reforms. **1988** The Hungarian Democratic Forum was formed by opposition groups. **1989** The communist dictatorship was dismantled, and a transitional constitution restored multiparty democracy. The opening of the border with Austria brought an end to the 'Iron Curtain'. **1990** Elections were won by a centre-right coalition. **1991** The withdrawal of Soviet forces was completed. **1996** A friendship treaty with the Slovak Republic was signed, as was a cooperation treaty with Romania. **1997** Hungary was invited to join NATO and to begin negotiations for membership of the European Union. A referendum showed clear support in favour of joining NATO. **1998** Viktor Orban, leader of right-of-centre Fidesz, became prime minister after the general election. **1999** Hungary became a full member of NATO.

Iceland Republic of

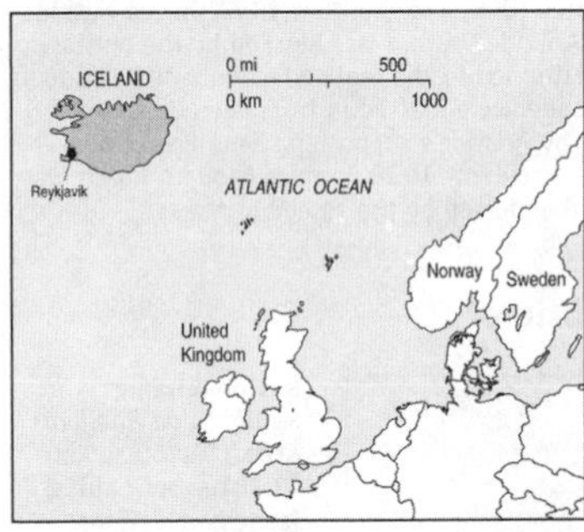

National name *Lýdveldid Ísland* **Area** 103,000 sq km/39,768 sq mi **Capital** Reykjavik **Major towns/cities** Akureyri, Akranes, Kópavogur, Hafnerfjördur, Vestmannaeyjar

Government

Head of state Ólafur Ragnar Grímsson from 1996 **Head of government** Davíd Oddsson from 1991 **Political system** liberal democracy **Armed forces** no defence forces of its own; US forces under NATO are stationed there: 2,500 military personnel and a 130-strong coastguard (1997) **Education spend** (% GNP) 5.4 (1996) **Health spend** (% GDP) 6.8 (1996) **Death penalty** abolished in 1928

Population and society

Population 279,000 (1999 est) **Population growth rate** 0.9% (1995–2000) **Ethnic groups** most of the population is descended from Norwegians and Celts **Religion** Evangelical Lutheran **Life expectancy** 77 (men); 81 (women) (1995–2000) **Literacy rate** 99% (men); 99% (women) (1997 est) **Unemployment** 2.8% (1998)

Economy and resources

GDP (US$) 8.2 billion (1998) **GNP** (US$) 7.7 billion (1998) **GNP per capita (PPP)** (US$) 22,830 (1998) **Real GDP growth** (% change on previous year) 3.7 (1998) **Consumer price inflation** 2.2% (1998) **Resources** aluminium, diatomite, hydroelectric and thermal power, fish **Exports** fish products, aluminium, ferrosilicon, diatomite, fertilizer, animal products. Principal market: UK 19% (1998) **Imports** machinery and transport equipment, motor vehicles, petroleum and petroleum products, foodstuffs, textiles. Principal source: Germany 11.5% (1998)

▪ Tourist information

Time difference GMT +/– 0 **Currency** krona **Language** Icelandic, the most archaic Scandinavian language **Visa requirements** UK: visa not required. USA: visa not required **Embassy in the UK** 1 Eaton Terrace, London SW1W 8EY. Tel: (020) 7730 5131/2; fax: (020) 7730 1683 **British embassy** PO Box 460, Laufásvegur 49, 101 Reykjavik. Tel: (354) 551 5883/4; fax: (354) 552 7940 **Chamber of commerce** Verzlunarráð Islands (Chamber of Commerce), Hús verslunarinnar, 103 Reykjavik. Tel: (354) 588 6666; fax: (354) 568 6564 **Office hours** 0900–1700 Mon–Fri. Most offices are closed Sat; some firms close down completely for a three-week holiday, usually in July **Banking hours** 0915–1600 Mon–Fri **Airports** international airport: Keflavik (45 km/28 mi southwest of Reykjavik); ten major domestic airports, 12 local airports; total passenger km: 3,216 million (1997 est) **Chief tourist attractions** rugged volcanic landscape with geysers **Major holidays** 1 January, 1 May, 17 June, 25–26 December; variable: Ascension Thursday, Good Friday, Easter Monday, Holy Thursday, First Day of Summer, August Holiday Monday

Chronology

7th century Iceland discovered by Irish seafarers. **874** First Norse settler, Ingólfr Arnarson, founded a small colony at Reykjavik. ***c.* 900** Norse settlers came in larger numbers, mainly from Norway. **930** Settlers established an annual parliament, the Althing, to make laws and resolve disputes. **985** Eric the Red left Iceland to found a settlement in Greenland. **1000** Icelanders adopted Christianity. **1263** Icelanders recognized the authority of the king of Norway after a brief civil war. **1397** Norway and Iceland were united with Denmark and Sweden under a single monarch. **15th century** Norway and Iceland were increasingly treated as appendages of Denmark, especially after Sweden seceded in 1449. **1783** Poisonous volcanic eruption caused great loss of life. **1814** Norway passed to the Swedish crown; Iceland remained under Danish rule. **1845** Althing was re-established in modernized form. **1874** New constitution gave Iceland limited autonomy. **1918** Iceland achieved full self-government under the Danish crown. **1940** British forces occupied Iceland after Germany invaded Denmark; US troops took over in 1941. **1944** Iceland became an independent republic under President Sveinn Björnsson. **1949** Iceland became a member of NATO. **1958** The introduction of an exclusive fishing limit led to the first 'Cod War', when Icelandic patrol boats clashed with British fishing boats. **1972–73** Iceland extended its fishing limit, renewing confrontations with Britain. **1975–76** The further extension of the fishing limit caused the third 'Cod War' with the UK. **1985** Iceland declared itself a nuclear-free zone. **1991** David Oddsson was appointed prime minister. **1992** Iceland defied a world ban to resume its whaling industry. **1996** Ólafur Ragnar Grímsson was elected president.

India Republic of

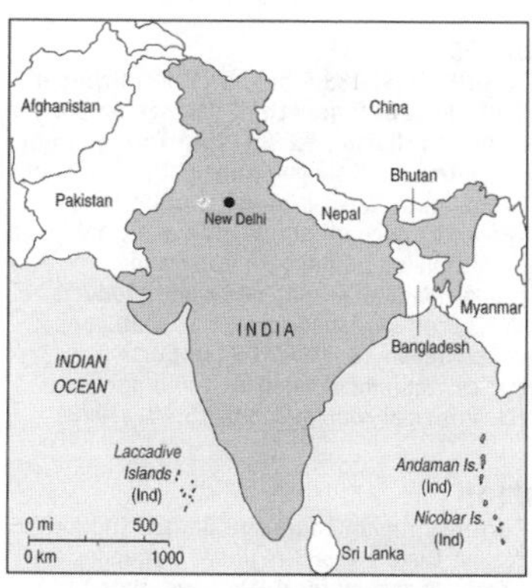

National name Hindi *Bharat* **Area** 3,166,829 sq km/1,222,713 sq mi **Capital** Delhi **Major towns/cities** Mumbai (Bombay), Calcutta, Chennai (Madras), Bangalore, Hyderabad, Ahmadabad, Kanpur, Pune, Nagpur, Bhopal, Jaipur, Lucknow, Surat

Government

Head of state Kocheril Raman Narayanan from 1997 **Head of government** Atal Behari Vajpayee from 1998 **Political system** liberal democracy federal republic **Armed forces** 1,145,000 (1997) **Conscription** none, although all citizens are constitutionally obliged to perform national service when called upon **Defence spend** (% GDP) 3.3 (1997) **Education spend** (% GNP) 3.5 (1995) **Health spend** (% GDP) 1.6 (1995) **Death penalty** retained and used for ordinary crimes

Population and society

Population 998,056,000 (1999 est) **Population growth rate** 1.6% (1995–2000) **Ethnic groups** 72% of Indo-Aryan descent; 25% (predominantly in south) Dravidian; 3% Mongoloid **Religion** Hindu 83%, Sunni Muslim 11%, Christian 2.5%, Sikh 2% **Life expectancy** 62 (men); 63 (women) (1995–2000) **Literacy rate** 67% (men); 39% (women) (1997 est) **Unemployment** 22% (1997 est)

Economy and resources

GDP (US$) 383.4 billion (1998) **GNP** (US$) 421.3 billion (1998) **GNP per capita (PPP)** (US$) 1,700 (1998) **Real GDP growth** (% change on previous year) 5.4 (1998) **Consumer price inflation** 7.5% (1998) **Foreign debt** (US$) 94.4 billion (1997) **Resources** coal, iron ore, copper ore, bauxite, chromite, gold, manganese ore, zinc, lead, limestone, crude oil, natural gas, diamonds **Exports** tea (world's largest producer), coffee, fish, iron and steel, leather, textiles, clothing, polished diamonds, handmade carpets, engineering goods, chemicals. Principal market: USA 22.8% (1998) **Imports** nonelectrical machinery, mineral fuels and lubricants, pearls, precious and semiprecious stones, chemicals, transport equipment. Principal source: USA 9.3% (1998)

▪ Tourist information

Time difference GMT +5.5 **Currency** rupee **Language** Hindi, English, and 17 other official languages: Assamese, Bengali, Gujarati, Kannada, Kashmiri, Konkani, Malayalam, Manipur, Marathi, Nepali, Oriya, Punjabi, Sanskrit, Sindhi, Tamil, Telugu, Urdu; more than 1,650 dialects **Visa requirements** UK: visa required. USA: visa required **Embassy in the UK** Office of the High Commissioner for India, India House, Aldwych, London WC2B 4NA. Tel: (020) 7836 8484; fax: (020) 7836 4331 **British embassy** British High Commission, Shanti Path, Chanakyapuri, New Delhi 110021. Tel: (11) 687 2161; fax: (11) 687 2882 **Chamber of commerce** India Exchange, 4 India Exchange Place, Calcutta 700001. Tel: (33) 220 3243; fax: (33) 220 4495 **Office hours** 0930–1730 Mon–Fri; 0930–1300 Sat **Banking hours** 1000–1400 Mon–Fri; 1000–1200 Sat **Airports** international airports: Ahmadabad, Bombay, Calcutta, Delhi (Indira Gandhi), Goa, Hyderabad, Madras, Thiruvanathapuram; over 70 domestic airports; total passenger km: 23,354 million (1997–98) **Major ports** Calcutta, Bombay, Chennai (Madras) **Chief tourist attractions** historic palaces, forts, and temples; Taj Mahal; varied scenery; wildlife **Major holidays** 1 (some states), 26 January, 1 May (some states), 30 June, 15 August, 2 October, 25, 31 December; variable: New Year (Parsi, some states)

Chronology

***c.* 2500–1500 BC** The earliest Indian civilization evolved in the Indus Valley with the city states of Harappa and Mohenjo Daro. ***c.* 1500–1200 BC** Aryan peoples from the northwest overran northern India and the Deccan; Brahmanism (a form of Hinduism) developed. **321 BC** Chandragupta, founder of the Mauryan dynasty, began to unite northern India in a Hindu Empire. **268–232 BC** Mauryan Empire reached its height under Asoka, who ruled two-thirds of India from his capital Pataliputra. ***c.* 180 BC** Shunga dynasty replaced the Mauryans; Hindu Empire began to break up into smaller kingdoms. **AD 320–480** Gupta dynasty reunified northern India. ***c.* 500** Raiding Huns from central Asia destroyed the Gupta dynasty; India reverted to many warring kingdoms. **11th–12th centuries** Rajput princes of northern India faced repeated Muslim invasions by Arabs, Turks, and Afghans, and in 1206 the first Muslim dynasty was established at Delhi. **14th–16th centuries** Muslim rule extended over northern India and the Deccan; south remained independent under the Hindu Vijayanagar dynasty. **1498** Explorer Vasco da Gama reached India, followed by Portuguese, Dutch, French, and English traders. **1526** Last Muslim invasion: Zahir ud-din Muhammad (Babur) defeated the Sultan of Delhi at Battle of Panipat and established the Mogul Empire, which was consolidated by Akbar the Great (1556–1605). **1600** East India Company founded by English merchants, who settled in Madras, Bombay, and Calcutta. **17th century** Mogul Empire reached its zenith under Jahangir (1605–27), Shah Jehan (1628–58), and Aurangzeb (1658–1707). **1739** Persian king Nadir Shah invaded India and destroyed Mogul prestige; the British and French supported rival Indian princes in subsequent internal wars. **1757** Battle of Plassey: Robert Clive defeated Siraj al-Daulah, nawab of Bengal; Bengal came under control of the British East India Company. **1772–85** Warren Hastings, British governor general of Bengal, raised the Indian army and pursued expansionist policies. **early 19th century** British took control (directly or indirectly) throughout India by defeating powerful Indian states in a series of regional wars. **1858** 'Indian Mutiny': mutiny in Bengal army erupted into widespread anti-British revolt; rebels sought to restore powers of Mogul emperor. **1858** British defeated the rebels; East India Company dissolved; India came under the British crown. **1885** Indian National Congress founded in Bombay as a focus for nationalism. **1909** Morley–Minto Reforms: Indians received the right to elect members of Legislative Councils; Hindus and Muslims formed separate electorates. **1919** British forces killed 379 Indian demonstrators at Amritsar; India Act (Montagu–Chelmsford Reforms) conceded a measure of provincial self-government. **1920–22** Mohandas Gandhi won control of the Indian National Congress, which launched a campaign of civil

India: States and Union Territories

State	Capital	Area sq km	Area sq mi	Population (1998 est)
Andhra Pradesh	Hyderabad	275,045	106,195	74,171,000
Arunachal Pradesh	Itanagar	83,743	32,333	1,128,000
Assam	Dispur	78,438	30,285	25,646,000
Bihar	Patna	173,877	67,134	96,955,000
Goa	Panaji	3,702	1,429	1,513,000
Gujarat	Gandhinagar	196,024	75,685	47,098,000
Haryana	Chandigarh	44,212	17,070	19,343,000
Himachal Pradesh	Shimla	55,673	21,495	6,423,000
Jammu and Kashmir[1]	Srinagar	222,236	85,805	9,535,000
Karnataka	Bangalore	191,791	74,051	50,983,000
Kerala	Trivandrum	38,863	15,005	31,780,000
Madhya Pradesh	Bhopal	443,446	171,215	77,400,000
Maharashtra	Mumbai	307,713	118,808	89,406,000
Manipur	Imphal	22,327	8,620	2,385,000
Meghalaya	Shillong	22,429	8,660	2,305,000
Mizoram	Aizawl	21,081	8,139	901,000
Nagaland	Kohima	16,579	6,401	1,591,000
Orissa	Bhubaneshwar	155,707	60,118	35,304,000
Punjab	Chandigarh	5,362	2,070	23,101,000
Rajasthan	Jaipur	342,239	132,138	52,005,000
Sikkim	Gangtok	7096	2,740	529,000
Tamil Nadu	Chennai	130,058	50,215	60,881,000
Tripura	Agartala	10,486	4,049	3,582,000
Uttar Pradesh	Lucknow	294,411	113,672	164,941,000
West Bengal	Calcutta	88,752	34,267	77,250,000
Union Territory				
Andaman and Nicobar Islands	Port Blair	8,249	3,185	365,000
Chandigarh	Chandigarh	114	44	840,000
Dadra and Nagar Haveli	Silvassa	491	190	180,000
Daman and Diu	Daman	112	43	132,000
Delhi	Delhi	1,483	573	13,040,000
Lakshadweep	Kavaratti	32	12	67,000
Pondicherry	Pondicherry	492	190	1,052,000

[1] Includes area occupied by Pakistan and China.

disobedience in support of the demand for complete self-rule. **1935** India Act provided for Indian control of federal legislature, with defence and external affairs remaining the viceroy's responsibility. **1940** Muslim League called for India to be partitioned along religious lines. **1947** British India partitioned into two independent dominions of India (mainly Hindu) and Pakistan (mainly Muslim) amid bloody riots; Jawaharlal Nehru of Congress Party became prime minister. **1950** India became a republic within the Commonwealth. **1962** India lost a brief border war with China; retained Kashmir in war with Pakistan in 1965. **1966** Indira Gandhi, daughter of Nehru, became prime minister. **1971** India defeated Pakistan in a war and helped East Pakistan become independent as Bangladesh. **1975** Found guilty of electoral corruption, Mrs Gandhi declared a state of emergency and arrested opponents. **1977–79** The Janata Party formed a government under Morarji Desai. **1980** Mrs Gandhi, heading a Congress Party splinter group, Congress (I) ('I' for Indira), was returned to power. **1984** Troops cleared Sikh separatists from the Golden Temple, Amritsar; Mrs Gandhi was assassinated by Sikh bodyguards; her son Rajiv Gandhi became prime minister. **1989** After financial scandals, Congress lost elections; V P Singh formed a Janata Dal minority government. **1990** Direct rule was imposed on Jammu and Kashmir after an upsurge in Muslim separatist violence; rising interethnic and religious conflict was seen in the Punjab and elsewhere. **1992** The destruction of a mosque at Ayodhya, northern India, by Hindu extremists resulted in widespread violence. **1996** Madras was renamed Chennai. Direct central rule was imposed on Uttar Pradesh after inconclusive assembly elections. **1997** Kocheril Raman Narayanan became the first 'untouchable' to be elected president. **1998** Atal Behari Vajpayee, leader of the Bharatiya Janata party, was elected prime minister. The creation of three new states was proposed. India carried out five underground nuclear explosions, meeting with international condemnation. There were floods in Uttar Pradesh. **1999** The Indian government renounced further nuclear weapons testing and promised to sign the Comprehensive Test Ban Treaty. India used air power to attack 'infiltrators' in Kashmir. In June Kashmir peace talks were offered to Pakistan. **2000** Relations with Pakistan worsened after India accused Pakistan of involvement (which it denied) of the hijacking of an Indian airliner by Kashmiri militants.

Indonesia Republic of

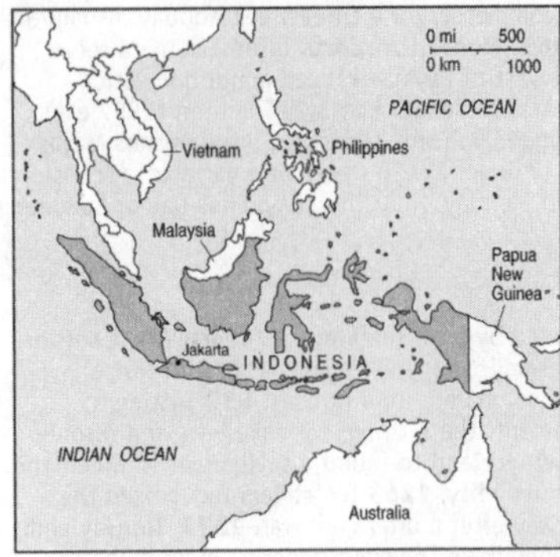

National name *Republik Indonesia* **Area** 1,904,569 sq km/ 735,354 sq mi **Capital** Jakarta **Major towns/ cities** Surabaya, Bandung, Yogyakarta (Java), Medan, Semarang (Java), Banda Aceh, Palembang (Sumatra), Ujung Pandang (Sulawesi), Denpasar (Bali), Kupang (Timor), Padang, Malang

Government

Head of state and government Abdurrahman Wahid from 1999 **Political system** emergent democracy **Armed forces** 284,000; paramilitary forces 200,000 (1997) **Conscription** 2 years (selective) **Defence spend** (% GDP) 2.2 (1997) **Education spend** (% GNP) 1.4 (1996) **Health spend** (% GDP) 0.7 (1990–95) **Death penalty** retained and used for ordinary crimes

Population and society

Population 210,126,000 (1999 est) **Population growth rate** 1.4% (1995–2000) **Ethnic groups** comprises more than 300 ethnic groups, the majority of which are of Malay descent; important Malay communities include Javanese (about 33% of the population), Sundanese (7%), and Madurese (3%); the largest non-Malay community is the Chinese (2%); substantial numbers of Indians, Melanesians, Micronesians, and Arabs **Religion** Muslim 88%, Christian 10%, Buddhist and Hindu 2% (the continued spread of Christianity, together with an Islamic revival, have led to greater religious tensions) **Life expectancy** 63 (men); 67 (women) (1995–2000) **Literacy rate** 91% (men); 80% (women) (1997 est) **Unemployment** 15.5% (1998 est)

Economy and resources

GDP (US$) 96.3 billion (1998) **GNP** (US$) 138.5 billion (1998) **GNP per capita (PPP)** (US$) 2,790 (1998) **Real GDP growth** (% change on previous year) –14.8 (1998) **Consumer price inflation** 9.8% (1998) **Foreign debt** (US$) 136.17 billion (1997) **Resources** petroleum (principal producer of petroleum in the Far East), natural gas, bauxite, nickel (world's third-largest producer), copper, tin (world's second-largest producer), gold, coal, forests **Exports** petroleum and petroleum products, natural and manufactured gas, textiles, rubber, palm oil, wood and wood products, electrical and electronic products, coffee, fishery products, coal, copper, tin, pepper, tea. Principal market: Japan 18.6% (1998) **Imports** machinery, transport and electrical equipment, manufactured goods, chemical and mineral products. Principal source: Japan 15.7% (1998)

▪ Tourist information

Time difference GMT +7/9 **Currency** rupiah **Language** Bahasa Indonesia (official), closely related to Malay; there are 583 regional languages and dialects; Javanese is the most widely spoken local language. Dutch is also spoken **Visa requirements** UK: visa not required. USA: visa not required **Embassy in the UK** 38 Grosvenor Square, London W1X 9AD. Tel: (020) 7499 7661; fax: (020) 7491 4993 **British embassy** Jalan M H Thamrin 75, Jakarta 10310. Tel: (21) 330 904; fax: (21) 314 1824 **Chamber of commerce** Indonesian Chamber of Commerce and Industry, 3rd–5th Floors, Chandra Building, Jalan M H Thamrin 20, Jakarta 10350. Tel: (21) 324 000; fax: (21) 310 6098 **Office hours** 0800–1600 or 0900–1700 Mon–Fri **Banking hours** 0800–1500 Mon–Fri **Airports** international airports: Jakarta (Sukarno-Hatta), Irian Jaya (Frans Kaisepo), Bali (Ngurah Rai), Surabaya, Manado (Sam Ratulangi); over 60 domestic airports; total passenger km: 26,516 million (1997 est) **Major ports** Tanjung Priok, Surabaya, Semarang (Java), Ujung Pandang (Sulawesi) **Chief tourist**

attractions Java, with its temples and volcanic scenery; Bali, with its Hindu-Buddhist temples and religious festivals; Lombok, Sumatra, and Celebes **Major holidays** 1 January, 17 August, 25 December; variable: Ascension Thursday, Eid-ul-Adha, end of Ramadan (2 days), Good Friday, New Year (Icaka, March), New Year (Muslim), Prophet's Birthday, Ascension of the Prophet (March/April), Waisak (May)

Chronology

3000–500 BC Immigrants from southern China displaced original Melanesian population. **6th century AD** Start of Indian cultural influence; small Hindu and Buddhist kingdoms developed. **8th century** Buddhist maritime empire of Srivijaya expanded to include all Sumatra and Malay peninsula. **13th century** Islam introduced to Sumatra by Arab merchants; spread throughout the islands over next 300 years. **14th century** Eastern Javanese kingdom of Majapahit destroyed Srivijaya and dominated the region. ***c.* 1520** Empire of Majapahit disintegrated; Javanese nobles fled to Bali. **16th century** Portuguese merchants broke the Muslim monopoly on the spice trade. **1602** Dutch East India Company founded; it displaced the Portuguese and monopolized trade with the Spice Islands. **1619** Dutch East India Company captured the port of Jakarta in Java and renamed it Batavia. **17th century** Dutch introduced coffee plants and established informal control over central Java through divide-and-rule policy among local rulers. **1749** After frequent military intervention, the Dutch East India Company obtained formal sovereignty over Mataram. **1799** The Netherlands took over interests of bankrupt Dutch East India Company. **1808** French forces occupied Java; British expelled them in 1811 and returned Java to the Netherlands in 1816. **1824** Anglo-Dutch Treaty: Britain recognized entire Indonesian archipelago as Dutch sphere of influence. **1825–30** Java War: Prince Dipo Negoro led unsuccessful revolt against Dutch rule; further revolt 1894–96. **19th century** Dutch formalized control over Java and conquered other islands; cultivation of coffee and sugar under tight official control made the Netherlands Indies one of the richest colonies in the world. **1908** Dutch completed conquest of Bali. **1927** Communist revolts suppressed; Achmed Sukarno founded Indonesian Nationalist Party (PNI) to unite diverse anti-Dutch elements. **1929** Dutch imprisoned Sukarno and tried to suppress PNI. **1942–45** Japanese occupation; PNI installed as anti-Western puppet government. **1945** When Japan surrendered, President Sukarno declared an independent republic, but the Dutch set about restoring colonial rule by force. **1947** Dutch 'police action': an all-out attack on Java and Sumatra conquered two-thirds of the republic. **1949** Under US pressure, the Dutch agreed to transfer sovereignty of the Netherlands Indies (except Dutch New Guinea or Irian Jaya) to the Republic of the United States of Indonesia. **1950** President Sukarno abolished federalism and proclaimed unitary Republic of Indonesia dominated by Java; revolts in Sumatra and South Moluccas. **1959** To combat severe political instability, Sukarno imposed authoritarian 'guided democracy'. **1963** The Netherlands ceded Irian Jaya to Indonesia. **1963–66** Indonesia tried to break up Malaysia by means of blockade and guerrilla attacks. **1965–66** Clashes between communists and army; Gen Raden Suharto imposed emergency administration and massacred up to 700,000 alleged communists. **1968** Suharto formally replaced Sukarno as president and proclaimed 'New Order' under strict military rule. **1970s** Rising oil exports brought significant agricultural and industrial growth. **1975** Indonesia invaded East Timor when Portuguese rule collapsed; 200,000 died in ensuing war. **1986** After suppressing a revolt on Irian Jaya, Suharto introduced a programme to settle 65,000 Javanese there and on outer islands. **1996** The government initiated a crackdown on its opponents. **1997** Hundreds were killed in ethnic riots in west Kalimantan province. There was a drought and a famine in Irian Jaya. Forest fires in Borneo and Sumatra blighted large areas of SE Asia with heavy smog, and caused catastrophic environmental damage. **1998** Following mass riots, Suharto stepped down as president. There was some withdrawal of troops from East Timor and partial autonomy was offered. The GDP contracted by 15%. Irian Jaya's status as a military occupation zone ended, following a ceasefire agreement with separatist rebels. Troops killed 16 student demonstrators in Jakarta. The repressive legislation of the Suharto era was repealed in a special legislature session and political parties were legalized. **1999** Ethnic violence continued in Borneo, with over 500 people killed in March and April. The government held its promised referendum on independence for East Timor on 30 August, but after an overwhelming vote in favour, pro-Indonesian militias rampaged through the country, killing hundreds and displacing thousands of citizens. Intervention was sought from United Nations (UN). Abdurrahman Wahid became president in October 1999. In November he felt separatist pressure from the Indonesian province of Aceh, but said that he would not rule out repression to solve the unrest. **2000** Following violence between Muslims and Christians in Maluku (Moluccas) in 1999, Indonesia was criticized for failing to stop the violence, while Indonesian Muslims called for a holy war in Maluku against the Christians.

East Timor: Key Events Leading to Independence

1520 Portuguese traders first land in Timor looking for the sandalwood tree. **1566** Portuguese Dominican friars establish a base for the conversion of the Timorese to Christianity. **1613** Dutch traders take possession of the western portion of the island, challenging Portugal's hegemony. **1860** The Dutch secure control of West Timor, leaving the Portuguese in control of EastTimor. This is confirmed by a further treaty of 1893, effective from 1914. **27 December 1949** Dutch Timor, in the west, becomes part of newly independent Indonesia. **May 1974** Nicolau Lobato forms the Timorese Social Democratic Association (ASDT), which becomes the communist Revolutionary Front for an Independent East Timor (FRETILIN) in September 1975 to fight for independence. **28 November 1975** FRETILIN seizes control of East Timor and declares independence, pre-empting a planned Portuguese withdrawal. Indonesia reacts by invading in early December. An estimated 100,000–200,000 Timorese, out of a total population of around 650,000, are killed in the military crackdown and the associated spread of famine and disease. However, resistance, led by FRETILIN, continues. **17 July 1976** The Indonesian President, TNJ Suharto, signs the Bill of Integration in corporating East Timor as Indonesia's 27th province, Lora Sae or TimorTimur. The UN refuses to recognize the annexation and calls for Indonesia's withdrawal. **20 January 1978** Australia becomes one of the first countries to recognize de facto Indonesia's incorporation of East Timor. **February 1983** The UN Commission on Human Rights adopts a resolution affirming East Timor's right to independence and self-determination. **1984** Famine and disease spread again when civil war, after a brief ceasefire in 1983, intensifies. **November 1988** Travel restrictions from East Timor (in force since 1976) are withdrawn by Indonesia. **January 1989** East Timor is opened to outsiders, including tourists and Indonesians, for the first time since December 1975. **October 1989** The Pope visits East Timor and makes a plea to the Indonesian government to halt human rights violations. **November 1990** The Indonesian government rejects proposals for unconditional peace negotiations by Jose Xanana Gusmão, commander-in-chief of FRETILIN's army, the National Liberation Armed Forces of East Timor (FALINTIL). **12 November 1991** The Indonesian army kills between 100 and 180 pro-independence peaceful demonstrators during the funeral ceremony for a separatist sympathizer at Santa Cruz cemetery in the EastTimor capital, Dili, and subsequently executes a further 60–100 'subversives'. **August 1992** The UN General Assembly adopts a resolution condemning Indonesia's violation of fundamental human rights in East Timor. **November 1992** FRETILIN leader Gusmão is arrested and taken to Jakarta, where he is tried and, in 1993, found guilty of conspiracy and rebellion and sentenced to 20 years' imprisonment. **July 1994** Indonesian troops kill at least three East Timorese in a further demonstration in Dili. **October 1994** Under UN auspices, FRETILIN Secretary for International Relations, José Ramos-Horta, for the first time meets Indonesia's foreign minister, Ali Alatas, in inaugural official talks on the island's status. **September–October 1995** Serious rioting in Dili, involving Timorese Roman Catholics and Muslim immigrants from Indonesia, is defused through the intervention of the Roman Catholic Bishop of Dili, Carlos Belo. **11 October 1996** Ramos-Horta and Belo are jointly awarded the Nobel Prize for Peace for their efforts to achieve a peaceful resolution to the East Timor conflict. **July 1998** The Indonesian president, BJ Habibie, who on 21 May had replaced the autocratic and unpopular TNJ Suharto, ending his 32 years in power, offers partial autonomy to East Timor, but rules out independence. **12 November 1998** The Indonesian army kills 44 civilians in a crackdown against pro-independence demonstrators and rebels in southern East Timor as delegates arrive for an Asia–Pacific Cooperation meeting. World attention is drawn to the oppression by the Indonesian authorities. **27 January 1999** The jailed Gusmão, head of the National Timorese Resistance Council (CNRT), calls for a ceasefire in the civil war in East Timor. This follows agreement by the Indonesian government to move Gusmão to house arrest (completed on 10 February) and consider granting independence after the June 1999 general election. Australia announces it will press Indonesia for an act of self-determination in East Timor that could lead to full independence. **5 May 1999** Following UN-brokered talks, Indonesia and Portugal sign an agreement in New York in which Indonesia agrees to hold a referendum in August 1999, offering the East Timorese voters the choice between 'special autonomy' within Indonesia or independence. **11 June 1999** A UN Mission in East Timor (UNAMET) is established to oversee the referendum. **30 August 1999** The East Timorese vote overwhelmingly (79%) for independence in a referendum.The turnout exceeds 90%. **1 September 1999** Pro-Indonesian militias, opposed to the pro-independence vote, rampage through Dili, placing the UN compound under siege for several hours and killing more than 20. Thousands of locals flee into the compound for safety as the armed anti-independence gangs embark on three weeks of violence, pillage, kidnappings, and rapes, which claim hundreds of lives, destroy 70% of buildings, and turn about 500,000 (three-quarters of the population) into displaced refugees. **6 September**

1999 Martial law isimposed, as militias continue to attack independence supporters. **12 September 1999** The Indonesian government yields to international pressure to allow a peacekeeping force into East Timor to assist UNAMET. This follows statements by the UN linking the Indonesian military to recent atrocities and a UN plan to set up a tribunal to deal with war crimes. **13 September 1999** The UN begins a mass evacuation of refugees from Dili to northern Australia. **20 September 1999** An Australian-led, 11,000-strong peacekeeping force, theInternational Force for East Timor (INTERFET), arrives to liberate East Timor from Indonesia and restore order. The anti-independence militias step up their activities. **October 1999** The Roman Catholic Bishop Carlos Belo and the independence leader Xanana Gusmão, return to East Timor, and refugees begin to return to Dili. **25 October 1999** The UN Security Council agrees to send up to 8,500 peacekeeping troops and 1,600 police to support a UN Transitional Administration in East Timor (UNTAET), with UN involvement expected to last up to three years. **30 October 1999** The last Indonesian troops leave East Timor. **November 1999** The Indonesian, multiparty government, headed by President Abdurraham Wahid, agrees to let East Timor become independent and a border is demarcated between East and West Timor. Further refugees return home from West Timor. **1 December 1999** Horta, the vice-president of the CNRT, returns to East Timor after 24 years of exile. **17 December 1999** International donors pledge US$522.5 million in aid for there construction of East Timor. **31 January 2000** Reports by the UN and by an Indonesian Commission to Investigate Human Rights Violations in East Timor conclude that the Indonesian military and police cooperated with the anti-independence gangs during the atrocities of September 1999. **23 February 2000** INTERFET is replaced by the UNTAET, commanded by General Jaime de los Santos of the Philippines, the handover being completed on 28 Febuary. However, 150,000 East Timorese remain in refugee camps in West Timor. **29 February 2000** Indonesia's President Wahid, on a visit to Dili, apologizes for Indonesia's past actions in the territory and signs a memorandum of understanding with UNTAET, paving the way for the resumption of trade and transport links.

Iran Islamic Republic of (formerly Persia)

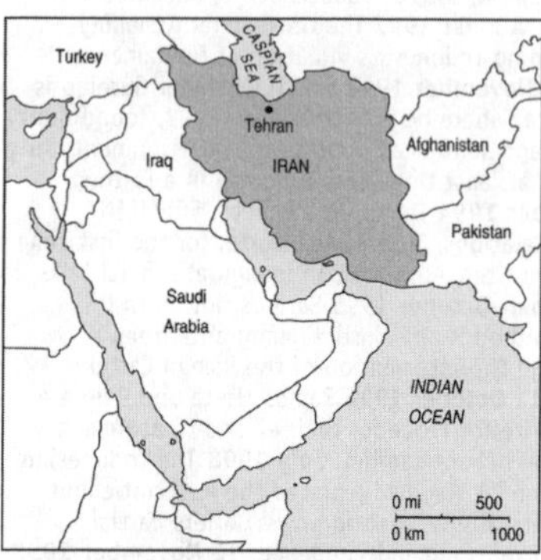

National name *Jomhori-e-Islami-e-Irân* **Area** 1,648,000 sq km/ 636,292 sq mi **Capital** Tehran **Major towns/ cities** Esfahan, Mashhad, Tabriz, Shiraz, Ahvaz, Bakhtaran, Qom, Kara

Government

Head of state and government Seyyed Muhammad Khatami from 1997 **Leader of the Islamic Revolution** Seyed Ali Khamenei from 1989 **Political system** Islamic nationalist **Armed forces** 518,000; plus 350,000 army reserves and 350,000 paramilitary forces (1997) **Conscription** military service is compulsory for two years **Defence spend** (% GDP) 6.6 (1997) **Education spend** (% GNP) 4.0 (1995) **Health spend** (% GDP) 1.4 (1995) **Death penalty** retained and used for ordinary crimes

Population and society

Population 66,796,000 (1999 est) **Population growth rate** 1.7% (1995–2000) **Ethnic groups** about 63% of Persian origin, 18% Turkic, 13% other Iranian, 3% Kurdish, and 3% Arabic **Religion** Shiite Muslim (official) 94%, Sunni Muslim, Zoroastrian, Christian, Jewish, Baha'i **Life expectancy** 69 (men); 70 (women) (1995–2000) **Literacy rate** 81% (men); 66% (women) (1997 est) **Unemployment** 11% (1998 est)

Economy and resources

GDP (US$) 90 billion (1998 est) **GNP** (US$) 109.6 billion (1998) **GNP per capita (PPP)** (US$) 3,920 (1998 est) **Real GDP growth** (% change on previous year) –2.1 (1998) **Consumer price inflation** 20% (1998) **Foreign debt** (US$) 11.8 billion (1997) **Resources** petroleum, natural gas, coal, magnetite, gypsum, iron ore, copper, chromite, salt, bauxite, decorative stone **Exports** crude petroleum and petroleum products, agricultural goods, carpets, metal ores. Principal market: Japan 15.1% (1997) **Imports** machinery and motor vehicles, paper, textiles, iron and steel and mineral products, chemicals and chemical products. Principal source: Germany 12.8% (1997)

▪ Tourist information

Time difference GMT +3.5 **Currency** rial **Language** Farsi (official), Kurdish, Turkish, Arabic, English, French **Visa requirements** UK: visa required. USA: visa required **Embassy in the UK** 16 Prince's Gate, London SW7 1PT. Tel: (020) 7584 8101; fax: (020) 7589 4440 **British embassy** PO Box 11365–4474, 143 Ferdowsi Avenue, Tehran 11344. Tel: (21) 675 011; fax: (21) 678 021 **Chamber of commerce** Iran Chamber of Commerce, Industries and Mines, 254 Taleghani Avenue, Tehran. Tel: (21) 836 0319; fax: (21) 882 5111 **Office hours** 0800–1600 Sat–Wed **Banking hours** 0900–1600 Sat–Wed; 0900–1200 Thu **Airports** international airports: Tehran (Mehrabad), Abadan, Esfahan; over 20 domestic airports; total passenger km: 7,380 million (1997 est) **Major ports** Abadan **Chief tourist attractions** wealth of historical sites, notably Esfahan, Tabriz, Rasht, Persepolis, and Susa **Major holidays** 11 February, 20–25 March, 1–2 April, 5 June; variable: Eid-ul-Adha, Ashora, end of Ramadan, Prophet's Birthday, Prophet's Mission (April), Birth of the Twelfth Imam (April/May), Martyrdom of Imam Ali (May), Death of Imam Jaffar Sadegh (June/July), Birth of Imam Reza (July), Id-E-Gihadir (August), Death of the Prophet and Martyrdom of Imam Hassan (October/November)

Chronology

c. 2000 BC Migration from southern Russia of Aryans, from whom Persians claim descent. **612 BC** The Medes, from northwest Iran, destroyed Iraq-based Assyrian Empire to the west and established their own empire which extended into central Anatolia (Turkey-in-Asia). **550 BC** Cyrus the Great overthrew Medes' empire and founded the First Persian Empire, the Achaemenid, conquering much of Asia Minor, including Babylonia (Palestine and Syria) in 539 BC. Expansion continued into Afghanistan under Darius I, who ruled 521–486 BC. **499–449 BC** The Persian Wars with Greece ended Persian domination of the ancient world. **330 BC** Collapse of Achaemenid Empire following defeat by Alexander the Great. **AD 224** Sassanian Persian Empire founded by Ardashir, with its capital at Ctesiphon, in the northeast. **637** Sassanian Empire destroyed by Muslim Arabs at battle of Qadisiya; Islam replaced Zoroastrianism. **750–1258** Dominated by the Persianized Abbasid dynasty, who reigned as caliphs (Islamic civil and religious leaders), with a capital in Baghdad (Iraq). **1380s** Conquered by the Mongol leader, Tamerlane. **1501** Emergence of Safavids; the arts and architecture flourished, particularly under Abbas I, 'the Great', who ruled 1588–1629. **1736** The Safavids were deposed by the warrior Nadir Shah Afshar, who ruled until 1747. **1790** Rise of the Qajars, who transferred the capital from Esfahan in central Iran to Tehran, further north. **19th century** Increasing influence in the north of tsarist Russia, which took Georgia and much of Armenia 1801–28. Britain exercised influence in the south and east, and fought Iran 1856–57 over claims to Herat (western Afghanistan). **1906** Parliamentary constitution adopted after a brief revolution. **1925** Qajar dynasty overthrown, with some British official help, in a coup by Col Reza Khan, a nationalist Iranian Cossack military officer, who was crowned shah ('king of kings'), with the title Reza Shah Pahlavi. **1920s onwards** Economic modernization, Westernization, and secularization programme launched, which proved unpopular with traditionalists. **1935** Name changed from Persia to Iran. **1941** Pahlavi Shah was forced to abdicate during World War II by Allied occupation forces and was succeeded by his son Muhammad Reza Pahlavi, who continued the modernization programme. **1946** British, US, and Soviet occupation forces left Iran. **1951** Oilfields nationalized by radical prime minister Muhammad Mossadeq as anti-British and US sentiment increased. **1953** Mossadeq deposed, the nationalization plan changed, and the US-backed shah, Muhammad Reza Shah Pahlavi, took full control of the government. **1963** Hundreds of protesters, who demanded the release of the arrested fundamentalist Shiite Muslim leader Ayatollah Ruhollah Khomeini, were killed by troops. **1970s** Spiralling world oil prices brought rapid economic expansion. **1975** The shah introduced a single-party system. **1977** The mysterious death in An Najaf of Mustafa, eldest son of the exiled Ayatollah Ruhollah Khomeini, sparked demonstrations by students, which were suppressed with the loss of six lives. **1978** Opposition to the shah was organized from France by Ayatollah Ruhollah Khomeini, who demanded a return to the principles of Islam. Hundreds of demonstrators were killed by troops in Jaleh Square, Tehran. **1979** Amid mounting demonstrations by students and clerics, the shah left the country; Khomeini returned to create a nonparty theocratic Islamic state. Revolutionaries seized 66 US hostages at embassy in Tehran; US economic boycott. **1980** Iraq invaded Iran, provoking a bitter war. The exiled shah died. **1981** US hostages were released. **1985–87** Fighting intensified in the Iran–Iraq War, with heavy loss of life. **1989** Khomeini issued a fatwa (public order) for the death of British writer Salman Rushdie for blasphemy against Islam. **1990** Generous peace terms with Iraq were accepted to close the Iran–Iraq war. **1991** Nearly 1 million Kurds arrived from northwest Iraq, fleeing persecution by Saddam Hussein after the Gulf War between Iraq and UN forces. **1993** Free-market economic reforms were introduced. **1997** Moderate politician Seyyed Muhammad Khatami was elected president. **1998** There were signs of rapprochement with the West. There was increased tension with Afghanistan, after the murder of Iranian civilians by the Talibaan. **1999** Diplomatic relations with the UK were to be restored. **2000** Supporters of President Khatami won parliamentary elections.

Iraq Republic of

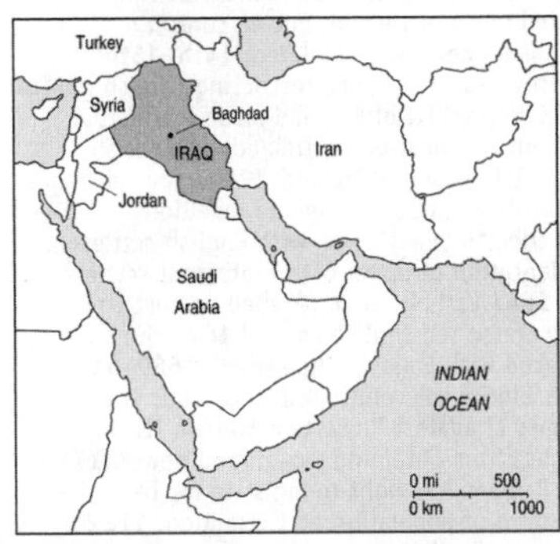

National name *al Jumhouriya al 'Iraqia* **Area** 434,924 sq km/ 167,924 sq mi **Capital** Baghdad **Major towns/ cities** Mosul, Basra, Kirkuk, Hilla, Najaf, Nasiriya

Government

Head of state and government Saddam Hussein from 1979 **Political system** nationalistic socialist **Armed forces** 387,500; plus 650,000 army reserves (1997) **Conscription** military service is compulsory for 18–24 months; it is waived on the payment of the equivalent of $800 **Defence spend** (% GDP) 7.4 (1997) **Education spend** (% GNP) 4.6 (1988) **Death penalty** retained and used for ordinary crimes

Population and society

Population 22,450,000 (1999 est) **Population growth rate** 2.8% (1995–2000); 2.8% (2000–05) **Ethnic groups** about 79% Arab, 16% Kurdish (mainly in northeast), 3% Persian, 2% Turkish **Religion** Shiite Muslim 60%, Sunni Muslim 37%, Christian 3% **Life expectancy** 61 (men); 64 (women) (1995–2000) **Literacy rate** 77% (men); 49% (women) (1995 est)

Economy and resources

GDP (US$) 42.8 billion (1997 est) **GNP** N/A **GNP per capita (PPP)** (US$) N/A **Real GDP growth** (% change on previous year) 15 (1998) **Consumer price inflation** 140% (1998) **Foreign debt** (US$) 21.2 billion **Resources** petroleum, natural gas, sulphur, phosphates **Exports** crude petroleum (accounting for more than 98% of total export earnings (1980–89), dates and other dried fruits. Principal market: Jordan 95% (1995) **Imports** machinery and transport equipment, basic manufactured articles, cereals and other foodstuffs, iron and steel, military goods. Principal source: Jordan 48.7% (1995)

▪ Tourist information

Time difference GMT +3 **Currency** Iraqi dinar **Language** Arabic (official); Kurdish, Assyrian, Armenian **Visa requirements** UK: visa required. USA: visa required **Embassy in the UK** Iraq has no diplomatic representation in the UK. The Embassy of the Hashemite Kingdom of Jordan deals with enquiries relating to Iraq: Iraq Interests Section, 21 Queen's Gate, London SW7 5JG. Tel: (020) 7584 7141/6; fax: (020) 7584 7716 **British embassy** the UK has no diplomatic representation in Iraq **Chamber of commerce** Federation of Iraqi Chambers of Commerce, Mustansir Street, Baghdad. Tel: (1) 888 6111 **Office hours** 0800–1400 Sat–Wed; 0800–1300 Thu **Banking hours** 0800–1200 Sat–Wed; 0800–1100 Thu; banks close at 1000 during Ramadan **Airports** international airports: Baghdad (Saddam), Basra, Bamerui; at least three domestic airports (many civilian airports sustained heavy damage during the 1991 Gulf War); total passenger km: 20 million (1994) **Major ports** Basra and Um Qass closed from 1980 **Major holidays** 1, 6 January, 8 February, 21 March, 1 May, 14, 17 July; variable: Eid-ul-Adha (4 days), Ashora, end of Ramadan (3 days), New Year (Muslim), Prophet's Birthday

Chronology

c. 3400 BC The world's oldest civilization, the Sumerian, arose in the land between the rivers Euphrates and Tigris, known as lower Mesopotamia, which lies in the heart of modern Iraq. Its cities included Lagash, Eridu, Uruk, Kish, and Ur. **c. 2350 BC** The confederation of Sumerian city-states was forged into an empire by the Akkadian leader Sargon. **7th century BC** In northern Mesopotamia, the Assyrian Empire, based around the River Tigris and formerly dominated by Sumeria and Euphrates-centred Babylonia, created a vast empire covering much of the Middle East. **612 BC** The Assyrian capital of Nineveh was destroyed by Babylon and Mede (in northwest Iran). **c. 550 BC** Mesopotamia came under Persian control. **AD 114** Conquered by the Romans. **266** Came under the rule of the Persian-based Sassanians. **637** Sassanian Empire destroyed by Muslim Arabs at battle of Qadisiya, in southern Iraq; Islam spread. **750–1258** Dominated by Abbasid dynasty, who reigned as caliphs (Islamic civil and religious leaders) in Baghdad. **1258** Baghdad invaded and burned by Tatars. **1401** Baghdad destroyed by Mongol ruler Tamerlane. **1533** Annexed by Suleiman the Magnificent, becoming part of the Ottoman Empire until the 20th century, despite recurrent anti-Ottoman insurrections. **1916** Occupied by Britain during World War I. **1920** Iraq became a British League of Nations protectorate. **1921** Hashemite dynasty established, with Faisal I installed by Britain as king. **1932** Independence achieved from British protectorate status, with Gen Nuri-el Said as prime minister. **1941–45** Occupied by Britain during World War II. **1955** Signed the Baghdad Pact collective security treaty with the UK, Iran, Pakistan, and Turkey. **1958** Monarchy overthrown in military-led revolution, in which King Faisal was assassinated; Iraq became a republic; joined Jordan in an Arab Federation; withdrew from Baghdad Pact as left-wing military regime assumed power. **1963** Joint socialist-nationalist Ba'athist-military coup headed by Col Salem Aref and backed by US Central Intelligence Agency; reign of terror launched against the left. **1968** Ba'athist military coup put Maj-Gen Ahmed Hassan al-Bakr in power. **1979** Al-Bakr was replaced by Saddam Hussein of the Arab Ba'ath Socialist Party. **1980** The war between Iraq and Iran broke out. **1985–87** Fighting in the Iran–Iraq war intensified, with heavy loss of life. **1988** There was a ceasefire and talks began with Iran. Iraq used chemical weapons against Kurdish rebels seeking greater autonomy in the northwest. **1989** There was an unsuccessful coup against President Hussein; Iraq successfully launched a ballistic test missile. **1990** A peace treaty favouring Iran was agreed. Iraq invaded and annexed Kuwait in August. US forces massed in Saudi Arabia at the request of King Fahd. The United Nations (UN) ordered Iraqi withdrawal and imposed total trade ban; further UN resolution sanctioned the use of force. All foreign hostages were released. **1991** US-led Allied forces launched an aerial assault on Iraq and destroyed the country's infrastructure; a land–sea–air offensive to free Kuwait was successful. Uprisings of Kurds and Shiites were brutally suppressed by surviving Iraqi troops. Allied troops established 'safe havens' for Kurds in the north prior to the withdrawal, and left a rapid-reaction force near the Turkish border. **1992** The UN imposed a 'no-fly zone' over southern Iraq to protect Shiites. **1993** Iraqi incursions into the 'no-fly zone' prompted US-led alliance aircraft to bomb strategic targets in Iraq. There was continued persecution of Shiites in the south. **1994** Iraq renounced its claim to Kuwait, but failed to fulfil the other conditions required for the lifting of UN sanctions. **1996** Iraqi-backed attacks on Kurds prompted US retaliation; these air strikes destroyed Iraqi military bases in the south. **1997** Iraq continued to resist the US and Allied pressure to allow UN weapons inspections. **1998** Iraq expelled UN weapons inspectors. In April the UN inspectors' report showed that Iraq had failed to meet UN requirements on the destruction of chemical and biological weapons. In December US and UK forces launched Operation Desert Fox which lasted four days; there were further clashes between US–UK forces and Baghdad over the no-fly zone, which continued in to 1999. **1999** In February US–UK air strikes resumed. The UK suggested the lifting of sanctions if Iraq resumed cooperation with the UN.

Ireland Republic of

National name *Eire* **Area** 70,282 sq km/27,135 sq mi **Capital** Dublin **Major towns/cities** Cork, Limerick, Galway, Waterford, Wexford

Government

Head of state Mary McAleese from 1997 **Head of government** Bertie Ahern from 1997 **Political system** liberal democracy **Armed forces** 12,700 (1997) **Conscription** military service is voluntary **Defence spend** (% GDP) 1.0 (1997) **Education spend** (% GNP) 5.8 (1996) **Health spend** (% GDP) 5.2 (1996) **Death penalty** abolished in 1990

Population and society

Population 3,705,000 (1999 est) **Population growth rate** 0.7% (1995–2000) **Ethnic groups** most of the population has Celtic origins **Religion** Roman Catholic 95%, Church of Ireland, other Protestant denominations **Life expectancy** 74 (men); 79 (women) (1995–2000) **Literacy rate** 99% (men); 99% (women) (1997 est) **Unemployment** 7.7% (1998)

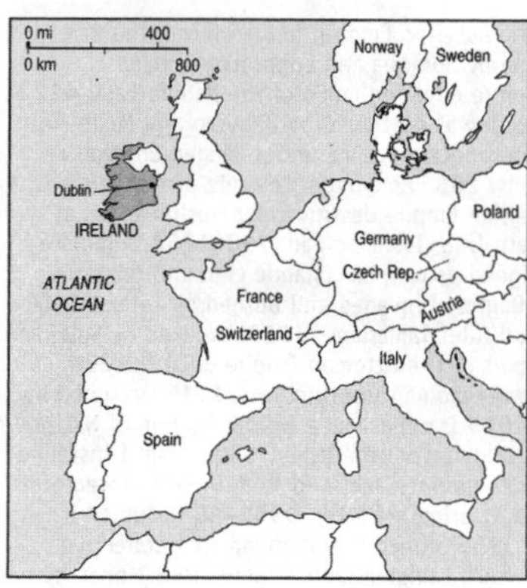

Economy and resources

GDP (US$) 80.9 billion (1998) **GNP** (US$) 67.5 billion (1998) **GNP per capita (PPP)** (US$) 18,340 (1998) **Real GDP growth** (% change on previous year) 9.4 (1998) **Consumer price inflation** 2.5% (1998) **Resources** lead, zinc, peat, limestone, gypsum, petroleum, natural gas, copper, silver **Exports** beef and dairy products, live animals, machinery and transport equipment, electronic goods, chemicals. Principal market: UK 22.2% (1998) **Imports** petroleum products, machinery and transport equipment, chemicals, foodstuffs, animal feed, textiles and clothing. Principal source: UK 33.6% (1998)

Tourist information

Time difference GMT +/– 0 **Currency** Irish pound (punt Eireannach) **Language** Irish Gaelic and English (both official) **Visa requirements** UK: visa not required. USA: visa not required **Embassy in the UK** 17 Grosvenor Place, London SW1X 7HR. Tel: (020) 7235 2171; fax: (020) 7245 6961 **British embassy** 31–33 Merrion Road, Dublin 4. Tel: (1) 269 5211; fax: (1) 283 8423 **Chamber of commerce** Chambers of Commerce of Ireland, 22 Merrion Square, Dublin 2. Tel: (1) 661 2888; fax: (1) 661 2811 **Office hours** 0900–1700 Mon–Fri **Banking hours** 1000–1600 Mon–Fri **Airports** international airports: Dublin, Shannon, Cork, Knock (Horan), Galway; five domestic airports; total passengers carried: 27.9 million (1996) **Major ports** Cork, Dun Laoghaire, Limerick, Waterford, Galway **Chief tourist attractions** scenery, notably the Killarney lakes and the west coast; Dublin, with its many literary associations and famous pub life **Major holidays** 1 January, 17 March, 25–26 December; variable: Good Friday, Easter Monday, June Holiday, August Holiday, October Holiday, Christmas Holiday

Republic of Ireland: Provinces and Counties

County	Administrative headquarters	Area sq km	Area sq mi	Population (1996)
Ulster Province				
Cavan	Cavan	1,890	729	52,900
Donegal	Lifford	4,830	1,864	129,900
Monaghan	Monaghan	1,290	498	51,300
Munster Province				
Clare	Ennis	3,190	1,231	94,000
Cork	Cork	7,460	2,880	420,300
Kerry	Tralee	4,700	1,814	126,100
Limerick	Limerick	2,690	1,038	177,902
Tipperary (North)	Nenagh	2,000	772	58,000
Tipperary (South)	Clonmel	2,260	872	75,500
Waterford	Waterford	1,840	710	94,600
Leinster Province				
Carlow	Carlow	900	347	41,600
Dublin	Dublin	920	355	1,056,700
Kildare	Naas	1,690	652	135,000
Kilkenny	Kilkenny	2,060	795	75,300
Laois (or Laoighis)	Port Laoise	1,720	664	52,900
Longford	Longford	1,040	401	30,200
Louth	Dundalk	820	316	92,200
Meath	Navan	2,340	903	109,700
Offaly	Tullamore	2,000	772	59,100
Westmeath	Mullingar	1,760	679	63,300
Wexford	Wexford	2,350	907	104,400
Wicklow	Wicklow	2,030	783	102,700
Connacht (or Connaught) Province				
Galway	Galway	5,940	2,293	188,600
Leitrim	Carrick-on-Shannon	1,530	590	25,100
Mayo	Castlebar	5,400	2,084	111,500
Roscommon	Roscommon	2,460	949	52,000
Sligo	Sligo	1,800	694	55,800

Chronology

3rd century BC The Gaels, a Celtic people, invaded Ireland and formed about 150 small kingdoms. **AD *c.* 432** St Patrick introduced Christianity. **5th–9th centuries** Irish Church was a centre of culture and scholarship. **9th–11th centuries** The Vikings raided Ireland until defeated by High King Brian Bóruma at Clontarf in 1014. **12th–13th centuries** Anglo-Norman adventurers conquered much of Ireland, but no central government was formed and many became assimilated. **14th–15th centuries** Irish chieftains recovered their lands, restricting English rule to the Pale around Dublin. **1536** Henry VIII of England made ineffectual efforts to impose the Protestant Reformation on Ireland. **1541** Irish parliament recognized Henry VIII as king of Ireland; Henry gave peerages to Irish chieftains. **1579** English suppressed Desmond rebellion, confiscated rebel lands, and tried to 'plant' them with English settlers. **1610** James I established plantation of Ulster with Protestant settlers from England and Scotland. **1641** Catholic Irish rebelled against English rule; Oliver Cromwell brutally reasserted English control 1649–50; Irish landowners evicted and replaced with English landowners. **1689–91** Williamite War: following the 'Glorious Revolution', the Catholic Irish unsuccessfully supported James II against Protestant William III in civil war. Penal laws barred Catholics from obtaining wealth and power. **1720** Act passed declaring British Parliament's right to legislate for Ireland. **1739–41** Famine killed one-third of population of 1.5 million. **1782** Protestant landlords led by Henry Grattan secured end of restrictions on Irish trade and parliament. **1798** British suppressed revolt by Society of United Irishmen (with French support) led by Wolfe Tone. **1800** Act of Union abolished Irish parliament and created United Kingdom of Great Britain and Ireland, effective 1801. **1829** Daniel O'Connell secured Catholic Emancipation Act, which permitted Catholics to enter parliament. **1846–52** Potato famine reduced population by 20% through starvation and emigration. **1870** Land Act increased security for tenants but failed to halt agrarian disorder; Isaac Butt formed political party to campaign for Irish home rule (devolution). **1885** Home-rulers, led by Charles Stewart Parnell, held balance of power in Parliament; first Home Rule Bill rejected 1886; second Home Rule Bill defeated in 1893. **1905** Arthur Griffith founded the nationalist movement Sinn Fein ('Ourselves Alone'). **1914** Ireland came close to civil war as Ulster prepared to resist implementation of Home Rule Act (postponed because of World War I). **1916** Easter Rising: nationalists proclaimed a republic in Dublin; British crushed revolt and executed 15 leaders. **1919** Sinn Fein MPs formed Irish parliament in Dublin in defiance of British government. **1919–21** Irish Republican Army (IRA) waged guerrilla war against British forces. **1921** Anglo-Irish Treaty partitioned Ireland; northern Ireland (Ulster) remained part of the United Kingdom; southern Ireland won full internal self-government with dominion status. **1922** Irish Free State proclaimed; IRA split over Anglo-Irish Treaty led to civil war 1922–23. **1932** Anti-Treaty party, Fianna Fáil, came to power under Éamon de Valera. **1937** New constitution established Eire (Gaelic name for Ireland) as a sovereign state and refused to acknowledge partition. **1949** After remaining neutral in World War II, Eire left the Commonwealth and became the Republic of Ireland. **1973** Ireland joined European Economic Community. **1985** The Anglo-Irish Agreement gave the Republic of Ireland a consultative role, but no powers, in the government of Northern Ireland. **1993** The Downing Street Declaration, a joint Anglo-Irish peace proposal for Northern Ireland, was issued. **1997** Mary McAleese was elected president; she appointed Bertie Ahern as her prime minister. **1998** A multiparty agreement (the Good Friday Agreement) was reached on the future of Northern Ireland. The subsequent referendum showed a large majority in favour of dropping Ireland's claim to Northern Ireland. Strict legislation was passed against terrorism. **1999** The IRA agreed to begin decommissioning discussions and a coalition government was established, with David Trimble as first minister. Powers were devolved to the province by the British government in December. **2000** After it was revealed that there had been no arms handover, the British secretary of state for Northern Ireland suspended the Northern Ireland Assembly and reintroduced direct rule. Within hours of the suspension of the Assembly, the British government announced a new IRA initiative on arms decommissioning.

Israel State of

National name *Medinat Israel* **Area** 20,800 sq km/8,030 sq mi (as at 1949 armistice) **Capital** Jerusalem (not recognized by United Nations) **Major towns/cities** Tel Aviv-Yafo, Haifa, Bat-Yam, Holon, Ramat Gan, Petach Tikva, Rishon Leziyyon, Beersheba

Government

Head of state Ezer Weizman from 1993 **Head of government** Ehud Barak from 1999 **Political system** liberal democracy **Armed forces** 175,000; 430,000 reservists (1997) **Conscription** voluntary for Christians, Circassians, and Muslims; compulsory for Jews and Druzes (men 36 months, women 21 months) **Defence spend** (% GDP) 11.5 (1997) **Education spend** (% GNP) 7.2 (1996) **Health spend** (% GDP) 2.1 (1990–95) **Death penalty** exceptional crimes only; last execution in 1962

Population and society

Population 6,101,000 (1999 est) **Population growth rate** 2.2% (1995–2000) **Ethnic groups** around 85% of the population is Jewish, the majority of the remainder Arab. Under the Law of Return 1950, 'every Jew shall be entitled to come to Israel as an immigrant'; those from the East and Eastern Europe are Ashkenazim, and those from Mediterranean Europe (Spain, Portugal, Italy, France, Greece) and Arab Africa are Sephardim (over 50% of the population is now of Sephardic descent); an Israeli-born Jew is a Sabra **Religion** Israel is a secular state, but the predominant faith is Judaism 85%; also Sunni Muslim, Christian, and Druze **Life expectancy** 76 (men); 80 (women) (1995–2000) **Literacy rate** 98% (men); 93% (women) (1997 est) **Unemployment** 8.6% (1998)

Economy and resources

GDP (US$) 100 billion (1998) **GNP** (US$) 95.2 billion (1998) **GNP per capita (PPP)** (US$) 17,310 (1997) **Real GDP growth** (% change on previous year) 1.6 (1998) **Consumer price inflation** 8.3% (1998) **Foreign debt** 39.3 billion (1997) **Resources** potash, bromides, magnesium, sulphur, copper ore, gold, salt, petroleum, natural gas **Exports** citrus fruits, worked diamonds, machinery and parts, military hardware, food products, chemical products, textiles and clothing. Principal market: USA 35.4% (1998) **Imports** machinery and parts, rough diamonds, chemicals and related products, crude petroleum and petroleum products, motor vehicles. Principal source: USA 19.6% (1998)

▪ Tourist information

Time difference GMT +2 **Currency** shekel **Language** Hebrew and Arabic (official); English, Yiddish, European, and western Asian languages **Visa requirements** UK: visa not required. USA: visa not required **Embassy in the UK** 2 Palace Green, London W8 4QB. Tel: (020) 7957 9500; fax: (020) 7957 9555 **British embassy** 192 Rehov Hayarkon, Tel Aviv 63405. Tel: (3) 524 9171/8; fax: (3) 524 3313 **Chamber of commerce** Federation of Israeli Chambers of Commerce, PO Box 20027, 84 Hahashmonaim Street, Tel Aviv 67011. Tel: (3) 563 1010; fax: (3) 561 9025 **Office hours** 0800–1300 and 1500–1800 Sun–Thu (November–May); 0730–1430 Sun–Thu (June–October) **Banking hours** 0830–1230 and 1600–1730 Mon, Tue, and Thu; 0830–1230 Wed; 0830–1200 Fri **Airports** international airports: Tel Aviv (Ben Gurion), Eilat; domestic airports in all major cities; total passenger km: 11,794 million (1997 est) **Major ports** Tel Aviv-Yafo, Haifa, 'Akko (formerly Acre), Eilat **Chief tourist attractions** resorts along Mediterranean coast, Red Sea coast (Eilat), and Dead Sea; ancient city of Jerusalem, with its four quarters (Armenian, Christian, Jewish, and Muslim) and many sites, including Temple Mount, the Cathedral of St James, Dome of the Rock, Al-Aqsa Mosque, and Church of the Holy Sepulchre; historic sites of Bethlehem, Nazareth, Masada, Megiddo, Jericho; caves of the Dead Sea scrolls **Major holidays** 1 January, 14 May; variable: New Year (Jewish, September/October), Purim (March), first day of Passover (April), last day of Passover (April), Pentecost (June), Fast of Av (August), Yom Kippur (October), Feast of Tabernacles (October, 2 days)

Chronology

***c.* 2000 BC** Abraham, father of the Jewish people, is believed to have come to Palestine from Mesopotamia. ***c.* 1225 BC** Moses led the Jews out of slavery in Egypt towards the promised land of Palestine. **11th century BC** Saul established a Jewish kingdom in Palestine; developed by kings David and Solomon. **586 BC** Jews defeated by Babylon and deported; many returned to Palestine in 539 BC. **333 BC** Alexander the Great of Macedonia conquered the entire region. **3rd century BC** Control of Palestine contested by Ptolemies of Egypt and Seleucids of Syria. **142 BC** Jewish independence restored after Maccabean revolt. **63 BC** Palestine fell to Roman Empire. **70 AD** Romans crushed Zealot rebellion and destroyed Jerusalem; start of dispersion of Jews (diaspora). **614** Persians took Jerusalem from Byzantine Empire. **637** Muslim Arabs conquered Palestine. **1099** First Crusade captured Jerusalem; Christian kingdom lasted a century before falling to sultans of Egypt. **1517** Palestine conquered by the Ottoman Turks. **1897** Theodor Herzl organized the First Zionist Congress at Basel to publicize Jewish claims to Palestine. **1917** The Balfour Declaration: Britain expressed support for the creation of a Jewish National Home in Palestine. **1918** British forces expelled the Turks from Palestine, which became a British League of Nations mandate in 1920. **1929** Severe violence around Jerusalem caused by Arab alarm at doubling of Jewish population in ten years. **1933** Jewish riots in protest at British attempts to restrict Jewish immigration. **1937** The Peel Report, recommending partition, accepted by most Jews but rejected by Arabs; open warfare ensued 1937–38. **1939** Britain postponed independence plans on account of World War II, and increased military presence. **1946** Resumption of terrorist violence; Jewish extremists blew up British headquarters in Jerusalem. **1947** United Nations (UN) voted for partition of Palestine. **1948** Britain withdrew; Independent State of Israel proclaimed with David Ben-Gurion as prime minister; Israel repulsed invasion by Arab nations; many Palestinian Arabs settled in refugee camps in the Gaza Strip and West Bank. **1952** Col Gamal Nasser of Egypt stepped up blockade of Israeli ports and support of Arab guerrillas in Gaza. **1956** War between Israel and Egypt; Israeli invasion of Gaza and Sinai followed by withdrawal in 1957. **1964** Palestine Liberation Organization (PLO) founded to unite Palestinian Arabs with the aim of overthrowing the state of Israel. **1967** Israel defeated Egypt, Syria, and Jordan in the Six-Day War; Gaza, West Bank, east Jerusalem, Sinai, and Golan Heights captured. **1969** Yassir Arafat became chair of the PLO; escalation of terrorism and border raids. **1973** Yom Kippur War: Israel repulsed surprise attack by Egypt and Syria. **1977** President Anwar Sadat of Egypt began peace initiative. **1979** Camp David talks ended with signing of peace treaty between Israel and Egypt; Israel withdrew from Sinai. **1980** United Jerusalem was declared the capital of Israel. **1982** Israeli forces invaded southern Lebanon to drive out PLO guerrillas; occupation continued until 1985. **1988** The Israeli handling of Palestinian uprising (Intifada) in the occupied territories provoked international criticism. **1990** The PLO formally recognized the state of Israel. **1991** Iraq launched missile attacks on Israel during the Gulf War; Middle East peace talks began in Madrid. **1992** A Labour government was elected under Yitzhak Rabin. **1993** Rabin and Arafat signed a peace accord; Israel granted limited autonomy to Gaza Strip and Jericho. Ezer Weizman was elected president. **1994** Arafat became the head of an autonomous Palestinian authority in Gaza and Jericho; a peace agreement was reached between Israel and Jordan. **1995** Rabin was assassinated by a Jewish opponent of the peace accord. **1996** A Likud government was elected under Binjamin Netanyahu, a critic of the peace accord. A revival of communal violence was seen and the peace process was threatened. **1997** A Jewish settlement in east Jerusalem was widely condemned. There were suicide bombs by Hamas in Jerusalem. There was partial and limited withdrawal from the West Bank. **1998** Violence flared on the West Bank between Palestinians and Israeli troops, again stalling the peace process. The Wye Peace Agreement was signed with the PLO. A land-for-security deal was approved by the Knesset, and the promised Israeli withdrawal from the Lebanon was subsequently placed in doubt. President Clinton attempted to restart the peace process. **1999** The South Lebanon 'security zone' was expanded. Yassir Arafat delayed the declaration of an independent state until after the Israeli elections. Ehud Barak (Labour) was elected prime minister and restarted peace negotiations. **2000** Ehud Barak and Syrian Foreign Minister Farouk Sharaa concluded peace talks in the US with only the outline of an agreement. The issue under negotiation was Israel's withdrawal from the Golan Heights. There was strong opposition to a withdrawal from the Golan Heights from Israeli politicians and civilians.

Italy Republic of

National name *Repubblica Italiana* **Area** 301,300 sq km/116,331 sq mi **Capital** Rome **Major towns/cities** Milan, Naples, Turin, Palermo, Genoa, Bologna

Government

Head of state Giuliano Amato from 2000 **Head of government** Massimo d'Alema from 2000 **Political system** liberal democracy **Armed forces** 325,200 (1997) **Conscription** 12 months **Defence spend** (% GDP) 1.9 (1997) **Education spend** (% GNP) 4.7 (1996) **Health spend** (% GDP) 5.5 (1996) **Death penalty** abolished in 1994

Population and society

Population 57,343,000 (1999 est) **Population growth rate** -0.01% (1995–2000); -0.2% (2000–05) **Ethnic groups** mainly Italian; some minorities of German origin **Religion** Roman Catholic 100% (state religion) **Life expectancy** 75 (men); 81 (women) (1995–2000) **Literacy rate** 99% (men); 98% (women) (1997 est) **Unemployment** 12.3% (1998)

Economy and resources

GDP (US$) 1,171 billion (1998) **GNP** (US$) 1,166.2 billion (1998) **GNP per capita (PPP)** (US$) 20,200 (1998) **Real GDP growth** (% change on previous year) 1.5 (1998) **Consumer price inflation** 2.4% (1998) **Resources** lignite, lead, zinc, mercury, potash, sulphur, fluorspar, bauxite, marble, petroleum, natural gas, fish **Exports** machinery and transport equipment, textiles, clothing, footwear, wine (leading producer and exporter), metals and metal products, chemicals, wood, paper and rubber goods. Principal market: Germany 16.5% (1998) **Imports** mineral fuels and lubricants, machinery and transport equipment, chemical products, foodstuffs, metal products. Principal source: Germany 18.8% (1998)

▪ Tourist information

Time difference GMT +1 **Currency** lira **Language** Italian; German, French, Slovene, and Albanian minorities **Visa requirements** UK: visa not required. USA: visa not required **Embassy in the UK** 14 Three Kings Yard, Davies Street, London W1Y 2EH. Tel: (020) 7312 2200; fax: (020) 7312 2230 **British embassy** Via XX Settembre 80A, 00187 Rome. Tel: (06) 482 5551; fax: (06) 487 3324 **Chamber of commerce** Unione Italiana delle Camere di Commercio, Industria, Artigianato e Agricoltura, Piazza Sallustio 21, 00187 Rome. Tel: (06) 47041; telex: 622 327 **Office hours** 0900–1300 and 1400–1800 Mon–Fri **Banking hours** generally 0830–1330 and 1530–1930 Mon–Fri **Airports** international airports: Bologna (G Marconi), Genoa (Cristoforo Colombo), Milan (Linate and Malpensa), Naples (Capodichino), Palermo (Punta Rais), Pisa (Galileo Galilei), Rome (Leonardo da Vinci and Ciampino), Turin, Venice (Marco Polo); over 30 domestic airports; total passenger km: 37,728 million (1997 est) **Major ports** Naples, Genoa, Palermo, Bari, Catania, Trieste **Chief tourist attractions** Alpine and Mediterranean scenery; ancient Greek and Roman archaeological remains; medieval, Renaissance, and baroque churches (including St Peter's, Rome); Renaissance towns and palaces; museums; art galleries; opera houses

Italy: Regions

Region	Capital	Area		Population (1997)
		sq km	sq mi	
Abruzzo	L'Aquila	10,794	4,168	1,276,000
Basilicata	Potenza	9,992	3,858	610,300
Calabria	Catanzaro	15,080	5,822	2,071,100
Campania	Naples	13,595	5,249	5,796,900
Emilia-Romagna	Bologna	22,123	8,542	3,947,100
Friuli-Venezia Giulia[1]	Trieste	7,846	3,029	1,184,700
Lazio	Rome	17,203	6,642	5,242,700
Liguria	Genoa	5,416	2,091	1,641,800
Lombardy	Milan	23,856	9,211	8,989,000
Marche	Ancona	9,694	3,743	1,450,900
Molise	Campobasso	4,438	1,714	329,900
Piedmont	Turin	25,399	9,807	4,291,400
Puglia	Bari	19,347	7,470	4,090,100
Sardinia[1]	Cagliari	24,090	9,301	1,661,400
Sicily[1]	Palermo	25,708	9,926	5,108,100
Trentino-Alto Adige[1]	Trento	13,613	5,256	924,300
Tuscany	Florence	22,992	8,877	3,527,300
Umbria	Perugia	8,456	3,265	831,700
Valle d'Aosta[1]	Aosta	3,262	1,259	119,600
Veneto	Venice	18,364	7,090	4,469,200

[1] Special autonomous region.

Major holidays 1, 6 January, 25 April, 1 May, 14 August (mid-August holiday, 2 days), 1 November, 8, 25–26 December; variable: Easter Monday

Chronology

4th and 3rd centuries BC Italian peninsula united under Roman rule. **AD 476** End of Western Roman Empire. **568** Invaded by Lombards. **756** Papal States created in central Italy. **800** Charlemagne united Italy and Germany in Holy Roman Empire. **12th and 13th centuries** Papacy and Holy Roman Empire contended for political supremacy; papal power reached its peak under Innocent III (1198–1216). **1183** Cities of Lombard League (founded in 1164) became independent. **14th century** Beginnings of Renaissance in northern Italy. **15th century** Most of Italy ruled by five rival states: the city-states of Milan, Florence, and Venice; the Papal States; and the Kingdom of Naples. **1494** Charles VIII of France invaded Italy. **1529–59** Spanish Habsburgs secured dominance in Italy. **17th century** Italy effectively part of Spanish Empire; economic and cultural decline. **1713** Treaty of Utrecht gave political control of most of Italy to Austrian Habsburgs. **1796–1814** France conquered Italy, setting up satellite states and introducing principles of French Revolution. **1815** Old regimes largely restored; Italy divided between Austria, Papal States, Naples, Sardinia, and four duchies. **1831** Giuseppe Mazzini founded the 'Young Italy' movement with the aim of creating a unified republic. **1848–49** Liberal revolutions occurred throughout Italy; reversed everywhere except Sardinia, which became centre of nationalism under leadership of Count Camillo di Cavour. **1859** France and Sardinia forcibly expelled Austrians from Lombardy. **1860** Sardinia annexed duchies and Papal States (except Rome); Giuseppe Garibaldi overthrew Neapolitan monarchy. **1861** Victor Emmanuel II of Sardinia proclaimed King of Italy in Turin. **1866** Italy gained Venetia after defeat of Austria by Prussia. **1870** Italian forces occupied Rome in defiance of Pope, completing unification of Italy. **1882** Italy joined Germany and Austria-Hungary in Triple Alliance. **1896** Attempt to conquer Ethiopia defeated at Battle of Adowa. **1900** King Umberto I assassinated by an anarchist. **1912** Annexation of Libya and Dodecanese after Italo-Turkish War. **1915** Italy entered World War I on side of Allies. **1919** Peace treaties awarded Trentino, South Tyrol, and Trieste to Italy. **1922** Mussolini established fascist dictatorship following period of strikes and agrarian revolts. **1935–36** Conquest of Ethiopia. **1939** Invasion of Albania. **1940** Italy entered World War II as ally of Germany. **1943** Allies invaded southern Italy; Mussolini removed from power; Germans occupied northern and central Italy. **1945** Allies completed liberation. **1946** Monarchy replaced by a republic. **1947** Peace treaty stripped Italy of its colonies. **1948** New constitution adopted; Christian Democrats emerged as main party of government in political system marked by ministerial instability. **1957** Italy became a founder member of European Economic Community (EEC). **1963** Creation of first of long series of fragile centre-left coalition governments. **1976** Communists attempt to join the coalition, the 'historic compromise', rejected by the Christian Democrats. **1978** Christian Democrat Aldo Moro, the architect of historic compromise, was murdered by Red Brigade guerrillas infiltrated by Western intelligence agents. **1983–87** Bettino Craxi, Italy's first Socialist prime minister, led the coalition. The economy improved. **1993** A major political crisis was triggered by the exposure of government corruption and Mafia links, and governing parties were discredited. A new electoral system replaced proportional representation, with 75% majority voting. **1998** Massimo d'Alema formed a new communist-led coalition and became prime minister. **1999** Carlo Azeglio Ciampi was elected president. Former prime minister Prodi became president of the new European Commission.

Jamaica

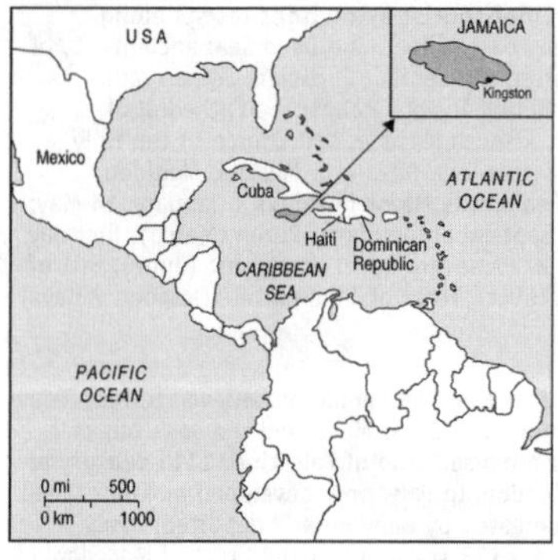

Area 10,957 sq km/ 4,230 sq mi **Capital** Kingston **Major towns/ cities** Montego Bay, Spanish Town, St Andrew, Portmore, May Pen

Government

Head of state Elizabeth II from 1962, represented by governor general Howard Felix Hanlan Cooke from 1991 /ITEM> **Head of government** Percival Patterson from 1992 **Political system** liberal democracy **Armed forces** 3,320 (1997)

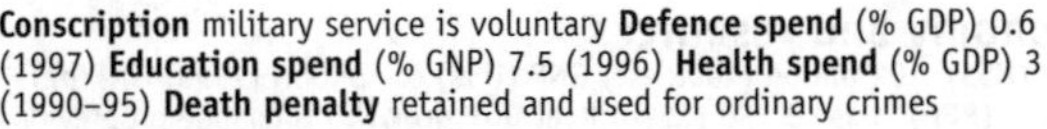

Conscription military service is voluntary **Defence spend** (% GDP) 0.6 (1997) **Education spend** (% GNP) 7.5 (1996) **Health spend** (% GDP) 3 (1990–95) **Death penalty** retained and used for ordinary crimes

Population and society

Population 2,561,000 (1999 est) **Population growth rate** 0.9% (1995–2000) **Ethnic groups** nearly 80% of African descent; about 15% of mixed African-European origin. There are also Chinese, Indian, and European minorities **Religion** Protestant 70%, Rastafarian **Life expectancy** 73 (men); 77 (women) (1995–2000) **Literacy rate** 81% (men); 90% (women) (1997 est) **Unemployment** 16.2% (1996)

Economy and resources

GDP (US$) 6.6 billion (1998) **GNP** (US$) 4.3 billion (1998) **GNP per capita (PPP)** (US$) 3,210 (1998) **Real GDP growth** (% change on previous year) –3.3% (1998) **Consumer price inflation** 34.7% (1998) **Foreign debt** (US$) 3.9 billion (1997) **Resources** bauxite (one of world's major producers), marble, gypsum, silica, clay **Exports** bauxite, alumina, gypsum, sugar, bananas, garments, rum. Principal market: USA 33.3% (1997) **Imports** mineral fuels, machinery and transport equipment, basic manufactures, chemicals, food and live animals, miscellaneous manufactured articles. Principal source: USA 47.7% (1997)

▪ Tourist information

Time difference GMT –5 **Currency** Jamaican dollar **Language** English, Jamaican creole **Visa requirements** UK: visa not required. USA: visa not required **Embassy in the UK** 1–2 Prince Consort Road, London SW7 2BZ. Tel: (020) 7823 9911; fax: (020) 7589 5154 **British embassy** British High Commission, PO Box 575, Trafalgar Road, Kingston 10. Tel: (809) 926 9050; fax: (809) 929 7869 **Chamber of commerce** PO Box 172, 7–8 East Parade, Kingston. Tel: (809) 922 0150; fax: (809) 924 9056 **Office hours** 0830–1630/1700 Mon–Fri **Banking hours** 0900–1400 Mon–Thu; 0900–1500 Fri **Airports** international airports: Kingston (Norman Manley), Montego Bay (Donald Sangster); four domestic airports; total passenger km: 2,720 million (1997 est) **Chief tourist attractions** climate; beaches; mountains; historic buildings **Major holidays** 1 January, 23 May, 5 August, 20 October, 25–26 December; variable: Ash Wednesday, Good Friday, Easter Monday

Chronology

c. AD 900 Settled by Arawak Indians, who gave the island the name Jamaica ('well watered'). **1494** The explorer Christopher Columbus reached Jamaica. **1509** Occupied by Spanish; much of Arawak community died from exposure to European diseases; black African slaves brought in to work sugar plantations. **1655** Captured by Britain and became its most valuable Caribbean colony. **1838** Slavery abolished. **1870** Banana plantations established as sugar cane industry declined in face of competition from European beet sugar. **1938** Serious riots during the economic depression and, as a sign of growing political awareness, the People's National Party (PNP) was formed by Norman Manley. **1944** First constitution adopted. **1958–62** Part of West Indies Federation. **1959** Internal self-government granted. **1962** Independence achieved within the Commonwealth, with Alexander Bustamante of the centre-right Jamaica Labour Party (JLP) as prime minister. **1981** Diplomatic links with Cuba were severed, and a free-market economic programme was pursued. **1988** The island was badly damaged by Hurricane Gilbert. **1992** Percival Patterson of the PNP became prime minister. **1998** Violent crime increased as the economy declined.

Japan

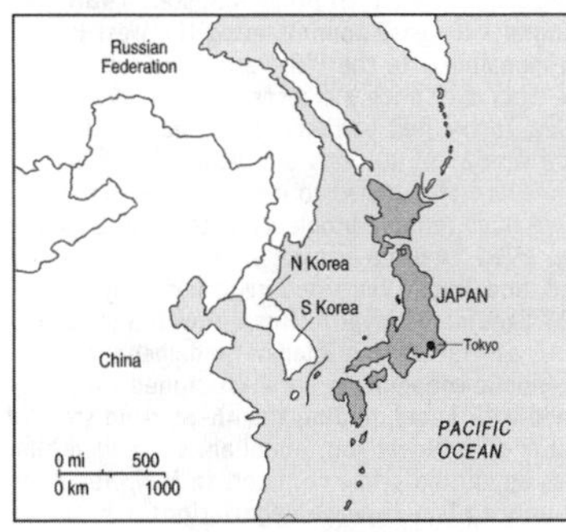

National name *Nippon* **Area** 377,535 sq km/ 145,766 sq mi **Capital** Tokyo **Major towns/ cities** Yokohama, Osaka, Nagoya, Fukuoka, Kitakyushu, Kyoto, Sapporo, Kobe, Kawasaki, Hiroshima

Government

Head of state (figurehead) Emperor Akihito (Heisei) from 1989 **Head of government** Yoshiro Mori from 2000 **Political system** liberal democracy **Armed forces** self-defence forces: 235,600; US forces stationed there: 44,800 (1997) **Conscription** military service is voluntary **Defence spend** (% GDP) 1 (1997) **Education spend** (% GNP) 3.6 (1996) **Health spend** (% GDP) 5.7 (1996) **Death penalty** retained and used for ordinary crimes

Population and society

Population 126,505,000 (1999 est) **Population growth rate** 0.2% (1995–2000); 0.1% (2000–05) **Ethnic groups** more than 99% of Japanese descent; Ainu (aboriginal people of Japan) in north Japan (Hokkaido, Kuril Islands) **Religion** Shinto, Buddhist (often combined), Christian **Life expectancy** 77 (men); 83 (women) (1995–2000) **Literacy rate** 99% (men); 99% (women) (1997 est) **Unemployment** 4.1% (1998)

Economy and resources

GDP (US$) 3,783.1 billion (1998) **GNP** (US$) 4,089.9 billion (1998) **GNP per capita (PPP)** (US$) 23,180 (1998) **Real GDP growth** (% change on previous year) –3 (1998) **Consumer price inflation** 1.1% (1998) **Resources** coal, iron, zinc, copper, natural gas, fish **Exports** motor vehicles, electronic goods and components, chemicals, iron and steel products, scientific and optical equipment. Principal market: USA 30.5% (1998) **Imports** mineral fuels, foodstuffs, live animals, bauxite, iron ore, copper ore, coking coal, chemicals, textiles, wood. Principal source: USA 23.9% (1998)

▪ Tourist information

Time difference GMT +9 **Currency** yen **Language** Japanese; also Ainu **Visa requirements** UK: visa not required. USA: visa not required for a stay of up to 90 days **Embassy in the UK** 101–104 Piccadilly, London W1V 9FN. Tel: (020) 7465 6500; fax: (020) 7491 9348 **British embassy** No. 1 Ichiban-cho, Chiyoda-ku, Tokyo 102. Tel: (3) 3265 5511; fax: (3) 5275 3164 **Chamber of commerce** 2nd Floor, Salisbury House, 29 Finsbury Circus, London EC2M 5QQ. Tel: (020) 7628 0069; fax: (020) 7628 0248. Nippon Shoko Kaigi-sho, 3-2-2, Marunouchi, Chiyoda-ku, Tokyo 10. Tel: (3) 3283 7851 **Office hours** 0900–1700 Mon–Fri **Banking hours** 0900–1500 Mon–Fri **Airports** international airports: Tokyo (Narita), Fukuoka, Kagoshima, Kansai, Nagoya, Osaka; one principal domestic services airport (Haneda), smaller airports cover connections between major towns and islands; total passenger km: 151,048 million (1997 est) **Major ports** Osaka, Nagoya, Yokohama, Kobe **Chief tourist attractions** ancient capital of Kyoto; Buddhist and Shinto temples; pagodas; forests and mountains; classical Kabuki theatre; traditional festivals **Major holidays** 1–3, 15 January, 11 February, 21 March, 29 April, 3, 5 May, 15, 23 September, 10 October, 3, 23 November

Chronology

660 BC According to legend, Jimmu Tenno, descendent of the Sun goddess, became the first emperor of Japan. **c. 400 AD** The Yamato, one of many warring clans, unified central Japan; Yamato chiefs are the likely ancestors of the imperial family. **5th–6th centuries AD** Writing, Confucianism, and Buddhism spread to Japan from China and Korea. **646** Start of Taika Reform: Emperor Kotoku organized central government on Chinese model. **794** Heian became imperial capital; later called Kyoto. **858** Imperial court fell under control of Fujiwara clan, who reduced the emperor to a figurehead. **11th century** Central government grew ineffectual; real power exercised by great landowners (daimyo) with private armies of samurai. **1185** Minamoto clan seized power under Yoritomo, who established military rule. **1192** Emperor gave Yoritomo the title of shogun (general); the shogun ruled in the name of the emperor. **1274** Mongol conqueror Kublai Khan attempted to invade Japan, making a second attempt in 1281; on both occasions Japan was saved by a typhoon. **1336** Warlord Takauji Ashikaga overthrew Minamoto shogunate; emperor recognized Ashikaga shogunate in 1338. **16th century** Power of Ashikagas declined; constant civil war. **1543** Portuguese sailors were the first Europeans to reach Japan; followed by Spanish, Dutch, and English traders. **1549** Spanish missionary St Francis Xavier began to preach Roman Catholic faith in Japan. **1585–98** Warlord Hideyoshi took power and attempted to conquer Korea in 1592 and 1597. **1603** Ieyasu Tokugawa founded new shogunate at Edo, reformed administration, and suppressed Christianity. **1630s** Japan adopted policy of isolation: all travel forbidden and all foreigners expelled except a small colony of Dutch traders in Nagasaki harbour. **1853** USA sent warships to Edo with demand that Japan open diplomatic and trade relations; Japan conceded in 1854. **1867** Revolt by isolationist nobles overthrew the Tokugawa shogunate. **1868** Emperor Mutsuhito assumed full powers, adopted the title *Meiji* ('enlightened rule'), moved imperial capital from Kyoto to Edo (renamed Tokyo), and launched policy of swift Westernization. **1894–95** Sino-Japanese War: Japan expelled Chinese from Korea. **1902–21** Japan entered a defensive alliance with Britain. **1904–05** Russo-Japanese War: Japan drove Russians from

Japan: Regions

Region	Chief city	Area sq km	Area sq mi	Population (1997 est)
Chubu	Nagoya	66,776	25,782	21,538,000
Chugoku	Hiroshima	31,908	12,320	7,768,000
Hokkaido	Sapporo	83,451	32,220	5,702,000
Kanto	Tokyo	32,418	12,517	39,839,000
Kinki	Osaka	33,094	12,778	22,554,000
Kyushu	Fukuoka	42,154	16,276	13,452,000
Okinawa	Naha	2,265	875	1,291,000
Shikoku	Matsuyama	18,798	7,258	4,177,000
Tohuku	Sendai	66,883	25,824	8,844,000

Manchuria and Korea; Korea annexed in 1910. **1914** Japan entered World War I and occupied German possessions in Far East. **1923** Earthquake destroyed much of Tokyo and Yokohama. **1931** Japan invaded Chinese province of Manchuria and created puppet state of Manchukuo; Japanese government came under control of military and extreme nationalists. **1937** Japan resumed invasion of China. **1940** After Germany defeated France, Japan occupied French Indo-China. **1941** Japan attacked US fleet at Pearl Harbor; USA and Britain declared war on Japan. **1942** Japanese conquered Thailand, Burma, Malaya, Dutch East Indies, Philippines, and northern New Guinea. **1945** USA dropped atomic bombs on Hiroshima and Nagasaki; Japan surrendered; US general Douglas MacArthur headed Allied occupation administration. **1947** MacArthur supervised introduction of democratic 'Peace Constitution', accompanied by demilitarization and land reform. **1952** Occupation ended. **1955** Liberal Democratic Party (LDP) founded with support of leading business people. **1956** Japan admitted to United Nations. **1950s–70s** Rapid economic development; growth of manufacturing exports led to great prosperity. **1993** An economic recession and financial scandals brought about the downfall of the LDP government in a general election. A coalition government was formed. **1995** An earthquake devastated Kobe. **1997** A financial crash occurred after bank failures. **1998** Keizo Obuchi, leader of the LDP, became prime minister, with Kiichi Miyazawa as finance minister. The government introduced a new $200 billion economic stimulus package, after GDP contracted 2% in 1998 in the worst recession since World War II. **2000** After Prime Minister Obuchi suffered a stroke, Yoshiro Mori was appointed in his place.

Jordan Hashemite Kingdom of

National name *Al Mamlaka al Urduniya al Hashemiyah* **Area** 89,206 sq km/34,442 sq mi (West Bank 5,879 sq km/2,269 sq mi) **Capital** Amman **Major towns/cities** Zarqa, Irbid, Saet, Ma'an

Government

Head of state King Abdullah ibn Hussein from 1999 **Head of government** Abdul-Raouf al-Rawabdeh from 1999 **Political system** emergent democracy **Armed forces** 104,100; plus paramilitary forces of approximately 30,000 (1997) **Conscription** selective **Defence spend** (% GDP) 6.4 (1997) **Education spend** (% GNP) 7.3 (1996) **Health spend** (% GDP) 3.7 (1990–95) **Death penalty** retained and used for ordinary crimes

Population and society

Population 6,483,000 (1999 est) **Population growth rate** 3% (1995–2000) **Ethnic groups** majority of Arab descent; small Circassian, Armenian, and Kurdish minorities **Religion** Sunni Muslim 80%, Christian 8% **Life expectancy** 69 (men); 72 (women) (1995–2000) **Literacy rate** 92% (men); 82% (women) (1997 est) **Unemployment** 20% (1997 est)

Economy and resources

GDP (US$) 7.02 billion (1998 est) **GNP** (US$) 6.9 billion (1998) **GNP per capita (PPP)** (US$) 3,230 (1998) **Real GDP growth** (% change on previous year) –1 (1998) **Consumer price inflation** 3.4% (1998) **Foreign debt** (US$) 8.2 billion (1997) **Resources** phosphates, potash, shale **Exports** phosphate, potash, fertilizers, foodstuffs, pharmaceuticals, fruit and vegetables, cement. Principal market: India 9.2% (1998) **Imports** food and live animals, basic manufactures, mineral fuels, machinery and transport equipment. Principal source: Germany 9.8% (1997)

▪ Tourist information

Time difference GMT +2 **Currency** Jordanian dinar **Language** Arabic (official), English **Visa requirements** UK: visa required. USA: visa required **Embassy in the UK** 6 Upper Phillimore Gardens, London W8 7HB. Tel: (020) 7937 3685; fax: (020) 7937 8795 **British embassy** PO Box 87, Abdoun, Amman. Tel: (6) 823 100; fax: (6) 813 759 **Chamber of commerce** Amman Chamber of Commerce, PO Box 287, Amman. Tel: (6) 666 151; telex: 21543 **Office hours** 0900–1700 Sat, Wed, and Thu **Banking hours** 0830–1230 and 1530–1730 Sat–Thu; generally 0830–1000 during Ramadan **Airports** international airports: Amman (charter flights only), Zizya (Queen Alia, 30 km south of Amman), Aqaba; internal flights operate between Amman and Aqaba; total passenger km: 4,900 million (1997 est) **Major ports** Aqaba **Chief tourist attractions** ancient cities of Petra and Jerash **Major holidays** 1 January, 1, 25 May, 10 June, 11 August, 14 November, 25 December; variable: Eid-ul-Adha (4 days), first day of Ramadan, end of Ramadan (4 days), New Year (Muslim), Prophet's Birthday

Chronology

13th century BC Oldest known 'states' of Jordan, including Gideon, Ammon, Moab, and Edom, established. **c. 1000 BC** East Jordan was part of kingdom of Israel, under David and Solomon. **4th century BC** Southeast Jordan occupied by the independent Arabic-speaking Nabataeans. **64 BC** Conquered by the Romans and became part of the province of Arabia. **AD 636** Became largely Muslim after the Byzantine forces of Emperor Heraclius were defeated by Arab armies at battle of Yarmuk, in northern Jordan. **1099–1187** Part of Latin Kingdom established by Crusaders in Jerusalem. **from early 16th century** Part of Turkish Ottoman Empire, administered from Damascus. **1920** Trans-Jordan (the area east of the River Jordan) and Palestine (which includes the West Bank) placed under British administration by League of Nations mandate. **1923** Trans-Jordan separated from Palestine and recognized by Britain as a substantially independent state under the rule of Emir Abdullah ibn Hussein, a member of the Hashemite dynasty of Arabia. **1946** Trans-Jordan achieved independence from Britain, with Abd Allah as king; name changed to Jordan. **1948** British mandate for Palestine expired, leading to fighting between Arabs and Jews, who each claimed the area. **1950** Jordan annexed West Bank; 400,000 Palestinian refugees flooded into Jordan, putting pressure on the economy. **1952** Partially democratic constitution introduced. **1958** Jordan and Iraq formed Arab Federation that ended when Iraqi monarchy was deposed. **1967** Israel defeated Egypt, Syria, and Jordan in Arab–Israeli Six-Day War, and captured and occupied the West Bank, including Arab Jerusalem. Martial law imposed. **1970–71** Jordanians moved against increasingly radicalized Palestine Liberation Organization (PLO), which had launched guerrilla raids on Israel from Jordanian territory, resulting in bloody civil war, before the PLO leadership fled abroad. **1976** Political parties were banned and elections postponed until further notice. **1980** Jordan emerged as an important ally of Iraq in its war against Iran, an ally of Syria, with whom Jordan's relations were tense. **1984** Women voted for the first time; the parliament was recalled. **1985** King Hussein ibn Tal Abdulla el Hashim and PLO leader Yassir Arafat put forward a framework for a Middle East peace settlement. There was a secret meeting between Hussein and the Israeli prime minister. **1988** Hussein announced his willingness to cease administering the West Bank as part of Jordan, passing responsibility to the PLO; parliament was suspended. **1989** There were riots over price increases of up to 50% following a fall in oil revenues. In the first parliamentary elections for 23 years the Muslim Brotherhood won 25 of 80 seats but were exiled from government. **1990** Hussein unsuccessfully tried to mediate after Iraq's invasion of Kuwait. There were huge refugee problems as thousands fled to Jordan from Kuwait and Iraq. **1991** 24 years of martial law ended, the ban on political parties was lifted, and Jordan remained neutral during the Gulf War involving Iraq. **1993** Candidates loyal to Hussein won a majority in the parliamentary elections; several leading Islamic fundamentalists lost their seats. **1994** An economic cooperation pact was signed with the PLO. A peace treaty was signed with Israel, ending the 46-year-old state of war. **1999** King Hussein died and his eldest son, Abdullah, succeeded him. Abdul-Raouf al-Rawabdeh was appointed prime minister. In May, Abdullah held talks with Yassir Arafat prior to Israeli peace negotiations.

Kazakhstan Republic of

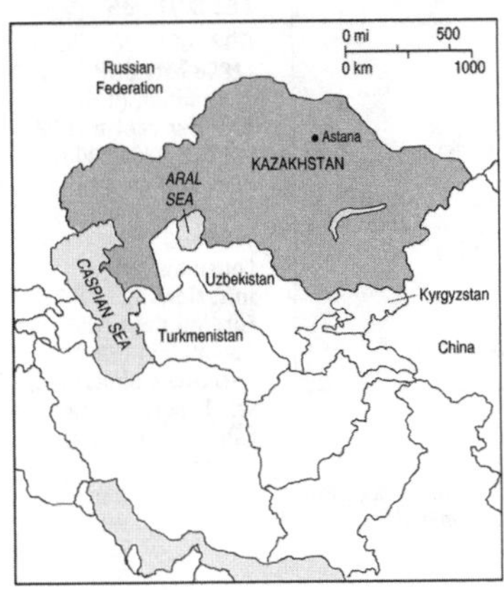

National name *Kazak Respublikasy* **Area** 2,717,300 sq km/ 1,049,150 sq mi **Capital** Astana (formerly called Akmola) **Major towns/ cities** Karaganda, Pavlodar, Semipalatinsk, Petropavlovsk, Chimkent

Government

Head of state Nursultan Nazarbayev from 1990 **Head of government** Nurlan Balgimbayev from 1997 **Political system** authoritarian nationalist **Armed forces** 35,100 (1997) **Defence spend** (% GDP) 2.3 (1997) **Education spend** (% GNP) 6.0 (1996) **Health spend** (% GDP) 2.5 (1996) **Death penalty** retained and used for ordinary crimes

Population and society

Population 16,269,000 (1999 est) **Population growth rate** –0.4% (1995–2000) **Ethnic groups** 40% of Kazakh descent, 38% ethnic Russian, 6% German, 5% Ukrainian, 2% Uzbek, and 2% Tatar **Religion** Sunni Muslim **Life expectancy** 63 (men); 73 (women) (1995–2000) **Literacy rate** 99% (men); 99% (women) (1997 est) **Unemployment** 8% (1998)

Economy and resources

GDP (US$) 21.03 billion (1998) **GNP** (US$) 20.6 billion (1998) **GNP per capita (PPP)** (US$) 3,400 (1998) **Real GDP growth** (% change on previous year) –2.5 (1998) **Consumer price inflation** 7.3% (1998) **Foreign debt** (US$) 4.27 billion (1997) **Resources** petroleum, natural gas, coal, bauxite, chromium, copper, iron ore, lead, titanium, magnesium, tungsten, molybdenum, gold, silver, manganese **Exports** ferrous and non-ferrous metals, mineral products (including petroleum and petroleum products), chemicals. Principal market: China 29.1% (1998) **Imports** energy products and electricity, machinery and transport equipment, chemicals. Principal source: Russia 39.4% (1998)

▪ Tourist information

Time difference GMT +6 **Currency** tenge **Language** Kazakh (official), related to Turkish; Russian **Visa requirements** UK: visa required. USA: visa required **Embassy in the UK** 3 Warren Mews, London W1P 5DJ. Tel/fax: (020) 7387 1047 **British embassy** 173 Furmanova Street, Almaty. Tel: (3272) 506 191; fax: (3272) 506 260 **Chamber of commerce** Chamber of Commerce and Industry of Kazakhstan, pr. Ablaikhana 93/95, 480091 Almaty. Tel: (3272) 621 446; fax: (3272) 620 594 **Office hours** 0900–1200/1300 and 1300/1400–1800 Mon–Fri **Banking hours** 0930–1300 and 1400–1730 Mon–Fri **Airports** international airports: Almaty, Aktau, Atyrau; 18 domestic airports; total passenger km: 2,429 million (1995) **Major holidays** 1, 28 January, 8, 22 March, 1, 9 May, 25 October, 31 December

Chronology

early Christian era Settled by Mongol and Turkic tribes. **8th century** Spread of Islam. **10th century** Southward migration into east Kazakhstan of Kazakh tribes, displaced from Mongolia by the Mongols. **13th–14th centuries** Part of Mongol Empire. **late 15th century** Kazakhs emerged as distinct ethnic group from Kazakh Orda tribal confederation. **early 17th century** The nomadic, cattle-breeding Kazakhs split into smaller groups, united in the three Large, Middle, and Lesser Hordes (federations), led by khans (chiefs). **1731–42** Faced by attacks from the east by Oirot Mongols, protection was sought from the Russian tsars, and Russian control was gradually established. **1822–48** Conquest by tsarist Russia completed; khans deposed. Large-scale Russian and Ukrainian peasant settlement of the steppes after the abolition of serfdom in Russia in 1861. **1887** Alma-Alta (now Almaty), established in 1854 as a fortified trading centre and captured by the Russians in 1865, destroyed by an earthquake. **1916** 150,000 killed as anti-Russian rebellion brutally repressed. **1917** Bolshevik coup in Russia followed by outbreak of civil war in Kazakhstan. **1920** Autonomous republic in USSR. **early 1930s** More than 1 million died of starvation during the campaign to collectivize agriculture. **1936** Joined USSR and became a full union republic. **early 1940s** Volga Germans deported to the republic by Soviet dictator Joseph Stalin. **1954–56** Part of Soviet leader Nikita Khrushchev's ambitious 'Virgin Lands' agricultural extension programme; large influx of Russian settlers made Kazakhs a minority in their own republic. **1986** There were nationalist riots in Alma-Alta (now Almaty) after the reformist Soviet leader Mikhail Gorbachev ousted the local communist leader and installed an ethnic Russian. **1989** Nursultan Nazarbayev, a reformist and mild nationalist, became leader of the Kazakh Communist Party (KCP) and instituted economic and cultural reform programmes, encouraging foreign inward investment. **1990** Nazarbayev became head of state; economic sovereignty was declared. **1991** Nazarbayev condemned the attempted anti-Gorbachev coup in Moscow; the KCP was abolished. The country joined the new Commonwealth of Independent States (CIS); and independence was recognized by the USA. **1992** Kazakhstan was admitted into the United Nations (UN) and the Conference on Security and Cooperation in Europe (CSCE; now the Organization on Security and Cooperation in Europe, OSCE). **1993** Presidential power was increased by a new constitution. A privatization programme was launched. START-1 (disarmament treaty) and Nuclear Non-Proliferation Treaty were both ratified by Kazakhstan. **1994** There was economic, social, and military union with Kyrgyzstan and Uzbekistan. **1995** An economic and military cooperation pact was signed with Russia. Kazakhstan achieved nuclear-free status. **1997** Nurlan Balgimbayev was appointed prime minister. Astana (formerly known as Akmola) was designated as the new capital. **1998** A treaty of 'eternal friendship' and a treaty of deepening economic cooperation was signed with Uzbekistan.

Kenya Republic of

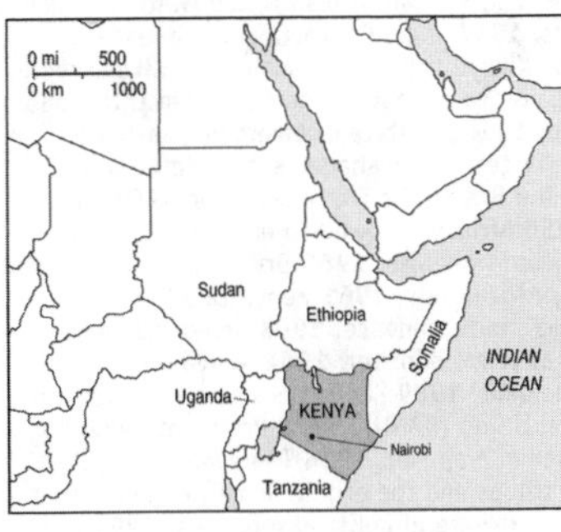

National name *Jamhuri ya Kenya* **Area** 582,600 sq km/224,941 sq mi **Capital** Nairobi **Major towns/cities** Mombasa, Kisumu, Nakuru, Eldoret, Nyeri

Government

Head of state and government Daniel arap Moi from 1978 **Political system** authoritarian nationalist **Armed forces** 24,200; paramilitary force 5,000 (1997) **Conscription** military service is voluntary **Defence spend** (% GDP) 2.4 (1997) **Education spend** (% GNP) 6.6 (1996) **Health spend** (% GDP) 1.9 (1990–95) **Death penalty** retained and used for ordinary crimes

Population and society

Population 29,549,000 (1999 est) **Population growth rate** 2% (1995–2000) **Ethnic groups** main ethnic groups are the Kikuyu (about 21%), the Luhya (14%), the Luo (13%), the Kalenjin (11%), the Kamba (11%), the Kisii (6%), and the Meru (5%); there are also Asian, Arab, and European minorities **Religion** Roman Catholic, Protestant, Muslim, traditional tribal religions **Life expectancy** 51 (men); 53 (women) (1995–2000) **Literacy rate** 87% (men); 72% (women) (1997 est) **Unemployment** 30% (urban, 1995 est)

Economy and resources

GDP (US$) 11.1 billion (1998) **GNP** (US$) 9.7 billion (1998) **GNP per capita (PPP)** (US$) 1,130 (1998) **Real GDP growth** (% change on previous year) 1 (1998) **Consumer price inflation** 11.5% (1998) **Foreign debt** (US$) 6.5 billion (1997) **Resources** soda ash, fluorspar, salt, limestone, rubies, gold, vermiculite, diatonite, garnets **Exports** coffee, tea, petroleum products, soda ash, horticultural products. Principal market: Uganda 16.1% (1998) **Imports** crude petroleum, motor vehicles, industrial machinery, iron and steel, chemicals, basic manufactures. Principal source: UK 12.3% (1997)

▪ Tourist information

Time difference GMT +3 **Currency** Kenya shilling **Language** Kiswahili (official), English; there are many local dialects **Visa requirements** UK: visa not required. USA: visa required **Embassy in the UK** 45 Portland Place, London W1N 4AS. Tel: (020) 7636 2371/5; fax: (020) 7323 6717

British embassy British High Commission, PO Box 30465, Bruce House, Standard Street, Nairobi. Tel: (2) 335 944; fax: (2) 333 196 **Chamber of commerce** Kenya National Chamber of Commerce and Industry, PO Box 47024, Ufanisi House, Hailé Sélassie Avenue, Nairobi. Tel: (2) 334 413 **Office hours** 0800–1300 and 1400–1700 Mon–Fri; in Mombasa offices usually open and close a half hour earlier **Banking hours** 0900–1500 Mon–Fri; 0900–1100 on the first and last Sat of every month **Airports** international airports: Mombasa (Moi), Nairobi (Jomo Kenyatta), Eldoret (opening date of 1997 delayed); three domestic airports; total passenger km: 1,802 million (1997 est) **Major ports** Mombasa **Chief tourist attractions** wildlife – 25 national parks and 23 game reserves, notably the Rift Valley, containing Aberdare National Park, overlooked by Mount Kenya, which also has a national park; Indian Ocean coast **Major holidays** 1 January, 1 May, 1 June, 10, 20 October, 12, 25–26 December; variable: Good Friday, Easter Monday, end of Ramadan

Chronology

8th century Arab traders began to settle along coast of East Africa. **16th century** Portuguese defeated coastal states and exerted spasmodic control over them. **18th century** Sultan of Oman reasserted Arab overlordship of East African coast, making it subordinate to Zanzibar. **19th century** Europeans, closely followed by Christian missionaries, began to explore inland. **1887** British East African Company leased area of coastal territory from sultan of Zanzibar. **1895** Britain claimed large inland region as East African Protectorate. **1903** Railway from Mombasa to Uganda built using Indian labourers, many of whom settled in the area; British and South African settlers began to farm highlands. **1920** East African Protectorate became crown colony of Kenya, with legislative council elected by white settlers (and by Indians and Arabs soon afterwards). **1923** Britain rejected demand for internal self-government by white settlers. **1944** First African appointment to legislative council; Kenyan African Union (KAU) founded to campaign for African rights. **1947** Jomo Kenyatta became leader of KAU, which was dominated by Kikuyu tribe. **1952** Mau Mau (Kikuyu secret society) began terrorist campaign to drive white settlers from tribal lands; Mau Mau largely suppressed by 1954 but state of emergency lasted for eight years. **1953** Kenyatta charged with management of Mau Mau activities and imprisoned by the British. He was released in 1959, but exiled to northern Kenya. **1956** Africans allowed to elect members of legislative council on a restricted franchise. **1960** Britain announced plans to prepare Kenya for majority African rule. **1961** Kenyatta allowed to return to help negotiate Kenya's independence. **1963** Kenya achieved independence with Kenyatta as prime minister. **1964** Kenya became a republic with Kenyatta as president. **1969** Kenya became one-party state under Kenyan African National Union (KANU). **1978** President Kenyatta died and was succeeded by Daniel arap Moi. **1984** There were violent clashes between government troops and the ethnic Somali population at Wajir. **1989** Moi announced the release of political prisoners. **1991** A multiparty system was conceded after an opposition group was launched. **1997** There were demonstrations calling for democratic reform. Constitutional reforms were adopted. **1998** A bomb exploded at the US embassy in Nairobi, killing over 230 people and injuring 5,000; an anti-American Islamic group claimed responsibility. **1999** A framework agreement was signed with the leaders of Uganda and Tanzania, intending to reestablish the East African Community (EAC) which had collapsed in 1977, hoping to lead to a Common market and political federation similar to that of the European Union (EU).

Kiribati Republic of (formerly part of the Gilbert and Ellice Islands)

National name *Ribaberikin Kiribati* **Area** 717 sq km/277 sq mi **Capital** Bairiki (on Tarawa Atoll) (and port) **Towns** principal atolls: North Tarawa, Gilbert group, Abaiang, Tabiteuea

Government

Head of state and government Teburoro Tito from 1994 **Political system** liberal democracy **Armed forces** no standing army **Education spend** (% GNP) 11.4 (1996) **Death penalty** abolished in 1979

Population and society

Population 77,000 (1999 est) **Population growth rate** 1.4% (1995–2000) **Ethnic groups** predominantly Micronesian, with a Polynesian minority; also European and Chinese minorities **Religion** Roman Catholic, Protestant (Congregationalist) **Life expectancy** 61 (men); 65 (women) (1998 est) **Literacy rate** 90% (men); 90%(women) (1993 est) **Unemployment** 2.2% (1992 est)

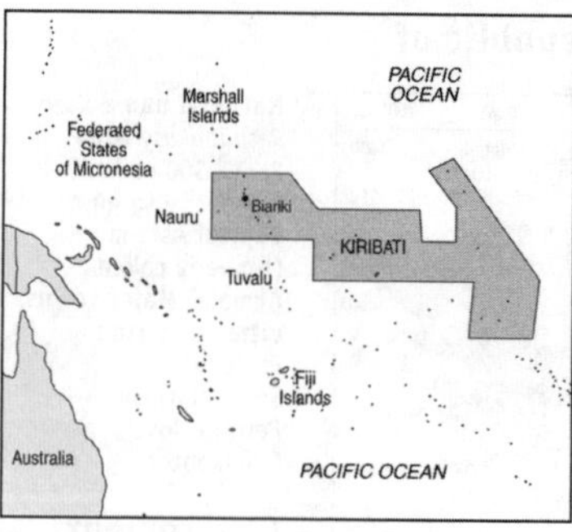

Economy and resources

GDP (US$) 76 million (1998 est) **GNP** (US$) 101 million (1998) **GNP per capita (PPP)** (US$) 3,480 (1998) **Real GDP growth** (% change on previous year) 1.5 (1998) **Consumer price inflation** 2% (1998) **Foreign debt** (US$) 11 million (1997) **Resources** phosphate, salt **Exports** copra, fish, seaweed, bananas, breadfruit, taro. Principal market: USA (1996) **Imports** foodstuffs, machinery and transport equipment, mineral fuels, basic manufactures. Principal source: Australia 46% (1996)

▪ Tourist information

Time difference GMT –10/11 **Currency** Australian dollar **Language** English (official), Gilbertese **Visa requirements** UK: visa not required for a stay of up to 28 days. USA: visa required **Embassy in the UK** Consulate of Kiribati, Faith House, 7 Tufton Street, London SW1P 3QN. Tel: (020) 7222 6952; fax: (020) 7976 7180 **British embassy** the British High Commission in Suva (see Fiji Islands) deals with enquiries relating to Kiribati **Chamber of commerce** none **Office hours** 0800–1230 and 1330–1615 Mon–Fri **Banking hours** 0930–1500 Mon–Fri **Airports** international airports: South Tarawa (Bonikri), Kiritimati Island (Cassidy), Butaritari Island (Antekana), Kanton Island, Tabuaeran Island; 15 domestic airports; total passenger km: 10 million (1995) **Major ports** Betio (on Tarawa) **Chief tourist attractions** remoteness; game-fishing; ecotourism, particularly birdwatching **Major holidays** 1 January, 12 June (3 days), 25–26 December; variable: Good Friday, Easter Monday, Holy Saturday, Youth (August)

Chronology

1st millennium BC Settled by Austronesian-speaking peoples. **1606** Visited by Spanish explorers. **late 18th century** Visited by British naval officers. **1857** Christian mission established. **1892** Gilbert (Kiribati) and Ellice (Tuvalu) Islands proclaimed a British protectorate. **1916–39** Uninhabited Phoenix Islands, Christmas Island, Ocean Island, and Line Island (Banaba) added to colony. **1942–43** While occupied by Japanese it was the scene of fierce fighting with US troops. **late 1950s** UK tested nuclear weapons on Christmas Island (Kiritimati). **1963** Legislative council established. **1974** Legislative council replaced by an elected House of Assembly. **1975** The mainly Melanesian-populated Ellice Islands separated to become Tuvalu. **1977** The predominantly Micronesian-populated Gilbert Islands were granted internal self-government. **1979** Independence was achieved within the Commonwealth, as the Republic of Kiribati, with Ieremia Tabai as president. **1985** Kiribati's first political party, the opposition Christian Democrats, was formed. **1994** The government resigned after losing a vote of confidence. Teburoro Tito of the MTM was elected president.

Korea, North People's Democratic Republic of

National name *Chosun Minchu-chui Inmin Konghwa-guk* **Area** 120,538 sq km/46,539 sq mi **Capital** Pyongyang **Major towns/cities** Hamhung, Chongjin, Nampo, Wonsan, Sinuiji

Government

Head of state Kim Jong Il from 1994 **Head of government** Hong Song Nam from 1997 **Political system** communist **Armed forces** 1,055,000 (1997) **Conscription** selective for 3–10 years **Defence spend** (% GDP) 27% (1997) **Death penalty** retained and used for ordinary crimes

Population and society

Population 23,702,000 (1999 est) **Population growth rate** 1.6% (1995–2000); 1.3% (2000–05) **Ethnic groups** entirely Korean, with the exception of a 50,000 Chinese minority **Religion** Chondoist, Buddhist, Christian, traditional beliefs **Life expectancy** 69 (men); 75 (women) (1995–2000) **Literacy rate** 99% (men); 99%(women) (1997 est)

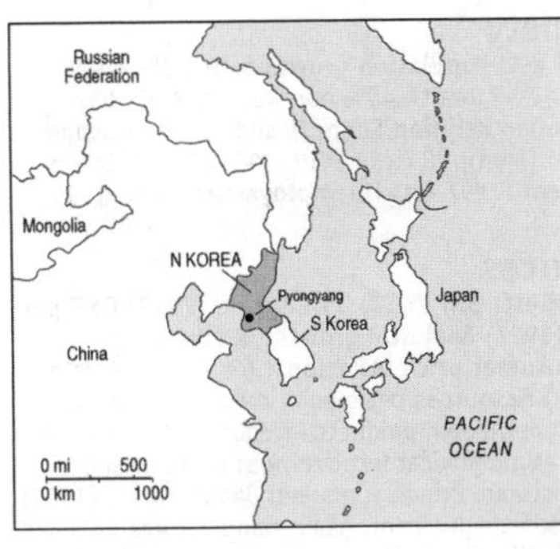

Economy and resources

GDP (US$) 21.8 billion (1997 est) **GNP** (US$) 17.7 billion (1997 est) **GNP per capita (PPP)** (US$) 845 (1997 est) **Real GDP growth** (% change on previous year) –6.8 (1997) **Consumer price inflation** N/A **Foreign debt** (US$) 7.5 billion (1997) **Resources** coal, iron, lead, copper, zinc, tin, silver, gold, magnesite (has 40–50% of world's deposits of magnesite) **Exports** base metals, textiles, vegetable products, machinery and equipment. Principal market: Japan 27.9% (1995 est) **Imports** petroleum and petroleum products, machinery and equipment, grain, coal, foodstuffs. Principal source: China 32.6% (1995 est)

▪ Tourist information

Time difference GMT +9 **Currency** won **Language** Korean **Visa requirements** UK: visa required. USA: visa required **Embassy for the UK** General Delegation of the DPRK, 104 boulevard Bineau, 92200 Neuilly-sur-Seine, France. Tel: (1) 4745 1797; fax: (1) 4738 1250 **British embassy** the UK has no diplomatic representation in North Korea **Chamber of commerce** DPRK Committee for the Promotion of External Economic Cooperation, Jungsongdong, Central District, Pyongyang. Tel: (2) 33974; fax: (2) 814 498 **Airports** international airport: Pyongyang (Sunan); two domestic airports (which foreigners are not allowed to use); total passenger km: 207 million (1995) **Chief tourist attractions** tourism is permitted only in officially accompanied parties **Major holidays** 1 January, 16 February, 8 March, 15 April, 9 September, 10 October, 27 December

Chronology

2333 BC Legendary founding of Korean state by Tangun dynasty. **1122 BC–4th century AD** Period of Chinese Kija dynasty. **668–1000** Peninsula unified by Buddhist Shilla kingdom, with capital at Kyongju. **1392–1910** Period of Chosun, or Yi, dynasty, during which Korea became a vassal of China and Confucianism became the dominant intellectual force. **1910** Korea formally annexed by Japan. **1920s and 1930s** Heavy industries developed in the coal-rich north, with Koreans forcibly conscripted as low-paid labourers; suppression of Korean culture led to the development of a resistance movement. **1945** Russian and US troops entered Korea at the end of World War II, forced surrender of Japanese, and divided the country in two at the 38th parallel. Soviet troops occupied North Korea. **1946** Soviet-backed provisional government installed, dominated by Moscow-trained Korean communists, including Kim Il Sung; radical programme of land reform and nationalization launched. **1948** Democratic People's Republic of Korea declared after pro-USA Republic of Korea founded in the south; Soviet troops withdrew. **1950** North Korea invaded South Korea to unite the nation, beginning the Korean War. **1953** Armistice agreed to end the Korean War, which had involved US participation on the side of South Korea, and Chinese on that of North Korea. The war ended in stalemate, at a cost of 2 million lives. **1961** Friendship and mutual assistance treaty signed with China. **1972** A new constitution, with an executive president, was adopted. Talks were held with South Korea about possible reunification. **1983** Four South Korean cabinet ministers were assassinated in Rangoon, Burma (Myanmar), by North Korean army officers. **1985** Relations improved with the Soviet Union. **1990** Diplomatic contacts with South Korea and Japan suggested a thaw in North Korea's relations with the rest of the world. **1991** North Korea became a member of the United Nations (UN). A nonaggression agreement with South Korea was signed. **1992** The Nuclear Safeguards Agreement was signed, allowing international inspection of nuclear facilities. A pact was also signed with South Korea for mutual inspection of nuclear facilities. **1994** Kim Il Sung died and was succeeded by his son, Kim Jong Il. An agreement was made to halt the nuclear-development programme in return for US aid, resulting in the easing of a 44-year-old US trade embargo. **1996** US aid was sought in the face of a severe famine caused by floods; rice was imported from South Korea and food aid provided by the UN. **1997** Kang Song San was replaced as prime minister by Hong Song Nam. Grave food shortages were revealed. **1998** A UN food-aid operation was instituted in an effort to avert widespread famine. A ballistic missile test was fired over Japan. Deceased former leader Kim Il Sung was declared 'president for perpetuity'. Relations with the USA deteriorated when the USA demanded access to an underground site in Kumchangri suspected of being part of a nuclear-weapons program. **1999** Japan lifted sanctions against North Korea.

Korea, South (Republic of Korea)

National name *Daehan Min-kuk* **Area** 98,799 sq km/38,146 sq mi **Capital** Seoul **Major towns/cities** Pusan, Taegu, Inchon, Kwangju, Taejon

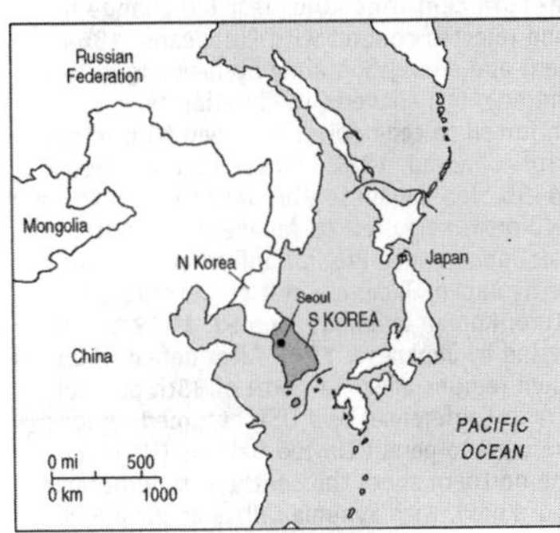

Government

Head of state Kim Dae Jung from 1998 **Head of government** Kim Jong Pil from 1998 **Political system** liberal democracy **Armed forces** 672,000 (1997) **Conscription** 26 months (army); 30 months (navy and air force) **Defence spend** (% GDP) 3.3 (1997) **Education spend** (% GNP) 3.7 (1996) **Health spend** (% GDP) 2.1 (1996) **Death penalty** retained and used for ordinary crimes

Population and society

Population 46,479,000 (1999 est) **Population growth rate** 0.8% (1995–2000) **Ethnic groups** with the exception of a small Nationalist Chinese minority, the population is almost entirely of Korean descent **Religion** Shamanist, Buddhist, Confucian, Protestant, Roman Catholic **Life expectancy** 69 (men); 76 (women) (1995–2000) **Literacy rate** 99% (men); 96% (women) (1997 est) **Unemployment** 6.8% (1998)

Economy and resources

GDP (US$) 297.9 billion (1998) **GNP** (US$) 369.9 billion (1998) **GNP per capita (PPP)** (US$) 12,270 (1998) **Real GDP growth** (% change on previous year) –7.6 (1998) **Consumer price inflation** 1.3% (1999) **Foreign debt** (US$) 143.3 billion (1997) **Resources** coal, iron ore, tungsten, gold, molybdenum, graphite, fluorite, natural gas, hydroelectric power, fish **Exports** electrical machinery, textiles, clothing, footwear, telecommunications and sound equipment, chemical products, ships ('invisible export' – overseas construction work). Principal market: USA 17.2% (1998) **Imports** machinery and transport equipment (especially electrical machinery), petroleum and petroleum products, grain and foodstuffs, steel, chemical products, basic manufactures. Principal source: USA 21.9% (1998)

▪ Tourist information

Time difference GMT +9 **Currency** won **Language** Korean **Visa requirements** UK: visa not required for a stay of up to 90 days. USA: visa not required **Embassy in the UK** 4 Palace Gate, London W8 5NF. Tel: (020) 7581 0247; fax: (020) 7581 8076 **British embassy** 4 Chung-dong, Chung-ku, Seoul 100. Tel: (2) 735 7341/3; fax: (2) 733 8368 **Chamber of commerce** Korean Chamber of Commerce and Industry, PO Box 25, 45 4-ka, Namdaemun-no, Chung-ku, Seoul 100.Tel: (2) 316 3114; fax: (2) 757 9475 **Office hours** 0830–1800 Mon–Fri; 0900–1300 Sat **Banking hours** 0930–1630 Mon–Fri; 0930–1330 Sat **Airports** international airports: Seoul (Kimpo), Pusan (Kim Hae), Cheju; three principal domestic airports; total passenger km: 61,011 million (1997 est) **Major ports** Pusan, Inchon **Chief tourist attractions** historic sites; mountain scenery; Cheju Island is a popular resort **Major holidays** 1–3 January, 1, 10 March, 5 May, 6 June, 17 July, 15 August, 1, 3, 9 October, 25 December; variable: New Year (Chinese, January/February), Lord Buddha's Birthday (May), Moon Festival (September/October)

Chronology

2333 BC Traditional date of founding of Korean state by Tangun (mythical son from union of bear-woman and god). **1122 BC** Ancient texts record founding of kingdom in Korea by Chinese nobleman Kija. **194 BC** Northwest

Korea united under warlord, Wiman. **108 BC** Korea conquered by Chinese. **1st–7th centuries AD** Three Korean kingdoms – Koguryo, Paekche, and Silla – competed for supremacy. **668** Korean peninsula unified by Buddhist Silla kingdom; culture combining Chinese and Korean elements flourished. **935** Silla dynasty overthrown by Wang Kon of Koguryo, who founded Koryo dynasty in its place. **1258** Korea accepted overlordship of Mongol Yüan Empire. **1392** Yi dynasty founded by Gen Yi Song-gye, vassal of Chinese Ming Empire; Confucianism replaced Buddhism as official creed; extreme conservatism characterized Korean society. **1592 and 1597** Japanese invasions repulsed by Korea. **1636** Manchu invasion forced Korea to sever ties with Ming dynasty. **18th–19th centuries** Korea resisted change in political and economic life and rejected contact with Europeans. **1864** Attempts to reform government and strengthen army by Taewongun (who ruled in name of his son, King Kojong); converts to Christianity persecuted. **1873** Taewongun forced to cede power to Queen Min; reforms reversed; government authority collapsed. **1882** Chinese occupied Seoul and installed governor. **1894–95** Sino-Japanese War: Japan forced China to recognize independence of Korea; Korea fell to Japanese influence. **1904–05** Russo-Japanese War: Japan ended Russian influence in Korea. **1910** Korea formally annexed by Japan; Japanese settlers introduced modern industry and agriculture; Korean language banned. **1919** 'Samil' nationalist movement suppressed by Japanese. **1945** After defeat of Japan in World War II, Russia occupied regions of Korea north of 38th parallel (demarcation line agreed at Yalta Conference) and USA occupied regions south of it. **1948** The USSR refused to permit United Nations (UN) supervision of elections in the northern zone; the southern zone became independent as the Republic of Korea, with Syngman Rhee as president. **1950** North Korea invaded South Korea; UN forces (mainly from the USA) intervened to defend South Korea; China intervened in support of North Korea. **1953** The Korean War ended with an armistice which restored the 38th parallel; no peace treaty was agreed and US troops remained in South Korea. **1961** Military coup placed Gen Park Chung Hee in power; a major programme of industrial development began. **1972** Martial law was imposed and presidential powers increased. **1979** The government of President Choi Kyu-Hah introduced liberalizing reforms. **1979** Gen Chun Doo Hwan assumed power after anti-government riots; Korea emerged as a leading shipbuilding nation and exporter of electronic goods. **1987** The constitution was made more democratic as a result of Liberal pressure; ruling Democratic Justice Party (DJP) candidate Roh Tae Woo Was elected president amid allegations of fraud. **1988** The Olympic Games were held in Seoul. **1991** Large-scale antigovernment protests were forcibly suppressed; South Korea joined the UN. **1992** South Korea established diplomatic relations with China. **1994** The US military presence was stepped up in response to the perceived threat from North Korea. **1997** South Korea was admitted to the OECD. Kim Dae Jung, former dissident and political prisoner, became the first opposition politician to lead South Korea. **1998** Kim Dae Jung was sworn in as president, with Kim Jong Pil as prime minister. New labour laws ended lifetime employment and the financial system was opened up. More than 2,000 prisoners were released, including 74 political prisoners. There was continuing labour unrest as GDP contracted by 5%. **1999** Talks on possible reunification with North Korea were suspended.

Kuwait State of

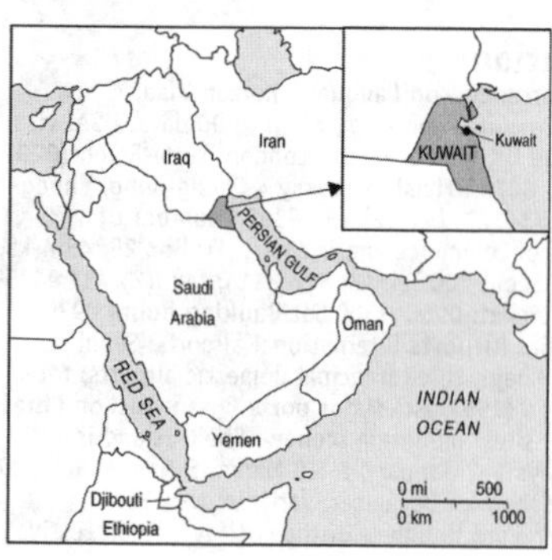

National name *Dowlat al Kuwait* **Area** 17,819 sq km/6,879 sq mi **Capital** Kuwait (also chief port) **Major towns/cities** as-Salimiya, Hawalli, Faranawiya, Abraq Kheetan, Jahra, Ahmadi, Fahaheel

Government

Head of state Sheikh Jabir al-Ahmad al-Jabir al-Sabah from 1977 **Head of government** Crown Prince Sheikh Saad al-Abdullah al-Salinas al-Sabah from 1978 **Political system** absolutist **Armed forces** 15,300 (1997) **Conscription** compulsory for two years **Defence spend** (% GDP) 11.4 (1997) **Education spend** (% GNP) 5.7 (1996) **Health spend** (% GDP) 3.6 (1990–95) **Death penalty** retained and used for ordinary crimes

Population and society

Population 1,897,000 (1999 est) **Population growth rate** 3.1% (1995–2000) **Ethnic groups** about 42% Kuwaiti, 40% non-Kuwaiti Arab, 5% Indian and Pakistani, 4% Iranian **Religion** Sunni Muslim, Shiite Muslim, Christian **Life expectancy** 74 (men); 78 (women) (1995–2000) **Literacy rate** 83% (men); 78% (women) (1997 est) **Unemployment** 1.8% (1996)

Economy and resources

GDP (US$) 30.4 billion (1998 est) **GNP** (US$) 35.1 billion (1997) **GNP per capita (PPP)** (US$) 24,270 (1997) **Real GDP growth** (% change on previous year) –2 (1998) **Consumer price inflation** 4.0% (1998) **Foreign debt** (US$) 9.4 billion (1997) **Resources** petroleum, natural gas, mineral water **Exports** petroleum and petroleum products (accounted for more than 93% of export revenue in 1994), chemical fertilizer, gas (natural and manufactured), basic manufactures. Principal market: Japan 24.1% (1997) **Imports** machinery and transport equipment, basic manufactures (especially iron, steel, and textiles) and other manufactured goods, live animals and food. Principal source: USA 22.2% (1997)

■ Tourist information

Time difference GMT +3 **Currency** Kuwaiti dinar **Language** Arabic (official) 78%, Kurdish 10%, Farsi 4%, English **Visa requirements** UK: visa required. USA: visa required **Embassy in the UK** 45–46 Queen's Gate, London SW7 5HR. Tel: (020) 7589 4533; fax: (020) 7589 7183 **British embassy** PO Box 2, Arabian Gulf Street, 13001 Safat, Kuwait City. Tel: (965) 240 3324/5/6; fax: (965) 240 7395 **Chamber of commerce** Kuwait Chamber of Commerce and Industry, PO Box 775, Chamber's Building, Ali as-Salem Street, 13008 Safat, Kuwait City. Tel: (965) 243 3864; fax: (965) 240 4110 **Office hours** 0700–1400 Sat–Wed (winter); 0730–1400 Sat–Wed (summer) **Banking hours** 0800–1200 Sun–Thu **Airports** international airports: Kuwait City; total passenger km: 5,997 million (1997 est) **Major holidays** 1 January, 25 February (3 days); variable: Eid-ul-Adha (3 days), end of Ramadan (3 days), New Year (Muslim), Prophet's Birthday, Ascension of the Prophet (March/April), Standing on Mount Arafat (August)

Chronology

***c.* 3000 BC** Archaeological evidence suggests that coastal parts of Kuwait may have been part of a commercial civilization contemporary with the Sumerian, based in Mesopotamia (the Tigris and Euphrates valley area of Iraq). ***c.* 323 BC** Visited by Greek colonists at the time of Alexander the Great. **7th century AD** Islam introduced. **late 16th century** Fell under nominal control of Turkish Ottoman Empire. **1710** Control was assumed by the Utab, a member of the Anaza tribal confederation in northern Arabia, and Kuwait city was founded, soon developing from a fishing village into an important port. **1756** Autonomous Sheikhdom of Kuwait founded by Abd Rahman of the al-Sabah family, a branch of the Utab. **1776** British East India Company set up a base in the Gulf. **1899** Concerned at the potential threat of growing Ottoman and German influence, Britain signed a treaty with Kuwait, establishing a self-governing protectorate in which the Emir received an annual subsidy from Britain in return for agreeing not to alienate any territory to a foreign power. **1914** Britain recognized Kuwait as an 'independent government under British protection'. **1922–33** Agreement on frontiers with Iraq, to the north, and Nejd (later Saudi Arabia) to the southwest. **1938** Oil discovered; large-scale exploitation after World War II transformed the economy. **1961** Full independence achieved from Britain, with Sheikh Abdullah al-Salem al-Sabah as emir. Attempted Iraqi invasion discouraged by dispatch of British troops to the Gulf. **1962** Constitution introduced, with franchise restricted to 10% of the population. **1977** Crown Prince Jabir al-Ahmad al-Jabir al-Sabah became emir. The National Assembly was dissolved. **1978** Sheikh Saad al-Abdullah al-Salem al-Sabah was appointed prime minister by the emir. **1981** The National Assembly was reconstituted. **1983** Shiite guerrillas bombed targets in Kuwait; 17 were arrested. **1986** The National Assembly was dissolved. **1987** Kuwaiti oil tankers were reflagged and received US Navy protection; there were missile attacks by Iran. **1988** Aircraft hijacked by pro-Iranian Shiites demanding the release of convicted guerrillas; Kuwait refused. **1989** Two of the convicted guerrillas were released. **1990** Prodemocracy demonstrations were suppressed. Kuwait was annexed by Iraq in August, causing extensive damage to property and environment. The emir set up a government in exile in Saudi Arabia. **1991** US-led coalition forces defeated Iraqi forces in Kuwait in the Gulf War. The new government omitted any opposition representatives. **1992** The reconstituted national assembly was elected, with opposition nominees, including Islamic candidates, winning the majority of seats. **1993** Incursions by Iraq into Kuwait were repelled by US-led air strikes on Iraqi military sites. **1994** The massing of Iraqi troops on the Kuwaiti border prompted a US-led response. Iraqi president Saddam Hussein publicly renounced any claim to Kuwait. **1999** A decree to secure a political voice for women in Kuwait was defeated in parliament, in the belief that female participation in politics would violate the principles of Islam and Kuwaiti traditions.

Kyrgyzstan Republic of

National name *Kyrgyz Respublikasy* **Area** 198,500 sq km/76,640 sq mi **Capital** Bishkek (formerly Frunze) **Major towns/cities** Osh, Przhevalsk, Kyzyl-Kiya, Tokmak, Djalal-Abad

Government

Head of state Askar Akayev from 1990 **Head of government** Amangeldy Mursadykovich Muraliyev from 1999 **Political system** emergent democracy **Armed forces** 12,200 (1997) **Conscription** compulsory for 12–18 months **Defence spend** (% GDP) 2.5 (1997) **Education spend** (% GNP) 5.7 (1996) **Health spend** (% GDP) 3.7 (1990–95) **Death penalty** retained and used for ordinary crimes

Population and society

Population 4,669,000 (1999 est) **Population growth rate** 0.6% (1995–2000) **Ethnic groups** 53% ethnic Kyrgyz, 22% Russian, 13% Uzbek, 3% Ukrainian, and 2% German **Religion** Sunni Muslim **Life expectancy** 63 (men); 72 (women) (1995–2000) **Literacy rate** 97% (men); 97% (women) (1995 est) **Unemployment** 3.2% (1998)

Economy and resources

GDP (US$) 1.7 billion (1998) **GNP** (US$) 1.6 billion (1998) **GNP per capita (PPP)** (US$) 2,200 (1998) **Real GDP growth** (% change on previous year) 3 (1998) **Consumer price inflation** 22% (1998) **Foreign debt** (US$) 928 million (1997) **Resources** petroleum, natural gas, coal, gold, tin, mercury, antimony, zinc, tungsten, uranium **Exports** wool, cotton yarn, tobacco, electric power, electronic and engineering products, non-ferrous metallurgy, food and beverages. Principal market: Germany 37.4% (1998) **Imports** petroleum, natural gas, engineering products, food products. Principal source: Russia 24.2% (1998)

▪ Tourist information

Time difference GMT +5 **Currency** som **Language** Kyrgyz, a Turkic language **Visa requirements** UK: visa not required. USA: visa not required **Embassy for the UK** 32 rue de Châtelain, 1050 Brussels, Belgium. Tel: (2) 627 1916; fax: (2) 627 1900 **British embassy** the British Embassy in Almaty (see Kazakhstan) deals with enquiries relating to Kyrgyzstan **Chamber of commerce** Kyrgyz Chamber of Commerce and Industry, Kievskaya 107, 720001 Bishkek. Tel: (3312) 210 574; fax: (3312) 210 575 **Office hours** 0900–1800 Mon–Sat **Banking hours** usually 0930–1730 Mon–Fri **Airports** international airports: Bishkek (Bishkek Manas), Osh; three domestic airports; total passenger km: 573 million (1995) **Chief tourist attractions** tourist facilities are limited – the country is visited mostly by mountaineers; spectacular and largely unspoilt mountain scenery; great crater lake of Issyk-Kul; several historical and cultural sites **Major holidays** 1, 7 January, 8, 21 March, 1, 9 May, 31 August

Chronology

8th century Spread of Islam. **10th century onwards** Southward migration of Kyrgyz people from upper Yenisey River region to Tian-Shan region; accelerated following rise of Mongol Empire in 13th century. **13th–14th centuries** Part of Mongol Empire. **1685** Came under control of Mongol Oirots following centuries of Turkic rule. **1758** Kyrgyz people became nominal subjects of Chinese Empire, following Oirots' defeat by Chinese rulers, the Manchus. **early 19th century** Came under suzerainty of Khanate (chieftaincy) of Kokand, to the west. **1864–76** Incorporated into tsarist Russian Empire. **1916–17** Many Kyrgyz migrated to China after Russian suppression of rebellion in Central Asia and outbreak of civil war following 1917 October Revolution in Russia, with local armed guerrillas (*basmachi*) resisting Bolshevik Red Army. **1917–1924** Part of independent Turkestan republic. **1920s** Land reforms resulted in settlement of many formerly nomadic Kyrgyz; literacy and education improved. **1924** Became autonomous republic within USSR. **1930s** Agricultural collectivization programme provoked *basmachi* resistance and local 'nationalist communists' were purged from Kyrgyz Communist Party (KCP). **1936** Became full union republic within USSR. **1990** A state of emergency was imposed in Bishkek after ethnic clashes. Askar Akayev, a reform communist, was chosen as president. **1991** Akayev condemned the attempted coup in Moscow against the reformist Mikhail Gorbachev; Kyrgyzstan joined the new Commonwealth of Independent States (CIS) and its independence was recognized by the USA. **1992** Kyrgyzstan joined the United Nations and Conference on Security and Cooperation in Europe (CSCE; now the Organization on Security and Cooperation in Europe, OSCE). A market-centred economic reform programme was instituted. **1994** he country joined the Central Asian Union, with Kazakhstan and Uzbekistan. **1996** A constitutional amendment increased the powers of the president. An agreement was made with Kazakhstan and Uzbekistan to create a single economic market. **1997** Private ownership of land was legalized but the privatization programme was suspended. An agreement was made on border controls with Russia. **1998** A referendum approved the private ownership of land. **1999** Amangeldy Muraliyev was appointed prime minister.

Laos (Lao People's Democratic Republic)

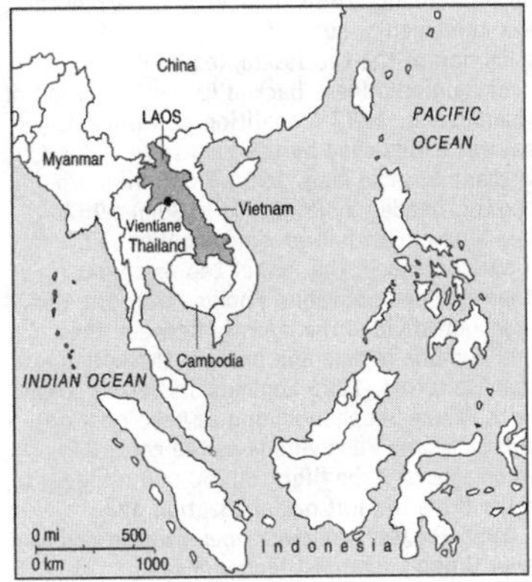

National name *Saathiaranagroat Prachhathippatay Prachhachhon Lao* **Area** 236,790 sq km/91,424 sq mi **Capital** Vientiane **Major towns/cities** Louangphrabang (the former royal capital), Pakse, Savannakhet

Government

Head of state Gen Khamtay Siphandon from 1998 **Head of government** Gen Sisavath Keobounphanh from 1998 **Political system** communist **Armed forces** 29,000 (1997) **Conscription** military service is compulsory for a minimum of 18 months **Defence spend** (% GDP) 3.9 (1997) **Education spend** (% GNP) 2.5 (1996) **Health spend** (% GDP) 1.3 (1990–95) **Death penalty** retained and used for ordinary crimes

Population and society

Population 5,297,000 (1999 est) **Population growth rate** 2.6% (1995–2000) **Ethnic groups** 60% Laotian, predominantly Lao Lum, 35% hill dwellers, and 5% Vietnamese and Chinese **Religion** Theravāda Buddhist 85%, animist beliefs among mountain dwellers **Life expectancy** 52 (men); 55 (women) (1995–2000) **Literacy rate** 71% (men); 47% (women) (1997 est) **Unemployment** 2.4% (1995)

Economy and resources

GDP (US$) 1.75 billion (1998) **GNP** (US$) 1.6 billion (1998) **GNP per capita (PPP)** (US$) 1,300 (1998 est) **Real GDP growth** (% change on previous year) 3 (1998) **Consumer price inflation** 55% (1998) **Foreign debt** (US$) 2.32 billion (1997) **Resources** coal, tin, gypsum, baryte, lead, zinc, nickel, potash, iron ore; small quantities of gold, silver, and precious stones **Exports** timber, textiles and garments, motorcycles, electricity, coffee, tin, gypsum. Principal market: Vietnam 42.7% (1997) **Imports** food (particularly rice and sugar), mineral fuels, machinery and transport equipment, cement, cotton yarn. Principal source: Thailand 56.2% (1997)

▪ Tourist information

Time difference GMT +7 **Currency** new kip **Language** Lao (official), French, English **Visa requirements** UK: visa required. USA: visa required **Embassy for the UK** 74 avenue Raymond Poincaré, 75116 Paris, France. Tel: (1) 4553 0298; fax: (1) 4727 5789 **British embassy** the UK has no diplomatic representation in Laos; the British Embassy in Bangkok (see Thailand) deals with enquiries relating to Laos **Chamber of commerce** Lao National Chamber of Commerce and Industry, BP 4596, rue Phonsay, Vientiane. Tel: (21) 412 392; fax: (21) 414 383 **Office hours** 0800–1200 and 1400–1700 Mon–Fri; 0800–1200 Sat **Banking hours** 0900–1630 Mon–Fri **Airports** international airports: Vientiane (Wattai); three domestic airports; total passenger km: 48 million (1995) **Chief tourist attractions** spectacular scenery; ancient pagodas and temples; wildlife **Major holidays** 24 January, 13–15 April, 1 May, 2 December

Chronology

c. 2000–500 BC Early Bronze Age civilizations in central Mekong River and Plain of Jars regions. **5th–8th centuries** Occupied by immigrants from southern China. **8th century onwards** Theravāda Buddhism spread by Mon monks. **9th–13th centuries** Part of the sophisticated Khmer Empire, centred on Angkor in Cambodia. **12th century** Small independent principalities, notably Louangphrabang, established by Lao invaders from Thailand and Yunnan, southern China; they adopted Buddhism. **14th century** United by King Fa Ngum; the first independent Laotian state, Lan Xang, formed. It was to dominate for four centuries, broken only by a period of Burmese rule 1574–1637. **17th century** First visited by Europeans. **1713** The Lan Xang kingdom split into three separate kingdoms, Louangphrabang, Vientiane, and Champassac, which became tributaries of Siam (Thailand) from the late 18th century. **1893–1945** Laos was a French protectorate, comprising the three principalities of Louangphrabang, Vientiane, and Champassac. **1945** Temporarily occupied by Japan. **1946** Retaken by France, despite opposition by the Chinese-backed Lao Issara (Free Laos) nationalist movement. **1950** Granted semi-autonomy in French Union, as an associated state under the constitutional monarchy of the king of Louangphrabang. **1954** Independence achieved from France under the Geneva Agreements, but civil war broke out between a moderate royalist faction of the Lao Issara, led by Prince Souvanna Phouma, and the communist Chinese-backed Pathet Lao (Land of the Lao) led by Prince Souphanouvong. **1957** A coalition government, headed by Souvanna Phouma, was established by the Vientiane Agreement. **1959** Savang Vatthana became king. **1960** Right-wing pro-Western government seized power, headed by Prince Boun Gum. **1962** Geneva Agreement established a new coalition government, led by Souvanna Phouma, but civil war continued, the Pathet Lao receiving backing from the North Vietnamese, and Souvanna Phouma from the USA. **1973** Vientiane ceasefire agreement divided the country between the communists and the Souvanna Phouma regime and brought the withdrawal of US, Thai, and North Vietnamese forces. **1975** Communists seized power; a republic was proclaimed, with Prince Souphanouvong as head of state and the Communist Party leader Kaysone Phomvihane as the controlling prime minister. **1979** Food shortages and the flight of 250,000 refugees to Thailand led to an easing of the drive towards nationalization and agricultural collectivization. **1985** Greater economic liberalization received encouragement from the Soviet Union's reformist leader Mikhail Gorbachev. **1989** The first assembly elections since communist takeover were held; Vietnamese troops were withdrawn from the country. **1991** A security and cooperation pact was signed with Thailand, and an agreement reached on the phased repatriation of Laotian refugees. **1995** The US lifted its 20-year aid embargo. **1996** The military tightened its grip on political affairs, but inward investment and private enterprise continued to be encouraged, fuelling economic expansion. **1997** Membership of the Association of South East Asian Nations (ASEAN) was announced. **1998** Khamtay Siphandon became president and was replaced as prime minister by Sisavath Keobounphanh.

Latvia Republic of

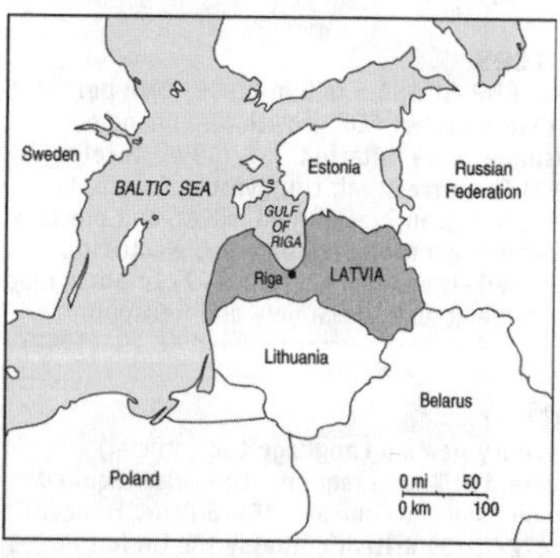

National name *Latvijas Republika* **Area** 63,700 sq km/24,594 sq mi **Capital** Riga **Major towns/cities** Daugavpils, Leipāja, Jurmala, Jelgava, Ventspils

Government

Head of state Vaira Vike-Freiberga from 1999 **Head of government** Andris Skele from 1999 **Political system** emergent democracy **Armed forces** 4,500 (1997) **Conscription** compulsory for 18 months **Defence spend** (% GDP) 4.6 (1997) **Education spend** (% GNP) 6.5 (1996) **Health spend** (% GDP) 4.4 (1990–95) **Death penalty** abolished for ordinary crimes 1999; laws provide for the death penalty for exceptional crimes only

Population and society

Population 2,389,000 (1999 est) **Population growth rate** –1.5% (1995–2000) **Ethnic groups** 53% of Latvian ethnic descent, 34% ethnic Russian, 4% Belorussian, 3% Ukrainian, 2% Polish, 1% Lithuanian **Religion** Lutheran, Roman Catholic, Russian Orthodox **Life expectancy** 63 (men); 74 (women) (1995–2000) **Literacy rate** 99% (men); 99% (women) (1997 est) **Unemployment** 14.4% (1997)

Economy and resources

GDP (US$) 5.5 billion (1998) **GNP** (US$) 5.9 billion (1998) **GNP per capita (PPP)** (US$) 4,820 (1998 est) **Real GDP growth** (% change on previous year) 4.5 (1998) **Consumer price inflation** 4.7% (1998) **Foreign debt** (US$) 503 million (1997) **Resources** peat, gypsum, dolomite, limestone, amber, gravel, sand **Exports** timber and timber products, textiles, food and agricultural products, machinery and electrical equipment, metal industry products. Principal market: Germany 5.6% (1998) **Imports** mineral fuels and products, machinery and electrical equipment, chemical industry products. Principal source: Germany 16.8% (1998)

▪ Tourist information

Time difference GMT +2 **Currency** lat **Language** Latvian **Visa requirements** UK: visa not required. USA: visa required **Embassy in the UK** 45 Nottingham Place, London W1M 3FE. Tel: (020) 7312 0040; fax: (020) 7312 0042 **British embassy** Alunana iela 5, LV-1010 Riga. Tel: (371) 782 8126; fax: (371) 733 8132 **Chamber of commerce** Latvian Chamber of Commerce and Industry, Brivibas bulvaris 21, LV-1849 Riga. Tel: (371) 722 5595; fax: (371) 782 0092 **Office hours** 0830–1730 Mon–Fri **Banking hours** 1000–1800 Mon–Fri **Airports** international airports: Riga (Spilva), Jelgava; total passenger km: 282.7 million (1996) **Major ports** Ventspils, Leipāja **Chief tourist attractions** historic centre of Riga, with medieval and art nouveau architecture; extensive beaches on Baltic coast; Gauja National Park; winter-sports facilities at Sigulda **Major holidays** 1 January, 1 May, 23–24 June, 18 November, 25–26 December; variable: Good Friday

Chronology

9th–10th centuries Invaded by Vikings and Russians. **13th century** Conquered by crusading German Teutonic Knights, who named the area Livonia and converted population to Christianity; Riga joined the Hanseatic League, a northern European union of commercial towns. **1520s** Lutheranism established as a result of the Reformation. **16th–17th centuries** Successively under Polish, Lithuanian, and Swedish rule. **1721** Tsarist Russia took control. **1819** Serfdom abolished. **1900s** Emergence of an independence movement. **1914–18** Under partial German occupation during World War I. **1918–19** Independence proclaimed and achieved after Russian Red Army troops expelled by German, Polish, and Latvian forces. **1920s** Land reforms introduced by Farmers' Union government. **1934** Democracy overthrown and, at time of economic depression, an autocratic regime was established; Baltic Entente mutual defence pact made with Estonia and Lithuania. **1940** Incorporated into USSR as constituent republic, following secret German–Soviet agreement. **1941–44** Occupied by Germany. **1944** USSR regained control; mass deportations of Latvians to Central Asia, followed by immigration of ethnic Russians; agricultural collectivization. **1960s and 1970s** Extreme repression of Latvian cultural and literary life. **1980s** Nationalist dissent began to grow, influenced by the Polish Solidarity movement and Mikhail Gorbachev's *glasnost* ('openness') initiative in the USSR. **1988** The Latvian Popular Front was established to campaign for independence. The prewar flag was readopted and official status was given to the Latvian language. **1989** The Latvian parliament passed a sovereignty declaration. **1990** The Popular Front secured a majority in local elections and its leader, Ivan Godmanir, became the prime minister. The Latvian Communist Party split into pro-independence and pro-Moscow wings. The country entered a 'transitional period of independence' and the Baltic Council was reformed. **1991** Soviet troops briefly seized key installations in Riga. There was an overwhelming vote for independence in a referendum. Full independence was achieved following the failure of the anti-Gorbachev coup attempt in Moscow; the Communist Party was outlawed. Joined United Nations (UN); a market-centred economic reform programme was instituted. **1992** The curbing of rights of non-citizens prompted Russia to request minority protection by the UN. **1993** The right-of-centre Latvian Way won the general election; a free-trade agreement was reached with Estonia and Lithuania. **1994** The last Russian troops departed. **1995** A trade and cooperation agreement was signed with the European Union (EU). A general election produced a hung parliament in which extremist parties received most support. Applied for EU membership. **1996** Guntis Ulmanis was re-elected president. The finance minister and deputy prime minister resigned from the eight-party coalition. **1997** A new political party was formed, the Latvian National Party of Reforms. Former Communist leader Alfreds Rubiks was released from prison. **1998** The DPS withdrew from the government, leaving the coalition as a minority. Citizenship laws were relaxed to make it easier for ethnic Russians to acquire citizenship. **1999** Andris Skele became prime minister. Vaira Vike-Freiberga was sworn in as president.

Lebanon Republic of

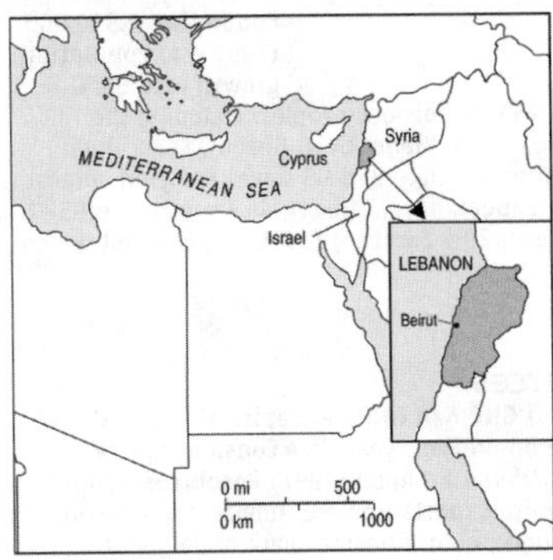

National name *Jumhouria al-Lubnaniya* **Area** 10,452 sq km/ 4,035 sq mi **Capital** Beirut (and port) **Major towns/cities** Tripoli, Zahlé, Baabda, Baalbek, Jezzine

Government

Head of state Emile Lahoud from 1998 **Head of government** Salim al-Hoss from 1998 **Political system** emergent democracy **Armed forces** 55,100 (1997); in 1995 there were 30,000 Syrian troops and the pro-Israeli South Lebanese army numbered 2,500 **Conscription** compulsory for 12 months **Defence spend** (% GDP) 4.5 (1997) **Education spend** (% GNP) 2.5 (1996) **Health spend** (% GDP) 2.1 (1990–95) **Death penalty** retained and used for ordinary crimes

Population and society

Population 3,236,000 (1999 est) **Population growth rate** 1.7% (1995–2000) **Ethnic groups** about 90% Arab, with Armenian, Assyrian, Jewish, Turkish, and Greek minorities **Religion** Muslim 58% (Shiite 35%, Sunni 23%), Christian 27% (mainly Maronite), Druze 3%; other Christian denominations including Orthodox, Armenian, and Roman Catholic **Life expectancy** 68 (men); 72 (women) (1995–2000) **Literacy rate** 91% (men); 78% (women) (1997 est) **Unemployment** 18% (1997 est)

Economy and resources

GDP (US$) 17.07 billion (1998) **GNP** (US$) 14.9 billion (1998) **GNP per capita (PPP)** (US$) 6,150 (1998) **Real GDP growth** (% change on previous year) 3.2 (1998) **Consumer price inflation** 6.0% (1998) **Foreign debt** (US$) 5.04 billion (1997) **Resources** there are no commercially viable mineral deposits; small reserves of lignite and iron ore **Exports** paper products, textiles, fruit and vegetables, jewellery. Principal market: Saudi Arabia 12.2% (1998) **Imports** electrical equipment, vehicles, petroleum, metals, machinery, consumer goods. Principal source: Italy 11.5% (1998)

▪ Tourist information

Time difference GMT +2 **Currency** Lebanese pound **Language** Arabic (official), French, Armenian, English **Visa requirements** UK: visa required. USA: visa required **Embassy in the UK** 21 Kensington Palace Gardens, London W8 4QH. (020) 7229 7265; fax: (020) 7243 1699 **British embassy** British Embassy in West Beirut, Shamma Building, Raoucheh, Ras Beirut. Tel: (1) 812 849; telex: 20465 **Chamber of commerce** Beirut Chamber of Commerce and Industry, PO Box 11-1801, Sanayeh, Beirut. Tel: (1) 349 530; fax: (1) 865 802 **Office hours** 0800–1300 Mon–Sat (June–October); 0830–1230 and 1500–1800 Mon–Fri; 0830–1230 Sat (November–May) **Banking hours** 0800–1400 Mon–Sat **Airports** international airports: Beirut (Khaldeh); most major cities have domestic airports; total passenger km: 2,173 million (1997 est) **Major ports** Tripoli, Tyre, Sidon, Jounie **Chief tourist attractions** sunny climate; scenery; historic sites **Major holidays** 1 January, 9 February, 1 May, 15 August, 1, 22 November, 25 December; variable: Eid-ul-Adha (3 days), Ashora, Good Friday, Easter Monday, end of Ramadan (3 days), New Year (Muslim), Prophet's Birthday

Chronology

5th century BC–1st century AD Part of the eastern Mediterranean Phoenician Empire. **1st century** Came under Roman rule; Christianity introduced. **635** Islam introduced by Arab tribes, who settled in southern Lebanon. **11th century** Druze faith developed by local Muslims. **1516** Became part of the Turkish Ottoman Empire. **1860** Massacre of thousands of Christian Maronites by the Muslim Druze led to French intervention. **1920–41** Administered by French under League of Nations mandate. **1943** Independence achieved as a republic, with a constitution that enshrined Christian and Muslim power-sharing. **1945** Joined the Arab League. **1948–49** Lebanon joined the first Arab war against Israel; Palestinian refugees settled in the south. **1958** Revolt by radical Muslims opposed to pro-Western policies of the Christian president, Camille Chamoun. **1964** Palestine Liberation Organization (PLO) founded in Beirut. **1967** More Palestinian refugees settled in Lebanon following the Arab-Israeli war. **1971** PLO expelled from Jordan; established headquarters in Lebanon. **1975** Outbreak of civil war between conservative Christians and leftist Muslims backed by PLO. **1976** Ceasefire agreed; Syrian-dominated Arab deterrent force formed to keep the peace, but considered by Christians as an occupying force. **1978** Israel launched a limited invasion of southern Lebanon in search of PLO guerrillas. An international United Nations peacekeeping force was unable to prevent further fighting. **1979** Part of southern Lebanon declared an 'independent free Lebanon' by a right-wing army officer. **1982** Israel again invaded Lebanon. Palestinians withdrew from Beirut under the supervision of an international peacekeeping force; the PLO moved its headquarters to Tunis. **1983** An agreement was reached for withdrawal of Syrian and Israeli troops but abrogated under Syrian pressure; intense fighting was seen between Christian Phalangists and Muslim Druze militias. **1984** Most of the international peacekeeping force were withdrawn. Radical Muslim militia took control of west Beirut. **1985** Lebanon was in chaos; many foreigners were taken hostage and Israeli troops withdrawn. **1987** Syrian troops were sent into Beirut. **1988** Gen Michel Aoun was appointed to head the caretaker military government; Premier Selim el-Hoss set up a rival government; the threat of partition hung over country. **1989** Gen Aoun declared a 'war of liberation' against Syrian occupation; Arab League-sponsored talks resulted in a ceasefire and a revised constitution recognizing Muslim majority; René Mouhawad was assassinated after 17 days as president; Maronite Christian Elias Hrawi was named as his successor; Aoun occupied the presidential palace, rejecting the constitution. **1990** The release of Western hostages began. Gen Aoun, crushed by Syrians, surrendered and legitimate government was restored. **1991** The government extended its control to the whole country. A treaty of cooperation with Syria was signed. **1992** The remaining Western hostages were released. A pro-Syrian administration was re-elected after many Christians boycotted general election. **1993** Israel launched attacks against Shia fundamentalist Hezbollah strongholds in southern Lebanon before the USA and Syria brokered an agreement to avoid the use of force. **1996** Israel launched a rocket attack on southern Lebanon in response to Hezbollah activity. USA, Israel, Syria, and Lebanon attempted to broker a new ceasefire. **1998** Army chief General Emile Lahoud was elected president. Salim al-Hoss became prime minister. **1999** Israeli withdrawal from southern Lebanon.

Lesotho Kingdom of

Area 30,355 sq km/ 11,720 sq mi **Capital** Maseru **Major towns/cities** Qacha's Nek, Teyateyaneng, Mafeteng, Hlotse, Roma, Quthing

Government

Head of state King Letsie III from 1996 **Head of government** Bethuel Pakulitha Mosisili from 1998 **Political system** emergent democracy **Armed forces** 2,000 (1997) **Conscription** military service is voluntary **Defence spend** (% GDP) 4.6 (1997) **Education spend** (% GNP) 7 (1996) **Health spend** (% GDP) 3.5 (1990–95) **Death penalty** retained and used for ordinary crimes

Population and society

Population 2,108,000 (1999 est) **Population growth rate** 2.2% (1995–2000) **Ethnic groups** almost entirely Bantus (of Southern Sotho) or Basotho **Religion** Protestant 42%, Roman Catholic 38%, indigenous beliefs **Life expectancy** 55 (men); 57 (women) (1995–2000) **Literacy rate** 72% (men); 93% (women) (1997 est) **Unemployment** 60% (1998 est)

Economy and resources

GDP (US$) 792 million (1998) **GNP** (US$) 1.2 billion (1998) **GNP per capita (PPP)** (US$) 2,320 (1998 est) **Real GDP growth** (% change on previous year) 8 (1998) **Consumer price inflation** 2.5% (1998) **Foreign debt** (US$) 660 million (1997) **Resources** diamonds, uranium, lead, iron ore; believed to have petroleum deposits **Exports** clothing, footwear, furniture, food and live animals (cattle), hides, wool and mohair, baskets. Principal market: Southern African Customs Union (SACU) 65.1% (1998) **Imports** food and live animals, machinery and transport equipment, electricity, petroleum products. Principal source: SACU 89.6% (1998)

▪ Tourist information

Time difference GMT +2 **Currency** loti **Language** Sesotho, English (official), Zulu, Xhosa **Visa requirements** UK: visa not required for visits of up to 30 days. USA: visa required **Embassy in the UK** 7 Chesham Place, Belgravia, London SW1 8HN. Tel: (020) 7235 5686; fax: (020) 7235 5023 **British embassy** British High Commission, PO Box Ms 521, Maseru 100. Tel: (266) 313 961; fax: (266) 310 120 **Chamber of commerce** Lesotho Chamber of Commerce and Industry, PO Box 79, Maseru 100. Tel: (266) 323 482 **Office hours** 0800–1245 and 1400–1630 Mon–Fri; 0800–1300 Sat **Banking hours** 0830–1530 Mon, Tue, Thu, and Fri; 0830–1300 Wed; 0830–1100 Sat **Airports** international airports: Maseru (Moshoeshoe I); 40 airstrips, of which 14 receive charter and regular scheduled air services; total passenger km: 8 million (1995) **Chief tourist attractions** mountain scenery **Major holidays** 1 January, 12, 21 March, 2 May, 4 October, 25–26 December; variable: Ascension Thursday, Good Friday, Easter Monday, Family (July), National Sports (October)

Chronology

18th century Formerly inhabited by nomadic hunter-gatherer San, Zulu-speaking Ngunis, and Sotho-speaking peoples settled in the region. **1820s** Under the name of Basutoland, Sotho nation founded by Moshoeshoe I, who united the people to repulse Zulu attacks from south. **1843** Moshoeshoe I negotiated British protection as tension with South African Boers increased. **1868** Became British territory, administered by Cape Colony (in South Africa) from 1871. **1884** Became British crown colony, after revolt against Cape Colony control; Basuto chiefs allowed to govern according to custom and tradition, but rich agricultural land west of the Caledon River was lost to South Africa. **1900s** Served as a migrant labour reserve for South Africa's mines and farms. **1952** Left-of-centre Basutoland African Congress, later Congress Party (BCP), founded by Ntsu Mokhehle to campaign for self rule. **1966** Independence achieved within Commonwealth, as Kingdom of Lesotho, with Moshoeshoe II as king and Chief Leabua Jonathan of the conservative Basotho National Party (BNP) as prime minister. **1970** State of emergency declared; king briefly forced into exile after attempting to increase his authority. **1973** State of emergency lifted; BNP won majority of seats in general election. **1975** Members of ruling party attacked by South African-backed guerrillas, who opposed African National Congress (ANC) guerrillas using Lesotho as a base. **1986** South Africa imposed a border blockade, forcing the deportation of 60 ANC members. **1990** Moshoeshoe II was dethroned and replaced by his son, as King Letsie III. **1993** Free multiparty elections ended the military rule. **1994** Fighting between rival army factions was ended by a peace deal, brokered by the Organization of African Unity. **1995** King Letsie III abdicated to restore King Moshoeshoe II to the throne. **1996** King Moshoeshoe II was killed in car accident; King Letsie III was restored to the throne. **1998** The LCD attained general election victory amidst claims of rigged polls; public demonstrations followed. South Africa sent troops to support the government. An interim political authority was appointed prior to new elections. Bethuel Mosisili became the new prime minister.

Liberia Republic of

Area 111,370 sq km/42,999 sq mi **Capital** Monrovia (and port) **Major towns/cities** Bensonville, Saniquillie, Gbarnga, Voinjama, Buchanan

Government

Head of state and government Charles Ghankay Taylor from 1997 **Political system** emergent democracy **Armed forces** 22,000 (1997) **Conscription** military service is voluntary **Defence spend** (% GDP) 3.9 (1997) **Education spend** (% GNP) 2.7 (1988) **Health spend** (% GDP) 3.5 (1990) **Death penalty** retained and used for ordinary crimes

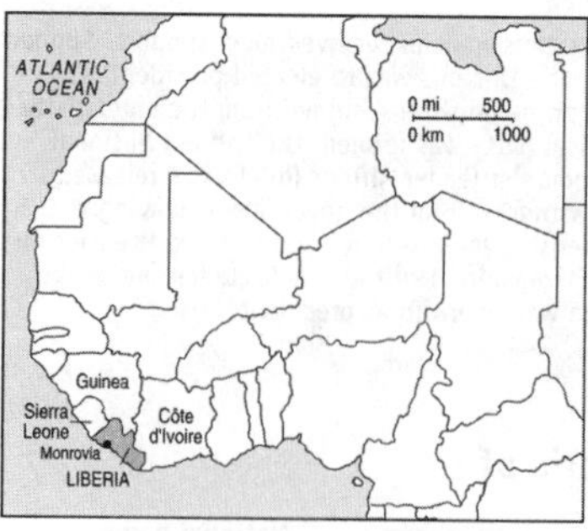

Population and society

Population 2,930,000 (1999 est) **Population growth rate** 8.2% (1995–2000) **Ethnic groups** 95% indigenous peoples, including the Kpelle, Bassa, Gio, Kru, Grebo, Mano, Krahn, Gola, Ghandi, Loma, Kissi, Vai, and Bella; 5% descended from repatriated US slaves **Religion** animist, Sunni Muslim, Christian **Life expectancy** 46 (men); 49 (women) (1995–2000) **Literacy rate** 50% (men); 29% (women) (1995 est) **Unemployment** 80% (1995 est)

Economy and resources

GDP (US$) 19.7 billion (1996) **GNP** N/A **GNP per capita (PPP)** (US$) N/A **Real GDP growth** (% change on previous year) N/A **Consumer price inflation** N/A **Foreign debt** (US$) 1.2 billion (1997) **Resources** iron ore, diamonds, gold, barytes, kyanite **Exports** iron ore, rubber, timber, coffee, cocoa, palm-kernel oil, diamonds, gold. Principal market: Belgium/Luxembourg 36.2% (1997) **Imports** machinery and transport equipment, mineral fuels, rice, basic manufactures, food and live animals. Principal source: South Korea 38.4% (1997)

▪ Tourist information

Time difference GMT +/– 0 **Currency** Liberian dollar **Language** English (official), over 20 Niger-Congo languages **Visa requirements** UK: visa required. USA: visa required **Embassy in the UK** 2 Pembridge Place, London W2 4XB. Tel: (020) 7221 1036 **British embassy** the British High Commission in Abidjan (see the Côte d'Ivoire) deals with enquiries relating to Liberia **Chamber of commerce** PO Box 92, Monrovia. Tel: (231) 223 738; telex: 44211 **Office hours** 0800–1200 and 1400–1600 Mon–Fri **Banking hours** 0900–1200 Mon–Thu; 0800–1400 Fri **Airports** international airports: Monrovia (Robertsfield and Spriggs Payne); regular services operate from Monrovia to major towns (most air services have been suspended since 1992); total passenger km: 7 million (1992) **Major ports** Buchanan, Greenville **Chief tourist attractions** sandy beaches along Atlantic coast; mountain scenery **Major holidays** 1 January, 11 February, 15 March, 12 April, 14 May, 26 July, 24 August, 29 November, 25 December; variable: Decoration (March), National Fast and Prayer (April), Thanksgiving (November)

Chronology

1821 Purchased by the philanthropic American Colonization Society and turned into settlement for liberated black slaves from southern USA. **1847** Recognized as an independent republic. **1869** The True Whig Party founded, which was to dominate politics for more than a century, providing all presidents. **1926** Large concession sold to Firestone Rubber Company as foreign indebtedness increased. **1980** President Tolbert was assassinated in military coup led by Sgt Samuel Doe, who banned political parties and launched an anticorruption drive. **1984** A new constitution was approved in a referendum. The National Democratic Party (NDPL) was founded by Doe as political parties were relegalized. **1985** Doe and the NDPL won decisive victories in the allegedly rigged elections. **1990** Doe was killed as bloody civil war broke out, involving Charles Taylor and Gen Hezekiah Bowen, who led rival rebel armies, the National Patriotic Front (NPFL) and the Armed Forces of Liberia (AFL). The war left 150,000 dead and 2 million homeless. A West African peacekeeping force was drafted in. **1992** Monrovia was under siege by Taylor's rebel forces. **1995** Ghanaian-backed peace proposals were accepted by rebel factions; an interim Council of State was established, comprising leaders of three main rebel factions. **1996** There was renewed fighting in the capital. A peace plan was reached in talks convened by the Economic Community of West African States (ECOWAS); Ruth Perry became Liberia's first female head of state. **1997** The National Patriotic Party (NPP) won a majority in assembly elections and its leader, Charles Taylor, became head of state. **1998** There was fighting in Monrovia between President Taylor's forces and opposition militias.

Libya (Great Socialist People's Libyan Arab Republic)

National name *Jamahiriya al-Arabiya al-Libya al-Shabiya al-Ishtirakiya al-Uzma* **Area** 1,759,540 sq km/ 679,358 sq mi **Capital** Tripoli **Towns and cities** Benghazi, Misurata, Az-Zaiwa, Tobruk, Ajdabiya, Derna

Government

Head of state Moamer al-Khaddhafi from 1969 **Head of government** Mubarak al-Shamikh from 2000 **Political system** nationalistic socialist **Armed forces** 65,000 (1997) **Conscription** conscription is selective for two years **Defence spend** (% GDP) 4.7 (1997) **Education spend** (% GNP) N/A **Death penalty** retained and used for ordinary crimes

Population and society

Population 5,470,000 (1999 est) **Population growth rate** 2.4% (1995–2000) **Ethnic groups** majority are of Berber and Arab origin, with a small number of Tebou and Touareg nomads and semi-nomads, mainly in south **Religion** Sunni Muslim **Life expectancy** 68 (men); 72 (women) (1995–2000) **Literacy rate** 89% (men); 63% (women) (1997 est) **Unemployment** 20% (1997 est)

Economy and resources

GDP (US$) 38 billion (1997 est) **GNP** (US$) 23.4 billion (1994 est) **GNP per capita (PPP)** (US$) 5,470 (1994 est) **Real GDP growth** (% change on previous year) -2 (1998 est) **Consumer price inflation** 24.2% (1998) **Foreign debt** (US$) 3.7 billion (1997) **Resources** petroleum, natural gas, iron ore, potassium, magnesium, sulphur, gypsum **Exports** crude petroleum (accounted for 94% of 1991 export earnings), chemicals and related products. Principal market: Italy 41.3% (1997) **Imports** machinery and transport equipment, basic manufactures, food and live animals, miscellaneous manufactured articles. Principal source: Italy 20.3% (1997)

▪ Tourist information

Time difference GMT +1 **Currency** Libyan dinar **Language** Arabic **Visa requirements** UK: visa required. USA: visa required **Embassy for the UK** British Interests Section, c/o Embassy of the Italian Republic, PO Box 4206, Sharia Uahran 1, Tripoli. Tel: (21) 333 1191; telex: 20296 (a/b BRITEMB LY) **British embassy** c/o Permanent Mission of the Socialist People's Libyan Arab Jamahiriya to the United Nations, 309–315 East 48th Street, New York, NY 10017, USA. Tel: (212) 752 5775; fax: (212) 593 4787. Paris Libyan People's Bureau. Tel: (1) 4720 1970 **Chamber of commerce** Tripoli Chamber of Commerce, Industry and Agriculture, PO Box 2321, Sharia al-Fatah September, Tripoli. Tel: (21) 333 3755; telex: 20181 **Office hours** generally 0700–1400 Sat–Wed **Banking hours** 0800–1200 Sat–Wed (winter); 0800–1200 Sat–Thu and 1600–1700 Sat and Wed (summer) **Airports** international airports: Tripoli, Benghazi (Benina), Sebhah (international civilian links with Libya have been suspended since April 1992, in accordance with a UN Security Council Resolution of March 1992); seven domestic airports; total passenger km: 398 million (1995) **Major ports** Benghazi, Misurata, Az-Zaiwa, Tobruk, Ajdabiya, Derna **Chief tourist attractions** Tripoli, with its beaches and annual International Fair; the ancient Roman towns of Leptis Magna, Sabratha, and Cyrene **Major holidays** 2, 8, 28 March, 11 June, 23 July, 1 September, 7 October; variable: Eid-ul-Adha (4 days), end of Ramadan (3 days), Prophet's Birthday

Chronology

7th century BC Tripolitania, in western Libya, was settled by Phoenicians, who founded Tripoli; it became an eastern province of Carthaginian kingdom, which was centred on Tunis to the west. **4th century BC** Cyrenaica, in eastern Libya, colonized by Greeks, who called it Libya. **74 BC** Became a Roman province, with Tripolitania part of Africa Nova province and Cyrenaica combined with Crete as a province. **19 BC** The desert region of Fezzan (Phazzania), inhabited by Garmante people, was conquered by Rome. **6th century AD** Came under control of Byzantine Empire. **7th century** Conquered by Arabs, who spread Islam: Egypt ruled Cyrenaica and Morrocan Berber Almohads controlled Tripolitania. **mid-16th century** Became part of Turkish Ottoman Empire, who combined the three ancient regions into one regency in Tripoli. **1711** Karamanli (Qaramanli) dynasty established virtual independence from Ottomans. **1835** Ottoman control reasserted. **1911–12** Conquered by Italy. **1920s** Resistance to Italian rule by Sanusi order and Umar al-Mukhtar. **1934** Colony named Libya. **1942** Italians ousted, and area divided into three provinces: Fezzan (under French control), Cyrenaica, and Tripolitania (under British control). **1951** Achieved independence as United Kingdom of Libya, under King Idris, former Amir of Cyrenaica and leader of Sanusi order. **1959** Discovery of oil transformed economy, but also led to unsettling social changes. **1969** King deposed in military coup led by Col Moamer al Khaddhafi. Revolution Command Council set up and Arab Socialist Union (ASU) proclaimed the only legal party in a new puritanical Islamic-socialist republic which sought Pan-Arab unity. **1970s** Economic activity collectivized, oil industry nationalized, opposition suppressed by Khaddhafi's revolutionary regime. **1972** Proposed federation of Libya, Syria, and Egypt abandoned. **1980** A proposed merger with Syria was abandoned. Libyan troops began fighting in northern Chad. **1986** The US bombed Khaddhafi's headquarters, following allegations of his complicity in terrorist activities. **1988** Diplomatic relations with Chad were restored, political prisoners were freed, and the economy was liberalized. **1989** The US navy shot down two Libyan planes. There was a reconciliation with Egypt. **1992** Khaddhafi came under international pressure to extradite the suspected Lockerbie and UTA (Union de Transports Aérians) bombers for trial outside Libya. United Nations sanctions were imposed; several countries severed diplomatic and air links with Libya. **1995** There was an antigovernment campaign of violence by Islamicists. Hundreds of Palestinians and thousands of foreign workers were expelled. **1999** Lockerbie suspects were handed over for trial in the Netherlands, to be tried by Scottish judges, who ruled that the suspects should be tried on every count. Having handed over the suspects, and after Libya paid compensation to the family of PC Yvonne Fletcher, who was murdered outside the Libyan embassy in London in 1984, full diplomatic relations with the UK were restored. **2000** Khaddhafi surprised the outside world by installing a head of government other than himself, Prime Minister Mubarak al-Shamikh.

Liechtenstein Principality of

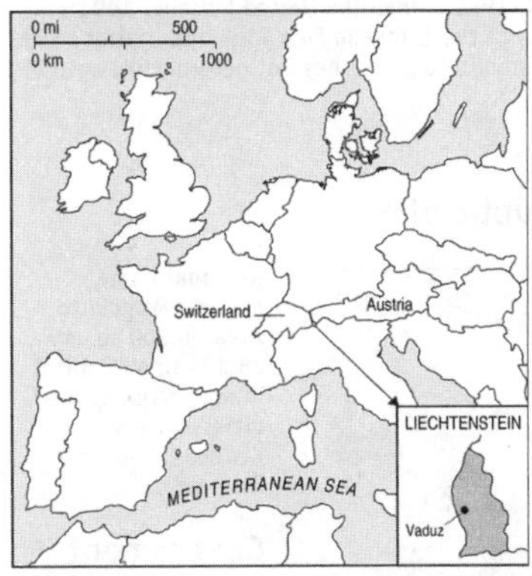

National name *Fürstentum Liechtenstein* **Area** 160 sq km/62 sq mi **Capital** Vaduz **Major towns/ cities** Balzers, Schaan, Ruggell, Triesen, Eschen

Government

Head of state Prince Hans Adam II from 1989 **Head of government** Mario Frick from 1993 **Political system** liberal democracy **Armed forces** no standing army since 1868; there is a police force of 59 men and 19 auxiliaries **Conscription** in an emergency Liechtensteiners under the age of 60 are liable to military service **Death penalty** abolished in 1987 (last execution in 1785)

Population and society

Population 32,000 (1999 est) **Population growth rate** 1.3% (1995–2000) **Ethnic groups** indigenous population of Alemannic origin; one-third of the population are foreign-born resident workers **Religion** Roman Catholic (87%), Protestant **Life expectancy** 78 (men); 83 (women) (1995–2000) **Literacy rate** 99% (men); 99% (women) (1999 est) **Unemployment** 1.6% (1997)

Economy and resources

GDP (US$) 1.3 billion (1995) **GNP** (US$) 1.35 billion (1995 est) **GNP per capita (PPP)** (US$) 25,100 (1995 est) **Real GDP growth** (% change on previous year) 0.7 (1995) **Consumer price inflation** 0.5% (1997)

Resources hydro power **Exports** small machinery, artificial teeth and other material for dentistry, stamps, precision instruments, ceramics. Principal market: Switzerland 14.5% (1996) **Imports** machinery and transport equipment, foodstuffs, textiles, metal goods. Principal source: European Economic Area (EEA) 45.4% (1996)

▪ Tourist information

Time difference GMT +1 **Currency** Swiss franc **Language** German (official); an Alemannic dialect is also spoken **Visa requirements** UK: visa not required. USA: visa not required **Embassy in the UK** Liechtenstein is generally represented overseas by Switzerland **British embassy** enquiries relating to Liechtenstein are dealt with by the British Consulate General, Dufourstrasse 56, CH-8008 Zürich, Switzerland. Tel: (1) 261 1520–6; fax: (1) 252 8351 **Chamber of commerce** Liechtenstein Industrie-und Handeslkammer (Chamber of Industry and Commerce), Postfach 232, Josef Rheinberger-Strasse 11, FL-9490 Vaduz. Tel: (4175) 232 2744; fax: (4175) 233 1503 **Office hours** generally 0800–1200 and 1400–1800 Mon–Fri **Banking hours** 0800–1630 Mon–Fri **Airports** international airports: none, the nearest is at Zürich, Switzerland **Chief tourist attractions** Alpine setting; postal museum; Prince's castle; National Museum and State Art Collection at Vaduz **Major holidays** 1, 6 January, 2 February, 19 March, 1 May, 15 August, 1 November, 8, 24–26, 31 December; variable: Ascension Thursday, Carnival, Corpus Christi, Good Friday, Easter Monday, Whit Monday

Chronology

c. AD 500 Settled by Germanic-speaking Alemanni tribe. **1342** Became a sovereign state. **1434** Present boundaries established. **1719** Former independent lordships of Schellenberg and Vaduz were united by Princes of Liechtenstein to form the present state. **1815–66** A member of the German Confederation. **1868** Abolished standing armed forces. **1871** Liechtenstein was the only German principality to stay outside the newly formed German Empire. **1918** Patriotic Union (VU) party founded, drawing most support from the mountainous south. **1919** Switzerland replaced Austria as the foreign representative of Liechtenstein. **1921** Adopted Swiss currency; constitution created a parliament. **1923** United with Switzerland in customs and monetary union. **1938** Prince Franz Josef II came to power. **1970** After 42 years as the main governing party, the northern-based Progressive Citizens' Party (FBP) was defeated by VU which, except for 1974–78, became a dominant force in politics. **1978** Joined the Council of Europe. **1984** The franchise was extended to women in the national elections. **1989** Prince Franz Josef II died; he was succeeded by Hans Adam II. **1990** Joined the United Nations. **1991** Became the seventh member of the European Free Trade Association. **1993** Mario Frick of VU became Europe's youngest head of government, aged 28, after two general elections.

Lithuania Republic of

National name *Lietuvos Respublika* **Area** 65,200 sq km/ 25,173 sq mi **Capital** Vilnius **Major towns/ cities** Kaunas, Klaipeda, Siauliai, Panevezys

Government

Head of state Valdas Adamkus from 1998 **Head of government** Andrius Kubelius from 1999 **Political system** emergent democracy **Armed forces** 5,300 (1997) **Conscription** military service is compulsory for 12 months **Defence spend** (% GDP) 4.4 (1997) **Education spend** (% GNP) 5.6 (1996) **Health spend** (% GDP) 5.1 (1990–95) **Death penalty** abolished in 1998

Population and society

Population 3,682,000 (1999 est) **Population growth rate** –0.3% (1995–2000) **Ethnic groups** 80% Lithuanian ethnic descent, 9% ethnic Russian, 7% Polish, 2% Belarussian, 1% Ukrainian **Religion** predominantly Roman Catholic; Lithuanian Lutheran Church **Life expectancy** 64 (men); 76 (women) (1995–2000) **Literacy rate** 99% (men); 99% (women) (1997 est) **Unemployment** 14.1% (1997)

Economy and resources

GDP (US$) 10.5 billion (1998) **GNP** (US$) 9.02 billion (1998) **GNP per capita (PPP)** (US$) 4,310 (1998) **Real GDP growth** (% change on previous year) 4.2 (1998) **Consumer price inflation** 5.1% (1998) **Foreign debt** (US$) 1.54 billion (1997) **Resources** small deposits of petroleum, natural gas, peat, limestone, gravel, clay, sand **Exports** textiles, machinery and equipment, non-precious metals, animal products, timber. Principal market: Russia 16.5 (1998) **Imports** petroleum and natural gas products, machinery and transport equipment, chemicals, fertilizers, consumer goods. Principal source: Russia 21.2% (1998)

▪ Tourist information

Time difference GMT +2 **Currency** litas **Language** Lithuanian (official) **Visa requirements** UK: visa not required for a stay of up to 90 days. USA: visa not required for a stay of up to 90 days **Embassy in the UK** 17 Essex Villas, London W8 7BP. Tel: (020) 7938 2481; fax: (020) 7938 3329 **British embassy** PO Box 863, Anta Kalnio 2, 2055 Vilnius. Tel: (2) 222 070; fax: (2) 357 579 **Chamber of commerce** Association of Lithuanian Chambers of Commerce and Industry, Kudirkos 18, 2600 Vilnius. Tel: (2) 222 630; fax: (2) 222 621 **Office hours** 0900–1300 and 1400–1800 Mon–Fri **Airports** international airports: Vilnius, Kaunas, Siauliai; few domestic flights; total passenger km: 308 million (1995) **Chief tourist attractions** historic cities of Vilnius, Klaipeda, Kaunas, and Trakai; coastal resorts such as Palanga and Kursiu Nerija; picturesque countryside **Major holidays** 1 January, 16 February, 5 May, 6 July, 1 November, 25–26 December; variable: Easter Monday

Chronology

late 12th century Became a separate nation. **1230** Mindaugas united Lithuanian tribes to resist attempted invasions by German and Livonian Teutonic Knights, and adopted Christianity. **14th century** Grand Duchy formed by Gediminas, founder of Vilnius and Jogaila dynasty, and his son, Algirdas; absorbing Ruthenian territories to east and south, it stretched from the Baltic to the Black Sea and east, nearly reaching Moscow. **1410** Led by Duke Vytautas, and in alliance with Poland, the Teutonic Knights were defeated decisively at the Battle of Tannenberg. **1569** Joined Poland in a confederation, under the Union of Lublin, in which Poland had the upper hand and Lithuanian upper classes were Polonized. **1795** Came under control of Tsarist Russia, following partition of Poland; 'Lithuania Minor' (Kaliningrad) fell to Germany. **1831 and 1863** Failed revolts for independence. **1880s** Development of organized nationalist movement. **1914–18** Occupied by German troops during World War I. **1918–19** Independence declared and, after uprising against attempted imposition of Soviet Union (USSR) control, was achieved as a democracy. **1920–39** Province and city of Vilnius occupied by Poles. **1926** Democracy overthrown in authoritarian coup by Antanas Smetona, who became president. **1934** Baltic Entente mutual-defence pact signed with Estonia and Latvia. **1939–40** Secret German–Soviet agreement brought most of Lithuania under Soviet influence as a constituent republic. **1941** Lithuania revolted and established own government, but during World War II Germany again occupied the country and 210,000, mainly Jews, were killed. **1944** USSR resumed rule. **1944–52** Lithuanian guerrillas fought USSR, which persecuted the Catholic Church, collectivized agriculture, and deported half a million Balts to Siberia. **1972** Demonstrations against Soviet government. **1980s** There was a growth in nationalist dissent, influenced by the Polish Solidarity movement and the *glasnost* ('openness') initiative of reformist Soviet leader Mikhail Gorbachev. **1988** An independence movement, the Sajudis, was formed to campaign for increased autonomy; the parliament declared Lithuanian the state language and readopted the flag of the interwar republic. **1989** The Communist Party split into pro-Moscow and nationalist wings, and lost the local monopoly of power; over 1 million took part in nationalist demonstrations. **1990** Nationalist Sajudis won elections; their leader, Vytautas Landsbergis, became the president; a unilateral declaration of independence was rejected by the USSR, who imposed an economic blockade. **1991** Soviet paratroopers briefly occupied key buildings in Vilnius, killing 13; the Communist Party was outlawed; Lithuanian independence was recognized by the USSR and Western nations; the country was admitted into the United Nations. **1992** Economic restructuring caused a contraction in GDP. **1993** A free-trade agreement was reached with other Baltic states. The last Russian troops departed. **1994** A friendship and cooperation treaty was signed with Poland. **1994** A trade and cooperation agreement was reached with the European Union. **1997** A border treaty was signed with Russia. **1998** Valdas Adamkus became president. **1999** Andrius Kubelius became prime minister.

Luxembourg Grand Duchy of

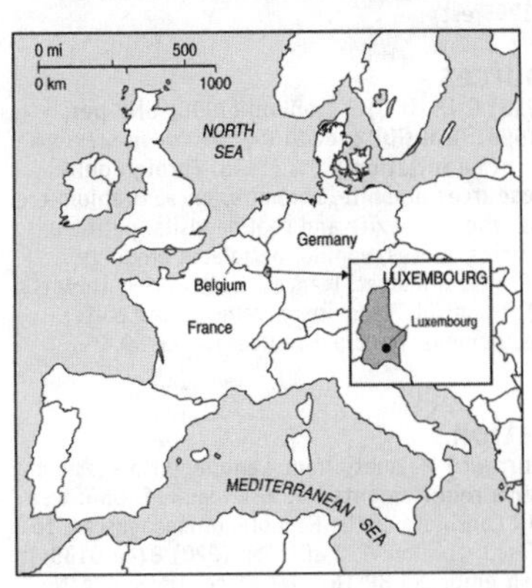

National name *Grand-Duché de Luxembourg* **Area** 2,586 sq km/998 sq mi **Capital** Luxembourg **Major towns/cities** Esch-Alzette, Differdange, Dudelange, Petange

Government

Head of state Grand Duke Jean from 1964 **Head of government** Jean-Claude Juncker from 1995 **Political system** liberal democracy **Armed forces** 800; gendarmerie 600 (1997) **Conscription** military service is voluntary **Defence spend** (% GDP) 0.8 (1997) **Education spend** (% GNP) 4.1 (1996) **Health spend** (% GDP) 6.2 (1996) **Death penalty** abolished in 1979

Population and society

Population 426,000 (1999 est) **Population growth rate** 1.1% (1995–2025) **Ethnic groups** majority descended from the Moselle Franks **Religion** Roman Catholic **Life expectancy** 73 (men); 80 (women) (1995–2000) **Literacy rate** 99% (men); 99% (women) (1997 est) **Unemployment** 2.8% (1998)

Economy and resources

GDP (US$) 16.5 billion (1998) **GNP** (US$) 18.6 billion (1998) **GNP per capita (PPP)** (US$) 37,420 (1998) **Real GDP growth** (% change on previous year) 4.5 (1998) **Consumer price inflation** 1.6% (1998) **Resources** iron ore **Exports** base metals and manufactures, mechanical and electrical equipment, rubber and related products, plastics, textiles and clothing. Principal market: Germany 19% (1998) **Imports** machinery and electrical apparatus, transport equipment, mineral products. Principal source: Germany 17.9% (1998)

■ Tourist information

Time difference GMT +1 **Currency** Luxembourg franc **Language** French, German, local Letzeburgesch (all official) **Visa requirements** UK: visa not required. USA: visa not required for a stay of up to 90 days **Embassy in the UK** 27 Wilton Crescent, London SW1X 8SD. Tel: (020) 7235 6961; fax: (020) 7235 9734 **British embassy** 14 boulevard Roosevelt, L-2450 Luxembourg-Ville. Tel: (352) 229 864/5/6; fax: (352) 229 867 **Chamber of commerce** 7 rue Alcide de Gasperi, L-2981 Luxembourg-Kirchberg. Tel: (352) 435 853; fax: (352) 438 326 **Office hours** generally 0830–1200 and 1400–1800 Mon–Fri **Banking hours** generally 0900–1200 and 1330–1630 Mon–Fri **Airports** international airports: Luxembourg (Findel); no domestic airports; total passenger km: 380 million (1995) **Chief tourist attractions** Luxembourg-Ville, with its historic monuments and many cultural events; medieval castles (Clerf, Esch/Sauer, Vianden, Wietz); Benedictine abbey at Echternach; thermal centre at Mandorf-les-Bains; footpaths and hiking trails **Major holidays** 1 January, 1 May, 23 June, 15 August, 1–2 November, 25–26, 31 December; variable: Ascension Thursday, Easter Monday, Whit Monday, Shrove Monday

Chronology

963 Luxembourg became autonomous within Holy Roman Empire under Siegfried, Count of Ardennes. **1060** Conrad, descendent of Siegfried, took the title Count of Luxembourg. **1354** Emperor Charles IV promoted Luxembourg to the status of duchy. **1441** Luxembourg ceded to dukes of Burgundy. **1482** Luxembourg came under Habsburg control. **1555** Luxembourg became part of Spanish Netherlands on division of Habsburg domains. **1684–97** Much of Luxembourg occupied by France. **1713** Treaty of Utrecht transferred Spanish Netherlands to Austria. **1797** Conquered by revolutionary France. **1815** Congress of Vienna made Luxembourg a grand duchy, under King William of the Netherlands. **1830** Most of Luxembourg supported Belgian revolt against the Netherlands. **1839** Western part of Luxembourg assigned to Belgium. **1842** Luxembourg entered the Zollverein (German customs union). **1867** Treaty of London confirmed independence and neutrality of Luxembourg to allay French fears about possible inclusion in a unified Germany. **1870s** Development of iron and steel industry. **1890** Link with Dutch crown ended on accession of Queen Wilhelmina, since Luxembourg's law of succession did not permit a woman to rule. **1912** Revised law of succession allowed Marie-Adelaide to become grand duchess. **1914–18** Occupied by Germany. **1919** Plebiscite overwhelmingly favoured continued independence; Marie-Adelaide abdicated after allegations of collaboration with Germany; Charlotte became grand duchess. **1921** Entered into close economic links with Belgium. **1940** Invaded by Germany. **1942–44** Annexed by Germany. **1948** Luxembourg formed Benelux customs union with Belgium and the Netherlands. **1949** Luxembourg became founding member of North Atlantic Treaty Organization (NATO). **1958** Luxembourg became founding member of European Economic Community (EEC). **1964** Grand Duchess Charlotte abdicated in favour of her son Jean. **1994** Former premier Jacques Santer became the president of the European Commission (EC). **1995** Jean-Claude Juncker became prime minister.

Macedonia Former Yugoslav Republic of (official international name); Republic of Macedon (official internal name)

National name *Republika Makedonija* **Area** 25,700 sq km/ 9,922 sq mi **Capital** Skopje **Major towns/cities** Bitolj, Prilep, Kumanovo, Tetovo

Government

Head of state Kiro Gligonov from 1991 **Head of government** Ljubco Georgievski from 1998 **Political system** emergent democracy **Armed forces** 15,400; plus paramilitary force of 7,500 (1997) **Conscription** military service is compulsory for nine months **Defence spend** (% GDP) 10.2 (1997) **Education spend** (% GNP) 5.6 (1996) **Health spend** (% GDP) 7.3 (1990–95) **Death penalty** laws do not provide for the death penalty for any crime

Population and society

Population 2,011,000 (1999 est) **Population growth rate** 0.6% (1995–2000) **Ethnic groups** 66% Macedonian ethnic descent, 22% ethnic Albanian, 5% Turkish, 3% Romanian, 2% Serb, and 2% Muslim, comprising Macedonian Slavs who converted to Islam during the Ottoman era, and are known as Pomaks. This ethnic breakdown is disputed by Macedonia's ethnic Albanian population, who claim that they form 40% of the population and seek autonomy, and by ethnic Serbs, who claim that they form 11.5% **Religion** Christian, mainly Orthodox; Muslim 2.5% **Life expectancy** 71 (men); 75 (women) (1995–2000) **Literacy rate** 94% (men); 94% (women) (1997 est) **Unemployment** 38.8% (1997)

Economy and resources

GDP (US$) 2.2 billion (1998) **GNP** (US$) 2.6 billion (1998) **GNP per capita (PPP)** (US$) 3,660 (1998) **Real GDP growth** (% change on previous year) 2.9 (1998) **Consumer price inflation** 9% (1998) **Foreign debt** (US$) 1.54 billion (1997) **Resources** coal, iron, zinc, chromium, manganese, lead, copper, nickel, silver, gold **Exports** manufactured goods, machinery and transport equipment, miscellaneous manufactured articles, sugar beet, vegetables, cheese, lamb, tobacco. Principal market: Germany 21.4% (1998) **Imports** mineral fuels and lubricants, manufactured goods, machinery and transport equipment, food and live animals, chemicals. Principal source: Germany 13.3% (1998)

■ Tourist information

Time difference GMT +1 **Currency** Macedonian denar **Language** Macedonian, closely allied to Bulgarian and written in Cyrillic **Visa requirements** UK: visa not required. USA: visa required **Embassy in the UK** 10 Harcourt House, 19A Cavendish Square, London W1M 9AD. Tel: (020) 7499 5152; fax (020) 7499 2864 **British embassy** Office of the British Government Representative, Ul Veljko Vlahovic 26, 91000 Skopje. Tel: (91) 116 772; fax: (91) 117 005 **Chamber of commerce** Economic Chamber of

Macedonia, PO Box 324, Dimitrie Cupovski 13, 91000 Skopje. Tel: (91) 233 215; fax: (91) 116 210 **Office hours** 0700/0800–1500/1600 Mon–Fri **Airports** international airports: Skopje, Ohrid; domestic services between Skopje and Ohrid; total passenger km: 340 million (1995) **Chief tourist attractions** mountain scenery **Major holidays** 1–2 January, 1–2 May, 2 August, 11 October

Chronology

4th century BC Part of ancient great kingdom of Macedonia, which included northern Greece and southwest Bulgaria and, under Alexander the Great, conquered a vast empire; Thessaloniki founded. **146 BC** Macedonia became a province of the Roman Empire. **395 AD** On the division of the Roman Empire, came under the control of Byzantine Empire, with its capital at Constantinople. **6th century** Settled by Slavs, who later converted to Christianity. **9th–14th centuries** Under successive rule by Bulgars, Byzantium, and Serbia. **1371** Became part of Islamic Ottoman Empire. **late 19th century** The 'Internal Macedonian Revolutionary Organization', through terrorism, sought to provoke Great Power intervention against Turks. **1912–13** After First Balkan War, partitioned between Bulgaria, Greece, and the area that constitutes the current republic of Serbia. **1918** Serbian part included in what was to become Yugoslavia; Serbian imposed as official language. **1941–44** Occupied by Bulgaria. **1945** Created a republic within Yugoslav Socialist Federation. **1967** The Orthodox Macedonian archbishopric of Skopje, forcibly abolished 200 years earlier by the Turks, was restored. **1980** The rise of nationalism was seen after the death of Yugoslav leader Tito. **1990** Multiparty elections produced an inconclusive result. **1991** Kiro Gligorov, a pragmatic former communist, became president. A referendum supported independence. **1992** Independence was declared, and accepted by Serbia/Yugoslavia, but international recognition was withheld because of Greece's objections to the name. **1993** Sovereignty was recognized by the UK and Albania; United Nations membership was won under the provisional name of the Former Yugoslav Republic of Macedonia; Greece blocked full European Union (EU) recognition. **1994** Independence was recognized by the USA; a trade embargo was imposed by Greece, causing severe economic damage. **1995** Independence was recognized by Greece and the trade embargo lifted. President Gligorov survived a car bomb assassination attempt. **1997** Plans to reduce the strength of the UN Preventive Deployment Force (UNPREDEP) were abandoned. The government announced compensation for the public's losses in failed investment schemes. **1998** The UN extended the mandate of UNPREDEP. A general election resulted in Ljubco Georgievski, the VRMO-DPMNE leader, becoming prime minister. A 1,700-strong NATO force was deployed in Macedonia to safeguard the 2,000 ceasefire verification monitors in neighbouring Kosovo, Yugoslavia.

Madagascar Democratic Republic of

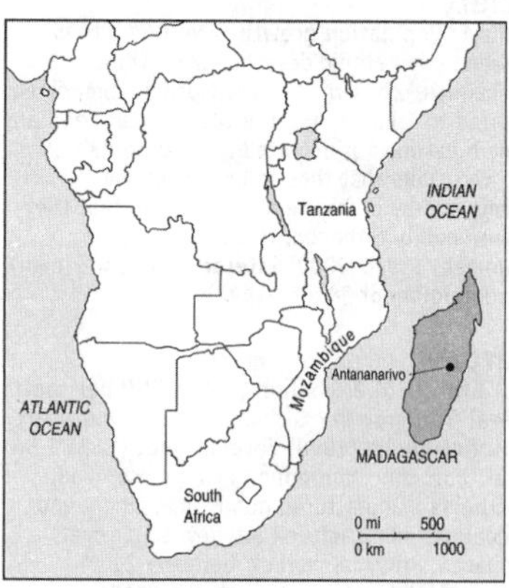

National name *Repoblika Demokratika n'i Madagaskar* **Area** 587,041 sq km/226,656 sq mi **Capital** Antananarivo **Major towns/cities** Antsirabe, Mahajanga, Fianarantsoa, Toamasina, Ambatondrazaka

Government

Head of state Didier Ratsiraka from 1996 **Head of government** René Tantely Gabrio Andrianarivo from 1998 **Political system** emergent democracy **Armed forces** 21,000; plus paramilitary gendarmerie of 7,500 (1997) **Conscription** military service is compulsory for 18 months **Defence spend** (% GDP) 0.8 (1997) **Education spend** (% GDP) 1.9 (1996) **Health spend** (% GDP) 1.1 (1990–95) **Death penalty** retains the death penalty for ordinary crimes but can be considered abolitionist in practice (last known execution in 1958)

Population and society

Population 15,496,000 (1999 est) **Population growth rate** 2.9% (1995–2000) **Ethnic groups** 18 main Malagasy tribes of Malaysian–Polynesian origin; also French, Chinese, Indians, Pakistanis, and Comorans **Religion** traditional beliefs, Roman Catholic, Protestant **Life expectancy** 56 (men); 59 (women) (1995–2000) **Literacy rate** 88% (men); 73% (women) (1995 est) **Unemployment** 6% (1995 est)

Economy and resources

GDP (US$) 3.75 billion (1998) **GNP** (US$) 3.8 billion (1998) **GNP per capita (PPP)** (US$) 900 (1998) **Real GDP growth** (% change on previous year) 3.9 (1998) **Consumer price inflation** 8.0% (1998) **Foreign debt** (US$) 4.1 billion (1997) **Resources** graphite, chromite, mica, titanium ore, small quantities of precious stones, bauxite and coal deposits, petroleum reserves **Exports** coffee, shrimps, cloves, vanilla, petroleum products, chromium, cotton fabrics. Principal market: France 39.5% (1998) **Imports** minerals (crude petroleum), chemicals, machinery, vehicles and parts, metal products, electrical equipment. Principal source: France 39.4% (1998)

▪ Tourist information

Time difference GMT +3 **Currency** Malagasy franc **Language** Malagasy (official); French, English **Visa requirements** UK: visa required. USA: visa required **Embassy in the UK** Consulate of the Republic of Madagascar, 16 Lanark Mansions, Pennard Road, London W12 8DT. Tel: (020) 8746 0133; fax: (020) 8746 0134 **British embassy** BP 167, 1er Etage, Immeuble 'Ny Havana', Cité de 67 Ha, 101 Antananarivo. Tel: (2) 27749; fax: (2) 26690 **Chamber of commerce** Fédération des Chambres de Commerce, d'Industrie et d'Agriculture de Madagascar, BP 166, 20 rue Colbert, 101 Antananarivo. Tel: (2) 21567 **Banking hours** 0800–1100 and 1400–1600 Mon–Fri **Airports** international airports: Antananarivo (Ivato), Mahajunga (Amborovi); two domestic airports and 57 airfields open to public air traffic; total passenger km: 631 million (1995) **Major ports** Toamasina, Antsiranana, Toliary, Mahajanga **Chief tourist attractions** unspoilt scenery; unusual wildlife; much of Madagascar's flora and fauna is unique to the island – there are 3,000 endemic species of butterfly **Major holidays** 1 January, 29 March, 1 May, 26 June, 15 August, 1 November, 25, 30 December; variable: Ascension Thursday, Good Friday, Easter Monday, Whit Monday

Chronology

c. 6th–10th centuries AD Settled by migrant Indonesians. **1500** First visited by European navigators. **17th century** Development of Merina and Sakalava kingdoms in the central highlands and west coast. **1642–74** France established a coastal settlement at Fort-Dauphin, which they abandoned after a massacre by local inhabitants. **late 18th–early 19th century** Merinas, united by their ruler Andrianampoinimerina, became dominant kingdom; court converted to Christianity. **1861** Ban on Christianity (imposed in 1828) and entry of Europeans lifted by Merina king, Radama II. **1885** Became French protectorate. **1895** Merina army defeated by French and became a colony; slavery abolished. **1942–43** British troops invaded to overthrow French administration allied to the pro-Nazi Germany Vichy regime and install anti-Nazi Free French government. **1947–48** Nationalist uprising brutally suppressed by French. **1960** Independence achieved from France, with Philibert Tsiranana, the leader of the Social Democratic Party (PSD), as president. **1972** Merina-dominated army overthrew Tsiranana's government, dominated by the cotier (coastal tribes), as the economy deteriorated. **1975** Martial law imposed; new one-party state Marxist constitution adopted, with Lt-Commander Didier Ratsiraka as president. **1978** More than 1,000 people were killed in race riots in Majunga city in the northwest. **1980** Ratsiraka abandoned the Marxist experiment, which had involved nationalization and the severing of ties with France. **1990** Political opposition was legalized and 36 new parties were created. **1991** Antigovernment demonstrations were held. Ratsiraka formed a new unity government, which included opposition members. **1992** Constitutional reform was approved by a referendum. **1995** A referendum backed the appointment of a prime minister by the president, rather than the assembly. **1996** Didier Ratsiraka was elected president again. **1998** ARES largest party following election. Tantely Andrianarivo appointed prime minister. **2000** Around 600,000 people were made homeless when cyclones swept through the island.

Malawi Republic of (formerly Nyasaland)

National name *Malawi* **Area** 118,484 sq km/45,735 sq mi **Capital** Lilongwe **Major towns/cities** Blantyre, Lilongwe, Mzuzu, Zomba

Government

Head of state and government Bakili Muluzi from 1994 **Political system** emergent democracy **Armed forces** 5,000 (1997) **Conscription** military service is voluntary **Defence spend** (% GDP) 1.1 (1997) **Education spend**

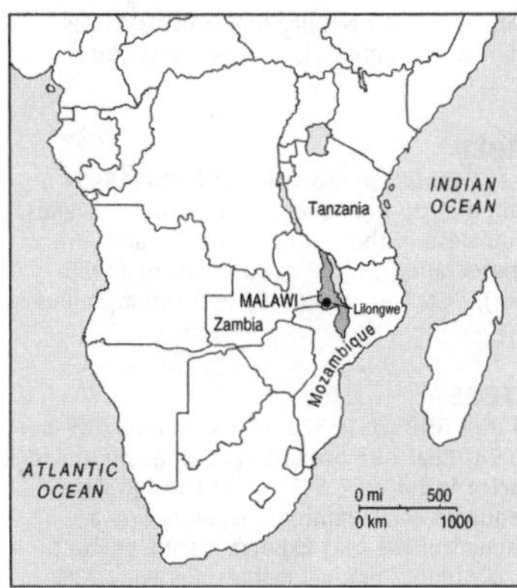

(% GNP) 5.5 (1996) **Health spend** (% GDP) 2.3 (1990–95) **Death penalty** retained and used for ordinary crimes

Population and society

Population 10,640,000 (1999 est) **Population growth rate** 2.4% (1995–2000) **Ethnic groups** almost all indigenous Africans, divided into numerous ethnic groups, such as the Chewa, Nyanja, Tumbuka, Yao, Lomwe, Sena, Tonga, and Ngoni. There are also Asian and European minorities **Religion** Christian 75%, Muslim 20% **Life expectancy** 39 (men); 40 (women) (1995–2000) **Literacy rate** 73% (men); 43% (women) (1997 est) **Unemployment** N/A

Economy and resources

GDP (US$) 1.6 billion (1998) **GNP** (US$) 2.1 billion (1998) **GNP per capita (PPP)** (US$) 730 (1998) **Real GDP growth** (% change on previous year) 3.8 (1998) **Consumer price inflation** 15% (1998) **Foreign debt** (US$) 2.2 billion (1997) **Resources** marble, coal, gemstones, bauxite and graphite deposits, reserves of phosphates, uranium, glass sands, asbestos, vermiculite **Exports** tobacco, tea, sugar, cotton, groundnuts. Principal market: South Africa 12.8% (1997) **Imports** petroleum products, fertilizers, coal, machinery and transport equipment, miscellaneous manufactured articles. Principal source: South Africa 34.1% (1998)

▪ Tourist information

Time difference GMT +2 **Currency** Malawi kwacha **Language** English, Chichewa (both official) **Visa requirements** UK: visa not required. USA: visa not required **Embassy in the UK** 33 Grosvenor Street, London W1X 0DE. Tel: (020) 7491 4172/7; fax: (020) 7491 9916 **British embassy** British High Commission, PO Box 30042, Lingadzi House, Lilongwe 3. Tel: (265) 782 400; fax: (265) 782 657 **Chamber of commerce** Associated Chambers of Commerce and Industry of Malawi, PO Box 258, Chichiri Trade Fair Grounds, Blantyre. Tel: (265) 671 988; fax: (265) 671 147 **Office hours** 0730–1700 Mon–Fri **Banking hours** 0800–1300 Mon–Fri **Airports** international airports: Lilongwe (Kamuzu), Blantyre (Chileka); three domestic airports; total passenger km: 110 million (1995) **Chief tourist attractions** beaches on Lake Malawi; varied scenery; big game; excellent climate **Major holidays** 1 January, 3 March, 14 May, 6 July, 17 October, 22, 25–26 December; variable: Good Friday, Easter Monday, Holy Saturday

Chronology

1st–4th centuries AD Immigration by Bantu-speaking peoples. **1480** Foundation of Maravi (Malawi) Confederacy, which covered much of central and southern Malawi and lasted into the 17th century. **1530** First visited by the Portuguese. **1600** Ngonde kingdom founded in northern Malawi by immigrants from Tanzania. **18th century** Chikulamayembe state founded by immigrants from east of Lake Nyasa; slave trade flourished and Islam introduced in some areas. **mid-19th century** Swahili-speaking Ngoni peoples, from South Africa, and Yao entered the region, dominating settled agriculturists; Christianity introduced by missionaries, such as David Livingstone. **1891** Became British protectorate of Nyasaland; cash crops, particularly coffee, introduced. **1915** Violent uprising, led by Rev John Chilembwe, against white settlers who had moved into the fertile south, taking land from local population. **1953** Became part of white-dominated Central African Federation, which included South Rhodesia (Zimbabwe) and North Rhodesia (Zambia). **1958** Dr Hastings Kamuzu Banda returned to the country after working abroad and became head of the conservative-nationalist Nyasaland/Malawi Congress Party (MCP), which spearheaded the campaign for independence. **1963** Central African Federation dissolved. **1964** Independence achieved within Commonwealth as Malawi, with Banda as prime minister. **1966** Became one-party republic, with Banda as president. **1967** Banda became pariah of Black Africa by recognizing racist, white-only republic of South Africa. **1971** Banda was made president for life. **1970s** There were reports of human-rights violations and the murder of Banda's opponents. **1980s** The economy began to deteriorate after nearly two decades of expansion. **1986–89** There was an influx of nearly a million refugees from Mozambique. **1992** There were calls for a multiparty political system. Countrywide industrial riots caused many fatalities. Western aid was suspended over human-rights violations. **1993** A referendum overwhelmingly supported the ending of one-party rule. **1994** A new multiparty constitution was adopted. Bakili Muluzi, of the United Democratic Front (UDF), was elected president in the first free elections for 30 years. **1995** Banda and the former minister of state John Tembo were charged with conspiring to murder four political opponents in 1983, but were cleared.

Malaysia Federation of

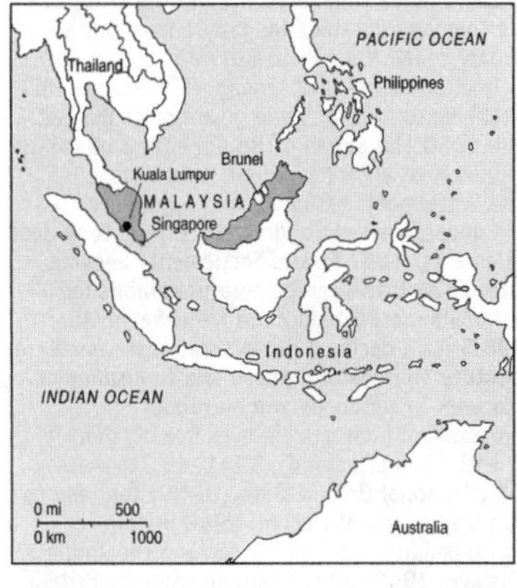

National name *Persekutuan Tanah Malaysia* **Area** 329,759 sq km/127,319 sq mi **Capital** Kuala Lumpur **Major towns/cities** Johor Baharu, Ipoh, George Town (Penang), Kuala Trengganu, Kuala Baharu, Petalong Jaya, Kelang, Kuching in Sarawak, Kota Kinabalu in Sabah

Government

Head of state Tuanku Salehuddin Abdul Aziz Shan bin al-Marhum Hisamuddin Alam Shah from 1999 **Head of government** Mahathir bin Muhammad from 1981 **Political system** liberal democracy **Armed forces** 111,500; reserve force 37,800; paramilitary force 20,100 (1997) **Conscription** military service is voluntary **Defence spend** (% GDP) 3.7 (1997) **Education spend** (% GNP) 5.2 (1996) **Health spend** (% GDP) 1.4 (1990–95) **Death penalty** retained and used for ordinary crimes

Population and society

Population 21,830,000 (1999 est) **Population growth rate** 2.0% (1995–2000); 1.7% (2000–05) **Ethnic groups** 58% of the population is Malay, four-fifths of whom live in rural areas; 32% is Chinese, four-fifths of whom are in towns; 9% is Indian, mainly Tamil **Religion** Muslim (official), Buddhist, Hindu, local beliefs **Life expectancy** 70 (men); 74 (women) (1995–2000) **Literacy rate** 90% (men); 81% (women) (1997 est) **Unemployment** 2.5% (1997)

Economy and resources

GDP (US$) 71.3 billion (1998) **GNP** (US$) 79.8 billion (1998) **GNP per capita (PPP)** (US$) 6,990 (1998 est) **Real GDP growth** (% change on previous year) –6 (1998) **Consumer price inflation** 5.3% (1998) **Foreign debt** (US$) 47.2 billion (1997) **Resources** tin, bauxite, copper, iron ore, petroleum, natural gas, forests **Exports** palm oil, rubber, crude petroleum, machinery and transport equipment, timber, tin, textiles, electronic goods. Principal market: USA 21.6% (1998) **Imports** machinery and transport equipment, chemicals, foodstuffs, crude petroleum, consumer goods. Principal source: Singapore 24.7% (1998)

▪ Tourist information

Time difference GMT +8 **Currency** ringgit **Language** Malay (official), English, Chinese, Tamil, Iban **Visa requirements** UK: visa not required. USA: visa not required **Embassy in the UK** 45 Belgrave Square, London SW1X 8QT. Tel: (020) 7235 8033; fax: (020) 7235 5161 **British embassy** British High Commission, PO Box 11030, 185 Jalan Ampang, 50450 Kuala Lumpur. Tel: (3) 248 2122; fax: (3) 248 0880 **Chamber of commerce** Malaysian International Chamber of Commerce and Industry, PO Box 12921, Wisma Damansara, 10th Floor, Jalah Semantan, 50792 Kuala Lumpur. Tel: (3) 254 2677; fax: (3) 255 4946 **Office hours** vary between Peninsular Malaysia and East Malaysia; generally 0830–1200/1300 and 1400/1500–1600/1730 Mon–Fri; 0830–1200 Sat **Banking hours** 1000–1500 Mon–Fri; 0930–1130 Sat **Airports** international airports: Kuala Lumpur (Subang), Penang (Bayan Lepas), Kota Kinabalu, Kuching; 15 domestic airports; total passenger km: 28,762 million (1997 est) **Major ports** Kelang **Chief tourist attractions** cultures of the country's many ethnic groups; tranquil beaches backed by dense rainforest **Major holidays** 1 January (in some states), 1 May, 3 June, 31 August, 25 December; variable: Eid-ul Adha, Diwali (in most states), end of Ramadan (2 days),

New Year (Chinese, January/February, most states), New Year (Muslim), Prophet's Birthday, Wesak (most states), several local festivals

Chronology

1st century AD Peoples of Malay peninsula influenced by Indian culture and Buddhism. **8th–13th centuries** Malay peninsula formed part of Buddhist Srivijaya Empire based in Sumatra. **14th century** Siam (Thailand) expanded to included most of Malay peninsula. **1403** Muslim traders founded port of Malacca, which became a great commercial centre, encouraging the spread of Islam. **1511** The Portuguese attacked and captured Malacca. **1641** The Portuguese were ousted from Malacca by the Dutch after a seven-year blockade. **1786** The British East India Company established a trading post on island of Penang. **1795–1815** Britain occupied the Dutch colonies after France conquered the Netherlands. **1819** Stamford Raffles of East India Company obtained Singapore from Sultan of Johore. **1824** Anglo-Dutch Treaty ceded Malacca to Britain in return for territory in Sumatra. **1826** British possessions of Singapore, Penang, and Malacca formed the Straits Settlements, ruled by the governor of Bengal; ports prospered and expanded. **1840** The Sultan of Brunei gave Sarawak to James Brooke, whose family ruled it as an independent state until 1946. **1851** Responsibility for Straits Settlements assumed by the governor general of India. **1858** British government, through India Office, took over administration of Straits Settlements. **1867** Straits Settlements became crown colony of British Empire. **1874** British protectorates established over four Malay states of Perak, Salangor, Pahang, and Negri Sembilan, which federated in 1896. **1888** Britain declared protectorate over northern Borneo (Sabah). **late 19th century** Millions of Chinese and thousands of Indians migrated to Malaya to work in tin mines and on rubber plantations. **1909–14** Britain assumed indirect rule over five northern Malay states after agreement with Siam (Thailand). **1941–45** Japanese occupation. **1946** United Malay National Organization (UMNO) founded to oppose British plans for centralized Union of Malaya. **1948** Britain federated nine Malay states with Penang and Malacca to form the single colony of the Federation of Malaya. **1948–60** Malayan emergency: British forces suppressed insurrection by communist guerrillas. **1957** Federation of Malaya became independent with Prince Abdul Rahman (leader of UMNO) as prime minister. **1963** Federation of Malaya combined with Singapore, Sarawak, and Sabah to form Federation of Malaysia. **1963–66** 'The Confrontation' – guerrillas supported by Indonesia opposed federation with intermittent warfare. **1965** Singapore withdrew from the Federation of Malaysia. **1968** Philippines claimed sovereignty over Sabah. **1969** Malay resentment of Chinese economic dominance resulted in race riots in Kuala Lumpur. **1971** *Bumiputra* policies which favoured ethnic Malays in education and employment introduced by Tun Abul Razak of UMNO. **1981** Mahathir bin Muhammad (UMNO) became prime minister; the government became increasingly dominated by Muslim Malays. **1987** Malay–Chinese relations deteriorated; over 100 opposition activists were arrested. **1991** An economic development policy was launched which aimed at 7% annual growth. **1997** The currency was allowed to float. Parts of Borneo and Sumatra were covered by thick smog for several weeks following forest-clearing fires. **1998** The repatriation of foreign workers commenced. Currency controls were introduced as the GDP contracted sharply. **1999** Mahathir bin Muhammad's ruling coalition party was elected to retain power. Tuanku Salehuddin Abdul Aziz Shan bin al-Marhum Hisamuddin Alam Shah was appointed president.

Maldives Republic of the

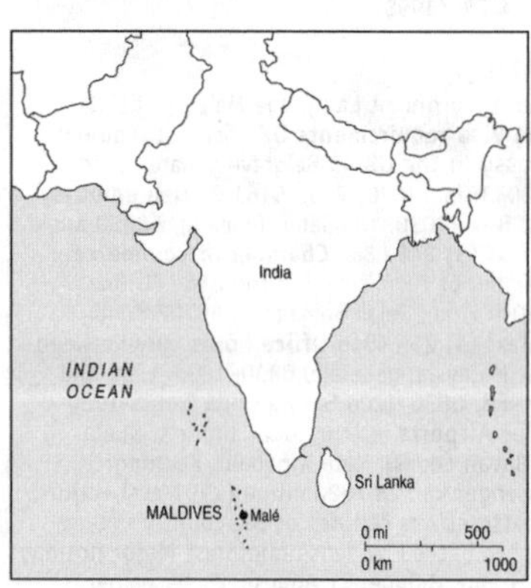

National name *Divehi Raajjeyge Jumhooriyaa* **Area** 298 sq km/115 sq mi **Capital** Malé **Major towns/cities** Seenu, Kurehdhu, Kunfunadhoo, Dhiggiri, Anthimatha

Government

Head of state and government Maumoon Abd Gayoom from 1978 **Political system** authoritarian nationalist **Armed forces** no standing army **Education spend** (% GNP) 6.4 (1996) **Health spend** (% GDP) 5 (1990) **Death penalty** retains the death penalty for ordinary crimes but can be considered abolitionist in practice (last known execution in 1952)

Population and society

Population 278,000 (1999 est) **Population growth rate** 2.8% (1995–2025) **Ethnic groups** four main groups: Dravidian in the northern islands, Arab in the middle islands, Sinhalese in the southern islands, and African **Religion** Sunni Muslim **Life expectancy** 66 (men); 63 (women) (1995–2000) **Literacy rate** 96% (men); 96% (women) (1997 est) **Unemployment** 0.9% (1997 est)

Economy and resources

GDP (US$) 342 million (1998 est) **GNP** (US$) 323 million (1998) **GNP per capita (PPP)** (US$) 3,100 (1998) **Real GDP growth** (% change on previous year) 6.8 (1998) **Consumer price inflation** 7.6% (1997) **Foreign debt** (US$) 200 million (1997) **Resources** coral (mining was banned as a measure against the encroachment of the sea) **Exports** marine products (tuna bonito ('Maldive Fish'), clothing. Principal market: Germany 33% (1996) **Imports** consumer manufactured goods, petroleum products, food, intermediate and capital goods. Principal source: Singapore 29.1% (1996)

▪ Tourist information

Time difference GMT +5 **Currency** rufiya **Language** Divehi (Sinhalese dialect), English **Visa requirements** UK: visa required. USA: visa required **Embassy in the UK** Honorary Tourism Representative for the Maldives Republic in the UK, 3 Esher House, 11 Edith Terrace, London SW10 0TH. Tel: (020) 7352 2246; fax: (020) 7351 3382 **British embassy** the British High Commission in Colombo (see Sri Lanka) deals with enquiries relating to the Maldives **Chamber of commerce** State Trading Organisation, STO Building, 7 Haveeree Higun, Malé 20-02. Tel: (960) 323 279; fax: (960) 325 218 **Office hours** 0730–1330 Sat–Thu **Banking hours** 0900–1300 Sun–Thu **Airports** international airports: Malé, Gan; total passenger km: 71 million (1995) **Chief tourist attractions** white sandy beaches; multi-coloured coral formations; water and underwater sports/activities **Major holidays** 1 January, 26 July (2 days), 11 November (2 days); variable: Eid-ul-Adha (4 days), end of Ramadan (3 days), New Year (Muslim), Prophet's Birthday, first day of Ramadan (2 days), Huravee (February), Martyrs (April), National (October/November, 2 days)

Chronology

12th century AD Islam introduced by seafaring Arabs, who displaced the indigenous Dravidian population. **14th century** Ad-Din sultanate established. **1558–73** Under Portuguese rule. **1645** Became a dependency of Ceylon (Sri Lanka), which was ruled by the Dutch until 1796 and then by the British, with Sinhalese and Indian colonies being established. **1887** Became an internally self-governing British protectorate, which remained a dependency of Sri Lanka until 1948. **1932** The sultanate became an elected position when the Maldives' first constitution was introduced. **1953** Maldive Islands became a republic within the Commonwealth, as the ad-Din sultanate was abolished. **1954** Sultan restored. **1959–60** Secessionist rebellion in Suvadiva (Huvadu) and Addu southern atolls. **1965** Achieved full independence outside Commonwealth. **1968** Sultan deposed after referendum; republic reinstated with Ibrahim Nasir as president. **1975** The closure of a British airforce staging post on the southern island of Gan led to a substantial loss in income. **1978** The autocratic Nasir retired and was replaced by the progressive Maumoon Abd Gayoom. **1980s** Economic growth was boosted by the rapid development of the tourist industry. **1982** Rejoined the Commonwealth. **1985** Became a founder member of the South Asian Association for Regional Cooperation. **1988** A coup attempt by Sri Lankan mercenaries, thought to have the backing of former president Nasir, was foiled by Indian paratroops. **1998** Gayoom was re-elected for a further presidential term.

Mali Republic of

National name *République du Mali* **Area** 1,240,142 sq km/478,818 sq mi **Capital** Bamako **Major towns/cities** Mopti, Kayes, Ségou, Timbuktu, Sikasso

Government

Head of state Alpha Oumar Konare from 1992 **Head of government** Ibrahim Boubaker Keita from 1994 **Political system** emergent democracy **Armed forces** 7,400; plus paramilitary forces of 7,800 (1997) **Conscription** selective conscription for two years **Defence spend** (% GDP) 1.7 (1997) **Education spend** (% GNP) 2.2 (1996) **Health spend** (% GDP) 2.0 (1990–95) **Death penalty** retains the death penalty for ordinary crimes but can be considered abolitionist in practice (last execution 1980)

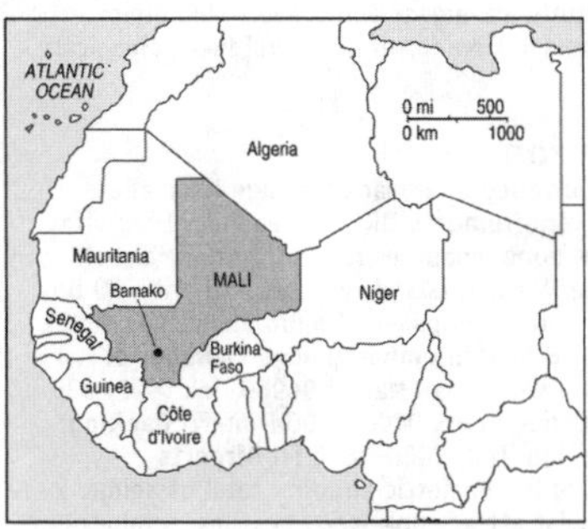

Population and society

Population 10,960,000 (1999 est) **Population growth rate** 2.4% (1995–2000) **Ethnic groups** around 50% belong to the Mande group, including the Bambara, Malinke, and Sarakole; other significant groups include the Fulani, Minianka, Senutu, Songhai, and the nomadic Tuareg in the north **Religion** Sunni Muslim 90%, animist, Christian **Life expectancy** 52 (men); 55 (women) (1995–2000) **Literacy rate** 43% (men); 28% (women) (1997 est)

Economy and resources

GDP (US$) 2.7 billion (1998) **GNP** (US$) 2.6 billion (1998) **GNP per capita (PPP)** (US$) 720 (1998) **Real GDP growth** (% change on previous year) 5.0 (1998) **Consumer price inflation** 3.0% (1998) **Foreign debt** (US$) 2.9 billion (1997) **Resources** iron ore, uranium, diamonds, bauxite, manganese, copper, lithium, gold **Exports** cotton, livestock, gold, miscellaneous manufactured articles. Principal market: Thailand 20.3% (1997) **Imports** machinery and transport equipment, food products, petroleum products, other raw materials, chemicals, miscellaneous manufactured articles. Principal source: Côte d'Ivoire 19% (1997)

▪ Tourist information

Time difference GMT +/− 0 **Currency** franc CFA **Language** French (official), Bambara **Visa requirements** UK: visa required. USA: visa required **Embassy for the UK** 487 avenue Molière, B-1060 Brussels, Belgium. Tel: (2) 345 7432; fax: (2) 344 5700 **British embassy** British Consulate, BP 1598, Plan International, Bamako. Tel: (223) 230 583; fax: (223) 228 143 **Chamber of commerce** Chambre de Commerce et d'Industrie de Mali, BP 46, place de la Liberté, Bamako. Tel: (223) 225 036; fax: (223) 222 120 **Office hours** 0730–1230 and 1300–1600 Mon–Thu; 0730–1230 and 1430–1730 Fri **Banking hours** 0730–1200 and 1315–1500 Mon–Thu; 0730–1230 Fri **Airports** international airports: Bamako (Senou), Mopti; ten domestic airports; total passenger km: 223 million (1995) **Chief tourist attractions** cultural heritage, including the historic town of Timbuktu, with its 13th–15th-century mosques; oases along the ancient trans-Sahara camel route **Major holidays** 1, 20 January, 1, 25 May, 22 September, 19 November, 25 December; variable: Eid-ul-Adha, end of Ramadan, Prophet's Birthday, Prophet's Baptism (November)

Chronology

5th–13th centuries Ghana Empire founded by agriculturist Soninke people, based on the Saharan gold trade for which Timbuktu became an important centre. At its height in the 11th century it covered much of the western Sahel, comprising parts of present-day Mali, Senegal, and Mauritania. Wars with Muslim Berber tribes from the north led to its downfall. **13th–15th centuries** Ghana Empire superseded by Muslim Mali Empire of Malinke (Mandingo) people of southwest, from which Mali derives its name. At its peak, under Mansa Musa in the 14th century, it covered parts of Mali, Senegal, Gambia, and southern Mauritania. **15th–16th centuries** Muslim Songhai Empire, centred around Timbuktu and Gao, superseded Mali Empire. It covered Mali, Senegal, Gambia, and parts of Mauritania, Niger, and Nigeria, and included a professional army and civil service. **1591** Songhai Empire destroyed by Moroccan Berbers, under Ahmad al-Mansur, who launched an invasion to take over western Sudanese gold trade and took control over Timbuktu. **18th–19th centuries** Niger valley region was divided between the nomadic Tuareg, in the area around Gao in the northeast, and the Fulani and Bambara kingdoms, around Macina and Bambara in the centre and southwest. **late 18th century** Western Mali visited by Scottish explorer Mungo Park. **mid-19th century** The Islamic Tukolor, as part of a jihad (holy war) conquered much of western Mali, including Fulani and Bambara kingdoms, while in the south, Samori Ture, a Muslim Malinke (Mandingo) warrior, created a small empire. **1880–95** Region conquered by French, who overcame Tukolor and Samori resistance to establish colony of French Sudan. **1904** Became part of the federation of French West Africa. **1946** French Sudan became an overseas territory within the French Union, with its own territorial assembly and representation in the French parliament; the pro-autonomy Sudanese Union and Sudanese Progressive Parties founded in Bamako. **1959** With Senegal, formed the Federation of Mali. **1960** Separated from Senegal and became independent Republic of Mali, with Modibo Keita, an authoritarian socialist of the Sudanese Union party, as president. **1968** Keita replaced in army coup by Lt Moussa Traoré, as economy deteriorated: constitution suspended and political activity banned. **1974** A new constitution made Mali a one-party state, dominated by Traoré's nationalistic socialist Malian People's Democratic Union (UDPM), formed in 1976. **1979** More than a dozen were killed after a student strike was crushed. **1985** There was a five-day conflict with Burkina Faso over a long-standing border dispute which was mediated by the International Court of Justice. **late 1980s** Closer ties developed with the West and free-market economic policies were pursued, including privatization, as the Soviet influence waned. **1991** Violent demonstrations and strikes against one-party rule led to 150 deaths; Traoré was ousted in a coup. **1992** A referendum endorsed a new democratic constitution. The opposition Alliance for Democracy in Mali (ADEMA) won multiparty elections; Alpha Oumar Konare was elected president. A peace pact was signed with Tuareg rebels fighting in northern Mali for greater autonomy. **1993–94** Ex-president Traoré was sentenced to death for his role in suppressing the 1991 riots. **1997** President Konare was re-elected.

Malta Republic of

National name *Repubblika Ta'Malta* **Area** 320 sq km/124 sq mi **Capital** Valletta (and port) **Major towns/cities** Rabat, Birkirkara, Qormi, Sliema, Zetjun, Zabor

Government

Head of state Guido de Marco from 1999 **Head of government** Edward Fenech Adami from 1998 **Political system** liberal democracy **Armed forces** 2,000 (1997) **Conscription** military service is voluntary **Defence spend** (% GDP) 0.9 (1997) **Education spend** (% GNP) 5.2 (1995) **Death penalty** laws provide for the death penalty only for exceptional crimes such as crimes under military law or crimes committed in exceptional circumstances such as wartime (last execution 1943)

Population and society

Population 386,000 (1999 est) **Population growth rate** 0.7% (1995–2000) **Ethnic groups** essentially European, supposedly originated from ancient North African kingdom of Carthage **Religion** Roman Catholic 98% **Life expectancy** 75 (men); 79 (women) (1995–2000) **Literacy rate** 91% (men); 92% (women) (1997 est) **Unemployment** 5% (1997)

Economy and resources

GDP (US$) 3.7 billion (1998) **GNP** (US$) 3.56 billion (1998) **GNP per capita (PPP)** (US$) 13,610 (1998) **Real GDP growth** (% change on previous year) 4.1 (1998) **Consumer price inflation** 2.4% (1998) **Foreign debt** (US$) 1.03 billion (1997) **Resources** stone, sand; offshore petroleum reserves were under exploration 1988–95 **Exports** machinery and transport equipment, manufactured articles (including clothing), beverages, chemicals, tobacco. Principal market: France 20.7% (1998) **Imports** machinery and transport equipment, basic manufactures (including textile yarn and fabrics), food and live animals, mineral fuels. Principal source: Italy 19.3% (1998)

▪ Tourist information

Time difference GMT +1 **Currency** Maltese lira **Language** Maltese, English (both official) **Visa requirements** UK: visa not required. USA: visa not required **Embassy in the UK** Malta House, 36–38 Piccadilly, London W1V OPP. Tel: (020) 7292 4800; fax: (020) 7734 1832 **British embassy** British High Commission, PO Box 506, 7 St Anne Street, Floriana, Valetta. Tel: (356) 233 134; fax: (356) 242 001 **Chamber of commerce** Exchange Building, Republic Street, Valetta VLT 05. Tel: (356) 247 233; fax: (356) 245 223 **Office hours** 0830–1245 and 1430–1730 Mon–Fri; 0830–1200 Sat **Banking hours** 0800–1200 Mon–Thu; 0800–1200 and 1430–1600 Fri; 0800–1130 Sat **Airports** international airports: Luqa (Malta, 8 km/5 mi from Valetta); helicopter service between Malta and Gozo; total passenger km: 1,681 million (1997 est) **Major ports** Marsaxlokk, Valletta **Chief tourist attractions** fine climate; sandy beaches and rocky coves; Blue Lagoon of Comino; prehistoric temples and Ta' Pinh church of Gozo; Valetta, with its 16th-century churches, palaces, hospitals, and aqueducts, and its yachting centre **Major holidays** 1 January, 31 March, 1 May, 15 August, 13, 25 December; variable: Good Friday

Chronology

7th century BC Invaded and subjugated by Carthaginians from North Africa. **218 BC** Came under Roman control. **AD 60** Converted to Christianity by the apostle Paul. **395** On the division of the Roman Empire, became part of Eastern (Byzantine) portion, dominated by Constantinople. **870** Came under Arab rule. **1091** Arabs defeated by Norman Count Roger I of Sicily; Roman Catholic Church re-established. **1530** Handed over by Holy Roman Emperor Charles V to a religious military order, the Hospitallers (Knights of St John of Jerusalem). **1798–1802** Occupied by French. **1814** Annexed to Britain by the Treaty of Paris on condition that Roman Catholic Church was maintained and Maltese Declaration of Rights honoured. **later 19th century–early 20th century** Became vital British naval base, with famous dockyard that developed as the island's economic mainstay. **1942** Awarded theGeorge Cross for valour in resisting severe Italian aerial attacks during World War II. **1947** Achieved self-government. **1956** Referendum approved MLP's proposal for integration with UK. Plebiscite opposed and boycotted by right-of-centre Nationalist Party (PN). **1958** MLP rejected final British integration proposal. **1964** Independence achieved from Britain, within Commonwealth. A ten-year defence and economic-aid treaty with the UK was signed. **1971** Prime Minister Mintoff adopted a policy of nonalignment and declared the 1964 treaty invalid; negotiations began for leasing NATO base in Malta. **1972** Seven-year NATO agreement signed. **1974** Became a republic. **1979** British military base closed; closer links were established with communist and Arab states, including Libya. **1987** Edward Fenech Adami (PN) was narrowly elected prime minister; he adopted a more pro-European and pro-American policy stance than the preceding administration. **1990** A formal application was made for European Community membership. **1998** The PN was returned to power after a snap election, with Edward Fenech Adami returning as prime minister. **1999** Guido de Marco was elected president.

market: USA **Imports** foodstuffs, beverages and tobacco, building materials, machinery and transport equipment, mineral fuels, chemicals. Principal source: USA

■ Tourist information

Time difference GMT +12 **Currency** US dollar **Language** Marshallese, English (both official) **Visa requirements** UK: visa required. USA: visa required **Embassy in the UK** none; enquiries relating to the Marshall Islands are dealt with by the Marshall Islands Visitors Authority, PO Box 1727, Ministry of Resources and Development, Majuro 96960. Tel: (692) 625 3206; fax: (692) 625 3218 **British embassy** none **Chamber of commerce** Majuro Chamber of Commerce, Majuro 96960. Tel: (692) 625 3051; fax: (692) 625 3343 **Office hours** 0800–1700 Mon–Fri **Banking hours** generally 1000–1500 Mon–Thu; 1000–1800 Fri **Airports** international airports: Majuro; ten domestic airports; total passenger km: 57 million (1995) **Chief tourist attractions** sandy beaches; coral atolls; tropical vegetation **Major holidays** 1 January, 1 March, 1 May, 1 July, 21 October, 17 November, 4, 25 December

Chronology

after c. 1000 BC Micronesians first settled the islands. **1529** Visited by Spanish navigator Miguel de Saavedra and thereafter came under Spanish influence. **1875** Spanish rule formally declared in face of increasing encroachment by German traders. **1885** German protectorate established. **1914** Seized by Japan on the outbreak of World War I. **1920–44** Administered under League of Nations mandate by Japan and vigorously colonized. **1944** Japanese removed after heavy fighting with US troops during World War II. **1946–63** Eniwetok and Bikini atolls used for US atom-bomb tests; islanders later demanded rehabilitation and compensation for the damage. **1947** Became part of United Nations (UN) Pacific Islands Trust Territory, administered by USA. **1979** Amata Kabua was elected president as internal self-government was established. **1986** The Compact of Free Association with the USA granted the islands self-government, with the USA retaining the responsibility for defence and security until 2001. **1990** UN trust status was terminated. **1991** Independence was agreed with Kabua as president; UN membership was granted. **1997** Imata Kabua, cousin of Amata, was elected president after his Amata's death in 1996.

Marshall Islands Republic of the

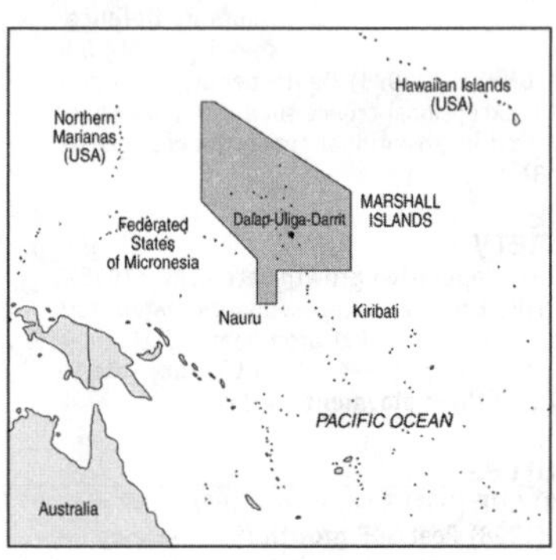

Area 181 sq km/70 sq mi **Capital** Dalap-Uliga-Darrit (on Majuro atoll) **Major towns/cities** Ebeye (the only other town)

Government

Head of state and government Kessai H Note from 2000 **Political system** liberal democracy **Armed forces** the USA maintains a military presence on the Kwajalein Atoll (the Compact of Free Association gave the USA responsibility for defence in return for US assistance) **Education spend** (% GDP) 6 (1994) **Death penalty** abolished in 1991

Population and society

Population 62,000 (1999 est) **Population growth rate** 3.2% (1995–2025) **Ethnic groups** 97% Marshallese, of predominantly Micronesian descent **Religion** Christian (mainly Protestant) and Baha'i **Life expectancy** 63 (men); 66 (women) (1998 est) **Literacy rate** 91% (men); 90% (women) (1994 est) **Unemployment** 16% (1991 est)

Economy and resources

GDP (US$) 97 million (1998 est) **GNP** (US$) 95 million (1998) **GNP per capita (PPP)** (US$) 1,780 (1998 est) **Real GDP growth** (% change on previous year) –5 (1998) **Consumer price inflation** 4% (1998) **Foreign debt** (US$) 125 million (1997 est) **Resources** phosphates **Exports** coconut products, trochus shells, copra, handicrafts, fish, live animals. Principal

Mauritania Islamic Republic of

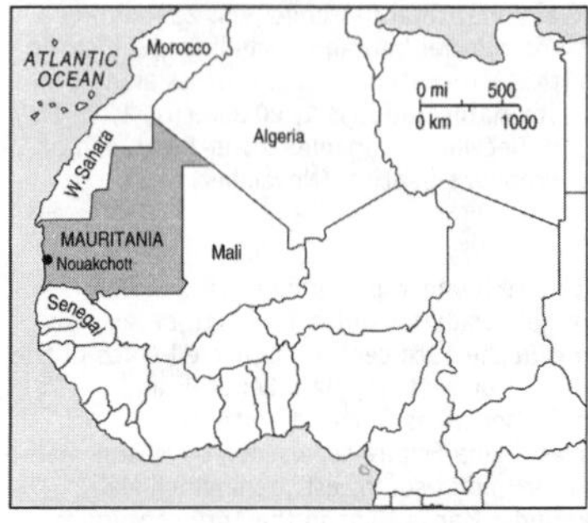

National name *République Islamique Arabe et Africaine de Mauritanie* **Area** 1,030,700 sq km/ 397,953 sq mi **Capital** Nouakchott (port) **Major towns/cities** Nouâdhibou, Kaédi, Zouerate, Kiffa, Rosso, Atar

Government

Head of state Maaoya Sid'Ahmed Ould Taya from 1984 **Head of government** Cheik el Avia Ould Muhammad Khouna from 1998 **Political system** emergent democracy **Armed forces** 15,700; plus paramilitary force of around 5,000 (1997) **Conscription** military service is by authorized conscription for two years **Defence spend** (% GDP) 2.2 (1997) **Education spend** (% GNP) 5.0 (1995) **Health spend** (% GDP) 1.8 (1990–95) **Death penalty** retained and used for ordinary crimes

Population and society

Population 2,598,000 (1999 est) **Population growth rate** 2.7% (1995–2000) **Ethnic groups** over 80% of the population is of Moorish or Moorish-black origin; about 18% is black African (concentrated in the south); there is a small European minority **Religion** Sunni Muslim **Life expectancy** 52 (men); 55 (women) (1995–2000) **Literacy rate** 49% (men); 28% (women) (1997 est) **Unemployment** 23% (1995 est)

Economy and resources

GDP (US$) 971 million (1998) **GNP** (US$) 1.04 billion (1998) **GNP per capita (PPP)** (US$) 1,660 (1998 est) **Real GDP growth** (% change on previous year) 4.2 (1998) **Consumer price inflation** 5.0% (1998) **Foreign debt** (US$) 2.45 billion (1997) **Resources** copper, gold, iron ore, gypsum, phosphates, sulphur, peat **Exports** fish and fish products, iron ore. Principal market: Japan 23.9% (1997) **Imports** machinery and transport equipment, foodstuffs, consumer goods, building materials, mineral fuels. Principal source: France 25.9% (1997)

▪ Tourist information

Time difference GMT +/– 0 **Currency** ouguiya **Language** French and Hasaniya Arabic (both official), African languages including Pulaar, Soninke, and Wolof **Visa requirements** UK: visa required. USA: visa required **Embassy in the UK** Honorary Consulate of the Islamic Republic of Mauritania, 140 Bow Common Lane, London E3 4BH. Tel: (020) 8980 4382; fax: (020) 8980 2232 **British embassy** the British Embassy in Rabat (see Morocco) deals with enquiries relating to Mauritania **Chamber of commerce** Chambre de Commerce, d'Agriculture, d'Elevage, d'Industrie et des Mines de Mauritanie, BP 215 Nouakchott. Tel: (222) 52214; telex: 581 **Office hours** 0800–1500 Sat–Wed; 0800–1300 Thu **Banking hours** 0700–1500 Sun–Thu **Airports** international airports: Nouakchott, Nouâdhibou; six domestic airports; total passenger km: 301 million (1995) **Major ports** Nouâdhibou **Chief tourist attractions** game reserves; national parks; historic sites, several of which have been listed by UNESCO under its World Heritage programme **Major holidays** 1 January, 1, 25 May, 10 July, 28 November; variable: Eid-ul-Adha, end of Ramadan, New Year (Muslim), Prophet's Birthday

Chronology

early Christian era A Roman province with the name Mauritania, after the Mauri, its Berber inhabitants who became active in the long-distance salt trade. **7th–11th centuries** Eastern Mauritania was incorporated in the larger Ghana Empire, centred on Mali to the east, but with its capital at Kumbi in southeast Mauritania. The Berbers were reduced to vassals and converted to Islam in the 8th century. **11th–12th centuries** The area's Sanhadja Berber inhabitants, linked to the Morocco-based Almoravid Empire, destroyed the Ghana Empire and spread Islam among neighbouring peoples. **13th–15th centuries** Southeast Mauritania formed part of the Muslim Mali Empire, which extended to the east and south. **1441** Coast visited by Portuguese, who founded port of Arguin and captured Africans to sell as slaves. **15th–16th centuries** Eastern Mauritania formed part of Muslim Songhai Empire, which spread across western Sahel, and Arab tribes migrated into the area. **1817** Senegal Treaty recognized coastal region (formerly disputed by European nations) as French sphere of influence. **1903** Formally became French protectorate. **1920** Became French colony, within French West Africa. **1960** Independence achieved, with Moktar Ould Daddah, leader of Mauritanian People's Party (PPM), as president. New capital built at Nouakchott. **1968** Underlying tensions between agriculturalist black population of south and economically dominant semi-nomadic Arabo-Berber peoples, or Moors, of desert north became more acute after Arabic was made an official language (with French). **1976** Western Sahara, to the northwest, ceded by Spain to Mauritania and Morocco. Mauritania occupied the southern area and Morocco the mineral-rich north. Polisario Front formed in Sahara to resist this occupation and guerrilla war broke out, with the Polisario receiving backing from Algeria and Libya. **1979** A peace accord was signed with the Polisario Front in Algiers, in which Mauritania renounced its claims to southern Western Sahara and recognized the Polisario regime; diplomatic relations were restored with Algeria. **1981** Diplomatic relations with Morocco were broken after it annexed southern Western Sahara. **1984** Col Maaoya Sid'Ahmed Ould Taya became president. **1985** Relations with Morocco were restored. **1989** There were violent clashes in Mauritania and Senegal between Moors and black Africans, chiefly of Senegalese origins; over 50,000 Senegalese were expelled. **1991** An amnesty was called for political prisoners. Political parties were legalized and a new multiparty constitution was approved in a referendum. **1992** The first multiparty elections were largely boycotted by the opposition; Taya and his Social Democratic Republican Party (DSRP) were re-elected. Diplomatic relations with Senegal resumed. **1998** Cheik el Avia Ould Muhammad Khouna was appointed prime minister.

Mauritius Republic of

Area 1,865 sq km/720 sq mi; the island of Rodrigues is part of Mauritius; there are several small island dependencies **Capital** Port Louis (port) **Major towns/cities** Beau Bassin-Rose Hill, Curepipe, Quatre Bornes, Vacoas-Phoenix

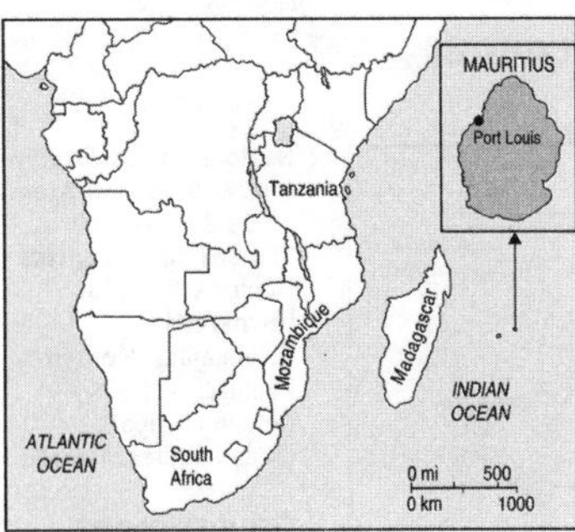

Government

Head of state Cassam Uteem from 1992 **Head of government** Navin Ramgoolam from 1995 **Political system** liberal democracy **Armed forces** no standing defence forces; 1,800-strong police mobile unit (1997) **Defence spend** (% GDP) 2.1 (1997) **Education spend** (% GNP) 4.3 (1995) **Health spend** (% GDP) 2.2 (1990–95) **Death penalty** abolished in 1985

Population and society

Population 1,149,000 (1999 est) **Population growth rate** 0.8% (1995–2000) **Ethnic groups** five principal ethnic groups: French, black Africans, Indians, Chinese, and Mulattos (or Creoles). Indo-Mauritians predominate, constituting 67% of the population, followed by Creoles (29%), Sino-Mauritians (3.5%), and Europeans (0.5%) **Religion** Hindu, Christian (mainly Roman Catholic), Muslim **Life expectancy** 68 (men); 75 (women) (1995–2000) **Literacy rate** 87% (men); 79% (women) (1997 est) **Unemployment** 9.8% (1995)

Economy and resources

GDP (US$) 4.2 billion (1998) **GNP** (US$) 4.29 billion (1998) **GNP per capita (PPP)** (US$) 9,400 (1998) **Real GDP growth** (% change on previous year) 5.5 (1998) **Consumer price inflation** 8.0% (1998) **Foreign debt** (US$) 2.47 billion (1997) **Exports** raw sugar, clothing, tea, molasses, jewellery. Principal market: UK 32.1% (1997) **Imports** textile yarn and fabrics, petroleum products, industrial machinery, motor vehicles, manufactured goods. Principal source: France 18.6% (1997)

▪ Tourist information

Time difference GMT +4 **Currency** Mauritian rupee **Language** English (official), French, Creole, Indian languages **Visa requirements** UK: visa not required. USA: visa not required **Embassy in the UK** 32/33 Elvaston Place, London SW7 5NW. Tel: (020) 7581 0294; fax: (020) 7823 8437 **British embassy** British High Commission, PO Box 186, Les Cascades Building, Edith Cavell Street, Port Louis. Tel: (230) 211 1361; fax: (230) 211 1369 **Chamber of commerce** Mauritius Chamber of Commerce and Industry, 3 Royal Street, Port Louis. Tel: (230) 208 3301; fax: (230) 208 0076 **Office hours** 0900–1600 Mon–Fri; 0900–1200 Sat (some offices only) **Banking hours** 0930–1430 Mon–Fri; 0900–1130 Sat (except Bank of Mauritius) **Airports** international airport: Plaisance (Sir Seewoosagur Ramgoolam, 48 km/30 mi southeast of Port Louis); two domestic airports; total passenger km: 3,875 million (1997 est) **Chief tourist attractions** fine scenery and beaches; pleasant climate; blend of cultures **Major holidays** 1–2 January, 12 March, 1 May, 1 November, 25 December; variable: Eid-ul-Adha, Diwali, end of Ramadan, Prophet's Birthday, Chinese Spring Festival (February)

Chronology

1598 Previously uninhabited, the island was discovered by the Dutch and named after Prince Morris of Nassau. **1710** Dutch colonists withdrew. **1721** Reoccupied by French East India Company, who renamed it Île de France, and established sugar cane and tobacco plantations worked by imported African slaves. **1814** Ceded to Britain by the Treaty of Paris. **1835** Slavery abolished; indentured Indian and Chinese labourers imported to work the sugar-cane plantations, which were later hit by competition from beet sugar. **1903** Formerly administered with Seychelles, it became a single colony. **1936** Mauritius Labour Party (MLP) founded, drawing strong support from sugar workers. **1957** Internal self-government granted. **1968** Independence achieved from Britain within Commonwealth, with Seewoosagur Ramgoolam of centrist Indian-dominated MLP as prime minister. **1971** A state of emergency was temporarily imposed as a result of industrial unrest. **1982** Aneerood Jugnauth, of the moderate socialist Mauritius Socialist Movement (MSM), became prime minister, pledging a programme of nonalignment, nationalization, and the creation of a republic. **1992** Became a republic within the Commonwealth, with Cassam Uteem elected as president. **1995** The MLP and the cross-community Mauritian Militant Movement (MMM) coalition won election victory; Navin Ramgoolam (MLP) became the prime minister.

Mexico United States of

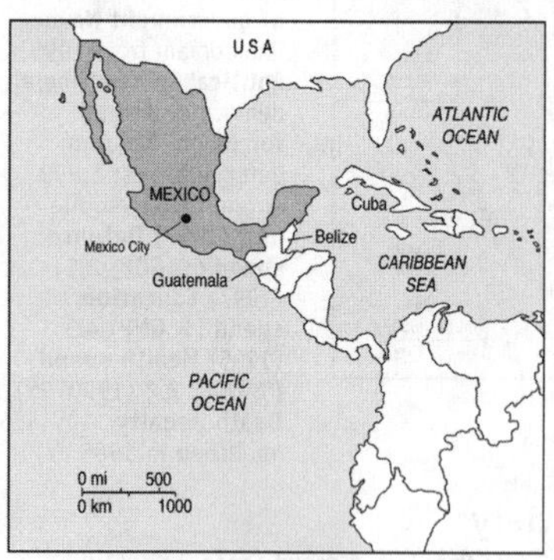

National name *Estados Unidos Mexicanos* **Area** 1,958,201 sq km/ 756,061 sq mi **Capital** Mexico City **Major towns/cities** Guadalajara, Monterrey, Puebla, Netzahualcóyotl, Ciudad Juárez, Tijuana

Government

Head of state and government Ernesto Zedillo Ponce de León from 1994 **Political system** liberal democracy **Armed forces** 175,000; rural defence militia of 15,000 (1997) **Conscription** one year, part-time (conscripts selected by lottery) **Defence spend** (% GDP) 1 (1997) **Education spend** (% GNP) 4.9 (1996) **Health spend** (% GDP) 2.7 (1996) **Death penalty** only for exceptional crimes; last execution 1937

Population and society

Population 97,366,000 (1999 est) **Population growth rate** 1.6% (1995–2000); 1.5% (2000–05) **Ethnic groups** around 60% mestizo (mixed American Indian and Spanish descent), 30% American Indians, remainder mainly of European origin **Religion** Roman Catholic **Life expectancy** 70 (men); 76 (women) (1995–2000) **Literacy rate** 92% (men); 88% (women) (1997 est) **Unemployment** 3.2% (1998)

Economy and resources

GDP (US$) 393.2 billion (1998) **GNP** (US$) 380.9 billion (1998) **GNP per capita (PPP)** (US$) 8,190 (1998 est) **Real GDP growth** (% change on previous year) 4.3 (1998) **Consumer price inflation** 13.1% (1998) **Foreign debt** (US$) 149.7 billion (1997) **Resources** petroleum, natural gas, zinc, salt, silver, copper, coal, mercury, manganese, phosphates, uranium, strontium sulphide **Exports** petroleum and petroleum products, engines and spare parts for motor vehicles, motor vehicles, electrical and electronic goods, fresh and preserved vegetables, coffee, cotton. Principal market: USA 81.9% (1998) **Imports** motor vehicle chassis, industrial machinery and equipment, iron and steel, telecommunications apparatus, organic chemicals, cereals and cereal preparations, petroleum and petroleum products. Principal source: USA 73.9% (1998)

▪ Tourist information

Time difference GMT –6/8 **Currency** Mexican peso **Language** Spanish (official); Nahuatl, Maya, Zapoteco, Mixteco, Otomi **Visa requirements** UK: visa (tourist card) required. USA: visa (tourist card) required **Embassy in the UK** 42 Hertford Street, London W1Y 7TF. Tel: (020) 7499 8586; fax: (020) 7495 4053 **British embassy** Apartado 96 bis, Rió Lerma 71, Colonia Cuauhtémoc, 06500 Mexico Distrito Federal. Tel: (5) 207 2089; fax: (5) 207 7672 **Chamber of commerce** Confederacíon de Cámaras Nacionales de Comercio, Servicios y Turismo, Apartado 113 bis, 2° y 3°, Balderas 144, Centro Curuhtémoc, 06079 Mexico Distrito Federal. Tel: (5) 709 1559; fax: (5) 709 1152 **Office hours** vary considerably; usually 0900–1600 Mon–Fri **Banking hours** 0900–1330 Mon–Fri; some banks open Sat afternoon **Airports** international airports: Mexico City (Benito Juárez), Guadalajara (Miguel Hidalgo), Acapulco (General Juan N Alvarez), Monterrey (General Mariano Escobeno), and 40 others; 39 domestic airports; total passenger km: 22,243 million (1997 est) **Major ports** 49 ocean ports **Chief tourist attractions** coastal scenery; volcanoes; Sierra Nevada (Sierra Madre) mountain range; Mayan and Aztec monuments and remains; Spanish colonial churches and other buildings **Major holidays** 1 January, 5 February, 21 March, 1, 5 May, 1, 16 September, 12 October, 2, 20 November, 12, 25, 31 December; variable: Holy Thursday, Good Friday

Chronology

c. 2600 BC Mayan civilization originated in Yucatán peninsula. **1000–500 BC** Zapotec civilization developed around Monte Albán in southern Mexico. **4th–10th centuries AD** Mayan Empire at its height. **10th–12th centuries** Toltecs ruled much of Mexico from their capital at Tula. **12th century** Aztecs migrated south into the valley of Mexico. **c. 1325** Aztecs began building their capital Tenochtitlán on site of present-day Mexico City. **15th century** Montezuma I built up the Aztec Empire in central Mexico. **1519–21** Hernán Cortes conquered Aztec Empire and secured Mexico for Spain. **1520** Montezuma II, last king of the Aztecs, was killed. **1535** Mexico became Spanish viceroyalty of New Spain; plantations and mining developed with Indian labour. **1519–1607** Indigenous population reduced from 21 million to 1 million, due mainly to lack of resistance to diseases transported from Old World. **1810** Father Miguel Hidalgo led unsuccessful revolt against Spanish. **1821** Independence proclaimed by Augustín de Iturbide with support of Church and landowners. **1822** Iturbide overthrew provisional government and proclaimed himself Emperor Augustín I. **1824** Federal republic established amid continuing public disorder. **1824–55** Military rule of Antonio López de Santa Anna, who imposed stability (he became president in 1833). **1846–48** Mexican War: Mexico lost California and New Mexico to USA. **1848** Revolt of Mayan Indians suppressed. **1855** Benito Juárez aided overthrow of Santa Anna's dictatorship. **1857–60** Sweeping liberal reforms and anti-clerical legislation introduced by Juárez led to civil war with conservatives. **1861** Mexico suspended payment on foreign debt leading to French military intervention; Juárez resisted with US support. **1864** Supported by conservatives, France installed Archduke Maximilian of Austria as emperor of Mexico. **1867** Maximilian shot by republicans as French troops withdrew; Juárez resumed presidency. **1872** Death of Juárez. **1876** Gen Porfirio Diaz established dictatorship; Mexican economy modernized through foreign investment. **1911** Revolution overthrew Diaz; liberal president Francisco Madero introduced radical land reform and labour legislation but political disorder increased. **1914 and 1916–17** US military intervened to quell disorder. **1917** New constitution, designed to ensure permanent democracy, adopted with US encouragement. **1924–35** Government dominated by anti-clerical Gen Plutarco Calles, who introduced further social reforms. **1929** Foundation of National Revolutionary Party (PRFN), renamed PRI in 1946. **1938** President Lázaro Cárdenas nationalized all foreign-owned oil wells in face of US opposition. **1942** Mexico declared war on Germany and Japan (and so regained US favour). **1946–52** Miguel Alemán first of succession of authoritarian PRI presidents to seek moderation and stability rather than further radical reform. **1960s** Rapid industrial growth partly financed by borrowing. **1976** Huge oil reserves were discovered in the southeastern state of Chiapas; oil production tripled in six years. **1982** Falling oil prices caused a grave financial crisis; Mexico defaulted on debt. **1985** An earthquake in Mexico City killed thousands. **1994** There was an uprising in Chiapas by the Zapatista National Liberation Army (EZLN), seeking rights for the Mayan Indian population; Mexico formed the North American Free

Mexico: States

State	Capital	Area sq km	Area sq mi	Population (1995)
Aguascalientes	Aguascalientes	5,589	2,157	862,700
Baja California Norte	Mexicali	70,113	27,071	2,112,100
Baja California Sur	La Paz	73,677	28,447	375,500
Campeche	Campeche	51,833	20,013	642,500
Chiapas	Tuxtla Gutiérrez	73,887	28,528	3,584,800
Chihuahua	Chihuahua	247,087	95,400	2,793,500
Coahuila	Saltillo	151,571	58,522	2,173,800
Colima	Colima	5,455	2,106	488,000
Durango	Victoria de Durango	119,648	46,196	1,431,700
Guanajuato	Guanajuato	30,589	11,810	4,406,600
Guerrero	Chilpancingo	63,794	24,631	2,916,600
Hidalgo	Pachuca de Soto	20,987	8,103	2,112,500
Jalisco	Guadalajara	80,137	30,941	5,991,200
México	Toluca de Lerdo	21,461	8,286	11,708,000
Michoacán	Morelia	59,864	23,113	3,870,600
Morelos	Cuernavaca	4,941	1,908	1,442,700
Nayarit	Tepic	27,621	10,664	896,700
Nuevo León	Monterrey	64,555	24,925	3,550,100
Oaxaca	Oaxaca de Juárez	95,364	36,820	3,228,900
Puebla	Puebla de Zaragoza	33,919	13,096	4,624,400
Querétaro	Querétaro	11,769	4,544	1,250,500
Quintana Roo	Chetumal	50,350	19,440	703,500
San Luis Potosí	San Luis Potosí	62,848	24,266	2,200,800
Sinaloa	Culiacán Rosales	58,092	22,429	2,425,700
Sonora	Hermosillo	184,934	71,403	2,085,500
Tabasco	Villahermosa	24,661	9,522	1,748,800
Tamaulipas	Ciudad Victoria	79,829	30,821	2,527,300
Tlaxcala	Tlaxcala	3,914	1,511	883,900
Veracruz	Jalapa Enríquez	72,815	28,114	6,737,300
Yucatán	Mérida	39,340	15,189	1,556,600
Zacatecas	Zacatecas	75,040	28,973	1,336,500

Trade Area (NAFTA) with the USA and Canada. Presidential elections were won by Ernesto Zedillo Ponce de León. **1995** The government agreed to offer greater autonomy to Mayan Indians in Chiapas. **1996** There were short-lived peace talks with the EZLN; and violent attacks against the government by the new leftist Popular Revolutionary Army (EPR) increased. **1997** The PRI lost its assembly majority. A civilian counterpart to the Zapatista rebels, the Zapatista National Liberation Front (EZLN), was formed. **1998** A lapsed peace accord with Zapatist rebels was reactivated, but talks between the government and the rebels broke down.

Micronesia Federated States of

Area 700 sq km/270 sq mi **Capital** Kolonia, in Pohnpei state **Major towns/cities** Weno, in Chuuk state; Lelu, in Kosrae state

Government

Head of state and government Jacob Nena from 1997 **Political system** liberal democracy **Armed forces** USA is responsible for country's defence **Death penalty** laws do not provide for the death penalty for any crime

Population and society

Population 116,000 (1999 est) **Population growth rate** 2% (1995–2000) **Ethnic groups** main ethnic groups are the Trukese (41%) and Pohnpeian (26%), both Micronesian **Religion** Christianity (mainly Roman Catholic in Yap state, Protestant elsewhere) **Life expectancy** 67 (men); 71 (women) (1995–2000) **Literacy rate** 91% (men); 88% (women) (1980 est) **Unemployment** 18.2% (1994)

Economy and resources

GDP (US$) 213 million (1998 est) **GNP** (US$) 203 million (1998) **GNP per capita (PPP)** (US$) 3,920 (1998 est) **Real GDP growth** (% change on previous year) 1.1 (1998 est) **Consumer price inflation** 3% (1996) **Exports** copra, pepper, fish. Principal market: Japan 84.8% (1996) **Imports** manufactured goods, machinery and transport equipment, mineral fuels. Principal source: USA 73.2% (1996)

▪ Tourist information

Time difference GMT +10 (Chuuk and Yap); +11 (Kosrae and Pohnpei) **Currency** US dollar **Language** English (official) and eight local languages **Visa requirements** UK: visa not required for a stay of up to 30 days. USA: visa not required **Embassy in the UK** Micronesia has no diplomatic representation in the UK; the Department of Trade and Industry has a Pacific Islands Desk. Tel: (020) 7215 4760; fax: (020) 7215 4398 **British embassy** the UK has no diplomatic representation in Micronesia **Chamber of commerce** Resources and Development Department, Pohnpei 96941. Tel: (691) 320 5133. Resources and Development Department, Chuuk 96942. Tel: (691) 330 2552; fax: (691) 330 4194 **Airports** international airports: Pohnpei (5 km/3 mi from Kolonia), Chuuk, Yap, Kosrae; domestic services also operate between these airports **Major ports** Teketik, Lepukos, Okak **Chief tourist attractions** excellent conditions for scuba-diving (notably in Chuuk Lagoon); ancient ruined city of Nan Madol on Pohnpei; World War II battle sites and relics (many underwater) **Major holidays** 1 January, 10 May, 24 October, 3 November, 25 December (some variations from island to island)

Chronology

***c.* 1000 BC** Micronesians first settled the islands. **1525** Portuguese navigators first visited Yap and Ulithi islands in the Carolines (Micronesia). **later 16th century** Fell under Spanish influence. **1874** Spanish rule formally declared in face of increasing encroachment by German traders. **1885** Yap seized by German naval forces, but was restored to Spain after arbitration by Pope Leo XIII on the condition that Germany was allowed freedom of trade. **1899** Purchased for $4.5 million by Germany from Spain, after the latter's defeat in the Spanish–American War. **1914** Occupied by Japan at the outbreak of World War I. **1919** Administered under League of Nations mandate by Japan, and vigorously colonized. **1944** Occupied by USA after Japanese forces defeated in World War II. **1947** Administered by USA as part of the United Nations (UN) Trust Territory of the Pacific Islands, under the name of the Federated States of Micronesia (FSM). **1979** A constitution was adopted that established a federal system for its four constituent states (Yap, Chuuk, Pohnpei, and Kosrae) and internal self-government. **1986** The Compact of Free Association was entered into with the USA, granting the islands self-government with the USA retaining responsibility for defence and security until 2001. **1990** UN trust status was terminated. **1991** Independence agreed, with Bailey Olter as president. Entered into United Nations (UN) membership. **1997** Jacob Nena was sworn in as president after the existing president, Bailey Olter, was incapacitated by a stroke.

Moldova Republic of

National name *Republica Moldoveneasca* **Area** 33,700 sq km/13,011 sq mi **Capital** Chişinău (Kishinev) **Major towns/cities** Tiraspol, Beltsy, Bendery

Government

Head of state Petru Lucinschi from 1997 **Head of government** Vladimir Voronin from 1999 **Political system** emergent democracy **Armed forces** 11,000 (1997) **Conscription** military service is compulsory for up to 18 months **Defence spend** (% GDP) 4.4 (1997) **Education spend** (% GNP) 9.7 (1996) **Health spend** (% GDP) 4.9 (1990–95) **Death penalty** abolished in 1995

Population and society

Population 4,379,000 (1999 est) **Population growth rate** 0.02% (1995–2000) **Ethnic groups** 65% ethnic Moldovan (Romanian), 14% Ukrainian, 13% ethnic Russian, 4% Gagauzi, 2% Bulgarian, 2% Jewish **Religion** Russian Orthodox **Life expectancy** 64 (men); 72 (women) (1995–2000) **Literacy rate** 99% (men); 97% (women) (1997 est) **Unemployment** 10.4% (1998 est)

Economy and resources

GDP (US$) 1.9 billion (1998 est) **GNP** (US$) 1.8 billion (1998) **GNP per capita (PPP)** (US$) 1,510 (1998 est) **Real GDP growth** (% change on previous year) –7 (1998) **Consumer price inflation** 7.7% (1998) **Foreign debt** (US$) 1.04 billion (1997) **Resources** lignite, phosphorites, gypsum, building materials; petroleum and natural gas deposits discovered in the early 1990s were not yet exploited in 1996 **Exports** food and agricultural products, machinery and equipment, textiles, clothing. Principal market: Russia 53% (1998) **Imports** mineral fuels, energy and mineral products, mechanical engineering products, foodstuffs, chemicals, textiles, clothing. Principal source: Russia 21.7% (1998)

▪ Tourist information

Time difference GMT +2 **Currency** leu **Language** Moldovan **Visa requirements** UK: visa required. USA: visa required **Embassy in the UK** 219 Marsh Wall, Isle of Dogs, London E14 9PD. Tel: (020) 7538 8600; fax: (020) 7538 5967 **British embassy** the British Embassy in Moscow (see Russian Federation) deals with enquiries relating to Moldova **Chamber of commerce** Chamber of Commerce and Industry of the Republic of Moldova, 28 Emineskou, 277012 Chişinău. Tel: (2) 221 552; fax: (2) 233 810 **Airports** international airports: Chişinău; no domestic services; total passenger km: 211 million (1995) **Major holidays** 1, 7–8 January, 8 March, 9 May, 27, 31 August; variable: Mertsishor (Spring Festival, first week in March), Good Friday, Easter Monday

Chronology

AD 106 The current area covered by Moldova, which lies chiefly between the Prut River, bordering Romania in the west, and the Dniestr River, with Ukraine in the east, was conquered by the Roman Emperor Trajan and

became part of the Roman province of Dacia. It was known in earlier times as Bessarabia. **mid-14th century** Formed part of an independent Moldovan principality, which included areas, such as Bukovina to the west, that are now part of Romania. **late 15th century** Under Stephen IV the Great the principality reached the height of its power. **16th century** Became a tributary of the Ottoman Turks. **1774–75** Moldovan principality, though continuing to recognize Turkish overlordship, was placed under Russian protectorship; Bukovina was lost to Austria. **1812** Bessarabia ceded to tsarist Russia. **1856** Remainder of Moldovan principality became largely independent of Turkish control. **1859** Moldovan Assembly voted to unite with Wallachia, to the southwest, to form the state of Romania, ruled by Prince Alexandru Ion Cuza. The state became fully independent in 1878. **1918** Following the Russian Revolution, Bessarabia was seized and incorporated within Romania. **1924** Moldovan autonomous Soviet Socialist Republic (SSR) created, as part of Soviet Union, comprising territory east of Dniestr River. **1940** Romania returned Bessarabia, east of Prut River, to Soviet Union, which divided it between Moldovan SSR and Ukraine, with Trans-Dniestr region transferred from Ukraine to Moldova. **1941** Moldovan SSR occupied by Romania and its wartime ally Germany. **1944** Red Army reconquered Bessarabia. **1946–47** Widespread famine as agriculture was collectivized; rich farmers and intellectuals were liquidated. **1950** Immigration by settlers from Russia and Ukraine as industries were developed. **late 1980s** There was an upsurge in Moldovan nationalism, encouraged by the *glasnost* initiative of reformist Soviet leader Mikhail Gorbachev. **1988** The Moldovan Movement in Support of Perestroika (economic restructuring) campaigned for accelerated political reform. **1989** There were nationalist demonstrations in Kishinev (now Chişinău). The Moldovan Popular Front (MPF) was founded; Moldovan was made the state language. There were campaigns for autonomy among ethnic Russians, strongest in industrialized Trans-Dniestr region, and Turkish-speaking but Orthodox Christian Gagauz minority in southwest. **1990** The MPF polled strongly in parliamentary elections and Mircea Snegur, a reform-nationalist communist, became president. Economic and political sovereignty was declared. **1991** Independence was declared and the Communist Party outlawed after a conservative coup in Moscow against Gorbachev; joined Commonwealth of Independent States (CIS). There was insurrection in the Trans-Dniestr region. **1992** Admitted into United Nations and the Conference on Security and Cooperation in Europe; a peace agreement was signed with Russia to end the civil war in Trans-Dniestr, giving special status to the region. The MPF-dominated government fell; A 'government of national accord' was formed, headed by Andrei Sangheli and dominated by the ADP. **1993** A new currency, the leu, was introduced. A privatization programme was launched and closer ties were established with Russia. **1994** Parliamentary elections were won by the ADP. Plebiscite rejected nationalist demands for a merger with Romania. Russia agreed to withdraw Trans-Dniestr troops by 1997. **1995** Joined Council of Europe; economic growth resumed. **1996** Petru Lucinschi was elected president. **1997** A cooperation agreement was signed with the Dniestr region. A law was passed that provided for elections using proportional representation. **1999** A new coalition government was formed, headed by Ion Sturza. It fell in November, and Vladimir Voronin, a communist, succeeded as prime minister.

Monaco Principality of

National name *Principauté de Monaco* **Area** 1.95 sq km/0.75 sq mi **Capital** Monaco-Ville **Major towns/cities** Monte Carlo, La Condamine; heliport Fontvieille

Government

Head of state Prince Rainier III from 1949 **Head of government** Michel Leveque from 1998 **Political system** liberal democracy **Armed forces** no standing defence forces; defence is the responsibility of France **Education spend** (% GNP) 5.6 (1992) **Death penalty** abolished in 1962

Population and society

Population 32,200 (1999 est) **Population growth rate** 1.1% (1995–2025) **Ethnic groups** 58% French; 19% Monegasque **Religion** Roman Catholic **Life expectancy** 75 (men); 82 (women) (1998 est) **Literacy rate** 99% (men); 99% (women) (1997 est) **Unemployment** 2.8% (1998 est)

Economy and resources

GDP (US$) 850 million (1996 est) **GNP** N/A (there are no available data for GNP separate from the figures for France) **GNP per capita (PPP)** (US$) 26,170 (1996 est) **Real GDP growth** (% change on previous year) N/A **Imports and exports** largely dependent on imports from France; full customs integration with France

▪ Tourist information

Time difference GMT +1 **Currency** French franc **Language** French (official); English, Italian **Visa requirements** UK: visa not required. USA: visa not required **Embassy in the UK** Embassy and Consulate General, 4 Cromwell Place, London SW7 2JE. Tel: (020) 7225 2679; fax: (020) 7581 8161 **British embassy** British Consulate, BP 265, 33 boulevard Princesse Charlotte, MC-98005, Monaco, Cedex. Tel: 9350 9966; fax: 9350 1447 **Chamber of commerce** Conseil Economique, 8 rue Louis Notari, MC-98000, Monaco, Cedex. Tel: 9330 2082; fax: 9350 0596 **Office hours** 0900–1200 and 1400–1800 Mon–Fri **Banking hours** 0900–1200 and 1400–1630 Mon–Fri **Airports** international airports: none – helicopter services link the principality with the nearest airport, Nice (Nice-Côte d'Azur); total passenger km: 1 million (1995) **Chief tourist attractions** dramatic scenery; Mediterranean climate; 13th-century Palais du Prince; numerous entertainment facilities, including casinos, Jardin Exotique, Musée Océanographique, world championship Grand Prix motor race and annual car rally at Monte Carlo **Major holidays** 1, 27 January, 1, 8 May, 14 July, 15 August, 3 September, 1, 11, 19 November, 8, 25 December; variable: Easter Monday, Whit Monday

Chronology

1191 The Genoese took control of Monaco, which had formerly been part of the Holy Roman Empire. **1297** Came under the rule of the Grimaldi dynasty, the current ruling family, who initially allied themselves to the French. **1524–1641** Came under Spanish protection. **1793** Annexed by France during French Revolutionary Wars. One member of the ruling family was guillotined; the rest imprisoned. **1815** Placed under protection of Sardinia. **1848** The towns of Menton and Roquebrune, which had formed the greater part of the principality, seceded and later became part of France. **1861** Franco-Monegasque treaty restored Monaco's independence under French protection; the first casino was built. **1865** Customs union established with France. **1918** France given veto over succession to throne and established that if a reigning prince dies without a male heir, Monaco is to be incorporated into France. **1941–45** Occupied successively by Italians and Germans during World War II. **1949** Prince Rainier III ascended the throne. **1956** Prince Rainier married US actor Grace Kelly. **1958** Birth of male heir, Prince Albert. **1962** A new, more liberal constitution was adopted. **1982** Princess Grace died in a car accident. **1993** Joined United Nations. **1998** Michel Leveque was appointed head of government.

Mongolia State of (formerly Outer Mongolia, People's Republic of Mongolia)

National name *Mongol Uls* **Area** 1,565,000 sq km/604,246 sq mi **Capital** Ulaanbaatar (Ulan Bator) **Major towns/cities** Darhan, Choybalsan, Erdenet

Government

Head of state Natsagiyn Bagabandi from 1997 **Head of government** Janlaviyn Narantsatsralt from 1998 **Political system** emergent democracy **Armed forces** 9,000; plus a paramilitary force of around 5,900 (1997) **Conscription**

military service is compulsory for 12 months **Defence spend** (% GDP) 1.7 (1996) **Education spend** (% GNP) 6.4 (1996) **Health spend** (% GDP) 4.8 (1990–95) **Death penalty** retained and used for ordinary crimes

Population and society

Population 2,621,000 (1999 est) **Population growth rate** 1.7% (1995–2000) **Ethnic groups** 90% Mongol, 4% Kazakh, 2% Chinese, and 2% Russian **Religion** officially none (Tibetan Buddhist Lamaism suppressed in 1930s) **Life expectancy** 64 (men); 67 (women) (1995–2000) **Literacy rate** 89% (men); 79% (women) (1997 est) **Unemployment** 7.6% (1997 est)

Economy and resources

GDP (US$) 1.04 billion (1998) **GNP** (US$) 1 billion (1998) **GNP per capita (PPP)** (US$) 1,520 (1998) **Real GDP growth** (% change on previous year) 3.5 (1998) **Consumer price inflation** 10.1% (1998) **Foreign debt** (US$) 718 million (1997) **Resources** copper, nickel, zinc, molybdenum, phosphorites, tungsten, tin, fluorospar, gold, lead; reserves of petroleum discovered 1994 **Exports** minerals and metals (primarily copper concentrate), consumer goods, foodstuffs, agricultural products. Principal market: China 30.1% (1998) **Imports** engineering goods, mineral fuels and products, industrial consumer goods, foodstuffs. Principal source: Russia 30.6% (1998)

▪ Tourist information

Time difference GMT +8 **Currency** tugrik **Language** Khalkha Mongolian (official); Chinese, Russian, and Turkic languages **Visa requirements** UK: visa required. USA: visa required **Embassy in the UK** 7 Kensington Court, London W8 5DL. Tel: (020) 7937 0150; fax: (020) 7937 1117 **British embassy** PO Box 703, 30 Enkh Taivny Gudammzh, Ulaanbaatar 13. Tel: (1) 358 133; fax: (1) 358 036 **Chamber of commerce** Mongolian Chamber of Commerce and Industry, Sambuugiyn Gudamj 11, Ulaanbaatar 38. Tel: (1) 324 620; telex: 79336 **Office hours** 0900–1800 Mon–Fri; 0900–1500 Sat **Banking hours** 1000–1500 Mon–Fri **Airports** international airports: Ulaanbaatar (Buyant Ukha); six domestic airports; total passenger km: 516 million (1995) **Chief tourist attractions** spectacular scenery, including Gobi Desert and Altai chain; wildlife; historical relics; tourism is relatively undeveloped **Major holidays** 1–2 January, 8 March, 1 May, 1 June, 10 July (3 days), 7 November; variable: Tsagaan (Lunar New Year, January/February, 2 days)

Chronology

AD 1206 Nomadic Mongol tribes united by Genghis Khan to form nucleus of vast Mongol Empire which, stretching across central Asia, reached its zenith under Genghis Khan's grandson, Kublai Khan. **late 17th century** Conquered by China to become province of Outer Mongolia. **1911** Independence proclaimed by Mongolian nationalists after Chinese 'republican revolution'; tsarist Russia helped Mongolia to secure autonomy, under a traditionalist Buddhist monarchy in the form of a reincarnated lama. **1915** Chinese sovereignty reasserted. **1921** Chinese rule overthrown with Soviet help. **1924** People's Republic proclaimed on death of king, when the monarchy was abolished; defeudalization programme launched, entailing collectivization of agriculture and suppression of lama Buddhism. **1932** Armed antigovernment uprising suppressed with Soviet assistance; 100,000 killed in political purges. **1946** China recognized Mongolia's independence. **1952** Death of Marshal Horloogiyn Choybalsan, the dominant force in the ruling communist Mongolian People's Revolutionary Party (MPRP) since 1939. **1958** Yumjaagiyn Tsedenbal became the dominant figure in MPRP and country. **1962** Joined Comecon. **1966** 20-year friendship, cooperation, and mutual-assistance pact signed with Soviet Union (USSR). Relations with China deteriorated. **1987** There was a reduction in the number of Soviet troops; Mongolia's external contacts broadened. The tolerance of traditional social customs encouraged a nationalist revival. **1989** Further Soviet troop reductions. **1990** A demonstrations and democratization campaign was launched, influenced by events in Eastern Europe. Ex-communist MPRP elected in the first free multiparty elections; Punsalmaagiyn Ochirbat was indirectly elected president. Mongolian script was readopted. **1991** A privatization programme was launched. GDP declined by 10%. **1992** The MPRP returned to power in assembly elections held under a new, noncommunist constitution. The economic situation worsened; GDP again declined by 10%. **1993** Ochirbat won the first direct presidential elections. **1996** The economy showed signs of revival. The Union Coalition won assembly elections, defeating the MPRP and ending 75 years of communist rule. A defence cooperation agreement was signed with the USA. **1997** The ex-communist Natsagiyn Bagabandi was elected MPRP chairman and then became president. An economic shock therapy programme, supervised by IMF and World Bank, created unemployment and made the government unpopular. All taxes and tariffs on trade were abolished. **1998** National Democratic Party (DU) leader Tsakhiagiin Elbegdorj became prime minister. His government was toppled after losing a no-confidence vote. Attempts to form a new DU-led government, led by Rinchinnyamiin Amarjargal, failed. Janlaviyn Narantsatsralt, member of the MNDP, became prime minister.

Morocco Kingdom of

National name *al-Mamlaka al-Maghrebia* **Area** 458,730 sq km/ 177,115 sq mi (excluding Western Sahara) **Capital** Rabat **Major towns/cities** Casablanca, Marrakesh, Fez, Oujda, Kenitra, Tetouan, Meknès

Government

Head of state Hassan II from 1961 **Head of government** Abderrahmane Youssoufi from 1998 **Political system** emergent democracy **Armed forces** 196,300; paramilitary forces of 42,000 (1997) **Conscription** 18 months **Defence spend** (% GDP) 4.2 (1997) **Education spend** (% GNP) 5.3 (1996) **Health spend** (% GDP) 1.6 (1990–95) **Death penalty** retained and used for ordinary crimes

Population and society

Population 27,866,000 (1999 est) **Population growth rate** 1.8% (1995–2000); 1.6% (2000–05) **Ethnic groups** majority indigenous Berbers; sizeable Jewish minority **Religion** Sunni Muslim **Life expectancy** 65 (men); 69 (women) (1995–2000) **Literacy rate** 59% (men); 33% (women) (1997 est) **Unemployment** 17.8% (1996)

Economy and resources

GDP (US$) 33.5 billion (1998) **GNP** (US$) 34.8 billion (1998) **GNP per capita (PPP)** (US$) 3,120 (1998) **Real GDP growth** (% change on previous year) 6.1 (1998) **Consumer price inflation** 2.9% (1998) **Foreign debt** (US$) 19.3 billion (1997) **Resources** phosphate rock and phosphoric acid, coal, iron ore, barytes, lead, copper, manganese, zinc, petroleum, natural gas, fish **Exports** phosphates and phosphoric acid, mineral products, seafoods and seafood products, citrus fruit, tobacco, clothing, hosiery. Principal market: France 31.7% (1997) **Imports** crude petroleum, raw materials, wheat, chemicals, sawn wood, consumer goods. Principal source: France 26.6% (1997)

▪ Tourist information

Time difference GMT +/– 0 **Currency** dirham (DH) **Language** Arabic (official) 75%; Berber 25%, French, Spanish **Visa requirements** UK: visa not required. USA: visa not required **Embassy in the UK** 49 Queen's Gate Gardens, London SW7 5NE. Tel: (020) 7581 5001–4; fax: (020) 7225 3862 **British embassy** BP 45, 17 Boulevard de la Tour Hassan, Rabat. Tel: (7) 720 905/6; fax: (7) 704 531 **Chamber of commerce** La Fédération des Chambres de Commerce et de l'Industrie du Maroc, 6 rue d'Erfoud, Rabat-Agdal. Tel: (7) 767 078; fax: (7) 767 076 **Office hours** generally 0830–1200 and 1430–1830 Mon–Fri (September–July, except Ramadan); 0900–1500/1600 Mon–Fri (Ramadan and July–early September) **Banking hours** 0830–1130 and 1430–1700 Mon–Fri (winter); 0800–1530 Mon–Fri (summer) (hours may vary during Ramadan) **Airports** international airports: Casablanca (Mohammed V), Rabat (Salé), Tangier (Boukhalef Sohahel), Agadir (Al Massira), Fez (Sais), Marrakesh, Oujda, Al-Hocina el-Aaiun, Ouarzazate; domestic services operate between these; total passenger km: 5,247 million (1997) **Major ports** Casablanca, Tangier, Agadir **Chief tourist attractions** sunny climate; ancient sites and cities (notably Marrakesh , Fez, Meknès, Rabat); spectacular scenery; resorts on Atlantic and Mediterranean coasts **Major holidays** 1 January, 3 March, 1, 23 May, 9 July, 14 August, 6, 18 November; variable: Eid-ul-Adha (2 days), end of Ramadan (2 days), New Year (Muslim), Prophet's Birthday

Chronology

10th–3rd centuries BC Phoenicians from Tyre settled along north coast. **1st century AD** Northwest Africa became Roman province of Mauritania.

5th–6th centuries Invaded by Vandals and Visigoths. **682** Start of Arab conquest, followed by spread of Islam. **8th century** King Idris I established small Arab kingdom. **1056–1146** The Almoravids, a Berber dynasty based at Marrakesh, built an empire embracing Morocco and parts of Algeria and Spain. **1122–1268** After a civil war, the Almohads, a rival Berber dynasty, overthrew the Almoravids; Almohads extended empire but later lost most of Spain. **1258–1358** Beni Merin dynasty supplanted Almohads. **14th century** Moroccan Empire fragmented into separate kingdoms, based in Fez and Marrakesh. **15th century** Spain and Portugal occupied Moroccan ports; expulsion of Muslims from Spain in 1492. **16th century** Saadian dynasty restored unity of Morocco and resisted Turkish invasion. **1649** Foundation of current Alaouite dynasty of sultans; Morocco remained an independent and isolated kingdom. **1856** Under British pressure, the sultan opened Morocco to European commerce. **1860** Spain invaded Morocco, which was forced to cede the southwestern region of Ifni. **1905** A major international crisis was caused by German objections to increasing French influence in Morocco. **1911** Agadir Crisis: further German objections to French imperialism in Morocco were overcome by territorial compensation in central Africa. **1912** Morocco was divided into French and Spanish protectorates; the sultan was reduced to puppet ruler. **1921** Moroccan rebels, the Riffs, led by Abd el-Krim, defeated a large Spanish force at Anual. **1923** The city of Tangier was separated from Spanish Morocco and made a neutral international zone. **1926** French forces crushed Riff revolt. **1944** A nationalist party, Istiqlal, was founded to campaign for full independence. **1948** Consultative assemblies introduced. **1953–55** Serious anti-French riots. **1956** French and Spanish forces withdrew; Morocco regained effective independence under Sultan Muhammad V, who took title of king in 1957. **1961** Muhammad V succeeded by Hassan II. **1962** First constitution adopted; replaced in 1970 and 1972. **1965–77** King Hassan suspended the constitution and ruled by decree. **1969** Spanish overseas province of Ifni returned to Morocco. **1975** Spain withdrew from Western Sahara, leaving Morocco and Mauritania to divide it between themselves. **1976** Polisario Front, supported by Algeria, began guerrilla war in Western Sahara with the aim of securing its independence as the Sahrahwi Arab Democratic Republic. **1979** Mauritania withdrew from its portion of Western Sahara, which Morocco annexed after major battles with Polisario. **1984** Morocco signed mutual defence with Libya, which had previously supported Polisario. **1991** A UN-sponsored ceasefire came into effect in the Western Sahara. **1992** The constitution was amended in an attempt to increase the influence of parliament. **1996** A new two-chamber assembly was approved. **1998** Prime Minister Abderrahmane Youssoufi formed a centre-left coalition.

Mozambique People's Republic of

National name *República Popular de Moçambique* **Area** 799,380 sq km/308,640 sq mi **Capital** Maputo (and chief port) **Major towns/cities** Beira, Nampula, Nacala, Chimoio

Government

Head of state Joaquim Alberto Chissano from 1986 **Head of government** Pascoal Mocumbi from 1994 **Political system** emergent democracy **Armed forces** 6,100 (1997) **Conscription** early 1996 government was seeking to reintroduce compulsory military service, which had been suspended under the General Peace Accord **Defence spend** (% GDP) 3.9 (1997) **Education spend** (% GNP) 6.2 (1992) **Health spend** (% GDP) 4.6 (1990–97) **Death penalty** abolished in 1990

Population and society

Population 19,286,000 (1999 est) **Population growth rate** 2.5% (1995–2000); 2.8% (2000–05) **Ethnic groups** the majority belong to local groups, the largest being the Makua-Lomue, who comprise about 38% of the population; the other significant group is the Tsonga (24%) **Religion** animist, Roman Catholic, Muslim **Life expectancy** 44 (men); 47 (women) (1995–2000) **Literacy rate** 57% (men); 25% (women) (1997 est) **Unemployment** N/A

Economy and resources

GDP (US$) 3.96 billion (1998) **GNP** (US$) 3.6 billion (1998) **GNP per capita (PPP)** (US$) 850 (1998 est) **Real GDP growth** (% change on previous year) 10 (1998) **Consumer price inflation** –1.3% (1998) **Foreign debt** (US$) 5.9 billion (1997) **Resources** coal, salt, bauxite, graphite; reserves of iron ore, gold, precious and semi-precious stones, marble, natural gas (all largely unexploited in 1996) **Exports** shrimps and other crustaceans, cashew nuts, raw cotton, sugar, copra, lobsters. Principal market: Spain 17.1% (1996) **Imports** foodstuffs, capital goods, crude petroleum and petroleum products, machinery and spare parts, chemicals. Principal source: South Africa 54.6% (1996)

▪ Tourist information

Time difference GMT +2 **Currency** metical **Language** Portuguese (official); 16 African languages **Visa requirements** UK: visa required. USA: visa required **Embassy in the UK** 21 Fitzroy Square, London W1P 5HJ. Tel: (020) 7383 3800; fax: (020) 7383 3801 **British embassy** Caixa Postal 55, Avenida Vladimir I Léuine 310, Maputo. Tel: (1) 420 111/2/5/6/7; fax: (1) 421 666 **Chamber of commerce** Câmara de Comercio de Mozambique, CP 1836, Rua Mateus Sansão Mutemba 452, Maputo. Tel: (1) 491 970; telex: 6498 **Office hours** 0730–1200 and 1400–1730 Mon–Fri; 0800–1330 Sat **Banking hours** 0745–1115 Mon–Fri **Airports** international airports: Maputo (Mavalane), Beira, Nampula; five domestic airports; total passenger km: 290 million (1995) **Major ports** Beira, Nacala, Quelimane **Chief tourist attractions** Indian Ocean coastline with beaches bordered by lagoons, coral reefs, and strings of islands (travel within Mozambique can be dangerous due to risk of armed robbery and unexploded landmines) **Major holidays** 1 January, 3 February, 7 April, 1 May, 25 June, 7, 25 September, 25 December

Chronology

1st–4th centuries AD Bantu-speaking peoples settled in Mozambique. **8th–15th century** Arab gold traders established independent city-states on the coast. **1498** Portuguese navigator Vasco da Gama was the first European visitor; at this time the most important local power was the Maravi kingdom of the Mwene Matapa peoples, who controlled much of the Zambezi basin. **1626** The Mwene Matapa formally recognized Portuguese sovereignty. Portuguese soldiers set up private agricultural estates and used slave labour to exploit gold and ivory resources. **late 17th century** Portuguese temporarily pushed south of Zambezi by the ascendant Rozwi kingdom. **1752** First Portuguese colonial governor appointed; slave trade outlawed. **late 19th century** Concessions given by Portugal to private companies to develop and administer parts of Mozambique. **1930** Colonial Act established more centralized Portuguese rule, ending concessions to monopolistic companies and forging closer integration with Lisbon. **1951** Became an overseas province of Portugal and, economically, a cheap labour reserve for South Africa's mines. **1962** Frelimo (National Front for the Liberation of Mozambique) established in exile in Tanzania by Marxist guerrillas, including Samora Machel, to fight for independence. **1964** Fighting broke out between Frelimo forces and Portuguese troops, starting a ten-year liberation war; Portugal despatched 70,000 troops to Mozambique. **1969** Eduardo Mondlane, leader of Frelimo, was assassinated. **1975** Following revolution in Portugal, independence was achieved as a socialist republic, with Machel as president, Joaquim Chissano as prime minister, and Frelimo as the sole legal party; Portuguese settlers left the country. Lourenço Marques renamed Maputo. Key enterprises were nationalized. **1977** Renamo resistance group formed, with covert backing of South Africa. **1979** Machel encouraged Patriotic Front guerrillas in Rhodesia to accept Lancaster House Agreement, creating Zimbabwe. **1983** Good relations were restored with Western powers. **1984** The Nkomati Accord of nonaggression was signed with South Africa. **1986** Machel was killed in air crash near the South African border and was succeeded by Chissano. **1988** Tanzanian troops withdrawn from Mozambique. **1989** Renamo continued attacks on government facilities and civilians. **1990** One-party rule officially ended, and Frelimo abandoned Marxist–Leninism and embraced market economy. **1992** A peace accord was signed with Renamo. **1993** There were price riots in Maputo as a result of the implementation of IMF-promoted reforms to restructure the economy, which was devastated by war and drought. **1994** The demobilization of contending armies was completed. Chissano and Frelimo were re-elected in the first multiparty elections; Renamo (now a political party) agreed to cooperate with the government. Pascoal Mocumbi was appointed prime minister by President Chissano. **1995** Admitted to Commonwealth. **2000** Severe flooding was estimated to involve the loss of 10,000 lives and 1 million homes.

Myanmar Union of (formerly Burma)

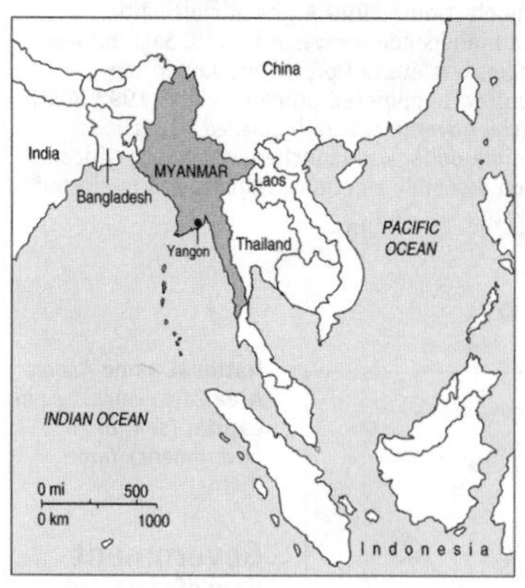

National name *Thammada Myanmar Naingngandaw* **Area** 676,577 sq km/261,226 sq mi **Capital** Yangon (formerly Rangoon) (and chief port) **Major towns/cities** Mandalay, Mawlamyine, Bago, Bassein, Taunggyi, Sittwe, Manywa

Government

Head of state and government Than Shwe from 1992 **Political system** military **Armed forces** 429,000; plus two paramilitary units totalling 85,300 (1997) **Conscription** military service is voluntary **Defence spend** (% GDP) 7.7 (1997) **Education spend** (% GNP) 1.3 (1995) **Health spend** (% GDP) 0.5 (1990–95) **Death penalty** retained and used for ordinary crimes

Population and society

Population 45,039,000 (1999 est) **Population growth rate** 1.2% (1995–2000) **Ethnic groups** Burmans, who predominate in the fertile central river valley and southern coastal and delta regions, constitute the ethnic majority, comprising 72% of the total population. Out of more than 100 minority communities, the most important are the Karen (7%), Shan (6%), Indians (6%), Chinese (3%), Kachin (2%), and Chin (2%). The indigenous minority communities, who predominate in mountainous border regions, show considerable hostility towards the culturally and politically dominant Burmans, undermining national unity **Religion** Hinayāna Buddhist 85%, animist, Christian, Muslim **Life expectancy** 59 (men); 62 (women) (1995–2000) **Literacy rate** 89% (men); 79% (women) (1997 est) **Unemployment** 4.1% (1997)

Economy and resources

GDP (US$) 261 billion (1998 est) **GNP** (US$) 134.1 billion (1996 est) **GNP per capita (PPP)** (US$) 1,280 (1996 est) **Real GDP growth** (% change on previous year) 4 (1998) **Consumer price inflation** 51% (1998) **Foreign debt** (US$) 5.07 billion (1997) **Resources** natural gas, petroleum, zinc, tin, copper, tungsten, coal, lead, gems, silver, gold **Exports** teak, rice, pulses and beans, rubber, hardwood, base metals, gems, cement. Principal market: India 13.1% (1998) **Imports** raw materials, machinery and transport equipment, tools and spares, construction materials, chemicals, consumer goods. Principal source: Singapore 31.2% (1998)

▪ Tourist information

Time difference GMT +6.5 **Currency** kyat **Language** Burmese (official), English **Visa requirements** UK: visa required. USA: visa required **Embassy in the UK** 19a Charles Street, Berkeley Square, London W1X 8ER. Tel: (020) 7629 6966; fax: (020) 7629 4169 **British embassy** PO Box 638, 80 Strand Road, Yangon. Tel: (1) 95300; fax: (1) 89566 **Chamber of commerce** Myanmar Foreign Trade Bank, PO Box 203, 80–86 Maha Bandoola Garden Street, Yangon. Tel: (1) 83129; fax: (1) 89585 **Office hours** 0930–1630 Mon–Fri **Banking hours** 1000–1400 Mon–Fri **Airports** international airports: Yangon (Mingaladon); 21 domestic airports; total passenger km: 147 million (1995) **Chief tourist attractions** palaces; Buddhist temples and shrines in Yangon, Mandalay, Taunggyi, and Pagan (notably Yangon's ancient Sule, Botataung, and Shwedagon pagodas); Indian Ocean coast; mountainous interior **Major holidays** 4 January, 12 February, 2, 27 March, 1 April, 1 May, 19 July, 1 October, 25 December; variable: New Year (Burmese), Thingyan (April, 4 days), end of Buddhist Lent (October), Full Moon days

Chronology

3rd century BC Sittoung valley settled by Mons; Buddhism introduced by missionaries from India. **3rd century AD** Arrival of Burmans from Tibet. **1057** First Burmese Empire established by King Anawrahta, who conquered Thaton, established capital inland at Pagan, and adopted Theravāda Buddhism. **1287** Pagan sacked by Mongols. **1531** Founding of Toungoo dynasty, which survived until mid-18th century. **1755** Nation reunited by Alaungpaya, with port of Rangoon as capital. **1824–26** First Anglo-Burmese war resulted in Arakan coastal strip, between Chittagong and Cape Negrais, being ceded to British India. **1852** Following defeat in second Anglo-Burmese war, Lower Burma, including Rangoon, was annexed by British. **1886** Upper Burma ceded to British after defeat of Thibaw in third Anglo-Burmese war; British united Burma, which was administered as a province of British India. **1886–96** Guerrilla warfare waged against British in northern Burma. **early 20th century** Burma developed as a major rice, teak and, later, oil exporter, drawing in immigrant labourers and traders from India and China. **1937** Became British crown colony in Commonwealth, with a degree of internal self-government. **1942** Invaded and occupied by Japan, who installed anti-British nationalist puppet government headed by Ba Maw. **1945** Liberated from Japanese control by British, assisted by nationalists Aung San and U Nu, formerly ministers in puppet government, who had formed the socialist Anti Fascist People's Freedom League (AFPFL). **1947** Assassination of Aung San and six members of interim government by political opponents. **1948** Independence achieved from Britain as Burma, with U Nu as prime minister. Left Commonwealth. Quasi-federal state established. **1958–60** Administered by emergency government, formed by army chief of staff Gen Ne Win. **1962** Gen Ne Win reassumed power in left-wing army coup; he proceeded to abolish federal system and follow the 'Burmese way to socialism', involving sweeping nationalization and international isolation, which crippled the economy. **1973–74** Adopted presidential-style 'civilian' constitution. **1975** The opposition National Democratic Front was formed by regionally-based minority groups, who mounted guerrilla insurgencies. **1987** There were student demonstrations in Rangoon as food shortages worsened. **1988** The government resigned after violent student demonstrations and workers' riots. Gen Saw Maung seized power in a military coup; over 2,000 were killed. **1989** Martial law was declared; thousands were arrested including advocates of democracy and human rights. The country was renamed Myanmar, and its capital Yangon. **1990** The landslide general election victory for opposition National League for Democracy (NLD) was ignored by the military junta; NLD leaders U Nu and Suu Kyi, the daughter of Aung San, were placed under house arrest. **1991** Martial law and human-rights abuses continued. Suu Kyi, still imprisoned, was awarded the Nobel Peace Prize. There was a pogrom against the Muslim community in the Arakan province in southwest Myanmar. Western countries imposed sanctions. **1992** Saw Maung was replaced as head of state by Than Shwe. Several political prisoners were liberated. Martial law was lifted, but restrictions on political freedom remained. **1993** A ceasefire was agreed with Kachin rebels in the northeast. **1995** Suu Kyi was released from house arrest, but her appointment as NLD leader was declared illegal. NLD boycotted the constitutional convention. **1996** Suu Kyi held the first party congress since her release; 200 supporters were detained by the government. There were major demonstrations in support of Suu Kyi. **1997** Admission to Association of South East Asian Nations (ASEAN) granted, despite US sanctions for human-rights abuses. **1998** Japan resumed a flow of aid, which had been stopped in 1988. The military junta ignored pro-democracy roadside protests by Aung San Suu Kyi and broke up student demonstrations. 300 members of the opposition NLD were released from detention.

Namibia Republic of (formerly South West Africa)

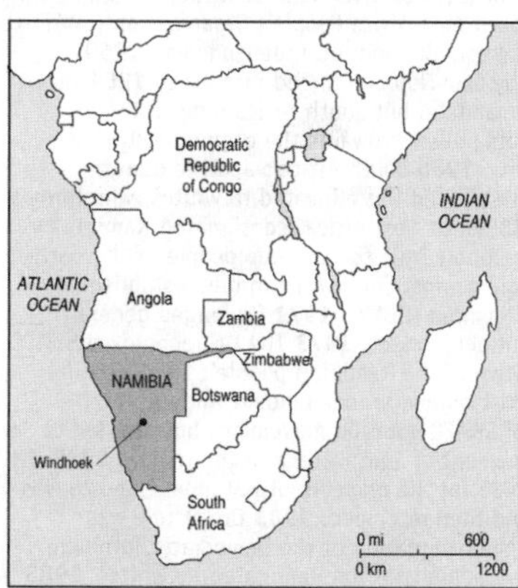

Area 824,300 sq km/318,262 sq mi **Capital** Windhoek **Major towns/cities** Swakopmund, Rehoboth, Rundu

Government

Head of state Sam Nujoma from 1990 **Head of government** Hage Geingob from 1990 **Political system** emergent democracy **Armed forces** 5,800 (1997) **Conscription** military service is voluntary **Defence spend** (% GDP) 3.5 (1997) **Education spend** (% GNP) 9.1 (1996) **Health spend** (% GDP) 3.7 (1990–95) **Death penalty** abolished in 1990

Population and society

Population 1,695,000 (1999 est) **Population growth rate** 2.2% (1995–2000) **Ethnic groups** 85% black African, of which 51% belong to the Ovambo tribe; the remainder includes the pastoral Nama and hunter-gatherer groups. There is a 6% white minority **Religion** mainly Christian (Lutheran, Roman Catholic, Dutch Reformed Church, Anglican) **Life expectancy** 52 (men); 53 (women) (1995–2000) **Literacy rate** 81% (men); 79% (women) (1997 est) **Unemployment** 38% (1997 est)

Economy and resources

GDP (US$) 3.1 billion (1998) **GNP** (US$) 3.2 billion (1998) **GNP per capita (PPP)** (US$) 4,950 (1998 est) **Real GDP growth** (% change on previous year) 3 (1998) **Consumer price inflation** 10% (1998) **Foreign debt** (US$) 141 million (1997 est) **Resources** uranium, copper, lead, zinc, silver, tin, gold, salt, semi-precious stones, diamonds (one of the world's leading producers of gem diamonds), hydrocarbons, lithium, manganese, tungsten, cadmium, vanadium **Exports** diamonds, fish and fish products, live animals and meat, uranium, karakul pelts. Principal market: UK 33% (1998) **Imports** food and live animals, beverages, tobacco, transport equipment, mineral fuels, chemicals, electrical and other machinery. Principal source: South Africa 87% (1998)

▪ Tourist information

Time difference GMT +1 **Currency** Namibia dollar **Language** English (official), Afrikaans, German, indigenous languages **Visa requirements** UK: visa not required. USA: visa not required **Embassy in the UK** 6 Chandos Street, London W1M 0LQ. Tel: (020) 7636 6244; fax: (020) 7637 5694 **British embassy** British High Commission, PO Box 22202, 116 Robert Mugabe Avenue, Windhoek. Tel: (61) 223 022; fax: (61) 228 895 **Chamber of commerce** Namibia National Chamber of Commerce and Industry, PO Box 9355, Windhoek. Tel: (61) 228 809; fax: (61) 228 009 **Office hours** 0800–1700 Mon–Fri **Banking hours** 0900–1530 Mon–Fri; 0830–1100 Sat **Airports** international airports: Windhoek; all major towns have domestic airports or landing strips; total passenger km: 906 million (1997 est) **Major ports** Walvis Bay **Chief tourist attractions** game parks; nature reserves (notably the Etosha National Park and Game Reserve); the government is promoting the development of ecotourism **Major holidays** 1 January, 21 March, 1, 4, 16, 25 May, 26 August, 10, 25–26 December; variable: Good Friday, Easter Monday

Chronology

1480s Coast visited by European explorers. **16th century** Bantu-speaking Herero migrated into northwest and Ovambo settled in northernmost areas. **1840s** Rhenish Missionary Society began to spread German influence; Jonkar Afrikaner conquest state dominant in southern Namibia. **1884** Germany annexed most of the area, calling it South West Africa, with Britain incorporating a small enclave around Walvis Bay in the Cape Colony of South Africa. **1892** German farmers arrived to settle in the region. **1903–04** Uprisings by the long-settled Nama (Khoikhoi) and Herero peoples brutally repressed by Germans, with over half the local communities slaughtered. **1908** Discovery of diamonds led to a larger influx of Europeans. **1915** German colony invaded and seized by South Africa during World War I and the Ovambo, in the north, were conquered. **1920** Administered by South Africa, under League of Nations mandate. **1946** Full incorporation in South Africa refused by United Nations (UN). **1949** White voters in South West Africa given representation in the South African parliament. **1958** South West Africa People's Organization (SWAPO) formed to campaign for racial equality and full independence. **1960** Radical wing of SWAPO, led by Sam Nujoma, forced into exile. **1964** UN voted to end South Africa's mandate, but South Africa refused to relinquish control or soften its policies towards the economically disenfranchised black majority. **1966** South Africa's apartheid laws extended to the country; 60% of land was allocated to whites, who formed 10% of the population. **1968** South West Africa redesignated Namibia by UN; SWAPO, drawing strong support from the Ovambo people of the north, began armed guerrilla struggle against South African rule, establishing People's Liberation Army of Namibia (PLAN). **1971** Prolonged general strike by black Namibian contract workers. **1973** The UN recognized SWAPO as the 'authentic representative of the Namibian people'. **1975–76** The establishment of a new Marxist regime in independent Angola strengthened the position of SWAPO guerrilla movement, but also led to the increased military involvement of South Africa in the region. **1978** UN Security Council Resolution 435 for the granting of full independence was accepted by South Africa, and then rescinded. **1983** Direct rule was reimposed by Pretoria after the resignation of the Democratic Turnhalle Alliance (DTA), a conservative administration dominated by whites. **1985** South Africa installed a new puppet administration, the Transitional Government of National Unity (TGNU), which tried to reform the apartheid system, but was not recognized by the UN. **1988** Peace talks between South Africa, Angola, and Cuba led to an agreement on troop withdrawals and full independence for Namibia. **1989** UN peacekeeping force were stationed to oversee free elections to the assembly to draft a new constitution; SWAPO won the elections. **1990** A liberal multiparty constitution was adopted and independence was achieved. Sam Nujoma, SWAPO's former guerrilla leader, was elected president. Joined the Commonwealth. Hage Geingob was appointed prime minister. **1993** South Africa, with its new multiracial government, relinquished its claim to Walvis Bay sovereignty. Namibia dollar was launched with South African rand parity. **1994** SWAPO won assembly elections; Nujoma was re-elected president.

Nauru Republic of

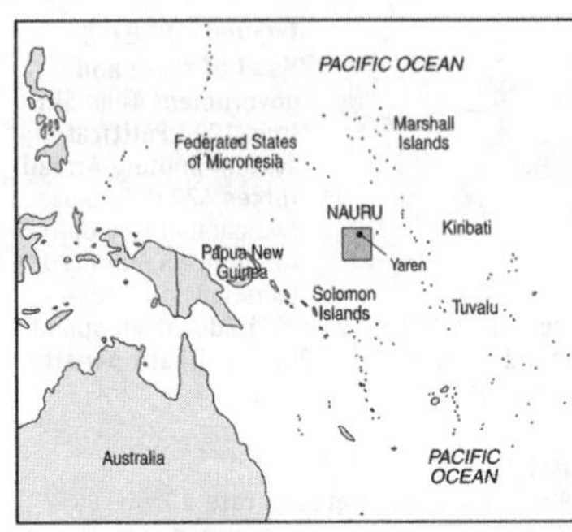

National name *Naoero* **Area** 21 sq km/8.1 sq mi **Capital** (seat of government) Yaren District

Government

Head of state and government Rene Harris from 1999 **Political system** liberal democracy **Armed forces** no standing army; Australia is responsible for Nauru's defence **Death penalty** retains the death penalty for ordinary crimes but can be considered abolitionist in practice (no executions since independence)

Population and society

Population 11,200 (1999 est) **Population growth rate** 1.8% (1995–2025) **Ethnic groups** about 87% of European origin (mostly British), about 9% Maori, and about 2% Pacific Islander **Religion** Protestant, Roman Catholic **Life expectancy** 64 (men); 69 (women) (1998 est) **Literacy rate** 99% (men); 99% (women) (1997 est) **Unemployment** 0% (1996)

Economy and resources

GDP (US$) 368 million (1995) **GNP** (US$) 304 million (1994 est) **GNP per capita (PPP)** (US$) 11,800 (1994 est) **Consumer price inflation** 10.1% (1996) **Resources** phosphates **Exports** phosphates. Principal market: Australia **Imports** food and live animals, building construction materials, petroleum, machinery, medical supplies. Principal source: Australia

▪ Tourist information

Time difference GMT +12 **Currency** Australian dollar **Language** Nauruan (official), English **Visa requirements** UK: visa required. USA: visa required **Embassy in the UK** Nauru Government Office, 3 Chesham Street, London SW1X 8ND. Tel: (020) 7235 6911; fax: (020) 7235 7423 **British embassy** the British Embassy in Suva (see Fiji Islands) deals with enquiries relating to Nauru **Chamber of commerce** Central Bank of Nauru, PO Box 289, Nauru. Tel: 444 3238; fax: 444 3203 **Airports** international airports: Nauru Island; total passenger km: 216 million (1995) **Chief tourist attractions** beautiful beaches interspersed by coral pinnacles **Major holidays** 1, 31 January, 17 May, 1 July, 27 October, 25–26 December; variable: Good Friday, Easter Monday, Easter Tuesday

Chronology

1798 British whaler Capt John Fearn first visited Nauru and named it Pleasant Island. **1830s–80s** The island was a haven for white runaway convicts and deserters. **1888** Annexed by Germany at the request of German settlers who sought protection from local clan unrest. **1899** Phosphate deposits discovered; mining began eight years later, with indentured Chinese labourers brought in to work British Australian-owned mines. **1914** Occupied by Australia on the outbreak of World War I. **1920** Administered by Australia on behalf of itself, New Zealand, and the UK until independence, except 1942–43, when occupied by Japan, and two-thirds of the population were deported briefly to Micronesia. **1951** Local Government Council set up to replace Council of Chiefs. **1956** Hammer DeRoburt became head chief of Nauru. **1968** Independence achieved, with 'special member' British Commonwealth status. Hammer DeRoburt elected president. **1987** Kennan Adeang established the Democratic Party of Nauru. **1994** Australia agreed to an out-of-court settlement of A$107

million, payable over 20 years, for environmental damage caused by phosphate mining which had left 80% of land agriculturally barren. **1998** Bernard Dowiyogo became president.

Nepal Kingdom of

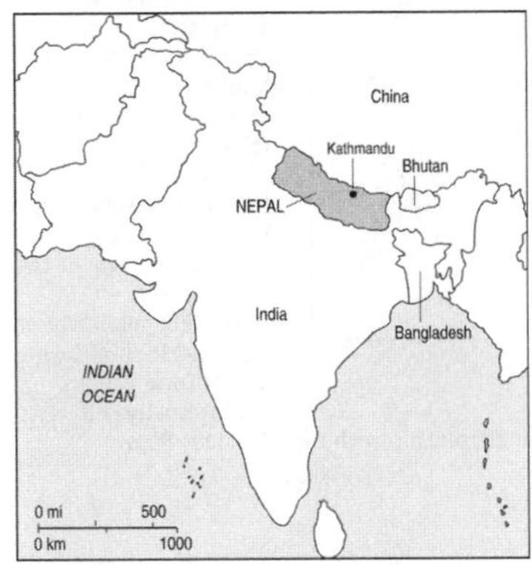

National name *Nepal Adhirajya* **Area** 147,181 sq km/56,826 sq mi **Capital** Kathmandu **Major towns/cities** Pátan, Moráng, Bhádgáon, Biratnagar, Lalitpur, Bhaktapur, Pokhara

Government

Head of state King Birendra Bir Bikram Shah Dev from 1972 **Head of government** Krishna Prasad Bhattarai from 1999 **Political system** emergent democracy **Armed forces** 46,000 (1997) **Conscription** military service is voluntary **Defence spend** (% GDP) 0.9 (1997) **Education spend** (% GNP) 3.1 (1996) **Health spend** (% GDP) 1.2 (1990–95) **Death penalty** abolished in 1997

Population and society

Population 23,386,000 (1999 est) **Population growth rate** 2.4% (1995–2000) **Ethnic groups** 80% of Indo-Nepalese origin, including the Gurkhas, Paharis, Newars, and Tharus; 20% of Tibeto-Nepalese descent (concentrated in the north and east) **Religion** Hindu 90%; Buddhist, Muslim, Christian **Life expectancy** 58 (men); 57 (women) (1995–2000) **Literacy rate** 56% (men); 21% (women) (1997 est) **Unemployment** 4.9% (1990); 40%–50% underemployment (1997)

Economy and resources

GDP (US$) 4.48 billion (1998) **GNP** (US$) 4.8 billion (1998) **GNP per capita (PPP)** (US$) 1,090 (1998) **Real GDP growth** (% change on previous year) 2.3 (1998) **Consumer price inflation** 2.9% (1997) **Foreign debt** (US$) 2.4 billion (1997) **Resources** lignite, talcum, magnesite, limestone, copper, cobalt **Exports** woollen carpets, clothing, hides and skins, food grains, jute, timber, oil seeds, ghee, potatoes, medicinal herbs, cattle. Principal market: India 32.8% (1998) **Imports** basic manufactures, machinery and transport equipment, chemicals, pharmaceuticals. Principal source: India 30.7% (1998)

▪ Tourist information

Time difference GMT +5.5 **Currency** Nepalese rupee **Language** Nepali (official); 20 dialects spoken **Visa requirements** UK: visa required. USA: visa required **Embassy in the UK** 12a Kensington Palace Gardens, London W8 4QV. Tel: (020) 7229 1594; fax: (020) 7792 9861 **British embassy** PO Box 106, Lainchaur, Kathmandu. Tel: (1) 410 583; fax: (1) 411 789 **Chamber of commerce** PO Box 198, Chamber Bhavan, Kantipath, Kathmandu. Tel: (1) 222 890; fax: (1) 229 998 **Office hours** 1000–1700 Sun–Fri (summer); 1000–1600 Sun–Fri (winter) **Banking hours** 1000–1450 Sun–Thu; 1000–1230 Fri **Airports** international airports: Kathmandu (Tribhuvan); 37 domestic airports and airfields; total passenger km: 953 million (1997 est) **Chief tourist attractions** Lumbini, birthplace of Buddha; the Himalayas, including Mount Everest, the world's highest peak; the lake city of Pokhara; wildlife includes tigers, leopards, elephants, buffalo, and gaur **Major holidays** 11 January, 19 February, 8 November, 16, 29 December; variable: New Year (Sinhala/Tamil, April), Maha Shivarata (February/March)

Chronology

8th century BC Kathmandu Valley occupied by Ahirs (shepherd kings), Tibeto-Burman migrants from northern India. **c. 563 BC** In Lumbini in far south, Prince Siddhartha Gautama, the historic Buddha, was born. **AD 300** Licchavis dynasty immigrated from India and introduced caste system. **13th–16th centuries** Dominated by Malla dynasty, great patrons of the arts. **1768** Nepal emerged as a unified kingdom after the ruler of the principality of the Gurkhas in the west, King Prithwi Narayan Shah, conquered Kathmandu Valley. **1792** Nepal's expansion halted by defeat at the hands of Chinese in Tibet; commercial treaty signed with Britain. **1815–16** Anglo-Nepali 'Gurkha War'; Nepal became British-dependent buffer state with British resident stationed in Kathmandu. **1846** Fell under sway of Rana family, who became hereditary chief ministers, dominating powerless monarchy and isolating Nepal from outside world. **1923** Full independence formally recognized by Britain. **1951** Monarchy restored to power and Ranas overthrown in 'palace revolution' supported by Nepali Congress Party (NCP). **1959** Constitution created an elected legislature. **1960–61** Parliament dissolved by King Mahendra; political parties banned after NCP's pro-India socialist leader B P Koirala became prime minister. **1962** New constitution provided for tiered, traditional system of indirectly elected local councils (*panchayats*) and an appointed prime minister. **1972** King Mahendra died; succeeded by his son, King Birendra Bikram Shah Dev. **1980** A constitutional referendum was held, following popular agitation led by B P Koirala, resulted in the introduction of direct, but nonparty, elections to the National Assembly. **1983** The monarch-supported prime minister was overthrown by directly elected deputies to the National Assembly. **1986** New assembly elections returned a majority opposed to the *panchayat* system of partyless government. **1988** Strict curbs were placed on opposition activity; over 100 supporters of the banned NCP were arrested, and censorship was imposed. **1989** A border blockade was imposed by India during a treaty dispute. **1990** The *panchayat* system collapsed after mass NCP-led violent prodemocracy demonstrations; a new democratic constitution was introduced, and the ban on political parties lifted. **1991** The Nepali Congress Party, led by Girija Prasad Koirala, won the general election. **1992** Communists led antigovernment demonstrations in Kathmandu and Pátan. **1994** Koirala's government was defeated on a no-confidence motion; parliament was dissolved. A minority communist government was formed under Man Mohan Adhikari. **1995** Parliament was dissolved by King Birendra at Prime Minister Adhikari's request; fresh elections were called but the supreme court ruled the move unconstitutional. **1998** G P Koirala of the NCP became prime minister and formed a new coalition government.

Netherlands, the Kingdom of (popularly referred to as Holland)

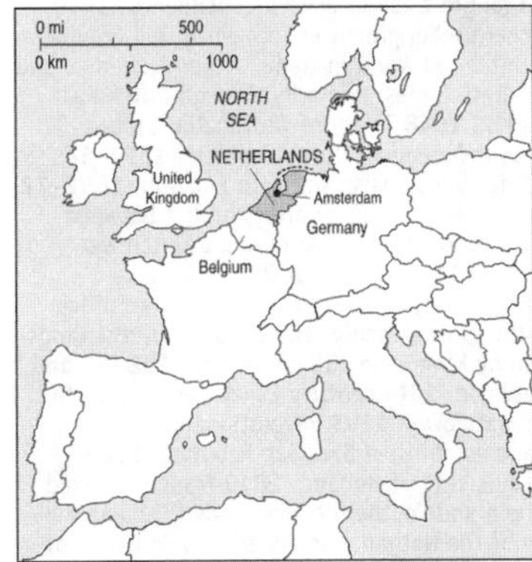

National name *Koninkrijk der Nederlanden* **Area** 41,863 sq km/16,163 sq mi **Capital** Amsterdam **Major towns/cities** Rotterdam, The Hague (seat of government), Utrecht, Eindhoven, Groningen, Tilburg, Maastricht, Haarlem, Apeldoorn, Nijmegen, Enschede **Territories** Aruba, Netherlands Antilles (Caribbean)

Government

Head of state Queen Beatrix Wilhelmina Armgard from 1980 **Head of government** Wim Kok from 1994 **Political system** liberal democracy **Armed forces** 57,200 (1997) **Conscription** military service is voluntary **Defence spend** (% GDP) 1.9 (1997) **Education spend** (% GNP) 5.2 (1996) **Health spend** (% GDP) 6.2 (1996) **Death penalty** abolished in 1982

Population and society

Population 15,735,000 (1999 est) **Population growth rate** 0.4% (1995–2000) **Ethnic groups** primarily Germanic, with some Gallo-Celtic mixtures; sizeable Indonesian and Surinamese minorities **Religion** Roman Catholic, Dutch Reformed Church **Life expectancy** 75 (men); 81 (women) (1995–2000) **Literacy rate** 99% (men); 99% (women) (1997 est) **Unemployment** 4.2% (1998)

Economy and resources

GDP (US$) 382.5 billion (1998) **GNP** (US$) 388.7 billion (1998) **GNP per capita (PPP)** (US$) 21,620 (1998) **Real GDP growth** (% change on previous year) 3.8 (1998) **Consumer price inflation** 2% (1998) **Resources**

petroleum, natural gas **Exports** machinery and transport equipment, foodstuffs, live animals, petroleum and petroleum products, natural gas, chemicals, plants and cut flowers, plant-derived products. Principal market: Germany 26.5% (1997) **Imports** electrical machinery, cars and other vehicles, mineral fuels, metals and metal products, plastics, paper and cardboard, clothing and accessories. Principal source: Germany 20.1% (1998)

▪ Tourist information

Time difference GMT +1 **Currency** guilder **Language** Dutch **Visa requirements** UK: visa not required. USA: visa not required **Embassy in the UK** 38 Hyde Park Gate, London SW7 5DP. Tel: (020) 7584 5040; fax: (020) 7581 3458 **British embassy** Lange Voorhout 10, 2514 ED The Hague. Tel: (70) 364 5800; fax: (70) 427 0345 **Chamber of commerce** The Hague Chamber of Commerce and Industry, Konigskade 30, 2596 AA The Hague. Tel: (70) 328 7100; fax: (70) 324 0684 **Office hours** 0830–1700 Mon–Fri **Banking hours** 0900–1600 Mon–Fri **Airports** international airports: Amsterdam (Schipol), Rotterdam (Zestienhoven), Eindhoven (Welschap), Maastricht (Beck), Groningen (Eelde), Enschede (Twente); domestic services operate between these; total passenger km: 70,702 million (1997 est) **Major ports** Rotterdam **Chief tourist attractions** the lively, cosmopolitan city of Amsterdam, with its museums and historical buildings; old towns; canals; the bulb fields in spring; art galleries; modern architecture; outlying islands **Major holidays** 1 January, 30 April, 5 May, 25–26 December; variable: Ascension Thursday, Good Friday, Easter Monday, Whit Monday

Chronology

55 BC Julius Caesar brought lands south of River Rhine under Roman rule. **4th century AD** Region overrun by Franks and Saxons. **7th–8th centuries** Franks subdued Saxons north of Rhine and imposed Christianity. **843–12th centuries** Division of Holy Roman Empire: the Netherlands repeatedly partitioned, not falling clearly into either French or German kingdoms. **12th–14th centuries** Local feudal lords, led by count of Holland and bishop of Utrecht, became practically independent; Dutch towns became prosperous trading centres, usually ruled by small groups of merchants. **15th century** Low Countries (Holland, Belgium, and Flanders) came under rule of dukes of Burgundy. **1477** Low Countries passed by marriage to Habsburgs. **1555** The Netherlands passed to Spain upon division of Habsburg domains. **1568** Dutch rebelled under leadership of William the Silent, Prince of Orange, and fought a long war of independence. **1579** Union of Utrecht: seven northern rebel provinces formed United Provinces. **17th century** 'Golden Age': Dutch led world in trade, art, and science, and founded colonies in East and West Indies, primarily through Dutch East India Company, founded in 1602. **1648** Treaty of Westphalia: United Provinces finally recognized as independent Dutch Republic. **1652–54** Commercial and colonial rivalries led to naval war with England. **1652–72** Johann de Witt ruled Dutch Republic as premier after conflict between republicans and House of Orange. **1665–67** Second Anglo-Dutch war. **1672–74** Third Anglo-Dutch war. **1672** William of Orange became stadholder (ruling as chief magistrate) of the Dutch Republic, an office which became hereditary in the Orange family. **1672–78** The Netherlands fought to prevent domination by King Louis XIV of France. **1688–97 and 1701–13** War with France resumed. **18th century** Exhausted by war, the Netherlands ceased to be a Great Power. **1795** Revolutionary France conquered the Netherlands and established Batavian Republic. **1806** Napoleon made his brother Louis king of Holland. **1810** France annexed the Netherlands. **1815** Northern and southern Netherlands (Holland and Belgium) unified as Kingdom of the Netherlands under King William I of Orange, who also became grand duke of Luxembourg. **1830** Southern Netherlands rebelled and declared independence as Belgium. **1848** Liberal constitution adopted. **1890** Queen Wilhelmina succeeded to throne; dynastic link with Luxembourg broken. **1894–96** Dutch suppressed colonial revolt in Java. **1914–18** The Netherlands remained neutral during World War I. **1940–45** Occupied by Germany during World War II. **1948** The Netherlands formed Benelux customs union with Belgium and Luxembourg; Queen Wilhelmina abdicated in favour of her daughter Juliana. **1949** Became a founding member of the North Atlantic Treaty Organization (NATO); most of Dutch East Indies became independent as Indonesia after four years of war. **1953** Dykes breached by storm; nearly two thousand people and tens of thousands of cattle died in flood. **1954** Remaining Dutch colonies achieved internal self-government. **1958** The Netherlands became a founding member of the European Economic Community (EEC). **1963** The Dutch colony of Western New Guinea was ceded to Indonesia. **1975** Dutch Guiana became independent as Suriname. **1980** Queen Juliana abdicated in favour of her daughter Beatrix. **1994** Following an inconclusive general election, a three-party coalition was formed under PvdA leader Wim Kok. **1999** The coalition government resigned in May after the smallest party, Democrats 66 (D-66), withdrew.

New Zealand Dominion of

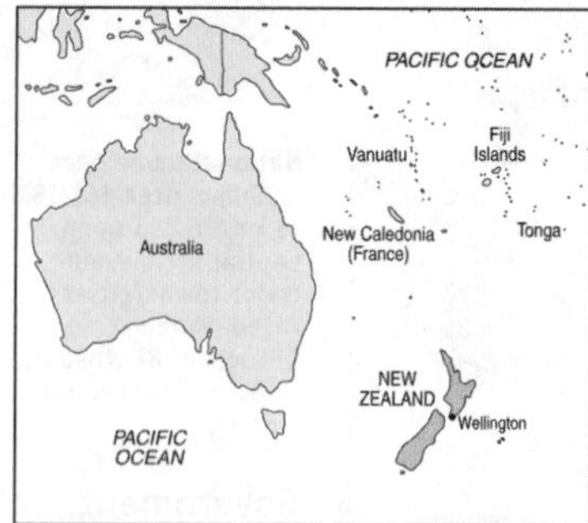

Area 268,680 sq km/103,737 sq mi **Capital** Wellington (and port) **Major towns/cities** Auckland, Hamilton, Palmerston North, Christchurch, Dunedin, Napier-Hastings **Territories** Tokelau (three atolls transferred in 1926 from former Gilbert and Ellice Islands colony); Niue Island (one of the Cook Islands, separately administered from 1903: chief town Alafi); Cook Islands are internally self-governing but share common citizenship with New Zealand; Ross Dependency in Antarctica

Government

Head of state Queen Elizabeth II from 1952, represented by governor general Catherine Tizard from 1990 **Head of government** Helen Clark from 1999 **Political system** liberal democracy **Armed forces** 9,600; around 7,000 reserves (1997) **Conscription** military service is voluntary **Defence spend** (% GDP) 1.6 (1997) **Education spend** (% GNP) 7.3 (1996) **Health spend** (% GDP) 5.7 (1996) **Death penalty** abolished in 1989

Population and society

Population 3,828,000 (1999 est) **Population growth rate** 1% (1995–2000); 0.8% (2000–05) **Ethnic groups** around 87% of European origin, 9% Maori, 2% Pacific Islander **Religion** Christian **Life expectancy** 74 (men); 80 (women) (1995–2000) **Literacy rate** 99% (men); 99% (women) (1997 est) **Unemployment** 7.5% (1998)

Economy and resources

GDP (US$) 54.1 billion (1998) **GNP** (US$) 55.8 billion (1998) **GNP per capita (PPP)** (US$) 15,840 (1998) **Real GDP growth** (% change on previous year) −0.3 (1998) **Consumer price inflation** 1.3% (1998) **Resources** coal, clay, limestone, dolomite, natural gas, hydroelectric power, pumice, iron ore, gold, forests **Exports** meat, dairy products, wool, fish, timber and wood products, fruit and vegetables, aluminium, machinery. Principal market: Australia 21.2% (1998) **Imports** machinery and mechanical appliances, vehicles and aircraft, petroleum, fertilizer, consumer goods. Principal source: Australia 22% (1998)

▪ Tourist information

Time difference GMT +12 **Currency** New Zealand dollar **Language** English (official), Maori **Visa requirements** UK: visa not required. USA: visa not required **Embassy in the UK** New Zealand House, 80 Haymarket, London SW1Y 4TQ. Tel: (020) 7930 8422; fax: (020) 7839 4580 **British embassy** British High Commission, PO Box 1818, 44 Hill Street, Wellington 1. Tel: (4) 472 6049; fax: (4) 471 1974 **Chamber of commerce** New Zealand Chambers of Commerce and Industry, PO Box 1590, 9th Floor, 109 Featherston Street, Wellington. Tel: (4) 472 2725; fax: (4) 471 1767 **Office hours** 0900–1700 Mon–Fri **Banking hours** 0900–1630 Mon–Fri **Airports** international airports: Auckland (Mangere), Christchurch, Wellington (Rongotai); 32 domestic airports; total passenger km: 23,020 million (1997 est) **Major ports** Auckland **Chief tourist attractions** trout- and deep-sea fishing and generally idyllic setting, including beaches, hot springs, mountains, lakes, and forests **Major holidays** 1, 2 January, 6 February, 25 April, 25–26 December; variable: Good Friday, Easter Monday, Queen's Birthday (June), Labour (October)

Chronology

1642 Dutch explorer Abel Tasman reached New Zealand but indigenous Maoris prevented him from going ashore. **1769** English explorer James Cook surveyed coastline of islands. **1773 and 1777** Cook again explored coast. **1815** First British missionaries arrived in New Zealand. **1826** New Zealand Company founded in London to establish settlement. **1839** New Zealand Company relaunched, after initial failure, by Edward Gibbon Wakefield. **1840** Treaty of Waitangi: Maoris accepted British sovereignty;

colonization began and large-scale sheep farming developed. **1845–47** Maori revolt against loss of land. **1851** Became separate colony (was originally part of the Australian colony of New South Wales). **1852** Colony procured constitution after dissolution of New Zealand Company; self-government fully implemented in 1856. **1860–72** Second Maori revolt led to concessions, including representation in parliament. **1891** New Zealand took part in Australasian Federal Convention in Sydney but rejected the idea of joining the Australian Commonwealth. **1893** Became the first country to give women the right to vote in parliamentary elections. **1898** Liberal government under Richard Seddon introduced pioneering old-age pension scheme. **1899–1902** Volunteers from New Zealand fought alongside imperial forces in Boer War. **1907** New Zealand achieved dominion status within British Empire. **1912–25** Government of Reform Party, led by William Massey, reflected interests of North Island farmers and strongly supported imperial unity. **1914–18** 130,000 New Zealanders fought for the British Empire in World War I. **1916** Labour Party of New Zealand established. **1931** Statute of Westminster affirmed equality of status between Britain and dominions, effectively granting independence to New Zealand. **1935–49** Labour governments of Michael Savage and Peter Fraser introduced social reforms and encouraged state intervention in industry. **1936** Liberal Party merged with Reform Party to create National Party. **1939–45** New Zealand troops fought in World War II, notably in Crete, North Africa, and Italy. **1947** Parliament confirmed independence of New Zealand within British Commonwealth. **1951** New Zealand joined Australia and USA in ANZUS Pacific security treaty. **1965–72** New Zealand contingent took part in Vietnam War. **1973** British entry into European Economic Community (EEC) forced New Zealand to seek closer trading relations with Australia. **1985** Non-nuclear military policy led to disagreements with France and USA. **1986** The USA suspended defence obligations to New Zealand after it banned the entry of US warships. **1988** A free-trade agreement was signed with Australia. **1991** The Alliance Party was formed to challenge the two-party system. **1998** The government was ordered to return more than £2 million worth of land confiscated from its Maori owners more than 30 years earlier. **1999** The conservative government was replaced by a centre-left coalition of the Labour Party and New Zealand Alliance, with Helen Clark, leader of the Labour Party, as the new prime minister.

Nicaragua Republic of

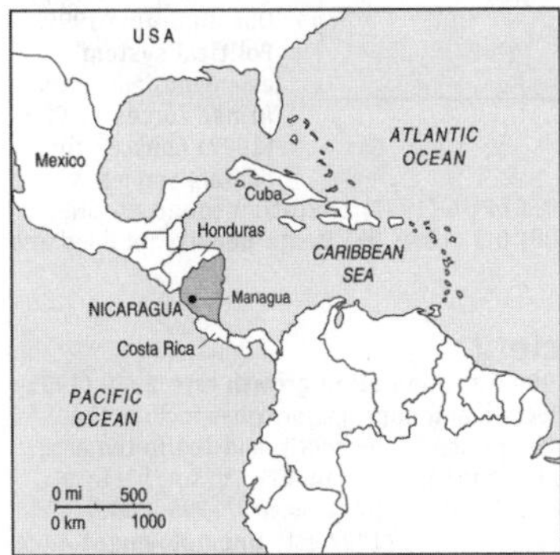

National name *República de Nicaragua* **Area** 127,849 sq km/ 49,362 sq mi **Capital** Managua **Major towns/ cities** León, Chinandega, Masaya, Granada

Government

Head of state and government Arnoldo Aleman from 1997 **Political system** emergent democracy **Armed forces** 17,000 (1997) **Conscription** military service is voluntary (since 1990) **Defence spend** (% GDP) 1.4 (1997) **Education spend** (% GNP) 3.6 (1996) **Health spend** (% GDP) 4.3 (1990–95) **Death penalty** abolished in 1979

Population and society

Population 4,938,000 (1999 est) **Population growth rate** 2.7% (1995–2000) **Ethnic groups** over 70% of mixed Indian, Spanish, and African origin; about 9% African; 5% Indian **Religion** Roman Catholic 95% **Life expectancy** 66 (men); 71 (women) (1995–2000) **Literacy rate** 63% (men); 63% (women) (1997 est) **Unemployment** 13.3% (1997)

Economy and resources

GDP (US$) 1.97 billion (1998) **GNP** (US$) 1.87 billion (1998) **GNP per capita (PPP)** (US$) 1,790 (1998 est) **Real GDP growth** (% change on previous year) 4 (1998) **Consumer price inflation** 13% (1998) **Foreign debt** (US$) 5.7 billion (1997) **Resources** gold, silver, copper, lead, antimony, zinc, iron, limestone, gypsum, marble, bentonite **Exports** coffee, meat, cotton, sugar, seafood, bananas, chemical products. Principal market: USA 34.8% (1998) **Imports** machinery and transport equipment, food and live animals, consumer goods, mineral fuels and lubricants, basic manufactures, chemicals and related products. Principal source: USA 30.7% (1998)

▪ Tourist information

Time difference GMT –6 **Currency** cordoba **Language** Spanish (official), Indian, English **Visa requirements** UK: visa not required for a stay of up to 90 days. USA: visa not required for a stay of up to 90 days **Embassy in the UK** 2nd Floor, 36 Upper Brook Street, London W1Y 1PE. Tel: (020) 7409 2536; fax: (020) 7409 2593 **British embassy** Apartado A-169, El Reparto 'Los Robles', Primera Etapa, Entrada principal de la Carretera a Massaya, 4a Casa a Mano Derecha, Managua. Tel: (2) 780 014; fax: (2) 784 085 **Chamber of commerce** Cámara de Comercio de Nicaragua, Apartado 135, Frente a Lotería Popular, C C Managua JR. Tel: (2) 670 718 **Office hours** 0800–1600 Mon–Fri **Banking hours** 0800–1600 Mon–Fri; 0830–1130 Sat **Airports** international airports: Managua (Augusto Cesar Sandino); total passenger km: 80 million (1995) **Major ports** Corinto, Puerto Cabezas, El Bluff **Chief tourist attractions** Lake Nicaragua, with its 310 beautiful islands; the Momotombo volcano; the Corn Islands (Islas de Maiz) in the Caribbean, fringed with white coral and palm trees **Major holidays** 1 January, 1 May, 19 July, 14–15 September, 8, 25 December; variable: Good Friday, Holy Thursday

Chronology

10th century AD Indians from Mexico and Mesoamerica migrated to Nicaragua's Pacific lowlands. **1522** Visited by Spanish explorer Gil Gonzalez de Avila, who named the area Nicaragua after local Indian chief, Nicarao. **1523–24** Colonized by the Spanish, under Francisco Hernandez de Cordoba, who was attracted by local gold deposits and founded cities of Granada and León. **17th–18th centuries** British were the dominant force on the Caribbean side of Nicaragua, while Spain controlled the Pacific lowlands. **1821** Independence achieved from Spain; Nicaragua was initially part of Mexican Empire. **1823** Became part of United Provinces (Federation) of Central America, also embracing Costa Rica, El Salvador, Guatemala, and Honduras. **1838** Became fully independent when it seceded from the Federation. **1857–93** Ruled by succession of Conservative Party governments. **1860** The British ceded control over Caribbean ('Mosquito') Coast to Nicaragua. **1893** Liberal Party leader, José Santos Zelaya, deposed the Conservative president and established a dictatorship which lasted until overthrown by US marines in 1909. **1912–25** At the Nicaraguan government's request, with political situation deteriorating, USA established military bases and stationed marines. **1927–33** Re-stationed US marines faced opposition from anti-American guerrilla group led by Augusto César Sandino, who was assassinated in 1934 on the orders of the commander of the US-trained National Guard, Gen Anastasio Somoza Garcia. **1937** Gen Somoza elected president; start of near-dictatorial rule by Somoza family, which amassed a huge personal fortune. **1961** Left-wing Sandinista National Liberation Front (FSLN) formed to fight the Somoza regime. **1978** The Nicaraguan Revolution: Pedro Joaquin Chamorro, a popular publisher and leader of the anti-Somoza Democratic Liberation Union (UDEL), was assassinated, sparking a general strike and mass movement in which moderates joined with the FSLN to overthrow the Somoza regime. **1979** The Somoza government was ousted by the FSLN after a military offensive. **1980** A FSLN junta took power in Managua, headed by Daniel Ortega Saavedra; lands held by Somozas were nationalized and farming cooperatives established. **1982** There was subversive activity against the government by right-wing Contra guerrillas, promoted by the USA, attacking from bases in Honduras. A state of emergency was declared. **1984** US troops mined Nicaraguan harbours. The action was condemned by the World Court in 1986 and $17 billion in reparations ordered. FSLN won the assembly elections. **1985** The US president Ronald Reagan denounced the Sandinista government, vowing to 'remove it', and imposed a US trade embargo. **1987** A Central American peace agreement was cosigned by Nicaraguan leaders. **1988** The peace agreement failed. Nicaragua held talks with the Contra rebel leaders. A hurricane left 180,000 people homeless. **1989** Demobilization of rebels and release of former Somozan supporters; the ceasefire ended but the economy was in ruins after the Contra war; there was 60% unemployment. **1990** The FSLN was defeated by right-of-centre National Opposition Union (UNO), a US-backed coalition; Violeta Barrios de Chamorro, widow of the murdered Pedro Joaquin Chamorro, was elected president. There were antigovernment riots. **1992** Around 16,000 people were made homeless by an earthquake. **1994** A peace accord was made with the remaining Contra rebels. **1996** Right-wing candidate Arnoldo Aleman won the presidential elections. **1998** Daniel Ortega was re-elected FSLN leader.

Niger Republic of

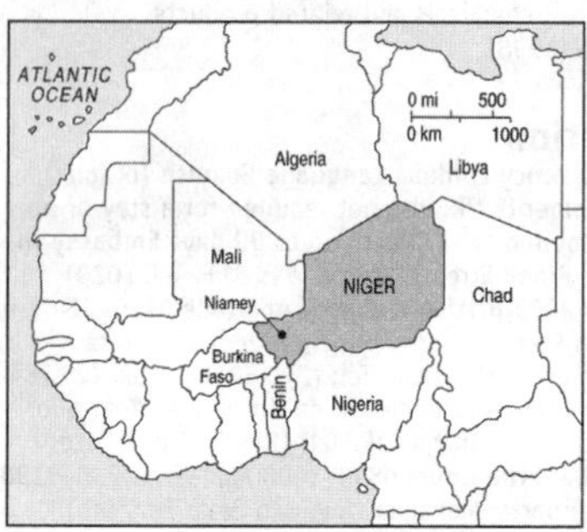

National name *République du Niger* **Area** 1,186,408 sq km/ 458,072 sq mi **Capital** Niamey **Major towns/ cities** Zinder, Maradi, Tahoua, Agadez, Birui N'Konui

Government

Head of state Daouda Mallam Wanke from 1999 **Head of government** Ibrahim Hassane Mayaki from 1997 **Political system** military **Armed forces** 5,300; plus paramilitary forces of 5,400 (1997) **Conscription** conscription is selective for two years **Defence spend** (% GDP) 1.4 (1997) **Education spend** (% GNP) 3.1 (1993/94) **Health spend** (% GDP) 1.6 (1990–95) **Death penalty** retains the death penalty for ordinary crimes but can be considered abolitionist in practice (last known execution in 1976)

Population and society

Population 10,401,000 (1999 est) **Population growth rate** 3.2% (1995–2000) **Ethnic groups** three ethnic groups make up over 75% of the population: the Hausa (mainly in central areas and the south), Djerma-Songhai (southwest), and Beriberi-Manga (east); there is also a significant number of the mainly nomadic Fulani people, and the Tuareg in the north **Religion** Sunni Muslim; also Christian, and traditional animist beliefs **Life expectancy** 47 (men); 50 (women) (1995–2000) **Literacy rate** 22% (men); 7% (women) (1999 est) **Unemployment** N/A

Economy and resources

GDP (US$) 2.05 billion (1998) **GNP** (US$) 1.9 billion (1998) **GNP per capita (PPP)** (US$) 830 (1998) **Real GDP growth** (% change on previous year) 4 (1998) **Consumer price inflation** 4.5% (1998) **Foreign debt** (US$) 1.58 billion (1997) **Resources** uranium (one of world's leading producers), phosphates, gypsum, coal, cassiterite, tin, salt, gold; deposits of other minerals (including petroleum, iron ore, copper, lead, diamonds, and tungsten) have been confirmed **Exports** uranium ore, live animals, hides and skins, cow-peas, cotton. Principal market: USA 29.7% (1997) **Imports** machinery and transport equipment, miscellaneous manufactured articles, cereals, chemicals, refined petroleum products. Principal source: France 15.4% (1997)

▪ Tourist information

Time difference GMT +1 **Currency** franc CFA **Language** French (official), Hausa, Djerma, and other minority languages **Visa requirements** UK: visa required. USA: visa required **Embassy for the UK** 154 rue du Longchamps, 75116 Paris, France. Tel: (1) 4504 8060; fax: (1) 4504 6226 **British embassy** Honorary British Vice-Consulate, BP 11168, Niamey. Tel: (227) 732 015/539 **Chamber of commerce** Chambre de Commerce, d'Agriculture, d'Industrie et d'Artisanat du Niger, BP 209, place de la Concertation, Niamey. Tel: (227) 732 210; telex: 5242 **Office hours** 0730–1230 and 1530–1830 Mon–Fri; 0730–1230 Sat **Banking hours** 0800–1100 and 1600–1700 Mon–Fri **Airports** international airports: Niamey, Agadez; four major domestic airports; total passenger km: 223 million (1995) **Chief tourist attractions** the Aïr and Ténéré Nature Reserve, covering 77,000 sq km/ 29,730 sq mi; Agadez, surrounded by green valleys and hot springs, and still a major terminus for trans-Saharan caravans **Major holidays** 1 January, 15 April, 1 May, 3 August, 18, 25 December; variable: Eid-ul-Adha, end of Ramadan, Prophet's Birthday

Chronology

10th–13th centuries Kanem-Bornu Empire flourished in southeast, near Lake Chad, spreading Islam from the 11th century. **15th century** Tuareg sultanate of Agades dominant in the north. **17th century** Songhai-speaking Djerma established an empire on Niger River. **18th century** Powerful Gobir kingdom founded by Hausa people, who had migrated from the south in the 14th century. **late 18th–early 19th centuries** Visited by European explorers, including the Scottish explorer, Mungo Park; Sultanate of Sokoto formed by Islamic revivalist Fulani, who had defeated the Hausa in a jihad (holy war). **1890s** French conquered the region and ended the local slave trade. **1904** Became part of French West Africa, although Tuareg resistance continued until 1922. **1946** Became French overseas territory, with its own territorial assembly and representation in the French parliament. **1958** Became an autonomous republic within the French community. **1960** Achieved full independence; Hamani Diori of Niger Progressive Party (NPP) elected president, but maintained close ties with France. **1971** Uranium production commenced. **1974** Diori was ousted in an army coup; the military government launched a drive against corruption. **1977** A cooperation agreement was signed with France. **1984** There was a partial privatization of state firms due to further drought and increased government indebtedness as world uranium prices slumped. **1989** Ali Saibu was elected president without opposition. **1991** Saibu was stripped of executive powers, and a transitional government was formed amid student and industrial unrest. **1992** The transitional government collapsed amid economic problems and ethnic unrest among secessionist Tuareg in the north. A referendum approved of a new multiparty constitution. **1993** The Alliance of the Forces for Change (AFC), a left-of-centre coalition, won an absolute majority in assembly elections. Mahamane Ousmane, a Muslim Hausa, was elected president in the first free presidential election. **1994** A peace agreement was signed with northern Tuareg. **1996** President Ousmane was ousted in a military coup led by Ibrahim Barre Mainassara. Civilian government was restored with Boukary Adji as premier; Mainassara was formally elected president. **1997** Ibrahim Hassane Mayaki was appointed prime minister. **1999** President Mainassara was assassinated in a coup; Major Daouda Mallam Wanke, the commander of Niger's presidential guard, assumed power.

Nigeria Federal Republic of

Area 923,773 sq km/ 356,668 sq mi **Capital** Abuja **Major towns/ cities** Ibadan, Lagos, Ogbomosho, Kano, Oshogbo, Ilorin, Abeokuta, Zaria, Ouitsha, Iwo, Kaduna

Government

Head of state and government Olusegun Obasanjo from 1999 **Political system** emergent democracy **Armed forces** 77,000 (1997) **Conscription** military service is voluntary **Defence spend** (% GDP) 4 (1997) **Education spend** (% GNP) 0.9 (1996) **Health spend** (% GDP) 0.3 (1990–95) **Death penalty** retained and used for ordinary crimes

Population and society

Population 108,945,000 (1999 est) **Population growth rate** 2.4% (1995–2000) **Ethnic groups** over 250 tribal groups; major tribes include the Hausa and Fulani in the north, Yoruba in the south, and Ibo in the east **Religion** Sunni Muslim 50% (in north), Christian 40% (in south), local religions 10% **Life expectancy** 49 (men); 52 (women) (1995–2000) **Literacy rate** 69% (men); 51% (women) (1997 est) **Unemployment** 4.5% (1997)

Economy and resources

GDP (US$) 41.4 billion (1998) **GNP** (US$) 36.4 billion (1998) **GNP per capita (PPP)** (US$) 820 (1998) **Real GDP growth** (% change on previous year) 1.6 (1998) **Consumer price inflation** 25.6% (1998) **Foreign debt** (US$) 28.4 billion (1997) **Resources** petroleum, natural gas, coal, tin, iron ore, uranium, limestone, marble, forest **Exports** petroleum, cocoa beans, rubber, palm products, urea and ammonia, fish. Principal market: USA 36.9% (1997) **Imports** machinery and transport equipment, basic manufactures, cereals, chemicals, foodstuffs. Principal source: UK 13.2% (1997)

▪ Tourist information

Time difference GMT +1 **Currency** naira **Language** English (official), Hausa, Ibo, Yoruba **Visa requirements** UK: visa required. USA: visa required **Embassy in the UK** Nigeria House, 9 Northumberland Avenue, London WC2N 5BX. Tel: (020) 7839 1244; fax: (020) 7839 8746 **British embassy** British High Commission, Private Mail Bag 12136, 11 Eleke Crescent, Victoria Island, Lagos. Tel: (1) 619 531; fax: (1) 666 909

Chamber of commerce The Nigerian Association of Chambers of Commerce, Industry, Mines and Agriculture; Private Mail Bag 12816; 15a Ikorodu Road, Maryland, Lagos. Tel: (1) 496 4737; telex 21368 **Office hours** 0730–1530 Mon–Fri **Banking hours** 0800–1500 Mon; 0800–1330 Tue–Fri **Airports** international airports: Lagos (Murtala Mohammed), Kano, Abuja, Port Harcourt, Calabar; 14 domestic airports; total passenger km: 819 million (1995) **Major ports** Lagos, Port Harcourt, Warri, Calabar **Chief tourist attractions** fine coastal scenery; dense forests; rich diversity of arts **Major holidays** 1 January, 1 May, 1 October, 25–26 December; variable: Eid-ul-Adha (2 days), end of Ramadan (2 days), Good Friday, Easter Monday, Prophet's Birthday

Chronology

4th century BC–2nd century AD Highly organized Nok culture flourished in northern Nigeria. **9th century** Northeast Nigeria became part of empire of Kanem-Bornu, based around Lake Chad. **11th century** Creation of Hausa states, including Kano and Katsina. **13th century** Arab merchants introduced Islam in the north. **15th century** Empire of Benin at its height in south; first contact with European traders. **17th century** Oyo Empire dominant in southwest; development of slave trade in Niger delta. **1804–17** Islamic Fulani (or Sokoto) Empire established in north. **1861** British traders procured Lagos; spread of Christian missionary activity in south. **1884–1904** Britain occupied most of Nigeria by stages. **1914** North and south protectorates united; growth of railway network and trade. **1946** Nigerians allowed a limited role in decision-making in three regional councils. **1951** The introduction of elected representation led to the formation of three regional political parties. **1954** New constitution increased powers of the regions. **1958** Oil discovered in the southeast. **1960** Achieved independence from Britain, within the Commonwealth. **1963** Became a republic, with Nnamdi Azikiwe as president. **1966** Gen Aguiyi-Ironsi of Ibo tribe seized power and imposed unitary government; massacre of Ibo by Hausa in north; Gen Gowon seized power and restored federalism. **1967** Conflict over oil revenues led to secession of eastern region as independent Ibo state of Biafra; ensuing civil war claimed up to a million lives. **1970** Surrender of Biafra and end of civil war; development of the oil industry financed more effective central government. **1975** Gowon ousted in military coup; second coup put Gen Olusegun Obasanjo in power. **1979** Civilian rule restored under President Shehu Shagari. **1983** A bloodless coup was staged by Maj-Gen Muhammadu Buhari. **1985** Buhari was replaced by Maj-Gen Ibrahim Babangida; Islamic northerners were dominant in the regime. **1992** Multiparty elections were won by Babangida's SDP. **1993** Moshood Abiola (SDP) won the first free presidential election; the results were suspended. Gen Sani Abacha restored military rule and dissolved political parties. **1995** Commonwealth membership was suspended in protest at human-rights abuses by the military regime. **1998** General Abdulsalam Abubakar took over as president. Nigeria's most prominent political prisoner, Moshood Abiola, died suddenly on the eve of his expected release. There were moves towards political liberalization, with the formation of new political parties and the release of some dissidents. **1999** The People's Democratic Party won a Senate majority. Olusegun Obasanjo was elected president. Nigeria rejoined the Commonwealth.

North Korea *see* Korea, North

Norway Kingdom of

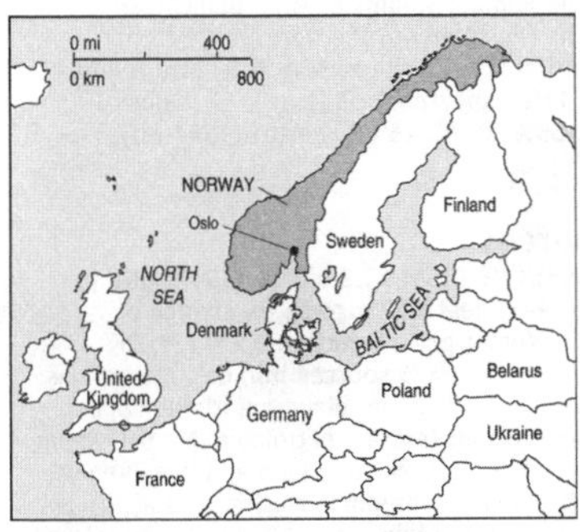

National name *Kongeriket Norge* **Area** 387,000 sq km/ 149,420 sq mi (includes Svalbard and Jan Mayen) **Capital** Oslo **Major towns/ cities** Bergen, Trondheim, Stavanger, Kristiansand, Drammen **Territories** dependencies in the Arctic (Svalbard and Jan Mayen) and in Antarctica (Bouvet and Peter I Island, and Queen Maud Land)

Government

Head of state Harald V from 1991 **Head of government** Jens Stoltenberg from 2000 **Political system** liberal democracy **Armed forces** 33,600; 234,000 reservists (1997) **Conscription** 12 months, with 4–5 refresher training periods **Defence spend** (% GDP) 2.3 (1997) **Education spend** (% GNP) 7.5 (1996) **Health spend** (% GDP) 6.5 (1996) **Death penalty** abolished in 1979

Population and society

Population 4,442,000 (1999 est) **Population growth rate** 0.5% (1995–2000) **Ethnic groups** majority of Nordic descent; Saami minority in far north **Religion** Evangelical Lutheran (endowed by state) **Life expectancy** 75 (men); 81 (women) (1995–2000) **Literacy rate** 99% (men); 99% (women) (1997 est) **Unemployment** 3.2% (1998)

Economy and resources

GDP (US$) 145.9 billion (1998) **GNP** (US$) 152.1 billion (1998) **GNP per capita (PPP)** (US$) 24,290 (1998) **Real GDP growth** (% change on previous year) 3 (1998) **Consumer price inflation** 2.3% (1998) **Resources** petroleum, natural gas, iron ore, iron pyrites, copper, lead, zinc, forests **Exports** petroleum, natural gas, fish products, non-ferrous metals, wood pulp and paper. Principal market: UK 16.9% (1998) **Imports** machinery and transport equipment, chemicals, clothing, fuels and lubricants, iron and steel, office machines and computers, telecommunications and sound apparatus and equipment. Principal source: Sweden 14.7% (1998)

▪ Tourist information

Time difference GMT +1 **Currency** Norwegian krone **Language** Norwegian (official); there are Saami- (Lapp) and Finnish-speaking minorities **Visa requirements** UK: visa not required. USA: visa not required **Embassy in the UK** 25 Belgrave Square, London SW1X 8QD. Tel: (020) 7235 7151; fax: (020) 7245 6993 **British embassy** Thomas Heftyesgate 8, 0244 Oslo 2. Tel: (22) 552 400; fax: (22) 434 005 **Chamber of commerce** Norwegian Trade Council, Drammensveien 40, 0243 Oslo. Tel: (22) 926 300; fax: (22) 926 400 **Office hours** 0800–1600 Mon–Fri **Banking hours** 0900–1700 Mon–Thu in major cities and 0900–1530 Fri **Airports** international airports: Oslo (Fornebu), Stavanger (Sola), Bergen (Flesland); 54 domestic airports with scheduled services; total passenger km: 14,646 million (1996) **Chief tourist attractions** rugged landscape with fjords, forests, lakes, and rivers; winter sports **Major holidays** 1 January, 1, 17 May, 25–26 December; variable: Ascension Thursday, Good Friday, Easter Monday, Holy Thursday, Whit Monday

Chronology

5th century First small kingdoms established by Goths. ***c.* 900** Harald Fairhair created united Norwegian kingdom; it dissolved after his death. **8th–11th centuries** Vikings from Norway raided and settled in many parts of Europe. ***c.* 1016–28** Olav II (St Olav) reunited the kingdom and introduced Christianity. **1217–63** Haakon VI established royal authority over nobles and church and made the monarchy hereditary. **1263** Iceland submitted to the authority of the king of Norway. **1397** Union of Kalmar: Norway, Denmark, and Sweden united under a single monarch. **15th century** Norway, the weakest of the three kingdoms, was increasingly treated as an appendage of Denmark. **1523** Secession of Sweden further undermined Norway's status. **16th century** Introduction of the sawmill precipitated the development of the timber industry and the growth of export trade. **1661** Denmark restored formal equality of status to Norway as a twin kingdom. **18th century** Norwegian merchants profited from foreign wars which increased demand for naval supplies. **1814** Treaty of Kiel: Denmark ceded Norway (minus Iceland) to Sweden; Norway retained its own parliament but cabinet appointed by the king of Sweden. **19th century** Economic decline followed slump in timber trade due to Canadian competition; expansion of merchant navy and whaling industry. **1837** Democratic local government introduced. **1884** Achieved internal self-government when the king of Sweden made the Norwegian cabinet accountable to the Norwegian parliament. **1895** Start of constitutional dispute over control of foreign policy: Norway's demand for a separate consular service refused by Sweden. **1905** Union with Sweden dissolved; Norway achieved independence under King Haakon VII. **1907** Norway became first the European country to grant women the right to vote in parliamentary elections. **early 20th century** Development of industry based on hydroelectric power; long period of Liberal government committed to neutrality and moderate social reform. **1940–45** German occupation with Vidkun Quisling as puppet leader. **1945–65** Labour governments introduced economic planning and permanent price controls. **1949** Became a founding member of the North Atlantic Treaty Organization (NATO). **1952** Joined the Nordic Council. **1957** Olaf V succeeded his father King Haakon VII. **1960** Joined European Free Trade Association (EFTA). **1972** A national referendum rejected membership of

European Economic Community (EEC). **1975** The export of North Sea oil began. **1981** Gro Harlem Brundtland (Labour) became Norway's first woman prime minister. **1986** Falling oil prices caused a recession. **1991** Olaf V was succeeded by his son Harald V. **1994** A national referendum rejected membership of European Union (EU). **1997** Kjell Magne Bondevik (Christian People's Party) became prime minister. **1998** There was a decline in the state of the economy. **2000** Bondevik resigned as prime minister and was succeeded by Jens Stoltenberg.

Oman Sultanate of

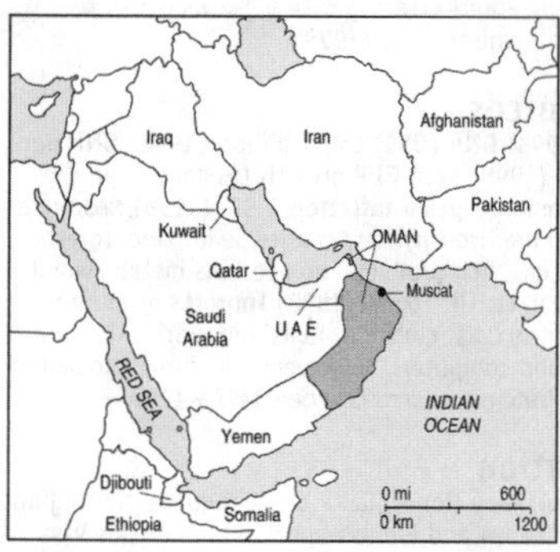

National name *Saltanat 'Uman* **Area** 272,000 sq km/105,019 sq mi **Capital** Muscat **Major towns/cities** Salalah, Ibri, Sohar, Al-Buraimi, Nizwa

Government

Head of state and government Qaboos bin Said from 1970 **Political system** absolutist **Armed forces** 43,500 (1997) **Conscription** military service is voluntary **Defence spend** (% GDP) 10.9 (1997) **Education spend** (% GNP) 4.6 (1995) **Health spend** (% GDP) 2.5 (1990–95) **Death penalty** retained and used for ordinary crimes

Population and society

Population 2,460,000 (1999 est) **Population growth rate** 3.3% (1995–2000) **Ethnic groups** predominantly Arab, with substantial Iranian, Baluchi, Indo-Pakistani, and East African minorities **Religion** Ibadhi Muslim 75%, Sunni Muslim, Shiite Muslim, Hindu **Life expectancy** 69 (men); 73 (women) (1995–2000) **Literacy rate** 77% (men); 55% (women) (1997 est) **Unemployment** 11.9% (1993)

Economy and resources

GDP (US$) 14.96 billion (1998) **GNP** (US$) 10.6 billion (1997) **GNP per capita (PPP)** (US$) 8,690 (1997) **Real GDP growth** (% change on previous year) –2.5 (1998) **Consumer price inflation** 1.0% (1998) **Foreign debt** (US$) 3.6 billion (1997) **Resources** petroleum, natural gas, copper, chromite, gold, salt, marble, gypsum, limestone **Exports** petroleum, metals and metal goods, textiles, animals and products. Principal market: Japan 23.3% (1997) **Imports** machinery and transport equipment, basic manufactures, food and live animals, beverages, tobacco. Principal source: UAE 24.2% (1997)

▪ Tourist information

Time difference GMT +4 **Currency** Omani rial **Language** Arabic (official); English, Urdu, other Indian languages **Visa requirements** UK: visa required. USA: visa required **Embassy in the UK** 167 Queen's Gate, London SW7 5HE. Tel: (020) 7225 0001; fax: (020) 7589 2505 **British embassy** PO Box 300, 113 Muscat. Tel: (968) 693 077; fax: (968) 693 087 **Chamber of commerce** Oman Chamber of Commerce and Industry, PO Box 1400, 112 Ruwi. Tel: (968) 707 684; fax: (968) 708 497 **Office hours** 0830–1300 and 1600–1900 Sat–Wed; 0800–1300 Thu **Banking hours** 0800–1200 Sat–Wed and 0800–1130 Thu **Airports** international airports: Muscat (Seeb), Salalah; domestic services operate between these; total passenger km: 3,226 million (1995) **Major ports** Mina Qaboos, Mina Raysut **Chief tourist attractions** the old towns of Muscat, Nizwa (ancient capital of the interior), and Dhofar; the forts of Nakhl, Rustaq, and Al-Hazm – tourism was introduced in 1985 and is strictly controlled **Major holidays** 18 November (2 days), 31 December; variable: Eid-ul-Adha (5 days), end of Ramadan (4 days), New Year (Muslim), Prophet's Birthday, Lailat al-Miraj (March/April)

Chronology

***c.* 3000 BC** Archaeological evidence suggests Oman may have been the semilegendary Magan, a thriving seafaring state at the time of the Sumerian civilization of Mesopotamia (the Tigris and Euphrates region of Iraq). **9th century BC** Migration of Arab clans to Oman, notably the Qahtan family from southwest Arabia and the Nizar from northwest Arabia, between whom rivalry has continued. **4th century BC–AD 800** North Oman under Persian control. **AD 630** Converted to Islam. **751** Julanda ibn Masud was elected imam (spiritual leader); Oman remained under imam rule until 1154. **1151** Dynasty established by Banu Nabhan. **1428** Dynastic rule came under challenge from the imams. **1507** Coastal area, including port city of Muscat, fell under Portuguese control. **1650** Portuguese ousted by Sultan ibn Sayf, a powerful Ya'ariba leader. **early 18th century** Civil war between the Hinawis (descendents of the Qahtan) and the Ghafiris (descendents of the Nizar). **1749** Independent Sultanate of Muscat and Oman established by Ahmad ibn Said, founder of the Al Bu Said dynasty that still rules Oman. **first half of 19th century** Muscat and Oman was the most powerful state in Arabia, ruling Zanzibar until 1861, and coastal parts of Persia, Kenya, and Pakistan; came under British protection. **1951** The Sultanate of Muscat and Oman achieved full independence from Britain. Treaty of Friendship with Britain signed. **1964** Discovery of oil led to the transformation of the undeveloped kingdom into a modern state. **1970** After 38 years' rule, Sultan Said bin Taimur was replaced in a bloodless coup by his son Qaboos bin Said. Name was changed to the Sultanate of Oman and a modernization programme was launched. **1975** Left-wing rebels in Dhofar in the south, who had been supported by South Yemen, defeated with UK military assistance, ending a ten-year insurrection. **1981** The Consultative Council was set up; Oman played a key role in the establishment of a six-member Gulf Cooperation Council. **1982** The Memorandum of Understanding with the UK was signed, providing for regular consultation on international issues. **1991** Joined the US-led coalition opposing Iraq's occupation of Kuwait.

Pakistan Islamic Republic of

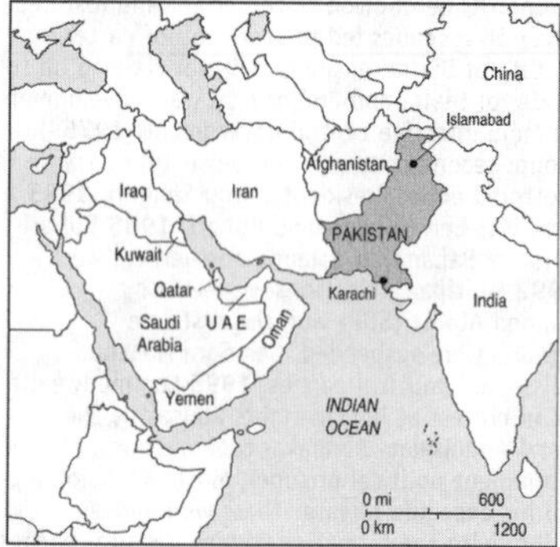

National name *Islami Jamhuriya e Pakistan* **Area** 803,940 sq km/310,321 sq mi; one-third of Kashmir under Pakistani control **Capital** Islamabad **Major towns/cities** Lahore, Rawalpindi, Faisalabad, Karachi, Hyderabad, Multan, Peshawar, Gujranwala, Sialkot, Sargodha, Quetta, Islamabad

Government

Head of state and government General Pervez Musharraf from 1999 **Political system** military **Armed forces** 587,000; paramilitary forces 247,000 (1997) **Conscription** military service is voluntary **Defence spend** (% GDP) 5.8 (1997) **Education spend** (% GNP) 3.0 (1996) **Health spend** (% GDP) 0.8 (1990–95) **Death penalty** retained and used for ordinary crimes

Population and society

Population 152,330,000 (1999 est) **Population growth rate** 2.8% (1995–2000) **Ethnic groups** four principal, regionally based, antagonistic communities: Punjabis in the Punjab; Sindhis in Sind; Baluchis in Baluchistan; and the Pathans (Pushtans) in the Northwest Frontier Province **Religion** Sunni Muslim 75%, Shiite Muslim 20%; also Hindu, Christian, Parsee, Buddhist **Life expectancy** 63 (men); 65 (women) (1995–2000) **Literacy rate** 55% (men); 25% (women) (1997 est) **Unemployment** 5.4% (1996)

Economy and resources

GDP (US$) 63.9 billion (1998) **GNP** (US$) 63.2 billion (1998) **GNP per capita (PPP)** (US$) 1,560 (1998) **Real GDP growth** (% change on previous year) 4.3 (1998) **Consumer price inflation** 6.2% (1998) **Foreign debt** (US$) 29.6 billion (1997) **Resources** iron ore, natural gas, limestone, rock salt, gypsum, silica, coal, petroleum, graphite, copper, manganese, chromite **Exports** cotton, textiles, petroleum and petroleum products, clothing and accessories, leather, rice, food and live animals. Principal market: USA 21.5% (1998–99) **Imports** machinery and transport equipment, mineral fuels and lubricants, chemicals and related products, edible oil. Principal source: USA 8.2%, Japan 8.2% (1998–99)

Tourist information

Time difference GMT +5 **Currency** Pakistan rupee **Language** Urdu (official); English, Punjabi, Sindhi, Pashto, Baluchi, other local dialects **Visa requirements** UK: visa required. USA: visa required **Embassy in the UK** 40 Lowndes Square, London SW1X 9JN. Tel: (020) 7235 2044 **British embassy** British High Commission, PO Box 1122, Diplomatic Enclave, Ramna 5, Islamabad. Tel: (51) 822 131/5; fax: (51) 823 439 **Chamber of commerce** Chamber of Commerce and Industry, PO Box 4833, Talpur Road, Karachi. Tel: (21) 241 0814; fax: (21) 242 7315 **Office hours** 0900–1700 Sat–Thu **Banking hours** 0900–1300 and 1500–2000 Sun–Thu (some banks open on Sat) **Airports** international airports: Karachi (Civil), Lahore, Islamabad, Peshawar, Quetta, Rawalpindi; 30 domestic airports; total passenger km: 10,940 million (1997 est) **Major ports** Karachi, Port Qasim **Chief tourist attractions** Himalayan scenery; fine climate; mountaineering; trekking; winter sports; archaeological remains and historic buildings **Major holidays** 23 March, 1 May, 1 July, 14 August, 6, 11 September, 9 November, 25, 31 December; variable: Eid-ul-Adha (3 days), Ashora (2 days), end of Ramadan (3 days), Prophet's Birthday, first day of Ramadan

Chronology

2500–1600 BC The area was the site of the Indus Valley civilization, a sophisticated, city-based ancient culture. **327 BC** Invaded by Alexander the Great of Macedonia. **1st–2nd centuries** North Pakistan was the heartland of the Kusana Empire, formed by invaders from Central Asia. **8th century** First Muslim conquests, in Baluchistan and Sind, followed by increasing immigration by Muslims from the west, from the 10th century. **1206** Establishment of Delhi Sultanate, stretching from northwest Pakistan and across northern India. **16th century** Sikh religion developed in Punjab. **16th–17th centuries** Lahore served intermittently as a capital city for the Mogul Empire, which stretched across the northern half of the Indian subcontinent. **1843–49** Sind and Punjab annexed by British and incorporated within empire of 'British India'. **late 19th century** Major canal irrigation projects in West Punjab and the northern Indus Valley drew in settlers from the east, as wheat and cotton production expanded. **1933** The name 'Pakistan' (Urdu for 'Pure Nation') invented by Choudhary Rahmat Ali, as Muslims within British India began to campaign for the establishment of an independent Muslim territory that would embrace the four provinces of Sind, Baluchistan, Punjab, and the Northwest Frontier. **1940** The All-India Muslim League (established in 1906), led by Karachi-born Muhammad Ali Jinnah, endorsed the concept of a separate nation for Muslims in the Lahore Resolution. **1947** Independence achieved from Britain, as a dominion within the Commonwealth. Pakistan, which included East Bengal, a Muslim-dominated province more than 1,600 km/1,000 mi from Punjab, was formed following the partition of British India. Large-scale and violent cross-border migrations of Muslims, Hindus, and Sikhs followed, and a brief border war with India over disputed Kashmir. **1956** Proclaimed a republic. **1958** Military rule imposed by Gen Ayub Khan. **1965** Border war with India over disputed territory of Kashmir. **1969** Power transferred to Gen Yahya Khan following strikes and riots. **1970** A general election produced a clear majority in East Pakistan for the pro-autonomy Awami League, led by Sheikh Mujibur Rahman, and in West Pakistan for Islamic socialist Pakistan People's Party (PPP), led by Zulfiqar Ali Bhutto. **1971** East Pakistan secured independence, as Bangladesh, following a civil war in which it received decisive military support from India. Power was transferred from the military to the populist Bhutto in Pakistan. **1977** Bhutto overthrown in military coup by Gen Zia ul-Haq following months of civil unrest; martial law imposed. **1979** Bhutto executed for alleged murder; tight political restrictions imposed by Zia regime. **1980** 3 million refugees fled to the Northwest Frontier Province and Baluchistan as a result of the Soviet invasion of Afghanistan. **1981** The broad-based Opposition Movement for the Restoration of Democracy was formed. The Islamization process was pushed forward by the government. **1985** Martial law and the ban on political parties was lifted. **1986** Agitation for free elections was launched by Benazir Bhutto, the daughter of Zulfiqar Ali Bhutto. **1988** An Islamic legal code, the Shari'a, was introduced; Zia was killed in a military plane crash. Benazir Bhutto became prime minister after the (now centrist) PPP won the general election. **1989** Tension with India was increased by outbreaks of civil war in Kashmir. Pakistan rejoined the Commonwealth, which it had left in 1972. **1990** Bhutto was dismissed as prime minister by President Ghulam Ishaq Khan on charges of incompetence and corruption. The conservative Islamic Democratic Alliance (IDA), led by Nawaz Sharif, won the general election and launched a privatization and economic deregulation programme. **1993** Khan and Sharif resigned. Benazir Bhutto and PPP were re-elected. Farooq Leghari (PPP) was elected president. **1994** There was regional sectarian violence between Shia and Sunni Muslims, centred in Karachi. **1996** Benazir Bhutto was dismissed amid allegations of corruption. **1997** The right-of-centre Pakistan Muslim League won the general election, returning Nawaz Sharif to power as prime minister. President Leghari resigned. Rafiq Tarar was elected president. **1998** Pakistan conducted its first ever nuclear tests, provoking international condemnation and sanctions by the USA. Benazir Bhutto and her husband were charged with corruption. Federal rule was imposed on Sindh as a result of escalating violence. A $5.5 billion economic bailout package was agreed with the IMF and World Bank. **1999** Benazir Bhutto and her husband were found guilty of corruption, sentenced to five years in prison, and fined £5.3 million. India agreed to enter peace talks on Kashmir. Pakistan's army overthrew the government after Sharif tried to sack general Pervez Musharraf from the top military job. General Musharraf, who appointed himself the country's chief executive, declared a state of emergency. **2000** Relations with India worsened as India accused Pakistan of involvement in the hijacking of an Indian airliner by Kashmiri militants. Pakistan denied any involvement.

Palau Republic of (or Belau)

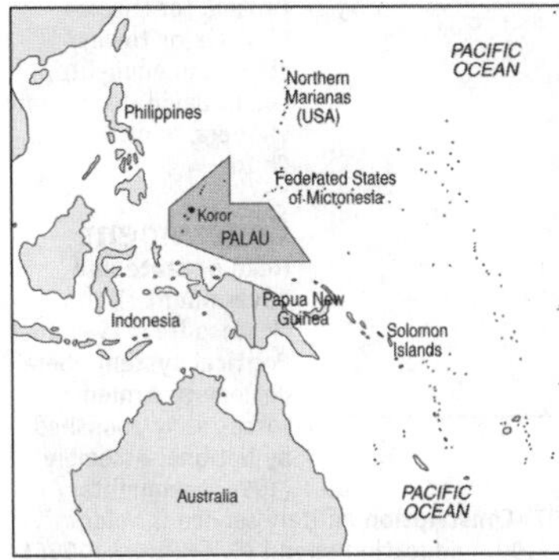

Area 508 sq km/196 sq mi **Capital** Koror (on Koror Island) **Major towns/cities** Melekeiok, Garusuun, Malakal

Government

Head of state and government Kuniwo Nakamura from 1992 **Political system** liberal democracy **Armed forces** no defence forces of its own; under the Compact of Free Association, the USA is responsible for the defence of Palau; two US military bases operate on the islands **Death penalty** laws do not provide for the death penalty for any crime

Population and society

Population 19,000 (1999 est) **Population growth rate** 2.4% (1995–2000) **Ethnic groups** predominantly Micronesian **Religion** Christian, principally Roman Catholic **Life expectancy** 65 (men); 71 (women) (1998 est) **Literacy rate** 95% (1995 est) **Unemployment** 7% (1997 est)

Economy and resources

GDP (US$) 145 million (1998 est) **GNP** N/A **GNP per capita (PPP)** (US$) N/A **Consumer price inflation** N/A **Foreign debt** (US$) 100 million (1990) **Exports** copra, coconut oil, handicrafts, trochus, tuna **Imports** food and live animals, crude materials, mineral fuels, beverages, tobacco, chemicals, basic manufactures, machinery and transport equipment

Tourist information

Time difference GMT +9 **Currency** US dollar **Language** Palauan and English **Visa requirements** UK: visa not required for a stay of up to 30 days. USA: visa not required for a stay of up to 30 days **Embassy in the UK** Palau has no diplomatic representation in the UK; the UK Department of Trade and Industry has a Pacific Islands Desk. Tel: (020) 7215 4760; fax: (020) 7215 4398 **British embassy** the UK has no diplomatic representation in Palau **Chamber of commerce** Palau Visitors Authority, PO Box 6028, Koror 96940. Tel: (680) 488 2920; fax: (680) 488 2911 **Office hours** generally 0730–1130 and 1230–1630 Mon–Fri **Banking hours** 1000–1500 Mon–Thu; 1000–1800 Fri **Airports** international airports: Koror (Palau International, on Babelthaup Island, near Koror Island); two domestic airfields **Chief tourist attractions** rich marine environment; the myriad Rock Islands, known as the Floating Garden Islands **Major holidays** 1 January, 15 March, 5 May, 1 June, 9 July, 5 September, 24 October, 24 November, 25 December

Chronology

c. 1000 BC Micronesians first settled the islands. **1543** First visited by Spanish navigator Ruy Lopez de Villalobos. **16th century** Colonized by Spain. **1899** Purchased from Spain by Germany. **1914** Occupied by Japan at the outbreak of World War I. **1920** Administered by Japan under League of Nations mandate. **1944** Occupied by USA after Japanese removed during World War II. **1947** Became part of United Nations (UN) Pacific Islands Trust Territory, administered by USA. **1981** Acquired autonomy as the Republic of Belau (Palau) under a constitution which prohibited the entry, storage, or disposal of nuclear or biological weapons. **1982** The Compact of Free Association signed with the USA, providing for the right to maintain US military facilities in return for economic aid. The compact could not come into force since it contradicted the constitution, which could only be amended by a 75% vote in favour. **1992** Kuniwo Nakamura was elected president. **1993** A referendum approved a constitutional amendment allowing the implementation of the Compact of Free Association with the USA. **1994** Independence was achieved and UN membership granted.

Panama Republic of

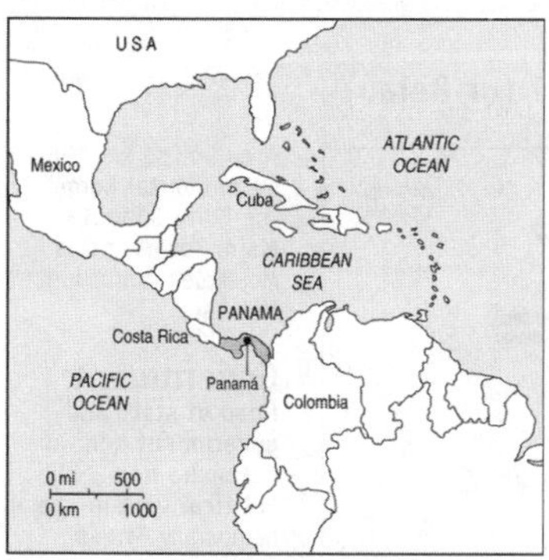

National name *República de Panamá* **Area** 77,100 sq km/ 29,768 sq mi **Capital** Panamá (or Panama City) **Major towns/ cities** San Miguelito, Colón, David, La Chorrera, Santiago, Chitré

Government

Head of state and government Mireya Moscoso from 1999 **Political system** liberal democracy **Armed forces** army abolished by National Assembly (1994); paramilitary forces numbered 11,800 (1997) **Conscription** military service is voluntary **Defence spend** (% GDP) 1.3 (1997) **Education spend** (% GNP) 4.6 (1996) **Health spend** (% GDP) 5.4 (1990–95) **Death penalty** laws do not provide for the death penalty for any crime (last known execution in 1903)

Population and society

Population 2,812,000 (1999 est) **Population growth rate** 1.6% (1995–2000); 1.4% (2000–05) **Ethnic groups** about 70% mestizos (of Spanish-American and American-Indian descent), 14% West Indian, 10% white American or European, and 6% Indian **Religion** Roman Catholic **Life expectancy** 72 (men); 76 (women) (1995–2000) **Literacy rate** 92% (men); 90% (women) (1997 est) **Unemployment** 13.4% (1997)

Economy and resources

GDP (US$) 9.2 billion (1998) **GNP** (US$) 8.5 billion (1998) **GNP per capita (PPP)** (US$) 6,940 (1998) **Real GDP growth** (% change on previous year) 3 (1998) **Consumer price inflation** 0.6% (1998) **Foreign debt** (US$) 6.3 billion (1997) **Resources** limestone, clay, salt; deposits of coal, copper, and molybdenum have been discovered **Exports** bananas, shrimps and lobsters, sugar, clothing, coffee. Principal market: USA 39.9% (1998) **Imports** machinery and transport equipment, petroleum and mineral products, chemicals and chemical products, electrical and electronic equipment, foodstuffs. Principal source: USA 39.7% (1998)

■ Tourist information

Time difference GMT –5 **Currency** balboa **Language** Spanish (official), English **Visa requirements** UK: visa not required (business visitors need a business visa). USA: visa required **Embassy in the UK** 48 Park Street, London W1Y 3PD. Tel: (020) 7493 4646; fax: (020) 7493 4333 **British embassy** Apartado 889, Zona 1, 4th and 5th Floors, Torre Banco Sur, Calle 53 Este, Panama 1. Tel: (2) 690 866; fax: (2) 230 730 **Chamber of commerce** Cámara de Comercio, Industrias y Agricultura de Panamá, Apartado 74, Edificio Comosa, Avenida Samuel Lewis, Planta Baja, Panamá 1. Tel: (2) 271 233; fax: (2) 274 186 **Office hours** 0800–1200 and 1400–1700 Mon–Fri **Banking hours** 0800–1330 Mon–Fri; 0830–1200 Sat **Airports** international airports: Panamá (Tocumen); two domestic airports; total passenger km: 1,094 million (1997 est) **Major ports** Colón, Cristóbal, Balboa **Chief tourist attractions** Panamá; ruins of Portobelo; San Blas Islands, off the Atlantic coast; 800 sandy tropical islands in Gulf of Panama **Major holidays** 1, 9 January, 1 May, 11–12 October, 3–4, 28 November, 8, 25 December; variable: Carnival (2 days), Good Friday

Chronology

1502 Visited by Spanish explorer Rodrigo de Bastidas, at which time it was inhabited by Cuna, Choco, Guaymi, and other Indian groups. **1513** Spanish conquistador Vasco Núñez de Balboa explored Pacific Ocean from Darien isthmus; he was made governor of Panama (meaning 'abundance of fish'). **1519** Spanish city established at Panama, which became part of the Spanish viceroyalty of New Andalucia (later New Granada). **1572–95 and 1668–71** Spanish settlements sacked by British buccaneers Francis Drake and Henry Morgan. **1821** Achieved independence from Spain; joined confederacy of Gran Colombia, which included Colombia, Venezuela, Ecuador, Peru, and Bolivia. **1830** Gran Colombia split up and Panama became part of Colombia. **1846** Treaty signed with USA, allowing it to construct a railway across the isthmus. **1880s** French attempt to build a Panama canal connecting the Atlantic and Pacific Oceans failed as a result of financial difficulties and the death of 22,000 workers from yellow fever and malaria. **1903** Full independence achieved with US help on separation from Colombia; USA bought rights to build Panama Canal, and were given control of a 10-mile strip, the Canal Zone, in perpetuity. **1914** Panama Canal opened. **1939** Panama's status as a US protectorate was terminated by mutual agreement. **1968–81** Military rule of Gen Omar Torrijos Herrera, leader of the National Guard, who deposed the elected president and launched a costly programme of economic modernization. **1977** USA–Panama treaties transferred the canal to Panama (effective from 2000), with the USA guaranteeing protection and annual payment. **1987** Gen Manuel Noriega (head of the National Guard and effective ruler since 1983) resisted calls for his removal, despite suspension of US military and economic aid. **1988** Noriega, charged with drug smuggling by the USA, declared a state of emergency after a coup against him failed. **1989** 'State of war' with USA announced, and US invasion (codenamed 'Operation Just Cause') deposed Noriega; 4,000 Panamanians died in the fighting. Guillermo Endara, who had won earlier elections, was installed as president in December. **1991** Constitutional reforms were approved by the assembly, including the abolition of the standing army; a privatization programme was introduced. **1992** Noriega was found guilty of drug offences and given a 40-year prison sentence in USA. A referendum rejected the proposed constitutional reforms. **1994** The constitution was amended by assembly; the army was formally abolished. **1998** Voters rejected a proposed constitutional change to allow the president to run for a second term. **1999** Mireya Moscoso, widow of former president Arnulfo Arias, became Panama's first female head of state. Panama formally took control of its canal.

Papua New Guinea

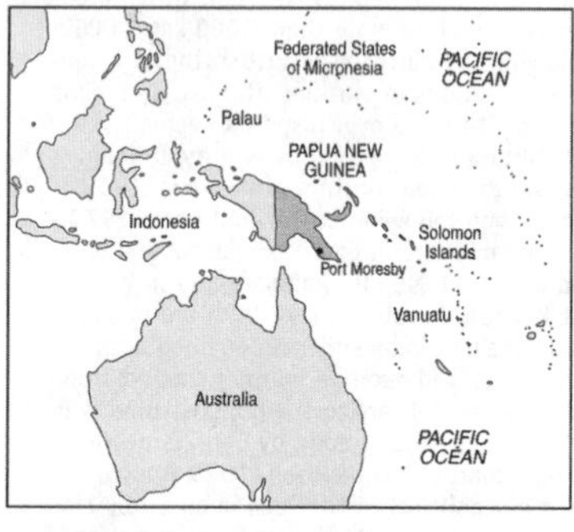

Area 462,840 sq km/ 178,702 sq mi **Capital** Port Moresby (on East New Guinea) (also port) **Major towns/ cities** Lae, Madang, Arawa, Wewak, Goroka, Rabaul, Mount Hagen

Government

Head of state Queen Elizabeth II, represented by governor general Silas Atopare from 1997 **Head of government** Mekere Morauta from 1999 **Political system** liberal democracy **Armed forces** 4,300 (1997) **Conscription** military service is voluntary **Defence spend** (% GDP) 1.2 (1997) **Education spend** (% GNP) 6.3 (1993 est) **Health spend** (% GDP) 2.8 (1990–95) **Death penalty** retains the death penalty for ordinary crimes but can be considered abolitionist in practice (last execution 1950)

Population and society

Population 4,702,000 (1999 est) **Population growth rate** 2.2% (1995–2000); 2.1% (2000–05) **Ethnic groups** mainly Melanesian, particularly in coastal areas; inland (on New Guinea and larger islands), Papuans predominate. On the outer archipelagos and islands, mixed Micronese-Melanesians are found. A small Chinese minority also exists **Religion** Protestant, Roman Catholic, local faiths **Life expectancy** 57 (men); 59 (women) (1995–2000) **Literacy rate** 82% (men); 65% (women) (1997 est)

Economy and resources

GDP (US$) 4.64 billion (1998) **GNP** (US$) 4.1 billion (1998) **GNP per capita (PPP)** (US$) 2,700 (1998 est) **Real GDP growth** (% change on previous year) 1.6 (1998) **Consumer price inflation** 13.6% (1998) **Foreign**

debt (US$) 2.27 billion (1997) **Resources** copper, gold, silver; deposits of chromite, cobalt, nickel, quartz; substantial reserves of petroleum and natural gas (petroleum production began in 1992) **Exports** gold, copper ore and concentrates, crude petroleum, timber, coffee beans, coconut and copra products. Principal market: Australia 19.8% (1998) **Imports** machinery and transport equipment, manufactured goods, food and live animals, miscellaneous manufactured articles, chemicals, mineral fuels. Principal source: Australia 51.5% (1998)

▪ Tourist information

Time difference GMT +10 **Currency** kina **Language** English (official); pidgin English, 715 local languages **Visa requirements** UK: visa required. USA: visa required **Embassy in the UK** 14 Waterloo Place, London SW1Y 4AR. Tel: (020) 7930 0922/7; fax: (020) 7930 0828 **British embassy** British High Commission, PO Box 4778, Kiroki Street, Waigani, Boroko, Port Moresby. Tel: (675) 325 1677; fax: (675) 325 3547 **Chamber of commerce** Papua New Guinea Chamber of Commerce and Industry, PO Box 1621, Port Moresby. Tel: (675) 213 057; fax: (675) 214 203 **Office hours** 0800–1630 Mon–Fri **Banking hours** 0900–1500 Mon–Thu; 0900–1700 Fri **Airports** international airports: Port Moresby (Jackson); 177 domestic airports and airstrips with scheduled services; total passenger km: 830 million (1995) **Major ports** Rabaul **Chief tourist attractions** spectacular scenery; the greatest variety of ecosystems in the South Pacific; abundant wildlife – birds include 38 species of birds of paradise, also the megapode and cassowary; two-thirds of the world's orchid species come from Papua New Guinea **Major holidays** 1 January, 15 August, 16 September, 25–26 December; variable: Good Friday, Easter Monday, Holy Saturday, Queen's Birthday (June), Remembrance (July)

Chronology

c. 3000 BC New settlement of Austronesian (Melanesian) immigrants. **1526** Visited by Portuguese navigator Jorge de Menezes, who named the main island the Ilhos dos Papua. **1545** Spanish navigator Ynigo Ortis de Retez gave the island the name of New Guinea, as a result of a supposed resemblance of the peoples with those of the Guinea coast of Africa. **17th century** Regularly visited by Dutch merchants. **1828** Dutch East India Company incorporated the western part of New Guinea into Netherlands East Indies (becoming Irian Jaya, in Indonesia). **1884** Northeast New Guinea annexed by Germany; the southeast was claimed by Britain. **1870s** Visits by Western missionaries and traders increased. **1890s** Copra plantations developed in German New Guinea. **1906** Britain transferred its rights to Australia, which renamed the lands Papua. **1914** German New Guinea occupied by Australia at the outbreak of World War I; from the merged territories Papua New Guinea was formed. **1920–42** Held as League of Nations mandate by Australia. **1942–45** Occupied by Japan, which lost 150,000 troops resisting Allied counterattack. **1947** Held as United Nations Trust Territory by Australia. **1951** Legislative Council established. **1964** Elected House of Assembly formed. **1967** Pangu Party (Pangu Pati; PP) formed to campaign for home rule. **1975** Independence achieved from Australia, within Commonwealth, with Michael Somare (PP) as prime minister. **1985** Somare challenged by deputy prime minister Paias Wingti, who later left the PP and formed the People's Democratic Movement (PDM); he became head of a five-party coalition government. **1988** Joined Solomon Islands and Vanuatu to form the Spearhead Group, aiming to preserve Melanesian cultural traditions. **1989** State of emergency imposed on copper-rich Bougainville in response to separatist violence. **1990** The Bougainville Revolutionary Army (BRA) issued a unilateral declaration of independence. **1991** There was an economic boom as gold production doubled. **1994** There was a short-lived peace agreement with the BRA. **1996** The prime minister of Bougainville was murdered, jeopardizing the peace process. Gerard Sinato was elected president of the transitional Bougainville government. **1997** The army and police mutinied following the government's use of mercenaries against secessionist rebels. Silas Atopare was appointed governor general. **1998** There was a truce with Bougainville secessionists. At least 1,500 people died and thousands were left homeless when tidal waves destroyed villages on the north coast. **1999** A coalition of parties headed by Mekere Morauta won a parliamentary majority to form a new government. Bougainville Transitional Government (BTG) was replaced by the new interim Bougainville Reconciliation Government (BRG), headed by former rebel leader Joseph Kabui and BTG leader Gerard Sinato.

Paraguay Republic of

National name *República del Paraguay* **Area** 406,752 sq km/157,046 sq mi **Capital** Asunción (and port) **Major towns/cities** Ciudad del Este, Pedro Juan Caballero, San Lorenzo, Fernando de la Mora, Lambare, Concepción, Villartica, Encaración

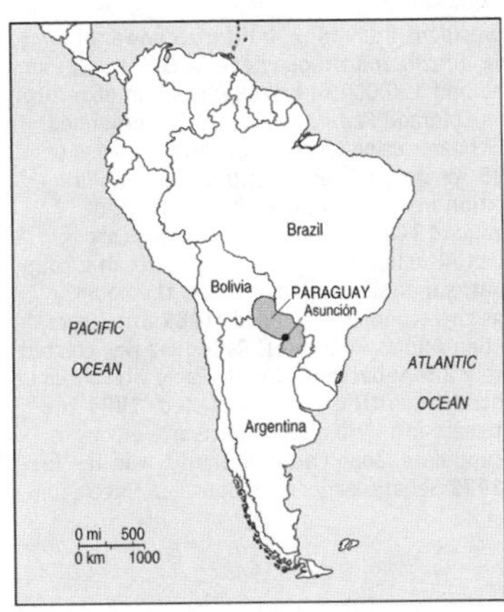

Government

Head of state and government Luis Gonzalez Macchi from 1999 **Political system** emergent democracy **Armed forces** 20,200 (1997) **Conscription** 12 months (army); 24 months (navy) **Defence spend** (% GDP) 1.5 (1997) **Education spend** (% GNP) 3.9 (1996) **Health spend** (% GDP) 1.0 (1990–95) **Death penalty** abolished in 1992

Population and society

Population 5,359,000 (1999 est) **Population growth rate** 2.6% (1995–2000); 2.3% (2000–05) **Ethnic groups** predominantly mixed-race mestizos; less than 5% Spanish or Indian **Religion** Roman Catholic (official religion); Mennonite, Anglican **Life expectancy** 68 (men); 72 (women) (1995–2000) **Literacy rate** 94% (men); 91% (women) (1997 est) **Unemployment** 8.2% (1997)

Economy and resources

GDP (US$) 8.57 billion (1998) **GNP** (US$) 9.2 billion (1998) **GNP per capita (PPP)** (US$) 3,650 (1998) **Real GDP growth** (% change on previous year) 0.2 (1998) **Consumer price inflation** 11.5% (1998) **Foreign debt** (US$) 2.05 billion (1997) **Resources** gypsum, kaolin, limestone, salt; deposits (not commercially exploited) of bauxite, iron ore, copper, manganese, uranium; deposits of natural gas discovered in 1994; exploration for petroleum deposits ongoing mid-1990s **Exports** soybeans (and other oil seeds), cotton, timber and wood manufactures, hides and skins, meat. Principal market: Brazil 37.1% (1998) **Imports** machinery, vehicles and parts, mineral fuels and lubricants, beverages, tobacco, chemicals, foodstuffs. Principal source: Brazil 31.8% (1998)

▪ Tourist information

Time difference GMT –3/4 **Currency** guaraní **Language** Spanish 6% (official), Guaraní 90% **Visa requirements** UK: visa not required. USA: visa not required **Embassy in the UK** Braemar Lodge, Cornwall Gardens, London SW7 4AQ. Tel: (020) 7937 1253; fax: (020) 7937 5687 **British embassy** Casilla 404, Calle Presidente Franco 706, Asunción. Tel: (21) 444 472; fax: (21) 446 385 **Chamber of commerce** Cámara y Bolsa de Comercio, Estrella 540, Asunción. Tel: (21) 493 321; fax: (21) 440 817 **Office hours** 0800–1200 and 1500–1730/1900 Mon–Fri **Banking hours** 0845–1215 Mon–Fri **Airports** international airports: Asunción (Silvio Pettirossi), Ciudad del Este (Guaraní); three domestic airports; total passenger km: 283 million (1995) **Major ports** Concepción **Chief tourist attractions** the Iguaçu Falls; the sparsely populated Gran Chaco; Asunción (La Encaración church, the Pantheon of Heroes) **Major holidays** 1 January, 3 February, 1 March, 1, 14–15 May, 12 June, 15, 25 August, 29 September, 12 October, 1 November, 8, 25, 31 December; variable: Corpus Christi, Good Friday, Holy Thursday

Chronology

1526 Visited by Italian navigator Sebastian Cabot, who travelled up Paraná River; at this time the east of the country had long been inhabited by Guaraní-speaking Amerindians, who gave the country its name, which means 'land with an important river'. **1537** Spanish made an alliance with Guaraní Indians against hostile Chaco Indians, enabling them to colonize interior plains; Asunción founded by Spanish. **1609** Jesuits arrived from Spain to convert local population to Roman Catholicism and administer the country. **1767** Jesuit missionaries expelled. **1776** Formerly part of Spanish Viceroyalty of Peru, which covered much of South America, became part of Viceroyalty of La Plata, with capital at Buenos Aires (Argentina). **1808** With Spanish monarchy overthrown by Napoleon Bonaparte, La Plata Viceroyalty became autonomous, but Paraguayans revolted against rule from Buenos Aires. **1811** Independence achieved from Spain. **1814** Under dictator Gen José Gaspar Rodriguez Francia ('El Supremo'), Paraguay became an isolated state. **1840** Francia was succeeded by his nephew, Carlos Antonio Lopez, who opened country to foreign trade and whose son,

Francisco Solano Lopez, as president from 1862, built up a powerful army. **1865–70** War with Argentina, Brazil, and Uruguay over access to sea; more than half the population died and 150,000 sq km/58,000 sq mi of territory lost. **late 1880s** Conservative Colorado Party and Liberal Party founded. **1912** Liberal leader Edvard Schaerer came to power, ending decades of political instability. **1932–35** Territory in west won from Bolivia during Chaco War (settled by arbitration in 1938). **1940–48** Presidency of autocratic Gen Higinio Moríñigo. **1948–54** Political instability; six different presidents. **1954** Gen Alfredo Stroessner seized power in a coup. He ruled as a ruthless autocrat, suppressing civil liberties; the country received initial US backing as the economy expanded. **1989** Stroessner was ousted in a coup led by Gen Andrés Rodríguez. Rodríguez was elected president; the right-of-centre military-backed Colorado Party won assembly elections. **1992** A new democratic constitution was adopted. **1993** The Colorado Party won the most seats in the first free multiparty elections, but no overall majority; its candidate, Juan Carlos Wasmosy, won the first free presidential elections. **1999** Senate leader Luis Gonzalez Macchi became president.

Peru Republic of

National name *República del Perú* **Area** 1,285,200 sq km/ 496,216 sq mi **Capital** Lima **Major towns/ cities** Arequipa, Iquitos, Chiclayo, Trujillo, Cuzco, Piura, Chimbote

Government

Head of state Alberto Fujimori from 1990 **Head of government** Alberto Pandolfi from 1998 **Political system** liberal democracy **Armed forces** 125,000; plus paramilitary forces numbering 78,000 (1997) **Conscription** conscription is selective for two years **Defence spend** (% GDP) 2.2 (1997) **Education spend** (% GNP) 2.9 (1996) **Health spend** (% GDP) 2.6 (1990–95) **Death penalty** retains the death penalty only for exceptional crimes such as crimes under military law or crimes committed in exceptional circumstances such as wartime (last execution 1979)

Population and society

Population 25,230,000 (1999 est) **Population growth rate** 1.7% (1995–2000); 1.7% (2000–05) **Ethnic groups** about 45% South American Indian, 37% mestizo, 15% European, and 3% African **Religion** Roman Catholic (state religion) **Life expectancy** 66 (men); 71 (women) (1995–2000) **Literacy rate** 94% (men); 84% (women) (1997 est) **Unemployment** 7.7% (1997)

Economy and resources

GDP (US$) 64.1 billion (1998) **GNP** (US$) 61.1 billion (1998) **GNP per capita (PPP)** (US$) 4,910 (1998 est) **Real GDP growth** (% change on previous year) 2 (1998) **Consumer price inflation** 7.3% (1998) **Foreign debt** (US$) 30.5 billion (1997) **Resources** lead, copper, iron, silver, zinc (world's fourth-largest producer), petroleum **Exports** copper, fishmeal, zinc, gold, refined petroleum products. Principal market: USA 24.9% (1997) **Imports** machinery and transport equipment, basic foodstuffs, basic manufactures, chemicals, mineral fuels, consumer goods. Principal source: USA 19.1% (1997)

▪ Tourist information

Time difference GMT –5 **Currency** nuevo sol **Language** Spanish, Quechua (both official), Aymara **Visa requirements** UK: visa not required for a stay of up to 90 days. USA: visa not required for a stay of up to 90 days **Embassy in the UK** 52 Sloane Street, London SW1X 9SP. Tel: (020) 7235 1917; fax: (020) 7235 4463 **British embassy** PO Box 854, Natalio Sanchez 125, Edificio El Pacifico, Pisos 11/12, Plaza Washington, Lima 100. Tel: (1) 433 5032; fax: (1) 433 4738 **Chamber of commerce** Confederación de Cámaras de Comercio y Producción del Perú, Avenida Gregorio Escobedo 398, Lima 11. Tel: (1) 463 3434; fax: (1) 463 2820 **Office hours** 0900–1700 Mon–Fri **Banking hours** 0930–1600 Mon–Fri (some banks open 0930–1230 Sat) **Airports** international airports: Lima (Jorge Chávez), Iquitos (Colonel Francisco Secada Vignetta), Cuzco (Velasco Astete), Arequipa (Rodríguez Ballón); 27 domestic airports; total passenger km: 2,561 million (1997 est) **Major ports** Callao, Chimbote, Salaverry **Chief tourist attractions** Lima, with its Spanish colonial architecture; Cuzco, with its pre-Inca and Inca remains, notably Machu Picchu; Lake Titicaca; Amazon rainforest in northeast **Major holidays** 1 January, 1 May, 29–30 June, 28 July (2 days), 30 August, 8 October, 1 November, 8, 25, 31 December; variable: Good Friday, Holy Thursday

Chronology

4000 BC Evidence of early settled agriculture in Chicama Valley. **AD 700–1100** Period of Wari Empire, first expansionist militarized empire in Andes. **1200** Manco Capac became the first emperor of South American Indian Quechua-speaking Incas, who established a growing and sophisticated empire centred on the Andean city of Cuzco, and believed their ruler was descended from the Sun. **late 15th century** At its zenith, the Inca Empire stretched from Quito in Ecuador to beyond Santiago in southern Chile. It superseded the Chimu civilization, which had flourished in Peru 1250–1470. **1532–33** Incas defeated by Spanish conquistadores, led by Francisco Pizarro. Empire came under Spanish rule, as part of the Viceroyalty of Peru, with capital in Lima, founded in 1535. **1780** Tupac Amaru, who claimed to be descended from the last Inca chieftain, led a failed native revolt against Spanish. **1810** Peru became the headquarters for the Spanish government as European settlers rebelled elsewhere in Spanish America. **1820–22** Fight for liberation from Spanish rule led by Gen José de San Martín and Army of Andes which, after freeing Argentina and Chile, invaded southern Peru. **1824** Became last colony in Central and South America to achieve independence from Spain after attacks from north by Field Marshal Sucre, acting for freedom fighter Simón Bolívar. **1836–39** Failed attempts at union with Bolivia. **1849–74** Around 80,000–100,000 Chinese labourers arrived in Peru to fill menial jobs such as collecting guano. **1866** Victorious naval war fought with Spain. **1879–83** Pacific War fought in alliance with Bolivia and Chile over nitrate fields of the Atacama Desert in the south; three provinces along coastal south lost to Chile. **1902** Boundary dispute with Bolivia settled. **mid-1920s** After several decades of civilian government, a series of right-wing dictatorships held power. **1927** Boundary dispute with Colombia settled. **1929** Tacna province, lost to Chile in 1880, was returned. **1941** A brief war with Ecuador secured Amazonian territory. **1945** Civilian government, dominated by left-of-centre American Popular Revolutionary Alliance (APRA, formed 1924), came to power after free elections. **1948** Army coup installed military government led by Gen Manuel Odría, who remained in power until 1956. **1963** Return to civilian rule, with centrist Fernando Belaúnde Terry as president. **1968** Return of military government in bloodless coup by Gen Juan Velasco Alvarado, following industrial unrest. Populist land reform programme introduced. **1980** Return to civilian rule, with Fernando Belaúnde as president; agrarian and industrial reforms pursued. Sendero Luminoso ('Shining Path') Maoist guerrilla group active. **1981** Boundary dispute with Ecuador renewed. **1985** Belaúnde succeeded by Social Democrat Alan García Pérez, who launched campaign to remove military and police 'old guard'. **1988** García was pressured to seek help from International Monetary Fund (IMF) as the economy deteriorated. Sendero Luminoso increased its campaign of violence. **1990** Right-of-centre Alberto Fujimori defeated ex-communist writer Vargas Llosa in presidential elections. Inflation rose to 400%; a privatization programme was launched. **1992** Fujimori allied himself with the army and suspended the constitution, provoking international criticism. The Sendero Luminoso leader was arrested and sentenced to life imprisonment. A new single-chamber legislature was elected. **1993** A new constitution was adopted. **1994** 6,000 Sendero Luminoso guerrillas surrendered to the authorities. **1995** A border dispute with Ecuador was resolved after armed clashes. Fujimori was re-elected. A controversial amnesty was granted to those previously convicted of human-rights abuses. **1996** Hostages were held in the Japanese embassy by Marxist Tupac Amaru Revolutionary Movement (MRTA) guerrillas. **1997** The hostage siege ended. **1998** Alberto Pandolfi was appointed prime minister. A border dispute that had lasted for 157 years was settled with Ecuador.

Philippines Republic of the

National name *Republika ng Pilipinas* **Area** 300,000 sq km/115,830 sq mi **Capital** Manila (on Luzon) (and chief port) **Major towns/cities** Quezon City (on Luzon), Davao, Caloocan, Cebu, Zamboanga

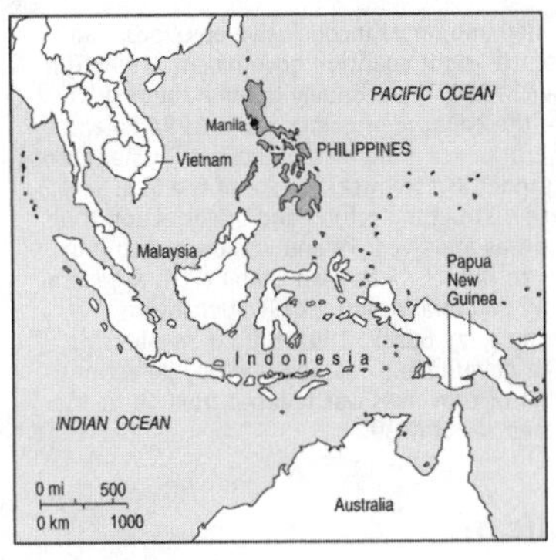

Government

Head of state and government Joseph Ejercito Estrada from 1998 **Political system** liberal democracy **Armed forces** 110,500 (1995); reserve forces 131,000; paramilitary forces around 42,500 (1997) **Conscription** military service is voluntary **Defence spend** (% GDP) 1.7 (1997) **Education spend** (% GNP) 2.2 (1996) **Health spend** (% GDP) 1.3 (1990–95) **Death penalty** retained in law, but considered abolitionist in practice; last execution in 1976

Population and society

Population 74,454,000 (1999 est) **Population growth rate** 2.1% (1995–2000); 1.8% (2000–05) **Ethnic groups** comprises more than 50 ethnic communities, although 95% of the population is designated 'Filipino', an Indo-Polynesian ethnic grouping **Religion** mainly Roman Catholic; Protestant, Muslim, local religions **Life expectancy** 67 (men); 70 (women) (1995–2000) **Literacy rate** 95% (men); 94% (women) (1997 est) **Unemployment** 7.9% (1997)

Economy and resources

GDP (US$) 65.1 billion (1998) **GNP** (US$) 78.9 billion (1998) **GNP per capita (PPP)** (US$) 3,540 (1998) **Real GDP growth** (% change on previous year) −1.6 (1998) **Consumer price inflation** 10.1% (1998) **Foreign debt** (US$) 45.4 billion (1997) **Resources** copper ore, gold, silver, chromium, nickel, coal, crude petroleum, natural gas, forests **Exports** electronic products (notably semiconductors and microcircuits), garments, agricultural products (particularly fruit and seafood), woodcraft and furniture, lumber, chemicals, coconut oil. Principal market: USA 34.2% (1998) **Imports** machinery and transport equipment, mineral fuels, basic manufactures, food and live animals, textile yarns, base metals, cereals and cereal preparations. Principal source: USA 21.8% (1998)

▪ Tourist information

Time difference GMT +8 **Currency** peso **Language** Tagalog (Filipino, official); English and Spanish; Cebuano, Ilocano, and more than 70 other indigenous languages **Visa requirements** UK: visa not required for a stay of up to 21 days. USA: visa not required for a stay of up to 21 days **Embassy in the UK** 9a Palace Green, London W8 4QE. Tel: (020) 7937 1600; fax: (020) 7937 2925 **British embassy** 15th–17th Floors, LV Locsin Building, 6752 Ayala Avenue, Makati, Metro Manila 1226. Tel: (2) 816 7116; fax: (2) 819 7206 **Chamber of commerce** Philippine Chamber of Commerce and Industry, Ground Floor, CCP Complex, Roxas Boulevard, Makati, Metro Manila 2801. Tel: (2) 833 8591; fax: (2) 816 1946 **Office hours** usually 0800–1200 and 1300–1700 Mon–Fri; some offices open 0800–1200 Sat **Banking hours** 0900–1600 Mon–Fri **Airports** international airports: Manila (Ninoy Aquino), Cebu (Mactan), Laoag City, Davao, Zamboanga, Puerto Princesa City, Subic Bay, Freeport; comprehensive internal services; total passenger km: 16,872 million (1997 est) **Major ports** Cebu, Davao (on Mindanao), Iloilo, Zamboanga (on Mindanao) **Chief tourist attractions** thousands of islands and islets, some ringed by coral reefs; Mindanao; the Visayas Islands **Major holidays** 1 January, 1 May, 12 June, 4 July, 1, 30 November, 25, 30–31 December; variable: Good Friday, Holy Thursday

Chronology

14th century Traders from Malay peninsula introduced Islam and created Muslim principalities of Manila and Jolo. **1521** Portuguese navigator Ferdinand Magellan reached the islands, but was killed in battle with islanders. **1536** Philippines named after Charles V's son (later Philip II of Spain) by Spanish navigator Ruy López de Villalobos. **1565** Philippines conquered by Spanish army led by Miguel López de Lagazpi. **1571** Manila was made capital of the colony, which was part of the Viceroyalty of Mexico. **17th century** Spanish missionaries converted much of the lowland population to Roman Catholicism. **1762–63** British occupied Manila. **1834** End of Spanish monopoly on trade; British and American merchants bought sugar and tobacco. **1896–97** Emilio Aguinaldo led a revolt against Spanish rule. **1898** Spanish-American War: US navy destroyed Spanish fleet in Manila Bay; Aguinaldo declared independence, but Spain ceded Philippines to USA. **1898–1901** Nationalist uprising suppressed by US troops; 200,000 Filipinos killed. **1907** Americans set up elected legislative assembly. **1916** Bicameral legislature introduced based on the US model. **1935** Philippines gained internal self-government with Manuel Quezon as president. **1942–45** Occupied by Japan. **1946** Philippines achieved independence from USA under President Manuel Roxas; USA retained military bases and supplied economic aid. **1957–61** 'Filipino First' policy introduced by President Carlos García to reduce economic power of Americans and Chinese; official corruption increased. **1972** President Ferdinand Marcos declared martial law and ended the freedom of the press; economic development financed by foreign loans, of which large sums were diverted by Marcos for personal use. **1981** Martial law officially ended but Marcos retained sweeping emergency powers, ostensibly needed to combat long-running Muslim and communist insurgencies. **1983** Opposition leader Benigno Aquino was murdered at Manila airport while surrounded by government troops. **1986** Corazon Aquino (widow of Benigno Aquino) used 'people's power' to force Marcos to flee the country. **1987** A 'Freedom constitution' was adopted; Aquino's People's Power won congressional elections. **1989** A state of emergency was declared after the sixth coup attempt was suppressed with US aid. **1991** The Philippine senate called for the withdrawal of US forces; US renewal of Subic Bay naval base lease was rejected. **1992** Fidel Ramos was elected to succeed Aquino; a 'Rainbow Coalition' government was formed. **1995** Imelda Marcos (the widow of Ferdinand Marcos) was elected to the House of Representatives while on bail from prison on a sentence for corruption. **1996** The LDP withdrew from the LDP–DFSP coalition. A peace agreement was made between the government and the Moro National Liberation Front (MNLF) after 25 years of civil unrest on Mindanao. **1997** Preliminary peace talks took place between the government and the Muslim secessionist Moro Islamic Liberation Front (MILF). The Supreme Court rejected a proposal to allow a second presidential term. **1998** Joseph Estrada was inaugurated as president and Gloria Macapagal Arroyo as vice-president. Imelda Marcos was acquitted of corruption charges. A dispute with China over the mineral-rich Spratly Islands was resolved with an agreement on the joint use of the resources.

Poland Republic of

National name *Rzeczpospolita Polska* **Area** 312,683 sq km/ 120,726 sq mi **Capital** Warsaw **Major towns/ cities** Łódź, Kraków (Cracow), Wrocław (Breslau), Poznań (Posen), Gdańsk (Danzig), Szczecin (Stettin), Katowice (Kattowitz), Bydgoszcz (Bromberg), Lublin

Government

Head of state Aleksander Kwaśniewski from 1995 **Head of government** Jerzy Buzek from 1997 **Political system** liberal democracy **Armed forces** 241,800 (1997) **Conscription** military service is compulsory **Defence spend** (% GDP) 2.3 (1997) **Education spend** (% GNP) 4.6 (1996) **Health spend** (% GDP) 4.8 (1990–95) **Death penalty** abolished in 1997

Population and society

Population 38,741,000 (1999 est) **Population growth rate** 0.08% (1995–2000) **Ethnic groups** 98% ethnic Western-Slav ethnic Poles; small ethnic German, Ukrainian, and Belarussian minorities **Religion** Roman Catholic 95% **Life expectancy** 68 (men); 77 (women) (1995–2000) **Literacy rate** 99% (men); 99% (women) (1997 est) **Unemployment** 10.3% (1998)

Economy and resources

GDP (US$) 148.9 billion (1998) **GNP** (US$) 150.8 billion (1998) **GNP per capita (PPP)** (US$) 6,740 (1998) **Real GDP growth** (% change on previous year) 5.5 (1998) **Consumer price inflation** 12.0% (1998) **Foreign debt** (US$) 39.88 billion (1997) **Resources** coal (world's fifth-largest producer), copper, sulphur, silver, petroleum and natural gas reserves **Exports**

machinery and transport equipment, textiles, chemicals, coal, coke, copper, sulphur, steel, food and agricultural products, clothing and leather products, wood and paper products. Principal market: Germany 36% (1998) **Imports** electro-engineering products, fuels and power (notably crude petroleum and natural gas), textiles, food products, iron ore, fertilizers. Principal source: Germany 19.5% (1998)

▪ Tourist information

Time difference GMT +1 **Currency** złoty **Language** Polish **Visa requirements** UK: visa not required for a stay of up to six months. USA: visa not required **Embassy in the UK** 47 Portland Place, London W1N 3AG. Tel: (020) 7580 4324/9; fax: (020) 7323 4018 **British embassy** Aleje Róż 1, 00-556 Warsaw. Tel: (228) 628 1001–5; fax: (228) 217 161 **Chamber of commerce** Krajowa Izba Gospodarcza (Polish Chamber of Commerce), PO Box 361, Trębacka 4, 00-077 Warsaw. Tel: (22) 260 221; fax: (22) 274 673 **Office hours** 0700–1600 Mon–Fri **Banking hours** 0800–1800 Mon–Fri **Airports** international airports: Warsaw (Okęcie), Kraków (Balice), Wrocław (Strachowice), Gdańsk; four domestic airports; total passenger km: 4,204 million (1997 est) **Major ports** Gdańsk (Danzig), Szczecin (Stettin), Gdynia (Gdingen) **Chief tourist attractions** historic cities of Gdańsk, Wrocław, Kraków, Poznań, and Warsaw; numerous health and climatic resorts; mountain and forest scenery **Major holidays** 1 January, 1, 3, 9 May, 15 August, 1, 11 November, 25–26 December; variable: Corpus Christi, Easter Monday

Chronology

966 Polish Slavic tribes under Mieszko I, leader of Piast dynasty, adopted Christianity and united region around Poznań to form first Polish state. **1241** Devastated by Mongols. **13th–14th centuries** German and Jewish refugees settled among Slav population. **1386** Jagellonian dynasty came to power: golden age for Polish culture. **1569** Poland united with Lithuania to become the largest state in Europe. **1572** Jagellonian dynasty ended; future kings were elected by nobility and gentry, who formed 10% of the population. **mid-17th century** Defeat in war against Russia, Sweden, and Brandenburg (in Germany) set in a process of irreversible decline. **1772–95** Partitioned between Russia, which ruled the northeast; Prussia, the west, including Pomerania; and Austria in the south-centre, including Galicia, where there was greatest autonomy. **1815** After Congress of Vienna, Russian eastern portion of Poland re-established as kingdom within Russian Empire. **1830 and 1863** Uprisings against repressive Russian rule. **1892** Nationalist Polish Socialist Party (PPS) founded. **1918** Independent Polish republic established after World War I, with Marshal Józef Piłsudski, founder of the PPS, elected president. **1919–21** Abortive advance into Lithuania and Ukraine. **1926** Piłsudski seized full power in coup and established an autocratic regime. **1935** On Piłsudski's death, a military regime held power under Marshal Śmigły-Rydz. **1939** Invaded by Germany; western Poland incorporated into Nazi Reich (state) and the rest became a German colony; 6 million Poles – half of them Jews – were slaughtered in the next five years. **1944–45** Liberated from Nazi rule by USSR's Red Army; boundaries redrawn westwards at the Potsdam Conference. One half of 'old Poland', 180,000 sq km/70,000 sq mi in the east, was lost to the USSR; 100,000 sq km/40,000 sq mi of ex-German territory in Silesia, along the Oder and Neisse rivers, was added, shifting the state 240 km/150 mi westwards; millions of Germans were expelled. **1947** Communist people's republic proclaimed after manipulated election. **1949** Joined Comecon. **early 1950s** Harsh Stalinist rule under communist leader Bolesław Bierut: nationalization; rural collectivization; persecution of Catholic Church members. **1955** Joined Warsaw Pact defence organization. **1956** Poznań strikes and riots. The moderate Władysław Gomułka installed as Polish United Workers' Party (PUWP) leader. **1960s** Private farming reintroduced and Catholicism tolerated. **1970** Gomułka replaced by Edward Gierek after Gdańsk riots against food price rises. **1970s** Poland heavily indebted to foreign creditors after a failed attempt to boost economic growth. **1980** Solidarity, led by Lech Wałęsa, emerged as free trade union following Gdańsk disturbances. **1981** Martial law imposed by General Wojciech Jaruzelski, trade-union activity banned, and Solidarity leaders and supporters arrested. **1983** Martial law ended. **1984** Amnesty for 35,000 political prisoners. **1988** Solidarity-led strikes and demonstrations for pay increases. Reform-communist Mieczysław Rakowski became prime minister. **1989** Agreement to relegalize Solidarity, allow opposition parties, and adopt a more democratic constitution, after talks involving Solidarity, the Communist Party, and the Catholic Church. Widespread success for Solidarity in first open elections for 40 years; noncommunist 'grand coalition' government was formed, headed by Tadeusz Mazowiecki of Solidarity; an economic austerity and free-market restructuring programme began. **1990** The PUWP was dissolved and re-formed as the Democratic Left Alliance (SLD). Wałęsa was elected president and Jan Bielecki became prime minister. **1991** A shock-therapy economic restructuring programme, including large-scale privatization, produced a sharp fall in living standards and a rise in the unemployment rate to 11%. The unpopular Bielecki resigned and, after inconclusive elections, Jan Olszewski formed a fragile centre-right coalition government. **1992** The political instability continued. **1993** The economy became the first in Central Europe to grow since the collapse of communism. **1994** Poland joined the NATO 'partnership for peace' programme; the last Russian troops left the country. **1995** Aleksander Kwaśniewski, leader of the SLD, was elected president. **1997** Further structural reform and privatization took place and a new constitution was approved. Poland was invited to join NATO and begin negotiations to join the European Union (EU). A general election was won by Solidarity Electoral Action (AWS). A coalition government was formed, led by Jerzy Buzek. **1998** Full EU membership negotiations commenced. The government was weakened by defections to the opposition. The number of provinces was reduced from 49 to 16. **1999** Poland became a full member of NATO.

Portugal Republic of

National name *República Portuguesa* **Area** 92,000 sq km/ 35,521 sq mi (including the Azores and Madeira) **Capital** Lisbon **Major towns/ cities** Porto, Coimbra, Amadora, Setúbal, Guarde, Portalegre

Government

Head of state Jorge Sampaio from 1996 **Head of government** Antonio Guterres from 1995 **Political system** liberal democracy **Armed forces** 59,300 (1997) **Conscription** 4–18 months **Defence spend** (% GDP) 2.6 (1997) **Education spend** (% GNP) 4.9 (1996) **Health spend** (% GDP) 4.5 (1990–95) **Death penalty** abolished in 1976

Population and society

Population 9,873,000 (1999 est) **Population growth rate** 0.04% (1995–2000) **Ethnic groups** most of the population is descended from peoples who inhabited the Iberian peninsula in classical and pre-classical times; there are a number of minorities from Portugal's overseas possessions and former possessions **Religion** Roman Catholic 97% **Life expectancy** 72 (men); 79 (women) (1995–2000) **Literacy rate** 94% (men); 88% (women) (1997 est) **Unemployment** 4.9% (1998)

Economy and resources

GDP (US$) 106.6 billion (1998) **GNP** (US$) 106.4 billion (1998) **GNP per capita (PPP)** (US$) 14,380 (1998) **Real GDP growth** (% change on previous year) 3.8 (1998) **Consumer price inflation** 2.4% (1998) **Resources** limestone, granite, marble, iron, tungsten, copper, pyrites, gold, uranium, coal, forests **Exports** textiles, clothing, footwear, pulp and waste paper, wood and cork manufactures, tinned fish, electrical equipment, wine, refined petroleum. Principal market: Germany 19.8% (1998) **Imports** foodstuffs, machinery and transport equipment, crude petroleum, natural gas, textile yarn, coal, rubber, plastics, tobacco. Principal source: Spain 24% (1998)

▪ Tourist information

Time difference GMT +/– 0 **Currency** escudo **Language** Portuguese **Visa requirements** UK: visa not required for a stay of up to three months. USA: visa not required for a stay of up to two months **Embassy in the UK** 11 Belgrave Square, London SW1X 8PP. Tel: (020) 7235 5331/4; fax: (020) 7245 1287 **British embassy** Rua de São Bernardo 33, 1200 Lisbon. Tel: (1) 396 1191; fax: (1) 397 6768 **Chamber of commerce** Confederação do Comércio Português, Rua dos Correeiros 79, 1° Andar, 1100 Lisbon. Tel: (1) 301 0192; fax: (1) 301 0626 **Office hours** 0900–1300 and 1500–1900 Mon–Fri **Banking hours** generally 0830–1500 Mon–Fri **Airports** international airports: Lisbon (Portela de Sacavem), Faro, Oporto (Oporto Sá Carneiro), Madeira (Funchal), Azores (Santa Maria), São Miguel; domestic services operate between these; total passenger km: 9,343 million (1997 est) **Major ports** Porto, Setúbal **Chief tourist attractions** mild climate; historic town of Lisbon; summer resorts in the Algarve; winter resorts on Madeira and the Azores **Major holidays** 1 January,

25 April, 10 June, 15 August, 5 October, 1 November, 1, 8, 24–25 December; variable: Carnival, Corpus Christi, Good Friday

Chronology

2nd century BC Romans conquered Iberian peninsula. **5th century AD** Iberia overrun by Vandals and Visigoths after fall of Roman Empire. **711** Visigoth kingdom overthrown by Muslims invading from North Africa. **997–1064** Christians resettled northern area, which came under rule of Léon and Castile. **1139** Afonso I, son of Henry of Burgundy, defeated Muslims; the area became an independent kingdom. **1340** Final Muslim invasion defeated. **15th century** Age of exploration: Portuguese mariners surveyed coast of Africa, opened sea route to India (Vasco da Gama), and reached Brazil (Pedro Cabral). **16th century** 'Golden Age': Portugal flourished as commercial and colonial power. **1580** Philip II of Spain took throne of Portugal. **1640** Spanish rule overthrown in bloodless coup; Duke of Braganza proclaimed as King John IV. **1668** Spain recognized Portuguese independence. **1755** Lisbon devastated by earthquake. **1807** Napoleonic France invaded Portugal; Portuguese court fled to Brazil. **1807–11** In the Peninsular War British forces played a leading part in liberating Portugal from the French. **1820** Liberal revolution forced King John VI to return from Brazil and accept constitutional government. **1822** First Portuguese constitution adopted. **1828** Dom Miguel blocked the succession of his niece, Queen Maria, and declared himself absolute monarch; civil war ensued between liberals and conservatives. **1834** Queen Maria regained the throne with British, French, and Brazilian help; constitutional government restored. **1840s** Severe disputes between supporters of radical 1822 constitution and more conservative 1826 constitution. **late 19th century** Government faced severe financial difficulties; rise of socialist, anarchist, and republican parties. **1908** Assassination of King Carlos I. **1910** Portugal became republic after a three-day insurrection forced King Manuel II to flee. **1911** New regime adopted liberal constitution, but republic proved unstable, violent, and corrupt. **1916–18** Portugal fought in World War I on Allied side. **1926–51** Popular military coup installed Gen António de Fragoso Carmona as president. **1933** Authoritarian 'Estado Novo' ('New State') constitution adopted. **1949** Portugal became founding member of North Atlantic Treaty Organization (NATO). **1974** Army seized power to end stalemate situation in African colonial wars. **1975** Portuguese colonies achieved independence. **1976** First free elections in 50 years. **1986** Soares became the first civilian president in 60 years; Portugal joined the European Community (EC). **1989** The Social Democrat government started to dismantle the socialist economy and privatize major industries. **1995** Antonio Gutteres was elected prime minister in the legislative elections. **1996** Jorge Sampaio (PS) was elected president.

Qatar State of

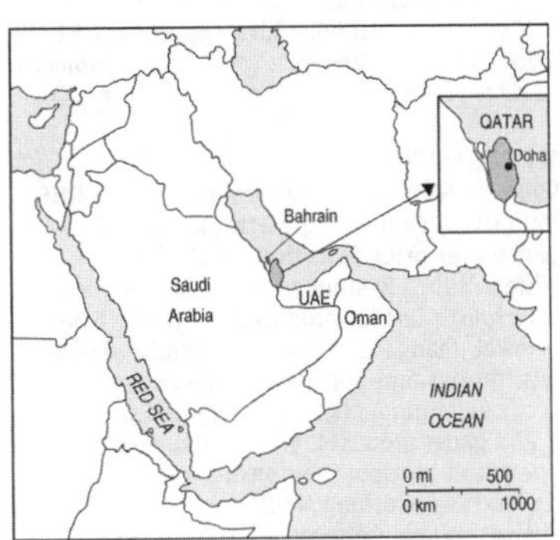

National name *Dawlat Qatar* **Area** 11,400 sq km/4,401 sq mi **Capital** Doha (and chief port) **Major towns/cities** Dukhan, centre of oil production; Halul, terminal for offshore oilfields; Umm Said, Ruwais, Wakra, Al-Khour

Government

Head of state and government Sheikh Hamad bin Khalifa al-Thani from 1995 **Political system** absolutist **Armed forces** 11,800 (1997) **Conscription** military service is voluntary **Defence spend** (% GDP) 13.7 (1997) **Education spend** (% GNP) 3.4 (1996) **Health spend** (% GDP) 3.4 (1995) **Death penalty** retained and used for ordinary crimes

Population and society

Population 589,000 (1999 est) **Population growth rate** 1.8% (1995–2025) **Ethnic composition** only about 25% of the population are indigenous Qataris; 40% are Arabs, and the others Pakistanis, Indians, and Iranians **Religion** Sunni Muslim **Life expectancy** 70 (men); 75 (women) (1995–2000) **Literacy rate** 80% (men); 81% (women) (1997 est) **Unemployment** dependent on immigrant workers – shortage of indigenous labour

Economy and resources

GDP (US$) 7.6 billion (1998 est) **GNP** (US$) 7.4 billion (1997) **GNP per capita (PPP)** (US$) 20,100 (1997 est) **Real GDP growth** (% change on previous year) 2 (1998) **Consumer price inflation** 3.1% (1998) **Foreign debt** (US$) 7.99 billion (1997) **Resources** petroleum, natural gas, water resources **Exports** petroleum. Principal market: Japan 49.7% (1997) **Imports** machinery and transport equipment, basic manufactures, food and live animals, miscellaneous manufactured articles, chemicals. Principal source: UK 25.2% (1997)

▪ Tourist information

Time difference GMT +3 **Currency** Qatari riyal **Language** Arabic (official); English **Visa requirements** UK: visa not required for a stay of up to 30 days. USA: visa required **Embassy in the UK** 1 South Audley Street, London W1Y 5DQ. Tel: (020) 7493 2200; fax: (020) 7493 3894 **British embassy** PO Box 3, Doha. Tel: (974) 421 991; fax: (974) 438 692 **Chamber of commerce** PO Box 402, Doha. Tel: (974) 425 131; fax: (974) 425 186 **Office hours** 0730–1230 and 1430–1800 Sat–Thu **Banking hours** 0730–1130 Sat–Thu **Airports** international airports: Doha; total passenger km: 2,766 million (1995) **Major holidays** 3 September, 31 December; variable: Eid-ul-Adha (4 days), end of Ramadan (4 days)

Chronology

7th century AD Islam introduced. **8th century** Developed into important trading centre during time of Abbasid Empire. **1783** The al-Khalifa family, who had migrated to northeast Qatar from west and north of the Arabian Peninsula, foiled Persian invasion and moved their headquarters to Bahrain Island, while continuing to rule the area of Qatar. **1867–68** After the Bahrain-based al-Khalifa had suppressed a revolt by their Qatari subjects, destroying the town of Doha, Britain intervened and installed Muhammad ibn Thani al-Thani, from the leading family of Qatar, as the ruling sheikh (or emir). A British Resident was given power to arbitrate disputes with Qatar's neighbours. **1871–1914** Nominally part of Turkish Ottoman Empire, although in 1893 sheik's forces inflicted a defeat on Ottomans. **1916** Qatar became British protectorate after treaty signed with Sheikh Adbullah al-Thani. **1949** Oil production began at onshore Dukhan field in west. **1960** Sheikh Ahmad al-Thani became new emir. **1968** Britain's announcement that it would remove its forces from the Persian Gulf by 1971 led Qatar to make an abortive attempt to arrange a federation of Gulf states. **1970** Constitution adopted, confirming emirate as absolute monarchy. **1971** Independence achieved from Britain. **1991** Qatar forces joined the United Nations (UN) coalition in the Gulf War against Iraq. **1995** Sheikh Khalifa was ousted by his son, Crown Prince Sheikh Hamad bin Khalifa al-Thani. **1996** The announcement of plans to introduce democracy were followed by an assassination attempt on Sheikh Hamad.

Romania

National name *România* **Area** 237,500 sq km/91,698 sq mi **Capital** Bucharest **Major towns/cities** Braşov, Timişoara, Cluj-Napoca, IaşI, Constanţa, Galaţi, Craiova, Ploieşti

Government

Head of state Emil Constantinescu from 1996 **Head of government** Mugur Isarescu from 1999 **Political system** liberal democracy **Armed forces** 227,000 (1997) **Conscription** military service is compulsory for 12–18 months **Defence spend** (% GDP) 2.3 (1997) **Education spend** (% GNP) 3.6 (1996) **Health spend** (% GDP) 3.6 (1990–95) **Death penalty** abolished in 1989

Population and society

Population 22,402,000 (1999 est) **Population growth rate** –0.4% (1995–2000) **Ethnic groups** 89% non-Slavic ethnic Romanian; substantial Hungarian, German, and Serbian minorities **Religion** mainly Romanian Orthodox **Life expectancy** 66 (men); 74 (women) (1995–2000) **Literacy rate** 99% (men); 97% (women) (1997 est) **Unemployment** 8.8% (1997)

Economy and resources

GDP (US$) 34.8 billion (1998 est) **GNP** (US$) 31.3 billion (1998) **GNP per capita (PPP)** (US$) 3,970 (1998) **Real GDP growth** (% change on previous year) –5 (1998) **Consumer price inflation** 59% (1998) **Foreign debt** (US$) 10.4 billion (1997) **Resources** brown coal, hard coal, iron ore, salt, bauxite, copper, lead, zinc, methane gas, petroleum (reserves expected to be exhausted by mid to late 1990s) **Exports** base metals and metallic articles, textiles and clothing, machinery and equipment, mineral products, foodstuffs. Principal market: Italy 19.5% (1997) **Imports** mineral products, machinery and mechanical appliances, textiles, motor cars. Principal source: Germany 16.4% (1997)

▪ Tourist information

Time difference GMT +2 **Currency** leu **Language** Romanian (official), Hungarian, German **Visa requirements** UK: visa required. USA: visa not required for a stay of up to 30 days **Embassy in the UK** Arundel House, 4 Palace Green, London W8 4QD. Tel: (020) 7937 9666/8; fax: (020) 7937 8069 **British embassy** Strada Jules Michelet 24, 70154 Bucharest. Tel: (1) 312 0305; fax: (1) 312 0229 **Chamber of commerce** Chamber of Commerce and Industry of Romania, Boulevard Nicolae Balcescu 22, 79502 Bucharest. Tel: (1) 615 4703; fax: (1) 312 2091 **Office hours** 0700–1530 Mon–Fri **Banking hours** 0900–1200 Mon–Fri; 1300–1500 Mon–Fri (currency exchange only) **Airports** international airports: Bucharest (Otopeni), Constanţa (Mihail Kogăiniceanu), Timişoara, Arad; 12 domestic airports; total passenger km: 1,857 million (1997) **Major ports** Galaţi, Constanţa, Brăila **Chief tourist attractions** Black Sea resorts (including Mangalia, Mamaia, and Eforie); Carpathian Mountains; Danube delta **Major holidays** 1–2 January, 15 April, 1 May, 1, 25–26 December

Chronology

106 Formed heartland of ancient region of Dacia, which was conquered by Roman Emperor Trajan and became a province of Roman Empire; Christianity introduced. **275** Taken from Rome by invading Goths, a Germanic people. **4th–10th centuries** Invaded by successive waves of Huns, Avars, Bulgars, Magyars, and Mongols. *c.* 1000 Transylvania, in north, became an autonomous province under Hungarian crown. **mid-14th century** Two Romanian principalities emerged, Wallachia in south, around Bucharest, and Moldova in northeast. **15th–16th centuries** The formerly autonomous principalities of Wallachia, Moldova, and Transylvania became tributaries to Ottoman Turks, despite peasant uprisings and resistance from Vlad Tepes ('the Impaler'), ruling prince of Wallachia. **late 17th century** Transylvania conquered by Austrian Habsburgs. **1829** Wallachia and Moldova brought under tsarist Russian suzerainty. **1859** Under Prince Alexandru Ion Cuza, Moldova and Wallachia united to form Romanian state. **1878** Romania's independence recognized by Great Powers in Congress of Berlin. **1881** Became kingdom under Carol I. **1916–18** Fought on Triple Entente side (Britain, France, and Russia) during World War I; acquired Transylvania and Bukovina, in north, from dismembered Austro-Hungarian Empire, and Bessarabia, in east, from Russia. This made it the largest state in Balkans. **1930** King Carol II abolished democratic institutions and established dictatorship. **1940** Forced to surrender Bessarabia and northern Bukovina, adjoining Black Sea, to Soviet Union, and northern Transylvania to Hungary; King Carol II abdicated, handing over effective power to Gen Ion Antonescu, who signed Axis Pact with Germany. **1941–44** Fought on Germany's side against Soviet Union; thousands of Jews massacred. **1944** Romania joined war against Germany. **1945** Occupied by Soviet Union; communist-dominated government installed. **1947** Paris Peace Treaty reclaimed Transylvania for Romania, but lost southern Dobruja to Bulgaria and northern Bukovina and Bessarabia to Soviet Union; King Michael, son of Carol II, abdicated and People's Republic proclaimed. **1955** Romania joined Warsaw Pact. **1958** Soviet occupation forces removed. **1965** Nicolae Ceauşescu became Romanian Communist Party leader, and pursued foreign policy autonomous of Moscow. **1975** Ceauşescu made president. **1985–87** Winter of austerity and power cuts as Ceauşescu refused to liberalize the economy. Workers' demonstrations against austerity programme are brutally crushed at Braşov. **1989** Bloody overthrow of Ceauşescu regime in 'Christmas Revolution'; Ceauşescu and wife tried and executed; estimated 10,000 dead in civil war. Power assumed by Centre-left National Salvation Front, headed by Ion Iliescu. **1990** Securitate secret police was replaced by new Romanian Intelligence Service; Eastern Orthodox Church and private farming were re-legalized. **1994** A military cooperation pact was made with Bulgaria. Far-right parties were brought into the governing coalition. **1996** There were signs of economic growth; parliamentary elections were won by the centre-right Democratic Convention Pasonic, who formed a coalition government with the reformist Social Democratic Union. **1997** An economic reform programme and drive against corruption were announced; there was a sharp increase in inflation. Former King Michael returned from exile. **1998** The Social Democrats withdrew support from ruling coalition, criticizing the slow pace of reform. Full EU membership negotiations commenced. The economy deteriorated sharply. **1999** Roadblocks were imposed by tanks north of Bucharest to prevent 10,000 striking miners entering Bucharest. Mugur Isarescu became prime minister.

Russian Federation (formerly Russian Soviet Federal Socialist Republic)

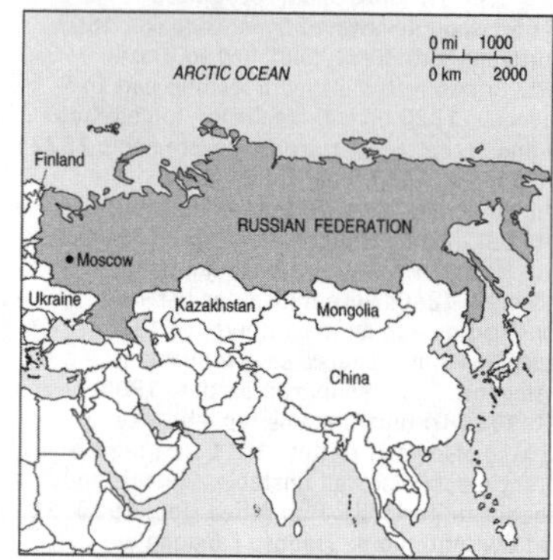

National name *Rossiskaya Federatsiya* **Area** 17,075,400 sq km/6,592,811 sq mi **Capital** Moscow **Major towns/cities** St Petersburg (Leningrad), Nizhniy Novgorod (Gorky), Rostov-na-Donu, Samara (Kuibyshev), Tver (Kalinin), Volgograd, Vyatka (Kirov), Yekaterinburg (Sverdlovsk), Novosibirsk, Chelyabinsk, Kazan, Omsk, Perm, Ufa

Government

Head of state Vladimir Putin from 2000 (acting president and prime minister from 1999) **Head of government** Mikhail Kasyanov from 2000 **Political system** emergent democracy **Armed forces** 1,240,000; paramilitary forces of 583,000 (1997) **Conscription** two years **Defence spend** (% GDP) 5.8 (1997) **Education spend** (% GNP) 4.1 (1996) **Health spend** (% GDP) 3.6 (1998) **Death penalty** retained and used for ordinary crimes

Population and society

Population 147,195,000 (1999 est) **Population growth rate** –0.2% (1995–2000) **Ethnic groups** predominantly ethnic Russian (eastern Slav); significant Tatar, Ukranian, Chuvash, Belarussian, Bashkir, and Chechen minorities **Religion** traditionally Russian Orthodox **Life expectancy** 61 (men); 73 (women) (1995–2000) **Literacy rate** 99% (men); 99% (women) (1997 est) **Unemployment** 13.3% (1998)

Economy and resources

GDP (US$) 446.9 billion (1998 est) **GNP** (US$) 337.9 billion (1998) **GNP per capita (PPP)** (US$) 3,950 (1998) **Real GDP growth** (% change on previous year) –4.6 (1998) **Consumer price inflation** 27.8% (1998) **Foreign debt** (US$) 125.6 billion (1997) **Resources** petroleum, natural gas, coal, peat, copper (world's fourth-largest producer), iron ore, lead, aluminium, phosphate rock, nickel, manganese, gold, diamonds, platinum, zinc, tin **Exports** mineral fuels, ferrous and non-ferrous metals and derivatives, precious stones, chemical products, machinery and transport equipment, weapons, timber and paper products. Principal market: Ukraine 9.1% (1998) **Imports** machinery and transport equipment, grain and foodstuffs, chemical products, textiles, clothing, footwear, pharmaceuticals, metals. Principal source: Germany 11.7% (1998)

▪ Tourist information

Time difference GMT +2–12 **Currency** rouble **Language** Russian **Visa requirements** UK: visa required. USA: visa required **Embassy in the UK** 13 Kensington Palace Gardens, London W8 4QX. Tel: (020) 7229 3628; fax: (020) 7727 8625 **British embassy** Sofiyskaya Naberezhnaya 14, Moscow 72. Tel: (095) 956 7200; fax: (095) 956 7420 **Chamber of commerce** Chamber of Commerce and Industry of the Russian Federation, Ulitsa Ilynka 6, 103684 Moscow. Tel: (095) 925 3581 **Office hours** 0900–1800/1900 Mon–Fri **Banking hours** 0930–1730 Mon–Fri **Airports** international airports: Moscow (Sheremetyevo), St Petersburg (Pulkovo); six principal domestic airports operate services to all major cities; total passenger km: 62,016 million (1997 est) **Chief tourist attractions** historic cities of Moscow and St Petersburg, with their cathedrals, fortresses, and art

Russian Federation: Republics

Republic	Capital	Area		Population (1997)
		sq km	sq mi	
Adygeya	Maikop	7,600	2,934	449,000
Alania (or North Ossetia)	Vladikavkaz	8,000	3,089	664,000
Altai	Gorno-Altaisk	92,600	35,753	202,000
Bashkortostan	Ufa	143,600	55,444	4,134,000
Buryatia	Ulan-Ude	351,300	135,637	1,050,000
Chechnya	Grozny	16,064	6,202	862,000
Chuvashia	Cheboksary	18,300	7,066	1,359,000
Dagestan	Makhachkala	50,300	19,421	2,121,000
Ingushetia	Nazran	3,236	1,249	303,000
Kabardino-Balkaria	Nalchik	12,500	4,826	789,000
Kalmykia	Elista	76,100	29,382	317,000
Karachai-Cherkessia	Cherkessk	14,100	5,444	436,000
Karelia	Petrozavodsk	172,400	66,564	780,000
Khakassia	Abakan	61,900	23,900	584,000
Komi	Syktyvkar	415,900	160,579	1,172,000
Mari El	Yoshkar-Ola	23,200	8,958	764,000
Mordovia	Saransk	26,200	10,116	950,000
Sakha	Yakutsk	3,103,200	1,198,146	1,032,000
Tatarstan	Kazan	68,000	26,255	3,763,000
Tuva	Kyzyl	170,500	65,830	310,000
Udmurtia	Izhevsk	42,100	16,255	1,636,000

treasures – the Hermitage in St Petersburg has one of the world's largest art collections; the Great Palace at Petrodvorets (formerly Peterhof); Trans-Siberian Railway; the Tver region is famed for its rivers, lakes, reservoirs, and other waterways; the Yaroslavl region has several historic towns including Yaroslavl and Uglich; the Nizhegorodskaya region has the medieval cities of Nizhniy Novgorod and Gordets, Vladimir, and Novgorod, one of Russia's oldest and grandest cities, with its famous early churches; the country's landscape includes forests, lakes, marshes, and pasture, with a rich variety of wildlife and geological formations including the volcanoes of Kamchatka and the cave formations near Archangelsk **Major holidays** 1, 7 January, 8 March, 15 April, 1–2, 9 May, 12 June, 22 August, 7 November

Chronology

9th–10th centuries Viking chieftains established own rule in Novgorod, Kiev, and other cities. **10th–12th centuries** Kiev temporarily united Russian peoples into its empire. Christianity introduced from Constantinople 988. **13th century** Mongols (Golden Horde) overran the southern steppes in 1223, compelling Russian princes to pay tribute. **14th century** Byelorussia and Ukraine came under Polish rule. **1462–1505** Ivan the Great, grand duke of Muscovy, threw off Mongol yoke and united lands in the northwest. **1547–84** Ivan the Terrible assumed title of tsar and conquered Kazan and Astrakhan; colonization of Siberia began. **1613** First Romanov tsar, Michael, elected after period of chaos. **1667** Following Cossack revolt, eastern Ukraine reunited with Russia. **1682–1725** Peter the Great modernized the bureaucracy and army; he founded a navy and a new capital, St Petersburg, introduced Western education, and wrested the Baltic seaboard from Sweden. By 1700 colonization of Siberia had reached the Pacific. **1762–96** Catherine the Great annexed the Crimea and part of Poland and recovered western Ukraine and Byelorussia. **1798–1814** Russia intervened in Revolutionary and Napoleonic Wars (1798–1801, 1805–07); repelled Napoleon, and took part in his overthrow (1812–14). **1827–29** Russian attempts to dominate the Balkans led to a war with Turkey. **1853–56** Crimean War. **1856–64** Caucasian War of conquest completed the annexation of northern Caucasus, causing more than a million people to emigrate. **1858–60** Treaties of Aigun (1858) and Peking (1860) imposed on China, annexing territories north of the Amur and east of the Ussuri rivers; Vladivostok founded on Pacific coast. **1861** Serfdom abolished. Rapid growth of industry followed, a working-class movement developed, and revolutionary ideas spread, culminating in the assassination of Alexander II in 1881. **1877–78** Russo-Turkish War **1898** Social Democratic Party founded by Russian Marxists; split into Bolshevik and Menshevik factions in 1903. **1904–05** Russo-Japanese War caused by Russian expansion in Manchuria. **1905** A revolution, though suppressed, forced tsar to accept parliament (Duma) with limited powers. **1914** Russo-Austrian rivalry in Balkans was a major cause of outbreak of World War I; Russia fought in alliance with France and Britain. **1917** Russian Revolution: tsar abdicated, provisional government established; Bolsheviks seized power under Vladimir Lenin. **1918** Treaty of Brest-Litovsk ended war with Germany; murder of former tsar; Russian Empire collapsed; Finland, Poland, and Baltic States seceded. **1918–22** Civil War between Red Army, led by Leon Trotsky, and White Russian forces with foreign support; Red Army ultimately victorious; control regained over Ukraine, Caucasus, and Central Asia. **1922** Former Russian Empire renamed Union of Soviet Socialist Republics. **1924** Death of Lenin. **1928** Joseph Stalin emerged as absolute ruler after ousting Trotsky. **1928–33** First five-year plan collectivized agriculture by force; millions died in famine. **1936–38** The Great Purge: Stalin executed his critics and imprisoned millions of people on false charges of treason and sabotage. **1939** Nazi-Soviet nonaggression pact; USSR invaded eastern Poland and attacked Finland. **1940** USSR annexed Baltic States. **1941–45** 'Great Patriotic War' against Germany ended with Soviet domination of eastern Europe and led to 'Cold War' with USA and its allies. **1949** Council for Mutual Economic Assistance (Comecon) created to supervise trade in Soviet bloc. **1953** Stalin died; 'collective leadership' in power. **1955** Warsaw Pact created. **1956** Nikita Khrushchev made 'secret speech' criticizing Stalin; USSR invaded Hungary. **1957–58** Khrushchev ousted his rivals and became effective leader, introducing limited reforms. **1960** Rift between USSR and Communist China. **1962** Cuban missile crisis: Soviet nuclear missiles installed in Cuba but removed after ultimatum from USA. **1964** Khrushchev ousted by new 'collective leadership' headed by Leonid Brezhnev and Alexei Kosygin. **1968** USSR and allies invaded Czechoslovakia. **1970s** 'Détente' with USA and western Europe. **1979** USSR invaded Afghanistan; fighting continued until Soviet withdrawal ten years later. **1985** Mikhail Gorbachev became leader and announced wide-ranging reform programme (*perestroika*). **1986** Chernobyl nuclear disaster. **1988** Special All-Union Party Congress approved radical constitutional changes and market reforms; start of open nationalist unrest in Caucasus and Baltic republics. **1989** Multi-candidate elections held in move towards 'socialist democracy'; collapse of Soviet satellite regimes in eastern Europe; end of Cold War. **1990** Baltic and Caucasian republics defied central government; Boris Yeltsin became president of Russian Federation and left the Communist Party. **1991** There was an unsuccessful coup by hardline communists; republics declared independence; communist rule dissolved in the Russian Federation; the USSR was replaced by a loose Commonwealth of Independent States (CIS). **1992** Russia assumed former USSR seat on the United Nations (UN) Security Council; a new constitution was devised; end of price controls. **1993** There was a power struggle between Yeltsin and the Congress of People's Deputies; congress was dissolved; an attempted coup was foiled; a new parliament was elected. **1994** Russia joined NATO 'Partnership for Peace'; Russian forces invaded the breakaway republic of Chechnya. **1997** A peace treaty was signed with Chechnya. Yeltsin signed an agreement on cooperation with NATO. Russia gained effective admission to the G-7 group. **1998** President Yeltsin sacked the government and appointed Sergei Kiriyenko as prime minister. The rouble was heavily devalued. Yevgeny Primakov replaced Kiriyenko as prime minister and market-centred reform was abandoned. The USA pledged aid of over 3 million tonnes of grain and meat, after a 5% contraction in GDP in 1998. **1999** Yeltsin dismissed first Primakov's government, and then Stepashin's government, appointing Vladimir Putin as prime minister. Troubles with Chechnya continued and Russian forces made a fresh onslaught on Grozny, the capital. President Yeltsin resigned on 31 December, and Putin took over as acting president. **2000** Vladimir Putin was elected president.

Rwanda Republic of

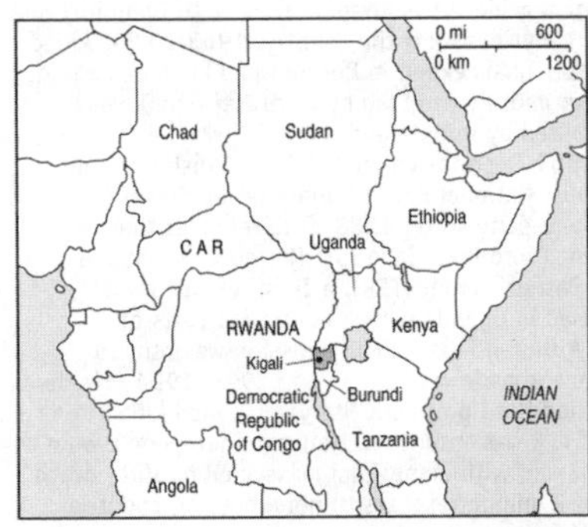

National name *Republika y'u Rwanda* **Area** 26,338 sq km/10,169 sq mi **Capital** Kigali **Major towns/cities** Butare, Ruhengeri, Gisenyi

Government

Head of state Paul Kagame from 2000 **Head of government** Pierre Celestin Rwigema from 1995 **Political system** authoritarian nationalist **Armed forces** 55,000 (1997) **Conscription** military service is voluntary **Defence spend** (% GDP) 5.5 (1997) **Education spend** (% GNP) 3.8 (1992) **Health spend** (% GDP) 1.9 (1990–95) **Death penalty** retains the death penalty for ordinary crimes but can be considered abolitionist in practice (last execution 1982)

Population and society

Population 7,235,000 (1999 est) **Population growth rate** 7.7% (1995–2000) **Ethnic groups** about 84% belong to the Hutu tribe, most of the remainder being Tutsis; there are also Twa and Pygmy minorities **Religion** Roman Catholic 54%, animist 23%, Protestant 12%, Muslim 9% **Life expectancy** 39 (men); 42 (women) (1995–2000) **Literacy rate** 71% (men); 56% (women) (1997 est)

Economy and resources

GDP (US$) 2.08 billion (1998) **GNP** (US$) 1.9 billion (1998) **GNP per capita (PPP)** (US$) 690 (1998) **Real GDP growth** (% change on previous year) 7 (1998) **Consumer price inflation** 10% (1998) **Foreign debt** (US$) 1.11 billion (1997) **Resources** cassiterite (a tin-bearing ore), wolframite (a tungsten-bearing ore), natural gas, gold, columbo-tantalite, beryl **Exports** coffee, tea, tin ores and concentrates, pyrethrum, quinquina. Principal market: Belgium–Luxembourg 36.1% (1997) **Imports** food, clothing, mineral fuels and lubricants, construction materials, transport equipment, machinery, tools, consumer goods. Principal source: Tanzania 14.8% (1997)

▪ Tourist information

Time difference GMT +2 **Currency** Rwanda franc **Language** Kinyarwanda, French (official); Kiswahili **Visa requirements** UK: visa required. USA: visa required **Embassy in the UK** 42 Aylmer Road, London N2. Tel/fax: (020) 7347 6967 **British embassy** the British Embassy in Kampala (see Uganda) deals with enquiries relating to Rwanda; British Consulate, BP 356, Avenue Paul VI, Kigali. Tel: 75219 or 75905; telex: 509 (a/b 09 RWANDEX RW) **Chamber of commerce** Chambre de Commerce et de l'Industrie du Rwanda, BP 319, Kigali. **Office hours** 0800–1600 Mon–Fri; 0800–1200 Sat **Banking hours** 0800–1200 and 1400–1800 Mon–Fri; 0800–1300 Sat **Airports** international airports: Kigali (Kanombe), Kamembe; four domestic airfields; total passenger km: 2 million (1994) **Chief tourist attractions** people are advised against all but essential travel to Rwanda; random violence and robbery continue **Major holidays** 1, 28 January, 1 May, 1, 5 July, 1, 15 August, 25 September, 26 October, 1 November, 1, 8, 24–25 December; variable: Carnival, Corpus Christi, Good Friday

Chronology

10th century onwards Hutu peoples settled in region formerly inhabited by hunter-gatherer Twa Pygmies, becoming peasant farmers. **14th century onwards** Majority Hutu community came under dominance of cattle-owning Tutsi peoples, immigrants from the east, who became a semi-aristocracy and established control through land and cattle contracts. **15th century** Ruganzu Bwimba, a Tutsi leader, founded kingdom near Kigali. **17th century** Central Rwanda and outlying Hutu communities subdued by Tutsi mwami (king) Ruganzu Ndori. **late 19th century** Under the great Tutsi king, Kigeri Rwabugiri, a unified state with a centralized military structure was established. **1890** Known as Ruandi, the Tutsi kingdom, along with neighbouring Burundi, came under nominal German control, as Ruanda-Urundi. **1916** Occupied by Belgium during World War I. **1923** Belgium granted League of Nations mandate to administer Ruanda-Urundi; they were to rule 'indirectly' through Tutsi chiefs. **1959** Interethnic warfare between Hutu and Tutsi, forcing mwami Kigeri V into exile. **1961** Republic proclaimed after mwami deposed. **1962** Independence from Belgium achieved as Rwanda, with Hutu Grégoire Kayibanda as president; many Tutsis left the country. **1963** 20,000 killed in interethnic clashes, after Tutsis exiled in Burundi had launched a raid. **1973** Kayibanda ousted in military coup led by Hutu Maj-Gen Juvenal Habyarimana; this was caused by resentment of Tutsis, who held some key government posts. **1981** Elections created civilian legislation, but dominated by Hutu socialist National Revolutionary Development Movement (MRND), in a one-party state. **1988** Hutu refugees from Burundi massacres streamed into Rwanda. **1990** The government was attacked by the Rwanda Patriotic Front (FPR), a Tutsi refugee military-political organization based in Uganda, which controlled parts of northern Rwanda. **1993** A United Nations (UN) mission was sent to monitor the peace agreement made with the FPR in 1992. **1994** President Habyarimana and Burundian Hutu president Ntaryamira were killed in an air crash; involvement of FPR was suspected. Half a million people were killed in the ensuing civil war, with many Tutsi massacred by Hutu death squads and the exodus of 2 million refugees to neighbouring countries. The government fled as FPR forces closed in. An interim coalition government was installed, with moderate Hutu and FPR leader, Pasteur Bizimungu, as president. **1995** A war-crimes tribunal opened and government human-rights abuses were reported. Pierre Rwigema was appointed prime minister by President Bizimungu. **1996–97** Rwanda and Zaire (Democratic Republic of Congo) were on the brink of war after Tutsi killings of Hutu in Zaire. A massive Hutu refugee crisis was narrowly averted as thousands were allowed to return to Rwanda. **1998** 378 rebels were killed by the Rwandan army. **2000** President Bizimungu resigned after disagreeing with his party, the RPF. Paul Kagame, the vice-president, became interim president.

St Kitts and Nevis (or St Christopher and Nevis) Federation of

Area 262 sq km/101 sq mi (St Kitts 168 sq km/65 sq mi, Nevis 93 sq km/36 sq mi) **Capital** Basseterre (on St Kitts) (and chief port) **Major towns/cities** Charlestown (largest on Nevis), Newcastle, Sandy Point Town, Dieppe Bay Town

Government

Head of state Queen Elizabeth II from 1983, represented by Governor General Dr Cuthbert Montraville Sebastian from 1996 **Head of government** Denzil Douglas from 1995 **Political system** liberal democracy **Armed forces** army disbanded in 1981 and absorbed by Volunteer Defence Force; participates in US-sponsored Regional Security System established in 1982 **Education spend** (% GNP) 3.8 (1996) **Health spend** (% GDP) 3.8 (1998) **Death penalty** retained and used for ordinary crimes

Population and society

Population 42,000 (1999 est) **Population growth rate** −0.8% (1995–2000) **Ethnic groups** almost entirely of African descent **Religion** Anglican 36%, Methodist 32%, other Protestant 8%, Roman Catholic 10% **Life expectancy** 65 (men); 71 (women) (1998 est) **Literacy rate** 99% (men); 97% (women) (1998 est) **Unemployment** 4.5% (1996 est)

Economy and resources

GDP (US$) 272 million (1998) **GNP** (US$) 250 million (1998) **GNP per capita (PPP)** (US$) 7,940 (1998) **Real GDP growth** (% change on previous year) 3 (1998) **Consumer price inflation** 1% (1998) **Foreign debt** (US$) 62 million (1997) **Exports** sugar, manufactures, postage stamps; sugar and sugar products accounted for approximately 40% of export earnings in 1992. Principal market: USA 46.6% (1996) **Imports** foodstuffs, basic manufactures, machinery, mineral fuels. Principal source: USA 45% (1996)

▪ Tourist information

Time difference GMT −4 **Currency** East Caribbean dollar **Language** English (official) **Visa requirements** UK: visa not required. USA: visa not required **Embassy in the UK** High Commission for Eastern Caribbean States, 10 Kensington Court, London W8 5DL. Tel: (020) 7937 9522; fax: (020) 7937 5514 **British embassy** the British High Commission in St John's (see Antigua and Barbuda) deals with enquiries relating to St Kitts and Nevis **Chamber of commerce** St Kitts and Nevis Chamber of Industry and Commerce, PO Box 332, South Square Street, Basseterre. Tel: (809) 465 2980; fax: (809) 465 4490 **Office hours** 0800–1200 and 1300–1600 Mon–Fri **Banking hours** 0800–1500 Mon–Thu; 0800–1500/1700 Fri and 0830–1100 Sat **Airports** international airports: Basseterre (Golden Rock), Charlestown on Nevis (Newcastle Airfield); domestic services operate between these **Chief tourist attractions** coral beaches on St Kitts' north and west coasts; coconut forests; spectacular mountain scenery on Nevis; St Kitts' historical Brimstone Hill Fort and associations with Lord Nelson and Alexander Hamilton **Major holidays** 1 January, 19 September, 25–26, 31 December; variable: Good Friday, Easter Monday, Whit Monday, Labour (May), Queen's Birthday (June), August Monday

Chronology

1493 Visited by the explorer Christopher Columbus, after whom the main island is named, but for next two centuries the islands were left in the possession of the indigenous Caribs. **1623 and 1628** St Kitts and Nevis islands successively settled by British as their first Caribbean colony, with 2,000 Caribs brutally massacred in 1626. **1783** In the Treaty of Versailles France, which had long disputed British possession, rescinded its claims to the islands, on which sugar cane plantations developed, worked by imported African slaves. **1816** Anguilla was joined politically to the two islands. **1834** Abolition of slavery. **1871–1956** Part of the Leeward Islands Federation. **1937** Internal self-government granted. **1952** Universal adult suffrage granted. **1958–62** Part of the Federation of the West Indies. **1967** St Kitts, Nevis, and Anguilla achieved internal self-government, within the British Commonwealth, with Robert Bradshaw, Labour Party leader, as prime minister. **1970** NRP formed, calling for separation for Nevis. **1971** Anguilla returned to being a British dependency after rebelling against domination by St Kitts. **1980** People's Action Movement (PAM) and NRP centrist coalition government, led by Kennedy Simmonds, formed after inconclusive general election. **1983** Full independence was achieved within the Commonwealth. **1994** A three-week state of emergency was imposed after violent antigovernment riots by Labour Party supporters in Basseterre. **1995** Labour Party won a general election; Denzil Douglas became prime minister. **1997** Nevis withdrew from the federation. **1998** Nevis referendum on secession failed to secure support.

St Lucia

Area 617 sq km/238 sq mi **Capital** Castries **Major towns/cities** Soufrière, Vieux-Fort, Laborie

Government

Head of state Queen Elizabeth II from 1979, represented by Governor General Dr Perlette Louisy from 1997 **Head of government** Kenny Anthony from 1997 **Political system** liberal democracy **Armed forces** none; participates in the US-sponsored Regional Security System established in 1982; police force numbers around 300 **Education spend** (% GNP) 9.8 (1996) **Health spend** (% GDP) 2.5 (1995) **Death penalty** retained and used for ordinary crimes

Population and society

Population 154,000 (1999 est) **Population growth rate** 1.4% (1995–2000) **Ethnic groups** great majority of African descent **Religion** Roman Catholic 90% **Life expectancy** 68 (men); 75 (women) (1998 est) **Literacy rate** 81% (men); 82%(women) (1997 est) **Unemployment** 15% (1996 est)

Economy and resources

GDP (US$) 610 million (1998) **GNP** (US$) 546 million (1998) **GNP per capita (PPP)** (US$) 4,610 (1998) **Real GDP growth** (% change on previous year) 3 (1998) **Consumer price inflation** 2.8% (1998) **Foreign debt** (US$) 151.7 million (1997) **Resources** geothermal energy **Exports** bananas, coconut oil, cocoa beans, copra, beverages, tobacco, miscellaneous articles. Principal market: UK 50% (1995) **Imports** machinery and transport equipment, foodstuffs, basic manufactures, mineral fuels. Principal source: USA 36% (1995)

▪ Tourist information

Time difference GMT –4 **Currency** East Caribbean dollar **Language** English; French patois **Visa requirements** UK: visa not required. USA: visa not required **Embassy in the UK** High Commission for Eastern Caribbean States, 10 Kensington Court, London W8 5DL. Tel: (020) 7937 9522; fax: (020) 7937 5514 **British embassy** British High Commission, PO Box 227, Derek Walcott Square, Castries. Tel: (809) 452 2484; fax: (809) 453 1543 **Chamber of commerce** St Lucia Chamber of Commerce, Industry and Agriculture, PO Box 482, Micond Street, Castries. Tel: (809) 452 3165; fax: (809) 453 6907 **Office hours** 0800–1600 Mon–Fri **Banking hours** generally 0800–1500 Mon–Thu; 0800–1700 Fri (some banks open 0800–1200 Sat) **Airports** international airports: Castries (Vigie), Vieux Fort (Hewanorra); domestic flights operate between these; aircraft arrivals: 42,436 (1993) **Major ports** Vieux-Fort **Chief tourist attractions** tropical climate; sandy beaches; mountain scenery; rich birdlife; historical sites; sulphur baths at Soufrière **Major holidays** 1–2 January, 22 February, 1 May, 13, 25–26 December; variable: Carnival, Corpus Christi, Good Friday, Easter Monday, Whit Monday, Emancipation (August), Thanksgiving (October)

Chronology

1502 Sighted by the explorer Christopher Columbus on St Lucia's day but not settled for more than a century due to hostility of the island's Carib Indian inhabitants. **1635** Settled by French, who brought in slaves to work sugar cane plantations as the Carib community was annihilated. **1814** Ceded to Britain as a crown colony, following Treaty of Paris; African slaves brought in to work sugar cane plantations. **1834** Slavery abolished. **1860s** A major coal warehousing centre until the switch to oil and diesel fuels in 1930s. **1871–1956** Part of Leeward Islands Federation. **1951** Universal adult suffrage granted. **1967** Acquired internal self-government as a West Indies associated state. **1979** Independence achieved within Commonwealth with John Compton, leader of United Workers' Party (UWP), as prime minister. **1991** Integration with other Windward Islands (Dominica, Grenada, and St Vincent) was proposed. **1993** Unrest and strikes by farmers and agricultural workers arose as a result of depressed prices for the chief cash crop, bananas.

St Vincent and the Grenadines

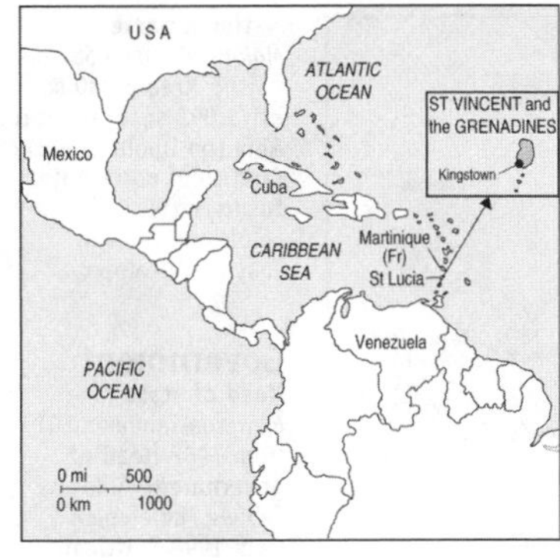

Area 388 sq km/150 sq mi, including islets of the Northern Grenadines 43 sq km/ 17 sq mi **Capital** Kingstown **Major towns/ cities** Georgetown, Châteaubelair, Layon, Baronallie

Government

Head of state Queen Elizabeth II from 1979, represented by governor general David Jack from 1989 **Head of government** James Mitchell from 1984 **Political system** liberal democracy **Armed forces** none – police force only; participates in the US-sponsored Regional Security System established in 1982 **Education spend** (% GNP) 6.7 (1993/ 94) **Health spend** (% GDP) 4.4 (1990) **Death penalty** retained and used for ordinary crimes

Population and society

Population 120,000 (1999 est) **Population growth rate** 0.7% (1995–2000) **Ethnic groups** largely of African origin; most of the original indigenous Caribs have disappeared **Religion** Anglican, Methodist, Roman Catholic **Life expectancy** 72 (men); 76 (women) (1998 est) **Literacy rate** 93% (men); 88% (women) (1997 est) **Unemployment** 38% (1995 est)

Economy and resources

GDP (US$) 275 million (1998 est) **GNP** (US$) 274 million (1998) **GNP per capita (PPP)** (US$) 4,090 (1998) **Real GDP growth** (% change on previous year) 4 (1998) **Consumer price inflation** 3.8% (1998) **Foreign debt** (US$) 257.8 million (1997) **Exports** bananas, eddoes, dasheen, sweet potatoes, flour, ginger, tannias, plantains. Principal market: UK 38.5% (1996) **Imports** basic manufactures, machinery and transport equipment, food and live animals, mineral fuels, chemicals, miscellaneous manufactured articles. Principal source: USA 38.6% (1996)

▪ Tourist information

Time difference GMT –4 **Currency** East Caribbean dollar **Language** English; French patois **Visa requirements** UK: visa not required. USA: visa not required **Embassy in the UK** High Commission for East Caribbean States, 10 Kensington Court, London W8 5DL. Tel: (020) 7937 9522; fax: (020) 7937 5514 **British embassy** British High Commission, PO Box 132, Granby Street, Kingstown. Tel: (809) 457 1701/2; fax: (809) 456 2720 **Chamber of commerce** St Vincent and the Grenadines Chamber of Industry and Commerce, PO Box 134, Halifax Street, Kingstown. Tel: (809) 457 1464; fax: (809) 456 2944 **Office hours** generally 0800–1600 Mon–Fri **Banking hours** 0800–1500 Mon–Thu; 0800–1700 Fri **Airports** international airports: Kingstown (E T Joshua); four domestic airports; visitor arrivals: 87,951 (1996) **Chief tourist attractions** famous white beaches, clear waters, lush vegetation; excellent yachting facilities **Major holidays** 1, 22 January, 27 October, 25–26 December; variable: Carnival

(July), Good Friday, Easter Monday, Whit Monday, Labour (May), Caricom (July), Emancipation (August)

Chronology
1498 Main island visited by the explorer Christopher Columbus on St Vincent's day. **17th–18th centuries** Possession disputed by France and Britain, with fierce resistance from the indigenous Carib community. **1783** Recognized as British crown colony by Treaty of Versailles. **1795–97** Carib uprising, with French support, resulted in deportation of 5,000 to Belize and Honduras. **1834** Slavery abolished. **1902** Over 2,000 killed by the eruption of La Soufrière volcano. **1951** Universal adult suffrage granted. **1958–62** Part of West Indies Federation. **1969** Achieved internal self-government. **1979** Achieved full independence within Commonwealth. **1981** General strike against new industrial-relations legislation at a time of economic recession. **1984** James Mitchell, of the centre-right New Democratic Party (NDP) became prime minister.

Samoa Independent State of

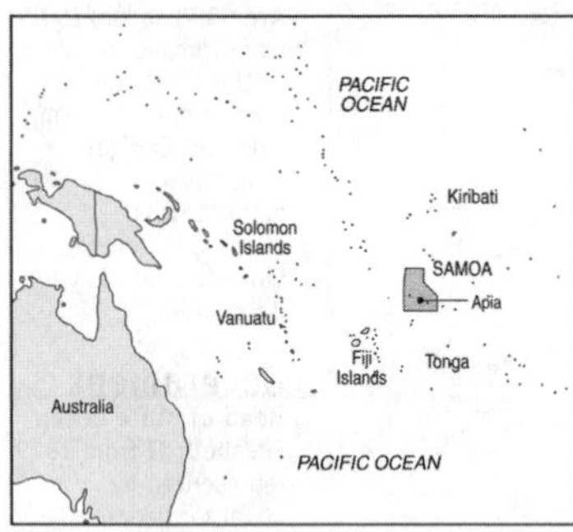

National name *Malotutu'atasi o Samoa i Sisifo* **Area** 2,830 sq km/1,092 sq mi **Capital** Apia (on Upolu island) (and chief port) **Major towns/cities** Lalomanu, Falevai, Tuasivi, Falealupo

Government
Head of state King Malietoa Tanumafili II from 1962 **Head of government** Tuila'epa Sa'ilele Malielegaoi from 1998 **Political system** liberal democracy **Armed forces** no standing defence forces; under Treaty of Friendship signed with New Zealand in 1962, the latter acts as sole agent in Samoa's dealings with other countries and international organizations **Education spend** (% GNP) 4.2 (1993/94) **Health spend** (% GDP) 5.3 (1995) **Death penalty** retains the death penalty for ordinary crimes, but can be considered abolitionist in practice

Population and society
Population 177,000 (1999 est) **Population growth rate** 1.4% (1995–2000) **Ethnic groups** 90% of Samoan (Polynesian) origin; 10% Euronesian (mixed European and Polynesian) **Religion** Congregationalist; also Roman Catholic, Methodist **Life expectancy** 69 (men); 74 (women) (1995–2000) **Literacy rate** 98% (men); 95% (women) (1997 est)

Economy and resources
GDP (US$) 194 million (1998 est) **GNP** (US$) 180 million (1998) **GNP per capita (PPP)** (US$) 3,440 (1998) **Real GDP growth** (% change on previous year) 2.5 (1998) **Consumer price inflation** 9% (1998) **Foreign debt** (US$) 169 million (1997) **Exports** coconut cream, beer, cigarettes, taro, copra, cocoa, bananas, timber. Principal market: Australia 69.8% (1997) **Imports** food and live animals, machinery and transport equipment, mineral fuel, clothing and other manufactured goods. Principal source: Australia 26.9% (1997)

▪ Tourist information
Time difference GMT −11 **Currency** tala, or Samoa dollar **Language** English, Samoan (official) **Visa requirements** UK: visa not required. USA: visa not required **Embassy for the UK** avenue Franklin D Roosevelt 123, B-1050 Brussels, Belgium. Tel: (2) 660 8454; fax: (2) 675 0336 **British embassy** Office of the Honorary British Representative, c/o Kruse Va'ai and Barlow, PO Box 2029, Apia. Tel: (685) 21895, fax: (685) 21407 **Chamber of commerce** c/o Pacific Forum Line, Matantu-tai, PO Box 655, Apia. Tel: (685) 20345 **Office hours** 0800–1200 and 1300–1630 Mon–Fri **Banking hours** 0900–1500 Mon–Fri; some banks open 0830–1130 Sat **Airports** international airports: Apia (Faleolo); two domestic airstrips **Chief tourist attractions** pleasant climate; spectacular scenery **Major holidays** 1–2 January, 25 April, 1 June (3 days), 12 October, 25–26 December; variable: Good Friday, Easter Monday, Holy Saturday

Chronology
c. 1000 BC Settled by Polynesians from Tonga. **AD 950–1250** Ruled by Tongan invaders; the Matai (chiefly) system was developed. **15th century** United under the Samoan Queen Salamasina. **1722** Visited by Dutch traders. **1768** Visted by the French navigator Louis Antoine de Bougainville. **1830** Christian mission established and islanders were soon converted to Christianity. **1887–89** Samoan rebellion against German attempt to depose paramount ruler and install its own puppet regime. **1889** Under the terms of the Act of Berlin, Germany took control of the nine islands of Western Samoa, while the USA was granted American Samoa, and Britain Tonga and the Solomon Islands. **1900s** More than 2,000 Chinese brought in to work coconut plantations. **1914** Occupied by New Zealand on the outbreak of World War I. **1918** Nearly a quarter of the population died in an influenza epidemic. **1920s** Development of nationalist movement, the Mau, which resorted to civil disobedience. **1920–61** Administered by New Zealand under League of Nations and, later, United Nations mandate. **1959** Local government established, headed by chief minister Fiame Mata'afa Mulinu'u. **1961** Referendum favoured independence. **1962** King Malietoa Tanumafili succeeded to the throne. **1962** Independence achieved within Commonwealth, with Mata'afa as prime minister, a position he retained (apart from a short break 1970–73) until his death in 1975. **1990** Universal adult suffrage was introduced and the power of Matai (elected clan leaders) reduced. **1991** Major damage was caused by 'Cyclone Val'. **1998** Name was changed officially to 'Samoa'. Tuila'epa Sa'ilele Malielegaoi, became the new prime minister.

San Marino Most Serene Republic of

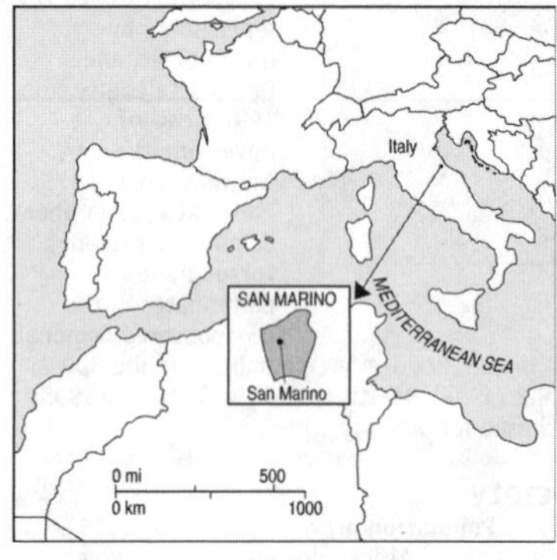

National name *Serenissima Repubblica di San Marino* **Area** 61 sq km/24 sq mi **Capital** San Marino **Major towns/cities** Serravalle (industrial centre), Faetano, Fiorentino, Monte Giardino

Government
Head of state and government two captains regent, elected for a six-month period **Political system** liberal democracy **Armed forces** voluntary military forces and a paramilitary gendarmerie **Conscription** military service is not compulsory, but all citizens between the ages of 15 and 55 may be enlisted in certain circumstances to defend the state **Death penalty** abolished in 1865

Population and society
Population 25,000 (1999 est) **Population growth rate** 1.3% (1995–2000) **Ethnic groups** predominantly Italian **Religion** Roman Catholic 95% **Life expectancy** 78 (men); 85 (women) (1998 est) **Literacy rate** 99% (men); 98% (women) (1998 est) **Unemployment** 4.4% (1997)

Economy and resources
GDP (US$) 500 million (1997 est) **GNP** (US$) 490 million (1997 est) **GNP per capita (PPP)** (US$) 20,000 (1997 est) **Real GDP growth** (% change on previous year) 3.0 (1995) **Consumer price inflation** 2% (1997) **Resources** limestone and other building stone **Exports** wood machinery, chemicals, wine, olive oil, textiles, tiles, ceramics, varnishes, building stone, lime, chestnuts, hides. Principal market: Italy **Imports** consumer goods, raw materials, energy supply. Principal source: Italy

▪ Tourist information
Time difference GMT +1 **Currency** Italian lira **Language** Italian **Visa requirements** UK: visa not required. USA: visa not required **Embassy in the UK** San Marino has no diplomatic representation in the UK; the UK Department of Trade and Industry has an Italy desk. Tel: (020) 7215 4385; fax (020) 7215 4711 **British embassy** British Consulate, Lungarno Corsini 2, 50123 Florence, Italy. Tel: (55) 284 133; fax: (55) 219 112 **Office hours** see Italy **Banking hours** see Italy **Airports** international airports: none (the closest are at Rimini and Bologna, in Italy; a bus service connects San Marino with Rimini) **Chief tourist attractions** mild climate; varied

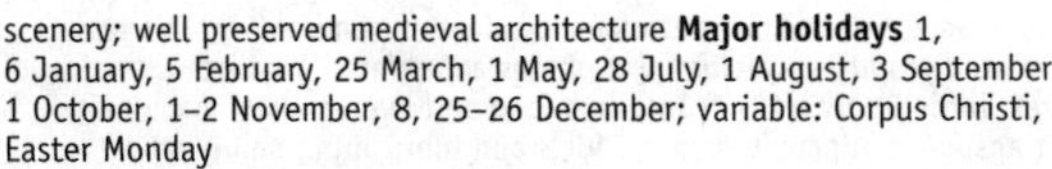
scenery; well preserved medieval architecture **Major holidays** 1, 6 January, 5 February, 25 March, 1 May, 28 July, 1 August, 3 September, 1 October, 1–2 November, 8, 25–26 December; variable: Corpus Christi, Easter Monday

Chronology

c. AD 301 Founded as a republic (the world's oldest surviving) by St Marinus and a group of Christians who settled there to escape persecution. **12th century** Self-governing commune. **1600** Statutes (constitution) provided for a parliamentary form of government, based around the Great and General Council. **1815** Independent status of the republic recognized by the Congress of Vienna. **1862** Treaty with Italy signed; independence recognized under Italy's protection. **1945–57** Communist-Socialist administration in power, eventually ousted in a bloodless 'revolution'. **1957–86** Governed by a series of left-wing and centre-left coalitions. **1971** Treaty with Italy renewed. **1992** San Marino joined the United Nations (UN). **1998** The ruling PDCS–PSS coalition remained in power after a general election.

São Tomé and Príncipe Democratic Republic of

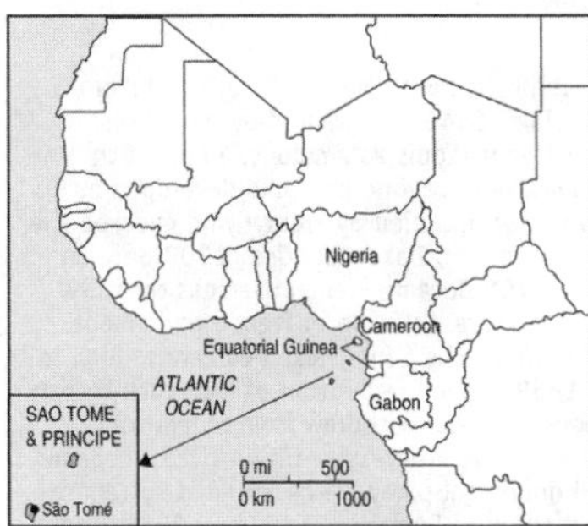

National name *República Democrática de São Tomé e Príncipe* **Area** 1,000 sq km/386 sq mi **Capital** São Tomé **Major towns/cities** São António, Santana, Porto-Alegre

Government

Head of state Miguel Trovoada from 1991 **Head of government** Carlos da Graca from 1994 **Political system** emergent democracy **Armed forces** no proper army; reorganization of island's armed forces (estimated at 900) and police into two separate police forces (one for public order, the other for criminal investigations) was initiated in 1992 **Education spend** (% GNP) N/A **Health spend** (%GDP) 6.2 (1995) **Death penalty** abolished in 1990

Population and society

Population 154,000 (1999 est) **Population growth rate** 2% (1995–2000) **Ethnic groups** predominantly African **Religion** Roman Catholic 80%, animist **Life expectancy** 63 (men); 66 (women) (1998 est) **Literacy rate** 85% (men); 62% women (1991 est) **Unemployment** 28% (1996 est)

Economy and resources

GDP (US$) 44 million (1998) **GNP** (US$) 40 million (1998) **GNP per capita (PPP)** (US$) 1,350 (1998) **Real GDP growth** (% change on previous year) 2.5 (1998 est) **Consumer price inflation** 42.3% (1998) **Foreign debt** (US$) 273 million (1997) **Exports** cocoa, copra, coffee, bananas, palm oil. Principal market: the Netherlands 50.9% (1997) **Imports** capital goods, food and live animals (of which 60.7% were donations in 1994), petroleum and petroleum products. Principal source: Portugal 26.3% (1997)

▪ Tourist information

Time difference GMT +/– 0 **Currency** dobra **Language** Portuguese (official); Fang (a Bantu language) **Visa requirements** UK: visa required. USA: visa required **Embassy in the UK** 42 avenue Brugmann, 1060 Brussels, Belgium. Tel: (2) 347 5375; fax: (2) 347 5408; Honorary Consulate of the Democratic Republic of São Tomé e Príncipe, 42 North Audley Street, London W1A 4PY. Tel: (020) 7499 1995; fax: (020) 7629 6460 **British embassy** British Consulate, c/o Hull Blythe (Angola) Ltd, BP 15, São Tomé. Telex: 220 (a/b HBALTD ST) (the British Embassy in Luanda, Angola deals with enquiries relating to São Tomé e Príncipe) **Chamber of commerce** the British Embassy in Luanda (see Angola) deals with queries relating to São Tomé and Príncipe **Banking hours** 0730–1130 Mon–Fri **Airports** international airports: São Tomé; one domestic airport (Príncipe); total passenger km: 8 million (1995) **Chief tourist attractions** unspoilt beaches; spectacular mountain scenery; unique species of flora and fauna **Major holidays** 1 January, 3 February, 1 May, 12 July, 6, 30 September, 21, 25 December; variable: Corpus Christi, Good Friday, Easter Monday

Chronology

1471 First visited by the Portuguese, who imported convicts and slaves to work on sugar plantations in the formerly uninhabited islands. **1522** Became a province of Portugal. **1530** Slaves successfully revolted, forcing plantation owners to flee to Brazil; thereafter became a key staging post for Congo-Americas slave trade. **19th century** Forced contract labour used to work coffee and cocoa plantations. **1953** More than 1,000 striking plantation workers gunned down by Portuguese troops. **1960** First political party formed, the forerunner of the socialist-nationalist Movement for the Liberation of São Tomé e Príncipe (MLSTP). **1974** Military coup in Portugal led to strikes, demonstrations, and army mutiny in São Tomé; thousands of Portuguese settlers fled the country. **1975** Independence achieved, with Manuel Pinto da Costa (MLSTP) as president; close links developed with communist bloc, and plantations nationalized. **1984** Formally declared a nonaligned state as economy deteriorated. **1988** Coup attempt against da Costa foiled by Angolan and East European troops. **1990** Influenced by collapse of communism in Eastern Europe, MLSTP abandoned Marxism; a new pluralist constitution was approved in a referendum. **1991** First multiparty elections. **1994** MLSTP returned to power with Carlos da Graca as prime minister. **1998** MLSTP–PSD won an absolute majority in the assembly.

Saudi Arabia Kingdom of

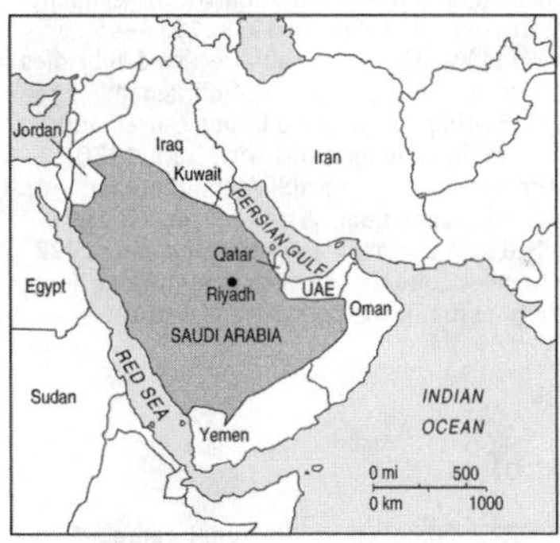

National name *Mamlaka al-'Arabiya as-Sa'udiya* **Area** 2,200,518 sq km/ 849,620 sq mi **Capital** Riyadh **Major towns/ cities** Jiddah, Mecca, Medina, Taif, Dammam, Hufuf

Government

Head of state and government King Fahd Ibn Abdul Aziz from 1982 **Political system** absolutist **Armed forces** 162,500; paramilitary forces 15,500 (1997) **Conscription** military service is voluntary **Defence spend** (% GDP) 12.4 (1997) **Education spend** (% GNP) 5.5 (1990–95) **Health spend** (% GDP) 3.1 (1990–95) **Death penalty** retained and used for ordinary crimes

Population and society

Population 20,899,000 (1999 est) **Population growth rate** 3.4% (1995–2000); 3.1% (2000–05) **Ethnic groups** around 90% Arab; 10% Afro-Asian **Religion** Sunni Muslim; there is a Shiite minority **Life expectancy** 70 (men); 73 (women) (1995–2000) **Literacy rate** 81% (men); 63% (women) (1997 est)

Economy and resources

GDP (US$) 125.8 billion (1998) **GNP** (US$) 120 billion (1998 est) **GNP per capita (PPP)** (US$) 9,200 (1998 est) **Real GDP growth** (% change on previous year) 1.6 (1998) **Consumer price inflation** 1.5% (1999) **Foreign debt** US $ 21.35 billion (1997) **Resources** petroleum, natural gas, iron ore, limestone, gypsum, marble, clay, salt, gold, uranium, copper, fish **Exports** crude and refined petroleum, petrochemicals, wheat. Principal market: Japan 17% (1997) **Imports** machinery and transport equipment, foodstuffs, beverages, tobacco, chemicals and chemical products, base metals and metal manufactures, textiles and clothing. Principal source: USA 23.3% (1997)

▪ Tourist information

Time difference GMT +3 **Currency** rial **Language** Arabic **Visa requirements** UK: visa required. USA: visa required **Embassy in the UK** 30 Charles Street, London W1X 7PH. Tel: (020) 7917 3000; fax: (020) 7917 3330 **British embassy** PO Box 94351, Riyadh 11693. Tel: (1) 488 0077; fax: (1) 488 2373 **Chamber of commerce** Riyadh Chamber of Commerce and Industry, PO Box 596, Riyadh 11421. Tel: (1) 404 0044; fax: (1) 402 1103 **Office hours** 0900–1300 and 1630–2000 Sat–Thu (2000–0100 during Ramadan) **Banking hours** 0830–1200 and 1700–1900 Sat–Wed; 0830–1200 Thu **Airports** international airports: Riyadh (King Khaled), Dhahran (Al Khobar), Jiddah (King Abdul Aziz); 20 domestic airports; total passenger km: 18,949 million (1997 est) **Major ports** Jiddah, Dammam,

Jubail, Jizan, Yanbu **Chief tourist attractions** the holy cities of Medina, Jiddah, and Mecca – notably Mecca's Al-Harram Mosque and large bazaars, and Medina's numerous mosques and Islamic monuments **Major holidays** 23 September; variable: Eid-ul-Adha (7 days), end of Ramadan (4 days)

Chronology

622 Muhammad began to unite Arabs in Muslim faith. **7th–8th centuries** Muslim Empire expanded, ultimately stretching from India to Spain, with Arabia itself being relegated to a subordinate part. **12th century** Decline of Muslim Empire; Arabia grew isolated and internal divisions multiplied. **13th century** Mameluke sultans of Egypt became nominal overlords of Hejaz in western Arabia. **1517** Hejaz became a nominal part of the Ottoman Empire after the Turks conquered Egypt. **18th century** Al Saud family united tribes of Nejd in central Arabia in support of the Wahhabi religious movement. ***c*.1830** The Al Saud established Riyadh as the Wahhabi capital. ***c*.1870** Turks took effective control of Hejaz and also Hasa on Persian Gulf. **late 19th century** Rival Wahhabi dynasty of Ibn Rashid became leaders of Nejd. **1902** Ibn Saud organized Bedouin revolt and regained Riyadh. **1913** Ibn Saud completed the reconquest of Hasa from Turks. **1915** Britain recognized Ibn Saud as emir of Nejd and Hasa. **1916–18** British-backed revolt, under aegis of Sharif Hussein of Mecca, expelled Turks from Arabia. **1919–25** Ibn Saud fought and defeated Sharif Hussein and took control of Hejaz. **1926** Proclamation of Ibn Saud as king of Hejaz and Nejd. **1932** Hejaz and Nejd renamed the United Kingdom of Saudi Arabia. **1933** Saudi Arabia allowed US-owned Standard Oil Company to prospect for oil, which was discovered in Hasa in 1938. **1939–45** Although officially neutral in World War II, Saudi Arabia received subsidies from USA and Britain. **1940s** Commercial exploitation of oil began, bringing great prosperity. **1987** Rioting by Iranian pilgrims caused 400 deaths in Mecca and a breach in diplomatic relations with Iran. **1990** Iraqi troops invaded Kuwait and massed on the Saudi Arabian border, prompting King Fahd to call for assistance from US and UK forces. **1991** Saudi Arabia fought on the Allied side against Iraq in the Gulf War. **1992** Under international pressure to move towards democracy, King Fahd formed a 'consultative council' to assist in the government of the kingdom.

Senegal Republic of

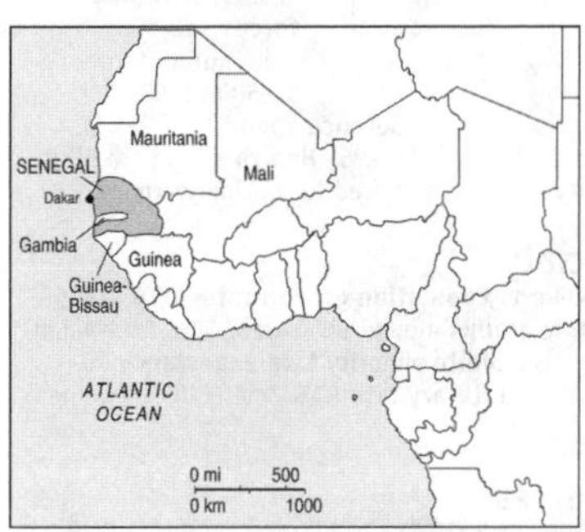

National name *République du Sénégal* **Area** 196,200 sq km/ 75,752 sq mi **Capital** Dakar (and chief port) **Major towns/cities** Thiès, Kaolack, Saint-Louis, Ziguinchor, Diourbel

Government

Head of state Abdoulaye Wade from 2000 **Head of government** Mamadou Lamine Loum from 1998 **Political system** nationalistic socialist **Armed forces** 13,400 (1997) **Conscription** military services is by selective conscription for two years **Defence spend** (% GDP) 1.6 (1997) **Education spend** (% GNP) 3.5 (1996) **Health spend** (% GDP) 1.2 (1995) **Death penalty** retains the death penalty for ordinary crimes but can be considered abolitionist in practice (last execution 1967)

Population and society

Population 9,240,000 (1999 est) **Population growth rate** 2.6% (1995–2000) **Ethnic groups** the Wolof group are the most numerous, comprising about 36% of the population; the Fulani comprise about 21%; the Serer 19%; the Diola 7%; and the Mandingo 6% **Religion** mainly Sunni Muslim **Life expectancy** 51 (men); 54 (women) (1995–2000) **Literacy rate** 45% (men); 25% (women) (1997 est) **Unemployment** 10.2% (1993)

Economy and resources

GDP (US$) 4.8 billion (1998) **GNP** (US$) 4.8 billion (1998) **GNP per capita (PPP)** (US$) 1,710 (1998) **Real GDP growth** (% change on previous year) 5 (1998) **Consumer price inflation** 2.0% (1998) **Foreign debt** (US$) 3.67 billion (1997) **Resources** calcium phosphates, aluminium phosphates, salt, natural gas; offshore deposits of petroleum to be developed **Exports** fresh and processed fish, refined petroleum products, chemicals, groundnuts and related products, calcium phosphates and related products. Principal market: India 25.6% (1997) **Imports** food and live animals, machinery and transport equipment, mineral fuels and lubricants (mainly crude petroleum), basic manufactures, chemicals. Principal source: France 30.6% (1997)

▪ Tourist information

Time difference GMT +/– 0 **Currency** franc CFA **Language** French (official); Wolof **Visa requirements** UK: visa not required. USA: visa not required **Embassy in the UK** 11 Phillimore Gardens, London W8 7QG. Tel: (020) 7937 0925/6; fax: (020) 7937 8130 **British embassy** BP 6025, 20 rue du Docteur Guillet, Dakar. Tel: (221) 237 392; fax: (221) 232 766 **Chamber of commerce** Chambre de Commerce et d'Industrie et d'Agriculture de la Région de Dakar, BP 118, 1 place de l'Indépendence, Dakar. Tel: (221) 237 189; telex: 61112 **Office hours** 0800–1200 and 1430–1800 Mon–Fri; 0800–1200 Sat **Banking hours** 0800–1115 and 1430–1630 Mon–Fri **Airports** international airports: Dakar (Dakar-Yoff); three domestic airports and 12 smaller airfields; total passenger km: 224 million (1995) **Chief tourist attractions** fine beaches; six national parks; the island of Gorée, near Dakar, a former centre for the slave trade **Major holidays** 1 January, 1 February, 4 April, 1 May, 15 August, 1 November, 25 December; variable: Eid-ul-Adha, Easter Monday, end of Ramadan, New Year (Muslim), Prophet's Birthday, Whit Monday

Chronology

10th–11th centuries Links established with North Africa; the Tukolor community was converted to Islam. **1445** First visited by Portuguese explorers. **1659** French founded Saint-Louis as a colony. **17th–18th centuries** Export trades in slaves, gums, ivory, and gold developed by European traders. **1854–65** Interior occupied by French who checked the expansion of the Islamic Tukulor Empire; Dakar founded. **1902** Became territory of French West Africa. **1946** Became French overseas territory, with own territorial assembly and representation in French parliament. **1948** Leopold Sedar Senghor founded the Senegalese Democratic Bloc to campaign for independence. **1959** Formed Federation of Mali with French Sudan. **1960** Achieved independence and withdrew from federation. Senghor, leader of socialist Senegalese Progressive Union (UPS), became president. **1966** UPS declared only legal party. **1974** Pluralist system re-established. **1976** UPS reconstituted as Socialist Party (PS). **1980** Troops sent to defend The Gambia against suspected Libyan invasion. **1981** Military help again sent to The Gambia to thwart coup attempt. Abdou Diouf was appointed president. **1982** Confederation of Senegambia came into effect. **1988** Mamadou Lamine Loum was appointed prime minister. **1989** Diplomatic links with Mauritania severed after 450 died in violent clashes; over 50,000 people repatriated from both countries. Senegambia federation abandoned. **1992** Diplomatic links with Mauritania were re-established. **1993** Assembly and presidential elections were won by the ruling PS. **1998** PS won the general election despite claims of fraud. Abdou Diouf became 'president for life'. **1999** A new 60-member Senate was created as Senegal's second legislative chamber. **2000** In presidential elections, Abdou Diouf lost to Abdoulaye Wade.

Seychelles Republic of

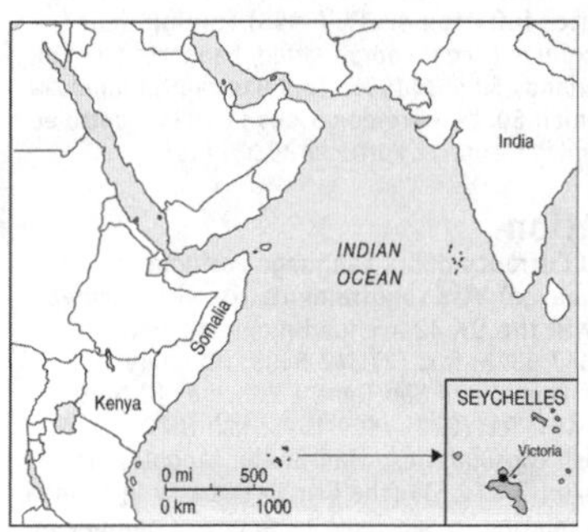

Area 453 sq km/174 sq mi **Capital** Victoria (on Mahé island) (and chief port) **Major towns/cities** Cascade, Port Glaud, Misere

Government

Head of state and government France-Albert René from 1977 **Political system** emergent democracy **Armed forces** 200; 300 paramilitary forces; plus 1,000-strong national guard (1997) **Conscription** military service is voluntary **Defence spend** (% GDP) 2.9 (1997) **Education spend** (% GNP) 7.6 (1996) **Health spend** (% GDP) 4.1 (1995) **Death penalty** retains death penalty only for exceptional crimes such as crimes under military law or crimes committed in exceptional circumstances such as wartime

Population and society
Population 79,000 (1999 est) **Population growth rate** 1.1% (1995–2000) **Ethnic groups** predominantly Creole (of mixed African and European descent); small European minority (mostly French and British) **Religion** Roman Catholic **Life expectancy** 66 (men); 76 (women) (1998 est) **Literacy rate** 86% (men); 82% (women) (1994 est) **Unemployment** 8.3% (1993)

Economy and resources
GDP (US$) 537 million (1998) **GNP** (US$) 507 million (1998) **GNP per capita (PPP)** (US$) 10,530 (1998) **Real GDP growth** (% change on previous year) 3 (1998) **Consumer price inflation** 1.5% (1998) **Foreign debt** (US$) 149.1 million (1997) **Resources** guano; natural gas and metal deposits were being explored mid-1990s **Exports** fresh and frozen fish, canned tuna, shark fins, cinnamon bark, refined petroleum products. Principal market: France 18.7% (1997) **Imports** machinery and transport equipment, food and live animals, petroleum and petroleum products, chemicals, basic manufactures. Principal source: South Africa 15.5% (1997)

▪ Tourist information
Time difference GMT +4 **Currency** Seychelles rupee **Language** creole (Asian, African, European mixture) 95%, English, French (all official) **Visa requirements** UK: visa not required. USA: visa not required **Embassy in the UK** 2nd Floor, Eros House, 111 Baker Street, London W1M 1FE. Tel: (020) 7224 1660; fax: (020) 7487 5756 **British embassy** British High Commission, PO Box 161, 3rd Floor, Victoria House, Victoria, Mahé. Tel: (248) 225 225; fax: (248) 225 127 **Chamber of commerce** Seychelles Chamber of Commerce and Industry, PO Box 443, 38 Premier Building, Victoria, Mahé. Tel: (248) 223 812 **Office hours** 0800–1200 and 1300–1600 Mon–Fri **Banking hours** 0830–1430 Mon–Fri; 0830–1100 Sat **Airports** international airports: Mahé Island (Seychelles); five domestic airports; total passenger km: 847 million (1997 est) **Chief tourist attractions** fine coral beaches; lush tropical vegetation; mountain scenery; rainforest; many unique plant and animal species; national parks and reserves; Aldabra, the largest atoll in the world **Major holidays** 1–2 January, 1 May, 5, 29 June, 15 August, 1 November, 8, 25 December; variable: Corpus Christi, Good Friday, Holy Saturday

Chronology
early 16th century First sighted by European navigators. **1744** Became French colony. **1756** Claimed as French possession and named after an influential French family. **1770s** French colonists brought African slaves to settle the previously uninhabited islands; plantations established. **1794** Captured by British during French Revolutionary Wars. **1814** Ceded by France to Britain; incorporated as dependency of Mauritius. **1835** Slavery abolished by British, leading to influx of liberated slaves from Mauritius and Chinese and Indian immigrants. **1903** Became British crown colony, separate from Mauritius. **1963–64** First political parties formed. **1976** Independence achieved from Britain as republic within Commonwealth, with a moderate, James Mancham, of the centre-right Seychelles Democratic Party (SDP) as president. **1977** More radical France-Albert René ousted Mancham in armed bloodless coup and took over presidency; white settlers emigrated. **1979** Nationalistic socialist Seychelles People's Progressive Front (SPPF) became sole legal party under new constitution; became nonaligned state. **1981** An attempted coup by South African mercenaries was thwarted. **1993** A new multiparty constitution was adopted. René defeated Mancham, who had returned from exile, in competitive presidential elections; SPPF won parliamentary elections. **1998** President René was re-elected.

Sierra Leone Republic of

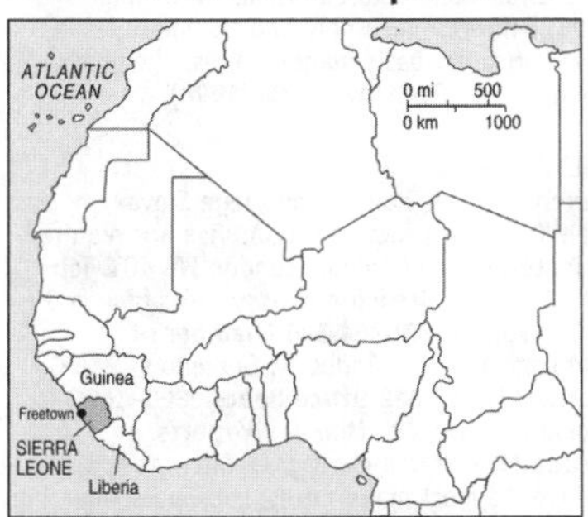

Area 71,740 sq km/ 27,698 sq mi **Capital** Freetown **Major towns/ cities** Koidu, Bo, Kenema, Makeni

Government
Head of state and government Ahmad Tejan Kabbah from 1998 **Political system** transitional **Armed forces** 15,000 (1997) **Conscription** military service is voluntary **Defence spend** (% GDP) 6.9 (1997) **Education spend** (% GNP) 1.4 (1992) **Health spend** (% GDP) 1.6 (1990–95) **Death penalty** retained and used for ordinary crimes

Population and society
Population 4,717,000 (1999 est) **Population growth rate** 3.0% (1995–2000) **Ethnic groups** 18 ethnic groups, 3 of which (the Mende, Tenne, and Limbe) comprise almost 70% of the population **Religion** animist 52%, Muslim 39%, Protestant 6%, Roman Catholic 2% (1980 est) **Life expectancy** 36 (men); 39 (women) (1995–2000) **Literacy rate** 48% (men); 20% (women) (1997 est) **Unemployment** N/A

Economy and resources
GDP (US$) 647 million (1998) **GNP** (US$) 680 million (1998) **GNP per capita (PPP)** (US$) 390 (1998) **Real GDP growth** (% change on previous year) –3.5 (1998) **Consumer price inflation** 37.4% (1998 est) **Foreign debt** (US$) 1.15 billion (1997) **Resources** gold, diamonds, bauxite, rutile (titanium dioxide) **Exports** rutile, diamonds, bauxite, gold, coffee, cocoa beans. Principal market: Belgium and Luxembourg 48.9% (1997) **Imports** machinery and transport equipment, food and live animals, basic manufactures, chemicals, miscellaneous manufactured articles. Principal source: UK 16% (1997)

▪ Tourist information
Time difference GMT +/– 0 **Currency** leone **Language** English (official), Krio (a creole language) **Visa requirements** UK: visa required. USA: visa required **Embassy in the UK** 33 Portland Place, London W1N 3AG. Tel: (020) 7636 6483/6; fax: (020) 7323 3159 **British embassy** British High Commission, Standard Chartered Bank Building, Lightfoot-Boston Street, Freetown. Tel: (232) 223 961/5; telex: 3235 (a/b 3235 UKREP SL) **Chamber of commerce** Sierra Leone Chamber of Commerce, Industry and Agriculture, PO Box 502, 5th Floor, Guma Building, Lamina, Sankoh Street, Freetown. Tel: (232) 226 305; fax: (232) 228 005 **Office hours** 0800–1200 and 1400–1645 Mon–Fri **Banking hours** 0800–1330 Mon–Thu; 0800–1400 Fri **Airports** international airports: Freetown (Lungi); six domestic airports; total passenger km: 24 million (1995) **Major ports** Bonthe-Sherbro **Chief tourist attractions** mountains; game reserves; coastline **Major holidays** 1 January, 19 April, 25–26 December; variable: Eid-ul-Adha, end of Ramadan, Good Friday, Easter Monday, Prophet's Birthday

Chronology
15th century Mende, Temne, and Fulani peoples moved from Senegal into region formerly populated by Bulom, Krim, and Gola peoples. The Portuguese, who named the area Serra Lyoa, established a coastal fort, trading manufactured goods for slaves and ivory. **17th century** English trading posts established on Bund and York islands. **1787–92** English abolitionists and philanthropists bought land to establish settlement for liberated and runaway African slaves (including 1,000 rescued from Canada), known as Freetown. **1808** Became a British colony and Freetown a base for British naval operations against slave trade, after Parliament declared it illegal. **1896** Hinterland conquered and declared British protectorate. **1951** First political party, Sierra Leone People's Party (SLPP), formed by Milton Margai, who became 'leader of government business', in 1953. **1961** Independence achieved within Commonwealth, with Margai as prime minister. **1965** Free-trade area pact signed with Guinea, Liberia, and the Côte d'Ivoire. **1967** Election won by All People's Congress (APC), led by Siaka Stevens, but disputed by army, who set up National Reformation Council and forced governor general to leave the country. **1968** Army revolt brought back Stevens as prime minister. **1971** New constitution made Sierra Leone a republic, with Stevens as president. **1978** New constitution made APC the only legal party. **1985** Stevens retired and was succeeded as president and APC leader by Maj-Gen Joseph Momoh. **1991** referendum endorsed multiparty politics and new constitution. A Liberian-based rebel group began guerrilla activities. **1992** President Momoh was overthrown by the military, and party politics were suspended as the National Provisional Ruling Council was established under Capt Valentine Strasser; 500,000 Liberians fled to Sierra Leone as a result of the civil war. **1995** The ban on political parties was lifted. **1996** Ahmad Tejan Kabbah became president after multiparty elections. **1997** President Kabbah's civilian government was ousted in a bloody coup. Maj Johnny Paul Koroma seized the presidency and the Revolutionary Council was formed. **1998** A Nigerian-led peacekeeping force drove out Maj Koroma's junta; President Kabbah returned from exile. Former members of military government were executed for treason. **1999** Fighting between government and rebel forces continued. Diplomatic efforts were spearheaded by the Organization of African Unity; a ceasefire and peace agreement were reached with rebels, and in November the first unit of what would become a 6,000-strong United Nations (UN) peacekeeping force arrived in Sierra Leone.

Singapore Republic of

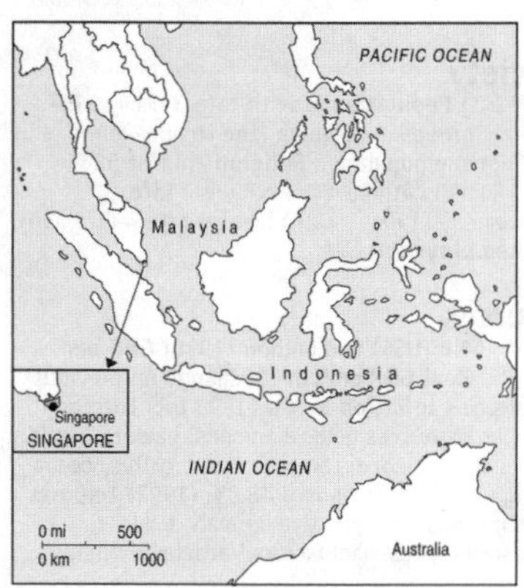

Area 622 sq km/240 sq mi **Capital** Singapore City **Major towns/cities** Jurong, Changi

Government

Head of state Ong Teng Cheong from 1993 **Head of government** Goh Chok Tong from 1990 **Political system** liberal democracy **Armed forces** 70,000; 263,800 reservists (1997) **Conscription** two years **Defence spend** (% GDP) 4.3 (1997) **Education spend** (% GNP) 3.0 (1996) **Health spend** (% GDP) 1.5 (1995) **Death penalty** retained and used for ordinary crimes

Population and society

Population 3,522,000 (1999 est) **Population growth rate** 1.4% (1995–2000) **Ethnic groups** 77% of Chinese ethnic descent, predominantly Hokkien, Teochew, and Cantonese; 15% Malay; 7% Indian, chiefly Tamil **Religion** Buddhist, Taoist, Muslim, Hindu, Christian **Life expectancy** 75 (men); 80 (women) (1995–2000) **Literacy rate** 96% (men); 87% (women) (1997 est) **Unemployment** 3.2% (1998)

Economy and resources

GDP (US$) 85.4 billion (1998) **GNP** (US$) 95.1 billion (1998) **GNP per capita (PPP)** (US$) 28,260 (1998) **Real GDP growth** (% change on previous year) 0.3 (1998) **Consumer price inflation** 2.4 (1998) **Foreign debt** (US$) 12.5 billion (1997) **Resources** granite **Exports** electrical and nonelectrical machinery, transport equipment, petroleum products, chemicals, rubber, foodstuffs, clothing, metal products, iron and steel, orchids and other plants, aquarium fish. Principal market: USA 19.9% (1998) **Imports** electrical and nonelectrical equipment, crude petroleum, transport equipment, chemicals, food and live animals, textiles, scientific and optical instruments, paper and paper products. Principal source: Japan 16.7% (1998)

▪ Tourist information

Time difference GMT +8 **Currency** Singapore dollar **Language** Malay (national tongue), Chinese, Tamil, English (all official) **Visa requirements** UK: visa not required. USA: visa not required **Embassy in the UK** 9 Wilton Crescent, London SW1X 8SA. Tel: (020) 7235 8315; fax: (020) 7245 6583 **British embassy** British High Commission, Tanglin Road, Singapore 1024. Tel: (65) 473 9333; fax: (65) 475 2320 **Chamber of commerce** Singapore International Chamber of Commerce, 10-001 John Hancock Tower, 6 Raffles Quay, Singapore 0104. Tel: (65) 224 1255; fax: (65) 224 2785 **Banking hours** 1000–1500 Mon–Fri; 1100–1600 Sat **Airports** international airports: Singapore (Changi); total passenger km: 55,459 million (1997 est) **Chief tourist attractions** blend of cultures; excellent shopping facilities; Singapore City, with its Tiger Balm Gardens, Sultan Mosque, Buddhist temples, House of Jade, bird park, botanical gardens, and national museum **Major holidays** 1 January, 1 May, 9 August, 25 December; variable: Eid-ul-Adha, Diwali, end of Ramadan, Good Friday, New Year (Chinese, January/February, 2 days), Vesak

Chronology

12th century First trading settlement established on Singapore Island. **14th century** Settlement destroyed, probably by Javanese Empire of Mahapahit. **1819** Stamford Raffles of British East India Company obtained Singapore from sultan of Johore. **1826** Straits Settlements formed from British possessions of Singapore, Penang, and Malacca ruled by governor of Bengal. **1832** Singapore became capital of Straits Settlements; the port prospered, attracting Chinese and Indian immigrants. **1851** Responsibility for Straits Settlements fell to governor general of India. **1858** British government, through the India Office, took over administration of Straits Settlements. **1867** Straits Settlements became crown colony of British Empire. **1922** Singapore chosen as principal British military base in Far East. **1942** Japan captured Singapore, taking 70,000 British and Australian prisoners. **1945** British rule restored after defeat of Japan. **1946** Singapore became separate crown colony. **1959** Internal self-government achieved as State of Singapore with Lee Kuan Yew (PAP) as prime minister. **1960s** Rapid development as leading commercial and financial centre. **1963** Singapore combined with Federation of Malaya, Sabah, and Sarawak to form Federation of Malaysia. **1965** Became independent republic after withdrawing from Federation of Malaysia in protest at alleged discrimination against ethnic Chinese. **1971** Last remaining British military bases closed. **1984** Two opposition members elected to national assembly for first time. **1988** Ruling PAP won all but one of available assembly seats; increasingly authoritarian rule. **1990** Lee Kuan Yew retired from the premiership after 31 years and was succeeded by Goh Chok Tong. **1993** Ong Teng Cheong was elected president with increased powers. **1996** Constitutional change was introduced, allowing better representation of minority races. **1997** The PAP, led by Prime Minister Goh Chok Tong, won a general election. **1998** Pay cuts were introduced as Singapore slipped into recession for the first time in 13 years.

Slovak Republic

National name *Slovenská Republika* **Area** 49,035 sq km/ 18,932 sq mi **Capital** Bratislava **Major towns/cities** Košice, Nitra, Prešov, Banská Bystrica, Žilina, Trnava

Government

Head of state Rudolf Schuster from 1999 **Head of government** Mikulas Dzurinda from 1998 **Political system** emergent democracy **Armed forces** 41,200 (1997) **Conscription** military service is compulsory for 18 months **Defence spend** (% GDP) 2.1 (1997) **Education spend** (% GNP) 4.7 (1996) **Health spend** (% GDP) 6.1 (1995) **Death penalty** abolished in 1990

Population and society

Population 5,381,000 (1999 est) **Population growth rate** 0.1% (1995–2000) **Ethnic groups** 87% ethnic Slovak, 11% ethnic Hungarian (Magyar); small Czech, Moravian, Silesian, and Romany communities **Religion** Roman Catholic (over 50%), Lutheran, Reformist, Orthodox **Life expectancy** 69 (men); 77 (women) (1995–2000) **Literacy rate** 99% (men); 99% (women) (1997 est) **Unemployment** 14% (1998)

Economy and resources

GDP (US$) 19.5 billion (1998 est) **GNP** (US$) 20 billion (1998) **GNP per capita (PPP)** (US$) 6,600 (1998 est) **Real GDP growth** (% change on previous year) 4.8 (1998) **Consumer price inflation** 6.7% (1998) **Foreign debt** (US$) 9.98 billion (1997) **Resources** brown coal, lignite, copper, zinc, lead, iron ore, magnesite **Exports** basic manufactures, machinery and transport equipment, miscellaneous manufactured articles. Principal market: Germany 28.9% (1998) **Imports** machinery and transport equipment, mineral fuels and lubricants, basic manufactures, chemicals and related products. Principal source: Germany 25.9% (1998)

▪ Tourist information

Time difference GMT +1 **Currency** Slovak koruna **Language** Slovak (official) **Visa requirements** UK: visa not required. USA: visa not required **Embassy in the UK** 25 Kensington Palace Gardens, London W8 4QY. Tel: (020) 7243 0803; fax: (020) 7727 5824 **British embassy** Grösslingova 35, 811 09 Bratislava. Tel: (7) 364 420; fax: (7) 364 396 **Chamber of commerce** Slovak Chamber of Commerce and Industry, Gorkéno 9, 816 03 Bratislava. Tel: (7) 362 787; fax: (7) 362 222 **Office hours** 0800–1600 Mon–Fri **Banking hours** generally 0800–1700 Mon–Fri **Airports** international airports: Bratislava (M R Stefanik), Poprad-Tatry, Košice, Piešťany, Sliač; domestic services to most major cities; total passenger km: 231 million (1997) **Chief tourist attractions** ski resorts in the High and

Low Tatras and other mountain regions; historic towns, including Bratislava, Košice, Nitra, and Bardejov; numerous castles and mansions; over 20 spa resorts with thermal and mineral springs **Major holidays** 1, 6 January, 1 May, 5 July, 29 August, 1, 15 September, 1 November, 24–26 December; variable: Good Friday, Easter Monday

Chronology

9th century Part of kingdom of Greater Moravia, in Czech lands to west, founded by Slavic Prince Sviatopluk; Christianity adopted. **906** Came under Magyar (Hungarian) domination and adopted Roman Catholicism. **1526** Came under Austrian Habsburg rule. **1867** With creation of dual Austro-Hungarian monarchy, came under separate Hungarian rule; policy of forced Magyarization stimulated a revival of Slovak national consciousness. **1918** Austro-Hungarian Empire dismembered; Slovaks joined Czechs to form independent state of Czechoslovakia. Slovak-born Tomas Masaryk remained president until 1935, but political and economic power became concentrated in Czech lands. **1939** Germany annexed Czechoslovakia, which became Axis puppet state under the Slovak autonomist leader Monsignor Jozef Tiso; Jews persecuted. **1944** Popular revolt against German rule ('Slovak Uprising'). **1945** Liberated from German rule by Soviet troops; Czechoslovakia re-established. **1948** Communists assumed power in Czechoslovakia. **1950s** Heavy industry introduced into previously rural Slovakia; Slovak nationalism and Catholic Church forcibly suppressed. **1968–69** 'Prague Spring': political reforms introduced by Slovak-born Communist Party leader Alexander Dubček; Warsaw Pact forces invaded Czechoslovakia to stamp out reforms; Slovak Socialist Republic, with autonomy over local affairs, created under new federal constitution. **1989** Prodemocracy demonstrations in Bratislava; new political parties, including centre-left People Against Violence (PAV), formed and legalized; Communist Party stripped of powers; new government formed, with ex-dissident playwright Václav Havel as president. **1990** Slovak nationalists polled strongly in multiparty elections, with Vladimir Meciar (PAV) becoming prime minister. **1991** There was increasing Slovak separatism as the economy deteriorated. Meciar formed a PAV splinter group, Movement for a Democratic Slovakia (HZDS), pledging greater autonomy for Slovakia. Pro-Meciar rallies in Bratislava followed his dismissal. **1992** Meciar returned to power following an electoral victory for the HZDS. Slovak parliament's declaration of sovereignty led to Havel's resignation. **1993** The Slovak Republic joined the United Nations (UN) and Council of Europe as a sovereign state, with Meciar as prime minister and Michal Kovac, formerly of HZDS, as president. /ITEM> **1994** The Slovak Republic joined NATO's 'Partnership for Peace' programme. **1995** Slovak was made the sole official language; a Treaty of Friendship and Cooperation was signed with Hungary. **1996** An anti-Meciar coalition, the Slovak Democratic Coalition, was formed, comprising five opposition parties. **1997** A referendum on NATO membership and presidential elections was declared invalid after confusion over voting papers. **1998** Presidential powers were assumed by Meciar after failure to elect new president. The national council chair, Ivan Gasparović, became acting head of state. Meciar stepped down as prime minister after the opposition Slovak Democratic Coalition (SDC) polled strongly in a general election. A new SDC-led coalition was formed under Mikulas Dzurinda. The koruna was devalued by 6%. **1999** Rudolf Schuster was elected president.

Slovenia Republic of

National name *Republika Slovenija* **Area** 20,251 sq km/ 7,818 sq mi **Capital** Ljubljana **Major towns/ cities** Maribor, Kranj, Celji, Velenje, Koper (Capodistria)

Government

Head of state Milan Kučan from 1990 **Head of government** Andrej Bajuk from 2000 from 2000 **Political system** emergent democracy **Armed forces** 9,600; plus reserve forces of 53,000 and a paramilitary police force of 4,500 (1997) **Conscription** military service is compulsory for seven months **Defence spend** (% GDP) 1.7% (1997) **Education spend** (% GNP) 5.8% (1996) **Health spend** (% GDP) 7.1 (1995) **Death penalty** abolished in 1989

Population and society

Population 1,989,000 (1999 est) **Population growth rate** –0.05% (1995–2000) **Ethnic groups** 98% of Slovene origin, 3% ethnic Croat, 2% Serb **Religion** Roman Catholic **Life expectancy** 71 (men); 78 (women) (1995–2000) **Literacy rate** 99% (men); 99% (women) (1997 est) **Unemployment** 14% (1997)

Economy and resources

GDP (US$) 18.2 billion (1998 est) **GNP** (US$) 19.4 billion (1998) **GNP per capita (PPP)** (US$) 12,730 (1998 est) **Real GDP growth** (% change on previous year) 3.3 (1998) **Consumer price inflation** 8.0% (1998) **Foreign debt** (US$) 4.76 million (1997) **Resources** coal, lead, zinc; small reserves/deposits of natural gas, petroleum, salt, uranium **Exports** raw materials, semi-finished goods, machinery, electric motors, transport equipment, foodstuffs, clothing, pharmaceuticals, cosmetics. Principal market: Germany 28.4% (1998) **Imports** machinery and transport equipment, raw materials, semi-finished goods, foodstuffs, chemicals, miscellaneous manufactured articles, mineral fuels and lubricants. Principal source: Germany 20.7% (1998)

■ Tourist information

Time difference GMT +1 **Currency** tolar **Language** Slovene, resembling Serbo-Croat, written in Roman characters **Visa requirements** UK: visa not required. USA: visa not required **Embassy in the UK** Suite 1, Cavendish Court, 11–15 Wigmore Street, London W1H 9LA. Tel: (020) 7495 7775; fax: (020) 7495 7776 **British embassy** 4th Floor, Trg Republike 3, 61000 Ljubljana. Tel: (61) 125 7191; fax: (61) 125 0174 **Chamber of commerce** Chamber of Economy of Slovenia, Slovenska 41, 61000 Ljubljana. Tel: (61) 125 0122; fax: (61) 219 536 **Office hours** 0700–1500 Mon–Fri **Banking hours** 0800–1800 Mon–Fri **Airports** international airports: Ljubljana (Brnik), Maribor, Portorož; two domestic airports; total passenger km: 677 million (1997) **Major ports** Koper **Chief tourist attractions** Alps in north; Mediterranean beaches; Karst limestone regions, with more than 6,000 caves; Ljubljana, with its castle, cathedral, Tivoli sports park, fairs, and festivals **Major holidays** 1–2 January, 8 February, 27 April, 1–2 May, 25 June, 15 August, 31 October, 1 November, 25–26 December; variable: Good Friday, Easter Monday

Chronology

1st century BC Came under Roman rule. **AD 395** In the division of the Roman Empire, stayed in the west, along with Croatia and Bosnia. **6th century** Settled by the Slovene South Slavs. **7th century** Adopted Christianity as Roman Catholics. **8th–9th centuries** Under successive rule of Franks and dukes of Bavaria. **907–55** Came under Hungarian domination. **1335** Absorbed in Austro-Hungarian Habsburg Empire, as part of Austrian crownlands of Carniola, Styria, and Carinthia. **1848** Slovene struggle for independence began. **1918** On collapse of Habsburg Empire, Slovenia united with Serbia, Croatia, and Montenegro to form the 'Kingdom of Serbs, Croats and Slovenes', under Serbian Karageorgevic dynasty. **1929** Kingdom became known as Yugoslavia. **1941–45** Occupied by Nazi Germany and Italy during World War II; anti-Nazi Slovene Liberation Front formed and became allies of Marshal Tito's communist-led partisans. **1945** Slovenia became a constituent republic of the Yugoslav Socialist Federal Republic. **mid-1980s** The Slovenian Communist Party liberalized itself and agreed to free elections. Yugoslav counterintelligence (KOV) began repression. **1989** The constitution was changed to allow secession from the federation. **1990** A Nationalist Democratic Opposition of Slovenia (DEMOS) coalition secured victory in the first multiparty parliamentary elections; Milan Kučan, a reform communist, became president. Sovereignty was declared. Independence was overwhelmingly approved in a referendum. **1991** Slovenia seceded from the Yugoslav federation, along with Croatia; 100 people were killed after the Yugoslav federal army intervened; a ceasefire brokered by the European Community (EC) brought the withdrawal of the Yugoslav army. **1992** Janez Drnovšek, a centrist Liberal Democrat, was appointed prime minister; independence was recognized by the EC and the USA. Slovenia was admitted into the United Nations (UN). **1997** A new government was formed by the ruling LDS, led by Prime Minister Janez Drnovsek. President Kucan was re-elected. The European Union (EU) agreed to open membership talks with Slovenia. **2000** Andrej Bajuk was elected prime minister.

Solomon Islands

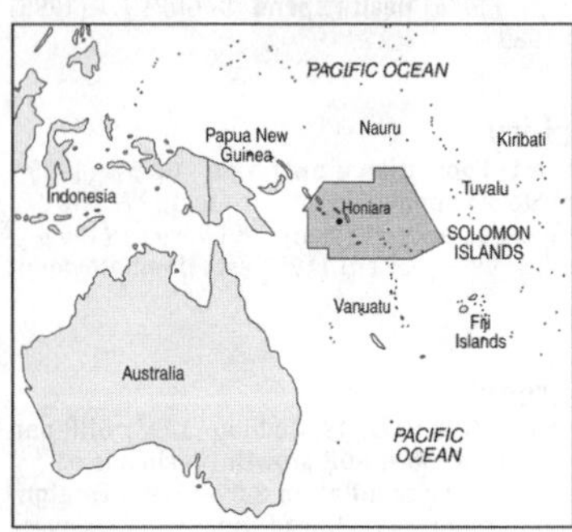

Area 27,600 sq km/ 10,656 sq mi **Capital** Honiara (on Guadalcanal) (and chief port) **Major towns/ cities** Gizo, Kieta, Auki

Government

Head of state Queen Elizabeth II, represented by governor general Moses Pitakaka from 1994 **Head of government** Bartholomew Ulufa'alu from 1997 **Political system** emergent democracy **Armed forces** no standing army; 80-strong marine wing of police force (1995) **Education spend** (% GNP) 4.2 (1993/94) **Health spend** (% GDP) 4.9 (1995) **Death penalty** laws do not provide for the death penalty for any crime

Population and society

Population 430,000 (1999 est) **Population growth rate** 3.1% (1995–2000) **Ethnic groups** 93% Melanesian, 4% Polynesian, 1.5% Micronesian, 0.7% European, 0.2% Chinese **Religion** Anglican, Roman Catholic, South Sea Evangelical, other Protestant **Life expectancy** 70 (men); 74 (women) (1995–2000) **Literacy rate** 60% (men); 60% (women) (1994 est)

Economy and resources

GDP (US$) 374 million (1998 est) **GNP** (US$) 311 million (1998) **GNP per capita (PPP)** (US$) 2,080 (1998) **Real GDP growth** (% change on previous year) –1 (1998) **Consumer price inflation** 13.5% (1998) **Foreign debt** (US$) 164 million (1997) **Resources** bauxite, phosphates, gold, silver, copper, lead, zinc, cobalt, asbestos, nickel **Exports** timber, fish products, oil palm products, copra, cocoa, coconut oil. Principal market: Japan 59.2% (1997) **Imports** rice, machinery and transport equipment, meat preparations, refined sugar, mineral fuels, basic manufactures, construction materials. Principal source: Australia 41.5% (1997)

▪ Tourist information

Time difference GMT +11 **Currency** Solomon Island dollar **Language** English (official); there are some 120 Melanesian dialects spoken by 85% of the population, and Papuan and Polynesian languages **Visa requirements** UK: visa not required. USA: visa not required **Embassy for the UK** BP 3, avenue de l'Yser 13, B-1040 Brussels, Belgium. Tel: (2) 732 7082; fax: (2) 732 6885; Solomon Islands Honorary Consulate, 19 Springfield Road, London SW19 7AL. Tel: (020) 8296 6232; fax: (020) 8946 1744 **British embassy** British High Commission, PO Box 676, Telekom House, Mendana Avenue, Honiara. Tel: 21705/6; fax: 20765 **Chamber of commerce** PO Box 64, Honiara. Tel: 22960 **Office hours** 0800–1200 and 1300–1630 Mon–Fri; 0730–1200 Sat **Banking hours** 0830–1500 Mon–Fri **Airports** international airport: Honiara (Henderson); 26 domestic airports; total passenger km: 89 million (1995) **Major ports** Yandina **Chief tourist attractions** tourism restricted by relative inaccessibility of country and inadequacy of tourist facilities **Major holidays** 1 January, 7 July, 25–26 December; variable: Good Friday, Easter Monday, Holy Saturday, Whit Monday, Queen's Birthday (June)

Chronology

1568 The islands were first sighted by Spanish navigator Alvaro de Mendana, journeying from Peru. **1595 and 1606** Unsuccessful Spanish efforts to settle the islands, which had long been peopled by Melanesians. **later 18th century** Visited again by Europeans. **1840s** Christian missions established. **1870s** Development of copra export trade and shipment of islanders to work on sugar cane plantations in Australia and Fiji Islands. **1886** Northern Solomon Islands became German protectorate. **1893** Southern Solomon Islands placed under British protection. **1899** Germany ceded Solomon Islands possessions to Britain in return for British recognition of its claims to Western Samoa. **1900** Unified British Solomon Islands Protectorate formed and placed under jurisdiction of Western Pacific High Commission (WPHC), with its headquarters in Fiji Islands. **1942–43** Occupied by Japan. Site of fierce fighting, especially on Guadalcanal, which was recaptured by US forces, with the loss of 21,000 Japanese and 5,000 US troops. **1943–50** Development of Marching Rule (Ma'asina Ruru) cargo cult populist movement on Malaita island, campaigning for self-rule. **1945** Headquarters of WPHC moved to Honiara. **1960** Legislative and executive councils established by constitution. **1974** Became substantially self-governing, with Solomon Mamaloni of centre-left People's Progressive Party (PPP) as chief minister. **1976** Became fully self-governing, with Peter Kenilorea of right-of-centre Solomon Islands United Party (SIUPA) as chief minister. **1978** Independence achieved from Britain within Commonwealth, with Kenilorea as prime minister. **1988** The Solomon Islands joined Vanuatu and Papua New Guinea to form the Spearhead Group, aiming to preserve Melanesian cultural traditions. **1997** Bartholomew Ulufa'alu was elected prime minister. **1998** Ulufa'alu's Alliance for Change government narrowly survived a no-confidence vote.

Somalia (Somali Democratic Republic)

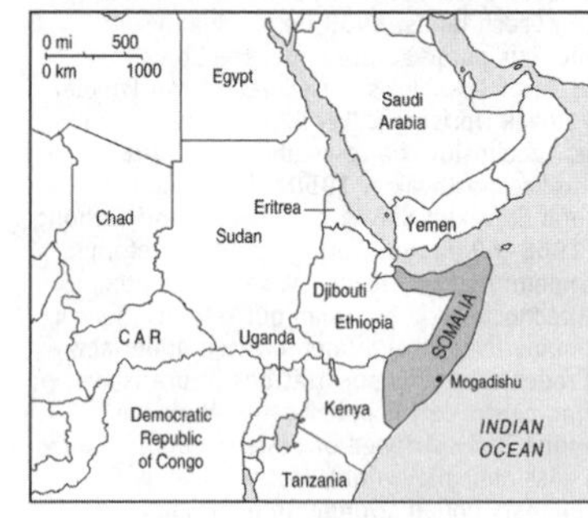

National name *Jamhuriyadda Dimugradiga ee Soomaliya* **Area** 637,700 sq km/246,215 sq mi **Capital** Mogadishu (and port) **Major towns/cities** Hargeysa, Berbera, Kismayo, Marka

Government

Head of state and government (interim) Hussein Aidid from 1996 **Political system** military **Armed forces** 225,000 (1997) **Defence spend** (% GDP) 4.8 (1997) **Education spend** (% GNP) N/A **Health spend** (% GDP) 0.9 (1990) **Death penalty** retained and used for ordinary crimes

Population and society

Population 9,672,000 (1999 est) **Population growth rate** 4.2% (1995–2000) **Ethnic groups** 98% indigenous Somali (about 84% Hamitic and 14% Bantu); population is divided into around 100 clans **Religion** Sunni Muslim **Life expectancy** 45 (men); 49 (women) (1995–2000) **Literacy rate** 36% (men); 14% (women) (1995 est)

Economy and resources

GDP (US$) 8 billion (1996 est) **GNP** (US$) N/A **GNP per capita (PPP)** (US$) 620 (1996 est) **Real GDP growth** (% change on previous year) 4 (1996 est) **Consumer price inflation** 363% (1995) **Foreign debt** (US$) 2.05 billion (1997) **Resources** chromium, coal, salt, tin, zinc, copper, gypsum, manganese, iron ore, uranium, gold, silver; deposits of petroleum and natural gas have been discovered but remain unexploited **Exports** livestock, skins and hides, bananas, fish and fish products, myrrh. Principal market: Saudi Arabia 57.9% (1997) **Imports** petroleum, fertilizers, foodstuffs, machinery and parts, manufacturing raw materials. Principal source: Kenya 27.8% (1997)

▪ Tourist information

Time difference GMT +3 **Currency** Somali shilling **Language** Somali, Arabic (both official), Italian, English **Visa requirements** UK: visa required. USA: visa required **Embassy in the UK** no diplomatic representation at present **British embassy** all staff have been withdrawn for the present; the British Embassy in Addis Ababa (see Ethiopia) deals with enquiries relating to Somalia **Office hours** 0800–1400 Sat–Thu **Banking hours** 0800–1130 Sat–Thu **Airports** international airports: Mogadishu, Berbera; seven domestic airports and airfields; passengers carried: 46,000 (1991) **Major ports** Berbera, Marka, Kismayo **Chief tourist attractions** beaches protected by a coral reef, among the longest in the world **Major holidays** 1 January, 1 May, 26 June, 1 July, 21 October (2 days); variable: Eid-ul-Adha (2 days), end of Ramadan (2 days), Prophet's Birthday

Chronology

8th–10th centuries Arab ancestors of Somali clan families migrated to the region and introduced Sunni Islam; coastal trading cities, including Mogadishu, were formed by Arabian immigrants and developed into sultanates. **11th–14th century** Southward and westward movement of Somalis and Islamization of Christian Ethiopian interior. **early 16th century** Portuguese contacts with coastal region. **1820s** First British contacts with northern Somalia. **1884–87** British protectorate of

Somaliland established in north. **1889** Italian protectorate of Somalia established in south. **1927** Italian Somalia became a colony and part of Italian East Africa from 1936. **1941** Italian Somalia occupied by Britain during World War II. **1943** Somali Youth League (SYL) formed as nationalist party. **1950** Italy resumed control over Italian Somalia under UN trusteeship. **1960** Independence achieved from Italy and Britain as Somalia, with Aden Abdullah Osman as president. **1963** Border dispute with Kenya; diplomatic relations broken with Britain for five years. **1969** President Ibrahim Egal assassinated in army coup led by Maj-Gen Muhammad Siad Barre; constitution suspended, political parties banned, Supreme Revolutionary Council set up, and socialist-Islamic state formed. **1972** 20,000 died in severe drought. **1978** Defeated in eight-month war with Ethiopia fought on behalf of Somali guerrillas in Ogaden to the southwest. Armed insurrection began in north and hundreds of thousands became refugees. **1979** New constitution for socialist one-party state dominated by Somali Revolutionary Socialist Party (SRSP). **1982** The antigovernment Ethiopian-backed Somali National Movement (SNM) was formed in the north, followed by oppressive countermeasures by the government. **late 1980s** Guerrilla activity increased in the north as the civil war intensified. **1991** Mogadishu was captured by rebels; Ali Mahdi Muhammad was named president; free elections were promised. The secession of northeast Somalia, as the Somaliland Republic, was announced but not recognized internationally. **1992** There was widespread famine. Western food-aid convoys were hijacked by 'warlords'. United Nations (UN) peacekeeping troops, led by US Marines, were sent in to protect relief operations. **1993** Leaders of armed factions (except the Somaliland-based faction) agreed to a federal system of government. US-led UN forces destroyed the headquarters of warlord Gen Muhammad Farah Aidid after the killing of Pakistani peacekeepers. **1994** Ali Mahdi Muhammad and Aidid signed a truce. Most Western peacekeeping troops were withdrawn, but clan-based fighting continued. **1996** Aidid was killed in renewed faction fighting; his son Hussein Aidid succeeded him as interim president. **1998** A peace plan was agreed. **1999** In June the Ethiopian army, supporting opponents of Aidid, invaded Somalia.

South Africa Republic of

National name *Republiek van Suid-Afrika* **Area** 1,222,081 sq km/471,845 sq mi **Capital** Cape Town (legislative) (and port), Pretoria (administrative), Bloemfontein (judicial) **Major towns/cities** Johannesburg, Durban, Port Elizabeth, Vereeniging, East London, Pietermaritzburg, Kimberley **Territories** Marion Island and Prince Edward Island in the Antarctic

Government

Head of state and government Thabo Mbeki from 1999 **Political system** emergent democracy **Armed forces** 79,400 (1997) **Conscription** none **Defence spend** (% GDP) 1.8 (1997) **Education spend** (% GNP) 7.9 (1996) **Health spend** (% GDP) 3.6 (1990–95) **Death penalty** abolished in 1998

Population and society

Population 39,900,000 (1999 est) **Population growth rate** 1.5% (1995–2000) **Ethnic groups** 77% of the population is black African, 12% white (of European descent), 9% of mixed African-European descent, and 2% Asian **Religion** Dutch Reformed Church and other Christian denominations, Hindu, Muslim **Life expectancy** 52 (men); 58 (women) (1995–2000) **Literacy rate** 85% (men); 83% (women) (1997 est) **Unemployment** 5.1% (1996)

Economy and resources

GDP (US$) 116.7 billion (1998) **GNP** (US$) 119 billion (1998) **GNP per capita (PPP)** (US$) 6,990 (1998 est) **Real GDP growth** (% change on previous year) 2.0 (1997) **Consumer price inflation** 6.5% (1998) **Foreign debt** (US$) 25.2 billion (1997) **Resources** gold (world's largest producer), coal, platinum, iron ore, diamonds, chromium, manganese, limestone, asbestos, fluorspar, uranium, copper, lead, zinc, petroleum, natural gas **Exports** metals and metal products, gold, precious and semiprecious stones, mineral products and chemicals, natural cultured pearls, machinery and mechanical appliances, wool, maize, fruit, sugar. Principal market: UK 10.1% (1997) **Imports** machinery and electrical equipment, transport equipment, chemical products, mechanical appliances, textiles and clothing, vegetable products, wood, pulp, paper and paper products. Principal source: Germany 13.7% (1997)

▪ Tourist information

Time difference GMT +2 **Currency** rand **Language** English and Afrikaans (both official); main African languages: Xhosa, Zulu, and Sesotho (all official) **Visa requirements** UK: visa not required. USA: visa not required **Embassy in the UK** South Africa House, Trafalgar Square, London WC2N 5DP. Tel: (020) 7930 4488; fax: (020) 7451 7284 **British embassy** British High Commission, 255 Hill Street, Arcadia, Pretoria 0002. Tel: (12) 433 121; fax: (12) 433 207 **Chamber of commerce** South African Chamber of Business, PO Box 91267, Auckland Park 20006. Tel: (11) 482 2524; fax: (11) 726 1344 **Office hours** 0830–1630 Mon–Fri **Banking hours** 0830–1530 Mon–Fri; 0800–1130 Sat **Airports** international airports: Cape Town (D F Malan), Durban (Louis Botha), Johannesburg (Jan Smuts); six domestic airports, 212 public aerodromes; total passenger km: 17,103 million (1997 est) **Major ports** Durban, Port Elizabeth, East London **Chief tourist attractions** fine climate; varied scenery; wildlife reserves **Major holidays** 1 January, 21 March, 27 April, 1 May, 16 June, 9 August , 24 September, 16, 25–26 December; variable: Good Friday

Chronology

1652 Dutch East India Company established colony at Cape Town as a port of call. **1795** Britain occupied Cape after France conquered the Netherlands. **1814** Britain bought Cape Town and hinterland from the Netherlands for £6 million. **1820s** Zulu people established military kingdom under Shaka. **1836–38** The Great Trek: 10,000 Dutch settlers (known as Boers, meaning 'farmers') migrated north to escape British rule. **1843** Britain established colony of Natal on east coast. **1852–54** Britain recognized Boer republics of Transvaal and Orange Free State. **1872** The Cape became self-governing colony within British Empire. **1877** Britain annexed Transvaal. **1879** Zulu War: Britain destroyed power of Zulus. **1881** First Boer War: Transvaal Boers defeated British at Majuba Hill and regained independence. **1886** Disovery of gold on Witwatersrand attracted many migrant miners (uitlanders) to Transvaal, which denied them full citizenship. **1895** Jameson Raid: uitlanders, backed by Cecil Rhodes, tried to overthrow President Paul Kruger of Transvaal. **1899–1902** Second South African War (also known as Boer War): dispute over rights of uitlanders led to conflict which ended with British annexation of Boer republics. **1907** Britain granted internal self-government to Transvaal and Orange Free State on a whites-only franchise. **1910** Cape Colony, Natal, Transvaal, and Orange Free State formed Union of South Africa, with Louis Botha as prime minister. **1912** Gen Barry Hertzog founded (Boer) Nationalist Party; The African National Congress (ANC) was formed to campaign for rights of black majority. **1914** Boer revolt in Orange Free State suppressed; South African troops fought for British Empire in World War I. **1919** Jan Smuts succeeded Botha as premier; South West Africa (Namibia) became South African mandate. **1924** Hertzog became prime minister, aiming to sharpen racial segregation and loosen ties with British Empire. **1939–45** Smuts led South Africa into World War II despite neutralism of Hertzog; South African troops fought with Allies in Middle East, East Africa, and Italy. **1948** Policy of apartheid ('separateness') adopted when National Party (NP) took power under Daniel Malan; continued by his successors Johannes Strijdom 1954–58, Hendrik Verwoerd 1958–66, B J Vorster 1966–78, and P J Botha 1978–89. **1950** Entire population classified by race; Group Areas Act segregated blacks and whites; ANC responded with campaign of civil disobedience. **1960** 70 black demonstrators killed at Sharpville; ANC banned. **1961** South Africa left Commonwealth and became republic. **1964** ANC leader Nelson Mandela sentenced to life imprisonment. **1967** Terrorism Act introduced indefinite detention without trial. **1970s** Over 3 million people forcibly resettled in black 'homelands'. **1976** Over 600 killed in clashes between black protesters and security forces in Soweto. **1984** New constitution gave segregated representation to coloureds and Asians, but continued to exclude blacks. **1985** Growth of violence in black townships led to proclamation of a state of emergency. **1986** USA and Commonwealth imposed limited economic sanctions against South Africa. **1989** F W de Klerk succeeded P W Botha as president; public facilities were desegregated; many ANC activists were released. **1990** The ban on the ANC was lifted; Mandela was released; talks began between the government and the ANC; there was a daily average of 35 murders. **1991** De Klerk repealed the remaining apartheid laws; sanctions were lifted; however, there was severe fighting between the ANC and the Zulu Inkatha movement. **1993** An interim majority rule constitution was adopted; de Klerk and Mandela agreed to form a government of national unity after free elections. **1994** The ANC were victorious in the first nonracial elections; Mandela became president; Commonwealth membership was restored. **1996** De Klerk withdrew the NP from the coalition after the new constitution failed to provide for power-sharing after 1999. **1997** A new constitution was signed by President Mandela. De Klerk announced his retirement from politics. **1999** Mandela retired as state president; he was succeeded by Thabo Mbeki; ANC won assembly majority in election.

South Korea *see* Korea, South

Spain Kingdom of

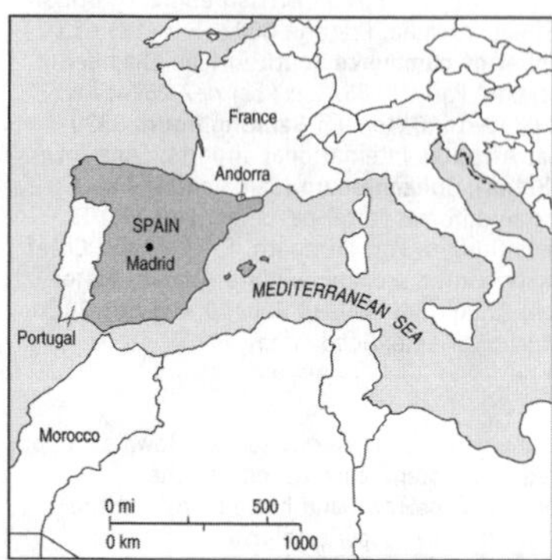

National name *Reino de España* **Area** 504,750 sq km/194,883 sq mi **Capital** Madrid **Major towns/cities** Barcelona, Valencia, Zaragoza, Seville, Málaga, Bilbao, Las Palmas de Gran Canarias, Murcia, Córdoba, Palma de Mallorca, Granada **Territories** Balearic and Canary Islands; in North Africa: Ceuta, Melilla, Alhucemas, Chafarinas Islands, Peñón de Vélez

Government

Head of state King Juan Carlos I from 1975 **Head of government** José Maria Aznar from 1996 **Political system** liberal democracy **Armed forces** 197,500 (1997) **Conscription** nine months **Defence spend** (% GDP) 1.4 (1997) **Education spend** (% GNP) 4.9 (1996) **Health spend** (% GDP) 5.8 (1996) **Death penalty** abolished in 1995

Population and society

Population 39,633,000 (1999 est) **Population growth rate** 0.03% (1995–2000) **Ethnic groups** mostly of Moorish, Roman, and Carthaginian descent **Religion** Roman Catholic **Life expectancy** 75 (men); 82 (women) (1995–2000) **Literacy rate** 98% (men); 96% (women) (1997 est) **Unemployment** 18.8% (1998)

Economy and resources

GDP (US$) 551.9 billion (1998) **GNP** (US$) 553.7 billion (1998) **GNP per capita (PPP)** (US$) 16,060 (1998) **Real GDP growth** (% change on previous year) 3.8 (1998) **Consumer price inflation** 1.8% (1998) **Resources** coal, lignite, anthracite, copper, iron, zinc, uranium, potassium salts **Exports** motor vehicles, machinery and electrical equipment, vegetable products, metals and their manufactures, foodstuffs. Principal market: France 19.6% (1998) **Imports** machinery and transport equipment, electrical equipment, petroleum and petroleum products, chemicals, consumer goods. Principal source: France 18.2% (1998)

▪ Tourist information

Time difference GMT +1 **Currency** peseta **Language** Spanish (Castilian, official), Basque, Catalan, Galician **Visa requirements** UK: visa not required. USA: visa not required **Embassy in the UK** 24 Belgrave Square, London SW1X 8SB. Tel: (020) 7235 5555/6/7; fax: (020) 7235 9905 **British embassy** Calle de Fernando el Santo 16, 28010 Madrid. Tel: (9) 319 0200, fax: (9) 319 0423 **Chamber of commerce** Consejo Superior de Cámaras Officiales de Comercio, Industria y Navigación de España, Calle Claudio Coello 19, 1°, 28001 Madrid. Tel: (9) 575 3400; fax: (9) 435 2392 **Office hours** 0800–1500, or 0900–1300 and 1600/1630–1900/1930 Mon–Fri **Banking hours** 0900–1400 Mon–Fri; 0900–1300 Sat (except during summer) **Airports** international airports: Alicante (Altet), Barcelona (del Prat), Bilbao, Tenerife (2), Madrid (Barajas), Málaga, Santiago de Compostela, Gerona, Gran Canaria, Lanzarote, Palma de Mallorca, Mahon, Valladolid, Seville, Valencia, Zarragoza; domestic services to all major towns; total passenger km: 36,950 million (1997 est) **Major ports** Barcelona, Valencia, Cartagena, Málaga, Cádiz, Vigo, Santander, Bilbao **Chief tourist attractions** climate; beaches; mountain scenery; winter resorts on the Canary Islands; many cities of historical interest, including Madrid, Seville, Córdoba, Barcelona, and Valencia, with their cathedrals, churches, palaces, fortresses, and museums **Major holidays** 1, 6 January, 19 March (most areas), 1 May, 25 July, 15 August, 12 October, 1 November, 8, 25 December; variable: Corpus Christi, Good Friday, Holy Saturday, Holy Thursday

Spain: Regions

(– = not applicable.)

Region	Capital	Area sq km	Area sq mi	Population (1996 est)
Andalusia	Seville	87,268	33,694	7,234,900
Aragon	Zaragoza	47,669	18,405	1,187,500
Asturias	Oviedo	10,565	4,079	1,087,900
Balearic Islands	Palma de Mallorca	5,014	1,935	760,400
Basque Country	Vitoria	7,261	2,803	2,098,100
Canary Islands	Las Palmas and Santa Cruz de Tenerife	7,273	2,808	1,606,500
Cantabria	Santander	5,289	2,042	527,400
Castilla-La Mancha	Toledo	79,226	30,589	1,712,500
Castilla-León	Valladolid	94,147	36,350	2,508,500
Catalonia	Barcelona	31,930	12,328	6,090,000
Extremadura	Mérida	41,602	16,063	1,070,200
Galicia	Santiago de Compostela	29,434	11,364	2,742,600
La Rioja	Longroño	5,034	1,944	264,900
Madrid	Madrid	7,995	3,087	5,022,300
Murcia	Murcia[1]	11,317	4,369	1,097,200
Navarra	Pamplona	10,421	4,024	520,600
Valencia	Valencia	23,305	8,998	4,009,300
Ceuta[2]	–	18	7	68,800
Melilla[2]	–	14	5	59,600

[1] Regional parliament is in Cartagena.
[2] Spanish enclave on the north coast of Morocco.

Chronology

2nd century BC Roman conquest of the Iberian peninsula, which became the province of Hispania. **5th century AD** After the fall of the Roman Empire, Iberia was overrun by Vandals and Visigoths. **711** Muslims invaded from North Africa and overthrew Visigoth kingdom. **9th century** Christians in northern Spain formed kingdoms of Asturias, Aragón, Navarre, and Léon, and county of Castile. **10th century** Abd-al-Rahman III established caliphate of Córdoba; Muslim culture at its height in Spain. **1230** Léon and Castile united under Ferdinand III, who drove the Muslims from most of southern Spain. **14th century** Spain consisted of Christian kingdoms of Castile, Aragón, and Navarre, and the Muslim emirate of Granada. **1469** Marriage of Ferdinand of Aragón and Isabella of Castile; kingdoms united on their accession in 1479. **1492** Conquest of Granada ended Muslim rule in Spain. **1494** Treaty of Tordesillas; Spain and Portugal divided newly discovered America; Spain became a world power. **1519–56** Emperor Charles V was both King of Spain and Archduke of Austria; he also ruled Naples, Sicily, and the Low Countries; Habsburgs dominant in Europe. **1555** Charles V divided his domains between Spain and Austria before retiring; Spain retained the Low Countries and southern Italy as well as South American colonies. **1568** Dutch rebelled against Spanish rule; Spain recognized independence of Dutch Republic in 1648. **1580** Philip II of Spain inherited the throne of Portugal, where Spanish rule lasted until 1640. **1588** Spanish Armada: attempt to invade England defeated. **17th century** Spanish power declined amid wars, corruption, inflation, and loss of civil and religious freedom. **1701–14** War of the Spanish Succession: allied powers fought France to prevent Philip of Bourbon inheriting throne of Spain. **1713–14** Treaties of Utrecht and Rastat: Bourbon dynasty recognized, but Spain lost Gibraltar, southern Italy, and Spanish Netherlands. **1793** Spain declared war on revolutionary France; reduced to a French client state in 1795. **1808** Napoleon installed his brother Joseph as King of Spain. **1808–14** Peninsular War: British forces played a large part in liberating Spain and restoring Bourbon dynasty. **1810–30** Spain lost control of its South American colonies. **1833–39** Carlist civil war: Don Carlos (backed by conservatives) unsuccessfully contested the succession of his niece Isabella II (backed by liberals). **1870** Offer of Spanish throne to Leopold of Hohenzollern-Sigmaringen sparked Franco-Prussian War. **1873–74** First republic ended by military coup which restored Bourbon dynasty with Alfonso XII. **1898** Spanish-American War: Spain lost Cuba and Philippines. **1923–30** Dictatorship of Gen Primo de Rivera with support of Alfonso XIII. **1931** Proclamation of Second Republic, initially dominated by anticlerical radicals and socialists. **1933** Moderates and Catholics won elections; insurrection by socialists and Catalans in 1934. **1936** Left-wing Popular Front narrowly won fresh elections; General Francisco Franco launched military rebellion. **1936–39** Spanish Civil War: Nationalists (with significant Italian and German support) defeated Republicans (with limited Soviet support); Franco became dictator of nationalist-fascist regime. **1941** Though officially neutral in World War II, Spain sent 40,000 troops to fight USSR. **1955** Spain admitted to the United Nations (UN). **1975** Death of Franco; he was succeeded by King Juan Carlos I. **1978** A referendum endorsed democratic constitution. **1982** Socialists took office under Felipe González; Spain joined the North Atlantic Treaty Organization (NATO); Basque separatist organization (ETA) stepped up its terrorist campaign. **1986** Spain joined the European Economic Community (EEC). **1997** 23 Basque nationalist leaders were jailed for terrorist activities. **1998** ETA announced an indefinite ceasefire. The government announced that it would begin peace talks. **2000** Prime Minister Aznar was re-elected.

Sri Lanka Democratic Socialist Republic of (formerly Ceylon)

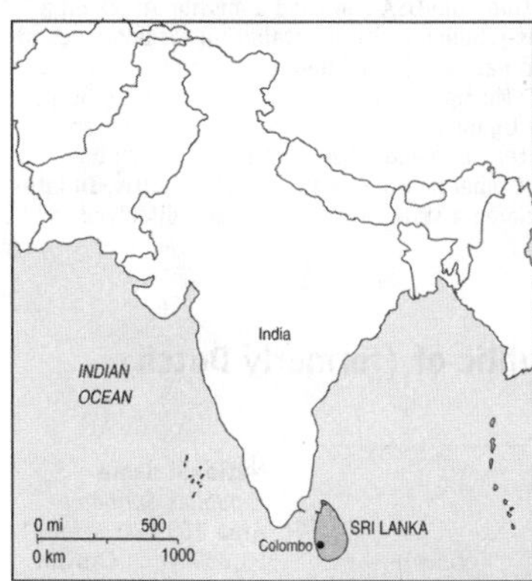

National name *Sri Lanka Prajathanthrika Samajawadi Janarajaya* **Area** 65,610 sq km/ 25,332 sq mi **Capital** Colombo (and chief port) **Major towns/ cities** Kandy, Dehiwala-Mount Lavinia, Moratuwa, Jaffna, Kotte

Government

Head of state Chandrika Bandaranaike Kumaratunga from 1994 **Head of government** Sirimavo Bandaranaike from 1994 **Political system** liberal democracy **Armed forces** 117,000 plus paramilitary forces numbering around 110,200 (1997) **Conscription** military service is voluntary **Defence spend** (% GDP) 6.1 (1997) **Education spend** (% GNP) 3.4 (1996) **Health spend** (% GDP) 3.7 (1995) **Death penalty** retains the death penalty for ordinary crimes but can be considered abolitionist in practice (last execution 1976)

Population and society

Population 18,639,000 (1999 est) **Population growth rate** 1.0% (1995–2000) **Ethnic groups** 73% Sinhalese, 19% Tamil, and 7% Moors or Muslims (concentrated in east); the Tamil community is divided between the long-settled 'Sri Lankan Tamils' (11% of the population), who reside in northern and eastern coastal areas, and the more recent immigrant 'Indian Tamils' (8%), who settled in the Kandyan highlands during the 19th and 20th centuries **Religion** Buddhist 69%, Hindu 15%, Muslim 8%, Christian 7% **Life expectancy** 71 (men); 75 (women) (1995–2000) **Literacy rate** 94% (men); 88% (women) (1997 est) **Unemployment** 10.7% (1998 est)

Economy and resources

GDP (US$) 15.1 billion (1998 est) **GNP** (US$) 15.2 billion (1998) **GNP per capita (PPP)** (US$) 2,300 (1998 est) **Real GDP growth** (% change on previous year) 5 (1998) **Consumer price inflation** 9% (1998) **Foreign debt** (US$) 7.6 billion (1997) **Resources** gemstones, graphite, iron ore, monazite, rutile, uranium, iemenite sands, limestone, salt, clay **Exports** clothing and textiles, tea (world's largest exporter and third-largest producer), precious and semi-precious stones, coconuts and coconut products, rubber. Principal market: USA 39.9% (1998) **Imports** machinery and transport equipment, petroleum, food and live animals, beverages, construction materials. Principal source: Japan 9.4% (1998)

▪ Tourist information

Time difference GMT +5.5 **Currency** Sri Lankan rupee **Language** Sinhala, Tamil, English **Visa requirements** UK: visa only required by business visitors. USA: visa only required by business visitors **Embassy in the UK** 13 Hyde Park Gardens, London W2 2LU. Tel: (020) 7262 1841; fax: (020) 7262 7970 **British embassy** PO Box 1433, 190 Galle Road, Kollupitiya, Colombo 3. Tel: (1) 437 336; fax: (1) 430 308 **Chamber of commerce** Federation of Chambers of Commerce and Industry of Sri Lanka, 29 Gregory's Road, Colombo 7. Tel: (1) 698 225; fax: (1) 699 530 **Office hours** 0830/0900–1615/1700 Mon–Fri **Banking hours** 0900–1300 Mon and Sat; 0900–1500 Tue–Fri **Airports** international airports: Colombo (Katunayake); five domestic airports; total passenger km: 4,249 million (1997 est) **Major ports** Jaffna, Galle, Negombo, Trincomalee **Chief tourist attractions** Buddhist festivals and ancient monuments; scenery **Major holidays** 14 January, 4 February, 1, 22 May, 30 June, 25, 31 December; variable: Eid-ul-Adha, Diwali, end of Ramadan, Good Friday, New Year (Sinhala/Tamil, April), Prophet's Birthday, Maha Sivarathri (February/March), Full Moon (monthly)

Chronology

***c.* 550 BC** Arrival of the Sinhalese, led by Vijaya, from northern India, displacing long-settled Veddas. **5th century BC** Sinhalese kingdom of Anuradhapura founded by King Pandukabaya. ***c.* 250–210 BC** Buddhism, brought from India, became established in Sri Lanka. **AD 992** Downfall of Anuradhapura kingdom, defeated by South Indian Colas. **1070** Overthrow of Colas by Vijayabahu I and establishment of the Sinhalese kingdom of Polonnaruva, which survived for more than two centuries before a number of regional states arose. **late 15th century** Kingdom of Kandy established in central highlands. **1505** Arrival of Portuguese navigator Lorenço de Almeida, attracted by spice trade developed by Arab merchants who had called the island Serendip. **1597–1618** Portuguese controlled most of Sri Lanka, with the exception of Kandy. **1658** Dutch conquest of Portuguese territories. **1795–98** British conquest of Dutch territories. **1802** Treaty of Amiens recognized island as British colony of Ceylon. **1815** British won control of Kandy, becoming the first European power to rule whole island. **1830s** Immigration of south Indian Hindu Tamil labourers to work central coffee plantations. **1880s** Tea and rubber become chief cash crops after blight ended production of coffee. **1919** Formation of the Ceylon National Congress to campaign for self rule; increasing conflicts between Sinhalese majority community and Tamil minority. **1931** Universal adult suffrage introduced for elected legislature and executive council in which power was shared with British. **1948** Ceylon achieved independence from Britain within Commonwealth, with Don Senanayake of conservative United National Party (UNP) as prime minister. **1949** Indian Tamils disenfranchised. **1956** Sinhala established as official language. **1960** Sirimavo Bandaranaike, the widow of assassinated prime minister Solomon Bandaranaike, won general election and formed an SLFP government, which nationalized oil industry. **1971** Sinhalese Marxist uprising, led by students and People's Liberation Army (JVP). **1972** Socialist Republic of Sri Lanka proclaimed; Buddhism given 'foremost place' in new state, antagonizing Tamils. **1976** Tamil United Liberation Front formed to fight for independent Tamil state ('Eelam') in north and east Sri Lanka. **1978** Presidential constitution adopted by new free-market government headed by Junius Jayawardene of UNP. **1983** Ethnic riots as Tamil guerrilla violence escalated; state of emergency imposed; more than 1,000 Tamils killed by Sinhalese mobs. **1987** President Jayawardene and Indian prime minister Rajiv Gandhi signed Colombo Accord aimed at creating new provincial councils, disarming Tamil militants ('Tamil Tigers'), and stationing 7,000-strong Indian Peace Keeping Force. Violence continued despite ceasefire policed by Indian troops. **1988** Left-wing JVP guerrillas campaigned against Indo-Sri Lankan peace pact. Prime Minister Ranasinghe Premadasa elected president. **1989** Dingiri Banda Wijetunga became prime minister. Leaders of Tamil Tigers and banned Sinhala extremist JVP assassinated. **1990** The Indian peacekeeping force was withdrawn. Violence continued, with a death toll of over a thousand a month. **1991** The Sri Lankan army killed 2,552 Tamil Tigers at Elephant Pass in the northern Jaffna region. A new party, the Democratic National United Front (DUNF), was formed by former members of UNP. **1992** Several hundred Tamil Tiger rebels were killed in an army offensive, code-named 'Strike Force Two'. **1993** President Premadasa was assassinated by Tamil Tiger terrorists; he was succeeded by Dingiri Banda Wijetunge. **1994** The UNP were narrowly defeated in a general election; Chandrika Kumaratunga became prime minister in an SLFP-led left-of-centre coalition. Peace talks opened with the Tamil Tigers. Kumaratunga was elected the first female president; her mother, Sirimavo Bandaranaike, became prime minister. **1995** Renewed bombing campaign by Tamil Tigers. A major offensive drove out Tamil Tigers from Jaffna city. **1996** A state of emergency was extended nationwide after Tamils bombed the capital. **1998** The Tamil Tigers were outlawed after the bombing of Sri Lanka's holiest Buddhist site. In September over 1,300 Sri Lankan soldiers and Tamil Tiger rebels died in renewed fighting in the north. In October the Tamil Tigers captured the strategic northern town of Kilinochchi, killing more than 600 government troops. **1999** In late 1999, the government lost a large amount of territory, including military bases, to Tamil guerrillas. In the December presidential elections, President Kumaratunga was re-elected, just days after she survived an assasination attempt by a Tamil suicide bomber.

Sudan Democratic Republic of

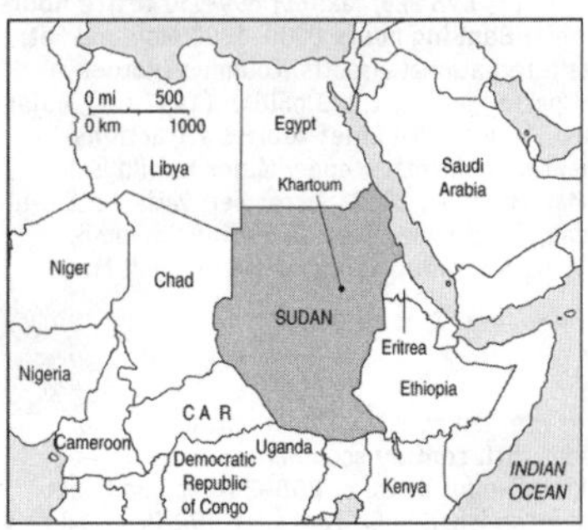

National name *Jamhuryat es-Sudan* **Area** 2,505,800 sq km/ 967,489 sq mi **Capital** Khartoum **Major towns/cities** Omdurman, Port Sudan, Juba, Wadi Medani, al-Obeid, Kassala, Atbara, al-Qadarif, Kosti

Government

Head of state and government Gen Omar Hassan Ahmed al-Bashir from 1989 **Political system** military **Armed forces** 79,700 (1997) **Conscription** military service is compulsory for three years **Defence spend** (% GDP) 5.6 (1997) **Education spend** (% GNP) N/A **Health spend** (% GDP) 0.5 (1990) **Death penalty** retained and used for ordinary crimes

Population and society

Population 28,882,000 (1999 est) **Population growth rate** 2.1% (1995–2000) **Ethnic groups** over 50 ethnic groups and almost 600 subgroups; the population is broadly distributed between Arabs in the north and black Africans in the south **Religion** Sunni Muslim; also animist and Christian **Life expectancy** 54 (men); 56 (women) (1995–2000) **Literacy rate** 65% (men); 41% (women) (1997 est) **Unemployment** 30% (1993 est)

Economy and resources

GDP (US$) 10.4 billion (1998) **GNP** (US$) 8.2 billion (1998) **GNP per capita (PPP)** (US$) 1,360 (1998) **Real GDP growth** (% change on previous year) 2.3 (1998) **Consumer price inflation** 50% (1998) **Foreign debt** (US$) 16.3 billion (1997) **Resources** petroleum, marble, mica, chromite, gypsum, gold, graphite, sulphur, iron, manganese, zinc, fluorspar, talc, limestone, dolomite, pumice **Exports** cotton, sesame seed, gum arabic, sorghum, livestock, hides and skins. Principal market: Saudi Arabia 21.3% (1997) **Imports** basic manufacture, crude materials (mainly petroleum and petroleum products), foodstuffs, machinery and equipment. Principal source: Libya 16.7% (1997)

▪ Tourist information

Time difference GMT +2 **Currency** Sudanese dinar **Language** Arabic 51% (official), local languages **Visa requirements** UK: visa required. USA: visa required **Embassy in the UK** 3 Cleveland Row, St James Street, London SW1A 1DD. Tel: (020) 7839 8080; fax: (020) 7839 7560 **British embassy** PO Box 801, Street 10, off Sharia Al Baladiya, Khartoum East. Tel: (11) 770 769; telex: 22189 (a/b PRDRM SD) **Chamber of commerce** PO Box 81, Khartoum. Tel: (11) 72346 **Office hours** 0800–1430 Sat–Thu **Banking hours** 0830–1200 Sat–Thu **Airports** international airports: Khartoum (civil); 20 domestic airports; total passenger km: 681 million (1995) **Major ports** Port Sudan **Major holidays** 1 January, 3 March, 6 April, 25 December; variable: Eid-ul-Adha (5 days), end of Ramadan (5 days), New Year (Muslim), Prophet's Birthday, Sham al-Naseem (April/May)

Chronology

c. 600 BC–AD 350 Meroë, near Khartoum, was capital of the Nubian Empire, which covered southern Egypt and northern Sudan. **6th century** Converted to Coptic Christianity. **7th century** Islam first introduced by Arab invaders, but did not spread widely until the 15th century. **16th–18th centuries** Arab-African Fur and Fung Empires established in central and northern Sudan. **1820** Invaded by Muhammad Ali and brought under Egyptian control. **1881–85** Revolt led to capture of Khartoum by Sheik Muhammad Ahmed, a self-proclaimed Mahdi ('messiah'), and the killing of British general Charles Gordon. **1898** Anglo-Egyptian offensive led by Lord Kitchener subdued Mahdi revolt at Battle of Omdurman in which 20,000 Sudanese died. **1899** Sudan administered as Anglo-Egyptian condominium. **1923** White Flag League formed by Sudanese nationalists in north; British instituted policy of reducing contact between northern and southern Sudan, with the aim that the south would eventually become part of federation of eastern African states. **1955** Civil war between the dominant Arab Muslim north and black African Christian and animist south broke out. **1956** Sudan achieved independence from Britain and Egypt as a republic. **1958** Military coup replaced civilian government with Supreme Council of the Armed Forces. **1964** Civilian rule reinstated after October Revolution of student demonstrations. **1969** Coup led by Col Gaafar Mohammed al-Nimeri abolished political institutions and concentrated power in a leftist Revolutionary Command Council. **1971** Nimeri confirmed as president and the Sudanese Socialist Union (SSU) declared the only legal party by a new constitution. **1972** Plans to form Federation of Arab Republics, comprising Sudan, Egypt, and Syria, abandoned due to internal opposition. To end 17-year-long civil war, Nimeri agreed to give south greater autonomy. **1974** National assembly established. **1980** Country reorganized into six regions, each with own assembly and effective autonomy. **1983** Shari'a (Islamic law) imposed. Sudan People's Liberation Movement (SPLM) formed in south as civil war broke out again. **1985** Nimeri deposed in a bloodless coup led by Gen Swar al-Dahab following industrial unrest in north. **1986** Coalition government formed after general election, with Sadiq al-Mahdi, great-grandson of the Mahdi, as prime minister. **1987** Civil war with Sudan People's Liberation Army (SPLA); drought and famine in south and refugee influx from Ethiopa and Chad. **1988** A peace pact was signed with SPLA, but fighting continued. **1989** Al-Mahdi was overthrown in a coup led by Islamic fundamentalist Gen Omar Hassan Ahmed el-Bashir. All political activity was suspended. **1991** A federal system was introduced, with division of the country into nine states as the civil war continued. **1998** Civil war continued between the SPLA and the the Islamist government. There was famine in the south, where millions faced starvation. The USA launched a missile attack on a suspected chemical weapons-producing site in retaliation for bombings of US embassies in Nairobi and Dar es Salaam. There was a temporary ceasefire by the SPLA. **1999** Multiparty politics were reintroduced. Steps to restore diplomatic ties with Uganda were taken when in December an agreement was signed to attempt to end rebel wars across the mutual border by ceasing to support rebel factions in the other's country. In late December the president declared a state of emergency and dissolved parliament.

Suriname Republic of (formerly Dutch Guiana)

National name *Republiek Suriname* **Area** 163,820 sq km/ 63,250 sq mi **Capital** Paramaribo **Major towns/cities** Nieuw Nickerie, Moengo, Pontoetoe, Brokopondo, Nieuw Amsterdam

Government

Head of state Jules Wijdenbosch from 1996 **Head of government** Prataapnarain Shawh Radhecheran Radhakishun from 1996 **Political system** emergent democracy **Armed forces** 1,800 (1997) **Conscription** military service is voluntary **Defence spend** (% GDP) 4.4 (1997) **Education spend** (% GNP) 3.5 (1995) **Health spend** (% GDP) 2 (1995) **Death penalty** retains the death penalty for ordinary crimes but can be considered abolitionist in practice (last execution 1982)

Population and society

Population 416,000 (1998 est) **Population growth rate** 0.4% (1995–2000) **Ethnic groups** a wide ethnic composition, including Creoles, East Indians, Indonesians, Africans, American Indians, Europeans, and Chinese **Religion** Christian, Hindu, Muslim **Life expectancy** 68 (men); 73 (women) (1995–2000) **Literacy rate** 95% (men); 92% (women) (1997 est) **Unemployment** 20% (1997)

Economy and resources

GDP (US$) 535 million (1998 est) **GNP** (US$) 685 million (1998) **GNP per capita (PPP)** (US$) 3,680 (1997 est) **Real GDP growth** (% change on previous year) 2 (1998) **Consumer price inflation** 25% (1998) **Foreign debt** (US$) 183 million (1997) **Resources** petroleum, bauxite (one of the world's leading producers), iron ore, copper, manganese, nickel, platinum, gold, kaolin **Exports** alumina, aluminium, shrimps, bananas, plantains, rice, wood and wood products. Principal market: USA 16.4% (1997) **Imports** raw materials and semi-manufactured goods, mineral fuels and

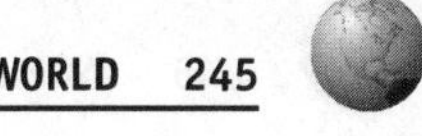

lubricants, investment goods, foodstuffs, cars and motorcycles, textiles. Principal source: USA 35.4% (1997)

▪ Tourist information

Time difference GMT −3.5 **Currency** Suriname guilder **Language** Dutch (official), Sranan (creole), English, Hindi, Javanese, Chinese. Spanish is the main working language **Visa requirements** UK: visa not required. USA: visa required **Embassy for the UK** Alexander Gogelweg 2, 2517 JH The Hague, The Netherlands. Tel: (70) 365 0844; fax: (70) 361 7445 **British embassy** British Honorary Consulate, c/o VSH United Buildings, PO Box 1860, Van't Hogerhuysstraat 9–11, Paramaribo. Tel: (597) 472 870; fax: (597) 475 515 **Chamber of commerce** Suriname Chamber of Commerce and Industry, PO Box 149, Dr J C de Mirandasstraat 10, Paramaribo. Tel: (597) 473 527; fax: (597) 474 779 **Office hours** 0700–1500 Mon–Thu; 0700–1430 Fri **Banking hours** 0730–1400 Mon–Fri **Airports** international airport: Paramaribo (Johan A Pengel); one domestic airport and 35 airstrips; total passenger km: 1,068 million (1997 est) **Chief tourist attractions** numerous historical sites; varied cultural activities; unspoiled interior with varied flora and fauna; 13 nature reserves and a nature park **Major holidays** 1 January, 25 February, 1 May, 1 July, 25 November, 25–26 December; variable: Good Friday, Easter Monday, end of Ramadan, Holi (March)

Chronology

AD 1593 Visited and claimed by Spanish explorers; the name Suriname derived from the country's earliest inhabitants, the Surinen, who were driven out by other Amerindians in the 16th century. **1602** Dutch settlements established. **1651** British colony founded by settlers sent from Barbados. **1667** Became a Dutch colony, received in exchange for New Amsterdam (New York) by Treaty of Breda. **1682** Coffee and sugar cane plantations introduced, worked by imported African slaves. **1795–1802 and 1804–16** Under British rule. **1863** Slavery abolished and indentured labourers brought in from China, India, and Java. **1915** Bauxite discovered and gradually became main export. **1954** Achieved internal self-government as Dutch Guiana. **1958–69** Politics dominated by Johan Pengel, charismatic leader of the mainly Creole Suriname National Party (NPS). **1975** Independence achieved, with Dr Johan Ferrier as president and Henck Arron (NPS) as prime minister; 40% of population emigrated to the Netherlands. **1980** Arron's government overthrown in an army coup. The army replaced Ferrier with Dr Chin A Sen. **1982** The army, led by Lt Col Desi Bouterse, seized power, setting up a Revolutionary People's Front; economic aid from the Netherlands and US was cut off after opposition leaders, charged with plotting a coup, were executed. **1985** Ban on political activities lifted. **1989** Bouterse rejected a peace accord reached by President Shankar with guerrilla insurgents, the Bush Negro (descendents of escaped slaves) maroons, and vowed to continue fighting. **1991** A New Front opposition alliance won an assembly majority. **1992** A peace accord was reached with guerrilla groups. **1996** Jules Wijdenbosch was elected president. He appointed Prataapnarain Shawh Radhecheran Radhakishun as his prime minister.

Swaziland Kingdom of

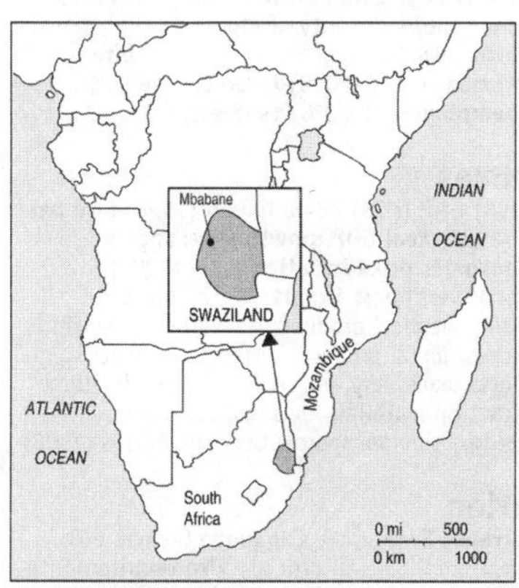

National name *Umbuso we Swatini* **Area** 17,400 sq km/6,718 sq mi **Capital** Mbabane **Major towns/cities** Manzini, Big Bend, Mhlume, Havelock Mine, Nhlangano

Government

Head of state King Mswati III from 1986 **Head of government** Barnabas Sibusiso Dlamini from 1996 **Political system** absolutist **Armed forces** 127,280 (1995) **Conscription** military service is compulsory for two years **Defence spend** (% GDP) 2.5 (1993 est) **Education spend** (% GNP) 7.3 (1996) **Health spend** (% GDP) 3 (1995) **Death penalty** retained and used for ordinary crimes

Population and society

Population 980,000 (1999 est) **Population growth rate** 2.9% (1995–2000); 2.6% (2000–05) **Ethnic groups** about 90% indigenous African, comprising the Swazi, Zulu, Tonga, and Shangaan peoples; there are European and Afro-European (Eurafrican) minorities numbering around 22,000 **Religion** Christian, animist **Life expectancy** 58 (men); 63 (women) (1995–2000) **Literacy rate** 79% (men); 76% (women) (1997 est) **Unemployment** 40% (1995 est)

Economy and resources

GDP (US$) 1.21 billion (1998) **GNP** (US$) 1.38billion (1998) **GNP per capita (PPP)** (US$) 3,580 (1998) **Real GDP growth** (% change on previous year) 2.6 (1998) **Consumer price inflation** 8% (1998) **Foreign debt** (US$) 382 million (1997) **Resources** coal, asbestos, diamonds, gold, tin, kaolin, iron ore, talc, pyrophyllite, silica **Exports** sugar, wood pulp, cotton yarn, canned fruits, asbestos, coal, diamonds, gold. Principal market: South Africa 74% (1997) **Imports** machinery and transport equipment, minerals, fuels and lubricants, manufactured items, food and live animals. Principal source: South Africa 82.9% (1997)

▪ Tourist information

Time difference GMT +2 **Currency** lilangeni **Language** Swazi, English (both official) **Visa requirements** UK: visa not required. USA: visa not required **Embassy in the UK** 20 Buckingham Street, London SW1E 6LB. Tel: (020) 7630 6611; fax: (020) 7630 6564 **British embassy** British High Commission, Allister Miller Street, Private Bag, Mbabane. Tel: (268) 42581; fax: (268) 42585 **Chamber of commerce** Swaziland Chamber of Commerce and Industry, PO Box 72, Mbabane. Tel: (268) 44408; fax: (268) 45442 **Office hours** 0800–1300 and 1400–1700 Mon–Fri; 0800–1300 Sat **Banking hours** 0830–1430 Mon–Fri; 0830–1100 Sat **Airports** international airport: Manzini (Matsapha); total passenger km: 49 million (1995) **Chief tourist attractions** magnificent mountain scenery; game reserves **Major holidays** 1 January, 25 April, 22 July, 6 September, 24 October, 25–26 December; variable: Ascension Thursday, Good Friday, Easter Monday, Commonwealth (March)

Chronology

late 16th century King Ngwane II crossed Lubombo mountains from the east and settled in southeast Swaziland; his successors established a strong centralized Swazi kingdom, dominating the long-settled Nguni and Sothi peoples. **mid-19th century** Swazi nation was ruled by the warrior King Mswati who, at the height of his power, controlled an area three times the size of the present-day state. **1882** Gold was discovered in the northwest, attracting European fortune hunters, who coerced Swazi rulers into granting land concessions. **1894** Came under joint rule of Britain and the Boer republic of Transvaal. **1903** Following the South African War, Swaziland became a special British protectorate, or High Commission territory, against South Africa's wishes. **1922** King Sobhuza II succeeded to the Swazi throne. **1968** Independence achieved within the Commonwealth, as the Kingdom of Swaziland, with King (or Ngwenyama) Sobhuza II as head of state. **1973** The king suspended the constitution, banned political activity, and assumed absolute powers after the opposition deputies had been elected to parliament. **1977** The king announced substitution of traditional tribal communities (*tinkhundla*) for the parliamentary system, arguing it was more suited to Swazi values. **1982** King Sobhuza II died; his place was taken by one of his wives, Queen Dzeliwe, until his son, Prince Makhosetive, was old enough to become king. **1983** Queen Dzeliwe ousted by a younger wife, Queen Ntombi, as real power passed to the prime minister, Prince Bhekimpi Dlamini. **1986** The crown prince was formally invested as King Mswati III. **1993** Direct elections of *tinkhundla* candidates were held for the first time. **1996** Barnabas Sibusiso Dlamini was appointed prime minister.

Sweden Kingdom of

National name *Konungariket Sverige* **Area** 450,000 sq km/173,745 sq mi **Capital** Stockholm (and chief port) **Major towns/cities** Göteborg, Malmö, Uppsala, Norrköping, Västerås, Linköping, Orebro, Jönköping, Helsingborg, Borås

Government

Head of state King Carl XVI Gustaf from 1973 **Head of government** Goran Persson from 1996 **Political system** liberal democracy **Armed forces** 53,400 (1997) **Conscription** 7–15 months (army and navy); 8–12 months (air force) **Defence spend** (% GDP) 2.4 (1997) **Education spend** (% GNP) 8.3 (1996) **Health spend** (% GDP) 7.2 (1996) **Death penalty** abolished in 1972

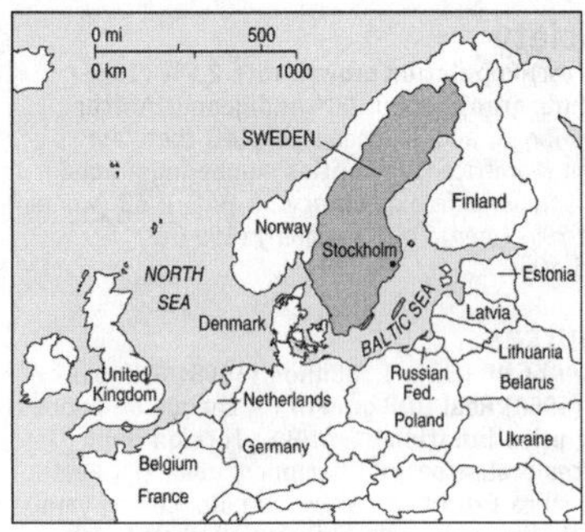

Population and society

Population 8,892,000 (1999 est) **Population growth rate** 0.3% (1995–2000); 0.3% (2000–05) **Ethnic groups** predominantly of Teutonic descent, with small Saami (Lapp), Finnish, and German minorities **Religion** Evangelical Lutheran (established national church) **Life expectancy** 76 (men); 81 (women) (1995–2000) **Literacy rate** 99% (men); 99% (women) (1997 est) **Unemployment** 8.2% (1998)

Economy and resources

GDP (US$) 224.9 billion (1998) **GNP** (US$) 226.9 billion (1998) **GNP per capita (PPP)** (US$) 19,480 (1998) **Real GDP growth** (% change on previous year) 2.8 (1998) **Consumer price inflation** 2.3% (1998) **Resources** iron ore, uranium, copper, lead, zinc, silver, hydroelectric power, forests **Exports** forestry products (wood, pulp, and paper), machinery, motor vehicles, power-generating non-electrical machinery, chemicals, iron and steel. Principal market: Germany 11.2% (1998) **Imports** machinery and transport equipment, chemicals, mineral fuels and lubricants, textiles, clothing, footwear, food and live animals. Principal source: Germany 19% (1998)

▪ Tourist information

Time difference GMT +1 **Currency** Swedish krona **Language** Swedish; there are Finnish- and Saami-speaking minorities **Visa requirements** UK: visa not required. USA: visa not required **Embassy in the UK** 11 Montagu Place, London W1H 2AL. Tel: (020) 7917 6400; fax: (020) 7724 4174 **British embassy** PO Box 27819, Skarpögatan 6–8, 115 93 Stockholm. Tel: (8) 671 9000; fax: (8) 662 9989 **Chamber of commerce** Federation of Swedish Commerce and Trade, PO Box 5512, Grevgatan 34, 114 85 Stockholm. Tel: (8) 666 1100; fax: (8) 662 7457 **Office hours** flexible, with lunch break 1200–1300 **Banking hours** generally 0930–1500 Mon–Fri **Airports** international airports: Stockholm (Arlanda), Göteborg (Landvetter), Malmö (Sturup); over 30 domestic airports; total passenger km: 8,615 million (1995) **Major ports** Helsingborg, Malmö, Göteborg **Chief tourist attractions** varied landscape – mountains north of Arctic Circle, white sandy beaches in south, lakes, waterfalls, and forests; Stockholm, with its modern architecture and cultural activities **Major holidays** 1, 6 January, 1 May, 1 November, 24–26, 31 December; variable: Ascension Thursday, Good Friday, Easter Monday, Whit Monday, Midsummer Eve and Day (June)

Chronology

8th century Kingdom of the Svear, based near Uppsala, extended its rule across much of southern Sweden. **9th–11th centuries** Swedish Vikings raided and settled along the rivers of Russia. *c.* 1000 Olaf Skötkonung, king of the Svear, adopted Christianity and united much of Sweden (except south and west coasts, which remained Danish until 17th century). **11th–13th centuries** Sweden existed as isolated kingdom under the Stenkil, Sverker, and Folkung dynasties; series of crusades incorporated Finland. **1397** Union of Kalmar: Sweden, Denmark, and Norway united under a single monarch; Sweden effectively ruled by succession of regents. **1448** Breach with Denmark: Sweden alone elected Charles VIII as king. **1523** Gustavus Vasa, leader of insurgents, became king of a fully independent Sweden. **1527** Swedish Reformation: Gustavus confiscated Church property and encouraged Lutherans. **1544** Swedish crown became hereditary in House of Vasa. **1592–1604** Sigismund Vasa, a Catholic, was king of both Sweden and Poland until ousted from Swedish throne by his Lutheran uncle Charles IX. **17th century** Sweden, a great military power under Gustavus Adolphus 1611–32, Charles X 1654–60, and Charles XI 1660–97, fought lengthy wars with Denmark, Russia, Poland, and Holy Roman Empire. **1720** Limited monarchy established; political power passed to *Riksdag* (parliament) dominated by nobles. **1721** Great Northern War ended with Sweden losing nearly all its conquests of the previous century. **1741–43** Sweden defeated in disastrous war with Russia; further conflict 1788–90. **1771–92** Gustavus III increased royal power and introduced wide-ranging reforms. **1809** Russian invaders annexed Finland; Swedish nobles staged coup and restored powers of Riksdag. **1810** Napoleonic marshal, Jean-Baptiste Bernadotte, elected crown prince of Sweden, as Charles XIII had no heir. **1812** Bernadotte allied Sweden with Russia against France. **1814** Treaty of Kiel: Sweden obtained Norway from Denmark. **1818–44** Bernadotte reigned in Sweden as Charles XIV John. **1846** Free enterprise established by abolition of trade guilds and monopolies. **1866** Series of liberal reforms culminated in new two-chambered *Riksdag* dominated by bureaucrats and farmers. **late 19th century** Development of large-scale forestry and iron-ore industry; neutrality adopted in foreign affairs. **1905** Union with Norway dissolved. **1907** Adoption of proportional representation and universal suffrage. **1920s** Economic boom transformed Sweden from an agricultural to an industrial economy. **1932** Social Democrat government of Per Halbin Hansson introduced radical public-works programme to combat trade slump. **1940–43** Under duress, neutral Sweden permitted limited transit of German forces through its territory. **1946–69** Social Democrat government of Tage Erlander developed comprehensive welfare state. **1959** Sweden joined European Free Trade Association. **1971** Constitution amended to create single-chamber Riksdag. **1975** Remaining constitutional powers of monarch removed. **1976–82** Centre-right coalition government under Prime Minister Thorbjörn Fälldin ended 44 years of Social Democrat dominance. **1991** The leader of the Moderate Party, Carl Bildt, headed up a coalition of the Moderate, Centre, Liberal, and Christian Democratic parties. **1995** Sweden became a member of the European Union. **1996** Goran Persson of the Social Democratic Labour Party (SAP) became prime minister. **1998** The SAP were narrowly re-elected in a general election.

Switzerland (Swiss Confederation)

National name German *Schweiz*, French *Suisse*, Romansch *Svizra*, Italian *Svizzera* **Area** 41,300 sq km/15,945 sq mi **Capital** Bern (Berne) **Major towns/cities** Zürich, Geneva, Basel, Lausanne, Luzern, St Gallen

Government

Head of state and government Adolf Ogi from 2000 **Government** liberal democracy **Armed forces** 26,300 (1997) **Conscription** 17 weeks' recruit training, followed by refresher training of varying length according to age **Defence spend** (% GDP) 1.5 (1997) **Education spend** (% GNP) 5.3 (1996) **Health spend** (% GDP) 7.1 (1996) **Death penalty** abolished in 1992

Population and society

Population 7,345,000 (1999 est) **Population growth rate** 0.7% (1995–2000); 0.5% (2000–05) **Ethnic groups** majority of Alpine descent; sizeable Nordic element **Religion** Roman Catholic 50%, Protestant 48% **Life expectancy** 75 (men); 82 (women) (1995–2000) **Literacy rate** 99% (men); 99% (women) (1997 est) **Unemployment** 4.1% (1998 est)

Economy and resources

GDP (US$) 264.4 billion (1998) **GNP** (US$) 284.8 billion (1998) **GNP per capita (PPP)** (US$) 26,620 (1998) **Real GDP growth** (% change on previous year) 2.2 (1998) **Consumer price inflation** 0.1% (1998) **Resources** salt, hydroelectric power, forest **Exports** machinery and equipment, pharmaceutical and chemical products, foodstuffs, precision instruments, clocks and watches, metal products. Principal market: Germany 23.6% (1998) **Imports** machinery, motor vehicles, agricultural and forestry products, construction material, fuels and lubricants, chemicals, textiles and clothing. Principal source: Germany 32.7% (1998)

▪ Tourist information

Time difference GMT +1 **Currency** Swiss franc **Language** German 64%, French 19%, Italian 8%, Romansch 0.6% (all official) **Visa requirements** UK: visa not required. USA: visa not required **Embassy in the UK** 16–18 Montagu Place, London W1H 2BQ. Tel: (020) 7616 6000; fax: (020) 7724 7001 **British embassy** Thunstrasse 50, CH-3005 Bern 15. Tel: (31) 352 5021/6; fax: (31) 352 0583 **Chamber of commerce** Schweizerischer Handels- und Industrie-Verein (Swiss Federation of Commerce and

Industry), PO Box 690, Mainaustrasse 49, CH-8034 Zürich. Tel: (1) 382 2323; fax: (1) 382 2332 **Office hours** 0800–1200 and 1400–1700 Mon–Fri **Banking hours** 0830–1630 Mon–Fri **Airports** international airports: Zürich (Kloten), Geneva, Bern (Belp), Basel (Basel-Mulhouse); domestic services operate between these; total passenger km: 26,396 million (1997 est) **Major ports** river port Basel (on the Rhine) **Chief tourist attractions** the Alps; lakes and lake resorts; walking; mountaineering; winter sports **Major holidays** 1 January, 1, 15 August (many cantons), 1 November (many cantons), 24–26 December; variable: Ascension Thursday, Corpus Christi (many cantons), Good Friday, Easter Monday, Whit Monday; many local holidays

Chronology

58 BC Celtic Helvetii tribe submitted to Roman authority after defeat by Julius Caesar. **4th century AD** Region overrun by Germanic tribes, Burgundians, and Alemannians. **7th century** Formed part of Frankish kingdom and embraced Christianity. **9th century** Included in Charlemagne's Holy Roman Empire. **12th century** Many autonomous feudal holdings developed as power of Holy Roman Empire declined. **13th century** Habsburgs became dominant as overlords of eastern Switzerland. **1291** Cantons of Schwyz, Uri, and Lower Unterwalden formed Everlasting League, a loose confederation to resist Habsburg control. **1315** Battle of Morgarten: Swiss Confederation defeated Habsburgs. **14th century** Luzern, Zürich, Basel, and other cantons joined Swiss Confederation, which became independent of Habsburgs. **1523–29** Zürich, Bern, and Basel accepted Reformation but rural cantons remained Roman Catholic. **1648** Treaty of Westphalia recognized Swiss independence from Holy Roman Empire. **1798** French invasion established Helvetic Republic, a puppet state with centralized government. **1803** Napoleon's Act of Mediation restored considerable autonomy to cantons. **1814** End of French domination; Switzerland reverted to loose confederation of sovereign cantons with a weak federal parliament. **1815** Great Powers recognized 'Perpetual Neutrality' of Switzerland. **1845** Seven Catholic cantons founded Sonderbund league to resist any strengthening of central government by Liberals. **1847** Federal troops defeated Sonderbund in brief civil war. **1848** New constitution introduced greater centralization; Bern chosen as capital. **1874** Powers of federal government increased; principle of referendum introduced. **late 19th century** Development of industry, railways, and tourism led to growing prosperity. **1920** League of Nations selected Geneva as its headquarters. **1960** Joined European Free Trade Association (EFTA). **1971** Women gained right to vote in federal elections. **1986** A proposal for membership of the United Nations (UN) was rejected in a referendum. **1992** Closer ties with the European Community (EC) were rejected in a national referendum. **1998** Ruth Dreifuss was elected president, the first woman to hold the post in Switzerland. **2000** Adolf Ogi was elected president.

Syria (Syrian Arab Republic)

National name *al-Jamhuriya al-Arabya as-Suriya* **Area** 185,200 sq km/71,505 sq mi **Capital** Damascus **Major towns/cities** Aleppo, Homs, Latakia, Hama

Government

Head of state Bashar al-Assad from 2000 **Head of government** Muhammad Mustafa Miro from 2000 **Political system** nationalistic socialist **Armed forces** 320,000; reserve forces 500,000; paramilitary forces 8,000 (1997) **Conscription** 30 months **Defence spend** (% GDP) 6.3 (1997) **Education spend** (% GNP) 4.2 (1996) **Health spend** (% GDP) 0.4 (1990) **Death penalty** retained and used for ordinary crimes

Population and society

Population 15,725,000 (1999 est) **Population growth rate** 2.5% (1995–2000) **Ethnic groups** predominantly Arab, with many differences in language and regional affiliations **Religion** Sunni Muslim 90%; other Islamic sects, Christian **Life expectancy** 67 (men); 71 (women) (1995–2000) **Literacy rate** 87% (men); 57% (women) (1997 est) **Unemployment rate** 12% (1997 est)

Economy and resources

GDP (US$) 17.9 billion (1998 est) **GNP** (US$) 15.6 billion (1998) **GNP per capita (PPP)** (US$) 3,000 (1998) **Real GDP growth** (% change on previous year) –1.5 (1998) **Consumer price inflation** 18.2% (1998) **Foreign debt** (US$) 20.86 billion (1997) **Resources** petroleum, natural gas, iron ore, phosphates, salt, gypsum, sodium chloride, bitumen **Exports** crude petroleum, textiles, vegetables, fruit, raw cotton, natural phosphate. Principal market: Italy 17.5% (1997) **Imports** crude petroleum, wheat, base metals, metal products, foodstuffs, machinery, motor vehicles. Principal source: Ukraine 13.1% (1997)

▪ Tourist information

Time difference GMT +2 **Currency** Syrian pound **Language** Arabic 89% (official); Kurdish 6%, Armenian 3% **Visa requirements** UK: visa required. USA: visa required **Embassy in the UK** 8 Belgrave Square, London SW1X 8PH. Tel: (020) 7245 9012; fax: (020) 7235 4621 **British embassy** PO Box 37, Quarter Malki, 11 rue Mohammed Kurd Ali, Immeuble Kotob, Damascus. Tel: (11) 712 561/2/3; fax: (11) 713 592 **Chamber of commerce** Federation of Syrian Chambers of Commerce, PO Box 5909, rue Mousa Ben Nousair, Damascus. Tel: (11) 333 7344; fax: (11) 333127 **Office hours** 0830–1430 Sat–Thu (Christian firms generally open Mon–Sat) **Banking hours** 0800–1400 Sat–Thu (banks tend to close early on Thu) **Airports** international airports: Damascus, Aleppo (Nejrab), Latakia (chartered flights); four domestic airports; total passenger km: 1,409 million (1997 est) **Major ports** Latakia **Chief tourist attractions** antiquities of Damascus and Palmyra; bazaars; Mediterranean coastline; mountains **Major holidays** 1 January, 8 March, 17 April, 1, 6 May, 23 July, 1 September, 6 October, 25 December; variable: Eid-ul-Adha (3 days), end of Ramadan (4 days), Easter Sunday, New Year (Muslim), Prophet's Birthday

Chronology

***c.*1750 BC** Syria became part of Babylonian Empire; during the next millennium it was successively conquered by Hittites, Assyrians, Chaldeans, and Persians. **333 BC** Alexander the Great of Macedonia conquered Persia and Syria. **301 BC** Seleucus I, one of the generals of Alexander the Great, founded the kingdom of Syria, which the Seleucid dynasty ruled for over 200 years. **64 BC** Syria became part of Roman Empire. **4th century AD** After division of Roman Empire, Syria came under Byzantine rule. **634** Arabs conquered most of Syria and introduced Islam. **661–750** Damascus was the capital of Muslim Empire. **1055** Seljuk Turks overran Syria. **1095–99** First Crusade established Latin states on Syrian coast. **13th century** Mameluke sultans of Egypt took control. **1516** Ottoman Turks conquered Syria. **1831** Egyptians led by Mehemet Ali drove out Turks. **1840** Turkish rule restored; Syria opened up to European trade. **late 19th century** French firms built ports, roads, and railways in Syria. **1916** Sykes-Picot Agreement: secret Anglo-French deal to partition Turkish Empire allotted Syria to France. **1918** British expelled Turks with help of Arab revolt. **1919** Syrian national congress called for independence under Emir Faisal and opposed transfer to French rule. **1920** Syria became League of Nations protectorate, administered by France. **1925** People's Party founded to campaign for independence and national unity; insurrection by Druze religious sect against French control. **1936** France promised independence within three years, but martial law imposed in 1939. **1941** British forces ousted Vichy French regime in Damascus and occupied Syria in conjunction with Free French. **1944** Syrian independence proclaimed but French military resisted transfer of power. **1946** Syria achieved effective independence when French forces withdrew. **1948–49** Arab–Israeli War: Syria joined unsuccessful invasion of newly independent Israel. **1958** Syria and Egypt merged to form United Arab Republic (UAR). **1959** USSR agreed to give financial and technical aid to Syria. **1961** Syria seceded from UAR. **1964** Ba'ath Socialist Party established military dictatorship. **1967** Six-Day War: Syria lost Golan Heights to Israel. **1970–71** Syria invaded Jordan in support of Palestinian guerrillas. **1971** Hafez al-Assad was elected president. **1973** Yom Kippur War: Syrian attack on Israel repulsed. **1976** Start of Syrian military intervention in Lebanese civil war. **1978** Syria opposed peace deal between Egypt and Israel. **1986** Britain broke off diplomatic relations, accusing Syria of involvement in international terrorism. **1990** Diplomatic links with Britain were restored. **1991** Syria contributed troops to a US-led coalition in the Gulf War against Iraq. A US Middle East peace plan was approved by Assad. **1994** Israel offered a partial withdrawal from the Golan Heights in return for peace, but Syria remained sceptical. **1995** A security framework agreement was made with Israel. **2000** Israeli prime minister Ehud Barak and Syrian foreign minister Farouk Sharaa returned to the US for peace talks on the issue of Israel's withdrawal from the Golan Heights. President Assad died and was succeeded by his son, Bashar al-Assad.

Taiwan (Republic of China): many countries do not recognize Taiwan

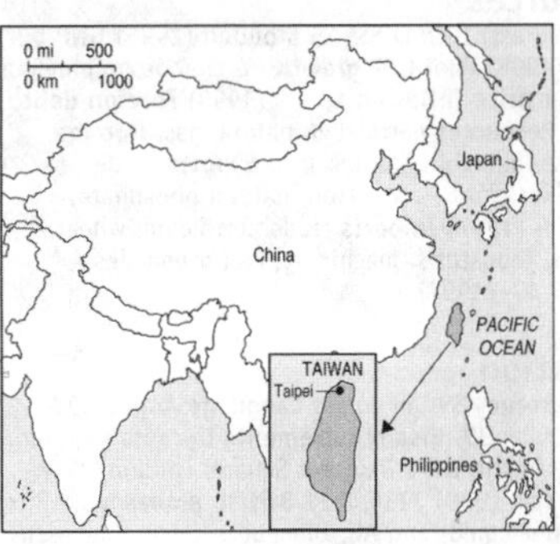

National name *Chung Hua Min Kuo* **Area** 36,179 sq km/13,968 sq mi **Capital** Taipei **Major towns/cities** Kaohsiung, Taichung, Tainan, Panchiao, Yunlin

Government

Head of state Chen Shui-bian from 2000 **Head of government** Tang Fei from 2000 **Political system** emergent democracy **Armed forces** 376,000; plus paramilitary forces numbering 26,700 and reserves totalling 1,657,500 (1997) **Conscription** military service is compulsory for two years **Defence spend** (% GDP) 4.7 (1997) **Education spend** (% GDP) 2.5 (1994) **Death penalty** retained and used for ordinary crimes

Population and society

Population 22,113,000 (1999 est) **Population growth rate** 1.0% (1995–2000) **Ethnic groups** 98% Han Chinese and 2% aboriginal by descent; around 87% are Taiwan-born and 13% are 'mainlanders' **Religion** officially atheist; Taoist, Confucian, Buddhist, Christian **Life expectancy** 74 (men); 80 (women) (1998 est) **Literacy rate** 95% (men); 93% (women) (1997 est) **Unemployment** 2.7% (1998)

Economy and resources

GDP (US$) 261.4 billion (1998) **GNP** (US$) 272 billion (1998 est) **GNP per capita (PPP)** (US$) 18,950 (1998 est) **Real GDP growth** (% change on previous year) 4.8 (1998) **Consumer price inflation** 1.8% (1998) **Foreign debt** (US$) 33.5 billion (1997) **Resources** coal, copper, marble, dolomite; small reserves of petroleum and natural gas **Exports** electronic products, base metals and metal articles, textiles and clothing, machinery, information and communication products, plastic and rubber products, vehicles and transport equipment, footwear, headwear, umbrellas, toys, games, sports equipment. Principal market: USA 26.6% (1998) **Imports** machinery and transport equipment, basic manufactures, chemicals, base metals and metal articles, minerals, textile products, crude petroleum, plastics, precision instruments, clocks and watches, musical instruments. Principal source: Japan 25.8% (1998)

▪ Tourist information

Time difference GMT +8 **Currency** New Taiwan dollar **Language** Mandarin Chinese (official); Taiwan, Hakka dialects **Visa requirements** UK: visa not required for a stay of up to 14 days. USA: visa not required for a stay of up to 14 days **Embassy in the UK** Taipei Representative Office in the UK, 50 Grosvenor Gardens, London SW1W 0EB. Tel: (020) 7396 9152; fax: (020) 7396 9151 **British embassy** the UK has no diplomatic representation in Taiwan **Chamber of commerce** General Chamber of Commerce, 6th Floor, 390 Flushing South Road, Section 1, Taipei. Tel: (2) 701 2671; fax: (2) 755 5493 **Office hours** 0830–1730 Mon–Fri; 0830–1230 Sat **Banking hours** 0900–1530 Mon–Fri; 0900–1230 Sat **Airports** international airports: Taipei (Chaing Kai-shek), Kaohsiung; 14 domestic airports; total passenger km: 39,878 million (1997) **Major ports** Kaohsiung, Keelung **Chief tourist attractions** island scenery; festivals; ancient art treasures **Major holidays** 1–3 January, 29 March, 5 April, 1 July, 28 September, 10, 25, 31 October, 12 November, 25 December; variable: New Year (Chinese, January/February, 3 days), Dragon Boat Festival (June), Mid-Autumn Festival (September/October)

Chronology

7th century AD Island occupied by aboriginal community of Malayan descent; immigration of Chinese from mainland began, but remained limited before 15th century. **1517** Sighted by Portuguese vessels en route to Japan and named Ilha Formosa ('beautiful island'). **1624** Occupied and controlled by Dutch. **1662** Dutch defeated by Chinese Ming general, Cheng Ch'eng-kung (Koxinga), whose family came to rule Formosa for a short period. **1683** Annexed by China's rulers, the Manchu Qing. **1786** Major rebellion against Chinese rule. **1860** Ports opened to Western trade. **1895** Ceded 'in perpetuity' to Japan under Treaty of Shominoseki at end of Sino-Japanese war. **1945** Recovered by China's Nationalist Guomindang government at end of World War II. **1947** Rebellion against Chinese rule brutally suppressed. **1949** Flight of Nationalist government, led by Generalissimo Jiang Jie Shi (Chiang Kai-shek), to Taiwan after Chinese communist revolution. They retained the designation of Republic of China (ROC), claiming to be the legitimate government for all China, and were recognized by USA and United Nations (UN). **1950s onwards** Rapid economic growth as Taiwan became a successful export-orientated Newly Industrializing Country (NIC). **1954** US–Taiwanese mutual defence treaty. **1971** Expulsion from UN as USA adopted new policy of détente towards communist China. **1972** Commencement of legislature elections as a programme of gradual democratization and Taiwanization was launched by the mainlander-dominated Guomindang. **1975** President Jiang Jie Shi died; replaced as Guomindang leader by his son, Jiang Ching-kuo. **1979** USA severed diplomatic relations and annulled the 1954 security pact. **1986** Centrist Democratic Progressive Party (DPP) formed as opposition to nationalist Guomindang. **1987** Martial law lifted; opposition parties legalized; press restrictions lifted. **1988** President Jiang Ching-kuo died; replaced by Taiwanese-born Lee Teng-hui. **1990** Chinese-born Guomindang members became a minority in parliament. **1991** President Lee Teng-hui declared an end to the civil war with China. The constitution was amended. Guomindang won a landslide victory in elections to the new National Assembly, the 'superparliament'. **1993** A cooperation pact was signed with China. **1996** Lee Teng-hui was elected president in the first ever Chinese democratic elections. **1997** The government narrowly survived a no-confidence motion. Vincent Siew became prime minister. **1998** President Lee Teng-hui announced that reunion with mainland China was impossible until Beijing adopted democracy. The ruling KMT increased its majority in parliamentary and local elections. **2000** Despite threats of invasion from China if Taiwan made moves towards independence, a pro-independence president, Chen Shui-bian, was elected, who appointed a member of the former government, Tang Fei, as prime minister.

Tajikistan Republic of

National name *Respublika i Tojikiston* **Area** 143,100 sq km/55,250 sq mi **Capital** Dushanbe **Major towns/cities** Khodzhent (formerly Leninabad), Kurgan-Tyube, Kulyab

Government

Head of state Imamali Rakhmanov from 1994 **Head of government** Yahya Azimov from 1996 **Political system** authoritarian nationalist **Armed forces** 9,000; paramilitary forces around 1,200 (1997) **Defence spend** (% GDP) 12.1 (1997) **Education spend** (% GNP) 2.2 (1996) **Health spend** (% GDP) 5.8 (1995) **Death penalty** retained and used for ordinary crimes

Population and society

Population 6,104,000 (1999 est) **Population growth rate** 1.5% (1995–2000) **Ethnic groups** 62% ethnic Tajik, 24% Uzbek, 8% ethnic Russian, 1% Tatar, 1% Kyrgyz, and 1% Ukrainian **Religion** Sunni Muslim **Life expectancy** 64 (men); 70 (women) (1995–2000) **Literacy rate** 99% (men); 98% (women) (1997 est) **Unemployment** 2.7% (1997)

Economy and resources

GDP (US$) 2 billion (1998 est) **GNP** (US$) 2.1 billion (1998) **GNP per capita (PPP)** (US$) 1,310 (1998 est) **Real GDP growth** (% change on previous year) 2 (1998) **Consumer price inflation** 40% (1998) **Foreign debt** (US$) 901 million (1997) **Resources** coal, aluminium, lead, zinc, iron, tin, uranium, radium, arsenic, bismuth, gold, mica, asbestos, lapis lazuli; small reserves of petroleum and natural gas **Exports** aluminium, cotton lint. Principal market: Uzbekistan 36.8% (1997) **Imports** industrial products and machinery (principally for aluminium plants), unprocessed agricultural products, food and beverages, petroleum and chemical products, consumer goods. Principal source: Netherlands 31.9% (1997)

▪ Tourist information

Time difference GMT +5 **Currencies** Tajik and Russian rouble **Language** Tajik (official), similar to Farsi (Persian) **Visa requirements** UK: visa required. USA: visa required **Embassy in the UK** Tajikistan has no diplomatic representation in the UK **British embassy** the British Embassy in Tashkent (see Uzbekistan) deals with all enquiries relating to Tajikistan **Chamber of commerce** Chamber of Commerce and Industry, Ulitsa Mazayeva 21, Dushanbe 7340012. Tel: (3772) 279 519 **Office hours** 0900–1800 Mon–Fri **Banking hours** 0900–1730 Mon–Fri **Airports** international airport: Dushanbe; three domestic airports; total passenger km: 2,231 million (1995) **Chief tourist attractions** spectacular mountain scenery; sites of historical interest in the Ferghana Valley, notably the city of Khojand **Major holidays** 1 January, 8, 21 March, 9 May, 9 September, 14 October; variable: end of Ramadan

Chronology

c. **330** Formed an eastern part of empire of Alexander the Great of Macedonia. **8th century** Tajiks established as distinct ethnic group, with semi-independent territories under the tutelage of the Uzbeks, to the west; spread of Islam. **13th century** Conquered by Genghis Khan and became part of Mongol Empire. **1860–1900** Northern Tajikistan came under tsarist Russian rule, while the south was annexed by Emirate of Bukhara, to the west. **1917–18** Attempts to establish Soviet control after Bolshevik revolution in Russia resisted initially by armed guerrillas (basmachi). **1921** Became part of Turkestan Soviet Socialist Autonomous Republic. **1924** Tajik Autonomous Soviet Socialist Republic formed. **1929** Became constituent republic of Soviet Union (USSR). **1930s** Stalinist era of collectivization led to widespread repression of Tajiks. **1978** 13,000 participated in anti-Russian riots. **late 1980s** Resurgence in Tajik consciousness, stimulated by the *glasnost* initiative of Soviet leader Mikhail Gorbachev. **1989** Rastokhez ('Revival') Popular Front established and Tajik declared state language. New mosques constructed. **1990** Violent interethnic Tajik–Armenian clashes in Dushanbe; a state of emergency was imposed. **1991** President Kakhar Makhkamov, local communist leader since 1985, was forced to resign after supporting the failed anti-Gorbachev coup in Moscow. Independence was declared. Rakhman Nabiyev, communist leader 1982–85, was elected president. Joined new Commonwealth of Independent States (CIS). **1992** Joined Muslim Economic Cooperation Organization, the Conference on Security and Cooperation in Europe (CSCE; now the Organization on Security and Cooperation in Europe, OSCE), and the United Nations (UN). Violent demonstrations by Islamic and prodemocracy groups forced Nabiyev to resign. Civil war between pro- and anti-Nabiyev forces claimed 20,000 lives, made 600,000 refugees, and wrecked the economy. Imamali Rakhmanov, a communist sympathetic to Nabiyev, took over as head of state. **1993** Government forces regained control of most of the country. CIS peacekeeping forces were drafted in to patrol the border with Afghanistan, the base of the pro-Islamic rebels. **1994** A ceasefire was agreed. Rakhmanov was popularly elected president under a new constitution. **1995** Parliamentary elections were won by Rakhmanov's supporters. There was renewed fighting on the Afghan border. **1996** Pro-Islamic rebels captured towns in the southwest. There was a UN-sponsored ceasefire between government and pro-Islamic rebels. President Rakhmanov appointed Yahya Azimov as his prime minister. **1997** A four-stage peace plan was signed. There was a peace accord with the Islamic rebel group the United Tajik Opposition (UTO). **1998** Members of UTO were appointed to the government as part of a peace plan. The UN military observer mission (UNMOT) suspended its operations, following the killing of four UN workers. More than 200 people were killed in clashes in Leninabad between the army and rebel forces loyal to the renegade Tajik army commander Col Makhmud Khudoberdiyev; the deputy leader of the Islamic-led UTO, Ali Akbar Turadzhonzada, was appointed first deputy prime minister.

Tanzania United Republic of

National name *Jamhuri ya Muungano wa Tanzania* **Area** 945,000 sq km/ 364,864 sq mi **Capital** Dodoma (since 1983) **Major towns/cities** Zanzibar Town, Mwanza, Tabora, Mbeya, Tanga

Government

Head of state Benjamin Mkapa from 1995 **Head of government** Cleoopa Msuya from 1994 **Political system** emergent democracy **Armed forces** 34,600; citizen's militia of 80,000 (1997) **Conscription** two years **Defence spend** (% GDP) 3.4 (1997) **Education spend** (% GNP) 5.0 (1993/94)

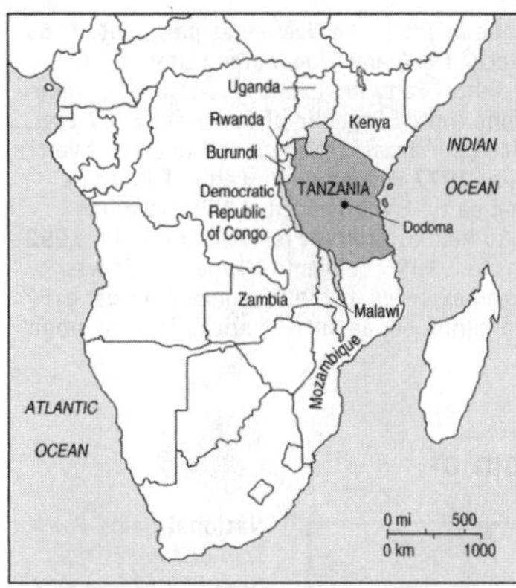

Health spend (% GDP) 2.5 (1995) **Death penalty** retained and used for ordinary crimes

Population and society

Population 32,793,000 (1999 est) **Population growth rate** 2.3% (1995–2000) **Ethnic groups** 99% of the population are Africans, ethnically classified as Bantus, and distributed among over 130 tribes; main tribes are Bantu, Nilotic, Nilo-Hamitic, Khoisan, and Iraqwi **Religion** Muslim, Christian, traditional religions **Life expectancy** 50 (men); 53 (women) (1995–2000) **Literacy rate** 82% (men); 62% (women) (1997 est)

Economy and resources

GDP (US$) 7.9 billion (1998) **GNP** (US$) 6.7 billion (1998) **GNP per capita (PPP)** (US$) 490 (1998) **Real GDP growth** (% change on previous year) 3.9 (1998) **Consumer price inflation** 20% (1998) **Foreign debt** (US$) 7.2 billion (1997) **Resources** diamonds, other gemstones, gold, salt, phosphates, coal, gypsum, tin, kaolin (exploration for petroleum in progress) **Exports** coffee beans, raw cotton, tobacco, tea, cloves, cashew nuts, minerals, petroleum products. Principal market: India 11.6% (1997) **Imports** machinery and transport equipment, crude petroleum and petroleum products, construction materials, foodstuffs, consumer goods. Principal source: South Africa 12.8% (1997)

▪ Tourist information

Time difference GMT +3 **Currency** Tanzanian shilling **Language** Kiswahili, English (both official) **Visa requirements** UK: visa required. USA: visa required **Embassy in the UK** 43 Hertford Street, London W1Y 8DB. Tel: (020) 7499 8951; fax: (020) 7499 8954 **British embassy** British High Commission, PO Box 9200, Hifadhi House, Samora Avenue, Dar es Salaam. Tel: (51) 46300/4; fax: (51) 46301 **Chamber of commerce** Dar es Salaam Chamber of Commerce, PO Box 41, Kelvin House, Samora Machel Avenue, Dar es Salaam. Tel: (51) 21893 **Office hours** 0730–1430 Mon–Fri **Banking hours** 0830–1600 Mon–Fri; 0830–1300 Sat **Airports** international airports: Dar es Salaam, Kilimanjaro, Zanzibar; 50 domestic airports and landing strips; total passenger km: 189 million (1995) **Major ports** (former capital) Dar es Salaam **Chief tourist attractions** national parks and game and forest reserves comprise one-third of the country; beaches and coral reefs along the Indian Ocean coast **Major holidays** 1, 12 January, 5 February, 1 May, 7 July, 9, 25 December; variable: Eid-ul-Adha, Good Friday, Easter Monday, end of Ramadan (2 days), Prophet's Birthday

Chronology

8th century Growth of city states along coast after settlement by Arabs from Oman. **1499** Portuguese navigator Vasco da Gama visited island of Zanzibar. **16th century** Portuguese occupied Zanzibar, defeated coastal states, and exerted spasmodic control over them. **1699** Portuguese ousted from Zanzibar by Arabs of Oman. **18th century** Sultan of Oman reasserted Arab overlordship of East African coast, which became subordinate to Zanzibar. **1744–1837** Revolt of ruler of Mombasa against Oman spanned 93 years until final victory of Oman. **1822** Moresby Treaty: Britain recognized regional dominance of Zanzibar, but protested against the slave trade. **1840** Sultan Seyyid bin Sultan moved his capital from Oman to Zanzibar; trade in slaves and ivory flourished. **1861** Sultanates of Zanzibar and Oman separated on death of Seyyid. **19th century** Europeans started to explore inland, closely followed by Christian missionaries. **1884** German Colonization Society began to acquire territory on mainland in defiance of Zanzibar. **1890** Britain obtained protectorate over Zanzibar, abolished slave trade, and recognized German claims to mainland. **1897** German East Africa formally established as colony. **1905–06** Maji Maji revolt suppressed by German troops. **1916** Conquest of German East Africa by British and South African forces, led by Gen Jan Smuts. **1919** Most of German East Africa became British League of Nations mandate of Tanganyika. **1946** Britain continued to govern Tanganyika as United Nations (UN) trusteeship. **1954** Julius Nyerere organized the Tanganyikan African National Union (TANU) to campaign for independence. **1961–62** Tanganyika achieved independence from Britain with Nyerere as prime

minister, and became a republic in 1962 with Nyerere as president. **1963** Zanzibar achieved independence. **1964** Arab-dominated sultanate of Zanzibar overthrown by Afro-Shirazi Party in violent revolution; Zanzibar merged with Tanganyika to form United Republic of Tanzania. **1967** East African Community (EAC) formed by Tanzania, Kenya, and Uganda; Nyerere pledged to build socialist state. **1977** Revolutionary Party of Tanzania (CCM) proclaimed as only legal party; EAC dissolved. **1979** Tanzanian troops intervened in Uganda to help overthrow President Idi Amin. **1992** Multiparty politics were permitted. **1995** Benjamin Mkapa of CCM was elected president. **1998** A bomb exploded at the US embassy in Dar es Salaam, killing 6 people and injuring 60; an anti-American Islamic group claimed responsibility.

Thailand Kingdom of

National name *Prathet Thai* or *Muang Thai* **Area** 513,115 sq km/ 198,113 sq mi **Capital** Bangkok (and chief port) **Major towns/ cities** Chiangmai, Hat Yai, Khon Kaen, Songkhla, Chon Buri, Nakhon Si Thammarat, Lampang, Phitsannlok, Ratchasima

Government

Head of state King Bhumibol Adulyadej from 1946 **Head of government** Chavalit Yongchaiyudh from 1996 **Political system** emergent democracy **Armed forces** 266,000 (1997) **Conscription** two years **Defence spend** (% GDP) 2.1 (1997) **Education spend** (% GNP) 4.1 (1996) **Health spend** (% GDP) 2 (1995) **Death penalty** retained and used for ordinary crimes

Population and society

Population 60,858,000 (1999 est) **Population growth rate** 0.9% (1995–2000) **Ethnic groups** 75% of the population is of Thai descent; 14% ethnic Chinese, one-third of whom live in Bangkok; Thai Malays constitute the next largest minority, followed by hill tribes; a substantial Kampuchean (Khmer) refugee community resides in border camps **Religion** Buddhist **Life expectancy** 66 (men); 72 (women) (1995–2000) **Literacy rate** 97% (men); 93% (women) (1997 est) **Unemployment** 4% (1998 est)

Economy and resources

GDP (US$) 154 billion (1998) **GNP** (US$) 134.4 billion(1998) **GNP per capita (PPP)** (US$) 5,840 (1998) **Real GDP growth** (% change on previous year) –8 (1998) **Consumer price inflation** 7.8% (1998) **Foreign debt** (US$) 93.4 billion (1997) **Resources** tin ore, lignite, gypsum, antimony, manganese, copper, tungsten, lead, gold, zinc, silver, rubies, sapphires, natural gas, petroleum, fish **Exports** textiles and clothing, electronic goods, rice, rubber, gemstones, sugar, cassava (tapioca), fish (especially prawns), machinery and manufactures, chemicals. Principal market: USA 22.3% (1998) **Imports** petroleum and petroleum products, machinery, chemicals, iron and steel, consumer goods. Principal source: Japan 23.7% (1998)

■ Tourist information

Time difference GMT +7 **Currency** baht **Language** Thai and Chinese (both official); Lao, Chinese, Malay, Khmer **Visa requirements** UK: visa not required. USA: visa not required **Embassy in the UK** 1/3 Yorkshire House, Grosvenor Crescent, London SW1X 7ET. Tel: (020) 7371 7621; fax: (020) 7235 9808 **British embassy** Wireless Road, Bangkok 10200. Tel: (2) 253 0191; fax: (2) 255 8619 **Chamber of commerce** 150 Thanon Rajbopit, Bangkok 10200. Tel: (2) 225 0086; fax: (2) 225 3372 **Office hours** 0800–1700 Mon–Fri **Banking hours** 0830–1530 Mon–Fri **Airports** international airports: Bangkok (Don Muang), Chiangmai, Phuket, Hat Yai, U-tapao; domestic services to all major towns; total passenger km: 30,987 million (1997 est) **Major ports** Nakhon Sawan **Chief tourist attractions** temples, pagodas, palaces; islands **Major holidays** 1 January, 6, 13 April, 1, 5 May, 1 July, 12 August, 23 October, 5, 10, 31 December; variable: end of Ramadan, Makha Bucha (February), Visakha Bucha (May), Buddhist Lent (July)

Chronology

13th century Siamese (Thai) people migrated south and settled in valley of Chao Phraya River in Khmer Empire. **1238** Siamese ousted Khmer governors and formed new kingdom based at Sukhothai. **14th and 15th centuries** Siamese expanded at expense of declining Khmer Empire. **1350** Siamese capital moved to Ayatthaya (which also became name of kingdom). **1511** Portuguese traders first reached Siam. **1569** Conquest of Ayatthaya by Burmese ended years of rivalry and conflict. **1589** Siamese regained independence under King Naresuan. **17th century** Foreign trade under royal monopoly developed with Chinese, Japanese, and Europeans. **1690s** Siam expelled European military advisers and missionaries and adopted policy of isolation. **1767** Burmese invaders destroyed city of Ayatthaya, massacred ruling families, and withdrew, leaving Siam in a state of anarchy. **1782** Reunification of Siam after civil war under Gen Phraya Chakri, who founded new capital at Bangkok and proclaimed himself King Rama I. **1824–51** King Rama III reopened Siam to European diplomats and missionaries. **1851–68** King Mongkut employed European advisers to help modernize the government, legal system, and army. **1856** Royal monopoly on foreign trade ended. **1868–1910** King Chulalongkorn continued modernization and developed railway network using Chinese immigrant labour; Siam became major exporter of rice. **1896** Anglo-French agreement recognized Siam as independent buffer state between British Burma and French Indo-China. **1932** Bloodless coup forced King Rama VII to grant a constitution with a mixed civilian-military government. **1939** Siam changed its name to Thailand (briefly reverting to Siam 1945–49). **1941** Japanese invaded; Thailand became puppet ally of Japan under Field Marshal Phibun Songkhram. **1945** Japanese withdrawal; Thailand compelled to return territory taken from Laos, Cambodia, and Malaya. **1947** Phibun regained power in military coup, reducing monarch to figurehead; Thailand adopted strongly pro-American foreign policy. **1955** Political parties and free speech introduced. **1957** State of emergency declared; Phibun deposed in bloodless coup; military dictatorship continued under Gen Sarit Thanarat (1957–63) and Gen Thanom Kittikachorn (1963–73). **1967–72** Thai troops fought in alliance with USA in Vietnam War. **1973** Military government overthrown by student riots. **1974** Adoption of democratic constitution, followed by civilian coalition government. **1976** Military reassumed control in response to mounting strikes and political violence. **1978** Gen Kriangsak Chomanan introduced constitution with mixed civilian–military government. **1980** Gen Prem Tinsulanonda assumed power. **1983** Prem relinquished army office to head civilian government; martial law maintained. **1988** Chatichai Choonhavan succeeded Prem as prime minister. **1991** A military coup imposed a new military-oriented constitution despite mass protests. **1992** A general election produced a five-party coalition; riots forced Prime Minister Suchinda Kraprayoon to flee; Chuan Leekpai formed a new coalition government. **1995–96** The ruling coalition collapsed. A general election in 1996 resulted in a new six-party coalition led by Chavalit Yongchaiyudh. **1997** A major financial crisis led to the floating of currency. An austerity rescue plan was agreed with the International Monetary Fund (IMF). **1998** Repatriation of foreign workers commenced, as the economy contracted sharply due to the resuce plan. The opposition Chart Patthana party was brought into the coalition government of Chuan Leekpai, increasing its majority to push through reforms.

Togo Republic of (formerly Togoland)

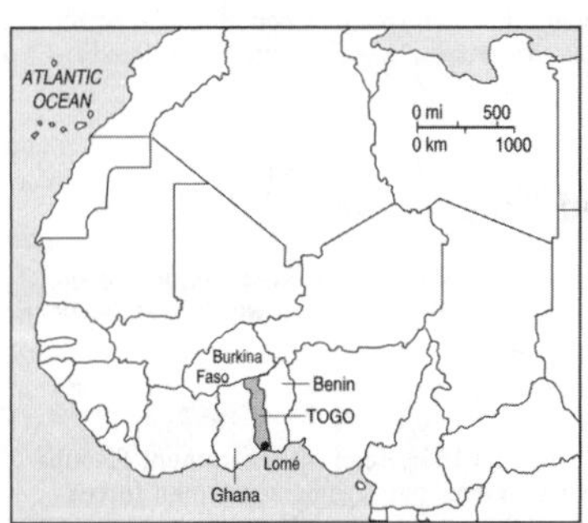

National name *République Togolaise* **Area** 56,800 sq km/ 21,930 sq mi **Capital** Lomé **Major towns/ cities** Sokodé, Kpalimé, Kara, Atakpamé, Bassar, Tsévié

Government

Head of state Etienne Gnassingbé Eyadéma from 1967 **Head of government** Kwasi Klutse from 1996 **Political system** emergent democracy

Armed forces 7,000 (1997) **Conscription** military service is by selective conscription for two years **Defence spend** (% GDP) 2.1 (1997) **Education spend** (% GNP) 4.7 (1996) **Health spend** (% GDP) 1.6 (1995) **Death penalty** retains the death penalty for ordinary crimes, but can be considered abolitionist in practice

Population and society

Population 4,512,000 (1999 est) **Population growth rate** 2.6% (1995–2000) **Ethnic groups** predominantly of Sudanese Hamitic origin in the north, and black African in the south; they are distributed among 37 different ethnic groups. There are also European, Syrian, and Lebanese minorities **Religion** animist, Catholic, Muslim, Protestant **Life expectancy** 48 (men); 50 (women) (1995–2000) **Literacy rate** 69% (men); 38% (women) (1997 est) **Unemployment** N/A

Economy and resources

GDP (US$) 1.5 billion (1998) **GNP** (US$) 1.5 billion (1998) **GNP per capita (PPP)** (US$) 1,390 (1998) **Real GDP growth** (% change on previous year) 2.5 (1998) **Consumer price inflation** 1% (1998) **Foreign debt** (US$) 1.34 billion (1997) **Resources** phosphates, limestone, marble, deposits of iron ore, manganese, chromite, peat; exploration for petroleum and uranium was under way in the early 1990s **Exports** phosphates (mainly calcium phosphates), ginned cotton, green coffee, cocoa beans. Principal market: Canada 7.6% (1997) **Imports** machinery and transport equipment, cotton yarn and fabrics, cigarettes, antibiotics, food (especially cereals) and live animals, chemicals, refined petroleum products, beverages. Principal source: Ghana 19.1% (1997)

▪ Tourist information

Time difference GMT +/− 0 **Currency** franc CFA **Language** French (official), Ewe, Kabre, Gurma **Visa requirements** UK: visa not required. USA: visa not required **Embassy in the EU** 8 rue Alfred Roll, 75017 Paris, France. Tel: (1) 4380 1213; fax: (1) 4380 9071 **British embassy** British Honorary Consulate, BP 20050, British School of Lomé, Lomé. Tel: (228) 264 606; fax: (228) 214 989 **Chamber of commerce** Chambre de Commerce, d'Agriculture et d'Industrie du Togo, BP 360, angle avenue de la Présidence, Lomé. Tel: (228) 217 065; fax: (228) 214 730 **Office hours** 0700–1730 Mon–Fri **Banking hours** 0800–1600 Mon–Fri **Airports** international airports: Lomé, Niamtougou; four domestic airports and several smaller airfields; total passenger km: 223 million (1995) **Chief tourist attractions** long sandy beaches shaded by palm trees along the coast between Lomé and Cotonou (Benin) **Major holidays** 1, 13, 24 January, 24, 27 April, 1 May, 15 August, 1 November, 25 December; variable: Ascension Thursday, Eid-ul-Adha, end of Ramadan

Chronology

15th–17th centuries Formerly dominated by Kwa peoples in southwest and Gur-speaking Voltaic peoples in north, Ewe clans immigrated from Nigeria and the Ane (Mina) from Ghana and the Côte d'Ivoire. **18th century** Coastal area held by Danes. **1847** Arrival of German missionaries. **1884–1914** Togoland was a German protectorate until captured by Anglo-French forces; cocoa and cotton plantations developed, using forced labour. **1922** Divided between Britain and France under League of Nations mandate. **1946** Continued under United Nations trusteeship. **1957** British Togoland, comprising one-third of the area and situated in the west, integrated with Ghana, following a referendum. **1960** French Togoland, situated in the east, achieved independence from France as the Republic of Togo with Sylvanus Olympio, leader of the United Togolese (UP) party, as head of state. **1967** Lt-Gen Etienne Gnassingbé Eyadéma became president in a bloodless coup; political parties were banned. **1969** Assembly of the Togolese People (RPT) formed by Eyadéma as the sole legal political party. **1975** EEC Lomé convention signed in Lomé, establishing trade links with developing countries. **1977** An assassination plot against Eyadéma, allegedly involving the Olympio family, was thwarted. **1979** Eyadéma returned in election. Further EEC Lomé convention signed. **1986** Attempted coup failed and situation stabilized with help of French troops. **1990** There were casualties as violent antigovernment demonstrations in Lomé were suppressed; Eyadéma relegalized political parties. **1991** Eyadéma was forced to call a national conference that limited the president's powers, and elected Joseph Kokou Koffigoh head of an interim government. Three attempts by Eyadéma's troops to unseat the government failed. **1992** There were strikes in southern Togo. A referendum showed overwhelming support for multiparty politics. A new constitution was adopted. **1993** Eyadéma won the first multiparty presidential elections amid widespread opposition. **1994** An antigovernment coup was foiled. The opposition CAR polled strongly in assembly elections. Eyadéma appointed Edem Kodjo of the minority UTD prime minister. **1996** Kwasi Klutse was appointed prime minister. **1998** President Eyadéma was re-elected.

Tonga Kingdom of (or Friendly Islands)

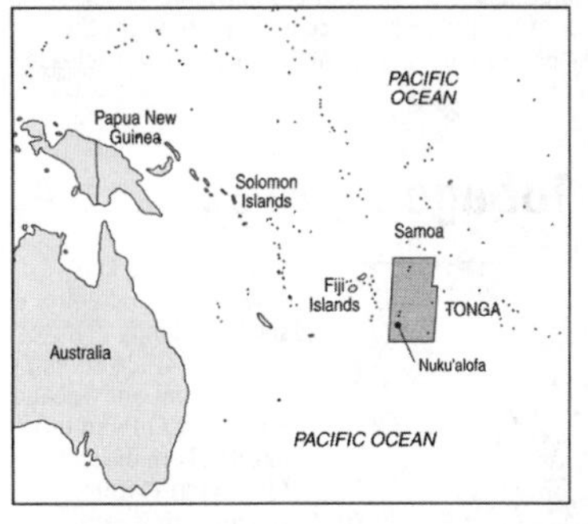

National name *Pule'anga Fakatu'i 'o Tonga* **Area** 750 sq km/ 290 sq mi **Capital** Nuku'alofa (on Tongatapu Island) **Major towns/cities** Pangai, Neiafu

Government

Head of state King Taufa'ahau Tupou IV from 1965 **Head of government** Baron Vaea of Houma from 1991 **Political system** absolutist **Armed forces** 125-strong naval force (1995) **Conscription** military service is voluntary **Education spend** (% GNP) 4.8 (1992) **Health spend** (% GDP) 4.1 (1991 est) **Death penalty** retains the death penalty for ordinary crimes, but can be considered abolitionist in practice (last execution 1982)

Population and society

Population 98,000 (1999 est) **Population growth rate** 0.3% (1995–2000) **Ethnic groups** 98% of Tongan ethnic origin, a Polynesian group with a small mixture of Melanesian; the remainder is European and part-European **Religion** Free Wesleyan Church **Life expectancy** 68 (men); 72 (women) (1998 est) **Literacy rate** 98% (men); 99% (women) (1997 est) **Unemployment** 13.3% (1996)

Economy and resources

GDP (US$) 180 million (1998 est) **GNP** (US$) 167 million (1998) **GNP per capita (PPP)** (US$) 3,860 (1998) **Real GDP growth** (% change on previous year) 0.2 (1998 est) **Consumer price inflation** 2.5% (1998) **Foreign debt** (US$) 70 million (1997) **Exports** vanilla beans, pumpkins, coconut oil and other coconut products, watermelons, knitted clothes, cassava, yams, sweet potatoes, footwear. Principal market: Japan 52.9% (1997) **Imports** foodstuffs, basic manufactures, machinery and transport equipment, mineral fuels. Principal source: New Zealand 29.7% (1997)

▪ Tourist information

Time difference GMT +13 **Currency** Tongan dollar or pa'anga **Language** Tongan (official); English **Visa requirements** UK: visa required (issued on arrival). USA: visa required (issued on arrival) **Embassy in the UK** 36 Molyneux Street, London W1H 6AB. Tel: (020) 7724 5828; fax: (020) 7723 9074 **British embassy** British High Commission, PO Box 56, Vuna Road, Nuku'alofa. Tel: (676) 21020/1; fax: (676) 24109 **Chamber of commerce** Office of the Minister of Labour, Commerce and Industries, PO Box 110, Nuku'alofa. Tel/fax: (676) 23688 **Office hours** 0830–1630 Mon–Fri; 0800–1200 Sat **Banking hours** 0930–1530 Mon–Fri; 0830–1130 Sat **Airports** international airports: Fua'amotu (15 km/9 mi from Nuku'alofa); five domestic airstrips; total passenger km: 11 million (1995) **Chief tourist attractions** mild climate; scenic beauty; beautiful beaches; high volcanic and low coral forms give the islands a unique character **Major holidays** 1 January, 25 April, 5 May, 4 June, 4 July, 4 November, 4, 25–26 December; variable: Good Friday, Easter Monday

Chronology

c. 1000 BC Settled by Polynesian immigrants from the Fiji Islands. *c.* AD 950 The legendary Aho'eitu became the first hereditary Tongan king (Tu'i Tonga). **13th–14th centuries** Tu'i Tonga kingdom at the height of its power. **1643** Visited by the Dutch navigator, Abel Tasman. **1773** Islands visited by British navigator Capt James Cook, who named them the 'Friendly Islands'. **1826** Methodist mission established. **1831** Tongan dynasty founded by a Christian convert and chief of Ha'apai, Prince Taufa'ahau Tupou, who became king 14 years later. **1845–93** Reign of King George Tupou I, during which the country was reunited after half a century of civil war; Christianity was spread and a modern constitution adopted in 1875. **1900** Friendship ('Protectorate') treaty signed between King George Tupou II and Britain, establishing British control over defence and foreign affairs, but leaving internal political affairs under Tongan control. **1918** Queen Salote Tupou III ascended the throne. **1965** Queen Salote died; she was succeeded by her son, King Taufa'ahau Tupou IV, who had been prime minister since 1949. **1970** Tonga achieved independence from Britain, but

remained within the Commonwealth. **1991** Baron Vaea was appointed prime minister. **1993** Six prodemocracy candidates were elected. There were calls for reform of absolutist power. **1996** A prodemocracy movement led by the People's Party won a majority of the 'commoner' seats in the legislative assembly. Prodemocracy campaigner Akilisis Pohiva was released after a month's imprisonment.

Trinidad and Tobago Republic of

Area 5,130 sq km/ 1,980 sq mi including smaller islands (Trinidad 4,828 sq km/ 1,864 sq mi and Tobago 300 sq km/115 sq mi) **Capital** Port-of-Spain (and port) **Major towns/cities** San Fernando, Arima, Point Fortin

Government

Head of state A N R Robinson from 1997 **Head of government** Basdeo Panday from 1995 **Political system** liberal democracy **Armed forces** 2,100; plus a paramlitary force of 4,800 (1997) **Conscription** military service is voluntary **Defence spend** (% GDP) 1.4 (1997) **Education spend** (% GNP) 3.7 (1996) **Health spend** (% GDP) 2.1 (1995) **Death penalty** retained and used for ordinary crimes

Population and society

Population 1,288,000 (1999 est) **Population growth rate** 0.8% (1995–2000) **Ethnic groups** the two main ethnic groups are Africans and East Indians; there are also European, Afro-European, and Chinese minorities. The original Carib population has largely disappeared **Religion** Roman Catholic, Anglican, Hindu, Muslim **Life expectancy** 72 (men); 76 (women) (1995–2000) **Literacy rate** 99% (men); 97% (women) (1997 est) **Unemployment** 16.2% (1997)

Economy and resources

GDP (US$) 6.16 billion (1998) **GNP** (US$) 5.8 billion (1998) **GNP per capita (PPP)** (US$) 6,720 (1998) **Real GDP growth** (% change on previous year) 4 (1998) **Consumer price inflation** 5.6% (1998) **Foreign debt** (US$) 2.16 billion (1997) **Resources** petroleum, natural gas, asphalt (world's largest deposits of natural asphalt) **Exports** mineral fuels and lubricants, chemicals, basic manufactures, food. Principal market: USA 39.7% (1997) **Imports** machinery and transport equipment, manufactured goods, mineral fuel products, food and live animals, chemicals. Principal source: USA 52.2% (1997)

▪ Tourist information

Time difference GMT −4 **Currency** Trinidad and Tobago dollar **Language** English (official); Hindi, French, Spanish **Visa requirements** UK: visa not required for a stay of up to three months. USA: visa not required for a stay of up to three months **Embassy in the UK** 42 Belgrave Square, London SW1X 8NT. Tel: (020) 7245 9351; fax: (020) 7823 1065 **British embassy** British High Commission, PO Box 778, 19 Clair Avenue, St Clair, Port of Spain. Tel: (809) 622 2748; fax: (809) 622 4555 **Chamber of commerce** Trinidad and Tobago Chamber of Industry and Commerce, PO Box 499, Room 950–952, Hilton Hotel, Port of Spain. Tel: (809) 627 4461; fax: (809) 627 4376 **Office hours** 0800–1600 Mon–Fri **Banking hours** 0900–1400 Mon–Thu; 0900–1200 and 1500–1700 Fri **Airports** international airports: Port of Spain, Trinidad (Piarco), Crown Point (near Scarborough, Tobago); domestic services between these; total passenger km: 2,790 million (1997 est) **Major ports** Scarborough, Point Lisas **Chief tourist attractions** sunny climate; attractive coastline (especially Tobago); the annual pre-Lenten carnival **Major holidays** 1 January, 19 June, 1, 31 August, 24 September, 25–26 December; variable: Corpus Christi, Good Friday, Easter Monday, Whit Monday

Chronology

1498 Visited by the explorer Christopher Columbus, who named Trinidad after the three peaks at its southeastern tip and Tobago after the local form of tobacco pipe. Carib and Arawak Indians comprised the indigenous community. **1532** Trinidad colonized by Spain. **1630s** Tobago settled by Dutch, who introduced sugar-cane growing. **1797** Trinidad captured by Britain and ceded by Spain five years later under Treaty of Amiens. **1814** Tobago ceded to Britain by France. **1834** Abolition of slavery resulted in indentured labourers being brought in from India, rather than Africa, to work sugar plantations. **1889** Trinidad and Tobago amalgamated as a British colony. **1956** The People's National Movement (PNM) founded by Eric Williams, a moderate nationalist. **1958–62** Part of West Indies Federation. **1959** Achieved internal self-government, with Williams as chief minister. **1962** Independence achieved within Commonwealth, with Williams as prime minister. **1970** Army mutiny and violent Black Power riots directed against minority East Indian population; state of emergency imposed for two years. **1976** Became a republic, with former Governor General Ellis Clarke as president and Williams as prime minister. **1986** Tobago-based National Alliance for Reconstruction (NAR), headed by A N R Robinson, won the general election. **1990** An attempted antigovernment coup by Islamic fundamentalists was foiled. **1991** A general election resulted in victory for PNM, with Patrick Manning as prime minister. **1995** The UNC and PNM tied in general election; a UNC–NAR coalition was formed, led by Basdeo Panday. **1997** Former Prime Minister Robinson was elected president.

Tunisia (Tunisian Republic)

National name *al-Jumhuriya at-Tunisiya* **Area** 164,150 sq km/ 63,378 sq mi **Capital** Tunis (and chief port) **Major towns/cities** Sfax, Ariana, Bizerte, Djerba, Gabès, Sousse, Kairouan, Bardo, La Goulette

Government

Head of state Zine el-Abidine Ben Ali from 1987 **Head of government** Hamed Karoui from 1989 **Political system** nationalistic socialist **Armed forces** 35,000; plus paramilitary forces numbering 12,000 (1997) **Conscription** military service is by selective conscription for 12 months **Defence spend** (% GDP) 1.8 (1997) **Education spend** (% GNP) 6.7 (1996) **Health spend** (% GDP) 3.0 (1990–95) **Death penalty** retained and used for ordinary crimes

Population and society

Population 9,460,000 (1999 est) **Population growth rate** 1.4% (1995–2000) **Ethnic groups** about 10% of the population is Arab; the remainder are of Berber-Arab descent. There are small Jewish and French communities **Religion** Sunni Muslim; Jewish, Christian **Life expectancy** 68 (men); 71 (women) (1995–2000) **Literacy rate** 78% (men); 56% (women) (1997 est) **Unemployment** 15% (1998 est)

Economy and resources

GDP (US$) 22.04 billion (1998) **GNP** (US$) 19.2 billion (1998) **GNP per capita (PPP)** (US$) 5,160 (1998) **Real GDP growth** (% change on previous year) 5 (1998) **Consumer price inflation** 3.2% (1998) **Foreign debt** (US$) 11.3 billion (1997) **Resources** petroleum, natural gas, phosphates, iron, zinc, lead, aluminium fluoride, fluorspar, sea salt **Exports** textiles and clothing, crude petroleum, phosphates and fertilizers, olive oil, fruit, leather and shoes, fishery products, machinery and electrical appliances. Principal market: France 27% (1998) **Imports** machinery, textiles, food (mainly cereals, dairy produce, meat, and sugar) and live animals, petroleum and petroleum products. Principal source: France: 27.1% (1998)

▪ Tourist information

Time difference GMT +1 **Currency** Tunisian dinar **Language** Arabic (official); French **Visa requirements** UK: visa not required. USA: visa not required **Embassy in the UK** 29 Prince's Gate, London SW7 1QG. Tel: (020) 7584 8117; fax: (020) 7225 2884 **British embassy** 5 place de la Victoire, Tunis. Tel: (1) 341 444; fax: (1) 354 877 **Chamber of commerce** Chambre de Commerce et d'Industrie de Tunis, 1 rue des Entrepreneurs, 1000 Tunis. Tel: (1) 242 872; fax: (1) 354 744 **Office hours** 0800–1230 and 1430–1800 Mon–Fri; 0800–1200 Sat (winter); 0800–1300 Mon–Sat (summer) **Banking hours** 0730–1100 Mon–Fri (summer); 0800–1100 and 1400–1615

Mon–Thu; 0800–1130 and 1300–1515 Fri (winter) **Airports** international airports: Tunis (Carthage), Monastir (Skanes), Djerba (Melita), Sfax, Tozeur (Nefta), Tabarka; domestic services operate between these; total passenger km: 2,539 million (1997 est) **Major ports** Sfax, Sousse, Bizerte **Chief tourist attractions** Moorish architecture; Roman remains; the ancient Phoenician city of Carthage; sandy beaches **Major holidays** 1, 18 January, 20 March, 9 April, 1 May, 1–2 June, 25 July, 3, 13 August, 3 September, 15 October; variable: Eid-ul-Adha (2 days), end of Ramadan (2 days), New Year (Muslim), Prophet's Birthday

Chronology

814 BC Phoenician emigrants from Tyre, in Lebanon, founded Carthage, near modern Tunis, as a trading post. By 6th century BC Carthaginian kingdom dominated western Mediterranean. **146 BC** Carthage destroyed by Punic Wars with Rome, which began in 264 BC; Carthage became part of Rome's African province. **AD 533** Came under control of Byzantine Empire. **7th century** Invaded by Arabs, who introduced Islam. Succession of Islamic dynasties followed, including Aghlabids (9th century), Fatimids (10th century), and Almohads (12th century). **1574** Became part of Islamic Turkish Ottoman Empire and a base for 'Barbary Pirates' who operated against European shipping until 19th century. **1705** Husayn Bey founded local dynasty, which held power under rule of Ottomans. **early 19th century** Ahmad Bey launched programme of economic modernization, which nearly bankrupted the country. **1881** Became French protectorate, with bey retaining local power. **1920** Destour (Constitution) Party, named after the original Tunisian constitution of 1861, founded to campaign for equal Tunisian participation in French-dominated government. **1934** Habib Bourguiba founded a radical splinter party, the Neo-Destour Party, to spearhead the nationalist movement. **1942–43** Brief German occupation during World War II. **1956** Independence achieved as monarchy under bey, with Bourguiba as prime minister. **1957** Bey deposed; Tunisia became one-party republic with Bourguiba as president. **1975** Bourguiba made president for life. **1979** Headquarters for Arab League moved to Tunis after Egypt signed Camp David Accords with Israel. **1981** Multiparty elections held, as a sign of political liberalization, but were won by Bourguiba's Destourian Socialist Party (DSP). **1982** Government allowed Palestine Liberation Organization (PLO) to use Tunis for its headquarters. **1985** Diplomatic relations with Libya severed; Israel attacked PLO headquarters. **1987** Zine el-Abidine Ben Ali, the new prime minister, declared Bourguiba (now aged 84) incompetent for government and seized power as president. **1988** 2,000 political prisoners freed; privatization initiative. Diplomatic relations with Libya restored. DSP renamed RCD. **1990** The Arab League's headquarters returned to Cairo, Egypt. **1991** There was opposition to US actions during the Gulf War, and a crackdown on religious fundamentalists. **1992** Human-rights transgressions provoked Western criticism. **1994** Ben Ali and the RCD were re-elected. The PLO transferred its headquarters to Gaza City in Palestine.

Turkey Republic of

National name *Türkiye Cumhuriyeti* **Area** 779,500 sq km/300,964 sq mi **Capital** Ankara **Major towns/cities** Istanbul, Izmir, Adana, Bursa, Antakya, Gaziantep, Konya, Mersin, Kayseri, Edirne, Antalya

Government

Head of state Ahmet Necdet Sezer from 2000 **Head of government** Bülent Ecevit from 1999 **Political system** liberal democracy **Armed forces** 639,000 (1997) **Conscription** 18 months **Defence spend** (% GDP) 4.2 (1997) **Education spend** (% GNP) 2.2 (1996) **Health spend** (% GDP) 2.7 (1996) **Death penalty** retained for ordinary crimes, but considered abolitionist in practice; last execution in 1984

Population and society

Population 65,546,000 (1999 est) **Population growth rate** 1.7% (1995–2000) **Ethnic groups** over 90% of the population are Turks, although only about 5% are of Turkic or Western Mongoloid descent; most are descended from earlier conquerors, such as the Greeks **Religion** Sunni Muslim; Orthodox, Armenian churches **Life expectancy** 67 (men); 72 (women) (1995–2000) **Literacy rate** 92% (men); 74% (women) (1997 est) **Unemployment** 6.3% (1998)

Economy and resources

GDP (US$) 189.9 billion (1998 est) **GNP** (US$) 200.5 billion (1998) **GNP per capita (PPP)** (US$) 5,830 (1998 est) **Real GDP growth** (% change on previous year) 2.9 (1998) **Consumer price inflation** 83.1% (1998) **Foreign debt** (US$) 91.2 billion (1997) **Resources** chromium, copper, mercury, antimony, borax, coal, petroleum, natural gas, iron ore, salt **Exports** textiles and clothing, agricultural products and foodstuffs (including figs, nuts, and dried fruit), tobacco, leather, glass, refined petroleum and petroleum products. Principal market: Germany 20.3% (1998) **Imports** machinery, construction material, motor vehicles, consumer goods, crude petroleum, iron and steel, chemical products, fertilizer, livestock. Principal source: Germany 15.9% (1998)

▪ Tourist information

Time difference GMT +3 **Currency** Turkish lira **Language** Turkish (official); Kurdish, Arabic **Visa requirements** UK: visa not required for a stay of up to three months. USA: visa not required for a stay of up to three months **Embassy in the UK** 43 Belgrave Square, London SW1X 8PA. Tel: (020) 7393 0202; fax: (020) 7393 0066 **British embassy** Senit Ersan Caddesi 46/A, Cankaya, Ankara. Tel: (312) 468 6230; fax: (312) 468 3214 **Chamber of commerce** Union of Chambers of Commerce, Industry, Maritime Commerce and Commodity Exchanges of Turkey, Atatürk Bul 149, Bakanhliklar, 06640, Ankara. Tel: (312) 417 7700; fax: (312) 418 3568 **Office hours** 0830–1200 and 1300–1730 Mon–Fri **Banking hours** 0830–1200 and 1300–1700 Mon–Fri **Airports** international airports: Ankara (Esenboga), Istanbul (Atatürk), Izmir (Adnan Menderes), Adana, Trabzon, Dalaman, Antalya; 15 domestic airports; total passenger km: 12,379 million (1997 est) **Major ports** Istanbul and Izmir **Chief tourist attractions** sunny climate; fine beaches; ancient monuments; historic Istanbul, with its 15th-century Topkapi Palace, 6th-century Hagia Sophia basilica, Blue Mosque, mosque of Suleiman the Magnificent, covered bazaars, and Roman cisterns **Major holidays** 1 January, 23 April, 19 May, 30 August, 29 October; variable: Eid-ul-Adha (4 days), end of Ramadan (3 days)

Chronology

1st century BC Asia Minor became part of Roman Empire, later passing to Byzantine Empire. **6th century AD** Turkic peoples spread from Mongolia into Turkestan, where they adopted Islam. **1055** Seljuk Turks captured Baghdad; their leader Tughrul took the title of sultan. **1071** Battle of Manzikert: Seljuk Turks defeated Byzantines and conquered Asia Minor. **13th century** Ottoman Turks, driven west by Mongols, became vassals of Seljuk Turks. ***c.* 1299** Osman I founded small Ottoman kingdom, which quickly displaced Seljuks to include all Asia Minor. **1354** Ottoman Turks captured Gallipoli and began their conquests in Europe. **1389** Battle of Kossovo: Turks defeated Serbs to take control of most of Balkan peninsula. **1453** Constantinople, capital of Byzantine Empire, fell to the Turks; became capital of Ottoman Empire as Istanbul. **16th century** Ottoman Empire reached its zenith under Suleiman the Magnificent 1520–66; Turks conquered Egypt, Syria, Arabia, Mesopotamia, Tripoli, Cyprus, and most of Hungary. **1683** Failure of Siege of Vienna marked the start of the decline of the Ottoman Empire. **1699** Treaty of Karlowitz: Turks forced out of Hungary by Austrians. **1774** Treaty of Kuchuk Kainarji: Russia drove Turks from Crimea and won the right to intervene on behalf of Christian subjects of the sultan. **19th century** 'The Eastern Question': Ottoman weakness caused intense rivalry between powers to shape future of Near East. **1821–29** Greek war of independence: Greeks defeated Turks with help of Russia, Britain, and France. **1854–56** Crimean War: Britain and France fought to defend Ottoman Empire from further pressure by Russians. **1877–78** Russo-Turkish War ended with Treaty of Berlin and withdrawal of Turks from Bulgaria. **1908** Young Turk revolution forced sultan to grant constitution; start of political modernization. **1911–12** Italo-Turkish War: Turkey lost Tripoli (Libya). **1912–13** Balkan War: Greece, Serbia, and Bulgaria expelled Turks from Macedonia and Albania. **1914** Ottoman Empire entered World War I on German side. **1919** Following Turkish defeat, Mustapha Kemal launched nationalist revolt to resist foreign encroachments. **1920** Treaty of Sèvres partitioned Ottoman Empire, leaving no part of Turkey fully independent. **1922** Kemal, having defied Allies, expelled Greeks, French, and Italians from Asia Minor; sultanate abolished. **1923** Treaty of Lausanne recognized Turkish independence; secular republic established by Kemal, who imposed rapid Westernization. **1935** Kemal adopted surname Atatürk ('Father of the Turks'). **1938** Death of Kemal Atatürk; succeeded as president by Ismet Inönü. **1950** First free elections won by opposition Democratic Party; Adnan Menderes became prime minister. **1952** Turkey became a member of NATO. **1960** Military coup led by Gen Cemal Gürsel deposed Menderes, who was executed in 1961. **1961** Inönü returned as prime minister; politics dominated by the issue of Cyprus. **1965** Justice Party came to power under Suleyman Demirel. **1971–73** Prompted by strikes and student unrest, the army imposed military rule. **1974** Turkey invaded northern Cyprus. **1980–83** Political violence led to further military rule. **1984** Kurds began guerrilla war in a quest for greater autonomy. **1989** Application to join European Community rejected. **1990–91** Turkey joined the UN coalition against Iraq in the Gulf War. **1995** Turkish offensives against Kurdish bases in northern Iraq; the Islamicist Welfare Party won the largest number of seats in general election. **1997** Plans were agreed for the curbing of Muslim fundamentalism. Mesut Yilmaz was appointed prime minister. An agreement was reached with Greece on the peaceful resolution of disputes. **1998** The Islamic Welfare Party (RP) was banned by Constitutional Court, and regrouped as the Virtue Party (FP). **1999** Bülent Ecevit became prime minister. Ecevit's ruling centre-left party won the majority of seats in the general election. Turkey suffered two devastating earthquakes, causing extensive loss of life and structural damage. At a European Union (EU) summit, Turkey was at last declared an EU candidate, but to become a full member would first have to settle its territorial dispute with Greece and satisfy EU human rights regulations. **2000** Ahmet Necdet Sezer was inaugrated as president. He urged reforms to push Turkey close to EU membership.

Turkmenistan Republic of

Area 488,100 sq km/ 188,455 sq mi **Capital** Ashgabat **Major towns/ cities** Chardzhov, Mary (Merv), Nebit-Dag, Krasnovodsk

Government

Head of state and government Saparmurad Niyazov from 1990 **Political system** authoritarian nationalist **Armed forces** 18,000 (1997) **Conscription** military service is compulsory for 18 months **Defence spend** (% GDP) 2.7 (1997) **Education spend** (% GNP) 7.9 (1993/94) **Health spend** (% GDP) 1.2 (1995) **Death penalty** retained and used for ordinary crimes

Population and society

Population 4,384,000 (1999 est) **Population growth rate** 1.8% (1995–2000) **Ethnic groups** 72% ethnic Turkmen, 10% ethnic Russian, 9% Uzbek, 3% Kazakh, 1% Ukrainian **Religion** Sunni Muslim **Life expectancy** 62 (men); 69 (women) (1995–2000) **Literacy rate** 99% (men); 98% (women) (1997 est) **Unemployment** 5% (1996 est)

Economy and resources

GDP (US$) 2.1 billion (1998 est) **GNP** (US$) 2.5 billion (1998 est) **GNP per capita (PPP)** (US$) 1,480 (1998 est) **Real GDP growth** (% change on previous year) –1 (1998) **Consumer price inflation** 24.8% (1998) **Foreign debt** (US$) 1.8 billion (1997) **Resources** petroleum, natural gas, coal, sulphur, magnesium, iodine-bromine, sodium sulphate and different types of salt **Exports** natural gas, cotton yarn, electric energy, petroleum and petroleum products. Principal market: Ukraine 43.6% (1997) **Imports** machinery and metalwork, light industrial products, processed food, agricultural products. Principal source: Ukraine 14.9% (1997)

■ Tourist information

Time difference GMT +5 **Currency** manat **Language** West Turkic, closely related to Turkish **Visa requirements** UK: visa required. USA: visa required **Embassy in the UK** Turkmenistan has no diplomatic representation in the UK; the Department of Trade and Industry has a desk which deals with enquiries relating to Turkmenistan. Tel: (020) 7215 8427; fax: (020) 7215 4817 **British embassy** the UK has no diplomatic representation in Turkmenistan **Chamber of commerce** Commission for International Economic Affairs of the Office of the President of Turkmenistan, Ulitsa Kemine 92, Ashgabat 744000. Tel: (3632) 298 770; fax: (3632) 297 524 **Airports** international airports: Ashgabat; three domestic airports; total passenger km: 1,562 million (1995) **Major ports** Turkmenbashi **Chief tourist attractions** ruins of the 12th-century Seljuk capital at Merv (now Mary); hot springs at Bacharden, on the Iranian border; the bazaar at Ashgabat **Major holidays** 1, 12 January, 19, 22 February, 8 March, 29 April, 9, 18 May, 27–28 October

Chronology

6th century BC Part of the Persian Empire of Cyrus the Great. **4th century BC** Part of the empire of Alexander the Great of Macedonia. **7th century** Spread of Islam into Transcaspian region, followed by Arab rule from 8th century. **10th–13th centuries** Immigration from northeast by nomadic Oghuz Seljuk and Mongol tribes, whose Turkic-speaking descendants now dominate the country; conquest by Genghis Khan. **16th century** Came under dominance of Persia, to the south. **1869–81** Fell under control of tsarist Russia after 150,000 Turkmen were killed in Battle of Gok Tepe in 1881; became part of Russia's Turkestan Governor-Generalship. **1916** Turkmen revolted violently against Russian rule; autonomous Transcaspian government formed after Russian Revolution of 1917. **1919** Brought back under Russian control following invasion by the Soviet Red Army. **1921** Part of Turkestan Soviet Socialist Autonomous Republic. **1925** Became constituent republic of USSR. **1920s–30s** Soviet programme of agricultural collectivization and secularization provoked sporadic guerrilla resistance and popular uprisings. **1960–67** Lenin Kara-Kum Canal built, leading to dramatic expansion in cotton production in previously semidesert region. **1985** Saparmurad Niyazov replaced Muhammad Gapusov, local communist leader since 1971, whose regime had been viewed as corrupt. **1989** Stimulated by the *glasnost* initiative of reformist Soviet leader Mikhail Gorbachev, Agzybirlik 'popular front' formed by Turkmen intellectuals. **1990** Economic and political sovereignty was declared. Niyazov was elected state president. **1991** Niyazov initially supported an attempted anti-Gorbachev coup in Moscow. Independence was later declared; Turkmenistan joined the new Commonwealth of Independent States (CIS). **1992** Joined the Muslim Economic Cooperation Organization and the United Nations; a new constitution was adopted. **1993** A new currency, the manat, was introduced and a programme of cautious economic reform introduced, with foreign investment in the country's huge oil and gas reserves encouraged. The economy continued to contract. **1994** A nationwide referendum overwhelmingly backed Niyazov's presidency. Ex-communists won most seats in parliamentary elections. **1997** Private land ownership was legalized.

Tuvalu South West Pacific State of (formerly Ellice Islands)

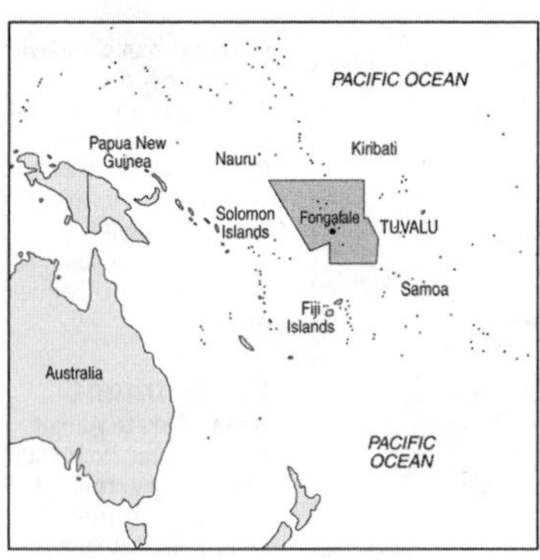

Area 25 sq km/9.6 sq mi **Capital** Fongafale (on Funafuti atoll) **Major towns/cities** Vaitupu, Niutao, Nanumea

Government

Head of state Queen Elizabeth II from 1978, represented by governor general Tulaga Manuella from 1994 **Head of government** Ionatana Ionatana from 1999 **Political system** liberal democracy **Armed forces** no standing defence force **Death penalty** laws do not provide for the death penalty for any crime

Population and society

Population 11,000 (1999 est) **Population growth rate** 0.9% (1995–2025) **Ethnic groups** almost entirely of Polynesian origin, maintaining close ties with Samoans and Tokelauans to the south and east **Religion** Christian (mainly Protestant) **Life expectancy** 63 (men); 66 (women) (1998 est) **Literacy rate** N/A

Economy and resources
GDP (US$) 8 million (1995 est) **GNP** (US$) 14 million (1996) **GNP per capita (PPP)** (US$) 1,435 (1996) **Real GDP growth** (% change on previous year) 20.4 (1996) **Consumer price inflation** 0.8 (1998) **Foreign debt** (US$) N/A **Exports** copra. Principal market: Australia **Imports** food and live animals, beverages, tobacco, consumer goods, machinery and transport equipment, mineral fuels. Principal source: Australia

▪ Tourist information
Time difference GMT +12 **Currency** Australian dollar **Language** Tuvaluan, English **Visa requirements** UK: visa not required. USA: visa required **Embassy for the UK** Honorary Consulate General of Tuvalu, Klövensteenweg 115A, 22559 Hamburg, Germany. Tel: (40) 810 580; fax: (40) 811 016 **British embassy** the British Embassy in Suva (see Fiji Islands) deals with enquiries relating to Tuvalu **Chamber of commerce** Development Bank of Tuvalu, PO Box 9, Vaiaku, Funafuti. Tel: (688) 20198; telex: 4800 **Office hours** 0730–1615 Mon–Thu and 0730–1245 Fri **Banking hours** 0930–1300 Mon–Thu; 0830–1200 Fri **Airports** international airport: Funafuti; no internal air service **Chief tourist attractions** Funafuti lagoon; sandy beaches; development of tourism has been limited due to Tuvalu's remote location and lack of amenities **Major holidays** 1 January, 4 March, 15 June, 5 August, 1–2 October, 14 November, 25–26 December; variable: Good Friday, Easter Monday

Chronology
c. 300 BC First settled by Polynesian peoples. **16th century** Invaded and occupied by Samoans. **1765** Islands first reached by Europeans. **1850–75** Population decimated by European slave traders capturing Tuvaluans to work in South America and by exposure to European diseases. **1856** The four southern islands, including Funafuti, claimed by USA. **1865** Christian mission established. **1877** Came under control of British Western Pacific High Commission (WPHC), with its headquarters in the Fiji Islands. **1892** Known as the Ellice Islands, they were joined with Gilbert Islands (now Kiribati) to form a British protectorate. **1916** Gilbert and Ellice Islands colony formed. **1942–43** Became a base for US airforce operations when Japan occupied the Gilbert Islands during World War II. **1975** Following a referendum, the predominantly Melanesian-peopled Ellice Islands, fearing domination by Micronesian-peopled Gilbert Islands in an independent state, were granted separate status. **1978** Independence achieved within Commonwealth, with Toaripi Lauti as prime minister; reverted to former name Tuvalu ('eight standing together'). **1979** The USA signed a friendship treaty, relinquishing its claim to the four southern atolls in return for continued access to military bases. **1986** Islanders rejected proposal for republican status. **1995** The union flag was removed from the national flag, presaging a move towards republican status. **1999** Ionatana Ionatana became prime minister.

Uganda Republic of

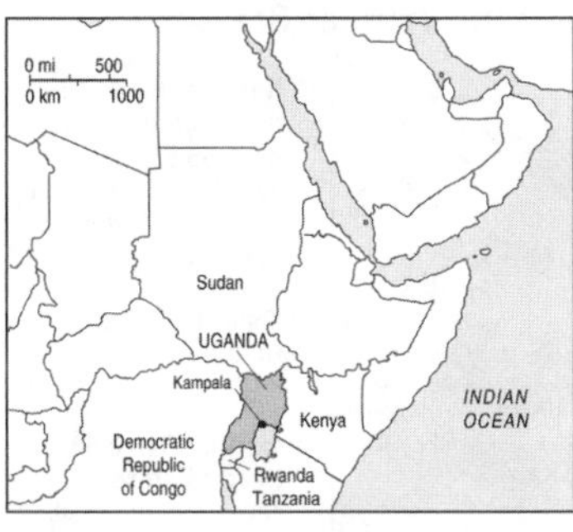

Area 236,600 sq km/ 91,351 sq mi **Capital** Kampala **Major towns/ cities** Jinja, Mbale, Entebbe, Masaka, Bugembe

Government
Head of state Yoweri Museveni from 1986 **Head of government** Apolo Nsibambi from 1999 **Political system** authoritarian nationalist **Armed forces** 55,000 (1997) **Conscription** military service is voluntary **Defence spend** (% GDP) 2.4 (1997) **Education spend** (% GNP) 2.6 (1996) **Health spend** (% GDP) 1.2 (1995) **Death penalty** retained and used for ordinary crimes

Population and society
Population 21,143,000 (1999 est) **Population growth rate** 2.8% (1995–2000) **Ethnic groups** about 40 different peoples concentrated into four main groups; the Bantu (the most numerous), Eastern Nilotic, Western Nilotic, and Central Sudanic; there are also Rwandan, Sudanese, Zairean, and Kenyan minorities **Religion** Christian 50%, animist 40%, Muslim 10% **Life expectancy** 39 (men); 40 (women) (1995–2000) **Literacy rate** 75% (men); 53% (women) (1997 est)

Economy and resources
GDP (US$) 6.65 billion (1998) **GNP** (US$) 6.7 billion (1998) **GNP per capita (PPP)** (US$) 1,170 (1998 est) **Real GDP growth** (% change on previous year) 5.5 (1998) **Consumer price inflation** 0% (1998) **Foreign debt** (US$) 3.7 billion (1997) **Resources** copper, apatite, limestone; believed to possess the world's second-largest deposit of gold (hitherto unexploited); also reserves of magnetite, tin, tungsten, beryllium, bismuth, asbestos, graphite **Exports** coffee, cotton, tea, tobacco, oil seeds and oleaginous fruit; hides and skins, textiles. Principal market: Spain 14.4% (1997) **Imports** machinery and transport equipment, basic manufactures, petroleum and petroleum products, chemicals, miscellaneous manufactured articles, iron and steel. Principal source: Kenya 31.1% (1997)

▪ Tourist information
Time difference GMT +3 **Currency** Uganda new shilling **Language** English (official), Kiswahili, Bantu and Nilotic languages **Visa requirements** UK: visa not required. USA: visa not required **Embassy in the UK** Uganda House, 58–59 Trafalgar Square, London WC2N 5DX. Tel: (020) 7839 5783; fax: (020) 7839 8925 **British embassy** British High Commission, PO Box 7070, 101–12 Parliament Avenue, Kampala. Tel: (41) 257 301/4; telex: 61202 (a/b UKREP KAMPALA) **Chamber of commerce** Uganda Investment Authority, PO Box 7418, Investment Center, Kampala Road, Kampala. Tel: (41) 234 105; fax: (41) 242 903 **Office hours** 0800–1230 and 1400–1630 Mon–Fri **Banking hours** 0830–1400 Mon–Fri **Airports** international airports: Entebbe; domestic services operate to all major towns; total passenger km: 103 million (1995) **Chief tourist attractions** good year-round climate; lakes; forests; wildlife; varied scenery includes tropical forest and tea plantations on the slopes of the snow-capped Ruwenzori Mountains and the arid plains of the Karamoja **Major holidays** 1 January, 1 April, 1 May, 9 October, 25–26 December; variable: Good Friday, Easter Monday, Holy Saturday, end of Ramadan

Chronology
16th century Bunyoro kingdom founded by immigrants from southeastern Sudan. **17th century** Rise of kingdom of Buganda people, which became particularly powerful from 17th century. **mid-19th century** Arabs, trading ivory and slaves, reached Uganda; first visits by European explorers and Christian missionaries. **1885–87** Uganda Martyrs: Christians persecuted by Buganda ruler, Mwanga. **1890** Royal Charter granted to British East African Company, a trading company whose agent, Frederick Lugard, concluded treaties with local rulers, including the Buganda and the western states of Ankole and Toro. **1894** British protectorate established, with Buganda retaining some autonomy under its traditional prince (Kabaka) and other resistance being crushed. **1904** Cotton growing introduced by Buganda peasants. **1958** Internal self-government granted. **1962** Independence achieved from Britain, within Commonwealth, with Milton Obote of Uganda People's Congress (UPC) as prime minister. **1963** Proclaimed federal republic with King Mutesa II (of Buganda) as president and Obote as prime minister. **1966** King Mutesa, who opposed creation of a one-party state, ousted in coup led by Obote, who ended federal status and became executive president. **1969** All opposition parties banned after assassination attempt on Obote; key enterprises nationalized. **1971** Obote overthrown in army coup led by Maj-Gen Idi Amin Dada; constitution suspended and ruthlessly dictatorial regime established; nearly 49,000 Ugandan Asians expelled; over 300,000 opponents of regime killed. **1976** Relations with Kenya strained by Amin's claims to parts of Kenya. **1979** After annexing part of Tanzania, Amin forced to leave the country by opponents backed by Tanzanian troops. Provisional government set up. **1978–79** Fighting broke out against Tanzanian troops. **1980** Provisional government overthrown by army. Elections held and Milton Obote returned to power. **1985** After opposition by pro-Lule National Resistance Army (NRA), and indiscipline in army, Obote ousted by Gen Tito Okello; constitution suspended; power-sharing agreement entered into with NRA leader Yoweri Museveni. **1986** Museveni became president, heading broad-based coalition government. **1993** The King of Buganda was reinstated as formal monarch, in the person of Ronald Muwenda Mutebi II. **1996** A landslide victory was won by Museveni in the first direct presidential elections. **1997** Allied Democratic Forces (ADF) led uprisings by rebels. **1999** The leaders of Uganda and Sudan signed an agreement to bring an end to rebel wars across their mutual border by ceasing to support rebel factions in the other's country. President Museveni appointed Apolo Nsibambi as prime minister. **2000** Despite the peace deal, rebels with bases in Sudan attacked towns in northern Uganda in January, while others continued to battle the Ugandan army along the border with the Democratic Republic of Congo.

Ukraine

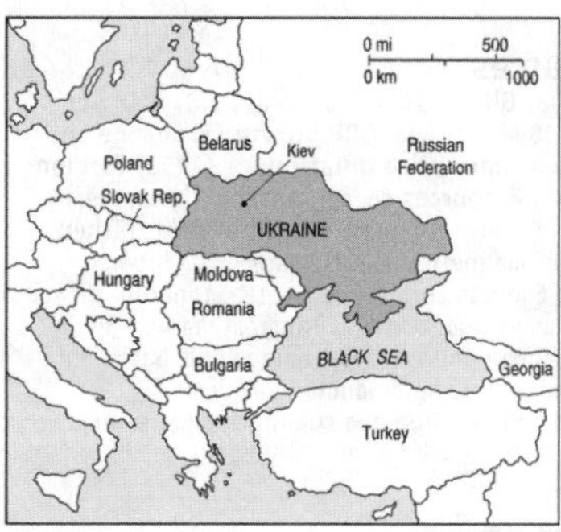

Area 603,700 sq km/ 233,088 sq mi **Capital** Kiev **Major towns/ cities** Kharkov, Donetsk, Dnepropetrovsk, Lugansk (Voroshilovgrad), Lviv (Lvov), Mariupol (Zhdanov), Krivoy Rog, Zaporozhye, Odessa

Government

Head of state Leonid Kuchma from 1994 **Head of government** Valery Pustovoitenko from 1997 **Political system** emergent democracy **Armed forces** 387,400 (1997) **Conscription** 18 months (males over 18) **Defence spend** (% GDP) 2.7 (1997) **Education spend** (% GNP) 7.2 (1996) **Health spend** (% GDP) 4.9 (1995) **Death penalty** moratorium placed on executions since 1991 as condition for application to join Council of Europe (joined in 1995); despite continued demands by Council to uphold moratorium, executions have continued

Population and society

Population 50,658,000 (1999 est) **Population growth rate** –0.4% (1995–2000) **Ethnic groups** 73% of the population is of Ukrainian descent; 22% ethnic Russian; 1% Jewish; 1% Belarussian **Religion** traditionally Ukrainian Orthodox; also Ukrainian Catholic **Life expectancy** 64 (men); 74 (women) (1995–2000) **Literacy rate** 99% (men); 99% (women) (1997 est) **Unemployment** 4.1% (1998)

Economy and resources

GDP (US$) 49.7 billion (1998 est) **GNP** (US$) 42.7 billion (1998) **GNP per capita (PPP)** (US$) 2,420 (1998 est) **Real GDP growth** (% change on previous year) –1.6 (1998) **Consumer price inflation** 11% (1998) **Foreign debt** (US$) 10.9 billion (1997) **Resources** coal, iron ore (world's fifth-largest producer), crude oil, natural gas, salt, chemicals, brown coal, alabaster, gypsum **Exports** grain, coal, oil, various minerals. Principal market: Russia 23% (1998) **Imports** mineral fuels, machine-building components, chemicals and chemical products. Principal source: Russia 48.1% (1998)

▪ Tourist information

Time difference GMT +2 **Currency** hryvna **Language** Ukrainian (a Slavonic language) **Visa requirements** UK: visa required. USA: visa required **Embassy in the UK** 78 Kensington Park Road, London W11 2PL. Tel: (020) 7727 6312; fax: (020) 7792 1708 **British embassy** vul Desyatinna 9, 252025 Kiev. Tel: (044) 228 0504; fax: (044) 228 3972 **Chamber of commerce** Chamber of Commerce and Industry, vul Velyka Zhytomyrska 33, 254655 Kiev. Tel: (044) 212 2911; fax: (044) 212 3353 **Office hours** 0900–1800 (lunch breaks tend to last at least 1 hr 30 mins) **Airports** international airports: Kiev (Borispol); four principal domestic airports; total passenger km: 1,534 million (1995) **Chief tourist attractions** popular Black Sea resorts, including Odessa and Yalta; the Crimean peninsula; cities of historical interest, including Kiev and Odessa **Major holidays** 1, 7 January, 8 March, 1–2, 9 May, 24 August

Chronology

9th century Rus' people established state centred on Kiev and adopted Eastern Orthodox Christianity 988. **1199** Reunification of southern Rus' lands, after period of fragmentation, under Prince Daniel of Galicia-Volhynia. **13th century** Mongol-Tatar Golden Horde sacked Kiev and destroyed Rus' state. **14th century** Poland annexed Galicia; Lithuania absorbed Volhynia and expelled Tatars; Ukraine peasants became serfs of Polish and Lithuanian nobles. **1569** Poland and Lithuania formed single state; clergy of Ukraine formed Uniate Church, which recognized papal authority but retained Orthodox rites, to avoid Catholic persecution. **16th and 17th centuries** Runaway serfs known as Cossacks ('outlaws') formed autonomous community in eastern borderlands. **1648** Cossack revolt led by Gen Bogdan Khmelnitsky drove out Poles from central Ukraine; Khmelnitsky accepted Russian protectorate in 1654. **1660–90** 'Epoch of Ruins': Ukraine devastated by civil war and invasions by Russians, Poles, and Turks; Poland regained western Ukraine. **1687** Gen Ivan Mazepa entered into alliance with Sweden in effort to regain Cossack autonomy from Russia. **1709** Battle of Poltava: Russian victory over Swedes ended hopes of Cossack independence. **1772–95** Partition of Poland: Austria annexed Galicia, Russian annexations included Volhynia. **1846–47** Attempt to promote Ukrainian national culture through formation of Cyril and Methodius Society. **1899** Revolutionary Ukrainian Party founded. **1917** Revolutionary parliament (Rada), proclaimed Ukrainian autonomy within a federal Russia. **1918** Ukraine declared full independence; civil war ensued between Rada (backed by Germans) and Reds (backed by Russian Bolsheviks). **1919** Galicia united with Ukraine; conflict escalated between Ukrainian nationalists, Bolsheviks, anarchists, White Russians, and Poles. **1921** Treaty of Riga: Russia and Poland partitioned Ukraine. **1921–22** Several million people perished in famine. **1922** Ukrainian Soviet Socialist Republic (Ukrainian SSR) became part of Union of Soviet Socialist Republics (USSR). **1932–33** Enforced collectivization of agriculture caused another catastrophic famine with more than 7.5 million deaths. **1939** USSR annexed eastern Poland and added Galicia-Volhynia to Ukrainian SSR. **1940** USSR seized northern Bukhovina from Romania and added it to Ukrainian SSR. **1941–44** Germany occupied Ukraine; many Ukrainians collaborated; millions of Ukrainians and Ukrainian Jews were exterminated by Nazis. **1945** USSR annexed Ruthenia from Czechoslovakia and added it to Ukrainian SSR, which became a nominal member of the United Nations (UN). **1946** Uniate Church forcibly merged with Russian Orthodox Church. **1954** Crimea transferred from Russian Federation to Ukrainian SSR. **1986** Major environmental disaster caused by explosion of nuclear reactor at Chernobyl, north of Kiev. **1989** Rukh (nationalist movement) established as political party; ban on Uniate Church lifted. **1990** Ukraine declared its sovereignty under President Leonid Kravchuk, leader of the CP. **1991** Ukraine declared its independence from USSR; President Kravchuk left the CP; Ukraine joined the newly formed Commonwealth of Independent States (CIS). **1992** Crimean sovereignty was declared but then rescinded. **1994** Election gains were made by radical nationalists in western Ukraine and by Russian unionists in eastern Ukraine; Leonid Kuchma succeeded Kravchuk as president. **1996** A new constitution replaced the Soviet system, making the presidency stronger; remaining nuclear warheads were returned to Russia for destruction; a new currency was introduced. **1997** New government appointments were made to speed economic reform. A treaty of friendship was signed with Russia, solving the issue of the Russian Black Sea fleet. A loan of $750 million from the International Monetary Fund (IMF) was approved. **1998** The communists won the largest number of seats in parliamentary elections, but fell short of an absolute majority. The value of the hryvnya fell by over 50% against the US dollar after the neighbouring Russian currency crisis. The government survived a no-confidence vote tabled by left-wing factions that opposed the government's economic program. **1999** Viktor Andriyovych Yushchenko became prime minister.

United Arab Emirates (federation of the emirates of Abu Dhabi, Ajman, Dubai, Fujairah, Ras al Khaimah, Sharjah, Umm al Qaiwain)

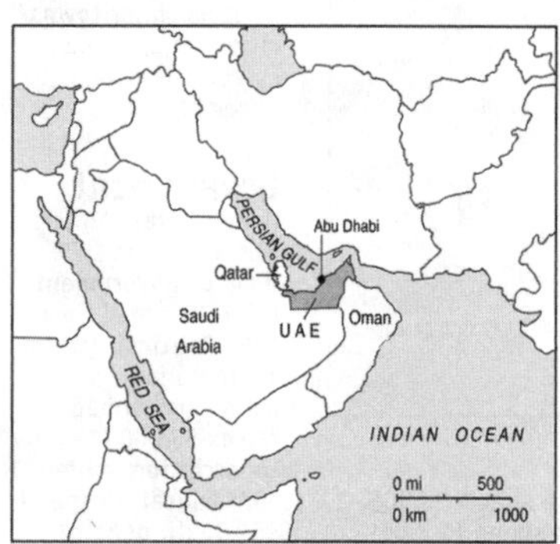

National name *Ittihad al-Imarat al-Arabiyah* **Area** 83,657 sq km/ 32,299 sq mi **Capital** Abu Dhabi **Major towns/cities** Dubai, Sharjah, Ras al-Khaimah, Ajman, Fujairah

Government

Head of state Sheikh Zayed bin Sultan al-Nahayan of Abu Dhabi from 1971 **Head of government** Maktum bin Rashid al-Maktum of Dubai from 1990 **Supreme council of rulers** *Abu Dhabi* Sheikh Zayed bin Sultan al-Nahayan, president (1966); *Ajman* Sheikh Humaid bin Rashid al-Nuami (1981); *Dubai* Sheikh Maktoum bin Rashid al-Maktoum (1990); *Fujairah* Sheikh Hamad bin Muhammad al-Sharqi (1974); *Ras al Khaimah* Sheikh Saqr bin Muhammad al-Quasimi (1948); *Sharjah* Sheikh Sultan bin Muhammad al-Quasimi (1972); *Umm al Qaiwain* Sheikh Rashid bin Ahmad al-Mu'alla (1981) **Political system**

absolutist **Armed forces** 64,500 (1997) **Conscription** military service is voluntary **Defence spend** (% GDP) 5.5 (1997) **Education spend** (% GNP) 1.8 (1995) **Health spend** (% GDP) 2.0 (1990–95) **Death penalty** retained and used for ordinary crimes

Population and society

Population 2,397,000 (1999 est) **Population growth rate** 2.0% (1995–2000); 1.8% (2000–05) **Ethnic groups** 75% Iranians, Indians, and Pakistanis; about 25% Arabs **Religion** Muslim 96%; Christian, Hindu **Life expectancy** 74 (men); 77 (women) (1995–2000) **Literacy rate** 74% (men); 77% (women) (1997 est)

Economy and resources

GDP (US$) 47.2 billion (1998) **GNP** (US$) 48.66 billion (1998) **GNP per capita (PPP)** (US$) 19,720 (1998) **Real GDP growth** (% change on previous year) –1.8 (1998) **Consumer price inflation** 4.7% (1998) **Foreign debt** (US$) 12.3 billion (1997) **Resources** petroleum and natural gas **Exports** crude petroleum, natural gas, re-exports (mainly machinery and transport equipment). Principal market: Japan 36.3% (1997) **Imports** machinery and transport equipment, food and live animals, fuels and lubricants, chemicals, basic manufactures. Principal source: USA 9.6% (1997)

▪ Tourist information

Time difference GMT +4 **Currency** UAE dirham **Language** Arabic (official), Farsi, Hindi, Urdu, English **Visa requirements** UK: visa not required for a stay of up to 30 days. USA: visa required **Embassy in the UK** 30 Prince's Gate, London SW7 1PT. Tel: (020) 7581 1281; fax: (020) 7581 9616 **British\,embassy** PO Box 248, Abu Dhabi. Tel: (2) 326 600; fax: (2) 341 744 **Chamber of commerce** Dubai Chamber of Commerce and Industry, PO Box 1457, Diera, Dubai. Tel: (4) 221 181; fax: (4) 211 646 **Office hours** 0800–1300 and 1600–1900 Sat–Wed and 0800–1200 Thu **Banking hours** 0800–1200 Sat–Wed and 0800–1100 Thu in Abu Dhabi (0800–1200 Thu in the Northern States). Some are also open 1600–1730 **Airports** international airports: Abu Dhabi (Nadia), Dubai, Ras al-Khaimah, Sharjah, Fujairah; domestic services operate between Abu Dhabi and Dubai; total passenger km: 9,958 million (1995) **Major ports** Dubai **Chief tourist attractions** Dubai, popularly known as the 'Pearl of the Gulf', with its 16 km/10 mi deep-water creek **Major holidays** 1 January, 6 August, 2 December (2 days); variable: Eid-ul-Adha (3 days), end of Ramadan (4 days), New Year (Muslim), Prophet's Birthday, Lailat al-Miraj (March/April)

Chronology

7th century AD Islam introduced. **early 16th century** Portuguese established trading contacts with Persian Gulf states. **18th century** Rise of trade and seafaring among Qawasim and Bani Yas, respectively in Ras al-Khaimah and Sharjah in north and Abu Dhabi and Dubai in desert of south. Emirates' current ruling families are descended from these peoples. **early 19th century** Britain signed treaties ('truces') with local rulers, ensuring that British shipping through the Gulf was free from 'pirate' attacks and bringing Emirates under British protection. **1892** Trucial Sheiks signed Exclusive Agreements with Britain, agreeing not to cede, sell, or mortgage territory to another power. **1952** Trucial Council established by seven sheikdoms of Abu Dhabi, Ajman, Dubai, Fujairah, Ras al Khaimah, Sharjah, and Umm al Qawain, with a view to later forming a federation. **1958** Large-scale exploitation of oil reserves led to rapid economic progress. **1968** Britain's announcement that it would remove its forces from the Persian Gulf by 1971 led to an abortive attempt to arrange federation between seven Trucial States and Bahrain and Qatar. **1971** Bahrain and Qatar ceded from the Federation of Arab Emirates, which was dissolved. Six Trucial States formed the United Arab Emirates, with the ruler of Abu Dhabi, Sheikh Zayed, as president. A provisional constitution was adopted. The UAE joined the Arab League and the United Nations (UN). **1972** Seventh state, Ras al Khaimah, joined the federation. **1976** Sheikh Zayed threatened to relinquish presidency unless progress towards centralization became more rapid. **1985** Diplomatic and economic links with the Soviet Union and China were established. **1987** Diplomatic relations with Egypt were restored. **1990** Maktum bin Rashid al-Maktum of Dubai was appointed prime minister. **1990–91** UAE opposed the Iraqi invasion of Kuwait, and UAE troops fought as part of the UN coalition. **1991** The Bank of Commerce and Credit International (BCCI), partly owned and controlled by Abu Dhabi's ruler Zayed bin Sultan al-Nahayan, collapsed at a cost to the UAE of $10 billion. **1992** There was a border dispute with Iran. **1994** Abu Dhabi agreed to pay BCCI creditors $1.8 billion.

United Kingdom of Great Britain and Northern Ireland

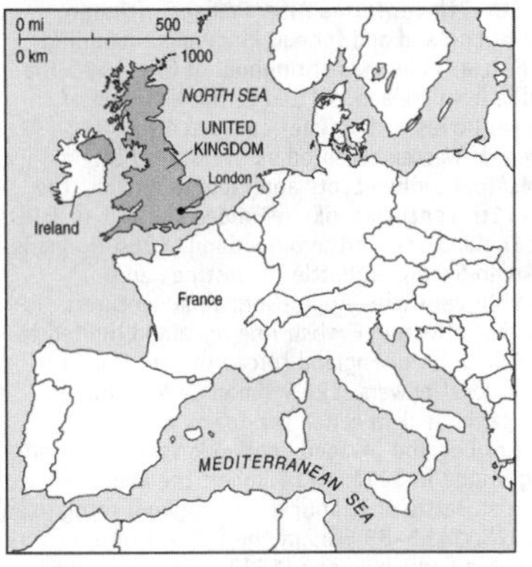

Area 244,100 sq km/ 94,247 sq mi **Capital** London **Major towns/ cities** Birmingham, Glasgow, Leeds, Sheffield, Liverpool, Manchester, Edinburgh, Bradford, Bristol, Coventry, Belfast, Newcastle upon Tyne, Cardiff **Territories** Anguilla, Bermuda, British Antarctic Territory, British Indian Ocean Territory, British Virgin Islands, Cayman Islands, Falkland Islands, Gibraltar, Montserrat, Pitcairn Islands, St Helena and Dependencies (Ascension, Tristan da Cunha), Turks and Caicos Islands; the Channel Islands and the Isle of Man are not part of the UK but are direct dependencies of the crown

Government

Head of state Queen Elizabeth II from 1952 **Head of government** Tony Blair from 1997 **Political system** liberal democracy **Armed forces** 213,800 (1997) **Conscription** military service is voluntary **Defence spend** (% GDP) 2.8 (1997) **Education spend** (% GNP) 5.4 (1996) **Health spend** (% GDP) 5.8 (1996) **Death penalty** abolished in 1998

Population and society

Population 58,744,000 (1999 est) **Population growth rate** 0.2% (1995–2000) **Ethnic groups** 81.5% English; 9.6% Scots; 2.4% Irish; 1.9% Welsh; 2% West Indian, Asian, and African **Religion** Church of England (established Church); other Protestant denominations, Roman Catholic, Muslim, Jewish, Hindu, Sikh **Life expectancy** 75 (men); 80 (women) (1995–2000) **Literacy rate** 99% (men); 99% (women) (1997 est) **Unemployment** 6.3% (1998)

Economy and resources

GDP (US$) 1,357.4 billion (1998) **GNP** (US$) 1,263.8 billion (1998) **GNP per capita (PPP)** (US$) 20,640 (1998) **Real GDP growth** (% change on previous year) 2.3 (1998) **Consumer price inflation** 2.6% (1998) **Resources** coal, limestone, crude petroleum, natural gas, tin, iron, salt, sand and gravel **Exports** industrial and electrical machinery, automatic data-processing equipment, motor vehicles, petroleum, chemicals, finished and semi-finished manufactured products, agricultural products and foodstuffs. Principal market: USA 13.3% (1998) **Imports** industrial and electrical machinery, motor vehicles, food and live animals, petroleum, automatic data processing equipment, consumer goods, textiles, paper, paper board. Principal source: USA 13.5% (1998)

▪ Tourist information

Time difference GMT +/– 0 **Currency** pound sterling (£) **Language** English, Welsh, Gaelic **Visa requirements** USA: visa not required **Chamber of commerce** Association of British Chambers of Commerce, 9 Tufton Street, London SW1P 3QB. Tel: (020) 7222 1555; fax: (020) 7799 2202 **Office hours** 0900/0930–1700/1730 Mon–Fri **Banking hours** 0930–1530/1630 Mon–Fri (some banks open Sat morning) **Airports** international airports: London (Heathrow, Gatwick, London City, Stansted, Luton), Birmingham, Manchester, Newcastle, Bristol, Cardiff, Norwich, Derby, Edinburgh, Glasgow, Leeds/Bradford, Liverpool, Southampton; 22 domestic airports; total passenger km: 157,614 million (1997 est) **Major ports** London, Grimsby, Southampton, Liverpool **Chief tourist attractions** London, with its many historic monumments, cathedrals, churches, palaces, parks, and museums; historic towns, including York, Bath, Edinburgh, Oxford, and Cambridge; the Lake District in the northwest; the mountains of North Wales; varied coastline includes sandy beaches, cliffs, and the fjord-like inlets of northwest Scotland **Major holidays** 1 January, 25–26 December; variable: Good Friday, Easter Monday (not Scotland), Early May, Late May and Summer (August) Bank Holidays; Northern Ireland also has 17 March, 29 December; Scotland has 2 January

Chronology

c. **400–200 BC** British Isles conquered by Celts. **55–54 BC** Romans led by Julius Caesar raided Britain. **AD 43–60** Romans conquered England and Wales, which formed the province of Britannia; Picts stopped them penetrating further north. **5th–7th centuries** After Romans withdrew, Anglo-Saxons overran most of England and formed kingdoms, including Wessex, Northumbria, and Mercia; Wales was stronghold of Celts. **500** The Scots, a Gaelic-speaking tribe from Ireland, settled in the kingdom of Dalriada (Argyll). **5th–6th centuries** British Isles converted to Christianity. **829** King Egbert of Wessex accepted as overlord of all England. ***c.* 843** Kenneth McAlpin unified Scots and Picts to become the first king of Scotland. **9th–11th centuries** Vikings raided the British Isles, conquering north and east England and northern Scotland. **1066** Normans led by William I defeated Anglo-Saxons at Battle of Hastings and conquered England. **12th–13th centuries** Anglo-Norman adventurers conquered much of Ireland, but effective English rule remained limited to area around Dublin. **1215** King John of England forced to sign Magna Carta, which placed limits on royal powers. **1265** Simon de Montfort summoned the first English parliament in which the towns were represented. **1284** Edward I of England invaded Scotland; Scots defeated English at Battle of Stirling Bridge in 1297. **1314** Robert the Bruce led Scots to victory over English at Battle of Bannockburn; England recognized Scottish independence in 1328. **1455–85** Wars of the Roses: House of York and House of Lancaster disputed English throne. **1513** Battle of Flodden: Scots defeated by English; James IV of Scotland killed. **1529** Henry VIII founded Church of England after break with Rome; Reformation effective in England and Wales, but not in Ireland. **1536–43** Acts of Union united Wales with England, with one law, one parliament, and one official language. **1541** Irish parliament recognized Henry VIII of England as king of Ireland. **1557** First Covenant established Protestant faith in Scotland. **1603** Union of crowns: James VI of Scotland became James I of England also. **1607** First successful English colony in Virginia marked the start of three centuries of overseas expansion. **1610** James I established plantation of Ulster in Northern Ireland with Protestant settlers from England and Scotland. **1642–52** English Civil War between king and Parliament, with Scottish intervention and Irish rebellion, resulted in victory for Parliament. **1649** Execution of Charles I; Oliver Cromwell appointed Lord Protector in 1653; monarchy restored in 1660. **1689** 'Glorious Revolution' confirmed power of Parliament; replacement of James II by William III resisted by Scottish Highlanders and Catholic Irish. **1707** Act of Union between England and Scotland created United Kingdom of Great Britain, governed by a single parliament. **1721–42** Cabinet government developed under Robert Walpole, in effect the first prime minister. **1745** 'The Forty-Five': rebellion of Scottish Highlanders in support of Jacobite pretender to throne; defeated 1746. *c.* 1760–1850 Industrial Revolution: Britain became the first industrial nation in the world. **1775–83** American Revolution: Britain lost 13 American colonies; empire continued to expand in Canada, India, and Australia. **1793–1815** Britain at war with revolutionary France, except for 1802–03. **1800** Act of Union created United Kingdom of Great Britain and Ireland, governed by a single parliament; effective 1801. **1832** Great Reform Act extended franchise; further extensions in 1867, 1884, 1918, and 1928. **1846** Repeal of Corn Laws reflected shift of power from landowners to industrialists. **1870** Home Rule Party formed to campaign for restoration of separate Irish parliament. **1880–90s** Rapid expansion of British Empire in Africa. **1906–14** Liberal governments introduced social reforms and curbed the power of the House of Lords. **1914–18** The UK played a leading part in World War I; the British Empire expanded in Middle East. **1919–21** The Anglo-Irish war ended with the secession of southern Ireland as the Irish Free State; Ulster remained within the United Kingdom of Great Britain and Northern Ireland with some powers devolved to a Northern Irish parliament. **1924** The first Labour government was led by Ramsay MacDonald. **1926** A general strike arose from a coal dispute. Equality of status was recognized between the UK and Dominions of the British Commonwealth. **1931** A National Government coalition was formed to face a growing economic crisis; unemployment reached 3 million. **1939–45** The UK played a leading part in World War II. **1945–51** The Labour government of Clement Attlee created the welfare state and nationalized major industries. **1947–71** Decolonization brought about the end of the British Empire. **1969** Start of the Troubles in Northern Ireland; the Northern Irish Parliament was suspended in 1972. **1973** The UK joined the European Economic Community. **1979–90** The Conservative government of Margaret Thatcher pursued radical free-market economic policies. **1982** Unemployment reached over 3 million. The Falklands War with Argentina over the disputed sovereignty of the Falkland Islands cost more than a thousand lives but ended with the UK retaining control of the islands. **1983** Coal pits were closed by the Conservative government and the miners went on strike. **1991** British troops took part in a US-led war against Iraq under a United Nations (UN) umbrella. Following the economic successes of the 1980s there was a period of severe economic recession and unemployment. **1993** A peace proposal for Northern Ireland, the Downing Street Declaration, was issued jointly with the Irish government. **1994** The IRA and Protestant paramilitary declared a ceasefire in Northern Ireland. **1996** The IRA renewed its bombing campaign in London. **1997** The Labour Party won a landslide victory in a general election; Tony Blair became prime minister. Blair launched a new Anglo-Irish peace initiative. Blair met with Sinn Fein leader Gerry Adams; all-party peace talks began in Northern Ireland. Scotland and Wales voted in favour of devolution. Princess Diana was killed in a car crash. **1998** A historic multiparty agreement (the 'Good Friday Agreement') was reached on the future of Northern Ireland; a peace plan was approved by referenda in Northern Ireland and the Irish Republic. The Ulster Unionist Party (UUP) leader, David Trimble, was elected first minister. **1999** The Scottish Parliament and the Welsh Assembly opened, with Labour the largest party in both. The IRA agreed to begin decommissioning discussions and a coalition government was established. In December, the British government announced that it would write off its third world debts. **2000** After it was revealed that there had been no arms handover by the IRA, the secretary of state for Northern Ireland suspended the Northern Ireland Assembly.

United States of America

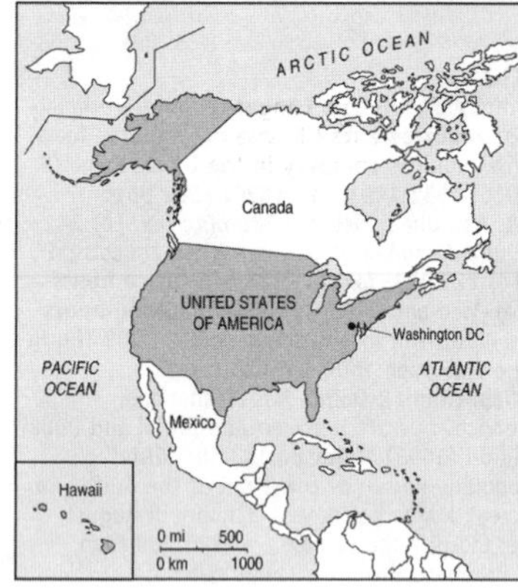

Area 9,372,615 sq km/ 3,618,766 sq mi
Capital Washington DC
Major towns/cities New York, Los Angeles, Chicago, Philadelphia, Detroit, San Francisco, Washington, Dallas, San Diego, San Antonio, Houston, Boston, Baltimore, Phoenix, Indianapolis, Memphis, Honolulu, San José
Territories the commonwealths of Puerto Rico and Northern Marianas; Guam, the US Virgin Islands, American Samoa, Wake Island, Midway Islands, and Johnston and Sand Islands

Government

Head of state and government Bill Clinton from 1993 **Political system** liberal democracy **Armed forces** 1,447,600 (1997) **Conscription** military service is voluntary **Defence spend** (% GDP) 3.4 (1997) **Education spend** (% GNP) 5.4 (1996) **Health spend** (% GDP) 6.3 (1996) **Death penalty** retained and used for ordinary crimes

Population and society

Population 276,219,000 (1999 est) **Population growth rate** 0.8% (1995–2000); 0.8% (2000–05) **Ethnic groups** approximately three-quarters of the population are of European origin, including 29% who trace their descent from Britain and Ireland, 8% from Germany, 5% from Italy, and 3% each from Scandinavia and Poland; 12% are African-Americans, 8% Hispanic, and 3% Asian and Pacific islander; African-Americans form 30% of the population of the states of the 'Deep South', namely Alabama, Georgia, Louisiana, Mississippi, and South Carolina **Religion** Christian 86.5% (Roman Catholic 26%, Baptist 19%, Methodist 8%, Lutheran 5%); Jewish 1.8%; Muslim 0.5%; Buddhist and Hindu less than 0.5% **Life expectancy** 73 (men); 80 (women) (1995–2000) **Literacy rate** 99% (men); 99% (women) (1995 est) **Unemployment** 4.5% (1998)

Economy and resources

GDP (US$) 8,210.6 billion (1998) **GNP** (US$) 7,921.3 billion (1998) **GNP per capita (PPP)** (US$) 29,340 (1998) **Real GDP growth** (% change on previous year) 3.5 (1998) **Consumer price inflation** 1.6% (1998) **Resources** coal, copper (world's second-largest producer), iron, bauxite, mercury, silver, gold, nickel, zinc (world's fifth-largest producer), tungsten, uranium, phosphate, petroleum, natural gas, timber **Exports** machinery, motor vehicles, agricultural products and foodstuffs, aircraft, weapons, chemicals, electronics. Principal market: Canada 23.3% (1998) **Imports** machinery and transport equipment, crude and partly refined petroleum, office machinery, textiles and clothing. Principal source: Canada 19.3% (1998)

▪ Tourist information

Time difference GMT -5-11 **Currency** US dollar **Language** English, Spanish **Visa requirements** UK: visa not required for a stay of up to 90 days **Embassy in the UK** 24 Grosvenor Square, London W1A 1AE, Tel: (020) 7499 9000; fax: (020) 7629 9124 **British embassy** 3100 Massachusetts Avenue, NW, Washington DC 20008. Tel: (202) 462 1340; fax: (202) 898 4255 **Chamber of commerce** 1615 H Street, NW, Washington DC 20062-0001. Tel: (202) 659 6000; fax: (202) 463 5836 **Office hours** 0900-1730 Mon-Fri **Banking hours** variable, but generally 0900-1500 Mon-Fri **Airports** international airports: Anchorage, Atlanta (Hartsfield), Baltimore (Baltimore/Washington), Boston (Logan), Chicago (O'Hare), Cincinnati (Northern Kentucky), Cleveland (Hopkins), Dallas/Fort Worth, Denver (Stapleton), Detroit Metropolitan, Honolulu, Houston Intercontinental, Kansas City, Las Vegas (McCarran), Los Angeles, Miami, Minneapolis/St Paul, New Orleans, New York (John F Kennedy, La Guardia, Newark), Orlando, Philadelphia, Phoenix (Sky Harbor), Pittsburgh, Portland, St Louis (Lambert), Salt Lake City, San Diego (Lindbergh Field), San Francisco, Seattle-Tacoma, Tampa, Washington DC (Dulles, National); about 800 domestic airports; total passenger km: 964,430 million (1997 est) **Chief tourist attractions** many cities of interest, including New York, with its skyscrapers, Washington DC, with its monuments, Boston, San Francisco, and New Orleans; enormous diversity of geographical features – the Rocky

United States of America: States

State	Nickname(s)	Abbreviation	Capital	Area sq km	Area sq mi	Population (1998)	Joined the union
Alabama	Heart of Dixie/Camellia State	AL	Montgomery	134,700	51,994	4,352,000	1819
Alaska	Mainland State/The Last Frontier	AK	Juneau	1,531,100	591,005	614,000	1959
Arizona	Grand Canyon State/Apache State	AZ	Phoenix	294,100	113,523	4,669,000	1912
Arkansas	Bear State/Land of Opportunity	AR	Little Rock	137,800	53,191	2,538,000	1836
California	Golden State	CA	Sacramento	411,100	158,685	32,667,000	1850
Colorado	Centennial State	CO	Denver	269,700	104,104	3,971,000	1876
Connecticut	Constitution State/Nutmeg State	CT	Hartford	13,000	5018	3,274,000	1788
Delaware	First State/Diamond State	DE	Dover	5,300	2,046	744,000	1787
Florida	Sunshine State/Everglade State	FL	Tallahassee	152,000	58,672	14,916,000	1845
Georgia	Empire State of the South/ Peach State	GA	Atlanta	152,600	58,904	7,642,000	1788
Hawaii	Aloha State	HI	Honolulu	16,800	6,485	1,193,000	1959
Idaho	Gem State	ID	Boise	216,500	83,569	1,229,000	1890
Illinois	Inland Empire/Prairie State/ Land of Lincoln	IL	Springfield	146,100	56,395	12,045,000	1818
Indiana	Hoosier State	IN	Indianapolis	93,700	36,168	5,899,000	1816
Iowa	Hawkeye State/Corn State	IA	Des Moines	145,800	56,279	2,862,000	1846
Kansas	Sunflower State/Jayhawker State	KS	Topeka	213,200	82,295	2,629,000	1861
Kentucky	Bluegrass State	KY	Frankfort	104,700	40,414	3,936,000	1792
Louisiana	Pelican State/Sugar State/ Creole State	LA	Baton Rouge	135,900	52,457	4,369,000	1792
Maine	Pine Tree State	ME	Augusta	86,200	33,273	1,244,000	1812
Maryland	Old Line State/Free State	MD	Annapolis	31,600	12,198	5,135,000	1788
Massachusetts	Bay State/Old Colony	MA	Boston	21,500	8,299	6,147,000	1788
Michigan	Great Lakes State/Wolverine State	MI	Lansing	151,600	58,518	9,817,000	1837
Minnesota	North Star State/Gopher State	MN	St Paul	218,700	84,418	4,725,000	1858
Mississippi	Magnolia State	MS	Jackson	123,600	47,710	2,752,000	1817
Missouri	Show Me State/Bullion State	MO	Jefferson City	180,600	69,712	5,439,000	1821
Montana	Treasure State/Big Sky Country	MT	Helena	381,200	147,143	880,000	1889
Nebraska	Cornhusker State/Beef State	NE	Lincoln	200,400	77,354	1,663,000	1867
Nevada	Sagebrush State/Silver State/ Battleborn State	NV	Carson City	286,400	110,550	1,747,000	1864
New Hampshire	Granite State	NH	Concord	24,000	9,264	1,185,000	1788
New Jersey	Garden State	NJ	Trenton	20,200	7,797	8,115,000	1787
New Mexico	Land of Enchantment/ Sunshine State	NM	Santa Fé	315,000	121,590	1,737,000	1912
New York	Empire State	NY	Albany	127,200	49,099	18,175,000	1788
North Carolina	Tar Heel State/Old North State	NC	Raleigh	136,400	52,650	7,546,000	1789
North Dakota	Peace Garden State	ND	Bismarck	183,100	70,677	638,000	1889
Ohio	Buckeye State	OH	Columbus	107,100	41,341	11,209,000	1803
Oklahoma	Sooner State	OK	Oklahoma City	181,100	69,905	3,347,000	1907
Oregon	Beaver State/Sunset State	OR	Salem	251,500	97,079	3,282,000	1859
Pennsylvania	Keystone State	PA	Harrisburg	117,400	45,316	12,001,000	1787
Rhode Island	Little Rhody/Ocean State	RI	Providence	3,100	1,197	988,000	1790
South Carolina	Palmetto State	SC	Columbia	80,600	31,112	3,836,000	1788
South Dakota	Coyote State/Mount Rushmore State	SD	Pierre	199,800	77,123	738,000	1889
Tennessee	Volunteer State	TN	Nashville	109,200	42,151	5,431,000	1796
Texas	Lone Star State	TX	Austin	691,200	266,803	19,760,000	1845
Utah	Beehive State/Mormon State	UT	Salt Lake City	219,900	84,881	2,100,000	1896
Vermont	Green Mountain State	VT	Montpelier	24,900	9,611	591,000	1791
Virginia	Old Dominion State/Mother of Presidents	VA	Richmond	105,600	40,762	6,791,000	1788
Washington	Evergreen State/Chinook State	WA	Olympia	176,700	68,206	5,689,000	1889
West Virginia	Mountain State/Panhandle State	WV	Charleston	62,900	24,279	1,811,000	1863
Wisconsin	Badger State/America's Dairyland	WI	Madison	145,500	56,163	5,224,000	1848
Wyoming	Equality State	WY	Cheyenne	253,400	97,812	481,000	1890
District of Columbia (Federal District)	–	DC	Washington	180	69	523,000	established by Act of Congress 1790-91

Mountains, the Everglades of Florida, the Grand Canyon; hundreds of national parks, historical parks, and reserves, including Redwood, Yosemite, and Death Valley (all in California); Disneyland (California) and Walt Disney World (Florida) **Major holidays** 1 January, 4 July, 12 October (not all states), 11 November, 25 December; variable: Martin Luther King's birthday (January, not all states), George Washington's birthday (February), Memorial (May), Labor (first Mon in September), Columbus (October), Thanksgiving (last Thu in November); much local variation

Chronology

***c.* 15,000 BC** First evidence of human occupation in North America. **1513** Ponce de Léon of Spain explored Florida in search of the Fountain of Youth; Francisco Coronado explored southwest region of North America 1540–42. **1565** Spanish founded St Augustine (Florida), the first permanent European settlement in North America. **1585** Sir Walter Raleigh tried to establish an English colony on Roanoke Island in what he called Virginia. **1607** English colonists founded Jamestown, Virginia, and began growing tobacco. **1620** The Pilgrim Fathers founded Plymouth Colony (near Cape Cod); other English Puritans followed them to New England. **1624** Dutch formed colony of New Netherlands; Swedes formed New Sweden in 1638; both taken by England in 1664. **17th–18th centuries** Millions of Africans were sold into slavery on American cotton and tobacco plantations. **1733** Georgia became thirteenth British colony on east coast. **1763** British victory over France in Seven Years' War secured territory as far west as Mississippi River. **1765** British first attempted to levy tax in American colonies with Stamp Act; protest forced repeal in 1767. **1773** 'Boston Tea Party': colonists boarded ships and threw cargoes of tea into sea in protest at import duty. **1774** British closed Boston harbour and billeted troops in Massachusetts; colonists formed First Continental Congress. **1775** American Revolution: colonies raised Continental Army led by George Washington to fight against British rule. **1776** American colonies declared independence; France and Spain supported them in a war with Britain. **1781** Americans defeated British at Battle of Yorktown; rebel states formed loose confederation, codified in Articles of Confederation. **1783** Treaty of Paris: Britain accepted loss of colonies. **1787** 'Founding Fathers' devised new constitution for United States of America. **1789** Washington elected first president of USA. **1791** Bill of Rights guaranteed individual freedom. **1803** Louisiana Purchase: France sold former Spanish lands between Mississippi River and Rocky Mountains to USA. **1812–14** War with Britain arose from dispute over blockade rights during Napoleonic Wars. **1819** USA bought Florida from Spain. **19th century** Mass immigration from Europe; settlers moved westwards, crushing Indian resistance and claiming 'manifest destiny' of USA to control North America. By end of century, the number of states in the Union had increased from 17 to 45. **1846–48** Mexican War: Mexico ceded vast territory to USA. **1854** Kansas–Nebraska Act heightened controversy over slavery in southern states; abolitionists formed Republican Party. **1860** Abraham Lincoln (Republican) elected president. **1861** Civil war broke out after 11 southern states, wishing to retain slavery, seceded from USA and formed the Confederate States of America under Jefferson Davis. **1865** USA defeated Confederacy; slavery abolished; President Lincoln assassinated. **1867** Alaska bought from Russia. **1869** Railway linked east and west coasts; rapid growth of industry and agriculture 1870–1920 made USA very rich. **1876** Sioux Indians defeated US troops at Little Big Horn; Indians finally defeated at Wounded Knee in 1890. **1898** Spanish–American War: USA gained Puerto Rico and Guam; also Philippines (until 1946) and Cuba (until 1901); USA annexed Hawaii. **1917–18** USA intervened in World War I; President Woodrow Wilson took leading part in peace negotiations in 1919, but USA rejected membership of League of Nations. **1920** Women received right to vote; sale of alcohol prohibited, until 1933. **1924** American Indians made citizens of USA by Congress. **1929** 'Wall Street Crash': stock market collapse led to Great Depression with 13 million unemployed by 1933. **1933** President Franklin Roosevelt launched the 'New Deal' with public works to rescue the economy. **1941** Japanese attacked US fleet at Pearl Harbor, Hawaii; USA declared war on Japan; Germany declared war on USA, which henceforth played a leading part in World War II. **1945** USA ended war in Pacific by dropping two atomic bombs on Hiroshima and Nagasaki, Japan. **1947** 'Truman Doctrine' pledged US aid for nations threatened by communism; start of Cold War between USA and USSR. **1950–53** US forces engaged in Korean War. **1954** Racial segregation in schools deemed unconstitutional; start of campaign to secure civil rights for black Americans. **1962** Cuban missile crisis: USA forced USSR to withdraw nuclear weapons from Cuba. **1963** President Kennedy assassinated. **1964–68** President Lyndon Johnson introduced the 'Great Society' programme of civil-rights and welfare measures. **1961–75** USA involved in Vietnam War. **1969** US astronaut Neil Armstrong was first person on the Moon. **1974** 'Watergate' scandal: evidence of domestic political espionage compelled President Richard Nixon to resign. **1979–80** Iran held US diplomats hostage, humiliating President Jimmy Carter. **1981–89** Tax-cutting policies of President Ronald Reagan led to large federal budget deficit. **1986** 'Irangate' scandal: secret US arms sales to Iran illegally funded Contra guerrillas in Nicaragua. **1990** President George Bush declared an end to the Cold War. **1991** USA played leading part in expelling Iraqi forces from Kuwait in the Gulf War. **1992** Democrat Bill Clinton won presidential elections, beginning his term of office in 1993. **1996** US launched missile attacks on Iraq in response to Hussein's incursions into Kurdish safe havens. **1998** The House of Representatives voted to impeach Clinton on the grounds of perjury and obstruction of justice, due to his misleading the public about his relationship with a White House intern. Clinton's national approval rating remained high, and he was acquitted in 1999. In response to bombings of US embassies in Tanzania and Kenya by an Islamic group, the USA bombed suspected sites in Afghanistan and Sudan. The USA also led air strikes against Iraq following the expulsion of UN weapons inspectors by Saddam Hussein. **1999** US forces led NATO air strikes against Yugoslavia in protest against Serb violence against ethnic Albanians in Kosovo.

Uruguay Oriental Republic of

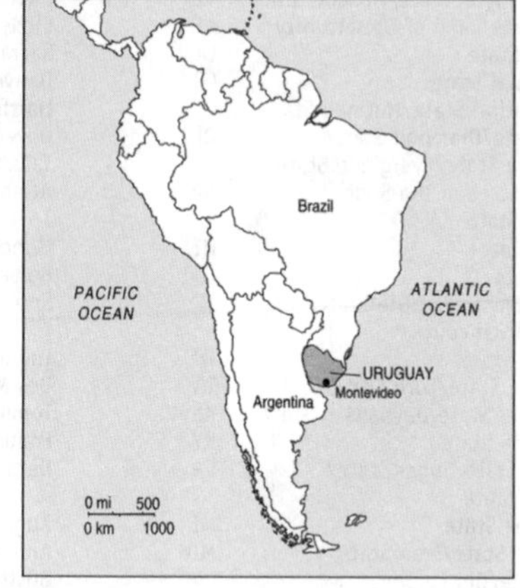

National name *República Oriental del Uruguay* **Area** 176,200 sq km/68,030 sq mi **Capital** Montevideo **Major towns/cities** Salto, Paysandú, Las Piedras

Government

Head of state and government Jorge Batlle from 2000 **Political system** liberal democracy **Armed forces** 25,600 (1997) **Conscription** military service is voluntary **Defence spend** (% GDP) 2.3 (1997) **Education spend** (% GNP) 3.3 (1996) **Health spend** (% GDP) 1.9 (1995) **Death penalty** abolished in 1907

Population and society

Population 3,313,000 (1999 est) **Population growth rate** 0.7% (1995–2000) **Ethnic groups** predominantly of European descent: about 54% Spanish, 22% Italian, with minorities from other European countries **Religion** mainly Roman Catholic **Life expectancy** 71 (men); 78 (women) (1995–2000) **Literacy rate** 97% (men); 98% (women) (1997 est) **Unemployment** 10.1% (1998 est)

Economy and resources

GDP (US$) 20.15 billion (1998) **GNP** (US$) 20.3 billion (1998) **GNP per capita (PPP)** (US$) 9,480 (1998) **Real GDP growth** (% change on previous year) 3 (1998) **Consumer price inflation** 10.8% (1998) **Foreign debt** (US$) 6.6 billion (1997) **Resources** small-scale extraction of building materials, industrial minerals, semi-precious stones; gold deposits are being developed **Exports** textiles, meat (chiefly beef), live animals and by-products (mainly hides and leather products), cereals, footwear. Principal market: Brazil 34.7% (1998) **Imports** machinery and appliances, transport equipment, chemical products, petroleum and petroleum products, agricultural products. Principal source: Brazil 28.5% (1998)

▪ Tourist information

Time difference GMT –3 **Currency** Uruguayan peso **Language** Spanish (official) **Visa requirements** UK: visa not required. USA: visa not required **Embassy in the UK** 2nd Floor, 140 Brompton Road, London SW3 1HY. Tel: (020) 7584 8192; fax: (020) 7581 9585 **British embassy** PO Box 16024, Calle Marco Bruto 1073, 1130 Montevideo. Tel: (2) 623 630; fax: (2) 627 815 **Chamber of commerce** Cámara Nacional de Comercio, Edificio de la Bolsa de Comercio, Misiones 1400, Casilla 1000, 11000 Montevideo. Tel: (2) 961 277; fax: (2) 961 243 **Office hours** 0830–1200 and 1430–1830/1900 Mon–Fri **Banking hours** 1330–1730 Mon–Fri (summer); 1300–1700 Mon–Fri (winter) **Airports** international airport: Montevideo (Carrasco); seven domestic airports; total passenger km: 636 million (1995) **Chief tourist attractions** sandy beaches; forests; tropical swamps on the coast;

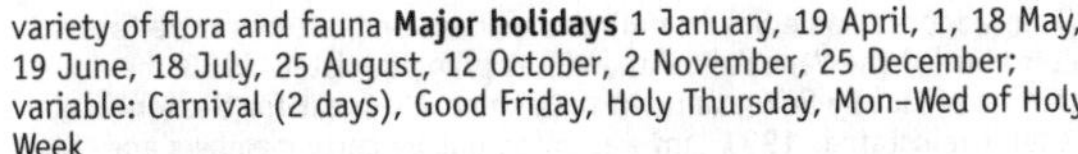

variety of flora and fauna **Major holidays** 1 January, 19 April, 1, 18 May, 19 June, 18 July, 25 August, 12 October, 2 November, 25 December; variable: Carnival (2 days), Good Friday, Holy Thursday, Mon–Wed of Holy Week

Chronology

1516 Río de la Plata visited by Spanish navigator Juan Diaz de Solis, who was killed by native Charrua Amerindians. This discouraged European settlement for more than a century. **1680** Portuguese from Brazil founded Nova Colonia do Sacramento on Río de la Plata estuary. **1726** Spanish established fortress at Montevideo and wrested control over Uruguay from Portugal, with much of the Amerindian population being killed. **1776** Became part of Viceroyalty of La Plata, with capital at Buenos Aires. **1808** With Spanish monarchy overthrown by Napoleon Bonaparte, La Plata Viceroyalty became autonomous, but Montevideo remained loyal to Spanish Crown and rebelled against Buenos Aires control. **1815** Dictator José Gervasio Artigas overthrew Spanish and Buenos Aires control. **1820** Artigas ousted by Brazil, which disputed control of Uruguay with Argentina. **1825** Independence declared after fight led by Juan Antonio Lavalleja. **1828** Independence recognized by country's neighbours. **1836** Civil war between Reds and Whites, after which Colorado and Blanco parties were named. **1840** Merino sheep introduced by British traders, who later established meat processing factories for export trade. **1865–70** Fought successfully alongside Argentina and Brazil in war against Paraguay. **1903** After period of military rule, José Battle y Ordonez, a progressive from centre-left Colorado Party, became president. As president 1903–07 and 1911–15, he gave women the franchise and created an advanced welfare state as a successful ranching economy developed. **1930** First constitution adopted, but period of military dictatorship followed during Depression period. **1958** After 93 years out of power, the right-of-centre Blanco Party returned to power. **1967** The Colorado Party were in power, with Jorge Pacheco Areco as president. A period of labour unrest and urban guerrilla activity by left-wing Tupamaros. **1972** Juan María Bordaberry Arocena of the Colorado Party became president. **1973** Parliament dissolved and Bordaberry shared power with military dictatorship, which crushed Tupamaros and banned left-wing groups. **1976** Bordaberry deposed by army; Aparicio Méndez Manfredini became president. **1981** Gen Grigorio Alvárez Armellino became new military ruler. **1984** Violent antigovernment protests after ten years of repressive rule and deteriorating economy. **1985** Agreement reached between army and political leaders for return to constitutional government and freeing of political prisoners. **1986** Government of national accord established under President Sanguinetti. **1992** The public voted against privatization in a national referendum. **2000** Jorge Batlle, of the Colorado Party, was elected president.

Uzbekistan Republic of

National name *Ozbekistan Respublikasy* **Area** 447,400 sq km/ 172,741 sq mi **Capital** Tashkent **Major towns/ cities** Samarkand, Bukhara, Namangan, Andizhan

Government

Head of state Islam Karimov from 1990 **Head of government** Otkir Sultonov from 1995 **Political system** authoritarian nationalist **Armed forces** 70,000 (1997) **Conscription** military service is compulsory for 18 months **Defence spend** (% GDP) 3.9 (1997) **Education spend** (% GNP) 8.1 (1996) **Health spend** (% GDP) 3.5 (1990–95) **Death penalty** retained and used for ordinary crimes

Population and society

Population 23,941,000 (1999 est) **Population growth rate** 1.6% (1995–2000) **Ethnic groups** 71% Uzbek, 8% ethnic Russian, 4% Tajik, 3% Kazakh, 2% Tatar **Religion** Sunni Muslim **Life expectancy** 64 (men); 71 (women) (1995–2000) **Literacy rate** 98% (men); 96% (women) (1997 est) **Unemployment** 0.4% (officially registered 1997; true level believed to be considerably higher)

Economy and resources

GDP (US$) 14.2 billion (1998) **GNP** (US$) 20.9 billion (1998) **GNP per capita (PPP)** (US$) 2,900 (1998) **Real GDP growth** (% change on previous year) 1 (1998) **Consumer price inflation** 17.8% (1998) **Foreign debt** (US$) 2.76 billion (1997) **Resources** petroleum, natural gas, coal, gold (world's seventh-largest producer), silver, uranium (world's fourth-largest producer), copper, lead, zinc, tungsten **Exports** cotton fibre, textiles, machinery, food and energy products, gold. Principal market: Russia 14.9% (1998) **Imports** machinery, light industrial goods, food and raw materials. Principal source: Russia 16% (1998)

▪ Tourist information

Time difference GMT +5 **Currency** som **Language** Uzbek, a Turkic language **Visa requirements** UK: visa required. USA: visa required **Embassy in the UK** 72 Wigmore Street, London W1H 9DL. Tel: (020) 7935 1899; fax: (020) 7935 9554 **British embassy** 6 Ulitsa Murtazayeva, Tashkent 700084. Tel: (3712) 345 652; fax: (873) 340 465 **Chamber of commerce** Tashkent International Business Centre, Ulitsa Pushkina 17, Tashkent. Tel: (3712) 323 231; fax: (3712) 334 414 **Office hours** 0900–1700 Mon–Fri **Banking hours** 0900–1700 Mon–Fri **Airports** international airport: Tashkent; eight domestic airports; total passenger km: 4,855 million (1995) **Chief tourist attractions** over 4,000 historical monuments, largely associated with the ancient 'Silk Route'; many historical sites and cities, including Samarkand (Tamerlane's capital), Bukhara, and Khiva **Major holidays** 1–2 January, 8, 21 March, 1 September, 8 December

Chronology

6th century BC Part of the Persian Empire of Cyrus the Great. **4th century BC** Part of the empire of Alexander the Great of Macedonia. **1st century BC** Samarkand (Maracanda) developed as transit point on strategic Silk Road trading route between China and Europe. **7th century** City of Tashkent founded; spread of Islam. **12th century** Tashkent taken by Turks; Khorezem (Khiva), in northwest, became centre of large Central Asian polity, stretching from Caspian Sea to Samarkand in the east. **13th–14th centuries** Conquered by Genghis Khan and became part of Mongol Empire, with Samarkand serving as capital for Tamerlane. **18th–19th centuries** Dominated by independent emirates and khanates (chiefdoms) of Bukhara in southwest, Kokand in east, and Samarkand in centre. **1865–67** Tashkent was taken by Russia and made capital of Governor-Generalship of Turkestan. **1868–76** Tsarist Russia annexed emirate of Bukhara (1868); and khanates of Samarkand (1868), Khiva (1873), and Kokand (1876). **1917** Following Bolshevik revolution in Russia, Tashkent soviet ('people's council') established, which deposed the emir of Bukhara and other khans in 1920. **1918–22** Mosques closed and Muslim clergy persecuted as part of secularization drive by new communist rulers, despite nationalist guerrilla (basmachi) resistance. **1921** Part of Turkestan Soviet Socialist Autonomous Republic. **1925** Became constituent republic of USSR. **1930s** Skilled ethnic Russians immigrated into urban centres as industries developed. **1944** About 160,000 Meskhetian Turks forcibly transported from their native Georgia to Uzbekistan by Soviet dictator Joseph Stalin. **1950s–80s** Major irrigation projects stimulated cotton production, but led to desiccation of Aral Sea. **late 1980s** Upsurge in Islamic consciousness stimulated by *glasnost* initiative of Soviet Union's reformist leader Mikhail Gorbachev. **1989** Birlik ('Unity'), nationalist movement, formed. Violent attacks on Meskhetian and other minority communities in Ferghana Valley. **1990** Economic and political sovereignty was declared by the increasingly nationalist UCP, led by Islam Karimov, who became president. **1991** An attempted anti-Gorbachev coup by conservatives in Moscow was initially supported by President Karimov. Independence was declared. Uzbekistan joined the new Commonwealth of Independent States (CIS); Karimov was re-elected president. **1992** There were violent food riots in Tashkent. Uzbekistan joined the Economic Cooperation Organization and the United Nations (UN). A new constitution was adopted. **1993** There was a crackdown on Islamic fundamentalists as the economy deteriorated. **1994** Economic, military, and social union was forged with Kazakhstan and Kyrgyzstan, and an economic integration treaty was signed with Russia. Links with Turkey were strengthened and foreign inward investment encouraged. **1995** The ruling People's Democratic Party of Uzbekistan (PDP) (formerly UCP) won a general election, from which the opposition was banned from participating, and Otkir Sultonov was appointed prime minister. Karimov's tenure as president was extended for a further five-year term by national referendum. **1996** An agreement was made with Kazakhstan and Kyrgyzstan to create a single economic market. **1998** A treaty of eternal friendship and deepening economic cooperation was signed with Kazakhstan. **1999** Uzbekistan threatened to end participation in a regional security treaty, accusing Russia of seeking to integrate the former Soviet republics into a superstate.

Vanuatu Republic of

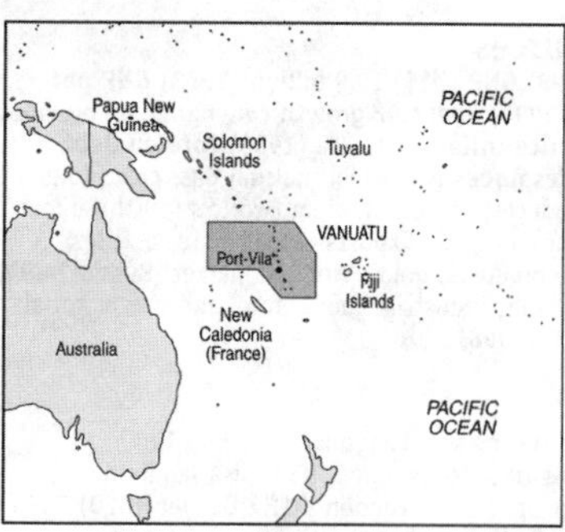

National name *Ripablik blong Vanuatu* **Area** 14,800 sq km/5,714 sq mi **Capital** (and chief port) Port-Vila (on Efate) **Major towns/cities** Luganville (on Espíritu Santo)

Government

Head of state John Bernard Bani from 1999 **Head of government** Donald Kalpokas from 1998 **Political system** liberal democracy **Armed forces** no standing defence force; paramilitary force of around 300; police naval service of around 50 (1995) **Education spend** (% GNP) 4.9 (1996) **Health spend** (% GDP) 2.9 (1990) **Death penalty** laws do not provide for the death penalty for any crime

Population and society

Population 186,000 (1999 est) **Population growth rate** 2.4% (1995–2000) **Ethnic groups** 95% Melanesian, 3% European or mixed European, 2% Vietnamese, Chinese, or other Pacific islanders **Religion** Christian 80%, animist **Life expectancy** 66 (men); 70 (women) (1995–2000) **Literacy rate** 54% (men); 23% (women) (1995 est)

Economy and resources

GDP (US$) 252 million (1998 est) **GNP** (US$) 231 million (1998) **GNP per capita (PPP)** (US$) 3,160 (1998 est) **Real GDP growth** (% change on previous year) 2.5 (1998) **Consumer price inflation** 3% (1998) **Foreign debt** (US$) 48 million (1997) **Resources** manganese; gold, copper, and large deposits of petroleum have been discovered but have hitherto remained unexploited **Exports** copra, beef, timber, cocoa, shells. Principal market: Japan 32.1% (1997) **Imports** machinery and transport equipment, food and live animals, basic manufactures, miscellaneous manufactured articles, mineral fuels, chemicals, beverages, tobacco. Principal source: Japan 52.6% (1997)

▪ Tourist information

Time difference GMT +11 **Currency** vatu **Language** Bislama 82%, English, French (all official) **Visa requirements** UK: visa not required. USA: visa not required **Embassy in the UK** Vanuatu has no diplomatic representation in the UK; the UK Department of Trade and Industry has a Pacific Islands Desk. Tel: (020) 7215 4985; fax: (020) 7215 4398 **British embassy** British High Commission, PO Box 567, KPMG House, rue Pasteur, Port-Vila. Tel: (678) 23100; fax: (678) 23651 **Chamber of commerce** PO Box 189, Port-Vila. Tel/fax: (678) 23255 **Office hours** 0730–1130 and 1330–1630 Mon–Fri **Banking hours** generally 0830–1500 Mon–Fri (some banks close for lunch at midday) **Airports** international airports: Port-Vila (Banerfield); 28 domestic airports and airstrips; total passenger km: 146 million (1995) **Major ports** Santo **Chief tourist attractions** unspoilt landscape **Major holidays** 1 January, 5 March, 1 May, 30 July 15 August, 25–26 December; variable: Ascension, Good Friday, Easter Monday, Constitution (October), Unity (November)

Chronology

1606 First visited by Portuguese navigator Pedro Fernandez de Queiras, who named the islands Espíritu Santo. **1774** Visited by British navigator Capt James Cook, who named them the New Hebrides, after the Scottish islands. **1830s** European merchants attracted to islands by sandalwood trade. Christian missionaries arrived, but many were attacked by the indigenous Melanesians who, in turn, were ravaged by exposure to European diseases. **later 19th century** Britain and France disputed control; islanders were shipped to Australia, the Fiji Islands, Samoa, and New Caledonia to work as plantation labourers. **1906** The islands were jointly administered by France and Britain as the Condominium of the New Hebrides. **1963** Indigenous Na-Griamel (NG) political grouping formed on Espíritu Santo to campaign against European acquisition of more than a third of the land area. **1975** A representative assembly was established following pressure from the VP, formed in 1972 by English-speaking Melanesian Protestants. **1978** A government of national unity was formed, with Father Gerard Leymang as chief minister. **1980** A revolt on the island of Espíritu Santo by French settlers and pro-NG plantation workers delayed independence but it was achieved within the Commonwealth, with George Kalkoa (adopted name Sokomanu) as president and left-of-centre Father Walter Lini (of the Vanua'ahu Pati, VP) as prime minister. **1988** The dismissal of Lini by Sokomanu led to Sokomanu's arrest for treason. Lini was later reinstated. **1991** Lini was voted out by party members and replaced by Donald Kalpokas. A general election produced a coalition government of the Francophone Union of Moderate Parties (UMP) and Lini's new National United Party (NUP) under Maxime Carlot Korman. **1993** A cyclone caused extensive damage. **1995** The governing UMP–NUP coalition won a general election, but Serge Vohor of the VP-dominated Unity Front became prime minister in place of Carlot Korman. **1996** The VP, led by Donald Kalpokas, joined the governing coalition. **1997** Prime Minister Vohor formed a new coalition. The legislature was dissolved and new elections called after a no-confidence motion against Vohor. **1998** A two-week state of emergency followed rioting in the capital. Donald Kalpokas was elected prime minister after an early election, heading a VP–NUP coalition. **1999** John Bernard Bani elected president.

Vatican City State

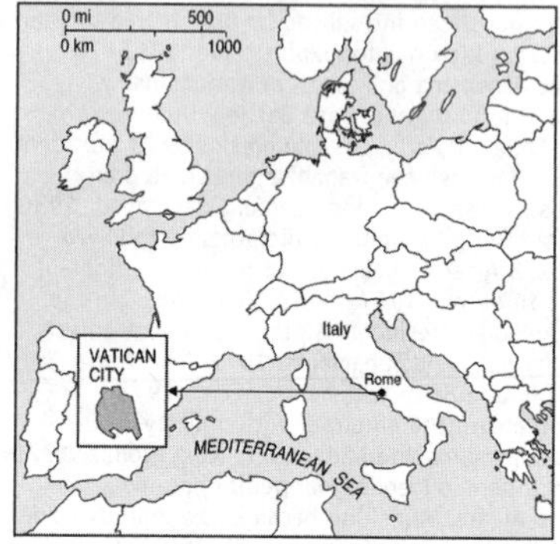

National name *Stato della Città del Vaticano* **Area** 0.4 sq km/0.2 sq mi

Government

Head of state John Paul II from 1978 **Head of government** Cardinal Sebastiano Baggio **Political system** theocratic **Death penalty** abolished in 1969

Population and society

Population 1,000 (1999 est) **Religion** Roman Catholic **Life expectancy** see Italy **Literacy rate** see Italy

Economy and resources

GDP see Italy **GNP** (US$) see Italy **GNP per capita (PPP)** see Italy **Real GDP growth** (% change on previous year) see Italy

▪ Tourist information

Time difference GMT +1 **Currency** Vatican City lira; Italian lira **Language** Latin (official), Italian **Visa requirements** see Italy. There is free access to certain areas, including St Peter's Church and Square, the Vatican Museum, and Vatican Gardens; special permission is required to visit all other areas **Embassy in the UK** Apostolic Nunciature, 54 Parkside, London SW19 5NE. Tel: (020) 8946 1410; fax: (020) 8947 2494 **British embassy** Via Condotti 91, 00187 Rome. Tel: (6) 678 9462; fax: (6) 994 0684 **Chamber of commerce** Prefecture of the Economic Affairs of the Holy See, Palazzo delle Congregazioni, Largo del Colonnato 3, 00193 Rome. Tel: (6) 6988 4263; fax: (6) 6988 5011 **Airports** international airports: one heliport serves visiting heads of state and Vatican officials; the closest international airport is Rome (see Italy) **Chief tourist attractions** St Peter's Church; St Peter's Square; Vatican Museum; the Pope's Sunday blessing **Major holidays** see Italy

Chronology

AD 64 Death of St Peter, a Christian martyr who, by legend, was killed in Rome and became regarded as the first bishop of Rome. The Pope, as head of the Roman Catholic Church, is viewed as the spiritual descendent of St Peter. **756** The Pope became temporal ruler of the Papal States, which stretched across central Italy, centred around Rome. **11th–13th centuries** Under Gregory VII and Innocent III the papacy enjoyed its greatest temporal power. **1377** After seven decades in which the papacy was based in Avignon (France), Rome once again became the headquarters for the Pope, with the Vatican Palace becoming the official residence. **1860** Umbria, Marche, and much of Emilia Romagna which, along with Lazio formed the Papal States, were annexed by the new unified Italian state. **1870** First Vatican Council defined as a matter of faith the absolute primacy of the Pope and the infallibility of his pronouncements on 'matters of faith and morals'. **1870–71** French forces, which had been protecting the Pope, were withdrawn, allowing Italian nationalist forces to capture Rome, which became the capital of Italy; Pope Pius IX retreated into the Vatican Palace, from which no Pope was to emerge until 1929. **1929** The Lateran Agreement, signed by the Italian fascist leader Benito Mussolini and Pope Pius XI, restored full sovereign jurisdiction over the Vatican City State to the bishopric of Rome (Holy See) and declared the new state to be a neutral and inviolable territory. **1947** A new Italian constitution confirmed the sovereignty of the Vatican City State. **1962** The Second Vatican Council was called by Pope John XXIII. **1978** John Paul II became the first non-Italian pope for more than 400 years. **1985** A new concordat was signed under which Roman Catholicism ceased to be Italy's state religion. **1992** Relations with East European states were restored.

Venezuela Republic of

National name *República de Venezuela* **Area** 912,100 sq km/ 352,161 sq mi **Capital** Caracas **Major towns/ cities** Maracaibo, Maracay, Barquisimeto, Valencia, Ciudad Guayana, San Cristobál

Government

Head of state and government Hugo Chávez Frías from 1998 **Political system** liberal democracy **Armed forces** 56,000 (1997) **Conscription** military service is by selective conscription for 30 months **Defence spend** (% GDP) 1.1 (1997) **Education spend** (% GNP) 5.2 (1996) **Health spend** (% GDP) 1 (1995) **Death penalty** abolished in 1863

Population and society

Population 23,706,000 (1999 est) **Population growth rate** 2.0% (1995–2000); 1.8% (2000–05) **Ethnic groups** 67% mestizos (of Spanish-American and American-Indian descent), 21% Europeans, 10% Africans, 2% Indians **Religion** Roman Catholic **Life expectancy** 70 (men); 76 (women) (1995–2000) **Literacy rate** 93% (men); 92% (women) (1997 est) **Unemployment** 12.8% (1998 est)

Economy and resources

GDP (US$) 105.7 billion (1998) **GNP** (US$) 81.3 billion (1998) **GNP per capita (PPP)** (US$) 8,190 (1998) **Real GDP growth** (% change on previous year) –0.9 (1998) **Consumer price inflation** 35.8% (1998 est) **Foreign debt** (US$) 21.6 billion (1997) **Resources** petroleum, natural gas, aluminium, iron ore, coal, diamonds, gold, zinc, copper, silver, lead, phosphates, manganese, titanium **Exports** petroleum and petroleum products, metals (mainly aluminium and iron ore), natural gas, chemicals, basic manufactures, motor vehicles and parts. Principal market: USA 56.7% (1997) **Imports** machinery and transport equipment, chemicals, food and live animals, basic manufactures, crude materials. Principal source: USA 53.4% (1997)

▪ Tourist information

Time difference GMT –4 **Currency** bolívar **Language** Spanish (official), Indian languages 2% **Visa requirements** UK: visa not required. USA: visa not required **Embassy in the UK** 1 Cromwell Road, London SW7 2HW. Tel: (020) 7584 4206/7; fax: (020) 7589 8887 **British embassy** Apartado 1246, Edificio Torre Las Mercedes, 3°, Avenida la Estancia, Chuao, Caracas 1060. Tel: (2) 993 4111; fax: (2) 993 9989 **Chamber of commerce** Federación Venezolana de Cámaras y Associaciones de Comercio y Producción, Apartado 2568, Edificio Fedecámaras, 5°, Avenida El Empalme, Urb El Bosque, Caracas. Tel: (2) 731 1711; fax: (2) 731 0220 **Office hours** 0800–1800 Mon–Fri (there is a long midday break) **Banking hours** 0830–1130 and 1400–1630 Mon–Fri **Airports** international airports: Caracas (Simón Bolívar), Cabello, Maracaibo; domestic services operate to most large towns; total passenger km: 5,800 million (1997 est) **Major ports** Maracaibo **Major holidays** 1, 6 January, 19 March, 19 April, 1 May, 24, 29 June, 5, 24 July, 15 August, 12 October, 1 November, 8, 25 December; variable: Ascension Thursday, Carnival (2 days), Corpus Christi, Good Friday, Holy Thursday

Chronology

1st millennium BC Beginnings of settled agriculture. AD **1498–99** Visited by explorers Christopher Columbus and Alonso de Ojeda, at which time the principal indigenous Indian communities were the Caribs, Arawaks, and Chibchas; it was named Venezuela ('little Venice') since the coastal Indians lived in stilted thatched houses. **1521** Spanish settlement established on the northeast coast and was ruled by Spain from Santo Domingo (Dominican Republic). **1567** Caracas founded by Diego de Losada. **1739** Became part of newly created Spanish Viceroyalty of New Granada, with capital at Bogotá (Colombia), but, lacking gold mines, retained great autonomy. **1749** First rebellion against Spanish colonial rule. **1806** Rebellion against Spain, led by Francisco Miranda. **1811–12** First Venezuelan Republic declared by patriots, taking advantage of Napoleon Bonaparte's invasion of Spain, but Spanish Royalist forces re-established their authority. **1813–14** The Venezuelan, Simón Bolívar, 'El Libertador' (the Liberator), created another briefly independent republic, before being forced to withdraw to Colombia. **1821** After the battle of Carabobo, Venezuelan independence achieved within Republic of Gran Colombia (which also comprised Colombia, Ecuador, and Panama). **1829** Became separate state of Venezuela after leaving Republic of Gran Colombia. **1830–48** Gen José Antonio Páez, the first of a series of caudillos (military leaders), established political stability. **1870–88** Antonio Guzmán Blanco ruled as benevolent liberal-conservative dictator, modernizing infrastructure and developing agriculture (notably coffee) and education. **1899** International arbitration tribunal found in favour of British Guiana (Guyana) in long-running dispute over border with Venezuela. **1902** Ports blockaded by British, Italian, and German navies as a result of Venezuela's failure to repay loans. **1908–35** Harsh rule of dictator Juan Vicente Gómez, during which period Venezuela became world's largest exporter of oil, which had been discovered in 1910. **1947** First truly democratic elections held, but the new president, Rómulo Gallegos, was removed within eight months by the military in the person of Col Marcos Pérez Jimenez. **1958** Overthrow of Pérez and establishment of an enduring civilian democracy, headed by left-wing Romulo Betancourt of Democratic Action Party (AD). **1964** Dr Raúl Leoni (AD) became president in first-ever constitutional handover of civilian power. **1974** Carlos Andrés Pérez (AD) became president, with economy remaining buoyant through oil revenues. Oil and iron industries nationalized. **1984** Social pact established between government, trade unions, and business; national debt rescheduled as oil revenues plummetted. **1987** Widespread social unrest triggered by inflation; student demonstrators shot by police. **1989** An economic austerity programme was instigated. Price increases triggered riots known as 'Caracazo'; 300 people were killed. Martial law was declared and a general strike followed. Elections were boycotted by opposition groups. **1992** An attempted antigovernment coups failed, at a cost of 120 lives. **1996** Former President Carlos Andrés Pérez was found guilty on corruption charges and imprisoned. **1999** Hugo Chávez was inaugurated as president. Flooding and mudslides swamped Venezuela's Caribbean coast in late December, resulting in death tolls as high as 30,000, at least 150,000 homeless civilians from 23,000 destroyed homes, 70,000 evacuees, and 96,000 damaged homes.

Vietnam Socialist Republic of

National name *Công Hòa Xã Hôi Chu Nghia Viêt Nam* **Area** 329,600 sq km/127,258 sq mi **Capital** Hanoi **Major towns/cities** Ho Chi Minh City (formerly Saigon), Haiphong, Da Nang, Can Tho, Nha Trang, Nam Dinh

Government

Head of state Tran Duc Luong from 1997 **Head of government** Phan Van Khai from 1997 **Political system** communist **Armed forces** 492,000; plus paramilitary forces numbering 65,000 and around 3 million reserves (1997) **Conscription** military service is compulsory for two years **Defence spend** (% GDP) 4.1 (1997) **Education spend** (% GNP) 2.7 (1996)

Health spend (% GDP) 1.1 (1990–95) **Death penalty** retained and used for ordinary crimes

Population and society

Population 78,705,000 (1999 est) **Population growth rate** 1.6% (1995–2000) **Ethnic groups** 88% Viet (also known as Kinh), 2% Chinese, 2% Khmer, 8% consists of more than 50 minority nationalities, including the Hmong, Meo, Muong, Nung, Tay, Thai, and Tho tribal groups **Religion** Taoist, Buddhist, Roman Catholic **Life expectancy** 65 (men); 70 (women) (1995–2000) **Literacy rate** 95% (men); 89% (women) (1997 est) **Unemployment** 7% (1994 est)

Economy and resources

GDP (US$) 24.8 billion (1998 est) **GNP** (US$) 25.6 billion (1998) **GNP per capita (PPP)** (US$) 1,690 (1998) **Real GDP growth** (% change on previous year) 5.5 (1998) **Consumer price inflation** 8.8% (1998) **Foreign debt** (US$) 21.6 billion (1997) **Resources** petroleum, coal, tin, zinc, iron, antimony, chromium, phosphate, apatite, bauxite **Exports** rice (leading exporter), crude petroleum, coal, coffee, marine products, handicrafts, light industrial goods, rubber, nuts, tea, garments, tin. Principal market: Japan 18.2% (1997) **Imports** petroleum products, machinery and spare parts, steel, artificial fertilizers, basic manufactures, consumer goods. Principal source: Singapore 18.2% (1997)

■ Tourist information

Time difference GMT +7 **Currency** dong **Language** Vietnamese (official); French, English, Khmer, Chinese, local languages **Visa requirements** UK: visa required. USA: visa required **Embassy in the UK** 12–14 Victoria Road, London W8 5RD. Tel: (020) 7937 1912; fax: (020) 7937 6108 **British embassy** 16 Pho Ly Thuong Kiet, Hanoi. Tel: (4) 252 349; fax: (4) 265 762 **Chamber of commerce** Vietcochamber (Chamber of Industry and Commerce of Vietnam), 33 Ba Trieu, Hanoi. Tel: (4) 253 023; fax: (4) 256 446 **Office hours** 0730–1200 and 1300–1630 Mon–Sat **Airports** international airports: Hanoi (Noi Bai), Ho Chi Minh City (Tan Son Nhat); seven domestic airports; total passenger km: 3,785 million (1997 est) **Major ports** Ho Chi Minh City (formerly Saigon), Da Nang, Haiphong **Chief tourist attractions** Hanoi, with its 11th-century Temple of Literature, Mot Cot Pagoda, 3rd-century Co Loa citadel, and museums (many historical sites were destroyed by war); tropical rainforest **Major holidays** 1 January, 30 April, 1 May, 1–2 September; variable: Têt, Lunar New Year (January/February, 3 days)

Chronology

300 BC Rise of Dong Son culture. **111 BC** Came under Chinese rule. **1st–6th centuries AD** Southern Mekong delta region controlled by independent Indianized Funan kingdom. **939** Chinese overthrown by Ngo Quyen at battle of Bach Dang River; first Vietnamese dynasty founded. **11th century** Theravāda Buddhism promoted. **15th century** North and South Vietnam united, as kingdom of Champa in the south was destroyed in 1471. **16th century** Contacts with French missionaries and European traders as political power became decentralized. **early 19th century** Under Emperor Nguyen Anh authority was briefly recentralized. **1858–84** Conquered by France and divided into protectorates of Tonkin (North Vietnam) and Annam (South Vietnam). **1887** Became part of French Indo-China Union, which included Cambodia and Laos. **late 19th–early 20th century** Development of colonial economy based in south on rubber and rice, drawing migrant labourers from north. **1930** Indochinese Communist Party (ICP) formed by Ho Chi Minh to fight for independence. **1941** Occupied by Japanese during World War II; ICP formed Vietminh as guerrilla resistance force designed to overthrow Japanese-installed puppet regime headed by Bao Dai, Emperor of Annam. **1945** Japanese removed from Vietnam at end of World War II; Vietminh, led by Ho Chi Minh, in control of much of the country, declared independence. **1946** Vietminh war began against French, who tried to reassert colonial control and set up noncommunist state in south in 1949. **1954** France decisively defeated at Dien Bien Phu. Vietnam divided along 17th parallel between communist-controlled north and US-backed south. **1963** Ngo Dinh Diem, leader of South Vietnam, overthrown in military coup by Lt-Gen Nguyen Van Thieu. **1964** US combat troops entered Vietnam War as North Vietnamese army began to attack South and allegedly attacked US destroyers in the Tonkin Gulf. **1969** Death of Ho Chi Minh, who was succeeded as Communist Party leader by Le Duan. US forces, which numbered 545,000 at their peak, gradually began to be withdrawn from Vietnam as a result of domestic opposition to the rising casualty toll. **1973** Paris ceasefire agreement provided for the withdrawal of US troops and release of US prisoners of war. **1975** Saigon captured by North Vietnam, violating Paris Agreements. **1976** Socialist Republic of Vietnam proclaimed. Hundreds of thousands of southerners became political prisoners; many more fled abroad. Collectivization extended to south. **1978** Diplomatic relations severed with China. Admission into Comecon. Vietnamese invasion of Cambodia. **1979** Sino-Vietnamese 17-day border war; 700,000 Chinese and middle-class Vietnamese fled abroad as refugee 'boat people'. **1986** Death of Le Duan and retirement of 'old guard' leaders; pragmatic Nguyen Van Linh became Communist Party leader. **1987–88** Over 10,000 political prisoners were released. **1989** Troops were fully withdrawn from Cambodia. **1991** A Cambodia peace agreement was signed. Relations with China were normalized. **1992** A new constitution was adopted, guaranteeing economic freedoms. Relations with South Korea were normalized. **1994** The US 30-year trade embargo was removed. **1995** Full diplomatic relations were re-established with the USA. Vietnam became a full member of ASEAN. **1997** Diplomatic relations with the USA were restored. Tran Duc Luong and Phan Van Khai were elected president and prime minister respectively. The size of the standing army was reduced. **1998** The Vietnamese currency was devalued. A new emphasis was placed on agricultural development after export and GDP growth slumped to 3%.

Yemen Republic of

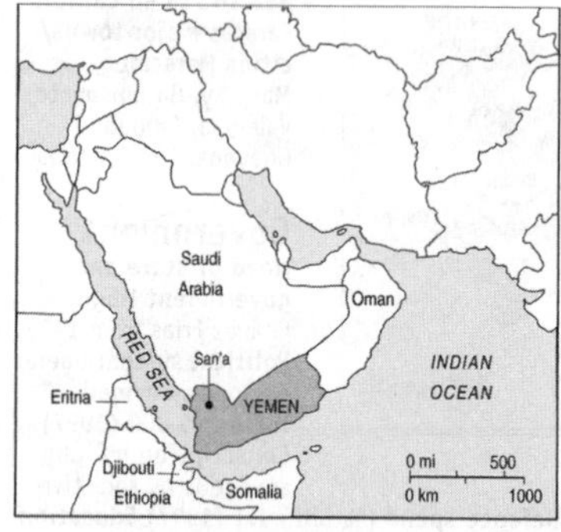

National name *Jamhuriya al Yamaniya* **Area** 531,900 sq km/ 205,366 sq mi **Capital** San'a **Major towns/cities** Aden, Ta'izz, Al Mukalla, Hodeida, Ibb, Dhamar

Government

Head of state Ali Abdullah Saleh from 1990 **Head of government** Abdul Ali al-Rahman al-Iryani from 1998 **Political system** emergent democracy **Armed forces** 66,300; plus paramilitary forces numbering at least 80,000 (1997) **Conscription** military service is compulsory for two years **Defence spend** (% GDP) 7 (1997) **Education spend** (% GNP) 6.5 (1996) **Health spend** (% GDP) 1.8 (1995) **Death penalty** retained and used for ordinary crimes

Population and society

Population 17,488,000 (1999 est) **Population growth rate** 3.7% (1995–2000); 3.1% (2000–05) **Ethnic groups** predominantly Arab **Religion** Sunni Muslim 63%, Shiite Muslim 37% **Life expectancy** 57 (men); 58 (women) (1995–2000) **Literacy rate** 64% (men); 21% (women) (1997 est) **Unemployment** 25% (1997 est)

Economy and resources

GDP (US$) 4.3 billion (1998) **GNP** (US$) 4.9 billion (1998) **GNP per capita (PPP)** (US$) 740 (1998) **Real GDP growth** (% change on previous year) 1.8 (1998) **Consumer price inflation** 8% (1998) **Foreign debt** (US$) 3.85 billion (1997) **Resources** petroleum, natural gas, gypsum, salt; deposits of copper, gold, lead, zinc, molybdenum **Exports** petroleum and petroleum products, cotton, basic manufactures, clothing, live animals, hides and skins, fish, rice, coffee. Principal market: China 30.9% (1997) **Imports** textiles and other manufactured consumer goods, petroleum products, sugar, grain, flour, other foodstuffs, cement, machinery, chemicals. Principal source: UAE 9% (1997)

■ Tourist information

Time difference GMT +3 **Currency** riyal (North); dinar (South), both legal currency throughout the country **Language** Arabic **Visa requirements** UK: visa required. USA: visa required **Embassy in the UK** 57 Cromwell Road, London SW7 2ED. Tel: (020) 7584 6607; fax: (020) 7589 3350 **British embassy** PO Box 1287, 129 Haddah Road, Sana'a. Tel: (1) 215 630; fax: (1) 263 059 **Chamber of commerce** Federation of Chambers of Commerce, PO Box 16992, Sana'a. Tel: (1) 221 765; telex: 2229 **Office hours** 0800–1230 and 1600–1900 Mon–Wed; 0800–1100 Thu **Banking hours** 0800–1200 Sat–Wed; 0800–1130 Thu **Airports** international airports: Sana'a (El-Rahaba), Ta'izz (al-Jahad), Hodeida, Aden (Khormaksar), Mukalla (Riyan), Seybun; domestic services operate between these; total passenger km: 486 million (1995) **Major ports** Aden **Chief tourist attractions** sandy beaches along coastal plains; Hadramaut mountain range; Aden; San'a's old city, with its medieval mosques and other buildings; hillside villages of Kawkaban, Thulla, and Shiban **Major holidays** 1 May, 26 September; variable: Eid-ul-Adha (5 days), end of Ramadan (4 days), New Year (Muslim), Prophet's Birthday

Chronology

1st millennium BC South Yemen (Aden) divided between economically advanced Qataban and Hadramawt kingdoms. ***c.* 5th century BC** Qataban fell to the Sabaeans (Shebans) of North Yemen (Sana). ***c.* 100 BC–AD 525** All of Yemen became part of the Himyarite kingdom. **AD 628** Islam introduced. **1174–1229** Under control of Egyptian Ayyubids. **1229–1451** 'Golden age' for arts and sciences under the Rasulids, who had served as governors of Yemen under the Ayyubids. **1538** North Yemen came under control of Turkish Ottoman Empire. **1636** Ottomans left North Yemen and power fell into hands of Yemeni Imams, based on local Zaydi tribes, who also held South Yemen until 1735. **1839** Aden became a British territory. Port developed into an important ship refuelling station after opening of Suez Canal in 1869; protectorate was gradually established over 23 Sultanates inland. **1870s** The Ottomans re-established control over North Yemen. **1918** North Yemen became independent, with Imam Yahya from the Hamid al-Din family as king. **1937** Aden became a British crown colony. **1948** Imam Yahya assassinated by exiled Free Yemenis nationalist movement, but the uprising was crushed by his son, Imam Ahmad. **1959** Federation of South Arabia formed by Britain between city of Aden and feudal sultanates (Aden Protectorate). **1962** Military coup on death of Imam Ahmad; North Yemen declared Yemen Arab Republic (YAR), with Abdullah al-Sallal as president. Civil war broke out between royalists (supported by Saudi Arabia) and republicans (supported by Egypt). **1963** Armed rebellion by National Liberation Front (NLF) began against British rule in Aden. **1967** Civil war ended with republicans victorious. Sallal deposed and replaced by Republican Council. The Independent People's Republic of South Yemen was formed after the British withdrawal from Aden. Many fled to the north as the repressive communist NLF regime took over in south. **1970** People's Republic of South Yemen renamed People's Democratic Republic of Yemen. **1971–72** War between South Yemen and YAR; union agreement brokered by Arab League signed but not kept. **1974** The pro-Saudi Col Ibrahim al-Hamadi seized power in North Yemen; Military Command Council set up. **1977** Hamadi assassinated; replaced by Col Ahmed ibn Hussein al-Ghashmi. **1978** Constituent people's assembly appointed in North Yemen and Military Command Council dissolved. Ghashmi killed by envoy from South Yemen; succeeded by Ali Abdullah Saleh. War broke out again between the two Yemens. The South Yemen president was deposed and executed; the Yemen Socialist Party (YSP) was formed in the south by communists. **1979** A ceasefire was agreed with a commitment to future union. **1986** There was civil war in South Yemen; the autocratic head of state Ali Nasser was dismissed. A new administration was formed under the more moderate Haydar Abu Bakr al-Attas, who was committed to negotiating union with the north because of the deteriorating economy in the south. **1989** A draft multiparty constitution for a single Yemen state was published. **1990** The border between the two Yemens was opened; the countries were formally united on 22 May as the Republic of Yemen. Ali Abdullah Saleh, president of North Yemen since 1978, was appointed president of the new unified Yemen. **1991** The new constitution was approved; Yemen opposed US-led operations against Iraq in the Gulf War. **1992** There were antigovernment riots. **1993** Saleh's General People's Congress (GPC) won most seats in a general election but no overall majority; a five-member presidential council was elected, including Saleh as president, YSP leader Ali Salim al-Baidh as vice-president, and Bakr al-Attas as prime minister. **1994** Fighting erupted between northern forces, led by President Saleh, and southern forces, led by Vice-president al-Baidh, as southern Yemen announced its secession. Saleh inflicted crushing defeat on al-Baidh and a new GPC coalition was appointed. **1998** A new government was headed by Abdul Ali al-Rahman al-Iryani.

Yugoslavia Federal Republic of

National name *Federativna Republika Jugoslavija* **Area** 58,300 sq km/ 22,509 sq mi **Capital** Belgrade **Major towns/cities** Priština, Novi Sad, Niš, Rijeka, Kragujevac, Podgorica (formerly Titograd), Subotica

Government

Head of state Slobodan Milošević from 1997 **Head of government** Momir Bulatović from 1998 **Political system** emergent democracy **Armed forces** 114,200 (1997) **Conscription** military service is compulsory for 12–15 months; voluntary military service for women introduced in 1983 **Defence spend** (% GDP) 7.8 (1997) **Education spend** (% GNP) 6.1 (1992; former Yugoslavia) **Death penalty** retained and used for ordinary crimes

Population and society

Population 10,637,000 (1999 est) **Population growth rate** 0.1% (1995–2000) **Ethnic groups** according to the 1991 census, 62% of the population of the rump federal republic is ethnic Serb, 17% Albanian, 5% Montenegrin, 3% 'Yugoslav', and 3% Muslim. Serbs predominate in the

republic of Serbia, where they form (excluding the autonomous areas of Kosovo and Vojvodina) 85% of the population; in Vojvodina they comprise 55% of the population. Albanians constitute 77% of the population of Kosovo; Montenegrins comprise 69% of the population of the republic of Montenegro; and Muslims predominate in the Sandzak region, which straddles the Serbian and Montenegrin borders. Since 1992 an influx of Serb refugees from Bosnia and Kosovo has increased the proportion of Serbs in Serbia, while many ethnic Hungarians have left Vojvodina, and an estimated 500,000 Albanians have left Kosovo **Religion** Serbian and Montenegrin Orthodox; Muslim in southern Serbia **Life expectancy** 70 (men); 76 (women) (1995–2000) **Literacy rate** 97% (men); 88% (women) (1995 est) **Unemployment** 26.1% (1996)

Economy and resources

GDP (US$) 15.8 billion (1998 est) **GNP** (US$) 17.9 billion (1997 est) **GNP per capita (PPP)** (US$) 5,880 (1997 est) **Real GDP growth** (% change on previous year) 4 (1998) **Consumer price inflation** 23% (1998) **Foreign debt** (US$) 15.1 billion (1997 est) **Resources** petroleum, natural gas, coal, copper ore, bauxite, iron ore, lead, zinc **Exports** basic manufactures, machinery and transport equipment, clothing, miscellaneous manufactured articles, food and live animals. Principal market: Italy 11.5% (1997) **Imports** machinery and transport equipment, electrical goods, agricultural produce, mineral fuels and lubricants, basic manufactures, foodstuffs, chemicals. Principal source: Germany 13.4% (1997)

▪ Tourist information

Time difference GMT +1 **Currency** new Yugoslav dinar **Language** Serbo-Croatian; Albanian (in Kosovo) **Visa requirements** UK: visa required. USA: visa required **Embassy in the UK** 5–7 Lexham Gardens, London W8 5JJ. Tel: (020) 7370 6105; fax: (020) 7370 3838 **British embassy** Ulica Generala Zdanova 46, 11000 Belgrade. Tel: (1) 645 055; fax: (1) 659 651 **Chamber of commerce** Chamber of Economy of Serbia, Ulica Generala Zdanova 13–15, 11000 Belgrade. Tel: (1) 340 611; fax: (1) 330 949. Chamber of Economy of Montenegro, Novaka Miloseva 29/II, 81000 Podgorica. Tel: (81) 31071; fax: (81) 34926 **Office hours** 0700–1430 Mon–Fri **Banking hours** 0700–1500 Mon–Fri **Airports** international airports: Belgrade (Surcin), Podgorica; three domestic airports; total passenger km: 3,443 million (1991) **Chief tourist attractions** Montenegro's Adriatic coastline and its great lake of Scutari; varied scenery – rich alpine valleys, rolling green hills, bare, rocky gorges, thick forests, limestone mountains **Major holidays** 1–2 January, 1–2 May, 4, 7 (Serbia only), 13 (Montenegro only) July, 29–30 November; Orthodox Christian holidays may also be celebrated throughout much of the region

Chronology

3rd century BC Serbia (then known as Moesia Superior) conquered by Romans; empire was extended to Belgrade centuries later by Emperor Augustus. **6th century AD** Slavic tribes, including Serbs, Croats, and Slovenes, crossed River Danube and settled in Balkan Peninsula. **879** Serbs converted to Orthodox Church by St Cyril and St Methodius. **mid-10th–11th centuries** Serbia broke free briefly from Byzantine Empire to establish independent state. **1217** Independent Serbian kingdom re-established, reaching its height in mid-14th century under Stefan Dushan, when it controlled much of Albania and northern Greece. **1389** Serbian army defeated by Ottoman Turks at Battle of Kosovo; area became Turkish *pashalik* (province). Montenegro in southwest survived as sovereign principality. Croatia and Slovenia in northwest became part of Habsburg Empire. **18th century** Vojvodina enjoyed protection from the Austrian Habsburgs. **1815** Uprisings against Turkish rule secured autonomy for Serbia. **1878** Independence achieved as Kingdom of Serbia, after Turks defeated by Russians in war over Bulgaria. **1912–13** During Balkan Wars, Serbia expanded its territory at expense of Turkey and Bulgaria. **1918** Joined Croatia and Slovenia, formerly under Austrian Habsburg control, to form Kingdom of Serbs, Croats, and Slovenes under Serbian Peter

Karageorgević (Peter I); Montenegro's citizens voted to depose their ruler, King Nicholas, and join the union. **1929** New name of Yugoslavia ('Land of the Southern Slavs') adopted; Serbian-dominated military dictatorship established by King Alexander I as opposition mounted from Croatian federalists. **1934** Alexander I assassinated by a Macedonian with Croatian terrorist links; his young son Peter II succeeded, with Paul, his uncle, as regent; Nazi Germany and fascist Italy increased their influence. **1941** Following a coup by pro-Allied air-force officers, Nazi Germany invaded. Peter II fled to England. Armed resistance to German rule began, spearheaded by pro-royalist, Serbian-based Chetniks ('Army of the Fatherland'), led by Gen Draza Mihailović, and communist Partisans ('National Liberation Army'), led by Marshal Tito. An estimated 900,000 Yugoslavs died in the war, including more than 400,000 Serbs and 200,000 Croats. **1943** Provisional government formed by Tito at liberated Jajce in Bosnia. **1945** Yugoslav Federal People's Republic formed under leadership of Tito; communist constitution introduced. **1948** Split with USSR after Tito objected to Soviet 'hegemonism'; expelled from Cominform. **1953** Workers' self-management principle enshrined in constitution and private farming supported; Tito became president. **1961** Nonaligned movement formed under Yugoslavia's leadership. **1971** In response to mounting separatist demands in Croatia, new system of collective and rotating leadership introduced. **1980** Tito died; collective leadership assumed power. **1981–82** Armed forces suppressed demonstrations in Kosovo province, southern Serbia, by Albanians demanding full republic status. **1986** Slobodan Milošević, a populist-nationalist hardliner who had the ambition of creating a 'Greater Serbia', became leader of communist party in the Serbian republic. **1988** Economic difficulties: 1,800 strikes, 250% inflation, 20% unemployment. Ethnic unrest in Montenegro and Vojvodina, and separatist demands in rich northwestern republics of Croatia and Slovenia; 'market socialist' reform package, encouraging private sector, inward investment, and liberalizing prices combined with austerity wage freeze. **1989** Reformist Croatian Ante Marković became prime minister. Ethnic riots in Kosovo province against Serbian attempt to end autonomous status of Kosovo and Vojvodina; at least 30 were killed and a state of emergency imposed. **1990** Multiparty systems were established in the republics; Kosovo and Vojvodina were stripped of autonomy. In Croatia, Slovenia, Bosnia, and Macedonia elections brought to power new noncommunist governments seeking a looser confederation. **1991** Demonstrations against Serbian president Slobodan Milošević in Belgrade were crushed by riot police and tanks. Slovenia and Croatia declared their independence, resulting in clashes between federal and republican armies; Slovenia accepted a peace pact sponsored by the European Community (EC), but fighting intensified in Croatia, where Serb militias controlled over a third of the republic; Federal President Stipe Mesic and Prime Minister Marković resigned. **1992** There was an EC-brokered ceasefire in Croatia; the EC and the USA recognized Slovenia's and Croatia's independence. Bosnia-Herzegovina and Macedonia then declared their independence, and Bosnia-Herzegovina's independence was recognized by the EC and the USA. A New Federal Republic of Yugoslavia (FRY) was proclaimed by Serbia and Montenegro but not internationally recognized; international sanctions were imposed and UN membership was suspended. Ethnic Albanians proclaimed a new 'Republic of Kosovo', but it was not recognized. **1993** Pro-Milošević Zoran Lilic became Yugoslav president. There was antigovernment rioting in Belgrade. Macedonia was recognized as independent under the name of the Former Yugoslav Republic of Macedonia. The economy was severely damaged by international sanctions. **1994** A border blockade was imposed by Yugoslavia against Bosnian Serbs; sanctions were eased as a result. **1995** Serbia played a key role in the US-brokered Dayton peace accord for Bosnia-Herzegovina and accepted the separate existence of Bosnia and Croatia. **1996** Diplomatic relations were restored between Serbia and Croatia, and UN sanctions against Serbia were lifted. Allies of Milošević were successful in parliamentary elections. Diplomatic relations were established with Bosnia-Herzegovina. There was mounting opposition to Milošević's government following its refusal to accept opposition victories in municipal elections. **1997** Milošević was elected president and the pro-democracy mayor of Belgrade was ousted. The validity of Serbian presidential elections continued to be questioned. The anti-Milošević candidate was elected president of Montenegro. **1998** A Serb military offensive against ethnic Albanian separatists in Kosovo led to a refugee and humanitarian crisis. The offensive against the Kosovo Liberation Army (KLA) was condemned by the international community and NATO military intervention was threatened. President Milošević appointed Momir Bulatović as prime minister. **1999** Fighting continued between Serbians and Albanian separatists in Kosovo. In March, following the failure of efforts to reach a negotiated settlement, NATO began a bombing campaign against the Serbs; the ethnic cleansing of Kosovars by Serbs intensified and the refugee crisis in neighbouring countries worsened as hundreds of thousands of ethnic Albanians fled Kosovo. In May President Milošević was indicted for crimes against humanity by the International War Crimes Tribunal in The Hague. A peace was agreed on NATO terms in June. Refugees began returning to Kosovo.

Zambia Republic of (formerly Northern Rhodesia)

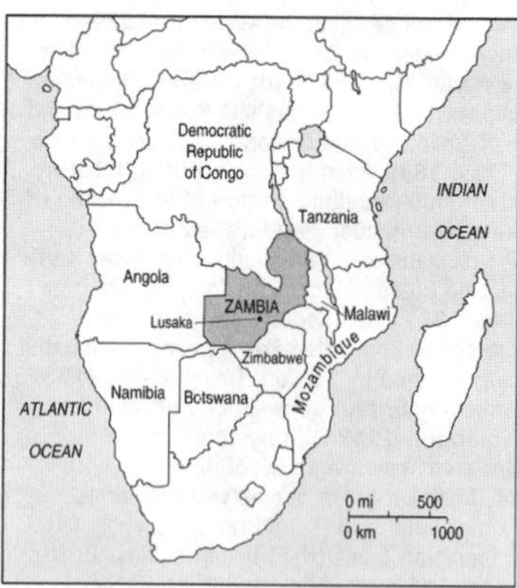

Area 752,600 sq km/ 290,578 sq mi **Capital** Lusaka **Major towns/ cities** Kitwe, Ndola, Kabwe, Mufulira, Chingola, Luanshya, Livingstone

Government

Head of state and government Frederick Chiluba from 1991 **Political system** emergent democracy **Armed forces** 21,600; plus paramilitary forces of 1,400 (1997) **Conscription** military service is voluntary **Defence spend** (% GDP) 1.7 (1997) **Education spend** (% GNP) 2.2 (1996) **Health spend** (% GDP) 2.9 (1995) **Death penalty** retained and used for ordinary crimes

Population and society

Population 8,976,000 (1999 est) **Population growth rate** 2.3% (1995–2000) **Ethnic groups** over 95% indigenous Africans, belonging to more than 70 different ethnic groups, including the Bantu-Botatwe and the Bemba **Religion** Christian, animist, Hindu, Muslim **Life expectancy** 40 (men); 41 (women) (1995–2000) **Literacy rate** 83% (men); 68% (women) (1997 est)

Economy and resources

GDP (US$) 3.6 billion (1998) **GNP** (US$) 3.2 billion (1998) **GNP per capita (PPP)** (US$) 860 (1998) **Real GDP growth** (% change on previous year) –3 (1998) **Consumer price inflation** 28.0% (1998) **Foreign debt** (US$) 6.75 billion (1997) **Resources** copper (world's fourth-largest producer), cobalt, zinc, lead, coal, gold, emeralds, amethysts and other gemstones, limestone, selenium **Exports** copper, zinc, lead, cobalt, tobacco. Principal market: Japan 11.6% (1997) **Imports** machinery and transport equipment, mineral fuels, lubricants, electricity, basic manufactures, chemicals, food and live animals. Principal source: South Africa 48.3% (1997)

▪ Tourist information

Time difference GMT +2 **Currency** Zambian kwacha **Language** English (official); Bantu languages **Visa requirements** UK: visa not required. USA: visa required **Embassy in the UK** 2 Palace Gate, London W8 5NG. Tel: (020) 7589 6655; fax: (020) 7581 1353 **British embassy** British High Commission, PO Box 50050, Independence Avenue, 15101 Ridgeway, Lusaka. Tel: (1) 251 133; fax: (1) 253 798 **Chamber of commerce** Ministry of Commerce, Trade and Industry, PO Box 31968, Kwacha Annex, Cairo Road, Lusaka. Tel: (1) 228 301; fax: (1) 226 727 **Office hours** 0800–1300 and 1400–1700 Mon–Fri **Banking hours** 0815–1430 Mon–Fri **Airports** international airports: Lusaka; over 127 domestic airports, aerodromes, and airstrips; total passenger km: 428 million (1994) **Chief tourist attractions** unspoilt scenery; wildlife; 19 national parks, including the magnificent Luangava and Kafue National Parks, which have some of the most prolific animal populations in Africa; Victoria Falls **Major holidays** 1 January, 1, 25 May, 24 October, 25 December; variable: Good Friday, Holy Saturday, Youth (March), Heroes (July), Unity (July), Farmers (August)

Chronology

16th century Immigration of peoples from Luba and Lunda Empires of Zaire, to the northwest, who set up small kingdoms. **late 18th century** Visited by Portuguese explorers. **19th century** Instability with immigration of Ngoni from east, Kololo from west, establishment of Bemba kingdom in north, and slave-trading activities of Portuguese and Arabs from East Africa. **1851** Visited by British missionary and explorer David Livingstone. **1889** As Northern Rhodesia, came under administration of British South Africa Company of Cecil Rhodes, and became involved in copper mining, especially from 1920s. **1924** Became a British protectorate. **1948** Northern Rhodesia African Congress (NRAC) formed by black Africans to campaign for self-rule. **1953** Became part of Central African Federation, which included South Rhodesia (Zimbabwe) and Nyasaland (Malawi). **1960** The United National Independence Party (UNIP) was formed by Kenneth Kaunda as a breakaway from NRAC, as African socialist body to campaign for independence and dissolution of federation dominated by South Rhodesia's white minority. **1963** The federation was dissolved and internal self-government achieved. **1964** Independence was achieved within the Commonwealth as the Republic of Zambia, with Kaunda of the UNIP as president. **later 1960s** Key enterprises were brought under state control. **1972** UNIP was declared the only legal party. **1975** The opening of the Tan-Zam railway from the Zambian copperbelt, 322 mi/200 km north of Lusaka, to port of Dar es Salaam in Tanzania, reduced Zambia's dependence on the rail route via Rhodesia (Zimbabwe) for its exports. **1976** Zambia declared its support for Patriotic Front (PF) guerrillas fighting to topple the white-dominated regime in Rhodesia (Zimbabwe). **1980** There was an unsuccessful South African-promoted coup against President Kaunda; relations with Zimbabwe improved when the PF came to power. **1985** Kaunda was elected chair of African Front Line States. **1991** A new multiparty constitution was adopted. The MMD won a landslide election victory, and its leader Frederick Chiluba became president in what was the first democratic change of government in English-speaking black Africa. **1993** A state of emergency was declared after rumours of a planned antigovernment coup. A privatization programme was launched. **1996** Kaunda was effectively barred from future elections by an amendment to the constitution. **1997** There was an abortive antigovernment coup. **1998** Former president Kaunda was placed under house arrest after alleged involvement in the antigovernment coup. Kaunda was charged but the charges were subsequently dropped.

Zimbabwe Republic of (formerly Southern Rhodesia)

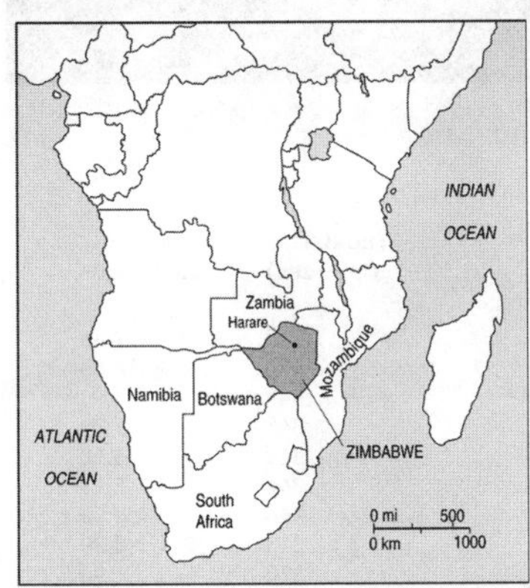

Area 390,300 sq km/ 150,694 sq mi **Capital** Harare **Major towns/ cities** Bulawayo, Gweru, Kwekwe, Mutare, Hwange, Chitungwiza

Government

Head of state and government Robert Mugabe from 1987 **Political system** nationalistic socialist **Armed forces** 39,000; 21,800 paramilitary forces (1997) **Conscription** military service is voluntary **Defence spend** (% GDP) 4.7 (1997) **Education spend** (% GNP) 8.3 (1996) **Health spend** (% GDP) 1.7 (1995) **Death penalty** retained and used for ordinary crimes

Population and society

Population 11,529,000 (1999 est) **Population growth rate** 1.4% (1995–2000) **Ethnic groups** four distinct ethnic groups: indigenous Africans, who account for about 95% of the population, Europeans (mainly British), who account for about 3.5%, and Afro-Europeans and Asians, who each comprise about 0.5% **Religion** Christian, Muslim, Hindu, animist **Life expectancy** 44 (men); 45 (women) (1995–2000) **Literacy rate** 94% (men); 88% (women) (1997 est) **Unemployment** 45% (1995 est)

Economy and resources

GDP (US$) 5.9 billion (1998) **GNP** (US$) 7.1 billion (1998) **GNP per capita (PPP)** (US$) 2,150 (1998) **Real GDP growth** (% change on previous year) 1.4 (1998) **Consumer price inflation** 31.7% (1998) **Foreign debt** (US$) 4.96 billion (1997) **Resources** gold, nickel, asbestos, coal, chromium, copper, silver, emeralds, lithium, tin, iron ore, cobalt **Exports** tobacco, metals and metal alloys, textiles and clothing, cotton lint. Principal market: South Africa 12.1% (1997) **Imports** machinery and transport equipment, basic manufactures, mineral fuels, chemicals, foodstuffs. Principal source: South Africa 36.6% (1997)

■ Tourist information

Time difference GMT +2 **Currency** Zimbabwe dollar **Language** English (official), Shona, Sindebele **Visa requirements** UK: visa not required. USA: visa not required **Embassy in the UK** Zimbabwe House, 429 Strand, London WC2R 0SA. Tel: (020) 7836 7755; (020) 7379 1167 **British embassy** British High Commission, PO Box 4490, Stanley House, Jason Moyo Avenue, Harare. Tel: (4) 793 781; fax: (4) 728 380 **Chamber of commerce** Zimbabwe National Chambers of Commerce, PO Box 1934, Equity House, Rezende Street, Harare. Tel: (4) 753 444; fax: (4) 753 450 **Office hours** 0800–1630 Mon–Fri **Banking hours** 0800–1500 Mon, Tue, Thu, Fri; 0800–1300 Wed; 0800–1130 Sat **Airports** international airports: Harare, Bulowayo, Victoria Falls; domestic air services operate between most of the larger towns; total passenger km: 874 million (1997 est) **Chief tourist attractions** Victoria Falls; Kariba Dam; mountain scenery, including Mount Inyanganai; some of southern Africa's best wildlife parks, notably Hwange, Matapos, and Nyanga national parks; ruins of old Zimbabwe, near Fort Victoria; World's View in the Matapos Hills **Major holidays** 1 January, 18–19 April, 1, 25 May, 11 August (2 days), 25–26 December; variable: Good Friday, Easter Monday

Chronology

13th century Shona people settled Mashonaland (eastern Zimbabwe), erecting stone buildings (hence name Zimbabwe, 'stone house'). **15th century** Shona Empire reached its greatest extent. **16th–17th centuries** Portuguese settlers developed trade with Shona states and achieved influence over kingdom of Mwanamutapa in northern Zimbabwe in 1629. **1837** Ndebele (or Matabele) people settled in southwest Zimbabwe after being driven north from Transvaal by Boers; Shona defeated by Ndebele led by King Mzilikazi who formed military empire based at Bulawayo. **1870** King Lobengula succeeded King Mzilikazi. **1889** Cecil Rhodes's British South Africa Company (SA Co) obtained exclusive rights to exploit mineral resources in Lobengula's domains. **1890** Creation of white colony in Mashonaland and founding of Salisbury (Harare) by Leander Starr Jameson, associate of Rhodes. **1893** Matabele War: Jameson defeated Lobengula; white settlers took control of country. **1895** Matabeleland, Mashonaland, and Zambia named Rhodesia after Cecil Rhodes. **1896** Matabele revolt suppressed. **1898** Southern Rhodesia (Zimbabwe) became British protectorate administered by BSA Co; farming, mining, and railways developed. **1922** Union with South Africa rejected by referendum among white settlers. **1923** Southern Rhodesia became self-governing colony; Africans progressively disenfranchised. **1933–53** Prime Minister Godfrey Huggins (later Lord Malvern) pursued 'White Rhodesia' policy of racial segregation. **1950s** Immigration doubled white population to around 250,000, while indigenous African population stood at around 6 million. **1953** Southern Rhodesia formed part of Federation of Rhodesia and Nyasaland. **1961** Zimbabwe African People's Union (ZAPU) formed with Joshua Nkomo as leader; declared illegal a year later. **1962** Rhodesia Front party of Winston Field took power in Southern Rhodesia, pledging to preserve white rule. **1963** Federation of Rhodesia and Nyasaland dissolved as Zambia and Malawi moved towards independence; Zimbabwe African National Union (ZANU) formed, with Robert Mugabe as secretary; declared illegal a year later. **1964** Ian Smith became prime minister; he rejected British terms for independence which required moves towards black majority rule; Nkomo and Mugabe imprisoned. **1965** Smith made unilateral declaration of independence (UDI); Britain broke off all relations. **1966–68** United Nations (UN) imposed economic sanctions on Rhodesia, which still received help from South Africa and Portugal. **1969** Rhodesia declared itself a republic. **1972** Britain rejected draft independence agreement as unacceptable to African population. **1974** Nkomo and Mugabe released and jointly formed Patriotic Front to fight Smith regime in mounting civil war. **1975** Geneva Conference between British, Smith regime, and African nationalists failed to reach agreement. **1978** At height of civil war, whites were leaving Rhodesia at rate of 1,000 per month. **1979** Rhodesia became Zimbabwe-Rhodesia with new 'majority' constitution which nevertheless retained special rights for whites; Bishop Abel Muzorewa became premier; Mugabe and Nkomo rejected settlement; Lancaster House Agreement temporarily restored Rhodesia to British rule. **1980** Zimbabwe achieved independence from Britain with full transition to African majority rule; Mugabe became prime minister with Rev. Canaan Banana as president. **1984** A ZANU–PF party congress agreed to the principle of a one-party state. **1987** Mugabe combined the posts of head of state and prime minister as executive president; Nkomo became vice-president. **1989** ZANU–PF and ZAPU formally merged; the Zimbabwe Unity Movement was founded by Edgar Tekere to oppose the one-party state. **1992** The United Party was formed to oppose ZANU–PF. Mugabe declared drought and famine a national disaster. **1996** Mugabe was re-elected president. **1998** Mugabe issued new rules banning strikes and restricting political and public gatherings. The government's radical land distribution plans were watered down after pressure from aid donors. There were violent antigovernment demonstrations. **1999** Further violent antigovernment protests took place. In June the human rights group African Rights produced a scathing report on Mugabe's government.

Largest and Smallest Countries

Largest Countries by Area

Rank	Country	Area sq km	Area sq mi
1	Russian Federation	17,075,400	6,592,811
2	Canada	9,970,610	3,849,652
3	China	9,572,900	3,696,000
4	USA	9,372,615	3,618,766
5	Brazil	8,511,965	3,286,469
6	Australia	7,682,300	2,966,136
7	India	3,166,829	1,222,713
8	Argentina	2,780,092	1,073,393
9	Kazakhstan	2,717,300	1,049,150
10	Sudan	2,505,800	967,489
11	Algeria	2,381,741	919,590
12	Congo, Democratic Republic of	2,344,900	905,366
13	Saudi Arabia	2,200,518	849,620
14	Mexico	1,958,201	756,061
15	Indonesia	1,904,569	735,354
16	Libya	1,759,540	679,358
17	Iran	1,648,000	636,292
18	Mongolia	1,565,000	604,246
19	Peru	1,285,200	496,216
20	Chad	1,284,000	495,752

Smallest Countries by Area

Rank	Country	Area sq km	Area sq mi
1	Vatican City State	0.4	0.2
2	Monaco	2.0	0.8
3	Nauru	21	8.1
4	Tuvalu	25	9.6
5	San Marino	61	24
6	Liechtenstein	160	62
7	Marshall Islands	181	70
8	St Kitts and Nevis	262	101
9	Maldives	298	115
10	Malta	320	124
11	Grenada	344	133
12	St Vincent and the Grenadines	388	150
13	Barbados	430	166
14	Antigua and Barbuda	440	169
15	Seychelles	453	174
16	Andorra	468	181
17	Palau	508	196
18	St Lucia	617	238
19	Singapore	622	240
20	Bahrain	688	266

Population

Largest Countries by Population Size

Countries with a population of over 100 million, 1999 and 2050.

Rank	Country	Population (millions)	% of world population
1999			
1	China	1,274	21.31
2	India	998	16.69
3	United States	276	4.62
4	Indonesia	209	3.10
5	Brazil	168	2.81
6	Pakistan	152	2.54
7	Russian Federation	147	2.45
8	Bangladesh	127	2.12
9	Japan	127	2.12
10	Nigeria	109	1.82
World total		5,978	

Rank	Country	Population (millions)	% of world population
2050 (projected)			
1	India	1,529	17.16
2	China	1,478	16.58
3	United States	349	3.91
4	Pakistan	346	3.88
5	Indonesia	312	3.50
6	Nigeria	244	2.73
7	Brazil	244	2.73
8	Bangladesh	213	2.39
9	Ethiopia	170	1.90
10	Congo, Democratic Republic of	160	1.79
11	Mexico	147	1.65
12	Philippines	131	1.47
13	Vietnam	127	1.42
14	Russian Federation	122	1.42
15	Iran	115	1.29
16	Egypt	115	1.29
17	Japan	105	1.17
18	Turkey	101	1.13
World total		8,909	

Smallest Countries by Population Size

Rank	Country	Population (1999 est)
1	Vatican City State	1,000
2	Tuvalu	11,000
3	Nauru	11,200
4	Palau	19,000
5	San Marino	25,000
6 =	Liechtenstein	32,000
	Monaco	32,000
8	St Kitts and Nevis	42,000
9	Marshall Islands	62,000
10	Andorra	66,000
11	Antigua and Barbuda	69,000
12	Dominica	75,000
13	Kiribati	77,000
14	Seychelles	79,000
15	Grenada	97,000
16	Tonga	98,000
17	Micronesia, Federated States of	116,000
18	St Vincent and the Grenadines	120,000
19 =	São Tomé and Príncipe	154,000
	St Lucia	154,000

Population Growth

It is projected that the world's annual population growth rate will continue declining from 1.33% in 1995–2000 to 0.34% in 2045–50. According to UN Population Division estimates, 97% of the world population increase takes place in less developed regions. Every year the population of Asia is increasing by 50 million, the population of Africa by 17 million, and that of Latin America and the Caribbean by nearly 8 million. Europe, on the other hand, has the lowest growth rate (0.03%); Eastern Europe has a negative rate (−0.2%).

World Population Milestones

World population reached:

Number	Year
1 billion	1804
2 billion	1927 (123 years later)
3 billion	1960 (33 years later)
4 billion	1974 (14 years later)
5 billion	1987 (13 years later)
6 billion	1999 (12 years later)
World population may reach:	
7 billion	2013 (14 years later)
8 billion	2028 (15 years later)
9 billion	2054 (26 years later)

Source: United Nations Population Division, Department of Economic and Social Affairs

Growth of the World's Largest Cities

Data refer to urban agglomerations. The concept of agglomeration defines the population contained within the contours of contiguous territory inhabited at urban levels of residential density without regard to administrative boundaries.

Rank	City	Population (millions)
1955		
1	New York (NY), USA	13.22
2	London, UK	8.93
3	Tokyo, Japan	8.82
4	Shanghai, China	6.86
5	Paris, France	6.27
6	Buenos Aires, Argentina	5.84
7	Essen, Germany	5.82
8	Moscow, Russia	5.75
9	Chicago (IL), USA	5.44
10	Los Angeles (CA), USA	5.15
1975		
1	Tokyo, Japan	19.77
2	New York (NY), USA	15.88
3	Shanghai, China	11.44
4	Mexico City, Mexico	11.24
5	São Paulo, Brazil	10.05
6	Osaka, Japan	9.84
7	Buenos Aires, Argentina	9.14
8	Los Angeles (CA), USA	8.93
9	Paris, France	8.88
10	Beijing, China	8.55

Rank	City	Population (millions)
1995		
1	Tokyo, Japan	26.95
2	Mexico City, Mexico	16.56
3	São Paulo, Brazil	16.53
4	New York (NY), USA	16.33
5	Mumbai, India	15.14
6	Shanghai, China	13.58
7	Los Angeles (CA), USA	12.47
8	Calcutta, India	11.92
9	Buenos Aires, Argentina	11.80
10	Seoul, South Korea	11.61
2015		
1	Tokyo, Japan	28.90
2	Mumbai, India	26.20
3	Lagos, Nigeria	24.60
4	São Paulo, Brazil	20.30
5	Dhaka, Bangladesh	19.50
6	Karachi, Pakistan	19.40
7	Mexico City, Mexico	19.20
8	Shanghai, China	18.00
9	New York (NY), USA	17.60
10	Calcutta, India	17.30

Source: United Nations Population Division, Department of Economic and Social Affairs

Largest Cities in the World

Urban agglomerations with populations of over 7 million.

2000

Rank	City	Population (millions)
1	Tokyo, Japan	28.0
2	Mexico City, Mexico	18.1
3	Mumbai, India	18.0
4	São Paulo, Brazil	17.7
5	New York (NY), USA	16.6
6	Shanghai, China	14.2
7	Lagos, Nigeria	13.5
8	Los Angeles (CA), USA	13.1
9	Calcutta, India	12.9
10	Buenos Aires, Argentina	12.4
11	Seoul, South Korea	12.2
12	Beijing, China	12.0
13	Karachi, Pakistan	11.8
14	Delhi, India	11.7
15	Dhaka, Bangladesh	11.0

Rank	City	Population (millions)
16=	Cairo, Egypt	10.8
	Metro Manila, Philippines	10.8
18=	Osaka, Japan	10.6
	Rio de Janeiro, Brazil	10.6
20	Tianjin, China	10.2
21	Jakarta, Indonesia	9.8
22	Paris, France	9.6
23	Istanbul, Turkey	9.4
24	Moscow, Russian Federation	9.3
25	London, UK	7.6
26=	Lima, Peru	7.4
	Tehran, Iran	7.4
28	Bangkok, Thailand	7.2

Source: United Nations Population Division, Department of Economic and Social Affairs

World Population Growth by Major Area

Percentage of world population by area, and total world population.

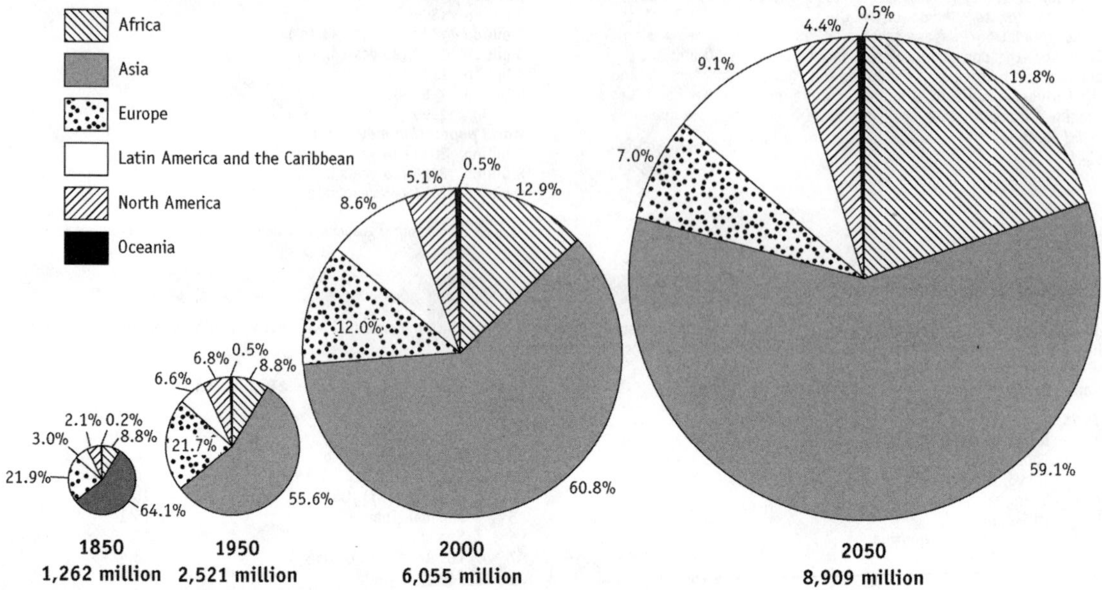

Demographic Impact of AIDS

The AIDS epidemic has dramatically affected population growth rates and life expectancy in a number of the world's developing countries. Of the 30 million people currently infected by HIV in the world, 26 million (85%) reside in 34 developing countries. Among these countries, 29 are in Sub-Saharan Africa, 3 are in Asia (Cambodia, India, and Thailand), and 2 in Latin America and the Caribbean (Brazil and Haiti). In the 29 African countries in which the impact of AIDS was studied, life expectancy at birth was estimated to decrease to 47 years in 1995–2000, whereas it would have been expected to reach 54 years in the absence of the AIDS epidemic. This represents a loss of 7 years. By 2010–15, the average life expectancy at birth in the nine hardest-hit countries is projected to be 17 years less than it would have been in the absence of AIDS.

Even in the worst cases, however, the toll of AIDS is not expected to lead to declines of population, because fertility in these countries is high. In Botswana, with an adult HIV/AIDS prevalence of 25%, the population in 2025 is expected to be 23% smaller than it would be in the absence of AIDS; nevertheless, the population is still expected to double between 1995 and 2050.

Top 10 Contributors to World Population Growth

60% of the world population increase is contributed by only ten countries, with 20.6% contributed by India and 14.7% by China.

1995–2000

Rank	Country	Net addition (in thousands)	Percentage of world population increase
1	India	15,999	20.6
2	China	11,408	14.7
3	Pakistan	4,048	5.2
4	Indonesia	2,929	3.8
5	Nigeria	2,511	3.2
6	USA	2,267	2.9
7	Brazil	2,154	2.8
8	Bangladesh	2,108	2.7
9	Mexico	1,547	2.0
10	Philippines	1,522	2.0
Total		46,494	59.8
WORLD TOTAL		77,738	100

Source: United Nations Population Division, Department of Economic and Social Affairs

Countries with the Fastest- and Slowest-growing Populations

Data represent average annual growth of national populations for the period 1995–2000.

1995–2000

Rank	Country	Average population growth rate %
Fastest-growing populations		
1	Liberia	8.2
2	Rwanda	7.7
3	Somalia	4.2
4	Eritrea	3.8
5	Yemen	3.7
6	Saudi Arabia	3.4
7	Oman	3.3
8=	Angola	3.2
	Niger	3.2
10	Kuwait	3.1
11=	Bosnia-Herzegovina	3.0
	Jordan	3.0
	Madagascar	3.0
	Sierra Leone	3.0
15	Afghanistan	2.9
16=	Bhutan	2.8
	Congo, Republic of the	2.8
	Iraq	2.8
	Uganda	2.8

Rank	Country	Average population growth rate %
Slowest-growing populations		
1	Latvia	–1.5
2	Estonia	–1.2
3	Georgia	–1.1
4	Bulgaria	–0.7
5=	Albania	–0.4
	Hungary	–0.4
	Kazakhstan	–0.4
	Romania	–0.4
	Ukraine	–0.4
10=	Armenia	–0.3
	Belarus	–0.3
	Lithuania	–0.3
13=	Czech Republic	–0.2
	Russian Federation	–0.2
15=	Croatia	–0.1
	Slovenia	–0.1
17=	Italy	0.0
	Moldova	0.0
	Portugal	0.0
	Spain	0.0

Source: The State of the World Population 1999, © *United Nations Population Fund*

Urban Population Growth

Regional totals and selected countries.

Region/country	Level of urbanization: % of total population in urban settlements 1975	2000	2025	Urban population: Total number in millions 1975	2000	2025	% annual growth rate 1975–2000	2000–25
Africa								
Total	25.15	37.30	53.77	104.1	310.1	804.2	4.37	3.81
Algeria	40.33	59.65	74.05	6.4	18.5	33.6	4.23	2.38
Angola	17.79	36.17	55.59	1.1	4.7	14.8	5.88	4.56
Cameroon	26.87	49.33	66.86	2.0	7.5	19.5	5.25	3.81
Congo, Democratic Republic of	29.50	31.03	49.82	6.8	15.8	52.1	3.35	4.76
Côte d'Ivoire	32.09	46.95	64.13	2.1	7.8	23.6	5.16	4.40
Egypt	43.45	46.36	62.20	16.8	32.0	60.5	2.57	2.54
Ghana	30.06	39.17	57.74	2.9	7.9	21.9	3.93	4.08
Kenya	12.92	31.76	51.48	1.7	10.3	32.6	7.05	4.59
Libya	60.95	88.35	92.75	1.5	5.6	11.9	5.32	3.00
Mozambique	8.62	41.07	61.09	0.9	7.8	21.5	8.62	4.05
Nigeria	23.38	43.29	61.64	14.6	55.7	146.9	5.34	3.88
Tanzania	10.08	28.20	48.25	1.6	9.6	30.3	7.17	4.60
Asia								
Total	24.62	37.68	54.81	592.3	1,407.8	2,718.4	3.46	2.63
Bangladesh	9.28	21.28	39.99	7.1	28.6	78.4	5.57	4.03
China	17.25	34.49	54.51	106.0	443.0	831.8	4.07	2.52
India	21.31	28.56	45.24	132.3	291.9	629.7	3.17	3.08
Indonesia	19.36	40.34	60.74	26.2	85.8	167.4	4.74	2.67
Iran	45.82	61.86	74.86	15.3	46.2	92.5	4.42	2.78
Japan	75.69	78.39	84.86	84.4	99.1	103.2	0.64	0.16
Korea, South	48.04	86.22	93.70	16.9	40.6	50.9	3.50	0.91
Pakistan	26.40	37.85	56.73	19.7	61.2	161.6	4.53	3.88
Philippines	35.56	59.01	74.26	15.3	44.0	77.6	4.23	2.27
Thailand	15.10	21.90	39.08	6.2	13.5	28.7	3.10	3.01
Europe								
Total	67.07	75.14	83.22		453.4	548.4	597.6	0.76
Latin America								
Total	61.32	76.61	84.67	196.2	401.1	600.9	2.86	1.61
Argentina	80.73	89.40	93.39	21.0	32.7	43.0	1.77	1.10
Bolivia	41.51	65.23	78.97	1.9	5.4	10.4	4.05	2.59
Brazil	61.15	81.21	88.94	66.0	141.9	204.8	3.06	1.47
Colombia	60.71	75.21	84.14	14.4	28.4	41.5	2.71	1.51
Mexico	62.76	77.71	85.82	36.9	79.6	117.2	3.07	1.55
Paraguay	38.98	56.44	71.82	1.0	3.2	6.5	4.44	2.86
Peru	61.46	74.52	83.54	9.3	19.4	30.6	9.94	1.82
Venezuela	77.83	94.45	97.17	9.9	22.8	33.8	3.34	1.57
North America								
Total	73.85	77.44	84.78	176.7	237.2	313.3	1.18	1.11

(*continued*)

Urban Population Growth (*continued*)

Region/country	Level of urbanization			Urban population				
	% of total population in urban settlements			Total number in millions			% annual growth rate	
	1975	2000	2025	1975	2000	2025	1975–2000	2000–25
Canada	75.61	77.16	83.67	17.5	23.9	32.0	1.24	1.16
USA	73.65	77.46	84.91	159.0	213.1	281.2	1.17	1.11
Oceania								
Total		71.78	70.25	74.86		15.4	21.5	30.7
Australia	85.92	84.69	88.59	11.9	16.3	21.8	1.24	1.18
New Zealand	82.78	87.20	91.64	2.5	3.3	4.0	1.00	0.81
World								
Total	37.73	47.52	61.07	1,538.3	2,926.4	5,065.3	2.57	2.19
More developed regions	69.84	76.52	83.98	729.3	904.2	1,040.0	0.86	0.56
Less developed regions	26.68	40.52	57.05	809.0	2,022.1	4,025.3	3.66	2.75

Source: United Nations Population Division, Department of Economic and Social Affairs

Median Age of World Population by Major Area

Area	Median age (years)		
	1950	2000	2050
Africa	18.7	18.4	30.7
Asia	21.9	26.3	39.3
Europe	29.2	37.5	47.4
Latin America and the Caribbean	20.1	24.5	37.8
North America	29.8	35.9	42.1
Oceania	27.9	31.1	39.3
Less developed regions	21.3	24.4	36.7
More developed regions	28.6	37.5	45.6
World total	23.5	26.6	37.8

Source: United Nations Population Division, Department of Economic and Social Affairs

Highest and Lowest Urban Populations

1999

Rank	Country	Population living in urban areas (%)
Highest urban population		
1=	Monaco	100
	Nauru	100
	Singapore	100
	Vatican City State	100[1]
5=	Belgium	97[2]
	Kuwait	97[2]
7=	Andorra	95[3]
	San Marino	95[3]
9=	Iceland	92[3]
	Qatar	92[3]
11=	Bahrain	91[3]
	Israel	91[2]
	Luxembourg	91[2]
	Uruguay	91[2]
15	Malta	90[3]
16=	Argentina	89[2]
	Lebanon	89[2]
	Netherlands	89[2]
	UK	89[2]
20	Bahamas	88[3]

Rank	Country	Population living in urban areas (%)
Lowest urban population		
1	Rwanda	6[2]
2	Bhutan	7
3	Burundi	8[2]
4	Nepal	11
5	Uganda	14[2]
6	Malawi	15[2]
7=	Burkina Faso	17[2]
	Ethiopia	17[2]
	Papua New Guinea	17
10	Eritrea	18[2]
11	Solomon Islands	19
12=	Niger	20[2]
	Vanuatu	20
	Vietnam	20
15=	Bangladesh	21
	Liechtenstein	21[1]
	Samoa	21
18	Afghanistan	22

[1] 1995. [2] 1998. [3] 1997.

Source: World Health Organization

Highest and Lowest Population Densities

1999

Rank	Country	Population per sq km
Highest density		
1	Monaco	16,074
2	Singapore	5,662
3	Vatican City State	2,500
4	Malta	1,206
5	Maldives	933
6	Bahrain	882
7	Bangladesh	881
8	Taiwan	685
9	Barbados	625
10	Mauritius	616
11	Nauru	524
12	Korea, South	473
13	Tuvalu	423
14	San Marino	417
15	Netherlands	376
16	Comoros	363
17	St Vincent and the Grenadines	355
18	Marshall Islands	343
19	Japan	335
20	Belgium	333

(continued)

Highest and Lowest Population Densities *(continued)*

Rank	Country	Population per sq km
Lowest density		
1=	Australia	2
	Mongolia	2
	Namibia	2
4=	Botswana	3
	Canada	3
	Iceland	3
	Libya	3
	Mauritania	3
	Suriname	3
10=	Gabon	4
	Guyana	4
12=	Central African Republic	6
	Chad	6
	Kazakhstan	6
15	Bolivia	7
16	Congo, Republic of the	8
17=	Mali	9
	Niger	9
	Oman	9
	Russian Federation	9
	Saudi Arabia	9
	Turkmenistan	9

Source: US Bureau of the Census

Youngest and Oldest Populations

1999

Rank	Country	% of population
Youngest populations (aged under15)		
1	Uganda	50
2	Marshall Islands	49
3=	Angola	48
	Congo, Democratic Republic of	48
	Niger	48
	SãoTomé and Príncipe	48
	Somalia	48
	Yemen	48
9=	BurkinaFaso	47
	Burundi	47
	Malawi	47
	Zambia	47
13=	Benin[1]	46
	Chad	46
	Congo, Republic of the	46
	Ethiopia	46
	Mali	46
	Rwanda	46
	Tanzania	46
	Togo	46

Rank	Country	% of population
Oldest populations (aged 60 orover)		
1=	Greece	24
	Italy	24
3=	Germany	23
	Japan	23
5=	Belgium	22
	Spain	22
	Sweden	22
8=	Bulgaria	21
	Portugal	21
	Ukraine	21
	UK	21
12=	Austria	20
	Croatia	20
	Denmark	20
	Finland	20
	France	20
	Hungary	20
	Latvia	20
	Norway	20

[1] 1998.

Source: US Bureau of the Census

Senior citizens enjoying the sunshine in the Botanic Gardens, Glasgow, Scotland. It is forecast that by 2050 there will be more older people worldwide than children. *Syndication International*

Population Ageing

The figures for 2050 are from the medium-fertility variant of the United Nations population estimates and projections revised in 1998.

Area	Population aged 60 years or older				Percentage 80 years or older	
	Number (thousands)		Percentage of total population			
	1999	2050	1999	2050	1999	2050
More developed regions	228,977	375,516	19	33	16	27
Less developed regions	364,133	1,594,293	8	21	9	17
Least developed countries	30,580	180,983	5	12	7	10
World total	593,111	1,969,809	10	22	11	19

Source: United Nations Population Division

A Silver World: The Ageing Population

by Anna Farkas

Introduction A gradual raising of the average age of the global population in the decades to come is all but certain. The reasons for this trend reflect the substantial medical and social advances of the 20th century – lowered infant and child mortality; a fall in death rates from infectious diseases; improvements in sanitation, housing, education, and nutrition; better health care and access to family planning – all of which have led to longer life expectancies. In 1950 average life expectancy was 46 years; in 2050 average life expectancy is projected to be 76, and the median (or average) age is projected to be 38. Even the average age of the oldest part of the population, 80 years and above, is increasing. The oldest old are the fastest-growing segment of the older population– by 2050, 16% of the older population will be aged 80 years or over compared with 11% in 1999, and the number of centenarians will have risen from approximately 145,000 to 2.2 million. On average, people have never been this healthy or lived this long.

Outnumbering the Young The number of people aged 60 years or older was estimated to be nearly 600 million in 1999 and is projected to grow to almost 2 billion by 2050, at which time the world population of older people will be larger than the population of children (0–14) for the first time in human history. In the world as a whole, there are still three times as many children (30%) as older people (10%). However, in the more developed regions, where fertility rates have fallen, the number of older people exceeded that of children for the first time in 1988. Italy has the oldest population, with 60% more older people than children. By the year 2050 in the more developed regions there will be more than twice as many older people as children. In terms of actual numbers, however, the majority of the world's older population resides in Asia (53%), while Europe has the next largest share (25%). According to the World Health Organization (WHO), more than 60% of elderly people live in developing countries. The rate of growth is extremely fast in some countries; in China, for example, the proportion of elderly people is expected to double between the years 2000 and 2025 – from 7% to 14%.

The Support Ratio – Facing the Issues As the percentage of young dependants declines, the proportion of older dependants will increase. Demographic support ratios, or dependency ratios, are used as indicators of the relative sizes of the working and nonworking-age populations. The older-person support ratio (the number of people aged 15–64 years per person aged 65 years or older) indicates the dependency burden on potential workers. The impact of demographic ageing is visible in the support ratio, which is falling in both more and less developed regions. Support ratios have important implications for social security schemes, particularly pay-as-you-go systems, in which current workers pay for the benefits of current retirees. In the UK, the ratio of people of working age to people over 65 could fall from the current 3.7:1 to 2.1:1 by 2040. UK organizations for the elderly, such as Help the Aged, have come together as part of a Millennium Debate of the Age to discuss the various issues related to the ageing population. They want to see wider discussion of issues such as who funds long-term care, rationing of care – particularly in the light of increasing technological change – and promoting healthy living. In March 1999 the government's commission on long-term care for the elderly recommended that all nursing and personal care should be provided free (and paid for by taxation), though the government has yet to respond to the report's recommendations.

Active Ageing The WHO has warned that the health impact of the world's ageing population could be enormous, predicting a huge rise in cancers, coronary heart disease, diabetes, dementia, and other age-related illnesses. These chronic diseases are expected to become 'the main contributors to the burden of disease' in developing countries by 2020. The WHO has, therefore, launched a campaign to promote good health in old age as well as a positive approach to the elderly, saying that they should be viewed as active citizens with a great deal to contribute to society rather than as a burden. 'Active ageing' was the focus of the WHO's 1999 World Health Day.

In the USA, over 3 million people aged over 65 currently take part in voluntary activities in schoos and religious, health, and political organizations, and more than 2 million children are cared for by their grandparents. As increasing numbers of the elderly enjoy many years of active life through better healthcare, there is every reason to believe that societies in both the more- and less-developed regions can adjust to and benefit from this new era.

Employment

Agricultural and Non-agricultural Employment for Selected Countries

The minimum age for population base varies as follows: USA, France, Sweden, and UK, 16 years; Australia, Canada, Germany, Italy (1996), and Japan, 15 years; and Italy (1990), 14 years. For Italy the data are not comparable between 1990 and 1996.
(N/A = not available.)

Sector		Australia	Canada	France	Germany	Italy	Japan	Sweden	UK	USA[3]
Employment (thousands)										
1990 Agriculture, forestry, fishing		440	551	1,248	965	1,879	4,270	178	573	3,394
Industry[1]	manufacturing	1,170	2,105	4,708	8,839	4,755	15,010	943	5,971	21,346
Total		1,865	3,117	6,425	10,875	6,842[2]	20,890	1,268	8,128	29,834
Services		5,554	9,497	14,425	16,112	12,355	36,550	3,056	18,117	85,565
Total		7,859	13,165	22,098	27,952	21,080	61,710	4,501	26,818	118,793
1998 Agriculture, forestry, fishing		428	551	976[4]	N/A	1,332	3,330[4]	119	511[5]	3,509
Industry[1]	manufacturing	1,104	2,254	N/A	N/A	4,908	13,790[4]	774	5,066[5]	20,733
Total		1,814	3,189	5,421[4]	N/A	6,464[2]	20,430[4]	1,005	7,006[5]	29,871
Services		6,354	10,587	15,954[4]	N/A	12,373	40,800[4]	2,899	18,571[5]	98,083
Total		8,597	14,326	22,350[4]	N/A	20,167	64,550[4]	4,023	26,088[5]	131,463
Percentage distribution										
1990 Agriculture, forestry, fishing		6	4	6	3	9	7	4	2	3
Industry[1]	manufacturing	15	16	21	32	23	24	21	22	18
Total		24	24	29	39	32[2]	34	28	30	25
Services		71	72	65	58	59	59	68	68	72
Total		100	100	100	100	100	100	100	100	100
1998 Agriculture, forestry, fishing		5	4	4[4]	N/A	7	5[4]	3	2[5]	3
Industry[1]	manufacturing	13	16	N/A	N/A	24	21[4]	19	19[5]	16
Total		21	22	24[4]	N/A	32[2]	32[4]	25	27[5]	23
Services		74	74	71[4]	N/A	61	63[4]	72	71[5]	75
Total		100	100	100[4]	N/A	100	100[4]	100	100[5]	100

[1] Includes mining and construction.
[2] Public utilities included in industry.
[3] Data not comparable between years.
[4] Preliminary.
[5] Data are for 1996.

Source: US Bureau of Labor Statistics

Civilian Labour Force and Employment for Selected Countries

Data are based on OECD-Secretariat estimates; for Germany and Italy, data are from the European Labour Force Survey.
(N/A = not available.)

Year	Australia	Canada	France	Germany	Italy	Japan	Korea	Poland	Sweden[1]	Switzerland[2]	UK	USA
Civilian labour force (millions)[3]												
1990	8.4	14.3	24.3	29.4[4]	23.9[4]	63.8	18.5	N/A	4.5	3.6	28.2	125.8[4]
1995	9.0	14.9	24.9	29.8	22.7	66.7	20.8	17.0	4.3	3.9	28.3	132.3
1997	9.2	15.4	25.2	39.4	22.7	67.8	21.7	17.1	4.2	3.9	28.8	136.3
1998	9.3	15.6	25.3	39.4	23.0	67.9	21.5	17.2	4.2	N/A	28.9	137.7
Labour force participation rate (%)[5]												
1990	73.0	76.8	66.0	69.1[4]	59.8[4]	70.1	62.8	N/A	84.6	81.1	77.8	76.5[4]
1995	73.5	74.7	66.8	70.5	57.3	71.5	65.1	67.4	79.5	80.8	75.9	76.9
1997	72.4	74.9	67.1	70.6	57.7	72.6	65.4	66.4	78.7	81.5	76.2	77.4
1998	73.0	75.4	67.4	70.1	57.8	72.6	64.0	66.1	78.1	82.3	75.9	77.4
Civilian employment (millions)[6]												
1990	7.9	13.2	22.1	27.9[4]	21.2[4]	62.5	18.1	N/A	4.5	3.8	26.6	118.8[4]
1995	8.2	13.5	21.9	35.9	19.9	64.6	20.4	14.8	4.0	3.8	25.8	124.9
1997	8.4	13.9	22.0	35.5	20.0	65.5	21.1	15.2	3.9	3.8	26.8	129.6
1998	8.6	14.3	22.4	35.7	20.2	65.1	19.9	15.4	4.0	3.8	27.0	131.5
Employment–population ratio (%)[7]												
1990	67.9	70.5	59.9	66.4[4]	53.9[4]	68.6	61.2	N/A	83.1	79.6	72.4	72.2[4]
1995	67.5	67.5	59.0	64.7	50.5	69.2	63.7	58.1	72.2	78.1	69.3	72.5
1997	66.3	67.9	58.8	63.6	50.5	70.0	63.7	58.8	70.7	78.1	70.8	73.5
1998	67.2	69.0	59.4	64.1	50.8	69.5	59.5	58.9	71.5	79.3	71.2	73.8

[1] Refers to persons aged 16–64.
[2] The year 1990 refers to 1991.
[3] The civilian labour force corresponds to the total labour force minus the armed forces.
[4] Break in series. Data not comparable with prior years.
[5] Civilian labour force as a percentage of the working age population.
[6] Civilian employment corresponds to the civilian labour force minus the unemployed.
[7] Civilian employment as a percentage of the civilian working-age population.

Youth Employment

Despite a generally improving economic environment in the world's industrialized countries as a whole, in many countries employment prospects remain worrying, particularly for young people. The average youth unemployment rate in the OECD area rose from 10% in 1979 to 13% in 1998, and in 1998 one out of every five unemployed young people lived in a household where no one else had a job.

Many young people leave school without the requisite skills and competency. Many are also experiencing falling relative (and sometimes real) wages and considerable uncertainty as to whether or not they will be able to settle into good careers. However, on a more positive note, more young people are staying longer in school and the proportion of dropouts has declined in most OECD countries.

Employment by Gender in Selected Countries

(N/A = not available.)

Country	Civilian Employment–Population Ratio[1]							
	Women				Men			
	1980	1990	1995	1998	1980	1990	1995	1998
Australia	41.9	49.3	50.3	50.8	75.1	71.2	68.1	67.8
Canada	46.7	54.0	52.1	53.4	73.1	70.1	65.5	66.2
France	40.3	41.6	41.1	N/A	68.9	61.3	57.3	N/A
Germany	38.9[2]	40.9[3]	39.6[4]	N/A	69.9[2]	65.6[3]	60.4[4]	N/A
Italy	27.9	29.2	28.3	29.3[3]	66.0	60.0	56.5[3 4]	55.6
Japan	45.7	48.0	47.7	47.4[4]	77.9	75.4	75.0	73.9[4]
Sweden	58.0	61.8[3]	54.7	53.6[4]	73.6	70.6[3]	62.1	62.2[4]
UK	44.8	49.6	49.6	N/A	72.8	70.3	65.5	N/A
USA	47.7	54.3[3]	55.6[3]	57.1[3]	72.0	72.0[3]	70.8[3]	71.6[3]

[1] Civilian employment as a percentage of the civilian working-age population.
[2] Former West Germany.
[3] Break in series. Data not comparable with prior years.
[4] Preliminary.

Source: US Bureau of Labor Statistics

Part-time Employment by Gender in Selected Countries

This table shows part-time employment as a proportion of employment. Part-time employment refers to persons who usually work less than 30 hours per week in their main job.
(In percentages. N/A = not available.)

Country	Men		Women	
	1990	1998	1990	1998
Australia[1 2]	11.3	14.4	38.5	40.7
Austria	N/A	2.7	N/A	22.8
Belgium	4.6	4.9	29.8	32.2
Canada	9.1	10.5	26.8	28.6
Czech Republic	N/A	1.7	N/A	5.4
Denmark	10.2	9.9	29.6	25.4
Finland	4.8	6.8	10.6	13.0
France	4.4	5.8	21.7	25.0
Germany	2.3	4.6	29.8	32.4
Greece	4.0	5.3	11.5	15.9
Hungary	N/A	1.9	N/A	5.0
Iceland[3]	7.5	9.8	39.7	38.6
Ireland, Republic of	4.2	N/A	20.5	N/A
Italy	3.9	5.5	18.2	22.7
Japan[1 4]	9.5	12.9	33.2	39.0
Luxembourg	1.6	2.6	19.1	29.6
Mexico	N/A	8.2	N/A	28.3
Netherlands	13.4	12.4	52.5	54.8
New Zealand	7.9	10.6	34.6	37.6
Norway	6.7	8.1	39.1	35.9
Poland[1]	N/A	8.0	N/A	16.6
Portugal	3.1	5.2	11.8	15.8
Spain	1.4	2.9	11.5	16.6
Sweden	5.3	5.6	24.5	22.0
Switzerland[3]	6.8	7.2	42.6	45.8
Turkey	4.9	3.4	18.8	13.3
UK	5.3	8.2	39.5	41.2
USA[5]	8.3[6]	8.2	20.0	19.1
EU[7]	4.2	5.9	27.0	28.1
OECD Europe[7]	4.4	5.6	26.8	26.1
Total OECD[7]	6.0[6]	7.0	23.6	24.0

[1] Data are based on actual hours worked.
[2] Data are based on hours worked at all jobs.
[3] 1990 refers to 1991.
[4] Less than 35 hours per week.
[5] Estimates are for wage and salary workers only.
[6] Indicates break in series.
[7] For above countries only.

Source: OECD Employment Outlook June 1999, *OECD 1999*

The Rise of Part-time Employment

Part-time work has been one of the major sources of employment growth in recent years, particularly in Japan and many European countries, but much less so in the USA. In most countries, part-timers tend to receive lower levels of hourly earnings, as well as training, compared with their full-time counterparts. Part-time working is very heterogeneous, varying significantly across countries and between men and women. Despite this, most part-time workers say that they are happy working part-time, preferring it to other forms of 'non-standard' employment, such as temporary employment and shift-working. Attitudes to part-time working tend to be more favourable, on average, in those countries where it is more strongly developed.

Female Labour Force Participation Rates for Selected Countries: 1980–97

Data are for female labour force of all ages divided by female population 15–64 years old.
(N/A = not available. In percentages.)

Country	1980	1990	1995	1997
Australia	52.1	62.9	64.8	64.7
Austria	48.7	55.4	62.3	61.9
Belgium	47.0	52.4	56.1	N/A
Canada	59.1	67.8	67.6	67.8
Czech Republic	N/A	69.1	65.4[1]	64.4
Denmark	71.4	78.5	73.6	75.1
Finland	70.1	72.9	70.3	71.3
France	54.4	57.6	59.4	59.8
Germany[2]	52.8	57.4	61.7	61.8
Greece	33.0	43.6	45.9	N/A
Hungary	N/A	N/A	50.5	49.4
Iceland	N/A	N/A	82.4	N/A
Ireland, Republic of	36.3	38.9	47.8	50.4
Italy	39.1	45.9	43.3[1]	44.1
Japan	54.9	60.4	62.1	63.7
Korea, South	N/A	51.3	53.2	54.8
Luxembourg	39.9	50.7	58.0	60.9
Mexico	33.7	23.6	40.1	42.8
Netherlands	35.5	53.1	59.0[1]	62.2
New Zealand	44.5	62.9	63.3	64.9
Norway	62.3	71.2	72.4	75.8
Poland	N/A	N/A	61.1	60.0
Portugal	54.3	62.9	62.4	65.1
Spain	32.2	41.2	45.1	47.1
Sweden	74.1	80.1[1]	76.1	74.5

(continued)

Female Labour Force Participation Rates for Selected Countries: 1980–97 *(continued)*

Country	1980	1990	1995	1997
Switzerland	54.1	59.6	67.8[1]	69.4
Turkey	N/A	36.7	34.2	30.2
UK	58.3	65.5	66.0	67.5
USA	59.7	68.8	70.7	71.3

[1] Break in series. Data not comparable with prior years.
[2] Prior to 1991 data are for former West Germany.

Source: Labour Force Statistics, © *OECD*

Standardized Unemployment Rates for Selected Countries

Data are annual averages. The standardized unemployment rates shown here are calculated as the number of unemployed persons as a percentage of the civilian labour force. The unemployed are persons of working age who, in the reference period, are without work, are available for work, and have taken specific steps to find work.
(N/A = not available.)

Country	1997	1998	1999	Country	1997	1998	1999
Australia	8.5	8.0	7.2	Luxembourg	2.8	2.8	2.8
Austria	4.5	4.7	4.3	Netherlands	5.2	4.0	3.1
Belgium	9.4	9.5	9.0	Norway	4.1	3.3	N/A
Canada	9.1	8.3	7.6	Poland	11.2	10.6	N/A
Czech Republic	4.8	6.5	N/A	Portugal	6.8	5.1	4.5
Denmark	5.6	5.1	4.5	Spain	20.8	18.8	15.8
Finland	12.6	11.4	10.2	Sweden	9.9	8.3	7.0
France	12.3	11.7	11.0	Switzerland	4.2	3.5	N/A
Germany	9.9	9.4	9.1	UK	7.0	6.3	N/A
Hungary	8.9	8.0	7.1	USA	4.9	4.5	4.2
Ireland, Republic of	9.8	7.7	6.5	EU-15	10.6	9.9	9.2
Italy	11.7	11.9	N/A	OECD	7.4	7.1	6.8

Unemployment

OECD projections indicate that unemployment in OECD economies is likely to decline slightly over 1999–2001, and to decline even more rapidly within Europe. Despite these improvements, eight OECD countries are projected to have double-digit unemployment rates in 2000, and a total of 35 million persons remained unemployed in the OECD area in 1999.

International Political Organizations

Amazon Pact

(Amazon Cooperation Treaty) Agreement to protect and control the industrial or commercial development of the Amazon River region. The pact provides for technical and scientific cooperation in exploiting the natural resources of this ecologically important area.

Date established 1978

Founding members Bolivia, Brazil, Colombia, Ecuador, Guyana, Peru, Suriname, Venezuela

Current members same

Address Tratado de Cooperación Amazónica, Avda Prolongación Primavera 654, Chacarilla, Surco, Lima 33, Peru; phone: +51 (14) 499 084; fax: +51 (14) 499 718

Andean Community

(Communidad Andino; full name: Junta del Acuerdo di Cartagena [JUNAC]) South American organization aimed at economic and social cooperation between member states. Its ultimate aim is to create a free-trade area.

Date established 1969

Founding members Bolivia, Chile, Colombia, Ecuador, Peru

Current members Bolivia, Colombia, Ecuador, Peru, Venezuela. Observer: 1

Address Av Paseo de la Republica 3895, Casilla 18–1177, Lima 21, Peru; phone: +51 (14) 221 2222; fax: +51 (14) 221 3329; e-mail: info@junta.org.pe

Web site www.comunidadandina.org

Arab League

(League of Arab States) Organization of Arab states established to promote Arab unity, primarily in opposition to Israel.

Date established 1945

Founding members Egypt, Iraq, Lebanon, Saudi Arabia, Syria, Transjordan, Yemen

Current members Algeria, Bahrain, Comoros, Djibouti, Egypt, Iraq, Jordan, Kuwait, Lebanon, Libya, Mauritania, Morocco, Oman, Palestine, Qatar, Saudi Arabia, Somalia, Sudan, Syria, Tunisia, United Arab Emirates, Yemen

Address Arab League Building, Tahrir Square, Cairo, Egypt; phone: +20 (2) 575 0511; fax: +20 (2) 577 5626

Arab Maghreb Union (AMU)

Association formed to promote cooperation among the Arab states in North Africa. It aims to formulate common policies on military, economic, international, and cultural issues.

Date established 1989

Founding members Algeria, Libya, Mauritania, Morocco, Tunisia

Current members same

Address 26–27 Rue Okba Agdal, Rabat, Morocco; phone: +212 (7) 777 2668; fax: +212 (7) 777 2693

Association of Caribbean States (ACS)

Organization sponsored by the Caribbean Community and Common Market (CARICOM) formed to promote social, political, and economic cooperation in the region, and eventual integration.

Date established 1994

Founding members Antigua and Barbuda, Bahamas, Barbados, Belize, Colombia, Costa Rica, Cuba, Dominica, Dominican Republic, El Salvador, Grenada, Guatemala, Guyana, Haiti, Honduras, Jamaica, Mexico, Nicaragua, Panama, St Kitts and Nevis, St Lucia, St Vincent and the Grenadines, Suriname, Trinidad and Tobago, Venezuela

Current members same. Associate members: 11 dependent territories in the region

Address 11–13 Victoria Avenue, Port of Spain, Trinidad and Tobago; phone: +1868 623 2783; fax: +1868 623 2679

Web site www.acs-aec.org

Association of South East Asian Nations (ASEAN)

Regional alliance formed to promote peace and economic, social, and cultural development. It took over the nonmilitary role of the Southeast Asia Treaty Organization in 1975.

Date established 1967

Founding members Indonesia, Malaysia, Philippines, Singapore, Thailand

Current members Brunei, Indonesia, Laos, Malaysia, Myanmar, Philippines, Singapore, Thailand, Vietnam

Address ASEAN Secretariat, PO Box 2072, 7-A Jl, Sisingamangaraja, Jakarta 12110, Indonesia; phone: +62 (21) 726 2991/724 3372; fax: +62 (21) 739 8234/724 3504

Web site www.asean.or.id

Caribbean Community and Common Market (CARICOM)

Organization for economic and foreign policy coordination, and political and cultural unity in the Caribbean region. It replaced the Caribbean Free Trade Association.

Date established 1973

Founding members Barbados, Guyana, Jamaica, Trinidad and Tobago

Current members Antigua and Barbuda, Bahamas (a member of the Community but not of the Common Market), Barbados, Belize, Dominica, Grenada, Guyana, Haiti, Jamaica, Montserrat, St Kitts and Nevis, St Lucia, St Vincent and the Grenadines, Suriname, and Trinidad and Tobago. Associate members: British Virgin Islands, Turks and Caicos Islands. Observers: Dominican Republic, Mexico, Puerto Rico, and Venezuela

Address The Caribbean Community Secretariat, PO Box 10827, Georgetown, Guyana; phone: +592 (2) 69280; fax: +592 (2) 67816

Web site www.caricom.org

Commonwealth of Independent States (CIS)

Successor body to the Union of Soviet Socialist Republics, formed to ensure continued cooperation in trade and military policy, and recognition of borders. It has no formal political institutions, and its role is uncertain.

Date established 1991

Founding members Belarus, Russia, Ukraine

Current members Armenia, Azerbaijan, Belarus, Georgia, Kazakhstan, Kyrgyzstan, Moldova, Russia, Tajikistan, Turkmenistan, Ukraine, Uzbekistan

Address 220000 Minsk, Kirava 17, Belarus; phone: +375 (172) 293 517; fax: +375 (172) 272 339

Council of the Baltic Sea States

Organization founded to foster closer economic and political cooperation between states in the Baltic region.

Date established 1992

Founding members Denmark, Estonia, Finland, Iceland, Germany, Latvia, Lithuania, Norway, Poland, Russia, Sweden, the European Union (EU)

Current members same

Address CBSS Secretariat, Strömsborg, PO Box 2010, 10311 Stockholm, Sweden; phone: +46 (8) 440 1920; fax: +46 (8) 440 1944; e-mail: cbss@baltinfo.org

Web site www.baltinfo.org

Council of the Entente (CE)

(Conseil de l'Entente) Organization of West African states for strengthening economic links and promoting industrial development.

Date established 1959

Founding members Benin, Burkina Faso, Côte d'Ivoire, Niger

Current members Benin, Burkina Faso, Côte d'Ivoire, Niger, Togo

Address Mutual Aid and Loan Guarantee Fund, 01 BP 3734, Abidjan 01, Côte d'Ivoire; phone: +225 33 2835/1001; fax: +225 33 1149

Council of Europe

Intergovernmental body set up to achieve greater unity between European countries, to facilitate their economic and social progress, and to uphold the principles of parliamentary democracy and respect for human rights.

Date established 1949

Founding members Belgium, Denmark, France, Greece, Republic of Ireland, Italy, Luxembourg, Netherlands, Norway, Sweden, Turkey, UK

Current members Albania, Andorra, Austria, Belgium, Bulgaria, Croatia, Cyprus, Czech Republic, Denmark, Estonia, Finland, France, Germany, Greece, Hungary, Iceland, Republic of Ireland, Italy, Latvia, Liechtenstein, Lithuania, Luxembourg, Former Yugoslav Republic of Macedonia, Malta, Moldova, Netherlands, Norway, Poland, Portugal, Romania, Russia, San Marino, Slovenia, Slovak Republic, Spain, Sweden, Switzerland, Turkey, UK, Ukraine

Address Conseil de l'Europe/Council of Europe, F-67075 Strasbourg, CEDEX, France; phone: +33 (3) 88 41 20 00; fax: +33 (3) 88 41 27 81; e-mail: pointi@coe.int

Web site www.coe.fr

Group of Seven (G7)

The seven leading industrial nations of the world. The aim of their meetings was initially to coordinate international management of exchange rates. They now meet annually to discuss topical issues rather than to formulate policy. From 1991 Russia participated increasingly in G7 summits; the 1997 and 1998 summits were termed 'The Summit of the Eight', with full Russian participation, giving rise to the G8.

Date established 1975

Founding members Canada, France, West Germany, Italy, Japan, UK, USA

Current members Canada, France, Germany, Italy, Japan, UK, USA

Address no permanent secretariat

International Organization for Migration (IOM)

Intergovernmental body set up to help resettle refugees and displaced persons, and encourage social and economic development through migration. It also aims to advance understanding of migration issues. IOM works closely with the United Nations and the International Catholic Migration Commission.

Date established founded in 1951 as the Intergovernmental Committee for European Migration; became the IOM in 1989

Founding members Australia, Austria, Belgium, Bolivia, Brazil, Canada, West Germany, Greece, Italy, Luxembourg, Netherlands, Switzerland, Turkey, USA

Current members Albania, Angola, Argentina, Armenia, Australia, Austria, Bangladesh, Belgium, Bolivia, Canada, Chile, Colombia, Costa Rica, Croatia, Cyprus, Czech Republic, Denmark, Dominican Republic, Ecuador, Egypt, El Salvador, Finland, France, Germany, Greece, Guatemala, Haiti, Honduras, Hungary, Israel, Italy, Japan, Kenya, South Korea, Luxembourg, Netherlands, Nicaragua, Norway, Pakistan, Panama, Paraguay, Peru, Philippines, Poland, Portugal, Senegal, Slovak Republic, Sri Lanka, Sweden, Switzerland, Tajikistan, Thailand, Uganda, Uruguay, USA, Venezuela, Zambia. Observers: 49

Address 17 Route de Morillons, CP 71, CH-1211 Geneva 19, Switzerland; phone: +41 (22) 717 9111; fax: +41 (22) 798 6150; e-mail: info@iom.int

Web site www.iom.int

Organization of African Unity (OAU)

Association formed to eradicate colonialism and improve economic, cultural, and political cooperation in Africa. It also aims to coordinate military, scientific, and health policies.

Date established 1963

Founding members Cameroon, Central African Republic, Chad, Republic of the Congo, Côte d'Ivoire, Dahomey, Ethiopia, Gabon, Liberia, Madagascar, Mauritania, Niger, Nigeria, Senegal, Sierra Leone, Somalia, Togo, Tunisia, Upper Volta

Current members Algeria, Angola, Benin, Botswana, Burkina Faso, Burundi, Cameroon, Cape Verde, Central African Republic, Chad, Comoros, Democratic Republic of Congo, Republic of the Congo, Côte d'Ivoire, Djibouti, Egypt, Equatorial Guinea, Eritrea, Ethiopia, Gabon, Gambia, Ghana, Guinea, Guinea-Bissau, Kenya, Lesotho, Liberia, Libya, Madagascar, Malawi, Mali, Mauritania, Mauritius, Mozambique, Namibia, Niger, Nigeria, Rwanda, São Tomé and Príncipe, Senegal, Seychelles, Sierra Leone, Somalia, South Africa, Sudan, Swaziland, Tanzania, Togo, Tunisia, Uganda, Zambia, Zimbabwe

Address PO Box 3243, Addis Ababa, Ethiopia; phone: +251 (1) 517 700; fax: +251 (1) 512 622

Web site www.oau-oua.org

Organization of the Islamic Conference (OIC)

Association of states in the Middle East, Africa, and Asia, formed to promote Islamic solidarity between member countries, to consolidate economic, social, cultural, and scientific cooperation, and to eliminate racial discrimination.

Date established 1971

Founding members Afghanistan, Algeria, Bahrain, Bangladesh, Benin, Brunei, Burkina Faso, Cameroon, Chad, Comoros, Djibouti, Egypt, Gabon, Gambia, Guinea, Guinea-Bissau, Indonesia, Iran, Iraq, Jordan, Kuwait, Lebanon, Libya, Malaysia, Maldives, Mali, Mauritania, Morocco, Niger, Nigeria, Oman, Pakistan, Palestine, Qatar, Saudi Arabia, Senegal, Sierra Leone, Somalia, Sudan, Syria, Tunisia, Uganda, United Arab Emirates, Zanzibar

Current members Afghanistan, Albania, Algeria, Azerbaijan, Bahrain, Bangladesh, Benin, Brunei, Burkina Faso, Cameroon, Chad, Comoros, Djibouti, Egypt, Gabon, Gambia, Guinea, Guinea-Bissau, Indonesia, Iran, Iraq, Jordan, Kazakhstan, Kuwait, Kyrgyzstan, Lebanon, Libya, Malaysia, Maldives, Mali, Mauritania, Morocco, Mozambique, Niger, Nigeria, Oman, Pakistan, Palestine, Qatar, Saudi Arabia, Senegal, Sierra Leone, Somalia, Sudan, Suriname, Syria, Tajikistan, Tunisia, Turkey, Turkmenistan, Uganda, United Arab Emirates, Yemen. Observers: Central African Republic, Turkish Northern Cyprus, Côte d'Ivoire

Address PO Box 5925, Jeddah, Saudi Arabia; phone: +966 (2) 636 1400; fax: +966 (2) 636 6871; e-mail: idb.archive@mail.oicisnet.org

Web site www.oicis.net

Nordic Council

Consultative body founded to discuss mutual interests and increase cooperation in the Nordic region.

Date established 1952

Founding members Denmark, Iceland, Norway, Sweden

Current members Denmark, Finland, Iceland, Norway, Sweden; and representatives from the Faroe Islands, the Aland Islands, and Greenland

Address PB 3043, DK 1021 Copenhagen, Denmark; phone: +45 33 960 400; fax: +45 33 111 870; e-mail: nordisk-rod@nordisk-rod.dk

Web site www.norden.org

North Atlantic Treaty Organization (NATO)

Military and political association set up to provide for the collective defence of the main western European and North American states against the perceived threat from the USSR. It maintains troops and weapons, including nuclear weapons, in Europe. In 1994 NATO launched a 'Partnership for Peace' programme, inviting ex-Soviet republics and ex-Warsaw Pact countries to take part in a range of military cooperation agreements; by October 1997, 28 countries had joined the Partnership. Poland, Hungary, and the Czech Republic became full members of NATO in April 1999.

Date established 1949

Founding members Belgium, Canada, Denmark, France, Iceland, Italy, Luxembourg, Netherlands, Norway, Portugal, UK, USA

Current members Belgium, Canada, Czech Republic, Denmark, France, Germany, Greece, Hungary, Iceland, Italy, Luxembourg, Netherlands, Norway, Poland, Portugal, Spain, Turkey, UK, USA

Address NATO, Boulevard Leopold III, 1110 Brussels, Belgium; phone: +32 (2) 707 4111; fax: +32 (2) 707 4117; e-mail: natodoc@hq.nato.int

Web site www.nato.int/

Organization of American States (OAS)

Association founded to maintain peace and solidarity within the western hemisphere, also concerned with the social, cultural, and economic development of Latin America.

Date established 1948

Founding members Antigua and Barbuda, Argentina, Bahamas, Barbados, Bolivia, Brazil, Chile, Colombia, Costa Rica, Cuba, Dominica, Dominican Republic, Ecuador, El Salvador, Grenada, Guatemala, Guyana, Haiti, Honduras, Jamaica, Mexico, Nicaragua, Panama, Paraguay, Peru, St Kitts and Nevis, St Lucia, St Vincent and the Grenadines, Suriname, Trinidad and Tobago, Uruguay, USA, Venezuela

Current members Antigua and Barbuda, Argentina, Bahamas, Barbados, Belize, Bolivia, Brazil, Canada, Chile, Colombia, Costa Rica, Cuba, Dominica, Dominican Republic, Ecuador, El Salvador, Grenada, Guatemala, Guyana, Haiti, Honduras, Jamaica, Mexico, Nicaragua, Panama, Paraguay, Peru, St Kitts and Nevis, St Lucia, St Vincent and the Grenadines, Suriname, Trinidad and Tobago, Uruguay, USA, Venezuela. Observers: 40

Address 17th Street and Constitution Avenue NW, Washington, DC 20006, USA; phone: +1 (202) 458 3000; fax: +1 (202) 458 3967; e-mail: info@oas.org

Web site www.oas.org

Organization for Security and Cooperation in Europe (OSCE)

International forum set up to reach agreement in security, economics, science, technology, and human rights. It was originally known (until 1994) as the Conference on Security and Cooperation in Europe (CSCE).

Date established 1972

Founding members Albania, Austria, Belgium, Bulgaria, Canada, Cyprus, Czechoslovakia, Denmark, Finland, France, East Germany, West Germany, Greece, Hungary, Iceland, Republic of Ireland, Italy, Liechtenstein, Luxembourg, Malta, Monaco, Netherlands, Norway, Poland, Portugal, Romania, San Marino, Spain, Sweden, Switzerland, Turkey, UK, USA, USSR, Yugoslavia

Organization for Security and Cooperation in Europe (OSCE) *(continued)*

Current members Albania, Andorra, Armenia, Austria, Azerbaijan, Belarus, Belgium, Bosnia-Herzegovina, Bulgaria, Canada, Croatia, Cyprus, Czech Republic, Denmark, Estonia, Finland, France, Georgia, Germany, Greece, Hungary, Iceland, Republic of Ireland, Italy, Kazakhstan, Kyrgyzstan, Latvia, Liechtenstein, Lithuania, Luxembourg, Former Yugoslav Republic of Macedonia, Malta, Moldova, Monaco, Netherlands, Norway, Poland, Portugal, Romania, Russia, San Marino, Slovakia, Slovenia, Spain, Sweden, Switzerland, Tajikistan, Turkey, Turkmenistan, UK, Ukraine, USA, Uzbekistan, the Vatican, Yugoslavia (suspended)

Address OSCE Secretariat, Kärntner Ring 5–7, 1010 Vienna, Austria; phone: +43 (1) 5143 6180; fax: +43 (1) 5143 6105

Web site www.osce.org

Schengen Group

Association of states within the European Union that in theory adhere to the ideals of the Schengen Convention, notably the abolition of passport controls at common internal borders and the strengthening of external borders.

Date established 1995

Founding members Belgium, France, Germany, Luxembourg, Netherlands

Current members Austria, Belgium, Germany, Greece, Italy, Luxembourg, Netherlands, Portugal, Spain. Observers: 5

Address c/o Benelux Union Economique, Rue de la Régence 39, B-1000 Brussels, Belgium; phone: +32 (2) 519 3811; fax: +32 (2) 513 4206

Secretariat of the Pacific Community (SPC)

Organization (known until 1998 as the South Pacific Commission) formed to promote economic and social cooperation between Pacific countries and those with dependencies in the region. A nuclear-free zone in the Pacific is another aim.

Date established 1947

Founding members Australia, France, Netherlands, New Zealand, UK, USA

Current members American Samoa, Australia, Cook Islands, Fiji Islands, France, French Polynesia, Guam, Kiribati, Marshall Islands, Federated States of Micronesia, Nauru, New Caledonia, New Zealand, Niue, Northern Marianas, Palau, Papua New Guinea, Pitcairn Islands, Samoa, Solomon Islands, Tokelau, Tonga, Tuvalu, UK, USA, Vanuatu, Wallis and Futuna

Address B.P. D5, 98848 Noumea Cedex, New Caledonia; phone: +687 262 000; fax: +687 263 818; e-mail: spc@spc.org.nc

Web site www.spc.org.nc/

South Asian Association for Regional Cooperation (SAARC)

Organization aiming to promote the welfare and economic, social, and cultural development of the region.

Date established 1985

Founding members Bangladesh, Bhutan, India, Maldives, Nepal, Pakistan, Sri Lanka

Current members same

Address PO Box 4222, Kathmandu, Nepal

Unrepresented Nations' and Peoples' Organization (UNPO)

International association founded to represent ethnic and minority groups unrecognized by the United Nations and to defend the right to self-determination of oppressed peoples around the world.

Date established 1991

Founding members representatives of American Indians, Armenia, Australian Aborigines, the Crimea, Estonia, Georgia, the Greek minority in Albania, the Kurds, the minorities of the Cordillera in the Philippines, the non-Chinese in Taiwan, Tibet, Turkestan, the Volga region, West Irians, West Papuans

Current members 47 ethnic and minority groups, including the above

Address 40A Javastraat, NL-2585, The Hague, The Netherlands; phone: +31 (70) 360 3318; fax: +31 (70) 360 3346; e-mail: unponl@unpo.org

Web site www.unpo.org

Western European Union (WEU)

Organization set up as a consultative forum for military issues, in close cooperation with NATO. The WEU is the defence component of the European Union and the potential basis of a common European defence policy.

Date established 1954

Founding members Belgium, France, West Germany, Italy, Luxembourg, Netherlands, UK

Current members Belgium, France, Germany, Greece, Italy, Luxembourg, Netherlands, Portugal, Spain, UK

Address Secretariat-General, 4 Rue de la Régence, B-1000 Brussels, Belgium; phone: +32 (2) 500 4455; fax: +32 (2) 511 3519; e-mail: weu.info@ping.be

Web site www.weu.int

See also **Leaders of Selected Organizations**, p 743.

The European Union

European Union (EU)

The European Union is an organization working towards political and monetary union, a common foreign and security policy, and cooperation on justice and home affairs. The Maastricht Treaty established a single market with free movement of goods and capital in 1993, and a Charter of Social Rights.

In 1997 the European Commission agreed that Estonia, Poland, the Czech Republic, Hungary, Slovenia, and Cyprus, should commence entry talks for the EU's expansion into Central and Eastern Europe. Further negotiations began in April 1998.

In March 1998 the European Commission announced details of the widest ranging shake-up in the 35-year history of its common farm policy, launching a move to phase out price supports, the bedrock of the Common Agricultural Policy (CAP) since its creation in 1962. The new goal was to allow Europe's most efficient farmers, who had been shielded from world trends by artificially high prices, to compete globally for food sales. One of the keystones of the farm policy, a ban on member states subsidizing their own farmers from national coffers, would fall away for the first time. The move appeared to mark the first stage of the dismemberment of the original CAP.

On 1 January 1999 the euro – the world's newest and second most important currency – was successfully launched by the 11 participating countries (all EU members except Denmark, Greece, Sweden, and the UK), with euro notes and coins to begin circulating in 2002.

In March 1999 the Amsterdam Treaty – the EU's new constitution – was ratified by all 15 members and came into effect 1 May 1999. The new treaty amended the 1957 founding treaty of Rome by lifting internal border controls and setting forth additional citizen rights.

Date established 1957 (as the European Economic Community)

Founding members Belgium, France, West Germany, Italy, Luxembourg, Netherlands

European Union (EU) *(continued)*

Current members Austria, Belgium, Denmark, Finland, France, Germany, Greece, Republic of Ireland, Italy, Luxembourg, Netherlands, Portugal, Spain, Sweden, UK

Address c/o European Commission, Rue de la Loi 200, B-1049 Brussels, Belgium; phone: +32 (2) 299 1111; e-mail: address-information@cec.eu.int;

Web site www.europa.eu.int and www.eurunion.org

Some Key Dates in the Growth of the European Union

17 March 1948 Benelux Treaty enters into force.

1948 Creation of the Organization for European Economic Cooperation (OEEC) to administer Marshall Plan aid.

1949 Creation of the Council of Europe based in Strasbourg.

9 May 1950 Schuman Declaration; Robert Schuman proposes pooling Europe's coal and steel industries.

18 April 1951 European Coal and Steel Community (ECSC) Treaty signed.

1952–54 Development and failure of the plan for a European Defence Community (EDC).

25 March 1957 Signing of the Treaties of Rome establishing the European Economic Community (EEC) and European Atomic Energy Community (Euratom).

1967 Merger of the executive institutions of the three European Communities (ESCS, EEC, and Euratom).

1 July 1968 Completion of the Customs Union 18 months early.

1 January 1973 Denmark, Ireland, and the UK join the European Community (EUR 9).

13 March 1979 European Monetary System (EMS) becomes operative.

1 January 1981 Greece joins the European Community (EUR 10).

29 June 1985 European Council endorses 'White Paper' plan to complete single market by the end of 1992.

1 January 1986 Spain and Portugal join the European Community (EUR 12).

1 July 1987 Single European Act enters into force.

26–27 June 1989 Madrid European Council endorses plan for Economic and Monetary Union.

3 October 1990 Unification of Germany; the states of the former German Democratic Republic enter the European Community.

7 February 1992 The Maastricht Treaty setting up the European Union is signed.

2 May 1992 European Community and European Free Trade Association (EFTA) agree to form the European Economic Area (EEA).

1 January 1993 European single market is achieved on time.

1 November 1993 Treaty on European Union (Maastricht) enters into force after ratification by the member states.

1 January 1994 Establishment of the European Economic Area.

1 January 1995 Austria, Finland, and Sweden join the European Union (EUR 15).

17 June 1997 Treaty of Amsterdam is concluded.

12 March 1998 European Conference in London launches Europe-wide consultations on issues related to Common Foreign and Security Policy and Justice and Home Affairs.

30–31 March 1998 EU opens membership negotiations with Cyprus, Czech Republic, Estonia, Hungary, Poland, and Slovenia.

2 May 1998 Eleven EU member states qualify to launch the euro on 1 January 1999: Austria, Belgium, Finland, France, Germany, Republic of Ireland, Italy, Luxembourg, the Netherlands, Portugal, and Spain.

1 July 1998 European Central Bank inaugurated in Frankfurt, Germany.

1 January 1999 EMU and euro launched in the 11 qualifying EU countries.

1 May 1999 The Amsterdam Treaty enters into force after ratification by the member states.

15 January 2000 EU opens accession negotiations with Bulgaria, Latvia, Lithuania, Malta, Romania, and Slovakia.

European Parliament: Composition by Seats

Although the number of seats allocated to each country takes account of population size, representation is not strictly proportional and favours the smaller countries.

Member state	Number of seats
Austria	21
Belgium	25
Denmark	16
Finland	16
France	87
Germany	99
Greece	25
Ireland, Republic of	15
Italy	87
Luxembourg	6
Netherlands	31
Portugal	25
Spain	64
Sweden	22
UK	87
Total	626

European Union: Central Organs

European Commission initiates EU action. Its 20 members (two each from France, Germany, Italy, Spain, and UK; and one each from Austria, Belgium, Denmark, Finland, Greece, Republic of Ireland, Luxembourg, Netherlands, Portugal, and Sweden) are pledged to independence of national interests. Headquarters: Rue de la Loi 200, B-1049 Brussels, Belgium; phone: +32 (2) 299 1111; e-mail: address-information@cec.eu.int; Web site: www.europa.eu.int/en/comm/index

Council of Ministers of the European Union makes decisions on the Commission's proposals. Headquarters: Rue de la Loi 200, B-1049 Brussels, Belgium; phone: +32 (2) 285 6522; Web site: www.ne.eu.int/en.summ.htm

Committee of the Regions represents the regions within the EU, with 222 members serving a four-year term. Headquarters: Rue Belliard 79, B-1040 Brussels, Belgium; phone: +32 (2) 282 2211; fax: +32 (2) 282 2325; e-mail: info@cor.eu.int; Web site: www.cor.eu.int

Committee of Permanent Representatives (COREPER) consists of permanent officials (one group comprising ambassadors to the EU and one comprising deputy permanent representatives of member states) temporarily seconded by member states to work for the European Commission. Headquarters: Rue Ravenstein 2, B-1000 Brussels, Belgium; phone: +32 (2) 546 9011; fax: +32 (2) 513 4893; e-mail: info@esc.eu.int; Web site: www.ces.eu.int

Economic and Social Committee established 1957, a consultative body with 222 members drawn from employers, workers, consumers, and other interest groups within member states. Headquarters: Rue Ravenstein 2, B-1000 Brussels, Belgium; phone: +32 (2) 546 9011; fax: +32 (2) 513 4893; e-mail: info@esc.eu.int; Web site: www.ces.eu.int

European Union: Central Organs (*continued*)

European Parliament assembly of the EU, directly elected from 1979, which comments on the legislative proposals of the European Commission. Members are elected for a five-year term. The European Parliament has 626 seats, apportioned on the basis of population. It can dismiss the whole Commission and reject the EU budget in its entirety. Full sittings are in Strasbourg, most committees meet in Brussels, and the seat of the secretariat is in Luxembourg. Headquarters: Allée du Printemps, BP 1024, F-67070 Strasbourg, CEDEX, France; phone: +33 (3) 8817 4001; fax: +33 (3) 8825 6501; Web site: www.europarl.eu.int

European Court of Justice established 1957 to safeguard interpretation of the Rome Treaties that form the basis of the EU. It consists of 15 judges and 9 advocates-general drawn from member states for six-year terms. Headquarters: Court of Justice to the European Communities, Palais de la Coeur de Justice, Boulevard Konrad Adenauer, Kirchberg, L-2925 Luxembourg, Luxembourg; phone: +352 43031; fax: +352 43032; e-mail: info@curia.eu.int; Web site: www.europa.eu.int/cj/en

European Union: Selected Specialized Organizations

European Atomic Energy Community (Euratom) established 1957 to promote cooperation of EU member states in nuclear research and the rapid and large-scale development of nonmilitary nuclear energy. Headquarters: c/o European Commission, Rue de la Loi 200, B-1049 Brussels, Belgium; e-mail: eesd@cec.eu.int; Web site: www.cordis.lu/fp5-euratom/home.html

European Coal and Steel Community (EDSC) established 1952 to coordinate the coal and steel industries of member countries and eliminate tariffs and other restrictions. Headquarters: Bâtiment Jean Monnet, Rue Alcide de Gasperi, Plateau du Kirchberg, L-3424 Luxembourg, Luxembourg.

European Investment Bank (EIB) established 1957 to provide interest-free, long-term financing of approved capital projects. Headquarters: 100 Boulevard Konrad Adenauer, Kirchberg, L-2950 Luxembourg, Luxembourg; phone: +352 43 793 142; fax: +352 43 793 189; e-mail: info@eib.org; Web site: www.eib.eu.int//

European Monetary System (EMS) established in 1979 to promote financial cooperation and monetary stability. Central to the EMS is the Exchange Rate Mechanism (ERM), a voluntary system of semi-fixed exchange rates based on the European currency unit (ECU), planned as a stepping stone towards the introduction of a common currency, the euro. Headquarters: D-2-ecu, Rue de la Loi 200, B-1049 Brussels, Belgium.

Principal EC and EU Treaties and Selected Agreements

Treaty establishing the European Coal and Steel Community (ECSC) Signed in Paris 18 April 1951; entered into force 23 July 1952. Laid the foundation of the European Union. Six countries – Germany, France, Belgium, Luxembourg, Italy, and the Netherlands – agreed to place control of the coal and steel industries under a central authority. As the first European supranational organization, the ECSC was primarily intended to ensure peace in Europe and 'lay the bases for a broader and deeper Community', as stated in the preamble. It is the only one of the three founding treaties with a limited lifespan. It was concluded for 50 years and will expire 2002, after which it will probably be incorporated into the EC Treaty.

Treaty establishing the European Economic Community (EEC) (commonly known as the Treaty of Rome) Signed in Rome 25 March 1957; entered into force 1 January 1958. Created the EEC. New members were added: Denmark, Ireland, and the UK in 1973; Greece in 1981; Spain and Portugal in 1986; Austria, Finland, and Sweden in 1995. The preamble to the EEC Treaty expressed the resolve of the partners to create 'an ever closer union among the peoples of Europe'. Its initial goals of establishing a common market and common agricultural, transport, competition, and economic policies, were gradually followed by new fields of activity such as environment, social, regional, education, and research and technology areas. The Treaties of Rome served to set up a Joint Parliamentary Assembly and a Court common to all three Communities.

The Treaty of Rome was amended in some important respects by the Single European Act, and was extensively remodelled by the Maastricht Treaty and revised by the Amsterdam Treaty.

Treaty establishing the European Atomic Energy Community (Euratom) Signed in Rome 25 March 1957; entered into force 1 January 1958. Original signatories were Belgium, Germany, France, Italy, Luxembourg, and the Netherlands. The task of this Community is to contribute towards raising the living standards in member states by creating conditions necessary to the establishment and growth of nuclear industries.

Merger Treaty (usually known as the EC treaty) Signed in Brussels 8 April 1965; entered into force 1 July 1967. Brought about the merger of the Council of Ministers of the three Communities and of the High Authority of the ECSC, establishing a single Council and a single Commission of the European Communities.

First Accession Treaty Signed 22 January 1972. Concerned the accession of Denmark, Ireland, and the UK. For the UK, the Treaty entered into force 1 January 1973. From the date of accession the provisions of the original Treaties and the acts adopted by the institutions were made binding on the new member states.

Second Accession Treaty Signed in Athens 28 May 1979; entered into force 1 January 1981. Concerned the accession of Greece. Detailed transitional provisions are set out in the Treaty, most of which deal with agriculture. The Community provisions on free movement of workers did not come into effect until 1 January 1988.

Third Accession Treaty Signed in Lisbon and Madrid 12 January 1985; came into force 1 January 1986. Concerned the accession of Spain and Portugal. Detailed provisions are set out in the Treaty, but most of these interim arrangements were spent by January 1993, and Spanish and Portuguese workers have full free movement rights within the Community.

Single European Act Signed in Luxembourg 17 February 1986, and at The Hague 28 February 1986; entered into force 1 July 1987. Made extensive amendments to the other basic Community legislation, regarding voting procedures in the Council of Ministers and somewhat enlarging the legislative powers of the European Parliament. The main objective was to facilitate the adoption of nearly 300 measures to complete the Community's internal market.

Treaty on European Union (also known as the Maastricht Treaty) Signed in Maastricht 7 February 1992; came into force 1 November 1993. Created the European Union, European citizenship, and endowed the European Parliament with additional powers under a co-decision procedure. A much more thorough-going revision of the Treaty of Rome, it comprises two major sets of provisions: those aiming at the establishment of an economic and monetary union (EMU), at the latest by 1 January 1999; and those defined as steps towards the achievement of a political union, involving common foreign and defence policies. It renamed the EC to the European Union (EU). The Maastricht Treaty contains a number of fundamental opt-outs such as that granted to the UK under the Social Protocol attached to the Treaty.

The Treaty established three pillars for the European Union:

Pillar 1 incorporates the original three Treaties described above, with amendments. This covers the ongoing process of economic integration to create a single market for the movement of goods, capital, labour, and services. Added to this is a detailed plan for economic and monetary Union and supplementary powers in certain policy areas such as environment, research and technology, education and training.

Pillar 2 gives statutory authority to the Common Foreign and Security Policy (CFSP), and sets out the procedures for policy making and joint action in foreign and security affairs.

Pillar 3 deals with Justice and Home Affairs (JHA), including issues of asylum, immigration, combating drug addiction and fraud on an international scale, judicial cooperation in civil and criminal matters, and customs and police cooperation in areas such as terrorism.

Principal EC and EU Treaties and Selected Agreements *(continued)*

Policy under Pillars 2 and 3 is handled by intergovernmental cooperation, with limitations on the roles of the Commission and Parliament, in comparison with those defined in the founding Treaties.

Treaty of Amsterdam Signed in Amsterdam 2 October 1997; came into force 1 May 1999. Revising the Treaties on which the EU is founded, the Treaty's main objectives are: to reinforce the Parliament's legislative power, strengthen cooperation in foreign and security policy and justice and home affairs, to develop a more coherent EU strategy to boost employment (introducing an Employment Chapter), and to remove remaining barriers to free movement of people across internal borders.

The Treaty reflects the need to make the EU's institutions more efficient in preparation for the next enlargement. It recognizes the fact that many of the potential new members are relatively new democracies with significant ethnic minorities. It therefore includes new Treaty articles making EU membership conditional on upholding the principles of liberty, democracy, respect for human rights, and fundamental freedoms, with the possibility of suspension of right, including voting rights, for any member state which breaches these principles in the treatment of its citizens.

Treaty reforms of institutions aimed at making the EU more effective focus on simplifying decision-making procedures.

• The elected European Parliament (EP) will have increased decision-making powers:

extended co-decision: this means it can adopt decisions jointly with the Council of Ministers or reject proposals, in more areas, including transport policy, research, development aid, Trans-European Networks, and new Treaty areas such as employment policy, public health, the fight against fraud, equal opportunities;

consultation: for unanimous decisions within the Council, the EP may be consulted;

assent: in the case of international agreements, Treaty decisions, and accession of new members.

• The appointment of the Commission President is made subject to the European Parliament's formal approval. The Treaty limits the size of the Parliament to 700 (compared to 626 at present) in anticipation of enlargement.

• The size of the European Commission will be reduced to one commissioner per member state as soon as the Union enlarges (the larger countries currently have two). The Treaty does not change the distribution of voting shares within the Council of Ministers to compensate the larger countries (a protocol commits the EU to reopen discussions after enlargement takes place).

• Within the Council of Ministers, the Treaty extends the areas where decisions can be taken by a qualified majority, including anti-fraud measures, research, and employment. Unanimity remains the rule, however, in respect of constitutional matters and core sensitive areas such as taxation.

• The Treaty encourages closer ties with the national parliaments. A protocol allows a six week interval between the tabling of any legislative proposal and placing on Council agenda for decision, giving national parliaments a chance to hold a debate at the start of the legislative procedure. New measures to tackle fraud include increased cooperation between the customs authorities of the member states and enabling anti-fraud measures to be taken by majority voting.

Social Charter

In order to take account of the social dimension of the single market, the European Council on 9 December 1989 adopted a Charter of Fundamental Social Rights for Workers – known as the Social Charter – setting out minimum standards in a 47-point list. It covers basic rights for all EU citizens as regards freedom of movement, equal treatment, social protection, and fair wages. Although the Social Charter is not legally binding, the UK voted against it. The Charter was adopted by 11 of the then 12 member states. The Charter's initiatives were based on Articles of the Treaty of Rome, as amended by the Single European Act, which the UK has signed and implemented. Therefore any directive or regulation adopted by the Council of Ministers needs to be implemented by all member states, including the UK.

What is the 'Social Charter'?

One proposal at the 1991 Intergovernmental Conference (Maastricht) was to replace the existing Social Chapter of the Treaty of Rome with a new Chapter. The UK did not sign the Social Charter in 1989, and, at Maastricht, did not agree to the adoption into the Treaty of the draft Social Chapter. Therefore the other member states adopted a separate Agreement on Social Policy with a text almost identical to the proposed new Social Chapter. The agreement, often referred to as the 'Social Chapter' was appended to a protocol (the 'Social Protocol') which was agreed by all member states. The original chapter of the Treaty of Rome still remains in force.

The Protocol makes clear that any action the other member states take under the Agreement, and any financial consequences, will not apply to the UK. On their accession in 1995, Austria, Finland, and Sweden agreed to accept the Social Protocol and the Agreement on Social Policy. The UK is not party to either the Social Charter or the Social Chapter, though it agreed to the Social Protocol, which allows the other member states to use Community institutions. Measures from the action programme intended to implement the Social Charter apply to the UK if they have been adopted under the Treaty of Rome (as amended), whereas initiatives under the Social Chapter do not, at present.

Legislation introduced under the Treaty of Rome (basis for the Social Charter and Social Action programmes) applies to all 15 member states. For example, the Working Time Directive was introduced through the health and safety provisions in the Treaty of Rome, before the existence of the Social Chapter, and therefore applies to all 15 member states.

Legislation introduced under the Social Chapter – that is, as and when the UK does not wish to participate – is not binding on the UK, at present. So far, only two EU directives have been introduced in this way: the Working Time Directive and the Directive on parental leave agreed in 1996. Numerous UK companies have decided to introduce Works Councils even though they are exempted through the UK opt-out.

Schengen Agreement Concluded in Schengen, Luxembourg 1990 by Germany, France, Belgium, the Netherlands, and Luxembourg, this agreement is aimed at the gradual removal of controls at internal frontiers between the member states. There is also a further agreement on arrangements for processing asylum applications and cross-border cooperation between police forces. Since 1990 Spain, Portugal, and Italy have joined these arrangements; Austria, Greece, Denmark, Sweden, and Finland are signatories but not the UK and Ireland; whilst Norway and Iceland, who are not EU members, also participate in the Schengen area. The Schengen Agreement was incorporated into the Amsterdam Treaty. This will remove frontier checks between member states as the common area is progressively established.

What will this mean for the UK?

Because of their common travel area and the fact that they are both islands with common external and internal EU frontiers, a special arrangement has been agreed for the UK and Ireland in this area of cooperation. Both countries will maintain frontier checks at their own borders, although they can participate in individual initiatives taken by the other member states, on asylum or visa policy for example, if they wish to do so. For constitutional reasons there is also a special arrangement for Denmark.

Voting Procedure in the EU Council of Ministers

The Council of Ministers adopts legislation either by simple majority, qualified majority, or unanimity. In most cases, however, either unanimity or qualified majority is stipulated (by the EC and Euratom Treaties), in order to facilitate Community decision-making and protect the interests of the smaller member states. It eliminates the risk of two of the larger member states constituting a blocking minority. A qualified majority is 62 votes out of a total of 87. A blocking minority is 26 votes.

Qualified Majority Voting System

A weighted voting system gives each member state a vote roughly proportional to its population and economic strength.

Country	Population (1999 est)	Number of votes
France	58,886,000	10
Germany	82,177,000	10
Italy	57,343,000	10
UK	58,744,000	10
Spain	39,633,000	8
Belgium	10,152,000	5
Greece	10,626,000	5
Netherlands	15,735,000	5
Portugal	9,873,000	5
Austria	8,177,000	4
Sweden	8,892,000	4
Denmark	5,283,000	3
Finland	5,165,000	3
Ireland, Republic of	3,705,000	3
Luxembourg	426,000	2

Presidency of the Council of Ministers

Year	1 January–30 June	1 July–31 December
2000	Portugal	France
2001	Sweden	Belgium
2002	Spain	Denmark
2003	Greece	Italy
2004	Ireland, Republic of	Netherlands
2005	Luxembourg	UK
2006	Austria	Germany

The European Commission: Division of Portfolios 1999–2004

In March 1996 the Commission was hit by a damning report by independent investigators into fraud, nepotism, and mismanagement within the Commission. While not individually accused of lining their own pockets, the Commissioners were collectively accused of having lost control of a bureaucracy that enriched others and of mishandling taxpayers' money, and the report concluded that it was difficult to find anyone with any sense of responsibility for what had happened. Following the report, and a motion of censure by the European Parliament, all 20 EU Commissioners resigned.

Romano Prodi, the former Italian prime minister, was invited to accept the EU presidency, in succession to Jacques Santer. On 9 July 1999 Prodi announced the names and portfolios of the 19 proposed Commissioners, and the new Commission was scheduled to take office following approval by the European Parliament in September 1999.

Under the Treaty of Amsterdam, the 19 designated Commissioners were for the first time agreed between the governments of the member states and the incoming president.

The new Commission will include five women, one of them a vice-president, and will seek to promote equal opportunities between men and women throughout its mandate, as well as reflecting the political complexion of the European Parliament. It will be subjected to the highest standards of probity in public life. Each prospective Commissioner has given a personal undertaking that he or she will resign if asked by the President to do so. Prodi underlined his determination to introduce strict rules on conflict of interest for Commissioners once they have left office.

The 20 Commissioners

Romano Prodi (Italian) President
Neil Kinnock (British) Vice-president; Administrative Reform
Loyola de Palacio (Spanish) Vice-president; Relations with the European Parliament; Transport and Energy
Mario Monti (Italian) Competition
Franz Fischler (Austrian) Agriculture and Fisheries
Erkki Liikanen (Finnish) Enterprise and Information Society
Frits Bolkestein (Dutch) Internal Market
Philippe Busquin (Belgian) Research
Pedro Solbes Mira (Spanish) Economic and Monetary Affairs
Poul Nielson (Danish) Development and Humanitarian Aid
Gunter Verheugen (German) Enlargement
Chris Patten (British) External Relations
Pascal Lamy (French) Trade
David Byrne (Irish) Health and Consumer Protection
Michel Barnier (French) Regional Policy
Viviane Reding (Luxembourguese) Education and Culture
Michaele Schreyer (German) Budget
Margot Wallström (Swedish) Environment
Antonio Vitorino (Portuguese) Justice and Home Affairs
Anna Diamantopoulou (Greek) Employment and Social Affairs

The European Union: Citizenship and Rights

Citizens' rights
(Information from the European Parliament and European Union.)

The EU has gradually been conferring on people new rights which can be upheld by national courts and by the European Court of Justice. These rights were written into the EC Treaty at various stages, reflecting the development of Union activities. The Treaty of Rome began by outlawing discrimination based on nationality in matters connected with the free movement of workers. Subsequently three other instruments – the Single Act (1987) and the Maastricht (1992) and Amsterdam (1997) Treaties – added further rights.

According to the EC Treaty, every person holding the nationality of a member state is a citizen of the EU. Nationality is defined according to the national laws of the member state. Citizenship of the EU is complementary to national citizenship and comprises a number of rights and duties in addition to those stemming from citizenship of a member state.

For all citizens of the EU, citizenship implies:

- the right to move and reside freely within the territory of the member states
- the right to vote, and to stand as a candidate in elections to the European Parliament and in municipal elections in the member state in which they reside, under the same conditions as nationals of that state
- the right to diplomatic protection in the territory of a third country (non-EU state) by the diplomatic or consular authorities of another member state, if their own country does not have diplomatic representation there
- the right to petition the European Parliament and the right to apply to the Ombudsman appointed by the European Parliament concerning instances of maladministration in the activities of the Community institutions or bodies, with the exception of the Court of Justice and the Court of First Instance.

The Amsterdam Treaty, which came into force 1 May 1999, builds on this and gives new prominence to the rights of individuals, including:

- a new article permitting the Council to take action by unanimity to combat discrimination based on sex, racial or ethnic origin, religion or belief, disability, age, or sexual orientation
- a strong commitment to eliminate inequalities between men and women, in particular through application of the principle of equal pay for equal work or for work of equal value
- protection against the misuse of personal data held by the Community institutions
- new or strengthened cooperation in areas of particular concern to the Union's citizens: public health, environmental protection and sustainable development, and consumer protection.

Most importantly, the Amsterdam Treaty also takes specific steps to open up the Union's decision-making procedures to closer public scrutiny. Anyone in the EU now has right of access to documents originating from the European Parliament, Council, and Commission, within reasonable limits. Moreover, whenever the Council takes a decision which has legal effect, the voting results will be made public. This will make it much easier for people to see how the decisions which affect them have been taken.

How to get your rights recognized and enforced
If you consider that national, regional, or local authorities have wrongly interpreted your rights under Community law, or that they have discriminated against you or members of your family, you should assert your rights by complaining to the administration concerned. If you are not satisfied with the response, there are other ways to enforce your rights.

You should start by following national procedures. National courts must ensure that rights based on Community law are respected and, where necessary, set aside any measure which infringes it.

In addition, there are also ways of raising your case at Community level. Firstly, you can complain to the European Commission. If the Commission considers your complaint well-founded, it can contact the national authorities concerned to ask for an explanation and to request that the infringement of Community law be terminated. If the Commission is not satisfied with the response of the national authorities, it can open infringement proceedings against the country concerned. This may lead to the case being referred to the European Court of Justice in Luxembourg.

You may also present a petition to the European Parliament (see below) or raise your complaint with a Member of the European Parliament, who can put questions to the Commission and the Council. Their reply to the question must be made public.

You can also contact the European Ombudsman, but only if your complaint concerns maladministration by one of the Community institutions (for example, the European Parliament, the Council, or the European Commission), or by any decentralized body of the Community (for example, the European Training Foundation). Generally speaking, 'maladministration' means administrative irregularities or omissions. The European Ombudsman cannot deal with complaints concerning national or local administrations.

Petitioning European Parliament
The right to petition (added by the Treaty of Maastricht) was introduced to provide European citizens with a new way of sorting out situations which are doing them harm. But petitions are also a valuable source of information for parliamentary business, because they draw Parliament's attention to cases where the principles and rules of European integration are being infringed.

- Any citizen of the Union, and any natural or legal person residing or having its registered office in a member state, may petition Parliament, either individually or in association with others.
- Petitions must concern matters that come within the Community's fields of activity and affect the petitioners directly.
- Petitions must be addressed to the European Parliament.

How to submit your petition – You should state your name, occupation, nationality, and the place of residence of each petitioner.
- The petition must be written in one of the official languages of the European Union. A petition in another language will not be considered unless the petitioner has attached a translation or a summary of the petition's content in an official EU language, which will serve as the basis for Parliament's work on the petition.

The petition can be submitted in either written or electronic form.

- If you wish to submit a petition in paper form, there is no form to be filled in or standard format to be followed. However, your petition must: bear your name, nationality, occupation, and place of residence (in the case of a group petition, it must bear the name, nationality, occupation, and place of residence of the presenter or, at least, the first signatory); be written clearly and legibly; be signed. Your petition may include annexes, including copies of any supporting documents you may have.

- If you wish to submit a petition via the Internet you should: go to the European Parliament Petition site, www.europarl.eu.int/dg1/en/petition/htm; read the instructions that will appear on the screen; complete the on-screen form. As soon as you have sent your petition you will receive electronic confirmation that it has been received. To enable the European Parliament to register your petition, you must send them written confirmation. For this purpose simply click on the 'Print' button which will appear once the form has been sent to the European Parliament. Your form will then be displayed on the screen in standard format and can be printed. Then simply send the document by post with all signatures and relevant annexes. When the paper version of your petition has been received it will be officially registered and the consideration procedure will begin.

Admissibility
The Committee on Petitions first decides whether the petition is admissible, by checking that the matter comes within the European Union's fields of activity. If it does not, the committee declares the petition inadmissible and informs petitioners accordingly, giving the reasons and usually suggesting they apply to another authority that can take up the matter.

During the 1998–99 parliamentary year, the Committee on Petitions judged 693 petitions admissible and 540 inadmissible.

Examination of petitions
The Committee then asks the Commission to provide information. It sometimes also consults other parliamentary committees and Parliament's Directorate-General for Research. When sufficient information has been collected the petition is put on the agenda for a committee meeting, to

The European Union: Citizenship and Rights *(continued)*

which the Commission is also invited. At the meeting the Commission makes an oral statement and comments on its written reply to the issues raised in the petition. Members of the Committee on Petitions then have an opportunity to put questions to the Commission representative.

Further action

This depends on the case:

– If the petition is a special case requiring individual treatment, the Commission contacts the appropriate authorities or puts the case to the permanent representative of the member state concerned, as this approach is likely to settle the matter. In some cases the committee asks the President of Parliament to make representations to the national authorities in person.

– If the petition concerns a matter of general importance, for instance if the Commission finds that Community law has been infringed, the Commission can institute legal proceedings, and this is likely to result in a ruling by the Court of Justice to which the petitioner can then refer.

– If the petition is a political issue, Parliament or the Commission may use it as the basis for a political initiative. Petitions of this kind are dealt with jointly in a report and become part of the political work of Parliament; the individual cases are not taken up. The issues raised in petitions are thus a way of prompting action by Parliament.

In each case the petitioner receives a reply setting out the result of the action taken.

Publication of petitions

Petitions entered in the general register and the main decisions taken on them during the consideration procedure are announced at plenary sittings of the European Parliament. These announcements appear in the minutes of the sitting. The texts of petitions entered in the register and of opinions of the Committee accompanying forwarded petitions are stored in the European Parliament archives, where they may be consulted by any Member of the European Parliament.

See also  **Citizenship and Immigration**, pp 308–314.

The European Union – What Are the Benefits?

(Information from the European Commission Representation in the UK.)

What has Europe got to do with me?

As a result of the UK's membership of the European Community (or European Union, as it is now officially known), you can now live, work, or study in any of the 15 member states – that is Austria, France, Germany, Spain, Portugal, Belgium, Luxembourg, Denmark, Sweden, Finland, Ireland, Greece, the Netherlands, Italy, and the UK. As of 1 January 1994 these opportunities also apply to Iceland and Norway who have signed the European Economic Area (EEA) Agreement with the European Union member states. If you have recently crossed the Channel or visited another EU country, you will have noticed that routine passport checks are less frequent and import restrictions on personal goods have been lifted. This means there are no limits on what you can bring back from another member state – including alcohol and tobacco – provided that the goods have been bought, tax paid, for your personal use. (In July 1999 the purchase of duty-free tobacco and alcohol when travelling between member states, was discontinued, although duty-free perfume and gifts can still be purchased.) These are some of the more visible examples of the benefits of EU membership to ordinary people.

But what if I don't want to go abroad?

If you have no interest in travelling to other EU countries, you might well think the European Union has nothing to do with you. In fact, almost every aspect of daily life in the UK is affected in some way by the UK's membership of the European Union.

In the home

EU water quality standards ensure that lead, nitrates, and other unwanted residues are kept to safe levels. EU regulations ensure that all electrical appliances are safe. An eco-labelling scheme has been introduced to highlight products which cause least damage to the environment (for example washing machines). Some products will carry energy consumption ratings. All foodstuffs are labelled with clear price markings, sell-by dates, and lists of ingredients, permitted additives, and nutritional information. Unsafe additives, colourings, or flavourings are banned.

If you have children, their toys must pass EU fire-safety standards to protect them from accidents.

To protect you from unscrupulous door-to-door salesmen, EU rules give you the right to a one week cooling-off period during which you may cancel any contract agreed at home or on the doorstep.

Similarly, if you have been misled by a dishonest advertisement in a magazine or on television, EU rules give you rights to quicker redress when disputes occur.

These rules do not mean that European institutions are trying to standardize all aspects of British life. They simply set out the essential safety, quality, and hygiene standard requirements that should be met before they are placed on the market, for your own protection. It is also important to bear in mind that no major decisions are taken without agreement reached in the Council of Ministers, where all national governments (including the UK) take the decisions affecting us.

In the street

The EU has taken the lead in tightening emissions standards for cars, lorries, and other means of transport. Such environmental action also helps reduce global warming.

In the classroom

Even if you have no interest in foreign travel or learning another language, your children might. A range of EU programmes are in place to encourage language learning, study visits, and exchanges which can lead to job opportunities abroad in the future. Under EU rules, qualifications gained in one country must be recognized in another.

In the town centre

As a direct result of the single market, a wider variety of high-quality produce is available on supermarket shelves than ever before, with guaranteed standards of food and product safety.

If you buy a household appliance such as a stereo system, cooker, or fridge, you are protected by EU rules from unfair terms in customer contracts. Credit offers must also be clear and fair and if a product doesn't work or causes injury, EU rules make sure that the producer is liable for any damage caused. If you stop for a snack, EU rules ensure that all food premises and food handling staff meet minimum standards of hygiene and cleanliness.

Managing your money

If you are looking for a mortgage, savings plan, or other financial product, you will soon find more choice in the high street as foreign companies take advantage of the single market to offer their products in the UK. This might enable you to secure a loan at a lower rate of interest than offered by UK institutions, but with the same guarantees.

In the town hall

Like all local authorities in the UK, your local town or county council will be looking to attract funding from one of the Community structural funds to create jobs, boost the local economy, and attract investment. Substantial financial help is also given to the regions, especially run-down areas, to help them face industrial change and restructuring problems. Examples of projects include the construction of industrial sites on formerly derelict land, rejuvenation of inner cities to attract tourists, and initiatives to diversify economies in rural areas. Many councils are also forging closer economic as well as social ties with localities in other EU countries.

In the workplace

If you work in any form of manufacturing or service industry, you may find your business prospects are affected by the need to export products and win contracts in other member states. Until the single market was completed, all sorts of hidden barriers to trade, such as different technical standards, made it difficult to market goods outside the country of origin. Now anything that can be legally marketed and sold in one member state must, in principle, be allowed onto the market of all member states.

The European Union – What Are the Benefits? *(continued)*

On a personal level, EU health and safety rules protect you from hazards in the workplace, such as excessive noise, exposure to dangerous substances, or prolonged work at computer screens. Other rules also ensure that women receive adequate maternity leave and that conditions of employment are safeguarded if your company is taken over.

You are also protected from sexual discrimination wherever it occurs and EU laws have been passed on equal pay, equal employment rights, and equal social security entitlements between men and women.

On holiday
When booking a holiday, your rights as a consumer have been extended by the package travel directive, which obliges the tour operator to provide clear information, comply with the terms of the contract, and offer a refund or compensation if the service cannot be fully provided. If you buy an air ticket, travel agents are now obliged to inform you of the lowest available fare. To protect your family from health risks caused by dirty water, tough EU standards have been set to ensure high-quality bathing water at beaches and lakes. Should you fall ill abroad, you are entitled to health care and emergency treatment on the same terms as offered to locals. Before you leave the UK, you should obtain an E111 form from any main post office.

But are we still British?
Despite popular rumour, the Community is not looking to interfere in the nooks and crannies of national life in any of the member states. Under the so-called 'subsidiarity principle', joint action is only taken when a problem can be dealt with more effectively at EU level than by national governments alone. This principle was enshrined in EU law by the Maastricht Treaty.

To help clarify the areas in which the Community does and does not play a role in a member state's affairs, the London Office of the European Commission has produced a leaflet entitled 'Do you believe all you read in the newspapers?' As a citizen of an EU country, you have no fewer national rights, you have simply acquired additional rights as citizens of Europe as well.

So what are these rights?

- The right to set up business in any EU country.
- The right to study in any EU country.
- The right to the same treatment in terms of employment, healthcare, social security.
- The right to consular protection from the embassies of other EU countries, for example if you lose your passport in a non-EU country where your home country is not represented.
- The right to complain to your Member of the European Parliament (MEP) or the European Ombudsman about any aspect of EU policy.
- The right to vote and stand as a candidate in local and European Parliament elections.

The European Union: Useful Addresses

For information and advice to do with working or studying in another EU country you can dial the freephone number (0800) 581591 or visit the Europa Internet site (www.europa.eu.int). You can use the freephone number or the Internet site to obtain guides on working, living, and studying in an another EU country, as well as consumer issues, travelling, and equal opportunities in the EU. Information and useful addresses relevant to national taxation, voting rights, and residence permits in the other member states are contained in factsheets, which can be obtained by ringing the freephone number given above.

You can also seek assistance from the embassy or consulate of the country concerned in order to obtain details of relevant national authorities in other member states.

In addition, information on European policies and programmes is available at or through your local library.

Useful addresses
Information can be obtained from:

European Commission Offices in the UK
Jean Monnet House, 8 Storey's Gate, London SW1P 3AT; phone: (020) 7973 1992; fax: (020) 7973 1900; Windsor House, 9/15 Bedford Street, Belfast BT2 7EG; phone: (028) 9024 0708; fax: (028) 9024 8241; 4 Cathedral Road, Cardiff CF11 9SG; phone: (029) 2037 1631; fax: (029) 2039 5489; 9 Alva Street, Edinburgh EH2 4PH; phone: (0131) 225 2058; fax: (0131) 226 4105

European Parliament Office in the UK
2 Queen Anne's Gate, London SW1H 9AA; phone: (020) 7227 4300; fax: (020) 7227 4302

European Ombudsman
M Jacob Söderman, 1, avenue du Président Robert Schuman, BP 403, F-67001 Strasbourg Cedex; phone: +33 (3) 88 17 40 01; fax: +33 (3) 88 17 90 62; e-mail: euro-ombudsman@europarl.eu.int; Web site: www.euro-ombudsman.eu.int

Citizenship of the EU – voting rights, European elections, civil protection in the EU
The Home Office, 50 Queen Anne's Gate, London SW1H 9AT; phone: (020) 7273 3000

EFTA
All queries relating to the exercise of your rights in European Economic Area (EEA) countries which are not members of the European Union (Norway, Iceland, and Liechtenstein) should be addressed to:

EFTA Secretariat; 74 rue de Trèves, B-1040 Brussels; phone: +32 (2) 286 1711

The United Nations

The United Nations (UN)

The UN is an association of states for international peace, security, and cooperation. The UN was established as a successor to the League of Nations, and has played a role in many areas, such as refugees, development assistance, disaster relief, cultural cooperation, and peacekeeping.

The principal institutions are the General Assembly, the Security Council, and the Economic and Social Council, and the International Court of Justice.

The UN operates many specialized agencies, involved either in promoting communication between states (such as the International Telecommunication Union, ITU), or concerned with the welfare of states, such as the World Health Organization (WHO), the UN Educational, Scientific, and Cultural Organization (UNESCO), and the International Bank for Reconstruction and Development (World Bank). Much of the work of the specialized welfare agencies concerns developing countries, and consists mainly of research and fieldwork. However, they also provide international standards relevant to all countries in their respective fields. Though autonomous, the specialized agencies are related to the UN by special arrangements and work with the UN and each other through the coordinating machinery of the Economic and Social Council.

At a July 1998 UN conference in Rome, a treaty was agreed to set up a permanent international criminal court to try individuals accused of war crimes, genocide, and crimes against humanity.

Date established 1945

Founding members 51 states: Argentina, Australia, Belgium, Bolivia, Brazil, Belorussian Soviet Socialist Republic, Canada, Chile, China, Colombia, Costa Rica, Cuba, Czechoslovakia, Denmark, Dominican Republic, Ecuador, Egypt, El Salvador, Ethiopia, France, Greece, Guatemala, Haiti, Honduras, India, Iran, Iraq, Lebanon, Liberia, Luxembourg, Mexico, Netherlands, New Zealand, Nicaragua, Norway, Panama, Paraguay, Peru, Philippines, Poland, Saudi Arabia, South Africa,

The United Nations (UN) *(continued)*

Syria, Turkey, UK, Ukrainian Soviet Socialist Republic, Uruguay, USA, USSR, Venezuela, Yugoslavia
Current members 188 states as of May 2000

Budget The total operating expenses for the entire UN system – including the World Bank, International Monetary Fund, and all the UN funds, programmes, and specialized agencies – come to $18.2 billion a year.

The budget for the UN's core functions – the Secretariat operations and five regional commissions – is $1.25 billion a year. The UN and its agencies, programmes, and funds – mainly UNICEF, UNDP, UNFPA, WFP, and WHO – have a budget of $4.8 billion a year for economic and social development.

The top six contributors to the UN are the USA (25%); Japan (20.57%); Germany (9.86%); France (6.55%); Italy (5.44%); and the UK (5.09%). Collectively, they account for more than 72% of the regular UN budget.

The USA owes more in unpaid assessments than any other member state: over $1.6 billion.

Address United Nations, 1 United Nations Plaza, New York, NY 10017, USA; phone: +1 (212) 963 4475

Web site www.un.org

United Nations Secretaries-General

Term	Secretary-General	Nationality
1946–53	Trygve Lie	Norwegian
1953–61	Dag Hammarskjöld	Swedish
1961–71	U Thant	Burmese
1972–81	Kurt Waldheim	Austrian
1982–92	Javier Pérez de Cuéllar	Peruvian
1992–96	Boutros Boutros-Ghali	Egyptian
1997–	Kofi Annan	Ghanaian

United Nations Charter: Preamble

The Charter of the United Nations (UN) was signed on 26 June 1945 in San Francisco, at the conclusion of the UN Conference on International Organization, and came into force on 24 October 1945. The Statute of the International Court of Justice is an integral part of the charter.

Preamble

We the peoples of the UN determined to save succeeding generations from the scourge of war, which twice in our lifetime has brought untold sorrow to mankind, and

to reaffirm faith in fundamental human rights, in the dignity and worth of the human person, in the equal rights of men and women and of nations large and small, and

to establish conditions under which justice and respect for the obligations arising from treaties and other sources of international law can be maintained, and

to promote social progress and better standards of life in larger freedom,

and for these ends to practise tolerance and live together in peace with one another as good neighbours, and

to unite our strength to maintain international peace and security, and

to ensure, by the acceptance of principles and the institution of methods, that armed force shall not be used, save in the common interest, and

to employ international machinery for the promotion of the economic and social advancement of all peoples,

have resolved to combine our efforts to accomplish these aims.

Accordingly, our respective governments, through representatives assembled in the city of San Francisco, who have exhibited their full powers found to be in good and due form, have agreed to the present Charter of the United Nations and do hereby establish an international organization to be known as the United Nations.

United Nations: Members and Contributions

Country	Year of admission	Scale of assessments 2000 (%)	Gross contributions for 2000 (US $)
Afghanistan	1946	0.003	36,037
Albania	1955	0.003	36,037
Algeria	1962	0.086	1,033,065
Andorra	1993	0.004	48,050
Angola	1976	0.010	120,124
Antigua and Barbuda	1981	0.002	24,025
Argentina[1]	1945	1.103	13,249,659
Armenia	1992	0.006	72,074
Australia[1]	1945	1.483	17,814,365
Austria	1955	0.942	11,315,665
Azerbaijan	1992	0.011	132,136
Bahamas	1973	0.015	180,186
Bahrain	1971	0.017	204,211
Bangladesh	1974	0.010	120,124
Barbados	1966	0.008	96,099
Belarus[1]	1945	0.057	684,706
Belgium[1]	1945	1.104	13,261,672
Belize	1981	0.001	12,012
Benin	1960	0.002	24,025
Bhutan	1971	0.001	12,012
Bolivia[1]	1945	0.007	84,087
Bosnia-Herzegovina	1992	0.005	60,062
Botswana	1966	0.010	120,124
Brazil[1]	1945	1.471	17,670,216
Brunei	1984	0.020	240,248
Bulgaria	1955	0.011	132,136
Burkina Faso	1960	0.002	24,025
Burundi	1962	0.001	12,012
Cambodia	1955	0.001	12,012
Cameroon	1960	0.013	156,161
Canada[1]	1945	2.732	32,817,832
Cape Verde	1975	0.002	24,025
Central African Republic	1960	0.001	12,012
Chad	1960	0.001	12,012
Chile[1]	1945	0.136	1,633,684
China[1]	1945	0.995	11,952,322
Colombia[1]	1945	0.109	1,309,350
Comoros	1975	0.001	12,012
Congo, Democratic Republic of	1960	0.007	84,087
Congo, Republic of the	1960	0.003	36,037
Costa Rica[1]	1945	0.016	192,198
Côte d'Ivoire	1960	0.009	108,112
Croatia	1992	0.030	360,372
Cuba[1]	1945	0.024	288,297
Cyprus	1960	0.034	408,421
Czech Republic	1993	0.107	1,285,325
Denmark[1]	1945	0.692	8,312,570

(continued)

United Nations: Members and Contributions *(continued)*

Country	Year of admission	Scale of assessments 2000 (%)	Gross contributions for 2000 (US $)
Djibouti	1977	0.001	12,012
Dominica	1978	0.001	12,012
Dominican Republic[1]	1945	0.015	180,186
Ecuador[1]	1945	0.020	240,248
Egypt[1]	1945	0.065	780,805
El Salvador[1]	1945	0.012	144,149
Equatorial Guinea	1968	0.001	12,012
Eritrea	1993	0.001	12,012
Estonia	1991	0.012	144,149
Ethiopia[1]	1945	0.006	72,074
Fiji Islands	1970	0.004	48,050
Finland	1955	0.543	6,522,724
France[1]	1945	6.545	78,621,051
Gabon	1960	0.015	180,186
Gambia	1965	0.001	12,012
Georgia	1992	0.007	84,087
Germany[2]	1973/1990	9.857	118,406,065
Ghana	1957	0.007	84,087
Greece[1]	1945	0.351	4,216,347
Grenada	1974	0.001	12,012
Guatemala[1]	1945	0.018	216,223
Guinea	1958	0.003	36,037
Guinea-Bissau	1974	0.001	12,012
Guyana	1966	0.001	12,012
Haiti[1]	1945	0.002	24,025
Honduras[1]	1945	0.003	36,037
Hungary	1955	0.120	1,441,486
Iceland	1946	0.032	384,396
India[1]	1945	0.299	3,591,703
Indonesia	1950	0.188	2,258,328
Iran[1]	1945	0.161	1,933,994
Iraq[1]	1945	0.032	384,396
Ireland, Republic of	1955	0.224	2,690,774
Israel	1949	0.350	4,204,334
Italy	1955	5.437	65,311,330
Jamaica	1962	0.006	72,074
Japan	1956	20.573	247,130,768
Jordan	1955	0.006	72,074
Kazakhstan	1992	0.048	576,594
Kenya	1963	0.007	84,087
Kiribati	1999	0.001	12,012
Korea, North	1991	0.015	180,186
Korea, South	1991	1.006	12,084,458
Kuwait	1963	0.128	1,537,585
Kyrgyzstan	1992	0.006	72,074
Laos	1955	0.001	12,012
Latvia	1991	0.017	204,211
Lebanon[1]	1945	0.016	192,198
Lesotho	1966	0.002	24,025
Liberia[1]	1945	0.002	24,025
Libya	1955	0.124	1,489,536
Liechtenstein	1990	0.006	72,074
Lithuania	1991	0.015	180,186
Luxembourg[1]	1945	0.068	816,842
Macedonia, Former Yugoslav Republic of	1993	0.004	48,050
Madagascar	1960	0.003	36,037
Malawi	1964	0.002	24,025
Malaysia	1957	0.183	2,198,266
Maldives	1965	0.001	12,012
Mali	1960	0.002	24,025
Malta	1964	0.014	168,173
Marshall Islands	1991	0.001	12,012
Mauritania	1961	0.001	12,012
Mauritius	1968	0.009	108,112
Mexico[1]	1945	0.995	11,952,322
Micronesia, Federated States of	1991	0.001	12,012
Moldova	1992	0.010	120,124
Monaco	1993	0.004	48,050
Mongolia	1961	0.002	24,025
Morocco	1956	0.041	492,508
Mozambique	1975	0.001	12,012
Myanmar	1948	0.008	96,099
Namibia	1990	0.007	84,087
Nauru	1999	0.001	12,012
Nepal	1955	0.004	48,050
Netherlands[1]	1945	1.632	19,604,210
New Zealand[1]	1945	0.221	2,654,737
Nicaragua[1]	1945	0.001	12,012
Niger	1960	0.002	24,025
Nigeria	1960	0.032	384,396
Norway[1]	1945	0.610	7,327,554
Oman	1971	0.051	612,632
Pakistan	1947	0.059	708,731
Palau	1994	0.001	12,012
Panama[1]	1945	0.013	156,161
Papua New Guinea	1975	0.007	84,087
Paraguay[1]	1945	0.014	168,173
Peru[1]	1945	0.099	1,189,226
Philippines[1]	1945	0.081	973,003
Poland[1]	1945	0.196	2,354,427
Portugal	1955	0.431	5,177,337
Qatar	1971	0.033	396,409
Romania	1955	0.056	672,694
Russian Federation[3]	1945	1.077	12,937,337
Rwanda	1962	0.001	12,012
St Kitts and Nevis	1983	0.001	12,012
St Lucia	1979	0.001	12,012
St Vincent and the Grenadines	1980	0.001	12,012
Samoa	1976	0.001	12,012
San Marino	1992	0.002	24,025
São Tomé and Príncipe	1975	0.001	12,012
Saudi Arabia[1]	1945	0.562	6,750,960
Senegal	1960	0.006	72,074
Seychelles	1976	0.002	24,025
Sierra Leone	1961	0.001	12,012
Singapore	1965	0.179	2,150,217
Slovak Republic	1993	0.035	420,434
Slovenia	1992	0.061	732,755
Solomon Islands	1978	0.001	12,012
Somalia	1960	0.001	12,012
South Africa[1]	1945	0.366	4,396,532
Spain	1955	2.591	31,124,086
Sri Lanka	1955	0.012	144,149
Sudan	1956	0.007	84,087
Suriname	1975	0.004	48,050
Swaziland	1968	0.002	24,025
Sweden	1946	1.079	12,961,362
Syria[1]	1945	0.064	768,793
Tajikistan	1992	0.004	48,050
Tanzania	1961	0.003	36,037
Thailand	1946	0.170	2,042,105
Togo	1960	0.001	12,012
Tonga	1999	0.001	12,012
Trinidad and Tobago	1962	0.016	192,198
Tunisia	1956	0.028	336,347
Turkey[1]	1945	0.440	5,285,449
Turkmenistan	1992	0.006	72,074
Uganda	1962	0.004	48,050
UK[1]	1945	5.092	61,167,058
Ukraine[1]	1945	0.190	2,282,353
United Arab Emirates	1971	0.178	2,138,204
Uruguay[1]	1945	0.048	576,594
USA[1]	1945	25.000	300,309,591
Uzbekistan	1992	0.025	300,310
Vanuatu	1981	0.001	12,012
Venezuela[1]	1945	0.160	1,921,981
Vietnam	1977	0.007	84,087
Yemen[2]	1947	0.010	120,124
Yugoslavia[4]	1945	0.026	312,322
Zambia	1964	0.002	24,025

(continued)

United Nations: Members and Contributions (*continued*)

Country	Year of admission	Scale of assessments 2000 (%)	Gross contributions for 2000 (US $)
Zimbabwe	1980	0.009	108,112
Total		100.003	1,201,274,400

[1] Founder member.
[2] Represented by two countries until unification in 1990.
[3] Became a separate member upon the demise of the USSR which was a founder member in 1945.
[4] Founder member, but suspended from membership in 1993.

Source: United Nations Secretariat

Principal UN Institutions, Programmes, and Agencies

United Nations: Secretariat

The Secretariat is headed by the secretary general, who has under- and assistant-secretaries general and a large international staff of civil servants with loyalties to the organization and the international community rather than to any government. The secretary general is appointed by the General Assembly on the recommendation of the Security Council for a renewable five-year term.

Secretary-General

Kofi Annan (Ghana)] Deputy Secretary-General: Louise Fréchette (Canada) Under-Secretary-General, Department of Economic and Social Affairs: Nitin Desai (India) Under-Secretary-General, Department of General Assembly Affairs and Conference Services: Jongjian Jin (China) Assistant Secretary-General, Special Adviser on Gender Issues and Advancement of Women: Angela King (Jamaica)

Political, Security and Humanitarian Affairs

Under-Secretaries-General Under-Secretary-General for Humanitarian Affairs and Emergency Relief Co-ordinator: Sergio Vieira de Mello (Brazil) Under-Secretary-General, Peacekeeping Operations: Bernard Miyet (France) Under-Secretary-General, Political Affairs: Kieran Prendergast (UK) **Assistant Secretaries-General** Assistant Under-Secretary-General, Peacekeeping Operations: Renée Carrier (Canada) Assistant Secretary-General, Political Affairs: Ibrahima Fall (Senegal)

Legal, Administrative Affairs, and Public Information

Under-Secretaries-General Under-Secretary-General, Office of Legal Affairs: Hans Corell (Sweden) Under-Secretary-General, Department of Public Information: Kensaku Hogen (Japan) Under-Secretary-General, Department of Management: Joseph Connor (USA) **Assistant Secretaries-General** Assistant Secretary-General, Controller, Office of Programme Planning, Budget and Accounts: Jean-Pierre Halbwachs (Mauritius) Assistant Secretary-General, Office of Human Resources Management: Rafiah Salim (Malaysia) Assistant Secretary-General, Department of General Assembly Affairs and Conference Services: Federico Riesco-Quintana (Chile) Special Assistant to the Under-Secretary-General, Department of Public Information: Paula Refolo (USA) Executive Director, Office of the Iraq Programme: Benon Sevan (Cyprus)

Secretary-General's Executive Office] Chef de cabinet and Under-Secretary-General: S Iqbal Riza (Pakistan) Assistant Secretary-General for External Relations: Gillian Sorensen (USA) Spokesman for the Secretary-General: Fred Eckhard (USA)

United Nations: Security Council

The most powerful body of the UN, responsible for maintaining international peace and security. UN member states undertake to accept and carry out its decisions. Any permanent member of the council can veto a decision. The council may investigate disputes, make recommendations, and call on members to take economic or military measures to enforce its decisions, and if these measures are deemed inadequate it may take military action.

Date established 1945

Founding members China, France, UK, USA, USSR

Current members permanent members: China, France, Russia, UK, USA; rotating members (1997–98): Costa Rica, Japan, Kenya, Portugal, Sweden; (1999–2000): Argentina, Bahrain, Brazil, Canada, Gabon, Gambia, Malaysia, Namibia, Netherlands, Slovenia; (2000–01): Argentina, Bangladesh, Canada, Jamaica, Malaysia, Mali, Namibia, Netherlands, Tunisia, Ukraine

Address United Nations, Room S-3520A, New York, NY 10017, USA; phone: +1 (212) 963 1234; fax: +1 (212) 758 2718

Web site www.un.org/Overview/Organs/sc.html

United Nations: General Assembly

The largest decision-making body of the UN, consisting of one representative from each of the member states. The General Assembly meets annually. It controls UN finances and approves the budget. Other decisions are not binding; it merely makes recommendations to the Security Council or a member state. It elects the nonpermanent members of the Security Council.

Date established 1945

Current members 188 states

Address United Nations, 1 United Nations Plaza, New York, NY 10017, USA; phone: +1 (212) 963 1234; fax: +1 (212) 963 4879; Web site: www.un.org/ga/54

United Nations: International Court of Justice

The main judicial organ of the UN. Only states, not individuals, can be parties to cases before the court. There is no appeal. Decisions of the court are binding, but states are not obliged to submit cases to it. The court gives advisory opinions at the request of UN bodies.

Date established 1945

Members 15 independent judges, elected by the Security Council and the General Assembly on the basis of their competence in international law and irrespective of their nationalities, except that no two judges can be nationals of the same state

Address Peace Palace, NL-2517 KJ The Hague, The Netherlands; phone: +31 (70) 302 2323; fax: +31 (70) 364 9928; e-mail: information@icj-cij.org; Web site: www.icj-cij.org

United Nations: Economic and Social Council (ECOSOC)

Organ of the UN that guides and coordinates the General Assembly's economic programme. It initiates studies of international economic, social, cultural, educational, health, and related matters. It also coordinates the activities of the Food and Agriculture Organization.

Date established 1945

Founding members Belgium, Canada, Chile, China, Colombia, Cuba, Czechoslovakia, France, Greece, India, Lebanon, Norway, Peru, UK, Ukrainian Soviet Socialist Republic, USA, USSR, Yugoslavia

Current members 54 members elected for three years, one-third retiring in rotation

Address United Nations, 1 United Nations Plaza, New York, NY 10017, USA; phone: +1 (212) 963 1234; fax: +1 (212) 758 2718

Web site www.ces.eu.int

The council includes five regional commissions:

Economic Commission for Africa (ECA) established 1958 to promote and facilitate concerted action for the economic and social development of Africa through research and the coordination of national policies. Headquarters: Africa Hall, PO Box 3001, Addis Ababa, Ethiopia; phone: +251 (1) 51 5826; fax: +251 (1) 51 0365; e-mail: ecainfo@un.org

Web site www.un.org/depts/eca

Economic and Social Commission for Asia and the Pacific (ESCAP) established 1947 (present name from 1974) to promote regional economic cooperation, poverty alleviation through economic growth and social development, and environmentally sustainable development. Headquarters: UN Building, Rajadamnern Nok Avenue, Bangkok 10200, Thailand; phone: +66 (2) 288 1234; fax: +66 (2) 288 100; e-mail: webmaster@unescap.org; Web site: www.unescap.org

Economic Commission for Europe (UN/ECE) established 1947 to generate and improve economic relations between member and other countries and to strengthen cooperation between governments, particularly in environment, transport, statistics, trade facilitation, and economic analysis. Headquarters: Palais des Nations, 8–14 Avenue de la Paix, CH-1211 Geneva 10, Switzerland; phone: +41 (22) 917 4444; fax: +41 (22) 917 0505; e-mail: info.ece@unece.org; Web site: www.unec.org

Economic Commission for Latin America and the Caribbean (ECLAC) established 1948 to raise the level of economic activity in the region and strengthen the economic relations of member countries with one another and with other countries. Headquarters: Avenida Vitacura 3030, PO Box 179-D, Santiago, Chile; e-mail: webmaster@eclac.cl; Web site: www.eclac.org

Economic and Social Commission for Western Asia (ESCWA) established 1973 to raise the level of economic activity in the Middle East and northern Africa, and strengthen the economic relations of member countries with one another and with other countries. Headquarters: PO Box 927115, Amman, Jordan; e-mail: library@escwa.org.ib; Web site: www.escwa.org.ib

United Nations: Selected Programmes and Organs

International Atomic Energy Agency (IAEA) established 1957 to advise and assist member countries in the development and peaceful application of nuclear power, and to guard against its misuse. It is an independent intergovernmental organization under the aegis of the UN. Headquarters: Wagramerstrasse 5, PO Box 100, A-1400 Vienna, Austria; phone: +43 (1) 20600; e-mail: eesd@cec.eu.int; Web site: www.cordis.lu/fp5-euratom/home.html

United Nations Centre for Human Settlements (UNCHS, Habitat) established 1978 to service the intergovernmental Commission on Human Settlements by providing planning, construction, land development, and finance. It is a standing committee under the Economic and Social Council and the General Assembly. Headquarters: 2 United Nations Plaza, Room DC-2-0943, New York, NY 10017, USA; phone: +1 (212) 963 420; fax: +1 (212) 963 8721; e-mail: infohabitat@igc.apc.org; Web site: www.undp.org/un/habitat

United Nations Children's Fund (UNICEF) established 1946 to improve the lives of children throughout the world. It carries out programmes in health, nutrition, education, water and sanitation, the environment, women in development, and other areas of importance to children. Headquarters: 3 United Nations Plaza, New York, NY 10017, USA; phone: +1 (212) 326 7000; fax: +1 (212) 888 7465; e-mail: addresses@unicef.org; Web site: www.unicef.org

United Nations Conference on Trade and Development (UNCTAD) established 1964 to promote international trade, particularly in developing countries. Headquarters: Palais des Nations, 8–14 Avenue de la Paix, CH-1211 Geneva 10, Switzerland; phone: +41 (22) 917 1234; fax: +41 (22) 907 0057; Web site: www.unicc.org/unctad

United Nations Development Fund for Women (UNIFEM) established 1976 to help women achieve equality through economic and social development. It provides direct technical and financial support to women's initiatives. Headquarters: 304 East 45th Street, 6th Floor, New York, NY 10017, USA; phone: +1 (212) 906 6400; fax: +1 (212) 906 6705; e-mail: unifem@undp.org; Web site: www.unifem.undp.org

United Nations Development Programme (UNDP) established 1965 to eradicate poverty, especially in the least developed countries, and to achieve sustainable human development, the empowerment of women, and the protection and regeneration of the environment. Headquarters: 1 United Nations Plaza, New York, NY 10017, USA; phone: +1 (212) 906 5788; fax: +1 (212) 906 5365; e-mail: mborg@undp.org.fi; Web site: www.undp.org

United Nations Environment Programme (UNEP) established 1972 to monitor the state of the environment and promote environmentally sound developments throughout the world. Headquarters: PO Box 30552, Nairobi, Kenya; phone: +254 (2) 230 800; fax: +254 (2) 226 890; e-mail: ipainfo@unep.org; Web site: www.unep.ch/unepright

United Nations High Commissioner for Refugees (UNHCR) established 1951 to help refugees and displaced people worldwide, to give them international protection, and to find solutions to their problems. Headquarters: 8–14 Avenue de la Paix, 1211 Geneva 10, Switzerland; phone: +41 (22) 917 9000; fax: +41 (22) 917 9016; Web site: www.unhcr.ch

United Nations Institute for Training and Research (UNITAR) established 1965 to improve the effectiveness of the UN through training and research. It is a standing committee under the Economic and Social Council and the General Assembly. Headquarters: Palais des Nations, CH-1211 Geneva 10, Switzerland; phone: +41 (22) 917 1234; fax: +41 (22) 917 8047; e-mail:info@unitar.org; Web site: www.unitar.org

United Nations Population Fund (UNFPA) established 1972 under the umbrella of UNDP to help countries, at their request, to address issues of reproductive health and population, and to raise awareness of this in all countries. Headquarters: 220 East 42nd Street, 19th Floor, Room DN 1901, New York, NY 10017, USA; phone: +1 (212) 297 5000; fax: +1 (212) 557 6416; e-mail: hq@unfpa.org; Web site: www.unfpa.org/index.htm

United Nations Research Institute for Social Development (UNRISD) established 1964 to conduct research into problems and policies of social and economic development. It is a standing committee under the Economic and Social Council and the General Assembly. Headquarters: Palais des Nations, 1211 Geneva 10, Switzerland; phone: +41 (22) 917 3020; fax: +41 (22) 917 0650; e-mail: info@unrisd.org; Web site: www.unrisd.org

World Food Programme (WFP) established 1963 to improve economic and social development through food aid and to provide emergency relief. It is a standing committee under the Economic and Social Council and the General Assembly. Headquarters: C G Viola 68, Parco de Medici, 00148 Rome, Italy; phone: +39 (06) 6513 2628; fax: +39 (06) 6513 2840; e-mail: wfpinfo@wfp.org; Web site: www.wfp.org

United Nations: Specialized Agencies

Food and Agriculture Organization (FAO) established 1945 to coordinate activities to improve food and timber production and levels of nutrition throughout the world. It is also concerned with investment in agriculture and dispersal of emergency food supplies. Headquarters: Viale delle Terme di Caracalla, I-00100 Rome, Italy; phone: +39 (06) 57051; fax: +39 (06) 5705 3152; Web site: www.fao.org

International Civil Aviation Organization (ICAO) established 1947 to promote safety and efficiency in aviation, international facilities, and air law. Headquarters: 999 University Street, Montréal, H3C 5H7, Canada; phone: +1 (514) 954 8219; fax: +1 (514) 954 6376; e-mail: dgca@icao.int; Web site: www.icao.int

International Fund for Agricultural Development (IFAD) established 1977 to provide additional funds for benefiting the poorest in developing countries. Headquarters: Via del Serafico 107, I-00142 Rome, Italy; phone: +39 (06) 54591; fax: +39 (06) 504 3463; e-mail: ifad@ifad.org; Web site: www.ifad.org

International Labour Organization (ILO) established 1919 to formulate standards for labour and social conditions. Headquarters: 4 Route des Morillons, CH-1211 Geneva, Switzerland; phone: +41 (22) 799 6026; fax: +41 (22) 799 8533; e-mail: cabinet@ilo.org; Web site: www.ilo.org

International Maritime Organization (IMO) established 1958 to promote safety at sea, pollution control, and the abolition of restrictive practices. Headquarters: 4 Albert Embankment, London SE1 7SR, UK; phone: (020) 7735 7611; fax: (020) 7587 3210; e-mail: info@imo.org; Web site: www.imo.org

International Monetary Fund (IMF) established 1944 to promote world trade and to smooth loan repayments among member states; the IMF also makes loans to members in balance-of-payments difficulties, on certain conditions. Headquarters: 700 19th Street NW, Washington, DC 20431, USA; phone: +1 (202) 623 7000; fax: +1 (202) 623 4661; Web site: www.imf.org

International Telecommunication Union (ITU) established 1934 to promote international regulations for telephone, radio, and telegraph communications, and to allocate radio frequencies. Headquarters: Palais des Nations, 8–14 Avenue de la Paix, CH-1211 Geneva 10, Switzerland.

United Nations Educational, Scientific, and Cultural Organization (UNESCO) established 1946 to promote cooperation among nations through education, science, and culture, and to further respect for justice, the rule of law, and human rights and fundamental freedoms. It pays special attention to women's issues and youth development. Headquarters: 7 Place de Fontenoy, F-75352 Paris 075P, France; Web site: www.unesco.org

United Nations Industrial Development Organization (UNIDO) established 1966 to promote industrial development and coordination. It acts as the chief coordinating body for industrial activities within the UN system. Headquarters: Vienna International Centre, PO Box 300, A-1400 Vienna, Austria; phone: +43 (1) 211 310; fax: +43 (1) 232 156; Web site: www.unido.org

Universal Postal Union (UPU) established 1875 to coordinate international collaboration of postal services. It became an agency of the UN in 1947. Headquarters: Bureau International de l'UPU, Weltpoststrasse 4, CH-3000 Bern 15, Switzerland; phone: +41 (31) 350 3111; fax: +41 (31) 350 3110; e-mail: ib.info@ib.upu.org; Web site: www.ibis.ib.upu.org

World Health Organization (WHO) established 1946 to assist all peoples in attaining the highest possible levels of health, to prevent the spread of diseases, and to eradicate them. It is creating a worldwide early-warning system for infectious diseases. Headquarters: 20 Avenue Appia, CH-1211 Geneva 27, Switzerland; phone: +41 (22) 791 2111; fax: +41 (22) 791 0746; Web site: www.who.ch

World Intellectual Property Organization (WIPO) established 1974 to protect copyright, patents, and trademarks in the arts, science, and industry. Headquarters: 34 Chemin des Colombettes, CP 18, CH-1211 Geneva 20, Switzerland; phone: +41 (22) 338 9111; fax: +41 (22) 733 5428; Web site: www.wipo.int

World Meteorological Organization (WMO) established 1951 to facilitate worldwide cooperation in the creation and maintenance of a network of stations for making meteorological observations and to ensure the rapid exchange of information. Headquarters: 7 bis Avenue de la Paix, CP 2300, CH-1211 Geneva 2, Switzerland; phone: +41 (22) 730 8111; fax: +41 (22) 730 8181; e-mail: ipa@www.wmo.ch; Web site: www.wmo.ch

United Nations: World Bank Group

International Bank for Reconstruction and Development (IBRD, World Bank) established 1945 to promote economic development by lending money to countries in need. The loans are on commercial terms and guaranteed by member states. Headquarters: 1818 H Street NW, Washington, DC 20433, USA; phone: +1 (202) 477 1234; fax: +1 (202) 477 6391; e-mail: knewcombe@worldbank.org; Web site: www.worldbank.org

International Development Association (IDA) established 1960 to meet the need for lending to poor countries on easy terms; administered by the World Bank. Headquarters: 1818 H Street NW, Washington, DC 20433, USA; phone: +1 (202) 477 1234; fax: +1 (202) 477 6391; Web site: www.worldbank.org/html/extdr/ida.html

International Finance Corporation (IFC) established 1956 to encourage private enterprise in developing countries. It is affiliated to the World Bank. Headquarters: 2121 Pennsylvania Avenue NW, Washington, DC 20433, USA; phone: +1 (202) 473 7711; fax: +1 (202) 974 4384; e-mail: ifc-webmaster@ifc.org; Web site: www.ifc.org

Multilateral Investment Guarantee Agency (MIGA) established 1988 to encourage the flow of private investment to developing member countries. Headquarters: 1818 H Street NW, Washington, DC 20433, USA; phone: +1 (202) 477 1234; fax: +1 (202) 477 0741; Web site: www.miga.org

International Human Rights

Universal Declaration of Human Rights

On 10 December 1948 the General Assembly of the United Nations adopted and proclaimed the Universal Declaration of Human Rights. Following this historic act, the Assembly called upon all member countries to publicize the text of the declaration and 'to cause it to be disseminated, displayed, read, and expounded principally in schools and other educational institutions, without distinction based on the political status of countries or territories'.

Preamble

Whereas recognition of the inherent dignity and of the equal and inalienable rights of all members of the human family is the foundation of freedom, justice, and peace in the world,

Whereas disregard and contempt for human rights have resulted in barbarous acts which have outraged the conscience of mankind, and the advent of a world in which human beings shall enjoy freedom of speech and belief and freedom from fear and want has been proclaimed as the highest aspiration of the common people,

Whereas it is essential, if man is not to be compelled to have recourse, as a last resort, to rebellion against tyranny and oppression, that human rights should be protected by the rule of law,

Whereas it is essential to promote the development of friendly relations between nations,

Whereas the peoples of the United Nations have in the Charter reaffirmed their faith in fundamental human rights, in the dignity and worth of the human person and in the equal rights of men and women and have

Universal Declaration of Human Rights (*continued*)

determined to promote social progress and better standards of life in larger freedom,

Whereas member states have pledged themselves to achieve, in cooperation with the United Nations, the promotion of universal respect for and observance of human rights and fundamental freedoms,

Whereas a common understanding of these rights and freedoms is of the greatest importance for the full realization of this pledge,

Now, therefore, the General Assembly proclaims this Universal Declaration of Human Rights as a common standard of achievement for all peoples and all nations, to the end that every individual and every organ of society, keeping this Declaration constantly in mind, shall strive by teaching and education to promote respect for these rights and freedoms and by progressive measures, national and international, to secure their universal and effective recognition and observance, both among the peoples of member states themselves and among the peoples of territories under their jurisdiction.

Universal Declaration of Human Rights: Articles

Article 1 All human beings are born free and equal in dignity and rights. They are endowed with reason and conscience and should act towards one another in a spirit of brotherhood.

Article 2 Everyone is entitled to all the rights and freedoms set forth in this Declaration, without distinction of any kind, such as race, colour, sex, language, religion, political or other opinion, national or social origin, property, birth, or other status. Furthermore, no distinction shall be made on the basis of the political, jurisdictional, or international status of the country or territory to which a person belongs, whether it be independent, trust, non-self-governing, or under any other limitation of sovereignty.

Article 3 Everyone has the right to life, liberty, and security of person.

Article 4 No one shall be held in slavery or servitude; slavery and the slave trade shall be prohibited in all their forms.

Article 5 No one shall be subjected to torture or to cruel, inhuman, or degrading treatment or punishment.

Article 6 Everyone has the right to recognition everywhere as a person before the law.

Article 7 All are equal before the law and are entitled without any discrimination to equal protection of the law. All are entitled to equal protection against any discrimination in violation of this Declaration and against any incitement to such discrimination.

Article 8 Everyone has the right to an effective remedy by the competent national tribunals for acts violating the fundamental rights granted him by the constitution or by law.

Article 9 No one shall be subjected to arbitrary arrest, detention, or exile.

Article 10 Everyone is entitled in full equality to a fair and public hearing by an independent and impartial tribunal, in the determination of his rights and obligations and of any criminal charge against him.

Article 11 1. Everyone charged with a penal offence has the right to be presumed innocent until proved guilty according to law in a public trial at which he has had all the guarantees necessary for his defence.

2. No one shall be held guilty of any penal offence on account of any act or omission which did not constitute a penal offence, under national or international law, at the time when it was committed. Nor shall a heavier penalty be imposed than the one that was applicable at the time the penal offence was committed.

Article 12 No one shall be subjected to arbitrary interference with his privacy, family, home, or correspondence, nor to attacks upon his honour and reputation. Everyone has the right to the protection of the law against such interference or attacks.

Article 13 1. Everyone has the right to freedom of movement and residence within the borders of each state.

2. Everyone has the right to leave any country, including his own, and to return to his country.

Article 14 1. Everyone has the right to seek and to enjoy in other countries asylum from persecution.

2. This right may not be invoked in the case of prosecutions genuinely arising from nonpolitical crimes or from acts contrary to the purposes and principles of the United Nations (UN).

Article 15 1. Everyone has the right to a nationality.

2. No one shall be arbitrarily deprived of his nationality nor denied the right to change his nationality.

Article 16 1. Men and women of full age, without any limitation due to race, nationality, or religion, have the right to marry and to found a family. They are entitled to equal rights as to marriage, during marriage, and at its dissolution.

2. Marriage shall be entered into only with the free and full consent of the intending spouses.

3. The family is the natural and fundamental group unit of society and is entitled to protection by society and the state.

Article 17 1. Everyone has the right to own property alone as well as in association with others.

2. No one shall be arbitrarily deprived of his property.

Article 18 Everyone has the right to freedom of thought, conscience, and religion; this right includes freedom to change his religion or belief, and freedom, either alone or in community with others and in public or private, to manifest his religion or belief in teaching, practice, worship, and observance.

Article 19 Everyone has the right to freedom of opinion and expression; this right includes freedom to hold opinions without interference and to seek, receive and impart information and ideas through any media and regardless of frontiers.

Article 20 1. Everyone has the right to freedom of peaceful assembly and association.

2. No one may be compelled to belong to an association.

Article 21 1. Everyone has the right to take part in the government of his country, directly or through freely chosen representatives.

2. Everyone has the right of equal access to public service in his country.

3. The will of the people shall be the basis of the authority of government; this will shall be expressed in periodic and genuine elections which shall be by universal and equal suffrage and shall be held by secret vote or by equivalent free voting procedures.

Article 22 Everyone, as a member of society, has the right to social security and is entitled to realization, through national effort and international cooperation and in accordance with the organization and resources of each state, of the economic, social, and cultural rights indispensable for his dignity and the free development of his personality.

Article 23 1. Everyone has the right to work, to free choice of employment, to just and favourable conditions of work, and to protection against unemployment.

2. Everyone, without any discrimination, has the right to equal pay for equal work.

Universal Declaration of Human Rights: Articles (*continued*)

3. Everyone who works has the right to just and favourable remuneration ensuring for himself and his family an existence worthy of human dignity, and supplemented, if necessary, by other means of social protection.

4. Everyone has the right to form and to join trade unions for the protection of his interests.

Article 24 Everyone has the right to rest and leisure, including reasonable limitation of working hours and periodic holidays with pay.

Article 25 1. Everyone has the right to a standard of living adequate for the health and wellbeing of himself and of his family, including food, clothing, housing, and medical care and necessary social services, and the right to security in the event of unemployment, sickness, disability, widowhood, old age, or other lack of livelihood in circumstances beyond his control.

2. Motherhood and childhood are entitled to special care and assistance. All children, whether born in or out of wedlock, shall enjoy the same social protection.

Article 26 1. Everyone has the right to education. Education shall be free, at least in the elementary and fundamental stages. Elementary education shall be compulsory. Technical and professional education shall be made generally available and higher education shall be equally accessible to all on the basis of merit.

2. Education shall be directed to the full development of the human personality and to the strengthening of respect for human rights and fundamental freedoms. It shall promote understanding, tolerance, and friendship among all nations, racial or religious groups, and shall further the activities of the UN for the maintenance of peace.

3. Parents have a prior right to choose the kind of education that shall be given to their children.

Article 27 1. Everyone has the right freely to participate in the cultural life of the community, to enjoy the arts, and to share in scientific advancement and its benefits.

2. Everyone has the right to the protection of the moral and material interests resulting from any scientific, literary, or artistic production of which he is the author.

Article 28 Everyone is entitled to a social and international order in which the rights and freedoms set forth in this Declaration can be fully realized.

Article 29 1. Everyone has duties to the community in which alone the free and full development of his personality is possible.

2. In the exercise of his rights and freedoms, everyone shall be subject only to such limitations as are determined by law solely for the purpose of securing due recognition and respect for the rights and freedoms of others and of meeting the just requirements of morality, public order, and the general welfare in a democratic society.

3. These rights and freedoms may in no case be exercised contrary to the purposes and principles of the UN.

Article 30 Nothing in this Declaration may be interpreted as implying for any state, group, or person any right to engage in any activity or to perform any act aimed at the destruction of any of the rights and freedoms set forth herein.

Human Rights and Relief Organizations

ACTIONAID

International charity focusing on long-term development by working with communities in the developing world to strengthen human resources to alleviate poverty and improve quality of life. ACTIONAID operates in 24 countries.

Date established 1972

Funding private donations, child and community sponsorship, contributions from official bodies such as the British government and the European Union, and income from trading, such as the sale of merchandise

Address: Headquarters ACTIONAID UK, Chataway House, Leach Road, Chard, Somerset TA20 1FR, UK; phone: (01460) 62972; fax: (01460) 67191; e-mail: mail@actionaid.org.uk

Address in Ireland ACTIONAID Ireland, Unity Buildings, 16–17 Lower O'Connell Street, Dublin 1, Republic of Ireland; phone: +353 (1) 878 7911; fax: +353 (1) 878 6245

Web site www.actionaid.org

Amnesty International

Independent, politically-unaligned organization for the protection of human rights worldwide, as set out in the Universal Declaration of Human Rights. Amnesty campaigns for the release of prisoners of conscience; fair trials for political prisoners; and an end to torture, extrajudicial executions, 'disappearances', and the death penalty. It organizes fact-finding missions and human-rights education. Amnesty operates in more than 100 countries.

Date established 1961

Funding private donations and membership fees

Addresses in UK Headquarters: International Secretariat, 1 Easton Street, London WC1X 0DJ, UK; phone: (020) 7413 5500; fax: (020) 7950 1157; e-mail: amnestyis@amnesty.org; UK branch: 99–119 Rosebery Avenue, London EC1R 4RE, UK; phone: (020) 7814 6200; fax: (020) 7833 1510; e-mail: info@amnesty.org.uk

Web site www.amnesty.org

CARE International

Nonprofit, nongovernmental organization aiming to relieve human suffering, to provide economic opportunity, and to build sustained capacity for self-help. CARE International operates in 77 countries.

Date established 1946

Funding corporate and private donations, government grants, contributions in kind, such as agricultural produce donated by governments

Address: Headquarters Boulevard de Régent 58/10, B-1000 Brussels, Belgium; phone: +32 (2) 502 4333; fax: +32 (2) 502 8202

Address in UK CARE UK, Tower House 8–14, Southampton Street, London WC2E 7HA; phone: (020) 7379 5247; fax: (020) 7379 0543

Web site www.careinternational.org.uk

Concern Worldwide

Nongovernmental organization providing relief, assistance, and advancement to people in need in less developed areas of the world. Concern operates in 13 countries throughout Asia, Africa, and Latin America.

Date established 1968

Funding private donations and co-funding

Address: Headquarters 52–55 Lower Camden Street, Dublin 2, Ireland; phone: +353 (1) 417 7700; fax: +353 (1) 475 7362; e-mail: info@concern.ie

Address in UK Concern Worldwide UK, 1st Floor, 248–250 Lavender Hill, London SW11 1LJ, UK; phone: (0171) 738 1033; fax: (0171) 738 1032; e-mail: infolondon@concernworldwide.org

Web sites www.irishnet.com/concern.htm and www.concern.org.uk

Human Rights Watch

Politically unaligned charity that reports on practices affecting human rights. It documents and publicizes imprisonments, censorship, violation of human-rights laws, and abuses of internationally recognized human rights. It covers more than 70 countries.

Date established 1978 (as Helsinki Watch)

Funding grants from foundations; private donations

Address: Headquarters 34th Floor, 350 Fifth Avenue, New York, NY 10118-3299, USA; phone: +1 (212) 290 4700; fax: +1 (212) 736 1300; e-mail: hrwnyc@hrw.org

Address in UK 33 Islington High Street, London N1 9LH, UK; phone: (020) 7713 1995; fax: (020) 7713 1800; e-mail: hrwuk@hrw.org

Web site www.hrw.org

International Committee of the Red Cross (ICRC)

Umbrella body for national Red Cross and Red Crescent societies. It is a neutral, impartial, and independent humanitarian institution. The Red Cross was set up to help all victims of war and internal violence, by providing medical assistance, organizing humanitarian relief, and attempting to ensure implementation of rules restricting armed violence. It also helps victims of natural disasters. The Red Cross operates in more than 50 countries.

Date established 1863

Funding grants from the states party to the Geneva Convention and from international organizations such as the European Union, public funds, money from national Red Cross and Red Crescent societies, private donations

Address: Headquarters Public Information Centre, 19 Avenue de la Paix, CH 1202 Geneva, Switzerland; phone: +41 (22) 734 6001; fax: +41 (22) 733 2057; e-mail (press or operational information): press.gva@icrc.org

Web site www.icrc.org

Médecins Sans Frontières International (MSF)

Nonprofit humanitarian organization offering assistance to populations in distress and to victims of disasters or armed conflict. MSF volunteers provide primary health care, operate emergency nutrition and sanitation programmes, and train local medical staff. MSF observes strict impartiality and neutrality in the name of universal medical ethics and demands full freedom in exercising its functions. MSF is independent of political, religious, or economic influence, and operates in 80 countries.

Date established 1971

Funding private donations and grants from international organizations and governments

Address: Headquarters 39 Rue de la Tourelle, B-1040, Brussels, Belgium; phone: +32 (2) 280 1881; fax: +32 (2) 280 0173

Address in UK 124–132 Clerkenwell Road, London EC1R 5DJ, UK; phone: (020) 7713 5600; fax: (020) 7713 5004

Web sites www.msf.org and www.dwb.org

Oxfam

Charity aiming to put an end to poverty worldwide. It provides assistance for development and relief by working in partnership with local groups, helping poor people to help themselves. Oxfam campaigns internationally, gives poor people channels to voice their concerns, funds long-term projects such as education and training, and provides emergency aid. The organization operates in over 70 countries. Oxfam UK is a member of Oxfam International.

Date established 1942

Funding donations from individuals, groups, companies, and trusts; grants from the UK Department for International Development, the European Union, United Nations agencies, and governments

Address: Headquarters 274 Banbury Road, Oxford OX2 7DZ, UK; phone: (01865) 311 311; fax: (01865) 313 770; e-mail: oxfam@oxfam.org.uk

Web site www.oxfam.org.uk

Save the Children Fund

Charity aiming to achieve lasting benefits for children within the communities in which they live by influencing policy and practice in tackling the underlying causes of poverty. The organization operates in more than 50 countries.

Date established 1919

Funding government grants, private and corporate donations, shops and trading, donations from sister charities

Address: Headquarters 17 Grove Lane, London SE5 8RD, UK; phone: (020) 7703 5400; fax: (020) 7703 2278; e-mail: enquiries@scfuk.org.uk

Web site www.savethechildren.org.uk

Survival International

Charity supporting tribal peoples worldwide. It stands for their right to decide their own future and helps them protect their lives, lands, and human rights. It works closely with local indigenous organizations and focuses especially on tribal peoples most recently in contact with the outside world.

Date established 1969

Funding donations from members, private individuals, and organizations

Address: Headquarters 11–15 Emerald Street, London WC1N 3QL, UK; phone: (020) 7242 1441; fax: (020) 7242 1771; e-mail: info@survival-international.org

Web site www.survival-international.org

Voluntary Service Overseas (VSO)

Organization aiming to enable men and women to work alongside people in poorer countries in order to share skills, build capabilities, and promote international understanding and action, in the pursuit of a more equitable world. VSO has recruitment offices in the UK, Canada, and the Netherlands, and operates in 59 countries, with more than 1,950 volunteers overseas in 1997.

Date established 1958

Funding private donations and foundation grants

Address: Headquarters 317 Putney Bridge Road, London SW15 2PN, UK; phone: (020) 8780 7200; fax: (020) 8780 1236; e-mail: enquiry@vso.org.uk

Web site www.vso.org.uk

WomenAid International

International humanitarian aid and development agency aiming to provide relief and assistance to women and children suffering distress caused by war, disasters, or poverty; to empower women through education, training, and provision of credit; and to campaign against violations of women's human rights.

Date established 1988

Funding various international, national, and individual sources

Address 3 Whitehall Court, Whitehall, London SW1A 2EL, UK; phone: (020) 7839 1790; fax: (020) 7839 2929; e-mail: womenaid@womenaid.org

Web site www.womenaid.org/

Refugees

Numbers of Refugees Worldwide

The total number of people of concern to the United Nations High Commissioner for Refugees (UNHCR) rose from 21.5 million as of 1 January 1999 to 22.3 million as of 1 January 2000. This represents 1 out of every 269 persons on Earth. The conflicts in Kosovo and the Balkan region were largely responsible for the latest annual increase.

The 1990s were a roller coaster decade for the agency in many areas. In 1990, UNHCR was helping an estimated 17 million people before a series of major crisis in northern Iraq, the former Yugoslavia, Rwanda, and Africa's Great Lakes region. Reflecting these new emergencies, the number of persons needing assistance rocketed to an all-time high of 27 million in 1995 before gradually tapering off towards the end of the century.

Region	Refugees	Returned refugees	Asylum seekers	Internally displaced people and others of concern	Total of concern to UNHCR (as of 1 Jan 2000)
Africa	3,523,250	933,890	61,110	1,732,290	6,250,540
Asia	4,781,750	617,620	24,750	1,884,740	7,308,860
Europe	2,608,380	952,060	473,060	3,252,300	7,285,800
Latin America and the Caribbean	61,200	6,260	1,510	21,200	90,170
North America	636,300	–	605,630	–	1,241,930
Oceania	64,500	–	15,540	–	80,040
Total	11,675,500	2,509,830	1,181,600	6,890,530	22,257,340

Source: United Nations High Commissioner for Refugees

See also **Asylum Seekers in the UK,** p 103.

Web Sites

Amnesty International Online

http://www.amnesty.org/

Home page of the world's foremost human rights organization, with information on its structure, current campaigns, and how you can help, as well as a library of documents on human rights for all parts of the world.

Commonwealth Institute

http://www.commonwealth.org.uk/

Full outline of the role of the Commonwealth Institute, with details of current exhibitions and links to embassies, tourist offices, and other institutions in Commonwealth states.

Commonwealth of Independent States (CIS)

http://www.rochester.k12.mn.us/kellogg/rodgers/cis/thecis.htm

Educational site featuring maps and regional guides for the CIS, as well as an analysis of the history of the area.

Council of Europe

http://www.coe.int/

Home page of the 50-year-old Strasbourg-based organization charged with strengthening democracy, human rights, and the rule of law among its 40 member states. Includes a large documentary archive.

Earthrise

http://earthrise.sdsc.edu/

Earthrise is a growing database of Earth images taken by astronauts from space over the last 15 years. Users can search the image database by keyword or by topographical and political maps.

European and Asian Documents on Fourth World Affairs

http://www.cwis.org/eurasia.html

Extensive text archive on the indigenous people of Europe and Asia maintained by the Fourth World Documentation Project and intended to educate the international community about the problems that these largely unrecognized national populations face within their states.

European Union

http://europa.eu.int/

Official, multilingual site for the European Union, with information on all aspects of the EU, including policy, the various institutions and post-holders, and up-to-date news.

G8 Information Center

http://www.g7.utoronto.ca/

Run by the University of Toronto, this site details the economic summits and meetings of the Group of Eight, and provides copies of relevant documents.

Geographia

http://www.geographia.com/

Site designed for travellers but containing a vast amount of information on countries all over the world. Five regional sections are accompanied by special features on selected locations.

Greatest Places

http://www.greatestplaces.org/

This site takes you on a journey to seven of the most geographically dynamic locations on earth.

Great Globe Gallery

http://hum.amu.edu.pl/ zbzw/glob/glob1.htm

Over 200 globes and maps, showing the Earth from all angles, including space shots, political maps, the ancient world, geographical features, and animated spinning globes.

Hunger Site

http://www.thehungersite.com/index.html

At this site dedicated to alleviating hunger throughout the world, you can donate a meal to a starving person with one click on the 'Donate free food' button. The food is paid for by corporate sponsors and distributed by international food agencies.

International Committee of the Red Cross

http://www.icrc.org/

Home page of the Red Cross Movement, with frequently updated reports on the charity's operations worldwide, and extensive coverage of issues surrounding international humanitarian law.

Médecins Sans Frontières (MSF)

http://www.msf.org/

Home page of MSF, the humanitarian medical aid agency dedicated to providing medical aid wherever it is needed, and to raising awareness of the plight of the people it helps.

Metropolis – World Association of the Major Metropolises

http://www.metropolis.org/eng/menu.html

Information on the world's major cities, providing comparisons of urban strategies and development in the world's leading metropolitan areas. The site includes a directory of member cities and details of the work of Metropolis' four standing commissions.

National Geographic Online

http://www.nationalgeographic.com/

Features include the *Map Machine Atlas*, which allows you to nd maps, ags, facts, and proles for the countries of the world, discussion forums on a variety of subjects, and a wealth of multimedia items.

Oceania – Documents on Fourth World Affairs

http://www.cwis.org/melpac.html

Extensive text archive on the indigenous people of Oceania. This database aims to increase knowledge and understanding of the problems that these largely unrecognized national populations face within their states.

Organization for Security and Cooperation in Europe

http://www.osce.org/

Site of the UN organization charged with keeping the peace in Europe, with regularly updated information on its work on such issues as arms control, election monitoring, and conflict prevention.

Our Modern Commonwealth

http://www.rhouse.co.uk/rhouse/rcs/modcom/

Useful general guide to the Commonwealth organized by the Royal Commonwealth Institute. The materials for teachers and students are designed for use in schools in all Commonwealth countries.

Oxfam UK and Ireland

http://www.oxfam.org/

Site of the UK's foremost non-governmental development and relief agency, giving comprehensive information on Oxfam's work around the world and regular updates of its current campaigns.

Royal Geographical Society

http://www.rgs.org/

Mine of information for both geographers and non-specialists, including events organized by the RGS, online exhibitions, field expeditions and research projects, publications, and links to other geographical organizations.

Save the Children Fund

http://www.oneworld.org/scf/

Home page of the UK's leading children's charity, with extensive information on its work nationally and in more than 50 countries, and on key topics in international development.

6 Billion Human Beings

http://www.popexpo.net/english.html

From the Musée de l'Homme in Paris, an interactive site about population growth. It explains the causes for the rapid growth over the last 200 years, and the reasons why global population may stabilize over this century. You can find out the world's population in the year you were born, and see a ticking counter of the current population.

Treaty Establishing the European Community

http://europa.eu.int/abc/obj/treaties/en/entoc05.htm

Complete text of the founding document of the European Economic Community. This is provided by the European Union and includes all associated protocols and documents of ratification.

UNICEF United Nations Children's Fund

http://www.unicef.org/

Comprehensive guide to the work of the agency and the mission it has set itself. The site includes excellent statistical data, narrative information, and a section on 'Voices of Youth', with quizzes, discussion forums, and educational activities. UNICEF's annual 'State of the World's Children' report can also be accessed here.

United Nations Home Page

http://www.un.org/

Official site providing a general overview of the United Nations, with news, photographs, key documents, and links to all UN departments and information resources.

VolcanoWorld

http://volcano.und.edu/

Comprehensive site on volcanoes, with details of the most recent eruptions, currently active volcanoes, a glossary, images and video clips, and even a list of extraterrestrial volcanoes.

Voluntary Service Overseas (VSO)

http://www.vso.org.uk/

Opportunities to work as a volunteer in the developing world, as well as information about VSO campaigns, events, and publications. The site includes volunteers' reports from all over the globe for those considering applying to the scheme.

Women Aid International

http://www.womenaid.org/

Home page of the organization that seeks to promote women's human rights around the world, through education, training, and provision of credit.

World Factbook

http://www.odci.gov/cia/publications/factbook/

Annual factbook produced by the CIA on countries of the world. Provides exhaustive information on each country, divided into sections on geography, people, government, economy, communications, transportation, and transnational issues. There are also flags and maps.

World Population Estimates

http://www.popin.org/pop1998/

Online edition of the United Nations' *1998 Revision of the World Population Estimates and Projections*, which outlines the standard set of population figures used throughout the UN system. The site includes a projected estimate of the world population in 2050, and an assessment of the global demographic impact of HIV/AIDS.

World Village

http://www.worldvillage.org/e_index.html

What if the world were a village inhabited by 1,000 people? This site provides some thought-provoking answers, by scaling down statistics to figures that are easier to comprehend.

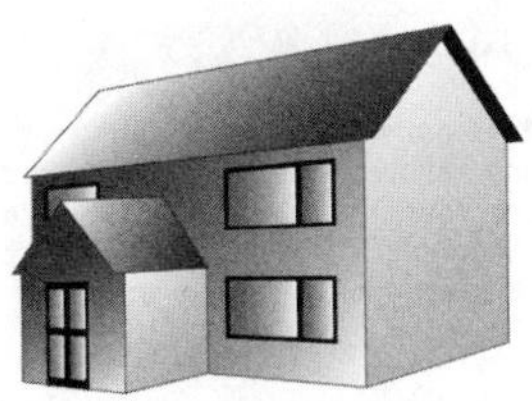

Consumer and Citizenship

Consumer Information

Consumer Rights and Protection

Consumers' Statutory Rights in the UK

As a customer purchasing goods (including purchases made over the Internet), you have certain statutory rights, whether what you are buying is new or second-hand. Under the Sale and Supply of Goods Act 1994, goods must:

- fit any description given
- be in good condition, free from faults, and capable of doing the job expected of them for a reasonable length of time
- correspond with any samples you have been shown.

If goods fail to meet the above criteria, you are legally entitled to reject them and receive your money back. The supplier cannot issue a credit note unless you agree to this. If the goods are not rejected in 'reasonable time' (not specified by law), you may only be able to insist on the item being repaired at no extra cost.

Under hire purchase or conditional sale agreement terms, you have the same basic rights as if you had paid cash, but your contract is with the finance company, not the retailer. If, however, the goods are faulty, your rights last for the length of time of the hire purchase agreement, not just for a 'reasonable' length of time.

Source: Office of Fair Trading, © Crown copyright 1998; with Helicon updates

Before You Buy

In general, before you buy, ask yourself:

Is it what I am looking for?
Can I afford it?
Is this the best place to buy it?
Can I take it back if I do not like it?
How will I pay for it?
Have I seen what other shops have to offer?
Does the trader have a good reputation for treating customers fairly?

Extended Warranties

Extended warranties are a particular type of guarantee offered by retailers when you buy goods. The warranties are sold by specialist insurance or warranty companies and cover the goods once the manufacturer's guarantee expires. As with manufacturer's guarantees you must comply with the terms and conditions to obtain any benefit from them. They do not cover failures due to wear and tear. Warranties can add significantly to the cost of goods.

Guarantees

Guarantees provide you with additional rights over and above your statutory rights. A guarantee does not take away or replace your statutory rights. Guarantees are required by law to state that your 'statutory rights are not affected'.

Traditional guarantees (those provided by manufacturers with their new products) are often subject to conditions of use. They promise to repair any faults that occur due to defects from the manufacture of an item, during a specified period. These guarantees are dependent on the proper use, servicing, maintenance, and so on, of a product. It is not a legal requirement for manufacturers to provide a guarantee with their products.

Guarantees are also sometimes given with second-hand goods, but may only be a verbal statement by the seller, or be written on the receipt. If something goes wrong with a second-hand product, there is no legal way to enforce a verbal or even a written guarantee, but you could sue for breach of contract under civil law. It is not a criminal offence to renege on a verbal agreement.

Guarantees usually last for one year, during which time the manufacturer of a product is legally obliged to repair any faults that are due to manufacturing or material defects. If faults occur very soon after purchasing an item, you can claim your money back, under your statutory rights, without having to have the item repaired under guarantee.

When you have to complete a registration card to return to the manufacturer, make sure that:

- the seller fills in the purchase details
- you return the card to the stated address
- you retain the documents supplied with the goods outlining how to make a claim.

Otherwise the guarantee may not be effective.

Source: Office of Fair Trading, © Crown copyright 1998; with Helicon updates

Untrue Claims

It is a criminal offence for a trader to say or write something untrue about what is being offered for sale. If, when you have bought the goods, you feel that you have been seriously misled, tell your local Trading Standards or Consumer Protection Department, which may decide to prosecute the trader. If the trader is convicted, a claim for compensation may be considered in court, except in Northern Ireland, where you would have to sue separately.

Source: Office of Fair Trading, © Crown copyright 1998

Trade Associations

Trade associations and professional bodies can develop and enforce their own codes of conduct, or practice guidelines, for their members. If a trader, for example a builder, carries out unsatisfactory work, he or she can be reported to the trade association of which he or she is a member. If traders are found to be in breach of their trade association's code of conduct, they can be excluded from the association. However, membership of a trade association is not always a guarantee of quality; not all trade associations regulate their members. It is always advisable to check the membership status of a trader and to find out any benefits there may be in choosing a supplier belonging to a particular trade association or professional body.

Source: Office of Fair Trading, © Crown copyright 1998

Counterfeit Products

An increasing range of products are being copied and sold, including video and audio tapes, 'designer' clothes, perfume, cosmetics, toys, computer software, etc. The practice of counterfeiting is illegal and it infringes on the intellectual property rights of those who own the copyright, designs, patents, and trade marks of these products. The production, distribution, and sale of fake goods purporting to be original is viewed very seriously by Trading Standards departments; counterfeit goods can be seized and those responsible prosecuted, resulting in large fines and prison sentences.

To control counterfeiting, UK trade marks, copyright, and trade descriptions legislation is provided for under the Trades Descriptions Act of 1968 and specifies the following:

A trade mark can be a name, logo, word, or signature that connects a person/company to a product; therefore, they have the right to use the mark.

Copyright provides rights to the creator of literary, dramatic, musical, or artistic work.

A trade description can be applied to anything that a person is likely to think applies to the goods and which conduces to a belief in the authenticity of a product's origin or the quality of an item.

Under UK trade descriptions legislation it is therefore illegal to:

apply a registered trade mark to goods or packaging without the consent or licence of the trade mark owner
infringe copyright by copying work without the authorization or licence of the copyright owner
apply any kind of identity to products or packaging which is likely to mislead a consumer as to the origin of manufacture or the identity of the producer.

For more information, contact the Office of Fair Trading's Consumer Information Line on (08457) 224499. This number is available for anyone seeking information about their rights as consumers or on where they should turn to for assistance with a particular problem. The Office is unable to help customers on individual cases but it maintains close contacts with a wide range of official, voluntary, and trade associations which may be able to intervene. Calls from within the UK are charged at local rates; the number is available during UK office hours. The OFT Web site is www.oft.gov.uk.

Source: Office of Fair Trading, © Crown copyright 1998; with Helicon updates

Consumer Information

Shopping by Mail, Telephone, Television, and Internet: Some Tips

- When ordering, check that the source you use (such as Web site or newspaper) is not obsolete or out of date.
- Avoid sending cash by post – use credit cards, postal orders, or cheques.
- When giving your card details make sure you know who and where the trader is. If purchasing on the Internet, ask the trader for an e-mail reply and get as many concrete details as you can about the trader.
- Keep a copy or record of the order and note the date on which it was made and sent. Do not delete e-mails received from the trader.
- Keep a copy of the advertisement if possible; if not, make a note of where and when it appeared and any other details. Be wary of any company that only has a post office box number.
- If you intend to purchase a product based on a telephone call from a company, make sure you obtain the company's name, address, and telephone number, and the name of the sales representative who contacted you, before you call and place your order.
- If you are joining a book or record club make sure you know what commitment you are making and the cancellation terms.
- Before you buy, check the cost of the same items sold in other places.

(*See also* **Internet Shopping: Fraud and Security,** p 331.)

Delivery of Goods

If you insist on, or are given, a delivery date when you send for the goods, and this date is not met, you can cancel your order and ask for your money back. Even if no definite date is given, goods should be delivered within a reasonable time, usually 28 days, or as specified in the advertisement or by the telephone sales representative. If they are not delivered within such a time, contact the seller to say that if the goods have not arrived by a certain date (for example, within two weeks) you will not accept them and will ask for your money back. But if you agree to give the seller extra time (for example, another month), you cannot change your mind and try to cancel your order before that extra time is up.

Unsolicited goods

If you receive goods you have not ordered, you do not have to accept them. If you do nothing and do not hear any more from the trader for six months, the goods will become yours. Or you can write to the trader saying that the goods were 'unsolicited' (unasked for). If the trader does not then collect them within 30 days, the goods are yours. You must, of course, allow unsolicited goods to be collected, provided that the trader comes to collect them at a reasonable time after prior notice. You must also take care of the goods until they are collected.

Price

Make sure you know all the conditions regarding price. You may have agreed to pay any increase that takes place between ordering and delivery, or perhaps you will have agreed a fixed price. Be sure you know whether there are extra charges for postage and packing, and if so, what they are.

Source: Office of Fair Trading, © Crown copyright 1998; with Helicon updates

Unfair Contract Terms

If you have entered into a contract on the trader's standard terms of business, the law says that certain types of terms that act against the consumer's interest may be unfair and unenforceable. If you think a term is unfair, you may wish to seek advice from your local Trading Standards service or Citizens' Advice Bureau. You can also write to the Director General of Fair Trading. He or she can take court action to stop the use of an unfair term in future contracts. He or she cannot, however, get involved with individual cases.

How to Complain

If you have to make a complaint, the following gives advice on how to proceed and who to contact for further advice or to take the matter further. When you complain, get your facts right and always keep calm. You are probably more likely to get matters resolved if you do not lose your temper.

Goods

- Return to the shop as soon as possible with your receipt or proof of purchase (bank or credit card statement showing the amount paid through your account).
- Explain the problem and what you expect to be done, setting a deadline.
- If the outcome is not satisfactory, put your complaint in writing; address your letter to the customer services manager, chairperson, or, where the shop is part of a chain, the head office.
- If the problem is still not resolved, get further advice and/or consider going to court.

Services

- Complain verbally to the supplier and provide an opportunity for the supplier to resolve the problem.
- Complain in writing if the matter is not resolved and provide a deadline for it to be corrected.
- Consider withholding payment until the problem is resolved, but beware: check the small print of any contract you have signed and obtain further advice before refusing to pay, especially if you have a credit agreement. Note: if you continue to pay for a service you are not happy with under a credit agreement, you still have legal redress against the lender for providing an unsatisfactory service.
- Keep a diary of events, notes of telephone calls, and copies of any relevant documentation, such as letters. Also take photographs where necessary. These records will all help in case you have to bring legal action to resolve the matter.
- Consider obtaining an expert opinion to support your complaint.

Complaints over the phone

- Make a note beforehand of what you want to say.
- Have receipts and any other documents handy.
- Note the name of the person you speak to.
- Write down the date and time of the call and what was said.
- Follow up your call with a letter, particularly if the complaint is a serious one.

Complaints in writing

- Type your letter if possible; if your letter is handwritten, make sure it is clear and legible.
- Include your name, address, and home and work telephone numbers.
- Keep your letter brief, polite, and to the point, avoid repetition and personal remarks.
- Describe the item or service; say where and when you bought the item, or when the service was done, and how much it cost.
- Explain what is wrong, any action you have already taken, to whom you spoke, and what happened.
- Say what you want done to remedy the situation – for example, a refund or repair, or the job done again without charge.
- Set a deadline by which you want a response from the other party.

How to Complain (*continued*)

- Use special delivery so you can check that your letter has been delivered; keep copies of any letters you send; do not send original documents, such as receipts and guarantees – send copies instead.
- Be persistent: if you fail to get what you want at your first attempt, write another letter of complaint setting out your dissatisfaction.

Model complaint letter

[Your name and address]
[Date]

[Name of person, if known, or 'Customer Services Manager' or 'Chairman'] [The person's title, if name is known] [Company name] [Full address, including postal code]

Dear [Person's surname, if known, or 'Dear Sir or Madam']

Re: [Order, account, or reference number]

On [full date], I [ordered, bought, rented, leased, had repaired, sought a service] [a name of the product with its serial and/or model number or service performed] at/from [company, location, catalogue, and other important details relevant to the transaction] price [£...].

Unfortunately, your product [does not correspond with its description, was damaged in transit, showed serious defects, etc.] [or the service was inadequate]. I am disappointed because [describe why the product or service was faulty or inadequate, misrepresented, and so on, or why you believe the billing was incorrect].

To resolve this problem, I would appreciate your [state the specific action you want: reimbursement, charge-card credit, replacement, repair, exchange, the service done or improved, etc.] within [... days]. Enclosed are copies of my records (include copies, not originals, of any relevant documents).

I look forward to [your reply, your cheque for £..., receiving a replacement, etc.]. I will wait until [date] before seeking help from [my local trading standards or consumer protection department]. Please contact me at the above address or by telephone at [give home and work numbers with their area codes].

Yours sincerely/faithfully

[Your name]

Enclosure(s)

cc: [Name(s) of any person(s) to whom you are sending a copy of this letter]

Taking further action

If you are struggling to get a complaint addressed satisfactorily, you can take further action. Just telling a trader who is being unhelpful or obstructive that you will go to court could be enough to get your complaint resolved. If you do have to take legal action, it can be much easier than it sounds and could well be worth the effort.

Before going to arbitration or to court, you may wish to seek an impartial opinion on the merits of your case. This opinion is best obtained from a solicitor. Some solicitors work in law centres or advice agencies that offer free advice. Many solicitors in private practice offer a low-cost initial interview. Your local Citizens' Advice Bureau can help you find such a solicitor.

Conciliation and arbitration

If the trader is a member of a trade association, there may be a conciliation or arbitration scheme you can use. Some associations have both. Such schemes are informal and generally inexpensive. However, arbitration may not necessarily be cheaper than going to court under the small claims procedure. Check what fees you will be expected to pay if you lose the case.

You have to choose between court and arbitration – you cannot do both. If you do not like an arbitrator's decision, you cannot then go to court (except in special circumstances). Under the Consumer Arbitration Agreements Act 1996, a clause in a contract which says that you have to go to arbitration cannot bind you as long as the value of your dispute is not greater than the small claims limit.

Going to court

If, after trying to resolve your complaint by telephone and in writing, you remain unsatisfied, you can take further action by going to court. If the threat of court action is not sufficient to make a trader/service provider address your problem seriously, you can proceed with legal action and go to court to sue for the return of your money or for compensation. In England and Wales, a claim of £5,000 or less can be dealt with in the County Court as a 'small claim'; in Northern Ireland, the limit is £1,000; in Scotland, small claims of up to £750 can be taken to the Sheriff Court. You do not require the services of a solicitor to pursue a small claim, and even if your opponent employs the services of one, you are not liable for their legal costs if you lose the case (unless you are found to have made an unreasonable claim, caused unnecessary expense costs, or do not attend a hearing).

The necessary forms for filing a small claim are available from County Court offices (Sheriff Court in Scotland). The court will then serve the summons and advise you on what to do next.

There are court fees, but these are payable by your opponent if you win your case. In England and Wales the fees for the issue of small claims proceedings are graduated. Fees start from £27 for claims that do not exceed £200, rising to £60 for claims between £400 and £500. For claims between £500 but less than £1,000 the fee is £80. Claims that exceed £1,000 but not £5,000 attract a fee of £115.

In Northern Ireland the fees start at £13 for claims under £150, going up to a maximum of £55.

In Scotland the fees are £6 for claims up to £50, and £36 for claims over £50 to £750. The court will serve the summons on the defendant and tell you what to do next. If the value of your claim does not exceed £200, and has been defended, there will normally be no award of expenses. If the value of the claim is more than £200 but not more than £750, and has been defended, the maximum amount of expenses that will normally be awarded by the court is £75.

The necessary forms and leaflets explaining court procedure are available from court offices (look under Courts in the telephone book for the address), and from the Court Service (England and Wales only) Web site: www.courtservice.gov.uk/forms/formmenu.htm. You can get advice and help filling in the court forms from your local Citizens' Advice Bureau or consumer advice centre. Some of these can provide free legal advice as well, and someone from there may even be able to go to court with you.

Source: Office of Fair Trading, © Crown copyright 1999; with Helicon updates

See also Legal Aid, pp 471–472.

Main Consumer Organizations and Bodies in the UK

Major Consumer Organizations

Citizens' Advice Bureaux (CAB)

CABs provide a wide range of advice and can help resolve many consumer problems, including complaints about goods and services. Details on contacting your nearest branch can be found in the telephone book under Citizens' Advice Bureaux.

Trading Standards departments

Trading Standards (or consumer protection) departments have the powers to investigate complaints about goods and services and can advise on everyday consumer issues. Details on contacting your local Trading Standards department can be found in the telephone book under Trading Standards Service. In Northern Ireland, contact the trading standards branch of the Department of Economic Development.

Office of Fair Trading

The Office of Fair Trading is a non-ministerial government department responsible for a wide range of issues of fair trading in the UK. It has powers to protect consumers in the following ways:

- identifying and correcting trading practices which are against the consumer's interests
- regulating the provision of consumer credit
- investigating and acting to prevent anti-competitive practices
- encouraging competitive behaviour.

Major Consumer Organizations (*continued*)

Utilities regulators

If you have a complaint about utilities services, that is gas, electricity, water, or telephones, you can take the matter to the relevant regulatory body if your problem is not resolved by the company. Each of the four utilities has a regulator that can help solve consumer problems: OFFER, Office of Electricity Regulation; OFWAT, Office of Water Services; OFTEL, Office of Telecommunications; Gas Consumers' Council. Contact information for these bodies can be found in the telephone book.

The Ombudsmen

Ombudsmen exist to deal with complaints from citizens about certain public bodies or private sector services. There are 23 recognized Ombudsman schemes, most of which are established by statute. The schemes vary in the procedures they use and the powers that they have.

Using the services of an Ombudsman is a last resort. The party against which a complaint is being made must first be given reasonable time to resolve the complaint; indeed, many organizations have their own complaints procedures, which normally resolve problems satisfactorily. It is only if and when a complaint has not been resolved by going through the normal channels that an Ombudsman will consider it.

Ombudsmen schemes include: The Health Service Ombudsman; Police Complaints Authority; The Legal Services Ombudsman; Broadcasting Standards Commission; The Independent Housing Ombudsman; The Parliamentary Ombudsman. There are also Ombudsmen schemes for banking, pensions, and investments.

Other organizations

Other organizations from which help and advice can be obtained include environmental health departments (for advice on health matters), law centres, and trade associations. Contact information for many consumer organizations can be found here, or consult your telephone book.

Directory of Consumer Bodies in the UK

- **Arbitration**

Chartered Institute of Arbitrators 24 Angel Gate, City Road, London EC1V 2RS; phone: (020) 7837 4483; fax: (020) 7837 4185; e-mail: info@arbitrators.org; Web site: www.arbitrators.org

Scottish Council for Arbitration 27 Melville Street, Edinburgh EH3 7JF; phone: (0131) 220 4776; fax: (0131) 226 2501; e-mail: maildesk@mcroberts.co.uk

- **Ombudsmen**

Banking Ombudsman 70 Gray's Inn Road, London WC1X 8NB; phone: (020) 7404 9944; fax: (020) 7405 5052; e-mail: banking.ombudsman@obo.org.uk; Web site: www.obo.org.uk

Building Societies Ombudsman Millbank Tower, Millbank, London SW1P 4XS; phone: (020) 7931 0044; fax: (020) 7931 8485; e-mail: bldgsocombudsman@easynet.co.uk; Web site: www.lambeth.com/lbsomb.htm

Ombudsman for Estate Agents Beckett House, 4 Bridge Street, Salisbury, Wiltshire SP1 2LX; phone: (01722) 333306; fax: (01722) 332296; Web site: www.oea.co.uk

The Funeral Ombudsman 26–28 Bedford Row, London WC1R 4HE; phone: (020) 7430 1112; fax: (020) 7430 1012; e-mail: fos@dircon.co.uk

The Insurance Ombudsman Scheme Bureau City Gate One, 135 Park Street, London SE1 9EA; phone: (08456) 006666; fax: (020) 7902 8197; e-mail: complaint@theiob.org.uk; Web site: www.theiob. org.uk

Legal Services Ombudsman 22 Oxford Court, Oxford Street, Manchester M2 3WQ; phone: (0161) 236 9532; fax: (0161) 236 2651; e-mail: enquires.olso@gtnet.gov.uk

Pensions Ombudsman 11 Belgrave Road, London SW1V 1RB; phone: (020) 7834 9144; fax: (020) 7821 0065; e-mail: pensions-ombudsman@iclweb.kit.co.uk

Personal Investment Authority Ombudsman Hertsmere House, Hertsmere Road, London E14 4AB; phone: (020) 7216 0016; fax: (020) 7712 8742; e-mail: postsort@piaomb.demon.co.uk

- **Doorstep and party plan selling**

Direct Selling Association Ltd 29 Floral Street, London WC2E 9DP; phone: (020) 7497 1234; fax: (020) 7497 3144; Web site: www.dsa.org.uk

- **Electrical goods**

The Association of Manufacturers of Domestic Electrical Appliances Rapier House, 40–46 Lambs Conduit Street, London WC1N 3NW; phone: (020) 7405 0666; fax: (020) 7405 6609

The Radio, Electrical, and Television Retailers' Association Ltd RETRA House, St John's Terrace, 1 Ampthill Street, Bedford MK42 9EY; phone: (01234) 269110; fax: (01234) 269609; e-mail: retra@retra.co.uk; Web site: www.retra.co.uk

- **Furniture**

Qualitas National Conciliation Service Chief Conciliation Officer, Maxwell Street, Stevenage, Herts SG1 2EW; phone: (01438) 777777; fax: (01438) 777780; e-mail: qualitas@fira.co.uk

- **Holidays**

Air Travel Organizer's Licence (ATOL) Civil Aviation Authority, CAA House, 45–59 Kingsway, London WC2B 6TE; phone: (020) 7832 5620/6600; fax: (020) 7832 6692; Web site: www.caa.co.uk

Association of British Travel Agents (ABTA) 68–71 Newman Street, London W1P 4AH; phone: (020) 7637 2444; fax: (020) 7307 1992; e-mail: dashby@abta.co.uk; Web site: www.abtanet.com

Association of Independent Tour Operators (AITO) 133a St Margarets Road, Twickenham, Middlesex TW1 1RG; phone: (020) 8744 9280; fax: (020) 8744 3187; e-mail: aito@martex.co.uk; Web site: www.aito.co.uk

The Timeshare Council 23 Buckingham Gate, London SW1E 6LB; phone: (020) 7291 0901; fax: (020) 7828 0739; Web site: www.timesharecouncil.com

- **Home maintenance and improvements**

Glass and Glazing Federation 44–48 Borough High Street, London SE1 1XB; phone: (020) 7403 7177; fax: (020) 7357 7458; e-mail: info@ggf.org.uk; Web site: www.ggf.org.uk

- **Mail order**

Direct Marketing Association Haymarket House, 1 Oxendon Street, London SW1Y 4EE; phone: (020) 7321 2525; fax: (020) 7321 0191; e-mail: dma@dma.org.uk; Web site: www.dma.org.uk

Mailing/Telephone Preference Service FREEPOST 22, London W1E 7EZ; phone: (020) 7766 4410; fax: (020) 7976 1886; e-mail: mps@dma.org.uk

Mail Order Protection Scheme 16 Tooks Court, London EC4A 1LB; phone: (020) 7269 0520; fax: (020) 7404 0106; Web site: www.mops.org.uk

Mail Order Traders' Association 40 Waterloo Road, Birkdale, Southport PR8 2NG; phone: (01704) 563787; fax: (01704) 551247; e-mail: malcolmlandau@compuserve.com

Telephone Preference Services BT: phone: (0800) 398893. For general public to stop receiving cold calls. Customers of other companies should call the customer services number on their bill.

- **Motor trade**

Complaints about used cars, repairs, and servicing in England, Wales, and Northern Ireland

The National Conciliation Service, Retail Motor Industry Federation 9 North Street, Rugby CV21 2AB; phone: (01788) 538316; fax: (01788) 538337

Complaints about cars still under a manufacturer's warranty

The Customer's Relation Adviser, Society of Motor Manufacturers and Traders Forbes House, Halkin Street, London SW1X 7DS; phone: (020) 7235 7000; fax: (020) 7235 7112; Web site: www.smmt.co.uk

Complaints about car body repair

The Conciliation Service, The Vehicle Builders' and Repairers' Association Belmont House, 102 Finkle Lane, Gildersome, Leeds LS27 7TW; phone: (0113) 253 8333; fax: (0113) 238 0496; e-mail: vbra@vbra.co.uk; Web site: www.vbra.co.uk

Complaints about used cars, repairs, and servicing in Scotland

Customer Complaints Service, Scottish Motor Trade 3 Palmerston Place, Edinburgh EH12 5AF; phone: (0131) 225 3643; fax: (0131) 220 0446

- **Vehicle checks**

Equifax HPI Autodata PO Box 61, Dolphin House, New Street, Salisbury, Wiltshire SP1 1TB; phone: (01722) 422422; fax: (01722) 412164; Web site: www.hpicheck.com

Directory of Consumer Bodies in the UK *(continued)*

- **Small claims procedure**

Court Service Customer Services Unit Southside, 105 Victoria Street, London SW1E 6QT; phone: (020) 7210 1689; fax: (020) 7210 1797; e-mail: cust.ser.cs@gtnet.gov.uk; Web site: www.courtservice.gov.uk/contact

Scottish Courts Service Hayweight House, 23 Lauriston House, Edinburgh EH3 9DQ; phone: (0131) 229 9200; fax: (0131) 221 6890; e-mail: enquiries@scotcourts.gov.uk; Web site: www.scotcourts.gov.uk

- **General consumer and advisory bodies**

Advice Services Alliance (ASA) 4 Deans Court, St Paul's Churchyard, London EC4V 5AA; phone: (020) 7236 6022; fax: (020) 7248 3367; Web site: www.asa.mcmail.com

Citizens' Advice Scotland (CAS) 26 George Square, Edinburgh EH8 9LD; phone: (0131) 667 0156; fax: (0131) 668 4359; Web sites: www.natcab.org.uk and www.adviceguide.org.uk

Consumers' Association (CA) 2 Marylebone Road, London NW1 4DF; phone: (020) 7830 6000; e-mail: which@which.net; Web site: www.which.net

Department of Trade and Industry (DTI) Consumer Affairs Enquiry Unit DTI, 1 Victoria Street, London SW1H 0ET; phone: (020) 7215 5000; fax: (020) 7215 0315; Web site: www.dti.gov.uk

Federation of Independent Advice Centres (FIAC) 4 Deans Court, St Paul's Churchyard, London EC4V 5AA; phone: (020) 7489 1800; fax: (020) 7489 1804; e-mail: national@fiac.org.uk; Web site: www.fiac.org.uk

General Consumer Council for Northern Ireland (GCCNI) Elizabeth House, 116 Holywood Road, Belfast BT4 1NY; phone: (028) 9067 2488; fax: (028) 9065 7701; e-mail: info@gccni.org.uk; Web site: www.gccni.org.uk

Institute of Trading Standards Administration 3–5 Hadleigh Business Centre, 351 London Road, Hadleigh, Essex SS7 2BT; phone: (01702) 559922; fax: (01702) 556336; e-mail: institute@itsa.org.uk; Web site: www.tradingstandards.gov.uk

Law Centres Federation Duchess House, 18–19 Warren Street, London W1P 5DB; phone: (020) 7387 8570; fax: (020) 7387 8368; e-mail: info@lawcentres.org.uk; Web site: www.lawcentres.org.uk

National Association of Citizens' Advice Bureaux (NACAB) Myddleton House, 115–123 Pentonville Road, London N1 9LZ; phone: (020) 7833 2181; fax: (020) 7833 4371; Web site: www.nacab.org.uk

National Consumer Council (NCC) 20 Grosvenor Gardens, London SW1W 0DH; phone: (020) 7730 3469; fax: (020) 7730 0191; e-mail: info@ncc.org.uk; Web site: www.ncc.org.uk

National Federation of Consumer Groups 527 Leeds Road, Scholes, Leeds LS15 4RD; phone: (0113) 264 8341; Web site: www.nfcg.org.uk

Office of Fair Trading (OFT) Head Office, Fleetbank House, 2–6 Salisbury Square, London EC4Y 8JX; phone: (020) 7211 8000; fax: (020) 7211 8800; e-mail: enquiries@oft.gov.uk; Web site: www.oft.gov.uk

Office of Fair Trading Consumer Information Line (0345) 224499 (local call rates apply on BT lines within the UK)

Scottish Consumer Council (SCC) Royal Exchange House, 100 Queen Street, Glasgow G1 3DN; phone: (0141) 226 5261; fax: (0141) 221 0731; e-mail: scc@scotconsumer.org.uk; Web site: www.scotconsumer.org.uk

Welsh Consumer Council (WCC)/Cyngor Defnyddwyr Cymru (CDC) 5th Floor, Longcross Court, 47 Newport Road, Cardiff CF24 0WL; phone: (029) 2025 5454; fax: (029) 2025 5464; e-mail: info@wales.consumer.org.uk; Web site: www.wales.consumer.org.uk

Postal Information

First and Second Class Mail in the UK

As of July 2000.

First Class costs 27p up to 60 g, and 41p up to 100 g. Rates increase by weight up to 1 kg, which costs £3.32; each extra 250 g over 1 kg costs 81p.

Second Class costs 19p up to 60 g, and 33p up to 100 g. Rates increase by weight up to 750 g, which costs £1.85 and is the maximum weight that can be sent by Second Class.

The Post Office: Threats and Lifelines

Government plans to pay Social Security benefits directly into bank accounts rather than over the Post Office counter led to fears in 2000 that many post offices in rural areas and inner cities would close. However, the government changed its mind, proposing instead to offer Social Security recipients the option of having benefits paid directly into their bank accounts. The government also announced the creation of the post office based Universal Bank which will offer basic banking facilities to 3.5 million people in the UK who do not have bank accounts. Another key element to the future success of the Post Office is how well it adapts to e-commerce.

Threats

- Social Security recipients to be given the option of having benefits paid directly into their bank accounts, removing some Post Office business, especially in poorer areas
- Threat to letter monopoly from regulator and EC commission which applies to all letters costing under £1
- Increased use of e-mail to communicate
- Competition in parcel delivery from international companies

Lifelines

- The creation of Universal Bank based in post offices
- Revenue potential from invoice processing and delivery of goods bought online – the Post Office forecasts growth of up to 75% in five years as net shopping takes off
- The government now permits the Post Office to acquire overseas companies, allowing commercial operations to be set up outside the UK
- Potential from Internet kiosks installed in post offices

Royal Mail Domestic Services in the UK

As of July 2000.

Sending mail

When using first class and second class mail services, a certificate of posting is available free on request; with the Recorded service proof of posting is given automatically. Compensation for a lost item is either the market value of the item or up to £27, whichever is lower.

First class costs from 27p, and is usually delivered the next working day after posting.

Second class costs from 19p, and is usually delivered within 3 working days after posting.

Recorded costs 63p plus the first or second class postage, and is delivered within the usual first or second class period.

Special delivery costs from £3.50, and delivery to all UK addresses is guaranteed by 12.00 p.m. on the next working day. Proof of posting and delivery is provided; standard compensation is £250 for loss of, or damage to, an item; a Consequential Loss service is available at extra cost.

Receiving mail

Callers service allows you to collect items from your local delivery office before the delivery round begins and costs 26p per collection.

Keepsafe Royal Mail stores your mail while you are away from 1 day to 2 months and delivers it on your return. It costs £5.25–£15.75, depending on length of time.

Poste restante allows you to select a Post Office from which to collect your mail while travelling in the UK. There is a maximum duration of 3 months in any town, and there is no charge.

■ Postal Information

Royal Mail Domestic Services in the UK *(continued)*

Private box (PO Box) provides you with an alternative address and holds your mail for collection from your local delivery office. There is no maximum duration, and the cost is £42 for 6 months and £52 for 1 year.

Redirection Royal Mail forwards your personal mail to a new permanent or temporary address, either in the UK or abroad. There is a maximum duration of 2 years, and the cost (per surname) ranges from £6.30 for 1 month to £31.50 for 1 year (redirection within the UK) and £12.60 for 1 month to £63 for 1 year (redirection abroad).

International Letter Rates from the UK

As of July 2000.

Surface mail and postcards outside Europe only items up to 20 g cost 36p, up to 60 g cost 58p, and up to 100 g cost 83p. Rates increase with each extra 50 g up to 500 g, which costs £3.14; thereafter rates increase with each extra 50 g up to a maximum of 2 kg, which costs £13.37.

Airmail Europe items up to 20 g cost 36p. Items over 20 g are charged at the same rate for both areas, and rates increase with each extra 20 g up to a maximum of 2 kg, which costs £15.20.

Airmail zone 1 items up to 10 g cost 45p, and 65p up to 20 g. Rates increase with each extra 20 g up to a maximum of 2 kg, which costs £35.30.

Airmail zone 2 items up to 10 g cost 45p, and 65p up to 20 g. Rates increase with each extra 20 g up to a maximum of 2 kg, which costs £42.23.

(For details of Airmail zones 1 and 2 consult the booklet *The Easy Way to Mail Abroad,* obtainable from Royal Mail Customer Services, phone: (08457) 740740.)

International Small Packets Service from the UK

As of July 2000.

The International Small Packets service is for sending gifts or goods worldwide. Items intended for this service should be marked 'Small Packet', and those sent by Airmail should be marked 'Par Avion – By Airmail'. It is permissible to include a letter in the Small Packet if it relates to the contents. Delivery times are normally the same as for letters.

Customs declarations are obligatory for all Small Packets unless they are sent within the European Union. The required declaration varies according to the value of the Packet's contents; information is available from a Post Office.

Rates

Surface mail costs 57p up to 100 g. Rates increase by 19p for each extra 50 g to a maximum of 2 kg, which costs £7.79; for books and pamphlets only, each extra 50 g costs 19p (to a maximum of 5 kg).

Airmail Europe costs 87p up to 100 g. Rates increase by 9p for each extra 20 g to a maximum of 2 kg, which costs £9.42.

Airmail zone 1 costs £1.15 up to 100 g. Rates increase by 17p for each extra 20 g to a maximum of 2 kg, which costs £17.30.

Airmail zone 2 costs £1.15 up to 100 g. Rates increase by 19p for each 20 g to a maximum of 2 kg, which costs £19.20.

(For details of Airmail zones 1 and 2 consult the booklet *The Easy Way to Mail Abroad,* obtainable from Royal Mail Customer Services, phone: (08457) 740740.)

Royal Mail Special International Services from the UK

As of July 2000.

International Recorded costs £2.60 plus Airmail postage. Advice of delivery (a copy of the signature taken on delivery) is available for an extra 40p. Maximum compensation for a lost item is £28. Items must have an International Recorded label, available from a Post Office.

International Registered is for items of monetary value, and costs £3.15 plus Airmail or Surface mail postage for compensation cover up to £500; and £4.20 plus Airmail or Surface mail postage for compensation cover up to £2,200. Advice of delivery (a copy of the signature taken on delivery) is available for an extra 40p. Items must have an International Registered label attached, with 'Insured for xxx pounds' written in ink above the address. Secure sealing is advisable, and for some countries a signed customs declaration is required. The maximum weight is 2 kg.

Swiftair is for packages that require priority handling, so that they are sent on the first available flight to their destination countries. It is not a guaranteed courier service. It costs £2.85 per item plus Airmail postage. Maximum compensation is £27. Items must have a Swiftair label attached, available from a Post Office. The maximum weight for letters and Small Packages is 2 kg, and for books and pamphlets 5 kg. Swiftair is available from the UK to most destinations worldwide.

Swiftair Plus Recorded combines Swiftair with International Recorded, and costs £3.50 plus Airmail postage. Maximum compensation is £28. Advice of delivery is available for an extra 40p. The maximum weight is 2 kg for letters and Small Packets, and 5 kg for books and pamphlets.

Swiftair Plus Registered combines Swiftair with International Registered, and costs £4.00 for compensation cover up to £500 and £4.75 for compensation cover up to £2,200. Advice of delivery is available for an extra 40p. The maximum weight is 2 kg.

International Printed Papers Service from the UK

As of July 2000.

The International Printed Papers service is an economical way to send printed material, such as books, newspapers, magazines, and pamphlets. Personal correspondence cannot be included. Items intended for this service should be marked 'Printed Papers', and those sent by Airmail should be marked 'Par Avion – By Airmail'. Delivery times are normally the same as for letters.

Customs labels are not usually needed for mail containing only letters or documents. For items just containing books, a Customs declaration is required for the following countries: Algeria; Dominican Republic. For all Printed Papers items a Customs declaration is required for the following countries: Bangladesh; Djibouti; India; Japan; Zimbabwe. For Venezuela, please consult a Post Office. Customs labels are available from a Post Office.

Rates

Surface mail costs 57p up to 100 g. Rates increase by 19p for each extra 50 g up to 2 kg, which costs £7.79; for books and pamphlets only, each extra 50 g costs 19p (to a maximum of 5 kg).

Airmail Europe costs 75p up to 100 g. Rates increase by 8p for each extra 20 g up to 2 kg, which costs £8.35; for books and pamphlets only, each extra 20 g costs 8p (to a maximum of 5 kg).

Airmail zone 1 costs £1.15 up to 100 g. Rates increase by 17p for each extra 20 g up to 2 kg, which costs £17.30; for books and pamphlets only, each extra 20 g costs 17p (to a maximum of 5 kg).

Airmail zone 2 costs £1.15 up to 100 g. Rates increase by 19p for each extra 20 g up to 2 kg, which costs £19.20; for books and pamplets only, each extra 20 g costs 19p (to a maximum of 5 kg).

(For details of Airmail zones 1 and 2 consult the booklet *The Easy Way to Mail Abroad,* obtainable from Royal Mail Customer Services, phone: (08457) 740740.)

International Delivery Times from the UK

As of July 2000.

Surface mail delivery times noted by Royal Mail are 2 weeks within Western Europe (all European countries not part of the former USSR or Eastern Europe); 4 weeks to other parts of Europe; and up to 8–12 weeks for places outside Europe.

Airmail delivery times are 2 days within Western Europe; 3 days to Eastern Europe; 4 days outside Europe.

Airmail distinctions outside Europe are categorized as either Zone 1 or Zone 2. The Post Office supplies full lists of the zones into which individual countries fall.

Telephone Information

Public Telecommunications Operators in the UK

The UK was one of the first countries in the world to break up telecommunications and postal services within its state-owned monopoly and allow competition by issuing licences to new Public Telecommunications Operators (PTOs) of fixed networks and mobile networks.

Two events in 1981 heralded the beginning of deregulation and increased competition in the UK telecommunications industry: the government sold shares in Cable, and postal and telecommunications services, which had both been run by the Post Office, were separated and British Telecommunications plc (BT) was formed.

Privatization of BT took place in stages, beginning in 1984 when the government sold 51% of its shares in BT to the public. In the same year, BT lost its monopoly on telecommunications provision and services in the UK when Mercury Communications was granted an operator's licence. The introduction of Vodafone and Cellnet cellular radio networks in 1985 provided the BT and Mercury duopoly with some competition, encouraging the development of new markets. Cable television operators were also granted licences to provide telecommunications services, but only as agents for BT and Mercury.

The BT/Mercury duopoly on fixed services continued until 1991 when the government decided to accept applications for licences from new operators. Vodafone and Cellnet were issued with licences to provide fixed services, and cable television networks were allowed to offer services in their own right.

Restrictions on the use of leased lines for the provision of international services were lifted in 1991. Further competition was encouraged with the creation of International Simple Resale (ISR). This system allows operators of international leased lines to interconnect with public networks between designated countries and re-sell their services to both residential and business customers.

In 1996, the Department of Trade and Industry removed the BT/Mercury duopoly on the provision of international telecommunications services and opened the telecommunications industry to full competition.

Data from Oftel

See also **Computing and Telecommunications**, pp 491–498.

BT General Services in the UK

Service		Details	Contact (service is free unless stated otherwise)
Customer services	residential customers	to enquire about any BT service or product, to change your phone book entry, or to make a complaint; 8 a.m. to 6 p.m., Monday to Saturday	from a BT line: 150; from a mobile phone or non-BT line: 0800 800150
	business customers	Sales Office: to make an enquiry about a BT product or service; Service Centre: to make an after-sales enquiry, to change your phone book entry or to make a complaint; 8 a.m. to 6 p.m., Monday to Saturday	from a BT line: 152; from a mobile phone or non-BT line: 0800 800152
	general enquiries	to enquire about BT media relations, schools liaison, building services, land planning, wayleaves (concerning access to properties for building work, etc), or personnel; 8 a.m. to 6 p.m., Monday to Friday	from any line: 0800 309409
Fault reporting	residential customers	24 hours a day, 7 days a week	from a BT line: 151; from a mobile phone or non-BT line: 0800 800151
	business customers	24 hours a day, 7 days a week	from any line: 0800 800154
Bill enquiries	residential customers	8 a.m. to 6 p.m., Monday to Saturday	from a BT line: 150; from a mobile phone or non-BT line: 0800 800150
	business customers	8 a.m. to 6 p.m., Monday to Saturday	from any line: 0800 800156; from a mobile phone: 0800 800156
Making a complaint		contact customer services (see above) for complaints about any BT services	contact customer services (see above)
Operator services		for help making a call, 24 hours a day, 7 days a week	local and national calls, and calls to the Republic of Ireland: 100; international calls: 155
Directory enquiries		for help finding a number or code, 24 hours a day, 7 days a week	local and national numbers and numbers for the Republic of Ireland: 192[1]; international numbers: 153[1]; for those who cannot hold, handle, or read *The Phone Book*, contact 195 for free directory enquiry service

(continued)

BT General Services in the UK (*continued*)

Service	Details	Contact (service is free unless stated otherwise)
Customers with special needs	details of BT services for customers with special needs, including people with impaired hearing, speech difficulties, restricted vision, and limited mobility, can be found in *The Phone Book; free guide: (0800) 800150*	
Malicious calls	customer services will provide simple advice on the most suitable action to take	150
	adviceline: BT provides information on how to deal with unwanted phone calls and what BT can offer to help tackle the problem, 24 hours a day, 7 days a week	0800 666700
	specialist bureau: specially trained investigators will help tackle the problem. In extreme cases, they can work with the police to trace calls	0800 661441
Telephone number changes	information on telephone number changes introduced in April 2000, affecting Cardiff, Coventry, London, Northern Ireland, Portsmouth, and Southampton	0808 224 2000

[1] Unless calls are made from a public payphone, users are charged 35p (for two searches) for directory enquiries services for both residential and business lines.

Data from British Telecommunication, plc.

Operator-connected Calls in the UK

Help making calls

The Operator can provide help in making calls, 24 hours a day, 7 days a week. For help making local and national calls and calls to the Republic of Ireland, call free on 100. For help with international calls, call free on 155.

The operator can help with the following services:

- calls to someone else in the UK
- calls to someone abroad
- calls from abroad
- calls to or from a ship
- reverse charges (collect): the operator can arrange a phone call from you if the recipient agrees to accept the cost of the call and vice versa, both within the UK and internationally.

Alarm calls

The Operator can arrange for you to be called at a set time. Users of this service will be charged £2.70.

Telemessages

The Operator can arrange for a message given over the phone to be delivered by post the next day. Telemessages within the UK cost £8.99 for 50 words. For special occasions, such as weddings or birthdays, a telemessage greeting card with up to 50 words can be sent for £9.99. For more information, contact Freefone: 0800 190190.

Mobile Telephones

The quality and range of services on offer from mobile phones are on the increase: they can be compatible with PCs, used to send and receive e-mails, and even to access the Internet. However, the majority of users in the UK – nearly one-third of the population – still use them in the traditional way, for making and receiving telephone calls.

Choosing a mobile phone

Establish which operators provide good network coverage in your area. Ask friends with mobile phones how good they find coverage for their network. You also need to decide which tariff type you want:

With a 'prepay' tariff you buy calls up front and there is no monthly line rental but calls are generally more expensive and the phones themselves are usually more expensive. These are usually the cheapest option if not many calls are made.

Conventional tariffs charge for line rental with a certain amount of calls free after which calls are charged at the tariff rate chosen. The phones themselves are usually cheaper than with prepay tariffs but you are tied into a 12-month contract.

All inclusive tariffs charge a higher amount up front – perhaps as much as £200. This will include rental for at least a year, handset, connection, and some calls.

Identify the most suitable tariff structure that is available on each tariff type – there will be several to suit different types of user. This will depend upon what time of the day and week calls are made, time spent, and call destination – local or international for example.

Dangers of using a mobile phone

Lurid tabloid headlines of irradiated brains have helped distort the true picture of mobile phone safety. The fear is that radio waves emitted by mobile phones can cause health problems such as cancer. In actual fact research to date has not produced any concrete findings. If you are worried, cut down on mobile phone usage until further research casts some light on the issue. If a risk is established children are likely to be more vulnerable, so some doctors are recommending that the use of mobile phones by those under 16 should be restricted to essential calls only.

Emergency Telephone Numbers in the UK

Dial 999 for:

- Fire
- Police
- Ambulance
- Coastguard (sea and cliff rescue)
- Mountain Rescue
- Cave Rescue
- 112 can also be dialled as an alternative

The operator asks callers which emergency service they require and then connects the caller to the service. Callers should tell the emergency service:

- where the trouble is
- what the trouble is
- where the caller is
- the number of the telephone they are using.

Textphone users should contact Typetalk's emergency relay service on: 0800 112999 text. It is against the law to make false calls to the emergency services. Callers making false calls can be traced immediately to the telephone that they are calling from.

Citizenship and Immigration

Customs Allowances of the UK

If travellers are entering the UK from another European Union (EU) country, they no longer need to go through the red ('something to declare') or green ('nothing to declare') channels at Customs. EU travellers usually go through a separate exit, sometimes called the blue channel, and do not have to pass through Customs at all.

While travellers may not see any Customs officers on arrival in the UK, it is important to remember that Customs do carry out selective checks to look for prohibited and restricted goods.

The EU countries are: Austria, Belgium, Denmark, Finland, France, Germany, Greece, the Republic of Ireland, Italy, Luxembourg, the Netherlands, Portugal, Spain (but not the Canary Islands), Sweden, and the UK (but not the Channel Islands).

Prohibited and restricted goods

Certain goods are restricted or banned completely from being brought into the UK from any country. Restricted goods are those which cannot be imported into the UK without an appropriate authority, such as a licence. Within the EU, these restrictions may vary slightly. Travellers are advised to contact the Customs departments of the countries they are leaving to enquire whether particular goods are banned or restricted in the UK. The table opposite provides examples of banned and restricted goods from outside the EU, together with contact details for enquiries.

Goods bought in the EU

You do not have to pay any tax or duty in the UK on goods you have bought in other EU countries for your own use. Own use includes gifts, but you may be breaking the law if you sell goods that you have bought. If you are caught selling the goods, they will be taken off you and you could get up to seven years in prison. Any vehicle you used to transport the goods could also be taken off you.

The law sets out guidelines for the amount of alcohol and tobacco you can bring into the UK. If you bring in more than this, you must be able to satisfy Customs officers that the goods are for your own use. Otherwise the goods may be taken off you.

The guidelines for goods you can buy in the EU for your own use are:

- 800 cigarettes
- 400 cigarillos
- 200 cigars
- 1 kg of smoking tobacco
- 10 litres of spirits
- 20 litres of fortified wine (such as port or sherry)
- 90 litres of wine (of which not more than 60 litres can be sparkling wine)
- 110 litres of beer

People under 17 are not allowed to bring tobacco and alcohol into the UK.

Goods bought outside the EU

Travellers arriving in the UK from a country that is not part of the EU must go through customs; through the red channel if they have something to declare; through the green channel if they are confident that they have no more than the Customs allowances and are not carrying any prohibited, restricted, or commercial goods.

For travellers arriving from outside the EU, the following allowances apply:

- 200 cigarettes or 100 cigarillos or 50 cigars or 250 g of tobacco
- 2 litres of still table wine
- 1 litre of spirits or strong liqueurs over 22% volume or 2 litres of fortified wine, sparkling wine, or other liqueurs
- 60 cc/ml of perfume
- 250 cc/ml of toilet water
- £145 worth of all other goods including souvenirs and gifts.

Note: people aged under 17 do not have a tobacco or alcohol allowance, they are not allowed to bring tobacco or alcohol into the country.

Money

There are no legal limits to the amount of money that travellers can bring into the UK from either within or outside the EU. However, if a traveller is found be in possession of more than £10,000 sterling in cash or items transferable to cash, such as traveller's cheques or share certificates, they will be challenged to explain why and to provide proof of their explanation.

If you have a complaint

If you have a complaint, contact Customs at your local office or at the port or airport. If they cannot sort out the problem, you should contact the Collector, the head of Customs for the region. Your local office will tell you how to do this. If the Collector does not sort out your complaint, you can then ask the independent Adjudicator to look into it. The Adjudicator's services are free.

Address: The Adjudicator's Office, Haymarket House, 28 Haymarket, London SW1Y 4SP; phone: (020) 7930 2292; fax: (020) 7930 2298.

Further information

For further information about UK Customs rules and allowances, contact one of the Excise and Inland Customs Advice Centres below:

Belfast Custom House, Queens Square, Belfast BT1 3ET; phone: (028) 9056 2972; fax: (028) 9056 2971; Web site: www.hmce.gov.uk; open: 9.00 a.m.–5.00 p.m.

Wolverhampton Deansgate, 62–70 Tettenhall Road, Wolverhampton WV1 4TZ; phone: (01902) 771921; fax: (01902) 392202; Web site: www.hmce.gov.uk; open: 9.00 a.m.–4.00 p.m.

Cardiff Portcullis House, 21 Cowbridge Road East, Cardiff CF1 9SS; phone: (029) 2038 6400; fax: (029) 2038 6444; Web site: www.hmce.gov.uk; open: 9.00 a.m.–4.30 p.m.

Cheadle Boundary House, Cheadle Point, Cheadle, Cheshire SK8 2JZ; phone: (0161) 261 7997; fax: (0161) 261 7399; Web site: www.hmce.gov.uk; open: 9.00 a.m.–4.30 p.m.

Dundee Caledonian House, Greenmarket, Dundee DD1 1HD; phone: (01382) 200822; fax: (01382) 313247; Web site: www.hmce.gov.uk; open: 9.00 a.m.–4.00 p.m.

Glasgow Portcullis House, 21 India Street, Glasgow G2 4PZ; phone: (0345) 442266; fax: (0141) 308 3402; Web site: www.hmce.gov.uk; open: 9.30 a.m.–4.30 p.m.

Ipswich Haven House, 17 Lower Brook Street, Ipswich, Suffolk IP4 1DN; phone: (01473) 235951; fax: (01473) 235921; Web site: www.hmce.gov.uk; open: 9.00 a.m.–4.30 p.m.

London Central Berkeley House, 304 Regents Park Road, Finchley, London N3 2JY; phone: (020) 7865 4400; fax: (020) 8346 9154; Web site: www.hmce.gov.uk; open: 9.00 a.m.–4.30 p.m.

London South Dorset House, Stamford Street, London SE1 9PY; phone: (020) 7202 4227; fax: (020) 7202 4131; Web site: www.hmce.gov.uk; open: 9.00 a.m.–5.00 p.m.; non-UK phone: (44) 20 7202 4227; non-UK fax: (44) 20 7202 4216

Newcastle upon Tyne Dobson House, Regent Centre, Gosforth NE3 3PF; phone: (0191) 201 1719; fax: (0191) 201 1594; open: 8.30 a.m.–5.00 p.m.

Nottingham Bowman House, 100–102 Talbot Street, Nottingham NG1 5NF; phone: (0115) 971 2107; fax: (0115) 971 2219; open: 9.00 a.m.–4.00 p.m.

Plymouth Crownhill Court, Tailyour Road, Crownhill, Plymouth PL6 5BZ; phone: (01752) 777123; fax: (01752) 765828; open: 9.00 a.m.–4.00 p.m.

Reading Eldon Court, 75 London Road, Reading RG1 5BS; phone: (0118) 964 4355; fax: (0118) 964 4206; open: 9.00 a.m.–5.00 p.m.

Customs Allowances of the UK *(continued)*

Redhill Warwick House, 67 Station Road, Redhill, Surrey RH1 1QU; phone: (08450) 199199; fax: (01737) 734600; open: 9.00 a.m.–5.00 p.m.

Southampton Custom House, Orchard Place, Southampton SO14 3NS; phone: (023) 8033 0330; fax: (023) 8082 7546; open: 9.00 a.m.–5.00 p.m.

Contact details can also be found in the phone book under Customs and Excise.

For advice on Air Passenger Duty, please contact the Excise and Inland Customs Advice Centre office: 1 Park Road, Uxbridge, Middx UB8 1RW; phone: (0189) 584 2226; fax: (0189) 581 4305 (not open to the public); Web site: www.hmce.gov.uk

Source: HM Customs and Excise, © *Crown copyright 1999; with Helicon updates*

Prohibited and Restricted Goods

(– = not applicable.)

Type of goods	Details	Contact for further information
Prohibited (banned) goods		
Unlicensed drugs	such as heroin, morphine, cocaine, cannabis, amphetamines, barbiturates, and LSD	–
Offensive weapons	such as flick knives, swordsticks, knuckledusters, and some martial arts equipment	–
Obscene material	such as pornographic material in the form of books, magazines, films, video tapes, laser discs, and computer software, and indecent or obscene material featuring children	–
Counterfeit and copied goods	such as watches, clothes, and CDs. Also any fake goods with false marks of their origin, e.g. fake designer labels on clothes	–
Restricted goods		
Firearms, explosives, and ammunition	including electric shock devices (such as stunguns) and gas canisters	Excise and Inland Customs Advice Centre (see below)
Dogs, cats, and other animals	including rabbits, gerbils, rats, and mice; a British import (rabies) licence is vital	Ministry of Agriculture, Fisheries and Food: (020) 8330 4411; fax: (020) 7270 8419; Web site: www.maff.gov.uk/maffhome.htm
Live birds	including family pets, unless they are covered by a British health import licence	Ministry of Agriculture, Fisheries and Food: (020) 8330 4411; fax: (020) 7270 8419; Web site: www.maff.gov.uk/maffhome.htm
Endangered species	including birds and plants, whether alive or dead. Also goods, such as fur, ivory, or leather, that have been taken from endangered species	Department of the Environment: (0117) 987 8202; Web site: www.detr.gov.uk
Meat and poultry	including most products made from them, such as bacon, ham, sausages, paté, eggs, milk, and cream; 1 kg of meat per person is allowed as long as it is fully cooled and in airtight containers	Ministry of Agriculture, Fisheries and Food: (020) 8330 4411; fax: (020) 7270 8419; Web site: www.maff.gov.uk/maffhome.htm
Certain plants and their produce	including trees, shrubs, potatoes, certain fruit, bulbs, and seeds	Ministry of Agriculture, Fisheries and Food: (01904) 455195; fax: (01904) 455199; Web site: www.maff.gov.uk/maffhome.htm
Radio transmitters	such as CB radios that are not approved for use in the UK	Radio Communications Agency: (020) 7211 0502; fax: (020) 7211 0507; Web site: www.radio.gov.uk

Source: HM Customs and Excise, © *Crown copyright*

The Pet Travel Scheme in the UK (PETS)

The Pet Travel Scheme (PETS) allows you to bring your pet cat or dog into the UK without quarantine as long as the pet meets all the conditions of the scheme. PETS was introduced with a pilot scheme which started on 28 February 2000. This applies only to pet cats and dogs coming into the UK from Western Europe, and to guide dogs and hearing dogs coming from Australia and New Zealand. The scheme will be extended in 2001 to include other species of pets and other countries.

Preparing your pet

For your pet to be able to enter the UK without quarantine, it has to meet certain conditions.

Your pet has to be:

- microchipped
- vaccinated
- blood tested
- treated against ticks and tapeworms

You also need to get an official PETS certificate from a government-approved vet to verify that these procedures have been carried out.

The six month rule

You should note that you will have to wait six months from the date your vet took the blood sample which gave a successful blood test result before your pet can enter or re-enter the UK. Pets resident in the UK are exempt from this rule if the blood sample was taken before 28 February 2000.

Routes

The only valid routes for the PETS pilot scheme are:

By sea

- Calais–Dover
- Cherbourg–Portsmouth
- Caen–Portsmouth
- St Malo–Portsmouth
- Le Havre–Portsmouth

Through the Channel Tunnel Calais (Coquelles)–Folkestone (Cheriton)

By air As of May 2000 there were three confirmed routes: British Midland Airways from Amsterdam (Schiphol) to Heathrow, Finnair from Helsinki to Heathrow, and Lufthansa from Frankfurt to Heathrow.

Citizenship and Immigration ■

The Pet Travel Scheme in the UK (PETS) *(continued)*

There are additional permitted routes for guide dogs and hearing dogs from Australia or New Zealand arriving at London Heathrow Airport.

Taking pets out of the UK

Some of the qualifying countries also require another, separate, certificate (known as an export health certificate), to show that your pet meets certain health conditions set out by that country. These requirements are separate from those of the Pet Travel Scheme.

As of May 2000, an export health certificate is required for pets entering France, Gibraltar, Greece, Iceland, Italy, Liechtenstein, Netherlands, Norway, Portugal, Spain, Sweden, or Switzerland. Your pet may be refused entry if you do not have one. For details of how to get an official export health certificate, contact your local Animal Health Divisional Office.

Before you travel to other countries with your pet, you are advised to check what documentation is required for your pet to enter that country.

Certificate for treatment against parasites

Before your pet can enter or re-enter the UK without quarantine it will have to be treated against certain ticks and tapeworms. This treatment will have to be carried out every time your pet enters the UK.

For more information on PETS and quarantine, contact: Ministry of Agriculture, Fisheries, and Food, 1A Page Street, London SW1P 4PQ; phone: (0870) 241 1710; fax: (020) 7904 6834; e-mail: pets@ahvg.maff.gsi.gov.uk; Web site: www.maff.gov.uk/animalh/quarantine/index.htm.

Source: Ministry of Agriculture, Fisheries and Food,

Passport Regulations and Requirements of the UK

Eligibility for a UK passport

As of 1 January 1983, under the British Nationality Act 1981, UK passports are issued to: British citizens; British subjects; British Dependent Territories citizens; British Overseas citizens; British Protected Persons; British Nationals (Overseas). British Nationals (Overseas) passports can be acquired only by people with a connection to Hong Kong.

The most usual ways to qualify as one of the above (excluding British Nationals (Overseas)), are:

- by birth in the UK or a British Colony
- by naturalization in the UK or a British Colony
- by registration as a citizen of the UK and Colonies
- by legitimate descent from a father to whom one of the above applies

Women who marry UK citizens do not automatically acquire British nationality by marriage (*see* **Visiting and Immigration to the UK** p 312).

Anyone who is unsure about their eligibility to hold a UK passport should contact a Passport Office for advice (see below).

While the holder of a UK passport can generally travel anywhere in the world, travellers are not exempt from immigration rules in other countries. Nor are they exempt from obtaining any necessary visas.

Passport applications

UK passports are issued in the UK by the six Regional Passport Offices of the United Kingdom Passport Agency, an Executive Agency of the Home Office. Passport application forms can be obtained from the Regional Passport Offices (see below), main Post Offices, Lloyds Bank, and ARTAC WorldChoice Travel Agents. Until recently, three types of passport were available in the UK: the standard ten-year passport, the British Visitor's Passport, valid for travel to EU countries for one year, and the Collective Passport, valid for a single journey for sponsored parties of young people under the age of 18. The British Visitor's Passport has been abolished, and the standard ten-year passport is now required to travel abroad. The Collective Passport is still available. The following table gives details of the current types of passports available, together with information on validity, postal application fees, and the forms required to make applications. (Fees are current as of May 2000.)

Notes

Family passports have now been discontinued, but existing ones may still be used until they expire. Applications that are made in person to Passport Offices will incur a handling charge of £10 per application in addition to the fees listed opposite. Personal applications do not guarantee a priority service.

Women who are getting married and want to change their names on their passports in time for their honeymoon can do so by requesting special forms PD1 and PD2. Applications must not be made more than three months before the wedding. For further information, contact a Passport Office (see table). It should be noted that some countries will not grant visas on these passports. Travellers are advised to contact the Embassy or High Commission of the country concerned for further information. Married women can also amend their passport details after their marriage to show their new name, if applicable, using Form C.

If a passport is lost or stolen, an application for a replacement can be made using Forms A or B. Details of the lost passport will need to be given and photographs, relevant documents, and the usual fee will have to be submitted. Initially, a replacement passport, valid for one year, might be issued, to enable enquiries about the lost passport to be made. Since October 1998, all children who were not already on a valid 10-year passport now need to hold their own passport if they are to travel abroad. It is no longer possible to add or re-include children on British passports. This includes newborn babies and all children up to the age of 16. Children aged 16 and over already have to hold their own passports and are unaffected by these changes.

Completing passport applications

Instructions for completing applications are provided on the forms. Original documents proving status and eligibility for a UK passport must be sent with an application; copies are not acceptable. The type of documents required with an application are detailed on application forms and vary according to the type of application. Documents to be produced may include any of the following:

- birth certificate
- marriage certificate
- proof of a name change
- adoption certificate
- divorce decree
- old passport
- registration document
- naturalization document

Where photographic evidence of identity is required with a passport application, two identical copies of a recent photograph should be included. These should be unmounted, printed on normal thin photographic paper, and should measure 45 mm x 35 mm/1.77 in x 1.38 in. The photograph should show the full face, without a hat, and should be taken against a white background. One copy of the photograph must be signed by someone else to confirm the identity of the applicant. This person must be one of the following: Member of Parliament; Justice of the Peace; minister of religion; professionally qualified person (for example, doctor, lawyer, teacher, etc); local councillor; bank officer; civil servant; police officer; or someone of similar standing who has known you for at least two years, and who is either a British citizen, British Dependent Territories citizen, British National (Overseas), British Overseas citizen, British Subject, or a citizen of a Commonwealth country. A relative cannot countersign a passport application.

Passport applications should be made at least one month before the passport is needed. The time of year that an application is made can affect the speed with which it is processed. The UK Passport Agency explains in its leaflet *Answers to Questions People Ask Us* (included with all passport application forms) that passports can be issued within two weeks between the months of September and December. Between January and August, applications can take up to four weeks to be processed. If a passport is needed more quickly than in two to four weeks, it is possible to process properly completed applications if they are submitted together with a photocopy of proof of travel, for example, a flight ticket. It is not normally possible to obtain a passport on the day of application. However, in cases of emergency, travellers are advised to contact a Passport Office for advice (see below).

■ Citizenship and Immigration

Passport Regulations and Requirements of the UK (*continued*)

Regional passport offices

(Minicom numbers are for the deaf and hard of hearing.)

Liverpool Passport Office 5th Floor, India Buildings, Water Street, Liverpool L2 0QZ; phone: (0870) 521 0410; minicom: (0151) 236 6292; open: 8.00 a.m.–6.00 p.m

London Passport Office Clive House, 70 Petty France, London SW1H 9HD; phone: (0870) 521 0410; minicom: (020) 7271 8808; open: Monday to Friday 7.30 a.m.–4 p.m. The London Office only deals with personal callers. Postal applications from residents of Greater London should be sent to the Glasgow Passport Office.

Newport Passport Office Olympia House, Upper Dock Street, Newport, Gwent NP20 1XA; phone: (01633) 473701; minicom: (01633) 473701; open: 8.00 a.m.–6.00 p.m.

Peterborough Passport Office, Aragon Court, Northminster Road, Peterborough PE1 1QG; phone: (01733) 555644; minicom: (01733) 555688; open: 8.00 a.m.–6.00 p.m.

Belfast Passport Office, Hampton House, 47–53 High Street, Belfast BT1 2QS; phone: (028) 9031 9500; minicom: (028) 9033 0214; open: 8.30 a.m.–6.00 p.m. The Belfast Passport Office deals with all applications in Northern Ireland.

Glasgow Passport Office, 3 Northgate, 96 Milton Street, Cowcaddens, Glasgow G4 0BT; phone: (0141) 322 4621; minicom: (0141) 332 4621; open: 8.30 a.m.–6.00 p.m. The Glasgow Passport Office deals with all applications in Scotland and those from Greater London.

Source: The UK Passport Agency, © Crown copyright 1998; with Helicon updates

Would-be travellers queuing outside the Passport Office in Glasgow, Scotland. A huge backlog of applications during the summer of 1999 left Passport Offices throughout the UK unable to process requests for passports quickly enough, and Home Secretary Jack Straw introduced emergency measures to cope with the demand. *Syndication International*

UK Passports

Type of passport	Validity/details	Application fee (£)	Application form required
New passports			
Standard passport (32 pages)	normally valid for 10 years	28	Form A
Large standard passport (48 pages)	for persons who travel widely, valid for 10 years	38	Form A
Standard passport for minors under 16	valid initially for 5 years	14.80	Form B
Collective passports	valid on a single journey for organized trips for school children or young people under the age of 18	40	contact Passport Office for application form
Additions/amendments to existing passports			
Standard passport	if replacing and surrendering a ten-year passport	17	Form R
Standard passport	to make changes	17[1]	Form C
Standard passport for minors under 16	to extend a passport (total possible life is ten years)	no fee[2]/11[3]	Form D

[1] It is cheaper to buy a new passport for a child.
[2] For passports issued before 28 March 1998.
[3] For passports issued after 28 March 1998.

Source: The UK Passport Agency, © Crown copyright 1998; with Helicon updates

Visa Requirements for Travel to and from the UK

Foreign visitors travelling to the UK

All overseas nationals wishing to enter the UK must satisfy immigration officers on arrival in this country that they meet the requirements of UK immigration law. Where necessary, people must have a valid entry clearance (visa or entry certificate) before arriving in the UK. Nationals of the countries or territories listed below must have a valid UK visa each time they enter the country:

Afghanistan; Albania; Algeria; Angola; Armenia; Azerbaijan; Bahrain; Bangladesh; Belarus; Benin; Bhutan; Bosnia-Herzegovina; Bulgaria; Burkina Faso; Burundi; Cambodia; Cameroon; Cape Verde; Central African Republic; Chad; China; Colombia; Comoros; Congo, Democratic Republic of Congo; Republic of the Côte d'Ivoire; Cuba; Cyprus, Turkish Republic of Northern; Djibouti; Dominican Republic; Ecuador; Egypt; Equatorial Guinea; Eritrea; Ethiopia; Fiji Islands; Gabon; Gambia; Georgia; Ghana; Guinea; Guinea-Bissau; Guyana; Haiti; India; Indonesia; Iran; Iraq; Jordan; Kazakhstan; Kenya; Kyrgyzstan; Korea, North; Kuwait; Laos; Lebanon; Liberia; Libya; Macedonia, Former Yugoslav Republic of; Madagascar; Maldives; Mali; Mauritania; Mauritius; Moldova; Mongolia; Morocco; Mozambique; Myanmar; Nepal; Niger; Nigeria; Oman; Pakistan; Papua New Guinea; Peru; Philippines; Qatar; Romania; Russia; Rwanda; São Tomé and Príncipe; Saudi Arabia; Senegal; Sierra Leone; Slovak Republic; Somalia; Sri Lanka; Sudan; Suriname; Syria; Taiwan; Tajikistan; Tanzania; Thailand; Togo; Tunisia; Turkey; Turkmenistan; Uganda; Ukraine; United Arab Emirates; Uzbekistan; Vietnam; Yemen; Yugoslavia (documents issued by former SFR of Yugoslavia or by present Yugoslav authorities); Zambia.

Nationals of any country not listed above do not need a UK visa for a visit or to study in the UK. However, an entry clearance must be obtained if they wish to do one of the following:

- settle in the UK
- work in the UK (unless a work permit is held)
- set up business in the UK
- live in the UK as a person of independent means
- accompany or join someone going to the UK for any of the above purposes.

Applicants for entry clearance to the UK must fill in all necessary official forms. These forms are available from British Missions in foreign countries offering entry clearance services. Applicants should check with their nearest British Mission for information and advice.

For more information about British immigration and visa requirements, see the Internet service of the Foreign and Commonwealth Office: www.fco.gov.uk/travel/im_visa.asp, or contact the Immigration and Nationalisation Directorate (IND) at:

Lunar House, Wellesley Road, Croydon, Surrey CR9 1AT; phone: (0870) 706 7766; fax: (020) 8760 3017; Web site: www.homeoffice.gov.uk/ind/hpg.htm

Alternatively, contact the Immigration Advisory Service or the Refugee Legal Centre. Both are independent charities that give free and confidential advice, assistance, and representation to anyone applying for an entry clearance to the UK. Their addresses are:

Immigration Advisory Service, County House, 190 Great Dover Street, London SE1 4YB; phone: (020) 7357 6917; fax: (020) 7378 0665

Refugee Legal Centre, Sussex House, 39–45 Bermondsey Street, London SE1 3XF; phone: (020) 7378 6242.

British Nationals travelling overseas

British nationals wishing to travel abroad should enquire about any visa requirements at the Embassy, High Commission, or consulate of the country they plan to visit. Tourists can check with their travel agents. Business and tourist visa requirements in foreign countries change constantly, sometimes at short notice. They also vary according to the length of stay and purpose of the visit.

There are some countries to which UK nationals are advised against travelling. As at July 2000, the Travel Advice Unit of the Foreign and Commonwealth Office advises against all travel to the following destinations: Afghanistan, Burundi, Comoros (Anjovan and Moheli), the Democratic Republic of Congo (except Kinshasa), the Republic of the Congo (except Brazzaville and Pointe Noire), Ecuador, Ethiopia (East of the Harar to Gode line), Fiji Islands, India (Jammu and Kashmir only), Indonesia (Maluku Province), Iraq, Liberia (except Monrovia), Namibia (Caprivi and Kavango regions), Nigeria (Kaduna), Pakistan (federally administered tribal areas and all areas bordering Afghanistan), Philippines (Mindanao, the Southern Zamboanga Peninsula and islands southwest of Mindanao), Russian Federation (Chechen Republic and North Caucasus region), Sierra Leone, Solomon Islands, Southern Somalia, north and east Sri Lanka, Tajikistan, southeastern Turkey.

Unless on essential business, the Travel Advice Unit advises against travel to the following destinations: northeast Albania, Algeria, Angola, Central African Republic, the Democratic Republic of Congo (Kinshasa), Republic of the Congo (Brazzaville and Pointe Noire), East Timor, Eritrea, Ethiopia (Tigray and Afar), Indonesia (Aceh), Liberia (Monrovia), Philippines (Maguidanoa, Lanao del Sur, Lanao del Norte, Sultan Kudaraat, and North and South Cotabato), Rwanda (northwest and border areas to the southwest, south, and southeast), Yemen, Federal Republic of Yugoslavia (Serbia including Kosovo).

Travellers wanting up-to-date information or advice from the Foreign and Commonwealth Office about travelling abroad can use the Internet Service of the Foreign and Commonwealth Office – www.fco.gov.uk/travel/ – or contact the British Embassy of the country to which they wish to travel.

Source: Foreign and Commonwealth Office; Home Office Immigration and Nationality Directorate, © Crown copyright 1997; with Helicon updates

Visiting and Immigration to the UK

General information

People wishing to visit the UK must be able to prove that they wish to visit the country for no more than six months, that they plan to leave the UK at the end of their visit, and that they have enough funds to finance their visit without applying for social security benefits. Multiple-entry visas (valid for two years) can be applied for by frequent business visitors.

People wishing to visit the UK on business can do so if they satisfy the criteria above, with an additional proviso that they live and work abroad and do not intend to move their business base to this country, or plan to take employment, produce goods, or provide services in the UK.

There is no strict limit to the number of visits to the UK. However, a visitor is not normally expected to spend more than six months out of any twelve month period in the country.

Students

People who wish to come to the UK to study must show that they have been accepted for a course of study at a publicly funded institution of further or higher education, a bona fide private education institution, or an independent fee-paying school.

They must also show that they will be undertaking an appropriate educational course, such as a recognized full-time degree course, a weekday course with a minimum of 15 hours' organized daytime study per week, or a full-time course of study at an independent fee-paying school.

Students must be able to meet the costs of their course and maintain and accommodate themselves (and any dependants) without working or applying for benefits. Students must be intending to leave the UK on completion of their studies.

Au pairs

An au pair placement is an arrangement whereby a single person aged between 17 and 27 comes to the UK to study English and live as a member of an English-speaking family. The au pair helps in the home for a maximum of five hours a day with a minimum of two full days off each week. In return, the au pair receives a reasonable allowance and the use of his or her own room. An au pair placement is for a maximum of two years.

Nationals of the European Economic Area (EEA) can enter the UK to work or study without any formalities (see details on the European Economic Area below).

The following non-EEA places are included in the au pair scheme:

Andorra; Bosnia-Herzegovina; Croatia; Cyprus; Czech Republic; Faroe Islands; Greenland; Hungary; Macedonia; Malta; Monaco; San Marino; Slovak Republic; Slovenia; Switzerland; Turkey.

Citizenship and Immigration

Visiting and Immigration to the UK *(continued)*

Visas have to be obtained by nationals of the following countries applying to work in the UK as an au pair:

Bosnia-Herzegovina; Former Yugoslav Republic of Macedonia; Slovak Republic; Turkey.

Anyone who wishes to come to the UK as an au pair must show that they want to enter the country having arranged an au pair placement and that: they are not married; they have no dependants; they do not intend to stay in the UK for more than two years as an au pair; they are able to maintain and accommodate themselves without applying for benefits; they intend to leave the country on completion of their stay as an au pair.

Permission to extend a stay in the UK for more than the normal two-year period will only be granted to someone who entered the UK as an au pair; permission will not be granted to anyone who did not enter the UK as an au pair.

Working holidaymakers

In the UK, there is a working holidaymaker scheme. This is an arrangement whereby a single person aged between 17 and 27 comes to the UK for an extended holiday (maximum two years) before settling down in their own country. Part-time or casual employment is allowed as part of the conditions of being in the UK as a working holidaymaker.

Working holidaymakers must show that they:

- are a Commonwealth citizen, British Dependent Territories citizen, or British Overseas citizen
- are seeking entry for an extended holiday
- are unmarried or married to a person who at the same time qualifies for entry as a working holidaymaker, and that they intend to take a holiday together
- do not have any dependent children who are five years of age or over, or who will reach five years of age before they complete their holiday
- only intend to take employment that will be incidental (casual or part-time) to their holiday
- are able to support and accommodate themselves without applying for benefits
- have the means to pay for their onward journey
- intend to leave the UK on completion of their holiday

Spouses and fiancé(e)s

A person's spouse or fiancé(e) can apply to join or accompany the person in the UK so long as the person is lawfully living in the UK themselves. Alternatively, they must be returning to settle in the UK on the same occasion as their spouse or fiancé(e).

Spouses must show that they:

- are lawfully married
- intend to live together permanently
- have met each other
- can support themselves and any dependants without applying for benefits
- have adequate accommodation where they and their dependants can live without applying for benefits
- are not under the age of 16

On arrival in the UK, a spouse will be given permission to stay and work for 12 months. Near the end of the 12 months, if the couple are still married and intend to live together, the spouse may apply to remain here permanently.

Fiancé(e)s must show that they:

- plan to marry within a reasonable time (usually six months)
- both plan to live together permanently after they are married
- have met each other
- have somewhere to live until they are married, without needing to apply for benefits
- are able to support themselves and any dependants without applying for benefits

A fiancé(e) will be given permission to stay in the UK for six months without permission to work. Once married, the fiancé(e) can apply to stay. If granted, permission will be given to stay and work for 12 months after which time an application to stay in the UK permanently can be made.

Children

To qualify to bring children to the UK, the parents must show that they: are present and settled in the UK, meaning that they live here lawfully, with no time limit on their stay; have adequate accommodation in which the family can all live without applying for benefits; are the child's parent (this includes the stepfather/mother of a child whose father/mother is dead; both the father and mother of an illegitimate child; and an adoptive parent in certain defined circumstances).

For children to qualify to join their parents in the UK, children must show that they: are not leading a life independent of their parents, are not married, or have not formed an independent family unit; are less than 18 years old.

Children cannot normally come to live in the UK if one parent lives abroad, unless the parent here has had sole responsibility for the child's upbringing, or there are serious and compelling reasons which make it undesirable not to allow the child to come here.

Provided that the parents of children are settled in the UK, or that the person applying for children to be allowed into the country has sole responsibility for the children, children will normally be allowed to remain permanently in the UK from the date of their arrival.

If children are accompanying a spouse into the country, they will normally be given permission to remain in the country for one year, the same period as the spouse. If the spouse is given permission to remain in the country permanently, the children will normally also be allowed to remain permanently in the country.

Adopted children

Different rules apply to the admission of adopted children into the UK. For information, contact the Immigration and Nationality Directorate of the Home Office: (020) 8686 0688.

Right of abode in the UK (British citizenship)

The right of abode means that a person is entirely free from UK immigration control; they do not need to obtain the permission of an immigration officer to enter the UK; and they may live and work without restriction.

To apply for or to obtain further information about British citizenship contact:

Home Office, Nationality Directorate, 3rd Floor, India Buildings, Water Street, Liverpool L2 0QN; phone: (0151) 237 5200; fax: (0151) 237 5380; Web site: www.homeoffice.gov.uk

Relatives

Immigration rules in the UK allow for the admission of widowed mothers and fathers aged 65 or over and the parents or grandparents travelling together, of whom at least one is aged 65 or over. In certain circumstances sons, daughters, sisters, brothers, uncles, and aunts over the age of 18, and also parents and grandparents under 65 may be granted entrance to the UK.

People who would like relatives to join them in the UK must be lawfully living in the country with no time limit on their stay. They must be able to show that they have sufficient funds to support and accommodate their relatives without applying for benefits, and that their relatives are: wholly or mainly financially dependent on them; without other close relatives to turn to for financial support.

Children over 18, sisters, brothers, aunts, uncles, and other parents and grandparents may come if they meet the requirements set out above, and if they can show that they live alone in 'exceptional circumstances'.

Nationals of the European Economic Area (EEA)

If you are a national of one of the following countries, you are a national of the EEA: Austria; Belgium; Denmark; Finland; France; Germany; Greece; Iceland; Ireland, Republic of; Italy; Liechtenstein; Luxembourg; Netherlands; Norway; Portugal; Spain; Sweden.

Note: Iceland, Liechtenstein, and Norway are not members of the European Union (EU). However, under the European Economic Area Agreement, nationals of these countries have the same rights as EU citizens.

European Community law grants EEA nationals a right to live and work in the UK. This right is called a right of residence.

EEA nationals have a right of residence in the UK if they are working in the UK, or if they are not working in the UK, but have enough funds to support themselves throughout their stay in the country without needing assistance through applying for benefits. Family members of EEA nationals in the UK have the same rights to live and work here.

Further information about rights of residence of EEA nationals and their family members can be obtained by writing to:

EC Group, European Directorate, Immigration and Nationality Directorate, Room 1204, Apollo House, 36 Wellesley Road, Croydon CR9 3RR.

Visiting and Immigration to the UK *(continued)*

Further information

For further information about immigration rules on the above and other categories of immigrants to the UK, contact the Immigration and Nationality Directorate (IND) at:

Immigration and Nationality Directorate, Block C, Whitgift Centre, Wellesley Road, Croydon CR9 1AT. Web site: www.homeoffice.gov.uk/ind/hpg.htm.

The IND's Telephone Enquiry Bureau (TEB) deals with general enquiries: phone: (08706) 067 766; for application forms: (0870) 241 0645.

The TEB is open from 9 a.m. to 4.45 p.m., Monday to Wednesday, 10 a.m. to 4.45 p.m. Thursday, and from 9 a.m. to 4.30 p.m. on Fridays.

In addition, there are a number of public recorded-information lines: overseas visitors phone: (020) 8760 1600; overseas students phone: (020) 8760 1622; work-permit holders phone: (020) 8760 1644.

There are also regional offices which deal with personal enquiries only:

Belfast Belfast Immigration Office, Olive Tree House, Fountain Street, Belfast BT1 5EA; phone: (028) 9032 2547; open: Tuesday to Thursday 2.00 p.m.–4.00 p.m.

Birmingham Birmingham Public Enquiry Office, Dominion Court, 41 Station Road, Solihull B91 3RT; phone: (0121) 606 7345; open: Monday to Friday 9.00 a.m.–3.00 p.m.

Glasgow Glasgow Immigration Office, Dumbarton Court, Argyll Avenue, Glasgow Airport, Paisley PA3 2TD; phone: (0141) 887 2255; open: Monday to Friday 9.30 a.m.–12.30 p.m. and 2.00 p.m–4.00 p.m

Liverpool Liverpool Immigration Office, Graeme House, Derby Square, Liverpool L2 7SF; phone: (0151) 236 4909; open: Monday to Friday 9.00 a.m.–12.00 p.m.

Source: Home Office Immigration and Nationality Directorate, © Crown copyright 1997; with Helicon updates

See also **Asylum Seekers in the UK,** p 103.

Birth, Marriage, and Death

See also **Population, Demography, and Society,** pp 99–105.

Birth, Marriage, and Death Registration and Records in the UK

Births

In England, Wales, and Northern Ireland, a child's birth must be registered within six weeks of the date of birth. In Scotland, a birth must be registered within three weeks. If the parents are married, either parent should go to their district Registrar of Births, Deaths, and Marriages and provide details of the child and of both parents. It is not a requirement to provide proof of the birth. If the parents are not married, both parents must visit the Registrar if they wish both their details to appear on the birth certificate. Otherwise, only the mother's details will be entered on the certificate. Alternatively, the father can send a sworn testimonial stating that he is the father of the child.

Marriages

Marriages are registered at the time of the event, and a certificate is given to the couple getting married.

Deaths

A death must be registered with the local Registrar of Births, Marriages, and Deaths within five days of the event. When registering a death, the registrar will require the following information about the deceased:

- full name (including maiden name if applicable) and home address
- full details of date and place of birth, and sex
- date of birth of surviving husband or wife, if applicable
- occupation of the deceased
- date and place of death

The registrar will also need the following documents:

- a doctor's certificate of cause of death
- the deceased's NHS card
- details of any state benefits the deceased was receiving
- war pension order book, if applicable

Whoever goes to register a death with the registrar must also supply their own details. Certificates registering the death and allowing a burial are then issued.

How to obtain a copy of a birth, death, or marriage certificate

Copies of birth, marriage, and death certificates can be obtained from the Register Office in the area where the event took place. This can be done by post or in person. If you don't know where the event occurred, you can obtain copies of certificates by searching the indexes to records held at the Family Records Centre. All the indexes to births, deaths, and marriages from 1837 in England and Wales are held at the Centre and are available for public searches.

The address of the Family Records Centre is: 1 Myddleton Street, London EC1R 1UW.

Obtaining a copy of a certificate from the Family Records Centre can be done in one of four ways:

In person The Family Records Centre is open Monday–Friday, between 8.30 a.m. and 4.30 p.m. (except for public holidays), and you can search the indexes of records held there. If you make your application in person, there are two services available: a 24-hour priority service allows you to collect a certificate one clear working day after the day of application; alternatively, you can collect the certificate on the fourth working day. Otherwise, it will be posted to you within four working days.

By post You can make an order for certificates by post. Again, there are two services available: a priority service, through which your order will be posted to you within two working days, and a standard service, through which the order will be posted within 22 working days. If you can provide the volume reference number for the certificate from the General Register Office index, your order will be posted to you within ten working days.

By telephone Certificates can be ordered by telephone at the following number: (0151) 471 4816. Telephone orders must be paid for by credit or debit card when the order is placed. Again, there are priority and standard services, and dispatch times are the same as orders by post.

By fax Orders can also be made by fax on (01704) 550013. You must quote your credit or debit card details.

By e-mail priority.certificates@ons.gov.uk

Web site www.ons.gov.uk/regist_f.htm

Cost of certificates By post: £11; priority service £27. In person: £6.50; priority service £22.50

For an application form and a full list of fees, contact:

General Register Office, PO Box 2, Southport, Merseyside PR8 2JD; phone: (0151) 471 4800.

Many public libraries and local public record offices keep microfilm copies of the indexes that are available for public use.

Source: Office for National Statistics, © Crown copyright 2000

Marriage Laws and Procedure in the UK

(This article includes some information on Guernsey, Jersey, and the Isle of Man. Please note that these territories are not part of the UK, but are British Crown Dependencies.)

Minimum age and parental consent

The minimum legal age for getting married throughout the UK is 16. In England, Wales, Northern Ireland, Guernsey, and the Isle of Man, the written consent of parents or legal guardians is required if you are under 18 years of age. In Jersey, parental consent is required if you under 20 years of age. In Scotland, no parental consent is required.

Marriage in England and Wales

As long as the legal requirements are met, anyone from anywhere in the world can get married in England or Wales, either by civil or religious ceremony. Marriages in England and Wales must take place between 8 a.m. and 6 p.m. Most ceremonies, civil or religious, are governed by the opening times of register offices and the times of church services.

Civil marriage in England and Wales Marriage at a register office or other licensed venue (see below) can take place anywhere in England or Wales and does not have to be the place of residence of one or both of the people wishing to marry. If you wish to marry by civil ceremony you should contact the Superintendent Registrar of the district in which you wish to get married to discuss any arrangements that must be made. Details of your nearest register office can be found in your local telephone directory under 'Registration of Births, Deaths, and Marriages'.

To start civil marriage proceedings, you must 'give notice' at your local register office. This can be done in one of three ways and up to 12 months before your marriage:

Marriage by certificate without licence. This is the most common form of notice. After 21 days, you will be issued with a certificate of marriage to enable you to get married. You must get married within 12 months of the date of entry in the notice book.

Marriage by certificate and licence. This allows couples to marry more quickly, but it is more expensive. One whole day after giving notice, the Superintendent Registrar will issue a certificate of marriage. One of you must meet a 15-day residency requirement when you give notice. Your marriage must then take place within 12 months of the date of entry in the notice book.

Marriage by Registrar General's licence. This licence is available for couples where one partner cannot attend a place where marriages can be legally solemnized. This situation would apply to those who are seriously ill at home or in hospital, or those who are in prison. The marriage can take place at any time and at any place, as long as it is within three months of the date of entry in the notice book (one month for the seriously ill). No residency requirement needs to be fulfilled.

Civil marriage in England and Wales: at a licensed venue Since April 1995, it has been possible to arrange for a civil marriage ceremony to take place at a specially licensed venue. As at July 1999, there were over 2,700 approved premises, such as hotels, stately homes, and castles licensed for civil ceremonies. No religious content is allowed at all, but in addition to the statutory declaratory and contracting words that you are required to say in a civil ceremony, it is also possible to have your own choice of vows and promises and to include readings, poems, and live music. The legal requirements for getting married at such a venue are the same as those for getting married by civil ceremony at a register office, but with the additional requirement of arranging for the attendance of a Superintendent Registrar at the venue. You do not have to give formal notice of your marriage to the Superintendent Registrar of the registration district in which the venue is situated. However, once you have chosen your venue and made a provisional booking, you should contact the local Superintendent Registrar as his or her attendance is required to solemnize the marriage.

You can obtain a full list of the addresses and telephone numbers of approved premises by sending a cheque or postal order for £5.00, made payable to 'Office for National Statistics', to:

Local Services Office for National Statistics, ONS Smedley Hydro, Trafalgar Road, Birkdale, Southport PR8 2HH; phone: (0151) 471 4458; fax: (0151) 471 4549; Web site: www.ons.gov.uk (major credit cards accepted.)

Civil marriage in England and Wales: further information For more information on legal civil marriage issues in England and Wales, you can contact the Marriages Section of the Registrar General for England and Wales by telephoning: (01704) 569824. Alternatively you can write to the Marriages Section at the same address as the Office for National Statistics (above).

Religious marriage in England and Wales You don't have to be regular churchgoer to be married in the Church of England or the Church in Wales. If you wish to be married in either Church, you should visit the minister of the church in which you want to get married to discuss your plans. There are four ways of getting married in accordance with the procedures of the Church of England:

Publication of banns. This simply means announcing aloud your intention to marry. It is the traditional and most popular method, used by most couples, and is equivalent to the civil method of getting married by certificate. Church congregations are invited to register objections, if they have any. Couples are usually required to be in attendance on at least one of the three occasions when banns are read. If couples live in different parishes, the banns are read in both parishes.

Marriage by common licence. This is equivalent in timing to the civil method of getting married by certificate and licence. Banns are not required to be published. The bishop of the diocese in which you wish to marry approves the application to marry, and one whole day's notice is required before the ceremony can take place. To be married by common licence, one of the couple must have lived in the parish during the 15 days before the application for the licence. One of the couple must also have been baptized. A common licence lasts for three months from the date of issue.

Marriage by special licence. Approved by the Archbishop of Canterbury, a special licence allows couples to get maried in a church of a parish where neither live. If granted, you can get married at any time within three months without meeting any residency requirement. For more information on getting married by special licence, you should contact the Registrar of Court Faculties: 1 The Sanctuary, London SW1P 3JT; phone: (020) 7222 5381; fax: (020) 7222 7502; Web site: www.facultyoffice.org.uk

Marriage by Superintendent Registrar's certificate without licence. This is a rarely used method of getting married in church, as ministers will prefer you to marry by either publication of banns or by common licence.

Religious marriage in England and Wales: further information If you would like more information about getting married in a church of the Church of England or Church in Wales, you should either see your minister, or you can contact the Enquiry Centre of the General Synod of the Church of England. The address is: Church House, Great Smith Street, London SW1P 3NZ; phone: (020) 7898 1000; fax: (020) 7222 6672; Web site: www.cofe.anglican.org

Religious marriage in England and Wales: Roman Catholic marriages The legal requirements that have to be fulfilled for a Roman Catholic wedding are the same that apply to civil marriages. However, if the church is in a different registration district and you cannot prove the church is your normal place of worship, you will be required to give notice in the registration district in which the church is situated after having met the necessary residency requirement.

For more information, you should talk to your priest or contact either of the following organizations:

Marriage Care, 1 Blythe Mews, Blythe Road, London W14 0NW; phone: (020) 7371 1341; fax: (020) 7371 4921; Web site: www.marriagecare.org.uk

The Catholic Enquiry Office, The Chase Centre, 114 West Heath Road, London NW3 7TX; phone: (020) 8458 3316; fax: (020) 8905 5780; Web site: www.cms.org.uk

Cost of marriage in England and Wales By civil ceremony: from April 2000, for a civil ceremony where you both live in the same registration district, giving notice costs £25. If you live in different districts you each have to pay £25 when giving notice. The registrar's attendance fee for solemnizing your marriage at a register office is £34. If you are getting married by a superintendent registrar's certificate and licence, an additional £46.50 is payable. The cost of a special licence is £15. Each extract of your marriage entry in the register of marriages (your marriage certificate) costs £3.50 (£6.50 if purchased at a later date). Therefore, the minimum you can pay for a civil ceremony (by certificate without licence) at a register office, where you both live in the same registration district, is £59.50 (including a marriage certificate).

Marriage Laws and Procedure in the UK *(continued)*

If you are getting married at a licensed venue (an approved premise), an additional fee is payable for the registrar to attend and solemnize your marriage. This fee is set by your local authority and you should expect to pay between £100–200 (varies depending upon the day of the week).

By religious ceremony: the fee payable for a religious marriage is not fixed and is decided by the religious celebrant solemnizing your marriage. The fees for getting married in the Church of England or Church in Wales also depend upon the method used, that is whether by banns, common licence, or special licence. However, you should expect to pay between £200–300 but this will vary depending upon whether you have bells, an organist, a choir, and heating, which are all extra. There may also be an additional fee if you wish to have your service videoed.

If your religious celebrant is not authorized to solemnize marriages and you have to get married at a register office beforehand, you will also have to pay the appropriate civil ceremony fees. If a superintendent registrar needs to attend your religious ceremony, a further attendance fee will be payable.

Marriage in Scotland

Civil marriage in Scotland A civil marriage can only be solemnized in a register office by a Registrar or an Assistant Registrar who has been authorized by the Registrar General. In Scotland, there are no time-of-day restrictions for marriage ceremonies, although ceremonies are restricted to the opening times of register offices. Some remote Scottish communities have their own Parlour Registrars, who are authorized to perform civil marriages in their home. These marriages can take place at any time, at the discretion of the Parlour Registrar.

Religious marriage in Scotland Religious ceremonies can take place at any time and in any place in Scotland, as long as an authorized celebrant can attend and officiate, and there are two witnesses present. Scottish churches make no provision for marriage by the publication of banns.

Marriage in Scotland: residency requirements Scotland is the only country in the UK where there is no residency requirement to be fulfilled. Instead, at least one of the couple must visit the Registrar from the district in which the marriage is to take place during the seven days before the date of the wedding. In the case of civil marriages, this is to make arrangements with the Registrar; in the case of religious marriages, it is to collect the marriage schedule.

Marriage in Scotland: giving notice Couples must both submit a marriage notice to the Registrar for the district in which they intend to marry during the three months before the wedding date, and not later than 15 days before the date.

The marriage schedule in Scotland No marriage can take place in Scotland without a marriage schedule (the licence to marry), which must be presented to the person performing the ceremony before it commences.

Marriage at Gretna Green

Possibly the world's most famous wedding venue, Gretna Green is a small town in Dumfriesshire. In 1998, it was host to more than 5,500 weddings, about 19% of all weddings held in Scotland. The minimum age for getting married in Scotland has been 16, without parental consent, since the 18th century. Once the first stage-coach stop over the English/Scottish border, Gretna Green became the place for young English couples wishing to elope and marry without their parents' consent.

Cost of marriage in Scotland From April 1999, the cost of giving notice to get married by either civil or religious ceremony is £12 each. For the solemnization of a civil marriage, the fee is £45. For Saturday afternoon ceremonies, there is sometimes a surcharge which can be in the region of £50. The marriage certificate will cost £8.

The cost of marriage by religious ceremony is not fixed and is decided by the religious celebrant solemnizing the marriage. Couples should speak to the minister in charge of their chosen venue to discuss fees.

Marriage in Scotland: further information
For further information and advice about getting married in Scotland and to obtain a list of all register offices in Scotland, contact the General Register Office: Marriages Section, New Register House, Edinburgh EH1 3YT; phone: (0131) 314 4447; fax: (0131) 314 4400; e-mail: marriage@gro-scotland.gov.uk; Web site: www.gro-scotland.gov.uk

Marriage in Northern Ireland

Civil marriage in Northern Ireland Civil marriages can take place in Northern Ireland by either a registrar's certificate or by a registrar's licence. The marriage of house-bound or detained persons can only take place on the authority of a licence issued by the Registrar General.

By certificate A registrar's certificate authorizes you to marry in a register office, church, or other registered building, providing at least one of you resides in the district in which you wish to marry. A certificate allowing the marriage to take place is issued 21 days after notice of intent to marry is given. You must both meet a seven-day residency requirement when you give notice.

By licence A registrar's licence allows you to get married a little quicker: seven days after giving notice. One of you must meet a 15-day residency requirement when you give notice.

By Registrar General's licence This licence allows you to marry if one of you is either house-bound or detained as a prisoner. A Registrar General's licence cannot be issued for a marriage between two people of the Roman Catholic, Jewish, or Quaker religions.

Religious marriage in Northern Ireland

Church of Ireland: marriage according to the rites and ceremonies of the Church of Ireland can take place by the publications of banns, licence, special licence, or a registrar's certificate.

Provided that one or both people are members of the Church of Ireland, or other Protestant Episcopal Church, a licence is available from a Church of Ireland licensing minister. Names and addresses of licensing ministers can be obtained from any member of the Church of Ireland clergy.

Special licences may be granted by a bishop of the Church of Ireland, provided that one or both of you are members of that Church or other Protestant Episcopal Church. The marriage may then take place at any time and in any place within the diocese of the bishop granting the licence.

To obtain a registrar's certificate to authorize your marriage, one or both of you must belong to the Church of Ireland.

Marriage by any of these means can be advised on by your minister.

Presbyterian Church Marriages: the governing bodies of the Presbyterian Church in Northern Ireland are the General Assembly of the Presbyterian Church in Ireland, the Remonstrant Synod of Ulster (non-subscribing), the Presbytery of Antrim, and the Reformed Presbyterian Synod of Ireland. Marriages according to the disciplines of these bodies can take place by licence, special licence, or publication of banns. You should discuss with your Presbyterian minister which method would be most suitable, according to your circumstances.

Roman Catholic Church: where both of you are Roman Catholics, the marriage procedure is governed by the laws of the Roman Catholic Church. Information and guidance on your marriage should be obtained from a member of the Roman Catholic clergy.

According to the Irish Marriage Acts, marriage in a Roman Catholic church can also take place by licence or registrar's certificate. These methods apply where one of you is not a Roman Catholic.

Other Church marriages: marriages according to the customs of other religious bodies can take place in Northern Ireland by registrar's licence (except for Jews and Quakers), by registrar's certificate, or by special licence. Information about these marriages can be obtained from the registrar in the district in which you wish to marry.

Cost of marriage in Northern Ireland If your marriage is on the authority of a licence issued by a licensing minister of the Church of Ireland or Presbyterian Church. There is no charge for giving notice. However, the licence will cost between £13 and £15, depending on region.

From November 1998, to give notice to marry by licence or certificate issued by a Registrar of Marriages costs £8.50. A registrar's certificate costs £5.50; a registrar's licence costs £10.50. The solemnization of your marriage in the presence of a registrar will cost £12.50. There is a £7 charge for your marriage certificate and any additional copies cost £4 each.

For ceremonies taking place in a church, the celebrant will charge a fee for the church service. These fees are set by the relevant

Birth, Marriage, and Death

Marriage Laws and Procedure in the UK *(continued)*

church authorities. Couples should consult their church minister for information.

Marriage in Northern Ireland: further information For information about getting married in Northern Ireland, contact the registrar of marriages in the registration district in which you wish to get married. Alternatively, contact the General Register Office:
Oxford House, 49–55 Chichester Road, Belfast BT1 4HH; phone: (028) 9025 2000; fax: (028) 9025 2044; open 9.30 a.m.–4.00 p.m.

Other religions and interfaith marriages

For information and advice about Jewish weddings, contact the Jewish Marriage Council:

23 Ravenhurst Avenue, London NW4 4EE; phone: (020) 8203 6311; fax: (020) 8203 8727; e-mail: jmc@dircon.co.uk; Web site: www.jmc-uk.org

For information about Quaker marriages, contact the Religious Society of Friends:

173–177 Euston Road, London NW1 2BJ; phone: (020) 7663 1000; fax: (020) 7663 1001; Web site: www.quaker.org.uk

For advice when partners are practising members of different Churches, contact:

Association of Interchurch Families, 35–41 Lower Marsh, London SE1 7RL; phone: (020) 7620 4444; fax: (020) 7620 0719; Web site: www.christian-aid.org.uk

Documents required for marriage in the UK

To be married in the UK you must produce your birth certificate. If you have been married before, you must produce your decree absolute of divorce (dissolution or annulment papers in Northern Ireland) or, if you are widowed, the death certificate of your former spouse. If you are travelling to the UK to get married, you will have to prove your identity and that you have met the necessary residency requirements. For marriages in Scotland and Northern Ireland you must obtain from your own country's marriage authority a certificate stating that there is no impediment to marry, i.e. that you are both free to marry. If you are under 18 you must produce written permission from your parents or legal guardian.

For further information, contact the registrar of the registration district in which you wish to get married.

Same-sex marriages in the UK

It is not possible for gay and lesbian couples to have a legally solemnized marriage. UK marriage laws prohibit people of the same sex at birth from marrying.

Marriage prohibitions (forbidden degrees of relationship)

A man may not marry his: mother, (including step-mother, former step-mother, mother-in-law, former mother-in-law, adoptive mother, or former adoptive mother); daughter (including step-daughter, former step-daughter, daughter-in-law, former daughter-in-law, adoptive daughter, or former adoptive daughter); sister (including half-sister or step-sister); father's mother (grandmother); mother's mother (grandmother); father's father's former wife (step-grandmother); mother's father's former wife (step-grandmother); son's daughter (granddaughter); daughter's daughter (granddaughter); wife's son's daughter (step-granddaughter); wife's daughter's daughter (step granddaughter); son's son's wife (grandson's wife); daughter's son's wife (grandson's wife); father's sister (aunt); mother's sister (aunt); brother's daughter (niece); sister's daughter (niece).

A woman may not marry her: father (including step-father, former step-father, father-in-law, former father-in-law, adoptive father, or former adoptive father); son (including step-son, former step-son, son-in-law, former son-in-law, adoptive son, or former adoptive son); brother (including half-brother or step-brother); father's father (grandfather); mother's father (grandfather); mother's mother's former husband (step-grandfather); father's mother's former husband (step-grandfather); son's son (grandson); daughter's son (grandson); husband's daughter's son (step-grandson); husband's son's son (step-grandson); son's daughter's husband (granddaughter's husband); daughter's daughter's husband (granddaughter's husband); father's brother (uncle); mother's brother (uncle); brother's son (nephew); sister's son (nephew).

In Scotland, a man may not marry his great-grandmother or great-granddaughter and a woman may not marry her great-grandfather or great-grandson.

Exceptions for step-relatives and relatives-in-law: In England, Scotland, and Wales (not Northern Ireland, Isle of Man, Guernsey, or Jersey), the Marriage Act of 1986 allows for the following relatives to marry:

Step-relatives can marry provided they are at least 21 years of age. The younger of the couple must not ever have lived in the same house as the older of the couple before the age of 18, nor must they ever have been treated as the child of the older person's family. Although a man may marry his sister-in-law and a woman may marry her brother-in-law, other relatives-in-law may marry only if they are at least 21 years of age and the family members involved in creating the in-law relationship are both dead. For example, if a man wishes to marry his daughter-in-law, both his son and his son's mother must be dead. In England and Wales, marriages under this Act are not permitted with the calling of banns but can take place in a church on the authority of a licence issued by a superintendent registrar.

Marriage of cousins: It is not illegal to marry a cousin. However, cousins who wish to marry should visit their GP to ensure there are no factors in their family health records that might make a decision to have children inadvisable on medical grounds.

Source: WeddingGuideUK.com

Marriages in the UK

Category	1985	1990	1991	1992	1993	1994	1995	1996	1997[1]
Men									
under 21	30,243	15,930	13,271	11,031	8,767	7,091	6,302	5,497	5,126
21–24	123,242	92,270	79,877	74,458	65,129	56,877	48,432	42,488	36,875
25–29	109,896	122,800	115,637	118,255	114,101	111,108	105,218	101,647	97,345
30–34	47,594	56,966	56,970	62,470	63,848	65,490	68,245	69,867	70,904
35–44	46,265	49,984	48,147	51,125	50,553	51,310	53,350	56,513	58,292
45–54	19,652	21,996	20,915	23,290	23,841	24,136	24,786	26,252	26,472
55 and over	16,225	15,464	14,922	15,384	15,369	15,220	14,918	15,250	15,204
Women									
under 21	82,209	45,626	38,305	32,618	26,839	22,903	20,643	18,485	17,254
21–24	137,437	119,037	105,505	102,494	93,125	84,171	75,071	66,191	59,549
25–29	80,105	103,209	99,851	105,223	104,517	102,803	100,644	99,651	97,932
30–34	33,424	42,794	43,617	48,514	49,546	52,359	54,819	57,752	58,589
35–44	35,380	38,983	37,582	40,075	40,090	41,213	43,115	45,969	47,267
45–54	14,892	16,825	16,473	18,504	18,800	19,280	19,720	21,025	21,038
55 and over	9,670	8,936	8,406	8,585	8,691	8,503	8,239	8,441	8,589
Total	393,117	375,410	349,739	356,013	341,608	331,232	322,251	317,514	310,218
Persons marrying per 1,000 resident population	13.9	13.1	12.1	12.3	11.7	11.3	11.0	10.8	10.5
Previous marital status									
Bachelors	291,171	276,512	256,538	258,567	245,996	236,619	227,717	221,826	216,237
Divorced men	88,981	88,199	83,069	87,419	85,824	85,261	85,743	87,113	85,625

(continued)

Marriages in the UK (*continued*)

Category	1985	1990	1991	1992	1993	1994	1995	1996	1997[1]
Widowers	12,965	10,699	10,132	10,027	9,788	9,352	8,791	8,575	8,356
Spinsters	296,797	279,442	259,084	260,252	248,063	237,241	228,462	221,697	216,776
Divorced women	83,921	85,608	81,224	86,361	84,268	85,220	85,396	87,618	85,648
Widows	12,399	10,360	9,431	9,400	9,277	8,771	8,393	8,199	7,794
First marriage for both partners	256,594	240,729	222,369	222,142	210,567	200,910	192,078	185,293	181,135
First marriage for one partner only	74,780	74,496	70,884	74,535	72,925	72,040	72,023	72,937	70,743
Remarriage for both partners	61,743	60,185	56,486	59,336	58,116	58,282	58,150	59,284	58,340

[1] Provisional. Later figures not available.

Source: Annual Abstract of Statistics 2000, *© Crown copyright 2000*

Marriage and Divorce Rates in Selected Countries

(– = not applicable.)

Country	Marriages (per thousand people)		Divorces (per thousand people)	
	1987	1997	1987	1997
Austria	10.0	5.1	1.9	2.2[1]
Belgium	5.7	4.7	2.0	2.1
Canada	6.9	5.2[1]	3.0	2.4[1]
Denmark	6.1	6.5	2.8	2.1[1]
Finland	5.3	4.6	2.0	2.6
France	4.8	4.9	1.9	2.1[1]
Germany	6.7	5.1	2.3	2.1[1]
Greece	6.6	6.0	0.9	0.9
Iceland	4.7	5.4	1.9	1.8
Ireland, Republic of	5.2	4.3	–[2]	–[2]
Italy	5.4	4.8	0.5	0.6[1]
Japan	5.7	6.4[1]	1.4	1.7[1]
Luxembourg	5.3	4.8	1.8	2.0[1]
Netherlands	6.0	5.5	1.9	2.2
Norway	5.0	5.3[1]	2.0	2.4[1]
Portugal	7.2	6.4[1]	0.9	1.4[1]
Spain	5.6	4.8	0.5	0.8[1]
Sweden	4.9	3.6	2.2	2.4
Switzerland	6.6	5.5	1.8	2.4
UK	7.0	5.4[1]	2.9	2.9[1]
USA	9.9	8.9	4.8	4.3

[1] 1996.
[2] Divorce was not allowed in the Republic of Ireland until 1997.

Making a Will

Most people die without leaving a will. In such cases 'rules of intestacy' determine who benefits, and the beneficiaries will be a spouse, blood relations, or adopted children.

The most obvious advantage to making a will is that you choose who benefits when you die. But making a will can also reduce the amount of inheritance tax your beneficiaries will be liable for, and it allows you to choose executors to deal with your affairs. Before drawing up a will:

Draw up a list of your assets and think who you want to benefit from them.

Decide who you want to appoint as executors (those who administer your estate). They can be members of your family, solicitors, or banks.

If you are liable for inheritance tax (charged at 40% on estates with a value in excess of £234,000 in the 2000–01 tax year), ensure any professional you see can assist you with tax planning. For instance no tax is payable if all your estate is left to your spouse (although they will be liable to tax upon death).

When your will is drawn up it should be stored securely – if it is lost you will be intestate. It is important to keep your will up to date, so review it every few years.

You can write the will yourself if your arrangements are straightforward. But if, for instance, you live or own property abroad, are liable to inheritance tax, or own your own business, you should seek professional help with writing your will. This may be obtained from:

- some banks and life insurance companies
- solicitors
- professional will writers.

The Economics of Cohabitation

No tax benefits arise from cohabitation – and married couples have not benefited from the married couples' tax allowance since it was abolished in April 2000. If you are unmarried, but have cohabited as man and wife, your partner has no claim on your assets if you separate or die; so if you want your partner to benefit in the event of your death you must make a will.

The machinations of home economics offer much more scope when it comes to taking financial advantage of living together, whether married or not. Some of the many areas couples living together can save money on through lowering the per head outlay are:

- standing charges on utility bills
- TV licence
- council tax
- banking costs if joint accounts held (if bank charges apply)
- necessary consumer durables, such as washing machines
- mortgage/rent payments
- insurance premiums
- motoring costs (if one car is given up)

On top of this there is more scope for discounts and deals on larger purchases (for example, two for one offers).

Divorce Laws and Procedure in the UK

According to UK divorce law, there is essentially one basis for divorce: that a marriage has 'irretrievably broken down'. To satisfy a court that a marriage has reached this condition, one or more of the following five grounds must be proved:

- A spouse has committed adultery. It is no longer necessary to name a third party in this case. If no third party is named, a defendant can admit to adultery on a form called an 'Acknowledgement of Service'. If a defendant will not admit to adultery, other forms of proof may be necessary to satisfy a court that adultery has been committed.
- The couple have been living apart for two years or more, and both agree to a divorce.

Birth, Marriage, and Death

Divorce Laws and Procedure in the UK *(continued)*

- The couple have lived apart for five years, and one partner wants a divorce.
- One partner deserted the marriage more than two years before. (Note: desertion is not the same as agreed separation.)
- One partner has behaved in such a way that the other partner can no longer be expected to tolerate living with them. 'Unreasonable behaviour' covers a very broad range of acts: physical and/or verbal abuse, drunkenness, public humiliation, mental cruelty, financial irresponsibility, excessive jealousy, and even excessive DIY, and failure to help with household work.

It is not possible to get divorced unless you have been married for at least one year. The legal procedure for obtaining a divorce in England begins with issuing a divorce petition to any divorce county court, or, in London, the Principle Registry. In Scotland, divorces are generally conducted in the Sheriff Court. Less commonly, they can also be issued in the Court of Session in Edinburgh, Scotland's supreme court. In Northern Ireland, the majority of divorces are issued in the High Court, although it is possible to seek divorce through the county courts.

After a divorce petition is successful, a Decree Nisi is granted, and a further six or more weeks after this, a Decree Absolute, which finalizes the dissolution of the marriage.

It is not a legal requirement to employ the services of a solicitor when you wish to get divorced. A free booklet on obtaining an undefended divorce, 'DIY Divorce', can be obtained from any county court. Professional advice is recommended, however. The advice of a professional can help determine whether there are grounds for a divorce. Legal advice can also be essential in guiding couples through the legal processes involved in divorce, as well as settling matters such as financial support for children. It is not recommended that you pursue a divorce without professional advice if children are involved, and/or extra financial settlement is being sought.

Common-law marriage

Contrary to popular and widespread belief, there is no such thing as common-law marriage. It is often believed that if man and a woman live together, after a certain length of time they acquire similar rights to an actual wife or husband. Where cohabiting couples (both heterosexual or same-sex partnerships) end their relationship, the law in the UK is not the same as for married couples. Property rights are unaffected between unmarried couples, i.e. the distinction between 'his', 'hers', and 'theirs' remains the same as beforehand when a relationship breaks down; each is entitled to keep their own property. The position for married couples is that the courts can divide all property whichever way they think best, regardless of who actually owns it.

If a couple live together, and they have children, the situation can become more complex if the relationship fails. An unmarried mother has legal responsibility for her children; an unmarried father has to ask the courts to give him joint responsibility. However, whether the father has joint responsibility or not, he is still responsible for maintaining his children, and this responsibility can be enforced.

Arrangements for children

The Children Act resulted in a change in the arrangements for children of divorced parents. Parents are now encouraged to agree access and living arrangements without the need for the courts to step in. If this attempt fails, the courts will intervene to make a decision on behalf of the children; the Children Act requires that courts put the good of the children first. Children now have the right to have their wishes heard when decisions are made about them.

In 1993 a system for child maintenance was introduced in England, Wales, Scotland, and Northern Ireland. A government agency called the Child Support Agency (CSA) operates the scheme. Under the Child Support Act, 1991, child support maintenance is an amount of money that absent parents pay regularly as a contribution to the financial support of their children. Absent parents must now, by law, support their children, whether the couple are married, divorced, separated, formerly lived together, or had a child during a very brief relationship. The courts no longer decide on the financial contributions that absent parents must make towards their children; the CSA has been given these decision-making powers. The amount that absent parents pay is calculated by the CSA; the agency also assesses and reviews the amounts of child support maintenance needed. The CSA is empowered to collect money from an absent parent and pass it on to the guardian parent.

The Child Support Agency can be contacted at the following address:

PO Box 55, Brierley Hill, West Midlands DY5 1YL; National Enquiry Line: (0345) 133133; Web site: www.dss.gov.uk/csa

Counselling

The National Marriage Guidance Council (Relate), Herbert Gray College, Little Church Street, Rugby, Warwickshire CV21 3AP; phone: (01788) 573241; fax: (01788) 535007; Web site: www.relate.org.uk

Relate provides help with marital and relationship problems. There are over 130 branches nationwide. For your nearest branch, look in your local telephone directory.

Marriage Care, Clitherow House, 1 Blythe Mews, Blythe Road, London W14 0NW; phone: (020) 7371 1341; fax: (020) 7371 4921; Web site: www.marriagecare.org.uk. Relationship counselling service for the Roman Catholic community.

Divorces in England and Wales, and Scotland

(N/A = not available.)

Item	1985	1990	1991	1992	1993	1994	1995	1996	1997	1998
England and Wales										
Decrees absolute, granted[1] (rate per 1,000 married couples[1])	13.4	13.0	13.5	13.7	13.9	13.4	13.1	13.8	13.0	N/A
Total[1]	160,300	153,386	158,745	160,385	165,018	158,175	155,499	157,107	146,689	N/A
Duration of marriage (years)										
0–4	45,776	36,299	37,779	36,898	37,252	35,695	34,507	34,924	31,767	N/A
5–9	41,537	42,061	42,735	43,745	46,536	44,769	44,304	44,609	41,260	N/A
10–14	27,087	27,310	28,791	29,285	30,156	28,073	27,365	27,332	26,215	N/A
15–19	18,460	19,819	20,127	20,160	20,233	19,200	18,943	19,321	18,027	N/A
20 and over	26,427	27,881	29,294	30,290	30,836	30,431	30,370	30,912	29,408	N/A
Not stated	13	16	19	7	5	7	10	9	12	N/A
Age of wife at marriage (years)										
16–19	52,858	41,116	40,594	39,731	38,810	34,068	31,319	29,927	25,579	N/A
20–24	69,663	71,489	74,050	74,698	76,580	73,287	71,355	71,123	66,167	N/A
25–29	18,689	21,701	24,025	25,172	27,177	28,358	29,439	31,396	31,022	N/A
30–34	8,544	8,909	9,608	9,939	10,593	11,007	11,585	12,335	12,094	N/A
35–39	4,612	4,880	5,024	5,200	5,673	5,615	5,800	6,051	5,767	N/A
40–44	2,609	2,598	2,727	2,872	3,091	3,064	3,121	3,254	3,156	N/A
45 and over	3,325	2,693	2,717	2,766	2,819	2,769	2,870	3,021	2,904	N/A

(continued)

Divorces in England and Wales, and Scotland *(continued)*

Item	1985	1990	1991	1992	1993	1994	1995	1996	1997	1998
Age of wife at divorce (years)										
16–24	26,170	15,454	14,960	13,482	12,924	10,956	9,783	8,615	6,871	N/A
25–29	35,680	35,121	35,582	34,853	35,362	32,608	30,563	30,075	26,435	N/A
30–34	28,668	31,295	33,195	34,901	36,300	35,848	35,538	36,274	33,967	N/A
35–39	26,554	24,421	25,661	26,577	28,162	27,195	27,550	28,727	27,715	N/A
40–44	17,767	21,263	21,979	21,783	21,891	20,765	20,739	20,774	20,125	N/A
45 and over	25,448	25,816	27,349	28,782	30,374	30,796	31,316	32,633	31,564	N/A
Not stated	13	16	19	7	5	7	10	9	12	N/A
Divorces involving no children[2]	51,912	47,119	48,115	46,979	47,652	48,286	48,560	48,800	45,556	N/A
Divorces involving one or more children[2]	108,388	106,267	110,630	113,406	117,366	109,889	106,939	108,307	101,133	N/A
Scotland										
Decrees absolute, granted[3] [4] (rate per 1,000 married couples[5])	11.1	10.5	10.6	10.8	11.1	11.5	10.8	10.9	11.0	11.2
Total[1]	13,371	12,272	12,399	12,479	12,787	13,133	12,249	12,308[6]	12,222	12,384
Duration of marriage (years)										
0–4	2,364	2,208	2,142	2,085	2,092	2,095	1,908	1,914	1,793	1,766
5–9	3,882	3,546	3,508	3,610	3,722	3,790	3,399	3,432	3,224	3,360
10–14	2,684	2,361	2,484	2,454	2,539	2,592	2,407	2,310	2,385	2,456
15–19	1,868	1,617	1,718	1,675	1,745	1,786	1,698	1,709	1,804	1,729
20 and over	2,573	2,540	2,547	2,655	2,689	2,870	2,837	2,934	3,016	3,073
Age of wife at marriage (years)										
16–20	7,143	5,600	5,592	5,378	5,406	5,306	4,600	4,420	4,142	3,984
21–24	3,914	4,185	4,147	4,198	4,252	4,532	4,336	4,341	4,321	4,414
25–29	1,246	1,377	1,545	1,685	1,812	1,926	1,887	1,933	2,151	2,314
30–34	461	497	514	575	612	628	654	697	791	824
35–39	247	275	249	301	312	329	338	393	360	382
40–44	143	139	148	138	152	163	196	234	199	198
45 and over	170	159	142	153	164	166	166	198	173	185
Not stated	49	40	62	51	77	83	72	92	85	83
Age of wife at divorce (years)										
16–24	1,881	1,199	1,038	963	844	767	622	583	426	377
25–29	3,152	2,938	2,932	2,807	2,775	2,750	2,353	2,269	2,021	1,957
30–34	2,628	2,611	2,741	2,785	3,037	3,045	2,747	2,708	2,736	2,767
35–39	2,183	1,891	2,037	2,092	2,212	2,390	2,290	2,307	2,469	2,562
40–44	1,440	1,614	1,665	1,685	1,771	1,788	1,734	1,761	1,819	1,951
45 and over	2,040	1,979	1,924	2,096	2,071	2,310	2,431	2,587	2,667	2,687
Age not stated	49	40	62	51	77	83	72	93	84	83
Actions involving no children[7]	6,040	6,555	6,521	6,927	6,951	7,390	7,515	8,167	9,761	9,231
Actions involving one or more children[7]	7,331	5,717	5,878	5,552	5,836	5,743	4,734	4,141	2,461	3,153

[1] Data include decrees of divorce and of nullity.
[2] Children of the family as defined by the Matrimonial Causes Act, 1973.
[3] For divorces under pre-1976 legislation, these figures relate only to persons who were married in Scotland, and obtained their decree of divorce from the Court of Session. Also with effect from 1 May 1984, the jurisdiction of the Sheriff Courts was extended to include divorce.
[4] With effect from 1984, these statistics have been collected on the basis of divorces granted only, and any difference in the number of divorces brought and granted relates to nullity of marriages.
[5] Rates are calculated using the average of the estimated married male and female populations.
[6] Includes 9 cases where the duration of marriage was not recorded.
[7] These actions relate to all persons divorced or separated in Scotland, irrespective of the country of marriage.

Source: Annual Abstract of Statistics 2000,

Personal Finance

Saving and Investing

An Introduction to Saving and Investing

Savings and investment decisions can have a huge impact on our current and future financial well-being. It pays to plan, and putting these affairs in order now can reap rewards. Your strategy will depend on a variety of factors, including your age, your existing savings and investments, your pension arrangements, your tax position, and your attitude to risk.

There is a bewildering array of options and products, so it is always sensible to seek the advice of a qualified financial advisor, who is obliged to gather all relevant details and find the solution that best suits your personal circumstances.

One way to differentiate types of investment is to separate those that carry no risk to the value of the capital invested from those where there is a risk to some or all of it.

Saving Where Capital is Guaranteed

Deposit-based saving

Deposit-based savings accounts are available from banks and building societies, as well as from supermarkets, insurance companies, and National Savings. They fall into two broad categories: instant-access accounts and notice accounts. They can often be operated by post and, increasingly, on the Internet. Interest rates usually vary with the base rate.

Some accounts, called 'Monthly Interest' accounts, pay interest monthly. Others, known as 'regular savings' accounts (traditionally the preserve of building societies), pay a yearly bonus that makes their rate attractive in comparison with most other deposit-based accounts – provided that regular savings are made, and withdrawals limited.

It is important to ensure that you are getting a good rate of interest on your savings, especially if the current rate of inflation is higher than the interest being paid, which may well be the case if savings are kept in a current account. Consider switching to a better-paying account if the rate is low. One place to keep abreast of the best rates is in the financial supplements of the weekend newspapers.

Other ways of saving

For savers who can hold onto their money for longer periods, or who can save regularly, there are a number of additional options.

- **Guaranteed income and growth bonds** Issued by insurance companies. A lump sum must be invested for a specified period, which can be as long as ten years. During this period a fixed rate of return is paid. Some companies insist that the investment is held until maturity; others allow early encashment, but the return may be very poor.
- **National Savings Certificates** These are either fixed-rate or indexed-linked to inflation. The minimum that can be invested is £100, the maximum £10,000. The investment runs for between two and five years, and returns are tax-free.
- **National Savings Capital Bonds** Interest is fixed for the five-year life of the bond when it is purchased. There are penalties for early encashment. Up to £250,000 may be invested in these bonds.
- **Gilts** Issued by the government. A regular income is paid, as set at the outset. If the gilt is held until its maturity date then a guaranteed amount is repaid. However, during the life of the gilt its value fluctuates – so if it is redeemed early the investor may not recoup the investment.

It is also possible to invest in unit trusts and investment trusts (see below) which invest in low- or no-risk areas such as gilts or bank and building society accounts.

Standard Deposit-based Savings Accounts: For and Against

For

- There is no risk to the original capital.
- There is convenient, immediate, and penalty-free access to instant-access accounts.
- There is convenient and penalty-free access to notice accounts if the requisite notice is given.
- Closing and switching accounts is free and straightforward.

Against

- Inflation can erode the real value of your savings, especially if the interest received is low.
- Historically, returns have been lower than from investment-based savings such as shares or unit trusts.
- The interest rate is normally not guaranteed and could fall – although some types of account are index-linked to inflation.

Individual Savings Accounts (ISAs)

One efficient way to make savings and investments, if you pay tax, is in a tax-free Individual Savings Account (ISA). These were launched by the government in 1999 to replace TESSAs and PEPs. They are not investments in their own right, but rather an account for holding savings and investments in a tax-free way. Each year the government decides the maximum limits for each type of holding – cash, investment-linked life insurance, and stocks and shares. Accounts must be operated by an approved manager who will normally make a charge. Most high street banks and building societies offer their customers an ISA.

Investing Where Capital Is Not Guaranteed

In this form of investment the capital is invested in stocks and shares, and the amount of return depends upon how well these perform. Although such investments can be used to make a quick profit, for most investors they will be viewed as a long-term investment. The longer the investment is held, the lower is the risk to the investment from stock market volatility.

Charges and commissions made on purchases mean that in the short term actual returns may be poor. For instance, £100 invested in a unit trust might initially be worth only £95 after a £5 charge has been deducted. If the investment grows by 12% per year, then after one year it will be worth about the same as the return on a savings account paying 6%; but after seven years it will be worth £210 – £60 more than the savings account.

Major ways of investing

An investor may invest directly in stocks and shares of one or more companies by instructing a stockbroker, or perhaps their bank, or even building society, who often act as the stockbrokers' agents. However, this can be a relatively expensive way to invest, especially if the amount is small, as the minimum broker charge can be as high as £30. Moreover, when one considers the need to spread investments to reduce risk, the costs associated with this method will soon mount and could seriously diminish the return.

Investors may instead invest indirectly into a unit trust or investment trust. In both cases investments – whether regular payments starting from as little as £20 per month, or lump-sum (as the provider permits) – are invested on behalf of the investor by a fund manager who pools the funds of all other investors in the trust. With a unit trust the investor buys 'units' in the trust and the value of these fluctuates. With an investment trust the investor buys shares in an investment trust company whose business it is to invest on behalf of the investor. The investor gains or loses not only from the fluctuating share price of the investment trust company itself, but also from the value of the shares in which it invests (known as the underlying assets). Investing in such schemes can be a good way to spread risk, as most funds invest in a number of different companies.

An equity-based unit-linked endowment policy (*see also* **Mortgages: Repayment Methods,** p 326.) is another way to invest indirectly into the stock market. Policies can be in the form of a one-off, lump-sum, single-premium bond, or a unit-linked, regular-premium plan. In either case the insurance company takes part of the premium to cover its expenses, leaving the remainder to provide the investor with life insurance and units in a chosen investment fund. In a with-profits endowment policy a minimum lump sum is guaranteed at maturity, and additional growth is dependent upon the performance of the investment element. To gain maximum benefit this type of policy should be held for the full term, which is normally anything between 10 and 25 years. Early surrender often means that returns will be poor – perhaps, because of the charging structure, even lower than the payments into them. They are not designed to provide the investor with income.

Gilts (see above) may also be considered, as their value fluctuates during their lifetime. One advantage is that there is a guaranteed return if held until maturity.

Corporate bonds work in a similar way to gilts, but because a company, rather than the government, backs the investor's loan, and the loan is not secured on the assets of the company, there is a slightly higher risk of default. Consequently they tend to pay higher interest rates than gilts. A debenture works in the same way, but is secured on the assets of a company, so the rate tends to be lower.

Investment: The Risks

Generally speaking, there is a trade-off in investment between risk and return: the higher the risk, the greater the potential gain or loss. Investments will be exposed to some or all of the following types of risk:

- from inflation
- to capital, as the value of the share price fluctuates
- to income, as the dividend varies according to the performance of the company
- provider risk associated with the investment management company

To reduce risks, investments can be spread over a number of different types of company. Some pooled investments, such as unit trusts, are required by law to invest in predefined sectors. Some of these sectors are regarded as high-risk – emerging market sectors, for example – whilst others are less risky – as, say, the UK Growth or UK Income sectors.

To allow the ups and downs – or volatility – of the stock market to even out, investors should be prepared to invest for a minimum of five years.

Saving and Investing: Protection

Bank and building society savings accounts in the UK are covered by the Deposit Protection Scheme, which guarantees that if a savings institution goes bankrupt, savers will receive 90% of their investment back. This is subject, however, to a maximum limit of £18,000.

The Investors' Compensation Scheme protects investors if their investment company goes bankrupt. The scheme repays in full the first £30,000 invested, and then 90% of the next £20,000. Amounts above this are not covered. The scheme does not protect against poor performance of the investment.

The Effect of Inflation on Your Saving

£100 invested at a rate of 5% would grow to £163 in ten years if inflation is zero. But if inflation runs at 3% a year, your return is effectively reduced to £128. If it runs at 7% per year £100 would only be worth £82.
(In pounds.)

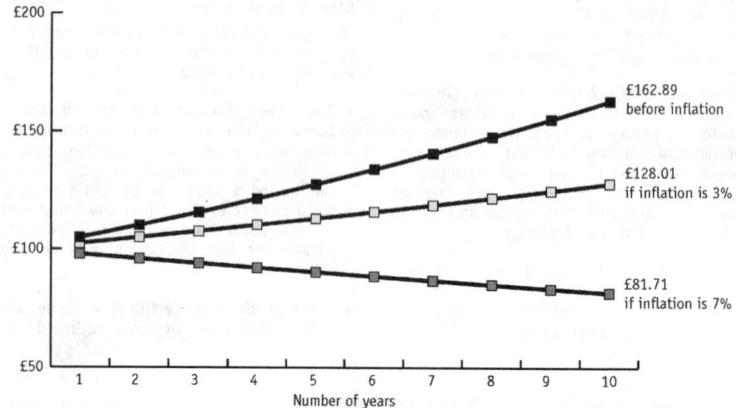

Saving and Investing: Comparative Returns on Investment Over the Last Five Years

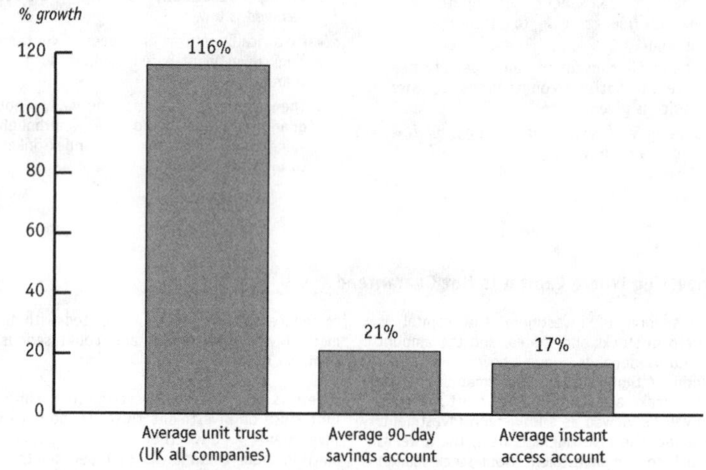

Compound Interest

This table assumes that interest is calculated annually and takes no account of taxation.

Value of £100 after:	Interest rate											
	4%	5%	6%	7%	8%	9%	10%	11%	12%	13%	14%	15%
3 months	101.0	101.3	101.5	101.8	102.0	102.3	102.5	102.8	103.0	103.3	103.5	103.8
6 months	102.0	102.5	103.0	103.5	104.0	104.5	105.0	105.5	106.0	106.5	107.0	107.5
1 year	104.0	105.0	106.0	107.0	108.0	109.0	110.0	111.0	112.0	113.0	114.0	115.0
2 years	108.2	110.3	112.4	114.5	116.6	118.8	121.0	123.2	125.4	127.7	130.0	132.3
3 years	112.5	115.8	119.1	122.5	126.0	129.5	133.1	136.8	140.5	144.3	148.2	152.1
4 years	117.0	121.6	126.2	131.1	136.0	141.2	146.4	151.8	157.4	163.0	168.9	174.9
5 years	121.7	127.6	133.8	140.3	146.9	153.9	161.1	168.5	176.2	184.2	192.5	201.1
6 years	126.5	134.0	141.9	150.1	158.7	167.7	177.2	187.0	197.4	208.2	219.5	231.3
7 years	131.6	140.7	150.4	160.6	171.4	182.8	194.9	207.6	221.1	235.3	250.2	266.0
8 years	136.9	147.7	159.4	171.8	185.1	199.3	214.4	230.5	247.6	265.8	285.3	305.9
9 years	142.3	155.1	168.9	183.8	199.9	217.2	235.8	255.8	277.3	300.4	325.2	351.8
10 years	148.0	162.9	179.1	196.7	215.9	236.7	259.4	283.9	310.6	339.5	370.7	404.6
15 years	180.1	207.9	239.7	275.9	317.2	364.2	417.7	478.5	547.4	625.4	713.8	813.7
20 years	219.1	265.3	320.7	387.0	466.1	560.4	672.7	806.2	964.6	1,152.3	1,374.3	1,636.7
25 years	266.6	338.6	429.2	542.7	684.8	862.3	1,083.5	1,358.5	1,700.0	2,123.1	2,646.2	3,291.9

Borrowing

An Introduction to Borrowing

(For mortgage borrowing, *see* **Mortgages and Housing,** p 326–328.)

There are many ways to borrow money, and choosing the right one can save you hundreds or even thousands of pounds in interest payments. Make sure that repayments are affordable, as the penalty for over-borrowing can be heavy, sometimes extending to house repossession in cases where a loan is taken out using a home as security.

Card-based borrowing

Most credit cards have an interest-free period of up to 56 days. If you pay your bill in full within this period no interest is charged; otherwise interest is applied at a monthly rate. For cardholders who do not pay their bill in full each month a minimum of between 3% and 5% of the balance must be paid. On top of interest, some issuers also charge an annual fee. Credit cards are good for flexibility and short-term borrowing, but high interest rates make them unsuitable for borrowing in the long term. (*See also* **Internet Shopping: Fraud and Security,** p 331.)

Charge cards give the holder a high or no limit to monthly spending. Unlike credit cards, the balance must be paid in full each month, so they are only suitable for short-term borrowing. They tend to have higher annual fees than credit cards.

A Gold Card can be either a credit or a charge card. Normally the holder needs to earn £20,000 per annum or more to be eligible for one. They often have a high annual fee, and a higher limit than standard credit cards.

Store cards can work like a credit card or charge card, or like a budget account where the holder agrees to pay a certain amount each month and can then borrow a multiple of that amount. Annual Percentage Rates (APRs) on these cards are usually higher than on other types of card, making them an expensive way to borrow. Additionally, they can only be used in certain stores.

Unsecured personal loans

Amounts borrowed range from as little as £500 to £15,000. The borrower usually pays a fixed monthly payment for a set amount of time, typically between one and five years. The fixed payment may help the borrower to budget, but this is not the cheapest form of borrowing, and is normally not flexible – although some providers do permit the borrower more leeway in repaying the loan, provided that a minimum amount is repaid each month (in a similar way to a credit card).

Overdrafts

Arranging an overdraft on a current account is a cheap way of borrowing if the provider does not charge fees for arranging it and for maintenance. Otherwise charges, even on a small overdraft, can run into hundreds of pounds a year, making the cost of borrowing very high. Either way, slipping into unauthorized overdraft will mean very high charges, and interest rates that top 30% a year.

Secured personal loans

If the borrower has sufficient equity in their property it may be used as security against a loan. Rates will be considerably lower than on unsecured loans. It is also possible to take a further advance on a mortgage at the existing lender's standard rate, which will be lower still – but the borrower may have to pay extra costs such as valuation and legal fees. Similarly, an endowment policy holder may use the policy to obtain a loan from their insurance company, or even from a bank or other lender. Although this is undoubtedly the cheapest form of borrowing over the long term, the clear drawback is that the borrower's assets are at risk if repayments cannot be met.

Borrowing Tips

- If you pay your credit card bill in full each month, and it has an interest-free period, then use it for free borrowing.
- As a general rule, use windfalls or lump sums to pay off outstanding credit before investing; but beware of early redemption clauses.
- If you are not interested in perks, then where possible use a credit or charge card rather than a store card, as you will almost certainly pay less interest.
- If your credit card charges a high Annual Percentage Rate (APR) then switch to a lower-charging one: transferring it is free, and often you pay an even lower rate on the balance transferred for the first six months or permanently.
- If you think that you may be able to repay all or some of a loan early then ask the lender what redemption penalties apply before taking the loan: some lenders make a charge, others do not.

Annual Percentage Rates (APRs)

To make the costs of borrowing comparable, everybody offering credit (with the exception of overdrafts on bank accounts) is compelled to quote an APR. This stands for annual percentage rate, and it shows the cost of credit expressed as an annual rate, taking *what* you pay, *when* you pay it, and for *how long* it is paid, into account.

For example, on the face of it, borrowing £1,000 now and paying back £1,200 in one year's time seems the same as borrowing £1,000 now and repaying £100 per month for the next 12 months. But the former has an APR of 20%, and the latter 41.3% because the repayment methods are different.

Buying on Credit

Most people at some time will enter an agreement with a supplier to purchase goods or services on credit. Before doing so it is wise to:

- Check if other forms of borrowing are cheaper.
- If credit is interest free, check the price elsewhere in case the retailer has bumped it up, as sometimes happens. If so, will it be cheaper to buy elsewhere even if interest is charged?
- Ensure you can afford the repayments.
- Read all the credit agreements and ask if you do not understand anything.
- When the agreement has been signed you should be given a copy of the credit agreement which sets out your cancellation rights. A copy of your cancellation rights should also be sent by post. You can legally withdraw from the deal if:
- The deal was made in the last few days.
- You talked to the lender or supplier in person (not on the telephone).
- You were not on the lender's premises (including exhibition stands) when the deal was signed.
- You signed the deal in your own home.
- The lender has not yet signed the agreement.

Extra protection is afforded if an item is purchased using a credit card and cost between £100 and £30,000. If you have a claim against the seller because, for example, the item purchased is faulty or not what you asked for you may also have a claim against the credit card company: both are liable for misrepresentation and breach of contract. In spite of widely held misconceptions such protection also extends to purchases made over the Internet although this is more difficult to enforce if you buy from outside the UK. (*See also* **Internet Shopping: Fraud and Security,** p 331.)

Your Credit Reference

No one has a right to credit. Before giving you credit, lenders – such as banks, loan companies, and shops – want to check whether you are an acceptable risk. To help them do this, they may check with firms called credit reference agencies to get some details about you and your credit record. The main credit reference agencies keep information on their computers about almost every adult in the UK. These agencies do not keep 'blacklists' or give any opinion about whether or not you should be given credit. They simply provide information about your credit record. The credit reference agency will not be able to tell you why you were refused credit. It is the lender who decides whether you are an acceptable risk.

The two main credit reference agencies in the UK are:

Experian Ltd, PO Box 8000, Nottingham NG1 5GX; phone: (0115) 976 8747

Equifax Europe, Dept 1E, PO Box 3001, Glasgow G81 2DT; phone: (0990) 783783

The Office of the Data Protection Commissioner has responsibility for credit reference agencies and produces a leaflet *No Credit?* on how to consult your credit record and correct any mistakes. You can order copies of it by phoning (0870) 442 1211. For more information, see the Data Protection Web site: www.dataprotection.gov.uk

Refused Credit?

If you are refused credit you have the right:

- to know the name and address of the Credit Reference Agency contacted by the lender
- to see the information the agency holds about you
- to correct inaccurate information held about you.

Banking

Bank Accounts: An Introduction

Today, the act of popping out to the local bank branch to pay bills or set up direct debits is beginning to seem positively antiquated, as technology rapidly opens up more and more ways to allow banking business to be conducted. Many banks provide operator or touchtone telephone banking services for their current accounts; and a new generation of accounts removes branches from the picture altogether, enabling customers to bank remotely using the Internet, or even interactive digital television. This information revolution is, however, still in its infancy; problems relating to key issues such as security remain to be resolved, and not all providers as yet offer the full range of facilities that customers have become used to.

Current accounts

A current account will offer some or all of the following facilities:

- overdraft
- direct debits and standing orders
- transfer of funds within and between institutions (less common with telephone and Internet banking)
- cheque book and guarantee card (subject to status)
- access to a reasonable cash machine (ATM) network
- balance statements and records of recent transactions
- deposit of cash and cheques: for obvious reasons it will not be possible to do this remotely

In addition to normal current accounts there are other options:

High-interest cheque accounts, combining features of savings and current accounts, often paying a good rate of interest, and providing instant access to money and a cheque book and cheque card. Some also allow direct debits and standing orders to be set up and maintained.

Packaged current accounts have a high monthly fee, and in return the customer receives a package of benefits such as discounts at certain shops or free insurance. Banks claim that the benefits gained outweigh the costs, but before deciding to open one of these accounts it is worth considering what the benefit amounts to, as it could be cheaper to open a normal current account.

Costs of operating a current account

The costs of operation can vary considerably between providers. Most do not charge if you are in credit, but many charge arrangement and maintenance fees for overdrafts. The cost of going overdrawn without agreement is universally high, and it is always wise to avoid this. Some banks charge a monthly fee in return for benefits (see packaged current accounts).

When opening or switching an account it is always sensible to assess how expensive it will be, and whether a cheaper alternative is available.

Key Dates in the History of Cash Dispensers and Automated Teller Machines (ATMs)

27 June 1967 World's first off-line automated cash dispenser is opened by Barclays Bank in Enfield, North London. Unlike later cash dispensers, which use magnetic cards, these first cash dispensers require customers to use paper vouchers which are then exchanged for £10 notes.

1968 Automated cash dispensers are installed in France, in Sweden, and in Switzerland, which has the world's first 'national' cash dispenser network, accepting thin plastic cards, for a given amount, which the machine retains at the end of the transaction. The machines are off-line and not connected to the bank's computers.

1969 First automated cash dispenser is opened in the United States at the Long Island branch of the Chemical Bank in New York; first automated cash dispenser is installed in Japan.

1972 Lloyds Bank in the UK install the first second-generation automated cash dispenser, an on-line 'Cash-Point' machine. Developed by IBM, it uses plastic cards with a magnetic strip that identifies the customer's account and is connected directly to the bank's central computer. Also in the UK, Barclays Bank pilot a new 'Touch Bank' Automated Teller Machine (ATM) which uses touch screens.

1973 Automated cash dispensers are developed in Japan where a passbook with a magnetic strip is used to access cash.

Early 1970s Docutel, an American electronics corporation from Texas, develops a new generation of machines able to perform services additional to cash dispensing, including enabling customer enquiries on bank balances, deposits, and transfers between accounts. These are the first true ATMs and spread from the mid 1970s.

1983 The worldwide number of ATMs reaches 100,000; they provide 24-hour banking at convenient locations and are twice as efficient as cashiers.

Key Dates in the History of Cash Dispensers and Automated Teller Machines (ATMs) *(continued)*

1986 In the UK, the Interchange Network Limited (Link) is established as a national network of machines for customers of more than 30 leading banks and building societies, including the Cooperative Bank, Girobank, Abbey National, and Bank of Scotland.

1991 Number of ATMs tops 300,000 as they become a worldwide phenomenon, with the highest densities in Japan (98,500), where a large proportion of salaries are paid in cash, the USA (83,500), and Europe (82,000).

Mid 1990s Low-price cash dispensers designed for use at retailers and other indoor locations are introduced. Selling at under US$10,000, compared with $20,000 for earlier machines, they lead to a surge of installations.

1994 The company CyberCash is founded. It is one of several companies to develop e-cash (or electronic cash) as a way of purchasing items over the Internet securely. Subscribers are given an electronic account (protected by encryption to prevent fraud) and the company manages payment transfers.

October 1997 Death of Luther Simjian (born 1905), a Turkish-born US inventor who held the ATM patent.

April 1998 A new dispenser that incorporates 'iris recognition' is given a trial run at Nationwide Building Society, Swindon, England – the process does not require plastic cards.

January 1999 Worldwide number of ATMs and cash dispensers exceeds 800,000, with more than a third in the Asia-Pacific region (including 145,000 in Japan), 189,000 in the USA, and 218,000 in Western Europe, where Finns and Swedes are the heaviest users per capita. In Europe, usage per machine per month averages 3,500 withdrawals. The NCR Corporation, based in Dayton, Ohio,manufactures about half of these ATMs.

May 1999 A new 'mobile ATM' is launched by Proton World International, allowing cardholders to reload e-cash cards via their mobile phones.

July 1999 ICL, a subsidiary of Fujitsu, launches the first cash dispenser with a bill-paying facility using barcode scanning. The system is adopted by Banque de Caire, Egypt's third largest bank.

29 February 2000 In the UK, the Link ATM network announces that it will allow members to surcharge their customers if they wish – a number of banks are already charging a 'disloyalty fee' of varying levels. This raises fears of double charging.

March 2000 The Link Board abolishes the possibility of two machine charges (disloyalty and surcharge) being imposed in a single transaction, operational from 1 July 2000.

May 2000 The Halifax announces that it will not introduce cash machine charges for customers or non-customers next year.

June 2000 Abbey National announces that, like the Halifax, it will not be introducing cash machine charges in 2001 for customers or non-customers. Abbey National's decision means that the owners of cash machines in the UK Link network will not be introducing charges.

See also 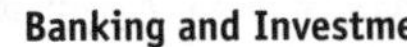 **Banking and Investment**, pp 669–675.

Pensions

Types of Pensions

State pensions

Demographics and transformations in working patterns have led to a number of changes in pensions provided by the state and the way in which these are funded.

Anyone who has paid sufficient National Insurance Contributions (or NICs) is entitled to a basic state pension. This increases in line with price inflation, and in the tax year 2000–01 is £67.50 per week for a single pensioner. Anyone with a weekly income of less than £78.45 can have it topped up to this level.

Employees earning above the weekly Lower Earnings Limit of £67 (in the 2000–01 tax year) pay National Insurance Contributions and can benefit from the additional State Earnings-Related Pension Scheme (SERPS). This provides an additional element of pension which depends on income earned up to the Upper Earnings Limit of £535 per week (2000–01 tax year). It is possible to contract out of SERPs into an employer's pension scheme. If this is done then a smaller percentage of National Insurance Contributions goes towards the state pension scheme.

From April 2002 the government will gradually replace SERPs with the Second State Pension. This pension is targeted at low earners (everyone earning more than £9,500 will get the same pension from this scheme). The plan is that employees earning above this amount will 'contract out' into personal pension plans. The government is also considering extending the scheme to the self-employed.

Employers' pension schemes

If you are working, your employer may offer a voluntary pension scheme. The scheme will be either contributory (meaning that you and your employer both make contributions into the scheme), or non-contributory (where your employer pays all the contributions). The contributions you make are tax-free. The two most common types of employers' pension scheme are:

Final salary schemes, where the amount you get depends upon how long you have been in the scheme and your income at the time of retirement. Typically this will be one-sixtieth or one-eightieth for each year in the scheme, subject to a maximum of two-thirds of your final salary. If you leave the scheme before retirement then the pension must be increased to provide at least partial protection against inflation.

Money-purchase schemes, where you and/or your employer pay contributions that are a fixed percentage of your earnings. These are invested, and the proceeds are used to buy an annuity (a policy bought from an insurer for a lump sum in return for a guaranteed income for life).

Employers' pension schemes must allow members to make Additional Voluntary Contributions (AVCs) to enable extra pension and scheme benefits to be built up. However, the final pension amount is still capped at two-thirds of final salary. Any fund built up above this amount is returned at retirement with tax deducted. Employees can make these payments into their own employer's scheme or other pension provider, in which case they are called Freestanding Additional Voluntary contributions (FSAVCs).

An increasing number of employers are offering a Group Personal Pension Scheme (GPPS) instead of these schemes. These are personal pension schemes in which the employer and not the employee makes the arrangement with a personal pension plan provider. Although they have the characteristics of a personal pension, they may offer advantages such as lower charges and variable contributions.

Personal pension plans

Personal pension plans allow the individual to set up their own plan with an insurer. Premiums are invested and the holder's pension will depend at least partly upon how well the investments perform.

Pensions: Personal vs Employers'

Personal pension plans

Advantages

- The holder can choose the provider.
- The holder can retain the same plan when changing jobs.
- There is no limit on benefits, so if the investments perform well the holder does well; the Inland Revenue stipulates maximum benefits permissible in employers' pension schemes.

Disadvantages

High administration and running costs impact heavily on fund value, especially in early years.

Employers' pensions

Advantages

- They provide certainty, as the pension is based on final salary with a final salary scheme.
- The employer pays running and maintenance costs, so all contributions go directly into the plan.
- The employer contributes to the plan.

Disadvantages

- The employee cannot choose the provider.
- Benefits are limited to two-thirds of final salary.
- They are non-transferable.

Mortgages and Housing

Mortgages: Repayment Methods

Repayment mortgage

Also known as a capital and interest mortgage, a repayment mortgage is designed to allow the sum borrowed to be paid off by the end of the mortgage term, typically 25 years. Each repayment consists of two elements: interest on the loan, and the repayment of capital. Initially, nearly all of the monthly payment will consist of interest, with only a small fraction of it going towards reducing the capital owed. Over time, as the balance falls, the interest element of the repayment reduces, leaving proportionately increasing instalments of repayment of the capital, until the final payment, when the balance becomes zero and the mortgage is repaid in full.

Interest only mortgage

The borrower makes interest payments on the entire loan until the end of the mortgage term, at which point the proceeds of a maturing investment-linked product are used to repay the loan. There are a number of such products that the lender may offer or permit to be used for this purpose:

- endowment policies
- pension-linked mortgages
- ISAs

Endowment policies are the most popular option. The borrower pays a monthly premium into an endowment insurance policy, commonly a with-profits or unit-linked policy. In the case of a with-profits policy profits are normally added each year. These bonuses cannot be removed or reduced. In the case of a unit-linked policy the premiums are paid into investments such as stocks and shares. Another form of endowment policy is a unitized policy – a combination of the with-profits and unit-linked policies. Part of the premium is invested in a with-profits endowment and the rest is invested in stocks and shares.

The potential benefit of investing premiums in such investments is clear, but investing this way can be risky. Insurers conduct regular reviews in order to assess whether the investment is on course for paying off the loan, and, if it is not, the insurer will ask the borrower to increase premiums to make up for the forecast shortfall. Because of the poor returns from endowment policies in recent years, an increasing number of insurers are asking their policyholders to do this. (*See also* **Endowment Mortgages: For and Against,** p 327.)

Mortgages can also be linked to a pension plan. At the end of the term part of the proceeds of the pension fund are used to repay the mortgage. The tax relief that is available on pension contributions makes this an attractive option. However, it is important to remember that this type of scheme will reduce the amount of pension available to the borrower at retirement.

With a mortgage linked to a stocks and shares Individual Savings Account (ISA) (*see* **Individual Savings Accounts (ISAs)**, p 321), which replaced Personal Equity Plans (PEPs) in 1999, the tax-free proceeds should be sufficient to repay the mortgage at the end of the term. However, as with all investment products, there is no guarantee that this will be the case.

Choosing a Mortgage in the UK

There are a number of different types of product which a borrower can choose for making repayments on either a repayment or an interest-only loan.

Standard variable-rate mortgage

Interest on the loan is charged at the lender's standard rate. These deals are often offered with cashbacks, which can be as high as 5 or 6% of the amount borrowed, subject to a maximum limit.

Fixed-rate mortgage

Many lenders offer mortgages with a fixed rate of interest over a set term, usually between one and five years. At the end of the term the interest rate normally reverts to the lender's standard rate, but some lenders may offer another fixed rate. Generally, the shorter the set period, the lower the fixed rate will be.

The advantage of a fixed-rate mortgage is that the level of monthly mortgage payments is guaranteed, allowing borrowers to budget more easily. On the other hand, although fixed interest rates protect the borrower against increases in interest rates, borrowers lose out if rates decrease.

Discount-rate mortgage

These are particularly popular with first-time buyers. The lender guarantees that the rate charged will be at a set level below the standard rate – typically 2% for a 2-year discount. They normally last from 6 months to 5 years, with larger discounts available on shorter periods. The rate reverts to the lender's standard rate at the end of the period. The advantage of discounted deals is that monthly payments will be reduced when the lender's standard rate is lowered; but conversely they will increase when the lender's standard rate increases.

Capped-rate mortgage

These combine elements of both fixed and discounted rates: the rate the borrower pays is guaranteed not to rise above a certain level specified at the outset, but when interest rates fall the rate the borrower pays falls too. This gives the borrower more certainty over future payments while also allowing benefit to be derived from rate reductions.

With the exception of mortgages taken out at the lender's standard rate without cashback, these products generally carry heavy charges if the loan is fully or partially redeemed during the deal period. Any benefit received is often clawed back in full. In some cases this extends well beyond the deal period, effectively tying the borrower to the lender for years. To be eligible for a deal the borrower may also be required to take out the lender's contents and buildings, and accident, sickness, and unemployment insurance, which can be considerably more expensive than insurance available elsewhere.

Another, more recently developed, type of mortgage is the flexible mortgage. Although conditions vary from lender to lender, it is designed to allow borrowers to be flexible

Choosing a Mortgage in the UK (*continued*)

– allowing, for instance, extra payments to be made, or payments to be missed or reduced. Interest is generally charged at the lender's standard rate, although some deals are of the type discussed above; redemption penalties may still apply. For borrowers who can afford to make extra payments, flexible mortgages can reduce the mortgage term by years and save thousands of pounds in interest.

Endowment Mortgages: For and Against

For

- Endowments are portable: if the borrower moves house the endowment may be transferred to cover a loan.
- In theory, if the endowment performs well enough a surplus could be generated.

Against

- Endowments are risky: if the endowment is not performing well enough to cover the loan then the borrower will have to increase premiums, take out a new policy, or take out a repayment mortgage on the expected shortfall.
- Endowments are inflexible: because of poor surrender values the borrower cannot cash in a policy or switch to another endowment. This, combined with high charges, means that it often takes years for the fund even to reach a level equivalent to the amount paid in.

Monthly Repayments on a £30,000 Mortgage at Various Rates

(In pounds unless otherwise indicated.)

Mortgage rate (%)	20-year term	25-year term	30-year term
4.00	181.79	158.35	143.22
4.50	189.79	166.75	152.01
5.00	197.99	175.38	161.05
5.50	206.37	184.23	170.34
6.00	214.93	193.29	179.87
6.50	223.67	202.56	189.62
7.00	232.59	212.03	199.59
7.50	241.68	221.70	209.76
8.00	250.93	231.54	220.13
8.50	260.35	241.57	230.67
9.00	269.92	251.76	241.39
9.50	279.64	262.11	252.26
10.00	289.51	272.61	263.27
10.50	299.51	283.25	274.42
11.00	309.66	294.03	285.70
11.50	319.93	304.94	297.09
12.00	330.33	315.97	308.58

Mortgage Rates: Banks vs Building Societies

Building societies tend to have lower mortgage rates than banks, so offering borrowers a better deal. This is because building societies act in the interest of their members – the majority of their borrowers and savers, whilst banks reduce margins on savings and mortgage rates to pay their shareholders. The table gives the average standard mortgage rates charged by banks and building societies from March 1999 to January 2000.

Month	Average mortgage rate	
	Banks	Building societies
March 1999	6.99	6.66
April 1999	6.99	6.65
May 1999	6.88	6.65
June 1999	6.88	6.63
July 1999	6.85	6.60
August 1999	6.85	6.59
September 1999	6.85	6.58
October 1999	6.97	6.62
November 1999	6.99	6.67
December 1999	7.02	6.88
January 2000	7.23	6.92

Data from the Council of Mortgage Lenders

Average House Prices in the UK by Region

As of May 2000.

Region	Average price: 1st quarter 1995 (£)	Average price: 1st quarter 1999 (£)	Average price: 1st quarter 2000 (£)	Increase since 1st quarter 1995 (%)	Increase since 1st quarter 1999 (%)
East Anglia	59,479	68,953	81,309	36.701	17.919
East Midlands	53,569	61,531	68,174	27.263	10.796
Greater London	78,373	114,830	148,676	89.702	29.475
North	50,499	54,152	56,706	12.291	4.716
Northern Ireland	43,074	63,324	65,871	52.926	4.022
North West	54,871	57,863	61,653	12.359	6.55
Scotland	57,889	59,953	64,671	11.716	7.87
South East	77,594	102,765	123,733	59.463	20.404
South West	62,356	76,372	93,284	49.599	22.144
Wales	52,233	58,066	62,940	20.499	8.394
West Midlands	60,814	67,960	78,806	29.586	15.96
Yorkshire and Humberside	51,113	53,462	57,301	12.107	7.18
Average	58,489	69,936	96,312	34.52	12.95

Data from Halifax plc

Regional House Prices

House prices inflation in the UK stood at just over 14% in the UK in the first quarter of 2000. Although each of the regions has recorded an increase, this figure masks significant variations between and within regions. For instance Greater London experienced the highest increase, with house price inflation running at over double the national average at a staggering 29.5%; whereas the lowest increase was in Northern Ireland where prices increased by a more modest 4%.

It is difficult to be certain what will happen to house prices, but overall the signs are that house price inflation is set to fall – that is prices will increase at a decreasing rate. This will be caused by a number of factors which may have varying impacts in each region. These factors include:

- A dampening of demand in more expensive areas as many buyers, particularly first-time buyers, simply cannot afford to buy.
- The abolition of mortgage interest relief, which will increase the mortgage bill. This will have a disproportionately large effect in less expensive regions.
- Interest rate increases, which will affect all regions similarly.
- Increase in stamp duty on higher priced properties. Although this will not affect the vast majority of sales, it will have a disproportionately large effect in the more expensive regions of southern England.

House Prices in the UK – How To Invest Wisely

by Anthony Bailey

Owning a home is seen as an ideal way both to provide a place to live and to invest for the future. Rising house prices are viewed as a good thing in the UK – in stark contrast to, for example, the high price of new cars that has been at the centre of an ongoing debate over 'rip-off' Britain. Yet in many areas, skilled and white-collar workers (let alone the unskilled and other lower income groups) stand little chance of buying a decent family home or of renting one at a manageable rent. It is a kind of economic failure, a huge mismatch between supply and demand.

The House Market Cycle There is no doubt that falling house prices can be a bad thing. In the recession of the early 1990s, 'negative equity' became a hot topic of conversation. It brought the misery of either chronic immobility or serious debt to a homeowner whose property's value fell to less than the outstanding mortgage. House price falls had occurred before, in the 1970s for example, but the falls were concealed by high general inflation. There is every chance prices will fall again. The housing market moves in cycles. The long-term price trend has been upwards and it may yet continue that way, but the possibility of short- or even medium-term price falls should never be ruled out – and house price falls could be painful in today's climate of low inflation.

House vs Retail Price Inflation Over the 25 years to 2000, house price inflation more or less matched retail price inflation. In the first quarter of 2000, house price inflation stood at 14.5% – with regional variations from 4% in Northern Ireland to 29.5% in Greater London. Yet in March 2000 retail price inflation stood at 2.6%. Annual pay inflation was higher at 5.6%, but still well below house price inflation. If history is any guide, house prices will at some point adjust (and possibly fall) to resume the longer-term trend of simply matching retail price inflation.

Highs, Lows, and Averages Even in 2000 the euphoria of homeowners in property hot spots contrasted with the gloom of those stranded in properties whose value was falling, in areas caught in a spiral of decline. The contrast was often starkest in northern English cities. Trendy city-centre flats in converted warehouses were all the rage but no one wanted old-fashioned terraced properties a stone's throw away. The annual report of the Land Registry, published in 2000, showed a small decline in the average price of all properties in England and Wales as early as the second half of 1999. It is hard to get an accurate picture of average house prices because of different methodologies in computing them. The two most widely quoted house price indices – from mortgage lenders Halifax and Nationwide – showed a continuing rise in average prices throughout 1999. These two indices can produce different figures, occasionally brought into sharp relief when one index shows a slight rise and the other a slight fall in prices. However, both indices tend to show the same general trend in house prices, and changes in the trend can act as an early warning sign to homebuyers.

Avoiding the Pitfalls Following a few rules can help avoid the downside of homeownership: never forget that the housing market moves in cycles. If house prices have been rising for several years, there is a good chance that prices will soon start levelling off or even falling – unfortunately, judging your position in the cycle is well nigh impossible. Be sceptical of professionals' forecasts of house price movements published enthusiastically by newspapers. Journalists do not usually compare current with earlier forecasts from the same source. The track record of the forecasters is poor. Be cautious in how much you borrow in relation to the value of a property. At the height of a boom, some lenders will give 100% loans – a potential disaster if house prices fall and you want to move. If there is a good chance that you will want to move again in a year or two, high value loans are high risk. High value loans are less of a worry if you expect to stay put in a new home for, say, five years. Be cautious if a lender is happy to lend you a high multiple of your earnings, for example four times what you earn. Could you manage if mortgage rates shoot up, or if you get ill, or become unemployed? A good time to buy property purely as an investment is when house prices have stabilized or fallen and when the professionals have been gloomy for at least a year or two. The huge growth in the buy-to-let mortgage market has allowed individuals to become private landlords, but becoming a landlord does not guarantee that you will make easy money.

■ Mortgages and Housing

Consumer Expenditure

Households and their Expenditure in the UK

(N = nil or negligible.)

Category	1990	1992	1994–95	1996–97	1998–99
Number of households supplying data	7,046	7,418	6,853	6,415	6,630
Total number of persons supplying data	17,437	18,174	16,617	15,732	16,218
Total number of adults supplying data[1]	12,939	13,563	12,365	11,495	11,886
Household percentage distribution by tenure					
Rented unfurnished	29	28	28	28	28
Rented furnished	3	4	4	5	3
Rent-free	1	2	1	2	2
Owner-occupied	66	66	67	66	67
Average number of persons per household					
All persons	2.5	2.5	2.4	2.5	2.4
Men	1.2	1.2	1.2	1.2	1.2
Women	1.3	1.3	1.3	1.3	1.3
Adults[1]					
persons under 65	1.5	1.5	1.4	1.4	1.5
persons 65 and over	0.4	0.4	0.4	0.4	0.4
Total	1.8	1.8	1.8	1.8	1.8
Children[1]					
children under 2	0.1	0.1	0.1	0.1	0.1
children 2 and under 5	0.1	0.1	0.1	0.1	0.1
children 5 and under 18	0.4	0.4	0.4	0.5	0.4
Total	0.6	0.6	0.6	0.7	0.5
Persons economically active	1.2	1.2	1.2	1.2	1.2
Persons not economically active					
men 65 and over, women 60 and over	0.4	0.4	0.4	0.4	0.4
others	0.9	0.9	0.9	0.9	0.8
Total	1.3	1.3	1.3	1.3	1.2
Average weekly household expenditure on commodities and services (£)[4]					
Housing[2 3]	44.42	47.36	46.42	49.10	57.20
Fuel and power	11.11	13.02	12.95	13.35	11.70
Food	44.81	47.66	50.43	55.15	58.90
Alcoholic drink	10.01	11.06	12.32	12.41	14.00
Tobacco	4.82	5.38	5.61	6.07	5.80
Clothing and footwear	16.03	16.39	17.13	18.27	21.70
Household goods[3]	20.00	21.90	22.66	26.74	29.60
Household services[3]	12.28	13.40	15.08	16.36	18.90
Personal goods and services	9.47	10.18	10.78	11.64	13.30
Motoring expenditure	33.83	35.66	36.17	41.20	51.70
Fares and other travel costs	6.19	7.20	6.64	7.45	8.30
Leisure goods	11.28	13.32	13.89	15.17	17.80
Leisure services[3]	21.54	27.56	31.20	33.95	41.90
Miscellaneous	1.37	1.75	2.30	2.21	1.20
Total	247.16	271.83	289.86	309.07	352.20
Expenditure on commodity or service as a percentage of total expenditure[4]					
Housing[2 3]	18	17	16	16	16
Fuel and power	5	5	5	4	3
Food	18	18	18	18	17
Alcoholic drink	4	4	4	4	4
Tobacco	2	2	2	2	2
Clothing and footwear	7	6	6	6	6
Household goods[3]	8	8	8	9	8
Household services[3]	5	5	5	5	5
Personal goods and services	4	4	4	4	4
Motoring expenditure	14	13	13	13	15
Fares and other travel costs	3	3	2	2	2
Leisure goods	5	5	5	5	5
Leisure services[3]	9	10	11	11	12
Miscellaneous	1	1	1	1	N

[1] Adults = all persons 18 and over and married persons under 18; children = all unmarried persons under 18.

[2] Until 1992 excludes mortgage payments but includes imputed rent of owner-occupancy and of rent-free occupancy. Imputed expenditure is the weekly equivalent of the rateable value which is adjusted to allow for general increases in rents since date of valuation. 1985 assessments of rateable values in Scotland were used from 1 April 1985 in the calculation of imputed income and housing expenditure of owner-occupiers and those living rent-free. In 1992 values of income and expenditure pertaining to households in owner-occupied and rent-free housing were no longer imputed. From 1992 onwards the interest element of mortgage payments is recorded as part of housing expenditure.

[3] Expenditure on certain items was recorded on a retrospective basis from 1989 and 1990.

[4] A new classification system for expenditure was introduced in April 1994. There have been some minor adjustments to the coverage of the following expenditure groups: leisure goods and services, motoring expenditure and fares, household goods and services, personal goods and services. As a result, figures for these expenditure groups, and for total expenditure, are not directly comparable with figures for earlier years.

Source: Annual Abstract of Statistics 2000, Family Expenditure Survey,

Working Hours Needed to Buy Selected Commodities in the UK

Figures indicate the length of time necessary for a person on average hourly adult earnings for all industries and services to work so that his/her net income pays for various goods. The earnings figures are based on full-time employees on adult rates whose pay was not affected for the survey period by absence. Net income also includes child benefit payments.

Commodity	Married couple with husband only working[1]		Working single mother with child	
	1971	1998	1971	1998
800 g white sliced wrapped bread	9 min	4 min	14 min	5 min
1 pint milk	5 min	3 min	8 min	3 min
Dozen eggs, first quality, size 2	21 min	11 min	32 min	14 min
1 kg potatoes	4 min	6 min	6 min	7 min
1 kg cod fillets	1 hr 1 min	48 min	1 hr 30 min	59 min
1 kg rump steak	1 hr 54 min	1 hr 5 min	2 hr 49 min	1 hr 19 min
1 pint of beer (bitter)	14 min	13 min	20 min	15 min
20 cigarettes (king size filter)	22 min	24 min	33 min	29 min
Road fund tax	40 hr 1 min	18 hr 25 min	59 hr 54 min	22 hr 31 min
First class stamp	3 min	2 min	4 min	2 min

[1] Married man with non-earning wife and two children under 11.

Source: Office for National Statistics; Inland Revenue; DVLA; Postal Museum, © Crown copyright 1999

E-Shopping

The importance of shopping over the Internet has grown with the huge rise in the number of users connected to it. In March 1999, an NOP survey reported that nearly 11,000 adult users in the UK were being added to the online community every day. During June of the same year, according to another NOP survey report, nearly 1.5 million adults had gone online to purchase a product or service and had spent £239 million in the process. This indicated that the number of online shoppers had increased by 44% in the first six months of 1999. The survey findings indicated a growing confidence among users in shopping online, with 79% prepared to disclose their credit card details over the Internet.

Survey findings published in February 2000 showed that more than 3 million out of the 12 million people who regularly access the World Wide Web had shopped online at some time during the four weeks before Christmas 1999. This was a threefold increase over the same period in 1998. Based on these findings, NOP estimated that online shopping in the UK would pass £10 billion in 2000. In the light of such trends, the UK Government has been making its own efforts to stimulate growth in e-commerce. In his March 2000 budget, Chancellor of the Exchequer Gordon Brown announced special tax concessions to small businesses buying computer equipment to trade online, and also promoted Internet training courses for employees.

There is no doubt that online shopping is now offering a credible alternative to the high street retailers. What do online shoppers buy? The most popular purchases appear to be books, music CDs and tapes, groceries, and computer equipment, software, and accessories.

Shopping on the Internet: Some Tips

Over 25 million homes in Western Europe have access to the Internet; in the UK 17% of homes are connected, and this figure is expected to double in the next two years. With such a potential market only a mouse click away it is no surprise that the new-style and traditional high-street and supermarket retailers have been stampeding to set up online shops.

Internet shopping can offer most of the advantages of shopping in person: goods can be viewed, bought, and ordered for delivery. Moreover, rival prices can be easily compared; there is no queuing, and no pestering by shop assistants; you can enjoy an inexpensive cup of tea and a cake in your own kitchen when you fancy a breather; and you don't have to worry about the state of the shop's toilet either. The downside, of course, is that you cannot physically examine what you are buying; you may have to wait some time for delivery; slow connection speeds can be frustrating; and, if you register with the Web site, you may find yourself receiving junk e-mail.

As on the high street, some online shops and malls (sites with many online shops) are better than others when it comes to service, availability, product or service information, and finding and ordering items. Here are some tips for ensuring that your online experience is as safe, cheap, fast, and stress-free as possible.

Your consumer rights are the same as on the high street, but to avoid rogue traders gather as much information as possible. Call the company if you are unsure. Buying from overseas sites can be problematic, so use a UK site if possible.

- To avoid unauthorized disclosure of your credit card details, make sure that you buy from a secure site that uses encryption.
- Remember that if you buy goods from abroad they will probably be liable to customs and excise duty and VAT – imports of less than £18 are exempted, except for tobacco, alcohol, and perfume.
- Before buying, ensure that the price you have been quoted includes VAT, duty, and delivery. High delivery charges can significantly increase item costs.
- Shop around several sites to find what you are looking for, as prices vary considerably.
- Some sites are more useful and easier to navigate around than others; so, if you are happy with other aspects of a site, bookmark it for future use.
- If buying from overseas, make sure that the goods are legal in the UK, and also that they are UK-compatible – some products, such as digital video discs (DVDs) may not be compatible.
- Check to see when the Web site was last updated.
- Find out what the retailer's refund policy is before you buy.

See also **Shopping by Mail, Telephone, Television, and Internet: Some Tips**, p 301.

Consumer Expenditure

Internet Shopping: Fraud and Security

One of the major Internet issues is the security of credit card details sent over the medium. Most retailers use encryption to scramble the details that you send them. Although there is an element of risk – powerful computers are capable of cracking some types of encryption codes – in practice, the chances of this happening to you are remote, and certainly much lower than the likelihood of your card being used fraudulently in other situations. Nevertheless, it pays to be cautious, so never send your details to a site that does not use encryption, and never e-mail your credit card details to anyone.

A greater threat stems from the possibility that the site to which you send your details is fraudulent. Never send details to a site about which you have doubts, and always gather as much concrete information as you can about the trader – details such as their postal address and telephone number. The Consumers' Association has launched a scheme called 'Which? Web Trader', which vets traders, and allows reputable ones to display the scheme's logo. A list of accredited traders can be found at the scheme's Web site: www.which.net/webtrader/wt5.html.

Taxation

Estimated Average Incomes of Households Before and After Tax in the UK

Original income is the total income in cash and kind of household before the deduction of taxes or the addition of state benefits. The addition of cash benefits (retirement pensions, child benefit, etc) and the deduction of income tax, council tax, water charges, domestic rates, and employees' National Insurance contributions give disposable income. By further allowing for taxes paid on goods and services purchased, such as value added tax (VAT), an estimate of 'post-tax' income is derived.

1997–98

Households	Retired households[1]		Non-retired households								All households
	One adult	Two or more adults	One adult	Two adults	Three or more adults	One adult with children[2]	Two adults with one child[2]	Two adults with two children[2]	Two adults with three or more children[2]	Three or more adults with children[2]	
Number of households in population (thousands)	3,477	2,787	3,692	4,909	2,283	1,453	1,887	2,249	882	937	24,550
	Average per household (£ per year)										
Original income	3,219	9,693	13,793	27,241	35,439	4,943	28,337	30,047	24,437	31,721	19,680
Disposable income	7,132	14,100	12,183	22,699	30,628	9,408	23,646	24,934	23,007	28,604	18,402
Post-tax income	5,893	11,035	9,775	18,270	24,214	7,164	18,989	20,219	18,409	21,721	14,685

[1] A retired household is defined as one where the combined income of retired members amounts to at least half the total gross income of the household, where a retired person is defined as anyone who describes themselves as 'retired' or anyone over the minimum National Insurance pension age describing themselves as 'unoccupied' or 'sick or injured but not intending to seek work'.

[2] Children are defined as persons aged under 16 or aged between 16 and 18, unmarried and receiving non-advanced further education.

Source: Annual Abstract of Statistics 2000, © *Crown copyright 2000*

Income Tax in the UK

Taxes on individual incomes are generally progressive in that larger incomes are subject to a greater amount of tax. Income tax is imposed for the year of assessment beginning on 6 April. A new 10% starting rate of income tax took effect in April 1999, and the basic rate was reduced from 23% to 22% with effect from April 2000. The higher rate of tax remains at 40%.

Allowances and reliefs reduce an individual's income tax liability. All taxpayers are entitled to a personal allowance against income from all sources. The married couple's allowance (MCA) and associated allowances were abolished from April 2000; however, couples in which at least one of the spouses was aged 65 or over on 5 April 2000 are able to keep the MCA. In April 2000, the under-16 child credit in the Working Families Tax Credit was increased by £4.35 with effect from June 2000. From 6 April 2000 there was a further increase of £1.10 above indexation in the credit for children under 11 years. A tax credit worth up to £442 per year will be introduced from 6 April 2001 for families with children; the credit will be tapered away from families where one or both parents are higher rate taxpayers.

Relief on mortgage interest repayments was removed with effect from 6 April 2000. Employees' contributions to their pension schemes continue to qualify for tax relief.

In general, income tax is charged on all income that originates in the UK – although some forms of income are exempt, such as child benefit – and on all income arising abroad of people resident in the UK. The UK has entered into agreements with many countries to provide relief from double taxation; where such agreements are not in force, unilateral relief is often allowed. British residents working abroad for the whole year may benefit from 100% tax relief.

Most wage and salary earners pay their income tax under the Pay-As-You-Earn (PAYE) system whereby tax is deducted and accounted for to the Inland Revenue by the employer, in a way that enables most employees to pay the correct amount of tax during the year.

A self-assessment system for collecting personal taxation has been introduced. Around 9 million people – primarily higher-rate taxpayers, the self-employed, and those receiving investment income (particularly where this is paid without tax being deducted) – are required to complete an annual tax return for the Inland Revenue. Taxpayers are now able to calculate their own tax liability, although they can choose to have the calculations done by the Inland Revenue if they return the form by the end of September.

Source: Britain 2000: The Official Yearbook of the United Kingdom, © *Crown copyright 1999; with Helicon updates*

Income Tax Bands in the UK

1999–2000 Rate	Taxable income (£ a year)
Starting rate 10%	0–1,500
Basic rate 23%	1,501–28,000
Higher rate 40%	over 28,000
***2000–01* Rate**	**Taxable income (£ a year)**
Starting rate 10%	0–1,520
Basic rate 22%	1,521–28,400
Higher rate 40%	over 28,400

Income Tax Allowances in the UK

Allowance	£ per year 1999–2000	2000–01
Personal allowance		
age under 65	4,335	4,385
age 65–74	5,720	5,790
age 75 and over	5,980	6,050
Married couple's allowance[1]		
age 65 before 6 April 2000	5,125	5,185
age 75 and over	5,195	5,255
Income limit for age-related allowances	16,800	17,000
Widow's bereavement allowance[2]	1,970	2,000
Blind person's allowance	1,380	1,400

[1] Married couple's allowance was abolished from April 2000; however the allowance is still available for couples in which at least one of the spouses was aged 65 or over on 5 April 2000. Tax relief for these allowances is restricted to 10%.

[2] This will not be available in respect of deaths occurring after 5 April 2000.

National Insurance Contributions in the UK

Entitlement to National Insurance benefits such as Retirement Pension, Incapacity Benefit, contributory Jobseeker's Allowance, Maternity Allowance, and Widow's Benefit, is dependent upon the payment of contributions. There are five classes of National Insurance contributions. The rates given below are effective from April 2000 to April 2001.

Class 1

Class 1 contributions are paid by employers and their employees. Employees who earn less than £67 a week do not pay Class 1 contributions. For earnings above £67 per week the rate of contributions is 10% up to the upper earnings limit of £535 per week. Employees who are contracted out of SERPS pay a lower rate of 8.4%. The employer pays contributions at the rate of 12.2% for all earnings above £84 per week. For employees who are contracted out of SERPS the employer pays 9.2% up to the upper earnings limit of £535 per week, and 12.2% for earnings above £535 per week.

Class 1A

Class 1A contributions are paid by employers who provide their employees with fuel and/or a car for private use. A Class 1A contribution is payable on the cash equivalent of the benefit provided.

Class 2

Class 2 contributions are paid by the self-employed. The self-employed may claim exemption from Class 2 contributions if their profits are expected to be below £3,825 for the 2000–01 tax year. A flat rate of £2 per week is payable for earnings between £3,825 and £4,385. For earnings between £4,385 and £27,820 7% of profit is payable in addition to the flat rate of £2 per week.

Class 3

Class 3 contributions are paid voluntarily to safeguard rights to some benefits and for pension purposes. Contributions are at a flat rate of £6.45 a week.

Class 4

Class 4 contributions are paid by self-employed people on their taxable profits between £7,530 and £26,000 a year (in addition to their Class 2 contribution). Class 4 contributions are payable at the rate of 6%.

Employees who work after pensionable age (60 for women and 65 for men) do not pay contributions but the employer continues to be liable. Self-employed people over pensionable age do not pay contributions.

Source: Britain 1999: The Official Yearbook of the United Kingdom, © *Crown copyright 1998; with Helicon updates*

Capital Gains Tax in the UK

Capital gains tax (CGT) is payable by individuals and trusts on gains realized from the disposal of assets. It is payable on the amount by which total chargeable gains for a year exceed the exempt amount (£7,200 for individuals and £3,600 for trusts in 2000–01). For individuals, CGT is calculated at income tax rates, as if the amount were additional taxable income, while there are special rates for trusts. From 6 April 2000, capital gains falling within the starting rate band benefit from the 10p starting rate. Only gains arising since 1982 are subject to tax. Indexation relief is given to take account of the effects of inflation. Gains on some types of asset are exempt from CGT. These include the principal private residence, government securities, certain corporate bonds, and gains on shares and corporate bonds owned under Personal Equity Plans (PEPs). For companies, capital gains are charged to corporation tax, although there is no annual exempt amount.

The table gives the annual amount exempt from tax. The rate of tax chargeable on the excess of gains over the annual exempt amount was 30% from 1980–81 to 1987–88. Thereafter the rate has been the same as income tax.

For 2000–01, gains below the starting rate limit will be taxed at 10%, gains between the starting rate and basic rate limits will be taxed at 20%, and gains above the basic rate limit will be taxed at 40%.

Capital Gains Tax in the UK

Tax year	Annual exempt amount (£) Individuals	Trusts	Tax year	Annual exempt amount (£) Individuals	Trusts
1980–81 and 1981–82	3,000	1,500	1991–92	5,500	2,750
1982–83	5,000	2,500	1992–93 to 1994–95	5,800	2,900
1983–84	5,300	2,650	1995–96	6,000	3,000
1984–85	5,600	2,800	1996–97	6,300	3,150
1985–86	5,900	2,950	1997–98	6,500	3,250
1986–87	6,300	3,150	1998–99	6,800	3,400
1987–88	6,600	3,300	1999–2000	7,100	3,550
1988–89 to 1990–91	5,000	2,500	2000–01	7,200	3,600

Taxation

Stamp Duty in the UK

Certain kinds of transfer are subject to stamp duty. Transfers of shares attract duty at 0.5% of the cost, while certain instruments, such as declarations of trust, have small fixed duties of 50p or £1, though in practice (from 1 October 1999) stamp duty is collected in multiples of £5. Transfers by gift and transfers to charities are exempt. Recent budgets have raised the rate of stamp duty on the transfers of property (except shares) over £250,000 in order to encourage stability in the housing market. Duty on land and property is now payable at 1% of the total price above £60,000, 3% for property above £250,000, and 4% for property where the price exceeds £500,000.

Source: Inland Revenue Statistics 1997 *and* Britain 2000: The Official Yearbook of the United Kingdom, © *Crown copyright 1997 and 1999; with Helicon updates*

Inheritance Tax in the UK

Inheritance tax is essentially charged on estates at the time of death and on gifts made within seven years of death; most other lifetime transfers are not taxed. There are several important exemptions. Generally, transfers between spouses are exempt, and gifts and bequests to UK charities, major political parties, and heritage bodies are also normally exempt. In general, business assets and farmland are exempt from inheritance tax, so that most family businesses can be passed on without a tax charge. Tax is charged at a single rate of 40% above a threshold: currently £234,000 in 2000–01. Only about 3% of estates a year become liable for an inheritance tax bill.

Source: Britain 2000: An Official Yearbook of the United Kingdom, © *Crown copyright 1999; with Helicon updates*

Value Added Tax in the UK

Value Added Tax (VAT) is a broadly based expenditure tax, with a standard rate of 17.5% and a reduced rate of 5% on domestic fuel and power and on the installation of energy-saving materials in low-income households under government schemes. It is collected at each stage in the production and distribution of goods and services by taxable persons. The final tax is payable by the consumer.

The annual level of turnover above which traders must register for VAT is £52,000. Certain goods and services are relieved from VAT, either by being charged at a zero rate or by being exempt.

Zero Rating

Under zero rating, a taxable person does not charge tax to a customer but reclaims any input tax paid to suppliers. Among the main categories where zero-rating applies are:

- goods exported to other countries
- most food
- water and sewerage for non-business use
- domestic and international passenger transport
- books, newspapers, and periodicals
- construction of new residential buildings
- young children's clothing and footwear
- drugs and medicines supplied on prescription
- specified aids for handicapped people
- certain supplies by or to charities

Exemptions

For exempt goods or services, a taxable person does not charge any output tax but is not entitled to reclaim the input tax. The main categories where exemption applies are:

- many supplies of land and buildings
- insurance and other financial services
- postal services
- betting
- gaming (with certain important exceptions)
- lotteries
- much education and training
- health and welfare

Source: Britain 2000: The Official Yearbook of the United Kingdom, © *Crown copyright 1999; with Helicon updates*

See also **Council Tax Bands in England, Scotland, and Wales**, p 74.

The National Lottery

Introduction

Parliament

In 1993, the National Lottery Act was passed by parliament, enabling a national lottery to be set up in the UK. Eight consortia submitted bids to run the UK lottery. The licence was awarded to the Camelot consortium by Sir Peter Davies of the lottery regulatory body OFLOT (now the National Lottery Commission). The licence is up for review in 2001 and Camelot is expected to put in a bid. Parliament also decided the five 'good causes' to benefit from the lottery: arts, sport, heritage, charities, and celebrating the millennium; a sixth Good Cause is the new health, education, and environment cause. The National Lottery was launched on 14 November 1994.

National Lottery Commission (OFLOT)

The National Lottery Act 1998 brought in the new commission, including members with expertise in consumers' views, business, the lottery market, and lottery distribution. The status of the Commission is as a non-departmental government body. The Commission's principal duties are to protect the interests of National Lottery players and ensure that the lottery is run fairly and properly. It is also a legal objective to maximize the money raised for good causes. The Commission will select the next operator when the current licence expires in September 2001. The 1998 legislation also gives the Commission powers to impose financial penalties for breaches of the current licence.

Camelot

The Camelot consortium was set up with five shareholder companies, of which there are now only four (GTECH's shares were bought out by the other four shareholders in April 1998):

- Cadbury Schweppes – consumer product marketing
- De La Rue – security printing
- ICL – computer systems, field service, and retailer training
- Racal – data communication

Camelot's profit is expected to remain under 1% of sales during the period of the licence. Under the terms of the licence, as sales increase, a higher percentage of earnings go to the Good Causes, and a smaller percentage to Camelot to cover operating costs.

Retailers

There are over 36,000 National Lottery retailers of which 24,000 are online. 68.87% of retailers are independently owned. The average weekly lottery sales for an online independent retailer is

Introduction *(continued)*

£2,259. Retailers earn 5% commission on all sales and 1% commission on all prizes paid out between £10–200. In the year to end March 1998 retailer commission totalled £281 million.

National Lottery Distribution Fund (NLDF)

Camelot is legally obliged to maximize the funds raised by the National Lottery for the Good Causes. Camelot is not responsible for the distribution of funds to the Good Causes, which are distributed by the NLDF. Camelot aims to raise £10 billion for the Good Causes by 2001.

Good Causes

Out of every pound spent on the National Lottery, some 28p goes to the six Good Causes. These receive weekly funds from the NLDF. Some £7.5 billion had been raised for Good Causes by the end of May 1999 and over 38,000 awards for £6.7 billion had been distributed. The Good Causes have a specific agenda to promote:

- *The Arts Councils of England, Northern Ireland, Scotland, and Wales* To help people to take part in and enjoy the broadest range of arts activities, helping young people to develop their talent, as well as capital projects.
- *The Millennium Commission* To fund millennium projects that make a substantial contribution to their community, as well as promoting a nationwide programme of events in the year 2000. It will cease existing on 31 December 2000.
- *National Heritage Lottery Fund* To safeguard and enhance the heritage of the UK.
- *National Lottery Charities Board* Gives grants to help those at the greatest disadvantage and to improve the quality of life in the community. The first three programmes focused on poverty, community involvement, and health and social research.
- *The Sports Councils of England, Northern Ireland, Scotland, and Wales* To help people across the UK enjoy sports of all kinds. They give awards to initiatives as well as individuals.
- *New Opportunities Fund* The New Opportunities Fund is a non-departmental public body sponsored by the Department for Culture, Media, and Sports. This was created by the National Lottery Act 1998 and is responsible for distributing National Lottery grants throughout the UK, for health, education, and environment initiatives. The initiatives are determined by government after consultation. An initial £1 billion was given to fund three grant programmes: healthy living centres; out of school hours childcare and out of school hours learning; and ICT training for teachers, school librarians, and librarians' activities. When the Millennium Commission ceases to exist on 31 December 2000, the New Opportunties Fund will receive one third of the total Good Causes amount.
- *National Endowment for Science, Technology and the Arts (NESTA)* This was set up by the Government as part of the National Lottery Act 1998. It has a one-off grant of £200 million from the lottery to be used as an endowment. The interest from this capital, an estimated £12 million per year, will be given out as grants to relevant organizations. Unlike other grant-giving bodies, NESTA's primary activity will be the support of individuals, rather than organizations.

Thunderball

Ticket sales of the original Lottery game fell by 5.6% to £5.2 billion between 1998 and 1999 and in order to revitalize lottery sales, a new game, Thunderball, was launched, in June 1999, with the aim of attracting those who want a greater chance of winning, even if the amount of the prizes is smaller.

(*See also* **Major Millennium Commission Projects in the UK**, p 97.)

Spending on the National Lottery and Scratch Cards in the UK

Between April 1998 and March 1999, 56% of households participated in the Saturday or Wednesday night draws in a two-week diary-keeping period following an interview. According to the Family Expenditure Survey, participating households spent an average of £3.80 a week on the National Lottery draws in 1998–99.

Social group	Saturday or Wednesday draw 1988–99 (£)
Professional	1.80
Managerial and technical	2.10
Skilled non-manual	2.00
Skilled manual	3.20
Partly skilled	2.80
Unskilled	2.50
Economically inactive	1.70
Average	2.30

Source: Social Trends 30,

■ The National Lottery

Top 10 Awards from the National Lottery Distribution Fund

As of May 2000.

Rank	Recipient	Project name	Award amount (£)	Award date	Distributing body
1	English National Stadium Trust	English National Stadium, Wembley	120,000,000	17 October 1997	English Sports Council
2	Royal Opera House Covent Garden Ltd	Restoration, refurbishment, and extension of Royal Opera House	55,000,000	17 July 1995	Arts Council of England
3=	Tate Gallery	Tate Gallery of Modern Art, Bankside	50,000,000	18 October 1995	Millennium Commission
	The Earth Centre Millennium Partnership	The Earth Centre, Doncaster	50,000,000	20 September 1995	Millennium Commission
	Birmingham City Council	Digbeth Millennium Campus	50,000,000	16 October 1996	Millennium Commission
6	Welsh Rugby Union and South Glamorgan	Welsh National Stadium	46,000,000	23 February 1996	Millennium Commission
7	The Ulster Museum and Sheridan Group	The Odyssey Project	45,000,000	11 June 1997	Millennium Commission
8	Sustrans	National Cycle Network	43,500,000	6 September 1995	Millennium Commission
9	Bristol 2000 Ltd	Bristol 2000	41,300,000	16 May 1996	Millennium Commission
10	Salford City Council	Creation of The Lowry Centre	41,000,000	21 February 1996	Arts Council of England

Source: National Lottery Commission, © Crown copyright 1999

See also **Major Millennium Commission Projects in the UK**, p 97.

National Lottery Totals

Cumulative totals as of 3 May 2000.

Total	Amount (£)
Sales since launch	>27.3 billion
Amount passed to Good Causes[1]	>8.2 billion
Paid to lottery retailers in sales commission	>1.3 billion
Paid to the Government in lottery duty	>3.2 billion
National Lottery Game, Instants, and Thunderball prizes	13.1 billion
Charitable donations (separate from Good Causes)	23.8 million[2]

[1] Includes unclaimed prizes and contribution from Instants.
[2] To December 1999.

The National Lottery: Thunderball Odds

The exact value of prizes depends on the number of winners overall and per prize category.

Winning selection	Odds
Match 5 and the 'Thunderball'	1 in 3,895,584
Match 5	1 in 299,661
Match 4 and the 'Thunderball'	1 in 26,866
Match 4	1 in 2,067
Match 3 and the 'Thunderball'	1 in 960
Match 3	1 in 74
Match 2 and the 'Thunderball'	1 in 107
Match 1 and the 'Thunderball'	1 in 33

The National Lottery: The Odds

The exact value of prizes depends on how many tickets are sold and how many people match the same quantity of numbers as you. For example, if two or more people match the six numbers drawn, then the jackpot is split between them.

Winning selection	Odds
Jackpot – match 6 main numbers	1 in 13,983,816
Match 5 main numbers plus the bonus number	1 in 2,330,636
Match 5 main numbers	1 in 55,492
Match 4 main numbers	1 in 1,033
Match 3 main numbers	1 in 57

Web Sites

British Immigration and Visa Requirements

http://193.114.50.10/travel/visa.asp

Clear explanation of UK entry requirements provided by the Foreign and Commonwealth Office. Addresses of all British consular offices are provided, and application forms and leaflets can be downloaded.

British Official Publications: Library and Information Resources

http://www-sul.stanford.edu/depts/jonsson/brit.html

Comprehensive set of resources available for viewing UK government documents, including Her Majesty's Stationery Office (HMSO), the Public Record Office, and the Central Statistical Office.

Budget

http://www.hm-treasury.gov.uk/pub/html/budget.html

Frequently updated information on the UK's budget from the Treasury. Accompanying documents provide a picture of the state of Britain's public finances.

Child Support Agency (CSA)

http://www.dss.gov.uk/csa/

The CSA is a UK government agency that helps children whose parents live apart by assessing how much money the absent parent should contribute to supporting those children.

Consumer Reports

http://www.consumerreports.org/

Online consumer magazine with articles and test results across a range of products and services, including cars and trucks, electronics, house and home, money, health and food, personal, and leisure.

Consumers International

http://193.128.6.150/consumers/

Worldwide non-profit federation of consumer organizations. The site includes news, campaigns and issues, global newsletters, and a members' directory.

Consumer World

http://www.consumerworld.org/

A non-commercial resource for consumers, with news, information on consumer agencies worldwide, and consumer internet resources.

Copyright Licensing Agency

http://www.cla.co.uk/

UK Reproduction Rights Organization site, with full online documentation about UK copyright laws.

Her Majesty's Customs and Excise

http://www.hmce.gov.uk/

Information for businesses and the public about UK Customs regulations and allowances. There is also comprehensive advice for travellers.

HM Land Registry

http://www.landreg.gov.uk

Explains the role of the land registration agency for England and Wales, with reports on property prices, links to regional offices, and details of how to obtain online access to registry documents.

HSE – Health and Safety Executive

http://www.open.gov.uk/hse/hsehome.htm

Explains the HSE's role in protecting the health of the British workforce, with reports on particular dangers in the workplace and ways of minimizing occupational risks.

Inland Revenue and National Insurance Contributions Office

http://www.inlandrevenue.gov.uk

Detailed information on individual and business tax, including a separate section on self-assessment.

Mortgages Online

http://www.mortgages-online.co.uk

Independent mortgage advice online with links to other independent financial organizations; the site also has a mortgage calculator.

Office of Fair Trading

http://www.oft.gov.uk/

Site of the agency charged with protecting consumers and enforcing UK competition policy. Contains advice to consumers, information on publications, and news items on current investigations and issues.

Oftel

http://www.oftel.gov.uk/

Information on the watchdog agency overseeing Britain's telecommunications industry, with advice to consumers and industry guidelines.

Ofwat – Office of Water Services

http://www.open.gov.uk/ofwat/index.htm

Information on the watchdog agency charged with monitoring and regulating the supply of water in the UK. Includes reports on the efficiency of water and sewerage services, and assistance for aggrieved customers of water companies.

Patent Office – Home Page

http://www.patent.gov.uk/

Guide to the complexity of issues surrounding rights and intellectual property, covering such aspects as patents, trade marks, designs, and copyright. Also gives advice on intellectual property rights on the Internet.

Royal Mail

http://www.royalmail.co.uk

Comprehensive coverage of postal services in the UK, including a postal rates calculator and postal services guide.

Source, The

http://www.statistics.gov.uk/

UK government site that provides easy access to statistics, including demographics.

Trading Standards Central

http://www.tradingstandards.gov.uk/index.htm

Maintained by ITSA, the Institute of Trading Standards Administration, the site includes sections on 'Safety warnings', 'For business', 'For consumers', 'For schools', 'Legislation', and 'Europe'.

UK Passport Agency

http://www.open.gov.uk/ukpass/ukpass.htm

Comprehensive information on eligibility criteria, how to obtain or renew a passport, and regular updates on the approximate waiting time to have one issued.

UK PAYE Tax Calculator

http://listen.to/taxman

A quick, unofficial calculator to work out your personal tax liability. Based on gross income per annum, it includes tax allowances and National Insurance contributions, and provides a breakdown by year, month, and week.

Welsh Consumer Council

http://www.wales.consumer.org.uk/

National consumer body for Wales.

EDUCATION

The Year in Review

July 1999 A study of 20,000 11-year-olds in the UK finds that too much homework may cause primary school pupils to achieve poorer rather than better results, challenging the 'more is better' philosophy of extramural work.

July 1999 The UK government responds to a recruitment crisis in modern language teaching by the launch of 'golden hello' incentives to entice more trainees. One-third of new teaching bursaries go to candidates from overseas.

July 1999 The Catholic Church and the Church of England criticize the lack of spiritual and moral content in the new National Curriculum which will affect pupils from September 2000. They argue that marriage should be mentioned in the areas of personal, social, health, and citizenship education.

16 July 1999 The *Times Educational Supplement* launches an 'Open All Hours' campaign to reverse cuts and improve services at the UK's 4,187 public libraries. Spending on books has declined by more than one-fifth since the late 1980s, and, since 1976, the number of libraries open for 60 hours or more per week has decreased from 173 to 6.

August 1999 The UK government's Disability Rights Task Force announces its proposals that schools not suitably adapted for disabled students may be taken to special needs tribunals.

August 1999 In the UK, this month's record high A level pass rate marks the 17th successive year of improving results, but examiners say that the rise is levelling off.

September 1999 A survey by the National Employer's Organisation for School Teachers reveals that 600 teachers have been dismissed, redeployed, or retired, and 3,000 are under investigation for incompetence.

September 1999 In the UK, new externally assessed Advanced Extension exams for the ablest sixth formers are announced in an experimental launch of 'world class tests' by the government.

October 1999 Conservative Party leader William Hague makes educational reform a key part of the party conference in Blackpool, attacking Labour policies for their 'unnecessary bureaucracy', in an effort to appeal to teachers and parents. A 'Common Sense Education' document released by the Conservative Party proposes that league tables of seven-year-olds' Key stage 1 test scores be published by a future Conservative government.

22 October 1999 According to the *Times Educational Supplement*, a trial scheme returning A level and GCSE papers to students in August found that most pupils seemed reluctant to read them, jeopardizing plans to extend the scheme nationally.

November 1999 In the UK, new figures reveal that primary schools receive an average of £700 less per pupil than secondary schools.

25 November 1999 The Talibaan government of Afghanistan opens the first state schools for girls, around the capital, Kabul.

30 November 1999 The Guru Nanak Sikh primary and secondary school in Hayes, West London, becomes the first state-funded Sikh school in Europe, after a two-year local campaign.

December 1999 Film-maker and Labour peer David Puttnam is chosen by the UK government for the part-time post of chairing the General Teaching Council. The role requires Lord Puttnam, a champion of education, to be an advocate of and encouragement to teachers.

December 1999 Four out of five teachers involved in the UK government's 'zero tolerance' approach to failing schools say they believe the policy is working, but that it is also increasing stress.

3 December 1999 The borough of Islington in London announces a scheme in which 14-year-olds will be paid £3.50 per hour to attend lessons on Saturday mornings to boost their GCSE scores.

January 2000 UK chief inspector of schools Chris Woodhead admits in his New Year Annual Report that longer school hours have not led to an improvement in results.

January 2000 Curriculum advisors ask UK education secretary David Blunkett to allow 14-year-olds to choose vocational courses, currently only available to sixth form and college students, instead of GCSEs.

January 2000 A teaching pack called 'Beyond the Phase: A Practical Guide to Challenging Homophobia in Schools', becomes the centre of controversy in Avon, England, where it is made available in 180 schools. Campaigners in favour of section 28, the law that forbids the promotion of homosexuality in schools, use the pack – which encourages among students an open attitude to homosexuality – to bolster their arguments against the government's plans to scrap the section.

28 January 2000 At its annual conference in Swanwick, Derbyshire, the National Association for the Teaching of English urges teachers to boycott new mathematics tests for student teachers. The same organization spearheaded a successful tests boycott in 1993.

February 2000 In conjunction with the government, the Church of England makes daily school assembly plans available free on the Internet, to help headteachers meet the legal requirement of 200 acts of collective worship per school year.

February 2000 Dr Ian Chalmers of University College London warns that pupils sitting exams in the future may be required to take urine or blood tests if new 'smart drugs', designed to improve intelligence and memory, become available.

March 2000 The UK Qualifications and Curriculum Authority announces that it is considering creating a course similar to the International Baccalaureate, in which students aim for a US-style graduation at age 19.

March 2000 A new UK government initiative is anticipated in which one-stop education, health, and welfare centres are created, based on the model of 'full-service schools' in the USA.

March 2000 Three 'superheads' resign their posts in London schools during a period of less than a week. Ten 'superheads' were appointed as part of the UK government's fresh-start programme for reviving failing schools.

1 March 2000 UK education secretary David Blunkett announces a new policy for schools with low GCSE results – schools failing to meet new targets for three successive years will face the possibility of being relaunched, with all teachers being forced to reapply for their jobs.

21 March 2000 UK chancellor Gordon Brown's budget for 2000 includes an extra £1 billion for schools.

31 March 2000 The continuing teaching recruitment crisis prompts UK government ministers to offer postgraduates up to £10,000 per year while training. This is the first time a salary has been offered to student teachers.

April 2000 Increased anxiety and stress at facing OFSTED inspections is linked to the death by suicide or alcoholism of at least four UK teachers in less than two years.

April 2000 In a £47 million UK government initiative, it is announced that over 1,000 learning support units, or 'sin-bins', for violent and disruptive pupils at risk of exclusion, will be set up in schools by 2002.

April 2000 A new Internet link being pioneered at a comprehensive school in Islington, London, enables parents to track their children's schoolwork and attendance, and e-mail teachers with any questions.

April–May 2000 A United Nations-sponsored education conference in Dakar, Senegal, calls for free, universal access to education by the year 2015. The campaign for better educational opportunities worldwide says there are 125 million children in the world who do not have a school to attend, and that basic education must be funded by the state if education is to be universal. The campaign calculates the cost of achieving global primary education at $8 billion – the amount spent on weapons in a week.

May 2000 In the UK, the Nuffield Inquiry recommends that primary school pupils be taught foreign languages from the age of eight.

May 2000 New statistics reveal that more than one out of six teachers have been verbally or physically threatened by pupils, and one out of eight threatened by parents. There have been approximately one thousand calls to a new helpline by teachers worried about aggressive children or parents.

June 2000 Estelle Morris, UK minister for school standards, tells a conference of educationalists that state schools are failing to identify and improve standards for thousands of gifted and talented children.

21 June 2000 All 12 teachers at a primary school in Chessington, London, resign from their jobs in protest following a critical OFSTED inspection.

29 June 2000 The findings of a United Nations survey reveal that at least 7 million adults in the UK are functionally illiterate.

30 June 2000 Loch Choire Primary in Sutherland, Scotland, the smallest and most remote school in the UK, with the highest per capita cost (£27,000 each year), closes with the departure of 11-year-old Eileen Grant, its only pupil.

19 August 2000 UK A level results are announced: there are a record number of A and B grades and the pass rate reached 88.5% – its highest ever.

25 August 2000 A record 98% pass rate is announced for GCSEs with the proportion of A and A* grades also reaching a record 15.2%.

David Blunkett, UK education secretary, continued his attack on grammar schools in 2000, saying that selection of pupils would increasingly be seen as an anachronism and that he expects grammar schools to have disappeared by 2011. *Syndication International*

World Education

Introduction

This section gives a snapshot of the vast differences in provision of education around the world. In sub-Saharan Africa 43% of children do not attend primary school, whereas in the industrialized countries of the West 98% of children receive primary education. Wealthy countries like the USA and Japan can be seen to put most of their children and young people through an expensive course of education and training, while poorer countries in Africa, which may be spending the same proportion of their wealth on education as the richer countries, spend only a fifth of the world average per inhabitant, and less than one-twentieth of European per capita spending. A similar picture emerges when class sizes are compared.

In some poor countries girls are even more disadvantaged in terms of schooling than boys. Low spending on education at all levels is accompanied by high levels of illiteracy around the world.

Percentage of Children Attending School Around the World

Figures show the number of children enrolled in primary school as a percentage of the total number of children in the primary school age group. Data are for around 1995.

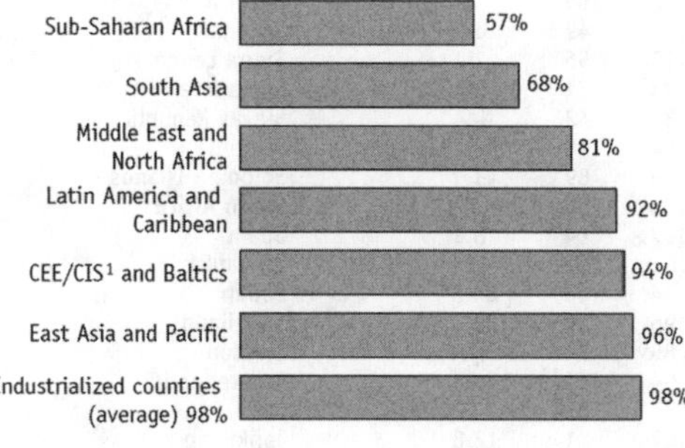

Source: State of the World's Children 1999, © *UNICEF*

Enrolment in Education Worldwide

The data in this table are for the latest year available. Only those countries for which data are available are listed. In some countries a relatively high number of pupils outside the official age range for the respective levels of education attends classes of these levels. Since the enrolment ratio given is for the total enrolment, regardless of age, divided by the population of the official age group, if a country has almost universal education among the school-age population at the first level, the enrolment ratio given will exceed 100. As the school year, in a number of countries, does not coincide with the UK academic year, the year shown in this table is the one in which the school or academic year in that country starts.
(In percentages. N/A = not available.)

Country	Year	1st level[1]	2nd level[2]	3rd level[3]
Afghanistan	1995	49	22	N/A
Albania	1996	107[4]	38[4]	12
Algeria	1996	107	63	12[4]
Angola	1991	88	14	0.7
Argentina	1996	113	77	36.2
Armenia	1996	87	90	12
Australia	1997	101	153	80
Austria	1996	100	103	48
Azerbaijan	1996	106	77	17
Bahamas	1996	98	87	N/A
Bahrain	1996	106	94	20.2[5]
Bangladesh	1990	69	21	4.4
Barbados	1991	90	85[6]	29.4[5]
Belarus	1996	98	93	44
Belgium	1995	103	146	56
Belize	1994	121	49	N/A
Benin	1997	78[10]	18	3[10]
Bolivia	1990	95	37	22.2
Botswana	1996	112	66	5.8
Brazil	1997	125	62	15[10]
Brunei	1996	107	77	6.6
Bulgaria	1996	99	77	41.2
Burkina Faso	1996	40[4]	8[5]	0.9
Burundi	1995	51	7[7]	0.8[13]
Cambodia	1997	113	24	1
Cameroon	1996	85	27[7]	N/A
Canada	1995	102[7]	106	90.2
Cape Verde	1997	148	55	N/A
Central African Republic	1991	58	10	1.4
Chad	1996	65	10	0.6[4]
Chile	1996	101	75	30.3
China	1997	123	70	6
Colombia	1996	113	67	17
Comoros	1995	74	22	0.6
Congo, Democratic Republic of	1994	72	26	2.3
Congo, Republic of the	1995	114	53	N/A
Costa Rica	1998	104	49	30[7]
Côte d'Ivoire	1997	71[10]	25	6[7]
Croatia	1996	87	82	28
Cuba	1996	106	77	12.4
Cyprus	1996	100	97	23
Czech Republic	1995	104	99	24
Denmark	1995	101	121	48
Djibouti	1996	38	14	0.3

(continued)

Enrolment in Education Worldwide *(continued)*

Country	Year	1st level[1]	2nd level[2]	3rd level[3]
Dominican Republic	1996	94	52	23
Ecuador	1996	127	54[7]	N/A
Egypt	1997	101	78	N/A
El Salvador	1997	97	37	18[10]
Eritrea	1996	54	21	1
Estonia	1996	94	104	41.8
Ethiopia	1996	43	12	0.8
Fiji Islands	1992	128	64	11.9[8]
Finland	1996	99	118	74
France	1996	105	111	51
Gambia	1995	77	25	1.7[7]
Georgia	1996	88	77	42
Germany	1996	104	104	47
Ghana	1994	79	36	19
Greece	1996	93	95	47
Guatemala	1997	88	26	8.1[4]
Guinea	1996	53	13	1
Guinea-Bissau	1994	64	N/A	N/A
Guyana	1996	96	73	11
Haiti	1990	56	22	N/A
Honduras	1994	111	32[5]	10
Hong Kong	1995	96	75	21.9[5]
Hungary	1995	104	99	23.8
Iceland	1996	98	109	37
India	1996	101	49	6.9
Indonesia	1996	113	56	11
Iran	1996	98	77	18
Iraq	1995	85	42	N/A
Ireland, Republic of	1996	104	118	41
Israel	1995	99	89	41.1
Italy	1996	101	95	47
Jamaica	1996	107	64[9]	8.1
Japan	1997	101	103[4]	41[7]
Jordan	1992	94	63[6]	24.5[6]
Kazakhstan	1996	96	85	32.7[4]
Kenya	1995	85	24	N/A
Korea, South	1997	94	102[10]	68
Kuwait	1997	77	65	19[10]
Kyrgyzstan	1995	107	81	12.2
Laos	1996	111	29	2.8
Latvia	1996	96	84	33.3
Lebanon	1996	111	82	27[4]
Lesotho	1996	97	29	2.4
Libya	1993	111	98[13]	17[8]
Lithuania	1996	98	86	31.4
Luxembourg[11]	1996	99	88	10
Macedonia, Former Yugoslav Republic of	1996	99	63	20
Madagascar	1995	73	13	2.1
Malawi	1995	135	16	0.6
Malaysia	1997	101	64	12[8]
Maldives	1997	128	69	N/A
Mali	1997	49	13	1
Malta	1996	107	84	29
Mauritania	1996	83	16[4]	3.9[4]
Mauritius	1996	107	65	6.5
Mexico	1996	114	64	16
Moldova	1996	97	80	27
Mongolia	1996	89	56	17
Morocco	1996	84	39	11.1[7]
Mozambique	1995	60	7	0.5
Myanmar	1995	121	30[7]	5.4[7]
Namibia	1997	131	62	8.1[4]
Nepal	1996	113	42	5
Netherlands	1996	108	132	47
New Zealand	1997	101	113	63
Nicaragua	1998	101	57	12
Niger	1997	29	7[10]	N/A
Nigeria	1994	89	30	4.1[5]
Norway	1996	100	118	62
Oman	1997	76	67	8
Pakistan	1991	65	23	3
Panama	1996	105	69	32
Papua New Guinea	1995	80	14	3.2
Paraguay	1997	111	47	10[10]
Peru	1997	123	72	26
Philippines	1997	117	78	29[4]
Poland	1995	96	98	24.7
Portugal	1995	128	111	39
Qatar	1996	86[4]	80[4]	27
Romania	1996	104	78	22.5
Russia	1996	102	94	22
Rwanda	1991	82	11	0.6[6]
Samoa	1997	100	62[10]	N/A
Saudi Arabia	1996	76	61	16.3
Senegal	1997	71	16	3.4[7]
Sierra Leone	1990	50	17	1.3
Singapore	1996	94	72	38.5
Slovak Republic	1996	102	94	22.1
Slovenia	1996	98	92	36
Solomon Islands	1994	97	17	N/A
South Africa	1996	116	84	17.3
Spain	1996	109	120	51
Sri Lanka	1996	109	75[4]	5.1[4]
Sudan	1996	53	20	N/A
Swaziland	1997	117	54[10]	6[10]
Sweden	1996	107	140	50
Switzerland	1995	N/A	N/A	33
Syria	1996	101	42	15.7[7]
Tajikistan	1996	93	76	19.9
Tanzania	1997	66	6	0.6
Thailand	1996	87	56	22
Togo	1996	119	27	3.6
Trinidad and Tobago	1996	99	74[4]	8
Tunisia	1997	118	64	14[10]
Turkey	1996	107	58	21
Turkmenistan	1990	N/A	N/A	21.8
Uganda[12]	1995	74	12	2
UK	1996	116	129	52
Ukraine	1995	87[5]	91[5]	42
United Arab Emirates	1996	89	80	12
Uruguay	1996	109	85	30
USA	1995	102	97	81
Uzbekistan	1994	78	94	32[8]
Vanuatu	1992	98	20	N/A
Venezuela	1996	91	40	28[8]
Vietnam	1997	113	57	7[10]
Yemen	1996	70	34	4.2
Yugoslavia	1996	69	62	22
Zambia	1995	89	28[7]	2.5[7]
Zimbabwe	1997	112	50	7[10]

[1] These figures are for education at the first level, of which the main function is to provide the basic elements of education (for example, at elementary school and primary school).
[2] These figures are for education at the second level, provided at middle school, secondary school, high school, teacher training school at this level, and schools of a vocational or technical nature. This level of education is based upon at least four years' previous instruction at first level and provides general and/or specialized instruction.
[3] These figures are for education at the third level, which is provided at universities, teachers' colleges, and higher professional schools, and which requires, as a minimum condition of entry, the successful completion of education at the second level, or evidence of the attainment of an equivalent level of knowledge.
[4] Figures for 1995.
[5] Figures for 1993.
[6] Figures for 1989.
[7] Figures for 1994.
[8] Figures for 1991.
[9] Figure for 1990.
[10] Figures for 1996.
[11] Some students study in neighbouring countries.
[12] These figures are for government maintained and aided schools.
[13] Figures for 1992.

Source: UNESCO Statistical Yearbook 1999, © *UNESCO 1999*

Public Expenditure on Education by Region of the World

Data for countries of the former USSR are not included in either the world total or regional totals because there is insufficient information to calculate valid estimates for these countries.

Region	Public expenditure on education ($ thousand millions)				Public expenditure on education (% of GNP)				Public expenditure on education per inhabitant ($)			
	1980	1985	1990	1995	1980	1985	1990	1995	1980	1985	1990	1995
Africa	22.9	22.0	25.7	29.1	5.3	5.7	5.6	5.9	48	40	41	41
America	188.6	249.5	374.9	481.7	4.9	4.9	5.2	5.3	307	375	521	623
Asia	93.8	107.6	199.8	302.1	4.0	3.9	3.7	3.6	37	39	66	93
Europe	200.6	165.8	367.5	492.6	5.1	5.1	5.1	5.4	418	340	741	982
Oceania	10.4	10.6	18.6	24.5	5.6	5.6	5.6	6.0	467	439	715	878
World total	516.4	555.6	986.5	1,329.9	4.8	4.8	4.8	4.9	126	124	202	252

Source: UNESCO Statistical Yearbook 1997, © *UNESCO 1997*

Countries with the Most Pupils Per Teacher at First Level of Education

These figures are for education at the first level, of which the main function is to provide the basic elements of education (for example, at elementary school and primary school). Data for each country are for the school year in parentheses and are the most recent available.

Rank	Country	Pupils per teacher
1	Central African Republic (1990–91)	77
2	Congo, Republic of the (1995–96)	70
3	Chad (1996–97)	67
4	Bangladesh (1990)	63
5	Malawi (1995–96)	59
6=	Afghanistan (1994)	58
	Mozambique (1995)	58
	Rwanda (1991–92)	58
9	Benin (1996–97)	56
10	Equatorial Guinea (1993–94)	55

Source: UNESCO Statistical Yearbook 1999, © *UNESCO 1999*

Countries with the Lowest Percentage of Female Enrolment at First Level of Education

These figures are for education at the first level, of which the main function is to provide the basic elements of education (for example, at elementary school and primary school). Data for each country are for the school year in parentheses and are the most recent available.

Rank	Country	Female enrolment (%)
1	Senegal (1995–96)	26
2	Yemen (1996–97)	28
3	Pakistan (1993–94)	31
4	Afghanistan (1995)	32
5	Chad (1996–97)	34
6	Ethiopia (1996–97)	36
7=	Benin (1996–97)	37
	Guinea (1997–98)	37
	Guinea-Bissau (1994–95)	37
10	Niger (1997–98)	39

Source: UNESCO Statistical Yearbook 1999, © *UNESCO 1999*

Literacy Levels in Selected Developed Countries

In England, about one adult in five is not functionally literate and many more people have problems with numeracy. Some seven million adults in England (one in five adults) if given the alphabetical index of the Yellow Pages, cannot locate the page reference for plumbers. That is an example of functional illiteracy. It means that one in five adults has a lower level of literacy than that expected of an 11-year-old child. The data in this table (based on official surveys) are inevitably estimates, and may be a little on the high side: but the order of magnitude is certainly right.

1998

Country	% of adults with low literacy
Poland	44
Ireland, Republic of	24
UK	23
USA	22
New Zealand	20
Switzerland (German)	19
Australia	17
Belgium	17
Canada	17
Switzerland (French)	17
Germany	12
Netherlands	10
Sweden	7

Source: The Moser Report, © *Crown copyright 1999*

Countries with the Fewest Pupils Per Teacher at First Level of Education

These figures are for education at the first level, of which the main function is to provide the basic elements of education (for example, at elementary school and primary school). Data for each country are for the year in parentheses and are the most recent available.

Rank	Country	Pupils per teacher
1	San Marino (1996–97)	5
2	Qatar (1995–96)	9
3	Denmark (1994–95)	10
4=	Hungary (1994–95)	11
	Italy (1995–96)	11
6=	Austria (1996–97)	12
	Belgium (1993–94)	12
	Bermuda (1996–97)	12
	Cuba (1996–97)	12
	Libya (1992–93)	12
	Portugal (1993–94)	12
	Sweden (1996–97)	12
13=	Martinique (1995–96)	13
	Saudi Arabia (1996–97)	13

Source: UNESCO Statistical Yearbook 1999, © *UNESCO 1999*

World Illiteracy Rates: Highest 25 Countries

The percentages in this table are all estimates.

2000

Rank	Country	Illiterates (%)
1	Niger	84.3
2	Burkina Faso	77.0
3=	Afghanistan	63.7
	Sierra Leone	63.7
5	Gambia	63.5
6	Guinea-Bissau	63.2
7	Senegal	62.7
8	Benin	62.5
9	Ethiopia	61.3
10	Mauritania	60.1
11	Mali	59.7
12	Bangladesh	59.2
13	Guinea	58.9
14	Nepal	58.6
15	Pakistan	56.7
16	Mozambique	56.2
17	Yemen	53.8
18	Central African Republic	53.5
19	Côte d'Ivoire	53.2
20	Bhutan	52.7
21	Burundi	51.9
22	Haiti	51.4
23	Morocco	51.1
24	Djibouti	48.6
25	Liberia	46.6

Source: UNESCO Statistical Yearbook 1999, © *UNESCO 1999*

Number of Illiterate Adults by Gender and Region

Figures given are estimated. Percentages given are percentages of illiterate population.

	1980	1990	2000
World			
Total (millions)	880	882	876
Male (percentage)	37	36	36
Female (percentage)	63	64	64
Southern Asia			
Total (millions)	345	389	429
Male (percentage)	40	39	37
Female (percentage)	60	61	63
Eastern Asia/Pacific			
Total (millions)	277	233	185
Male (percentage)	32	30	27
Female (percentage)	68	70	73
Sub-Saharan Africa			
Total (millions)	126	138	142
Male (percentage)	40	39	39
Female (percentage)	60	61	61
Middle East and North Africa			
Total (millions)	56	63	68
Male (percentage)	38	37	36
Female (percentage)	62	63	64
Latin America/Caribbean			
Total (millions)	44	42	42
Male (percentage)	44	44	45
Female (percentage)	56	56	55
Developed countries			
Total (millions)	29	17	11
Male (percentage)	28	33	38
Female (percentage)	72	67	62

Source: UNESCO Statistical Yearbook 1999, © *UNESCO 1999*

UK Schools and Teachers

Organization of Schools in the UK

School education in the UK is a national service administered locally. This means that policies enacted by the national government at Westminster are put into practice by local education authorities (LEAs) in England and Wales, education authorities (EAs) in Scotland, and education and library boards in Northern Ireland. These are part of the democratic system of borough and county councils.

Under the 1979–97 Conservative administration some schools were given greater autonomy, but the Labour government brought these grant-maintained schools back into a more direct relationship with their LEAs as 'foundation' schools. Funding advantages for such schools have been phased out.

State schools have boards of governors drawn from parents, the LEA, and the local community. The governors are responsible for school policy and for overseeing the school's budget. The head teacher is responsible for the day-to-day running of the school and for discipline.

Seven per cent of British children attend fee-paying private schools, which range from famous 'public' schools like Eton and Harrow, run as non-profit making charities, to small private establishments run as businesses. Many private schools have a highly selective intake and are very successful in public examinations.

Number of Primary, Secondary, and Special Schools in the UK

(N/A = not available.)

Type of school	1986–87	1988–89	1990–91	1992–93	1993–94	1994–95	1995–96	1996–97[1]	1997–98[1]
Public Sector Mainstream									
Primary									
Total	24,609	24,344	24,135	23,829	23,673	23,516	23,426	23,306	23,213
of which grant maintained	N/A	N/A	N/A	75	265	415	453	489	514
Secondary[2]									
Total	5,091	4,894	4,790	4,648	4,496	4,479	4,462	4,439	4,435
of which grant maintained	N/A	N/A	50	266	564	634	654	665	686
of which sixth form colleges	N/A	N/A	N/A	119	N/A	N/A	N/A	N/A	N/A
Non-maintained mainstream									
Total	2,544	2,542	2,508	2,476	2,478	2,433	2,436	2,523	2,501
of which City Technology Colleges (CTCs)	N/A	N/A	N/A	14	15	15	15	15	15
Special									
Total	1,915	1,873	1,830	1,768	1,742	1,749	1,567	1,529	1,518
Maintained									
Total	N/A	N/A	N/A	N/A	1,670	1,638	1,458	1,429	1,420
of which grant maintained	N/A	N/A	N/A	N/A	N/A	2	9	18	21
Non-maintained	N/A	N/A	N/A	N/A	72	111	109	100	98
Pupil Referral Units									
Total	N/A	N/A	N/A	N/A	N/A	N/A	287	333	333

[1] Figures are provisional. They include 1995–96 schools data for Wales.
[2] From 1 April 1993, figures exclude sixth form colleges in England and Wales as these colleges were reclassified as further education colleges.

Source: Annual Abstract of Statistics 2000, © *Crown copyright 2000*

Public Examinations and Testing in the UK

British schoolchildren are subjected to more external assessment than any others in the world. Since the introduction of the National Curriculum, pupils have been assessed at the ages of 7 (8 in Northern Ireland), 11, and 14, by a combination of teacher assessment and national tests that are externally marked. Public examinations follow at 16 and 18 (in Scotland at 16 and 17).

From September 1999 a new level of assessment was introduced for children starting school at the age of five. This 'base-line assessment', conducted in the reception class by teachers, covers six areas: personal and social development, language and literacy, mathematical development, knowledge and understanding of the world, physical development, and creative development. Schemes are being developed locally, but must be accredited by the national body responsible for the implementation of the National Curriculum and assessment regulations.

There is some debate about the desirability of introducing children under 5 to the more formal aspects of literacy. This introduction is becoming more widespread, as just over half of 4-year-olds now join primary school reception classes rather than traditional nursery classes or pre-school groups.

The Key Stage tests are related to the attainment targets in the National Curriculum for English and mathematics at the age of 7, and for English, mathematics, and science at 11 and 14. Other National Curriculum subjects are not tested. The expectation is that a typical 7-year-old will have reached Level 2, a typical 11-year-old Level 4, and a typical 14-year-old Level 5 or 6. Special arrangements are made to accommodate the minority of children who are unlikely to reach these levels, or will significantly exceed them. A National Literacy Hour and a National Numeracy Hour have been introduced to primary schools as a means of ensuring that children reach government targets of 80% at Level 2 in English and 75% at Level 2 in mathematics by 2002.

British children go through a dual system of school-leaving examination. This consists of General Certificate of Secondary Education (GCSE) examinations (Scottish Certificate of Education (SCE) Standard grade in Scotland) taken at 16, and General Certificate of Education (GCE) A Level examinations taken at 18 (SCE Highers at 17 in Scotland). There is also a parallel system of vocational qualifications: General National Vocational Qualifications (GNVQs) and General Scottish Vocational Qualifications (GSVQs). The Scottish school system is in the course of introducing a joint system of academic and vocational qualifications at 17.

It is expected that the majority of children will sit a GCSE examination in most of the ten National Curriculum subjects. Young people intending to study at university usually require three A Levels or five Scottish Higher subjects, and entry to a degree course is dependent upon their performance in these. Vocational qualifications are also accepted as a qualification for higher education and are regarded as particularly appropriate for students wanting to study for a vocational diploma or degree course.

The Best- and Worst-Performing Local Education Authorities at SATs for 11-Year-Olds

English local education authorities, ranked by the aggregate of the average scores achieved by their primary schools in 1999's National Curriculum tests for 11-year-olds. The first three columns show the average proportion of pupils who achieved the expected level for their age in English, mathematics, and science. This is followed by their aggregate score. Ties are broken alphabetically.

Rank	LEA	English %	Maths %	Science %	Aggregate
Best					
1	Isles of Scilly	89.3	89.3	96.4	275.0
2	London, City of	81.5	81.5	96.3	259.3
3	Richmond-upon-Thames	82.5	80.4	87.9	250.7
4	Wokingham	80.8	77.2	87.3	245.3
5	Rutland	78.4	77.6	85.3	241.4
6	Surrey	77.9	76.0	86.3	240.2
7	Bury	77.4	75.9	85.1	238.4
8	Havering	78.2	75.7	84.3	238.3
9	Sefton	77.0	76.9	83.4	237.3
10	Hertfordshire	77.3	74.9	85.0	237.2
Worst					
1	Hackney	53.4	54.8	59.2	167.4
2	Nottingham, City of	53.9	53.2	63.6	170.6
3	Newham	53.9	59.0	65.0	177.8
4	Bradford	59.3	55.0	65.5	179.8
5	Sandwell	58.7	55.9	65.8	180.4
6	Southwark	57.7	57.4	67.1	182.2
7	Greenwich	58.4	59.0	70.6	187.9
8=	Haringey	60.2	60.4	68.0	188.6
	Tower Hamlets	57.3	62.1	69.2	188.6
10	Kingston-upon-Hull	58.2	60.6	71.2	190.0

Source: The Telegraph

The Best- and Worst-Performing Local Education Authorities at GCSE

Best

Rank	LEA	% of pupils gaining five or more GCSEs grade A* to C
1	Isles of Scilly	66.7
2	Buckinghamshire	59.5
3	Kingston-upon-Thames	58.6
4	Sutton	57.9
5	Windsor and Maidenhead	57.2
6=	North Yorkshire	56.3
	Barnet	56.3
8	Wokingham	56.2
9	Bromley	55.4
10=	Redbridge	54.7
	Gloucestershire	54.7

Worst

Rank	LEA	% of pupils gaining five or more GCSEs grade A* to C
1	Kingston-upon-Hull	22.8
2	Knowsley	22.9
3	Islington	23.3
4	Nottingham	26.1
5	Hackney	26.5
6	Haringey	26.6
7	Middlesbrough	27.5
8	Tower Hamlets	27.6
9=	Manchester	28.7
	Sandwell	28.7

Source: The Audit Commission, © *Crown copyright 1999*

Comprehensive or Selective Education – Who Gets to Choose?

by Maureen O'Connor

The change from selective to nonselective secondary education in England, from a system of secondary modern and grammar schools to comprehensive schools, is one of the great pieces of unfinished political business that has spilled from the 20th to the 21st century. It is a curiously English problem. Scotland and Wales have provided secondary education through a wholly comprehensive system for 30 years. Northern Ireland has retained the Eleven Plus examination and grammar schools, and the issue only became a live one during the recent power-sharing executive.

The Size of the Issue The 'problem' of grammar schools generates political heat out of all proportion to its size. There are now only 164 grammar schools remaining in a secondary system of more than 2,000 schools in England. Only 36 local education authorities out of more than 100 have any grammar schools at all, and only 15 have sufficient to be able to run a system that separates out significant numbers of 'academic' children from the rest.

Arguments Against Selection The abolition of grammar schools began in the 1960s for two main reasons: firstly, because the Eleven Plus testing system, which divided children between different kinds of schools, was proving extremely inaccurate and was widely regarded as unfair; and secondly, educationists and politicians of all parties realized that, in a rapidly changing society, a system which excluded many children from the opportunity of taking certain public examinations and studying some subjects, was not in the national interest. The objective was to provide schools which would allow children of all abilities to achieve their full potential.

Into the Political Arena The move towards comprehensive education was not at first politically contentious, with only middle-class parents campaigning against what they regarded as second-class schools. Amongst the most enthusiastic supporters of comprehensive reform were some of the rural, mainly Conservative-controlled, local education authorities, who saw good sense in running fewer, larger secondary schools catering for all the children in a district. During her time as secretary of state for education, Margaret Thatcher approved the closure of more grammar schools than any other education minister. However, by the 1970s some local authorities had taken issue with a Labour government keen to complete the reform by legislation, and under the Conservative administration of the 1980s and 1990s the surviving grammar schools were protected.

Education by Ballot It might have been expected that the Labour government elected in 1997 would have completed the reform to which the party had become deeply committed while in opposition. It might also have been expected that opposition to change might have become more muted, as all secondary schools became more similar with the introduction of a National Curriculum and a national system of Standard Assessment Tests (SATs) at key stages. However, support for grammar schools remained strong in areas like Kent and Buckinghamshire where they survived. To the disappointment of many of Labour's supporters, including some parents in areas where grammar schools remain, the Labour government did not choose to impose abolition. Instead it introduced a complex system of parental ballots in areas which still had grammar schools. The first of these, in the North Yorkshire town of Ripon, saw the local grammar school survive by a significant majority of the votes cast. Further ballots are expected later in 2000, although concerns have been raised regarding the balloting system, which excludes some parents affected by grammar school selection from voting.

Does Selection Work? Forty years after comprehensive education in England entered the political debate, the two questions that sparked the reform in the first place remain unresolved: is the Eleven Plus a fair method of selection and does selective education improve the performance of children where it is practised? Argument on both issues continues and the latest evidence does not give comfort to grammar school supporters. In Northern Ireland, where the future of grammar schools has recently moved up the political agenda, new research by Professor John Gardner at Queen's University in Belfast, entitled 'Testing the Test', suggests that more than two-thirds of children taking the Eleven Plus examination may be wrongly classified. As to improved performance, the supporters of grammar schools have long claimed that teaching children of proven academic ability in separate schools boosts their results. This is difficult to substantiate because of the different social composition in the local authority areas, and it is increasingly under question according to recent evidence. The local authorities with the most grammar schools do not necessarily do well in the 'league tables' of local authority performance. The county of Kent, for instance, which is wholly selective, boasts high-achieving grammar schools along-side very poorly performing secondary modern schools, producing average results for the county overall. A new study by Professor David Jesson at York University of progress made by 500,000 children in the two years between Key Stage 3 SATs and General Certificate of Secondary Education (GCSE) examinations, suggests that children in selective areas do significantly less well than those in comprehensive areas. In terms of 'value added' between the two tests of performance, none of the 15 authorities with large numbers of grammar schools was in the top ten local authorities and four were in the bottom ten.

Grammar Schools of the Future? If past conflicts are anything to go by, the debate of comprehensive versus grammar school education will not be resolved by reason alone. Passions still run high where grammar schools are concerned. What is perhaps most interesting is that no local authority that has closed them has ever persuaded parents or its electors that it is a good idea to introduce them again.

Inspection of Schools in the UK

Schools in England are regularly inspected by the Office for Standards in Education (OFSTED). Scotland, Wales, and Northern Ireland have their own systems of inspection. Inspections in Scotland are organized by the Scottish Office Education and Industry Department (SOEID), in Wales by the Education and Culture Department of the National Assembly for Wales, and in Northern Ireland by the Department of Education for Northern Ireland (DENI). However, the processes of inspection are broadly similar throughout the UK. OFSTED is an independent government department separate from the Department for Education and Employment (DfEE), and headed by Her Majesty's Chief Inspector of Schools. Its main task is to manage a system of regular inspection for England's 24,000 schools. All state schools, and pre-schools in receipt of public funds, are inspected on a four-year cycle, and inspection reports are published.

Inspections are carried out by independent teams of inspectors led by OFSTED-trained registered inspectors; the teams include one lay member. Teams will vary in number according to the size of a school, but as many as 14 may be needed for a large secondary school inspection. Inspection contracts are won by competitive tender and inspections are carried out according to a published national framework. Parents are involved in the process by invitation to a pre-inspection meeting and by being sent a summary copy of the inspection report. Inspection covers all aspects of a school's life from financial management and governance to teaching quality. A school is required to respond to its inspection report by producing an action plan to rectify any areas deemed below standard.

The inspection process is underpinned by Her Majesty's Inspectorate, employed by OFSTED, to regulate and monitor the education system, and to inspect other aspects of the system such as independent schools, teacher training, LEAs, and aspects of further education.

Consultation began in autumn 1998 on a new system of school inspection, which would allow schools that are recognized to be performing well to operate with a lighter inspection regime.

School League Tables

The publication of school examination and test results was introduced by the Conservative government in the early 1990s. The theory was that if performance became public knowledge, failing schools would either make greater efforts to improve, or parents would abandon them in favour of more successful institutions, and the under-achieving schools would eventually wither and die.

Almost a decade later, it is clear that the mass of information now made available to parents about SATs, GCSE, and A level results, and about such matters as truancy and rates of improvement, has not affected education in the ways anticipated.

There are several reasons for this. The first is that the mechanisms of school choice have simply never allowed a genuine market (whether or not such a thing is desirable) to work. Successful schools often cannot expand because they do not have the space to accommodate more children. Less successful schools continue to attract pupils either because for some families, particularly in rural areas or for those without a car, they are the only practical choice, or because some parents do not regard academic results as the only mark of a good school.

Secondly, statistics that present raw examination results produce a table that has the most selective (and often private) schools at the top, and those that admit children with the greatest problems at the bottom. At first, every school was included in the tables. Highly selective independent and state grammar schools, and some semi-comprehensive schools, dominated the top of the tables, while at the bottom were special schools for learning-disabled and disturbed children. Since then, the Department for Education and Employment (DfEE) and Her Majesty's Inspectorate, through OFSTED, have accepted that, if comparisons are to be made and be meaningful, like must be compared with like. Even the newspapers have responded by drawing up leagues of 'best' independent and state schools separately, and by distinguishing between selective private and grammar schools and comprehensive schools.

Beacon Schools

Beacon schools are schools selected by the government as those that, in its judgement, provide high-quality education for their pupils. The Beacon schools then disseminate information and advice on their methods to other schools. Factors other than examination results are taken into account in the selection of Beacon schools – for example, the location of a school, and the social background of the majority of its pupils. In order to be eligible for Beacon status, a school can be reported as a high-performing school by OFSTED, show improvement in performance relative to the school's circumstances, or be nominated by a Local Education Authority. There are currently 250 Beacon schools; another 300 will join the scheme in 2000.

The real difficulty in using the tables as some sort of indication of school quality is what to make of apparently similar schools that produce dissimilar results.

Only about a quarter of comprehensive schools have pupils from a representatively wide range of socio-economic groups. Intakes reflect the communities served by the schools. A school in a leafy suburb will admit a disproportionate number of children from middle-class homes, who are very likely to do well in exams. An inner-city school will take in a disproportionate number of children who, for example, live in poor housing, or who may not speak English at home.

As a result, it is possible to conclude that an inner-city school half of whose pupils gain five good GCSE passes is excelling, while a suburban school with the same results is probably under-achieving. LEAs in prosperous areas consistently perform better in these leagues than do those in areas with serious social problems.

As children are now tested at regular intervals during their school careers, and will soon be assessed when they enter school, it should, in theory, be easier to assess how much progress they are making between tests. This should allow judgements to be made more fairly about whether or not a school is enabling its pupils to do better than expected. In experimental league tables that take social factors into account, the higher performers seldom come out as well, and some apparent failures look distinctly successful.

All that can be certain from the data produced by the DfEE is that performance at GCSE and A Level continues to improve. However, the best-performing LEAs are actually improving more quickly than the poor performers, so the gap is widening. In primary schools, improvement in literacy and numeracy, as measured by the National Curriculum tests, has not been consistent.

Improving Schools in England

If a school is deemed to be 'failing', it is put under 'special measures' by OFSTED, and is required to produce and implement a detailed action plan. Inspectors return to assess progress, and standards are generally expected to improve rapidly if the school is to avoid closure. Two years is generally accepted as the maximum time allowed to demonstrate clear improvement.

The reasons for these differences in performance still seem to be much more closely related to the sort of children admitted by schools than to any other factor defined by league tables.

The Top 10 State Schools at A level

The average point score is calculated by assigning points to each pass grade at A level per pupil.

Rank	School	Average point score in 1999
1	Colchester Royal Grammar School (Colchester, Essex)	34.6
2	King Edward VI Camp Hill School (Boys) (Birmingham)	33.6
3	Chelmsford County High School for Girls (Chelmsford, Essex)	33.5
4	King Edward VI Grammar School (Chelmsford, Essex)	33.2
5	Lancaster Royal Grammar School (Lancaster, Lancashire)	33.0
6	Colyton Grammar School (Colyton, Devon)	32.0
7	Colchester County High School for Girls (Colchester, Essex)	31.0
8	King Edward VI Handsworth School (Birmingham)	30.9
9	Pate's Grammar School (Cheltenham, Gloucestershire)	30.7
10	King Edward VI Camp Hill Girls' School (Birmingham)	30.6

Source: © *The Independent 2000*

The Worst 10 State Schools at A level

The average point score is calculated by assigning points to each pass grade at A level per pupil.

Rank	School	Average point score in 1999
1=	William Farr Church of England Comprehensive School (Lincoln, Lincolnshire)	22.7
	Droitwich Spa High School (Droitwich Spa, Worcestershire)	22.7
	Chosen Hill School (Gloucester, Gloucestershire)	22.7
4	High School for Girls (Gloucester, Gloucestershire)	22.8
5=	The Judd School (Tonbridge, Kent)	22.9
	Lady Lumley's School (Pickering, North Yorkshire)	22.9
	King Edward VI School Lichfield (Lichfield, Staffordshire)	22.9
8=	St Nicholas Catholic High School (Northwich, Cheshire)	23.0
	Sir Henry Floyd Grammar School (Aylesbury, Buckinghamshire)	23.0
10	The Chase (Malvern, Worcestershire)	23.1

Source: © *The Independent 2000*

The Top 10 State Schools at GCSE

Rank	School (LEA)	% of pupils with 5 A*–C GCSEs in 1999
1	Brooke Weston City Technology College (Corby, Northamptonshire)	82.1
2	Thomas Telford School (Telford, Telford and Wrekin)	72.6
3	Emmanuel City Technology College (Gateshead)	70.2
4	The Coopers' Company and Coborn School (Upminster, Havering)	61.2
5	Millais School (Horsham, West Sussex)	61.1
6	Lady Margaret School (London, Hammersmith and Fulham)	60.5
7	The London Oratory School (London, Hammersmith and Fulham)	59.3
8	The King's School (Peterborough)	59.0
9	Old Swinford Hospital (Stourbridge, Dudley)	58.6
10	The Hertfordshire and Essex High School (Bishop's Stortford, Hertfordshire)	58.5

Source: © *The Independent 2000*

The Worst 10 State Schools at GCSE

Rank	School (LEA)	% of pupils with 5 A*–C GCSEs in 1999
1	Gillingham Community College (Medway)	0
2	William Crane Comprehensive School (Nottingham)	2
3	Amy Johnson School (Hull)	2
4	Merrywood School (Bristol)	3
5	Copperfields College (Leeds)	3
6	All Hallows Roman Catholic High School (Liverpool)	4
7	High View School and Technology Centre (Derby)	4
8	Battersea Technical College (London, Wandsworth)	4
9	Windsor High School (Salford)	4
10	Herries School (Sheffield)	4

Source: © *The Independent 2000*

Inspecting the Inspectors

Most schools are satisfied with the way they have been inspected by OFSTED, but the consequences of a bad report can be devastating. Some schools have felt that the inspection process and the inspectors have treated them unfairly or have provided a poor level of service. To register a complaint about an OFSTED inspection you can:

complain to the team leader during the inspection;

complain to the inspection contractor;

make a formal written complaint to OFSTED.

If you are dissatisfied by the way your complaint has been handled you can contact the OFSTED complaints adjudicator, and, finally, the parliamentary ombudsman.

There are OFSTED telephone helplines: (020) 7421 6673 (advice about procedures); (020) 7421 6680 (for concerns about inspectors' conduct).

For further information you can telephone the OFSTED publications centre on (020) 7510 0180.

Education Action Zones

Growing concern about the performance of schools in some deprived inner-city areas has led the Labour government to set up Education Action Zones. Schools in these areas are run by partnerships that involve business and industry as well as the local education authority (LEA). The schools are encouraged to innovate and experiment in an effort to raise standards.

National Curriculum Key Stages

Pupils' year groups are labelled year 1 to year 11 and within these years learning is divided into four key stages.

Key stage	School year	Age
1	reception	4–5
	year 1	5–6
	year 2	6–7
2	year 3	7–8
	year 4	8–9
	year 5	9–10
	year 6	10–11
3	year 7	11–12
	year 8	12–13
	year 9	13–14
4 (GCSE)	year 10	14–15
	year 11	15–16

The National Curriculum

A National Curriculum was established by the Education Reform Act of 1988. This laid down detailed programmes of study for all the ten main subjects, together with a system of levels of performance that a typical child might be expected to attain between the ages of 5 and 16. Learning is divided into four key stages: for children aged between 5 and 7, 7 and 11, 11 and 14, and 14 and 16.

The amount of work demanded by the National Curriculum was reduced after an inquiry conducted by Sir Ron Dearing in 1996. In 1997 the Labour government relaxed the requirements for humanities and arts subjects in primary schools in order to allow more time to be spent on English, mathematics, and science. The whole National Curriculum was revised for the year 2000.

■ UK Schools and Teachers

Standard Assessment Tests (SATs)

There are three formal 'key stages' of assessment for school pupils in England, Wales, and Northern Ireland before the General Certificate of Secondary Education (GCSE). Key Stage 1 tests are taken at the age of 7 (8 in Northern Ireland), Key Stage 2 at 11, and Key Stage 3 at 14. The tests at all key stages include the core subjects of English, mathematics, and science (and Welsh in Welsh-speaking schools in Wales). An average 7-year-old is expected to attain level 2, an 11-year-old level 4, and a 14-year-old between levels 5 and 6. National tests in English and mathematics are taken at five stages in Scottish Schools.

In 1999 boys did not perform as well as girls at all key stages in all subjects in teacher assessments. However, roughly the same proportions of boys and girls achieved the expected level in tests for mathematics at Key Stages 2 and 3. The proportion of pupils reaching expected levels tends to fall with age for both genders, with the biggest drop between Key Stages 1 and 2.

SATs Results by Key Stage and Gender in England

According to government targets, a typical 11-year-old is expected to achieve level 4 on the National Curriculum scale. By 2002, 75% are expected to attain level 4 in mathematics and 80% to attain level 4 in English. Figures indicate pupils reaching or exceeding expected standards by key stage and gender.
(In percentages. – = not applicable.)

Subject	1994				1997				1998				1999			
	Teacher assessments		Tests		Teacher assessments		Tests		Teacher assessments		Tests		Teacher assessments		Tests	
	Males	Females	Males	Females	Males	Females	Males	Females	Males	Females	Males	Females	Males	Females	Males	Females
Key Stage 1[1]																
English	75	88	–	–	75	85	–	–	76	86	–	–	78	87	–	–
Maths	79	83	–	–	82	86	82	85	83	87	83	86	84	88	85	88
Science	85	87	–	–	84	86	–	–	85	87	–	–	85	88	–	–
Key Stage 2[2]																
English	–	–	–	–	57	70	57	70	59	72	57	73	61	73	64	75
Maths	–	–	–	–	63	65	63	61	64	66	59	58	68	69	68	68
Science	–	–	–	–	68	70	68	69	70	72	70	69	74	75	78	78
Key Stage 3[3]																
English	55	72	49	69	52	70	48	67	53	71	56	73	55	73	54	72
Maths	62	67	60	63	62	65	60	60	62	65	60	59	63	65	62	62
Science	63	65	64	63	60	63	61	60	60	63	57	55	59	62	55	55

[1] Percentage of pupils achieving level 2 or above.
[2] Percentage of pupils achieving level 4 or above.
[3] Percentage of pupils achieving level 5 or above.

Data from *the Department for Education and Employment.*

GCE, GCSE, SCE, and GNVQ/GSVQ Qualifications Attained by Pupils and Students in the UK

Qualifications attained	1995–96[2]	1996–97[2]	1997–98[3]
All pupils[1]			
Pupils with GCE Advanced (A) level/SCE Higher (H) grade passes or equivalent[4]			
2 or more A, 3 or more H[5]	204,000	219,000	260,000
1 A, 1 or 2 H	78,000	77,000	70,000[6]
Pupils with GCSE or equivalent[7]			
5 or more A*–C/1–3 grades[7]	331,000	333,000	335,000
1–4 A*–C/1–3 grades[8 9]	372,000	359,000	336,000
No grade A*–C but at least 1 grade D–G[10 11]	237,000	240,000	234,000
No graded results	51,000	53,000	47,000
Females			
Pupils with GCE A Level/SCE H grade passes or equivalent[4]			
2 or more A, 3 or more H[5]	109,000	118,000	141,000
1 A, 1 or 2 H	44,000	43,000	40,000[6]
Pupils with GCSE or equivalent[7]			
5 or more A*–C/1–3 grades[7]	180,000	181,000	182,000
1–4 A*–C/1–3 grades[8 9]	196,000	189,000	174,000
No grade A*–C but at least 1 grade D–G[10 11]	106,000	107,000	104,000
No graded results	26,000	26,000	24,000
Males			
Pupils with GCE A Level/SCE H grade passes or equivalent[4]			
2 or more A, 3 or more H[5]	95,000	101,000	119,000
1 A, 1 or 2 H	34,000	33,000	30,000[6]

(continued)

GCE, GCSE, SCE, and GNVQ/GSVQ Qualifications Attained by Pupils and Students in the UK (*continued*)

Qualifications attained	1995–96[2]	1996–97[2]	1997–98[3]
Pupils with GCSE or equivalent[7]			
5 or more A*–C/1–3 grades[7]	151,000	152,000	153,000
1–4 A*–C/1–3 grades[8] [9]	175,000	170,000	162,000
No grade A*–C but at least 1 grade D–G[10] [11]	131,000	134,000	129,000
No graded results	25,000	26,000	23,000

[1] Of all ages.
[2] Schools only for Scotland and Northern Ireland.
[3] GCSE data for Northern Ireland relate to schools only; figures, other than 5 or more grades A*–C, refer to 1996–97.
[4] 2 AS level count as 1 A level pass. A levels only counted for Northern Ireland.
[5] Includes Advanced level GNVQ/GSVQ. An Advanced GNVQ/GSVQ is equivalent to 2 GCE A levels or AS equivalent/3 SCE Higher grades.
[6] Data for Northern Ireland relate to FE colleges only.
[7] Includes Intermediate and Foundation level GNVQ/GSVQ.
[8] GNVQ/GSVQ Intermediate Part 1, Full, and language unit are equivalent to 2, 4, and 0.5 GCSE grades A*–C/SCE Standard grades 1–3 respectively. Figures include those with 4.5 GCSEs.
[9] Includes pupils with 1 AS level for England and Wales and 1 SCE Higher grade for Scotland.
[10] Grades D–G at GCSE and Scottish SCE Standard grades 4–7.
[11] GNVQ/GSVQ Foundation Part 1, Full, and language unit are equivalent to 2, 4, and 0.5 GCSE grades D–G/SCE Standard grades 4–7 respectively.

Source: Annual Abstract of Statistics 2000, © *Crown copyright 2000*

A Level and Highers Results by Gender in the UK

Figures indicate pupils with GCE A level/SCE H grade passes or equivalent.

Grades	1976–77[1]	1986–87	1991–92	1993–94	1995–96[2]	1997–98[3]
Males						
2 or more A, 3 or more H	63,000	66,000	75,000	67,000	95,000	119,000
1 A, 1 or 2 H	16,000	16,000	15,000	23,000	34,000	30,000
Females						
2 or more A, 3 or more H	51,000	62,000	82,000	72,000	109,000	141,000
1 A, 1 or 2 H	17,000	18,000	16,000	27,000	44,000	40,000

[1] Excluding Northern Ireland.
[2] Data for Scotland and Northern Ireland relate to schools only.
[3] Data for Northern Ireland relate to FE colleges only.

Source: Annual Abstract of Statistics 2000, © *Crown copyright 2000*

Examination Achievements of Pupils in Schools by Region

In percentages.

1997–98 Region	2 or more GCE A levels[1]		5 or more GCSEs grades A*–C[2]		No graded GCSEs[2]	
	Males	Females	Males	Females	Males	Females
North East	19	25	35	43	10	7
North West	25	31	39	49	9	6
Yorkshire and the Humber	22	27	36	46	10	7
East Midlands	26	32	40	51	7	5
West Midlands	25	31	38	48	8	6
East	31	36	46	56	6	4
London	26	33	40	51	8	5
South East	32	39	47	58	7	5
South West	28	37	46	57	6	4
England	27	33	41	52	8	5
Wales	23	30	40	51	11	8
Scotland	25	33	50	61	5	4
GREAT BRITAIN	26	33	42	52	8	5

[1] Pupils aged 17 to 19 at the end of the school year in England and Wales as a percentage of the 18-year-old population. For Scotland the figures relate to pupils in years S5/S6 gaining three or more SCE Higher passes as a percentage of the 17-year-old population.
[2] Pupils aged 16 at the end of the school year in England and Wales as a percentage of the 15-year-old population at the start of the school year. For Scotland, pupils are in year S4.

Data from *the Department for Education and Employment.*

School Testing and Examinations in England and Wales: Key Dates

1944 The Butler Education Act introduces universal secondary education to the age of 15 (raised to 16 in 1972), with three types of secondary schools: selective grammar schools (for around 20% of pupils), technical schools (for around 5%), for 'technically minded' pupils, and less intellectually rigorous secondary moderns (for the remaining 75%). Entrance to the state-funded grammar schools is by means of an '11-plus' examination, taken at the age of 11.

1948 Middlesex County Council establishes 3 'comprehensive' schools, in Hillingdon and Potters Bar, modelled on the US high school system. Entrance to the new type of school is not based on the '11-plus'.

■ UK Schools and Teachers

School Testing and Examinations in England and Wales: Key Dates *(continued)*

1951 General Certificate of Education (GCE) is introduced. First announced in April 1948 it replaces School and Higher School certificates.

1964 The Schools Council for the Curriculum and Examinations (SCCE) is set up.

1965 Certificate of Secondary Education (CSE) is introduced. The Labour government issues *Circular 10/65* calling upon all local authorities to submit proposals for establishing secondary-level, non-selective comprehensive schools, absorbing existing state grammar, secondary modern, and technical schools.

1970 The new Conservative government issues *Circular 10/70* which stresses that reorganization of secondary education is entirely a matter for local authorities.

1974 Labour's education secretary, Reg Prentice, proposes abolition of the 11-plus examination and establishment of a fully comprehensive school system.

1976 Labour's Education Act in England and Wales requires those Local Education Authorities (LEAs) who have not introduced comprehensive education to plan to do so.

1977 The Department of Education floats the idea of national testing of children in mathematics, reading, and writing.

1978 The Waddell Committee recommends a new examination in England and Wales to replace the CSE and GCE O level, taken at the age of 16.

1980 The Conservative government's Education Act repeals Labour's 1976 comprehensive school legislation, freeing LEAs from the obligation to introduce non-selective comprehensive education in England and Wales. At this date, around four-fifths of the secondary school population attend comprehensives. The Act also introduces an assisted places scheme, subsidising independent (private) school places for able children from disadvantaged backgrounds.

1983 The advisory SCCE is abolished.

1987 The Advanced Supplementary (AS) level is introduced. It covers half the syllabus of a full A level.

1988 The General Certificate of Secondary Education (GCSE), involving written examinations and continuous assessment, replaces the CSE and GCE O level. Its grades range from A to G and the syllabus includes more practical and course work than the O level. The Education Reform Act reduces teacher and pupil choice over subjects taught and studied by introducing a National Curriculum for all schoolchildren. It covers ten subject areas and involves tests, against expected national levels of performance, via Standard Assessment Tests (SATs) at four key stages at the ages of 7, 11, 14, and 16, with the results to be made public. A new School Examinations and Assessment Council (SEAC) is set up to help develop the National Curriculum and assessment system.

1991 Testing of 7-year-olds is introduced, despite opposition from the teaching profession.

1992 The Office for Standards in Education (OFSTED) is established by the Education (Schools) Act. A non-ministerial government department, it includes Her Majesty's Inspectors and has a remit to improve standards of achievement in schools. First performance league tables are published for secondary schools.

1993 SEAC is abolished and replaced by the School Curriculum and Assessment Authority (SCAA).

February and May 1993 Teachers' unions support ballots calling for a boycott of tests.

April 1993 The education minister's chief curriculum adviser, who had warned against tests distorting the curriculum, is replaced at the end of his contract by Sir Ron Dearing, the former head of the Post Office.

May 1993 More than three-quarters of schools boycott the tests for 14-year-olds in English, mathematics, and science.

August 1993 A review of tests, carried out by Dearing, results in extensive cuts in the testing programme.

November 1993 There are criticisms of the latest 'league tables' on secondary school performance in examinations, as critics say they take no account of a school's intake and the 'value added' by the school.

1994 An additional 'Starred A Grade' is introduced for GCSE high attainers.

July 1994 Education secretary, John Patten, threatens to bring in external markers should the teachers' boycott of test marking continue in 1995.

December 1994 The chief executive of the SCAA admits that the results of national curriculum tests, which cost the government £30 million a year, are 'not particularly helpful to parents'.

May 1995 Statutory tests in English, mathematics, and science are introduced for 11-year-olds. They last for four hours, spread over four days, and, like tests for 14-year-olds (which last seven hours), are marked by external examiners.

August 1995 The National Curriculum is revised and reduced for key stages 1 to 3 (for pupils aged five to 14 years).

August 1996 The National Curriculum is revised and reduced for key stage 4 (for pupils aged 14–16 years).

November 1996 Results of the 1996 National Curriculum tests show that two-fifths of pupils aged 11 and 14 failed to reach the expected levels of achievement in English, mathematics, and science (the SCAA had set a target for more than three-quarters to reach the level). Performance improves by ten points over 1995 for 11-year-olds, as teachers ensure pupils are given more revision time, but still a third leave primary school with a reading age two or more years below their calendar age.

March 1997 The government publishes the first league tables of primary schools based on National Curriculum test scores by 11-year-olds and comparing pupils' progression since tests taken at the age of seven.

May 1997 The new Labour government sets challenging targets that, by 2002, three-quarters of 11-year-olds will attain level 4 in mathematics and four-fifths attain the same level in English. It looks to schools to set their own targets.

October 1997 The Qualification and Curriculum Authority (QCA) is formed by the Education Act through the amalgamation of the SCAA and National Council for Vocational Qualifications (NCVQ). An independent government agency, it has a remit to promote quality in education and advise the education secretary on pupil assessment and the curriculum. The consultation paper 'Qualifying for Success' makes proposals for improvements to the A level and GNVQ programmes.

January 1998 The published annual league tables of tests in literacy and numeracy of 11-year-olds in state schools show an overall improvement. Education secretary David Blunkett announces a relaxation of the National Curriculum in order to focus on English and mathematics.

August 1998 GCSE results reveal a slight increase in pupils achieving C grades and above but a 50% increase in the number of failures. Critics blame the recent emphasis on school performance league tables for encouraging schools to concentrate on more able students to improve the overall results of the school, with low achievers receiving less attention.

September 1998 Baseline assessment by teachers of the language, mathematical, and personal and social skills of children aged four to five, within seven weeks of entering primary school, is made statutory (in Wales from September 1999).

September 1998 Higher education minister Baroness Blackstone announces that A levels will be made less elitist, broader, and more flexible to encourage more pupils, particularly from working class families, to stay at school and go to university. These changes in the way sixth-form study is structured form the initiative known as Curriculum 2000. In 1998, 88% of pupils passed A levels.

October 1998 The government increases the mark needed to pass National Curriculum reading tests for 7-year-olds. Under the new criteria, 40% of 7-year-olds will be classified as unable to read.

December 1998 Chris Woodhead, the chief inspector of schools, condemns National Curriculum testing as unreliable, particularly when making comparisons across years. His views are rejected by the National Foundation for Education Research, which plays a key role in developing the tests.

September 1999 Results of National Curriculum tests for 11-year-olds show improvement, with 70% achieving the required level 4 in English and 69% in mathematics.

September 2000 Curriculum 2000, an overhaul of post-16 education, is introduced. Revisions include a revised A level syllabus, a new Advanced Subsidiary (AS) level which will represent the first half of a full A level (students being expected to take 4–6 AS levels in the first year of A-level study), and a new Key Skills qualification covering communication, application of number, and information technology.

School Pupils in the UK: Issues of Gender, Social Class, and Ethnic Group

In the days when all children in the UK took the 11-plus examination, which allocated the most successful to grammar schools and the rest to secondary moderns and technical schools, the results were adjusted to ensure that an even number of girls and boys were offered places, as girls outperformed boys. Although girls got off to a good start at school, they tended to fall behind later; and in the adult population, women remain less highly qualified than men.

In the primary schools performance has been generally improving since the introduction of the National Curriculum in 1989. Girls do particularly well in English, with 83% of 7-year-old girls performing at the 'expected' level, compared with 73% of boys. In English, girls outperform boys throughout their schooling, often by a significant margin. In mathematics, the gap in favour of girls is less marked at 7, and has closed by the age of 11. In science boys have begun to pull ahead slightly at 11.

By the time pupils take their GCSE examinations at 16 the picture has become more complicated. In general terms, more boys than girls leave school without any qualifications, and girls do rather better than boys in the overall number of GCSE passes they gain. However, there are different trends between the genders in the choice of subjects, so like-with-like comparisons become more difficult. Most pupils take English and mathematics at GCSE: girls still perform significantly better than boys in English, but performance is much the same in mathematics. In science, boys have tended to maintain a slight advantage.

At A level, where the choice of subjects is wide and one gender tends to dominate certain subject areas, girls have eliminated the gap which used to exist between their performance and that of boys.

At university level the picture changes. Women and men have been almost equally represented in higher education for 15 years or more. Participation has almost doubled over the same period, so boys and girls seem to have been equally motivated towards higher education throughout its expansion in the UK. However, in terms of performance at degree level, women congregate around the middle of the degree tables, while men take a majority of the first class degrees – and a majority of the thirds.

There seems to be little doubt that boys and girls learn in different ways: boys are more assertive in class, girls more attentive; girls do better on sustained tasks while boys prefer memorizing and fact-based learning; girls favour language activities, boys like mathematics and science; boys prefer 'sudden death' examinations and do well on multiple choice tests, while girls have an advantage in coursework.

Other factors considered at one time or another to be significant are now regarded as less so. Major studies have shown little difference in the performance of boys and girls in single sex and co-educational schools, if the prior level of attainment of the pupils is taken into account. However, in August 2000 the government announced plans to reintroduce single-sex classes to try to improve the performance of boys, who, for the first time, performed worse than girls at A level. Both boys and girls perform better on tasks where they are familiar with the content either at home or at school. There is evidence that in English and mathematics, examiners answered the need to present materials and problems that are not biased in favour of one gender or the other.

There is no evidence of discrimination in tests and exams. When the Associated Examining Board commissioned research on 'blind' marking, offering A Level scripts that might be assigned to the 'wrong' sex, the results remained consistent.

The issue of gender in education is complicated by factors external to the schools and colleges. It is difficult to isolate the influence of gender from those of race, family, and social class. Boys are over-represented amongst children with learning difficulties generally, with reading difficulties specifically, and with emotional and behavioural difficulties (EBDs). However, white boys are more heavily represented in the first two groups while black boys dominate those with EBDs.

The 1990 Youth Cohort Study looked at examination scores amongst white, Asian, and Afro-Caribbean boys and girls in three social class groups. Top performers were white girls, followed by Asian boys, and then white boys, all from professional families. Fourth in this particular league table were Asian girls from manual working-class homes. The lowest scores were obtained by Afro-Caribbean boys, and then girls, from working-class families.

Level of Education Held by Gender and Ethnic Group in Great Britain

Data are for men aged 16–64 and women aged 16–59, and are for combined quarters: Spring 1997 to Winter 1997–98. (In percentages.)

1997–98	Degree or equivalent	Higher education qualification[1]	GCE A-level or equivalent	GCSE grades A* to C or equivalent	Other qualification	No qualification
Men						
Indian/Pakistani/Bangladeshi	18	5	16	14	25	22
Black	14	6	22	18	24	16
White	14	8	32	18	14	15
Other groups[2]	20	5	17	15	27	15
Women						
Indian/Pakistani/Bangladeshi	9	5	11	18	25	33
Black	9	12	14	27	22	16
White	11	9	16	29	15	20
Other groups[2]	12	8	15	17	33	15

[1] Below degree level.
[2] Includes those who did not state their ethnic group.

Source: Social Trends 29, © *Crown copyright 1999*

■ UK Schools and Teachers

Adult Literacy Levels by Gender in the UK

The abilities of working people (aged 16 to 65) were measured on three types of literacy: prose literacy (the ability to understand text), document literacy (the ability to locate and use information in charts and timetables), and quantitative literacy (the ability to perform basic arithmetic operations on numbers embedded in text). Performance on each dimension is grouped into five literacy levels, level 1 being the lowest and level 5 the highest. (In percentages.)

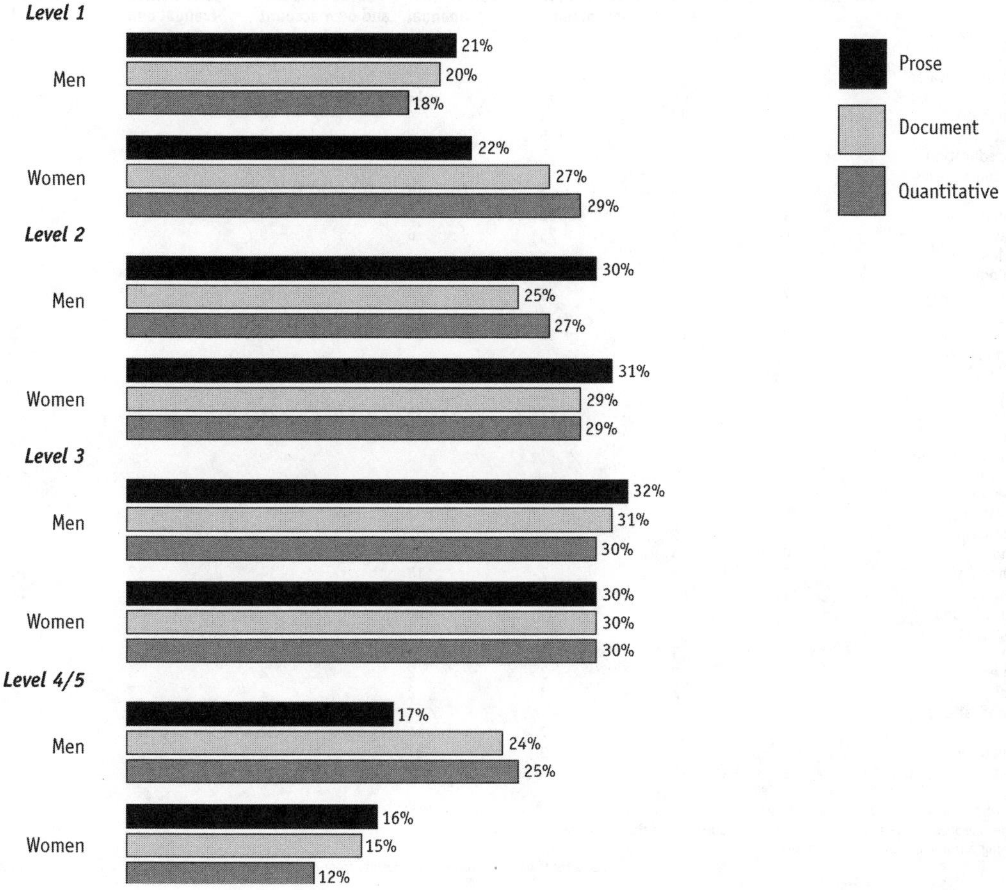

		Prose	Document	Quantitative
Level 1	Men	21%	20%	18%
Level 1	Women	22%	27%	29%
Level 2	Men	30%	25%	27%
Level 2	Women	31%	29%	29%
Level 3	Men	32%	31%	30%
Level 3	Women	30%	30%	30%
Level 4/5	Men	17%	24%	25%
Level 4/5	Women	16%	15%	12%

Source: Social Trends 28, © *Crown copyright 1998*

We found that 11- to 14-year-olds believed you could not be masculine and be seen to be working hard at school ... It is the same whether the boys are white, black, Asian, working-class or middle-class. They think that to be properly masculine you have to be good at sport, particularly football ... You need to be seen not to work. Those who are clever – swots, stiffs, boffs or whatever you want to call them – are unpopular and seen as not male.

Dr Ann Phoenix, English educationalist at Birkbeck College, London.

Highest Qualification Levels

In the UK, 23% of adults of working age have a qualification at level 4 (degree level qualifications, or a professional qualification such as accountancy) or above. This equates to 6.9 million adults out of a total of 30.1 million. 24% of men of working age have achieved a qualification at level 4 or above, compared with 22% of women of working age. Attainment levels vary greatly by economic activity, with 25% of unemployed people having no qualifications, compared with 11% of employees.

Highest Qualification by Gender and Socio-Economic Group in Great Britain

Data are for economically active persons aged 25–69 not in full-time education and are for 1995 and 1996 combined. (In percentages.)

Highest qualification level attained[1]	Socio-economic group[2]							
	Professional	**Employers and managers**	**Intermediate non-manual**	**Junior non-manual**	**Skilled manual and own account non-professional**	**Semi-skilled manual and personal service**	**Unskilled manual**	**Total**
Degree or equivalent								
men	65	24	30	12	2	1	1	16
women	68	22	24	4	4	1	0	11
Total	66	24	26	5	2	1	0	14
Higher education below degree level								
men	17	19	20	13	10	7	2	14
women	11	19	28	5	4	4	1	11
Total	16	19	25	6	9	5	1	12
GCE A level or equivalent[3]								
men	7	17	16	24	15	10	7	15
women	7	13	9	12	10	8	4	10
Total	7	16	12	14	14	9	5	12
GCSE grades A–C or equivalent[3]								
men	5	19	20	29	24	22	20	21
women	4	23	21	39	28	23	14	27
Total	5	20	20	37	25	23	16	24
GCSE grades D–G or equivalent/ commercial qualifications/ apprenticeship								
men	0	5	4	7	14	12	12	9
women	3	8	7	18	14	12	10	12
Total	1	6	6	16	14	12	11	10
Foreign or other qualifications								
men	3	3	3	2	2	3	4	3
women	7	2	3	2	2	4	2	2
Total	4	2	3	2	2	3	2	2
No qualifications								
men	2	12	7	14	33	45	55	23
women	0	13	9	21	38	47	69	26
Total	2	12	8	20	34	46	64	25

[1] Those who never went to school are excluded.
[2] Excludes members of the armed forces, full-time students, and those who had never worked.
[3] Including further-education qualifications.

Source: Living in Britain 1996: Results from the 1996 General Household Survey, © *Crown copyright 1998*

School Funding in the UK

The main funding for state schools in the UK is provided by central government grants to local education authorities (LEAs), with a smaller proportion coming from local taxes. Many schools also raise funds through their parent-teacher associations (PTAs) and, increasingly, through sponsorship from business and industry. Individual school budgets are determined by the LEA, but governors have responsibility for allocating funds internally. The proportion of gross domestic product (GDP) spent on the education service in the UK has decreased since the 1970s from a high of 6.6% to a low of 4.6% in 1998, despite a rapid expansion of higher education in the 1980s and 1990s, and a gradual increase in school pupil numbers in the 1990s. This has led to significantly higher pupil-teacher ratios in maintained schools, and wide disparities in class sizes.

The reduction of class sizes to 30 or under for pupils aged five to seven was one of the Labour government's priorities when it came to power in 1997, but there is still concern about class sizes for older children. Teacher supply became an increasing problem in the 1990s, with difficulties in recruiting trainees, particularly in mathematics, science, and foreign languages. In July 2000 Gordon Brown, the chancellor of the Exchequer, announced that an extra £12 billion would be spent on education over the next three years.

■ UK Schools and Teachers

Government Spending on Education in the UK

Data are for years ending 31 March. Due to rounding constituent figures may not sum to totals. (N/A = not available. In millions of pounds.)

Expenditure	1986–87	1987–88	1988–89	1989–90	1990–91	1991–92	1992–93[1]	1993–94[2]	1994–95[2]	1995–96[3]	1996–97[16]
Current expenditure											
Nursery and primary schools	4,238	4,743	5,259	5,889	6,458	7,247	8,262	8,712	9,094	9,349	9,676
Secondary schools	5,583	5,991	6,437	6,832	7,147	7,787	8,347	8,615	8,875	8,987	9,253
Special schools	727	812	888	1,008	1,121	1,245	1,354	1,420	1,451	1,492	1,567
Universities[4]	1,654	1,824	1,958	2,104	2,265	2,437	3,361	N/A	N/A	N/A	N/A
Other higher, further, and adult education[5]	2,716	2,971	3,277	3,729	4,128	4,454	4,136	N/A	N/A	N/A	N/A
Higher Education Funding Council[5 6]	N/A	N/A	N/A	N/A	N/A	N/A	N/A	4,908	5,192	5,455	5,738
Further Education Funding Council[7]	N/A	N/A	N/A	N/A	N/A	N/A	N/A	3,072	3,200	3,374	3,712
Continuing education	N/A	N/A	N/A	N/A	N/A	N/A	N/A	380	294	266	273
Other education expenditure	871	900	1,009	1,191	1,325	1,361	1,009	905	963	1,045	1,153
Related current expenditure											
Training of teachers: residence[8]	19	N/A	N/A	N/A	N/A	N/A	N/A	N/A	N/A	N/A	N/A
School welfare[9]	40	57	70	91	155	214	270	346	359	330	344
Meals and milk[10]	559	547	469	485	506	556	161	149	147	148	148
Youth service and physical training	211	246	277	328	348	360	393	392	401	399	390
Maintenance grants and allowances to pupils and students[11 12]	806	843	900	934	1,028	1,379	1,705	1,972	2,204	2,180	2,026
Transport of pupils	290	302	311	335	393	442	417	444	486	506	569
Miscellaneous expenditure	5	6	10	17	2	3	8	10	31	31	49
Current expenditure total[13]	17,719	19,240	20,865	22,943	24,876	27,485	29,424	31,325	32,697	33,562	34,898
Capital expenditure											
Nursery and primary schools	187	192	246	314	353	376	384	414	517	525	525
Secondary schools	187	213	195	397	465	493	518	485	565	574	588
Special schools	23	11	33	38	36	35	32	31	37	51	52
Universities[4]	156	158	172	196	211	231	236	N/A	N/A	N/A	N/A
Other higher, further, and adult education[5]	152	177	180	248	230	293	285	N/A	N/A	N/A	N/A
Higher Education Funding Council[5 6]	N/A	N/A	N/A	N/A	N/A	N/A	N/A	406	412	453	74
Further Education Funding Council[7]	N/A	N/A	N/A	N/A	N/A	N/A	N/A	194	201	213	19
Continuing education	N/A	N/A	N/A	N/A	N/A	N/A	N/A	6	8	10	4
Other education expenditure	10	32	22	41	39	33	25	12	45	25	17
Related capital expenditure	24	21	25	32	26	20	17	23	25	17	18
Capital expenditure total	739	804	873	1,266	1,359	1,481	1,496	1,571	1,810	1,868	1,287
VAT refunds to local authorities	345	357	399	455	493	584	656	648[13]	886	923	801
Total government expenditure											
Central government	2,567	2,746	3,025	4,337	4,582	4,288	4,722	8,186	9,490	10,234	10,426
Local authorities	16,235	17,655	19,112	20,325	22,146	25,261	26,853	25,354[13]	25,900	26,118	25,877
Total government expenditure on education[14]	18,803	20,401	22,137	24,664	26,728	29,550	31,576	33,544[13]	35,393	36,352	36,986
Total government expenditure as % of GDP[15]	4.84	4.75	4.62	4.72	4.75	5.01	5.15	5.18	5.16	5.03	4.92

(continued)

Government Spending on Education in the UK (*continued*)

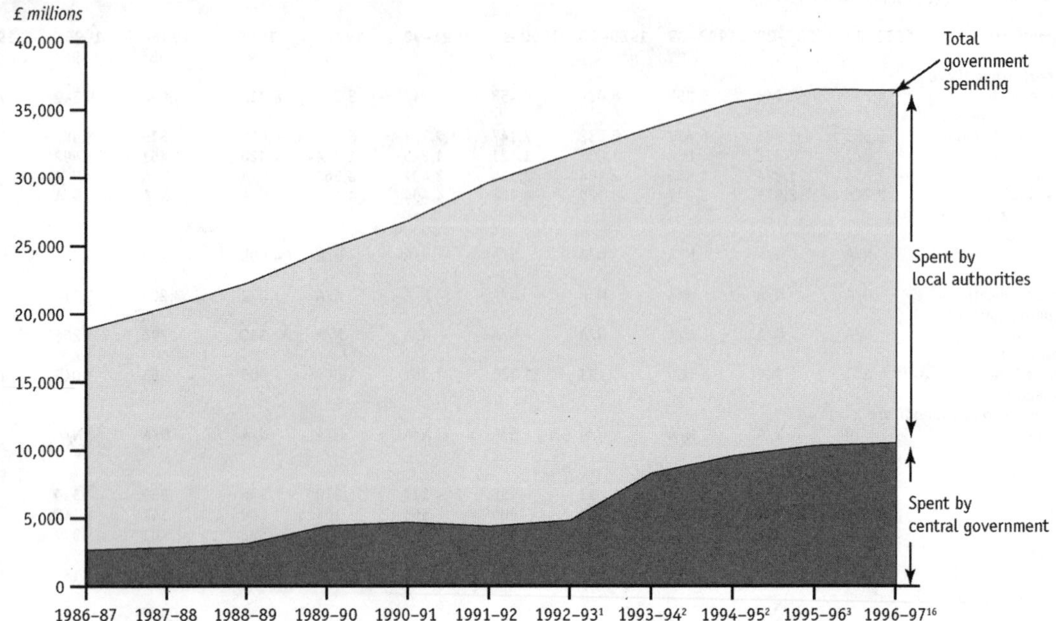

[1] Includes 1991–92 data for Wales.
[2] Includes 1993–94 data for Wales.
[3] Provisional data. Includes 1994–95 data for Wales.
[4] Includes expenditure on University departments of Education for England and Wales.
[5] Including tuition fees.
[6] Includes expenditure on Higher Education Institutions in Northern Ireland.
[7] Includes expenditure for Further Education in Northern Ireland.
[8] With effect from 1987–88 included with maintenance grants and allowances.
[9] Expenditure on the school health service is included in the National Health Service.
[10] From 1992–93 expenditure on meals and milk in England has been recharged across other expenditure headings.
[11] From 1986–87, excludes the secondment of teachers on further training.
[12] From 1990–91, includes student loans expenditure.
[13] Revised figure.
[14] Excludes additional adjustment to allow for Capital consumption made for National Accounts purposes amounting to £1,013 million in 1995–96.
[15] GDP includes adjustments to remove the distortion caused by abolition of domestic rates which have led to revisions of the historical series.
[16] Provisional data. Includes 1995–96 data for Wales and Scotland.

Source: Annual Abstract of Statistics, 2000,

Educational Expenditure as a Percentage of GDP in the UK

Financial year	Expenditure (£ millions)	% GDP
1970–71	2,740	5.2
1971–72	3,140	5.3
1972–73	3,708	5.6
1973–74	4,237	5.7
1974–75	5,528	6.3
1975–76	7,020	6.4
1976–77	7,849	6.2
1977–78	8,305	5.5
1978–79	9,169	5.3
1979–80	10,617	5.1
1980–81	13,051	5.5
1982–83	15,037	5.26
1983–84	15,946	5.14
1984–85	16,517	4.97
1986–87	19,042	4.90
1988–89	22,137	4.66
1989–90	24,664	4.77
1990–91	26,728	4.80
1991–92	29,550	5.08

(*continued*)

Spending per Pupil on Key Items in LEA-Maintained Schools in England

The expenditure data are drawn from the figures submitted annually by local authorities (in the form of RO1 spending returns) to the Department of the Environment, Transport, and Regions (DETR). The pupil data are drawn from the Department of Education and Employment annual Form 7 survey. The real-terms index has been calculated at 1998–99 prices using March 1999 Gross Domestic Product (GDP) deflators, and shows the percentage increase in real-terms spending compared with a base year of 1992–93.

Spending per pupil on:		1993–94	1994–95	1995–96	1996–97	1997–98[1]
Teaching staff	cash (£)	1,290	1,311	1,330	1,342	1,355
	real-terms index	100	100	99	97	95
Support staff	cash (£)	145	162	175	199	212
	real-terms index	100	110	115	127	131
Books and equipment	cash (£)	78	79	78	81	89
	real-terms index	100	100	96	97	104
Repairs and maintenance	cash (£)	79	82	76	77	69
	real-terms index	100	102	92	91	80

[1] Data for 1997–98 are provisional and are based on a combination of actual and estimated expenditure.

Source: The Government's Expenditure Plans 1999–00 to 2001–02,

UK Schools and Teachers

Educational Expenditure as a Percentage of GDP in the UK *(continued)*

Financial year	Expenditure (£ millions)	% GDP
1992–93	31,576	5.20
1993–94	33,544	5.24
1994–95	35,367	5.21
1995–96	36,171	5.07
1996–97	36,986	4.92

Source: Annual Abstract of Statistics 2000, © *Crown copyright 2000*

Computers in Schools

The National Grid for Learning (launched on 12 January 1998) is a government plan to connect every UK classroom to the Internet by 2002. A draft report from the Department for Education and Employment, released in July 2000, indicated that the use of computers in schools helped to raise standards of literacy and numeracy, especially among underachieving pupils from poorer areas. Despite the success of private initiatives, such as Tesco's 'Computers for Schools' scheme, a huge amount of public money is still needed to equip schools adequately.

Use of Information Technology in Schools

(N = nil or negligible. ICT = information and communications technology.)

Item	Primary		Secondary		Special	
	1998	1999	1998	1999	1998	1999
Computers in schools						
average computers per school	13	16	101	101	19	21
average pupils per computer	18	13	9	8	4	4
Expenditure on ICT						
Estimated total (£ millions)						
teaching and learning	49	105	119	136	7	12
school management and administration	19	20	24	25	2	4
Average per school (£)						
teaching and learning	2,600	5,700	33,300	38,200	6,034	9,674
school management and administration	1,000	1,100	6,800	7,200	1,523	3,668
Average per pupil (£)						
teaching and learning	11	27	38	45	73	124
school management and administration	4	5	8	8	18	47
Connected to the Internet						
percentage of schools	17	62	83	93	31	60
Percentage with personal e-mail address						
teachers	2	15	9	32	2	14
pupils	N	4	3	12	N	4
ICT development plan						
percentage of schools with a plan	53	79	83	90	31	85
Teacher use of ICT						
percentage who feel confident to use ICT within the curriculum	65	68	61	66	65	68
percentage who have received some training in ICT	90	92	85	88	89	92
percentage who have received updated training within the last two years	45	46	36	39	46	45

Source: Statistics of Education 1999, © *Crown copyright 1999*

Types of School in the UK

Schooling in the UK is divided into primary and secondary sectors, with the change of school at 11 (12 in Scotland). The state system includes a few middle schools taking children from 9 to 13, and private sector secondary schools commonly admit pupils at 13.

Compulsory schooling begins at the age of five, (four in Northern Ireland) although an increasing proportion of four-year-olds are being accommodated in reception classes of primary schools. Nursery education for three- and four-year-olds is not compulsory but has been expanding in recent years. The Labour government has expanded provision to provide places in either pre-schools or reception classes for all four-year-olds whose parents want it.

The state school system allows some schools to be run in partnership with religious denominations. The majority of these voluntary-aided schools are associated with the Roman Catholic Church and the Church of England. There are a small number of Jewish schools; approval was given in 1998 for the first Muslim schools to receive government funding, and in 1999 for the first Sikh school.

The vast majority of state secondary schools are comprehensive, admitting children regardless of ability. A few LEAs still maintain selective (grammar) schools that admit children according to their results in an entrance test. The Labour government elected in 1997 has legislated to allow parents of affected children to participate in a ballot on whether local grammar schools should remain selective or become comprehensive. In the first ballot, in Ripon, North Yorkshire, parents voted to retain selection.

Some other forms of specialization at secondary level were encouraged by the previous Conservative government and have been continued by the Labour government. A minority of schools specialize, for example, in technology, languages, or the performing arts. Additional funding is provided for such schools and admission is by an assessment of aptitude.

When a school is unable to admit all the children who have applied for places, decisions are generally made on the basis of how close a family lives to the school. There is an appeal system for families who are not satisfied with admissions decisions.

Pupil–Teacher Ratios by Type of School in the UK

As of January, except for Scotland and Wales where data are as of September, for the year shown.

	1988	1990	1992	1993	1994[1]	1995[1]	1996[1]	1997[1]	1998[2]
All schools or departments[3 4 5]									
England	17.2	17.0	17.2	17.4	17.7	18.1	18.2	18.3	18.5
Wales	18.0	18.1	18.2	18.2	18.4	18.7	18.7	18.8	18.8
Scotland	15.8	15.3	15.3	15.4	15.5	15.4	15.5	15.8	15.8
Northern Ireland	18.4	18.3	18.3	18.1	17.8	17.3	17.1	16.7	16.7
UK Average	17.1	16.9	17.1	17.3	17.5	17.8	18.0	18.1	18.3
Public sector mainstream schools or departments									
Nursery	21.4	21.8	21.6	21.6	21.6	21.9	21.3	21.3	20.7
Primary	21.9	21.7	21.8	21.9	22.2	22.4	22.7	22.8	23.1
Secondary	15.1	14.8	15.2	15.4	15.7	16.0	16.1	16.2	16.4
Special schools[4]									
Total	6.3	5.8	5.7	5.8	5.9	6.0	6.2	6.2	6.3

[1] From 1 April 1993, figures exclude sixth form colleges in England and Wales that were reclassified as further education colleges.
[2] Figures are provisional. They include 1996–97 data for Wales.
[3] Figures include non-maintained schools or departments, including independent schools in Scotland.
[4] Up to 1993–94, figures include unqualified teachers for England and Scotland. From 1994–95, figures include qualified teachers only for all countries.
[5] Figures take account of the full-time equivalent of part-time teachers.

Source: Annual Abstract of Statistics 2000, © *Crown copyright 2000*

Numbers of Teachers by Type of School in the UK

Data are for January of each year except Scotland and Wales, where data are for September.

Type of school	1988	1990	1992	1993	1994[1]	1995[1]	1996[1]	1997[1]	1998[2]
Public sector mainstream schools or departments									
Nursery[3 4]	2,700	2,700	2,800	2,900	2,800	2,800	2,900	2,900	3,000
Primary[3 4]	210,100	219,000	222,600	224,400	225,500	225,900	227,300	226,900	225,600
Secondary[3 4]	244,900	236,600	232,700	233,600	228,400	228,400	228,200	228,900	228,700
Special schools									
Total[4]	19,300	19,600	19,600	19,600	19,200	19,200	18,600	18,300	18,100
TOTAL[3 5]	531,100	532,500	534,900	537,800	533,200	532,600	534,000	533,000	532,800

[1] From 1 April 1993, figures exclude sixth form colleges in England and Wales as these colleges were reclassified as further education colleges.
[2] Figures are provisional. This column includes 1996–97 data for Wales.
[3] Figures of teachers take account of the full-time equivalent of part-time teachers.
[4] Up to 1993–94, figures include unqualified teachers for England and Scotland. From 1994–95, figures include qualified teachers only for all countries.
[5] Figures include non-maintained schools or departments, including independent schools in Scotland.

Source: Annual Abstract of Statistics 2000, © *Crown copyright 2000*

Number of School Pupils by Type of School in the UK

There were over 10 million full-time and part-time pupils and 33,500 schools in the academic year 1998–99, compared with 9.6 million pupils and 34,600 schools in 1990–91. Since a low in the 1980s, pupil numbers have increased, but are still below their peak level of the 1970s.

(– = not applicable. N/A = not available.)

School	1970–71	1980–81	1990–91	1995–96	1998–99[1]
Public sector schools[2]					
Nursery[3]	50,000	89,000	105,000	84,000	109,000
Primary[3]	5,902,000	5,171,000	4,955,000	5,338,000	5,376,000
Secondary					
modern	1,164,000	233,000	94,000	78,000	92,000
grammar	673,000	149,000	156,000	189,000	203,000
comprehensive[4]	1,313,000	3,730,000	2,843,000	3,129,000	3,205,000
other	403,000	434,000	300,000	282,000	291,000
All public sector schools	9,507,000	9,806,000	8,453,000	9,099,000	9,276,000
Non-maintained schools[2]	621,000	619,000	613,000	603,000	616,000
Special schools[5]	103,000	148,000	114,000	115,000	115,000
Pupil referral units	–	–	–	N/A	9,000
All schools	10,230,000	10,572,000	9,180,000	9,816,000	10,016,000

[1] Data for Wales and for nursery schools in Scotland are for 1997–98.
[2] Excludes special schools.
[3] Nursery classes within primary schools are included in primary schools except for Scotland in 1990–91, in which instance they are included in nursery schools.
[4] Excludes sixth form colleges from 1980–81.
[5] Includes maintained and non-maintained sectors.

Source: Social Trends 30, © *Crown copyright 2000*

Special Schools in the UK

Roughly 2% of children have serious disabilities or learning difficulties that cannot be catered for in mainstream education, and are taught in special day or residential schools. Most children with special needs are given additional help within mainstream classrooms.

There is a five-stage process of assessing special needs and the help that children require to enable them to benefit from their education. Children with the most serious difficulties at the fifth stage of the assessment process may be eligible for a statement of Special Educational Needs (SEN), which spells out the help that must be provided by their school, whether mainstream or special. Parents may appeal to an official tribunal if they are not happy with the assessment of their child.

UK Schools and Teachers

Recruitment to and Targets for Initial Teacher Training Courses in England

Includes intakes for PGCE courses at the Open University, and entrants to school-centred ITT. (N/A = not available.)

	1997–98		1998–99		% change in recruitment
	Actual	Target	Actual[1]	Target	1997–98 to 1998–99[1]
Primary and secondary					
Undergraduate	9,620	N/A	8,790	N/A	−9
Postgraduate	18,100	N/A	17,130	N/A	−5
Total	27,720	30,550	25,920	30,600	−6
Primary					
Undergraduate	7,070	N/A	6,710	N/A	−5
Postgraduate	4,680	N/A	4,840	N/A	+3
Total	11,750	11,050	11,550	11,500	−2
Secondary					
Undergraduate	2,540	N/A	2,090	N/A	−18
Postgraduate	13,420	N/A	12,290	N/A	−8
Total	15,960	19,500	14,380	19,100	−10
Secondary by subject					
Mathematics	1,460	2,370	1,120	2,270	−23
English and drama	2,140	2,270	2,160	2,545	+1
Science	2,790	3,460	2,290	3,230	−18
Languages[2]	1,800	2,860	1,660	2,510	−8
Design and technology[3]	1,980	3,380	1,680	3,190	−15
History	960	980	900	980	−7
Geography	850	960	750	1,070	−12
Physical education	1,640	1,610	1,490	1,540	−9
Art	900	1,020	900	1,170	0
Music	500	650	490	640	−2
Religious education	640	740	610	790	−5
Other	300	370	330	420	+10

[1] Provisional.
[2] Includes Welsh.
[3] Includes business studies, computing, and home economics.

Data from School Teachers' Review Body Eighth Report 1999, © *Crown copyright 1999*

Pupils Under Five Years of Age in Nursery and Primary Schools in England

As of January for the year shown.

Year	All pupils under 5	Number of pupils per teacher in nursery schools and classes	% of population under 5 at previous 31 December
1989	547,564	24	45
1991	603,586	25	48
1993	656,711	26	51
1995	699,844	27	53
1997	713,509	29	56
1999	722,004	30	58

Source: Statistics of Education: Schools in England 1998, © *Crown copyright 1998, and DfEE Statistical First Release: pupils under five years of age in maintained schools in England,* © *Crown Copyright 1999*

Pupils with Special Educational Needs in Public Sector and Assisted Schools in England, by Type of School

The data in this table are for full-time and part-time pupils with statements of Special Educational Needs (SEN) as of January for the year shown. (N/A = not available.)

Category	1993	1994	1995	1996	1997	1998	1998–99[7]
Maintained schools							
Nursery schools	332	318	416	425	488	440	400
Primary schools[1 2]	43,464	50,112	55,768	61,698	63,551	67,014	69,800
Secondary schools[1 2 3]	41,114	50,142	57,040	65,137	70,080	73,956	77,300
Special schools[2 4 5]	82,855	83,673	85,879	87,458	87,330	87,931	87,300
Pupil referral units[5]	N/A	N/A	1,325	1,828	1,693	1,798	1,900
Other schools							
Independent schools[6]	5,227	5,458	5,826	5,810	6,461	6,450	6,900
Non-maintained special schools[5]	5,037	4,838	5,053	4,992	5,026	4,705	4,400
Total	178,029	194,541	211,307	227,348	234,629	242,294	248,000

[1] Includes middle schools as deemed.
[2] Includes grant-maintained schools.
[3] Excludes sixth-form colleges from 1994.
[4] Includes general and special hospital schools.
[5] Excludes dually registered pupils.
[6] Includes direct grant nursery schools and city technology colleges.
[7] Provisional.

Source: Statistics of Education: Schools in England 1998, © *Crown copyright 1998, and Educational and Training Statistics for the UK 1999,* © *Crown copyright 1999*

UK Further and Higher Education

Further Education in the UK

Compulsory education in the UK ends at the age of 16. Further education (FE) refers to courses taken after age 16 up to, but not beyond, GCE A level (or equivalent). FE students may remain in a school sixth form or move to a sixth form college for the two-year General Certificate of Education (GCE) A Level course. (In Scotland, Scottish Certificate of Education (SCE) Highers are taken at 17). Those seeking vocational courses may opt to switch to a college of further education. A growing number of sixth-form and FE colleges offer 16- to 18-year-olds a range of academic and vocational courses in the same institution.

Higher Education in the UK

Higher Education (HE) is study undertaken at a more advanced level than GCE A level (or equivalent), including both academic and vocational courses. The participation rate in higher education has been rising steadily as colleges and universities have expanded and the current government's target is to see 50% of young people gaining degrees and diplomas. However, as student numbers have risen, staff numbers have not kept pace. Women outnumber men in further education but the situation is reversed in the universities and women lag particularly in full-time postgraduate study. However, in 1994–95 for the first time more women than men obtained first degree and postgraduate qualifications.

Students in Further and Higher Education Aged 16 and Over in the UK

The data in this table are provisional. Full-time includes sandwich, and for Scotland, short full-time. Part-time comprises both day and evening, including block release (except Scotland) and open/distance learning.
(N/A = not available.)

1997–98 Mode of study	All ages[1]		Age at 31 August 1997				
	1996–97	1997–98	16	18	20+	25+	30+
Full-time students							
Postgraduate	138,300	140,800	N/A	100	800	12,200	36,900
First degree[2]	875,800	899,300	500	146,500	182,400	16,200	73,500
Other undergraduate[3]	143,700	152,700	800	18,300	20,900	4,800	26,800
All higher education[4]	1,194,600	1,230,400	2,100	168,900	208,600	34,300	146,800
All further education[5]	859,600	863,600	247,600	103,500	23,600	11,200	119,000
Total FE/HE students	2,054,200	2,094,000	249,700	272,400	232,200	45,500	265,800
Part-time students							
Postgraduate	214,400	207,000	N/A	100	100	9,200	140,500
First degree[2]	174,700	88,100	N/A	400	2,500	3,800	49,500
Other undergraduate[3]	217,000	321,000	200	3,200	500	8,600	223,200
All higher education[4]	696,900	708,000	400	5,500	11,200	25,400	462,900
All further education[5]	1,575,700	1,616,400	57,400	59,900	38,700	44,900	903,000
Total FE/HE students	2,272,600	2,324,400	57,800	65,400	49,900	70,300	1,365,900
TOTAL	4,326,800	4,418,400	307,500	337,800	282,100	115,800	1,631,700

[1] Includes students aged under 16.
[2] For 1996–97 first degree includes most Open University students.
[3] From 1997–98 includes most Open University students. Figures for 1996 exclude qualifiers at Department of Health establishments not recorded by HESA.
[4] Data are not available by level for higher education students in further education institutions in England and are included in total higher education figures only.
[5] Excludes approximately 177,000 students in further education institutions in England. External institutions and specialist designated colleges are also excluded.

Source: Annual Abstract of Statistics 2000, © *Crown copyright 2000*

Curriculum 2000

Curriculum 2000 is intended to introduce greater flexibility to sixth-form study programmes and to encourage students to take a wider range of subjects, especially vocational subjects.

- **advanced subsidiary (AS) level qualification** new qualification equivalent to approximately half an A level
- **advanced extension (AE) tests** new qualification equivalent to the current special (S) level.
- **A level** new syllabus offering linear (end-of-course) or modular (staged) assessment courses; new coursework limits for A levels (no more than 30% in most subjects); and a requirement for tests covering the entire syllabus at the end of all courses.
- **GNVQ** to be tested more systematically; a new advanced GNVQ equivalent to a single A level.
- **key skills qualification** a new optional qualification in communication skills and the application of number and information technology.

Full-Time Academic Teaching and Research Staff at Higher Education Institutions in the UK

(- = not applicable. N/A = not available.)

Academic years	Professors	Readers and senior lecturers	Lecturers and assistant lecturers	Researchers	Other	Total	% annual change
1979–80[1]	4,337	8,734	20,518	N/A	661	34,250	1.6
1980–81[1]	4,382	8,809	20,460	N/A	646	34,297	0.1
1981–82[1]	4,351	8,777	20,045	N/A	562	33,735	– 1.6
1982–83[1]	4,017	8,284	18,885	N/A	456	31,642	– 6.2
1983–84[1]	3,893	8,145	18,595	N/A	463	31,096	– 1.7
1984–85[1 2]	3,807	7,942	18,737	N/A	557	31,043	– 0.2
1985–86[1]	3,959	8,025	18,850	N/A	578	31,412	1.2
1986–87[1]	4,070	8,074	18,711	N/A	577	31,432	0.1
1987–88[1]	4,160	8,291	18,268	N/A	542	31,261	– 0.5
1988–89[1]	4,093	8,266	17,778	N/A	484	30,621	– 2.0
1989–90[1]	4,261	8,618	17,903	N/A	558	31,340	2.3
1990–91[1]	4,520	8,842	17,830	N/A	669	31,861	1.7
1991–92[1]	4,872	9,270	17,824	N/A	672	32,638	2.4
1992–93[1]	5,226	9,650	17,854	N/A	717	33,447	2.5
1993–94[1]	5,545	9,890	18,275	N/A	787	34,497	3.1
1994–95[3]	6,762	16,949	39,295	4,662	4,842	72,510	–
1995–96[3]	7,947	17,457	41,503	5,412	5,582	77,901	7.4
1996–97[3 4]	8,222	17,591	39,820	4,809	5,589	76,031	– 2.4
1997–98[3 4]	8,441	17,293	39,497	4,999	5,684	75,914	– 0.2

[1] Includes full-time teaching and research staff in posts wholly financed from general university funds but excludes the Open University and the former polytechnics and central institutions who obtained university status in 1992.

[2] Includes Ulster Polytechnic, which merged with the University of Ulster in October 1984.

[3] Includes full-time academic staff of at least 25% full-time equivalence who are wholly institutionally financed for all publicly funded higher education institutions (including the Open University and the former polytechnics and colleges).

[4] Due to changes in the definition of the HESA standard staff population for 1996–97, it is not advisable to make direct comparisons with figures for 1994–95 and 1995–96.

Source: Annual Abstract of Statistics 2000,

Numbers of Students, Teachers, and Researchers in UK Higher Education Institutions

	1990–91	1991–92[1 2]	1992–93[1 2]	1993–94[1 2]	1994–95[3 4]	1995–96[3 4]	1996–97[3 4 5]	1997–98[3 4]
Full-time students								
Overseas	43,496	45,462	47,278	49,817	123,620	144,777	160,056	172,316
Postgraduates	65,282	73,579	78,490	85,105	129,711	135,348	140,916	143,521
Men	208,359	223,823	238,278	255,065	546,090	574,152	557,176	560,367
Women	161,895	177,834	197,339	215,500	530,540	533,689	581,419	605,760
Total	370,254	401,657	435,617	470,565	1,076,630	1,107,841	1,138,595	1,166,127
Part-time students								
Postgraduates	46,912	53,283	61,046	67,388	205,614	234,771	222,656	243,480
Total	58,604	66,438	75,506	83,311	490,683	612,253	617,584	633,937
Full-time academic teaching and research staff								
Total	31,340[6]	31,861[6]	32,638[6]	34,497[6]	72,510[7]	77,901[7,8]	76,031	75,914

[1] Excluding the Open University and the former polytechnics and central institutions that obtained university status in 1992.

[2] Overseas students defined by fee-paying status. From 1980–81 most European Union students paid home fees and are therefore excluded from the overseas figures and are shown as home students.

[3] Students in all publicly-funded higher education institutions.

[4] Full-time includes sandwich students.

[5] From 1996–97 onwards the HESA standard higher education population excludes those students studying for the whole of their programme outside the UK.

[6] Full-time teaching and research staff in posts wholly financed from general university funds for all publicly-funded higher education institutions.

[7] Full-time academic staff of at least 25% full-time equivalence who are wholly institutionally financed for all publicly-funded higher education institutions.

[8] Due to changes in the definition of the HESA standard staff population from 1996–97 onwards, it is not advisable to make direct comparisons with figures for 1994–95 and 1995–96.

Source: Annual Abstract of Statistics 2000,

The Top 10 Universities for Quality of Teaching

Rank	University	% mark for excellence
1	Cambridge	95.20
2	York	84.80
3	Imperial College, London	83.20
4	Oxford	81.20
5	LSE	77.60
6	University College, London	68.00
7	Nottingham	66.80
8 =	Durham	66.66
	School of Oriental and African Studies, London	66.66
10	Warwick	62.50

Data from 1999 Sunday Times League Table

The Top 10 Universities for Research

Rank	University	% mark for excellence
1	Cambridge	91.00
2 =	Oxford	87.50
	LSE	87.50
4	Warwick	77.50
5	Imperial College, London	77.00
6	University College, London	76.00
7	Edinburgh	72.50
8=	Lancaster	72.00
	UMIST	72.00
	York	72.00

Data from 1999 Sunday Times League Table

The Worst 10 Universities for Quality of Teaching

Rank	University	% mark for excellence
1=	Bradford	0.00
	Lincolnshire and Humberside	0.00
	Napier	0.00
	Paisley	0.00
5	Derby	4.00
6	Leeds Metropolitan	5.60
7	Teesside	6.40
8	Heriot-Watt	6.80
9	Abertay Dundee	7.20
10	Wolverhampton	8.00

Data from 1999 Sunday Times League Table

Research Grants and Contracts to Higher Education Institutions in the UK

The financial data in this table relate to the institutions' financial year of 1 August 1997 to 31 July 1998. Research grants and contracts include all income in respect of externally sponsored research carried out by the institution for which directly related expenditure has been incurred. The data are for the 30 higher education institutions receiving the largest grants from the research councils that come under the Office of Science and Technology. These councils include the Biotechnology and Biological Sciences Research Council, the Natural Environment Research Council, the Engineering and Physical Sciences Research Council, the Economic and Social Sciences Research Councils, the Particle Physics and Astronomy Research Council, and the Medical Research Council. The data also include income from the British Academy. Other sources of research grants and contracts include UK based charities, UK industry, health and hospital authorities, UK industry, commerce and public corporations, as well as EU and other overseas sources.

1997–98

Rank	Institution	Research council grant (£)
1	The University of Oxford	101,430,000
2	Imperial College of Science, Technology and Medicine	98,105,000
3	University College London	91,717,000
4	The University of Cambridge	87,689,000
5	The University of Edinburgh	51,617,000
6	The Victoria University of Manchester	45,845,000
7	King's College, London	43,247,000
8	The University of Glasgow	42,713,000
9	The University of Leeds	42,549,000
10	The University of Birmingham	40,122,000
11	The University of Southampton	38,010,000
12	The University of Sheffield	36,092,000
13	The University of Bristol	33,899,000
14	The University of Nottingham	32,595,000
15	The University of Liverpool	31,024,000
16	The University of Newcastle-upon-Tyne	29,921,000
17	United Medical and Dental Schools, Guys and St Thomas's Hospital	26,343,000
18	Cranfield University	24,805,000
19	Queen Mary and Westfield College	23,553,000
20	The University of Leicester	22,172,000
21	The University of Dundee	21,855,000
22	The University of Warwick	18,903,000
23	University of Aberdeen	18,239,000
24	The Queen's University of Belfast	18,159,000
25	University of Wales, Cardiff	17,448,000
26	The University of York	17,367,000
27	The University of Strathclyde	14,935,000
28	The University of Durham	13,897,000
29	The University of Reading	13,614,000
30	The University of Manchester Institute of Science and Technology	13,121,000

Source: Resources of Higher Education Institutions 1997–98, *Higher Education Statistics Agency,* © *Crown copyright 1999*

The Worst 10 Universities for Research

Rank	University	% mark for excellence
1	Thames Valley	4.00
2=	Bournemouth	6.00
	Paisley	6.00
4=	Luton	7.00
	Anglia	7.00
	Glamorgan	7.00
	Wolverhampton	7.00
8=	Napier	7.50
	Lincolnshire and Humberside	7.50
10	Teesside	8.00

Data from 1999 Sunday Times League Table

Overseas Students

There are many reasons why students from other countries choose to study in the UK. Some countries actively promote educational exchanges, and in many places English language skills are highly valued, as English is seen as the language of international commerce. Students from countries other than the UK number 213,264 and represent 11.8% of the total student body. Overseas students make up 36.1% of all full-time postgraduates. Students from outside the UK are well-represented in: agriculture and related subjects; architecture, building, and planning; languages; engineering and technology; and law and business studies. These subjects reflect the skills and knowledge that are considered especially valuable. Overseas students from outside the European Union pay high fees and so are important to educational institutions.

Top 10 Universities for Number of Applications

Rank	University	Applications per place in 1999
1	Bristol	12.4
2	LSE	12.1
3	Nottingham	11.5
4=	Bath	10.7
	Sheffield	10.7
6	City	10.1
7	King's College, London	9.8
8	York	9.6
9	Manchester	9.5
10	Warwick	9.2

Data from UCAS

Top 20 Countries with Overseas Students in Higher Education in the UK

1997–98

Rank	Country of origin	Postgraduate	First degree	Other undergraduate	Total
1	Greece	7,993	16,484	1,125	25,602
2	Malaysia	3,970	12,857	553	17,380
3	Ireland, Republic of	3,288	8,980	3,626	15,894
4	Germany	4,072	5,071	3,894	13,037
5	France	3,341	5,583	3,920	12,844
6	USA	3,930	1,322	4,865	10,117

(continued)

Top 20 Countries with Overseas Students in Higher Education in the UK (*continued*)

1997–98

Rank	Country of origin	Postgraduate	First degree	Other undergraduate	Total
7	Hong Kong	3,210	4,454	313	7,977
8	Spain	1,726	3,142	2,352	7,220
9	Singapore	1,635	4,328	118	6,081
10	Japan	2,499	1,759	1,074	5,332
11	Italy	2,095	1,854	1,305	5,254
12	Norway	789	2,630	312	3,731
13	Sweden	762	1,512	1,067	3,341
14	Cyprus	1,036	2,117	83	3,236
15	Taiwan	2,152	891	190	3,233
16	Canada	1,995	522	453	2,970
17	India	2,111	639	215	2,965
18	Netherlands	1,256	1,041	520	2,817
19	China	2,322	353	208	2,883
20	Thailand	2,082	452	131	2,665

Source: Students in Higher Education Institutions, 1997–98, *Higher Education Statistics Agency, © Crown copyright 1999*

Students in Further and Higher Education, by Type of Course and Gender, in the UK

Enrolments include home and overseas students.

Course	Men					Women				
	1970–71	1980–81	1990–91	1995–96[1]	1997–98[2]	1970–71	1980–81	1990–91	1995–96[1]	1997–98[2]
Further education[3]										
Full-time	116,000	154,000	219,000	375,000	416,000	95,000	196,000	261,000	393,000	448,000
Part-time	891,000	697,000	768,000	735,000	654,000	630,000	624,000	986,000	1,104,000	962,000
Total	1,007,000	851,000	987,000	1,110,000	1,070,000	725,000	820,000	1,247,000	1,497,000	1,410,000
Higher education[4]										
Undergraduate										
full-time	241,000	277,000	345,000	519,000	498,000	173,000	196,000	319,000	529,000	554,000
part-time	127,000	176,000	193,000	221,000	174,000	19,000	71,000	148,000	310,000	235,000
Postgraduate										
full-time	33,000	41,000	50,000	76,000	75,000	10,000	21,000	34,000	60,000	66,000
part-time	15,000	32,000	50,000	98,000	105,000	3,000	13,000	36,000	89,000	102,000
Total[5]	416,000	526,000	638,000	914,000	918,000	205,000	301,000	537,000	988,000	1,021,000

[1] Further education data for the UK and higher education in further education institutions data for England and Wales are for 1994–95.
[2] The figures for 1997–98 refer to headcounts and so are not comparable with earlier years, which refer to enrolments. Further education institutions data for England and Wales relate to 1996–97.
[3] Excludes adult education centres.
[4] Includes Open University.
[5] Data include students whose level of study is unknown.

Awards and Loans Provision for Students in the UK

(– = not applicable. In pounds.)

Academic years	Standard maintenance grant	Maximum amount of loan	Standard maintenance grant plus student loan
1979–80			
home	985	–	–
London	1,485	–	–
elsewhere	1,245	–	–
1980–81			
home	1,125	–	–
London	1,695	–	–
elsewhere	1,430	–	–
1981–82			
home	1,180	–	–
London	1,825	–	–
elsewhere	1,535	–	–
1982–83			
home	1,225	–	–
London	1,900	–	–
elsewhere	1,595	–	–
1983–84			
home	1,275	–	–
London	1,975	–	–
elsewhere	1,660	–	–
1984–85			
home	1,435	–	–
London	2,100	–	–
elsewhere	1,775	–	–
1985–86			
home	1,480	–	–
London	2,165	–	–
elsewhere	1,830	–	–
1987–88			
home	1,567	–	–
London	2,330	–	–
elsewhere	1,972	–	–
1988–89			
home	1,630	–	–
London	2,425	–	–
elsewhere	2,050	–	–
1990–91			
home	1,795	330	2,125
London	2,845	460	3,305
elsewhere	2,265	420	2,685
1991–92			
home	1,795	460	2,255
London	2,845	660	3,505
elsewhere	2,265	580	2,845

(*continued*)

Awards and Loans Provision for Students in the UK *(continued)*

Academic years	Standard maintenance grant	Maximum amount of loan	Standard maintenance grant plus student loan
1992–93			
home	1,795	570	2,368
London	2,845	830	3,675
elsewhere	2,265	715	2,980
1993–94			
home	1,795	640	2,435
London	2,845	940	3,785
elsewhere	2,265	800	3,065
1994–95			
home	1,615	915	2,530
London	2,560	1,375	3,935
elsewhere	2,040	1,150	3,190
1995–96			
home	1,530	1,065	2,595
London	2,340	1,695	4,035
elsewhere	1,885	1,385	3,270
1996–97			
home	1,400	1,260	2,660
London	2,105	2,035	4,140
elsewhere	1,710	1,645	3,355
1997–98			
home	1,435	1,290	2,725
London	2,160	2,085	4,245
elsewhere	1,755	1,685	3,440

Data from *the Department for Education and Employment*

Loans to Students in the UK

Up to and including the academic year 1997–98, students were funded under the system introduced in 1990–91, when non-income-assessed student loans were initiated to provide extra resources for living expenses, partially replacing grants. The main grants were frozen at the 1990–91 values until 1994–95, when their level was reduced, and that of loans increased. Broad parity between the main rates of grant and loans was achieved in the academic year 1996–97.

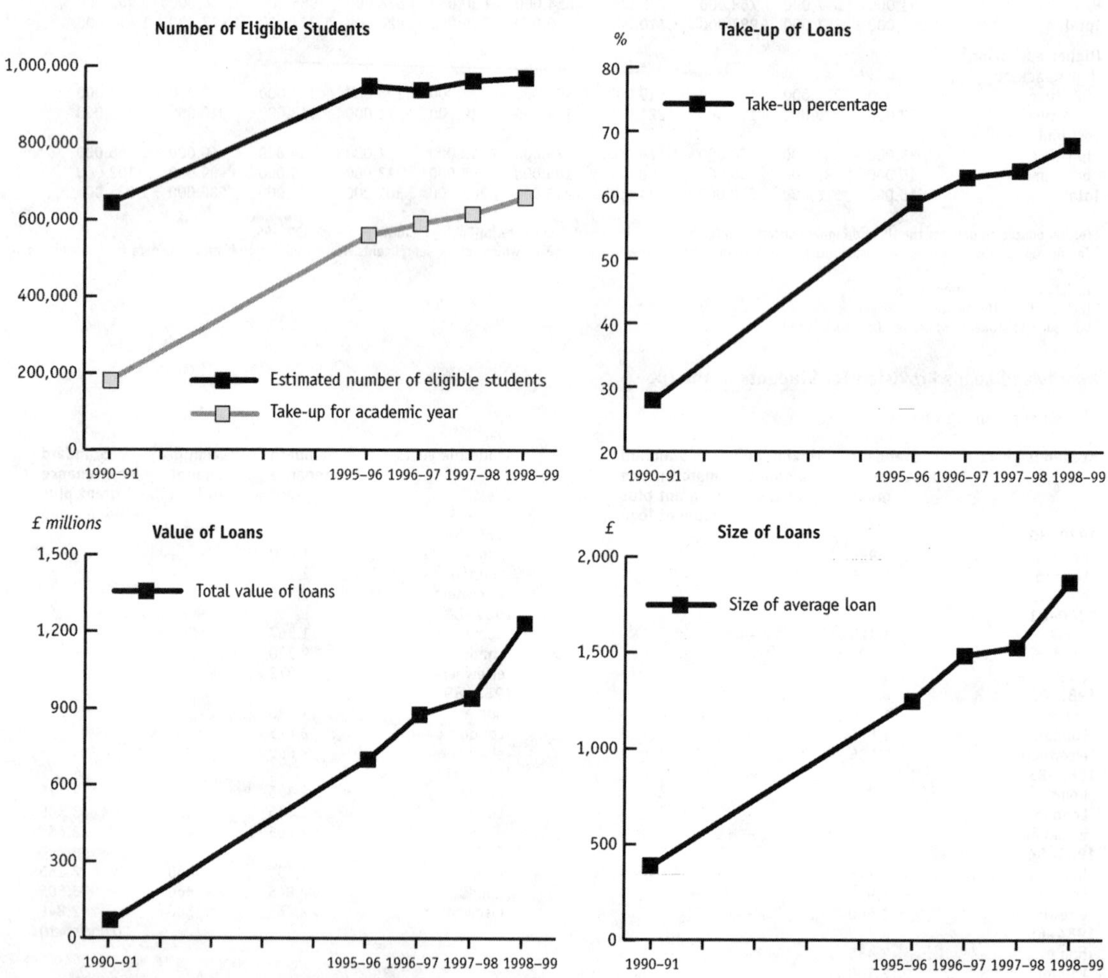

Higher Education Funding and Student Support in the UK

Finance has been a continuing problem for universities in the UK and since 1999 students have been expected to pay fees for higher education courses, maintenance grants have been phased out, and student loans have been introduced as the main form of financial assistance for undergraduates. For the universities themselves, overseas students, who pay full fees if they come from outside the European Union, have become a major source of income. There is also fierce competition for research funding both from the Research Councils and from other sources.

Degrees and Diplomas Obtained by Full-Time Students in the UK

The data in this table are for calendar years.
(N/A = not available.)

Degrees	1986[1]	1987[1]	1988[1]	1989[1]	1990[1]	1991[1]	1992[1]	1993[1]	1994–95[2 3]	1995–96[2 3]	1996–97[2 3]	1997–98[2 3]
First degrees												
Honours												
men	35,823	35,845	36,735	37,473	38,342	39,360	41,908	43,624	N/A	N/A	N/A	N/A
women	25,988	26,601	27,799	28,578	30,121	31,659	34,423	36,983	N/A	N/A	N/A	N/A
Ordinary[4]												
men	5,405	5,518	5,520	5,301	4,973	4,879	4,980	4,891	N/A	N/A	N/A	N/A
women	3,696	3,853	3,702	3,601	3,745	3,739	3,582	3,591	N/A	N/A	N/A	N/A
Totals												
men	N/A	N/A	N/A	N/A	N/A	N/A	N/A	N/A	104,977	111,050	111,027	111,152
women	N/A	N/A	N/A	N/A	N/A	N/A	N/A	N/A	106,864	115,576	119,388	122,458
Higher degrees												
men	17,354	18,559	19,176	20,424	20,905	22,689	24,929	27,568	19,634[5]	23,743	24,404	26,294
women	7,219	8,008	8,676	9,794	10,419	11,912	14,034	16,374	20,973[5]	25,283	26,743	29,469
All degrees												
men	58,582	60,059	61,431	63,198	64,202	66,928	71,817	76,101	124,611	133,793	135,431	137,446
women	36,903	38,475	40,177	41,973	44,285	47,310	52,039	56,948	127,837	140,859	146,131	151,927
Diplomas and Certificates												
men	5,867	6,800	6,659	6,621	6,712	7,914	8,811	9,470	16,606[6]	15,661	15,201	14,608
women	5,706	6,303	6,611	6,599	7,000	8,997	9,881	11,584	17,199[6]	16,975	19,000	18,880

[1] Figures exclude the Open University and former polytechnics and central institutions that obtained university status in 1992.
[2] Figures include students in all publicly funded higher education institutions including the Open University and former polytechnics and colleges.
[3] Data are for the academic year, not the calendar year.
[4] Includes some degrees where the class is not recorded.
[5] Figures include all postgraduate qualifications.
[6] Figures include other undergraduate qualifications.

Source: Annual Abstract of Statistics 2000, *© Crown copyright 2000*

Selected Degree Abbreviations in the UK

BA Bachelor of Arts

BA (Econ) Bachelor of Arts in Economics and Social Studies

BAgr Bachelor of Agriculture

BA(Lan) Bachelor of Languages

BAO Bachelor of Obstetrics

BArch Bachelor of Architecture

BChD Bachelor of Dental Surgery

BCL Bachelor of Civil Law

BCom Bachelor of Commerce

BCommunications Bachelor of Communications

BCS Bachelor of Combined Studies

BD Bachelor of Divinity

BDS Bachelor of Dental Surgery

BEd Bachelor of Education

BEng Bachelor of Engineering

BLing Bachelor of Linguistics

BLitt Bachelor of Letters

BMedSci Bachelor of Medical Science

BMet Bachelor of Metallurgy

BMus Bachelor of Music

BPharm Bachelor of Pharmacy

BPhil Bachelor of Philosophy

BSc Bachelor of Science

BSc(Econ) Bachelor of Science in Economics

BscEng Bachelor of Science in Engineering

BscTech Bachelor of Technical Science

BSocSc Bachelor of Social Sciences

BTech Bachelor of Technology

BVSc Bachelor of Veterinary Science

ChB Bachelor of Surgery

ChM Master of Surgery

DCL Doctor of Civil Law

DD Doctor of Divinity

DDS Doctor of Dental Surgery

DDSc Doctor of Dental Science

DLitt Doctor of Letters

DM Doctor of Medicine

DMus Doctor of Music

DPhil Doctor of Philosophy

DSc Doctor of Science

LittD Doctor of Letters

LLB Bachelor of Law

LLD Doctor of Law

LLM Master of Law

MA Master of Arts

(continued)

Selected Degree Abbreviations in the UK *(continued)*

MArb Master of Arboriculture

MArch Master of Architecture

MB Bachelor of Medicine

MBA Master of Business Administration

MCD Master of Civic Design

MCh Master of Surgery

MChD Master of Dental Surgery

MChemA Master in Chemical Analysis

MCom Master of Commerce

MD Doctor of Medicine

MDS Master of Dental Surgery

MEd Master of Education

MEng Master of Engineering

MLitt Master of Letters

MMus Master of Music

MPharm Master of Pharmacy

MPhil Master of Philosophy

MPhys Master of Physics

MSc Master of Science

MSc(Econ) Master of Science in Economics

MSW Master in Social Work

MTech Master of Technology

MTh Master of Theology

MVSc Master of Veterinary Science

PhD Doctor of Philosophy

Graduate Destinations in the UK

Most new graduates go into employment on finishing their course. Unemployment rates are low, with the most popular profession being teaching, closely followed by business and research activities, then by health and social work. Of those working in this last sector, 90% held associate professional and technical posts in 1998. Overseas students are generally more likely to find employment overseas, particularly those with postgraduate qualifications. One in five graduates go on to further study or training, with female first degree graduates forming the largest group of these.

First Destinations of Higher Education Graduates in the UK

This table provides data on all qualifiers by first destination, level of qualification obtained, domicile, and gender.

1997–98 Level of qualification	Employment in the UK	Employment overseas	Undertaking study	Not available for employment, study, or training	Assumed to be unemployed	Others	Total
Postgraduate							
Home							
women	15,467	554	1,156	493	663	117	18,450
men	12,103	887	1,405	261	664	112	15,432
Overseas							
women	894	1,921	801	68	140	3,954	7,778
men	773	3,300	951	157	115	5,241	10,760
First degree							
Home							
women	62,955	2,386	18,289	4,749	4,408	1,138	93,925
men	52,248	1,952	14,428	3,510	5,514	1,085	78,737
Overseas							
women	1,186	1,080	2,168	134	274	5,529	10,371
men	1,004	1,352	2,453	166	244	7,658	12,877
Other undergraduate							
Home							
women	6,775	40	3,717	236	267	56	11,091
men	3,329	57	4,541	174	385	75	8,561
Overseas							
women	224	51	180	8	5	361	829
men	50	28	173	9	7	391	658
Total	157,231	13,608	50,262	9,965	12,686	25,717	269,469

Source: First Destinations of Students Leaving Higher Education Institutions 1997–98, *Higher Education Statistics Agency,* *© Crown copyright 1999*

Employment Destinations of Graduates by Business Sector in the UK

1997–98 Business sector	Postgraduate		First degrees		Other undergraduate		Total
	Women	Men	Women	Men	Women	Men	
Education	10,477	5,634	9,222	2,998	79	84	28,494
Property development, renting, business, and research activities	1,481	2,409	11,068	14,017	293	497	29,765
Health and social work	1,272	698	11,317	4,442	4,975	720	23,424
Manufacturing	667	1,170	5,599	7,364	205	362	15,367
Wholesale and retail trade/repair of motor vehicles, motorcycles, and general and household goods	213	236	7,127	4,760	315	337	12,988

(continued)

UK Further and Higher Education

Employment Destinations of Graduates by Business Sector in the UK *(continued)*

1997–98 Business sector	Postgraduate		First degrees		Other undergraduate		Total
	Women	Men	Women	Men	Women	Men	
Financial activities	333	664	4,412	4,556	163	160	10,288
Public administration and defence/social security	883	942	3,975	3,280	337	253	9,760
Other community, social, and personal service activities	573	361	4,157	3,482	173	252	8,938
Transport, storage, and communication	151	319	2,473	2,692	106	141	5,882
Hotels and restaurants	39	24	2,395	1,528	211	185	4,382
Construction	24	109	440	1,764	17	114	2,468
Not known	117	144	653	718	39	65	1,736
Electricity, gas, and water supply	79	146	739	822	15	35	1,836
Agriculture and forestry	37	57	239	395	59	155	942
Mining and quarrying	53	164	189	366	5	14	791
Private households with employed persons	8	4	93	29	7	4	145
International organizations and bodies	12	9	33	21	0	1	76
Fishing	2	9	10	18	0	0	39
Total	16,361	13,099	64,141	53,252	6,999	3,379	157,321

Source: First Destinations of Students Leaving Higher Education Institutions 1997–98, *Higher Education Statistics Agency,* © *Crown copyright 1999*

Directory of Local Education Authorities in the UK

England

Barking and Dagenham Alan Larbalestier, Chief Education Officer, Education Offices, Town Hall, Barking, Essex IG11 7LU; phone: (020) 8592 4500; fax: (020) 8227 8235; e-mail: alarbalestier@barking-dagenham.gov.uk; Web site: www.bardaglea.org.uk

Barnet Martyn Kempson, Director of Education and Children, Educational Services (formerly Friern Barnet Town Hall), Friern Barnet Lane, London N11 3DL; phone: (020) 8359 2000; fax: (020) 8359 3057; e-mail: adrian.ley@barnet.gov.uk; Web site: www. barnet.gov.uk

Barnsley Mrs Jean Potter, Acting Programme Director of Education and Leisure, Education Offices, Berneslai Close, Barnsley, South Yorkshire S70 2HS; phone: (01226) 770770; fax: (01226) 773599; e-mail: derek.dalton@barnsley.gov.uk; Web site: www.barnsley.gov.uk

Bath and North East Somerset David Williams, Education Director, Bath and North East Somerset Council, PO Box 25, Riverside, Temple Street, Keynsham, Bristol BS31 1DN; phone: (01225) 477000; fax: (01225) 394011; e-mail: roy_jones@bathnes.gov.uk; Web site: www.bathnes.gov.uk

Bedfordshire *(see also Luton)* Paul Brett, Director of Education, Arts and Libraries, County Hall, Cauldwell Street, Bedford MK42 9AP; phone: (01234) 363222; fax: (01234) 228619; e-mail: brettp@bedforshire.gov.uk; Web site: www.bedfordshire.gov.uk

Bexley Paul McGee, Director of Education and Leisure Services, Bexley Council, Hill View, Hill View Drive, Welling, Kent DA16 3RY; phone: (020) 8303 7777; fax: (020) 8319 4302; e-mail: paul.mcgee@bexley.gov.uk; Web site: www.bexley.gov.uk

Birmingham Tim Brighouse, Chief Education Officer, Education Department, Council House Extension, Margaret Street, Birmingham B3 3BU; phone: (0121) 303 2872; fax: (0121) 303 1318; e-mail: ceoffice@lea.birmingham.gov.uk; Web site: www.birmingham.gov.uk

Blackburn with Darwen *(formerly in Lancashire)* Mark Pattison, Director of Education and Training, Blackburn with Darwen Borough Council, Town Hall, King William Street, Blackburn, Lancashire BB1 7DY; phone: (01254) 585585; fax: (01254) 698388; Web site: www.blackburn.gov.uk

Blackpool *(formerly in Lancashire)* Dr David Saunders, Director of Education, Blackpool Borough Council, Progress House, Clifton Road, Blackpool FY4 4US; phone: (01253) 476555; fax: (01253) 476504; Web site: www.blackpool.gov.uk

Bolton Mrs Margaret Blenkinsop, Director of Education and Arts, PO Box 53, Paderborn House, Civic Centre, Bolton, Lancashire BL1 1JW; phone: (01204) 333333; fax: (01204) 365492; e-mail: bolton.educ.arts@lclweb.com; Web site: www.bolton.gov.uk

Bournemouth *(formerly in Dorset)* Kabir Shaikh, Director of Education, Bournemouth Borough Council, Dorset House, 20–22 Christ Church Road, Bournemouth BH1 3NL; phone: (01202) 456219; fax: (01202) 456191; Web site: www.bournemouth.gov.uk

Bracknell Forest *(formerly in Berkshire)* Tony Eccleston, Director of Education, Bracknell Forest Council, Edward Elgar House, Skimpedhill Lane, Bracknell RG12 1LY; phone: (01344) 424642; fax: (01344) 354001; e-mail: 1103001.2213@compuserve.com; Web site: www.bracknell-forest.gov.uk

Bradford Mrs Diana Cavanagh, Strategic Director (Education), Flockton House, Flockton Road, Bradford, West Yorkshire BD4 7RY; phone: (01274) 751840; fax: (01274) 740612; e-mail: education.info@bradford.gov.uk; Web site: www.bradford.gov.uk

Brent Jacqueline Griffin, Education Offices, Brent London Borough Council, Chesterfield House, 9 Park Lane, Wembley, Middlesex HA9 7RW; phone: (020) 8937 3190; fax: (020) 8937 3023; e-mail: john.simpson@brent.gov.uk; Web site: www2.brent.gov.uk

Brighton and Hove David Hawker, Director of Educational Services, Brighton and Hove Council, King's House, Grand Avenue, Hove, East Sussex BN3 2LS; phone: (01273) 290000; fax: (01273) 293456; e-mail: peter.walker@brighton.hove.gov.uk; Web site: www.brighton-hove.gov.uk

Bristol Richard Riddell, Director of Education, Bristol City Council, Avon House, The Haymarket, Bristol BS99 7EB; phone: (0117) 922 2000; fax: (0117) 903 7963; e-mail: richard_riddell@bristol_city.gov.uk; Web site: www.bristol-city.gov.uk

Bromley Ken Davis, Director of Education, London Borough of Bromley, Education Department, Bromley Civic Centre, Stockwell Close, Bromley BR1 3UH; phone: (020) 8464 3333; fax: (020) 8313 4049; e-mail: jjackson@lea.bromley.sch.uk; Web site: www.bromley.gov.uk

Buckinghamshire *(see also Milton Keynes)* David McGahey, Director of Education, County Hall, Aylesbury, Bucks HP20 1UZ; phone: (01296) 395000; fax: (01296) 383367; e-mail: dmcgahey@buckscc.gov.uk; Web site: www.buckscc.gov.uk

Bury Harold Williams, Borough Education Officer, Education Department, Athenaeum House, Market Street, Bury, Lancashire BL9 0BN; phone: (0161) 253 5000; fax: (0161) 253 5653; e-mail: bhargreaves@bury.gov.uk; Web site: www.bury.gov.uk

Calderdale Ms Carol White, Director of Education, Education Department, PO Box 33, Northgate House, Northgate, Halifax, West Yorkshire HX1 1UN; phone: (01422) 357257; fax: (01422) 392515; e-mail: edcit@dial.pipex.com; Web site: www.calderdale.gov.uk

Cambridgeshire *(see also Peterborough)* Andrew Baxter, Director of Education, Libraries, and Heritage, Castle Court, Shire Hall, Castle Hill, Cambridge CB3 0AP; phone: (01223) 717111; fax: (01223) 717971; e-mail: andrew.baxter@education.camcity.gov.uk; Web site: www.camcnty.gov.uk

Camden Bob Litchfield, Director of Education, London Borough of Camden, Education Department, Crowndale Centre, 218–220 Eversholt Street, London NW1 1BD; phone: (020) 7911 1525; fax: (020) 7911 1536; e-mail: b.glass@camden.gov.uk; Web site: www.camden.gov.uk

Cheshire *(see also Halton; Warrington)* David Cracknell, Group Director of Educational Services, County Hall, Chester CH1 1SQ; phone: (01244) 602424; fax: (01244)

Directory of Local Education Authorities in the UK (*continued*)

603821; e-mail: cracknell@cheshire-cc.btx400.co.uk; Web site: www.cheshire.gov.uk

Cornwall Jonathan Harris, Secretary for Education, Education Offices, County Hall, Treyew Road, Truro, Cornwall TR1 3AY; phone: (01872) 322000; fax: (01872) 323818; e-mail: rrandall@cornwall.gov.uk; Web site: www.cornwall.gov.uk

Corporation of London David Smith, City Education Officer, Corporation of London Education Department, PO Box 270, Guildhall, London EC2P 2EJ; phone: (020) 7332 1750; fax: (020) 7332 1621; e-mail: david.smithcity@campus.bt.com; Web site: www.cityoflondon.gov.uk

Coventry Mrs Cathy Goodwin, Chief Education Officer, New Council Offices, Earl Street, Coventry CV1 5RS; phone: (024) 7683 3333; fax: (024) 7683 1620; e-mail: cgoodwin@coventry.gov.uk; Web site: www.coventry.gov.uk

Croydon Dr David Sands, Director of Education, Taberner House, Park Lane, Croydon CR9 1TP; phone: (020) 8686 4433; fax: (020) 8760 0871; e-mail: david_sands@croydon.gov.uk; Web site: www.croydon.gov.uk

Cumbria John Nellist, Director of Education, Education Offices, 5 Portland Square, Carlisle CA1 1PU; phone: (01228) 606060; fax: (01228) 606896; e-mail: jennet@nellist.demon.co.uk; Web site: www.cumbria.gov.uk

Darlington Geoffrey Pennington, Director of Education, Darlington Borough Council, Town Hall, Darlington DL1 5QT; phone: (01325) 380651; fax: (01325) 382032; Web site: www.darlington.gov.uk

Derby, City of Tony Lenney, Acting Director of Education, Derby City Council, Middleton House, 27 St Mary's Gate, Derby DE1 3NN; phone: (01332) 293111; fax: (01332) 716920; Web site: www.derby.gov.uk

Derbyshire *(see also Derby, City of)* Ms Valerie Hannon, Director of Education, County Offices, Matlock, Derbyshire DE4 3AG; phone: (01629) 580000; fax: (01629) 580350; e-mail: colin@derbyslea.demon.co.uk; Web site: www.derbyshire.gov.uk

Devon *(see also Plymouth; Torbay)* Tony Smith, Chief Education Officer, County Hall, Exeter EX2 4QG; phone: (01392) 382000; fax: (01392) 382203; e-mail: education@ched.devon-cc.gov.uk; Web site: www.devon-cc.gov.uk

Doncaster Matthew Simpson, Director of Education and Leisure Services, PO Box 266, The Council House, Doncaster, South Yorkshire DN1 3AD; phone: (01302) 737222; fax: (01302) 737223; e-mail: matthew.simpson@doncaster.gov.uk; Web site: www.doncaster.gov.uk

Dorset *(see also Bournemouth; Poole)* Richard Ely, Director of Education, Libraries and Arts, Education Department, County Hall, Colliton Park, Dorchester, Dorset DT1 1XJ; phone: (01305) 251000; fax: (01305) 224499; e-mail: t.r.phillips@dorset-cc.gov.uk; Web site: www.dorset-cc.gov.uk

Dudley Richard Colligan, Chief Education Officer, Westox House, 1 Trinity Road, Dudley, West Midlands DY1 1JB; phone: (01384) 818181; fax: (01384) 814216; e-mail: edcent@dudley.gov.uk; Web site: www.dudley.gov.uk

Durham *(see also Darlington)* Keith Mitchell, Director of Education, Education Department, County Hall, Durham DH1 5UJ; phone: (0191) 386 4411; fax: (0191) 386 0487; e-mail: keith.mitchell@durham.gov.uk; Web site: www.durham.gov.uk

Ealing Alan Parker, Director of Education, Perceval House, 5th Floor, 14–16 Uxbridge Road, Ealing, London W5 2HL; phone: (020) 8579 2424; fax: (020) 8280 1291; e-mail: Aparker@ealing.gov.uk; Web site: www.ealing.gov.uk

East Riding of Yorkshire John Ginnever, Director of Education, Leisure and Libraries, East Riding of Yorkshire Council, County Hall, Beverley, East Riding of Yorkshire HU17 9BA; phone: (01482) 887700; fax: (01482) 884920; e-mail: john.ginnever@east-riding-of-yorkshire.gov.uk; Web site: www.east-riding-of-yorkshire.gov.uk

East Sussex *(see also Brighton and Hove)* Mrs Denise Stokoe, Director of Education, East Sussex County Council, PO Box 4, County Hall, St Anne's Crescent, Lewes, East Sussex BN7 1SG; phone: (01273) 481000; fax: (01273) 481261; Web site: www.eastsussexcc.gov.uk

Enfield Ms Liz Graham, Director of Education, Education Department, PO Box 56, Civic Centre, Silver Street, Enfield, Middlesex EN1 3XQ; phone: (020) 8366 6565; fax: (020) 8982 7375; e-mail: phillipson_mir@yahoo.com; Web site: www.enfield.gov.uk

Essex *(see also Southend-on-Sea; Thurrock)* Paul Lincoln, Director of Learning Services, Essex County Council Learning Services, PO Box 47, Chelmsford CM2 1WN; phone: (01245) 492211; fax: (01245) 492759; e-mail: stella.cox@essexcc.gov.uk; Web site: www.essexcc.gov.uk

Gateshead Brian Edwards, Director of Education, Education Offices, Civic Centre, Regent Street, Gateshead, Tyne and Wear NE8 1HH; phone: (0191) 477 1011; fax: (0191) 490 1168; e-mail: gmbc_educ_dept@infman.demon.co.uk; Web site: www.gatesheadmbc.gov.uk

Gloucestershire Roger Crouch, Chief Education Officer, Shire Hall, Gloucester GL1 2TP; phone: (01452) 425300; fax: (01452) 425496; e-mail: educ@gloscc.gov.uk; Web site: www.gloscc.gov.uk

Greenwich George Gyte, Director of Education, London Borough of Greenwich, 9th Floor, Riverside House, Beresford Street, London SE18 6DF; phone: (020) 8854 8888; fax: (020) 8855 2427; e-mail: education@greenwich.gov.uk; Web site: www.greenwich.gov.uk

Hackney Ms Elizabeth Reid, Director of Education, Hackney Education Directorate, Edith Cavell House, Enfield Road, London N1 5BA; phone: (020) 8356 5000; fax: (020) 8356 7295; Web site: www.hackney.gov.uk

Halton Graham Talbot, Director of Education, Education Department, Halton Borough Council, Grosvenor House, Halton LEA, Runcorn, Cheshire WA7 2GW; phone: (0151) 424 2061; fax: (0151) 471 7321; Web site: www.halton-web-directory.co.uk

Hammersmith and Fulham Ms Christine Whatford, Director of Education, London Borough of Hammersmith and Fulham, Town Hall, King Street, London W6 9JU; phone: (020) 8748 3020 (x 3621); fax: (020) 8576 5686; e-mail: 106737.326@compuserve.com; Web site: www.lbhf.gov.uk

Hampshire *(see also Portsmouth; Southampton)* Andrew Seber, County Education Officer, Hampshire County Council, The Castle, Winchester, Hampshire SO23 8UG; phone: (01962) 841841; fax: (01962) 842355; e-mail: edhqmail@hants.gov.uk; Web site: www.hants.gov.uk

Haringey Ms Frances Magee, Director of Education Services, London Borough of Haringey, Education Offices, 48 Station Road, Wood Green, London N22 4TY; phone: (020) 8975 9700; fax: (020) 8862 3864; Web site: www.haringey.gov.uk

Harrow Paul Osburn, Director of Education, PO Box 22, Civic Centre, Harrow, Middlesex HA1 2UW; phone: (020) 8863 5611; fax: (020) 8427 0810; e-mail: posburn@harrow.gov.uk; Web site: www.harrowlb.demon.co.uk

Hartlepool Jeremy Fitt, Director of Education and Community Services, Hartlepool Council, Civic Centre, Victoria Road, Hartlepool TS24 8AY; phone: (01429) 266522; fax: (01429) 523777; e-mail: education@hartlepool.gov.uk

Havering Stephen Evans, Executive Director of Children and Lifelong Learning, London Borough of Havering, The Broxhill Centre, Broxhill Road, Harold Hill, Romford RM14 1XN; phone: (01708) 772222; fax: (01708) 773850; e-mail: colin.hardy@havering.gov.uk; Web site: www.havering.gov.uk

Herefordshire *(formerly in Hereford and Worcester)* Dr Eddie Oram, Director of Education, Hereford Education and Conference Centre, Herefordshire Council, PO Box 185, Blackfriars Street, Hereford HR4 9ZR; phone: (01432) 260000; fax: (01432) 264348

Hertfordshire Ray Shostak, Director of Education, County Hall, Hertford SG13 8DF; phone: (01992) 555555; fax: (01992) 588674; e-mail: ray.shostak@hertscc.gov.uk; Web site: www.hertscc.gov.uk

Hillingdon Phillip O'Hear, Corporate Director of Education, Youth and Leisure, London Borough of Hillingdon, Civic Centre, Uxbridge, Middlesex UB8 1UW; phone: (01895) 250111; fax: (01895) 250878; e-mail: dwalker@lbhill.gov.uk; Web site: www.hillingdon.gov.uk

Hounslow Douglas Trickett, Director of Education, Civic Centre, Lampton Road, Hounslow, Middlesex TW3 4DN; phone: (020) 8862 5352; fax: (020) 8862 5249; e-mail: info@education.hounslow.gov.uk; Web site: www.hounslow.gov.uk

Islington Andy Roberts, Director of Education, London Borough of Islington, Laycock Street, London N1 1TH; phone: (020) 7226 1234; fax: (020) 7457 5555; e-mail: suehammond@islington.gov.uk; Web site: www.islington.gov.uk

Kensington and Chelsea Roger Wood, Executive Director of Education and Libraries, Royal Borough of Kensington and Chelsea, Town Hall, Hornton Street, London W8 7NX; phone: (020) 7361 3334; fax: (020) 7361 2078; e-mail: director@rbkc.gov.uk; Web site: www.rbkc.gov.uk

Kent Nick Henwood, Strategic Director of Education and Libraries, Education Department, Sessions House, County Hall, Maidstone, Kent ME14 1XQ; phone: (01622) 671411; fax: (01622) 694091; e-mail: ed-mgt-info@kent.gov.uk; Web site: www.kent.gov.uk

UK Further and Higher Education

Directory of Local Education Authorities in the UK *(continued)*

Kingston upon Hull, City of Miss Joan Taylor, Director of Education, Kingston upon Hull City Council, Essex House, Manor Street, Kingston upon Hull HU1 1YD; phone: (01482) 610610; fax: (01482) 613407; e-mail: kuhedc@karoo.co.uk; Web site: www. hullcc. gov.uk

Kingston upon Thames John Braithwaite, Director of Education and Leisure, Royal Borough of Kingston upon Thames, Guildhall, High Street, Kingston upon Thames, Surrey KT1 1EU; phone: (020) 8546 2121; fax: (020) 8547 5296; e-mail: john.braithwaite@rbk.kingston.gov.uk; Web site: www.kingston.gov.uk

Kirklees Gavin Tonkin, Chief Education Officer, Kirklees Metropolitan Council, Oldgate House, 2 Oldgate, Huddersfield HD1 6QW; phone: (01484) 221000; fax: (01484) 225264; e-mail: rob.vincent@geo2.poptel.gov.uk; Web site: www.kirkleesmc.gov.uk

Knowsley Peter Wylie, Director of Education, Knowsley Metropolitan Borough Council, Education Office, Huyton Hey Road, Huyton, Merseyside L36 5YH; phone: (0151) 489 6000; fax: (0151) 449 3852; e-mail: directorofeducation.de@knowsley.gov.uk; Web site: www.knowsley.gov.uk

Lambeth Mrs Heather du Quesnay, Executive Director of Education, Lambeth Education Department, London Borough of Lambeth, Blue Star House, 234/244 Stockwell Road, London SW9 7QE; phone: (020) 7926 1000; fax: (020) 7926 2296; e-mail: lambeth@rmplc.co.uk; Web site: www.lambeth.gov.uk

Lancashire *(see also Blackburn with Darwen; Blackpool)* Christopher Trinick, Director of Education and Cultural Studies, Lancashire County Council, PO Box 61, County Hall, Preston PR1 8RJ; phone: (01772) 254868; fax: (01772) 261630; e-mail: stephen.clark@educ.lancscc.gov.uk; Web site: www.lancashire.com

Leeds Keith Burton, Director of Education, Leeds Education Department, Selectapost 17, Merrion House, Merrion Centre, Leeds LS2 8DT; phone: (0113) 234 8080; fax: (0113) 234 1394; e-mail: jean.potter@leeds.gov.uk; Web site: www.leeds.gov.uk

Leicester City Anthony Webster, Acting Director of Education, Leicester City Council, Marlborough House, 38 Welford Road, Leicester LE2 7AA; phone: (0116) 254 9922; fax: (0116) 233 9922; e-mail: warrtoo1@leicester.gov.uk; Web site: www.leicester.gov.uk/city/

Leicestershire *(see also Leicester City; Rutland)* Ms Jackie Strong, Director of Education, Education Department, County Hall, Glenfield, Leicester LE3 8RF; phone: (0116) 232 3232; fax: (0116) 265 6634; e-mail: jturner@leics.gov.uk; Web site: www.leics.gov.uk

Lewisham Ms Althea Erunshile, Director of Education and Culture, London Borough of Lewisham, Laurence House, Town Hall, Catford, London SE6 4SW; phone: (020) 8695 6000; fax: (020) 8690 4392; e-mail: martin.meredith@lewisham.gov.uk; Web site: www.lewisham.gov.uk

Lincolnshire Norman Riches, Director of Education and Cultural Services, County Offices, Newland, Lincoln LN1 1YQ; phone: (01522) 552222; fax: (01522) 553257; e-mail: caroline.turner@lincolnshire.gov.uk; Web site: www.lincolnshire.gov.uk

Liverpool Colin Hilton, Director of Education & Lifelong Learning, Education Offices, 14 Sir Thomas Street, Liverpool L1 6BJ; phone: (0151) 225 2882; fax: (0151) 225 3029; e-mail: postroom@connect.bt.com; Web site: www.liverpool.gov.uk

London, Inner see separate entries for the former Inner London Education Authority (ILEA) London Boroughs: Camden, Corporation of London (covering the one square mile of the City of London), Greenwich, Hammersmith and Fulham, Hackney, Islington, Kensington and Chelsea, Lambeth, Lewisham, Southwark, Tower Hamlets, Wandsworth, Westminster

London, Outer see separate entries for the following London Boroughs: Barking and Dagenham, Barnet, Bexley, Brent, Bromley, Croydon, Ealing, Enfield, Haringey, Harrow, Havering, Hillingdon, Hounslow, Kingston upon Thames, Merton, Newham, Redbridge, Richmond upon Thames, Sutton, Waltham Forest

Luton Tony Dessent, Director of Education, Luton Borough Council, Unity House, 111 Stuart Street, Luton, Bedfordshire LU1 5NP; phone: (01582) 548001; fax: (01582) 548454; e-mail: dessentt@luton.gov.uk; Web site: www.luton.gov.uk

Manchester David Johnson, Chief Education Officer, Education Offices, Crown Square, Manchester M60 3BB; phone: (0161) 234 5000; fax: (0161) 234 7147; e-mail: tkeane@manchester.gov.uk; Web site: www.manchester.gov.uk

Man, Isle of Ralf Cowin, Director of Education, Education Department, 2nd Floor, Murray House, Mount Hevelock, Douglas, Isle of Man IM1 2SG; phone: (01624) 685820; fax: (01624) 685834; e-mail: admin@doe.gov.im; Web site: www.gov.im

Medway *(formerly in Kent)* Richard Bolsin, Director of Education, Medway Council, Compass Centre, Chatham Maritime, Chatham, Kent ME4 4YN; phone: (01634) 306000; fax: (01634) 890120; Web site: www.medway.gov.uk

Merton Mrs Jenny Cairns, Director of Education, Leisure and Libraries, London Borough of Merton, Crown House, London Road, Morden, Surrey SM4 5DX; phone: (020) 8543 2222; fax: (020) 8545 3443; e-mail: 106001.2536@compuserve.com

Middlesbrough Dr Cheryle Berry, Corporate Director of Education and Leisure, Middlesbrough Borough Council, PO Box 191, 2nd Floor, Civic Centre, Middlesbrough TS1 2XS; phone: (01642) 262001; fax: (01642) 262038; e-mail: malcolm_shorney@middlesbrough.gov.uk; Web site: www.middlesbrough.gov.uk

Milton Keynes Jill Stansfield, Learning and Development Strategic Director, Milton Keynes Council, Saxon Court, 502 Avebury Boulevard, Milton Keynes MK9 3HS; phone: (01908) 691691; fax: (01908) 253289; e-mail: jill.stansfield@milton-keynes.gov.uk; Web site: www.mkweb.co.uk

Newcastle upon Tyne David Bell, Director of Education and Libraries, Education Offices, Civic Centre, Barras Bridge, Newcastle upon Tyne NE1 8PU; phone: (0191) 232 8520; fax: (0191) 211 4983; e-mail: dbell@ceo-newcastle.demon.co.uk; Web site: www.newcastle.gov.uk

Newham Ian Harrison, Director of Education, London Borough of Newham, Education Offices, Broadway House, 322 High Street, Stratford, London E15 1AJ; phone: (020) 8555 5552; fax: (020) 8503 0014; e-mail: peter.aylmer@newham.gov.uk; Web site: www.newham.gov.uk

Norfolk Bryan Slater, Director of Education, Norfolk County Council, County Hall, Martineau Lane, Norwich NR1 2DL; phone: (01603) 222300; fax: (01603) 222119; e-mail: bryan.slater.edu@norfolk.gov.uk; Web site: www.norfolk.gov.uk

Northamptonshire Mrs Brenda Bignold, Director of Education and Community Learning, PO Box 149, County Hall, Guildhall Road, Northampton NN1 1AU; phone: (01604) 236236; fax: (01604) 236188; e-mail: education@northamptonshire.gov.uk; Web site: www.northamptonshire.gov.uk

North East Lincolnshire Geoff Hill, Head of Professional Service – Education, North East Lincolnshire Council, Eleanor Street, Grimsby DN32 9DU; phone: (01472) 313131; fax: (01472) 323020; e-mail: geoff.hill@nelincs.gov.uk; Web site: www.nelincs.gov.uk

North Lincolnshire Dr Trevor Thomas, Director of Education and Personal Development, North Lincolnshire Council, PO Box 35, Hewson House, Station Road, Brigg DN20 8JX; phone: (01724) 297241; fax: (01724) 297242; e-mail: lesley.blackburn@northlincs.gov.uk; Web site: www.northlincs.gov.uk

North Somerset John Simpson, Director of Education, North Somerset Council, PO Box 51, Town Hall, Weston-Super-Mare BS23 1ZZ; phone: (01934) 888888; fax: (01934) 888834; e-mail: mo.waters@n-somerset.gov.uk; Web site: www.n-somerset.gov.uk

North Tyneside Les Walton, Executive Director for Education, School Services, North Tyneside Council, Stephenson House, Stephenson Street, North Shields NE30 1QA; phone: (0191) 200 5151; fax: (0191) 200 6090; e-mail: Nteaiu@rmplc.co.uk; Web site: www.northtyneside.gov.uk

Northumberland Dr Lindsey Davies, Director of Education, Education Department, Northumberland County Council,County Hall, Morpeth, Northumberland NE61 2EF; phone: (01670) 533677; fax: (01670) 533750; e-mail: education@northumberland.gov.uk; Web site: www.northumberland.gov.uk

North Yorkshire *(see also York)* Cynthia Welbourn, Director of Education, County Hall, Northallerton, North Yorkshire DL7 8AE; phone: (01609) 780780; fax: (01609) 778611; e-mail: cynthia.welbourn@northyorks.gov.uk; Web site: www.northyorks. gov.uk

Nottingham, City of *(formerly in Nottinghamshire)* Paul Roberts, Director of Education, Nottinghamshire City Council, Sandfield Centre, Sandfield Road, Lenton, Nottingham NG7 1QH; phone: (0115) 915 5555; fax: (0115) 915 0603; Web site: www.nottinghamcity.gov.uk

Nottinghamshire *(see also Nottingham, City of)* Rob Valentine, Director of Education, Nottinghamshire County Council, County Hall, West Bridgford, Nottingham NG2 7QP; phone: (0115) 982 3823; fax: (0115) 981 2824; e-mail: edcomm@nottscc.gov.uk; Web site: www.nottscc.gov.uk

Directory of Local Education Authorities in the UK *(continued)*

Oldham Michael Willis, Director of Education and Leisure Services, Oldham Metropolitan Borough Council, Level 5, PO Pox 40, Civic Centre, West Street, Oldham OL1 1XJ; phone: (0161) 911 4260; fax: (0161) 911 3221; e-mail: els.mwillis@oldham.gov.uk; Web site: www.oldham.gov.uk

Oxfordshire Graham Badman, Chief Education Officer, Education Department, Macclesfield House, New Road, Oxford OX1 1NA; phone: (01865) 792422; fax: (01865) 791637; e-mail: occlea01@rmplc.co.uk; Web site: www.oxfordshire.gov.uk

Peterborough, City of *(formerly in Cambridgeshire)* Bill Goodwin, Director of Education, Peterborough City Council, Bayard Place, Broadway, Peterborough PE1 1FB; phone: (01733) 563141; fax: (01733) 748111; Web site: www.peterborough.gov.uk

Plymouth, City of *(formerly in Devon)* Sohail Faruqi, Director of Education, City of Plymouth Council, Civic Centre, Plymouth PL1 2AA; phone: (01752) 307400; fax: (01752) 307403; Web site: www.plymouth.gov.uk

Poole *(formerly in Dorset)* Dr Shirley Goodwin, Policy Director Education, Borough of Poole, Civic Centre, Poole, Dorset BH15 2RU; phone: (01202) 633633; fax: (01202) 633706; e-mail: l.guppy@poole.gov.uk; Web site: www.poole.gov.uk

Portsmouth John Gaskin, City Education Officer, Portsmouth City Council, Civic Offices, Guildhall Square, Portsmouth PO1 2EA; phone: (023) 9282 2251; fax: (023) 9283 4159; Web site: www.portsmouthcc.gov.uk

Reading Andrew Daykin, Director of Education, Reading Borough Council, Civic Offices, Civic Centre, Reading RG1 7TD; phone: (0118) 939 0900; fax: (0118) 958 9770; Web site: www.reading.gov.uk

Redbridge Don Capper, Director of Education, Education Office, London Borough of Redbridge, Lynton House, 255–259 High Road, Ilford, Essex IG1 1NY; phone: (020) 8478 3020; fax: (020) 8478 9044; Web site: www.redbridge.gov.uk

Redcar and Cleveland Patrick Scott, Director of Education, Redcar and Cleveland Borough Council, Redcar Council Offices, PO Box 83, Kirkleatham Street, Redcar TS10 1YA; phone: (01642) 444000; fax: (01642) 444122; e-mail: redcareduc@aol.com; Web site: www.redcar-cleveland.gov.uk

Richmond upon Thames Vincent McDonnell, Director of Education, London Borough of Richmond upon Thames, Education Department, Regal House, London Road, Twickenham TW1 3QB; phone: (020) 8891 1411; fax: (020) 8891 7714; e-mail: education@richmond.gov.uk; Web site: www.richmond.gov.uk

Rochdale Brian Atkinson, Director of Education, Education Department, PO Box 70, Municipal Offices, Smith Street, Rochdale OL16 1YD; phone: (01706) 647474; fax: (01706) 658560; e-mail: council@rochdale.gov.uk; Web site: www.rochdale.gov.uk

Rotherham Harry Bower, Director of Education Services, Norfolk House, Walker Place, Rotherham S60 1QT; phone: (01709) 382121; fax: (01709) 372056; e-mail: harry.bower@rotherham.gov.uk; Web site: www.rotherham.gov.uk

Rutland Mrs Carole Chambers, Director of Education & Community Services, Rutland Council, Catmose, Oakham, Rutland LE15 6HP; phone: (01572) 722577; fax: (01572) 758307; e-mail: rutland@connect.bt.com; Web site: www.rutnet.co.uk

St Helens Ms Judith Godley, Acting Director of Community Education, Community Education and Leisure Services Department, The Rivington Centre, Rivington Road, St Helens, Merseyside WA10 4ND; phone: (01744) 456000; fax: (01744) 455350; e-mail: facet.sthelens@cableinet.co.uk; Web site: www.sthelens.gov.uk

Salford Mark Carriline, Director of Education and Leisure, Education Office, Chapel Street, Salford M3 5LT; phone: (0161) 832 9751/8; fax: (0161) 835 1561; Web site: www.salford.gov.uk

Sandwell Stuart Gallacher, Director of Education and Community Services, Sandwell Metropolitan Borough Council, PO Box 41, Shaftesbury House, 402 High Street, West Bromwich, West Midlands B70 9LT; phone: (0121) 525 7366; fax: (0121) 553 1528; e-mail: vale.r@sandwell.gov.uk; Web site: www.sandwell.gov.uk

Scilly, Isles of Philip Hygate, Secretary for Education, Education Department, Town Hall, St Mary's, Isles of Scilly TR21 0LW; phone: (01720) 422537; fax: (01720) 422202; e-mail: steve@scilly.demon.co.uk

Sefton Brynley Marsh, Director of Education, Sefton Borough Council, Education Department, Town Hall, Bootle, Merseyside L20 7AE; phone: (0151) 933 6003; fax: (0151) 934 3349; Web site: www.sefton. gov.uk

Sheffield Jonathon Crossley-Holland, Director of Education, PO Box 67, Leopold Street, Sheffield S1 1RJ; phone: (0114) 272 6444; fax: (0114) 273 6279; e-mail: ses@connect.bt.com; Web site: www.sheffield.gov.uk

Shropshire *(see also Telford and Wrekin)* Liz Nicholson, Corporate Director of Education, Shropshire County Council, The Shirehall, Abbey Foregate, Shrewsbury SY2 6ND; phone: (01743) 251000; fax: (01743) 254415; e-mail: janet.rigby@shropshire-cc.gov.uk; Web site: www.shropshire-cc.gov.uk

Slough *(formerly in Berkshire)* John Christie, Chief Education Officer, Slough Borough Council, Town Hall, Bath Road, Slough SL1 3UQ; phone: (01753) 552288; fax: (01753) 692499

Solihull David Nixon, Director of Education, Libraries and Arts, PO Box 20, Council House, Solihull, West Midlands B91 3QU; phone: (0121) 704 6656; fax: (0121) 704 6669; e-mail: pmayhew@solihull.gov.uk; Web site: www.solihull.gov.uk

Somerset Michael Jennings, Corporate Director of Education, County Hall, Taunton, Somerset TA1 4DY; phone: (01823) 355455; fax: (01823) 355332; e-mail: educ.ses@somerset.gov.uk; Web site: www.somerset.gov.uk

Southampton Bob Hogg, Director of Education, Southampton City Council, Frobisher House, Nelson Gate, Commercial Road, Southampton SO15 1GX; phone: (023) 8022 3855; fax: (023) 8083 3224; e-mail: sesgsog1@hants.gov.uk; Web site: www.southampton.gov.uk

Southend-on-Sea *(formerly in Essex)* Stephen Hay, Director of Education and Libraries Services, Southend on Sea Borough Council, PO Box 6, Civic Centre, Victoria Avenue, Southend on Sea SS2 6ER; phone: (01702) 215921; fax: (01702) 432273; Web site: www.southend.gov.uk

South Gloucestershire Ms Therese Gillespie, Director of Education, South Gloucestershire Offices, Bowling Hill, Chipping Sodbury BS37 6JX; phone: (01454) 863333; fax: (01454) 863263; e-mail: educ_service@southglos.gov.uk; Web site: www.southglos.gov.uk

South Tyneside Ian Reid, Director of Education, Education Department, Town Hall Civic Offices, Westoe Road, South Shields, Tyne and Wear NE33 2RL; phone: (0191) 427 1717; fax: (0191) 427 0584; Web site: www.nof.co.uk/stmbc

Southwark Gordon Mott, Director of Education and Library Services, London Borough of Southwark, 1 Bradenham Close (off Albany Road), London SE17 2QA; phone: (020) 7525 5050/5051; fax: (020) 7525 5200; e-mail: fn64@dial.pipex.com; Web site: www.southwark.gov.uk

Staffordshire *(see also Stoke-on-Trent)* Dr Philip Hunter, Director of Education, County Buildings, Tipping Street, Stafford ST16 2DH; phone: (01785) 278610; fax: (01785) 278639; e-mail: p.hunter@staffordshire.gov.uk; Web site: www.staffordshire.gov.uk

Stockport Max Hunt, Chief Education Officer, Education Division, Stopford House, Piccadilly, Stockport SK1 3XE; phone: (0161) 480 4949; fax: (0161) 953 0012; Web site: www.stockportmbc.gov.uk

Stockton-on-Tees Stanley Bradford, Chief Education Officer, Stockton-on-Tees Council, PO Box 228, Municipal Buildings, Church Road, Stockton-on-Tees TS18 1XE; phone: (01642) 393939; fax: (01642) 393479; e-mail: education.services@sbcss3.stockton-bc.gov.uk; Web site: www.stockton-bc.gov.uk

Stoke-on-Trent Nigel Rigby, Director of Education, Stoke-on-Trent City Council, Swann House, Boothen Road, Stoke-on-Trent ST4 4SY; phone: (01782) 236100; fax: (01782) 236102; e-mail: nigel.rigby@ stoke01.stoke-cc.gov.uk; Web site: www.stoke.gov.uk

Suffolk David Peachey, County Director of Education, Education Department, St Andrew House, County Hall, Ipswich IP4 1LJ; phone: (01473) 583000; fax: (01473) 584624; e-mail: annedn@educ.suffolkcc.gov.uk; Web site: www.suffolkcc.gov.uk

Sunderland Dr John Williams, Director of Education and Community Services, Education Department, PO Box 101, Town Hall and Civic Centre, Sunderland SR2 7DN; phone: (0191) 553 1000; fax: (0191) 553 1410; e-mail: eileen.jennings@sunderland.gov.uk; Web site: www.sunderland.gov.uk

Surrey Dr Paul Gray, Director of Education, County Hall, Penrhyn Road, Kingston upon Thames KT1 2DJ; phone: (020) 8 541 9501; fax: (020) 8541 9502; e-mail: eanderson@surreycc.gov.uk; Web site: www.surreycc.gov.uk

Sutton Dr Ian Birnbaum, Director of Education, London Borough of Sutton, The Grove, Carshalton SM5 3AL; phone: (020) 8770 5000; fax: (020) 8770 6548; e-mail: janice.hamilton@sutton.gov.uk; Web site: www.sutton.gov.uk

Swindon Mike Lusty, Chief Education Officer, Swindon Borough Council, Sanford House, Sanford Street, Swindon SN1 1QH; phone: (01793) 463000; fax: (01793) 488597; Web site: www.swindon.gov.uk

UK Further and Higher Education

Directory of Local Education Authorities in the UK *(continued)*

Tameside Paul Lawday, Director of Education, Tameside Metropolitan Borough Council, Education Department, Council Offices, Wellington Road, Ashton under Lyne, Lancashire OL6 6DL; phone: (0161) 342 8355; fax: (0161) 342 3260; e-mail: educ.dept@educ.tameside.gov.uk; Web site: www.tameside.gov.uk

Telford and Wrekin *(formerly in Shropshire)* Mrs Christine Davis, Corporate Director of Education and Training, Telford and Wrekin Council, PO Box 440, Civic Offices, Telford TF3 4LD; phone: (01952) 202100; fax: (01952) 293946; e-mail: education@wrekin.gov.uk; Web site: www.telford.gov.uk

Thurrock *(formerly in Essex)* Raphael Wilkins, Director of Education, Thurrock Council, Civic Offices, New Road, Grays, Essex RM17 6SL; phone: (01375) 652652; fax: (01375) 652792; Web site: www.thurrock-community.org.uk

Torbay *(formerly in Devon)* Graham Cane, Director of Education Services, Torbay Borough Council, Oldway Mansion, Paignton, Devon TQ3 2TE; phone: (01803) 208208; fax: (01803) 208225; Web site: www.torbay.gov.uk

Tower Hamlets Ms Christine Gilbert, Director of Education and Community Services, London Borough of Tower Hamlets, Education Department, Mulberry Place, 5 Clove Crescent, London E14 2BG; phone: (020) 7364 5000; fax: (020) 7364 4296; Web site: www.tower-hamlets.gov.uk

Trafford Chris Pratt, Director of Education, Arts and Leisure, Trafford Metropolitan Borough Council, PO Box 19, Tatton Road, Sale, Cheshire M33 7YR; phone: (0161) 912 3251; fax: (0161) 912 4184

Wakefield John McLeod, Chief Education Officer, Education Department, County Hall, Bond Street, Wakefield, West Yorkshire WF1 2QL; phone: (01924) 306090; fax: (01924) 305632; e-mail: jpotts@wakefield.gov.uk; Web site: www.wakefield.gov.uk

Walsall Humphrey Smith, Chief Education Services Officer, The Civic Centre, Darwall Street, Walsall, West Midlands WS1 1DQ; phone: (01922) 650000; fax: (01922) 722322; Web site: www.walsall.gov.uk

Waltham Forest Andrew Lockhart, Chief Education Officer, London Borough of Waltham Forest, Municipal Offices, High Road, Leyton, London E10 5QJ; phone: (020) 8527 5544; fax: (020) 8556 8720; Web site: www.lbwf.gov.uk

Wandsworth Paul Robinson, Director of Education, London Borough of Wandsworth, Town Hall, Wandsworth High Street, London SW18 2PU; phone: (020) 8871 8013; fax: (020) 8871 8011; Web site: www.wandsworth.gov.uk

Warrington *(formerly in Cheshire)* Malcolm Roxburgh, Director of Education, Education Department, Warrington Borough Council, New Town House, Buttermarket Street, Warrington WA1 2LS; phone: (01925) 444400; fax: (01925) 442705; Web site: www.warrington.gov.uk

Warwickshire Eric Wood, County Education Officer, PO Box 24, 22 Northgate Street, Warwick CV34 4SR; phone: (01926) 410410; fax: (01926) 412746; e-mail: warkslea@dial.pipex.com; Web site: www.warwickshire.gov.uk

West Berkshire *(formerly in Berkshire)* Jay Mercer, Corporate Director (Education), West Berkshire Council, Avonbank House, West Street, Newbury RG14 1BZ; phone: (01635) 519723; fax: (01635) 519725; Web site: www.westberks.gov.uk

Westminster John Harris, Director of Education and Leisure, City of Westminster, PO Box 240, Westminster City Hall, 64 Victoria Street, London SW1E 6QP; phone: (020) 7641 6000; fax: (020) 7641 3404; e-mail: zlo1@dial.pipex.com; Web site: www.westminster.gov.uk

West Sussex Richard Bunker, Director of Education, County Hall, West Street, Chichester, West Sussex PO19 1RF; phone: (01243) 777100; fax: (01243) 777229; e-mail: rbunker@westsussex.gov.uk; Web site: www.westsussex.gov.uk

Wigan Bob Clark, Director of Education, Education Offices, Gateway House, Standishgate, Wigan WN1 1AE; phone: (01942) 828891; fax: (01942) 828811; e-mail: m.aspey@wiganmbc.gov.uk; Web site: www.wiganmbc.gov.uk

Wight, Isle of Alan Kaye, Director of Education, County Hall, Newport, Isle of Wight PO30 1UD; phone: (01983) 821000; fax: (01983) 826099; e-mail: aseawardiw@aol.com; Web site: www.iwight.gov.uk

Wiltshire *(see also Swindon)* Robert Wolfson, Chief Education Officer, County Hall, Bythesea Road, Trowbridge, Wiltshire BA14 8JB; phone: (01225) 713000; fax: (01225) 713982; e-mail: wiltsgovsupport@cableinet.co.uk; Web site: www.wiltshire.gov.uk

Windsor and Maidenhead, Royal Borough of *(formerly in Berkshire)* Malcolm Peckham, Director of Education, Royal Borough of Windsor and Maidenhead, Town Hall, St Ives Road, Maidenhead SL6 1RF; phone: (01628) 798888; fax: (01628) 796408

Wirral Christopher Rice, Director of Education, Wirral Metropolitan Borough Council, Hamilton Building, Conway Street, Birkenhead L41 4FD; phone: (0151) 666 2121; fax: (0151) 666 4207; e-mail: educ@wirral.gov.uk; Web site: www.wirral.gov.uk

Wokingham *(formerly in Berkshire)* Andy Roberts, Director of Education and Cultural Services, Wokingham District Council, PO Box 156, Shute End, Wokingham RG40 1WN; phone: (0118) 974 6100; fax: (0118) 974 6103; Web site: www.wokingham.gov.uk

Wolverhampton Roy Lockwood, Director of Education, Education Department, Civic Centre, St Peter's Square, Wolverhampton WV1 1RR; phone: (01902) 556556; fax: (01902) 554218; e-mail: directorofeducation@dial.pipex.com; Web site: www.wolverhampton.gov.uk

Worcestershire Julien Kramer, Director of Education Services, Worcestershire County Council, County Hall, Spetchley Road, Worcester WR5 2NP; phone: (01905) 763763; fax: (01905) 768400; Web site: www.worcestershire.gov.uk

York, City of Mike Peters, Director of Education, City of York Council, 10–12 George Hudson Street, York YO1 6ZG; phone: (01904) 613161; fax: (01904) 554206; Web site: www.york.gov.uk

Scotland

Aberdeen John Stodter, Director of Education, Aberdeen City Council, Sumerhill Education Centre, Stronsay Drive, Aberdeen AB15 6JA; phone: (01224) 522000; fax: (01224) 346061; e-mail: lmilne@aberdeen-education.org.uk

Aberdeenshire M White, Director of Education, Woodhill House, Westburn Road, Aberdeen AB16 5GB; phone: (01224) 665420; fax: (01224) 665445; Web site: www.aberdeenshire.gov.uk

Angus Jim Anderson, Director of Education, Angus Council, County Buildings, Market Street, Forfar DD8 3WE; phone: (01307) 461460 (x 3236); fax: (01307) 461848; e-mail: education@angus.gov.uk; Web site: www.angus.gov.uk

Argyll and Bute Archibald Morton, Director of Education, Argyll House, Alexandra Parade, Dunoon, Argyll PA23 8AJ; phone: (01369) 704000; fax: (01369) 708584; Web site: www.argyll-bute.gov.uk

Clackmannanshire Keir Bloomer, Director of Education and Community Services, Lime Tree House, Castle Street, Alloa FK10 1EX; phone: (01259) 450000; fax: (01259) 452440; e-mail: info@education.clacks-gov.uk; Web site: www.education.clacks.gov.uk

Dumfries and Galloway Frazer Sanderson, Acting Director of Education, 30 Edinburgh Road, Dumfries DG1 1NW; phone: (01387) 260000; fax: (01387) 260453; Web site: www.dumgal.gov.uk

Dundee Mrs Anne Wilson, Director of Education, Floor 8 Tayside House, Crichton Street, Dundee DD1 3RJ; phone: (01382) 434000; fax: (01382) 433080; e-mail: anne.wilson@dundeecity.gov.uk; Web site: www.dundeecity.gov.uk

East Ayrshire John Mulgrew, Director of Education, Council Headquarters, London Road Centre, London Road, Kilmarnock KA3 7DG; phone: (01563) 576017; fax: (01563) 576210; e-mail: john.mulgrew@east-ayrshire.gov.uk; Web site: www.east-ayrshire.gov.uk

East Dunbartonshire Ian Mills, Director of Education and Leisure Services, Boclair House, 100 Milngavie Road, Bearsden, Glasgow G61 2TQ; phone: (0141) 578 8000; fax: (0141) 578 8653; e-mail: ian.mills@eastdunbarton.gov.uk

East Lothian Alan Blackie, Director of Education and Community Services, Council Buildings, Haddington EH41 4BU; phone: (01620) 827588; fax: (01620) 827291; Web site: www.eastlothian.gov.uk

East Renfrewshire Mrs Eleanor Currie, Director of Education, East Renfrewshire Council, Eastwood Park, Rouken Glen Road, Giffnock, Glasgow G46 6UG; phone: (0141) 577 3430; fax: (0141) 577 3405; e-mail: mathisonm@eastrenfrewshire.gov.uk; Web site: www.eastrenfrewshire.gov.uk

Edinburgh Roy Jobson, Director of Education, Council Headquarters, Wellington Court, 10 Waterloo Place, Edinburgh EH1 3EG; phone: (0131) 469 3000; fax: (0131) 469 3320; e-mail: roy.jobson@educ.edin.gov.uk; Web site: www.educ.edin.gov.uk

Directory of Local Education Authorities in the UK *(continued)*

Falkirk Dr G Young, Director of Education, McLaren House, Marchmont Avenue, Polmont FK2 0NZ; phone: (01324) 506600; fax: (01324) 506664; Web site: www.falkirk-ents.demon.co.uk

Fife Alex McKay, Head of Education, Fife House, North Street, Glenrothes, Fife KY7 5LT; phone: (01592) 413656; fax: (01592) 413696; e-mail: amckay@itasdarc.demon.co.uk; Web site: www.fife.gov.uk

Glasgow K Corsar, Director of Education, House 1, Charing Cross Complex, 20 India Street, Glasgow G2 4PF; phone: (0141) 287 2000; fax: (0141) 287 6892; Web site: www.glasgow.gov.uk

Highland Bruce Robertson, Director of Education, Glenurquhart Road, Inverness IV3 5NX; phone: (01463) 702802; fax: (01463) 702808; Web site: www.highland.gov.uk

Inverclyde Bernard McLeary, Director of Education Services, Department of Education Services, 105 Dalrymple Street, Greenock PA15 1HT; phone: (01475) 882828; fax: (01475) 712875; e-mail: bernard.mcleary@ecsumail1.ecsu.org

Midlothian Donald MacKay, Director of Education, Midlothian Council, Midlothian House, Buccleuch Street, Dalkeith EH22 1DJ; phone: (0131) 270 7500; fax: (0131) 271 3751; Web site: www.midlothian.gov.uk

Moray Donald Duncan, Acting Director of Education, High Street, Elgin IV30 1BX; phone: (01343) 563134; fax: (01343) 563478; Web site: www.moray.org/

North Ayrshire John Travers, Director of Education, Cunninghame House, Friars Croft, Irvine KA12 8EE; phone: (01294) 324400; fax: (01294) 324444; e-mail: adv@naceducation.prestel.co.uk; Web site: www.ers.north-ayrshire.gov.uk

North Lanarkshire Michael O'Neill, Director of Education, Municipal Building, Kildonan Street, Coatbridge ML5 3BT; phone: (01236) 812336; fax: (01236) 812335; Web site: www.northlan.gov.uk

Orkney Islands L Manson, Director of Education, School Place, Kirkwall, Orkney KW15 1NY; phone: (01856) 873535 (x 2401); fax: (01856) 870302

Perth and Kinross Bill Frew, Director of Education, Blackfriars, Perth PH1 5LT; phone: (01738) 476200; fax: (01738) 476210; e-mail: bfrew@pkc.gov.uk

Renfrewshire Mrs Sheila Rae, Director of Education, Cotton Street, Paisley PA1 1LE; phone: (0141) 842 5000; fax: (0141) 842 5699; Web site: www.renfrewshire.gov.uk

Scottish Borders John Christie, Director of Education, Council Headquarters, Newtown St Boswells, Melrose TD6 0SA; phone: (01835) 824000 (x 451); fax: (01835) 825091; e-mail: jchristie@scotborders.gov.uk

Shetlands Islands Jim Halcrow, Director of Education, Hayfield House, Hayfield Lane, Lerwick ZE1 0QD; phone: (01595) 744300; fax: (01595) 692810

South Ayrshire Mike McCabe, Director of Educational Services, Wellington Square, Ayr KA7 1DR; phone: (01292) 612208; fax: (01292) 612258; e-mail: mike.mccabe@south-ayrshire.gov.uk

South Lanarkshire Mrs Maggi Allan, Director of Education, Floor 5, Council Offices, Almada Street, Hamilton ML3 0AE; phone: (01698) 454379; fax: (01698) 454465; Web site: www.southlanarkshire.gov.uk

Stirling Gordon Jeyes, Director of Education, Viewforth, Stirling FK8 2ET; phone: (01786) 442000; fax: (01786) 442782

West Dunbartonshire Ian McMurdo, Director of Education, Council Offices, Garshake Road, Dumbarton G82 3PU; phone: (01389) 737301; fax: (01389) 737348

Western Isles Council Murdo MacLeod, Acting Director of Education and Leisure Services, Sandwick Road, Stornoway, Isle of Lewis HS1 2BW; phone: (01851) 703773 (x 430); fax: (01851) 705796; Web site: www.cne-siar.gov.uk

West Lothian Roger Stewart, Corporate Manager of Education Services, Lindsay House, South Bridge Street, Bathgate EH48 1TS; phone: (01506) 776000; fax: (01506) 776378; e-mail: roger.stewart@westlothian.gov.uk; Web site: www.westlothian.gov.uk

Wales

Blaenau Gwent Brian Mawby, Director of Education, Victoria House, Victoria Business Park, Ebbw Vale NP3 6ER; phone: (01495) 350555; fax: (01495) 355495; e-mail: education.department@blaenau-gwent.gov.uk

Bridgend David Matthews, Director of Education and Leisure Services, Education Department, County Council Offices, Sunnyside, Bridgend CF31 4AR; phone: (01656) 642200; fax: (01656) 642646; Web site: www.bridgend.gov.uk

Caerphilly Neil Harries, Director of Education and Leisure Services, County Offices, Caerphilly Road, Ystrad Mynach, Hengoed CF82 7EP; phone: (01443) 864948; fax: (01443) 816998; e-mail: harrijno@caerphilly.gov.uk; Web site: www.caerphilly.gov.uk

Cardiff Hugh Knight, Director of Education, County Hall, Atlantic Wharf, Cardiff CF10 4UW; phone: (029) 2087 2000; fax: (029) 2087 2777; Web site: www.cardiff.gov.uk

Carmarthenshire John Ellis, (Interim) Director of Education and Community Development, Pibwrlwyd, Carmarthen SA31 2NH; phone: (01267) 234567; fax: (01267) 221692; e-mail: carmsleahq@satproj.org.uk; Web site: www.carmarthenshire.gov.uk

Ceredigion Roger Williams, Director of Education and Community Services, Education Department, County Offices, Marine Terrace, Aberystwyth SY23 2DE; phone: (01970) 617581; fax: (01970) 633663; Web site: www.ceredigion.gov.uk

Conwy Elwyn Williams, Director of Education, Education Department, Government Buildings, Dinerth Road, Colwyn Bay LL28 4UL; phone: (01492) 544261 (x 4561); fax: (01492) 541311; Web site: www.conwy.gov.uk

Denbighshire Edgar Lewis, Director of Education, Denbighshire County Council, c/o Phase 4 of County Hall, Mold CH7 6GR; phone: (01824) 706777; fax: (01824) 706780; Web site: www.denbighshire.gov.uk

Flintshire Keith McDonogh, Director of Education, Libraries, and Information, County Hall, Mold CH7 6ND; phone: (01352) 704010; fax: (01352) 754202; Web site: www.flintshire.gov.uk

Gwynedd Dafydd Whittall, Director of Education, Shire Hall Street, Caernarfon LL55 1SH; phone: (01286) 679162; fax: (01286) 677347; Web site: www.gwynedd.gov.uk

Isle of Anglesey Richard Jones, Director of Education, Ffordd Glan Hwfa, Llangefni, Ynys Mon LL77 7EY; phone: (01248) 752920; fax: (01248) 752999/750533; Web site: www.ynysmon.gov.uk

Merthyr Tydfil Dewi Jones, Director of Education, Ty Keir Hardie, Riverside Court, Avenue de Clichy, Merthyr Tydfil CF47 8XD; phone: (01685) 724600; fax: (01865) 721965; Web site: www.mnet2000.org.uk

Monmouthshire David Young, Director of Education, County Hall, Cwmbran NP44 2XH; phone: (01633) 644644; fax: (01633) 644488/ 644525; e-mail: gwenphillips@monmouthshire.gov.uk; Web site: www.monmouthshire.gov.uk

Neath Port Talbot Vivian Thomas, Director of Education, Civic Centre, Port Talbot SA13 1PJ; phone: (01639) 763333; fax: (01639) 763000; Web site: www.neath-porttalbot. gov.uk

Newport Graham Bingham, Director of Education, Civic Centre, Newport NP9 4UR; phone: (01633) 232206; fax: (01633) 232326; Web site: www.newport.gov.uk

Pembrokeshire Gerson Davies, Director of Education, Cambria House, PO Box 27, Haverfordwest SA61 1TP; phone: (01437) 764551 (x 5860); fax: (01437) 775838; Web site: www.pembrokeshire.gov.uk

Powys R J Barker, Director of Education, Llandridnod Wells LD1 5LG; phone: (01597) 826433; fax: (01597) 826475; Web site: www.powys.gov.uk

Rhondda Cynon Taff C Berry, Director of Education, Education Centre, Grawen Street, Porth CF39 0BU; phone: (01443) 687666; fax: (01443) 680286; Web site: www.rhondda-cynon-taff.gov.uk

Swansea Richard Parry, Acting Director of Education, County Hall, Swansea SA1 3SN; phone: (01792) 636000; fax: (01792) 636333; Web site: www.swansea.gov.uk

Torfaen Mike de Val, Director of Education, County Hall, Cwmbran NP44 2WN; phone: (01495) 762200; fax: (01495) 648165

Vale of Glamorgan Alun Davies, Director of Education, Civic Offices, Holton Road, Barry CF63 4RU; phone: (01446) 700111; fax: (01446) 745566

Wrexham Terry Garner, Director of Education and Leisure Services, Roxburgh House, Hill Street, Wrexham LL11 1SN; phone: (01978) 297471; fax: (01978) 297422; Web site: www.wrexham.gov.uk

Northern Ireland Education and Library Boards

Belfast David Cargo, Chief Executive of the Education and Library Board, 40 Academy Street, Belfast BT1 2NQ; phone (028) 9056 4000; fax: (028) 9033 1714

North-Eastern Gordon Topping, Chief Executive of the Education and Library Board, County Hall, 182 Galgorm Road, Ballymena, Co Antrim BT42 1HN; phone: (01266) 653333; fax: (01266) 44299

South-Eastern Jackie Fitzsimons, Chief Executive of the Education and Library Board, 16 Grahamsbridge Road, Dundonald, Belfast BT16 2HS; phone: (01232) 566200; fax: (01232) 483297

Southern Mrs Helen McClenaghan, Chief Executive of the Education and Library Board, 3 Charlemont Place, The Mall, Armagh BT61 9AX; phone: (01861) 512200; fax: (01861) 512390

UK Further and Higher Education

Directory of Local Education Authorities in the UK *(continued)*

Western Joseph Martin, Chief Executive of the Education and Library Board, Campsie House, 1 Hospital Road, Omagh, Co Tyrone BT79 0AW; phone: (01662) 411411; fax: (01662) 243557

The Channel Islands

Guernsey Derek Neale, Director of Education, Education Department, Grange Road, St Peter Port, Guernsey, Channel Islands GY1 1RQ; phone: (01481) 710821; fax: (01481) 714475

Jersey Tom McKeon, Director of Education, Education Department, PO Box 142, St Saviour, Jersey JE4 8QJ; phone: (01534) 509500; fax: (01534) 509800; e-mail: educdept@super.net.uk

Web Sites

Advisory Centre for Education

http://www.ace-ed.org.uk

The Advisory Centre for Education (ACE) is a charity funded by a variety of organizations, including Local Education Authorities (LEAs), which runs discussion forums for concerned parents. Parents can also submit confidential questions to ACE.

BBC Education Home Page

http://www.bbc.co.uk/education/

Resources for teachers and schoolchildren, including a 'learning station' with age- and key stage-related games, and exercises for primary and secondary schoolchildren.

Biology for Children

http://www.kapili.com/biology4kids/index.html

Fun, interactive introduction to biology.

British Council Virtual Education Campus

http://www.britcoun.org/eis/index.htm

This guide to British education is an essential source of information for those wishing to study in Britain or to learn more about the British educational system.

Chemistry for Children

http://www.chem4kids.com/

Fun introduction to chemistry.

Computer Assisted Learning in Chemistry

http://members.aol.com/ChangChem/

Extensive range of online activities, plus downloadable worksheets.

Department for Education and Employment

http://www.dfee.gov.uk/

Official government site which includes contact details of UK Local Education Authorities, school and college performance tables, and recent news from the department.

GCSE Answers – English

http://www.gcse.com/recep.htm

GCSE preparation material, including full details of syllabus requirements, and interactive tutorials.

GCSE Answers – Maths

http://www.gcse.com/Maths/pre.htm

GCSE preparation material, including interactive tutorials on topics such as negative numbers, probability, and trigonometry.

GCSE French Revision

http://www.canonave.ndirect.co.uk/gcse/

Comprehensive French revision pages.

Geographical Study Resources

http://www.m8i.net/

Extensive geographical resource, with downloadable maps and photos, and a guide to writing coursework and essays.

History Channel UK

http://www.thehistorychannel.co.uk/index.htm

History articles targeted at A-level and GCSE students, and a debating chamber for historical issues.

Home Education Advisory Service

http://www.heas.org.uk

Service set up by home educators to publicize education options for parents, including educating children at home.

Independent Schools Information Service

http://www.isis.org.uk/

Official site of the organization that represents all of the UK's independent schools, with advice on how to choose one for your child, and information for non-UK residents.

Information Technology Revision

http://www.doc.mmu.ac.uk/schools/bramhall/it.htm

Comprehensive reference source for the GCSE IT-theory exam, covering the key revision areas and skills needed to pass the course.

Learning Through Play

http://www.topmarks.co.uk/parents/words.htm

Contains advice and activities for parents wanting to give their children a head start at school.

Literacy

http://www.literacytrust.org.uk/Database/index.html

Information on UK literacy statistics, details of government initiatives, and advice for parents on how to help their children learn to read.

Maths Tuition

http://www.maths-help.co.uk

Write in with your maths problem and have a response by a qualified maths teacher within 24 hours. There is also a maths chat room with scheduled, themed sessions.

Montessori Education

http://www.lfpm.com/montess.html#phil

Introduction to the main principles and practices of Montessori education, with an annotated bibliography, and a list of public Montessori schools.

National Information Services and Systems

http://www.niss.ac.uk/

Education pages of the National Information Services and Systems agency, with links to directories, funding, educational resources, and reports and evaluation of higher education institutions.

National Union of Students

http://www.nus.org.uk/

Information about the NUS and its current executive. Includes 'Student News', the magazine *NUS Network*, and articles about student welfare, entertainment, financial issues, media, and the NUS's fees campaign.

NUT Online

http://www.teachers.org.uk

Official site of the National Union of Teachers (NUT), with help for student teachers, discussions of pay and conditions, health and safety articles, and details of NUT policies on major issues.

OFSTED Reports Database

http://www.ofsted.gov.uk/reports/index.htm

Includes OFSTED Reports Database with the full text of reports from OFSTED inspections, searchable by school name, education authority, or postcode.

Open University

http://www.open.ac.uk/

Site of Britain's largest teaching institution (in terms of student numbers), with information on the university's distance-learning programmes, an online prospectus, and details of BBC programmes used as part of many of the courses.

Physics Factory – GCSE

http://physics.digiweb.com/gcse.htm

Aimed at GCSE students, this site would be useful for anyone with an interest in physics. As well as regularly changing pages on major topics in physics, there is a screen saver you can download to help you remember the important equations.

Qualifications and Curriculum Authority

http://www.qca.org.uk/menu.htm

This site offers a clear explanation of the curriculum, as well as details about all the educational qualifications up to A Level, including GCSE, NVQ, and GNVQ.

Schools Online Science Cafe

http://www.shu.ac.uk/schools/sci/sol/experts/exptin.htm

This site has suggestions for science experiments, a facility for posting questions to scientists, and a chance to participate in online experiments by submitting your own data.

Schools on the Internet

http://schools.sys.uea.ac.uk/schools/schools.html

Developed from a project run by the School of Information Services, this site provides links to all schools with Web sites, searchable by area.

Student Advice

http://www.studentzone.org.uk/

Maintained for students by the National Information Services and Systems agency, this site contains information about academic resources, grants and scholarships, as well as links to news, sports, and entertainment sites.

Student Loans Company Ltd

http://www.slc.co.uk/

Site of government-owned company that administers the student loans scheme; a must-see for anyone considering entering university.

Student World UK

http://www.student-world.co.uk/main.htm

Resource for students, graduates, and academic staff, with sections on education, finance, jobs, sport, shopping, and culture.

Times Educational Supplement

http://www.tes.co.uk

Online version of the education sector's chief publication, with a searchable version of the current edition, plus archives and a discussion forum for teachers.

UCAS Home Page

http://www.ucas.ac.uk/

Official site for the organization that handles admissions to universities and colleges in the UK. There is a search facility for all universities, colleges, and courses; an advice centre for prospective students; information for higher education staff; and 'studentUK', with news, views, and advice.

RELIGION AND BELIEF

The Year in Review

July 1999 Scottish Episcopal bishop Richard Holloway causes controversy by declaring that the only moral absolute concerning sex is that it be consensual, and that even sodomy and sadomasochism can be acceptable.

July 1999 Sarvodyan Kurien, a Catholic pharmacist inspired by Mahatma Ghandi and Mother Theresa, dies in the southern Indian town of Cochin at the age of 80. He was famed as a 'Good Samaritan', for rescuing nearly 600 abandoned babies from the streets since 1952, and keeping them until adoptive parents were found.

August 1999 Former Pakistani prime minister Benazir Bhutto calls on the government of the Punjab to stop the dispossession of poor Christians by religious extremists using the threat of blasphemy charges to steal land.

19 August 1999 In the USA, the evangelical Lutheran church, with 5 million members, and the Episcopal church, with 2.4 million members, agree to join in full communion with each other. Although the denominations will retain their own structures, they will recognize each other's sacraments, hold joint worship services, and accept each other's clergy.

20 August 1999 The *Church of England Newspaper* calls for Bishop Richard Holloway to resign because of his controversial views on sex and drugs, and his recommendations that God be 'left out' of moral debate.

September 1999 In the USA, an international group of scholars of Indian religions issue an open letter condemning 'hate crime' in religion, with particular reference to the Australian missionary Graham Staines and his two children who were burnt alive in their car in Pakistan by men chanting Hindu slogans.

September 1999 In the UK, Siobhan McDonagh raises a 10-Minute-Rule Bill in the House of Commons, asking the government to revoke a ban on Catholic, Anglican, and Orthodox clergy acting as members of Parliament. The present law prevents such clergy, but not ministers of other denominations and religions, from being MPs.

September 1999 The National Conference of Priests overwhelmingly calls on the Catholic Church to allow divorced people in second marriages to take communion.

28 November 1999 English pop singer Cliff Richard has his 14th number one single with 'The Millennium Prayer', the Lord's Prayer played to the tune of 'Auld Lang Syne'. Many popular radio stations refuse to play it.

November 1999 Archbishop of Canterbury Dr George Carey pleads with Anglo-Catholic opponents of women's ordination to 'stay in the fold' of the Anglican church, as more than 500 traditionalists meet in Westminster.

11 December 1999 Roman Catholic Archbishop of Glasgow, Cardinal Thomas Winning urges retention of Section 28 of the Local Government Act which forbids the promotion of homosexuality in schools.

31 December 1999 Archbishop of Canterbury Dr George Carey leads the UK in prayer at 11.15 p.m. in a New Year's Eve event broadcast from the Millennium Dome in Greenwich, followed by a national 'Millennium Moment' with candles and prayers, televised at 11.50 p.m.

January 2000 Chinese premier Zhu Ronghi informs religious leaders in Beijing that religion must come under tighter government control.

January 2000 A decision not to include questions on religious belief in the 2001 Scottish census is criticized by church leaders and the Muslim community.

January 2000 Michael Scott-Joynt, Bishop of Winchester, announces that the Church of England is preparing to change its law in order to let divorcees marry in church.

5 January 2000 14-year-old religious leader Ugyen Trinley Dorje, Tibet's third-ranking lama, leader of the Kagyupa sect, defects from China to India, trekking for a week across the Himalayas.

25 January 2000 Anglican bishops unanimously agree that ministers may use their discretion to officiate at marriages of divorcees who have a former spouse still living.

February 2000 The Vatican releases a document of repentance asking forgiveness for sins of the church during the Inquisition and wars of religion, anti-Semitism, persecution of scientists, and failure to oppose violent dictatorships. The aim is to purify the church for the Jubilee year celebrations.

February 2000 Pope John Paul II urges Italian couples to have more children in an effort to counter the country's demographic decline and discourage abortions.

February 2000 In Sudan, a young teacher and at least 14 pupils are killed when the Kunda Catholic School is bombed by the air force of the Islamic government in Khartoum. Most of the children killed are Muslim.

February 2000 The Catholic church in the Czech Republic forbids priests and bishops secretly ordained into the underground church during the communist era to celebrate mass unless they are officially re-ordained.

February 2000 In the UK, television presenter Joan Bakewell announces her departure from

the religious debate programme *Heart of the Matter*, criticizing the BBC's marginalization of religious programming. This follows a call from the general synod of the Church of England for the BBC to increase religious broadcasting, especially at peak times.

February–March 2000 In Kaduna, Nigeria, over 1,000 people die in clashes between Christian Ibos and Hausa-speaking Muslim immigrants. Three hundred more are killed in Aba and around 30 churches are burned down.

March 2000 Leading physicist Freeman Dyson wins the prestigious Templeton prize for religion for his writing on technology and society and the relation of science to religion and ethics.

12 March 2000 In a speech unprecedented for its sweeping apology, Pope John Paul II seeks forgiveness for the Catholic church for 2,000 years of violence against and persecution of Jews and other minority groups and women.

17 March 2000 Hundreds of people are burned to death in a church in what is first thought to be a mass suicide by members of the Restoration of the Ten Commandments of God sect at Kanungo, Uganda. It is later treated as mass murder as the leaders of the sect are investigated.

21 March 2000 Pope John Paul II makes a six-day visit to Israel and the West Bank, the first papal visit to the area since 1964.

April 2000 Senior bishops in Portugal aver that the survival of the Anglican communion is 'profoundly threatened' by the ordination of homosexuals and the blessing of same-sex unions, but warn traditionalists against forming rebel groups.

April 2000 Prime Minister Tony Blair encourages Muslims to share their beliefs with people of other faiths, and describes Islam as 'deeply reflective, peaceful, and very beautiful' in an interview with *Muslim News*.

April 2000 More than 5,000 Muslims call for a jihad (holy war) against Christians in Maluka province, at a rally in the Indonesian capital Jakarta. It is estimated that 3,000 people may already have been killed in violent struggles since January 1999, and tens of thousands are believed to have fled into the surrounding forests.

April 2000 The organization Christian Research reports that church-going figures are still plunging despite a huge interest in spirituality, saying, 'What people want is Christianity, not the church.'

1 April 2000 There are mixed reactions to the appointment of the first dalit (low-caste) archbishop in India.

May 2000 Christian leaders in Pakistan deplore the decision of head of state General Pervez Musharraf to yield to pressure from Muslim groups and revoke measures preventing abuse of the blasphemy laws.

3 June 2000 Reports emerge that Hindu extremists have stabbed a Jesuit seminarian at a mission camp near Bangalore in south India.

Major Religions and Faiths

For religions other than Christianity, the abbreviations CE and BCE have been used for dates, instead of AD and BC, in accordance with multi-faith practice.

The Baha'i Faith

Introduction

The Baha'i faith originated in the mid-19th century in the area of present-day Iran. It is based on the belief that the man born as Mirza Husayn Ali in 1817 was the prophet sent by God to the present age. He is now known as Baha'u'llah – 'the Glory of God'.

Baha'is believe that humanity is constantly evolving and growing more adult in its understanding and behaviour, and thus gradually becoming capable of forming one world rather than diverse nations, races, and religions. Baha'is also believe in One God, creator of all, and that humanity is a special creation, essentially good.

The Baha'i teachings stress economic justice, equal rights, and education for all, and the breaking down of traditional barriers of race, class, and creed.

The Baha'i Community in the UK

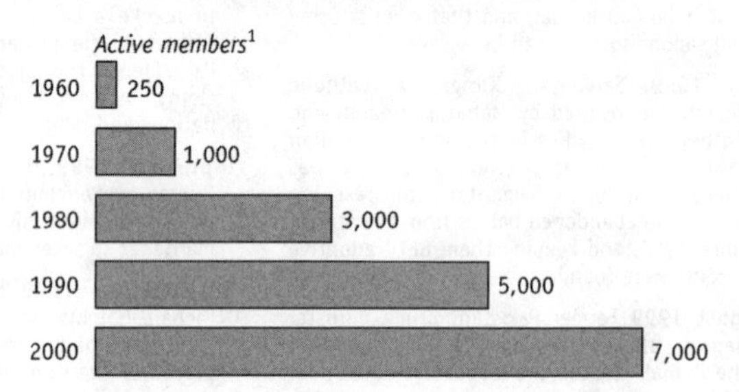

[1] Figures are estimates.

Source: UK Christian Handbook, Religious Trends No 2 2000/01 (*Christian Research, London*), © *PW Brierley 1999*

Scripture
Baha'is believe that there have been revelations from God appropriate to each era, including the Torah, the New Testament, the Koran, and the words of the Buddha and the Hindu god Krishna. Baha'is maintain that these revelations have been superseded, although not contradicted, by the writings of Baha'u'llah and his successor Abdul Baha. These writings form the main body of Baha'i scripture. The claim that the Baha'i sacred texts are the successor to the Koran has led to criticism of Baha'i in many Muslim lands, including Iran, where the faith began.

Organization
The Baha'i international headquarters is in Haifa, Israel, and includes an International House of Justice in preparation for the time when there will be one world government, guided by the Baha'i faith. The Baha'i community meet in local spiritual assemblies whose structure is democratic and participatory, intended as a model for universal government.

Adherents
There are approximately 6.7 million Baha'is worldwide with the largest concentrations in Asia and Africa. The estimated number of Baha'i groups in the UK rose from 200 in 1980 to 440 in 2000.

Information on the Baha'i Faith in the UK

The Baha'i Information Office 27 Rutland Gate, London SW7 1PD; phone: (020) 7584 2566; Web site: www.bahai.org.uk

Buddhism

Introduction

Buddhists follow the teachings of Siddhartha Gautama, given the title of the Buddha – the 'enlightened' or 'awakened' one. He was born the son of a nobleman in northern India in the 6th century BCE and at the age of 29 left his life of luxury to search for understanding of suffering and the way to end it. After six years of austerity he realized that asceticism, like overindulgence, was futile, and achieved enlightenment through the middle way of meditation. He began teaching at Varanasi and founded the Sangha, an order of monks to carry on his teachings.

His teachings are summarized as the Four Noble Truths and the way to end suffering is through the Eightfold Path. By learning and practising this path one can eventually escape the cycle of birth and death. Buddhists believe that all beings are reborn into many different forms because of the ties of desire. When desire is allowed to cool like a fire going out, the attachment to the cycle of birth and death is loosened. Buddhists try to perfect the qualities of wisdom, compassion, and harmlessness in order to achieve enlightenment, leading to the highest peace and freedom, which is 'nirvana'.

The Four Noble Truths

Suffering exists

There is a reason for suffering

There is a way to end suffering.

The way to end suffering is through the Eightfold Path

The Eightfold Path

Right views

Right thoughts

Right speech

Right action

Right livelihood

Right effort

Right mindfulness

Right concentration

Scripture

The teachings of the Buddha were handed down orally and eventually written in the 1st century BCE in a collection of writings called the *Tripitaka* – 'three baskets'. Different versions survive in Chinese, Tibetan, and Pali (an ancient south Indian language), and they are now translated into hundreds of languages worldwide. There are also important Buddhist scriptures written by later sages and scholars, many of them in the ancient Indian language Sanskrit.

Important sites of pilgrimage

Early Buddhist scriptures mention four destinations in Nepal or India that a Buddhist pilgrim might visit:

- The Buddha's birthplace at Lumbini in Nepal
- Bodh Gaya in India where the Buddha found enlightenment
- Sarnath where the Buddha preached his first sermon
- Kusingara where the Buddha died

As the traditions of Buddhism have developed and spread, hundreds of sites have become pilgrimage destinations, including temples, pagodas, mountains, and bodhi-trees (traditionally a religious and spiritual tree). Important sites include Siripada (Adam's Peak) in Sri Lanka, which attracts not only Buddhists but also Hindu, Muslim, and Christian pilgrims. According to Sri Lankan Buddhist traditions, the Buddha left his footprint on the peak of this mountain. In China there are four main sacred mountains visited by Buddhist pilgrims, and Mount Kailas in western Tibet is an important destination for Tibetan Buddhist pilgrims.

Branches

There are three main branches of Buddhism: Theravada, found mainly in southeast Asia, Sri Lanka, and India; Tibetan Mahayana; and Chinese/Japanese Mahayana. There is also a wide variety of new Buddhist movements. There is no central authority in Buddhism, each school having its own teachers and spiritual guides, although figures such as the Dalai Lama have raised the worldwide profile of Buddhism and voiced a Buddhist viewpoint on world affairs.

Teachings

Buddhism is still taught by personal instruction from teacher to pupil, but the means for its transmission are now more diverse than ever. The last two decades of the 20th century saw a flowering of books and magazines on the subject and the increasing availability of information, teachings, and scriptures in electronic formats and the existence of Internet networks of Buddhists, have made Buddhism a global religion for the 21st century.

Adherents

There are approximately 350 million followers of Buddhism worldwide. The majority live in Asia, although Buddhism is growing rapidly beyond Asia, particularly in the USA and UK. The number of Buddhist groups in the UK rose from approximately 50 in 1980 to an estimated 234 in 2000.

See also **Major Religous Festivals**, p 392.

Adherents to Buddhism in the UK

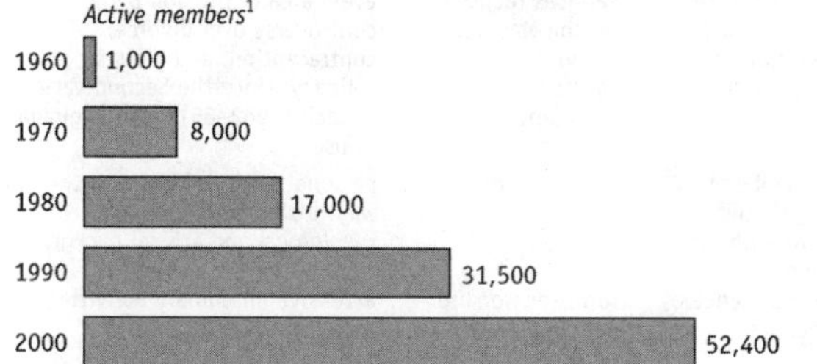

[1] Figures are estimates.

Source: UK Christian Handbook, Religious Trends No 2 2000/01 (*Christian Research, London*), © *PW Brierley 1999*

Information about Buddhism in the UK

The Buddhist Society 58 Eccleston Square, London SW1V 1PH; phone: (020) 7834 5858; fax: (020) 7976 5238; Web site: www.buddsoc.org.uk

Christianity

Introduction

Christians believe in one God who created the universe, and created human beings to have a special relationship with him. Through human wilfulness, exemplified in the story of Adam and Eve, this relationship was broken. Christians believe that because of his love for humanity, God took on the form of a man, Jesus, in order to bring them back into a relationship with him. The Gospels relate that Jesus was conceived by a virgin, Mary, through the power of God, and was born as a baby in Bethlehem. Modern scholarship now puts his birth around 4 BC. Christians take their name from the title given to Jesus: 'the Christ', meaning the anointed one of God. After three years of teaching, Jesus was crucified and died, but Christians believe that through the power of God he came to life again. This belief was spread by Jesus' closest followers, the Apostles, and Christianity grew rapidly in the first three centuries AD.

Scripture
The Christian Bible consists of the Old Testament, originally written in Hebrew (the same book as the Hebrew Bible read by Jews), and the New Testament, originally written in Greek, which contains accounts of the life and teachings of Jesus, and letters from early Christians. The Bible is translated into many different languages.

Important sites of pilgrimage
Some pilgrimage sites are specific to a local community, and some are associated with the historic area of Palestine, where Jesus lived. This area is now divided between parts of the modern states of Israel, Jordan, and Syria, and is known in Christianity as the Holy Land. The main focus of a pilgrimage to the Holy Land is Jerusalem, where Jesus died and rose again. Other important sites in the Holy Land are Bethlehem, where Jesus was born, Nazareth where he grew up, and the River Jordan where he was baptized.

Rome is a centre of pilgrimage, particularly for Catholics, as the Vatican is the seat of the papacy, but other Christians visit because of Rome's association with St Peter and St Paul, two of the greatest early Christian leaders.

Santiago de Compostela in northern Spain is believed to be the burial place of St James, one of Jesus' disciples. It was especially popular as a pilgrimage centre in medieval Europe and there are still routes to the shrine from many different countries in Europe. Thousands of pilgrims still walk all or part of the route.

Thousands of people make pilgrimage to Lourdes in France because of a series of visions seen by St Bernadette in 1854, and the healing believed to be associated with the spring of water which arose there.

Denominations
Christianity has many different branches, referred to as churches or denominations. Catholicism is the largest with approximately 900 million followers under the leadership of the Pope, who is based in Rome. Other major branches are Orthodox and Protestant. The Orthodox churches are self-governing, each led by a Patriarch. There are a large number of Protestant denominations, each with a different organization and authority. The World Council of Churches provides a forum for dialogue amongst the major Protestant Churches.

Adherents
There are nearly two billion Christians worldwide, with the largest concentrations in Europe, North and South America, southern Africa, and Australasia.

About 65% of the population of the UK regards itself as broadly Christian, but active church membership is estimated at about 5.9 million (approximately 10% of the population).

Major Denominations of the Christian Religion

From the beginning of its history, the Christian church has had divisions over teachings or organization. Many smaller divisions died out or were re-united. The Great Schism of 1054 gave rise to the Roman Catholic and the Orthodox churches. The Reformation in the 16th century gave rise to the Protestant denominations which rejected the teaching and authority of the Roman Catholic church. In the following centuries there were further divisions between these denominations, and new Christian groups are still being formed.

Denomination	Organization	Characteristics	Special rites	Orientation
Anglican	episcopal; the archbishop of Canterbury recognized as 'first among equals' in the various Anglican churches	central doctrine derived from the Thirty-Nine Articles promulgated at the Reformation, but in practice accommodates a broad range of belief	ritual derives from the *Book of Common Prayer*	numerically the predominant denomination in the UK, but with a significant international presence and missionary activities
Baptist	self-governing churches; congregational	only adult Christians, capable of own choice, should be baptized	baptism by total immersion	missionary activities; supports separation of church and state
Catholic	strict hierarchy with the pope (the bishop of Rome) as leader	emphasis on teachings of the pope and church authorities; belief in the factual presence of Christ in bread and wine offerings; veneration of Mary, the mother of Jesus Christ	wide range of services focused on the Mass; seven sacraments; rich theological tradition	authority of the church regulates every area of life and belief; controversy over divorce, contraception, and priests' celibacy; since the Second Vatican Council (1962–65) local languages in use
Lutheran	congregational or episcopal	belief in the symbolic presence of Christ in bread and wine offerings; Bible as the only source of authority; no belief in predestination	simple services; infant baptism	personal faith perceived as the only way to salvation; strong theological and ethical background
Methodist	superintendent system and conferences	scripture, tradition, and experience are at the core of the church's practices	forms of worship vary depending on local tradition; infant or adult baptism	extensive missionary activities and social involvement

(continued)

Major Denominations of the Christian Religion *(continued)*

Denomination	Organization	Characteristics	Special rites	Orientation
Orthodox	independent and autonomous national churches governed by synods of bishops; the Patriarch of Constantinople recognized as 'first among equals'	emphasis on Christ's resurrection; belief that the Holy Spirit descends from God the Father only; tradition as a source of authority; rich traditions of worship; veneration of Mary, the mother of God	elaborate liturgy; seven sacraments; veneration of icons	traditional orientation, usually little social involvement
Pentecostal	a wide range of groups; allows for freedom of organization	emphasis on the personal teachings of the Holy Spirit	spirit baptism; healing; adult baptism; 'speaking in tongues'	charismatic
Presbyterian	government by elders (lay people or ordained ministers)	emphasis on self-control and self-discipline; belief in the symbolic presence of Christ in bread and wine offerings	simple services with emphasis on the sermon; infant baptism	strong belief in justice and supremacy of God

Adherents to Christianity Worldwide by Denomination and Continent

(In millions.)

2000

Continent	Anglican	Baptist	Lutheran	Methodist	Orthodox	Pentecostal	Presbyterian
Africa	20.4	9.9	6.7	8.0	29.5	20.5	11.6
Asia	0.5	8.5	5.7	3.0	101.3[1]	14.4	15.3
Europe	25.1	2.9	53.5	1.5		3.6	12.3
North America	4.7	46.8	13.9	12.9	7.9	34.2	8.3
Oceania	5.2	0.5	1.0	0.5	0.5	1.3	0.9
South America	0.2	3.1	1.4	0.5	0.5	45.2	0.8
World total	56.0	71.5	83.1	26.4	140.2	122.4	49.3

[1] Combined figure for Asia and Europe.

Christianity: Key Dates

1st century The Christian church is traditionally said to have originated at Pentecost, and separated from the parent Jewish religion by the declaration of saints Barnabas and Paul that the distinctive rites of Judaism are not necessary for entry into the Christian church.

3rd century Christians are persecuted under the Roman emperors Septimius Severus, Decius, and Diocletian.

312 Emperor Constantine establishes Christianity as the religion of the Roman Empire.

4th century A settled doctrine of Christian belief evolves, with deviating beliefs condemned as heresies. Questions of discipline threaten disruption within the church; to settle these, Constantine calls the Council of Arles in 314, followed by the councils of Nicaea (325) and Constantinople (381).

5th–7th centuries Councils of Ephesus (431) and Chalcedon (451). Christianity is carried northwards by such figures as St Columba (521–597) and St Augustine (died 605), who became the first archbishop of Canterbury.

800 Holy Roman Emperor Charlemagne is crowned by the pope. The church assists the growth of the feudal system of which it forms the apex.

1054 The Eastern Orthodox Church splits from the Roman Catholic Church.

11th–12th centuries Secular and ecclesiastical jurisdiction are often in conflict; for example, Emperor Henry IV and Pope Gregory VII, Henry II of England and his archbishop Becket.

1096–1291 The church supports the Crusades, a series of wars in the Middle East.

1233 The Inquisition is established to suppress heresy.

14th century Increasing worldliness (against which the foundation of the Dominican and Franciscan monastic orders is a protest) and ecclesiastical abuses leads to dissatisfaction and the appearance of the reformers Wycliffe and Huss.

15th–17th centuries Thousands of women are accused of witchcraft, tortured, and executed.

early 16th century The Renaissance brings a re-examination of Christianity in northern Europe by the humanists Erasmus, More, and Colet.

1517 The German priest Martin Luther becomes leader of the Protestant movement and precipitates the Reformation.

1519–64 In Switzerland the Reformation is carried on by Calvin and Zwingli.

1529 Henry VIII renounces papal supremacy and proclaims himself head of the Church of England.

1545–63 The Counter-Reformation is initiated by the Catholic church at the Council of Trent.

1560 The Church of Scotland is established according to Calvin's Presbyterian system.

17th century Jesuit missionaries establish themselves in China and Japan. Puritans, Quakers, and other sects seeking religious freedom establish themselves in North America.

18th century During the Age of Reason, Christian dogmas are questioned, and intellectuals begin to examine society in purely secular terms. In England and America, religious revivals occur among the working classes in the form of Methodism and the Great Awakening. In England the Church of England suffers the loss of large numbers of Nonconformists.

19th century The evolutionary theories of Darwin and the historical criticism of the Bible challenge the Book of Genesis. Missionaries convert people in Africa and Asia, suppressing indigenous faiths and cultures.

1948 The World Council of Churches is founded as part of the ecumenical movement to reunite various Protestant sects and, to some extent, the Protestant churches and the Catholic Church.

1950s–80s Protestant evangelicism grows rapidly in the USA, spread by television.

1969 A liberation theology of freeing the poor from oppression emerges in South America, and attracts papal disapproval.

1972 The United Reformed Church is formed by the union of the Presbyterian Church in England and the Congregational Church. In the USA, the 1960s–70s sees the growth of cults, some of them nominally Christian, which are a source of social concern.

1980s The Roman Catholic Church plays a major role in the liberalization of the Polish government; in the USSR the Orthodox Church and other sects are tolerated and even encouraged under Gorbachev.

1988 The Holy Shroud of Turin, claimed by some to be Christ's mortuary cloth, is shown by carbon dating to date from about 1330.

1990s The Christian church grapples with the question of its attitude to homosexuality; the policy of most churches is to oppose its public acceptance, declaring that homosexual behaviour conflicts with Christian teachings.

Christianity: Key Dates *(continued)*

1992 After 359 years, the Roman Catholic Church accepts that Galileo was right: the Earth does go round the Sun.

1993 Legislation to allow the Church of England to ordain women priests gains royal assent in Britain.

1997 The Roman Catholic church issues a statement called the 'Declaration of Repentance', in which it formally apologizes for its silence when the French government deported Jews to Nazi death camps in German and Poland during World War II.

1998 US archaeologists in Aqaba, Jordan, announce the discovery of the world's oldest Christian church, built by the Christian community of Ayla in the late 3rd century.

1999 British rabbis and Catholic leaders at the Vatican agree to form an amicable partnership and accept the legitimacy of each other's beliefs. Until now, relations were hindered by the Catholic belief that the coming of Jesus Christ superseded the Jewish Covenant between God and Abraham.

Books of the Bible

Name of book	Chapters	Date written
Books of the Old Testament		
Genesis	50	mid-8th century BC
Exodus	40	950–586 BC
Leviticus	27	mid-7th century BC
Numbers	36	850–650 BC
Deuteronomy	34	mid-7th century BC
Joshua	24	*c.* 550 BC
Judges	21	*c.* 550 BC
Ruth	4	late 3rd century BC
1 Samuel	31	*c.* 900 BC
2 Samuel	24	*c.* 900 BC
1 Kings	22	550–600 BC
2 Kings	25	550–600 BC
1 Chronicles	29	*c.* 300 BC
2 Chronicles	36	*c.* 300 BC
Ezra	10	*c.* 450 BC
Nehemiah	13	*c.* 450 BC
Esther	10	*c.* 200 BC
Job	42	600–400 BC
Psalms	150	6th–2nd century BC
Proverbs	31	350–150 BC
Ecclesiastes	12	*c.* 200 BC
Song of Solomon	8	3rd century BC
Isaiah	66	late 3rd century BC
Jeremiah	52	604 BC
Lamentations	5	586–536 BC
Ezekiel	48	6th century BC
Daniel	12	*c.* 166 BC
Hosea	14	*c.* 732 BC
Joel	3	*c.* 500 BC
Amos	9	775–750 BC
Obadiah	1	6th–3rd century BC
Jonah	4	600–200 BC
Micah	7	late 3rd century BC
Nahum	3	*c.* 626 BC
Habakkuk	3	*c.* 600 BC
Zephaniah	3	3rd century BC
Haggai	2	*c.* 520 BC
Zechariah	14	*c.* 520 BC
Malachi	4	*c.* 430 BC
Books of the New Testament		
Matthew	28	before AD 70
Mark	16	before AD 70
Luke	24	AD 70–80
John	21	AD 90–100
Acts	28	AD 70–80
Romans	16	AD 355–358
1 Corinthians	16	AD 57
2 Corinthians	13	AD 57
Galatians	6	AD 53
Ephesians	6	AD 140
Philippians	4	AD 63
Colossians	4	AD 140
1 Thessalonians	5	AD 50–54
2 Thessalonians	3	AD 50–54
1 Timothy	6	before AD 64
2 Timothy	4	before AD 64
Titus	3	before AD 64
Philemon	1	AD 60–62
Hebrews	13	AD 80–90
James	5	before AD 52
1 Peter	5	before AD 64
2 Peter	3	before AD 64
1 John	5	AD 90–100
2 John	1	AD 90–100
3 John	1	AD 90–100
Jude	1	AD 75–80
Revelation	22	AD 81–96

The Ten Commandments

1 To have no other gods besides Jehovah
2 To make no idols
3 Not to misuse the name of God
4 To keep the sabbath holy
5 To honour one's parents
6 Not to commit murder
7 Not to commit adultery
8 Not to commit theft
9 Not to give false evidence
10 Not to be covetous

The Seven Deadly Sins

In Christian theology seven vices are considered fundamental to all other sins:

anger
avarice
envy
gluttony
lust
pride
sloth

New Saints

By the beginning of the year 2000 Pope John Paul II had canonized over 290 saints, more than all other 20th century popes put together. Before 1978 when Pope John Paul II was elected, the Roman Catholic Church had canonized a total of 302 saints since official Vatican records began under Pope Clement VIII in 1592.

Pope John Paul II has also carried out over 820 beatifications (the first step towards canonization), more than a third of the total since records began.

New rules introduced by the Vatican in 1983 streamlined the canonization process and diminished the role of the 'Devil's Advocate', the person appointed to set forth possible objections to any person whom the Catholic Church proposed to canonize.

The Patron Saints of Britain and Ireland

St George (died *c.* 303) is the patron saint of England. The story of St George rescuing a woman by slaying a dragon, evidently derived from the Greek Perseus legend, first appears in the 6th century. The cult of St George was introduced into western Europe by the Crusaders and his association with England probably began when his story became popular among medieval Crusaders. His feast day is 23 April.

St David (lived 5th–6th century) is the patron saint of Wales. A Christian abbot and bishop, he was, according to legend, the son of a prince of Dyfed and uncle of King Arthur. He was responsible for the adoption of the leek as the national emblem of Wales, but his own emblem is a dove. His feast day is 1 March.

St Andrew (lived 1st century) is the patron saint of Scotland. A New Testament apostle, according to tradition he was martyred at Patrai in Greece on an X-shaped cross (St Andrew's cross). Some time before the 8th century bones claimed to be his were brought to St Andrews in Scotland. The X-shaped cross represents Scotland in the Union Jack. His feast day is 30 November.

St Patrick (*c.* 389–*c.* 461) is the patron saint of Ireland. Born in Britain, probably in South Wales, he was carried off by pirates to six years' slavery in Antrim, Ireland, before escaping either to Britain or Gaul to train as a missionary. He landed in Ireland again in 432 or 456, and his work was a vital factor in the spread of Christian influence there. St Patrick is said to have used a shamrock to illustrate the doctrine of the Holy Trinity, and it was made the national badge of Ireland. His feast day 17 March.

Major Religions and Faiths

Popes

Name	Date reign began
St Peter	*c.* 42
St Linus	*c.* 67
St Anacletus (Cletus)	*c.* 76
St Clement I	*c.* 88
St Evaristus	*c.* 97
St Alexander I	*c.* 105
St Sixtus I	*c.* 115
St Telesphorus	*c.* 125
St Hyginus	*c.* 136
St Pius I	*c.* 140
St Anicetus	*c.* 155
St Soterus	*c.* 166
St Eleutherius	175
St Victor I	189
St Zephyrinus	199
St Callistus I	217
St Urban I	222
St Pontian	230
St Anterus	235
St Fabius	236
St Cornelius	251
St Lucius I	253
St Stephen I	254
St Sixtus II	257
St Dionysius	259
St Felix I	269
St Eutychian	275
St Caius	283
St Marcellinus	296
St Marcellus I	308
St Eusebius	309
St Melchiades	311
St Sylvester I	314
St Marcus	336
St Julius I	337
Liberius	352
St Damasus I	366
St Siricius	384
St Anastasius I	399
St Innocent I	402
St Zosimus	417
St Boniface I	418
St Celestine I	422
St Sixtus III	432
St Leo I the Great	440
St Hilary	461
St Simplicius	468
St Felix III	483
St Gelasius I	492
Anastasius II	496
St Symmachus	498
St Hormisdas	514
St John I	523
St Felix IV	526
Boniface II	530
John II	533
St Agapetus I	535
St Silverius	536
Vigilius	537
Pelagius I	556
John III	561
Benedict I	575
Pelagius II	579
St Gregory (I) the Great	590
Sabinianus	604
Boniface III	607
St Boniface IV	608
St Deusdedit (Adeodatus I)	615
Boniface V	619
Honorius I	625
Severinus	640
John IV	640
Theodore I	642
St Martin I	649
St Eugene I	654
St Vitalian	657
Adeodatus II	672
Donus	676
St Agatho	678
St Leo II	682
St Benedict II	684
John V	685
Conon	686
St Sergius I	687
John VI	701
John VII	705
Sisinnius	708
Constantine	708
St Gregory II	715
St Gregory III	731
St Zachary	741
Stephen II (III)[1]	752
St Paul I	757
Stephen III (IV)	768
Adrian I	772
St Leo III	795
Stephen IV (V)	816
St Paschal I	817
Eugene II	824
Valentine	827
Gregory IV	827
Sergius II	844
St Leo IV	847
Benedict III	855
St Nicholas (I) the Great	858
Adrian II	867
John VIII	872
Marinus I	882
St Adrian III	884
Stephen V (VI)	885
Formosus	891
Boniface VI	896
Stephen VI (VII)	896
Romanus	897
Theodore II	897
John IX	898
Benedict IV	900
Leo V	903
Sergius III	904
Anastasius III	911
Landus	913
John X	914
Leo VI	928
Stephen VII (VIII)	928
John XI	931
Leo VII	936
Stephen VII (IX)	939
Marinus II	942
Agapetus II	946
John XII	955
Leo VIII	963
Benedict V	964
John XIII	965
Benedict VI	973
Benedict VII	974
John XIV	983
John XV	985
Gregory V	996
Sylvester II	999
John XVII	1003
John XVIII	1004
Sergius IV	1009
Benedict VIII	1012
John XIX	1024
Benedict IX[2]	1032
Gregory VI	1045
Clement II	1046
Benedict IX[2]	1047
Damasus II	1048
St Leo IX	1049
Victor II	1055
Stephen IX (X)	1057
Nicholas II	1059
Alexander II	1061
St Gregory VII	1073
Victor III	1086
Urban II	1088
Paschal II	1099
Gelasius II	1118
Callistus II	1119
Hororius II	1124
Innocent II	1130
Celestine II	1143
Lucius II	1144
Eugene III	1145
Anastasius IV	1153
Adrian IV	1154
Alexander III	1159
Innocent III	1179
Lucius III	1181
Urban III	1185
Gregory VIII	1187
Clement III	1187
Celestine III	1191
Innocent III	1198
Honorius III	1216
Gregory IX	1227
Celestine IV	1241
Innocent IV	1243
Alexander IV	1254
Urban IV	1261
Clement IV	1265
Gregory X	1271
Innocent V	1276
Adrian V	1276
John XXI[3]	1276
Nicholas III	1277
Martin IV	1281
Honorius IV	1285
Nicholas IV	1288
St Celestine V	1294
Boniface VIII	1294
Benedict XI	1303
Clement V	1305
John XXII	1316
Benedict XII	1334
Clement VI	1342
Innocent VI	1352
Urban V	1362
Gregory XI	1370
Urban VI	1378
Boniface IX	1389
Innocent VII	1404
Gregory XII	1406
Martin V	1417
Eugene IV	1431
Nicholas V	1447
Callistus III	1455
Pius II	1458
Paul II	1464
Sixtus IV	1471
Innocent VIII	1484
Alexander VI	1492
Pius III	1503
Julius II	1503
Leo X	1513
Adrian VI	1522
Clement VII	1523
Paul III	1534
Julius III	1550
Marcellus II	1555
Paul IV	1555
Pius IV	1559
St Pius V	1566
Gregory XIII	1572
Sixtus V	1585
Urban VII	1590
Gregory XIV	1590
Innocent IX	1591
Clement VIII	1592
Leo XI	1605
Paul V	1605
Gregory XV	1621
Urban VIII	1623
Innocent X	1644
Alexander VII	1655
Clement IX	1667
Clement X	1670
Innocent XI	1676
Alexander VIII	1689
Innocent XII	1691
Clement XI	1700
Innocent XIII	1721
Benedict XIII	1724
Clement XII	1730
Benedict XIV	1740
Clement XIII	1758
Clement XIV	1769
Pius VI	1775
Pius VII	1800
Leo XII	1823
Pius VIII	1829
Gregory XVI	1831
Pius IX	1846
Leo XIII	1878
St Pius X	1903
Benedict XV	1914
Pius XI	1922
Pius XII	1939
John XXIII	1958
Paul VI	1963
John Paul I[4]	1978
John Paul II	1978

[1] The original Stephen II died before consecration, and was dropped from the list of popes in 1961; Stephen III became Stephen II and the numbers of the other popes named Stephen were also moved up.

[2] Benedict IX was driven from office for scandalous conduct but returned briefly in 1047.

[3] There was no John XX.

[4] John Paul I died after only 33 days as Pontiff.

Selected Patron Saints and their Feast Days

The recognition of saints and the choice of their feast (saint's) day varies between different denominations of Christianity, as well as between different countries and calendars.

Saint	Protector of	Feast day
Adelard	gardeners	2 January
Agatha	nurses	5 February
Agnes	girls	21 January
Albert the Great	scientists	15 November
Alphonsus Liguori	theologians	1 August
Amand	brewers, hotelkeepers	6 February
Andrew	fishermen	30 November
Anthony of Padua	lost articles, poor	13 June
Apollonia	dentists	9 February
Augustine	theologians, printers	28 August
Barbara	architects, builders	4 December
Bartholomew	plasterers	24 August
Camillus de Lellis	nurses	18 July
Catherine of Alexandria	philosophers, preachers, students	25 November
Catherine of Bologna	art, artists	9 March
Cecilia	musicians, poets, singers	22 November
Christopher	travellers	25 July
David	poets	29 December
Dismas	prisoners	25 March
Dominic	astronomers	8 August
Eligius	jewellers, metalworkers	1 December
Florian	firefighters	4 May
Francis de Sales	authors, editors, journalists	24 January
Francis of Assisi	animals, merchants	4 October
Francis Xavier	missions	3 December
Gabriel	messengers, postal workers, radio and television workers	29 September
Genesius	actors, secretaries	25 August
George	soldiers	23 April
Giles	disabled, beggars	1 September
Gregory the Great	musicians, teachers	3 September
Isidore	farmers	15 May
Ivo (St Yves in French)	lawyers	19 May
Jean Vianney	priests	4 August
Jerome	librarians	30 September
Joan of Arc	soldiers	30 May
John Baptist de la Salle	teachers	7 April
John Chrysostom	orators	13 September
John of God	book trade, nurses, printers	8 March
Joseph	carpenters, dying, fathers	19 March
Jude	desperate situations, lost causes	28 October
Luke	artists, butchers, doctors, glassworkers, sculptors, surgeons	18 October
Martha	cooks, housewives, servants, waiters	29 July
Martin de Porres	barbers, hairdressers	3 November
Martin of Tours	soldiers	11 November
Matthew	accountants, bookkeepers, tax collectors, bankers	21 September
Michael	grocers, police officers	29 September
Monica	mothers	27 August
Nicholas of Myra	children, brides	6 December
Paula	widows	26 January
Peter	fishermen	29 June
Raymond Nonnatus	midwives	31 August
Raphael	blind, lovers, travellers	29 September
Roch	invalids	16 August
Sebastian	athletes, soldiers	20 January
Thomas Aquinas	philosophers, scholars, students, theologians	28 January
Thomas More	lawyers	22 June
Valentine	lovers	14 February
Vincent de Paul	charities	27 September
Vincent Ferrer	builders	5 April

Christianity in the UK

The Church of England

The Church of England, the mother church of the Anglican Communion, is the established (state) form of Christianity in England. It was dissociated from the Roman Catholic Church in 1534 under Henry VIII; the British monarch is still the supreme head of the Church of England today.

Two archbishops head the provinces of Canterbury and York, which are subdivided into 44 dioceses. The Church Assembly (established in 1919) was replaced in 1970 by a General Synod with three houses (bishops, other clergy, and laity) to regulate church matters, subject to Parliament and the royal assent. The Archbishops' Council was established in 1998 to oversee the affairs of the Church of England and coordinate the work of all of its central institutions.

General Synod of the Church of England and the Archbishops' Council Secretary-General, P Mawer; Church House, Great Smith Street, London SW1P 3NZ; phone: (020) 7898 1000; fax: (020) 7898 1369

Archbishop of Canterbury The Most Reverend and Right Honourable the Lord Archbishop of Canterbury, Dr George Carey; Lambeth Palace, Lambeth Palace Road, London SE1 7JU; phone: (020) 7898 1000; fax: (020) 7261 9836; Web site: www.archbishopofcanterbury.org

Archbishop of York The Most Reverend and Right Honourable the Lord Archbishop of York, Dr David Hope; Bishopthorpe Palace, Bishopthorpe, York YO23 2GE; phone: (01904) 707021; fax: (01904) 709204; Web site: www.bishopthorpepalace.co.uk

Archbishops of Canterbury

Date elected	Name
597	Augustine
604	Laurentius
619	Mellitus
624	Justus
627	Honorius
655	Deusdedit
668	Theodore
693	Berthwald
731	Tatwine
735	Nothelm
740	Cuthbert
761	Bregowine
765	Jaenbert
793	Ethelhard
805	Wulfred
832	Feologeld
833	Ceolnoth
870	Ethelred
890	Plegmund
914	Athelm
923	Wulfhelm
942	Oda
959	Aelfsige
959	Brithelm
960	Dunstan
c. 988	Ethelgar

(continued)

Archbishops of Canterbury *(continued)*

Date elected	Name
990	Sigeric
995	Aelfric
1005	Alphege
1013	Lyfing
1020	Ethelnoth
1038	Eadsige
1051	Robert of Jumieges
1052	Stigand
1070	Lanfranc
1093	Anselm
1114	Ralph d'Escures
1123	William de Corbeil
1139	Theobald
1162	Thomas à Becket
1174	Richard (of Dover)
1184	Baldwin
1193	Hubert Walter
1207	Stephen Langton
1229	Richard le Grant
1234	Edmund of Abingdon
1245	Boniface of Savoy
1273	Robert Kilwardby
1279	John Peckham
1294	Robert Winchelsey
1313	Walter Reynolds
1328	Simon Meopham
1333	John de Stratford
1349	Thomas Bradwardine
1349	Simon Islip
1366	Simon Langham
1368	William Whittlesey
1375	Simon Sudbury
1381	William Courtenay
1396	Thomas Arundel
1398	Roger Walden
1399	Thomas Arundel[1]
1414	Henry Chichele
1443	John Stafford
1452	John Kempe
1454	Thomas Bourchier
1486	John Morton
1501	Henry Deane
1503	William Warham
1533	Thomas Cranmer
1556	Reginald Pole
1559	Matthew Parker
1576	Edmund Grindal
1583	John Whitgift
1604	Richard Bancroft
1611	George Abbot
1633	William Laud
1660	William Juxon
1663	Gilbert Sheldon
1678	William Sancroft
1691	John Tillotson
1695	Thomas Tenison
1716	William Wake
1737	John Potter
1747	Thomas Herring
1757	Matthew Hutton
1758	Thomas Secker
1768	Frederick Cornwallis
1783	John Moore
1805	Charles Manners-Sutton
1828	William Howley
1848	John Bird Sumner
1862	Charles Thomas Longley
1868	Archibald Campbell Tait
1883	Edward White Benson
1896	Frederick Temple
1903	Randall Thomas Davidson
1928	William Cosmo Gordon Lang
1942	William Temple
1945	Geoffrey Francis Fisher
1961	Arthur Michael Ramsey
1974	Frederick Donald Coggan
1980	Robert Alexander Kennedy Runcie
1991	George Leonard Carey

[1] Restored.

Women Clergy in the Church of England

In 1992 the Church of England General Synod and the Anglican church in Australia voted in favour of the ordination of women priests. In November 1993, legislation to allow the Church of England to ordain women priests gained the royal assent in Britain.

As of mid-1998.

Diocese	Total full-time diocesan clergy	Women as % of total
Lincoln	237	16.9
Southwark	379	16.6
Southwell	188	15.4
Bristol	157	15.3
Ripon	160	15.0
Oxford	460	14.6
St Albans	290	14.5
Birmingham	220	14.1
Liverpool	254	13.4
Guildford	195	13.3
Durham	236	12.7
Hereford	118	12.7
Ely	161	12.4
Sheffield	197	11.7
Leicester	158	11.4
Lichfield	374	11.2
Worcester	162	11.1
Coventry	148	10.8
Rochester	233	10.7
Bath and Wells	248	10.1
Manchester	295	9.5
Chelmsford	414	9.4
Peterborough	162	9.3
York	282	9.2
Wakefield	175	9.1
St Edmundsbury and Ipswich	166	9.0
London	548	8.8
Gloucester	161	8.7
Salisbury	233	8.2
Portsmouth	112	8.0
Carlisle	152	7.9
Norwich	195	7.7
Bradford	121	7.4
Newcastle	152	7.2
Canterbury	184	7.1
Derby	183	7.1
Chester	285	6.7
Winchester	245	6.1
Exeter	258	5.0
Blackburn	245	4.9
Truro	128	2.3
Chichester	343	2.0
Sodor and Man	22	0

Membership of the Christian Churches in the UK

According to research carried out in the UK by Christian Research, membership of the institutional Christian churches (Anglican, Roman Catholic, Orthodox, and Presbyterian) fell overall by almost 27% between 1980 and 2000; however, whilst membership of the Anglican, Catholic, and Presbyterian churches fell, membership of the institutional Orthodox churches increased by 21%.

During the same period, membership of the Free Churches (including Baptist, Methodist, Pentecostal, and New Churches) increased slightly overall (by 0.8%), but membership of the Baptist and Methodist churches declined, by 12% and 28% respectively. Membership of the Pentecostal churches increased by 98%. Membership of the New Churches increased by 1,267%, from 10,037 in 1980 to an estimated 137,225 in 2000.

In the 20th century church membership in the UK peaked in 1930, when there were more than 10 million church members – 31% of the adult population. By 2000 church membership had dropped to 5,861,796 – 12% of the adult population – with a fall in membership of 40% since 1960.

Christian Churchgoers in England by Denomination

Figures show estimates of the number of adults (taken as aged 15 or over) regularly attending a Christian church.

Denomination	1980	1990	2000	% change 1980–2000
Anglican	968,000	917,600	793,700	– 18
Baptist	201,300	197,700	223,700	11
Catholic	1,601,400	1,346,400	1,030,700	– 36
Independent	164,200	179,700	128,200	– 22
Methodist	437,900	395,200	313,100	– 28
New Churches	50,300	114,200	187,500	273
Orthodox	7,200	9,600	21,100	193
Pentecostal	147,200	164,700	163,100	11
United Reformed	139,000	104,100	100,000	– 28
Other churches	97,700	83,000	75,500	– 23
Total	3,814,200	3,512,200	3,036,600	– 20

Source: UK Christian Handbook, Religious Trends No 2, 2000/01, © *Christian Research, London, 2000*

Church Attendance in England

1998

Frequency of attendance	% of the population
Every Sunday	7.5
At least every fortnight	8.3
At least every month	10.2
At least once a quarter	11.3
At least twice a year	12.6
At least once a year	16.2

Data from the English Church Attendance Survey conducted by Christian Research, London

Belief in God in Great Britain

In a 1998 British Social Attitudes survey conducted by the National Centre for Social Research, respondents were asked to identify the statement that came closest to describing their beliefs.

1998

Statement	%
I know God really exists and I have no doubt about it	21
While I have doubts, I feel that I do believe in God	23
I find myself believing in God some of the time, but not at others	14
I don't believe in a personal God, but I do believe in a Higher Power of some kind	14
I don't know whether there is a God and I don't believe there is any way to find out	15
I don't believe in God	10
Not answered	3

Source: Social Trends 30, © *Crown copyright 2000*

The Decline in Church Attendance and Membership in the UK

According to research carried out by Christian Research, London, between 1980 and 2000 the average number of adults in Britain who regularly attended a Christian church fell by more than a million, from 4,770,800 to 3,755,100 – an average fall of approximately 977 people a week. A net 6,065 churches closed between 1960 and 2000 and the number of ministers fell from 41,211 to 33,709.

The Church of Ireland

The Church of Ireland, an autonomous church of the Anglican Communion, is divided into two provinces, Armagh and Dublin; the provinces are subdivided into 12 dioceses.

The Church of Ireland, Central Office Church Avenue, Rathmines, Dublin 6; phone: (00 353) 1497 8422; fax: (00 353) 1497 8821; e-mail: hostmaster@ireland.anglican.org; Web site: www.ireland.anglican.org

Archbishop of Armagh and Primate of All Ireland The Most Reverend Dr R H A Eames; The See House, Cathedral Close, Armagh BT61 7EE; phone: (028) 3752 7144; fax: (028) 3752 7823; e-mail: archbishop@armagh.anglican.org

Archbishop of Dublin, Bishop of Glendalough, and Primate of Ireland The Most Reverend Dr Walton Empey; The See House, Milltown, Dublin 6; phone: (00 353) 1497 7849; fax: (00 353) 1497 6355; e-mail: archbishop@dublin.anglican.org

The Scottish Episcopal Church

The Scottish Episcopal Church is an autonomous church within the Anglican Communion; it has seven dioceses and is governed by the General Synod, presided over by the elected diocesan bishop known as the Primus.

The General Synod of the Scottish Episcopal Church 21 Grosvenor Crescent, Edinburgh EH12 5EE; phone: (0131) 225 6357; fax: (0131) 346 7247; Web site: www.scotland.anglican.org

Primus of the Scottish Episcopal Church 21a Grosvenor Crescent, Edinburgh EH12 5EL; phone: (0131) 538 7044; fax: (0131) 538 7088

The Church in Wales

The Church in Wales is an autonomous province of the Anglican Communion, consisting of six dioceses (with bishops elected by an electoral college of clergy and lay people) with an archbishop elected from among the six bishops.

The Governing Body of the Church in Wales 39 Cathedral Road, Cardiff CF11 9XF; phone: (029) 2023 1638; fax: (029) 2038 7835; e-mail: information@rb.churchinwales.org.uk; Web site: www.churchinwales.org.uk

Archbishop of Wales The Most Reverend Dr Rowan Williams; Bishopstow, Stow Hill, Newport NP20 4EA; phone: (01633) 263510; fax: (01633) 259946

The Church of Scotland

The Church of Scotland is the established (national) form of Christianity in Scotland, first recognized by the state in 1560. It is based on the Protestant doctrines of the reformer Calvin and governed on Presbyterian lines.

The government of the Church of Scotland is by kirk sessions, presbyteries, synods, and the General Assembly, the supreme court. The kirk session consists of the parish minister and ruling elders, elected by the congregation. The presbyteries consist of all parish ministers in a specified district, with one ruling elder from every congregation. The provincial synods, of which there are 12, comprise three or more presbyteries. The presbyteries elect the two commissioners who sit in the General Assembly.

The Church of Scotland, Church Office 121 George Street, Edinburgh EH2 4YN; phone: (0131) 225 5722; fax: (0131) 220 3133; Web site: www.cofs.org.uk

■ Major Religions and Faiths

The Roman Catholic Church in the UK

In the UK the Roman Catholic Church is governed by the Bishops' Conference of England and Wales, of Scotland, and of Ireland.

Apostolic Nuncio to Great Britain The Most Reverend Pablo Puente; 54 Parkside, London SW19 5NE; phone: (020) 8946 1410

Bishops' Conference England and Wales 39 Eccleston Square, London SW1V 1BX; phone: (020) 7630 8220; fax: (020) 7630 5166; e-mail: cbcew@aol.com; Web site: www.tasc.ac.uk

Bishops' Conference Scotland 64 Aitken Street, Airdrie, Lanarkshire ML6 6LT; phone: (01236) 764061; fax: (01236) 762489; e-mail: gensec@bpsconfscot.com

Bishops' Conference Ireland 65 Newry Road, Dundalk, County Louth; phone: (00 353) 42 933 8087; fax: (00 353) 42 933 3575

Orthodox Churches in the UK

Patriarchate of Antioch Father Samir Gholam, Antiochan Priest for London, 30 Chatsworth Gardens, New Malden, Surrey KT3 6DW; phone: (020) 8942 9676

Eastern Orthodox Churches

Greek Orthodox Church, Patriarchate of Constantinople His Eminence Archbishop Gregorios of Thyateira, Archdiocese of Thyateira and Great Britain; 5 Craven Hill, London W2 3EN; phone: (020) 7723 4787; fax: (0171) 224 9301

Russian Orthodox Church, Patriarchate of Moscow Diocesan Secretary, Gillian Crow; 6 Maiden Place, Dartmouth Park, Highgate, London NW5 1HZ; phone: (020) 7272 9898; fax: (020) 7272 4227; e-mail: gillian@crow.co.uk

Oriental Orthodox Churches

The Council of Oriental Orthodox Churches Deacon Aziz M A Nour; 34 Chertsey Road, Church Square, Shepperton, Middlesex TW17 9LF; phone: (020) 8368 8447; fax: (020) 8368 8447

Other Christian Churches in the UK

Associated Presbyterian Churches The Minister, St Stevens, Old Edinburgh Road, Inverness; phone: (01463) 223983; fax: (01463) 226939

Baptist Union of Great Britain Baptist House, PO Box 44, 129 Broadway, Didcot OX11 8RT; phone: (01235) 517700; fax: (01235) 517715; e-mail: baptistuniongb@baptist.org.uk

Congregational Federation 4–8 Castle Gate, Nottingham NG1 7AS; phone: (0115) 911 1460; fax: (0115) 911 1462

Free Church of England The Bishop Primus Right Reverend K Powell; 9 Kingsleigh Drive, Castle Bromwich, Birmingham B36 9DQ; phone/fax: (0121) 747 3052; Web site: www.fce.org.uk

Free Church of Scotland Free Church Offices, The Mound, Edinburgh EH1 2LS; phone: (0131) 226 5286/4978; fax: (0131) 220 0597; e-mail: offices@freechurchofscotland.org.uk; Web site: www.freechurch.org

Free Presbyterian Church of Scotland 16 Matheson Road, Stornoway HS1 2LA; phone: (01463) 220304

Lutheran Council of Great Britain 5 Kings Croft Road, London NW2 3QE; phone: (020) 8450 9557; fax: (020) 8904 2849

Methodist Church 25 Marylebone Road, London NW1 5JR; phone: (020) 7486 5502; fax: (020) 7935 1507; e-mail: co-ordsec@methodistchurch.org.uk

Pentecostal Revival Church of Christ 220 Ellison Road, Streatham, London SW16 5DJ; phone: (020) 8764 2643.

Presbyterian Church in Ireland Church House, Fisherwick Place, Belfast BT1 6DW; phone: (01232) 322284; fax: (01232) 236609; e-mail: info@presbyterianireland.org; Web site: www.presbyterianireland.org

Presbyterian Church of Wales (or **Calvinic Methodist Church of Wales**) 53 Richmond Road, Cardiff CF24 3WJ; phone: (029) 2049 4913; fax: (029) 2046 4293

Religious Society of Friends (Quakers) in Britain Quaker Communications Department, Friends House, 173–177 Euston Road, London NW1 2BJ; phone: (020) 7663 1000; fax: (020) 7663 1001; Web site: www.quaker.org

The Salvation Army UK Territorial Headquarters, 101 Queen Victoria Street, London EC4P 4EP; phone: (020) 7236 5222; fax: (020) 7332 0101; Web site: www.salvationarmy.org.uk

Seventh-Day Adventist Church British Union Conference, Stanborough Park, Watford WD2 6JP; phone: (01923) 672251; fax: (01923) 893212; e-mail: buc@adventist.org.uk; Web site: www.adventist.org.uk

United Reformed Church in the United Kingdom 86 Tavistock Place, London WC1H 9RT; phone: (0171) 916 2020; fax: (020) 7916 2021; e-mail: urc@urc.org.uk; Web site: www.urc.org.uk

Inter-Church and Inter-Faith Organizations

The World Council of Churches is an international organization that aims to bring together the diverse movements within the Christian church. Established in 1945, it has a membership of 330 churches in more than 120 countries.

The World Council of Churches PO Box 2100, 1211 Geneva 2, Switzerland; phone: +41 (22) 791 6111; fax: +41 (22) 791 0361; e-mail: info@wcc-coe.org; Web site: http://wcc-coe.org

Churches Together in Britain and Ireland is an ecumenical organization that promotes cooperation between the Christian churches in the UK and also works to promote effective inter-faith relations in Britain and Ireland.

Churches Together in Britain and Ireland, Inter Church House, 35–41 Lower Marsh, London SE1 7SA; phone: (020) 7523 2121; fax: (020) 7928 0010; e-mail: info@ctbi.org.uk; Web site: www.ctbi.org.uk

Inter Faith Network for the United Kingdom promotes cooperation between communities of all faiths in the UK and has over 85 member bodies.

The Inter Faith Network, 5–7 Tavistock Place, London WC1H 9SN; phone: (020) 7388 0008; fax: (020) 7387 7968; e-mail: ifnet@interfaith.org.uk; Web site: www.interfaith.org.uk

Hinduism

Introduction

Hinduism encompasses a wide variety of beliefs originating in India, and is regarded by some as not constituting a formal religion at all. No precise dates can be given for its origins, although the Vedas, the earliest texts of Hinduism, arose from a culture that was probably established in India during the second millennium BCE.

Most Hindus believe that God takes many forms and is worshipped by many different names, so the multitude of gods and goddesses in Hindu belief are aspects of the same godhead. God has three main male forms, Brahma the Creator, Vishnu the Preserver, and Shiva the Destroyer. Each of these has a female counterpart: respectively Sarasvati, Lakshmi, and Parvati. God may also come to Earth in human form: the best known of these are Krishna and Rama, both incarnations of Vishnu. Each person and each animal embodies a spark (atman) of the universal soul, which is God. After death the atman is reborn in a new body. Therefore God is in every object in the universe, and everything that exists is part of God.

Hindus believe that every action, good or bad, has an effect (karma) on this life and on future lives. By accumulating positive karma one can eventually break free from the cycles of birth and death to achieve liberation or moksha, which is complete union with God.

Scripture

There are many sacred books, all written in the ancient Indian language Sanskrit. The oldest are the Vedas, first written in the second millennium BCE, followed by the Upanishads, more philosophical writings. Two great epics, the *Mahābhārata* and the *Rāmayāna*, existed in oral form long before they were written down around 2,000 years ago. The *Mahābhārata* contains the best-loved Hindu scripture, the Bhagavad Gītā, or 'Song of the Blessed', about the god Krishna.

Important sites of pilgrimage

Pilgrimages are an important part of Hindu devotion, and there are hundreds of pilgrimage sites throughout India. Hindus celebrate many local festivals, often associated with pilgrimage sites or shrines not known outside their own area. The River Ganges is regarded as holy throughout its length, but particularly at Benares (Varanasi), where pilgrims bathe, and the ashes of the dead are scattered. Hindus regard the whole range of the Himalayas as sacred, especially Mount Kailas, where it is said that the god Shiva sits in meditation, and where Arjuna (a hero of the *Mahābhārata*) went to visit him.

Vrindavan, on the sacred River Yamuna, is revered as the birthplace of the god Krishna, and attracts pilgrims from all over India and beyond, especially at Janmashtami, the festival celebrating Krishna's birth.

Adherents

There are nearly 760 million Hindus worldwide, almost all living in south Asia. In India there are over 650 million Hindus, and other large Hindu communities live in countries where colonial or trading ties encouraged migration from India: the UK, Guyana, Kenya, South Africa, and Indonesia.

In the UK, the number of active members of the Hindu faith increased by approximately 37% (from 120,000 to 165,000) between 1980 and 2000 and by 2000 there were nearly 170 Hindu temples in the UK. The largest communities in the UK are in Leicester, London, Birmingham, and Bradford.

See also **The Hindu Calendar**, p 12 and **Major Religious Festivals**, p 392.

Hindu Religious Organization in the UK

National Council of Hindu Temples Bhaktiventa Manor, Hilfield Lane, Aldenham, Watford WD2 8EZ; phone/fax: (01923) 856269/857244; e-mail: bimal.krsna.bcs@pamho.net

Hindu Gods

The Hindu pantheon is dominated by the primary gods Shiva and Vishnu, and, to a lesser extent Brahma, the creator, who control the powers of destruction and preservation. Throughout India, Hinduism is organized around the two main sects, Vaishnavism and Shaivism, whose followers regard either Vishnu or Shiva as the pre-eminent deity. Vishnu is also worshipped in up to 22 earthly incarnations. The best-known deities and their aspects or incarnations are listed below.

Agni	god of fire; a three-headed god who rides on aram
Balarama	brother of Krishna
Bhairava	incarnation of Shiva
Brahma	god of creation
Durga	wife of Shiva, the inaccessible
Ganesh	elephant-headed son of Shiva
Garuda	bird on which Shiva rides
Hanuman	monkey god
Indra	storm god, bringer of rain
Iswara	collectively represented as Trimurti by Brahma, Vishnu, and Shiva; Iswara corresponds to nature and the human soul
Kali	goddess of destruction; evil wife of Shiva
Kalki	incarnation of Vishnu as a giant with a horse's head
Kama	god of desire and sexual lust
Karaikkal-Ammaiyar	mother goddess and teacher, often shown playing the cymbals
Karrttikeya	six-headed, twelve-armed god who rides on a peacock
Krishna	incarnation of Vishnu which corresponds to the perfect deification of life
Kurma	incarnation of Vishnu as a tortoise
Lakshmana	half-brother of Rama

(continued)

Hindu Gods (*continued*)

Lakshmi	(Sri) goddess of wealth and good fortune; wife of Vishnu
Mahadevi Shakti	(Mahasakti) supreme goddess; corresponds to the Absolute (Brahman) and facilitates its self-manifestation
Mahishasuramardini	consort of Shiva
Matsya	incarnation of Vishnu as a fish
Nandin	bull vehicle of Shiva
Narada	incarnation of Vishnu
Narasimha	incarnation of Vishnu as a man-lion
Nataraja	aspect of Shiva as the lord of dance and rhythm
Parashurama	incarnation of Vishnu
Parvati	good wife of Shiva; opposite of Kali
Pidari	consort of Shiva
Pushan	the enhancer, prosperer, and enlightener
Radha	consort of Krishna; represents romantic love
Rama	incarnation of Vishnu
Rudra	the violent, terrifying aspect of Shiva
Sarasvati	mother goddess of art, music, and learning; female counterpart of Brahma
Savitri	creator of the true and the just
Shakti	female symbol of power or energy
Shani	astral god and bringer of ill-luck
Shiva	god of creation and destruction; lord of the dance
Shatrughna	half brother of Rama
Sita	wife of Rama
Skanda	formed from the discarded semen of Shiva
Surya	sun god; the illuminator
Uma	the gracious; ascetic goddess
Vamana	incarnation of Vishnu as a dwarf
Varaha	incarnation of Vishnu as a boar
Virabhadra	incarnation of Shiva
Vishnu	god of creation
Yashoda	foster mother of Krishna

Active Members of the Hindu Faith in the UK

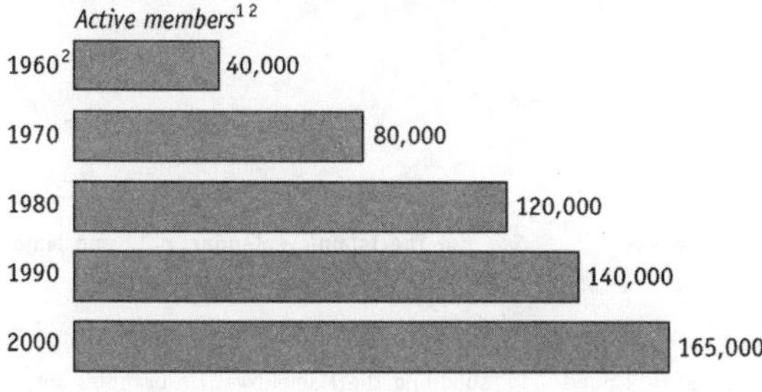

[1] Active members are taken as one third of the community.
[2] Figures are estimates.

Source: UK Christian Handbook, Religious Trends No 2 2000/01 (*Christian Research, London*), © *PW Brierley 1999*

Islam

Introduction

The beliefs of Islam are summed up in the Declaration of Faith: 'There is no god but God, and Muhammad is the Prophet of God'.

Islam means 'peace' or 'submission', and a Muslim is 'one who submits' (to the will of God). In Islam there is one God (Arabic Allah), who is creator of the universe and the only absolute power. According to Muslim belief, God has sent many prophets, from Adam onwards, to give his message to humanity, but their message was partially lost or misunderstood. The complete message is believed to have been given by the Prophet Muhammad, who lived in Arabia in the 6th century CE. Although this message marked the beginning of a formal religion, Muslims believe that all previous prophets were Muslims, and that Islam is the primordial faith. Muslims regard Muhammad with deep love and respect as God's final prophet, and seek to follow his example, but worship is due only to God.

Scripture

Muslims believe that the Koran was dictated to the Prophet Muhammad by the angel Jibra'il, a messenger from God, and, because it was committed to memory and written down almost immediately, that it is the final and complete revelation from God. The Koran is believed to have been written by God, in Arabic, before time began. Muslims point to the beauty of the language as evidence of its divine origin, and it is always recited in Arabic.

Important sites of pilgrimage

All Muslims who can afford it are expected to perform the *hajj*, or pilgrimage, to Mecca (Arabic Makkah) during the month of pilgrimage at least once in a lifetime; however, the Koran specifically states that one must not put one's own or one's family's health or well-being at risk by going.

Muslims believe that the Kaaba at Mecca was first built by Adam as a house of worship, and subsequently rebuilt by Ibrahim (Abraham) and his son Isma'il. It is a simple cube-shaped stone building, and has been a religious site since very early times. Every year between two and three million Muslims make their pilgrimage there, and no non-Muslim is allowed to enter the city.

Before entering Mecca the pilgrims set aside their normal clothes and wear a simple white garment as a mark of equality with others and humility before God. Each pilgrim performs seven circuits round the Kaaba, touching or kissing the black stone in the Kaaba wall if it is possible to do so in the vast throng of pilgrims. Over six days the pilgrims visit several different sites in and around Mecca, performing special ceremonies at each.

The mosque at Medina, Saudi Arabia, which contains Muhammad's tomb, and the Dome of the Rock in Jerusalem, which is built on the place from which Muhammad began his ascent into heaven, are also important sites of pilgrimage.

Organization

There is no overall world organization of Islam, but several bodies have been set up to promote contact and to give Islam a voice in international affairs. These bodies include the World Muslim Congress, the Muslim World League, and the Organization of the Islamic Conference.

Introduction (*continued*)

Adherents
There are over a billion Muslims worldwide, concentrated in the Middle East, North and West Africa, southeastern Europe, Indonesia, and Malaysia. There are two main branches of Islam: Sunni who make up 80% of all Muslims, and Shia, who are found mainly in Iran, Iraq, Yemen, and Bahrain. In the UK, the estimated number of active members of the Muslim faith rose approximately 120% (from 306,000 to 675,000) between 1980 and 2000.

The Five Pillars of Islam

1 Repeating the creed

2 Daily prayer or salat

3 Giving alms

4 Fasting during the month of Ramadan

5 The hajj, or pilgrimage to Mecca, once in a lifetime

Muslim Religious Organizations in the UK

Imams and Mosques Council 20–22 Creffield Road, London W5 3RP; phone: (020) 8992 6636

Union of Muslim Organizations in the UK and Eire 109 Campden Hill Road, London W8 7TL; phone: (020) 7229 0538

Active Members of the Muslim Faith in the UK

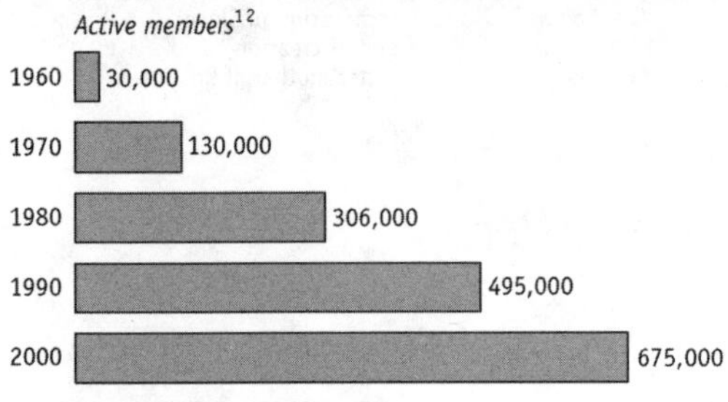

[1] Figures are estimated and include non-South Asians.
[2] Taken as 50% of the estimated Muslim community.

Source: UK Christian Handbook, Religious Trends No 2 2000/01 (*Christian Research, London*), © *PW Brierley 1999*

See also **The Islamic Calendar**, p 12 and **Major Religious Festivals**, p 392.

Islam: Key Events

3rd–6th centuries The eastern Roman Empire and the Persian Sassanians are in continuous conflict for the domination of Syria, Egypt, and Asia Minor.

571 Birth of Muhammad, the prophet of Islam, in Mecca.

6th–7th centuries Islam begins in Arabia, calling for a new way of life based on submission to God. An Islamic state is established that develops further during the formative period of the four Orthodox caliphs or successors to the prophet, Abu Bakr, Umar, Uthman, and Ali. During this period the Persians are defeated (637) and their capital Cteisphon is captured.

8th century Islam expands under the Umayyad and Abbasid dynasties to Spain and Sind; southern France is invaded; Southern Italy is occupied. The early schools of Islamic law continue to develop during this period and legal doctrine becomes integrated into the legal practices of the courts.

9th century Turkish slave Mamelukes rise to power in Baghdad and a dictatorship is established in Egypt that occupies Syria, in a move towards the fragmentation of the main Islamic state.

10th century The Fatimid Shiite Isma'ili sect conquers Cairo in 969. Al-Azhar University is founded in 972. With the insanity of the Fatimid caliph (who believes himself God) and his death in 1018, a new religion appears in the form of the Druze Shia subsect, comprised of those adherents who believe in the caliph's divinity.

11th century The Abbasid and Fatimid dynasties and the Byzantine empire decline. The central Asian Turkish nomads known as the Seljuks emerges. Islamic law becomes stagnant. The first Christian Crusade captures Muslim-held Jerusalem in 1099.

12th century Muslims are reunited in a jihad or holy war, and recapture Jerusalem under the leadership of Saladin. The Mongols emerge as a new force in the Middle East, seizing Persia and part of Syria.

13th century The Mongols continue their march, sacking Baghdad. With the fall of the city 1258 and the death of the caliph Mustasim, the Abbasid caliphate ends. Only two years later the Mongols are defeated by Qutuz at the decisive Battle of Ayn Jalut on the way to Damascus, ending their expansion towards the heartland of the Muslim world. Thirty years later the Mongol khan converts to Islam. This is followed by the emergence of the first Ottomans in Turkey.

14th century Ottoman Turks invade Bulgarian territory up to the Balkans.

15th century In the Second Battle of Kossova in 1446 Serbia is annexed to Turkey, with Bosnia as its vassal. Muhammad al-Fath conquers Constantinople in 1453. Albania is annexed to the Ottoman Turkish empire. In 1492, Granada, the last Muslim state in Spain, falls to the monarchs of Spain, Ferdinand and Isabella. The Safavid dynasty is founded in Persia.

16th–17th centuries Ottoman power reaches its height during the reign of the Ottoman Suleiman the Magnificent 1520–65. The first unsuccessful Ottoman siege of Vienna is in 1529, and the second in 1683. With the defeat of the Ottomans in the naval battle of Lepanto, their dominance of the Mediterranean ends. The forcible conversion of Muslims to Catholicism begins in Spain.

18th century In Arabia, Muhammad ibn-Abd-al-Wahab (1703–1792) preaches a return to fundamental Muslim values.

19th century Muhammad Ali is appointed pasha of Egypt by the Turks in 1805, after subduing the Mamelukes. He occupies Mecca and Taif in 1813 and continues across Arabia, expelling the Saudis from their capital Dariyya in 1818. European powers take control of many territories that previously came under Muslim rule. In 1876 Britain purchases shares in the Suez Canal and becomes involved in Egypt, with military occupation following in 1882. In 1878 Turkey hands Cyprus to Britain and a year later, after the Treaty of Berlin, Turkey loses 80 percent of its European territory.

20th century European expansion continues in the Middle East. During World War I, the Arabs revolt against Ottoman Turkish rule. In 1921, the British make kings of two sons of the Sharif of Mecca, Abdullah ibn Hussein of Transjordan and Faisal of Iraq. Mustafa Kemal abolishes the Turkish sultanate in 1922 and becomes the first president of Turkey. Reza Shah seizes the government in Persia in 1925. Abdul Aziz Ibn Saud captures Riyadh and Mecca, assuming the title of king in 1926. Hasan al-Banna founds the Muslim Brotherhood in Egypt in 1928. Egyptian president Gamal Abdel Nasser nationalizes the Suez Canal in 1956 and executes Sayyid Qutb, the leader of the Muslim Brotherhood. The secular Pahlavi dynasty in Iran ends in 1979 with the return from exile of Ayatollah Khomeini, who declares Iran an Islamic Republic. The Iraq–Iran War is followed by Saddam Hussein's invasion of Kuwait (1990) and the Gulf War. Revivalist movements arise, calling for a return to fundamental Islamic values; in Algeria this leads to violent unrest. Islamic regimes are established in Iran, Afghanistan, Sudan, and Pakistan.

Jainism

Introduction

The word Jain means follower of the Jinas – 'those who overcome', in the sense of achieving discipline over one's own desires, thoughts, and actions. There were 24 Jinas, also known as Tirthankaras ('bridge-builders'), the last of whom was Mahavira who lived in India in the 5th century BCE. The first is believed to have lived millions of years ago and to have invented human culture. The example of the Jinas helps others to achieve freedom from reincarnation. The belief in non-violence (ahimsa) is central to the Jain tradition, and Jains try to avoid violence to life in every form, including animals and plants as well as humans. Jain monks and nuns wear a cloth over the mouth and nose to avoid harming any flying insects, and sweep the ground in front of them to avoid treading on any creature. This central teaching of nonviolence has had a powerful effect on Indian culture and thought and was highlighted by the teachings of Mahatma Gandhi.

Organization

The Jain tradition is divided into two groups: Svetambaras, who are concentrated in northeast India, and Digambaras, who mainly live in southern India. There are Jain temples in all the major Indian cities.

Adherents

There are an estimated 4 million Jains worldwide, over 98% of them in India. The two largest Jain communities outside India are in the UK and the USA. Estimates suggest that the number of active members of the tradition in the UK doubled between 1980 and 2000.

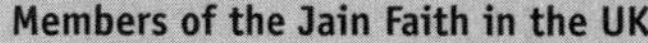

Members of the Jain Faith in the UK

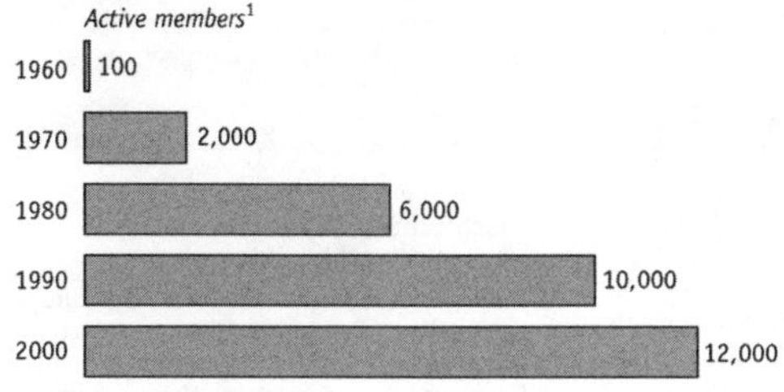

[1] Figures are estimates.

Source: UK Christian Handbook, Religious Trends No 2 2000/01 (*Christian Research, London*), © *PW Brierley 1999*

Jain Organizations in the UK

Federation of Jain Organizations in the UK
11 Lindsay Drive, Harrow HA3 0TA; phone: (020) 8204 2871

Judaism

Introduction

Jews believe in one God, the Creator and Ruler of the universe. They believe that God made a Covenant, or agreement, with Abraham, who is regarded as the father of the Jewish people, and is believed by some scholars to have lived around 1900 BCE. Keeping the law is the Jewish people's part in this Covenant. Jews look forward to the coming of the Messiah, a leader from God, who will bring peace, fruitfulness, and security to the whole world. At the Messiah's coming, the dead will be brought back to life and judged by God.

Study of the law is an important part of Jewish life. The fifth commandment lays down that no work must be done on the seventh day of the week, the Sabbath, or Shabbat. Since Jewish days are reckoned from nightfall to nightfall, the Sabbath begins as it gets dark on Friday evening, and ends at dusk on Saturday evening. Jewish food laws (kashrut) relate to what is eaten, and how it is slaughtered, prepared, cooked, and eaten. Food is either permitted (kosher) or forbidden (terefah).

Scripture

The Hebrew Bible consists of the Torah (Five Books of Moses), the Prophets, and other writings, including the Psalms. It was written in Hebrew, and is still read in Hebrew. The Torah tells the early history of the Jewish people, and contains laws and guidance on one's way of life.

Important sites of pilgrimage

The land of Israel has a special status for Jews. In the Bible, God promised the land of Canaan to Abraham and his descendants. Although there is no injunction to travel to Israel, many Jews like to visit as often as they can.

In ancient times the Temple in Jerusalem was the place of worship for all Jews, with the presence of God signified by the Ark of the Covenant in the most sacred place inside. The Western Wall in Jerusalem is all that remains of the last great Temple, destroyed in 70 CE. It is a centre of pilgrimage and prayer for Jews from all over the world, both for private prayer, which is said facing the wall, and for public services and bar mitzvahs.

Many Jews also visit Yad Vashem ('a place and a name') in Jerusalem, a memorial to the Jews who died in the Nazi Holocaust.

Jewish law and traditions

Questions of belief and practice are debated by Rabbis who are trained in Jewish law and its interpretation. The most traditional form of Judaism is known as Orthodox. Orthodox Jews use only Hebrew in services, and interpret the laws quite strictly. Conservative Judaism, mainly found in the USA, seeks to interpret the law in the light of changing circumstances, while remaining true to tradition. Reform, or Liberal, Judaism arose in the 19th century and observes fewer dietary laws, as well as holding services in the vernacular rather than in Hebrew. Bodies such as the World Jewish Congress, which represents around 70% of all Jews, provide a forum for debate and a Jewish voice in world affairs.

Adherents

There are approximately 14 million Jews worldwide, in the sense that a Jew is the child of a Jewish mother, although not all are religious Jews who follow the laws given by God to Moses. Approximately 48% live in North America, 30% in Israel, and 20% in Europe and Russia. Estimates suggest that the number of Jewish households in the UK fell by almost 20% between 1980 and 2000.

Members of the Jewish Faith in the UK

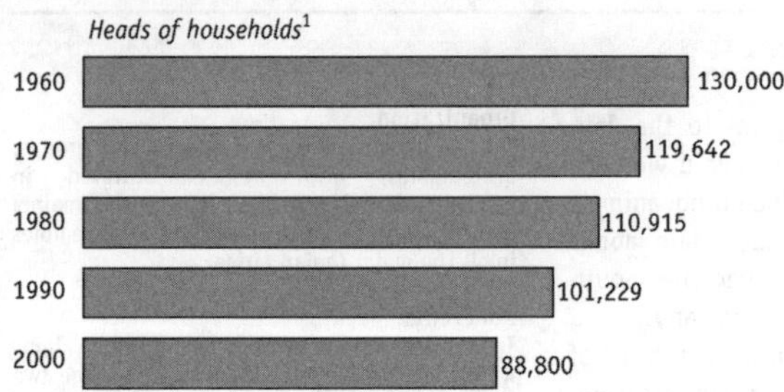

[1] Figures are estimates.

Source: UK Christian Handbook, Religious Trends No 2 2000/01 (*Christian Research, London*), © PW Brierley 1999

Jewish Religious Organizations in the UK

Office of the Chief Rabbi Chief Rabbi, Professor Jonathan Sacks; Executive Director, Mrs S Weinberg; Adler House, 735 High Road, London N12 0US; phone: (020) 8343 6301; fax: (020) 8343 6310; e-mail: info@chiefrabbi.org; Web site: www.chiefrabbi.org

Board of Deputies of British Jews E Tabachnik, President; Commonwealth House, 1–19 New Oxford Street, London WC1A 1NF; phone: (020) 7543 5400; fax: (020) 7543 0010

Federation of Synagogues G Kushner, Administrator; 65 Watford Way, London NW4 3AQ; phone: (020) 8202 2263; fax: (020) 8203 0610

Reform Synagogues of Great Britain Rabbi T Bayfield, Chief Executive; The Sternberg Centre for Judaism, 80 East End Road, London N3 2SY; phone: (020) 8349 4731; fax: (020) 8343 0901

United Synagogue Head Office J M Lew, Chief Executive; 753 High Road, London N12 0US; phone: (020) 8343 8989; fax: (020) 8343 6262; Web site: www.brijnet.org/us

Judaism: Key Events

***c.* 2000 BCE** Led by Abraham, the ancient Hebrews emigrate from Mesopotamia to Canaan.

18th century BCE–1580 BCE Some settle on the borders of Egypt and are put to forced labour.

13th century BCE They are rescued by Moses, who leads them out of Egypt to Canaan, the 'Promised Land'. Moses receives the Ten Commandments from God and brings them to the people. The main invasion of Canaan is led by Joshua in about 1274.

12th–11th centuries BCE During the period of Judges, ascendancy is established over the Canaanites.

***c.* 1000 BCE** Complete conquest of Palestine and the union of all Judea is achieved under David, and Jerusalem becomes the capital.

10th century BCE Solomon succeeds David and enjoys a reputation for great wealth and wisdom, but his lack of a constructive policy leads, after his death, to the secession of the north of Judea (Israel) under Jeroboam, with only the tribe of Judah remaining under the house of David as the southern kingdom of Judah.

9th–8th centuries BCE Assyria becomes the dominant power in the Middle East. Israel purchases safety by tribute, but the basis of the society is corrupt, and prophets such as Amos, Isaiah, and Micah predict destruction. At the hands of Tiglathpileser and his successor Shalmaneser IV, the northern kingdom (Israel) is made into Assyrian provinces after the fall of Samaria in 721 BCE, although the southern kingdom of Judah is spared as an ally.

586–458 BCE Nebuchadnezzar takes Jerusalem and carries off the major part of the population to Babylon. Judaism is retained during exile, and is reconstituted by Ezra on the return to Jerusalem.

520 BCE The Temple, originally built by Solomon, is restored.

***c.* 444 BCE** Ezra promulgates the legal code that is to govern the future of the Jewish people.

4th–3rd centuries BCE After the conquest of the Persian Empire by Alexander the Great, the Syrian Seleucid rulers and the Egyptian Ptolemaic dynasty struggle for control of Palestine, which comes under the government of Egypt, although with a large measure of freedom.

2nd century BCE With the advance of Syrian power, Antiochus IV attempts to intervene in the internal quarrels of the Hebrews, even desecrating the Temple, and a revolt breaks out in 165 BCE led by the Maccabee family.

63 BCE Judea's near-independence ends when internal dissension causes the Roman general Pompey to intervene, and Roman suzerainty is established.

1st century CE A revolt leads to the destruction of the Temple (66–70) by the Roman emperor Titus. Judean national sentiment is encouraged by the work of Rabbi Johanan ben Zakkai (*c.* 20–90), and, following him, the president of the Sanhedrin (supreme court) is recognized as the patriarch of Palestinian Jewry.

2nd–3rd centuries Greatest of the Sanhedrin presidents is Rabbi Judah Ha-Nasi, who codifies the traditional law in the *Mishnah*. The Palestinian *Talmud* (*c.* 375) adds the *Gemara* to the *Mishnah*.

4th–5th centuries The intellectual leadership of Judaism passes to the descendants of the 6th century BCE exiles in Babylonia, who compile the Babylonian *Talmud*.

8th–13th centuries Judaism enjoys a golden era, producing the philosopher Saadiah, the poet Jehudah Ha-levi (*c.* 1075–1141), the codifier Moses Maimonides, and others.

14th–17th centuries Where Christianity becomes the dominant or state religion, the Jews are increasingly segregated from mainstream life and trade by the Inquisition, anti-Semitic legislation, or by expulsion. The Protestant and Islamic states and their colonies allow for refuge. Persecution leads to messianic hopes, strengthened by the 16th-century revival of Kabbalism, culminating in the messianic movement of Shabbatai Sevi in the 17th century.

18th–19th centuries Outbreaks of persecution increase with the rise of European nationalism. Reform Judaism, a rejection of religious orthodoxy and an attempt to interpret it for modern times, begins in Germany in 1810 and is soon established in England and the USA. In the late 19th century, large numbers of Jews fleeing persecution (pogroms) in Russia and Eastern Europe emigrate to the USA, leading to the development of large Orthodox, Conservative, and Reform communities there. Many become Americanized and lose interest in religion.

20th century Zionism, a nationalist movement dedicated to achieving a secure homeland where the Jewish people would be free from persecution, is founded in 1896; this leads to the establishment of the state of Israel in 1948. Liberal Judaism (more radical than Reform) develops in the USA. In 1911 the first synagogue in the UK is founded. The Nazi German regime (1933–45) exterminates 6 million European Jews. Hundreds of thousands of survivors take refuge in pre-existing Jewish settlements in what eventually becomes the new state of Israel. Although most Israeli and American Jews are not affiliated with synagogues after the 1950s, they continue to affirm their Jewish heritage. Both Orthodox and Hasidic Judaism, however, flourish in their new homes and grow rapidly in the 1970s and 1980s. Conflict with Palestinian separatists (1987–93) and the subsequent peace process increase tensions between secular and Orthodox Jews in Israel. The Catholic Church apologizes (1997) for its silence during the Holocaust. The German government establishes (1998) a fund to compensate Holocaust survivors.

Major Religions and Faiths

The Chief Rabbinate of Britain

The Chief Rabbinate of Britain has developed from the position of the Rabbi of the Great Synagogue, London. From the early years of the 18th century until recently, he was acknowledged as the spiritual leader of the London Ashkenazi Community and this recognition was also accepted in the provinces and overseas. To conform with constitutional practice, the official designation (1845–1953) was 'Chief Rabbi of the United Hebrew Congregations of the British Commonwealth of Nations' and subsequently 'Chief Rabbi of the United Hebrew Congregations of the Commonwealth'.

The Chief Rabbinate of Britain

Dates of appointment	Name
1709–56	Aaron Hart
1756–64	Hart Lyon
1765–92	David Tevele Schiff
1802–42	Solomon Herschell
1845–90	Nathan Marcus Adler
1891–1911	Hermann Adler
1913–46	Joseph Herman Hertz
1948–65	Israel Brodie
1967–91	Immanuel Jakobovits
1991–	Jonathan Sacks

See also **The Jewish Calendar**, p 11 and **Major Religious Festivals**, p 392.

Sikhism

Introduction

The Sikh faith began in the Punjab in India in the 15th century. Guru Nanak, the founder of Sikhism, taught this new faith that rejected both Hindu and Muslim religious and social practices of the time. The Punjabi word *Sikh* means 'follower' or 'disciple'. Guru Nanak was succeeded by nine further Gurus, or teachers, each of whom was chosen by his predecessor, and each of whom made a distinctive contribution to the development of the Sikh faith.

Sikhs believe in one God, described as 'timeless and without form', creator and director of the universe. He cannot be found by religious practices, but makes himself known to those who are ready, as they seek him through prayer and service to others. Sikh teachings emphasize equality, service, and protection of the weak against injustice. Sikhs wear five distinctive marks of their faith, known as the 'five Ks' because their names in Punjabi all begin with K.

The Five Ks

Kesh – uncut hair; devout Sikhs do not cut their hair or beard at any time

Kanga – a comb to keep the hair in place; the hair is also kept tidy under a turban in imitation of the great Sikh Guru, Gobind Singh

Kara – a steel bangle, a complete circle symbolizing one God and one truth

Kirpan – a small sword or dagger, a reminder of the need to fight injustice

Kacchera – short trousers or breeches, indicating readiness to ride into battle

Scripture

In 1708 the collection of Sikh writings was instituted as the Guru for all time to come. Sikhs revere their scripture, the Guru Granth Sahib, as they would a living teacher.

The Guru Granth Sahib contains hymns written by some of the Sikh Gurus. These were collected by Guru Arjan, the fifth Guru, who also added hymns and poems written by devout Muslims and Hindus, saying that God's revelation is not confined to Sikhs. This collection was known as the Adi Granth, or 'first book'. Guru Gobind Singh, the tenth Guru, instituted this collection as the Guru for the Sikhs for all time. It is written in Gurmukhi, a form of written Punjabi.

Important sites of pilgrimage

Guru Ram Das, the fourth Guru of Sikhism, began building the holy city of Amritsar in the Punjab. Here the House of God (Golden Temple) houses the first copy of the Guru Granth Sahib, the Sikh scripture. The city is the spiritual centre of Sikhism.

Anandpur, the site of the founding of the Khalsa, the community of committed Sikhs, is a popular destination, and many items important to Sikh history can be seen in the Gurdwara there.

Other major pilgrimage sites include places of martyrdom, such as the remains of the building at Sarhind in which the two youngest sons of Guru Gobind Singh were immured and killed.

Adherents

There are approximately 22 million Sikhs worldwide. Most of them live in India, mainly in the Punjab in northwest India, but Sikhs have migrated to many parts of the world, and there are sizeable communities in the UK, the USA, and Canada, and smaller ones in East Africa, Europe, Malaysia, Indonesia, Australia, and New Zealand. The Sikh World Council was formed in 1995 to provide a forum and an international voice for Sikhs. Estimates suggest that the numbers of Sikhs in the UK rose from 150,000 to 400,000 between 1980 and 2000, a rise of 166%.

See also **Major Religious Festivals**, p 392.

The Ten Gurus

Guru Nanak, the founder of the Sikh faith, was succeeded by nine further gurus, or teachers, each of whom was chosen by his predecessor. In 1708 the collection of Sikh writings was instituted as the Guru for all time to come, and Sikhs revere their scripture, the Guru Granth Sahib, as they would a living teacher.

Guru Nanak Dev (1469–1539)

Guru Angad Dev (b. 1504, guru 1539–52)

Guru Amar Das (b. 1479, guru 1552–1574)

Guru Ram Das (b. 1534, guru 1574–81)

Guru Arjan Dev (b. 1563, guru 1581–1606)

Guru Hargobind (b. 1595, guru 1606–1644)

Guru Har Rai (b. 1630, guru 1644–61)

Guru Harkrishan (b. 1656, guru 1661–64)

Guru Tegh Bahadur (b. 1621, guru 1664–75)

Guru Gobind Singh (b. 1666, guru 1675–1708)

Sikh Religious Organizations in the UK

Sikh Missionary Society UK 10 Featherstone Road, Southall UB2 5AA; phone: (020) 8574 1902; fax: (020) 8574 1912

The World Sikh Foundation (Sikh Cultural Society of Great Britain) 33 Wargrave Road, South Harrow HA2 8LL; phone/fax: (020) 8864 9228

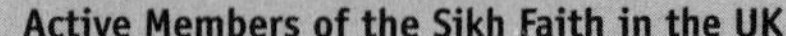

Active Members of the Sikh Faith in the UK

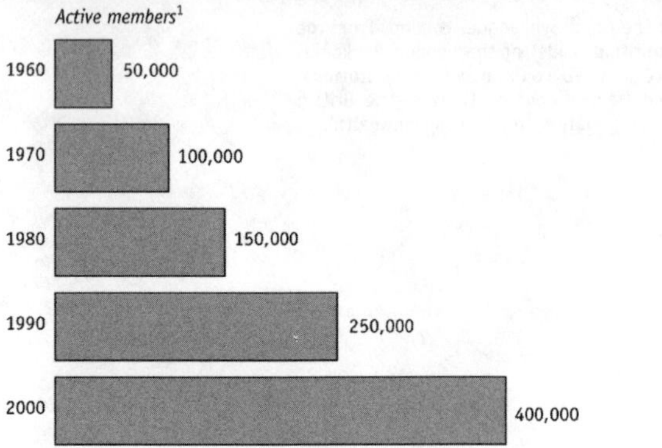

[1] All figures based on the Sikh Cultural Society's estimates.

Source: UK Christian Handbook, Religious Trends No 2 2000/01 (*Christian Research, London*), © *PW Brierley 1999*

Taoism

Introduction

Taoism emerged in China around the 1st century CE, and is named after the Chinese word *Tao* (Way or Path). The Tao is a natural force, the Way of the Universe, which guides all life. Living in harmony with the Tao brings peace and happiness; struggling against it brings suffering.

The balance of the universe is created by the forces of yin and yang – opposite forces in continual interaction and change, giving order to all life. Yin is heavy, dark, moist, earthy, and is associated with the feminine. Yang is airy, light, dry, hot, heavenly, and associated with the masculine. All forms of life are either predominantly yin or yang, but never exclusively so. The yin/yang symbol represents the two forces in balance, but each containing a speck of the other.

Traditional Taoist practices include the exorcism of evil spirits and ghosts, divination in various forms, and the worship of deities, many of whom have specific roles such as help in childbirth or different illnesses. The art of *feng shui*, or geomancy, is also practised in order to build in accordance with the Tao of the landscape.

Scripture

From the 5th to the 3rd century BCE, much was written on the significance of the Tao, most significantly the *Tao Te Ching* of Lao Tzu, the book of the sage Chuang Tzu, and the writings of Kung Fu Tzu (Confucius). They are still influential to this day, but there are also hundreds of other Taoist texts. By the 14th century CE, over 1,440 of these had been collected together to form the Taoist Canon.

Important sites of pilgrimage

The major pilgrimage sites for Taoism are the five Taoist sacred mountains:

Hua Shan
Heng Shan
Heng Shan
Tai Shan
Song Shan

The Tao (Path) that leads the pilgrim up these mountains passes temples, statues of deities and heroes, and commemorations of myths and legends. The sacred mountains are especially associated with sages and those who achieve immortality through rigorous practices and training.

Adherents

Because of the repression of religion in China, it is not possible to estimate the number of Taoists. However, the number of male and female Taoist priests in China is growing rapidly, and now stands at around 15,000. New temples are being opened and old ones restored. Taoist traditions are followed by members of Chinese communities throughout the world, and Taoist thought, literature, and philosophy is becoming increasingly popular with non-Chinese followers. The China Taoist Association promotes Taoism in China, although its function is partly political rather than religious.

Taoist Organization in the UK

British Taoist Association 16 Birchview, Epping, Essex CM16 6TJ

New Religious Movements

by Charlotte Hardman

The Terms 'Cult' and 'New Religious Movement' Hardly any religious group would describe itself as a cult. The word 'cult' is used mainly by those who wish to identify particular groups as dangerous. This definition of the term has been mainly promoted by the Christian counter-cult movement (who see 'cults' as everything that departs from their version of Christianity) and by secular anti-cultists (whose definition of 'cult' emerged from the active campaigns of parents worried by how their children changed when they joined particular religious groups).

To avoid the negative connotations implicit in the word 'cult', sociologists of religion prefer the term 'new religious movement' (NRM) for any of those broadly religious groups that have come into being in the second half of the 20th century. However, the more widespread use of the term 'NRM' is beginning to carry with it some of the negativity and sinister overtones that 'cult' conveys.

Members Disclaim Terms Members of NRMs often deny the organization is new or religious or a movement. They emphasize instead that their beliefs are based on old traditions, and that they offer a philosophy, an education, a healing process, or a particular 'way of life'.

The wish to disclaim the terms 'cult' and 'new religious movement' has become particularly strong since the Branch Davidian tragedy in Texas, which reaffirmed the Jonestown message of 15 years ago that 'cults' and 'cult leaders' are dangerous. (Strikingly, however, the People's Temple was not labelled a cult until after the mass suicide of the members in Guyana, and the Branch Davidians could be said to have been closer to a fundamentalist sect – one of several splinter groups whose extremist leader broke with the main Davidic Seventh-Day Adventists.)

Recent Rapid Growth of NRMs New religious movements or cults are not a new phenomenon. Throughout history, small, unconventional religious groups have emerged, as Christianity and other now accepted mainstream religions once did.

What is new is the rapid growth in the number of these groups in the 1960s and 1970s, with some 1,000 now in existence in the UK (though inevitably there are problems of definition). To put the groups in perspective, the number of committed members of all NRMs in the UK – those who have dedicated their whole lives to a movement – is unlikely to exceed 15,000.

The Diverstiy of NRMs It is impossible to generalize about the beliefs and practices of the NRMs. They have adopted ideas from a wide range of traditions, many of which were, until recently, strange to the West.

Of all the new religious groups, a few may be said to be benevolent and a few malevolent but the majority have both positive and negative attributes. Moreover, the individual members may be said to share characteristics with the rest of the population; if anything, they have a larger proportion of young people with high ideals who want to bring about improvements to themselves and the world.

Popular Image against Factual Reality The popular image of a cult, and one that has been adopted by the tabloid press in particular, is of a group of brainwashed followers of a corrupt leader who encourages them to use deceptive practices to secure more members to satisfy his or her greed for money, power, or sexual gratification, and who allows or even encourages the abuse of children, political conspiracy, drug-trafficking, and even murder.

Although a few of these activities may be practised by some of the new groups or may have been practised in the past, the implication that this is standard practice of all NRMs is inaccurate and highly misleading. Many of the groups have changed, and continue to develop in response to internal and external influences.

The disaster at Waco, Texas, with its armed fortress and zealot leader, David Koresh, has been much publicized and is remembered by the public as typical of a cult, whereas the morally acceptable activities of members of many of the new religious movements remain unseen.

Recruitment and Membership One of the most widely accepted notions about cults is that their members are all innocent victims who are members because they were rendered incapable of making a decision about joining. Much has been written by sociologists of religion on this topic. They point out, for example, the high turnover rate, which is incompatible with the notion of brainwashing.

Although recruitment practices may sometimes be deceptive or highly persuasive (such as 'love-bombing', by which prospective members are showered with affection, attention, and instant friendship), research shows that most people are capable of resisting the encouragements to join if they do not wish to do so.

Once they have joined, some members are subjected to techniques that may affect their powers of reasoning, yet even in these situations people do leave the group. The attachment of a particular member to a particular group is a process far more complex than the brainwashing thesis suggests, and to understand why any individual has joined a new religious movement it is crucial to look closely at both the individual and the group he or she has joined.

Major Religious Festivals

Major Religious Festivals

Festival	Description	Normally held	2001	2002
Theravada Buddhism (Southern Buddhism)[1]				
New Year Festival	images of the Buddha are bathed in scented water and stupas of sand are built on river banks or in temple grounds to be washed away at New Year, symbolizing the clearing away of negative deeds	beginning of Citta	April 2001[2]	April 2002[2]
Vesakha	celebrates the Buddha's birth, enlightenment, and passing into nirvana; processions take place in the temple, bodhi trees are sprinkled with scented water, lanterns are lit, and street stalls are erected	full moon of Vesakha	7 May 2001	27 April 2002
Asalha	commemorates the Buddha's first sermon and marks the beginning of the three-month rainy season, a period of temple retreat known as Vassa	full moon of Asalha	5 July 2001	24 June 2002
Assayuja	celebrates the return of the Buddha from heaven after passing on the teachings to his mother; Assayuja marks the end of Vassa	third full moon of Vassa	October 2001[2]	October 2002[2]
Kattika	commemorates the first Buddhist missionaries who went out to spread the Buddha's teachings; this is also the date for the end of Vassa if the rains continue longer than usual	full moon of Kattika	November 2001[2]	November 2002[2]
Kathina	offerings, especially robes, are presented to the monasteries in elaborate ceremonies	end of Vassa	October/November 2001[2]	October/November 2002[2]
Mahayana (East) Buddhism (Eastern Buddhism)[3]				
Birth of the Buddha	images of the Buddha as a child are bathed in scented water or tea, and offerings are made at temples and shrines	eighth day of the fourth lunar month	8 April 2001 (Japan)	8 April 2002 (Japan)
Birth of Kuan Yin	the Bodhisattva of Mercy; offerings and prayers are made to her by those who seek help in times of need	19th day of second lunar month	February/March 2001[2]	February/March 2002[2]
Enlightenment of Kuan Yin		19th day of sixth lunar month	June/July 2001[2]	June/July 2002[2]
Death of Kuan Yin		19th day of ninth lunar month	September/October 2001[2]	September/October 2002[2]
Hungry Ghost Festival	unsettled spirits of the dead are calmed with chanting and offerings to enable them to pass peacefully into the next world	8–15th days of the Chinese seventh lunar month	July/August 2001[2]	July/August 2002[2]
O-Bon	families reunite to remember and honour their ancestors; offerings are made to the Buddha and monks visit home shrines to read Buddhist scriptures	13–15 July (Japan)	13–15 July 2001 (Japan)	13–15 July 2002 (Japan)
Mahayana (North) Buddhism (Northern Buddhism)[4]				
Tibetan New Year	houses are cleaned to sweep away any negative aspects from the last year; costumed monks perform new year rituals and chants; people light firecrackers or torches to chase away the spirits	new moon of February	23 February 2001[6]	12 February 2002[6]
Modlam Chenmo	the Great Prayer Festival is celebrated with traditional stories, puppet shows, and butter sculptures in the monasteries	8–15th of the first lunar month	February 2001[2]	February 2002[2]
The Buddha's Enlightenment and Passing into Nirvana	pilgrims visit monasteries to make offerings; traditional Chan dancing is performed	15th day of the fourth lunar month	May 2001[2]	May 2002[2]
Guru Rinpoche's Birthday	commemorates the Indian teacher who helped establish Buddhist teachings in Tibet towards the end of the 8th century CE	tenth day of the sixth lunar month	July 2001[2]	July 2002[2]
Chokhor Duchen	celebrates the Buddha's first sermon after his enlightenment	fourth day of the sixth lunar month	July 2001[2]	July 2002[2]
Lhabab Duchen	commemorates the descent of the Buddha from heaven after giving the teachings to his mother	22nd day of the ninth lunar month	October 2001[2]	October 2002[2]
Christianity[5]				
Christmas Day	celebration of the birth of Jesus in Bethlehem; Christians meet for worship, often at midnight, when the events are retold through words, music, drama, and pictures		25 December 2001	25 December 2002
Epiphany	celebrates the arrival of the three wise men from the east who came looking for a newborn king and were led by a bright star to Bethlehem; they brought Jesus gifts of gold, frankincense, and myrrh		6 January 2001	6 January 2002

(continued)

Major Religious Festivals *(continued)*

Festival	Description	Normally held	2001	2002
Ash Wednesday	in many churches, people come forward to be marked with ashes, an ancient symbol of sorrow and repentance; Lent is a time of reflection and fasting which recalls the 40 days Jesus spent fasting and praying in the desert	start of Lent (six weeks before Easter)	28 February 2001	13 February 2002
Palm Sunday	Christians recall Jesus' entry into Jerusalem during the last week of his life, when he was welcomed by people waving palm fronds; other important days of Holy Week are Maundy Thursday, when Jesus shared the last supper with his disciples, and Good Friday, when he was crucified	start of Holy Week (one week before Easter)	8 April 2001	24 March 2002
Easter Sunday	time of rejoicing that recalls the disciples' discovery that Jesus was alive, and that he had been resurrected; many churches keep a vigil throughout Saturday night so that they can greet Easter Day with services, family meals, and the exchange of flowers and eggs	between 23 March and 24 April in the Roman Catholic and Protestant churches	15 April 2001	31 March 2002
Ascension Day	this day commemorates the disciples witnessing Jesus being lifted up to heaven 40 days after Easter Day	40 days after Easter	24 May 2001	9 May 2002
Pentecost or Whitsun	when Jesus left his disciples for the last time after his resurrection, he promised them a 'comforter' who would be with them forever; Pentecost celebrates the coming of the Holy Spirit upon the disciples	seventh Sunday after Easter	3 June 2001	19 May 2002
Hinduism				
Mahashivaratri	'Great Night of Shiva' when Shiva, his wife Parvati, and their child Ganesh are honoured; offerings are made to Shiva between midnight and sunrise and the 24-hour fast is broken at dawn	13th or 14th day of dark half of Magh	21 February 2001	12 March 2002
Sarasvati Puja	Sarasvati, the patron of the arts and learning, is celebrated with music and by wearing yellow clothes, symbolizing the warmth of spring	first day of spring season (Phalgun)	29 January 2001[6]	17 February 2002[6]
Holi	the pranks that Krishna played as a child are celebrated, and the story of Prahalad, a prince who was willing to sacrifice himself for Vishnu, is remembered; offerings are made around bonfires and coloured water or powder is sprayed in high-spirited games	full moon day of Phalgun	9 March 2001[6]	28 March 2002
Rama Naumi	celebrates the birthday of the god Rama, hero of the epic *Rāmayāna* that is recited during the festival; offerings are also made in temples to a statue of the baby Rama	ninth day of the bright half of Caitra	2 April 2001	21 April 2002
Ratha Yatra	a statue of Vishnu, also called Jagganath, Lord of the Universe, is placed on a large wooden chariot and pulled through the streets where lamps, flowers, and other offerings are laid in his path	16th day of Asadha	23 June 2001	12 July 2002
Raksha Bandhan	sisters tie rakhis, silk threads decorated with flowers, onto their brothers' wrists as a symbol of protection	full moon day of Sravana	3 August 2001	22 August 2002
Janamashtarni	the birth of Krishna is celebrated as an image of the child Krishna is washed with yoghurt, ghee, honey, and milk, and then placed on a swing	eighth day of Bhadrapada	12 August 2001	31 August 2002
Navaratri Dusshera	the festival of Dusshera follows immediately after Navaratri; over nine nights different manifestations of the goddess Durga are honoured; in the form of Durga she is the destroyer of evil, as Kali she is the destroyer of time, and as Parvati she is the faithful wife of Shiva; at Dusshera, an effigy of the demon Ravana is burnt to celebrate Durga's power over demons	first ten days of the bright half of Aswin	26 October 2001	15 October 2002
Diwali	accounts are settled at this time and worship is given to Lakshmi, goddess of wealth and good fortune; coloured patterns are made on the ground; windows are illuminated with lamps and candles; this festival also celebrates the return of Rama and Sita from exile, a story told in the *Rāmayāna*	13th day of the dark half of Aswin	14 November 2001	4 November 2002
Islam[7]				
Festival of Ashura	festival commemorating both the escape of the Israelites from Egypt, and also the day Noah's ark touched ground after the flood; in Shia Islam, Ashura also celebrates the martyrdom of Ali	10 Muharram	4 April 2001	24 March 2002[6]

(continued)

Major Religious Festivals *(continued)*

Festival	Description	Normally held	2001	2002
Ramadan	this month of fasting is one of the Five Pillars of Islam, when adult Muslims refrain from drinking, eating, smoking, and conjugal relations from dawn until dusk	ninth month of the year	17 November 2001	6 November 2002[6]
The Night of Power–Lailat ul Qadr	during the last ten days of Ramadan many Muslims spend time praying in the mosque since prayers made on the Night of Power are said to be 'better than a thousand months'	around 27 Ramadan	3 December 2001	2 December 2002[6]
Eid ul-Fitr	important time of communal prayer and celebration when families and friends gather to share special foods and exchange gifts	end of Ramadan, heralded by the sight of a new moon	16 December 2001	5 December 2002[6]
Pilgrimage to Mecca	in the Five Pillars of Islam, this is the most important time, but only those who have sufficient finances and are physically able are expected to make the journey	8–13 Dhu al-Hijjah	4–9 March 2001	21–26 February 2002
Eid-ul-Adha	the willingness of the prophet Ibrahim to sacrifice his son Ishmael is remembered; at God's command a lamb was sacrificed instead, an act commemorated at this time in the sacrifice of a lamb or goat	10 Dhu al-Hijjah	6 March 2001	23 February 2002
Birthday of the Prophet Muhammad (Milad-un-Nabi)	the scale of celebrations varies according to country; for example, thousands of pilgrims gather on Lamu island off the coast of Kenya for processions, speeches, and prayers	month of Rabi I	24 May 2001	14 May 2002
Judaism				
Rosh Hashanah	Jewish New Year, a ten-day period of repentance leading up to Yom Kippur	1 Tishri	18–19 September 2001	7–8 September 2002
Yom Kippur	Day of Atonement, a time when Jews seek forgiveness of those who have been wronged; also the major fast of the year	10 Tishri	27 September 2001	16 September 2002
Succoth	Feast of Tabernacles, a time when families build and eat in open-air shelters in commemoration of the temporary desert shelters built by the Israelites during their journey to the Promised Land	15–23 Tishri	2–3 October 2001	21–22 September 2002
Simhat Torah	end of Succoth and the end of the annual reading of the Torah, which is processed around the synagogue on this day	24 Tishri	10 October 2001	29 September 2002
Hanukkah	Dedication of the Temple, a time when the eight-branched Hanukkah candle is lit commemorating the rededication of the Temple in Jerusalem in the 2nd century BCE, when the Temple lamp miraculously stayed alight for ten days, even though there was only enough oil to last one day	25 Kislev–3 Tebet	10–17 December 2001	30 November–7 December 2002
Purim	celebration of the story of Esther who saved her people from destruction at the hands of Haman; the congregation dress in unusual clothes for the synagogue service and boo when Haman's name is read out from the scrolls of Esther	14 Adar	9 March 2001	26 February 2002
Pesach	Passover, celebrating God's deliverance of the Israelites from captivity in Egypt; families gather for the first evening of the festival to share the Seder meal, which recalls in words and symbols the departure of the Israelites from Egypt	15–22 Nisan	8–15 April 2001	28 March–4 April 2002
Shavuot	also known as the Pentecost or the Feast of Weeks, this is both a harvest festival and a thanksgiving for the gift of Torah to Moses on Mount Sinai	6–7 Sivan	28–29 May 2001	17–18 May 2002
Sikhism				
Baisakhi	commemorates the founding of the Order of the Khalsa in 1699, the community of committed Sikhs who undertake to uphold their faith and defend the weak; it is the usual time for Sikhs to join the Khalsa	13 April (occasionally on the 14 April), first day of the solar month of Baisākh (Sanskrit Vaiśakha)	13 April 2001[6]	13 April 2002[6]
Martyrdom of the Guru Arjan Dev	time of celebration and sorrow when Sikhs remember those who have suffered for their faith; there is a continuous reading of the Guru Granth Sahib in the gurdwara	fourth Jaistha	June 2001[2]	June 2002[2]
Diwali	Diwali lamps are lit at home, and the release from prison of Guru Hargobind is commemorated	second day of Kartik	25 October 2001[6]	25 October 2002[6]
Guru Nanak's Birthday	colourful street processions are held and hymns honouring Guru Gobind Singh (1469–1539), the founder of the Khalsa, are sung in the gurdwara	full moon day of Kartik	November 2001[2 8]	November 2002[2 8]

(continued)

Major Religious Festivals *(continued)*

Festival	Description	Normally held	2001	2002
Hola Mohalla	falls at the same time as the Hindu festival of Holi; celebrated with games and pranks; sporting contests take place as well as religious congregations, political conferences, pilgrimages, and administration of baptism	starting a day earlier and finishing a day later than Holi; full moon day of Phalgun	17 March 2001[6]	17 March 2002[6]

[1] Predominant mainly in Sri Lanka and Southeast Asia.
[2] Date unknown.
[3] Predominant mainly in China, Taiwan, Korea, and Japan.
[4] Predominant mainly in Tibet, Nepal, Bhutan, Mongolia, parts of western China, southern Siberia, and northern India.
[5] The calendar reform by pope Gregory XIII in 1582 was rejected by the Orthodox Church. Since 1923, the Orthodox Church has been divided over the calendar. The Greek Church adopted the new calendar except the days that depend on Easter. Others (mostly Slavic) have retained the Julian calendar and therefore remain 13 days behind in their dating (Christmas: 7 January, New Year: 14 January).
[6] Unconfirmed.
[7] The Islamic calendar is entirely lunar, and unlike most other lunar calendars, is not adjusted to keep in step with the solar year. Some dates are therefore approximate and some are not yet known by the relevant authorities; this applies particularly to movable feasts, based on lunar reckonings.
[8] Date CE varies from year to year in accordance with traditional dates of the Indian Calendar (Bikrami Sambat); often falls in November.

See also  **Time and Calendars,** pp 7–15.

Web Sites

About Islam and Muslims

http://www.unn.ac.uk/societies/islamic/

UK-based site offering extensive information about the Islamic faith and culture.

Atheist Express

http://www.hti.net/www/atheism

Site dedicated to atheism, free thought, humanism, ethics, religious criticism, and state-church separation. It includes history, articles, cartoons, and milestones of and about atheism, as well as a different slant on church history.

Baha'i Faith Page

http://www.bcca.org/bahaivision/

Introduction to this religion founded in the 19th century, with an overview explaining the faith, a collection of religious writings, and links to Baha'i groups around the world.

Bible Gateway

http://bible.gospelcom.net/

Full text of a number versions of the Bible, fully searchable by passage, phrase, or word, and with hyperlinked footnotes and cross-references. The user can choose from several languages.

Book of Mormon

http://www.jefflindsay. com/BOMIntro.shtml

Introduction to the holy book of The Church of Jesus Christ of Latter-Day Saints.

Brief Introduction to Taoism

http://www.geocities.com/HotSprings/2426/Ttaointro.html

Good objective introduction to Taoism and its evolution within Chinese philosophy.

British Humanist Association

http://www.humanism. org.uk/

Explains the principles of Humanism, and has a comprehensive list of links to relevant sites.

Celtic Myth and Lore

http://www.witchhaven.com/shadowdrake/lore.html

Information about the herbology, astronomy, law, stories, and folk practices of the Celtic people. The site includes many stories and poems, as well as graphics and audio clips.

Chinese Religion

http://birmingham.gov.uk/epislive/citywide.nsf/437194deb01c293b802564d60047624b/e6615e702e28ffa88025662f00525bc7?OpenDocument

All-text site from Birmingham University containing a lot of information about the three main strands of religion in China – Buddhism, Taoism, and Confucianism. The site also focuses on some of the important religious festivals, including New Year.

Church of Christ, Scientist (Christian Science)

http://www.religioustolerance.org/cr-sci.htm

Description of the history, beliefs, and attitudes towards healing of the Church of Christ, Scientist. Splits and schisms within the sect are described, together with the views of those who condemn Christian Science as a heretic cult.

Church of England

http://www.church-of-england.org/

The structure of the church, a guide to prayer, and links to non-English churches within the Anglican communion.

Classical Mythology Home Page

http://www.princeton.edu/~rhwebb/myth.html

Course materials from the Princeton University's Classics Department; informative and academically rigorous, but easy for the casual reader to use.

Confucius (Kung Fu Tzu)

http://www.confucius.org/main01.htm

Some background information on Confucius and Confucianism as well as images and versions of most of his famous texts on morality.

Fundamentals of Jainism

http://www.angelfire.com/co/jainism/

Comphrehensive introduction to the monastic and ascetic religion of Jainism.

Gnosticism

http://www.newadvent.org/cathen/06592a.htm

Extended source of information on the doctrine of salvation by knowledge, including gnosticism's extensive pre-Christian roots in a variety of cultural and historical contexts, and its influence on the development of Christianity.

Hinduism Today

http://www.HinduismToday.kauai.hi.us/ashram/

Online magazine produced by Sanatana Dharma's Electronic Ashram. It explores India's ancient spiritual path by providing nine informative sections related to Hinduism.

His Holiness the Dalai Lama

http://www.dalailama.com/

Profile of Tenzin Gyatso, the 14th incarnation of the Dalai Lama. It traces his childhood, escape from Tibet, and efforts to preserve Tibetan culture in exile.

Holy See (Vatican City)

http://www.vatican.va/

Multilingual, searchable site, with recent news reports and press releases from the Vatican Information Service.

Islam at a Glance

http://www.iad.org/books/WAMY1.html

Clear and concise introduction to the key beliefs of Islam. It covers Muhammad, the Koran, prayer, Islam in the modern world, and the Five Pillars of Islam.

Jewish Culture and History

http://www.igc.apc.org/ddickerson/judaica.html

Wide-ranging collection of information on Judaism, including links to online Hebrew texts.

Koran

http://etext.virginia.edu/koran.html

Full text of the Koran in searchable form, offered by the Electronic Centre at the University of Virginia, USA.

List of Norse Beings

http://www.ugcs.caltech.edu/~cherryne/list.html

Alphabetical listing of all the main Norse gods and other beings found in Scandinavian mythology, plus links to other Norse mythology resources.

Multifaithnet

http://www.multifaith.org/

Run by the University of Derby, this site gives in-depth descriptions of all the main world religions.

Mysticism in World Religions

http://www.digiserve.com/mystic/

Explores mystical experience in six world religions, by comparing and contrasting quotations from their respective sacred literatures.

Religious Society of Friends

http://www.quaker.org/

Quaker beliefs and ethics, a detailed history of the faith, and information on Quaker societies throughout the world and their activities.

Salvation Army

http://www.salvationarmy.org/

International headquarters of the evangelical mission. There is a history of the Salvation Army, an outline of its structure, and details of its many charitable activities in more than a hundred countries.

Shinto – The Way of the Gods

http://www.trincoll.edu/_tj/tj4.4.96/articles/cover.~html

Guide to Shinto beliefs and practices, explaining the link between Shintoism and Japanese mythology, and the significance of Shinto rituals in modern Japanese life. There is also a guide to the main Shinto shrines.

Sikhism Home Page

http://www.sikhs.org/

Overview of the main principles of Sikhism, with a description of the religion's philosophy and scriptures, ceremonies, and important dates, as well as bibliographic guidance and a glossary of terms.

Vedas and Upanishads

http://www.san.beck.org/EC7-Vedas.html

Thorough source of information on the Hindu mystical texts, including links to English-language versions of the full texts of the major Upanishads.

Voodoo Information Pages

http://members.aol.com/racine125/index1.html

General information on the religion of vodou, more commonly known as voodoo.

What is Theravada Buddhism?

http://www.accesstoinsight.org/theravada.html

Full introduction to the school of Buddhism that is based on the record of the Buddha's teachings known as the Pali Canon.

What Sufism Is

http://www.sufism.org/books/livinex.html

Essay by Kabir Edmund Helminski which describes the nature of the mystical religion of Sufism.

World Council of Churches

http://www.wcc-coe.org/

Site of the organization bringing together over 300 Christian churches in 120 countries. It contains comprehensive information on the ecumenical movement, evangelism, and the role of Christian churches in development.

World Scripture

http://unification.net/ws/

A good source of scriptural and religious material for scholars and people of all faiths, this site has a comparative anthology of sacred texts containing over 4,000 scriptural passages from 268 sacred texts and 55 oral traditions, organized under 164 different themes.

Worldwide Study Bible

http://www.ccel.org/wwsb/index.html

Exhaustive guide to the Bible, with the full text of all the books of the Old and New Testaments, synopses of important sections, and a biblical dictionary.

Zen Buddhism

http://www.iijnet.or.jp/iriz/index_e.html

Largest collection of Buddhist primary text materials on the Internet, together with many examples of Zen art, and information on Zen centres and masters.

Zoroastrianism

http://www.religioustolerance.org/zoroastr.htm

Objective account of the beliefs, history, and practices of the ancient monotheistic faith, as well as the legends associated with Zoroaster.

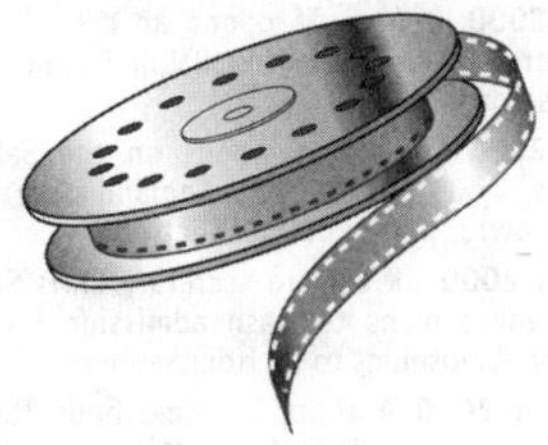

ARTS AND MEDIA

The Year in Review

July 1999 English writer J K Rowling publishes *Harry Potter and the Prisoner of Azkaban*, the third book of her best-selling children's series about a schoolboy wizard.

3 July 1999 The marriage of English pop singer Victoria Adams, known as 'Posh Spice' of the Spice Girls, and English Manchester United footballer David Beckham takes place at a castle near Dublin, Ireland.

8 July 1999 A collection of arts and antiques stolen by the Nazis from the wealthy Jewish banking family, the Rothschilds, is sold at auction by Christie's in London.

September 1999 An exhibition of Flemish painter Anthony Van Dyck is held at the Royal Academy, London.

24 September 1999 The Broadway musical hit *The Lion King* opens at the Lyceum Theatre, London. It is adapted from the Disney film, with additional songs by Tim Rice and Elton John.

28 September–7 November 1999 The first British Biennial of Contemporary Art, including 280 exhibitions from around the world, is held in Liverpool.

October 1999 Irish poet Seamus Heaney publishes *Beowulf: A New Translation*.

October 1999 The six-part documentary *Walking with Dinosaurs*, featuring state-of-the-art computer animation and costing £6 million to produce, is aired on television by the British Broadcasting Corporation (BBC).

19 October 1999 A UK parliamentary committee is set up to look into the matter of returning the Elgin marbles to Greece. It is the first time that the government considers returning the ancient Greek sculptures since they were acquired by Britain almost 200 years ago.

19 October 1999 The entire *Encyclopaedia Britannica*, with the addition of archived news updates from current media sources, is launched on the Internet, with free access.

25 October 1999 South African writer J M Coetzee wins the Booker Prize for his novel *Disgrace*. He is the only writer to win the award twice, having also won in 1983 for his novel *The Life and Times of Michael K*.

26 October 1999 The Cathedral of St John the Divine in New York City, the world's largest cathedral, bars US poet Ezra Pound from its poets' corner because of his anti-Semitic broadcasts from Italy during World War II.

November 1999 English writer Alan Sillitoe publishes his novel *The German Numbers Woman*.

28 November 1999 The Basilica of St Francis of Assisi in the town of Assisi, Italy reopens after a £20 million restoration, two years after an earthquake destroyed its ceiling of Renaissance frescoes.

30 November 1999 English artist Steve McQueen wins the Turner Prize for his black-and-white silent film *Deadpan*, inspired by the comedian Buster Keaton.

6 December 1999 Graham Vick's new production of the opera *Falstaff* by Giuseppe Verdi opens at the Royal Opera House, Covent Garden, London, the first opera to be performed since the reopening of the opera house.

22 December 1999 The film *Onegin* is released, based on the verse novel by Russian writer Alexander Pushkin, starring Ralph Fiennes, Liv Tyler, Lena Headey, Martin Donovan, and Alun Armstrong.

31 December 1999 After much controversy and fanfare, the Millennium Dome opens in Greenwich, London.

January 2000 *Fantasia 2000*, a remake of the 1940 animated Disney film, is released, directed by Hendel Butoy, Francis Glebas, Paul Brizzi, Gaetan Brizzi, and Eric Goldberg.

January 2000 English writer Zadie Smith publishes her debut novel *White Teeth*, for which she reportedly received an advance of £250,000.

1 January 2000 The Pompidou Centre in Paris reopens after a two-year, £55 million/$88 million renovation.

1 January 2000 Thieves break through a glass panel in the roof of the Ashmolean Museum, Oxford, and steal the painting *Auvers-sur-Oise* by French impressionist Paul Cézanne, worth £3 million.

21 January 2000 The film *Angela's Ashes*, based on the Pulitzer Prize-winning memoir by Irish-born US writer Frank McCourt, is

released, directed by Alan Parker and starring Robert Carlyle, Shane Murray-Corcoran, and Emily Watson.

21 January 2000 The film *Topsy-Turvy* is released, directed by Mike Leigh and starring Allan Corduner, Dexter Fletcher, Sukie Smith, Roger Heathcott, and Wendy Nottingham.

February 2000 Fur makes a comeback at the New York fashion week, with designers such as Oscar de la Renta and Ralph Lauren showing a range of fur clothing in their new collections. Animal rights activists stage protests against the designers.

23 February 2000 The rock band Santana, making a comeback after its wide popularity in the late 1960s and early 1970s, wins eight Grammy awards (which ties with singer Michael Jackson for the highest number of Grammys won in a year).

March 2000 The Soho Theatre Company moves to its new building on Dean Street, Soho, London, refurbished by British architects Richard Paxton and Heidi Locher.

March 2000 Harold Pinter's new play *Celebration* opens at the Almeida Theatre, London.

March 2000 The *Journals of Sylvia Plath 1950–62* are published posthumously, edited by Karen V Kukil.

12 March 2000 The Oxford English Dictionary goes online. At 60 million words, it is the largest reference book available on the Internet to date.

April 2000 The 'Art Nouveau 1890–1914' exhibition is held at the Victoria and Albert Museum, London.

April 2000 The Whitney Biennial is held at the Whitney Museum of American Art, New York City.

April 2000 *The Graduate*, a theatrical adaptation by Terry Johnson of Charles Webb's novel (1963) and Mick Nichols's film (1967), starring Kathleen Turner and Matthew Rhys, opens at the Gielgud Theatre, London.

April 2000 *Richard II* opens at the Almeida Theatre, London, starring Ralph Fiennes and Linus Roache.

April 2000 The Lowry opens on the Salford Quays, near Manchester, England (*see also* **The Lowry**, p 420; **colour section**).

3 April 2000 UK culture secretary Chris Smith announces plans to slash admission fees to national museums to £1 from September 2001.

13 April 2000 A court in Rome finds Italian opera singer Luciano Pavarotti guilty of tax evasion and he is ordered to pay a £3 million fine.

18 April 2000 The opera *The Last Supper*, written by English composer Harrison Birtwistle, premieres at the Linden-Opera, Berlin.

19 April 2000 An exhibition of US architect Frank Gehry's models for a new $450 million/£285 million Guggenheim museum on Wall Street opens at the museum's main site on 5th Avenue, New York City.

9 May 2000 The Internet company Napster is held liable for damages sought by the US record industry, in the controversy over downloaded music. MP3 Inc and Napster had been charged with music piracy by Warner Brothers and the Recording Industry Association of America (RIAA).

12 May 2000 Tate Modern, London's new gallery of modern art, opens in the converted Bankside power station on the South Bank of the Thames. Over 3,000 people per hour visit the collection (*see also* **colour section**).

14 May 2000 The Guggenheim Museum in Bilbao, northern Spain, is named as the European Museum for 2000 by the Council of Europe in Bonn.

25 May 2000 Somerset House on the Strand in London is opened to the public for the first time. Designed in the 18th century as government offices, the building features the Gilbert Collection, a £100 million display of gold and silver artefacts.

June 2000 The Experience Music Project, an interactive Jimi Hendrix music museum designed by US architect Frank Gehry, opens in Seattle, Washington.

8 June 2000 The Frankfurt eBook Award, worth $100,000, is launched to recognize achievements in electronic publishing. The winner will be announced at the Frankfurt Book Fair in October.

14 June 2000 The Turner Prize shortlist is announced: Glenn Brown, Michael Raedecker, Tomoko Takahashi, and Wolfgang Tillmans. Of the four nominees, only Brown is British-born. Untypically for recent nominees, whose work has tended to use photography, videos, and installations, two of the artists are painters.

21 June 2000 After a so-called 'super-waif summit' in London called by the UK minister for women, Tessa Jowell, fashion editors, designers, and modelling agencies agree to stop using images of unnaturally thin models. Such images have been shown to be linked with eating disorders and problems of self-esteem in women.

8 July 2000 The fourth Harry Potter book *Harry Potter and the Goblet of Fire*, is published and becomes the fastest selling book of all time in the UK. The children's series by J K Rowling about a schoolboy wizard had already sold over 30 million copies in 33 different languages.

Funding the Arts: Annual Grants from the Arts Councils

1998–99

Region	Total grants (£)
Arts Council of England	127,974,000
Arts Council of Wales	12,706,000
Scottish Arts Council	27,443,500

Source: Data from the Arts Councils of England and Wales, and the Scottish Arts Council

Italian tenor Luciano Pavarotti speaks to the media before his concert in the grounds of Stormont Castle, Belfast, Northern Ireland, in September 1999. Some 14,000 people attended the performance, which ended with an audience sing-along. *Syndication International*

Arts Festivals

Calendar of Major Arts Festivals in the UK

Some 500 professional arts festivals are held in the UK each year. The table lists some of the largest of the annual festivals.

Date	Event	Features
February–March	Bath Literature Festival	international literary festival
April	Cheltenham International Jazz Festival	jazz
May	Brighton Festival	England's largest arts festival; music, drama, comedy, opera, street theatre
May	Chelmsford Cathedral Festival	classical music, jazz, opera
May	Manchester Streets Ahead Festival	theatre, music, dance
May	Newbury International Spring Festival	classical and world music, opera, jazz, film, visual arts
May–June	Bath International Music Festival	jazz, early, classical, contempory, and world music
May–June	BOC Covent Garden Festival	opera and music theatre, with over 100 performances
May–June	Hay Festival	one of the largest literary festivals in the world
May–June	Salisbury Festival	classical, jazz, circus, theatre, visual arts
May–August	Glyndebourne Festival	opera
June	Aldeburgh Festival	music, visual arts, film
June	Glastonbury Festival	rock and pop
June	Spitalfields Festival (London)	early, contemporary, world music
June–July	City of London Festival	opera, theatre, poetry, jazz, dance
June–July	LIFT (London International Festival of Theatre)	avant-garde theatre
June–July	Ludlow Festival	opera, ballet, jazz, theatre
June–July	Opera at Garsington (Oxfordshire)	opera
July	Buxton Festival	rarely performed operas, chamber music, jazz, fringe events
July	Cheltenham International Festival of Music	contemporary and classical music
July	Chichester Festivities	classical music, jazz
July	Fishguard Music Festival (Pembrokeshire)	choral, jazz, orchestral music
July	Greenwich and Docklands International Festival	theatre, dance, visual arts, music
July	International Music Eisteddfod at Llangollen	six-day festival of music
July	York Early Music Festival	early and world music
July–August	Dartington International Summer School	five-week programme of music and dance performances and masterclasses
July–August	Edinburgh International Jazz and Blues Festival	jazz and blues
July–August	Harrogate International Festival	jazz, classical music, dance, comedy, street theatre, fringe
July–September	BBC Proms	classical music (over 70 concerts)
August	Edinburgh Festival Fringe	UK's largest fringe festival
August	Edinburgh International Book Festival	literary
August	Edinburgh International Film Festival	film
August	Royal National Eisteddfod	alternating each year in south and north Wales
August	Three Choirs Festival at Hereford, Gloucester, and Worcester	oldest choral festival in Europe (rotates between three cities)
August–September	Arundel Festival	jazz and orchestral concerts, drama, street theatre
August–September	Edinburgh International Festival	opera, music, dance, theatre
September–October	Windsor Festival	baroque, opera, jazz, contemporary music
October	Ballymena Arts Festival	classical music, jazz, dance, theatre, comedy, visual arts
October	Canterbury Festival	drama, dance, opera, jazz, folk, cabaret
October	Cheltenham Festival of Literature	two-week literary festival
October	Norfolk and Norwich Festival	music, theatre, dance, opera, comedy, visual arts, street theatre
October	Royal National Mod	music, dance, drama, and literature, at a different venue each year in the Highlands, Scotland
October	Southwark Festival	contemporary arts, ethnic and classical music, dance
October–November	Belfast Festival at Queen's	theatre and dance, jazz, classical, folk, world music
October–November	Dance Umbrella	London's annual seven-week international festival of contemporary dance
November	Huddersfield Festival	contemporary music, film, opera, dance
November	London Film Festival	shows some 250 international films, hosted by the British Film Institute

Television and Radio

Households with TV Sets, VCRs, Satellite, and Cable Television in the UK

(– = not applicable.)

Year	All households	TV households	TV households (%)	Receiving colour (%)	2+ TV sets (%)	VCR (%)	Satellite households	Cable households
1970	18,364,000	16,895,000	92	2	3	–	–	–
1975	19,144,000	18,570,000	97	40	6	–	–	–
1980	20,322,000	19,916,000	98	71	19	–	–	–
1985	21,242,000	20,605,000	97	86	39	28	–	–

(continued)

Households with TV Sets, VCRs, Satellite, and Cable Television in the UK *(continued)*

Year	All households	TV households	TV households (%)	Receiving colour (%)	2 + TV sets (%)	VCR (%)	Satellite households	Cable households
1990	22,122,000	21,458,000	97	93	46	61	–	–
1995	23,902,000	23,212,000	97	98	55	76	–	–
1999	24,741,000	23,988,000	97	99	60	84	4,116,000	3,160,000

Source: © *Taylor Nelson SOFRES TV Research*

Proportion of UK-Produced Programmes Shown on Television in the UK

Figures are for peak-time viewing.
(In percentages. – = not applicable.)

Channel	1996–97	1997–98	1998–99
BBC1	82	84	85
ITV	80	82	86
BBC2	64	63	63
Channel 4	60	64	64
Channel 5	–	46	49
All BBC	73	74	74
ITV/Channel 4	70	73	75
All commercial including Channel 5	–	64	66

Source: BBC Annual Report 1999, © *BBC 1999, with permission*

Proportion of Factual Programmes in Peak-Time Television in the UK

(In percentages. – = not applicable.)

Channel	1996–97	1997–98	1998–99
BBC1	46	51	52
BBC2	51	50	49
ITV	29	32	34
Channel 4	49	50	51
Channel 5	–	36	32

Source: BBC Annual Report 1999, © *BBC 1999, with permission*

Average Daily Television Usage per Household in the UK

(– = not applicable. In hours.)

Year	Total[1]	ITV	BBC1	BBC2	Channel 4	Channel 5	Other
1969	4.5	2.4	2.1	–	–	–	–
1972	4.8	2.7	1.9	0.3	–	–	–
1976	5.1	2.7	2.1	0.4	–	–	–
1980	5.1	2.5	2.0	0.6	–	–	–
1982	4.9	2.4	1.9	0.6	–	–	–
1986	5.3	2.4	1.9	0.6	0.5	–	–
1990	5.1	2.3	1.9	0.5	0.5	–	–
1995	5.9	2.2	1.9	0.7	0.7	–	–
1998	5.8	1.9	1.7	0.7	0.6	0.3	0.6
1999	5.8	1.8	1.7	0.7	0.6	0.3	0.7

[1] Totals may not add due to rounding and the small percentage of other (non-terrestrial) viewing.

Source: © *Taylor Nelson SOFRES TV Research*

BBC World Service Radio Audience Figures

Figures are for an average weekly audience. Figures cover those countries where formal audience data collection is possible. Global totals are shown rounded to whole numbers; regional figures are shown rounded to the nearest half million. The regional figures, therefore, may appear not to add up to the global total.

Region	1996–97	1997–98	1998–99
Asia and Pacific	62.0	60.5	63.5
Africa and Middle East	45.5	41.0	42.0
Eurasia	9.0	12.0	12.0
Europe	17.5	16.0	16.0
Americas	9.0	8.0	9.0
Total	143.0	138.0	143.0

Source: BBC Annual Report 1999, © *BBC 1999, with permission*

Average Daily Hours of Viewing by Age and Social Grade in the UK

The A–E scale of socio-economic group represents a breakdown of the population based on selected economic and social criteria. Group A represents those with the highest incomes and group E represents those with the lowest income (In hours.)

Category	1994	1998	1999
Socio-economic group			
adults ABC1	3.2	3.3	3.3
adults C2	3.7	3.9	3.9
adults DE	4.2	4.6	4.7
Age			
4–9	2.6	2.5	2.6
10–15	2.7	2.5	2.7
16–24	2.8	2.7	2.9
25–34	3.5	3.5	3.4
35–44	3.4	3.3	3.4
45–54	3.6	3.6	3.7
55 or over	4.8	4.9	4.9
All individuals	3.6	3.6	3.7

Source: © *Taylor Nelson SOFRES TV Research*

Top 10 Countries by Number of Television Sets

1996

Rank	Country	TV sets per 1,000 people
1	USA	805
2	Malta	751
3	Monaco	727
4	Canada	714
5	Japan	684
6	El Salvador	675
7	Oman	660
8	Finland	605
9	Denmark	592
10	France	591

Source: UNESCO Statistical Yearbook, 1999, © *UNESCO 1999*

See also **Media**, pp 754–758.

Interactive TV

Lack of a computer may not be a bar to surfing the Internet and taking part in online shopping and banking. With the advent of interactive digital television, the much heralded interactive TV revolution is here. ntl: launched the first interactive TV service in the UK in March 1999. This was an analogue service. In 2000 ntl: produced its first digital service. In 1999, Sky Digital launched Open, its interactive TV network, offering e-mail, online shopping, and games through the television using a special keyboard.

See also **Key Dates for Digital Television in the UK**, p 401.

■ Television and Radio

Key Dates for Digital Television in the UK

1991 The European Launching Group (ELG), an independent voluntary industry group, is established to oversee development of a digital television system for Europe.

1993 The ELG becomes Digital Video Broadcasting (DVB).

1996 The BBC begins a limited trial service of Digital Terrestrial Television (DTT).

1997 DVB is making digital television a reality, using a system that delivers programmes of standard (analogue phase alternate line (PAL) system) quality. Its technology and standards are adopted by Europe's governments and official bodies, and services begin to roll out across Europe. The same technology is being adopted in many other countries round the world – with the exception of the USA where digital TV is seen as a way of delivering a few channels of high definition (HD) pictures to viewers willing to buy new HD receivers. In the UK the new pay broadcaster ONdigital (the trading name for British Broadcasting plc owned by Granada and Carlton) is granted a DTT licence.

September 1998 The BBC launch BBC Choice a week before the necessary receiving equipment is available in the shops.

October 1998 Rupert Murdoch's British Sky Broadcasting Group (BSkyB) launches its Sky Digital satellite service with a unique offer. Anyone who agrees to connect the receiver to a telephone line pays a reduced price for the set-top receiver box, or digibox, and dish aerial. The service allows BSkyB's sister company, British Interactive Broadcasting, to offer its online shopping service, Open, through an ordinary television set.

November 1998 Launch of FilmFour, a new DTT film subscription channel. ONdigital launches its 30 channel DTT service. Viewers who sign up for ONdigital's pay channels pay a reduced price for the set-top box, which connects the aerial to an ordinary television set.

December 1998 Channel ITV2, a new DTT service for England and Wales, is launched.

February 1999 The cable company Telewest Communications plc launches its DTT service in the Midlands, promising rapid expansion.

April 1999 S2, Scotland's second ITV channel, is launched on DTT.

May 1999 BSkyB announces that from June it will give away set-top boxes for free to anyone who signs up for a subscription; the cost to BSkyB is an estimated £400 million. ONdigital quickly matches the offer. Just like the cellphone companies, which have long given away free phones, digital broadcasters must now make their money from customer use.

June 1999 BBC Knowledge is launched (available through ONDigital Channel 13, via a set-top box; Sky Digital Channel 573, via a set-top box and satellite dish; and Digital Cable). Northern Ireland's second ITV channel, TV-YOU, is launched on DTT.

July 1999 The music channel MTV becomes available through ONDigital.

August 1999 Sky Digital launches British Eurosport. The government-appointed Davies Panel recommends a digital supplement of £24 on top of the licence fee for those buying digital services, in order to support BBC digital television. 60% of viewers say this would put them off buying the technology. The supplement is rejected by parliament in February 2000.

September 1999 UK culture secretary Chris Smith announces that the government expects to switch off the existing analogue service between 2006 and 2010, but only if at least 95% of viewers have digital television sets or set-top boxes, and if providers can reach 99.4% of the population. At this time 70% of households have analogue sets and 1.5 million households have digital television. A survey conducted for the BBC by media consultancy ECON concludes that only just over 55% of households are interested in pay television, interest being lowest among older age and lower income groups. Using Sky's interactive digital TV channel, Open, Abbey National is the first UK financial service to launch its services on DTT.

February 2000 Chris Smith announces that a white paper overhauling the regulations governing broadcasting and telecommunications services will be published in the autumn, in order to pave the way for a switch to digital television.

March 2000 Around three million households have signed up to digital television in the last 18 months, but an independent television commission says that the switch to digital television in six years is unrealistic.

April 2000 NTL, the UK's biggest cable company, begins its digital services in Scotland, Northern Ireland, and Wales, including pay per view and full Internet access. HSBC becomes the first bank to make its digital banking service (launched autumn 1999) fully interactive on digital television screens (using Open).

May 2000 According to researchers at Oxford University's environmental change unit, digital television will increase domestic power consumption in UK homes by 7% by 2010 and so add significantly to global warming. This is because set-top boxes have to be on full power all the time in order to receive.

Top 50 Programmes on Terrestrial Television in the UK

1999

Rank	Programme	Channel	Transmission date	Number of viewers
1	*Coronation Street*	ITV	7 March	19,815,000
2	*Who Wants to be a Millionaire?*	ITV	7 March	19,207,000
3	*Coronation Street*	ITV	4 January	19,029,000
4	*Coronation Street*	ITV	13 January	18,218,000
5	*Heartbeat*	ITV	28 February	17,008,000
6	*Touch of Frost*	ITV	21 March	16,849,000
7	*Coronation Street*	ITV	8 January	16,747,000
8	*EastEnders*	BBC1	7 January	15,719,000
9	*Big Match/League Final*	ITV	26 May	15,616,000
10	*Coronation Street*	ITV	25 December	15,505,000
11	*EastEnders*	BBC1	25 October	15,402,000
12	*EastEnders*	BBC1	26 January	15,382,000
13	*Walking with Dinosaurs*	BBC1	4 October	14,996,000
14	*Big Match: Champions' League*	ITV	17 November	14,600,000
15	*EastEnders*	BBC1	5 September	14,393,000
16	*Vicar of Dibley*	BBC1	27 December	14,367,000
17	*New You've Been Framed*	ITV	7 November	13,903,000
18	*EastEnders*	BBC1	31 December	13,440,000
19	*Emmerdale*	ITV	20 January	13,351,000
20	*Goldeneye*	ITV	10 March	13,228,000
21	*Emmerdale*	ITV	19 January	13,206,000
22	*TV Nightmares*	ITV	9 January	13,099,000
23	*Casualty*	BBC1	13 February	13,090,000
24	*Emmerdale*	ITV	14 January	12,986,000
25	*EastEnders Special*	BBC1	14 February	12,966,000
26	*2000 Today*	BBC1	31 December	12,803,000

(*continued*)

Top 50 Programmes on Terrestrial Television in the UK (*continued*)

1999 Rank	Programme	Channel	Transmission date	Number of viewers
27	*Mission Impossible*	BBC1	26 December	12,798,000
28	*Neighbours from Hell*	ITV	7 January	12,769,000
29	*Comic Relief Launch*	BBC1	4 February	12,468,000
30	*EastEnders*	BBC1	25 December	12,435,000
31	*Who Wants to be a Christmas Millionaire?*	ITV	25 December	12,433,000
32	*Stars in their Eyes: Result*	ITV	5 June	12,393,000
33	*Weather*	BBC1	25 December	12,351,000
34	*ITV News Bulletin*	ITV	17 November	12,305,000
35	*Before They Were Famous*	BBC1	25 December	12,250,000
36	*Lost for Words*	ITV	3 January	12,226,000
37	*Stars in their Eyes: Final*	ITV	5 June	12,214,000
38	*Total Eclipse*	BBC1	10 August	12,186,000
39	*Police, Camera, Action*	ITV	6 January	12,003,000
40	*Forgotten*	ITV	15 February	12,002,000
41	*Airline*	ITV	5 February	11,993,000
42	*Ground Force*	BBC1	5 March	11,986,000
43	*Coronation Street/After Hours*	ITV	13 November	11,951,000
44	*Changing Rooms Christmas Special*	BBC1	27 December	11,877,000
45	*James Bond: Tomorrow Never Dies*	ITV	13 October	11,860,000
46	*News and Weather*	BBC1	25 December	11,767,000
47	*Where the Heart Is*	ITV	18 April	11,699,000
48	*BBC News*	BBC1	25 December	11,693,000
49	*Emmerdale*	ITV	25 December	11,671,000
50	*Emmerdale*	ITV	12 November	11,553,000

Source: © *Taylor Nelson SOFRES TV Research*

Top 30 Light Entertainment Programmes on Terrestrial Television in the UK

1999 Rank	Programme	Channel	Transmission date	Number of viewers
1	*Who Wants to be a Millionaire?*	ITV	7 March	19,207,000
2	*Vicar of Dibley*	BBC1	27 December	14,367,000
3	*New You've Been Framed*	ITV	7 November	13,903,000
4	*TV Nightmares*	ITV	9 January	13,099,000
5	*2000 Today*	BBC1	31 December	12,803,000
6	*Comic Relief/Launch*	BBC1	4 February	12,468,000
7	*Who Wants to be a Christmas Millionaire?*	ITV	25 December	12,433,000
8	*Stars in their Eyes: Result*	ITV	5 June	12,393,000
9	*Stars in their Eyes: Final*	ITV	5 June	12,214,000
10	*National TV Awards*	ITV	26 October	10,917,000
11	*Stars in their Eyes*	ITV	17 April	10,821,000
12	*British Soap Awards*	ITV	19 May	10,795,000
13	*Audience with Cliff Richard*	ITV	13 November	10,727,000
14	*Royal Variety Performance*	ITV	4 December	10,604,000
15	*Harry Enfield and Kevin/Teenager*	BBC1	27 December	10,590,000
16	*The Royle Family*	BBC1	25 December	10,438,000
17	*Stars in their Eyes: Champion*	ITV	30 October	10,359,000
18	*Dinner Ladies*	BBC1	30 December	10,345,000
19	*One Hour to Go ...*	BBC1	31 December	10,326,000
20	*The National Lottery – We've Got Your Number*	BBC1	27 February	10,301,000
21	*Celebrity Stars in their Eyes*	ITV	9 October	10,299,000
22	*Tarrant on TV*	ITV	24 January	10,267,000
23	*Blind Date*	ITV	6 March	10,265,000
24	*This is Your Life*	BBC1	11 January	10,142,000
25	*It'll be Alright on the Night 11*	ITV	2 October	10,116,000
26	*Stars in their Eyes: Result*	ITV	30 October	10,111,000
27	*It'll be Alright on the Night 7*	ITV	20 March	9,993,000
28	*The Way They Were*	ITV	17 April	9,950,000
29	*The 1999 Brit Awards*	ITV	17 February	9,864,000
30	*Barbara*	ITV	27 June	9,804,000

Source: © *Taylor Nelson SOFRES TV Research*

Top 30 Drama Programmes Shown on Terrestrial Television in the UK

1999 Rank	Programme	Channel	Transmission date	Number of viewers
1	*Coronation Street*	ITV	17 March	19,815,000
2	*Coronation Street*	ITV	4 January	19,029,000
3	*Coronation Street*	ITV	13 January	18,218,000
4	*Heartbeat*	ITV	28 February	17,008,000
5	*Touch of Frost*	ITV	21 March	16,849,000
6	*Coronation Street*	ITV	8 January	16,747,000
7	*EastEnders*	BBC1	7 January	15,719,000
8	*Coronation Street*	ITV	25 December	15,505,000

(*continued*)

Top 30 Drama Programmes Shown on Terrestrial Television in the UK *(continued)*

1999 Rank	Programme	Channel	Transmission date	Number of viewers
9	*EastEnders*	BBC1	25 October	15,402,000
10	*EastEnders*	BBC1	26 January	15,382,000
11	*EastEnders*	BBC1	5 September	14,393,000
12	*EastEnders*	BBC1	31 December	13,440,000
13	*Emmerdale*	ITV	20 January	13,351,000
14	*Emmerdale*	ITV	19 January	13,206,000
15	*Casualty*	BBC1	13 February	13,090,000
16	*Emmerdale*	ITV	14 January	12,986,000
17	*EastEnders Special*	BBC1	14 February	12,966,000
18	*EastEnders*	BBC1	25 December	12,435,000
19	*Lost For Words*	ITV	3 January	12,226,000
20	*Forgotten*	ITV	15 February	12,002,000
21	*Coronation Street/After Hours*	ITV	13 November	11,951,000
22	*Where the Heart Is*	ITV	18 April	11,699,000
23	*Emmerdale*	ITV	25 December	11,671,000
24	*Emmerdale*	ITV	12 November	11,553,000
25	*Jonathan Creek*	BBC1	28 December	11,446,000
26	*London's Burning*	ITV	28 February	11,377,000
27	*The Bill*	ITV	5 January	11,246,000
28	*Extremely Dangerous*	ITV	11 November	11,135,000
29	*Grafters*	ITV	8 November	11,127,000
30	*Emmerdale*	ITV	8 November	11,105,000

Source: © *Taylor Nelson SOFRES TV Research*

Top 30 Films Shown on Terrestrial Television in the UK

1999 Rank	Film	Channel	Transmission date	Number of viewers
1	*Goldeneye*	ITV	10 March	13,228,000
2	*Mission Impossible (FM)*	BBC1	26 December	12,798,000
3	*James Bond: Tomorrow Never Dies*	ITV	13 October	11,860,000
4	*Jingle all the Way*	ITV	22 December	11,295,000
5	*The Nutty Professor*	ITV	1 December	11,073,000
6	*Twister*	ITV	6 October	10,669,000
7	*The Specialist*	ITV	11 March	10,578,000
8	*Never Say Never Again*	ITV	18 August	10,136,000
9	*Apollo 13*	BBC1	1 January	10,103,000
10	*Dr No*	ITV	2 June	10,025,000
11	*The Spy Who Loved Me*	ITV	21 July	9,954,000
12	*All the King's Men*	BBC1	14 November	9,672,000
13	*For Your Eyes Only*	ITV	4 August	9,303,000
14	*Home Alone 2*	ITV	3 January	9,282,000
15	*The Man with the Golden Gun*	ITV	14 July	9,280,000
16	*Diamonds are Forever*	ITV	30 June	9,231,000
17	*K-9*	BBC1	1 January	9,215,000
18	*While You Were Sleeping*	ITV	13 March	9,196,000
19	*Executive Decision*	ITV	24 April	9,091,000
20	*Live and Let Die*	ITV	7 July	9,011,000
21	*Matilda*	BBC1	26 December	8,991,000
22	*Goldfinger*	ITV	16 June	8,977,000
23	*Moonraker*	ITV	28 July	8,846,000
24	*In the Line of Fire*	ITV	2 January	8,801,000
25	*You Only Live Twice*	ITV	23 June	8,706,000
26	*Eraser*	ITV	23 October	8,668,000
27	*David Copperfield*	BBC1	25 December	8,650,000
28	*Forrest Gump*	BBC1	4 April	8,647,000
29	*Octopussy*	ITV	14 August	8,436,000
30	*Braveheart*	BBC1	7 January	8,422,000

Source: © *Taylor Nelson SOFRES TV Research*

Top 30 Sports Programmes on Terrestrial Television by Rating in the UK

1999 Rank	Programme	Channel	Transmission date	Number of viewers
1	*Big Match: Champions' League Final*	ITV	26 May	15,616,000
2	*Big Match: Champions' League*	ITV	17 November	14,600,000
3	*Big Match: Champions' League*	ITV	3 March	11,914,000
4	*Big Match: Champions' League*	ITV	17 March	11,527,000
5	*Big Match: Champions' League*	ITV	21 April	11,314,000
6	*Big Match Live*	ITV	7 April	11,251,000
7	*Grand National*	BBC1	10 April	10,103,000
8	*Big Match: Champions' League*	ITV	29 September	9,691,000
9	*Big Match: FA Cup Final*	ITV	22 May	9,632,000
10	*Euro 2000: Scotland v England*	BBC1	13 November	9,372,000

(continued)

Top 30 Sports Programmes on Terrestrial Television by Rating in the UK (*continued*)

1999 Rank	Programme	Channel	Transmission date	Number of viewers
11	*Big Match: Champions' League*	ITV	8 December	9,367,000
12	*Big Match: Champions' League*	ITV	22 September	8,824,000
13	*Big Match: Champions' League*	ITV	15 September	8,510,000
14	*Big Match: Champions' League*	ITV	27 October	8,375,000
15	*Big Match: Champions' League*	ITV	3 November	8,262,000
16	*Big Match: Champions' League*	ITV	24 November	8,163,000
17	*Big Match: Champions' League*	ITV	20 October	8,030,000
18	*Brazilian Grand Prix*	ITV	11 April	7,519,000
19	*Big Match*	ITV	16 February	7,402,000
20	*World Athletics 99*	BBC1	24 August	7,384,000
21	*Match of the Day Live*	BBC1	22 April	7,323,000
22	*Big Match Live*	ITV	27 January	7,294,000
23	*Grand National Rerun*	BBC1	10 April	7,027,000
24	*Men's Singles Final*	BBC1	4 July	6,962,000
25	*Big Match Live*	ITV	7 March	6,651,000
26	*World Athletics 99*	BBC1	26 August	6,647,000
27	*Rugby 99: Post-Match Analysis*	ITV	6 November	6,638,000
28	*Rugby 99: Post-Match Analysis*	ITV	24 October	6,614,000
29	*Rugby 99: England v New Zealand*	ITV	9 October	6,602,000
30	*World Athletics 99*	BBC1	25 August	6,465,000

Source: © *Taylor Nelson SOFRES TV Research*

Top 20 Programmes Shown on Satellite Television in the UK

1999 Rank	Programme	Channel	Transmission date	Number of viewers
1	*Football Special Live*	Sky Sports 1	5 May	2,578,000
2	*Friends*	Sky 1	7 January	2,408,000
3	*International Football Live*	Sky Sports 2	13 November	2,073,000
4	*FA Cup Semi-final (Replay)*	Sky Sports 2	14 April	2,044,000
5	*Super Sunday Live*	Sky Sports 1	16 May	2,026,000
6	*Men in Black*	Sky Premier	6 February	2,025,000
7	*FA Cup Review*	Sky Sports 2	11 April	1,941,000
8	*FA Cup*	Sky Sports 2	3 January	1,827,000
9	*Super Sunday Review*	Sky Sports 1	10 January	1,698,000
10	*Football Analysis*	Sky Sports 1	16 May	1,687,000
11	*FA Cup Special*	Sky Sports 2	10 March	1,658,000
12	*Worthington Cup Final*	Sky Sports 2	21 March	1,645,000
13	*FA Cup Special Live*	Sky Sports 2	11 April	1,596,000
14	*Sky Sports Centre*	Sky Sports 1	5 May	1,569,000
15	*Lost World: Jurassic Park*	Sky Premier	30 January	1,544,000
16	*The Simpsons*	Sky 1	5 December	1,449,000
17	*Monday Night Football*	Sky Sports 1	12 April	1,355,000
18	*Rebel Sports*	Sky Sports 2	30 May	1,311,000
19	*Football Review*	Sky Sports 2	30 May	1,265,000
20	*The Fifth Element*	Sky Premier	2 January	1,179,000

Source: © *Taylor Nelson SOFRES TV Research*

Top 20 Films Shown on Satellite Television in the UK

1999 Rank	Programme	Channel	Transmission date	Number of viewers
1	*Men in Black*	Sky Premier	6 February	2,025,000
2	*Lost World: Jurassic Park*	Sky Premier	30 January	1,544,000
3	*The Fifth Element*	Sky Premier	2 January	1,179,000
4	*Bean*	Sky Premier	7 February	1,142,000
5	*Volcano*	Sky Premier	1 May	1,122,000
6=	*Air Force One*	Sky Premier	27 March	1,121,000
	The Full Monty	Sky Premier	13 March	1,121,000
8	*Con Air*	Sky Premier	16 January	1,024,000
9	*Contact*	Sky Premier	3 April	1,008,000
10	*GI Jane*	Sky Premier	22 May	979,000
11	*Speed 2: Cruise Control*	Sky Premier	6 March	951,000
12	*Face/Off*	Sky Premier	15 May	941,000
13	*Austin Powers*	Sky Premier	17 April	903,000
14	*Alien Resurrection*	Sky Premier	5 June	891,000
15	*Deep Impact*	Sky Premier	20 November	863,000
16	*The Peacemaker*	Sky Premier	3 July	862,000
17	*Event Horizon*	Sky Premier	10 April	836,000
18	*Letters from a Killer*	Sky Premier	9 January	825,000
19	*Titanic*	Sky Premier	23 October	780,000
20	*The Jackal*	Sky Premier	17 July	769,000

Source: © *Taylor Nelson SOFRES TV Research*

■ Television and Radio

Top 20 Sports Programmes Shown on Satellite Television in the UK

1999

Rank	Programme	Channel	Transmission date	Number of viewers
1	*Football Special Live*	Sky Sports 1	5 May	2,578,000
2	*International Football Live*	Sky Sports 2	13 November	2,073,000
3	*FA Cup Semi-final Replay*	Sky Sports 2	14 April	2,044,000
4	*Super Sunday Live*	Sky Sports 1	16 May	2,026,000
5	*FA Cup Review*	Sky Sports 2	11 April	1,941,000
6	*Super Sunday Live*	Sky Sports 1	22 August	1,883,000
7	*Super Sunday Live*	Sky Sports 1	9 May	1,854,000
8	*FA Cup*	Sky Sports 2	3 January	1,827,000
9	*International Football Live*	Sky Sports 2	27 March	1,769,000
10	*Super Sunday Live*	Sky Sports 1	31 January	1,742,000
11	*Football Special Live*	Sky Sports 1	11 May	1,728,000
12	*Super Sunday Live*	Sky Sports 1	3 October	1,727,000
13	*International Football Live*	Sky Sports 2	10 February	1,725,000
14	*Football Special Live*	Sky Sports 1	12 May	1,723,000
15	*International Football Live*	Sky Sports 2	5 June	1,715,000
16	*Super Sunday Live*	Sky Sports 1	8 August	1,713,000
17	*FA Cup*	Sky Sports 2	24 January	1,702,000
18	*Super Sunday Review*	Sky Sports 1	10 January	1,698,000
19	*Football Special Live*	Sky Sports 1	17 February	1,691,000
20	*Football Analysis*	Sky Sports 1	16 May	1,687,000

Source: © Taylor Nelson SOFRES TV Research

Television Companies in the UK

Anglia Television Ltd Anglia House, Norwich NR1 3JG; phone: (01603) 615151; fax: (01603) 631032; e-mail: pr@angliatv.com; Web site: www.angliatv.com

BBC Television BBC Broadcasting House, London WIA IAA; phone: (020)7580 4468; BBC Information, PO Box 1116, Belfast BT2 7AJ; phone: (0870) 010 0222; fax: (028) 9032 6453; Web site: www.bbc.co.uk

Border Television The Television Centre, Carlisle CA1 3NT; phone: (01228) 541384; fax: (01228) 541384; Web site: www.border-tv.com

Carlton Broadcasting 101 St Martin's Lane, London WC2N 4AZ; phone: (020) 7615 1515; fax: (020) 7615 1778; Web site: www.carlton.com

Carlton Broadcasting (Westcountry Broadcasting) Language Science Park, Western Wood Way, Plymouth PL7 5BQ; phone: (01752) 333333; fax: (01752) 333444; Web site: www.carlton.com

Channel 4 124 Horseferry Road, London SW1P 2TX; phone: (020) 7396 4444; fax: (020) 7306 8347; e-mail: viewerenqs@channel4.co.uk; Web site: www.channel4.com

Channel 5 Broadcasting 22 Longacre, London WC2E 9LY; phone: (020) 7550 5555; fax: (020) 7550 5554; e-mail: dutyoffice@channel5.co.uk; Web site: www.channel5.co.uk

Channel Television Television Centre, La Pouquelaye, St Helier, Jersey, Channel Islands JE1 3ZD; phone: (01534) 816816; fax: (01534) 816817; e-mail: broadcast@channeltv.co.uk; Web site: www.channeltv.co.uk

GMTV London Television Centre, Upper Ground, London SE1 9TT; phone: (020) 7827 7000; fax (press office): (020) 7827 7009; Web site: www.gmtv.co.uk

Grampian Television Queen's Cross, Aberdeen AB15 4XJ; phone: (01224) 846846; fax: (01224) 846800; e-mail: gtv@grampiantv.co.uk; Web site: www.scot.scottishmediagroup.com

Granada Television The Television Centre, Quay Street, Manchester M60 9EA; phone: (0161) 832 7211; fax: (0161) 827 2029; e-mail: officers.duty@gmg.co.uk; Web site: www.granadatv.co.uk

HTV (Cymru) Wales Television Centre, Culverhouse Cross, Cardiff CF5 6XJ; phone: (029) 2059 0590; fax: (029) 2059 7183; e-mail: htv@htv.co.uk; Web site: www.htv.co.uk

London Weekend Television (LWT) London Television Centre, Upper Ground, London SE1 9LT; phone: (020) 7620 1620; fax (duty office): (020) 7261 3307; Web site: www.g-wizz.net/lwt

Meridian Broadcasting Television Centre, Southampton SO14 0PZ; phone: (01380) 222555; fax: (01380) 335050; Web site: www.meridian.tv.co.uk

Scottish Television Cowcaddens, Glasgow G2 3PR; phone: (0141) 300 3000; fax: (0141) 300 3519; Web site: www.scottishmediagroup.com

Tyne Tees Television The Television Centre, City Road, Newcastle upon Tyne NE1 2AL; phone: (0191) 261 0181; fax: (0191) 261 2302; e-mail: tyne.tees@granadamedia.com; Web site: www.granadatv.co.uk

Ulster Television (UTV) Havelock House, Ormeau Road, Belfast BT7 1EB; phone: (028) 9032 8122; fax: (028) 9024 6695; Web site: www.utvlive.com

Yorkshire Television The Television Centre, Kirkstall Road, Leeds LS3 1JS; phone: (0113) 243 8283; fax: (0113) 244 0213; Web site: www.granadamedia.com

Satellite and Cable Television Companies in the UK

Bloomberg International TV Citygate House, 39–45 Finsbury Square, London EC2A 1PQ; phone: (020) 7330 7500; fax: (020) 7392 6000; Web site: www.bloomberg.com/uk

Bravo, Flextech, The Discovery Channel, Trouble, UK Gold, UK Living 160 Great Portland St, London W1N 5TB; phone: (020) 7299 5000; fax: (020) 7299 6000; Web site: www.flextech.co.uk

Carlton Digital, Carlton Food Network 27–35 Mortimer St, London W1N 7RJ; phone: (020) 7725 4600; fax: (020) 7725 4700; Web site: www.carltontv.com

Channel Broadcasting Cartoon Network 18 Soho Square, London W1V 5FD; phone: (020) 7478 1000; fax: (020) 7478 1010; Web site: www.cartoonnetwork.co.uk

CNN International CNN House, 19–22 Rathbone Place, London W1P 1DF; phone: (020) 7637 6700; fax: (020) 7307 6682; Web site: www.cnn.com

Disney Channel UK Centre West, 3 Queen Caroline Street; London W6 9PE; (020) 8222 1300; fax: (020) 8222 1144; Web site: www.disneychannel.co.uk

Eurosport UK 55 Drury Lane, London WC2B 5SQ; phone: (020) 7468 7777; fax: (020) 7468 0023; Web site: www.eurosport.com

Granada Breeze, Granada Men and Motors, Granada Plus Granada Sky Broadcasting, Franciscan Court, 16 Hatfields, London SE1 8DJ; phone: (020) 7578 4040; fax: (020) 7578 4035; Web site: www.gsb.co.uk

MTV Europe 180 Oxford St, London W1N 0DS; phone: (020) 7284 7777; fax: (020) 7284 7788; Web sites: www.mtveurope.com and www.mtv.co.uk

News 24 BBC Information, PO Box 1116, Belfast BT2 7AJ; phone: (0870) 010 0222; fax: (028) 9032 6453; Web site: www.bbc.co.uk

Nickleodeon 15–18 Rathbone Place, London W1P 1DF; phone: (020) 7462 1000; fax: (020) 7462 1020; Web site: www.nick.com

The Sci-Fi Channel 77 Charlotte Street, London W1P 2DD; phone: (020) 7805 6100; fax: (020) 7805 6150; Web site: www.uk.scifi.com

Sky (including the Movie Channel, Sky 1, Sky Movies 1, Sky Movies Gold, Sky Sports (1, 2 and 3), Sky News, National Geographic Channel) BSkyB Ltd, Grant Way, Isleworth, Middlesex TW7 5QD; phone: (020) 7705 3000; Web site: www.sky/com

Digital Television Companies in the UK

BBC Digital TV Television Centre, Wood Lane, London W12 7RJ; phone: (020) 8743 8000; Web site: www.bbc.co.uk/digital

British Interactive Broadcasting BIB (Platform) Company, 47 Cannon Street, London EC4M 5SQ; phone (020) 7332 7083

Cable and Wireless Caxton Way, Watford Business Park, Watford, Herts WD1 8XH; phone: (020) 8528 2000; Web site: www.cwcom.co.uk

Digital 3 and 4 Ltd Unit 4, 56 Norwich Road, Wymondham, Norfolk NR18 0NT; phone: (01953) 608040

FilmFour 124 Horseferry Road, London SW1P 2TX; phone: (020) 7396 4444

Flextech Television 160 Great Portland Street, London W1N 5TB; phone: (020) 7299 6000

GMTV2 The London Television Centre, Upper Ground, London SE1 9TT; phone: (020) 7827 7000

Granada Sky Broadcasting (DTT) Franciscan Court, 16 Hatfields, London SE1 8DJ; phone: (020) 7578 4040; Web site: www.gsb.co.uk

Home Shopping Channel Sir John Moores Building, 100 Old Hall Street, Liverpool L70 1AB; phone: (0151) 235 2055

ITV2 200 Gray's Inn Road, London WC1X 8HF; phone: (020) 7843 8000

Microsoft Endeavour House, 189 Shaftesbury Avenue, London WC2H 8JB; phone: (020) 7632 5500; Web site: www.microsoft.com/tv

ONdigital 346 Queenstown Road, London SW8 4DG; phone: (020) 7819 8000; Web site: www.ondigital.co.uk

SDN The Media Centre, Culverhouse Cross, Cardiff CF5 6XJ; phone: (01222) 405 600

Sky Digital BSkyB Ltd, Grant Way, Isleworth TW7 5QD; phone: (020) 7705 3000; Web site: www.sky.com/skydigital

National Radio Stations in the UK

BBC Network Radio BBC Information, PO Box 1116, Belfast BT2 7AJ; phone: (0870) 010 2222; fax: (028) 9032 6453; Web site: www.bbc.co.uk

Radio 1 phone (press office): (0870) 0100 100; Web site: www.bbc.co.uk/radio1

Radio 2 phone (press office): (0870) 0100 200; Web site: www.bbc.co.uk/radio2

Radio 3 phone (press office): (0870) 0100 300; Web site: www.bbc.co.uk/radio3

Radio 4 phone (press office): (0870) 0100 400; Web site: www.bbc.co.uk/radio4

Radio 5 Live phone (press office): (0870) 0100 500; Web site: www.bbc.co.uk/radio5

Classic FM PO Box 2834, London W1A 5NT; phone: (020) 7343 9000; fax: (020) 7344 2700; Web site: www.classicfm.com

Talk Sport PO Box 1089, London SE1 8WQ; phone: (020) 7636 1089; fax: (020) 7636 1053; Web site: www.talksport.co.uk

Ginger TV/Virgin Radio 1 Golden Square, London W1R 4DJ; phone: (020) 7434 1215; fax: Virgin (020) 7434 1197, Ginger TV (020) 7663 2001; Web site: www.virginradio.com

Newspapers and Magazines

The UK's Newspaper and Magazine Industry

Traditional print media in the UK faces increasing competition from the Internet, the proliferation of television and satellite channels, and radio stations, and the wide circulation of free print: there are over 300 free customer magazines and several hundred free newspapers funded by advertising. In 1990 the circulation of the national dailies was more than 15 million but by the end of the 20th century daily circulation had fallen to 13 million. However, two-thirds of the UK's 1,400 or so regional and local newspapers increased their circulation at the end of the 1990s.

Nine out of ten adults read a weekly local paper, and the number of periodicals increased by one-third over the last decade to around 7,000.

In general the newspaper industry has reacted to competition by including more colour, lifestyle, leisure columns, and sport, and establishing their own online newspapers. Advertising earns a large part of their income and newspapers and magazines form the largest advertising medium in the UK (*see* **Advertising Expenditure in the UK by Media Sector**, p 416). Although there is no state censorship or control and few imprints are financially dependent on political parties (though many are regarded as having a political bias), ownership and, to a varying extent, editorial control of many of the main national and regional newspapers now lie in the hands of large corporations. Further control is exercised by the major wholesalers and outlets. With the perceived decline of editorial independence and growth in commercialization, only 15% of the public say that they trust national newspaper journalists to place truth above telling a good story, although trust in local coverage remains the highest of all media.

National Newspapers in the UK

Newspaper	First publication	Ownership
Daily		
The Times	1785	News International
The Guardian	1821	Guardian Media Group
The Daily Telegraph	1855	Telegraph Group
Financial Times	1888	Pearson
Daily Mail	1896	Daily Mail & General Trust
The Express	1900	United News & Media
Mirror	1903	Mirror Group
The Sun	1964	News International
Daily Star	1978	United News & Media
The Independent	1986	Irish Independent Newspapers
Sunday		
The Observer	1791	Guardian Media Group
The Sunday Times	1822	News International
News of the World	1843	News International
Sunday People	1881	Mirror Group
The Express on Sunday	1918	United News & Media
The Sunday Telegraph	1961	Telegraph Group
Sunday Mirror	1963	Mirror Group
The Mail on Sunday	1982	Daily Mail & General Trust
Independent on Sunday	1990	Irish Independent Newspapers

Online Newspapers

Since *The Daily Telegraph* first launched its *Electronic Telegraph* on the Internet in November 1994, many newspaper publishers have established free online versions. Online newspapers are used heavily as an advertising medium and offer a wide range of interactive features. These may include links to other sites of interest, keyword searching, photograph and text archives, regular 'online only' updates and comment, and a wide range of other services, from personal online networks to property sales and job search. Major news sites such as the *Electronic Telegraph*, *Guardian Unlimited*, *FT.com*, and *The Times* contain extensive backdated archives, while others offer a rolling archive covering a limited period. Although acknowledging the benefits of online newspapers – which include their global accessibility – critics point out that it can currently cost more in telephone charges to read a page on the Internet than it does to buy a copy of the whole hard-copy newspaper. There are also concerns over the Internet's effect on the continuing viability of traditional print media.

Online UK Newspapers

Newspaper	Online address	Other information
National		
Electronic Telegraph	www.telegraph.co.uk	first online national newspaper, launched November 1994; free archive dating from 12 December 1994 with search facilities and links to other sites
The Daily Express	www.express.co.uk	online version of the mid-market tabloid
FT.com	www.newsft.com	online site of the *Financial Times*; free archive and search facilities; Global Archive link to 4,000 business and global news sources with over 6 million articles
Guardian Unlimited	www.guardianunlimited.co.uk	online site of *The Guardian* and *The Observer* launched in January 1999; free archive dating from 1 September 1998
The Independent	www.independent.co.uk	online site of *The Independent*; free archive dating from 18 October 1999
Megastar	www.megastar.co.uk	online version of the *Daily Star*; free archive dating from 1997
Mirror	www.mirror.com	online version of the *Mirror*; interactive features include an online picture library link (www.mirrorpix.com)
News of the World	www.newsoftheworld.co.uk	online version of the Sunday tabloid
The Sun	www.the-sun.co.uk	online version of the daily tabloid
Sunday Mirror	www.sundaymirror.co.uk	online version of the Sunday tabloid
The Sunday Times	www.sunday-times.co.uk	online version of *The Sunday Times*; the library offers access to full text of back issues from 1 January 1996
The Times	www.the-times.co.uk	the library offers access to full-text of back issues from 1 January 1996; linked sites include the *Times Educational Supplement*, *The Sunday Times*, the the library offers access to full-text of back issues from 1 January 1996; linked sites include the *Times Higher Education Supplement* with a searchable archive from 1994 (available only to subscribers), and the *Times Literary Supplement*
Other online press		
Ananova	www.ananova.com	continually updated news site of the Press Association (formerly the PA Newscentre); features Ananova, the world's first virtual newscaster; includes search facility
Belfast Telegraph	www.belfasttelegraph.co.uk	daily news and free archive dating from November 1995
Daily Record	www.record-mail.co.uk	online version of Scotland's highest-selling daily newspaper
The Economist	www.economist.co.uk	weekly news and reviews; free archive dating from 1995; free weekly newsletter; book reviews with first chapters
NISS News	www.niss.ac.uk/cr/uknews.html	links to the main UK national newspapers and other news sources (newswires and press agencies), and local UK newspapers by area
The Paper Boy	www.thepaperboy.com/uk	compendium with links to almost 300 UK national, regional, and local papers, and other media sites; home page gives access to nearly 4,000 online newspapers from over 135 countries
This is London	www.thisislondon.co.uk	online site of the *London Evening Standard*; includes picture gallery archive, with contents dating from 1901, and news archive from late 1997
Y Cymro	www.nwn.co.uk	online version of the Welsh language newspaper of North Wales Newspapers

The Press Complaints Commission

In response to growing public criticism of standards, and allegations of inaccuracy, misrepresentation, harassment, discrimination, and bias, the newspaper industry established the Press Complaints Commission (PCC) in 1991, a self-regulatory body that upholds an agreed Code of Practice, and deals with complaints about the contents and conduct of newspapers and magazines. The Commission deals with between 2,500 and 3,000 complaints each year, most of which involve inaccuracy. The Commission also conducts formal adjudications on others, and all adjudications are published in full.

Following the death of Diana, Princess of Wales, in 1997, substantial changes to the industry's Code of Practice were introduced in the light of increased public concern about media intrusion. The following were among the significant revisions to the Code that came into effect in January 1998:

- a recognition that everyone has a right of respect for their private lives
- stipulations against the taking of pictures of people in 'private places' (defined as 'public or private property where there is reasonable expectation of privacy')
- a ban on the publication of pictures obtained as a result of 'persistent pursuit'
- a stipulation that children should be free to complete their time at school without unnecessary press intrusion
- a ban on payments to minors, except where they are in the interests of the child

Contact information

Press Complaints Commission 1 Salisbury Square, London EC4 8AE; phone (020) 73531248; fax: (020) 7353 8355; e-mail: pcc@pcc.org.uk; Web site: www.pcc.org.uk

Newspaper Readership Figures in the UK

Figures are from an unweighted sample of 35,816 adults aged 15 and over. An unweighted sample is 'raw' data which have not been 'weighted' to represent the full population (that is, taking into account age, social grades, and so on). For this survey, the estimated population was 46.5 million and did not include Northern Ireland. Adult coverage is the percentage of the total population aged 15 and over in Great Britain, but not Northern Ireland.

January–December 1999

Newspaper	Adult readers	Adult coverage (%)
National daily		
The Sun	9,799,000	21.1
Mirror	6,095,000	13.1
Daily Mail	5,820,000	12.5
The Daily Telegraph	2,468,000	5.3
The Express	2,412,000	5.2
Daily Record	1,756,000	3.8
The Times	1,846,000	4.0
Daily Star	1,591,000	3.4
The Guardian	1,105,000	2.4
Financial Times	614,000	1.3
The Independent	587,000	1.3
Racing Post	235,000	0.5
Any national daily	25,771,000	55.4
National Sunday		
News of the World	10,592,000	22.8
The Mail on Sunday	6,256,000	13.5
Sunday Mirror	6,141,000	13.2
Sunday People	3,837,000	8.3
The Sunday Times	3,302,000	7.1
The Express on Sunday	2,391,000	5.1
The Sunday Telegraph	2,171,000	4.7
The Mail on Sunday	1,953,000	4.2
The Sunday Post	1,809,000	3.9
The Observer	1,076,000	2.3
Independent on Sunday	737,000	1.6
Scotland on Sunday	319,000	0.7
Any national Sunday	27,478,000	59.1
Regional daily		
London Evening Standard	989,000	2.1
Liverpool Echo	394,000	0.8
The Herald	309,000	0.7
Newcastle Evening Chronicle	307,000	0.7
Glasgow Evening Times	302,000	0.6
Leeds Yorkshire Evening Post	270,000	0.6
Yorkshire Post	232,000	0.5
The Scotsman	225,000	0.5
Dundee Courier and Advertiser	192,000	0.4
Edinburgh Evening News	185,000	0.4
Dundee Evening Telegraph	73,000	0.2
Any regional morning/evening	11,928,000	25.7
Any regional evening	10,074,000	21.7
Regional Sunday		
Newcastle Sunday Sun	399,000	0.9
Any regional Sunday	713,000	1.5

Source: National Readership Surveys

General Magazine Readership Figures in the UK

Figures are from an unweighted sample of 35,816 adults aged 15 and over. An unweighted sample is 'raw' data which have not been 'weighted' to represent the full population (that is, taking into account age, social grades, and so on). For this survey, the estimated population was 46.5 million and did not include Northern Ireland. Adult coverage is the percentage of the total population aged 15 and over in Great Britain, but not Northern Ireland. Magazines that are classifed by the magazine industry as 'women's' magazines are listed separately.

January–December 1999

Periodical	Adult readers	Adult coverage (%)
Weekly		
What's on TV	4,492,000	9.7
Radio Times	3,779,000	8.1
TV Times	3,066,000	6.6
TV Quick	2,133,000	4.6
Auto Trader	2,017,000	4.3
The Big Issue	1,150,000	2.5
Exchange & Mart	874,000	1.9
TV & Satellite Week	737,000	1.6
TES (Times Educational Supplement)	575,000	1.2
Motorcycle News	568,000	1.2
NME (New Musical Express)	455,000	1.0
New Scientist	436,000	0.9
The Weekly News	429,000	0.9
The Economist	414,000	0.9
Angling Times	388,000	0.8
Auto Express	380,000	0.8
Time Out	357,000	0.7
Autocar	347,000	0.7
Shoot	335,000	0.7
Match	333,000	0.7
Country Life	308,000	0.7
Horse & Hound	300,000	0.6
Amateur Gardening	290,000	0.6
Autosport	240,000	0.5
Time	235,000	0.5
Angler's Mail	224,000	0.5
Garden News	222,000	0.5
Melody Maker	194,000	0.4
Kerrang!	174,000	0.4
Any general weekly	18,442,000	39.7
Fortnightly		
Smash Hits	732,000	1.6
Private Eye	601,000	1.3
Bike Trader	325,000	0.7
Big!	194,000	0.4
Monthly		
Skyview TV Guide	4,803,000	10.3
Reader's Digest	3,780,000	8.1
FHM (For Him Magazine)	3,765,000	8.1
Cable Guide	3,230,000	6.9
Loaded	2,192,000	4.7
National Geographic	1,912,000	4.1
Saga Magazine	1,872,000	4.0
BBC Gardeners' World	1,785,000	3.8
Sky View Digital TV Guide	1,696,000	3.6
Max Power	1,464,000	3.1
BBC Top Gear	1,418,000	3.0
What Car?	1,348,000	2.9
Maxim	1,186,000	2.6
Sky	913,000	2.0
Men's Health	898,000	1.9
Classic Cars	830,000	1.8
Top of the Pops Magazine	757,000	1.6
BBC Match of the Day	724,000	1.6
GQ	717,000	1.5
Golf Monthly	703,000	1.5
FourFourTwo	667,000	1.4
Q	642,000	1.4
TV Hits	606,000	1.3
F1 Racing	578,000	1.2
Empire	567,000	1.2
Mixmag	558,000	1.2
Superbike	554,000	1.2
Revs	552,000	1.2
OnDigital	531,000	1.1
Performance Bikes	522,000	1.1
What Hi-Fi?	514,000	1.1

(continued)

General Magazine Readership Figures in the UK *(continued)*

January–December 1999

Periodical	Adult readers	Adult coverage (%)
Garden Answers	504,000	1.1
Fast Car Magazine	497,000	1.1
Golf World	475,000	1.0
Classic and Sportscar	448,000	1.0
BBC Wildlife	439,000	0.9
High Life	435,000	0.9
Bike	420,000	0.9
Rugby World	411,000	0.9
Bizarre	403,000	0.9
The Garden	388,000	0.8
Esquire	373,000	0.8
Classic Bike	362,000	0.8
Front	358,000	0.8
Land Rover Owner International	342,000	0.7
Practical Caravan	341,000	0.7
Flicks	310,000	0.7
Select	306,000	0.7
Total Sport	302,000	0.7
Practical Classics (incorporating Popular Classics)	300,000	0.6
Fore!	295,000	0.6
Ride	289,000	0.6
Practical Photography	285,000	0.6
Car	284,000	0.6
Total Football	282,000	0.6
Sea Angler	272,000	0.6
Your Garden	258,000	0.6
Classic FM Magazine	250,000	0.5
Mojo	250,000	0.5
Practical Boat Owner	249,000	0.5
Today's Golfer	248,000	0.5
Choice	236,000	0.5
Sporting Gun	232,000	0.5
The Face	223,000	0.5
BBC Music Magazine	211,000	0.5
Yachting Monthly	211,000	0.5
The Field	206,000	0.4
Cars/Car Conversions	206,000	0.4
Moneywise	201,000	0.4
Trout & Salmon	195,000	0.4
Arena	190,000	0.4
The Scot's Magazine	173,000	0.4
Street Machine	167,000	0.4
Practical Woodworking	159,000	0.3
Focus	156,000	0.3
Fiesta	141,000	0.3
Classic CD	134,000	0.3
Geographical Magazine	112,000	0.2
Any general monthly	23,609,000	50.8
Bi-monthly		
Viz	1,166,000	2.5
The Countryman	174,000	0.4
Quarterly		
AA Member's Magazine	3,642,000	7.8
The Ford Magazine	989,000	2.1
Homebase Living	855,000	1.8

Source: National Readership Surveys

Women's Magazine Readership Figures in the UK

The following table lists those magazines that are classified as 'women's' magazines by the magazine industry. Readership figures, howevers, are for all adults. Figures are from an unweighted sample of 35,816 adults aged 15 and over. An unweighted sample is 'raw' data which have not been 'weighted' to represent the full population (that is, taking into account age, social grades, and so on). For this survey, the estimated population was 46.5 million and did not include Northern Ireland. Adult coverage is the percentage of the total population aged 15 and over in Great Britain, but not Northern Ireland.

January–December 1999

Periodical	Readers	Coverage (%)
Weekly		
Take a Break	4,462,000	9.6
Woman's Own	2,504,000	5.4
Bella	2,444,000	5.3
Hello!	2,288,000	4.9
Woman	2,063,000	4.4
Chat	1,947,000	4.2
Best	1,700,000	3.7
Woman's Weekly	1,629,000	3.5
OK!	1,330,000	2.9
That's Life	1,179,000	2.5
The People's Friend	1,111,000	2.4
My Weekly	1,048,000	2.3
Woman's Realm	669,000	1.4
Now	550,000	1.2
The Lady	129,000	0.3
Any women's weekly	11,063,000	23.8
Fortnightly		
More!	916,000	2.0
Inside Soap	742,000	1.6
Mizz	285,000	0.6
Monthly		
Asda Magazine	4,291,000	9.2
Safeway Magazine	3,916,000	8.4
Sainsbury's Magazine	2,765,000	5.9
The Somerfield Magazine	2,578,000	5.5
Good Housekeeping	1,994,000	4.3
Cosmopolitan	1,890,000	4.1
Marie Claire	1,592,000	3.4
Ideal Home	1,526,000	3.3
Prima	1,375,000	3.0
Homes & Gardens	1,355,000	2.9
Vogue	1,264,000	2.7
House & Garden	1,242,000	2.7
Sugar	1,209,000	2.6
Woman & Home	1,201,000	2.6
BBC Good Food	1,008,000	2.2
House Beautiful	939,000	2.0
Bliss	922,000	2.0
Elle	873,000	1.9
Family Circle	871,000	1.9
Mother & Baby	796,000	1.7
Candis	787,000	1.7
Country Living	780,000	1.7
Just Seventeen	751,000	1.6
Homes & Ideas	739,000	1.6
Country Homes and Interiors	703,000	1.5
Essentials	702,000	1.5
She	682,000	1.5
BBC Homes & Antiques	664,000	1.4
Company	627,000	1.3
New Woman	599,000	1.3
Red	596,000	1.3
Practical Parenting	584,000	1.3
'19'	528,000	1.1
Yours	521,000	1.1
Health & Fitness Magazine	519,000	1.1
Top Santé Health & Beauty	415,000	0.9
BBC Good Homes Magazine	405,000	0.9
The Real Homes Magazine	394,000	0.8
Inspirations	381,000	0.8

(continued)

Women's Magazine Readership Figures in the UK *(continued)*

January–December 1999

Periodical	Readers	Coverage (%)
'B'	357,000	0.8
Woman's Journal	351,000	0.8
Home & Country	348,000	0.7
Perfect Home	343,000	0.7
Period Living/Traditional Homes	326,000	0.7
Harpers & Queen	318,000	0.7
Minx	313,000	0.7
BBC Vegetarian Good Food	311,000	0.7
Looks	310,000	0.7
25 Beautiful Homes	306,000	0.7
Slimming	301,000	0.6
Tatler	253,000	0.5
Vanity Fair	251,000	0.5
Babycare & Pregnancy	250,000	0.5
World of Interiors	238,000	0.5
Expecting Our Baby	236,000	0.5
Your Home	231,000	0.5
Elle Decoration	201,000	0.4
Any women's monthly	18,178,000	39.1
Bi-monthly		
Weight Watchers	1,172,000	2.5
Hair	956,000	2.1
Slimming World Magazine	517,000	1.1
R Conley Diet/Fitness Magazine	440,000	0.9
Prima Baby	265,000	0.6
You & Your Wedding	257,000	0.6
Brides/Set Up Home	191,000	0.4
Wedding & Home	186,000	0.4
Slimmer	135,000	0.3

Source: National Readership Surveys

Top 10 Countries by Number of Daily Newspapers

1996

Rank	Country	Number of daily newspapers
1	USA	1,520
2	Brazil	380
3	Germany	375
4	Mexico	295
5	Russian Federation	285
6	Pakistan	264
7	Argentina	181
8	Greece	156
9	Japan	122
10	France	117

Source: UNESCO Statistical Yearbook 1999, *© UNESCO 1999*

Newspaper Facts

One of the earliest newspapers was the Roman *Acta Diurna*; it is said to have been started by Julius Caesar and contained announcements of marriages, deaths, and military appointments.

In England by 1645 there were 14 news weeklies on sale in London, but the first daily was the subsidized pro-government *Daily Courant* (1702).

The Times is the UK's oldest national daily; it was the first newspaper to print a photograph (1842) and published the first generally available daily weather forecast (1875).

The Mirror was originally conceived as a newspaper for gentlewomen, and was run by mainly female staff; a free hand mirror was issued with the first copy.

The world's most widely read newspaper is Japan's *Yomiuri Shimbun*, with a daily circulation of 10 million.

See also **Media,** pp 754–758.

Books

The UK Book Industry

In 1999 publishers in the UK issued almost 110,000 new titles, and the contribution of book publishing to the UK economy was £4,080 million – 0.46% of GDP. The resurgence in the popularity of books, and media hype of blockbuster stars and prize-winners, increasingly lend an air of Hollywood to the industry, with a succession of high-profile deals – from Nick Hornby's £2 million transfer from Gollancz to Penguin to footballer Michael Owen's £2 million three-book deal with HarperCollins. Areas of growth include children's books, the self-help genre, 'new age' material (over 150 books on the art of Feng Shui appeared in the late 1990s), and narrative non-fiction.

Books and the Internet

The greatest transformation in the book world has been initiated by the Internet. Many publishers are now operating their own Web sites, and, in the case of reference publishing, extending their markets by placing entire works online, either for free access or through subscription. With the advantages of constant updating, greater subject penetration through Web-links, lower overheads, and regular cash flow from subscription or advertising, a number of works will cease to appear in hard copy.

In the marketplace online bookshops are now big business, from giants through to thousands of small specialist sites. Books are the most popular item purchased on the Internet. Figures released in July 2000 by Whitaker BookTrack indicated that between February and May 2000 Internet booksellers accounted for 6% of all book purchases in the UK, a threefold increase on the same period in 1999.

The UK Book Industry *(continued)*

The UK's high street retailers have met the competition by setting up their own electronic outlets, such as WHSmith.co.uk and Blackwell's Online Bookshop. With global Internet trading, the traditional division of the English-speaking world into British and US publishing territories is becoming obsolete; in 1999 and 2000 advance Internet sales of J K Rowling's third and fourth Harry Potter novels made them bestsellers even before their publication.

The e-book

The biggest revolution in the publishing industry in the early 21st century, is expected to be the electronic or e-book. In March 2000 Stephen King, the world's top-selling novelist, published his novella *Riding the Bullet* straight onto the Internet, and in the first 24 hours sold the equivalent of 2.5 books per second. With the recent development of font-enhancing software, portability in the form of hand-held devices, and advances in electronic 'paper' that can be charged to show print, the e-book and self-publishing will offer further challenges to traditional publishing media. (*See also* **Language and Dictionaries Online**, p 433.)

Number of New Titles Published in the UK by Category

Category	1998	1999
Adult fiction	9,111	9,730
Children's	8,399	9,043
Adult non-fiction	29,480	30,994
Academic/professional	51,839	55,104
School	4,096	3,963
Total	102,925	108,744

Source: The Publishers' Association 2000

The Potter Phenomenon

By July 2000 some 35 million copies of the first three books in J K Rowling's multi-award winning Harry Potter series had been sold worldwide and the books had been translated into 33 languages. The fourth book in the series, *Harry Potter and The Goblet of Fire*, was published on 8 July 2000 (its title was kept secret until 27 June). A record-breaking 5.3 million copies of the hardback edition were printed – 1.5 million in the UK and 3.8 million in the USA. On the day it was published the book became the fastest selling book of all time in the UK: over 370,000 copies were sold in one day, breaking the record set by *How To Cook 2*, by Delia Smith, which sold 110,425 in the first three days after publication. The profits and turnover of Bloomsbury (the publisher of all four Harry Potter books in the UK) doubled between 1998 and 2000 and the value of its shares by July 2000 had risen eightfold in two years. With an income of an estimated £14.5 million in 1999, J K Rowling was third in the list of the highest UK women earners.

The Nation's Top 50 Favourite Authors

The table presents results of a poll conducted for World Book Day in January–February 2000 in over 4,000 bookshops and libraries, through schools and on the Internet. About 40,000 people took part in the poll. Roald Dahl, at the top of the list, received 4.5% of the total vote. Sales of the UK editions of his books amount to some 30 million. J K Rowling, at number 2, received 3.5% of the vote. Among adults alone, the top three authors were Catherine Cookson, Terry Pratchett, and Maeve Binchy.

Rank	Author
1	Roald Dahl
2	J K Rowling
3	Terry Pratchett
4	Catherine Cookson
5	Jacqueline Wilson
6	Maeve Binchy
7	Jane Austen
8	Dick Francis
9	Stephen King
10	Danielle Steel
11	J R R Tolkien
12	R L Stine
13=	Charles Dickens
	Wilbur Smith
15	Patricia Cornwell
16	John Grisham
17	Enid Blyton
18=	Dick King Smith
	Thomas Hardy
20	Josephine Cox
21	Rosamund Pilcher
22	Bernard Cornwell
23	Agatha Christie
24	C S Lewis
25	Joanna Trollope
26	Patrick O'Brian
27=	Bill Bryson
	Georgette Heyer
	Ruth Rendell
30=	Iain Banks
	Jack Higgins
	Lucy Daniels
	Mary Higgins Clark
34=	Anne McCaffrey
	Brian Jacques
	Ellis Peters
	Ian Rankin
	Robert Goddard
39=	Sebastian Faulks
	Tom Clancy
41=	Barbara Erskine
	Margaret Forster
43=	Dean R Koontz
	George Orwell
45=	Graham Greene
	James Patterson
	Colin Forbes
48=	Judy Blume
	P G Wodehouse
	Colin Dexter

Source: © World Book Day 2000

Top 10 Best-Selling Paperback Fiction Titles of the Year in the UK

1999

Rank	Title	Author (publisher)	Quantity sold	Total value
1	*Tara Road*	Maeve Binchy (Orion)	288,131	£1,526,012.47
2	*Charlotte Gray*	Sebastian Faulks (Vintage)	228,362	£1,364,183.51
3	*About a Boy*	Nick Hornby (Indigo)	226,407	£1,344,679.16
4	*Point of Origin*	Patricia Cornwell (Warner)	212,236	£978,796.44
5	*Long Road Home*	Danielle Steel (Corgi)	205,553	£887,303.47
6	*Street Lawyer*	John Grisham (Arrow Books)	204,672	£990,303.79
7	*Captain Corelli's Mandolin*	Louis De Bernières (Vintage)	195,249	£1,322,197.88
8	*When the Wind Blows*	James Patterson (Headline Feature)	186,136	£798,642.25
9	*Mirror Image*	Danielle Steel (Corgi)	181,323	£754,286.30
10	*Other People's Children*	Joanna Trollope (Black Swan)	175,033	£1,065,268.69

Source: Whitaker BookTrack

Top 10 Best-Selling Hardback Fiction Titles of the Year in the UK

1999

Rank	Title	Author (publisher)	Quantity sold	Total value
1	*Hannibal*	Thomas Harris (Heinemann)	286,797	£3,850,085.16
2	*Bridget Jones: Edge of Reason*	Helen Fielding (Picador)	228,115	£2,496,792.51
3	*Adrian Mole: The Cappuccino Years*	Sue Townsend (Michael Joseph)	168,957	£2,124,252.87
4	*Fifth Elephant*	Terry Pratchett (Doubleday)	114,392	£1,648,222.13
5	*Monsoon*	Wilbur Smith (Macmillan, London)	87,990	£1,227,843.53
6	*Crisis Four*	Andy McNab (Bantam Press)	86,408	£1,176,204.06
7	*Remorseful Day*	Colin Dexter (Macmillan, London)	83,884	£1,182,744.17
8	*Black Notice*	Patricia Cornwell (Little, Brown)	82,859	£1,169,619.53
9	*Second Wind*	Dick Francis (Michael Joseph)	81,186	£1,156,653.78
10	*The Testament*	John Grisham (Century)	73,721	£1,002,557.67

Source: Whitaker BookTrack

Top 10 Best-Selling Paperback Non-Fiction Titles of the Year in the UK

1999

Rank	Title	Author (publisher)	Quantity sold	Total value
1	*'Who Wants to be a Millionaire?': The Quiz Book*	Question Masters (Boxtree)	309,199	£1,759,658.97
2	*Angela's Ashes: A Memoir of a Childhood*	Frank McCourt (Flamingo)	212,781	£1,586,463.51
3	*Notes from a Small Island*	Bill Bryson (Black Swan)	177,508	£1,147,328.45
4	*Notes from a Big Country*	Bill Bryson (Black Swan)	133,246	£800,664.22
5	*Georgiana, Duchess of Devonshire*	Amanda Foreman (Flamingo)	107,136	£924,708.75
6	*Driving Over Lemons: An Optimist in Andalucia*	Chris Stewart (Sort of Books)	96,806	£651,274.80
7	*Lillian Too's Little Book of Feng Shui*	Lillian Too (Element Books)	90,051	£179,125.93
8	*Neither Here Nor There*	Bill Bryson (Black Swan)	67,443	£466,897.99
9	*Falling Leaves Return to Their Roots*	Adeline Yen Mah (Penguin)	67,036	£454,654.95
10	*Things Can Only Get Better*	John O'Farrell (Black Swan)	65,047	£448,833.08

Source: Whitaker BookTrack

Top 10 Best-Selling Hardback Non-Fiction Titles of the Year in the UK

1999

Rank	Title	Author (publisher)	Quantity sold	Total value
1	*Guinness World Records: 2000: Millennium Edition*	(Guinness)	364,586	£3,942,404.13
2	*Delia's How to Cook: Book 2*	Delia Smith (BBC)	321,026	£3,632,147.70
3	*Managing My Life: My Autobiography*	Alex Ferguson (Hodder)	194,024	£2,785,866.77
4	*Delia's How to Cook: Book 1*	Delia Smith (BBC)	192,673	£2,135,662.98
5	*'Tis*	Frank McCourt (Flamingo)	121,958	£1,921,328.11
6	*New British Classics*	Gary Rhodes (BBC)	110,167	£1,830,856.07
7	*Naked Chef*	Jamie Oliver (Michael Joseph)	108,590	£1,747,696.07
8	*If Only*	Geri Halliwell (Bantam Press)	105,940	£1,456,994.23
9	*Parcel Arrived Safely: Tied with String*	Michael Crawford (Century Publishing Co)	70,816	£1,052,708.53
10	*The Broons: 2000*	(D C Thomson)	68,124	£318,604.46

Source: Whitaker BookTrack

Top 10 Best-Selling Children's Paperbacks of the Year in the UK

1999

Rank	Title	Author (publisher)	Quantity sold	Total value
1	*Harry Potter and the Philosopher's Stone*	J K Rowling (Bloomsbury)	503,473	£2,457,408.69
2	*Harry Potter and the Chamber of Secrets*	J K Rowling (Bloomsbury)	417,171	£2,034,180.12
3	*Children's Book of Books*	(HarperCollins)	246,049	£227,289.42
4	*Star Wars Episode One: Phantom Menace: a Junior Novelisation*	(Scholastic)	76,519	£377,180.14
5	*Girls in Love*	Jacqueline Wilson (Corgi)	64,437	£255,037.59
6	*Buried Alive!*	Jacqueline Wilson (Yearling)	63,129	£248,385.53
7	*Lottie Project*	Jacqueline Wilson (Yearling)	60,295	£237,209.51
8	*Double Act*	Jacqueline Wilson (Yearling)	57,735	£226,040.19
9	*A Bug's Life: Disney Read-to-me*	(Ladybird Books)	54,073	£107,422.70
10	*A Bug's Life: A Bug's Life Colouring Book*	(Ladybird Books)	53,278	£73,090.80

Source: Whitaker BookTrack

Top 10 Best-Selling Children's Hardbacks of the Year in the UK

1999

Rank	Title	Author (publisher)	Quantity sold	Total value
1	*Harry Potter and the Prisoner of Azkaban*	J K Rowling (Bloomsbury)	343,579	£3,282,128.71
2	*'Beano' Book: 2000*	(D C Thomson)	177,094	£921,206.56
3	*Bug's Life: Book of the Film*	(Ladybird Books)	73,024	£144,924.06
4	*'Dandy' Book: 2000*	(D C Thomson)	71,841	£393,595.50
5	*'Star Wars' Annual: 2000*	(Egmont World)	46,898	£250,214.38
6	*'Rupert' Annual: Number 64, 2000*	I Robinson (Pedigree Books)	45,985	£283,890.09
7	*Spooky Stories: Small Book*	(Mustard)	43,755	£218,326.34
8	*Children's Bedtime Treasury*	(Parragon)	43,239	£215,890.59
9	*Thomas Pocket Library: Volume 2: Photo Mini Board Book Collection*	W Awdry (Heinemann Young Books)	33,330	£99,575.56
10	*Very Hungry Caterpillar*	Eric Carle (Hamish Hamilton)	32,666	£162,790.99

Source: Whitaker BookTrack

Some of the World's Most Reprinted Books

All figures are approximate.
(– = not applicable.)

Title	Author	Number of copies
The Bible	Various translations	over 6,000,000,000
Little Red Book	Mao Zedong (Mao Tse Tung) (1893–1976)	over 800,000,000
Eclectic Readers (*The McGuffey Readers*)	William Holmes McGuffey (1800–1873)	up to 122,000,000
A Grammatical Institute of the English Language (*Webster's Spelling Book*, or *American Spelling Book*)	Noah Webster (1758–1843)	100,000,000
The Guinness Book of Records	–	79,000,000[1]
A Message to Garcia	Elbert Hubbard (1856–1915)	up to 50,000,000
The World Almanac	–	over 40,000,000[1]
The Common Sense Book of Baby and Child Care	Benjamin Spock (1903–1998)	over 39,200,000
The Valley of the Dolls	Jacqueline Susann (*c.* 1926–1974)	30,000,000
In His Steps: What Would Jesus Do?	Charles Monroe Sheldon (1857–1946)	28,500,000

[1] Figures represent aggregate sales of annual publication.

Source: Index Translationem, © *UNESCO*

Some of the World's Most Translated Authors

(– = not applicable.)

Name	Dates
Vladimir Ilyich Lenin	1870–1924
Agatha Christie	1890–1976
Jules Verne	1828–1905
William Shakespeare	1564–1616
Enid Blyton	1897–1968
Leo Nikolaievich Tolstoy	1828–1910
Charles Perrault	1628–1703
Georges Simenon	1903–1989
Karl Marx	1818–1883
Fyodor Mikhailovich Dostoyevsky	1821–1881
Barbara Cartland	1901–2000
Hans Christian Andersen	1805–1875
Jacob and Wilhelm Grimm	1785–1863 and 1786–1859
Konstantin Ustinovich Chernenko	1911–1985
Isaac Asimov	1920–1992
Friedrich Engels	1820–1895
Jack London (John Griffith Chaney)	1876–1916
Arthur Conan Doyle	1859–1930
Mark Twain (Samuel Langhorne Clemens)	1835–1910
Charles Dickens	1812–1870
Robert Louis Stevenson	1850–1894
Graham Greene	1904–1991
Pope John Paul II (Karol Wojtyła)	1920–

Source: Index Translationem, © *UNESCO*

The World's Top 10 Producers of Books

1996

Rank	Country	Number of titles
1	China	110,283
2	UK	107,263
3	Germany	71,515
4	USA	68,175
5	Japan	56,221
6	Spain	46,330
7	Russian Federation	36,237
8	Italy	35,236
9	France	34,766[1]
10	Korea, South	30,487

[1] Figures are for 1995.

Source: UNESCO Statistical Yearbook 1999, © *UNESCO 1999*

See also  **Literature,** pp 758–759.

Libraries

Public Libraries in the UK

Provision of the UK's public library system, inaugurated under the 1850 Public Libraries Act, is a statutory duty of local authorities and boards. The service, incorporating over 4,160 central and branch libraries and over 660 mobile libraries, plays a key role in life-long educational, personal, social, and community development and in the dissemination of news and information. Around 60% of the population are public library members, and over 480 million books are borrowed each year along with over 35 million audio-visual items; in 1999 visiting the library was listed as the UK's 4th most popular pastime.

Funding

Local authorities in the UK spend nearly £820 million annually on the library service, a cost of 26p per person per week.

In March 2000 the new *Comprehensive and Efficient Standards* for public libraries were published by the Department of Culture, Media, and Sport (DCMS) for consultation; suggested measures include that all authorities should spend no less than £2,000 per annum per 1,000 population on new books, and that all authorities should have at least one service point open for 60 or more hours

Public Libraries in the UK (*continued*)

per week, with other major libraries to be open for 45 hours per week.

The People's Network

In 1999 the library service received a cash boost of £200 million from the National Lottery's New Opportunities fund to enable it to complete the People's Network, a scheme that aims to link every public library in the UK electronically by 2002, and which is intended to give libraries access over the Internet to specially created material for their role in supporting lifelong learning. The People's Network will also connect public libraries to the National Grid for Learning (national learning networks using the Internet), and part of the New Opportunities funding will help develop Community Grids for Learning (local learning networks using the Internet). Some libraries, along with schools and colleges, may benefit from a £470 million Capital Modernization Fund initiative to create a network of up to 2,000 Information and Communication Technology (ICT) based learning centres.

Some Library Firsts

- Since 1850 advances in the content, accessibility, and operation of the public library service have far outstripped the imagination of the system's original founders.
- The first public library was opened in Athens in 330 BC.
- In the UK, the first documented free public library was established in Manchester in 1852, after the 1850 Public Library Act.
- The first free, tax-supported library in the USA was opened in Boston in 1854.
- Microfilm was used by public libraries for the first time in 1884.
- The first motorized mobile library service in the UK was launched in 1920 in Perthshire.
- In 1935 Middlesex County Library was the first in the UK to loan gramophone records.
- In 1974 Kentish Town Library became the first in the UK to use a barcode loan system.
- Somerset became the first UK public library with an online catalogue in 1982.
- Marylebone, London, launched its Input Output Centre in 1995 giving public access to the Internet.
- In 1998 Hendon Library opened the UK's first complete library multimedia centre.

150 Years of Public Libraries in the UK

The Public Libraries Act, enabling local councils to provide free public libraries funded by a levy of a 1/2d rate, received royal assent in August 1850. Although its initial provision was limited, the Act established a system that would provide democratic access to a wide range of information for the entire population.

Celebrations spearheaded by the Library Association to mark the 150th anniversary of the Act include a commemorative 50p piece, and a wide range of local, national, and media events, from the opening in May 2000 of Peckham's futuristic, state-of-the-art public library in the London Borough of Southwark, to Wrexham's year-long programme of themed months and activities.

Top 10 Most Borrowed Fiction Titles of the Year in the UK

July 1998–June 1999

Rank	Title	Author	Publisher and year of publication
1	*The Solace of Sin*	Catherine Cookson	Bantam Press, 1998
2	*The Bondage of Love*	Catherine Cookson	Bantam Press, 1997
3	*The Bonny Dawn*	Catherine Cookson	Bantam Press, 1996
4	*The Desert Crop*	Catherine Cookson	Bantam Press, 1997
5	*A Ruthless Need*	Catherine Cookson	Bantam Press, 1995
6	*The Lady on My Left*	Catherine Cookson	Bantam Press, 1997
7	*Justice is a Woman*	Catherine Cookson	Bantam Press, 1994
8	*The Obsession*	Catherine Cookson	Bantam Press, 1995
9	*The Branded Man*	Catherine Cookson	Bantam Press, 1996
10	*10 Lb. Penalty*	Dick Francis	Michael Joseph, 1997

Source: Registrar of Public Lending Right

Top 10 Most Borrowed Non-Fiction Titles in the UK

July 1998–June 1999

Rank	Title	Author	Publisher and year of publication
1	*A Kentish Lad*	Frank Muir	Bantam Press, 1997
2	*Notes from a Small Island*	Bill Bryson	Doubleday, 1995
3	*Immediate Action*	Andy McNab	Bantam Press, 1995
4	*The Official Theory Test for Car Drivers and Motorcyclists*	Driving Standards Agency	Stationery Office, 1998
5	*Delia Smith's Winter Collection*	Delia Smith	BBC Books, 1995
6	*Menopause*	Miriam Stoppard	Dorling Kindersley, 1994
7	*Men are from Mars: Women are from Venus*	John Gray	Thorsons, 1993
8	*The Internet*	Terry Burrows, Brian Cooper, and Simon Collins	Dorling Kindersley, 1996
9	*Wild Swans: Three Daughters of China*	Jung Chang	HarperCollins, 1991
10	*Windows 95 for Dummies*	Andy Rathbone	IDG Books, 1995

Source: Registrar of Public Lending Right

■ Libraries

Top 10 Most Borrowed Children's Non-Fiction Titles in the UK

July 1998–June 1999

Rank	Title	Author/illustrator	Publisher and year of publication
1	*Dark Knights and Dingy Castles*	Terry Deary	Scholastic, 1997
2	*Eyewitness Guide: Ancient Egypt*	George Hart	Dorling Kindersley, 1990
3	*The Groovy Greeks*	Terry Deary	Hippo, 1996
4	*The 20th Century*	Terry Deary	Andre Deutsch, 1996
5	*Cruel Kings and Mean Queens*	Terry Deary	Andre Deutsch, 1995
6	*The Measly Middle Ages*	Terry Deary	Hippo, 1996
7	*The Awesome Egyptians*	Terry Deary	Scholastic, 1993
8	*The Angry Aztecs*	Terry Deary	Hippo, 1997
9	*The Slimy Stuarts*	Terry Deary	Hippo, 1996
10	*Eyewitness Guide: Ancient Rome*	Simon James	Dorling Kindersley, 1990

Source: Registrar of Public Lending Right

Library Loans by Category in the UK

(In percentages.)

Category	1988–89	1998–99
Adult fiction		
General fiction	17.8	22.2
Historical	3.5	2.6
Mystery and detection	12.8	13.0
Horror	0.7	0.4
Science fiction	0.8	0.9
War	1.8	1.3
Humour	0.7	0.2
Light romance	14.1	10.5
Westerns	1.2	0.7
Short stories	0.5	0.2
Adult fiction total	53.9	52.0
Adult non-fiction		
Science and technology	1.3	1.0
History	3.5	2.5
Travel and foreign countries	2.9	2.4
Social sciences	2.5	1.8
Religion	0.9	0.8
Nature and country life	1.5	1.0
Domestic and leisure	4.7	4.0
Health	1.7	1.7
Arts	1.2	0.9
Biography	2.6	2.4
Humour	0.7	0.2
Literature	0.9	0.7
Adult non-fiction total	24.4	19.4
Adult total	78.3	71.4
Children's books		
Children's fiction	17.5	22.2
Children's non-fiction	4.2	6.4
Children's total	21.7	28.6
ALL BOOKS TOTAL	100.0	100.0

Source: Registrar of Public Lending Right

Top 20 Most Borrowed Adult Fiction Authors in the UK

July 1998–June 1999

Rank	Author
1	Catherine Cookson
2	Danielle Steel
3	Dick Francis
4	Josephine Cox
5	Jack Higgins
6	Ruth Rendell
7	Agatha Christie
8	Emma Blair
9	Audrey Howard
10	Terry Pratchett
11	Barbara Taylor Bradford
12	Harry Bowling
13	Patricia Cornwell
14	Maeve Binchy
15	Virginia Andrews
16	Mary Higgins Clark
17	John Grisham
18	Bernard Cornwell
19	Dean R Koontz
20	Mary Jane Staples

Source: Registrar of Public Lending Right

Top 20 Most Borrowed Classic Authors in the UK

July 1998–June 1999

Rank	Author
1	Ernest Hemingway
2	Beatrix Potter
3	A A Milne
4	Daphne Du Maurier
5	J R R Tolkein
6	William Shakespeare
7	Charles Dickens
8	Jane Austen
9	Thomas Hardy
10	Anthony Trollope
11	George Orwell
12	E M Forster
13	C S Forrester
14	Arthur Conan Doyle
15	Rudyard Kipling
16	D H Lawrence
17	Louisa M Alcott
18	John Buchan
19	Edith Nesbit
20	Wilkie Collins

Source: Registrar of Public Lending Right

Top 10 Most Borrowed Children's Fiction Titles in the UK

July 1998–June 1999

Rank	Title	Author/illustrator	Publisher and year of publication
1	*Where's Wally?: The Wonder Book*	Martin Hanford	Walker, 1997
2	*The BFG*	Roald Dahl/Quentin Blake	Puffin, 1984
3	*A Quiet Night In*	Jill Murphy	Walker, 1993
4	*The Witches*	Roald Dahl/Quentin Blake	Puffin, 1985
5	*George's Marvellous Medicine*	Roald Dahl/Quentin Blake	Penguin, 1982
6	*The Twits*	Roald Dahl	Puffin, 1982
7	*Scarecrow Walks at Midnight*	R L Stine	Hippo, 1995
8	*Say Cheese and Die Again*	R L Stine	Hippo, 1997
9	*Ghost Beach*	R L Stine	Hippo, 1996
10	*Egg Monsters from Mars*	R L Stine	Hippo, 1997

Source: Registrar of Public Lending Right

Top 10 Most Borrowed Children's Authors in the UK

July 1998–June 1999

Rank	Author
1	R L Stine
2	Janet and Allan Ahlberg
3	Roald Dahl
4	Enid Blyton
5	Ann M Martin
6	Dick King-Smith
7	Lucy Daniels
8	John Cunliffe
9	Mick Inkpen
10	Eric Hill

Source: Registrar of Public Lending Right

Copyright Libraries in the UK and Ireland

Under copyright laws, UK publishers are required to deliver one free copy of every book published (including sheet music and maps) to the British Library. The other copyright libraries have the right to request a free copy of any book within 12 months of its publication.

British Library Board Headquarters, British Library, 96 Euston Road, London NW1 2DB; phone: (020) 7412 7332 (visitor enquiries), (020) 7412 7000 (switchboard); fax: (020) 7412 7609; e-mail: reader-services-enquiries@bl.uk; Web site: www.bl.uk

Bodleian Library University of Oxford, Broad Street, Oxford OX1 3BG; phone: (01865) 277000 (enquiries), (01865) 277182 (administration); fax: (01865) 277182; e-mail: enquiries@bodley.ox.ac.uk; Web site: www.bodley.ox.ac.uk

University Library University of Cambridge, West Road, Cambridge CB3 9DR; phone: (01223) 333000; fax: (01223) 333160; e-mail: library@ula.cam.ac.uk; Web site: www.lib.cam.ac.uk/libraries

National Library of Scotland George IV Bridge, Edinburgh EH1 1EW; phone: (0131) 226 4531; fax: (0131) 620 6662; e-mail: enquiries@nls.uk; Web site: www.nls.uk

Trinity College Dublin Library College Street, Dublin 2, Republic of Ireland; phone: +353 (1) 608 1127 (general enquiries), +353 (1) 608 1661 (librarian's office); fax: +353 (1) 671 9003; e-mail: library@tcd.ie; Web site: www.tcd.ie/library

National Library of Wales: Llyfrgell Genedlaethol Cymru Aberystwyth, Ceredigion SY23 3BU; phone: (01970) 632800; fax: (01970) 615709; e-mail: holi@llgc.org.uk; Web site: www.llgc.org.uk

Advertising

Advertising Expenditure in the UK

Advertising expenditure in the UK has increased by over 40% since 1990. In 1999 it was almost £1 billion more than in 1998, exceeding £15 billion for the first time. At 1.95%, advertising also accounted for its highest-ever share of Gross Value Added (formerly GDP) in 1999. Online companies spent more than £150 million on advertising in traditional media in 1999 – three times that spent in 1998.

Advertising Expenditure in the UK by Media Sector

(In billions of pounds at current prices.)

1999

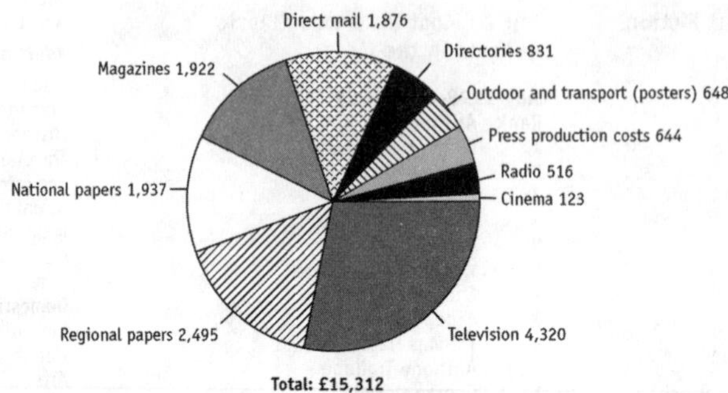

Source: Advertising Association

The Rise of Advertising Expenditure in the UK

(In billions of pounds at current prices).

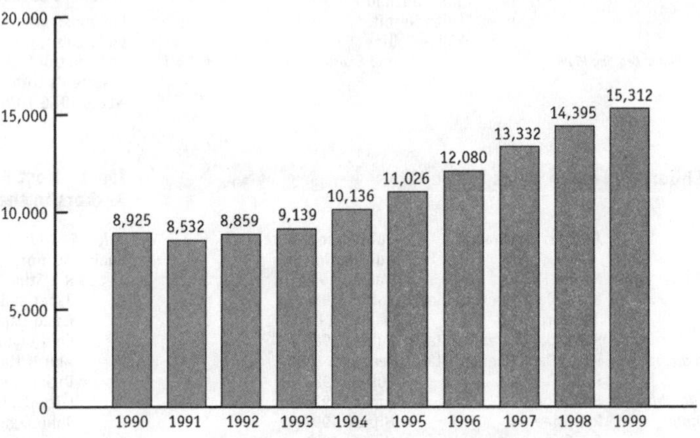

Source: Advertising Association

Advertising Firsts

The first known printed advertisement is a handbill produced in 1478 by the English printer Caxton to advertise his book *Salisbury Pye*.

One of the first recorded advertisements for a commodity was for tea, and appeared in the *Publick Adviser* of September 1658. It read: That excellent, and by all Physitians approved China drink, called by the Chineans, Tcha, by other nations Tay alias Tee, is sold at the Sultaness-Head, a Cophee-house in Sweetings Rents by the Royal Exchange, London.

Top 10 TV Adverts of All Time

The table presents results of a survey carried out in March 2000 by *The Sunday Times* and Channel 4, which invited readers and viewers to vote for 'the best advertisement of all time'.

Rank	Advertisement	Year
1	Guinness: Horses and Surfers	1999
2	Smash: Martians	1973
3	Tango: Orange Man	1992
4	Electricity Association: Heat (Creature Comforts)	1992
5	Boddingtons: Ice Cream	1997
6	Levi's Launderette	1985
7	R Whites: Secret Lemonade Drinker	1972
8	Hamlet: Photo Booth	1986
9	Walker's Crisps: Gary Lineker	1993
10	Impulse: Chance Encounter	1998

Top 20 Advertisers by Spend Across All Media in the UK

Figures include press, television, radio, cinema, and outdoor. Outdoor excludes tobacco advertising and 'moving transport advertising'.

1999

Rank	Company	Amount (£)
1	Procter & Gamble Ltd	165,367,025
2	Central Office of Information	92,466,215
3	Renault UK Ltd	84,453,509
4	British Telecom Ltd	84,422,805
5	L'Oréal Golden Ltd	67,085,354
6	Mars Confectionery	63,628,997
7	Ford Motor Company Ltd	57,274,102
8	Kellogg Company of GB Ltd	53,062,378
9	Elida Fabergé Ltd	52,432,104
10	Lever Brothers Ltd	50,315,549
11	One2One Communications	49,319,212
12	Peugeot Motor Company plc	47,624,692
13	Rover Group Ltd	44,547,881
14	McDonald's Restaurants Ltd	42,404,799
15	BT Cellnet	36,145,904
16	Nestlé Rowntree Division	36,043,595
17	DFS Northern Upholstery	35,011,994
18	British Gas plc	34,966,809
19	Orange plc	34,744,825
20	Pedigree Masterfoods	34,452,897

Source: ACNielsen MMS, 2000

Top 20 Brands by Advertising Spend Across All Media in the UK

Figures include press, television, radio, cinema, and outdoor. Excludes outdoor tobacco advertising and 'moving transport advertising'.

1999

Rank	Brand	Amount (£)
1	McDonald's	42,367,671
2	ONdigital	33,425,024
3	Sainsbury's	29,114,944
4	One2One Phone Network	27,920,252
5	B&Q	26,188,451
6	Time Computers	25,030,998
7	PC World	24,917,092
8	DFS	21,571,283
9	Renault (Megane/Megane range)	21,372,380
10	Homebase	20,621,740
11	Curry's	19,299,497
12	Tesco	18,144,635
13	Tiny Computers	17,786,966
14	Vauxhall (Zafira range)	16,526,557
15	Royal Mail	16,423,812
16	Asda	16,004,149
17	Guinness	15,974,366
18	British Gas	15,658,887
19	Renault (Clio/Clio range)	15,558,386
20	Rover (75)	14,922,747

Source: ACNielsen MMS, 2000

Top 10 Advertising Agencies in the UK

1999

Rank	Agency	Billings (£ in millions)
1	BMP DDB Ltd	440.00
2	Abbott Mead Vickers BBDO Ltd	399.00
3	Grey Advertising Ltd	390.00
4	Saatchi & Saatchi	354.62
5	Lowe Lintas	325.00
6	WWAV Rapp Collins	319.61
7	McCann-Erickson London	305.00
8	TBWA GGT Simons Palmer	300.00
9	J Walter Thompson Company Ltd	280.92
10	Publicis Ltd	260.00

Source: Advertisers Annual *(Hollis Directories) (020) 8977 7711*

Advertising Standards and Complaints

The British Codes of Advertising and Sales Promotion

The rules laid down in the British Codes of Advertising and Sales Promotion are designed to protect the consumer from being misled or offended. The basic principles of the Codes are that advertisements should be:

- legal, decent, honest and truthful
- prepared with a sense of responsibility to consumers and to society
- in line with the principles of fair competition generally accepted in business.

Advertising in the press and other non-broadcast media

- The Advertising Standards Authority (ASA) was set up in 1962 to enforce the British Codes of Advertising and Sales Promotion in non-broadcast media. This includes:
- press (national, regional, magazines, and free newspapers)
- screen (cinema commercials and advertisements in electronic media such as computer games, video, viewdata services, CD-ROM, and Internet)
- outdoor (posters, transport, and aerial announcements)
- direct marketing (direct mail, leaflets, brochures, catalogues, circulars, inserts, and facsimiles)
- sales promotions (on-pack promotions, reader offers, competitions, and prize draws)

The Advertising Standards Authority resolved 12,141 complaints relating to 8,617 advertisements during 1999. A total of 851 – just under 10% of the total – were found to break the codes. Of the total number resolved, about 12% related to ten advertisements.

Television advertising

The Division of Advertising and Sponsorship Regulation of the Independent Television Commission (ITC) is responsible for regulating advertising and programme sponsorship on commercial television according to an agreed set of codes.

After a continuous steep rise in the number of complaints submitted to the ITC since 1994, the overall number of complaints received in 1999 fell by 7% to 6,700 compared with 1998. A total of 113 advertisements had complaints upheld against them (5% of those about which viewers had complained and about 0.4% of all commercials shown during 1999).

Whilst the number of people claiming to have been offended by an advertisement fell by nearly 30% in 1999, 32% more people claimed to have been misled by a television advertisement than in 1998, and the number of complaints about the possible harmful effects of advertisements rose by 21%.

Radio

The Radio Authority, a statutory body established by the government, has been responsible for regulating advertising on UK commercial radio since 1991.

How to complain

Complaints about a UK non-broadcast advertisement should be submitted in writing to the ASA at the address on the next page, with details of the complaint and a copy of the advertisement if possible. Complaints may also be submitted via the complaints form on the ASA Web site (www.asa.org.uk).

(continued)

Advertising Standards and Complaints *(continued)*

The Advertising Standards Authority Complaints Team, 2 Torrington Place, London WC1E 7HW; phone: (020) 7580 5555; fax: (020) 7631 3051

Complaints about an advertisement shown on commercial television in the UK may be submitted directly to the television company concerned or to one of the national or regional offices of the ITC. Complaints may also be submitted via the complaints form on the ITC Web site (www.itc.org.uk). Further information can be obtained from the Web site or from the ITC's head office:

ITC Head Office 33 Foley Street, London W1P 7LB; phone: (020) 7255 3000; fax: (020) 7306 7800

Complaints about an advertisement that appeared on radio in the UK should be submitted to:

The Radio Authority Holbrook House, 14 Great Queen Street, Holborn, London WC2B 5DG; phone: (020) 7430 2724; fax: (020) 7405 7062

Complaints about advertising that has appeared outside the UK should be directed to the advertising regulator of the country concerned – further details may be obtained from:

The European Advertising Standards Alliance 10a Rue de la Pépinière, B-1000 Brussels, Belgium; phone: +32 (2) 523 78 06; fax: +32 (2) 153 28 61

Complaints About Television Advertising in the UK

1999

Complaint	Number of complaints	Number of advertisements	Number of advertisements about which complaints were upheld wholly or in part
Misleading	2,074	967	72
Offensive	3,092	603	9
Harmful	1,213	419	9
Miscellaneous	464	177	23
Total	6,843	2,166	113

Source: Independent Television Commission

Films and Videos

New Initiatives in the Film Industry

At the end of the 1990s, certain sectors of the UK film industry were thriving: construction of multiplex cinema sites progressed, with 98 multi-screen centres due for completion 1999–2001, and the UK's film services industry continued to attract UK and overseas contracts, particularly in the fields of digital technology and computer-generated special effects. However, despite lottery funding and tax incentives, the UK film production industry was stagnating under a preponderance of low-budget, poor-quality films. The UK audience for British films declined from 23% to 14% during 1997–99 and less than 10% of lottery funding was recouped at the box-office.

The Film Council

On 1 April 2000 UK film production and its public funding were given a radical shake-up and new commercial edge with the launch of the Film Council, a government-sponsored body to develop film culture, restructure the industry, and distribute lottery film funding. Its £22 million package of initiatives included £10 million to support 'popular, mainstream' films, £4.2 million for European co-productions, £5 million for avant-garde film-making, and £5 million for the development of screenplays – the largest fund of its type in Europe. The British Film Institute's annual grant was set at £16 million to facilitate the Council's objectives for film culture and education.

Worldwide developments

Developments in the industry worldwide included the growth of the rental première (films going straight to video or satellite movie channels), and films made specially for video – Disney has set up a studio for its video-only sequels. Film distribution has been further revolutionized by the Internet, with dedicated Web sites streaming home-made animations and digital shorts. In January 2000 MGM and Blockbuster announced their joint development of a system for the digital streaming and downloading of films on the Web, a move that may supersede traditional video rental. Technological advances and cheaper equipment have also opened the industry to a new set of film-makers, bypassing traditional studio production; in 1999 *The Blair Witch Project*, a $30,000 film shot on digital video cameras and hyped on the Internet, became the most profitable film of all time.

Trends in Cinema-Going in the UK

Year	Total admissions (millions)[1]
1983	64
1984	54
1985	70
1986	73
1987	75
1988	78
1989	88
1990	89
1991	93
1992	98
1993	113
1994	124
1995	115
1996	123
1997	139
1998	131
1999	139

[1] Admissions figures are for those cinemas taking advertising.

Source: The Cinema Advertising Association/ACNielsen EDI

Top 20 Grossing Films of All Time at the Worldwide Box Office

Total box office figures given include theatrical box office receipts and do not include video rentals, television rights, and other revenues. Totals may include theatrical re-release receipts. Figures are not adjusted for inflation, and all are estimated and subject to change.

Rank	Film	Total box office ($)
1	*Titanic (1997)*	1,835,300,000
2	*Star Wars: Episode I – The Phantom Menace (1999)*	923,000,000
3	*Jurassic Park (1993)*	919,700,000
4	*Independence Day (1996)*	810,400,000
5	*Star Wars (1977)*	780,000,000
6	*The Lion King (1994)*	766,700,000
7	*ET the Extra-Terrestrial (1982)*	704,800,000
8	*Forrest Gump (1994)*	679,400,000
9	*The Sixth Sense (1999)*	660,700,000
10	*The Lost World: Jurassic Park (1997)*	614,300,000
11	*Men in Black (1997)*	586,200,000
12	*Armageddon (1998)*	554,400,000
13	*The Empire Strikes Back (1980)*	533,800,000
14	*Home Alone (1990)*	533,700,000
15	*Ghost (1990)*	517,600,000
16	*Terminator 2: Judgment Day (1991)*	516,800,000
17	*Indiana Jones and the Last Crusade (1989)*	494,700,000
18	*Twister (1996)*	493,200,000
19	*Toy Story 2 (1999)*	482,300,000
20	*Saving Private Ryan (1998)*	479,300,000

Source: © 1990–2000 The Internet Movie Database Ltd (an amazon.com company)

Top 20 Films at the UK Box Office

This ranking includes films released in the UK between 1 January 1999 and 30 December 1999.

Rank	Title	Distributor	Box office (£)
1	*Star Wars: Episode I The Phantom Menace*	Twentieth Century Fox	51,031,269
2	*Notting Hill*	Universal Pictures	31,006,109
3	*A Bug's Life*	Buena Vista	29,425,409
4	*The World is Not Enough*	UIP	28,576,504
5	*Austin Powers 2*	Entertainment	25,772,822
6	*The Sixth Sense*	Buena Vista	25,688,864
7	*Shakespeare in Love*	UIP	20,805,890
8	*Tarzan*	Buena Vista	18,041,615
9	*The Mummy*	UIP	17,796,828
10	*The Matrix*	Warner	17,285,889
11	*The Blair Witch Project*	Pathé Distribution Ltd	14,988,404
12	*American Pie*	UIP	13,998,175
13	*The Rugrats Movie*	UIP	13,543,471
14	*East is East*	Film Four Distribution	10,355,621
15	*Little Voice*	Buena Vista	8,495,496
16	*Inspector Gadget*	Buena Vista	8,460,402
17	*Deep Blue Sea*	Warner	8,148,636
18	*Star Trek: Insurrection*	UIP	7,656,690
19	*Runaway Bride*	Buena Vista	7,567,030
20	*Waking Ned*	Twentieth Century Fox	7,055,261

Source: ACNielsen EDI

Top 10 Video Rentals in the UK

1999

Rank	Title	Distributor
1	*There's Something About Mary*	Fox Pathé
2	*Armageddon*	Buena Vista
3	*Saving Private Ryan*	CIC
4	*Enemy of the State*	Buena Vista
5	*Lock, Stock & Two Smoking Barrels*	Universal
6	*Blade*	EV
7	*Lethal Weapon 4*	Warner
8	*The Truman Show*	CIC
9	*Payback*	Warner
10	*Dr Dolittle*	Fox Pathé

Source: © MRIB, 2000

See also Film and Theatre, pp 747–753.

Top 10 Retail Videos in the UK

1999

Rank	Title	Label
1	*A Bug's Life*	Walt Disney
2	*The Lion King II – Simba's Pride*	Walt Disney
3	*The Matrix*	Warner Home Video
4	*Notting Hill*	Universal Pictures
5	*Saving Private Ryan*	Paramount Home Entertainment
6	*Lock, Stock & Two Smoking Barrels*	Universal Pictures
7	*Mulan*	Walt Disney
8	*Antz*	Dreamworks
9	*Dr Dolittle*	Fox Video
10	*Flubber*	Walt Disney

Source: © Chart Information Network, 2000

Art, Museums, and Galleries

Top 10 Most Popular Art Exhibitions Around the World

Rankings are for total, not daily, attendance figures.

1993–99

Rank	Name	Museum and date	Total attendance number
1	Cézanne to Matisse: Paintings from the Barnes Foundation	Musée d'Orsay, Paris (8 September 1993–2 January 1994)	1,500,000
2	Claude Monet: 1840–1926	Art Institute of Chicago (22 July–26 November 1995)	964,895
3	Van Gogh's Van Goghs	Los Angeles County Museum, Los Angeles (17 January–16 May 1999)	821,004

(continued)

Top 10 Most Popular Art Exhibitions Around the World (*continued*)

Rank	Name	Museum and date	Total attendance number
4	The Origins of Impressionism	Metropolitan Museum of Modern Art, New York (27 September 1994–8 January 1995)	794,108
5	Monet in the 20th Century	Royal Academy, London (23 January–18 April 1999)	739,324
6	Flemish Artists in Rome: 1508–1608	Palais des Beaux-Arts, Brussels (24 February–21 May 1995)	675,658
7	Treasures from Mount Athos	Museum of Byzantine Culture, Thessaloniki (21 June 1997–30 April 1998)	675,208
8	Richard Serra	Bilbao Guggenheim, Bilbao (30 March–17 October 1999)	675,071
9	The Greeks in the West	Palazzo Grassi, Venice (24 May–8 December 1996)	600,000
10	Monet in the 20th Century	Museum of Fine Arts, Boston (20 September–27 December 1998)	565,992

Source: The Art Newspaper *(London and New York)*

Top 10 Most Popular Art Exhibitions in the UK

Rankings are for total, not daily attendance figures, and include only exhibitions for which an entrance fee was levied.

1994–99

Rank	Name	Museum and date	Total attendance
1	Monet in the 20th Century	Royal Academy, London (23 January–18 April 1999)	739,324
2	Cézanne	Tate Gallery, London (8 February–28 April 1996)	408,688
3	Picasso: Sculptor-Painter	Tate Gallery, London (16 February–8 May 1994)	296,648
4	Sensation: Young British Artists	Royal Academy, London (18 September–28 December 1997)	285,737
5	Degas: Beyond Impressionism	National Gallery, London (22 May–26 August 1996)	283,000
6	Bonnard	Tate Gallery, London (12 February–17 May 1998)	276,202
7	From Manet to Gaugin: Impressionism and Post-Impressionism from Swiss Private Collections	Royal Academy, London (30 June–8 October 1995)	253,221
8	Van Dyck 1599–1641	Royal Academy, London (11 September–10 December 1999)	250,703
9	Africa: The Art of a Continent	Royal Academy, London (4 October 1995–21 January 1996)	250,280
10	The Glory of Venice	Royal Academy, London (15 September–14 December 1994)	230,279

Source: The Art Newspaper *(London and New York)*

Tate Modern

The UK's new national museum of international modern art from 1900 to the present day, housed in London's former Bankside Power Station, Southwark, was opened under the directorship of Nicholas Serota on 12 May 2000. A Millennium Project funded by the National Lottery, the £134 million transformation of Giles Gilbert Scott's original structure, designed in 1947, was achieved by Swiss architects Herzog & de Meuron, to accommodate a collection that had been kept mainly in storage at the Tate Gallery, Millbank (now Tate Britain). The collection is innovatively displayed in four themed groups – Landscape/Matter/Environment, Still Life/Object/Real Life, The Nude/Action/Body, and History/Memory/Society – allowing an unusual juxtaposition of works. Artists represented include Bacon, Dalí, Braque, Picasso, Matisse, Monet, Rothko, and Warhol, along with contemporary names such as Damien Hirst, Gillian Wearing, and Steve McQueen. *See also* **colour section.**

Top 10 Highest Prices Paid for Oil Paintings Sold at Auction

As of May 2000.

Rank	Work	Artist	Place and date of sale	Price ($)
1	*Portrait du Dr Gachet*	Vincent van Gogh	Christie's, New York, 15 May 1990	75,000,000
2	*Au Moulin de la Galette*	Pierre-Auguste Renoir	Sotheby's, New York, 17 May 1990	71,000,000
3	*Portrait de l'artiste sans barbe*	Vincent van Gogh	Christie's, New York, 19 November 1998	65,000,000
4	*Rideau, cruchon et compotier*	Paul Cézanne	Sotheby's, New York, 10 May 1999	55,000,000
5	*Les noces de Pierette*	Pablo Picasso	Binoche et Godeau, Paris, 30 November 1989	51,671,920
6	*Irises*	Vincent van Gogh	Sotheby's, New York, 11 November 1987	49,000,000
7	*Femme assise dans un jardin*	Pablo Picasso	Sotheby's, New York, 10 November 1999	45,000,000
8	*Le Rêve*	Pablo Picasso	Christie's, New York, 10 November 1997	44,000,000
9	*Self Portrait: Yo Picasso*	Pablo Picasso	Christie's, New York, 9 May 1989	43,500,000
10	*Nu au fauteuil noir*	Pablo Picasso	Christie's, Rockefeller, New York, 9 November 1999	41,000,000

Source: Art Sales Index Ltd

The Lowry

The first purpose-built cultural centre in the UK to integrate the visual and performing arts opened at Salford Quays, on the Manchester Ship Canal on 28 April 2000. Named after local artist L S Lowry, celebrated for his scenes of northern industrial life peopled by 'matchstick men', it features a study centre and gallery housing the city of Salford's extensive collection of his work. It also houses temporary exhibition galleries; Artworks, an interactive creative attraction; the Lyric Theatre, with the largest stage in England oustide London; a 466-seat flexible theatre, and shops, restaurants, and bars. The £106 million complex, an irregular oval structure of shimmering stainless steel and glass designed by Michael Wilford, will be linked by footbridge to the Imperial War Museum North across the canal.

The centre is a National Landmark Millennium Project for the Arts, financed by such bodies as the National Lottery Fund, Arts Council, and European Regional Development Fund as part of a programme for the economic regeneration of the docks area of Salford.

See also **Major Millennium Commission Projects in the UK**, p 97; **colour section.**

See also **Art and Architecture,** pp 763–764.

Art, Museums, and Galleries

Made-to-Order Theft – The Art World's Worst Nightmare

by Anna Farkas

Introduction The daring 'made-to-order' art theft that has plagued the art world over the years, often the work of a professional thief hired to steal a particular work, has become a billion-dollar industry linked to drugs cartels and illicit arms dealing. Stolen artworks are easy to transport around the world and have become a very valuable commodity in the hands of criminal organizations where, as well as being a means of laundering money, they can be traded as collateral in making deals with one another.

The Master Criminal The theft of a $4.8 million Cézanne from the Ashmolean Museum in Oxford, England, on New Year's Day 2000 was believed to be another incident in this underworld trade in stolen art, now estimated to be worth more than £3 billion a year. The oil on canvas, *Auvers-sur-Oise*, was painted between 1879 and 1882 and marked an important transition between Paul Cézanne's early and later work. The thief, striking at 1.30 a.m., apparently clambered over the rooftops of other university buildings before reaching the museum. He then reportedly smashed a skylight and lowered himself down a rope, before tossing a smoke canister onto the floor of the Hindley Smith Gallery. The room was instantly filled with smoke, obscuring the view from the security cameras. Less than 10 minutes later the intruder, carrying the Cézanne, slipped out of the Ashmolean Museum and quickly blended into the crowds celebrating the new year around the city.

The Criminals' Masters According to experts there is virtually no chance of the Cézanne coming on the legitimate market without being identified as a stolen work. Not only is it listed on the databases of stolen art that auction houses and dealers consult every time an important new item comes up for sale, but it is also immediately identifiable as the Ashmolean's. The painting could pass from hand to hand in the vast art underworld, where it could be sold for a fraction of its value until it finally emerges, years later, in a legitimate sale. Art crime specialists have emphasized how art and cultural property crime has become inextricably connected to organized crime. Groups as diverse as the US, Italian, and Russian mafia, the IRA, and Colombian cocaine cartels have been identified as being involved. Investigators believe that the J M W Turner masterpieces *Shade and Darkness: The Evening of the Deluge and Light* and *Colour: The Morning After the Deluge*, stolen from the Frankfurt gallery Schirn Kunsthalle in 1994, have passed on to Serbian gangsters connected to Balkan war criminals, and that the paintings were being used as collateral for drug deals – particularly as a £160,000 reward for their return has been ignored; many of the gangs operating in Frankfurt and the north of Germany have Serbian connections.

Lost and Found Thousands of institutions and private art collectors have been successfully struck by art thieves in the last several decades. There have been a spate of raids on British art collections, in which the total value of art and antiques being stolen is estimated at £300–500 million each year. The Art Loss Register and the Thesaurus Group, organizations that track down stolen art and antiquities, each has a database of more than 100,000 missing items ranging from the smallest antiques of sentimental value to the biggest of old masters. These include items taken in general burglaries, not just works targeted by art thieves. The international police organization Interpol has about 14,000 major art works on its files that are missing around the world. According to the Art Loss Register, among the missing are 47 works by Edgar Degas, 54 by Auguste Rodin, 142 by Rembrandt, 355 by Pablo Picasso, 271 by Joan Miró, and 250 by Marc Chagall. One of the most shocking art thefts of the last decade took place in 1990, when two men dressed as policemen talked their way into the Isabella Stewart Gardner Museum in Boston in the middle of the night, bound and gagged the guards, and left with a treasure trove of items, including *The Concert* by Jan Vermeer and Rembrandt's *Storm on the Sea of Galilee*. The stolen works worth £130 million, which were uninsured, have not been recovered. Another sensational art raid occurred at Stockholm's Museum of Modern Art in 1993, when thieves copied Jules Dassin's film *Rififi* (1954) in which the gangsters cut through a roof to steal jewellery. They stole six works by Picasso (three of which were recovered a month later) and two by Georges Braque, the whole totalling more than £40 million. Although some works are never recovered, others reappear in the legitimate market after five to seven years. Some paintings have been recovered after the thieves demanded a ransom, as in the case of Edvard Munch's *Scream* (1893), which was stolen from the National Gallery in Oslo in 1994 by intruders who propped a ladder against a wall, smashed a window, and reportedly left a note saying, 'Thanks for the poor security'. The painting was recovered when the police foiled the ransom plot. There has also been the occasional happy ending. In 1991 two thieves broke into the Van Gogh Museum in Amsterdam and stole 20 paintings. The works, worth an estimated £320 million, were recovered less than an hour later by police who found them in a car near a railway station.

Top 10 Highest Prices Paid for Sculptures Sold at Auction

As of May 2000.

Rank	Work	Artist	Place and date of sale	Price ($)
1	*Petite danseuse de quatorze ans*	Edgar Degas	Sotheby's, New York, 11 November 1999	11,250,000
2	*Petite danseuse de quatorze ans* (resold later, see above)	Edgar Degas	Sotheby's, New York, 12 November 1996	10,800,000
3	*The dancing faun*	Adriaen de Vries	Sotheby's, London, 7 December 1989	9,796,000
4	*Petite danseuse de quatorze ans* (resold later, see above)	Edgar Degas	Christie's, New York, 14 November 1988	9,250,000
5	*Petite danseuse de quatorze ans* (resold later, see above)	Edgar Degas	Sotheby's, New York, 10 May 1988	9,200,000

(*continued*)

Top 10 Highest Prices Paid for Sculptures Sold at Auction (*continued*)

Rank	Work	Artist	Place and date of sale	Price ($)
6	*Nu couche, Aurore*	Henri Matisse	Christie's, Rockefeller, New York, 9 November 1999	8,400,000
7	*La negresse blonde*	Constantin Brancusi	Sotheby's, New York, 16 May 1990	8,000,000
8	*La muse endormie III*	Constantin Brancusi	Christie's, New York, 14 November 1989	7,500,000
9	*La forêt-sept figures et une tête*	Alberto Giacometti	Sotheby's, New York, 16 November 1998	6,800,000
10	*Mlle Pogany II*	Constantin Brancusi	Christie's, New York, 14 May 1997	6,400,000

Source: Art Sales Index Ltd

Top 5 Highest Prices Paid for Paintings at Auction by Living Artists

As of May 2000.

Rank	Work	Artist	Place and date of sale	Price ($)
1	*False start*	Jasper Johns	Sotheby's, New York, 10 November 1988	15,500,000
2	*Rebus*	Robert Rauschenberg	Sotheby's, New York, 30 April 1991	6,600,000
3	*Large interior, W11*	Lucian Freud	Sotheby's, New York, 14 April 1998	5,300,000
4	*Untitled*	Cy Twombly	Sotheby's, New York, 8 May 1990	5,000,000
5	*Tomlinson Court Park*	Frank Stella	Sotheby's, New York, 8 November 1989	4,600,000

Source: Art Sales Index Ltd

Top 10 Single-Owner Art Sales

As of May 2000.

Rank	Collection	Place and date of sale	Price (£)
1	The collection of Victor and Sally Ganz	Christie's, New York, 10 November 1997	111,022,783
2	Impressionist and modern art from the collection of Mr and Mrs John Whitney	Sotheby's, New York, 10 May 1999	71,943,825
3	John T Dorrance's collection of oil paintings and watercolours	Sotheby's, New York, 18 October 1989	70,624,937
4	Paintings and watercolours from Madame Bourdon's collection	Guy Loudmer, Paris, 25 March 1990	61,843,177
5	The collection of John and Frances L Loeb	Christie's, New York, 12 May 1997	51,714,727
6	The Reader's Digest collection	Sotheby's, New York, 16 November 1999	47,659,396
7	The collection of Lydia Winston Malbin	Sotheby's, New York, 16 May 1990	39,684,024
8	The collection of Eleanore and Daniel Saidenberg	Sotheby's, New York, 10 November 1999	39,537,887
9	Jaime Ortiz-Patino's collection of Impressionist paintings	Sotheby's, New York, 9 May 1989	37,834,358
10	Impressionist and modern paintings and sculpture, the Stralem collection	Sotheby's, New York, 8 May 1995	37,703,822

Source: Art Sales Index Ltd

Top 10 Highest Prices Paid for Books and Manuscripts Sold at Auction

As of May 2000.

Rank	Work	Place and date of sale	Price ($)
1	*The Codex Leicester*, Leonardo da Vinci's autographed manuscript with drawings and diagrams	Christie's, New York, 11 November 1994	30,802,500
2	*The Rothschild Prayerbook*, illuminated manuscript	Christie's, London, 8 July 1999	13,400,000[1]
3	*The Gospels of Henry the Lion*, 12th-century illuminated manuscript on vellum with 31 full-page miniatures	Sotheby's, London, 6 December 1983	11,000,920
4	John James Audubon's *The Birds of America* (1827–38)	Christie's London, 10 March 2000	8,800,000[2]
5	Chaucer's *Canterbury Tales* (printed by William Caxton *c.* 1476)	Christie's, London, 8 July 1998	7,565,396
6	*The Northumberland Bestiary* (*c.*1250–60)	Sotheby's, London, 29 November 1990	5,900,000
7	*The Gutenberg Bible* (1455)	Christie's, New York, 22 October 1987	5,390,000
8	*The Cornaro Missal* (*c.*1503)	Christie's, London, 8 July 1999	4,461,078
9	Autographed manuscript of nine symphonies by Wolfgang Amadeus Mozart (*c.*1773–74)	Sotheby's, London, 22 May 1987	4,316,950
10	John James Audubon's *The Birds of America* (1827–38) (resold later, see above)	Sotheby's, New York, 6 June 1989	3,960,000

[1] This was a record price for an illuminated manuscript.
[2] This was a record price for any printed book.

Data from Christie's and Sotheby's

Music, Theatre, and Dance

Music

Top 40 Singles of the Year in the UK

1999

Rank	Title	Artist (label)
1	'Baby One More Time'	Britney Spears (Jive)
2	'Blue (Da Ba Dee)'	Eiffel 65 (Eternal)
3	'The Millennium Prayer'	Cliff Richard (Papillon)
4	'Mambo No 5 (A Little Bit of ...)'	Lou Bega (RCA)
5	'9 PM (Till I Come)'	ATB (Ministry of Sound)

(*continued*)

Top 40 Singles of the Year in the UK *(continued)*

Rank	Title	Artist (label)
6	'Livin' La Vida Loca'	Ricky Martin (Columbia)
7	'That Don't Impress Me Much'	Shania Twain (Mercury)
8	'Sweet Like Chocolate'	Shanks & Bigfoot (Pepper)
9	'Flat Beat'	Mr Oizo (F Communications)
10	'When the Going Gets Tough'	Boyzone (Polydor)
11	'Bring It All Back'	S Club 7 (Polydor)
12	'Better Off Alone'	Alice Deejay (Positiva)
13	'Genie in a Bottle'	Christina Aguilera (RCA)
14	'Perfect Moment'	Martine McCutcheon (Innocent)
15	'Boom, Boom, Boom, Boom!!'	Vengaboys (Positiva)
16	'No Scrubs'	TLC (Laface)
17	'If I Could Turn Back the Hands of Time'	R Kelly (Jive)
18	'When You Say Nothing At All'	Ronan Keating (Polydor)
19	'Heartbeat/Tragedy'	Steps (Jive)
20	'I Try'	Macy Gray (Epic)
21	'2 Times'	Ann Lee (Neo/Systematic)
22	'My Love Is Your Love'	Whitney Houston (Arista)
23	'Beautiful Stranger'	Madonna (Maverick)
24	'Turn Around'	Phats & Small (Multiply)
25	'It's Not Right But It's OK'	Whitney Houston (Arista)
26	'I Have a Dream/Seasons in the Sun'	Westlife (RCA)
27	'Witch Doctor'	Cartoons (EMI)
28	'King of my Castle'	Wamdue Project (AM:PM)
29	'We Like to Party! (The Vengabus)'	Vengaboys (Positiva)
30	'Pretty Fly (For a White Guy)'	Offspring (Columbia)
31	'Everybody's Free (To Wear Sunscreen)'	Baz Luhrmann (EMI)
32	'Wild Wild West'	Will Smith (Columbia)
33	'Sometimes'	Britney Spears (Jive)
34	'Maria'	Blondie (RCA/Beyond)
35	'I Want It That Way'	Backstreet Boys (Jive)
36	'Keep on Movin''	Five (RCA)
37	'Re-Rewind the Crowd Say Bo Selecta'	Artful Dodger (Relent/Public Demand)
38	'We're Going to Ibiza!'	Vengaboys (Positiva)
39	'Tender'	Blur (Food)
40	'You Get What You Give'	New Radicals (MCA)

Source: Chart Information Network, 2000

Top 40 Albums of the Year in the UK

1999

Rank	Title	Artist (label)
1	*Come On Over*	Shania Twain (Mercury)
2	*By Request*	Boyzone (Polydor)
3	*The Man Who*	Travis (Independiente)
4	*Gold – Greatest Hits*	Abba (Polydor)
5	*Performance and Cocktails*	Stereophonics (V2)
6	*I've Been Expecting You*	Robbie Williams (Chrysalis)
7	*Steptacular*	Steps (Jive)
8	*Talk on Corners*	Corrs (Atlantic)
9	*Westlife*	Westlife (RCA)
10	*On How Life Is*	Macy Gray (Epic)
11	*The Hush*	Texas (Mercury)
12	*All the Way ... A Decade of Song*	Céline Dion (Epic)
13	*You've Come a Long Way, Baby*	Fatboy Slim (Skint)
14	*Baby One More Time*	Britney Spears (Jive)
15	*My Love Is Your Love*	Whitney Houston (Arista)
16	*Step One*	Steps (Jive)
17	*The Miseducation of Lauryn Hill*	Lauryn Hill (Columbia)
18	*Songs from the Last Century*	George Michael (Virgin)
19	*Forgiven, Not Forgotten*	Corrs (Atlantic)
20	*The Party Album!*	Vengaboys (Positiva)
21	*S Club*	S Club 7 (Polydor)
22	*Ladies and Gentlemen – The Best of*	George Michael (Epic)
23	*Reload*	Tom Jones (Gut)
24	*Synkronized*	Jamiroquai (Sony S2)
25	*You, Me and Us*	Martine McCutcheon (Innocent)
26	*Greatest Hits III*	Queen (Parlophone)
27	*Invincible*	Five (RCA)
28	*Fanmail*	TLC (Laface)
29	*Ray of Light*	Madonna (Maverick)
30	*The Greatest Hits*	Cher (WEA/Universal TV)
31	*Unplugged*	Corrs (Atlantic)
32	*This Is My Truth Tell Me Yours*	Manic Street Preachers (Epic)
33	*Life Thru A Lens*	Robbie Williams (Chrysalis)
34	*Surrender*	Chemical Brothers (Virgin)
35	*Ricky Martin*	Ricky Martin (Columbia)
36	*Charlotte Church*	Charlotte Church (Sony Classical)
37	*Millennium*	Backstreet Boys (Jive)
38	*Gran Turismo*	Cardigans (Stockholm)
39	*Schizophonic*	Geri Halliwell (EMI)
40	*Turn It On Again – The Hits*	Genesis (Virgin)

Source: © Chart Information Network, 2000

Music Online

The Internet is set to have a profound influence on recorded music. Already, CDs can be bought more cheaply from Web sites outside the UK than from high street shops. According to a Mintel report published in August 1999, the value of music sales online is expected to soar from a 1998 figure of $29 million to $3.9 billion in 2005. However, the development of even cheaper ways of acquiring music threatens to undermine the traditional recording industry.

Top 40 Classical Albums of the Year in the UK

1999

Rank	Title	Artist (label)
1	*Charlotte Church*	Charlotte Church (Sony Classical)
2	*Sacred Arias*	Andrea Bocelli (Philips)
3	*Relax ...*	Various Artists (Classic FM)
4	*Voice of an Angel*	Charlotte Church (Sony Classical)
5	*Best Clasical Album of the Millennium*	Various Artists (Virgin/EMI)
6	*Star Wars – The Phantom Menace* (soundtrack)	LSO/Williams (Sony Classical)
7	*Titanic* (soundtrack)	James Horner (Sony Classical)
8	*Classical Kennedy*	Kennedy/English Chamber Orchestra (EMI Classics)
9	*The Only Opera Album You'll Ever Need*	Various Artists (RCA Victor)
10	*Most Relaxing Classical Album ... Ever! II*	Various Artists (Virgin/EMI)
11	*Viaggio Italiano*	Andrea Bocelli (Philips)
12	*Love Songs*	Luciano Pavarotti (Decca)
13	*Only Classical Album You'll Ever Need*	Various Artists (BMG Conifer)
14	*Back to Titanic* (soundtrack)	James Horner (Sony Classical)
15	*Midsummer Classics*	Various Artists (Global Television)
16	*Most Relaxing Classical Album ... Ever!*	Various Artists (Virgin/EMI)
17	*Lesley Garrett*	Lesley Garrett (BBC/BMG Conifer)
18	*Braveheart* (soundtrack)	LSO/Horner (Decca)
19	*From the Heart*	Lesley Garrett (Silva Treasury)
20	*The Very Best of Classical Experience*	Various Artists (Virgin/EMI)
21	*The Beyondness of Things*	English Chamber Orchestra/Barry (Decca)

(continued)

MP3

MP3 (short for Motion Picture Experts Group Audio Level 3) is a technology that allows the storage of CD-quality digital sound in a compact file format; it can be replayed on a computer or on a special MP3 player, and can be copied onto compact disc. MP3 compresses each minute of music into one megabyte of computer-readable digital data, so downloading a five-minute pop track can be done quickly, especially on a modern Pentium processor. MP3 could pose a challenge to big record producers and famous labels, because the ease with which MP3 tracks can be transmitted over the Internet is an open invitation to piracy and copyright infringement, or at least to the free acquisition of music. But many artists, especially those lesser known, may welcome MP3 as a means of promoting themselves or reaping more directly the profits of their talents.

Top 40 Classical Albums of the Year in the UK *(continued)*

Rank	Title	Artist (label)
22	*Best Choral Album in the World ... Ever!*	Various Artists (Virgin/EMI)
23	*The Vivaldi Album*	Cecilia Bartoli (Decca)
24	*Requiem – Spiritual Music to Uplift*	Various Artists (Decca)
25	*Cecilia & Bryn – Duets*	Bartoli/Terfel/Chung (Decca)
26	*Songs of Praise – The Christmas Album*	Various Artists (BBC Music)
27	*The Best of Carl Orff*	Munich Radio Orchestra/Eichhorn (RCA Victor)
28	*100 Popular Classics*	Various Artists (Castle Music)
29	*Elgar, Cello Concerto/Sea Pictures*	Du Pré/Baker/LSO/Barbirolli (EMI Classics)
30	*Aria – The Opera Album*	Andrea Bocelli (Philips)
31	*The Piano* (soundtrack)	Michael Nyman (Venture)
32	*Desert Island Discs*	Various Artists (BBC Music)
33	*Mnemosyne*	Jan Garbarek/Hilliard Ensemble (ECM New Series)
34	*With a Song in My Heart*	Mario Lanza (Camden)
35	*100 Relaxing Classics*	Various Artists (Pulse)
36	*Brassed Off* (soundtrack)	Grimethorpe Colliery Band (RCA Victor)
37	*Paul McCartney's Working Classical*	Loma Mar Quartet/LSO/Foster/Quinn (EMI Classics)
38	*Simply the Best Classical Anthems*	Various Artists (Warner ESP)
39	*A Soprano in Love*	Lesley Garrett (Silva Screen)
40	*Adverts Hall of Fame*	Various Artists (Classic FM)

Source: © Chart Information Network, 2000

Selected Symphony and Chamber Orchestras in the UK

As of May 2000.

Orchestra	Director/conductor
The Academy of Ancient Music	Christopher Hogwood
Academy of London	Robert Hamwell
Academy of St Martin in the Fields	Neville Marriner (president)
The Ambache	Diana Ambache
BBC Concert Orchestra	Barry Wordsworth
BBC National Orchestra of Wales	Mark Wigglesworth
BBC Philharmonic Orchestra	Yan Pascal Tortelier
BBC Scottish Symphony Orchestra	Osmo Vänskä
BBC Symphony Orchestra	Andrew Davis
Birmingham Contemporary Music Group	Thomas Adès
Bournemouth Symphony Orchestra	Yakov Kreizberg
Brandenburg Consort	Roy Goodman
Britten Sinfonia	Nicholas Cleobury
BT Scottish Ensemble	Clio Gould
CBSO (City of Birmingham Symphony Orchestra)	Sakari Oramo
Charivari Agréable Simfonie	Kah-Ming Ng
City of London Sinfonia	Stephen Carpenter
City of Oxford Orchestra	Roger Payne
City of Stoke-on-Trent Chamber Orchestra	Frank Wadkin
Corydon Orchestra	Matthew Best
East of England Orchestra	Nicholas Kok
English Camerata	Elizabeth Altman
English Classical Players	Jonathan Brett
English Northern Philharmonia	Jonathan Brett
English Sinfonia	Nicolae Moldoveanu
English String Orchestra	William Boughton
English Symphony Orchestra	William Boughton
Foundation Philharmonic Orchestra	Bill Starling
Guildford Philharmonic Orchestra	En Shao
Guildhall Strings	Robert Salter
The Hallé	Mark Elder
The Hanover Band	Caroline Brown
The King's Consort	Robert King
London Chamber Orchestra	Christopher Warren-Green
London Mozart Players	Matthias Bamert
London Philharmonic Orchestra	Bernard Haitink
London Pro Arte Orchestra	Murray Stewart
London Sinfonietta	Oliver Knussen
London Symphony Orchestra	Colin Davis
Manchester Camerata	Nicholas Kraemer
Milton Keynes City Orchestra	Hilary Davan Wetton
Mozart Orchestra	Gordon Heard
New London Orchestra	Ronald Corp
New Queen's Hall Orchestra	John Boyden
Northern Sinfonia	Richard Hickox
Orchestra da Camera	Howard Griffiths
Orchestra of St John's Smith Square	John Lubbock
Orchestra of the Age of Enlightenment	Frans Buiggen and Simon Rattle
Orchestre Révolutionnaire et Romantique	John Eliot Gardiner
Philharmonia Orchestra	Christoph von Dohnányi
Royal Liverpool Philharmonic Society	Petr Altrichter
Royal Philharmonic Orchestra	Danielle Gatti
Royal Scottish National Orchestra	Simon Crookall
Scottish Chamber Orchestra	Joseph Swensen
Sinfonia 21	Martyn Brabbins
Taverner Players	Andrew Parrott
Ulster Orchestra	Dmitry Sitkovetsky
Welsh Chamber Orchestra	Anthony Hose
Welsh Philharmonic Orchestra	G J Harries

Some Major Opera Companies in the UK

Company	Director
Central Festival Opera Ltd	Tom Hawkes
City of Birmingham Touring Opera	Graham Vick
Dorset Opera	Patrick Shelley
English Festival Opera	Simon Gray
English National Opera	Paul Daniel
English Touring Opera	Andrew Greenwood
European Chamber Opera	Stefan Paul Sanchez
First Act Opera International	Elaine Holden
Garsington Opera Ltd	Leonard Ingrams
Glyndebourne Festival Opera	Andrew Davis
Glyndebourne Touring Opera	Louis Langrée
Music Theatre London	Tony Britten
National Youth Music Theatre	Jeremy James Taylor
New Chamber Opera	Gary Cooper
New Sussex Opera	Michael Fulcher
Northern Opera Ltd	Richard Bloodworth
Opera Box Ltd	Fraser Goulding
Opera da Camera	Derek Barnes
Opera Europa	John Gibbons

(continued)

Some Major Opera Companies in the UK *(continued)*

Company	Director	Company	Director
Opera Factory	David Freeman	The Royal Opera	Bernard Haitink
Opera North	Richard Mantle	Scottish Opera	Richard Armstrong
Opera Restor'd	Peter Holman	Surrey Opera	Jonathan Butcher
Pimlico Opera	Wasfi Kani	Welsh National Opera	Carlo Rizzi

See also  **Music**, pp 760–763.

Theatre and Dance

Theatre and Dance in the UK

Crisis in regional theatre

In May 2000 the Arts Council of England published a report describing regional theatre as an 'art form in crisis', where lack of funding since the mid-1980s had led to less challenging plays, fewer performances and tours (down 25% in 6 years), an audience drop of 28%, less employment (the average actor working for only 11 weeks a year), and soaring deficits of £4.4 million in producing theatres. It estimated that regeneration, including a more flexible theatre network, education and community schemes, and a more diverse and relevant range of high-quality productions to attract wider, younger, and multicultural audiences, would require additional funding of £25 million.

West End trends

At the same time London's West End was swamped with a preponderance of big budget musicals, including the £6.5 million *Lion King* and £6 million *The King and I* which joined long runners such as *Starlight Express* (1984) and *Les Misérables* (1985). The trend reflected the consolidation of London's theatres in fewer hands, and the need to create big productions to fill London's large Victorian and Edwardian theatres. Although the West End was apparently booming, some critics argued that there were too many London theatres with unexceptional productions chasing insufficient audiences, many openings being fillers to cover fixed costs and runaway successes being a rarity.

However, British theatre was still regarded as among the best in the world and remained a billion-pound success story – *Titanic*'s £925 million worldwide box office was little more than half that taken by Andrew Lloyd-Webber's *Phantom Of The Opera*.

Closer concord for dance forms

In dance, the formerly disparate worlds of classical ballet and modern dance achieved closer concord, classical choreographers experimenting in fringe and mainstream modern groups, modern dancers choreographing for classical companies, and fundraising initiatives, such as the rebuilding of the Place, London's foremost centre for the teaching and performance of modern dance, being jointly undertaken.

Top 10 Longest-Running West End Theatre Productions

As of May 2000.

Rank	Production	Category	Years	Months
1	*The Mousetrap*	whodunnit	47	5
2	*Cats*	musical	19	0
3	*Starlight Express*	musical	16	2
4	*Les Misérables*	musical	14	8
5	*The Phantom of the Opera*	musical	13	8
6	*Blood Brothers*	musical	11	11
7	*The Woman in Black*	thriller	11	3
8	*Miss Saigon*	musical	10	9
9	*Buddy*	musical	10	8
10	*An Inspector Calls*	play	4	8

Source: © Society of London Theatre

See also **Film and Theatre**, pp 747–753.

Theatres and Theatre-Going in the UK

There are six key organizations representing the people who put on theatre shows in the UK: Theatrical Management Association (TMA), Society of London Theatre (SOLT), Apollo Theatres, Independent Theatre Council (ITC), Little Theatre Guild, and National Operatic and Dramatic Society (NODA).

1998	
Number of performances[1]	104,340
Number of tickets sold	31,597,000
Value of tickets sold (£)[2]	105,600,000
VAT to government on tickets alone (£)[2]	15,800,000
VAT to government on additional sales (eg ice cream, drinks, programmes) (£)[2]	4,000,000
Average ticket price (£)	11.80

[1] Figures are for TMA, SOLT, ITC, and Little Theatre Guild members only.
[2] Figures are for TMA members only.

Source: Theatrical Management Association

Top 5 Dance Companies by Budget in the UK

2000–01

Rank	Company	Address	Artistic director	Budget (£)
1	The Royal Ballet	Royal Opera House, Covent Garden, London WC2E 9DD; phone: (020) 7240 1200	Anthony Dowell	9,000,000
2	Birmingham Royal Ballet	Birmingham Hippodrome, Thorp Street, Birmingham B5 4AU; phone: (0121) 622 2555	David Bintley	5,650,087
3	English National Ballet	Markova House, 39 Jay Mews, London SW7 2ES; phone: (020) 7581 1245	Derek Deane	4,171,070
4	The Scottish Ballet	261 West Princes Street, Glasgow G4 9EE; phone: (0141) 331 2931	Ken Burke	2,228,376
5	Northern Ballet Theatre	West Park Centre, Spen Lane, Leeds LS16 5BE; phone: (0113) 274 5355	vacant	1,388,205

Source: Arts Councils of England, Scotland, Wales, and Northern Ireland

Media Groups and Watchdogs

Main Media Groups in the UK

BBC Corporate HQ BBC Information, PO Box 1116, Belfast BT2 7AJ; phone: (0870) 0100 222; fax: (028) 9032 6453; Web site: www.bbc.co.uk

Capital FM/Capital Gold 30 Leicester Square, London WC2H 7LA; phone: (020) 7766 6000; fax: (020) 7766 6100; Web site: www.capitalradio.co.uk

Carlton Communications 25 Knightsbridge, London SW1X 7RZ; phone: (020) 7663 6363; fax: (020) 7663 6300; Web site: www.carlton.com

Daily Mail North Cliff House, 2 Derry Street, London W8 5TT; phone: (020) 7938 6000; fax: (020) 7937 3251; Web site: www. dailymail.co.uk

Flextech 160 Great Portland Street, London W1N 5TB; phone: (020) 7299 5000; fax: (020) 7299 6000; Web site: www.flextech.co.uk

Granada Media The London Television Centre, Upper Ground, London SE1 9LT; phone: (020) 7620 1620; fax: (020) 7261 3115; The Television Centre, Quay Street, Manchester M60 9EA; phone: (0161) 832 7211; fax: (0161) 827 2029; Web site: www.g-wizz.net

Guardian/Observer News Services 119 Farringdon Road, London EClR 3ER; phone: (020) 7278 2332; fax: (020) 7837 1192; Web site: www.guardian.co.uk

Johnston Press 53 Manor Place, Edinburgh EH3 7EG; phone: (0131) 225 3361; fax: (0131) 225 4580; Web site: www.johnston.co.uk

News International Plc 1 Virginia Street, London E1 9BD; phone: (020) 7782 6000; fax: *Sun* (020) 7782 5605; *News of the World*: (020) 7782 4433; *The Times*: (020) 7782 5988; *The Sunday Times*: (020) 7782 5542; Web sites: *Sun* and *News of the World*: www.lineone.net; *The Times*: www.the-times.co.uk; *The Sunday Times*: www.sunday-times.co.uk

Newsquest Media Group Newspaper House, 33–44 London Road, Morden, Surrey SM4 5BR; phone: (020) 8640 8989; fax: (020) 8646 3997; Web site: www.newsquest.co.uk

Pearson 3 Burlington Gardens, London W1X 1LE; phone: (020) 7411 2000; fax: (020) 7411 2390; Web site: www.pearson.com

Telegraph 1 Canada Square, Canary Wharf, London E14 5DT; phone: (020) 7538 5000; fax: (020) 7538 6242; Web site: www.telegraph.co.uk

Trinity Mirror Group 1 Canada Square, Canary Wharf, London E14 5AP; phone: (020) 7510 3000; fax: (020) 7293 3405; Web site: www.mirror.co.uk

Trinity Mirror Plc Kings Field Court, Chester Business Park, Chester CH4 9RE; phone: (01244) 687000; fax: (01244) 687100; Web site: www.trinity.plc.uk

United News and Media Floodgate House, 245 Blackfriars Road, London SE1 9UY; phone: (020) 7921 5000; fax: (020) 7633 0244; Web site: www.unm.com

Media Watchdogs in the UK

Advertising Standards Authority deals with complaints about advertisements in newspapers, magazines, and other non-broadcast media; Brook House, 2 Torrington Place, London WC1E 7HW; phone: (020) 7580 5555; fax: (020) 7631 3051; Web site: www.asa.org.uk

BBC Feedback listener response programme; Feedback, c/o Testbed Productions Limited, 5th Floor, 14–16 Great Portland Street, London W1N 5AB; phone: (020) 7436 0555; fax: (020) 7436 2800; e-mail: mail@testbed.co.uk

BBC Information Offices general information: if possible give the programme title, transmission date, and time; a daily summary of comments is seen by senior programme-makers, and written comments will be answered; *TV and radio*: BBC Information, PB Box 1116, Belfast BT2 7AJ; phone: (0870) 010 0222 (national rate), open 24 hours; fax: (020) 8749 8258; e-mail: info@bbc.co.uk; Web site: www.bbc.co.uk/info

BBC Points of View TV programme (broadcast weekly) takes complaints and comments to be broadcast about BBC television; Points of View, BBC Television Centre, London W12 7RJ; phone: (020) 8811 1050; fax: (020) 8811 1050

BBC Programme Complaints Unit deals with complaints of specific and serious injustice or inaccuracy, or a serious breach of accepted standards in a BBC broadcast; Fraser Steel, Head of the BBC Programme Complaints Unit, BBC Information, PO Box 1116, Belfast BT2 7AJ; phone: (0870) 010 0222

BBC Reception Advice for TV and radio reception advice; Monday–Friday 8 a.m.–7 p.m., Engineering and Information Department, PO Box 1116, Belfast BT2 7AJ; phone: (0870) 0100 123; fax: (020) 8576 7466; e-mail: reception@bbc.co.uk

BBC Viewer and Listener Correspondence deals with all BBC output, and all written comments receive a reply; Viewer and Listener Correspondence, PO Box 1116, Belfast BT2 7AJ; phone: (0870) 0100 123

Broadcasting Standards Commission for complaints about violence, sexual conduct, decency, and taste in TV and radio programmes and advertisements; 7 The Sanctuary, London SW1P 3JS; phone: (020) 7233 0544; fax: (020) 7233 0397; Web site: www.bsc.org.uk

Channel 4 *Right to Reply* takes complaints and suggestions about television programmes for discussion at 6.30 p.m. on Saturdays; Right to Reply, 124 Horseferry Road, London SW1P 2TX; phone: (020) 7306 8582; fax: (020) 7306 8373; e-mail: righttoreply@channel4.co.uk

Independent Television Commission regulates television advertising and programmes on all commercial channels; 33 Foley Street, London W1P 7LB; phone: (020) 7255 3000; fax: (020) 7306 7800; e-mail: publicaffairs@itc.org.uk; Web site: www.itc.org.uk

Oftel the watchdog for the telecommunications industry; 50 Ludgate Hill, London EC4M 7JJ; phone: (020) 7634 8700

Press Complaints Commission self-regulatory body concerned with all editorial material in newspapers and magazines; 1 Salisbury Square, London EC4Y 8JB; Helpline: (020) 7353 3732; Scottish helpline: (0131) 220 6652; text phone: (020) 7583 2264; fax: (020) 7353 8355; e-mail: pcc@pcc.org.uk; Web site: www.pcc.org.uk

Radio Authority deals with programmes and advertising on independent (non-BBC) radio; Holbrook House, 14 Great Queen Street, London WC2B 5DG; phone: (020) 7430 2724; fax: (020) 7405 7062; e-mail: info@radioauthority.org.uk; Web site: www.radioauthority.org.uk

Web Sites

American Ballet Theater

http://www.abt.org/

Site of the US ballet company, with details of current performances, profiles of dancers and choreographers, and the history of the company.

Art Crime

http://museum-security.org/artcrime.html

Latest news about 'cultural property incidents, such as art theft, looting of art in wartime, fire, and forgery'.

Art London.Com

http://www.artlondon.com/

Here you can search for particular works of art, artists, galleries, antique dealers, designers, interior decorators, art colleges, and everything else to do with arts and culture in London and the UK.

Arts Council of England

http://www.artscouncil.org.uk/

Details of the council's work in funding and promoting the arts, as well as sections on 'The arts in the UK' and 'The wider context' of cultural diversity.

Arts Council of Wales

http://www.ccc-acw.org.uk/

Covering the aims, structure, meetings, and publications of the Welsh arts council, and a guide to grants.

Ashmolean Museum

http://www.ashmol.ox.ac.uk/

Guide to the museum in Oxford, England, founded by Elias Ashmole, with details of permanent collections, exhibitions, and talks.

BalletWeb

http://www.novia.net/~jlw/index.html

Site devoted to classical ballet, with commentary on dance issues, photo-essays, and the Electronic Ballerina – a computer animation illustrating ballet steps.

BBC Symphony Orchestra

http://www.bbc.co.uk/orchestras/so/

Highlights of the current season's performances, as well as a 'Spotlight' on individual musicians in the orchestra.

Bigmouth

http://www.bigmouth.co.uk/festivals/

The most comprehensive and up-to-date site on the Web for information on summer music festivals in the UK.

Bodleian Library, University of Oxford

http://www.bodley.ox.ac.uk/

Practical information for visitors and readers, and information on a range of online services offered by the library.

Bolshoi in History

http://www.bolshoi.ru/eng/frame.html

History of the Bolshoi Theatre in Moscow, Russia, from its inception in 1776 up to the present day.

British Arts Festivals Association

http://www.artsfestivals.co.uk/

A directory of leading professional arts festivals in the UK, with information on, and links to, all the major festivals.

British Library

http://www.bl.uk/

Extensive information for users of the library's many services, including the facility to search through all the 9.5 million books catalogued since 1977.

Edinburgh Festival Online

http://www.go-edinburgh.co.uk/

The official Edinburgh festival site, with full details of all the contributing arts.

English National Ballet

http://www.ballet.org.uk/ballet/cgi-bin/index.cgi

The site includes a 'Tour schedule' and 'Company news', as well as the opportunity to contribute to the 'Online think tank' and 'Performance reviews'. There is also a 'Ballet school' for aspiring dancers.

English National Opera

http://www.eno.org/

Details of the company, its current productions, and the low-price ticket scheme 'Enjoy opera for schools'.

Getty

http://www.getty.edu/

Site of the Getty Institute in California, home to one of the largest art collections in the world.

Glossary of Musical Terms

http://www.hnh.com/mgloss.htm

A–Z glossary of musical terms, with links to articles on composers, including a list of recommended works.

Guggenheim Museum Bilbao

http://www.bm30.es/homegug.uk.html

Includes the background to the building of the Guggenheim museum, which opened in 1997, as well as gallery plans and details of exhibitions.

London Theatre Guide

http://www.officiallondontheatre.co.uk/

Complete and current information on London's theatreland, from ticket availability to awards and reviews.

Louvre Museum and Palace

http://mistral.culture.fr/louvre/louvrea.htm

Comprehensive guide to the Louvre Museum and Palace, Paris, France, including the history of the institution, floor plans of the collections, and pictures of major works.

MTV UK

http://www.mtv.co.uk/

Pop news, charts, and features, and show information for the UK edition of MTV.

Musée d'Orsay

http://www.musee-orsay.fr:8081/ORSAY/orsaygb/HTML.NSF/By+Filename/mosimple+index?OpenDocument

Guide to the Musée d'Orsay in Paris, France, and its major collections of Impressionist and post-Impressionist works of art.

Museumsworld News

http://www.museumsworld.com/news.htm

Articles from the world of museums, including the latest discoveries and acquisitions, and attempts by some countries to regain treasures looted or removed by others.

National Gallery, London

http://www.nationalgallery.org.uk/

Comprehensive guide to the National Gallery in London, with full details on current and future exhibitions. There is also a 'Puzzling pictures' section which looks at works with an unusual history.

National Museum of Photography, Film, and Television

http://www.nmsi.ac.uk/nmpft/

Details of collections, events, and forthcoming exhibits at the National Museum of Photography, Film, and Television, in Bradford, England.

NME (New Musical Express)

http://www.nme.com/

Weekly guide to the UK rock and pop scene, with news, reviews, charts, and a searchable gig database.

Opera for the Culturally Illiterate

http://www.dn.net/schultz/opera.html

Irreverent and entertaining introduction to opera's 'wonderful world of sex, alcohol, and profound carnage' by tenor singer John Schultz.

Royal Opera House

http://www.royalopera.org/

Site of Britain's leading opera house, with information on current performances and bookings, and a history of the Royal Opera. An educational section offers practical activities designed to interest young people in opera and ballet.

Royal Philharmonic Orchestra

http://www.rpo.co.uk/

Performance and education are the main themes of this site from the Royal Philharmonic Orchestra, with a full programme for adults and children.

Scottish Arts Council

http://www.sac.org.uk/

As well as reporting on the Council's work, the site showcases Scottish art, with an 'Image of the Month' and 'Poem of the Month'.

UK Arts

http://www.ukarts.co.uk

Site with links to arts and media associations, providing a free listing for all art galleries, museums, arts festivals, and other artistic activities in the UK.

Victoria and Albert Museum

http://www.vam.ac.uk/

Guide to the world's largest museum of the decorative arts, with information on permanent displays, exhibitions, public events, publications, and talks. Other museums operated by the V&A are described and there are good summaries of the museum's main collections.

What's On Stage

http://www.whatsonstage.com/

Comprehensive listing of theatre and classical music performances throughout the UK, with a searchable database, news, seating plans, and online ticket ordering.

Language and Languages

World Languages

The communications revolution has propelled humankind across a new threshold in the development of speech and of human society itself. Conversations now span the globe in millions, and the recording and propagation of the spoken word are no longer dependent on the written word. Homes with access to the Internet have more knowledge at their disposal than the largest libraries only a few decades ago. The power of nation states to limit the global awareness of their citizens decreases every day, and the twin poles of human society are now the individual person and the planetary community of humankind. At the outset of a new millennium, there is an accelerating need for the development of one or more languages of global communication. Yet there is an equally important need for the maintenance and development of the thousands of spoken and written languages that constitute the framework of human diversity, providing humankind with a communal structure more profound and ancient than that of the nation state.

David Dalby, Linguasphere Press

The World's Most Spoken Languages

Chinese (Putonghua or 'Mandarin') and English appear more or less 'neck and neck' as the planet's two most spoken languages, breaking the barrier of around 1 billion speakers each at the turn of the millennium.

The world's most widely spoken language alternates daily. When the Sun is over the western Pacific, the national language of China is the most in use. When the Sun is over the Atlantic and China sleeps, English takes the lead. The world's second most spoken language also alternates daily, between Hindi-Urdu and Spanish.

English as a Global Language

English is the official or primary language of 60 countries. It is estimated that nearly 400 million people speak English as their first language; that 600 million have learned it as a second language; and that one in three of the world's population routinely encounter it.

Languages of the World: Glossary

alternate (as in alternate language or 'voice') second language, as opposed to a primary (first) language

arterial language language spoken by at least 1% of humankind, that is, by at least 60 million in the year 2000

autonym indigenous name of a language and/or its speech community, that is, as used in that language (noted in brackets in the list of arterial languages, where it differs from the English name)

endangered language language in steady demographic decline, its component voices being no longer replaced in proportion to those dying

linguasphere global continuum of languages, extended by humankind around the world since the onset of speech

macrolanguage language with an estimated total of between 10 and 100 million primary and alternate voices

megalanguage language with an estimated total of more than 100 million primary and alternate voices

net layer of close relationships among languages, in which all component languages normally share a majority of their basic vocabulary

primary (as in primary language or 'voice') first (mother-tongue) language, as opposed to an alternate (second) language

Languages of the World: Glossary *(continued)*

translingual person able to navigate with reasonable competence between two or more closely related languages

voice total linguistic repertoire and performance of an individual person in any language or languages of which they have experience (in preference to the technical term 'idiolect')

Source: David Dalby, The Linguasphere Register of the World's Languages and Speech Communities *(Linguasphere Press, Hebron, Wales, 2000)*

The Linguasphere

by David Dalby

The time has now passed when individual communities could afford to regard their own languages and cultures as separate from or even superior to those of others.

Humankind is acquiring a new global view of itself and of its planetary environment, and it can now be seen that the very concept of the individual language, as distinct and separate from other languages, is misleading. All forms of all languages are integral parts of a fluid continuum of human speech, which has evolved within and among individual communities since speech first made human beings human.

This planetary mantle of communication, or *linguasphere*, includes the words of every communicating human in every language, embracing not only speech itself but all written, electronic, and other derivatives of speech.

The ultimate component of the linguasphere is and always has been the unique 'voice' of the individual person, each spanning an average of only a few decades. Speech communities, composed of successive generations of voices, have migrated, overlapped, merged, and divided through time and across all continents and oceans, providing humankind with a continuous web of multilingual speech, with a continuously shifting kaleidoscope of interrelated and interacting languages. The abstract concept of 'language' may itself be misleading, and it is more useful to concentrate on the concrete reality of speech.

Rather than the 'gift of language' itself, it is the combined 'hardware' of the human brain, of the human vocal apparatus, and of the human hand that may be regarded as humankind's distinctive attribute. The combination of the first two of these faculties enabled humans to develop the 'software' of speech, based on the vocal labelling and communication of complex messages and ideas. Use of the hand led to the extension of this software to manual labelling or 'writing', including the development of subsidiary communicational hardware, from pens to printing presses, telephones, and computers. These in their turn have allowed the creation of permanent copies of speech, from clay tablets to compact discs.

Speech, the most fundamental by-product of humankind's intellectual and vocal powers, has served not only to establish networks of communication among individual brains, and to create and demarcate communities, but also to program those brains for participation – passive, creative, or destructive – in a continuously and rapidly evolving society.

Over the last 5,000 years, inherited written texts in hundreds of languages have influenced the natural fluidity and variability of speech within and among human brains, and have sometimes created prisons of the mind. Yet they have also permitted the accumulation and acceleration of human knowledge, inspiration, and creativity across successive generations of voices. The time has come for a reappraisal of the study and development of human languages and communication, embracing speech communities of all sizes. It would be appropriate if the first decade of a new century were devoted to the consideration and design of new approaches to education in all languages, adapted to the realities and perspectives of a new era of global communication.

Counting the number of languages in the world today depends on how one distinguishes so-called 'languages' from so-called 'dialects' within the continuum of the linguasphere. If an individual language is defined very broadly, the approximate total is around 5,000, whereas a finer distinction gives a total of over 13,000 (in addition to component dialects). Within this vast array, attention is drawn below to the opposite extremes of size: to the *endangered* languages spoken by very tiny communities and to the small number of *arterial* languages spoken by a significant proportion of humankind.

World Languages

Endangered Languages

A language may be classified as 'endangered' when the annual number of new speakers (normally children) is substantially less than the number of those dying or abandoning that language.

The most endangered category of speech communities today is that of hunter-gatherers or former hunter-gatherers in the Americas, Asia, Africa, and Australasia.

The population of such hunter-gatherer communities has always been very small but their extinction has accelerated greatly during the last 500 years, under pressure from the worldwide expansion of speech communities from Europe. In particular, the traditional languages of Australia have accounted for just over one third of all cases of linguistic extinction recorded for the world as a whole during the 20th century. It should be noted that speakers of the English language have accounted for the most extensive *ethnic clearance* of other speech communities in human history, including the conquest of two continents.

During the 1990s, much publicity was given to claims that more than half the languages of the world would become extinct during the 21st century. Fortunately, this estimate is likely to prove a considerable exaggeration, as can be seen by comparison with the proportion of languages – less than 10% – that are known to have become extinct during the 20th century. Nevertheless, members of truly endangered speech communities deserve support in the preservation of their languages, and should be encouraged to record as much as possible of their linguistic and cultural heritage in audio-visual form, for the benefit of their own descendants and of the wider world.

Finally, the children of endangered speech communities should be given the opportunity to receive a bilingual education, including their own and an international language. Such education needs to provide an interface between these two languages, and the encouragement of literary creativity in both. The creation of written literature is one of the most important actions to be taken in the defence of any endangered or potentially endangered language, as witnessed by the successful defence and development of the Welsh language on the doorstep of English itself.

Arterial Languages

In lists of the most spoken languages of the world, it has been customary to rank them by order of their total numbers of speakers, although there are considerable difficulties in estimating more than very approximate totals. For statistical purposes, a distinction can be made between languages comprising more than 100 million voices (or speakers) each, and those comprising between 10 and 100 million. The first category comprises 12 major 'megalanguages' at the beginning of the 21st century (see the first 12 entries in the table **The World's Arterial Languages in 2000–01**, p 432), and the second category comprises more than 60 'macrolanguages'.

Whereas macrolanguages and megalanguages are measured in absolute terms, however, a valuable intermediate category is that of *arterial languages*, measured in relative proportion to the current world population. These may be defined as all those languages spoken by at least 1% each of the current world population (that is, 60 million or more voices in 1999/2000). This category at present totals at least 28 languages.

The following independent estimates have taken totals from other sources into account, and the demography of the countries involved, although the most difficult estimate is that relating to English. In an era of increasing telecommunication and travel, the number of voices for most arterial languages is still expanding, and this is particularly true for English. The estimates relate not only to the *primary* voices (or 'first language speakers') of each language but also to its *alternate* voices (or 'second language speakers'). The first of these categories includes all who acquire native or 'native-like' competence in a language, usually their 'mother tongue', whereas the category of alternate voices includes those whose speaking of the language in question is influenced by their knowledge of one or more other languages, especially their own mother tongue. Alternate voices are a frequent medium of enrichment for a language, and should not be therefore regarded as 'secondary' in status to primary voices.

In many cases, totals of primary voices alone would have presented a false picture of linguistic reality – only 6 million voices for Swahili, for example, (as opposed to 55 million including alternate voices) or only 400 million voices for English (as opposed to around 1 billion).

Estimates of primary speakers may be based to a large extent on the latest census figures for relevant nation states, updated to allow for population growth, although specific linguistic totals are not available for the majority of countries. The assessment of 'alternate' speakers, on the other hand, must depend on the personal judgement of informed observers, and also on where one draws the line in terms of adequate competence in a language. If it were possible to measure and count every 'voice' concerned, it would be reasonable to include only those with the ability to 'get by in a language' – to follow the main points of a televised drama or news bulletin, for example, or to ask and reply to straightforward questions about everyday subjects.

Not to be overlooked is the fact that most of the world's principal languages belong to one of a small number of 'nets' of closely related languages. In most cases, such relationships enable speakers of one language to acquire, with relative ease, at least a partial understanding of one or more other languages. For certain languages in the following table therefore, modest allowance has been made for 'translingual' voices alternating between languages in the same net, as in the ability of many Ukrainian and Belarussian voices to adapt themselves to Russian, of Czech and Slovak voices to Polish, or of Portuguese voices to Spanish (although less in the reverse direction, in each of these cases). A further important example is provided by Hindi, reinforced by the popularity of Hindi-speaking films in South Asia. Many millions of voices alternate regularly between Hindi and their own languages in the same Central Indic net, often within the same conversation or same sentence.

For the purpose of assessing realistic totals, two or more very closely related languages have sometimes been treated together as a single unit. Examples from the table (see **The World's Arterial Languages in 2000–01**, p 432) include Hindi and Urdu, Malay and Indonesian, and Turkish and Azeri. This is not to imply that such associated languages are the 'same' language but that they are sufficiently close to form an extended transnational speech-community. In contrast, individual language-names sometimes cover wide degrees of internal spoken variation (often bridged by a standardized and/or common vehicular idiom, as in the case of Arabic or German).

Spoken languages, which are being measured here, must **not** be confused with corresponding written languages – not only because of varying literacy rates, but also because of the differential distribution of certain writing systems. In Asia, Hindi and Urdu overlap as spoken languages but are written in different scripts (Devanagari and Perso-Arabic). In contrast, the major Chinese languages (not readily interintelligible when spoken) are the 'same' language in writing, through the use of identical 'meaning-based' characters. For this reason, the estimates below take no account of those able to read a particular language. On the other hand, it should be noted that the majority of today's major spoken languages (megalanguages and macrolanguages) are either closely related to or have been heavily influenced by one of a small number of classical written languages, notably Classical Chinese, Sanskrit and Pali, Classical Arabic, Latin, and Church Slavonic.

Of the 12 megalanguages at the top of the following table, 8 are classified within the Indo-European language-family. All 12 are national state-languages, and all include a more or less important intercontinental diaspora of speakers. No less than 8 interrelated Chinese languages (sometimes misleadingly called 'dialects') are megalanguages or macrolanguages in their own right.

The figure presented here for English, of approximately 1 billion (1,000 million) primary and alternate voices in the year 2000, is lower than some previous estimates, although it is clear that the demand to learn English and the consequent supply of teaching are increasing rapidly in many parts of the world. It is likely that the total numbers of alternate (especially young) speakers of English are now expanding worldwide at a rate of well above one million a month, having already overtaken the estimated 400 million primary speakers of the language.

In terms of geographical spread, English already occupies an unrivalled position in the world, and a steady expansion in its learning and use around the globe will see it taking an

(continued)

increasing lead over all other languages during the early part of the 21st century. Moreover, within a decade or two, it is reasonable to assume that there will be more speakers of English in Asia than in any other continent: India is an increasingly important source of literary creativity in English, and China will not be far behind. Asia will play an important role in helping to ensure that English serves as a transnational auxiliary language, against a multilingual background.

In terms of its place in the world, French is also unique. Measured in terms of primary speakers only, it falls below the level of 100 million speakers and lies in 12th position among the 12 megalanguages. And yet it is the only language that currently provides an alternative to English as a transnational vehicular language around the world, being used as an official or semi-official language in 44 countries in 5 continents.

The natural diversity of humankind requires the development of one or more global languages that are at the service of a multilingual world society, and that do not function as the vehicles of dominant monolingual cultures.

Source: David Dalby, The Linguasphere Register of the World's Languages and Speech Communities *(Linguasphere Press, Hebron, Wales, 2000)*

The World's Arterial Languages in 2000–01

An arterial language is a language that is spoken by at least 1% of humankind, that is, by at least 60 million in the year 2000.

Arterial language	Total speakers (primary + alternate voices) (in millions)	Principal countries and areas where spoken
Standard Chinese (Putonghua)	(800 + 200) = 1,000	China; Taiwan; Thailand; Malaysia; Singapore; Vietnam
English	(400 + 600) = 1,000	UK; Republic of Ireland; Canada; USA; Australia; New Zealand; South Africa; Botswana; Lesotho; Malawi; Namibia; Swaziland; Zambia; Zimbabwe; Kenya; Tanzania; Uganda; Rwanda; Ethiopia; Somalia; Sudan; Cameroon; Gambia; Ghana; Liberia; Nigeria; Sierra Leone; Gibraltar; Malta; Cyprus; Bahrain; Egypt; Israel and Palestine; Jordan; Kuwait; United Arab Emirates; Mauritius; Seychelles; Bangladesh; Burma; China (Hong Kong); India; Malaysia; Pakistan; Singapore; Sri Lanka; Fiji; Kiribati; Federated States of Micronesia; Nauru; Papua New Guinea; Philippines; Samoa; Solomon Islands; Tonga; Tuvalu; Vanuatu; Bahamas; Belize; Bermuda; Barbados; Dominica; Grenada; Guyana; Jamaica; Puerto Rico; St Lucia; St Kitts and Nevis; St Vincent; Trinidad and Tobago; Virgin Islands
Hindi + Urdu	(550 + 350) = 900	India; Pakistan; Nepal; Fiji; Mauritius; South Africa; UK
Spanish (Español)	(400 + 50) = 450	Spain; Mexico; Venezuela; Colombia; Ecuador; Peru; Bolivia; Chile; Argentina; Paraguay; Uruguay; Panama; Costa Rica; Nicaragua; Honduras; El Salvador; Guatemala; Cuba; Dominican Republic; Puerto Rico; Canary Islands; Morocco; Equatorial Guinea; USA
Russian (Russkiy)	(170 + 150) = 320	Russian Federation; Ukraine; Belarus; Latvia; Estonia; Lithuania; Georgia; Azerbaijan; Armenia; Kazakhstan; Kyrgyzstan; Turkmenistan; Uzbekistan; Tajikistan; Moldova; Poland; Slovakia; other states of central Europe; USA; Canada; Brazil
Maghribi Arabic + Mashriqi Arabic ('Arabiyya)	(200 + 50) = 250	Morocco; Algeria; Tunisia; Malta; Mauritania; Senegal; Mali; Niger; Cameroon; Chad; Libya; Sudan; Egypt; Israel and Palestine; Lebanon; Syria; Saudi Arabia; Yemen; United Arab Emirates; Oman; Kuwait; Bahrain; Qatar; Iraq; Iran; Djibouti; Somalia; Comoros; France
Bengali (Bangla)	(190 + 60) = 250	Bangladesh; India; UK
Portuguese (Português)	(180 + 20) = 200	Portugal; Brazil; Angola; Cape Verde; Guinea-Bissau; Macau; Mozambique; São Tomé and Príncipe
Malay + Indonesian	(50 + 110) = 160	Indonesia; Malaysia; Singapore
Japanese (Nihongo)	(120 + 10) = 130	Japan; USA; Brazil; Peru
German (Deutsch)	(100 + 25) = 125	Germany; Austria; Switzerland; France; Italy; Belgium; Luxembourg; Liechtenstein; USA; Canada; Namibia; Kazakhstan; Romania; Russian Federation; Brazil; Argentina
French (Français)	(90 + 35) = 125	France; Canada; Belgium; Luxembourg; Switzerland; Monaco; St Pierre and Miquelon; Canada; Haiti; Guadeloupe; Martinique; French Guiana; French Polynesia; New Caledonia; Vanuatu; Laos; Cambodia; Vietnam; Réunion; Mauritius; Seychelles; Lebanon; Syria; Tunisia; Algeria; Morocco; Mali; Mauritania; Benin; Burkina Faso; Burundi; Cameroon; Central African Republic; Chad; Comoros; Democratic Republic of Congo; Republic of the Congo; Côte d'Ivoire; Djibouti; Gabon; Guinea; Madagascar; Niger; Rwanda; Senegal; Togo
Thai + Lao, including Isan and Huang + Buyi	90	Thailand; Laos; Vietnam; China
Punjabi	85	Pakistan; India; Malaysia; Fiji; UK
Wu Chinese	85	China
Javanese (Jawa)	80	Indonesia; Malaysia; Singapore; New Caledonia/Kanaky; French Guiana; Suriname
Marathi	80	India
Korean (Hankukmal)	75	North Korea; South Korea; China; Japan; USA
Vietnamese (Viêt)	75	Vietnam; Cambodia; USA
Italian (Italiano)	70	Italy; Switzerland; USA; Canada; Argentina; Brazil
Tamil	70	India; Sri Lanka; Malaysia; Singapore; Fiji; Mauritius; Trinidad and Tobago
Telugu	70	India; Malaysia

(continued)

The World's Arterial Languages in 2000–01 (*continued*)

Arterial language	Total speakers (primary + alternate voices) (in millions)	Principal countries and areas where spoken
Yue Chinese or Cantonese	70	China; Malaysia; Vietnam; Singapore; Indonesia; USA
Bhojpuri + Maithili	60	India; Nepal; Bangladesh; Mauritius; South Africa; Trinidad; Guyana; Suriname; UK
Turkish + Azeri (Türkçe + Azeri), including Turkmen	60	Turkey; Bulgaria; Greece; Cyprus; Turkmenistan; Kazakhstan; Uzbekistan; Iran; Azerbaijan; Russian Federation; Germany
Ukrainian + Belorussian (Ukrainska + Belarusskaya)	60	Ukraine; Belarus; Russian Federation; Moldova; Kazakhstan; Kyrgyzstan; Turkmenistan; Uzbekistan; Azerbaijan; Georgia; Armenia; Latvia; Lithuania; Poland; Slovakia; Hungary; Israel; USA; Canada; Brazil
Swahili	(7 + 53) = 60	Tanzania; Kenya; Uganda; Rwanda; Burundi; Democratic Republic of Congo; Somalia; Comoros
Tagalog, including Filipino	(25 + 35) = 60	Philippines; USA; Canada

Source: David Dalby, The Lingusphere Register of the World's Languages and Speech Communities *(Linguasphere Press, Hebron, Wales, 2000)*

New Words in English

English is a growing and global language, and the process of lexical innovation – the coinage of new words and phrases, and the use of existing ones in new senses – continues at a great, if not readily quantifiable, rate. Attempts to measure change in word stock must rely on the historical data of dictionaries, and are consequently distorted by the research bias of dictionary-makers, who might concentrate heavily on the language of a given period at the expense of others, and exaggerate the extent of linguistic growth for that period. However, the rapidity and scale of change in 20th-century life and developments in technology and the media, politics, and leisure culture, have had a corresponding impact on the language. One estimate, based on the resources of the *Oxford English Dictionary (OED)*, is that the vocabulary of English has grown by 25% since 1900.

New Words of the 1970s, 1980s, and 1990s

Below is a small sample of the verbal inventions of the last three decades, drawn from both formal language and slang; the date given is that of the earliest printed or other record of usage held in the files of the *OED*.

1970s		1980s		1990s	
action replay	1973	alternative comedy	1980	alcopop	1995
bulimia	1976	balti	1984	bad hair day	1991
car bomb	1972	cashback	1988	Britpop	1995
chairperson	1971	chat line	1984	cybercafé	1994
cling film	1975	download	1980	docusoap	1998
environmentalism	1972	empower	1986	DVD	1994
flexitime	1972	ghetto-blaster	1981	ethnic cleansing	1991
flip-flop	1970	gridlock	1981	GM	1996
gentrify	1972	hip-hop	1982	home page	1993
industrial action	1971	lager lout	1987	jobseeker	1993
junk food	1973	lap-top	1984	laddish	1991
passive smoking	1971	multiplex	1982	off-message	1993
psycho-babble	1976	OTT	1982	out (verb)	1990
quality time	1977	pear-shaped	1983	prebuttal	1997
reflexology	1976	rave	1989	puffa jacket	1991
sell-by date	1973	road rage	1988	rebrand	1994
speed bump	1975	safe sex	1983	screen saver	1990
squat (noun)	1975	shell suit	1989	slacker	1994
teletext	1974	sound bite	1980	twoc	1990
user-friendly	1977	yuppie	1982	Web	1994

Language and Dictionaries Online

The information age is set to transform dictionaries and dictionary-making. Lexicographers are now able to hold a vast corpus of information on and illustrations of contemporary and historical language use in databases capable of future expansion. At the same time, electronic publication is opening up new possibilities for dictionaries.

(*continued*)

The Greek Alphabet

Letter		Name	Transliteration
Α	α	alpha	a
Β	β	beta	b
Γ	γ	gamma	g
Δ	δ	delta	d
Ε	ϵ	epsilon	e
Ζ	ζ	zeta	z
Η	η	eta	e, ē
Θ	θ	theta	th
Ι	ι	iota	i
Κ	κ	kappa	k
Λ	λ	lambda	l
Μ	μ	mu	m
Ν	ν	nu	n
Ξ	ξ	xi	x
Ο	ο	omicron	o
Π	π	pi	p
Ρ	ρ	rho	r
Σ	σ, ς	sigma	s
Τ	τ	tau	t
Υ	υ	upsilon	u
Φ	ϕ	phi	ph
Χ	χ	chi	ch, kh
Ψ	ψ	psi	ps
Ω	ω	omega	o, ō

The Cyrillic Alphabet

The Cyrillic alphabet is used for writing Russian and various other Slavic languages.

Letter		Transliteration
а	А	a
б	Б	b
в	В	v
г	Г	g, gh
д	Д	d
е	Е	ye
ё	Ё	yo
ж	Ж	zh
з	З	z
и	И	i
й	Й	i
к	К	k
л	Л	l
м	М	m
н	Н	n
о	О	o
п	П	p
р	Р	r
с	С	s
т	Т	t
у	У	ou
ф	Ф	f
х	Х	kh
ц	Ц	ts

(*continued*)

Language and Dictionaries Online *(continued)*

English dictionaries online
In July 1999 the *Encarta World English Dictionary* appeared on CD-ROM alongside a print version; produced by Microsoft in collaboration with international publishing houses, it lays claim to global scope in recording the variety of contemporary international English. The well-established US *Merriam-Webster Collegiate Dictionary* is available at www.m-w.com. And in March 2000 the *Oxford English Dictionary*, first initiated in 1857, went online to subscribers at www.oed.com. The more than 500,000 entries of its 2nd edition are now searchable, with a promise of quarterly updates of 1,000 new and revised entries, and a complete revision by 2010.

Specialist and multilingual dictionaries online
There is a proliferation of online dictionaries dealing with specialist language, from architecture, at www.masshomes.com/michaeldurkin/glossary.html, to printing, at www.uniprint.com/terms.htm. And this is matched by the development of online multilingual dictionaries: www.yourDictionary.com for example, a portal supporting dictionary resources for 224 languages.

The Cyrillic Alphabet *(continued)*

Letter		Transliteration
ч	Ч	ch
ш	Ш	sh
щ	Щ	shch
ъ	Ъ	hard symbol
ы	Ы	y
ь	Ь	soft (or mute)
э	Э	e
ю	Ю	yu
я	Я	ya

Judgement Day for Legal Latin?

Under civil justice reforms introduced in the UK in April 1999, the language used in civil courts was simplified, and many old Latin phrases and other archaic legal terms were replaced. For example, the Latin terms 'ex parte', 'inter partes', and 'inter camera', were replaced by 'with notice', 'without notice', and 'in private', respectively, and 'Mareva injunctions' (whereby a defendant's assets are frozen pending the outcome of litigation) became 'freezing orders'. Other archaic terms were also replaced: for example, 'plaintiffs' became 'claimants' and 'writs' became 'claim forms'. In December 1999 the Lord Chancellor, Lord Irvine, announced that there would be a similar review of the criminal court system, conclusions of which were expected in December 2000.

Indo-European Languages: Common Roots

Similarities between six words in Indo-European languages contrasted with their differences in other language groups.

Indo-European languages						
English	month	mother	new	night	nose	three
Welsh	mis	mam	newydd	nos	trwyn	tri
Gaelic	mí	máthair	nua	oíche	srón	trí
French	mois	mère	nouveau	nuit	nez	trois
Spanish	mes	madre	nuevo	noche	nariz	tres
Portuguese	mês	mãe	novo	noite	nariz	três
Italian	mese	madre	nuovo	notte	naso	tre
Latin	mensis	mater	novus	nox	nasus	tres
German	Monat	Mutter	neu	Nacht	Nase	drei
Dutch	maand	moeder	nieuw	nacht	neus	drie
Icelandic	mánudur	módir	nýr	nótt	nef	brír
Swedish	månad	moder	ny	natt	näsa	tre
Polish	miesiąc	matka	nowy	noc	nos	trzy
Czech	měść	matka	nový	noc	nos	tři
Romanian	lună	mamă	nou	noapte	nas	trei
Albanian	muaj	nënë	iri	natë	hundë	tre,tri
Greek	men	meter	neos	nux	rhïs	treis
Russian	mesyats	mat	novy	noch	nos	tri
Lithuanian	menuo	motina	naujas	naktis	nosis	trys
Armenian	amis	mayr	nor	kisher	kit	yerek
Persian	māh	mādar	nau	shab	bini	se
Sanskrit	mās	matar	nava	nakt	nās	trayas
Non-Indo-European languages						
Basque	hilabethe	ama	berri	gai	sādār	hirur
Finnish	kuukausi	äiti	uusi	yö	nenä	kolme
Hungarian	hónap	anya	új	éjszaka	orr	három
Turkish	ay	anne	yeni	gece	burun	úç

A Selection of Latin Phrases

ad astra per aspera to the stars through difficulties
addendum something to be added, usually in writing, that qualifies a foregoing thesis or statement
ad infinitum to infinity, endlessly
ad nauseam to the point of disgust
carpe diem 'seize the day'; live for the present
casus belli justification for war, grounds for a dispute
caveat emptor 'let the buyer beware'; dictum that professes the buyer is responsible for checking that the goods or services they purchase are satisfactory
cave canem beware of the dog
cogito, ergo sum 'I think, therefore I am'; quotation from French philosopher René Descartes
compos mentis of sound mind
curriculum vitae (CV) 'the course of life'; account of a person's education and previous employment, attached to a job application
de facto in fact
de gustibus non est disputandum there is no accounting for taste
de jure according to law; legally
deus ex machina 'a god from the machinery'; far-fetched or unlikely event that resolves an intractable difficulty
dramatis personae the characters in a play
emeritus someone who has retired from an official position but retains their title on an honorary basis, for example, a professor emeritus
ergo therefore; hence
et alia or **et al.** and other things
ex libris 'from among the books of'; used on bookplates to identify the owner
in loco parentis 'in place of a parent'; in a parental capacity
in situ in place, on the spot, without moving from position
inter alia among other things
in vino veritas in wine (there is) the truth
ipse dixit '(he) himself said (it)'; the master has spoken
ipso facto by that very fact
literati educated or cultured people; literary persons
magnum opus a great work of art or literature
mea culpa 'my fault'; an admission of guilt
modus operandi a method of operating
modus vivendi 'way of living'; a compromise between opposing points of view
mores the customs and manners of a society
mutatis mutandis with changes being made; with alterations to fit a new set of circumstances
nil desperandum never despair
nolo contendere plea of no defence; no contest; equivalent to plea of guilty
non sequitur 'it does not follow'; statement that has little or no relevance to the one that preceded it
passim 'in many places'; indicates that a reference occurs repeatedly throughout the work

■ World Languages

A Selection of Latin Phrases (*continued*)

per se in itself
postmortem 'after death'; autopsy
post scriptum (ps) something written below the signature on a letter
prima facie at first sight
pro rata in proportion
pro tem (pore) for the time being
quidnunc 'what now?'; gossip; busybody
quid pro quo 'something for something'; an exchange of one thing in return for another
quod erat demonstrandum (QED) 'which was to be proved'; added at the end of a geometry proof
quo vadis? where are you going?
q.v. abbreviation for **quod vide** ('which see'), indicating a cross-reference
sic 'thus', 'so'; sometimes found in brackets within a printed quotation to show that the original has been quoted accurately even though it contains an apparent error
sine die 'without a day being appointed'; indefinitely
sine qua non 'without which not'; absolutely essential
status quo 'the state in which'; the current situation, without change
sub judice 'under a judge'; of judicial proceedings, not yet decided by a court of law or judge: as long as a matter is sub judice all discussion is prohibited elsewhere
tabula rasa 'scraped tablet' (from the Romans' use of wax-covered tablets which could be written on with a pointed stick and cleared by smoothing over the surface); a mind without any preconceived ideas
tempus fugit time flies
terra firma dry land; solid ground
vade mecum 'go with me'; a useful handbook carried about for reference
vice versa the other way around
viva voce 'with living voice'; by word of mouth; an oral examination

Sign Language

Language used by deaf people involves movements of the hands, face, and the upper part of the body, not the voice. The meaning of signs also depends on the 'speaker's' movements and facial expressions. There are as many sign languages as there are spoken ones. British Sign Language is used by an estimated 50,000 people in the UK.

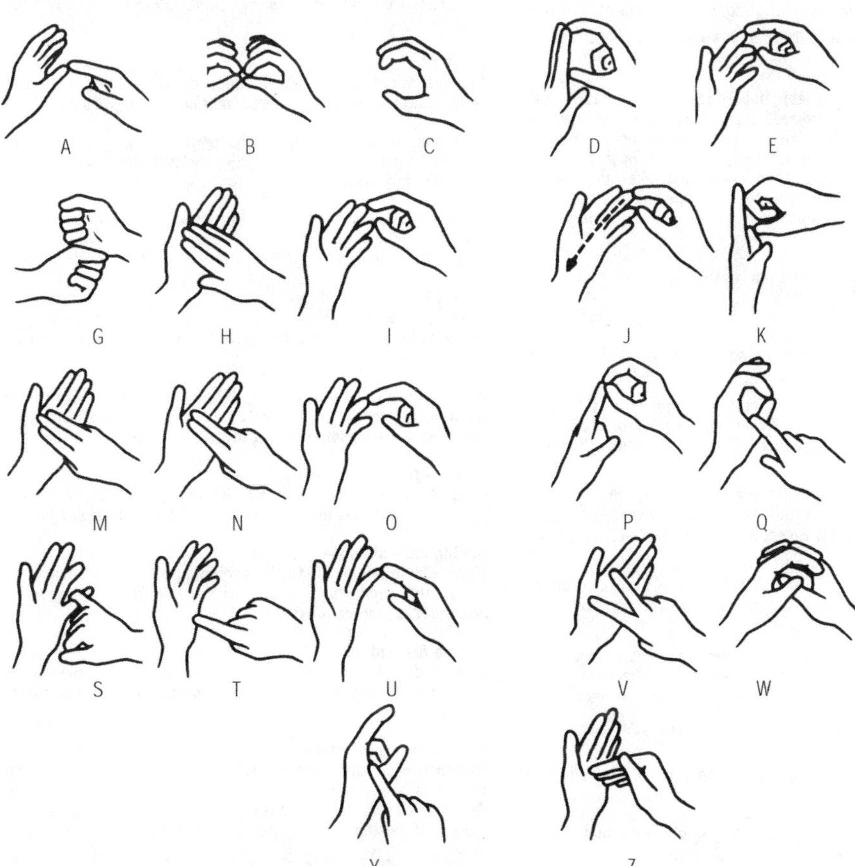

The Phonetic Alphabet Used in Radio Communications

The phonetic alphabet is used in radio communications to ensure accurate transmission of information. The use of well-known words instead of letters helps to avoid confusion, as it is easier to distinguish between Papa, Victor, and Bravo than it is between p, v, and b.

A Alpha
B Bravo
C Charlie
D Delta
E Echo

(continued)

The Phonetic Alphabet Used in Radio Communications (*continued*)

F Foxtrot
G Golf
H Hotel
I India
J Juliet
K Kilo
L Lima
M Mike
N November
O Oscar
P Papa
Q Quebec
R Romeo
S Sierra
T Tango
U Uniform
V Victor
W Whisky
X X-ray
Y Yankee
Z Zulu

The International Phonetic Alphabet

The International Phonetic Alphabet (IPA) is a system of codified symbols that makes possible the identification, description, and classification of sounds used in articulate speech. The IPA is a highly modified version of the Roman alphabet. It is based on ordinary Roman letters, along with modified forms, letters from other alphabets, and some invented letters. There are also a number of accents and other diacritics. Each symbol stands for a particular sound, but the interpretation of a sequence of symbols also depends on a number of conventions and on the phonetic context.

Usage

A Brief Guide to English Spelling

English is one of the least consistently phonetic of all languages. Different spelling patterns have evolved through the long history of the language's development, and have been inherited from its many source languages. Consequently, there are many spelling rules – and almost as many exceptions.

Spelling origins
In Old English (5th–12th centuries) and Middle English (11th–16th centuries) spelling was not standardized. *Feax, feaxe, fex*, and *fexe* are four Old English spellings for 'hair' found in the same book. Chaucer, writing in Middle English, used *neigh, negh, ney*, and *nygh* for 'near'. Modern English, which had approached something like its present, standardized form in the 18th century, contains spelling patterns that also include accepted variations (*organize, organise; enquiry, inquiry*).

Vowels
All English words must contain at least one vowel, *a, e, i, o*, or *u*; *y* as used in *hymn* also counts as a vowel.

Plurals
Many nouns become plural simply by adding an *s*: *bird, birds; lake, lakes*.

The plural of words ending in *y* are formed by changing the *y* to an *i* and adding *es*: *party, parties; fairy, fairies*. However, if the *y* is preceded by a vowel the *y* is retained and an *s* added: *chimney, chimneys; storey, storeys*.

Plurals of words ending in *o* require the additon of *es*: *tomato, tomatoes; embargo, embargoes*, but if a vowel precedes the *o*, only an *s* is added: *radio, radios; zoo, zoos*. Exceptions to this rule include *albino, albinos* and *logo, logos*.

Words ending in *s, x, z, ch*, or *sh*, which would be difficult to pronounce if an *s* were added, use *es*: *princess, princesses; fox, foxes; watch, watches*.

Irregular plurals include nouns where the stem changes: *foot, feet; tooth, teeth; mouse, mice*; nouns where there is no change: *sheep, sheep; fish, fish*; and some Latinate nouns: *appendix, appendices; spectrum, spectra*.

Doubling rules
When adding suffixes like *–ed, –ing*, or *–er* to a word, the following rules apply:

Most short words of one syllable ending with a single consonant double the last letter: *hop, hopping; win, winner; chop, chopped*.

Words of more than one syllable ending with a single consonant double the last letter if the word is stressed on the last syllable: *begin, beginner; commit, committed; occur, occurring*. However, if the stress is not on the last syllable, but an earlier one, the last letter is not doubled: *benefit, benefited; gallop, galloping; pardon, pardoned*. Exceptions include *handicap, handicapped; kidnap, kidnapped; worship, worshipped*.

Words of more than one syllable ending in *l* double the *l* even if the stress does not fall on the last syllable: *cancel, cancelled; travel, trav-elled; jewel, jeweller*. (These words take a single l in US spelling.) Exceptions include appealing and paralleled.

Words ending with more than one consonant do not double the last letter: *thump, thumped; halt, halting*.

Final consonants are not doubled before suffixes beginning with a consonant: *commit, commitment; fulfil, fulfilment; quarrel, quarrelsome; rival, rivalry*.

Keep *e*?
The final silent *e* of words is dropped when adding a suffix beginning with a vowel: *care, caring; tease, teasing; value, valuable; love, lovable*.

Exceptions occur where the *e* is preceded by a *g* or *c*, when it is sometimes retained: *knowledge, knowledgeable; age, ageing; trace, traceable* (but *tracing*).

If the suffix begins with a consonant the *e* is kept: *bare, barely; woe, woeful; refine, refinement; care, careless*. Exceptions include *argue, argument; awe, awful; due, duly; true, truly*; and *whole, wholly*.

***y* or *i*?**
When adding the endings *ed, ing*, or *er*, words ending in *y* and preceded by a vowel keep the *y*: *obey, obeyed; annoy, annoying; play, player*.

Words ending in *y* and preceded by a consonant, change the *y* to an *i* when adding *ed* or *er*: *apply, applied; occupy, occupied; fly, flier*; but keep the *y* when adding *ing*: *carry, carrying; fly, flying*.

***–ful* or *–full*?**
Used at the end of a word *full* becomes *ful*: *beautiful, hopeful, joyful, spoonful*. Other combinations include *fulfill, fulfilment* but *full, fullness*.

Adding *mis–* and *dis–*
When adding *mis* or *dis* to the beginning of a word, there is only one *s* unless the word itself begins with *s*: *misheard, disagree, disappear, misspelled, disservice, dissimilar*.

Adding *in–* and *un–*
When adding *in* or *un* to the beginning of a word, there is only one *n* unless the word itself begins with *n*: *inseparable, unending, innumerable, unnecessary*.

i* before *e* except after *c
This rhyme is a good general guide to the use of *ie* or *ei*, especially if the sound is *ee*: *fiend, siege, believe, niece, pier*, and *receipt, ceiling, deceive*. However, there are always exceptions: *weird, neither, protein, species*. If the sound is *ay*, the spelling is always *ei*: *freight, neighbour, weigh*.

Adding *–ly* and *–ally*
When *ly* is added to a word ending in *y*, the *y* is changed to an *i*: *crazy, crazily; funny, funnily; wary, warily*. Words ending in *ic* require the addition of *ally*: *enthusiastic, enthusiastically; basic, basically*. An exception is *publicly*.

–ize* or *–ise
In British English many verbs can be spelled either *–ize* or *–ise*; *–ize* is the usual US spelling. Words that can only be spelled *–ize* are *capsize* and *prize* (to value). A number of words can only be spelled *–ise*, including *disguise, surprise, exercise, advertise, arise, improvise, despise*.

Some Commonly Misspelled Words

accommodation
achieve
acquittal
address
aggressive
amount
anemone
appearance
asphalt
attach
banister
beautiful
beginning
bicycle
biscuit
budgeted
business
cemetery
cigarette
collapsible
committee
competition
conscientious
controversial
definitely
dependant (noun)
dependent (adjective)
describe
desiccate
desperate
detach
diarrhoea
diphtheria
disappear
disappoint
dissect
dissipate
ecstasy
eighth
embarrass
exaggerate
excellent
excitement
exercise
exhilarate
extravagant
February
foreign
friend
fulfil
gauge
gazetteer
government
grammar
guarantee
guard
handkerchief
harass
height
hygiene
hypocrisy
idiosyncrasy
immediately
independent (noun and adjective)
install
instalment
jewellery
league
liaise
library
liquefy
literature
longitude
manoeuvre
Mediterranean
millennium
millionaire
mischievous
mortgage
necessary
neither
niece
noticeable
nuisance
occasion
occurrence
omit
oneself
parallel
paraphernalia
permissible
personnel
Pharaoh
poisonous
possess
potatoes
practice (noun)
practise (verb)
precede
prejudice
privilege
profession
pronunciation
publicly
questionnaire
receive
repellent
seize
separate
sergeant
siege
sieve
sincerely
soldier
solemn
supersede
targeted
terrestrial
tomatoes
tranquillity
traveller
unnecessary
until
unusual
unwieldy
vetoed
vicious
videoed
Wednesday
yield

A Brief Guide to English Punctuation

The purpose of punctuation – a system of marks and spaces – is to make text readable, clear, and logical, to direct pause and emphasis, to denote possession, and to indicate dialogue. Without adequate punctuation, words may be incorrectly construed or the meaning of a sentence rendered ambiguous.

Full stop or period (.)
Used to mark the end of a sentence and to indicate that a word has been abbreviated, as in *No.* for *number*. Acronyms and contractions incorporating the last letter of a word may not always employ full stops: *NATO* rather than *N.A.T.O.*, *Dr* for *Doctor*.

Comma (,)
Used to demarcate a phrase or noun in apposition: *Billy, the striker, was sent off*; to define a subordinate phrase: *Mrs Parsons, who drank 20 cups of coffee a day, suffered from chronic insomnia*; or to separate elements in sequence or items in a list: *his steady, heavy, menacing footsteps*; *bacon, egg, and beans*. Commas are also used to mark off sentence connectors such as *however* and *moreover*: *Nevertheless, the public continued to walk on the grass*. Commas can introduce and terminate direct speech: *She asked, 'Shall we go?' 'I think we should,' he replied.*

Colon (:)
Used before a list or as a substitute for 'namely': *The contents of the hamper tumbled out: apples, ham sandwiches, and a chocolate cake*; or after a complete statement to specify or add related detail: *That's her cat: the fluffy white one*. A colon is another way to introduce a passage of direct speech or quotation: *I heard the announcement: 'Please exit immediately'*; *Remember the saying: 'Love is blind'*.

Semicolon (;)
Used to link two independent sentences where they form a related statement and where a full stop would be too abrupt: *We watched the fireworks; it was a dazzling display*. Semicolons are also used to separate items in a complex list that already includes commas: *pens, pencils, and paper; tools, various; and rope*.

Hyphen (-)
Used to join words as an aid to sense. Adjectival compounds are hyphenated because they affect the noun together, the sense being changed if they are separated: *a small-town boy* is a boy from a small town, whereas *a small town boy* is a small boy from a town. Hyphens are used with adverbs only if an identical adjective exists (*well*, *long*), as in *late-blooming plant* but *brightly blooming flower*. Generally speaking, phrasal verbs are not hyphenated unless used adjectivally: *things turned out well* but *a well-turned-out crowd*. The hyphenation of compound nouns and certain prefixes is not clear cut, although modern style is moving towards omitting the hyphen, as in *noncooperation*.

Apostrophe (')
Used either to indicate a missing letter: *mustn't* for *must not* and *it's* for *it is*, or with the addition of 's' to show possession: *Amy's camera*, *James's coat*, *the clock's hands*, *children's books*. Plurals ending in 's' do not have an additional 's': *girls' watches*, *babies' cots*.

Quotation marks (' ';" ")
Used in pairs to mark off dialogue or quotations, around the titles of works (when not in italics), or to indicate a word used in an unusual or ironic way: *Our 'learned' friend appears to be lost*. In the UK single quotes are commonly used, and double quotes within single: *Mother said, 'Let's sing "Humpty Dumpty" together'*; in the USA normal practice is the other way round. Full stops and commas come before the closing quotation marks when the quotation is a full sentence: *'Humpty Dumpty,' she recited, 'sat on the Wall.'*; and after when the quotation is a fragment: *She described the egg as 'large, speckled, and free-range'*.

Parenthesis ( )
Used around a phrase to indicate that it is an aside or interruption to the normal flow of text; pairs of brackets (round ( ) and square [ ]), commas, and dashes may be employed. Parenthetical commas are the gentlest device: *He climbed Everest, so he said, because it was there*; dashes the most emphatic; and brackets the clearest and most clinical. Round brackets are used generally; square are employed in the editing and insertion of text.

Dash (–)
Used singly a dash represents an abrupt change of subject or a sudden break in dialogue: *'Not that one – this one!'* and will emphasize a point: *Smoking is harmful to your health – even life threatening*. Used in pairs, dashes act as parentheses marking off a clearly subordinate part of a sentence where commas would not be appropriate: *A heckler from the back – trouble always comes from the back – shouted abuse at the speaker*.

Question mark (?)
Used to indicate an enquiry at the end of a direct question: *Where is my reward?* or implied query: *This is my reward?* It is never needed at the end of an indirect question: *He asked us who was coming*, since this is a statement.

Exclamation mark (!)
Used mainly in dialogue to indicate emphasis, urgency, or strong emotion, particularly with interjections, greetings, or orders: *'That's terrible!' 'How embarrassing!' 'Bye now!' 'Let me out!' 'Shut up!'* Overuse reduces impact.

Asterisk (*)
Used to link the asterisked word with a note at the bottom of the page, and in place of letters in expletives – *'Go to H*ll!'* was employed when 'Hell' was a taboo word.

Ellipsis (...)
Used to denote the omission of one or more words in a sentence; to signify uncertainty in dialogue: *'Perhaps I'll wear the blue... no, maybe the red'*; or to indicate that a sentence has not been completed or leads to an unknown conclusion.

A Brief Guide to Letter Writing

There are generally agreed ways of laying out a letter, and people expect to find certain information, such as the sender's address and the date, in certain places.

General layout
Regard should be given to the overall appearance of the letter on the page. Space should be left at the top, bottom, and sides to form a frame around the text. The text, whether handwritten, typed, or set, should be clear and evenly spaced – a line guide may be used beneath the paper to avoid sloping when handwriting.

Writer's address and date information
The writer's address should be placed in the top righthand corner of the page. The address may be either laid out in a sloping style, each line beginning a few characters to the right of the previous line; or in block style, with all lines of the address aligned from the same point. When using a sloping style, a comma may be put at the end of each line of the address except the last, which has a full stop. However, the modern tendency is for 'open punctuation', with no punctuation in the address, date, and opening and closing phrases. The style of address in the letter should be used on the envelope.

If including a telephone number, this should be placed below the address (in line with the first line of the address) or in the top lefthand corner of the page. If fax and e-mail numbers are given, they should be placed beneath the telephone number; such contact information is then best placed in the top lefthand corner. Telephone is usually abbreviated to *Tel*, with a full stop or colon if punctuation is used, followed by the full dialling code; other numbers should follow style.

The date should appear below the address and any other contact details, in line with the first line of the address. Its most common form is *31 July 2000*. The use of *1st*, *2nd*, *3rd*, *4th* and so on has declined, but may appear in handwritten letters or copperplate print styles. The name of the month and date of the year should be given in full. Another form gives the name of the month first, and then the number of the day separated from the year by a comma: *July 31, 2000*. All-number dates such as *31.7.00* are used only in informal writing.

Leaving a line space between the address, telephone number, and date will make the information clearer.

Setting out the main text
After writing the address and date, leave a few blank lines and move down to the left, remembering to leave an imaginary margin. Open the letter *Dear So-and-so* and then leave another line space before beginning the first paragraph.

In formal letters each paragraph will deal with a separate aspect of the writer's correspondence. Even in informal letters it is helpful to the reader for example to put information about a reunion in one paragraph, and details of a future holiday in another. The most usual way to begin a paragraph in a handwritten letter is to indent the first line. Another way to distinguish paragraphs is to leave a line space between them, a method often used in typewritten letters. When leaving a line space it is not necessary to indent. Following the last paragraph, leave a line space before signing off the letter.

Closing words
It is usual to finish a letter with a conventional phrase of goodwill. For people known personally but not closely, a phrase such as *Best wishes* is suitable. In formal personal letters the standard phrase is *Yours sincerely*. Only the first word in these phrases has a capital letter. The phrase can be placed in the centre or on the left of the page. This is also the place for the writer to sign the letter. For family and friends, just the first name is usual, otherwise the first name (or initials) and surname should be written. It is courteous and sensible to sign off clearly. There is no full stop after the signature.

Business letters
The general rules governing the layout of a letter should be followed. Additionally the 'inside address', comprising the name or position of the addressee, department, and company address, should appear on the left hand side of the letter, below the level of the date and before the opening phrase. The inside address, and that on the envelope, should always be in block style. In a letter to a business, the date is sometimes written on the left above the inside address.

Business letters often include reference numbers that need to be quoted to ensure that correspondence on a particular issue is kept together. The usual place to quote references is on the left above the inside address, followed by a line space.

Headings are helpful in directing the reader to the purpose of the letter. These should appear to the left beneath the opening phrase, with a line space above and below, and can be emphasized by underlining or using bold type. The word *Re* (Latin 'on the subject of') may introduce the heading: *Re: purchase of 57 Manor Road, Beccles*.

The body of the letter, set out in paragraphs, should begin with what prompted the letter, such as a complaint or response to an advertisement. Related information should be detailed, and finally any action being sought, such as further information or compensation. If the letter requires more than one page, continue on a new sheet; never write on the back of a page. Put the page number in the top lefthand corner, and add the date and addressee's name on separate lines below. Leave a line space before continuing the letter.

If the addressee's name is unknown, *Dear Sir or Madam* is used. When beginning a letter in this way, the conventional ending is *Yours faithfully*. If the addressee's name is known, it should be used at the beginning of the actual letter: *Dear Mr Brown*; and the ending will be *Yours sincerely*. When addressing a woman, *Ms* may be used for married or single women, or where marital status is unknown; *Mrs* and *Miss* denote married and single respectively. The closing phrase commonly appears on the left. On a typewritten letter the writer's name should be typed below, leaving space for a signature.

When enclosing documents with a letter, write *Enc* in the bottom lefthand corner of the page, followed by a list of the items enclosed.

See also **How to Complain**, p 301; **Forms of Address in the UK**, p 441.

A Brief Guide to Corresponding by Fax

Material sent by fax should always be covered by a facsimile cover or transmittal sheet containing details of the addressee, sender, date, and the number of sheets being transmitted – the latter is essential to ensure that the receiver can assess whether all the material has arrived. Facsimile transmittal sheets usually take the form of a structured document headed *Facsimile Transmittal* or *Fax*, with subheadings and spaces left for entering the appropriate information.

The standard headings are: *To:* for the addressee's name, followed by *Fax:* for the addressee's fax number; *From:* for the sender's name, followed by *Tel:* for the sender's telephone number – important if the addressee experiences difficulty receiving the fax; *Date:*; *Re:* for the subject of the fax; and *Total of pages:* for the number of sheets transmitted, usually shown as 'Covering sheet + 3', for example. Other headings may include *Company:*, *Sender's Ref No:*, *Your Ref No:*, and *cc:* to indicate that others have been sent the same information.

Many word processing programs contain templates for facsimile transmittal sheets which may be used as they stand or personalized, for instance for use with a company letterheading. Some templates include instruction boxes, such as *Urgent*, *Please comment*, *Please recycle*. If the message itself is to be written on the facsimile transmittal sheet, the sender's full address details should be included in the subheadings or as a letterheading.

A Brief Guide to 'Netiquette'

Although electronic mail (e-mail), is relatively new in the history of correspondence, an informal code of practice and presentation for Internet users has emerged, often referred to as 'netiquette'.

If the e-mail system being used allows the addition of a **personal name string** to the address, such as *2001@mailbox.com (Geoffrey Chaucer)*, always use this facility; it enables the recipient to identify the sender more rapidly, and may help the postmaster to sort out an invalid address.

It is helpful to insert a brief but explanatory **subject heading** in the e-mail heading to enable the recipient to sort and search a list of messages in their mailbox more easily. If the subject changes over a chain of correspondence using the reply facility, either change the subject heading to make it relevant or start a new message.

When sending a large attachment that may take a long time to download, it is polite to warn the recipient in advance. Avoid typing a message in upper-case throughout – apart from being difficult to read, this is considered **shouting** in netiquette. Limited use of upper-case to accentuate a point is acceptable. Emphasis or emotion may also be indicated by the use of 'emoticons'.

In business correspondence create separate e-mails for separate topics where appropriate, as this helps the recipient to sort and file their information. If answering a message by reply, return the minimum amount of correspondence, and use quotation marks around any material quoted from a previous message used in the reply. Messages can easily be forwarded, so do not send sensitive or confidential information by e-mail.

Spamming is a term used for the sending of mass or bulk mailings – the equivalent of direct mailshots. Unsolicited junk e-mails, especially if they involve advertising, can be irritating to the recipient, so avoid forwarding e-mails of this kind.

Sending a message of abuse or outrage is known as **flaming**. Errors of netiquette, such as losing or forgetting to save instructions that someone has sent you, 'shouting' in capitals, or passing on junk mail (especially if it involves advertising) may attract flaming.

An e-mail program can be set up to apply a **signature message** automatically (check the instructions). This should include such information as name, business name, postal address, e-mail address, telephone and fax numbers, and Internet home page address.

Emoticons

An emoticon or 'smiley' is a symbol designed to communicate emotion in text using punctuation marks and other symbols. Most emoticons take the form of a human face and should be viewed sideways. Below is a selection of some of the growing number of emoticons now in use online.

<table>
<tr><th>Emoticon</th><th>Interpretation</th></tr>
<tr><td>:-)
:)
:-〉
: 〉</td><td>happy</td></tr>
<tr><td>:-(
: (
:-〈
: 〈</td><td>sad</td></tr>
<tr><td>;-)
;)
;-〉
; 〉</td><td>winking</td></tr>
<tr><td>:-t
~:-(</td><td>cross, angry</td></tr>
<tr><td>:-|</td><td>indifferent</td></tr>
<tr><td>:-o
8-0</td><td>suprised, amazed, shocked</td></tr>
</table>

<table>
<tr><th>Emoticon</th><th>Interpretation</th></tr>
<tr><td>:-D</td><td>laughing</td></tr>
<tr><td>:,-(
:'-(
;-(</td><td>crying</td></tr>
<tr><td>8-|</td><td>in suspense</td></tr>
<tr><td>|-|</td><td>asleep (bored)</td></tr>
<tr><td>:-&</td><td>tongue-tied</td></tr>
<tr><td>:-#
:-x</td><td>lips are sealed</td></tr>
<tr><td>:-\</td><td>undecided</td></tr>
<tr><td>:-/</td><td>sceptical</td></tr>
<tr><td>:-P</td><td>poking tongue out</td></tr>
<tr><td>$-)</td><td>greedy</td></tr>
<tr><td>〉:-)
〉:-〉</td><td>devilish</td></tr>
</table>

<table>
<tr><th>Emoticon</th><th>Interpretation</th></tr>
<tr><td>〉;-)
〉;-〉</td><td>devilish</td></tr>
<tr><td>0:-)</td><td>angelic</td></tr>
<tr><td><:-)</td><td>dunce (stupid question?)</td></tr>
<tr><td>:-#</td><td>smiling with beard</td></tr>
<tr><td>8-)
8)
8-〉
8 〉</td><td>smiling with glasses</td></tr>
<tr><td>(-:</td><td>left-handed, Australian</td></tr>
<tr><td>:-*
:-X</td><td>kiss</td></tr>
<tr><td>(8(|)</td><td>Homer Simpson</td></tr>
<tr><td>@@@@8 (|)</td><td>Marge Simpson</td></tr>
</table>

See also **Some Internet Terms,** p 491.

A Selection of Acronyms and Abbreviations in Use Online

Acronym/abbreviation	Meaning
AFAICT	As Far As I Can Tell
AFAIK	As Far As I Know
AFAIR	As Far As I Recall/Remember
AIUI	As I Understand It
ATM	At The Moment
B4	Before
BCNU	Be Seeing You
BTDT	Been There Done That
BTW	By The Way
CUL	See You Later
DQM	Don't Quote Me
FAQ	Frequently Asked Question
FOAF	Friend Of A Friend
FOC	Free Of Charge
FOCL	Falls Off Chair Laughing
F2F	Face To Face
FUD	Fear, Uncertainty, and Doubt
FWIW	For What It's Worth
FYI	For Your Information
GIGO	Garbage In Garbage Out
HTH	Hope That Helps
IIRC	If I Recall/Remember Correctly
IKWYM	I Know What You Mean
IME	In My Experience
IMHO	In My Humble Opinion
IMNSHO	In My Not So Humble Opinion
IMO	In My Opinion

Acronym/abbreviation	Meaning
IOW	In Other Words
ISTM	It Seems To Me
ISTR	I Seem To Recall/Remember
ISWYM	I See What You Mean
IYKWIM	If You Know What I Mean
JAM	Just A Minute
LCW	Loud, Confident, and Wrong
LOL	Lots Of Luck/Laughing Out Loud
NAFAIK	Not As Far As I Know
NALOPKT	Not A Lot Of People Know That
OIC	Oh I See
OTOH	On The Other Hand
OTT	Over The Top
PD	Public Domain
PMFJI	Pardon Me For Jumping In
POV	Point Of View
ROTFL	Rolling On The Floor Laughing
TIC	Tongue In Cheek
TPTB	The Powers That Be
TTBOMK	To The Best of My Knowledge
TTFN	Ta Ta For Now
TTYL	Talk To You Later
TYVM	Thank You Very Much
WRT	With Respect To
WYSIWYG	What You See Is What You Get
YHM	You Have Mail
YKWIM	You Know What I Mean

Names and Forms of Address

Popular Names of 1999

In 1999 Jack was the most popular name given to boys in England and Wales for the fifth year running and Chloe was the most popular girls' name for the third year in a row. Chloe was also the most popular girls' name in Scotland and Northern Ireland and Jack was the most popular boys' name in Scotland, replacing Ryan which had held on to the top position for five years.

Imogen was the highest new entry in the top 50 girls' names in England and Wales, and Niamh showed the greatest increase in popularity, rising 22 places from 1998. Niamh rose 21 places to number 26 in Scotland and 3 places to number 9 in Northern Ireland.

Louis was the only new entry in the top 50 boys' names in England and Wales and Owen climbed the most places, up 11 to 33. Owen also entered the top 50 in Scotland, rising 13 places to number 49, but the name did not appear in the Northern Ireland top 50.

John, consistently very popular in the first half of the 20th century, dropped out of the boys top 50 in England and Wales in 1998; Jonathan dropped out in 1999.

From 1899 to 1999
Although many of the most popular girls' names of 1899 have fallen from favour, Alice and Elizabeth still appear in the top 50. Five of the most popular boys' names of 1899 still appear in the top 50 and Thomas and James appear in the top 10 for both 1899 and 1999.

Top 50 Girls' and Boys' Names in England and Wales

(+/– indicates movement since 1998; – indicates no change since 1998.)

1999 Girls Rank	Name		*Boys* Rank	Name	
1	Chloe	–	1	Jack	–
2	Emily	–	2	Thomas	–
3	Megan	–	3	James	–
4	Olivia	+12	4	Joshua	+1
5	Sophie	–	5	Daniel	–1
6	Charlotte	–	6	Matthew	–
7	Lauren	+1	7	Samuel	–
8	Jessica	–4	8	Joseph	+1
9	Rebecca	–	9	Callum	–1
10	Hannah	–3	10	William	+4
11	Bethany	+3	11	Ryan	+1
12	Lucy	–2	12	Luke	+1
13	Georgia	–1	13	Lewis	+5
14	Amy	–3	14	Harry	+1
15	Katie	–2	15	Jordan	–5
16	Ellie	+6	16	Benjamin	–
17	Emma	–2	17	Liam	+6
18	Courtney	–1	18	George	–1
19	Eleanor	–	19	Alexander	–
20	Abigail	+1	20	Adam	+1
21	Shannon	–3	21	Oliver	–1
22	Molly	+1	22	Connor	–11
23	Jade	–3	23	Jake	–1
24	Caitlin	+4	24	Cameron	+5
25	Alice	–	25	Michael	–1
26	Ella	+12	26	Nathan	–1
27	Grace	+9	27	Jacob	–
28	Laura	–4	28	Kieran	–2
29	Rachel	–	29	Mohammed	+5
30	Holly	–3	30	Ben	–2
31	Sarah	–5	31	Jamie	+4
32	Leah	+8	32	Charlie	+1
33	Elizabeth	–3	33	Owen	+11
34	Amber	–3	34	Bradley	–3
35	Jasmine	+12	35	Brandon	+1
36	Natasha	+1	36	Aaron	–6
37	Amelia	+11	37	Kyle	+1
38	Phoebe	+5	38	Christopher	–6
39	Victoria	+3	39	Robert	–2
40	Anna	+1	40	Ethan	+7
41	Nicole	–6	41	David	–2
42	Paige	–10	42	Alex	+3
43	Chelsea	–4	43	Charles	–2
44	Georgina	–11	44	Reece	–2
45	Danielle	–11	45	Edward	–2
46	Zoe	–2	46	Andrew	–6
47	Imogen	new entry[1]	47	Dylan	–1
48	Niamh	new entry[2]	48	Max	+2
49	Lydia	+1	49	Sam	–
50	Alexandra	–4	50	Louis	new entry[3]

[1] Ranked 59 in 1998.
[2] Ranked 70 in 1998.
[3] Ranked 53 in 1998.

Source: Office for National Statistics, © Crown copyright 1999

Top 10 Girls' and Boys' Names in Scotland

(+/– indicates movement since 1998; – indicates no change since 1998.)

1999 Girls Rank	Name		*Boys* Rank	Name	
1	Chloe	–	1	Jack	+1
2	Rebecca	+1	2	Lewis	+2
3	Lauren	+5	3	Ryan	–2
4	Emma	–	4	Cameron	+1
5	Amy	–	5	Ross	–2
6	Megan	–4	6	James	–
7	Caitlin	–1	7	Andrew	+1
8	Rachel	–1	8	Liam	+7
9	Erin	+5	9	Scott	–
10	Sophie	+1	10	Connor	–3

Source: General Register Office for Scotland, © Crown copyright 1999

Top 10 Girls' and Boys' Names in Northern Ireland

(+/– indicates movement since 1998; – indicates no change since 1998.)

1999 Girls Rank	Name		*Boys* Rank	Name	
1	Chloe	–	1	Matthew	–
2	Rebecca	+1	2	Ryan	–
3	Emma	–1	3	James	–
4	Caitlin	+7	4	Jack	–
5	Megan	+5	5	Adam	+1
6	Amy	–3	6	Conor[1]	–1
7	Lauren	–2	7	Michael	+1
8	Sarah	–	8	Jordan	–2
9	Niamh	+3	9	Daniel	+3
10	Rachel	–1	10	Aaron	+3

[1] 247 boys were registered with the name Conor, but another 70 boys had the alternative spelling Connor which was ranked 47th.

Source: General Register Office, Northern Ireland, © Crown copyright 1999

Top 10 Girls' and Boys' Names in 1899

The table shows the most popular names for babies born in England and Wales in 1899 and the ranking of these names in 1999. The names of people who died before 1991 were not included in the statistics used to compile the rankings for 1899.

(– = an insignificant number or not in use.)

Girls 1899 Rank	Name	1999 Rank	*Boys* 1899 Rank	Name	1999 Rank
1	Mary	146	1	William	10
2	Florence	166	2	John	57
3	Edith	693	3	George	18
4	Dorothy	1,198	4	Thomas	2
5	Elsie	641	5	Frederick	122
6	Annie	130	6	Charles	43
7	Alice	25	7	Arthur	178
8	Elizabeth	33	8	James	3
9	Ethel	–	9	Albert	253
10	Margaret	532	10	Alfred	145

Source: Office for National Statistics, © Crown copyright 1999

TOTAL SOLAR ECLIPSE
A total solar eclipse, which lasted for two minutes, was visible from southwestern England on 11 August 1999. It was the first total solar eclipse to be visible from the UK since 1927, and the next will occur in 2090. *Above* a view of the eclipse over the Old Bailey in London. *Right* observers in Cornwall watching the eclipse through protective sunglasses. *Syndication International; Morgan-Moore/Rex*

PADDINGTON RAIL CRASH
Rescue teams, fire, police, and ambulance crews at the scene of the train crash near Paddington station in London, on 5 October 1999. Thirty-one people were killed in the crash and hundreds injured when a train failed to stop at a red signal in the morning rush hour. In the ensuing enquiry, it emerged that the driver was newly qualified and had not been given specific instruction about the complex track close to the scene of the disaster. *Syndication International*

HAROLD SHIPMAN CASE
English GP Harold Shipman being escorted to court in Preston, Lancashire, on 5 October 1999. Shipman was convicted of murdering 15 of his elderly female patients. *Syndication International*

HOPE FOR PARAPLEGICS
Italian paraplegic Gabriele Tronconi is able to stand with the help of electrodes – attached to his legs – that stimulate his paralysed muscles. His hope for regaining mobility lies with a radical new implant therapy that may allow him to stand and walk with a frame without external wires. He is seen here in Brussels on 20 March 2000. *Benoit Doppagne/Popperfoto*

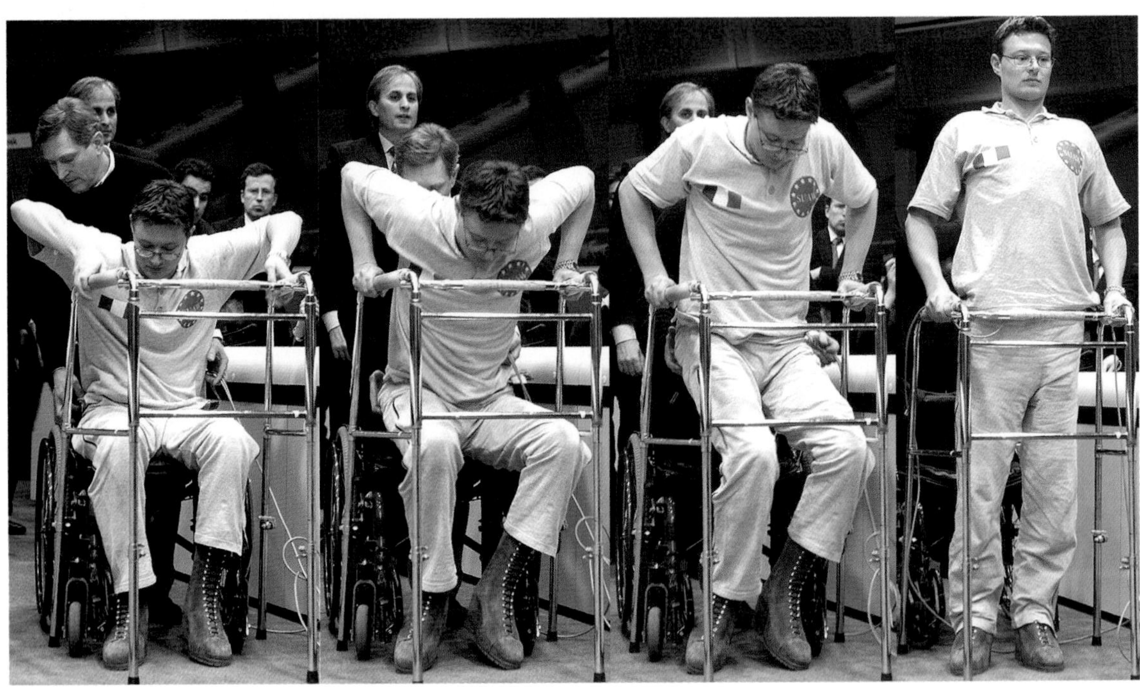

SAM MENDES (*left*)
English film director Sam Mendes at the Academy Awards ceremony in Los Angeles CA, USA on 27 March 2000. His feature film directorial debut, *American Beauty*, won five Academy Awards, including those for Best Film and Best Director.
Richard Young/Rex

ALL SAINTS (*right*)
Three members of the pop band All Saints – Natalie and Nicole Appleton and Melanie Blatt – and Dave Stewart, of the band The Eurythmics. The three All Saints starred in the film *Honest*, which was set in London's swinging sixties and was directed by Stewart. The film was a box-office (and critical) flop. *Rex*

HUMAN GENOME
Director of the Sanger Centre Dr John Sulston speaks at the Human Genome Project press conference at the Wellcome Trust in London, on 26 June 2000. The announcement that scientists had completed a working draft of the human genetic code was made simultaneously by publicly and privately funded ventures. The achievement – seen as one of the greatest milestones in human history – was met with both hope for new treatments for disease, and fear over ethical issues and the possible abuse of genetic information. *Popperfoto*

LONDON EYE
The London Eye, a vertical wheel 151 m/495 ft in diameter, opened to the public on 1 March 2000 after much publicized delays due to technical difficulties. It forms part of the UK's millennium celebrations, together with such projects as the Millennium Dome, and is situated opposite the Houses of Parliament on the River Thames. Intended to symbolize the turning of the century, the London Eye was conceived and designed by the architects David Marks and Julia Barfield and its construction was undertaken by British Airways.
Sean Aidan

THE LOWRY (*top left*)
Part of the old Salford Quays just outside Manchester has been transformed into The Lowry, a spectacular National Landmark Millennium Project for the Arts, which opened in April 2000. It houses two art galleries, one dedicated to the local artist, L S Lowry, the other showing work by contemporary artists; the 1,730-seat Lyric Theatre and a second, studio theatre The Quays with 466 seats; and Art Works a high-tech interactive experience designed to encourage individual creativity. The National Lottery was the main sponsor for the project, donating £68.9 million of the £105.9 million total cost. *Len Grant/The Lowry*

TATE MODERN (*below, far left* exterior view; *below left* interior view)
The new Tate Modern gallery was opened by the Queen on the south bank of the Thames on 12 May 2000. Housed in the old power station at Bankside, the gallery cost £134 million, approximately £50 million of which came from the National Lottery's Millennium Fund. *Tate London 2000*

POLAR BEARS UNDER THREAT (*below*)
A polar bear on the coast of Hudson Bay, Canada. Polar bears living on the Arctic icecap may be in danger of starving to death, according to the Canadian Wildlife Service. This warning follows data published by scientists from the University of Washington indicating that the Arctic icecap has shrunk by approximately 40% over the last 50 years, probably due to global warming. *Daniel J Cox/Oxford Scientific Films*

CHAOS IN ZIMBABWE
Right Zimbabweans brandishing agricultural tools, attempting to occupy land seized by force from white farmers in April 2000. Over 900 mainly white-owned farms were illegally invaded following the government's defeat in a constitutional referendum and ahead of parliamentary elections. *Below* police and guards at the gate of the farm owned by Rob Marshall, who was being prevented from entering his property.
Joe Alexander/Popperfoto; Howard Burditt/Popperfoto

CHANDRIKA KUMARATUNGA SURVIVES *(above)*
Sri Lanka's president Chandrika Kumaratunga (*left*), who survived an assassination attempt shortly before winning another term of office in elections in December 1999. Here she is seen with her mother, Sri Lankan prime minister Sirimavo Bandaranaike, at her official residence in Colombo. *David Loh/Popperfoto*

DEATH OF PRESIDENT ASSAD *(right)*
The funeral of Syrian president Hafez al-Assad took place in Damascus on 13 June 2000, with thousands of people thronging the procession route. President for 30 years, Assad was the only leader that many Syrians had ever known. *Popperfoto*

VIOLENCE IN EAST TIMOR *(below right)*
Refugees fleeing the turmoil in East Timor. On 1 September 1999, the day after the referendum that approved East Timorese independence, pro-Indonesian militiamen killed more than 20 people in the capital Dili. This followed a six-month campaign of violence and intimidation against advocates of independence. UN troops were sent in to stop the militiamen on 4 September. *Rex*

COUP IN FIJI *(below left)*
Colleagues of murdered Fijian police officer Filipo Seavula carry his coffin as it is taken for burial in Fiji's capital city, Suva, on 6 June 2000. Seavula was shot dead on 28 May during a riot led by rebel supporters of coup leader George Speight, who took 31 hostages, including the former prime minister Mahendra Chaudhry and his ministers. *David Gray/Popperfoto*

FLOODS IN MOZAMBIQUE
Severe flooding in Mozambique in March 2000 – the country's worst in 40 years – left thousands dead and hundreds of thousands homeless. Victims were stranded on rooftops and in trees, while helicopter crews attempted rescue operations in appalling weather conditions. *Syndication International*

CONFLICT IN SIERRA LEONE
On 24 May 2000 Prime Minister Tony Blair ordered the UK High Commissioner in Freetown to make a formal protest to the Sierra Leone government, after photographs were released of child soldiers wearing British uniforms and carrying British Army rifles.This child soldier is 14 years old. *Syndication International*

FOOTBALL: FRANCE'S LAST-MINUTE VICTORY
In the final of the European Championship 2000, held in Rotterdam on 2 July, France beat Italy 2–1 with an extra-time golden goal, scored by David Trezeguet (*far left*). *Popperfoto*

EUROPE

Abbr.	Nation	Capital city
A.	**Andorra**	Andorra la Vella
AL.	**Albania**	Tiranë
AU.	**Austria**	Vienna
B.	**Belgium**	Brussels
B.H.	**Bosnia-Herzegovina**	Sarajevo
	Bulgaria	Sofia
C.	**Croatia**	Zagreb
CZ.	**Czech Republic**	Prague
D.	**Denmark**	Copenhagen
E.	**Estonia**	Tallinn
H.	**Hungary**	Budapest
LA.	**Latvia**	Riga
L.	**Liechtenstein**	Vaduz
LI.	**Lithuania**	Vilnius
LU.	**Luxembourg**	Luxembourg
MA.	**Macedonia**	Skopje
	Malta	Valletta
M.	**Monaco**	Monaco
MO.	**Moldova**	Chişinău
N.	**Netherlands**	Amsterdam
	Romania	Bucharest
S.	**San Marino**	San Marino
S.R.	**Slovak Republic**	Bratislava
SL.	**Slovenia**	Ljubljana
SW.	**Switzerland**	Bern
V.	**Vatican City**	
Y.	**Yugoslavia**	Belgrade

ASIA

Abbr.	Nation	Capital city
AR.	**Armenia**	Yerevan
AZ.	**Azerbaijan**	Baku
B.	**Bahrain**	Al Manamah
	Brunei	Bandar Seri Begawan
C.	**Cyprus**	Nicosia
G.	**Georgia**	Tbilisi
I.	**Israel**	Jerusalem
	Jordan	Amman
K.	**Kuwait**	Kuwait
L.	**Lebanon**	Beirut
	Maldives	Malé
Q.	**Qatar**	Doha
SI.	**Singapore**	Singapore
	Syria	Damascus
	Tajikistan	Dushanbe
U.A.E.	**United Arab Emirates**	Abu Dhabi

OCEANIA

Nation	Capital city
Fiji Islands	Suva
Kiribati	Bairiki
Marshall Islands	Dalap-Uliga-
Micronesia, Federated States of	Palikir
Nauru	Yaren
Palau	Koror
Samoa	Apia
Solomon Islands	Honiara
Tonga	Nuku'alofa
Tuvalu	Fongafale
Vanuatu	Port-Vila

THE WORLD: POLITICAL

Key

◇ capital city

○ other major city

—— international boundary

NORTH AND CENTRAL AMERICA

Abbr.	Nation	Capital city
A.	**Antigua and Barbuda**	St John's
	Barbados	Bridgetown
	Belize	Belmopan
	Costa Rica	San José
D.	**Dominica**	Roseau
	Dominican Republic	Santo Domingo
	El Salvador	San Salvador
G.	**Grenada**	St George's
	Guatemala	Guatemala
	Haiti	Port-au-Prince
	Honduras	Tegucigalpa
	Jamaica	Kingston
	Nicaragua	Managua
	Panama	Panamá
S.K.	**St Kitts and Nevis**	Basseterre
S.L.	**St Lucia**	Castries
S.V.	**St Vincent and the Grenadines**	Kingstown
	Trinidad and Tobago	Port-of-Spain

AFRICA

Abbr.	Nation	Capital city
BE.	**Benin**	Porto Novo
B.F.	**Burkina Faso**	Ouagadougou
B.	**Burundi**	Bujumbura
	Cape Verde	Praia
	Comoros	Moroni
C.I.	**Côte d'Ivoire**	Yamoussoukro
D.	**Djibouti**	Djibouti
E.G.	**Equatorial Guinea**	Malabo
	Eritrea	Asmara
	Gabon	Libreville
	Gambia	Banjul
G.	**Ghana**	Accra
	Guinea-Bissau	Bissau
	Liberia	Monrovia
	Mauritius	Port Louis
R.	**Rwanda**	Kigali
S.T.	**São Tomé and Príncipe**	São Tomé
	Senegal	Dakar
	Seychelles	Victoria
	Swaziland	Mbabane
T.	**Togo**	Lomé

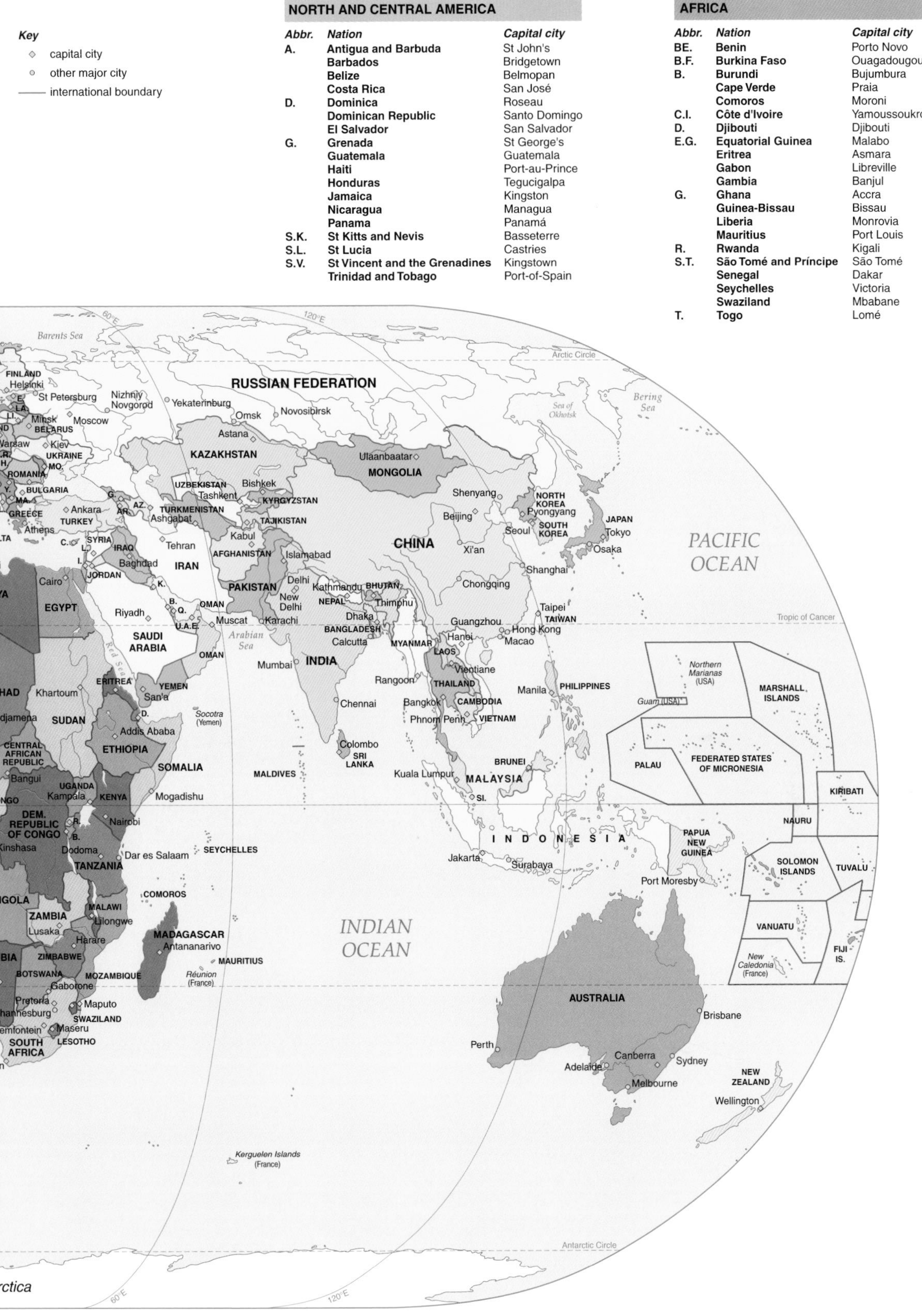

THE WORLD: PHYSICAL

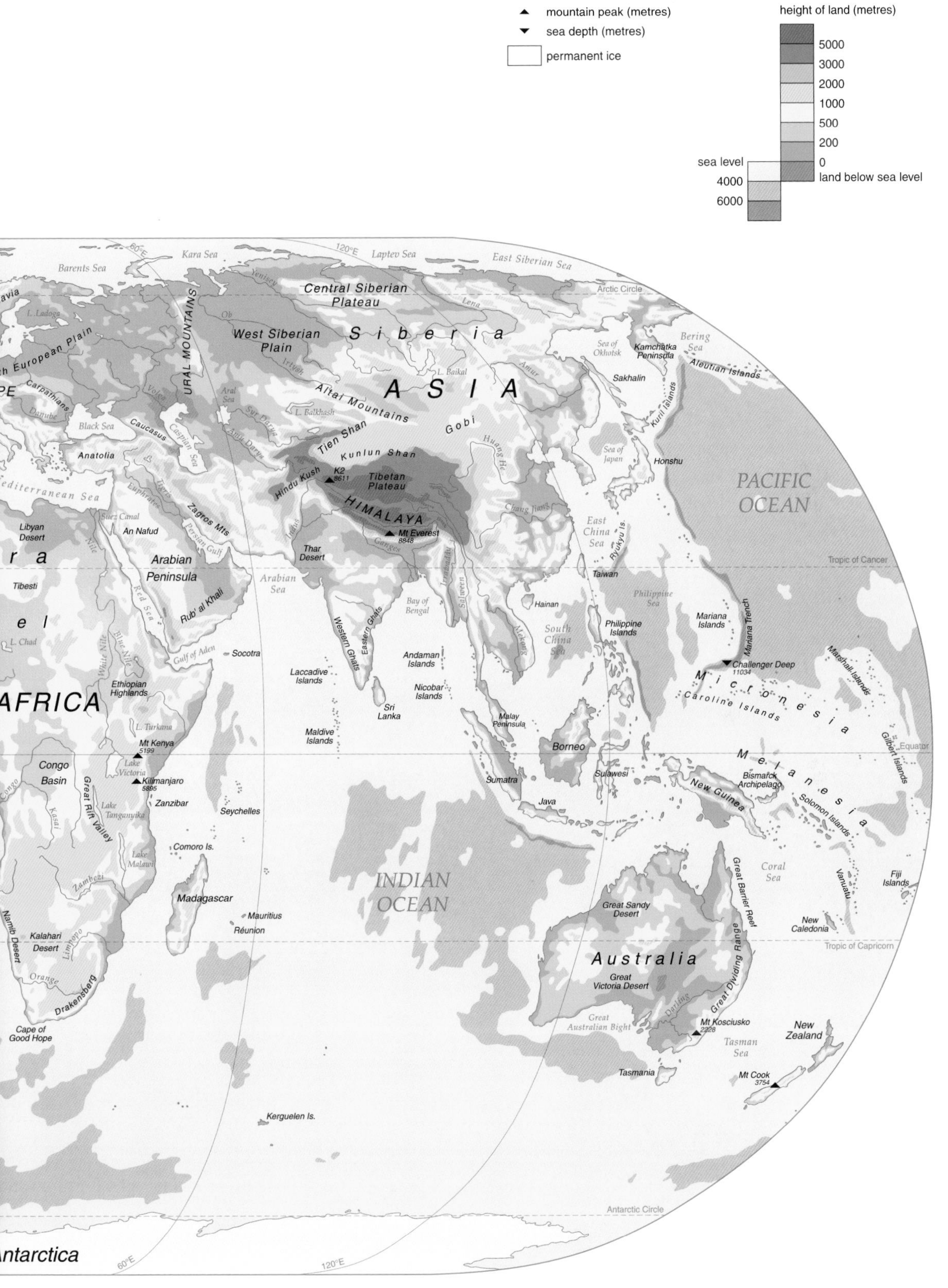

Key
mountain peak (metres)
sea depth (metres)
permanent ice
height of land (metres)
5000
3000
2000
1000
500
200
0
land below sea level
sea level
4000
6000
Barents Sea
Kara Sea
Laptev Sea
East Siberian Sea
Arctic Circle
Central Siberian Plateau
West Siberian Plain
URAL MOUNTAINS
Siberia
ASIA
Altai Mountains
Tien Shan
Kunlun Shan
Gobi
Hindu Kush
K2 8611
Tibetan Plateau
HIMALAYA
Mt Everest 8848
Black Sea
Caucasus
Caspian Sea
Aral Sea
L. Balkhash
L. Baikal
Anatolia
Mediterranean Sea
Zagros Mts
Persian Gulf
Suez Canal
An Nafud
Arabian Peninsula
Rub' al Khali
Libyan Desert
Tibesti
L. Chad
Ethiopian Highlands
AFRICA
L. Turkana
Mt Kenya 5199
Lake Victoria
Kilimanjaro 5895
Congo Basin
Great Rift Valley
Lake Tanganyika
Lake Malawi
Zanzibar
Seychelles
Comoro Is.
Madagascar
Mauritius
Réunion
Kalahari Desert
Namib Desert
Drakensberg
Cape of Good Hope
Kerguelen Is.
Antarctica
Antarctic Circle
Thar Desert
Arabian Sea
Gulf of Aden
Socotra
Laccadive Islands
Maldive Islands
Western Ghats
Eastern Ghats
Bay of Bengal
Sri Lanka
Andaman Islands
Nicobar Islands
Malay Peninsula
Sumatra
Java
Borneo
Sulawesi
INDIAN OCEAN
Sea of Okhotsk
Kamchatka Peninsula
Bering Sea
Aleutian Islands
Sakhalin
Kuril Islands
Sea of Japan
Honshu
PACIFIC OCEAN
East China Sea
Ryukyu Is.
Taiwan
Tropic of Cancer
Hainan
South China Sea
Philippine Sea
Philippine Islands
Mariana Islands
Mariana Trench
Challenger Deep 11034
Micronesia
Caroline Islands
Marshall Islands
Gilbert Islands
Equator
Melanesia
Bismarck Archipelago
New Guinea
Solomon Islands
Coral Sea
Vanuatu
Fiji Islands
New Caledonia
Great Barrier Reef
Great Sandy Desert
Australia
Great Victoria Desert
Great Dividing Range
Great Australian Bight
Mt Kosciusko 2228
Tasman Sea
Tasmania
New Zealand
Mt Cook 3754
Tropic of Capricorn

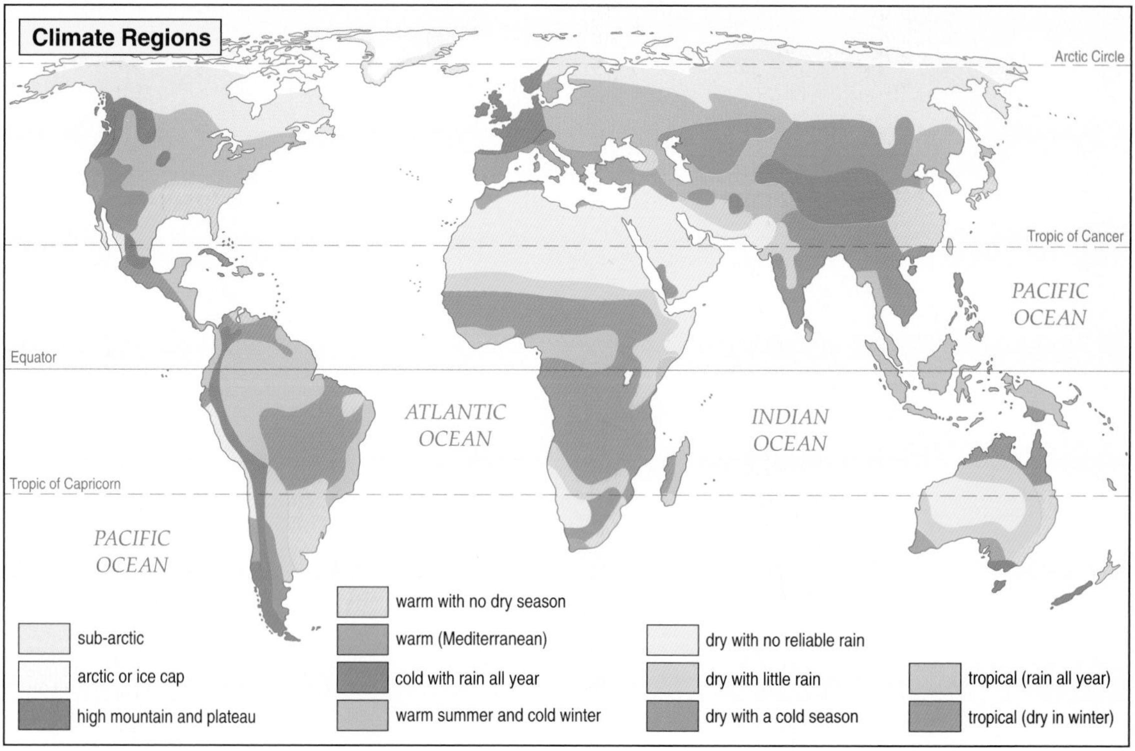

Climate Regions

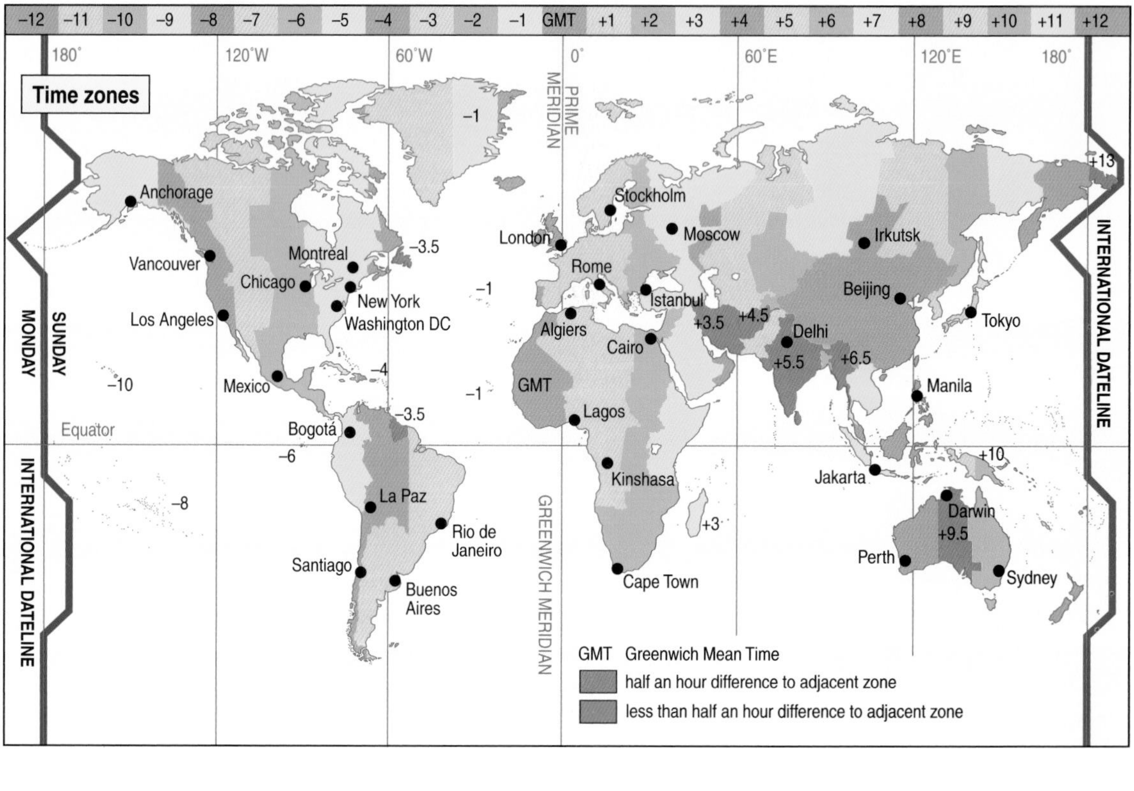

Time zones

Forms of Address in the UK

Two dashes indicate first name and surname; one dash indicates surname or place; C – indicates first name only. Honourable is abbreviated to Hon. Formal ceremonial styles for closing letters are provided where appropriate. Spoken address is provided where a special style is followed, and only in selected instances. For the royal family, it is normal practice to address letters to the private secretary, lady-in-waiting, or equerry of the relevant member of the family. Both formal and social forms of address are given for the peerage, where usage differs in some cases. In general, the social form is now generally preferred to the formal. For formal forms of address used for official documents and on very formal occasions, as well as for more detailed information on forms of address, see Debrett's *Correct Form* and Black's *Titles and Forms of Address*.

Addressee	Address	Salutation (opening of letter)
Government officers		
Cabinet minister	The Right Hon – –	Dear Minister
Member of Parliament	– –, Esq, adding MP after title or name and honours	Dear Minister
Minister of the Crown	if a Privy Counsellor, see relevant section below; otherwise, see Member of Parliament or grade of peerage below	Dear Secretary of State, or Dear Minister if the matter concerns the department
Prime Minister	The Right Hon – –	Dear (Mr) Prime Minister
Privy Counsellor	The Right Hon – –, if not a peer; The Right Hon, the Earl of –, PC (PC after all orders and decorations)	according to rank
Secretary of State	The Right Hon – –, MP, Secretary of State for –, or The Secretary of State for –; otherwise according to rank	Dear Secretary of State
Diplomatic officials		
Ambassador	His/Her Excellency the Ambassador of –, or HM Ambassador to –	Your Excellency; close letter: I have the honour to be, Sir/Madam (or according to rank), Your Excellency's obedient servant; spoken address: Your Excellency at least once, and then Sir or Madam by name
Consul	– –, Esq, HM Consul-General (Consul, or Vice-Consul, as the case may be)	Sir
Governor of a country	His Excellency (preceding all ranks and titles); if knighted: His Excellency Mr – –	according to rank; close letter: have the honour to be, Sir (or My Lord, if a peer), Your Excellency's obedient servant; spoken address: Your Excellency
Governor-General	His Excellency (preceding all ranks and titles) followed by ordinary designation, Governor-General of –. (The Governor-General of Canada has the rank of Right Hon, which he retains for life)	as for Governor
Governor-General's wife	the style Her Excellency is confined to wives of Governor-Generals of Commonwealth countries within the country administered by her husband	
High Commissioner	His Excellency (preceding all ranks and titles) the High Commissioner of –	as for Ambassador
Lieutenant-Governor, Isle of Man, Jersey, and Guernsey	as for Governor	as for Governor
Civic titles		
Lady Mayoress	as for Lord Mayor's wife	
Lord Mayor	the Lord Mayors of London, York, Belfast, Cardiff, Dublin, and also Sydney, Melbourne, Adelaide, Brisbane, and Hobart are styled: The Right Hon the Lord Mayor of –. Other Lord Mayors are styled: The Right Worshipful the Lord Mayor of –	My Lord Mayor, or Dear Lord Mayor
Lord Mayor's wife	The Lady Mayoress of –	My Lady Mayoress
Mayor	The Right Worshipful the Mayor of – (if mayor of a city); The Worshipful the Mayor of – (if mayor of a borough or town mayor)	Dear Mr Mayor (may be used for a man or woman); Mr Mayor, or Sir/Madam
Lord Provost	the Lord Provosts of Edinburgh and Glasgow are styled: The Right Hon the Lord Provost; the Lord Provosts of Perth, Aberdeen, and Dundee are styled: The Lord Provost of –	My Lord Provost
Provost	The Provost of –	Dear Lord Provost
Aldermen	Mr/Miss/Mrs Alderman –	Dear Sir; Dear Alderman; Dear Alderman –
Councillor	Councillor –; Miss/Mrs Councillor –	Dear Councillor; Dear Councillor –; Dear Miss/Mrs Councillor –; never Mr Councillor
The bench		
Judge of City of London Court	as for Circuit Judge	
Judge, Circuit	His or Her Honour Judge –; if a Knight, His Honour Judge Sir – –	Dear Sir or Madam; spoken address: when on the bench, Your Honour; otherwise Sir
Judge of High Court (men)	The Hon Mr Justice –	Dear Sir; spoken address: when on the bench, My Lord or Your Lordship; otherwise Sir
Judge of High Court (women)	The Hon Mrs (or Miss) Justice –	Dear Madam; spoken address: when on the bench, My Lady or Your Ladyship; otherwise Madam
Justice of the Peace	as for Esquire (see Peerage)	spoken address: when on the bench, Your Worship; otherwise as for Esquire
Lord Advocate	The Right Hon the Lord Advocate, or The Right Hon – –	as for Esquire (see Peerage)
Lord Chancellor	The Right Hon the Lord High Chancellor	as for peer, according to rank (see Peerage)
Lord Chief Justice	The Lord Chief Justice of England or The Right Hon Lord –, Lord Chief Justice of England	Dear Lord Chief Justice
Lord Justice Clerk and Lord Justice General	The Right Hon the Justice Clerk, and The Right Hon the Lord Justice General	My Lord, Dear Lord Justice General/Clerk, or Dear Lord –

(continued)

Forms of Address in the UK *(continued)*

Addressee	Address	Salutation (opening of letter)
Lord Justice of Appeal	The Right Hon Lord Justice –, or The Right Hon Sir – –	as for Judge of High Court
Lord of Appeal-in-Ordinary	as for Baron (see Peerage)	
Lord of Session, Scottish	The Hon Lord/Lady –	My Lord/Lady/Madam, or Dear Lord/Lady/ Madam –
Lord of Session's wife or widow	Lady –	as for a Baron's wife (see Peerage)
Master of the Rolls	The Right Hon the Master of the Rolls, or The Right Hon –, according to rank	Dear Sir; spoken address: when on the bench, My Lord or Your Lordship; otherwise Sir
Queen's Counsel	– – Esq, QC	as for Esquire (see Peerage)
Sheriff	Sheriff Principal –	Dear Sheriff
Peerage and other titles		
Baron	The Right Hon Lord – (formal), The Lord – (social)	The Lord – (formal), Dear Lord – (social); spoken address: Lord –
Baroness in her own right	The Right Hon the Baroness – (formal), The Baroness – (social)	My Lady (formal), Dear Lady – (social); spoken address: Lady –
Baron's wife	The Right Hon Lady – (formal), The Lady – (social)	as for Baroness in her own right
Baron's children	The Hon – –	Dear Mr/Miss/Madam –
Baronet	Sir – –, Bt	Dear Sir (formal), Dear Sir C– (social); spoken address: Sir C–
Baronet's wife	Lady –	Dear Madam (formal), Dear Lady – (social); spoken address: Lady –
Countess	The Right Hon the Countess of –	as for Baroness in her own right
Courtesy titles	while his father is alive, the heir apparent to a Duke, Earl, or Marquess takes the highest of his father's other titles as a courtesy title; these courtesy titles are not preceded by The Most Hon or The Right Hon; in correspondence the title is not preceded by The	
Dames of Orders of Chivalry	Dame – –, followed by appropriate post-nominal letters	Dear Madam (formal), Dear Dame C– (social); spoken address: Dame C–
Duchess	Her Grace the Duchess of – (formal), The Duchess of – (social)	Dear Madam (formal), Dear Duchess (social); spoken address: Your Grace (formal), Duchess (social)
Duke	His Grace the Duke of – (formal), The Duke of – (social)	My Lord Duke (formal), Dear Duke (social); spoken address: Your Grace (formal), Duke (social)
Duke's daughter	Lady – – (formal), Dear Madam (social)	Dear Lady C–; spoken address: Lady C–
Duke's eldest son	see Courtesy titles	
Duke's younger son	Lord – –	My Lord (formal); Dear Lord C– (social); spoken address: My Lord (formal), Lord C– (social)
Earl	The Right Hon the Earl of – (formal), The Earl of – (social)	My Lord (formal), Dear Lord – (social); spoken address: My Lord (formal), Lord – (social)
Earl's daughter	as for Duke's daughter	
Earl's eldest son	see Courtesy titles	
Earl's wife	The Right Hon the Countess of – (formal), The Countess of – (social)	Madam (formal), Lady – (social); spoken address: Madam (formal), Lady – (social)
Earl's younger son	The Hon – –	as for Baron's children
Esquire	– – Esq	Sir; spoken address: Sir
Knight Bachelor	Sir – –	Dear Sir (formal), Dear Sir C– (social); spoken address: Sir C–
Knight's wife	as for a Baronet's wife	
Knight of an Order of Chivalry	Sir – –, followed by appropriate post-nominal letters	as for Knight Bachelor
Life Peer	as for Baron	
Life Peeress	as for Baroness in her own right	
Life Peer's children	as for Baron's children	
Life Peer's wife	as for Baron's wife	
Marchioness	The Most Hon the Marchioness of – (formal), The Marchioness of – (social)	as for Baroness
Marquess	The Most Hon the Marquess of – (formal), The Marquess of – (social)	My Lord (formal), Dear Lord – (social); spoken address: My Lord (formal), Lord – (social)
Marquess's daughter	Lady – –	as for Duke's daughter
Marquess's eldest son	see Courtesy titles	
Marquess's younger son	Lord – –	as for Duke's younger son
Master	The Master of –; the title is used in Scottish peerage by the heir apparent or presumptive of a peer; heirs apparent of the senior grades of the peerage usually use a courtesy title	Dear Sir (formal), Dear Master of – (social); spoken address: Master, or Sir (formal), Master, or Mr – (social)
Master's wife	according to her husband's rank	
Prince	His Royal Highness the Duke of –, if a duke; His Royal Highness the Prince C–, if the son of a sovereign; otherwise His Royal Highness Prince C–	Sir; close letter: I have the honour to be (or remain), Your Royal Highness's most humble and obedient servant; spoken address: Your Royal Highness

(continued)

Forms of Address in the UK *(continued)*

Addressee	Address	Salutation (opening of letter)
Princess	Her Royal Highness the Duchess of –, if the wife of a Royal duke; Her Royal Highness The Princess C–; otherwise Her Royal Highness the Princess C–	Madam; close letter: I have the honour to be (or remain), Madam, Your Royal Highness's most humble and obedient servant; spoken address: Your Royal Highness
Queen Mother	Her Gracious Majesty Queen Elizabeth The Queen Mother, for state and formal documents; otherwise Her Majesty Queen – The Queen Mother	as for Queen Regent
Queen Regent	The Queen's Most Excellent Majesty, for state and formal documents; otherwise Her Majesty The Queen	Madam, May it please your Majesty; close letter: I have the honour to be (or remain) Madam, Your Majesty's most humble and obedient servant; spoken address: Your Majesty
Viscount	The Right Hon the Viscount – (formal), The Viscount – (social)	My Lord (formal), Dear Lord – (social); spoken address: Lord –
Viscount's wife	The Right Hon the Viscountess – (formal), The Viscountess – (social)	Madam (formal), Dear Lady – (social); spoken address: Lady –
Viscount's children	as for Baron's children	
Widow and divorcee	widows and divorcees keep their husbands' titles until remarriage; the wife of the holder of a peerage becomes a dowager on the death of her husband or on the marriage of the new peer if unmarried at the time of succession; she is addressed as The Dowager Lady; the same title can be held by more than one person, hence the term is used less frequently today, and an alternative form, eg, The Right Hon C–, Countess of – is used, distinction being made by the use of the first name; the ex-wives of Marquesses and below are not styled The Most Hon or The Right Hon	
Clerical titles		
Archbishop (Anglican)	The Most Reverend the Lord Archbishop of –; (the Archbishops of Canterbury and York are Privy Counsellors, and should be addressed as The Most Reverend and Right Hon the Lord Archbishop of –)	Your Grace (more formal), Dear Archbishop, or My Lord Archbishop; spoken address: Your Grace
Archbishop (Roman Catholic)	His Grace the Archbishop of –	My Lord Archbishop; spoken address: Your Grace
Archdeacon	The Venerable the Archdeacon of –	Dear Archdeacon, Dear Mr Archdeacon, or Venerable Sir; spoken address: Archdeacon
Bishop (Anglican)	The Right Reverend the Lord Bishop of –; (the Bishop of London is a Privy Counsellor and should be addressed as The Right Reverend and Right Hon the Lord Bishop of London; the Bishop of Meath is styled The Most Reverend)	Dear Bishop or My Lord; spoken address: Bishop
Bishop (Episcopal Church in Scotland)	The Right Reverend – –, Bishop of –	as for Anglican bishop
Bishop (Roman Catholic)	His Lordship the Bishop of –, or The Right Reverend – –, Bishop of –; in Ireland, The Most Reverend is used instead of The Right Reverend	My Lord, or My Lord Bishop; spoken address: My Lord, or My Lord Bishop
Canon (Anglican)	The Reverend Canon – –	Dear Canon, or Dear Canon –; spoken address: Canon, or Canon –
Canon (Roman Catholic)	The Very Reverend Canon – –	Very Reverend Sir; spoken address: Canon –
Cardinal	His Eminence Cardinal –; if an archbishop, His Eminence the Cardinal Archbishop of –	Your Eminence, My Lord Cardinal, or Dear Cardinal –; spoken address: Your Eminence
Clergy		
Anglican Communion	The Reverend ––	Dear Sir/Madam, Dear Mr/Mrs/Miss –
Roman Catholic	The Reverend –– (add initials of the religious order, if applicable)	Dear Reverend Father
Other churches	The Reverend – –	Dear Sir/Madam, Dear Mr/Mrs/Miss –
Dean (Anglican)	The Very Reverend the Dean of –	Dear Dean; Very Reverend Sir; spoken address: Very Reverend Sir (formal); Dean (social)
Monsignor	The Very Reverend Monsignor – –	Reverend Sir or Dear Monsignor; spoken address: Monsignor –
Pope	His Holiness the Pope	Your Holiness or Most Holy Father; close letter: if Roman Catholic: I have the honour to be Your Holiness's most devoted and obedient child (or, most humble child); if not Roman Catholic: I have the honour to be (or remain) Your Holiness's obedient servant; spoken address: Your Holiness
Prebendary (Anglican)	The Very Reverend Prebendary – –	Dear Prebendary, or Dear Prebendary –; spoken address: Prebendary, or Prebendary –
Prebendary (Roman Catholic)	The Very Reverend Prebendary – –	Very Reverend Sir; spoken address: Prebendary –
Rabbi	Rabbi – –; with a doctorate, Rabbi Doctor – –	Dear Sir, Dear Rabbi, or Dear Doctor; spoken address: Rabbi –, or Doctor –
Armed forces	professional rank always precedes any other rank or title, for example Admiral the Right Hon the Earl of –, Air-Marshal Sir –; officers below the rank of Rear-Admiral and Marshall of the Royal Air Force are entitled to RN and RAF respectively after their name; officers in the women's services add WRNS, WRAF, or WRAC	

(continued)

Forms of Address in the UK *(continued)*

Addressee	Address	Salutation (opening of letter)
Academic		
Chancellor of University	The Chancellor of the University of –	Dear Sir/Madam, My Lord (if a peer), or Dear Chancellor
Dean, Director, Master, Mistress, President, Principal, Provost, Rector, and Warden of university college	The Dean/Director, etc, of – College, University of –, or title/status – – (position) of – College, University of –	as for Chancellor, substituting relevant position
High Steward	The High Steward of the University of –	Dear High Steward
Professor	Professor – –; if in holy orders, The Reverend Professor	Dear Sir/Madam, or Dear Professor; spoken address: according to rank
Vice-Chancellor	The Vice-Chancellor of the University of –; The Reverend the Vice-Chancellor of Oxford, and The Right Worshipful the Vice-Chancellor of the University of Cambridge	Dear Vice-Chancellor

Web Sites

Acronyms and Abbreviations

http://www.ucc.ie/acronyms/

Enormous database of abbreviations, acronyms, and their expanded forms, searchable by abbreviation or keyword.

Anagram Insanity

http://anagram.avatartech.com/pages/anagram.html

Anagram-producing page: key in a string of characters and the server will return an exhaustive list of possible permutations of letters.

Arabic

http://philae.sas.upenn.edu/Arabic/arabic.html

Twelve dialogue lessons for learning Arabic; the site also has a library of Arabic images.

Arabic Writing

http://www.islam.org/Mosque/ihame/Ref3.htm

Informative pages on the history of the Arabic script, with examples of Arabic writing and photographs of different calligraphic styles found in ancient texts.

Braille and Moon

http://www.rnib.org.uk/braille/welc.htm

Comprehensive information about Braille and Moon from Britain's Royal National Institute for the Blind. You can see how Braille works by typing text and seeing it translated, and can download Braille and Moon true-type fonts.

Brief History of the English Language

http://www.m-w.com/about/look.htm

Part of a site maintained by Merriam-Webster, this page features a brief history of the English language, showing its evolution through the three periods of Old, Middle, and Modern English.

Chinese Characters

http://zhongwen.com/

This etymological dictionary for learning Chinese characters covers over 4,000 characters, including several types of pronunciation for each and a 'family tree' diagram to demonstrate the characters' genealogy. The site also includes a Chinese-English dictionary.

Chomsky, Noam

http://www.thirdworldtraveler.com/Chomsky/Noam_Chomsky.html

Substantial collection of the political work and thought of the US academic and philosopher Noam Chomsky, with books, articles, an archive of his correspondence, and numerous interviews.

Elements of Style

http://www.bartleby.com/141/index.html

William Strunk's classic provides a succinct and practical guide to the elementary rules and principles of English grammar.

Esperanto – The International Language

http://espeiranto.org/angle/

Official source of information (in many languages) on the international language spoken by around two million people, including details of national societies and Esperanto language courses.

Etymological Dictionary of the Gaelic Language

http://www.smo.uhi.ac.uk/gaidhlig/faclair/macbain

Text of an etymology of Gaelic compiled by Alexander MacBain and published by Gairm Publications, Glasgow.

Euskara – Language of the Basques

http://students.washington.edu/buber/Basque/Euskara/

Thorough introduction to the language, with lessons, dictionary, information on software, advice for those learning the language, and a guide to Euskara media.

Finno-Ugrian Languages

http://www.helsinki.fi/hum/sugl/fgrlang.html

Guide to the Finno-Ugric (Uralian) language group, with information on Hungarian, Finnish, and Estonian, and many of the more minor languages in danger of extinction. Lexical and morphological similarities between the languages are examined.

Foundation for Endangered Languages

http://www.bris.ac.uk/Depts/Philosophy/CTLL/FEL/

Bristol University site bringing together the latest information and research on the world's endangered languages. There are online editions of the foundation's newsletter, and contact addresses for scholars and indigenous peoples struggling to preserve their language.

Gaelic and Gaelic Culture

http://sunsite.unc.edu/gaelic/gaelic.html

Dedicated to the Gaelic and Celtic culture and language, this site includes information on the three Gaelic languages – Irish, Manx, and Scottish – along with audioclips of examples of each.

Glossary of Rhetorical Terms With Examples

http://www.uky.edu/ArtsSciences/Classics/rhetoric.html

If you are ever confused about how to distinguish synecdoche, litotes, and prolepsis, then this is the site for you; there are also links to other rhetoric and classicist sites.

Hindi Language and Literature

http://www.cs.colostate.edu/~malaiya/hindiint.html

Exploration of Hindi language and culture with links to information about Hindi-speaking regions, dialects, traditional songs, authors, and poets.

Journal of Pidgin and Creole Languages

http://www.siu.edu/departments/cola/ling/

Results of current research into the theory and description of these languages, supported by an interactive glossary of pidgin and Creole terms and audio samples.

Learn Chinese

http://pasture.ecn.purdue.edu/~agenhtml/agenmc/china/ctutor.html

Audio tutorial of basic Mandarin Chinese, with over 200 phrases presented in written and audio form.

Linguasphere

http://www.linguasphere.com/

Site of the Linguasphere Observatory, presenting information on the languages of the world and on the Register of the World's Languages and Speech Communities.

Little Venture's Latin Pages

http://www.compassnet.com/mrex/index.html

Online aid to learning or brushing up Latin. You can send grammar and vocabulary enquiries, and the site includes sections on FAQs, a Latin quiz, a fun etymology section, an explanation of the Roman calendar system.

Mercator Project

http://www.troc.es/mercator/

Site of the European Union initiative to preserve minority languages and cultures within the EU. There is general information on a wide variety of languages, as well as details of the activities of a number of language promotion organizations and academic institutions throughout Europe.

Modern English to Old English Vocabulary

http://www.mun.ca/Ansaxdat/vocab/wordlist.html

Comprehensive online dictionary of modern English words paired with their Old English counterparts.

Punctuation Made Simple

http://www.cas.usf.edu/JAC/pms/

Handbook aimed at writers and editors, but useful to anyone wanting to improve their punctuation.

Pun Page

http://punpunpun.com/

Puns in every shape and form.

Roget's Thesaurus

http://humanities.uchicago.edu/forms_unrest/ROGET.html

Online, public domain version of *Roget's Thesaurus* (last updated in 1991).

Runes, Alphabet of Mystery

http://members.aol.com/cbsunny/index.html

Introduction to the ancient Germanic alphabet, with information on both the alphabet and the stones the letters were traditionally carved upon.

Sapir, Edward

http://kroeber.anthro.mankato.msus.edu/information/biography/pqrst/sapir_edward.html

Profile of the German linguist and anthropologist and his pioneering research into Native American languages and the insights derived from it.

Semiotics for Beginners

http://www.aber.ac.uk/~dgc/sem01.html

Clear introduction to the theories and roots of what some theorists have called the 'science of signs'.

Sign Writing Site

http://www.signwriting.org/

Information about sign language with lessons, dictionaries, stories, and computer programs in sign language.

Traveller's Japanese With Voice

http://www.ntt.co.jp/japan/japanese/

Introduction to Japanese at a level suitable for the business traveller or the occasional visitor to the country.

Welsh Course

http://www.cs.brown.edu/fun/welsh/home.html

Course on the Welsh language that contains a lexicon and glossary as well as a set of graded lessons. It also includes other related cultural and linguistic resources.

Wordbot

http://www.cs.washington.edu/homes/kgolden/wordbot.html

Linguistic site that allows you to load pages from the Internet and run them through a variety of filters. These filters can translate foreign language pages into your own language, link words to dictionary definitions, or look up synonyms and antonyms.

Word Page

http://users.aol.com/jomnet/words.html

This page offers ten different English words per week – their definitions, origins, words of similar/opposite meaning, and examples of each one in use.

World Wide Words

http://www.quinion.demon.co.uk/words/index.htm

The latest neologisms (new words) in the English language – topical words, turns of phrase, and weird words too new to be found in dictionaries are listed and defined. There are also articles on the latest developments of the language.

LAW AND CRIME

The Year in Review

2–4 July 1999 US white supremacist group member Benjamin Nathanial Smith goes on a racially motivated shooting spree through Illinois. He shoots and wounds six Jewish men in Chicago, then kills African-American Ricky Byrdsong, and fires at two Asian Americans. On 3 July he shoots at two black people in Springfield and at a group of Asian students in Urbana. On 4 July he fires into a group of Koreans, killing one. Smith shoots himself while pursued by police.

3 July 1999 Former UK futures trader Nick Leeson is released from prison in Singapore, after serving a little more than half of a six-and-a-half-year prison sentence for fraud and forgery when his losses led to the collapse of Barings Bank in 1995.

29 July 1999 US securities trader Mark Barton kills nine people and injures 13 during a shooting spree in two office buildings in Atlanta, Georgia. He killed his wife and two children a few days before and kills himself after the shootings.

9 August 1999 A court in Aden, Yemen, convicts eight British men, all of Pakistani or Arab origin, for their roles in bomb attacks on the British consulate in Yemen in 1998.

12 August 1999 The UN International Criminal Tribunal for Rwanda indicts Pauline Nyiramasuhuko, minister of family and women's affairs during the massacre of Tutsis in 1994, for allowing her subordinates to rape Tutsi women. She is the first woman to be tried in an international tribunal on a rape charge.

2 September 1999 UK home secretary Jack Straw appoints the first Muslim adviser to the prison service. The move follows a twofold increase in the number of Muslims in prisons over the past six years.

3 September 1999 Nine press photographers who were charged with manslaughter and negligence for their role in chasing the car in which Diana, Princess of Wales, died in 1997, are cleared of all charges by a French court in Paris.

16 September 1999 A court in Myanmar sentences UK human-rights campaigner Rachel Goldwyn to seven years' labour in prison for chaining herself to a lamp post and handing out leaflets. The prosecution claims that she threatened national security by attracting a large crowd. However, she is released less than two months later.

16 September 1999 A gunman opens fire on a group of teenagers listening to a Christian rock band at a Baptist church in Fort Worth, Texas, killing seven and injuring many more before finally shooting himself.

1 October 1999 UK childminder Manjit Basuta is convicted of causing the death of 13-month-old Oliver Smith, a boy in her care, in San Diego, California, and is sentenced to serve at least 25 years in prison.

8 October 1999 A UK court rules that former Chilean dictator Augusto Pinochet can be extradited to be tried for 35 torture charges during his 17-year rule of Chile. The final ruling will be made by Home Secretary Jack Straw.

26 October 1999 The Dutch parliament votes 49–26 to end the ban on brothels imposed in 1912. The law, which will go into effect in 2000, will legalize the Netherlands' sex industry.

27 October 1999 A court in Los Angeles, California, rules that both partners of a British gay couple can be named as legal parents on the birth certificates of surrogate twin babies.

8 November 1999 An inquest jury in Fulham, London, delivers an open verdict on the death of Asian student Ricky Reel in 1997, rejecting Scotland Yard claims that it was accidental. His parents led a two-year campaign to reopen the case, insisting he was a victim of a racial attack.

12 November 1999 English rock star Gary Glitter is sentenced to four months in prison after pleading guilty to charges of downloading hundreds of images of child pornography from the Internet.

28 November 1999 Computer expert Eden Strang bursts naked into St Andrew's church, Thornton Heath, London, during Sunday Mass, and attacks the congregation with a samurai sword, injuring 11 people. He is stopped by off-duty police officer Tom Tracey, who hits Strang over the head with an organ pipe.

30 November 1999 Mexican police and troops and the FBI begin exhuming bodies from sites on two ranches south of Ciudad Juarez, Mexico. The victims are believed to be rivals of the Ciudad Juarez drug cartel.

December 1999 In the USA 98 people on death row are recorded to have been executed in 1999, bringing the total number of executions since the death penalty was re-established to 598.

6 December 1999 An international court in Arusha, Tanzania, convicts Hutu leader George Rutaganda of genocide, extermination, and murder for his role in the deaths of thousands of Tutsis in Rwanda in 1994. He is sentenced to life in prison.

7 December 1999 Abdelbaset Ali Muhammad al-Megrahi and Al Amin Khalifa Fhimah, the two Libyans accused of murdering 270 people in the aeroplane explosion over Lockerbie, Scotland, in 1988, appear before a Scottish court in the Netherlands. It is their first public court appearance following the crash 11 years ago.

8 December 1999 The French government decides not to lift its ban against British beef. The UK government contacts the European Commission to take legal proceedings against the French government.

16 December 1999 The European Court of Human Rights rules that the two boys who murdered two-year-old James Bulger in 1993, Robert Thompson and Jon Venables, were not given a fair trial. Ruling that the boys, then aged ten, were subjected to an adult hearing, the court awards costs and expenses of £15,000 to Thompson and £29,000 to Venables.

7 January 2000 Former Conservative MP Jonathan Aitken is released from Elmley Prison in Kent after serving seven months of an 18-month sentence for perjury and perverting the course of justice during his libel action against *The Guardian* newspaper and Granada Television.

10 January 2000 Despite international human rights protests, Chris Thomas, a 26-year-old US prisoner who at age 17 killed his girlfriend's parents, is executed by lethal injection at the Greensville Correctional Center, Virginia. Only four other countries – Iran, Nigeria, Pakistan, and Saudi Arabia – allow the execution of juvenile offenders.

13 January 2000 UK home secretary Jack Straw announces that he will allow US boxer Mike Tyson to enter the UK for a scheduled fight against English boxer Julius Francis on 29 January. Tyson is on a list of undesirable visitors to the UK because of his 1992 conviction for rape.

14 January 2000 In what is described as the first significant judgement on ethnic cleansing, five Bosnian Croats are found guilty of crimes against humanity for the massacre of more than 100 Muslims during the war in Bosnia in 1993, at the Hague, the Netherlands.

28 January 2000 Andy Pennington, the personal assistant to Liberal Democrat MP Nigel Jones, is stabbed to death while trying to protect Jones from a sword-wielding attacker in Cheltenham, England.

31 January 2000 English GP Harold Shipman is convicted of 15 murders and sentenced to life imprisonment (*see also* **colour section**).

4 February 2000 The UK Conservative Party expels novelist and politician Jeffrey Archer for five years, after an internal inquiry finds that he had perverted the course of justice in his 1987 libel case against the *Daily Star* newspaper, which had alleged that he had made payments to a prostitute. Archer is found to have convinced a friend to act as an alibi for him during the case and then continued to conceal the truth when the fake alibi was discovered in November 1999.

7 February 2000 Section 28, the law that bans local authorities from promoting homosexuality in schools, is supported in the House of Lords by 210 votes to 165. The vote undermines the Labour government pledge to repeal the ban.

10 February 2000 All of the hostages on an Afghan Boeing 727, which was hijacked on 6 February, are released at Stansted Airport, England. Police arrest 21 people who were apparently directly involved in the hijacking. They also investigate the possibility that the hijack was a ploy for some of the passengers to seek political asylum in the UK.

29 February 2000 After a playground argument, a six-year-old boy shoots and kills six-year-old Kayla Rolland in front of their classmates and teacher at Buell Elementary School in Morris Mount Township, near Flint, Michigan.

10 March 2000 Three gunmen shoot dead Iqbal Raad, the lawyer of former Pakistani prime minister Nawaz Sharif, who is standing trial on charges of treason and kidnapping.

16 March 2000 A Pakistani judge convicts Javed Iqbal, Pakistan's most notorious serial killer, of murdering 100 children and sentences him to be strangled, chopped up into pieces, and dissolved in acid in front of the parents of his victims.

11 April 2000 English historian David Irving loses his libel suit against US academic Deborah Lipstadt and her publisher Penguin Books. The judge rules that a claim in her book that he is a Holocaust denier is justified.

13 April 2000 A court in Rome, Italy, orders Italian opera singer Luciano Pavarotti to pay a £3 million fine for tax evasion.

14 April 2000 English criminal Kenneth Noye is convicted of stabbing 21-year-old electrician Stephen Cameron in a road rage incident in 1996 and sentenced to life in prison. Noye had fled to Spain after the incident and was brought back after a massive search by the Kent police.

19 April 2000 In a controversial verdict, English farmer Tony Martin is found guilty of murder for shooting 16-year-old Fred Barras, who was trying to burgle his isolated farmhouse.

June 2000 In the UK, the Lord Chancellor's department produces a report admitting that the appointment of judicial candidates is based on patronage and 'secret soundings' of existing judges and senior lawyers, thus deterring applications from women and ethnic minorities.

8 June 2000 In Kansas, USA, John Robinson, a man who used the code name 'Slavemaster' in Internet chat rooms, is arrested for sexual assault, but the charge is upgraded to murder when the remains of five bodies are found in barrels. He lured his victims after meeting them on the Web, and is believed by police to be the first Internet serial killer.

18 June 2000 UK home secretary Jack Straw orders an inquiry into a computer blunder in which the records of 140,000 young offenders were wiped off the national police database.

19 June 2000 Lawyers for 3,000 South African asbestos workers suffering from asbestosis and mesothelioma begin hearings at the House of Lords against a UK company, Cape Asbestos. The case, dubbed a 'British Bhopal', is hoped to win compensation not only for sufferers but for an environmental clean-up in Prieska, the affected town.

21 June 2000 The UK Home Office reports that cases of sex attackers drugging their victims with amnesia-inducing substances have increased, but a breakthrough in hair analysis by forensic scientists means that evidence of drug use is now being used in prosecution of date-rape cases.

29 June 2000 UK Home Office minister Mike O'Brien announces that relatives of young women forced into marriage against their will can now be prosecuted for sex offences committed after the wedding. Laws regarding abduction, threatening behaviour, and assault also will be more vigorously implemented.

30 June 2000 Suggestions by Prime Minister Tony Blair that the police could start to impose on-the-spot fines for 'drunken louts', are reacted to sceptically by senior police officers and other groups.

World Law and Crime

Number of Recorded Crimes in Selected Countries

Definitions of offences vary between countries both due to legal differences and statistical recording methods; comparisons may be affected by these differences.
(N/A = not available.)

Crime	1998	% change 1997–98
England and Wales		
Homicide	750	0
Violent crime	331,843	−6
Theft of a motor vehicle	390,891	−2
Domestic burglary	472,960	−6
Drug trafffiicking	21,306	−9
Northern Ireland		
Homicide	75	53
Violent crime	9,496	21
Theft of a motor vehicle	9,705	20
Domestic burglary	7,725	8
Drug trafficking	193	10
Scotland		
Homicide	100	5
Violent crime	25,725	9
Theft of a motor vehicle	28,433	−1
Domestic burglary	38,033	3
Drug trafficking	8,490	4
Australia		
Homicide	333	−8
Violent crime	173,250	8
Theft of a motor vehicle	131,572	1
Domestic burglary	295,699	4
Drug trafficking	23,348	−4
Austria		
Homicide	77	17
Violent crime	48,200	3
Theft of a motor vehicle	4,092	6
Domestic burglary	11,811	−8
Drug trafficking	15,906	−5
Belgium		
Homicide	218	2
Violent crime	61,882	2
Theft of a motor vehicle	36,555	4
Domestic burglary	63,022	N/A
Drug trafficking	10,158	−8
Canada		
Homicide	555	−5
Violent crime	295,369	−1
Theft of a motor vehicle	165,799	−6
Domestic burglary	220,889	−5
Drug trafficking	17,727	2
Czech Republic		
Homicide	313	8
Violent crime	23,464	1
Theft of a motor vehicle	27,889	−5
Domestic burglary	12,752	−2
Drug trafficking	1,029	30
Denmark		
Homicide	49	−44
Violent crime	13,754	−1
Theft of a motor vehicle	37,565	−9
Domestic burglary	101,933	−9
Drug trafficking	178	4
Finland		
Homicide	113	−19
Violent crime	28,293	3
Theft of a motor vehicle	26,404	20
Domestic burglary	10,291	−9
Drug trafficking	9,461	14
France		
Homicide	961	0
Violent crime	193,480	2
Theft of a motor vehicle	415,930	0
Domestic burglary	207,274	3
Drug trafficking	92,858	7
Germany		
Homicide	975	−17
Violent crime	186,306	N/A
Theft of a motor vehicle	162,518	−15
Domestic burglary	166,742	−8
Drug trafficking	68,994	0
Greece		
Homicide	176	−13
Violent crime	9,312	6
Theft of a motor vehicle	7,510	14
Domestic burglary	43,228	−2
Drug trafficking	6,574	10
Hungary		
Homicide	289	0
Violent crime	28,414	7
Theft of a motor vehicle	15,255	6
Domestic burglary	30,515	−2
Drug trafficking	2,068	119
Ireland, Republic of		
Homicide	51	−4
Violent crime	4,515	−17
Theft of a motor vehicle	13,793	2
Domestic burglary	15,840	−7
Drug trafficking	1,766	8
Italy		
Homicide	924	0
Violent crime	71,752	11
Theft of a motor vehicle	309,113	3
Domestic burglary	246,804	4
Drug trafficking	43,014	4
Japan		
Homicide	1,388	8
Violent crime	41,751	3
Theft of a motor vehicle	705,431	1
Domestic burglary	237,703	7
Drug trafficking	2,712	15
Netherlands		
Homicide	244[1]	4[1]
Violent crime	76,600	3
Theft of a motor vehicle	37,308[2]	1[2]
Domestic burglary	487,300	0
Drug trafficking	5,700[2]	−14[2]
New Zealand		
Homicide	64	−28
Violent crime	42,590	1
Theft of a motor vehicle	29,731	−3
Domestic burglary	49,481	0
Drug trafficking	15,158	4
Norway		
Homicide	38	0
Violent crime	18,445	6
Theft of a motor vehicle	21,672	8
Domestic burglary	15,106	−11
Drug trafficking	38,774	12
Poland		
Homicide	759	−6
Violent crime	70,001	5
Theft of a motor vehicle	65,399	15
Domestic burglary	74,137	6
Drug trafficking	676	−32
Portugal		
Homicide	152	16
Violent crime	15,463	−8
Theft of a motor vehicle	26,965	18
Domestic burglary	21,515	−11
Drug trafficking	3,538	4

(continued)

Number of Recorded Crimes in Selected Countries (*continued*)

Crime	1998	% change 1997–98
Russian Federation		
Homicide	29,551	9
Violent crime	92,697	−22
Theft of a motor vehicle	35,448	−1
Domestic burglary	40,219	12
Drug trafficking	190,127	2
South Africa		
Homicide	24,877	1
Violent crime	661,779	2
Theft of a motor vehicle	107,513	7
Domestic burglary	249,375[2]	1[2]
Drug trafficking	39,830	−7
Spain		
Homicide	1,040	1
Violent crime	91,099	4
Theft of a motor vehicle	136,084	2
Domestic burglary	82,335	−2
Drug trafficking	13,263	−7
Sweden		
Homicide	187	20
Violent crime	72,080	6
Theft of a motor vehicle	76,921	−2
Domestic burglary	17,645	−4
Drug trafficking	502	−11
Switzerland		
Homicide	76	−13
Violent crime	7,939	8
Theft of a motor vehicle	21,534[2]	3[2]
Domestic burglary	83,416	1
Drug trafficking	3,734	15
USA		
Homicide	16,914	−7
Violent crime	1,531,044	−6
Theft of a motor vehicle	1,240,754	−8
Domestic burglary	2,329,950	−5
Drug trafficking	37,322	13

[1] 1994 and 1994–96 percentage changes.
[2] 1997 and 1996–97 percentage changes.

Source: International Comparisons of Criminal Justice Statistics 1998,

Homicide Rates in Selected Countries

Definitions of offences vary between countries both due to legal differences and statistical recording methods; comparisons may be affected by these differences.

Country	1998	Homicides per 100,000 population 1998
South Africa	24,877	57.52
Russian Federation	29,551	20.20
USA	16,914	6.26
Northern Ireland	75	4.44
Czech Republic	313	3.04
Hungary	289	2.85
Spain	1,040	2.61
Finland	113	2.19
Belgium	218	2.14
Sweden	187	2.11
Poland	759	1.96
Scotland	100	1.95
Greece	176	1.93
Canada	555	1.83
Australia	333	1.78
New Zealand	64	1.68
France	961	1.64
Italy	924	1.60
Netherlands	244[1]	1.57[1]
Portugal	152	1.52
England and Wales	750	1.43
Ireland	51	1.41
Germany	975	1.19
Japan	1,388	1.10
Switzerland	76	1.07
Austria	77	0.95
Denmark	49	0.93
Norway	38	0.86

[1] In 1996.

Source: International Comparisons of Criminal Justice Statistics 1998,

Homicide Rates in Selected Cities

City	Number of homicides 1996–98	Homicides per 100,000 population of the city Average 1996–98
Washington, DC	958	59.90
Pretoria	1512[1]	41.12[1]
Moscow	4201	17.85
Amsterdam	171[2]	7.90[2]
Belfast	54	6.10
Warsaw	277	5.67
Copenhagen	66	4.56
Berlin	431	4.17
Prague	119	3.28
Madrid	269	3.12
Budapest	159	2.82
Stockholm	52	2.67
Helsinki	42	2.65
Lisbon	146	2.65
Paris	159	2.52
Dublin	71	2.23
London	488	2.15
Wellington	10	2.10
Oslo	29	1.93
Vienna	87	1.83
Edinburgh	24	1.78
Rome	131	1.51
Brussels	59	1.47
Athens	46	1.32
Geneva	13	1.08
Tokyo	380	1.07
Ottawa	24	1.02
Canberra	6	0.64

[1] 1995–97.
[2] 1994–96.

Source: International Comparisons of Criminal Justice Statistics 1998,

The Death Penalty

As of April 2000, over half the countries of the world had abolished capital punishment in law or practice. Of these, 73 countries had abolished the death penalty for all crimes, 13 for ordinary crimes only, and 22 in practice. There were still 87 countries that retained the death penalty, including the USA (38 states).

The UK abolished the death penalty for all crimes as recently as 1998, although it was abolished in 1965 for all crimes except treason and piracy.

In the USA, 98 people were executed in 1999. The USA has carried out the greatest number of known executions of prisoners under 18 – 13 since 1990.

The Death Penalty: Sentences and Executions in 1999

During 1999 at least 1,813 prisoners were executed in 31 countries and 3,857 people were sentenced to death in 64 countries. Five countries alone accounted for 85% of all executions recorded by Amnesty International (AI) worldwide: China 1,077; Iran 165; Saudi Arabia 103; USA 98; Democratic Republic of Congo 100.

These figures include only cases known to AI; the true figures are certainly higher. AI received reports of hundreds of executions in Iraq but was unable to confirm most of these reports or give an exact figure.

Executions are known to have been carried out in the following countries in 1999:

Afghanistan
Belarus
Burundi
China
Congo, Democratic Republic of
Cuba
Egypt
Iran
Iraq
Japan
Jordan
Mongolia
Nigeria
Pakistan
Palestinian Authority
Philippines
Russian Federation
Saudi Arabia
Singapore
Somalia
Syria
Taiwan
Tajikistan
Thailand
Trinidad and Tobago
Uganda
United Arab Emirates
USA
Uzbekistan
Vietnam
Yemen

Source: Amnesty International

Countries that Have Abolished the Death Penalty for All Crimes

(As of 27 April 2000. N/A = not available. – = not applicable.)

Country	Date of abolition	Date of last execution
Andorra	1990	1943
Angola	1992	N/A
Australia	1985	1967
Austria	1968	1950
Azerbaijan	1998	1993
Belgium	1996	1950
Bulgaria	1998	1989
Cambodia	1989	N/A
Canada	1998	N/A
Cape Verde	1981	1835
Colombia	1910	1909
Costa Rica	1877	N/A
Croatia	1990	N/A
CzechRepublic	1990[1]	N/A
Denmark	1978	1950
Djibouti	1995	N/A
Dominican Republic	1966	N/A
East Timor	1999	N/A
Ecuador	1906	N/A
Estonia	1998	1991
Finland	1972	1944
France	1981	1977
Georgia	1997	1994
Germany	1949/1987[2]	1949[2]
Greece	1993	1972
Guinea-Bissau	1993	1986[3]
Haiti	1987	1972[3]
Honduras	1956	1940
Hungary	1990	1988
Iceland	1928	1830
Ireland, Republic of	1990	1954
Italy	1994	1947
Kiribati[4]	N/A	–
Liechtenstein	1987	1785
Lithuania	1998	N/A
Luxembourg	1979	1949
Macedonia, Former Yugoslav Republic of	N/A	N/A
Marshall Islands[4]	N/A	–
Mauritius	1995	1987
Micronesia, Federated States of[4]	N/A	–
Moldova	1995	N/A
Monaco	1962	1847
Mozambique	1990	1986
Namibia	1990	1988[3]
Nepal	1997	1979
Netherlands	1982	1952
New Zealand	1989	1957
Nicaragua	1979	1930
Norway	1979	1948
Palau	N/A	N/A
Panama	N/A	1903[3]
Paraguay	1992	N/A
Poland	1997	1988
Portugal	1976	1849[3]
Romania	1989	1989
San Marino	1865	1468[3]
São Tomé and Príncipe[4]	1990	–
Seychelles	1993	N/A
Slovak Republic	1990[1]	N/A
Slovenia	1989	N/A
Solomon Islands[4]	N/A	–
South Africa	1997	N/A
Spain	1995	1975
Sweden	1972	1910
Switzerland	1992	1944
Turkmenistan	1999	N/A
Tuvalu[4]	N/A	–
UK	1998	1968
Ukraine	1999	N/A
Uruguay	1907	N/A
Vanuatu[4]	N/A	–
Vatican City State	1969	N/A
Venezuela	1863	N/A

[1] The death penalty was abolished in the Czech and Slovak Federal Republic in 1990. On 1 January 1993 the Czech and Slovak Federal Republic divided into two states, the Czech Republic and the Slovak Republic. The last execution in the Czech and Slovak Federal Republic was in 1988.

[2] The death penalty was abolished in the Federal Republic of Germany (FRG) in 1949 and in the German Democratic Republic (GDR) in 1987. The last execution in the FRG was in 1949; the date of the last execution in the GDR is not known. The FRG and the GDR were unified in October 1990.

[3] Date of last known execution.

[4] No executions since independence.

Source: Amnesty International

Prison Population in Selected Countries

(– = not applicable.)

Country	1988	1993	1998
England and Wales	50,099	45,633	65,771
Northern Ireland	1,901	1,902	1,516
Scotland	5,229	5,637	6,018
UK total	57,229	53,172	73,305
Australia	11,849	15,003	18,344
Austria	6,565	7,099	6,891
Belgium	6,497	7,489	7,860
Canada	26,634	31,709	32,970
Czech Republic	23,615	16,567	22,067
Denmark	3,362	3,370	3,340
Finland	4,054	3,432	2,836
France	46,423	51,134	53,607
Germany	52,076	65,838	78,324

(continued)

Prison Population in Selected Countries *(continued)*

Country	1988	1993	1998
Greece	4,178	7,135	7,129
Hungary	20,821	13,196	14,366
Ireland	1,953	2,801	2,620
Italy	34,675	51,231	49,864
Japan	54,344	45,057	52,830
Netherlands	6,254	8,037	11,699
New Zealand	3,458	4,600	5,450
Norway	2,113	2,650	2,466
Poland	75,995	61,895	59,180
Portugal	8,168	11,079	14,330
Russian Federation	–	844,870	1,009,172
South Africa	111,481	111,798	141,441
Spain	28,917	46,076	44,370
Sweden	5,427	5,697	5,290
Switzerland	4,679	5,627	5,648
USA	949,659	1,369,185	1,802,496

Source: International Comparisons of Criminal Justice Statistics 1998,

Policing the Internet

by Paul Bray

Introduction Every society has its rogues and chancers who must be kept in check by the rule of law. The Internet is no exception and, as it evolves from an enthusiasts' playground into a backbone of international commerce, it too will have to be policed.

Is the Internet a Law Unto Itself? The glib response is that existing laws – such as contract, copyright, libel, and obscenity – apply online as much as off. But whose laws? If you buy goods from a Web site, the sale is probably governed by the laws of the country in which the site is based. These may be very different from those in your home country – especially if the site is hosted under a virtual 'flag of convenience', in a country with relaxed legislation and little desire to enforce it. The same dilemma arises with dubious activities, such as publishing pornography or disseminating computer viruses. In May, the 'Love Bug' virus caused billions of pounds worth of disruption to computer systems worldwide. However, when the suspected perpetrators were traced to the Philippines by Interpol and the FBI and arrested, there was doubt as to whether any Philippines law had been broken – even though spreading the virus was an offence in the USA, where much of the damage was done.

Wielding the Arm of the Law Even when the law is clear, who should enforce it? In February 2000, after anarchists temporarily disabled several high-profile Web sites by overloading them with messages, the European Union proposed several measures. These included better police training, coordination of international police efforts by Interpol, and making the police work more closely with Internet service providers (ISPs), the companies that provide Internet connections and host Web sites. ISPs complain that making them responsible for the actions of their customers is merely shooting the messenger. Their opponents argue that, since they have the capability to delete offensive material or close down dodgy sites, they should do so. This was the argument used by physicist Laurence Godfrey when he won damages from ISP Demon Internet in an out-of-court settlement in March 2000, after Demon failed to remove material written by third parties that libelled Dr Godfrey. The authorities are worried about criminals using the Internet for drug trafficking, money-laundering, paedophilia, and terrorism, especially if they encrypt (encode) their communications. Legislation like the UK government's Regulation of Investigatory Powers Bill (February 2000) and the EU directive on cybercrime is attempting to regularize surveillance of suspects' use of e-mails and newsgroups, and to enable the authorities to read encrypted messages. However, there is stiff opposition. Civil liberties campaigners fret about infringements of personal freedom. ISPs resent the potential cost of installing 'wire-tapping' equipment for the authorities to use. And business groups worry that legitimate Internet commerce will be driven abroad to countries with less strict legislation.

Self Help Net-savvy businesses have formed their own police forces like the Business Software Alliance, which successfully investigates software 'piracy' (using software without paying for it). They also use the services of companies like Virtual Internet, which monitor infringements of copyright. Private individuals are best advised to follow the old Latin maxim *caveat emptor*, 'let the buyer beware'. Good rules of thumb include: only buying from well known businesses whose Web sites run on secure servers; paying by personal credit card (not debitcard), so that the credit card company may be liable for losses; ignoring 'get rich quick' offers in unsolicited e-mails; and carefully monitoring children's use of the Internet.

UK Law and Crime

Crimes and Offences

Notifiable Offences Recorded by the Police and Clear-up Rates

Due to different legal systems, differences in classification, and different counting rules, recorded crime statistics in England and Wales, Scotland, and Northern Ireland cannot be directly compared. Notifiable offences provide a measure of the amount of crime committed. In England and Wales the counting rules were revised from 1 April 1998 to include all indictable and triable-either-way offences together with a few closely linked summary offences. Before 1 April 1998 notifiable offences broadly covered the most serious offences. In Northern Ireland notifiable offences are broadly the more

Notifiable Offences Recorded by the Police and Clear-up Rates *(continued)*

serious offences including most indictable, triable-either-way offences, and some summary offences. Scottish figures of 'crime' have been grouped in an attempt to approximate to the classification of notifiable offences in England, Wales, and Northern Ireland.
Combined primary and secondary clear-up rates for England and Wales; primary only in Scotland and Northern Ireland as secondary means of clear-up are not used.
(N = nil or negligible. N/A = not available.)

	England and Wales				Scotland				Northern Ireland			
	Notifiable offences			Clear-up rates (%)	Notifiable offences			Clear-up rates (%)	Notifiable offences			Clear-up rates (%)
	1981	1991	1998–99[1]	1998–99	1981	1991	1998–99[1]	1998–99	1981	1991	1998–99[1]	1998–99
Theft and handling stolen goods, of which:	1,603,000	2,761,000	2,127,000	22	201,000	284,000	192,000	31	25,000	32,000	35,000	23
theft of vehicles	333,000	582,000	391,000	18	33,000	44,000	28,000	28	5,000	8,000	10,000	13
theft from vehicles	380,000	913,000	681,000	10	N/A	N/A	50,000	15	7,000	7,000	6,000	6
Burglary	718,000	1,220,000	952,000	19	96,000	116,000	57,000	21	20,000	17,000	15,000	17
Criminal damage[2]	387,000	821,000	834,000	17	62,000	90,000	79,000	23	5,000	2,000	10,000	14
Violence against the person	100,000	190,000	231,000	71	8,000	16,000	16,000	80	3,000	4,000	7,000	57
Fraud and forgery	107,000	175,000	174,000	36	21,000	26,000	24,000	76	3,000	5,000	5,000	44
Robbery	20,000	45,000	66,000	23	4,000	6,000	5,000	33	3,000	2,000	1,000	19
Sexual offences, of which:	19,000	29,000	35,000	68	2,000	3,000	5,000	77	N	1,000	1,000	76
rape	1,000	4,000	8,000	64	N	1,000	1,000	77	N	N	N	76
Drug offences[3]	N/A	11,000	21,000	97	2,000	12,000	31,000	100	N	N	N	90
Other notifiable offences[4]	9,000	23,000	42,000	78	12,000	20,000	22,000	95	3,000	1,000	2,000	71
All notifiable offences	2,964,000	5,276,000	4,482,000	29	408,000	573,000	432,000	41	62,000	63,000	77,000	29

[1] Estimates of the number of offences under the old counting rules.
[2] In Northern Ireland excludes criminal damage valued at £200 or less. For clear-up rates, all criminal damage in Northern Ireland is recorded.
[3] In England and Wales trafficking was the only notifiable drugs offence counted under the old counting rules to 1 April 1998. In Scotland, trafficking was the only recorded drugs crime in 1981.
[4] In Northern Ireland includes 'possession of controlled drugs' and 'offences against the state'. In Scotland excludes 'offending while on bail' from 1991 onwards.

Source: Social Trends 30, © *Crown copyright 2000*

Murder and Manslaughter Recorded by the Police in England and Wales

Offence	*Offences recorded*			*Offences cleared up 1999–2000*[1]	
	1997–98	1998–99[4]	1999–2000	Number	% of total
Homicide (murder, manslaughter, infanticide)	748	750	765	693	90.6
Attempted murder	661	676	749	626	83.6
Threat or conspiracy to murder	9,661	11,212	13,434	8,053	59.9
Child destruction[2]	6	9	1	1	100.0
Causing death by dangerous driving or by careless driving when under the influence of drink and drugs	325	349	317	293	92.4
Causing death by aggravated vehicle taking[3]	18	30	37	21	56.8

[1] Offences cleared up in current year may have been initially recorded in an earlier year.
[2] The statutory crime of killing any child capable of being born alive (ie after 28 weeks gestation) before it has an existence independent of its mother; it overlaps with the offence of procuring the miscarriage of a viable child.
[3] Offence introduced on 1 April 1992.
[4] Revised counting procedures introduced from April 1998.

Cases of Homicide Recorded in Scotland

This table shows the status of cases currently recorded as homicide as of 12 November 1999.

Crime and status		1990	1992	1994	1996	1998
Convictions	murder	22	36	40	43	37
	culpable homicide	41	59	37	48	20
	Total	63	95	77	91	57
Other[1]	murder	11	29	22	19	29
	culpable homicide	4	6	5	3	11
	Total	15	35	27	22	40
Solved cases		78	130	104	113	97
All homicide cases		80	131	108	116	98

[1] Includes cases which were either unsolved or pending at 12 November 1999, or where the accused had no proceedings taken against them or were aquitted.

Source: The Scottish Office, © *Crown copyright 1999*

Race and the Criminal Justice System

- The latest population estimates indicate that 2% of those aged ten and over in England and Wales were of black ethnic origin, 3% of Asian origin, and 1% 'other' non-white ethnic groups.
- Of the 1 million stop and search procedures carried out by the police under the Police and Criminal Evidence Act (PACE), 9% were of black people, 5% Asian, and 1% 'other' non-white origin. Black people were, on average, six times more likely to be stopped and searched than white people.
- Of the 1.3 million arrests for notifiable offences that took place, 7% were of black people, 4% Asian, and 1% 'other' non-white origin. Black people were more likely to be arrested than white or other ethnic groups.
- Racist incidents recorded by the police rose by 66% to just over 23,000. This is thought to reflect improved police documentation of such incidents. Full recording of the new racially motivated offences was not introduced until 1 April 1999.
- Ethnic minorities are under-represented in the police service, prison service, lay magistracy, and senior posts in all the criminal justice agencies.

See also **Key Dates in the Reform of the Metropolitan Police after the Stephen Lawrence Inquiry,** p 459.

■ UK Law and Crime

Racial Incidents in England and Wales

Police force area	1994–95	1995–96	1996–97	1997–98	1998–99	% change 1997/98–1998/99
England						
Avon and Somerset	286	318	310	409	626	53
Bedfordshire	41	43	77	75	134	79
Cambridgeshire	75	160	141	147	205	39
Cheshire	62	27	92	78	158	103
Cleveland	62	112	68	76	147	93
Cumbria	24	27	37	46	45	– 2
Derbyshire	291	192	208	174	208	20
Devon and Cornwall	44	73	82	90	116	29
Dorset	37	41	67	86	145	69
Durham	26	23	24	37	75	103
Essex	127	178	116	160	229	43
Gloucestershire	37	34	34	32	83	159
Greater Manchester	637	776	595	624	1,197	92
Hampshire	210	279	178	219	271	24
Hertfordshire	183	234	295	288	325	13
Humberside	75	58	55	72	111	54
Kent	173	129	256	276	273	– 1
Lancashire	222	320	337	311	450	45
Leicestershire	366	270	299	237	367	55
Lincolnshire	2	0	7	6	14	133
London, City of	6	2	10	6	28	367
Merseyside	131	130	162	241	324	34
Metropolitan Police	5,480	5,011	5,621	5,862	11,050	89
Norfolk	39	41	56	89	94	6
Northamptonshire	146	214	195	318	282	– 11
Northumbria	508	475	488	444	623	40
North Yorkshire	30	37	43	41	64	56
Nottinghamshire	259	362	330	391	475	21
South Yorkshire	156	194	169	213	293	38
Staffordshire	164	253	225	214	220	3
Suffolk	73	74	74	54	150	178
Surrey	39	77	55	45	126	180
Sussex	247	263	260	298	399	34
Thames Valley	233	266	233	279	486	74
Warwickshire	114	99	66	107	111	4
West Mercia	35	46	64	57	83	46
West Midlands	375	489	725	632	988	56
West Yorkshire	254	355	623	644	1,068	66
Wiltshire	64	37	35	59	101	71
Wales						
Dyfed-Powys	3	23	18	17	37	118
Gwent	22	32	60	45	98	118
North Wales	3	5	4	12	36	200
South Wales	517	443	357	367	734	100
England and Wales total	11,878	12,222	13,151	13,878	23,049	66

Source: Statistics on Race and the Criminal Justice System, © *Crown copyright 1999*

Selected Sex Offences Recorded by the Police in England and Wales

(– = not applicable.)

Offence	Offences recorded					Offences cleared up 1998–99	
	1987	1991	1995	1997	1998–99[2]	Number	%
Buggery[1]	929	1,127	818	645	566	503	89
Indecent assault on a male	2,425	3,070	3,150	3,503	3,683	3,092	84
Indecent assault on a female	13,340	15,792	16,876	18,674	19,524	12,172	62
Indecency between males	1,127	965	727	520	354	326	92
Rape of a female	2,471	4,045	4,986	6,281	7,132	4,544	64
Rape of a male[1]	–	–	150	347	504	340	67
Unlawful sexual intercourse with a girl under 13	312	315	178	148	153	126	82
Unlawful sexual intercourse with a girl under 16	2,699	1,949	1,260	1,112	1,135	937	83
Incest	511	389	185	183	139	113	81
Procuration	175	138	207	131	215	204	95
Abduction	268	411	364	277	240	87	36
Bigamy	66	75	86	75	129	70	54
Soliciting or importuning by a man	–	–	–	–	1,107	1,021	92
Gross indecency with a child	831	1,147	1,287	1,269	1,293	1,022	79
Total	25,154	29,423	30,274	33,165	605,797	397,740	66

[1] The Criminal Justice and Public Order Act 1994 introduced a specific offence of rape of a male. Following this change in legislation, male victims of forced buggery are now classified as male rape.

[2] The number of crimes reported in that financial year using the expanded offence coverage and revised counting rules which came into effect 1 April 1998.

Source: Criminal Statistics, England and Wales 1998, © *Crown copyright 1999*

Incidence of Violent Crime in England and Wales

Total violent crimes recorded by the police, by police force area per 100,000 population. Violent crimes comprise violence against the person, sexual offences, and robbery.

1998–99

Police force area	Total violent crime	Police force area	Total violent crime	Police force area	Total violent crime
Metropolitan Police[1]	2,516	South Wales	1,018	North Yorkshire	718
Gwent	2,151	Derbyshire	991	West Mercia	707
Greater Manchester	1,774	Northamptonshire	982	Gloucestershire	688
West Midlands	1,533	Kent	897	Suffolk	655
Nottinghamshire	1,387	Durham	883	South Yorkshire	629
Leicestershire	1,261	Cambridgeshire	872	Surrey	626
Humberside	1,237	Lancashire	855	Thames Valley	623
Cumbria	1,199	Devon and Cornwall	844	Essex	620
Sussex	1,117	Wiltshire	832	Dorset	484
Merseyside	1,112	Hampshire	809	Warwickshire	482
Staffordshire	1,055	Norfolk	790	Hertfordshire	446
Dyfed-Powys	1,054	North Wales	787	England	1,159
Northumbria	1,033	Cheshire	776	Wales	1,188
Bedfordshire	1,026	Lincolnshire	772	England and Wales	1,160
West Yorkshire	1,020	Cleveland	762		
Avon and Somerset	1,014				

[1] Including City of London.

Source: Criminal Statistics, England and Wales 1998, © *Crown copyright 1999*

The Law on Drugs

A first offender who is caught in possession of a controlled (illegal) drug, and admits that he/she has committed a criminal offence, may receive a formal warning from the police or a formal caution. If a person between the ages of 10 and 17 commits further criminal offences, including selling or smuggling drugs, they could be charged by the police and dealt with by a Youth Court. This court has a number of options open to it, such as fining parents or putting the offender in a Young Offenders Institution (but not prison).

Keeping drugs for another person and handing them back could result in a charge of unlawful supply. On premises you are responsible for (ie you occupy or are concerned in the management of) it is an offence to knowingly allow anyone to produce, give away, or sell illegal drugs. It is an offence even to offer the drug free of charge. So if a parent knows that their child is sharing illegal drugs with a friend in their home and does nothing to stop it, the parent may have committed an offence. Knowingly allowing the smoking of cannabis in your home is an offence.

If you take illegal drugs from someone to prevent them from committing an offence, you must either destroy them or take the drugs to the police as soon as possible. The Misuse of Drugs Act divides illegal drugs into three classes and provides for maximum penalties as follows.

Class of drug	Drug type	Maximum penalties
Class A	amphetamines (speed) if prepared for injection, cocaine and crack, ecstasy, heroin, LSD (acid), magic mushrooms (if prepared for use)	possession: 7 years' prison and/or a fine possession with intent to supply, or supply: life imprisonment and/or a fine
Class B	amphetamines (speed), cannabis	possession: 5 years' prison and/or a fine possession with intent to supply, or supply: 14 years' prison and/or a fine
Class C	anabolic steroids, benzodiazepines (eg temazepam, valium)	possession: 2 years' prison and/or a fine possession with intent to supply, or supply: 5 years' prison and/or a fine

The Cannabis Debate

Despite the threat of prosecution, many people from all backgrounds and social classes in the UK are thought to use cannabis. Pressure is now mounting to re-examine the legislation that makes using the drug a crime. As one of the oldest known drugs, cannabis has been used medicinally for thousands of years. Taken from the hemp plant, it can induce feelings of relaxation, well-being, and drowsiness. However, in 1925 it was outlawed in the UK following an agreement of the Geneva Convention. This international body was won over by an Egyptian delegate who claimed that 'Indian hemp' was the main cause of insanity in his country.

There is scientific evidence to suggest that cannabis may be useful in treating a wide range of conditions. For example, cannabis is an antiemetic and so can apparently reduce the vomiting and nausea that are side effects of chemotherapy treatment given to cancer patients. There is evidence that extracts of cannabis can relieve the symptoms of some chronic conditions, such as multiple sclerosis (MS), and the UK government has commissioned research on the substances in cannabis that may have this effect. The drug can apparently also help stop muscle spasms and reduce tremors, help in the treatment of glaucoma, and may stimulate the appetites of AIDS patients with wasting disease. In the USA, the Food and Drug Administration has approved the oral use of dronabinol, a cannabis derivative, for people with AIDS.

Some people believe that cannabis is safer than alcohol and should be fully legalized for recreational use. It is not known to cause deaths and, unlike alcohol, is rarely blamed for aggressive mood swings. Advocates believe that, in moderation, it can be enjoyed socially like alcohol without serious harm. And rather than force recreational users into the world of drug dealing, the market should be legalized and regulated.

However, opponents of the use of cannabis point to the fact that it damages the ability to concentrate, and may lead to memory loss, anxiety, or depression. It is also thought to adversely affect unborn babies if taken during pregnancy and is known to impair driving and motor skills. Critics argue that any relaxation of the law would send out a message that the drug is safe, despite these risks. It would also breach international obligations

The Cannabis Debate (*continued*)

under UN conventions which commit the global community to work in unison against the drug trade.

The side effects of the drug vary considerably and are highly unpredictable, partly because cannabis has more than 400 active ingredients. A report by the House of Lords Science and Technology Committee recommended its use for medicinal purposes, but the British Medical Association (BMA) did not entirely support the report's findings and recommendations. The BMA believes only cannabinoids – the active ingredients of the cannabis plant – should be used in medicine, pointing out that crude cannabis contains many toxic ingredients as well. The BMA is also worried about how cannabis would be prescribed, as it has been shown that smoking the drug is harmful to health.

The first clinical trials testing the safety and efficacy of cannabis-based medicines, involving patients suffering from MS, spinal cord injury, and other forms of severe pain, were given the go-ahead in the UK in April 2000. The government said it would not consider legalizing cannabis for medical use until clinical trials had been completed, but indicated that if the trials were successful it would be prepared to amend the Misuse of Drugs Act 1971 to allow the prescribing of cannabis-based medicine. If successful, the clinical trials could lead to cannabis-based drugs being made widely available by 2003.

Cautions and Convictions for Possession of Cannabis in the UK

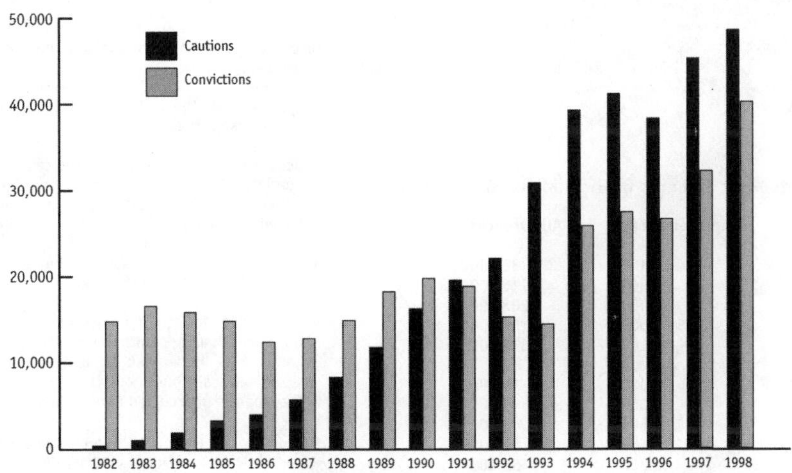

Source: Home Office Research, Development, and Statistics Directorate

Fighting Crime with Modern Technology

Modern technology is helping the police to detect crime faster and to win more convictions in court. Millions of pounds are being invested in computer expertise and high-tech equipment in the effort to ensure that lawbreakers are brought to justice.

One of the most important advances is in the development of DNA technology. It once required a pool of blood or clump of hair to identify a culprit at the scene of a crime. Now, the saliva from a sneeze found on a window sill or fleck of dandruff could be enough to trace a criminal. £34 million is being invested in expanding the country-wide DNA database which will eventually hold profiles from every known active criminal in the UK. The database holds over 750,000 criminal justice samples taken from suspects charged, reported, cautioned, or convicted for a recordable offence. The database also holds around 73,000 DNA profiles from DNA found at scenes of crime. Profiles from suspects not subsequently proceeded against or acquitted at court are removed from the database.

Even computer crime is becoming more difficult to perpetrate. Disks containing illegal material, such as pornography, are often encrypted so that only those with the right 'cyber keys' can access them. However, computer experts at a new Government Technical Assistance Centre are working to break the codes and reveal the material.

A police force in West Yorkshire has even gone online to tackle local crime. Bradford Police have set up a Web site encouraging Internet surfers to pass on information about people breaking the law in their communities. The Crimebeat site is part of a growing campaign styled 'e-policing'.

High-tech cameras are also proving a great success in the UK and are attracting interest from countries across the globe. Developed for the Cleveland force, new miniature cameras half the size of a button have been fitted into the protective helmets of mounted officers. Originally devised for policing brawls between football fans, the hidden lens takes video footage of crowd violence, which has been used repeatedly as corroborative evidence in court to convict criminals. Previously, officers found it difficult to arrest suspects at the same time as attempting to break up fights involving hundreds of people, but now they can concentrate on controlling the violence while letting the camera do the rest of the work.

Burglaries of Domestic Dwellings by Time of Day in England and Wales

In percentages.

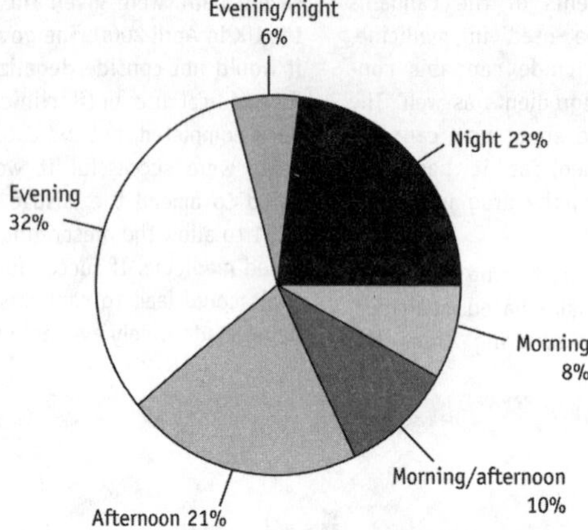

Source: Social Trends 30, © *Crown copyright 2000*

Proportion of Households which were Victims of Crime in England and Wales

In percentages.

1997	Inner city	Urban	Rural
Vehicle crime (owners)			
all thefts	23.7	16.2	12.0
vandalism	9.2	7.2	4.9
Bicycle thefts (owners)	8.9	5.2	2.4
Burglary	8.5	5.9	3.4
Home vandalism	4.3	3.7	2.6
Other household	8.4	6.8	5.4
Any household offence	32.2	28.6	22.8

Source: Social Trends 30, © *Crown copyright 2000*

Is Your Home a Target for Burglars?

There were 952,000 offences of burglary recorded by the police in England and Wales in 1998–99.

The findings of the British Crime Survey in 1998 suggested that:

- people were more likely to be victims of burglary during the evening or night (three-fifths of burglaries took place between 6pm and 6am)
- the risk of burglary was no higher at weekends than during the week
- people who left their homes unoccupied for more than a month during the year had a 43% higher risk of being burgled than identical households that never left their homes unoccupied during the night
- as levels of home security increase, the risk of being a victim of burglary decreases
- detached houses are at higher risk of burglary than other types of home and flats are the least likely to be burgled
- homes that had been burgled within the previous four years were more likely to be burgled again than those that had not.

Motoring Offences Detected by Automatic Cameras in England and Wales

	Fixed penalty[1]	All prosecutions	All offences
Speeding			
1993	25,800	6,400	32,200
1994	95,500	20,600	116,100
1995	170,000	36,900	206,900
1996	212,600	49,600	262,200
1997	288,600	48,100	336,700
Traffic lights			
1993	19,200	20,300	39,500
1994	25,900	14,000	40,000
1995	33,300	14,800	48,100
1996	33,400	19,400	52,800
1997	34,600	18,800	53,300

[1] Fixed penalty paid and no further action taken.

Source: Social Trends 30, © *Crown copyright 2000*

Young Offenders and Juvenile Crime

Young Offenders under an Immediate Custodial Sentence in England and Wales

Age and offence group	1992	1994	1996	1998
Men				
Aged under 18				
violence against the person	385	424	665	781
sexual offences	35	33	62	65
burglary	1,056	1,211	1,284	1,315
robbery	293	378	704	706
theft and handling 874	726	1,192	1,219	1,232
fraud and forgery	4	10	14	25
drugs offences	36	26	63	101
other offences	543	625	789	964
offence not recorded	266	72	271	94
Total	3,344	3,971	5,365	5,283
Aged 18–20				
violence against the person	1,208	1,378	1,623	1,999
sexual offences	102	81	90	135
burglary	2,552	2,535	2,468	2,482

(continued)

Young Offenders under an Immediate Custodial Sentence in England and Wales (*continued*)

Age and offence group	1992	1994	1996	1998
robbery	731	669	977	981
theft and handling	1,737	2,586	2,693	3,165
fraud and forgery	45	79	123	134
drugs offences	299	296	518	605
other offences	1,901	2,516	2,833	3,546
offence not recorded	911	336	485	198
Total	9,486	10,476	11,810	13,245
Total men	12,830	14,447	16,881	18,528
Women				
Aged under 18				
violence against the person	18	54	68	96
sexual offences	0	0	0	0
burglary	8	15	15	25
robbery	15	28	40	50
theft and handling	15	31	43	56
fraud and forgery	2	0	2	2
drugs offences	4	3	4	15
other offences	6	13	31	42
offence not recorded	11	5	11	16
Total	79	149	214	302
Aged 18–20				
violence against the person	41	74	81	114
sexual offences	2	0	0	1
burglary	18	30	34	49
robbery	17	30	46	55
theft and handling	72	113	179	290
fraud and forgery	10	9	23	39
drugs offences	23	31	58	81
other offences	45	56	61	120
offence not recorded	37	17	16	20
Total	265	360	498	769
Total women	344	509	712	1,071
TOTAL	13,174	14,956	17,593	19,599

Source: Prison Statistics, England and Wales 1998, © *Crown copyright 1999*

Prison Population of Young Offenders in Scotland

Average daily population of under-21 offenders by type and length of sentence.

Type/length of sentence	1994	1995	1996	1997	1998	% change 1997–98[1]
Less than 6 months	209	249	194	144	131	– 9
6 months–less than 2 years	223	227	282	301	264	– 12
2 years–less than 4 years	160	114	132	146	123	– 16
4 years or over (excluding life)	103	98	131	154	154	0
Life	15	14	17	19	17	– 11
Section 205 sentences (indeterminate)	9	14	10	18	20	11
Section 206 sentences (fixed)	1	2	4	4	3	– 25
Total[2]	720	719	770	787	712	– 10

[1] Based on rounded figures.
[2] Components may not add to totals due to rounding.
Source: Prison Statistics Scotland 1998, Scottish Office Statistical Bulletin, CrJ/1999, © *Crown copyright 2000*

Peak Age of Offenders

Police and court figures suggest that the peak age for males offending in England and Wales was 18 in 1997–98. Rates of females offending were lower and the peak age was 15. Before 1972 the peak age for both genders was 14. This peak rose to 15 for males when, in 1972, the school leaving age was raised from 15 to 16. The peak age had gone up to 18 for males by 1988, but that for female offenders remained around 14 or 15. In Northern Ireland, the peak age for males in 1997–98 was 19; 14% of this group were found guilty of an offence. The peak age for females was 18.

Juveniles Found Guilty at All Courts in Northern Ireland

Offence	1991	1992	1993	1994	1995	1996	1997
Violence against the person	38	46	43	49	51	75	49
Sexual offences	8	11	7	8	7	4	8
Burglary	194	165	155	180	170	137	124
Robbery	7	8	4	9	22	13	18
Theft	328	247	280	283	345	338	334
Fraud and forgery	10	16	14	14	21	14	11
Criminal damage	92	82	94	117	116	121	136
Offences against the state	5	6	1	8	9	6	10
Other indictable	11	8	2	6	14	24	10
Total indictable[1]	693	589	600	674	755	732	700
Summary[2]	111	113	125	131	180	182	198
Motoring[3]	71	40	44	74	74	58	57
TOTAL[4]	875	742	769	879	1,009	972	955

[1] Excludes indictable motoring offences.
[2] A summary offence is an offence that is triable in a magistrate's court.
[3] Includes indictable motoring offences.
[4] Juveniles are aged 10–16 years inclusive.

Source: Annual Abstract of Statistics 2000, © *Crown copyright 2000*

The Police

The Police Caution and the Right to Silence

When a suspect is questioned by the police, he or she must first be cautioned. Under the provisions of the Criminal Justice and Public Order Act 1994, the police caution has been amended so that the suspect is now reminded of the right to silence, while at the same time warned that silence may lead to adverse comment by the judge or the prosecution during trial, who may invite the jury to draw an adverse inference from silence.

The new caution now reads as follows:

'You do not have to say anything. But it may harm your defence if you do not mention when questioned something which you later rely on in court. Anything you do say may be given in evidence.'

The Code of Practice states that a minor change in the wording is permitted so long as the overall meaning is retained. At the beginning of a police interview at a police station, it is necessary for the interviewing officer to refer the suspect to any significant statement or silence the suspect made in response to questions prior to the interview. The officer should then check that the suspect confirms or denies the prior silence or statement, and whether he or she wishes to add anything.

Where there is a break in questioning, the suspect should be reminded that he or she is still under caution. If the suspect is in any doubt, he or she should be cautioned again before the interview continues.

Strength of the Police Service in England and Wales

As of 31 March 1999.

	Rank	Strength
Men	Chief Constables	47
	Assistant Chief Constables	142
	Superintendents	1,156
	Chief Inspectors	1,511
	Inspectors	5,602
	Sergeants	17,196
	Constables	78,302
	Total	103,956
Women	Chief Constables	2
	Assistant Chief Constables	9
	Superintendents	57
	Chief Inspectors	93
	Inspectors	334
	Sergeants	1,542
	Constables	17,848
	Total	19,885
TOTAL		123,841
Total officers per 100,000 population		237.2

Source: Home Office Statistical Bulletin, *Issue 14/99*

Strength of the Police Service in Scotland

As of 31 March 1999.

Force	Regular police		Special constables	
	Men	Women	Men	Women
Central	619	100	40	22
Dumfries and Galloway	361	76	139	48
Fife	718	128	71	31
Grampian	1,040	209	98	23
Lothian and Borders	2,222	393	148	50
Northern	578	82	360	122
Strathclyde	6,050	1,085	240	70
Tayside	957	192	132	56
Total	12,545	2,265	1,229	422

Source: Her Majesty's Chief Inspector of Constabulary for Scotland Report for 1998/99, *Scottish Executive October 1999,*

Royal Ulster Constabulary Staffing Levels

As of 31 March 2000.

Position	Effective strength
Chief constable	1
Deputy chief constable	1
Assistant chief constable	8
Chief superintendent	39
Superintendent	123
Chief inspector	170
Inspector	498
Sergeant	1,390
Constable	6,163
Total	8,393
Full-time reserve	2,688
Part-time reserve	1,152

Source: Annual Report,Chief Constable of Royal Ulster Constabulary 1999/2000,

Police Complaints Authority

The Police Complaints Authority was set up on 29 April 1985 under the provisions of the Police and Criminal Evidence Act 1984, to supervise the investigation of complaints against the police by members of the public. It replaced the Police Complaints Board.

The Authority has three basic functions: to supervise the investigation of the most serious complaints against police officers; to supervise investigations into non-complaint matters voluntarily referred by police forces because of their potential gravity; and to review the outcome of every investigation, whether supervised or not, and to decide whether disciplinary action should be taken against any offence.

The more serious matters investigated by the Authority include the use of firearms by the police; death in police custody or care; cases of corruption; alleged miscarriages of justice; misuse of police records; public order incidents; and child abuse allegations.

Information from the Police Complaints Authority.

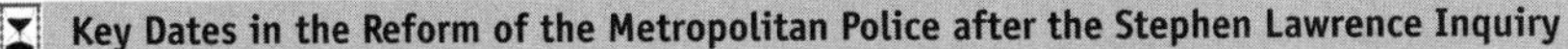

Key Dates in the Reform of the Metropolitan Police after the Stephen Lawrence Inquiry

22 April 1993 Stephen Lawrence, an 18-year-old black student, is subjected to verbal racial abuse and stabbed to death by five white youths at 10.30 p.m. near a bus stop in Eltham, southeast London. The subsequent police investigation fails to produce sufficient evidence to mount a successful prosecution.

April 1995 The parents of Stephen Lawrence start a private prosecution against four youths for the murder of their son.

September 1995 The prosecution of two of the four suspects fails at the committal stage, but the others are to stand trial at the Old Bailey in December 1995, along with a fifth youth who is also charged with murder.

April 1996 The private prosecution against the three youths collapses after vital eyewitness evidence is ruled as inadmissable. As 'not guilty' verdicts are entered, no further action can be taken against them.

February 1997 The inquest jury returns a unanimous verdict that Stephen Lawrence had been unlawfully killed in an unprovoked racist attack by five white youths. Kent Police, under the supervision of the Police Complaints Authority, investigate the Metropolitan Police Services' (MPS) handling of the murder investigation, at the request of the Lawrence family. The investigation, which takes a year to complete, is critical of the MPS investigation but finds 'no evidence of racist conduct by any MPS officer'.

July 1997 Jack Straw, Home Secretary in the new Labour government, appoints Sir William Macpherson, a retired High Court judge, to investigate matters arising from Stephen Lawrence's death and lessons to be learned for the investigation and prosecution of racially motivated crimes. The Inquiry holds 69 days of hearings, between October 1997 and November 1998, taking evidence from senior MPS officers and the five murder suspects.

April 1998 The MPS begins piloting a new, more targeted and ethnically balanced, approach to 'stop and search'.

June 1998 MPS Commissioner (head) Sir Paul Condon and Assistant Commissioner Ian Johnston, the head of MPS crime, apologise to the Lawrence family for letting them down over the police investigation.

August 1998 The MPS forms a Racial and Violent Crimes Task Force under the command of Deputy Assistant Commissioner John Grieve, formerly head of Anti-Terrorism, and with a mandate to monitor and review investigations of racial and violent crimes. It also begins to establish Community Safety Units in every borough to deal with 'hate crimes' (racist, homophobic, and domestic violence incidents).

December 1998 MPS issue *Protect and Respect*, a policing diversity strategy which aims to provide better protection to ethnic communities from racial and violent crime and demonstrate fairness in policing.

January 1999 DAC John Grieve takes personal charge of the continuing investigation into the Lawrence murder; the MPS launches *Operation Spectrum*, a menu of options for the proactive prevention and investigation of racist crime.

24 February 1999 Publication of 335-page *The Stephen Lawrence Inquiry* report by Sir William Macpherson, which criticises the MPS's 'professional incompetence, institutional racism[1] and failure of leadership' which allowed Lawrence's white murderers to escape justice. The government accepts all the inquiry's 70 recommendations, which include setting targets for the recruitment, promotion and retention of black and Asian police officers, and the extension of the 1976 Race Relations Act to the police. The Home Secretary, Jack Straw, produces an action plan and orders Her Majesty's Inspectorate of Constabulary (HMIC) to make an immediate inspection of the MPS and, after Macpherson shows that black people are on average five times more likely to be stopped and searched than whites, declares that the police will use their powers to 'stop and search' with more restraint.

25 February 1999 Sir Paul Condon announces the creation of quick reaction units to deal with murders in the first critical hour and also 'random integrity spot checks' of officers' behaviour and victims' views of their conduct to help diagnose racism in the MPS.

March 1999 The MPS adopts the 15 recommendations of its multi-agency Ethnic Minority (Recruitment and Advancement) Working Group to help achieve the Macpherson and Home Secretary's goal of, within a decade, raising its proportion of non-white officers from its current level of 3.4% to one in line with the proportion of ethnic minorities (25–30%) in London at large.

April 1999 The MPS reports that recorded racist crime has more than doubled since 1997–98 to 9,230 offences in 1998–99, largely reflecting improved reporting and recording, and that the detection rate for racial crime has also increased. New Area Murder Review Units are established. New police Code of Conduct makes racist language or behaviour a breach. New targets are set for the number of ethnic minority officers in proportion to the community served.

November 1999 The Home Secretary declares increasing trust and confidence in policing among minority ethnic communities and announces a new Ministerial Priority for the Police Service.

3 December 1999 A Race Relations (Amendment) Bill is introduced to Parliament.

10 January 2000 The HMIC publishes its report *Policing London: Winning Consent* on its investigation into the MPS, finding progress has been made in responding to the community and race relations issues highlighted in the *Macpherson Report*.

1 February 2000 Sir Paul Condon retires as MPS Commissioner and is succeeded by Sir John Stevens who issues a new 10-point *Policing Pledge for Londoners* and vows to make London the safest major city in the world.

1 April 2000 The MPS is re-organised to provide for borough-based policing; a new Code of Practice is put in place for the reporting and recording of racist incidents.

May 2000 MPS figures show a further doubling in the number of 'racist incidents', to 23,346 in 1999–2000, these crimes now being classified according to the Macpherson definition of a 'racist crime[2]'. The Home Secretary publishes a consultation on complaints against the police in which the government's consultants, KPMG, suggest replacing the existing Police Complaints Authority with a regionally-based Independent Agency for Complaints.

3 July 2000 MPS comes under the control of a new Metropolitan Police Authority (MPA), the majority of whose 23 members will be elected representatives, having previously been directly accountable to the Home Secretary. Whether the MPA can continue to deliver improvements remains to be seen.

[1] The *Macpherson Report* gives the following definition of institutional racism: 'the collective failure of an organisation to provide an appropriate and professional service to people because of their colour, culture, or ethnic origin. It can be seen or detected in processes, attitudes and behaviour which amount to discrimination through unwitting prejudice, ignorance, thoughtlessness, and racist stereotyping which disadvantages minority ethnic groups'.

[2] The *Macpherson Report* defines a racist crime as 'any incident which is perceived to be racist by the victim or any other person'.

Complaints against the Police in England and Wales

Year	Total complaints	Complaints investigated		Withdrawn/not proceeded with		Informally resolved	
1994	36,521	9,590	26%	14,658	40%	12,273	34%
1995–96	35,840	8,653	24%	15,535	43%	11,652	33%
1996–97	36,731	10,820	29%	14,286	39%	11,625	32%
1997–98	35,834	9,840	27%	13,714	38%	12,280	34%
1998–99	31,653	9,202	29%	11,423	36%	11,028	35%

Source: Police Complaints and Discipline 1999, © *Crown copyright 1999*

Complaints Cases and Allegations Against the Police in Scotland

	Complaints and allegations		
	Total complaint allegations	Allegations referred to procurators' fiscal	Criminal proceedings taken
1996–97	2,113	1,215	23
1997–98	2,129	1,112	23
1998–99	2,128	1,030	22

	Outcome of hearings		
	Disciplinary hearings 1998–99	Misconduct hearings 1998–99	Total
Dismissed	0	1	1
Required to resign	0	6	6
Reduced in rank	0	2	2
Reduced in pay	0	9	9
Fined	1	49	15
Reprimanded	1	15	60
Cautioned	0	5	5
Total	2	87	89

Source: Annual Report of Her Majesty's Chief Inspectorate of Constabulary, *© Crown copyright 1999*

Complaints Against the Police in Northern Ireland

1999–2000 **Offence alleged**	**Substantiated**	**Not substantiated**	**Informally resolved**	**Withdrawn**	**Incapable of investigation**	**Total**
Assault	8	764	52	545	277	1,646
Incivility	9	363	263	95	79	809
Oppressive conduct/harassment	1	121	127	54	69	372
Irregularity in procedure	14	82	60	30	22	208
Neglect of duty	15	225	208	44	39	531
Unlawful arrest/detention	2	63	5	14	112	196
Irregularity in search of premises	2	18	19	9	24	72
Mishandling of property	1	14	0	5	6	26
Irregularity in relation to evidence/perjury	0	38	6	6	6	56
Traffic offence	0	5	19	1	1	26
Corrupt practice	0	2	0	0	1	3
Discriminatory behaviour	0	5	6	2	0	13
Other	2	115	15	25	44	201
Total	54	1,815	780	830	680	4,159

Source: Annual Report, Chief Constable of Royal Ulster Constabulary 1999/00, *© Crown copyright 2000*

The Prisons

Population in Prison Under Sentence in England and Wales

(N/A = not available.)

Offence group		**1994**	**1995**	**1996**	**1997**	**1998**
	Men					
Offences with immediate custodial sentence	violence against the person	7,715	8,491	9,230	10,033	10,524
	rape	1,638	1,781	1,926	2,080	2,369
	other sexual offences	1,629	1,875	2,013	1,989	2,410
	burglary	5,096	5,896	6,342	7,976	8,538
	robbery	5,090	5,264	5,591	6,277	6,449
	theft and handling	3,030	3,450	3,591	3,929	4,097
	fraud and forgery	879	1,071	1,099	1,104	1,080
	drugs offences	3,186	3,858	5,269	6,483	7,099
	motoring offences	1,527	1,660	1,720	N/A	N/A
	other offences[1]	2,301	2,514	2,952	5,046	5,208
	offence not recorded	1,869	1,547	1,454	1,694	2,019
	All offences	33,960	37,407	41,187	46,611	49,793
In default of payment of a fine		514	490	136	128	109
Total		34,474	37,897	41,323	46,739	49,902
	Women					
Offences with immediate custodial sentence	violence against the person	277	290	355	391	420
	rape	1	2	3	3	4
	other sexual offences	11	10	9	5	12
	burglary	39	57	80	101	118
	robbery	95	108	124	161	177
	theft and handling	227	279	314	334	395
	fraud and forgery	65	96	119	121	119

(continued)

Population in Prison Under Sentence in England and Wales *(continued)*

Offence group		1994	1995	1996	1997	1998
	Women					
	drugs offences	326	398	486	691	794
	motoring offences	20	18	14	N/A	N/A
	other offences[1]	112	114	150	190	217
	offence not recorded	93	84	73	66	110
	All offences	1,266	1,456	1,727	2,063	2,366
In default of payment of a fine		23	26	5	3	1
Total		1,289	1,482	1,732	2,066	2,367
TOTAL		35,763	39,379	43,055	48,805	52,269

[1] Motoring offences are included in 'other offences' for 1997 and 1998.

Source: Prison Statistics of England and Wales 1998, © *Crown copyright 1999*

Expenditure on Penal Establishments in Scotland

Figures are for 31 March in year shown and are in thousands of pounds.

Expenditure	1991–92	1992–93	1993–94	1994–95	1995–96	1996–97	1997–98	1998–99
Manpower and associated services	124,898	129,597	135,301	140,009	135,941	143,107	137,890	144,690
Prisoner and associated costs	8,504	10,274	10,795	11,679	12,373	13,377	16,313	18,891
Capital expenditure	13,032	13,681	11,845	15,636	15,377	22,577	22,136	23,697
Total gross expenditure	146,434	153,552	157,941	167,324	163,691	179,061	176,339	187,248

Source: Annual Abstract of Statistics 2000, © *Crown copyright 2000*

Average Daily Prison Population and Receptions in Scotland

Components may not add to totals due to rounding. (N = nil or negligible. – = not applicable.)

	1988	1990	1992	1994	1996[1]	1998
Average daily population						
Men	5,057	4,587	5,099	5,408	5,673	5,825
Women	172	137	158	177	189	193
Total	5,229	4,724	5,257	5,585	5,862	6,018
Analysis by type of custody						
Remand	844	751	876	1,015	1,000	938
Persons under sentence						
adult prisoners	3,434	3,201	3,552	3,785	4,026	4,281
young offenders	817	708	769	720	770	712
detention centre inmates[2]	85	N	N	N	N	N
persons recalled from supervision/licence	28	39	32	37	46	67
Total	4,381	3,961	4,375	4,569	4,861	5,077
Persons sentenced by court martial	3	11	6	1	N	2
Civil prisoners	1	1	1	1	1	1
Receptions to penal establishments[3]						
Remand						
men	14,225	14,323	12,722	13,985	13,976	13,887
women	775	845	824	937	1,001	1,108
Total	15,000	15,168	13,546	14,922	14,977	14,995
Persons under sentence						
men	19,427	16,235	18,856	19,697	20,869	19,517
women	1,113	899	1,110	1,414	1,286	1,238
imprisoned directly	7,984	7,551	8,543	9,349	10,040	9,607
imprisoned in default of fine	7,234	5,182	6,603	7,377	7,432	6,862
imprisoned in default of compensation order[4]	46	23	40	26	–	–
Total	20,540	17,134	19,966	21,111	22,155	20,755
Persons sentenced to young offenders' institution						
directly	2,160	2,719	3,041	2,855	3,111	2,748
in default of fine	2,466	1,653	1,736	1,498	1,567	1,538
in default of compensation order[4]	6	3	2	6	–	–
Persons sentenced to detention centre[2]	642	N	N	N	N	N
Persons recalled from supervision/licence	2	3	1	N	5	N
Persons sentenced by court martial	10	10	2	5	4	5
Civil prisoners[5]	8	21	34	27	32	11

[1] From 1 April 1996 there was a change in the method of collection of statistical information from Scottish Prison Service establishments. In summary, there are changes in the population categorization of prisoners, the coverage of receptions, and the main crime/offence classification for reception purposes.
[2] From 1 November 1988 detention centre sentences were no longer available.
[3] Total receptions cannot be calculated by adding together receptions in each category because there is double counting. This arises because a person received on remand and then under sentence in relation to the same set of charges is counted in both categories.
[4] From 1996 compensation orders are included in the figures for default of fine.
[5] Data for 1996 are estimated.

Source: Annual Abstract of Statistics 2000, © *Crown copyright 2000*

Population in Prison Establishments in Northern Ireland

	Type of prisoner		1994	1995	1996	1997	1998
Men	Remand	aged under 21	106	72	69	70	71
		aged 21 or over	321	240	249	288	291
		Total	427	312	318	358	362
	Fine defaulter	aged under 21	4	5	5	6	7
		aged 21 or over	23	23	19	23	22
		Total	27	28	24	29	29
	Immediate custody	young offenders' centre	133	118	115	104	114
		young prisoners	91	87	66	57	44
		adult prisoners	1,179	1,177	1,076	1,044	921
		Total	1,403	1,382	1,257	1,205	1,079
	non-criminal		1	5	11	10	10
	Total		1,858	1,727	1,610	1,602	1,480
Women	Remand	aged under 21	5	2	2	3	4
		aged 21 or over	7	3	6	5	7
		Total	12	5	8	8	11
	Fine defaulter	aged under 21	1	0	0	0	0
		aged 21 or over	2	1	0	1	1
		Total	3	1	0	1	1
	Immediate custody	young offenders' centre	4	6	4	3	1
		young prisoners	3	2	1	0	0
		adult prisoners	19	21	16	18	14
		Total	26	29	21	21	15
	non-criminal		0	0	0	0	0
	Total		41	35	29	30	27
All prisoners	Remand		439	317	326	366	373
	Fine defaulter		30	29	24	30	30
	Immediate custody		1,429	1,411	1,278	1,266	1,094
	Non-criminal		1	5	11	10	10
TOTAL			1,899	1,762	1,639	1,632	1,507

Source: The Northern Ireland Prison Population in 1998, © *Crown copyright 1999*

The UK Legal System and Judiciary

The Law in Britain: Useful Addresses

Lord Advocate's Department Dover House, Whitehall, London SW1A 2AU; phone: (020) 7270 3000 (switchboard for all government offices); Crown Office, 25 Chambers Street, Edinburgh EH1 1LA; phone: (0131) 226 2626; **Lord Chancellor's Department** Selborne House, 54–60 Victoria Street, London SW1E 6QW; phone: (020) 7210 8500; fax: (020) 7210 0647; **Law Officers' Department** 9 Buckingham Gate, London SE1E 6JP; **The Law Society** 113 Chancery Lane, London WC2A 1PL; phone: (020) 7242 1222; fax: (020) 7831 0344; Web site: www.lawsociety.org.uk; **The Inns of Court School of Law** 4 Gray's Inn Place, London WC1R 5DX; phone: (020) 7404 5787; fax: (020) 7831 4188; Web site: www.icsl.ac.uk; **The British Institute of International and Comparative Law** Charles Clore House, 17 Russell Square, London WC1B 5DR; phone: (020) 7636 5802; fax: (020) 7323 2016; **Institute of Advanced Legal Studies** University of London, Charles Clore House, 17 Russell Square, London WC1B 5DR; phone: (020) 7637 1731; fax: (020) 7580 9613.

The Pinochet Extradition: Key Dates

11 September 1973 General Augusto Pinochet (1915–), commander-in-chief of the Chilean army, ousts President Salvador Allende in a military coup and 'purges' thousands of his left-wing supporters.

1987 A decree is issued granting officials of the Pinochet regime immunity from prosecution for any human rights abuses.

11 March 1990 The 17-year Pinochet dictatorship is ended when, following free elections in 1989, power is handed over to President Patricio Aylwin; but Pinochet remains head of the armed forces.

4 March 1991 The Rettig Commission for Truth and Reconciliation in Chile, set up in 1990 and headed by the investigative lawyer Raúl Rettig (1909–2000), reports that at least 1,319 people were killed by state agencies and 979 'disappeared' during the Pinochet dictatorship.

1992 The Rettig Commission's findings are confirmed in a report by its successor body, the Corporation for Reparation and Reconciliation, established 8 February 1992.

February 1995 The findings of the Corporation for Reparation and Reconciliation amount to 1,102 disappearances and 2,095 extra judicial executions and deaths under torture, making a total of 3,197 cases officially recognised by the state.

March 1998 Pinochet steps down as armed forces' commander-in-chief and becomes a special 'senator-for-life' in the Chilean parliament.

21 September 1998 Pinochet flies to the UK for medical treatment for his back.

16 October 1998 Pinochet is arrested in London on a provisional warrant issued by Baltazar Garzon, a Spanish magistrate, who seeks his extradition on 35 charges of murder, torture, and hostage-taking during his period in power.

28 October 1998 The London High Court rules that, as a former head of state and current senator-for-life, Pinochet enjoys immunity from prosecution and that his arrest is unlawful. The decision is appealed, on Spain's behalf, to the highest court, the House of Lords, and Pinochet is forced to remain in the UK, living in a rented mansion in Surrey.

11 November 1998 The UK receives from Spain a formal request for Pinochet's extradition.

25 November 1998 The judicial committee of the House of Lords, the 'Law Lords', rules in a landmark 3:2 verdict that, as murder and torture are not acceptable functions of a head of state, Pinochet does not have immunity from prosecution and that extradition proceedings can continue.

9 December 1998 British Home Secretary Jack Straw rejects appeals by Pinochet's lawyers and gives the British courts 'authority to proceed' with the hearing on the general's extradition for crimes against humanity.

The Pinochet Extradition: Key Dates *(continued)*

Anti-Pinochet protesters demonstrate outside the Houses of Parliament in London following the UK government's decision in January 2000 to let former Chilean dictator Augusto Pinochet fly back to Chile, on the grounds that he was medically unfit to stand trial for alleged violations of human rights. *Syndication International*

10 December 1998 Pinochet's lawyers appeal to the House of Lords to review their 25 November decision on the grounds of possible bias, as one of the judges, Lord Hoffman, had failed to declare that he was an unpaid director of Amnesty International, which had presented evidence against Pinochet.

17 December 1998 The Law Lords concur with this request and overturn their 25 November judgement and agree to re-hear the case from January 1999.

24 March 1999 In a confusing second ruling by the Law Lords, Pinochet loses his appeal for immunity from prosecution, but the number of charges against him are substantially reduced, to those of torture committed after 8 December 1988, when a British law implementing the 1984 International Convention Against Torture came into effect. As a consequence, the Lords ask Home Secretary Straw to reconsider the case for extradition.

15 April 1999 Home Secretary Straw signs a second 'authority to proceed' with Spain's extradition request.

27 May 1999 The High Court dismisses a request by Pinochet's lawyers for a judicial review of Straw's decision.

1 October 1999 Belgium renews its arrest warrant for Pinochet.

8 October 1999 London's Bow Street Magistrates Court approves Spain's extradition request on all 35 charges against him, and the case is passed to Home Secretary Straw for a final decision on whether to extradite.

14 October 1999 Chile formally requests Pinochet's return because of his deteriorating health.

21 October 1999 Spain says it will not appeal if Pinochet is released on humanitarian grounds.

5 November 1999 The Home Office asks Pinochet to have a medical examination.

11 January 2000 Home Secretary Straw announces to the UK Parliament that the government will not extradite Pinochet because the unanimous conclusion of a four-member medical team was that the 84-year-old Pinochet was medically unfit to follow or participate in a trial. Medical tests carried out on 5 January found that Pinochet, who had suffered strokes in October 1999, had irrecoverable mental impairment.

15 February 2000 The High Court orders Straw to hand over the confidential medical reports to the four countries (Spain, Belgium, Switzerland, and France) requesting Pinochet's extradition.

2 March 2000 Despite protests from the countries seeking Pinochet's extradition, and from human rights campaigners, Pinochet's 17-month detention in the UK ends and he is allowed to fly back to Chile. There the military stage a public welcome, but thousands of Chilean opponents demonstrate for his prosecution.

26 April 2000 The Santiago Appeals Court, in Chile, begins hearings on a petition to remove the immunity from prosecution that Pinochet enjoys as a senator. This is at the request of the state prosecutor, Judge Juan Guzman, after the government, on a review of the medical evidence from the UK, declares Pinochet physically able to stand trial in a Chilean court, as health requirements to stand trial in Chile are less strict than in the UK.

23 May 2000 Pinochet is stripped of his immunity from prosecution as a senator-for-life by the Santiago Appeals Court, by a vote of 13 to 9. The decision, on 5 June, leaves Pinochet facing 110 lawsuits.

A Glossary of the Law in Britain: Courts, Professionals, and Important Bodies

admiralty court English court that tries and gives judgement in maritime causes: the court is now incorporated within the Queen's Bench Division of the High Court and deals with such matters as salvage and damages arising from collisions between ships

advocate a Scottish lawyer, also referred to as counsel, who has passed or won exemption from professional exams and whose main function is to plead for a client in court (similar to an English barrister)

attorney general principal law officer of the crown and head of the English Bar: the post is one of great political importance

barrister a lawyer qualified by study at the Inns of Court to plead for a client in court: barristers also undertake the writing of opinions on the prospects of a case before trial; they act for clients through the intermediary of solicitors

central criminal court crown court in the City of London, able to try all treasons and serious offences committed in the City or Greater London

chambers in the UK, rented offices used by a group of barristers: chambers in London are usually within the precincts of one of the four law courts

Chancery a division of the High Court that deals with such matters as the administration of the estates of deceased persons, the execution of trusts, the enforcement of sales of land, and foreclosure of mortgages

circuit the geographic district that constitutes a particular area of jurisdiction in England and Wales: the six different centres to which High Court and circuit judges travel to try civil and criminal cases are: Midland and Oxford, Northeastern, Northern, Southeastern, Wales and Chester, and Western

circuit judge full-time judicial officer; sits as court judge in civil cases and presiding judge in the crown court: circuit judges must have been barristers for ten years or recorders for three years

A Glossary of the Law in Britain: Courts, Professionals, and Important Bodies *(continued)*

commissioner for oaths a person appointed by the Lord Chancellor with power to administer oaths or take affidavits: all practising solicitors have these powers but must not use them in proceedings in which they are acting for any of the parties or in which they have an interest

common law that part of the English law not embodied in legislation: consists of rules of law based on common custom and usage and on judicial decisions; English common law became the basis of law in the USA and many other English-speaking countries

coroner official who investigates the deaths of persons who have died suddenly by acts of violence or under suspicious circumstances, by holding an inquest or ordering a post-mortem examination (autopsy)

county court English court of law; exists to try civil cases; presided over by one or more circuit judges

Court of Appeal UK law court comprising a Civil Division and a Criminal Division, set up under the Criminal Appeals Act 1968: the Criminal Division of the Court of Appeal has the power to revise sentences or quash a conviction on the grounds that in all the circumstances of the case the verdict is unsafe or unsatisfactory, or that the judgement of the original trial judge was wrong in law, or that there was a material irregularity during the course of the trial

Court of Arches in the UK, ecclesiastical court of the archbishop of Canterbury; the presiding judge is the dean of the Arches

Court of Protection in English law, a department of the High Court that deals with the estates of people who are incapable, by reason of mental disorder, of managing their own property and affairs

Court of Session supreme civil court in Scotland, established 1532: the court sits in Edinburgh

Criminal Injuries Compensation Board UK board established in 1964 to administer financial compensation by the state for victims of crimes of violence

Crown court in England and Wales, any of several courts that hear serious criminal cases referred from magistrates' courts after committal proceedings

Crown Prosecution Service body established by the Prosecution of Offences Act 1985, responsible for prosecuting all criminal offences in England and Wales; headed by the Director of Public Prosecutions (DPP)

defamation an imputation against a person's character or reputation in a spoken or written, published statement

Director of Public Prosecutions the head of the Crown Prosecution Service (established 1985), responsible for the conduct of all criminal prosecutions in England and Wales

district court a Scottish court covering a local government district and dealing with minor criminal cases (similar to a magistrate's court)

ecclesiastical law in England, the Church of England has special ecclesiastical courts to administer church law

European Court of Human Rights court that hears cases referred from the European Commission of Human Rights, if the Commission has failed to negotiate a friendly settlement in a case where individuals' rights have been violated by a member state, as defined in the 1950 European Convention on Human Rights; the court sits in Strasbourg and comprises one judge for every state that is a party to the 1950 convention: the UK has never incorporated the Human Rights Convention into its laws, which means that a statute that directly contradicts the convention will always prevail over a Strasbourg decision in a British court; in practice, however, the UK has always passed the necessary legislation to make its laws comply with the court's decisions

European Court of Justice the court of the European Union (EU); it sits in Luxembourg with judges from the member states

Faculty of Professional Advocates organization for Scottish advocates incorporated in 1532

Inns of Court four private legal societies in London, England: Lincoln's Inn, Gray's Inn, Inner Temple, and Middle Temple; all barristers (advocates in the English legal system) must belong to one of the Inns of Court the main function of each Inn is the education, government, and protection of its members; each is under the administration of a body of Benchers (judges and senior barristers)

judge person invested with power to hear and determine legal disputes in the UK, judges are chosen from barristers of long standing, but solicitors can be appointed circuit judges; the independence of the higher judiciary is ensured by the principle that they hold their office during good behaviour and not at the pleasure of the crown; they can be removed from office only by a resolution of both houses of Parliament

jury body of 12 (15 in Scotland) lay people sworn to decide the facts of a case and reach a verdict in a court of law in England, jurors are selected at random from the electoral roll; certain people are ineligible for jury service (such as lawyers and clerics), and others can be excused (such as members of Parliament and doctors) if the jury cannot reach a unanimous verdict it can give a majority verdict (at least 10 of the 12)

justice of the peace an unpaid magistrate; in Scotland, a judge presiding over a district court who receives no salary

Land Registry, HM official body set up in 1925 to register legal rights to land in England and Wales; the records are open to public inspection (since December 1990)

Law Commission either of two statutory bodies established in 1965 (one for England and Wales and one for Scotland) which consider proposals for law reform and publish their findings: they also keep British law under constant review, systematically developing and reforming it by, for example, the repeal of obsolete and unnecessary enactments

Law Lords in England, the ten Lords of Appeal who, together with the Lord Chancellor and other peers, make up the House of Lords in its judicial capacity: the House of Lords is the final court of appeal in both criminal and civil cases; Law Lords rank as life peers

Law Society professional governing body of solicitors: it also functions as a trade union for its members; the society, incorporated in 1831, regulates training, discipline, and standards of professional conduct

Lord Advocate chief law officer of the crown in Scotland who has ultimate responsibility for criminal prosecutions in Scotland

Lord Chancellor head of the judiciary a political appointment, the Lord Chancellor is also a member of the cabinet and holds the office of Keeper of the Great Seal

Lord Chief Justice of England head of the Queen's Bench: ranks second only to the Lord Chancellor

Lord Justice of Appeal in England and Wales, one of 14 lords justices who form, together with the Lord Chancellor, the Lord Chief Justice of England, the Master of the Rolls, and the president of the Family Division as ex officio members, the penultimate court of appeal (the Court of Appeal) for England and Wales

Lord Lieutenant the sovereign's representative in a county, who recommends magistrates for appointment: it is an unpaid position and the retirement age is 75

magistrate a person who presides in a magistrates' court: either a justice of the peace or a stipendiary magistrate

magistrates' court in England and Wales, a local law court that mainly deals with minor criminal cases: a magistrates' court consists of between two and seven lay justices of the peace (who are advised on the law by a clerk to the justices), or a single paid lawyer called a stipendiary magistrate

Master of the Rolls English judge who is the president of the civil division of the Court of Appeal, besides being responsible for Chancery records and for the admission of solicitors

notary public legal practitioner who attests or certifies deeds and other documents. British diplomatic and consular officials may exercise notarial functions outside the UK

Old Bailey popular term for the Central Criminal Court

Police Complaints Authority an independent group set up under the Police and Criminal Evidence Act 1984 to supervise the investigation of complaints against the police by members of the public

probate formal proof of a will

procurator fiscal officer of a Scottish sheriff's court who (combining the role of public prosecutor and coroner) inquires into suspicious deaths and carries out the preliminary questioning of witnesses to crime

Queen's Counsel (QC) in England and Scotland, a barrister of senior rank: the title QC is awarded by the Queen on the recommendation of the Lord Chancellor; a QC wears a silk gown, and takes precedence over a junior member of the Bar: when the monarch is a king, the title is King's Council

recorder in the English legal system, a part-time judge who usually sits in the crown courts in less serious cases but may also sit in the county courts or the High Court

royal assent formal consent given by a British sovereign to the passage of a bill through Parliament: last instance of a royal refusal was the rejection of the Scottish Militia Bill of 1702 by Queen Anne

royal prerogative powers, immunities, and privileges recognized in common law as

The UK Legal System and Judiciary

A Glossary of the Law in Britain: Courts, Professionals, and Important Bodies *(continued)*

belonging to the crown: most prerogative acts in the UK are now performed by the government on behalf of the crown

Serious Fraud Office set up in 1987 to investigate and prosecute serious or complex criminal fraud cases

sheriff in England and Wales, the crown's chief executive officer in a county for ceremonial purposes; in Scotland, the equivalent of the English county-court judge, but also dealing with criminal cases

sheriff court a Scottish court presided over by a sheriff covering the more serious criminal and civil cases and fatal accident inquiries in its area

silk in UK law, a Queen's Counsel, a senior barrister entitled to wear a silk gown in court

slander spoken defamatory statement: if written, or broadcast on radio or television, it constitutes libel

solicitor member of one of the two branches of the English legal profession who provides all-round legal services (making wills, winding up estates, conveyancing, divorce, and litigation): a solicitor cannot appear at High Court level, but must brief a barrister on behalf of his or her client; solicitors may become circuit judges and recorders

Solicitor General a law officer of the Crown, deputy to the Attorney General, a political appointee with ministerial rank

stipendiary magistrate paid, qualified lawyers, working mainly in London and major cities

the Bar the profession of barristers collectively; to be 'called to the Bar' is to become a barrister

Treasury counsel in the UK, a group of barristers who receive briefs from the DPP to appear for the prosecution in criminal trials at the Central Criminal Court

Treasury solicitor the official representing the crown in matrimonial, probate, and admiralty cases: Queen's Proctor is an obsolete term for treasury solicitor

tribunal in English law, a body appointed by the government to arbitrate in disputes, or investigate certain matters: tribunals usually consist of a lawyer as chair, sitting with two lay assessors

Writers to the Signet society of Scottish solicitors

UK Law and the European Convention on Human Rights

The government has made a number of pledges to modernize British politics and increase the rights of citizens. These include the incorporation of the European Convention on Human Rights into UK law for the first time. The legislation looks set to generate a new culture in the UK of individual rights and freedoms enforceable in court. Established to protect the people of Europe following the atrocities of World War II, the Convention has been embraced by 41 countries since its inception in 1950. The UK has long been a party to it, but, believing its own domestic law to be sufficient, has never fully incorporated it in legislation. This has meant that people whose Convention rights were infringed have faced a lengthy battle to reach the European Court in Strasbourg. They needed first to exhaust the UK appeal system, and then wait an average of five years, and sustain a cost of around £30,000, before their case could be heard in France. Moreover, the European Commission of Human Rights has found the UK in violation of the Convention – over matters such as the treatment of children in the criminal courts and the banning of homosexuals from the armed forces – more often than any other country except Italy.

Under the Human Rights Act, UK citizens will now be able to invoke the Convention in domestic courts. Public authorities, including local government and privatized utilities, will also be bound by the Convention's articles. If they fall foul of the legislation, they could be ordered to pay compensation to victims.

The Convention protects many basic rights, without discrimination, including the rights to life, liberty, security, education, marriage, and a fair trial; to free elections, freedom from torture or slavery, and freedom of thought, religion, expression, and assembly; and to respect for home, family, correspondence, and property. It also abolishes the death penalty.

Its incorporation could impact on a wide range of issues, and looks set to strengthen the protection of both property and privacy – especially in the face of press intrusion – and to force the police to be more accountable for their actions. Police forces will be required to justify any invasion of Convention rights. This might mean that more questions will be asked before a search warrant is granted, a surveillance operation is set up, or a person is detained at a police station.

See also **The European Union – How does it Affect Us?**, p 286.

The Law in Britain: The Courts

In England and Wales the court system was reorganized under the Courts Act 1971. The higher courts are:

House of Lords
The highest court for the whole of Britain, deals with both civil and criminal appeals.

Court of Appeal
This court is divided between criminal and civil appeal courts; it sits in London at the Royal Courts of Justice. The criminal division deals with appeals from the Crown Court and is presided over by the Lord Chief Justice who is the most senior judge in England and Wales. The Lord Justices of Appeal are assisted by High Court judges when required.

High Court of Justice
This court deals with important civil cases, it sits at the Royal Courts of Justice and at County Courts around the country; land, patent issues, industrial disputes, property and inheritance matters are dealt with by its Chancery Division. The Queen's Bench Division deals with common law business such as tort and contractual disputes. There is also a Family Division. Appeal is to the Court of Appeal (Civil Division), which also hears appeals from the County Courts and from tribunals.

Crown Courts
These courts sit in over 90 permanent centres throughout England and Wales, each centre being designated as first, second, or third tier, reflecting the seriousness of the offences tried. Trial of cases is by a jury of 12 people selected at random from the electoral register. They are directed on matters of law by a judge, who may be any one of the 84 High Court Judges, 478 Circuit Judges, 787 Recorders and 454 Assistant Recorders (the latter two being part-time appointments), which handle criminal cases.

County Courts
There are 250 county courts which deal with civil matters. Cases are heard before District Judges, who hear uncontested and smaller value claims; higher value claims being dealt with by Circuit Judges. Each court is assigned at least one District and one Circuit Judge.

Magistrates' Courts
The lowest tier of criminal court in England and Wales, dealing with about 98% of all criminal cases. The 450 courts are funded jointly by local and central government and deal with minor criminal cases and are served by Justices of the Peace or stipendiary (paid) magistrates.

The Law in Britain: The Courts (*continued*)

Juvenile Courts
These courts are presided over by specially qualified justices. There are also special courts, such as the Restrictive Practices Court and the Employment Appeal Tribunal.

The Courts in Scotland
The supreme civil court is the House of Lords, below which comes the Court of Session, and then the Sheriff's Court (in some respects similar to the English county court, but with criminal as well as civil jurisdiction). More serious criminal cases are heard by the High Court of Justiciary which also sits as a Court of Criminal Appeal (with no appeal to the Lords). Juries have 15 members, and a verdict of 'not proven' can be given. There is no coroner, inquiries into deaths being undertaken by the procurator fiscal.

Judiciary System: The Lords of Appeal

The House of Lords, Westminster, London SW1A 0PW; phone: (020) 7219 5979

The Lord High Chancellor of Great Britain
The Right Honourable The Lord Irvine of Lairg

The Lords of Appeal in Ordinary
The Right Honourable The Lord Browne-Wilkinson, The Right Honourable The Lord Slynn of Hadley, The Right Honourable The Lord Lloyd of Berwick, The Right Honourable The Lord Nicholls of Birkenhead, The Right Honourable The Lord Steyn, The Right Honourable The Lord Hoffmann, The Right Honourable The Lord Hope of Craighead, The Right Honourable The Lord Clyde, The Right Honourable The Lord Hutton, The Right Honourable The Lord Saville of Newdigate, The Right Honourable The Lord Hobhouse of Woodborough, The Right Honourable The Lord Millett.

Registrar, The Clerk of the Parliaments
J M Davies, Esquire

The Midland and Oxford Circuit

Circuit Office The Priory Courts, 33 Bull Street, Birmingham B4 6DW; phone: (0121) 681 3206; fax: (0121) 681 3210; **Circuit Administrator** Peter Handcock.

The North Eastern Circuit

Circuit Office 17th Floor, West Riding House, Albion Street, Leeds LS1 5AA; phone: (0113) 251 1200; fax: (0113) 251 1247; **Circuit Administrator** Peter Farmer.

The Northern Circuit

Circuit Office 15 Quay Street, Manchester M60 9FD; phone: (0161) 833 1004/1005; fax: (0161) 832 8596; **Circuit Administrator** Robin Vincent.

The South Eastern Circuit

Circuit Office – London Courts New Cavendish House, 18 Maltravers Street, London WC2R 3EU; phone and fax: (020) 7947 7230; **Circuit Administrator** Bob Clark.

The Wales and Chester Circuit

Circuit Office 2nd Floor, Churchill House, Churchill Way, Cardiff CF10 2HH; phone: (029) 2041 5500; fax: (029) 2041 5511; **Circuit Administrator** Peter Risk.

The Western Circuit

Circuit Office Bridge House, Sion Place, Clifton, Bristol BS8 4BN; phone: (0117) 974 3763; fax: (0117) 974 4133; **Circuit Administrator** David Ryan.

The Supreme Court of Judicature, Court of Appeal

Royal Courts of Justice, The Strand, London WC2A 2LL; phone:(020) 7947 6000 **Civil Appeals Office** Registrar: J D R Adams; phone: (020) 7947 6409 **Criminal Appeal and Courts Martial Appeal Office** Registrar: Master McKenzie (Michael McKenzie); phone: (020) 7947 6103; fax: (020) 7947 6900

Ex-officio Judges
The Lord High Chancellor of Great Britain The Right Honourable The Lord Irvine of Lairg (President) **The Lord Chief Justice of England** The Right Honourable The Lord Bingham of Cornwall **The Right Honourable The Master of The Rolls** The Right Honourable The Lord Woolf **The Right Honourable The President of the Family Division** The Right Honourable Sir Stephen Brown **The Right Honourable The Vice-Chancellor** The Right Honourable Sir Richard Scott.

Lords Justices
Years of appointment are given in brackets.
The Right Honourable Sir Martin Nourse (1985)
The Right Honourable Dame Elizabeth Butler-Sloss (1988)
The Right Honourable Sir Murray Stuart-Smith (1988)
The Right Honourable Sir Roy Beldam (1989)
The Right Honourable Sir David Hirst (1992)
The Right Honourable Sir Simon Brown (1992)
The Right Honourable Sir Anthony Evans (1992)
The Right Honourable Sir Christopher Rose (1992)
The Right Honourable Sir John Roch (1993)
The Right Honourable Sir Peter Gibson (1993)
The Right Honourable Sir Denis Henry (1993)
The Right Honourable Sir Swinton Thomas (1994)
The Right Honourable Sir Andrew Morritt (1994)
The Right Honourable Sir Philip Otton (1994)
The Right Honourable Sir Robin Auld (1995)
The Right Honourable Sir Malcolm Pill (1995)
The Right Honourable Sir William Aldous (1995)
The Right Honourable Sir Alan Ward (1995)
The Right Honourable Sir Michael Hutchison (1995)
The Right Honourable Sir Konrad Schiemann (1995)
The Right Honourable Sir Nicholas Phillips (1995)
The Right Honourable Sir Mathew Thorpe (1995)
The Right Honourable Sir Mark Potter (1996)
The Right Honourable Sir Henry Brooke (1996)
The Right Honourable Sir Igor Judge (1996)
The Right Honourable Sir Mark Waller (1996)
The Right Honourable Sir John Mummery (1996)
The Right Honourable Sir Charles Mantell(1997)
The Right Honourable Sir John Chadwick (1997)
The Right Honourable Sir Richard Buxton (1997)
The Right Honourable Sir Robert Walker (1997)
The Right Honourable Sir Antony May (1997)
The Right Honourable Sir Simon Tuckey (1997)
The Right Honourable Sir Anthony Clarke (1998)

Appeals Entered in Appellate Courts in England and Wales

(– = not applicable.)

Nature of court		1938	1958	1968	1978	1988	1998
Judicial Committee of the Privy Council		107	44	37	52	61	78
House of Lords	from courts in England and Wales	32	29	41	77	75	77
	elsewhere	11	23	11	6	15	6
Court of Appeal	Civil Division	574	668	948	1,401	1,645	1,640
	Criminal Division[1]	–	–	6,414	6,099	7,235	8,649
High Court	Chancery Division	–	27	119	74	111	186
	Queen's Bench Division[2]	263	186	394	510	1,800	5,215
	Family Division	–	102	263	247	240	19
Total		987	1,079	8,227	84,66	11,182	15,870

[1] Includes applications.
[2] Includes judicial review, appeals by way of case stated, and statutory appeals.

Source: Judicial Statistics, England and Wales 1998, *© Crown copyright 1999*

The High Court of Justice

Chancery Division
Royal Courts of Justice, The Strand, London WC2A 2LL; phone: (020) 7947 6000 **Chancery Chambers** Chief Master: Mr Winegarten; Court Manager: G C Robinson; phone: (020) 7947 6167 **Bankruptcy and Companies Courts** Chief Registrar: M C B Buckley; Court Manager: Ms Flaxman; phone: (020) 7947 7343; fax: (020) 7947 6378 **Restrictive Practices Court** Clerk to the Court: M C B Buckley; Court Manager: M A Brown; phone: (020) 7947 6037.

Chancery Division: Judges
The Lord High Chancellor of Great Britain The Right Honourable The Lord Irvine of Lairg (President) **The Right Honourable The Vice-Chancellor** The Right Honourable Sir Richard Scott.

Years of appointment are given in brackets.
The Honourable Sir Donald Rattee (1989)
The Honourable Sir Francis Ferris (1990)
The Honourable Sir Jonathan Parker (1991)
The Honourable Sir John Lindsay (1992)
The Honourable Dame Mary Arden (Chairman of The Law Commission) (1993)
The Honourable Sir Edward Evans-Lombe (1993)
The Honourable Sir William Blackburne (1993)
The Honourable Sir Gavin Lightman (1994)
The Honourable Sir Robert Carnwath (1994)
The Honourable Sir Colin Rimer (1994)
The Honourable Sir Hugh Laddie (1995)
The Honourable Sir Timothy Lloyd (1996)
The Honourable Sir David Neuberger (1996)
The Honourable Sir Andrew Park (1997)
The Honourable Sir Nicolas Pumphrey (1997)
The Honourable Sir Michael Hart (1998)

Queen's Bench Division
Royal Courts of Justice, The Strand, London WC2A 2LL; phone:(020) 7936 6474 Senior Master and Queen's Rememberance: R L Turner; phone: (020) 7947 6105; fax: (020) 7947 6237 **Crown Office** Master of the Crown Office, Queen's Coroner and Attorney: Master McKenzie (Michael McKenzie); phone: (020) 7947 6108; fax: (020) 7947 6747.

Queen's Bench Division: Judges
The Lord Chief Justice of England The Right Honourable The Lord Bingham of Cornwall (President).

Years of appointment are given in brackets.
The Honourable Sir Oliver Popplewell (1983)
The Honourable Sir Richard Tucker (1985)
The Honourable Sir Patrick Garland (1985)
The Honourable Sir Michael Turner (1985)
The Honourable Sir John Alliott (1986)
The Honourable Sir Harry Ognall (1986)
The Honourable Sir John Owen (1986)
The Honourable Sir Humphrey Potts (1986)
The Honourable Sir Richard Rougier (1986)
The Honourable Sir Ian Kennedy (1986)
The Honourable Sir Stuart McKinnon (1988)
The Honourable Sir Edwin Jowitt (1988)
The Honourable Sir Scott Baker (1988)
The Honourable Sir Douglas Brown (1989)
The Honourable Sir Michael Morland (1989)
The Honourable Sir Roger Buckley(1989)
The Honourable Sir Anthony Hidden (1989)
The Honourable Sir Michael Wright (1990)
The Honourable Sir John Blofeld (1990)
The Honourable Sir Peter Cresswell (1990)
The Honourable Sir John Laws (1992)
The Honourable Dame Ann Ebsworth (1992)
The Honourable Sir Simon Tuckey (Judge in charge of the Commerical List) (1992)
The Honourable Sir David Latham (1992)
The Honourable Sir Christopher Holland (1992)
The Honourable Sir John Kay (1992)
The Honourable Sir Richard Curtis (1992)
The Honourable Sir Stephen Sedley (1992)
The Honourable Dame Janet Smith (1992)
The Honourable Sir Anthony Colman (1992)
The Honourable Sir John Dyson (1993)
The Honourable Sir Thayne Forbes (1993)
The Honourable Sir Michael Sachs (1993)
The Honourable Sir Stephen Mitchell (1993)
The Honourable Sir Roger Bell (1993)
The Honourable Sir Michael Harrison (1993)
The Honourable Sir Bernard Rix (1993)
The Honourable Dame Heather Steele (1993)
The Honourable Sir William Gage (1993)
The Honourable Sir Jonathan Mance (1993)
The Honourable Sir Andrew Longmore (1993)
The Honourable Sir Thomas Morison (1993)
The Honourable Sir David Keene (1994)
The Honourable Sir Andrew Collins (1994)
The Honourable Sir Maurice Kay (1994)
The Honourable Sir Brian Smedley (1995)
The Honourable Sir Anthony Hooper (1995)
The Honourable Sir Neil Butterfield (1995)
The Honourable Sir George Newman (1995)
The Honourable Sir David Poole (1995)
The Honourable Sir Martin Moore-Bick (1995)
The Honourable Sir Gordon Langley (1995)
The Honourable Sir John Thomas (1995)
The Honourable Sir Roger Toulson (1996)
The Honourable Sir Robert Nelson (1996)
The Honourable Sir Michael Astill (1996)
The Honourable Sir Alan Moses (1996)
The Honourable Sir Timothy Walker (1996)
The Honourable Sir David Eady (1996)
The Honourable Sir Jeremy Sullivan (1997)
The Honourable Sir David Penry-Davey (1997)
The Honourable Sir Stephen Richards (1997)
The Honourable Sir David Steel (1998)
The Honourable Sir Rodney Klevan (1998)
The Honourable Sir Charles Gray (1998)

Family Division
Royal Courts of Justice, The Strand, London WC2A 2LL; phone: (020) 7947 6000.

The High Court of Justice (*continued*)

Family Division: Judges
The President of the Family Division The Right Honourable Sir Stephen Brown **Senior District Judge of the Family Division** G B N A Aspel; phone: (020) 7947 6934.

Years of appointment are given in brackets.
The Honourable Sir Edward Cazalet (1988)
The Honourable Sir Robert Johnson (1989)
The Honourable Dame Joyanne Bracewell (1990)
The Honourable Sir Michael Connell (1991)
The Honourable Sir Peter Singer (1993)
The Honourable Sir Nicholas Wilson (1993)
The Honourable Sir Nicholas Wall(1993)
The Honourable Sir Andrew Kirkwood (1993)
The Honourable Sir Christopher Stuart-White (1993)
The Honourable Dame Brenda Hale (1994)
The Honourable Sir Hugh Bennett (1995)
The Honourable Sir James Holman (1995)
The Honourable Dame Mary Claire Hogg (1995)
The Honourable Sir Christopher Summer (1996)
The Honourable Sir Andrew Hughes (1997)
The Honourable Sir Arthur Charles (1998)

The Crown Prosecution Service

The Crown Prosecution Service (CPS) is responsible for the independent review and conduct of criminal proceedings instituted by police forces in England and Wales.

In April 1999 the CPS was reorganized, moving from 14 to 42 areas that correspond with the police forces of England and Wales (there are 43 police forces in total but the City of London and Metropolitan Police Forces became one CPS area – London).

Each area has its own Chief Crown Prosecutor (CCP) and an area business manager (ABM). The Chief Crown Prosecutor reports to the Director of Public Prosecutions (DPP) and is locally accountable to the public for the way cases are handled. Each area has one or more local branches headed by a Branch Crown Prosecutor; the Branch Crown Prosecutors supervise the management of cases at the local magistrates' courts and the Crown Court.

The restructuring followed the recommendations of the Glidewell Report on the reorganization of the CPS, and aims to make the CPS more accountable to the local population and to enable good working relationships between other agencies in the criminal justice system.

CPS Headquarters 50 Ludgate Hill, London EC4M 7EX; phone: (020) 7796 8000; fax: (020) 7796 8002; public enquiry point: (020) 7796 8500; e-mail (enquiries and comments): enquiries@cps.gov.uk; e-mail (complaints): complaints@cps.gov.uk; Web site: www.cps.gov.uk/

Director of Public Prosecutions (Grade 1) David Calvert-Smith

CPS Avon and Somerset CCP: David Archer; ABM: Lesley Burton. 1st Floor, Froomsgate House, Rupert Street, Bristol BS1 2QJ; phone: (0117) 930 2800; fax: (0117) 930 2810

CPS Bedfordshire CCP: Monica Townsend; ABM: Janet Altham. Sceptre House, 7–9 Castle Street, Luton, Bedfordshire LU1 3AJ; phone: (01582) 816600; fax: (01582) 816678

CPS Cambridgeshire CCP: Richard Crowley; ABM: Ian Farrell. Justinian House, Spitfire Close, Ermine Business Park, Huntingdon, Cambridgeshire PE18 6XY; phone: (01480) 825200; fax: (01480) 925205

CPS Cheshire CCP: Barry Hughes; ABM: Edwina Sherwood. 2nd Floor, Windsor House, Pepper Street, Chester CH1 1TD; phone: (01244) 408600; fax: (01244) 408658

CPS Cleveland CCP: David Magson; ABM: Margaret Phillips. 5 Linthorpe Road, Middlesbrough, Cleveland TS1 1TX; phone: (01642) 204500; fax: (01642) 204503

CPS Cumbria CCP: David Farmer; ABM: John Pears. 1st Floor, Stocklund House, Castle Street, Carlisle, Cumbria CA3 8SY; phone: (01228) 882900; fax: (01228) 882910

CPS Derbyshire CCP: David Adams; ABM: Adele Clarke. 7th Floor, St Peter's House, Gower Street, Derby DE1 1SB; phone: (01332) 614000; fax: (01332) 614009

CPS Devon and Cornwall CCP: Andrew Cresswell; ABM: John Nettleton. Hawkins House, Pynes Hill, Rydon Lane, Exeter, Devon EX2 5SS; phone: (01392) 288000; fax: (01392) 288002

CPS Dorset CCP: John Revell; ABM: Jason Putman. 1st Floor, Oxford House, Oxford Road, Bournemouth BH8 8HA; phone: (01202) 498700; fax: (01202) 556513

CPS Durham CCP: Jeff Corringhan; ABM Brian Feetham. Elvet House, Hallgarth Street, Durham DH1 3AT; phone: (0191) 383 5800; fax: (0191) 383 5801

CPS Dyfed-Powys CCP: Simon Rowlands; ABM: Christine Jones. Heol Penlanffos, Tanerdy, Carmarthen, Dyfed SA31 2EZ; phone: (01267) 242100; fax: (01267) 242111

CPS Essex CCP: John Bell; ABM: Paul Overett. County House, 100 New London Road, Chelmsford, Essex CM2 0RG; phone: (01245) 455800; fax: (01245) 455809

CPS Gloucestershire CCP: Withiel Cole; ABM: Will Hollins. 2 Kimbrose Way, Gloucester, Glos GL1 2DB; phone: (01452) 872400; fax: (01452) 872406

CPS Greater Manchester CCP: Tony Taylor; ABM: Kevin Fox. PO Box 237, 8th Floor, Sunlight House, Quay Street, Manchester M60 3PS; phone: (0161) 827 4700; fax: (0161) 827 4930

CPS Gwent CCP: Chris Woolley; ABM: Bill Fullerton. 7th Floor, Chartist Tower, Dock Street, Newport NP9 1DW; phone: (01633) 261100; fax: (01633) 261106

CPS Hampshire CCP: Roger Daw; ABM: Mark Sunderland. 3rd Floor, Black Horse House, 8–10 Leigh Road, Eastleigh, Hants SO50 9FH; phone: (023) 8067 3800; fax: (023) 8067 3854

CPS Hertfordshire CCP: Charles Ingham; ABM: Liam Carroll. Queen's House, 58 Victoria Street, St Albans, Herts AL1 3HZ; phone: (01727) 798700; fax: (01727) 798796

CPS Humberside CCP: Bob Marshall; ABM: Caron Skidmore. 2nd Floor, King William House, Lowgate, Kingston-Upon-Hull HU1 1RS; phone: (01482) 621000; fax: (01482) 596500

CPS Kent CCP: Elizabeth Howe; ABM: Ken Mitchell. Priory Gate, 29 Union Street, Maidstone, Kent ME14 1PT; phone: (01622) 356300; fax: (01622) 356340

CPS Lancashire CCP: Dickie Dickenson; ABM: Glynn Rankin. 3rd Floor, Unicentre, Lord's Walk, Preston PR1 1DH; phone: (01772) 208100; fax: (01772) 208144

CPS Leicestershire CCP: Martin Howard; ABM: Laraine Jones. Princes Court, 34 York Road, Leicester LE1 5TU; phone: (0116) 204 6700; fax: (0116) 204 6777

CPS Lincolnshire CPP: Alison Kerr; ABM: Angela Garbett. Crosstread House, 10a Newport, Lincoln LN1 3DF; phone: (01633) 261000

CPS London CCP: Peter Boeuf; ACCPs: Howard Cohen, Alison Saunders, Melanie Werrett; ABM: Alex Machray. 4th Floor, 50 Ludgate Hill, London EC4M 7EX; phone: (020) 7796 8000; fax: No general number

CPS Merseyside CCP: John Holt; ABM: Deborah King. 7th Floor (south), Royal Liver Building, Pier Head, Liverpool L3 1HN; phone: (0151) 239 6400; fax: (0151) 255 0642

CPS Norfolk CCP: Peter Tidey; ABM: Adrian Mardell. Haldin House, Old Bank of England Court, Queen Street, Norwich, Norfolk NR2 4SX; phone: (01603) 693000; fax: (01603) 693001

CPS Northamptonshire CCP: Colin Chapman; ABM: John Stephenson. Beaumont House, Cliftonville, Northampton NN1 5BE; phone: (01604) 823600; fax: (01604) 823656

CPS Northumbria CCP: Nicola Reasbeck; ABM: Steve Guy. 1st Floor, Benton House, 136 Sandyford Road, Newcastle upon Tyne NE2 1QE; phone: (0191) 260 4200; fax: (0191) 260 4240

CPS North Wales CCP: Paul Whittaker; ABM: Angela Walsh. Bromfield House, Ellice Way, Wrexham LL13 7YW; phone: (01978) 346000; fax: (01978) 346001

CPS North Yorkshire CCP: Bob Turnbull; ABM: Richard Cragg. 6th Floor, Ryedale Building, 60 Piccadilly, York, North Yorks YO1 1NS; phone: (01904) 731700; fax: (01904) 610394

CPS Nottinghamshire CCP: Peter Lewis; ABM: Gail Pessol. 2 King Edward Court, King Edward Street, Nottingham NG1 1EL; phone: (0115) 852 3300; fax: (0115) 852 3380

The UK Legal System and Judiciary

The Crown Prosecution Service (*continued*)

CPS South Wales CCP: Huw Heycock; ABM: Ian Edmondson. 20th Floor, Capital House, Greyfriars Road, Cardiff CF1 3PL; phone: (029) 2080 3800; fax: (029) 2064 4453

CPS South Yorkshire CCP: Judith Bermingham; ABM: Christopher Day. Greenfield House, 32 Scotland Street, Sheffield S3 7DQ; phone: (0114) 229 8600; fax: (0114) 229 8653

CPS Staffordshire CCP: Harry Ireland; ABM: Brian Laybourne. 11a Princes Street, Stafford ST16 2EU; phone: (01785) 272200; fax: (01785) 272290

CPS Suffolk CCP: Chris Yule; ABM: Diane Waddington. Saxon House, 1 Cromwell Square, Ipswich, Suffolk IP1 1TS; phone: (01473) 282100; fax: (01473) 282101

CPS Surrey CCP: Sandie Hebblethwaite; ABM: Martyn Wray. One Onslow Street, Guildford, Surrey GU1 4YA; phone: (01483) 468200; fax: (01483) 882603/4

CPS Sussex CCP: Michael Kennedy; ABM: Barry Shepherd. Unit 3, Clifton Mews, Clifton Hill, Brighton, East Sussex BN1 3HR; phone: (01273) 765600; fax: (01273) 765605

CPS Thames Valley CCP: Simon Clements; ABM: Graham Choldcroft. The Courtyard, Lombard Street, Abingdon, Oxon OX14 5SE; phone: (01235) 551900; fax: (01235) 554144

CPS Warwickshire CCP: Mark Lynn; ABM: Sue Petyt. Rossmore House, 10 Newbold Terrace, Leamington Spa, Warks CV32 4EA; phone: (01926) 455000; fax: (01926) 455002/3

CPS West Mercia CCP: Jim England; ABM: Lawrence Sutton. Artillery House, Heritage Way, Droitwich, Worcester WR9 8YB; phone: (01905) 825000; fax: (01905) 796793

CPS West Midlands CCP: David Blundell; ABM: Mike Grist. 14th Floor, Colmore Gate, 2 Colmore Row, Birmingham B3 2QA; phone: (0121) 262 1300; fax: (0121) 629 7351

CPS West Yorkshire CCP: Neil Franklin. Oxford House, Oxford Row, Leeds LS1 3BE; phone: (0113) 290 2700; fax: (0113) 242 1302; ABM: Robert Stevenson. 4/5 South Parade, Wakefield, West Yorks WF1 1LR; phone: (01924) 205200; fax: (01924) 369470

CPS Wiltshire CCP: Nick Hawkins; ABM: Nadeem Nabi. Fox Talbot House, Bellinger Close, Malmesbury Road, Chippenham, Wiltshire SN15 1BN; phone: (01249) 766100; fax: (01249) 766101

The Supreme Court of Scotland

The Supreme Courts in Scotland comprise the Court of Session and the High Court of Justiciary.

Court of Session The Civil Court, comprising the Inner House with its two divisions, and the Outer House. Parliament House, Parliament Square, Edinburgh EH1 1RQ; phone: (0131) 225 2595; fax: (0131) 240 6746.

Addresses High Court of Justiciary Lawnmarket, Edinburgh EH1 2NS; phone: (0131) 225 2595; fax: (0131) 240 6915

Council on Tribunals Scottish Committee, 44 Palmerston Place, Edinburgh EH12 5BJ; phone: (0131) 220 1236; fax: (0131) 225 4271

Crown Office 25 Chambers Street, Edinburgh EH1 1LA; phone: (0131) 226 2626; fax: (0131) 247 2650

Faculty of Advocates 11 Parliament House, Edinburgh EH1 1RF; phone: (0131) 226 5071; fax: (0131) 225 3642

The Law Society of Scotland Law Society's Hall, 26 Drumsheugh Gardens, Edinburgh EH3 7YR; phone: (0131) 226 7411; fax: (0131) 225 2934

Secretary of Commissions For Scotland Saughton House, Broomhouse Drive, Edinburgh EH11 3XD; phone: (0131) 244 2691; fax: (0131) 244 2623

Scottish Courts Administration Hayweight House, 23 Lauriston Street, Edinburgh EH3 9DQ; phone: (0131) 229 9200; fax: (0131) 221 6890

Scottish Land Court: 1 Grosvenor Crescent, Edinburgh EH12 5ER; phone: (0131) 225 3595; fax: (0131) 226 4812

Sheriff Court of Chancery 27 Chambers Street, Edinburgh EH1 1LB; phone: (0131) 225 2525; fax: (0131) 225 8899

The Sheriff Courts of Scotland

Central Scotland

Sheriff Principal R A Dunlop, QC

Alloa Sheriff Court House, Mar Street, Alloa FK10 1HR; phone: (01259) 722734; fax: (01259) 219470

Dumfries and Galloway

Sheriff Principal Peter McGonigle **Dumfries** Sheriff Court House, Buccleuch Street, Dumfries DG1 2AN; phone: (01387) 262334; fax: (01387) 262357

Fife

Sheriff Principal R A Dunlop; (covered by Tayside)

Cupar Sheriff Court House, Cupar KY15 4LX; phone: (01334) 652121; fax: (01334) 656807

Grampian

Sheriff Principal Douglas Risk, QC

Aberdeen Sheriff Court House, Castle Street, Aberdeen AB10 1AP; phone: (01224) 648316; fax: (01224) 657234

Lothian and Borders

Sheriff Principal Gordon Nicholson, QC

Edinburgh Sheriff Court House, 27 Chambers Street, Edinburgh EH1 1LB; phone: (0131) 225 2525; fax: (0131) 225 2288

Northern

Sheriff Principal Douglas Risk, QC

Dingwall Sheriff Court House, Ferry Road, Dingwall IV15 9QX; phone: (01349) 863153

Strathclyde

Sheriffs Principal Edward Bowen, QC; Sheriff Court House, PO Box 23, 1 Carlton Place, Glasgow G5 9DA; phone: (0141) 418 5234; fax: (0141) 418 5185 (Glasgow and Strathkelvin); Bruce Kerr, QC; Sheriff Court House, St James Street, Paisley PA3 2AW; phone: (0141) 887 5291; fax: (0141) 889 1748 (North Strathclyde); John Conor McInness, QC; Graham Street, Airdrie, ML6 6EE; phone: (01236) 751121; fax: (01236) 750980 (South Strathclyde, Dumfries, and Galloway)

Tayside

Sheriff Principal R A Dunlop, QC;

Perth Sheriff Court House, Tay Street, Perth PH2 8NL; phone: (01738) 620546; fax: (01738) 445181

The Courts of Northern Ireland

The Supreme Court of Judicature comprises the Court of Appeal, the High Court, and the Crown Court. All matters relating to these courts are under the jurisdiction of the UK Parliament.

The Supreme Court Royal Courts of Justice, Chichester Street, Belfast BT1 3JF; phone: (028) 9023 5111; fax: (028) 9031 3508.

Offices Queen's Bench, Appeals' and Clerk of the Crown in Northen Ireland Master: J W Wilson, QC; High Court Master: Mrs D M Kennedy

Office of Care and Protection Master: F B Hall

Bankruptcy and Companies Office Master: C W G Redpath

Chancery Office Master: R A Ellison

Probate and Matrimonial Office Master: Mrs Melody McReynolds

Taxing Office Master: J C Napier

Court Funds Office Accountant General: H G Thompson

Official Solicitor Miss Brenda M Donnelly

Recorders His Honour Judge Hart, QC; His Honour Judge Burgess; His Honour Judge Martin, QC

Northern Ireland Court Service Headquarters: Windsor House, 7–15 Bedford Street, Belfast BT2 7LT; phone: (028) 9032 8594; fax: (028) 9043 9110.

Civil Proceedings

Bankruptcy Proceedings in England and Wales

Summary of bankruptcy proceedings in the Chancery Division of the High Court.

1998

Applications filed	bankruptcy petitions by creditors	9,885
	bankruptcy petitions by debtors	431
	other applications and summonses	12,854
Total		23,170
Number of appointments before registrars	listed	21,179
	unlisted	17,779
Orders made	bankruptcy orders on creditors' petitions	4,614
	bankruptcy orders on debtors' petitions	429
Total		5,043
Withdrawn/dismissed		4,580
Transfers to county courts		3,763
Others		23,716

Source: Judicial Statistics, England and Wales 1998, *© Crown copyright 1999*

County Court Actions for Mortgage Repossessions in England, Wales, and Northern Ireland

Data are for local authority and private actions. The figures do not indicate the number of houses repossessed through the courts; not all warrants will have resulted in the issue and execution of warrants of possession. The regional breakdown relates to the location of the court rather than the address of the property. Data exclude Scotland.
(N/A = not available.)

Region	1994			1996			1998		
	Actions entered	Suspended orders	Orders made	Actions entered	Suspended orders	Orders made	Actions entered	Suspended orders	Orders made
North East	3,200	2,400	1,200	3,500	2,000	1,100	4,300	2,300	1,200
North West	9,700	5,400	3,100	9,900	6,300	3,500	14,200	6,500	3,700
Merseyside	2,500	800	600	2,800	1,400	500	2,100	1,000	600
Yorkshire and the Humber	5,700	7,600	3,200	7,600	3,900	2,600	8,200	4,300	3,100
East Midlands	6,000	3,200	2,400	5,900	3,000	2,000	6,400	3,100	1,700
West Midlands	8,600	4,400	2,600	7,600	3,900	2,100	8,100	3,700	2,300
Eastern	9,300	4,200	3,600	8,300	4,000	3,400	8,500	3,900	2,600
London	15,500	8,400	6,800	11,400	6,400	4,800	11,400	5,300	3,500
South East	13,600	7,900	5,600	11,600	6,600	4,000	11,200	5,800	3,400
South West	7,400	3,500	2,500	6,300	3,300	2,400	7,300	3,000	2,100
England total	83,500	43,300	30,700	74,900	40,700	26,400	79,600	37,900	23,600
Wales total	4,400	2,300	1,500	4,900	2,700	1,400	5,400	2,800	1,700
Northern Ireland total[1]	1,400	N/A	N/A	1,200	N/A	N/A	1,600	200	500

[1] Mortgage possession actions are heard in the Chancery Division of the Northern Ireland High Court.

Source: Regional Trends 34, *© Crown copyright 1999*

Cases Brought to the Employment Appeal Tribunal

The Employment Appeal Tribunal was set up by the Employment Protection Act 1975 and hears appeals on a question of law arising from any decisions of, or any proceeedings before, an industrial tribunal. For example, it deals with unfair dismissal and redundancy matters and allegations of discriminatory acts. It may also hear applications for compensation from persons unreasonably excluded from unions. The Tribunal has wide discretion regarding costs.

During 1998, the Tribunal recieved 1,511 cases, an increase of 7% on the 1997 figure of 1,409. A total of 1,292 cases were disposed of in 1998, 86 fewer than in 1997. The great majority of cases received and dealt with related to claims of unfair dismissal.

1998

Class	Number of cases received	Cases disposed of				
		by hearing				
		dismissed	allowed	remitted	withdrawn	Total
EP(C)A 1978[1]						
unfair dismissal	440	282	28	49	94	453
interim relief	0	0	0	0	0	0
redundancy pay	31	16	3	9	7	35
contract of employment	53	25	3	3	19	50
trade union activities	2	2	0	1	2	5
other	248	84	10	11	39	144
Equal Pay Act 1970	6	3	0	0	1	4
Sex Discrimination Act 1975	89	49	4	10	32	95
Race Relations Act 1976	174	67	6	14	24	111

(continued)

Cases Brought to the Employment Appeal Tribunal *(continued)*

Class	Number of cases received	Cases disposed of: by hearing: dismissed	allowed	remitted	withdrawn	Total
Employment Act 1980	0	0	0	0	0	0
Employment Act 1988	0	0	0	0	0	0
Wages Act 1986	60	24	7	5	10	46
European Communities Act 1972[2]	26	11	6	2	7	26
Jurisdiction/Preliminary	133	74	7	16	23	120
Interlocutories	109	63	24	6	20	113
Reserve Forces Act	0	0	0	0	0	0
Employment Rights Act 1996	140	46	8	8	28	90
Total	1,511	746	106	134	306	1,292

[1] Employment Protection (Consolidation) Act 1978.
[2] Transfers of undertakings.

Source: Judicial Statistics, England and Wales 1998, *© Crown copyright 1999*

Matrimonial Suits in England and Wales

Suits		1938	1958	1968	1978	1988	1998
Dissolution of marriage	petitions filed	9,970	25,584	54,036	162,450	182,804	165,870
	decrees nisi	7,621	23,456	47,959	151,533	154,788	144,231
	decrees absolute	6,092	22,195	45,036	142,726	152,139	141,543
Nullity of marriage	petitions filed	263	655	971	1,117	604	505
	decrees nisi	170	496	819	959	389	281
	decrees absolute	158	459	758	941	494	267
Judicial separation	petitions filed	71	158	233	2,611	2,925	916
	decrees granted	25	88	105	1,228	1,917	519

Source: Judicial Statistics, England and Wales 1998, *© Crown copyright 1999*

Legal Aid

Legal Aid in the UK

The justice system in the UK provides legal aid to allow people to seek legal advice, assistance, or representation, according to their means. To qualify for free legal aid, a person must be in receipt of income support, or an equivalent level of income. Those who are not entitled to free legal aid as a result of their income make a contribution towards their legal costs. Any person granted legal aid may be required to repay all or part of it, should they be awarded damages or have their costs paid by a third party. The opponent of a legally aided party may recover costs from the Legal Aid Board in certain circumstances.

In civil law cases legal aid payments are made to lawyers through the Legal Aid Fund, administered by the Legal Aid Board. In Scotland legal aid is administered by the Scottish Legal Aid Board, whilst the Law Society for Northern Ireland performs that role in Northern Ireland.

In criminal proceedings in England, Wales, and Northern Ireland, the court may decide that it is in the interests of justice to grant legal aid. Where a defendant is considered to require financial assistance, this may be provided either in whole or in part. In addition, the Legal Aid Board provides duty solicitors to offer assistance to unrepresented defendants in magistrates' courts. Duty solicitors are available to provide advice and assistance 24 hours a day to suspects questioned by the police at police stations. In Northern Ireland legal aid in criminal cases is provided free of charge.

In Scotland there is a duty solicitor scheme for representing people in custody and at court, provided free of charge. In less serious, summary criminal proceedings an application for monetary assistance can be made to the Scottish Legal Aid Board. The Board will pay for an accused person's legal expenses if it is satisfied that it would be in the interest of justice and that he or she could not meet the expenses without undue hardship. For more serious, solemn proceedings, the court itself considers an application and bases its decision on the accused person's financial circumstances alone. When a grant is made in a criminal case, the applicant is not required to make a contribution.

Tackling the Rising Cost of Legal Aid in Scotland

Scotland's per capita legal aid budget is one of the highest in Europe and has attracted criticism in recent years for its soaring cost. Expenditure jumped by over £50 million during the 1990s, making it 50% higher per head of population than in England and Wales. It is now hoped that a new initiative will help to trim the current £138 million annual expense. A five-year pilot scheme of public defenders on a fixed salary was launched in Edinburgh on 1 October 1998. Usually, private solicitors apply for legal aid on behalf of clients, and, if it is granted, submit their bill on a case-by-case basis. Under the scheme, six public solicitors are each being paid between £22,500 and £32,000 a year to deal with some of the less serious criminal cases in Edinburgh, irrespective of the outcome or length of proceedings.

Tackling the Rising Cost of Legal Aid in Scotland (*continued*)

Every person entitled to legal aid for non-jury cases heard in the city can use the public defence solicitors' office. However, in the early stages of the scheme, if the person was born in either January or February, he or she normally had no choice, but had to be represented by a public defender in order to receive legal aid. The rule, which was laid down to ensure that the pilot scheme was successfully initiated, was criticized by civil rights campaigners, who believed that it is discriminatory to base a mandatory system on birth date. Although by May 2000 more than 20% of the office's clients had made contact through personal choice rather than compulsion, in June the Scottish Legal Aid Board announced an end to the rule. From 1 July 2000 any person facing criminal charges in Edinburgh could be represented by the solicitor of their choice.

The Law Society of Scotland opposes the initiative, as it restricts clients' choice of representation, and believes that money can be better saved by simpler measures, such as more efficient timetabling, and increased use of information technology.

The scheme is on trial and will be evaluated after three years, when a report examining cost, quality, and client satisfaction will be submitted to the Scottish Parliament. It will be the politicians' responsibility to decide whether the project has succeeded and should be extended beyond Edinburgh to other parts of Scotland. It has already sparked interest throughout the UK and abroad.

Trends in Legal Aid Expenditure

(In millions of pounds.)

Payment		1994–95	1995–96	1996–97	1997–98	1998–99
Gross payments		1,383	1,507	1,614	1,670	1,731
Recoveries		298	350	397	436	433
Net payments		1,085	1,157	1,217	1,235	1,298
Net payments in	matrimonial and family proceedings	351	374	393	390	424
	other civil proceedings	379	400	415	403	413
	criminal proceedings	307	330	355	384	402
	administration	49	52	54	58	60

Source: Legal Aid Board Annual Report 1998–99, © *Crown copyright 1999*

Web Sites

Bentham Archive of British Law

http://www.ndirect.co.uk/~law/bentham.htm

Law resource for research and guidance. It includes introductions to Roman, property, European, media, and computer law; the full text of recent Acts of Parliament and of European Union courts; and legal contacts and addresses.

Bill of Rights

http://earlyamerica.com/earlyamerica/freedom/bill/index.html

Full text of the US Bill of Rights, with background information.

Court of Justice of the European Communities

http://europa.eu.int/cj/en/index.htm

Official guide to the history and structure of Europe's highest court. Full texts of judgements and lists of cases pending are available, and the site indicates the great range of issues involved in the interpretation and application of EU treaties.

Crime Library

http://crimelibrary.com/index.html

Collection of stories about infamous criminals and crimes.

Crime Prevention Initiatives

http://www.crime-prevention.org.uk/home_office/guide/

Practical advice on protecting yourself, your family, home, and personal possessions against crime, reproduced from the Home Office publication, *Your Practical Guide to Crime Prevention*.

Crown Prosecution Service – Working in the Interests of Justice

http://www.cps.gov.uk/

Official site of the body responsible for criminal prosecutions in Britain and Wales (data also provided in Welsh). This is a good introduction to the work of this organization with practical information for defendants, victims, and witnesses.

Death Penalty Information

http://sun.soci.niu.edu/%7Ecritcrim/dp/dp.html

US-based site that gives both sides of the argument surrounding the death penalty.

General Council of the Bar

http://www.barcouncil. org.uk/

Professional body for barristers in England and Wales. The site outlines the role of barristers within the UK legal system, and their education and training, and provides a 'Bar council directory'.

Her Majesty's Prison Risley

http://www.hmp-risley.freeserve.co.uk

Outlines the mission of Her Majesty's Prison Service as a whole, as well as that of Risley prison.

International Law Association (ILA)

http://www.ila-hq.org/

Detailing the ILA's objectives and activities in studying, elucidating, and advancing international law, and promoting the unification of law.

Interpol

http://193.123.144.14/interpol-pr/

International Criminal Police Organization site, with a wealth of information about the organization, including a detailed explanation of its structure and history, and also includes exhibitions on the work of Interpol.

Law Commission – Working for Better Law

http://www.gtnet.gov.uk/lawcomm/misc/about.htm

Comprehensive information on the role of the Law Commission in England and Wales. There are full details on all the laws currently under review, and recent judgements of the commission can also be easily accessed.

Law Society of England and Wales

http://www.lawsoc.org.uk/

Professional body for solicitors in England and Wales. The site contains details about 'Legal education', 'Professional training and accreditation', and 'Law and policy'.

Legal Aid (England and Wales)

http://www.legal-aid.gov.uk/

Covering provision of legal aid in England and Wales, with helpful guidelines on how to qualify and the procedure to follow.

Met Police

http://www.met.police.uk/

New Scotland Yard online that includes a complete history of the police in the UK, latest news, recruitment, and information about crime prevention. There is also a 'Youth page' section that includes several 'Streetwise' guides to safety.

Organized Crime

http://www.crime.org/

Crime statistics tutorial, offering guidance on evaluating crime statistics. The site includes analysis of the process of compiling crime statistics and their reliability, plus lots of links to crime data on the web.

Organized Crime Registry

http://members.tripod.com/~orgcrime/index.htm

Articles, links, and news about organized crime syndicates, including the US mafia, Russian mafia, Japanese yakuza, Triads, South American drug cartels, and other crime syndicates.

Right of Way

http://www.ramblers.org.uk/campaigns/rowfaq.html

Practical information about rights of way in Britain from Britain's Rambler's Association. The legal status of a right of way, how paths can become rights of way, and the duties and responsibilities of walkers, farmers, and public authorities are clearly spelt out.

The Scottish Courts Website

http://www.scotcourts.gov.uk/

Information relating to all civil and criminal courts within Scotland, including location details, contact numbers, advice, and details of recent significant judgments.

Scottish Legal Aid Board

http://www.slab.org.uk/

Details on how to obtain legal aid in Scotland, as well as news, publications, and statistics about the use of legal aid.

Stephen Lawrence Inquiry

http://www.official-documents.co.uk/document/cm42/4262/4262.htm

Full text of the report produced by the inquiry into the murder of black British teenager Stephen Lawrence, published by the Stationery Office.

United Nations Crime and Justice Information Network

http://www.icj-cij.org/

Global crime prevention and criminal justice information network on the Web. It provides access to United Nations documents, links to other UN organizations, and country-specific information.

Web Journal of Current Legal Issues

http://webjcli.ncl.ac.uk/

Bi-monthly electronic legal journal featuring case comments, book reviews, and articles on subjects such as legal education, information technology, law reform, and legal research.

Science and Technology

The Year in Review

1 July 1999 Details of the Rosetta space probe, to be sent up in 2003, are released by the European Space Agency at the Royal Society in London. It is to travel more than 5 billion kilometres and take samples from the comet Wirtanen in 2012.

8 July 1999 A study by the US department of Agriculture, published in *New Scientist*, suggests that GM crops do not necessarily improve productivity or decrease the need for pesticides.

16 July 1999 Russia launches its final *Mir* supply craft, after a delay of two days because of a dispute with Kazakhstan over the explosion previously of a satellite, which had scattered debris over the country.

July 23 1999 Colonel Eileen Collins of the US Air Force is the first woman to command a space crew, commanding the space shuttle *Columbia* on a 5-day mission, putting into orbit the powerful Chandra X-ray observatory.

July 31 1999 The National Aeronautics and Space Administration (NASA) crash-lands the spacecraft *Lunar Prospector* on the Moon, in order to stir up debris that can be analysed for evidence of water vapour.

August 1999 Sterols (fatty molecules) are reported to have been discovered in shale in northwest Australia by scientists from the University of Sydney. They give evidence of the existence of complex life forms on Earth 2.7 billion years ago, up to 1 billion years earlier than had been previously estimated.

August 1999 A new four-part classification system of the plant kingdom is presented at the 16th International Botanical Congress in St Louis, Missouri.

28 August 1999 The last crew members of the Russian space station *Mir* return to Earth.

2 September 1999 The journal *Nature* reports that the mice implanted with a single gene gained a greater capacity for learning and remembering. The research is hoped to apply eventually to dementia treatment.

6 September 1999 The Royal Society of Chemistry is told by science historian Walter Sneader of the University of Strathclyde that the discovery of aspirin in 1897 should be rightly attributed to Jewish chemist Arthur Eichengrun, rather than Felix Hoffman. The Nazis had later forced Eichengrun from his post, preventing him from asserting his discovery.

23 September 1999 NASA's *Mars Climate Orbiter* breaks up before entering orbit around Mars.

30 September 1999 Japan suffers the most serious nuclear accident in its history when a nuclear leak at a uranium processing plant in Tokaimura, 160 km/100 mi northeast of Tokyo, causes radiation levels around the plant to rise to 15,000 times the normal level, and exposes 14 workers to very high levels of radiation.

October 1999 Ahmed Zewail of the US is awarded the Nobel Prize for Chemistry for research into femtosecond spectroscopy, using lasers to study the movement of molecules in chemical reactions. Martinus Veldtman and Gerardus t'Hooft of the Netherlands are awarded the Nobel Prize for Physics for their mathematical work in particle physics, which confirmed the existence of the 'top quark' in 1995. Gunter Blobel, a German-born biologist, wins the Nobel Prize for Physiology or Medicine for demonstrating how signalling mechanisms in cells control the movement of proteins.

October 1999 A Russian expedition led by scientist Bernard Buigues discovers the carcass of a 23,000 year-old woolly mammoth frozen in Siberia. The carcass is flown to Khatanga, Russia, where scientists plan to clone the mammoth using an elephant as a surrogate mother.

4 October 1999 US multinational Monsanto yields to pressure from 'green' campaigners and advocates of farmers in developing countries, and agrees not to market sterile seeds modified by the Terminator gene,

which makes farmers dependent on purchasing the company's seeds each year.

15 October 1999 The exhibition 'Leonardo' in London, featuring large-scale working models of Leonardo da Vinci's sketched inventions, opens at the Science Museum.

November 1999 The journal *Nature Genetics* publishes the genome (genetic map) of the most virulent parasitic transmitter of malaria. This should advance the search for vaccines against the disease.

3 November 1999 Scientists from the UK and China announce that they have identified fossils of two previously unknown species of fish in southern China, which are 530 million years old. The find proves that vertebrates are at least 50 million years older than previously thought.

16 November 1999 Six bodies found by British scientists in frozen ground in 1998 on Spitsbergen, an arctic Norwegian island, are discovered to have traces of the 'Spanish flu' virus, responsible for the 1819 epidemic that left 40 million dead. The researchers hope to map the RNA of the virus within 18 months.

20 November 1999 China launches its first spacecraft, an uncrewed vehicle that travels for 21 hours in space, from the Jinquan satellite centre in the northwest province of Gansu.

December 1999 'A Story of Time', an exhibition of more than 500 items that reflect changing concepts of time, opens at the National Maritime Museum at Greenwich, London.

2 December 1999 Scientists in London, Washington, DC, and Tokyo, announce that they have deciphered the string of 34 million chemical bases in chromosome 22 in human DNA. Chromosome 22 provides the code for at least 679 genes, 27 of which are linked to diseases, including cancer.

2 December 1999 The US space probe *Mars Polar Lander*, launched on 3 January 1999, fails to land on Mars as planned. It was intended to photograph and take samples from the planet.

9 December 1999 US scientists at the Institute for Genomic Research (TIGR) in Rockville, Maryland, announce plans to create a new life form in the laboratory. They will use a microbe called *Mycoplasma genitalium*, which contains the smallest number of genes of any living creature known.

19 December 1999 After repeated delays, the space shuttle *Discovery* launches successfully from the Kennedy Space Centre at Cape Canaveral, Florida, on a mission to repair the Hubble Space Telescope.

January 2000 UK patents are awarded jointly to the Ministry of Agriculture, Fisheries and Food, and the Biotechnology and Biosciences Research Council for the technique used to create 'Dolly', the sheep cloned from adult cells at the Roslin Institute in Edinburgh. It is also reported that scientists in Japan have cloned six calves from an older male animal.

1 January 2000 British Prime Minister Tony Blair and MP Patricia Hewitt launch GeT, Greenwich Electronic Time, which will act as an international standard for all electronic commerce.

1 January 2000 The 'Millennium Bug' does not cause widespread computer malfunction; whether this is due to preventative measures or not remains controversial.

18 January 2000 Richard Cook, the *Mars Polar Lander* project manager at NASA's jet propulsion laboratory, announces that NASA scientists are giving up their search for the craft, which disappeared on 3 December 1999.

20 January 2000 Discovery of the remains of the largest dinosaur, an unclassified herbivore around 100 m/328 ft long, is reported by palaeontologists in Argentina.

10 February 2000 Physicists at CERN laboratory in Geneva announce they have simulated the Big Bang in the nuclear accelerator, creating temperatures more than 100,000 times hotter than the Sun's core, and a quark-gluon plasma called 'quagma', providing the first observational evidence of gluons, the particles that hold quarks together.

11 February 2000–22 February 2000 The space shuttle *Endeavour* carries out a mission in which it scans the Earth's surface with radar signals to create a detailed topographical map of the world.

14 March US President Bill Clinton and British Prime Minister Tony Blair issue a joint statement that encourages scientists deciphering the human genetic code to make their research freely available to the scientific community.

Patricia Hewitt, MP, who, with Prime Minister Tony Blair, launched Greenwich Electronic Time, in January 2000. *Pic: Andy McCartney*

16 March 2000 Reports are published of the discovery of 45-million-year-old fossils of the earliest higher primates (anthropoids), the order that now includes humans and chimpanzees, by a team of Chinese and US palaeontologists in China.

26 June 2000 Scientists at the Human Genome Project announce they have completed a working draft of the human genetic code. The rival private US company, Celera Genomics, claims its first draft is close to completion (*see also* **colour section**).

1 July 2000 The Øresund Fixed Link bridge, linking Malmö in Sweden to Copenhagen, Denmark, opens. It is the longest cable-stayed bridge carrying both rail and road traffic in the world, with a free span of 492 m/1,608 ft.

The Elements

The Chemical Elements

An element is a substance that cannot be split chemically into simpler substances. The atoms of a particular element all have the same number of protons in their nuclei (their atomic number).
(– = not applicable.)

Name	Symbol	Atomic number	Atomic mass (amu)[1]	Relative density[2]	Melting or fusing point (°C)
Actinium	Ac	89	227[3]	–	–
Aluminium	Al	13	26.9815	2.58	658
Americium	Am	95	243[3]	–	–
Antimony	Sb	51	121.75	6.62	629
Argon	Ar	18	39.948	gas	– 188
Arsenic	As	33	74.9216	5.73	volatile, 450
Astatine	At	85	210[3]	–	–
Barium	Ba	56	137.34	3.75	850
Berkelium	Bk	97	249[3]	–	–
Beryllium	Be	4	9.0122	1.93	1,281
Bismuth	Bi	83	208.9806	9.80	268
Bohrium	Bh	107	262[3]	–	–
Boron	B	5	10.81	2.5	2,300
Bromine	Br	35	79.904	3.19	– 7.3
Cadmium	Cd	48	112.40	8.64	320
Caesium	Cs	55	132.9055	1.88	26
Calcium	Ca	20	40.08	1.58	851
Californium	Cf	98	251[3]	–	–
Carbon	C	6	12.011	3.52	infusible
Cerium	Ce	58	140.12	6.68	623
Chlorine	Cl	17	35.453	gas	– 102
Chromium	Cr	24	51.996	6.5	1,510
Cobalt	Co	27	58.9332	8.6	1,490
Copper	Cu	29	63.546	8.9	1,083
Curium	Cm	96	247[3]	–	–
Dubnium	Db	105	262[3]	–	–
Dysprosium	Dy	66	162.50	–	–
Einsteinium	Es	99	254[3]	–	–
Erbium	Er	68	167.26	4.8	–
Europium	Eu	63	151.96	–	–
Fermium	Fm	100	253[3]	–	–
Fluorine	F	9	18.9984	gas	– 223
Francium	Fr	87	223[3]	–	–
Gadolinium	Gd	64	157.25	–	–
Gallium	Ga	31	69.72	5.95	30
Germanium	Ge	32	72.59	5.47	958
Gold	Au	79	196.9665	19.3	1,062
Hafnium	Hf	72	178.49	12.1	2,500
Hassium	Hs	108	265[3]	–	–
Helium	He	2	4.0026	gas	– 272
Holmium	Ho	67	164.9303	–	–
Hydrogen	H	1	1.0080	gas	– 258
Indium	In	49	114.82	7.4	155
Iodine	I	53	126.9045	4.95	114
Iridium	Ir	77	192.22	22.4	2,375
Iron	Fe	26	55.847	7.86	1,525
Krypton	Kr	36	83.80	gas	– 169
Lanthanum	La	57	138.9055	6.1	810
Lawrencium	Lr	103	260[3]	–	–
Lead	Pb	82	207.2	11.37	327
Lithium	Li	3	6.941	0.585	186
Lutetium	Lu	71	174.97	–	–
Magnesium	Mg	12	24.305	1.74	651
Manganese	Mn	25	54.9380	7.39	1,220
Meitnerium	Mt	109	266[3]	–	–
Mendelevium	Md	101	256[3]	–	–
Mercury	Hg	80	200.59	13.596	– 38.9
Molybdenum	Mo	42	95.94	10.2	2,500
Neodymium	Nd	60	144.24	6.96	840
Neon	Ne	10	20.179	gas	– 248.6
Neptunium	Np	93	237[3]	–	–
Nickel	Ni	28	58.71	8.9	1,452
Niobium	Nb	41	92.9064	8.4	1,950
Nitrogen	N	7	14.0067	gas	– 211
Nobelium	No	102	254[3]	–	–
Osmium	Os	76	190.2	22.48	2,700
Oxygen	O	8	15.9994	gas	– 227
Palladium	Pd	46	106.4	11.4	1,549
Phosphorus	P	15	30.9738	1.8–2.3	44
Platinum	Pt	78	195.09	21.5	1,755
Plutonium	Pu	94	242[3]	–	–
Polonium	Po	84	210[3]	–	–
Potassium	K	19	39.102	0.87	63
Praseodymium	Pr	59	140.9077	6.48	940
Promethium	Pm	61	145[3]	–	–
Protactinium	Pa	91	231.0359	–	–
Radium	Ra	88	226.0254	6.0	700
Radon	Rn	86	222[3]	gas	– 150
Rhenium	Re	75	186.2	21	3,000
Rhodium	Rh	45	102.9055	12.1	1,950
Rubidium	Rb	37	85.4678	1.52	39
Ruthenium	Ru	44	101.07	12.26	2,400
Rutherfordium	Rf	104	262[3]	–	–
Samarium	Sm	62	150.4	7.7	1,350
Scandium	Sc	21	44.9559	–	–
Seaborgium	Sg	106	263[3]	–	–
Selenium	Se	34	78.96	4.5	170–220
Silicon	Si	14	28.086	2.0–2.4	1,370
Silver	Ag	47	107.868	10.5	960
Sodium	Na	11	22.9898	0.978	97
Strontium	Sr	38	87.62	2.54	800
Sulphur	S	16	32.06	2.07	115–119
Tantalum	Ta	73	180.9479	16.6	2,900
Technetium	Tc	43	99[3]	–	–
Tellurium	Te	52	127.60	6.0	446
Terbium	Tb	65	158.9254	–	–
Thallium	Tl	81	204.37	11.85	302
Thorium	Th	90	232.0381	11.00	1,750
Thulium	Tm	69	168.9342	–	–
Tin	Sn	50	118.69	7.3	232
Titanium	Ti	22	47.90	4.54	1,850
Tungsten	W	74	183.85	19.1	2,900–3,000
Ununbium	Uub[4]	112	277[3]	–	–
Ununhexium	Uuh[4]	116	289[3]	–	–
Ununnilium	Uun[4]	110	269[3]	–	–
Ununoctium	Uuo[4]	118	293[3]	–	–
Ununquadium	Uuq[4]	114	289[3]	–	–
Unununium	Uuu[4]	111	272[3]	–	–
Uranium	U	92	238.029	18.7	–
Vanadium	V	23	50.9414	5.5	1,710
Xenon	Xe	54	131.30	gas	– 140
Ytterbium	Yb	70	173.04	–	–
Yttrium	Y	39	88.9059	3.8	–
Zinc	Zn	30	65.37	7.12	418
Zirconium	Zr	40	91.22	4.15	2,130

[1] Atomic mass units.
[2] Also known as specific gravity. Relative density is the density (at 20°C/68°F) of a solid or liquid relative to the maximum density of water (at 4°C/39.2°F).
[3] The number given is that for the most stable isotope of the element.
[4] Elements as yet unnamed; temporary identification assigned until a name is approved by the International Union for Pure and Applied Chemistry.

Periodic Table of the Elements

Key (*element*): 1 — atomic number; Hydrogen — name; H — symbol; 1.00794 — relative atomic mass

Period	I	II											III	IV	V	VI	VII	0
1	1 Hydrogen **H** 1.00794																	2 Helium **He** 4002.60
2	3 Lithium **Li** 6.941	4 Beryllium **Be** 9.012											5 Boron **B** 10.81	6 Carbon **C** 12.011	7 Nitrogen **N** 14.0067	8 Oxygen **O** 15.9994	9 Fluorine **F** 18.99840	10 Neon **Ne** 20.179
3	11 Sodium **Na** 22.98977	12 Magnesium **Mg** 24.305											13 Aluminium **Al** 26.98154	14 Silicon **Si** 28.066	15 Phosphorus **P** 30.9738	16 Sulphur **S** 32.06	17 Chlorine **Cl** 35.453	18 Argon **Ar** 39.948
4	19 Potassium **K** 30.098	20 Calcium **Ca** 40.06	21 Scandium **Sc** 44.9559	22 Titanium **Ti** 47.90	23 Vanadium **V** 50.9414	24 Chromium **Cr** 51.996	25 Manganese **Mn** 54.9380	26 Iron **Fe** 55.847	27 Cobalt **Co** 58.9332	28 Nickel **Ni** 58.70	29 Copper **Cu** 63.546	30 Zinc **Zn** 65.38	31 Gallium **Ga** 69.72	32 Germanium **Ge** 72.59	33 Arsenic **As** 74.9216	34 Selenium **Se** 78.96	35 Bromine **Br** 79.904	36 Krypton **Kr** 83.80
5	37 Rubidium **Rb** 85.4678	38 Strontium **Sr** 87.62	39 Yttrium **Y** 88.9059	40 Zirconium **Zr** 91.22	41 Niobium **Nb** 92.9064	42 Molybdenum **Mo** 95.94	43 Technetium **Tc** 97.9072	44 Ruthenium **Ru** 101.07	45 Rhodium **Rh** 102.9055	46 Palladium **Pd** 106.4	47 Silver **Ag** 107.868	48 Cadmium **Cd** 112.40	49 Indium **In** 114.82	50 Tin **Sn** 118.69	51 Antimony **Sb** 121.75	52 Tellurium **Te** 127.75	53 Iodine **I** 126.9045	54 Xenon **Xe** 131.30
6	55 Caesium **Cs** 132.9054	56 Barium **Ba** 137.34	**La**	72 Hafnium **Hf** 178.49	73 Tantalum **Ta** 180.9479	74 Tungsten **W** 183.85	75 Rhenium **Re** 186.207	76 Osmium **Os** 190.2	77 Iridium **Ir** 192.22	78 Platinum **Pt** 195.09	79 Gold **Au** 196.9665	80 Mercury **Hg** 200.59	81 Thallium **Tl** 204.37	82 Lead **Pb** 207.37	83 Bismuth **Bi** 207.2	84 Polonium **Po** 210	85 Astatine **At** 211	86 Radon **Rn** 222.0176
7	87 Francium **Fr** 223.0197	88 Radium **Ra** 226.0254	**Ac**	104 Rutherfordium **Rf** 261.109	105 Dubnium **Db** 262.114	106 Seaborgium **Sg** 263.120	107 Bohrium **Bh** 262	108 Hassium **Hs** 265	109 Meitnerium **Mt** 266	110 Ununnilium **Uun** 269	111 Unununium **Uuu** 272	112 Ununbium **Uub** 277		114 Ununquadium **Uuq** 277		116 Ununhexium **Uuh** 277		118 Ununoctium **Uuo** 277

Lanthanide series

57 Lanthanum **La** 138.9055	58 Cerium **Ce** 140.12	59 Praeseodymium **Pr** 140.9077	60 Neodymium **Nd** 144.24	61 Promethium **Pm** 144.9128	62 Samarium **Sm** 150.36	63 Europium **Eu** 151.96	64 Gadolinium **Gd** 157.25	65 Terbium **Tb** 158.9254	66 Dysprosium **Dy** 162.50	67 Holmium **Ho** 164.9304	68 Erbium **Er** 167.26	69 Thulium **Tm** 168.9342	70 Ytterbium **Yb** 173.04	71 Lutetium **Lu** 174.97

Actinide series

89 Actinium **Ac** 227.0278	90 Thorium **Th** 232.0381	91 Protactinium **Pa** 231.0359	92 Uranium **U** 238.029	93 Neptunium **Np** 237.0482	94 Plutonium **Pu** 244.0642	95 Americium **Am** 243.0614	96 Curium **Cm** 247.0703	97 Berkelium **Bk** 247	98 Californium **Cf** 251.0786	99 Einsteinium **Es** 252.0828	100 Fermium **Fm** 257.0951	101 Mendelevium **Md** 258.0986	102 Nobelium **No** 259.1009	103 Lawrencium **Lr** 260.1054

The periodic table of the elements arranges the elements into horizontal rows (called periods) and vertical columns (called groups) according to their atomic numbers. The elements in a group or column all have similar properties – for example, all the elements in the far right-hand column are inert gases.

Common Alloys

Name	Approximate composition	Uses
brass	35–10% zinc, 65–90% copper	decorative metalwork, plumbing fittings, industrial tubing
bronze – common	2% zinc, 6% tin, 92% copper	machinery, decorative work
bronze – aluminium	10% aluminium, 90% copper	machinery castings
bronze – coinage	1% zinc, 4% tin, 95% copper	coins
cast iron	2–4% carbon, 96–98% iron	decorative metalwork, engine blocks, industrial machinery
dentist's amalgam	30% copper, 70% mercury	dental fillings
duralumin	0.5 % magnesium, 0.5% manganese, 5% copper, 94% aluminium	framework of aircraft
gold – coinage	10% copper, 90% gold	coins
gold – dental	14–28% silver, 14–28% copper, 58% gold	dental fillings
lead battery plate	6% antimony, 94% lead	car batteries
manganin	1.5% nickel, 16% manganese, 82.5% copper	resistance wire
nichrome	20% chromium, 80% nickel	heating elements
pewter	20% lead, 80% tin	utensils
silver – coinage	10% copper, 90% silver	coins
solder	50% tin, 50% lead	joining iron surfaces
steel – stainless	8–20% nickel, 10–20% chromium, 60–80% iron	kitchen utensils
steel – armour	1–4% nickel, 0.5–2% chromium, 95–98% iron	armour plating
steel – tool	2–4% chromium, 6–7% molybdenum, 90–95% iron	tools

Hazard Labels

harmful/irritant

toxic

radioactive

explosive

flammable

corrosive

oxidizing/supports fire

biohazardous/infectious

environmentally dangerous

Inventions

Selected Inventions

Invention	Date	Inventor	Nationality
Achromatic lens	1733	Chester Moor Hall	British
Adding machine	1642	Blaise Pascal	French
Aeroplane, powered	1903	Orville and Wilbur Wright	US
Air conditioning	1902	Willis Carrier	US
Air pump	1654	Otto Guericke	German
Airship, first successful	1852	Henri Giffard	French
Airship, rigid	1900	Ferdinand von Zeppelin	German
Amniocentesis test	1952	Douglas Bevis	British
Aqualung	1943	Jacques Cousteau	French
Arc welder	1919	Elihu Thomson	US
Armillary ring	125	Zhang Heng	Chinese
Aspirin	1899	Felix Hoffman	German
Assembly line	1908	Henry Ford	US
Autogiro	1923	Juan de la Cierva	Spanish
Automatic pilot	1912	Elmer Sperry	US
Babbitt metal	1839	Isaac Babbitt	US
Bakelite, first synthetic plastic	1909	Leo Baekeland	US
Ballpoint pen	1938	Lazlo Biró	Hungarian
Barbed wire	1874	Joseph Glidden	US
Bar code system	1970	Monarch Marking, Plessey Telecommunications	US, British
Barometer	1642	Evangelista Torricelli	Italian
Bathysphere	1934	Charles Beebe	US
Beaufort scale for wind velocity	1806	Francis Beaufort	Irish-born British
Bessemer process	1856	Henry Bessemer	British
Bicycle	1839	Kirkpatrick Macmillan	British
Bifocal spectacles	1784	Benjamin Franklin	US
Binary calculator	1938	Konrad Zuse	German
Bottling machine	1895	Michael Owens	US
Braille	1837	Louis Braille	French
Bunsen burner	1850	Robert Bunsen	German
Calculator, pocket	1971	Texas Instruments	US
Camera film (roll)	1888	George Eastman	US
Camera obscura	1560	Battista Porta	Italian
Carbon fibre	1963	Leslie Phillips	British
Carbon–zinc battery	1841	Robert Bunsen	German
Carburettor	1893	Wilhelm Maybach	German
Car, four-wheeled	1887	Gottlieb Daimler	German
Car, petrol-driven	1885	Karl Benz	German
Carpet sweeper	1876	Melville Bissell	US
Cash register	1879	James Ritty	US
Cassette tape	1963	Philips	Dutch
Catapult	*c.* 400 BC	Dionysius of Syracuse	Greek
Cathode ray oscilloscope	1897	Karl Braun	German
CD-ROM	1984	Sony, Fujitsu, Philips	Japanese, Japanese, Dutch

(continued)

Selected Inventions (*continued*)

Invention	Date	Inventor	Nationality
Cellophane	1908	Jacques Brandenberger	Swiss
Celluloid	1869	John Wesley Hyatt	US
Cement, Portland	1824	Joseph Aspidin	British
Centigrade scale	1742	Anders Celsius	Swedish
Charge-coupled device (CCD)	1969	George Smith and Willard Boyle, Bell Laboratories	US
Chemical symbols	1811	Jöns Jakob Berzelius	Swedish
Chronometer, accurate	1762	John Harrison	British
Cinematograph	1895	Auguste and Louis Lumière	French
Clock, pendulum	1656	Christiaan Huygens	Dutch
Clockwork radio	1992	Trevor Baylis	British
Colt revolver	1835	Samuel Colt	US
Compact disc	1972	RCA	US
Compact disc player	1984	Sony, Philips	Japanese, Dutch
Compass, simple	1088	Shen Kua	Chinese
Computer, bubble memory	1967	A H Bobeck and Bell Telephone Laboratories team	US
Computer, first commercially available (UNIVAC 1)	1951	John Mauchly, John Eckert	US
Computerized axial tomography (CAT) scanning	1972	Godfrey Hounsfield	British
Contraceptive pill	1954	Gregory Pincus, Min Chueh Chang, and John Rock	US
Cotton gin	1793	Eli Whitney	US
Cream separator	1878	Carl de Laval	Swedish
Crookes tube	1878	William Crookes	British
Cyclotron	1931	Ernest O Lawrence	US
DDT	1940	Paul Müller	Swiss
Diesel engine	1892	Rudolf Diesel	German
Difference engine (early computer)	1822	Charles Babbage	British
Digital versatile disk or digital video disk (DVD)	1995	Consortium of companies including Toshiba, Time Warner, Sony, and Philips	Japanese, US, Dutch
Diode valve	1904	Ambrose Fleming	British
Dynamite	1866	Alfred Nobel	Swedish
Dynamo	1831	Michael Faraday	British
Electric cell	1800	Alessandro Volta	Italian
Electric fan	1882	Schuyler Wheeler	US
Electric generator, first commercial	1867	Zénobe Théophile Gramme	French
Electric light bulb	1879	Thomas Edison	US
Electric motor	1821	Michael Faraday	British
Electric motor, alternating current	1888	Nikola Tesla	Croatian-born US
Electrocardiography	1903	Willem Einthoven	Dutch
Electroencephalography	1929	Hans Berger	German
Electromagnet	1824	William Sturgeon	British
Electron microscope	1933	Ernst Ruska	German
Electrophoresis	1930	Arne Tiselius	Swedish
Fahrenheit scale	1714	Gabriel Fahrenheit	Polish-born Dutch
Felt-tip pen	1955	Esterbrook	British
Floppy disk	1970	IBM	US
Flying shuttle	1733	John Kay	British
Fractal images	1962	Benoit Mandelbrot	Polish-born French
Frozen food	1929	Clarence Birdseye	US
Fuel cell	1839	William Grove	British
Galvanometer	1820	Johann Schwiegger	German
Gas mantle	1885	Carl Welsbach	Austrian
Geiger counter	1908	Hans Geiger, Ernest Rutherford	German, New Zealand-born British
Genetic fingerprinting	1985	Alec Jeffreys	British
Glider	1877	Otto Lilienthal	German
Gramophone	1877	Thomas Edison	US
Gramophone (flat discs)	1887	Emile Berliner	German
Gyrocompass	1911	Elmer Sperry	US
Gyroscope	1852	Jean Foucault	French
Heart, artificial	1982	Robert Jarvik	US
Heart-lung machine	1953	John Gibbon	US
Helicopter	1939	Igor Sikorsky	US
Holography	1947	Dennis Gabor	Hungarian-born British
Hovercraft	1955	Christopher Cockerell	British
Hydrogen bomb	1952	US government scientists	US
Hydrometer	1675	Robert Boyle	Irish
Iconoscope	1923	Vladimir Zworykin	Russian-born US
Integrated circuit	1958	Jack Kilby, Texas Instruments	US
Internal-combustion engine, four-stroke	1877	Nikolaus Otto	German
Internal-combustion engine, gas-fuelled	1860	Etienne Lenoir	Belgian
In vitro fertilization	1969	Robert Edwards	British
Jet engine	1930	Frank Whittle	British
Jumbo jet	1969	Joe Sutherland, Boeing team	US
Laser, prototype	1960	Theodore Maiman	US
Lightning rod	1752	Benjamin Franklin	US
Linoleum	1860	Frederick Walton	British
Liquid crystal display (LCD)	1971	Hoffmann-LaRoche Laboratories	Swiss
Lock (canal)	980	Ciao Wei-yo	Chinese
Lock, Yale	1851	Linus Yale	US
Logarithms	1614	John Napier	British
Loom, power	1785	Edmund Cartwright	British
Machine gun	1862	Richard Gatling	US
Magnifying glass	1250	Roger Bacon	British
Map	*c.* 510 BC	Hecataeus	Greek
Map, star	*c.* 350 BC	Eudoxus	Greek
Maser	1953	Charles Townes, Arthur Schawlow	US
Mass-spectrograph	1918	Francis Aston	British
Microscope	1590	Zacharias Janssen	Dutch
Miners' safety lamp	1813	Humphry Davy	British
Minidisk	1991	Sony	Japanese
Mobile telephone communication	1921	Detroit Police Department	US
Modem	1958	Bell Laboratories	US
Mohs scale for mineral hardness	1822	Frederick Mohs	German
Morse code	1838	Samuel Morse	US
Motorcycle	1885	Gottlieb Daimler	German
Neutron bomb	1977	US military	US
Nylon	1934	Wallace Carothers	US
Paper chromatography	1944	Archer Martin, Richard Synge	British
Paper, first	AD 105	Ts'ai Lun	Chinese
Particle accelerator	1932	John Cockcroft, Ernest Walton	British, Irish
Pasteurization (wine)	1864	Louis Pasteur	French
Pen, fountain	1884	Lewis Waterman	US
Personal stereo (Walkman™)	1979	Akio Morita, head of Sony	Japanese
Photoelectric cell	1904	Johann Elster	German
Photograph, first colour	1881	Frederic Ives	US
Photograph, first (on a metal plate)	1827	Joseph Niepce	French
Piano	1704	Bartolommeo Cristofori	Italian
Planar transistor	1959	Robert Noyce	US
Plastic, first (Parkesine)	1862	Alexander Parkes	British
Plough, cast iron	1785	Robert Ransome	British
Punched-card system for carpet-making loom	1805	Joseph-Marie Jacquard	French
Radar, first practical equipment	1935	Robert Watson-Watt	British
Radio	1901	Guglielmo Marconi	Italian

(continued)

Selected Inventions *(continued)*

Invention	Date	Inventor	Nationality
Radio interferometer	1955	Martin Ryle	British
Radio, transistor	1952	Sony	Japanese
Razor, disposable safety	1895	King Gillette	US
Recombinant DNA, technique	1973	Stanley Cohen, Herbert Boyer	US
Refrigerator, domestic	1918	Nathaniel Wales, E J Copeland	US
Richter scale	1935	Charles Richter	US
Road locomotive, steam	1801	Richard Trevithick	British
Road vehicle, first self-propelled (steam)	1769	Nicolas-Joseph Cugnot	French
Rocket, powered by petrol and liquid oxygen	1926	Robert Goddard	US
Rubber, synthetic	1909	Karl Hoffman	German
Scanning tunnelling microscope	1980	Heinrich Rohrer, Gerd Binning	Swiss, German
Seed drill	1701	Jethro Tull	British
Seismograph	1880	John Milne	British
Shrapnel shell	1784	Henry Shrapnel	British
Silicon transistor	1954	Gordon Teal	US
Silk, method of producing artificial	1887	Hilaire, Comte de Chardonnet	French
Spinning frame	1769	Richard Arkwright	British
Spinning jenny	1764	James Hargreaves	British
Spinning mule	1779	Samuel Crompton	British
Stainless steel	1913	Harry Brearley	British
Steam engine	50 BC	Hero of Alexandria	Greek
Steam engine, first successful	1712	Thomas Newcomen	British
Steam engine, improved	1765	James Watt	British
Steam locomotive, first effective	1814	George Stephenson	British
Steam turbine, first practical	1884	Charles Parsons	British
Steel, open-hearth production	1864	William Siemens, Pierre Emile Martin	German, French
Submarine	1620	Cornelius Drebbel	Dutch
Superheterodyne radio receiver	1918	Edwin Armstrong	US
Tank	1914	Ernest Swinton	British
Telephone	1876	Alexander Graham Bell	British-born US
Telescope, binocular	1608	Johann Lippershey	Dutch
Telescope, reflecting	1668	Isaac Newton	British
Television	1926	John Logie Baird	British
Terylene (synthetic fibre)	1941	John Whinfield, J T Dickson	British
Thermometer	1607	Galileo	Italian
Thermometer, alcohol	1730	René Antoine Ferchault de Réaumur	French
Thermometer, mercury	1714	Gabriel Fahrenheit	Polish-born Dutch
TNT	1863	J Willbrand	German
Toaster, pop-up	1926	Charles Strite	US
Toilet, flushing	1778	Joseph Bramah	British
Transistor	1948	John Bardeen, Walter Brattain, William Shockley	US
Triode valve	1906	Lee De Forest	US
Tunnel diode	1957	Leo Esaki, Sony	Japanese
Tupperware	1944	Earl Tupper	US
Type, movable earthenware	1045	Pi Shêng	Chinese
Type, movable metal	1440	Johannes Gutenberg	German
Ultrasound, first use in obstetrics	1958	Ian Donald	British
Velcro	1948	Georges de Mestral	Swiss
Video, home	1975	Matsushita, JVC, Sony	Japanese
Viscose	1892	Charles Cross	British
Vulcanization of rubber	1839	Charles Goodyear	US
Wind tunnel	1932	Ford Motor Company	US
Wireless telegraphy	1895	Guglielmo Marconi	Italian
Word processor	1965	IBM	US
World Wide Web	1990	Tim Berners-Lee	British
Zinc–carbon battery	1868	George Leclanché	French
Zip	1891	Whitcombe Judson	US

Gene Technology

Genetically Modified Foods

Genetically modified (GM) foods are produced using genetic engineering technology. Individual genes can be copied or transferred from one living organism to another, to incorporate specific characteristics into the organism or remove undesirable characteristics. The technology may be used, for example, to produce crops with higher yields, enhanced taste, resistance to pests, or a longer growing season. The higher yields and increased nutritional content produced by the new technology may help in feeding the world's rapidly increasing population, and it may be possible in future to produce healthier foods such as oil seeds that produce oils with lower saturated fat content. Other advantages are that higher yields mean that less land will need to be given over to farmland in order to produce more food, and that reliance on pesticides will be reduced by creating crops that are themselves resistant to pests.

However, there remain some reservations about GM products, and some companies and countries, including the UK, have taken steps to delay the commercial growing of GM crops until risks have been assessed, and to introduce legislation forcing GM products to be declared as such. While traditional agriculture uses selective breeding to produce desired characteristics in crops and animals produced, there is controversy over the use of the more direct and precise methods of genetic modification. Opponents of the technology argue that there is as yet insufficient knowledge of the possible side-effects of the process to declare GM food safe. For example, GM foods may cause more allergic reactions (triggered by the genes introduced from other foods and thus unanticipated by the consumer). An international agreement, termed the Biosafety Protocol, was approved by 130 governments in January 2000. The protocol enables nations to ban imports of GM seeds and crops as a precautionary measure while scientific proof of the safety of the crops is obtained. In September 1999 legislation was passed in the UK to make compulsory the labelling of GM foods by all establishments selling food, including supermarkets, restaurants, and fast food outlets. On 17 March 2000 the environment minister, Michael Meacher, announced details of the test sites that will be used to evaluate the effects of GM crops on the environment. The farm-scale evaluations will be carried out until 2003 and there will be no commercial growing of GM crops until the risks to the environment have been assessed.

■ **Gene Technology**

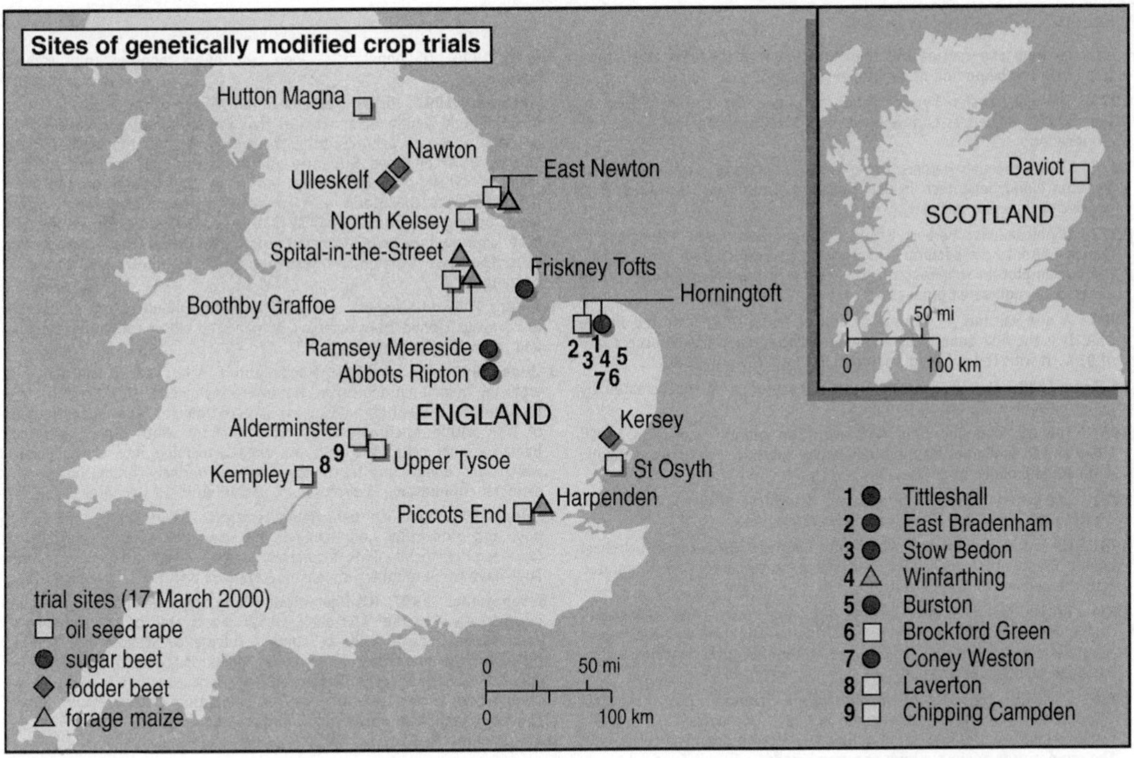

Sites of genetically modified crop trials

Hutton Magna
Nawton
Ulleskelf
East Newton
North Kelsey
Spital-in-the-Street
Friskney Tofts
Boothby Graffoe
Horningtoft
Ramsey Mereside
Abbots Ripton
ENGLAND
Alderminster
Kersey
Upper Tysoe
St Osyth
Kempley
Harpenden
Piccots End
Daviot
SCOTLAND

trial sites (17 March 2000)
- □ oil seed rape
- ● sugar beet
- ◆ fodder beet
- △ forage maize

1 ● Tittleshall
2 ● East Bradenham
3 ● Stow Bedon
4 △ Winfarthing
5 ● Burston
6 □ Brockford Green
7 ● Coney Weston
8 □ Laverton
9 □ Chipping Campden

See also **GM Crops**, p 700.

Genetics: Key Dates

1856 Austrian monk and botanist Gregor Mendel begins experiments breeding peas, research that will lead him to discover the laws of heredity.

1865 Gregor Mendel publishes a paper in the *Proceedings* of the Natural Science Society of Brünn that outlines the fundamental laws of heredity.

1869 Swiss biochemist Johann Miescher discovers a nitrogen and phosphorous material in cell nuclei that he calls nuclein but which is now known as the genetic material DNA.

1888 Dutch geneticist Hugo Marie de Vries uses the term 'mutation' to describe varieties that arise spontaneously in cultivated primroses.

1902 US geneticist Walter Sutton and German zoologist Theodor Boveri find the chromosomal theory of inheritance when they show that cell division is connected with heredity.

1906 English biologist William Bateson introduces the term 'genetics'.

1910 US geneticist Thomas Hunt Morgan discovers that certain inherited characteristics of the fruit fly *Drosophila melanogaster* are sex linked. He later argues that because all sex-related characteristics are inherited together they are linearly arranged on the X chromosome.

1934 Norwegian biochemist Asbjrn Fölling discovers the genetic metabolic defect phenylketonuria, which can cause retardation; his discovery stimulates research in biochemical genetics and the development of screening tests for carriers of deleterious genes.

1944 The role of deoxyribonucleic acid (DNA) in genetic inheritance is first demonstrated by US bacteriologist Oswald Avery, US biologist Colin MacLeod, and US biologist Maclyn McCarthy; it opens the door to the elucidation of the genetic code.

25 April 1953 English molecular biologist Francis Crick and US biologist James Watson announce the discovery of the double helix structure of DNA, the basic material of heredity. They also theorize that if the strands are separated then each can form the template for the synthesis of an identical DNA molecule. It is one of the most important discoveries in biology.

1954 Russian-born US cosmologist George Gamow suggests that the genetic code consists of the order of nucleotide triplets in the DNA molecule.

1958 US geneticists George Beadle, Edward Tatum, and Joshua Lederberg share the Nobel Prize for Physiology or Medicine: Beadle and Tatum for their discovery that genes act by regulating definite chemical events; and Lederberg for his discoveries concerning genetic recombination.

1961 French biochemists François Jacob and Jacques Monod discover messenger ribonucleic acid (mRNA), which transfers genetic information to the ribosomes, where proteins are synthesized.

1967 US scientist Charles Caskey and associates demonstrate that identical forms of messenger RNA produce the same amino acids in a variety of living beings, showing that the genetic code is common to all life forms.

October 1968 US geneticists Mark Ptashne and Walter Gilbert separately identify the first repressor genes.

1969 US geneticist Jonathan Beckwith and associates at Harvard Medical School isolate a single gene for the first time.

1970 US geneticist Hamilton Smith discovers type II restriction enzyme that breaks the DNA strand at predictable places, making it an invaluable tool in recombinant DNA technology.

1970 US biochemists Howard Temin and David Baltimore separately discover the enzyme reverse transcriptase, which allows some cancer viruses to transfer their RNA to the DNA of their hosts turning them cancerous – a reversal of the common pattern in which genetic information always passes from DNA to RNA.

1972 US microbiologist Daniel Nathans uses a restriction enzyme that splits DNA molecules to produce a genetic map of the monkey virus (SV40), the simplest virus known to produce cancer; it is the first application of these enzymes to an understanding of the molecular basis of cancer.

1973 US biochemists Stanley Cohen and Herbert Boyer develop the technique of recombinant DNA. Strands of DNA are cut by restriction

Genetics: Key Dates *(continued)*

enzymes from one species and then inserted into the DNA of another; this marks the beginning of genetic engineering.

1975 The gel-transfer hybridization technique for the detection of specific DNA sequences is developed; it is a key development in genetic engineering.

1976 US biochemist Herbert Boyer and US venture capitalist Robert Swanson found Genentech in San Francisco, California, the world's first genetic engineering company.

1977 US biochemist Herbert Boyer, at Genentech, fuses a segment of human DNA into the bacterium *Escherichia coli*, which begins to produce the human protein somatostatin; this is the first commercially produced genetically engineered product.

1980 A new vaccine for the prevention of hepatitis B is tested in the USA. It is the first genetically engineered vaccine and has a success rate of 92%. It wins Federal Drug Administration approval in 1986.

16 June 1980 The US Supreme Court rules that a microbe created by genetic engineering can be patented.

1981 The US Food and Drug Administration grants permission to Eli Lilley and Co to market insulin produced by bacteria, the first genetically engineered product to go on sale.

1981 The genetic code for the hepatitis B surface antigen is discovered, creating the possibility of a bioengineered vaccine.

1981 US geneticists Robert Weinberg, Geoffrey Cooper, and Michael Wigler discover that oncogenes (genes that cause cancer) are integrated into the genome of normal cells.

1984 British geneticist Alec Jeffreys discovers that a core sequence of DNA is almost unique to each person; this examination of DNA, known as 'genetic fingerprinting', can be used in criminal investigations and to establish family relationships.

1986 The US Department of Agriculture permits the Biological Corporation of Omaha to market a virus produced by genetic engineering; it is the first living genetically altered organism to be sold. The virus is used against a form of swine herpes.

1986 The US Department of Agriculture permits the first outdoor test of genetically altered high-yield plants (tobacco plants).

1987 The first genetically altered bacteria are released into the environment in the USA; they protect crops against frost.

10 October 1987 The *New York Times* announces US geneticist Dr Helen Donis-Keller's mapping of all 23 pairs of human chromosomes, allowing the location of specific genes for the prevention and treatment of genetic disorders.

April 1988 The US Patent and Trademark Office grants Harvard University a patent for a mouse developed by genetic engineering.

1991 British geneticists Peter Goodfellow and Robin Lovell-Badge discover the gene on the Y chromosome that determines sex.

May 1994 The first genetically engineered food goes on sale in the USA in California and Chicago, Illinois. The 'Flavr Savr' tomato is produced by the US biotechnology company Calgene.

April 1995 US surgeons report the successful transplant of genetically altered hearts of pigs into baboons, a notable advance in trans-species operations.

July 1995 The US government approves experimentation of genetically altered animal organs in humans.

August 1995 The US Environmental Protection Agency approves the sale of genetically modified maize, which contains a gene from a soil bacterium that produces a toxin fatal to the European corn borer, a pest that causes approximately $1 billion-worth of damage annually.

9 May 1996 Scientists at the National Institute of Allergy and Infectious Disease discover a protein, fusin, that allows the HIV virus to fuse with a human immune system cell's outer membrane and inject genetic material. Its presence is necessary for the AIDS virus to enter the cell.

August 1996 US geneticists clone two rhesus monkeys from embryo cells.

27 February 1997 British researcher Ian Wilmut of the Roslin Institute in Edinburgh, Scotland, announces that British geneticists have cloned an adult sheep. A cell was taken from the udder of the mother sheep and its DNA combined with an unfertilized egg that had had its DNA removed. The fused cells were grown in the laboratory and then implanted into the uterus of a surrogate mother sheep. The resulting lamb, Dolly, came from an animal that was six years old. This is the first time cloning has been achieved using cells other than reproductive cells. The news is met with international calls to prevent the cloning of humans.

February 1997 US genetic scientist Don Wolf announces the production of monkeys cloned from embryos. It is a step closer to cloning humans and intensifies ethical debate.

3 June 1997 US geneticist Huntington F Wilard constructs the first artificial human chromosome. He inserts telomeres (DNA and protein found on the tips of chromosomes) and centromeres (specialized regions of DNA within a chromosome) removed from white blood cells into human cancer cells. The cells are then assembled into chromosomes, which are about one-tenth the size of normal chromosomes. The artificial chromosome is successfully passed on to all daughter cells.

11 June 1997 English behavioural scientist David Skuse claims that boys and girls differ genetically in the way they acquire social skills. Girls acquire social skills intuitively and are 'pre-programmed', while boys have to be taught. This has important implications for education.

18 September 1997 US geneticist Bert Vogelstein and colleagues demonstrate that the *p53* gene, which is activated by the presence of carcinogens, induces cells to commit suicide by stimulating them to produce large quantities of poisonous chemicals, called 'reactive oxygen species' (ROS). The cells literally poison themselves. It is perhaps the human body's most effective way of combating cancer. Many cancers consist of cells with a malfunctioning *p53* gene.

October 1998 US scientist French Anderson announces a technique that could cure inherited diseases by inserting a healthy gene to replace a damaged one. He calls for a full debate on the issue of gene therapy, which brings with it the dilemma of whether it is ethical to enable the choice of physical attributes such as eye colour and height.

8 December 1998 The Human Fertilization and Embryology Authority and the Human Genetics Advisory Commission publish a joint report in the UK on cloning. While they oppose cloning for reproductive purposes, they leave the door open for cloning for curing intractable diseases.

10 December 1998 In a joint effort by scientists around the world, the first genetic blueprint for a whole multicellular animal is completed. The 97 million-letter code, which is published on the Internet, is for a tiny worm called *Caenorhabditis elegans*. The study began 15 years ago and cost £30 million.

24 January 1999 US scientist Craig Venter of the Institute for Genomic Research in Maryland announces the possibility of creating a living, replicating organism from an artificial set of genes, at a meeting of the American Association for the Advancement of Science, in Anaheim, California. The experiment is put on hold until the moral question is discussed by religious leaders and ethicists at the University of Pennsylvania.

April 1999 European Union legislation is implemented in the UK, requiring that some foods containing genetically modified (GM) protein or DNA be labelled in restaurants and food shops. In September the UK passes its own legislation to make labelling compulsory at all food outlets.

2000 First working draft of the Human Genome Project, which maps the composition and sequence of all human genes, is released. The publicly funded Human Genome Project and the commercial Celera Genomics compete to be the first to complete the sequencing. In June the Human Genome Project announces it has completed a working draft; Celera claims its own first draft is in a more ordered state.

Gene Technology

The Role of Genetics in Conservation

Human population growth has led to increasing exploitation of our environment. It is now evident that active conservation measures are required to prevent the permanent loss of much of our flora and fauna.

The genetic make-up of plant and animal populations is constantly changing through the effects of, for example, migration, inbreeding, and chance. Genetic analyses form a key part of many conservation plans since the genetic composition of an organism can reveal a great deal of information about its past. One goal of conservation is preventing the loss of distinctive sets of organisms. A genetic evaluation can provide good evidence as to whether or not an expensive recovery programme is justified.

Many zoos and botanical gardens have greatly aided conservation by rearing rare animals and plants. However, some captive populations represent an unwanted mix of separate groups through unintentional cross-breeding. Although the introduction of new individuals may be essential to prevent a serious decline in numbers, conservationists can maintain the genetic integrity of a group by carrying out a genetic study of potential donor organisms prior to breeding. Sometimes an endangered plant or animal is widely dispersed and thus, for economic or political reasons, it may not be possible to protect every individual. Where it is difficult to actually follow individual creatures, such as in the marine environment, a genetic approach may be the only method available to form management plans.

While we can provide a safeguard to many organisms by stopping a decline in numbers or the destruction of their habitat, a species often depends upon its store of genetic variability to withstand a change in the environment. Lost genetic variation may never be regained, but we cannot be sure which genetic regions will be useful in the future. Many conservation strategies use genetics to preserve a variety of plants or animals.

Genetic signatures of species are used to identify products that illegally contain endangered organisms. Genetic markers have confirmed suspicions that minke whale meat legally sold in Japan also contains flesh from protected whale and dolphin species. Genetic markers may also be used to determine whether a protected organism has been bred from captivity or illegally taken from the wild.

The conservation of every endangered organism is impracticable and unfeasible. Genetic analyses provide a framework for decision-making and prioritizing suitable groups for conservation. There is, however, particular concern about the amount of genetic variation that needs to be maintained for future use. At present a large amount of DNA has been sequenced for many species, although the actual 'meaning' of most of this is unknown. Because DNA may be extracted from museum specimens, it is now possible to obtain the genetic code of extinct species. In the future, therefore, there may be an emphasis on trying to preserve and recreate genetic variation using the genetic code itself.

See also  **Conservation,** pp 636–638.

Understanding Cloning

by Paul Wymer

Sexual reproduction is the means by which genetic variability is introduced in a population. A clone, however, refers to one or more offspring derived from a single ancestor, whose genetic composition is identical to that of the ancestor. Hence the offspring of organisms that reproduce asexually, such as microbes, some insects, and corals are clones, as are identical twins produced by the splitting of a single embryo. Long before anyone understood the mechanism of heredity, the genetic make-up of successive generations of certain plants was preserved by taking cuttings, because cloning in this way bestowed on the plants qualities such as disease-resistance, high yield, and predictable growth.

Although there is nothing unnatural about cloning per se, colloquial use of the term generally refers to the procedures used by modern science to create mammalian clones. This can be achieved by substituting the nucleus, which contains the genes, from one of the cells making up a mammal's body, for the nucleus of a fertilized egg, that is then brought to term. This technique was first used in 1997 to produce Dolly the sheep.

Genetic modification Interest in cloning livestock is largely allied to genetic modification – the ability to add new genes to an animal's normal repertoire or to modify one of its own genes. This might enable cloned farm animals to provide not only traditional products such as meat, milk, and hide, but also natural proteins for pharmaceutical use, or to serve as organ donors for human transplants. Also of interest is the rapid production of large animals carrying genetic defects that mimic human illnesses, such as cystic fibrosis. Although mice have provided some information, mice and humans have very different genes for cystic fibrosis. Sheep are expected to be more valuable for research into this condition because their lungs resemble those of humans. Moreover, because sheep live for years, scientists can evaluate their long-term responses to treatments.

Gene therapy Cloning could also help curtail transmission of genetic disease. Many scientists are now working on therapies that would supplement or replace defective genes in cells, but even successfully treated patients will still pass on defective genes to their offspring. If a couple was willing to produce an embryo that could be treated by advanced forms of gene therapy, nuclei from modified embryonic cells could be transferred to eggs to create children who would be entirely free of a given disease.

UNDERSTANDING CLONING *(continued)*

Some of the most ambitious projects concerning cloning involve the production of human stem cells (embryonic cells from which all others are derived), that might be used to repair or replace tissue damaged by illness. Stem cells matched to an individual patient could theoretically be made by creating an embryo by nuclear transfer just for that purpose, using one of the patient's cells as the donor and a human egg as the recipient. Embryo-derived cells might be used to treat a variety of serious diseases caused by damage to cells, perhaps including Acquired Immune Deficiency Syndrome (AIDS) as well as Parkinson's disease, muscular dystrophy, and diabetes.

Ethical concerns All of these developments raise difficult ethical issues. It is important, however, to realize that in many cases it is genetic modification, and not cloning, that has opened the way for such practices. Cloning would be of limited interest, and certainly be of little commercial value, without genetic modification. Nonetheless, creating animals with genetic defects and human babies without them raises challenging problems. It seems on balance that society supports research on animals, provided that the illnesses being studied are serious and efforts are made to avoid unnecessary suffering. Opinion on gene therapy of human embryos is more opaque. Furthermore, the possibility of growing human embryos for their cells is deeply disturbing to some people who consider life to be sacred from conception, while others regard the embryo as a cluster of cells that does not become a sentient being until much later in development.

Human cloning Perhaps the most troubling question concerns the cloning of humans, which is technically feasible, although not yet a reality. Arguments in favour of permitting human cloning, for example to overcome human infertility, seem few and far between. Significantly, it is quite possible that cloned individuals would turn out to be at risk. The long-term effects of asking an 'old' adult cell nucleus to begin life again in an egg are not known. The nucleus of a skin cell, for example, could have accumulated many genetic mistakes of no consequence to its role in the skin, but when required to make a brand new organism these could prove disastrous in other tissues, or greatly increase the probability of developing cancer.

The UK government regards the deliberate cloning of human beings as ethically unacceptable. Under UK law, cloning of individual humans cannot take place whatever the origin of the material and whatever technique is used. The recent joint Human Fertilization and Embryology Authority/Human Genetics Advisory Commission report, 'Cloning Issues in Reproduction, Science and Medicine', concurred with this view, citing serious ethical concerns about reproductive cloning as a means to relieve infertility, or for any other reason.

Astronomy

Exploring the Solar System

After three close flybys of Jupiter's moons Io and Europa between October 1999 and February 2000, the NASA spacecraft *Galileo* has sent back stunning images of these two very different worlds. Io is a volcanically active satellite, while Europa has an ice-covered surface beneath which there may be an ocean supporting primitive life. NASA has extended the *Galileo* mission to explore Jupiter and its moons to at least the end of 2000. Meanwhile, the NASA craft *Cassini* successfully skirted Venus and Earth to gain momentum for its journey to Jupiter and Saturn. The probe is scheduled to reach Jupiter in late 2000 and Saturn in 2004. Another NASA probe, *Near Earth Asteroid Rendezvous* (*NEAR*), went into orbit around the asteroid Eros in February 2000 for a year-long scientific investigation of this body. However, NASA's long-term exploration of Mars has been jeopardized by the loss in 1999 of two costly probes, the *Mars Climate Orbiter* and the *Mars Polar Lander*. The next Mars mission, planned for early 2001, has now been indefinitely postponed.

The Hubble Space Telescope continues to penetrate the remotest parts of the universe. Both Hubble and various ground-based observatories have continued the search for planets outside our Solar System. Since the discovery in 1995 of a planet orbiting the star 51 Pegasi, astronomers in many countries have detected more than 30 other extrasolar planets. Most appear to be huge worlds, three or four times the mass of Jupiter, orbiting close to their stars.

May 2000 saw a rare alignment of the planets. On 5 May, at 8:08 Universal Time (9:08 BST), the planets Mercury, Venus, Mars, Jupiter, and Saturn all lay close to each other in the sky. Unfortunately, the Sun was also in the grouping and made the spectacle unobservable.

Looking further afield, two X-ray astronomy satellites launched in 1999, NASA's Chandra X-ray observatory and the European Space Agency's XMM-Newton X-ray observatory, began to reveal the universe in a new light. Chandra was programmed to send back X-ray images of stars and galaxies, while XMM-Newton was designed to analyse spectra in the X-ray wavelength range. In 2000, the two satellites began sending back impressive data. Notably, they were helping astronomers to understand how the energy released from an exploding star expands into the universe. (*See also* **Space Exploration**, p 488.)

The Planets

(– = not applicable.)

Planet	Main constituents	Atmosphere	Average distance from the Sun km (millions)	Average distance from the Sun mi (millions)	Orbital period (Earth yrs)	Diameter km (thousands)	Diameter mi (thousands)	Average density (water = 1 unit)
Mercury	rock, ferrous	–	58	36	0.241	4.88	3.03	5.4
Venus	rock, ferrous	carbon dioxide	108	67	0.615	12.10	7.51	5.2
Earth	rock, ferrous	nitrogen, oxygen	150	93	1.000	12.76	7.92	5.5
Mars	rock	carbon dioxide	228	141	1.880	6.78	4.21	3.9
Jupiter	liquid hydrogen, helium	–	778	483	11.860	142.80	88.73	1.3
Saturn	hydrogen, helium	–	1,427	886	29.460	120.00	74.56	0.7
Uranus	ice, hydrogen, helium	hydrogen, helium	2,870	1,783	84.000	50.80	31.56	1.3
Neptune	ice, hydrogen, helium	hydrogen, helium	4,497	2,794	164.800	48.60	30.20	1.6
Pluto	ice, rock	methane	5,900	3,666	248.500	2.27	1.41	~2.0

Largest Natural Planetary Satellites

Planet	Satellite	Diameter km	Diameter mi	Mean distance from centre of primary planet km	Mean distance from centre of primary planet mi	Orbital period (Earth days)
Jupiter	Ganymede	5,262	3,300	1,070,000	664,898	7.16
Saturn	Titan	5,150	3,200	1,221,800	759,226	15.95
Jupiter	Callisto	4,800	3,000	1,883,000	1,170,096	16.69
Jupiter	Io	3,630	2,240	421,600	261,982	1.77
Earth	Moon	3,476	2,160	384,400	238,866	27.32
Jupiter	Europa	3,138	1,900	670,900	416,897	3.55
Neptune	Triton	2,700	1,690	354,300	220,162	5.88

Largest Asteroids

An asteroid is a small body, composed of rock and iron, that orbits the Sun. Most lie in a belt between the orbits of Mars and Jupiter, and are thought to be fragments left over from the formation of the Solar System.

Name	Diameter km	Diameter mi	Average distance from Sun (Earth = 1)	Orbital period (years)
Ceres	940	584	2.77	4.6
Pallas	588	365	2.77	4.6
Vesta	576	358	2.36	3.6
Hygeia	430	267	3.13	5.5
Interamnia	338	210	3.06	5.4
Davida	324	201	3.18	5.7

Asteroids

Most asteroids lie within the main asteroid belt between the orbits of Mars and Jupiter, but there are many that have orbits that cross that of Earth – these are known as the near-earth asteroids (NEAs). NEAs with a diameter of more than 1 km/0.6 mi pose the greatest threat to Earth – they are known as potentially hazardous asteroids (PHAs). It is estimated that there are between 500 and 1,000 of these and on average an asteroid in this size range collides with Earth every 100,000 years.

Astronomical Facts

All Uranus' moons are named after characters from Shakespeare. The five visible from Earth are Miranda, Ariel, Umbriel, Titania, and Oberon.

The tail of a comet can be more than 100 million km long yet has less density than a vacuum created under laboratory conditions.

Neutron stars are so condensed that a fragment the size of a sugar cube would weigh as much as all the people on Earth put together.

An explosion in Northern Ireland in December 1997 was blamed on terrorists, but was later discovered to be caused by a meteorite. It left a 1.2-m/4-ft wide crater.

Astronauts in space cannot burp. It is gravity that causes bubbles to rise to the top of a liquid, so space shuttle crews were forced to request less gas in their fizzy drinks to avoid discomfort.

How Brightly do the Stars Shine?

A star's brightness is referred to as its **magnitude** and is affected by the amount of light it gives out and by the distance at which it lies. **Apparent magnitude** is brightness as seen from Earth. **Absolute magnitude** is brightness as measured at a standard distance of 32.6 light years (10 parsecs) from the star.

In 129 BC, the Greek astronomer Hipparchus listed about 850 stars classified by magnitude. He created a system of classification from 1st magnitude (the brightest stars visible to the naked eye) to 6th magnitude (the faintest stars visible to the naked eye). In the mid 19th century the English astronomer Norman Pogson developed the scale. Pogson defined a star of magnitude 1 as being exactly 100 times brighter than a star of magnitude 6; hence, a change in one magnitude represented a change of a factor of 2.512 in brightness. The larger the number denoting the magnitude, the fainter the object. Zero or first magnitude indicates some of the brightest stars. Still brighter are those of negative magnitude, such as Sirius, whose magnitude is −1.46.

The **Brightest Stars** table excludes the Sun – which is the nearest and brightest star visible from Earth – and is ordered by apparent magnitude, the lowest numbers indicating the greatest brightness.

The measurement of the magnitudes of celestial bodies is known as photometry, originally carried out by expertise of eye alone (visual photometry), but now generally making use of photographic or photoelectric apparatus (photographic photometry).

In October 1997 astronomers at the University of California identified the biggest and brightest star in the universe so far and named it the Pistol Star. The star was detected using NASA's Hubble Space Telescope. Its distance from the Earth is yet to be determined, although its diameter is estimated as 4 light years.

Solar System

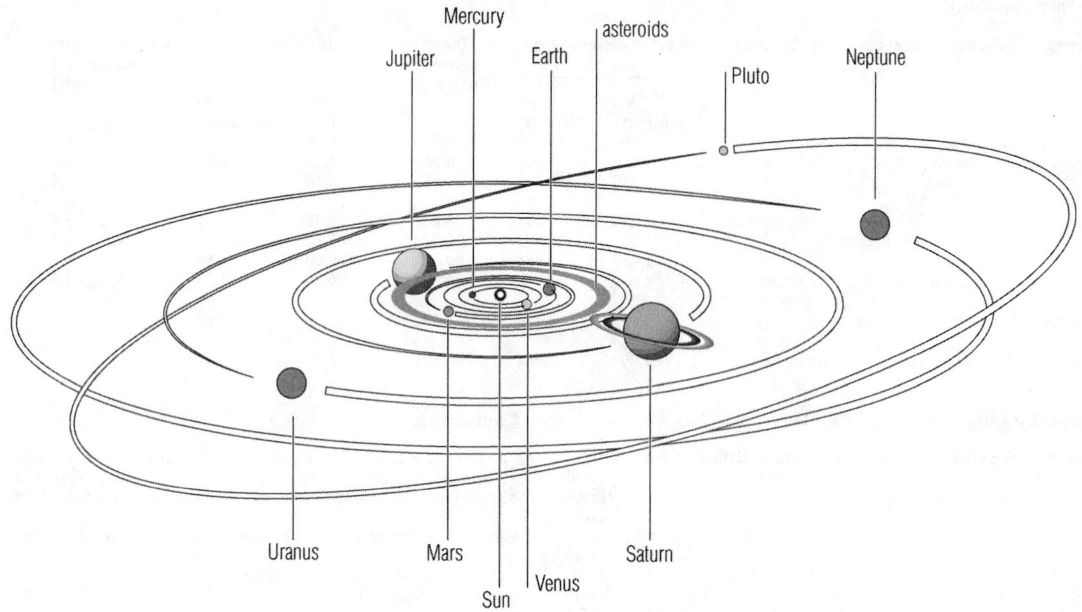

Most of the objects in the Solar System lie close to the plane of the ecliptic. The planets are tiny compared to the Sun. If the Sun were the size of a basketball, the planet closest to the Sun, Mercury, would be the size of a mustard seed 15 m/48 ft from the Sun. The most distant planet, Pluto, would be a pinhead 1.6 km/1 mi away from the Sun. The Earth, which is the third planet out from the Sun, would be the size of a pea 32 m/100 ft from the Sun.

Brightest Stars

Scientific name	Common name	Distance from Sun (light years)	Apparent magnitude	Absolute magnitude
Alpha Canis Majoris	Sirius	9	−1.46	1.4
Alpha Carinae	Canopus	1,170	−0.72	−2.5
Alpha Centauri	Rigil Kent	4	−0.27	4.4
Alpha Boötis	Arcturus	36	−0.04	0.2
Alpha Lyrae	Vega	26	0.03	0.6
Alpha Aurigae	Capella	42	0.08	0.4
Beta Orionis	Rigel	910	0.12	−8.1
Alpha Canis Minoris	Procyon	11	0.38	2.6
Alpha Eridani	Achernar	85	0.46	−1.3
Alpha Orionis	Betelgeuse	310	0.50[1]	−7.2
Beta Centauri	Hadar	460	0.61[1]	−4.4
Alpha Aquilae	Altair	17	0.77	2.3
Alpha Crucis	Acrux	360	0.83	−4.6
Alpha Tauri	Aldebaran	68	0.85[1]	−0.3
Alpha Scorpii	Antares	330	0.96[1]	−5.2
Alpha Virginis	Spica	260	0.98[1]	−3.2
Beta Geminorum	Pollux	36	1.14	0.7
Alpha Piscis Austrini	Fomalhaut	22	1.16	2.0
Beta Crucis	Mimosa	490	1.25[1]	−4.7
Alpha Cygni	Deneb	1,830	1.25	−7.2

[1] Variable star.

See also **The Sun,** p 488.

Constellations

A constellation is one of the 88 areas into which the sky is divided for the purposes of identifying and naming celestial objects. The first constellations were simple, arbitrary patterns of stars in which early civilizations visualized gods, sacred beasts, and mythical heroes.
(– = not applicable.)

Constellation	Abbreviation	Popular name
Andromeda	And	–
Antlia	Ant	Airpump
Apus	Aps	Bird of Paradise
Aquarius	Aqr	Water-bearer
Aquila	Aqi	Eagle
Ara	Ara	Altar
Aries	Ari	Ram
Auriga	Aur	Charioteer
Boötes	Boo	Herdsman
Caelum	Cae	Chisel
Camelopardalis	Cam	Giraffe
Cancer	Cnc	Crab
Canes Venatici	CVn	Hunting Dogs
Canis Major	CMa	Great Dog
Canis Minor	CMi	Little Dog
Capricornus	Cap	Goat
Carina	Car	Keel
Cassiopeia	Cas	–
Centaurus	Cen	Centaur
Cepheus	Cep	–
Cetus	Cet	Sea Monster, Whale
Chamaeleon	Cha	Chameleon
Circinus	Cir	Compasses
Columba	Col	Dove
Coma Berenices	Com	Berenice's Hair
Corona Australis	CrA	Southern Crown
Corona Borealis	CrB	Northern Crown

(continued)

Constellations (*continued*)

Constellation	Abbreviation	Popular name
Corvus	Crv	Crow
Crater	Crt	Cup
Crux	Cru	Southern Cross
Cygnus	Cyn	Swan
Delphinus	Del	Dolphin
Dorado	Dor	Goldfish
Draco	Dra	Dragon
Equuleus	Equ	Foal
Eridanus	Eri	River
Fornax	For	Furnace
Gemini	Gem	Twins
Grus	Gru	Crane
Hercules	Her	–
Horologium	Hor	Clock
Hydra	Hya	Watersnake
Hydrus	Hyi	Little Snake
Indus	Ind	American Indian
Lacerta	Lac	Lizard
Leo	Leo	Lion
Leo Minor	LMi	Little Lion
Lepus	Lep	Hare
Libra	Lib	Balance
Lupus	Lup	Wolf
Lynx	Lyn	–
Lyra	Lyr	Harp
Mensa	Men	Table
Microscopium	Mic	Microscope
Monoceros	Mon	Unicorn
Musca	Mus	Fly
Norma	Nor	Level, Square
Octans	Oct	Octant
Ophiuchus	Oph	Serpent-bearer
Orion	Ori	–
Pavo	Pav	Peacock
Pegasus	Peg	Flying Horse
Perseus	Per	–
Phoenix	Phe	Phoenix
Pictor	Pic	Painter
Pisces	Psc	Fishes
Piscis Austrinus	PsA	Southern Fish
Puppis	Pup	Poop, Stern
Pyxis	Pyx	Compass
Reticulum	Ret	Net
Sagitta	Sge	Arrow
Sagittarius	Sgr	Archer
Scorpius	Sco	Scorpion
Sculptor	Scl	Sculptor's Tools
Scutum	Sct	Shield
Serpens	Ser	Serpent
Sextans	Sex	Sextant
Taurus	Tau	Bull
Telescopium	Tel	Telescope
Triangulum	Tri	Triangle
Triangulum Australe	TrA	Southern Triangle
Tucana	Tuc	Toucan
Ursa Major	UMa	Great Bear
Ursa Minor	UMi	Little Bear
Vela	Vel	Sails
Virgo	Vir	Virgin
Volans	Vol	Flying Fish
Vulpecula	Vul	Fox

Some Major Comets

A comet is a small, icy body orbiting the Sun, usually on a highly elliptical path. Comets consist of a central nucleus a few kilometres across, and are often likened to dirty snowballs because they consist mostly of ice mixed with dust. As a comet approaches the Sun, it warms up, releasing gas and dust to form a coma (halo). Many comets have tails – these always point away from the Sun and are made up of gas and dust particles.
(– = not applicable.)

Name	First recorded sighting	Orbital period (yrs)	Interesting facts
Halley's comet	240 BC	76	parent of Eta Aquarid and Orionid meteor
Comet Tempel-Tuttle	1366	33	parent of Leonid meteors
Biela's comet	1772	6.6	broke in half in 1846; not seen since 1852
Encke's comet	1786	3.3	parent of Taurid meteors
Comet Swift-Tuttle	1862	130	parent of Perseid meteors; reappeared 1992
Comet Ikeya-Seki	1965	880	so-called 'Sun-grazing' comet, passed 500,000 km/300,000 mi above surface of the Sun on 21 October 1965
Comet Kohoutek	1973	–	observed from space by *Skylab* astronauts
Comet West	1975	500,000	nucleus broke into four parts
Comet Bowell	1980	–	ejected from Solar System after close encounter with Jupiter
Comet IRAS-Araki-Alcock	1983	–	passed only 4.5 million km/2.8 million mi from the Earth on 11 May 1983
Comet Austin	1989	–	passed 32 million km/20 million mi from the Earth in 1990
Comet Shoemaker-Levy 9	1993	–	made up of 21 fragments; crashed into Jupiter in July 1994
Comet Hale-Bopp	1995	3,500	produces a coma, a surrounding hazy cloud of gas and dust, of greater volume than the Sun; the bright coma is due to an outgassing of carbon monoxide; clearly visible with the naked eye in March 1997
Comet Hyakutake	1996	–	passed 15 million km/9.3 million mi from the Earth in 1996; has the longest-known comet tail (550 million km/342 million mi)

Solar and Lunar Eclipses

This table does not include partial eclipses of the Moon.
(– = not applicable.)

Month	Day	Type of eclipse	Duration of totality	Region for observation
2001				
January	9	lunar total	1 hr 2 min	Africa, Europe, Asia
June	21	solar total	4 min 57 sec	central and southern Africa
December	14	solar annular	3 min 53 sec	Pacific Ocean
2002				
June	10	solar annular	0 min 23 sec	Pacific Ocean
December	4	solar total	2 min 4 sec	southern Africa, Indian Ocean, Australia

(*continued*)

Solar and Lunar Eclipses *(continued)*

Month	Day	Type of eclipse	Duration of totality	Region for observation
2003				
May	16	lunar total	0 hr 53 min	the Americas, eastern and western Africa
May	31	solar annular	3 min 37 sec	Iceland, Greenland
November	9	lunar total	0 hr 24 min	the Americas, Africa, Europe
November	23	solar total	1 min 57 sec	Antarctica
2004				
April	19	solar partial	–	Antarctica, southern Africa
May	4	lunar total	1 hr 16 min	South America, Africa, Europe, Asia, Australia
October	14	solar partial	–	northeast Asia, north Pacific as far south as Hawaii, Alaska
October	28	lunar total	1 hr 21 min	the Americas, Europe, Africa, central Asia

See also **Phases of the Moon,** p 8.

The Sun

The Sun is the star at the centre of the Solar System and is the nearest and brightest star visible from Earth. It is composed of about 70% hydrogen and 30% helium, with other elements making up less than 1%. The Sun's energy is generated by nuclear fusion reactions that turn hydrogen into helium at its centre. The gas core is far denser than mercury or lead on Earth.

The Sun is about 4.6 billion years old, with a predicted lifetime of 10 billion years. At the end of its life, it will expand to become a red giant (a large bright star with a cool surface) the size of Mars's orbit, then shrink to become a white dwarf (a small, dense, hot star).

Diameter 1,392,000 km/865,000 mi

Temperature at the surface approx. 5,800 K/5,530°C/9,986°F

Temperature at the centre approx. 15 million K/15 million°C/27 million°F

Apparent magnitude − 26.9

Absolute magnitude 4.71

Surface gravity (Earth = 1) 27.9

The Moon

The Moon is a natural satellite of Earth, with a mass 0.012 (approximately one-eightieth) that of Earth. Its average distance from Earth is 384,400 km/238,855 mi, and it orbits in a west-to-east direction every 27.32 days (the sidereal month). It spins on its axis with one side permanently turned towards Earth. The Moon has no atmosphere and was thought to have no water till ice was discovered on its surface in 1998.

The Moon is illuminated by sunlight, and goes through a cycle of phases of shadow, waxing from new (dark) via first quarter (half Moon) to full, and waning back again to new every 29.53 days (the synodic month, also known as a lunation).

Diameter 3,476 km/2,160 mi

Maximum distance from Earth (apogee) 406,740 km/252,736 mi

Minimum distance from Earth (perigee) 356,410 km/221,463 mi

Maximum surface temperature 110°C/230°F

Minimum surface temperature − 170°C/ − 274°F

Surface gravity (Earth = 1) 0.16

Space Flight

Space Exploration

The spectacular images from the Hubble Space Telescope have excited people all over the world. Shuttle servicing missions will extend its lifetime to at least 2010, while new generations of space telescopes are being launched and developed. Although planetary exploration received a blow with the loss of two Mars spacecraft in 1999, new projects are underway – one to revisit Mercury after an interval of 30 years. About 70 new satellite and space probe launches are made each year, and every planet in the Solar System except Pluto has been explored by spacecraft. There have been 215 crewed space flights and 390 people have experienced space flight. By 2050, there could be space hotels, bases on the Moon, and expeditions to Mars.

Successful Satellite Launches

As of March 2000.

Country	Launch site	First success date	Number of successes 1957–99
Russia/CIS	Tyuratam (Baikonur), Kazakhstan	4 October 1957	1,050
	Kapustin Yar, Russia	16 March 1962	84
	Plesetsk, Russia	17 March 1966	1,468
	Svobodny, Russia	8 March 1997	2
USA	Cape Canaveral (Eastern Test Range) and Kennedy Space Center	1 February 1958	609
	Vandenberg AFB (Western Test Range)	28 February 1959	565
	Wallops Island	16 February 1961	35
	US operated air-launch	5 April 1990	24
	Sea Launch offshore platform	28 March 1999	2
France	Hammaguir	26 November 1965 (closed since April 1967)	4
USA/Italy	Indian Ocean Platform (San Marco)	26 April 1967	9

(continued)

Successful Satellite Launches (*continued*)

Country	Launch site	First success date	Number of successes 1957–99
Australia/UK	Woomera	29 November 1967 (closed since 1976)	2
Japan	Uchinoura (Kagoshima)	11 February 1970	23
	Tanegashima (Osaki)	9 September 1975	31
France/Europe	Kourou	10 March 1970	129
China	Jiuquan	24 April 1970	24
	Xichang	29 January 1984	25
	Taiyuan	6 September 1988	15
India	Sriharikota	18 July 1980	9
Israel	Palmachim	19 September 1988	3

Space Probes: Recent Key Dates

4 July 1997 The NASA *Mars Pathfinder* becomes the third spacecraft to soft land on Mars. It deploys a micro-roving vehicle called *Sojourner*. The *Mars Pathfinder* images are posted on Internet Web sites and accessed by millions of people all over the world.

11 September 1997 NASA's *Mars Global Surveyor* enters orbit around the Red Planet to begin a highly successful mission which continues into 2000, taking high resolution images of almost the entire Martian surface, as well as gathering vital climate data.

15 October 1997 The NASA–European Space Agency (ESA) *Cassini-Huygens* mission gets underway with the successful launch of a Titan IV Centaur booster from Cape Canaveral. *Cassini* will enter orbit around Saturn in July 2004 and will deploy the ESA *Huygens* spacecraft to land on Titan, the largest moon of the ringed planet.

6 January 1998 NASA's *Lunar Prospector* is launched by an Athena 2 rocket from Cape Canaveral and enters orbit around the Moon to conduct a comprehensive survey of the Moon's chemical composition, including a discovery, announced in March 1998, that there could be water ice beneath the surface of the polar regions. *Lunar Prospector* later impacts the south pole of the Moon on 31 July 1999 but no trace of water is found in the resulting impact plume.

April 1998 Daniel Goldin, the administrator of NASA, gives the go-ahead for the development of the fourth and last *Great Observatory* series spacecraft, the Space Infrared Telescope Facility, to be launched in 2001. The *Great Observatory* series includes the Hubble Space Telescope which was launched in 1990.

4 July 1998 Japan launches its first probe to explore Mars using an M5 booster from Kagoshima. Called *Planet B* or *Nozomi*, the spacecraft was scheduled to reach the Red Planet via flybys of the Moon in October and December 1998 and a flyby of the Earth in October 1999 but will not reach Mars until 2003 due to flight path deviations.

24 October 1998 The first spacecraft in NASA's New Millennium programme, called *Deep Space 1*, is launched aboard a Delta II booster from Cape Canaveral, to demonstrate a range of new technologies needed for future Solar System exploration, including ion propulsion and 'intelligent spacecraft' systems during a flight that featured a flyby of an asteroid in 1999.

11 December 1998 The *Mars Climate Orbiter* is launched by a Delta II from Cape Canaveral as part of NASA's long-term exploration of Mars. However, due to a metric–imperial value data error – made during the manufacture of the spacecraft – the craft makes a wrong approach to Mars and crashes into the Martian surface during the planned orbital insertion burn on 23 September 1999.

3 January 1999 The second programme spacecraft, the *Mars Polar Lander*, is launched by another Delta II from Cape Canaveral but is also lost (on 6 December 1999) as it attempts to make a soft landing in a region close to the Red Planet's south pole. The dual loss of the Mars missions is a major blow to NASA and to the future exploration of Mars.

> *This is so dumb. There seems to have developed across the whole space community a systematic problem of insufficient attention to detail.*
>
> John Logsdon, Director of the Space Policy Unit, George Washington University, on the loss of NASA's Mars probe as a result of a mix-up between metric and imperial measurements, *Daily Telegraph*, 2 October 1999.

7 April 1999 The European Space Agency's *Mars Express* mission is given formal approval with a contract to build the Mars orbiting spacecraft. *Mars Express* will be launched in 2003, entering orbit in December of that year. A UK piggy-back spacecraft, *Beagle 2*, will land on the Martian surface.

June 1999 NASA gives formal approval to the development of the Next Generation Space Telescope (NGST) to succeed the Hubble Space Telescope and to be launched in about 2008. NASA also says that Hubble will remain operational until 2010 and may be brought back to Earth aboard the space shuttle.

23 July 1999 The space shuttle *Columbia* STS 93 is launched and deploys the Chandra X-Ray Observatory, NASA's third *Great Observatory* series spacecraft, into orbit.

July 1999 NASA gives approval for two new Discovery programme spacecraft: *Messenger*, which will make two close flybys of the planet Mercury in 2008, the first such mission since *Mariner 10* in 1974; and *Deep Impact*, a mission to penetrate the comet P/Tempel in July 2005.

10 December 1999 The European Space Agency's 'X-Ray Multi Mirror' telescope is launched by an Arianespace *Ariane 5* booster from Kourou, French Guiana.

March 2000 NASA scientists announce that they may have to crash the *Galileo* probe in order to prevent it from contaminating Europa, one of Jupiter's moons, with microbes from Earth. They believe their best chance of locating extraterrestrial life within our Solar System is on Europa.

Astronauts: Selected Biographies

Neil Armstrong (1930–) US astronaut and the first person to walk on the Moon. Armstrong was a former US Navy fighter pilot and civilian rocket plane test pilot who joined NASA's astronaut corps in 1962. He flew the first space docking mission, *Gemini 8* in 1966, and commanded *Apollo 11*, piloting the first crewed lunar landing. On 21 July 1969 Armstrong became the first person to walk on the Moon, famously saying 'That's one small step for [a] man, one giant leap for mankind.'

Sergei Avdeyev (1956–) Russian cosmonaut. A civilian flight engineer selected in 1985, Avdeyev has clocked up a world record 748 days of space flight time during three missions aboard the *Mir* space station, *Soyuz* TM15, 22, and 28 in 1992, 1995, and 1998.

Frank Borman (1928–) US astronaut. A former US Air Force test pilot and NASA 1962 astronaut class member, Borman commanded a record-breaking 14-day *Gemini 7* Earth orbit mission in December 1965 and the first human mission to the Moon. *Apollo 8* was launched on 21 December 1968 and made ten Moon orbits.

Eileen Collins (1956–) US astronaut and the first female space flight commander. A NASA Group 13 astronaut and US Air Force pilot, Collins piloted two space shuttle missions before leading the space shuttle STS 93 mission launched on 23 July 1999.

Pete Conrad (1930–1999) US astronaut. Conrad flew two Gemini missions in 1965–66, became the third man on the Moon on *Apollo 12* in 1969, and commanded the first *Skylab* space station mission in May 1973. During this mission he made a heroic spacewalk to save the project by freeing a jammed solar panel. Conrad died in a motorcycle accident.

Micheal Foale (1957–) British-born US astronaut. Selected as an astronaut candidate in 1987, Foale spent 134 days on the *Mir* space

Astronauts: Selected Biographies *(continued)*

station in 1997, helping to carry out repairs and maintenance to the mechanical systems. In December 1999 he served on the STS 103 mission to repair and upgrade the Hubble Space Telescope.

Yuri Gagarin (1934–1968) Soviet cosmonaut and the first person in space. A Soviet Air Force pilot, Gagarin was selected in 1959 among the first cosmonaut detachment. He became a world hero as the first person in space, making one orbit aboard *Vostok 1* launched on 12 April 1961. He did not make another space flight and was killed in an air crash.

John Glenn (1921–) US astronaut and politician. A former US Marine pilot and member of the original Mercury Seven astronauts, Glenn became the first American to orbit the Earth, on the third Mercury mission on 20 February 1962. After a distinguished Congressional career, Glenn returned to space aboard Space Shuttle STS 95 in November 1998 at the age of 77, becoming the oldest person in space.

Gus Grissom (1926–1967) US astronaut. A former US Air Force test pilot and one of the Mercury Seven astronauts selected in 1959, Grissom flew the second *Mercury* sub-orbital mission in July 1961, and commanded the first crewed *Gemini* mission, *Gemini 3*, in March 1965. He died in the *Apollo 1* spacecraft fire on 27 January 1967.

Vladimir Komarov (1927–1967) Soviet cosmonaut. One of the first cosmonauts selected in 1959, Komarov flew as commander of the three-person *Voskhod* mission in October 1964. He piloted the ill-fated and trouble-plagued *Soyuz 1* orbital flight which ended in disaster on 24 April 1967 when a parachute failed to open and plummeted to the ground with Komarov inside the capsule.

Alexei Leonov (1934–) Soviet cosmonaut. A member of the first cosmonaut detachment in 1959, as pilot of *Voskhod 2*, Leonov became the first person to make a spacewalk on 18 March 1965. He was earmarked as the first Soviet to walk on the Moon had the cancelled programme gone ahead. Leonov also commanded the Soviet side of the *Apollo–Soyuz* Test Project mission in 1975 in which a *Soyuz* and *Apollo* spacecraft docked in orbit.

James Lovell (1928–) US astronaut. Lovell flew *Gemini* missions *7* and *12* in 1965–66 and *Apollo 8* around the Moon in December 1968. He commanded the mission of *Apollo 13* which was launched on 11 April 1970. *Apollo 13* entered the history books as the 'great space rescue'. The crippled craft made it safely back to the Earth after an aborted Moon landing mission. A commercially successful film *Apollo 13* was made in 1995.

Shannon Lucid (1943–) US astronaut. Lucid was selected as a NASA Group 8 Shuttle mission specialist astronaut in 1978. She flew five space shuttle missions between 1985 and 1996, the last of which, launched on 26 March 1996, delivered her to the *Mir* space station for a mission in which she clocked up a record-breaking 188 days in space, the most time by a female and by any US astronaut on a single mission. Lucid has also flown in space for a US record 223 days on her five space flights.

Bruce McCandless (1937–) US astronaut. A Group 5 NASA astronaut selected in 1966 for a potential *Apollo* mission, McCandless did not get into space until 3 February 1984 as a mission specialist on space shuttle STS 41B. McCandless helped develop the Manned Manoeuvring Unit which he used to become the first person to fly as an independent satellite during a spacewalk on the 41B mission.

Valeri Poliakov (1942–) Soviet cosmonaut and physician. Poliakov joined the cosmonaut team in 1972 and was launched aboard *Soyuz* TM18 on 8 January 1994, flying a record-breaking mission lasting 478 days, the longest single mission flight time. Having already made an earlier spaceflight, Poliakov has accumulated 678 days of space experience.

Sally Ride (1951–) US astronaut, astrophysicist, and the first US woman in space. A NASA Group 8 mission specialist astronaut, Ride was selected in 1978 and became the first US female in space aboard space shuttle STS 7 launched on 18 June 1983. Ride also flew another mission in 1984.

Svetlana Savitskaya (1948–) Soviet cosmonaut and the first woman to make a spacewalk. A record-breaking test pilot, Savitskaya joined the cosmonaut team in 1980 and made two *Soyuz* missions in 1982 and 1984. On her second mission she became the first female to make a spacewalk; it lasted 3 hours, 35 minutes.

Helen Sharman (1963–) British astronaut and the first Briton in space. A research chemist, Sharman was chosen from 13,000 applicants for a 1991 joint UK–Soviet space flight. She was launched on 18 May 1991 aboard *Soyuz TM-12* and spent six days on the *Mir* space station.

Alan Shepard (1923–1998) US astronaut and the first American in space. Shepard was the first 1959 Group 1 NASA astronaut to fly into space on a sub-orbital *Mercury Redstone* mission on 5 May 1961. He subsequently commanded *Apollo 14*, becoming the fifth man to walk on the Moon in February 1971. He died of leukaemia.

Anatoli Solovyov (1938–) Soviet cosmonaut. Solovyov was selected in 1979 and flew five missions to the *Mir* space station between 1988 and 1997 – including a launch aboard space shuttle STS 71 in June 1995 – on which he made a record 14 spacewalks, accumulating over 60 hours of EVA experience.

Valentina Tereshkova (1937–) Soviet cosmonaut and the first woman in space. An amateur parachutist, Tereshkova became the first woman to make a space flight when she was launched in *Vostok 6* on 16 June 1963. The flight lasted 70 hours 50 minutes. She never made another flight.

John Young (1930–) US astronaut. Young forged a career spanning four decades and is still an active astronaut. He flew as pilot of *Gemini 3* in 1965, commander of *Gemini 10* in 1966, command module pilot of *Apollo 10* in 1969, commander of *Apollo 16* – becoming the seventh man on the Moon – in 1972, commander of the first space shuttle mission in 1981, and commander of STS 9 in 1983.

Selected Forthcoming Missions of the European Space Agency

As of March 2000.

Proposed date	Mission	Remarks
June–July 2000	Cluster II	four identical satellites designed to provide the first three-dimensional images of events in the Earth's space environment
2001	Integral	international gamma-ray laboratory; a satellite for observations at gamma-ray wavelengths
late 2001	Smart-1	experimental space probe; the first European project to demonstrate solar electric propulsion
January 2003	Rosetta	space probe to rendezvous with Comet Wirtanen in 2011; Rosetta will release two landers which will sample the comet's nucleus
2003	Mars Express	Mars orbiter that will land craft to analyse the surface
2004	Columbus	pressurized laboratory 6.7 m/22 ft long and 4.5 m/15 ft in diameter, to be launched by the space shuttle
2007	FIRST/ Planck	far infrared and submillimetric space telescope and cosmic ray observatory combined into one mission

Most Space Flights and Walks

As of March 2000.

Record	Name	Country	Number
Space flights			
Men	Curt Brown	USA	6
	Franklin Chang-Díaz	USA	
	Story Musgrave	USA	
	Jerry Ross	USA	
	John Young	USA	
Women	Bonnie Dunbar	USA	5
	Tamara Jernigan	USA	
	Shannon Lucid	USA	
	Janice Voss	USA	
Spacewalks			
Men	Anatoli Solovyov	USSR/Russia/CIS	14
Women	Kathryn Thornton	USA	3

■ Space Flight

Selected World Space Agencies

Commonwealth of Independent States (CIS)
Russian Space Agency (RKA), Shchepkin Street 42, 129857 Moscow; phone: +7 095 971 9176; Web site: www.rka.ru/english

Europe
European Space Agency (ESA), 8–10 rue Mario-Nikis, 75738 Paris Cedex 15; phone: +33 1 5369 7654; fax: +33 1 5369 7560; e-mail: esaweb@esrin.esa.it; Web site: www.esrin.esa.it

France
Office National d'Études et de Recherches Aérospatiales (ONERA) (The French National Aerospace Research Establishment), Toulouse Research Center (ONERA-CERT), BP 4025-31055, Toulouse Cedex 4, France; phone: +33 562 25 25 25; Web site: www.cert.fr

Germany
Deutsches Zentrum für Luft- und Raumfahrt (DLR) (German Aerospace Centre), Linder Hoehe, 51147 Köln (Cologne), Germany; phone: +49 2203 601 2116; fax: +49 2203 601 3249; e-mail: info@dlr.de; Web site: www.dlr.de

Ireland, Republic of
Enterprise Ireland, Glasnevin, Dublin 9; phone +353 1 808 2000; fax: +353 1 808 2020; e-mail: client.service@enterprise-ireland.com; Web site: www.enterprise-ireland.com

Italy
Agenzia Spaziale Italiana (ASI), Via di Villa Patrizi 13, 00161 Rome; phone: +39 06 85 679; fax: +39 06 44 04 212; Web site: www.asi.it

UK
British National Space Centre (BNSC), 151 Buckingham Palace Road, London SW1W 9SS; phone: 020 7215 0806/7; fax: 020 7215 0936; e-mail: information@BNSC-HQ.cc.Mail.compuserve.com; Web site: www.bnsc.gov.uk/

USA
National Aeronautics and Space Administration (NASA), 300 East Street SW, Washington, DC; phone: +1 202 358 0000; fax: +1 202 358 0037; e-mail: library@hq.nasa.gov; Web site: www.nasa.gov

Computing and Telecommunications

Getting onto the Net

The number of people who can connect to the Internet at home or at work keeps rising, but according to the government, Internet usage in the UK is still not high enough. At the start of 2000, one in every two people in the USA was an Internet user; in the UK, the figure was reported to be one in five. The government announced plans to widen PC ownership and Internet access to include poorer families as a means of increasing opportunities in both education and work.

One barrier to increased Internet use is cost. Most home PC users get online by dialling an Internet Service Provider (ISP). They often pay a monthly subscription to the ISP for the Internet connection. In addition, they pay their telephone company's local-rate call charge for all the time they spend online. The relatively high cost of making a local call in the UK has deterred many people from using the Internet on a regular basis. In the USA, most Internet subscribers pay a flat fee every month to their phone company for an unlimited amount of local-call time and a monthly subscription to their ISP for an Internet connection. As a result, people do not run up big bills surfing the Net.

Since 1998, there has been a growth in the number of UK ISPs offering free connection to the Net. Such providers make their money through offering an expensive telephone helpline, through receiving a cut from the telephone companies whenever their service is accessed, and from advertising. But even with free connection, the expense of using the phone still remains. In March 2000, the UK branch of the California-based company AltaVista announced virtually free Internet access via a toll-free (0800) telephone number. Users signing up to AltaVista's service – scheduled to begin in summer 2000 – would have to pay a start-up fee (between £35 and £50) and a modest annual subscription. The telecommunications provider ntl: subsequently offered unmetered Internet access to anyone signing up with its telephone service. Prompted by these developments and by demands for lower call charges from the UK telecommunications regulator OFTEL, BT, the main fixed-line telecoms provider, announced a package of its own. However, demand for these services has been so great that the communications companies have struggled to provide the promised services.

BT controls the 'local loop', the link between a customer's telephone and the local telephone exchange, so ultimately it controls the price of all Internet surfing by BT telephone customers, whichever ISP they use. In July 2001 BT is due to give up this monopoly and allow competitors to use the local loop: this should bring prices down.

Some Internet Terms

acceptable use set of rules enforced by a service provider or backbone network restricting the use to which their facilities may be put

access provider another term for Internet Service Provider

address a unique series of numbers and letters identifying where information is stored on the Internet. It is usually an e-mail address (identifiable by the @ sign separating the individual account from the server on which it is stored) or an Internet address, a URL

anonymous remailer service that allows Internet users to post to USENET and send e-mail without revealing their true identity or e-mail address

bang path list of routing that appears in the header of a message sent across the Internet, showing how it travelled from the sender to its destination

bitmap the description of an image in terms of a series of coloured pixels or 'bits'. All Web page images are bitmaps, usually in a compressed format such as GIFs or JPEGs

blocking software any of various software programs that work on the World Wide Web to block access to categories of information considered offensive or dangerous

blue-ribbon campaign campaign for free speech launched to protest against moves towards censorship on the Internet

bookmark facility for marking a specific place in electronic documentation to enable easy return to it. It is used in several types of software, including electronic help files and tutorials. Bookmarks are especially important on the World Wide Web, where it can be difficult to remember a uniform resource locator (URL) in order to return to it. Most Web browsers therefore have built-in bookmark facilities, where by the browser stores the URL with the page name attached. To return directly to the site, the user picks

Some Internet Terms *(continued)*

the page name from the list of saved bookmarks

Boolean logic a mathematically-based logic system that uses **Boolean operators** such as 'AND', 'OR', or 'NOT'. On the Internet it is used in search engines where it enables the user to streamline a request

'bot (short for robot) automated piece of software that performs specific tasks on the Internet. 'Bots are commonly found on multi-user dungeons (MUDs) and other multi-user role-playing game sites, where they maintain a constant level of activity even when few human users are logged on

browser any program that allows the user to search for and view data; Web browsers allow access to the World Wide Web

bulletin board centre for the electronic storage of messages. Bulletin board systems (BBSs) are usually dedicated to specific interest groups, and may carry public and private messages, notices, and programs

chat real-time exchange of messages between users of a particular system. Chat allows people who are geographically far apart to type messages to each other which are sent and received instantly. Users may join public or private 'chat rooms' to talk with other users

client any computer connected to a network or the Internet that accesses files or other data from a central computer called a server or host

cookie any piece of data, usually a variable, that is passed from a World Wide Web document to a Web browser and persists even after the browser has moved on to download another page and would have normally destroyed the variable. Typical cookies include visitor counts or visitor e-mail addresses and are designed to facilitate access to a Web site

crawler automated indexing software that scours the Web for new or updated sites

cybersex online sexual fantasy spun by two or more participants via live, online chat

cyberspace the imaginary, interactive 'worlds' created by networked computers; often used interchangeably with 'virtual world'

dialup service Internet access over an ordinary telephone line offered by an Internet Service Provider (ISP)

digital city area in cyberspace, either text-based or graphical, that uses the model of a city to make it easy for visitors and residents to find specific types of information

domain name the part of a URL, which identifies the location of the server on which the Web site is maintained. Domain names use suffixes to denote the nature of the site, and sometimes the geographical location. The most common suffixes are **.ac** (academic community), **.co**, **.com** (commercial sites), **.edu** (educational), **.net** (networks), and **.org** (non-profit organizations), although InterNIC, the company that registers and controls domain names has recently introduced more. Locator suffixes include **.uk** and **.ie** (for Ireland); there is no locator suffix for the USA, being the default location. 'www.helicon.co.uk' is thus identified as a commercial Web site operating from within the UK

dot com term for businesses operating wholly or substantially over the Internet. Taken from the **.com** suffix in many of their domain names

download the transfer of files or data from a remote computer to the user's computer. The Internet is entirely based on the downloading of information (usually HTML) to be resolved by a browser. A **download**, used as a noun, usually refers to a substantial file, or one which needs an additional program (or 'plug-in') besides the browser to be viewed or run

Dynamic HTML (or **DHTML**) a version of HTML that directly incorporates Java, and allows greater control by Web site designers. Being relatively new, it is not supported by older Web browsers

e-commerce (also known as **e-business**) selling and buying goods and services online through sites on the World Wide Web that have been set up by companies or other commercial organizations

e-mail (contraction of **electronic mail**) system for sending messages over the Internet from one user to another or to a list of users

emoticon (contraction of **emotion** and **icon**) symbol composed of punctuation marks designed to express some form of emotion in the form of a human face

e-zine (contraction of **electronic magazine**) periodical sent by e-mail

FAQ (abbreviation for **frequently asked questions**) file of answers to commonly asked questions on any topic

firewall security system built to block access to a particular computer or network while still allowing some types of data to flow in and out on to the Internet

flame angry public or private electronic mail message used to express disapproval of breaches of netiquette or the voicing of an unpopular opinion

frames the division of a browser window into two or more sections that can load different Web pages independently. Frames are frequently used to aid the navigation of a large Web site, where one frame retains a menu or contents page

freeware software made available for download on the Internet for free usage and redistribution with no conditions attached, as opposed to **shareware**, which requires a fee to be paid after a 'trial' period. Freeware is distributed for a range of reasons from altruism though to the supply of a free, low-level version of a product to encourage its use, whilst more sophisticated elements must be purchased

GIF (acronym for **Graphics Interchange Format**) the most common image format on Web sites; compressed for storage and rapid download, but limited to 256 colours. GIFs are frequently used, despite the faster downloads and greater colour facility of other image formats, because they can be 'transparent' or 'animated'; allowing a smoother look to a Web page

FTP (abbreviation for **File Transfer Protocol**) protocol that controls the transfer of computer files between a server and a client over the Internet. FTP is similar to HTTP but is not limited to the World Wide Web

gateway the point of contact between two wide-area networks

Gopher menu-based server on the Internet that indexes resources and retrieves them according to user choice via any one of several built-in methods such as FTP or Telnet. Gopher servers can also be accessed via the World Wide Web and searched via special servers called Veronicas

Gopherspace name for the knowledge base composed of all the documents indexed on all the Gophers in the world

hit request sent to a file server. Sites on the World Wide Web often measure their popularity in numbers of hits

home page opening page on a particular site on the World Wide Web

hop intermediate stage of the journey taken by a message travelling from one site to another on the Internet

host (or host computer) large computer that supports a number of smaller computers or terminals that are connected to it via a network. Hosts may be mainframe computers that service large number of terminals or green screens, or, for example, Internet hosts that serve Web pages and files to personal computers attached via the Internet

HTML (abbreviation for **Hypertext Markup Language**) procedure for coding documents so that they can be read by a Web browser. It uses a system of tags (special codes placed between angle brackets) that format text, set up links to other documents, or add multimedia content

HTTP (abbreviation for **Hypertext Transfer Protocol**) protocol used for communications between client (the Web browser) and server on the World Wide Web

hypermedia system that uses links to lead users to related graphics, audio, animation, or video files in the same way that hypertext systems link related pieces of text

in-line graphics images included in Web pages that are displayed automatically by Web browsers without any action required by the user

Internet Relay Chat (IRC) service that allows users connected to the Internet to chat with each other over many channels

Internet Service Provider (ISP) any company that sells access to the Internet over the ordinary telephone or a dedicated connection called a leased line

The World's Top IT Companies by Market Capitalization

Rank	Company	Country[1]	Market capitalization ($ millions)[2]
1	Microsoft	USA	375,522.0
2	Intel	USA	221,394.4
3	IBM	USA	162,974.1
4	Cisco Systems	USA	161,161.1
5	Lucent Technologies	USA	140,838.3
6	Dell Computer	USA	107,982.4
7	America Online	USA	80,788.0
8	Nokia	Finland	80,190.4
9	Ericsson	Sweden	54,160.1
10	Oracle	USA	52,364.3

[1] Includes telecommunications equipment companies.
[2] Based on share price at 22 February 1999.

Source: © Financial Times 1999

Computing and Telecommunications

Some Internet Terms (*continued*)

Java an object-oriented programming language that, among other things, allows designers of pages on the World Wide Web to embed small applications called applets in their documents so as to add certain features such as animation. Java should not be confused with **Javascript**, a plain-text scripting language that can also be embedded in a Web document to accomplish certain tasks such as formatting a menu or counting visitors to a site

JPEG (pronounced 'jay-peg') with GIFs, the most common standard for image compression, named after the Joint Photographic Experts Group, who designed it. JPEG files are fast to download from Web pages but the compression system, designed around photography and naturalistic images, can cause problems with lettering

Jughead (acronym for **Jonzy's Universal Gopher Hierarchy Excavation and Display)** search engine enabling users of the Internet server Gopher to find keywords in Gopherspace directories

killfile file specifying material that you do not wish to see when accessing a newsgroup. By entering names, subjects, or phrases into a killfile, users can filter out tedious threads, offensive subject headings, spamming, or contributions from specific subscribers

link image or item of text in a World Wide Web document that acts as a route to another Web page or file on the Internet

lurk read a USENET newsgroup without making a contribution

MBONE (contraction of **multicast backbone**) layer of the Internet designed to deliver packets of multimedia data, enabling video and audio communication

MIME (acronym for **Multipurpose Internet Mail Extensions**) standard for transferring multimedia e-mail messages and World Wide Web hypertext documents over the Internet

moderator person or group of people that screens submissions to certain newsgroups and mailing lists before passing them on for wider circulation

MP3 (abbreviated for **MPEG 3rd Layer**) a type of highly compressed audio file which allows CD-quality sound to be downloaded from the Internet in reasonably short periods of time

MPEG (from **Motion Pictures Expert Group**) a file format for downloading audio-visual (multimedia) files from the Internet. Web browsers do not automatically support MPEG, and to view the downloaded file an additional application, or 'plug-in' is required

MUD (acronym for **multi-user dungeon**) interactive multi-player game, played via the Internet or modem connection to one of the participating computers. MUD players typically have to solve puzzles, avoid traps, fight other participants, and carry out various tasks to achieve their goals. Also **MUSE** (**multi-user shared environment**) and **MUSH** (**multi-user shared hallucination**)

netiquette behaviour guidelines evolved by users of the Internet including: no messages typed in upper case (considered to be the equivalent of shouting); new users, or new members of a newsgroup should read the frequently asked questions (FAQ) file before asking a question; and no advertising via USENET newsgroups

net police USENET readers who monitor and 'punish' postings which they find offensive or believe to be in breach of netiquette. Many newsgroups are policed by these self-appointed guardians

network a method of connecting computers so that they can share data and peripheral devices, such as printers. The main types are classified by the pattern of the connections – star or ring network, for example – and by the degree of geographical spread allowed; for example, local area networks (LANs) for communication within a room or building, and wide area networks (WANs) for more remote systems. The Internet is the computer network that connects online servers and computers throughout the world, with around 300 million users

newbie insulting term for a new user of a USENET newsgroup, sometimes widened to include anyone new to the Internet

newsgroup discussion group on the Internet's USENET. Newsgroups are organized in seven broad categories (the 'Big Seven'): **comp.** – computers and programming; **news.** – newsgroups themselves; **rec.** – sports and hobbies; **sci.** – scientific research and ideas; **talk.** – discussion groups; **soc.** – social issues; and **misc.** – everything else. In addition, there are alternative hierarchies such as the wide-ranging and anarchic **alt.** (alternative). Within these categories there is a hierarchy of subdivisions

newsreader program that gives access to USENET newsgroups, interpreting the standard commands understood by news servers in a simple, user-friendly interface

news server computer that stores USENET messages for access by users. Most Internet Service Providers (ISPs) offer a news server as part of the service

off-line browser program that downloads and copies Web pages onto a computer so that they can be viewed without being connected to the Internet

off-line reader program that downloads e-mail or information from newsgroups, FTP servers, or other Internet resources, storing it locally on a hard disk so that it can be read without running up a large phone bill

plug-in a smaller, additional program that runs with a Web browser to allow enhanced functionality. Most currently available Web browsers come with a series of in-built plug-ins; additional ones can be downloaded usually free of charge, and many Web sites with content which requires plug-ins offer a direct link to the relevant software

portal Web site designed to be used as a start-up site for browsing sessions and to provide a gateway to the rest of the Web

posting sending a message to a USENET newsgroup

Pretty Good Privacy (PGP) strong encryption program that runs on personal computers and is distributed on the Internet free of charge

proxy server server on the World Wide Web that 'stands in' for another server, storing and forwarding files on behalf of a computer which might be slower or too busy to deal with the request itself

router any machine that helps the efficient movement of electronic data between two computers on a network or on the Internet

search engine a program that scans the Internet for specific information by searching for keywords given by the user. Search engines vary in the manner in which they retrieve the information, and so different engines are suited to different types of information. There are a large number of Web sites given over to commercial search engines, and most recent Web browsers incorporate a search facility

server large-capacity computer that holds files centrally on a network and can be accessed by client computers connected to the network. The Internet is a global system of networks that all consist of servers and clients

signature (or **.sig**) personal information appended to a message by the sender of an e-mail message or USENET posting in order to add a human touch

shareware software available on the Internet for downloading and may be used for a limited 'trial' period, before the user is requested to pay a fee for continued usage, which also usually includes technical support and updates

spamming advertising on the Internet by broadcasting to many or all newsgroups regardless of relevance

spider program that combs the Internet for new documents such as Web pages and FTP files. Spiders start their work by retrieving a document such as a Web page and then following all the links and references contained in it

surfing exploring the Internet, especially by following a series of links rather then going straight to a specific site

TELNET program that allows an authorized user at his or her own computer to connect to another computer over the Internet and operate it remotely to access data

trolling mischievously posting a deliberately erroneous or obtuse message to a newsgroup in order to tempt others to reply – usually in a way that makes them appear gullible, intemperate, or foolish

upload the transfer of files or data from a computer to a remote server or host. It is mainly used in the maintenance and amendment of Web sites

URL (abbreviation for **Uniform Resource Locator**) series of letters and/or numbers specifying the location of a document on the World Wide Web (the 'address'). Every URL consists of a domain name, a description of the document's location within the host computer, and the name of the document itself, separated by full stops and forward strokes or slashes (/)

USENET (acronym for **users' network**) the world's largest bulletin board system, which brings together people with common interests to exchange views and information. It consists

The UK's Leading Computer Software Developers by Market Share

1999

Software developer	Market share %
Microsoft	9.0
IBM	8.0
ICL	3.5
Oracle	3.4
Misys	2.7
Computer Associates	2.5
SAP	2.2
JBA	1.9
Sage	1.4
MDIS	1.2
Others	64.2
Total	100.0

Source: UK Computer Market Review 2000, © *Key Note Ltd*

Some Internet Terms (*continued*)

of e-mail messages and articles organized into newsgroups

virus a piece of software that can replicate and transfer itself from one computer to another, without the user being aware of it. Some viruses are relatively harmless, but others can damage or destroy data. Viruses are written by anonymous programmers, often maliciously, and are spread on floppy disks, CD-ROMs, and via networks and e-mail (**worm viruses**). Antivirus software can be used to detect and destroy well-known viruses, but new viruses continually appear and these may bypass existing antivirus programs

WAP (abbreviation for **Wireless Application Protocol**) internationally recognized protocol used for communications between the Internet and a mobile phone or other wireless network, allowing the user access to e-mail and certain Web-based services

wAreZ slang for pirated games or other applications that can be downloaded using FTP

Web authoring tool program for creating Web pages. The basic Web authoring tool is HTML, the source code that determines how a Web page is constructed and how it looks when viewed with a browser. New generation versions of HTML include DHTML and the recent development, XML

Web browser client software that allows you to access the World Wide Web

Webmaster system administrator for a server or site on the World Wide Web

Web page hypertext document on the World Wide Web

Web ring a group of Internet Web sites with a common theme or interest joined together with connecting links

Web site set of related Web pages designed and set up on a Web server by a person, company, or organization and used as a point of contact with the Internet community

webzine magazine published on the World Wide Web, instead of on paper

World Wide Web (WWW) hypertext system for publishing information on the Internet. World Wide Web documents (Web pages) are text files coded using HTML to include text and graphics, stored on a special computer (Web server) connected to the Internet. Web pages may also contain Java applets for enhanced animation, video, sound, and interactivity

worm virus designed to spread from computer to computer across a network or by e-mail. Worms replicate themselves while hiding in a computer's memory, causing systems to slow down, but do not infect other programs or destroy data directly

XML (acronym for **eXtensible Mark-up Language**) a programming language for Web authoring similar to HTML, but more flexible in that it allows the designer to define tags to provide customized functionality. Whilst it has not yet replaced HTML as the Internet standard, as few Web browsers currently support it, most observers believe it will not be long before it does

(*See also* **A Selection of Acronyms and Abbreviations in Use Online,** p 439.)

Number of Hosts on the Internet

The following figures are taken from the Internet Domain Survey, carried out every six months by Network Wizards for the Internet Software Consortium. The annual figures in the table relate to the survey taken in July of each year. Each figure represents the number of computers or networks throughout the world that have a unique Internet Protocol address and have been officially assigned a name. Such a computer or network is called an Internet host. As of January 2000, Network Wizards reported that there were 72,398,092 hosts on the Internet. Since most computers have more than one user and networks consist of a varying number of individual computers, it is not possible to gain an accurate estimate of the number of individual users on the Internet. At best, such a figure would be immediately out of date because of the Internet's continual growth. (As of July 1999.)

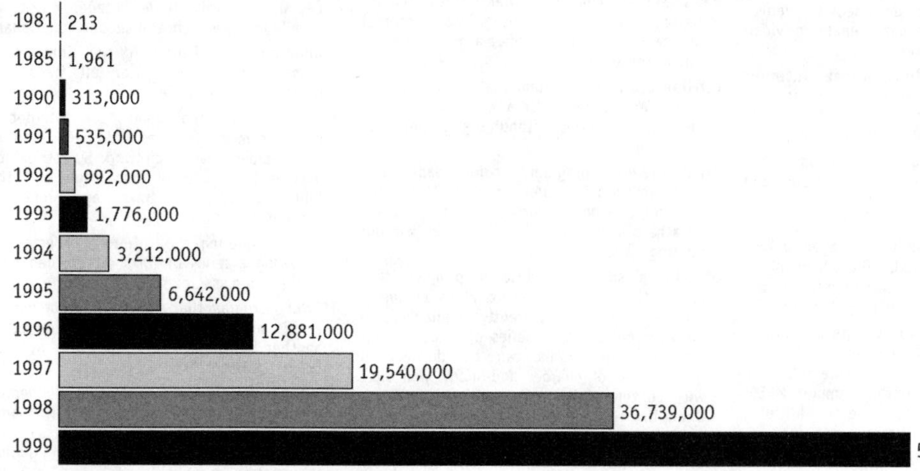

Source: Internet Software Consortium (http://www.isc.org)

Internet Service Providers

In 1999 there were about 300 Internet Service Providers (ISPs) in the UK. ISPs are of two types. One type provides a basic connection to the Internet together with technical support and certain access features, and the other type (known also as an online service provider or online content provider) offers proprietary content available only to subscribers. This content takes the form of entertainment, news and sport, information services, commercial databases, and members' forums. Online service providers (OSPs) offer access to the Internet, but this access may be limited. There were an estimated 4.3 million Internet subscribers in the UK at the end of January 2000. But the Internet is growing at a vast rate. Euromonitor forecasts that there will be 9 million subscribers by 2002. The UK ISP with the largest customer base is Freeserve, with about 1.5 million subscribers. It is followed by the UK arm of America Online (AOL), a global online content provider with a worldwide membership of more than 22 million. Some 600,000 of them are in the UK. AOL, which

Internet Service Providers *(continued)*

merged with Time Warner in January 2000, also owns CompuServe, another global online content provider with a significant share of the UK market. The third largest ISP is Demon, owned by the telecoms company Thus plc. Demon serves subscribers in the UK and the Netherlands. BT Internet and MSN Freeweb (part of the Microsoft Network) rank fourth and fifth respectively. Freeserve, owned by the electrical store chain Dixons, was an early UK example of a high street retailer offering Internet access. Others include WHSmith, Boots, and Tesco. Many ISPs offer a range of Internet connection packages. The information given in the following table relates to standard dialup accounts.

Selected Internet Service Providers

As of March 2000.

ISP	Web address	Subscription	E-mail addresses	Proprietary Content	Free Web space (MB)	Helpline
AOL	www.aol.co.uk	monthly sub	5	yes	10	free
BT Internet	www.btinternet.com	monthly sub	5	no	10	local rate
Cable & Wireless Lite	www.cwcom.net	free to C&W customers	5	yes	20	national rate
CompuServe	www.compuserve.co.uk	monthly sub	5	yes	10	national rate
ClaraNET	www.clara.net	monthly sub	unlimited	no	25	free
Demon	www.demon.net	monthly sub	unlimited	no	20	national rate
Easynet	www.easynet.co.uk	monthly sub	5	no	unlimited	free
Freeserve	www.freeserve.net	free	unlimited	yes	15	50p per minute
LineOne	www.lineone.net	free	unlimited	yes	10	50p per minute
MSN Freeweb	www.msn.co.uk	free	1	yes	none	national rate
Virgin Net	www.virgin.net	free	5	yes	10	50p per minute
Which? Online	www.which.net	monthly sub	5	yes	5	£1 per minute
WHSmith Online	www.whsmith.co.uk	free	unlimited	yes	12	national rate

The Future for Microsoft

Microsoft topped the list of global IT companies again in 1999–2000, keeping a firm hold on the PC market with the introduction of Windows 2000, the latest version of its Windows operating system. But in April 2000, its long-running anti-trust battle with the US government took another turn when a US judge found against Bill Gates's mighty corporation and ruled that it should be broken up. Microsoft, which already dominates the market in operating systems with Windows, was accused of seeking to control people's access to the World Wide Web by making its Web browser Microsoft Internet Explorer (MSIE) part of the Windows operating software. With MSIE included on their Windows CD, customers would not need to buy or obtain anyone else's browser to start Web surfing. The US government challenged Microsoft's actions as anti-competitive and won its case.

Has this shaken Microsoft's dominance? Its share price fell by 14% around the time that the court decision was announced, and Bill Gates – the richest man in the world – saw his personal fortune fall by hundreds of millions of dollars. Gates was set to appeal against the decision, seeing it as an attack upon the innovative spirit of his company and an overturning of the global development of personal computing. Since its foundation in 1977, Microsoft has played the leading role in the history of that development. It is hard to imagine a world in which Microsoft did not continue to be an active and ubiquitous player.

The UK's Leading Computer Services Companies by Market Share

1999

Company	Market share %
EDS	8.6
IBM	7.9
Cap Gemini	4.9
ICL	4.2
Reuters Group	4.0
Andersen Consulting	3.5
Computer Sciences Corporation	3.5
Compaq/Digital	2.7
Sema Group	2.4
Siemens	2.3
Oracle	1.9
Syntegra	1.8
Computercenter	1.8
KPMG Consulting	1.8
Capita Group	1.7
Unisys	1.7
Logica	1.6
Delphi Group	1.6
PriceWaterhouseCoopers	1.6
Others	40.5
Total	100.0

Source: UK Computer Market Review 2000, © *Key Note Ltd*

Household Penetration of Computers in Selected Countries

Country	Household penetration %	Year
Austria	30.8	1998
Belgium	33.0	1998
Denmark[1]	46.7	1999
Finland	44.0	1999
France	22.8	1998
Germany	39.0	1999
Ireland, Republic of	22.0	1997
Italy	26.6	1998
Luxembourg	44.0	1998
Netherlands	58.8	1998
Norway	53.0	1998
Portugal[2]	33.1	1998
Slovenia	34.1	1998
Spain	28.4	1998
Sweden	59.8	1998
Turkey	20.0	1997
UK	35.2	1998

[1] Figure relates to fixed PCs only.
[2] Figure relates to adult (15+) population in mainland Portugal.

Source: European Marketing Pocket Book 2000, *NTC Publications Ltd*

The UK's Leading Computer Hardware Manufacturers by Market Share

1999

Manufacturer	Market share %
Compaq/Digital	13.7
IBM	7.4
Hewlett-Packard	7.4
Dell	6.0
ICL	5.0
Toshiba	3.5
NEC/Packard Bell	3.3
OT Group	2.5
Seagate Technology	2.4
Siemens	2.4
3Com	2.3
Canon	1.7
Sun Microsystems	1.5
Granville Technology (Time)	1.1
Gateway 2000	1.0
Others	38.8
Total	100.0

Source: UK Computer Market Review 2000, © *Key Note Ltd*

See also **The Dot-Com Bubble,** p 677.

Use of Computers by UK Adults by Socio-economic Breakdown

The reasons given represent the first response of adults surveyed. In percentages.

2000

Category	Educational purposes	Using e-mail	Accessing Internet	Playing games	Hobbies	Using CD-ROMs	Working from home	Faxes	Household expenditure
All adults[1]	10	8	7	7	6	5	5	4	2
Sex									
male	9	10	8	9	6	6	4	5	2
female	11	7	7	5	5	3	5	3	2
Age									
16–24	23	11	11	17	3	9	9	1	1
25–34	11	12	9	11	6	6	6	4	3
35–44	12	9	12	8	7	6	6	7	2
45–64	6	6	5	3	8	3	4	6	3
65+	3	2	1	1	2	1	1	1	1
Social grade									
AB	13	12	9	4	7	6	9	6	3
C1	12	13	8	8	8	5	5	4	4
C2	8	6	7	12	5	6	4	4	0
DE	8	3	5	5	4	3	3	2	1
Region									
Scotland/North	11	7	4	10	5	5	4	3	1
Midlands/Wales	8	6	9	7	6	3	5	5	2
South	10	10	8	5	6	6	5	5	3

[1] A base of 1,054 adults was used for the above table.

Source: The Gallup Organization

Telephone Ownership in Selected Countries

1998

Country	Total number of lines (thousands)	Per hundred inhabitants
Luxembourg	293.1	69.17
Sweden	5,965.0	67.37
USA	179,822.1	66.10
Canada	19,206.0	63.50
Germany	46,530.0	56.72
Singapore	1,777.9	56.20
UK	32,829.0	55.69
Australia	9,540.0	50.93
Japan	63,580.0	50.26
Argentina	7,132.0	19.74
South Africa	3,075.4	12.47
China	87,420.9	6.96
Congo, Democratic Republic of	22.0	0.79
Chad	8.6	0.12

Source: Industry Overview, © *International Telecommunication Union 1998, reproduced by permission of the ITU*

■ Computing and Telecommunications

The UK Computer Hardware Market by Sector and Value

(In millions of pounds.)

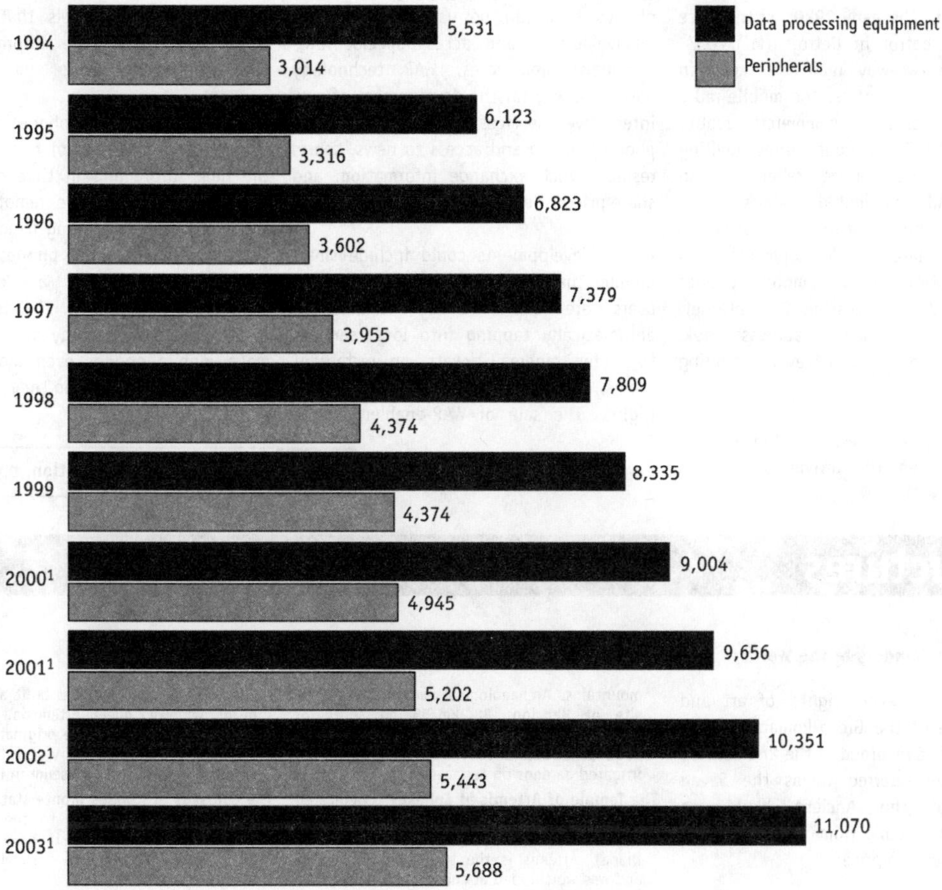

Year	Data processing equipment	Peripherals
1994	5,531	3,014
1995	6,123	3,316
1996	6,823	3,602
1997	7,379	3,955
1998	7,809	4,374
1999	8,335	4,374
2000[1]	9,004	4,945
2001[1]	9,656	5,202
2002[1]	10,351	5,443
2003[1]	11,070	5,688

[1] Data for 2000-03 are forecast.

Source: UK Computer Market Review 2000, © *Key Note Ltd*

See also **Music Online,** p 423; **E-Shopping,** p 330; **A Brief Guide to 'Netiquette',** p 439; **Emoticons,** p 439; **A Selection of Acronyms and Abbreviations in Use Online,** p 439; **B2B: Trading and the Internet,** p 660.

Mobile Phone Ownership in Selected Countries

(N/A = not available.)

Country	Cellular mobile subscribers (thousands)			Per hundred inhabitants
	1997	1998	1999	1999
Finland	2,148.1	2,946.9	3,416.0	66.14
Norway	1,676.8	2,107.0	2,744.8	61.75
Sweden	3,169.0	4,108.0	5,125.0	57.83
Singapore	848.6	1,094.7	1,531.7	47.50
Japan	38,253.9	47,307.6	56,849.0	44.94
UK	8,933.0	14,874.0	23,944.0	40.76
Australia	4,893.0	5,342.0	6,501.0	34.38
USA	55,312.3	69,209.3	86,047.0	31.15
Germany	8,170.0	13,913.0	23,470.0	28.56
Canada	4,207.0	5,320.0	7,000.0	22.96

Source: Industry Overview, © *International Telecommunication Union 1999, reproduced by permission of the ITU*

The Mobile Phenomenon

In 1990 there were just over 11 million mobile phones worldwide. In 2000 there are nearly 400 million. By 2004 there may be as many as 1 billion, exceeding the number of fixed phones.

Two out of every five people in the UK own a mobile phone.

The Rise and Rise of the Mobile Phone

The birth of mobile telecommunications dates back to the early 1920s when police officers on patrol in Detroit (MI), USA, used bulky two-way radios to keep in touch with headquarters. The mobile radio telephone became a commercial reality in 1946, but without direct-dialling capabilities the service relied on an operator and was limited. Today's digital mobile telephones marry cellular radio to the latest developments in computerization. Modern mobile phones can be used for accessing the Internet, managing an electronic address book, checking e-mail, and even sending pictures.

The industry's biggest development in 2000 has been the arrival of wireless application protocol (WAP)-enabled mobile phones that can be used to send and receive e-mail and access special WAP-compliant Web sites. WAP technology paves the way for the development of new interactive services, including mobile-phone banking and access to news, sports results, stock exchange information, and share prices, no matter where you are.

Future developments could include smart mobiles that will know exactly where their users are and will be capable of automatically tapping into local services to order cinema tickets or restaurant tables, call taxis, or book train journeys or flights. The sale of WAP-enabled mobile phones started in the UK during summer 2000, but newer models that download faster and store more information are already being developed.

The number of mobile phones is destined to surpass the number of fixed phones in the near future and in time could make them obsolete. In some remote parts of the world where installing fixed telephone lines is difficult, mobile phones are laying the foundations of a local telecommunications system. The development of WAP-based technology seems likely to make mobile phones even more popular and more ubiquitous than they are now.

See also **Telephone Information**, pp 306–307.

Structures

The Seven Wonders of the World

The canon of seven 'sights' of art and architecture of the Greco-Roman classical world was first recorded in the 2nd century BC. Generally referred to as the Seven Wonders of the Ancient World, to distinguish them from more recent wonders, they comprise:

The Pyramids of Egypt are the three pyramids at Gîza, near Cairo. Pyramids were used in ancient Egypt to enclose a royal tomb; for example, the Great Pyramid of Khufu/Cheops at El Gîza, which measures 230 m/755 ft square and 147 m/481 ft high.

The Hanging Gardens of Babylon in the capital of Mesopotamia. According to legend, King Nebuchadnezzar constructed the gardens in the 6th century BC for one of his wives who was homesick for her birthplace in the Iranian mountains. Archaeological excavations at the site of Babylon, 88 km/55 mi south of Baghdad in modern Iraq, have uncovered a huge substructure that may have supported irrigated gardens on terraces.

The Temple of Artemis at Ephesus is dedicated to the Greek goddess of chastity, the young of all creatures, the Moon, and the hunt (Roman Diana). Artemis is the twin sister of Apollo and was worshipped at cult centres throughout the Greek world, one of the largest of which was at Ephesus.

The Statue of Zeus at Olympia, in gold and ivory, was made by the Greek sculptor Phidias. It was later removed to Constantinople, where it was destroyed in a fire. It is thought that the face of Zeus might possibly have served as a model for the face of Christ Pantocrator in the dome of St Sophia there.

The Mausoleum at Halicarnassus the ancient city in Asia Minor (now Bodrum in Turkey). The tomb of Mausolus was built about 350 BC by his widowed queen Artemisia. Today, little remains at the site of the original monument, although some fragmentary sculptures from it are kept in the British Museum in London.

The Colossus of Rhodes bronze statue of Apollo erected at the entrance to the harbour at Rhodes 292–280 BC. Said to have been about 30 m/100 ft high, in 225 BC it fell as a result of an earthquake.

The Lighthouse of Pharos a gigantic lighthouse at the entrance to the harbour of Alexandria. It was built in the early 3rd century BC by the Macedonian kings of Egypt, Ptolemy I and Ptolemy II, and took its name from the island on which it stood. The lighthouse was repeatedly damaged by earthquakes, and any remains of the ancient structure are now concealed under the medieval fortress of Kait Bey.

Tallest Buildings in the World

Uninhabited structures, such as radio masts, are not included.
As of March 2000. (– = not applicable.)

Building/structure	City	Height m	Height ft	Storeys	Year completed
Petronas Tower 1	Kuala Lumpur, Malaysia	452	1,483	88	1996
Petronas Tower 2	Kuala Lumpur, Malaysia	452	1,483	88	1996
Sears Tower[1]	Chicago (IL), USA	443	1,454	110	1973
Jin Mao Building	Shanghai, China	420	1,379	88	1997
One World Trade Center	New York (NY), USA	417	1,368	110	1972
Two World Trade Center	New York (NY), USA	415	1,362	110	1973
Empire State Building	New York (NY), USA	381	1,250	102	1931
Central Plaza	Hong Kong, China	374	1,227	78	1992
Bank of China	Hong Kong, China	369	1,209	70	1989
The Centre	Hong Kong, China	350	1,149	73	1998

[1] Height excludes TV antennas.

Which is the World's Tallest Building?

Throughout the 20th century the race has been on to build the world's tallest building and for most of that time the USA has dominated the competition. The Sears Tower in Chicago was completed in 1973 and was generally considered to be the world's tallest for more than 20 years. However, in 1996 the twin Petronas Towers in Kuala Lumpur, Malaysia, stole the title. Or did they?

If Petronas and Sears stood alongside each other, Sears would appear taller. It has more storeys and its antennas reach a higher point. The Petronas Towers are widely regarded as the world's tallest because tradition dictates that spires count and antennas do not. The Petronas–Sears debate inspired the Council on Tall Buildings and Urban Habitat to establish four categories for measuring tall buildings and structures:

1. Height to structural or architectural top.
2. Height to highest occupied floor.
3. Height to top of roof.
4. Height to tip of antenna.

Sears already held the title in categories 2 and 3. On 5 June 2000 an extension was built on to a Sears antenna, pushing it 24 inches above the One World Trade Centre, New York, and snatching the title for category 4. But in the most important category, height to structural or architectural top, the two Petronas Towers still hold the title of the world's two tallest buildings.

Tallest Buildings in the World by Continent

As of March 2000. (N/A = not available.)

Building	City	Height m	Height ft	Storeys	Year completed
Asia					
Petronas Tower I	Kuala Lumpur, Malaysia	452	1,483	88	1996
Petronas Tower II	Kuala Lumpur, Malaysia	452	1,483	88	1996
Jin Mao Building	Shanghai, China	420	1,379	88	1997
Central Plaza	Hong Kong, China	374	1,227	78	1992
Bank of China	Hong Kong, China	369	1,209	70	1989
The Centre	Hong Kong, China	350	1,149	73	1998
Emirates Tower 1	Dubai, United Arab Emirates	350	1,149	54	1999
T&C Tower	Kaohsiung, Taiwan	347	1,140	85	1997
Shun Hing Square	Shenzhen, China	325	1,066	69	1996
CITIC Plaza	Guangzhou, China	322	1,056	80	1996
Australia					
Rialto Towers	Melbourne, Australia	251	823	61	1985
MLC Centre	Sydney, Australia	228	748	65	1978
Governor Philip Tower	Sydney, Australia	227	745	54	1993
Central Park Tower	Perth, Australia	226	742	52	1992
Bourke Place	Melbourne, Australia	224	735	48	1991
BHP Petroleum Plaza	Melbourne, Australia	220	722	52	1991
Chifley Tower	Sydney, Australia	215	705	50	1992
BankWest Tower	Perth, Australia	214	702	52	1988
Melbourne Central	Melbourne, Australia	211	692	55	1991
101 Collins Street	Melbourne, Australia	195	640	50	1991
Europe					
Commerzbank	Frankfurt, Germany	299	981	63	1997
Messeturm	Frankfurt, Germany	257	843	64	1991
MV Lomonosov State University	Moscow, Russian Federation	239	784	39	1953
1 Canada Square, Canary Wharf	London, England	236	774	56	1991
Palace of Culture and Science	Warsaw, Poland	231	758	42	1955
Tour Maine, Montparnasse	Paris, France	209	686	58	1973
DG Bank	Frankfurt, Germany	208	682	53	1993
Millennium Tower	Vienna, Austria	202	663	50	1999
Currency Stock Exchange	Moscow, Russian Federation	200	656	36	1999
Ukraine Tower	Moscow, Russian Federation	198	650	34	1961
Main Tower	Frankfurt, Germany	198	650	56	1999
North America					
Sears Tower[1]	Chicago (IL), USA	443	1,454	110	1973
One World Trade Center	New York (NY), USA	417	1,368	110	1972
Two World Trade Center	New York (NY), USA	415	1,362	110	1973
Empire State Building	New York (NY), USA	381	1,250	102	1931
Amoco Building	Chicago (IL), USA	346	1,136	80	1973
John Hancock Center	Chicago (IL), USA	344	1,127	100	1968
Chrysler Building	New York (NY), USA	319	1,046	77	1930
NationsBank Plaza	Atlanta (GA), USA	312	1,023	55	1992
Library Tower	Los Angeles (CA), USA	310	1,018	75	1990
AT&T Corporate Center	Chicago (IL), USA	306	1,007	60	1989
Rest of the world					
Carlton Centre	Johannesburg, South Africa	222	730	50	1973
Parcque Central Torre Officinas I	Caracas, Venezuela	221	725	56	1978
Parcque Central Torre Officinas II	Caracas, Venezuela	221	725	56	1979
Colpatria Tower	Bogotá, Colombia	192	630	50	1979
Coltejer	Medellín, Colombia	175	574	37	1972
Las Americas	Bogotá, Colombia	174	571	47	1974

(continued)

Tallest Buildings in the World by Continent *(continued)*

Building	City	Height (m)	Height (ft)	Storeys	Year completed
Ponte Investments Apartments	Johannesburg, South Africa	173	567	54	1973
La Nacional	Bogotá, Colombia	171	561	47	N/A
Palacio Zarzur Kogan	São Paulo, Brazil	170	557	50	1960
Edificio Italia	São Paulo, Brazil	165	542	45	1965

[1] Height excludes TV antennas.

Longest Bridges by Span in the World

Bridge	Location	Date built/opened	Length m	Length ft
Suspension spans				
Akashi-Kaikyo	Honshu–Awaji Islands, Japan	1998	1,990	6,529
Store Baelt	Zealand–Funen, Denmark	1998	1,624	5,328
Humber Bridge	Kingston-upon-Hull, England	1973–81	1,410	4,626
Jiangyin	Chang Jiang River, China	1999	1,385	4,543
Tsing Ma	Hong Kong	1997	1,377	4,518
Verrazono Narrows	Brooklyn–Staten Island, New York Harbor (NY), USA	1959–64	1,298	4,260
Golden Gate	San Francisco (CA), USA	1937	1,280	4,200
Höga Kusten	Veda, Sweden	1997	1,210	3,970
High Coast Bridge	Västernorrland, Sweden	1997	1,210	3,969
Mackinac Straits	Michigan (MI), USA	1957	1,158	3,800
Minami Bisan-Seto	Kojima-Sakaide, Japan	1988	1,100	3,609
Second Bosporus	Istanbul, Turkey	1988	1,090	3,576
First Bosporus	Golden Horn, Istanbul, Turkey	1973	1,074	3,524
George Washington	Hudson River, New York (NY), USA	1927–31	1,067	3,500
Ponte 25 Abril (Salazar)	Tagus River, Lisbon, Portugal	1966	1,013	3,323
Firth of Forth (road)	South Queensferry, Scotland	1958–64	1,006	3,300
Kita Bisan-Seto	Japan	1988	990	3,248
Severn Bridge	Beachley, England	1961–66	988	3,240
Cable-stayed spans				
Tatara	Onomichi-Imabari, Japan	1999	890	2,920
Pont de Normandie	Seine Estuary, France	1995	856	2,808
Qingzhou Minjiang	Fuzhou, China	1996	605	1,985
Yangpu	Shanghai, China	1993	602	1,975
Xupu	Shanghai, China	1997	590	1,936
Meiko Chuo	Nagoya, Japan	1997	590	1,936
Skarnsundet	near Trondheim, Norway	1991	530	1,740
Cantilever spans				
Pont de Quebec (railroad)	St Lawrence, Canada	1918	549	1,800
Firth of Forth (rail)	South Queensferry, Scotland	1882–90	521	1,710
Minato Ohashi	Osaka, Japan	1974	510	1,673
Commodore Barry	Delaware River at Chester (PA), USA	1974	501	1,644
Greater New Orleans	Mississippi River (LA), USA	1958	480	1,575
Howrah	Hooghly River, Calcutta, India	1943	457	1,500
Steel-arch spans				
New River Gorge	Fayetteville (WV), USA	1977	518	1,700
Bayonne (Killvan Kull)	New Jersey–Staten Island (NY), USA	1932	504	1,652
Sydney Harbour	Sydney, Australia	1923–32	503	1,500

Highest Railway Bridges in the World

The world's highest railway bridge (above ground) spans the Mala Rijeka Gorge near Kolasin in Yugoslavia. It consists of five steel spans on concrete piers and took 25 years to build. This table shows other bridges that are over 100 m/328 ft above ground level. (N/A = not available.)

Bridge	Railway	Location	Date opened	Height m	Height ft
Mala Rijeka Viaduct	Yugoslav Railways	Kolasin on Belgrade–Bar line	1976	198	650
Vresk	Iranian State	220 km/137 mi from Bandar Shah on Caspian Sea Trans Iranian line	1938	152	500
Fades Viaduct	French National	Clermont-Ferrand–Montluçon line	1909	133	435
Khotur	Iranian State	Khotur River near Khoi	1973	131	430
Victoria Falls	Rhodesia Railways	Livingstone	1904	128	420
Pfaffenberg–Zwenberg	Austrian Federal	Mallnitz–Spittal	1971	120	394
Viaur	French National	Tanus, Rodez–Albi	1902	116	381
Garabit Viaduct	French National	Neussargues–Béziers	1884	112	367
Müngstner	German Federal	Mügsten, over River Wupper	1897	107	350
Rio Grande	Costa Rica	near San José	N/A	105	346
Vance Creek	Simpson Timber Co	Shelton, west of Tacoma (WA), USA	1928	105	346

(continued)

■ Structures

(continued)

Bridge	Railway	Location	Date opened	Height	
				m	ft
Tramo Sobre	Former Buenos Aires Great Southern, Argentina	Rio Negro	N/A	104	344
Viaduct No 2	Turkish State	between Konakler and Günaykoy on Izmir–Afyonkarahisar line, 199.3 km/123.8 mi from Izmir	1900	103	338
Faux-Mau-Ti	China	Yunnan section	1910	102	335
Rio Chinipas	Chihuahua–Pacific Mexico	on Ojinago–Topolobampo line	N/A	101	330
Corte	Corsica	Corte	1894	100	328
Lindischgraben	Austrian Federal	Tauern Railway Obervellach–Penk	1977	100	328
Ten Tze	China	Yunnan section	1910	approx. 100	approx. 328

See also **Rail Transport**, pp 596–601.

The Highest Dams in the World

This table includes dams registered with the International Commission on Large Dams (ICOLD). Dams registered with ICOLD must be 15 m/49 ft in height or more.

Dam	Location	Height above lowest formation	
		m	ft
Rogun	Tajikistan	335	1,099
Nurek	Tajikistan	300	984
Grand Dixence	Switzerland	285	935
Inguri	Georgia	272	892
Vajont	Italy	262	869
Manuel M Torres	Mexico	261	856
Tehri	India	261	856
Avlvaro Obregon	Mexico	260	853
Mauvoisin	Switzerland	250	820
Alberto Lleras C	Colombia	243	797
Mica	Canada	243	797
Sayano-Shushenskaya	Russian Federation	242	794
Ertan	China	240	787
La Esmeralda	Colombia	237	778
Kishau	India	236	774
Oroville	USA	235	770
El Cajon	Honduras	234	768
Chirkey	Russian Federation	233	765
Bhakra	India	226	741
Cyprus	USA	226	741

Source: 1998 World Register of Dams, *International Commission on Large Dams*

Longest Vehicular Tunnels in the World

Tunnel	Location	Year opened	Length	
			km	mi
Saint Gotthard	Switzerland	1980	16.3	10.1
Arlberg	Austria	1978	14.0	8.7
Fréjus	France–Italy	1980	12.9	8.0
Mont Blanc	France–Italy	1965	11.7	7.2
Gudvangen	Norway	1992	11.4	7.1
Kan-Etsu	Japan	1991	11.0	6.8
Kan-Etsu	Japan	1985	10.9	6.8
Gran Sasso	Italy	1984	10.2	6.3
Gran Sasso	Italy	1976	10.0	6.2
Seelisberg	Switzerland	1979	9.3	5.8

Longest Railway Tunnels in the World

Tunnel	Location	Year completed	Length	
			km	mi
Seikan	Japan	1985	54	34
Channel Tunnel	UK–France	1994	50	31
Dai-Shimizu	Japan	1979	22	14
Simplon Nos 1 and 2	Switzerland–Italy	1906, 1922	20	12
Shin-Kanmon	Japan	1975	19	12
Apennine	Italy	1934	19	12
Rokko	Japan	1972	16	10
Sciliar	Italy	1993	16	10
Haruna	Japan	1982	15	10
Furka	Switzerland	1981	15	10

Largest Reservoirs by Volume in the World

Reservoir	Location	Year completed	Volume	
			cubic m (millions)	cubic yd (millions)
Kariba	Zambia/Zimbabwe	1959	180,600	236,207
Bratsk	Russian Federation	1964	169,000	221,035
High Aswan	Egypt	1970	162,000	211,880
Akosombo	Ghana	1965	150,000	196,185
Daniel Johnson	Canada	1968	141,851	185,527
Xinfeng	China	1960	138,960	181,746
Guri	Venezuela	1986	135,000	176,567

(continued)

Largest Reservoirs by Volume in the World *(continued)*

Reservoir	Location	Year completed	Volume	
			cubic m (millions)	cubic yd (millions)
Bennett W A C	Canada	1967	74,300	97,177
Krasnoyarsk	Russian Federation	1967	73,300	95,869
Zeya	Russian Federation	1978	68,400	89,460
La Grande 2 Barrage	Canada	1978	61,715	80,717
La Grande 3 Barrage	Canada	1981	60,020	78,500
Ust-Ilim	Russian Federation	1977	59,300	77,558
Boguchany[1]	Russian Federation		58,200	76,120
Kuibyshev	Russian Federation	1955	58,000	75,858
Serra de Mesa	Brazil	1998	54,400	71,150
Canapiscau Barrage KA-3	Canada	1980	53,790	70,352
Cahora Bassa	Mozambique	1974	52,000	68,011
Bukhtarma	Kazakhstan	1960	49,800	65,089
Tucuruí	Brazil	1984	49,536	64,788

[1] Under construction.

Source: 1998 World Register of Dams, *International Commission on Large Dams*

Scientific Associations and Societies

Scientific Associations in the UK

Astronomical Society, Royal, Burlington House, Piccadilly, London W1V 0NL; phone: (020) 7734 4582/3307; fax: (020) 7494 0166; e-mail: ronw@ras.org.uk; Web site: www.ras.org.uk

Chemistry, Royal Society of, Burlington House, Piccadilly, London W1V 0BN; phone: (020) 7437 8656; fax: (020) 7437 8883; Web site: www.rsc.org and www.chemsoc.org (all chemical societies)

Computer Professionals, Association of, 204 Barnett Wood Lane, Ashtead KT21 2DB; phone: (01372) 273442; fax: (01372) 277778; e-mail: acp@btinternet.com; Web site: www.btinternet.com/~acp

Computer Society, British, 1 Sanford Street, Swindon SN1 1HJ; phone: (01793) 417417; fax: (01793) 480270; e-mail: bcshq@bcs.org.uk; Web site: www.bcs.org.uk

Engineering Council, 10 Maltravers Street, London WC2R 3ER; phone: (020) 7240 7891; fax: (020) 7240 7517; e-mail: staff@engc.org.uk; Web site: www.engc.org.uk

Engineers' & Managers' Association, Flaxman House, Gogmore Lane, Chertsy KT16 9JS; phone: (01932) 577007; fax: (01932) 567707; e-mail: hq@ema.org.uk; Web site: www.ema.org.uk

Forensic Science Society, Clarke House, 18a Mount Parade, Harrogate HG1 1BX; phone: (01423) 506068; fax: (01423) 566391; e-mail: president@fscisoc.demon.co.uk; Web site: www.demon.co.uk/forensic

Human Genome Mapping Project Resource Centre, UK MRC HGMP Resource Centre, Hinxton, Cambridge CB10 1SB; phone: (01223) 494500; fax: (01223) 494512; e-mail: admin@hgmp.mrc.ac.uk; Web site: www.hgmp.mrc.ac.uk

Mathematical Association, 259 London Road, Leicester LE2 3BE; phone: (0116) 221 0013; fax: (0116) 212 2835; e-mail: office@m-a.org.uk; Web site: www.m-a.org.uk

Mining & Metallurgy, Institution of, 77 Hallam Street, London W1N 5LR; phone: (020) 7580 3802; fax: (020) 7436 5388; e-mail: hq@imm.org.uk; Web site: www.imm.org.uk

Physics, Institute of, 76 Portland Place, London W1N 3DH; phone: (020) 7470 4800; fax: (020) 7470 4848; e-mail: physics@iop.org; Web site: www.iop.org

Plant Engineers, Institution of, 77 Great Peter Street, London SW1P 2EZ; phone: (020) 7233 2855; fax: (020) 7233 2604; e-mail: mail@iplante.org.uk; Web site: www.iplante.org.uk

Royal Society, 6 Carlton House Terrace, London SW1Y 5AG; phone: (020) 7839 5561; fax: (020) 7930 2170; e-mail: webmanager@royalsoc.ac.uk; Web site: www.royalsoc.ac.uk

Sanger Centre, Wellcome Trust Genome Campus, Hinxton, Cambridge CB10 1SA; phone: (01223) 834244; fax: (01223) 494919; Web site: www.sanger.ac.uk

Soil Association, Bristol House, 40–46 Victoria Street, Bristol BS1 6BY; phone: (0117) 929 0661; fax: (0117) 925 2504; e-mail: info@soilassociation.org; Web site: www.soilassociation.org

Statistical Society, Royal, 12 Errol Street, London EC1Y 8LX; phone: (020) 7638 8998; fax: (020) 7256 7598; Web site: www.rss.org.uk

Web Sites

Analytical Chemistry Basics

`http://www.scimedia.com/chem-ed/analytic/ac-basic.htm`

Online course designed for those at undergraduate level.

Beginners' Guide to Linux

`http://home.earthlink.net/~michaelburns/`

Aimed at first-time users of the operating system Linux. Also includes information on common commands, firewalls, and Xwindows.

Biology Timeline

`http://www.zoologie.biologie.de/history.html`

Chronology of important developments in the biological sciences.

Breaking The Genetic Code

`http://www.nih.gov/od/museum/neir1.htm`

The Nobel prize-winning work of US biochemist Marshall Nirenberg on genetics.

Brief History of Cosmology

`http://www-history.mcs.stand.ac.uk/~history/HistTopics/Cosmology.html`

The history of cosmology from the Babylonians to the Hubble Space Telescope.

Chemical Elements.com

`http://www.chemicalelements.com/`

Searchable, interactive version of the periodic table.

Chemistry of the Ozone Layer

`http://pooh.chem.wm.edu/chemWWW/courses/chem105/projects/group2/page1.html`

Introduction to the ozone layer and ozone depletion: the role of chlorofluorocarbons, the consequences of increased radiation for life on Earth, and actions to tackle the problem.

Classification of Living Things

`http://daphne.palomar.edu/animal/default.htm`

Introduction to the principles of classification established by Swedish botanist Carolus Linnaeus.

Darwin and Evolution

`http://landow.stg.brown.edu/victorian/darwin/darwin5.html`

Clear introduction to the evolutionary theories of Charles Darwin.

Dictionary of Cell Biology

http://www.mblab.gla.ac.uk/dictionary/

Searchable database of more than 5,000 terms frequently encountered in modern biology literature.

Elementary Particles

http://www.neutron.anl.gov/Particles.htm

Elementary particles explained.

Evolution: Theory and History

http://www.ucmp.berkeley.edu/history/evolution.html

Explores topics on classification, taxonomy, and dinosaur discoveries, and looks at key figures in the field and reviews their contributions.

Frequently Asked Questions in Mathematics

http://www.cs.unb.ca/~alopez-o/math-faq/mathtext/math-faq.html

Experts' answers to FAQs, from 'Why is there no Nobel prize in mathematics?' to 'What is the current status of Fermat's last theorem?'

Galileo Project Information

http://nssdc.gsfc.nasa.gov/planetary/galileo.html

NASA site about the Galileo spacecraft mission.

History of Mathematics

http://www-groups.dcs.st-andrews.ac.uk/history/HistTopics/History_overview.html

Overview of the history of mathematics, including sections on the problems of notation and communication.

History of Space Exploration

http://www.solarviews.com/eng/history.htm

Includes information on the history of rocketry, and chronologies of exploration by the USA, Russia, Japan, and Europe.

History of the Royal Society

http://www-history.mcs.stand.ac.uk/~history/Societies/RShistory.html

Includes biographies of the founding members of the Society, and information on the main prizes the society awards for scientific achievement.

Human Genome Project Information

http://www.ornl.gov/TechResources/Human_Genome/home.html

News, progress reports, a molecular genetics primer, and links to other sites related to this mammoth project.

Introduction to Evolutionary Biology

http://www.talkorigins.org/faqs/faq-intro-to-biology.html

Good explanation of the subject, including the 'evolution versus creation' debate, and how changes to the environment can affect the way in which a species evolves.

Look Inside the Atom

http://www.aip.org/history/electron/jjhome.htm

Part of the American Institute of Physics site, this page examines J J Thomson's 1897 experiments that led to the discovery of the electron.

NASA Home Page

http://www.nasa.gov/

Information on the US National Aeronautics and Space Administration; includes media galleries (video, audio, stills), latest news, and the most recent images from the Hubble Space Telescope.

NASA Shuttle Web

http://spaceflight.nasa.gov/shuttle/index.html

Official NASA site for all shuttle missions. Questions can be sent to shuttle crew members during missions.

Nuclear Energy: Frequently Asked Questions

http://www-formal.stanford.edu/jmc/progress/nuclear- faq.html

Answers to the most commonly asked questions about nuclear energy.

Nuclear Physics

http://www.scri.fsu.edu/~jac/Nuclear/

'Hyper-textbook' of nuclear physics, with a graphical description of the properties of nuclei, as well as information on the uses and applications of nuclear physics.

Physics 2000

http://www.colorado.edu/physics/2000/

Fun place to learn about 20th-century physics and familiar high-tech devices. This site is designed to make physics more accessible to people of all ages.

Practical Guide to Astronomy

http://www.aardvark.on.ca/space/

Well-illustrated guide covering such aspects as the 'Big Bang' theories of English physicist Stephen Hawking, early astronomers and their key discoveries, and an in-depth look at the elements of our Solar System.

Project Skylab

http://www.ksc.nasa.gov/history/skylab/skylab.html

Official NASA archive of the project that launched the USA's first experimental space station in 1973.

Royal Institution of Great Britain

http://www.ri.ac.uk/

Profile of the history and role of the world's longest established independent research organization, with information on the RI's ongoing scientific research and its many activities aimed at educating the public about science.

Royal Society of Chemistry

http://www.rsc.org/

Work of the UK society to promote understanding of chemistry and assist its advancement, with details of the society's research work, online and print publications, and a comprehensive educational programme.

SETI Institute

http://www.seti-inst.edu/

SETI (Search for ExtraTerrestrial Intelligence) Institute conducts research designed to answer the question 'Are we alone in the universe?' You can even help the search by devoting some of your own computer's time to 'crunching' the enormous amounts of data the Institute collects.

Solar System

http://www.hawastsoc.org/solar/eng/homepage.htm

Educational tour of the Solar System.

Space Telescope Electronic Information Service

http://www.stsci.edu/

Home page of the Hubble Space Telescope, with an archive and images of its observations, a description of the instruments aboard, and a section for educators, students, and the general public.

Strange Science

http://www.turnpike.net/~mscott/index.htm

Examines some of the medieval discoveries that led to the growth of interest in modern-day science.

Tree of Life

http://phylogeny.arizona.edu/tree/phylogeny.html

Project designed to present information about the phylogenetic relationships and characteristics of organisms, illustrating their diversity and unity.

What's New in Mathematics?

http://www.ams.org/new-in-math/

Section of the American Mathematical Society's Web site aimed at the general public, with features on latest developments and buzz words.

World Atom – International Atomic Energy Agency

http://www.iaea.org/

Public information source of the UN agency charged with monitoring and assisting the peaceful uses of nuclear energy.

Your Genes, Your Choices: Exploring the Issues Raised by Genetic Research

http://www.ornl.gov/hgmis/publicat/genechoice/index.html

Illustrated e-book that describes the science of genetic research, as well as the ethical, legal, and social issues that it raises.

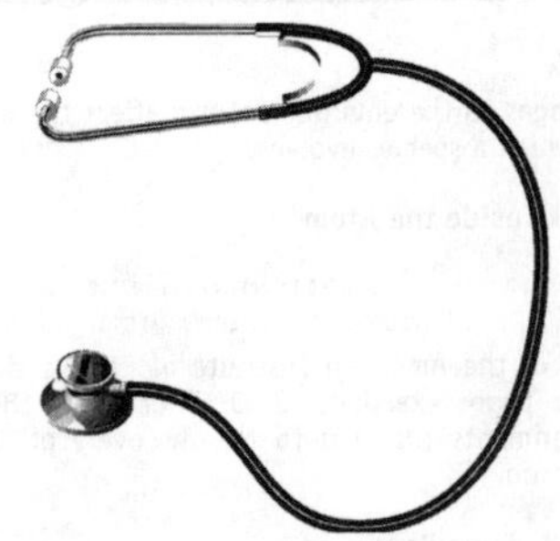

MEDICINE AND HEALTH

The Year in Review

July 1999 Researchers at Elan Pharmaceuticals in California report the development of a vaccine that both prevents and reduces deposits of plaque in the brain that are associated with Alzheimer's disease.

July 1999 A group of leaders in legal, medical, and ethical fields object to the use of embryos for stem cell research on ethical grounds, calling on the US Congress to continue banning federal funding for embryo research.

7 July 1999 Major tobacco companies are held liable for smoking-related illnesses in a class-action suit on behalf of smokers in Florida, USA. The jury determines that the companies misled the public on the hazards of cigarettes, which are judged to be addictive and to cause more than 20 diseases.

14 July 1999 The European Commission votes to formally end its ban on beef exports from the UK after veterinary officials reported that the epidemic of bovine spongiform encephalopathy (BSE) is under control.

27 July 1999 Australian premier Bob Carr announces that the country's first legal heroin injecting room will be set up in Sydney by the New South Wales government. The centre will be operated for 18 months beginning in early 2000, permitting addicts to inject themselves under medical supervision, with the aim of reducing deaths from disease and overdoses.

August 1999 Delegates at a conference at Sarum College, Salisbury, petition for South African companies to be permitted to produce cheap forms of drug compounds used to keep AIDS under control. This is a response to efforts by US pharmaceutical firms to protect their 'intellectual property rights', despite World Trade Organization rules that patent rights may be waived in cases of extreme urgency. Eight percent of the South African population is HIV positive, and millions are predicted to die of AIDS by 2005, leaving hundreds of thousands of children orphaned.

October 1999 A study by a drug safety research unit in Southampton, UK, indicates that young women smokers are dying prematurely of heart attacks, with the risk increasing with the greater number of cigarettes smoked.

20 October 1999 A programme to immunize vulnerable groups against the C strain of meningitis is announced by the UK government.

4 August 1999 The German government announces that it will continue its ban on British beef while it determines whether it is safe from BSE, despite the EU's decision in July to end the ban.

October 1999 The humanitarian group Médicins Sans Frontières receives the Nobel Peace Prize for its emergency medical care around the world, particularly in Kosovo and East Timor.

20 October 1999 Scientists from Johns Hopkins University, Baltimore, Maryland, announce a genetically-engineered vaccine that stimulates the entire immune system of men with prostate cancer. It is one of several new gene therapy trials that bring hope for new treatments for various forms of cancer.

3 November 1999 Gro Harlem Brundtland, director general of the World Health Organization, spearheads plans to raise a fund of $500–600 million to combat the worldwide spread of tuberculosis.

3 December 1999 UK health secretary Alan Milburn orders an inquiry into the Alder Hey children's hospital in Liverpool, after claims that up to 850 organs from the bodies of children were removed and stored following post-mortem examinations, without consent from parents.

January 2000 England's flu epidemic forces cancellations of non-urgent surgery, causing waiting lists for surgery at National Health Service (NHS) hospitals to increase sharply.

10 January 2000 The UK government announces that the official number of cases of influenza has risen to 200 per 100,000. The chief medical officer declares a national epidemic.

10 January 2000 The UK government launches a research unit at Oxford University to test a new AIDS vaccine. Trials will be held in the UK and Kenya.

11 January 2000 The youngest victim of new variant Creutzfeldt-Jacob Disease (CJD), 15-year-old Claire McVey from Barstaple, north Devon, dies.

13 January 2000 Less than two years after the first successful arm transplant, a team of 20 surgeons performs a 17-hour operation to transplant two arms onto a victim of an explosion, in Lyon, France.

16 January 2000 UK prime minister Tony Blair announces a plan to spend an extra £12 billion on the National Health Service over the next six years, bringing health spending up to the European average.

17 January 2000 The UK government announces pay rises above inflation for all health workers.

31 January 2000 English doctor Harold Shipman is convicted of murdering 15 elderly female patients in his care, by injecting them with a lethal dose of morphine and claiming that they died of natural causes. He remains under investigation for the deaths of up to 135 more of his patients. (*See also* **colour section**).

8 February 2000 In one of the most detailed speeches on medical research issues given by a US president, Bill Clinton prevents US federal government agencies from discriminating against employees on the basis of genetic tests.

March 2000 A new inplant therapy that uses electrodes to stimulate paralysed muscles is tested. (*See also* **colour section**).

May 2000 An outbreak of legionnaire's disease in Melbourne, Australia, affects at least 58 people, of whom two die.

May–June 2000 A mystery illness of heroin-injecting addicts causes up to 40 fatalities in the UK and Ireland. The contaminant is eventually identified as *Clostridium novyi* type A, a bacterium that caused outbreaks of gas gangrene in the two world wars.

June 2000 Microbiologists at Edinburgh University find that babies living in a smoky environment are at greater risk of developing meningitis, because tobacco smoke helps the meningococcal bacteria adhere to the tissues lining the throat.

June 2000 Researchers at the Wolfson Institute of preventive medicine in London publish evidence that taking an aspirin a day to prevent heart attacks doubles the risk of stomach ulcers and bleeding, and should be avoided by those people who have never had a heart attack or stroke.

8 June 2000 UK public health minister Yvette Cooper tells the Royal College of Physicians that seven out of ten adults take too little exercise and publishes radical new guidelines permitting doctors to prescribe bicycles or gym sessions on the National Health Service.

13 June 2000 A new register, intended to provide an early warning system for medical errors, is proposed for England. This follows the inquiry into over 200 misdiagnoses by Dr James Elwood, a 78-year-old pathologist, and the controversy surrounding disgraced consultant gynaecologist Richard Neale.

14 June 2000 European Parliament MPs approve strong new anti-tobacco rulings which will mean greatly enlarged health warnings on cigarette packs and lower limits on tar and nicotine. The use of graphic images to warn against smoking-related diseases is rejected, however.

21 June 2000 The UK National Health Service is ranked 18th in a league table of 191 member states produced by the World Health Organization; France is in first place. The assessment is based on five criteria, and indicates that long waiting lists and problems obtaining care are the weakest features of the UK health service.

30 June 2000 US biomedical scientists announce the success of an experiment artificially transmitting the malaria parasite through fruit flies, which may revolutionize understanding of the disease that kills over a million people a year. Fruit flies are much easier to work with than mosquitoes, the natural hosts of malaria.

General Medical Information

First Aid Advice

First aid is the controlled application of tried and tested methods and techniques using the knowledge and resources available at the time of injury or onset of illness until expert help arrives. In other words, the provider of first aid is the casualty's firsthand assistance and, in an emergency situation, this could mean the difference between life and death.

There are hundreds of thousands of personal injury accidents each year. In many cases, first aid knowledge could save lives. At the very least, casualties can be made comfortable and minor injuries attended to before the emergency services arrive. Vital time can be saved, with unnecessary pain and anxiety avoided.

In the UK, the leading first aid organizations are the British Red Cross and St John Ambulance. Both offer training, and first aid courses for children, the general public, and the workforce. Both organizations believe that everyone should obtain at least a basic knowledge of first aid through a two-hour or one-day introductory course.

Authoritative first aid manuals provide good basic guidelines and instructions on how to care for victims of accident, injury, or illness. The British Red Cross supplies the following essential and practical first aid and care guides:

First Aid Manual
ISBN: 0 7513 0707 6
£10.99

Practical First Aid
ISBN: 0 7513 0546 4
£5.99

First Aid for Children Fast
ISBN: 0 7513 0138 8
£8.99

Carer's Handbook
ISBN: 0 7513 0464 6
£9.99

The Babysitter's Handbook
ISBN: 0 7513 0217 1
£9.99

The Basic Responsible Reactions
In an emergency:

Keep calm Remaining calm while helping the victim will help them to keep calm and cooperate. If the victim becomes anxious or excited the extent of damage from the injury could be increased.

Plan quickly what you need to do Learn basic procedures, or have your first aid manual available, so you can care for the victim.

Send for professional help Reaching help quickly could save a life. Know your local emergency telephone numbers. (999 in the UK or 112 – the international emergency number – in Ireland or your local emergency telephone number.)

Be an encouragement to the injured person Let the victim know that help is on the way and try to make them as comfortable as possible. Showing care and concern for the victim can give them hope whilst awaiting help.

Phobias

Fear	Name of phobia
animals	zoophobia
bacteria	bacteriophobia, bacillophobia
beards	pogonophobia
bees	apiphobia, melissophobia
being alone	monophobia, autophobia, eremophobia
being buried alive	taphophobia
being seen by others	scopophobia
being touched	haphephobia, aphephobia
birds	ornithophobia
blood	h(a)ematophobia, h(a)emophobia
blushing	ereuthrophobia, erythrophobia
books	bibliophobia
cancer	cancerophobia, carcinophobia
cats	ailurophobia, gatophobia
chickens	alektorophobia
childbirth	tocophobia, parturiphobia
children	paediphobia
cold	cheimatophobia, frigophobia
colour	chromatophobia, chromophobia, psychrophobia
criticism	enissophobia
crossing bridges	gephyrophobia
crossing streets	dromophobia
crowds	demophobia, ochlophobia
darkness	achluophobia, nyctophobia, scotophobia
dawn	eosophobia
daylight	phengophobia
death, corpses	necrophobia, thanatophobia
defecation	rhypophobia
deformity	dysmorphophobia
dirt, contamination	mysophobia
disease	nosophobia, pathophobia
disorder	ataxiophobia
dogs	cynophobia
draughts	anemophobia
dreams	oneirophobia
drinking	dipsophobia
drugs	pharmacophobia
dust	amathophobia, koniphobia
eating	phagophobia
enclosed spaces	claustrophobia
everything	pan(t)ophobia
facial hair	trichopathophobia
faeces	coprophobia
failure	kakorraphiaphobia
fatigue	kopophobia, ponophobia
fears	phobophobia
fire	pyrophobia
fish	ichthyophobia
flying, the air	aerophobia
fog	homichlophobia
food	sitophobia
foreign languages	xenoglossophobia
freedom	eleutherophobia
germs	spermophobia
ghosts	phasmophobia
glass	hyalophobia
god	theophobia
going to bed	clinophobia
graves	taphophobia
hair	chaetophobia, trichophobia, hypertrichophobia
heart conditions	cardiophobia
heat	thermophobia
heaven	ouranophobia
heights	acrophobia, altophobia
hell	hadephobia, stygiophobia
horses	hippophobia
human beings	anthropophobia
ice, frost	cryophobia
illness	nosemaphobia, nosophobia
imperfection	atelophobia
infinity	apeirophobia
inoculations, injections	trypanophobia
insanity	lyssophobia, maniaphobia
insects	entomophobia
itching, or the insects that cause itching	acarophobia
jealousy	zelophobia
knowledge	epistemophobia
lakes	limnophobia
large objects	macrophobia
leaves	phyllophobia
leprosy	leprophobia
lice	pediculophobia
lightning	astraphobia
machinery	mechanophobia
many things	polyphobia
marriage	gamophobia
meat	carnophobia
men	androphobia
metals	metallophobia
mice	musophobia
mirrors	eisoptrophobia, catoptrophobia
money	chrometophobia
monsters, monstrosities	teratophobia
motion	kinesophobia, kinetophobia
music	musicophobia
names	onomatophobia
needles, sharp objects	belonephobia
night, darkness	achluophobia
noise	phonophobia
novelty	cainophobia, cenotophobia, neophobia
nudity	gymnotophobia
number 13	triskaidekaphobia, terdekaphobia
odours	osmophobia
open spaces	agoraphobia
pain	algophobia, odynophobia
parasites	parasitophobia
physical love	erotophobia
pleasure	hedonophobia
pointed instruments	aichmophobia
poison	toxiphobia, toxophobia, iophobia
poverty	peniaphobia
pregnancy	maieusiophobia
punishment	poinephobia
rain	ombrophobia
responsibility	hypegiaphobia
ridicule	katagalophobia
rivers	potamophobia
robbery	harpaxophobia
rust	iophobia
sacred things	hierophobia
satan	satanophobia
school	scholionophobia
sea	thalassophobia
semen	spermatophobia
sex	genophobia
sexual intercourse	coitophobia
shadows	sciophobia
shock	hormephobia
sin	hamartiophobia
sinning	peccatophobia
skin	dermatophobia
sleep	hypnophobia
small objects	microphobia
smell	olfactophobia
smothering, choking	pnigerophobia
snakes	ophidiophobia, ophiophobia
snow	chionophobia
sound	akousticophobia
speaking	laliophobia, lalophobia
speed	tachophobia
spiders	arachn(e)ophobia
standing	stasiphobia
stars	siderophobia
stillness	eremophobia
stings	cnidophobia
strangers	xenophobia
sun	heliophobia
symbols	symbolophobia
technology	technophobia
teeth	odontophobia
thinking	phronemophobia

(continued)

■ General Medical Information

Phobias (*continued*)

Fear	Name of phobia	Fear	Name of phobia
thunder	astraphobia, brontophobia, keraunophobia	weakness	asthenophobia
travel	hodophobia	wind	ancraophobia
trees	dendrophobia	women	gynophobia
vehicles	amaxophobia, ochophobia	words	logophobia
venereal disease	cypridophobia	work	ergophobia, ergasiophobia
vomiting	emetophobia	worms	helminthophobia
walking	basiphobia	wounds, injury	traumatophobia
wasps	spheksophobia	writing	graphophobia
water	hydrophobia, aquaphobia		

Compatibility of Blood Groups

Blood group	Antigen on red blood cell	Antibody in plasma	Blood groups that can be received by this individual	Blood groups that can receive donations from this individual
A	A	anti-B	A, 0	A, AB
B	B	anti-A	B, 0	B, AB
AB	A and B	none	any	AB
0	neither A nor B	anti-A and anti-B	0	any

Medical Transplants: Key Dates

1682 A Russian doctor uses bone from a dog to repair the skull of an injured nobleman. The graft is reportedly successful, though it angers the Russian Orthodox Church.

1771 Scottish surgeon John Hunter describes his experiments in the transplantation of tissues, including a human tooth into a cock's comb in *Treatise on the Natural History of Human Teeth*.

1905 Corneal grafting, which may restore sight to a diseased or damaged eye, is pioneered.

1950s Kidneys are first transplanted successfully; kidney transplants are pioneered by British surgeon Roy Calne. British immunologist Peter Medawar conducts vital research into the body's tolerance of transplanted organs and skin grafts.

1964 Chimpanzee kidneys are transplanted into humans in the USA, but with little success; in the UK a pig's heart valve is transplanted successfully and the operation becomes routine.

1967 South African surgeon Christiaan Barnard performs the first human heart transplant. The 54-year-old patient lives for 18 days.

1969 The world's first heart and lung transplant is performed at the Stanford Medical Center, California, USA.

1970 The first successful nerve transplant is performed in West Germany.

1978 Cyclosporin, an immunosuppressive drug derived from a fungus, revolutionizes transplant surgery by reducing the incidence and severity of rejection of donor organs.

1982 Jarvik 7, an artificial heart made of plastic and aluminium is transplanted; the recipient lives for 112 days.

1986 British surgeons John Wallwork and Roy Calne perform the first triple transplant – heart, lung, and liver – at Papworth Hospital, Cambridge, England.

1987 The world's longest-surviving heart-transplant patient dies in France, 18 years after his operation. A three-year-old girl in the USA receives a new liver, pancreas, small intestine, and parts of the stomach and colon; the first successful five-organ transplant.

1989 Grafts of fetal brain tissue are first used to treat Parkinson's disease.

1995 The first experiments to use genetically altered animal organs in humans are given US government approval in July – genetically altered pig livers are attached to the circulatory systems of patients whose livers have failed. An AIDS patient receives a bone marrow transplant from a baboon but the graft fails to take.

23 June 1998 Cultured human neural cells are injected into the brain of a stroke victim. This is the first transplant of brain tissue used in stroke treatment and the first use of cultured cells rather than fetal tissue.

24 September 1998 An international team of surgeons in Lyon, France, performs the first hand-and-forearm transplant operation on a man whose arm was amputated 14 years earlier. Although doctors have been able to attach severed limbs for years, they have been unable to successfully move a limb from a dead donor to a living recipient. This was the first successful transplant of a limb from a dead donor.

18 February 1999 Brazilian doctors say they have performed the world's first successful liver and kidney transplant from a live donor. The operation, in which surgeons gave a 53-year-old man a kidney and part of the liver of his 26-year-old son, was carried out at the Hospital Israelita Albert Einstein in Sao Paolo two months earlier. The operation raises ethical concerns about the limits of live organ donors and the medical risk to donors.

24 August 1999 For the first time, US doctors manage to get the body of a transplant patient to tolerate its donor kidney without the aid of medication to suppress the immune system. The technique used by doctors at Massachusetts General Hospital is called 'mixed chimerism', which, although used before to allow the use of imperfectly matched bone marrow transplants in frail cancer patients, had never been successfully used in the field of organ transplantation.

23 September 1999 Dr Oktay of New York Methodist Hospital carries out the first successful ovary transplant, restoring ovulation to a 30-year-old woman who had had both her ovaries removed. It is still uncertain whether the eggs she releases can be fertilized and lead to a successful pregnancy. The team of British and US doctors who devised the new medical treatment say that it could delay the effects of female menopause and even, eventually, lead to a way of extending female fertility into the 60s.

30 September 1999 A US man who received a baboon liver in an operation hailed as a breakthrough contracts a virus thought only to affect the animal. The man, a 35-year-old HIV patient, dies from liver disease just two months after the transplant. It is seen as a major setback for doctors who hope that animal to human transplantation will be the answer to donor shortages.

17 January 2000 A team of US doctors announces an artificial eye (known as the Dobelle Eye) comprising a video camera, radio antenna, and microchip has been implanted into the eye socket of a blind patient for trials.

10 February 2000 A former docker from Swansea, who is Europe's longest heart transplant survivor, celebrates the 20th anniversary of his operation.

14 March 2000 The world's first pig clones are announced. Millie, Christa, Alexis, Carrel, and Dotcom are hailed as a breakthrough in the efforts to find more organs for human transplant operations. The news immediately leads to controversy, with ethical and health issues being raised.

3 May 2000 A team of scientists from a Seattle cancer centre announce they have developed a technique that may prevent or reduce the risk of rejection of transplanted bone marrow. The method, which blocks T-cells, a type of white blood cell, and has been successfully tested on mice, could lead to safer and more effective bone marrow transplant operations.

Medical Prefixes

a(n)- lacking
ab- away from
abdomin(o)- abdominal
ad- towards, near
andr(o)- male
angi(o)- blood or lymph vessel
ant(i)- against, counteracting
ante- before
arthr(o)- joint
aut(o)- self
bi- twice, two
brachi(o)- arm
brachy- shortness
brady- slowness
bronch(o)- bronchial tube
carcin(o)- cancer
cardi(o)- heart
cerebr(o)- brain
cholecyst- gall bladder
circum- surrounding
colp(o)- vagina
contra- against
crani(o)- skull
cry(o)- cold
crypt- hidden, concealed
cyst(o)- bladder
cyt(o)- cell
dent- tooth
derm- skin
di- double
dys- difficult, painful, abnormal
end(o)- within, inner
enter(o)- intestine
epi- above, upon
ex(o)- outside, outer
extra- outside, beyond
gastr(o)- stomach
gyn- female
haem- blood
hepat(o)- liver
hist(o)- tissue
hyper- above
hypno- sleep
hypo- below
hyster(o)- uterus
immuno- immunity
infra- below
intra- within
laryng(o)- larynx
mal- abnormal, diseased
mast- breast
muco- mucus
my(o)- muscle
necro- death
neo- new
nephr(o)- kidney
neur(o)- nerve
noct- night
oculo- eye
olig(o)- deficiency, few
ophthalm(o)- eye
oro- mouth
ortho- straight, normal
osteo- bone
ot(o)- ear
paed- children
path(o)- disease
peri- around, enclosing
pharmac(o)- drugs
phleb(o)- vein
phot(o)- light
pneumon- lung
poly- many, excessive
post- after
pre- (pro-) before
ren- kidney
retro- behind
rhin- nose
sclero- thickening
ser(o)- serum
spondyl- vertebra, spine
supra- above
syn- together, union
tachy- fast
tetra- four
therm(o)- heat, temperature
trache(o)- trachea
uni- one
urin- urine, urinary system
utero- uterus
vaso- vessel
vesico- bladder

Medical Suffixes

-aemia condition of blood
-algia pain
-ase enzyme
-blast formative cell
-cele tumour, swelling
-centesis puncture
-cide destructive, killing
-coccus spherical bacterium
-cyte cell
-derm skin
-dynia pain
-ectasis dilation, extension
-ectomy surgical removal of
-facient making, causing
-fuge expelling
-genesis origin, development
-genic causing, produced by
-gram tracing, record
-iasis diseased condition
-iatric practice of healing
-itis inflammation of
-kinesis movement
-lith calculus, stone
-lysis breaking down, dissolution
-malacia softening
-megaly enlargement
-oid likeness, resemblance
-oma tumour
-opia eye defect
-osis disease, condition
-ostomy surgical opening or outlet
-otomy surgical incision into an organ or part
-pathy disease
-penia lack of, deficiency
-pexy surgical fixation
-phage ingesting
-philia affinity for, morbid attraction
-phobia fear
-plasty reconstructive surgery
-plegia paralysis
-pnoea condition of breathing
-poiesis formation
-ptosis prolapse
-scopy visual examination
-stasis stagnation, stoppage of flow
-tome cutting instrument
-uria condition of urine

Medical Abbreviations and Acronyms

A&E accident and emergency department
ABP arterial blood pressure
ADLs activities of daily living
adm. admission
aet. aetiology
AI artificial insemination
AIDS acquired immune deficiency syndrome
ALG antilymphocyte globulin
ALS antilymphocyte serum
ARM artificial rupture of membranes (for delivery)
BCG bacille Calmette-Guérin (TB vaccine)
BMI body mass index
BMR basal metabolic rate
BP blood pressure
BPD bronchopulmonary dysplasia
CA cancer
CABG coronary artery bypass graft
CAPD continuous ambulatory peritoneal dialysis
CAT computerized axial tomography
CCU coronary care unit
CJD Creutzfeldt-Jakob disease
CMV cytomegalovirus
CNS central nervous system
COAD chronic obstructive airways disease
CPAP continuous positive airways pressure

(*continued*)

General Medical Information

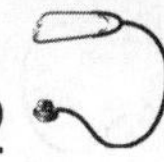

Medical Abbreviations and Acronyms (*continued*)

CPR cardiopulmonary resuscitation
CSF cerebrospinal fluid
CT computerized tomography
CV cardiovascular
CVA cardiovascular accident
CVP central venous pressure
CVS chorionic villus sampling
CXR chest X-ray
D&C dilation and curettage
DHA district health authority
DI donor insemination
DIC disseminated intravascular coagulation
disch. discharge
DL danger list
DMD Duchenne's muscular dystrophy
DNA deoxyribonucleic acid
DOA dead on arrival
DPT combined vaccine against diphtheria, pertussis (whooping cough), and tetanus
Dr doctor
DRG diagnostic related group
DTs delirium tremens
DVT deep vein thrombosis
ECG electrocardiogram
ECT electroconvulsive therapy
EEG electroencephalograph
EMG electromyograph
ENT ear, nose, and throat
EPO erythropoietin
ET endotracheal tube (used for patient on ventilator)
GH growth hormone
GIFT gamete intrafallopian transfer
GP general practitioner
GVHD graft-versus-host disease
HBIG hepatitis B immunoglobulin
HCG human chorionic gonadotrophin
HIV human immunodeficiency virus
HLA human leucocyte antigen
HMO health maintenance organization
HRT hormone replacement therapy
IBS irritable bowel syndrome
ICD international classification of diseases
ICP intracranial pressure
ICU intensive care unit
IHD ischaemic heart disease
IMR infant mortality rate
IMV intermittent mandatory ventilation
IOP intraocular pressure
IPPV intermittent positive pressure ventilation
IQ intelligence quotient
IUD intrauterine device
IV intravenous
IVP intravenous pyelogram
IZS insulin zinc suspension
K&M kaolin and morphine
LBW low birth weight
LP lumbar puncture
LSD lysergic acid diethylamide
MAB monoclonal antibody
MAOI monoamine oxidase inhibitor
MAP mean arterial pressure
MBD minimal brain dysfunction
MD doctor of medicine
ME myalgic encephalomyelitis
MHC major histocompatibility complex
MI myocardial infarction
MLD minimum lethal dose
MMR combined vaccine against measles, mumps, and rubella (German measles)
MND motor neurone disease
MO medical officer
MRI magnetic resonance imaging
MRS magnetic resonance spectroscopy
MRSA methicillin-resistant *Staphylococcus aureus*
MS multiple sclerosis
MSU mid-stream urine specimen
NHS National Health Service (in the UK)
NPO nil per orem (nothing by mouth)
NTD neural tube defect
O&G obstetrics and gynaecology
OA osteoarthritis
OD overdose
OP outpatient
ORT oral rehydration therapy
OT occupational therapy
PA physician's assistant
paed. paediatrics
path. pathology
PCOD polycystic ovary disease
PE pleural effusion
PET positron-emission tomography
PICU paediatric intensive care unit
PID pelvic inflammatory disease
PIH pregnancy-induced hypertension
PKU phenylketonuria
PM postmortem
PMS premenstrual stress disorder
PO per orem (by mouth)
PoP plaster of Paris
pre-op pre-operative
PTA post-traumatic amnesia
RA rheumatoid arthritis
RDS respiratory distress syndrome
REM sleep rapid eye movement sleep
RES reticuloendothelial system
RN registered nurse
RNA ribonucleic acid
RQ respiratory quotient
RSI repetitive strain injury
RSV respiratory syncytial virus
Rx treatment/prescription
SAD seasonal affective disorder
SAH subarachnoid haemorrhage
SIDS sudden infant death syndrome
SLE systemic lupus erythematous
STD sexually transmitted disease
TAB combined vaccine against typhoid, paratyphoid A, and paratyphoid B
TAT thematic apperception test
TATT tired all the time
TB tuberculosis
TENS transcutaneous electrical nerve stimulation
TIA transient ischaemic attack
tPA tissue plasminogen activator (heart drug)
TPR temperature, pulse, and respiration
TS Tourette's syndrome
TSH thyroid-stimulating hormone
Tx transfusion, transplant
URTI upper respiratory tract infection
UTI urinary tract infection
VA visual acuity
VD venereal disease
VF ventricular fibrillation
WHO World Health Organization

Bones of the Human Body

Bone	Number
Cranium (skull)	
Occipital	1
Parietal: 1 pair	2
Sphenoid	1
Ethmoid	1
Inferior nasal conchae	2
Frontal: 1 pair, fused	1
Nasal: 1 pair	2
Lacrimal: 1 pair	2
Temporal: 1 pair	2
Maxilla: 1 pair, fused	1
Zygomatic: 1 pair	2
Vomer	1
Palatine: 1 pair	2
Mandible (jawbone): 1 pair, fused	1
Total	21
Ear	
Malleus (hammer)	1
Incus (anvil)	1
Stapes (stirrups)	1
Total (2 x 3)	6
Vertebral column (spine)	
Cervical vertebrae	7
Thoracic vertebrae	12
Lumbar vertebrae	5
Sacral vertebrae: 5, fused to form the sacrum	1
Coccygeal vertebrae: between 3 and 5, fused to form the coccyx	1
Total	26
Ribs	
Ribs, 'true': 7 pairs	14
Ribs, 'false': 5 pairs, of which 2 pairs are floating	10
Total	24
Sternum (breastbone)	
Manubrium, sternebrae ('body'), and xiphisternum	
Total	3

(continued)

Bones of the Human Body (*continued*)

Bone	Number
Throat	
Hyoid	1
Total	1
Pectoral girdle	
Clavicle: 1 pair (collarbone)	2
Scapula (including coracoid): 1 pair (shoulder-blade)	2
Total	4
Upper extremity (each arm)	
Forearm	
humerus	1
radius	1
ulna	1
Carpus (wrist)	
scaphoid	1
lunate	1
triquetral	1
pisiform	1
trapezium	1
trapezoid	1
capitate	1
hamate	1
metacarpals	5
Phalanges (fingers)	
first digit	2
second digit	3
third digit	3
fourth digit	3
fifth digit	3
Total (2 x 30)	60
Pelvic girdle	2
Ilium, ischium, and pubis (combined): 1 pair of hip bones, innominate	
Total	2
Lower extremity (each leg)	
Leg	
femur (thighbone)	1
tibia (shinbone)	1
fibula	1
patella (kneecap)	1
Tarsus (ankle)	
talus	1
calcaneus	1
navicular	1
cuneiform, medial	1
cuneiform, intermediate	1
cuneiform, lateral	1
cuboid	1
metatarsals (foot bones)	5
Phalanges (toes)	
first digit	2
second digit	3
third digit	3
fourth digit	3
fifth digit	3
Total (2 x 30)	60
TOTAL	207

Human Body: Composition

Chemical element or substance	Body weight (%)
Pure elements	
Oxygen	65
Carbon	18
Hydrogen	10
Nitrogen	3
Calcium	2
Phosphorus	1.1
Potassium	0.35
Sulphur	0.25
Sodium	0.15
Chlorine	0.15
Pure elements (continued)	
Magnesium, iron, manganese, copper, iodine, cobalt, zinc	traces
Water and solid matter	
Water	60–80
Total solid material	20–40
Organic molecules	
Protein	15–20
Lipid	3–20
Carbohydrate	1–15
Other	0–1

Skull

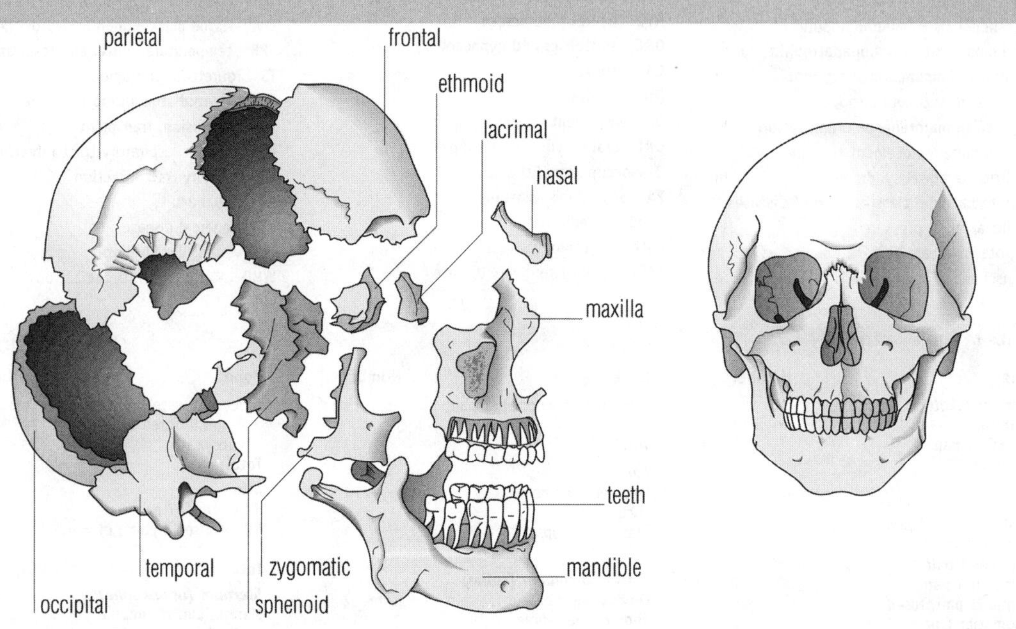

The skull is a protective box for the brain, eyes, and hearing organs. It is also a framework for the teeth and flesh of the face.

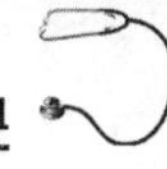

Skeleton

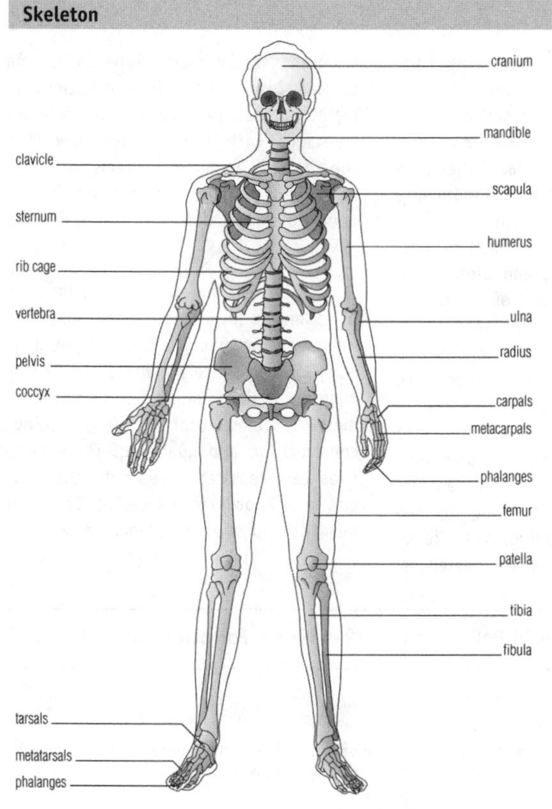

Human Body

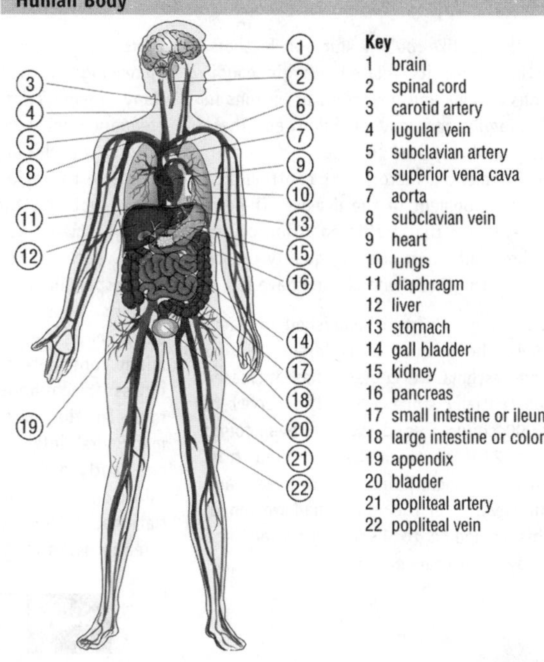

The adult human body has approximately 650 muscles, 100,000 km/60,000 mi of blood vessels, and 13,000 nerve cells.

Do You Have a Cold or the Flu?

This table is meant as a guide only. Always consult a qualified doctor if you have concerns or doubts.

		Cold	Flu
Definition		minor disease of the upper respiratory tract, caused by a variety of common viruses that can easily be transmitted from person to person	viral infection primarily affecting the air passages, accompanied by systemic effects such as fever, chills, aches and pains; there is always the risk of secondary (bacterial) infection of the lungs (pneumonia)
Symptoms	aches and pains	slight	common, often severe
	cough	occasional	can become severe
	fever	rare	common, high
	headache	rare	prominent
	fatigue/exhaustion	mild/never	can last for several weeks/early and prominent
	runny or stuffy nose	common	sometimes
	sneezing	common	sometimes
	sore throat	common	sometimes
Prevention		none	annual vaccination
Treatment		temporary relief of symptoms; there is little immediate hope of an effective cure as the viruses transform so rapidly	bed rest and analgesic drugs such as aspirin or paracetamol

See also **Flu Outbreaks and Epidemics**, p 527.

Asthma

Asthma is a controllable but not curable disease. The World Health Organization estimates that 100–150 million people around the world are asthmatic, and the number is growing by 50% every decade. Asthma causes 180,000 deaths a year worldwide. The UK has amongst the highest incidences of asthma in the world. Asthma symptoms or attacks can be triggered by many different factors. Common triggers include colds or flu, cigarette smoke, exercise, and allergies

Asthma *(continued)*

to things like pollen, fur, or feathers. Asthma, like its related allergic conditions eczema and hay fever, often runs in the family and may be inherited. There are probably a number of other, environmental, factors that contribute to the development of the disease. There is no evidence that traffic pollution causes asthma, although poor air quality can be a trigger in those who already have it.

According to a study published in March 2000, the number of children suffering from asthma in England has increased substantially since 1992. The survey of 3,000 children aged six and seven found that 23% of them had suffered from asthma at some point in their lives – and the severity of the illness had worsened. This compared to 13% of children in a study eight years earlier.

There are several reasons for the increasing incidence of the disease. Many women continue to smoke during pregnancy, increasing the chance of their children developing asthma. Although a definitive cause for the lung abnormality at the root of asthma continues to elude doctors, many aspects of modern lifestyles, such as housing and diet, might be responsible. Aspects of living in modern housing – little ventilation, damp, more carpeting, and more dust – might contribute to asthma. Exposure to illness in childhood could also play a role. In the past, when children had many viral infections, their bodies were constantly defending themselves against infection. But now, according to the National Asthma Campaign, with fewer infections and weakened defences, children may be more prone to asthma instead. In a similar vein, some scientists maintain that parents are so hygiene-conscious with their babies now that the babies' immune systems are not developing properly and that it is in fact good for small children to be exposed to low levels of dirt.

Some scientists have linked the increase in asthma to an increase in air pollution. However, this theory is hotly disputed. If true, the most likely culprits are PM10s, microscopically small particles emitted by diesel engines, coal burning, mining, construction, and quarrying. These particles can penetrate deep into the lung and are known to exacerbate existing heart or respiratory problems.

See also **World Pollution** pp 629–633; **UK Pollution**, pp 633–635.

Common Allergies

Allergy is extremely widespread and now affects 1 in 4 of the UK population at some time during their lifetime. Each year the numbers are increasing by 5%. The most common allergy in the UK is hay fever which can occur at any age and in early 2000 affected 20% of all allergy sufferers.

This table is meant as a guide only. Always consult a qualified doctor if you have any concerns or doubts.

Allergy	Cause	Symptoms/comments
Pollen allergy (hay fever)	mainly grass and tree pollen	allergic rhinitis (running eyes and nose, sneezing, nasal congestion), eczema, urticaria (nettlerash or hives), and asthma; asthma symptoms range from mild to moderate or severe and can be life-threatening; people with the disease suffer 'attacks', or acute episodes, when the air passages in their lungs narrow and breathing becomes difficult; affects more than 3 million people in the UK, including one in every seven school children and one in every 25 adults
Dust-mite allergy	enzymes in the faeces of mites in house dust, feathers, pillows, and mattresses	symptoms as above, though they tend to be primarily respiratory in nature; affects about 5% of the UK population (1999)
Pet allergy	allergens in the pet's saliva, urine, or skin flakes, carried on its fur	symptoms as above
Mould allergy	spores from moulds growing in damp living spaces and on hay and cereal grain	symptoms as above, though they tend to be primarily respiratory in nature; moulds can be found both indoors and outdoors and allergies are often associated with pollen allergies
Insect bite or sting allergy	proteins in the venom	severe and prolonged swelling at the site of the sting, pain, and – in extreme cases – anaphylactic shock (respiratory difficulties, a rapid fall in blood pressure, and collapse, followed by loss of consciousness and even death); sufferers may also experience abdominal pain, vomiting, and diarrhoea
Food allergy	most commonly to proteins in dairy foods, eggs, peanuts, true nuts, wheat and soya products, and shellfish, or to chemicals such as monosodium glutamate, tartrazine, sulphur dioxide, and sodium benzoate in food additives	eczema, urticaria, asthma, itching around the mouth, vomiting, diarrhoea, and – in extreme cases – anaphylactic shock (see above); the most visible signs of the onset of anaphylactic shock resulting from food allergies are often swelling and rashes on the lips and tongue; food allergy is often confused with food intolerance, which is not caused by the body's immune response but by its inability to digest a particular food (for example, lactose intolerance) or by adverse reactions to druglike chemicals such as caffeine in coffee and amines in chocolate and cheese; peanut allergies affect about 0.5% of the UK population
Drug allergy	most commonly to the antibiotics penicillin and tetracycline, sulfonamides, streptomycin, and local anaesthetics such as novocaine and lidocaine	signs of an allergic reaction include fever, urticaria, itchy nose, throat or ears, and flushed skin; symptoms of a stronger reaction may include coughing, swelling – especially of the eyes or tongue, and cyanosis, a bluish tint of the skin; anaphylactic shock can be triggered by drugs like morphine or the dye injected prior to X-raying; the horse serum used in the makeup of some vaccines can also cause anaphylactic shock

(continued)

Common Allergies (*continued*)

Allergy	Cause	Symptoms/comments
Latex allergy	latex, the processed form of the milky sap derived from natural rubber trees, used mainly in gloves and many other medical products such as IV tubing and catheters, as well as in condoms, shoe soles, and swimming goggles	early symptoms include eczema, urticaria, and flushing, often followed by itching, congestion, eye irritation, wheezing, asthma, and progression into anaphylaxis; while direct skin contact is a problem, the allergen can also be inhaled – this occurs primarily when the gloves are removed and the protein which has combined with the powder inside the glove becomes airborne; those allergic to the following foods may also be sensitive to latex: avocados, bananas, potatoes, tomatoes, hazelnuts, chestnuts, kiwi, and papayas

World Health

Projected Figures for World Deaths by Age Group

Age group	1975–2000		2000–2025	
	Number (thousands)	Percentage of total	Number (thousands)	Percentage of total
0–4	304,970	25	181,024	12
5–19	96,127	8	63,400	4
20–64	349,719	28	422,028	29
65 +	482,479	39	787,202	54
Total	1,233,295	100	1,453,654	100

Source: World Health Report 1998, *World Health Organization*

Newly Recognized Infectious Diseases

Year of recognition	Agent	Type	Disease/comments
1973	Rotavirus	virus	major cause of infantile diarrhoea worldwide
1975	Parvovirus B19	virus	aplastic crisis in chronic haemolytic anaemia
1976	*Cryptosporidium parvum*	parasite	acute and chronic diarrhoea
1977	Ebola virus	virus	Ebola haemorrhagic fever
1977	*Legionella pneumophila*	bacterium	legionnaires' disease
1977	Hantaan virus	virus	haemorrhagic fever with renal syndrome (HRFS)
1977	*Campylobacter jejuni*	bacterium	enteric pathogen distributed globally
1980	human T-lymphotropic virus 1 (HTLV-1)	virus	T-cell lymphoma-leukaemia
1981	toxin-producing strains of *Staphylococcus aureus*	bacterium	toxic shock syndrome
1982	*Escherichia coli* 0157:H7	bacterium	haemorrhagic colitis; haemolytic uraemic syndrome
1982	HTLV-2	virus	hairy cell leukaemia
1982	*Borrelia burgdorferi*	bacterium	Lyme disease
1983	human immunodeficiency virus (HIV)	virus	acquired immunodeficiency syndrome (AIDS)
1983	*Helicobacter pylori*	bacterium	peptic ulcer disease
1985	*Enterocytozoon bieneusi*	parasite	persistent diarrhoea
1986	*Cyclospora cayetanensis*	parasite	persistent diarrhoea
1986	BSE agent (uncertain)	prion	bovine spongiform encephalopathy in cattle and possibly variant Creutzfeldt-Jakob disease (vCJD) in humans
1988	human herpes virus 6 (HHV-6)	virus	exanthem subitum, characterized by high fever and skin rash.
1988	hepatitis E virus	virus	enterically transmitted non-A, non-B hepatitis
1989	*Ehrlichia chaffeensis*	bacterium	human ehrlichiosis
1989	hepatitis C virus	virus	parenterally transmitted non-A, non-B liver hepatitis
1991	Guanarito virus	virus	Venezuelan haemorrhagic fever
1991	*Encephalitozoon hellem*	parasite	conjunctivitis, disseminated disease
1991	new species of *Babesia*	parasite	atypical babesiosis
1992	*Vibrio cholerae* 0139	bacterium	new strain associated with epidemic cholera
1992	*Bartonella henselae*	bacterium	cat-scratch disease causing flu-like fever; bacillary angiomatosis
1993	Sin Nombre virus	virus	Hantavirus pulmonary syndrome
1993	*Encephalitozoon cuniculi*	parasite	disseminated disease
1994	Sabia virus	virus	Brazilian haemorrhagic fever
1995	human herpes virus 8	virus	associated with Kaposi's sarcoma in AIDS patients
1996	NvCJD	prion	new variant Creutzfeldt-Jakob disease
1997	Avian influenza	Type A(9H5N1) virus	influenza; can cause Reye syndrome
1999	Nipah virus	virus	encephalitis cases and deaths caused by the virus have almost exclusively occurred in persons in close contact with pigs

Source: World Health Organization

Leading Causes of Death

There were 53.9 million deaths from all causes worldwide in 1998.

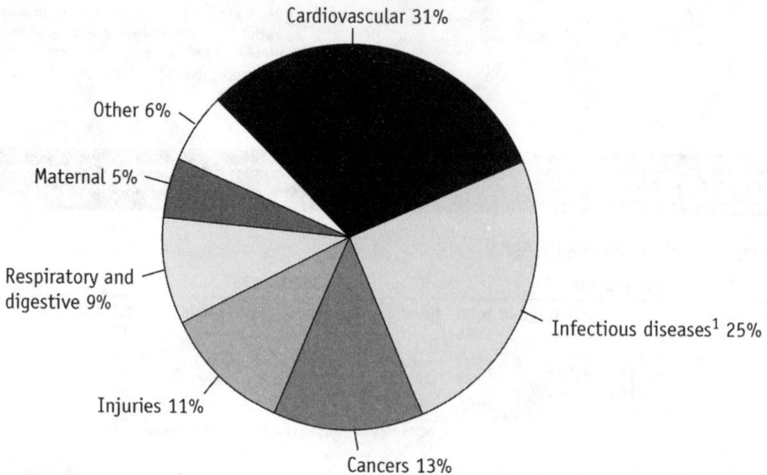

[1] Cancers, cardiovascular, and respiratory/digestive deaths can also be caused by infections and raise the percentage of deaths due to infectious diseases even more.

Source: WHO Infectious Diseases Report, © *World Health Organization 1999*

Mortality, Morbidity, and Disability for Selected Infectious Diseases in the World

(N/A = not available or not applicable. In thousands.)

1997 (estimates) **Disease by main mode of transmission**	**Deaths**	**New cases (incidence)**	**All cases (prevalence)**	**Persons with severe activity limitation[1]**
Person to person				
Acute lower respiratory infection (ALR)	3,745	395,000	N/A	N/A
Tuberculosis	2,910	7,250	16,300	8,420
Hepatitis B, viral	605	67,730	N/A	N/A
Measles	960	31,075	N/A	N/A
HIV/AIDS	2,300	5,800	30,600	N/A
Whooping cough (pertussis)	410	45,050	N/A	N/A
Meningococcal meningitis	50	N/A	500	60
Poliomyelitis, acute	2	35	N/A	10,600
Leprosy	2	570	1,150	3,000
Gonorrhoea	N/A	62,000	23,000	N/A
Syphilis, venereal	N/A	12,000	28,000	N/A
Chancroid	N/A	2,000	2,000	N/A
Trachoma	N/A	N/A	152,420	5,600
Food-, water-, and soil-borne				
Diarrhoea (including dysentery)	2,455	4,000,000[2]	N/A	N/A
Neonatal tetanus	275	415	N/A	N/A
Amoebiasis	70	48,000	N/A	N/A
Hookworm diseases	65	N/A	151,000[3]	N/A
Ascariasis	60	N/A	250,000[4]	N/A
Schistosomiasis	20	N/A	200,000	120,000
Cholera[5]	10	145	N/A	N/A
Trichuriasis	10	N/A	45,530[6]	N/A
Trematode infections (food-borne only)	10	N/A	40,000	N/A
Dracunculiasis (guinea-worm infection)	N/A	70	70	N/A
Insect-borne				
Malaria	1,500–2,700	300,000–500,000	N/A	N/A
Leishmaniasis	80	2,000	12,000	N/A
Onchocerciasis (river blindness)	45	N/A	17,655	770
Chagas' disease (American trypanosomiasis)	45	300	18,000	N/A
Dengue/dengue haemorrhagic fever	140	3,100	N/A	N/A
Sleeping sickness (African trypanosomiasis)	100	150	400	200
Japanese encephalitis	10	45	N/A	N/A
Plague[7]	0.14	2.9	N/A	N/A
Yellow fever	30	200	N/A	N/A

(continued)

 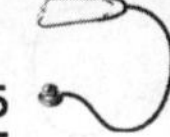

Mortality, Morbidity, and Disability for Selected Infectious Diseases in the World *(continued)*

1997 (estimates) Disease by main mode of transmission	Deaths	New cases (incidence)	All cases (prevalence)	Persons with severe activity limitation[1]
Filariasis (lymphatic)	N/A	N/A	119,100	119,100
Animal-borne				
Rabies (dog-mediated)	60	60	N/A	N/A
Others[8]	740	N/A	N/A	N/A
Total	17,310	N/A	N/A	N/A

[1] Permanent and long-term.
[2] Incidence figure refers to episodes.
[3] Number of infected persons is 1.25 billion.
[4] Number of infected persons is 1.38 billion.
[5] 1996 notifications.
[6] Number of infected persons is 1 billion.
[7] 1995 notifications.
[8] Includes noma (an infection of the mouth occurring in malnourished children) and emerging diseases eg influenza, Ebola, and lassa.

Source: The World Health Report 1998, *World Health Organization*

Percentages of Populations with Access to Safe Water and Adequate Sanitation in Selected Countries

Regional and world averages are based on latest data available 1990–98.
(– = not applicable.)

Region/area	% of population with access to safe water			% of population with access to adequate sanitation		
	Total	Urban	Rural	Total	Urban	Rural
Sub-Saharan Africa	50	77	39	45	70	35
Middle East and North Africa	85	97	72	74	92	53
South Asia	80	86	78	33	73	20
East Asia and Pacific	69	95	58	33	73	20
Latin America	78	88	42	71	82	44
CEE/CIS and Baltic States	–	–	–	–	–	–
Industrialized countries	–	–	–	–	–	–
Developing countries	72	89	62	44	79	25
Least developed countries	57	79	51	37	67	29
World	72	90	62	44	79	25

Maternal Mortality Ratio for Selected Countries by Region

Maternal mortality ratio represents the number of deaths to women per 100,000 live births, which result from conditions related to pregnancy, delivery, and related complications.

Region		Maternal mortality ratio
Africa		
Eastern Africa	Mozambique	1,500
	Eritrea	1,400
	Ethiopia	1,400
	Burundi	1,300
	Rwanda	1,300
Middle Africa	Angola	1,500
	Chad	900
	Congo, Republic of the	890
	Central African Republic	700
	Cameroon	550
Northern Africa	Morocco	372
	Sudan	370
	Libya	220
	Egypt	170
	Algeria	140
Southern Africa	Lesotho	610
	Botswana	250
	South Africa	230
	Namibia	220
Western Africa	Sierra Leone	1,800
	Nigeria	1,000
	Burkina Faso	930
	Guinea-Bissau	910
	Guinea	880

Region		Maternal mortality ratio
Asia		
Eastern Asia	China	115
	Mongolia	65
	Korea, South	30
	Japan	8
Southeastern Asia	Cambodia	900
	Laos	650
	Myanmar	580
	Indonesia	390
	Philippines	208
South-central Asia	Nepal	1,500
	Bangladesh	850
	India	437
	Pakistan	340
	Iran	120
Western Asia	Yemen	1,400
	Iraq	310
	Lebanon	300
	Turkey	180
	Syria	179
Europe		
Eastern Europe	Romania	41
	Bulgaria	20
	Hungary	14
	Poland	10
	Slovak Republic	8

(continued)

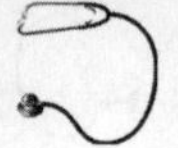

Maternal Mortality Ratio for Selected Countries by Region *(continued)*

Region		Maternal mortality ratio
Northern Europe	Estonia	52
	Latvia	15
	Lithuania	13
	Finland	11
	Ireland, Republic of	10
Southern Europe	Albania	28
	Macedonia, Former Yugoslav Republic of	22
	Portugal	15
	Croatia	12
	Italy	12
	Yugoslavia	12
Western Europe	Germany	22
	France	15
	Netherlands	12
	Austria	10
	Belgium	10
Latin America and Caribbean		
Caribbean	Haiti	600
	Jamaica	120
	Dominican Republic	110
	Trinidad and Tobago	90
	Cuba	36
Central America	El Salvador	300
	Honduras	220
	Guatemala	190
	Nicaragua	160
	Mexico	110
South America	Bolivia	370
	Peru	280
	Venezuela	200
	Paraguay	190
	Chile	180
Northern America		
	USA	12
	Canada	6
Oceania		
	Papua New Guinea	930
	New Zealand	25
	Australia	99
Former USSR		
	Tajikistan	74
	Kazakhstan	53
	Russian Federation	53
	Azerbaijan	44
	Turkmenistan	44

Source: World Development Indicators 1999, *The World Bank*

Births to Teenage Mothers in Developing Countries

Data are for women aged 15–19, showing regional averages and countries with the highest birth rate for teenage mothers. The measure does not indicate the full dimensions of teen pregnancy as only live births are included in the numerator; stillbirths and spontaneous or induced abortions are not reflected.

1995–2000

Region/country	Number of births per 1,000 women aged 15–19
Eastern Africa	
Average	132
Somalia	213
Uganda	180
Malawi	162
Ethiopia	152
Madagascar	137
Middle Africa	
Average	196
Angola	219
Congo, Democratic Republic of	217
Chad	185
Gabon	172
Cameroon	140
Northern Africa	
Average	50
Egypt	65
Libya	56
Sudan	52
Tunisia	13
Southern Africa	
Average	71
Namibia	105
Botswana	78
South Africa	68
Western Africa	
Average	136
Liberia	213
Sierra Leone	202
Niger	199
Guinea	193
Guinea-Bissau	190
Mali	181
Burkina Faso	157
Senegal	119
Southeastern Asia	
Average	48
Laos	104
Thailand	70
Indonesia	58
Philippines	43
Cambodia	14
South-central Asia	
Average	103
Afghanistan	153
Nepal	120
Bangladesh	115
India	112
Pakistan	90
Bhutan	71
Iran	29
Western Asia	
Average	57
Saudi Arabia	113
Yemen	102
Oman	80
United Arab Emirates	73
Iraq	45
Syria	44
Latin America and the Caribbean	
Average	76
Nicaragua	152
Guatemala	119
Honduras	115
Venezuela	98
El Salvador	95
Jamaica	91
Dominican Republic	89
Colombia	88
Costa Rica	85
Bolivia	79
Haiti	70

Source: World Population Prospects: The 1998 Revision, *United Nations Population Division, DESA*

Births to Teenage Mothers in Developed Countries

Data for women aged 15–19, for selected countries. The measure does not indicate the full dimensions of teen pregnancy as only live births are included in the numerator; stillbirths and spontaneous or induced abortions are not reflected.

1995–2000

Country	Number of births per 1,000 women aged 15–19
USA	59
Bulgaria	49
Russian Federation	45
Macedonia, Former Yugoslav Republic of	42
Yugoslavia	39
Estonia	38
Lithuania	37
Belarus	36
Romania	36
Ukraine	36
New Zealand	34
Moldova	32
Slovak Republic	32
Bosnia-Herzegovina	29
Hungary	29
UK	29
Latvia	27
Canada	23
Czech Republic	23
Poland	23
Australia	20
Portugal	20
Croatia	19
Ireland, Republic of	19
Israel	19
Austria	18
Slovenia	17
Greece	13
Norway	13
Belgium	11
Germany	11
Finland	10
Denmark	9
France	9
Spain	8
Italy	7
Sweden	7
Japan	4
Netherlands	4
Switzerland	4

Source: World Population Prospects: The 1998 Revision, *United Nations Population Division, DESA*

Infant Mortality and Female Fertility Rates

Fertility rate is the average number of children per woman; figures show regional averages and countries ranked by highest infant mortality rate.

1995–2000

Region	Country	Infant mortality rate (per thousand births)	Fertility rate
Africa			
Average		87	5.06
Eastern Africa	Burundi	119	6.28
	Ethiopia	116	6.30
	Malawi	138	6.75
	Mozambique	114	6.25
	Somalia	122	7.25
	Zimbabwe	69	3.80
	Average	101	5.79
Central Africa	Angola	125	6.80
	Cameroon	74	5.30
	Chad	112	6.07
	Gabon	87	5.40
	Average	95	6.17
Northern Africa	Algeria	44	3.81
	Egypt	51	3.40
	Libya	28	3.80
	Sudan	71	4.61
	Average	52	3.58
Southern Africa	Botswana	59	4.35
	Lesotho	93	4.75
	South Africa	59	3.25
	Average	62	3.43
Western Africa	Benin	88	5.80
	Guinea-Bissau	130	5.75
	Nigeria	81	5.15
	Sierra Leone	170	6.06
	Average	90	5.47
Asia			
Average		57	2.60
Eastern Asia	China	41	1.80
	Japan	4	1.43
	Korea, South	10	1.65
	Mongolia	51	2.60
	Average	38	1.77
South-central Asia	Afghanistan	152	6.90
	Bangladesh	79	3.11
	India	72	3.13
	Iran	35	2.80
	Pakistan	74	5.03
	Average	73	3.36
Southeast Asia	Cambodia	103	4.60
	Philippines	36	3.62
	Singapore	5	1.68
	Thailand	29	1.74
	Average	46	2.69
Western Asia	Azerbaijan	36	1.99
	Iraq	95	5.25
	Israel	8	2.68
	Turkey	45	2.50
	Yemen	80	7.60
	Average	51	3.77
Europe			
Average		12	1.45
Eastern Europe	Czech Republic	6	1.19
	Moldova	29	1.76
	Poland	15	1.53
	Russian Federation	18	1.35
	Ukraine	19	1.38
	Average	18	1.42
Northern Europe	Denmark	7	1.72
	Estonia	19	1.29
	Ireland, Republic of	7	1.90
	Sweden	5	1.57
	UK	7	1.72
	Average	8	1.72

(continued)

Infant Mortality and Female Fertility Rates *(continued)*

1995–2000

Region	Country	Infant mortality rate (per thousand births)	Fertility rate
Southern Europe	Albania	30	2.50
	Greece	8	1.28
	Italy	7	1.20
	Macedonia, Former Yugoslav Republic of	23	2.06
	Portugal	9	1.37
	Average	10	1.31
Western Europe	Austria	6	1.41
	France	6	1.71
	Germany	5	1.30
	Switzerland	6	1.47
	Average	6	1.48
Latin America and Caribbean			
Average		36	2.70
Caribbean	Cuba	9	1.55
	Dominican Republic	34	2.80
	Haiti	68	4.38
	Martinique	7	1.75
	Average	36	2.55
Central America	Costa Rica	12	2.83
	Mexico	31	2.75
	Nicaragua	43	4.42
	Panama	21	2.63
	Average	33	3.05
South America	Argentina	22	2.62
	Bolivia	66	4.36
	Brazil	42	2.27
	Chile	13	2.44
	Peru	45	2.98
	Average	37	2.58
North America			
Average		7	1.94
	Canada	6	1.55
	USA	7	1.99
Oceania			
Average		24	2.38
	Australia	6	1.79
	Fiji Islands	20	2.73
	New Zealand	7	2.01
	Papua New Guinea	61	4.60
	Samoa	23	4.15
World average			
Total		57	2.71
Least developed countries		99	5.05
Less developed regions		63	3.00
More developed regions		9	1.57

Source: The State of World Population 1999, © *United Nations Population Fund*

Numbers and Rates of Abortions for Selected Countries

Data represent rates of legally-induced abortions that are ranked for selected countries. Abortion rate is defined here as the number of abortions per 1,000 women aged 15–44. The very high levels of abortion in some countries, notably in Eastern Europe, are a legacy of deficiencies in family planning services, which have led to abortions being used almost as a routine method of family planning. Governments' abortion policies vary greatly, and while saving the woman's life is considered grounds on which abortion is permitted in almost all countries where abortion is legal, other factors, such as economic, social, or personal reasons, are likely to be considered sufficient grounds only in the world's more developed nations. Clinically-undertaken abortions are a safe procedure in contrast to the many illegal abortions in other countries, especially in less developed regions, which contribute substantially to higher rates of maternal mortality.

1996

Country	Rate (per 1,000 women)
Uzbekistan	83.3
Vietnam	83.3[1]
Romania	78.0
Cuba	77.7
Russian Federation	68.4[2]
Belarus	67.5
Estonia	53.8
Bulgaria	51.3
Latvia	44.1
Kazakhstan	43.9
Moldova	38.8
Armenia	35.4
Hungary	34.7
Lithuania	34.4
Macedonia, Former Yugoslav Republic of	28.5
Albania	27.2
China	26.1[2]
Mongolia	25.9
USA	22.9
Slovenia	22.8
Kyrgyzstan	22.3
Australia[3]	22.2
Georgia	21.9
Czech Republic	20.7
Slovakia	19.7
Sweden	18.7
New Zealand	16.4[2]
Denmark	16.1[2]
Azerbaijan	16.0
Singapore	15.9
Norway	15.6
Canada	15.5[4]
Israel	14.3[2]
Japan	13.4[2]
Croatia	12.9
France	12.4[2]
Ukraine	11.8
Italy	11.4
Finland	9.9
Switzerland	8.4[5]
Germany	7.6
Belgium	6.8[6]
Netherlands	6.5
Ireland, Republic of	5.9[7]
Spain	5.7
Bangladesh	3.8
India	2.7
South Africa	2.7[8]

[1] Excludes an estimated 500,000 private sector abortions.
[2] 1995.
[3] Abortion law in Australia is determined at the state level and is governed by various state laws and, in some states, court decisions. The most restrictive laws allow abortion to be performed to save the life of the woman and to preserve her physical or mental health; the most liberal law (Western Australia) allows abortion on request.
[4] Including abortions in the USA.
[5] Includes estimates for 2 of the 26 cantons.
[6] Including abortions obtained in the Netherlands.
[7] Based on the Irish residents who obtained abortions in England.
[8] 1997.

Source: United Nations Development Program/United Nations/Population Division, DESA

See also **Abortions in England and Wales by Age Group**, p 526.

■ World Health

Dependency Ratios Worldwide

Dependency ratio is the ratio of the population under 15 and over 65 to the population aged 15–64 (per 100 persons aged 15–64).

Region	Age	*Dependency ratio (per 100)* 1995–2000	2020–25	2045–50
Africa				
Eastern Africa	0–14	89.7	69.0	38.6
	65+	5.5	4.6	7.7
	Total	95.2	73.7	46.3
Central Africa	0–14	91.6	75.5	40.6
	65+	6.2	5.5	7.3
	Total	97.7	81.0	48.0
Northern Africa	0–14	66.4	39.7	31.8
	65+	6.6	8.7	18.3
	Total	73.0	48.3	50.1
Southern Africa	0–14	62.1	46.2	34.7
	65+	5.7	6.5	11.2
	Total	67.8	52.7	45.8
Western Africa	0–14	87.8	65.4	37.4
	65+	5.6	5.7	9.1
	Total	93.4	71.1	46.5
Total	0–14	81.8	61.1	37.2
	65+	5.9	6.0	10.0
	TOTAL	87.7	67.2	47.3
Asia				
Eastern Asia	0–14	37.5	27.1	26.5
	65+	10.1	18.3	37.1
	Total	47.6	45.4	63.7
South-central Asia	0–14	63.1	38.3	30.9
	65+	7.3	9.7	18.8
	Total	70.4	48.0	49.7
Southeast Asia	0–14	55.1	34.8	30.8
	65+	7.0	10.3	23.5
	Total	62.1	45.0	54.3
Western Asia	0–14	62.4	46.3	33.3
	65+	7.5	9.9	17.9
	Total	69.9	56.2	51.3
Total	0–14	50.5	34.1	29.7
	65+	8.5	13.0	25.1
	TOTAL	59.0	47.1	54.8
Europe				
Eastern Europe	0–14	31.4	22.7	23.2
	65+	18.4	24.4	39.4
	Total	49.8	47.1	62.6
Northern Europe	0–14	29.8	25.9	27.0
	65+	23.7	31.3	42.3
	Total	53.6	57.2	69.3
Southern Europe	0–14	24.9	20.1	23.6
	65+	22.1	32.4	58.2
	Total	46.9	52.5	81.8

Region	Age	*Dependency ratio (per 100)* 1995–2000	2020–25	2045–50
Western Europe	0–14	26.3	22.9	25.2
	65+	22.4	32.3	47.4
	Total	48.7	55.2	72.6
Total	0–14	28.6	22.7	24.3
	65+	20.8	28.8	45.2
	TOTAL	49.4	51.5	69.5
Latin America and the Caribbean				
Caribbean	0–14	50.0	35.7	30.7
	65+	10.6	15.1	27.5
	Total	60.6	50.8	58.2
Central America	0–14	62.9	39.8	32.2
	65+	7.1	10.8	23.5
	Total	70.0	50.6	55.7
South America	0–14	52.9	36.3	32.0
	65+	8.5	12.7	24.0
	Total	61.3	49.0	56.0
Total	0–14	55.1	37.2	32.0
	65+	8.3	12.3	24.1
	TOTAL	63.4	49.6	56.0
North America				
	0–14	33.5	28.0	27.9
	65+	19.0	25.8	35.5
	TOTAL	52.5	53.8	63.4
Oceania				
Australia and New Zealand	0–14	32.9	28.4	28.7
	65+	18.1	25.6	36.3
	Total	51.0	54.0	65.0
Total	0–14	40.4	34.0	30.5
	65+	15.3	20.4	28.8
	TOTAL	55.7	54.4	59.3
World				
More developed regions[1]	0–14	29.3	24.4	25.8
	65+	20.3	29.3	42.7
	Total	49.6	53.7	68.4
Less developed regions[2]	0–14	56.2	39.2	31.7
	65+	7.7	11.2	21.1
	Total	63.9	50.4	52.8
Least developed countries[3]	0–14	81.0	61.2	37.2
	65+	5.7	8.0	10.2
	Total	86.7	67.2	47.4
Total	0–14	50.2	36.9	31.0
	65+	10.5	14.1	23.8
	TOTAL	60.7	50.9	54.8

[1] More developed regions comprise Northern America, Japan, Europe, and Australia and New Zealand.
[2] Less developed regions comprise all regions of Africa, Asia (excluding Japan), Latin America and the Caribbean, Melanesia, Micronesia, and Polynesia.
[3] Least developed countries according to standard UN designation.

Source: United Nations Population Division, Department of Economic and Social Affairs

UK Health and Health Care

Health Authorities Face Tough Tests and Deeper Debt

The 41 performance indicators that measure health authority performance, published in July 2000, highlighted great regional variations. The new measures – known as Higher Level Performance Indicators – look first at background quality of health in an area and work through a series of indicators in order to determine what effect the area's health services have on health problems. As might be expected, some figures suggest that where you live plays a large part in your chances of good health. For example, in the case of the indicator for deaths from all circulatory disease – where a low score is good and a high score is bad – prosperous West Sussex scored 97.2, compared to industrial Manchester's 201.8. In the indicator for number of GPs (in which higher numbers reflect higher number of GPs in the health authority), Kingston and Richmond scored 71.2, compared with Sunderland's 43.1. The indicator for patient satisfaction – in which higher numbers indicate a higher proportion of patients who had complained or felt like complaining about surgery staff – reported a score of 8 for Gloucestershire, compared with 19 for Liverpool.

In the March 2000 Budget, Chancellor Gordon Brown promised the NHS an extra £2 billion for the next four years – an annual increase of more than 6% above inflation. Prime Minister Tony Blair set the health service five challenges in return for the additional funding announced in the Budget. Blair said the need for new cash for the NHS was clear – but added

Health Authorities Face Tough Tests and Deeper Debt *(continued)*

that it must be accompanied by 'fundamental reforms', and urged the health service to meet challenges on partnership, performance, professions, patient care, and prevention. It was also clear that there were too many discrepancies in standards between different hospitals and NHS Trusts.

However, the financial deficits facing health authorities and hospitals were set to worsen, according to figures contained in the National Audit Office's summary of NHS accounts published in April 2000. It appeared likely that a large share of the extra funds would be used to pay off a proportion of NHS debts. Although the debt situation improved slightly in the year up to March 1999, predictions for 1999–2000 showed a huge increase in debt. In the 1998–99 financial year, NHS authorities and hospital trusts ended up with a combined deficit of £18 million. Predictions for the following year suggest that this is about to escalate to almost £200 million. Half of the 100 health authorities recorded a deficit in 1998–99, and one in four NHS trusts. In fact, one in five health authorities and one in eight hospital or community trusts were officially classed as being in 'serious financial difficulty'.

NHS Reforms

Under the NHS reforms which took effect in April 1999, GP fundholding would be replaced by a system of Primary Care Groups (PCG). Individual GP fundholding practices would no longer purchase care from trusts. Instead, groups of approximately 50 GPs would be organized into local collectives (PCGs) and have responsibility for purchasing health care for around 100,000 patients in their local area. They would be able to buy most hospital and community care for their patients, and would have to decide how to spend local NHS resources in consultation with other health and social services workers.

The government's reforms were outlined in its Health White Paper for England, unveiled in December 1997, which announced a reduction in the number of NHS trusts and health authorities, and a limitation on the internal market system introduced by the Conservatives in 1990. The health secretary claimed the changes would save £1 billion by cutting unnecessary red tape.

PCGs were the government's response to the Conservatives' market-led division of GPs into fundholders and non-fundholders. The 600 PCGs would bring together local health professionals including GPs, managers, and patients. They would make decisions about spending on local health services and each would have a member of the public on its board.

Health minister Alan Milburn averted the threat of industrial action by GPs in June 1998 after agreeing to a package of changes to the government's proposed reforms of the NHS. GPs across the country had expressed increasing disquiet with the proposal that the PCGs would control a single budget for drugs, hospital procedures, and GP surgery costs, but, after intensive negotiations, said they were satisfied that the proposals to establish a network of PCGs were workable, and the major threats to patient care and GP morale had been addressed.

As no new money had been promised for the NHS, GPs faced the prospect of being blamed by the public for lack of resources. Their biggest fear was that, once operations and drugs had been paid for, there would be nothing left to develop family doctors' surgeries. In June 1998, the health minister personally guaranteed that the level of investment in primary care infrastructure would be maintained and uplifted to take account of inflation.

Key Dates in the UK's National Health Service

1828 The UK's first hospital providing free medical treatment for the poor is opened in London by the surgeon William Marsden. It is later known as the Royal Free Hospital.

1911 The Liberal government's National Insurance Act provides state-funded medical treatment to lower paid workers (but not their families). The workers contribute four pence a week, employers three pence, and the state two pence. Ten million workers are covered by this National Health Insurance Scheme.

1917 Free treatment of venereal disease is introduced for civilians as well as soldiers.

1929 The Local Government Act gives local authorities powers to transform Poor Law infirmaries (providing treatment to the destitute) into municipal hospitals.

1939 Emergency medical servces introduced, initially to cover air raid casualties.

December 1942 The Beveridge Report on *Social Insurance and Allied Services* advocates a comprehensive health service available to all. Its estimates of annual cost (£170 million) and prediction of a fall in demand for treatment as the nation's health improves are to prove wildly wrong.

February 1944 Winston Churchill's wartime coalition government issues a consultative white paper, *A National Health Service*, suggesting GPs be under contract to a central medical board (later a local committee).

6 November 1946 The Labour government, with Aneurin Bevan (1897–1960) as health minister, secures passage of a National Health Act. The Act provides for free medical and dental services for all, establishes local health centres and state control over (formerly local authority and voluntary) hospitals.

February 1948 The British Medical Association (BMA), the representative body of general practitioners (GPs), or family doctors, organizes a poll of its members, of whom eight times more vote against the National Health Act than in its favour.

5 July 1948 The National Health Service (NHS) comes into effect, and nine-tenths of GPs agree to join.

22 April 1951 Bevan, now minister for labour, and Harold Wilson, president of the board of trade, resign from the Labour government in opposition to the imposition of charges for dentures and spectacles while defence spending increases.

1952 Prescription charges of one shilling (5p) and a flat rate charge of £1 for NHS dental treatment are introduced as health costs rise, in line with growing demand and new types of operations.

1961 An oral contraceptive pill becomes available on the NHS.

1962 The Conservative Party, with Enoch Powell as health minister, launches a 10-year programme of building new district general hospitals.

1965 The Labour government abolishes prescription and dental charges.

1968 The Labour government re-imposes prescription and dental charges, setting them at half the cost of the treatment.

1974 Under the National Health Service Reorganization Act 1973, NHS management is reorganized in response to the creation of a new local government structure in England and Wales, and a new needs-based resource allocation system is introduced. A three-tier structure of health authorities is created – Regional Health Authorities, Area Health Authorities, and District Management Teams –, to coordinate administration of hospital, GP, and local authority health services. Hospitals' waiting lists (for those waiting more than three months for treatment) rise to 550,000.

July 1974 to April 1975 NHS employees carry out sporadic industrial action against pay beds (where private patients pay for advantages such as individual rooms in NHS hospitals) and wage conditions. At the end

UK Health and Health Care

 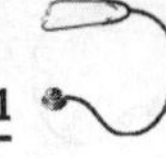

Key Dates in the UK's National Health Service (*continued*)

of the dispute Labour's social services secretary, Barbara Castle, announces that 'pay beds' will be abolished.

1979 The Area Health Authorities are abolished, and District Health Authorities replace the District management Teams.

1980 The new Conservative government's Health Services Act restores pay beds and eases controls on private hospitals.

1983 NHS hospitals are required to allow private contractors to tender for cleaning, catering, and laundry services, as part of the Conservative government's 'compulsory competitive tendering' initiative. New tier of general management introduced into NHS.

1988 Charges for (formerly free) eye tests and dental checks are introduced under the Health and Medicines Act 1988. Despite recent real increases in expenditure, the House of Commons Social Services Select Committee estimates that the NHS has been underfunded since 1981 by £2 billion as demand outstrips capacity and waiting lists grow.

1989 The White Paper, *Working for Patients*, foreshadows sweeping changes in the NHS. Tax relief is given on private health insurance premiums paid by the over 60s, boosting the private sector.

1990 The NHS is fundamentally reformed by the Conservatives' National Health Service and Community Care Act. Hospitals are given the right to become self-governing trust hospitals, independent of local health authorities, and are able to borrow and fix their own wages; larger general practices are given control of their budgets; and local authorities now have a responsibility to provide care for the elderly and handicapped in the community as well as in institutions. Despite BMA opposition, an NHS competitive 'internal market' is created in which 'fund-holding GPs' purchase non-acute treatments and operations for their patients from hospital 'providers'.

1992 Patients' Charter introduced (first published 1991), setting out service standards and rights for patients. An expanded version is published in 1995. The charter covers dental, optical, and pharmaceutical services, and hospital treatment.

1993 The number on hospital waiting lists for operations rises to over one million for the first time. The BMA lifts its opposition to GP fundholding. NHS treatment dental charges rise to 80% of costs.

1995 Following the passage of the Health Authorities Act, all health care is now provided by NHS Trusts.

April 1996 Regional Health Authorities are abolished and replaced by the eight offices of the NHS Executive. District Health Authorities and Family Health Service Authorities are merged to form 100 unified Health Authorities in England.

1997 NHS (Primary Care) Act allows flexibility in the delivery of primary healthcare services to patients. The National Institute of Clinical Excellence (NICE) is established to develop standards for NHS clinical care.

May 1997 A new Labour government, led by Tony Blair, comes to power, and pledges to abolish the internal market and reduce waiting lists by 100,000 over the lifetime of the Parliament.

December 1997 The government, in its White Paper, *The New NHS*, announces a reduction in the number of NHS trusts and health authorities and limitations on the internal market.

1998 Following a pilot project in three areas in March, NHS Direct, a new 24-hour telephone helpline staffed by nurses, is launched to give people fast access to health information. The service aims to cover 60% of the country by December 1999. (In 1999 an NHS Direct Online Internet site is Created.) The first 'Health Action Zones' are established in 11 areas of deprivation (15 more are set up in April 1999).

February 1999 The Labour government announces large pay increases for NHS workers, including a 12% increase in the salary of newly qualified nurses to counter growing recruitment difficulties.

April 1999 Under the Health Care Act 1999, GP practices are reorganized into primary care groups (comprising around 50 GPs) and fundholding status is abolished. An independent Commission for Health Improvement is to be set up to monitor local provision of clinical services. Free eye tests are restored to those over 60.

July 1999 The white paper *Saving Lives: Our Healthier Nation* is published, setting out targets in the four main areas of illness – heart disease and stroke, accidents, cancer, and mental health – to be achieved by 2010.

16 January 2000 After a flu epidemic, which leads to a rise in waiting lists, prime minister Tony Blair announces a plan to spend an extra £12 billion on the NHS over the next six years, with the goal of bringing UK health spending up to the European average.

July 2000 The government publishes its 'National Plan' for a new NHS. Proposals include greater NHS use of private care facilities to reduce waiting lists.

Government Spending on the National Health Service in the UK

Years ending 31 March.
(N = nil or negligible. In millions of pounds.)

Expenditure	1988–89	1990–91	1992–93	1994–95	1996–97	1998–99
Current expenditure						
Central government						
hospitals, community health services,[1] and family health services[2]	21,110	25,276	32,195	37,698	39,425	43,600
administration[3]	682	979	1,258	N	N	N
less payments by patients						
hospital services	– 347	– 510	– 505	– 111	– 42	– 84
pharmaceutical services	– 202	– 247	– 297	– 342	– 376	– 390
dental services	– 282	– 441	– 470	– 464	– 447	– 470
ophthalmic services	N	N	N	N	N	N
Total	– 831	– 1,198	– 1,272	– 917	– 865	– 944
Departmental administration	206	268	319	256	265	227
Other central services	604	738	1,301	2,304	3,124	3,357
Total current expenditure	21,771	26,063	33,801	39,341	41,949	45,346
Capital expenditure						
Central government	1,309	1,848	1,612	538	434	233

(*continued*)

Government Spending on the National Health Service in the UK *(continued)*

Expenditure	1988–89	1990–91	1992–93	1994–95	1996–97	1998–99
Total expenditure						
Central government	23,080	27,911	35,413	39,879	42,383	45,579
Total government expenditure as % of GDP[4]	4.82	4.96	5.78	5.81	5.53	5.36

[1] Includes the school health service.
[2] General medical services have been included in the expenditure of the Health Authorities. Therefore, hospitals and community health services and family practitioner services (now family health services) are not identifiable separately.
[3] Administration costs are not separately identifiable from 1993–94.
[4] GDP is adjusted to take account of change from rates to community charge.

Source: Annual Abstract of Statistics 2000, © *Crown copyright 2000*

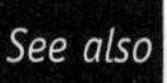

See also **Government Spending and Social Protection,** pp 111–115.

More Cash for the NHS – A Nurse's View

by Jane DeVille-Almond

In 2000, the National Health Service (NHS) saw the advent of the largest sustained government investment since it was founded in 1948. Chancellor Gordon Brown, in his March 2000 budget, gave the NHS an annual rise of more than 6% above inflation, a 35% increase in funding in real terms. NHS spending will rise from £49.3 billion in the financial year 1999–2000 to £54.2 billion in 2000–01 (£2 billion more than planned), and will reach £68.7 billion in 2003–04. Aiming to bring the UK closer to the average level of spending on health in the rest of Europe, government spending per household on the NHS will rise from £1,850 in 1999 to £2,800 by 2004.

NHS Reform Following the 2000 budget, Prime Minister Tony Blair stressed the need for 'fundamental reform' of the NHS to ensure effective use of the extra funding, with challenges for improvement being set in five areas: partnership, performance, professions, patient care (services and self care), and prevention. To address these challenges six modernization action teams of health professionals, managers, and health ministers are drawing up a national plan for the NHS, a ten-year government strategy for radical and real beneficial change to be unveiled at the end of July 2000. £500,000 has also been spent on 12 million public questionnaires on NHS reform, over 210,000 replies being returned by mid-June. The three top priorities expressed by the public are greater capacity (more doctors, nurses, and more pay); less waiting; and generally doing things differently. Better hospital food, medical records on smart cards, more information in waiting areas, and changes in the attitudes of medical personnel delivering services to patients were also noted as important. It was felt that children's provision should be given priority, followed by services for the elderly. However, will following the ideas of the public give the UK an improved NHS? Many health professionals think such decisions are best left to the professionals themselves, who have a deeper understanding of the issues. Possible targets in the national plan include renegotiation of NHS consultants' contracts to eradicate variations in productivity and improve commitment to NHS time; annual appraisal of doctors and consultants; revalidation approximately every five years; early warning systems for reporting incompetence or malpractice; the creation of dedicated centres for elective surgery; and increased use of spare private capacity (for instance, private theatres being rented but staffed by NHS personnel). Many health professionals, however, express concern regarding possible over-centralization in the national plan, preferring flexibility in management and spending to suit local circumstances. The possibility of performance-related pay for hospitals that achieve certain targets has also raised fears that people living close to badly run hospitals will be punished twice – firstly by receiving a poor service, and secondly by having a hospital with less money to improve.

Tackling Waiting Lists and Error The most popular target for funding, amongst NHS employees and the public, is the recruitment and training of more doctors and nurses on the wards to reduce waiting lists; part of the increase in NHS funding is already pledged to the recruitment of up to 10,000 more nurses. There are also calls for three-shift working to cut down the backlog of patients awaiting surgery. The government would like to see a maximum three-month waiting period, but to achieve this will require all, if not more, of the new money, since it will necessarily involve increasing wages, pensions, and so on. However, investment in personnel will bring economic savings, too, with fixed assets used more efficiently and a larger and better-trained workforce bringing about a significant reduction in costly negligence actions. Figures up to June 2000 indicate that outstanding claims for victims of medical accidents have reached £3.4 billion, a rise of £600 million on the previous year. Errors in the use of prescribed drugs count for 20% of cases annually, while 50% of the annual bill is for obstetric and gynaecological claims. The British Medical Association has stated that an immediate increase in the number of consultants employed in obstetrics and gynaecology would reduce litigation in this area (in April 2000 there were 150 newly qualified obstetrics and gynaecology consultants unable to find a consultancy).

Public Health and Inequality There needs to be big investment in public health, a poor vote catcher as this area offers no short-term solutions but is the foundation stone of a lasting, improved NHS. It is also clear that the many discrepancies in standards between different hospitals and NHS Trusts across the UK must be addressed. The 41 performance indicators that measure health authority performance, published in June 1999, greatly highlighted regional variations and, not surprisingly, suggested that where you live plays a large part in your chances of good health. For example, in the case of the indicator for avoidable deaths – where a

More Cash for the NHS – A Nurse's View (*continued*)

low score is good and a high score is bad – prosperous West Surrey got 33 compared to industrial Manchester's 80. However, tackling problems of poverty and inequality will take more than just the provision of a shiny new health centre and more staff; there needs to be proper investment to solve the issues surrounding bad housing, unemployment, and poor education, all of which have long-term effects on health.

Leadership and a Common Vision An improved NHS requires a fundamental shake-up of the way professionals are organized, motivated, and led, and a change in traditional demarcations, with nurses and physiotherapists, for instance, providing a greater share of clinical services to free up doctors' and consultants' time. What will really make such changes come about is a dedicated workforce that shares in a common vision. The NHS cannot afford a workforce confused by focus groups arguing over how best to spend this money. Most staff in the NHS do not need a manager – they can manage themselves – however leadership is crucial to develop, communicate, and ensure acceptance of a shared realistic vision. Sadly, it seems that such leadership is sorely lacking in today's NHS, and without leadership and a clear strategy an improved NHS may be an unfulfilled dream, no matter how much money is thrown into its coffers.

The Backlog of Debt In the meantime, there is a real likelihood that a large share of the extra money will be eaten up paying off debts incurred by health authorities and trusts during years of inefficient spending on overpriced management and red tape. According to the National Audit Office's summary of NHS accounts published in April 2000, the combined deficits of NHS health authorities and hospital trusts are predicted to rocket from £18 million in the financial year 1998–99 to almost £200 million in 1999–2000. Half the 100 health authorities recorded a deficit in 1998–99, as did one in four NHS trusts. In fact, one in five health authorities and one in eight hospital or community trusts were officially classed as being in 'serious financial difficulty'.

Employment in Health and Personal Social Services in Britain

At 30 September each year.
(N/A = not available.)

Summary		1988	1998
Health Service staff and practitioners			
Medical staff[1]	hospital	45,438	65,088
	community health[2]	3,435	2,320
	Total	48,873	67,408
Dental staff	hospital[1]	1,465	1,807
	community health[2]	1,663	1,386
	Total	3,128	3,193
Nursing and midwifery staff[3]		489,574	409,738
Professional and technical staff[3]		95,521	123,833
Health care assistants		N/A	21,887
Support staff		N/A	71,025
Ancillary, works and maintenance[3]		167,185	36,265
Administrative and clerical staff[3]		137,899	159,351
Ambulance staff[3]		22,302	18,526
Others[3]		N/A	3,014
Family Health services			
GPs		32,890	35,611
Dentists		17,440	20,216
Ophthalmic medical practitioners		930	855
Ophthalmic opticians		6,381	8,160
Personal Social Services staff			
Management, administration, and ancillary staff		24,993	N/A
Home help service		60,435	50,417
Field social workers		22,924	33,400
Day care establishments staff		27,962	30,300
Residential care staff		88,496	62,100
All other staff		3,502	N/A

[1] Whole-time equivalent. Excludes locums and GPs participating in Hospital Staff Fund.
[2] Whole-time equivalent. Excludes locums and occasional seasonal staff.
[3] A new system for classifying NHS mon-medical staff was used for the first time in September 1995.

Source: Annual Abstract of Statistics 2000, *© Crown copyright 2000*

Life Expectancy in the UK

Figures show the average future lifespan of a person at the age given in the first column. Data give interim life tables, 1996–98.
(In years.)

Age	Life expectancy	
	men	women
0	74.6	79.6
5	70.2	75.1
10	65.2	70.2
15	60.3	65.2
20	55.5	60.3
25	50.7	55.4
30	45.9	50.5
35	41.1	45.6
40	36.4	40.8
45	31.7	36.0
50	27.2	31.4
55	22.8	26.9
60	18.8	22.6
65	15.0	18.5
70	11.8	14.7
75	9.0	11.4
80	6.7	8.5
85	5.0	6.2

Source: Annual Abstract of Statistics 2000, *© Crown copyright 2000*

Health Information Service

The National Health Service provides a freephone Health Information Service for the public. Calls will automatically be routed to a local information centre, providing access to local information as well as details of national organizations and services.

Calls are answered by trained information staff and are in complete confidence. Medical advice and counselling are not provided. Health Information Service centres are open at least from 9.00 a.m. to 5.00 p.m., and in some areas there are longer hours.

Phone the Health Information Service free of charge for information on:

- NHS services
- self-help and support organizations
- keeping healthy
- illnesses and treatments
- waiting times
- rights and how to complain

0800 66 55 44 covers England and Wales. In Scotland similar information is provided on 0800 22 44 88.
Details of the Health Information Service and other national helplines are given on the Department of Health Web site: www.doh.gov.uk; e-mail: info@netsoct.co.uk

Staff in the National Health Service in England by Gender and Ethnic Group

Data are correct to September 1998 and include statistics for directly employed personnel only.

Staff description	% of staff						
	Gender		Ethnic group				
	Men	Women	White	Black	Asian	Other	Unkown
All directly employed staff	24.5	75.5	87.1	3.1	3.2	2.6	4.0
Nursing, midwifery, and health-visiting staff	12.2	87.8	86.4	3.9	1.3	2.4	6.0
of which: qualified staff	11.4	88.6	87.4	4.0	1.5	2.5	4.6
Medical and dental staff	66.6	33.4	64.7	3.9	17.3	8.3	5.8
Other direct-care staff	23.7	76.3	89.9	4.6	1.7	1.8	1.9
Administration and estates staff	25.1	74.9	93.4	2.0	1.6	1.3	1.7
Other management and support staff	42.5	57.5	92.2	2.8	1.0	2.0	2.0

Source: Health and Personal Social Services Statistics for England 1999, *© Crown copyright 2000*

NHS Direct

NHS Direct is a 24-hour telephone advice and information service staffed by experienced nurses. NHS Direct is currently available to 30 million people and aims to cover the whole of England by the end of 2000.

If you feel that there is something wrong with you, or with someone you are calling about, an NHS Direct nurse will be able to:

- tell you whether the symptoms can be managed safely at home, and advise you on what to do
- advise you if you do need to seek further professional help, and direct you to the right service at the right time – telling you, for instance, whether you need to contact your doctor or go to your local hospital's accident and emergency department

Phone: 0845 4647 (calls are charged at local rate)

Web site: www.nhsdirect.nhs.uk

National Health Service Hospital Waiting Lists by Region

Data include people waiting for admission as either an in-patient or a day case. As of 31 March 1999. Data are in percentages unless otherwise stated. (N/A = not available. N = nil or negligible.)

Region	Less than 6 months	6 months, but less than 12	12 months or longer	Average time spent waiting (months)
England				
Northern and Yorkshire	77	22	N	3.9
North West	76	20	4	4.1
Trent	74	21	5	4.3
West Midlands	79	18	3	3.8
Anglia and Oxford	74	22	5	4.3
North Thames	69	24	7	4.8
South Thames	69	25	6	4.8
South and West	76	20	4	4.1
England total	74	22	4	4.3
Wales	N/A	11	N/A	N/A
Scotland[1]	86	12	1	2.4
Northern Ireland	63	19	18	N/A

[1] Figures are as at 31 March 1998.

Source: Social Trends 30, *© Crown copyright 2000*

Deaths Analysed by Cause in the UK

(N = nil or negligible.)

Cause	1992[1]	1994	1996[4]	1998
England and Wales				
Deaths from natural causes[2]				
infectious and parasitic diseases[3]	2,633	3,318	3,636	3,410
neoplasms	145,963	141,747	139,459	138,306
endocrine, nutritional, and metabolic diseases and immunity disorders	10,605	7,430	7,502	7,542
diseases of the blood and blood-forming organs	2,417	1,898	1,986	1,937
mental disorders	12,950	8,042	9,296	10,430
diseases of the nervous system and sense organs	11,577	9,010	9,772	10,035
diseases of the circulatory system	254,683	242,213	237,669	226,677
diseases of the respiratory system	60,388	81,485	88,630	90,192
diseases of the digestive system	18,742	18,635	19,946	21,025
diseases of the genito-urinary system	5,306	6,812	6,752	6,946
complications of pregnancy, childbirth, etc	45	50	41	43
diseases of the skin and subcutaneous tissue	907	1,107	1,075	1,070
diseases of the musculo-skeletal system	5,376	3,406	3,517	3,566
congenital anomalies	1,565	1,301	1,227	1,247

(continued)

 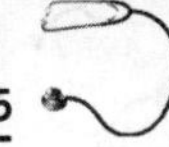

Deaths Analysed by Cause in the UK *(continued)*

Cause	1992[1]	1994	1996[4]	1998
certain conditions originating in the perinatal period	242	147	149	124
signs, symptoms, and ill-defined conditions	5,278	7,754	10,772	13,846
Total	538,677	534,354	541,429	536,396
Deaths from injury and poisoning[2]				
all accidents	12,729	10,219	10,479	10,351
of which motor vehicle accidents	4,114	3,279	3,184	2,946
suicide and self-inflicted injury	3,952	3,619	3,445	3,614
all other external causes	2,294	2,253	2,137	2,236
Total	17,074	16,091	16,061	16,201
TOTAL	555,358	553,194	560,135	555,015
Scotland				
Deaths from natural causes[2]				
infectious and parasitic diseases[3]	270	306	493	486
neoplasms	15,312	15,394	15,419	14,907
endocrine, nutritional, and metabolic diseases and immunity disorders	742	768	722	797
diseases of the blood and blood-forming organs	183	121	180	222
mental disorders	1,133	1,306	1,595	1,725
diseases of the nervous system and sense organs	877	853	852	894
diseases of the circulatory system	28,776	27,138	26,728	25,253
diseases of the respiratory system	6,999	6,981	7,863	8,011
diseases of the digestive system	2,122	2,192	2,440	2,578
diseases of the genito-urinary system	888	816	839	890
complications of pregnancy, childbirth, etc	7	9	6	5
diseases of the skin and subcutaneous tissue	82	101	75	94
diseases of the musculo-skeletal system	306	279	252	284
congenital anomalies	209	170	192	176
certain conditions originating in the perinatal period	216	191	181	165
signs, symptoms, and ill-defined conditions	280	311	337	398
Total	58,098	56,710	57,941	56,579
Deaths from injury and poisoning[2]				
all accidents	1,580	1,413	1,497	1,388
of which motor vehicle accidents	468	354	363	387
suicide and self-inflicted injury	569	624	596	649
all other external causes	386	335	404	342
Total	2,535	2,372	2,497	2,379
TOTAL	60,937	59,328	60,671	59,164
Northern Ireland				
Deaths from natural causes[2]				
infectious and parasitic diseases[3]	41	39	54	53
neoplasms	3,621	3,665	3,715	3,769
endocrine, nutritional, and metabolic diseases and immunity disorders	38	47	81	85
diseases of the blood and blood-forming organs	18	29	22	24
mental disorders	52	91	100	145
diseases of the nervous system and sense organs	181	187	236	240
diseases of the circulatory system	7,112	7,011	6,633	6,367
diseases of the respiratory system	2,423	2,398	2,749	2,627
diseases of the digestive system	405	424	483	499
diseases of the genito-urinary system	238	250	254	265
complications of pregnancy, childbirth, etc	N	N	1	1
diseases of the skin and subcutaneous tissue	27	27	29	36
diseases of the musculo-skeletal system	43	31	35	30
congenital anomalies	77	87	72	70
certain conditions originating in the perinatal period	63	69	68	64
signs, symptoms, and ill-defined conditions	46	44	88	149
Total	14,303	14,325	14,528	14,271
Deaths from injury and poisoning[2]				
all accidents	376	430	402	381
of which motor vehicle accidents	165	172	121	129
suicide and self-inflicted injury	107	138	124	126
all other external causes	98	120	72	62
Total	581	688	598	569
TOTAL	14,988	15,633	15,218	14,933
UK TOTAL	631,283	627,636	638,896	629,112

[1] On 1 January 1986, a new certificate for deaths within the first 28 days of life was introduced. It is not possible to assign one underlying cause of death from this certificate. The 'cause' figures in this table exclude all deaths at ages under 28 days.
[2] Within certain main categories only selected causes of death are shown.
[3] Deaths assigned to AIDS and AIDS-related diseases are included in immunity disorders for England and Wales up to 1992 and Scotland up to 1995. Northern Ireland has always assigned such deaths to infectious diseases. England and Wales adopted this practice from 1993 onwards.
[4] Data for 1995 and 1996 have been amended to show the number of deaths that occurred during the calendar year. Data up to 1992 give the number of deaths that were registered in the calendar year and subsequent years give the number that occurred during the calendar year.

Source: Annual Abstract of Statistics 2000, *© Crown copyright 2000*

See also **Death Rates per 1,000 Population in the UK**, p 101.

Infant and Maternal Mortality in the UK

(Per 1,000 live births.)

Year	Deaths of infants under one year	Maternal deaths in pregnancy and childbirth
1900–02	142	4.71
1910–12	110	3.95
1920–22	82	4.37
1930–32	67	4.54
1940–42	59	3.29
1950–52	30	0.88
1960–62	22	0.36
1970–72	18	0.17
1980–82	12	0.09
1990–92	7	0.07
1998	5.7	0.07

Source: Annual Abstract of Statistics 2000, © *Crown copyright 2000*

See also **Births in the UK**, p 100.

Abortions in Britain

1998

Age	England and Wales	Scotland[1]
Under 15	1,103	73
15	2,656	212
16–19	33,236	2,694
20–24	45,766	3,404
25–29	40,366	2,740
30–34	30,449	1,799
35–39	18,174	1,143
40–44	5,576	338
45 and over	511	21
All ages	177,871	12,424

[1] Provisional data.

Source: Annual Abstract of Statistics 2000, © *Crown copyright 2000*

Abortions in England and Wales by Age Group

This shows numbers of abortions, in thousands, for all women resident in England and Wales.

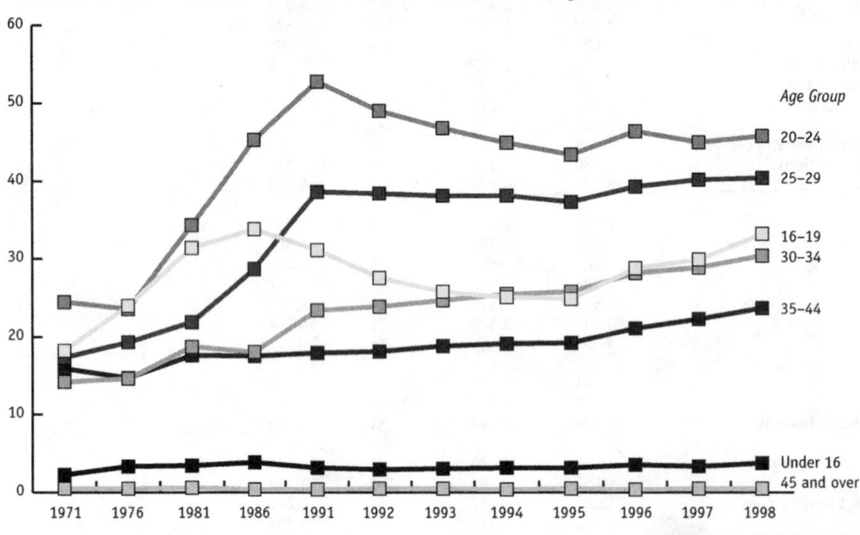

Source: Health Statistics Quarterly, Spring 2000, ©*Crown copyright 2000*

Mental Health

One in four people in Britain will experience some form of mental health problem at some point in their life. There are many types of problem, including anxiety, depression, schizophrenia, and personality disorders, and problems can vary greatly in severity and duration.

Mental health is most often mentioned in the media in relation to violence and crime, and the popular image this creates is a distortion of the facts. For example, research has shown that you are 14 times more likely to be attacked by someone without a diagnosed mental health problem than by someone with a mental illness. Equally, one of the most significant, yet overlooked, features of mental health problems is the danger posed not to others but to the self: about 1,000 people with mental health problems commit suicide each year in Britain, and suicide is the leading cause of death for men under 25 in Britain.

Mental health problems affect people from all social backgrounds. Most researchers agree that serious mental health problems are caused by an interplay of genetic predisposition and environmental stresses. Social stress from poverty, unemployment, and bereavement can be a factor in the development of problems, and in turn the problems can cause difficulties in employment and housing for sufferers, and can result in their social exclusion.

There has been a general trend in recent years towards care in the community. The government promised an extra £510 million in funding for mental health services in 1999 as a preliminary to a new national framework of service provision. The Mental Health Act is currently being reformed, and there are proposals for compulsory treatment orders to allow the legal enforcement of treatment in the community instead of detention in a psychiatric ward. Some campaigning groups are concerned that this may lead to an infringement of civil liberties.

In April 2000, a top psychiatrist, Professor Louis Appleby, was appointed to spearhead the government's drive to modernize mental health services. Appleby, professor of psychiatry at the University of Manchester and director of the National Confidential Inquiry into Suicides and Homicides by People with

Mental Health *(continued)*

Mental Illness, was named national director of mental health for the NHS in England. The mental health `tsar' will also coordinate government policies on issues that affect people with mental health problems.

The National Service Framework for Mental Health, launched in April 2000, sets seven standards for mental health services nationally, and aims to improve quality and reduce variations in provision to service users. It will include round-the-clock crisis teams for emergencies, more mental health beds, and improved training for GPs. The Framework is backed by government funding of £700 million over three years.

Suicide Rates by Gender and Age in the UK

Data include deaths that are undetermined whether accidentally or purposely inflicted.
(Rate per 100,000 population.)

Gender and age		1971	1976	1981	1986	1991	1996
Men	15–24	6.9	9.6	10.6	12.7	15.9	16.4
	25–44	13.5	15.0	19.5	20.1	24.3	21.8
	45–64	19.8	21.0	23.1	22.6	20.4	17.5
	65 and over	25.4	23.8	23.7	26.4	18.4	15.4
Women	15–24	3.3	4.6	3.4	3.4	4.0	4.0
	25–44	7.7	8.9	7.7	6.6	5.9	6.2
	45–64	15.9	14.3	15.0	12.0	8.2	6.9
	65 and over	16.5	15.0	15.5	13.6	8.6	6.3

Source: Social Trends 30, © *Crown copyright 2000*

Flu Outbreaks and Epidemics

Influenza viruses, or flu, and complications related to it, kill thousands of people in the UK each year. But despite massive investment in research into the virus, there is still no cure. There are, however, vaccines which have some protective effect and are normally administered to the elderly and the vulnerable each year. Yet every few years a new strain of flu appears which spreads so rapidly that vaccines to protect against it cannot be developed in time. This can lead to pandemics which threaten millions of lives. The worst 20th-century flu pandemic was that of Spanish flu in 1918, which killed an estimated 40 million people – more than World War I.

The 1999–2000 flu crisis in the UK stretched NHS hospitals to the limit, with large numbers of seriously ill patients; it led also to some political controversy when it appeared that the NHS might not be equipped to cope with the crisis. The flu outbreak of 1998/99 was even more severe, and more than 3,200 people in England died from flu and other respiratory diseases in the first week of 1999, according to the Association for Influenza Monitoring and Surveillance (AIMS). Neither of these two flu outbreaks, however, actually hit epidemic levels, according to the figures from the Royal College of General Practitioners, which has responsibility for counting flu cases. During the last officially declared epidemic in the UK in 1989, 29,000 flu-related deaths were reported. At its peak, there were 534 recorded cases in every 100,000 – well above the 400 threshold which officially defines an epidemic.

Rates of between 50 and 200 cases per 100,000 are usual when influenza viruses are circulating. Rates exceeding 200 represent above-average influenza incidence, and rates above 400 are exceptional. While the national average for 1999/2000 flu figures peaked at 203 per 100,000, the incidence was greatest in the north, where it reached 259; and incidence was generally higher in persons aged between 45 and 64, and 65 and over.

Peak Flu Figures in England and Wales, 1989/90–1999/2000

	Cases per 100,000
1989/90	534
1990/91	139
1991/92	125
1992/93	104
1993/94	235
1994/95	159
1995/96	160
1996/97	229
1997/98	76
1998/99	272
1999/2000	203

Data from Royal College of General Practitioners

Cancer

The global incidence of cancer is soaring due to rapidly ageing populations in most countries. By the year 2020, there will be, according to WHO estimates, 20 million new cancer patients each year. However, 70% of them will live in countries that between them will have less than 5% of the resources for cancer control. To cope with increased disease burden, very significant advances in prevention, screening, and treatment will need to be made.

Dramatic technological change is likely in surgery, radiotherapy, and chemotherapy, leading to increased cure rates, but at a price that not all countries or patients will be able to afford. The completion of the Human Genome Project will almost certainly bring sophisticated genetic risk assessment methods which will need to be carefully integrated into existing screening programmes. But the greatest efforts to control cancer during the next 20–25 years will have to come through organized preventive strategies and detection programmes. Reducing cigarette consumption, dietary modification, and significant reduction in the incidence of infection (which causes around 15% of cancer worldwide) – changes that would be difficult to achieve in many of the world's economic environments – represent some of the most effective ways to reduce the global incidence, morbidity, and mortality from cancer.

In the UK, 5,000 people are diagnosed with cancer each week. Doctors estimate that one in three UK citizens will get some form of cancer at some point in their lives; one in four will eventually die from the disease.

Major Causes of Death from Cancer in England and Wales

Figures are from weighted data where a sample of the population has been used to represent the full population. Percentages do not add up to 100 for each gender due to rounding.

1998

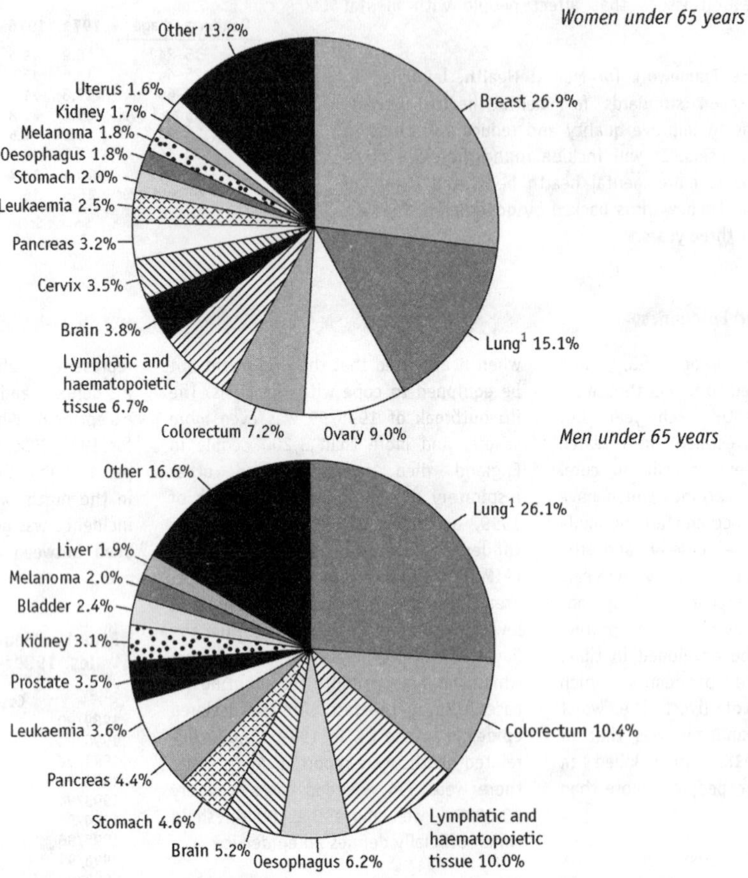

[1] Malignant neoplasm of trachea, bronchus, and lung.

Source: Mortality Statistics: Cause, England and Wales, © *Crown copyright 1999*

World Mortality from Cancer and Measures to Reduce the Risk of Cancer

1998

Cancers	Deaths	Dietary and lifestyle measures to reduce the risk of cancer
Trachea, bronchus, and lung	1,244,000	eliminate smoking
Stomach	822,000	increase fruit and vegetable consumption; reduce salt intake
Liver	609,000	reduce alcohol consumption; vaccinate against hepatitis B
Colon and rectum	556,000	reduce fat and protein consumption; increase vegetable consumption
Oesophagus	436,000	eliminate smoking; reduce alcohol consumption
Breast (female)	412,000	reduce fat and animal protein consumption; avoid obesity
Mouth and pharynx	352,000	eliminate smoking; reduce alcohol consumption
Bladder	158,000	eliminate smoking; reduce alcohol consumption

Source: The World Health Report 1999, *World Health Organization*

Prevalence of Smoking: Top Countries

Data are for men and women 15 years or older.

1997 (estimates)
Male smoking prevalence

Rank	Country	men (% of population)	women (% of population)
1	Korea, South	68.2	6.7
2	Latvia	67.0	12.0
3	Russian Federation	67.0	30.0
4	Dominican Republic	66.3	13.6

(continued)

Prevalence of Smoking: Top Countries (*continued*)

1997 (estimates)

Male smoking prevalence

Rank	Country	men (% of population)	women (% of population)
5	Tonga	65.0	14.0
6	Turkey	63.0	24.0
7	China	61.0	7.0
8	Bangladesh	60.0	15.0
9	Fiji	59.3	30.6
10	Japan	59.0	14.8

Female smoking prevalence

Rank	Country	women (% of population)	men (% of population)
1	Denmark	37.0	37.0
2	Norway	35.5	36.4
3	Czech Republic	31.0	43.0
4	Fiji	30.6	59.3
5=	Israel	30.0	45.0
	Russian Federation	30.0	67.0
7=	Canada	29.0	31.0
	Netherlands	29.0	36.0
	Poland	29.0	51.0
10=	Greece	28.0	46.0
	Iceland	28.0	31.0
	Ireland	28.0	29.0
	Papua New Guinea	28.0	46.0

Source: Tobacco or Health: A Global Status Report, *World Health Organization 1997*

Trends in Smoking in the UK by Age

Age group	Year % 1994[1]	1995	1996	1997	1998[2]
Men					
16–24	34	22	39	31	39
25–34	34	39	39	35	39
35–44	34	29	29	27	28
45–54	26	34	26	26	28
55–64	24	25	23	26	24
65–74	19	21	15	18	18
>74	14	14	10	8	13
Total	28	28	28	26	29
Women					
16–24	33	33	36	26	29
25–34	30	30	34	35	32
35–44	28	28	32	31	28
45–54	28	35	27	28	26
55–64	24	22	27	23	22
65–74	20	21	22	23	14
>74	8	10	10	8	9
Total	26	27	28	27	26

[1] Data from General Household Survey of Great Britain 1994.

[2] Data for England only.

Smoking: Trends in Starting and Giving Up

It is unlikely that individuals who avoid starting to smoke in adolescence or young adulthood will ever become smokers. Currently, the overwhelming majority of smokers started before the age of 25, and often in childhood or adolescence; in the high-income countries, eight out of ten began in their teens. In middle- and low-income countries for which data are available, it appears that smokers start by the early twenties, but the trend is toward younger ages. For example, in China between 1984 and 1996 there was a significant increase in the number of young men aged between 15 and 19 years who took up smoking. A similar lowering of the age of starting has been observed in the high-income countries.

The earlier in life a smoker starts, the greater the risk of disabling illnesses. In high-income countries with long-term data, researchers have concluded that smokers who start early and smoke regularly are much more likely to develop lung cancer than smokers who quit while they are still young. In the UK, a survey of male doctors showed that those who stop smoking before the age of 35 survive about as well as those who never smoked. Those who quit between the ages of 35 and 44 also gain substantial benefits, and there are benefits at older ages too.

While there is evidence that smoking begins in youth worldwide, the proportion of smokers who quit appears to vary sharply between high-income countries and the rest of the world. In environments of steadily increased knowledge about the health effects of tobacco, the prevalence of smoking has gradually fallen, and a significant number of former smokers has accumulated over the decades. In most high-income countries, about 30% of the male population are former smokers. In contrast, only 2% of Chinese men had quit in 1993, only 5% of Indian men at around the same period, and only 10% of Vietnamese men had quit in 1997.

Smoking: Some Facts

Since the middle of the 20th century, tobacco products have killed more than 60 million people in developed countries alone.

Currently, tobacco is responsible for 3.5 million deaths worldwide – or about 7% of all deaths – per year.

By 2020, tobacco use will cause 17.7% of all deaths in developed countries, and 10.9% of all deaths in developing countries.

In absolute figures, the biggest and sharpest increases in disease burden are expected in India and China, where the use of tobacco has grown most steeply. In China alone, where there are about 300 million smokers, and cigarette consumption is estimated at around 1,900 cigarettes per adult per year, around 50 million Chinese people now under 20 years of age will eventually be killed by tobacco.

Cigarette Smoking Trends of Children in England

Data present the prevalence of smoking cigarettes among secondary school children aged 11 to 15 years.

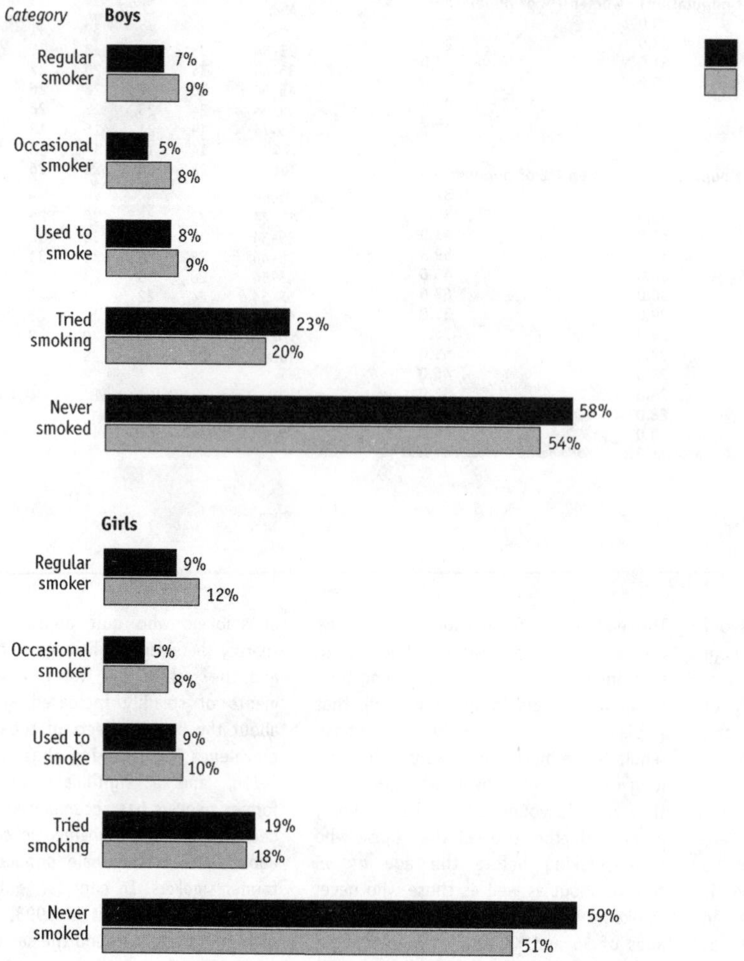

Category	Boys 1988	Boys 1998	Girls 1988	Girls 1998
Regular smoker	7%	9%	9%	12%
Occasional smoker	5%	8%	5%	8%
Used to smoke	8%	9%	9%	10%
Tried smoking	23%	20%	19%	18%
Never smoked	58%	54%	59%	51%

Source: Health and Personal Services Statistics for England 1999, *© Crown copyright 1999*

AIDS and Other Sexually Transmitted Diseases

New Cases of Sexually Transmitted Diseases in England by Year of Report

(NC = data not collected.)

Disease	Number of cases						
	1977	**1987**	**1994**	**1995**	**1996**	**1997**	**1998**
Syphilis[1]	2,759	589	304	132	116	147	126
Gonorrhoea[2]	58,109	25,254	9,644	9,938	11,710	12,462	12,393
Chlamydia[3]	NC	NC	27,698	29,213	32,092	38,981	44,196
Herpes simplex[4]	NC	NC	15,347	14,999	15,071	15,126	15,706
Genital warts[4]	NC	NC	49,052	51,166	54,029	58,812	59,973
Non-specific genital infection	95,491	131,383	111,049	104,547	111,315	125,299	137,561

[1] Infectious syphilis, primary and secondary.
[2] Uncomplicated gonorrhoea.
[3] Uncomplicated chlamydia.
[4] First attacks only.

Source: Communicable Disease Surveillance Centre

■ **AIDS and Other Sexually Transmitted Diseases**

Global Summary of the HIV/AIDS Epidemic

Children are below 15 years.

1999

Category	Group	Number (millions)
New HIV infections	adults	5.0
	of which women	2.3
	children	0.6
	Total	5.6
People living with HIV/AIDS	adults	32.4
	of which women	14.8
	children	1.2
	Total	33.6
HIV/AIDS associated deaths	adults	2.1
	of which women	1.1
	children	0.5
	Total	2.6
Cumulative HIV/AIDS deaths[1]	adults	12.7
	of which women	6.2
	children	3.6
	Total	16.3
Cumulative AIDS orphans[1 2]	children	11.2

[1] From the beginning of the epidemic to the end of 1999.
[2] Orphans are defined as HIV-negative children having lost their mother or both parents due to AIDS before reaching the age of 15 (end 1997).

Source: United Nations Programme on AIDS, World Health Organization

Estimated Cumulative Deaths Due to HIV/AIDS to End 1999

This table shows estimated adult and child deaths due to HIV/AIDS from the beginning of the epidemic to end 1999.

Region	Cumulative deaths (estimated)
Sub-Saharan Africa	13,700,000
North Africa and Middle East	70,000
Western Europe	210,000
Eastern Europe and Central Asia	17,000
East Asia and Pacific	40,000
South and South-East India	1,100,000
Australia and New Zealand	8,000
North America	450,000
Caribbean	160,000
Latin America	520,000

Source: AIDS Epidemic Update: December 1999, *UNAIDS/World Health Organization*

AIDS: Key Dates

1977 Two homosexual men in New York are diagnosed as having the rare cancer Kaposi's sarcoma. They are thought to be the first victims of AIDS.

1979 The Center for Disease Control in Atlanta, Georgia, reports the first cases of the disease later known as AIDS.

1981 The Center for Disease Control in Atlanta, Georgia, first conclusively identifies AIDS; doctors realize they have previously seen similar cases among drug users and homosexuals.

1983 US medical researcher Robert Gallo at the US National Cancer Institute, Maryland, and French medical researcher, Luc Montagnier, at the Pasteur Institute in Paris, isolate the virus thought to cause AIDS; it becomes known as HIV (human immunodeficiency virus).

20 March 1987 The AIDS treatment drug AZT is given approval by the US Food and Drug Administration. Treatment costs $10,000 per year per patient. The treatment does not cure the disease but it does relieve some symptoms and extend victims' lives.

31 December 1994 The number of AIDS cases worldwide exceeds 1 million for the first time, when the World Health Organization (WHO) announces that there are 1,025,073 officially reported AIDS cases.

1995 US researchers estimate that HIV reproduces at a rate of a billion viruses a day, even in otherwise healthy individuals, but is held at bay by the immune system producing enough white blood cells to destroy them. Gradually the virus mutates so much that the immune system is overwhelmed and the victim develops AIDS.

9 May 1996 Scientists discover a protein, 'fusin', which allows the HIV virus to fuse with a human immune system cell's outer membrane and inject genetic material. Its presence is necessary for the AIDS virus to enter the cell.

September 1996 The first three protease inhibitors are approved by the US Food and Drug Administration (FDA). Protease inhibitors are a new type of antiretroviral (a drug that stops the reproduction of HIV in the body).

January 1997 WHO estimates that 22.6 million men, women, and children have to date been infected by HIV, the virus responsible for causing AIDS. Approximately 42% of adult sufferers are female, with the proportion of women infected steadily increasing.

February 1997 The Centers for Disease Control and Prevention in Atlanta, Georgia, report that deaths among people with AIDS declined 13% during the first six months of 1996 over the same period the year before.

8 May 1997 US AIDS researcher David Ho and colleagues show how aggressive treatment of HIV-1 infection with a cocktail of three antiviral drugs can drive the virus to below the limits of conventional clinical detection within eight weeks.

9 February 1998 David Ho reports the discovery of the AIDS virus in a 1959 blood sample and suggests that a transfer of the virus from ape to human occurred in the late 1940s or early 1950s.

March 1998 According to a new study, a protein found in the urine of pregnant women could stop the reproduction of HIV, the virus that causes AIDS. The protein is known as human chorionic gonadotropin, or hcg. It also boosts the immune system and, because it is produced by the human body, is nontoxic and has very few side effects.

30 June 1998 Doctors report for the first time the ominous spread of a strain of the AIDS virus that is resistant to protease inhibitors, the medicines that have revolutionized care of the disease.

October 1998 Children born today in 29 sub-Saharan African nations face a life expectancy of just 47 years because of the toll the AIDS pandemic is taking on the region, according to a UN population report.

December 1998 Researchers report they have identified an inherited gene variation that in some patients causes an HIV infection to accelerate rapidly to AIDS. The identification of all the gene variations involved in both the rapid acceleration of HIV and in the slow progress of the disease would help in the design and testing of vaccines.

January 1999 WHO estimates that 33.4 million adults and children are living with AIDS at the end of 1998. Deaths due to HIV/AIDS in 1998 totalled 2.5 million, while the cumulative number of deaths reached 13.9 million.

January 1999 Researchers say they have conclusive evidence that the HIV virus has spread on at least three separate occasions from chimpanzees to humans in Africa. Chimps, which probably carried the virus for hundreds of thousands of years, apparently do not become ill from it. Understanding why, say AIDS experts, could help in a search for a cure and in the development of a vaccine.

February 1999 Thailand gives permission to the US company VaxGen Inc. to begin advance testing of an AIDS vaccine on about 2,500 people. The California-based company has already done preliminary trials of AIDSVAX vaccine on up to 90 Thai drug users. About 30 possible AIDS vaccines are in development, but AIDSVAX is the first to undergo massive testing to determine if it prevents AIDS infection.

February 1999 The first trial of an AIDS vaccine in Africa begins in a group of Ugandans considered at low risk of the disease.

16 March 1999 US scientists report they have isolated an enzyme present in tears, which they believe has a powerful anti-HIV effect.

19 April 1999 The AIDS epidemic in South Africa reaches alarming new levels, with 10% of the population now infected with HIV. A national survey confirmed that the country has one of the highest rates of infection in the world.

21 April 1999 Hundreds of demonstrators rally in Washington, DC, to protest at policies

AIDS: Key Dates (*continued*)

which they say protect drug companies but make AIDS drugs too expensive for people in Africa.

April 1999 Scientists at Yerkes Regional Primate Center in Georgia, USA, announce that a 'safe' HIV vaccine has been successfully tested on monkeys. The vaccine, that uses harmless parts of HIV, protected monkeys from extremely virulent strains of the virus for at least 62 weeks.

12 May 1999 AIDS is now the leading cause of death in Africa, overtaking malaria as the continent's main killer disease, according to the UN.

1 June 1999 A new easier-to-take AIDS drug – Efavirenz – which has been hailed as 'a major advance in the treatment of HIV infection', is granted a licence for sale in the EU. It was approved in the USA the previous summer.

16 July 1999 Researchers in the USA and Uganda say they have identified a cheap and effective drug – called Nevirapine – which could control the spread of AIDS. The drug could prevent up to 400,000 children each year being born with the disease.

23 September 1999 Drug-resistant strains of HIV are on the increase, with as many as 3.8% of newly infected Americans failing to respond to a variety of different treatments, according to a study carried out by the AIDS Research Center at Rockerfeller University in New York.

November 1999 More than 50 million people are infected with the HIV virus, according to UN and WHO estimates. More than 16 million have died from AIDS-related illnesses.

7 March 2000 Virologists at Thomas Jefferson University in Philadelphia say they have developed an HIV vaccine using a weakened rabies virus to carry a piece of the HIV virus safely into the cells of laboratory mice. The cells respond by creating immune system antibodies to attack the fragment, thus increasing their long-term capacity to fight off the HIV virus.

31 March 2000 A combination of drugs introduced in 1997 to treat HIV is said to have dramatically increased the lifespan of patients, according to a comprehensive study carried out in Europe. The study shows that the drug combination known as Haart (highly-active antiretroviral therapy) is responsible for an overall decline of 64% in the risk of dying from AIDS within 10 years of developing the virus.

30 April 2000 The US government formally designates AIDS as a threat to international security and orders a major reassessment of its efforts against the disease. The Clinton administration acts after intelligence reports warned that the AIDS epidemic could trigger wars and genocide and undermine democratic governments, particularly in Africa.

2 May 2000 More than four out of every five deaths in Rwanda are now AIDS-related, according to government officials. The figure – which covers the preceding three months – was given at an international conference on AIDS by Rwanda's health minister.

10 July 2000 The annual world AIDS conference opens in Durban, South Africa, where President Mbeki comes under fire for his poor handling of the HIV emergency affecting an estimated 4.2 million South Africans. Between one fifth and one quarter of the adult population is affected.

HIV/AIDS: Regional Statistics and Features

As of end November 1999

	Epidemic started	Adults and children living with HIV/AIDS	Adults and children newly infected with HIV	Adult prevalence rate (%)[1]	HIV-positive adults who are women (%)	Main mode(s) of transmission for those living with HIV/AIDS[2]
Sub-Saharan Africa	late 1970s–early 1980s	23,300,000	3,800,000	8.0	55	hetero
South and Southeast Asia	late 1980s	6,000,000	1,300,000	0.69	30	hetero
Latin America	late 1970s–early 1980s	1,300,000	150,000	0.57	20	MSM, IDU, hetero
North America	late 1970s–early 1980s	920,000	44,000	0.56	20	MSM, IDU, hetero
Caribbean	late 1970s–early 1980s	360,000	57,000	1.96	35	hetero, MSM
Eastern Europe, Central Asia	early 1980s	360,000	95,000	0.14	20	IDU, MSM
East Asia, Pacific	late 1980s	530,000	120,000	0.07	15	IDU, hetero, MSM
North Africa, Middle East	late 1980s	220,000	19,000	0.13	20	IDU, hetero
Western Europe	late 1970s–early 1980s	520,000	30,000	0.25	20	MSM, IDU
Australia, New Zealand	late 1970s–early 1980s	12,000	500	0.1	10	MSM, IDU
World totals	–	33,600,000	5,600,000	1.1	46	–

[1] The proportion of adults (15–49 years) living with HIV/AIDS in 1999, using 1998 population figures.
[2] IDU: transmission through injecting drugs; hetero: heterosexual transmission; MSM: men who have sex with men.

Source: Global AIDS Surveillance, World Health Organization

AIDS Cases in the UK by Age Group at Diagnosis and Gender

Correct to December 1999.

Age group	Men		Women		Total	
	number of cases[1]	% of cases	number of cases[1]	% of cases	number of cases[1]	% of cases
0–14	215	1	188	9	343	2
15–24	550	3	165	8	715	4
25–34	5,525	38	1,055	51	6,580	39
35–44	5,241	36	463	23	5,764	34
45–54	2,302	16	130	6	2,432	15
55–64	734	5	51	3	785	5
>64	159	1	13	0	172	1
Total	14,726	100	2,065	100	16,791	100

[1] Total number of cases from 1982 or earlier to December 1999.

Source: Communicable Disease Surveillance Centre

AIDS and Other Sexually Transmitted Diseases

HIV Cases by Exposure Category in the UK

At end December 1999.

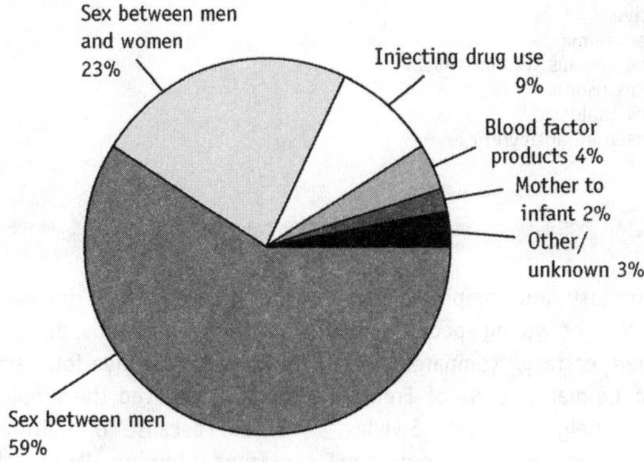

Source: Communicable Disease Surveillance Centre

Percentage of Adults in England Who Have Changed Their Behaviour Because of Concern About AIDS

The Health Education Monitoring Survey (HEMS) is carried out by the Social Survey Division of the Office of National Statistics on behalf of the Health Education Authority.
(In percentages.)

	Age					
	16–24	25–34	35–44	45–54	Total[1]	HEMS 1995 Total[1]
Using a condom	17	13	6	2	9	13
Sticking to one partner	11	13	9	5	10	12
Finding out more about someone	16	9	4	2	7	10
Having fewer partners	6	6	2	1	4	4
Not having sex	2	1	1	1	2	2
Avoiding some sexual practices	1	3	1	0	1	2
Other changes	2	0	0	0	1	1
Not changed behaviour	63	66	78	88	74	67
Changed, but not because of AIDS	4	7	6	4	5	6
Number of respondents	491	1,039	1,010	855	3,395	3,147

[1] Totals add to more than 100% because respondents may have changed in more than one way.

Source: Health in England 1998: Investigating the Links Between Social Inequalities and Health,

Drug and Alcohol Use and Abuse

Common Drugs Derived from Plants

Many of these plants are poisonous and if swallowed can cause serious illness or unconsciousness. They should only be used if administered by a medically trained professional.

Plant	Drug	Use
Amazonian liana	curare	muscle relaxant
Annual mugwort	artemisinin	antimalarial
Autumn crocus	colchicine	antitumour agent
Camphor tree	camphor	rubefacient; used in insect repellents and medicinal inhalants and liniments
Coca	cocaine	local anaesthetic
Common thyme	thymol	antifungal
Deadly nightshade (belladonna)	atropine	anticholinergic
Dog button (nux-vomica)	strychnine	central nervous system stimulant
Ergot fungus	ergotamine	analgesic
Foxglove	digitoxin, digitalis	cardiotonic
Indian snakeroot	reserpine	antihypertensive
Meadowsweet	salicylate	analgesic
Mexican yam	diosgenin	birth control pill
Mint, peppermint	menthol	rubefacient
Opium poppy	codeine, morphine	analgesic (codeine is also antitussive)

(*continued*)

Common Drugs Derived from Plants *(continued)*

Plant	Drug	Use
Pacific yew	taxol	antitumour agent
Recured thornapple	scopolamine	sedative
Rosy periwinkle	vincristine, vinblastine	antileukaemia
Tea, coffee, and kola nuts	caffeine	central nervous system stimulant
Velvet bean	L-dopa	antiparkinsonian
White willow	salicylic acid	topical analgesic
Yellow cinchona	quinine	antimalarial, antipyretic

The Rise of Drug Use in the UK

In recent years, the availability of drugs has become more widespread, particularly with the advent of recreational drugs like ecstasy. Drug use in Britain is thought to have risen by 30% in the last five years, and use of hard drugs like heroin and cocaine – estimated to be used by 2% of the population – is also rising as they become cheaper and more accessible.

Young people in Britain are reported to be taking up to five times more illegal drugs than their European counterparts – particularly ecstasy and amphetamines. In the UK, 9% of young people said they had tried ecstasy, compared with only 2.8% of Germans, 3.1% of French, and 1% of Belgians and Swedes. According to the latest annual report of the European Monitoring Centre for Drugs and Drug Addiction, as many as one in 12 British 12-year-olds is said to have taken drugs.

Britain's Standing Conference on Drug Abuse said at the end of 1999 that use of illegal drugs had increased eight-fold among 15-year-olds during the previous 10 years and five-fold among 12-year-olds. It believed the problem was bad in Britain because of cultural and supply reasons. Turning Point, the drug and alcohol abuse charity, said much of the rise in UK abuse was due to the advent of recreational drugs, such as ecstasy, which target a much younger age group.

Number of New Drug Addicts in the UK

Data are for users presenting to drug misuse services for the first time.

Main drug	Six months ending							
	March 1994	Sept 1995	March 1996	Sept 1996	March 1997	Sept 1997	March 1998	Sept 1998
Heroin	8,546	11,793	12,623	14,334	15,597	12,392	13,635	16,081
Methadone	3,232	3,469	3,484	3,574	3,704	2,852	2,925	3,088
Other opiates	574	560	507	493	454	436	461	633
Amphetamines	1,786	2,215	2,216	2,248	2,009	1,999	2,141	2,490
Cannabis	1,205	1,677	1,623	1,533	1,660	1,934	2,201	2,775
Cocaine	714	1,046	977	870	1,020	925	1,143	1,663
Benzodiazepines	743	910	717	659	558	598	616	693
Ecstasy	175	289	335	268	246	223	141	196
Solvents	172	175	176	166	158	148	167	157
Other drugs	483	498	368	576	398	412	417	471
Not known	234	216	287	158	121	77	69	347
Total number of users	17,864	22,848	23,313	24,879	25,925	21,996	23,916	28,599

Source: Health and Personal Services Statistics for England 1999, © *Crown copyright 1999*

Alcohol Strengths and Recommended Daily Alcohol Intake in the UK

The most recent UK government guidelines on alcohol consumption, published in 1995, advise that drinking up to three to four units a day for men and up to two to three units a day for women poses no significant risk to health, but that regularly consuming at or beyond the maximum level incurs a progressive risk of damage. Women who are or are intending to become pregnant should not drink more than one to two units once or twice a week. Units of alcohol are used to compare the amounts of alcohol in different types of drinks: each contains 10 ml/0.35 fl oz of pure alcohol (ethanol).

Drink	% alcohol by volume (ABV)[1]	Measure constituting one unit
Normal-strength beer, lager, or cider	3.5–4.0	284 ml/½ pint
Strong beer, lager, or cider	8.0–9.0	¼ of a large, 440 ml/15.5 fl oz can
Low-alcohol beer or lager	1.0	1,136 ml/2 pints
Alcopops	4.7–5.5	⅔ of a 330 ml/11.6 fl oz bottle
Wine	8.0–9.0	small glass (125 ml/4.4 fl oz)
Fortified wine, such as sherry or port	15.0–18.0	small glass (50 ml/1.8 fl oz)
Spirits, such as gin, vodka, whisky, rum, or brandy	40.0	single pub measure (25 ml/0.9 fl oz)

[1] The alcohol content of beers and wines can vary greatly – some wines, for example, can be as strong as 13% ABV.

Source: Sensible Drinking, © *Crown copyright 1995*

■ Drug and Alcohol Use and Abuse

 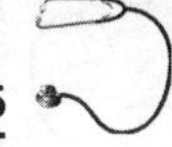

Alcohol Use

Scientists claimed in late 1999 that small amounts of alcohol may protect the heart from damage caused during heart attacks, and that it may even help people who have undergone open heart surgery or heart transplants. Working with rats, researchers at Stanford University in California found that small amounts of alcohol could reduce the overall damage caused by heart attacks by 70%. British experts, however, have warned patients not to try to drink alcohol if they think they are having an attack, as it could react badly with other medication given to patients when they arrive at hospital.

Other studies have already shown that moderate alcohol consumption provides some protection against heart disease. It was reported in the *Proceedings of the National Academy of Sciences* that alcohol protects cells against the damage caused by oxygen starvation by activating a chemical called epsilon protein. However, a spokesman for the British Heart Foundation said that the message from such studies might confuse the public.

In fact, earlier in the year, the British Medical Association (BMA) had recommended that alcoholic drinks should carry health warnings, and that an independent regulator should ensure that the industry does not target the young. The BMA published a policy document in which it called for a raft of measures to cut alcohol abuse amongst the young, and urged the government to take concerted action to address the problems of underage and teenage drinking.

The present regulators, the Portman Group, attacked the BMA's position, saying its views were out of date and that strong regulations were already in place. However, recent studies indicate a rise in drinking amongst those aged 11 to 15, and show that the appeal of 'designer' drinks – or alcopops – is greatest amongst teenagers aged between 13 and 16.

Alcohol Consumption Levels for Adults in the UK

Data is for alcohol consumption among people aged 16 or over. Columns showing consumption levels are in percentage and columns showing average weekly consumption are in numbers.

1996–97

Region	Men					Women				
	Consumption levels (units per week)				Average weekly consumption (number of units)	Consumption levels (units per week)				Average weekly consumption (number of units)
	Non-drinker	1–10	11–21	22 or more		Non-drinker	1–7	8–14	15 or more	
England										
North East	9	34	24	33	19	17	55	15	13	6
North West and Merseyside	7	40	22	31	19	11	54	17	18	8
Yorkshire and the Humber	7	41	23	30	17	12	55	18	15	7
East Midlands	6	43	25	26	15	10	59	19	12	6
West Midlands	9	39	24	28	16	16	55	16	12	6
East	7	48	21	24	14	13	59	16	12	6
London	11	45	19	25	15	20	56	12	13	6
South East	5	45	23	27	16	10	57	18	14	7
South West	6	46	24	25	15	9	60	17	13	6
Average England	7	43	23	27	16	13	57	16	14	6
Wales	6	50	19	25	15	13	56	15	16	7
Scotland	7	41	28	25	16	13	60	16	11	5
Northern Ireland	22	38	17	22	14	31	48	12	8	4
Average UK	7	43	23	27	16	13	57	16	14	6

Source: Regional Trends 34, © *Crown copyright 1999*

Trends in Alcohol Consumption in the UK

Data are estimated averages of alcohol consumption per person over 14 during the year given. The figures for 1991–98 are not strictly comparable to those for previous years.
(In litres per person aged over 14.)

Year	Beer	Spirits	Wine	Cider	Total
1956	3.86	0.82	0.29	0.10	5.07
1960	4.09	0.96	0.42	0.10	5.57
1965	4.42	1.07	0.54	0.10	6.13
1970	4.96	1.21	0.67	0.15	7.00
1975	5.64	1.90	1.07	0.19	8.80
1980	5.45	2.24	1.35	0.21	9.25
1985	4.98	2.13	1.66	0.29	9.05
1990	5.02	2.10	1.83	0.33	9.28
1995	4.66	1.69	2.03	0.57	8.92
1996	5.00	1.70	2.13	0.57	9.40
1997	5.20	1.80	2.14	0.50	9.60
1998	5.00	1.70	2.18	0.56	9.44

Behaviour Related to Alcohol Use in Adults in Britain Aged 16–24

This table shows summary results from the HEA/BRMB Sexual Health Matters Research 1998 Survey of 736 adults aged 16–24 living in Britain, conducted in homes using a face-to-face questionnaire, Oct/Nov 1998. (In percentages.)

Which, if any, of the following have you done after drinking alcohol?

	Total	Men	Women	16–19 yrs	20–24 yrs
Had sex you later regretted	19	22	15	19	20
Had unsafe sex	14	16	10	10	16
Not been able to have sex because you were too drunk	9	11	4	7	10
Not been able to remember whether you had sex the night before	10	14	4	7	10
Been involved in an argument	43	46	38	42	44
Been involved in a fight	20	29	6	22	18
Been sick	62	62	62	57	66
Been in trouble with the police	13	18	4	13	12
None of these	17	13	23	24	12
Don't know	1		2	1	1
Refused to answer	1	1	1	1	1

Reproduced by permission of Health Promotion England. Information correct at time of going to press.

Commonly Abused Drugs

This table is intended to give general information only. If required, proper medical or legal advice should be taken from other sources. This table is not intended to condone drug use. The only safe option is not to take drugs.

Name	Source	Forms and appearance	Legal position	Methods of use	Effects of use
Alkyl nitrites (poppers) (also called amyl nitrite, nitro, nitrite)	various synthetic volatile chemicals	in small glass bottles under trade names of Liquid Gold, Hi-Tech, Rave, Locker Room, Ram, Rush, etc	controlled by the Medicines Act	inhalation	feelings of excitement and exhilaration; sexual arousal and increased sensitivity of sexual organs
Amphetamine (also called speed, uppers, whizz, billy, amph, sulphate)	a totally synthetic product	grey or white powder; tablets and capsules	class B, schedule 2 controlled substance (but class A if prepared for injection)	powder is snorted, swallowed, injected, or dissolved in a drink; tablets are swallowed	increased energy, strength, concentration, feelings of euphoria and elation; suppression of appetite; reduction in the need for sleep
Anabolic steroids (also called 'roids; product names include: Sustanon 250, Deca-Durabolin, Dianabol, Anavar, Stanozolol)	synthetic products designed to imitate certain natural hormones within the human body	capsules and tablets; liquid	can only be sold lawfully by a pharmacist by doctor's prescription; supply is illegal and class C penalties apply	injections; also taken orally	increase in body bulk and muscle growth; feelings of stamina and strength
Cannabis (also called marijuana, dope, grass, hash, ganja, blow, weed, draw, puff, spliff, wacky backy)	plants of the genus *Cannabis saliva*	herbal: dried plant material, similar to a coarse cut tobacco (marijuana); resin: blocks of various colours and texture (hashish); oil: extracted from resin, with a distinctive smell	class B, schedule 1 controlled substance, but class A penalties can apply to cannabis oil	smoked in a variety of ways; can be put into cooking or made into a drink; occasionally eaten on its own	relaxation, feelings of happiness, congeniality, increased appetite
Cocaine (also called coke, charlie, snow, white lady, C)	leaves of the coca bush, *Erythroxylum coca*	white crystalline powder; very rarely in paste form	class A, schedule 2 controlled substance	sniffed; injected; smoked (paste)	feelings of energy, strength, exhilaration, confidence; talkativeness; sexual arousal; craving for more of the drug
Crack and freebase cocaine (also called rock, wash, stone, cloud nine; base, freebase)	derived from cocaine hydrochloride	small, raisin-sized crystals (crack cocaine); powder (freebase cocaine)	class A, schedule 2 controlled substances	smoking	effects are those of cocaine, but both shorter and more intense
Ecstasy (chemical name MDMA; also called disco biscuits, burgers, hug drug, Dennis the Menace, diamonds, New Yorkers, E, Adam, XTC, Fantasy, Doves, rhubarb and custard (red and yellow capsules))	a totally synthetic product	tablets and capsules of different shape, size, and colour; rarely, powder; ecstasy is not always available in pure form, which increases the risks	class A, schedule 1	orally	feelings of euphoria, energy, stamina, sociability, sexual arousal; these effects last three to six hours
Gammahydroxybutyrate (GHB) (also called GBH, liquid X)	pre-operation anaesthetic	liquid	controlled by the Medicines Act	orally	relaxation, sleepiness, short-term memory loss; reported sexual arousal
Heroin (also called smack, junk, H, skag, brown, horse, gravy)	from raw opium produced by the opium poppy	brownish-white powder	class A, schedule 2 controlled substance	smoking; injections in solution; also sniffed or taken orally	feelings of euphoria, inner peace, freedom from fear and deprivation

(continued)

■ **Drug and Alcohol Use and Abuse**

Commonly Abused Drugs *(continued)*

Adverse effects	Tolerance potential	Habituation potential	Withdrawal effects	Overdose potential
nausea and vomiting; headaches and dizziness; skin problems; damage to vision if touches the eyes; poisonous if swallowed	tolerance develops quickly	no significant physical or psychological dependence	no significant effects	little risk of overdose
increased blood pressure with risk of stroke; diarrhoea or increased urination; disturbance of sleep patterns; weight loss; depression; paranoia; psychosis	tolerance develops rapidly	physical dependence: rare; psychological dependence: common	mental agitation, depression, panic; no physical symptoms	fatal overdose possible, even at low doses
bone growth abnormalities; hypertension and heart disease; liver and kidney malfunction; hepatitis; sexual abnormalities and impotence (for men); growth of facial hair, deepening voice, shrinking breasts, and damage to fetal development (for women)	tolerance may develop	no physical dependence; profound psychological dependence	sudden collapse of muscle strength and stamina; irritability, violent mood swings	overdose can lead to collapse, convulsions, coma, and death
impaired judgement and concentration; loss of short-term memory; dizziness; confusion; lethargy and apathy; anxiety; paranoia; potential for cigarette addiction, and cancer and breathing disorders through long-term smoking	tolerance develops rapidly	true physical dependence: rare; psychological dependence: common	disturbed sleep patterns; anxiety, panic	it is not thought possible to overdose fatally
agitation, panic, feelings of being threatened; damage to nasal passages, exhaustion, weight loss; collapsed veins, ulceration; delusions; violence	tolerance develops rapidly	strong physical and psychological dependence	severe cravings; feelings of anxiety and panic; depression	it is possible to overdose fatally
depression, feelings of being threatened; paranoia, psychosis; violence	some tolerance develops	strong physical and psychological dependence; babies born to pregnant users may also be dependent	severe depression; aggression, panic; risk of suicide	overdose can lead to coma and death
mood swings; perhaps neurological damage, and associated depression, in the long term; liver and kidney problems; nausea and vomiting; overheating, dehydration, convulsions, sudden death	tolerance develops	physical dependence: none; psychological dependence: low	no physical symptoms; irritability, depression	overdose can lead to coma and death
nausea and vomiting; muscle stiffness; disorientation; collapse; risks from mixing with alcohol and unknown concentration of the drug	little tolerance develops	little dependence	few withdrawal symptoms	overdose can lead to convulsions and collapse, and, rarely, death
addictive (even when smoked); depressed breathing, severe constipation, nausea, and vomiting; adverse effect on general state of health, with lower immunity; vein collapse and ulceration; risk of infection from needles	tolerance develops rapidly	profound physical and psychological dependence	sweating, flu-like symptoms 'going cold turkey'; severe cravings; professional assistance necessary	overdose can lead to coma and death

(continued)

Commonly Abused Drugs (*continued*)

Name	Source	Forms and appearance	Legal position	Methods of use	Effects of use
Lysergic acid diethylamide (LSD) (also called acid, trips, tab, blotters, dots, microdots)	derived from ergot (a fungus of certain cereal grains)	colourless crystals; for street use, mainly impregnated into squares of blotted paper or into squares of clear gelatine; or into tiny pills	class A, schedule 1 controlled substance	orally (paper squares and pills); under the eyelid (gelatine squares)	hallucinations and sensory distortion; sense of movement and time may speed up or slow down; a 'trip' may last for 8–12 hours
Magic (hallucinogenic) mushrooms (also called shrooms, mushies)	natural mushrooms (mainly fly agaric and liberty cap)	several varieties; identification is difficult	possession and eating of fresh mushrooms is not an offence; preparation is[1]	eaten; infused to make a drink	hallucinations; feelings of euphoria, well-being, gaiety
Methadone (also called doll, dolly, red rock, tootsie roll; phy-amps, phy (ampoules))	a totally synthetic product	powder; tablets, ampoules, linctus, mixture	class A, schedule 2 controlled substance	orally; injections	feelings of relaxation, bodily warmth, freedom from pain and worry
Methylamphetamine (also called ice, meth, crystal, glass, ice-cream (crystal form); meth, Methedrine (powder or tablets))	a totally synthetic drug, closely related to amphetamine sulphate	crystals or, less commonly, tablets or powder	class B, schedule 2 controlled substance	burning crystals and inhaling the fumes; drinking, sniffing, licking off the finger (powder and tablets)	feelings of euphoria, great strength and energy, sustained for long periods without rest or food
Over-the-counter medicines	range of proprietary medicines	mostly tablets	some are controlled	taken orally; injected	vary
Solvents (also called glue, gas, can, cog (depending on substance and container))	domestic and commercial products	liquid petroleum gases (LPGs): aerosols, camping gas cylinders, lighter gas refills; liquid solvents: fire extinguisher fluid, corrective fluids, certain paints and removers, nail polish and remover, anti-freeze, petrol; solvent-based glues: impact adhesives used for wood, plastic, laminate surfaces, vinyl floor tiles	sale to those under 18, or to people acting for them, is illegal if it is suspected that the product is intended for abuse	sniffed or inhaled from a cloth or sleeve; gas products sometimes sprayed into the throat	heavy, alcohol-like intoxication; sometimes hallucinations, excitability; effects short-lived, but users may repeat doses through day
Tranquillizers (chemical names include: diazepam, lorazepam, nitrazepam, chlordiazepoxide, flunitrazepam, temazepam; also called tranx, barbs, barbies, blockers, tueys, traffic lights, golf balls (tranquillizers); jellies, jelly beans, M&Ms, rugby balls (temazepam in jelly capsules))	pharmaceutical drugs aimed at treating patients with problems of anxiety, insomnia, and depression; based on benzodiazepine or barbiturate	tablets or capsules	although possession without prescription is not illegal (except for temazepam), supply is, and class C penalties apply	taken orally or injected	in higher doses: feelings of euphoria, elimination of fear and feelings of deprivation

(*continued*)

Commonly Abused Drugs *(continued)*

Adverse effects	Tolerance potential	Habituation potential	Withdrawal effects	Overdose potential
risk of accident while hallucinating; flashbacks; risk of developing a latent psychiatric disorder, or complicating a current one	tolerance develops and disappears rapidly	no physical dependence; some psychological dependence	no physical effect; few psychological effects	it is not thought possible to overdose
stomach pains, and sickness and diarrhoea; risk of complicating mental health problems; risks from eating wrongly identified mushrooms	tolerance develops rapidly	no dependence	few withdrawal effects	little overdose potential
sweating, nausea, itching, tiredness; disruption of menstrual cycle in women	tolerance develops slowly	strong physical and psychological dependence	fever, flu-like symptoms; diarrhoea; aggression	overdose can lead to respiratory depression, collapse, coma, and death
increased blood pressure with risk of stroke and heart failure; diarrhoea or increased urination; severe disturbance of sleep patterns; hallucinations, aggression, psychosis, delusions, paranoia	tolerance develops rapidly	physical dependence: not uncommon; psychological dependence: profound	severe cravings; depression; fear; panic and mental agitation	serious risk of fatal overdose, even at very low levels
vary	tolerance may develop	physical and psychological dependence may develop	possible effects	overdose can lead to health disturbances and death
over-stimulation of the heart, and death; asphyxiation from swelling of throat tissues or inhalation of vomit; danger of accidents whilst hallucinating; problems with speech, balance, short-term memory, cognitive skills; possible personality changes; danger of death through flooding of lungs if gas is sprayed into throat; damage to brain, liver, and kidney from long-term solvent abuse	tolerance may develop	no physical dependence; strong psychological dependence	no physical symptoms; anxiety and mood swings	overdose can lead to collapse, coma, and death
drowsiness; short-term memory loss; violent mood swings; bizarre sexual behaviour; deep depression, disorientation, lethargy; extremely dangerous if combined with alcohol or injected	tolerance develops rapidly	profound physical and psychological dependence	confusion, violent headaches, deep depression; sudden withdrawal may lead to convulsions and death	overdose can lead to convulsions, depression of breathing, collapse, coma, and death (more common for barbiturate-based products; generally increased if combined with alcohol)

[1]Preparation (such as crushing, slicing, drying, etc) is punishable as an offence relating to psilocin and psilocybin – the active ingredients of most hallucinogenic mushrooms, both class A, schedule 1 controlled substances.

See also **The Law on Drugs**, p 454.

Food and Nutrition

A Billion Thin and a Billion Fat

For the first time in history, the number of overweight people worldwide equals those who are underfed, and both groups, according to a Worldwatch Institute report published in March 2000, are victims of malnutrition. Citing statistics from the World Health Organization and other UN bodies, the report said that, whilst the world's underfed population had dropped slightly since 1980 to 1.2 billion, the number of overweight people had surged to 1.2 billion. The hungry and the overweight share high levels of sickness and disability, shortened life expectancies, and lower levels of productivity.

According to the report, 790 million people – roughly one out of every five people in the developing world – are chronically hungry, down from 918 million in 1970 (a drop of 14%). In contrast, 55% of adults in the USA are overweight by international standards, and 23% of US adults are obese. Surprisingly, the problem of obesity is advancing rapidly in some developing countries. In Brazil and Colombia, for example, 36% and 41% respectively of the population are overweight. According to Brian Halweil, a co-author of the report, nations have often 'simply traded hunger for obesity and diseases of poverty for diseases of excess.'

Prevalence of Undernourishment in Developing Countries

Region	Number of undernourished people (millions)	Proportion of total population (%)		
	1995	1979–81	1990–92	1995–97
Sub-Saharan Africa	180	37	35	33
Near East and North Africa	33	9	8	9
Asia and Pacific	526	32	21	17
Latin America and Caribbean	53	13	13	11
Developing world	792	29	30	18

Body Mass by Gender in England

Data are for men and women aged 16 or over.

1997

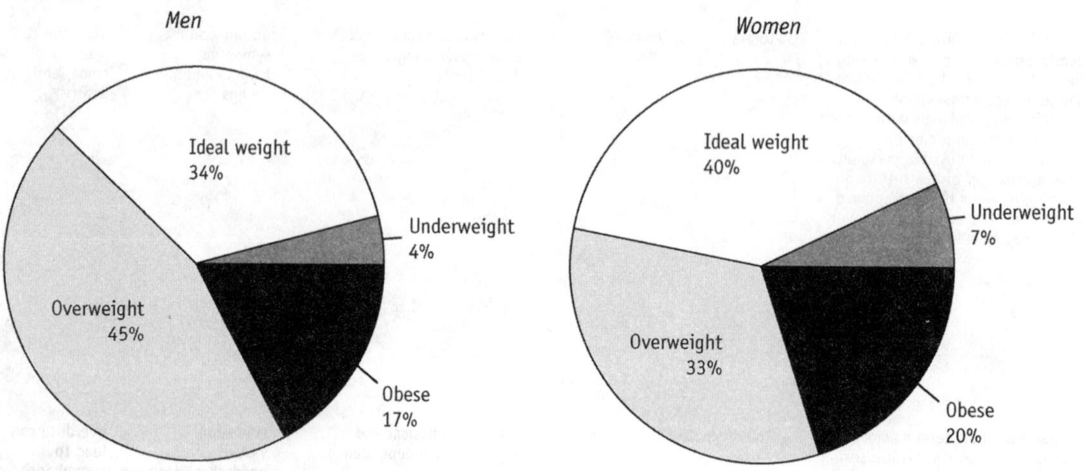

Source: Social Trends 30, © *Crown copyright 2000*

Obesity and Eating Habits in the UK

Obesity is one of the most significant, and fastest-growing, public health problems in the world. In the UK, 17% of men and 20% of women are currently obese, and over half the adult population is overweight. The rapid increase in the incidence of obesity in the UK parallels what is occurring in the USA, and if current trends continue more than one quarter of British adults will be obese by the year 2010.

According to researchers, obese heart patients live an average four years less than their slim counterparts. Being seriously overweight also hastens the onset of heart disease by an average of seven years compared with people who stay slim.

Nearly half the UK population could be at higher risk of heart disease and cancer because they eat less than half the recommended daily portions of fruit and vegetables, according to a survey published in late 1999. The survey also revealed regional variations, with southerners more likely to meet the target than those in the north. 23% of

Obesity and Eating Habits in the UK *(continued)*

southerners managed to eat five portions a day, compared to only 8% of those living in Yorkshire and Humberside. Another report, *Health Survey for England '98*, found that there was also a clear socio-economic component with regard to fat and fibre intake in both sexes: high fat and low fibre intake was more common amongst people in the lowest and low-income groups.

Five daily portions of fruit and vegetables are considered essential to provide optimum levels of minerals and vitamins, including antioxidants – which have been shown to reduce disease. Eating more fruit and vegetables can reduce the risk of some cancers. It is also known that eating too many fatty foods can be harmful, as high levels of cholesterol are strongly linked to heart disease. In January 2000 a British medical expert, Dr Tom Marshall, proposed that the government put value-added tax (VAT) on fatty foods, thereby preventing between 900 and 1,000 premature deaths per year in the UK. Although it successfully highlighted the impact that diet has on cholesterol concentrations in the UK population, the proposal was not considered feasible.

Obesity Trends by Age in England

Obesity – having a high proportion of one's body mass in the form of fat – is commonly measured using the body mass index (BMI), which relates a person's weight in kilograms to their height in metres squared. The UK Department of Health's Health of the Nation programme defines obesity as having a BMI greater than 30, though other thresholds – sometimes differentiating between mild, moderate, and severe obesity – are used elsewhere.
Data are percentages of people having a BMI greater than 30 kg/m^2. Figures are from weighted data where a sample of the population has been used to represent the full population.

Age	1993	1994	1995	1996	1997	1998
			Men			
16–24	4.9	5.7	5.8	6.1	5.0	5.2
25–34	10.0	9.8	11.8	12.5	13.1	15.9
35–44	14.3	15.5	16.0	16.2	17.5	16.8
45–54	16.5	17.2	19.4	21.1	21.6	21.2
55–64	19.9	17.8	21.5	23.6	27.4	23.3
65–74	15.2	17.9	17.8	19.6	18.4	21.2
>74	10.8	14.7	14.2	16.1	11.9	15.9
Total	13.2	13.8	15.3	16.4	17.0	17.3

Age	1993	1994	1995	1996	1997	1998
			Women			
16–24	7.8	7.9	8.0	7.9	8.6	10.7
25–34	11.1	12.9	13.3	14.9	14.5	16.3
35–44	17.1	16.9	16.6	17.5	18.2	20.5
45–54	18.9	17.8	21.5	19.2	22.5	23.9
55–64	24.0	25.5	23.2	27.5	30.1	28.6
65–74	21.5	25.3	24.1	24.5	24.8	29.0
>74	15.8	16.3	17.0	19.9	21.9	20.7
Total	16.4	17.3	17.5	18.4	19.7	21.2

Source: Health Survey of England 1997, ©*Crown copyright 1997;* Health Survey for England: Cardiovascular Disease 1998, ©*Crown copyright 1999*

Main Dietary Minerals

Mineral	Main dietary sources	Major functions in the body	Deficiency symptoms
calcium	milk, cheese, green vegetables, dried legumes	constituent of bones and teeth; essential for nerve transmission, muscle contraction, and blood clotting	tetany
chromium	vegetable oils, meat	involved in energy metabolism	impaired glucose metabolism
copper	drinking water, meat	associated with iron metabolism	anaemia
fluoride	drinking water, tea, seafoods	helps to keep bones and teeth healthy	increased rate of tooth decay
iodine	seafoods, dairy products, many vegetables, iodized table salt	essential for healthy growth and development	goitre
iron	meat (especially liver), legumes, green vegetables, whole grains, eggs	constituent of haemoglobin; involved in energy metabolism	anaemia
magnesium	whole grains, green vegetables	involved in protein synthesis	growth failure, weakness, behavioural disturbances
manganese	widely distributed in foods	involved in fat synthesis	not known in humans
molybdenum	legumes, cereals, offal	constituent of some enzymes	not known in humans
phosphorus	milk, cheese, meat, legumes, cereals	formation of bones and teeth, maintenance of acid-base balance	weakness, demineralization of bone
potassium	milk, meat, fruits	maintenance of acid-base balance, fluid balance, nerve transmission	muscular weakness, paralysis
selenium	seafoods, meat, cereals, egg yolk	role associated with that of vitamin E	not known in humans
sodium	widely distributed in foods	as for potassium	cramp, loss of appetite, apathy
zinc	widely distributed in foods	involved in digestion	growth failure, underdevelopment of reproductive organs

Vitamins

Vitamin	Name	Main dietary sources	Established benefit	Deficiency symptoms
A	retinol	dairy products, egg yolk, liver; also formed in body from β-carotene, a pigment present in some leafy vegetables	aids growth; prevents night blindness and xerophthalmia (a common cause of blindness among children in developing countries); helps keep the skin and mucous membranes resistant to infection	night blindness; rough skin; impaired bone growth
B_1	thiamin	germ and bran of seeds and grains, yeast	essential for carbohydrate metabolism and health of nervous system	beriberi; Korsakov's syndrome

(continued)

Vitamins (*continued*)

Vitamin	Name	Main dietary sources	Established benefit	Deficiency symptoms
B_2	riboflavin	eggs, liver, milk, poultry, broccoli, mushrooms	involved in energy metabolism; protects skin, mouth, eyes, eyelids, mucous membranes	inflammation of tongue and lips; sores in corners of the mouth
B_6	pyridoxine/ pantothenic acid/biotin	meat, poultry, fish, fruits, nuts, whole grains, leafy vegetables, yeast extract	important in the regulation of the central nervous system and in protein metabolism; helps prevent anaemia, skin lesions, nerve damage	dermatitis; neurological problems; kidney stones
B_{12}	cyanocobalamin	liver, meat, fish, eggs, dairy products, soybeans	involved in synthesis of nucleic acids, maintenance of myelin sheath around nerve fibres; efficient use of folic acid	anaemia; neurological disturbance
	folic acid	green leafy vegetables, liver, peanuts; cooking and processing can cause serious losses in food	involved in synthesis of nucleic acids; helps protect against cervical dysplasia (precancerous changes in the cells of the uterine cervix)	megaloblastic anaemia
	nicotinic acid (or niacin)	meat, yeast extract, some cereals; also formed in the body from the amino acid tryptophan	maintains the health of the skin, tongue, and digestive system	pellagra
C	ascorbic acid	citrus fruits, green vegetables, tomatoes, potatoes; losses occur during storage and cooking	prevents scurvy, loss of teeth; fights haemorrhage; important in synthesis of collagen (constituent of connective tissue); aids in resistance to some types of virus and bacterial infections	scurvy
D	calciferol, cholecalciferol	liver, fish oil, dairy products, eggs; also produced when skin is exposed to sunlight	promotes growth and mineralization of bone	rickets in children; osteomalacia in adults
E	tocopherol	vegetable oils, eggs, butter, some cereals, nuts	prevents damage to cell membranes	anaemia
K	phytomenadione, menaquinone	green vegetables, cereals, fruits, meat, dairy products	essential for blood clotting	haemorrhagic problems

Nutritive Value of Foods

The energy value of each food is given in kilojoules (kJ) and kilocalories (kcal), and both have been calculated from the protein, fat, and carbohydrate content per 100 g of edible portion.

Food	Energy		Protein (g)	Fat (g)	Saturated fat (g)	Carbohydrate (g)
	kJ	kcal				
Cereal and cereal products						
Bread, brown	927	218	8.5	2.0	0.4	44.3
Bread, white	1,002	235	8.4	1.9	0.4	49.3
Flour, plain, white	1,450	341	9.4	1.3	0.2	77.7
Flour, wholemeal	1,318	310	12.7	2.2	0.3	63.9
Oats, porridge, raw	1,587	375	11.2	9.2	1.6	66.0
Rice, brown, boiled	597	141	2.6	1.1	0.3	32.1
Rice, white, boiled	587	138	2.6	1.3	0.3	30.9
Spaghetti, white, boiled	442	104	3.6	0.7	0.1	22.2
Dairy products						
Butter	3,031	737	0.5	81.7	54.0	0.0
Cheddar cheese	1,708	412	25.5	34.4	21.7	0.1
Cottage cheese	413	98	13.8	3.9	2.4	2.1
Cream, fresh, heavy	1,849	449	1.7	48.0	30.0	2.7
Cream, fresh	817	198	2.6	19.1	11.9	4.1
Eggs, boiled	612	147	12.5	10.8	3.1	0.0
Low-fat spread	1,605	390	5.8	40.5	11.2	0.5
Margarine, polyunsaturated	3,039	739	0.2	81.6	16.2	1.0
Milk, semi-skimmed	195	46	3.3	1.6	1.0	5.0
Milk, skimmed	140	33	3.3	0.1	0.1	5.0
Milk, whole	275	66	3.2	3.9	2.4	4.8
Yoghurt, whole milk, plain	333	79	5.7	3.0	1.7	7.8
Fish/Seafood						
White fish, steamed, flesh only	417	98	22.8	0.8	0.2	0.0
Shrimps, boiled	451	107	22.6	1.8	0.4	0.0
Fruit						
Apples	199	47	0.4	0.1	0.0	11.8
Apricots	674	158	4.0	0.6	0.0	36.5
Avocados	784	190	1.9	19.5	4.1	1.9
Bananas	403	95	1.2	0.3	0.1	23.2
Cherries	203	48	0.9	0.1	0.0	11.5
Grapefruit	126	30	0.8	0.1	0.0	6.8
Grapes	257	60	0.4	0.1	0.0	15.4
Mangoes	245	57	0.7	0.2	0.1	14.1
Melon	119	28	0.6	0.1	0.0	6.6
Oranges	158	37	1.1	0.1	0.0	8.5
Peaches	142	33	1.0	0.1	0.0	14.0
Pears	169	40	0.3	0.1	0.0	10.0

(*continued*)

 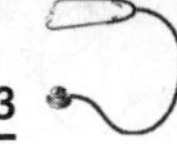

Nutritive Value of Foods *(continued)*

Food	Energy kJ	Energy kcal	Protein (g)	Fat (g)	Saturated fat (g)	Carbohydrate (g)
Plums	155	36	0.6	0.1	0.0	8.8
Raspberries	109	25	1.4	0.3	0.1	4.6
Strawberries	113	27	0.8	0.1	0.0	6.0
Meat						
Beef, lean only, raw	517	123	20.3	4.6	1.9	0.0
Chicken, meat and skin, raw	954	230	17.6	17.7	5.9	0.0
Lamb, lean only, raw	679	162	20.8	8.8	4.2	0.0
Pork, lean only, raw	615	147	20.7	7.1	2.5	0.0
Vegetables						
Aubergine	64	15	0.9	0.4	0.1	2.2
Beetroot	195	46	2.3	0.0	0.0	9.5
Cabbage	109	26	1.7	0.4	0.1	4.1
Celery	32	7	0.5	0.2	0.0	0.9
Courgettes	74	18	1.8	0.4	0.1	1.8
Cucumber	40	10	0.7	0.1	0.0	1.5
Lettuce	59	14	0.8	0.5	0.1	1.7
Mushrooms	55	13	1.8	0.5	0.1	0.4
Onions	150	36	1.2	0.2	0.0	7.9
Parsnips	278	66	1.6	1.2	0.2	12.9
Peas	291	69	6.0	0.9	0.2	9.7
Peppers	65	15	0.8	0.3	0.1	2.6
Potatoes, new, flesh only	298	70	1.7	0.3	0.1	16.1
Potatoes, old, flesh only	318	75	2.1	0.2	0.0	17.2
Spinach	90	21	301	0.8	0.1	0.5
Sweetcorn kernels	519	122	2.9	1.2	0.2	26.6
Sweet potatoes	358	84	1.1	0.3	0.1	20.5
Tofu, soybean, steamed	304	73	8.1	4.2	0.5	0.7
Watercress	94	22	3.0	1.0	0.3	0.4

Source: Manual of Nutrition, *© Crown copyright 1995*

Recommended Daily Intake of Nutrients

This table is meant as a guide only. Always consult a qualified dietician if you have any concerns or doubts. (– = not applicable.)

Sex and age			Energy MJ	Energy kcal	Protein (g)	Calcium (mg)	Iron (mg)	Vitamin A (µg)	Thiamine (retinol equivalent) (mg)	Riboflavin (mg)	Niacin (mg)	Vitamin C (mg)	Vitamin D[1] (µg)
Boys	<1		3.25	780	19	600	6	450	0.3	0.4	5	20	7.5
	1		5.00	1,200	30	600	7	300	0.5	0.6	7	20	10
	2		5.75	1,400	35	600	7	300	0.6	0.7	8	20	10
	3–4		6.50	1,560	39	600	8	300	0.6	0.8	9	20	10
	5–6		7.25	1,740	43	600	10	300	0.7	0.9	10	20	–
	7–8		8.25	1,980	49	600	10	400	0.8	1.0	11	20	–
	9–11		9.50	2,280	56	700	12	575	0.9	1.2	14	25	–
	12–14		11.00	2,640	66	700	12	725	1.1	1.4	16	25	–
	15–17		12.00	2,880	72	600	12	750	1.2	1.7	19	30	–
Girls	<1		3.00	720	18	600	6	450	0.3	0.4	5	20	7.5
	1		4.50	1,100	27	600	7	300	0.4	0.6	7	20	10
	2		5.50	1,300	32	600	7	300	0.5	0.7	8	20	10
	3–4		6.25	1,500	37	600	8	300	0.6	0.8	9	20	10
	5–6		7.00	1,680	42	600	10	300	0.7	0.9	10	20	–
	7–8		8.00	1,900	48	600	10	400	0.8	1.0	11	20	–
	9–11		8.50	2,050	51	700	12[2]	575	0.8	1.2	14	25	–
	12–14		9.00	2,150	53	700	12[2]	725	0.9	1.4	16	25	–
	15–17		9.00	2,150	53	600	12[2]	750	0.9	1.7	19	30	–
Men													
18–34		sedentary	10.50	2,510	62	500	10	750	1.0	1.6	18	30	–
		moderately active	12.00	2,900	72	500	10	750	1.2	1.6	18	30	–
		very active	14.00	3,350	84	500	10	750	1.3	1.6	18	30	–
35–64		sedentary	10.00	2,400	60	500	10	750	1.0	1.6	18	30	–
		moderately active	11.50	2,750	69	500	10	750	1.1	1.6	18	30	–
		very active	14.00	3,350	84	500	10	750	1.3	1.6	18	30	–
65–74			10.00	2,400	60	500	10	750	1.0	1.6	18	30	–
>74			9.00	2,150	54	500	10	750	0.9	1.6	18	30	–
Women													
18–54		most occupations	9.00	2,150	54	500	12[2]	750	0.9	1.3	15	30	–
		very active	10.50	2,500	62	500	12[2]	750	1.0	1.3	15	30	–
Pregnant			10.00	2,400	60	1,200	13	750	1.0	1.6	18	60	10
Lactating			11.50	2,750	69	1,200	15	1,200	1.1	1.8	21	60	10
55–74			8.00	1,900	47	500	10	750	0.8	1.3	15	30	–
>74			7.00	1,680	42	500	10	750	0.7	1.3	15	30	–

[1] Most people who go out in the sun need no dietary source of vitamin D, but children and adolescents in winter, and housebound adults, are recommended to take 10 µg vitamin D daily.

[2] These iron recommendations may not cover heavy menstrual losses.

Rules for Safe Food Production

The World Health Organization (WHO) regards illness due to contaminated food as one of the most widespread health problems in the contemporary world. For infants, immuno-compromised people, pregnant women, and the elderly, the consequences of such an illness can be fatal.

WHO data indicate that a small number of factors related to food handling are responsible for a large proportion of food-borne disease episodes everywhere. Common errors include:

- preparation of food several hours prior to consumption, combined with storage of that food at temperatures that favour growth of bacteria and/or formation of toxins;
- insufficient cooking or reheating of food and so failing to reduce or eliminate pathogens;
- cross contamination;
- handling of the food by people with poor personal hygiene.

The WHO has devised ten rules in response to these errors, offering advice that can reduce the risk of food-borne pathogens being able to contaminate, survive, or multiply. By following these basic rules, the risk of food-borne disease will be significantly reduced.

1. Choose foods processed for safety While many foods, such as fruits and vegetables, are best in their natural state, others simply are not safe unless they have been processed. For example, always buy pasteurized as opposed to unpasteurized milk, and if you have the choice, select fresh or frozen poultry treated with ionizing radiation. When shopping, keep in mind that food processing was invented to improve safety as well as to prolong shelf-life. Certain foods eaten raw, such as lettuce, need thorough washing.

2. Cook food thoroughly Many raw foods, most notably poultry, meats, eggs, and unpasteurized milk, may be contaminated with disease-causing organisms. Thorough cooking will kill the bacteria, but remember that the temperature of all parts of the food must reach at least 70°C/158°F. If cooked chicken is still raw, put it back in the oven until it is done – all the way through. Frozen meat, fish, and poultry must be thoroughly thawed before cooking.

3. Eat cooked foods immediately When cooked foods cool to room temperature, microbes begin to proliferate. The longer the wait, the greater the risk. To be on the safe side, eat cooked foods just as soon as they come off the heat.

4. Store cooked foods carefully If you must prepare foods in advance or want to keep leftovers, be sure to store them under either hot (near or above 60°C/140°F) or cool (near or below 10°C/50°F) conditions. This rule is of vital importance if you plan to store foods for more than four or five hours. Foods for infants should preferably not be stored at all. A common error, responsible for countless cases of food-borne disease, is putting too large a quantity of warm food in the refrigerator. In an overburdened refrigerator, cooked foods cannot cool to the core as quickly as they must. When the centre of food remains warm (above 10°C/50°F) for too long, microbes thrive, quickly proliferating to disease-causing levels.

5. Reheat cooked foods thoroughly This is your best protection against microbes that may have developed during storage (proper storage slows down microbial growth but does not kill the organisms). Once again, thorough reheating means that all parts of the food must reach at least 70°C/158°F.

6. Avoid contact between raw foods and cooked foods Safely cooked food can become contaminated through even the slightest contact with raw food. This cross-contamination can be direct, as when raw poultry meat comes into contact with cooked foods. It can also be more subtle. For example, do not prepare a raw chicken and then use the same unwashed cutting board and knife to carve the cooked bird. Doing so can reintroduce the disease-causing organisms.

7. Wash hands repeatedly Wash hands thoroughly before you start preparing food and after every interruption – especially if you have to change a baby or have been to the toilet. After preparing raw foods such as fish, meat, or poultry, wash again before you start handling other foods. And if you have an infection on your hand, be sure to bandage or cover it before preparing food. Remember too that household pets – dogs, cats, birds, and especially reptiles – often harbour dangerous pathogens that can pass from your hands into food.

8. Keep all kitchen surfaces meticulously clean Since foods are so easily contaminated, any surface used for food preparation must be kept absolutely clean. Think of every food scrap, crumb, or spot as a potential reservoir of germs. Cloths that come into contact with dishes and utensils should be changed frequently and boiled before re-use. Separate cloths for cleaning the floors also require frequent washing.

9. Protect foods from insects, rodents, and other animals Animals frequently carry pathogenic micro-organisms that cause food-borne disease. Storing foods in closed containers is your best protection against contamination from animals.

10. Use safe water Safe water is just as important for food preparation as for drinking. If you have any doubts about the water supply, boil water before adding it to food or making ice for drinks. Be especially careful with any water used to prepare an infant's meal.

Source: World Health Organization

Food Scares and Food Standards

The creation of the FSA had its beginnings with a government report on an outbreak of *E. coli* in Scotland at the end of 1996, which caused 20 deaths. The British government announced its plans for a new Food Standards Agency in January 1998, hoping to allay public disquiet which had grown following food scares during 1996–97. The FSA had been an election promise by Labour, and the recent food safety scares over salmonella, *E. coli*, BSE, and GM foods eventually pushed the issue of food safety to the top of the government's agenda. Figures from the Public Health Laboratory showed that 200 people die in England and Wales each year from food poisoning. The FSA, which would take the lead on policy related to food poisoning, was welcomed by health and food organizations alike.

The Draft Food Standards Bill was completed in January 1999 and the agency was set up on 1 April 2000. The government announced plans to charge an annual flat rate of £90 on all food outlets to fund the cost of setting up the agency. However, the plans were under review after the proposed rate provoked a strong protest from retailers and was dubbed a 'poll tax on food'. According to the Draft Bill, the new agency would help rebuild public confidence in the food industry. The new agency would have a long reach, with powers to trace food hygiene problems all the way back along the food chain. Consumers could expect to receive more and better information about food safety and standards, so that they can make informed choices. The agency would have powers to monitor food law enforcement by local authorities and ensure people can benefit from a more consistent application of the law.

 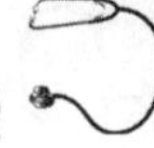

Useful Addresses

Helplines for Health and Related Issues

The National Health Service national phone advice lines include freephone numbers from the Department of Health.

AIDS Helpline phone: (0800) 567123 (24 hours); Web site: www.lovelife.hea.org.uk

Arthritis Care Helpline Freephone: (0808) 800 4050 (Monday–Friday 12 noon–4.00 p.m.)

Brook Advisory Centres sexual health service for young people; phone: (020) 7617 8000; Helpline: (020) 7713 9000; fax: (020) 7833 8182; e-mail: brookcentres@compuserve.com.uk

Cancer Helpline helpline of BACUP, a leading organization for people with cancer; Freephone: (0808) 800 1234 (9.00 a.m.–7.00 p.m.); Web site: www.cancerbacup.org.uk

Cerebral Palsy Helpline helpline from Scope for people with cerebral palsy and their carers; Freephone: (0808) 800 3333 (Monday–Friday 9.00 a.m.–9.00 p.m., Saturday and Sunday 2.00 p.m.–6.00 p.m.); Web site: www.scope.org.uk

Childline helpline for children in danger or distress; phone: (0800) 1111 (24 hours); Web site: www.childline.org.uk

Diabetes Careline run by the British Diabetic Association; phone: (020) 7636 6112 (Monday–Friday 9.00 a.m.–5.00 p.m.); e-mail: careline@diabetes.org.uk; Web site: www.diabetes.org.uk

Disability Benefits Enquiry Line phone: (0800) 882200 (Monday–Friday 8.30 a.m.–6.30 p.m., Saturday 9.00 a.m.–1.00 p.m.); Web site: www.dss.gov.uk

Drinkline national alcohol helpline; phone: (0345) 320202 (Monday–Friday 11.00 a.m.–11.00 p.m.)

Drugs Helpline national drugs helpline; phone: (0800) 776600 (24 hours); Web site: www.d-code.co.uk

Epilepsy Helpline helpline of the British Epilepsy Association; Freephone: (0808) 800 5050 (Monday–Thursday 9.00 a.m.–4.30 p.m., Friday 9.00 a.m.–4.00 p.m.); e-mail: epilepsy@bea.org.uk; Web site: www.epilepsy.org.uk

Gamblers Anonymous phone: (0114) 262 0026 (24 hours)

Heartline Association advice relating to all aspects of coronary heart disease and its prevention; phone: (01276) 675655 (Monday–Friday 12 noon–5.00 p.m.)

NHS Health Information Service information on health issues such as illness and disease, self-help groups, and treatments; phone: (0800) 665544 voice and minicom (Monday–Friday 9.00 a.m.–7.00 p.m.); Web site: www.doh.gov.uk

NSPCC child protection helpline of the National Society for the Prevention of Cruelty to Children; phone: (0800) 800500 (24 hours); Web site: www.nspcc.org.uk

Quitline help for people wanting to stop smoking; phone: (0800) 002200 (12 noon–9.00 p.m.)

Samaritans phone: (0345) 909090 (24 hours); e-mail: jo@samaritans.org.uk; Web site: www.samaritans.org.uk

Saneline for people with mental health problems and their families and carers; phone: (0345) 678000 (12 noon–2.00 a.m.)

Seniorline information line from Help the Aged; Freephone: (0808) 800 6565 (Monday–Friday 9.00 a.m.–4.00 p.m.)

Sexwise helpline for young people with concerns over sexual or relationship matters; phone: (0800) 282930 (7.00 a.m.–midnight)

Source: Department of Health

Charitable Societies and Associations for Health and Related Issues

Action for Blind People 14–16 Verney Road, London SE16 3DZ; phone: (020) 7732 8771; fax: (020) 7639 0948; e-mail: central@afbp.org; Web site: www.afbp.org

Age Concern England: Astral House, 1268 London Road, London SW16 4ER; phone: (020) 8679 8000; fax: (020) 8765 7211; Northern Ireland: 3 Lower Crescent, Belfast BT7 1NR; phone: (028) 9024 5729; fax: (028) 9023 5497; Scotland: 113 Rose Street, Edinburgh EH2 3DT; phone: (0131) 220 3345; fax: (0131) 220 2779; Wales: 1 Cathedral Road, Cardiff CF1 9SD; phone: (029) 2037 1566; Web site: www.ace.org.uk

Alcoholics Anonymous PO Box 1, Stonebow House, Stonebow, York YO1 7NJ; phone: (01904) 644026 (administration), (0845) 769 7555 (helpline, local rate); fax: (01904) 629091; Web site: www.alcoholics-anonymous.org.uk

Alzheimer's Disease Society Gordon House, 10 Greencoat Place, London SW1P 1PH; phone: (020) 7306 0606; fax: (020) 7306 0808; e-mail: info@alzheimers.org.uk; Web site: www.alzheimers.org.uk

Arthritis Care 18 Stephenson Way, London NW1 2HD; phone: (020) 7916 1500, phone: (0808) 800 4050 (free helpline, 12 noon–4.00 p.m.); fax: (020) 7916 1505

Association for Spina Bifida and Hydrocephalus (ASBAH) 42 Park Road, Peterborough PE1 2UQ; phone: (01733) 555988; fax: (01733) 555985; e-mail: postmaster@asbah.demon.co.uk; Web site: www.asbah.demon.co.uk

British Association of Cancer United Patients (BACUP) 3 Bath Place, Rivington Street, London EC2A 3DR; phone: (020) 7696 9003; Cancer Information Service (Freephone): (0808) 800 1234; fax: (020) 7696 9002; e-mail: info@cancerbacup.org; Web site: www.cancerbacup.org.uk

British Association of the Hard of Hearing *see* **Hearing Concern**

British Deaf Association 1–3 Worship Street, London EC2A 2AB; phone: (020) 7588 3520; fax: (020) 7588 3527; Web site: www.bda.org.uk

British Diabetic Association (BDA) 10 Queen Anne Street, London W1M 0BD; phone: (020) 7323 1531; fax: (020) 7637 3644; e-mail: bda@diabetes.org.uk; Web site: www.diabetes.org.uk

British Epilepsy Association (BEA) New Anstey House, Gate Way Drive, Yeadon, Leeds LS19 7XY; phone: (0113) 210 8800; Freephone: (0808) 800 5050; fax: (0113) 391 0300; e-mail: epilepsy@bea.org.uk; Web site: www.epilepsy.org.uk

British Health Care Association 24a Main Street, Garforth, Leeds LS25 1AA; phone: (0113) 232 0903; fax: (0113) 232 0904; e-mail: cbell@bhca.org.uk; Web site: www.bhca.org.uk

British Heart Foundation 14 Fitzhardinge Street, London W1H 4DH; phone: (020) 7935 0185; fax: (020) 7486 5820; Web site: www.bhf.org.uk

British Lung Foundation 78 Hatton Garden, London EC1N 8LD; phone: (020) 7831 5831; fax: (020) 7831 5832; Web site: www.lung.org.uk

British Migraine Association 178a High Road, Byfleet, West Byfleet, Surrey KT14 7ED; phone: (01932) 352468; fax: (01932) 351257; e-mail: info@migraine.org.uk; Web site: www.migraine.org.uk

British Polio Fellowship Ground Floor, Unit A, Eagle Office Centre, The Runway, South Ruislip, Middlesex HA4 6SE; phone: (020) 8842 4999; fax: (020) 8842 0555; e-mail: british.polio@dial.pipex.com

British Red Cross Society 9 Grosvenor Crescent, London SW1X 7EJ; phone: (020) 7235 5454; fax: (020) 7245 6315; e-mail: information@redcross.org.uk; Web site: www.redcross.org.uk

Cancer Research Campaign 10 Cambridge Terrace, London NW1 4JL; phone: (020) 7224 1333; fax: (020) 7487 4310; e-mail: enquiries@crc.org.uk; Web site: www.crc.org.uk

Chest, Heart and Stroke Association *see* **Stroke Association**

Children's Society Edward Rudolf House, 69–85 Margery Street, London WC1X 0JL; phone: (020) 7837 4299; fax: (020) 7841 4500; e-mail: communications@the-childrens-society.org.uk; Web site: www.the-childrens-society.org.uk

Commonwealth Society for the Deaf (Sound Seekers) 134 Buckingham Palace Road, London SW1W 9SA; phone: (020) 7259 0200; fax: (020) 7259 0300

Cystic Fibrosis Trust Alexandra House, 11 London Road, Bromley, Kent BR1 1BY; phone: (020) 8464 7211; fax: (020) 8313 0472; e-mail: enquiries@cftrust.org.uk; Web site: www.cftrust.org.uk

Downs Syndrome Association 155 Mitcham Road, London SW17 9PG; phone: (020) 8682 4001; fax: (020) 8682 4012; Web site: www.downs-syndrome.org.uk

Charitable Societies and Associations for Health and Related Issues *(continued)*

Dyslexia Institute Ltd 133 Gresham Road, Staines, Middlesex TW18 2AJ; phone: (01784) 463851; fax: (01784) 460747; Web site: www.dyslexia-inst.org.uk

Eating Disorders Association 1st Floor, Wensum House, 103 Prince of Wales Road,Norwich NR1 1DW; phone: (01603) 619090; helpline: (01603) 621414 (Monday–Friday 9.00 a.m.–6.30 p.m.); youth helpline: (01603) 765050 (Monday–Friday 4.00 p.m.–6.00 p.m.); fax: (01603) 664915; e-mail: info@edauk.com; Web site: www.edauk.com

ENABLE (Scottish Society for the Mentally Handicapped) 6th Floor, 7 Buchanan Street, Glasgow G1 3HL; phone: (0141) 226 4541; fax: (0141) 204 4398; e-mail: enable@enable.org.uk

Foundation for the Study of Infant Deaths 14 Halkin Street, London SW1X 7DP; phone: (020) 7222 8001; helpline: (020) 7235 1712; fax: (020) 7823 1986; e-mail: fsid@dial.pipex.com

Friends of the Elderly and Gentlefolk's Help 40–42 Ebury Street, London SW1W 0LZ; phone: (020) 7730 8263; fax: (020) 7259 0154

Guide Dogs for the Blind Hillfields, Burghfield Common, Reading, Berks RG7 3YG; phone: (0118) 983 5555; fax: (0118) 983 5433; Web site: www.gdba.org.uk

Haemophilia Society 3rd Floor, Chesterfield House, 385 Euston Road, London NW1 3AU; phone: (020) 7380 0600; fax: (020) 7387 8220; e-mail: info@haemophilia.org.uk; Web site: www.haemophilia.org.uk

Hearing Concern (British Association for the Hard of Hearing) 7–11 Armstrong Road, London W3 7JL; phone: (020) 8743 1110; fax: (020) 8742 9043; e-mail: hearing.concern@ukonline.co.uk; Web site: http://web.ukonline.co.uk/hearing.concern

Help the Aged 16–18 St James's Walk, Clerkenwell Green, London EC1R 0BE; phone: (020) 7253 0253; fax: (020) 7251 0747; e-mail: info@helptheaged.org.uk; Web site: www.helptheaged.co.uk

Imperial Cancer Research Fund PO Box 123, Lincoln's Inn Fields, London WC2A 3PX; phone: (020) 7242 0200; fax: (020) 7269 3100; Web site: www.icnet.uk

Leprosy Mission (England and Wales) Goldhay Way, Orton Goldhay, Peterborough PE2 5GZ; phone: (01733) 370505; fax: (01733) 404880; e-mail: post@glmew.org.uk; Web site: www.leprosymission.org

Leukaemia Research Fund 43 Great Ormond Street, London WC1N 3JJ; phone: (020) 7405 0101; fax: (020) 7242 1488; e-mail: info@leukaemia-research.org.uk; Web site: www.leukaemia.demon.co.uk

Macmillan Cancer Relief Anchor House, 15–19 Britten Street, London SW3 3TZ; phone: (020) 7351 7811; fax: (020) 7376 8098; Web site: www.macmillan.org.uk

Marie Curie Cancer Care 28 Belgrave Square, London SW1X 8QG; phone: (020) 7235 3325; fax: (020) 7823 2380; Web site: www.mariecurie.org.uk

Maternity Alliance 45 Beech Street, London EC2P 2LX; phone: (020) 7588 8583; fax: (020) 7588 8584; e-mail: info@maternityalliance.org.uk

ME Association 4 Corringham Road, Stanford-le-Hope, Essex SS17 0AH; phone: (01375) 642466; fax: (01375) 360256; Web site: www.meassociation.org.uk

MENCAP (The Royal Society for Mentally Handicapped Children and Adults) 123 Golden Lane, London EC1Y 0RT; phone: (020) 7454 0454; fax: (020) 7608 3254; e-mail: info@mencap.org.uk; Web site: www.mencap.org.uk

Mental After Care Association 25 Bedford Square, London WC1B 3HW; phone: (020) 7436 6194; fax: (020) 7637 1980; e-mail: maca-bs@maca.org.uk

Migraine Trust 45 Great Ormond Street, London WC1N 3HZ; phone: (020) 7831 4818; fax: (020) 7831 5174; e-mail: migrainetrust@ compuserve.com; Web site: www.migrainetrust.org

MIND (The National Association for Mental Health) Granta House, 15–19 Broadway, London E15 4BQ; phone: (020) 8522 1728, (0845) 766 0163; info line: (0345) 660163; fax: (020) 8522 1725; Web site: www.mind.org.uk

Multiple Sclerosis Society of Great Britain and Northern Ireland 25 Effie Road, London SW6 1EE; phone: (020) 7610 7171; helpline: (0808) 8000; fax: (020) 7736 9861; e-mail: info@mssociety.org.uk; Web site: www. mssociety.org.uk

National Association for Colitis and Crohn's Disease 4 Beaumont House, Sutton Road, St Albans, Hertfordshire AL1 5HH; phone: (01727) 830038; fax: (01727) 862550; e-mail: nacc@nacc.org.uk; Web site: www.nacc.org.uk

National Association for Maternal and Child Welfare Ltd 1st Floor, 40–42 Osnaburgh Street, London NW1 3ND; phone: (020) 7383 4117; fax: (020) 7383 4115; e-mail: valerie.forebrothernamcw@btinternet.com; Web site: www.charitynet.org/-namcw

National Association for Mental Health *see* **MIND**

National Asthma Campaign Providence House, Providence Place, London N1 0NT; phone: (020) 7226 2260; helpline: (0845) 701 0203; fax: (020) 7704 0740; Web site: www.asthma.org.uk

National Childbirth Trust Alexandra House, Oldham Terrace, London W3 6NH; phone: (020) 8992 8637; fax: (020) 8992 5929; Web site: www.nct-online.org

National Library for the Blind Far Cromwell Road, Bredbury, Stockport, Cheshire SK6 2SG; phone: (0161) 355 2000; fax: (0161) 355 2098; e-mail: enquiries@nlbuk.org; Web site: www.nlbuk.org

National Osteoporosis Society PO Box 10, Radstock, Bath, BA3 3YB; phone: (01761) 471771; helpline: (01761) 472721; fax: (01761) 471104; e-mail: info@nos.org.uk; Web site: www.nos.org.uk

National Schizophrenia Fellowship (NSF) 28 Castle Street, Kingston upon Thames, Surrey, KT1 1SS; phone: (020) 8547 3937, (020) 8974 6814 (advice); fax: (020) 8547 3862; e-mail: info@nsf.org.uk; Web site: www.nsf.org.uk

Nutrition Society 10 Cambridge Court, 210 Shepherds Bush Road, London W6 7NJ; phone: (020) 7602 0228; fax: (020) 7602 1756; e-mail: mail@nutsoc.org.uk; Web site: www.nutsoc.org.uk

Patients' Association PO Box 935, Harrow HA1 3JY; phone: (020) 8423 9111; helpline: (020) 8423 8999; fax: (020) 8423 9119; Web site: www.patients-association.com

Princess Royal Trust for Carers 142 Minories, London EC3N 1LB; phone: (020) 7480 7788; fax: (020) 7481 4729; e-mail: info@carers.org.uk; Web site: www.carers.org

Psoriasis Association 7 Milton Street, Northampton NN2 7JG; phone: (01604) 711129; fax: (01604) 792894

QUIT (society that helps people stop smoking) Victory House, 170 Tottenham Court Road, London W1P 0HA; phone: (020) 7388 5775; freephone quitline: (0800) 002200; fax: (020) 7388 5995; Web site: www.quit.org.uk

RADAR (Royal Association for Disability and Rehabilitation) 12 City Forum, 250 City Road, London EC1V 8AF; phone: (020) 7250 3222; fax: (020) 7250 0212; Web site: www.radar.org.uk

Red Cross Society *see* **British Red Cross**

Royal Association in Aid of Deaf People Walsingham Road, Colchester CO2 7BP; phone: (01206) 769755; fax: (01206) 509509; e-mail: info@royaldeaf.org.uk; Web site: www.royaldeaf.org.uk

Royal Cancer Hospital, Institute of Cancer Research 237 Fulham Road, Chelsea, London SW3 6JB; phone: (020) 7352 8133; fax: (020) 7352 3299

Royal Commonwealth Society for the Blind *see* **Sight Savers International**

Royal London Society for the Blind Dorton House, Seal, Sevenoaks, Kent TN15 0ED; phone: (01732) 761477; fax: (01732) 592506

Royal National College for the Blind College Road, Hereford, HR1 1EB; phone: (01432) 265725; fax: (01432) 353478; Web site: www.rncb.ac.uk

Royal National Institute for Deaf People 19–23 Featherstone Street, London EC1Y 8SL; phone: (020) 7296 8000; helpline: (0808) 808 0123; fax: (020) 7296 8199; Texthelp: (0808) 808 9000; e-mail: helpline@rnid.org.uk; Web site: www.rnid.org.uk

Royal National Institute for the Blind 224 Great Portland Street, London W1N 6AA; phone: (020) 7388 1266; fax: (020) 7388 2034; e-mail: rnib@rnib.org.uk; Web site: www.rnib.org.uk

Royal School for Deaf Children Victoria Road, Margate, Kent CT9 1NB; phone: (01843) 227561; fax: (01843) 227637

Royal Society for the Prevention of Accidents Edgbaston Park, 353 Bristol Road, Birmingham B5 7ST; phone: (0121) 248 2000; fax: (0121) 248 2001; Web site: www.rospa.co.uk

St John Ambulance 1 Grosvenor Crescent, London SW1X 7EF; phone: (020) 7235 5231; fax: (020) 7235 0796; Web site: www.sjal.demon.co.uk

SANE – The Mental Health Charity 2nd Floor, 199–205 Old Marylebone Road, London NW1 5QP; phone: (020) 7724 6520; helpline: (0345) 678000; fax: (020) 7724 6502

Save the Children Fund Griffin House, 161 Hammersmith Road, London W8 8SG; phone: (020) 8752 2800; fax: (020) 8752 2806

Scottish Association for Mental Health Cumbrae House, 15 Carlton Court, Glasgow G5 9JP; phone: (0141) 568 7000; fax: (0141) 568 7001

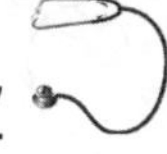

Charitable Societies and Associations for Health and Related Issues *(continued)*

Scottish Society for the Mentally Handicapped *see* **ENABLE**

SENSE (The National Deaf-Blind and Rubella Association) 11–13 Clifton Terrace, London N4 3SR; phone: (020) 7272 7774; fax: (020) 7272 6012; e-mail: enquiries@sense.org.uk; Web site: www.sense.org.uk

Sight Savers International (Royal Commonwealth Society for the Blind) Grosvenor Hall, Bolnore Road, Haywards Heath, West Sussex RH16 4BX; phone: (01444) 446600; fax: (01444) 446688; e-mail: information@sightsavers.int.org.uk; Web site: www.sightsavers.org.uk

Stroke Association Stroke House, 123 Whitecross Street, London EC1Y 8JJ; phone: (020) 7490 7999; fax: (020) 7490 2686; e-mail: stroke@stroke.org.uk; Web site: www.stroke.org.uk

Terrence Higgins Trust 52–54 Gray's Inn Road, London WC1X 8JU; phone: (020) 7831 0330, helpline: (020) 7242 1010; fax: (020) 7242 0121; e-mail: info@tht.org.uk; Web site: www.tht.org.uk

Web Sites

Action on Smoking and Health (ASH)

http://www.ash.org.uk/

ASH, the UK's leading pressure group against smoking, brings news and information of its campaigns plus opportunities to join in. There is also information and help with quitting smoking.

AIDS and HIV Information

http://www.thebody.com/index.shtml

AIDS and HIV site offering advice on safe sex and AIDS prevention, information about treatments and testing, and health and nutritional guidance for those with the disease.

Alcohol Concern

http://www.alcoholconcern.org.uk/

Huge resource addressing the problems surrounding alcohol abuse.

Allergy Facts

http://www.onlineallergycenter.com/about.htm

Information about the causes, symptoms, and treatment of allergy attacks, and helps clarify typical misunderstandings about allergy sufferers.

Alternative and Complementary Medicine Centre

http://www.healthy.net/clinic/therapy/

Guide to a range of disciplines within the field of complementary medicine, and their relationship to mainstream medical treatment.

Ancient Medicine/Medicina Antiqua

http://web1.ea.pvt.k12.pa.us/medant/

Ancient Greek and Roman medicine. Containing hypertext editions of Greco-Roman medical texts, this site forms a starting point for those wishing to study this section of the classics.

Animated Medical Graphics

http://www.animatedmedical.com/

Uses animations to explain medical terms and topics to those without a medical background. Non-medical analogies are used in the explanations, to make the topics as accessible as possible.

Babyworld.Com

http://www.babyworld.co.uk/

Help for all first-time parents that includes medical information – an extensive database of possible ailments, for example, but also covers such topics as pregnancy, daily care, development, and news.

Body Map: the Nervous System

http://library.thinkquest.org/10348/find/content/nervous.html

An overview of the way in which the brain sends, receives, and processes the nerve impulses that control everything we do. Part of a larger site on the human body, it explains the roles played by the central, peripheral, and autonomic nervous systems, and also provides experiments.

Bovine Spongiform Encephalopathy (BSE)

http://cahpwww.nbc.upenn.edu/bse/bse1.html

Collection of informative articles chronicling the BSE (or 'mad cow') controversy in the UK, including background information and official reports.

Breast Cancer Awareness

http://www.avoncrusade.com/

Promotes awareness of this disease through a library of FAQs about breast cancer and mammograms, as well as a glossary of common terms and access to support groups.

British Nutrition Society

http://www.nutrition.org.uk/

Offering educational resources for parents, schools and teachers, the British Nutrition Foundation Web site has a wide range of information about the nutritional value of your diet.

Cancer Help UK

http://medweb.bham.ac.uk/cancerhelp/indexg.html

UK cancer information – news, glossaries, treatments, research, help, and support.

Children's Health

http://www.kidshealth.org/

In-depth coverage of children's health issues, including infections, behaviour and emotions, food, and fitness; also includes an interactive map of the human body, designed for children to explore.

Department of Health Website

http://www.doh.gov.uk/

Produced by and for the UK Department of Health, this site is aimed primarily at health and social care professionals and academics, with links to more general information and other health-related sites.

Fitness Online

http://www.fitnessonline.com/

Guide to getting fit, featuring 'Searchable workouts'.

Healthy Ideas

http://www.healthyideas.com/

Online magazine with news and information about nutrition, natural healing, weight loss, fitness techniques, tips on healthy cooking, and lifestyle-related articles.

Heart: An Online Exploration

http://sln.fi.edu/biosci/heart.html

Explore the heart: discover its complexities, development, and structure; follow the blood on its journey through the blood vessels; and learn how to maintain a healthy heart.

Human Anatomy Online

http://www.innerbody.com/htm/body.html

Fun, interactive, and educational site on the human body, with hundreds of images and animations.

Immunology

http://www.nutramed.com/immunology/index.htm

Excellent and easy-to-understand introduction to the science of immunology.

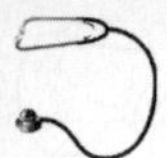

Institute for the Study of Drug Dependence (ISDD)

http://www.drugscope.org.uk/

Aiming to advance knowledge, understanding, and policy-making about drugs, this site from the ISDD contains an online drug encyclopedia and a FAQ section that tackles many of the main issues.

Internet Drug Index

http://www.rxlist.com/

Online list of prescription and non-prescription drugs, with a search engine to help find specific types or products, as well as information about indications and side effects.

MedicineNet

http://www.medicinenet.com/

US-based site dealing in plain language with all current aspects of medicine. It includes a dictionary of diseases, cures, and medical terms, as well as an 'Ask the experts' section, current medical news, and first aid advice.

Mental Health

http://www.mentalhealth.com/

This well-designed encyclopedia of mental disorders offers comprehensive information on diagnosing and treating mental health problems, and includes an online magazine.

National Health Service (NHS)

http://www.nhs50.nhs.uk/

Features a detailed history of the NHS, as well as a glimpse into the future with 'Technology for Tomorrow'.

NHS Direct

http://www.nhsdirect.nhs.uk/main.jhtml

Here you can search the NHS database for access to authoritative medical information and guidelines to healthy living; you can also call NHS Direct nurses for medical advice.

Patient Advice

http://www.patient.co.uk/

Excellent site offering advice and help on health issues.

Personal and Occupational Stress Management

http://www.stress.org.uk/

Information on the causes of stress, how to avoid it, and how to cope with it. The site also includes special features, including a study on 'Workplace bullying'.

Plainsense Men's Health

http://www.plainsense.com/Health/Mens/

Covers a wide range of issues specific to male physical and mental health, with practical advice on self-help and treatment options.

Plainsense Women's Health

http://www.plainsense.com/Health/Womens/index.htm

Covers a wide range of issues specific to female physical and mental health, with practical advice on self-help and treatment options.

Suicide Information and Education Center (SIEC)

http://www.siec.ca/

Extensive information on suicide prevention and intervention efforts and trends, drawn from the SIEC database, as well as details of organizations and crisis support.

Transplantation and Donation

http://www.transweb.org/index.htm

Information about organ and tissue transplantation and donation, the latest research developments, answers to FAQs, and articles and reports from medical professionals.

Trashed

http://www.trashed.co.uk/index2.html

Health Education Authority site designed for young people, offering objective information about drugs and their effects.

Visible Embryo

http://www.visembryo.com/

Learn about the first four weeks of human development.

Wired for Health

http://www.wiredforhealth.gov.uk/mainfram.html

Government health site targeting young people and teachers, with well-presented information on how to stay healthy and ways of promoting health education.

World Health Organization

http://www.who.ch/

Overview of the World Health Organization, including its major programmes, and recent world health reports.

You Are What You Eat

http://library.advanced.org/11163/gather/cgi-bin/wookie.cgi/

Includes interactive exercises designed to help visitors learn about their personal eating habits and how to improve them. Users can also search the food database for nutritional information.

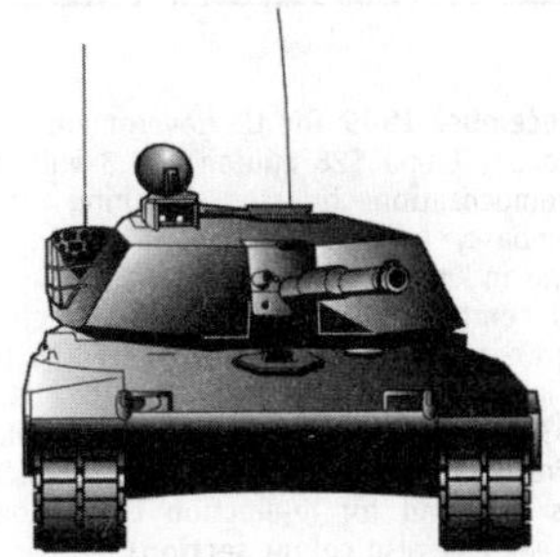

THE MILITARY AND DEFENCE

The Year in Review

4 July 1999 In a meeting with US president Bill Clinton, Pakistani prime minister Nawaz Sharif pledges to restore the line of ceasefire between Pakistani and Indian forces in the disputed region of Kashmir. Muslim forces, however, vow to continue fighting, and the Indian government rejects foreign intervention in solving the crisis.

5 July 1999 The North Atlantic Treaty Organization (NATO) and the Russian government reach an agreement in Moscow on the details of Russian participation in NATO's peacekeeping force in the Serbian province of Kosovo. Russian troops start to enter Kosovo on 6 July.

7 July 1999 Helicopter gunships and armoured vehicles are deployed by the Russian military to fight Chechen guerrillas armed with grenade launchers and mortars in Chechnya and Dagestan.

14 July 1999 China announces that it is now capable of producing neutron bombs.

20 July 1999 A militant group in Iran called Laskar-I-Toiba (Army of the Pure) is linked with the deaths of 15 Kashmiris in a village shooting.

3 August 1999 The Talibaan win a series of military victories in northern Afghanistan, prompting the flight of hundreds of thousands of civilians. On 5 August, the Afghan opposition retaliates, gaining back lost ground.

4 August 1999 NATO appoints British defence secretary George Robertson as its secretary general.

5 August 1999 Japan and South Korea carry out their first joint naval drills.

10 August 1999 An Indian fighter jet shoots down a Pakistani naval plane in a border area, killing all 16 people aboard. The incident increases the friction between the two nations over the disputed region of Kashmir.

12 August 1999 The Indonesian army in Ambon is accused by clergy of the killing of 25 Christians; an investigation by the armed forces follows.

13 August 1999 Japan agrees to consider entering into a joint anti-ballistic missile defence project with the USA. Taiwan later declares its interest in the program.

17–19 August 1999 Delegates from the USA and Russia meet in Moscow to discuss a new Strategic Arms Reduction Treaty (START III), which would limit the number of nuclear warheads possessed by each country.

1 September 1999 The United Nations compound in Dili, the capital of East Timor, is under siege for more than two hours as militiamen battle in the streets outside, killing one man. Thousands of local people flee into the compound for safety.

4 September 1999 In a referendum, the people of East Timor vote overwhelmingly for independence from Indonesia. Within hours of the announcement of the result, militiamen create roadblocks and enter the capital, Dili.

5 September 1999 Hours after the signing of a new peace accord that sets out a 12-month timetable to resolve almost all the major issues between the Israelis and Palestinians, two Israeli suicide bombers strike northern Israel in an apparent attempt by extremist groups to upset peace efforts.

5 September 1999 The day after the East Timorese vote for independence, militiamen kill more than 20 people in the capital, Dili. Mounting violence creates up to 150,000 refugees, a quarter of the population. The United Nations Security Council plans to send a mission to Jakarta to put pressure on the Indonesian government to halt the violence.

6 September 1999 Martial law is declared in East Timor, as militias continue to attack independence supporters.

12 September 1999 The Indonesian government yields to international pressure to allow a United Nations peacekeeping force into East Timor. The decision comes after statements by the UN linking the military to the recent atrocities, and a plan announced by the UN Human Rights Commissioner to set up a tribunal to deal with war crimes (*see also* **colour section**).

13 September 1999 The United Nations begins a mass evacuation of refugees from Dili, East Timor, to northern Australia. The evacuation follows fears that the violence against the East Timorese by the Indonesian army and militias might escalate.

20 September 1999 The first international peacekeepers arrive in East Timor from Australia and the UK to liberate the territory from Indonesia.

17 October 1999 Having overthrown the government in a military coup, the self-proclaimed new chief executive of Pakistan, Pervez Musharraf, makes his first public appearance and announces his intention that the country return to civilian rule.

> *I don't care if he is a politician or a prime minister, there should be no force to stop a father and a son from communicating.*
>
> Hassan Sharif, son of ousted Pakistani prime minister, Nawaz Sharif, after the military leaders of the coup refused to let them speak by telephone. *Newsweek*, 25 October 1999.

18 October 1999 Commonwealth foreign ministers meeting in Durban, South Africa, suspend Pakistan's membership in response to the coup.

2 November 1999 US president Bill Clinton, Israeli president Ehud Barak, and Palestinian National Authority leader Yasser Arafat meet in Oslo, Norway, to negotiate a final peace settlement in the Middle East.

7 November 1999 On the eve of talks planned to reach a final agreement for peace in the Middle East, three pipe bombs explode in Netanya, Israel, injuring 33 people. No group claims responsibility.

10 November 1999 Amnesty International, Pax Christi, UNICEF UK, and the Jesuit Refugee Service petition Downing Street on the eve of Remembrance Day to stop using child soldiers. The UK has the highest number of under-18-year-olds in its armed forces of any European country, deployed both in conflict situations and peacekeeping.

28 November 1999 Russian troops fire on the Chechen capital of Groznyy with bombs, rockets, and shells, killing hundreds of people and destroying large areas of the city, in their worst attack on the Chechen capital since the war began two months ago.

28 November 1999 The Basque separatist group ETA (Euskadi Ta Askatasuna/Basque Homeland and Freedom) announces that it is ending its 14-month ceasefire in its violent campaign against the Spanish government.

8 December 1999 The Serbian army takes control of Montenegro's main airport and bans civilian flights, raising fears that the government plans to prevent the republic's move toward independence.

15 December 1999 Chechen rebels resist a Russian assault on Groznyy, destroying tanks and armoured personnel carriers, and killing some 100 Russian soldiers.

15 December 1999 US president Bill Clinton opens peace talks between Israeli prime minister Ehud Barak and Syrian foreign minister Farouk al-Sharaa, in Washington, DC.

16 December 1999 The US government agrees to pay China $28 million/£17.3 million in compensation for the bombing of its embassy in Belgrade, Serbia, during the war in Kosovo.

18 December 1999 Two bombs, which the government suspects were planted by Tamil Tigers, explode in Colombo, Sri Lanka, killing 33 people and injuring some 150, including President Bandaranaike Kumaratunga, who is to stand for re-election the following week (see also **colour section**).

21 December 1999 Russian soldiers clash with 500 Chechen rebels near the village of Serzhen Yurt.

24 December 1999 Henri Konan Bedie, president of Côte d'Ivoire, is ousted in a military coup led by General Robert Guei. After a night of chaos and looting in Abidjan, Guei announces the formation of a 10-member military committee, headed by himself, to rule the country.

1 January 2000 A computer glitch caused by the millennium bug affects spy satellite operations in the USA, reducing the Pentagon's ability to monitor world events. From 7 p.m. to midnight Greenwich Mean Time, the system is covered by a back-up system.

12 January 2000 Under pressure from the European court of human rights, UK defence secretary Geoff Hoon announces the lifting of the ban on homosexuals in the armed forces.

February 2000 Fighting between the Talibaan and forces led by Ahmad Shah Masoud resumes in northern Afghanistan after a seven-month reprieve.

3 February 2000 Peter Mandelson, the Northern Ireland secretary, announces that the British government will reimpose direct rule over Northern Ireland unless the IRA begins decommissioning its weapons within a week.

5 February 2000 Former Rwandan army chief Tharcisse Muvunyi is arrested in London on charges of genocide during the civil war in Rwanda in 1994.

8 February 2000 The Palestinian National Authority reports that is has frozen peace talks with Israel, less than a week before the deadline for a framework for a peace agreement in the Middle East. Israel's withdrawal from the West Bank is a major factor in the breakdown of the talks.

March 2000 India announces an increase of 28% in defence spending, which is criticized by Pakistan as representing a 'war budget'.

March 2000 A report by the US military claims that secret details of the bombing campaign against Yugoslavia were leaked to the Serbs by a NATO-based spy.

April 2000 The Duma, Russia's lower parliamentary house, gives its approval to START II, an arms-control treaty with the USA that aims to reduce the nuclear capacity of both nations.

9 April 2000 A US Marine Corp MV-22 Osprey 'convertiplane', a new aircraft that the Pentagon hopes to play a leading role in 21st-century warfare and looks like a cross between an aeroplane and a helicopter, crashes during a test flight, killing all 19 marines aboard, at Marana, Arizona.

6 April 2000 Nawaz Sharif, the deposed prime minister of Pakistan, is sentenced to life in prison for terrorism and hijacking in a plot against General Pervez Musharraf, the military leader who ousted him from power in 1999.

21 April 2000 The Russian parliament ratifies the comprehensive nuclear test ban treaty with the USA. The US Senate refused to ratify the treaty in 1999.

May 2000 The British government shows support for the defence industry in Europe with £5 billion in orders, including Meteor air-to-air missiles and A400M Airbus transport aircraft.

June 2000 The largest haul of weapons yet found in Kosovo, including 67 tons of ammunition, 1,100 anti-tank rockets, and 45,000 hand grenades, was seized by a British Army battle group involved in anti-terrorist activities.

British troops training in Petrovac, Yugoslavia. The discovery of hidden weapons by a British army anti-terrorist group in June 2000 was evidence that the threat of instability in the region remains present. *Syndication International*

7 June 2000 The UK Ministry of Defence announces that it will be selling off large amounts of its vast landholdings to help meet targets for the development of brownfield land, partly in response to an earlier campaign by the *Independent on Sunday* to open up 'Out of Bounds Britain'.

13 June 2000 The decision of MI5, the UK security service, not to refer the case of spy Melita Norwood to the police for prosecution is condemned in Parliament. The 86-year-old woman had provided intelligence for the KGB for 40 years.

18 June 2000 The chief constable of Wiltshire asks the home secretary for emergency funding to widen an investigation into secret chemical warfare tests performed on approximately 20,000 workers in the 1950s and 1960s at Porton Down. If allegations are proved true, the Ministry of Defence will face multi-million pound claims for compensation.

19 June 2000 A massacre of 160 people occurs in the village of Duma on Halmahera, in the Moluccas, Indonesia. The 'Laskar Jihad' or Holy War Force, a Muslim paramilitary group thought to be supported by the former dictator Suharto, is behind the recent violence in the 18-month religious conflict.

World Defence and Weaponry

Biological, Chemical, and Nuclear Warfare

biological warfare the use of living organisms, or of infectious material derived from them, to bring about death or disease in humans, animals, or plants. At least ten countries have this capability.

chemical warfare use in war of gaseous, liquid, or solid substances intended to have a toxic effect on humans, animals, or plants. Together with biological warfare, it was banned by the Geneva Protocol in 1925, and the United Nations in 1989 also voted for a ban. In June 1990, the USA and USSR agreed bilaterally to reduce their stockpile to 5,000 tonnes each by 2002. The USA began replacing its stocks with new nerve-gas binary weapons. In 1993, over 120 nations, including the USA and Russian Federation, signed a treaty outlawing the manufacture, stockpiling, and use of chemical weapons. However, it was not until 1997 that the Russian parliament ratified the treaty.

nuclear warfare war involving the use of nuclear weapons. Nuclear-weapons research began in the UK in 1940, but was transferred to the USA after it entered World War II. The research programme, known as the Manhattan Project, was directed by J Robert Oppenheimer. (*See also* **Nuclear Weapons: Key Dates**, p 553.)

The SA80 Rifle

The SA80 Rifle was introduced into service in 1986, to replace the Self Loading Rifle (SLR), which had been in service since the 1960s. The new rifle was designed to be shorter and lighter, with a reduced calibre from 7.62 mm to 5.5 mm, and a correspondingly higher muzzle velocity. During the Gulf War, it emerged that soldiers complained that the rifle's bolt and magazine were prone to jamming in the extreme climatic conditions of the desert. Soldiers' complaints were confirmed by tests carried out in 1995. The German weapons manufacturer Heckler and Koch is set to win an £80 million contract to overhaul an initial batch of 22,000 of the 200,000 rifles in service.

Defence Research-and-Development Spending for Selected Countries

Includes only countries spending more than $50 million on military R&D and making figures available. Figures are in millions of constant 1995 dollars.

Country	R&D expenditure	Year
Nuclear weapon states		
USA	38,000	1997
France	4,000	1997
UK	3,300	1997
China[1]	1,000	1994
Russian Federation	970	1997
Non-nuclear weapon and threshold states		
Germany	2,100	1997
Japan	1,800	1997
India	630	1997
Spain	600	1997
Sweden	570	1996
Korea, South	510	1997
Taiwan	350	1994
Brazil	340	1997
Italy	300	1995
Australia	170	1994
South Africa	150	1996
Canada	120	1996
Ukraine	120	1994
Netherlands	100	1996
Switzerland	100	1995
Norway	69	1997
Poland	53	1997

[1] Figure accurate to one significant digit.

Source: Eric Arnett, in SIPRI Yearbook 1999: Armaments, Disarmament and International Security, *Stockholm International Peace Research Institute (Oxford University Press, 1999)*

The Leading Recipients of Major Conventional Weapons

Countries are ranked according to 1994–98 aggregate imports. Figures are trend-indicator values expressed in millions of constant 1990 dollars.

Rank 1994–98	Rank 1993–97	Recipient	1994	1995	1996	1997	1998	1994–98
1	2	Taiwan	731	1,162	1,451	5,311	4,656	13,311
2	1	Saudi Arabia	1,298	1,249	1,961	3,292	1,948	9,748
3	3	Turkey	1,386	1,327	1,132	1,394	1,376	6,615
4	4	Egypt	1,926	1,645	940	931	440	5,882
5	5	Korea, South	642	1,553	1,598	731	656	5,171
6	7	Greece	1,172	943	241	832	1,566	4,754
7	8	India	497	932	988	1,266	466	4,149
8	6	Japan	678	948	624	662	1,181	4,093
9	11	United Arab Emirates	629	442	600	840	756	3,267
10	12	Thailand	758	628	555	1,128	63	3,132
11	10	Kuwait	49	974	1,338	418	228	3,007
12	15	Malaysia	453	1,143	200	780	59	2,635

(continued)

The Leading Recipients of Major Conventional Weapons *(continued)*

Rank 1994–98	Rank 1993–97	Recipient	1994	1995	1996	1997	1998	1994–98
13	14	Pakistan	683	242	552	614	525	2,616
14	9	China	112	427	1,115	834	104	2,592
15	13	USA	711	459	431	696	223	2,520
16	20	Israel	796	229	73	46	1,285	2,429
17	18	Spain	646	395	441	230	402	2,114
18	19	Finland	196	162	581	439	647	2,025
19	26	Singapore	187	232	538	123	685	1,765
20	21	Indonesia	600	359	547	141	66	1,713

Source: Björn Hagelin, Pieter D Wezeman and Siemon T Wezeman, in SIPRI Yearbook 1999: Armaments, Disarmament and International Security, *Stockholm International Peace Research Institute (Oxford University Press, 1999)*

Defence Expenditure and Strength of Armed Forces – Global Trends

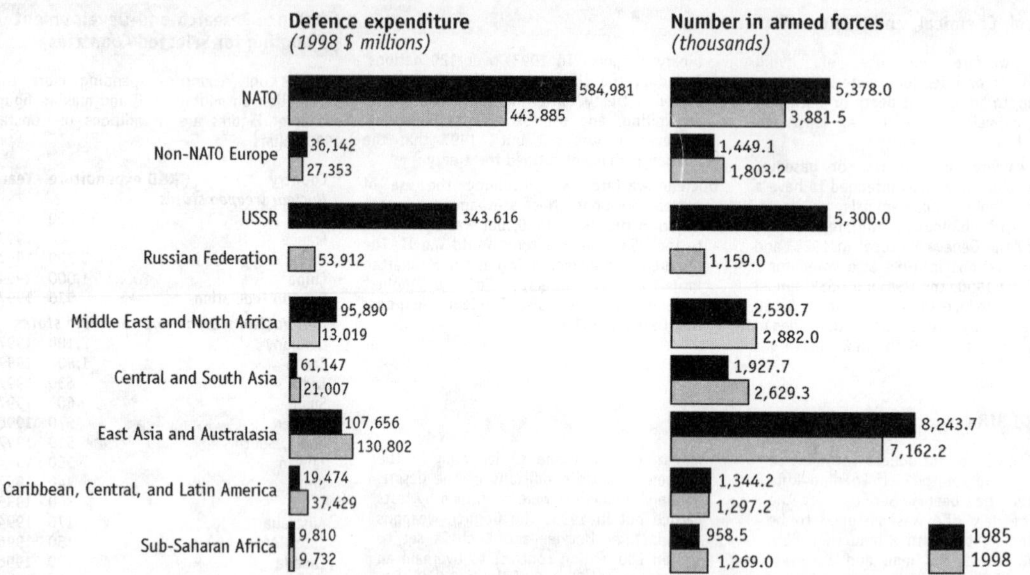

Source: The Military Balance 1999/2000, *International Institute for Strategic Studies, by permission of Oxford University Press and the IISS*

Selected Conventional Weapons Arsenals for Selected Countries

As of January 1999. (N/A = not available.)

Weapon type	Brazil	Canada	France	Germany	India	Iraq	Israel	Italy	Nigeria	Poland	Russian Federation	UK	USA	Yugoslavia
Sea forces														
Tactical submarines	4	1	8	14	16	0	4	8	0	3	44	12	57	4
Carriers	1	0	1	0	1	0	0	1	0	0	1	3	12	0
Cruisers	0	0	1	0	0	0	0	1	0	0	7	0	27	0
Destroyers	0	4	4	2	7	0	0	4	0	1	17	11	54	0
Frigates	18	12	35	12	13	2	0	24	1	1	10	20	37	4
Patrol/coastal	37	14	40	28	40	6	53	16	26	40	112	24	21	34
Mine warfare	6	2	22	34	18	4	0	13	2	24	72[4]	19	27	10
Amphibious[1]	4	0	9	0	9	0	1	3	1	5	25[4]	8	42	20
Support/logistics	25	7	36	42	31	3	0	82	5	18	436[4]	21	116	9
Land forces														
Main battle tanks	178	114	1,207	3,136	3,414[4]	2,200[4]	2,800	1,322	200	1,675	15,500[4]	542	8,087	785
Armoured reconnaisance vehicles	409	398	1,583	523	100[4]	N/A	400[4]	0	382[4]	510	2,000[4]	462	113	88
Armoured infantry fighting vehicles[2]	0	0	713	2,118	1,350	900[4]	0	0	0	1,405	6,725	747	6,715	718
Armoured personnel carriers	803	1,743	3,820	3,306	157	2,000[4]	9,900[4]	3,107	N/A	728[4]	3,337	3,016	17,800	169
Artillery pieces[3]	874[5]	289	1,055	2,068	5,487[4]	2,100[6]	2,570[5]	1,334	469	1,580	15,700[4]	425	6,629	4,453[5]

(continued)

Selected Conventional Weapons Arsenals for Selected Countries *(continued)*

Weapon type	Country and weapon strength													
	Brazil	Canada	France	Germany	India	Iraq	Israel	Italy	Nigeria	Poland	Russian Federation	UK	USA	Yugo-slavia
Anti-tank guided weapons	22	575	2,065	1,960	N/A	N/A	1,225[4]	1,426	0	403	N/A	841	42,428	N/A
Rocket launchers	405	N/A	19,540	0	N/A	N/A	N/A	1,810	N/A	N/A	N/A	N/A	N/A	3,200
Air defence guns	N/A	34	774	1,529	2,400[4]	N/A	850	275	N/A	1,116	N/A	0	0	1,850
Surface-to-air missiles	44	118	605	N/A	N/A	N/A	1,298	196	64	1,290	N/A	512	N/A	N/A
Air Forces														
Combat aircraft	296	140	592	503	853	316[7]	459	339	91	325	4,295[4]	495	4,565	238
Helicopters	156	213	657	765	250	500[4]	133	542	17	222	3,492[4]	537	6,323	52

[1] Ships specifically employed to disembark troops over unprepared beaches or to support amphibious operations.
[2] Armoured combat vehicles are designed to transport an infantry squad, armed with an integral cannon of at least 20-mm calibre.
[3] Weapons with a calibre of 100 mm and above, capable of engaging targets by delivering primarily indirect fire. Includes guns, howitzers, multiple rocket launchers, and mortars.
[4] Estimated.
[5] Estimated. Figure includes towed and self-propelled artillery but not multiple rocket launchers for which complete figures are not available.
[6] Does not include mortars, for which figures are not available.
[7] Estimated for bombers, ground attack, and fighter aircraft.

Source: Data from The Military Balance 1999/2000, *International Institute for Strategic Studies*

Strategic Nuclear Arsenals

The arsenals of the second-tier powers – UK, France, and China – are many orders of magnitude less than those of the USA and the Russian Federation. As current systems get older, the volume of deployed Russian strategic nuclear warheads will fall sharply over the next decade. ICBM = Inter Continental Ballistic Missile; SLBM = Submarine Launched Ballistic Missile.
As of January 1998. (– = not applicable.)

Country	Bombers		ICBMs		SLBMs		Total	
	deployed weapons	warheads[1]	deployed weapons	warheads[1]	deployed weapons	warheads[1]	deployed weapons	warheads[1]
USA	92/53[2]	1,750	550	2,000	432	3,456	1,074/1,035	7,206
Russian Federation	70	806	756	3,590	348	1,576	1,174	5,972
	Aircraft							
France	69	80	–	–	64	384	133	464
UK	–	–	–	–	48	185	48	185
	Aircraft		Land-based missiles					
China	150	150	128	128	12	12	290	290

[1] Warheads in stockpile for France, UK, and China.
[2] Hardware configured to carry various combinations of munitions.

Source: Robert S Norris and William M Arkin, in SIPRI Yearbook 1999: Armaments, Disarmament and International Security, *Stockholm International Peace Research Institute (Oxford University Press, 1999)*

Nuclear Weapons: Key Dates

1938 The German scientist Otto Hahn finds that uranium nuclei split when bombarded with neutrons, a discovery that later leads to the development of the nuclear bomb.

1940 Nuclear weapons research begins in the UK, but, known as the 'Manhattan Project', is transferred to the USA after it enters World War II in 1941. The work is carried out at Los Alamos, New Mexico, under the direction of US physicist, J Robert Oppenheimer.

16 July 1945 First test explosion of an atomic device takes place in the Nevada Desert at Alamogordo, New Mexico, USA.

August 1945 The USA drops the world's first atomic bombs on Hiroshima (6 August) and Nagasaki (9 August), Japan, killing more than 115,000 and hastening Japan's surrender and the end of World War II.

1949 The USSR test-explodes a nuclear device and becomes a nuclear power.

12 May 1951 The thermonuclear hydrogen bomb (H-bomb), much more powerful than the atomic bomb, is first tested by the USA, at Eniwetok Atoll, Pacific Ocean; the UK test-explodes its first nuclear device in the Monte Bello Islands, off Australia.

1957 The USSR introduces Intercontinental Ballistic Missiles (ICBMs), with a range of over 5,500 km: the USA soon follows. The International Atomic Energy Agency (IAEA) is set up as an autonomous intergovernmental organization within the United Nations to promote peaceful uses of nuclear energy and conduct inspections of nuclear installations in countries suspected of developing nuclear weapons.

1958 The Campaign for Nuclear Disarmament (CND) is formed in the UK to spearhead popular opposition to nuclear weapons and to campaign for nuclear disarmament.

1960 France test-explodes its first nuclear device; the USA deploys Polaris submarine-launched ballistic missiles (SLBMs).

October 1962 The Cuban Missile Crisis brings the USA and the USSR to the brink of nuclear war before the Soviets agree to withdraw 42 nuclear missiles recently installed in Cuba and capable of reaching US cities.

December 1962 The USA provides the UK with Polaris missiles under the Nassau Treaty.

August 1963 The USSR, UK, and USA sign the Nuclear Test Ban Treaty, prohibiting atmospheric tests and testing in space, but allowing underwater tests of nuclear weapons.

1964 China test-explodes a nuclear device to become the world's fifth nuclear power.

1968 ICBMs begin to be equipped with clusters of warheads (multiple independently targetable re-entry vehicles or MIRVs) capable of being directed at individual targets.

1969 Strategic Arms Limitation Talks (SALT) between the USA and the USSR begin as technological advances threaten the nuclear balance.

March 1970 The Nuclear Non-Proliferation Treaty (NPT), approved by the United Nations in June 1968 and signed by China, France, the USSR, UK, and USA, comes into effect, limiting the spread of nuclear weapons for 25

Nuclear Weapons: Key Dates *(continued)*

years. It is indefinitely extended in May 1995.

May 1972 The USA and the USSR sign, as part of SALT I, the Anti-Ballistic Missile (ABM) Treaty, restricting each to one land-based ABM system for defence of its capital system and one for defence of a single missile site.

June 1979 US President Jimmy Carter and Soviet leader Leonid Brezhnev sign the Strategic Arms Limitation Treaty (SALT) II, limiting arms levels. Although not ratified by the US Senate because of the USSR's occupation of Afghanistan, both countries abide by it.

1981 The USA begins to deploy Trident multiple-warhead SLBMs. On 12 December a 'peace camp' is established outside the US Air Force base at Greenham Common, Berkshire, England, by women protesters opposed to the proposed deployment of intermediate-range Cruise nuclear missiles. Nevertheless, Cruise missiles are deployed in Western Europe, 1983–91, the first arriving at Greenham Common in November 1983.

March 1983 US President Ronald Reagan announces the Strategic Defensive Initiative (SDI: 'Star Wars' programme) to provide a defensive shield against Soviet nuclear missiles, operative from 2000. Suggested components of the system include laser beams and microwaves directed from satellites in space.

November 1983 The first Cruise missiles are deployed at Greenham Common in the UK.

December 1987 The USA and the USSR agree the Intermediate-Range Nuclear Force (INF) Treaty to remove land-based intermediate-range nuclear missiles from Western and Central Europe, thus reducing US and Soviet nuclear arsenals by 4%.

1989 The UK agrees to purchase from the USA submarine-launched Trident missiles to replace, from the mid-1990s, its ageing Polaris SLBMs.

1989–91 The Cold War ends and the USSR breaks apart. US spending on SDI continues at $3–4 billion a year, for protection against accidental nuclear attack and defence against possible nuclear threat from 'rogue nations' (as personified by Iraq following the Gulf War 1991).

1990 The number of nuclear weapons worldwide is 50,000, distributed among five states: China, France, the USSR, the UK, and the USA. More powerful Trident II missiles are introduced in the USA.

1991 South Africa voluntarily dismantles its six nuclear bombs before signing the Nuclear Non-Proliferation Treaty.

1 August 1991 The USA and the USSR sign the Strategic Arms Reduction Treaty (START), limiting both sides to no more than 6,000 nuclear warheads.

December 1991 In the Minsk Agreement to disband the USSR, Belarus, Ukraine, and Kazakhstan declare they will become non-nuclear states.

1992 The first UK submarine designed to carry Trident missiles is launched; it is of the giant Vanguard class.

June 1992 Russian President Boris Yeltsin and US President George Bush agree to go beyond START and promise, by 2003, to cut US nuclear warheads from 9,986 to 3,500 and Russian warheads from 10,237 to 3,000. START II is signed January 1993.

1993 US defense secretary Les Aspin declares the SDI preoject dead (its technology could not be made to work), but the Pentagon continues to spend $3–4 billion a year on missile defence research.

January 1996 After completing six tests in French Polynesia during 1995, France announces an end to its nuclear testing programme and calls for a worldwide testing ban. The Comprehensive Test Ban Treaty is signed by 149 countries.

March 1996 US Republicans promote the development of a missile defence shield to combat nuclear threat from 'rogue nations' and defend all 50 US states by 2003 (later amended to 2005). Known as National Missile Defence (NMD) and dubbed 'son of Star Wars', it uses ground- rather than space-based interceptors, guided to their targets by early warning satellites, radar, and computers. Deployment would entail the establishment an ABM site in Alaska to supplement that in North Dakota, contravening the 1972 US–Soviet ABM treaty. US president Bill Clinton sets up the '3 + 3' development programme for NMD (3 years research and 3 years deployment if the president considers it necessary). The USA and the UK sign a treaty to make the South Pacific a nuclear free zone.

July 1996 The International Court of Justice, in response to a request for a ruling by the UN General Assembly in December 1994, declares that, in general, the use of nuclear weapons is contrary to the established rules of war.

May 1998 India becomes a nuclear power, carrying out five tests in the Rajasthan desert; Pakistan responds by successfully test-firing its own Ghauri nuclear missile to become the world's seventh nuclear power.

August 1998 North Korea tests a two-stage ballistic missile.

March 1999 Under the National Missile Defense Act, the USA states that deployment of NMD will begin as soon as technologically feasible.

June 1999 USA successfully tests its Theater High Altitude Area Defense (THAAD) missile, a new 'hit-to-kill' kinetic energy missile developed to protect troops in the field from medium range missiles, and a prime candidate for use in NMD.

July 1999 Concerns are raised that North Korea and Iran are close to developing nuclear weapons, despite earlier pledges by North Korea to abandon its atomic weapons programme.

October 1999 The US Senate votes against ratification of the Comprehensive Test Ban Treaty (CTBT). Russian Federation, China, India, and Pakistan are also yet to ratify the treaty.

November 1999 European powers voice increasing opposition to deployment of NMD, stating it would contravene the ABM treaty, downgrade the transatlantic alliance, and lead to a fresh arms race.

January 2000 An NMD test missile launched from the Marshall Islands fails to intercept a target launched from Santa Barbara, USA. Independent analysis of a previous 'successful' test in October 1999 by missile defence expert Theodore Postol (professor of science and national security policy at the Massachusetts Institute of Technology), had revealed that available technology cannot distinguish between real and decoy targets.

April 2000 START II is ratified by the Russian Duma (the US Senate had ratified the 1993 treaty in 1996), but a resolution is passed that this will be revoked if the 1972 ABM treaty is broken. Under START II Russian and US nuclear arsenals are to be halved to no more than 3,500 warheads each by 2007. The Duma also ratifies the CTBT.

June 2000 President Clinton offers to share NMD technology with 'civilized nations'. His summit with Russian president Vladimir Putin produces an agreement to cut military plutonium stores and develop a joint early warning system, but Putin continues to oppose NMD for contravention of the ABM treaty.

July 2000 The US Defense Department announces that its test of the controversial NMD system has failed, when an interceptor rocket failed to hit a dummy warhead over the Pacific Ocean. The failure is seen as a significant setback to the Pentagon's planned installation of a complete missile defence system over the USA by 2005.

The Leading Suppliers of Major Conventional Weapons

Countries are ranked according to 1994–98 aggregate exports. Figures are trend-indicator values expressed in millions of constant 1990 dollars. (N/A = not available.)

Rank		Supplier	1994	1995	1996	1997	1998	1994–98
1994–98	1993–97							
1	1	USA	9,844	9,580	9,712	12,404	12,342	53,882
2	2	Russia	1,155	3,271	3,602	2,956	1,276	12,260
3	5	France	756	806	1,924	3,284	3,815	10,585

(continued)

World Defence and Weaponry

The Leading Suppliers of Major Conventional Weapons *(continued)*

Rank 1994–98	Rank 1993–97	Supplier	1994	1995	1996	1997	1998	1994–98
4	3	UK	1,494	1,708	1,800	3,238	673	8,913
5	4	Germany	2,637	1,425	1,399	686	1,064	7,211
6	6	China	731	849	751	338	157	2,826
7	7	Netherlands	495	378	414	551	506	2,344
8	8	Italy	306	330	366	442	298	1,742
9	10	Ukraine	189	192	195	516	449	1,541
10	9	Canada	365	436	239	137	217	1,394
11	11	Spain	275	111	99	637	221	1,343
12	12	Israel	115	206	257	292	147	1,017
13	13	Czech Republic	378	188	132	30	16	744
14	14	Belarus	8	24	129	516	16	693
15	16	Belgium	20	296	144	89	51	600
16	17	Sweden	63	180	155	51	136	585
17	15	Moldova	165	N/A	N/A	392	N/A	557
18	20	Poland	131	184	65	20	1	401
19	19	Australia	24	22	15	318	3	382
20	18	Switzerland	70	75	122	62	35	364

Source: Björn Hagelin, Pieter D Wezeman and Siemon T Wezeman, in SIPRI Yearbook 1999: Armaments, Disarmament and International Security, *Stockholm International Peace Research Institute (Oxford University Press, 1999)*

Largest Arms-Producing Companies

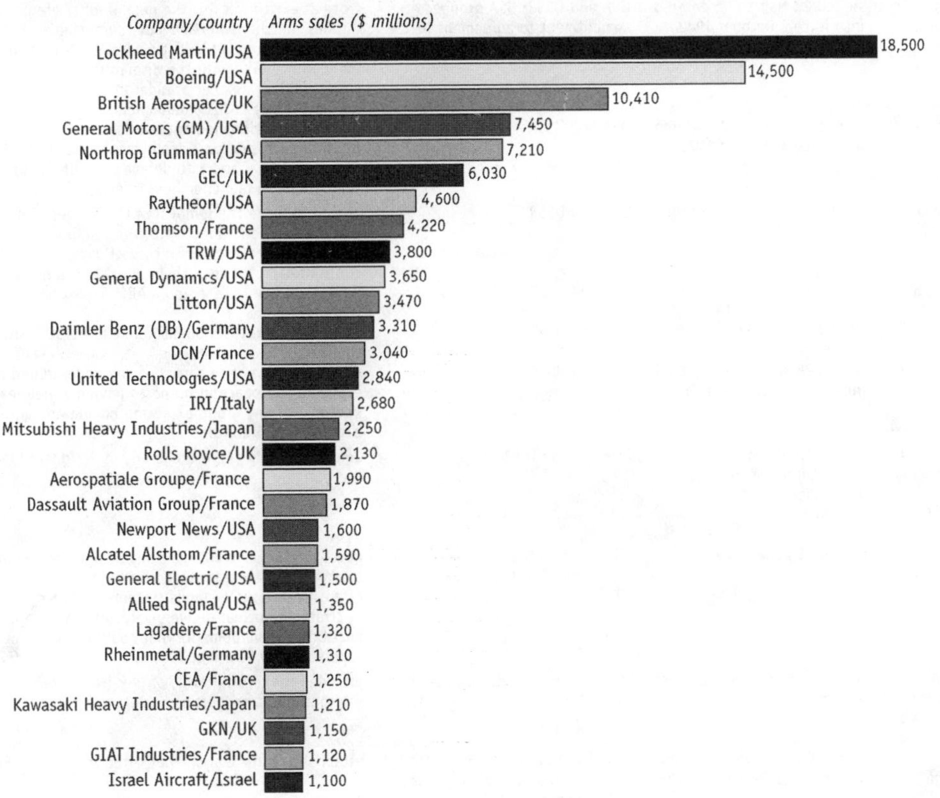

Source: Elisabeth Sköns, Reinhilde Weidacher, and the SIPRI Arms Industry Network, in SIPRI Yearbook 1999: Armaments, Disarmament and International Security, *Stockholm International Peace Research Institute (Oxford University Press, 1999)*

Arms Control Agreements

Treaty	Dates	Parties	Details
Agreements (nuclear)			
Antarctic Treaty	signed 1 December 1959; entered into force 23 June 1961	37 nations	prohibited any use of Antarctica for military purposes; specifically prohibited nuclear testing and nuclear waste
Partial Test Ban Treaty	signed 5 August 1963; entered into force 10 October 1963	125 nations; an additional 10 nations have signed the treaty, but have not ratified it	prohibited nuclear weapon tests in outer space, in the atmosphere, and underwater
Outer Space Treaty	signed 27 January 1967; entered into force 10 October 1967	96 nations; an additional 27 nations have signed the treaty, but have not ratified it	prohibited nuclear weapons in Earth orbit and outer space
Treaty of Tlatelolco	signed 14 February 1967; entered into force 22 April 1968	32 nations; the USA, the UK, France, Russian Federation, China, and the Netherlands have signed the relevant protocols to the treaty	prohibited nuclear weapons in Latin America and required safeguards on facilities
Non-proliferation Treaty	signed 1 July 1968; entered into force 5 March 1970; renewed indefinitely in 1995	188 nations; all nations that have signed have also formally adopted the treaty; the principal non-signatories are Israel, India, and Pakistan	divided the world into nuclear and non-nuclear weapon states based on status in 1968; obliged non-nuclear states to refrain from acquiring nuclear weapons and to accept International Atomic Energy Agency (IAEA) safeguards on their nuclear energy facilities; obliged nuclear states to refrain from providing nuclear weapons to non-nuclear states, to assist in the development of nuclear energy in non-nuclear states, and to work toward global nuclear disarmament
Seabed Arms Control Treaty	signed 11 February 1971; entered into force 18 May 1972	94 nations; an additional 20 nations have signed the treaty, but have not ratified it	prohibited placement of nuclear weapons on the seabed and ocean floor beyond a 19 km/12 mi coastal limit
Accident Measures Agreement	signed and entered into force 30 September 1971	USA and USSR	measures to prevent accidental nuclear war, including agreement to notify each other of planned missile launches and the detection of unidentified objects
SALT I – Interim Agreement	signed 26 May 1972; entered into force 3 October 1972	USA and USSR; USA dropped commitment to agreement in 1986	froze at existing levels the number of strategic ballistic missile launchers on each side; permitted an increase in submarine-launched ballistic missiles (SLBMs) up to an agreed level only with the dismantling or destruction of a corresponding number of older intercontinental ballistic missile (ICBM) or SLBM launchers
ABM Treaty	signed 26 May 1972; entered into force 3 October 1972	USA and USSR	prohibited nationwide anti-ballistic missile (ABM) defences, limiting each side to 2 deployment areas (1 to defend the national capital and 1 to defend an ICBM field) of no more than 100 ABM launchers and interceptor missiles each
Prevention of Nuclear War Agreement	signed and entered into force 22 June 1973	USA and USSR	agreed to make the removal of the danger of nuclear weapons and their use an 'objective of their policies'; committed to consult with each other in case of danger of nuclear confrontation between them or other countries
ABM Protocol	signed 3 July 1974; entered into force 24 May 1976	USA and USSR	limited each side to a single ABM deployment area
Threshold Test Ban Treaty	signed 3 July 1974; entered into force 11 December 1990	USA and USSR	limited nuclear tests on each side to a 150 kiloton threshold
Peaceful Nuclear Explosions Treaty	signed 28 May 1976; entered into force 11 December 1990	USA and USSR	an agreement not to carry out any underground nuclear explosion for peaceful purposes having a yield exceeding 150 kilotons, or any group explosion having an aggregate yield exceeding 150 kilotons
US–International Atomic Energy Agency Safeguards Agreement	signed 18 November 1977; entered into force 9 December 1980	USA and the IAEA	agreed to apply IAEA safeguards in designated facilities in the USA
SALT II Treaty	signed 18 June 1979	USA and USSR; USA dropped commitment to the agreement in 1986	never ratified, but both nations pledged to comply with the treaty's provisions; provided for broad limits on strategic offensive nuclear weapons systems, including equal numbers of strategic nuclear delivery vehicles, and restraints on qualitative developments that could threaten future stability; superseded by START in 1991
Convention on the Physical Protection of Nuclear Material	signed 3 March 1980; entered into force 8 February 1987	58 nations; an additional 7 nations have signed the treaty, but have not ratified it	provided for certain levels of physical protection during international transport of nuclear materials
Treaty of Rarotonga	signed 6 April 1985; entered into force 11 December 1986	12 nations are party to the treaty; all 5 declared nuclear weapons states have signed the relevant protocols to the treaty; the USA signed the protocols on 25 March 1996, but has yet to ratify the treaty	established a nuclear-weapons-free zone in the South Pacific

(continued)

Arms Control Agreements *(continued)*

Treaty	Dates	Parties	Details
Missile Technology Control Regime	informal association formed in April 1987	28 nations	established export control guidelines and annexed listing nuclear-capable ballistic missile equipment and technologies that would require export licences
Nuclear Risk Reduction Centres	signed and entered into force 15 September 1987	USA and USSR	established centres designed to reduce the risk of nuclear war
Intermediate-Range Nuclear Forces Treaty	signed 8 December 1987; entered into force 1 June 1988	USA and USSR	eliminated all US and Soviet ground-launched ballistic and cruise missiles with ranges of 500–5,500 km/310–3,418 mi, their launchers, associated support structures, and support equipment
Ballistic Missile Launch Notification Agreement	signed and entered into force 31 May 1988	USA and USSR	agreement to notify each other, through nuclear risk reduction centres, no less than 24 hours in advance, of the planned date, launch area, and area of impact for any launch of an ICBM or SLBM
START I Treaty	signed 31 July 1991; entered into force 5 December 1994	USA and USSR (Russian Federation)	Russian Federation formally accepted all of the USSR's arms control treaty obligations after the dissolution of the USSR. Because strategic nuclear weapons affected by the START I Treaty remained on the soil of Ukraine, Kazakhstan, and Belarus after the USSR's demise, an additional agreement was necessary to guarantee their removal; this was assured under the Lisbon protocol of May 1992. START established limits on deployed strategic nuclear weapons, and required the USA and Russian Federation to make phased reductions in their offensive strategic nuclear forces over a 7 year period
START II Treaty	signed 3 January 1993; ratified by USA 26 January 1996	USA and Russian Federation; still awaiting ratification by Russian Federation. Both sides committed to negotiating START III upon Russian Federation's ratification of START II	limited each side to 3,000–3,500 deployed strategic nuclear weapons each by the year 2003; banned multiple-warhead land-based missiles
Treaty of Bangkok	signed 15 December 1995; entered into force 27 March 1977	10 nations; none of the acknowledged nuclear powers have signed the relevant protocols. Brunei, Cambodia, Indonesia, Laos, Malaysia, Myanmar, Singapore, Thailand, and Vietnam have now ratified the treaty; the Philippines have signed but not ratified it	established a nuclear-weapons-free zone in Southeast Asia
Treaty of Pelindaba	signed 11 April 1996; the USA signed on 11 May 1996. Treaty open to signature by all states of Africa. It will enter into force upon the 28th ratification	54 signatories; the 5 acknowledged nuclear weapons states have signed the relevant protocols to the treaty and 8 states have now ratified it	established a nuclear-weapons-free zone in Africa
Comprehensive Test Ban Treaty	signed 24 September 1996	on 6 April 1998, the UK and France became the first of the five main nuclear powers to ratify the treaty. In October 1999 the US senate votes against ratification. China, India, and Pakistan are also yet to ratify the treaty. Russian Federation ratifies in April 2000	banned all explosive nuclear tests
Joint Statement on Parameters on Future Reductions in Nuclear Forces	signed 21 March 1997	USA and Russian Federation	USA and Russian Federation have agreed that negotiations for START III will begin as soon as START II enters into force
Agreements (non-nuclear)			
Geneva Protocol	signed 17 June 1925; entered into force 8 February 1928; ratified by USA 22 January 1975	132 nations	prohibited in war the use of asphyxiating or poisonous gas and liquids and all bacteriological (biological) methods of warfare; essentially a 'no first use' agreement, because many signatories ratified it with the reservation that it would cease to be binding if an enemy failed to observe the prohibitions
Biological and Toxic Weapons Convention	signed 10 April 1972; entered into force 26 March 1975	142 nations; 18 nations signed but not ratified	prohibited development, production, stockpiling, acquisition, or retention of biological agents not associated with peaceful uses, biological or toxin weapons, and their delivery systems; required destruction or diversion of all prohibited agents to peaceful purposes within 9 months after entry into force; prohibited transfer of, or assistance to manufacture, prohibited agents
Incidents at Sea Agreement	signed and entered into force 25 May 1972	USA and USSR	agreement on the prevention of incidents on and over the high seas, including steps to avoid collision and the avoidance of manoeuvres in areas of heavy sea traffic

(continued)

Arms Control Agreements *(continued)*

Treaty	Dates	Parties	Details
Environmental Modification Prevention	signed 18 May 1977; entered into force 5 October 1978	64 nations; an additional 17 nations have signed the treaty, but have not ratified it	prohibited deliberate manipulation of natural processes for hostile or other military purposes
Protocol (I) Additional to the 1949 Geneva Convention and Relating to the Protection of Victims of International Conflict	signed 12 December 1977; entered into force 7 December 1978	148 nations; in addition Cambodia acceded to Protocol on 14 January 1998, and UK ratified Protocol on 28 January 1998	Protocol prohibits the use of weapons or means of warfare that cause superfluous injury or unnecessary suffering
Convention on Certain Conventional Weapons (The Inhumane Weapons Convention)	opened for signature 10 April 1981; entered into force 2 December 1983; signed by the USA 2 April 1982 and ratified 24 March 1995	72 nations; 10 nations have signed the convention but not ratified it; 29 nations have signed the amended Protocol II; 34 nations have signed Protocol IV	banned the use of non-metallic fragmentation weapons and blinding lasers, and imposed restrictions on the use of land mines and incendiary weapons
Australia Group	informal association formed in 1984 in response to chemical weapons use in the Iran–Iraq War	30 nations	established voluntary export controls on certain chemicals
Stockholm Conference	signed and entered into force 19 September 1986	54 nations	established security and confidence-building measures designed to increase openness and predictability with regard to military activities in Europe
US–Soviet Bilateral Memorandum of Understanding	signed and entered into force September 1989	USA and USSR	agreement to exchange data on size, composition, and location of chemical weapon stockpiles and storage, production, and destruction facilities, and to conduct reciprocal visits and both routine and challenge inspections
US–Soviet Bilateral Destruction Agreement	signed June 1990; has not yet entered into force	USA and USSR; currently abandoned by Russian Federation	agreement to stop producing chemical weapons and to reduce their stockpiles to no more than 5,000 agent tons, with destruction to begin by 31 December 1992 and to be completed by 31 December 2002
Conventional Forces in Europe (CFE) Treaty	signed 19 November 1990; entered into force 9 November 1992	30 nations	established limits on the numbers of tanks, armoured combat vehicles, artillery combat aircraft, and helicopters in Europe
Open Skies Treaty	signed 24 March 1992	27 nations; the USA and 22 other nations have ratified the treaty; ratifications by Russia, Belarus, Ukraine, Kyrgyztan, and Georgia are still required for entry into force	permitted unarmed reconnaissance flights designed to promote military transparency and confidence among former NATO and Warsaw Pact adversaries
CFE 1A Treaty	signed 10 July 1992; entered into force 9 November 1992	30 nations	established limits on the number of troops in Europe
Chemical Weapons Convention	opened for signature 13 January 1993; entered into force 29 April 1997	169 nations; 121 signatories have ratified the treaty	prohibited the development, production, acquisition, stockpiling, retention, transfer, and use of chemical weapons – required declaration of chemical weapons or chemical weapon capabilities, including those primarily associated with commercial use; required destruction of declared chemical weapons and associated production facilities; provided for routine inspections of relevant facilities and challenge inspections upon request
Florence Agreement	signed 14 June 1996, entered into force immediately upon signature	Bosnia-Herzegovina, Bosnian Serb Republic, Croatia, Serbia, and Montenegro	negotiated under the Dayton Agreement; set limits on armaments of the warring parties of the conflict in Bosnia-Herzegovina; covered heavy conventional weapons including main battle tanks, armoured combat vehicles, heavy artillery (75 mm and above), combat aircraft, and attack helicopters
Ottawa Treaty	signed 3–4 December 1997	135 countries; 77 countries had ratified the treaty as of 29 April 1999	banned the production, use, and export of anti-personnel mines; also committed signatories to the destruction of stockpiles of mines within four years, and to clearing existing minefields as well as relieving the suffering of the victims of land mines

Arms Embargoes by International Organizations

(UNSCR = United Nations Security Council Resolution Resolution. – = not applicable.)

1994–98

Target	Entry into force[1]	Lifted	Legal basis	Organization
Afghanistan[2]	22 October 1996	–	UNSCR 1076	UN
Afghanistan[2 3]	17 December 1996	–	–	EU
Angola (UNITA)	15 September 1993	–	UNSCR 864	UN
Armenia[4]	28 February 1992	–	–	OSCE
Azerbaijan[4]	28 February 1992	–	–	OSCE
Bosnia-Herzegovina	1991	–	–	EU
Burundi	August 1996	–	–	neighbouring countries[5]
China	27 June 1989	–	–	EU
Congo, Democratic Republic of[3]	7 April 1993	–	–	EU
Croatia	1991	–	–	EU
Haiti	30 September 1991	15 October 1994	–	OAS
Haiti[6]	13 October 1993	15 October 1994	UNSCR 841	UN
Iraq	4 August 1990	–	–	EU
Iraq	6 August 1990	–	UNSCR 661	UN
Liberia	19 November 1992	–	UNSCR 788	UN
Libya	27 January 1986	–	–	EU
Libya	31 March 1992	–	UNSCR 748	UN
Myanmar[3]	29 July 1991	–	–	EU
Nigeria[3]	20 November 1995	–	–	EU
Nigeria	24 April 1996	–	–	Commonwealth
Rwanda	17 May 1994	16 August 1995[7]	UNSCR 918	UN
Rwanda (rebels)	16 August 1998	–	UNSCR 1011	UN
Sierra Leone	8 October	5 June 1998	UNSCR 1132	UN
Sierra Leone	8 December 1997	–	–	EU
Sierra Leone (rebels)	5 June 1998	–	UNSCR 1171	UN
Slovenia	1991	10 August 1998	–	EU
Somalia	23 January 1992	–	UNSCR 733	UN
South Africa[8]	4 November 1977	24 May 1994	UNSCR 418	UN
Sudan[3]	15 March 1994	–	–	EU
Yugoslavia	25 September 1991	1 October 1996	UNSCR 713	UN
Yugoslavia	1991	–	–	EU
Yugoslavia (Serbia and Montenegro)	31 March 1998	–	UNSCR 1160	UN

[1] All non-UN embargoes are voluntary.
[2] Voluntary (non-mandatory) embargo.
[3] The embargo does not apply to deliveries under existing contracts.
[4] Embargo on deliveries to forces engaged in combat in the Nagorno-Karabakh area.
[5] (Democratic Republic of Congo), Ethiopia, Kenya, Rwanda, Tanzania, and Uganda.
[6] Originally imposed in June 1993, but temporarily suspended until October 1993.
[7] The arms embargo was suspended on this date and formally ended on 1 September 1996.
[8] A voluntary arms embargo commenced on 7 August 1963 (UNSCR 181); a voluntary embargo on equipment and material for arms production on 4 November 1963 (UNSCR 182); and a voluntary embargo on arms imports from South Africa on 13 December 1985 (UNSCR 558).

Source: Björn Hagelin, Pieter D Wezeman and Siemon T Wezeman, in SIPRI Yearbook 1999: Armaments, Disarmament and International Security, *Stockholm International Peace Research Institute (Oxford University Press, 1999)*

Major Conflicts and Casualties

Location of Major Armed Conflicts

Conflict locations with at least one major armed conflict in 1998.
(N/A = no reliable figures available. – = not applicable.)
ADF = Alliance of Democratic Forces
ADFL = Alliance des forces démocratiques pour la libération du Congo-Kinshasa (Alliance of Democratic Forces for the Liberation of Congo-Kinshasa)
AFRC = Armed Forces Revolutionary Council
BdSF = Bodo Security Force
CNDD = Conseil national pour la défense de la démocratie (National Council for the Defence of Democracy)
ELN = Ejército de Liberación Nacional (National Liberation Army)
FARC = Fuerzas Armadas Revolucionarias Colombianas (Revolutionary Armed Forces of Colombia)
FDU = Forces démocratiques unies (United Democratic Forces)
FIS = Front Islamique du Salut, Jibhat al-Inqath (Islamic Salvation Front)
Fretilin = Frente Revolucionára Timorense de Libertação e Independência (Revolutionary Front for an Independent East Timor)
GIA = Groupe Islamique Armé (Armed Islamic Group)
JSS/SB = Parbatya Chattagram Jana Sanghati Samiti (Chittagong Hill Tracts People's Coordination Association/Shanti Bahini [Peace Force])
KNU = Karen National Union
LRA = Lord's Resistance Army
LTTE = Liberation Tigers of Tamil Eelam
MFDC = Mouvement des forces démocratiques de la Casamance (Casamance Movement of Democratic Forces)
MRTA = Movimiento Revolucionario Tupac Amaru (Tupac Amaru Revolutionary Movement)
NDA = National Democratic Alliance
NPA = New People's Army

(continued)

Location of Major Armed Conflicts (*continued*)

Palipehutu = Parti pour la libération du peuple Hutu (Party for the Liberation of the Hutu People)
PDK = Party of Democratic Kampuchea (Khmer Rouge)
PKK = Partiya Karkeren Kurdistan (Kurdish Worker's Party, or Apocus)
PLO = Palestine Liberation Organization
RUF = Revolutionary United Front
SAIRI = Supreme Assembly for the Islamic Revolution in Iraq
Sendero Luminoso = Shining Path
UCK = Ushtria Clirimtare e Kosoves (Kosovo Liberation Army, KLA)
ULFA = United Liberation Front of Assam
UNITA = Uniao Nacional Para a Independencia Total de Angola (National Union for the Total Independence of Angola)

Location	Incompatibility[1]	Year formed/ year joined[2]	Warring parties[3]	No of troops in 1997[4]	Total deaths[5] (including 1998)	Deaths in 1998
Europe						
Yugoslavia	Territory	1997/1998	Govt of Yugoslavia	115,000	1,000–2,000	1,000–2,000
			vs UCK	5,000–10,000		
Middle East						
Iran	Govt	1970/1991	Govt of Iran	500,000[6]	N/A	N/A
			vs Mujahideen e-Khalq	N/A		
Iraq	Govt	1980/1991	Govt of Iraq	430,000	N/A	N/A
			vs SAIRI	N/A		
Israel	Territory	1964/1964	Govt of Israel vs	170,000–180,000	>13,000 (1948–)	100 (military)
			non-PLO groups[7]	N/A		50 (civilian)
Turkey	Territory	1974/1984	Govt of Turkey	800,000[8]	>30,000	>1,000
			vs PKK	5,000–6,000		
Asia						
Afghanistan	Govt	1992/1992	Govt of Afghanistan	25,000–50,000	N/A	>2,000
			vs Jumbish-i Milli-ye Islami	40,000		
		1978/1978	vs Jamiat-i-Islami	N/A		
		1990/1990	vs Hezb-i-Wahdat	N/A		
Cambodia	Govt	1979/1979	Govt of Cambodia	140,000[9]	>25,500[10]	N/A
			vs PDK	1,000–4,000		
India	Territory	–/1989	Govt of India	1,175,000	>20,000[12]	>800
			vs Kashmir insurgents[11]	N/A		
		–/1992	vs BdSF	N/A		
		1982/1988	vs ULFA	N/A		
India–Pakistan	Territory	1947/1996	Govt of India	1,175,000	N/A	>300
			vs Govt of Pakistan	587,000		
Indonesia	Territory	1975/1975	Govt of Indonesia	500,000	15,000–16,000 (military)	50–200
			vs Fretilin	100–200		
Myanmar	Territory	1948/1948	Govt of Myanmar	300,000–400,000	8,000 (1948–50);5,000–8,000 (1981–88)	N/A
			vs KNU	2,000–4,000		
Philippines	Govt	1968/1968	Govt of the Philippines	110,000	21,000–25,000	<50
			vs NPA	6,000–7,000		
Sri Lanka	Territory	1976/1983	Govt of Sri Lanka	110,000	>40,000	>4,000
			vs LTTE	6,000–8,000		
Africa						
Algeria	Govt	1992/1992	Govt of Algeria	270,000[13]	40,000–100,000	>1,500 (military) >2,500 (civilian)
			vs FIS[14]	N/A		
		1993/1993	vs GIA	N/A		
Angola	Govt	1975/1998	Govt of Angola	110,000	N/A	1,000
			vs UNITA	30,000		
Burundi	Govt	1994/1994	Govt of Burundi	40,000	>2,000[15]	1,000
			vs CNDD	3,000–10,000		
			vs Palipehutu	2,000		
Congo (Brazzaville)	Govt	–/1997	Govt of Congo	10,000	4,000–7,000	4,000–7,000
			vs FDU,[16] Angola	1,500–3,000, 3,500		
Eritrea–Ethiopa	Territory	–/1998	Govt of Eritrea	40,000–55,000	>1,000	>1,000
			vs Govt of Ethiopia	80,000		
Guinea–Bissua	Govt	1998/1998	Govt of Guinea–Bissau, Senegal, Guinea	3,000–6,000, 2,000–3,000, 1,000–1,500	>1,000	>1,000
			vs Military faction	3,000–6,000		
Rwanda	Govt	–/1997	Govt of Rwanda	55,000	N/A	>1,500
			vs Opposition alliance	50,000–65,000		
Senegal	Territory	1982/1982	Govt of Senegal	13,000	1,000	>250
			vs MFDC	500–1,000		

(*continued*)

■ Major Conflicts and Casualties

Location of Major Armed Conflicts (*continued*)

Location	Incompatibility[1]	Year formed/ year joined[2]	Warring parties[3]	No of troops in 1997[4]	Total deaths[5] (including 1998)	Deaths in 1998
Sierra Leone	Govt	1991/1991	Govt of Sirerra Leone	30,000	>5,000	>1,500
			vs RUF, AFRC	15,000		
Sudan	Govt	1980/1983	Govt of Sudan	90,000	37,000–40,000 (military)[17]	>2,500
			vs NDA[18]	50,000	N/A	
Uganda	Govt	1993/1994	Govt of Uganda	45,000–60,000	>2,000	>800
			vs LRA	6,000		
		1996/1996	vs ADF	1,500		
Central and South America						
Colombia	Govt	1949/1978	Govt of Colombia	140,000	N/A[19]	1,000–1,500
			vs FARC	10,000		
		1965/1978	vs ELN	3,500		
Peru	Govt	1980/1981	Govt of Peru	125,000	>28,000	25–100
			vs Sendero Luminoso	500–1,500		
		1984/1986	vs MRTA	200		

[1] 'Govt' and 'Territory' refer to contested incompatibilities concerning government (type of political system, a change of central government or in its composition) and territory (control of territory [interstate conflict], secession, or autonomy), respectively.
[2] Year formed = year in which the incompatibility was stated. Year joined = year in which use of armed force began or recommenced.
[3] Non-governmental warring parties active during 1997 are listed by the name of the parties using armed force.
[4] Total armed forces of the government warring party, and for non-government parties from the conflict location. For government and non-government parties from outside the location, the figure is for total armed forces within the country that is the location of the armed conflict.
[5] Total battle-related deaths during the conflict.
[6] Including the Revolutionary Guard.
[7] Examples of these groups are Hamas, PFLP-GC (Popular Front for the Liberation of Palestine-General Command), Islamic Jihad, Hizbollah, and Amal.
[8] Including the Gendarmerie/National Guard.
[9] Including all militias.
[10] Regarding battle-related deaths in 1979–89, ie, not only involving the government and PDK, the only figure available is from official Vietnamese sources, indicating that 25,300 Vietnamese soldiers died in Cambodia. An estimated figure for the period 1979–89, based on various sources, is >50,000, and for 1989 >1,000. The figures for 1990, 1991, and 1992 were lower.
[11] Several groups are active, some of the most important being the Jammu and Kashmir Liberation Front (JKLF), the Hizb-e-Mujahideen, and the Harkat-ul-Ansar.
[12] Only the Kashmir conflict.
[13] Including the Gendarmerie and the National Security Forces.
[14] The Islamic Salvation Army (Armée Islamique du Salut, AIS) is considered to be the armed wing of the FIS. There are also several other armed Islamic groups under the FIS military command.
[15] Political violence in Burundi since 1993, involving other groups than the CNDD, has claimed a total of at least 100,000 lives.
[16] Armed action was primarily carried out by the Cobras, the private militia of FDU leader Sassou-Nguesso.
[17] Figure for up to 1991.
[18] The June 1995 Asmara Declaration forms the basis for the political and military activities of the NDA. The NDA is an alliance of several southern and northern opposition organizations, of which the SPLM (Sudan People's Liberation Movement) is the largest, with 30,000–50,000 troops. SPLM leader John Garang is also the leader of the NDA.
[19] In the past three decades the civil wars of Colombia have claimed a total of some 30,000 lives.

Source: Margareta Sollenberg, Staffan Angman, Ylva Blondel, Ann-Sofi Jakobsson and Andrés Jato, in SIPRI Yearbook 1999: Armaments, Disarmament and International Security, *Stockholm International Peace Research Institute (Oxford University Press, 1999)*

UK Military Casualties in Conflicts Since 1945

The number of wounded refers to those detained in hospital, and may represent a lower figure than that reported operationally; the number of wounded and killed refers to officers and soldiers in all services.
(N/A = not available.)

Conflict/campaign	Number killed	Number wounded	Total
Indonesia (1945–46)	50	N/A	N/A
Palestine (1945–48)	223	478	701
Malaya (1948–61)			
British units	340	613	953
Brigade of Gurkhas	169	308	477
Total	509	921	1,430
Korea (1950–53)	865	2,589	3,454
Egypt (1951–54)	53	N/A	N/A
Kenya (1952)	12	69	81
Cyprus (1955–58)	79	414	493
Egypt (1956)	12	63	75
Borneo and Malaya (1962–66)			
British units	16	36	52
Brigade of Gurkhas	43	87	130
Total	59	123	182
Radfan (1964–67)	24	188	212
Aden (1964–67)	68	322	390
Falklands (1982)	255[1]	777	1,032
Gulf (1991)	42[2]	43	85

[1] Includes five civilians.
[2] Includes nine killed accidentally by US 'friendly fire'.

Major Armed Conflicts Worldwide

Data show regional distribution of locations with at least one major armed conflict, for the period 1990–98.

Region	1990	1991	1992	1993	1994	1995	1996	1997	1998
Africa	10	10	7	7	6	6	5	8	11
Asia	10	8	11	9	9	9	10	9	8
Central and South America	5	4	3	3	3	3	3	2	2
Europe	1	2	4	5	4	3	2	1	1
Middle East	5	5	4	4	5	4	4	4	4
Total	31	29	29	28	27	25	24	24	26

Source: Margareta Sollenberg, Peter Wallensteen and Andrés Jato, in SIPRI Yearbook 1999: Armaments, Disarmament and International Security, *Stockholm International Peace Research Institute (Oxford University Press, 1999)*

Military Casualties in World War I

World War I casualty statistics vary greatly from source to source. Official records are often lacking and based on differing criteria and these figures remain open to interpretation and debate. Figures are for 1914–18 and are rounded to the nearest 250.
(N/A = not available.)

Country	Mobilized	Deaths (all causes)	Wounded	Total casualties	Prisoners/missing
Allied powers					
Belgium	207,000	13,750	44,000	57,750	67,750
British Empire[1]					
UK	5,397,000	702,500	1,662,750	2,365,250	170,500
Australia	330,000	59,250	152,250	211,500	4,000
Canada	552,000	56,750	149,750	206,500	3,750
India[2]	1,216,000	64,500	69,250	133,750	11,250
Newfoundland	N/A	1,250	2,250	3,500	250
New Zealand	N/A	16,750	41,250	58,000	500
South Africa	N/A	7,000	12,000	19,000	1,500
Other colonies	N/A	500	750	1,250	N/A
British Empire total	>7,495,000	908,500	2,090,250	2,998,750	191,750
France (including colonial territories)	7,500,000	1,385,250	2,675,000–4,266,000[3]	4,060,250–5,651,250	446,250
Greece	230,000	5,000	21,000	26,000	1,000
Italy	5,500,000	460,000	947,000	1,407,000	530,000
Japan	800,000	250	1,000	1,250	0
Montenegro	50,000	3,000	10,000	13,000	7,000
Portugal	100,000	7,250	15,000	22,250	12,250
Romania	750,000	200,000	120,000	320,000	80,000
Russia	12,000,000	1,700,000	4,950,000	6,650,000	2,500,000
Serbia	707,250	127,500	133,250	260,750	153,000
USA	4,272,500	116,750	204,000	320,750	4,500
Central powers					
Austria-Hungary	6,500,000	1,200,000	3,620,000	4,820,000	2,200,000
Bulgaria	400,000	101,250	152,500	253,750	11,000
Germany	11,000,000	1,718,250	4,234,000	5,952,250	1,073,500
Turkey	1,600,000	>335,750	>400,000	>735,750	>200,000

[1] Figures for the British Empire and constituent countries are for 1914–20.
[2] Includes 4,912 British casualties: British drafts and units serving with the Indian Army.
[3] Official records for the number of French wounded are not available.

Casualties in World War II

Figures are for 1939–45 and are rounded to the nearest 250.
(– = not applicable. N/A = not available.)

Country	Personnel[1]	Military killed	Military wounded	Prisoners of war	Civilian dead
Allied powers					
Australia	680,000	23,250	39,750	26,250	–
Belgium	800,000	7,750	14,500	N/A	75,000[2]
Brazil	200,000	1,000	4,250	–	–
Canada	780,000	37,500	53,250	9,750	–
China	5,000,000	1,324,500[3]	1,762,000	N/A	N/A[4]
Czechoslovakia	180,000	6,750	8,000	–	310,000[5]
Denmark	15,000	4,250	N/A	–	–
Estonia	–	–	–	–	140,000
France	5,000,000	205,750	390,000	765,000	300,000
Greece	150,000	16,250	50,000	N/A	337,000[6]
India	2,394,000	24,250	64,250	79,500	–
Latvia	–	–	–	–	120,000
Lithuania	–	–	–	–	170,000
Netherlands	500,000	13,750	2,750	N/A	236,250[7]
New Zealand	157,000	12,250	19,250	8,500	–
Norway	25,000	4,750	N/A	N/A	5,500[8]
Poland	1,000,000	320,000	530,000	–	6,028,000[9]

(continued)

Casualties in World War II *(continued)*

Country	Personnel[1]	Military killed	Military wounded	Prisoners of war	Civilian dead
South Africa	140,000	8,750	14,250	14,500	–
UK	4,683,000	264,500	277,000	172,500[10]	60,500
USA	16,353,750	405,500	671,750	105,000	–
USSR	20,000,000	13,600,000	5,000,000	N/A	7,720,000
Yugoslavia	3,741,000	305,000	425,000	–	1,355,000[11]
Axis powers					
Austria	800,000	380,000	N/A	N/A	145,000[12]
Finland	250,000	79,000	N/A	–	–
Germany	10,000,000	3,300,000	N/A	630,000[13]	3,063,000[14]
Hungary	350,000	147,500	N/A	–	280,000[15]
Italy	4,500,000	262,500	N/A	1,478,000	93,000[16]
Japan	N/A	1,140,500	N/A	11,600[17]	953,000[18]
Romania	600,000	300,000	N/A	N/A	145,000[19]

[1] Peak strength of armed forces during World War II.
[2] Includes approximately 25,000 Jews.
[3] Estimates vary for Chinese military killed.
[4] Estimates for Chinese civilian dead vary very widely, from 700,000 to 10,000,000.
[5] Includes approximately 250,000 Jews.
[6] Includes approximately 260,000 deaths due to starvation.
[7] Includes approximately 104,000 Jews, 25,000 civilian underground workers, and 15,000 deaths due to starvation.
[8] Includes approximately 2,000 resistance fighters and 750 Norwegians serving in the German army.
[9] Includes approximately 3,200,000 Jews.
[10] 7,250 British prisoners of war died while in German captivity; 12,500 died while in Japanese captivity.
[11] Includes approximately 55,000 Jews.
[12] Includes approximately 60,000 Jews.
[13] Excludes those in the USSR.
[14] Includes approximately 170,000 Jews.
[15] Includes approximately 200,000 Jews.
[16] Includes approximately 8,000 Jews.
[17] Excludes those in the USSR.
[18] Includes approximately 668,000 killed in air raids on home islands.
[19] Includes approximately 60,000 Jews.

NATO and European Defence

NATO International Commands

As of July 2000.

Command	Commander (branch of service)
Supreme Allied Commander, Europe (SACEUR)	General Joseph W Ralston (USAF)
Deputy Supreme Allied Commander, Europe (DSACEUR)	General Sir Rupert Smith (UK Army)
Supreme Allied Commander, Atlantic (SACLANT)	Admiral Harold W Gehman, Jr (US Navy)
Commander-in-Chief, Allied Forces, Southern Europe (AFSOUTH)	Admiral James O Ellis (US Navy)
Commander-in-Chief, Allied Forces, Northern Europe (AFNORTH)	Air Chief Marshall Sir John Cheshire KBE, CBE (RAF)
Chairman, Military Committee (MC)	Admiral Guido Venturoni (Italian Navy)

Defence Spending by NATO Countries

(In millions of dollars at 1995 prices and exchange rates.)

State	Item	1990	1994	1998
North America				
Canada	personnel	5,488	4,979	3,653
	equipment	1,866	1,685	952
USA	personnel	130,660	115,513	100,483
	equipment	88,535	86,487	62,455
Europe				
Belgium	personnel	4,062	3,147	2,943
	equipment	469	354	234
Denmark	personnel	1,884	1,849	1,885
	equipment	481	501	468
Germany	personnel	29,572	25,479	23,871
	equipment	10,047	4,568	4,899
Greece	personnel	3,243	3,119	3,751
	equipment	1,083	1,208	1,279
Italy	personnel	13,536	13,921	16,628
	equipment	3,845	3,289	2,897
Luxembourg	personnel	100	114	129
	equipment	4	3	8
Netherlands	personnel	5,189	4,809	3,961
	equipment	1,723	1,386	1,415
Norway	personnel	1,634	1,356	1,406
	equipment	853	1,107	909
Portugal	personnel	1,830	1,956	2,092
	equipment	258	104	210
Spain	personnel	5,901	5,526	5,686
	equipment	1,209	1,018	997
Turkey	personnel	2,657	3,285	3,619
	equipment	1,100	1,888	2,313
UK	personnel	16,800	15,199	12,249
	equipment	7,443	9,141	9,017
NATO Europe total	personnel	86,408	79,759	78,222
	equipment	28,515	24,567	24,645
TOTAL	personnel	222,555	200,251	182,358
	equipment	118,915	112,740	88,052

Source: Eric Arnett, in SIPRI Yearbook 1999: Armaments, Disarmament and International Security, *Stockholm International Peace Research Institute (Oxford University Press, 1999)*

See also **North Atlantic Treaty Organization (NATO)**, p 276.

European Defence: Expenditure and Strength of Armed Forces

(– = not applicable.)

Country	Defence expenditure (1997 $ millions)		% of GDP		Numbers in armed forces (thousands)		Estimated reservists (thousands)
	1985	1998	1985	1998	1985	1998	1998
NATO Europe							
Belgium	5,863	3,698	3.0	1.5	91.6	43.7	152.1
Denmark	2,978	2,799	2.2	1.6	29.6	32.1	100.0
France	46,522	39,807	4.0	2.8	464.3	358.8	292.5
Germany	50,220	32,387	3.2	1.5	478.0	333.5	315.0
Greece	3,317	5,720	7.0	4.8	201.5	168.5	291.0
Iceland[1]	–	–	–	–	–	–	–
Italy	24,471	22,633	2.3	2.0	385.1	298.4	304.0
Luxembourg	91	139	0.9	0.9	0.7	0.8	–
Netherlands	8,470	6,634	3.1	1.8	105.5	57.2	75.0
Norway	2,948	3,133	3.1	2.2	37.0	28.9	234.0
Portugal	1,746	2,334	3.1	2.3	73.0	53.6	210.9
Spain	10,731	7,272	2.4	1.3	320.0	194.0	447.9
Turkey	3,269	8,191	4.5	4.4	630.0	639.0	378.7
UK	45,408	36,613	5.2	2.8	327.1	210.9	319.6
NATO Europe total	206,033	171,359	3.1	2.1	3,143.4	2,419.3	3,120.7
Non-NATO Europe							
Albania	269	98	5.3	6.6	40.4	54.0	155.0
Armenia	–	146	–	8.4		53.4	300.0
Austria	1,839	1,764	1.2	0.8	54.7	45.5	100.7
Azerbaijan	–	189	–	4.6	–	72.2	575.7
Belarus	–	452	–	3.2	–	83.0	289.5
Bosnia-Herzegovina	327	389	–	8.1	–	40.0	100.0
Bulgaria	2,331	390	14.0	3.7	148.5	101.5	303.0
Croatia	–	1,371	–	8.3	–	56.2	220.0
Cyprus	124	489	3.6	5.5	10.0	10.0	88.0
Czech Republic	–	1,132	–	2.1	–	59.1	240.0
Czechoslovakia	3,338	–	8.2	–	203.3	–	–
Estonia	–	68	–	1.3	–	4.3	14.0
Finland	2,139	1,855	2.8	1.5	36.5	31.7	500.0
FRY (Serbia-Montenegro)[2]	1,489	1,523	3.8	9.1	241.0	114.2	400.0
Georgia	–	108	–	2.5	–	33.2	250.0
Hungary	3,380	647	7.2	1.4	106.0	43.3	90.3
Ireland, Republic of	456	780	1.8	1.0	13.7	11.5	14.8
Latvia	–	157	–	2.5	–	5.0	14.6
Lithuania	–	134	–	1.3	–	11.1	27.7
Macedonia, Former Yugoslav Republic of	–	136	–	9.9	–	20.0	102.0
Malta	23	29	1.4	0.9	0.8	1.9	–
Moldova	–	51	–	4.3	–	11.1	66.0
Poland	8,202	3,356	8.1	2.2	319.0	240.7	406.0
Romania	1,987	870	4.5	2.3	189.5	219.7	470.0
Slovakia	–	407	–	2.0	–	45.5	20.0
Slovenia	–	360	–	1.7	–	9.6	53.0
Sweden	4,564	5,531	3.3	2.5	65.7	53.1	570.0
Switzerland	2,749	3,556	2.1	1.4	20.0	26.3	390.0
Ukraine	–	1,361	–	2.9	–	346.4	1,000.0
Non-NATO Europe total	36,142	27,353	4.8	3.6	1,449.1	1,803.2	6,760.3
Russian Federation and USSR							
Russian Federation	–	53,912	–	5.2	–	1,159.0	2,400.0
USSR	343,616	–	16.1	–	5,300.0	–	–

[1] Iceland has no defence forces of its own.
[2] FRY = Federal Republic of Yugoslavia.

Source: The Military Balance 1999/2000, *International Institute for Strategic Studies, by permission of Oxford University Press and the IISS*

Conventional Armed Forces in Europe (CFE)

Data show personnel and Treaty-limited equipment (TLE) current holdings and CFE limits on the forces of the treaty members. Current holdings are derived from data declared as of 1 January 1999.

Country	Personnel		Tanks[1]		Armoured combat vehicles[1]		Artillery[1]		Attack helicopters		Combat aircraft[2]	
	holding	limit	holding	limit	holding	limit	holding	limit	holding	limit	holding	limit
Budapest/Tashkent Group												
Armenia	60,000	60,000	102	220	204	220	225	285	7	50	6	100
Azerbaijan	69,920	70,000	262	220	331	220	303	285	15	50	48	100
Belarus	83,020	100,000	1,778	1,800	2,513	2,600	1,515	1,615	62	80	252	294
Bulgaria	80,779	104,000	1,475	1,475	1,986	2,000	1,744	1,750	43	67	233	235

(continued)

Conventional Armed Forces in Europe (CFE) *(continued)*

Country	Personnel		Tanks[1]		Armoured combat vehicles[1]		Artillery[1]		Attack helicopters		Combat aircraft[2]	
	holding	limit	holding	limit	holding	limit	holding	limit	holding	limit	holding	limit
Czech Republic[3]	58,193	93,333	938	957	1,219	1,367	754	767	34	50	114	230
Georgia	29,191	40,000	79	220	113	220	106	285	3	50	7	100
Hungary[3]	43,743	100,000	807	835	1,332	1,700	839	840	59	108	136	180
Moldova	10,677	20,000	0	210	209	210	153	250	0	50	0	50
Poland[3]	210,555	234,000	1,675	1,730	1,437	2,150	1,580	1,610	104	130	298	460
Romania	185,092	230,000	1,373	1,375	2,100	2,100	1,411	1,475	16	120	360	430
Russia[4]	605,171	1,450,000	5,510	6,400	10,064	11,480	6,299	6,415	761	875	2,870	3,431
Slovak Republic	44,880	46,667	478	478	683	683	383	383	19	40	94	100
Ukraine	320,000	450,000	4,014	4,080	4,902	5,050	3,739	4,040	265	330	964	1,090
North Atlantic Treaty Group												
Belgium	39,756	70,000	155	334	526	1,005	243	320	46	46	137	232
Canada[5]	0	10,660	0	77	0	263	0	32	0	13	0	90
Denmark	30,426	39,000	337	353	286	336	503	503	12	18	76	106
France	242,169	325,000	1,207	1,306	3,653	3,820	1,050	1,292	314	390	596	800
Germany	273,535	345,000	3,096	4,069	2,480	3,281	2,056	2,445	204	293	534	900
Greece	158,621	158,621	1,735	1,735	2,364	2,498	1,886	1,920	20	30	522	650
Italy	229,535	315,000	1,256	1,348	2,917	3,339	1,595	1,955	134	142	535	650
Netherlands	37,054	80,000	359	743	640	1,080	398	607	10	50	164	230
Norway	20,581	32,000	170	170	180	275	192	491	0	24	73	100
Portugal	35,178	75,000	187	300	355	430	359	450	0	26	101	160
Spain	160,372	300,000	676	891	1,181	2,047	1,150	1,370	28	90	201	310
Turkey[4]	512,922	530,000	2,554	2,795	2,515	3,120	2,811	3,523	26	103	346	750
UK	217,525	260,000	542	1,015	2,396	3,176	429	636	249	371	533	900
USA	101,724	250,000	846	4,006	1,704	5,152	558	2,742	136	404	223	784

[1] Includes TLE with land-based maritime forces (Marines, Naval Infantry, etc).
[2] Does not include land-based maritime aircraft, for which a separate limit has been set.
[3] Czech Republic, Hungary, and Poland became NATO members on 12 March 1999.
[4] Personnel and TLE are for the Atlantic to the Urals (ATTU) zone only.
[5] Canada has now withdrawn all its TLE from the ATTU.

Source: The Military Balance 1999/2000, *International Institute for Strategic Studies, by permission of Oxford University Press and the IISS*

Peacekeeping

Peacekeeping in Africa

A proud 50-year history has been tarnished by the failure of recent UN peacekeeping operations in Africa. The collapse of the UN peacekeeping mission in Sierra Leone, which caused the hurried despatch of British Paratroops to the region, was the latest and most dramatic example of the failure of the UN's policy of using African forces to police African disputes and conflicts.

The end of the global ideological struggle characteristic of the Cold War, has lifted the lid off a series of armed conflicts and long running disputes in Africa. Meanwhile, the attention of the USA and Europe has been focused on the Balkan conflicts fought out in Bosnia, Croatia, and Kosovo. Western governments have been keen to promote the use of African peacekeeping forces to police African disputes. The former colonial powers – keen to avoid renewed involvement in the continent – have been training African military forces for peacekeeping operations. Of the two main military powers in the region, South Africa has been reluctant to take the lead, whilst Nigeria has taken an active role in peacekeeping with mixed success. Bungled operations have led to high casualties and resentment from neighbouring states. It was Nigeria's withdrawal from Sierra Leone that precipitated the recent crisis.

For the success of future peacekeeping operations in Africa, it is essential that they should continue to be principally African missions. However, it is important that Western governments provide the necessary assistance in terms of funding and training. The character of peacekeeping operations must change from a purely traditional peacekeeping role. Peacekeeping forces in future will need to be trained, armed, and ready to fight on the ground if necessary to enforce peace resolutions. The credibility of the UN, and its tradition of peacekeeping, is at stake.

United Nations Peacekeeping Operations

United Nations peacekeeping operations come within the jurisdiction of the Security Council. This table gives operations current as of February 2000. Strength figures include military and civilian police personnel. Fifteen UN missions were underway in February 2000, with 26,743 peacekeepers serving in them.

Operation	Date of establishment	Area of operation	Strength (as of November 1998)	Budget estimate ($ millions)[1]
UNTSO United Nations Truce Supervision Organization	1948	Middle East	140	23.0
UNMOGIP United Nations Military Observer Group in India and Pakistan	1949	India and Pakistan	45	8.3
UNFICYP United Nations Peacekeeping Force in Cyprus	1964	Cyprus	1,306	45.3[1]
UNDOF United Nations Disengagement Observer Force	1974	Syria	1,029	35.3
UNIFIL United Nations Interim Force in Lebanon	1978	Lebanon	4,483	148.9
UNIKOM United Nations Iraq-Kuwait Observation Mission	1991	Iraq/Kuwait	1,102	50.8
MINURSO United Nations Mission for the Referendum in Western Sahara	1991	Western Sahara	316	37.3[2]
UNOMIG United Nations Observer Mission in Georgia	1993	Georgia	102	19.4[3]
UNMOT United Nations Mission of Observers in Tajikistan	1994	Tajikistan	29	18.7
UNMIBH United Nations Mission in Bosnia-Herzegovina	1995	Bosnia-Herzegovina	1,995	168.2
UNMOP United Nations Mission of Observers in Prevlaka	1996	Croatia	28	[4]
UNAMSIL United Nations Mission of Observers in Sierra Leone	1999	Sierra Leone	4,508[5]	200[6]
UNMIK United Nations Mission in Kosovo	1999	Kosovo	3,132	456.4
MONUC United Nations Organization Mission in the Democratic Republic of the Congo	1999	Democratic Republic of Congo	83	41.0
UNTAET United Nations Transitional Administration in East Timor	1999	East Timor	8,445[7]	386.3[8]

[1] 1 July 1999–30 June 2000.
[2] 1 November 1998–30 June 1999.
[3] Data for 1998/1999.
[4] Included in UNMIBH budget. Estimated cost of $2,000,000 for the period 1 July 1998–30 June 1999.
[5] As at 5 January 2000.
[6] Initial appropriation.
[7] Strength at 23 March 2000.
[8] Proposed budget for 1 December 1999–30 June 2000.

Source: UN Department of Public Information

Average Strength and Cost of United Nations Peacekeeping Forces

1991–99

Year	Troops	Other UN personnel	Total	UN costs ($ millions)
1991	9,000	5,000	14,000	380
1992	33,000	12,000	45,000	1,330
1993	67,000	22,000	89,000	3,000
1994	72,000	13,000	85,000	3,400
1995	61,000	12,000	73,000	3,300
1996	21,000	7,000	28,000	1,600
1997	20,000	10,000	30,000	1,300
1998	15,000	9,000	24,000	1,400
1999	9,000	3,000	12,000	900

Source: The Military Balance 1999/2000, *International Institute for Strategic Studies, by permission of Oxford University Press and the IISS*

Leading Troop Contributions to United Nations Operations

As of 30 June 1999.

Country	Strength
Poland	990
Bangladesh	810
Austria	669
Ghana	657
Ireland, Republic of	627
India	621
Nepal	601
Fiji Islands	596
Finland	504
Argentina	496
Egypt	328
UK	306
France	247
Côte d'Ivoire	235
Canada	219

Source: The Military Balance 1999/2000, *International Institute for Strategic Studies, by permission of Oxford University Press and the IISS*

See also  **The United Nations,** pp 287–292.

Selected Non-United Nations Peacekeeping Operations

Data taken from *The Military Balance 1999/2000*, International Institute for Strategic Studies, by permission of Oxford University Press and the IISS.

Operation	Date of establishment	Area of operation	Strength	Cost to June 1999 ($ millions)
MFO Multinational Force and Observers	1981	Egypt	1,872	1,334
SFOR II Stablization Force for Bosnia-Herzegovina	1998	Bosnia-Herzegovina	20,000	9,000
AFOR NATO Albania Force	1999	Albania	5,500	650
KFOR NATO Kosovo Force	1999	Kosovo	55,000	10,000

■ Peacekeeping

UK Armed Forces and Defence Expenditure

Are Our Armed Forces Overstretched?

The armed forces of the UK are under great strain in attempting to fulfil an increasing number of missions around the world, without adequate resources. Concerns have been raised by the House of Commons Defence Select Committee that the UK's armed forces are over-stretched by increasing commitments around the world.

In addition to the deployment of forces at home and in Northern Ireland, the UK's forces are currently deployed in Belize, Bosnia, Brunei, Canada, Cyprus, the Falkland Islands, Germany, Gibraltar, Kenya, Kosovo, Albania, and in the Middle East (to enforce the Iraq no-fly zone). Despite the peace dividend, following the end of the Cold War, the UK's most important deployment overseas is in Germany, where an armoured division is stationed as part of NATO's Rapid Reaction Corps. There are over 4,000 military personnel stationed in Bosnia as part of the Stabilisation Force (SFOR). The UK contributed over 6,000 troops to the NATO-led peacekeeping force in Kosovo (KFOR). Garrison forces are maintained in Brunei, Gibraltar, and the Falkland Islands, in addition to the UK's long term peace-keeping commitments in Cyprus.

The increasing role of the UK's armed forces in international peacekeeping operations reflects their reputation for professionalism, as well as a political will on the part of the UK government to take on an international 'policing' role. It also reflects the UK's status as a former colonial power. Elite units such as the Parachute Regiment and the Royal Marines are coming under increasing strain. The Parachute Regiment led NATO's forces into Kosovo, and restored order in Sierra Leone. There is a real danger that without significantly increased resources and manpower, the UK's armed forces could struggle to meet its international commitments as well as the nation's own defence needs.

Armed Forces in the UK

General information
The armed forces of the UK are made up of the Army, the Royal Navy, and the Royal Air Force. The Queen is the commander-in-chief for all branches of the armed forces. The Ministry of Defence (MoD) is concerned with the control, administration, equipment, and support of the armed forces of the Crown. The research, development, production, and purchase of weapons is the concern of the Procurement Executive of the MoD.

The chief of staff of the defence staff is the professional head of the armed forces and under the chief of staff each service's chief of staff is responsible for the fighting effectiveness, efficiency, and morale of that particular service. They and other senior officers and officials at the head of the department's main functions form the MoD's corporate board, chaired by the permanent under-secretary. The secretary of state chairs the Defence Council (established 1964) and is responsible to Parliament for the formulation and conduct of defence policy, and the provision of the means to implement it.

The defence and security of the UK are pursued through membership of the European Union (EU), the Western European Union (WEU), the Organization for Security and Cooperation in Europe (OSCE), and the United Nations (UN). The UK contributes significantly to the peacekeeping work of the UN both financially and in terms of the deployment of personnel.

All three armed services are professionals, with no conscript element.

Royal Navy
Control of the Royal Navy is vested in the Defence Council and is exercised through the Admiralty Board, chaired by the Secretary of State for Defence. Naval members of the Defence Council are the Chief of Naval Staff (First Sea Lord), responsible for management, planning, fighting efficiency, and operational advice; the combined Second Sea Lord and Commander-in-Chief Naval Home Command, responsible for procurement of ships, their weapons, and equipment; the Chief of Fleet Support, responsible for logistic support, fuels and transport, naval dockyards, and auxiliary services; the Commander-in-Chief Fleet; and the Assistant Chief of Staff, responsible for coordinating advice on certain policy and operational matters.

The principal roles of the Royal Navy are to deploy the national strategic nuclear deterrent, to provide maritime defence of the UK and its dependent territories, to contribute to the maritime elements of NATO forces, and to meet national maritime objectives outside the NATO area. The Commander-in-Chief Fleet, with headquarters at Northwood, is responsible for the command of the fleet, while command of naval establishments in the UK is exercised by the Commander-in-Chief Home Command from Portsmouth.

Royal Marines The British Corps of Royal Marines was founded in 1664. It is primarily a military force also trained for fighting at sea, and providing commando units, landing craft, crews, and divers. The Royal Marines corps provides a commando brigade comprising three commando groups. Each commando group is approximately 1,000 strong, with artillery, engineering, and logistic support, air defence, and three helicopter squadrons. The Royal Marine corps' strength is completed by the Special Boat Squadron and specialist defence units.

Royal Naval Reserve and Royal Marines Reserve The Royal Naval Reserve (RNR) and the Royal Marines Reserve (RMR) are volunteer forces that provide trained personnel in war to supplement regular forces. The RMR principally provides reinforcement and other specialist tasks with the UK-Netherlands Amphibious Force.

Personnel who have completed service in the Royal Navy and the Royal Marines have a commitment to serve in the Royal Fleet Reserve.

Queen Alexandra's Royal Naval Nursing Service Nursing sisters were first appointed to naval hospitals in 1884. The Queen Alexandra's Royal Nursing Service (QARNNS) gained its title in 1902. Men were integrated into the Service in 1982; female medical assistants were introduced in 1987.

Army
Control of the British Army is vested in the Defence Council and is exercised through the Army Board. The Secretary of State is Chairman of the Army Board. The military members of the Army Board are the Chief of the General Staff, the Adjutant General, the Quartermaster General, the Master General of the Ordnance, the Commander-in-Chief Land Command, and the Assistant Chief of the General Staff.

Women serve throughout the Army in the same regiments and corps as men. There are only a few roles in which they are not employed, such as the Infantry and Royal Armoured Corps.

Territorial Army The Territorial Army (TA) is a force of volunteer soldiers, created from volunteer regiments (incorporated in 1872) as the Territorial Force in 1908. It was raised and administered by county associations, and intended primarily for home defence. It was renamed the Territorial Army in 1922. Merged with the Regular Army in World War II, it was revived in 1947, and replaced by a smaller, more highly trained Territorial and Army Volunteer Reserve, again renamed Territorial Army in 1979. The Army Chief of the General Staff is responsible for the TA.

The role of the TA is to act as a general reserve for the Army, reinforcing it, as required, with individuals, sub-units, and other units, both overseas and in the UK. It also provides the framework and basis for regeneration and reconstruction in the event of unforeseen needs in times of national emergency.

Armed Forces in the UK *(continued)*

Queen Alexandra's Royal Army Nursing Corps Founded in 1902 as Queen Alexandra's Imperial Military Nursing Service, the Queen Alexandra's Royal Army Nursing Corps (QARANC) gained its current title in 1949. The Corps has trained nurses and trains and employs health care assistants. Members of the QARANC serve in Ministry of Defence hospital units in the UK and in military hospitals both in the UK and abroad. Service in the Corps was opened to men in 1992.

Royal Air Force
The Royal Air Force (RAF) was formed in 1918 by the merger of the Royal Naval Air Service and the Royal Flying Corps. The RAF is administered by the Air Force Board, which is chaired by the Secretary of State for Defence. Other members of the Board include the Chief of the Air Staff, Air Member for Personnel, Air Member for Logistics, and Air Officer Commanding-in-Chief Strike Command. The RAF is organized into three commands: Strike Command, Personnel and Training Command, and Logistics Command.

Royal Auxiliary Air Force The Royal Auxiliary Air Force (RAUXAF) was formed in 1924, and merged with the Royal Air Force Volunteer Reserve in 1997. It supports the RAF in air and ground defence of airfields, air movements, maritime air operations, and medical evacuations by air.

Princess Mary's Royal Air Force Nursing Service The Princess Mary's Royal Air Force Nursing Service (PMRAFNS) offers commissions to Registered General Nurses.

Formation of the UK Armed Forces: Front Line and Support Units

The number of personnel and the amount of equipment in each vessel, regiment, battalion, or squadron vary according to the roles currently assigned. As of 1 April 1999.

Front line units			
Royal Navy			
Trident/Polaris submarines		vessels	3
Fleet submarines		vessels	12
Submarines total		vessels	15
Carriers		vessels	3
Assault ships		vessels	3
Destroyers		vessels	12
Frigates		vessels	23
Mine counter measure vessels		vessels	20
Patrol ships and craft		vessels	24
Fixed wing aircraft		squadrons	3
Helicopters		squadrons	12
Royal Marines			
Commandos			3
Army			
Combat arms	armour	regiments	11
	infantry	battalions	40
	special forces	regiments	1
	aviation	regiments	5
Combat support	artillery	regiments	15
	engineers	regiments	10
	signals	regiments	11
Home Service Forces[1]			
Combat arms	infantry	battalions	7
Territorial Army			
Combat arms	armour	regiments	6
	infantry	battalions	33
	special forces	regiments	2
	aviation	regiment	1
Combat support	artillery[2]	regiments	6
	engineers	regiments	9
	signals	regiments	11
Royal Air Force			
Strike/attack		squadrons	5
Offensive support		squadrons	5
Reconnaissance		squadrons	5
Maritime patrol		squadrons	3
Air defence		squadrons	5
Airborne Early Warning		squadrons	2
Air transport, tankers, and helicopters		squadrons	14
Search and Rescue		squadrons	2
Royal Air Force regiments	surface to air missiles	squadrons	4
	ground defence	squadrons	5
Support units			
Royal Navy and Royal Fleet Auxiliary Service			
Support ships		vessels	0
Survey ships		vessels	6
Ice patrol ships		vessels	1
Tankers[3]		vessels	9
Fleet replenishment ships[3]		vessels	4
Aviation training ship[3]		vessels	1
Landing ships[3]		vessels	5
Forward repair ships[3]		vessels	1
Royal Marines			
Logistic Unit		regiments	1
Army			
Combat service support	equipment support[4]	battalions	6
	logistics	regiments	24
	field ambulances/ field hospitals	number	12
Territorial Army			
Combat service support	equipment support[4]	battalions	5
	logistics	regiments	19
	field ambulances/ field hospitals	number	18
Royal Auxiliary Air Force			
Ground defence		squadrons	3
Role support		squadrons	5
Air movements		squadrons	1
Aeromedical/air transportable surgical		squadrons	2
Royal Air Force Reserve			
Meteorological		squadrons	1

[1] Includes Royal Irish Regiment (Home Service) battalions (formed under the Ulster Defence Regiment in 1992) and home defence units raised in the Dependent Territories. Excludes the Home Service Force which was not organized into battalion-size units.
[2] Includes the Honourable Artillery Company.
[3] Ships of the Royal Fleet Auxiliary Service.
[4] The REME Order of Battle did not include regiment or battalion equivalents until 1993.

Source: UK Defence Statistics 1999, *Defence Analytical Services Agency,* © *Crown copyright 1999*

■ UK Armed Forces and Defence Expenditure

Armed Forces in Northern Ireland

As of 1 April for the year shown.
(N/A = not available.)

		1975	1980	1985	1990	1995	1996	1997	1998	1999
Army[1]										
Major combat units[2]	long tour units	5	6	6	6	6	6	6	6	6
	short tour units	10	6	2	4	5	5	6	6	6
	Total	15	12	8	10	11	11	12	12	12
Total units serving[3]		50	32	18	25	22	22	28	26	N/A
Royal Irish Regiment (Home Service)[4]										
Full-time personnel	male	1,394	2,416	2,552	2,697	2,755	2,702	2,515	2,468	2,361
	female	12	138	195	242	301	312	247	233	244
	Total	1,406	2,554	2,717	2,939	3,056	3,014	2,762	2,701	2,605
Part-time personnel	male	5,708	4,267	3,224	2,819	1,943	1,819	1,777	1,750	1,698
	female	577	552	508	478	314	303	229	211	208
	Total	6,285	4,819	3,732	3,297	2,257	2,122	2,006	1,961	1,906
Service personnel deaths										
Royal Irish Regiment (Home Service)		6	9	4	8	0	0	0	0	N/A
Total		20	17	6	15	0	1	5	2	N/A

[1] Includes Royal Marine commandos in the Infantry role, but excludes the battalions of the Royal Irish Regiment (Home Service).
[2] Excludes temporary deployments.
[3] Includes one unit that served two separate tours in Northern Ireland during 1990 and another in 1997.
[4] The Royal Irish Regiment was formed on 1 July 1992 by the merger of the Ulster Defence Regiment and the Royal Irish Rangers. The Home Service element of the Royal Irish Regiment corresponds to the former Ulster Defence Regiment. These figures do not include long-term sick.

Source: UK Defence Statistics 1999, *Defence Analytical Services Agency, © Crown copyright 1999*

See also **Key Dates in the Northern Ireland Peace Process Since 1993**, p 66.

Deployment of UK Military Personnel Overseas

As of 1 April for the year shown. Figures include service personnel who are on loan to countries in the areas shown and naval services and civilian personnel at sea. All defence attachés and advisers and their staffs are included under 'Other locations' and not identified within specific areas.
(- = not applicable.)

Service	1975	1980	1985	1990	1995[1]	1999
Continental Europe						
Naval services	365	413	885	378	1,310	507
Army	58,470	58,782	59,850	56,635	26,465	24,952
Royal Air Force	10,110	11,365	12,194	12,338	5,974	5,243
Civilian	2,512	2,283	1,977	1,984	1,431	1,383
Gibraltar						
Naval services	618	643	733	487	407	245
Army	822	776	771	686	65	72
Royal Air Force	486	404	455	378	154	118
Civilian	318	299	109	108	80	57
Cyprus						
Naval services	14	17	19	6	2	111
Army	3,741	3,253	3,177	2,743	2,873	2,331
Royal Air Force	3,267	1,325	1,539	1,462	1,441	1,215
Civilian	465	370	293	254	236	295
Other Mediterranean, Near East, and Gulf						
Naval services	3,928	2,936	552	1,640	2,009	526
Army	282	232	238	152	191	229
Royal Air Force	1,778	76	104	263	364	836
Civilian	172	11	11	7	6	16
Hong Kong						
Naval services	272	326	272	223	185	–
Army	3,434	2,389	1,964	1,624	514	–
Royal Air Force	562	251	268	265	208	–
Civilian	213	383	298	262	94	–
Other Far East						
Naval services	2,734	56	114	1,106	343	42
Army	1,562	199	235	162	201	261
Royal Air Force	1,174	20	9	15	24	30
Civilian	119	27	15	22	26	20
Other locations						
Naval services	6,418	1,464	2,746	2,343	1,567	4,023
Army	1,558	1,862	4,406	2,854	2,869	3,567
Royal Air Force	776	770	2,633	1,834	1,728	1,208
Civilian	2,974	2,857	2,752	2,956	2,536	2,637

[1] From 1 April 1995, the method of counting part-time civilian staff changed to reflect the actual hours worked (on average about 60% of full time hours) rather than the notional 50% previously used.

(continued)

Deployment of UK Military Personnel Overseas *(continued)*

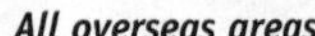

All overseas areas

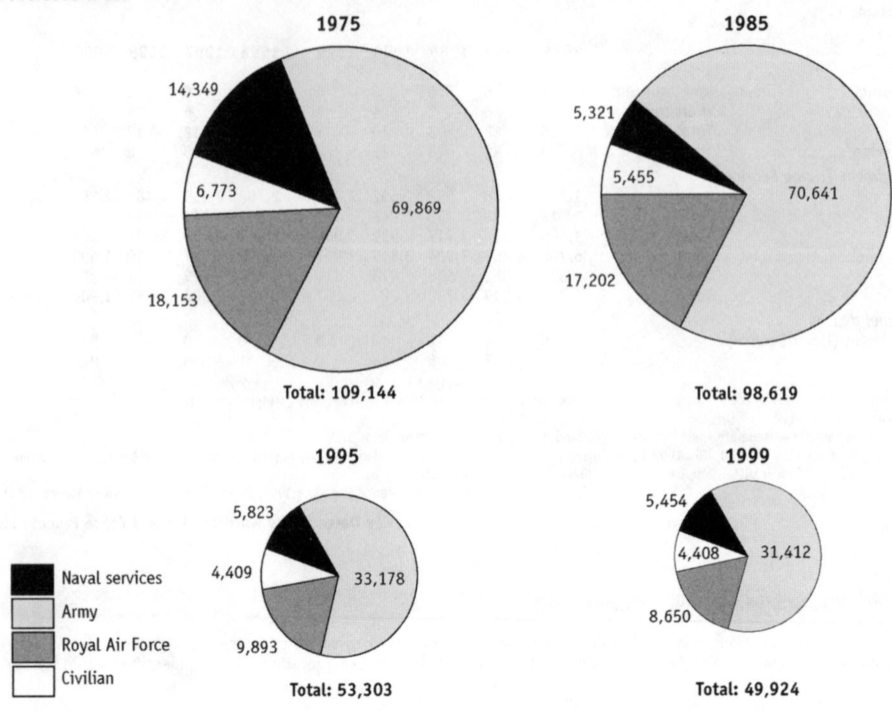

Source: UK Defence Statistics 1999, *Defence Analytical Services Agency,* © *Crown copyright 1999*

Deployment of UK Military Personnel in the UK

Figures show deployment of UK regular forces and Ministry of Defence civilians, including Royal Navy and Royal Marines personnel on board ships in home waters. As of 1 July for the year shown.

Personnel	1980	1985	1990	1994	1995	1996	1997	1998
UK[1]								
Service	238,100	229,600	215,900	199,500	182,200	177,400	171,600	173,400
Civilian	231,200	167,700	135,200	114,000	108,000	102,600	99,700	97,900
Total	496,300	397,200	351,100	313,500	290,200	280,000	271,300	271,300
England								
Service	200,000	193,300	179,600	162,100	149,400	146,600	142,600	144,600
Civilian	196,600	140,400	114,600	95,000	89,600	85,400	82,000	80,200
Total	396,700	333,700	294,200	257,000	239,000	232,000	224,600	224,700
Wales								
Service	6,900	6,300	5,300	5,500	5,200	4,300	3,300	3,200
Civilian	9,500	6,500	5,500	4,900	4,800	4,700	4,800	5,000
Total	16,400	12,800	10,800	10,400	10,000	9,100	8,200	8,300
Scotland								
Service	18,100	20,100	19,300	18,000	16,900	15,500	13,900	14,200
Civilian	21,900	18,100	12,300	11,200	10,600	9,500	9,800	9,500
Total	40,000	38,200	31,600	29,300	27,500	25,000	23,700	23,700
Northern Ireland[2]								
Service	11,900	9,700	11,500	11,600	9,900	10,500	11,500	11,000
Civilian	3,200	2,700	2,700	2,900	3,000	3,000	3,100	3,200
Total	15,100	12,400	14,200	14,600	12,900	13,500	14,600	14,200

[1] The figures for service personnel in England, Scotland, and Wales are obtained from a different source from that used to obtain the UK total; consequently, the sum of the national figures may differ from the UK total.

[2] Includes all personnel serving on emergency tours of duty, but excludes the former Ulster Defence Regiment, now the Home Service element of the Royal Irish Regiment.

Source: UK Defence Statistics 1999, *Defence Analytical Services Agency,* © *Crown copyright 1999*

■ UK Armed Forces and Defence Expenditure

UK Defence Expenditure

Figures are VAT-inclusive at current prices and are in millions of pounds, except for percentages.
(– = not applicable.)

Type of expenditure		1985–86	1990–91	1995–96	1997–98	1998–99[1]	1999–2000[1]
Expenditure on personnel	of the armed forces	3,510	4,811	6,150	5,938	6,064	6,232
	of the retired armed forces	899	1,406	–	–	–	–
	of civilian staff	1,970	2,594	2,374	2,321	2,196	2,247
	Total	6,379	8,811	8,524	8,259	8,259	8,479
Expenditure on equipment	sea	2,499	2,955	2,110	2,142	2,351	2,299
	land	1,887	1,927	1,576	1,658	1,702	1,652
	air	3,296	3,197	3,356	3,843	4,394	4,532
	other	511	759	1,495	1,360	1,339	1,321
	Total	8,193	8,838	8,537	9,003	9,785	9,803
Other expenditure	works, buildings, and land	1,413	2,067	2,065	1,253	1,806	1,744
	miscellaneous stores and services	1,958	2,582	2,391	2,395	2,389	2,254
	Total	3,371	4,649	4,456	3,862	4,195	3,998
Total expenditure/budget		18,263	22,207	21,517	21,610	22,549	22,280
Total expenditure at 1997–98 prices		30,391	27,575	22,725	21,610	21,999	21,207
% of total expenditure/budget							
Expenditure on personnel	of the armed forces	19.6	21.6	28.6	28.4	27.3	28.0
	of the retired armed forces	5.0	6.3	–	–	–	–
	of civilian staff	11.0	11.6	11.0	11.1	9.9	10.1
	Total	35.6	39.5	39.6	39.5	37.1	38.1
Expenditure on equipment	sea	13.9	13.3	9.8	10.2	10.6	10.3
	land	10.5	8.6	7.3	7.9	7.7	7.4
	air	18.4	14.3	15.6	18.4	19.8	20.3
	other	2.8	3.4	7.0	6.5	6.0	5.9
	Total	45.6	39.6	39.7	43.1	44.0	44.0
Other expenditure	works, buildings, and land	7.9	9.3	9.6	6.0	8.1	7.8
	miscellaneous stores and services	10.9	11.6	11.1	11.5	10.7	10.1
	Total	18.8	20.9	20.7	17.4	18.9	17.9

[1] Estimate.

Source: UK Defence Statistics 1999, *Defence Analytical Services Agency, © Crown copyright 1999*

See also **Government Expenditure as a Percentage of GDP in the UK**, p 112.

UK Armed Forces Weapons Arsenal

Weapon		Number
Strategic weapons		
Strategic submarines[1]		3
Conventional weapons		
Tactical submarines		12
Carriers		3
Destroyers		11
Frigates		20
Patrol ships		24
Mine warfare ships		19
Amphibious warfare ships		8
Landing/amphibious craft	Army	16
	Royal Navy	23
	Royal Marines	28
Support ships		21
Main battle tanks		542
Reconnaisance vehicles		462

Weapon		Number
Armoured infantry fighting vehicles		747
Armoured personnel carriers		3,016
Artillery pieces		425
Mortars		543
Anti-tank guided weapons		841
Surface to air missile systems	Army	512
	Royal Air Force	24
Combat aircraft	Royal Air Force	462
	Fleet Air Arm	54
Armed helicopters	Army	269
	Royal Air Force	167
	Royal Navy	138
	Royal Marines	18
Training helicopters		12

[1] Each capable of carrying 16 Trident DS missiles carrying 16 Multiple Independently-Targeted Re-entry Vehicles (MIRV).

Source: Data from The Military Balance 1999/2000, *International Institute for Strategic Studies*

UK Ministry of Defence Contracts over £100 Million

Data for 1998–99. (Includes suppliers of food, fuels, and services.)

Over £250 million
British Aerospace Aircraft Group
DERA
Devonport Royal Dockyard Ltd
General Electric Co plc
GKN plc
Hunting plc
Lockheed Martin Group
Matra BAE Dynamics (UK) Ltd
Rolls Royce plc
Vickers plc

£100–250 million
Annington Receivables Ltd
Babcock International Group Ltd
BMW (AG)
British Telecom plc
Building and Property Defence Ltd
EDS International Ltd
ICL plc
John Mowlem and Co
Other UK government departments
Racal Electronics Ltd
Serco Group plc

Source: UK Defence Statistics 1999, *Defence Analytical Services Agency, © Crown copyright 1999*

UK Service Personnel

Strengths of UK Regular Forces

Figures include trainees. As of 1 April in the year given.
(N/A = not available.)

Year[1]	Total	Officers			Other ranks		
		Total	men	women	Total	men	women
All services							
1993	274,849	40,403	37,599	2,804	234,446	218,333	16,113
1994	254,488	37,487	34,749	2,738	217,001	201,977	15,024
1995	233,340	35,545	32,956	2,589	197,795	183,776	14,019
1996	221,870	34,106	31,628	2,478	187,764	174,560	13,204
1997	210,823	32,675	30,295	2,380	178,148	165,697	12,451
1998	210,136	32,625	30,061	2,564	177,511	164,375	13,136
1999	208,636	32,235	29,578	2,657	176,401	162,911	13,490
Naval services							
1993	59,357	9,802	9,307	495	49,555	45,564	3,991
1994	55,779	9,182	8,688	494	46,597	42,841	3,756
1995	50,893	8,760	8,287	473	42,133	38,696	3,437
1996	48,307	8,370	7,913	457	39,937	36,763	3,174
1997	44,651	7,810	7,357	453	36,841	34,041	2,800
1998	44,466	7,752	N/A	N/A	36,714	N/A	N/A
1999	43,701	7,706	N/A	N/A	35,995	N/A	N/A
Army							
1993	134,583	16,129	14,959	1,170	118,454	112,030	6,424
1994	123,028	14,840	13,669	1,171	108,188	102,307	5,881
1995	111,693	13,956	12,851	1,105	97,737	92,265	5,472
1996	108,840	13,757	12,677	1,080	95,083	89,709	5,374
1997	110,140	13,971	12,831	1,140	96,169	90,074	6,095
1998	109,827	13,898	N/A	N/A	95,929	N/A	N/A
1999	109,722	13,620	N/A	N/A	96,102	N/A	N/A
Royal Air Force							
1993	80,909	14,472	13,333	1,139	66,437	60,739	5,698
1994	75,681	13,465	12,392	1,073	62,216	56,829	5,387
1995	70,754	12,829	11,818	1,011	57,925	52,815	5,110
1996	64,723	11,979	11,038	941	52,744	48,088	4,656
1997	56,256	11,010	10,096	914	45,246	41,155	4,091
1998	55,843	10,975	N/A	N/A	44,868	N/A	N/A
1999	55,213	10,909	N/A	N/A	44,304	N/A	N/A

Source: UK Defence Statistics 1999, *Defence Analytical Services Agency,* © *Crown copyright 1999*

Ethnic Composition of UK Regular Forces by Rank

For 'All services' the ranks are shown in army terms.
As of 1 April 1999.
(N = nil or negligible.)

Rank		Total	White		Ethnic minorities		Unknown[1]	
			number	%	number	%	number	%
All services								
Officers	Lieutenant Colonel and above	5,238	5,190	99.1	48	0.9	N	N
	Major and below	26,997	26,446	98.0	289	1.1	262	1.0
	Total	32,235	31,636	98.1	337	1.0	262	0.8
Other ranks	Sergeant and above	47,998	47,431	98.8	560	1.2	7	0.0
	Corporal and below	128,403	126,829	98.8	1,311	1.0	263	0.2
	Total	176,401	174,260	98.8	1,871	1.1	270	0.2
TOTAL		208,636	205,896	98.7	2,208	1.1	532	0.3
Naval services								
Officers	Commander and above	1,432	1,422	99.3	10	0.7	N	N
	Lieutenant Commander and below	6,274	6,209	99.0	65	1.0	N	N
	Total	7,706	7,631	99.0	75	1.0	N	N
Other ranks	Petty Officer and above	13,048	12,949	99.2	99	0.8	N	N
	Leading rate and below	22,947	22,758	99.2	189	0.8	N	N
	Total	35,995	35,707	99.2	288	0.8	N	N
TOTAL		43,701	43,338	99.2	363	0.8	N	N
Army								
Officers	Lieutenant Colonel and above	2,255	2,233	99.0	22	1.0	N	N
	Major and below	11,365	11,118	97.8	116	1.0	131	1.2
	Total	13,620	13,351	98.0	138	1.0	131	1.0

(continued)

Ethnic Composition of UK Regular Forces by Rank *(continued)*

Rank		Total	White		Ethnic minorities		Unknown[1]	
			number	%	number	%	number	%
Other ranks	Sergeant and above	22,100	21,794	98.6	300	1.4	6	0.0
	Corporal and below	74,002	72,966	98.6	807	1.1	229	0.3
	Total	96,102	94,760	98.6	1,107	1.2	235	0.2
TOTAL		109,722	108,111	98.5	1,245	1.1	366	0.3
Royal Air Force								
Officers	Wing Commander and above	1,551	1,535	99.0	16	1.0	N	N
	Squadron Leader and below	9,358	9,119	97.4	108	1.2	131	1.4
	Total	10,909	10,654	97.7	124	1.1	131	1.2
Other ranks	Sergeant and above	12,850	12,688	98.7	161	1.3	1	0.0
	Corporal and below	31,454	31,105	98.9	315	1.0	34	0.1
	Total	44,304	43,793	98.8	476	1.1	35	0.1
TOTAL		55,213	54,447	98.6	600	1.1	166	0.3

[1] Ethnic origin not held on the administrative system.

Source: UK Defence Statistics 1999, *Defence Analytical Services Agency,* © *Crown copyright 1999*

Strengths of UK Regular Forces by Gender and Rank

The ranks shown are in army terms. Prior to 1990 the figures relate to 1 January; from 1990 they relate to 1 April.

Rank		1975	1985	1990	1995	1999
Women						
Officers	Major General and above	0	0	0	0	0
	Brigadier	6	6	7	3	2
	Colonel	28	23	24	17	25
	Lieutenant Colonel	62	47	60	99	100
	Major	336	292	309	386	465
	Captain	864	936	1,172	1,330	1,193
	Lieutenant and below	783	853	965	754	872
	Total[1]	2,079	2,157	2,537	2,589	2,657
Other ranks	Warrant Officer	127	117	144	160	214
	Staff Sergeant	189	262	361	365	391
	Sergeant	682	963	1,386	1,313	1,203
	Corporal	1,481	2,903	2,979	2,982	2,357
	Lance Corporal	860	1,156	1,288	1,120	1,196
	Private (including juniors)	9,157	8,843	8,514	8,079	8,129
	Total	12,496	14,244	14,672	14,019	13,490
Men						
Officers	Major General and above	254	212	203	166	142
	Brigadier	414	381	381	323	367
	Colonel	1,587	1,421	1,459	1,209	1,061
	Lieutenant Colonel	4,841	4,378	4,556	3,972	3,757
	Major	12,457	11,660	11,491	9,907	9,495
	Captain	17,336	13,987	13,891	12,535	10,689
	Lieutenant and below	8,011	7,947	8,351	4,844	4,067
	Total[1]	44,900	39,986	40,332	32,956	29,578
Other ranks	Warrant Officer	11,777	11,416	11,407	9,084	8,562
	Staff Sergeant	27,102	23,241	22,352	18,302	16,109
	Sergeant	37,794	35,042	34,045	26,252	23,302
	Corporal	48,645	52,764	52,587	40,924	32,384
	Lance Corporal	22,100	22,973	22,553	16,127	14,186
	Private (including juniors)	135,628	125,026	105,226	73,087	68,368
	Total	283,046	270,462	248,170	183,776	162,911

[1] Prior to 1987, professionally qualified female officers serving in the medical, dental, veterinary, and legal specializations are included with the male officer numbers.

Source: UK Defence Statistics 1999, *Defence Analytical Services Agency,* © *Crown copyright 1999*

Relative Ranks in the UK Armed Forces

Royal Navy	Army	Royal Air Force
Admiral of the Fleet	Field Marshal	Marshal of the RAF
Admiral	General	Air Chief Marshal
Vice Admiral	Lieutenant General	Air Marshal
Rear Admiral	Major General	Air Vice Marshal
Commodore	Brigadier	Air Commodore
Captain	Colonel	Group Captain
Commander	Lieutenant Colonel	Wing Commander
Lieutenant Commander	Major	Squadron Leader
Lieutenant	Captain	Flight Lieutenant
Sub Lieutenant	Lieutenant	Flying Officer
Midshipman	Second Lieutenant	Pilot Officer

Source: Ministry of Defence, © *Crown copyright*

Strengths of UK Reserves and Auxiliary Forces

Volunteer reserves and auxiliary forces comprise personnel in civilian occupations who undertake to give a certain amount of their time to train in support of the regular forces. As of 1 April 1999.
(– = not applicable.)

Service/force		1985	1990	1995	1999
Regular Reserve					
Naval Service	Royal Fleet Reserve	11,000	13,600	9,800	10,600
	individuals liable to recall	14,700	13,600	13,500	14,100
	Total	25,700	27,200	23,300	24,700
Army	Army Reserve	61,900	65,800	53,400	34,800
	individuals liable to recall	88,200	117,700	141,900	145,600
	Total	150,200	183,500	195,300	180,400
Royal Air Force	Royal Air Force Reserve	2,500	10,100	15,900	14,700
	individuals liable to recall	27,300	30,100	29,600	27,700
	Total	29,800	40,100	45,500	42,400
Total		205,700	212,000	250,800	247,500
Volunteer Reserve	Naval Service	6,300	7,000	3,700	3,800
	Army[1]	81,000	81,900	59,900	51,800
	Royal Air Force[2]	1,200	1,700	1,300	1,700
Total		88,600	90,600	64,900	57,400

[1] Includes the Ulster Defence Regiment prior to 1 July 1992, when it merged with the Royal Irish Rangers and became the Home Service element of the Royal Irish Regiment, part of the Regular Forces. Includes non-regular permanent staff. For 1985 and 1990, includes the Home Service Force.
[2] Includes Officer Training Corps.

Source: UK Defence Statistics 1999, *Defence Analytical Services Agency,*

UK Military Orders, Decorations, and Medals in Common Use

VC Victoria Cross
CGC Conspicuous Gallantry Cross
GC George Cross
KG Knight of the Order of the Garter
KT Knight of the Order of the Thistle
GCB Knight Grand Cross or Dame Grand Cross of the Order of the Bath
OM Member of the Order of Merit
KCB Knight Commander of the Order of the Bath
CB Companion of the Order of the Bath
GCMG Knight Grand Cross or Dame Grand Cross of the Order of St Michael and St George
CMG Companion of the Order of St Michael and St George
GCVO Knight Grand Cross or Dame Grand Cross of the Royal Victorian Order
KCVO Knight Commander of the Royal Victorian Order
DCVO Dame Commander of the Royal Victorian Order
CVO Commander of the Royal Victorian Order
GBE Knight Grand Cross or Dame Grand Cross of the Order of the British Empire
CH Member of the Order of the Companion of Honour
KBE Knight Commander of the Order of the British Empire
DBE Dame Commander of the Order of the British Empire
CBE Commander of the Order of the British Empire
DSO Companion of the Distinguished Service Order
LVO Lieutenant of the Royal Victorian Order
OBE Officer of the Order of the British Empire
ISO Companion of the Imperial Service Order (obsolete)
MVO Member of the Royal Victorian Order
MBE Member of the Order of the British Empire
CGC Conspicuous Gallantry Cross
RRC Member of the Royal Red Cross
DSC Distinguished Service Cross
MC Military Cross
DFC Distinguished Flying Cross
AFC Air Force Cross
ARRC Associate of the Royal Red Cross
DCM Distinguished Conduct Medal (obsolete)
CGM Conspicuous Gallantry Medal (obsolete)
GM George Medal
DSM Distinguished Service Medal (obsolete)
MM Military Medal (obsolete)
DFM Distinguished Flying Medal (obsolete)
AFM Air Force Medal (obsolete)
QGM Queen's Gallantry Medal
BEM British Empire Medal (obsolete)
RVM Royal Victorian Medal
TD Territorial Decoration or Efficiency Decoration

Source: The Army List 1998,

Military Colleges in the UK

Royal College of Defence Studies Vice-Admiral J H S McNally, LVD Seaford House, 37 Belgrave Square, London SW1X 8NS; phone: (020) 7915 4800; fax: (020) 7915 2999

Joint Services Command and Staff College Air Vice Marshall B K BurridgeBroad Lane, Bracknell, Berkshire RG12 9DD; phone: (01344) 454593; fax: (01344) 357055

Royal Naval Military College
Britannia Royal Naval College Commodore M W G Kerr, Dartmouth, Devon TQ6 0HJ; phone: (01803) 832141; fax: (01803) 677015

Military Colleges (Army)
Royal Military College of Science, Shrivenham Major General J C B Sutherell, Swindon, Wiltshire SN6 8LA; phone: (01793) 784455; fax: (01793) 785555

Royal Military Academy Sandhurst Major General A G Denaro, CBE, Camberley, Surrey GU15 4PQ; phone: (01276) 633344; fax: (01276) 412249

Royal Air Force College
Royal Air Force Staff College Air Commodore T W Rimmer, OBE, Cranwell, Sleaford, Lincolnshire NG34 8HB; phone: (01400) 261201; fax: (01400) 261201 ext 7399

Source: Ministry of Defence,

UK Service Personnel

Web Sites

A-Bomb WWW Museum

http://www.csi.ad.jp/ABOMB/index.html

Commemorative and awareness-raising site of the nuclear catastrophe in Hiroshima and Nagasaki in 1945.

Arms Race – How Technology Defined Our Identity

http://icdweb.cc.purdue.edu/~phealy/arms.html

Illustrated account of the arms race as part of the Cold War, with links to associated issues such as the space race and the USA's relations with Cuba and Vietnam.

Battle of Britain

http://www.geocities.com/Pentagon/4143/

Informative tribute to the Battle of Britain. Includes the history of the battle, and details on key people, the technology, and the pilots and aircraft.

British Army

http://www.army.mod.uk/

Home page of the British Army, with extensive information on the structure of the army, weapons systems, current deployments, and career opportunities. An 'Army World Challenge' game asks what you would do if faced with five challenging scenarios developed from actual current operational missions.

Chemical and Biological Warfare Chronicle

http://www.stimson.org/cwc/index.html

Includes features on biological- and chemical-warfare issues, where policy, technology, and politics intersect; and has information on current treaties and maps of biological- and chemical-weapons sites.

Chronicle of the Falkland Islands History and War

http://www.yendor.com/vanished/falklands-war.html

The history of the Falkland Islands, from their discovery in 1592 to the British capture of the islands from Argentina in 1982. The main focus of this site is its detailed account of the 1982 conflict between the UK and Argentina.

D-Day

http://www.pbs.org/wgbh/pages/amex/dday/index.html

The story of the allied invasion of Normandy during World War II. The site includes a special feature on the paratrooper drop behind enemy lines, as well as newspaper accounts of the invasion and the text of letters written by soldiers at the front.

Federation of American Scientists, Nuclear Resources

http://www.fas.org/nuke/index.html

In-depth site from this official US source that covers nuclear forces worldwide. It includes details of the structure, design and history of nuclear, chemical, and biological weapons; and news and analysis of developments across the globe.

Great War and the Shaping of the 20th Century

http://www.pbs.org/greatwar/

A comprehensive multimedia exploration of the history and effects of World War I. An interactive timeline lets you examine the events leading up to and during World War I, as well as its aftermath; there is also an interactive gallery of maps and locations.

Ministry of Defence, United Kingdom

http://www.mod.uk/

Official site of the UK Ministry of Defence, this site gives complete information on the history of the MOD, its ministers and chiefs of staff, its various agencies, and other MOD-related bodies. There are separate pages for each of the armed forces and reserve forces, plus news and press releases, veterans' service records, and links to defence ministries in all other countries.

NATO

http://www.nato.int

Official site of the North Atlantic Treaty Organization. The site includes a guide to NATO's structure, its members and partners, and staff vacancies; a complete archive of all official documents and NATO publications; and a multimedia section with videos and virtual visits.

Naval Dockyards Society

http://www.canterbury.u-net.com/Dockyards/

The society provides information on all aspects of naval dockyards – construction, history, workforce, as well as the surrounding communities. The site also includes an online version of the society's newsletter.

Nuclear Test Ban Treaty

http://www.ctbt.rnd.doe.gov/ctbt/index.html

US Department of Energy site that explains the efforts to ensure that the signatories remain faithful to the letter of the comprehensive nuclear test ban treaty, with sections on the various monitoring methods as well as onsite inspections.

Royal Air Force

http://www.raf.mod.uk/

Site of the UK's air force, with information for would-be recruits, as well as extensive information on the role of the RAF and profiles of all RAF aircraft, weapons systems, and bases.

Royal British Legion

http://www.britishlegion.org.uk/

Site of Britain's leading war veterans' organization, with comprehensive information about the history of the British Legion, its current activities, and its annual Poppy Appeal. A 'Lost trails' section helps reunite ex-servicemen.

Royal Navy

http://www.royal-navy.mod.uk/

Official guide to the Royal Navy that includes information about the latest training, deployments worldwide, career opportunities, and a history of the navy.

Special Air Service (SAS)

http://www.ability.org.uk/intro.html

Unofficial information on the elite British Army regiment. Known facts about the SAS are presented, together with information gleaned from the press on their counterinsurgency and anti-terrorist operations.

START II Treaty Fact Sheet

http://www.state.gov/www/regions/nis/russia_start2_treaty.html

Site published by the US Bureau of Public Affairs explaining the START II treaty of 1993 which was designed to further reduce and limit strategic offensive weapons.

Stockholm International Peace Research Institute (SIPRI)

http://www.sipri.se

SIPRI's research areas include arms transfer and production, military expenditure, military technology, chemical and biological weapons, and European security. As well as details of SIPRI's findings in these areas, the site includes more general information about the institute's history and structure.

Treaties and Agreements

http://dosfan.lib.uic.edu/acda/treaties.htm

Text of international treaties provided by the US Arms Control and Disarmament Agency.

United Nations Institute for Disarmament Research

http://www.unog.ch/UNIDIR/webpage.htm

UNIDIR is an autonomous institution within the United Nations, researching disarmament, international security, and related issues. The site includes details of the organization's background and structure, as well as its current projects.

US Army Home Page

http://www.army.mil/

Full details on the the mission, structure, and activities of the US Army.

Vietnam – Stories Since the War

http://www.pbs.org/pov/stories/

Extensive repository of personal narratives about the Vietnam War, where visitors can read or listen to excerpts of selected stories.

War, Peace, and Security Guide

http://www.cfcsc.dnd.ca/links/index.html

Canadian Forces College guide to armed forces and conflicts worldwide, as well as peace-keeping organizations and treaties.

World War Electronic Passport

http://www.mrdowling.com/706wars.html

Concise accounts of World War I and II, provided by a teacher and written in a straightforward and readable style.

World War I Document Archive

http://www.lib.byu.edu/~rdh/wwi/

Archive of primary documents from World War I, including conventions, treaties, official papers, and memorials and personal reminiscences; plus an image archive, a biographical dictionary, and links to related resources.

World War II Timeline

http://www.historyplace.com/worldwar2/timeline/ww2time.htm

Detailed chronology of World War II, as well as the major interwar events leading up to it. It is divided by year and includes links to subsidiary pages with more details of all major events.

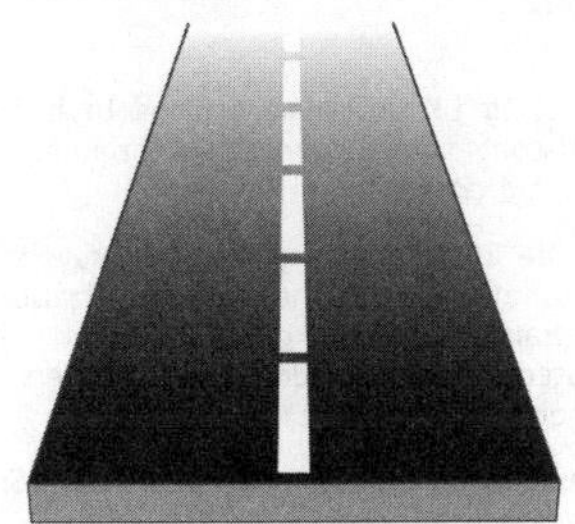

Travel, Transport, and Tourism

The Year in Review

2 July 1999 The UK High Court dismisses charges of manslaughter against Great Western Trains, whose passenger train collided with a freight train in London in 1997, killing seven people.

14 July 1999 The UK and Argentina agree that a Chilean airline may begin flights between Argentina and the Falkland Islands. There have not been commercial flights between the two since the Falklands War in 1982.

23 August 1999 The Dutch cruise ship *Norwegian Dream* collides with a 52,000-tonne cargo vessel, *Ever Decent*, 23 km/15 mi off the coast of Kent, England, injuring 21 people.

18 September 1999 UK deputy prime minister and transport minister John Prescott announces plans to reduce speed limits from 95 kph/60 mph to 80 kph/50 mph on rural roads, as well as a more widely imposed 30 kph/20 mph limit in urban areas. He also proposes to triple the number of roadside cameras used to monitor excess speed.

5 October 1999 In the UK's worst rail crash for ten years, two commuter trains crash near Paddington Station, London. The death toll stands at 26, but later rises to 31, with 150 injuries. The crash is blamed on human error; the driver went through a red warning signal (*see also* **colour section**).

21 October 1999 Paddington Station reopens with restricted services, after a two-week closure caused by the crash at Ladbroke Grove.

31 October 1999 An EgyptAir jet crashes into the Atlantic Ocean 105 km/65 mi southeast of the island of Nantucket, Massachusetts. All 217 people aboard are killed.

20 November 1999 The Jubilee Line extension of the London Underground is opened, 18 months late and at a cost of at least £3.5 billion, almost double the initial budget.

1 December 1999 UK deputy prime minister and transport minister John Prescott publishes a new transport bill that introduces several controversial changes, including the privatization of air-traffic control.

4 January 2000 Two trains collide in southern Norway, 160 km/100 mi north of Oslo, killing 33 people.

5 January 2000 Problems with the newly opened extension of the Jubilee Line of the London Underground compound visitors' difficulties in getting to the Millennium Dome at Greenwich. Signal failures lead to five-hour delays.

30 January 2000 A Kenya Airways Airbus 310 on its way to Lagos, Nigeria, crashes just after takeoff from Côte d'Ivoire, killing 169 out of 179 passengers and crew.

19 March 2000 Bill Morris, head of the Transport and General Workers Union, calls on the British public to buy Rover cars instead of BMW as a protest against BMW's intended sell-off of Rover.

9 April 2000 A survey reveals that lastminute.com is the most recognized travel brand on the Internet, overtaking British Airways. This reflects increasing public awareness of 'dot.com' companies in response to large-scale publicity campaigns.

9 May 2000 The World Wildlife Fund (WWF) produces a report into Europe's endangered species, including the lynx, brown bear, and wolves. It suggests that tourism may have a crucial role in maintaining these species, and that many business opportunities may arise as well, as companies practice sustainable development in areas with the now rare carnivores.

23 May 2000 Plans to cut the holidays of UK schoolchildren to one month are criticized by the travel industry as likely to lead to huge jams at UK airports.

24 May 2000 David Quarmby, chairman of the British Tourist Authority, is announced as the new chairman in charge of the Millennium Dome, after Bob Ayling's departure. Since its opening, the Dome has fallen short of its targets for visitors.

June 2000 UK pressure group Transport 2000 threatens to sue the police force for failing to prosecute motorists caught for speeding, claiming that this results in the deaths of hundreds of people each year in the UK through road accidents.

2 June 2000 A Web site is set up calling for a national boycott on petrol to campaign against increasing fuel prices. By 29 June it has registered over 82,000 'hits'.

15 June 2000 The European Union claims that VAT should be levied on all road tolls, affecting UK government plans to institute anti-congestion charges for bringing cars into big cities.

19 June 2000 The UK government says it will press ahead with the part-privatization of air-traffic control, despite recent chaos caused by the breakdown of computers with obsolete components.

21 June 2000 UK culture secretary Chris Smith opens the National Cycle Network, a 5,000-mile network through the UK. Only 2% of journeys taken in the UK are by bicycle, as opposed to 11% in Germany and 18% in Denmark.

23 June 2000 The Palace Backpackers Hostel in Childers, Queensland, Australia goes up in flames, causing the death of 15 people, including six Britons and an Irishwoman. The cause is later established as arson.

26 June 2000 French air-traffic controllers call a one-day strike to protest against possible European Union plans for privatization, causing disruption of air traffic throughout Europe.

26 June 2000 UK home secretary Jack Straw announces that British people who commit sex offences while abroad will have their names put on the national register of sex offenders. This move is part of a wider crackdown on 'sex tourism'.

25 July 2000 113 people are killed when an Air France Concorde aeroplane crashes just after taking off from Charles de Gaulle airport in Paris. A burst tyre is later confirmed to have caused the disaster.

Aviation

Airlines and Airports

International and domestic air travel has grown steadily worldwide since 1950 and more rapidly since 1980. In June 2000 the International Air Transport Association (IATA) predicted that air traffic would grow at a rate of nearly 6% in 2000, and over 5% in both 2001 and 2002. UK airlines flew almost 1.4 billion aircraft kilometres in 1999, over 5% more than in 1998. The number of passengers they carried rose from 93 million in 1998 to almost 98 million in 1999.

Until it was split up in 1992, the world's largest airline was the former USSR's state-owned Aeroflot, which operated 1,300 aircraft over 1 million km/620,000 mi of routes. It once carried over 110 million passengers a year, falling to 62 million by 1992. British Airways is now the world's largest international airline: it carried 30.3 million international passengers in 1999, more than 3 million more than its closest rival, Lufthansa.

The UK has more than 150 licensed civil airports. Seven of these – Heathrow, Gatwick, and Stansted (all serving London), Southampton, Edinburgh, Glasgow, and Aberdeen – are managed by the British Airports Authority (BAA), the world's largest commercial operator of airports (established in 1965).

Heathrow is the world's busiest airport for international travellers: it handled almost 55 million international passengers in 1999 – almost 16 million more than the world's second busiest, Paris Charles de Gaulle. In March 2000 the government announced that a decision about a proposed fifth terminal at Heathrow would not be made until after the next general election. The proposals for the terminal, originally put forward in 1995, were the subject of a four-year public enquiry that ended in March 1999; it was the longest public inquiry in British planning history. Gatwick is also one of the world's busiest airports in terms of international passenger traffic, and it has the busiest single runway in the world. The second runway at Manchester Airport, due for completion in 2000, is the first full-length runway to be built in the UK for 20 years.

The increase in the number of flights offered by 'no frills' budget airlines in recent years has contributed to the rapid growth of Stansted airport. It is now one of Europe's fastest growing airports, with year-on-year growth of more than 30%, and it handled more than 10 million passengers in the year 1999–2000. Over £200 million is being invested by BAA to increase the capacity of Stansted to 15 million passengers a year.

Top 5 Airlines by Number of Passengers

Rankings are for passengers carried on scheduled services.

1998 Rank	International		Domestic		Total	
	Airline	**Number of passengers**	**Airline**	**Number of passengers**	**Airline**	**Number of passengers**
1	British Airways	30,315,000	Delta Air Lines	98,298,000	Delta Air Lines	105,534,000
2	Lufthansa	27,287,000	United Airlines	75,675,000	United Airlines	87,049,000
3	Air France	20,743,000	American Airlines	64,055,000	American Airlines	81,452,000
4	American Airlines	17,397,000	US Airways	53,912,000	US Airways	57,478,000
5	KLM	15,322,000	Northwest Airlines	47,708,000	Northwest Airlines	55,812,000

Source: World Air Transport Statistics 2000, *IATA*

Top 30 UK International Airline Routes

1999

Rank	Route	Passengers carried
1	Heathrow to New York (JFK)	2,655,557
2	Heathrow to Amsterdam	2,247,239
3	Heathrow to Dublin	2,131,307
4	Heathrow to Paris (Charles de Gaulle)	1,883,927
5	Heathrow to Frankfurt am Main	1,584,111
6	Heathrow to Los Angeles International	1,406,493
7	Heathrow to Chicago (O'Hare)	1,264,794
8	Stansted to Dublin	1,125,537
9	Heathrow to Brussels	1,080,766
10	Heathrow to Rome (Fiumicino)	1,059,102
11	Heathrow to San Francisco	1,052,152
12	Heathrow to Washington (Dulles)	1,050,656
13	Heathrow to Toronto	1,024,567
14	Heathrow to Tokyo (Narita)	976,631
15	Heathrow to Zürich	943,676
16	Heathrow to Hong Kong	917,970
17	Heathrow to Madrid	907,556
18	Gatwick to Orlando	892,020
19	Heathrow to Singapore	882,154
20	Manchester to Tenerife (Surrei)	858,373
21	Heathrow to Johannesburg	856,568
22	Heathrow to Copenhagen	853,272
23	Gatwick to Malaga	844,765
24	Heathrow to Stockholm (Arla)	832,109
25	Manchester to Palma de Mallorca	814,084
26	Heathrow to Munich	792,052
27	Heathrow to Geneva	784,211
28	Heathrow to New York (Newark)	765,384
29	Gatwick to Palma de Mallorca	755,615
30	Gatwick to Tenerife (Surrei)	715,065

Source: UK Airports: Annual Statements of Movements, Passengers and Cargo 1999, *Civil Aviation Authority*

Charter Airline Punctuality League Table at UK Airports

The comparative punctuality of airlines is based on an analysis of statistics collected at the following airports: Birmingham, Edinburgh, Gatwick, Glasgow, Heathrow, Luton, Manchester, Newcastle, and Stansted. Airlines included are those that operated a total of at least 100 flights on 10 or more routes in the period April–October 1999. The charter airlines are ranked according to the percentage of flights that were more than one hour late during the summer of 1999.

April–October 1999

Rank	Airline	Average delay (minutes)	% more than one hour late
1	Britannia Airways	29	14.0
2	Futura Airlines	30	14.7
3	Eurocypria Airlines Ltd	33	15.4
4	Monarch Airlines	33	15.5
5	Caledonian Airways	35	15.7
6	Virgin Sun	30	15.8
7	British Airways	36	16.3
8	Air 2000	33	16.4
9	Virgin Express	37	16.8
10	Sabre Airways Ltd	41	17.7
11	Flying Colours Airlines	31	18.2
12	British World Airlines Ltd	56	22.6
13	TransAer	46	24.0
14	Iberworld	39	24.1
15	European Air Charter	51	24.8
16	Airtours International	57	28.2
17	British Midland	51	29.2
18	Air Foyle	66	30.7
19	Spanair	57	31.3
20	Air Europa	68	32.4
Total chartered		37	18.1

Source: Air Transport Users Council

Total Fleet for Major UK Airlines

This table shows the number of aircraft in service at the end of each year. (– = not applicable; N/A = not available.)

Fleet	1990	1992	1994	1996	1998
British Airways	233	225	227	212	229
British Airways (Euro Ops)[1]	40	12	16	28	34
Airtours International Airways Ltd	–	8	14	18	21
Britannia Airways	32	33	29	28	28
British World Airline[2]	17	19	21	17	11
British Midland	29	31	34	34	37
KLM UK[3]	25	28	36	41	41
Loganair	17	22	14	13	11
Monarch	17	21	18	24	17
Virgin Atlantic	6	8	13	15	25
Total[4]	690	718	695	722	837

[1] Dan Air Services until taken over by British Airways in November 1992.
[2] This was British Air Ferries until 1993.
[3] This was Air UK until taken over by KLM in 1997.
[4] Prior to 1994 the total includes Bond and Bristow Helicopters.

Source: Transport Statistics Great Britain 1999, © *Crown copyright 1999*

Punctuality of Flights at UK Airports

Figures are percentages of flights on time (within 15 minutes) for all reporting airports, including London and regional airports.

Year	Scheduled flights	Charter flights
1990	70	45
1991	73	46
1992	76	48
1993	81	53
1994	81	50
1995	79	53
1996	77	52
1997	74	51
1998	72	53
1999	71	52

Source: Transport Statistics Great Britain 1999, © *Crown copyright 1999; with Helicon updates*

Top 10 Busiest Airports by Passenger Traffic

The figures are for airports participating in the Airports Council International (ACI) monthly airport traffic statistics collection.

1999

Rank	Airport	Number of passengers (millions)[1 2]
1	Atlanta	77.94
2	Chicago O'Hare	72.57
3	Los Angeles International	63.88
4	London Heathrow	62.26
5	Dallas Fort Worth	60.00
6	Tokyo Honeda	54.34
7	Frankfurt	45.86
8	Paris Charles de Gaulle	43.60
9	San Francisco	40.39
10	Denver	38.03

[1] Results are preliminary (as of March 2000).
[2] This includes arriving and departing passengers (direct transit passengers counted once).

Source: Airports Council International (ACI), World Headquarters, Geneva, Switzerland, www.airports.org

The Busiest Airports in the World

Preliminary results released in March 2000 from almost 600 airports worldwide indicated that in 1999 passenger traffic went up 5%, cargo grew 6%, and aircraft movements were 4% higher than in 1998. Atlanta consolidated its position as the world's busiest airport, handling 77.9 million passengers, but international passenger traffic, in terms of four European airports continued to dominate: London Heathrow, Paris Charles de Gaulle, Frankfurt, and Amsterdam.

Top 5 Airports for Overall Passenger Satisfaction

In a survey of customer satisfaction at 57 major international airports conducted by the International Air Transport Association (IATA), over 60,000 international passengers were asked to rate their origin and destination airport on 24 service elements including speed of baggage delivery, availability of baggage carts, courtesy/friendliness of airport staff, comfortable waiting areas, and ease of finding one's way through the airport.

1999 Rank	Airport
International leisure passengers	
1	Copenhagen
2=	Helsinki
	Singapore
4	Vancouver
5	Manchester
International business passengers	
1	Singapore
2	Copenhagen
3	Vancouver
4	Helsinki
5	Kuala Lumpur
All passengers	
1	Copenhagen
2	Singapore
3	Helsinki
4	Vancouver
5	Manchester

Source: IATA Global Airport Monitor 2000, *IATA*

Top 10 Busiest Airports by Cargo Volume

The figures are for airports participating in the Airports Council International (ACI) monthly airport traffic statistics collection.

1999 Rank	Airport	Cargo (thousand tonnes)[1]
1	Memphis	2,412.9
2	Hong Kong	2,000.5
3	Los Angeles International	1,969.1
4	Tokyo Narita	1,841.6
5	New York Kennedy	1,728.2
6	Anchorage	1,657.6[2]
7	Seoul	1,655.3
8	Miami	1,651.1
9	Frankfurt	1,539.0
10	Singapore	1,531.8

[1] This includes both loaded and unloaded freight and mail.
[2] This includes transit freight.

Source: Airports Council International (ACI), World Headquarters, Geneva, Switzerland, www.airports.org

Top 10 Busiest Airports by International Passenger Traffic

1999 Rank	Airport	Number of international passengers (millions)
1	London Heathrow	54.80
2	Paris Charles de Gaulle	38.89
3	Frankfurt	37.10
4	Amsterdam	36.30
5	Hong Kong	28.40
6	London Gatwick	27.60
7	Singapore	24.50
8	Tokyo Narita	22.50
9	Bangkok	18.85
10	New York Kennedy	18.11

Source: Airports Council International (ACI), World Headquarters, Geneva, Switzerland, www.airports.org

Top 20 Busiest UK Airports

1999 Rank (by passengers)	Airport	Terminal[1] passengers (thousands)	% change from 1994	Cargo volume (thousand tonnes)	Take-offs and landings (thousands)
1	Heathrow	61,979	20.7	1,265.5	451.5
2	Gatwick	30,410	44.5	294.3	246.8
3	Manchester	17,419	21.5	108.0	169.9
4	Stansted	9,411	189.0	175.5	135.7
5	Birmingham	6,936	45.0	29.2	98.7
6	Glasgow	6,759	23.9	9.0	88.4
7	Luton	5,251	191.1	26.8	55.1
8	Edinburgh	5,090	69.8	18.2	84.8
9	Belfast International	3,012	47.7	26.0	44.8
10	Newcastle	2,934	21.4	0.8	43.6
11	Aberdeen	2,456	13.5	4.6	82.9
12	East Midlands	2,217	37.3	128.6	42.7
13	Bristol	1,966	54.1	0.1	35.0
14	Leeds/Bradford	1,451	78.7	0.3	26.2
15	London City	1,386	190.0	0.5	42.2
16=	Liverpool	1,303	196.1	25.1	27.1
	Cardiff	1,303	30.7	0.4	17.7
18	Belfast City	1,282	4.4	0.8	33.2
19	Southampton	752	58.3	0.7	25.4
20	Teesside	730	96.8	2.8	13.2

[1] Terminal refers to both embarking and disembarking passengers.

Source: UK Airports: Annual Statements of Movements, Passengers and Cargo, 1999, *Civil Aviation Authority*

International Aircraft Registration Prefixes

Most civil aircraft carry one or two letters or a number and a letter to identify their nationality. This nationality mark is painted on both sides of the fuselage or tail. It is also displayed on the underside of the wing. Numbers or letters following the nationality mark on a plane are the registration mark issued to that particular plane in its own country. Each country that belongs to the International Civil Aviation Organization (ICAO) reports its nationality mark to the organization.

Country	ICAO mark
Afghanistan	YA
Albania	ZA
Algeria	7T
Andorra	C3
Angola	D2
Antigua and Barbuda	V2
Argentina	LQ, LV
Armenia	EK
Australia	VH
Austria	OE
Azerbaijan	4K
Bahamas	C6
Bahrain	A9C
Bangladesh	S2, S3
Barbados	8P
Belarus	EW
Belgium	OO
Belize	V3
Benin	TY
Bhutan	A5
Bolivia	CP
Bosnia-Herzegovina	T9
Botswana	A2
Brazil	PP, PT
Brunei	V8
Bulgaria	LZ
Burkina Faso	XT
Burundi	9U
Cambodia	XU
Cameroon	TJ
Canada	C, CF
Cape Verde	D4
Central African Republic	TL
Chad	TT
Chile	CC
China	B
Colombia	HK
Comoros	D6
Congo, Democratic Republic of	9Q, 9T
Congo, Republic of the	TN
Costa Rica	TI
Côte d'Ivoire	TU
Croatia	9A
Cuba	CU
Cyprus	5B
Czech Republic	OK
Denmark	OY
Djibouti	J2
Dominica	J7
Dominican Republic	HI
Ecuador	HC
Egypt	SU
El Salvador	YS
Equatorial Guinea	3C
Eritrea	E3
Estonia	ES
Ethiopia	ET
Fiji Islands	DQ
Finland	OH
France	F
Gabon	TR
Gambia	C5
Georgia	4L
Germany	D
Ghana	9G
Greece	SX
Grenada	J3
Guatemala	TG
Guinea	3X
Guinea-Bissau	J5
Guyana	8R
Haiti	HH
Honduras	HR
Hungary	HA
Iceland	TF
India	VT
Indonsia	PK
Iran	EP
Iraq	YI
Ireland, Republic of	EI
Israel	4X
Italy	I
Jamaica	6Y
Japan	JA
Jordan	JY
Kazakhstan	UN
Kenya	5Y
Kiribati	T3
Korea, North	P
Korea, South	HL
Kuwait	9K
Kyrgyzstan	EX
Laos	RDPL
Latvia	YL
Lebanon	OD
Lesotho	7P
Liberia	EL
Libya	5A
Liechtenstein	HB
Lithuania	LY
Luxembourg	LX
Macedonia, Former Yugoslav Republic of	Z3
Madagascar	5R
Malawi	7Q
Malaysia	9M
Maldives	8Q
Mali	TZ
Malta	9H
Marshall Islands	V7
Mauritania	5T
Mauritius	3B
Mexico	XA, XB, XC
Micronesia, Federated States of	V6
Moldova	ER
Monaco	3A
Mongolia	BNMAU, MONGOL, MT
Morocco	CN
Mozambique	C9
Myanmar	XY, XZ
Namibia	V5
Nauru	C2
Nepal	9N
Netherlands	PH
New Zealand	ZK, ZL, ZM
Nicaragua	YN
Niger	5U
Nigeria	5N
Norway	LN
Oman	A40
Pakistan	AP
Panama	HP
Papua New Guinea	P2
Paraguay	ZP
Peru	OB
Philippines	RP
Poland	SP
Portugal	CS
Qatar	A7
Romania	YR
Russian Federation	RA
Rwanda	9XR
St Kitts and Nevis	V4
St Lucia	J6
St Vincent and the Grenadines	J8
Samoa	5W
San Marino	T7
São Tomé and Príncipe	S9
Saudi Arabia	HZ
Senegal	6W
Seychelles	S7
Sierra Leone	9L
Singapore	9V
Slovak Republic	OM
Slovenia	S5
Solomon Islands	H4
Somalia	6O
South Africa	ZS, ZT, ZU
Spain	EC
Sri Lanka	4R
Sudan	ST
Suriname	PZ
Swaziland	3D
Sweden	SE
Switzerland	HB
Syria	YK
Taiwan	B
Tajikistan	EY
Tanzania	5H
Thailand	HS
Togo	5V
Tonga	A3
Tunisia	TS
Turkey	TC
Turkmenistan	EZ
Tuvalu	T2
Uganda	5X
UK	G
Ukraine	UR
United Arab Emirates	A6
United Nations	4N
Uruguay	CX
USA	N
Uzbekistan	UK
Vanuatu	YJ
Vatican City State	HV
Venezuela	YV
Vietnam	VN
Yemen	7O
Yugoslavia	YU
Zambia	9J
Zimbabwe	Z

Source: International Civil Aviation Organization, used by permission

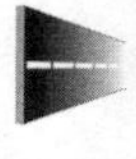

Air Distances Between Major World Cities

(In miles.)

City	Bangkok	Beijing	Berlin	Cairo	Cape Town	Caracas	Chicago	Hong Kong	London	Los Angeles	Madrid	Melbourne	Mexico City	Montreal	Moscow	New York	Paris	Rio de Janeiro	Rome	San Francisco	Singapore	Stockholm	Tokyo	Washington, DC
Bangkok		2,046	5,352	4,523	6,300	10,555	8,570	1,077	5,944	7,637	6,337	4,568	9,793	8,338	4,389	8,669	5,877	9,994	5,494	7,931	883	5,089	2,865	8,807
Beijing	2,046		4,584	4,698	8,044	8,950	6,604	1,217	5,074	6,250	5,745	5,643	7,753	6,519	3,607	6,844	5,120	10,768	5,063	5,918	2,771	4,133	1,307	6,942
Berlin	5,352	4,584		1,797	5,961	5,238	4,414	5,443	583	5,782	1,165	9,918	6,056	3,740	1,006	3,979	548	6,209	737	5,672	6,164	528	5,557	4,181
Cairo	4,523	4,698	1,797		4,480	6,342	6,141	5,066	2,185	7,520	2,087	8,675	7,700	5,427	1,803	5,619	1,998	6,143	1,326	7,466	5,137	2,096	5,958	5,822
Cape Town	6,300	8,044	5,961	4,480		6,366	8,491	7,376	5,989	9,969	5,308	6,425	8,519	7,922	6,279	7,803	5,786	3,781	5,231	10,248	6,008	6,423	9,154	7,895
Caracas	10,555	8,950	5,238	6,342	6,366		2,495	10,165	4,655	3,632	4,346	9,717	2,234	2,438	6,177	2,120	4,732	2,804	5,195	3,902	11,402	5,471	8,808	2,047
Chicago	8,570	6,604	4,414	6,141	8,491	2,495		7,797	3,958	1,745	4,189	9,673	1,690	745	4,987	714	4,143	5,282	4,824	1,859	9,372	4,331	6,314	596
Hong Kong	1,077	1,217	5,443	5,066	7,376	10,165	7,797		5,990	7,240	6,558	4,595	8,788	7,736	4,437	8,060	5,990	11,009	5,774	6,905	1,605	5,063	1,791	8,155
London	5,944	5,074	583	2,185	5,989	4,655	3,958	5,990		5,439	785	10,500	5,558	3,254	1,564	3,469	214	5,750	895	5,367	6,747	942	5,959	3,674
Los Angeles	7,637	6,250	5,782	7,520	9,969	3,632	1,745	7,240	5,439		5,848	7,931	1,542	2,427	6,068	2,451	5,601	6,330	6,326	347	8,767	5,454	5,470	2,300
Madrid	6,337	5,745	1,165	2,087	5,308	4,346	4,189	6,558	785	5,848		10,758	5,643	3,448	2,147	3,593	655	5,045	851	5,803	7,080	1,653	6,706	3,792
Melbourne	4,568	5,643	9,918	8,675	6,425	9,717	9,673	4,595	10,500	7,931	10,758		8,426	10,395	8,950	10,359	10,430	8,226	9,929	7,856	3,759	9,630	5,062	10,180
Mexico City	9,793	7,753	6,056	7,700	8,519	2,234	1,690	8,788	5,558	1,542	5,643	8,426		2,317	6,676	2,090	5,725	4,764	6,377	1,887	10,327	6,012	7,035	1,885
Montreal	8,338	6,519	3,740	5,427	7,922	2,438	745	7,736	3,254	2,427	3,448	10,395	2,317		4,401	331	3,432	5,078	4,104	2,543	9,203	3,714	6,471	489
Moscow	4,389	3,607	1,006	1,803	6,279	6,177	4,987	4,437	1,564	6,068	2,147	8,950	6,676	4,401		4,683	1,554	7,170	1,483	5,885	5,228	716	4,660	4,876
New York	8,669	6,844	3,979	5,619	7,803	2,120	714	8,060	3,469	2,451	3,593	10,359	2,090	331	4,683		3,636	4,801	4,293	2,572	9,534	3,986	6,757	205
Paris	5,877	5,120	548	1,998	5,786	4,732	4,143	5,990	214	5,601	655	10,430	5,725	3,432	1,554	3,636		5,684	690	5,577	6,673	1,003	6,053	3,840
Rio de Janeiro	9,994	10,768	6,209	6,143	3,781	2,804	5,282	11,009	5,750	6,330	5,045	8,226	4,764	5,078	7,170	4,801	5,684		5,707	6,613	9,785	6,683	11,532	4,779
Rome	5,494	5,063	737	1,326	5,231	5,195	4,824	5,774	895	6,326	851	9,929	6,377	4,104	1,483	4,293	690	5,707		6,259	6,229	1,245	6,142	4,497
San Francisco	7,931	5,918	5,672	7,466	10,248	3,902	1,859	6,905	5,367	347	5,803	7,856	1,887	2,543	5,885	2,572	5,577	6,613	6,259		8,448	5,399	5,150	2,441
Singapore	883	2,771	6,164	5,137	6,008	11,402	9,372	1,605	6,747	8,767	7,080	3,759	10,327	9,203	5,228	9,534	6,673	9,785	6,229	8,448		5,936	3,300	9,662
Stockholm	5,089	4,133	528	2,096	6,423	5,471	4,331	5,063	942	5,454	1,653	9,630	6,012	3,714	716	3,986	1,003	6,683	1,245	5,399	5,936		5,053	4,183
Tokyo	2,865	1,307	5,557	5,958	9,154	8,808	6,314	1,791	5,959	5,470	6,706	5,062	7,035	6,471	4,660	6,757	6,053	11,532	6,142	5,150	3,300	5,053		6,791
Washington, DC	8,807	6,942	4,181	5,822	7,895	2,047	596	8,155	3,674	2,300	3,792	10,180	1,885	489	4,876	205	3,840	4,779	4,497	2,441	9,662	4,183	6,791	

Air Safety

Flying is still one of the safest ways to travel (*see also* **Death Rates by Mode of Transport in Britain,** p 591), but as air traffic continues to increase, concerns are growing about the ability of air traffic control systems to cope. Air safety in the UK is regulated by the Civil Aviation Authority's (CAA) Safety Regulation Group which works closely with the Joint Aviation Authorities (JAA), a European grouping of aviation safety regulation authorities. It also collaborates with the International Civil Aviation Organization (ICAO), which was established in 1947 to ensure that international safety standards are agreed and applied.

1999 was one of the safest years since 1970 in terms of the number of fatalities resulting from civil aviation accidents. The ICAO reported 20 aircraft accidents involving passenger fatalities in scheduled air services worldwide in 1999. The number of fatalities was 492 compared to 905 from 20 accidents in 1998, and the rate of fatalities per 100 million passenger kilometres decreased from approximately 0.03 in 1998 to 0.02 in 1999. There were 24 accidents involving non-scheduled services in 1999, compared with 25 accidents in 1998. These accidents involved 142 fatalities, compared with 210 in 1998.

Recent World Aircraft Disasters

Only disasters in which ten or more persons have died are listed.
As of July 2000.

Date	Aircraft	Location	Details	Survivors	Fatalities
27 January 1998	F27, Myanmar Airways	Thandwe, Myanmar	caught fire during take-off	31	14
2 February 1998	DC-9-32, Cebu Pacific Air	near Claveria, Philippines	crashed into a mountain	none	104
16 February 1998	Airbus A300-600R, China Airlines	Taipei International Airport, Taiwan	crashed in thick fog during attempt to land	none	205[1]
18 March 1998	Saab 340B, Formosa Airlines	at sea near Hsinchu, Taiwan	crashed into the sea in turbulent weather conditions	none	13
19 March 1998	727-200, Ariana Afghan Airlines	Charasyab, Afghanistan	crashed into the Sharki Baratayi mountain	none	45
20 April 1998	727-200, Air France	Bogota, Colombia	crashed into a mountain shortly after take-off	none	53
30 July 1998	Beech 1900/Cessna, Proteus Air	Lorient, France	mid-air collision	none	15
24 August 1998	Fokker F27, Myanmar Airways	Manibagi, Myanmar	crashed in bad weather	none	39
29 August 1998	Tupolov 154M, Cubana	Quito, Ecuador	crashed shortly after take-off	21	78[1]
2 September 1998	MD11, Swissair	Halifax, Canada	crashed at night into the Atlantic Ocean	none	229
25 September 1998	BAe 146-100, Paukn Air	Melilla, Spain	crashed into a mountainous area	none	38
11 December 1998	A310-200, Thai Airways International	Surat Thani, Thailand	crashed on landing	50	96
24 February 1999	Tupolev 154, China Southwest Airlines	Ruian, China	exploded in mid-air	none	61
1 June 1999	MD80, America Airlines	Little Rock (AR), USA	crashed on landing in bad weather	134	11
16 June 1999	Airlink Bandeirante	Goroka, Papua New Guinea	crashed into high ground	none	17
24 July 1999	Air Fiji Bandeirante	near Suva, Fiji	crashed into a mountain	none	17
August 1999	Cabo Verde Airlines Dornier 228-200	Santo Antao Island, Cape Verde	crashed into high ground in bad weather	none	18
31 August 1999	LAPA 737-200	Buenos Aires, Argentina	overran the runway on take-off, hit two cars, and caught fire	38	67[2]
31 October 1999	Egypt Air 767-300ER	Atlantic Ocean near Nantucket Island, MA, USA	radar and radio contact with aircraft lost shortly after aircraft departed New York Kennedy Airport; aircraft last sighted about 96 km/60 mi southeast of Nantucket Island	none	217
9 November 1999	TAESA DC9-31	Uruapan, Mexico	exploded shortly after take-off	none	18
11 December 1999	SATA ATP	Azores, Portugal	crashed on Sao Jorge island	none	35
21 December 1999	Cubana DC10-30	Guatemala City, Guatemala	aircraft overran wet runway and came to rest in a residential neighbourhood near the airport	297	26[3]
24 December 1999	Cubana Yak42	near Valencia, Venezuela	aircraft struck high ground on approach to Valencia	none	22
10 January 2000	Crossair Saab 340	near Zurich, Switzerland	crashed shortly after take-off	none	10
30 January 2000	Kenya Airways A310-300	near Abidjan, Ivory Coast	aircraft crashed into Atlantic Ocean shortly after take-off	9	170
31 January 2000	Alaska Airlines MD83	near Pt Mugu (CA), USA	crashed into Pacific ocean	none	88
19 April 2000	Air Philippines 737-200	near Davao, Philippines	crashed on Samal Island during second approach to Davao's airport	none	131
8 July 2000	Aerocaribe BAe Jetstream 32	Villaharmosa, Mexico	crashed in bad weather about 30 minutes after take-off	none	19
17 July 2000	Alliance Air 737-200	near Patna, India	during second approach to Patna airport, crashed into a residential area about 2 km/1.25 mi from the airport	7	51[4]
25 July 2000	Air France Concorde	near Paris, France	aircraft caught fire on take-off from Charles de Gaulle airport, Paris, and crashed into a hotel near the airport	none	113[5]

[1] Figure includes nine on the ground. [2] Figure includes two of the occupants of the cars. [3] Figure includes nine people in the neighbourhood.
[4] Figure includes five people on the ground. [5] Figure includes four people on the ground.

The 10 Worst Aircraft Disasters in Aviation History

Fatalities	Date	Airline(s)	Aircraft	Location
582	27 March 1977	Pan American and KLM (Royal Dutch Airlines)	Two Boeing 747s	Tenerife, Canary Islands
520	12 August 1985	Japan Airlines	Boeing 747	Mount Ogura, Japan
349	12 November 1996	Saudi Arabian Air and Kazakhstan Airlines	Boeing 747 and Ilyushin 76TD	Charki Dadri, India
346	3 March 1974	Turkish Air	DC10	northeast of Paris
329	23 June 1985	Air India	Boeing 747	Republic of Ireland coast, Atlantic Ocean
301	19 August 1980	Saudi Arabian Air	Lockheed L-1011	Riyadh, Saudi Arabia
290	3 July 1988	Iran Air	A300 Airbus	Persian Gulf
275	25 May 1979	American Airlines	DC10	Chicago (IL), USA
270	21 December 1988	Pan American	Boeing 747	Lockerbie, Scotland
269	1 September 1983	Korean Airlines	Boeing 747	near Sakhalin Island, Okhokst Sea

Source: National Transportation Safety Board, US Department of Transportation

Recent International Airline Terrorism

Not every hijacking or bombing can be categorized as a terrorist act. This table excludes hijackings and bombings carried out for ransom or other personal motives rather than for political reasons.

Date	Terrorist act	Airline	Flight	Description
1 March 1988	bombing	BOP Air	Phadabawa–Johannesburg, South Africa	aircraft destroyed in flight; 17 killed
21 December 1988	bombing	Pan American, flight 103	London, UK–New York, USA	aircraft destroyed in flight over Lockerbie, UK; 270 killed
19 September 1989	bombing	Union des Transport	Brazzaville, Congo–Ndjamena, Chad–Paris, France	aircraft destroyed in flight; 171 killed
27 November 1989	bombing	Avianca	Bogotá–Cali, Colombia	aircraft destroyed in flight; 107 killed
18 March 1991	bombing	Aeroflot	Moscow–Novokuznetsk, Russia	incendiary device; aircraft landed safely
19 July 1994	bombing	Alas Airline	Colon City–Panama City, Panama	explosion in flight; aircraft crashed over the Santa Rita mountains; 21 killed
3 November 1994	hijacking	Scandinavian Airlines	Bardfoss–Oslo, Norway	80 passengers held hostage; hijacker demanded peace corridor in Bosnia and later surrendered
11 December 1994	bombing	Philippines Airlines 747	Manila, Philippines–Tokyo, Japan	explosion in flight; 1 killed, 10 injured; aircraft landed safely; Abu Sayyaf Group (ASG) responsible
24 December 1994	hijacking; bombing	Air France Airbus 400	Algiers, Algeria–Marseille, France	Algerian hijackers demanded that 2 leaders of Islamic Salvation Front be released; in Marseille police stormed the aircraft and killed all terrorists; dynamite discovered in cabin; 3 hostages had been killed by the terrorists
23 November 1996	hijacking	Ethiopian Airlines	Ethiopia–Kenya	aircraft ran out of fuel on redirected route and crashed near a beach on the Comoros Islands; 125 killed, including the hijackers
24 December 1999	hijacking	Indian Airlines Airbus	Katmandu, Nepal–New Delhi, India	five armed militants hijacked the aircraft carrying 189 passengers and 11 crew; after refuelling in Pakistan, the aircraft diverted via Dubai, United Arab Emirates, to Qandahar, Afghanistan; one hostage was killed and the remaining hostages were released on 31 December 1999, after the Indian government agreed to release three militants imprisoned in India

The Safest Airlines?

Statistics comparing the relative safety of airlines in terms of the number incidents they have had involving passenger fatalities, do not necessarily indicate that one airline is safer than another. An important indicator of safety is how an airline is regulated by its nation's civil aviation authority. Also important are the safety standards adhered to by the nation's airports and air traffic control systems.

Among the best safety records in terms of the number of incidents involving passenger fatalities (since 1970) is that of the US airline Southwest Airlines, which has not had an incident involving passenger fatalities in an estimated 9.5 million flights since 1970. Scandinavian Airlines System (SAS) has not had such an incident in an estimated 5.4 million flights; Finnair, has not had a fatal event in 1.7 million flights; and Qantas has not had an incident involving passenger fatalities in an estimated 1.02 million flights since 1970.

British Airways has had 2 fatal events in an estimated 6.35 million flights since 1970, giving it a rate of 0.32 fatal events per million flights; Air France has had 7 fatal events in 5.9 million flights since 1970, giving it a rate of 1.19.

Some airlines, however, have comparatively high rates: for example, Air Cubana has had 8 fatal events in an estimated 0.33 million flights since 1970, giving it a rate of 24 fatal events per million flights; Aero Peru has had 2 fatal events in 0.12 million flights, giving it a rate of 16.7; and Air Zimbabwe has had 2 fatal events in 0.16 million flights, giving it a rate of 12.5 fatal events per million flights.

Aviation

Worldwide Airline Fatalities

Data are for scheduled air transport operations.

Year	Fatal accidents	Passenger deaths	Death rate[1]
1990	25	495	0.03
1991	30	653	0.04
1992	29	1,097	0.06
1993	35	940	0.05
1994	28	941	0.04
1995	26	710	0.03
1996	23	1,135	0.05
1997	27	930	0.04
1998	20	905	0.03
1999	20	492	0.02

[1] Rate per 100 million passenger kilometres flown.

Source: Data from the International Civil Aviation Organization

Air Traffic Control in the UK

Air traffic control in the UK is undertaken by the National Air Traffic Services (NATS), a public body that employs around 5,200 people and has an annual turnover of over £500 million. With air traffic typically increasing more than 5% a year, and forecasters predicting a rise of 43% by 2010, NATS estimates that it needs investment of £1.3 billion over the next decade if it is to cope. In 1998 the Labour government announced plans to raise some of this revenue from a partial privatization of NATS. Under a 'private-public partnership' scheme, the government proposes to keep 49% of NATS in the public sector, with 5% going to staff, and 46% to the private sector.

Opponents of the controversial scheme, including the British Airlines Pilots Association, have warned that a private company would be likely to increase charges to customers and attempt to cut costs in a way that would jeopardize safety. In February 2000 a cross-party parliamentary committee also criticized the proposals, reporting that safety standards would be likely to suffer and that charges to airlines and airports would probably increase. In June 2000 the government rejected an offer by a consortium of airlines (including British Airways and Virgin Airlines) to take over NATS as a non-profit-making venture.

Air traffic operations in the UK are currently handled at three control centres: RAF West Drayton; Manchester Airport; and Prestwick, Scotland. It is planned that all air traffic operations will eventually be concentrated at two sites: air traffic over England and Wales will be handled at a new air traffic control centre at Swanwick, near Southampton; and air traffic over Northern Ireland and Scotland will be handled at a new centre in Prestwick which will replace the existing centre in 2005–06. In July 2000 it was announced that the new control centre at Swanwick was due to begin operating on 27 January 2002, six years later than originally estimated. The centre will have cost around £620 million, almost twice as much as predicted.

Airprox Incidents in the UK

An airprox is a situation in which the distance between aircraft, their relative positions, and speed have compromised or may have compromised the safety of the aircraft involved. The UK airprox board (UKAB), an organization formed in January 1999, publishes reports on air proximity incidents in UK airspace. The board analyses incidents that are reported by aircraft pilots and air traffic control officers and assesses them for their level of risk. It assigns one of four risk categories to each incident.

Category A incidents are those in which an actual risk of collision existed

Category B incidents are those in which the safety of the aircraft was compromised

Category C incidents are those in which there was no risk of collision

Category D incidents are those in which insufficient information was available to determine the risk involved, or inconclusive or conflicting evidence precluded such determination

In May 2000 the Air Accident Investigation Branch, which is normally called upon only to investigate crashes, began an inquiry into an incident in April 2000 in which two British passenger planes were said to have come within 30 m/100 ft of collision at Heathrow airport. It was reported that an incoming Boeing 747 was cleared to land by air traffic control at the same time and on the same runway as a British Midland plane had been cleared for take-off. Reports suggested that the landing was aborted when air traffic controllers instructed the pilot to take evasive action. The incident added to concerns felt by those campaigning against the government's plan partly to privatize air traffic control services.

Airprox Incidents in the UK: Monthly Averages

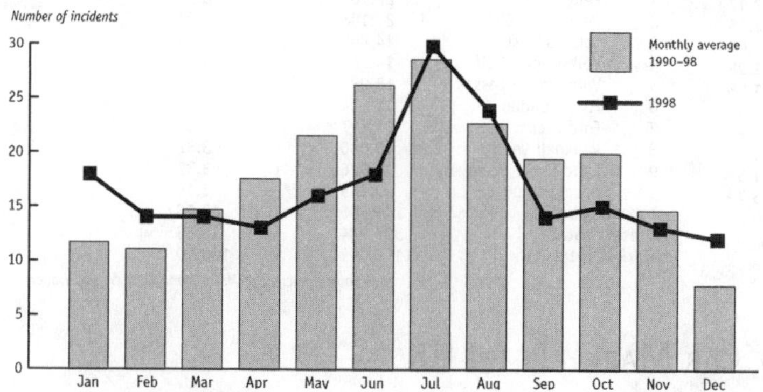

Source: United Kingdom Airprox Board, © CAA/MOD 2000

Airprox Incidents in UK Air Space

Figures are for commercial air transport (CAT) incidents only. Rates given are the number of airprox incidents per 100,000 hours flown.

	1990	1991	1992	1993	1994	1995	1996	1997	1998
Hours flown (thousands)	893	874	946	968	1,004	1,061	1,114	1,179	1,249
Rate for (A + B)	2.69	2.29	1.69	2.07	2.49	2.26	2.87	2.37	1.20
Rate for (A + B + C)	11.42	9.95	9.83	7.85	8.17	8.86	9.61	8.23	8.33
Risk A	6	1	5	3	5	3	7	9	1
Risk B	18	19	11	17	20	21	25	19	14
Risk C	78	67	77	56	57	70	75	69	89

Source: United Kingdom Airprox Board, © CAA/MOD 2000

Hijacked Aircraft at Stansted

On 6 February 2000, an Afghan Ariana Airlines Boeing 727 on an internal flight from Kabul to Mazar-e-Sharif in Afghanistan was hijacked and diverted to Tashkent, Uzbekistan. It then flew to Moscow, where nine passengers were released, and on to Stansted Airport where it landed at 2.01 a.m. on 7 February. The incident was brought to an end with the release of all hostages and the surrender of the hijackers, who had not made political demands. Over 70 of the passengers returned to Afghanistan and a number of others sought political asylum in the UK. It was the longest hijack in UK history, lasting a total of five days (of which the aircraft was at Stansted for four days). (*See also* **Asylum Seekers in the UK**, p 103.)

Stansted, now Britain's fourth busiest airport, is the designated London destination for hijacked aircraft. The February 2000 incident was the third major hijack situation at Stansted since 1982.

Road Transport

Cars and Motoring

UK Buyers' Favourite New Cars

In 1999 Ford held on to its 1998 position at the top of the new car registration figures – the Focus and the Fiesta taking 9.24% of the market with sales of 103,228 and 99,830 respectively. Mercedes C Class and E Class cars retained their first and second positions at the top of the sales league for automatics, while Peugeot held first and second places in the top 10 diesels list, in spite of the fact that the Peugeot 306 was more than 10,000 sales down from its 1998 total. Overall, the Vauxhall Astra was front runner for the title of 'most popular car in the UK', standing third in the top 20 registrations, fifth in the top 10 automatics, and third in the top 10 diesels.

Top 20 New Car Registrations in the UK

1999

Rank	Model range	Registrations	Market share (%)
1	Ford Focus	103,228	4.70
2	Ford Fiesta	99,830	4.54
3	Vauxhall Astra	92,050	4.19
4	Vauxhall Corsa	86,779	3.95
5	Vauxhall Vectra	77,479	3.53
6	Ford Mondeo	77,183	3.51
7	Renault Megane	65,127	2.96
8	Renault Clio	63,991	2.91
9	Volkswagen Golf	63,715	2.90
10	Peugeot 206	58,788	2.68
11	Peugeot 306	53,447	2.43
12	Nissan Micra	47,775	2.17
13	BMW 3 Series	47,265	2.15
14	Rover 200	45,728	2.08
15	Citroën Saxo	43,557	1.98
16	Volkswagen Polo	43,422	1.98
17	Ford Ka	42,607	1.94
18	Peugeot 406	42,242	1.92
19	Fiat Punto	38,597	1.76
20	Rover 400	33,343	1.52
Top 20 total		1,226,153	55.79
Market total		2,197,615	100.00

Source: Society of Motor Manufacturers and Traders Ltd

The Model T: Top Car of the 20th Century?

Henry Ford's Model T was the first car to be constructed solely by assembly-line methods and to be mass marketed. Some 15 million Model Ts were built between 1908 and 1927 and it has since been dubbed the 'car that put the world on wheels'. Production peaked in 1923 when more than 2 million Model Ts were built in factories worldwide. No car has ever broken or is ever likely to beat its record 50.4% share of world car production (set in 1918) and its record 56.5% share of world car registrations (set in 1921).

In 1927 a four-door, 2.8-litre Ford Model T cost £120 on the road. It had a top speed of 42 mph and would go from 0 to 40 mph in 35.8 seconds.

Top 10 Automatic Cars in the UK

1999

Rank	Model range	Sales	Market share (%)
1	Mercedes C Class	12,960	4.32
2	Mercedes E Class	12,519	4.18
3	BMW 3 Series	10,484	3.50
4	BMW 5 Series	9,513	3.17
5	Vauxhall Astra	9,053	3.02
6	Vauxhall Omega	7,932	2.65
7	Jaguar S Range	7,458	2.49
8	Honda Civic	7,269	2.42
9	Ford Mondeo	7,064	2.36
10	Honda Accord	7,032	2.35
Top 10 total		91,284	30.45
Automatics total		299,817	13.64
Market total		2,197,615	100.00

Source: Society of Motor Manufacturers and Traders Ltd

Top 10 Diesel Cars in the UK

1999

Rank	Model range	Sales	Market share (%)
1	Peugeot 306	27,101	8.92
2	Peugeot 406	21,188	6.97
3	Vauxhall Astra	14,869	4.89
4	Volkswagen Golf	14,666	4.83
5	Volkswagen Passat	13,036	4.29
6	Ford Mondeo	12,314	4.05
7	Ford Focus	11,717	3.86
8	Vauxhall Vectra	10,080	3.32
9	Land Rover Discovery	10,076	3.32
10	Peugeot 206	9,559	3.15
Top 10 total		144,606	47.58
Diesels total		303,924	13.83
Market total		2,197,615	100.00

Source: Society of Motor Manufacturers and Traders Ltd

The Car Market in the UK

by Tracey Kifford

The British Car – Then and Now In 1885 the German engineers Gottlieb Daimler and Karl Benz built the first petrol-engine motor car. It bore little resemblance to the vehicles of today until, in 1891, French inventor René Panhard put the engine at the front of the car, encased under a car bonnet and set on a wooden chassis. English car manufacturer Frederick Lanchester developed epicyclic gearing (the forerunner of automatic transmission) in 1896, and within ten years Britain's car industry had developed so fast that Rolls-Royce was considered one of the world's premier car marques. The UK car industry took off after World War I as Morris, Austin, Clyno, and Swift all began to mass-produce cheap cars for a wider market, while at the luxury end of the market were Rolls-Royce, Rover, Daimler, Jaguar, Bentley, Aston Martin, and Lotus. Similar advances were taking place in Europe and the USA, with a further explosion in demand after World War II. The zenith of the UK car industry came in 1959 when the British Motor Company (BMC) launched the Mini (designed by Alec Issigonis), with front-wheel drive, rubber suspension, and a transverse engine. Refined and upgraded, it was manufactured for years, and thousands are still on the road. However, the 1970s, a time of general industrial

The Car Market in the UK *(continued)*

unrest across the UK, hit the car industry hardest of all; while the industry imploded with strikes, the closure of works, and corporate mergers shrinking the manufacturing base, Japanese cars began to arrive in the UK. The Nissan Motor Company and Honda opened assembly plants in Washington, Dagenham, and Swindon, while UK production went overseas as UK marques were bought by European companies. The change has been considerable. Forty years ago 'foreign cars' were rarely seen outside London but now, while Ford, Rover, Jaguar, Rolls-Royce, and Vauxhall are still on the road, Audi, Volkswagen (VW), Nissan, Toyota, Mazda, Renault, Peugeot, Fiat, and, increasingly, Hyundai, Daewoo, Kia, and Proton all have significant shares of the UK market. In the first few months of the 21st century, UK car manufacturing experienced further setbacks fuelled by the strength of the pound against the euro and general over-capacity in European production (a 20 million construction capability compared to 15 million sales). In May 2000 the Phoenix rescue consortium saved Rover production at Longbridge (following its threatened closure by former owners BMW in March) and Ford announced substantial job losses at its Dagenham plant; the manufacture of Nissan's new Micra at Sunderland is also under question.

Car Buying in the UK As the car market has changed so, too, has the way that cars are bought. When cars first appeared they were ordered direct from the manufacturers, but soon dealers sprang up to handle sales and repairs. As the mass market grew, UK car buyers continued to buy from local dealerships. Computerized shipping systems meant that popular makes and models could be supplied within a few days, while the more unusual cars, or models packed with special features, could take longer to deliver. The advantages of buying through dealerships include the bargains that can be struck with eager sales staff, and the trade-in potential of an old car. In addition, dealers can offer one-stop shopping, with finance and insurance provided on the spot (not necessarily at the best prices). The growth of the variety of finance packages available has encouraged sales – a plethora of lease- hire schemes, and schemes involving options to buy the car outright or sell it back to the dealer, have been introduced, to join the more traditional hire purchase (HP) or cash methods of buying.

New Ways of Selling However, a growing realization that consumers were demanding lower prices led to further changes. The first step was to try to cut dealer commissions, but the next obvious step was to try to sell direct to the motorist. Daewoo premiered a form of this approach when they began selling in the UK; rather than develop a dealer network, the company sold cars via the Halfords chain, reducing commission prices and infrastructure costs. The next step came when car companies sold direct to consumers via the Internet; Japanese manufacturers, such as Nissan, have been selling cars via the Internet for some years. In the UK, Vauxhall has adopted the Japanese model, allowing vehicles to be bought online direct from the company, with finance and part-exchange deals as part of the package.

Getting the Buyer a Better Deal Over the past decade, more new cars have been imported, because buying abroad can save as much as £6,000, depending on the model, the country of purchase, and the exchange rates. Imported cars must meet UK specifications, but provided the vehicle matches such specifications, and dealers who have previously exported to the UK know what these are, there is no trouble ensuring this. Following a European Commission study published in 1998 showing that car prices in the UK were higher than elsewhere in Europe, a government inquiry was launched. The Competition Commission reported in April 2000 that car manufacturers should allow individual buyers to benefit from the same level of discount as that offered to bulk purchasers, such as fleet buyers. The government announced in June 2000 measures to ensure that this happens. However, it will be up to consumers and dealers to report unfair trading practices.

Number of Motor Vehicles Registered in the UK for the First Time

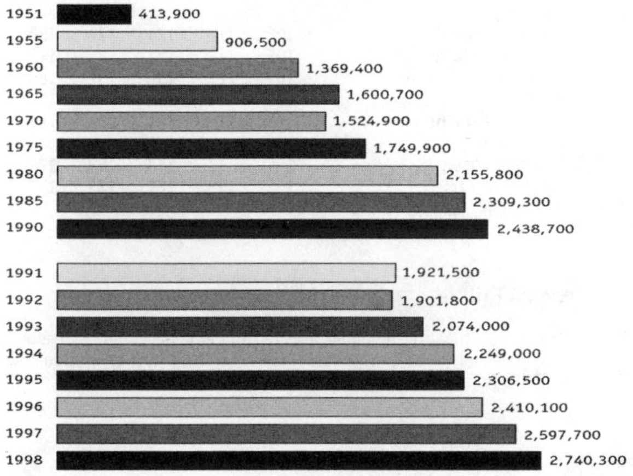

Source: Transport Statistics Great Britain 1999, © *Crown copyright 1999*

Car Ownership in Britain

- Between 1961 and 1998 the proportion of households in Britain with at least one car rose from 29% to 72%.
- The proportion of households with two or more cars grew from 2% to 28% over the same period.
- The number of private cars licensed in Britain rose from under 2 million in 1950 to over 22 million in 1998.

See also **Motor Vehicle Production in the UK**, p 688.

Motor Vehicles Registered in the UK for the First Time

(In thousands.)

1998	
Vehicle type	**Registrations**
Private and light goods	2,367.9
Goods vehicles	49.1
Motor cycles, etc	143.3
Public transport vehicles	7.4
Special machines and special concessionary	15.2
Other vehicles	157.0
Total	2,740.3

Source: Transport Statistics Great Britain 1999, © *Crown copyright 1999*

Households with Regular Use of a Car in Britain

(N = nil or negligible. In percentages.)

Number of cars in household	1961	1971	1981	1991	1998
No car	69	48	40	32	28
One car	29	44	45	45	44
Two cars	2	7	13	19	23
Three or more cars	N	1	2	4	5

Source: Transport Statistics Great Britain 1999, © *Crown copyright 1999*

Increase in the Number of Cars in Selected Countries

Countries are ranked by greatest percentage increase in vehicles between 1970–97.
(In thousands.)

Country	1970	1980	1990	1997	Increase 1970–97 (%)
Poland	479	2,383	5,261	8,533	1,681.4
Mexico	1,234	4,255	6,819	8,998	629.2
Czech Republic	685	1,779	2,411	3,392	395.2
Iceland	41	86	120	132	222.0
Austria	1,197	2,247	2,991	3,783	216.0
Italy	10,209	17,686	27,416	31,055	204.2
Germany	13,941	23,192	30,685	41,372	196.8
Ireland	394	734	796	1,134	187.8
Finland	712	1,226	1,939	1,948	173.6
Norway	694	1,234	1,613	1,758	153.3
Netherlands	2,405	4,240	5,196	5,810	141.6
Switzerland	1,380	2,247	3,012	3,323	140.8
Australia	3,835	5,801	7,672	8,908	132.3
UK	11,802	15,438	22,528	25,697	117.7
Canada	6,602	10,256	12,622	14,057	112.9
France	12,470	19,130	23,550	25,900	107.7
New Zealand	866	1,307	1,542	1,700	96.3
USA	103,454	149,477	181,975	202,323	95.6
Denmark	1,077	1,390	1,590	1,760	63.4
Sweden	2,288	2,883	3,601	3,703	61.8

Source: OECD Environmental Data 1999, © *OECD 1999*

Traffic in Britain

Road traffic in Britain reached all-time peak levels at the end of 1999, with motor vehicle traffic 1.8% higher than in 1998. The highest levels of traffic per head of population were in the south-east and east of England – levels in these regions were 30% higher and 25% higher respectively than the British average per head of population for 1998. The amount of traffic on motorways has grown more rapidly than on other roads: it more than quadrupled between 1975 and 1998 and was an estimated 4% higher in 1999 than in 1998. Estimates from the Commission for Integrated Transport suggest that the amount of traffic on many roads, especially in rural areas, will double by 2025. Congestion is set to increase by 65% overall and by 268% on motorways over the next 10 years.

In July 2000 the government announced plans to spend £180 billion of government and private sector money over the next ten years on reducing congestion and improving public transport: £59 billion would be spent on the roads, including some 100 new bypasses and the widening of motorways; £60 billion would be allocated to the railways; and £26 billion would be spent on local transport schemes.

John Prescott UK deputy Prime Minister and Secretary of State for the Environment, Transport, and the Regions, who in September 1999 announced plans for speed limit restrictions on certain roads across the UK. *Syndication International*

Road Traffic Forecasts for Great Britain

Traffic in Britain is forecast to grow to the levels indicated (1998 = 100).

Vehicle forecasts	2001	2006	2011	2016	2021	2026	2031
Road traffic and vehicles							
Cars and taxis	105	114	123	131	138	143	148
Goods vehicles[1]	105	113	121	131	143	154	167
Light goods vehicles	109	122	136	152	169	188	206
Buses and coaches	102	106	109	114	119	124	131
All motor traffic	105	115	124	133	141	148	154
Car ownership							
Cars per person	105	111	118	123	129	133	137
Number of cars	106	113	121	127	133	137	140

[1] Over 3.5 tonnes gross vehicle weight.

Source: Transport Statistics Great Britain 1999, © *Crown copyright 1999*

Signal Failure

The world's first traffic signal, erected in Parliament Square, London, in 1868, exploded and killed the police officer operating it. The first vehicle-activated traffic signals introduced in the UK in 1932 also exploded.

Road Transport

Principal Motorways in the UK

For roads consisting of motorway and other types of road, the length is given for the motorway part only.

Motorway	Destinations	Length
M1	London–Leeds	304 km/189 mi
M11	London–Cambridge	98 km/61 mi
M18	Rotherham–Goole	56 km/35 mi
M180	Doncaster–Grimsby	82 km/51 mi
M2	Gravesend–Faversham	53 km/33 mi
M20	London–Folkestone	117 km/73 mi
M23	London–Crawley	45 km/28 mi
M25	London orbital	188 km/117 mi
M27	Cadnam–Portsmouth	55 km/34 mi
M3	London–Southampton	129 km/80 mi
M4	London–Llanelli	325 km/202 mi
M40	London–Birmingham	193 km/120 mi
M42	Bromsgrove–Ashby-de-la-Zouch	79 km/49 mi
M5	Birmingham–Exeter	266 km/165 mi
M53	Wallasey–Chester	39 km/24 mi
M54	Wolverhampton–Telford	37 km/23 mi
M55	Preston–Blackpool	29 km/18 mi
M56	Manchester–Chester	39 km/24 mi
M6	Rugby–Carlisle	209 km/130 mi
M61	Manchester–Preston	50 km/31 mi
M62	Liverpool–Kingston Upon Hull	206 km/128 mi
M63	Salford–Stockport	32 km/20 mi
M65	Bamber Bridge–Colne	45 km/28 mi
M66	Ramsbottom–Stockport	35 km/22 mi
M74	Glasgow–Abington	129 km/80 mi
M8	Edinburgh–Greenock	109 km/68 mi
M9	Edinburgh–Dunblane	64 km/40 mi
M90	Rosyth–Perth	48 km/30 mi
A1(M)	London–Newcastle	230 km/143 mi
A74(M)	Gretna–Abington	59 km/37 mi
Northern Ireland		
M1	Belfast–Dungannon	66 km/41 mi
M2	Belfast–Ballymena	42 km/26 mi

Total Road Lengths in the UK

(In kilometres.)

Road type	Length				
	1990	**1992**	**1994**	**1996**	**1998**
Trunk roads	15,666	15,358	15,203	15,540	15,533
Class 1 or principal	35,226	35,712	35,867	35,901	36,002
Class 2 or B	29,838	30,227	30,347	30,196	30,278
Class 3 or C	80,716	81,334	82,105	82,528	83,152
Unclassified	196,588	199,679	201,445	204,656	206,635
Total roads	358,034	362,310	364,966	368,821	371,603
Of which					
trunk motorway	2,993	3,063	3,092	3,181	3,258
principal motorway	77	71	76	45	45
Total motorway	3,070	3,133	3,168	3,226	3,303

Source: Transport Statistics Great Britain 1999, © *Crown copyright 1999*

The First Motorways

The world's first motorway (85 km/53 mi) ran from Milan to Varese, Italy, and was completed in 1924; by 1939 some 500 km/300 mi of motorway had been built, although these did not attain the standards of later express highways. In Germany some 2,100 km/1,310 mi of Autobahnen had been completed by 1942.

The first motorway in the UK, the Preston by-pass (now part of the M6) was opened in 1958, and the first section of the M1 was opened in 1959.

Motor Vehicle Nationality Abbreviations

Many road vehicles display one or more letters to identify their nationality. These letters are in accordance with the 1968 United Nations (UN) Convention on Road Traffic and the 1949 UN Convention on Road Traffic.

Country	Abbreviation
Aden	ADN
Albania	AL
Alderney	GBA
Algeria	DZ
Andorra	AND
Argentina	RA
Australia	AUS
Austria	A
Bahamas	BS
Bahrain	BRN
Bangladesh	BD
Barbados	BDS
Belarus	BY
Belgium	B
Belize	BH
Benin	DY
Bosnia-Herzegovina	BIH
Botswana	RB
Brazil	BR
Brunei	BRU
Bulgaria	BG
Cambodia	K
Canada	CDN
Central African Republic	RCA
Chile	RCH
China	RC
Congo, Democratic Republic of	ZRE
Congo, Republic of the	RCB
Costa Rica	CR
Côte d'Ivoire	CI
Croatia	HR
Cyprus	CY
Czech Republic	CZ
Denmark	DK
Dominican Republic	DOM
Ecuador	EC
Egypt	ET
Estonia	EST
Faroe Islands	FO
Fiji Islands	FJI
Finland	FIN
France	F
Gambia	WAG
Georgia	GE
Germany	D
Ghana	GH
Gibraltar	GBZ
Greece	GR
Grenada	WG
Guatemala	GCA
Guernsey	GBG
Guyana	GUY
Haiti	RH
Hong Kong	HK
Hungary	H
Iceland	IS
India	IND
Indonesia	RI
Iran	IR
Ireland, Republic of	IRL
Isle of Man	GBM
Israel	IL
Italy	I
Jamaica	JA
Japan	J
Jersey	GBJ
Jordan	HKJ
Kazakhstan	KZ
Kenya	EAK
Korea, South	ROK
Kuwait	KWT
Kyrgyzstan	KS
Laos	LAO
Latvia	LV
Lebanon	RL
Lesotho	LS
Lithuania	LT
Luxembourg	L
Macedonia, Former Yugoslav Republic of	MK
Malawi	MW
Malaysia	MAL
Mali	RMM
Malta	M
Mauritius	MS
Mexico	MEX
Monaco	MC
Morocco	MA
Myanmar	BUR
Namibia	NAM
Netherlands	NL
Netherlands Antilles	NA
New Zealand	NZ
Nicaragua	NIC
Niger	RN
Nigeria	WAN
Norway	N

(continued)

Motor Vehicle Nationality Abbreviations *(continued)*

Country	Abbreviation	Country	Abbreviation	Country	Abbreviation
Pakistan	PAK	Singapore	SGP	Tunisia	TN
Papua New Guinea	PNG	Slovak Republic	SK	Turkey	TR
Paraguay	PY	Slovenia	SLO	Turkmenistan	TM
Peru	PE	South Africa	ZA	Uganda	EAU
Philippines	RP	Spain (including African localities and provinces)	E	UK and Northern Ireland	GB
Poland	PL			Ukraine	UA
Portugal	P	Sri Lanka	CL	Uruguay	ROU
Romania	RO	Suriname	SME	USA	USA
Russian Federation	RUS	Swaziland	SD	Uzbekistan	UZ
Rwanda	RWA	Sweden	S	Vatican City State	V
St Lucia	WL	Switzerland	CH	Venezuela	YV
St Vincent	WV	Syria	SYR	Yugoslavia	YU
Samoa	WS	Tajikistan	TJ	Zambia	RNR
San Marino	RSM	Tanzania	EAT	Zanzibar	EAZ
Senegal	SN	Thailand	T	Zimbabwe	ZW
Seychelles	SY	Togo	TG		
Sierra Leone	WAL	Trinidad and Tobago	TT		

Places that Drive on the Left

Anguilla
Antigua
Australia
Bahamas
Bangladesh
Barbados
Bermuda
Bhutan
Botswana
Brunei
Cook Islands
Cyprus
Dominica
Falkland Islands
Fiji Islands
Grenada
Guyana
Hong Kong
India
Indonesia
Ireland, Republic of
Jamaica
Japan
Kenya
Kiribati
Lesotho
Malawi
Malaysia
Malta
Mauritius
Montserrat
Mozambique
Namibia
Nepal
New Zealand
Norfolk Island
Pakistan
Papua New Guinea
St Kitts and Nevis
St Lucia
St Vincent and the Grenadines
Seychelles
Singapore
Solomon Islands
Somalia
South Africa
Sri Lanka
Suriname
Swaziland
Tanzania
Thailand
Tonga
Trinidad and Tobago
Tuvalu
Uganda
UK (including Guernsey, Jersey, and the Isle of Man)
Virgin Islands (British)
Zambia
Zimbabwe

Road Safety

Between 1990 and 1997, arguably as a result of positive policy changes, there was a significant decrease in road traffic deaths in most countries within the Organization for Economic Cooperation and Development (OECD). Exceptions were Portugal, Greece, the Czech Republic, and the Republic of Ireland.

An assortment of legally enforceable measures, including speed restrictions, traffic calming, and speed cameras, have been established in the UK in order to keep road traffic accidents to a low level. However, almost 5,000 child cyclists and pedestrians are still killed or seriously injured each year on the roads of Britain. In March 2000 the government announced measures to encourage local authorities to introduce more traffic-calmed 20 mph zones, particularly around schools and in residential areas. It set targets for a 40% reduction in the number of people killed or seriously injured in road accidents by 2010. However, it made no commitment to a lowering of national speed limits – a measure which some transport and road safety groups, including Transport 2000, believe would save lives. Other organizations, including the Association of British Drivers, do not accept that lower speed limits have been proven to reduce casualties significantly.

In May 2000 it was announced that UK police forces would be challenged in the High Court over the way they enforce speed limits. This legal challenge was to be brought by the pressure group Transport 2000 following the disclosure earlier in the year that police guidelines recommend that drivers breaking the 30 mph limit should not be prosecuted unless they were exceeding 35 mph.

Road Accident Death Rates for OECD Countries

Countries other than the UK are ranked by rate of road deaths (1997) per 100,000 population.
(N/A = not available.)

Country	Number of road deaths					Number of road vehicles in 1997 (thousands)	Rate of road deaths in 1997 per 100,000 population[1]
	1990	1992	1994	1996	1997		
Great Britain	5,217	4,229	3,650	3,598	3,599	26,200	6.3
Northern Ireland	185	150	157	142	144	744	8.6
Other countries							
Portugal	3,017	3,084	2,504	2,730	N/A	5,169	28.9
Greece	1,998	2,103	2,195	2,063	2,199	3,858	20.9
USA	44,529	39,235	40,716	41,907	41,967	211,579	15.7
Czech Republic	1,307	1,545	1,637	1,568	1,587	4,933	15.5
France	11,215	9,900	9,019	8,541	8,444	N/A	14.4
New Zealand	729	646	580	514	540	N/A	14.4
Luxembourg	70	73	74	N/A	60	263	14.3
Spain	9,032	7,818	5,615	5,483	5,640	19,880	14.3
Hungary	2,532	2,101	1,562	1,370	1,391	2,769	13.7
Austria	1,558	1,403	1,338	1,027	1,105	4,669	13.7
Belgium	1,976	1,672	1,692	1,356	1,364	5,091	13.4
Ireland, Republic of	478	415	404	453	472	1,240	12.8
Italy	7,151	8,029	7,104	6,688	6,724	38,646	11.7
Germany	11,046	10,631	9,814	8,758	8,549	46,488	10.4
Canada	3,960	3,501	3,260	3,082	3,064	N/A	10.2
Australia	2,331	1,981	1,937	1,973	1,767	N/A	9.5
Denmark	634	577	546	514	489	2,090	9.3
Japan	14,595	14,886	12,768	11,674	11,254	84,067	8.9
Finland	649	601	480	404	438	2,390	8.5
Switzerland	925	834	679	616	587	4,331	8.3
Netherlands	1,376	1,285	1,298	1,180	1,163	7,309	7.5
Norway	332	325	283	255	303	2,387	6.9
Sweden	772	759	589	537	541	4,284	6.1
Iceland	24	21	12	10	15	N/A	5.5

[1] Population taken from the Organization of Economic Cooperation and Development's (OECD's) International Road and Traffic Accidents Database.

Source: Transport Statistics Great Britain 1999, *© Crown copyright 1999*

Number of Road Accident Deaths in the UK

Road user type	1988	1998
Pedestrians		
children	282	103
adults	1,454	803
Total pedestrians	1,736	906
Cyclists		
children	62	32
adults	165	126
Total cyclists	227	158
Motorcyclists[1] and passengers	670	498
Car drivers and passengers	2,142	1,696
Bus/coach drivers and passengers	17	18
LGV and HGV drivers and passengers	219	127
TOTAL	5,011	3,403
All road users[2]	5,052	3,421

[1] These figures include mopeds and scooters.
[2] These figures include other motor or non-motor road users, and unknown vehicle type and casualty age.

Source: Transport Statistics Great Britain 1999, *© Crown copyright 1999*

Death Rates by Mode of Transport in Britain

Rates given are per billion passenger kilometres.
(N = nil or negligible.)

Mode	1981	1986	1991	1996	1997	Average 1988–97
Motorcycle	115.8	100.3	94.4	92.7	108.8	89.9
Walk	76.9	75.3	62.5	54.3	54.2	68.2
Pedal cycle	56.9	49.6	46.8	47.2	44.6	46.0
Car	6.1	5.1	3.7	3.1	3.1	3.6
Water[1]	0.4	0.5	N	0.8	0.4	2.6[2]
Van	3.8	3.8	2.2	1.1	1.2	1.9
Rail	1.0	0.9	0.8	0.4	0.5	0.7
Bus or coach	0.3	0.5	0.6	0.2	0.3	0.4
Air[1]	0.2	0.5	N	N	N	0.1

[1] Data are for United Kingdom.
[2] This includes the rate for 1989 when 51 people were killed when the dredger *The Bowbelle* collided with the pleasure cruiser *The Marchioness* on the River Thames, London.

Source: Social Trends 30, *© Crown copyright 2000*

Road Accidents in the UK by Road Class

Road class	Severity	1988	1998
Motorways/A (M) roads	fatal	216	157
	fatal and serious	1,285	1,148
	All severities	5,648	8,861
	rate[1]	11	11
Built-up roads			
A roads	fatal	1,267	629
	fatal and serious	17,733	10,466
	All severities	82,756	74,825
	rate[1]	112	94
Other roads	fatal	1,094	709
	fatal and serious	21,776	13,782
	All severities	101,626	98,844
	rate[1]	110	81
Non built-up roads			
A roads	fatal	1,480	1,159
	fatal and serious	11,106	7,735
	All severities	35,105	34,982
	rate[1]	35	26
Other roads	fatal	585	483
	fatal and serious	6,588	4,639
	All severities	21,838	21,411
	rate[1]	44	44
All roads	fatal	4,643	3,137
	fatal and serious	58,493	37,770
	All severities	246,994	238,923
	rate[1]	68	52

[1] Rate per 100 million vehicle kilometres.

Source: Transport Statistics Great Britain 1999, *© Crown copyright 1999*

Drink Driving and Breath Tests in Britain

The legal alcohol limits in the UK are as follows: 35 microgrammes of alcohol in 100 millilitres of breath, 80 milligrammes of alcohol in 100 millilitres of blood, and 107 milligrammes of alcohol in 100 millilitres of urine. Figures include cases in which a test focus refused or could not be provided. (N/A = not available.)

Incidents and breath tests		1994	1995	1996	1997	1998
Car drivers involved in injury accidents in Great Britain	number involved	322,946	318,083	331,091	338,924	337,794
	% of drivers involved tested	28	31	40	46	51
	% positive	7	7	5	5	4
Motorcycle riders in injury accidents in Great Britain	number involved	25,127	24,219	23,798	25,211	25,514
	% of drivers involved tested	21	24	33	39	45
	% positive	9	8	5	4	4
Screening breath tests administered in England and Wales	number of tests required	679,000	703,000	781,000	800,000	815,000
	% positive	14	13	13	13	12

Source: Transport Statistics Great Britain 1999, © *Crown copyright 1999*

Seat Belt Laws in the UK

(– = not applicable.)

Vehicle occupants	Front seat	Rear seat	Who is responsible
Driver	seat belt must be worn if available	–	driver
Children aged under 3 years	appropriate child restraint[1] must be used	appropriate child restraint[1] must be used if available	driver
Children aged 3–11 years, and under 1.5 m (approximately 5 ft) in height	appropriate child restraint[1] must be worn if available; if not, adult seat belt must be used	appropriate child restraint[1] must be worn if available; if not, adult seat belt must be worn if available	driver
Children aged 12 or 13 or younger children 1.5 m (approximately 5 ft) or more in height	adult seat belt must be worn if available	adult seat belt must be worn if available	driver
Adult passengers	seat belt must be worn if available	seat belt must be worn if available	passenger

[1] An appropriate child restraint is a baby carrier, child seat harness, or booster seat suitable for the weight of the child using it.

Speeding Facts

- Estimates suggest that 85% of pedestrians hit at 40 mph will die, 45% will die if hit at 30 mph, and 5% will die if hit at 20 mph.
- Results of a speed survey conducted in 1998 by the Department of the Environment, Transport, and the Regions, indicated that:
- The majority of cars on motorways break the speed limit – 55% of those surveyed were exceeding 70 mph, and 19% were travelling in excess of 80 mph.
- Less than 10% of HGVs keep to the speed limit on dual carriageways.
- On single carriageways, 28% of articulated HGVs exceed the speed limit, and over a quarter of them travel at over 50 mph. Almost half of articulated HGVs break the limit on 30 mph roads.
- More than two thirds of cars and light goods vehicles break the speed limit on 30 mph roads.
- 63% of motorcycles exceed the speed limit on 30 mph roads and more than a third break the limit on 40 mph roads.

Source: Vehicle Speeds in Great Britain 1998, © *Crown copyright 1999*

Vehicle Speeds on Non-Urban Roads in Britain

1998 Vehicle	Speed limit (mph)	Average speed (mph)	% over limit	% more than 10 mph over limit
Motorways				
Cars	70	69	55	19
Light goods	70	66	40	9
Buses/coaches	70	60	3	0
Articulated HGVs	60	55	7	0
Dual carriageways				
Cars	70	70	54	14
Light goods	70	66	38	7
Buses/coaches	60	59	49	3
Articulated HGVs	50	55	91	6
Single carriageways				
Cars	60	46	10	2
Light goods	60	46	8	1
Buses/coaches	50	42	19	2
Articulated HGVs	40	45	72	26

Source: Vehicle Speeds in Great Britain 1998, © *Crown copyright 1999*

Vehicle Speeds on Urban Roads in Britain

1998 Vehicle	Average speed	% over 30 mph	% over 35 mph
30 mph speed limit roads			
Motorcycles	32	63	40
Cars	32	69	33
Light goods	32	67	31
Buses/coaches	28	41	13
Articulated HGVs[1]	29	47	14
40 mph speed limit roads		**% over 40 mph**	**% over 45 mph**
Motorcycles	36	35	19
Cars	36	26	8
Light goods	35	22	6
Buses/coaches	31	7	1
Articulated HGVs[1]	32	7	1

[1] Three-axle.

Source: Vehicle Speeds in Great Britain 1998, © *Crown copyright 1999*

Travel and Transport Trends in the UK

Travel in the UK

On average each person in Britain makes over 1,000 journeys a year and a large proportion of these will be made by car. The motor industry, its subsidiaries, and the users of their products have been regarded by successive governments as a source of funds for the UK economy. It has, therefore, been difficult to promote public transport to motorists, most of whom are showing no signs of moving away from their own cars.

In November 1999 a report by the Commission for Integrated Transport advised that setting a traffic reduction target for the whole country would be too generalized and that phased benchmark targets might be more easily attainable. So far the UK government has not acted on this advice but, in any event, the public does not appear ready or willing to change its habits. In the years 1996 to 1998 the number of miles travelled by car per person, per year, was more than one and a half times greater than in the years 1975 to 1976. In recent times, in terms of public transport, only taxis or minicabs and the London Underground have enjoyed a rise in passenger numbers. Shared car occupancy, even by those commuting to the same workplace every day, has not grown in popularity, and public transport as the chosen alternative to private motoring has yet to gain ground. (*See also* **Traffic in Britain**, p 588.)

Average Number of Journeys Made per Person per Year in the UK

This table includes journeys under one mile.

1996–98	
Purpose	**Number of journeys**
Shopping	222
Visiting friends	187
Commuting	166
Education and escorting to education	119
Other personal business	105
Social/entertainment/holidays/day trips	91
Other escort	82
Other, including just walking	44
Business	37
Total	1,051

Source: Transport Statistics Great Britain 1999, © *Crown copyright 1999*

Household Expenditure on Transport in the UK

Overall household expenditure on transport has been rising in real terms, particularly for motoring costs and air travel, while expenditure on bus and coach fares has fallen. The cost of travel has roughly kept pace with inflation since 1981, though price increases outstripped inflation for rail, bus, and coach fares, and vehicle tax, insurance, and maintenance.
(In pounds per week at 1995 prices).

Expenditure	**1971**	**1981**	**1991**	**1998**
Motoring costs				
Motor vehicles and spares	4.25	4.78	6.18	8.16
Petrol and engine oil	2.46	3.26	4.30	3.89
Repairs and insurance	1.28	1.92	2.42	2.78
Vehicle tax	0.45	0.57	0.86	0.94
Other	0.38	0.83	2.28	2.36
Total motoring costs	8.82	11.22	16.03	18.13
Fares and other travel costs				
Air	0.27	0.82	1.28	2.26
Rail and tram fares	0.89	0.86	0.94	1.01
Bus and coach fares	1.82	1.27	1.04	0.97
Other	0.52	0.60	1.01	1.20
Total fares and other travel costs	2.69	3.31	4.17	5.43
Total expenditure on transport	11.52	14.55	20.19	23.55

Source: Social Trends 30, © *Crown copyright 2000*

Travel in Britain – Some Key Facts

- Residents of Britain each made an average of 1,051 journeys in 1998 – almost 3 a day.
- On average each person in Britain travelled 10,828 km/6,728 mi in 1998 – about 29 km/18 mi a day.
- Travel by car, van, and taxi rose from 536 to 616 billion passenger kilometres between 1985 and 1998, an increase of almost 15%.
- Travel by car in 1998 accounted for almost 79% of the total distance travelled in Britain and the average distance travelled by car was 39% more than in the mid-1980s.
- Residents of Britain walked an average of 310 km/193 mi in 1998 – about 3% of the average distance travelled. 80% of journeys under 1 mile were taken on foot but 62% of journeys between 1 and 2 miles were taken by car.

Data from National Travel Survey, Transport Statistics Bulletin 1999

Time Spent Travelling in Britain

- Residents of Britain each spent an average of 357 hours – just over two weeks – travelling within Britain in 1998. About 51% of this time, or approximately 9 days, was spent travelling by car.
- Whilst average journey lengths increased by 23% between 1985 and 1998, from 8.4 km/5.2 mi to 10.3 km/6.4 mi, the average journey time for all modes was 20 minutes – the same as it was 1985/86.
- On average, residents of Britain spent three days walking in 1998, or 12 minutes a day – a fall of 14% since 1986.

Data from National Travel Survey, Transport Statistics Bulletin 1999

Distance Travelled by Mode of Transport in Britain

(– = not appropriate. In miles per person per year.)

Mode of travel	1985–86	1996–98	% change[1]
Car	3,796	5,292	39
Surface rail	292	290	−1
Van/lorry	228	244	7
Local bus (excluding London)	258	197	−24
Walking (including short walks)	244	193	−21
Private hire bus	131	103	−21
Non-local bus	109	95	−13
Other public transport including air	22	57	159
Buses in London	39	52	31
London Transport Underground	44	51	17
Taxi/minicab	27	50	85
Bicycle	44	38	−13
Other private vehicle	33	35	6
Motorcycle/moped	51	30	−41
All modes total	5,317	6,728	27
% of mileage accounted for by car	76	82	–

[1]Percentage change from 1985–96.

Source: Transport Statistics Great Britain 1999, *© Crown copyright 1999*

Use of Public Transport in Britain

(In millions of passenger journeys. N/A = not available.)

Year	Local bus service	Non-local bus or coach	National rail network	London Underground	Light rail, other rail and metros[1]	Air passengers on domestic flights[2]
1950	12,734	260	1,010	695	N/A	N/A
1960	12,166	367	1,037	674	N/A	2.2
1970	8,643	467	824	672	18	5.4
1980	6,216	559	760	559	13	7.2
1990–91	4,844	619	809	775	66	13.1
1994–95	4,415	N/A	735	764	78	13.3
1998–99	4,243	N/A	892	866	100	16.8

[1] Light rail and metros comprise the Glasgow underground, Nexus (Tyne and Wear, from 1980), Docklands Light Railway (from 1988–89), Manchester Metrolink (from 1992–93), and Sheffield Supertram (from 1993–94).
[2] UK airlines, domestic passengers uplifted on scheduled and non-scheduled flights at calendar year end.

Source: Bulletin of Public Transport Statistics, *© Crown copyright 1999*

Car Users' Attitudes Towards Discouraging Car Use in Britain

In 1998 the British Social Attitudes Survey explored car users' views about measures to discourage car use. More people thought they were likely to reduce their car use because of 'gradually doubling the cost of petrol over the next ten years' or 'greatly improving the reliability of local public transport' than for other measures. This survey also found that three in ten agreed that 'many of the short journeys I make by car I could just as easily go by bus', but half disagreed.
(N = negligible. In percentages.)

1998

Measure	Might use car even more	Might use car a little less	Might use car quite a bit less	Might give up using car	No difference	All respondents[1]
Gradually doubling the cost of petrol over the next ten years	1	31	23	5	38	100
Greatly improving the reliability of local public transport	N	28	27	6	37	100
Greatly improving long distance rail and coach services	N	25	22	4	47	100
Charging all motorists around £2 each time they enter or drive through a city or town centre at peak times	0	23	21	7	45	100
Cutting in half long distance rail and coach fares	0	23	24	7	43	100
Cutting in half local public transport fares	N	21	28	6	42	100
Making parking penalties and restrictions much more severe	N	20	18	4	54	100
Charging £1 for every 50 miles motorists travel on motorways	N	18	15	6	58	100
Special cycle lanes on local roads	N	10	11	3	73	100

[1] All respondents includes 'don't know' and unanswered categories.

Source: Social Trends 30, *© Crown copyright 2000*

Travel and Transport Trends in the UK

Car Occupancy Rates in Britain

A National Travel Survey undertaken by the Department of Environment, Transport, and the Regions indicated that in 1998:

- 64% of journeys by car were made by the driver only
- the average occupancy rate per car was 1.2 on commuting trips, 1.1 on business trips, and 1.6 overall.

Data from The National Travel Survey, Transport Statistics Bulletin 1999

Bus Services in Britain

Since deregulation of the bus services in October 1986, most bus companies have been operated commercially but about 17% are subsidized, and 17 bus companies are owned by local authorities. There are five main groups operating bus services in Britain: Arriva, Go-Ahead Group, National Express, First Group, and Stagecoach. Some bus companies have been criticized for poor levels of service and for cutting or changing some of the more 'uneconomic' routes, particularly in rural areas. In 1999, rural bus services in the UK received a total of around £170 million in extra funds over three years, and in England the 'rural bus challenge' has been developed to encourage the development of improved services in rural areas.

About 10.5 million elderly people in Britain are eligible for concessionary fares on bus services, and about 97% of local authorities in England and Wales had a concessionary fare scheme for elderly people in 1999. Take up of concessionary fare schemes fell from 60% in 1989–91 to 52% in 1996–98.

Public Transport in Britain: Some Key Facts

- Between 1950 and 1999 the number of journeys that British residents made by bus fell by two thirds, from 12.7 billion journeys to 4.25 billion. However, buses still carry more passengers than all other forms of public transport put together.
- Use of the national rail network increased by 5.5% in 1998–99.
- Between 1980 and 1999 domestic air travel in Britain increased by 57%.
- Bus and coach drivers each earned an average of £286.20 a week in 1999; their earnings have remained static in real terms while the average wage for all occupations increased by 15% between 1989 and 1999 to £400.00 a week.
- Train drivers earned an average of £506.30 per week in 1999. Their earnings have increased by 27% in real terms since 1991.
- Bus and coach drivers worked an average of 48.5 hours per week including overtime, compared with 40 hours for all occupations. Train drivers worked an average of 41.3 hours a week in 1999.

Data from A Bulletin of Public Transport Statistics 1999

Time Taken to Walk to the Nearest Bus Stop in Britain

(In percentages. N = nil or negligible.)

Area	Time taken			
	6 minutes or less	7–13 minutes	14–26 minutes	27 minutes or more
London borough	89	9	1	1
Metropolitan built-up area	92	8	1	N
Large urban	90	9	1	N
Medium urban	91	7	2	N
Small urban	82	11	4	2
Rural	77	11	6	6
All areas	87	9	2	1

Source: Social Trends 30, © *Crown copyright 2000*

The National Cycle Network

In 1952 cycle traffic on public roads reached 23 billion passenger kilometres. By 1998 it had fallen to around 4 billion kilometres. The National Cycling Strategy, announced in 1996, aims to double cycle use by the year 2002 from the 1996 base of 16 bicycle journeys per person per year, and to double it again by 2012.

The transport charity Sustrans is coordinating the development of the National Cycle Network, a Millennium Commission project supported by £43.5 million of National Lottery funds. The first 5,000 miles of a linked series of traffic-free paths and traffic-calmed roads opened in June 2000, and a further 4,000 miles of the network will be open by 2005 when the network is expected to be complete.

Distance Travelled by Bicycle in Britain

(In miles per person per year.)

1998 Age range	Males	Females	All
5–10	14	9	12
11–17	119	27	74
18–29	98	13	53
30–49	86	17	50
50 and over	44	11	27
All aged 5 and over	70	14	41

Source: Social Trends 30, © *Crown copyright 2000*

Journeys to and from School in Britain

(N = nil or negligible. In percentages.)

Main mode of transport	Age 5–10		Age 11–16	
	1985–86	1996–98	1985–86	1996–98
Walk	67	55	52	43
Bicycle	1	N	6	2
Car/van	22	36	10	21
Private bus	5	3	9	7
Local bus	4	4	20	25
Rail	N	N	1	1
Other	2	2	1	2

Source: National Travel Survey, Transport Statistics Bulletin 1999, © *Crown copyright 1999*

The School Run

In urban areas in Britain, at 8.50 a.m. in term time in 1998, 18% of road traffic was generated by the school run. This proportion had increased from 14% in 1990.

In the period 1985–98:

- the proportion of primary-aged children walking to school in Great Britain fell by 12%
- the proportion of children walking to their secondary school fell by 9%
- the number of primary-aged children being taken to school by car rose by 14%
- the number of secondary-aged children travelling to school by car rose by 11%.

Data from National Travel Survey, Transport Statistics Bulletin 1999

Average Time Taken to Travel to Work by Region in Britain

Figures are for autumn 1998.

Area of workplace		Average time (minutes)
North East	Tyne and Wear	23
	rest of North East	18
	North East average	21
Yorkshire and Humberside	South Yorkshire	22
	West Yorkshire	24
	rest of Yorkshire and Humberside	20
	Yorkshire and Humberside average	22
North West and Merseyside	Greater Manchester	25
	Merseyside	22
	rest of North West	20
	North West and Merseyside average	22
East Midlands		19
West Midlands	Metropolitan County	25
	rest of West Midlands	19
	West Midlands average	22
East		21
South East		24
London	central London	55
	rest of inner London	41
	outer London	30
	London average	41
South West		20
England		25
Wales		19
Scotland	Strathclyde	23
	rest of Scotland	22
	Scotland average	23
Britain average		25

Source: Transport Statistics Great Britain 1999, © *Crown copyright 1999*

Rail Transport

Rail Transport in the UK

Following the Paddington rail crash on 5 October 1999 (when the driver of a Thames Train passed a signal set at 'danger', colliding with a Great Western London-bound express), public attention was immediately drawn to the subject of railway safety. Comparisons were made with previous rail crashes and their causes. Much of the criticism was aimed at Railtrack (owner of the track infrastructure, with responsibility for planning and coordinating the train paths and timetables), and at how it deals with complications arising from the operation of signalling systems.

The Department of the Environment, Transport, and the Regions (DETR) has been issuing monthly reports on 'Signals Passed at Danger' (SPAD incidents). The report for March 2000 recorded 52 SPAD incidents across the whole of the railway network, of which 12 were serious (Railtrack's severity category 3 to 8) – an increase on the same period in previous years. Of the 52 incidents, 25 were at signals that had previously been passed at danger, and of these, 12 signals had been passed at danger five or more times since the mid-1980s. In 14 instances the driver had passed a signal at danger on previous occasions. Nevertheless, the report concluded that the underlying trend in incidents was still downward.

Although Railtrack has asked the UK government for £20 billion for the further development of a high-speed rail infrastructure, critics say that enough money has already been spent on prestige projects such as the Ashford link in Kent. The Automobile Association (AA) claims that the public would be better served if this investment were made in road maintenance and bypass construction.

Railtrack and the Rail Network in the UK

Under the Conservative government's 1993 Railway Act the old British Rail was split up and sold off. This process was completed by November 1997, by which time British Rail had been divested of all its operating railway functions. The different functions of managing the track, the trains, services, and subsidiary aspects (such as property and policing) are now in a variety of hands.

The British Railways Board (BRB) has retained responsibility for non-operational land, and for the British Transport Police. It also advises the government on railway policy and improving accountability. Railtrack owns the track infrastructure, the stations, and access, and is the front-line provider for the freight and passenger services.

Railtrack runs 14 stations itself, the rest being leased to the 25 Train Operating Companies (TOCs). It also has responsibility for planning and coordinating the train paths and timetables.

The TOCs run the passenger services in specific regions and have to publish a Passengers' Charter to set out the minimum service standards.

The new rail network is accountable to the Office of the Rail Regulator (ORR) and the Shadow Strategic Rail Authority (SSRA). Set up in 1993, the ORR has a chief executive independent of ministerial control. Its main functions and duties are to issue the licences to operate trains, networks, and stations; the

Railtrack and the Rail Network in the UK *(continued)*

enforcement of domestic competition in rail services; consumer and passenger protection; and the promotion of the use of passenger and freight services. The SSRA monitors and manages the TOCs with a strong emphasis on protecting passengers' interests and investment in the services. The SSRA is a non-ministerial government department, and works closely with the ORR and with the BRB. The objectives of the SSRA are broadly to increase the number of rail passengers, and promote passenger services by managing the franchises of the train operators. This includes enforcing ticket pricing policy and imposing financial penalties on operators who fail to meet their passenger obligations.

UK Railways: Key Dates Since 1939

World War II The privately owned railways are taken under government control, by the Board of Trade.

1 January 1948 Under the Transport Act 1947, the main private railway companies are nationalized by Clement Attlee's Labour government and brought under the control of the British Transport Commission (BTC: also covering canals and road haulage). Six regions are formed from the former four main railway systems: London Midland; Western; Southern; Eastern; North Eastern; and Scottish.

1950s Railways continue to lose traffic share to roads as car ownership increases.

1955 Under the £1,240 million Modernization Plan, steam locomotives begin to be phased out and replaced by diesel and, in the 1960s, electric trains.

June 1961 Dr Richard Beeching is appointed chairman of the loss-making BTC with the brief to balance its books.

1962 The Conservative government's Transport Act sets up the British Railways Board (BRB), from 1963, to manage railways. Chaired by Beeching, it is accountable to the Transport Ministry.

1963 The Beeching Report, *The Reshaping of British Railways*, reveals that half of the UK's rail routes are unprofitable and recommends the closure of loss-making branch lines to reduce the rail network from 13,000 to 8,000 miles and greater concentration on containerized freight and inter-city passenger services. As head of the BRB until 1965, Beeching implements much of the plan, with the system stabilizing at 17,000 km/11,000 mi as 2,350 small stations are closed.

1968 The Labour government's Transport Act makes urban railways and unprofitable rural services eligible for government financial grants (subsidies) on social grounds.

6 October 1976 High-speed inter-city passenger services come into operation on the Paddington to Bristol–South Wales line.

12 December 1988 35 people are killed near Clapham Junction, London, in a crash involving an overcrowded commuter train and caused by a trailing wire interrupting the signalling system. The subsequent official inquiry recommends fitting all trains with automatic train protection (ATP) braking systems, but the idea is not adopted, on cost grounds.

November 1993 The Conservative government's Railways Act creates a new structure for British railways by separating the management of the railway infrastructure from the provision of train services, providing for the privatization of British Rail, and establishing a new regulatory regime.

December 1993 The Office of Passenger Rail Franchising (OPRAF) is set up to monitor and manage the 25 passenger Train Operating Companies (TOCs) holding franchises to operate on the British railway network, and the Office of the Rail Regulator (ORR), headed by John Swift QC, to monitor provision of the rail infrastructure, is set up. Minimum service levels and performance standards for incentive regimes are subsequently set.

1 April 1994 A new company, Railtrack, takes over management and ownership of British Rail's 11,000 miles of track, signalling, and other railway infrastructure, including 2,500 stations. BRB retains some functions, including responsibility for the British Transport Police.

6 May 1994 The Channel Tunnel rail link to France is opened, although the high speed train link to Fawkham Junction, Kent on the British side is not expected to be open before 2003; the stage from Fawkham Junction to St Pancras, London, is due for completion in 2007.

4 February 1996 The first privatized rail services since 1948 begin, with Great Western Trains and South West Trains securing the first TOC franchises.

20 May 1996 Railtrack is privatized via flotation on the London Stock Exchange.

30 March 1997 The last TOC franchise is secured by Scotrail.

1998 English, Welsh, and Scottish Railway (EWS) opens the first commercial 'piggyback' service in the UK carrying lorry trailers between Mossend, Glasgow, and Willesden, London.

July 1998 In the White Paper, *New Deal for Transport*, the new Labour government announces plans to establish an over arching Strategic Rail Authority (SRA) with powers to impose tougher sanctions against under performing private railway companies. The Rail Regulator announces he will tighten Rail track's funding regime from 2001 to secure improvements in the rail infrastructure.

February 1999 In a special 'National Rail Summit', the government increases the pressure on the rail industry to improve service quality; Sir Alastair Morton is appointed chairman of the BRB and chairman-designate of the SRA.

March 1999 Railtrack announces plans to spend £27 billion over the next 10 years on maintenance, renewal, and enhancement of the network.

April 1999 A Shadow Strategic Rail Authority (SSRA) begins work to provide strategic direction for British railways, take over the residual functions of the BRB, manage the passenger rail franchises until the SRA itself is constituted, and encourage increased use of rail for freight transport; Tom Winsor becomes the new Rail Regulator, heading the ORR.

May 1999 As part of its Integrated Transport strategy, the Labour government launches a Rail Passenger Partnership Scheme (RPP), providing support for innovative local services designed to attract people from cars to trains.

July 1999 The government's Railways Bill is published, which will give the SRA its full powers.

5 October 1999 More than 30 people are killed in a collision between a local train, which passed a stop signal, and an inter-city express at Ladbroke Grove, near Paddington, London. An official inquiry is set up, headed by a senior judge, Lord Cullen.

November 1999 Legislation is introduced to Parliament to establish the SRA by late 2000; the SSRA begins the process of franchise replacement.

February 2000 The Labour government announces measures to transfer some of Railtrack's safety responsibilities to the Health and Safety Executive.

March 2000 Railtrack, with South West Trains, announces a feasibility study for the introduction of double decker trains to cope with the 25% increase in commuter traffic coming into Waterloo, London.

9 March 2000 The SSRA reveals plans to create 'microfranchises' within existing network areas.

26 May 2000 The Rail Passengers Council claims that many fares have increased by several times the rate of inflation since privatization as the rail companies exploit loopholes in government regulation of fares.

Railtrack Profits and Turnover

Railtrack figures	1997–98 (£ millions)	1998–99 (£ millions)	% change (1997–98 to 1998–99)
Turnover	2,485	2,573	4
Profit after taxation	216[1]	425	51
Dividend	74.1	84.0	13

[1] This is after a one-off 'Windfall Tax' charge of £156 million.

Source: Railtrack

Operators' Bad Timing

Performance figures for January 1999 to January 2000, issued in March 2000 by the Shadow Strategic Rail Authority (SSRA), showed that almost 10% of trains were late in 1999 and 15 of the 25 train operating companies had more late trains than in the previous 12 months, but no operators remained in the bottom (E) grade.

Statistics published by the Central Rail Users' Consultative Committee in 1999 indicated that 437,000 trains ran late in the year 1998–99, an average of 1,200 a day.

Performance of Train Companies in Britain

The Shadow Strategic Rail Authority grades train operating companies on a scale A–E, based on their performance in terms of punctuality and reliability: those grade A are the best performing and those graded E are the worst. Silverlink, graded E in 1998, improved its performance in 1999 to grade C, leaving no train companies with the bottom E grade.

January 1999–January 2000

Overall grade[1]	Subsidy operator	% of trains late	Punctuality grade	% of trains cancelled	Reliability grade
A	Island Line	3.6	A	0.3	A
B	ScotRail	5.1	B	0.7	B
	Wales and West	6.9	B	0.5	A
	North Western Trains	7.0	B	0.8	B
	Anglia Railways	7.6	B	0.6	B
	Central Trains[2]	8.6	B	0.6	B
	Chiltern	9.3	B	0.2	A
	Great Eastern	9.8	B	0.3	A
	West Anglia Great Northern	9.9	B	0.7	B
C	Northern Spirit	7.1	B	1.1	C
	Silverlink	9.0	B	1.3	C
	Midland Main Line	10.5	C	0.4	A
	Great North Eastern	10.6	C	0.8	B
	South West Trains	10.6	C	1.2	C
	Great Western	10.7	C	1.4	C
	Gatwick Express	11.5	C	0.5	A
	Thames Trains	11.5	C	1.0	B
	Connex South Central	11.6	C	0.9	B
	Thameslink	12.0	C	1.1	C
	Connex South Eastern	14.2	C	1.1	C
	Virgin West Coast	14.6	C	0.9	B
	Merseyrail Electrics	7.2	B	1.7	D
D	LTS Rail	10.2	C	1.6	D
	Cardiff Railway	10.8	C	1.8	D
	Virgin CrossCountry	18.7	D	0.9	B

[1] The overall grade is determined by the lower of each company's grades (A to E).
[2] Central's figures exclude 'Centro' services.

Source: The Shadow Strategic Rail Authority (formerly OPRAF)

Rail Travel in Britain: How to Complain

In the first instance a customer wishing to complain about the performance of a train operating company should complain directly to the train operating company concerned. The rail regulator requires train operators to have an effective complaints handling system in place and to provide data on complaint resolution. The address of the train operator has to be displayed on the train and on notices inside stations. If a satisfactory response is not forthcoming from the train operator, a customer can refer the matter to the relevant Rail Users' Consultative Committee (RUCC). There are eight RUCCs in Britain – one for the six regions of England and one each for Scotland and Wales. They were set up under the Railways Act 1993 to protect and promote the interests of users of the services of Britain's rail network. In and around London, the London Regional Passengers' Committee represents the interests of rail users. The work if the RUCCs is coordinated by the London-based Central Rail Users' Consultative Committee.

More than a Million Complaints

Passenger train operators in the UK received a record total of 1,072,958 complaints in the year 1998–99 – an 8% rise on the figure for the previous year. Of the 25 train operating companies, Virgin West Coast and Virgin CrossCountry received the most complaints (around 240,000) and Island Line and Gatwick Express received the fewest.

Complaints to the Central Rail Users' Consultative Committee also reached an all-time-high in the year 1998–99; it received 27% more complaints than in the previous 12 months – an increase of 154% over two years.

Rail Transport

Types of Complaint Against Train Operating Companies in Britain

The Office of the Rail Regulator (ORR) requires train operating companies to break down the complaints they receive into 12 major subject categories. Over half of all complaint issues made in the year 1998–99 were about train service performance.

1998–99

Complaint category	%	Complaint category	%
Train service performance	54.9	Complaint handling	2.3
Train quality	11.0	National rail enquiry service	1.4
Fares, retailing, and refunds	10.1	Safety and security	1.2
Other	5.2	Timetable issues	1.1
Information at stations/on trains	5.0	Special needs	0.5
Staff conduct	3.2		
Station quality	2.4		

Source: © Office of the Rail Regulator (ORR), 2000

Complaints to Train Operating Companies

1 April 1998–3 March 1999

Train company	Total written complaints[1]	Written complaints on pre-printed forms[1]	Train operators' target response times	Percentage of written complaints closed within train operators' own target response time
Virgin CrossCountry	890	501	10 working days	46
Virgin West Coast	730	462	10 working days	47
Great North Eastern Railway	579	244	20 working days	67
Great Western	399	186	5 working days	36
Anglia Railways	323	258	10 calendar days	83
Midland Main Line	261	156	20 working days	91
Wales and West	183	79	10 working days	85
North Western Trains	97	50	5 working days	81
Central Trains	92	57	3 weeks	98
Chiltern Railways	81	47	10 working days	96
Silverlink	54	39	10 working days	59
Northern Spirit	48	24	1 month[4]	100
Great Eastern Railway[2]	45	39	10 working days[3]	94
Thames Trains	37	15	10 working days	77
ScotRail	34	16	20 working days	93
Thameslink	34	10	10 working days	92
West Anglia Great Northern	32	18	10 working days	97
Cardiff Railway	31	14	15 calendar days	68
South West Trains	31	17	10 working days	91
LTS Rail	26	17	5 working days	40
Connex South Central	21	10	10 working days	82
Connex South Eastern	19	7	10 working days	84
Gatwick Express	18	10	10 working days	89
Merseyrail Electrics	17	6	20 working days	100
Island Line	10	1	10 working days	96

[1] Per 100,000 journeys.
[2] First Great Eastern's complaints totals include Delay Repay claims.
[3] 10 days from January 1999.
[4] 15 days from January 1999.

Source: © Office of the Rail Regulator (ORR), 2000

Rail Users' Consultative Committees: Contact Information

- **England**

Central Rail Users' Consultative Committee Clements House, 14–18 Gresham Street, London EC2V 7NL; phone: (020) 7505 9090; fax: (020) 7505 9004; e-mail: crucc@gtnet.gov.uk

RUCC for North Eastern England Hilary House, 16 St Saviour's Place, York YO1 2PL; phone: (01904) 625615; fax: (01904) 643026; Web site: www.northeast-railusers.com

RUCC for North Western England Boulton House, 17–21 Chorlton Street, Manchester M1 3HY; phone: (0161) 228 6247; fax: (0161) 236 1476

RUCC for the Midlands 6th Floor, The McLaren Building, 35 Dale End, Birmingham B4 7LN; phone: (0121) 212 2133; fax: (0121) 236 6945; e-mail: secretary@mids-railusers.com; Web site: www.mids-railusers.com

RUCC for Eastern England Stuart House, City Road, Peterborough PE1 1QF; phone: (01733) 312188; fax: (01733) 891286

RUCC for Western England 10th Floor, Tower House, Fairfax: Street, Bristol BS1 3BN; phone: (0117) 926 5703; fax: (0117) 929 4140; Web site: www.west-railusers.com

RUCC for London Area London Regional Passengers' Committee (LRPC), Clements House, 14–18 Gresham Street, London EC2V 7PR; phone: (020) 7505 9000; fax: (020) 7505 9003

RUCC for Southern England Centric House, 390 Strand, London WC2R 0LT; phone: (020) 7240 5308; fax: (020) 7240 8923

- **Scotland**

RUCC for Scotland 5th Floor, Corrunna House, 29 Cardogan Street, Glasgow G27 7AB; phone: (0141) 221 7760; fax: (0141) 221 3393

- **Wales**

RUCC for Wales St David's House, East Wing, Wood Street, Cardiff CF1 1ES; phone: (01222) 227247; fax: (01222) 223992

Train Accidents in the UK

(N/A = not available.)

Type of accident	1989	1990	1991–92	1992–93	1993–94	1994–95	1995–96	1996–97[1]	1997–98	1998–99
Collisions	329	290	187	154	135	125	123	120	127	120
Derailments	192	183	144	205	113	149	104	119	93	119
Running into level crossing gates and other obstructions	510	473	340	532	445	397	488	741	680	589
Fires	283	257	225	202	247	217	256	302	344	336
Damage to drivers' cab windscreens[2]	N/A	N/A	N/A	N/A	N/A	N/A	N/A	468	619	564
Miscellaneous	120	80	64	59	37	19	18	3	0	0
Total	1,434	1,283	960	1,152	977	907	989	1,753	1,863	1,728

[1] New accident reporting regulations (RIDDOR 95) came into force on 1 April 1996.
[2] Category now reportable under RIDDOR 95.

Source: Transport Statistics Great Britain 1999, © *Crown copyright 1999*

National Rail Length and London Underground Statistics in the UK

(N/A = not available.)

Year	Length of National Rail[1] route			Passengers on National Rail[2]		London Underground	
	Total route (km)	Electrified route (km)	Open to passenger traffic (km)	Passenger journeys (millions)	Passenger kilometres (billions)	Passenger journeys (millions)	Passenger kilometres (billions)
1900	29,783	N/A	N/A	N/A	N/A	N/A	N/A
1923	32,462	1,122	N/A	1,772	N/A	N/A	N/A
1946	31,963	N/A	N/A	1,266	47.0	569	N/A
1955	30,676	1,577	23,820	994	32.7	676	5.6
1965	24,011	2,886	17,516	865	30.1	657	4.7
1975	18,118	3,655	14,431	730	30.9	601	4.8
1984–85	16,816	3,798	14,304	701	29.5	672	5.4
1989–90	16,587	4,546	14,318	758	33.3	765	6.0
1994–95	16,542	4,970	14,359	702	28.7	764	6.1
1995–96	16,666	5,163	15,002	788	30.0	784	6.3
1998–99	16,659	5,166	15,038	892	35.1	866	6.7

[1] From 1994–95 route length is for Railtrack.
[2] From 1995–96 passenger traffic is for National Rail and former British Rail Train Operating Companies.

International Comparisons of Rail Infrastructures

(N = nil or negligible. N/A = not available.)

Country	Rail network in operation (km thousands)		Of which electrified (km thousands)		Rail network per 1,000 sq km	
	1986	1996	1986	1996	1986	1996
Austria	5.7	5.7	3.1	3.4	68	68
Belgium	3.6	3.4	2.2	2.5	118	111
Croatia	2.4	2.7	0.8	1.0	42	48
Czech Republic	N/A	9.4	N/A	2.9	N/A	120
Denmark	2.5	2.3	0.2	0.4	58	55
Finland	5.9	5.9	1.5	2.1	18	17
France	34.6	31.9	11.6	14.3	63	58
Germany	44.6	40.8	14.5	18.4	125	114
Greece	2.5	2.5	–	–	19	19
Hungary	7.8	7.7	2.0	2.4	84	83
Ireland, Republic of	1.9	1.9	–	–	27	28
Italy	16.0	16.0	9.1	10.2	53	53
Japan	N/A	26.5	N/A	17.0	N/A	70
Luxembourg	0.3	0.3	0.2	0.3	116	106
Netherlands	2.8	2.7	1.8	2.0	69	67
Norway	4.2	4.0	2.5	2.4	13	12
Portugal	3.6	2.9	0.5	0.6	39	31
Slovak Republic	N/A	3.7	N/A	1.5	N/A	75
Spain	14.2	12.3	6.4	6.9	28	24
Sweden	11.7	10.9	7.5	7.4	26	24
Switzerland	5.1	5.1[1]	5.1	5.1[1]	124	124[1]
UK	17.0	17.0	4.2	5.2	70	70
USA	225.4	240.0	1.7	1.7	24	26

[1] 1995 data.

Source: Transport Statistics Great Britain 1999, © *Crown copyright 1999*

■ Rail Transport

Channel Tunnel Traffic to and from Europe

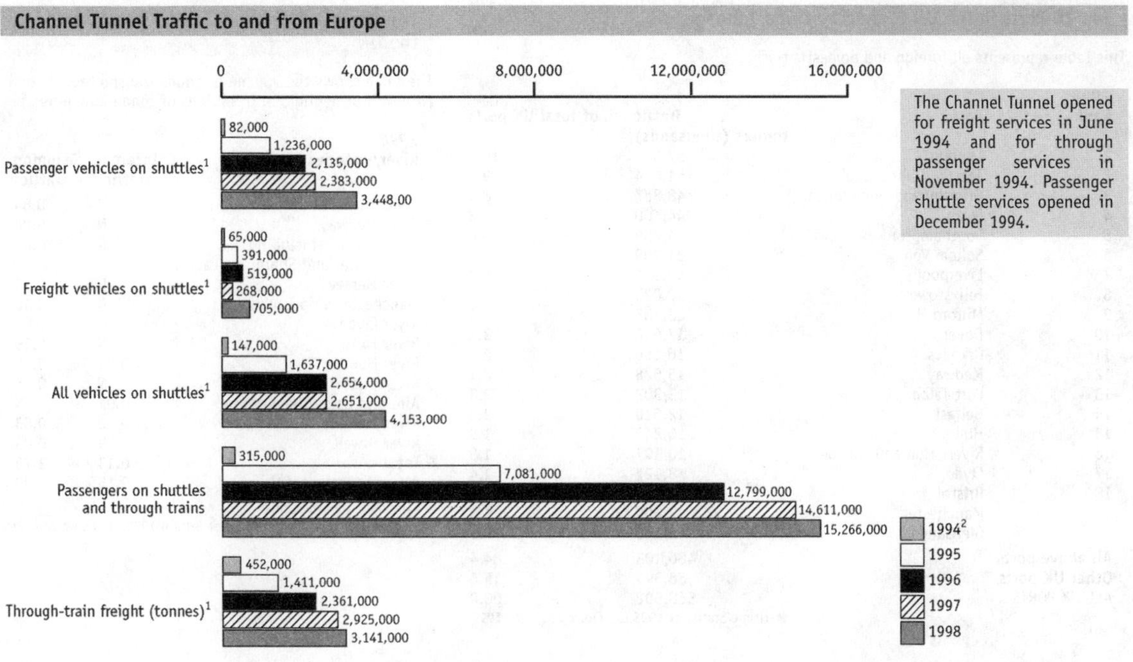

The Channel Tunnel opened for freight services in June 1994 and for through passenger services in November 1994. Passenger shuttle services opened in December 1994.

[1] The figures include non-commercial vehicles.
[2] The figures exclude non-commercial vehicles.

Source: Transport Statistics Great Britain 1999, © *Crown copyright 1999*

Shipping

Top 20 Merchant Fleets of the World

1998

Rank by total ships	Country of registry	Total number of ships	Number of container ships	Number of cruise/ passenger ships	Number of tankers	Number of bulk carriers[1]	Number of roll-on/ roll-off ships	Other[2]
1	Panama	4,456	469	51	971	1,293	68	1,604
2	Liberia	1,632	170	40	691	456	12	263
3	Russian Federation	1,472	25	7	273	113	11	1,043
4	China	1,465	96	34	244	332	14	745
5	Cyprus	1,436	121	15	173	488	20	619
6	Malta	1,305	45	7	349	371	39	494
7	Bahamas	1,029	53	60	241	151	37	487
8	Singapore	877	162	1	386	129	5	194
9	Saint Vincent	782	30	5	96	135	38	478
10	Greece	741	44	19	257	318	16	87
11	Japan	708	32	15	284	177	49	151
12	Norway (NIS)[3]	652	4	12	288	105	40	203
13	Philippines	533	11	8	68	211	18	217
14	Turkey	521	12	8	74	169	15	243
16	Netherlands	504	46	9	71	6	15	357
17	Germany	499	278	6	20	0	10	185
18	Indonesia	484	12	8	121	24	11	308
15	USA	473	91	12	156	15	58	141
19	Korea, South	435	45	3	107	112	1	167
20	Antigua and Barbuda	405	85	0	11	17	16	276
	UK[4]	142	23	21	63	4	5	26
World total		27,730	2,341	449	6,739	5,744	864	11,593

[1] Includes bulk/oil, ore/oil, and ore/bulk/oil carriers.
[2] Breakbulk ships, partial container ships, refrigerated cargo ships, barge, and specialized cargo ships.
[3] International Shipping Registry which is an open registry under which the ship flies the flag of the specified nation but is exempt from certain taxation and other regulations.
[4] The UK is ranked 35.

Source: Statistical Abstract of the United States 1999, *US Department of Transportation 1999*

Top 20 Ports in the UK Ranked by Cargo Tonnage

This table represents all foreign and domestic traffic.

1998

Rank	Port	Traffic tonnes (thousands)	% of total UK ports
1	London	57,311	10.1
2	Tees and Hartlepool	51,454	9.1
3	Grimsby and Immingham	48,387	8.5
4	Forth	44,400	7.8
5	Southampton	34,259	6.0
6	Sullom Voe	31,109	5.5
7	Liverpool	30,357	5.3
8	Felixstowe	30,025	5.3
9	Milford Haven	28,783	5.1
10	Dover	17,690	3.1
11	Orkneys	16,156	2.8
12	Medway	15,528	2.7
13	Port Talbot	13,302	2.3
14	Belfast	12,510	2.2
15	Hull	10,249	1.8
16	Rivers Hull and Humber	10,197	1.8
17	Clyde	8,127	1.4
18	Bristol	7,710	1.4
19	Manchester	7,409	1.3
20	Glensanda	5,140	0.9
All above ports		480,103	84.4
Other UK ports		88,399	15.6
ALL UK PORTS		568,502	100.0

Source: Maritime Statistics 1998, © *Crown copyright 1999*

The Busiest Rivers and Inland Waterways in the UK

The table shows the volume of goods transported.
(N = nil or negligible. In billions of tonne-kilometres.)

1998

River/waterway	Internal traffic[1]	Seagoing traffic[1]
River Thames	0.07	0.84
River Medway	N	0.06
River Severn (including Gloucester and Sharpness canal)	N	0.01
River Mersey	N	0.11
Manchester Ship Canal	N	0.10
River Clyde	N	0.06
River Forth	N	0.19
River Humber	0.01	0.29
River Ouse	N	0.05
Aire and Calder Navigation	0.02	N
River Trent	0.02	0.03
River Orwell	N	0.04
Total	0.13	1.76
All waterways total	0.15	1.80

[1] The data are provisional.

Source: Transport Statistics Great Britain 1999, © *Crown copyright 1999*

Tourism and Travel Tips

The World's Top 10 Tourism Destinations

Rank	Country	Number of arrivals (thousands) 1996	1999[1]	% change 1996–99
1	France	62,406	71,400	14.4
2	Spain	40,541	51,958	28.2
3	USA	46,489	46,983	1.1
4	Italy	32,853	35,839	9.1
5	China	22,765	27,047	18.8
6	UK	25,163	25,740	2.3
7	Mexico	21,405	20,216	−5.6
8	Canada	17,285	19,556	13.1
9	Poland	19,410	17,940	−7.6
10	Germany	15,205	17,093	12.4

[1] 1999 figures are preliminary.

Source: World Tourism Organization

Visits to and Expenditure in the UK by Overseas Residents

Year	Visits (millions)	Spending (£ millions)
1988	15.3	6,184
1989	17.3	6,945
1990	18.0	7,748
1991	17.1	7,386
1992	18.5	7,891
1993	19.9	9,487
1994	20.8	9,786
1995	23.5	11,763
1996	25.2	12,290
1997	25.5	12,244
1998	25.7	12,671
1999[1]	25.5	12,605

[1] Figures for 1999 are estimates.

Source: International Passenger Survey, © *Key Note Ltd 2000*

Tourism in the UK

Tourism is one of the UK's leading industries: the British Tourist Authority estimates that tourism is worth some £63 billion each year to the UK economy. It supports around 1.75 million jobs (6% of the work force and five times as many as the car industry) and it is forecast to grow by 4% per annum over the next ten years, making it one of the UK's fastest growing industries. Market analysts estimate that one in five of all new jobs created in the UK is created in the tourist industry.

In 1999 around 25.5 million overseas visitors came to the UK and they spent some £12.6 billion. The British Tourist Authority estimates that spending by overseas visitors will amount to some £18 billion by 2003.

Popular attractions in 1999

The *Monet in the 20th Century* exhibition, which ran from 23 January–18 April 1999, was the most popular art exhibition ever held in the UK: it attracted a daily average of 8,555 people and a total of some 813,000 visitors. As a result, the Royal Academy entered the top 10 UK attractions (charging admission) for the first time, rising 11 places from its 1998 position. However, indoor attractions were less popular overall in 1999 compared with 1998, with visits to historic properties falling by 0.5% and visits to museums falling by 1%. The UK's outdoor attractions, including country parks, gardens, steam railways, wildlife attractions, and farms all grew in popularity, with attendance up by between 4% and 7%.

In 1999 Blackpool Pleasure Beach maintained its 1998 position as the UK's most visited attraction not charging admission, with some 7.2 million visitors. The British Museum, London, was the second most popular free attraction in 1999, with almost 5.5 million visitors. London Zoo was the most popular wildlife attraction in the UK, with almost 1,068,000 visitors; Hampton Court Gardens, London, were the most visited gardens, attracting 1,200,000 visitors; and York Minster was the most visited cathedral, with 1,800,000 visitors.

The UK Travel and Tourism Market

The domestic market represents the travel and tourism market accounted for by UK residents travelling within the UK; the outbound market is that part accounted for by UK residents travelling overseas; and the inbound market represents that part of the market accounted for by overseas visitors to the UK.

1999		Trips/visits (millions)	Nights (millions)	Expenditure (£ millions)
Volume/value	domestic market	123.5	435	14,875
	outbound market	53.6	536	28,672
	inbound market	25.5	228	12,605
	Total	202.6	1,199	56,152
% of total	domestic market	61.0	36.3	26.5
	outbound market	26.5	44.7	51.1
	inbound market	12.6	19.0	22.4
	Total	100.0[1]	100.0	100.0

[1] Items do not sum to total due to rounding.

Source: © *Key Note Ltd 2000*

UK Travellers' Favourite Destinations in the UK

1998 Region	Trips (millions)	Nights (millions)	Spending (£ billions)
West Country	16	76	2.7
East	13	49	1.3
Heart of England	16	45	1.2
Southern	11	38	1.2
London	11	29	1.1
North West	8	24	1.0
Yorkshire	9	31	1.0
South West	10	31	0.9
Cumbria	3	10	0.4
Northumbria	4	14	0.3
England total	102	346	10.9
Scotland	10	44	1.5
Wales	10	38	1.2
Northern Ireland	1	5	0.2
TOTAL UK[1]	122	438	14.0

[1] Total columns may not add up due to rounding.

Source: United Kingdom Tourist Survey, © *Key Note Ltd 2000*

UK Travellers' Favourite Destinations in the World

Country	Number of travellers				% change
	1995	1996	1997	1998	1995–98
France	9,645,000	9,834,000	11,149,000	11,518,000	19.4
Spain	8,239,000	7,545,000	8,281,000	9,650,000	17.1
Ireland, Republic of	2,809,000	3,169,000	3,613,000	3,937,000	40.2
USA	2,657,000	3,079,000	3,028,000	3,542,000	33.3
Germany	1,899,000	1,898,000	2,023,000	2,062,000	8.6
Italy	1,600,000	1,558,000	1,801,000	2,012,000	25.8
Netherlands	1,364,000	1,532,000	1,756,000	1,952,000	43.1
Greece	2,056,000	1,460,000	1,512,000	1,860,000	– 9.5
Belgium	1,077,000	1,421,000	1,419,000	1,699,000	57.8
Portugal	1,211,000	1,102,000	1,304,000	1,299,000	7.3
Turkey	856,000	1,032,000	998,000	1,037,000	21.1
Cyprus	669,000	709,000	713,000	952,000	42.3
Switzerland	516,000	509,000	580,000	652,000	26.4
Austria	600,000	415,000	425,000	535,000	– 10.8
Others	6,147,000	6,787,000	7,355,000	8,165,000	32.8
Total	41,345,000	42,050,000	45,957,000	50,872,000	23.0

Source: International Passenger Survey, © *Key Note Ltd 2000*

The UK's Top 20 Tourist Attractions Charging Admission

(– = not applicable.)

Rank	Attraction	Number of visits	
		1998	1999
1	Alton Towers, Staffordshire	2,782,000	2,650,000
2	Madame Tussaud's, London	2,772,500	2,640,000

(continued)

Number of International Visitors to the UK by Country of Origin

Country	Number of visitors		% change 1995–98
	1995	1998	
USA	3,146,000	3,880,000	23.3
France	3,184,000	3,274,000	2.8
Germany	2,654,000	2,830,000	6.6
Ireland, Republic of	1,988,000	2,310,000	16.2
Netherlands	1,408,000	1,718,000	22.0
Belgium	1,296,000	1,183,000	– 8.7
Italy	924,000	1,090,000	18.0
Spain	772,000	879,000	13.9
Sweden	552,000	676,000	22.5
Canada	609,000	673,000	10.5

Source: International Passenger Survey, © *Key Note Ltd 2000*

The Millennium Dome

The Millennium Dome in Greenwich, southeast London, was the central venue on 31 December 1999 for London's official millennium celebrations and it opened to the public on 1 January 2000. Designed by the Richard Rogers Partnership, it is 320 m/1,050 ft in diameter, twice as big as the world's former largest dome, the Georgia Dome in Atlanta (GA), USA.

The Dome and exhibition were dogged by controversy from the start: the Greenwich site, the cost of the Dome itself, and the contents all caused disagreement, and poor ticket sales threatened the Dome's financial viability. In its opening month 366,420 people visited the Dome, just over half the number expected. Just over 3 million people had visited the Dome by the end of June 2000, putting it ahead of any fee-paying attraction for 1999, but falling short of expectations and of what was needed if the break-even figure of 10 million fee-paying visitors was to be met by the end of 2000. It was estimated in July 2000 that some 6 million people would have visited the Dome by the end of the year.

In March 1999 the government invited bids for sustainable alternative uses for the Dome on its present site after December 2000. In July 2000 it was announced that the Japanese financial group Nomura International had won the bid to take over the Dome, with their proposal for a Dome Europe theme park. Nomura announced plans to spend some £400 million turning the Dome into an amusement park and developing the Greenwich site with hotels, shopping complexes, restaurants, and a convention centre.

The London Eye

The London Eye forms part of the UK's millennium celebrations along with the Millennium Dome. The 135 m/450 ft diameter vertical wheel, located beside the River Thames and opposite the Houses of Parliament and Big Ben, opened on 1 February 2000 to ticket holders and to the public on 1 March. It is the world's biggest observation wheel and London's fourth highest structure. Its construction was undertaken by the airline British Airways, and it was designed by architects David Marks and Julia Barfield. The wheel has 32 fully enclosed capsules, each of which can hold 25 people, and it can take 1,500 visitors each hour.

The wheel has proved to be one of the London's most popular attractions in 2000; more than 600,000 advance tickets had already been sold by the beginning of February, and by the end of April more than 1 million people had taken the 30-minute ride. The wheel has planning permission for five years, but many believe it will stay in place for much longer. (*See also* **colour section**)

The UK's Top 20 Tourist Attractions Charging Admission *(continued)*

Rank	Attraction	Number of visits 1998	1999
3	Tower of London	2,551,459	2,422,181
4	Natural History Museum, London	1,904,539	1,739,591
5	Legoland, Windsor	1,510,363	1,620,000
6	Chessington World of Adventures, Surrey	1,650,000	1,550,000
7	Science Museum, London	1,599,817	1,480,000
8	Royal Academy, London	912,714	1,390,000
9	Canterbury Cathedral	1,500,000	1,350,000
10	Windsor Castle, Berkshire	1,495,465	1,280,000
11	Westminster Abbey, London	–	1,268,215
12	Edinburgh Castle	1,219,055	1,219,720
13	Flamingo Land Theme Park, Yorkshire	1,105,000	1,197,000
14	Drayton Manor Park, Staffordshire	1,003,802	1,174,448
15	Windermere Lake Cruises, Cumbria	1,060,600	1,140,207
16	St Paul's Cathedral, London	1,095,299	1,076,222
17	London Zoo	1,052,000	1,067,917
18	Chester Zoo	920,000	965,721
19	Victoria and Albert Museum, London	110,000	945,677
20	Thorpe Park, Chertsey, Surrey	852,000	926,000

Source: Visits to Tourist Attractions 1999, *English Tourism Council*

World Heritage Sites in the UK

There are 18 UK World Heritage sites, a term determined in 1972 by UNESCO. Their formal titles are, in order of designation:

1986 The Giant's Causeway and Causeway coast
1986 Durham Castle and Cathedral
1986 Ironbridge Gorge
1986 Studley Royal Park, including the ruins of Fountains Abbey
1986 Stonehenge, Avebury, and associated sites
1986 The castles and town walls of King Edward in Gwynedd
1986 St Kilda
1987 Blenheim Palace
1987 City of Bath
1987 Hadrian's Wall
1987 Palace of Westminster, Abbey of Westminster, and St Margaret's church
1988 Henderson Island (in the South Pacific)
1988 The Tower of London
1988 Canterbury Cathedral, St Augustine's Abbey, and St Martin's church
1995 Old and New Towns of Edinburgh
1995 Gough Island Wildlife Reserve (in the Atlantic)
1997 Maritime Greenwich
1999 The Heart of Neolithic Orkney

See also **Major Millennium Projects in the UK**, p 73.

Top 20 Most Visited Towns in the UK by Overseas Visitors

Between 1994 and 1998 there was an overall 20% increase in the number of nights stayed in the UK by overseas visitors, with most of this growth coming in the last two years. The most important markets continue to be France, which produces 20% of the UK's visitors, and the USA, which produces 20% of expenditure.

Town/city	Number of nights (millions) 1994	1998	% change 1994–98
London	74.3	91.7	23
Edinburgh	5.1	5.7	12
Oxford	2.9	4.0	38
Cambridge	2.4	3.7	54
Glasgow	3.0	3.7	23
Birmingham	2.9	3.5	21
Manchester	3.0	3.2	7
Brighton/Hove	2.8	2.9	4
Bournemouth	1.9	2.5	32
Newcastle upon Tyne	1.2	2.1	75
Bristol	1.5	2.0	33
Nottingham	1.0	1.7	70
Eastbourne	1.0	1.5	50
York	1.4	1.5	7
Bath	1.2	1.4	17
Leeds	0.8	1.4	75
Liverpool	1.3	1.4	8
Reading	1.0	1.3	30
Sheffield	1.0	1.2	20
Cardiff	0.9	1.1	22
Coventry	0.8	1.1	38

Source: *IPS/BTA [International Passenger Survey/British Tourist Authority] analysis*

Air Travel Tips

• Tickets

Shop around Look out for special deals and check the terms and conditions of the ticket before making a choice. Cheaper flights will often be more restrictive and less flexible.

When to travel The more flexible that you can be in your travel arrangements, the more chance you will have to make savings on the fare. There are variations in prices according to different seasons and there are also variations for different days of the week, and even times of the day.

What type of ticket The prices of charter flights vary according to season, day of the week, and time of day. Except for last-minute sales, tickets for charter flights are sold at the same price on a 'use it or lose it' basis. If you need to cancel, you will not receive a refund.

There is a wide range of different fares for scheduled flights, ranging from the 'full fare', which is fully flexible (allowing you to change or cancel your reservation), to the cheapest fare, which is very restrictive. Full fare tickets are often 'endorsable', which means that you can use the ticket on another airline. Cheaper tickets do not allow this facility. The less you pay, the less flexible the ticket will be. Many cheap return fares require you to stay for a Saturday night.

If you wish to buy a return ticket, but wish to specify the return date later, you should ask for an 'open date return' ticket (you may not be able to do this with cheaper fares). You should try to book your return flight as soon as possible, or consider a fare which will allow you to change your reservation, or use the ticket on another airline.

• Flights

Your choice of airline will depend on price and whether or not you have to travel on a particular day.

Non-stop, direct, or connecting flight On longer journeys, cheaper deals can involve a number of stops or the need to change planes. Direct flights may involve stops to take on fuel or passengers. If you are offered a connecting service, requiring you to change planes, check that there will be enough time to make the connection between flights. Where a connecting service involves an overnight stop, check if hotel accommodation and courtesy transport are included in the price. Check if a transit visa is needed for any country in which you have to stop.

In-flight food and drink Airlines are not obliged to provide food and drink during the flight, but most do. If you have special dietary needs, check before you book that the airline can satisfy them, and check if you will be expected to pay extra. Most airlines provide soft drinks; some airlines may refuse to serve alcohol (usually for religious reasons).

Smoking The trend is for airlines to provide more no-smoking flights in response to passengers' wishes. Check with the airline about the rules of the flight you intend to book.

• Luggage

When booking your ticket, check what baggage allowance is included in the price of the ticket. You will be allowed to carry 'checked-in' baggage carried in the hold, and 'cabin' luggage, which you can take onto the aircraft. If you need to carry more than the allowance, check what the airline will charge per kilogram of excess baggage; charges can be high. If you

Air Travel Tips *(continued)*

need to take connecting flights, check the allowance for each flight, as allowances vary.

Packing bags Do not pack things that you will need during the flight (e.g. medicine) in your checked-in luggage. Baggage may be searched for security reasons or screened using X-ray equipment; electronic equipment should be carried in hand luggage to avoid damage. Do not pack cash, valuables, or fragile goods in your luggage – airlines will not accept liability, and insurance companies will not provide cover. Certain 'dangerous' goods may not be carried; check with the airline for their rules.

Insurance Under the Warsaw Convention a cash limit is set for the value of compensation an airline has to pay for loss or damage to your luggage. As at March 1998, the ceiling was £14 per kilogram. Legal limits are usually set for domestic air travel in most countries. You should take out adequate insurance cover for yourself and your luggage.

• Passports, visas, and health

You are responsible for ensuring that you have the correct documentation (travel documents, passports, visas, inoculation certificates) for your journey. If you do not have the correct documentation, the airline may refuse to carry you, and you may not be entitled to a refund. Check with the embassy or high commission of the countries you intend to visit, which documents are required.

If you are concerned about your fitness to fly, check with your doctor before you travel. Most airlines will not carry women who are over 28 weeks into a pregnancy. A useful booklet *Health Advice for Travellers* is available from Post Offices. If you are taken ill abroad, limited treatment is available on production of form E111, in participating countries. You should ensure that you have adequate personal health insurance for your journey.

• Checking your ticket

When you receive your ticket, check that the date, time, flight number, and the name on the ticket are correct. Make sure that any errors are corrected before you travel. For scheduled airlines, check the reservation status box. If the box contains the letters 'OK', this means that your reservation has been confirmed. Anything else means that you do not have a confirmed reservation; check with the airline. If you have asked for special arrangements, check with the airline that these have been made for you.

• Check-in deadline

The check-in deadline is the latest time that you can check-in for your flight. If you miss the deadline, your place on the flight can be given to someone else on a waiting list. If this happens, you have no case for compensation or refund.

Driving in Europe

• Documents required

Passport European Union countries no longer make routine passport checks at internal land frontiers. Visitors must have a valid passport or identity card to prove their identity. Each person in the party must hold or be named on a current passport.

Motor insurance Third party motor vehicle insurance is compulsory throughout Europe. Most UK policies cover EU and certain non-EU countries. An International Motor Insurance Certificate or 'green card' provides evidence of third party cover. A green card is strongly advisable, especially when travelling to Spain, Portugal, Italy, Greece, and Turkey, and is required in Andorra. It is advisable to check with your insurer to ensure that you have adequate cover for the countries you intend to visit.

Driving licence A valid full driving licence must be carried by all motorists in Europe. A UK driving licence is recognized in most countries. An International Driving Permit is required for countries that do not recognize the UK licence. You must carry your driving licence at all times; you may be required to produce it on demand.

Vehicle registration document When driving a UK registered vehicle in Europe, it is necessary to carry a vehicle registration document, or a certificate of registration (V379). If the vehicle is not registered in your name, you should have the written permission of the owner (in Portugal a special form of authority is required). A Vehicle on Hire/Lease Certificate (VE 103) is required when driving a hire car abroad.

• Medical arrangements

When travelling within the European Economic Area (EEA), free or reduced price medical treatment is available on production of form E111. Cover provided under this reciprocal scheme is minimal; all travellers are advised to take out personal travel insurance. Further information can be found in the booklet *Health Advice for Travellers* (ref. T5) available from Post Offices.

• Accessories

Headlamp beam conversion kit Headlamp beams need to be adjusted for driving on the right hand side of the road. A conversion kit is a convenient way of carrying this out. Remember to remove the converters on returning to the UK.

Spare bulbs A spare set of bulbs is compulsory in some European Countries.

Snow chains These are a legal requirement in alpine countries.

Warning triangle A warning triangle is compulsory in several European countries. Regulations on the use and positioning of the warning triangle vary from country to country, and are normally printed on the cover of the triangle.

Immunization for Travellers

Details correct as of April 2000. This table is intended to give general advice only. Please take proper medical advice before travelling. (– = not applicable.)

Disease	Immunization	Timing	Reaction	Protection	Duration of protection	Other precautions	Notes
Cholera	2 injections not less than 1 week apart (the vaccine is not normally recommended)	1 week to 1 month before travel	soreness where injected, fever, headache, fatigue	50%	6 months	avoid food or water that may be dirty	low risk in reasonable tourist accommodation; vaccine should not be given to children under 2 months
Hepatitis A	injection of immunoglobulin	just before travel	soreness and swelling where injected, hives in some cases	prevents illness	3 months	avoid potentially contaminated food or water; drinking water of unknown purity and uncooked shellfish should be avoided	children under 2 years should receive a single dose of immunoglobulin
	vaccine consisting of 2 injections 1 month apart, then a 3rd injection 6–12 months later	2 months before travel	soreness where injected, headache, fatigue	lessens severity	10 years		

(continued)

Immunization for Travellers *(continued)*

Disease	Immunization	Timing	Reaction	Protection	Duration of protection	Other precautions	Notes
Hepatitis B	2 injections of vaccine 1 month apart, then booster 4 months later	last injection 1 month before travel	soreness where injected, fever	80–85%	about 5 years	–	usually only given to those at high risk, such as health workers; part of recommended childhood vaccination series
Malaria	none; take preventative tablets from 1 week before travel to 4 weeks after leaving malaria area	order tablets 2 weeks before travel	mild nausea, occasional vomiting	90%	only while tablets are taken	use anti-mosquito sprays, mosquito nets; keep arms and legs covered after sunset	some anti-malarial drugs are not recommended for pregnant mothers or children under 1 year
Polio	(a) oral vaccine – 3–4 doses (b) injection – 3–4 shots, the best way to be protected is to get 4 doses of polio vaccine immunized adults: 1 booster dose	for travellers who are not up to date, it may be necessary to allow as much as 7 months for the full recommended vaccination schedule, depending on other vaccines that may be necessary for the trip	minor local reactions (pain, redness) may occur after injection	>95%	10 years	–	(a) should not be given to pregnant mothers; (b) recommended only for people 18 years and older who have not yet been vaccinated; should not be given to people who have an allergy problem with the antibiotics neomycin or streptomycin; there is no risk of polio virus infection in any country of the western hemisphere
Rabies	3-dose series of injections, usually given on days 0, 7, and 21 or 28	5 weeks before travel	soreness where injected, headache, abdominal pain, muscle aches, nausea	opinion is divided as to whether vaccine prevents rabies or promotes a faster response to treatment	3 months	avoid bites, scratches, or licks from any animal; wash any bite or scratch with antiseptic or soap as quickly as possible and get immediate medical treatment	travellers to rabies-endemic countries should be warned about the risk of acquiring rabies, although rabies vaccination is not a requirement for entry into any country
Tetanus	normally given in childhood with booster every 10 years unimmunized adults: 2 injections 1 month apart then 3rd injection 6 months later	not critical	headache, lethargy in rare cases	>90%	about 10 years	wash any wounds with antiseptic	–
Typhoid	1–2 injections 4–6 weeks apart single injection 4 oral doses, every other day series on days 1, 2, 4, and 6	5–7 weeks before departure	soreness where injected, nausea, headache (worst in those over 35 and on repeat immunizations) may last 36 hours	70–70%	1–3 years 3 years 1 year	avoid food, milk, or water that may be contaminated by sewage or by flies; boil drinking water, eat foods that have been thoroughly cooked, peel raw vegetables and fruits yourself (with clean hands)	–
Yellow fever	1 injection	at least 10 days before departure	possible slight headache and low fever 5–10 days later, muscle ache	almost 100%	10 years	as malaria	may only be available from special centres

Tourism and Travel Tips

Travel Tips for People with Disabilities

Travel companies in the UK are required under the provisions of the Disability Discrimination Act 1995 not to treat customers with disabilities less favourably than other customers. In reality, there is great variation in the quality and range of services offered by travel agents and tour operators to travellers and holiday makers with disabilities. If you are a traveller with special needs, shop around to find a travel agent who is prepared to make the effort to ensure that you get what you want. You know best what your capabilities and needs are– don't just accept what a travel agent suggests as being 'suitable' for you. Independent travel can be very rewarding, if you are able to put the time and effort into researching thoroughly every aspect of your journey beforehand. The national tourist offices of the countries you wish to visit can provide advice and details of the major disability organizations for their country.

It is particularly important to get written confirmation of any arrangements or provisions (such as a ground-floor room) that you have specified when booking. Where wheelchair access is provided, check that it can accommodate the dimensions of your wheelchair, and that grab rails will be provided at a suitable height. Even if you are booking a package deal through a specialist operator, it is important to contact hotels, airlines, airports, and transport companies yourself to ensure that the necessary arrangements have been made.

Make sure that you have adequate travel and medical insurance cover. Ensure that the terms of the policy cover any claims arising from your disability.

Information sources

Royal Association for Disability and Rehabilitation (RADAR) RADAR publishes guides and can advise on travel in the UK and Europe. Address: 12 City Forum, 250 City Road, London EC1 8AF; phone: (020) 7250 3222; fax: (020) 7250 0212; e-mail: radar@radar.org.uk; Web site: www.radar.org.uk

Holiday Care Service Provides comprehensive advice on travel and holidays for people with disabilities. Address: 2nd Floor, Imperial Buildings, Victoria Road, Horley, Surrey RH6 7PZ; phone: (01293) 774 535; fax: (01293) 784 647; e-mail: holiday.care@virgin.net; Web site: www.holidaycare.org.uk

MENCAP Holiday Services MENCAP organize holidays for people with learning disabilities, staffed by volunteers. Address: MENCAP, Optimum House, Clippers Quay, Salford Quays, Salford M5 2XP; phone: (0161) 888 1200; fax: (0161) 888 1214; e-mail: AdrienWright@mencap.org.uk; Web site: www.mencap.org.uk

Royal National Institute for the Blind (RNIB) The RNIB can advise on hotels in the UK suitable for people with sight problems. They also organize tours to foreign countries. Address: RNIB Holiday Service, 224 Great Portland Street, London W1N6AA; phone: (020) 7388 1266; fax: (020) 7388 2034; e-mail: helpline@rnib.org.uk; Web site: www.rnib.org.uk

Triscope Triscope offers free advice about transport and travel for the elderly, people with disabilities, and for carers. Address: Alexandra House, Albany Road, Brentford, Middlesex TW8 0NE; phone: (020) 8580 7021; fax: (020) 8580 7022; e-mail: triscope@cableinet.co.uk; Web site: www.justmobility.co.uk/triscope

Public transport

For detailed information on public transport in the UK, contact the train and bus operators that operate services to your intended destination. Railtrack can provide contact information for train operators. Wheelchair access onto trains can normally be provided by portable ramps kept at railway stations. It is important to specify when booking your ticket that you need wheelchair access. Wheelchair spaces are provided on Eurostar services. Most licensed taxi firms in London and other cities can provide vehicles that can accommodate a wheelchair, again, specify your requirements when booking.

Transport for London Access and Mobility London Transport offers advice to visitors with disabilities on how best to use London's buses and underground services. Timetables and leaflets are available in large print and Braille formats. Address: Windsor House, 42–50 Victoria Street, London SW1H 0TL; phone: (020) 7941 4600; fax:(020) 7941 4605; Web site: www.londontransport.co.uk

Web Sites

Air Space

http://www.raes.org.uk/

Online magazine of the Royal Aeronautical Society, with information about the society, a diary of events, details of the 'Young members section', and pages of news and related links.

Allstar Network – Principles of Flight

http://www.allstar.u.edu/aero/princ1.htm

Guide to flight and aviation, with experiments to demonstrate the physics behind flight.

Automotive Learning Online

http://www.innerauto.com/innerauto/htm/auto.html

This fun and educational site on the automobile is a good training resource for engineering minds, but is also suited to anyone who simply wants to know how their car works.

Aviation Enthusiasts

http://www.runwayrats.com/

Forum dedicated to furthering interest in aviation-related hobbies. It includes links to museums and displays, features on key events in aviation history, and indexes of aircraft by type and manufacturer.

European Railway Server

http://mercurio.iet.unipi.it/home.html

Complete source of information about the railways of Europe. The needs of travellers, railway enthusiasts, and students of public transport are provided for, and there are links to all of Europe's railway operators.

EV Information Network

http://www.evadc.org/

Comprehensive information on electrically powered vehicles (EVs) – EV events, batteries, details of manufacturers and suppliers, and a forceful case for the advantages of EVs over the internal combustion engine.

Helicopter Aviation Home Page

http://www.copters.com/

Plentiful information (and images) on helicopters, including a history of their invention, their aerodynamics, a profile of mechanical components, advice to novice pilots, and manuals of various kinds of helicopters.

International Civil Aviation Organization

http://www.icao.int/

Site of the specialized UN agency regulating civil aviation, with information on the role and history of the ICAO, rules of the air, international conventions, and standardization of safety standards. There are links to all the online airlines, airports, and pilot training centres in the world.

National Railway Museum, York

http://www.nmsi.ac.uk/nrm/html/home_pb/menu.htm

Information for railway enthusiasts, both on the National Railway Museum and its exhibitions, and on railway matters from around the world.

Office of Passenger Rail Franchising (OPRAF)

http://www.opraf.gov.uk/

OPRAF is the organization that monitors the 25 passenger train franchises operating on the UK railway network, and is part of the larger Strategic Rail Authority. Their site contains relevant documents, news, and a list of FAQs.

164 Currency Converter

http://www.oanda.com/cgi-bin/ncc

Easy-to-use site that allows you to do automatic conversions to and from a wide range of currencies. You can select the amount to convert and also the date of the exchange rate you want to use.

Railtrack – The Heart of the Railway

http://www.railtrack.co.uk/

User-friendly Railtrack site which aims to simplify the planning of a railway journey in Britain. Input your destination and time of departure and you will quickly receive a schedule. The site also includes updates of operational difficulties and advice to travellers.

UK Travel Guide

http://www.uktravel.com/index.html

Essential resource for anyone planning to travel in the UK. It includes an A–Z of practical information, from accommodation to the weather, and an interactive map with features on towns and cities.

Welcome to IYHF

http://www.iyhf.org/iyhf/ehome.html

Site of the International Youth Hostel Federation, with information on the history and structure of the international youth hostel movement, and links to national organizations. Places in hostels around the world may also be booked through this site.

The Environment and Climate

The Year in Review

2 July 1999 US president Bill Clinton announces that the North American bald eagle will be removed from the official list of endangered species. The population of the bird is up to 5,800 pairs, compared to 417 in 1963.

19 July–1 August 1999 Record high temperatures are recorded in eastern USA, with over 200 deaths attributed to the heat. A serious drought affects farmers in five states which are declared disaster areas.

27 July 1999 A flash flood kills 21 people from Australia, the UK, New Zealand, South Africa, and Switzerland, who were canyoning (a sport involving jumping into fast-flowing water) at Saxeten Brook near Interlaken, Switzerland.

31 July 1999 In the USA, environmentalists from the Worldwatch Institute publish a study showing that global emissions of carbon from fossil fuels fell in 1998 for the first time since 1993.

August 1999 Torrential rains in the Philippines cause floods and landslides that kill at least 160 people.

4 August 1999 The 16th International Botanical Conference predicts the extinction of two-thirds of mammal, bird, butterfly, and plant species by the end of the 21st century due to human causes.

11 August 1999 Around 350 million people around the world view a solar eclipse. In the UK, the path of the eclipse passes over Cornwall – the first total solar eclipse visible in the UK since 1927 (*see also* **colour section**). Although local businesses have prepared for a large influx of tourists, only a fraction of the expected crowds arrive, and the eclipse is marred by poor visibility due to clouds and rain.

17 August 1999 An earthquake measuring 7.4 on the Richter scale strikes a densely populated industrial area of northwestern Turkey, near Izmit. The initial death toll rises to 2,000, but will exceed 13,000 by the following week, with at least 26,000 people injured.

3 September 1999 Eminent US marine biologists publish research warning that global warming, pollution, and overfishing have greatly increased levels of disease in oceans around the world, seriously threatening sea mammals, fish, coral reefs, and marine plantlife.

14 September 1999 Hurricane Floyd, one of the largest and most powerful storms on record, measuring more than 800 km/500 mi wide and with winds of up to 240 kph/150 mph, hits the Bahamas, causing widespread damage and flooding. It then threatens the coasts of Florida and Georgia, USA.

15 September 1999 Hurricane Floyd turns inland at North Carolina, USA, as more than 2 million people head for the border with South Carolina, forming one of the biggest evacuation programmes in US history.

15 September 1999 The *Global Environment Outlook 2000* report is published by the United Nations Environment Programme, criticizing the lack of sustainable development and pointing to problems such as inadequate sanitation for half of the world's population, global warming, and irreversible damage to rainforests.

21 September 1999 Taiwan is struck in the early morning by an earthquake measuring 7.6 on the Richter scale. More than 2,300 people are killed and 8,700 injured, with 100,000 left homeless.

30 September 1999 An earthquake in southern Mexico kills at least 20 people.

October 1999 Hundreds are killed by flooding and mudslides in Mexico along the Gulf Coast and the Sierra Madre Oriental Mountain range, and an estimated 200,000 made homeless.

17 October 1999 Hurricane Irene strikes Palm Beach, Florida, causing severe flooding. It then heads for North Carolina, where residents are evacuated from beach areas for the third time in two months.

30 October 1999 A cyclone hits the east coast of India, causing mass flooding which leaves hundreds dead and millions of people homeless.

25 October–5 November 1999 A UN conference on climate change, in Germany, attended by some 5,000 international delegates, works on the 1997 Kyoto protocol for restricting greenhouse gases.

14 November 1999 Severe floods in southwest France, the worst floods in France this century, kill at least 22 people.

17 November 1999 Scientists from the University of Washington in Seattle, Washington, publish data showing that the Arctic icecap has shrunk by around 40% over the past 50 years, probably due to global warming. The Canadian Wildlife Service reports that polar bears in the area are in danger of starving to death because of their shortened hunting season (*see also* **colour section**).

19 December 1999 Severe flash flooding washes away entire villages along the Caribbean coast of Venezuela in the country's worst national disaster this century. Within two days, the death toll has risen to 30,000.

16 December 1999 The World Meteorological Organization (WMO) reports that the 1990s was the warmest decade on record, and the 1900s was the warmest century in a millennium. The average surface temperature of the Earth has risen by more than one degree in the past century.

25 December 1999 A storm hits northern France, causing the most violent winds ever recorded in the area, killing at least 31 people, and causing severe damage in the capital, Paris.

29 December 1999 Severe storms hit western Europe, causing avalanches in several ski resorts. Avalanches in Austria kill 12 people in the mountains between Ischgl and Galtür.

6 January 2000 The last *Capra pyrenaica pyrenaica*, a species of Pyrenean mountain goat, dies after a tree falls on it, making the species extinct.

24–31 January 2000 A protocol on biosafety is agreed in Montreal, Canada, by delegates from over 140 nations, intended to control trade in genetically modified crops and food, particularly to developing countries.

27 January 2000 The World Wide Fund for Nature warns that the Iberian lynx, brown bear, harbour porpoise, monk seal, loggerhead sea turtle, and corncrake are among animals that are in serious decline in Europe. The Fund claims that the EU habitats and species directive, which was supposed to become law in all EU countries in 1994 but has not been fully implemented in any country, could save them.

30 January 2000 One hundred thousand tonnes of sludge containing heavy metals and cyanide are accidentally spilled in northern Romania, polluting the Somes river as well as the Tisza river in Hungary and the Danube in Yugoslavia. Over 100 tonnes of dead fish are washed up by the middle of February and serious long-term effects are anticipated from the heavy-metal contamination.

February 2000 Cyclone Eline hits Mozambique, causing two weeks of severe flooding which destroys much of the country's infrastructure. Hundreds are killed and at least 300,000 are left homeless (*see also* **colour section**).

6 February 2000 Italy has a national no-car day in which 150 cities participate, including Rome, Milan, Naples, and Florence.

11 February 2000 British Nuclear Fuels Ltd (BNFL) is told to take back a consignment of reprocessed plutonium–uranium mixed oxide fuel pellets delivered to Japan, after admitting giving false data on the pellets. Later in the month, plans by the UK government to partially privatize BNFL are thrown into doubt by revelations that safety data on its Sellafield plant had been falsified since 1996.

March 2000 The Ukraine government announces that it will shut down the Chernobyl nuclear power station by the end of the year. The worst nuclear accident in history occurred at Chernobyl in 1984.

14 March 2000 The World Commission on Water publishes a report calling for the annual investment in water facilities to more than double, and for controls to be put in place on over-extraction of water which is causing widespread environmental damage. It is anticipated that demand for water will increase by 40% between 2000 and 2040.

12 June 2000 English biologist Dr Roy Gambell, secretary of the International Whaling Commission, states that the international moratorium on commercial whaling, in effect since 1982, should end.

13 June 2000 Environment minister Michael Meacher announces that over 5 million acres classified as Areas of Outstanding Natural Beauty (AONBs) will be protected from development like national parks.

28 June 2000 A huge digital database incorporating electronic images and sounds of endangered species of animals and plants throughout the world is to be set up in the UK. The bank, called Arkive, is an initiative of the Wildscreen Trust, an educational charity based in Bristol.

29 June 2000 A brushfire caused by a car crash rages out of control in Washington state, dangerously near to the most contaminated nuclear site in the USA. This follows a brushfire earlier in the month that threatened nuclear weapons laboratories in New Mexico.

20 June 2000 A report into northeast Atlantic fisheries concludes that exotic deep-sea fish – including roughy, forkbeard, and the silky shark – as well as commercial fish such as cod and haddock are in serious danger of overexploitation.

Drought and famine again devastated large areas of Ethiopia. In May 2000, some eight million Ethiopians and a million Eritreans were at risk of starvation, a situation worsened by the ongoing war between the two countries. *Syndication International*

Animals and Plants

Classification of Living Things

Classification is the grouping of organisms based on similar traits and evolutionary histories. Taxonomy and systematics are the two sciences that attempt to classify living things. In taxonomy, organisms are generally assigned to groups based on their characteristics. In modern systematics, the placement of organisms into groups is based on evolutionary relationships among organisms. Thus, the groupings are based on evolutionary relatedness or family histories called phylogenies.

The groups into which organisms are classified are called taxa (singular, taxon). The taxon that includes the fewest members is the species which identifies a single type of organism. Closely related species are placed into a genus (plural, genera). Related genera are placed into families, families into orders, orders into classes, classes into phyla (singular, phylum) or – in the case of plants and fungi – into divisions, and phyla into divisions or kingdoms. The kingdom level, of which five are generally recognized, is the broadest taxonomic group and includes the greatest number of species. The table below provides an example of the classification of an organism representative of the animal kingdom and the plant kingdom.

■ Animals and Plants

Classification of Living Things (*continued*)

Taxonomic groups[1]

Common name	Kingdom	Phylum/division[2]	Class	Order	Family	Genus[3]	Species[3]
human	Animalia	Chordata	Mammalia	Primates	Hominoidea	*Homo*	*sapiens*
Douglas fir	Plantae	Tracheophyta	Gymnospermae	Coniferales	Pinaceae	*Pseudotsuga*	*douglasii*

[1] Intermediate taxonomic levels can be created by adding the prefixes 'super-' or 'sub-' to the name of any taxonomic level.
[2] The term division is generally used in place of phylum for the classification of plants and fungi.
[3] An individual organism is given a two-part name made up of its genus and species names. For example, Douglas fir is correctly known as *Pseudotsuga douglasii*.

The Five Kingdoms of Living Things

Kingdom	Main features of organisms	Number of species
Monera[1]	all are bacteria; single-celled; prokaryotic (lack a membrane-bound nucleus); autotrophic (feed on simple substances by photosynthesis and chemosynthesis) and heterotrophic (feed on complex substances); all reproduce asexually, some also reproduce sexually	›10,000
Protista	single-celled or multicelled; eukaryotic (have a membrane-bound nucleus and membrane-bound organelles); autotrophic (photosynthesis in algae and Euglenoids) and heterotrophic; may reproduce asexually or sexually	›100,000
Fungi	single-celled and multicellular; eukaryotic; heterotrophic; form spores at all stages of their life cycle; usually reproduce asexually, many reproduce by conjugation (a simple form of sexual reproduction)	about 100,000
Plantae	all are multicellular; eukaryotic; most are autotrophic (via photosynthesis); reproduce sexually; in some life cycle includes an alternation of generations (a haploid gametophyte stage when sex cells are created, these go on to produce spores in the diploid sporophyte stage, the spores then produce sex cells, and so on)	›250,000
Animalia	all are multicellular; eukaryotic; all are heterotrophic; reproduce sexually; develop from a blastula; most have tissues organized into organs	›1,000,000

[1] The Kingdom Monera is sometimes called the Kingdom Prokaryotae.

A light-emitting honey fungus can cause born owls to emit a ghostly glow. The owls accidentally pick up the fungus when perching on rotten tree stumps.

Native Species of Animals and Plants in Britain

As of 1997.

Species group	Number of native species
Animals	
Mammals breeding on land	44
Birds	551
Non-marine reptiles	6
Marine reptiles	1
Amphibians	6/7
Freshwater fish	38
Flies	*c.* 6,600
Bees, wasps, ants	542
Beetles	*c.* 4,000
Butterflies, moths	*c.* 2,600
Caddis flies	199
True bugs	540
Grasshoppers, crickets, cockroaches	30
Stoneflies	34
Dragonflies, damselflies	41
Mayflies	48
Spiders, harvestmen, pseudoscorpions	*c.* 687
Larger non-marine crustaceans	*c.* 70
Non-marine molluscs	*c.* 208
Leeches	16
Plants and other organisms	
Seed plants	*c.* 2,230
Ferns and related plants	70
Liverworts, mosses	*c.* 1,000
Lichens	›1,700
Stoneworts	30
Fungi	›20,000
Slime moulds	*c.* 350

Source: Digest of Environmental Statistics No 20; 1998, © *Crown copyright 1998*

Major Divisions in the Plant Kingdom

Phylum	Translation	Examples
Bryophyta	moss plant	mosses, liverworts, hornworts
Psilophyta	bare, smooth plant	whisk ferns
Lycophyta	wolf foot plant	club mosses
Sphenophyta	wedge plant	horsetails
Filicinophyta/ Pteridophyta	fern plant	ferns
Cycadophyta	palm plant	cycads
Ginkgophyta	silver apricot plant[1]	*Ginkgo*
Coniferophyta	cone bearing plant	cedar, cypress, juniper, pine, redwood
Gnetophyta	desert cone plant[2]	gnetum, welwitschia, ephedra
Angiospermophyta	little case seed plant	flowering plants[3]

[1] Japanese, not Latin, origin.
[2] Not literal translation.
[3] The Angiospermophyta, also called Angiosperms or Anthophyta, are the most successful land plants, found in almost every habitat. This phylum contains nearly every tree, shrub, grass, and plant that produces flowers and seeds. The phylum has two broad sub-divisions: Dicotyledons (Dicots) and Monocotyledons (Monocots). In the Dicots, the seedling emerges with a pair of seed leaves (cotyledons), whereas in Monocots, there is only the one. The Monocots include the grasses, rushes, and sedges, as well as many other flowering plants with long leaves with the veins running along the length. The Dicots include the majority of flowering plants and trees.

Birds support a vast variety of parasites. A curlew may carry over 1,000 feather lice, and a single grouse can harbour 10,000 nematode worms within its intestines.

Classification of Carnivorous Plants

Plants that obtain at least some of their nutrition by capturing and digesting prey are called carnivorous plants. Such plants have adaptations that allow them to attract, catch, and break down or digest prey once it is caught. Estimates of the number of species of carnivorous plants number from 450 to more than 600. Generally, these plants are classified into genera based upon the mechanism they have for trapping and capturing their prey. The major genera of these plants are listed in the table.

Classification of Carnivorous Plants (*continued*)

Common name	Genus	Scientific name	Trapping mechanism
bladderwort	*Utricularia*	*Utricularia vulgaris*	active trap; shows rapid motion during capture
butterwort	*Pinguicula*	*Pinguicula vulgaris*	semi-active trap; two-stage trap in which prey is initially caught in sticky fluid
calf's head pitcher plant	*Darlingtonia*	*Darlingtonia californica*	passive trap; attracts prey with nectar and then drowns prey in fluid contained within plant
flypaper plant	*Byblis*	*Byblis liniflora*	passive trap; attracts prey with nectar and then drowns prey in fluid contained within plant
sundew	*Drosera*	*Drosera linearis*	semi-active trap; two-stage trap in which prey is initially caught in sticky fluid
Venus flytrap	*Dionaea*	*Dionaea muscipula*	active trap; shows rapid motion during capture

Major Invertebrate and Vertebrate Groups

Phyla are listed in the order traditionally considered to be from the most primitive to the most advanced.

Taxon[1]	Name	Examples
Invertebrates		
P	Porifera	all sponges
P	Cnidaria	corals, sea anemones, *Hydra*, jellyfishes
P	Ctenophora	sea gooseberries, comb jellies
P	Platyhelminthes	flatworms, flukes, tapeworms
P	Nemertina	nemertine worms, ribbon worms
P	Rotifera	rotifers or wheel animals
P	Nematoda	roundworms
P	Ectoprocta	ectoprocts
P	Mollusca	clams, oysters, snails, slugs, octopuses, squids, cuttlefish
P	Annelida	ringed worms, including lugworms, earthworms, and leeches
P	Arthropoda	(subdivided into classes below)
C	Arachnida	spiders, ticks, scorpions, mites
C	Branchiopoda	water fleas
C	Cirripedia	barnacles
C	Malacostraca	crabs, lobsters, shrimp, woodlice
C	Diplopoda	millipedes
C	Chilopoda	centipedes
C	Insecta	silverfish, dragonflies, mayflies, stoneflies, cockroaches, earwigs, web spinners, termites, booklice, lice, grasshoppers, thrips, lace-wings, scorpion flies, caddis-flies, moths, butterflies, beetles, house flies, fleas, stylopids, ants, bees
P	Echinodermata	sea stars, brittle stars, sea urchins, sand dollars, sea cucumbers
P	Hemichordata	acorn worms, pterobranchs, graptolites
Vertebrates		
C	Agnatha	(jawless fishes) lampreys, hagfishes
C	Chondricthyes	(cartilaginous fishes) dogfishes, sharks, rays, skates
C	Osteichthyes	(bony fishes) sturgeons, eels, herrings, salmon, carps, catfishes, perches, flatfishes including flounder and halibut
C	Amphibia	caecilians, salamanders, newts, toads, frogs
C	Reptilia	turtles, tortoises, tuatara, lizards, snakes, crocodiles
C	Aves	ostriches, rheas, penguins, divers, pelicans, flamingoes, ducks, falcons, pheasants, cranes, gulls, pigeons, parrots, cuckoos, owls, swifts, kingfishers, sparrows
C	Mammalia	platypus, echidnas, kangaroos, opossums, shrews, bats, rats, anteaters, rabbits, dogs, whales, elephants, manatees, horses, tapirs, camels, pigs, lemurs, monkeys, humans

[1] P represents phylum; C represents class.

Classification of Mammals

Order	Number of species	Examples
Leading class: Mammalia		
Subclass: Prototheria (egg-laying mammals)		
Monotremata	3	echidna, platypus
Subclass: Theria		
Infraclass: Metatheria (pouched mammals)		
Marsupiala	266	kangaroo, koala, opossum
Infraclass: Eutheria (placental mammals)		
Rodentia	1,700	rat, mouse, squirrel, porcupine
Chiroptera	970	all bats
Insectivora	378	shrew, hedgehog, mole
Carnivora	230	cat, dog, weasel, bear
Primates	180	lemur, monkey, ape, human
Artiodactyla	145	pig, deer, cattle, camel, giraffe
Cetacea	79	whale, dolphin
Lagomorpha	58	rabbit, hare, pika
Pinnipedia	33	seal, walrus
Edentata	29	anteater, armadillo, sloth
Perissodactyla	16	horse, rhinoceros, tapir
Hyracoidea	11	hyrax
Pholidota	7	pangolin
Sirenia	4	dugong, manatee
Dermoptera	2	flying lemur
Proboscidea	2	elephant
Tubulidentata	1	aardvark

Classification of Major Bird Groups

Orders are listed from what is traditionally considered to be the most primitive to the most advanced.

Order	Examples
Struthioniformes	ostrich
Rheiformes	rhea
Casuariiformes	cassowary, emu
Apterygiformes	kiwi
Tinamiformes	tinamous
Sphenisciformes	penguin
Gaviiformes	loon
Podicipediformes	grebe
Procellariformes	albatross, petrel, shearwater, storm petrel
Pelecaniformes	pelican, booby, gannet, frigate bird
Ciconiiformes	heron, ibis, stork, spoonbill, flamingo
Anseriformes	duck, goose, swan
Falconiformes	falcon, hawk, eagle, buzzard, vulture
Galliformes	grouse, partridge, pheasant, turkey
Gruiformes	crane, rail, bustard, coot
Charadriiformes	wader, gull, auk, oyster-catcher, plover, puffin, tern
Columbiformes	dove, pigeon, sandgrouse
Psittaciformes	parrot, macaw, parakeet
Cuculiformes	cuckoo, roadrunner
Strigiformes	owl
Caprimulgiformes	nightjar, oilbird
Apodiformes	swift, hummingbird
Coliiformes	mousebird
Trogoniformes	trogon
Coraciiformes	kingfisher, hoopoe
Piciformes	woodpecker, toucan, puffbird
Passeriformes	finch, crow, warbler, sparrow, weaver, jay, lark, blackbird, swallow, mockingbird, wren, thrush

Classification of Fish

Order	Number of species	Examples
Class: Agnatha (jawless fishes)		
Subclass: Cyclostomota (scaleless fish with round mouths)		
Petromyzoniformes	30	lamprey
Myxiniformes	30	hagfish
Superclass: Pisces (jawed fishes)		
Class: Chondrichthyes (cartilaginous fishes)		
Subclass: Elasmobranchii (sharks and rays)		
Selachii	›200	shark
Batoidei	›300	skate, ray
Subclass: Holocephali (rabbitfishes)		
Chimaeriformes	20	chimaera, rabbitfish
Class: Osteichthyes (bony fishes)		
Subclass: Sarcopterygii (lobe-finned fishes)		
Coelacanthiformes	1	coelacanth
Ceratodiformes	1	Australian lungfish
Lepidosireniformes	4	South American and Africanlungfish
Subclass: Actinopterygii (ray-finned fishes)		
Polypteriformes	11	bichir, reedfish
Acipensiformes	25	paddlefish, sturgeon
Superorder: Teleostei		
Elopiformes	12	bonefish, tarpon, ladyfish
Anguilliformes	›500	eel
Clupeiformes	390	herring, anchovy
Osteoglossiformes	7	arapaima, African butterfly fish
Mormyriformes	150	elephant-trunk fish, featherback
Salmoniformes	160	salmon, trout, smelt, pike
Gonorhynchiformes	15	milkfish
Ostariophsi	6,000	carp, barb, characin, loach, catfish
Myctophiformes	300	deep-sea lantern fish, Bombay duck
Paracathopteryggi	853	toadfish, trout-perch, codfish
Atheriniformes	575	flying fish, toothcarp, halfbeak
Gasterosteiformes	150	stickleback, pipefish, seahorse
Pleuronectiformes	402	flatfish, flounder
Tetraodontiformes	250	puffer fish, triggerfish, sunfish
Perciformes	6,500	perch, cichlid, damsel fish, gobie, wrass, parrotfish, gourami, marlin, mackerel, tuna,swordfish, spiny eel, mullet, barracuda, sea bream, croaker, ice fish, butterfish

Barracudas are attracted to all things yellow. This means that they may be caught by the use of yellow-feathered lines.

Goldfish can change their colour according to their surroundings or mood. They will become pale in a white container or if they are angry or frightened.

There is a fish that can climb trees. The mudskipper spends three-quarters of its time out of water. Malaysian mudskippers live in mangrove swamps, where they climb among the tangled stems and roots, and sometimes into the branches.

Classification of Insects

Order	Number of species	Examples
Class: Insecta		
***Subclass: Apterygota** (**wingless insects**)*		
Collembola[1]	2,000	springtails
Diplura	660	two-pronged bristletails, campodeids, japygids
Protura	120	minute insects living in soil
Thysanura	600	three-pronged bristletails, silverfish
***Subclass: Pterygota** (**winged insects or forms secondary wingless**)*, incorporating two superorders:		
***Superorder: Exopterygota** (**young resemble adults but have externally-developing wings**)*		
Ephemeroptera	2,000	mayflies
Odonata	5,000	dragonflies, damselflies
Grylloblattodea	12	wingless soil-living insects of North America
Plecoptera	3,000	stoneflies
Zoraptera	20	tiny insects living in decaying plants
Isoptera	2,000	termites
Dermaptera	1,500	earwigs
Embioptera	200	web-spinners
Dictyoptera	3,700	cockroaches, praying mantises
Orthoptera	24,000	crickets, grasshoppers, locusts, mantids, roaches

(continued)

If alarmed, the bombardier beetle releases a boiling toxic chemical spray at 500–1,000 pulses per second. The chemicals are stored separately and only reach boiling point (100 °C) when they mix. Pulsing prevents the beetle's abdomen from exploding.

Once the female ground beetle has mated, she releases methacrylic acid, a chemical that not only deters other males but sends them into a death-like coma for up to three hours.

Darkling beetles living in the Namib desert in Africa drink by standing on their heads at the crests of sand dunes at dawn. Mists rolling in from the coast condense to form water on their bodies; the water then trickles down into their mouths.

The Costa Rican assassin bug has a cunning way of catching termites for food. Disguised as a piece of nesting material, it grabs a passing termite and sucks its body dry. It then uses the corpse as a lure, shaking it outside a termite burial chamber while concealed in a crack in the earth.

The caterpillars of some swallowtail butterflies deter predators by their uncanny resemblance to fresh bird droppings.

Classification of Insects *(continued)*

Order	Number of species	Examples
Phasmida	2,500	stick insects, leaf insects
Psocoptera	1,600	booklice, barklice, psocids
Mallophaga	2,500	biting lice, mainly parasitic on birds
Anoplura	250	sucking lice, mainly parasitic on mammals
Hemiptera	39,500	true bugs, including shield- and bedbugs, froghoppers, pond skaters, water boatmen
Homoptera	45,000	aphids, cicadas, hoppers, whiteflies
Thysanoptera	5,000	thrips
Superorder: Endopterygota (young are unlike adults and undergo sudden metamorphosis)		
Neuroptera	4,500	lacewings, alderflies, snakeflies
Mecoptera	450	scorpion flies
Lepidoptera	138,000	butterflies, moths
Trichoptera	7,000	caddisflies
Diptera	150,000	true flies, including bluebottles, mosquitoes, leatherjackets, midges
Siphonaptera	1,750	fleas
Hymenoptera	130,000	bees, wasps, ants, sawflies, chalcids
Coleoptera	250,000	beetles, including weevils, ladybirds, glow-worms, woodworms, chafers

[1] Some zoologists recognize the Collembola taxon as a class rather than an order.

Animal Lifespans

(N/A = not available.)

Animal	Average longevity (years)	Maximum longevity (years)[1]
Ass	12	35.8
Baboon	20	35.5
Bear (black)	18	36.8
Bear (grizzly)	25	47
Bear (polar)	20	34.7
Beaver	10	20.5
Buffalo (American)	15	N/A
Camel (Bactrian)	12	N/A
Cat (domestic)	12	28
Chimpanzee	40	44.5
Chipmunk	6	8
Cow	15	30
Deer (white-tailed)	8	N/A
Dog (domestic)	12	20
Elephant (African)	60	80
Elephant (Asian)	60	80
Elk	15	26.5
Fox (red)	7	14
Giraffe	25	33.5
Goat (domestic)	8	8
Gorilla	35	50
Guinea pig	4	7.5
Hippopotamus	45	49
Horse	20	46
Kangaroo	12	28
Leopard	12	19.3
Lion	15	25
Monkey (rhesus)	15	N/A
Moose	12	N/A
Mouse (domestic white)	1	3.5
Mouse (meadow)	3	N/A
Opossum (American)	2	8
Pig (domestic)	10	27
Puma	12	19
Rabbit (domestic)	5	13
Rhinoceros (black)	15	N/A
Rhinoceros (white)	20	N/A
Sea lion (California)	12	28
Sheep (domestic)	12	20
Squirrel (grey)	10	N/A

(continued)

As a flea jumps, its rate of acceleration is 20 times that of a space shuttle during launching. It reaches a speed of 100 m per sec within the first 500th of a second.

The tongue of the Malagasy hawk moth is more than twice the length of its body. This enables it to feed from flowers without having to land on them, thus avoiding predators waiting in ambush.

Green lacewing larvae feed on woolly alder aphids, but the aphids are guarded by ants who milk them for their honeydew. The larvae trick the ants by plucking the white waxy fluff from the aphids and sticking it over themselves. With this disguise, they move among the aphids and eat them without the ants noticing.

Australian researchers discovered in 1999 that orb spiders improve in their webspinning abilities as they grow older, indicating that they learn from experience.

Locust swarms can contain up to 10 billion individuals and cover a surface of 1,000 sq km/400 sq mi. The swarm can remain together for weeks, devastating crops and other vegetation for thousands of kilometres. Each square kilometre of locusts (up to 80 million) can consume 250 tonnes of food a day, the daily amount required to feed 80,000 people.

The eyelids of camels are transparent from the inside so the ships of the desert can see where they are going with their eyes closed.

Dolphins only sleep with half their brain at a time. Whilst one hemisphere goes to sleep, the other remains vigilant, with them swapping over several times a night. If both sides are put to sleep artificially, the dolphin stops breathing.

Elephants are highly social animals with strong family ties and research has shown that they are capable of complex emotions. Females assist each other in the birth of their calves, and families work together in the care of the young and sick members of the herd. If a family member dies they may cover its body with leaves, twigs, and branches, and sometimes stay by the 'grave' for some hours.

The average British fox obtains only about a third of its food from hunting. The remainder is acquired by scavenging.

One species of Hawaiian gecko reproduces without sex to create all-female populations. These females have fewer parasites (and thus better health) than their mixed-gender neighbours.

When a hippopotamus dies, other hippos surround the corpse and lick it. They may remain like this for a whole day, driving away any hungry crocodiles. They only abandon the corpse when the crocodiles become too numerous to deter.

The female spotted hyena has a higher level of the male sex hormone testosterone than the male.

A fully grown kangaroo can jump 13 m/14 yd. Mathematical calculations have shown that at speeds of over 29 kmph/18 mph, bouncing is a more energy-efficient way of moving for a kangaroo than running.

Animal Lifespans (*continued*)

Animal	Average longevity (years)	Maximum longevity (years)[1]
Tiger	16	26.3
Wolf (grey)	12	20
Zebra (Grant's)	15	35

[1] Maximum longevity figures refer to animals in captivity; an animal's potential lifespan is rarely attained in the wild.

Killer whales deliberately strand themselves by hurtling out of the sea on to the beach to capture elephant seal pups. This dangerous hunting technique (with a success rate of only 35%) takes the killer whale calves more than two years to learn.

Average Animal Gestation Periods and Incubation Times

Animal	Gestation[1]/incubation[2] (days)
Mammals	
Ass	365
Baboon	187
Bear (black)	210
Bear (grizzly)	225
Bear (polar)	240
Beaver	122
Buffalo (American)	270
Camel (Bactrian)	410
Cat (domestic)	58–65
Chimpanzee	230
Chinchilla	110–120
Chipmunk	31
Cow	279–292
Deer (white-tailed)	201
Dog (domestic)	58–70
Elephant (Asian)	645
Elk (Wapiti)	240–250
Fox (red)	52
Giraffe	420–450
Goat (domestic)	145–155
Gorilla	257
Guinea pig	68
Hippopotamus	225–250
Horse	330–342
Kangaroo	42
Leopard	92–95
Lion	108
Llama	330
Mink	40–75
Monkey (rhesus)	164
Moose	240–250
Mouse (domestic white)	19
Mouse (meadow)	21
Muskrat	28–30
Opossum (American)	12–13
Otter	270–300
Pig (domestic)	112–115
Porcupine	112
Puma	90
Rabbit (domestic)	30–35
Raccoon	63
Rhinoceros (black)	450
Seal	330
Sea lion (California)	350
Sheep (domestic)	144–151
Squirrel (grey)	30–40
Tiger	105–113
Whale (sperm)	480–500
Wolf	60–68
Zebra (Grant's)	365
Birds	
Chicken	20–22
Duck	26–28
Finch	11–14
Goose	25–28
Parrot	17–31
Pheasant	24
Pigeon	10–18
Quail	21–23
Swan	33–36
Turkey	28

[1] Mammals.
[2] Birds.

Speeds of Selected Animals

Animal	Speed kph	Speed mph
Cheetah	103	64
Wildebeest	98	61
Lion	81	50
Elk	72	45
Cape hunting dog	72	45
Coyote	69	43
Horse	69	43
Grey fox	68	42
Hyena	64	40
Zebra	64	40
Greyhound	63	39
Whippet	57	35.5
Rabbit (domestic)	56	35
Jackal	56	35
Reindeer	51	32
Giraffe	51	32
White-tailed deer	48	30
Wart hog	48	30
Grizzly bear	48	30
Cat (domestic)	48	30
Human	45	28
Elephant	40	25
Black mamba snake	32	20
Squirrel	19	12
Pig (domestic)	18	11
Chicken	14	9
Giant tortoise	0.27	0.17
Three-toed sloth	0.24	0.15
Garden snail	0.05	0.03

The koala sleeps on average 22 hours a day. It is the only animal more slothful than the sloth, which sleeps only 20 hours a day. Some say that the koala's diet of eucalyptus leaves means that it is in an almost permanently drugged sleep.

In the snow, a polar bear will put a paw over its black nose to lessen the chance of being seen by its prey.

The flatulence of a single sheep could power a small lorry for 40 km/25 mi a day. The digestive process produces methane gas, which can be burnt as fuel. According to one New Zealand scientist, the methane from 72 million sheep could supply the entire fuel needs of his country.

Nine-banded armadillos almost always produce litters of quadruplets. The one fertilized egg divides into four to produce a single-sex litter of identical babies.

While a male emu is incubating the eggs, he cannot move from the nest to eat or drink. He must survive on his existing fat reserves for eight weeks. When the chicks are hatched they remain in their father's care for at least seven months.

The kiwi produces the largest egg, proportionally to size, of any bird. The female lays one or two eggs, each weighing a quarter of her body weight.

Unusually for fish, sea horses are monogamous and have a relatively long courtship (3–7 days).

When pipefish mate it is the female who penetrates the male. She inserts her eggs into his internal pouch using her protruding ovarian duct. He then fertilizes the eggs and carries them as they develop.

Collective Names for Animals

Animal	Collective name
Ants	colony, swarm, nest
Badgers	cete
Bears	sleuth, sloth
Bees	grist, swarm, hive, nest, colony
Birds	flight, volery, flock
Boars	sounder
Cats	clowder, clutter, litter
Cattle	drove, herd
Chicks	brood, clutch
Clams	bed
Cranes	sedge, siege
Crows	murder
Deer	herd
Dogs	litter, kennel, pack (wild)
Ducks	brace, team, flock
Elephants	herd
Elks	gang
Fishes	school, shoal, draught
Foxes	leash, skulk
Geese	flock, gaggle, skein
Gnats	cloud, horde
Goats	tribe, trip, herd
Goldfinches	chirm, charm
Gorillas	band
Greyhounds	leash
Hares	down, husk
Hawks	cast
Horses	pair, team, herd, stable
Hounds	pack, cry, mute
Kangaroos	mob, troop, herd
Larks	exaltation
Leopards	leap
Lions	pride
Monkeys	troop
Mules	span
Nightingales	watch
Oxen	yoke, drove, herd
Oysters	bed
Partridge	covey
Peacocks	muster, ostentation
Pheasants	nest, nide
Pigs	litter
Plovers	congregation
Quails	bevy, covey
Rhinoceroses	crash
Rooks	parliament
Seals	pod, herd, rookery
Sheep	drove, flock, trip
Swans	bevy, wedge
Swine	drift, sounder
Teals	spring
Termites	colony, nest, swarm
Toads	knot
Turtles	bale, dole, rafter
Vipers	nest
Whales	gam, pod, herd
Wolves	pack

Names for Animal Young

Animal	Name for young
Antelope	calf
Bear	cub
Beaver	pup, kit, kitten
Bird	nestling, fledgling
Bobcat	kitten, cub
Buffalo	calf, yearling, spike-bull
Camel	calf, colt
Canary	chick
Cat	kitten
Cattle	calf
Chicken	chick
Chimpanzee	infant
Cod	codling, scrod, sprag
Condor	chick
Deer	fawn
Dog	pup, puppy, whelp
Duck	duckling
Elephant	calf
Fish	fry
Fox	cub
Frog	polliwog, tadpole
Giraffe	calf
Goat	kid
Goose	gosling
Hare	leveret
Hen	pullet
Hippopotamus	calf
Horse	foal, yearling, colt (male), filly (female)
Kangaroo	joey
Lion	cub
Louse	nit
Owl	owlet
Partridge	cheeper, chick
Penguin	fledgling, chick
Pig	piglet
Rabbit	bunny, kitten
Rhinoceros	calf
Seal	pup, whelp, cub
Sea lion	pup
Shark	cub
Sheep	lamb, lambkin
Squirrel	pup
Swan	cygnet
Tiger	cub, whelp
Turkey	chick, poult
Turtle	chicken
Walrus	calf
Whale	calf
Wolf	cub, pup
Zebra	colt, foal

Crufts Supreme Champions: Best in Show

(B – bitch. Ch – Champion. D – dog. N – neutered. Sh Ch – Show Champion.)

Year	Dog's name	Breed	Sex	Owner	Breeder
1980	Ch Shargleam Blackcap	Flat coated retriever	D	Miss P Chapman	owner
1981	Ch Astley's Portia of Rua	Irish setter	B	Mrs and Miss Tuite	Mrs M Korbel
1982	Ch Grayco Hazelnut	Toy poodle	B	Mrs L A Howard	owner
1983	Ch Montravia-Kaskarak Hitari	Afghan hound	D	Mrs P Gibbs	Mrs L Race
1984	Ch Saxonsprings Hackensack	Lhasa Apso	D	Mrs J Blyth	owner
1985	Ch Montravia Tommy-Gun	Standard poodle	D	Miss M Gibbs	Mrs C Coxall
1986	Ch Ginger Xmas Carol	Airedale terrier	B	Mrs A Livraghi	owner
1987	Ch Viscount Grant	Afghan hound	D	Mr C Amoo	owner
1988	Sh Ch Starlight Express of Valsett	English setter	B	Mr and Mrs J W Watkin	Mrs A R Wick
1989	Ch Potterdale Classic of Moonhill	Bearded collie	B	Mrs B R White	Mr and Mrs M Lewis
1990	Ch Olac Moon Pilot	West Highland white terrier	D	Mr D Tattersall	owner
1991	Sh Ch Raycroft Socialite	Clumber spaniel	D	Mr R Dunne	Mrs R Furness
1992	Ch Penglow Dutch Gold	Whippet	N	Miss Bolton	owner
1993	Sh Ch Dunnaway Debonair	Irish setter	N	Mrs Carrimer	owner
1994	Ch Perston Hit and Miss from Brocalita	Welsh terrier	N	Mrs B Halliwell	owner
1995	Sh Ch Starshell Chicago Bear	Irish setter	N	Miss Rachael Shaw	owner
1996	Sh Ch Canigou Cambrai	Cocker spaniel	N	Ms Tricia Bentley	owner
1997	Ch Ozmilion Mystification	Yorkshire terrier	D	Mr Osman Adam Sameja	owner
1998	Ch Saredon Forever Young	Welsh terrier	D	Mr D Scawthorn and Mrs J Averis	owner
1999	Sh Ch Caspians Intrepid	Irish setter	D	Mrs J Lorrimer	Mr and Mrs M Oakley
2000	Ch Torums Scarf Michael	Kerry blue terrier	D	Mr R Ramsay	owner

Source: The Kennel Club

Three out of ten dalmatian dogs suffer from some form of hearing disability, and 8% of all dalmatians are entirely deaf. Their spotty coats are a result of intense inbreeding, which has the side-effect of increasing genetic disorders – such as deafness.

Dogs Registered with the Kennel Club

Year	Sporting[1]	Non-sporting[2]	Total
1980	90,075	111,545	201,620
1981	75,398	96,960	172,358
1982	75,110	97,410	172,520
1983	78,663	106,236	184,899
1984	77,784	106,259	184,043
1985	84,608	113,682	198,290
1986	83,101	106,315	189,416
1987	79,674	101,762	181,436
1988	75,562	90,988	166,550
1989	135,016	148,899	283,915
1990	131,811	138,958	270,769
1991	126,997	125,527	252,524
1992	121,709	118,448	240,157
1993	119,689	116,204	235,893
1994	125,328	121,379	246,707
1995	136,679	127,412	264,091
1996	144,124	129,217	273,341
1997	142,296	126,194	268,490
1998	141,277	117,469	258,746
1999	133,858	108,524	242,382

[1] Hounds, gundogs, and terriers.
[2] Pastoral, toy, utility, and working dogs.

Source: The Kennel Club

Top 10 Pedigree Dog Breeds in the UK

1998 Rank	Breed
1	Labrador Retriever
2	German Shepherd Dog
3	West Highland White Terrier
4	Golden Retriever
5	Cocker Spaniel
6	English Springer Spaniel
7	Cavalier King Charles Spaniel
8	Boxer
9	Yorkshire Terrier
10	Staffordshire Bull Terrier

Source: www.petplanet.co.uk

Top 10 Names for Dogs in the UK

1998 Rank	Male	Female
1	Sam	Trixie
2	Spot	Polly
3	Pip	Jessie
4	Duke	Lucy
5	Piper	Bonnie
6	Max	Cassie
7	Charlie	Daisy
8	Rocky	Heidi
9	Zak	Susie
10	Tiny	Holly

Source: www.petplanet.co.uk

Animals and Plants: International Environmental Agreements

Convention on International Trade in Endangered Species (CITES) of Wild Fauna and Flora

Date of adoption 3 March 1973; Amendments: 22 June 1979; 30 April 1983
Place of adoption Washington, District of Columbia, USA; Amendments: Bonn, Germany; Gaborone, Botswana
Date of entry into force 1 July 1975; Amendments: 13 April 1987; Not yet
Number of signatory countries 110

Objectives To protect certain endangered species from over-exploitation by means of a system of import/export permits.

Summary of selected provisions Includes animals and plants whether dead or alive, and any recognizable parts or derivatives thereof. The Convention covers endangered species, trade in which is to be tightly controlled; species that may become endangered unless trade is regulated; and species that any Party wishes to regulate and requires international cooperation to control trade.

Convention on the Conservation of Migratory Species of Wild Animals

Date of adoption 23 June 1979
Place of adoption Bonn, Germany
Date of entry into force 1 November 1983
Number of signatory countries 39

Objective To protect those species of wild animals that migrate across or outside national boundaries.

Summary of selected provisions Listing of endangered migratory species; international agreements dealing with those aspects of the conservation and management of the migratory species concerned which serve to achieve the object of protection; establishment of a scientific council to provide advice on scientific matters.

International Plant Protection Convention

Date of adoption 6 December 1951; Amendment: November 1979
Place of adoption Rome, Italy
Date of entry into force 3 April 1952; Amendment: 4 April 1991
Number of signatory countries 97

Objectives To maintain and increase international cooperation in controlling pests and diseases of plants and plant products, and in preventing their introduction and spread across national boundaries.

Summary of selected provisions Parties undertake to adopt the legislative, technical and administrative measures specified in the Convention; specific and regional agreements to be made in conjunction with the Food and Agriculture Organization (FAO) of the United Nations; each Party to set up an official plant protection organization to inspect areas under cultivation and consignments of plants in international traffic for existence or outbreak of plant pests or diseases, and to carry out research in the field of plant protection; Parties to regulate very strictly the import and export of plants and plant products, by means, where necessary, of prohibitions, inspections, and destruction of consignments.

Endangered Species

Introduction

A species is described as being endangered if it is in danger of becoming extinct should its situation not improve; extinction means that a particular organism has not been seen in the wild for over 50 years. Threatened species are those at significant risk of becoming endangered; and a rare species is one that may also be at risk, and has a small population. Paleontologists estimate that as much as 90–99% of all species ever to have lived on Earth are extinct.

What are the benefits of preserving species?

In the field of medicine, certain plant and animal species have benefited technology and treatment enormously. Unfortunately, detailed experimentation with plant species has hardly begun. To preserve the potential of the botanical world, it is essential that variety within each species be conserved. It is also thought that much of the world's hunger could be reduced if more investment were made in developing unresearched crops. In addition to food and medicines, plants and animals produce other materials, including rubber, oils, wool, down, and dyes.

Introduction *(continued)*

Why are species becoming endangered?

Many factors may contribute to the extinction of a particular organism, including loss of natural habitat, exploitation (such as collecting, hunting, and trade in animal parts), pollution, and the introduction of non-native species (as predators or competitors, or bringing disease). The destruction of the natural habitat threatens the greatest number of species. The draining of wetlands, clearing of forests, and building of roads and dams are just some of the ways in which humans are destroying habitats. As habitats become smaller and more separate, species may begin to lose genetic diversity and become more vulnerable to extinction. International trade in live plants and animals, and in wildlife products such as skins, horns, shells, and feathers, has brought some species to the verge of extinction, and whole ecosystems (for example, coral reefs) are threatened. Species almost eradicated by trade in their products include many of the largest whales, crocodiles, marine turtles, and some wild cats.

While a steady rate of extinction is considered to be part of the process of evolution, the rate at which species are becoming extinct has accelerated as human populations have grown and levels of resource consumption increased.

Species	Observation
plants	a quarter of the world's plants are threatened with extinction by the year 2010
amphibians	worldwide decline in numbers; half of New Zealand's frog species are now extinct; 25% of species threatened with extinction (1996); 38% of US amphibians were endangered (1997)
birds	three-quarters of all bird species are declining; 11% are threatened with extinction (1996)
carnivores	almost all species of cats and bears are declining in numbers
fish	one-third of North American freshwater fish are rare or endangered; half the fish species in Lake Victoria, Africa's largest lake, are close to extinction due to predation by the introduced Nile perch; 33% of species are threatened with extinction (1996)
invertebrates	about 100 species are lost each day due to deforestation; half the freshwater snails in the southeastern USA are now extinct or threatened; 50% of crayfish and 56% of mussel species are endangered in the USA; a quarter of German invertebrates are threatened
mammals	half of Australia's mammals are threatened; 40% of mammals in France, the Netherlands, Germany, and Portugal are threatened; 25% of species are threatened with extinction (1996)
primates	two-thirds of primate species are threatened
reptiles	over 40% of reptile species are threatened; 20% with extinction (1996)

Selected Animals on the World Endangered and Threatened Species List

Common name	Scientific name	Range	When listed
Mammals			
Armadillo, giant	*Priodontes maximus* (= *giganteus*)	South America	24 June 1976
Bear, brown	*Ursus arctos arctos*	Europe	24 June 1976
Bear, brown	*Ursus arctos pruinosus*	Asia	24 June 1976
Bear, Mexican grizzly	*Ursus arctos* (= *U. a. nelsoni*)	North America	2 June 1970
Bison, wood	*Bison bison athabascae*	North America	2 June 1970
Bobcat	*Felis rufus escuinapae*	North America	24 June 1976
Camel, Bactrian	*Camelus bactrianus* (= *ferus*)	Asia	24 June 1976
Cat, leopard	*Felis bengalensis bengalensis*	Asia	24 June 1976
Deer, pampas	*Ozotoceros bezoarticus*	South America	24 June 1976
Dugong	*Dugong dugon*	Africa	2 December 1970
Duiker, Jentink's	*Cephalophus jentinki*	Africa	25 June 1979
Eland, western giant	*Taurotragus derbianus derbianus*	Africa	25 June 1979
Elephant, African	*Loxodonta africana*	Africa	12 May 1978
Elephant, Asian	*Elephas maximus*	Asia	24 June 1974
Gazelle, Clark's (Dibatag)	*Ammodorcas clarkei*	Africa	2 June 1970
Gorilla	*Gorilla gorilla*	Africa	2 June 1970
Kangaroo, Tasmanian forester	*Macropus giganteus tasmaniensis*	Australia	4 June 1973
Lemurs	*Lemuridae*	Africa	2 June 1970, 14 June 1976, 24 June 1976
Leopard	*Panthera pardus*	Africa, Asia	2 June 1970, 30 March 1972, 28 January 1982
Leopard, snow	*Panthera uncia*	Asia	30 March 1972
Manatee, Amazonian	*Trichechus inunguis*	South America	2 June 1970
Manatee, West African	*Trichechus senegalensis*	Africa	20 July 1979
Monkey, black howler	*Alouatta pigra*	North America	19 October 1976
Monkey, red-backed squirrel	*Saimiri oerstedii*	South America	2 June 1970
Monkey, spider	*Ateles geoffroyi frontatus*	South America	2 June 1970
Mouse, Shark Bay	*Pseudomys praeconis*	Australia	2 December 1970
Orangutan	*Pongo pygmaeus*	Asia	2 June 1970
Panda, giant	*Ailuropoda melanoleuca*	Asia	23 January 1984
Rat-kangaroo, Queensland	*Bettongia tropica*	Australia	2 December 1970
Rhinoceros, black	*Diceros bicornis*	Africa	14 July 1980
Rhinoceros, great Indian	*Rhinoceros unicornis*	Asia	2 December 1970
Seal, Saimaa	*Phoca hispida saimensis*	Europe	28 July 1993
Sloth, Brazilian three-toed	*Bradypus torquatus*	South America	2 June 1970
Tapir, Asian	*Tapirus indicus*	Asia	24 June 1974
Tapir, mountain	*Tapirus pinchaque*	South America	2 June 1970
Tiger	*Panthera tigris*	Asia	2 June 1970, 30 March 1972
Tiger, Tasmanian (thylacine)	*Thylacinus cynocephalus*	Australia	2 June 1970
Wallaby, banded hare	*Lagostrophus fasciatus*	Australia	2 December 1970
Whale, blue	*Balaenoptera musculus*	Oceanic	2 June 1970
Whale, bowhead	*Balaena mysticetus*	Oceanic	2 June 1970
Whale, finback	*Balaenoptera physalus*	Oceanic	2 June 1970
Whale, humpback	*Megaptera novaeangliae*	Oceanic	2 June 1970

(continued)

Selected Animals on the World Endangered and Threatened Species List (*continued*)

Common name	Scientific name	Range	When listed
Whale, right	*Balaena glacialis* (incl. *australis*)	Oceanic	2 June 1970
Whale, sperm	*Physeter macrocephalus* (= *catodon*)	Oceanic	2 June 1970
Wombat, hairy-nosed (Barnard's and Queensland hairy-nosed)	*Lasiorhinus krefftii* (formerly *L. Barnardi* and *L. gillespiei*)	Australia	2 December 1970, 4 June 1973
Zebra, Grevy's	*Equus grevyi*	Africa	21 August 1979
Zebra, mountain	*Equus zebra zebra*	Africa	24 June 1976, 10 February 1981
Birds			
Booby, Abbott's	*Sula abbotti*	Asia	24 June 1976
Condor, Andean	*Vultur gryphus*	South America	2 December 1970
Crane, hooded	*Grus monacha*	Asia	2 December 1970
Crane, Japanese	*Grus japonenis*	Asia	2 June 1970
Crane, whooping	*Grus americana*	North America	11 March 1967, and other dates
Eagle, harpy	*Harpia harpyja*	South America	24 June 1976
Egret, Chinese	*Egretta eulophotes*	Asia	2 June 1970
Falcon, American peregrine	*Falco peregrinus anatum*	North America	13 October 1970
Hawk, Galapagos	*Buteo galapagoensis*	South America	2 June 1970
Ibis, Japanese crested	*Nipponia nippon*	Asia	2 June 1970
Ibis, northern bald	*Geronticus eremita*	Africa, Asia, Europe	28 September 1990
Macaw, glaucous	*Anodorhynchus glaucus*	South America	24 June 1976
Macaw, indigo	*Anodorhynchus leari*	South America	24 June 1976
Ostrich, Arabian	*Struthio camelus syriacus*	Asia	2 June 1970
Ostrich, West African	*Struthio camelus spatzi*	Africa	2 June 1970
Parakeet, gold-shouldered (hooded)	*Psephotus chrysopterygius*	Australia	2 June 1970
Parakeet, Norfolk Island	*Cyanoramphus novaezelandiae cookii*	Australia	28 September 1990
Parrot, ground	*Pezoporus wallicus*	Australia	4 June 1973
Parrot, red-capped	*Pionopsitta pileata*	South America	24 June 1976
Stork, oriental white	*Ciconia ciconia boyciana*	Asia	2 June 1970
Woodpecker, imperial	*Campephilus imperialis*	North America	2 June 1970
Woodpecker, Tristam's	*Drycopus javenis richardsi*	Asia	2 June 1970
Reptiles			
Alligator, Chinese	*Alligator sinensis*	Asia	24 June 1976
Caiman, Apaporis River	*Caiman crocodilus apaporiensis*	South America	24 June 1976
Crocodile, African dwarf	*Osteolaemus tetraspis tetraspis*	Africa	24 June 1976
Crocodile, African slender-snouted	*Crocodylus cataphractus*	Africa	30 March 1972
Crocodile, Morelet's	*Crocodylus moreletii*	South America	2 June 1970
Iguana, Barrington land	*Conolophus pallidus*	South America	2 June 1970
Lizard, Hierro giant	*Gallotia simonyi simonyi*	Europe	29 February 1984
Lizard, Ibiza wall	*Podarcis pityusensis*	Europe	29 February 1984
Monitor, Bengal	*Varanus bengalensis*	Asia	24 June 1976
Monitor, desert	*Varanus griseus*	Africa	24 June 1976
Monitor, yellow	*Varanus flavescens*	Asia	24 June 1976
Python, Indian	*Python molurus molurus*	Asia	24 June 1976
Tartaruga	*Podocnemis expansa*	South America	2 June 1970
Tortoise, Bolson	*Gopherus flavomarginatus*	North America	17 April 1979
Tortoise, Galapagos	*Geochelone elephantopus*	South America	2 June 1970
Tuatara	*Sphenodon punctatus*	Australia	2 June 1970
Turtle, aquatic box	*Terrapene coahuila*	North America	4 June 1973
Turtle, green sea	*Chelonia mydas* (incl. *agassizi*)	North America (circumglobal)	28 July 1978
Viper, Lar Valley	*Vipera latiffi*	Asia	22 June 1983
Amphibians			
Frog, Goliath	*Conraua goliath*	Africa	8 December 1994
Frog, Israel painted	*Discoglossus nigriventer*	Europe	2 June 1970
Frog, Panamanian golden	*Atelopus varius zeteki*	South America	24 June 1976
Frog, Stephen Island	*Leiopelma hamiltoni*	Australia	2 June 1970
Salamander, Chinese giant	*Andrias davidianus davidianus*	western China	24 June 1976
Salamander, Japanese giant	*Andrias davidianus japonicus*	Japan	24 June 1976
Toad, African viviparous	*Nectophrynoides* spp.	Africa	24 June 1976
Toad, Cameroon	*Bufo superciliaris*	Africa	24 June 1976
Toad, Monte Verde	*Bufo periglenes*	South America	24 June 1976

Source: US Fish and Wildlife Service and World Conservation Monitoring Centre

Some Plants and Animals Removed from the World Endangered and Threatened Species List

Common name	Scientific name	Range	Reason removed from list
Dove, Palau	*Gallicolumba canifrons*	West Pacific–Palau Islands	recovered
Eagle, bald	*Haliaeetus leucocephalus*	North America	recovered
Falcon, Arctic peregrine	*Falco peregrinus tundris*	nests from northern Alaska to Greenland; winters to Central and South America	recovered
Fantail, Palau (Old World flycatcher)	*Rhipidura lepida*	West Pacific–Palau Islands	recovered
Kangaroo, eastern grey	*Macropus giganteus* (all subspecies except *tasmaniensis*)	Australia	recovered
Kangaroo, red	*Macropus rufus*	Australia	recovered
Kangaroo, western grey	*Macropus fuliginosus*	Australia	recovered
Owl, Palau	*Pyrroglaux podargina*	West Pacific–Palau Islands	recovered
Turtle, Indian flap-shelled	*Lissemys punctata punctata*	India, Pakistan, Bangladesh	better data
Whale, grey (eastern North Pacific population)	*Eschrichtius robustus*	North Pacific Ocean–coastal and Bering Sea, formerly North Atlantic Ocean	recovered

Source: US Fish and Wildlife Service and World Conservation Monitoring Center

Some Threatened Plants and Animals Used in the World Wildlife Trade

Common name	Scientific name	Range	Reason threatened
Alligator snapping turtle	*Macroclemys temminckii*	North America	used in canned turtle soup, a delicacy in some countries; also sold as pets
Asian elephant	*Elephas maximus*	Asia	poaching for ivory and other parts of the body; poaching increased sharply in 1995–96
Beluga sturgeon	*Huso huso*	Caspian Sea	caviar is a delicacy in many countries; the long cycle of the fish makes the population vulnerable
Big leaf mahogany	*Swietenia macrophylla king*	Central and South America	mahogany wood is used for furniture in many countries
Black rhino	*Diceros bicornis*	Africa	hunted for their horns, which are used in powdered form in oriental medicine
Bonobo	*Pan paniscus*	Congo, Democratic Republic of	habitat loss and hunting; occasionally hunted for traditional medicinal purposes or magical purposes; specific body parts are thought to enhance strength and sexual vigour
Chimpanzee	*Pan troglodytes*	Equatorial Africa	habitat loss, hunting of adults for bushmeat, capture of infants to supply the pet trade and entertainment industry, and the international biomedical trade
Giant panda	*Ailuropoda melanaleca*	China	destruction of the bamboo forests, the natural habitat for pandas, makes the population more vulnerable; as does poaching and demand as zoo animals
Goldenseal	*Hydrastis canadensis*	North America	used in herbal medicine as a natural antibiotic; demand has increased as herbal medicine becomes more widespread
Green-cheeked parrot	*Amazona viridigenalis*	Mexico	hunted and captured for pet trade; many birds die in transit
Hawksbill turtle	*Eretmochelys imbricata*	tropical seas	the shell is used as tortoiseshell, although under an official ban in most places; the slow reproductive cycle of the turtle makes the population more vulnerable
Mako shark	*Isurus oxyrinchus*	Atlantic, Pacific, and Indian Oceans	shark meat is a delicacy in some countries; the slow reproductive cycle makes the population more vulnerable
Tiger	*Panthera tigris*	Asia	destruction of jungle; hunted for bones and other parts for use in oriental medicine

Native Wildlife Species at Risk in Britain

In Great Britain there are just over 28,500 native species of invertebrates of which 15,000 have been assessed, 38 species of freshwater fish, 2,300 species of seed plants, ferns and related plants, and over 23,000 species of liverworts, mosses, lichens, stoneworts, fungi, and slime moulds. It is believed that a total of 155 native animal species and 107 native plant species have become extinct in Great Britain since 1900; these are included in the 'threatened' category in the table. As of 1997.

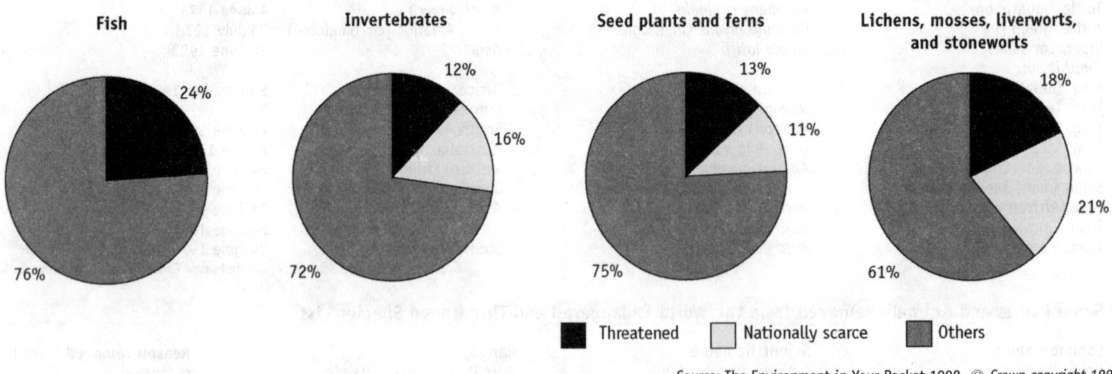

Source: The Environment in Your Pocket 1998, © *Crown copyright 1998*

■ Endangered Species

World Climate and Weather

World Weather Records

As of April 2000.
(N/A = not available.)

Record	Location	Details
Highest amount of rainfall in the northern hemisphere in 24 hours	Paishih, Taiwan	124 cm/49 in
Highest amount of rainfall in 24 hours (not induced by the presence of mountains)	Dharampuri, India	99 cm/39 in
Highest amount of rainfall in 24 hours	Cilaos, La Reunion Island	188 cm/74 in
Highest amount of rainfall over 5 days	Cilaos, La Reunion Island	386 cm/152 in
Highest amount of rainfall in 12 hours	Belouve, La Reunion Island	135 cm/53 in
Highest amount of rainfall in 20 minutes	Curtea-de-Arge, Romania	21 cm/8.1 in
Highest yearly number of days of rainfall	Bahia Felix, Chile	325 days
Longest period without rainfall	Arica, Chile	14 years
Highest yearly average period of thunderstorms	Kampala, Uganda	242 days per year
Highest sustained yearly average period of thunderstorms	Bogor, Indonesia	322 days per year from 1916 to 1919
Highest yearly average rainfall in Africa	Debundscha, Cameroon	1,029 cm/405 in (with an average variability of 191 cm/75 in)
Lowest yearly average rainfall in Africa	Wadt Halfa, Sudan	3 mm/0.1 in
Lowest yearly average rainfall in Asia	Aden, South Yemen	5 cm/1.8 in
Highest yearly average rainfall in Europe	Crkvice, Bosnia-Herzegovina	465 cm/183 in
Lowest yearly average rainfall in Europe	Astrakhan, Russian Federation	16 cm/6.4 in
Highest amount of rainfall in Australia in 24 hours	Crohamhurst, Queensland	91 cm/36 in
Highest yearly average rainfall in Australia	Bellenden Ker, Queensland	864 cm/340 in
Lowest yearly average rainfall in Australia	Mulka, South Australia	10 cm/4.1 in
Highest yearly average rainfall in South America	Quibdo, Colombia	899 cm/354 in
Lowest yearly average rainfall in South America	Arica, Chile	0.7 mm/0.03 in
Highest yearly average rainfall in North America	Henderson Lake, British Columbia, Canada	650 cm/256 in
Lowest yearly average rainfall in North America	Bataques, Mexico	3 cm/1.2 in
Highest temperature ever recorded in the world	El Aiziza, Libya	58°C/136°F
Lowest temperature ever recorded in the world	Vostok, Antarctica	−89°C/−129°F
Highest yearly average temperature in world	Dallol, Ethiopia	34°C/94°F
Highest yearly average temperature range	Eastern Sayan Region, Russian Federation	through 63°C/146°F
Highest average temperature sustained over a long period	Marble Head, Australia	38°C/100°F for 162 consecutive days
Highest temperature in Antarctica	Vanda Station, South Coast	near 15°C/59°F
Lowest temperature in Antarctica	Vostok, Antarctica	−89°C/−129°F
Highest temperature in Africa	El Aiziza, Libya	58°C/136°F
Lowest temperature in Africa	Ifrane, Morocco	−24°C/−11°F
Highest temperature in Asia	Tirat Tsvi, Israel	54°C/129°F
Lowest temperature in Asia	Verkhoyansk/Oimekon, Russian Federation	−68°C/−90°F
Highest temperature in Australia	Cloncurry, Queensland	53°C/128°F
Lowest temperature in Australia	Charlotte Press, New South Wales	−23°C/−9.4°F
Highest temperature in Europe	Seville, Spain	50°C/122°F
Lowest temperature in Europe	Ust 'Shchugor, USSR	−55°C/−67°F
Lowest temperature in Greenland	Northice	−66°C/−87°F
Highest temperature in North America	Death Valley (CA), USA	57°C/134°F
Lowest temperature in North America (excluding Greenland)	Snag, Yukon Territory, Canada	−63°C/−81°F
Lowest temperature in northern hemisphere	Verkhoyansk/Oimekon, Russian Federation	−68°C/−90°F
Highest temperature in South America	Rivadavia, Argentina	49°C/120°F
Lowest temperature in South America	Sarmiento, Argentina	−33°C/−27°F
Highest temperature in western hemisphere	Death Valley (CA)	57°C/134°F
Highest peak wind	Thule Air Base, Greenland	333 kph/207 mph
Highest average wind speed in 24 hours	Port Martin, Antarctica	173 kph/108 mph
Highest peak wind gust	Mt Washington (NH), USA	372 kph/231 mph
Highest monthly average wind speed	Port Martin, Antarctica	104 kph/65 mph

The World's Climates

Despite the complexity of climatic patterns produced by altitude, proximity to the oceans and aspect in relation to prevailing winds the world climates may be categorized. Broadly similar climates are found in different parts of the world in the same latitude and in similar positions on each continent.

Tropical Climates

These are grouped into two types:

- The equatorial climates are found within about 5° of latitude north and south of the equator, and the weather is hot and wet throughout the year.
- The hot tropical climates with a distinct wet and dry season are found roughly between 5° and 15° north and south of the equator. Parts of south and southeast Asia have a very clear division between the wet and dry seasons and are called tropical monsoon climates.

Dry Climates

There are three types of dry climate:

- Hot deserts with little rain at any season and no real cold weather, although the temperature drops sharply at night. The Sahara desert and much of the Arabian peninsula are the best examples of this type of climate.
- The second type is tropical steppe or semi-desert with a short rainy season during which the rains are unreliable and vary much from place to place. Examples are found in

The World's Climates *(continued)*

the drier parts of India and the Sahel region of Africa.

- The third type is deserts with a distinctly cold season which occur in higher latitudes in the interior of large continents. The best examples are parts of central Asia and western China.

Warm Temperate Climates

These fall into two groups:

- Rain occurs at all seasons, but summer is the wettest time of the year and temperatures then are warm to hot. Winters are mild with occasional cold spells. Much of eastern China and the southeastern states of the USA are in this category.
- Winters are generally mild and wet; summers are warm or hot with little or no rain. This type of climate is often called Mediterranean because of its wide extent around that sea. It also occurs in smaller areas elsewhere, for example central Chile, California, and Western Australia.

Cold Temperate Climates

These are categorized into two types:

- The cool temperate oceanic type of climate. Rain occurs in all months and there are rarely great extremes of heat or cold. This climate is found in much of northwest Europe, New Zealand, and coastal British Columbia.
- The second type is cold continental climates with a warm summer and a cold winter. Much of eastern and central Europe and eastern central Canada and the USA have this type of climate.

Sub-Arctic or Tundra Climates

- The winters are long and very cold. Summers are short, but during the long days temperatures sometimes rise surprisingly high. This type of climate occurs in central and northern Canada and much of northern and central Siberia.

Arctic or Icecap Climates

- In all months temperatures are near or below freezing point. Greenland and the Antarctic continents are the best examples of this type but it also occurs on some islands within the Arctic and Antarctic circles, such as South Georgia and Spitzbergen.

Climates of High Mountains and Plateaux

- Where land rises above or near the permanent snow line in any latitude, the climate resembles that of the Sub-Arctic and Arctic. The best examples are Tibet and the great mountain ranges of the Himalayas. In Africa only the isolated peaks of Mount Kenya and Kilimanjaro and the Ruwenzori range are high enough to carry permanent snow. Similar mountain climates are more extensive in North and South America.

Ultraviolet Index

The Ultraviolet (UV) Index is a measurement used to forecast the potential strength of the Sun's rays during specific periods.

There are four types of UV radiation (see table below), each having different wavelengths. Specifically, the UV Index measures UV-B radiation, the most dangerous and damaging type of ultraviolet radiation because it is not blocked by the Earth's ozone layer. Using these measurements, a forecast can be made indicating the potential danger resulting from exposure to UV radiation for peak hours of sunlight.

Wavelength is measured in nanometres (nm). A nanometre equals a millionth of a metre.

Wavelengths of UV Radiation by Type

UV category	Wavelengths (nm)
UV-A	320–400
UV-B	280–320
UV-C	200–280
UV-D	<200

The UV Index (UVI) uses a scale of 0–10+ to indicate the potential danger of the Sun's rays on a given day. The index is issued on a daily basis. From the index, a time estimate can be made of how long (in minutes) an individual can be exposed to the Sun's rays before damage to exposed skin may result. These values are presented in the following table.

UV Index and Skin Damage Estimates

UVI	Exposure level	Minutes before skin damage
0–2	minimal	>60
3–4	low	45
5–6	moderate	30
7–9	high	15
>10	very high	<10

Global Warming: Key Dates

1967 US scientists Syukuvo Manabe and R T Wetherald warn that the increase in carbon dioxide in the atmosphere, produced by human activities, is causing a 'greenhouse effect', which will raise atmospheric temperatures and cause a rise in sea levels.

1980 A ten-year World Climate Research Programme is launched to study and predict climate changes and human influence on climate change.

1989 The warmest year on record worldwide; environmentalists suggest this is due to the 'greenhouse effect'.

3 June 1992 The United Nations Conference on Environment and Development is held in Rio de Janeiro, Brazil, attended by delegates from 178 countries, most of whom sign binding conventions to combat global warming.

1993 An ice core drilled in Greenland provides evidence of climate change over 250,000 years, suggesting that sudden fluctuations have been common and that the recent stable climate is unusual.

1995 The Prince Gustav Ice Shelf and the northern Larsen Ice Shelf in Antarctica begin to disintegrate as a result of global warming.

11 December 1997 Delegates at the Kyoto, Japan, conference on global warming agree to cut emissions of greenhouse gases by 5.2% from 1990 levels during the years 2008 and 2012.

17 April 1998 An iceberg 40 km/25 mi long and 4.8 km/3 mi wide breaks off from the Larson B Ice Shelf in Antarctica

November 1998 A summit held in Buenos Aires, is attended by delegates from over 160 countries to discuss implementing the 1997 Kyoto Protocol to reduce global warming. Participants agree to devise strategies by 2000 for reducing emissions of greenhouse gases.

17 December 1998 The United Nations World Meteorological Organization (WMO) reports that 1998 is the warmest year on record, with a global average temperature of 14.4°C/58°F.

November 1999 Studies show that the Arctic icecap has shrunk by around 40% over the past 50 years, probably due to global warming. Reports show that polar bears in the region are in danger of starving to death because of their shortened hunting season.

16 December 1999 The WMO reports that the 1990s was the warmest decade and the 1900s the warmest century over the last 1,000 years.

■ World Climate and Weather

World Climate and Global Warming: International Environmental Agreements

UN Framework Convention on Climate Change (UNFCCC)

Also known as the Earth Summit or Rio Summit.

Date of adoption 14 June 1992
Place of adoption Rio de Janeiro, Brazil
Date of entry into force 15 March 1993
Number of signatory countries 176

Objectives Stabilization of greenhouse gas concentrations in the atmosphere at a level that would prevent dangerous anthropogenic interference with the climate system. Achievement of such a level within a time-frame sufficient to allow ecosystems to adapt naturally to climate change, to ensure that food production is not threatened, and to enable economic development to proceed in a sustainable manner.

Summary of selected provisions Developed countries to commit to stabilizing their emissions of carbon dioxide and other greenhouse gases at 1990 levels by 2000. To promote sustainable management, and promote and cooperate in the development, applications, and diffusion of technologies, practices, and processes that control, reduce or prevent emissions of greenhouse gases not controlled by the Montreal Protocol. Parties to make available to the Conference, and periodically update, national inventories of anthropogenic emissions by sources. Take climate change considerations into account, to the extent feasible, in their relevant social, economic, and environmental policies and actions. Promote and cooperate in scientific, technological, and other research related to the climate system. Commitments for developing countries are less – relating mostly to reporting requirements and development of national programmes – because of their lesser contribution to the problem to date and their lower levels of development.

At the first meeting of the Conference Parties in Berlin 1994, it was agreed that existing commitments were inadequate and negotiations to come up with a new agreement were initiated, culminating in the 'Kyoto Protocol' in December 1997. The 'Kyoto Protocol' sets out for the first time legally-binding emission targets for developed countries. These vary from country to country but, if achieved, are expected to result in an overall reduction in greenhouse gas emissions by an overall 8% by 2010 compared with 1990 levels. However, many other issues still remain unclear under the Protocol, and will be subject to further negotiations. As of 15 March 1999, the Protocol had been signed by 84 countries and was not yet in force.

Montreal Protocol on Substances that Deplete the Ozone Layer

Date of adoption 16 September 1987
Place of adoption Montreal, Canada
Date of entry into force 1 January 1989
Number of signatory countries 168

Objectives To reduce and eventually eliminate the emissions of artificial ozone-depleting substances

Summary of selected provisions Reductions in emissions of man-made ozone-depleting substances through controls on their production and supply. Stipulation of a 50% reduction in CFC consumption by 1999.

The Montreal Protocol on Substances that Deplete the Ozone Layer has been amended four times so far. Its control provisions were strengthened through four adjustments to the Protocol adopted in London 1990 (came into force 10 September 1992; ratified by 127 countries), Copenhagen 1992 (came into force 14 June 1994; ratified by 87 countries), and Montreal 1997 (not yet in force; ratified by 10 countries as of 15 March 1999).

Under the Protocol and its amendments, Parties agreed to:

- phase out production and consumption of CFCs, carbon tetrachloride, methyl chloroform, and HBFCs by 1996;
- phase out production and consumption of halons by 1994;
- phase out production and consumption of HCFCs by 2030 and of methyl bromide by 2005.

Within the Protocol and its amendments, special dispensations are given for essential uses and, in the case of methyl bromide, quarantine applications. A certain amount of production is also permitted to meet the needs of developing countries which have a 10-year grace period for compliance. There is no agreement on HFCs which are seen as long-term substitutes in some applications, which is significant as these are also greenhouse gases.

The Vienna Convention on the Protection of the Ozone Layer

Date of adoption 22 March 1985
Place of adoption Vienna, Austria
Date of entry into force 22 September 1988
Number of signatory countries 169

Objectives To protect the ozone layer and encourage governments to cooperate in developing scientific understanding of atmospheric processes.

Summary of selected provisions Agreement on specific measures to be taken to tackle ozone depletion, and on protocols that established specific controls.

UK Climate and Weather

Weather in the UK

The climate of the UK is notoriously variable and changeable from day to day. Weather is generally cool to mild with frequent cloud and rain but occasional settled spells of weather occur in all seasons. The frequent changes of weather affect all parts of the country in very much the same way; there are no great differences from one part of the country to another.

While the south is usually a little warmer than the north and the west wetter than the east, the continual changes of weather mean that, on occasions, these differences may be reversed. Extremes of weather are rare but they do occur. For example, in December 1981 and January 1982, parts of southern and central England experienced for a few days lower temperatures than central Europe and Moscow. During the long spells of hot, sunny weather in the summers of 1975 and 1976 parts of the UK were drier and warmer than many places in the western Mediterranean.

The greatest extremes of weather and climate occur in the mountains of Scotland, Wales, and northern England. Here at altitudes exceeding 600 m/2,000 ft conditions are wet and cloudy for much of the year with annual rainfall exceeding 1,500 mm/60 in and in places reaching as much as 5,000 mm/200 in. These are among the wettest places in Europe. Winter conditions may be severe with very strong winds, driving rain, or blizzards.

Virtually all permanent settlement in the UK lies below 300 m/1,000 ft, and at these levels weather conditions are usually much more congenial. As a general rule the western side is cloudier, wetter, and milder in winter, with cooler summers than the eastern side of the country. See tables for **Belfast**, Northern Ireland, and **Cardiff**, Wales.

The eastern side is drier the year round, with a tendency for summer rain to be heavier than that of winter. The east is a little colder in winter and warmer in summer. See the tables for **London**, England, and **Edinburgh**, Scotland.

The average number of hours of sunshine is greatest in the south and southeast of England and least in the north and west. Western Scotland, Wales, and Northern Ireland have rather less sunshine than most of England. In the UK daily sunshine hours range from between one and two in midwinter to between five and seven in midsummer. Winter sunshine is much reduced because of frequent fogs and low cloud. This is a consequence of winds from the Atlantic and seas surrounding the UK, which bring high humidity. For the same reason the mountain areas are particularly cloudy and wet.

Scotland is rarely much colder than England despite its more northerly latitude. Summers in Scotland, however, are usually shorter and rather cooler. Wales, western Scotland, and Northern Ireland are wetter the year round than most of England. Northwestern England and the Lake District are, however, particularly wet and cloudy.

Weather in the UK: Belfast, Northern Ireland

	Sunshine	Temperatures								Precipitation		Wet days (more than 0.25 mm/0.01 in)
	average hours per day	average daily minimum		average daily maximum		highest recorded		lowest recorded		average monthly		
		°C	°F	°C	°F	°C	°F	°C	°F	mm	in	
January	1	2	35	6	43	13	56	− 13	9	80	3.2	20
February	2	2	35	7	44	14	57	− 12	11	52	2.1	17
March	3	3	37	9	49	19	67	− 12	10	50	2.0	16
April	5	4	39	12	53	21	69	− 4	24	48	1.9	16
May	6	6	43	15	59	26	79	− 3	26	52	2.1	15
June	6	9	49	18	64	28	83	− 1	31	68	2.7	16
July	4	11	52	18	65	29	85	4	39	94	3.7	19
August	4	11	51	18	65	28	82	1	34	77	3.0	17
September	4	9	49	16	61	26	78	− 2	28	80	3.2	18
October	3	7	44	13	55	21	70	− 4	24	83	3.3	19
November	2	4	39	9	48	16	61	− 6	21	72	2.8	19
December	1	3	37	7	44	14	58	− 11	13	90	3.5	21

Weather in the UK: Cardiff, Wales

	Sunshine	Temperatures								Precipitation		Wet days (more than 0.25 mm/0.01 in)
	average hours per day	average daily minimum		average daily maximum		highest recorded		lowest recorded		average monthly		
		°C	°F	°C	°F	°C	°F	°C	°F	mm	in	
January	2	2	35	7	45	15	59	− 17	2	108	4.3	18
February	3	2	35	7	45	16	61	− 9	15	72	2.8	14
March	4	3	38	10	50	20	68	− 8	18	63	2.5	13
April	5	5	41	13	56	24	75	− 3	27	65	2.6	13
May	6	8	46	16	61	29	84	− 1	31	76	3.0	13
June	7	11	51	19	68	31	87	4	39	63	2.5	13
July	6	12	54	20	69	31	88	7	44	89	3.5	14
August	6	13	55	21	69	33	91	6	43	97	3.8	15
September	5	11	51	18	64	28	83	2	35	99	3.9	16
October	3	8	46	14	58	25	77	− 3	26	109	4.3	16
November	2	5	41	10	51	18	65	− 3	26	116	4.7	17
December	2	3	37	8	46	15	59	− 7	19	108	4.3	18

Weather in the UK: Edinburgh, Scotland

	Sunshine	Temperatures								Precipitation		Wet days (more than 0.25 mm/0.01 in)
	average hours per day	average daily minimum		average daily maximum		highest recorded		lowest recorded		average monthly		
		°C	°F	°C	°F	°C	°F	°C	°F	mm	in	
January	2	1	34	6	42	14	57	− 8	17	57	2.2	17
February	3	1	34	6	43	14	58	− 9	15	39	1.5	15
March	4	2	36	8	46	20	68	− 6	21	39	1.5	15
April	5	4	39	11	51	22	72	− 4	25	39	1.5	14
May	6	6	43	14	56	24	76	− 1	31	54	2.1	14
June	6	9	49	17	62	28	83	3	37	47	1.9	15
July	5	11	52	18	65	28	83	6	42	83	3.3	17
August	4	11	52	18	64	28	82	4	40	77	3.0	16
September	4	9	49	16	60	25	77	1	33	57	2.2	16
October	3	7	44	12	54	20	68	− 2	28	65	2.6	17
November	2	4	39	9	48	19	67	− 4	24	62	2.4	17
December	1	2	36	7	44	14	58	− 7	20	57	2.2	18

Weather in the UK: London, England

	Sunshine	Temperatures								Precipitation		Wet days (more than 0.25 mm/0.01 in)
	average hours per day	average daily				highest recorded		lowest recorded		average monthly		
		minimum		maximum								
		°C	°F	°C	°F	°C	°F	°C	°F	mm	in	
January	1	2	36	6	43	14	58	−10	15	54	2.1	15
February	2	2	36	7	44	16	61	−9	15	40	1.6	13
March	4	3	38	10	50	21	71	−8	18	37	1.5	11
April	5	6	42	13	56	26	78	−2	28	37	1.5	12
May	6	8	47	17	62	30	86	−1	30	46	1.8	12
June	7	12	53	20	69	33	91	5	41	45	1.8	11
July	6	14	56	22	71	34	93	7	45	57	2.2	12
August	6	13	56	21	71	33	92	6	43	59	2.3	11
September	5	11	52	19	65	30	86	3	37	49	1.9	13
October	3	8	46	14	58	26	78	−4	26	57	2.2	13
November	2	5	42	10	50	19	66	−5	23	64	2.5	15
December	1	4	38	7	45	15	59	−7	19	48	1.9	15

Current Weather Statistics for England and Wales

January 1999–June 2000

Figures in parentheses show relative difference from the average figures taken from the period 1961–90.

Month	Average rainfall (mm/in)	Average temperature (°C/°F)	Average sunshine (hours per day)	Remarks
1999				
January	120/4.7 (136%)	5.3/41.5 (+1.5°C)	2.11 (130%)	sunniest January since 1991
February	47/1.9 (74%)	4.9/40.8 (+1.1°C)	2.98 (123%)	tenth sunniest February since 1909
March	64/2.5 (89%)	6.9/44.4 (+1.2°C)	3.84 (110%)	third mild March in a row
April	71/2.8 (119%)	9.4/48.9 (−1.5°C)	5.61 (114%)	warmest April since 1993 and sunniest since 1995
May	53/2.1 (82%)	12.9/55.2 (+1.7°C)	5.71 (92%)	dullest May since 1994
June	78/3.1 (120%)	13.9/57.0 (−0.3°C)	7.00 (110%)	coolest June since 1991
July	22/0.9 (36%)	17.4/63.3 (+1.3°C)	7.87 (132%)	driest July since 1911 and sunniest since 1980
August	100/3.9 (132%)	16.2/61.2 (+0.4°C)	5.39 (96%)	wettest and dullest August since 1992
September	111/4.4 (144%)	15.4/59.7 (+1.8°C)	5.55 (122%)	warmest September since 1949 and sunniest since 1991
October	75/3.0 (88%)	10.6/51.1 (0°C)	4.36 (136%)	sunniest October since 1959 and 2nd sunniest since 1909
November	65/2.6 (73%)	7.7/45.9 (+1.2°C)	2.65 (122%)	driest November since 1989
December	139/5.5 (148%)	5.0/41.0 (+0.3°C)	2.06(141%)	sunniest December since 1962 and wettest since 1993
2000				
January	49/1.9 (52%)	4.7/40.5(+0.9°C)	2.31 (148%)	sunniest January since 1959
February	90/3.5 (140%)	6.0/42.8 (+2.2°C)	3.35 (146%)	sunniest February since 1989
March	34/1.3 (45%)	7.0/44.6 (+1.3°C)	3.89 (114%)	ninth consecutive month to be warmer than normal
April	143/5.6 (234%)	7.9/46.2 (0°C)	4.78 (99%)	wettest April since records began in 1766
May	95/3.7 (148%)	12.1/53.8 (+0.9°C)	6.39 (106%)	wettest May since 1988
June	38/1.5 (56%)	14.9/58.9 (+0.7°C)	5.89 (94%)	driest June since 1996 and warmest since 1993

UK Weather Records

Record	Location	Details	Date
Highest temperature	Cheltenham, Gloucestershire	37.1°C/98.8°F	3 August 1990
Lowest temperature	Braemar, Grampian	−27.2°C/−17°F	11 February 1895 and 10 January 1982
	Altnaharra, Highland	−27.2°C/−17°F	30 December 1995
Greatest temperature range in a single day	Tummel Bridge, Tayside	from −7°C/19.4°F to 22°C/71.6°F (a range of 29°C/55.2°F)	9 May 1978
Highest amount of rainfall in 24 hours	Martinstown, Dorset	280 mm/11 in	18 July 1955
Fastest gust of wind (high-level site)	Cairn Gorm station, Highland	150 knots/173 mph	20 March 1986
Fastest gust of wind (low-level site)	Fraserburgh, Aberdeenshire	123 knots/141mph	13 February 1989
Highest number of days with gale in a year	Lerwick, Shetlands	86 days	1949
Heaviest hailstone	Horsham, Sussex	141 g/5 oz; with diameters of up to 6 cm/2.4 in	1958
Highest amount of sunshine in one month	Eastbourne and Hastings, Sussex	384 hours	July 1911
Lowest amount of sunshine in one month	Westminster, Greater London	0 hours	December 1890

Extreme Weather and Natural Disasters

Retired Hurricane and Tropical Storm Names

The names of tropical storms and hurricanes that cause severe damage or result in great loss of life are retired and not used again. Storm names that have been retired appear in the table with the year of their retirement. The table covers Atlantic storms only.

Name	Year	Name	Year	Name	Year
Agnes	1972	Connie	1955	Hazel	1954
Alicia	1983	David	1979	Hilda	1964
Allen	1980	Diana	1990	Hortense	1996
Andrew	1992	Diane	1955	Hugo	1989
Anita	1977	Donna	1960	Inez	1966
Audrey	1957	Dora	1964	Ione	1955
Betsy	1965	Edna	1954	Janet	1955
Beulah	1967	Elena	1985	Joan	1988
Bob	1991	Eloise	1975	Klaus	1990
Camille	1969	Fifi	1974	Luis	1995
Carla	1961	Flora	1963	Marilyn	1995
Carmen	1974	Fran	1996	Mitch	1998
Carol	1954	Frederic	1979	Opal	1995
Celia	1970	Gilbert	1988	Roxanne	1995
Cesar	1996	Gloria	1985		
Cleo	1964	Gracie	1959		
		Hattie	1961		

The Naming of Hurricanes

A hurricane is defined as a storm with a wind speed of 75 mph. In the past, tropical storms and hurricanes were identified in various inconsistent and confusing ways. Major storms might be named after a holiday or saint's day, an area, or even a ship, but most never received any designation at all. During forecast operations identifications by latitude and longitude were used. This system was long, and confusing if more than one storm occurred at the same time.

The system of giving hurricanes short, distinctive names is quicker and less likely to be misinterpreted. The names are reused on a four- or six-year cycle, depending on the part of the world where the storm strikes. If a hurricane causes severe damage or has a serious impact on human lives or the economy, its name is retired and replaced by a new name beginning with the same letter.

Major Floods and Tsunamis Since 1981

A tsunami is an ocean wave generated by vertical movements of the sea floor resulting from earthquakes or volcanic activity. As of January 2000.

Year	Event	Location	Number of deaths
1981	floods	northern China	550
1982	floods	Peru	600
	floods	Guangdong, China	430
	floods	El Salvador/ Guatemala	›1,300
1983	tsunami	Japan/South Korea	107
1984	floods	South Korea	›200
1987	floods	northern Bangladesh	›1,000
1988	floods	Brazil	289
	floods	Bangladesh	›1,300
1990	tsunami	Bangladesh	370
	floods	Mexico	85
	floods	Tanzania	283
1991	floods	Afghanistan	1,367
	floods	Bangladesh	150,450
	floods	Benin	30
	floods	Chad	39
	floods/ storm	Chile	199
	floods	China	6,728
	floods	India	2,024
	floods	Malawi	1,172
	floods	Peru	40
	floods/ typhoon	Philippines	8,890
	floods	Romania	138
	floods	South Korea	54
	floods	Sudan	2,000
	floods	Turkey	30
	floods	Texas, USA	33
	floods	Vietnam	136
1992	floods	Afghanistan	450
	floods	Argentina	104
	floods	Chile	41
	floods	China	197
	floods	India	551
	floods	Pakistan	1,446
	floods	Vietnam	55
1993	floods	Indonesia	18
	floods	midwestern USA	48
1994	floods	Moldova	47
	floods	southern China	1,400
	floods	India	›600
	floods	Vietnam	›175
	floods	northern Italy	›60
1995	floods	Benin	10
	floods	Bangladesh	›200
	floods	Somalia	20
	floods	northwestern Europe	40
	floods	Hunan Province, China	1,200
	floods	southwestern Morocco	136
	floods	Pakistan	›120
	floods	South Africa	147
	floods	Vietnam	85
1996	floods	southern and western India	›300
	floods	Tuscany, Italy	30
	floods	North and South Korea	86
	floods	Pyrenees, France/ Spain	84
	floods	Yemen	324
	floods	central and southern China	2,300
1997	floods	west coast, USA	36
	floods	Sikkim, India	›50
	floods	Germany/Poland/ Czech Republic	›100
	floods	Somalia	›1,700
	floods	eastern Uganda	›30
	floods	Spain and Portugal	70
1998	tsunami	Papua New Guinea	›1,700
	floods/ mudslides	southern Italy	118
	floods	western Pakistan	›300
	floods	western Ukraine	17
	floods	Bangladesh	›400
	floods	northern India	›1,300
	floods	central, southeast, north, and northeast China	›3,650
	floods	Nepal	›250
	floods	South Korea	›195
	floods	Slovak Republic/ Poland	›34
	floods	Kyrgyzstan/ Uzbekistan border	›200

(continued)

Major Floods and Tsunamis Since 1981 *(continued)*

Year	Event	Location	Number of deaths
1998–99 (25 December–6 January)	floods	Sri Lanka	›5 (approximately 155,000 affected and 15,000 families initially displaced)
1999	floods	Chang Jiang River, China	›925
	floods	Bangladesh	30
	floods	Nepal	97
	floods	Mexico	341
	floods	Thua Thien-Hua, Vietnam	470
	floods	southern France	31
	floods	Venezuela	30–50,000
2000	floods	Mozambique	›500

Major Hurricanes, Typhoons, Cyclones, and Other Storms Since 1995

As of January 2000.

Date	Event/name	Location	Estimated number of deaths
23 January 1995	snowstorms	Kashmir, India	›200
5–7 September 1995	hurricane, Luis	Caribbean	14
2–3 November 1995	typhoon, Angela	Philippines	722
13 May 1996	tornado	Bangladesh	›600
27–28 July 1996	hurricane, César	Panama/El Salvador/Costa Rica	50
31 July–1 August 1996	typhoon, Herb	Taiwan	400
5–6 September 1996	hurricane, Fran	North Carolina and Virginia, USA	36
4 November 1996	cyclone	Andhra Pradesh, India	›1,000
4–5 January 1997	storms	Brazil	68
19 May 1997	cyclone	Bangladesh	112
27 September 1997	cyclone	Bangladesh	›47
9 October 1997	hurricane, Pauline/floods	Pacific coast of Mexico	128
2–3 November 1997	typhoon, Linda	southern Vietnam/Thailand	3,500
23 February 1998	tornadoes	central Florida, USA	38
8 April 1998	tornadoes	Alabama, Georgia, Mississippi, USA	›41
15 September–1 October 1998	hurricane, Georges	Caribbean	602
17 September–27 October 1998	three typhoons, Vickie, Zeb, and Babs	Philippines	›1,000
19 October–26 November 1998	three tropical storms, Chip, Dawn, and Elvis	central Vietnam	›265
22 October–5 November 1998	hurricane, Mitch	Central America and the Caribbean	›10,500
10–15 December 1998	typhoon, Faith	central Vietnam/Philippines	›45
15–19 January 1999	cyclone, Dani	Vanuatu/Fiji	›10
3 August 1999	typhoon, Olga	South Hwanghae province, North Korea	54
24 September 1999	typhoon	western Honchu, Japan	26
18 October 1999	typhoon	Orissa, India	66
29 October 1999	cyclone	Orissa, India	9,504
26 December 1999	storms	France	88

The Worst Storms, Floods, and Hurricanes in the UK

Date	Location	Details
26–27 November 1703	southwest England	storm: one of the worst in British history (called The Great Storm); it occurred before records were kept, but sources show that 125 people were killed on land and 8,000 at sea
16 January 1841	River Till	floods: following heavy snow in the first week of 1841, the temperature rose to 5°C/41°F and meltwater burst the banks of the River Till
29 December 1897	Tay Bridge	hurricane: part of the bridge collapsed during gale force winds, causing a train to plunge into the water below, drowning 75 people
26 August 1912	Norwich	floods: torrential rain amounting to the equivalent of three months' rainfall in a single day caused severe flooding, damaging or destroying about 3,650 buildings
29 May 1920	Louth	storms: where 115 mm/4.5 in of rain fell in 2.5 hours, caused severe flooding and devastated the town
28 January 1927	Glasgow	hurricane: gale force winds caused extensive damage and 11 people were killed and over 100 injured
6 January 1928	London	floods: torrential rain and meltwater from snow caused widespread flooding of the Thames and its tributaries
21 May 1950	Berkshire	tornado: with a wind speed of up to 370 kph/230 mph blazed a trail of destruction for nearly 161 km/100 mi in approximately four hours
15 August 1952	Lynmouth	torrential rainfall measuring 386 mm/15.2 in in 12 hours on Exmoor caused flood water to flow down the River Lyn and devastate Lynmouth; 34 people were killed
1–7 December 1952	London	anticyclone: prevented the passage of clean air from clearing fog over London; it is believed that up to 4,000 deaths in 1952 were a direct result of the black smoke from chimneys, or 'smog', that had settled in the air
4 November 1957	Hatfield	hurricane: gale force winds caused damage to 26 houses

(continued)

The Worst Storms, Floods, and Hurricanes in the UK (*continued*)

Date	Location	Details
16 February 1962	Sheffield	hurricane: severe gale with gusts of up to 154 kph/96 mph caused extensive damage to buildings; a crane was uprooted and crashed onto the new technical college and 100,000 homes were damaged, including 100 beyond repair
21 July 1965	Wisley	tornado: lasting about 10 minutes caused destruction 10–30 m/32–98 ft-wide for a distance of 3 km/2 mi
1 November 1965	Ferrybridge	gusting winds: caused three cooling towers to collapse
27 December 1965	Sea Gem Oil Rig	hurricane: high winds created waves 6 m/20 ft high, and caused oil rig to collapse; nine people died
24 June 1967	Mossdale	floods: heavy rains filled the caves, drowning six people inside
15 January 1968	Glasgow	hurricane: gale force winds gusting up to 161 km/100 mph caused extensive damage; over 100,000 homes were damaged
16 September 1968	River Mole	floods: 150–200 mm/5.9–7.9 in of rainfall over three days caused the River Mole to burst its banks
21 November 1971	Cairngorms	snow blizzard: caused deaths of six members of a school party on a climbing expedition
16 October 1987	south England	the worst storm since 1703, causing extensive damage to tree areas and a total of 17 deaths
24 December 1997	Scotland and northwest England	hurricane: widespread winds and severe gales seriously damaged many buildings, uprooted thousands of trees, and resulted in six deaths; electricity supply was disrupted for up to four days and Blackpool pier was breached
10 April 1998	eastern and central England	floods: the worst flooding in 50 years, resulting in five deaths and estimated damage of up to £500 million
21 October–2 November 1998	Wales and west England	floods: torrential rain and flooding submerged huge areas under several feet of water, caused over £100 million damage and claimed four lives; Manchester suffered its wettest October since records began in 1942 and Worcestershire suffered its worst floods for more than 30 years

Major Earthquakes Since 1980

As of March 2000.
(N/A = not available.)

Date	Location	Magnitude (Richter scale)	Estimated number of deaths
10 October 1980	northern Algeria	7.7	3,000
23 November 1980	southern Italy	7.2	4,800
13 December 1982	northern Yemen	6.0	1,600
30 October 1983	eastern Turkey	6.9	1,300
19, 21 September 1985	Mexico City, Mexico	8.1	5,000[1]
20 August 1988	Nepal/India	6.9	1,000
6 November 1988	southwestern China	7.6	1,000
7 December 1988	Armenia, USSR	6.8	25,000
17 October 1989	San Francisco (CA), USA	7.1	62
20–21 June 1990	northwestern Iran	7.7	50,000
16 July 1990	Luzon, Philippines	7.7	1,660
1 February 1991	Afghanistan/Pakistan	6.8	1,000
April 1991	northern Georgia	7.2	>100
20 October 1991	Uttar Pradesh, India	6.1	1,500
13, 15 March 1992	Erzincan, Turkey	6.7	2,000
12 December 1992	Flores Island, Indonesia	7.5	2,500
12 July 1993	western coast of Hokkaido, Japan	7.8	200
29 September 1993	Maharashtra, India	6.3	9,800
13–16 October 1993	Papua New Guinea	6.8	>60
6 June 1994	Cauca, Colombia	6.8	1,000
19 August 1994	northern Algeria	5.6	200
16 January 1995	Kobe, Japan	7.2	5,500
14 June 1995	Sakhalin Island, Russia	7.6	2,000
2 October 1995	southwestern Turkey	6.0	84
7 October 1995	Sumatra, Indonesia	7.0	>70
9 October 1995	Mexico	7.6	>66
3 February 1996	Yunnan Province, China	7.0	>250
17 February 1996	Irian Jaya, Indonesia	7.5	108
28 March 1996	Ecuador	5.7	21
4, 28 February 1997	Ardabil, Iran	N/A	>1,000
28 February 1997	Baluchistan Province, Pakistan	7.3	>100
10 May 1997	northeastern Iran (Khorasah Province)	7.1	>1,600
22 May 1997	India	6.0	>40
26 September 1997	central Italy	5.8	>11
28 September 1997	Sulawesi, Indonesia	6.0	>20
14 October 1997	north of Santiago, Chile	6.8	>10
21 November 1997	Chittagong, Bangladesh	6.0	17
11 January 1998	northeastern China	6.2	>47
4 February 1998	Takhar province, Afghanistan	6.1	>3,800
30 May 1998	north-east Afghanistan	6.9	4,000
27 June 1998	southern Turkey	6.2	145
19 November 1998	southwestern China	5.6 and 6.2	5
29 November 1998	Moluccas, Indonesia	6.5	>50

(continued)

Major Earthquakes Since 1980 (*continued*)

Date	Location	Magnitude (Richter scale)	Estimated number of deaths
25 January 1999	western Colombia	6.0	900
29 March 1999	India	6.8	110
17 August 1999	Turkey	7.4	14,095
21 September 1999	Taiwan	7.6	2,256
30 September 1999	Mexico	7.5	70
12 November 1999	Turkey	7.2	737
27 November 1999	Vanuatu	7.2	10

[1] Some estimates put the death toll as high as 20,000.

Most Destructive Earthquakes in the World

(N/A = not available.)

Date	Location	Estimated number of deaths	Magnitude (Richter scale)
23 January 1556	Shaanxi, China	830,000	N/A
11 October 1737	Calcutta, India	300,000	N/A
27 July 1976	Tangshan, China	255,000[1]	8.0
9 August 1138	Aleppo, Syria	230,000	N/A
22 May 1927	near Xining, China	200,000	8.3
22 December 856	Damghan, Iran	200,000	N/A
16 December 1920	Gansu, China	200,000	8.6
23 March 893	Ardabil, Iran	150,000	N/A
1 September 1923	Kwanto, Japan	143,000	8.3
30 December 1730	Hokkaido, Japan	137,000	N/A
September 1290	Chihli, China	100,000	N/A
November 1667	Caucasia, Russia	80,000	N/A
18 November 1727	Tabriz, Iran	77,000	N/A
28 December 1908	Messina, Italy	70,000–100,000	7.5
1 November 1755	Lisbon, Portugal	70,000	8.7
25 December 1932	Gansu, China	70,000	7.6
31 May 1970	northern Peru	66,000	7.8
1268	Cilicia, Asia Minor	60,000	N/A
11 January 1693	Sicily, Italy	60,000	N/A
4 February 1783	Calabria, Italy	50,000	N/A
20 June 1990	Iran	50,000	7.7
30 May 1935	Quetta, Pakistan	30,000–60,000	7.5

[1] This is the official casualty figure; the estimated death toll is as high as 750,000.

Major Volcanic Eruptions in the 20th Century

Volcano	Location	Year	Estimated number of deaths
Santa María	Guatemala	1902	1,000
Pelée	Martinique	1902	28,000
Taal	Philippines	1911	1,400
Kelut	Java, Indonesia	1919	5,500
Vulcan	Papua New Guinea	1937	500
Lamington	Papua New Guinea	1951	3,000
St Helens	USA	1980	57
El Chichon	Mexico	1982	1,880
Nevado del Ruiz	Colombia	1985	23,000
Lake Nyos	Cameroon	1986	1,700
Pinatubo	Luzon, Philippines	1991	639
Unzen	Japan	1991	39
Mayon	Philippines	1993	70
Loki[1]	Iceland	1996	0
Soufriere	Montserrat	1997	23
Merapi	Java, Indonesia	1998	38

[1] The eruption caused severe flooding, and melted enough ice to create a huge sub-glacial lake.

World Pollution

Air Pollution

Air pollution is contamination of the atmosphere caused by the discharge, accidental or deliberate, of a wide range of toxic airborne substances. Often the amount of the released substance is relatively high in a certain locality, so the harmful effects become more noticeable. The greatest single cause of air pollution in the UK is the car, which is responsible for 85% of the carbon monoxide and 45% of the oxides of nitrogen present in the atmosphere. According to a UK government report 1998, air pollution causes up to 24,000 deaths in Britain per year.

Possibly the world's worst ever human-made air pollution disaster occurred in Indonesia in September 1997. Caused by forest clearance fires, the smoke pollution spread to other countries of the region as far as the Philippines, Thailand, and Australia.

The 1997 Kyoto protocol committed the industrialized nations of the world to cutting their levels of harmful gas emissions to 5.2% by 2012. Europe is expected to take the biggest cut of 8%, the USA 7%, and Japan 6%. The agreement covers Russia and eastern Europe as well.

Acid rain

Acid rain is rain that has a value of less than 5 on the pH scale. The pollutants that cause acid rain are sulphur dioxide (formed by the burning of fossil fuels, such as coal) and oxides of nitrogen (contributed from various industrial activities and from car exhaust fumes). Acid rain is linked with damage to and the death of forests and lake organisms. It also results in damage to buildings and statues. Acid rain damages the chemical balance of soil, causing leaching of important minerals including magnesium and aluminium. Plants living in such soils, particularly conifers, suffer from mineral loss and become more prone to infection. The minerals from the soil pass into lakes and rivers, disturbing aquatic life, for instance, by damaging the gills of young fish and killing plant life. Lakes affected by acid rain are virtually clear due to the absence of green plankton.

The greenhouse effect and climate change

This is a phenomenon of the Earth's atmosphere by which solar radiation, trapped by the Earth and re-emitted from the surface as infrared radiation, is prevented from escaping by various gases in the air. Greenhouse gases trap heat because they readily absorb infrared radiation. The result is a rise in the Earth's temperature (global warming). The main greenhouse gases are carbon dioxide, methane, and chlorofluorocarbons (CFCs) as well as water vapour. Fossil-fuel consumption and forest fires are the principal causes of carbon dioxide build-up; methane is a by product of agriculture (rice, cattle, sheep).

Particulates or 'smog'

Smog is made up of particulates – clusters of small particles, such as carbon particles, in the air that come mostly from vehicle exhausts. Smog tends to form in urban areas where the air is not dispersed naturally. There is a link between increase in PM10 levels and a rise in death rate, increased hospital admissions, and asthma incidence. The elderly and those with chronic heart or lung disease are most at risk. The smaller the particulates the

Air Pollution (*continued*)

more dangerous they are: those below 2.5 µm across travel deep into the lungs and lodge there. The particulates themselves may be harmless but they may carry damaging chemicals, such as acids, into the lungs.

Indoor air pollution

The issue of pollution in offices and homes has become more recognized in recent years. Typically, people living in urban surroundings spend 90% of their time indoors, particularly those most at risk from the effects of pollution – the young, the old, and the infirm. Modern buildings, designed to be more energy-efficient and insulate more, tend to have greatly reduced ventilation rates. Sources of indoor air pollution include tobacco smoke, furnishings and building materials, computing equipment, and gas appliances.

Major Air Pollutants

Pollutant	Sources	Effects
Sulphur dioxide (SO_2)	oil, coal combustion in power stations	acid rain formed, which damages plants, trees, buildings, and lakes
Oxides of nitrogen (NO, NO_2)	high-temperature combustion in cars, and to some extent power stations	acid rain formed
Lead compounds	from leaded petrol used by cars	nerve poison
Carbon dioxide (CO_2)	oil, coal, petrol, diesel combustion	greenhouse effect
Carbon monoxide (CO)	limited combustion of oil, coal, petrol, diesel fuels	poisonous, leads to photochemical smog in some areas
Nuclear waste	nuclear power plants, nuclear weapon testing, war	radioactivity, contamination of locality, cancers, mutations, death
Ozone (O_3)	formed by the reaction between sunlight and NO_x compounds	greenhouse effect, acid rain by-product
Particulates (PM_{10}, 'smog')	vehicle exhausts, power generation, combustion processes	respiratory effects, acid rain
Volatile organic compounds (VOC)	industrial processes, vehicle emissions, petrol evaporation	greenhouse effect, ozone production

The World's Worst-Polluted Cities

A report published by the Washington-based World Resources Institute in January 1999 lists the ten cities in the world with the worst air pollution, finding that nine out of the ten were in China. The fifth-worst city is in India. Ranked number one is Lanzhou, in Gansu Province, northwest China. This is a region that has a large petrochemical industry and oil refineries.

According to World Health Organization (WHO) guidelines, the maximum permissible amount of total suspended particulates (TSPs) is 90 micrograms per cubic litre of air. Lanzhou has more than 700. The next worst ranked city is Jilin, which has almost 700, while Taiyun – ranked number three – has nearly 600. The remaining seven cities listed in the report, in order of descending TSP levels, are Jiaozuo, Rajkot in India, Wanxian, Urumqi, Yichang, Hanzhong, and Anyang.

The study, funded by the WHO, the US Environmental Protection Agency, and other groups, found that millions of children risked disease and death because they lived in these badly polluted cities. Children are more at risk because they breathe faster and because their lungs are still developing. The main problem is that these cities have rapidly growing economies, but lack the more modern and cleaner technology of developed countries.

Air Pollution in Selected Cities

'Total suspended particulates' refers to smoke, soot, dust, and liquid droplets from combustion that are in the air. Sulphur dioxide is produced when fossil fuels are burnt. Nitrogen dioxide is emitted by bacteria, fertilizers, motor vehicles, and industrial activities; both these dioxides contribute to acid rain formation. The World Health Organization (WHO) annual mean guidelines are 90 micrograms per cubic metre of total suspended particulates, and 50 for sulphur and nitrogen dioxide.

These data are the most recent available (1995). (N/A = not available.)

City	Country	Total suspended particulates (micrograms per cubic metre)	Sulphur dioxide (micrograms per cubic metre)	Nitrogen dioxide (micrograms per cubic metre)
Bangkok	Thailand	223	11	23
Beijing	China	377	90	122
Cairo	Egypt	N/A	69	N/A
Calcutta	India	375	49	34
Delhi	India	415	24	41
Jakarta	Indonesia	271	N/A	N/A
London	UK	N/A	25	77
Los Angeles	USA	N/A	9	74
Manila	Philippines	200	33	N/A
Mexico City	Mexico	279	74	130
Moscow	Russia	100	109	N/A
Mumbai	India	240	33	39
New York	USA	N/A	29	79
Osaka	Japan	43	19	63
Rio de Janeiro	Brazil	139	129	N/A
São Paulo	Brazil	86	43	83
Seoul	South Korea	84	44	60
Shanghai	China	246	53	73
Tokyo	Japan	49	18	68

Source: World Development Indicators 2000, *IBRD/World Bank, 2000*

■ World Pollution

Effect of Selected Indoor Air Pollutants on Human Health

Studies in Denmark and the USA have linked pollutants found in buildings with human symptoms such as dizziness, headaches, and fatigue. This is known as 'sick building syndrome'. New buildings are typically worse than old buildings, due to the release of chemicals from new furnishings, and reduced air exchange due to air conditioning. Some pollutants have a synergistic or 'cocktail' effect; for example, sulphur dioxide is much more harmful when particulates are present, as coated particles are transported directly to the lungs, where sulphur dioxide causes most harm.

Pollutant	Source	Potential threat
1,1,1-trichloroethane	aerosol sprays	dizziness, irregular breathing
asbestos	pipe insulation, ceiling and wall tiles	lung disease, lung cancer
carbon monoxide	faulty or unvented gas and paraffin heaters, wood stoves	headaches, drowsiness, irregular heartbeat; poisonous
formaldehyde	furniture stuffing, panelling, foam insulation	irritation of eyes, throat, skin and lungs; dizziness
methylene chloride	paint strippers and thinners	nerve disorders, diabetes
nitrogen oxides	unvented gas and paraffin heaters, wood stoves	irritated lungs, headaches
radon-222	radioactive soil and rock foundations, water supply	lung cancer
styrene	carpets, plastic products	kidney and liver damage
sulphur dioxide	solid fuel heaters	in asthmatics, reduced lung function, chest tightness, and coughing
tetrachloroethylene	dry-cleaning-fluid fumes on clothes and carpets	nerve disorders, liver and kidney damage, cancer threat
tobacco smoke	cigarettes, cigars	lung cancer, respiratory ailments, heart disease

Effect of Air Pollutants on Selected Materials

Air pollution is harmful not only to living creatures, but also to the materials around them. Acids are formed by the reaction of sulphur and nitrogen dioxides with atmospheric moisture. Damage to buildings in the USA from acid deposition alone is estimated at $5 billion annually.

Material	Effects	Pollutants responsible
ceramics and glass	surface erosion	particulates
leather	cracking, loss of strength	sulphur dioxide
metals	corrosion, tarnishing, loss of strength	sulphur dioxide, sulphuric acid, nitric acid, particulates
paints	surface erosion, discoloration, soiling	sulphur dioxide, ozone, particulates
paper	embrittlement, discoloration	sulphur dioxide
rubber	cracking, loss of strength	ozone
stone and concrete	surface erosion, discoloration, soiling	sulphur dioxide, sulphuric acid, nitric acid, particulates
textiles	deterioration, fading, soiling	sulphur dioxide, nitrogen dioxide, ozone, particulates
wood	discoloration, loss of strength, more prone to fungal diseases	sulphur dioxide, ozone

Nuclear Waste for Selected Countries

The table presents the annual spent fuel in nuclear power plants of selected OECD countries for selected years, and includes projections up to 2010 (as made in 1999).

Spent fuel arisings are one part of the radioactive waste generated at various stages of the nuclear fuel cycle (uranium mining and milling, fuel enrichment, reactor operation, spent fuel reprocessing). Radioactive waste also arises from decontamination and decommissioning of nuclear facilities, and from other activities using isotopes, such as scientific research and medical activities. Data in the table do not represent all radioactive waste generated; amounts of spent fuel arisings depend on the share of nuclear electricity in the energy supply and on the nuclear plant technologies adopted. The impact of nuclear waste on humans and the environment depends on the level of radioactivity and on the conditions under which the waste is handled, treated, stored, and disposed of.
(N/A = not available. N = nil or negligible.)

Rank (2000 figures)	Country	Spent fuel (tonnes of heavy metal)						
		1982	1992	1996	1998	2000	2005	2010
1	USA	1,100	2,300	2,300	2,700	2,300	2,000	1,700
2	Canada	856	1,690	1,690	1,510	1,500	1,900	1,900
3	UK	900	997	781	785	1,258	397	204
4	France	375	1,050	1,264	1,165	1,205	1,165	1,165
5	Japan	510	869	852	1,061	942	1,000	1,320
6	Korea	N/A	261	247	370	670	730	700
7	Germany	270	500	450	430	430	400	400
8	Sweden	100	250	235	232	230	200	200
9	Spain	60	168	158	97	148	160	150
10	Belgium	44	102	123	141	130	110	110
11	Finland	62	60	68	72	75	74	74
12	Switzerland	60	85	64	64	64	64	64
13	Hungary	N/A	N/A	55	53	53	53	53
14	Czech Republic	N/A	N/A	45	45	43	80	80
15	Mexico	N	N	39	43	22	40	20
16	Netherlands	16	15	14	12	12	N	N
17	Turkey	N	N	N	N	N	160	320

Source: OECD Environmental Data 1999, © *OECD 1999*

See also **Nuclear Energy Production in OECD Countries,** p 692; **Nuclear Power Plants in the UK,** p 696.

Major Oilspills Throughout the World

'Large' spills, defined as greater than 700 tonnes, are generally caused by ship accidents (such as grounding and collisions) or by oil-well blow-outs. Large ship spillages have decreased in number by approximately two-thirds between 1970 and 1998, now accounting for 3.3% of total ship spillages. As of March 1999.

Year	Location	Ship/oil well name	Amount	
			tonnes	millions of gallons
1991	Sea Island Terminal of Persian Gulf	deliberate release of oil by Iraqi troops at end of Persian Gulf war	799,120	240.0
1979	Gulf of Mexico	*Ixtoc 1* oil field	600,000	180.0
1983	Persian Gulf	*Nowruz* oil field	600,000	180.0
1979	off Tobago, West Indies	*Atlantic Empress* and *Aegean Captain*	370,000	111.0
1977	North Sea	*Ekofisk* oil well	270,000	81.0
1991	700 nautical miles off Angola	*ABT Summer*	260,000	78.0
1983	off Saldanha Bay, South Africa	*Castillo de Beliver*	252,000	75.6
1978	off Brittany, France	*Amoco Cadiz*	223,000	66.9
1991	Genoa, Italy	*Haven*	144,000	43.2
1988	700 nautical miles off Nova Scotia, Canada	*Odyssey*	132,000	39.6
1967	Scilly Isles, England	*Torrey Canyon*	119,000	35.7
1976	La Coruna, Spain	*Urquioia*	100,000	30.0
1977	300 nautical miles off Honolulu	*Haiwaiian Patriot*	95,000	28.5
1979	Bosphorus, Turkey	*Independenta*	95,000	28.5
1975	Oporto, Portugal	*Jakob Maersk*	88,000	26.4
1993	Shetland Islands, Scotland	*Braer*	85,000	25.5
1989	120 nautical miles off Atlantic Coast of Morocco	*Kharg 5*	80,000	24.0
1992	La Coruna, Spain	*Aegean Sea*	74,000	22.2
1996	Milford Haven, Wales	*Sea Empress*	72,000	21.6
1992	off Maputo, Mozambique	*Katina P*	72,000	21.6
1983	55 nautical miles off Muscat, Oman	*Assimi*	53,000	15.9
1974	Magellan Straits, Chile	*Metula*	50,000	15.0
1971	off Cape Agulhas, South Africa	*Wafra*	40,000	12.0
1989	Prince William Sound, Alaska, USA	*Exxon Valdez*	37,000	11.0

Household Waste Generated in Selected Countries

(N/A = not available)

Rank (by amount per capita)	Country	Household waste generated (thousands of tonnes)		Household waste, amounts per capita (kg/capita)[1]	
		1990	1997	1990	1997
1	Denmark	N/A	2,776	N/A	530
2	Netherlands	6,190	7,471	410	480
3=	Germany	N/A	35,402	N/A	440
	UK	2,000	26,000	350	440
5	USA	115,423	108,416	460	410
6	Switzerland	2,728	2,851	410	400
7	Ireland	N/A	1,325	N/A	370
8=	New Zealand	N/A	1,269	N/A	350
	France	20,420	20,800	350	350
10	Austria	2,504	2,775	320	340
11	Hungary	2,468	3,350	240	330
12	Norway	1,088	1,354	260	310
13=	Czech Republic	N/A	2,600	N/A	250
	Luxembourg	98	100	250	250
15=	Mexico	16,850	23,418	190	240
	Iceland	62	66	240	240
17	Poland	7,253	8,169	190	210
18=	Slovak Republic	N/A	1,100	N/A	200
	Canada	8,925	6,050	310	200
20	Finland	N/A	870	N/A	170

[1] National definitions may differ. Values per capita are rounded up.

Source: OECD Environmental Data 1999, © *OECD 1999*

■ World Pollution

Recycling Rates in Industrialized Countries

This table refers to municipal waste, waste handled by the scrapping industry, and other waste from economic activities. Material that is collected for recycling by private sources is also included. Recycling is defined as any reuse of material in a production process that diverts it from the waste stream, except reuse as fuel. 'Recycling rates' are the amounts recycled relative to apparent consumption (economic notion of domestic production of the respective material + imports − exports). It should be noted that definitions may vary from one country to another. In particular, total amounts of waste produced, rather than apparent consumption, may be used in some areas to derive recycling rates.
(N/A = not available.)

Country	Percentage of apparent consumption			
	Paper and cardboard		Glass	
	1990	1997	1990	1997
Austria	52	69	60	88
Belgium	13	16	55[1]	75
Canada	28	N/A	17[3]	N/A
Denmark	35	50	35[1]	70
Finland	43	N/A	36	62
France	34	41	41[1]	52
Germany	44	70	54	79
Greece	28	29	15	26
Ireland, Republic of	11[2]	12	23	38
Italy	27	31	53[1]	34
Japan	50	54	48	N/A
Korea, South	44	57	46	68
Mexico	2[1]	2	4[1]	4
Netherlands	50	62	67	82
Norway	20	44	22[1]	76
Portugal	40	40	27	44
Spain	39	42	27	37
Sweden	46	62	44[1]	76
Switzerland	49	63	65	91
Turkey	27	36	31	20
UK	33	40	21	26
USA	28	N/A	20	N/A

[1] Data are for 1991.
[2] Data are for 1992.
[3] Data are for 1987.

Source: OECD Environmental Data 1999, © *OECD 1999*

World Pollution: International Environmental Agreements

Conventions under Preparation, Brokered by United Nations Environmental Programme (UNEP)

As of May 2000.

- Convention on Trade in Dangerous Chemicals and Pesticides (PIC)
- Convention on Persistent Organic Pollutants (POPs)

Basel Convention on the Control of Transboundary Movements of Hazardous Wastes and Their Disposal

Date of adoption 1989
Place of adoption Basel, Switzerland
Date of entry into force 5 May 1992
Number of signatory countries 121

Objectives To minimize hazardous waste generation, regulate the transboundary movement of hazardous wastes, and provide obligations to its Parties to ensure that such wastes are managed and disposed of in an environmentally sound manner.

Summary of selected provisions Reduction of transboundary movements of hazardous watses to a minimum consistent with their environmentally sound management; to control the transboundary movement of hazardous wastes, monitor and prevent illegal traffic, provide assistance for the environmentally sound management of hazardous wastes; to promote cooperation between parties in the field and develop technical guidelines for the management of hazardous wastes.

UK Pollution

Air Pollution in the UK: Selected Pollutants and Cities

Air pollution levels in the UK depend on time of day, time of year, and location, hence summarizing pollution levels is difficult and often misleading. However, in order to give a brief summary of the measurements from automatic networks, and some idea of the sorts of levels measured in UK cities, this table gives annual means for 1997 for five pollutants.

- **Carbon monoxide (CO)** The sites with the highest annual means are measuring close to roads, since road traffic is one of the major sources of carbon monoxide.
- **Particulate matter (PM10)** There is a wide gradient in the concentrations of PM10 in the UK, from the southeast (higher levels) to the northwest (lower levels). Local effects from transport and industrial emissions increase PM10 concentrations.
- **Sulphur dioxide (SO_2)** Sulphur dioxide annual means are highest in areas where coal is used as a fuel, or where the site is influenced by a major power point source, such as a nuclear power station.
- **Nitrogen dioxide (NO_2)** Nitrogen dioxide means are highest in sites measuring close to roads, and lowest in rural areas.
- **Ozone (O_3)** Ozone annual means are actually higher in rural locations than in cities. This is because ozone is 'scavenged' in urban areas: reaction with emissions from motor vehicles leads to rapid, local removal from the atmosphere.
(N/A = not available.)

1997 City	Annual mean				
	Carbon monoxide (CO)[1]	Particulate matter (PM10)[2]	Sulphur dioxide (SO_2)[3]	Nitrogen dioxide (NO_2)[3]	Ozone (O_3)[3]
Belfast	0.7	25	12	20	17
Birmingham	0.6	22	5	23	16
Bristol	0.7	24	4	23	16
Cardiff	0.7	26	4	20	16
Coventry	0.4	N/A	7	12	16
Derry	0.3	21	6	11	22

(continued)

Air Pollution in the UK: Selected Pollutants and Cities (*continued*)

City	Annual mean				
	Carbon monoxide (CO)[1]	Particulate matter (PM10)[2]	Sulphur dioxide (SO_2)[3]	Nitrogen dioxide (NO_2)[3]	Ozone (O_3)[3]
Edinburgh	0.5	18	3	25	14
Exeter	1.6	N/A	3	23	N/A
Glasgow	0.8	21	4	29	14
Hull	0.7	24	6	21	16
Leeds	0.6	28	6	27	13
Leicester	0.6	20	4	21	16
Liverpool	0.5	25	7	23	16
London[4]	1.0	25	7	23	16
Manchester	0.5	24	6	27	12
Newcastle	0.5	21	5	21	17
Nottingham	0.6	23	6	26	13
Sheffield	0.5	25	8	25	15
Stoke-on-Trent	0.7	22	6	N/A	20
Swansea	0.4	24	5	20	19

[1] Measured in parts per million (ppm).
[2] Measured in micrograms per cubic metre ($\mu g\ m^{-3}$).
[3] Measured in parts per billion (ppb).
[4] Data for London are averages derived from statistics from several different Network stations. The top station/site in London for each type of pollutant is as follows: CO Marylebone Road – 2.5 ppm; PM10 Marylebone Road – 39 $\mu g\ m^{-3}$; SO_2 Marylebone Road – 9 ppb; NO_2 Marylebone Road – 50 ppb; O_3 Teddington – 20 ppb.

See also **Traffic in Britain,** p 588; **Car Users' Attitudes Towards Discouraging Car Use in Britain,** p 594.

The Worst-Polluting Companies in Britain

In 1998 British companies were fined a total of £2 million for pollution offences. The government's Environment Agency is calling on the courts to impose stiffer penalties in a bid to reduce pollution. Some specific examples of the pollution incidents in this year are given in the table footnotes.

Ranking	Company	Fines levied in pounds
1	ICI Chemicals	382,500[1]
2	Tyseley Waste Disposal Ltd	95,500
3	London Waste Ltd	38,500[2]
4	Wessex Water Ltd	36,500
5	Alco Waste Management	30,000
6	Anglian Water Services Ltd	24,250
7	EOM Construction Ltd	21,000
8=	Shell (UK) Ltd	20,000[3]
	BNFL	20,000[4]
10=	Celtic Energy	18,000
	European Vinyls Corporation Ltd	18,000

[1] A £300,000 fine was incurred in March 1998 for polluting groundwater with almost 150 tonnes of choloroform in April 1997. The company was also fined for releasing a metal-cleaning chemical that evaporated into the air and entered a nearby canal, and for a discharge at a site at Cleveland that sprayed across marshland and killed birds, fish and vegetation.
[2] The company was fined £95,000 after the disappearance of radioactive material during demolition work at an incinerator plant in Birmingham.
[3] Shell UK was fined £20,000 for polluting the Manchester Ship Canal with the equivalent of 10,500 household buckets of refined oil from the Stanlow Manufacturing Complex in Ellesmere Port.
[4] BNFL was fined £20,000 because of a discharge from a site in Preston into the River Ribble in 1997.

Source: The Environment Agency,

Quality of Seaside Bathing Waters in the UK

In order to comply with an EC Bathing Water Directive (76/160/EEC), at least 95% of samples taken during the bathing season must have no more than 10,000 coliform bacteria in total per 100 ml and no more than 2,000 faecal coliform bacteria per ml.

Region	Identified bathing waters			Number complying			% complying		
	1997	1998	1999	1997	1998	1999	1997	1998	1999
Anglia	35	36	36	35	36	34	100	100	94
North East	56	56	55	51	47	52	91	84	95
North West	34	34	34	17	21	23	50	62	68
South West	181	184	184	164	167	167	91	91	91
Southern	75	77	79	67	75	74	89	97	94
Thames	3	3	3	3	3	3	100	100	100
Welsh	64	68	70	60	64	69	94	94	99
England and Wales total	448	458	461	397	413	422	89	90	92
Scotland	23	23	60	18	12	54	78	52	90
Northern Ireland	16	16	16	14	15	15	88	94	94
UK total	487	497	537	429	440	491	88	89	91

Source: Environment Agency; Scottish Environmental Protection Agency; Northern Ireland Department of the Environment

■ UK Pollution

Water Pollution Incidents in the UK

The table shows data for substantiated water pollution incidents by source. A similar breakdown of incidents by type of pollutant is not available for Scotland.
(N/A = not available.)

1998

Region	Agriculture	Industry	Sewage and water	Domestic	Transport	Other	Total
Midlands	N/A	N/A	N/A	N/A	N/A	N/A	4,061
South West	N/A	N/A	N/A	N/A	N/A	N/A	2,603
North West	N/A	N/A	N/A	N/A	N/A	N/A	2,201
Anglian	N/A	N/A	N/A	N/A	N/A	N/A	2,163
North East	N/A	N/A	N/A	N/A	N/A	N/A	1,993
Wales	N/A	N/A	N/A	N/A	N/A	N/A	1,885
Thames	N/A	N/A	N/A	N/A	N/A	N/A	1,819
Southern	N/A	N/A	N/A	N/A	N/A	N/A	1,138
England and Wales Total	2,050	3,600	4,253	1,256	1,727	4,977	17,863
Scotland	N/A	N/A	N/A	N/A	N/A	N/A	1,821
Northern Ireland	467	435	276	227	64	172	1,641
Pollutant total	2,517[1]	4,035[1]	4,529[1]	1,483[1]	1,791[1]	5,149[1]	21,325

[1] Totals by source do not include Scotland.

Emissions in the UK

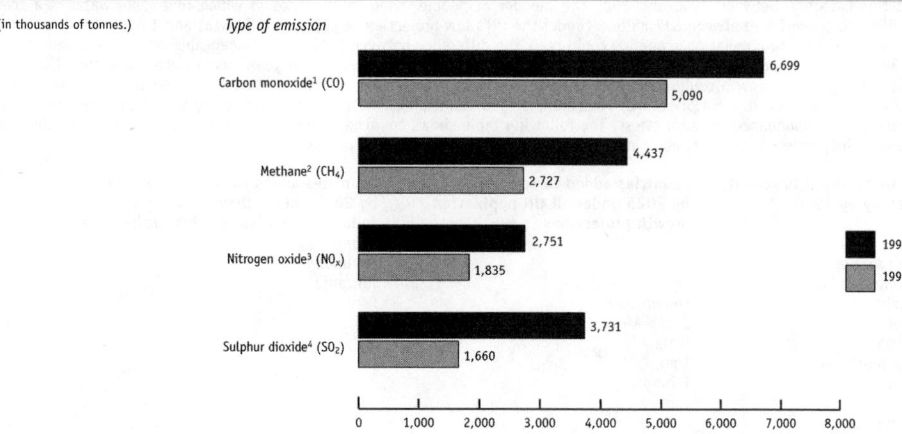

[1] Colourless, odourless gas formed when carbon is oxidized in a limited supply of air. It is a poisonous constituent of car exhaust fumes, forming a stable compound with haemoglobin in the blood, thus preventing the haemoglobin from transporting oxygen to the body tissues. The main source in the UK is road transport (3,797,000 tonnes in 1997).

[2] Methane burns with a bluish flame and explodes when mixed with air or oxygen. It is the chief constituent of natural gas and also occurs in the explosive firedamp of coal mines. Methane contributes to global warming. The main sources in the UK are landfill sites (823,000 tonnes in 1997) and livestock (1,004,000 tonnes in 1997).

[3] Gas compound that contains only nitrogen and oxygen. The nitrogen oxides, nitrogen monoxide and nitrogen dioxide, contribute to air pollution. The main source in the UK is road transport (883,000 tonnes in 1997).

[4] Pungent gas produced by burning sulphur in air or oxygen. It is widely used for disinfecting food vessels and equipment, and as a preservative in some food products. It occurs in industrial flue gases and is a major cause of acid rain. The main source in the UK is power stations (1,129,000 tonnes in 1997).

Source: Digest of United Kingdom Energy Statistics 1999, © *Crown copyright 1999*

Carbon Dioxide Emissions in the UK

Measurements are based on the methods established by the Intergovernmental Panel on Climate Change (IPCC).

1997

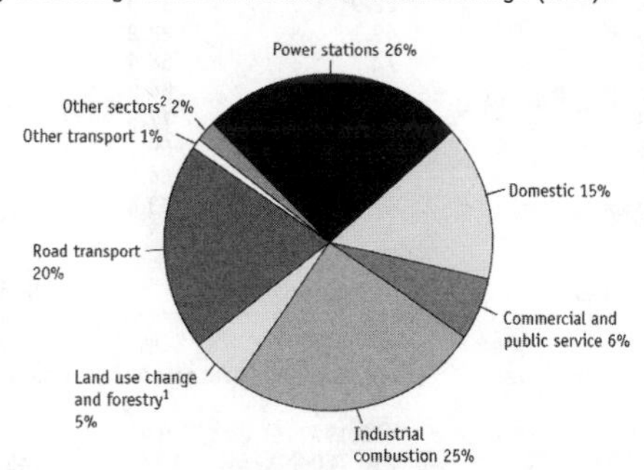

[1] Includes fuel combustion for agriculture, forestry, and fishing.
[2] Includes waste and fugitive emissions from other fuels.

Source: Digest of United Kingdom Energy Statistics 1999, © *Crown copyright 1999*

Conservation

Freshwater Resources and Withdrawals

Continent	Annual internal renewable water resources[1] Total (cubic km)	1998 per capita (cubic metres)	Year of data	Annual withdrawals Total (cubic km)	% of water resources[1]	Per capita (cubic metres)
Africa	3,996.0	5,133	1995	145.14	4	202
Asia	13,206.7	3,680	1987	1,633.85	12	542
Europe	6,234.6	8,547	1995	455.29	7	625
Central America	1,056.7	8,084	1987	96.01	9	916
North America	5,308.6	17,458	1991	512.43	10	1,798
Oceania	1,614.3	54,795	1995	16.73	1	591
South America	9,526.0	28,702	1995	106.21	1	335
World total	41,022.0	6,918	1987	3,240.00	8	645

[1] Annual internal renewable water resources usually include river flows from other countries.

Source: World Resources 1998–99: A Guide to the Global Environment, *World Resources Institute*

Water-Scarce Countries

In 1990, quantities of renewable fresh water qualified 20 nations as water-scarce, 15 of them with rapidly growing populations. By 2025 between 10 and 15 nations will be added to this category. Between 1990 and 2025 the number of people living in countries in which renewable water is a scarce resource will rise from 131 million to somewhere between 817 million (under the UN's low projection of population growth) and 1.079 billion (under the high projection). For several countries varying population scenarios could mark the difference between potentially manageable water stress and outright water scarcity in 2025. In 1990 Peru, for example, had 1,856 cubic metres of renewable water per person per year. Under almost any conditions, that figure will plunge, but the rate of population growth could determine whether Peru crosses into water scarcity or hovers in water stress in 2025. Similar possibilities face Tanzania, Zimbabwe, and Cyprus. For Sri Lanka, Mozambique, and Mauritania, the population trajectory will determine whether the threshold is crossed from relative water abundance to water stress. The following table shows countries experiencing water scarcity in 1955, 1990, and 2025 (projected), based on availability of less than 1,000 cubic metres of renewable water per person per year.

Water-scarce countries in 1955	Countries added to scarcity category by 1990	Countries added to scarcity category by 2025 under all UN population growth projections	Countries added to scarcity category by 2025 only if they follow UN medium or high projections
Malta	Qatar	Libya	Cyprus
Djibouti	Saudi Arabia	Oman	Zimbabwe
Barbados	United Arab Emirates	Egypt	Tanzania
Singapore	Yemen	Comoros	Peru
Bahrain	Israel	South Africa	
Kuwait	Tunisia	Syria	
Jordan	Cape Verde	Iran	
	Kenya	Ethiopia	
	Burundi	Haiti	
	Algeria		
	Rwanda		
	Malawi		
	Somalia		

Source: Sustaining Water, Population Action International

World Forest Ecosystems

1996
Closed forests

Continent/region	Land area (thousand ha)	Original forest as a % of land area[1]	Forest as a % of original forest: Current forests[2]	Forest as a % of original forest: Frontier forests[3]	% frontier forests threatened[3]
Africa	2,963,468	22.9	33.9	7.8	76.8
Asia	3,085,414	49.1	28.2	5.3	63.1
Europe	2,260,320	72.7	58.4	21.3	18.7
Central America	264,835	67.2	54.5	9.7	87.0
North America	1,838,009	59.7	77.3	34.1	26.2
South America	1,752,925	55.6	69.1	45.6	54.0
Oceania	849,135	16.9	64.9	22.3	76.3
World total	13,048,300	47.7	53.4	21.7	39.5

Forest ecosystems

Continent/region	Mangroves: Area (thousand ha)	Mangroves: % protected	Tropical forests: Area (thousand ha)	Tropical forests: % protected	Non-tropical forests: Area (thousand ha)	Non-tropical forests: % protected	Sparse trees and parkland: Area (thousand ha)	Sparse trees and parkland: % protected
Africa	3, 801	1.4	448,197	9.1	8,249	2.0	69,710	11.3
Asia	4,033	26.5	210,720	16.4	145,101	5.1	42,384	7.0
Europe	0	0	0	0	1,019,178	2.9	10,350	1.0
Central America	1,679	14.9	71,893	12.3	21,293	3.1	26	0
North America	199	60.0	443	6.7	683,700	8.9	148,827	5.7

(continued)

World Forest Ecosystems (*continued*)

Forest ecosystems

Continent/region	Mangroves		Tropical forests		Non-tropical forests		Sparse trees and parkland	
	Area (thousand ha)	% protected	Area (thousand ha)	% protected	Area (thousand ha)	% protected	Area (thousand ha)	% protected
South America	2,929	32.1	620,514	12.2	39,291	15.7	168,216	2.4
Oceania	5,466	6.6	53,560	9.1	27,088	18.7	102,126	6.1
World total	16,945	13.3	1,407,649	11.7	1,823,787	6.0	541,616	5.5

[1] Original forest is that estimated to have covered the planet 8,000 years ago given current climate conditions.
[2] Includes frontier and non-frontier forests.
[3] Frontier forests are large, relatively undisturbed forest ecosystems.

Source: World Resources 1998–99: A Guide to the Global Environment, *World Resources Institute*

Deforestation of Tropical and Temperate Forests Worldwide

(In hectares.)

Region	Forest area 1990	Forest area 1995	Total change 1990–95	Annual change	Annual change (%)
Africa	538,978,000	520,237,000	− 18,741,000	− 3,748,000	− 0.7
Asia	490,812,000	474,172,000	− 16,640,000	− 3,328,000	− 0.7
Europe[1]	144,044,000	145,988,000	1,944,000	389,000	0.3
Former USSR[1]	813,381,000	816,167,000	2,786,000	557,000	0.1
North and Central America	537,898,000	536,529,000	− 1,369,000	− 274,000	− 0.1
Oceania	91,149,000	90,695,000	− 454,000	− 91,000	− 0.1
South America	894,466,000	870,594,000	− 23,872,000	− 4,774,000	− 0.5

[1] No tropical forests exist in these regions, thus totals represent only temperate forests.

Source: State of the World's Forests 1999, *Food and Agriculture Organization of the United Nations*

Afforestation

Afforestation is the planting of trees in areas that have not previously held forests. (**Reafforestation** is the planting of trees in deforested areas.) Trees may be planted (1) to provide timber and wood pulp; (2) to provide firewood in countries where this is an energy source; (3) to bind soil together and prevent soil erosion; and (4) to act as windbreaks.

Afforestation is controversial because while many ancient woodlands of mixed trees are being lost, the new plantations consist almost exclusively of conifers. It is claimed that such plantations acidify the soil, replace more ancient and ecologically valuable species, and do not sustain wildlife.

Deforestation

Deforestation is the destruction of forest for timber, fuel, charcoal burning, and clearing for agriculture and extractive industries, such as mining, without planting new trees to replace those lost or allowing the natural forest to regenerate. Deforestation causes fertile soil to be blown away or washed into rivers, leading to soil erosion, drought, flooding, and loss of wildlife. It may also increase the carbon dioxide content of the atmosphere and intensify the greenhouse effect, as there are fewer trees absorbing carbon dioxide from the air for photosynthesis.

Many people are concerned about the damage deforestation does to the habitats of plants and animals. Deforestation ultimately leads to famine, and is thought to be partially responsible for the flooding of lowland areas because trees help to slow down water movement.

Countries Losing Greatest Areas of Forest

1990–95

Rank	Country	Area of lost forest (hectares)
1	Brazil	2,554,000
2	Indonesia	1,084,000
3	Congo, Democratic Republic of	740,000
4	Bolivia	581,000
5	Mexico	508,000
6	Venezuela	503,000
7	Malaysia	400,000
8	Myanmar	387,000
9	Sudan	353,000
10	Thailand	329,000
11	Paraguay	327,000
12	Tanzania	323,000
13	Zambia	264,000
14 =	Colombia	262,000
	Philippines	262,000
16	Angola	237,000
17	Peru	217,000
18	Ecuador	189,000
19	Cambodia	164,000
20	Nicaragua	151,000
21	Laos	148,000
22	Vietnam	135,000
23	Papua New Guinea	133,000
24	Madagascar	130,000
25	Cameroon	129,000
26	Central African Republic	128,000
27	Nigeria	121,000
28	Afghanistan	118,000
29	Ghana	117,000
30	Mozambique	116,000
31	Guinea-Bissau	114,000
32	Honduras	102,000
33	Chad	94,000
34	Gabon	91,000
35	Argentina	89,000
36	Hong Kong, China	87,000
37	Guatemala	82,000
38	Guinea	75,000
39	Botswana	71,000
40	Panama	64,000

Source: State of the World's Forests 1999, *Food and Agriculture Organization of the United Nations*

Top 10 Countries with the Fastest Forest Depletion Rates

1990–95 Rank	Country	Average (annual loss) (%)
1	Lebanon	7.8
2	Jamaica	7.2
3	Afghanistan	6.8
4	Comoros	5.6
5	Virgin Islands (British)	4.4
6	St Lucia	3.6
7	Philippines	3.5
8	Haiti	3.4
9	El Salvador	3.3
10=	Costa Rica	3.0
	Sierra Leone	3.0

Source: State of the World's Forests 1999, *Food and Agriculture Organization of the United Nations*

Conservation: International Environmental Agreements

Convention on Biological Diversity

Date of adoption 22 May 1992
Place of adoption Nairobi, Kenya
Date of entry into force 29 December 1993
Number of signatory countries 175

Objectives The conservation of biological diversity, the sustainable use of its components, and the fair and equitable sharing of benefits arising from the use of genetic resources.

Summary of selected provisions To promote scientific and technical cooperation, access to financial and genetic resources, and the transfer of ecologically sound technologies. Parties will develop national strategies or programmes for the conservation and sustainable use of biological diversity; identify and monitor components of biological diversity important for its conservation and sustainable use; and establish a system of protected areas to conserve biological diversity. The Convention is the first global, comprehensive agreement to address all aspects of biological diversity genetic resources, species and ecosystems.

United Nations Convention on the Law of the Sea

Date of adoption 10 December 1982
Place of adoption Montego Bay, Jamaica
Date of entry into force Not yet
Number of signatory countries 160

Objective To set up a comprehensive new legal regime for the sea and oceans and, as far as environmental provisions are concerned, to establish material rules concerning environmental standards as well as enforcement provisions dealing with pollution of the marine environment.

Summary of selected provisions Definition of the territorial sea and the contiguous zone; land-locked States to enjoy the right of access to and from the sea and freedom of transit; the sea bed and ocean floor and its subsoil are beyond the limits of national jurisdiction and its resources to be the common heritage of humankind. International rules and national legislation to be developed for the prevention, reduction, and control of pollution of the marine environment, and provisions set out concerning enforcement and responsibility and liability; rules set out to govern marine scientific research, the development and transfer of marine technology and the settlement of disputes.

Convention on Wetlands of International Importance

Date of adoption 2 February 1971
Place of adoption Ramsar, Iran
Date of entry into force 21 December 1975
Number of signatory countries 62

Objectives To stem the progressive encroachment on and loss of wetlands now and in the future, recognizing the fundamental ecological functions of wetlands and their economic, cultural, scientific, and recreational value.

Summary of selected provisions Parties to designate at least one national wetland for inclusion in a 'List of Wetlands of International Importance'; Parties to establish wetland nature reserves, cooperate in the exchange of information, and train personnel for wetland management.

International Convention for the Regulation of Whaling

Date of adoption 2 December 1946; Amendment: 19 November 1956
Place of adoption Washington, District of Columbia, USA
Date of entry into force 10 November 1948; Amendment: 4 May 1959
Number of signatory countries 49

Objectives To protect all species of whales from overfishing and safeguard for future generations the great natural resources represented by whale stocks. To establish a system of international regulation for the whale fisheries to ensure proper conservation and development of whale stocks.

Summary of selected provisions Establishment of an International Whaling Commission (IWC) to encourage research and investigation, to collect and analyse statistical information, and to appraise and disseminate information concerning whaling and whale stocks. The IWC meets annually to adopt regulations for the conservation and utilization of whale stocks, dealing with protected and unprotected species, size limits for species, maximum catches for any one season, types of gear and apparatus to be used, contracting Governments to take measures to enforce these regulations, and to report any infraction to them to the IWC.

United Nations Convention to Combat Desertification (UNCCD)

Date of adoption June 1994
Place of adoption Geneva, Switzerland
Date of entry into force 26 December 1996
Number of signatory countries 166 (of which 51 signed after ratification)

Objectives Strengthening the knowledge base and developing information and monitoring systems for regions prone to desertification and drought, including the social and economic aspects of these ecosystems.

Summary of selected provisions Develop and increase public awareness of desertification and drought; support local communities in their own efforts in combating desertification; promote true partnership between government authorities, at local and national levels, and land users, giving land users a responsible role in the planning and execution of development projects.

Land and Protected Areas

Top 10 Countries with the Greatest Protected Land Area

The International Union for the Conservation of Nature and Natural Resources (IUCN) identifies a protected area as an area of land and/or sea dedicated to the protection and maintenance of biological diversity and natural and associated cultural resources that are managed through legal or other effective means. The main purpose of management of a region or area as a protected area are: for scientific research; wilderness protection; preservation of species and genetic diversity; maintenance of environmental services; protection of specific natural and cultural features; tourism and recreation; education; sustainable use of resources from natural ecosystems; and maintenance of cultural and traditional attributes.

The number of protected areas in the UK is 515 and the total area protected is 50,001 sq km/19,305 sq mi. This represents 20.4% of the total land area.

1997 Rank	Country	Area		Number of protected areas	Protected area		Land area protected
		sq km	sq mi		sq km	sq mi	%
1	USA	9,372,614	3,618,766	3,333	1,988,444	767,738	21.22
2	Australia	7,682,300	2,966,152	5,647	1,045,686	403,739	13.61
3	Greenland	2,175,600	839,999	2	982,500	379,343	45.16
4	Canada	9,922,385	3,831,054	3,224	953,103	367,993	9.61
5	Saudi Arabia	2,400,900	926,987	78	825,620	318,772	34.39
6	China	9,597,000	3,705,402	810	682,407	263,477	7.11
7	Venezuela	912,045	352,141	194	560,404	216,372	61.44
8	Brazil	8,511,965	3,286,470	582	526,717	203,365	6.19
9	Russian Federation	17,075,400	6,592,812	216	516,688	199,493	3.03
10	Indonesia	1,919,445	741,098	1,069	345,118	133,250	17.98

Source: US Fish and Wildlife Service

Top 10 Countries with the Greatest Percentage of Protected Land Area

'Protected land area' can include marine habitats, such as the Great Barrier Reef Park in Australia, allowing for land area percentages to exceed 100%.

1997 Rank	Country	Protected land area %
1	Dominican Republic	173.5
2	Seychelles	111.1
3	Slovakia	75.6
4	Venezuela	61.4
5	Greenland	45.2
6	Hong Kong	43.4
7	Belize	39.8
8	Kiribati	39
9	Liechtenstein	38.1
10	Saudi Arabia	34.4

Source: US Fish and Wildlife Service

Protected Areas in the UK

As of August 1999.

Type of site[1]	Number of sites	Area (sq km)
National nature reserves	385	2,471
Local nature reserves (Great Britain only)	712	401
Sites of special scientific interest (SSSIs) (Great Britain only)	7,032	23,966
Areas of special scientific interest (ASSIs) (Northern Ireland)	149	873
Statutory marine nature reserves	3	196
Areas protected by international agreements		
Special Areas of Conservation (SACs)	340	17,660
Special Protection Areas (SPAs)	201	9,346
Ramsar sites	128	5,512

[1] Some sites may be included in more than one category.

Community Forests in England

Most countries in Europe have 20–25% of their landscape under trees. England has just 7.5%. The aim, in association with the Forestry Commission, is to double the figure to 15% by the year 2050.
(– = not applicable.)

Community forest	Area		Existing tree cover (%)	Population within 20 km (millions)	Contact phone number
	sq km	sq mi			
Forest of Avon	573	221	5.9	1.0	(0117) 953 2141
Forest of Mercia (south Staffordshire)	210	81	6.4	4.0	(01543) 505488
The Great North Forest (south Tyne and Wear/northeast Durham)	160	62	8.0	1.0	(0191) 460 6200
Great Western (Swindon)	390	151	3.0	0.3	(01793) 466324
The Greenwood (Nottingham)	414	160	11.3	1.0	(01623) 758231
Marston Vale (Bedford)	158	61	3.6	0.5	(01234) 767 0377
The Mersey Forest	925	357	4.0	5.0	(01925) 816217
Red Rose Forest (Greater Manchester West)	760	293	3.9	4.0	(0161) 872 1660
South Yorkshire	395	153	7.6	1.9	(0114) 257 1199
The Tees Forest (Cleveland)	255	98	6.9	1.0	(01642) 300716
Thames Chase (east of London)	98	38	9.7	3.0	(01708) 641880
Watling Chase (south Hertfordshire/North London)	163	63	7.9	3.0	(01923) 852641

See also **Forestry in the UK,** p 703.

Areas of Outstanding Natural Beauty and National Scenic Areas in the UK

The Countryside Agency designates Areas of Outstanding Natural Beauty in England. In Wales, similar areas are the responsibility of the Countryside Council for Wales. No Areas of Outstanding Natural Beauty are designated in Scotland; the Scottish Natural Heritage recognizes equivalent sites called National Scenic Areas.
(N/A = not available.)

Name	Region	Established (year)	Area	
			sq km	sq mi
England				
Arnside and Silverdale	Cumbria, Lancashire	1972	75	29
Blackdown Hills	Devon, Somerset	1991	370	143
Cannock Castle	Staffordshire	1958	68	26
Chichester Harbour	Hampshire, West Sussex	1964	74	29
Chilterns	Bedfordshire, Buckinghamshire, Hertfordshire, Oxfordshire	1965; extended 1990	833	322
Cornwall	Cornwall	1959; Camel estuary 1983	958	370
Cotswolds	south Gloucestershire, Bath and North East Somerset, Gloucestershire, Oxfordshire, Wiltshire, Warwickshire, Worcestershire	1966	2,038	787
Cranborne Chase and West Wiltshire Downs	Dorset, Hampshire, Somerset, Wiltshire	1983	983	379
Dedham Vale	Essex, Suffolk	1970; extended 1978, 1991	90	35
Dorset	Dorset, Somerset	1959	1,129	436
East Devon	Devon	1963	268	103
East Hampshire	Hampshire	1962	383	148
Forest of Bowland	Lancashire, North Yorkshire	1964	802	310
High Weald	Sussex, Kent, Surrey	1983	1,460	564
Howardian Hills	North Yorkshire	1987	204	79
Isle of Wight	Isle of Wight	1963	189	73
Isles of Scilly	Isles of Scilly	1976	16	6
Kent Downs	Bromley, Kent	1968	878	339
Lincolnshire Wolds	Northeast Lincolnshire	1973	558	215
Malvern Hills	Gloucestershire, Herefordshire, and Worcestershire	1959	105	40
Mendip Hills	North West Somerset, Bath and North East Somerset	1972	198	76
Nidderdale	North Yorkshire	1994	603	233
Norfolk Coast	Norfolk	1968	451	174
North Devon	Devon	1960	171	66
North Pennines	Cumbria, Durham, Northumberland	1988	1,983	766
Northumberland Coast	Northumberland	1958	135	52
North Wessex Downs	Berkshire, Hampshire, Oxfordshire, Wiltshire	1972	1,730	668
Quantock Hills	Somerset	1957	99	38
Shropshire Hills	Shropshire	1959	804	310
Solway Coast	Cumbria	1964	115	44
South Devon	Devon	1960	337	130
South Hampshire Coast	Hampshire	1967	77	30
Suffolk Coast and Heaths	Suffolk	1970	403	156
Surrey Hills	Surrey	1958	419	162
Sussex Downs	Sussex	1966	983	379
Tamar Valley	Devon, Cornwall	1995	195	115
Wye Valley (England)	Gloucestershire, Herefordshire, and Worcestershire	1971	209	126
Wales				
Anglesey	Anglesey	1967	221	85
Clwydian Range	Denbighshire, Flintshire	1985	157	60
Gower	Swansea	1956	189	73
Llyn	Gwynedd	1957	161	62
Scotland				
Assynt-Coigach	Highland	N/A	902	348
Ben Nevis and Glen Coe	Highland, Argyll and Bute, Perth and Kinross	N/A	1,016	392
Cairngorm Mountains	Highland, Aberdeenshire, Moray	N/A	672	259
Cuillin Hills	Highland	N/A	219	85
Deeside and Lochnagar	Aberdeenshire, Angus	N/A	400	154
Dornoch Firth	Highland	N/A	75	29
East Stewartry Coast	Dumfries and Galloway	N/A	45	17
Eildon and Leaderfoot	Scottish Borders	N/A	36	14
Fleet Valley	Dumfries and Galloway	N/A	53	20
Glen Affric	Highland	N/A	193	75
Glen Strathfarrar	Highland	N/A	38	15
Hoy and West Mainland	Orkney Islands	N/A	148	57
Jura	Argyll and Bute	N/A	218	84
Kintail	Highland	N/A	155	60
Knapdale	Argyll and Bute	N/A	198	76
Knoydart	Highland	N/A	395	153
Kyle of Tongue	Highland	N/A	185	71
Kyles of Bute	Argyll and Bute	N/A	44	17
Lochna Keal, Mull	Argyll and Bute	N/A	127	49
Loch Lomond	Argyll and Bute, Stirling, West Dunbartonshire	N/A	274	106
Loch Rannoch and Glen Lyon	Perth and Kinross, Stirling	N/A	484	187
Loch Shiel	Highland	N/A	134	52

(continued)

Areas of Outstanding Natural Beauty and National Scenic Areas in the UK *(continued)*

Name	Region	Established (year)	Area	
			sq km	sq mi
Loch Tummel	Perth and Kinross	N/A	92	36
Lynn of Lorn	Argyll and Bute	N/A	48	19
Morar, Moidart, and Ardnamurchan	Highland	N/A	135	52
Nith estuary	Dumfries and Galloway	N/A	93	36
North Arran	North Ayrshire	N/A	238	92
North-West Sutherland	Highland	N/A	205	79
River Earn	Perth and Kinross	N/A	30	12
River Tay	Perth and Kinross	N/A	56	22
St Kilda	Western Isles	N/A	9	3
Scarra, Lunga, and the Garvellachs	Argyll and Bute	N/A	19	7
Shetland	Shetland Islands	N/A	116	45
Small Isles	Highland	N/A	155	60
South Lewis, Harris, and North Uist	Western Isles	N/A	1,096	423
South Uist Machair	Western Isles	N/A	61	24
The Trossachs	Stirling	N/A	46	18
Trotternish	Highland	N/A	50	19
Upper Tweeddale	Scottish Borders	N/A	105	41
Wester Ross	Highland	N/A	1,453	561
Northern Ireland				
Antrim Coast and Glens	Co. Antrim	1988	706	273
Causeway Coast	Co. Antrim	1989	42	16
Lagan Valley	Co. Down	1965	21	8
Lecale Coast	Co. Down	1967	31	12
Mourne	Co. Down	1986	570	220
North Derry	Co. Londonderry	1966	130	50
Ring of Gullion	Co. Armagh	1991	154	59
Sperrin	Co. Tyrone, Co. Londonderry	1968	1,010	390
Strangford Lough	Co. Down	1972	186	72

National Parks in England and Wales

The Countryside Agency is responsible for designating areas in England and Wales as National Parks, and advises Government on policy towards them. There are seven National Parks in England which, together with The Broads, are managed by a special Authority and cover 7.6% (9,934 sq km/3,836 mi) of England.

Name	Region	Established (year)	Area		Natural features	Activities
			sq km	sq mi		
England						
The Broads[1]	between Norwich and Great Yarmouth, Norfolk	1989	303	117	fens, waterways, marshes, woodlands	walking, sailing, fishing, birdwatching
Dartmoor	Devon	1951	954	368	boggy plateaux, rocky land, river valleys; prehistoric remains	walking, fishing, riding
Exmoor	Somerset and Devon	1954	693	268	moorlands, cliffs; prehistoric remains	walking, riding, cycling, fishing
Lake District	Cumbria	1951	2,292	885	lakes, mountains, moorlands, fells	walking, climbing, sailing
The New Forest[2]	Hampshire	1990	376	117	forest, woodlands, heathlands	walking, riding, cycling
Northumberland	Northumberland	1956	1,049	405	grass moorlands, deep burn valleys, hills, mountains; Roman antiquities	walking, rock-climbing, canoeing, riding
North York Moors	North Yorkshire, Redcar, Cleveland	1952	1,436	554	open heather moorlands; unique wildlife	walking, riding
Peak District	Derbyshire, Staffordshire, South Yorkshire, Cheshire, west Yorkshire, Greater Manchester	1951	1,438	555	dales, hills, peat moorlands	walking, rock-climbing
Yorkshire Dales	North Yorkshire, Cumbria	1954	1,769	683	limestone cliffs, gorges, and pavements; valleys, waterfalls, caves	walking, caving
Wales						
Breacon Beacons	Powys, Carmarthenshire, Rhondda, Cynon, Taff, Merthyr Tydfil, Blaneau, Gwent, Monmouthshire	1957	1,351	522	mountains, valleys	walking, riding
Pembrokeshire Coast	Pembrokeshire	1952	584	225	cliffs, moorlands; includes Skomer Islands	walking, birdwatching, marine life watching

(continued)

National Parks in England and Wales *(continued)*

Name	Region	Established (year)	Area sq km	Area sq mi	Natural features	Activities
Snowdonia	Gwynedd, Conwy	1951	2,142	827	deep valleys, rugged mountains	hill walking, rock-climbing, riding

[1] The Broads are considered to have equivalent status to National Parks due to Statutory designation.
[2] The New Forest does not enjoy Statutory designation, despite planning protection that recognizes its high landscape qualities. Therefore the area does not have equivalent administration or funding to a National Park. 1990 is the date of the establishment of the New Forest Committee.

Heritage Coasts in England

England has many popular coastal resorts but 32% (1,027 km/638 mi) of scenic English coastline is conserved as Heritage Coasts. These special coastlines are managed so that their natural beauty is conserved and, where appropriate, the accessibility for visitors is improved. The first Heritage Coast to be defined was the famous white chalk cliffs of Beachy Head in Sussex.
(– = not applicable.)

Coast	Defined[1] (year)	Length km	Length mi	Location
Dover-Folkestone[2]	1975	7	4	Kent
East Devon	1984	27	17	Devon
Exmoor	1991	45	28	Devon/Somerset
Flamborough Headland	1989	19	12	East Riding of Yorkshire/north Yorkshire
Godrevy-Portreath	1986	9	6	Cornwall
Gribbin Head-Polperro	1986	24	15	Cornwall
Hamstead	1988	11	7	Isle of Wight
Hartland (Cornwall only)	1986	11	7	Cornwall
Hartland (Devon)	1990	37	23	Devon
Isles of Scilly	1974	64	40	Isles of Scilly
Lundy	1990	14	9	Devon
North Devon	1992	32	20	Devon
North Norfolk	1975	64	40	Norfolk
North Northumberland	1992	110	68	Northumberland
North Yorkshire and Cleveland	1981	57	35	North Yorkshire/Redcar and Cleveland
Pentire Point-Widemouth	1986	52	32	Cornwall
Penwith	1986	54	34	Cornwall
Purbeck	1981	50	31	Dorset
Rame Head	1986	8	5	Cornwall
St Agnes	1986	11	7	Cornwall
St Bees Head	1992	6	4	Cumbria
South Devon	1986	75	47	Devon
South Foreland[2]	1975	7	4	Kent
Spurn	1988	18	11	East Riding of Yorkshire
Suffolk	1979	57	35	Suffolk
Sussex	1973	13	8	Sussex
Tennyson	1988	34	21	Isle of Wight
The Lizard	1986	27	17	Cornwall
The Roseland	1986	53	33	Cornwall
Trevose Head	1986	4	2	Cornwall
West Dorset	1984	41	25	Dorset
Total	–	1,041	647	–

[1] Date of completion definition.
[2] Coastal frontage only defined.

National Trails in England

The first National Trail was the 412 km/256 mi Pennine Way opened in 1965. The longest is the 962 km/598 mi South West Coast Path which meanders through Somerset, Devon, Cornwall, and Dorset. The latest is the Thames Path (344 km/214 mi) which was opened in July 1997. It is unique in that it follows the course of a river – the Thames – from its source in Gloucestershire to its end at the Thames Barrier in London. Three new trails are currently being planned: the Cotswold Way, the Hadrian's Wall Path, and the Pennine Bridleway.
(– = not applicable.)

National Trail	Opened (year)	Length km	Length mi	Location
Cleveland Way	1969	176	109	north Yorkshire/Redcar and Cleveland; 44 km/27 mi of the trail is open to both horse riders and cyclists, while 3.4 km/2.1 mi is open to motorized vehicles
North Downs Way	1978	246	153	Surrey/Kent; 122 km/76 mi of the trail is open to both horse riders and cyclists, while 74 km/46 mi is open to motorized vehicles
Offa's Dyke Path	1971	285	177	Gloucestershire/Herefordshire/Shropshire (includes 198 km/123 mi in Wales); 22 km/14 mi of the trail is open to horse riders, 49 km/30 mi to cyclists, and 57 km/35 mi to motorized vehicles
Peddars Way/Norfolk Coast Path	1986	150	93	Norfolk/Suffolk; 70 km/43 mi of the trail is open to horse riders, cyclists, and motorized vehicles
Pennine Way	1965	412	256	Derby/north Yorkshire/Kirklees/Calderdale/Bradford/Rochdale/Oldham/Durham/ Cumbria/Northumberland (includes 16 km/10 mi in Scotland); 83 km/52 mi of the trail is open to both horse riders and cyclists, while 38 km/24 mi is open to motorized vehicles
Ridgeway	1973	137	85	Wiltshire/Oxfordshire/Berkshire/Buckinghamshire/Hertfordshire; 101 km/63 mi of the trail is open to both horse riders and cyclists, while 83 km/52 mi is open to motorized vehicles
South Downs Way	1972	171	106	Hampshire/west and east Sussex; 171 km/106 mi of the trail is open to both horse riders and cyclists, while 25 km/16 mi is open to motorized vehicles
South West Coast Path	1973–78	962	598	Somerset/Devon/Cornwall/Dorset; 35 km/22 mi of the trail is open to cyclists, while 45 km/28 mi is open to motorized vehicles
Thames Path	1997	344	214	Gloucestershire/Wiltshire/Oxfordshire/Berkshire/Buckinghamshire/Surrey/Greater London; 14 km/9 mi of the trail is open to horse riders, 16 km/10 mi to cyclists, and 0.6 km/0.4 mi to motorized vehicles
Wolds Way	1982	130	81	East Riding of Yorkshire/north Yorkshire; 44 km/27 mi of the trail is open to both horse riders and cyclists, while 20 km/12 mi is open to motorized vehicles
TOTAL	–	3,013	1,872	–

■ Land and Protected Areas

Land and Protected Areas: International Environmental Agreements

The Antarctic Treaty

Date of adoption 1 December 1959
Place of adoption Washington, District of Columbia, USA
Date of entry into force 23 June 1961
Number of signatory countries 40

Objectives To ensure that Antarctica is used for peaceful purposes, for international cooperation in scientific research, and does not become the scene or object of international discord.

Summary of selected provisions No military bases, military manoeuvres, or weapon testing in Antarctica; freedom of scientific investigation and cooperation in the exchange of information regarding plans for such investigation and of personnel engaged in such investigation, and of information resulting from such investigation; territorial claims in Antarctica not affected by the Convention; detailed agreed measures for the conservation of Antarctic fauna and flora.

Protocol to the Antartic Treaty on Environment Protectin

Date of adoption 3 October 1991
Place of adoption Madrid, Spain
Date of entry into force Not yet
Number of signatory countries 34

Objectives To reaffirm the status of the Antarctica as a special conservation area, and to enhance the framework for the protection of the Antarctic environment with its dependent and associated ecosystems.

Summary of selected provisions A statement of the environmental principles governing the conduct of States Parties in relation to the Antarctica. The basic principle is to protect the Antarctic environment and dependent and associated ecosystems as well as the intrinsic value of the Antarctica with its aesthetic values, as well as its status as a place of research; prohibition of mineral resource enterprises in the Antarctic Treaty area, save for purposes of scientific research; requirement of environmental impact assessment in the Antarctic Treaty area in respect of activities that are likely to entail significant adverse environmental consequences. The Protocol has the following annexes environment: impact assessment; conservation of Antarctic fauna and flora; waste disposal and waste management; prevention of marine pollution.

Environmental Groups and Initiatives

British Hydropower Association

Association that aims to protect and promote the use of water to generate energy. It is believed that it is in the nation's and the world's interest to extend the use of water power and to save fossil fuels. The association is affiliated with the European Small Hydro-Power Association and the Association of Independent Electricity Producers.

Date established 1996

Contact 60 Bramhall Lane South, Bramhall, Stockport, Cheshire SK7 2DU; phone: (0161) 440 9196; fax: (0161) 440 9273; e-mail: weal@mcmail.com; Web site www.bwea.com

British Trust for Conservation Volunteers

Major practical conservation organization and the largest in the UK. It has numerous affiliations including BCTV Enterprises, the National Trust, Green Alliance, Groundwork, Wildlife Link, and the Environmental Council.

Date established 1959

Contact 36 St Mary's Street, Wallingford, Oxfordshire OX10 0EU; phone: (01491) 839766; fax: (01491) 839646; e-mail: information@btcv.org.uk; Web site www.btcv.org.uk

Centre for Alternative Technology

Organization set up to invesigate, use, demonstrate, and promote environmentally and socially appropriate technologies for energy generation and conservation, food production, and building design.

Date established 1974

Contact Machynlleth, Powys SY20 9AZ; phone: (01654) 702400; fax: (01654) 702782; e-mail: info@cat.org.uk; Web site www.cat.org.uk

Conservation International

Organization established in order to conserve the Earth's living natural heritage and global biodiversity, and to demonstrate, through science, economics, policy, and community involvement, that human societies can live in harmony with nature. The organization has members in 22 countries.

Date established 1987

Contact 2501 M Street NW, Suite 200, Washington, DC 20037; phone: +1 (202) 429 5660; fax: +1 (202) 887 0192; e-mail: newmember@conservation.org; Web site www.conservation.org

Countryside Agency

Organization working to conserve the natural beauty of the English countryside. An advisory and promotional body, rather than an executive one, the Agency (formerly known as the Countryside Commission) owns no land and manages no facilities but achieves its objectives through collaboration with other organizations. It has seven regional offices.

Date established 1968

Contact John Dower House, Crescent Place, Cheltenham, Gloucestershire GL50 3RA; phone: (01242) 521381; fax: (01242) 584270; e-mail: info@countryside.gov.uk; Web site www.countryside.gov.uk

The Earth Council

Organization that aims to support and empower people in building a more secure, equitable, and sustainable future, to promote awareness and support, encourage public participation, and build bridges of understanding between citizens and government. Funding comes through the Earth Council Foundation's sponsoring institutions, foundations, corporations, and individuals.

Date established 1992

Contact Deputy Executive Director, Apartado 2323-1002, San José, Costa Rica; phone: +506 256 1611; fax: +506 255 2197; e-mail: eci@terra.ecouncil.ac.cr; Web site www.ecouncil.ac.cr

Earthwatch

Charity organization that aims to build a sustainable world through active partnership between scientists and citizens, by gathering data and communicating information to empower people and governments to act wisely as global citizens. It is funded through membership dues and donor organizations and individuals. The organization has members in over 118 countries.

Date established 1971

Contact Earthwatch Europe, Belsyre Court, 57 Woodstock Road, Oxford, OX2 6HJ, UK; phone: (44 1865) 311600; fax: (44 1865) 311383; e-mail: info@uk.earthwatch.org; Web site www.earthwatch.org

Friends of the Earth

Charity organization that aims to protect the planet from environmental degradation, to preserve biological, cultural, and ethnic diversity, and to empower citizens to have an influential voice in decisions affecting the quality of their environment and their lives. It is funded through membership dues, donations, and subsidies.

Date established 1969

Contact: Headquarters Friends of the Earth International, PO Box 19199, NL-1000 GD, Amsterdam; phone: (31 20) 622-1369; fax: (31 20) 639-2181; e-mail: foeint@antenna.nl; Web site www.foe.co.uk

Contact in UK Friends of the Earth, 26–28 Underwood Street, London, N1 7JQ; phone: (020) 7490 1555; fax: (020) 7490 0881; e-mail: info@foe.co.uk

Green Alliance

Organization that works on environmental policy and politics. Its main activities fall into three areas; greening government, greening business and finance, and greening science. It is affiliated with the European Environment Bureau, Wildlife Link, and the National Council for Voluntary Organizations.

Date established 1978

Contact 40 Buckingham Palace Road, London SW1W 0RE, phone: (020) 7233 7433; fax: (020) 7233 9033; e-mail: ga@green-alliance.demon.co.uk; Web site www.green-alliance.demon.co.uk

Greenpeace International

Independent organization that aims to protect biodiversity in all its forms, to prevent pollution and abuse of the Earth's ocean, land, air, and fresh water, to end all nuclear threats, and to promote peace, global disarmament, and non-violence. It is funded through donations, voluntary contributions from the public, and sales of merchandise. Greenpeace does not accept funds from business interests or governments. The organization has offices in 30 countries.

Date established 1971

Contact: Headquarters Keizersgracht 176, 1016 DW Amsterdam, The Netherlands; phone: +31 (20) 523 6222; fax: +31 (20) 523 6200; e-mail: greenpeace.international@greenz.dat.de

Address in UK Canonbury Villas, London N1 2PN; phone: (020) 7865 8100; Freephone: 0800 269065; fax: (020) 7865 8200; e-mail: info@uk.greenpeace.org; Web site www.greenpeace.org

International Energy Agency (IEA)

Autonomous agency linked with the OECD that aims to foster cooperation among participating countries to increase energy security through diversification of energy supply, more efficient and cleaner use of energy, energy conservation, and the development of alternative energy sources. The governments of the 23 OECD member states form the membership of the International Energy Agency.

Date established 1974

Contact: Headquarters 9 rue de la Fédération, 75739 Paris Cedex 15, France; phone: +33 (1) 4057 6551; fax: +33 (1) 4057 6559; Web site www.iea.org

International Wildlife Coalition

Organization that aims to preserve wildlife all over the world. It is also the headquarters of the Whale Adoption Project.

Date established 1983

Contact 141A High Street, Edenbridge, Kent TN8 5AX; phone: (01732) 866955; fax: (01792) 866955; e-mail: iwcuk@iwcmail.demon.co.uk; Web site www.iwc.org

Marine Conservation Society

Organization that aims to protect the marine environment for both wildlife and future generations by promoting its sustainable and environmentally sensitive management.

Date established 1983

Contact 9 Gloucester Road, Ross on Wye, Hereford HR9 5BU; phone: (01989) 566017; fax: (01989) 567815; e-mail: info@mcsuk.org; Web site www.mcsuk.org

National Association for Environmental Education

Association set up to promote and encourage environmental education through all levels of the education system.

Date established 1960

Contact Wolverhampton University, Walsall Campus, Gorway Road, Walsall WS1 3BD; phone: (01922) 631200; fax: (01922) 631200

New Economics Foundation

Organization that aims to build a just and sustainable economy, with ideas and action that put people and the environment first. The Foundation has close links with Friends of the Earth, GreenNet, and the Centre for Employment Initiatives.

Date established 1986

Contact Cinnamon House, 6–8 Cole Street, London SE1 4YH; phone: (020) 7407 7447; fax: (020) 7407 6473; e-mail: info@neweconomics.org; Web site www.neweconomics.org

Rainforest Action Network (RAN)

Non-profit volunteer and member-based organization that aims to protect tropical rainforests and support the rights of indigenous peoples. It is financed by membership dues, foundation grants and donations, and special events.

Date established 1985

Contact 221 Pine Street, Suite 500, San Francisco, CA 94104, USA; phone: +1 (415) 398 4404; fax: +1 (415) 398 2732; e-mail: rainforest@ran.org; Web site www.ran.org/ran

Royal Society for the Prevention of Cruelty to Animals (RSPCA)

Voluntary organization that aims to protect animals from cruelty. The organization's inspectors investigate cruelty complaints, and also undertake animal rescues, collections, and establishment visits. It also runs a number of hospitals and clinics, and campaigns for new laws to protect animal welfare.

Date established 1824

Address RSPCA, Causeway, Horsham, West Sussex RH12 1HG; phone: (0870) 444 3127; Web site: www.rspca.org.uk

Royal Society for the Protection of Birds (RSPB)

Organization acting for the protection of wild birds and their habitats. This includes the buying of land to create new nature reserves and protecting existing bird sites from any type of environmental encroachment.

Date established 1889

Contact The Lodge, Sandy, Bedfordshire SG19 2DL; phone: (01767) 680551; fax: (01767) 692365; e-mail: bird@rspb.demon.co.uk; Web site www.rspb.org.uk

Waste Management Information Bureau

The UK's national referral centre for advice and information on waste management.

Date established 1973

Contact AEA Technology Environment, F6 Culham, Abingdon, Oxfordshire OX14 3ED; phone: (01235) 463162; fax: (01235) 463004; e-mail: wmib@aeat.co.uk

Waste Watch

Organization that aims to promote recycling and waste reduction, with particular reference to the interests of the voluntary sector.

Date established 1987

Contact Europa House, Ground Floor, 13–17 Ironmonger Road, London EC1V 3QG; phone: (020) 7253 6266; Wasteline: (0870) 243 0136; fax: (020) 7253 5962; e-mail: info@wastewatch.org.uk; Web site www.wastewatch.org.uk

The Wildfowl and Wetlands Trust

Organization that aims to promote the conservation of wildfowl and their wetland habitats through research, conservation, and education programmes. The Trust's Mission Statement is to save wetlands for wildlife and people.

Date established 1946

Contact Slimbridge, Gloucestershire GL2 7BT; phone: (01453) 890333 ext 279; fax: (01453) 890827; e-mail: enquiries@wwt.org.uk; Web site www.wwt.org.uk

World Society for the Protection of Animals (WSPA)

Organization that aims to end the exploitation of animals through practical projects, educational campaigns, and representations at government level. WSPA policy states that it aims to 'encourage respect for animals, and responsible stewardship and laws and enforcement structures to provide legal protection for animals'. It is a charity that relies on member societies, individual membership dues, donations, and bequests. It accepts no financial aid from governments. It has a network of 350 member societies in more than 70 countries.

Date established 1981 (previously active in another name for over 40 years)

Contact: Eastern Hemisphere Headquarters 2 Langley Lane, London, SW8 1TJ, UK; phone: (020) 7793 0540; fax: (020) 7793 0208; e-mail: wspa@wspa.org.uk

Contact: Western Hemisphere Headquarters PO Box 190, 29 Perkins Street, Boston, MA 02130; phone: +1 (617) 522 7000; fax: +1 (617) 522 7077; Web site www.wspa.org.uk

World Wide Fund for Nature (WWF)

International organization that aims to protect the biological resources upon which human well-being depends and to preserve endangered and threatened species of wildlife and plants as well as habitats and natural areas of the world. It is funded through membership dues, legacies, bequests, corporate subscriptions, governments and aid agencies, foundation grants, and other earned income.

Date established 1961

Contact: Headquarters WWF International (World Wide Fund for Nature), Avenue du Mont-Blanc, CH-1196 Gland, Switzerland; phone: +41 (22) 364 9111; fax: +41 (22) 364 7850

Address in UK WWF-UK, Panda House, Weyside Park, Godalming, Surrey GU7 1XR; phone: (01483) 426444; fax: (01483) 426409; Web site www.wwf-uk.org

Web Sites

About the National Trust

http://www.nationaltrust.org.uk/aboutnt.htm

Information about the charity entrusted with the care of large parts of the British countryside and many historic buildings.

Alternative Technology

http://www.environment.gov.au/education/aeen/pd/tsw/mod23/mod23.htm

Part of a teachers' guide 'Teaching for a Sustainable World: International Edition', this site also contains useful information for students.

Bathing Water Quality

http://www.environment-agency.gov.uk/s-enviro/viewpoints/3compliance/5bathing/3-5.html

Regularly updated guide to the state of Britain's beaches provided by the Environment Agency.

Biodiversity: Introduction

http://kaos.erin.gov.au/life/general_info/op1.html#foreword

Introduction to a wider site on Australian biodiversity, which explains the global importance of maximum species' diversity. Also includes information on the use of plants for medicinal purposes.

Biodiversity: Measuring the Variety of Nature

http://www.nhm.ac.uk/science/projects/worldmap/

Exhibition on biodiversity and conservation from the Natural History Museum in London.

Biomass

http://www.nrel.gov/research/industrial_tech/biomass.html

Information on biomass from the US Department of Energy, with a clear explanation of the chemical composition of biomass and development of technologies to transform it into usable fuel sources.

British Trust for Conservation Volunteers (BTCV)

http://www.btcv.org/

The BTCV is the largest organization in the UK promoting practical conservation work by volunteers. The site gives information on volunteering, holidays, training, and employment, and on the organization's enterprises.

British Wind Energy Association

http://www.bwea.com/

Promoting the use of wind power as a clean, sustainable source of energy, this site includes a list of wind farms throughout the UK, as well as fact sheets on related issues.

Centre for Alternative Technology

http://www.cat.org.uk/

Site of the Centre For Alternative Technology in Wales, this includes a virtual tour of the site, pictures, and maps. It also includes a quiz, a question forum, and an extensive list of educational resources.

Coasts in Crisis

http://pubs.usgs.gov/circular/c1075/

Full text of a US Geological Survey publication, describing the various types of coastline, methods of shoring them up, and the human and meteorological forces attacking coasts.

Conservation International

http://www.conservation.org/

Nonprofit-making organization that uses science, economics, policy, and community involvement to promote biodiversity conservation worldwide.

Countryside Commission

http://www.countryside.gov.uk/

Guide to the work of the Commission and to the attractions of the British countryside, with information on all of the UK's national parks and officially-designated areas of outstanding beauty.

Earth Council

http://www.ecouncil.ac.cr/

Details the aims and activities of the Earth Council, a non-governmental organization promoting the implementation of the Earth Summit agreements.

Earthwatch Institute

http://www.earthwatch.org/

Earthwatch Institute promotes conservation through scientific field research, creating partnerships between scientists, educators, and the public. The site includes details of how to join and news of current expeditions and research.

Endangered Species

http://endangeredspecie.com/

Photos and information about endangered species and extinction rates. There is also a separate children's site.

English Heritage

http://www.english-heritage.org.uk/

Site of the public body charged with protecting England's historic environment.

English Nature – Facts and Figures

http://www.english-nature.org.uk/facts.htm

Site of the government agency charged with conserving wildlife and natural features in England. Includes information on Sites of Special Scientific Interest (SSSIs), national and marine nature reserves, and the protection of wetlands.

Environmental Education Network

http://envirolink.org/enviroed/

Collaborative effort to place environmental information on the Internet. The site is packed with multimedia items, and divided into sections for teachers and students.

Friends of the Earth Home Page

http://www.foe.co.uk/

Information on FoE campaigns on climate, industry, transport, and sustainable development, and tips for action. The site maintains an archive of FoE press releases on some of the most controversial environmental issues around the world.

Global Climate Change Information Programme (GCCIP)

http://www.doc.mmu.ac.uk/aric/arichome.html

The GCCIP provides an information link between scientists, politicians, economists, and the general public, on the subjects of climate change and air quality.

Global Warming

http://pooh.chem.wm.edu/chemWWW/courses/chem105/projects/group1/page1.html

An easy-to-follow explanation of global warming – its causes, the environmental effects, and the social and economic consequences.

Greenpeace

http://www.greenpeace.org/

Home page of Greenpeace, the world's largest environmental and ecological campaign group. The site includes detailed information on current campaigns and additional resources on issues such as the climate, nuclear power, oceans, genetic engineering, and forestry.

Met. Office Home Page

http://www.meto.govt.uk/

Authoritative account of global warming issues such as the ozone problem, El Niño, cyclones, and methods of forecasting. Scientific explanations alternate with images and film clips in an educational site which especially targets teachers and students.

National Wind Technology Centre

http://www.nrel.gov/wind/

US Department of Energy site, with information on the importance of tapping wind power, how it is done, and initiatives around the world that are generating energy from wind power.

Nature Explorer

http://www.naturegrid.org.uk/explorer/index.html

Wealth of information about water creatures. The presentation is fun and interactive, including a 'Virtual pond dip'.

Paul Ehrlich and the Population Bomb

http://www.pbs.org/kqed/population_bomb/

This site details US biologist Paul Ehrlich's crusade to warn and inform people that overconsumption of resources, environmental destruction, and unchecked population growth will destroy the Earth's ability to sustain life.

Rachel Carson Homestead

http://www.rachelcarson.org/

Information on the life and legacy of the pioneering ecologist, including a biography, details of Carson's publications, and details of the work of conservation organizations continuing her work.

Recycle City

http://www.epa.gov/recyclecity/

Site of the US Environmental Protection Agency designed to encourage and help people live more ecologically. The site includes games and activities to encourage children to think about waste disposal issues.

The Regional and Environmental Center for Central and Eastern Europe (REC)

www.rec.org/Default.shtml

Information on the issues and initiatives of the REC, a non-profit organization dedicated to helping solve environmental problems in central and eastern Europe.

Royal Society for the Protection of Birds

http://www.rspb.co.uk/

Europe's largest wildlife conservation charity provides news and local contact details, as well as a vast amount of information on birds and bird-watching in the UK, with descriptions and photographs of all common UK birds.

6 Billion Human Beings

http://www.popexpo.net/home.htm

From the Musée de l'Homme in Paris, France, an interactive site about population growth. It explains the causes for the rapid growth over the last 200 years, and why it might stabilize over the next century. You can find out the world's population in the year you were born, and see a ticking counter of the current global population.

State of the Climate: a Time for Action

http://www.panda.org/climate_event/intro.htm

Animated multimedia site from the Worldwide Fund for Nature (WWF) on climate change and its effects on the natural world, as well as details of WWF's campaigns on this issue.

State of the Environment

http://www.environment-agency.gov.uk/state_of_enviro/index3+.html

UK Environment Agency site, with access to data collected and studied by the Agency on such topics as bathing water quality, river habitats, and river gauging stations, as well as more general information on the state of the environment.

Sustainability Web Ring

http://sdgateway.net/webring/default.htm

Useful navigation tool for sites worldwide that deal with the principles, policies, and best practices for sustainable development.

Sustainable Development

http://iisd1.iisd.ca/

Looks at the issue from many points of view, with sections on trade and key topics such as forests and oceans. The site also reports on global initiatives to encourage sustainability.

The Greenhouse Effect: How the Earth Stays Warm

http://www.enviroweb.org/edf/ishappening/greeneffect/index.html

Explanation of the greenhouse effect, the process by which atmospheric gases trap heat, and how this is made harmful by pollutants put into the atmosphere.

What's it like where you live?

http://www.mobot.org/MBGnet/index2.htm

Aimed at younger children, this imaginative site has sections on different ecosystems from around the world, and includes related activities.

Worldwide Fund for Nature

http://www.panda.org/

Online base of the international wildlife charity, with information on current campaigns and on the natural world, including quizzes, interactive maps, and news.

ECONOMY AND BUSINESS

The Year in Review

1 July 1999 The euro reaches a new low of 1.0201 against the dollar.

5 July 1999 Centrica plc, the UK's largest natural-gas company, announces plans to acquire the Automobile Association (AA) for £1.1 billion.

12 July 1999 The annual *Human Development Index*, published by the United Nations, reports on the widening gap between the world's very rich and very poor. 20% of the world's population has 74 times the income of the poorest 20%.

19 July 1999 US computer company Hewlett-Packard announces that Carleton Fiorina will become its president and chief executive, making her the first woman to run one of the 20 largest companies in the USA.

22 July 1999 After a struggle for leadership, Mike Moore, former prime minister of New Zealand, is appointed director general of the World Trade Organization (WTO). His term is effective from 1 September 1999, and after three years will be turned over to the deputy prime minister of Thailand, Supachai Panitchpakdi.

26 July 1999 The WTO permits Canada and the USA to penalize European Union countries for their ban on hormone-treated beef by imposing trade sanctions on European exports.

30 July 1999 UK regional newspaper publisher Trinity plc announces plans to acquire the Mirror Group plc for £1.24 billion, which would create the UK's largest newspaper publisher.

20 August 1999 Three Japanese banks – Dai-Ichi Kangyo Bank Ltd, Fuji Bank Ltd, and Industrial Bank of Japan Ltd – announce plans to merge, which would form the world's largest financial institution.

20 August 1999 Camelot, the UK lottery-running company, forms an alliance with the Post Office to pursue a renewal of its contract.

30 August 1999 US software company Microsoft is forced to shut down its free e-mail service, Hotmail, when a hacker's Web page allows users to access the messages of any of its 40 million users.

7 September 1999 In the biggest media industry deal to date, US media company Viacom – owner of Paramount studios, the MTV music television channel, and the Blockbuster video rental chain – buys the CBS Corporation for $34 billion/£21 billion.

20 September 1999 The UK engineering company Rolls Royce announces plans to purchase Vickers plc for £576 million in cash. The merger is intended to create a world leader in the production of marine engine systems.

27 September 1999 James Wolfensohn is elected president of the World Bank for his second five-year term.

28–30 September 1999 The final details of the funding of a new debt-relief initiative for Highly Indebted Poor Countries (HIPCs) are finalized at the annual meeting of the International Monetary Fund (IMF) and the World Bank in Washington, DC. The initative was agreed at the G-7 meeting in Cologne, Germany, in June, after pressure from Jubilee 2000, the umbrella charity group campaigning for debt relief. Up to three-quarters of the eligible 38 countries are expected to benefit by the end of 2000.

13 October 1999 The Nobel Prize for Economics is awarded to Canadian-born Robert A Mundell for his work showing the effect of exchange rates on monetary and fiscal policy, and his contribution to the development of the euro, the common European currency.

5 October 1999 UN Secretary General Kofi Annan reveals to the UN's finance committee that the USA owes $1.739 billion in membership arrears, out of a total debt to the UN of $2.15 billion.

18 October 1999 Nissan, Japan's second largest car manufacturer, announces cutbacks of 21,000 jobs worldwide and the closure of five plants in Japan, in an effort to stem years of losses.

22 October 1999 UK agricultural minister Nick Brown urges British shoppers to boycott French food imports in response to the continued French ban on British beef. However, he does not ban French animal products, despite a EU report that found animal, and possibly human, waste in the feed that French farmers were giving to their livestock.

15 November 1999 The Chinese government agrees to a package of trade liberalization measures presented by the US government, a milestone in China's long transition into a free-market economy. Western businesses begin gearing up to export to the potential new consumer market.

22 November 1999 Thousands of BT customer service workers at call centres in the UK stage a national strike to protest against what they claim are poor working conditions and unrealistic targets.

26 November 1999 United News and Media and Carlton Communications announce that they are merging to form a company worth £8 billion.

30 November 1999 Activists protest against free trade in Seattle, Washington, disrupting the annual World Trade Organization meeting, in the biggest demonstration in the USA since the Vietnam War. Riot police use red pepper gas to disperse demonstrators, and a state of emergency is declared.

January 2000 Bill Gates, the world's richest man, resigns his position as chief executive of the computer company Microsoft to become the company's chief software architect.

9 January 2000 English composer Andrew Lloyd Webber announces his company's purchase of Stoll Moss theatres, London's biggest theatre empire – including 10 theatres such as the London Palladium, Garrick, and Theatre Royal Drury Lane – for £87.5 million.

10 January 2000 US media company Time Warner announces that it is merging with America Online, the world's largest Internet service provider, in a $350 billion/£220 billion deal, the largest ever merger, creating the world's fourth largest corporation.

18 January 2000 UK bank Schroders announces the sale of its investment banking division to US financial company Salomon Smith Barney (owned by Citigroup, the world's largest financial institution) for £1.3 billion/$2.8 billion.

24 January 2000 UK music company EMI and the record label division of US media company Time Warner merge in a £12 billion deal, which makes America Online, which acquired Time Warner earlier in the month, one of the world's largest music producers.

27 January 2000 The US biotech company Monsanto, at the centre of a backlash against genetically modified food, announces that it is merging with the US-Swiss pharmaceutical company Pharmacia and Upjohn to form a company worth $50 billion. The new company will be called Pharmacia.

February 2000 It is reported that Texas governor George W Bush has raised and spent more on his campaign for US president than anyone in the history of US politics. The *Washington Post* newspaper reports that he is spending $400,000 daily on his campaign and has nearly spent all of the $71 million/ £44 million he raised.

6 February 2000 Millennium Dome chief executive Jennie Page is sacked as the Dome struggles with a poor image and financial losses. Her replacement is Frenchman Pierre-Yves Gerbeau, previously an executive at Disneyland in Paris.

10 February 2000 UK telecommunications company Vodafone merges with its German rival Mannesmann in a £112 billion deal, in the largest corporate merger in Europe to date.

March 2000 The Computer Security Institute (CSI) publishes a survey that estimates that computer fraud and theft were responsible for $10 billion/£6.4 billion in losses for 1999.

10 March 2000 In the wake of heavy financial losses, Bob Ayling, the head of British Airways, resigns.

16 March 2000 German car manufacturer BMW announces plans to sell off Rover, a subsidiary, resulting in job losses at the Longbridge plant in Birmingham, England.

17 March 2000 Ecuador and the USA are awarded sanctions against the European Union by the World Trade Organization in retaliation for the EU's banana import policy, which favoured the mainly smaller former colonial producers in the Caribbean. The decision is condemned by Caribbean growers.

1 April 2000 US court-appointed mediator Richard Posner announces that efforts have failed to settle out of court the US government's monopoly case against software company Microsoft.

3 April 2000 US district judge Thomas Penfield Jackson rules against Microsoft in the anti-trust case brought by US state governments. Shares in the company fall by 15%.

5 April 2000 Hours before the tax deadline for the end of the financial year, the London stock exchange is paralysed by its worst computer failure to date. Trading hours are extended to 8 p.m. to get through the backlog of trades.

14 April 2000 Wall Street experiences a record one-day fall after a week of selling technology stocks knocked down share prices. The price slump wipes out $2 trillion/ £1,250 billion of the US economy.

15 April 2000 Finance ministers and heads of central banks from the Group of Seven (G-7) industrialized countries meet in Washington, DC, in the wake of Wall Street's record one-day fall the previous day. Economists fear that the fall in share prices could affect the world economy.

16 April 2000 Anti-globalization protesters demonstrate against the World Bank and International Monetary Fund (IMF) in Washington, DC. The protesters form a human barricade around the IMF headquarters, prompting a heavy show of force by the police, but failing to stop the IMF meetings.

28 April 2000 German car manufacturer BMW threatens to close down its Longbridge Rover plant in Birmingham, England, after Alchemy, the company planning to purchase the plant, pulls out of the deal hours before it was due to be signed.

May 2000 Most of Rover, the loss-making subsidiary of BMW, is sold to the Phoenix consortium for £10, including a £500 million loan. The consortium aims to minimize job losses at the car plant.

May 2000 A survey commissioned by accountants Price Waterhouse Coopers predicts that many so-called 'dot.coms' (new Internet companies) will run out of cash within 15 months of starting up due to high operating costs.

May 2000 Boo.com, an Internet fashion retailer, announces that it has been forced to liquidate remaining assets after being unable to raise necessary investment money.

May 2000 A computer virus called the Love Bug – since it appears in victims' mailboxes with the subject heading 'I love you' – hits millions of computers worldwide. A suspect is arrested in the Philippines, but is later released for lack of evidence.

May 2000 Liberty, the famous London department store family-run for 125 years, is bought by property company Marylebone Warwick Balfour, which says it will concentrate on refurbishing the flagship store and developing the Liberty brand.

May 2000 The UK mobile phone company Orange is to be bought out by France Telecom from Vodaphone-AirTouch for £25.1 billion, to create the second-largest mobile phone operator in Europe.

June 2000 Unison, the largest trade union in the UK, calls for a new tax rate of 50% in the pound for earnings in excess of £100,000 as a measure to alleviate poverty and improve public services; this follows a United Nations report that ranks the UK 20th out of 23 countries in the developed world according to relative poverty.

7 June 2000 A US court rules that the software company Microsoft must be split into two to break its monopoly over computer operating systems.

11 June 2000 A report published by the London Chamber of Commerce states that up to 19 million working days are lost because of bullying in the workplace, costing UK industry £2 billion per year.

14 June 2000 Zimbabwean president Robert Mugabe declares his intention to seize the assets of UK and other foreign mining companies in the country, following the widespread confiscation of white-owned farms.

14 June 2000 The UK supermarket chain Iceland reveals that it will be selling solely organic frozen vegetables, under its own label and at the same price as conventional produce. The organic food market is now growing at a rate of 40% per year, and a recent survey indicates that three out of four customers would prefer to buy organic products if they were more affordable.

15 June 2000 Dutch department store chain C&A announces plans to close all 109 of its high street branches in the UK and Ireland, threatening 4,800 jobs.

19 June 2000 The USA formally eases economic sanctions against North Korea for the first time in nearly 50 years, in response to the successful summit meeting between the leaders of North and South Korea.

19 June 2000 The Swedish furniture retailer Ikea reveals plans to open another 20 stores in the UK over the next decade, creating up to 12,000 jobs, while cutting its prices by up to 25%.

20 June 2000 The UK Post Office announces that nearly 4,000 jobs will be scrapped after experiencing its first financial loss in 24 years – an after-tax loss of £264 million. The chairman, Neville Bain, defends the decision to make bonus payments in 1999 to the three executive directors.

20 June 2000 Seagram, Vivendi, and Canal Plus announce their $34 billion merger, creating a new media giant called Vivendi Universal.

21–22 June 2000 Thousands of Cambodian factory workers take to the streets of Phnom Penh to protest against working conditions. The factories affected by the demonstrations produce clothes for western labels such as Gap and Osh Kosh.

27 June 2000 UK home office minister Charles Clarke and leaders in industry and banking meet to combat credit card fraud, which has increased by £54 million to £184 million in the previous 12 months.

29 June 2000 Barclays Bank says it is standing by its decision to charge for the use of its automatic teller machines (ATMs), despite the public outcry against charges which has forced most other banks to agree to scrapping them.

UK Chancellor Gordon Brown on Budget Day, March 2000. The Budget included £2 billion for the NHS, schools, and unemployment blackspots, and cut income tax for millions of low-income families. *Syndication International*

Economic Organizations of the World

African Development Bank (ADB)

Bank founded in 1964 by the Organization of African Unity to promote and finance economic development across the African continent. Its regional members are: Algeria, Angola, Benin, Botswana, Burkina Faso, Burundi, Cameroon, Cape Verde, Central African Republic, Chad, Comoros, Congo, Côte d'Ivoire, Democratic Republic of Congo, Djibouti, Egypt, Equatorial Guinea, Eritrea, Ethiopia, Gabon, Gambia, Ghana, Guinea, Guinea-Bissau, Kenya, Lesotho, Liberia, Libya, Madagascar, Malawi, Mali, Mauritania, Mauritius, Morocco, Mozambique, Namibia, Niger, Nigeria, Rwanda, São Tomé and Príncipe, Senegal, Seychelles, Sierra Leone, Somalia, South Africa, Sudan, Swaziland, Tanzania, Togo, Tunisia, Uganda, Zambia, Zimbabwe. Non-regional members are: Argentina, Austria, Belgium, Brazil, Canada, China, Denmark, Finland, France, Germany, India, Italy, Japan, Korea, Kuwait, Netherlands, Norway, Portugal, Saudi Arabia, Spain, Sweden, Switzerland, UK, USA. Address: Rue Joseph Anoma 01 BP 1387, Abidjan 01, Côte d'Ivoire; phone: +225 2020 4444; fax: +225 2021 7753; e-mail: comuadb@afdb.org; Web site: www.afdb.org

Arab Monetary Fund (AMF)

Money reserve established in 1976 by 20 Arab states to provide a mechanism for promoting greater stability in exchange rates and to coordinate Arab economic and monetary policies. It operates mainly by regulating petrodollars within the Arab community to make member countries less dependent on the West for the handling of their surplus money. Its members are: Algeria, Bahrain, Djibouti, Egypt, Iraq, Jordan, Kuwait, Lebanon, Libya, Mauritania, Morocco, Oman, Palestine, Qatar, Saudi Arabia, Somalia, Sudan, Syria, Tunisia, United Arab Emirates, Yemen, and the Palestine Liberation Organization. Address: PO Box 2818, Abu Dhabi, United Arab Emirates; phone: +971 (2) 215000; fax: +971 (2) 326454; Web site: www.imf.org/external/np/sec/decdo/amf.htm

Asian Development Bank (ADB)

Bank founded in 1966 to stimulate growth in Asia and the Far East by administering direct loans and technical assistance. Its regional members are: Afghanistan, Australia, Bangladesh, Bhutan, Cambodia, China, Cook Islands, Fiji Islands, Hong Kong (China), India, Indonesia, Japan, Kazakhstan, Kiribati, Krygyzstan, Laos, Malaysia, Maldives, Marshall Islands, Micronesia, Mongolia, Myanmar, Nauru, Nepal, New Zealand, Pakistan, Papua New Guinea, Philippines, Samoa, Singapore, Solomon Islands, South Korea, Sri Lanka, Tajikistan, Taipei (China), Thailand, Tonga, Tuvalu, Uzbekistan, Vanuatu, Vietnam. Its nonregional members are: Austria, Belgium, Canada, Denmark, Finland, France, Germany, Italy, Netherlands, Norway, Spain, Sweden, Switzerland, Turkey, UK, USA. Address: PO Box 789, 0980 Manila, Philippines; phone: +63 (2) 632 4444; fax: +63 (2) 636 2444; e-mail: business@adb.org; Web site: www.adb.org/mainpage.asp

Asia-Pacific Economic Cooperation (APEC)

Trade group of Pacific Asian countries, formed in 1989 to promote multilateral trade and economic cooperation between member states. Its members are Australia, Brunei, Canada, Chile, China, Hong Kong, Indonesia, Japan, Malaysia, Mexico, New Zealand, Papua New Guinea, Peru, the Philippines, Singapore, South Korea, Thailand, Taiwan, and the USA. Address: APEC Secretariat, 438 Alexandra Road, 14–00

Alexandra Point, Singapore 119958; phone: +65 276 1880; fax: +65 276 1775; e-mail: info@mail.apecsec.org.sg; Web site: www.apecsec.org.sg

Asociación Latino-Americana de Integración (ALADI)/Latin American Integration Association (LAIA)

Organization established to create a common market in Latin America. To promote trade, it applies tariff reductions preferentially on the basis of the different stages of economic development that individual member countries have reached. Formed in 1980 to replace the Latin American Free Trade Association, it has 11 members: Argentina, Bolivia, Brazil, Chile, Colombia, Ecuador, Mexico, Paraguay, Peru, Uruguay, and Venezuela. Address: Cebollati 1461, CP 11200, Montevideo, Uruguay; phone: +598 (2) 400 1121; fax: +598 (2) 409 0649; e-mail: sgaladi@aladi.org; Web site: www.aladi.org

Bank for International Settlements (BIS)

Organization established in 1930 whose function is to promote cooperation between central banks and to facilitate international financial settlements; it is also a centre for economic and monetary research. Central banks of the main trading states are members, each providing a director to the board, which meets at least ten times a year. The Bank was largely superseded by the International Monetary Fund. Its liaising role among central banks is its primary function today. Address: Centralbahnplatz 2, CH-4002 Basel, Switzerland; phone: +41 (61) 280 8080; fax: +41 (61) 280 9100; e-mail: emailmaster@bis.org; Web site: www.bis.org

Colombo Plan

Plan for cooperative economic and social development in Asia and the Pacific, established in 1950. Its member countries are Afghanistan, Australia, Bangladesh, Bhutan, Cambodia, Fiji Islands, India, Indonesia, Iran, Japan, South Korea, Laos, Malaysia, the Maldives, Myanmar, Nepal, New Zealand, Pakistan, Papua New Guinea, the Philippines, Singapore, Sri Lanka, Thailand, and the USA. Address: 12 Melbourne Avenue, PO Box 596, Colombo 4, Sri Lanka; phone: +94 (1) 581813; fax: +94 (1) 581754; e-mail: cplan@sri.lanka.net; Web site: www.tcol.co.uk/comorg/colplan.htm

Common Market for Eastern and Southern African Countries (COMESA)

Organization established in 1981 as the Preferential Trade Area of Eastern and Southern African States (PTA) with the objective of increasing economic and commercial cooperation between member states, harmonizing tariffs, and reducing trade barriers. The PTA developed into a common market in 1993. Its members are: Angola, Burundi, Comoros, Democratic Republic of Congo, Eritrea, Ethiopia, Kenya, Lesotho, Madagascar, Malawi, Mauritius, Mozambique, Namibia, Rwanda, Sudan, Swaziland, Tanzania, Uganda, Zambia, and Zimbabwe. Address: COMESA Centre, Ben Bella Road, PO Box 30051, Lusaka, Zambia; phone: +260 (1) 229725; fax: +260 (1) 225107; e-mail: comesa@comesa.int; Web site: www.comesa.int

Communauté Economique des Etats de l'Afrique Centrale (CEEAC)/Economic Community of Central African States

Organization formed in 1983 to foster economic cooperation between member states, which are Burundi, Cameroon, the Central African Republic, Chad, the Republic of the Congo, Equatorial Guinea, Gabon, Rwanda, São Tomé and Príncipe, and the Democratic Republic of Congo (formerly Zaire). Angola has observer status. Address: ECCAS-Kasasa Cinyanta Mutati, CEEAC, BP 2112, Libreville, Gabon; phone: +241 733547.

Communauté Economique des Etats de l'Afrique de l'Ouest/Economic Community of West African States (ECOWAS)

Organization promoting economic cooperation and development, established in 1975 by the Treaty of Lagos. Its members are Benin, Burkina Faso, Cape Verde, Côte d'Ivoire, the Gambia, Ghana, Guinea, Guinea-Bissau, Liberia, Mali, Mauritania, Niger, Nigeria, Senegal, Sierra Leone, and Togo. Address: Executive Secretariat, 6 King George V Road, Lagos, Nigeria; phone: +234 (1) 636841; fax: +234 (1) 636822.

Economic Cooperation Organization (ECO)

Islamic regional grouping formed in 1985 by Iran, Pakistan, and Turkey to reduce customs tariffs and promote commerce, with the aim of eventual customs union. In 1992 the newly independent republics of Azerbaijan, Kyrgyzstan, Tajikistan, Turkmenistan, and Uzbekistan were admitted into the ECO. Address: 1 Goulbou Alley, Kamraniyeh, PO Box 14155-6176, Tehran, Iran; phone: +98 (21) 283 1731; fax: +98 (21) 283 1733; e-mail: eco.org@neda.net

European Bank for Reconstruction and Development (EBRD)

International bank established in 1991, with an initial capital of 10 billion European Currency Units (ECUs), to assist the economic reconstruction of Central and Eastern Europe. The Bank aims to help Central and Eastern European countries to implement structural and sectoral economic reform, including demonopolization, decentralization, and privatization. The EBRD has 60 members: 58 countries, including 26 countries in Central and Eastern Europe and the Commonwealth of Independent States, the European Union, and the European Investment Bank. Each member appoints a Governor and an alternate. The Board of Governors delegates power to a Board of Directors, responsible for the direction of the general operations of the Bank. The president is elected by the Board of Governors. Address: 1 Exchange Square, London EC2A 2JN, UK; phone: (020) 7338 6000; fax: (020) 7338 6100; Web site: www.ebrd.com

European Free Trade Association (EFTA)

Organization established in 1960 consisting of Iceland, Norway, Switzerland, and Liechtenstein (from 1991), previously a nonvoting associate member. There are no import duties between members. Of the original EFTA members, the UK and Denmark left in 1972 to join the European Community (EC), as did Portugal in 1985; Austria, Finland, and Sweden joined the EC's successor, the European Union, in 1995. In 1973 the EC signed agreements with EFTA members, setting up a free-trade area of over 300 million consumers. Trade between the two groups amounted to over half of total EFTA trade. A further pact signed in 1991 between the EC and EFTA provided for a European Economic Area (EEA), allowing EFTA greater access to the EC market by ending many restrictions. The EEA came into effect in January 1994. Address: 9–11 rue de Varembé, 1211 Geneva 20, Switzerland; phone: +41 (22) 749 1111; fax: +41 (22) 733 9291; e-mail: efta-mailbox@secrbru.efta.be; Web site: www.efta.int/structure/main/index.html

Inter-American Development Bank (IDB)

Bank founded in 1959, at the instigation of the Organization of American States, to finance economic and social development, particularly in the less wealthy regions of the Americas. Its 46 members include the states of Central and Southern America, the Caribbean, and the USA, as well as Austria, Belgium, Canada, Denmark, Finland, France, Germany, Israel, Italy, Japan, the Netherlands, Norway, Portugal, Spain, Sweden, Switzerland, and the UK. Address: 1300 New York Avenue, NW, Washington DC 20577, USA; phone: +1 (202) 623 1000; Web site: www.iabd.org

International Monetary Fund (IMF)

Specialized agency of the United Nations with its headquarters in Washington, DC, established under the 1944 Bretton Woods agreement and operational since 1947. It seeks to promote international monetary cooperation and the growth of world trade, and to smooth multilateral payment arrangements among member states. IMF standby loans are available to members in balance-of-payments difficulties (the amount being governed by the member's quota), usually on the basis that the country must agree to take certain corrective measures. The IMF also operates other drawing facilities, including several designed to provide preferential credit to developing countries with liquidity problems. Having previously operated in US dollars linked to gold, since 1972 the IMF has used the special drawing right (SDR) as its standard unit of account, valued in terms of a weighted 'basket' of currencies. Since 1971, IMF rules have been progressively adapted to floating exchange rates. Address: 700 19th Street, NW, Washington DC 20431; phone: +1 (202) 623 7300; fax: +1 (202) 623 6278; e-mail: publicaffairs@imf.org; Web site: www.imf.org

Mercado Comun del Cono Sur (Mercosur)/Southern Cone Common Market

Free-trade organization, founded in 1991 on the signing of the Asunción Treaty by Argentina, Brazil, Paraguay, and Uruguay, and formally inaugurated on 1 January 1995. With a GNP of $800,000 million and a population of more than 190 million, Mercosur constitutes the world's fourth-largest free-trade bloc after the European Economic Area, the North American Free Trade Area, and the Asia-Pacific Economic Cooperation. Address: Secretariat, Rincón 575 piso 12, 11000 Montevideo, Uruguay; phone: +598 (2) 916 4590; fax: +598 (2) 916 4591; e-mail: info@mercosur.com; Web site: www.mercosur.com

North American Free Trade Agreement (NAFTA)

Trade agreement between the USA, Canada, and Mexico, agreed in August 1992 and effective from January 1994. The first trade pact of its kind to link two highly-industrialized countries to a developing one, it created a free market of 360 million people, with a total GDP of $6.45 trillion. Tariffs were to be progressively eliminated over a 10–15 year period and investment into low-wage Mexico by Canada and the USA progressively increased. Chile was invited to join in 1994, but its entry was delayed. Address: NAFTA Secretariat, US Section, Room 2061, 14th Street, Constitution Avenue NW, Washington DC 20230, USA; phone: +1 (202) 482 5438; fax: +1 (202) 482 0148; Web site: www.mac.doc.gov/nafta

Organization for Economic Cooperation and Development (OECD)

International organization of 30 industrialized countries that provides a forum for discussion and coordination of member states' economic and social policies. Founded in 1961, the OECD superseded the Organization for European Economic Cooperation, which had been established in 1948 to implement the Marshall Plan. The Commission of the European Union also participates in the OECD's work. The OECD's subsidiary bodies include the International Energy Agency, which was set up in 1974 in the face of a world oil crisis. The scope of the OECD also includes development aid. Members are: Australia, Austria, Belgium, Canada, the Czech Republic, Denmark, Finland, France, Germany, Greece, Iceland, the Republic of Ireland, Italy, Japan, Luxembourg, Mexico, the Netherlands, New Zealand, Norway, Portugal, Spain, Sweden, Switzerland, Turkey, the UK, and the USA; Hungary, Poland, and the Slovak Republic joined in 1996, and South Korea in 1997. Address: 2, rue André-Pascal, 75775 Paris Cedex 16, France; phone: +33 (1) 4524 8200; fax: +33 (1) 4524 8500; e-mail: webmaster@oecd.org; Web site: www.oecd.org

Organization of Arab Petroleum Exporting Countries (OAPEC)

Body established in 1968 to safeguard the interests of its members and encourage economic cooperation within the petroleum industry. Its members are Algeria, Bahrain, Egypt, Iraq, Kuwait, Libya, Qatar, Saudi Arabia, Syria, and the United Arab Emirates. Address: PO Box 20501, Safat 13066, Kuwait City, Kuwait; phone: +965 484 4500; fax: +965 481 5747; e-mail: oapec@qualitynet.net; Web site: www.kuwait.net/~oapec

Organization of Petroleum Exporting Countries (OPEC)

Body established in 1960 to coordinate price and supply policies of oil-producing states. Its concerted action in raising prices in the 1970s triggered worldwide recession but also lessened demand so that its influence was reduced by the mid-1980s. OPEC members in 1998 were: Algeria, Indonesia, Iran, Iraq, Kuwait, Libya, Nigeria, Qatar, Saudi Arabia, the United Arab Emirates, and Venezuela. Address: Obere Donaustrasse 93, A-1020 Vienna, Austria; phone: +43 (1) 211120; fax: +43 (1) 214 9827; Web site: www.opec.org

Southern African Development Community (SADC)

Formerly (to 1992) Southern African Development Coordination Conference (SADCC). Established in April 1980, SADCC's original aim was to promote regional independence from the economic dominance of the Republic of South Africa. With the adoption of the new name, the organization recast its objective as increased regional coordination and cooperation for mutual benefit. The community comprises 14 member states. Address: Private Bag 0095, Gaborone, Botswana; phone: +267 351863; fax: +267 372848; Web site: www.mbendi.co.za/orsodc.htm

South Asian Association for Regional Cooperation (SAARC)

Organization established in 1985 by India, Pakistan, Bangladesh, Nepal, Sri Lanka, Bhutan, and the Maldives to cover agriculture, telecommunications, health, population, sports, art, and culture. In 1993 a preferential trade agreement was adopted to reduce tariffs on intra-regional trade. Address: PO Box 4222, Kathmandu, Nepal; phone: +977 (1) 221785; fax: +977 (1) 227033; e-mail: saarc@mos.com.np; Web site: www.south-asia.com/saarc

World Bank

Popular name for the International Bank for Reconstruction and Development (IBRD), a specialized agency of the United Nations that borrows in the commercial market and lends on commercial terms. It was established in 1945 under the 1944 Bretton Woods agreement, which also created the International Monetary Fund. The International Development Association is an arm of the World Bank. Control of the bank is vested in a board of executives representing national governments, whose votes are apportioned according to the amount they have funded the bank. Thus, the USA has nearly 20% of the vote and always appoints the board's president. Address: 1818 H Street NW, Room J1 060, Washington DC 20433; phone: +1 (202) 477 1234; fax: +1 (202) 522 1500; e-mail: pic@worldbank.org; Web site: www.worldbank.org

World Trade Organization (WTO)

World trade monitoring body established in January 1995, on approval of the Final Act of the Uruguay round of the General Agreement on Tariffs and Trade (GATT). Under the Final Act, the WTO, a permanent trading body with a status commensurate with that of the International Monetary Fund or the World Bank, effectively replaced GATT. The WTO monitors agreements to reduce barriers to trade, such as tariffs, subsidies, quotas, and regulations that discriminate against imported products. All members of GATT were automatically to become members of the WTO on their parliaments' ratification of the Uruguay round; new members, without exception, would have to meet the criteria established by the Uruguay round. Address: 154 rue de la Lausanne, 1211 Geneva 21, Switzerland; phone: +41 (22) 739 5111; fax: +41 (22) 739 5458; e-mail: enquiries@wto.org; Web site: www.wto.org

See also  **The European Union**, pp 280–287; **International Political Organizations**, pp 277–280.

Economic Indicators

GDP and GNP

Gross domestic product (GDP) and gross national product (GNP) are the most commonly used economic indicators (statistical measures of a country's or region's economic activity).

GDP is the sum of all incomes earned by the production of all goods and services (the value of the output) within a nation's economic territory, normally given as a total for the year. It includes the production of foreign-owned firms within the country, but excludes the income from domestically owned firms located abroad.

GNP is the total value of all goods and services produced by firms owned by the country concerned. It is measured as the gross domestic product plus income from abroad, minus income earned during the same period by foreign investors within the country.

Countries with the Highest and Lowest Industrial Output Growth

1990–98

Country	Average annual % growth	Country	Average annual % growth
High growth		*Low growth*	
China	15.4	Tajikistan	– 17.2
Vietnam	13.0	Ukraine	– 15.5
Uganda	12.8	Latvia	– 12.8
Laos	11.8	Moldova	– 12.8
Myanmar	10.1	Kyrgyzstan	– 12.0
Cambodia	9.6	Congo, Democratic Republic of	– 11.7
Malaysia	9.4	Russian Federation	– 11.1
Lesotho	9.2	Kazakhstan	– 10.1
Mozambique	8.5	Lithuania	– 9.9
Singapore	8.4	Armenia	– 9.0

Source: World Development Indicators 2000, *The World Bank*

See also **Industrial Output of the UK**, p 684.

Economic Growth

Economic growth is the rate of growth of output of all goods and services in an economy, usually measured as the percentage increase in gross domestic product or gross national product from one year to the next. It is regarded as an indicator of the rate of increase or decrease (if economic growth is negative) in the standard of living.

Gross Domestic Product of the UK

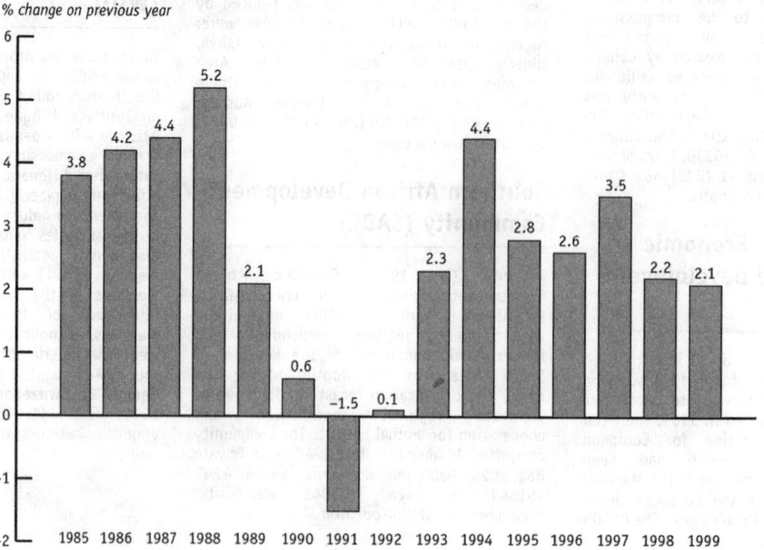

Source: HM Treasury, © *Crown copyright 2000*

Countries with the Highest and Lowest GDP

(In millions of dollars.)

1997

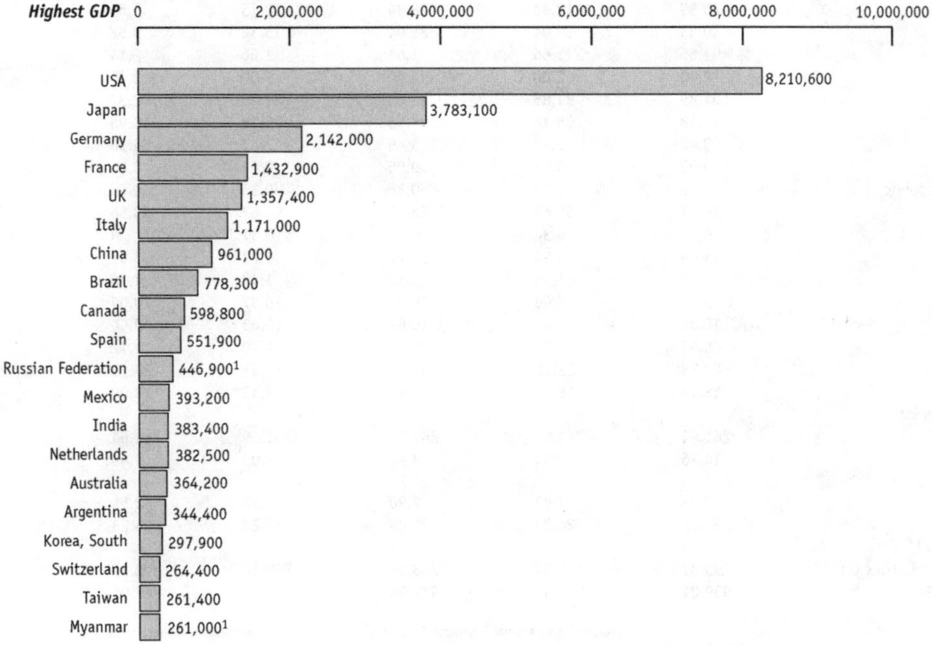

Highest GDP

USA	8,210,600
Japan	3,783,100
Germany	2,142,000
France	1,432,900
UK	1,357,400
Italy	1,171,000
China	961,000
Brazil	778,300
Canada	598,800
Spain	551,900
Russian Federation	446,900[1]
Mexico	393,200
India	383,400
Netherlands	382,500
Australia	364,200
Argentina	344,400
Korea, South	297,900
Switzerland	264,400
Taiwan	261,400
Myanmar	261,000[1]

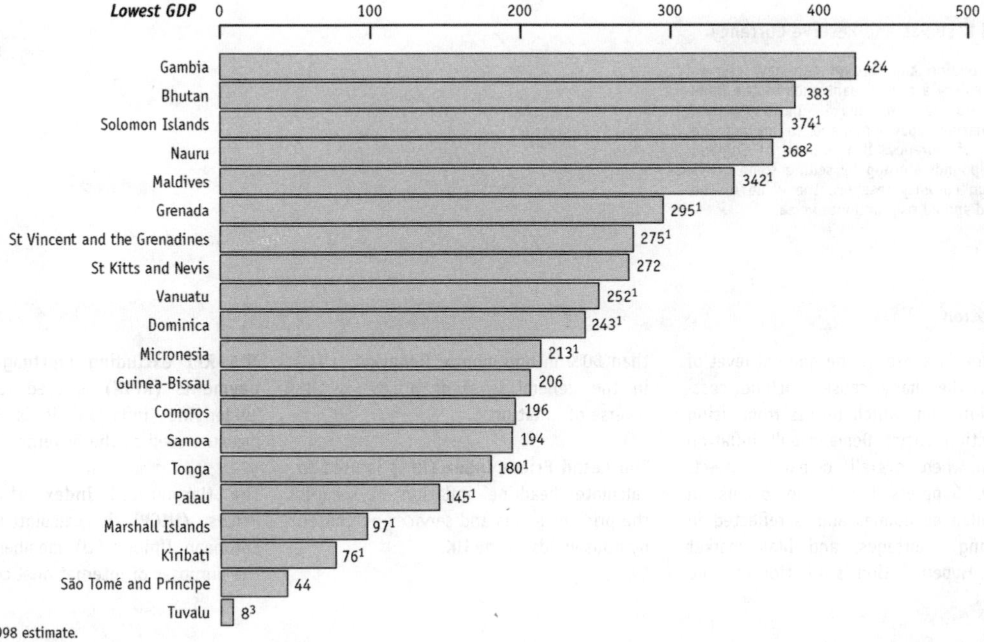

Lowest GDP

Gambia	424
Bhutan	383
Solomon Islands	374[1]
Nauru	368[2]
Maldives	342[1]
Grenada	295[1]
St Vincent and the Grenadines	275[1]
St Kitts and Nevis	272
Vanuatu	252[1]
Dominica	243[1]
Micronesia	213[1]
Guinea-Bissau	206
Comoros	196
Samoa	194
Tonga	180[1]
Palau	145[1]
Marshall Islands	97[1]
Kiribati	76[1]
São Tomé and Príncipe	44
Tuvalu	8[3]

[1] 1998 estimate.

[2] Figure for 1995.

[3] 1995 estimate.

See also **Government Expenditure as a Percentage of GDP in the UK**, p 112.

Gold Reserves: Industrial Countries

(– = not applicable. N = nil or negligible. In millions of fine troy ounces.)

Country	1990	1992	1994	1996	1998
Europe					
Austria	20.39	19.93	18.34	10.75	9.64
Belgium	30.23	25.04	25.04	15.32	9.52
Denmark	1.65	1.66	1.63	1.66	2.14
Finland	2.00	2.00	2.00	1.60	2.00
France	81.85	81.85	81.85	81.85	102.37
Germany	95.18	95.18	95.18	95.18	118.98
Greece	3.40	3.43	3.45	3.47	83.36
Iceland	0.05	0.05	0.05	0.05	0.06
Ireland, Republic of	0.36	0.36	0.36	0.36	0.45
Italy	66.67	66.67	66.67	66.67	83.36
Luxembourg	0.34	0.34	0.31	0.31	N
Netherlands	43.94	43.94	34.77	34.77	33.83
Norway	1.18	1.18	1.18	1.18	1.18
Portugal	15.83	16.06	16.07	16.07	20.09
Spain	15.61	15.62	15.62	15.63	19.54
Sweden	6.07	6.07	6.07	4.70	4.72
Switzerland	83.28	83.28	83.28	83.28	83.28
UK	18.94	18.61	18.44	18.43	23.00
North America					
USA	261.91	261.84	261.73	261.66	261.61
Canada	14.76	9.94	3.89	3.09	2.49
Pacific					
Australia	7.93	7.93	7.90	7.90	2.56
Japan	24.23	24.23	24.23	24.23	24.23
New Zealand	–	–	–	–	–
Industrial countries total	795.81	785.24	768.05	748.16	808.67
WORLD TOTAL	939.01	927.55	917.98	907.55	965.95

Source: International Financial Statistics April 2000, © *International Monetary Fund*

Gold Reserves and Reserve Currency

Gold bullion and foreign currency reserves are held by a central bank such as the Bank of England to make national and international payments and to protect the value of currency. If the Bank of England buys pounds sterling by selling some of its foreign currency reserves, the value of the pound should rise, and vice versa.

Inflation

Inflation is a rise in the general level of prices. The many causes include cost-push inflation, which results from rising production costs. Demand-pull inflation occurs when overall demand exceeds supply. Suppressed inflation occurs in controlled economies and is reflected in rationing, shortages, and black-market prices. Hyperinflation is inflation of more than 50% in one month. Deflation, a fall in the general level of prices, is the reverse of inflation.

The Retail Prices Index (RPI) is used to calculate 'headline' inflation; it records the price of goods and services purchased by households in the UK.

The RPI excluding mortgage interest payments (RPIX) is used to calculate 'underlying' inflation; it is the target measure used by the Government.

The Harmonized Index of Consumer Prices (HICP) is calculated in each European Union (EU) member state for the purposes of international comparison.

■ Economic Indicators

Countries with the Highest and Lowest Consumer Price Inflation

Country	Inflation rate (%)	Year
Highest inflation		
Angola	1,200.0	1998
Somalia	363.0	1995
Afghanistan	240.0[1]	1996
Iraq	140.0	1998
Belarus	127.0	1998
Turkey	83.1	1998
Congo, Democratic Republic of	65.0	1998
Romania	59.0	1998
Laos	55.0	1998
Myanmar	51.0	1998
Sudan	50.0	1998
Guinea-Bissau	49.1	1997
São Tomé and Príncipe	42.3	1998
Tajikistan	40.0	1998
Bosnia-Herzegovina	40.0	1998
Sierra Leone	37.4[1]	1998
Venezuela	35.8[1]	1998
Jamaica	34.7	1998
Bulgaria	32.0	1998
Zimbabwe	31.7	1998

Country	Inflation rate (%)	Year
Lowest inflation		
Mozambique	−1.3	1998
Brunei	−0.5[1]	1998
Uganda	0	1998
Switzerland	0.1	1998
Liechtenstein	0.5	1997
Panama	0.6	1998
Dominica	0.7	1998
Andorra	0.8	1998
Bahrain	0.8	1998
Belize	0.8	1997
Tuvalu	0.8	1998
Oman	1.0	1998
St Kitts and Nevis	1.0	1998
Togo, Republic of	1.0	1998
Japan	1.1	1998
Grenada	1.2	1998
New Zealand	1.3	1998
Korea, South	1.3	1999
Bahamas	1.5	1998
Finland	1.5	1998

[1]Estimate.

Retail Prices: Rates of Change in Selected Countries

Figures are consumer (retail) price percentage changes on previous year (not seasonally adjusted).

Country/Region	1990	1991	1992	1993	1994	1995	1996	1997	1998	1999
Austria	3.3	3.3	4.0	3.6	3.0	2.2	1.5	1.3	0.9	0.6
Belgium	3.4	3.2	2.4	2.8	2.4	1.5	2.1	1.6	1.0	1.1
Denmark	2.6	2.4	2.1	1.3	2.0	2.1	2.1	2.2	1.8	2.5
Finland	6.2	4.3	2.9	2.2	1.1	0.8	0.6	1.2	1.4	1.2
France	3.6	3.2	2.4	2.1	1.7	1.8	2.0	1.2	0.8	0.5
Germany[1]	2.7	4.0	5.1	4.4	2.8	1.7	1.4	1.9	0.9	0.6
Greece	20.4	19.5	15.9	14.4	10.7	8.9	8.2	5.5	4.8	2.6
Ireland, Republic of	3.3	3.2	3.1	1.4	2.3	2.5	1.7	1.4	2.4	1.6
Italy	6.5	6.3	5.3	4.6	4.1	5.2	4.0	2.0	2.0	1.7
Netherlands	2.5	3.2	3.2	2.6	2.8	1.9	2.0	2.2	2.0	2.2
Portugal	13.4	10.5	9.4	6.7	5.4	4.2	3.1	2.3	2.8	2.3
Spain	6.7	5.9	5.9	4.6	4.7	4.7	3.6	2.0	1.8	2.3
Sweden	10.4	9.4	2.3	4.6	2.2	2.5	0.5	0.5	−0.1	0.5
UK	9.5	5.9	3.7	1.6	2.5	3.4	2.5	3.1	3.4	1.6
EU-11[2] [3]	N/A	4.1	3.6	3.6	3.2	2.7	2.5	2.2	1.6	1.1	1.1
EU-15	5.8	5.2	4.5	3.6	3.1	3.1	2.5	2.1	1.7	1.3
Canada	4.8	5.6	1.5	1.9	0.2	2.2	1.6	1.6	1.0	1.7
Japan	3.1	3.3	1.7	1.2	0.7	−0.1	0.1	1.7	0.6	−0.3
USA	5.4	4.2	3.0	3.0	2.6	2.8	2.9	2.3	1.6	2.2

[1] From 1991 includes former East Germany.
[2] The 11 countries participating in the euro: Austria, Belgium, Finland, France, Germany, Republic of Ireland, Italy, Luxembourg, the Netherlands, Portugal, and Spain.
[3] Figures are aggregates calculated using 1997 consumption weights.

Source: HM Treasury, © Crown copyright 2000

Inflation in the UK

During the 1990s the annual inflation rate in the UK remained relatively low, and since 1993 it has been within a narrow range from 1.5–3.5%. In 1999 the underlying annual inflation rate averaged 2.3% (the Retail Prices Index (RPI) rate was 1.6%).

Relatively low world commodity prices and the sharp falls in import prices resulting from the appreciation in the value of sterling since the summer of 1996 have contributed to the low level of inflation in the UK.

In 1998 the Harmonized Index of Consumer Prices (HICP) for the UK was 1.5%. During most of 1998 and 1999 the UK's HICP was slightly above the EU average.

Higher levels of duty and increases in manufacturers' prices have caused tobacco to rise at well above the average RPI rate, but other products, including consumer durables, clothing and footwear, telephone services, and gas and electricity were cheaper in August 1999 than in 1998.

Retail Price Inflation in the UK

RPI = Retail Prices Index.

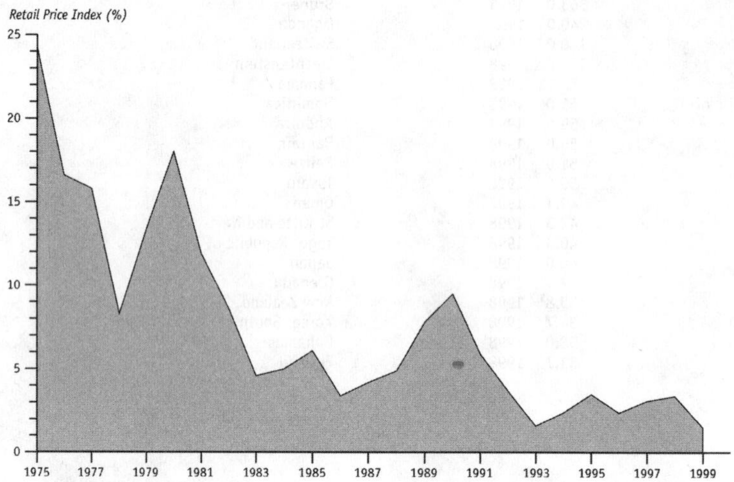

Source: HM Treasury, © Crown copyright 2000

See also  **Government Spending and Social Protection**, pp 111–115.

Retail Prices Index: Rates of Change in the UK

Item	% change on the previous year					
	1993	1994	1995	1996	1997	1998
Housing	−5.4	3.3	6.7	1.3	6.5	8.8
Food	1.8	1.0	3.9	3.2	0.1	1.3
Motoring expenditure	4.3	3.5	1.8	3.0	5.3	3.1
Alcoholic drink	4.5	2.5	3.8	2.9	2.8	3.4
Household goods	1.2	0.3	3.7	3.3	1.2	1.2
Leisure services	4.5	3.7	3.2	3.6	4.9	4.4
Clothing and footwear	0.8	0.5	0.2	−0.7	0.8	−0.6
Household services	3.6	0.1	−0.3	0.1	1.8	2.6
Catering	5.2	4.2	4.3	4.0	3.8	3.8
Leisure goods	1.4	−0.6	−0.1	1.6	0.2	−2.3
Fuel and light	−1.3	4.4	2.1	0.2	3.1	−4.3
Personal goods and services	4.0	3.7	3.2	3.7	3.6	4.7
Tobacco	8.5	7.5	6.7	6.7	7.4	8.6
Fares and other travel costs	5.2	2.6	2.5	3.0	3.4	2.2
Total	1.6	2.4	3.5	2.4	3.1	3.4
All items except housing	3.1	2.3	2.7	2.7	2.4	2.2
All items except mortgage interest payments	3.0	2.3	2.9	3.0	2.8	2.6

Source: Social Trends 30, © Crown copyright 2000

See also  **Consumer Expenditure**, pp 329–331.

Economic Indicators

Purchasing Power of the Pound within the UK

To find the purchasing power of the pound in 1993 compared with 100 pence in 1980, select the *column* headed 1980 and look at the 1993 *row*. The result is 48 pence, which means that the pound could purchase in 1993 less than half of what it could in 1980. These figures are calculated by taking the inverse ratio of the respective annual averages of the Retail Prices Index. In pence.

Year	1980	1981	1982	1983	1984	1985	1986	1987	1988	1989	1990	1991	1992	1993	1994	1995	1996	1997	1998
1980	100	112	122	127	133	142	146	152	160	172	189	200	207	210	216	223	228	236	244
1981	89	100	109	114	119	127	131	136	143	154	169	179	185	188	193	199	204	211	218
1982	82	92	100	105	110	116	120	125	132	142	155	164	171	173	177	184	188	194	201
1983	79	88	96	100	105	111	115	120	126	136	148	157	163	166	170	176	180	185	192
1984	75	84	91	95	100	106	110	114	120	129	141	150	155	158	162	167	171	177	183
1985	71	79	86	90	94	100	103	108	113	122	133	141	146	149	152	158	161	166	172
1986	68	76	83	87	91	97	100	104	109	118	129	136	142	144	147	152	156	161	167
1987	66	73	80	83	88	93	96	100	105	113	124	131	136	138	141	146	150	155	160
1988	63	70	76	79	83	88	92	95	100	108	118	125	130	132	135	139	143	147	152
1989	58	65	71	74	77	82	85	88	93	100	109	116	120	122	125	129	133	137	141
1990	53	59	64	67	71	75	78	81	85	91	100	106	110	112	114	118	121	125	129
1991	50	56	61	64	67	71	73	76	80	86	94	100	104	105	108	112	114	118	122
1992	48	54	59	61	64	68	71	74	77	83	91	96	100	102	104	108	110	114	118
1993	48	53	58	60	63	67	70	72	76	82	90	95	98	100	102	106	109	112	116
1994	46	52	56	59	62	66	68	71	74	80	88	93	96	98	100	103	106	109	113
1995	45	50	54	57	60	63	66	68	72	77	85	90	93	94	97	100	102	106	109
1996	44	49	53	56	58	62	64	67	70	75	83	87	91	92	94	98	100	103	107
1997	42	47	52	54	57	60	62	65	68	73	80	85	88	89	92	95	97	100	103
1998	41	46	50	52	55	58	60	63	66	71	77	82	85	86	88	92	94	97	100

Source: Annual Abstract of Statistics 2000,

See also **Working Hours Needed to Buy Selected Commodities in the UK**, p 330.

International Trade

Growth in International Trade

The International Monetary Fund (IMF) predicted in 1999 that the year 2000 would see strong growth in international trading. At its meeting in Washington, DC, USA, in April 2000 (chaired by British chancellor of the Exchequer, Gordon Brown), the 'remarkable' pace of expansion in the USA during 1999 was noted; growth had strengthened in western Europe, Asia, China, and India; and economic recovery in crisis-affected countries, including Japan, had gained significant momentum.

The Fund also reported that the predicted downturn in Latin America during 1999 had proved to be relatively mild, and that the Russian Federation's economic performance had improved but that it needed to strengthen its institutions and create an attractive environment for domestic and foreign investors.

Sustainable growth

The IMF advised in April 2000 that, although poorer countries still needed to direct their economic policies at providing support for recovery, the most advanced countries should now concentrate on strengthening the conditions for sustainable growth. The IMF stressed 'the critical importance of efforts to sustain growth and stability in the global economy, and to reduce poverty'. It welcomed the proposal of the World Trade Organization (WTO) of an early launch of a new round of multinational trade negotiations to bring benefits to all countries, including the poorest.

The Global Economy

The 'global economy' is now a familiar term in the developed world. Some see it as a wholly positive and liberating phenomenon, breaking down barriers between nations; others perceive in it a threat to the independence of governments and individuals.

What is the global economy?

For some, the global economy means Western market capitalism, now the world's dominant organizing economic principle following reforms in countries such as China and the collapse of the Soviet bloc. In this economic model, firms supply consumers in the marketplace; the state is confined to regulating this activity and providing those services the market cannot efficiently provide. For others, the term global economy also implies a greater role for international flows of trade, investment, and finance.

Why do we have a global economy?

The idea that countries concentrate on producing only those goods and services that they could produce relatively efficiently, and trade them for goods and services that they could only produce less efficiently, with the result that everyone might be better off, is a 19th-century concept. Without international trade, a vast number of foodstuffs and raw materials would not be available in the UK. In practice most trade, especially that between industrialized countries, is now in the same products (cars, for example). As consumers grow richer, international trade facilitates the wider choice of goods and services expected.

Free Trade: The Protests

Seattle and Washington

In November 1999 at the meeting of the World Trade Organization (WTO) in Seattle (WA), USA, some 5,000 people, from all backgrounds, were involved in protests against global free trade and the globalization of the economy.

In addition to concerns about the cultural imperialism associated with Western capitalism, protestors' objections were based on their fears that the world is becoming dominated by huge, unelected commercial conglomerates and corporate bodies that set up enterprises in least-developed countries (LDCs), taking advantage of the minimal environmental and employment legislation, low wages, and child labour in these countries.

Protestors were also demonstrating against the World Trade Organization's (WTO)

Free Trade: The Protests (*continued*)

perceived commitment to imposing western environmental standards and social rights on the LDCs.

Others argue that unless improved conditions are imposed on LDCs, the goods they produce can be retailed at such low cost that their export causes serious damage to the manufacturing industries of countries with higher environmental and social standards.

Protests in the UK

In June 1999 protestors targeted the London International Financial Futures and Options Exchange (LIFFE) building – home of the London futures market, causing some £2 million of damage. In November 1999, an anti-capitalist demonstration took place at Euston Station, and on May Day 2000, some 3,000 people demonstrated in London's Whitehall, causing damage to the Cenotaph and a statue of Winston Churchill.

See also **Third World Debt**, p 663.

Key Dates in the History of Free Trade: from GATT to WTO

30 October 1947 Twenty-three countries sign the General Agreement on Tariffs and Trade (GATT). The first round of trade negotiations result in 45,000 tariff concessions affecting one fifth of total world trade.

1 January 1949 GATT enters into force.

26 May 1956 Another trade round is completed, producing some $2.5 billion worth of tariff reductions.

1960–62 The fifth GATT round yields tariff concessions worth $4.9 billion of world trade and involves negotiations related to the creation of the European Economic Community (EEC).

1964–67 The Kennedy Round achieves tariff cuts worth $40 billion of world trade.

1973–79 The seventh GATT round, launched in Tokyo, Japan, reaches agreement to start reducing not only tariffs but trade barriers as well; tariff reductions worth more than $300 billion are achieved.

1986–94 GATT trade ministers launch the Uruguay Round, embarking on the most ambitious and far-reaching trade round so far.

1994 Ministers meet for the last time under GATT auspices at Marrakesh, Morocco, to establish the World Trade Organization (WTO) and sign other agreements.

1 January 1995 The World Trade Organization comes into force. The main differences between WTO and GATT are that GATT was a provisional legal agreement, whereas WTO is an organization with permanent agreements. GATT had only contracting parties and dealt only with trade in goods; WTO has members and covers services and intellectual property as well.

1997 Total world trade is now 14 times the level of 1950.

February 1997 Sixty-nine governments agree on widespread liberalization of telecommunications services which go beyond those agreed in the Uruguay Round.

May 1998 WTO members agree to study trade issues arising from global electronic commerce, made possible by the Internet.

1999 At a time when global economic growth is slowing and the 134-member WTO needs to focus on defending free trade, it faces splits in its membership, trade wars between the USA and other members, and a weakened credibility due to lack of compliance (notably by the EU) to its rulings.

November 1999 A summit is held in Seattle. It is designed to be the launchpad for the first global trade negotiations since the Uruguay Round ended in 1994. The talks, dubbed the Millennium Round, are expected to last three years. Anti-capitalist demonstrators, coordinated through the Internet, force cancelling of the summit's opening ceremony, as a local curfew is declared and the National Guard is called in. The USA presses for an agreement on labour rights, including the outlawing of child labour, while the European Union presses for environmental protection. China's entry into the WTO is agreed in principle, in exchange for improved access to China's market.

11 April 2000 Jordan becomes the 16th member of the WTO.

Leading Exporters and Importers of Commercial Services

(N/A = not available.)

1999

Rank	Country	Value ($ billions)	Share (%)	Annual change (%)
Exporters				
1	USA	251.7	18.8	5
2	UK	101.4	7.6	2
3	France	79.3	5.9	–6
4	Germany	76.8	5.7	–3
5	Italy	64.5	4.8	–3
6	Japan	59.8	4.5	–3
7	Spain	54.1	4.0	11
8	Netherlands	53.1	4.0	3
9	Belgium/Luxembourg	37.6	2.8	4
10	Hong Kong, China	35.4	2.6	3
11	Austria	32.6	2.4	3
12	Canada	32.4	2.4	7
13	Switzerland	27.2	2.0	5
14	China	26.6	2.0	N/A
15	Korea, Republic of	25.0	1.9	5
16	Singapore	22.9	1.7	25
17	Sweden	18.0	1.3	2
18	Australia	17.2	1.3	9
19=	Denmark	16.0	1.2	8
	Turkey	16.0	1.2	–31
21	Taipei, Chinese	14.8	1.1	–11
22	Thailand	14.1	1.1	8
23	Norway	13.7	1.0	–2
24	India	13.2	1.0	19
25	Mexico	11.6	0.9	–3
26	Malaysia	10.8	0.8	N/A
27	Greece	10.5	0.8	N/A
28	Israel	10.3	0.8	14
29	Poland	9.8	0.7	–10
30	Russian Federation	9.7	0.7	–25
Total		1,165.0	87.1	–
WORLD TOTAL		1,340.0	100.0	1.5

Rank	Country	Value ($ billions)	Share (%)	Annual change (%)
Importers				
1	USA	182.3	13.7	10
2	Germany	127.2	9.5	2
3	Japan	113.9	8.5	3
4	UK	81.4	6.1	4
5	Italy	62.7	4.7	0
6	France	59.2	4.4	–9
7	Netherlands	46.5	3.5	0
8	Canada	37.1	2.8	5
9	Belgium/Luxembourg	35.5	2.6	4
10	China	32.1	2.4	N/A
11	Spain	30.9	2.3	12
12	Austria	29.5	2.2	–2
13	Korea, Republic of	26.7	2.0	14
14	Ireland, Republic of	23.5	1.8	18
15	Taipei, Chinese	23.2	1.7	0
16	Sweden	22.8	1.7	5
17	Hong Kong, China	22.4	1.7	2
18	Singapore	19.3	1.4	8
19	Australia	18.0	1.3	6
20	India	17.3	1.3	22
21	Denmark	16.2	1.2	5
22	Switzerland	15.7	1.2	3
23	Norway	15.4	1.2	2
24	Thailand	13.9	1.0	17
25	Mexico	13.7	1.0	9
26	Malaysia	13.0	1.0	N/A
27	Indonesia	12.7	0.9	8
28	Russian Federation	11.7	0.9	–27
29	Brazil	11.6	0.9	–26
30	Israel	10.7	0.8	12
Total		1,145.0	85.9	–
WORLD TOTAL		1,335.0	100.0	2.5

Source: World Trade Organization, 2000

International Trade

Leading Exporters and Importers of Merchandise

1999

Rank	Country	Value ($ billions)	Share (%)	Annual change (%)
Exporters				
1	USA	695.0	12.4	2
2	Germany	540.5	9.6	0
3	Japan	419.4	7.5	8
4	France	299.0	5.3	–2
5	UK	268.4	4.8	–2
6	Canada	238.4	4.2	11
7	Italy	230.8	4.1	–5
8	Netherlands	204.1	3.6	2
9	China	194.9	3.5	6
10	Belgium/Luxembourg	184.1	3.3	3
11	Hong Kong, China	174.8	3.1	0
12	Korea, Republic of	144.2	2.6	9
13	Mexico	136.7	2.4	16
14	Taipei, Chinese	121.6	2.2	10
15	Singapore	114.6	2.0	4
16	Spain	109.4	2.0	0
17=	Malaysia	84.5	1.5	15
	Sweden	84.5	1.5	0
19	Switzerland	80.6	1.4	2
20	Russian Federation[1]	74.3	1.3	0
21	Ireland, Republic of	69.6	1.2	8
22	Austria	62.0	1.1	–1
23	Thailand	58.4	1.0	7
24	Australia	56.1	1.0	0
25	Saudi Arabia	50.5	0.9	27
26	Indonesia	48.5	0.9	–1
27	Brazil	48.0	0.9	–6
28	Denmark	47.8	0.9	–1
29	Norway	44.9	0.8	13
30	Finland	41.5	0.7	–4
Total[2]		4,927.0	87.8	-
WORLD TOTAL[2]		5,610.0	100.0	3

Rank	Country	Value ($ billions)	Share (%)	Annual change (%)
Importers				
1	USA	1059.9	18.0	12
2	Germany	472.6	8.0	0
3	UK	320.7	5.5	2
4	Japan	310.7	5.3	11
5	France	286.1	4.9	–1
6	Canada	220.2	3.7	7
7	Italy	216.0	3.7	0
8	Netherlands	188.9	3.2	1
9	Hong Kong, China	181.7	3.1	–3
10	Belgium/Luxembourg	169.4	2.9	2
11	China	165.7	2.8	18
12	Mexico	148.2	2.5	13
13	Spain	145.0	2.5	9
14	Korea, Republic of	119.7	2.0	28
15=	Taipei, Chinese	111.0	1.9	6
	Singapore	111.0	1.9	9
17	Switzerland	80.1	1.4	0
18	Australia	69.0	1.2	7
19	Sweden	68.2	1.2	0
20	Austria	67.8	1.2	0
21	Malaysia	65.5	1.1	12
22	Brazil	51.8	0.9	–15
23	Thailand	50.6	0.9	18
24	Ireland, Republic of	45.6	0.8	2
25	Poland	44.8	0.8	–5
26	India	44.6	0.8	4
27	Denmark	43.3	0.7	–6
28	Russian Federation[1]	41.1	0.7	–30
29	Turkey	39.2	0.7	–15
30	Portugal	37.6	0.6	2
Total[2]		4,976.0	84.7	-
WORLD TOTAL[2]		5,875.0	100.0	4

[1] Includes trade with the Baltic States and the CIS.
[2] Includes significant re-exports or imports for re-export.

Source: World Trade Organization, 2000

Top 20 European Union Trading Partners: Exports

Rank 1998	Partner	Value (billion ECU)				% of trading share			
		1995	1996	1997	1998	1995	1996	1997	1998
1	USA	103.3	114.4	141.3	160.1	18.0	18.3	19.6	21.9
2	Switzerland	51.0	51.4	53.0	56.9	8.9	8.2	7.4	7.8
3	Japan	32.9	35.7	36.1	31.4	5.7	5.7	5.0	4.3
4	Poland	15.3	19.9	25.1	28.1	2.7	3.2	3.5	3.8
5	Norway	17.3	19.7	23.3	24.9	3.0	3.2	3.2	3.4
6	Turkey	13.4	18.2	22.4	22.1	2.3	2.9	3.1	3.0
7	Russian Federation	16.1	19.1	25.5	21.0	2.8	3.1	3.5	2.9
8	China	14.7	14.7	16.5	17.4	2.6	2.4	2.3	2.4
9	Hong Kong	15.8	17.5	20.4	17.3	2.8	2.8	2.8	2.4
10	Czech Republic	11.7	14.0	15.8	17.1	2.0	2.2	2.2	2.3
11	Hungary	8.7	10.0	13.6	16.7	1.5	1.6	1.9	2.3
12	Brazil	11.4	11.7	14.9	15.6	2.0	1.9	2.1	2.1
13	Canada	10.3	10.7	14.1	14.9	1.8	1.7	2.0	2.0
14	Australia	10.5	11.5	13.1	12.9	1.8	1.8	1.8	1.8
15	Taiwan	10.1	9.9	12.7	12.1	1.8	1.6	1.8	1.7
16	Saudi Arabia	8.6	10.3	13.2	12.0	1.5	1.7	1.8	1.6
17	Singapore	10.9	12.3	13.5	10.9	1.9	2.0	1.9	1.5
18	Israel	9.7	10.4	11.5	10.9	1.7	1.7	1.6	1.5
19	South Africa	8.7	8.9	9.7	10.4	1.5	1.4	1.4	1.4
20	India	9.4	9.9	10.2	9.5	1.6	1.6	1.4	1.3
Total trade with partners outside the EU		572.8	625.1	720.7	729.6	100.0	100.0	100.0	100.0

Source: Eurostat Monthly Statistics, Main EU Trading Partners (Exports/Imports) *and* Eurostat Yearbook 1998/99, *© European Communities 1999*

Top 20 European Union Trading Partners: Imports

Rank 1998	Partner	Value (billion ECU)				% of trading share			
		1995	1996	1997	1998	1995	1996	1997	1998
1	USA	103.6	112.8	137.9	150.8	19.0	19.4	20.5	21.3
2	Japan	54.3	52.5	59.8	65.5	10.0	9.0	8.9	9.2
3	Switzerland	43.2	42.7	45.1	49.3	7.9	7.3	6.7	6.9
4	China	26.3	30.0	37.5	41.8	4.8	5.2	5.6	5.9
5	Norway	25.5	30.6	33.6	29.0	4.7	5.3	5.0	4.1
6	Russian Federation	21.5	23.3	27.0	23.1	3.9	4.0	4.0	3.2
7	Taiwan	11.8	12.9	15.7	18.1	2.2	2.2	2.3	2.6
8	Poland	12.3	12.3	14.2	16.1	2.2	2.1	2.1	2.3
9	Korea, South	10.9	11.1	13.1	15.6	2.0	1.9	2.0	2.2
10	Czech Republic	9.0	9.8	11.8	14.7	1.7	1.7	1.7	2.1
11	Hungary	7.6	8.8	11.7	14.5	1.4	1.5	1.7	2.0
12	Turkey	9.2	10.2	11.9	13.6	1.7	1.8	1.8	1.9
13	Brazil	10.8	10.4	12.6	13.2	2.0	1.8	1.9	1.9
14	Canada	11.7	11.5	12.5	12.7	2.1	2.0	1.9	1.8
15	Singapore	8.8	9.3	11.5	12.3	1.6	1.6	1.7	1.7
16	Malaysia	9.2	9.4	10.8	11.9	1.7	1.6	1.6	1.7
17	India	7.8	8.6	9.5	9.8	1.4	1.5	1.4	1.4
18	South Africa	7.8	8.2	9.1	9.7	1.4	1.4	1.4	1.4
19	Hong Kong	7.2	7.2	8.4	9.7	1.3	1.2	1.2	1.4
20	Thailand	6.6	7.5	8.6	9.3	1.2	1.3	1.3	1.3
Total trade with partners outside the EU		545.1	581.5	672.4	709.4	100.0	100.0	100.0	100.0

Source: Eurostat Monthly Statistics, Main EU Trading Partners (Exports/Imports) *and* Eurostat Yearbook 1998/99, © *European Communities 1999*

See also **Main Trading Partners of the UK**, p 662.

B2B: Trading and the Internet

The business world is finding considerable advantages in trading electronically; known as B2B (business to business) e-commerce. The UK Treasury claims that one in four British businesses are now trading electronically, and that the UK could ultimately save £27 billion a year if all enterprises used the e-business route in all their dealings.

E-commerce involves far more than just offering products and services for sale on the Internet. Many companies are expecting to source all their needs – equipment, components, and services – online, and to undertake entire transactions electronically. This means that they have needed totally to restructure their business procedures. Those which fail to do so are warned they could lose so much business that they may not survive, as companies that have harnessed e-commerce will be increasingly reluctant to trade with those that have not, as it means maintaining manual systems alongside electronic. As e-commerce enables buyers to identify suppliers in any part of the world, many British companies are sourcing globally to gain some advantage from the strength of the pound sterling. This is of course tough on their UK-based suppliers who have to accept that, unless their former customers can reduce their costs, they risk losing their business to end-product manufacturers in countries with weaker currencies.

Balance of Payments

A country's balance of payments is an account of its debit and credit transactions with other countries. Items are divided into the **current account**, which includes both visible trade (imports and exports of goods) and invisible trade (services such as transport, tourism, interest, and dividends), and the **capital account**, which includes investment in and out of the country, international grants, and loans. Deficits or surpluses on these accounts are brought into balance by buying and selling reserves of foreign currencies.

Balance of Payments of the UK

(In millions of pounds.)

Transactions	1989	1990	1991	1992	1993	1994	1995	1996	1997	1998
Trade in goods and services										
goods	– 24,724	– 18,707	– 10,223	– 13,050	– 13,319	– 11,091	– 11,724	– 13,086	– 11,910	– 20,765
services	3,917	4,010	4,471	5,674	6,623	6,528	8,915	8,897	12,414	12,253
net	– 20,807	– 14,697	– 5,752	– 7,376	– 6,696	– 4,563	– 2,809	– 4,189	504	– 8,512
Income										
compensation of employees	– 138	– 110	– 63	– 49	35	– 170	– 296	93	83	76
investment income	74	– 448	– 1,890	2,164	650	7,940	6,272	8,018	11,087	15,098
net	– 64	– 558	– 1,953	2,115	685	7,770	5,976	8,111	11,170	15,174
Current transfers	– 2,620	– 4,258	– 669	– 4,821	– 4,607	– 4,665	– 6,912	– 4,522	– 5,051	– 6,526
Current account balance	– 23,491	– 19,513	– 8,374	– 10,082	– 10,618	– 1,458	– 3,745	– 600	6,623	136
Capital account balance	270	497	290	421	309	33	534	736	804	421
Financial account balance	19,024	17,529	9,990	5,716	9,271	– 7,118	937	1,781	– 13,186	– 9,025
Net errors and omissions	4,197	1,487	– 1,906	3,945	1,038	8,543	2,274	– 1,917	5,759	8,468

Source: United Kingdom Balance of Payments. The Pink Book 1999, © *Crown copyright 1999*

■ International Trade

Imports and Exports of Commodities of the UK

(In millions of pounds.)

Category		1990	1992	1994	1996	1998
Import of goods						
Food and live animals	meat and meat preparations	1,890	2,030	1,976	2,663	2,092
	dairy products and eggs	916	1,113	1,144	1,246	1,163
	cereals and animal feeding stuffs	1,411	1,722	1,777	2,020	1,893
	vegetables and fruit	2,966	3,118	3,484	4,408	4,236
	Total	10,411	11,402	12,385	14,835	13,924
Beverages and tobacco	beverages	1,531	1,563	1,882	2,316	2,6701
	tobacco	377	462	382	626	485
	Total	1,908	2,027	2,262	2,945	3,156
Crude materials	wood, lumber, and cork	1,408	1,026	1,406	1,288	1,202
	pulp and waste paper	779	630	642	713	535
	textile fibres	549	480	633	691	494
	metal ores	1,478	1,164	1,165	1,619	1,485
	Total	5,721	4,667	5,547	6,357	5,619
Fuels	petroleum and petroleum products	6,286	5,325	4,843	5,730	3,532
	coal, gas, and electricity	1,581	1,689	1,311	1,310	1,182
	Total	7,866	7,018	6,154	7,040	4,715
Animal and vegetable oils and fats	**Total**	377	421	539	731	591
Chemicals	organic chemicals	2,630	2,794	3,544	4,890	4,724
	inorganic chemicals	964	952	1,105	1,288	1,074
	medicinal products	1,161	1,663	2,331	3,175	3,457
	plastics	3,228	3,038	3,775	4,478	4,051
	Total	10,833	11,618	14,623	18,746	18,145
Manufactures classified chiefly by material	wood and cork manufactures	951	847	1,039	1,121	1,138
	paper and paperboard manufactures	4,017	3,804	4,287	5,113	4,692
	textile manufactures	3,938	3,943	4,551	5,255	5,071
	iron and steel	2,688	2,515	2,975	3,716	3,335
	non-ferrous metals	3,004	2,592	3,032	3,860	3,851
	metal manufactures	2,592	2,579	2,925	3,625	3,908
	Total	21,903	20,671	24,551	29,611	28,748
Machinery and transport equipment	mechanical machinery	12,068	11,665	13,432	17,116	17,882
	electrical machinery	18,451	20,129	26,942	36,741	38,354
	road vehicles	12,597	12,120	16,287	20,851	23,210
	other transport equipment	4,052	3,410	4,279	3,723	6,240
	Total	47,164	47,319	60,931	78,426	85,681
Miscellaneous manufactures	clothing and footwear	5,074	5,629	6,368	8,097	9,190
	scientific and photographic	4,073	4,258	4,989	6,240	6,386
	Total	18,171	19,051	21,915	25,864	28,969
Other commodities and transactions	**Total**	1,740	1,679	991	1,613	1,742
IMPORTS TOTAL		126,090	125,867	149,890	186,151	191,278
Export of goods						
Food and live animals	meat and meat preparations	613	829	1,237	1,099	748
	dairy products and eggs	461	535	697	745	744
	cereals and animal feeding stuffs	1,302	1,543	1,528	2,044	1,721
	vegetables and fruit	265	333	399	480	410
	Total	4,344	5,291	6,352	7,117	6,322
Beverages and tobacco	beverages	2,116	2,448	2,876	3,183	2,910
	tobacco	656	971	871	1,213	1,071
	Total	2,774	3,417	3,745	4,399	3,980
Crude materials	wood, lumber, and cork	27	25	45	52	56
	pulp and waste paper	52	39	50	56	48
	textile fibres	496	489	574	620	497
	metal ores	634	459	666	668	559
	Total	2,163	1,880	2,405	2,626	2,293
Fuels	petroleum and petroleum products	7,544	6,665	8,520	10,424	6,494
	coal, gas, and electricity	326	308	416	661	494
	Total	7,867	6,970	8,936	11,085	6,990
Animal and vegetable oils and fats	**Total**	88	87	171	209	244
Chemicals	organic chemicals	3,353	3,701	4,749	5,234	4,960
	inorganic chemicals	954	1,185	1,125	1,210	1,170
	medicinal products	2,258	2,992	4,017	5,412	5,917
	plastics	2,123	2,139	2,811	3,348	3,222
	Total	13,183	14,977	18,859	22,504	22,311
Manufactures classified chiefly by material	wood and cork manufactures	116	131	172	229	247
	paper and paperboard manufactures	1,539	1,734	2,056	2,381	2,209
	textile manufactures	2,448	2,457	2,966	3,527	3,288
	iron and steel	3,035	3,006	3,676	4,130	3,355
	non-ferrous metals	2,192	1,751	2,235	2,723	2,456
	metal manufactures	2,117	2,212	2,654	3,415	3,630
	Total	15,824	15,485	19,635	23,495	21,397

(continued)

Imports and Exports of Commodities of the UK *(continued)*

Category		1990	1992	1994	1996	1998
Machinery and transport equipment	mechanical machinery	14,423	14,263	16,446	21,005	23,267
	electrical machinery	15,196	16,429	25,151	33,725	34,990
	road vehicles	7,300	8,895	9,736	14,609	14,788
	other transport equipment	4,935	4,837	4,849	5,492	6,007
	Total	41,852	44,422	56,176	74,824	79,049
Miscellaneous manufactures	clothing and footwear	1,973	2,426	3,219	4,029	3,560
	scientific and photographic	4,112	4,459	5,402	6,749	6,837
	Total	13,313	13,925	17,463	21,380	20,943
Other commodities and transactions	**Total**	2,299	2,070	1,460	1,940	1,883
EXPORTS TOTAL		103,691	108,509	135,189	169,569	165,387

Source: Annual Abstract of Statistics 2000, © *Crown copyright 2000*

Imports and Exports of Manufactured Goods of the UK

(In millions of pounds. N.e.c. = not elsewhere classified.)

Item	Imports[1]			Exports[2]		
	1997	**1998**	**1999**	**1997**	**1998**	**1999**
Food products and beverages	13,313	13,253	13,056	8,997	8,402	7,785
Tobacco products	209	165	142	1,206	1,047	1,012
Textiles	5,841	5,723	5,251	3,607	3,295	2,947
Wearing apparel; dressing and dyeing of fur	5,554	5,958	6,193	2,675	2,477	2,200
Tanning and dressing of leather; luggage, handbags, saddlery, harness, and footwear	2,694	2,645	2,772	1,082	959	928
Wood and products of wood and cork, except furniture; articles of straw and plaiting materials	2,393	2,267	2,266	284	289	308
Pulp and paper products; publishing, and printing	5,217	5,149	4,887	2,391	2,274	2,072
Publishing, printing, and reproduction of recorded media	1,473	1,519	1,530	2,442	2,353	2,233
Coke, petroleum products, and nuclear fuel	1,879	1,646	2,207	4,074	2,560	3,026
Chemicals and chemical products	18,494	18,428	18,858	22,636	22,837	23,385
Rubber and plastic products	4,638	4,823	4,748	4,111	4,199	3,934
Other non-mineral products	1,913	1,976	1,904	2,127	2,002	1,799
Basic metals	8,101	8,122	6,576	7,142	6,414	5,280
Fabricated metal products, except machinery	3,756	3,945	3,961	3,662	3,764	3,600
Machinery and equipment n.e.c.	15,551	15,715	15,237	18,436	18,230	16,115
Office machinery and computers	13,977	15,666	16,752	13,229	12,728	13,204
Electrical machinery and apparatus n.e.c.	7,185	7,154	7,256	6,709	6,691	6,582
Radio and television equipment	14,232	13,979	15,115	13,223	13,998	13,824
Medical and precision instruments	5,928	6,135	6,051	6,606	6,577	6,484
Motor vehicles, trailers, and similar vehicles	22,658	23,672	25,159	16,633	16,384	16,713
Other transport equipment	8,718	9,708	9,636	11,606	11,020	11,129
Furniture; manufacturing n.e.c.	6,176	6,279	6,418	4,040	3,766	3,477

[1] Calculated on a cost, insurance, and freight basis.
[2] Calculated on a free on board basis.

Source: Business Monitor MQ10, © *Crown copyright 2000*

Main Trading Partners of the UK

(N/A = not available. In millions of pounds.)

Country/region	Imports to the UK				Exports from the UK			
	1992	**1994**	**1996**	**1998**	**1992**	**1994**	**1996**	**1998**
European Union total	72,022	83,627	101,846	102,897	65,610	77,297	97,445	95,646
Germany	19,153	22,194	27,660	25,516	15,337	17,441	21,080	20,589
France	12,305	15,223	18,135	17,913	11,608	13,728	17,397	16,450
Italy	6,808	7,609	8,964	9,900	6,196	6,873	8,169	8,611
Netherlands	9,969	10,214	12,628	13,634	8,573	9,653	13,718	12,993
Belgium and Luxembourg	5,771	7,193	8,761	9,573	5,761	7,397	8,668	8,417
Denmark	2,397	2,203	2,397	2,188	1,573	1,830	2,254	2,046
Republic of Ireland	5,095	5,985	7,368	7,920	5,788	7,204	8,816	9,600
Greece	372	358	399	370	777	938	1,166	1,046
Portugal	1,177	1,305	1,690	1,812	1,176	1,269	1,707	1,718
Spain	3,039	3,735	5,131	5,836	4,552	5,161	6,842	7,164
Sweden	3,300	4,260	4,852	4,437	2,459	3,423	4,496	4,393
Finland	1,687	2,306	2,688	2,365	1,007	1,323	1,845	1,433
Austria	949	1,042	1,173	1,433	803	1,057	1,287	1,186
Other Western Europe total	8,602	9,657	11,829	10,309	4,318	5,727	7,383	7,879
Norway	3885	3,823	4,982	3,622	1,421	2,035	2,066	2,757
Switzerland	3,919	4,818	5,403	5,042	1,845	2,460	3,206	2,984
Turkey	456	630	933	1,165	691	815	1,566	1,657
Iceland	241	240	269	264	93	110	155	164

(continued)

Main Trading Partners of the UK *(continued)*

Country/region	Imports to the UK				Exports from the UK			
	1992	**1994**	**1996**	**1998**	**1992**	**1994**	**1996**	**1998**
North America total	15,872	19,937	25,743	28,782	14,262	19,525	22,436	25,061
USA	13,715	17,729	22,809	25,656	12,231	16,909	19,831	21,954
Canada	1,898	1,883	2,485	2,598	1,584	1,917	1,975	2,204
Mexico	154	241	334	379	292	390	319	550
Other OECD countries total	10,442	12,593	14,355	15,644	5,493	7,664	10,922	8,997
Japan	7,444	8,832	8,992	9,549	2,233	3,000	4,265	3,228
Australia	1,014	1,064	1,296	1,428	1,377	1,928	2,464	2,276
South Korea	932	1,097	2,039	2,308	660	972	1,303	692
Poland	356	546	601	686	606	701	1,353	1,220
New Zealand	429	542	632	543	263	416	473	353
Czech Republic	148	278	374	579	188	374	715	714
Oil exporting countries total	3,078	3,267	3,750	3,603	6,014	5,738	8,095	7,531
Saudi Arabia	964	812	753	893	1,966	1,519	2,484	2,694
Kuwait	128	239	181	186	263	314	580	336
Indonesia	538	783	981	982	314	366	830	380
Iran	163	134	119	37	583	290	398	333
Nigeria	166	124	296	141	622	459	433	469
Rest of the world total	15,549	20,385	28,213	29,193	12,534	18,701	22,660	19,964
Eastern Europe	1,022	1,767	2,535	2,786	747	1,485	2,272	2,393
Other America	2,226	2,470	3,167	2,909	1,469	2,378	2,677	3,129
China	953	1,642	2,202	2,962	428	846	739	870
Hong Kong	2,398	3,083	4,074	4,591	1,612	2,297	2,926	2,703
India	864	1,291	1,612	1,456	946	1,312	1,706	1,259
Israel	486	572	832	920	587	1,034	1,267	1,091
Malaysia	1,104	1,204	2,381	1,992	636	1,311	1,160	684
Pakistan	273	360	391	357	312	354	344	239
Philippines	241	245	896	901	204	356	397	307
Singapore	1,193	1,896	2,573	2,463	1,147	1,769	2,144	1,620
South Africa	866	971	1,222	1,422	1,079	1,415	1,880	1,546
Taiwan	1,395	1,583	2,090	2,330	559	736	941	880
Thailand	643	914	1,189	1,330	475	749	974	394

Source: Annual Abstract of Statistics 2000,

Aid and Debt

Third World Debt

A major role of the International Monetary Fund (IMF) is to provide credits and loans to member countries with balance of payment problems. At the end of 1999, 93 countries owed the IMF some $75 billion dollars, and vast amounts have also been borrowed from financial institutions. The Heavily Indebted Poor Countries (HIPC) Initiative was adopted in 1996 to provide exceptional assistance to 40 eligible countries for reducing their external debt burdens to sustainable levels, and an associate body, the Bank for International Settlements (BIS), is building a database to provide an accurate assessment of the indebtedness of individual countries.

There is increasing pressure from numerous groups worldwide to have these debts cancelled. Protestors argue that the amount least-developed countries (LDCs) are having to pay back, with interest, means they will probably never be in a position to become stable – politically, socially, and economically. The pressure group Third World 2000 argues that: 'The poorest countries are caught in a paradox – the more they repay, the greater their debt. By 2015 their debt to export ratio will be three times worse than it was in 1994, rising to over 1,000%.' The UK-based Jubilee 2000, which has members in over 60 countries, was responsible for some 70,000 people in 1998 forming a human chain around the venue in Birmingham UK of the G7 Summit – representing the world's seven most powerful countries. Protestors called on leaders to break the chains of debt, and this was repeated a year later in Cologne, when 50,000 people swarmed onto the streets, and a petition of 17 million signatures was presented to the G7 in support of the project's aim to cancel all such debts by the Millennium. Jubilee 2000 estimated then that 52 countries owed $356 billion, and it persuaded the major world powers to promise that this problem would be alleviated with up to $100 billion in debt relief. But only $13 billion had been cancelled by mid-May 2000, when the World Bank and the IMF announced that Uganda – which owed some $3.7 billion to international creditors in 1997 – would now owe 40% less. Jubilee 2000 was unimpressed; pointing out that Uganda will still have to pay some $1 million weekly in debt repayments, despite extreme poverty.

See also **Free Trade: The Protests**, p 657.

Top 20 Countries with the Highest Foreign Debt

(In billions of dollars.)

1997 Country	Debt
Brazil	193.60
Mexico	149.70
China	146.70
Korea, South	143.30
Indonesia	136.17
Russian Federation	125.60
Argentina	123.20
India	94.40
Thailand	93.40
Turkey	91.20
Malaysia	47.20
Philippines	45.40
Poland	39.88
Israel	39.30
Cuba	34.70
Taiwan	33.50
Colombia	31.80
Chile	31.40
Algeria	30.90
Peru	30.50

The Debt Burden of the 40 Heavily Indebted Poor Countries (HIPCs)

As of May 2000. (In US$ millions, unless otherwise stated.)

Country	Total debt
Angola	12,173
Benin	1,647
Bolivia	6,078
Burkina Faso	1,399
Burundi	1,119
Cameroon	9,829
Central African Republic	921
Chad	1,091
Congo, Democratic Republic of	12,929
Congo, Republic of the	5,119
Cote d'Ivoire	14,852
Ethiopia	10,352
Ghana	5,899
Guinea	3,442
Guinea-Bissau	964
Guyana	1,653
Honduras	5,002
Kenya	7,010
Laos	2,437
Liberia	2,103
Madagascar	4,394
Malawi	2,444
Mali	3,202
Mauritania	2,589
Mozambique	8,208
Myanmar	5,680
Nicaragua	5,968
Niger	1,659
Rwanda	1,226
São Tomé and Príncipe	246
Senegal	3,861
Sierra Leone	1,243
Somalia	2,635
Sudan	16,843
Tanzania	7,603
Togo	1,448
Uganda	3,935
Vietnam	22,359
Yemen	4,138
Zambia	6,865
Total (40 countries)	$212.6 billions

Source: Jubilee 2000

Loans and Grants to Developing Countries of the World

Net flow covers loans, grants, and grant-like flows minus amortization on loans (loan repayments). Military flows are excluded. Developing countries cover countries designated by the Development Assistance Committee (DAC) as developing.
(N/A = not available. In billions of dollars.)

Net flow to developing countries, by DAC country[1]	1980	1990	1995	1997
Australia	0.9	1.5	2.5	1.3
Austria	0.3	0.6	0.9	1.7
Belgium	2.9	0.1	−0.2	−11.5
Canada	3.2	3.5	5.1	10.0
Denmark	0.8	1.1	1.8	1.9
Finland	0.2	1.0	0.6	0.4
France	11.6	5.7	12.5	14.0
Germany[2]	10.6	13.6	21.2	19.7
Ireland, Republic of	[3]	0.2	0.2	0.3
Italy	4.0	3.2	2.8	8.1
Japan	6.8	17.2	42.3	29.5
Luxembourg	N/A	N/A	0.1	0.1
Netherlands	2.4	4.0	6.8	8.1
New Zealand	0.1	0.1	0.2	0.2
Norway	0.9	1.2	1.7	1.5
Portugal	N/A	0.3	0.4	1.3
Spain	N/A	1.0	2.0	7.4
Sweden	1.9	2.8	2.2	2.1
Switzerland	2.7	3.4	1.1	−3.5
UK	12.2	6.5	13.4	19.7
USA	13.9	11.1	47.0	75.0
Total	75.4	76.4	164.6	187.6

[1] Includes flows to OPEC countries: Algeria, Ecuador, Gabon, Iran, Iraq, Kuwait, Libya, Nigeria, Qatar, Saudi Arabia, United Arab Emirates, and Venezuela. Country totals may not add to DAC total because debt forgiveness of non-official development assistance claims is not included in DAC totals.
[2] Former West Germany.
[3] Less than $50 million.

Source: Statistical Abstract of the Unites States 1999

Top 20 Recipients of International Aid from the UK

Figures are for total bilateral gross public expenditure on aid: that is, aid provided directly to governments of recipient countries, or to institutions in the UK for work on behalf of such countries.
(In thousands of pounds.)

Region	1998–99
India	113,865
Tanzania	78,924
Bangladesh	69,918
Uganda	64,307
Ghana	63,844
Malawi	52,395
Kenya	43,011
China	39,541
South Africa	34,144
Zambia	33,134
Montserrat	32,068
Russian Federation	31,234
Zimbabwe	29,391
Mozambique	29,158
Pakistan	28,608
Indonesia	25,614
Sudan	24,706
Guyana	22,893
Nepal	17,209
Rwanda	13,776
Total	847,741
Total other countries	538,343
Regional totals	
Africa	584,766
America	153,532
Asia	358,004
Europe	86,823
Pacific	20,285
World unallocated[1]	182,673
TOTAL	1,386,084

[1] Most of the expenditure not allocable by region is for assistance provided through organizations in the UK.

Source: Annual Abstract of Statistics 2000,

■ **Aid and Debt**

Overseas Development Assistance

Bilateral assistance takes various forms:

Project aid is finance for investment schemes primarily designed to increase the physical capital of the recipient country, including contributions for local and recurrent costs.

Sector-wide programmes (typically in education, health or agriculture) comprise a combination of assistance including direct budgetary aid and technical cooperation.

Programme aid is financial assistance to fund imports, sector support programmes, or budgetary expenditure, usually as part of a World Bank/IMF-coordinated structural adjustment programme.

Technical cooperation is the provision of know-how in the form of personnel, training, research, and associated costs.

Grants and other aid in kind are used to provide equipment and supplies, and support to the development work of UK and international voluntary organizations.

Humanitarian assistance comprises food aid, disaster relief, short-term refugee relief, and disaster preparedness.

Aid and Trade Provision is a special allocation to soften the terms of credit to developing countries by mixing aid funds with private export credits.

The Commonwealth Development Corporation invests in productive public or private sector projects in developing countries.

Source: Annual Abstract of Statistics, © *Crown copyright 2000*

Public Expenditure on Overseas Aid in the UK

The UK overseas development assistance programme is administered by the department for International Development (DFID). Assistance is provided in two main ways: bilateral, that is directly to governments of recipient countries or to institutions in the UK for work on behalf of such countries, or multilateral, that is to international institutions for their economic development programmes.
(In millions of pounds.)

Expenditure	1990–91	1991–92	1992–93	1993–94	1994–95	1995–96	1996–97	1997–98	1998–99
Bilateral assistance									
Department for International Development									
Project or sector aid	173.9	140.9	122.8	11908	121.8	122.7	106.8	95.9	117.6
Programme aid	151.9	118.1	136.8	121.0	113.5	82.3	94.7	84.4	134.3
Technical cooperation projects	360.5	375,8	398,6	401.6	430.4	453.1	467.7	496.0	503.9
Grants and other aid in kind	133.3	139.0	155.9	171.7	149.6	179.6	181.66	167.6	186.3
Humanitarian assistance	60.2	138.4	142.8	179.6	205.4	141.2	121.8	93.6	116.4
Debt relief	0.6	0.5	20.1	23.7	28.1	27.3	23.5	23.1	24.0
Aid and trade provision	94.4	101.2	93.1	84.7	59.9	72.8	62.3	61.1	57.1
Commonwealth Development Corporation investments	158.8	124.2	223.3	183.4	215.3	280	189.1	268.7	159.3
Other government departments	50.7	38.7	60.5	22.8	33.0	61.6	34.2	170.2	87.1
Total bilateral assistance	1,184.4	1,176,8	1,353.9	1,308.3	1,357.2	1,420.7	1,281.8	1,460.65	1,386.1
Multilateral assistance									
European Community	338.0	459.9	476.1	529.8	612.1	693.7	636.4	557.3	724.5
World Bank Group	158.8	228.2	249.7	229.6	227.7	206.9	174.4	189.9	185.3
International Monetary Fund	1.5	1.5	10.0	20.0	90.0	30.0	20.0	20,0	18,0
UN agencies	94,2	112.9	122.4	142,5	127.9	117.0	130.9	141.3	131.3
Regional development banks	32.3	69.1	91.9	76.4	71.2	69.5	58.8	60.4	66.3
Other	20.8	20.7	21.4	17.8	27.9	27.0	30.6	30.8	30.7
Total multilateral assistance	645.8	892.4	971.4	1,016.2	1,156.8	1,144.1	1,051.2	999.6	1,155.9
Administrative costs	57.9	63.2	58.8	65.3	70.3	72,9	80.3	89.7	99.6
Total gross expenditure on aid	1,888.1	2,132.4	2,384,1	2,389.8	2,584.3	2,637,7	2,413.3	2,549.9	2,641.6

Source: Annual Abstract of Statistics 2000, © *Crown copyright 2000*

Debt of the Public Sector in the UK

(In millions of pounds unless otherwise stated.)

Item	1991–92	1992–93	1993–94	1994–95	1995–96	1996–97	1997–98	1998–99
Central government gross debt total	197,997	239,950	289,219	330,063	367,586	391,916	393,880	392,394
Local government gross debt total	55,281	49,897	50,239	50,229	50,552	51,598	51,932	52,793
Central government gross debt	253,278	289,847	339,458	380,292	418,138	443,514	445,812	445,187
Central government gross debt (consolidated)[1 2]	204,012	248,239	298,357	339,436	376,719	400,804	402,245	399,636
as percentage of GDP	33.9	39.5	44.8	48.2	50.7	50.7	48.1	46.5
Public corporations gross debt	11,510	16,194	23,867	26,916	26,595	26,158	26,044	26,775
Public sector gross debt (consolidated)	202,349	244,993	294,731	334,981	370,719	393,385	394,344	392,851
Public sector liquid assets	36,252	42,686	45,272	45,667	49,468	44,888	41,468	43,439
Public sector net debt	166,097	202,307	249,459	289,314	321,251	348,497	352,876	349,412
Public sector net debt as percentage of GDP	27.6	32.2	37.5	41.1	43.2	44.1	42.2	40.6

[1] General government gross debt as reported to the European Commission under the terms of the Maastricht Treaty.
[2] Consolidated general government gross debt equals general government gross debt less central government holdings of local government debt and local government holdings of central government debt.

Source: Annual Abstract of Statistics 2000, © *Crown copyright 2000*

The UK's Public Sector Debt

The UK's public sector net debt fell by almost £3.7 billion to £349.4 billion, during the financial year to end March 1999 – the first annual reduction since 1989/90.

At end of March 1999 public sector net debt stood at 40.6% of GDP, the lowest end-March figure since 1994, and almost 2% lower than at the end of March 1998.

Currencies of the World

Currencies of the World

Country	Currency	Country	Currency
Afghanistan	afghâni	Grenada	East Caribbean dollar
Albania	lek	Guatemala	quetzal
Algeria	Algerian dinar	Guinea	Guinean franc
Andorra	French franc and Spanish peseta	Guinea-Bissau	Guinean peso
Angola	kwanza	Guyana	Guyana dollar
Antigua and Barbuda	East Caribbean dollar	Haiti	gourde
Argentina	peso	Honduras	lempira
Armenia	dram (replaced Russian rouble in 1993)	Hungary	forint
Australia	Australian dollar	Iceland	krona
Austria	schilling	India	rupee
Azerbaijan	manat (left rouble zone in 1993)	Indonesia	rupiah
Bahamas	Bahamian dollar	Iran	rial
Bahrain	Bahraini dinar	Iraq	Iraqi dinar
Bangladesh	taka	Ireland, Republic of	Irish pound (punt Eireannach)
Barbados	Barbados dollar	Israel	shekel
Belarus	rouble and zaichik	Italy	lira
Belgium	Belgian franc	Jamaica	Jamaican dollar
Belize	Belize dollar	Japan	yen
Benin	franc CFA[1]	Jordan	Jordanian dinar
Bhutan	ngultrum; also Indian currency	Kazakhstan	tenge
Bolivia	boliviano	Kenya	Kenya shilling
Bosnia-Herzegovina	dinar	Kiribati	Australian dollar
Botswana	franc CFA[1]	Korea, North	won
Brazil	real	Korea, South	won
Brunei	Brunei dollar (ringgit)	Kuwait	Kuwaiti dinar
Bulgaria	lev	Kyrgyzstan	som
Burkina Faso	franc CFA[1]	Laos	new kip
Burundi	Burundi franc	Latvia	lat
Cambodia	Cambodian riel	Lebanon	Lebanese pound
Cameroon	franc CFA[1]	Lesotho	loti
Canada	Canadian dollar	Liberia	Liberian dollar
Cape Verde	Cape Verde escudo	Libya	Libyan dinar
Central African Republic	franc CFA[1]	Liechtenstein	Swiss franc
Chad	franc CFA[1]	Lithuania	litas
Chile	Chilean peso	Luxembourg	Luxembourg franc
China	yuan	Macedonia	Macedonian denar
Colombia	Colombian peso	Madagascar	Malagasy franc
Comoros	Comorian franc	Malawi	Malawi kwacha
Congo, Democratic Republic of	Congolese franc	Malaysia	ringgit
		Maldives	rufiya
Congo, Republic of	franc CFA[1]	Mali	franc CFA[1]
Costa Rica	colón	Malta	Maltese lira
Côte d'Ivoire	franc CFA[1]	Marshall Islands	US dollar
Croatia	kuna	Mauritania	ouguiya
Cuba	Cuban peso	Mauritius	Mauritian rupee
Cyprus	Cyprus pound and Turkish lira	Mexico	Mexican peso
Czech Republic	koruna (based on Czechoslovak koruna)	Micronesia, Federated States of	US dollar
Denmark	Danish krone		
Djibouti	Djibouti franc	Moldova	leu
Dominica, Commonwealth of	East Caribbean dollar; pound sterling; French franc	Monaco	French franc
		Mongolia	tugrik
Dominican Republic	Dominican Republic peso	Morocco	dirham (DH)
Ecuador	sucre; US dollar	Mozambique	metical
Egypt	Egyptian pound	Myanmar	kyat
El Salvador	Salvadorean colón	Namibia	Namibia dollar
Equatorial Guinea	franc CFA[1]	Nauru	Australian dollar
Eritrea	Ethiopian nakfa	Nepal	Nepalese rupee
Estonia	kroon	Netherlands	guilder
Ethiopia	Ethiopian birr	New Zealand	New Zealand dollar
Fiji Islands	Fiji dollar	Nicaragua	cordoba
Finland	markka	Niger	franc CFA[1]
France	franc	Nigeria	naira
Gabon	franc CFA[1]	Norway	Norwegian krone
Gambia	dalasi	Oman	Omani rial
Georgia	lari	Pakistan	Pakistan rupee
Germany	Deutschmark	Palau	US dollar
Ghana	cedi	Panama	balboa
Greece	drachma		

(*continued*)

Currencies of the World (*continued*)

Country	Currency
Papua New Guinea	kina
Paraguay	guaraní
Peru	nuevo sol
Philippines	peso
Poland	złoty
Portugal	escudo
Qatar	Qatari riyal
Romania	leu
Russian Federation	rouble
Rwanda	Rwanda franc
St Kitts and Nevis	East Caribbean dollar
St Lucia	East Caribbean dollar
St Vincent and the Grenadines	East Caribbean dollar
Samoa	tala, or Samoa dollar
San Marino	Italian lira
São Tomé and Príncipe	dobra
Saudi Arabia	rial
Senegal	franc CFA[1]
Seychelles	Seychelles rupee
Sierra Leone	leone
Singapore	Singapore dollar
Slovak Republic	Slovak koruna (based on Czechoslovak koruna)
Slovenia	tolar
Solomon Islands	Solomon Island dollar
Somalia	Somali shilling
South Africa	rand
Spain	peseta
Sri Lanka	Sri Lankan rupee
Sudan	Sudanese dinar
Suriname	Suriname guilder
Swaziland	lilangeni
Sweden	Swedish krona
Switzerland	Swiss franc
Syria	Syrian pound
Taiwan, China	New Taiwan dollar
Tajikistan	Tajik and Russian rouble
Tanzania	Tanzanian shilling
Thailand	baht
Togo	franc CFA[1]
Tonga	Tongan dollar or pa'anga
Trinidad and Tobago	Trinidad and Tobago dollar
Tunisia	Tunisian dinar
Turkey	Turkish lira
Turkmenistan	manat
Tuvalu	Australian dollar
Uganda	Uganda new shilling
Ukraine	hryvna
United Arab Emirates	UAE dirham
UK	pound sterling (£)
USA	US dollar
Uruguay	Uruguayan peso
Uzbekistan	som
Vanuatu	vatu
Vatican City State	Vatican City lira; Italian lira
Venezuela	bolívar
Vietnam	dong
Yemen	riyal (North); dinar (South), both legal currency throughout the country
Yugoslavia	new Yugoslav dinar
Zambia	Zambian kwacha
Zimbabwe	Zimbabwe dollar

[1] CFA = Communauté Financière Africaine.

Currency in the UK

The monetary unit in use in the UK is **pound sterling** (£). The unit is divided into 100 **pence** (p).

Notes

UK notes are issued by the Bank of England in the following denominations: £5, £10, £20, and £50. Series D £10 note was withdrawn on 20 May 1994. Series E £50 note came into circulation on 20 April 1994. A new £20 note was issued on 22 June 1999, featuring a portrait of Sir Edward Elgar on the reverse.

Coins

Coins in general circulation are: nickel brass £1, cupro-nickel 5p, 10p, 20p, and 50p, and bronze 1p and 2p. 1p and 2p coins are (from September 1992) issued in copper-plated steel. A bi-colour £2 coin was issued into general circulation on 15 June 1998. Another legal tender is a nickel brass £2 coin. It was, however, issued as a commemorative coin and as such is not intended for general circulation.

Coins that remain a legal tender and can sometimes be found in circulation are silver or cupro-nickel crowns dating from 1816 onwards. These had been equivalent to 25p; in 1990 the face value of the crown changed from 25p to £5.

Gold coins dating from 1838 onwards in denominations of £1, £2, £5, and 10 shilling (= 50p) are legal tender but only at face value. Gold coins introduced in October 1987 as Britannia Gold Bullion Coins, in denominations of £100, £50, £20, and £10, are not found in general circulation.

How to Check that a Banknote Is Genuine

The following checks can be carried out on all Bank of England banknotes.

1. What does the paper feel like?

It should feel crisp and slightly rough in the heavily printed areas. It should not feel waxy, limp, or shiny.

2. Can you see the watermark?

You should be able to see the watermark (a clearly defined portrait of the Queen) when you hold the note up to the light.

3. Can you see the thread?

On current notes, you should be able to see the thread – a series of silver dashes – as a bold continuous line when you hold the note up to the light. On the majority of notes the 'windowed' thread appears on the front. The exception is the new £20 note (featuring Edward Elgar) on which the thread appears on the back.

4. What is the quality of the printing?

The lines of print should be sharp and clearly defined with pure colours. They should not be soft or fuzzy.

5. Additional checks for the £20 and £50 notes

The £20 note has a foil hologram on the front which alternates between the number 20 and an image of Britannia. There is a line of very small lettering (the word and figure 20) under the image of the Queen which can only be read with the aid of a magnifying glass. The £50 banknote has a silver foil medallion and rose to the right of the portrait of the Queen.

Euro Conversion Rates for Participating Currencies

The conversion rates for the euro for the 11 participating currencies came into effect on 1 January 1999 as follows:

Currency	Units of national currency for 1€
Austrian schilling	13.7603
Belgian franc	40.3399
Deutschmark	1.95583
Dutch guilder	2.20371
Finnish markka	5.94573
French franc	6.55957
Irish punt	0.787564
Italian lira	1,936.27
Luxembourg franc	40.3399
Portuguese escudo	200.482
Spanish peseta	166.386

Source: European Central Bank

Exchange Rates for the Euro and Other Major Currencies

Currency	1999				2000	
	January	April	July	October	January	April
Australian dollar	1.839	1.668	1.576	1.641	1.542	1.588
Canadian dollar	1.765	1.594	1.540	1.581	1.469	1.389
Danish krone	7.44	7.43	7.44	7.43	7.44	7.45
Greek drachma	323.6	325.5	325.0	329.2	331.1	335.2
Hong Kong dollar	8.99	8.30	8.03	8.32	7.89	7.38
Japanese yen	131.3	128.2	123.7	113.5	106.5	99.9
Korean won	1,362.4	1,292.2	1,229.4	1,289.9	1,145.9	1,051.4
Norwegian krone	8.65	8.32	8.18	8.29	8.12	8.15
Singapore dollar	1.950	1.834	1.756	1.793	1.697	1.620
Swedish krona	9.08	8.91	8.74	8.73	8.60	8.27
Swiss franc	1.605	1.602	1.604	1.594	1.610	1.574
UK pound	0.703	0.665	0.658	0.646	0.618	0.598
US dollar	1.161	1.070	1.035	1.071	1.014	0.947

Source: ECB Monthly Bulletin June 2000, © *European Central Bank 2000*

Key Dates on the Road to the Euro

25 March 1957 The Treaties of Rome are signed, establishing the European Economic Community (EEC), and creating the Monetary Committee and the European Investment Bank.

1–2 December 1969 Summit in The Hague, the Netherlands, requests a report, under Pierre Werner (who later led the Christian Social Party in Luxembourg 1979–84), on the possibilities of developing the Community into an economic and monetary union (EMU), stipulating 1980 as target date for launch.

22 March 1971 The Council adopts the Werner Plan to strengthen coordination of economic policies. EEC Member States commit themselves to harmonize their budgetary policies and reduce the margins of fluctuation between their currencies.

10 April 1972 The six EEC countries agree to limit the margin of fluctuation between their currencies to 2.25% they are soon joined by sterling, the Irish punt, and Danish and Norwegian krone.

6–7 July 1978 The European Council meeting in Bremen, Germany, agrees the French-German proposal to launch the European Monetary System (EMS).

13 March 1979 The European Monetary System comes into force and the Exchange Rate Mechanism (ERM) is set up with eight participating member states (the UK stays outside) required to maintain their currencies within 2.25% fluctuation margins. The Spanish peseta, Italian lira, Portuguese escudo, and sterling are allowed a 'broad band' of 6%. The European currency unit (ECU) as a weighted average of all European currencies is introduced.

10 June 1985 Committee of Governors of Central Banks of Member States adopts measures designed to strengthen EMS.

10 June 1987 The Single European Act comes into force. It formalizes the single market programme.

27–28 June 1988 European Council in Hanover, Germany, appoints a committee (chaired by the president of the European Commission, Jacques Delors) to outline 'concrete stages' leading to economic and monetary union.

19 June 1989 Spanish peseta joins ERM with 6% fluctuation bands.

26–27 June 1989 Madrid European Council decides to liberalize capital movements in Europe. Heads of state or government approve the Delors Report, and decide to begin the first stage of EMU on 1 July 1990.

1 July 1990 The first phase of EMU comes into force. It involves the removal of most of the remaining restrictions on capital movements, more intensive cooperation between central banks, and increased coordination of economic policies.

6 October 1990 The UK joins ERM with 6% bands, at 2.95 Deutschmarks per pound sterling.

9–10 December 1991 A summit of European Community heads of government in Maastricht, the Netherlands, reaches agreement on a draft treaty on European union – known as the Maastricht Treaty – which calls for closer economic and political union. Britain obtains the right to abstain from social legislation and a single currency. The treaty requires completion of EMU and the introduction of the single European currency, the ecu, by 1999 at the latest.

4 April 1992 Portuguese escudo joins ERM with 6% bands.

16–17 September 1992 Speculators attack the weaker ERM currencies; sterling, the lira, and the peseta all fall below their ERM floors. 'Black Wednesday' in the UK; sterling is withdrawn from the ERM and allowed to 'float', and the base rate returns to 12% (cut to 9% on 22 September). The Italian lira is suspended from the ERM and the Spanish peseta is devalued by 5%.

1 January 1993 The single market establishing the free movement of capital enters into force.

2 August 1993 Following speculative pressure on currencies in the ERM, the French franc dips below the ERM floor and currencies are allowed to fluctuate within a broad band of 15% on either side of central rates.

1 November 1993 The Treaty on European Union enters into force.

1 January 1994 Stage II of EMU begins and the European Monetary Institute (EMI) is established. Final deadline of 1 January 1999 is agreed for the beginning of Stage III of EMU, regardless of the number of member states qualifying and of the general economic climate.

31 May 1995 The European Commission adopts a Green Paper on 'Practical Arrangements for the Introduction of the Single Currency'.

15–16 December 1995 The European Council meeting in Madrid, Spain, names the European currency unit 'euro' and confirms the EMI plan envisaging conversion to the euro over a four-year timetable, with its introduction on 1 January 1999.

October 1996 Finnish markka joins ERM with 15% fluctuation band. The Italian lira re-enters ERM in November.

13 December 1996 A European Council meeting summit in Dublin, Ireland, makes significant progress towards the introduction of a single currency.

January 1997 EMI specifies regulatory and organizational framework for the European Central Bank and the European System of Banks.

17 June 1997 The draft Amsterdam Treaty is agreed, including resolution on ERM II. Unemployment is a large issue in the talks.

27 October 1997 In a speech before Parliament, British chancellor of the exchequer Gordon Brown says that the government does not plan to join the economic and monetary union (EMU) until at least 2002.

25 March 1998 The European Commission officially recommends that all 11 applicant EU countries – Austria, Belgium, Finland, France, Germany, Ireland, Italy, Luxembourg, the Netherlands, Portugal, and Spain – qualify for monetary union. Of the other four EU countries, Greece would not meet the economic criteria in time, and Britain, Denmark, and Sweden had already chosen not to participate in EMU from the outset.

2 May 1998 EMU commences, six months ahead of schedule. European Union heads of state formalize the creation of the euro zone and confirm the 11 countries that qualify for EMU, fix bilateral conversion rates, and agree to maintain their economies in line with the Maastricht convergence criteria. A compromise is reached over a long-standing

Currencies of the World

Key Dates on the Road to the Euro *(continued)*

dispute over who will head the new European Central Bank (ECB): Wim Duisenberg of the Netherlands is appointed to the bank's presidency for the full eight years, but will voluntarily bow to the French candidate, Jean-Claude Trichet, halfway through the term, in 2002.

July 1998 London and Frankfurt stock exchanges agree a strategic alliance, laying the foundations for a pan-European stock exchange.

3 December 1998 Euroland central banks (except Italy) cut their interest rates to 3 percent, in preparation for the launch of the euro. European central bank governors fix euro conversion rates.

1 January 1999 The single European currency, the euro, is launched in 11 participating EU countries. It performs strongly when trading begins on 4 January, but subsequently falters.

1 January 1999 to 1 January 2002 Changeover to the euro by the banking and finance industry to take place.

23 February 1999 Britain's Labour prime minister announces a rough plan or timetable for adopting the euro. The Conservative opposition strengthen their opposition to the euro.

8 April 1999 The European Central Bank cuts interest rates for the euro for the first time.

30 April 2000 Germany's opposition Christian Democrats call for a European 'currency summit' to address the sharp devaluation of the euro, which was trading at 91 cents – a fall by a quarter since its launch.

3 May 2000 The Commission proposes Greece to become the 12th member of the 'Euro-zone'.

31 May 2000 France and Germany agree, at a meeting in Berlin, to increase the powers of the hitherto informal Euro-11 group of finance ministers, threatening to create a new 'euro axis'.

The next steps

1 January 2002 European System of Central Banks (ESCB) to start circulation of euro banknotes; member states to start circulation of euro coins and complete the changeover to the euro in public administration.

1 July 2002 Member states and the ESCB will cancel the legal-tender status of national banknotes and coins.

The Euro and the UK?

The UK government has set five economic tests that must be met before any decision to join the European single currency can be made. These are:

- whether the UK has achieved sustainable convergence with the economies of the single currency
- whether there is sufficient flexibility in the UK economy to adapt to economic change
- the effect membership would have on investment in the UK
- the impact membership would have on the UK financial services industry; and
- whether joining the single currency would be good for employment

Source: Britain 2000: An Official Handbook of the United Kingdom, © *Crown copyright 2000*

Production of Euro Banknotes

By 1 January 2002, when the euro banknotes will be put into circulation, around 13 billion euro banknotes, representing a value of EUR 600 billion, will have been printed for the 11 participating countries: 9 billion banknotes to replace national banknotes and 4 billion banknotes as logistical stocks.

See also  **The European Union**, pp 280–287.

The Euro: Banknotes and Coins

There will be 7 euro notes and 8 euro coins.

Banknotes	Coins
500 euro	2 euro
200 euro	1 euro
100 euro	50 euro cent
50 euro	20 euro cent
20 euro	10 euro cent
10 euro	5 euro cent
5 euro	2 euro cent
	1 euro cent

Banking and Investment

Top 25 Banks in the World

This table is ranked by market capitalization. Market capitalization is the market value of a company's issued share capital, that is the quoted price of its shares multiplied by the number of shares issued. As of 24 April 2000.

Rank	Company	Country	Market capitalization ($ millions)
1	Citigroup Inc	USA	207,466.81
2	HSBC Holdings	UK	95,882.81
3	Morgan Stanley Dean Witter	USA	87,857.63
4	Bank of America	USA	85,739.44
5	Wells Fargo	USA	70,747.56
6	American Express	USA	66,438.31
7	Fannie Mae	USA	64,923.03
8	Bank of Tokyo-Mitsubishi	Japan	63,681.52
9	Chase Manhattan	USA	61,130.01
10	Lloyds TSB	UK	57,222.93
11	UBS	Switzerland	54,612.62
12	Nomura Securities	Japan	53,063.46
13	Credit Suisse	Switzerland	50,556.16
14	BSCH	Spain	43,270.86
15	Deutsche Bank	Germany	42,923.21
16	BBV Argentaria	Spain	42,135.45
17	Sumitomo Bank	Japan	41,858.94

(continued)

Top 25 Banks in the World (*continued*)

Rank	Company	Country	Market capitalization ($ millions)
18	Royal Bank of Scotland	UK	39,248.11
19	Merrill Lynch	USA	39,071.09
20	Barclays	UK	38,509.91
21	Goldman Sachs Group	USA	38,354.09
22	BNP Paribas	France	37,012.25
23	Schwab (Charles)	USA	36,941.53
24	Bank One	USA	35,495.92
25	Freddie Mac	USA	34,788.95

Source: FT500, *FT.com 2000,* © *Financial Times 2000*

Top 20 Banks in Europe

This table is ranked by market capitalization. Market capitalization is the market value of a company's issued share capital, that is the quoted price of its shares multiplied by the number of shares issued. As of 4 May 2000.

Rank	Bank	Country	Market capitalization ($ millions)
1	HSBC Holdings	UK	113,869.0
2	Lloyds TSB Group	UK	65,067.6
3	UBS AG	Switzerland	56,801.7
4	Credit Suisse Group	Switzerland	52,478.4
5	Deutsche Bank	Germany	49,706.2
6	BSCH	Spain	42,026.8
7	BNP Paribas	France	41,730.8
8	Fortis	Belgium/Netherlands	41,546.9
9	Barclays	UK	40,841.3
10	National Westminster Bank	UK	35,393.8
11	ABN Amro	Netherlands	35,095.5
12	Bbv Argentaria	Spain	30,095.6
13	Dresdner Bank	Germany	26,620.5
14	Bayerische Hypotheken & Vereinsbank	Germany	26,530.1
15	Halifax	UK	24,165.6
16	Unicredito Italiano	Italy	23,965.0
17	Société Generale	France	23,806.4
18	Abbey National	UK	22,360.3
19	Banca Intesa	Italy	18,811.2
20	San Paolo-IMI	Italy	18,322.7

Source: FT500, *FT.com 2000,* © *Financial Times 2000*

Top 10 Banks in the UK

This table is ranked by market capitalization. Market capitalization is the market value of a company's issued share capital, that is the quoted price of its shares multiplied by the number of shares issued. As of 24 April 2000.

Rank	Bank	Market capitalization (£ millions)
1	HSBC Holdings	69,562.56
2	Lloyds TSB Group	39,749.77
3	Barclays	24,949.98
4	National Westminster Bank	21,622.06
5	Halifax	14,762.79
6	Abbey National	13,659.88
7	Standard Chartered	9,912.58
8	Royal Bank of Scotland Group	9,526.32
9	Bank of Scotland	8,259.76
10	Woolwich	4,911.27

Source: FT500, *FT.com 2000,* © *Financial Times 2000*

Banks and Building Societies in the UK

The explosive growth of Internet banking and the conversion of many building societies into banks has led many of the traditional banks to cut costs in order to compete. This is mainly being achieved through mergers and acquisitions, which enable duplicated branches and departments to be closed, and ancillary businesses such as insurance and mortgage services to be merged.

See also **Banking**, pp 324–325.

Barclays decided to close all branches deemed to be under-utilized – assuming that customers in small communities would travel to larger centres. Many angry customers changed banks, and the cost cutting caused much bad publicity.

On the building society scene, talk of demutualization is still very much to the fore. Several major building societies were able to convert to banks because customers voted in favour, having been promised substantial windfalls. Some societies, however, have remained mutual, convincing customers that demutualization would ultimately lead to a poorer deal for investors, as the emphasis would have to switch to maximizing profits.

Meanwhile, a wave of demutualization has engulfed the life assurance industry, with three of the largest being targeted by 'carpetbaggers' – those who invest solely to gain windfalls.

■ Banking and Investment

Assets and Liabilities of the Bank of England

(In millions of pounds.)

Year	Issue department					Banking department							
	Liabilities		Assets			Liabilities				Assets			
	Notes in circulation	Notes in Banking Department	Government securities	Other securities	Total	Public deposits	Bankers' deposits	Reserves and other accounts	Total	Government securities	Advances and other accounts	Premises, equip-ment, and other securities	Notes and coin
1990	17,283	7	14,672	2,618	8,613	44	1,842	6,713	8,615	1,432	2,146	5,030	7
1991	17,466	4	11,791	5,679	5,825	104	1,813	3,894	5,825	1,346	2,443	2,031	5
1992	17,542	8	7,808	9,742	5,623	97	1,553	3,959	5,623	1,237	3,935	443	8
1993	18,218	12	6,816	11,414	11,095	6,205	1,700	3,175	11,095	1,174	9,411	498	12
1994	20,055	5	11,468	8,592	6,192	938	1,855	3,385	6,192	1,050	4,696	441	5
1995	21,262	7	14,552	6,717	7,114	1,159	2,001	3,941	7,114	1,090	5,499	518	7
1996	22,407	12	16,524	5,896	6,229	1,001	2,021	3,193	6,229	1,232	2,339	2,646	12
1997	23,715	5	16,416	7,304	7,221	1,192	2,800	3,214	7,221	1,373	5,388	455	5
1998	24,573	7	15,826	8,754	6,802	237	1,388	5,163	6,802	1,352	3,302	2,141	7

Source: Annual Abstract of Statistics 2000, © *Crown copyright 2000*

Building Societies in the UK

The figures for each year relate to accounting years ending on dates between 1 February of that year and 31 January of the following year. (N/A = not available.)

Building societies		1990	1992	1994	1996[1]	1998
Societies on register (number)		117	105	96	88	74
Share investors (number)		36,948,000	37,533,000	38,150,000	37,768,000	21,195,000
Depositors (number)		4,299,000	3,879,000	5,369,000	6,718,000	820,000
Borrowers (number)		6,724,000	7,005,000	7,222,000	6,586,000	2,934,000
Liabilities (£ millions)	shares	160,538.2	187,108.4	201,812.2	196,546.4	103,289.8
	deposits and loans	40,695.5	57,067.5	69,925.2	73,919.1	33,311.2
	taxation and other	3,768.8	2,559.5	2,939.2	3,727.4	1,586.4
	general reserves	10,206.1	12,634.4	16,312.3	17,940.3	7,926.4
	other capital	1,639.7	3,144.7	4,125.7	4,762.3	1,550.7
Assets (£ millions)	mortgages	175,745.4	210,994.5	240,297.2	241,472.9	147,664.5
	investments	35,050.9	42,909.1	50,786.7	51,016.7	118,288.4
	cash/other	6,052.0	8,610.1	4,030.7	4,405.9	27,102.0
	Total	216,848.3	262,514.5	295,114.6	296,895.5	2,274.1

[1] The societies which have converted to the banking sector, namely Cheltenham and Gloucester (August 1995), National and Provincial (August 1996), Alliance and Leicester (April 1997), Halifax (June 1997), Woolwich (July 1997), Bristol and West (July 1997), and Northern Rock (October 1997) have been included in flow figures (using flows up to the date of conversion), but have been excluded from end year balances.

Source: Annual Abstract of Statistics 2000, © *Crown copyright 2000*

See also 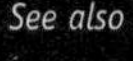 **Saving and Investing**, pp 320–322.

Average *Financial Times*/Stock Exchange (FTSE) Actuaries Share Indices

FTSE Actuaries share indices	1994	1995	1996	1997	1998
***FTSE 100*[1]**					
January	3,431.29	3,028.27	3,715.78	4,166.48	5,242.10
February	3,396.40	3,051.68	3,738.08	4,316.57	5,657.73
March	3,206.10	3,078.24	3,697.50	4,349.78	5,861.80
April	3,130.94	3,198.38	3,792.32	4,312.51	5,974.51
May	3,089.23	3,288.31	3,758.41	4,622.62	5,936.72
June	2,980.32	3,351.55	3,734.02	4,649.40	5,847.04
July	3,036.57	3,426.50	3,707.21	4,843.16	5,987.19
August	3,178.50	3,486.95	3,841.75	4,945.56	5,555.77
September	3,098.35	3,534.27	3,927.10	5,010.35	5,171.92
October	3,046.77	3,531.80	4,020.99	5,145.13	5,063.84
November	3,086.85	3,580.31	3,969.54	4,846.24	5,595.58
December	3,026.62	3,650.05	4,038.89	5,087.53	5,695.61
***FT Non-Financials*[1]**					
January	1,818.98	1,631.29	1,919.36	2,104.75	2,455.76
February	1,818.96	1,631.03	1,941.86	2,150.64	2,586.40
March	1,745.46	1,631.47	1,953.49	2,178.24	2,708.91
April	1,708.89	1,690.67	2,021.61	2,149.68	2,776.91

(*continued*)

Average *Financial Times*/Stock Exchange (FTSE) Actuaries Share Indices (*continued*)

FTSE Actuaries share indices	1994	1995	1996	1997	1998
May	1,690.44	1,738.74	2,013.00	2,219.45	2,847.14
June	1,618.42	1,767.52	1,999.60	2,231.81	2,833.04
July	1,642.28	1,806.86	1,958.89	2,284.21	2,859.68
August	1,726.77	1,846.24	2,002.27	2,326.86	2,658.60
September	1,680.38	1,868.17	2,043.06	2,369.90	2,480.53
October	1,639.72	1,851.30	2,069.12	2,439.08	2,413.68
November	1,654.73	1,854.75	2,040.44	2,332.02	2,630.55
December	1,622.39	1,879.54	2,056.24	2,401.00	2,651.00
Financials[1]					
January	2,619.71	2,084.15	2,916.24	3,674.44	4,968.04
February	2,607.79	2,125.71	2,942.72	3,919.61	5,542.60
March	2,324.02	2,170.51	2,837.38	3,876.31	5,732.81
April	2,240.03	2,264.66	2,866.93	3,825.30	5,801.80
May	2,164.18	2,350.00	2,898.78	4,331.40	5,497.77
June	2,111.15	2,411.52	2,867.16	4,281.17	5,274.89
July	2,129.92	2,466.78	2,886.69	4,468.02	5,352.53
August	2,197.58	2,526.20	3,078.43	4,647.61	4,914.36
September	2,181.71	2,599.72	3,149.04	4,634.33	4,410.37
October	2,137.44	2,691.46	3,292.82	4,787.52	4,319.56
November	2,188.27	2,805.33	3,300.68	4,407.61	4,877.76
December	2,134.40	2,879.80	3,418.82	4,756.91	4,955.84
Investment Trusts[1]					
January	3,058.15	2,609.12	3,079.31	3,198.05	3,436.17
February	3,056.69	2,604.17	3,142.90	3,328.88	3,635.46
March	2,901.35	2,583.43	3,106.91	3,340.35	3,855.17
April	2,844.45	2,648.57	3,216.41	3,234.90	3,935.37
May	2,812.57	2,762.00	3,237.58	3,377.50	4,036.89
June	2,709.20	2,791.09	3,170.26	3,422.71	3,976.40
July	2,725.64	2,874.20	3,075.76	3,453.98	3,960.55
August	2,882.04	2,938.91	3,147.91	3,512.81	3,606.48
September	2,831.12	2,969.59	3,182.58	3,493.30	3,166.36
October	2,732.79	2,924.52	3,204.46	3,534.96	3,118.92
November	2,732.46	2,932.60	3,137.47	3,275.77	3,478.60
December	2,686.29	2,998.07	3,129.25	3,370.41	3,480.98
FTSE All Share[1]					
January	1,710.35	1,501.87	1,818.72	2,041.99	2,455.05
February	1,709.09	1,506.17	1,839.78	2,105.82	2,624.19
March	1,619.80	1,511.04	1,836.04	2,121.89	2,740.51
April	1,582.06	1,566.98	1,892.47	2,092.74	2,799.69
May	1,559.27	1,614.69	1,889.96	2,203.40	2,814.73
June	1,497.44	1,643.59	1,875.05	2,207.24	2,775.66
July	1,517.70	1,680.80	1,844.67	2,269.94	2,804.19
August	1,591.47	1,718.13	1,899.46	2,324.27	2,597.71
September	1,554.01	1,743.26	1,938.37	2,357.80	2,397.79
October	1,516.65	1,739.84	1,973.94	2,422.75	2,338.00
November	1,533.46	1,755.17	1,951.91	2,293.45	2,571.19
December	1,502.42	1,783.30	1,976.41	2,388.17	2,595.88

[1] Working day average.

Source: Annual Abstract of Statistics 2000, © *Crown copyright 2000*

Share Ownership in the UK

(For the end of the given year. In billions of pounds.)

Share ownership	1990	1991	1992	1993	1994	1997	1998
Insurance companies[1]	91.0	110.2	119.8	159.8	167.2	298.8	325.5
Pension funds[1]	140.4	165.7	199.5	251.5	211.8	279.8	325.8
Individuals	90.5	105.3	125.4	141.1	154.6	208.8	250.8
Unit trusts[2]	27.3	30.4	38.0	52.7	51.8	85.2	45.6
Other financial institutions[2 3]	3.0	4.4	2.7	4.5	9.8	25.9	61.0
Charities, etc	8.2	12.8	11.2	12.5	9.9	24.3	20.4
Investments trusts	6.9	7.8	12.8	19.8	15.0	24.2	29.1
Private non-financial companies	12.7	17.6	11.3	11.7	8.7	14.8	20.9
Public sector	9.0	6.8	11.3	10.2	5.8	1.1	1.3
Banks[3]	3.2	1.1	3.0	4.7	3.0	0.8	8.4
Rest of the world	52.7	68.1	80.7	130.2	124.3	304.2	414.9
Total	444.9	530.2	615.7	798.7	761.9	1,267.9	1,503.7

[1] Data for pension funds and insurance companies were partially estimated in 1992 and 1993.
[2] For 1998 some Unit Trusts holdings have been classified to Other Financial Institutions leading to discontinuities in these sectors.
[3] Some holdings previously categorized to Bank holding companies (under Other Financial Institutions) may, for 1998, have been reclassified to Banks.

Source: Share Ownership, © *Crown copyright 2000*

■ Banking and Investment

Top 10 Most Active Stocks in the UK

1998

Rank	Company	Turnover value (£ millions)	Shares traded (millions)
1	HSBC Holdings	48,152.9	3,217.3
2	BP Amoco	39,105.9	3,948.7
3	Glaxo Wellcome	30,946.3	1,723.3
4	SmithKline Beecham	26,377.8	3,272.4
5	Shell Transport & Trading	25,496.9	6,491.3
6	Lloyds TSB	24,877.4	3,029.1
7	British Telecommunications	24,133.6	3,397.8
8	Barclays	20,325.3	1,361.0
9	Vodafone	20,011.5	2,741.5
10	National Westminster Bank	14,880.5	1,406.5

Source: London Stock Exchange Fact File 1999, © *London Stock Exchange Limited; reproduced with permission*

See also Saving and Investing, pp 320–322.

Average Rates on Representative British Government Stocks

Data show working day average.

Rate	1994	1995	1996	1997	1998
5-year conventional rate					
January	5.76	8.61	6.78	7.19	6.33
February	6.05	8.52	7.02	6.86	6.24
March	6.72	8.44	7.56	7.08	6.26
April	7.33	8.26	7.43	7.30	6.11
May	7.74	7.96	7.61	6.98	6.14
June	8.22	7.79	7.52	7.01	6.31
July	8.06	7.90	7.35	7.09	6.14
August	8.31	7.69	7.21	7.02	5.84
September	8.61	7.45	7.20	6.78	5.34
October	8.57	7.54	7.01	6.59	4.88
November	8.44	7.16	7.22	6.79	4.86
December	8.49	6.83	7.26	6.60	4.45
10-year conventional rate					
January	6.23	8.66	7.42	7.53	6.07
February	6.61	8.59	7.75	7.17	6.02
March	7.29	8.53	8.05	7.41	5.97
April	7.68	8.39	8.05	7.60	5.81
May	8.13	8.12	8.08	7.13	5.85
June	8.54	8.08	8.04	7.10	5.77
July	8.37	8.23	7.91	7.01	5.67
August	8.52	8.10	7.81	7.05	5.56
September	8.80	7.92	7.80	6.77	5.10
October	8.70	8.08	7.51	6.47	4.93
November	8.57	7.75	7.56	6.59	4.87
December	8.53	7.45	7.54	6.34	4.49
20-year conventional rate					
January	6.53	8.45	7.73	7.71	6.04
February	6.88	8.43	8.04	7.35	5.98
March	7.49	8.40	8.28	7.58	5.90
April	7.81	8.30	8.26	7.74	5.73
May	8.18	8.09	8.31	7.21	5.79
June	8.48	8.08	8.31	7.15	5.59
July	8.35	8.30	8.21	6.93	5.63
August	8.46	8.19	8.12	6.98	5.43
September	8.65	8.06	8.11	6.74	5.02
October	8.56	8.26	7.84	6.45	4.92
November	8.46	7.93	7.77	6.50	4.79
December	8.39	7.70	7.67	6.32	4.49
10-year index-linked rate					
January	2.70	3.89	3.42	3.44	3.01
February	2.81	3.87	3.57	3.23	2.94
March	3.07	3.86	3.70	3.41	2.89
April	3.25	3.79	3.66	3.55	2.80
May	3.51	3.58	3.74	3.52	2.83
June	3.78	3.58	3.80	3.62	2.81
July	3.85	3.61	3.82	3.68	2.67
August	3.82	3.52	3.59	3.59	2.55
September	3.85	3.46	3.57	3.47	2.59
October	3.84	3.65	3.41	3.17	2.66
November	3.84	3.54	3.42	3.23	2.39
December	3.85	3.45	3.41	3.01	2.11
20-year index-linked rate					
January	2.96	3.91	3.58	3.62	3.01
February	3.11	3.89	3.70	3.43	3.01
March	3.35	3.89	3.82	3.55	2.92
April	3.45	3.81	3.77	3.65	2.80
May	3.64	3.64	3.84	3.61	2.79
June	3.88	3.67	3.88	3.65	2.61
July	3.90	3.71	3.72	3.68	2.56
August	3.83	3.62	3.75	3.54	2.51
September	3.87	3.60	3.74	3.43	2.51
October	3.86	3.74	3.60	3.17	2.58
November	3.85	3.62	3.59	3.16	2.35
December	3.86	3.55	3.58	3.02	2.12

Source: Annual Abstract of Statistics 2000, © *Crown copyright 2000*

Investment of Overseas Companies in the UK

Data show net investment analysed by area and main country; includes unremitted profits. Unremitted profits are profits that are not repatriated for the UK home company.
(N = nil or negligible. A minus sign indicates a net disinvestment overseas, that is a decrease in the amount due to the investor's home country. In millions of pounds.)

Country/region	1994	1995	1996	1997	1998
Europe					
EU					
Austria	60	21	20	18	126
Belgium and Luxembourg	357	520	6	769	1,003
Denmark	76	68	151	229	197
Finland	32	−36	2	154	126
France	310	1,004	1,321	2,693	−470
Germany	71	2,090	835	1,170	205
Greece	N	N	N	N	2
Ireland, Republic of	224	−35	221	1,138	688
Italy	177	328	−184	−32	−1
Netherlands	1,915	−633	2,610	992	343
Portugal	N	N	N	N	−1

(continued)

Investment of Overseas Companies in the UK (*continued*)

Country/region	1994	1995	1996	1997	1998
Spain	21	17	66	71	80
Sweden	119	184	– 379	129	– 233
Total	3,367	3,555	4,673	7,330	2,061
EFTA					
Norway	– 131	124	1,060	– 71	– 122
Switzerland	– 44	912	1,151	1,321	12,366
Total	– 176	1,036	2,211	1,258	12,249
Other European countries					
Russian Federation[1]	0	19	61	19	N
UK offshore islands[2]	–	–	–	– 26	421
Total	– 125	36	47	24	395
Europe total	3,065	4,626	6,931	8,612	14,705
North America					
Canada	– 246	– 438	444	475	– 123
USA	2,138	9,293	6,742	10,708	21,533
North America total	1,891	8,853	7,481	N/A	21,757
Asia					
Near and Middle East countries	78	58	64	103	111
Other Asian countries					
Hong Kong	45	– 124	10	6	42
Japan	4	– 379	209	350	56
Singapore	2	40	1	17	16
South Korea	2	85	– 8	– 78	178
Total	110	– 248	348	327	382
Asia total	186	– 189	412	430	493
Australasia and Oceania					
Australia	260	– 708	1,096	1,219	940
New Zealand	127	60	– 104	– 7	– 113
Australasia and Oceania total	387	– 647	992	1,211	826
Africa					
South Africa	50	125	109	149	603
Africa total	63	117	118	161	853
OECD total	5,346	12,511	15,235	21,250	36,782
Central and Eastern Europe total	– 141	15	– 19	13	– 1
WORLD TOTAL	6,046	12,654	15,662	21,751	38,633

[1] Prior to 1995 Russian Federation covers other former USSR countries, the Baltic States, and Albania.
[2] The UK offshore islands consist of the Channel Islands and the Isle of Man, excluded from the definition of the economic territory of the UK from 1997.

Source: Business Monitor MA4, Overseas Direct Investment 1998, © *Crown copyright 1999*

See also **Major Foreign Acquisitions of UK Companies**, p 679.

Investment Overseas by UK Companies

Data show net investment analysed by area and main country; includes unremitted profits. Unremitted profits are profits that are not repatriated for the UK home company.
(A minus sign indicates a net disinvestment overseas, that is a decrease in the amount due to the UK. NA = not available. In millions of pounds.)

Country	1994	1995	1996	1997	1998
Europe					
EU					
Austria	102	90	102	10	26
Belgium and Luxembourg	132	438	991	1,521	– 703
Denmark	64	416	– 176	118	– 92
Finland	26	112	28	– 5	105
France	423	1,515	2,375	1,520	908
Germany	1,261	1,478	1,184	1,273	1,409
Greece	84	163	106	303	303
Ireland, Republic of	100	776	755	398	1,135
Italy	298	406	421	442	496
Netherlands	4,615	2,953	6,577	8,544	7,492
Portugal	169	159	56	86	– 15
Spain	460	431	735	911	– 169
Sweden	546	522	277	370	555
Total	8,278	9,457	13,432	15,489	11,444
EFTA					
Norway	662	– 255	96	1,999	627
Switzerland	– 16	– 338	– 110	320	8,016
Total	645	– 594	– 12	2,320	8,652
Other European countries					
Russian Federation[1]	115	39	132	456	– 170
UK offshore islands[2]	N/A	N/A	N/A	– 864	2,447
Total	317	322	– 97	1,927	2,708
Europe total	9,241	9,184	13,321	19,735	22,804

(continued)

Investment Overseas by UK Companies *(continued)*

Country	1994	1995	1996	1997	1998
America					
Bermuda	349	291	142	−44	460
Brazil	291	473	692	355	322
Canada	−4	244	−159	779	582
Chile	76	220	89	156	171
Colombia	204	123	100	242	N
Mexico	42	79	110	762	145
Panama	94	75	103	599	319
USA	6,549	11,840	1,837	11,288	45,709
America total	8,464	13,460	3,277	14,711	49,360
Asia					
Near and Middle East countries					
Gulf Arabian countries	250	116	30	280	1,534
Total	253	154	28	373	1,646
Other Asian countries					
Hong Kong	128	734	730	−348	1,525
India	87	61	110	182	208
Indonesia	92	−28	155	80	32
Japan	245	169	378	384	21
Malaysia	286	28	184	755	612
Singapore	590	−48	535	329	−5,581
South Korea	27	47	32	16	231
Thailand	177	245	194	106	187
Total	1,796	1,503	2,794	2,117	−2,388
Asia total	2,049	1,657	2,823	2,490	−742
Australasia and Oceania					
Australia	625	2,258	1,472	1,240	215
New Zealand	264	67	244	257	−116
Australasia and Oceania total	959	2,596	1,843	1,336	211
Africa					
Kenya	9	67	24	61	40
Nigeria	−197	−271	−94	234	−87
South Africa	170	466	−25	401	−210
Zimbabwe	28	16	25	7	42
Africa total	327	707	561	684	46
OECD total	16,880	23,686	17,545	32,743	67,449
Central and Eastern Europe total	168	194	201	1,695	460
WORLD TOTAL	21,040	27,604	21,823	38,957	71,678

[1] Prior to 1995 Russian Federation covers other former USSR countries, the Baltic States, and Albania.
[2] The UK offshore islands consist of the Channel Islands and the Isle of Man, excluded from the definition of the economic territory of the UK from 1997.

Source: Business Monitor MA4, Overseas Direct Investment 1998, *© Crown copyright 1999*

Business and Industry

Corporations and Companies

Top 25 Companies in the World

Market capitalization is the market value of a company's issued share capital, that is the quoted price of its shares multipled by the number of shares issued. As of 24 April 2000.

Rank	Company	Country	Market capitalization ($ millions)
1	General Electric	USA	534,046.40
2	Cisco Systems	USA	434,066.80
3	Intel	USA	388,089.40
4	Microsoft	USA	346,773.10
5	NTT DoCoMo	Japan	319,714.30
6	Vodafone Airtouch	UK	291,934.90
7	Exxon Mobil	USA	277,956.20
8	Wal-Mart Stores	USA	262,231.20
9	Nokia	Finland	241,308.10
10	Citigroup	USA	207,466.80
11	NTT	Japan	207,261.50
12	Oracle	USA	205,607.10
13	Deutsche Telekom	Germany	199,716.40

(continued)

Top 25 Companies in the World (*continued*)

Rank	Company	Country	Market capitalization ($ millions)
14	Toyota Motor	Japan	198,011.80
15	Royal Dutch/Shell	Netherlands/UK	195,801.50
16	Lucent Technologies	USA	193,240.80
17	BP Amoco	UK	191,071.50
18	International Business Machines	USA	191,035.50
19	American International Group	USA	172,343.70
20	Pfizer	USA	167,431.50
21	Merck	USA	166,648.50
22	Ericsson	Sweden	165,400.30
23	France Telecom	France	158,967.30
24	AT&T	USA	156,742.60
25	Sun Microsystems	USA	153,077.60

Source: FT500, *FT.com 2000,* © *Financial Times 2000*

Top 25 Companies in Europe

Market capitalization is the market value of a company's issued share capital, that is the quoted price of its shares multiplied by the number of shares issued.
(- = not applicable.) As of 4 May 2000.

Rank	Company	Country	Market capitalization ($ millions)
1	Deutsche Telekom	Germany	209,628.10
2	Nokia	Finland	208,077.40
3	Royal Dutch/Shell	Netherlands/UK	205,582.50
4	BP Amoco	UK	190,087.80
5	British Telecommunications	UK	151,549.40
6	Vodafone Airtouch	UK	150,081.50
7	France Telecom	France	131,035.70
8	Ericsson	Sweden	129,559.40
9	Mannesmann	Germany	117,315.80
10	HSBC Holdings	UK	113,869.00
11	Roche	Switzerland	108,390.10
12	Novartis	Switzerland	104,559.20
13	Glaxo Wellcome	UK	100,725.00
14	Total Fina	France	94,605.50
15	Telefonica	Spain	80,661.70
16	Allianz	Germany	80,567.70
17	DaimlerChrysler	Germany	75,625.80
18	Siemens	Germany	73,734.00
19	AstraZeneca	UK	71,275.80
20	T.I.M.	Italy	71,006.10
21	Nestlé	Switzerland	70,963.90
22	Telecom Italia	Italy	70,946.30
23	SmithKline Beecham	UK	69,639.40
24	Lloyds TSB Group	UK	65,067.60
25	Aegon	Netherlands	64,065.80

Source: FT500, *FT.com,* © *Financial Times 2000*

Top 25 Companies in the UK

Market capitalization is the market value of a company's issued share capital, that is the quoted price of its shares multiplied by the number of shares issued.
As of 24 April 2000.

Rank	Company	Market capitalization (£ millions)
1	BP Amoco	116,124.63
2	British Telecommunications	92,581.50
3	Vodafone Airtouch	91,684.81
4	HSBC Holdings	69,562.56
5	Glaxo Wellcome	61,532.88
6	Shell Transport & Trading Company	48,041.80
7	AstraZeneca	43,542.39
8	SmithKline Beecham	42,542.69
9	Lloyds TSB Group	39,749.77
10	Marconi	27,956.57
11	Cable & Wireless	25,249.39
12	Barclays	24,949.98
13	Prudential Corporation	22,353.77
14	National Westminster Bank	21,622.06
15	Colt Telecom Group	19,889.94
16	Diageo	17,094.08
17	British Sky Broadcasting Group	16,784.18
18	Anglo American	16,305.84
19	Rio Tinto	15,585.86
20	Halifax	14,762.79
21	Abbey National	13,659.88
22	Cable & Wireless Communications	13,289.88
23	Unilever	13,276.24
24	British Gas	12,749.43
25	Tesco	12,360.81

Source: FT500, *FT.com,* © *Financial Times 2000*

■ Business and Industry

The Dot-Com Bubble

In March 2000, the *Financial Times* Stock Exchange (FTSE) 100, the group of companies whose share performance serves as a barometer for the UK economy, underwent a shakeup. Out went several established, profitable, but seemingly old-fashioned companies from this index of blue-chip shares, and in came nine new technology companies and one media group. Among the 'casualties' were household names such as Hanson Trust and Imperial Tobacco, while the newcomers included the Internet service provider Freeserve and the palmtop computer manufacturer Psion. Freeserve, which was floated on the London Stock Exchange and New York's Nasdaq stock market in 1999 with a market value of £2.07 billion, had yet to make a profit. But their inclusion in the FTSE 100 was an indication that stock market investors were willing to believe that they had a bright profitable future and that e-commerce was the new way to do business.

Several Internet-based (so-called 'dot-com') companies went public in 2000, but none had quite the glamour that was associated with the company Lastminute.com. This Internet trader offers last-minute deals on everything from hotel rooms to opera tickets and flights. But like so many 'dot-com' businesses it had yet to make a profit at the time of flotation and its revenues in the last quarter of 1999 were only £409,000. Nevertheless, when it was launched on the London Stock Exchange on 14 March, Lastminute.com was valued at £733 million. Within three days, however, the value had fallen to £587 million. Some economists wondered whether such a fall indicated that investors were taking a more realistic view about the potential profitability of dot-com companies that had yet to prove themselves. In fact the fall had resulted from numerous private investors cashing in the 35 shares that they had each been allocated. For many, e-commerce represents a rosy economic future. At a European Union summit meeting in Lisbon, Portugal, held in March 2000, UK prime minister Tony Blair promoted plans to liberalize telecommunications and widen trade over the Internet in order to narrow the gap in e-commerce between Europe and the USA.

Major Companies by Industry Group in the UK

Rank	Company	Sales (£ millions)
Agriculture, forestry, and fishing		
1	PIC International Group plc	3,260.30
2	Grampian Foods Ltd	469,08
3	Linton Park plc	196.78
4	Moy Park Ltd	175.50
5	Hillesden Investments Ltd	150.69
6	Webbs Country Foods Ltd	136.47
7	Baker, F W, Ltd	132.63
8	Sovereign Food Group Ltd	131.05
9	Daylay Foods Ltd	120.10
10	Faccenda Group Ltd	119.14
Mining		
1	BP Amoco plc	44,731.00
2	BG plc	9,453.00
3	Shell UK Ltd	6,709.00
4	Rio Tinto plc	4,290.00
5	AMEC plc	2,721.90
6	Total Oil Holdings Ltd	2,453.47
7	Elf Petroleum UK plc	1,807.80
8	BP Exploration Operating Co Ltd	1,703.75
9	Hunting plc	981.80
10	BP Exploration Co Ltd	862.51
Construction		
1	BICC plc	3,670.00
2	Tarmac Holdings plc	2,912.60
3	Balfour Beatty Ltd	2,018.50
4	Mowlem, John, and Co Ltd	1,493.60
5	Laing, John, plc	1,476.50
6	Wimpey, George, plc	1,401.80
7	Taylor Woodrow plc	1,400.50
8	Carillion Construction Ltd	1,203.13
9	Laing Construction plc	1,197.50
10	Kvaerner Construction Group Ltd	1,066.46
Manufacturing of food and related products		
1	Unilever plc	27,094.00
2	Diageo plc	17,698.00
3	Tomkins plc	5,344.70
4	Bass plc	4,609.00
5	Wittington Investments Ltd	4,228.00
6	Associated British Foods plc	4,195.00
7	Tate & Lyle plc	4,117.30
8	Cadbury Schweppes plc	4,106.00
9	United Distillers & Vintners (ER) Ltd	3,607.00
10	Scottish & Newcastle plc	3,293.90

(continued)

Major Companies by Industry Group in the UK (*continued*)

Rank	Company	Sales (£ millions)
Transportation, communication, power generation and distribution, and other services		
1	British Telecommunications plc	16,953.00
2	British Airways plc	8,915.00
3	Centrica plc	7,481.00
4	The Post Office	6,759.00
5	British Gas Trading Ltd	6,327.00
6	Peninsular and Oriental Steam Navigation Co	5,911.70
7	Vodafone Airtouch plc	3,360.00
8	Swire, John & Sons, Ltd	3,249.00
9	Scottish Power UK plc	3,242.30
10	National Power plc	3,009.00
Communications		
1	British Telecommunications plc	16,953.00
2	Vodafone Airtouch plc	3,360.00
3	Cable & Wireless Communications plc	2,621.00
4	British Broadcasting Corporation	2,481.00
5	Cable & Wireless Communications (Mercury) Ltd	1,669.80
6	British Sky Broadcasting Group plc	1,545.00
7	British Sky Broadcasting Ltd	1,411.62
8	Vodafone Ltd	1,342.40
9	Orange plc	1,212.70
10	Cellnet Group Ltd	1,171.71
Wholesale trade durable goods		
1	Compaq Computer Group Ltd	4,258.19
2	Honda Motor Europe Ltd	2,809.10
3	Sony United Kingdom Ltd	2,173.78
4	Daimlerchrysler UK Ltd	2,066.69
5	Amalgamated Metal Corporation plc	2,010.23
6	Computacenter plc	1,586.23
7	Littlewoods Retail Ltd	1,533.59
8	BPB plc	1,315.30
9	Meyer International plc	1,282.20
10	Hitachi Europe Ltd	970.75
Wholesale trade non-durable goods		
1	Alliance Unichem plc	5,353.40
2	ABF Investments plc	4,195.00
3	Hillsdown Holdings Ltd	3,209.10
4	Booker Belmont Wholesale Ltd	2,395.93
5	Palmer & Harvey McLane (Holdings) Ltd	2,371.90
6	Palmer & Harvey McLane Ltd	2,294.10
7	Bunzl plc	1,939.30
8	AAH Pharmaceuticals Ltd	1,904.00
9	Aah Ltd	1,782.40
10	Nurdin & Peacock Cash & Carry Ltd	1,431.16
Retail trade		
1	Tesco plc	17,158.00
2	Tesco Stores Ltd	14,515.00
3	Sainsbury's Supermarkets Ltd	12,209.00
4	Asda Group plc	8,866.70
5	Marks & Spencer plc	8,224.00
6	Asda Stores Ltd	7,600.83
7=	Safeway Stores plc	7,510.70
	Safeway plc	7,510.70
9	Kingfisher plc	7,457.80
10	Somerfield plc	5,897.90

Source: Key British Enterprises, British Business Rankings 2000, *Dun and Bradstreet 2000*

Fastest-Growing Companies in Britain

Ranked by growth of turnover.

1998–99

Rank	Company	Business activity	Turnover (£ millions)	Profit (£ millions)	Profit (%)	Profit growth (%)	Turnover growth (%)
1	Posthouse Hotels Ltd	hoteliers	430,201,000	42,853,000	9.96	601	1,579
2	The Global Travel Group plc	travel agency franchising company	14,735,670	48,097	0.33	74	1,450
3	Action	holding company	172,095,000	5,084,000	2.95	637	1,432
4	D P Mann Ltd	insurance underwriters	14,595,108	7,343,426	50.31	799	1,287
5	Virgin Management Ltd	transportation services	397,198,000	13,541,000	3.41	233	765
6	Market Link Publishing plc	magazine and periodical publishers	4,956,106	763,331	15.40	311	664
7	Electronique Group Ltd	holding company – electrical components manufacturing companies	14,678,000	8,000	0.05	104	491

(*continued*)

Fastest-Growing Companies in Britain *(continued)*

Rank	Company	Business activity	Turnover (£ millions)	Profit (£ millions)	Profit (%)	Profit growth (%)	Turnover growth (%)
8	Incepta Group plc	financial and corporate communications group	88,171,000	5,611,000	6.36	248	424
9	NCR (UK) Group Ltd	holding company	559,433,000	39,178,000	7.00	154	419
10	UPM-Kymmene Ltd	paper wholesalers	437,132,000	2,083,000	0.48	291	383
11	Banks Hoggins O'Shea	advertising agents	28,462,348	678,737	2.38	26	317
12	Blane Leisure Ltd T/A Sports Division	sports wear and goods retailers	231,422,000	21,743,000	9.40	188	309
13	Roach Bridge Holdings plc	holding company	3,461,897	25,126	0.73	777	306
14	Morelock Signs Ltd	road signs manufacturers	4,417,829	60,315	1.37	5	303
15	Polestar Petty Ltd	intermediate holding company – printers	4,244,000	7,200,000	169.65	30	299
16	Avicore Ltd	holding company	17,755,000	2,456,000	13.83	264	283
17	Jordec Group plc	holding company	27,497,000	506,000	1.84	182	263
18	Planet Online Ltd	Internet access provider	24,729,026	535,503	2.17	170	252
19	Baan UK Ltd	computer software marketers	25,825,851	3,595,227	13.92	389	236
20	Solent & Pratt (Engineering) Ltd	butterfly valves manufacturers	5,380,374	783,501	14.56	604	235
21	Flights Travel Group Ltd	travel agents, holiday company, and conference organizers	13,173,742	273,435	2.08	328	228
22	Vocalis Group plc	holding company	6,232,000	72,000	1.16	104	211
23	J L A Group Ltd	holding company	13,684,367	897,549	6.56	78	189
24	Shotton Paper Co plc	newsprint manufacturers	182,981,000	34,804,000	19.02	113	184
25	Progressive Computer Recruitment Ltd	employment agency	31,009,286	2,784,870	8.98	659	177

Source: Reproduced from National Star Performers 1998–99, *with the permission of the publisher, Holcot Press Ltd*

Major Take-Overs and Mergers in the UK

Companies	Value (£ billions)	Date reported
SmithKline Beecham/Glaxo	130	18 January 2000
Vodafone Airtouch/Mannesmann	112	10 February 2000
BP/Amoco	67	31 December 1998
Vodafone/Airtouch	42	19 January 1999
Astra/Zeneca	24	6 April 1998
NatWest/Royal Bank of Scotland	21	11 February 2000
NatWest/Legal & General	11	5 September 1999
Glaxo/Wellcome	9.1	30 March 1995
Lloyds/Scottish Widows	7	23 June 1999
HSBC/Republic Bank of New York	6	31 December 1999
Lloyds/TSB	5	28 December 1995

Major Foreign Acquisitions of UK Companies

Major acquisitions, June 1998 to July 2000.

Target	Acquirer	Value (£ billions)	Date reported
Orange plc	Mannesmann AG (Germany)	19.8	23 November 1999
ASDA Group plc	Wal-Mart Stores Inc (USA)	6.72	26 July 1999
Arjo Wiggins Teape Appleton plc	Worms and Cie (France)	2.19	25 July 2000
Thomson Travel Group plc	Preussag AG (Germany)	1.8	27 July 2000
Racal Electronics plc	Thomson CSF (France)	1.32	15 June 2000
United Biscuits (Holdings) plc	Finalrealm (France/Europe)	1.26	17 April 2000
Select Appointments plc	Vedior NV (Netherlands)	1.15	21 October 1999
BTP plc	Clariant AG (Germany)	1.08	3 March 2000
Meyer International plc	Compagnie de Saint Goban (France)	1.04	14 March 2000
Kwik-Fit Holdings plc	FAH Investments (USA)	1.01	7 June 1999

See also **Investment of Overseas Companies in the UK**, p 673.

Rates of Corporation Tax in the UK

The rates of company tax in the UK are lower than in most other industrialized countries. Companies pay corporation tax on their income and capital gains after deduction of certain allowances and reliefs. A company that distributes profits to its shareholders is required to pay advance corporation tax (ACT) on these distributions to the Inland Revenue. ACT is set against the company's liability to corporation tax, subject to a limit. In the budget of March 1998 the government announced the abolition of advance corporation tax from April 1998, and its intention to introduce a new instalment system for the payment of large companies' corporation tax. Shareholders (except pension schemes and companies) resident in the UK receiving distributions from UK-resident companies are treated as having some or all their liability to income tax satisfied for such income.

Rates of Corporation Tax in the UK *(continued)*

The main rate of corporation tax was reduced from 31% to 30% from April 1999, and the reduced rate for smaller companies (those with profits below £300,000 a year) was reduced from 21% to 20%. Relief is allowed for companies with profits between £300,000 and £1.5 million, so that the company's overall rate is between the main rate and the small companies' rate. From April 2000 there was a new 10% rate of corporation tax for profits up to £10,000; this benefits companies with profits up to £50,000. The government announced in the budget of March 1999 its intention to introduce tax credits for research and development spending by small and medium-sized companies. Some capital expenditure may qualify for relief in the form of capital allowances. Examples include expenditure on machinery and plant, industrial buildings, agricultural buildings, and scientific research. Expenditure on machinery or plant by small or medium-sized businesses qualifies for a first-year allowance. This was introduced in 1997 and set at the rate of 50% if the expenditure was incurred in the year to July. This scheme was extended from 1 July 1999 to 1 July 2000 at the rate of 40%.
(– = not applicable.)

Financial year commencing 1 April	Full rate (%)	Advance rate on distributions	Small companies			
			Rate (%)	Range of profit for marginal relief		Marginal relief fraction
				Lower limit (£)	Upper limit (£)	
1990	34	$\frac{25}{75}$	25	200,000	1,000,000	$\frac{9}{400}$
1991	33	$\frac{25}{75}$	25	250,000	1,250,000	$\frac{1}{50}$
1992	33	$\frac{25}{75}$	25	250,000	1,250,000	$\frac{1}{50}$
1993	33	$\frac{9}{31}$	25	250,000	1,250,000	$\frac{1}{50}$
1994	33	$\frac{20}{80}$	25	300,000	1,500,000	$\frac{1}{50}$
1995	33	$\frac{20}{80}$	25	300,000	1,500,000	$\frac{1}{50}$
1996	33	$\frac{20}{80}$	24	300,000	1,500,000	$\frac{9}{400}$
1997	31	$\frac{20}{80}$	21	300,000	1,500,000	$\frac{1}{40}$
1998	31	$\frac{20}{80}$	21	300,000	1,500,000	$\frac{1}{40}$
1999	30	–[3]	20	300,000	1,500,000	$\frac{1}{40}$
2000	30	–[3]	20	300,000	1,500,000	$\frac{1}{40}$

[1] Chargeable gains realized after 16 March 1987 are taxed at the same rate as income.
[2] Normal corporation tax rates apply from 1985 after abolition of the special rate.
[3] Abolished April 1999.

Source: Inland Revenue Statistics 1999 *and* Britain 1999: The Official Yearbook of the United Kingdom, *© Crown copyright 1999; with Helicon updates*

See also 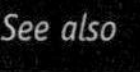 **Taxation,** pp 331–333.

Company Insolvencies by Industry in England and Wales

Industry		1994	1995	1996	1997	1998
Agriculture and horticulture		166	99	89	51	65
Manufacturing	food, drink, and tobacco	142	130	163	93	89
	chemicals	108	69	65	31	57
	metals and engineering	932	681	658	591	594
	textiles and clothing	736	567	568	596	526
	timber and furniture	252	267	249	181	149
	paper, printing, and publishing	579	452	438	364	426
	other	859	681	599	613	652
	Total	3,608	2,847	2,740	2,469	2,493
Construction and transport	construction	2,401	1,844	1,610	1,419	1,325
	transport and communication	774	706	682	540	504
	Total	3,175	2,550	2,292	1,959	1,829
Wholesaling	food, drink, and tobacco	244	205	183	158	139
	motor vehicles	112	83	95	41	60
	other	638	678	429	340	364
	Total	994	966	707	539	563
Retailing	food, drink, and tobacco	299	246	236	219	186
	motor vehicles and filling stations	226	195	227	132	120
	other	1,186	1,127	956	891	847
	Total	1,711	1,568	1,419	1,242	1,153
Services	financial institutions	259	198	222	111	101
	business services	1,807	1,525	1,500	1,528	1,617
	hotels and catering	777	692	708	609	626
	Total	2,843	2,415	2,430	2,248	2,344
	Other	4,231	4,091	3,784	4,102	4,756
TOTAL		16,728	14,536	13,461	12,610	13,203

Source: Annual Abstract of Statistics 2000, *© Crown copyright 2000*

See also **Bankruptcy Proceedings in England and Wales,** p 470.

Business and Industry

Business Sites by UK Region

In percentages unless otherwise stated.

1998 Region	Agriculture, hunting, forestry, and fishing	Mining and quarrying, energy, water supply, and manufacturing	Construction	Distribution hotels and catering; repairs	Transport and communication	Financial intermediation, real estate, renting, and business activities	Education and health	Public administration and other services	Total business sites (= 100%) (thousands)
North East	6.5	8.5	8.0	33.9	4.5	18.7	8.2	11.6	74.7
North West	5.7	9.2	8.2	34.0	4.5	22.0	6.6	9.8	251.9
Yorkshire and the Humber	7.6	9.8	8.8	33.6	4.8	19.1	6.7	9.6	186.8
East Midlands	8.4	11.6	9.5	30.8	4.8	19.8	6.3	8.8	168.2
West Midlands	7.1	12.0	9.1	31.2	4.3	20.8	6.4	9.1	206.4
East	6.9	9.1	11.0	27.7	4.8	25.7	5.6	9.2	238.5
London	0.3	7.2	5.9	27.6	4.0	36.8	5.4	12.8	370.6
South East	4.1	8.1	10.0	27.2	3.9	30.0	6.3	10.3	366.3
South West	12.3	8.0	9.8	29.9	3.8	20.6	6.5	9.1	227.1
England	5.9	9.0	8.8	29.9	4.3	25.6	6.2	10.2	2,090.4
Wales	16.7	7.4	9.4	30.9	4.2	14.9	6.2	10.3	115.7
Scotland	12.2	6.8	7.8	32.0	4.2	18.6	6.6	11.8	198.7
Northern Ireland	25.5	6.6	9.6	26.4	3.5	10.4	9.4	8.6	74.6
UK total	7.5	8.7	8.8	30.0	4.3	24.1	6.4	10.3	2,479.4

Source: Regional Trends 34, © *Crown copyright 1999*

See also 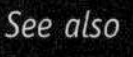 **Employment and Unemployment in the UK**, pp 105–111.

Business Registrations and Deregistrations in the UK

Figures show enterprises registered for VAT. An enterprise is defined as a legal unit, person, or group of people producing goods or services under their own control and with their own legal identity. A branch or office of a larger organization is not in itself an enterprise. There may be one or more VAT units within an enterprise.

Region	Registrations	Deregistrations	Net change (%)	Registration rates[1]	Deregistration rates[1]	End-year stock
1996						
England						
North East	4,100	4,500	−0.4	20	22	42,000
North West	16,500	17,200	−0.8	30	32	156,600
Yorkshire and the Humber	11,300	12,000	−0.7	28	30	117,700
East Midlands	10,800	11,400	−0.5	33	34	109,500
West Midlands	13,300	13,700	−0.4	32	33	134,800
Eastern	16,100	15,600	0.5	38	37	157,500
London	34,100	29,300	4.7	61	52	249,800
South East	27,100	25,700	1.4	43	41	241,800
South West	13,800	14,300	−0.5	35	37	147,100
Total	147,100	143,700	3.4	38	37	1,356,700
Wales	6,100	6,800	−0.6	26	29	75,400
Scotland	11,300	11,500	−0.3	28	28	117,500
Northern Ireland	3,700	3,100	0.6	30	25	53,500
TOTAL UK	168,200	165,100	3.1	36	35	1,603,200
1997						
England						
North East	4,200	4,400	−0.2	20	21	41,800
North West	18,100	17,100	1.0	33	32	157,600
Yorkshire and the Humber	11,800	12,300	−0.4	30	31	117,200
Est Midlands	11,700	11,200	0.5	36	34	110,000
West Midlands	13,600	13,900	−0.3	33	33	134,600
Eastern	18,300	15,800	2.5	43	37	160,000
London	37,200	28,300	8.9	66	50	258,700
South East	30,000	25,700	4.3	48	41	246,100
South West	15,300	14,400	0.9	39	37	148,000
Total	160,200	143,000	17.2	41	37	1,374,000
Wales	6,200	6,300	−0.1	27	27	75,300
Scotland	12,300	11,500	0.7	30	28	118,300
Northern Ireland	3,900	3,600	0.2	31	29	53,800
TOTAL UK	182,600	164,500	18.1	39	35	1,621,300

[1] Registrations and deregistrations during the year per 10,000 of the resident adult population.

Source: Regional Trends 34, © *Crown copyright 1999*

Companies Spending the Most on Research and Development in the UK

Total expenditure on scientific research and development in 1997 was £14.7 billion – 1.8% of GDP (compared to 1.94% in 1996). Expenditure on civil research and development was £12.5 billion in 1996, the rest going to defence projects. Research and development spending includes spending overseas.

1997

Rank	Company	Annual investment (£ millions)	As % of sales
1	Glaxo Wellcome	1,163	15
2	SmithKline Beecham	910	11
3	AstraZeneca[1]	708	13
4	Unilever	556	2
5	Shell	480	1
6	Ford Automotive	434	5
7	British Aerospace	430	6
8	General Electric	394	6
9	Pfizer	313	99[2]
10	BT	307	2

[1] Formed in 1999 from the merger of Astra of Sweden and Zeneca.
[2] Pfizer's UK sales have been low, but much of their research and development is in Britain.

Source: Britain 2000: The Official Yearbook of the United Kingdom, © *Crown copyright 1999*

Wealthiest Executives in the UK

(N/A = not available. – = not applicable.)

Director	Company	Financial year ending	Pay (£)	% change
Top 10 pay increases for directors of publicly quoted companies				
David Gruber	MEPC	September 1998	5,521,687	1,287.4
Dominic Cadbury	Cadbury Schweppes	December 1998	1,540,000	129.2
Jeremy Heath-Lewis	Eidos	March 1999	3,926,334	111.2
Greg Dyke	Pearson	December 1998	768,000	107.0
Stanley Fink	ED & F Man	March 1999	2,213,000	104.7
Ian Blackburn	Perkins Foods	December 1998	530,000	94.9
Douglas Fairservice	Candover Investments	December 1998	550,101	87.6
Charles Cornwall	Eidos	March 1999	1,121,153	87.5
Brian Wallace	Ladbroke	December 1998	858,000	86.5
Derek Wanless	National Westminster Bank	December 1998	832,000	84.9
Top 10 directors of publicly quoted companies (£1 million or more a year)				
David Gruber	MEPC	September 1998	5,521,687	1,287.4
Jeremy Heath-Lewis	Eidos	March 1999	3,926,334	111.2
Larry Fish	Royal Bank of Scotland	September 1998	3,224,000	49.1
Charles Brady	Amvescap	December 1998	2,761,000	11.1
Stanley Fink	ED & F Man	March 1999	2,213,000	104.7
Robert H Graham	Amvescap	December 1998	2,112,000	15.7
Ken Berry	EMI	March 1999	2,060,200	–
Martin Bandier	EMI	March 1999	2,052,200	–
Jan Leschly	SmithKline Beecham	December 1998	1,919,000	–20.3
Richard Sykes	Glaxo Wellcome	December 1998	1,863,000	8.1
The celebrity top 10				
Sting	Steerpike	July 1997	10,718,000	N/A
Elton John	Happenstance/J Bondi	July 1997	5,797,253	N/A
Phil Collins	Philip Collins	December 1997	5,460,000	N/A
Mark Knopfler	Chariscourt	March 1998	2,311,712	N/A
Paul McCartney	Apple Corps/MPL	January and December 1998	2,048,431	N/A
George Harrison	Apple Corps	January 1998	1,678,250	N/A
Yoko Ono	Apple Corps	January 1998	1,678,250	N/A
Ringo Starr	Apple Corps	January 1998	1,528,250	N/A
David Gilmour	David Gilmour Music	June 1998	1,513,626	N/A
Annie Lennox or Dave Stewart	DnA (the Eurythmics' company)	March 1998	1,483,702	N/A
Trevor Nunn	Awayvale/Homevale	March 1998	1,051,065	N/A

Source: Labour Research, *September 1999*

See also **Individual Distribution of Wealth in the UK**, p 103.

Industry

Industrial Sector

An industrial sector is any of the different groups into which industries may be divided: primary, secondary, and tertiary. **Primary industries** extract or use raw materials, for example, mining and agriculture. **Secondary industries** are manufacturing industries, where raw materials are processed or components are assembled. **Tertiary industries** supply services such as retailing, education, research and development, administration, and financial services such as accountancy.

■ **Business and Industry**

Top 10 Industrial Sectors Worldwide by Market Capitalization

As of May 2000.

Sector	Number of companies	Market capitalization ($ millions)
Information technology hardware	54	3,471,414.66
Telecommunication services	51	3,460,522.48
Banks	65	1,979,966.85
Software and computer services	42	1,920,752.53
Pharmaceuticals	21	1,466,651.25
Oil and gas	13	1,018,902.40
Electronic and electric equipment	17	977,346.18
Media and photography	32	706,559.17
General retailers	15	704,805.94
Insurance	14	663,133.41
Speciality and other finance	20	612,091.76

Source: FT500, FT.com, © *Financial Times 2000*

See also **Countries with the Highest and Lowest Industrial Output Growth**, p 652.

World Growth of Industrial Production (Selected Countries)

Figures are percentage change on the previous year. (N/A = not applicable).

Country/region	1990	1991	1992	1993	1994	1995	1996	1997	1998	1999
Austria	7.2	1.8	−1.5	−1.4	3.9	5.2	0.8	6.6	8.3	5.4
Belgium	1.3	−1.8	−0.6	−4.9	1.8	5.6	0.8	4.9	3.2	0.9
Denmark[1]	3.0	0.3	2.9	−2.4	10.2	4.4	1.8	5.8	2.1	2.6
Finland	−0.6	−8.7	1.3	5.6	11.3	7.2	3.6	10.2	7.0	5.5
France	1.5	−1.2	−1.2	−3.8	4.0	2.8	0.9	3.7	5.2	2.2
Germany	5.2	3.3	−2.6	−7.6	3.5	1.1	0.8	3.6	4.2	1.5
Greece	−2.3	−1.2	−1.4	−2.5	1.4	1.7	1.0	1.5	7.1	4.0
Italy	−0.5	−1.8	−0.9	−2.4	5.9	5.8	−1.6	3.8	1.3	0.0
Ireland, Republic of	4.7	3.2	9.1	5.6	11.9	18.9	7.9	15.3	15.8	N/A
Netherlands	2.5	1.7	−0.2	−1.1	4.9	3.5	2.5	3.1	1.4	0.4
Portugal	9.1	0.0	−2.6	−5.1	−0.1	11.7	5.2	2.6	5.7	3.0
Spain	−0.4	−0.6	−3.2	−4.7	7.8	4.8	−1.2	6.9	5.5	2.7
Sweden	3.7	−5.0	−2.3	−0.9	10.9	10.6	1.7	7.1	4.2	1.0
UK	−0.3	−3.4	0.4	2.2	5.4	1.7	1.1	1.0	0.6	0.5
EU-11[2]	1.4	4.7	5.0	2.8	0.1	−1.2	0.5	4.3	4.1	1.7
EU-15	2.1	−0.1	−1.4	−3.2	5.0	3.7	1.2	4.6	3.6	1.4
Canada	−2.8	−3.8	1.1	4.5	6.4	4.5	1.7	5.5	2.3	4.5
Japan	4.2	1.9	−5.7	−3.6	1.3	3.3	2.4	3.5	−6.6	0.4
USA	−0.2	−2.0	3.1	3.4	5.5	4.9	4.4	6.3	4.3	3.5

[1] Figures for Denmark are for manufacturing production.
[2] EU-11 = the 11 countries participating in the Euro: Austria, Belgium, Finland, France, Germany, Republic of Ireland, Italy, Luxembourg, the Netherlands, Portugal, and Spain.

Source: HM Treasury, © *Crown copyright 2000*

Business and Industry in the UK: A Stormy Climate

British business battled through the early months of the 21st century in a stormy climate. The continuing strength of the pound made it difficult for some companies to compete on their home ground, as well as overseas, and others that sought to mitigate their problems by manufacturing in underdeveloped countries have not always gained sufficient advantage to justify their investment. Publicity over 'sweat shop' working conditions in poor countries led to some shoppers boycotting imported clothing; but this proved too little too late to save the British textile industry.

Red tape condemned
Business leaders were increasingly outspoken over the growing level and complexity of legislation, with the support of the British Chambers of Commerce, which set up a 'burdens barometer' detailing the costs – particularly of new employment rights.

Many manufacturers were also worried by the Climate Change Levy, through which they would have to pay a premium on the energy they use from April 2001. Those which had already made considerable efforts to reduce energy usage claimed they would be hardest hit.

Despite the many apparent barriers to trading effectively, Britain entered its first summer of the Millennium with some optimism. 60% of 1,000 companies questioned by the Cranfield Management School forecast increasing demand for their products and services; with 42% stepping up recruitment campaigns to attract new personnel into most activities.

But during the same period, the Chartered Institute of Purchasing and Supply reported that manufacturers were not sharing this boom. In fact, it claimed that the sector would fall into recession unless sterling weakened substantially against the euro.

Industrial Output of the UK

Year	Manufacturing output		Industrial production		Total service industries	
	Index (1995 = 100)	% change on previous year	Index (1995 = 100)	% change on previous year	Index (1995 = 100)	% change on previous year
1980	80.9	−8.7	76.7	−6.5	67.8	−0.4
1985	82.6	2.9	82.8	5.5	76.3	3.1
1990	97.7	−0.2	94.1	−0.3	89.5	1.4
1991	92.8	−5.0	91.0	−3.3	89.3	−0.2
1992	92.8	0.0	91.3	0.3	89.7	0.4
1993	94.1	1.4	93.3	2.2	92.5	3.1
1994	98.5	4.7	98.3	5.4	96.8	4.6
1995	100.0	1.5	100.0	1.7	100.0	3.3
1996	100.4	0.4	101.1	1.1	103.3	3.3
1997	101.7	1.3	102.1	1.0	107.8	4.4
1998	102.0	0.3	102.7	0.6	111.7	3.6
1999	101.9	0.1	103.2	0.5	114.5	2.5

Source: HM Treasury,

Leading Producers of Selected Commodities

1997

World leading countries		Leading developing countries	
Country or area	Share (%)[1]	Country or area	Share (%)[2]
Food products			
USA	23.7	Brazil	12.9
Japan	14.4	Argentina	10.0
Germany (western part)	6.5	Indonesia	7.4
France	6.5	Mexico	6.6
UK	4.8	India	6.5
Italy	4.0	Korea, South	6.1
Spain	3.3	Philippines	4.5
Brazil	2.7	Turkey	4.1
Canada	2.7	Taiwan	3.3
Netherlands	2.2	Thailand	3.2
Argentina	2.1	Chile	2.6
Australia	1.6	Peru	2.1
Indonesia	1.6	Egypt	1.7
Belgium	1.5	Iran	1.6
Mexico	1.4	Colombia	1.6
Total	79.0	**Total**	74.2
Textiles			
USA	19.9	India	21.0
Italy	11.6	Taiwan	8.6
Japan	10.7	Turkey	8.4
India	7.1	Brazil	7.7
Germany (western part)	4.4	Korea, South	6.4
France	4.1	Pakistan	4.2
Taiwan	2.9	Iran	4.1
Turkey	2.8	Mexico	3.8
UK	2.8	Indonesia	3.4
Brazil	2.6	China (Hong Kong)	3.0
Spain	2.3	Argentina	2.8
Korea, South	2.2	Peru	2.3
Canada	2.1	Colombia	1.7
Iran	1.4	Egypt	1.4
Pakistan	1.4	Malaysia	1.2
Total	78.3	**Total**	80.0
Wearing apparel			
USA	25.3	Brazil	11.9
Japan	13.0	China (Hong Kong)	10.2
Italy	10.8	Indonesia	7.8
France	4.0	Korea, South	6.9
UK	3.8	Turkey	4.6
Brazil	3.2	Argentina	4.3
Germany (western part)	3.1	Tunisia	2.8
China (Hong Kong)	2.8	Taiwan	2.7
Spain	2.8	Mexico	2.6
Canada	2.6	Philippines	2.4
Indonesia	2.1	India	1.8
Korea, South	1.9	Morocco	1.8
Turkey	1.2	Iraq	1.6
Portugal	1.2	Sri Lanka	1.6
Argentina	1.2	Malaysia	1.2
Total	79.0	**Total**	64.2
Leather and fur products			
Italy	17.5	Mexico	14.9
USA	10.9	Argentina	14.7
Japan	10.5	Brazil	11.4
France	6.6	Korea, South	6.9
Mexico	5.2	India	5.7
Argentina	5.1	Bangladesh	5.5
Spain	4.9	Taiwan	3.2
Germany (western part)	4.0	Indonesia	2.7
Brazil	3.9	Uruguay	2.4
UK	3.2	Turkey	1.9
Korea, South	2.4	Paraguay	1.6
India	2.0	Iran	1.5
Bangladesh	1.9	Morocco	1.4
Portugal	1.3	Tunisia	1.2
Taiwan	1.1	Chile	1.1
Total	80.5	**Total**	76.1
Footwear			
Italy	23.9	Brazil	24.2
Brazil	8.0	Argentina	15.0
USA	7.9	Mexico	9.2
France	5.8	Taiwan	5.3
Japan	5.7	Indonesia	4.7
UK	5.2	Tunisia	2.6
Argentina	4.9	Korea, South	2.6
Spain	4.3	India	2.4
Portugal	3.1	Iraq	2.3
Mexico	3.0	Chile	2.0
Germany (western part)	3.0	Turkey	1.6
Taiwan	1.7	Colombia	1.5
Indonesia	1.6	Iran	1.4
South Africa	1.4	Venezuela	1.3
Austria	1.3	Morocco	1.0
Total	80.8	**Total**	77.1
Industrial chemicals			
USA	24.8	Taiwan	14.1
Japan	14.9	Korea, South	12.8
Germany (western part)	12.7	Brazil	11.9
France	5.0	Mexico	11.5
UK	4.9	India	10.8
Italy	4.0	Saudi Arabia	7.3
Netherlands	2.9	Turkey	4.5
Taiwan	2.7	Argentina	3.1
Korea, South	2.5	Malaysia	3.1
Brazil	2.3	Indonesia	2.2
Mexico	2.2	Venezuela	1.9
Belgium	2.2	Singapore	1.9
India	2.1	Pakistan	1.5
Spain	1.8	Egypt	1.1
Canada	1.6	Colombia	1.0
Total	86.6	Total	88.7

(continued)

Leading Producers of Selected Commodities *(continued)*

World leading countries: Country or area	Share (%)[1]	Leading developing countries: Country or area	Share (%)[2]
Other chemicals			
USA	26.2	Korea, South	15.8
Japan	17.4	Brazil	12.6
Germany (western part)	9.2	India	10.1
France	5.4	Argentina	10.0
UK	4.9	Mexico	9.8
Switzerland	4.1	Turkey	4.5
Spain	2.9	Taiwan	4.3
Korea, South	2.8	Philippines	3.3
Italy	2.5	Thailand	2.5
Brazil	2.2	Chile	2.4
Canada	2.0	Peru	2.1
India	1.8	Singapore	2.0
Argentina	1.8	Indonesia	1.8
Mexico	1.7	Egypt	1.7
Ireland, Republic of	1.6	Colombia	1.4
Total	86.5	**Total**	84.3
Iron and steel			
Japan	21.5	India	18.5
USA	15.1	Korea, South	15.2
Germany (western part)	8.1	Brazil	11.9
Italy	7.7	Mexico	11.7
India	4.8	Taiwan	11.6
France	4.4	Indonesia	6.1
Korea, South	4.0	Turkey	4.1
Brazil	3.1	Argentina	2.4
Mexico	3.1	Venezuela	1.9
Taiwan	3.0	Malaysia	1.4
UK	3.0	Philippines	1.2
Spain	2.8	Chile	1.0
Canada	1.6	Egypt	0.9
Indonesia	1.6	Peru	0.9
Austria	1.6	Colombia	0.8
Total	85.4	**Total**	89.6
Metal products			
USA	23.6	Korea, South	15.6
Japan	19.4	Taiwan	11.9
Germany (western part)	13.2	Brazil	11.5
France	6.8	Mexico	10.2
Italy	4.6	Argentina	6.7
UK	3.6	Malaysia	4.5
Spain	2.4	India	3.9
Canada	2.1	Turkey	3.1
Korea, South	1.8	Singapore	3.0
Austria	1.5	Chile	2.2
Sweden	1.5	Peru	2.1
Taiwan	1.4	Iran	2.0
Australia	1.3	China (Hong Kong)	1.5
Brazil	1.3	Indonesia	1.4
Netherlands	1.3	Colombia	1.2
Total	85.8	**Total**	80.8
Non-electrical machinery			
USA	41.1	Brazil	17.8
Japan	16.6	Korea, South	17.8
Germany (western part)	9.9	India	13.0
Italy	6.3	Singapore	9.3
UK	5.3	Taiwan	7.9
France	3.5	Turkey	6.5
Canada	1.8	Mexico	5.6
Brazil	1.3	Argentina	3.6
Korea, South	1.3	Iran	3.4
Spain	1.0	Malaysia	2.7
Finland	0.9	China (Hong Kong)	1.8
India	0.9	Chile	0.9
Netherlands	0.9	Egypt	0.7
Austria	0.8	Philippines	0.5
Singapore	0.7	Venezuela	0.4
Total	92.3	**Total**	91.9
Electrical machinery			
USA	35.5	Taiwan	23.4
Japan	22.3	Korea, South	21.3
Germany (western part)	9.0	Brazil	11.9
France	4.1	Malaysia	7.2
Italy	3.4	India	6.7
Taiwan	2.9	Mexico	6.2
UK	2.8	Singapore	4.1
Korea, South	2.6	Turkey	4.0
Brazil	1.5	Argentina	2.6
Spain	1.4	Philippines	1.9
Sweden	1.2	China (Hong Kong)	1.5
Austria	1.1	Iran	1.0
Canada	1.1	Indonesia	0.8
Netherlands	1.1	Colombia	0.4
Malaysia	0.9	Peru	0.4
Total	90.9	**Total**	93.4

[1] In world total value added (excluding eastern Europe and the former USSR) at constant 1990 prices.
[2] In total value added of developing countries at constant 1990 prices.

Source: International Yearbook of Industrial Statistics 2000, *United Nations Industrial Development Organization (UNIDO)*, and *Edward Elgar Publishing Ltd*

Summary of Industrial Production by Sector in the UK

(N = nil or negligible. N/A = not available. In millions of pounds.)

Category	Year	Gross output (production)[1]	Gross value added	Stocks and work in progress: At end of year	Stocks and work in progress: Change during year	Capital expenditure less disposals	Wages and salaries	Average number of persons employed[2]	Gross value added per person employed (£)
		Estimates for all firms							
Production and construction total	1995	N/A	176,754.7	72,058.7	N/A	23,798.6	76,335.9	5,667.2	31,189
	1996	576,309.5	185,760.7	68,398.2	430.3	23,672.2	88,606.3	5,470.0	33,960
	1997	591,462.2	193,254.7	68,974.9	614.4	27,185.4	94,429.7	5,502.6	35,121
Production industries total	1995	473,200.5	152,601.4	58,212.2	4,888.6	22,499.1	72,291.5	4,655.7	32,777
	1996	494,056.1	159,731.8	55,475.4	−5.6	22,485.7	74,137.1	4,454.1	35,862
	1997	503,731.0	163,793.2	55,902.4	−541.1	25,429.2	77,758.4	4,483.6	36,532
Mining and quarrying of energy producing materials	1995	2,447.6	888.2	364.8	−101.1	92.4	401.3	17.0	52,305
	1996	2,250.8	949.6	369.4	−12.3	157.1	443.0	18.8	50,460
	1997	1,997.7	891.7	355.2	−6.0	138.0	414.1	16.2	55,171

(continued)

Summary of Industrial Production by Sector in the UK *(continued)*

Category	Year	Estimates for all firms							
		Gross output (production)[1]	Gross value added	Stocks and work in progress		Capital expenditure less disposals	Wages and salaries	Average number of persons employed[2]	Gross value added per person employed (£)
				At end of year	Change during year				
except energy producing materials	1995	3,195.3	1,366.2	201.4	16.9	205.6	494.1	30.9	44,268
	1996	3,726.4	1,637.2	249.4	24.1	316.6	575.4	36.1	45,363
	1997	3,463.8	1,558.4	228.6	− 5.0	212.8	533.6	32.0	48,708
Mining and quarrying total	1995	5,643.0	2,254.4	566.2	− 84.1	298.0	895.4	47.8	47,120
	1996	5,977.2	2,586.8	618.8	11.9	473.7	1,018.4	54.9	47,110
	1997	5,461.5	2,450.1	583.8	− 11.0	350.7	947.7	48.2	50,877
Manufacturing of food, beverages, and tobacco	1995	72,609.9	17,640.0	6,765.6	377.2	2,444.2	7,366.7	533.1	33,092
	1996	75,880.6	19,345.2	6,984.5	501.9	2,346.5	7,529.3	498.0	38,845
	1997	76,355.6	19,616.4	7,449.8	259.2	2,561.7	8,110.5	494.3	39,686
of textiles and textile products	1995	16,982.8	6,374.2	2,869.8	197.4	467.0	3,720.5	380.1	16,768
	1996	17,306.4	6,803.5	2,786.1	15.3	575.3	3,872.0	356.6	19,077
	1997	18,307.3	7,128.6	3,087.8	44.6	482.0	4,103.0	364.4	19,560
of leather and leather products	1995	2,292.3	788.5	358.3	24.9	60.5	568.6	54.7	14,425
	1996	2,355.8	886.5	382.3	3.4	48.9	425.5	39.6	22,407
	1997	2,144.6	771.0	403.1	47.6	48.0	420.3	36.0	21,407
of wood and wood products	1995	5,777.1	1,814.1	713.5	14.1	158.3	1,094.9	87.4	20,758
	1996	5,601.0	1,799.9	629.6	− 6.7	170.1	1,080.1	87.0	20,696
	1997	5,761.2	2,034.0	670.4	24.6	235.2	1,110.4	91.1	22,331
of pulp, paper, and paper products; publishing and printing	1995	39,119.0	16,236.2	3,150.9	437.3	2,121.0	8,056.6	481.8	33,697
	1996	40,630.4	16,678.0	2,828.3	− 194.1	1,784.9	8,690.4	467.8	35,649
	1997	40,201.6	16,494.4	2,860.8	− 68.8	1,997.2	8,973.0	470.6	35,047
of coke, refined petroleum products, and nuclear fuel	1995	22,422.6	2,912.2	1,220.0	227.3	752.2	670.3	27.2	107,044
	1996	25,984.9	2,558.5	1,128.3	− 121.3	716.8	714.3	27.9	91,756
	1997	23,831.4	2,089.6	1,178.8	− 240.7	700.4	678.1	25.6	81,770
of chemicals, chemical products, and synthetic fibres	1995	44,721.5	15,411.9	5,808.8	447.2	2,285.9	5,735.7	281.7	54,707
	1996	45,588.4	15,440.3	5,717.1	264.8	2,758.2	5,702.1	267.1	57,810
	1997	46,359.1	14,802.0	5,540.7	− 46.6	2,830.2	5,996.0	269.2	54,990
of rubber and plastic products	1995	18,102.5	6,553.9	1,820.2	171.2	952.7	3,613.0	248.0	26,427
	1996	19,175.5	7,122.8	1,891.7	27.5	983.8	3,836.8	250.0	28.496
	1997	19,989.7	7,701.9	1,863.8	23.8	1,124.5	4,075.3	265.7	28,990
of other nonmetalic mineral products	1995	11,855.6	4,976.9	1,462.0	121.4	607.6	2,437.5	167.1	29,776
	1996	11,349.0	4,976.5	1,437.3	94.3	671.9	2,374.3	156.8	31,732
	1997	11,531.6	4,908.4	1,474.3	9.2	576.6	2,441.7	154.7	31,725
of basic iron and nonferro alloys	1995	43,489.1	15,889.6	4,711.8	515.9	1,369.6	8,647.9	582.8	27,263
	1996	43,725.9	15,344.2	4,452.6	7.7	1,572.2	8,860.9	551.8	27,806
	1997	41,867.9	15,580.0	4,246.0	− 21.9	1,653.0	8,822.1	538.8	28,915
of machinery and equipment not elsewhere specified	1995	33,839.5	12,014.6	5,661.6	376.1	1,080.1	6,993.0	423.1	28,397
	1996	34,700.4	12,478.2	5,198.5	69.0	1,177.8	6,993.3	400.2	31,177
	1997	36,531.9	13,541.9	5,510.1	137.9	1,141.7	7,476.5	404.7	33,465
of electrical and optical equipment	1995	50,427.2	16,717.5	7,373.7	733.2	2,370.1	8,472.2	537.5	31,102
	1996	54,777.8	17,480.6	6,975.1	− 213.2	2,193.6	8,977.3	533.0	32,797
	1997	58,459.6	18,048.2	6,956.5	− 50.8	2,810.1	9,536.3	544.1	33,174
of transport equipment	1995	47,033.2	13,425.3	12,335.0	1,305.9	2,303.0	7,418.3	408.3	32,885
	1996	51,840.5	14,833.4	11,493.3	− 432.7	2,414.9	7,867.0	406.3	36,512
	1997	55,880.4	16,080.5	10,808.1	− 682.2	3,302.9	8,600.2	414.6	38,786
not elsewhere classified	1995	13,514.3	4,631.2	1,704.2	125.5	433.5	2,722.9	220.8	20,976
	1996	13,882.5	5,151.1	1,607.9	74.3	421.8	2,829.9	214.0	24,074
	1997	14,787.8	5,721.1	1,869.2	60.8	567.6	3,130.8	225.6	25,363

(continued)

Summary of Industrial Production by Sector in the UK (*continued*)

Category	Year	Gross output (production)[1]	Gross value added	Stocks and work in progress: At end of year	Stocks and work in progress: Change during year	Capital expendi-ture less disposals	Wages and salaries	Average number of persons employed[2]	Gross value added per person employed (£)
Manufacturing total	1995	422,186.5	135,386.1	55,955.3	5,074.5	17,405.7	67,518.0	4,433.6	30,536
	1996	442,799.0	140,898.9	53,512.6	90.2	17,836.7	69,783.1	4,256.1	33,106
	1997	452,009.6	144,518.1	53,919.4	– 503.1	20,031.1	73,474.2	4,299.3	33,614
Electricity, gas, and water supply total	1995	45,371.0	15,14,960.9	1,690.7	– 101.8	4,795.5	3,878.1	174.3	85,841
	1996	45,279.9	16,246.1	1,344.0	– 107.7	4,175.3	3,335.5	143.2	113,483
	1997	46,259.9	16,824.9	1,399.2	– 27.0	5,047.4	3,336.6	136.1	123,597
Construction total	1995	N/A	24,153.3	13,846.6	N/A	1,299.5	4,044.4	1,011.5	23,879
	1996	82,253.4	26,028.8	12,922.8	435.9	1,186.5	14,469.3	1,015.9	25,621
	1997	87,731.2	29,461.6	13,072.5	1,155.5	1,756.2	16,671.3	1,019.0	28,912

Estimates for all firms.

[1] Figures for gross output include a substantial amount of duplication represented by the total value of partly manufactured goods sold by one industrial establishment to another. The extent of duplication varies from one census industry to another.

[2] The figures include working proprietors but exclude outworkers.

Source: Annual Abstract of Statistics 2000, © *Crown copyright 2000*

See also **Major Companies by Industry Group in the UK**, p 677.

Construction: Value of New Orders Obtained by Contractors in Great Britain

(In millions of pounds.)

Item	1990	1992	1994	1996	1997	1998
New housing						
Public housing	683	1,246	1,386	1,073	995	933
Private housing[1]	4,855	4,016	5,721	5,416	6,253	5,997
Total	5,538	5,263	7,106	6,487	7,248	6,930
Infrastructure						
Water	321	669	412	640	733	957
Sewerage	491	469	389	481	656	737
Electricity	187	281	170	294	382	359
Roads	1,425	1,322	1,356	1,710	928	821
Gas, communications, air	391	554	494	745	693	745
Railways	160	200	412	524	416	573
Harbours	216	252	218	270	182	287
Total Infrastructure						
public	2,029	1,690	2,211	1,671	1,352	1,505
private	1,161	2,056	1,240	2,993	2,639	2,974
Total	3,190	3,746	3,451	4,664	3,991	4,479
Other public non-housing						
Factories	149	128	111	91	72	84
Warehouses	14	54	38	14	27	20
Oil, steel, coal	81	47	12	4	4	2
Schools and colleges	527	584	658	707	749	770
Universities	146	203	376	355	273	405
Health	663	644	752	681	491	769
Offices	570	499	469	379	391	292
Entertainment	283	189	308	259	342	432
Garages	56	28	49	28	34	19
Shops	24	23	14	12	35	35
Agriculture	5	14	22	8	33	17
Other	601	351	844	419	441	660
Total	3,117	2,763	3,654	2,956	2,894	3,504
Private industrial[1]						
Factories	2,094	1,006	1,451	1,603	2,184	1,878
Warehouses	648	426	498	663	901	1,014
Oil, steel, coal	108	72	51	71	64	79
Total	2,850	1,503	1,999	2,337	3,149	2,971
Private commercial[1]						
Schools, universities	169	121	115	156	189	351
Health	271	193	255	277	356	651
Offices	4,215	1,691	1,777	2,169	2,506	3,472
Entertainment	1,195	747	928	1,407	1,847	2,244
Garages	364	234	300	265	344	315
Shops	1,345	1,034	1,453	1,795	1,937	2,154
Agriculture	127	94	120	123	148	146
Other	109	103	127	198	198	259
Total	7,796	4,218	5,075	6,390	7,525	9,593
TOTAL	22,491	17,493	21,285	22,834	24,806	27,477

[1] Figures for private sector include work to be carried out by contractors on their own initiative for sale.

Source: Annual Abstract of Statistics 2000, © *Crown copyright 2000*

See also **Government and Other Public Sector Expenditure on Housing in the UK**, p 115.

Motor Vehicle Production in Selected Countries

(N/A = not available. – = not applicable.)

Country	Cars				Commercial vehicles			
	1992	1994	1996	1998	1992	1994	1996	1998
Austria	23,479	45,785	97,386	91,264	18,493	6,795	8,703	11,942
Belgium	222,680	408,541	367,536	318,528	88,983	89,165	89,877	114,056
France[1]	3,329,490	3,175,213	2,087,505	2,582,260	438,310	383,225	303,116	341,103
Germany	4,863,721	4,093,685	4,539,583	5,348,115	330,221	262,453	303,326	378,673
Italy	1,476,627	1,340,878	1,317,995	1,402,382	209,860	193,591	227,370	290,355
Netherlands	94,019	92,044	145,206	242,989	13,701	12,352	18,532	27,471
Spain	1,790,615	1,821,696	1,941,716	2,216,386	331,272	320,566	470,593	609,656
Sweden	293,499	352,951	367,799	368,305	63,096	82,044	95,362	114,456
UK	1,291,880	1,466,823	1,686,134	1,748,258	248,453	227,815	238,314	227,379
EU total	13,386,010	12,797,616	12,550,860	14,318,487	1,742,389	1,578,006	1,755,193	2,115,091
Argentina	220,498	338,355	269,439	353,068	41,520	70,422	43,713	104,851
Australia[2]	270,170	309,512	304,741	335,653	14,235	25,354	27,328	N/A
Brazil	820,068	1,248,773	1,458,576	1,244,463	254,410	332,616	345,752	328,666
Canada	1,015,468	1,215,830	1,279,767	1,481,111	935,178	1,105,844	1,117,399	1,088,618
Czech Republic and Slovak Republic	202,455	179,713	270,197	491,262	27,129	11,286	37,523	42,599
Hungary	–	19,574	51,777	65,789	3,464	1,500	1,662	N/A
India	192,069	298,044	472,482	498,187	128,095	188,819	289,640	129,312
Japan[3]	9,378,694	7,802,037	7,863,763	8,055,763	3,120,590	2,752,082	2,482,023	1,994,029
Korea, South	1,306,752	1,805,895	2,239,497	1,625,125	422,944	505,768	573,217	329,369
Poland	218,808	337,600	433,620	581,000[4]	19,850	29,070	72,485	N/A
Romania	63,824	80,244	97,923	103,931	15,509	10,644	24,537	22,973
Russia[5]	1,095,401	891,657	874,241	860,726	117,952	273,776	188,515	204,478
Turkey	265,245	212,651	207,757	239,937	57,686	30,523	68,990	104,565
USA	5,664,203	6,613,983	6,080,410	5,547,116	4,064,587	5,648,767	5,749,410	6,451,689
Yugoslavia	25,271	7,648	–	–	5,856	1,557	–	–
TOTAL	34,124,936	34,159,132	34,455,050	35,801,618	10,971,394	12,566,034	12,777,387	12,916,240

[1] France has changed its way of reporting production statistics. Previously noncountable units already included in other overseas markets were in the totals. Historical information is not yet available.
[2] Includes partly finished vehicles.
[3] Excludes three-wheelers.
[4] Estimated.
[5] Includes Russia, Belarus, Ukraine, Latvia, and Armenia. Figures for 1998 only for Russia and Ukraine.

Source: Motor Industry of Great Britain 1999 World Automotive Statistics, *Society of Motor Manufacturers and Traders Ltd*

Motor Vehicle Production in the UK

(N/A = not available.)

Motor vehicle	1990	1992	1994	1995	1996	1997	1998
Passenger cars							
Cars < 1,001 cc	93,039	22,037	98,178	95,198	108,645	119,894	112,044
Cars 1,001 cc–1,600 cc	809,219	793,307	729,397	814,873	845,084	829,086	814,595
Cars 1,601 cc–2,800 cc	325,116	437,951	573,357	528,444	635,861	653,154	720,556
Cars > 2,800 cc	68,236	38,585	65,891	93,569	96,544	95,881	101,063
Total	1,295,610	1,291,880	1,466,823	1,532,084	1,686,134	1,698,001	1,748,258
Commercial vehicles							
Light commercial vehicles	230,510	216,477	197,285	199,346	205,372	210,942	203,629
Trucks							
trucks < 7.5 tonnes	10,515	9,558	8,154	9,523	9,812	6,254	5,006
trucks > 7.5 tonnes	13,674	11,113	10,016	11,717	9,229	7,930	7,002
Motive units for articulated vehicles	3,327	2,788	2,794	3,476	208	2,573	2,492
Buses, coaches, and minibuses	12,320	8,517	9,566	8,939	9,254	10,004	9,250
Total	270,346	248,453	227,815	233,001	238,314	237,703	227,379

Source: Annual Abstract of Statistics 2000, © *Crown copyright 2000*

See also 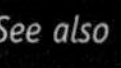 **Cars and Motoring**, pp 586–592.

Energy and Minerals

Energy Consumption and Production Worldwide

(– = not applicable. N/A = not available. N = nil or negligible. Btu = British thermal units. † = less than 0.5 trillion cubic feet, 500 barrels per day, or 500,000 short tons.)

Country	Primary energy consumed				Primary energy produced					
	Total (quadrillion Btu)		Per capita (million Btu)		Dry natural gas (triillion cubic feet)		Crude petroleum (1,000 barrels per day)		Coal (million short tons)	
	1990	1997[1]	1990	1997[1]	1990	1997[1]	1990	1997[1]	1990	1997[1]
Algeria	1.2	1.3	49	45	1.8	2.5	1,175	1,277	†	†
Argentina	1.9	2.5	59	71	0.6	1.0	483	834	†	†
Australia	3.7	4.5	217	241	0.7	1.0	575	588	226	293
Austria	1.2	1.3	150	160	0.1	0.1	22	19	3	1
Bahrain	0.3	0.3	520	452	0.2	0.2	42	40	N/A	N/A
Bangladesh	0.3	0.4	2	3	0.2	0.3	1	2	N/A	N/A
Belarus	–	1.1	–	106	–	†	–	36	–	N/A
Belgium	2.2	2.6	217	253	†	N	N/A	N/A	3	†
Brazil	5.7	7.6	39	48	0.1	0.2	631	841	5	5
Bulgaria	1.3	0.9	141	113	N	†	4	1	35	29
Canada	10.9	12.2	392	402	3.9	5.9	1,553	1,922	75	87
Chile	0.6	0.9	43	61	0.1	0.1	20	7	2	1
China	27.0	36.6	23	29	0.5	0.8	2,774	3,200	1,190	1,553
Colombia	0.9	1.2	28	33	0.2	0.2	440	652	23	36
Congo, Democratic Republic of	N/A	N/A	N/A	N/A	0	0	29	28	†	†
Cuba	0.5	0.4	46	40	†	†	14	30	N	†
Czech Republic	–	1.9	–	182	–	†	–	3	–	72
Denmark	0.8	1.0	156	184	0.1	0.3	121	230	N/A	N/A
Ecuador	N/A	N/A	N/A	N/A	†	†	285	388	N/A	N/A
Egypt	1.4	1.8	27	29	0.3	0.5	873	856	N	†
Finland	1.1	1.2	228	232	N/A	N/A	N/A	N/A	N/A	N/A
France	8.8	9.7	156	166	0.1	0.1	61	36	15	8
Germany	–	14.2	–	173	–	0.8	–	56	–	252
Hong Kong	0.5	0.6	84	94	N/A	N/A	N/A	N/A	N/A	N/A
Hungary	1.3	1.1	124	108	0.2	0.2	40	35	19	17
India	7.8	11.8	9	12	0.4	0.8	660	675	233	329
Indonesia	2.2	3.7	12	18	1.5	2.4	1,462	1,520	9	60
Iran	3.1	4.2	57	68	0.8	1.6	3,088	3,664	1	1
Iraq	0.9	1.2	51	56	0.2	0.1	2,040	1,155	N/A	N/A
Ireland, Republic of	0.4	0.5	105	133	0.1	0.1	N/A	N/A	†	†
Israel	0.5	0.7	97	118	†	†	†	†	N/A	N/A
Italy	7.0	7.7	122	131	0.6	0.7	87	112	1	†
Japan	18.1	21.3	147	169	0.1	0.1	11	10	11	5
Korea, North	2.1	1.9	103	81	N/A	N/A	N/A	N/A	71	68
Korea, South	3.7	7.5	86	162	N/A	N/A	N/A	N/A	19	5
Kuwait	0.5	0.7	210	359	0.2	0.3	1,175	2,083	N/A	N/A
Libya	0.5	0.6	123	102	0.2	0.2	1,375	1,446	N/A	N/A
Malaysia	1.0	1.7	55	78	0.7	1.4	619	746	†	†
Mexico	5.0	5.8	58	59	0.9	1.2	2,553	3,023	9	10
Morocco	0.3	0.4	13	13	†	†	†	†	1	1
Myanmar	N/A	N/A	N/A	N/A	†	0.1	13	10	†	†
Netherlands	3.4	3.9	225	249	2.7	3.0	70	53	N/A	N/A
New Zealand	0.7	0.8	217	210	0.2	0.2	40	58	3	3
Nigeria	0.7	0.9	7	7	0.1	0.2	1,810	2,332	†	†
Norway	1.6	1.8	373	404	1.0	1.6	1,704	3,143	†	†
Pakistan	1.2	1.7	10	13	0.5	0.7	62	57	3	4
Peru	N/A	N/A	N/A	N/A	†	†	129	118	†	†
Philippines	0.7	1.0	12	13	N	†	5	1	1	1
Poland	4.0	4.2	104	109	0.1	0.2	2	6	237	220
Portugal	0.7	0.9	75	92	N/A	N/A	N/A	N/A	†	N
Romania	2.9	1.9	125	85	1.0	0.5	163	134	42	41
Russian Federation	–	26.6	–	181	–	20.2	–	5,920	–	288
Saudi Arabia	3.2	4.2	212	215	1.1	1.5	6,410	8,562	N/A	N/A
Serbia	–	0.7	–	69	–	†	–	20	–	40
South Africa	3.4	4.3	91	99	N	0.1	N/A	N/A	193	243
Spain	3.9	4.5	101	114	0.1	†	16	8	40	29
Sweden	2.2	2.2	251	244	†	†	†	†	†	N
Switzerland	1.2	1.2	174	171	†	N	N/A	N/A	N/A	N/A
Syria	0.6	0.7	49	47	0.1	0.1	388	561	N/A	N/A
Taiwan	2.0	3.4	100	156	0.1	†	3	1	1	†
Tajikistan	–	N/A	–	N/A	–	†	–	1	–	†

(continued)

Energy Consumption and Production Worldwide (*continued*)

Country	Primary energy consumed				Primary energy produced					
	Total (quadrillion Btu)		Per capita (million Btu)		Dry natural gas (triillion cubic feet)		Crude pretroleum (1,000 barrels per day)		Coal (million short tons)	
	1990	1997[1]	1990	1997[1]	1990	1997[1]	1990	1997[1]	1990	1997[1]
Thailand	1.3	2.5	22	42	0.2	0.5	44	72	14	24
Trinidad and Tobago	N/A	N/A	N/A	N/A	0.2	0.3	150	124	N/A	N/A
Tunisia	N/A	N/A	N/A	N/A	†	0.1	93	90	N/A	N/A
Turkey	2.0	2.8	35	43	†	†	73	68	52	62
UK	9.4	10.1	164	171	1.8	3.2	1,820	2,518	106	54
Ukraine	–	6.6	–	130	–	0.6	–	58	–	87
United Arab Emirates	1.2	1.8	641	678	0.8	1.3	2,117	2,316	N/A	N/A
USA	84.1	94.2	337	352	17.8	18.9	7,355	6,452	1,029	1,090
Venezuela	2.1	2.7	108	115	0.8	1.0	2,137	3,315	2	6
Vietnam	0.3	0.6	4	8	†	†	50	191	5	11
World total	346.8	379.5	66	65	73.6	81.7	60,566	66,420	5,356	5,185

[1] Figures for 1997 are provisional.

Source: Statistical Abstract of the United States 1999

Crude Oil Production Worldwide

Data are for production of crude oil and natural gas liquids (NGL). (In thousands of metric tons.) (– = not applicable.)

Country/region	1994	1995	1996	1997	1998
OECD					
North America					
Canada	92,371	96,270	99,687	103,074	119,351
Mexico	158,104	153,555	160,776	168,376	172,799
USA	379,526	375,554	373,501	370,074	377,487
Total	630,001	625,379	633,964	641,524	669,637
Europe					
Austria	1,147	1,079	989	995	993
Czech Republic	128	146	152	163	194
Denmark	9,118	9,170	10,121	11,360	11,676
France	3,229	2,913	2,513	2,139	2,055
Germany	2,938	2,926	2,874	2,799	3,816
Greece	531	457	514	465	315
Hungary	1,955	2,302	2,119	2,172	1,846
Italy	4,895	5,236	5,452	6,006	5,843
Netherlands	4,323	3,479	3,103	2,925	2,663
Norway	128,514	138,500	156,804	155,549	150,529
Poland	284	292	317	250	450
Spain	948	783	512	371	529
Turkey	3,696	3,516	3,500	3,449	3,247
UK	126,939	130,324	129,838	128,212	132,876
Other	5	4	–	74	80
Total	288,650	301,127	318,808	316,855	317,112
Pacific					
Australia	25,067	26,870	26,366	27,025	29,349
Japan	710	704	683	684	638
Korea, South	–	–	–	476	671
New Zealand	1,955	1,668	2,177	2,840	2,282
Total	27,732	29,242	29,226	30,549	32,940
OECD TOTAL	946,383	955,748	981,998	988,928	1,019,689
Non-OECD					
Latin America					
Argentina	35,573	38,616	41,951	44,515	45,084
Bolivia	1,510	1,693	1,736	1,985	2,087
Brazil	34,786	35,727	40,378	43,148	49,973
Chile	860	732	575	670	473
Colombia	23,731	30,433	32,641	33,811	39,348
Cuba	1,426	1,643	1,649	1,758	1,836
Ecuador	19,974	20,160	20,096	19,647	20,529
Guatemala	366	468	730	1,323	1,158
Peru	6,345	6,072	6,000	5,862	5,725
Trinidad and Tobago	7,098	7,136	7,073	7,206	6,662
Venezuela	128,460	150,775	156,978	168,989	163,795
Other	334	338	338	349	451
Total	260,463	293,793	310,145	329,263	337,121
Europe					
Albania	535	522	489	386	412
Bulgaria	36	43	32	50	28

(continued)

Crude Oil Production Worldwide (*continued*)

Country/region	1994	1995	1996	1997	1998
Croatia	1,823	1,761	1,696	1,748	1,648
Romania	6,974	6,951	6,852	6,730	6,714
Slovak Republic	70	76	72	54	65
Yugoslavia	1,077	1,066	1,030	979	881
former Yugoslavia	2,902	2,829	2,727	2,728	2,530
other former Yugoslavia	2	2	1	1	1
Total	10,517	10,421	10,008	9,836	9,749
Former USSR					
Azerbaijan	9,563	9,162	9,100	9,022	11,459
Belarus	2,000	1,932	1,860	1,795	1,822
Georgia	74	47	128	299	93
Kazakhstan	20,279	20,450	22,975	26,436	25,696
Kyrgyzstan	88	89	100	50	85
Lithuania	93	128	155	155	224
Russia	315,767	305,107	301,214	303,424	303,076
Tajikistan	33	25	21	20	26
Turkmenistan	3,360	3,500	4,100	4,458	5,640
Ukraine	4,200	4,058	4,102	3,371	4,337
Uzbekistan	5,500	7,456	7,496	6,884	9,071
Total	360,957	351,954	351,251	355,914	361,529
Africa					
Algeria	55,369	55,719	58,722	60,909	59,498
Angola/Cabinda	24,237	25,437	34,689	35,632	35,750
Benin	310	228	193	150	66
Cameroon	6,267	5,495	5,325	5,976	5,285
Congo, Democratic Republic of	1,345	1,371	1,371	1,279	12,185
Congo, Republic of the	9,562	9,275	10,370	12,253	1,306
Egypt	46,497	46,734	45,174	43,733	43,599
Gabon	17,214	18,246	18,549	18,577	17,703
Ghana	304	304	355	250	355
Côte d'Ivoire	N/A	307	788	749	526
Libya	67,780	70,376	70,105	71,818	69,662
Morocco	8	5	5	5	12
Nigeria	96,217	97,541	98,651	103,924	106,013
South Africa	393	393	393	391	393
Sudan	N/A	N/A	102	499	282
Tunisia	4,450	4,352	4,291	4,078	3,991
Other	243	251	251	250	2,517
Total	330,196	336,034	349,334	360,473	359,143
Middle East					
Bahrain	2,421	2,375	2,329	2,168	2,238
Iran	180,950	182,919	183,802	181,764	182,755
Iraq	26,006	27,185	28,540	56,689	104,537
Israel	25	28	25	25	26
Jordan	2	2	2	2	–
Kuwait	105,162	106,556	106,758	108,178	107,788
Oman	40,629	42,788	44,328	44,785	45,543
Qatar	20,744	20,856	21,336	27,040	30,596
Saudi Arabia	428,721	430,844	432,231	438,996	442,655
Syria	29,000	31,329	30,745	29,658	28,753
United Arab Emirates	116,520	115,481	118,769	120,168	122,071
Yemen	17,138	17,472	17,631	16,787	19,333
Total	967,318	977,835	986,496	1,026,260	1,086,295
Asia					
Bangladesh	105	10	10	7	7
Brunei	9,459	9,578	9,354	9,407	9,419
India	33,213	37,180	34,142	34,719	36,011
Indonesia	76,268	75,517	77,043	75,023	74,463
Malaysia	35,469	36,637	35,078	35,915	36,422
Myanmar	681	474	402	411	360
Pakistan	2,813	2,755	2,947	2,669	2,751
Philippines	300	191	135	599	41
Taipei, Chinese	59	53	51	50	48
Thailand	4,291	4,173	5,205	4,105	5,817
Vietnam	7,259	8,502	9,586	8,829	12,253
Other	5,500	6,500	6,500	4,892	6,767
Total	175,417	181,570	180,453	176,626	184,359
China	146,082	150,044	157,334	160,158	160,943
NON-OECD TOTAL	2,250,950	2,301,651	2,345,021	2,418,530	2,499,139
WORLD TOTAL	3,197,333	3,257,399	3,327,019	3,407,458	3,518,828

Source: Oil Information 1998, © *OECD/International Energy Agency 1999*

See also **Major Oilspills Throughout the World**, p 632.

Electricity Production in OECD Countries

In gigawatt hours (GWh). A gigawatt is one thousand million watts, and a gigawatt hour means that a power station produces one thousand million watts of electrical power in one hour.

Country	1991	1993	1995	1997
Australia	156,851	163,747	173,384	183,069
Austria	52,355	52,638	56,587	56,850
Belgium	71,957	70,856	74,430	79,032
Canada	508,003	527,793	562,145	575,144
Czech Republic	60,530	58,881	60,847	64,598
Denmark	36,328	33,744	36,787	44,287
Finland	57,985	61,078	63,896	69,175
France	455,364	472,665	493,900	504,148
Germany	539,579	526,197	537,045	551,536
Greece	35,813	38,305	41,457	43,506
Hungary	29,964	32,915	34,017	35,396
Iceland	4,494	4,727	4,981	5,586
Ireland, Republic of	15,147	16,430	17,895	19,961
Italy	221,789	222,865	241,542	251,462
Japan	888,088	906,705	989,880	1,040,108
Korea, South	118,619	144,437	203,547	246,627
Luxembourg	1,415	1,068	1,237	1,264
Mexico	126,907	136,106	152,548	175,048
Netherlands	74,253	76,994	80,971	86,659
New Zealand	33,387	33,873	35,507	36,751
Norway	111,009	120,095	123,011	111,636
Poland	134,714	133,867	139,006	142,769
Portugal	29,872	31,206	33,265	34,188
Spain	155,819	156,808	167,084	186,982
Sweden	147,384	145,811	148,350	149,451
Switzerland	57,810	61,267	63,080	62,715
Turkey	60,246	73,808	86,247	103,296
UK	322,054	323,307	334,438	345,342
USA	3,273,210	3,411,280	3,582,114	3,698,949
OECD North America	3,908,120	4,075,179	4,296,807	4,449,141
OECD Pacific	1,196,945	1,248,762	1,402,318	1,506,555
OECD Europe	2,675,881	2,715,532	2,840,073	2,949,839
OECD TOTAL	7,780,946	8,039,473	8,539,198	8,905,535
EU total	2,217,114	2,229,972	2,328,884	2,423,843

Source: Energy Statistics of OECD Countries, 1996–1997, © *OECD/International Energy Agency 1999*

See also **Electricity Generation, Supply, and Consumption in UK**, p 695.

Nuclear Electricity Production in OECD Countries

(– = not applicable. In gigawatt hours.)

Country/region	1991	1993	1995	1997
Australia	–	–	–	–
Austria	–	–	–	–
Belgium	42,861	41,927	41,356	47,708
Canada	84,929	94,823	97,844	82,528
Czech Republic	12,132	12,627	12,230	12,494
Denmark	–	–	–	–
Finland	19,511	19,928	19,216	20,894
France	331,340	368,188	377,231	395,483
Germany	147,229	153,276	153,091	170,328
Greece	–	–	–	–
Hungary	13,726	13,796	14,026	13,968
Iceland	–	–	–	–
Ireland, Republic of	–	–	–	–
Italy	–	–	–	–
Japan	213,460	249,256	291,254	319,056
Korea	56,311	58,138	67,029	77,086
Luxembourg	–	–	–	–
Mexico	4,242	4,931	8,443	10,456
Netherlands	3,329	3,948	4,018	2,408
New Zealand	–	–	–	–
Norway	–	–	–	–
Poland	–	–	–	–
Portugal	–	–	–	–
Spain	55,578	56,060	55,455	55,299
Sweden	76,761	61,395	69,935	69,928
Switzerland	22,953	23,351	24,895	25,409
Turkey	–	–	–	–
UK	70,543	89,362	88,964	98,146
USA	649,399	646,987	713,806	666,363

(continued)

Nuclear Electricity Production in OECD Countries *(continued)*

Country/region	1991	1993	1995	1997
OECD North America	738,570	746,741	820,093	759,347
OECD Pacific	269,771	307,394	358,283	396,142
OECD Europe	795,963	843,858	860,417	911,765
OECD TOTAL	1,804,304	1,897,993	2,038,793	2,067,254
EU15	747,152	794,084	809,266	859,894

Source: Energy Statistics of OECD Countries 1996–1997, © *OECD/International Energy Agency 1999*

See also **Nuclear Power Plants in the UK**, p 696.

Global Distribution of Minerals

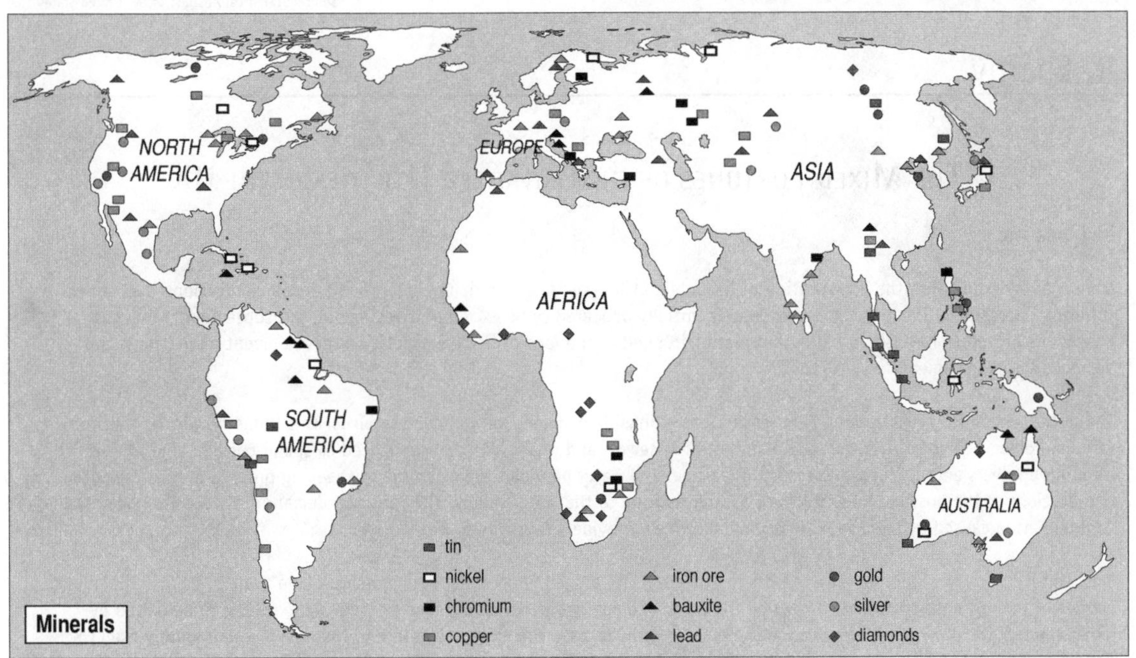

World Production of Major Mineral Commodities

(N/A = not available.)

Commodity	Units	1990	1995	1997	1998[1]	Leading producers, 1997
Mineral fuels						
Coal	million short tons	5,353	5,134	5,218	N/A	China, USA, India
Dry natural gas	trillion cubic feet	73.6	77.9	81.7	N/A	Russian Federation, USA, Canada
Natural gas plant liquids[2]	million barrels[3]	1,691	2,002	2,099	N/A	USA, Saudi Arabia, Canada
Petroleum, crude	million barrels[3]	22,107	22,752	24,243	N/A	Saudi Arabia, USA, Russian Federation
Nonmetallic minerals						
Cement, hydraulic	million metric tons	1,160	1,444	1,512	1,500	China, Japan, USA
Diamond, gem and industrial	million carats	111	113	118	N/A	Australia, Russian Federation, Democratic Republic of Congo
Nitrogen in ammonia	million metric tons	97.5	96.1	101.0	101.0	China, USA, India
Phosphate rock	million metric tons	162	130	138	141	USA, China, Morocco
Potash, marketable	million metric tons	27.5	24.7	25.7	24.9	Canada, Germany, Belarus
Salt	million metric tons	183	192	201	200	USA, China, Germany
Sulphur, elemental basis	million metric tons	57.8	53.2	53.6	54.0	USA, Canada, China
Metals						
Aluminium[4]	million metric tons	19.3	19.9	21.4	22.2	USA, Russian Federation, Canada
Bauxite, gross weight	million metric tons	113.0	107.0	123.0	125.0	Australia, Guinea, Brazil
Chromite, gross weight[2]	thousand metric tons	13,200	14,300	12,500	12,600	South Africa, Turkey, India
Copper, metal content[5]	thousand metric tons	8,950	10,100	11,400	11,900	Chile, USA, Canada
Gold, metal content	metric tons	2,180	2,220	2,410	2,400	South Africa, USA, Australia
Iron ore, gross weight[6]	million metric tons	983	1,030	1,040	1,020	China, Brazil, Australia
Lead, metal content[5]	thousand metric tons	3,370	2,780	3,010	3,080	Australia, China, USA
Manganese ore, gross weight	million metric tons	26.1	23.0	N/A	N/A	China, South Africa, Ukraine

(continued)

World Production of Major Mineral Commodities *(continued)*

Commodity	Units	1990	1995	1997	1998[1]	Leading producers, 1997
Nickel, metal content[5]	thousand metric tons	974	1,030	1,120	1,170	Russian Federation, Canada, New Caledonia (France)
Steel, crude	million metric tons	771	755	795	783	European Union, Japan, China
Tin, metal content[5]	thousand metric tons	221	195	211	216	China, Indonesia, Peru
Zinc, metal content[5]	thousand metric tons	7,150	7,240	7,460	7,800	Canada , Australia, China

[1] 1998 data are preliminary.
[2] Excludes China.
[3] Barrels hold 42 gallons.
[4] Unalloyed ingot metal.
[5] Mine output.
[6] Includes iron ore concentrates and iron ore agglomerates.

Source: Statistical Abstract of the United States 1999

UK Energy

The Mixed Fortunes of the Privatized Utilities in the UK

by Linda Wain

More than a decade after the privatization of UK public utilities – gas, electricity, water, and telecommunications – all sectors are suffering uncertainty. The new companies' shares initially appeared to be excellent investments, but subsequently industry watchdogs proved to have sharp teeth, and profits dropped in the face of fierce competition, development restrictions, and demands for improvement.

The water companies faced development restrictions alongside demands for improved services. This industry, which inherited serious problems of water pollution and disintegrating sewers and pipework, has been forced to spend considerable sums on cleaning up rivers and beaches, and reducing leakage. The water providers are also urgently seeking protection against legal ramifications of the possible side-effects of adding fluoride to the water supply. They are also demanding protection against the contamination caused by their being forced to allow new providers to use their pipework.

Most water companies reported lower profits in 2000 and threatened large-scale redundancies. Some want to merge (the objects of merger including those companies owned by the French company Vivendi), but these mergers are expected to be halted by legislation for the prevention of monopolies. Some 27 providers are therefore vulnerable to take-overs – particularly from UK energy suppliers, and from overseas water companies that are prevented from expanding at home. Some of these companies are most interested in the providers' ancillary businesses, such as waste and recycling services, so they may try to hive off water provision services as mutuals (nonprofit-making organizations) – although this is also likely to be blocked.

Many companies seeking to add water to their portfolios already supply gas and electricity through shared cabling and pipelines. One of the largest, PowerGen, has even linked up with the Safeway supermarket chain to supply energy nationally.

The fortunes of the other utilities have been similarly mixed. The imposition by Middle Eastern countries of a world oil embargo in 1973 led to intensive British exploration at sea, and many major deposits were found, along with substantial pockets of natural gas. Large-scale extraction of gas in UK coastal waters led to further problems for the British coal industry – already suffering from a decrease of coal-fired electricity generators in favour of nuclear power.

Electricity Generation, Supply, and Consumption in the UK

(– = not applicable. N/A = not available. N = nil or negligible. In gigawatt hours.)

Category		1990	1992	1994	1996	1997	1998
Electricity generated							
Major power producers[1]	conventional steam stations	230,376	217,228	174,943	160,565	133,132	134,317
	combined cycle gas turbine stations	N/A	2,991	36,971	65,880	86,974	93,832
	nuclear stations	61,306	73,269	88,282	91,040	98,146	100,140
	gas turbines and oil engines	432	358	244	226	459	221
	hydroelectric stations						
	natural flow	4,393	4,591	4,317	2,801	3,337	4,240
	pumped storage	1,982	1,697	1,463	1,556	1,486	1,624
	renewables other than hydro[2]	4	45	506	588	609	590
	Total	298,495	300,177	306,726	326,287	324,143	334,972
Other generators[3]	conventional steam stations[4]	15,014	15,049	14,866	17,200	16,606	16,559
	combined cycle gas turbine stations	292	409	902	1,232	1,500	2,848
	hydro-electric stations (natural flow)	814	840	777	560	790	986
	renewables other than hydro[2]	683	1,028	1,707	2,104	2,641	3,532
	Total	21,244	20,864	18,252	21,096	21,235	23,276
All generating companies	conventional steam stations	245,390	232,277	189,809	177,765	149,738	150,876
	combined cycle gas turbine stations	292	3,400	37,873	67,112	88,474	96,680
	nuclear stations	65,749	76,807	88,282	94,671	98,146	100,140
	gas turbines and oil engines	432	358	244	226	459	221
	hydroelectric stations						
	natural flow	5,207	5,431	5,094	3,361	4,127	5,226
	pumped storage	1,982	1,697	1,463	1,556	1,486	1,624
	renewables other than hydro[2]	687	1,073	2,213	2,692	3,250	4,122
	Total	319,739	321,043	324,978	347,383	345,378	358,248
Electricity used on works	major generating companies[1]	17,891	18,485	16,696	16,674	15,404	16,471
	other generators[3]	1,720	1,752	795	1,023	967	1,306
	Total	19,611	20,237	17,491	17,697	16,371	17,777
Electricity supplied							
Major power producers[1]	conventional steam stations	218,957	205,897	166,883	153,170	127,075	127,581
	combined cycle gas turbine stations	N/A	2,964	36,315	65,604	86,682	93,005
	nuclear stations	58,664	69,135	79,962	85,820	89,341	91,186
	gas turbines and oil engines	403	311	233	216	436	211
	hydroelectric stations						
	natural flow	4,384	4,579	4,265	2,763	3,299	4,228
	pumped storage	1,892	1,635	1,417	1,507	1,439	1,569
	renewables other than hydro[2]	3	37	455	533	540	722
	Total	280,604	281,692	290,030	309,612	308,812	318,501
Other generators[3]	conventional steam stations[4]	14,082	14,033	14,183	16,340	15,583	N/A
	combined cycle gas turbine stations	280	394	866	1,180	1,425	2,706
	hydroelectric stations (natural flow)	806	832	769	554	751	880
	renewables other than hydro[2]	656	987	1,639	1,999	2,509	3,123
	Total	19,524	19,112	17,457	20,073	20,268	21,970
All generating companies	conventional steam stations[4]	233,039	219,930	182,066	169,510	142,950	143,411
	combined cycle gas turbine stations	280	3,358	37,681	66,784	88,107	95,711
	nuclear stations	58,664	69,135	79,962	85,820	89,341	91,186
	gas turbines and oil engines	403	311	233	216	436	210
	hydroelectric stations						
	natural flow	5,190	5,411	5,034	3,317	4,050	5,108
	pumped storage	1,892	1,635	1,417	1,507	1,439	1,569
	renewables other than hydro[2]	659	1,024	2,094	2,532	3,049	3,845
	Total	300,128	300,804	307,487	329,686	329,080	340,471
Electricity used in pumping	Major power producers[1]	2,626	2,257	2,051	2,430	2,477	2,594
Electricity supplied (net)	major power producers[1]	277,978	279,435	287,979	307,181	306,335	315,907
	other generators[3]	19,524	19,112	17,457	20,073	20,268	21,970
	Total	297,502	298,547	305,436	327,254	326,603	337,877
Net imports		11,990	16,694	16,887	16,755	16,574	12,468
Electricity available		309,408	315,241	322,323	344,009	343,177	350,345
Losses in transmission, etc		24,988	23,788	30,541	29,724	25,691	26,076
Electricity consumption							
Fuel industries		9,986	9,984	7,518	8,629	8,235	7,575
Final users	industrial sector	100,643	95,277	95,067	103,129	104,743	107,226
	domestic sector	93,793	99,482	101,407	107,513	104,455	109,610
	other sectors	79,997	86,711	87,790	95,014	100,053	99,858
	Total final users	274,434	281,468	284,264	305,656	309,251	316,694
Total electricity consumption		284,420	291,453	291,782	314,285	317,486	324,269

[1] Represents generating companies corresponding to the old public sector supply system, i.e. National Power, PowerGen, Nuclear Electric, First Hydro Ltd, Scottish Power, Scottish Hydro-Electric, Scottish Nuclear, Premier Power Ltd, Coolkeeragh Power Ltd, Midland Power (UK) Ltd, South Western Electricity, NIGEN, and new independent generators, i.e. Teeside Power Ltd, Lakeland Power Ltd, Corby Power Ltd, Peterborough Power Ltd, Regional Power Ltd, Fibropower Ltd, Fibrogen Ltd, Fellside Heat and Power Ltd, Kead by Generation Ltd, Barking Power Ltd, Elm Energy and Recycling (UK) Ltd, South East London Combined Heat and Power Ltd, Derwent Cogeneration Ltd, Medway Power Ltd.

[2] Includes wind and biofuels.

[3] Represents larger establishments in the industrial and transport sectors generating one gigawatt-hour or more a year. Reactors operated by the United Kingdom Atomic Energy Authority and by British Nuclear Fuels plc are included.

[4] For other generators, conventional steam stations cover all types of station not separately listed.

Source: Annual Abstract of Statistics 2000,

Nuclear Power Plants in the UK

(Magnox – named after the magnesium oxide casing surrounding the uranium fuel rod. PWR – pressure water reactor; AGR – advanced gas reactor.)

Station name	Company	Fuel	Installed capacity (megawatts)	Year of commission
Hinkley Point B	Nuclear Electric	AGR	1,275	1978
Torness	Scottish Nuclear	AGR	1,250	1988
Heysham 2	Nuclear Electric	AGR	1,320	1989
Sizewell B	Nuclear Electric	PWR	1,200	1994
Hunterston B	Scottish Nuclear	AGR	1,150	1976
Heysham 1	Nuclear Electric	AGR	1,150	1989
Hartlepool	Nuclear Electric	AGR	1,200	1989
Dungeness B	Nuclear Electric	AGR	1,112	1985
Wylfa	Magnox Electric	Magnox	1,050	1971
Hinkley Point A	Magnox Electric	Magnox	475	1965
Dungeness A	Magnox Electric	Magnox	445	1965
Oldbury	Magnox Electric	Magnox	440	1967
Sizewell A	Magnox Electric	Magnox	430	1966
Brodwell	Magnox Electric	Magnox	240	1962
Calder Hall	British Nuclear Fuels	Magnox	192	1956
Chapelcross	British Nuclear Fuels	Magnox	196	1959

Source: Energy Report: Transforming Markets 1998, *© Crown copyright 1998*

See also **Nuclear Electricity Production in OECD Countries,** p 692.

Renewable Energy Utilization in the UK

Data include some waste of fossil fuel origin.
(In tonnes of oil equivalent.)

Source		1994	1996	1998
Used to generate electricity				
Onshore wind[1]		29,500	41,800	76,100
Hydro[1]	small scale	13,600	7,400	17,500
	large scale[2]	424,300	281,600	431,800
Biofuels	landfill gas	169,500	230,600	387,200
	sewage sludge digestion[3]	118,300	131,200	126,500
	municipal solid waste combustion[4]	304,800	324,500	545,700
	other[5]	114,500	131,300	140,900
	Total biofuels	707,100	817,500	1,200,300
TOTAL		1,174,600	1,148,300	1,725,800
Used to generate heat				
Active solar heating[6]		7,800	8,600	9,500
Biofuels	landfill gas	18,900	16,600	13,600
	sewage sludge digestion[3]	52,100	59,000	57,600
	wood combustion (domestic)[7]	204,200	204,200	204,200
	wood combustion (industrial)[7]	455,100	505,500	506,100
	straw combustion[8]	71,700	71,700	71,700
	municipal solid waste combustion[4]	46,800	44,200	22,000
	other[9]	46,600	43,700	43,700
	Total biofuels	895,400	944,900	918,900
Geothermal aquifiers		800	800	800
TOTAL		904,000	954,300	929,200
Total use of renewable sources				
Active solar heating[6]		7,800	8,600	9,500
Onshore wind		29,400	41,800	76,100
Hydro		437,900	289,000	449,300
Biofuels		1,602,600	1,762,400	2,119,100
Geothermal aquifiers		800	800	800
TOTAL		2,078,600	2,102,600	2,655,000

[1] For wind and hydro the figures represent the energy content of the electricity supplied, but for biofuels the figures represent the energy content of the fuel used.
[2] Excluding pumped storage stations.
[3] No estimate is made for digestors where gas is used to heat the sludge.
[4] Includes combustion of refuse-derived fuel pellets.
[5] Includes electricity from farm waste digestion, poultry litter combustion, and waste tyre combustion.
[6] Figures are based on a survey carried out in 1995 and are updated using data from the Solar Trade Association.
[7] Figures are an approximate estimate of domestic combustion based on a survey carried out in 1989; a moisture content of 50% is assumed.
[8] An approximate estimate based on a limited survey carried out in 1994 and on information collected in 1990.
[9] Includes heat from industrial wood waste combustion, waste tyre combustion, hospital waste combustion, general industrial waste combustion, and farm waste digestion.

Source: Digest of United Kingdom Energy Statistics 1999, *© Crown copyright 1999*

Total Inland Energy Consumption in the UK

(In millions of tonnes of oil equivalent.)

Category	1990	1992	1994	1996	1997	1998
Inland energy consumption of primary fuels and equivalents [1]						
Coal[2]	66.9	63.0	51.3	47.5	42.4	42.9
Petroleum[3]	78.3	78.3	77.6	77.9	75.3	74.8
Primary electricity[4]	17.7	20.4	23.2	23.6	25.1	25.1
Natural gas[5]	51.2	55.1	64.8	81.3	82.8	85.9
Less energy used by fuel producers and losses in conversion and distribution	67.6	66.8	66.2	70.9	71.0	72.5
Total consumption by final users[1]	146.4	150.0	153.2	162.0	154.5	156.2
Total internal energy consumption[1]	214.9	217.7	218.5	230.3	225.6	228.9
Final energy consumption by type of fuel						
Coal (direct use)[6]	8.1	8.1	6.9	4.9	4.4	3.8
Coke and breeze	4.3	3.9	1.2	1.0	0.9	0.9
Other solid fuel[6]	0.8	0.7	0.8	0.8	0.7	0.6
Coke oven gas	0.6	0.5	0.8	1.3	1.3	1.2
Natural gas (direct use)[5]	46.1	48.4	49.9	57.4	54.4	55.9
Electricity	23.6	24.2	24.4	26.2	26.5	27.1
Petroleum (direct use)[7]	63.3	64.6	65.2	66.1	65.4	65.8
Final energy consumption by class of consumer						
Agriculture	1.3	1.4	1.4	1.4	1.3	1.4
Iron and steel industry	6.9	6.5	7.7	4.7	4.6	4.4
Other industries	30.9	29.1	30.7	31.2	30.1	30.5
Railways[8]	0.7	0.7	0.7	1.3	1.2	0.5
Road transport	38.8	39.4	39.7	40.7	41.2	40.1
Water transport	1.4	1.4	1.3	1.3	1.3	1.2
Air transport	7.3	7.4	8.1	8.9	9.3	10.2
Domestic	40.8	44.0	44.0	48.1	44.9	46.0
Public administration	7.7	9.1	8.3	8.9	8.6	8.2
Commercial and other services[9]	10.3	10.5	11.0	12.0	12.1	12.1

[1] Includes, from 1988, small amounts of primary heat sources (solar, geothermal, etc). Up to 1988 includes natural gas used for non-energy purposes (e.g. petrochemicals).
[2] Includes net trade and stock change in other solid fuels. Includes, from 1988, solid renewable sources (wood, waste, etc).
[3] Figures give refinery throughput of crude oil, plus net foreign trade and stock change in petroleum products. Petroleum products not used as fuels (chemical feedstock, industrial and white spirits, lubricants, bitumen, and wax) are excluded.
[4] Primary electricity comprises nuclear, natural flow hydro, net imports of electricity, and, from 1988, generation of wind stations.
[5] Natural gas includes colliery methane, non-energy use of natural gas up to 1988, and, from 1988, landfill gas and sewage gas.
[6] Figures include solid renewable sources from 1988.
[7] Includes products such as briquettes, ovoids, Phurnacite, and Coalite, and, from 1988, wood, waste, and other materials used for heat generation.
[8] Figures include fuel used at transport premises from 1990.
[9] Figures include fuel used at transport premises prior to 1990.

Source: Annual Abstract of Statistics 2000,

Agriculture

Introduction

Arguments rage over whether intensive agriculture has helped or hindered poor countries, but experts are united in condemning the International Monetary Fund and the World Bank for backing the mass destruction of rainforests by multinationals to help pay off the debts of African countries. Some fear that this will speed the effects of global warming and rob rainforest dwellers of long-term survival through sustainable agriculture.

Some countries are further increasing their prosperity through genetically modified (GM) crops. But GM remains a contentious issue, particularly in Britain where protestors destroyed experimental plantings, and farmers unwittingly planted GM-contaminated seed.

Some livestock farmers in the UK have struggled to survive in the face of the mass slaughter of their stock, export bans, and of drastic revenue falls caused by cheap imports. Most feel they have been poorly treated by the European Union (EU), which has increased the cost of farming through legislation, such as new pollution controls for pig and poultry production (estimated to cost around £19,000 per farm). Legislation has also caused the closure of smaller slaughterhouses, forcing animals to be transported long distances – to the detriment of their welfare and the environment.

Agriculture: Intensive, Extensive, and Organic

Intensive agriculture
Intensive farming involves large quantities of inputs, such as labour or fertilizers, over a small area of land. Yields are often much higher than those obtained from extensive agriculture. The developed world achieves high production levels through mechanization, intensive farming, and scientific methods. The world's largest producer and exporter of food is the USA although less than 3% of its total workforce is employed in agriculture.

Extensive agriculture
Extensive farming is a system where the area of the farm is large but there are low inputs (such as labour or fertilizers). Extensive farming generally gives rise to lower yields per hectare than intensive

Agriculture: Intensive, Extensive, and Organic *(continued)*

agriculture. For example, in East Anglia, intensive use of land may give wheat yields as high as 53 tonnes per hectare, whereas an extensive wheat farm on the Canadian prairies may produce an average of 8.8 tonnes per hectare.

Organic farming

Organic farming does not involve the use of artificial fertilizers, pesticides (such as weedkillers or insecticides), or other agrochemicals (such as hormones, growth stimulants, or fruit regulators). In place of artificial fertilizers, compost, manure, seaweed, or other substances derived from living things are used (hence the name 'organic'). Growing a crop of a nitrogen-fixing plant, then ploughing it back into the soil, also fertilizes the ground. Weeds can be controlled by hoeing, mulching (covering with manure, straw, or black plastic), or burning off. Organic farming methods produce food with minimal pesticide residues and greatly reduce pollution of the environment. They are more labour intensive and therefore more expensive, but use less fossil fuel.

Global Food Production

(In millions of metric tons.)

Commodity	1990	1992	1994	1996	1998[1]
Grains					
wheat	588.0	562.3	524.6	582.4	586.6
coarse grains					
corn	482.3	538.5	561.8	591.4	593.7
Total	828.6	871.8	873.6	908.1	878.7
rice, milled	352.0	355.7	364.5	379.9	378.0
Total	1,768.6	1,789.8	1,762.7	1,870.4	1,843.2
Oils	58.3	61.7	70.1	74.9	80.2
Soybeans	104.2	117.4	137.7	131.6	158.1
Rapeseed	25.1	25.3	30.4	31.4	36.9
Pulses	58.4	51.0	57.2	55.3	56.8
Vegetables and melons	461.4	478.6	532.9	589.1	599.4
Fruits	352.2	379.0	390.4	426.7	431.2
Nuts	4.6	5.0	5.3	5.1	5.4
Red meat	116.0	118.6	119.9	128.6	133.3
Poultry	37.4	40.6	44.8	51.1	55.8
Milk	441.3	423.7	383.7	379.8	383.8

[1] Preliminary data.

Source: Statistical Abstract of the United States 1999

How Many Insects in your Food?

The US Food and Drug Administration (FDA) has guidelines for acceptable levels of insect contamination in food. For example it is acceptable to have up to 3 fruitfly maggots per 200 g/7 oz of tomato juice; 100 insect fragments per 25 g/0.8 oz of curry powder; and up to 13 insect heads per 100 g/3.5 oz of fig paste.

Food Facts

- It takes 500 l/880 pt of water to produce 1 kg/2.2 lb of potatoes.
- It takes 1,900 l/3,300 pt of water to produce 1 kg/2.2 lb of rice.
- It takes 3,500 l/6,200 pt of water to produce 1 kg/2.2 lb of chicken.
- It takes 100,000 l/176,000 pt of water to produce 1 kg/2.2 lb of beef.

Agriculture in the UK

About 75% of the UK's land area is in use for agriculture. The majority is grassland used for grazing animals, with just under 30% used for crops. UK farming employs around 2.3% of the country's workforce (around 615,000 people). The UK's main agricultural exports are livestock (reduced since 1995 because of the BSE crisis), food products, agrochemicals, and agricultural machinery.

Between 1990 and 1995 total income from farming in the UK doubled, but fell more than 60% between 1995 and 1999. The contribution made by agriculture to the UK's gross domestic product (GDP) has also been falling, and now stands at around 1% of the total.

Agricultural Land Use in the UK

(Figures are rounded so may not add up to 100.)

1998

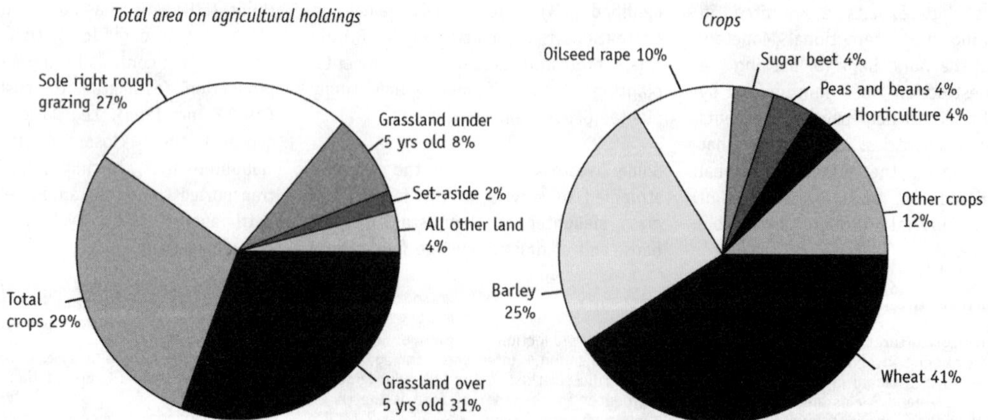

Source: Ministry of Agriculture, Fisheries, and Food, © Crown copyright 1999

■ **Agriculture**

Number and Size of Farms in the UK

As of June 1998.

Number and area of holdings

		Hectares				
		< 20	20–< 50	50–< 100	100 and over	Total[1]
England	number of holdings	63,600	31,600	24,000	25,800	145,100
	area of holdings (ha)	487,300	1,049,700	1,718,600	5,905,600	9,161,300
Scotland[2]	number of holdings	12,200	5,800	5,800	9,300	33,000
	area of holdings (ha)	86,600	194,900	419,300	4,498,700	5,199,500
Wales	number of holdings	11,100	7,600	5,500	3,700	27,900
	area of holdings (ha)	101,400	251,600	386,900	725,600	1,465,500
Northern Ireland	number of holdings	14,900	10,500	4,700	1,600	31,800
	area of holdings (ha)	145,300	339,700	321,800	261,600	1,068,400
Total UK	number of holdings	101,800	55,500	40,000	40,400	237,800
	area of holdings (ha)	820,600	1,835,900	2,846,600	11,391,500	16,894,700

[1] Totals may not necessarily agree with the sum of their components, due to rounding.

Source: Farm Incomes in the United Kingdom 1997/8, *© Crown copyright 1999*

The Price of Agricultural Land in England, by Region

Region	Average price (£ per hectare)		
	1996	1997[1]	1998[1]
North East	3,728	3,398	3,822
North West	5,511	5,972	6,189
Yorkshire and Humber	4,897	5,589	4,573
East Midlands	5,867	5,965	6,142
West Midlands	7,770	7,017	6,493
East	6,453	7,350	6,942
South East	6,845	7,934	8,168
South West	6,067	7,180	6,731
England	6,058	6,451	6,134

[1] Provisional estimates.

Source: Ministry of Agriculture, Fisheries, and Food, © Crown copyright 2000

Income from Farming in the UK

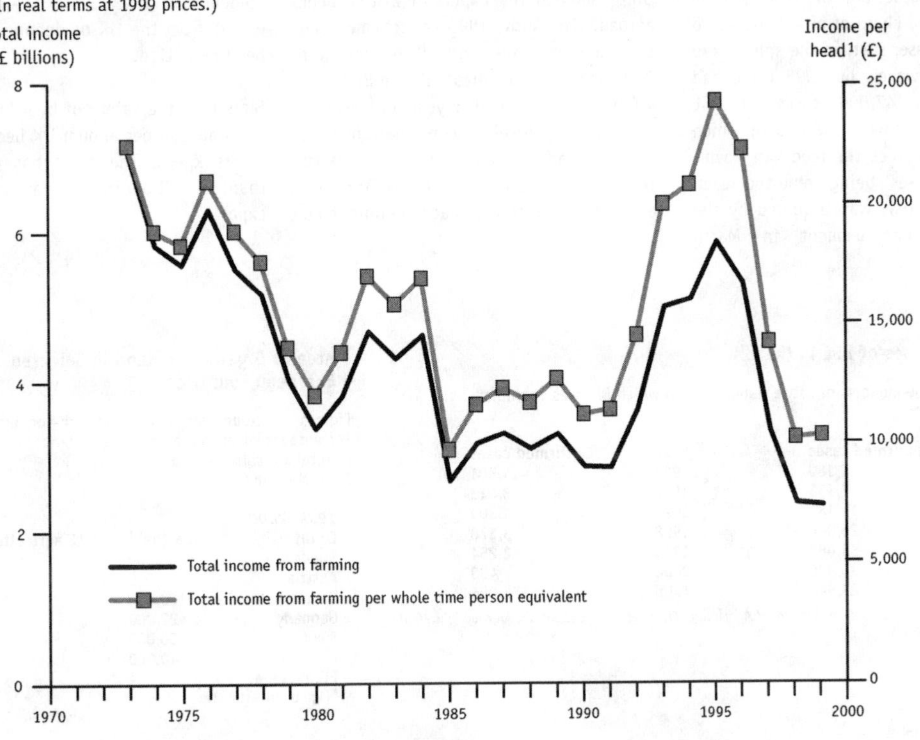

[1] Whole time person equivalent.

Source: Ministry of Agriculture, Fisheries, and Food, © Crown copyright 2000

Farm Income in the UK

Data are absolute levels of net farm income per farm at current prices.

Farm type[1]	Net farm income (£)			Annual % change	
	1997/98	1998/99	1999/00	1998/99	1999/00
Dairy	17,300	10,300	8,000	– 41	– 21
Cattle and sheep (hill)	7,500	3,600	2,500	– 52	– 26
Cattle and sheep (lowland)	1,400	– 500	1,500	2	2
Cereals	13,100	6,600	8,500	– 49	30
General cropping	17,200	29,700	15,500	73	– 48
Pigs and poultry	15,200	– 14,700	– 8,000	2	2
Mixed	6,400	1,300	4,000	– 79	179
All types (excluding horticulture)	11,000	7,200	6,000	– 34	– 16

[1] Full-time farms only.
[2] Percentage changes not given where income is negative.

Source: Ministry of Agriculture, Fisheries, and Food, © *Crown copyright 2000*

GM Crops

In April 2000 Advanta Seeds UK advised the Government that some of its supplies of conventional rapeseed, sold and sown in 1999 and 2000 in several EU Member States including the UK, contained about 1% of genetically modified rapeseed. In the UK, about 9,000 hectares were sown with affected stocks in 1999 and about 4,700 hectares were sown in the spring of 2000.

See also **Sites of Genetically Modified Crop Trials**, p 481.

BSE

The epidemic of bovine spongiform encephalopathy (BSE or 'mad cow disease') was first reported in beef cattle in Britain in 1985. It was later traced to cattle feed containing sheep carcasses infected with scrape. Government action to deal with the initial crisis involved a ban on animal remains (except fishmeal) being included in sheep and cattle feed, the slaughter of animals suspected of having the disease, and the removal from the human food chain of offal believed to carry the disease, such as the spinal cord and brain. However, by 1995 there had been around 147,000 cases of BSE recorded in UK cows – 18,000 of which had been born since the feed ban – with about 220 cases being reported each week. A new crisis was triggered by the government announcement in March 1996 that 10 young people had died from a variant of Creutzfeldt-Jakob Disease (CJD), probably caused by eating infected meat. However its statement that the risk from eating beef was only 'extremely small' did little to reduce people's fears.

Home-produced beef had been banned from UK schools and hospitals since May 1990 and in March 1996 the European Union banned the export of British beef abroad. In April 1996 a scheme was proposed by the agriculture minister Douglas Hogg to eradicate BSE in Britain – 4.6 million cattle over 6 years old were to be culled. Following confirmation that the new variant form of CJD belongs to the same group of diseases as BSE, the agriculture secretary Jack Cunningham announced a ban on the sale of beef on the bone.

By 1999 BSE had been detected in 175,000 cattle across Europe, 99.7% of them in the UK. However, the number of cases of BSE in Britain has declined and by mid-1999 about 55 new cases were being reported each week, compared with over 1,000 a week at the height of the epidemic in 1993. From 1 August 1999 export from the UK of deboned beef has been permitted.

Fears over the safety of beef brought the £500 million per annum UK beef industry to its knees. The crisis has cost more than £5 billion in eradication and lost exports.

Confirmed Cases of BSE in the UK

Figures are for the numbers of cattle slaughtered in which BSE was confirmed.
As of June 2000.

Year	Confirmed cases	Year	Confirmed cases
1988	2,180	1995	14,301
1989	7,133	1996	8,013
1990	14,181	1997	4,309
1991	25,026	1998	3,178
1992	36,680	1999	2,254
1993	34,370	2000	488
1994	23,943	**Total**	176,056

Source: Ministry of Agriculture, Fisheries, and Food, © *Crown copyright 2000*

Area of Organic Farmland in Selected European Countries

Figures include organic and in-conversion land. Percentages given represent organic land as a percentage of total agricultural land.
As of May 2000.

1999–2000

Country	Area (ha)[1]	% agricultural land
Sweden	268,000	11.2
Austria	345,000	10
Denmark	160,000	6
Germany	422,000	3
Italy	900,000	5.3
UK	540,000	3
EU average		2.2

[1] Figures are estimates.

Source: The Soil Association

Organic Farming in the UK

by GPF Lane

By the end of the 20th century organic farming had ceased to be a fringe activity and become a part of mainstream agriculture in the UK, with over 1,500 fully organic farmers farming almost half a million hectares (1.2 million acres) at the turn of the millennium. Conversion to organic farming experienced a sharp upturn towards the end of the 1990s, largely as a reaction to the bovine spongiform encephalopathy (BSE, or 'mad cow disease') epidemic and a decline in the fortunes of conventional farming. Public opposition to the introduction of genetically modified (GM) crops and the availability of financial assistance through Ministry of Agriculture, Fisheries, and Food (MAFF) schemes – such as the over subscribed Organic Farming Scheme (1999) – were also influential.

Organic produce is claimed to be healthier, as it contains lower levels of pesticide, fertilizer, and antibiotic residues, but there is no firm evidence to support this; the increased incidence of heart disease and cancer since the 1940s may be due to 'chemical' farming, or an increased preference for fatty foods. However, many people choosing organic produce are buying into the philosophy of organic farming – the idea of holistic, environmentally sustainable, non-intensive production, achieved with ecological principles to the fore.

Although organic crops normally yield about 60% of the same crop grown conventionally, current undersupply, with up to 70% of organic produce imported, means that substantial premiums are available for opportunists. Fears have already been expressed that the 'commoditization' of organic produce, which is starting to happen, will bring with it the familiar cycle of overproduction for maximum profit and subsequent decline in quality.

Organic Farming: Key Dates

1888 Biological pest control, later to become an important aspect of organic agriculture, is first used in California to control scale insects on citrus plants.

1924 Austrian philosopher and educationalist Rudolf Steiner gives a series of lectures on agriculture. These describe methods for achieving harmony with natural forces, derived from his theories of anthroposophy. The lectures inspire the development of what becomes known as biodynamic agriculture.

1930 Biodynamic pioneers form the Demeter Trading Association to market their produce in Germany. The Association is banned by the Nazis in 1941.

1940 The English agronomist Sir Albert Howard publishes *An Agricultural Testament*. This influential book describes a theory of farming based on the maintenance of soil fertility through composting, and avoidance of mineral or chemical fertilizers.

1942 Inspired by the work of Howard, J I Rodale launches *Organic Gardening and Farming* magazine in the USA. Rodale does much to popularize the term 'organic' in an agricultural context.

1943 *The Living Soil* by Lady Eve Balfour, an important figure in the development of organic farming in the UK, is published. She begins the 'Haughley Experiment' – a long-term (30 years) trial comparing the new intensive farming regime, reliant on chemicals, with the alternative organic methods championed by her and Howard.

1946 The Soil Association is launched in England. It supports extensive research into the 'vital relationships between soil, plant, animal, and man'. The Association is based on Balfour's experimental farm in Suffolk.

1954 The Demeter Association is re-established in Germany to promote and regulate biodynamic produce.

1962 US biologist Rachel Carson's book *Silent Spring* describes the environmental damage done by heavy pesticide use, fuelling widespread public concern. There is a general increase in interest in 'natural' farming methods throughout the 1960s and 1970s.

1975 British organic producers establish Organic Farmers and Growers, a cereal grain marketing cooperative.

1980 A new UK producers' self-help organization, the Organic Growers Association, is formed. It is followed in 1983 by a similar body, British Organic Farmers.

1986 The Organic Advisory Service is founded to assist British organic farmers. It is based at the Elm Farm Research Centre in Berkshire.

1987 The UK Register of Organic Food Standards (UKROFS) is established to oversee the certification of organic produce. At this time less than 0.1% of UK farmland is managed organically.

1989 Certification of organic producers in Britain is becoming more widespread, with 450 registered with the Soil Association, and 200 with Organic Farmers and Growers.

1991 European standards for organic production are agreed by the relevant national bodies of EC member states (e.g. UKROFS in the UK), via the EC (as it then was). EEC Regulation No. 2092/91 defines the basic standards for farming and food processing and the requirements for policing.

1995 The UK government introduces the Organic Aid Scheme, offering payments to conventional farmers wishing to convert to organic methods. The Organic Conversion Information Service is launched the following year to advise farmers wishing to convert. The UK organic food market is growing at a very rapid rate, and is worth £140 million, yet only comprising 0.4% of the total food market; organic fruit and vegetables are the most popular organic product. 70% of the produce supplying the organic market is imported.

1996 The USA has over 70,000 government certified organic farms; about 10% of Japan's farming villages have converted to organic production.

1997 The UK retail organic market is worth £273 million, having almost doubled in two years. Despite this, only 0.3% of British farmland is under organic methods, compared to 1.2% of the EU as a whole. Meanwhile, a poll indicates that over half of US consumers want organic methods to become the dominant form of agriculture in the USA.

1998 Controversy over the potential risks of genetic modification provides another boost for organic agriculture, which prohibits the use of GM crops. Sales of organic food are valued at £400 million in the UK, but 70% remains imported.

April 1999 The government opens its Organic Farming Scheme in England and Northern Ireland, which replaces the Organic Aid Scheme and raises payments to farmers wishing to convert to organic methods. The demand for the new scheme is so high that its entire 1999/2000 budget (£6.2 million) is allocated by August of the same year; a further £10 million is allocated in October 1999. Almost 1.5% of UK agricultural land is now organic, compared to 3% in Germany, 5% in Italy, 6% in Denmark, and 10% in Austria and Sweden. The EU average is 2.2%.

July 1999 Common standards for organic livestock and livestock products marketed in the EU are agreed.

October 1999 The Organic Targets bill is launched in parliament, setting goals of 30% of UK farmland and 20% of UK food to be organic by 2010.

March 2000 The rapid growth of organic agriculture continues, with 2.7% of British agricultural land managed organically or under conversion to organic.

Fishing Catches by Country

The data indicate annual catches in all regions.
(In thousands of tonnes live weight. – = not applicable.)

Country/region	1990	1992	1994	1996
European Union				
Austria	5	4	5	4
Belgium	42	37	36	32
Denmark	1,511	1,990	1,880	1,714
Finland	129	135	156	169
France	752	730	795	709
Germany	370	258	268	311
Greece	148	181	225	210
Italy	530	564	555	566
Ireland, Republic of	231	249	298	336
Luxembourg	–	–	–	–
Netherlands	406	433	422	415
Portugal	323	294	250	262
Spain	1,141	1,120	1,150	1,090
Sweden	254	310	390	374
UK	782	793	907	904
EU total	6,625	7,099	7,335	7,105
Iceland	1,522	1,583	1,571	2,076
Norway	1,603	2,431	2,334	2,638
European Economic Area total	9,750	11,113	11,240	11,819
Switzerland	4	4	3	3
USA	5,808	5,705	6,043	5,454
Canada	1,283	979	706	643
Japan	11,130	9,292	8,180	7,468

Source: Eurostat Yearbook 1998/9, © *European Communities*

Fishing Fleet of the UK

– = not applicable. N/A = not available.)

Fleet by size and segment	1993	1994	1995	1996	1997	1998
By size (metres)						
10 and under	7,666	7,194	6,319	5,606	5,474	5,487
>10						
10.00–12.19	1,361	1,167	1,016	800	732	628
12.20–17.00	751	680	622	540	523	491
17.01–18.29	220	193	187	164	162	154
18.30–24.38	657	610	574	509	471	443
24.39–30.48	210	211	212	223	227	226
30.49–36.58	124	126	127	114	104	89
>36.58	119	116	117	117	119	121
Total >10m	3,442	3,103	2,855	2,467	2,338	2,152
Total UK fleet (excluding islands)	11,108	10,297	9,174	8,073	7,812	7,639
By segment						
pelagic gears	69	68	67	58	49	50
beam trawls	240	212	220	215	153	123
demersal trawls	988	854	856	N/A	N/A	N/A
nephrop trawls	560	593	528	411	N/A	N/A
seines	203	197	165	N/A	N/A	N/A
demersal trawls and seines	N/A	N/A	N/A	1,040	N/A	N/A
demersal, seines, and nephrops	N/A	N/A	N/A	N/A	1,428	1,318
lines and nets	329	300	267	224	214	187
shellfish: mobile	181	206	194	265	227	241
shellfish: fixed	312	305	283	339	352	311
distant water	14	13	12	15	13	14
under 10 m	8,128	7,607	6,757	6,091	6,022	6,027
non-active/non-TAC[1]	668	472	371	–	–	–
other: mussel dredgers	N/A	N/A	N/A	N/A	3	2
Total UK fleet[2]	11,692	10,827	9,720	8,658	8,461	8,271

[1] TAC = total allowable catch; this is for fish species for which there are quotas.
[2] The UK figures here include Channel Islands and Isle of Man.

Source: Annual Abstract of Statistics 2000, © *Crown copyright 2000*

Forestry in Europe and the UK

Around 33% of the total land area of Europe is covered by woodland and the European Union's forests are increasing by an estimated 486 million cubic metres/17.6 billion cubic feet each year.

There are around 2.5 million hectares/6.2 million acres of woodland in the UK – about 10% of the total land area. Great Britain has around 2.2 million hectares/5.5 million acres of productive forest – 35% of this is managed by the Forestry Commission, a government department established in 1919. The UK imports around 85% of its timber and wood products.

Afforestation projects in the UK, aimed at increasing the area of woodland near cities to about 30% include the creation of 12 'community forests' covering 450,000 hectares/1.1 million acres, in and around major cities. Other afforestation schemes include the National Forest which is being developed in Staffordshire, Derbyshire, and Leicestershire, the Central Scotland Forest, and the Amman Gwendraeth scheme which is creating new woodlands in the Welsh valleys.

See also **Community Forests in England**, p 639.

■ Agriculture

International Forestry Comparisons

1997

Country	Forest area (million hectares)	Total land area (million hectares)	Forestry as % of land area
Austria	3.9	8.3	47
Belgium/Luxembourg	0.7	3.3	22
Denmark	0.4	4.2	10
Finland	20.0	30.5	66
France	15.0	55.0	27
Germany	10.7	34.9	31
Greece	6.5	12.9	51
Ireland, Republic of	0.6	6.9	8
Italy	6.5	29.4	22
Netherlands	0.3	3.4	10
Portugal	2.9	9.2	31
Spain	8.4	49.9	17
Sweden	24.4	41.2	59
UK	2.5	24.2	10
EU	102.9	313.2	33
China	133.0	932.6	14
Japan	25.0	37.7	67
Norway	8.1	30.7	26
Russian Federation	763.5	1,688.9	45
Switzerland	1.1	4.0	29
USA	212.5	915.9	23
World	3,454.4	12,981.0	27

Source: Britain 2000, The Official Yearbook of the United Kingdom,

See also **Countries Losing Greatest Areas of Forest**, p 637.

Forestry in the UK

(Years ending 31 March. Area: thousands of hectares; volume: millions of cubic metres.)

Item	1989–90	1990–91	1991–92	1992–93	1993–94	1994–95	1995–96	1996–97	1997–98	1998–99
***Forest area*[1]**										
Great Britain	2,326	2,336	2,350	2,361	2,377	2,390	2,405	2,423	2,440	2,659
Northern Ireland	74	75	77	77	78	79	80	81	81	2,577
Total UK	2,400	2,411	2,427	2,438	2,455	2,469	2,485	2,504	2,521	82
Forestry Commission (Great Britain)										
Productive woodland	864[5]	859	855	845	827	815	804	795	785	780
Net disposals of forestry land[2]	4.5	0.8	4.2	6.5	14.1	9.6	8.2	9.6	10.3	4.1
New planting[3]	4.1	3.5	3.0	2.4	1.4	0.9	0.4	0.5	0.1	0.1
Restocking[3]	7.9	7.6	8.3	8.5	7.9	7.9	7.5	7.9	7.8	7.9
Volume of timber removed[4]	3.5	3.4	3.9	4.1	4.3	4.3	4.2	4.7	4.7	5.3
Total estates	1,140	1,133	1,128	1,115	1,100	1,089	1,080	1,073	1,062	1,057
Private forestry (Great Britain)										
Productive woodland	1,266	1,281	1,298	1,317	1,344	1,367	1,392	1,417	1,444	1,542
New planting[3]	15.6	15.5	14.3	15.5	16.1	18.5	15.3	16.4	16.2	16.2
Restocking[3]	6.3	7.2	7.9	8.1	8.5	6.2	5.8	6.6	5.6	5.5
Volume of timber removed[4]	3.6	3.3	3.1	2.9	3.0	3.8	4.2	4.0	4.4	3.9
State afforestation in Northern Ireland										
Land under plantation	58.5	58.8	60.6	60.8	60.8	61.0	61.0	60.9	61.0	61.0
Plantable land acquired during year	0.6	0.4	0.3	0.4	0.4	0.1	0.1	0.1	0.1	0.3
Total area planted during year	1.0	1.0	0.9	0.9	0.8	0.8	0.8	0.6	0.7	0.7
Total estates	74.6	74.8	75.1	75.2	75.5	75.5	75.3	75.5	75.5	75.7

[1] Includes unproductive woodland.
[2] Data represent disposals less acquisitions, for plantations and plantable land.
[3] New planting is planting on ground not previously carrying forest; restocking is replacing trees after felling.
[4] Figures represent standing volume overbark; private forestry figures are for calendar years ending the previous December.
[5] The apparent decrease in 1989–90 is mainly the result of the reclassification of certain woodland types within the Forestry Commission.

Source: Annual Abstract of Statistics 2000,

Web Sites

APEC Secretariat Web Site

http://www.apecsec.org.sg/

Complete overview of the history and responsibilities of Asia-Pacific Economic Cooperation (APEC), as well as documentation from recent meetings.

Bank for International Settlements

http://www.bis.org/

Full information on the BIS and its role to promote cooperation among central banks, with links to all of the world's central banks that have Web sites.

Bank of England – Banknote Printing

http://www.bankofengland.co.uk/banknotes/index.htm

Easily-navigable site, with information on the origins of money and the complex printing process involved in the manufacture of new notes.

Budget

http://www.hm-treasury.gov.uk/pub/html/budget.html

Frequently updated information on the UK's budget from the Treasury. There is an index of official press releases relating to the budget, and wider information on the state of Britain's public finances.

Business Ethics Magazine Online

http://www.business-ethics.com/

Online version of the most comprehensive publication on corporate responsibility. It aims to promote ethical business practices, and to serve the community of professionals striving to live and work in responsible ways.

Capitalism.org

http://www.capitalism.org/home.htm

Philosophical, economic, and political examination of capitalism. Includes a 'Capitalism tour' and an online version of *Capitalism Magazine*.

Confederation of British Industry

http://www.cbi.org.uk/home.shtml

Representing over 250,000 public and private sector companies, the site has sections on 'News', 'CBI at work', and 'Business services'.

Cooperative Principles and History

http://www.wisc.edu/uwcc/prin.html

Clear exposition of the definition, values, principles, identity, and history of the co-operative movement, by the University of Wisconsin Center for Cooperatives.

Dow Jones Indexes

http://indexes.dowjones.com/

Latest readings from the Dow Jones Indexes, as well as explanations of the methodology used to compile them, and archives of previous readings.

European Bank for Reconstruction and Development

http://www.ebrd.com/english/index.htm

Explanation of the role and structure of the London-based group that assists in financing the economic transition in central and eastern Europe and the CIS.

European Free Trade Association

http://www.imf.org/external/np/sec/decdo/efta.htm

Introduction to the group of European states that are not levying import duties on one another, and its relationship with the European Union.

Federal Budget of the USA

http://www.access.gpo.gov/omb/index.html

Includes a citizens' guide with information about the budget and budget process for the general public, as well as the 'Economic Report of the President' for recent years.

Federal Reserve Board

http://www.bog.frb.fed.us/

Explains the complex functioning of the US central banking system, and is an invaluable source of information on the US economy in general.

Grameen Bank

http://www.citechco.net/grameen/bank/

Information about the pioneering work of the Grameen Bank, which extends credit without collateral to the poor of Bangladesh.

History of Money from Ancient Times to the Present Day

http://www.ex.ac.uk/~RDavies/arian/llyfr.html

Online version of a book about the history of money. It begins with a 'Comparative history of money' and ends with 'Third World money and debt in the 20th century'.

International Monetary Fund

http://www.imf.org/external/index.htm

Explains the role of the IMF in promoting international monetary cooperation and assisting states with balance-of-payments difficulties.

London Stock Exchange

http://www.londonstockexchange.com/

Explains how the exchange and its markets work, and how the stock market is regulated.

OECD – Organization for Economic Cooperation and Development

http://www.oecd.org/

As well as information on the OECD and the activities of its 29 member states, the site provides an excellent source of statistical information on the workings of the global economy.

164 Currency Converter

http://www.oanda.com/convert/classic

Here you can do automatic conversions to and from a wide range of currencies, from the Afghani to the złoty.

Reserve Bank of Australia

http://www.rba.gov.au/about/ab_ind.html

Home page of Australia's central bank; an essential site for anyone interested in monitoring the state of Australia's economy.

Secrets of Making Money

http://www.pbs.org/wgbh/nova/moolah/

This page investigates the science and art of minting money. There is a fun section that lets you try your hand at identifying bogus bills.

Stockmarket – the UK's Personal Finance Web Site

http://www.moneyworld.co.uk/stocks/index.html

Continually updated financial information from the leading stock exchanges.

United Nations Department of Economic and Social Affairs – Statistics Division

http://www.un.org/Depts/unsd/

Detailed, regularly updated, worldwide economic data.

US Securities and Exchange Commission

http://www.sec.gov/

Information on the US agency charged with the regulation of securities and financial markets. There is also advice for small businesses.

World Bank Home Page

http://www.worldbank.org/

Easy-to-use site includes sections on current events, press releases and bank news, country information, publications, and research studies.

World Economic Forum

http://www.weforum.org/

Independent international organization constituting a global partnership of business, political, and intellectual leaders, focusing on global economic development.

World Trade Organization

http://www.wto.org/wto/index.htm

Extensive information on the functions of the UN agency charged with administering international trade agreements; the full text of many of these agreements is included as well.

PEOPLE

People in the News

People in Court
Former Labour minister Lord Melchett, now head of the environmental group Greenpeace, is remanded in custody on **27 July 1999** after being charged with damaging a field of genetically modified (GM) wheat as part of a protest against trial plantings of GM crops.

Former Liverpool goalkeeper Bruce Grobbelaar wins a libel action against *The Sun* on **28 July 1999.** The paper had accused him of match fixing.

In **July 1999** a High Court judge rules that a 15-year-old girl (unnamed for legal reasons) should have a heart transplant against her wishes, as without the operation she would certainly die.

Former UK Conservative minister Neil Hamilton begins a libel action against Mohamed al-Fayed in **November 1999** over allegations that Mr al-Fayed had paid him 'cash for questions'.

Gary Glitter, the former English rock star, is jailed on **12 November 1999** for downloading child pornography from the Internet, but acquitted on eight charges of indecent assault. *News of the World* is later criticized for prejudicing the case by offering the complainant money for her story if Glitter is convicted, before the verdict is reached.

In **February 2000** British pop group the Spice Girls lose a legal battle with Aprilia, an Italian motorcycle company who estimate that they lost over £1 million in profits when a scooter sponsorship deal for a set of five scooters failed after Geri Halliwell left the group. The company claim that the rest of the group must have known that Halliwell was leaving when they signed the deal.

The Sultan of Brunei brings a suit against his youngest brother Prince Jefri and 70 others in **March 2000** for misuse of state funds. The Prince – who owns Bond Street jewellers Asprey & Garrard, hotels in London and Paris, homes in Brunei and abroad, and hundreds of luxury cars and a yacht – denies the charges.

English pop star **Noel Gallagher** and his wife, Meg, seperated amicably, nine months after the birth of their daughter in February 2000. *Syndication International*

Births in the News
In **July 1999** US model Cindy Crawford gives birth to a boy and calls him Presley, and in **October 1999** Danish model Helena Christensen gives birth to a boy and calls him Mingus. In **September 1999** English pop star Liam Gallagher and his wife, actress Patsy Kensit, have a son Lennon (named in tribute to Liam's musical idol, John Lennon). In **December 1999** English actress Emma Thompson and her partner, actor Greg Wise, have a baby girl they call Gaia. In **February 2000** English pop star Noel Gallagher and his wife, Meg Matthews, have a baby girl, Anaïs. On the other side of the Atlantic, US talk-show host Larry King, 66, and his seventh wife have a baby boy, Cannon, in **June 1999.**

On **19 October 1999** the symbolic six billionth person in the world is born to Fatima and Jasminko Nevic in a Sarajevo hospital; the child is later visited by UN Secretary General Kofi Annan.

On **1 January 2000** Jordan Doelling, born in Sydney, Australia, one second after midnight, is officially named as the first baby of the new millennium.

On **20 May 2000** Prime Minister Tony Blair's wife Cherie gives birth to a baby boy, Leo, the first child born to a serving UK prime minister for 150 years.

Children in the News
Prime Minister Tony Blair and his wife Cherie make a formal complaint in **December 1999** when *The Daily Sport* publishes a photograph of their eldest child, Euan, kissing a teenage girl at a Christmas ball. Euan returns to the limelight on **5 July 2000** when, in the same week that his father condemns 'drunken louts', he is arrested for being drunk and incapable after celebrating the end of his GCSE examinations. On **16 July 2000** the Press Complaints Commission upholds a complaint from the Blairs that *The Mail on Sunday* had invaded the privacy of their daughter Kathryn. The articles in question suggested that her school only offered her a place because of her family.

In **January 2000** English gay couple Tony Barlow and Barry Drewitt win their legal fight

to keep twins Aspen and Saffron Drewitt-Barlow in the UK. The twins were born to a surrogate mother in the USA.

A Burmese rebel group calling itself God's Army holds hundreds hostage in a Thai hospital in **January 2000**. The group is led by 12-year-old twins Johnny and Luther Htoo.

Rudy Donithan-Treat, an 11-year-old pupil at a middle school in Oakley, California, is awarded $1,500 compensation by a US court on **2 March 2000** after his Pokémon game cards were confiscated and lost by his school.

On **22 April 2000**, after weeks of frenzied media attention, six-year-old Cuban Elian Gonzalez is snatched by US federal agents from the house where he has been staying with relatives in Miami, Florida. The boy, after surviving a shipwreck in November 1999 while fleeing to the USA with his mother (who did not survive the journey), had become the centre of an international custody battle as his Cuban-American relatives in Miami fought to block his return to his father in Cuba. Along with his father, who had flown to the USA to join him, Elian finally returns to Cuba on **28 June 2000**.

Youngest and Oldest

In **July 1999** a 12-year-old girl pleads guilty to five charges of indecently assaulting young boys; in November she becomes the youngest girl in the UK to be put on a sex offenders list.

On **1 August 1999** Kin Narita and Gin Kanie, Japanese twin sisters who are thought to be the oldest twins in the world, celebrate their 107th birthdays. The pair became national favourites when their 'granny rap', released for their 100th birthdays, shot into the Japanese charts.

Diana Hoff, a 55-year-old Scotswoman, becomes the oldest person to row across the Atlantic solo on **4 January 2000**. She had hoped to become the first woman to row across the ocean single-handedly, but was beaten by Victoria Murden, a 36-year-old American, who left the Canary Islands on the same day as her.

Recognized for his theatrical achievements, English actor and director Kenneth Branagh, 39, becomes the youngest recipient of the Gielgud Award on **16 January 2000**. The Shakespeare Guild, a US organization, presents the award in the UK. John Andrews, president of the Guild, said 'Kenneth Branagh ... has revived the sagging fortunes of a 435-year-old has-been, and turned him into today's hottest screenwriter.'

Six-year-old child prodigy Justin Chapman becomes the youngest ever student at New York state's Rochester University, in **February 2000**. He plays the violin and has his own Web site.

Jenson Button becomes the UK's youngest ever starter of a Formula 1 race on **12 March 2000**, when he competes at the Australian Grand Prix in Melbourne at the age of 20.

In the *Sunday Times* list of the richest people in the UK under 30, published on **19 March 2000**, Charlotte Church, 14, is the youngest person to feature. She is ranked 42 on the list with an estimated £10 million earnings from her career as a classical singer.

At 79, Richard Farnsworth becomes the oldest man ever to be nominated for the Academy Award for best actor, for his leading role in David Lynch's *The Straight Story*. Also in **March 2000**, 11-year-old Haley Joel Osment becomes the youngest male to be nominated for the best supporting actor award for his role in *The Sixth Sense*.

Fred Moore, 107, from New Milton in Hampshire, is declared England's oldest learner in **May 2000**. He has been attending art classes once a week for more than 25 years.

On **11 May 2000** Iranian filmmaker Samira Makhmalbaf becomes the youngest ever director to compete for the prestigious Palme d'Or award at the Cannes Film Festival with her film *Blackboard*. She is 20 years old and directed her first film, *The Apple*, when she was only 17.

Prince William's 18th birthday on **21 June 2000** attracts international media attention and the press are no longer bound by the agreement, reached five years ago and largely adhered to, to respect his privacy while he reamains at school. However, Lord Wakeham, president of the Press Complaints Commission, issues a stern warning that he must not be subjected to harassment or photographed in places he could reasonably regard as private.

Political Embarrassment

On **1 July 1999** the UK government, following a personal apology by Home Secretary Jack Straw, announces emergency measures to cope with a passport crisis. New legislation requiring passports for children has left the passport offices with a backlog of 565,000 applications, and thousands of people are forced to cancel holidays or queue for their passports in person.

A US federal judge fines President Bill Clinton $90,000 on **29 July 1999**, for denying under oath that he had sexual relations with White House intern Monica Lewinsky.

Prime Minister Tony Blair's **August 1999** summer holiday in Tuscany embarrasses the UK and Italian governments when locals protest at the closure of 8 km/5 mi of beach around the villa, after it is revealed that renovations to the villa, lent by regional president Vannino Chiti, have cost Italian taxpayers £380,000. It is a further embarrassment when the Blairs attend the Palio, a traditional horse race in Siena, considered by animal lovers to be cruel.

UK Environment Minister John Prescott makes the headlines on **29 September 1999** when he uses two cars to travel 250 yards to a conference at which he urges motorists to cut down on their car use.

In **November 1999** UK Conservative leader William Hague is embarrassed by revelations that the Conservative Party may have broken a ban on foreign donations by accepting approximately £1 million from its treasurer Michael Ashcroft, who is based in Belize.

On **21 November 1999** the *News of the World* reveals that it has evidence that Tory peer Jeffrey Archer asked television producer Ted Francis to supply him with a false alibi in a libel case. The *Daily Star* had said that he had spent the night with a prostitute, but Archer asked Francis to say that he and Archer had had dinner together that night. Lord Archer subsequently resigns as candidate for London mayor.

In **January 2000** former German chancellor Helmut Kohl succumbs to pressure to stand down as honorary leader of the Christian Democrat party, after he refuses to reveal the sources of several donations made to the party during his time of office. Secret donations to political parties are illegal under German law.

Notorious

After four years in jail in Singapore, English trader Nick Leeson flies back to the UK on **4 July 2000**. Creditors of the collapsed Barings Bank have frozen his assets but he subsequently sells his story to the *Daily Mail* for a reported £100,000.

An unmade bed sparks controversy in **October 1999** when it is entered for the Turner Prize in London by English artist Tracey Emin. It doesn't win the prize.

In **March 2000** *The Times* receives one of a series of letters from prison from one of the UK's most notorious serial killers, Robert Maudsley. He asks for the means to commit suicide or for a change in his conditions, including that he be allowed to have a budgerigar, saying, 'I promise to love it and not eat it'.

A German magazine reports in **March 2000** that thousands of lost documents belonging to one of the most notorious Nazi war criminals, Adolf Eichmann, have been discovered in state archives. The documents are expected to help a new commission return property stolen from Jews during the war.

After a long legal battle, UK Home Secretary Jack Straw decides on **2 March 2000** that former Chilean dictator, General Augusto Pinochet, who is accused of thousands of murders and human-rights violations, is not well enough to be extradited to Spain to stand trial and can return home to Chile.

A computer graduate from a suburb of Manila in the Philippines, Onel de Guznam, leaps to fame on **4 May 2000** when it is revealed that he is responsible for the 'ILOVEYOU' computer virus. Quickly labelled the 'love bug' by the press, it is thought to be the most virulent computer virus in history, and estimates put the cost of the damage it does internationally at $15 billion.

Controversial Remarks

Dr Andrew Ness causes a stir on **8 July 1999** with an article for the *British Medical Journal* saying that there is too much emphasis on the risks of skin cancer from sunlight, and praising the sun's health benefits.

UK Home Secretary Jack Straw is accused of having made offensive remarks in a radio interview on **18 August 1999** in which he says New Age travellers 'seem to think because they label themselves as travellers that they have a licence to commit crimes'.

Prince Edward issues an apology on **2 September 1999** for remarks he made in an interview with *The New York Times*. Referring to the response in the USA to his ideas for television programmes, he had said that the British 'hate anyone who succeeds'.

In remarks that cause a storm of protest from the New York art world in **September 1999**, the mayor of New York City, Rudy Giuliani, describes the work of some British artists displayed in Brooklyn as 'sick and disgusting'. Among the exhibits is a picture of the Virgin Mary decorated with elephant dung, by British artist and Turner Prize winner Chris Ofili.

US president Bill Clinton offends people in Northern Ireland in **October 1999** when, referring to the lack of progress that has been made towards peace, he compares them to drunks trying to leave a bar, saying that 'when they get to the swing door they turn right round and go back in'; he later apologizes for the 'inappropriate' metaphor.

Little more than two weeks after the rail crash outside Paddington Station in London in **October 1999**, in which more than 30 people died, Railtrack's commercial director Richard Middleton is criticized when he refers in a Radio 4 interview to 'hysteria around rail safety'.

In **December 1999** Ian Jenkins, the British Museum's deputy curator of Greek and Roman antiquities, admits that the museum damaged the Elgin Marbles in a cleaning attempt in the 1930s, and then adds to the resulting furore by saying that the Greeks had left 'to rot' those carvings that had remained in Athens.

Harrods owner Mohamed al-Fayed claims in **December 1999** that Prince Philip masterminded the Paris car crash that killed his son Dodi and Diana, Princess of Wales. The Duke subsequently withdraws his royal warrant from Harrods.

It is reported on **1 February 2000** that US baseball player John Rocker has been fined an undisclosed amount and ordered to undergo 'sensitivity training', for telling a magazine that he would never play for a New York team because he did not want to sit next to gays, single mothers, or foreigners on the subway. A US baseball commissioner says the remarks had offended practically every element of society and had been a slur on baseball.

On a filmed visit to the White House in **May 2000**, Hollywood star Leonardo DiCaprio is said to have asked President Clinton some tough questions on the USA's poor record on global warming. When the interview is broadcast the 20 minutes are cut down to two.

English DJ Chris Evans causes Virgin Radio to be fined a record £75,000 in **May 2000** after he makes two on-air endorsements of Ken Livingstone's mayoral campaign. His remarks were prompted by disparaging comments made earlier by Labour candidate Frank Dobson about red-haired people.

Best and Worst

Australian Kerry Packer is thought to have had the worst gambling losses ever in the UK when he loses £11 million at blackjack in a three-week spree in a Mayfair club in **September 1999**. The loss, however, does not make much impact on his reputed £1.5 billion fortune.

The trial of English GP Harold Shipman begins in Preston on **5 October 1999**. He is subsequently convicted of the murder of 15 of his female patients, and in May Home Secretary Jack Straw gives the go-ahead for 23 further inquests. Shipman is thought to be the UK's worst ever serial killer.

English comedians Eric Morecambe and Ernie Wise are posthumously acknowledged as the best in their field when they are acclaimed as 'the century's finest double act' on a blue plaque in the Hall of Fame at Pinewood Studios in Buckinghamshire, in **October 1999**.

In the influential 'Mr Blackwell's 40th annual poll of the world's worst-dressed women in **January 2000**, the Queen comes in third, with singer Céline Dion in second place, and singer Cher in first.

The best-preserved Tyrannosaurus rex skeleton ever found – called Sue, after the US fossil hunter Sue Hendrickson who found it in 1990 – goes on display in Chicago on **17 May 2000**.

Narrow Escapes

Ferrari driver Michael Schumacher crashes into a tyre wall at high speed at the beginning of the British Grand Prix on **11 July 1999**. Despite extensive damage to the car, and the fact that it took rescue services 15 minutes to cut him free, he survived the crash due to recent developments in car safety.

Tim Westwood, a hip-hop and rap DJ on Radio 1, is shot in the arm while in his car at traffic lights in London on **18 July 1999**. He is kept in hospital under armed guard.

Ten people escape serious injury on **14 October 1999** when a double-decker bus crashes through a wall and down an embankment at Crystal Palace, falling some 12 m/40 ft into a children's play area.

In **October 1999** a high-powered motorbike collides with the car of BBC radio DJ Steve Wright, who manages to pull his six-year-old daughter Lucy from the wreckage seconds before it bursts into flames.

In **February 2000** English explorer Ranulph Fiennes calls off his latest attempt to reach the North Pole, suffering from severe frostbite in his left hand. He says that his survival was a 'very close run thing', as one of the two food supply sledges he was towing fell through thin ice.

Scott Durrant, 11, loses his footing while walking with his parents along Boulby Cliffs, near Saltburn, Cleveland, in **March 2000** and plunges 137 m/450 ft down England's highest cliff. The only injury he suffers is the loss of three front teeth.

On **2 May 2000**, the Formula 1 driver David Coulthard and his fiancée escape with minor injuries after the Learjet they are in crashes in France. The following month, on **1 June 2000**, top jockeys Frankie Dettori and Ray Cochrane survive after their light aircraft crashes in England. In both incidents, the pilots of the aircraft die.

First and Last

The British Open golf championship is won by a Scotsman for the first time in 68 years on **18 July 1999** when Paul Lawrie, then at 159 in the world golf rankings, beats Frenchman Jean van de Velde and Justin Leonard of the USA in a four hole play-off.

Colonel Eileen Collins becomes the first woman to command a US space mission. She commands the shuttle *Columbia*, which lifts off from Cape Canaveral on **23 July 1999**.

On **25 October 1999** the South African writer J M Coetzee becomes the first author to win the Booker Prize twice, this time for his novel *Disgrace*. His first win was for the 1983 *Life and Times of Michael K*.

Unemployed father of three Ian Woodley becomes the first person in the UK to win £1 million on a television quiz show in **December 1999**. The quiz was set up by multimillionaire presenter and DJ Chris Evans, as his rival, Chris Tarrant's show *Who Wants To Be A Millionaire?*, had not yet given away £1 million.

UK boy band Westlife celebrates in **December 1999** as it beats Cliff Richard at the last moment to make its double A-sided single *I Have A Dream/Seasons In The Sun* the last number one hit of the millennium.

Pop superstar Michael Jackson announces in **January 2000** that his forthcoming album, his first new work in more than five years, could be his last, since despite being in charts worldwide since the 1970s he is thinking of quitting the music business.

Saying that she finds fashion shows too stressful, US supermodel Naomi Campbell announces in **February 2000** that she has participated in her last London and New York shows. She says, however, that she will still consider appearing in the Milan show.

Despite recent ratings showing her programme has more than 7 million listeners, Radio 1 DJ Zoe Ball presents her last breakfast show on **10 March 2000**, saying that she wants to spend more time with her husband Norman Cook (also known as chart star Fatboy Slim).

One of the last pieces of music written by Johann Sebastian Bach is published for the first time in a biography of the composer in **April 2000**. It was discovered by Professor Christoph Wolff of Harvard University in an archive in Kiev, Ukraine.

On **1 June 2000** David Hempleman-Adams becomes the first person to fly a balloon solo across the Arctic Ocean. His journey ends 21 km/13 miles short of the North Pole itself due to light winds.

Entrepreneurs

Abraham Zapruder is $16 million richer on **3 August 1999**, when the US government is ordered to pay this sum for the 26-second film that he shot of the assassination of President Kennedy in 1963.

Predictions of millions of visitors to Cornwall in the UK for the total solar eclipse on **11 August 1999** lead entrepreneurs to lose large sums of money as damp and cloudy weather draws far fewer people to the event than anticipated.

In **October 1999**, Ron Harris, owner of a US Web site that offers models' eggs for sale for up to $150,000, does not entirely counter claims that the practice is distasteful when he says that purchasers will be able to combine their genes with those of 'the most beautiful and genetically advanced women'.

Richard Branson, the UK's most famous entrepreneur, is knighted in the New Year's honours list for 'services to entrepreneurship'.

Michelle Mone, creator of a new gel-filled bra, talks about the possibility of opening new

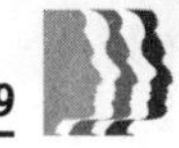

factories in Glasgow, saying, in **January 2000**, that the 'demand for our Ultimo bra has just gone haywire'.

Victor Kiam, the US entrepreneur whose Remington advertisements made him a household name in the 1970s, takes *The Mirror* to court in **March 2000** over the newspaper's allegations that his English company Ronson might be put into receivership at any time. An offer of £50,000 in damages is dismissed as too little too late. Kiam wins his case, and is awarded £105,000 in libel damages.

Having been unsuccessful in previous attempts to buy Marks and Spencer, in **March 2000** Monaco-based entrepreneur Philip Green buys UK department-store chain Bhs for £200 million instead.

Inventor and entrepreneur Paul Moller announces in **May 2000** that his revolutionary Skycar is about to begin tests in the USA. It is designed as a 'family car', with vertical take-off and landing capabilities, that runs on ordinary petrol, and which, it is hoped, could also be driven on ordinary roads.

The collapse of the Microsoft share price in **June 2000**, following a US court ruling that the company broke anti-monopoly laws, and the consequent drop in the personal fortune of Bill Gates, brings Larry Ellison, founder of the US computer company Oracle, a step closer to being the richest man in the world. He has an estimated personal fortune of £48 billion and has been an outspoken supporter of moves to break up Microsoft.

Prince William attending the Queen Mother's centennial service at St Paul's Cathedral, London, 11 July 2000. The previous month, Lord Wakeham, chairman of the Press Complaints Commission, had urged the media to exercise restraint in its coverage of Prince William. *Syndication International.*

Obituaries

July–December 1999

Al-Bayati Abdel Wahab, 73, Iraqi poet, who as a political dissident spent long periods in exile, and whose collection *The Broken Jug* (1954) laid the foundations for the modernist movement in Arab poetry; 3 August

Alberti Rafael Merello, 96, Spanish poet, painter, and performer, exiled during the Franco regime and hailed as a champion of liberty, and awarded the Cervantes Prize (Spain's most prestigious literary award) in 1983; 28 October

Allen Rex, 77, US actor, last of the 'singing cowboys', known as 'The Arizona Cowboy' after his film début in the 1950 western of the same name, and narrator of over 80 Disney films; 17 December

Anderson Marjorie Enid, 86, English broadcaster, best known as presenter of the BBC radio programme *Woman's Hour* 1958–73; 14 December

Archer Fred, 84, English writer and farmer, who produced almost 30 books about Worcestershire country life, including *A Lad of Evesham Vale* (1972); 22 September

Archer John (born Ralph Bowen), 84, US actor, who appeared in over 50 films, including the Hollywood space film *Destination* (1950), and in numerous radio plays; 5 December

Arkley Howard, 48, Australian artist, noted for his brightly coloured paintings, many of which explore Australian suburban culture; 22 July

Arnott William Melville, 90, Scottish cardiologist, who for his contributions to medicine, medical education, and medical research was awarded a knighthood in 1971; 17 September

Baker Kenny (Kenneth), 78, English trumpeter, bandleader, composer, and musical arranger; 7 December

Banks Eulalie Minfred, 104, English-born US illustrator and muralist, who illustrated over 50 children's books; 12 November

Bannen Ian, 71, Scottish actor, who appeared in many popular television series and in over 50 films, including *Flight of the Phoenix* (1965), for which he was nominated for an Academy Award, and *Waking Ned* (1998), and in 1996 received a BAFTA lifetime achievement award; 3 November

Barnes Alice Josephine Mary Taylor, 87, English obstetrician and gynaecologist, crusader for women's rights on such issues as birth control and abortion, and the first woman to be president of the British Medical Association 1979–80; 28 December

Baron Joseph Alexander, 82, English novelist and writer, whose 14 novels include *From the City, From the Plough* (1948), and who also adapted books for television; 6 December

Bate Walter Jackson, 81, US academic, a professor of English at Harvard 1949–86, who specialized in Augustan and Romantic English literature; 26 July

Baum John David, 59, English paediatrician, president of the Royal College of Paediatrics and Child Health from 1997; 5 September

Beaty Arthur David, 80, English writer, pilot, and psychologist, author of 30 novels, including the controversial *The Human Factor in Aircraft Accidents*, which helped generate research into aircraft safety, appointed MBE 1992; 4 December

Beer Patricia, 79, English poet and writer, whose publications include her *Collected Poems* (1988) and *Autumn* (1998); 15 August

Beesley Michael Edwin, 75, English industrial economist, who advocated the privatization of public utilities in the 1980s and who became an authority on their subsequent regulation, appointed CBE 1985; 24 September

Belsky Igor Dmitrievich, 74, Russian ballet dancer, choreographer, and director, one of the leading choreographers of Soviet ballet during the 1960s and 1970s, and artistic director of the Kirov Ballet 1973–77; 3 July

Berlin Sven, 88, English sculptor, painter, and writer, a member of the 'St Ives School' during the 1940s, and author of several novels, including *I Am Lazarus* (1961); 14 December

Berry John (born Jak Szold), 82, US film director, who directed *He Ran All the Way* (1951), and became a cult figure in France when he began a new career there after being blacklisted by the House Un-American Activities Committee in the early 1950s; 29 November

Black Robin, 93, Scottish colonial administrator, governor of Hong Kong 1958–64; 29 October

Boden Leonard Monro, 88, Scottish painter, noted for his portraits, which include ten of Queen Elizabeth II; 3 November

Bor Walter George, 83, Czech architect and town planner, a key figure in British post-war urban planning, who worked in particular in London, Liverpool, and Milton Keynes; 4 October

Bouchier Chili (born Dorothy Irene Boucher), 89, English actress, regarded as British cinema's first sex symbol, who appeared in both silent and talking films, including *Carnival* (1931), and played over 90 stage roles; 9 September

Bowerman Bill (William), 88, US athletics coach and businessman, co-founder of the company Nike 1968, and US head coach at the 1972 Munich Olympics; 24 December

Bowie William Lester, 58, US trumpet and flugelhorn player, composer and bandleader, whose jazz recordings include the album *All the Magic* (1982); 8 November

Bowles Paul Frederick, 88, US writer and composer, who publications include four novels, including *The Sheltering Sky* (1949), 11 collections of short stories, and poetry; 18 November

Bradley Marion Eleanor Zimmer, 69, US writer and editor, whose publications include nearly 50 science fiction and fantasy novels, 20 anthologies, and *Marion Zimmer Bradley's Fantasy Magazine*, which she founded in 1988; 25 September

Brass William, 78, Scottish demographer, noted for devising methods of estimating population statistics in the absence of census data, appointed CBE 1981; 11 November

Bresson Robert, 98, French film director, whose 13 minimalist films include *Lancelot du Lac* (1974) and *L'Argent* (1984); 18 December

Broackes Nigel, 65, English businessman, chairman of Trafalgar House 1969-92, and chairman of the London Docklands Development Corporation 1979–84, knighted 1984; 28 September

Bromwich John, 80, Australian tennis player, who won 15 grand slam titles, 13 of which were for doubles; 21 October

Brouwenstijn Gré, 84, Dutch opera singer, best known during her career (1941–71) for her portrayals of innocent characters, such as Desdemona in Verdi's *Otello*; 14 December

Brown Dennis Emanuel, 42, Jamaican singer, known as 'The Crown Prince of Reggae'; 1 July

Brown The Right Rev Leslie, 87, English Anglican priest, Bishop of Uganda 1953–60, Archbishop of Uganda, Rwanda, and Burundi 1961–65; 27 December

Bubis Ignatz, 72, German Jewish community leader, businessman, and politician, who was head of the Central Council of Jews in Germany from 1992; 13 August

Buffet Bernard, 71, French painter, successful internationally, particularly in Japan; 4 October

Burckhardt Rudy (Rudolph), 85, Swiss-born photographer, film-maker, painter, poet, and writer, best known for his black and white photographs of his adopted home, New York; 1 August

Burg Josef, 90, German-born Israeli politician, a member of the Israeli cabinet 1951–86, and leader of the National Religious Party 1977–86; 15 October

Burgess Vivienne, 85, English actress, whose career on stage and screen spanned 62 years; 26 August

Bury John Morley, 80, English landscape artist; 2 December

Byrd Charlie Lee, 74, US guitarist, best known for the 1962 album *Jazz Samba*, made with Stan Getz, which included the million-selling track *Desafinado* and helped popularize Bossa Nova music; 2 December

Cabral João Cabral de Melo Neto, 79, Brazilian poet and diplomat, the major poet of Brazil's post-war '1945 Generation', whose *Posias Completas/The Complete Poems* was published in 1968; 9 October

Cadícamo Enrique (General Rodriguez), 99, Argentine poet, lyricist, and scriptwriter, best known for his popular tango poems; 3 December

Cadmus Paul, 95, US artist for whose work the term 'symbolic realism' was coined, and whose early work was controversial because of its overt homosexuality; 19 December

Câmara Hélder Pessõa, 90, Brazilian priest, Auxiliary Bishop of Rio de Janeiro 1952–64 and Archbishop of Olinda and Recife 1964–85, who became known throughout the world as the inspirer of Latin America's 'liberation theology' movement; 27 August

Carter Peter, 69, English writer, whose books for children explore the experiences of young individuals living through periods of profound historical change; 21 July

Casson Hugh Maxwell, 89, English architect, artist, and writer, director of architecture (1948–51) for the 1951 Festival of Britain, for which he received a knighthood in 1952, and president of the Royal Academy 1976–84; 15 August

Castelli Leo (born Leo Krauss), 91, Italian-born US art dealer, who opened the Leo Castelli Gallery in New York, New York in 1957, and became known as the champion of pop art; 21 August

Chapman Marguerite, 79, US actress, among whose films was *Relentless* (1948); 31 August

Chaudhuri Nirad Chandra, 101, Indian writer, one of India's most distinguished writers in English, whose books include *The Autobiography of an Unknown Indian* (1951), *The Continent of Circe* (1965), and *Hinduism* (1979); 1 August

Clark Alan Kenneth McKenzie, 71, English military historian and politician, Conservative MP for Plymouth, Sutton 1974–92, and for Kensington and Chelsea 1997–99, and a junior government minister 1983–92, which included serving as minister of defence (1989–92), and who sparked controversy with the publication of his forthright *Diaries* (1993); 5 September

Clough Prunella (born Prunella Clough Taylor), 80, English painter; 26 December

Conrad Pete (Charles Peter), 69, US astronaut, commander of the second spacecraft to land on the moon (*Apollo 12*), and the third man to walk on the moon; 8 July

Couve de Murville Jacques Maurice, 92, French politician and diplomat, active in French politics 1930–86, who served as the last prime minister (1968–69) under General Charles de Gaulle; 24 December

Craigie Jill, 85, English film director, producer, and screenwriter, who was noted for her socialist, humanist, and feminist documentary films; 13 December

Crampton Arthur Edward Seán, 81, English sculptor, whose exhibitions included 17 one-man shows in London's West End; 16 July

Crichton Charles, 89, English film director, best known for the Ealing comedies *Hue and Cry* (1947), and *The Lavender Hill Mob* (1951), and for *A Fish Called Wanda* (1988); 14 September

Crisp Quentin: (Dennis Pratt) see extended obituary, p 720.

Croft Mary Jane, 83, US actress, who worked for many years in radio but is best known for her television role (1956–74) as Lucille Ball's sidekick in *I Love Lucy*, *The Lucy Show*, and *Here's Lucy*; 24 August

Danko Rick, 57, Canadian singer, bass player, and violinist, a founder member of The Band, whose teaming up with Bob Dylan helped produce Dylan's move from acoustic folk music into folk rock during the 1960s; 10 December

Darrow Whitney Jr, 89, US cartoonist, some 1500 of whose cartoons satirizing middle-class America appeared in the *New Yorker* 1932–82; 10 August

Davidson Victoria (born Lilli Ursula Barbara Commichau), 84, Bavarian-born British illustrator, cartoonist, and poster designer; 23 November

De Lima Sigrid, 77, US novelist, best known for *Praise for a Fine Day* (1960); 19 September

Dell Edmund, 78, English historian, politician, and businessman, Labour MP for Birkenhead 1964–79, during which time he held various cabinet posts, and founder Chairman of Channel 4 Television 1980–87, whose publications include *The Chancellors: a History of the Chancellors of the Exchequer 1945–90* (1996); 1 November

Demirchian Karen Serobovich, 67, Armenian politician, Communist Party first secretary 1974–88, and speaker of the Armenian parliament 1 999, where he was assassinated; 27 October

Denman Donald Robert, 88, English land economist, who in 1962 established land economy as a distinct academic discipline when he persuaded Cambridge University, England, to inaugurate a department of land economy; 2 September

Devlin Paddy (Patrick Joseph), 74, Northern Irish socialist politician, one of six Stormont MPs who founded the Social Democratic and Labour Party (SDLP) in 1970 (from which he was expelled in 1977), and who served as minister for health and social services in Northern Ireland's short-lived power-sharing government of 1974, appointed CBE 1999; 15 August

DeVol Frank, 88, US composer, arranger, and conductor, who worked with such leading vocalists as Ella Fitzgerald and Doris Day, won five Academy Awards and five Emmys for his film and television scores, and wrote the theme music for television's *The Brady Bunch*; 27 October

Dmytryk Edward, 90, Canadian film director, whose films include an adaptation of Raymond Chandler's *Farewell, My Lovely* (1944), and who in the late 1940s testified against colleagues before the Un-American Activities Committee; 1 July

Dorn Edward Merton, 70, US poet and teacher, whose works include 'Gunslinger' (1975), one of the major North American long poems; 10 December

Edison Harry, 79, US jazz trumpeter and bandleader, who was a member of the Count Basie Orchestra and performed on Frank Sinatra's best-selling Capitol albums; 26 July

Elrick George, 88, Scottish radio presenter and singer, known as 'The Smiling Voice of Radio',

whose songs included 'The Music Goes Round and Around' (1936); 15 December

Emmwood (pen-name of John Bertam Musgrave-Wood), 84, English cartoonist and painter, whose political cartoons appeared in the *Daily Mail* 1957–75; 30 August

Ewan Joseph Andorfer, 90, US naturalist and botanical historian, who established US natural history as a scholarly subject in the USA, and whose publications (numbering over 400) include *Rocky Mountain Naturalists* (1950, 1981); 5 December

Fanfani Amintore, 91, Italian politician, a leading member of the Christian Democratic Party, six times prime minister, and a senator from 1972; 20 November

Farmer James Leonard, 79, US civil rights campaigner and trade union leader, last surviving member of the 'Big Four' (Martin Luther King, Ray Wilkins, Whitney Young, Farmer) of the post-1945 civil rights movement in the USA; 9 July

Féraud Louis, 79, French fashion designer, who became prominent in the 1960s; 28 December

Ferguson Howard, 91, Northern Irish composer, pianist, and musicologist, whose small but highly regarded corpus was completed by 1958; 1 November

Ffinch Michael, 65, English poet, writer, and teacher, noted for his poems and for his acclaimed biography *G K Chesterton* (1986); 14 September

Figueiredo General João Baptista, 81, Brazilian soldier and politician, president of Brazil 1979–85, last of a succession of military presidents; 24 December

Forrest George (born George Forrest Chichester), 84, US songwriter, who in collaboration with Robert Wright wrote over 2,000 pieces for film, revue, and stage musicals, including *Kismet* (1953), which won a Tony Award; 10 October

Forrest Helen (born Helen Fogel), 82, US singer, who performed with big bands during World War II and was twice (1942, 1943) voted best female vocalist in the USA; 11 July

Francine Anne Hollingshead, 82, US actress and singer, best known for her Broadway roles; 3 December

Fredeman William Evan (born Richard Merill), 71, US academic and collector of Victoriana, one of the world's foremost scholars on the Pre-Raphaelite Brotherhood; 15 July

Frison-Roche Roger, 93, French writer and mountain guide, whose books include *Premier de cordée* ('First on the rope') (1941), one of the best-known modern novels in France; 17 December

Fuchs Vivian Ernest, 91, English explorer, leader of the Commonwealth Trans-Antarctic expedition 1955–58, for which he was knighted on his return, and director of the British Antarctic Survey 1958–73; 11 November

Funt Allen, 84, US television producer and presenter, who in 1948 created the long-running television show *Candid Camera*, which he produced and presented until 1993, when he was succeeded by his son Peter; 5 September

Gainham Sarah (pen-name of Rachel Stainer), 84, English writer and journalist, the best known of whose 12 novels is *Night Falls on the City* (1967); 24 November

Gilkyson Terry (born Hamilton Henry Gilkyson), 83, US singer and songwriter, among whose 300-plus published songs is 'The Bare Necessities', featured in Walt Disney's cartoon *The Jungle Book* (1967); 15 October

Gillies Mick (Michael Thomas), 79, English medical entomologist and expert in malaria transmission, son of the pioneer plastic surgeon Sir Harold Gillies; 10 December

Gironella Alberto, 69, Mexican artist, who was prominent in the public life of his country; 2 August

Gizikis General Phaedon, 82, Greek army officer, president of Greece 1973–74; 27 July

Goff Ivan, 89, Australian-born US screenwriter, who in partnership with Ben Roberts wrote 25 films, including the gangster classic *White Heat* (1949), and the television series *Charlie's Angels* (1976–80); 23 September

Goldstone James, 68, US television and film director, writer, and producer, best known for the pilot episode (1966) of the cult classic television series *Star Trek*; 5 November

Gorbachev Raisa Maksimovna Titorenko, 67, Soviet first lady, popular during the 1980s at the height of her husband Mikhail Gorbachev's reformist policies; 20 September

Gordon Alexander John, 82, Scottish-born Welsh architect, noted for numerous urban buildings in Wales, president of the Royal Institute of British Architects 1971–73, appointed OBE 1967 and CBE 1974, and knighted in 1988; 23 July

Graaff De Villiers, 85, South African politician, MP 1948–77 and leader of the opposition United Party 1956–77, during which time his party split and was brought to the brink of extinction; 4 October

Graham Ronny (born Ronald Montcrief Stringer), 79, US actor, writer, and composer, who wrote and performed for the stage, television, and film, collaborating on scripts for several Mel Brooks films; 4 July

Graves Ida Affleck (born Ida Florence Graves), 97, English poet, whose collections include *The Calfbearer* (1999); 14 November

Gray Edward George, 75, Welsh anatomist, noted for his 1957–58 discovery and classification of 'type 1' and 'type 2' synapses; 14 August

Greene Stephen, 82, US painter, noted for his abstract canvases; 18 November

Grey Ralph Francis Alnwick, 89, New Zealand-born British colonial administrator, who held various postings in Nigeria 1937–59, was governor of British Guiana 1959–64, of the Bahamas 1964–68, and of Northern Ireland 1968–73, appointed OBE 1951 and created Baron 1968; 17 October

Guizar Tito, 91, Mexican actor and singer, who starred in the first singing charro (cowboy in sombrero and bolero jacket) film *Alla en el Rancho Grande/Out There on the Big Ranch* (1936) and in the musicals *Brazil* (1944) and *Mexicana* (1945); 24 December

Hadid Muhammad, 91, Iraqi politician, economist, and industrialist, who was a key member of several politically progressive groups from 1931 until party politics was ended by the advent of the Ba'ath dictatorship in 1963; 3 August

Hale John Rigby, 75, English historian and cultural administrator, whose publications include *Civilisation of Europe in the Renaissance* (1993), knighted 1984; 12 August

Hall Theodore (born Theodore Alvin Holtzberg), 74, US physicist and spy, who while working on the Manhattan Project in 1944 passed secrets about the USA's atomic bomb project to the Soviet Union, and who later made important contributions to biophysics; 1 November

Harris Don, 61, African-American guitarist, violinist, and songwriter, who was half of the influential rock'n'roll duo Don and Dewey, and recorded several solo albums in the early 1970s; 1 December

Harrison Ginette, 41, English mountaineer and medical doctor, who in 1998 became the first woman to climb the 8,597-m, Himalayan mountain Kangchenjunga, and was killed while attempting to climb the world's seventh highest peak, Dhaulagiri I, in Nepal; 24 October

Hart-Davis Rupert Charles, 92, English publisher, writer, and editor, whose published writings include *The Lyttleton Hart-Davis Letters* (six volumes, 1978–84), knighted 1967; 8 December

Hartnett Michael, 57, Irish poet, whose collections in English and Gaelic include his *Selected and New Poems* (1994); 13 September

Hassan II, King of Morocco: see extended obituary, p 721.

Haydon Walter Robert, 79, English diplomat, foreign office spokesman and head of the foreign and commonwealth office news department 1967–71, high commissioner to Malawi 1971–73, 10 Downing Street's chief press secretary 1973–74, high commissioner to Malta 1974–76, and ambassador to the Republic of Ireland 1976–80; 1 December

Hegedüs András, 76, Hungarian politician and sociologist, Prime Minister 1955–56, during which time he was a signatory to the Warsaw Pact (1955) and requested the help of Soviet troops to quell domestic unrest (1956); 23 October

Heller Joseph: see extended obituary, p 722.

Hetherington Hector Alastair, 79, Welsh-born Scottish journalist, editor of *The Guardian* 1956–75; 3 October

Higgins George Vincent, 59, US writer and lawyer, best known for *The Friends of Eddie Coyle* (1972), the first of more than 20 thrillers; 6 November

Hill Robert, 62, English physicist, a leading expert on solar energy and photovoltaic technologies; 26 November

Hirson Baruch, 77, South African historian, physicist, and political activist, who was imprisoned (1964–73) for his membership of the African resistance movement, and whose publications include *Year of Fire, Year of Ash* (1980) and the magazine *Searchlight South Africa* (1988–95), which he founded and co-edited; 3 October

Hjul Peter Donald, 70, Northern Rhodesian-born British journalist and political activist, who left South Africa in 1965 after being banned for his anti-apartheid activities with the Liberal Party, and who became editor for the magazines *Fishing News International* and *Fish Farming International*; 8 September

Hollamby Edward Ernest, 78, English architect and town planner, appointed OBE 1970; 29 December

Holloway John, 79, English academic and poet, whose publications include 14 books of literary criticism and the long poem 'Civitatula' (1994); 29 August

Hopper Robert Thomas Cort, 53, English museum director, curator, and arts administrator, director of Bradford Art Galleries and Museums 1981–88, and director of the Henry Moore Sculpture Trust 1988–99; 18 December

Hughes William (Lord Hughes of Hawkhill, created Baron 1961), 88, Scottish politician and public servant, appointed OBE 1942 and CBE 1956; 31 December

Hull Michael George Raworth, 60, English obstetrician, gynaecologist, and reproductive endocrinologist, one of the world's leading experts in reproductive medicine; 22 November

Hunte Conrad Cleophas, 67, West Indian cricketer, who in 44 Test matches for the West Indies (the first of which was in 1958) scored 3,245 runs; 3 December

Hunter James Augustus ('Catfish'), 53, US baseball player, a highly successful pitcher, who in 1974 won a landmark legal case that paved the way for players to be freed of management-favouring contracts and so increased players' earning power; 9 September

Hyman Anthony George, 53, English writer and political scientist, an expert on the Muslim countries of Central Asia, whose publications include *Afghanistan Under Soviet Domination* (1982); 19 December

Hyman Joe, 77, English businessman, a major force in the British textile industry, particularly as chairman of Viyella International 1961–69; 6 July

Iotti Nilde (Leonilde), 79, Italian politician, a Communist Party MP; from 1991, a member of the Democratic Left Party 1946–99, and lower house speaker 1979–92; 4 December

Jackson Milt, 76, US vibraphone player and bandleader, a founding member of the Modern Jazz Quartet 1951–94; 9 October

Jakobovits Immanuel, 78, German-born English rabbi, Chief Rabbi of the United Hebrew Congregations of the British Commonwealth of Nations 1967–91, knighted 1981 and created a Baron 1988; 31 October

Jeffrey Peter, 70, English actor, who played numerous television parts, and whose stage career included 30 years with the Royal Shakespeare Company; 25 December

Jenkins David Clive, 73, Welsh trade unionist, who as general secretary (1970–88) increased the political influence of the Association of Scientific, Technical, and Managerial Staffs (now Manufacturing, Science, Finance); 22 September

Johnson Frank Minis Jr, 80, US judge, whose civil rights judgements, including his 1956 ruling (along with another member of a three-judge panel) that Alabama's segregated bus system was unconstitutional, helped to transform the American South; 23 July

Jones Geraint Dyfed Barri, 63, English archaeologist, who did much to popularize archaeology, one of whose chief interests was the archaeology of Roman Britain, on which subject his publications include *An Atlas of Roman Britain* (1990); 16 July

Jones Glyn, 71, English television producer and director, who in 1965 devised the long-running BBC science programme *Tomorrow's World*; 4 October

Jones Gwyn, 92, Welsh writer and academic, a scholar of Anglo-Saxon, Icelandic, and Welsh literature, whose publications include a number of novels and (in collaboration with Thomas Jones) a translation of *The Mabinogion* (1948), appointed CBE 1965; 6 December

Kahn Madeline, 57, US actress, whose films include Mel Brooks' comedy *Blazing Saddles* (1974), for which she earned an Academy Award nomination; 3 December

Keal Minna (born Minnie Nerenstein), 90, English composer, who came to prominence in 1989 with the performance of her symphony at the BBC Proms; 14 November

Kennedy John Fitzgerald Jr, 38, US journalist and publisher, whose father was US president 1961–63, and who in 1995 launched *George* magazine under his own editorship; 16 July

Kenny Michael, 58, English sculptor, who achieved some 50 solo exhibitions, and was treasurer and trustee of the Royal Academy 1995–99; 28 December

Kessler David Francis, 93, South African-born English newspaper proprietor, chairman and managing director of the *Jewish Chronicle* for 50 years, appointed OBE 1996; 24 November

Knight Curtis, 54, US singer, guitarist, and songwriter, who recorded with US guitarist Jimi Hendrix 1965–67; 29 November

Konsalik Heinz (pen-name of Heinz Günther), 78, German novelist, who wrote 155 novels, which were translated into over 40 languages, making him the most widely read author of post-war Germany; 2 October

Kraus Alfredo (born Alfredo Kraus Trujillo), 71, Spanish opera singer, whose tenor parts included his acclaimed performances in the title role of Massenet's *Werther*; 10 September

Lagoya Alexandre, 70, Egyptian-born French classical guitarist, who with his guitarist wife Ida Presti formed the internationally-renowned Presti-Lagoya Duo and made a number of innovations in guitar technique; 24 August

Lamerton Leonard Frederick, 84, English biophysicist, who made contributions to the medical fields of radiotherapy treatment and renewal systems; 19 September

Landowski Marcel, 84, French composer, conductor, administrator, and politician, whose works include the opera *Le Rire de Nils Halerius* (1948), appointed Commander of the Légion d'honneur 1987; 23 December

Larkin John, 57, US singer, pianist, and songwriter, known as 'Scatman John', who achieved two UK top 10 hits with songs which mixed dance rhythms with the jazz vocal technique of scat singing; 3 December

Lawrence John, 92, English writer on Russia and the history of his family, press attaché in Moscow, Russia 1942–45, founder and president of Keston Institute, Oxford, England, for the study of religion and communism, appointed OBE 1945; 30 December

Le Vien Jack Douglas, 81, US documentary maker and writer, best known for *The Black Fox* (1962), his Academy Award-winning documentary film on the rise of Hitler; 9 November

Liberman Alexander, 87, Russian-born US magazine art and editorial director, writer, photographer, painter, and sculptor, who for 58 years worked for Condé Nast, publishers of *Vogue*, where he was art director 1943–62, editorial director 1962–94, and deputy chairman (editorial) 1994–99; 19 November

Lionni Leonard ('Leo'), 89, Dutch-born US artist, graphic designer, writer, illustrator, and sculptor, who published more than 30 children's picture books; 11 October

Llewellyn Harry (Henry) Morton, 88, Welsh show jumper and jockey, who on his horse Foxhunter won 78 international competitions, including (as part of the British team) an Olympic show-jumping gold (1952), appointed OBE 1944 and CBE 1953, knighted in 1977; 15 November

Llewelyn Desmond Wilkinson, 85, Welsh actor, best known for his cameo role as Q in 17 of the 18 James Bond films produced 1963–99; 19 December

Lowe Len (Leonard), 83, English comedian, who with one of his brothers formed the double act Len and Bill Lowe (1938–50), and with his other brother subsequently formed the double act Lowe and Ladd (1950–56); 21 August

Lynch Jack: see extended obituary, p 722.

McCann Donal, 56, Irish actor, noted from the mid-1980s for his performances of Sean O'Casey's classic plays; 18 July

McFadden Roy, 77, Northern Irish poet, editor, and lawyer, whose *Collected Poems* appeared in1996; 15 September

McLachlan Peter John, 62, Northern Irish politician and charity administrator, Unionist Member

for South Antrim in the Northern Ireland Assembly 1973–75, appointed OBE 1983; 4 August

Maggio Pupella, 89, Italian actress, best known for her role in Federico Fellini's film *Amacord* (1973), and for her contributions to Neapolitan theatre; 8 December

Mahlathini (nickname of Simon Nkabinde), 61, South African singer, the leading exponent of 'mbaqanga' jive (a fast guitar and saxophone-based dance style); 27 July

March David, 74, English actor, best known for his work in radio drama, who won the 1985 Sony Award for best actor for his performance in an adaptation of *Mr Norris Changes Trains*; 25 August

Marchand Leslie Alexis, 99, US academic, whose work on the poet Byron includes his three-volume *Byron, A Biography* (1957), and a thirteen-volume edition of the complete *Byron's Letters and Journals* (1973–82, 1994); 11 July

Marshall Malcolm Denzil: see extended obituary, p 722.

Matthew Henry Colin Gray, 58, Scottish historian, who edited *The Gladstone Diaries* (1972–94), published a two-volume biography *Gladstone* (1986, 1995), and was editor (from 1992) of the *New Dictionary of National Biography*; 29 October

Mayfield Curtis: see extended obituary, p 723.

Mcwayizeni Prince (Mcwayizeni Israel Zulu), 68, South African politician, who was uncle of and sometime regent for Zulu King Goodwill Zwelithini, and who opposed Mangosuthu Buthelezi and his Inkatha movement in KwaZulu-Natal, South Africa. He was elected to the African National Congress' national executive committee in 1992 and to the South African parliament in 1994; 7 September

Mihail Archbishop (born Metodi Gogov), 87, Macedonian priest and archbishop of Ohrid and Macedonia, head (1994–99) of the independent Orthodox Church of Macedonia, which he helped establish in 1967; 6 July

Mills Donald Frederick, 84, US singer, who with his brothers John, Herbert, and Harry formed the Mills Brothers, known for vocally imitating instruments; 13 November

Mitchell Guy (born Al Cernick), 72, US popular singer, most successful during the 1950s; 2 July

Moondog (Louis Hardin), 83, US composer, whose eccentric orchestral works are collected on the album *Moondog* (1969); 8 September

Moore Clayton (born Jack Carlton Moore), 85, US actor, best known for his title-role in 169 episodes of *The Lone Ranger*, television's first Western series, 1949–57; 28 December

Morita Akio, 78, Japanese businessman, co-founder in 1946, with Maseru Ibuka, of the Sony Corporation, of which he was chief executive officer 1976–93 and chairman 1976–94; 3 October

Mortimer Penelope Ruth (born Penelope Ruth Fletcher), 80, Welsh writer, whose publications include the best-selling novel *The Pumpkin Eater* (1962) and the first volume of her autobiography, *About Time* (1979), which won the Whitbread Prize; 19 October

Moxon Jimmy (Roland James), 79, English colonial officer, civil servant, writer, bookseller, publisher, and restaurateur, resident from 1942 in the Gold Coast (later Ghana) where he became the only white traditional ruler and member of the house of chiefs; 24 August

Muirhead James Henry, 74, Australian judge, judge of the Federal Court of Australia 1977–87, who headed the controversial Royal Commission into Aboriginal deaths in custody 1987–89; 20 July

Munro David Ivor, 55, English film-maker, best known for the documentaries he made with the journalist John Pilger for ITV, especially *Year Zero: the silent death of Cambodia* (1979); 5 August

Nebiolo Primo, 76, Italian athletics administrator, president of the International Amateur Athletic Federation (IAAF) 1981–99; 7 November

Neurath Eva (born Eva Itzig), 91, German publisher, who settled in England during the 1930s where she became co-founder (with her husband Walter, in 1949) and chairman (from 1968) of Thames & Hudson, a leading publisher of art and illustrated books; 27 December

Nkomo Joshua Mqabuko Nyongolo: see extended obituary, p 723.

Nyerere Julius Kambarage: see extended obituary, p 724.

Ogilvy David Mackenzie, 88, English advertising copywriter and executive, founder of the advertising company Ogilvy & Mather (1948), of which he was chairman 1948–73, appointed CBE 1967; 21 July

Olney Richard, 71, US food and wine writer, whose publications include *Simple French Food* (1974); 3 August

Oram Albert Edward, 86, English politician, Labour and Co-operative MP for East Ham South 1955–74, created Baron Oram 1975; 4 September

Orr-Ewing Charles Ian, 87, English politician, Conservative MP for North Hendon 1950–70 and civil lord of the admiralty 1959–63, best known for his campaigning for the breaking of the BBC's television monopoly, appointed OBE 1945, created a Baronet 1963 and Baron 1971; 19 August

Owen Bill (William John Owen Rowbotham), 85, English actor, director, and writer, best known for his role as Compo Semini in the comedy television series *Last of the Summer Wine* 1974–99; 12 July

Paterson Jennifer Mary, 71, English professional cook, writer, and television presenter, best known for co-presenting (with Clarissa Dickson Wright) the BBC cookery programme *Two Fat Ladies* during the last three years of her life; 10 August

Paulucci Enrico (Enrico Paulucci delle Roncalle), 97, Italian artist, designer, and footballer; 22 August

Payton Walter Jerry, US American footballer, one of the game's greatest running backs, who during his 1975–87 career with the Chicago Bears team set a number of National Football League records; 1 November

Peyrefitte Alain, 74, French diplomat, politician, and writer, best known for his books on China, including *Quand la Chine s'éveillera/ When China Awakens* (1973), and for his best-selling biography of Charles de Gaulle, *C'était de Gaulle* (1994–97); 27 November

Pinseau Michel, 73, French architect and town-planner, best known for designing the Grand Mosque at Casablanca; 15 September

Pitfield Thomas Baron, 96, English composer, best known for his *Prelude, Minuet and Reel* for piano; 11 November

Polonsky Abraham Lincoln, 88, US screenwriter and director, best known for *Body and Soul* (1947) and *Force of Evil* (1948), and for his refusal to testify before the McCarthy hearings (1951); 26 October

Pontecorvo Guido, 91, Italian geneticist, one of the founders of modern genetics, professor of Genetics at Glasgow University, Scotland, 1955–68; 24 September

Powell Geoffry Charles Hamilton, 79, architect, of Chamberlin, Powell, and Bon, the architects of the Barbican development in London, England; 17 December

Puzo Mario: See extended obituary, p 724.

Radzinowicz Leon (born Leon Rabinowicz), 93, Polish-born criminologist, responsible for the establishment of academic criminology in Britain in the post-war years and an influential shaper of penal policy in England 1950–72, knighted 1970; 29 December

Rákos Sándor, 78, Hungarian poet, whose apolitical, introverted, and pessimistic poetry contravened Soviet-prescribed socialist realism in the 1950s, and whose later collections include *Társas-monológ/Soliloquy with Others* (1982); 25 December

Rapper Irving, 101, English-born US film director, whose films include *Now, Voyager* (1942) and *Deception* (1946), both starring Bette Davis; 20 December

Ravilious James, 60, English documentary photographer, best known for his photographs of north Devon, some of which are collected in *A Corner of England* (1995); 28 September

Reese 'Pee Wee' (Harold Henry), 81, US baseball player, who as a shortstop with the Brooklyn Dodgers (1940–58) advanced the racial integration of the game during the 1940s and earned his 1984 election to the Baseball Hall of Fame; 14 August

Riley Ralph, 74, English plant geneticist, a leading figure in crop genetics and biotechnology, knighted 1984; 27 August

Rodrigo Joaquín (Joaquín Rodrigo Vidre), 97, Spanish composer, teacher, and writer, best known for the *Concierto de Aranjuez* (1939); 6 July

Rodrigues Amália, 79, Portuguese singer, who from the 1940s was the greatest interpreter of the fado (a Portuguese popular song form), and whose recordings include the albums *Amália Rodrigues* (1962) and *Com Que Voz* (1970); 6 October

Rollason Helen, 43, English sports journalist, who in 1990 became the first woman to anchor the BBC sports programmes *Grandstand*, appointed MBE 1999; 9 August

Rowe Colin Frederick, 79, English architect, who in 1995 became only the second architectural scholar during the 20th century to be awarded the Royal Institute of British Architecture's gold medal; 5 November

Sallon Ralph David, 99, Polish-born English caricaturist, whose work appeared in the *Daily Mirror* (1948–91), appointed MBE 1977; 29 October

Sandman Mark, 46, US singer, bass-player, and songwriter, frontman of the group Morphine; 3 July

Sarkissian Vazgen, 40, Armenian politician, in charge of defence 1992–99, prime minister 1999 until his assassination in parliament; 27 October

Sarraute Nathalie (born Nathacha Tcherniak), 99, Russian-born French novelist and playwright, whose most successful book was her memoir *Enfance/Childhood* (1983); 19 October

Schottlander Bernard Moritz, 75, German-born English sculptor; 28 September

Scott George (Campbell): see extended obituary, p 724.

Scovell Edith Joy, 92, English poet, whose *Collected Poems* appeared in 1988; 19 October

Sendall Dennis Michael, 59, English physicist and information technologist, who worked on particle physics and did much to encourage the development of the World Wide Web from 1989; 15 July

Shamsher Haroon, 33, English musician, disc jockey, songwriter, and producer, who with his brother Farook in the mid-1980s formed the Joi Bangla Sound System, noted for their blend of Asian bhangra and Western beats; 8 July

Sidney Sylvia, 88, US actress, best known for her early roles in such films as *Street Scene* (1931), who made a comeback in the 1970s as a character actress; 1 July

Skelton John Stephen, 76, Scottish sculptor, noted particularly for his variations on the theme of the human figure, appointed MBE 1989; 29 November

Slavicky Klement, 88, Czech composer and conductor; 4 September

Smith David Thomas, 69, English painter, draughtsman, and printmaker, best known for his images of Antarctica; 1 September

Snow Hank (Clarence Eugene), 85, Canadian singer and guitarist, known as 'The Singing Ranger', who made over 80 albums; 20 December

Stafford-Clark David, 83, English psychiatrist, who did much to establish psychiatry in the mainstream of medicine, particularly through such books as *Psychiatry Today* (1951) and the early 1960s BBC television series *Lifeline*; 9 September

Starr Chester G, 84, US historian, who wrote 21 books, including *The Origins of Greek Civilization* (1961); 22 September

Stewart Payne, 42, US golfer, who had 11 victories on the US PGA Tour and seven others abroad, and represented his country in the Ryder Cup; 25 October

Storck Henri, 92, Belgian documentary film-maker, regarded as one of Europe's best makers of non-fiction films for such works as *Symphonie Paysanne* (1944) and *Rubens* (1948); 16 September

Stott Roger, 56, English post office engineer and politician, Labour MP for Westhoughton 1973–83 and for Wigan 1983–99, who was opposition front bench spokesman on transport 1980–83 and 1984–86, on information technology 1983–88, on trade and industry 1988–89, and on Northern Ireland 1990–97, appointed CBE 1979; 8 August

Strachey Barbara, 87, English broadcaster and writer, instrumental in the transformation of the BBC's General Overseas Service into the World Service in 1965, whose publications include *Remarkable Relations* (1980); 15 October

Stukelj Leon, 100, Slovenian gymnast, who, competing for Yugoslavia in the 1924 and 1928 Olympics, won three gold and three bronze medals, and in 1936 won an Olympic silver; 8 November

Swanson Robert, 52, US venture capitalist, founder of Genetech in San Francisco, California, the world's first genetic engineering company; 6 December

Timerman Jacobo, 76, Ukrainian-born Argentinian journalist and writer, founder (1971) of Argentina's daily tabloid *La Opinión*, which he edited until his political imprisonment 1977–79, writing the acclaimed *Prisoner Without a Name, Cell Without a Number* (1982) about his time in prison; 11 November

Tintner Georg, 82, Austrian conductor, who, during the last decade of his life, conducted performances for recordings of all 11 Anton Bruckner symphonies; 2 October

Tiruchelvam Neelan, 55, Sri Lankan politician and human rights campaigner, who as a representative of the Tamil United Liberation Front (TULF) pressed for peaceful radical change in his native country, and who made contributions to the field of human, and especially ethnic-minority, rights; 29 July

Tucker Albert, 84, Australian painter, longest surviving member of the Angry Penguins, a Melbourne avant-garde art group of the 1930s and early 1940s; 23 October

Tudjman Franjo: see extended obituary, p. 725.

Vaughan Frankie: see extended obituary, p. 725.

Vinson Helen (born Helen Rulfs), 92, US actress, best known for Hollywood films, including *The Power and the Glory* (1933); 7 October

Walker Colin John Shedlock, 64, English public servant and farmer, chairman of the Harwich Haven Authority 1988–99 and chairman of the National Blood Authority 1993–98, appointed OBE 1981 and knighted 1991; 1 September

Ward Bill (Ivor William), 83, English television producer and executive, whose career began with involvement in the inaugural television broadcasts of both the BBC (1936) and ITV (1955), appointed OBE 1976; 21 October

Washington Grover Jr, 56, US saxophonist and bandleader, who is regarded a key shaper of the 'smooth jazz' of the 1990s; 17 December

Watson Jack, 78, English actor, best known for playing tough men of action in films, and for his role as Petty Officer Bill Gregory in *Coronation Street* 1961–84; 4 July

Wazzan Chafic Dib, 74, Lebanese lawyer and politician, prime minister of Lebanon 1980–84; 8 July

Webster Katie (born Kathryn Jewel Thorne), 63, US pianist, who featured on more than 500 singles in the 1950s and 1960s, played in Otis Redding's band until his death in 1967, and released several solo albums; 5 September

West Morris Langlo, 83, Australian novelist, who sold over 60 million copies of some 30 novels published 1955–98, many of which tackle moral dilemmas within the context of Catholicism; 9 October

Westwood William John, 73, English Anglican priest, Bishop of Peterborough 1984–95, whose many media broadcasts included 'Thought for the Day' on BBC Radio 4's *Today* programme; 15 September

Wexler Norman, 73, US actor and screenwriter, best known for his screenplay for the hit film *Saturday Night Fever* (1977); 23 August

White Baroness Eirene Lloyd Jones, 90, Northern Irish-born Welsh politician, Labour MP for East Flint 1950–70, minister of state for foreign affairs 1966–67, minister of state in the Welsh office 1967–70, created Baroness 1970, deputy speaker of the House of Lords 1979–89; 23 December

Whitelaw Viscount (William Stephen Ian Whitelaw), 81, Scottish politician, Conservative MP, leader of the House of Commons 1970–72, secretary of state for Northern Ireland 1972–73, secretary of state for employment 1973–74, chairman of the Conservative Party 1974–75, deputy leader of the Conservative Party 1975–91, home secretary 1979–83, created Viscount 1983, leader of the House of Lords 1983–88; 1 July

Wildeblood Peter, 76, Italian-born English journalist, writer, and film producer, best known for his book *Against the Law* (1955), an account of his prosecution for homosexuality in 1954; 13 November

Wilkinson Kevin Michael, 41, English drummer, who played with rock bands China Crisis, Squeeze, Marillion, and the Waterboys; 17 July

Williams Shirley Anne, 54, US poet, novelist, and teacher, noted for her portrayal of African-Americans in such works as *The Peacock Poems* (1975) and the historical novel *Dessa Rose* (1986); 6 July

Willis Bobby (Robert), 57, English songwriter and show business manager, the manager and husband of Cilla Black, many of whose songs he wrote; 23 October

Wilson John Foster, 80, English campaigner for the blind, who in 1950 founded the Royal Commonwealth Society for the Blind (now Sight Savers International), of which he was director 1950–83, appointed OBE 1955 and CBE 1965, knighted 1975; 24 November

Wintour Charles Vere, 82, English journalist, editor of London's newspaper, the *Evening Standard* 1959–76 and 1978–80, appointed MBE 1945 and CBE 1978; 4 November

Wright Vincent, 61, English political scientist and historian, noted for his contributions to the study of 19th-century French history, contemporary French politics, and the politics of Western Europe; 8 July

Yulsman Jerry, 75, US photographer and writer, best known for his science fiction novel *Elleander Morning* (1984); 6 August

January–June 2000

Adderley Nat(haniel), 68, US cornet player and bandleader, whose jazz recordings include the 1995 album *Mercy, Mercy, Mercy*; 2 January

Alla Rakha (Ustad Alla Rakha Khan), 80, Indian musician, an internationally famous tabla player; 3 February

Allen (Alfred) Lewis, 94, English-born film director who made several Hollywood films, including *The Uninvited* (1944) and *So Evil My Love* (1948), later working for US television series such as *Perry Mason* and *Little House on the Prairie*; 3 May

Annan Noel Gilroy, 83, English writer and academic, appointed OBE 1946, created Baron Annan 1965, Provost, University College, London, England 1966–78, Vice-Chancellor, London University 1978–81; 21 February

Appelbee Leonard John, 85, English portrait and still-life painter; 12 June

Appleby Brigitte (born Brigitte Miriam Clare Goldschmidt), 73, German-born English potter, co-founder of Briglin Pottery; 12 April

Archdale Betty (Helen Elizabeth), 92, English-born women's cricketer and Australian educationist; 11 January

Archer Violet Balestreri, 86, Canadian composer, pianist, organist, and teacher, professor of music at the University of Alberta, Edmonton, Canada 1970–78; 21 February

Arkan (pseudonym of Zeljko Raznatovic), 47, Serbian paramilitary commander and businessman, said to be the leader of the Serbian Volunteer Guard (the Tigers), which carried out many of the worst atrocities during the Balkan conflicts of the 1990s, indicted for war crimes by an international tribunal in 1999, but assassinated before appearing before the tribunal; 15 January

Ashton Norman Henry, 86, English pathologist, director of pathology at the Institute of Ophthalmology, London 1948–78, who made many important sight-saving discoveries in ophthalmology, appointed CBE 1976; 4 January

Aspinall John Victor, 74, English zoologist and businessman, who established gambling clubs and zoos; 29 June

Assad Hafez-al: see extended obituary, p 720.

Atkins Vera May (born Vera Maria Rosenberg), 92, English intelligence agent, who worked for the Special Operations Executive, a British secret service, during World War II; 24 June

Auld Ian Hamilton, 74, English potter, and collector and teacher of arts and crafts; 10 February

Autant-Lara Claude, 98, French film director whose controversial films were often reviled by both the French government and by other directors, chiefly because of his far-right politics; 5 February

Bailey Jim (James Richard Abe), 80, English writer, poet, and publisher of the South African magazine *Drum* 29 February

Balderstone (John) Chris(topher), 59, English cricketer (for England, Leicester, and Yorkshire), footballer (for Carlisle, Queen of the South, and Doncaster), and umpire; 6 March

Bartali Gino, 85, Italian cyclist who won the Tour de France in 1938 and 1948; 5 May

Baskin Leonard, 77, US graphic artist, sculptor, and poet, whose work was inspired by William Blake; 4 June

Bassani Giorgio, 84, Italian writer, whose most famous novel is *Il giardino dei Finzi-Contini/The Garden of the Finzi-Continis* (1962); 13 April

Batchelor George Keith, 80, Australian physicist and mathematician, emeritus professor of applied mathematics, Cambridge University, England, and editor of the *Journal of Fluid Mechanics* 1956–2000; 30 March

Beneke 'Tex' (Gordon), 86, US tenor saxophonist, vocalist, and bandleader, who played with the Glenn Miller band both before and after the death of Miller in 1944; 30 May

Benson Mary, 80, South African anti-apartheid campaigner; 20 June

Bentzon Niels Viggo, 80, Danish composer and pianist, whose compositions total almost 700 works, including 24 symphonies and three operas; 25 April

Bernard Bruce Bonus, 72, English picture editor, writer, and scholar of photography; 29 March

Bertolucci Attilio, 88, Italian poet, editor, and television director on cultural issues; 14 June

Bhabra Hargurchet Singh, 44, Indian-born English writer and broadcaster, author of the novel *Gestures* (1986), and thriller novels under the pseudonym A M Kabal; 1 June

Bird Henry Arthur Richard, 90, English artist and teacher; 16 April

Bloom Freddy (born Elfrieden Wenzel), 86, English writer and journalist, of US-German descent, founder of the National Deaf Children's Society (NDCS); 20 May

Borovik Artem Genrikhovich, 40, Russian investigative journalist and television presenter; 9 March

Boudard Alphonse, 74, French novelist whose work was influenced by the streets and prisons of France, both thematically and stylistically; 14 January

Bourguiba Habib Ben Ali, 98, Tunisian politician and president 1957–87, considered to be the founder of modern Tunisia who struggled for its liberation from France in 1955; 6 April

Bowers Edgar, 75, US poet and university teacher; 4 February

Boxer Charles Ralph, 96, English historian, emeritus professor of London University, England, and Yale University, Connecticut, 27 April

Boycott Brian Blundell, 75, English neuroscientist and eye specialist, professor of biology, London University, England 1971–89; 22 April

Brae June (born June Bear), 82, English dancer, principal dancer in the pre-World War II Royal Ballet; 3 January

Brandys Kazimierz, 83, Polish novelist who experimented with form; 11 March

Brennan Shay (Seamus Anthony), 63, Irish footballer and football manager who played 19 times for the Republic of Ireland 1965–70; 9 June

Brück Hermann Alexander, 94, German-born astronomer and academic, Astronomer Royal for Scotland and Regius professor of astronomy, Edinburgh University, Scotland, 1957–75, appointed CBE 1966; 4 March

Budge (John) Donald: see extended obituary, p 720.

Burridge James Dugdale, 78, English solicitor and racehorse breeder, who bred the champion steeplechaser Desert Orchid; 27 February

Bursford Bruce, 41, English cyclist and cycling designer who set many records of speeds reached on self-designed and constructed cycles; 9 February

Buscetta Tommaso, 71, Italian gangster and the first boss of the Sicilian Mafia to confess and give evidence against the organization; 2 April

Capel Evelyn (born Evelyn Francis), 88, English priest, the first woman in Britain to be ordained in the Christian Community church; 5 January

Cartland (Mary) Barbara Hamilton: see extended obituary, p 720.

Casimir Hendrik Brugt Gerhard, 90, Dutch theoretical physicist and industrial research director, professor of physics, Leiden University, Netherlands, 1939–42; 4 May

Cassidy Frederic Gomes, 92, Jamaican-born US linguist and lexicographer, editor of *The Dictionary of Jamaican English* (1967, revised 1980) and *Dictionary of American Regional English* (ongoing); 14 June

Childs Barney Sanford, 74, US composer, poet, and academic specializing in literature and music; 11 January

Churchill Marguerite, 90, US actress, whose films include the 1930 Western *The Big Trail*, in which she was the first lead to play opposite John Wayne; 9 January

Claiborne Craig, 79, US food and cookery writer, food editor of *The New York Times* 1957–86; 22 January

Clay Nicholas, 53, English actor of film, stage, and television dramas; 25 May

Cliff Tony (born Ygael Gluckstein), 82, Palestinian-born socialist political activist who moved to England in 1950; 9 April

Coggan (Frederick) Donald, 90, English priest, ordained 1935, Bishop of Bradford 1956–61, Archbishop of York 1961–74, Archbishop of Canterbury 1974–80, created Baron 1980; 17 May

Cohen Alexander Henry, 79, US theatre producer, responsible for taking many British shows and actors to the New York stage; 22 April

Coley Doris, 58, US pop singer with the group the Shirelles, whose hits include 'Will You Love Me Tomorrow' and 'Dedicated to the One I Love'; 4 February

Colicos John, 71, Canadian actor who played many Shakespearean roles, and was the youngest ever actor to play King Lear with the Old Vic Company in England, as well as featuring in the television series *Battlestar Galactica*; 6 March

Collins Elisabeth (born Elisabeth Ward Ramsden), 95, English painter and sculptor, whose work is characteristically colourful and poetic, wife of the painter Cecil Collins; 17 January

Comfort Alexander, 80, English physician, academic, and writer, author of *The Joy of Sex* (1972); 26 March

Conzen Michael Robert Gunter, 93, German-born English geographer and emeritus professor of human geography, University of Newcastle upon Tyne, England; 4 February

Cooper Genevieve Hope St Clair, 55, English journalist, deputy editor of London's *Evening Standard* daily newspaper 1986–94; 26 June

Cossutta Carlo, 67, Italian opera singer, a tenor who sang in the leading opera houses of Europe, North, and South America; 22 January

Coulthard Jean, 92, Canadian composer and teacher, whose compositions number 350, in many genres, appointed Order of Canada 1978; 9 March

Coutts Charles Taylor, 79, Scottish communist activist and broadcaster who worked in Hungary from the 1956 uprising until his death; 6 April

Craxi Bettino (Benedetto), 65, Italian politician, prime minister 1983–87, who lived in self-imposed exile in Tunisia from 1994 to avoid charges of political corruption; 19 January

d'Agostino Giovanni Battista, 67, Italian artist and art teacher; 31 January

Daniels Henry Ellis, 87, English statistician, emeritus fellow of Birmingham University, England, and fellow of King's College, Cambridge 1975–76; 16 April

Dard Frédéric Charles Antoine, French writer and dramatist, who wrote crime and thriller novels under the pseudonym 'San-Antonio'; 6 June

David Tudor, 78, Welsh journalist, editor, and publisher, specializing in the subjects of education and Wales, appointed OBE 1984; 21 February

Davie (Alexander) Ian McNaughton, 76, Scottish poet and schoolmaster, whose publications include *Piers Prodigal* (1961) and *Roman Pentecost*; 4 June

Davies Donald Watts, 75, Scottish computer scientist whose 'packet switching' system forms the technological foundations of the Internet; 28 May

Dean Bill, 78, English actor most noted for his role as Harry Cross 1983–90 in the soap opera *Brookside*, and his role in the Ken Loach film *Kes* (1969); 21 April

Deutsch André, 82, Hungarian-born English publisher, appointed CBE 1989; 11 April

Dillon Carmen Joseph, 91, English art director who was the first woman to successfully design film sets in England, working on films such as Olivier's *Hamlet* (1948) and *The Browning Version* (1950); 12 April

Dlugoszewski Lucia, 68, US composer and choreographer, whose innovative work led her to music for film and stage as well as solo pieces; 11 April

Doyle Tony (Anthony), 57, Irish television and film actor, whose work included *Ballykissangel* (1996–99) and *Amongst Women* (1998); 28 January

Drake Frances (born Frances Dean), 91, US actress and Hollywood beauty who was acclaimed for her role in the film *Mad Love* (1935); 17 January

Dunbar Robert, 85, English film-maker and teacher whose films include *The Man Upstairs* (1959); 29 April

Durack Elizabeth, 84, Australian artist, who also worked under the name Eddie Burrup; 25 May

Durr Frank (Francis), 73, English jockey and horse trainer; 18 January

Dury Ian: see extended obituary, p. 721.

Edmond Lauris (born Lauris Dorothy Scott), 75, New Zealand poet and writer, appointed OBE in 1986; 28 January

Efremov Oleg Nikolaievich, 73, Russian actor and theatre director, artistic director of the Moscow Art Theatre during the Soviet Union regime; 24 May

Emery John Lewis, 84, English professor in paediatric pathology at Sheffield University, England, 1972–80 who did much work during his career in paediatric pathology on sudden death in infants (cot death); 1 May

Fairbanks Douglas Jr, 90, US actor who followed his father into films, but despite several roles in films, became more noteworthy for his romantic links than his acting; 7 May

Faulds Andrew Matthew William, 77, English actor and Labour Party politician, opposition spokesman for the arts 1970–73, 1979–82; 31 May

Fine Vivian, 86, US composer and pianist; 20 March

Fitzgerald Penelope (born Penelope Mary Knox), 83, English writer of fiction, who won the Booker Prize for her novel *Offshore* (1979), and in 1996 was awarded the Heywood Hill Prize for her career's achievement; 28 April

Forbes Meriel (stage name of Meriel Forbes-Robertson), 86, English film and theatre actress who often played opposite her husband, Ralph Richardson; 7 April

Fowler Eileen, 93, English fitness instructor who founded the Keep Fit Association, appointed MBE 1975; 7 March

Fryer Robert, 79, US theatre and film producer, whose theatre credits include *Chicago* (1975) and *Sweeney Todd* (1979), and whose films include *The Shining* (1979); 28 May

Fyodorov Svyatoslav Nikolayevich, 73, Ukrainian ophthalmologist who financed his own hospitals and agricultural enterprises; 2 June

Gertz Elmer, 93, US lawyer and writer, who won many landmark cases in US law, including his own libel case, and who opposed capital punishment and defended press freedom; 27 April

Gielgud (Arthur) John: see extended obituary, p 721.

Gifford Denis, 72, English film historian, film-maker, comic-strip artist, script-writer for television and radio, writer, and journalist; 18 May

Glock William Frederick, 92, English music critic, writer, and administrator, controller of music for the British Broadcasting Corporation (BBC) 1959–72, knighted 1970; 28 June

Golshiri Hoshang, 63, Iranian writer and political dissident, who demanded more freedom of thought and expression in the administrations of both the Shah and post-revolutionary Iran; 5 June

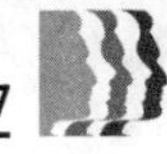

Gorey Edward St John, 75, US publisher, illustrator, writer, and designer, known for his Gothic themes; 15 April

Grant Bernie (Bernard Alexander Montgomery), 56, British engineer and politician born in Guyana, a Labour MP, the first Afro-Caribbean leader of a local authority in England; 8 April

Gray Charles (born Donald Marshall Gray), 71, English stage and film actor, probably most famous for his role as Blofeld in the James Bond film *Diamonds are Forever* (1971); 7 March

Gulda Friedrich, 69, Austrian pianist and composer who was internationally successful as both a classically trained and a jazz musician; 27 January

Gundry Inglis, 94, English composer and writer, whose compositions include the operas *Naaman, the Leprosy of War* (1937), and *The Prisoner Paul* (1970); 13 April

Gupta Radha Prasad, 78, Indian writer, translator, and collector; 9 March

Hale Kathleen, 101, English writer and illustrator, notably of children's books featuring Orlando the Marmalade Cat, appointed OBE in 1976; 26 January

Hall Arnold Alexander, 84, English aeronautical engineer and administrator, fulfilling managing positions of Hawker Siddeley Group plc 1955–84, knighted 1954; 9 January

Halsbury third Earl of (John Anthony Hardinge Giffard), 91, English mathematician and engineer, active in the House of Lords, especially initiating legislation on matters of science, chancellor of Brunel University, London, 1966–97; 14 January

Hamilton William Donald, 63, English biologist who formulated the concept of inclusive fitness as a way of explaining the biological theory of altruism, research professor and fellow of New College, Oxford University 1984–2000; 7 March

Hare Doris, 95, Welsh theatre and television actress, best known for her role as Mum in the television comedy *On the Buses* (1969–73); 30 May

Harris Gene (Eugene), 66, US blues pianist and jazz band leader; 16 January

Harris Margaret Frances, 95, English theatre designer, co-founder of the theatre design company Motley, and founder of a theatre design course at Sadler's Wells, London, England, at which she taught; 10 May

Hartling Poul, 85, Danish politician, prime minister of Denmark 1973–75, and United Nations high commissioner for refugees 1978–85; 30 April

Hawkins Jalacy J (Screamin' Jay Hawkins), 70, US rhythm and blues singer and songwriter whose live act was theatrical and controversial; 12 February

Herman Josef, 89, Polish-born painter and Jewish intellectual, English citizen since 1938, appointed OBE 1980; 19 February

Holroyd Bill (William Henry), 80, English cartoonist responsible for comic strips in such titles as *Beano, Dandy,* and *Topper;* 1 February

Hood Ann, 59, English opera singer; 3 February

Hosier John, 71, English musician and educator, principal of Guildhall School of Music and Drama 1978–89, appointed CBE 1984; 28 March

Hovhaness Alan (born Alan Vaness Chakmakjian), 89, US composer of Armenian descent, who composed prolifically, although destroyed much of his work himself in 1943; 21 June

Hoving Lucas (born Lukas Hovinga), 87, Dutch dancer, choreographer, and teacher, leading modern dancer in the company of José Limón; 5 January

Howell Jill (born Gillian Margaret Sarson), 72, English architect and teacher; 2 May

Hoy Agnete (born Agnete Blichfeldt), 85, Danish-born designer and potter who worked and taught in England; 1 April

Hundertwasser Friedensreich (born Friedrich Stowasser), 71, Austrian artist and architect whose work is characterized by its individuality; 19 February

Irons Evelyn, 99, Scottish-born journalist of London's *Evening Standard* 1935–55 and *The Sunday Times* 1955–70, one-time lover of the writer Vita Sackville-West; 3 April

Isaksson Ulla, 83, Swedish writer and feminist; 20 April

Jack Beau (born Sidney Walker), 78, US boxer, world lightweight champion 1942–43; 9 February

James Laurence William, 56, English writer of popular fiction, who wrote under his own name and several pseudonyms; 10 February

Jandl Ernst, 74, Austrian poet, known as a German surrealist in style, and modern in theme; 9 June

Jones Peter, 79, English actor, playwright, and broadcaster, performing in radio and television comedies from 1952 to his death; 10 April

Jones Philip Mark, 71, English trumpeter, appointed OBE in 1977 and CBE in 1986, principal of Trinity College of Music, London, 1988–1994; 17 January

Jones Ralph, 78, US drummer, who played with the group Bill Haley and his Comets; 1 June

Kane Gil (born Eli Katz), 73, Latvian-born US cartoonist who drew superheroes for Marvel comics, including Spiderman, the Incredible Hulk and Captain Marvel; 31 January

Kekwick Ralph Ambrose, 91, English biophysicist who pioneered the fractionation of human blood plasma for use in transfusions, emeritus professor of biophysics, London University, England; 17 January

Kelly Fred(eric), 83, US dancer and dance teacher, brother of Gene Kelly, with whom he sometimes appeared on stage and in films; 15 March

King Pee Wee (born Julius Frank Anthony Kuczynski), 86, US singer, songwriter, and country music bandleader; 7 March

Kirchschläger Rudolf, 85, Austrian politician and federal president 1974–86; 30 March

Kray Charlie (Charles James), 73, English criminal and brother of the renowned Kray twins; 4 April

Kung Pinmei Ignatius, 98, Chinese Roman Catholic priest, bishop of Shanghai 1959–2000, appointed cardinal 1979, installed 1991, imprisoned 1955–85 for allegiance to Rome; 12 March

Lamarr Hedy: see extended obituary, p 722.

Lamb Larry (Albert), 70, English journalist, editor of *The Sun* 1969–72 and 1975–81, *The Australian* 1982–83, and *Daily Express* 1983–86, knighted 1980; 18 May

Lasok Dominik, 78, Polish-born law scolar, emeritus professor of law, Exeter University, and expert in European Communities law, 11 April

Lastic Alain Basil de, The Most Reverend, 70, Indian Roman Catholic priest, auxiliary bishop of Calcutta 1979–84, bishop of Lucknow 1984–90, archbishop of Delhi 1991–2000; 20 June

Lederer Francis (Frantisek), 100, Czech actor who worked in German, English, and US film and theatre, and who also wrote, acted, and directed for television, as well as founding the World Peace Federation; 25 May

Leroy Eugène, 89, French painter and sculptor; 10 May

Levi Edward Hirsch, 88, US lawyer and academic, attorney general 1975–77, University of Chicago professor of law 1945–75 and president 1968–75; 7 March

Levi Peter Chad Tigar, 68, English writer, former Jesuit priest, Emeritus Fellow of St Catherine's College, Oxford, Professor of Poetry, Oxford University 1984–89; 1 February

Lewis Hylan Garnet, 88, US sociologist, researcher into racial integration in the USA, and teacher; 8 March

Lincoln Abraham, 93, US trombonist specializing in jazz; 9 June

Little Steve, 34, US boxer, super-middleweight World Boxing Association champion in 1994; 30 January

Lockley Ronald Mathias, 96, Welsh naturalist, writer, and conservationis; 12 April

Lombardi Mark, 48, US artist whose work was inspired by conspiracy theories and scandals; 22 March

Longrigg Roger Erskine, 70, English writer who worked in several different genres and under eight different pesudonyms; 26 February

MacSweeney Barry Patrick, 51, English poet and journalist, whose work includes *Pearl* (1995), and in 1997 won a Paul Hamlyn Award for his poetry; 9 May

Mannion Wilfred James, 81, English footballer who played for Middlesbrough 1936–54, Hull City 1954–55, and 26 times for England 1946–51; 14 April

Marchant Leonard, 70, South African-born English painter and printmaker, best known for his figurative mezzotints; 9 January

Markezinis Spyros, 90, Greek politician, who collaborated with the military regime of 1967–74 to become prime minister of Greece briefly in October 1973; 4 January

Martin Donald ('Don'), 68, US cartoonist, whose drawings appeared in the monthly cartoon magazine *Mad* 1954–87, and whose books of cartoons include *(Mad's Maddest Artist) Don Martin Steps Out!* (1962); 6 January

Martin Francis Xavier, 77, Irish priest, historian, and campaigner, professor of medieval history at University College, Dublin, 1962–88; 13 February

Martin Helen Dorothy, 90, US actress, one of the first African-American women to make her mark on the Broadway stage; 25 March

Matthau Walter (born Walter Matuschanskavasky), 79, US theatre and film actor of Russian descent, famed for his partnership with Jack Lemmon, notably in the play *The Odd Couple* (1965, filmed 1968), and in the *Grumpy Old Men* films (1993 and 1995); 1 July

Matthews Stanley: see extended obituary, p 723.

Maurer Ion Gheorghe, 97, Romanian politician, prime minister of Romania 1961–74; 8 February

Melville Harry Work, 92, Scottish chemist and academic administrator, science advisor for civil defence 1952–56, and for scientific and industrial research 1956–65, knighted 1958; 14 June

Mendieta Antonio Arguedas, 70, Bolivian politician, responsible for handing Che Guevara's diaries to Cuba; 22 February

Merrick David (born David Lee Margoulis), 89, US theatrical producer who produced successful shows such as *Hello, Dolly!* (1964) and took successful English shows to Broadway, including *Oliver!* (1963); 25 April

Mielke Erich, 92, German socialist politician, minister of state security, German Democratic Republic 1957–89, and head of the secret police, the Stasi; 22 May

Miller Merton Howard, 77, US economist who with Franco Modigliani, established the controversial 'Modigliani-Miller theorems' that combined economic theory and finance; 3 June

Mills Mervyn, 94, English novelist, historian, and writer for television, whose novel, *The Long Haul* (1956) was filmed in 1957; 11 May

Mitra Ramon, 82, Filipino politician and the first Speaker of the Filipino House of Representatives; 20 March

Mladenov Petar Toshev, 63, Bulgarian politician, minister of foreign affairs 1971–89, president 1990, the first president after the totalitarian regime was toppled; 31 May

Mommens Norman, 77, Flemish sculptor, painter, and writer; 8 February

Montero Germaine (born Germaine Heygel), 90, French singer and actress, who performed in Spain, France, and Switzerland during World War II; 29 June

Moore Vicki (born Victoria Lucille Seel), 43, English animal rights campaigner who worked to expose the cruelty of blood sports in Europe; 6 February

Nagako Dowager Empress of Japan (born Nagako Kuni), 97, Japanese Empress 1926–89; 16 June

Norberg-Schulz (Thorvald) Christian, 73, Norwegian architect, historian, and theorist on his subjects; 28 March

Nowakowski Marian Zygmunt, 87, Polish-born opera and concert singer and voice teacher, who sang in Britain for much of his career; 4 April

Nzo Alfred Baphethuxolo, 74, South African political activist and administrator, secretary-general, African National Congress 1969–91, and minister for foreign affairs in Nelson Mandela's government; 13 January

O'Brian (Richard) Patrick: see extended obituary, p 724.

Obuchi Keizo, 62, Japanese politician, prime minister of Japan 1998–2000, formerly cabinet secretary and foreign minister; 14 May

O'Connor John Joseph, US Roman Catholic priest, archbishop of New York, New York 1983–2000, named cardinal 1985; 3 May

Odone Michaela Teresa, US developer of Lorenzo's Oil, a treatment for adrenoleukodystrophy (ALD), and founder of the Myelin Project, for research into ALD; 10 June

Oliver Douglas Dunlop, 62, English poet, novelist and journalist, whose most famous poem is *The Infant and the Pearl*; 21 April

Pham Van Dong 94, Vietnamese politician, prime minister of the Democratic Republic of Vietnam 1954–76, and prime minister 1976–87 of the Socialist Republic of Vietnam, after the declaration of independence; 29 April

Pirt Stanley John, 77, English chemical microbiologist, and emeritus professor of microbiology at Queen Elizabeth (later King's) College, London; 22 February

Placzek Adolf Kurt, 87, Austrian-born art historian and librarian; 19 March

Powell Anthony Dymoke, 94, English writer and author of *A Dance to the Music of Time*, appointed CBE 1956; 28 March

Pryce-Jones Alan Payan, 91, English writer and critic, editor of the *Times Literary Supplement* 1948–59; 22 January

Puente 'Tito' (Ernesto Antonio), 75, US bandleader, percussionist, and composer, who successfully fused Latin rhythms with jazz; 31 May

Rampal Jean-Pierre, 78, French flautist, and one of the most recorded classical musicians in history; 20 May

Rankin John Morris, 40, US folk musician, who played with members of his family to acclaim in the UK and USA; 16 January

Rausing Gad, 77, Swedish industrialist whose father, Ruben, invented the Tetra Pak carton for liquids, and who was listed by *Forbes* magazine as the world's 31st richest individual in 1999; 28 January

Reeves Steven Lester, 74, US actor and bodybuilder, Mr America (1947), Mr World (1948), and Mr Universe (1950), and among his films is *Hercules* (1957); 1 May

Rey Henri, 87, French psychiatrist and psychoanalyst, at Maudsley Hospital, London, England 1945–77; 12 January

Richard (Joseph Henri) Maurice, 78, Canadian ice hockey player, known as 'The Rocket', who played for the Montreal Canadiens for 18 years; 27 May

Richardson Elliot, 79, US lawyer, who resigned as attorney general at the height of Watergate in 1973 after refusing President Nixon's request that he fire Archibald Cox, the special prosecutor; 1 January

Roberts Aldwyn ('Lord Kitchener'), 77, Trinidadian calypso singer; 11 February

Roberts William, 92, Welsh artist and honorary fellow of University College, Swansea, Wales; 11 March

Roosevelt Kermit, 83, US intelligence officer, famous for organizing a coup in Iran which overthrew Prime Minister Muhammad Mossadegh in 1953, and installed the Shah as absolute monarch; 8 June

Ross Arnold (born Arnold Rosenberg), 79, US jazz pianist who was sacked from the Glenn Miller band and went on to play for films and in Harry Janes' band; 5 June

Roy Jules, 92, French novelist, essayist, playwright, and poet, author of the novel sequence *Les Chevaux du Soleil/The Sun Horses* (1968–80); 15 June

Russell Ross, 90, US writer and record producer, regarded as a father-figure of jazz music; 31 January

Sainsbury Robert James, 93, English arts patron and businessman, son of the founder of the firm J Sainsbury; 2 April

Salam Saeb, 95, Lebanese politician and prime minister 1952, 1953, 1960–61, 1970–73; 21 January

Salter Lionel Paul, 85, English conductor, composer, pianist, harpsichordist, and writer; 1 March

Salzedo Leonard Lopès, 78, English composer and conductor, of Spanish descent, who wrote 17 ballet scores, the most famous of which is *The Witch Boy* (1956); 6 May

Sampney Ken(neth) Slater, 78, English trade unionist, president of the National Association of Colliery Overmen, Deputies, and Shotfirers (Nacods) 1980–85; 2 January

Sandys Pat (born Patricia Mary Trotter), 73, English television producer and actress, who later in her career worked on the programme *The Bill*; 19 May

Sayer Sylvia (born Sylvia Olive Pleadwell Munday), 95, English conservationist and environmental campaigner, chairman of the Dartmoor Preservation Society 1951–73, appointed KBE 1959; 4 January

Schulz Charles Monroe, 77, US cartoonist, creator of the *Peanuts* comic strip, and the

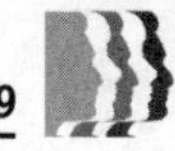

characters Charlie Brown, Snoopy, Lucy, Linus, and Schroeder; 12 February

Secunda Chelita (born Chelita Salvatori), 55, English journalist, fashion stylist, and PR; 7 March

Segal George, 75, US sculptor whose work was often more emotional than other art of the Pop Art era; 9 June

Sewell Fr Brocard (born Michael Seymour Sewell), 87, English Roman Catholic priest, who became a monk in 1952 and ordained in 1954, also a biographer and editor of *The Aylesford Review* (1955–68); 2 April

Shapiro Karl Jay, 86, US poet and teacher, who won the Pulitzer Prize in 1945 for his work *V-Letter and Other Poems*; 14 May

Shapiro Monte Bernard, 87, South African-born clinical psychologist who practised in England, senior lecturer at the Institute of Psychiatry, London, England, 1949–59, and honorary research fellow, University College, London, 1979–88; 29 April

Sharp George, 81, Scottish engine driver and politician, appointed OBE 1969, knighted 1976; 24 June

Shaw Jock, 87, Scottish footballer, with Glasgow Rangers throughout his career, as player, captain, and coach, and who played for Scotland; 13 June

Shaw (John) Giles Dunkerley, 68, English politician, Conservative MP and government minister 1979–87; 12 April

Sladkevicius Vincentas, 79, Lithuanian Roman Catholic priest, who fought for the rights of the Church during Soviet Control of Lithuania 1959–87, named cardinal 1988; 28 May

Sloane John Peter, 54, English pathologist, professor of breast pathology, Liverpool University, England, 1995–2000; 10 May

Sokolow Anna, 89, US dancer, choreographer, and teacher, of Russian-Jewish descent; 29 March

Squire (Jack Francis) Anthony, 86, English film director, producer, and writer, who specialized in filming aerial sequences; 15 May

Statham (John) Brian, 69, English cricketer famous for his accuracy in bowling, appointed CBE 1966; 11 June

Stephen Susan, 68, English film actress whose roles include playing opposite Dirk Bogarde in *For Better, For Worse* (1954); 16 July

Stobbs William, 85, English illustrator and teacher, principal, Maidstone College of Art, England 1958–79; 6 April

Stormonth Darling James Carlisle, 81, Scottish lawyer and conservationist, and influence behind the National Trust for Scotland, appointed CBE 1972 and knighted 1983; 17 April

Stuart (Henry) Francis Montgomery, 97, Irish writer who became involved with the poet Yeats through his marriage to the daughter of Yeats' lover Maud Gonne, and who taught and broadcast in Berlin throughout World War II; 2 February

Swanton Ernest William, 92, English sports writer and broadcaster, cricket commentator for *The Daily Telegraph* from 1946, appointed OBE in 1965 and CBE in 1994; 22 January

Swinburne Nora, 97, English film and stage actress, with a career that spanned from 1916 to 1975; 1 May

Takeshita Noboru, 76, Japanese politician, prime minister of Japan 1989–89; 19 June

Tayler Herbert, 87, English architect who worked with his partner David Green to provide housing in the Loddon district, southeast of Norwich, England; 3 February

Taylor Samuel, 87, US playwright and screenwriter, famous for his play *Sabrina Fair* (1953) and his script for Alfred Hitchcock's *Vertigo* (1958); 2 June

Thomas Bill, 78, US costume designer who worked on films such as *Mary Poppins* (1964) and *Bedknobs and Broomsticks* (1971); 30 May

Thompson (David) Brian, 73, English solicitor whose cases made a lasting contribution to workplace accident, employment, and trade union law; 26 February

Thompson Homer Armstrong, 93, US archaeologist, who worked on the excavation of the Athens agora from 1930 to World War II, and was field director of the site 1947–67, as well as teaching classical archaeology; 7 May

Tinker Hugh Russell, 78, English scholar of Southern Asia and political activist, with a particular interest in Myanmar (formerly Burma), emeritus professor of politics, Lancaster University, England; 14 April

Tomlinson David Cecil MacAlister, 83, English theatre and film actor, famous for his role as the father in *Mary Poppins* (1964), as well as other Disney films; 24 June

Tranter Nigel Godwin, 90, English writer, who published more than 130 books, best known for his historical novels set in Scotland, appointed OBE 1983; 9 January

Trevor Claire (born Claire Wemlinger), 88, US film, television, stage, and radio actress whose films include *Stagecoach* (1939), *Key Largo* (1948), and *The High and the Mighty* (1954); 8 April

Ugolini Nello, 94, Italian football and motor racing team manager; 20 February

Vadim Roger, 72, French film and theatre director, actor and writer, also famous as husband and lover to many of the actors he cast in his films, including Brigitte Bardot and Jane Fonda; 11 February

Vallejo Antonio Buero, 83, Spanish playwright who was regarded with suspicion for his activities during the Spanish Civil War (1936–39), and during Franco's dictatorship 1939–75; 29 April

Van den Bergh Tony (Edward Henry Coote), 83, writer and broadcaster for television and radio; 3 May

Van Vogt Alfred Elton, 87, Canadian-born US writer of science fiction; 26 January

Walter Nicolas Hardy, 65, English writer, journalist, and political activist; 7 March

Wharton Lady Ziki (born Myrtle Olive Felix Arbuthnot), 66, English photographer and animal welfare campaigner, succeeded as Baroness Wharton in 1990; 15 May

Wheldon Thomas, 56, Scottish oncologist and specialist in cancer therapy, professor of Glasgow University, Scotland 1999–2000; 4 June

Whitby (Lionel) Gordon, 73, English professor of clinical chemistry, at Edinburgh University 1963–91; 12 March

White Miles Edgren, 85, US costume designer who worked on such Broadway shows as *Oklahoma!* and such films as *Around the World in 80 Days* (1956); 17 February

Whitehouse Harold Leslie Keer, 82, English geneticist, botanist, and Emeritus Fellow of Darwin College, Cambridge, England; 18 January

Wicki Bernard, 80, German actor and director, who gained an international reputation in 1959 with his starkly realistic war film *Die Brücke/The Bridge*; 5 January

Widdowson Elsie May, 93, English nutritionist, whose influential work was carried out with Dr R A McCance, and influenced European dietary habits; 14 June

Wilkins Leslie Thomas, 85, English criminologist and statistician, emeritus professor of criminology at the State University of Albany, New York; 8 May

Willis (William) Rex, 75, Welsh rugby player, scrum half of both Cardiff and Wales, captain of Cardiff 1952–53; 18 January

Willmott Peter, 76, English sociologist and social researcher who co-wrote (with Michael Young) an influential study on the effect of living arrangements on families and individuals, *Family and Kinship in East London* (1957); 8 April

Wraight Robert Allen, 86, English writer, art critic and dealer, author of the best-selling *The Art Game* (1965); 1 April

Wright Judith Arundell, 85, Australian poet and campaigner for conservation and the rights of Aboriginal Australians; 25 June

Zevi Bruno, 81, Italian architect, historian, and critic, who argued that architecture should be democratic and organic; 9 January

Extended Obituaries

Assad, Hafez-al

(1930–2000)

President of Syria from 1970 to 2000, and leader of the Ba'ath Arab Socialist Party, Hafez-al Assad brought internal stability to his country and was respected for his shrewd international policy. Born in Qardaha, in northwestern Syria, into a peasant family Assad joined the air force and qualified at the top of his class as a pilot. Having joined the Ba'ath Arab Socialist Party as a schoolboy and become its student leader, he became party leader at the age of 40. In 1958 Syria had merged with Egypt to form the United Arab Republic (UAR) but three years later, after one of several army coups, it seceded and an independent Syrian Arab Republic was established. In 1963 a government was formed by the Ba'ath Party but three years later another army coup removed it. In 1970 the moderate wing of the party, led by Assad, seized power in yet another coup but this time stability was restored and Assad was elected president. A year later he ensured the longevity of this peace by forming the five main political parties into one broad group, the National Progressive Front. In external affairs, Assad was both feared and respected, and was regarded by most of his Western counterparts as the most skilful statesman in the Middle East, manoeuvring his country through several political minefields that events around him were creating: the 1973 Yom Kippur War fought by Egypt and Israel; the 1980–87 Iran–Iraq War; and the 1990–91 Gulf War. A major concern during his presidency was Israel's establishment of a security zone in Lebanon, which Assad viewed as a threat to Syria's territorial integrity. Towards the end of his life, however, Assad, with United States mediation, came close to securing a permanent peace with Israel. Assad's death left a political vacuum which his son, Bashar, would hope eventually to fill. *See also* **colour section**.

Budge, John Don(ald)

(1915–2000)

US tennis player, who in 1938 became the first person to achieve the Grand Slam of winning the Australian, French, US, and Wimbledon singles titles in the same calendar year. Renowned for his blistering serve and his brilliant service returns, he also pioneered the backhand as an attacking stroke. John Donald Budge was born in Oakland, California on 13 June 1915, the son of a former Glasgow Rangers footballer who had emigrated from Scotland. He did not take up tennis seriously until he was 17, yet in 1933, aged 18, he won the US junior championship. In 1935 he made his debut in the Davis Cup – in which competition he was to be undefeated in 21 of 23 singles matches and 6 of 8 doubles contests – and the following year, in partnership with Gene Mako, won the US doubles title. When Britain's Fred Perry decided to turn professional at the end of 1936 (thus rendering himself ineligible for Grand Slam championships, which at the time were strictly for amateurs), Budge took his place as the pre-eminent player in men's tennis. Between 1936 and 1938 he won a total of 14 Grand Slam titles, including triumphs in all three Wimbledon events in 1937 and his unique garnering of the Wimbledon singles, doubles, and mixed-doubles titles in successive years. Shortly after his 1938 achievement of the coveted Grand Slam, Budge himself turned professional and twice won the US pro championships before his career was interrupted by World War II. A shoulder injury sustained while serving in the US Army Air Corps hampered his game, but he remained on the pro circuit until 1950.

Cartland, (Mary) Barbara Hamilton

(1901–2000)

Dubbed the 'Queen of Romantic Fiction', Barbara Cartland was one of the world's most prolific writers, with 723 novels to her name, as well as many articles. Barbara Cartland's writing career began with a gossip column in the *Daily Express*, and was aided by the patronage of Lord Beaverbrook. Her first novel, *Jigsaw*, was published in 1923. Many of her earliest books were 'middle brow', but she soon turned to romantic novels that she produced at astounding speed, and to a standard formula, usually ending in marriage. In 1927, having herself received numerous proposals of marriage, Cartland married Alexander McCorquodale. They had one daughter, Raine, who later became stepmother to Princess Diana. Following divorce in 1936, Cartland married Hugh McCorquodale, Alexander's cousin, with whom she was to have two sons. During World War II she returned from initial flight to Canada to do war work, becoming a welfare officer with the Women's Voluntary Service and, in keeping with her romantic ethos, assembled a wardrobe of a thousand white wedding dresses for brides serving in the forces. At the end of the war she was asked to stand as a Conservative MP, but declined, choosing to concentrate on her writing and on launching her daughter into society. Cartland did serve, however, as a local councillor, and championed many causes, including the St John's Ambulance Brigade. In her later years, often elaborately dressed in her trademark pink, Cartland continued to make public appearances, in which she expressed her opinion on a wide range of social matters. She continued to write until the last. She was appointed Dame of the British Empire in 1991.

Barbara Cartland *Syndication International*

> *At fifty you have the choice of keeping your face or your figure, and it's much better to keep your face.*
>
> BARBARA CARTLAND, *Daily Mail*, 10 July 1981.

Crisp, Quentin (Dennis Pratt)

(1908–1999)

Renowned as much for his homosexuality as his wit, Quentin Crisp became a celebrity only at the age of 60, with the 1968 publication of his autobiography *The Naked Civil Servant*. Born Dennis Pratt in London on Christmas Day 1908, Crisp received a good schooling. He worked for a spell as a rent-boy, during which time he lost a string of regular jobs as he never bothered to conceal his sexual orientation. At one time he posed as an art model for government-sponsored drawing classes (hence a 'naked civil servant'). He finally settled down to working as a freelance commercial artist, and as he grew older was increasingly likely to be seen wearing makeup and a billowing yellow or white bouffant hairdo, tottering around on high-heeled shoes. *The Naked Civil Servant* caused a sensation when it appeared in 1968, for the publication of an openly and explicitly homosexual life-story, however well-written and amusingly sardonic, would only a few years or so before have brought its author a prison sentence, if it had been published at all. Crisp became something of a hero to the gay community for his incomparable demonstration that gays could be charming, witty, and worthy of admiration. In 1975 *The Naked Civil Servant* was made into a TV movie, starring John Hurt. Acclaimed by critics, it was a year later shown to TV audiences in the

USA, where it won several prestigious TV awards and turned Crisp into an international celebrity. His quick wit made him the doyen of US TV chat programmes. Crisp also managed to convert his writing style into a stage performance, creating a one-man show that successfully toured the USA. He additionally found himself giving lectures on cruise ships and even making cameo guest appearances in TV adverts. In the meantime he wrote more humorous books: *How to Have a Life-Style* (1979) and *How To Become A Virgin* (1981). Fame and fortune appealed to him, and he moved to New York in 1982, taking a permanent room in a Manhattan hotel. There he wrote *Manners From Heaven* (1984) and *How To Go To the Movies* (1989), and also appeared in several feature films. His last book, *Resident Alien: The New York Diaries* (1997), charted his reaction to the USA and revealed just how much he enjoyed it. It became a best-seller. Crisp died in Manchester, England, while preparing to take his one-man show on tour around his native country.

Quentin Crisp *Syndication International*

> *Though intelligence is powerless to modify character, it is a dab hand at finding euphemisms for its weaknesses.*
>
> Quentin Crisp, *The Naked Civil Servant*, ch. 29.

Dury, Ian

(1942–2000)

Often seen as the acceptable face of punk rock, Ian Dury was an accomplished singer, songwriter, and actor. Born into a working-class family in Upminster, at the age of seven Ian Dury contracted polio and spent two years in hospital before being sent to a special school. Despite the gap in his education, he made it to grammar school and the Royal College of Art and went on to lecture, briefly, at Canterbury College of Art. Dury formed his first band, Kilburn and the High Roads, in 1970. An album recorded for Warner Brothers was not released, while an album for Pye made little impact. The band split in 1976, largely due to Dury's health problems. Dury then became a solo artist, and formed the Blockheads as a backing band. His first solo single, 'Sex and Drugs and Rock'n'Roll', became his calling card but was not a hit; in 1987 it was enlisted for Aids education with his approval: 'Two of these just became more dangerous,' he said. He finally reached the Top 10 with 'What a Waste'. Dury's scatalogical poetry and rhyming slang were a more knowing take on the anarchy of punk, with references far wider than teenage rebellion. Musically, his hybrid sound was considerably more accomplished than the usual three-chord thrash. He achieved brief chart success before branching out into acting, making his acting debut opposite Bob Geldof in *Number One*. Further parts followed in Roman Polanski's *Pirates* and with Bob Dylan in *Hearts of Fire*. Dury had lost his first wife, Betty, to cancer, and he amazed everyone around him by the fortitude and good humour with which he bore his own illness – even appearing on stage attached to an intravenous drip just weeks before he died.

> *You don't have cancer; it has you.*
>
> Ian Dury, interviewed shortly before his death from cancer, *Daily Telegraph*, 28 March 2000.

Gielgud, (Arthur) John

(1904–2000)

For the last 40 years of his life, John Gielgud was revered as the 'grand old man' of theatre, cinema, and television. Arthur John Gielgud was born to a Polish father and English mother in London on 14 April 1904. He attended Westminster School, won a scholarship to the Royal Academy of Dramatic Art (RADA), and went on to make his professional debut at the Old Vic, London, in 1921. By the end of 1928 he had made the first of many appearances on the stages of New York's Broadway, and returned to the Old Vic to take the title roles in Shakespeare's *Richard II* and *Hamlet*. Within four years he was not only performing and directing at the Old Vic, but was also responsible for decisions on stage design – thus founding a tradition of directors of classic plays exerting a strong influence on the visual elements of production. Soon Gielgud was something of an impresario, assembling brilliant companies of actors and playing unlimited runs to packed houses in London and New York. As cinema was gaining in popularity, Gielgud appeared with Peter Lorre in Alfred Hitchcock's 1936 film *The Secret Agent*. Yet the stage remained his first priority, and in 1939, with Edith Evans, he starred in the celebrated London production of Wilde's *The Importance of Being Earnest*. It was not until the 1950s that his film career took off again with films of such Shakespeare plays as *Julius Caesar* and *Richard III*. In 1964, his Henry II in *Becket* saw him nominated for an Oscar. Gielgud then demonstrated his versatility with screen performances outside the classical repertoire – often with a great humour and even, on occasion, self-parody. He featured, for example, in the satirical *Oh What a Lovely War* (1969) and was Dudley Moore's imperturbable butler in *Arthur* (1981), which won him an Oscar for Best Supporting Actor. Gielgud gave his final stage performance in 1988, when he was already 83 years old. Ten years later he appeared in the Channel 4 TV production of *Merlin*. Within six weeks of his death on 21 May 2000 he was still filming Samuel Beckett's play *Catastrophe*. His companion of some 40 years, Martin Hensler, died a year or so before him. Gielgud was knighted in 1953, appointed Companion of Honour in 1977, and awarded the Order of Merit in 1996.

John Gielgud *Syndication International*

Hassan II

(1929–1999)

King of Morocco from 1961 until his death at the age of 70 on 23 July 1999, Moulay Hassan bin Mohammed maintained autocratic rule of his country, while in external affairs he helped bring about several international peace treaties. So daring were his political manoeuvres Moroccans liked to say Hassan had 'baraka', signifying that he had God on his side. From early in his reign, Hassan's authority was challenged by a series of attempted coups, to which he responded with a combination of repression and reform. Periods of emergency, during which the king effectively exercised absolute power, alternated with periods of political reform, in which Morocco enjoyed limited parliamentary government, with political parties and independent media operating within set bounds. Such reform, however, has been seen as merely a ploy to placate opposition, and Hassan's record is marred by the cruel, sometimes vengeful, treatment of political opponents and by the large-scale corruption it is alleged he encouraged among his subordinates in order to better control them. Nevertheless, if Hassan is judged by the effect, rather than the means, of his rule, it is arguable that his achievements are rather remarkable. Under Hassan, Morocco enjoyed continuity and relative stability, which facilitated economic development without momentous unrest or social trauma; and, within limits, Moroccans were allowed a measure of political freedom. Perhaps a weaker leader would have achieved less. In international affairs, moreover, Hassan's diplomacy helped bring about the 1979 peace treaty between Israel and Egypt, and subsequent agreements between Israel and the Palestine

Liberation Organisation. In addition, a summit of the world's Muslim leaders hosted by Hassan in 1994 resulted in a public statement against Islamic extremism. Hassan is succeeded by his son, Crown Prince Sidi Mohamed.

> *Morocco is like a tree nourished by roots deep in the soil of Africa which breathes through foliage rustling to the winds of Europe.*
>
> HASSAN II, *The Challenge*, 1979.

Heller, Joseph

(1923–1999)

Joseph Heller, who died in East Hampton, New York, on December 12, 1999, aged 76, made his name as a novelist with his 1961 best-seller *Catch-22*, a satirical depiction of modern warfare. The title of Heller's novel has passed into the English language to describe a situation of deadlock. Born and raised in Coney Island, Brooklyn, Heller saw active service in Italy with the US Army Air Force as a bombardier, and left with the rank of lieutenant. He then took a BA at New York University in 1948, and went on to Columbia for his MA, before studying at St. Catherine's College, Oxford, on a Fulbright scholarship, in 1949–50. Beginning to write he soon achieved literary success with stories appearing in such periodicals as *Atlantic Monthly*. Stylistically influenced by Hemingway and Chekhov, and drawing on his Jewish background, among Heller's best stories are *I Don't Love You Any More* and *Castle of Snow*. But it is with his first great work, *Catch-22* that Heller has always been associated, for he never achieved the same success with later works. He had a standard response to those who told him he hadn't written another novel as good as *Catch-22*: 'Who has?' Set on a tiny island in the Mediterranean, *Catch-22* features Captain Yossarian, a pilot who eventually deserts. The phrase *Catch-22* refers to a paralysing paradox with which airmen are confronted: the insane are excused from flying, but the sane are obliged to fly; yet not to want to fly is a clear indication of sanity, so to request to be excused from bombing missions on the grounds of insanity is to be obliged to go. In the words of Yossarian: 'That's some catch, that Catch-22.' Heller is survived by his second wife, Valerie, and the two children of his first marriage.

Lamarr, Hedy

(1914–2000)

As Hedy Keisler (an abbreviation of her birth name Hedwig Eva Maria Keisler), film actress Hedy Lamarr achieved international fame – and provoked a scandal – with her performance in the 1933 Czech film entitled *Ecstasy*, before moving on to Hollywood. *Ecstasy* caused a sensation because it featured an explicit love scene and a ten-minute nude swimming sequence. The film achieved further notoriety through attempts by her first husband, munitions manufacturer Friedrich Alexander Mandl, to buy up every copy and destroy them. Hollywood was decades away from such openness, but it recognized a beautiful face and the publicity value of nudity. Lamarr was promptly signed by MGM and brought to the USA in 1937. In 1938, cast alongside Charles Boyer in the film *Algiers*, Lamarr broke through as a major Hollywood star. Successful appearances with Clark Gable, in such films as *Boom Town* (1940) and *Comrade X* (1940), and in the role of Delilah, opposite Victor Mature's Samson, in the epic *Samson and Delilah* (1949) cemented her success. These triumphs, however, were followed by the gradual decline of her career in the middle 1950s. She gave an acclaimed performance as a drunken movie star on the skids in *The Female Animal* (1957), but this was to be her last film. Lamarr always maintained that her career dwindled because she would not sleep with the heads of film studios to get work. Her best-selling 1966 autobiography, *Ecstasy and Me*, is filled with lurid anecdotes; but she later sued, claiming that her publisher's ghost-writer had distorted her manuscript. Lamarr was married and divorced six times. With actor John Loder, she had a son (Anthony) and a daughter (Denise); she also adopted a boy (James).

Lynch, Jack

(1917–1999)

Leader (1966–79) of the Irish political party Fianna Fáil, Jack Lynch was twice Taoiseach (prime minister) of the Republic of Ireland, (1966–73 and 1977–79). Born in Cork, the youngest of five sons to middle-class parents, Lynch was educated at the city's Christian Brothers school and the North Cork monastery. At the age of 19 he joined the civil service, while studying part-time for the Bar at King's Inn, Dublin. As a young man he was a successful sportsman, winning medals in hurling and Gaelic football. It was his sporting celebrity that led to his being offered several parliamentary constituencies. He chose to stand in Cork, where he had a huge personal following, and won the seat for Fianna Fáil in 1948. Nine years later Lynch was given the education portfolio in Eamon de Valera's last cabinet. When Sean Lemass succeeded de Valera in 1959, Lynch moved to the department of industry and commerce and then, for a short period, was finance minister. When Lemass retired in 1966, Fianna Fáil was threatened with a split over the leadership, some backing the up-and-coming Charles Haughey while others favoured the old guard's George Colley. To avert such a split, the mild and softly-spoken Lynch was put forward as a compromise candidate and was elected leader. His mildness was viewed as a sign of weakness by such members of his party as Haughey, but it was precisely this characteristic that endeared him to many members of the general public. Meanwhile the situation in Northern Ireland was deteriorating, with thousands of Catholics fleeing to the south. In response, Lynch moved army medical units to the border and dispatched his foreign minister to the United Nations in an attempt to make the problem an international issue, much to the consternation of the British government. At the same time, some more forceful members of his cabinet had begun to take matters into their own hands, plotting to supply arms to the IRA. The exposure of this plot in October 1969 resulted in what became known as the 'arms crisis'. At first Lynch appeared to ignore the conspiracy until, finally convinced that it really was happening, he dealt decisively with the rebels. Perhaps because of these early problems, and despite such economic achievements as taking the Republic of Ireland into the European Economic Community in 1973, Lynch and Fianna Fáil were narrowly defeated in the 1973 general election. After four years in opposition, however, Lynch and his party were returned to power with an unprecedented majority of 20 seats in the Dáil. Lynch had already indicated that he wished to retire before the end of the parliamentary session, and two by-election defeats and criticisms of his handling of the north–south problems acted as catalysts. Lynch therefore stood down in 1979, and was succeeded by Charles Haughey.

> *I have never and never will accept the right of a minority who happen to be a majority in a small part of the country to opt out of a nation.*
>
> JACK LYNCH, *The Irish Times*, 14 November 1970.

Marshall, Malcolm Denzil

(1958–1999)

One of cricket's truly great fast bowlers, Malcolm Marshall was the most successful member of the formidable West Indian pace-bowling attack of the 1980s. Born in Pine, Bridgetown, Barbados on 18 April 1958, Marshall made his first-class debut for Barbados at the end of the 1977–78 season, and within 12 months he had made his way into the West Indies Test side. In 81 Test matches between 1978 and 1991 he amassed 376 wickets, a total only previously exceeded by Kapil Dev, Richard Hadlee, and Ian Botham, none of whom could match Marshall's average of a wicket every 20.94 runs. Between 1983 and 1986, moreover, he took 20 or more wickets in seven consecutive Test series; and in England in 1988 he captured 35 wickets at an average of only 12.65 to establish a new West Indian record for the most wickets in a series. Marshall was also a prolific wicket-taker in English county cricket for Hampshire between 1979 and 1992. In first-class cricket as a whole he took 1,651 wickets at an average of only 19. The key to Marshall's bowling success was his ability to swing the ball and seam it off the pitch without sacrificing speed or accuracy. He was also an accomplished batsman, and is the only West Indian other than Gary Sobers to have taken 100 wickets and scored over 1,000 runs in Test cricket. Marshall's Test career came to an end in 1991 but he continued to play first-class cricket for another three years.

Appointed West Indies coach in 1996, Marshall was preparing the team for the 1999 World Cup in England when he was diagnosed with cancer.

Matthews, Stanley

(1915–2000)

Dubbed the 'Wizard of Dribble', Stanley Matthews was perhaps the most famous, adored, and brilliant footballer England has produced. The inaugural winner of both English and European Footballer of the Year awards (in 1948 and 1956 respectively), and uniquely the only footballer to be knighted while still playing, Matthews was renowned both for his consummate skill and his exemplary conduct. Described by Pelé as 'the man who taught us the way football should be played', Matthews was never booked or sent off in his career. Born in Hanley, Staffordshire, on 1 February 1915, Matthews signed as a professional with Stoke City on his 17th birthday, and shortly afterwards made his league debut. In his first full season he scored 15 goals, helping Stoke to the 1932–33 Division Two title. He was awarded his first England cap in September 1934, but had to wait another three years before establishing himself in the side. Such brilliant individual displays as his performance against Czechoslovakia in December 1937, when he scored a hat-trick, helped build the Matthews legend. Playing on the right wing, Matthews delighted spectators but tormented defenders with his dazzling dribbling skills. Beautifully balanced, he liked to take the ball to an opponent, then – with sleight of foot, a sudden swerve, and burst of pace – he would accelerate away. Although a regular goalscorer early in his career, he preferred to create goals for his team-mates. He could pass or cross the ball with pin-point accuracy. In 1947, despite public protests by Stoke fans, Matthews was transferred to Blackpool for a fee of £11,500. He helped his new club reach the FA Cup finals of 1948 and 1951, but on both occasions he was on the losing side. However, when Blackpool made the final again in 1953, against Bolton Wanderers, and found themselves 3–1 down with just 20 minutes to go, Matthews inspired his side to an amazing comeback that gave them a 4–3 victory. The 'Matthews final', as it came to be known, is undoubtedly the most famous match in English football history after the 1966 World Cup final. In 1957, at the age of 42, Matthews made his 54th and final international appearance. Four years later, amid great rejoicing in the Potteries, he re-joined Stoke City. In 1963, after helping to inspire Stoke to win the Second Division title, he was named Footballer of the Year for a second time. On 6 February 1965, a month after being awarded a knighthood, he finally bowed out of the game. Always supremely fit, due in part to a daily exercise regime and an abstemious lifestyle, Matthews had played professional football for a total of 33 years from 1932 to 1965 – the longest career of any player in the English game. When he took part in his 710th and final league game he was 50 years and five days old. Matthews then worked for a time as general manager at Port Vale, but for most of the next three decades he undertook coaching assignments around the world, most notably in Malta and South Africa.

Stanley Matthews *Syndication International*

Mayfield, Curtis

(1942–1999)

An immensely talented soul singer, guitarist, and songwriter who was outspoken on civil rights and black pride, Curtis Mayfield became something of an African-American icon. Born in Chicago on 3 June 1942 into a literate and musical family, Mayfield was a member of a gospel choir as a child. He began writing songs during his early teens when his friend Jerry Butler formed a group called The Roosters. Shortly afterwards Eddie Thomas became their manager and renamed them The Impressions. The group's first successful record 'For Your Precious Love', entered the charts in 1958. Two years later Mayfield had his own R&B hit with 'He Will Break Your Heart', on the strength of which he took The Impressions to New York in search of a full-time recording contract. ABC Records signed them up, and Mayfield enjoyed a series of some 18 hits, including his 1965 release 'People, Get Ready'. This record became an anthem in African-Americans' struggle for equality and civil rights in a world apparently willing to resort to violence to deny them. Leaving ABC Records in 1968, Mayfield established his own record label (which was to feature several highly successful artists) before deciding to leave The Impressions and pursue a solo career. He issued two solo albums over 1970 and 1971, which were rapturously received. Mayfield was then invited to write the score for the film *Superfly*. Hit singles from the film's soundtrack went on to receive four Grammy nominations and sold well over a million copies. The full score is considered a classic of contemporary black music. Mayfield continued to issue albums, both solo and with other artists (including Gladys Knight and the Pips, Aretha Franklin, and Linda Clifford), and to work on film scores. Hit singles at this time included 'So In Love', 'Only You Babe', 'Show Me Love', and 'Baby, It's You'. Tours in Europe and Japan followed, and kept Mayfield busy through most of the 1980s. The end of the decade saw him once again concentrating on film scores. In August 1990, however, Mayfield suffered a catastrophic accident. In high wind, a heavy lighting rig high above the stage on which he was performing collapsed on top of him, permanently damaging his spine and confining him to a wheelchair. Nevertheless, he continued to work (his album *New World Order* was released in 1996) and was cared for by his wife and family in their home in Atlanta, Georgia, until his death.

Nkomo, Joshua Mqabuko Nyongolo

(1917–1999)

As leader (1961–88) of the Zimbabwe African People's Union (ZAPU), Joshua Nkomo helped end white minority rule in Zimbabwe, of which he became vice-president (1990–96). Born in Matabeleland, Nkomo grew up in what was (from 1923 to 1953) the self-governing British colony of Southern Rhodesia. In 1953 Southern Rhodesia joined Northern Rhodesia (now Zambia) and Nyasaland (now Malawi) to form the Central African Federation, which had a multi-racial constitution. When the Federation was dissolved ten years later, however, a group of white politicians formed the Rhodesian Front Party (RF) dedicated to securing white dominance in southern Rhodesia. Nkomo became a key figure in African nationalist opposition to the RF, and while in temporary exile in 1959 helped form the National Democratic Party (NDP). When the NDP was banned in 1961, Nkomo created the Zimbabwe African People's Union (ZAPU), which in 1962 was also declared unlawful. Meanwhile a split in ZAPU produced a rival organization, the Zimbabwe African National Union Patriotic Front (ZANU-PF), led by the Reverend Ndabaningi Sithole, and later by Robert Mugabe. When the British government refused to grant independence to Southern Rhodesia without a guarantee from the RF government of democratic multi-racial politics prime minister Ian Smith issued a Unilateral Declaration of Independence (UDI) in 1965, and in 1969 proclaimed a republic under a new constitution that guaranteed a white-dominated legislative assembly. ZAPU and ZANU then embarked upon a guerrilla war against the Smith regime. In 1979 a new British government, led by Margaret Thatcher, was persuaded to look once again at the situation in a by now war-devastated Southern Rhodesia, and convened a conference at Lancaster House in London. This resulted in a 1980 agreement (which became known as the Lancaster House Agreement) that granted full independence under a multi-racial constitution to Southern Rhodesia, which was henceforth to be known as Zimbabwe. Subsequent elections resulted in Robert Mugabe becoming Zimbabwe's first prime minister, with Nkomo given a cabinet post in the new government. However, tensions developed between the two political leaders and in

1982, when arms were discovered at his farm, Nkomo was dismissed. He left the country briefly, fearing assassination, but several months later he returned and was reinstated in the cabinet in 1988, a year which also saw the merging of ZANU and ZAPU. This reconciliation was of particular importance for the stability of Zimbabwe, since Nkomo was leader of the Ndebele, who comprise almost 20% of the country's 12 million people, while Mugabe leads the Shona, who comprise more than 70% of the population. In 1987 parliament had passed a new constitution, making Mugabe executive president, and in 1990 Nkomo became his deputy, an office he held until 1996, three years before his death.

Nyerere, Julius Kambarage

(1922–1999)

Having in 1954 formed the Tanganyika African National Union, which achieved Tanganyika's independence in 1961, Julius Nyerere became chief minister (1960), prime minister (1961), and then president (1962–85) of his country, which was renamed Tanzania in 1964. Born in Butiama village, Lake Victoria, Nyerere qualified as a teacher, and was still affectionately known as Mwalimu – or 'teacher' – even at the height of his political career. After taking a degree in history and economics at Edinburgh University, Nyerere returned to Tanganyika and in 1954 founded the Tanganyika African National Union (TANU), with himself as president, to campaign for independence. Tanganyika had been part of German East Africa and after World War I became a British protectorate. In 1961 the independence movement achieved internal self-government and, later in the year, full independence within the Commonwealth. Tanganyika became a republic, with Nyerere its first president. In 1964 it merged with the neighbouring island of Zanzibar and Nyerere became president of the new United Republic of Tanzania. During the next twenty years he was re-elected four times and became one of Africa's most respected politicians. Nyerere established himself as a genuine Christian-Socialist and in 1967, in the northern town of Arusha, made an historic statement, the Arusha Declaration. It committed his country to becoming a socialist state. A key component of Nyerere's plan was to raise the standard of living of millions of poor peasants by establishing village co-operatives. However, during the final years of his presidency, Nyerere was forced to compromise his ideology and accept limited capitalism. Nevertheless, he retained the respect of his people and the outside world, for his achievements were considerable: according to the UN, at the end of Nyerere's presidency, Tanzania, one of the most politically stable countries in Africa, boasted the best public health service in Africa and an excellent primary school system. Nyerere also took the lead in opposing colonial exploitation and misrule in Africa. He joined other African leaders in denouncing the racist policies of South Africa, playing host to such South African opposition movements as the African National Congress (ANC) and the Pan-African Congress (PAC), and was instrumental in exerting the political pressure that led to apartheid South Africa's exclusion from the Commonwealth in 1961. He also supported the movement opposing Portuguese rule in Mozambique, and broke off relations with Britain for its failure to use force when in 1965 Southern Rhodesia's white supremacist Ian Smith declared independence. In the late 1970s Nyerere condemned the brutal regime of Idi Amin in Uganda, and was courageous enough to send in Tanzanian troops to dislodge him. Nyerere, a practising Catholic and a man of austere habits, was much-loved and respected. He is also noted for his translations of Shakespeare into Swahili, and for a number of original poems.

> *Repaying debts is a matter of honour. We want to repay them. But before you can pay you have to live.*
> JULIUS NYERERE

O'Brian, (Richard) Patrick

(1914–2000)

A biographer and novelist, O'Brian is best-known as the creator of 18 tales about Captain Jack Aubrey, RN, and his physician friend Stephen Maturin, set during the Napoleonic Wars. O'Brian's first book, *Caesar* (1930), was an animal story published when he was only fifteen under his original name of Patrick Russ (he adopted the surname O'Brian in 1945). O'Brian had a flair for languages, and a decade later, during World War II, his fluency in French, Spanish, and Catalan found him employed in Intelligence – on which subject he remained discreet. After the war, a series of short stories, reviews, and early novels appeared, though it was his translations from French into English – including *Papillion* and all of Simone de Beauvoir – that provided the bulk of his income. He also wrote numerous biographies, including a vivid and perceptive portrait of Picasso (1976) – who was a friend and, for a time, a neighbour, of O'Brian's – and a biography of the naturalist and circumnavigator Sir Joseph Banks (1987). It was, however, for his historical naval adventures that O'Brian gained most recognition. In 1995 he was awarded the CBE, and was the first recipient of the Heywood Hill Prize for a lifetime's contribution to literature. At a dinner in the author's honour at the Royal Naval College, Greenwich, in 1996, William Waldegrave spoke persuasively of O'Brian as an epic writer, who had done for Nelson's Navy what Homer did for the siege of Troy, Kipling for British India, and Conrad for the mercantile empire of steam and iron. O'Brian was twice married, in 1936 and 1943. His second wife predeceased him in 1998. He is survived by a son from his first marriage.

Puzo, Mario

(1920–1999)

US writer Mario Puzo is best-known for his 1969 novel *The Godfather*, and for a film version of the book, on which he collaborated with Francis Ford Coppola. Born on 15 October 1920 in New York City, in 'Hell's Kitchen' on Manhattan's West Side, Puzo saw military service in World War II, before receiving his college education at the New School in New York and at Columbia University, courtesy of the GI Bill. Following the publication of several books, which received critical acclaim but poor sales, Puzo decided to write a more 'commercial' story. When published in 1969, *The Godfather*, a warm-hearted but brutally violent saga about a Mafia family, went to No 1 in the US best-seller lists and stayed on them for a year. Remarkably, although brought up in the shadow of Mafia territory, Puzo claimed: 'I wrote *The Godfather* entirely from research, I never met a real honest-to-god gangster.' The extraordinary success of Coppola's 1972 film version of the book, which starred Marlon Brando and Al Pacino, made much of the book's alternation between sudden violence, sentiment, and suspense, and portrayed such Mafia traditions as Omerta (oaths of silence) with an awful reverence. So successful was this blend that it spawned two sequels (1974, 1990), and for Puzo represented a rags-to-riches story that was pure Americana in its resonance. Puzo married Erika Broske in 1946 but was widowed in 1978. He died on 2 July 1999, at his home in Bay Shore, Long Island, and is survived by Carol Gino, his companion of 20 years, and by five children (three sons and two daughters). Puzo's last novel, *Omerta*, appeared posthumously in 2000.

Scott, George C(ampbell)

(1927–1999)

Renowned for movie roles that required forcefulness – tough guy, a mad airforce general, or a blackmailing thug, for example – George C Scott won two Emmys, three Oscar nominations, and one Oscar – which, famously, he declined. He was a master of the craft of incorporating into his characters little mannerisms and movements that emphasized personality. Born in Wise, Virginia, on 18 October 1927, Scott joined the Marine Corps and soon found himself assigned to the graves detail at Arlington Cemetery. It was in reaction to these duties, he later claimed, that he picked up a lifelong liking for alcohol in large quantities. He began studying journalism at the University of Missouri, but when he found himself acting in Rattigan's *The Winslow Boy* there, he knew at once that he wanted to be an actor. Amateur appearances in Detroit and Washington occupied him between 1950 and 1956, while all the time he was hoping to turn professional. When he moved to New York he almost immediately landed the title role in *Richard III* in the New York Shakespeare Festival. One critic described him as 'the meanest Richard III ever seen'. Bit-part TV work followed, until in 1959 he played opposite James Stewart in the film *Anatomy of a Murder*. Both Stewart and Scott received Oscar nominations. Two years later Scott was nominated again, this time for his part in the movie *The Hustler*, with Paul Newman. He declined the nomination – to general amazement. After appearing in the mystery

The List of Adrian Messenger (1963), with Kirk Douglas and Robert Mitchum, Scott gave a memorable performance in Stanley Kubrick's *Dr Strangelove* (1963) – a performance that was hilariously terrifying or, as another critic expressed it, 'compellingly lunatic'. Scott then spent some years combining movie acting with stage work, but at the same time became embroiled in an ever more complex personal life. It was not until 1970 that he really found himself a movie part to suit him, and the title role in *Patton* suited him so much that this time he was awarded an Oscar – which he declined to accept, as a mark of his disapproval of the Academy Awards. Further films followed, but he concentrated more on stage work and TV drama, and during the 1980s and 1990s his face and his voice became well known to US TV audiences. Scott died on 22 September 1999. He had been married five times – twice to the same wife – and fathered six children.

Tudjman, Franjo

(1922–1999)

President of Croatia from 1990 to 1999, Franjo Tudjman was a committed nationalist who also wrote prolifically on Croat and Yugoslav history. Born in Veliko Trgovisce, a hillside village north of Zagreb, Tudjman was son of the local leader of the nationalist Croatian Peasants Party. When Nazi Germany occupied Croatia in 1941 and installed the puppet Ustashe regime, Tudjman joined Tito's communist guerrilla army, the partisans. This began Tudjman's 20-year military career, which culminated in 1960 in his appointment as the youngest major-general in the Yugoslav National Army. Tudjman left the army in 1961, however, to embark on a new career as a Croat nationalist historian, founding his own Institute of the History of the Workers' Movement in Zagreb. He received a doctorate in 1965 for a dissertation on the history of the Yugoslav monarchy. Most controversially, in another work Tudjman painted a revisionist picture of the fascist Ustashe regime, claiming that fewer than 50,000 Serbs and others died at its Jasenovac concentration camp, rather than the 700,000 stated in Yugoslav history books. Elected to the Croatian parliament in 1965, Tudjman became associated with a resurgence in Croat nationalism, abandoned communism, and became an outspoken critic of Tito and what Tudjman regarded as a Serb-dominated regime. Expelled from the communist party in 1967 after supporting a campaign for recognition of Croatian as a distinct language, in 1971 he was sentenced to nine-months' imprisonment for anti-communist and anti-Yugoslav activities. After Tito's death in 1980, he received a second jail sentence of three years' hard labour in 1981, but was released after less than a year because of ill health.

In May 1990, with the Yugoslav federation fast disintegrating, Tudjman's Christian Democrat Union (HDZ), which he had founded in 1989 to advocate Croatian independence, won Croatia's first free elections. Tudjman became state president and immediately curbed the rights of the Serb minority in Croatia, provoking a revolt by Serbs in Slavonia and Krajina. When Croatia declared independence from Yugoslavia in 1991, it provoked a six-month-long war with the Serb-dominated Yugoslav National Army, which claimed 10,000 lives and led to Croatia losing temporarily the Serb-dominated Krajina and Slavonia territories. With independence achieved in 1992, however, Tudjman was directly elected president. Hoping to create a 'Greater Croatia', Tudjman then gave military backing to Bosnia's Croat population in the 1992–95 civil war in Bosnia-Herzegovina. However, although Tudjman failed to realize a 'Greater Croatia', he did recapture Western Slavonia and Krajina in 1995; and in January 1998 Croatia also gained Eastern Slavonia. Tudjman was re-elected president in June 1997 with 61% of the vote, aided by his control of the media. However, by the time of his death from cancer on 10 December 1999, charges of nepotism, repressive policies, and a deteriorating economy, had fuelled disillusionment with his regime.

Vaughan, Frankie

(1928–1999)

One of variety's great all-round entertainers, Frankie Vaughan, nicknamed 'Mr Moonlight' after his signature tune 'Give me the moonlight', also received recognition for his work in the community.

Born Frank Abelson in Liverpool on 3 February 1928, Vaughan won a scholarship to Lancaster College of Art and a place at Leeds University, before being called up to the Royal Army Medical Corps towards the end of World War II. During his three-and-a-half-year enlistment, he took his first steps into the world of entertainment, singing in camp concerts backed by station bands. Later, he made a successful debut at the Kingston Empire, and went on to become a household name with a recording career and appearances in films and on television. With the Public Record Office's release of 1969 files in January 2000, Vaughan was posthumously hailed as a hero for stamping out some of the most violent gang warfare in Britain. Government files show that crime in Glasgow fell sharply after the singer convinced gang leaders to surrender knives and other weapons. His 1968 peace mission, in which he met rival gang leaders in a pub, came at a time when Glasgow was living up to its 'No Mean City' image and such gangs as the Drummy, the Rebel, and Bal Toi clashed in nightly battles. Vaughan's efforts led to the setting up of the Easterhouse Project, a youth and community centre that is still open today. Vaughan married Stella Shock in 1951, and had two sons and a daughter. He was also awarded the OBE in 1965 and the CBE in 1997.

Frankie Vaughan *Syndication International*

Current World Leaders

Current World Leaders

As of July 2000.

Country	Head of State	Head of Government
Afghanistan	Muhammad Rabbani from 1996	Muhammad Rabbani from 1996
Albania	Rexhep Mejdani from 1998	Ilir Meta from 1999
Algeria	Abdel Aziz Bouteflika from 1999	Ahmed Benbitour from 1999
Andorra	Joan Marti i Alanis (bishop of Urgel, Spain) and Jacques Chirac (president of France)	Marc Forne from 1994
Angola	José Eduardo dos Santos from 1979	Fernando Franca van Dunem from 1996
Antigua and Barbuda	Queen Elizabeth II from 1981, represented by Governor General James B Carlisle from 1993	Lester Bird from 1994
Argentina	Fernando de la Rua from 1999	Fernando de la Rua from 1999
Armenia	Robert Kocharian from 1998	Amen Sarkisian from 1999
Australia	Queen Elizabeth II from 1952, represented by Governor General Sir William Deane from 1996	John Howard from 1996
Austria	Thomas Klestil from 1992	Wolfgang Schüssel from 2000
Azerbaijan	Geidar Aliyev from 1993	Artur Rasizade from 1996
Bahamas	Queen Elizabeth II from 1973, represented by Governor General Orville Turnquest from 1995	Hubert Ingraham from 1992
Bahrain	Sheikh Hamad bin Isa al-Khalifa from 1999	Sheikh Khalifa bin Salman al-Khalifa from 1970
Bangladesh	Abdur Rahman Biswas from 1991	Sheikh Hasina Wazed from 1996
Barbados	Queen Elizabeth II from 1966, represented by Governor General Sir Clifford Straughn Husbands from 1996	Owen Arthur from 1994
Belarus	Alexandr Lukashenko from 1994	Syargey Ling from 1996
Belgium	King Albert II from 1993	Guy Verhofstadt from 1999
Belize	Queen Elizabeth II from 1981, represented by Governor General Dr Norbert Colville Young from 1993	Said Musa from 1998
Benin	Mathieu Kerekou from 1996	vacant from 1998
Bhutan	Jigme Singye Wangchuk from 1972	Lyonpo Jigme Thimley from 1998
Bolivia	Hugo Banzer Suarez from 1997	Hugo Banzer Suarez from 1997
Bosnia-Herzegovina	Rotating chairman of the collective presidency, Ante Jelavic from 1999	Co-prime ministers Haris Silajdzic (from 1997) and Svetozar Mihajlovic (from 1998)
Botswana	Festus Mogae from 1998	Festus Mogae from 1998
Brazil	Fernando Henrique Cardoso from 1995	Fernando Henrique Cardoso from 1995
Brunei	HM Muda Hassanal Bolkiah Mu'izzaddin Waddaulah, Sultan of Brunei, from 1967	HM Muda Hassanal Bolkiah Mu'izzaddin Waddaulah, Sultan of Brunei, from 1967
Bulgaria	Petar Stoyanov from 1997	Ivan Kostov from 1997
Burkina Faso	Blaise Compaoré from 1987	Kadre Desire Ouedraogo from 1996
Burundi	Pierre Buyoya from 1996	Pascal-Firmin Ndimira from 1996
Cambodia	King Norodom Sihanouk from 1991	Hun Sen from 1998
Cameroon	Paul Biya from 1982	Simon Achidi Achu from 1992
Canada	Queen Elizabeth II from 1952, represented by Governor Adrienne Clarkson from 1999	Jean Chrétien from 1993
Cape Verde	Mascarenhas Monteiro from 1991	Carlos Viega from 1991
Central African Republic	Ange-Felix Patasse from 1993	Anicet Georges Dologuele from 1999
Chad	Idriss Deby from 1990	Nagoum Yamassoum from 1999
Chile	Ricardo Lagos from 2000	Dante Cordova from 1995
China	Jiang Zemin from 1993	Zhu Rongji from 1998
Colombia	Andres Pastrana from 1998	Andres Pastrana from 1998
Comoros	Azali Hassounani from 1999	Azali Hassounani from 1999
Congo, Democratic Republic of	Laurent Kabila from 1997	Laurent Kabila from 1997
Congo, Republic of the	Denis Sassou-Nguessou from 1997	Charles David Ganao from 1996
Costa Rica	Miguel Angel Rodriguez Echeverria, from 1998	Miguel Angel Rodriguez Echeverria, from 1998
Côte d'Ivoire	General Robert Guei from 1999	Kablan Daniel Duncan from 1993
Croatia	Stipe Mesic from 2000	Zlatko Matesa from 1995
Cuba	Fidel Castro Ruz from 1959	Fidel Castro Ruz from 1959
Cyprus	Glafkos Clerides (Greek) from 1993, Rauf Denktash (Turkish) from 1976	Glafkos Clerides (Greek) from 1993, Rauf Denktash (Turkish) from 1976
Czech Republic	Václav Havel from 1993	Miloš Zeman from 1998
Denmark	Queen Margrethe II from 1972	Poul Nyrup Rasmussen from 1993
Djibouti	Hassan Gouled Aptidon from 1977	Barkat Gourad from 1981
Dominica	Vernon Shaw from 1998	Edison James from 1995
Dominican Republic	Hipolito Majia from 2000	Hipolito Majia from 2000
Ecuador	Gustavo Noboa from 2000	Gustavo Noboa from 2000
Egypt	Hosni Mubarak from 1981	Atef Obeid from 1999
El Salvador	Francisco Guillermo Flores Pérez from 1999	Francisco Guillermo Flores Pérez from 1999
Equatorial Guinea	Teodoro Obiang Nguema Mbasogo from 1979	Angel Serafin Seriche Dougan, from 1996
Eritrea	Issaias Afwerki from 1993	Issaias Afwerki from 1993
Estonia	Lennart Meri from 1992	Mart Siimann from 1997
Ethiopia	Negasso Ghidada from 1995	Meles Zenawi from 1995
Fiji Islands	Leadership uncertain following a coup in May 2000	Leadership uncertain
Finland	Tarja Halonen from 2000	Paavo Lipponen from 1995
France	Jacques Chirac from 1995	Lionel Jospin from 1997

(continued)

Current World Leaders *(continued)*

Country	Head of State	Head of Government
Gabon	Omar Bongo from 1967	Jean-François Ntoutoume-Emane from 1999
Gambia	(interim) Yahya Jammeh from 1994	(interim) Yahya Jammeh from 1994
Georgia	Eduard Shevardnadze from 1992	Otar Patsatsia from 1993
Germany	Johannes Rau from 1999	Gerhard Schroeder from 1998
Ghana	Jerry Rawlings from 1981	Jerry Rawlings from 1981
Greece	Costis Stephanopoulos from 1995	Costas Simitis from 1996
Grenada	Queen Elizabeth II from 1974, represented by Governor General Daniel Williams from 1996	Keith Mitchell from 1995
Guatemala	Alfonso Portillo from 1999	Alfonso Portillo from 1999
Guinea	Lansana Conté from 1984	Lamine Sidime from 1999
Guinea-Bissau	Kumb Ialá from 2000	Caetano N'Tchama from 2000
Guyana	Bharrat Jagdeo from 1999	Samuel Hinds from 1992
Haiti	René Préval from 1996	Jacques Edouard Alexis from 1998
Honduras	Carlos Flores from 1998	Carlos Flores from 1998
Hungary	Arpád Göncz from 1990	Viktor Orban from 1998
Iceland	Ólafur Ragnar Grímsson from 1996	Davíd Oddsson from 1991
India	Kocheril Raman Narayanan from 1997	Atal Behari Vajpayee from 1998
Indonesia	Abdurrahman Wahid from 1999	Abdurrahman Wahid from 1999
Iran	Seyyed Muhammad Khatami from 1997	Seyyed Muhammad Khatami from 1997
Iraq	Saddam Hussein from 1979	Saddam Hussein from 1979
Ireland, Republic of	Mary McAleese from 1997	Patrick 'Bertie' Ahern from 1997
Israel	Ezer Weizman from 1993	Ehud Barak from 1999
Italy	Carlo Azeglio Ciampi from 1999	Giuliano Amato from 2000
Jamaica	Queen Elizabeth II from 1962, represented by Governor General Howard Felix Hanlan Cooke from 1991	Percival Patterson from 1992
Japan	Emperor Heisei (Akihito) from 1989	Yoshiro Mori from 2000
Jordan	King Abdullah ibn Hussein from 1999	Abdul-Raouf al-Rawabdeh from 1999
Kazakhstan	Nursultan Nazarbayev from 1990	Kasymzhomart Tokaev from 1999
Kenya	Daniel arap Moi from 1978	Daniel arap Moi from 1978
Kiribati	Teburoro Tito from 1994	Teburoro Tito from 1994
Korea, North	Kim Jong Il from 1994	Hong Song Nam from 1997
Korea, South	Kim Dae Jung from 1998	Kim Jong Pil from 1998
Kuwait	Sheikh Jabir al-Ahmad al-Jabir as-Sabah from 1977	Crown Prince Sheikh Saad al-Abdullah al-Salinas al-Sabah from 1978
Kyrgyzstan	Askar Akayev from 1990	Amangeldy Mursadykovich Muraliyev from 1999
Laos	Gen Khamtay Siphandon from 1998	Sisavath Keobounphanh from 1998
Latvia	Vaira Vike-Freiberga from 1999	Andris Skele from 1999
Lebanon	Emile Lahoud from 1998	Salim al-Hoss from 1998
Lesotho	King Letsie III from 1996	Bethuel Pakulitha Mosisili from 1998
Liberia	Charles Ghankay Taylor from 1997	Charles Ghankay Taylor from 1997
Libya	Moamer al-Khaddhafi from 1969	Mubarak al-Shamikh from 2000
Liechtenstein	Prince Hans Adam II from 1989	Mario Frick from 1993
Lithuania	Valdas Adamkus from 1998	Andrius Kubelius from 1999
Luxembourg	Grand Duke Jean from 1964	Jean-Claude Juncker from 1995
Macedonia, Former Yugoslav Republic of	Boris Trajkovski from 1999	Ljubco Georgievski from 1998
Madagascar	Didier Ratsiraka from 1996	René Tantely Gabrio Andrianarivo from 1998
Malawi	Bakili Muluzi from 1994	Bakili Muluzi from 1994
Malaysia	Tuanku Salehuddin Abdul Aziz Shan bin al-Marhum Hisamuddin Alam Shah from 1999	Mahathir bin Muhammad from 1981
Maldives	Maumoon Abd Gayoom from 1978	Maumoon Abd Gayoom from 1978
Mali	Alpha Oumar Konare from 1992	Ibrahim Boubaker Keita from 1994
Malta	Guido de Marco from 1999	Edward Fenech Adami from 1998
Marshall Islands	Kessai H Note from 2000	Kessai H Note from 2000
Mauritania	Maaoya Sid'Ahmed Ould Taya from 1984	Cheik el Avia Ould Muhammad Khouna from 1998
Mauritius	Cassam Uteem from 1992	Navin Ramgoolam from 1995
Mexico	Ernesto Zedillo Ponce de León from 1994	Ernesto Zedillo Ponce de León from 1994
Micronesia, Federated States of	Jacob Nena from 1997	Jacob Nena from 1997
Moldova	Petru Lucinschi from 1997	Vladimir Voronin from 1999
Monaco	Prince Rainier III from 1949	Michel Leveque from 1998
Mongolia	Natsagiyn Bagabandi from 1997	Rinchinnyamiyn Amarjagal from 1999
Morocco	Sayyid Muhammad VI ibn-Hassan from 1999	Abderrahmane Youssoufi from 1998
Mozambique	Joaquim Alberto Chissano from 1986	Pascoal Mocumbi from 1994
Myanmar	Than Shwe from 1992	Than Shwe from 1992
Namibia	Sam Nujoma from 1990	Hage Geingob from 1990
Nauru	Rene Harris from 1999	Rene Harris from 1999
Nepal	King Birendra Bir Bikram Shah Dev from 1972	Krishna Prasad Bhattarai from 1999
Netherlands	Queen Beatrix Wilhelmina Armgard from 1980	Wim Kok from 1994
New Zealand	Queen Elizabeth II from 1952, represented by Governor General Catherine Tizard from 1990	Helen Clark from 1999
Nicaragua	Arnoldo Aleman from 1997	Arnoldo Aleman from 1997
Niger	Tandja Mamadov from 1999	Hama Amadou from 1999
Nigeria	Olusegun Obasanjo from 1999	Olusegun Obasanjo from 1999
Norway	Harald V from 1991	Jens Stoltenberg from 2000
Oman	Qaboos bin Said from 1970	Qaboos bin Said from 1970

(continued)

Current World Leaders *(continued)*

Country	Head of State	Head of Government
Pakistan	General Pervez Musharraf from 1999	General Pervez Musharraf from 1999
Palau	Kuniwo Nakamura from 1992	Kuniwo Nakamura from 1992
Panama	Mireya Moscoso from 1999	Mireya Moscoso from 1999
Papua New Guinea	Head of state Queen Elizabeth II, represented by Governor General Silas Atopare from 1997	Mekere Morauta from 1999
Paraguay	Luis Gonzalez Macchi from 1999	Luis Gonzalez Macchi from 1999
Peru	Alberto Fujimori from 1990	Alberto Bustamante from 1999
Philippines	Joseph Ejercito Estrada from 1998	Joseph Ejercito Estrada from 1998
Poland	Aleksander Kwaśniewski from 1995	Jerzy Buzek from 1997
Portugal	Jorge Sampaio from 1996	Antonio Guterres from 1995
Qatar	Sheikh Hamad bin Khalifa al-Thani from 1995	Sheikh Abd Allah ibn Khalifah al-Thani from 1995
Romania	Emil Constantinescu from 1996	Mugur Isarescu from 1999
Russian Federation	Vladimir Putin from 2000 (acting president and prime minister 1999–2000)	Mikhail Kasyanov from 2000
Rwanda	(interim) Paul Kagame from 2000	Pierre Celestin Rwigema from 1995
St Kitts and Nevis	Queen Elizabeth II from 1983, represented by Governor General Dr Cuthbert Montraville Sebastian from 1996	Denzil Douglas from 1995
St Lucia	Queen Elizabeth II from 1979, represented by Governor General Dr Perlette Louisy from 1997	Kenny Anthony from 1997
St Vincent and the Grenadines	Queen Elizabeth II from 1979, represented by Governor General David Jack from 1989	James Mitchell from 1984
Samoa	King Malietoa Tanumafili II from 1962	Tuila'epa Sa'ilele Malielegaoi from 1998
San Marino	two captains regent, elected for a six-month period	two captains regent, elected for a six-month period
São Tomé and Príncipe	Miguel Trovoada from 1991	Carlos da Graca from 1994
Saudi Arabia	King Fahd Ibn Abdul Aziz from 1982	King Fahd Ibn Abdul Aziz from 1982
Senegal	Abdoulaye Wade from 2000	Mamadou Lamine Loum from 1998
Seychelles	France-Albert René from 1977	France-Albert René from 1977
Sierra Leone	Ahmad Tejan Kabbah from 1996	Ahmad Tejan Kabbah from 1996
Singapore	Sellapan Ramanathan Nathan from 1999	Goh Chok Tong from 1990
Slovak Republic	Rudolf Schuster from 1999	Mikulas Dzurinda from 1998
Slovenia	Milan Kučan from 1990	Andrej Bajuk from 2000
Solomon Islands	Queen Elizabeth II, represented by Governor General Moses Pitakaka from 1994	Leadership uncertain following a coup in June 2000
Somalia	(interim) Hussein Aidid from 1996	(interim) Hussein Aidid from 1996
South Africa	Thabo Mbeki from 1999	Thabo Mbeki from 1999
Spain	King Juan Carlos I from 1975	José Maria Aznar from 1996
Sri Lanka	Chandrika Bandaranaike Kumaratunga from 1994	Sirimavo Bandaranaike from 1994
Sudan	Omar Hassan Ahmed al-Bashir from 1989	Omar Hassan Ahmed al-Bashir from 1989
Suriname	Jules Wijdenbosch from 1996	Prataapnarain Shawh Radhecheran Radhakishun from 1996
Swaziland	King Mswati III from 1986	Barnabas Sibusiso Dlamini from 1996
Sweden	King Carl XVI Gustaf from 1973	Göran Persson from 1996
Switzerland	Adolf Ogi from 2000	Adolf Ogi from 2000
Syria	Bashar al-Assad from 2000	Muhammad Mustafa Miro from 2000
Taiwan	Chen Shui-bian from 2000	Tang Fei from 2000
Tajikistan	Imamali Rakhmanov from 1994	Akil Akilov from 1999
Tanzania	Benjamin Mkapa from 1995	Cleoopa Msuya from 1994
Thailand	King Bhumibol Adulyadej from 1946	Chavalit Yongchaiyudh from 1996
Togo	Etienne Gnassingbé Eyadéma from 1967	Kwasi Klutse from 1996
Tonga	King Taufa'ahau Tupou IV from 1965	Baron Vaea of Houma from 1991
Trinidad and Tobago	A N R Robinson from 1997	Basdeo Panday from 1995
Tunisia	Zine el-Abidine Ben Ali from 1987	Muhammad Ghannouchi from 1999
Turkey	Judeg Ahmet Necdet Sezer from 2000	Bülent Ecevit from 1999
Turkmenistan	Saparmurad Niyazov from 1990	Saparmurad Niyazov from 1990
Tuvalu	Queen Elizabeth II from 1978, represented by Governor General Tulaga Manuella from 1994	Ionatana Ionatana from 1999
Uganda	Yoweri Museveni from 1986	Apolo Nsibambi from 1999
UK	Queen Elizabeth II from 1952	Tony Blair from 1997
Ukraine	Leonid Kuchma from 1994	Viktor A Yuschenko from 1999
United Arab Emirates	Sheikh Zayed bin Sultan al-Nahayan of Abu Dhabi from 1971	Maktum bin Rashid al-Maktum of Dubai from 1990
Uruguay	Jorge Batlle from 2000	Jorge Batlle from 2000
USA	Bill Clinton from 1993	Bill Clinton from 1993
Uzbekistan	Islam Karimov from 1990	Otkir Sultonov from 1995
Vanuatu	John Bernard Bani from 1999	Barak Sope from 1999
Vatican City State	John Paul II from 1978	Cardinal Sebastiano Baggio
Venezuela	Hugo Chávez Frías from 1998	Hugo Chávez Frías from 1998
Vietnam	Tran Duc Luong from 1997	Phan Van Khai from 1997
Yemen	Ali Abdullah Saleh from 1990	Abdul Ali al-Rahman al-Iryani from 1998
Yugoslavia	Slobodan Milošević from 1997	Momir Bulatović from 1998
Zambia	Frederick Chiluba from 1991	Frederick Chiluba from 1991
Zimbabwe	Robert Mugabe from 1987	Robert Mugabe from 1987

Selected Historical Leaders

Africa

Kenyan Presidents from 1963

In 1963 Kenya achieved independence from Britain as a self-governing dominion. It became a republic within the Commonwealth in 1964.

Term	Name	Party
1963–78	Jomo Kenyatta	Kenya African National Union (KANU)
1978–	Daniel arap Moi	KANU

Nigerian Leaders from 1960

Nigeria achieved indpendence from Britain in 1960, and became a federal republic within the Commonwealth in 1963.

Term	Name	Party
Governor-Generals		
1960	James Robertson	independent
1960–63	Nnamdi Azikiwe	Nigerian National Democratic Party
Presidents[1]		
1963–66	Nnamdi Azikiwe	Nigerian National Democratic Party
1966	Johnson Aguiyi-Ironsi	military
1966–75	Yakubu Gowon	military
1975–76	Murtala Mohammed	military
1976–79	Olusegun Obasanjo	military
1979–83	Shehu Shagari	National Party of Nigeria
1983–85	Mohammed Buhari	military
1985–93	Ibrahim Babangida	military
1993	Ernest Shonekan	independent
1993–98	Sani Abacha	military
1998–99	Abdusalam Abubakar	military
1999–	Olusegun Obasanjo	People's Democratic Party

[1] Heads of state from January 1966 until October 1979 and from December 1983 did not officially use the title of president.

South African Prime Ministers and Presidents

In 1910 Cape Colony, Natal, Transvaal, and Orange Free State formed the self-governing Union of South Africa.

Term	Name
Prime Ministers	
1910–19	L Botha
1919–24	Jan Smuts
1924–39	James Hertzog
1939–48	Jan Smuts
1948–54	Daniel Malan
1954–58	J Strijdon
1958–66	Hendrik Verwoerd
1966–78	Balthazar Johannes Vorster
1978–84	Pieter Botha
Presidents[1]	
1984–89	Pieter Botha
1989–94	F W de Klerk
1994–99	Nelson Mandela
1999–	Thabo Mbeki

[1] The post of prime minister was abolished in 1984 and combined with that of president.

The Americas

Argentinian Presidents from 1943

In 1943 a pro-German right-wing military coup toppled Argentina's government and a military junta was formed.

Term	Name	Party
1943–44	Arturo Rawson	military
1944–46	Edelmiro Farrell	military
1946–55	Juan Perón	Justice Front of Liberation
1955	Eduardo Lonardi	military
1955–58	Pedro Aramburu	military
1958–62	Arturo Frondizi	Civic Radical Union-Intransigent
1962–63	José Guido	acting: independent
1963–66	Arturo Illía	Civic Radical Union of the People
1966–70	Juan Onganía	military
1970–71	Roberto Levingston	military
1971–73	Alejandro Lanusse	military
1973	Héctor Cámpora	Justice Front of Liberation
1973	Raúl Lastiri	acting: independent
1973–74	Juan Perón	Justice Front of Liberation
1974–76	Maria Estela de Perón	Justice Front of Liberation
1976–81	Jorge Videla	military
1981	Roberto Viola	military
1981–82	Leopoldo Galtieri	military
1982	Alfredo Saint-Jean	acting: military
1982–83	Reynaldo Bignone	military
1983–89	Raúl Alfonsín	Civic Radical Union
1989–99	Carlos Saúl Menem	Justice Party
1999–	Fernando de la Rua	Radical Civic Union (UCR)/Alianza

Aztec Emperors

According to Aztec tradition Acamapichtli was the founder of the Aztec royal house. The empire came to an end after the arrival of the Spanish conquistador Hernando Cortés in 1519.

Reign	Name
c. 1372– *c.* 91	Acamapichtli (chieftain at Tenochtitlán)
c. 1391– *c.* 1416	Huitzilihuitl (son)
c. 1416– *c.* 27	Chimalpopoca (son)
c. 1427– *c.* 40	Itzcoatl (son of Acamapichtli)
c. 1440– *c.* 68	(Huehue) Motecuhzoma
c. 1468–81	Axayacatl (grandson of Itzcoatl)
1481–86	Tizoc (brother)
1486–1502	Ahuitzotl (brother)
1502–20	Motecuhzoma Xocoyotl (son of Axayacatl); known as Montezuma II
1520	Cuitlahuac (brother)
1520–21	Cuauhtemoc (son of Ahuitzotl)

Brazilian Presidents from 1945

Term	Name	Party
1945–46	José Linhares	independent
1946–51	Eurico Dutra	Social Democratic Party
1951–54	Getúlio Vargas	Brazil Labour Party
1954–55	João Café	Social Progressive Party
1955	Carlos da Luz	independent
1955–56	Nereu Ramos	independent
1956–61	Juscelino Kubitschek	Social Democratic Party
1961	Jânio Quadros	Christian Democratic Party/Democratic National Union
1961–64	João Goulart	Brazil Labour Party
1964	Ranieri Mazzili	independent
1964–67	Humberto Branco	military
1967–69	Arthur da Costa e Silva	military
1969–74	Emilio Medici	military
1974–79	Ernesto Geisel	military
1979–85	João Figueiredo	military
1985–89	José Sarney	Social Democratic Party
1989–92	Fernando Collor de Mello	National Reconstruction Party
1992–94	Itamar Franco	National Reconstruction Party
1995–	Fernando Henrique Cardoso	Social Democratic Party

Mexican Presidents from 1946

In 1946 the National Revolutionary Party was renamed the Institutional Revolutionary Party (PRI).

Term	Name	Party	Term	Name	Party
1946–52	Miguel Alemán Valdés	PRI	1976–82	José López Portillo y Pacheco	PRI
1952–58	Adolfo Ruiz Cortines	PRI	1982–88	Miguel de la Madrid Hurtado	PRI
1958–64	Adolfo López Mateos	PRI	1988–94	Carlos Salinas de Gortari	PRI
1964–70	Gustavo Díaz Ordaz	PRI	1994–	Ernesto Zedillo Ponce de Léon	PRI
1970–76	Luís Echeverría Alvarez	PRI			

Canadian Prime Ministers from 1867

In 1867 the British North America Act established the Dominion of Canada.

Term	Name	Party
1867–73	John A Macdonald	Conservative
1873–78	Alexander Mackenzie	Liberal
1878–91	John A Macdonald	Conservative
1891–92	John J Abbott	Conservative
1892–94	John S D Thompson	Conservative
1894–96	Mackenzie Bowell	Conservative
1896	Charles Tupper	Conservative
1896–1911	Wilfred Laurier	Liberal
1911–20	Robert L Borden	Conservative
1920–21	Arthur Meighen	Conservative
1921–26	William L M King	Liberal
1926	Arthur Meighen	Conservative
1926–30	William L M King	Liberal
1930–35	Richard B Bennett	Conservative
1935–48	William L M King	Liberal
1948–57	Louis S St Laurent	Liberal
1957–63	John G Diefenbaker	Conservative
1963–68	Lester B Pearson	Liberal
1968–79	Pierre E Trudeau	Liberal
1979–80	Joseph Clark	Progressive Conservative
1980–84	Pierre E Trudeau	Liberal
1984	John Turner	Liberal
1984–93	Brian Mulroney	Progressive Conservative
1993	Kim Campbell	Progressive Conservative
1993–	Jean Chrétien	Liberal

Inca Emperors

According to Inca legend, Manco Capac, the first emperor, was sent to Earth by his father, the Sun, to found a city. The last Inca emperor of Peru, Atahualpa, was executed by the Spanish conquistador Francisco Pizarro in 1533. The Spanish installed a number of native puppet rulers until 1572.

Reign	Name	Reign	Name	Reign	Name
The Kingdom of Cuzco		until 1438	Viracocha Inca	*The Vilcabamba State*	
	Manco Capac[1]	*The Empire*		1533	Topa Hualpa
	Sinchi Roca[1]	1438–71	Pachacuti	1533–45	Manco Inca
	Lloque Yupanqui[1]	1471–93	Topa Inca	1545–60	Sayri Tupac
c. 1200–1400	Mayta Capac[1]	1493–1528	Huayna Capac	1560–71	Titu Cusi Yupanqui
	Capac Yupanqui[2]	1528–32	Huascar	1571–72	Tupac Amaru
	Inca Roca[2]	1532–33	Atahualpa		
	Yahuar Huacadc[2]				

[1] Mythical figure.
[2] Dates of reign are unknown.

US Presidents

Year elected /took office		President	Party	Losing candidate(s)	Party
1789	1	George Washington	Federalist	no opponent	
1792		George Washington[1]	Federalist	no opponent	
1796	2	John Adams	Federalist	Thomas Jefferson	Democrat-Republican
1800	3	Thomas Jefferson	Democrat-Republican	Aaron Burr	Democrat-Republican
1804		Thomas Jefferson[1]	Democrat-Republican	Charles Pinckney	Federalist
1808	4	James Madison	Democrat-Republican	Charles Pinckney	Federalist
1812		James Madison[1]	Democrat-Republican	DeWitt Clinton	Federalist
1816	5	James Monroe	Democrat-Republican	Rufus King	Federalist
1820		James Monroe	Democrat-Republican	John Quincy Adams	Democrat-Republican
				Andrew Jackson	Democrat-Republican
1824	6	John Quincy Adams	Democrat-Republican	Henry Clay	Democrat-Republican
				William H Crawford	Democrat-Republican
1828	7	Andrew Jackson	Democrat	John Quincy Adams	National Republican
1832		Andrew Jackson[1]	Democrat	Henry Clay	National Republican
1836	8	Martin Van Buren	Democrat	William Henry Harrison	Whig
1840	9	William Henry Harrison	Whig	Martin Van Buren	Democrat
1841	10	John Tyler[2]	Whig		
1844	11	James K Polk	Democrat	Henry Clay	Whig
1848	12	Zachary Taylor	Whig	Lewis Cass	Democrat
1850	13	Millard Fillmore[3]	Whig		

(continued)

Selected Historical Leaders

US Presidents (*continued*)

Year elected /took office		President	Party	Losing candidate(s)	Party
1852	14	Franklin Pierce	Democrat	Winfield Scott	Whig
1856	15	James Buchanan	Democrat	John C Fremont	Republican
1860	16	Abraham Lincoln	Republican	Stephen Douglas	Democrat
				John Breckinridge	Democrat
				John Bell	Constitutional Union
1864		Abraham Lincoln[1]	Republican	George McClellan	Democrat
1865	17	Andrew Johnson[4]	Democrat		
1868	18	Ulysses S Grant	Republican	Horatio Seymour	Democrat
1872		Ulysses S Grant[1]	Republican	Horace Greeley	Democrat–Liberal Republican
1876	19	Rutherford B Hayes	Republican	Samuel Tilden	Democrat
1880	20	James A Garfield	Republican	Winfield Hancock	Democrat
1881	21	Chester A Arthur[5]	Republican		
1884	22	Grover Cleveland	Democrat	James Blaine	Republican
1888	23	Benjamin Harrison	Republican	Grover Cleveland	Democrat
1892	24	Grover Cleveland	Democrat	Benjamin Harrison	Republican
				James Weaver	People's
1896	25	William McKinley	Republican	William J Bryan	Democrat–People's
1900		William McKinley[1]	Republican	William J Bryan	Democrat
1901	26	Theodore Roosevelt[6]	Republican		
1904		Theodore Roosevelt[1]	Republican	Alton B Parker	Democrat
1908	27	William Howard Taft	Republican	William J Bryan	Democrat
1912	28	Woodrow Wilson	Democrat	Theodore Roosevelt	Progressive
				William Howard Taft	Republican
1916		Woodrow Wilson[1]	Democrat	Charles E Hughes	Republican
1920	29	Warren G Harding	Republican	James M Cox	Democrat
1923	30	Calvin Coolidge[7]	Republican		
1924		Calvin Coolidge[1]	Republican	John W Davis	Democrat
				Robert M LaFollette	Progressive
1928	31	Herbert Hoover	Republican	Alfred E Smith	Democrat
1932	32	Franklin D Roosevelt	Democrat	Herbert C Hoover	Republican
				Norman Thomas	Socialist
1936		Franklin D Roosevelt[1]	Democrat	Alfred Landon	Republican
1940		Franklin D Roosevelt[1]	Democrat	Wendell Willkie	Republican
1944		Franklin D Roosevelt[1]	Democrat	Thomas E Dewey	Republican
1945	33	Harry S Truman[8]	Democrat		
1948		Harry S Truman[1]	Democrat	Thomas E Dewey	Republican
				J Strom Thurmond	States' Rights
				Henry A Wallace	Progressive
1952	34	Dwight D Eisenhower	Republican	Adlai E Stevenson	Democrat
1956		Dwight D Eisenhower[1]	Republican	Adlai E Stevenson	Democrat
1960	35	John F Kennedy	Democrat	Richard M Nixon	Republican
1963	36	Lyndon B Johnson[9]	Democrat		
1964		Lyndon B Johnson[1]	Democrat	Barry M Goldwater	Republican
1968	37	Richard M Nixon	Republican	Hubert H Humphrey	Democrat
				George C Wallace	American Independent
1972		Richard M Nixon[1]	Republican	George S McGovern	Democrat
1974	38	Gerald R Ford[10]	Republican		
1976	39	James Earl Carter	Democrat	Gerald R Ford	Republican
1980	40	Ronald Reagan	Republican	James Earl Carter	Democrat
				John B Anderson	Independent
1984		Ronald Reagan[1]	Republican	Walter Mondale	Democrat
1988	41	George Bush	Republican	Michael Dukakis	Democrat
1992	42	Bill Clinton	Democrat	Ross Perot	Independent
				George Bush	Republican
1996		Bill Clinton[1]	Democrat	Bob Dole	Republican
				Ross Perot	Reform

[1] Re-elected.
[2] Became president on death of Harrison.
[3] Became president on death of Taylor.
[4] Became president on assassination of Lincoln.
[5] Became president on assassination of Garfield.
[6] Became president on assassination of McKinley.
[7] Became president on death of Harding.
[8] Became president on death of F D Roosevelt.
[9] Became president on assassination of Kennedy.
[10] Became president on resignation of Nixon and Agnew.

US Presidents

Martin Van Buren, the eighth president of the United States (1837–41), was the first not to have been born a British subject. The first President to be born in a hospital was Jimmy Carter (in 1924), and the first President to be born in the twentieth century was John F Kennedy (born in 1917), who took office in 1961.

Asia

Chinese Dynasties

Period	Dynasty	Major events
c. 2205– c. 1776 BC	Hsia or Xia[1]	agriculture; use of bronze; first writing
c. 1776– c. 1027 BC	Shang or Yin	first major dynasty; first Chinese calendar
c. 1027– c. 256 BC	Zhou	developed society using money, iron, and written laws; age of Kung Fu Tzu (Confucius)
221–206 BC	Qin	unification after period of Warring States; building of Great Wall begun; roads built
206 BC– AD 220	Han	first centralized and effectively administered empire; introduction of Buddhism
220–265	Wei, Shu, Wu (Three Kingdoms)	division into three parts; prolonged fighting (Three Kingdoms) and eventual victory of Wei over Shu and Wu; Confucianism superseded by Buddhism and Taoism
265–317	Tsin	beginning of Hun invasions in the north
581–618	Sui	reunification; barbarian invasions stopped; Great Wall refortified
618–907	T'ang	centralized government; empire greatly extended; period of excellence in sculpture, painting, and poetry
907–960	Wu Tai (Five Dynasties)	economic depression and loss of territory in northern China, central Asia, and Korea; first use of paper money
960–1279	Song	period of calm and creativity; printing developed (movable type); central government restored; northern and western frontiers neglected and Mongol incursions begun
1279–1368	Yüan	beginning of Mongol rule in China, under Kublai Khan; Marco Polo visited China; dynasty brought to an end by widespread revolts, centred in Mongolia
1368–1644	Ming	Mongols driven out by native Chinese; Mongolia captured by 2nd Ming emperor; period of architectural development; Beijing flourished as new capital
1644–1912	Qing (Manchu)	China once again under non-Chinese rule, the Qing conquered by nomads from Manchuria; trade with the West; culture flourished, but conservatism eventually led to the dynasty's overthrow by nationalistic revolutionaries led by Sun Yat-sen

[1] This was a legendary and historically doubtful dynasty.

Chinese Prime Ministers and Communist Party Leaders

In 1949 the Guomindang government was overthrown by the Communists and the People's Republic of China declared. Although not officially the head of state, the leader of the Communust Party is usually comsidered to be the most politically influential person in China.

Term	Name
Prime Ministers	
1949–76	Zhou Enlai
1976–80	Hua Guofeng
1980–87	Zhao Ziyang
1987–98	Li Peng
1998–	Zhu Rongji

Term	Name
Communist Party Leaders	
1935–76	Mao Zedong
1976–81	Hua Guofeng
1981–87	Hu Yaobang
1987–89	Zhao Ziyang
1989–	Jiang Zemin[1]

[1] From 1993 Jiang Zemin has also been state president.

Indian Prime Ministers

In 1947 British India was partitioned into the independent dominions of India and Pakistan.

Term	Name	Party
1947–64	Jawaharlal Nehru	Congress
1964–66	Lal Bahadur Shastri	Congress
1966–77	Indira Gandhi	Congress (I)
1977–79	Morarji Desai	Janata
1979–80	Charan Singh	Janata/Lok Dal
1980–84	Indira Gandhi	Congress (I)
1984–89	Rajiv Gandhi	Congress (I)
1989–90	Viswanath Pratap Singh	Janata Dal
1990–91	Chandra Shekhar	Janata Dal (Socialist)
1991–96	P V Narasimha Rao	Congress (I)
1996	Atal Behari Vajpayee	Bharatiya Janata Party
1996–97	H D Deve Gowda	Janata Dal
1997–98	Inder Kumar Gujral	Janata Dal
1998–	Atal Behari Vajpayee	Bharatiya Janata Party

Indian Dynasties and Rulers

Only major dynasties and the most important rulers are included. The dates given for dynasties and rulers cover their periods of ascendancy.

Reign	Name
Saisunaga Dynasty (Magadhan ascendancy, northern India) 7th–4th centuries BC	
c. 543– c. 491 BC	Bimbisara (Srenika)
c. 491– c. 461 BC	Ajashatru (Kunika)
Nandas[1] 4th century BC	
c. 362– c. 334 BC	Mahapadma and eight sons
Mauryan Empire (India, except the area south of Karnataka) 4th–2nd centuries BC	
c. 321– c. 298 BC	Chandragupta Maurya
c. 298– c. 272 BC	Bindusara Amitraghata
c. 272– c. 232 BC	Asoka (-vardhana)
c. 232– c. 185 BC	later Mauryas
Shungas (Ganges Valley and part of central India) 2nd–1st centuries BC	
c. 185– c. 173 BC	Pushyamitra (Pushpamitra)
Indo-Greeks (northwest India) 2nd–1st centuries BC	
c. 180– c. 165 BC	Demetrius II
c. 155– c. 130 BC	Menander (Milinda)
Kanvas (northern India) c. 73–28 BC	
Satavahanas (north Deccan) 1st century BC–3rd century AD	
c. AD 120	Gautamiputra Satakarni
c. 130	Vashishthiputra Satakarni
c. 170– c. 200	Yajna Sri
Shakas (western India) 1st century BC–3rd century AD	
Kushanas (northern India and Central Asia) 1st century BC–3rd century AD	
c. 48– c. 78	Kadphises I
c. 78– c. 100	Kadphises II
c. 120– c. 162	Kanishka
c. 162– c. 182	Huvishka
c. 182– c. 220	Vasudeva
Guptas (northern India) 4th–6th centuries	
320–30	Chandragupta I
330–75	Samadragupta

(continued)

Indian Dynasties and Rulers *(continued)*

Reign	Name
375–415	Chandragupta II Vikramaditya
415–54	Kumaragupta I
454–67	Skandagupta
467–99	Buddhagupta
Hunas (northwest India and Central Asia) 5th–6th centuries	
Maukharis 6th–7th centuries	
Later Guptas of Magadha 6th–7th centuries	
Harsha 7th century	
606–47	Harshavardana
Pallavas (Tamil Nadu) c. 300–888	
630–68	Narasimhavaraman
730–96	Nandivarman II
Chalukyas of Vatapi (west and central Deccan) c. 556–757	
610–43	Pukaleshin II
Pandyas of Madurai (Tamil Nadu) 7th–10th centuries	
768–815	Varuguna I
815–62	Shrimara Shrivallabha
862–67	Varuguna II
Eastern Chalukyas of Vengi (Andhra Pradesh) c. 630–970	
Palas (Bengal and Bihar) c. 750–1100	
c. 750	Gopala
770–813	Dharmapala
813–55	Devapala
1005–55	Mahipala
Rashtrakutras (west and central Deccan) c. 753–973	
780–93	Dhruva
793–833	Govinda III
814–78	Amoghavarsha
878–914	Krishna II
914–72	Indra II
972–86	Krishna III
Pratiharas (west India and upper Ganges Valley) c. 773–1019	
773–93	Vatsaraja
793–833	Nagabhata
836–85	Bhoja
c. 908–42	Mahipala
Cholas of Thanjavur (Tamil Nadu) c. 850–1278	
984–1014	Rajaraja I
1014–44	Rajendra
1070–1118	Kulottunga I
Chandellas (Bundelkhand) c. 900–1203	
Kalachuris of Tripuri (Madhya Pradesh) c. 950–1195	
Chahamanis (east Rajasthan) c. 973–1192	
Chalukyas of Kalyani (west and central Deccan) 973–1189	
992–1008	Satyashraya
1043–68	Someshvara I
1076–1126	Vikramaditya VI
1181–89	Someshvara IV
Chaulukyas (Gujarat) c. 974–1238	
Gahadavalas (Qanauj) c. 974–1060	
Hoysalas of Dvarasamudra (central and south Deccan) c. 1110–1327	
Senas (Bengal) c. 1118–1199	
1158–69	Vallala Sena
Yadavas of Devagiri (north Deccan) c. 1190–1294	
Kakatiyas of Warangal (Andhra Pradesh) c. 1197–1323	
Sultans of Delhi 1206–1526	
1206–90	Slave Kings
1290–1320	Khaljis
1320–1413	Tughluqids
1414–51	Sayyids
1451–1526	Lodis
Sultans of Bengal 1336–1576	
1345–1414	line of Ilyas Shah
1414–36	line of Raja Ganesha
1437–87	line of Ilyas Shah (restored)
1487–94	line of Habashis
1494–1532	line of Sayyid Husain Shah
Sultans of Kashmir 1346–1589	
1346–1526	line of Shah Mirza Swati
Sultans of Gujarat 1391–1583	
1391–1411	Zafar Khan Muzaffar I
1411–42	Ahmad I
1458–1511	Mahmud I Begra
1511–26	Muzaffar II
Sharqi Sultans of Jaunpur 1394–1479	
Sultans of Malva 1401–1531	
Bahmanid Sultans of the Deccan and their successors 1347–1527	
Imadshahis of Berar 1484–1572	
Nizamshahis of Ahmadnagar 1490–1595	
Baridishahis of Bidar 1492– c. 1609	
Adilshahis of Bijapur 1489–1686	
Qutbshahis of Golconda 1512–1687	
Faruqi Sultans of Khandesh 1370–1601	
Pandyas of Madurai (Tamil Nadu) 1216–1327	
Rulers of Vijayanagar Empire 1336–1646	
1336–54	Harihara I
1354–77	Bukka I
1377– *c.* 1404	Harihara II
c. 1404–06	Bukka I
1406–22	Devaraya I
1422–25	Vira Vijaya
1425–47	Devaraya II
1447–65	Mallikarjuna
1465–85	Virupaksa
1485–86	Praudhadevaraya
c. 1486–92	Saluva Narasimha
c. 1492–1503	Immadi Narasimha
1503–09	Vira Narasimha
1509–30	Krishnadevaraya
c. 1530–42	Achyuta
1542– *c.* 70	Sadashiva
c. 1570–73	Tirumala
c. 1573–85	Rauga I
1585	Venkata I
1642–46	Ranga II
Chatrapati Bhonsles 1674–1707	
1674–80	Shivaji I
1680–89	Sambhaji
1689–1700	Rajaram
1700–07	Tara Bai
Mogul Emperors 1526–1858	
Great Moguls 1526–1707	
1526–30	Babur (Zahiruddin Muhammad)
1530–56	Humayun (Nasiruddin Muhammad)[2]
1556–1605	Akbar (Jalaluddin Muhammad)
1605–27	Jahangir (Nuruddin)
1627–28	Dewar Baksh
1628–58	Shah Jahan (Shihabuddin; dethroned)
1658–1707	Aurangzeb (Muhiyuddin)
Lesser Moguls 1707–1858	
1707–07	Azam Shah
1707–12	Shah Alam I (Muhammad Mu'azzam)
1712–12	Azim-ush Shan
1712–13	Jahandar Shah (Muhammad Muizzuddin)
1713–19	Farrukh Siyar (Jalaluddin Muhammad)
1719	Rafi ud-Darayat (Shamsuddin)
1719	Rafi ud-Daula Shah Jahan II
1719	Nikusiyar
1719–48	Muhammad Shah (Nasiruddin)
1748–54	Ahmad Shah Bahadur (Abu al-Nasir Muhammad)
1754–60	Alamgir II (Muhammad Azizuddin)
1760	Shah Jahan III
1760–1806	Shah Alam II (Jalaluddin Ali Jauhar; deposed briefly in 1788)
1806–37	Akbar Shah II (Muhiyuddin)
1837–58	Bahadur Shah II (Abul al-Zafar Muhammad Sirajuddin; banished)

[1] Low-caste Hindus, hostile to Brahmans and Kashatniyas; they were destroyed by Chandragupta Maurya.

[2] Humayun was defeated in 1540 and expelled from India until 1555, leaving northern India under the control of Sher Shah Suri (died 1545), Islam Shah, and Sikander Shah.

Japanese Emperors

Japanese chronology does not always match the emperor's reign dates. Rather, it is marked by occurrences, such as significant political events, military gains, and natural disasters. A date in parentheses indicates the date of enthronement, when it is later than the date of accession.

Reign dates[1] Probable	Traditional	Name
Legendary and Yamato Period 40 BC–592 AD		
40–10 BC	660–585 BC	Jimmu
10 BC– AD 20	581–49 BC	Suizei
20–50	549–11 BC	Annei
50–80	510–477 BC	Itoku
80–110	475–393 BC	Kōshō
110–40	392–291 BC	Kōan
140–70	290–15 BC	Kōrei
170–200	214–158 BC	Kōgen
200–30	157–98 BC	Kaika
230–58	97–30 BC	Sujin
259–90	29 BC–70 AD	Suinin
291–323	71–130	Keikō
323–56	131–90	Seimu
356–62	192–200	Chūai
363–80	201–269	Jingū Kōgō (regent)
380–95	270–310	Ōjin
395–428	313–99	Nintoku
428–33	400–05	Richū
433–38	406–10	Hanzei
438–55	412–53	Ingyō
455–57	454–56	Ankō
457–90	457–79	Yūryaku
490–95	480–84	Seinei
495–98	485–87	Kenzō
498–504	488–98	Ninken
504–10	499–506	Buretsu
510–34	507–31	Keitai
534–36	531–35	Ankan
536–39	535–39	Senka
539–71		Kimmei
572–85		Bidatsu
585–87		Yomei
587–92		Sushun
Asuka Period 592–710		
593–628		Suiko (empress)
629–41		Jomei
642–45		Kōgyoku (empress)
645–54		Kōtoku
655–61		Saimei (empress)
661–72	(668)	Tenji
6-2		Kōbun
672–86	(673)	Temmu
686–97	(690)	Jitō (empress)
697–707		Mommu
Nara Period 710–794		
707–15		Gemmei (empress)
715–24		Genshō (empress)
724–49		Shōmu
749–58		Kōken (empress)
758–64		Junnin
764–70		Shōtoku (empress)
770–81		Kōnin
Heian Period 794–1192		
781–806		Kammu
806–09		Heizei
809–23		Saga
823–33		Junna
833–50		Nimmyō
850–58		Montoku
858–76		Seiwa
876–84		Yōzei
884–87		Kōkō
887–97		Uda
897–930		Daigo
930–46		Suzaku
946–67		Murakami
967–69		Reizei
969–84		En'yū
984–86		Kazan
986–1011		Ichijō
1011–16		Sanjō
1016–36		Go-Ichijō
1036–45		Go-Suzaku
1045–68		Go-Reizei
1068–73		Go-Sanjō
1073–87		Shirakawa (1086–1129 cloistered rule)
1087–1107		Horikawa
1107–23	(1108)	Toba (1129–56 cloistered rule)
1123–42		Sutoku
1142–55		Konoe
1155–58		Go-Shirakawa (1158–92 cloistered rule)
1158–65	(1159)	Nijō
1165–68		Rokujō
1168–80		Takakura
1180–85		Antoku
Kamakura Period 1192–1333		
1183–98	(1184)	Go-Toba
1198–1210		Tsuchimikado
1210–21	(1211)	Juntoku
1221		Chūkyō
1221–32	(1222)	Go-Horikawa
1232–42	(1233)	Shijō
1242–46		Go-Saga
1246–60		Go-Fukakusa
1260–74		Kameyama
1274–87		Go-Uda
1287–98		Fushimi
1298–1301		Go-Fushimi
1301–08		Go-Nijo
1308–18		Hanazono
Namboku Period 1334–92[2]		
The Southern Court		
1318–39		Go-Daigo
1339–68		Go-Murakami
1368–83		Chōkei
1383–92		Go-Kameyama
The Northern Court		
1331–33	(1332)	Kōgon
1336–48	(1338)	Kōmyō
1348–51	(1350)	Sukō
1351–71	(1354)	Go-Kōgon
1371–82	(1375)	Go-En'yū
Muromachi Period 1392–1573[3]		
1382–1412	(1392)	Go-Komatsu
1412–28	(1415)	Shōkō
1428–64	(1430)	Go-Hanazono
1464–1500	(1466)	Go-Tsuchimikado
1500–26	(1521)	Go-Kashiwabara
1526–57	(1536)	Go-Nara
Momoyama Period 1573–1603		
1557–86	(1560)	Ōgimachi
Edo Period 1603–1867		
1586–1611	(1587)	Go-Yōzei
1611–29		Go-Mizunoo
1629–43	(1630)	Meishō (empress)
1643–54		Go-Kōmyō
1655–63	(1656)	Gosai
1663–87		Reigen
1687–1709		Higashiyama
1709–35	(1710)	Nakamikado
1735–47		Sakuramachi
1747–62		Momozono
1762–71	(1763)	Go-Sakuramachi (empress)
1771–79		Go-Momozono
1780–1817		Kōkaku
1817–46		Ninkō

(continued)

Japanese Emperors (*continued*)

Reign dates[1] Probable	Traditional	Name
1846–67	(1847)	Kōmei
Meiji Period 1868–1912		
1867–1912	(1868)	Meiji (Mutsuhito)
Taisho Period 1912–26		
1912–26	(1915)	Taisho (Yoshihito)
Showa Period 1926–89		
1926–89	(1928)	Showa (Hirohito)
1989–		Heisei (Akihito)

[1] Reign dates for the first 28 emperors are the subject of some doubt and speculation. The traditional view, upon which the National Calendar is based, places the accession of Jimmu at 660 BC. Modern research approximates the date to be much later at *c.* 40 BC. Both probable and traditional dates are given until 539.

[2] Although the Southern Court was set up in exile, it retained the imperial regalia and is considered to be the legitimate line.

[3] The Muromachi Period begins with the unification of the Southern and Northern Courts in 1392.

Japanese Prime Ministers from 1945

Term	Name	Party
1945–46	Kijurō Shidehara	coalition
1946–47	Shigeru Yoshida	Liberal
1947–48	Tetsu Katayama	coalition
1948	Hitoshi Ashida	Democratic
1948–54	Shigeru Yoshida	Liberal
1954–56	Ichirō Hatoyama	Liberal[1]
1956–57	Tanzan Ishibashi	LDP
1957–60	Nobusuke Kishi	LDP
1960–64	Hayato Ikeda	LDP
1964–72	Eisaku Satō	LDP
1972–74	Kakuei Tanaka	LDP
1974–76	Takeo Miki	LDP
1976–78	Takeo Fukuda	LDP
1978–80	Masayoshi Ohira	LDP
1980–82	Zenkō Suzuki	LDP
1982–87	Yasuhiro Nakasone	LDP
1987–89	Noboru Takeshita	LDP
1989	Sōsuke Uno	LDP
1989–91	Toshiki Kaifu	LDP
1991–93	Kiichi Miyazawa	LDP
1993–94	Morohiro Hosokawa	Japan New Party (JNP)-led coalition
1994	Tsutoma Hata	Shinseito-led coalition
1994–96	Tomiichi Murayama	Social Democratic Party of Japan (SDPJ)-led coalition
1996–98	Ryutaro Hashimoto	LDP
1998–00	Keizo Obuchi	LDP
2000–	Yoshiro Mori	LDP

[1] The conservative parties merged in 1955 to form the Liberal Democratic Party (LDP, Jiyū-Minshūtō).

Australasia

Australian Prime Ministers from 1901

The Commonwealth of Australia was created in 1901 when the six colonies of New South Wales, Victoria, Queensland, South Australia, Western Australia, and Tasmania federated as sovereign states.

Term	Name	Party
1901–03	Edmund Barton	Protectionist
1903–04	Alfred Deakin	Protectionist
1904	John Watson	Labor
1904–05	George Reid	Free Trade-Protectionist coalition
1905–08	Alfred Deakin	Protectionist
1908–09	Andrew Fisher	Labor
1909–10	Alfred Deakin	Fusion
1910–13	Andrew Fisher	Labor
1913–14	Joseph Cook	Liberal
1914–15	Andrew Fisher	Labor
1915–23	William Hughes	Labor (National Labor from 1917)
1923–29	Stanley Bruce	National-Country Coalition
1929–32	James Scullin	Labor
1932–39	Joseph Lyons	United Australia-Country coalition
1939	Earle Page	United Australia-Country coalition
1939–41	Robert Menzies	United Australia
1941	Arthur Fadden	Country–United Australia coalition
1941–45	John Curtin	Labor
1945	Francis Forde	Labor
1945–49	Joseph Chifley	Labor
1949–66	Robert Menzies	Liberal-Country coalition
1966–67	Harold Holt	Liberal-Country coalition
1967–68	John McEwen	Liberal-Country coalition
1968–71	John Gorton	Liberal-Country coalition
1971–72	William McMahon	Liberal-Country coalition
1972–75	Gough Whitlam	Labor
1975–83	Malcolm Fraser	Liberal-National coalition
1983–91	Robert Hawke	Labor
1991–96	Paul Keating	Labor
1996–	John Howard	Liberal-National coalition

New Zealand Prime Ministers from 1906

New Zealand has been self-governing from 1856. It gained dominion status within the British Empire under Joseph Ward in 1907; the country was granted autonomy by the 1931 Statute of Westminster, formally accepted in 1947.

Term	Name	Party
1906–12	Joseph Ward	Liberal
1912	Thomas MacKenzie	Liberal
1912–25	William Massey	Reform
1925–28	Joseph Coates	Reform
1925	Francis Bell	Reform
1928–30	Joseph Ward	United
1930–35	George Forbes	United
1935–40	Michael Savage	Labour
1940–49	Peter Fraser	Labour
1949–57	Sidney Holland	National
1957	Keith Holyoake	National
1957–60	Walter Nash	Labour
1960–72	Keith Holyoake	National
1972	John Marshall	National
1972–74	Norman Kirk	Labour
1974–75	Wallace Rowling	Labour
1975–84	Robert Muldoon	National
1984–89	David Lange	Labour
1989–90	Geoffrey Palmer	Labour
1990	Michael Moore	Labour
1990–97	Jim Bolger	National
1997–99	Jenny Shipley	National
1999–	Helen Clark	Labour

Europe

Belgian Monarchs

Leopold of Saxe-Coburg-Gotha was elected the first king of Belgium in 1831.

Reign	Name
1831–65	Leopold I
1865–1909	Leopold II
1909–14	Albert I
1914–18	German occupation
1918–34	Albert I (restored)
1934–40	Leopold III
1940–44	German occupation
1944–50	Prince Charles (regent)
1950–51	Leopold III (restored)
1951–93	Baudouin
1993–	Albert II

Belgian Prime Ministers from 1944

Term	Name	Party
1944–45	Hubert Pierlot	Catholic Party
1945–46	Achille van Acker	Socialist Party
1946	Paul-Henri Spaak	Socialist Party
1946	Achille van Acker	Socialist Party
1946–47	Camille Huysmans	Socialist Party
1947–49	Paul-Henri Spaak	Socialist Party
1949–50	Gaston Eyskens	Christian Social Party
1950	Jean Duvieusart	Christian Social Party
1950–52	Joseph Pholien	Christian Social Party
1952–54	Jean van Houtte	Christian Social Party
1954–58	Achille van Acker	Socialist Party
1958–61	Gaston Eyskens	Christian Social Party
1961–65	Théodore Lefèvre	Christian Social Party
1965–66	Pierre Harmel	Christian Social Party
1966–68	Paul van den Boeynants	Christian Social Party
1968–72	Gaston Eyskens	Christian Social Party
1972–74	Edmond Leburton	Socialist Party
1974–78	Léo Tindemans	Christian Social Party
1978–79	Paul van den Boeynants	Christian Social Party
1979–81	Wilfried Martens	Christian People's Party
1981	Mark Eyskens	Christian People's Party
1981–92	Wilfried Martens	Christian People's Party
1992–99	Jean-Luc Dehaene	Christian People's Party
1999–	Guy Verhofstadt	(Flemish) Liberal

Danish Prime Ministers from 1945

Term	Name	Party
1945	Vilhelm Buhl	Social Democratic Party
1945–47	Knud Kristensen	Agrarian Party
1947–50	Hans Hedtoft	Social Democratic Party
1950–53	Erik Eriksen	Agrarian Party
1953–55	Hans Hedtoft	Social Democratic Party
1955–60	Hans Hansen	Social Democratic Party
1960–62	Viggo Kampmann	Social Democratic Party
1962–68	Jens-Otto Krag	Social Democratic Party
1968–71	Hilmar Baunsgaard	Radical Party
1971–72	Jens-Otto Krag	Social Democratic Party
1972–73	Anker Jøgensen	Social Democratic Party
1973–75	Poul Hartling	Liberal Party
1975–82	Anker Jøgensen	Social Democratic Party
1982–93	Poul Schlüter	Conservative Party
1993–	Poul Nyrup Rasmussen	Social Democratic Party

Dutch Monarchs from 1806

In 1806 Louis Bonaparte was made King of Holland by his brother Napoleon I, Emperor of France, and ruled as Lodewijk I.

Reign	Name
1806–10	Lodewijk I
1810	Lodewijk II
1810–13	French annexation
1813–15	Provisional government
1815–40	Willem I
1840–49	Willem II
1849–90	Willem III
1890–1940	Wilhelmina
1940–45	German occupation
1945–48	Wilhelmina
1948–80	Juliana
1980–	Beatrix

Danish Monarchs from 1848

In 1848 Kristian VIII agreed to abolish monarchical absolutism. The decree was implemented by his son Frederick VII in 1849, and a liberal constitution established.

Reign	Name
House of Oldenburg	
1848–63	Frederick VII
Line of Glücksburg	
1863–1906	Christian IX
1906–12	Frederick VIII
1912–47	Christian X
1947–72	Frederick IX
1972–	Margrethe II

Dutch Prime Ministers from 1945

Term	Name	Party
1945	Pieter Gerbrandy	Anti-Revolutionary Party
1945–46	Willem Schermerhorn	Socialist Party
1946–48	Louis Beel	Catholic Party
1948–58	Willem Drees	Socialist Party
1958–59	Louis Beel	Catholic Party
1959–63	Jan de Quay	Catholic Party
1963–65	Victor Marijnen	Catholic Party
1965–66	Joseph Cals	Catholic Party
1966–67	Jelle Zijlstra	Anti-Revolutionary Party
1967–71	Petrus de Jong	Catholic Party
1971–73	Barend Biesheuvel	Anti-Revolutionary Party
1973–77	Johannes (Joop) den Uyl	Labour Party
1977–82	Andreas van Agt	Christian Democratic Appeal Party
1982–94	Rudolphus (Ruud) Lubbers	Christian Democratic Appeal Party
1994–	Wim Kok	Labour Party

Sovereigns of England and the United Kingdom from 899

Edward the Elder made the first major advances towards the unification of England under one sovereign and established the ascendancy of his dynasty.

Reign	Name	Relationship
West Saxon Kings		
899–924	Edward the Elder	son of Alfred the Great
924–39	Athelstan	son of Edward the Elder
939–46	Edmund	half-brother of Athelstan
946–55	Edred	brother of Edmund
955–59	Edwy	son of Edmund
959–75	Edgar	brother of Edwy
975–78	Edward the Martyr	son of Edgar
978–1016	Ethelred (II) the Unready	son of Edgar
1016	Edmund Ironside	son of Ethelred (II) the Unready
Danish Kings		
1016–35	Canute	son of Sweyn I of Denmark who conquered England in 1013

(continued)

Sovereigns of England and the United Kingdom from 899 (*continued*)

Reign	Name	Relationship
1035–40	Harold I	son of Canute
1040–42	Hardicanute	son of Canute
West Saxon Kings (restored)		
1042–66	Edward the Confessor	son of Ethelred (II) the Unready
1066	Harold II	son of Godwin
Norman Kings		
1066–87	William I	illegitimate son of Duke Robert the Devil
1087–1100	William II	son of William I
1100–35	Henry I	son of William I
1135–54	Stephen	grandson of William II
House of Plantagenet		
1154–89	Henry II	son of Matilda (daughter of Henry I)
1189–99	Richard I	son of Henry II
1199–1216	John	son of Henry II
1216–72	Henry III	son of John
1272–1307	Edward I	son of Henry III
1307–27	Edward II	son of Edward I
1327–77	Edward III	son of Edward II
1377–99	Richard II	son of the Black Prince
House of Lancaster		
1399–1413	Henry IV	son of John of Gaunt
1413–22	Henry V	son of Henry IV
1422–61, 1470–71	Henry VI	son of Henry V
House of York		
1461–70, 1471–83	Edward IV	son of Richard, Duke of York
1483	Edward V	son of Edward IV
1483–85	Richard III	brother of Edward IV
House of Tudor		
1485–1509	Henry VII	son of Edmund Tudor, Earl of Richmond
1509–47	Henry VIII	son of Henry VII
1547–53	Edward VI	son of Henry VIII
1553–58	Mary I	daughter of Henry VIII
1558–1603	Elizabeth I	daughter of Henry VIII
House of Stuart		
1603–25	James I	great-grandson of Margaret (daughter of Henry VII)
1625–49	Charles I	son of James I
1649–60 the Commonwealth		
House of Stuart (restored)		
1660–85	Charles II	son of Charles I
1685–88	James II	son of Charles I
1689–1702	William III and Mary	son of Mary (daughter of Charles I); daughter of James II
1702–14	Anne	daughter of James II
House of Hanover		
1714–27	George I	son of Sophia (granddaughter of James I)
1727–60	George II	son of George I
1760–1820	George III	son of Frederick (son of George II)
1820–30	George IV (regent 1811–20)	son of George III
1830–37	William IV	son of George III
1837–1901	Victoria	daughter of Edward (son of George III)
House of Saxe-Coburg		
1901–10	Edward VII	son of Victoria
House of Windsor		
1910–36	George V	son of Edward VII
1936	Edward VIII	son of George V
1936–52	George VI	son of George V
1952–	Elizabeth II	daughter of George VI

See also **Prime Ministers of Great Britain and the UK**, p 35.

French Rulers 751–1958

In 751 Pépin the Short deposed Childeric III, the last Merovingian ruler, to become king of the Franks. In 1958 the Algerian crisis caused the collapse of the Fourth Republic, and the establishment of a new constitution for the Fifth Republic.

Date of accession	Ruler
751	Pépin the Short
768	Charlemagne/Carloman
814	Louis I
840	Lothair I
843	Charles (II) the Bald
877	Louis II
879	Louis III
884	Charles (III) the Fat
888	Odo
893	Charles (III) the Simple
922	Robert I
923	Rudolf
936	Louis IV
954	Lothair II
986	Louis V
987	Hugues Capet
996	Robert II
1031	Henri I
1060	Philippe I
1108	Louis VI
1137	Louis VII
1180	Philippe II
1223	Louis VIII
1226	Louis IX
1270	Philippe III
1285	Philippe IV
1314	Louis X
1316	Jean I
1328	Philippe V
1322	Charles IV
1328	Philippe VI
1350	Jean II
1356	Charles V
1380	Charles VI
1422	Charles VII
1461	Louis XI
1483	Charles VIII
1498	Louis XII
1515	François I
1547	Henri II
1559	François II
1560	Charles IX
1574	Henri III
1574	Henri IV
1610	Louis XIII
1643	Louis XIV
1715	Louis XV
1774	Louis XVI
1792	National Convention
1795	Directory (five members)
1799	Napoléon Bonaparte (First Consul)
1804	Napoléon I (Emperor)
1814	Louis XVIII (King)
1815	Napoléon I (Emperor)
1815	King Louis XVIII
1824	Charles X
1830	Louis XIX
1830	Henri V (King)
1830	Louis-Philippe
1848	Philippe Buchez (President of the National Assembly)
1848	Louis Cavaignac (Minister of War)
1848	Louis Napoléon Bonaparte (President)
1852	Napoléon III (Emperor)
1871	Adolphe Thiers (President)
1873	Patrice MacMahon
1879	Jules Grevy
1887	François Sadui-Carnot
1894	Jean Casimir-Périer
1895	François Faure
1899	Emile Loubet
1913	Armand Fallières
1913	Raymond Poincaré
1920	Paul Deschanel
1920	Alexandre Millerand
1924	Gaston Doumergue
1931	Paul Doumer
1932	Albert Le Brun
1940	Philippe Pétain (Vichy government)
1944	provisional government
1947	Vincent Auriol (President)
1954	René Coty (President)

French Presidents and Prime Ministers from 1959 (the Fifth Republic)

Term	Name	Party
Presidents		
1959–69	General Charles de Gaulle	Gaullist
1969–74	Georges Pompidou	Gaullist
1974–81	Valéry Giscard d'Estaing	Republican/Union of French Democracy
1981–95	François Mitterand	Socialist
1995–	Jacques Chirac	Neo-Gaullist Rally for the Republic (RPR)
Prime Ministers		
1959–62	Michel Debré	Gaullist
1962–68	Georges Pompidou	Gaullist
1968–69	Maurice Couve de Murville	Gaullist
1969–72	Jacques Chaban-Delmas	Gaullist
1972–74	Pierre Messmer	Gaullist
1974–76	Jacques Chirac	Gaullist
1976–81	Raymond Barre	Union of French Democracy
1981–84	Pierre Mauroy	Socialist
1984–86	Laurent Fabius	Socialist
1986–88	Jacques Chirac	Neo-Gaullist RPR
1988–91	Michel Rocard	Socialist
1991–92	Edith Cresson	Socialist
1992–93	Pierre Bérégovoy	Socialist
1993–95	Edouard Balladur	Neo-Gaullist RPR
1995–97	Alain Juppé	Neo-Gaullist RPR
1997–	Lionel Jospin	Socialist

German Political Leaders from 1949

In 1949 the US, French, and British zones of occupation established after World War II became the Federal Republic of Germany, and the Soviet zone became the German Democratic Republic. The official reunification of the countries, with Helmut Kohl as chancellor, took place in 1990.

Term	Name	Party
Federal Republic of Germany		
Chancellors		
1949–63	Konrad Adenauer	Christian Democrat
1963–66	Ludwig Erhard	Christian Democrat
1966–69	Kurt Kiesinger	Christian Democrat
1969–74	Willy Brandt	Social Democrat
1974–82	Helmut Schmidt	Social Democrat
1982–90	Helmut Kohl	Christian Democrat
Democratic Republic		
Communist Party leaders		
1949–60	Wilhelm Pieck	
1960–71	Walter Ulbricht	
1971–89	Erich Honecker	
1989	Egon Krenz	
Prime Ministers		
1989–90	Hans Modrow	
1990–91	Lothar de Maizière	
Germany		
Chancellors		
1990–98	Helmut Kohl	Christian Democrat
1998–	Gerhard Schroeder	Social Democrat

Holy Roman Emperors

Reign	Name
Carolingian Kings and Emperors	
800–14	Charlemagne (Charles the Great)
814–40	Louis the Pious
840–55	Lothair I
855–75	Louis II
875–77	Charles (II) the Bald
881–87	Charles (III) the Fat
891–94	Guido of Spoleto
892–98	Lambert of Spoleto (co-emperor)
896–901	Arnulf (rival)
901–05	Louis III of Provence
905–24	Berengar
911–18	Conrad (I) of Franconia (rival)
Saxon Kings and Emperors	
918–36	Henry I the Fowler
936–73	Otto (I) the Great
973–83	Otto II
983–1002	Otto III
1002–24	Henry (II) the Saint
Franconian (Salian) Emperors	
1024–39	Conrad II
1039–56	Henry (III) the Black
1056–1106	Henry IV
1077–80	Rudolf of Swabia (rival)
1081–93	Hermann of Luxembourg (rival)
1093–1101	Conrad of Franconia (rival)
1106–25	Henry V
1126–37	Lothair II
Hohenstaufen Kings and Emperors	
1138–52	Conrad III
1152–90	Frederick Barbarossa
1190–97	Henry VI
1198–1215	Otto IV
1198–1208	Philip of Swabia (rival)
1215–50	Frederick II
1246–47	Henry Raspe of Thuringia (rival)
1247–56	William of Holland (rival)
1250–54	Conrad IV
1254–73	no ruler (the Great Interregnum)
Rulers from Various Noble Families	
1257–72	Richard of Cornwall (rival)
1257–73	Alfonso X of Castile (rival)
1273–91	Rudolf I, Habsburg
1292–98	Adolf I of Nassau
1298–1308	Albert I, Habsburg
1308–13	Henry VII, Luxembourg
1314–47	Louis IV of Bavaria
1314–25	Frederick of Habsburg (co-regent)
1347–78	Charles IV, Luxembourg
1378–1400	Wenceslas of Bohemia
1400	Frederick III of Brunswick
1400–10	Rupert of the Palatinate
1411–37	Sigismund, Luxembourg
Habsburg Emperors	
1438–39	Albert II
1440–93	Frederick III
1493–1519	Maximilian I
1519–56	Charles V
1556–64	Ferdinand I
1564–76	Maximilian II
1576–1612	Rudolf II
1612–19	Matthias
1619–37	Ferdinand II
1637–57	Ferdinand III
1658–1705	Leopold I
1705–11	Joseph I
1711–40	Charles VI
1742–45	Charles VII of Bavaria
Habsburg-Lorraine Emperors	
1745–65	Francis I of Lorraine
1765–90	Joseph II
1790–92	Leopold II
1792–1806	Francis II

Irish Prime Ministers from 1922

The Anglo-Irish Treaty which partitioned Ireland was signed in December 1921 and endorsed by election in 1922.

Term	Name	Party
1922	Michael Collins	Sinn Féin
1922–32	William T Cosgrave	Fine Gael
1932–48	Eamon de Valera	Fianna Fáil
1948–51	John A Costello	Fine Gael
1951–54	Eamon de Valera	Fianna Fáil
1954–57	John A Costello	Fine Gael
1957–59	Eamon de Valera	Fianna Fáil
1959–66	Seán Lemass	Fianna Fáil
1966–73	Jack Lynch	Fianna Fáil
1973–77	Liam Cosgrave	Fine Gael
1977–79	Jack Lynch	Fianna Fáil
1979–81	Charles Haughey	Fianna Fáil
1981–82	Garrett Fitzgerald	Fine Gael
1982	Charles Haughey	Fianna Fáil
1982–87	Garrett Fitzgerald	Fine Gael
1987–92	Charles Haughey	Fianna Fáil
1992–94	Albert Reynolds	Fianna Fáil
1994–97	John Bruton	Fine Gael
1997–	Patrick 'Bertie' Ahern	Fianna Fáil

Italian Kings

In 1861 Victor Emmanuelle II, King of Sardinia, was proclaimed the first king of a united Italy in Turin.

Reign	Name
1861–78	Victor Emmanuel II
1878–1900	Umberto I
1900–46	Victor Emmanuel III
1946	Umberto II (abdicated)

House of Habsburg 1804–1916

Francis II, the last Holy Roman Emperor, was the first to adopt the title Emperor of Austria, assuming it as Francis I in 1804. At the end of World War I Austria-Hungary collapsed and the empire dissolved.

Reign	Name
Emperors of Austria	
1804–35	Francis (Franz) I (of Austria) and II (as Holy Roman Emperor until 1806)
1835–48	Ferdinand I
Emperors of Austria-Hungary	
1848–1916	Franz Josef
1916–18	Charles (Karl Franz Josef)

Norwegian Monarchs from 1905

In 1905 Norway's union with Sweden was dissolved and Norway achieved independence.

Reign	Name
1905–40	Haakon VII (exiled)
1940–45	German occupation
1945–57	Haakon VII (restored)
1957–91	Olaf V
1991–	Harald V

Italian Prime Ministers from 1945

Term	Name	Party
1945–53	Alcide de Gasperi	Christian Democratic Party
1953–54	Giuseppe Pella	Christian Democratic Party
1954	Amintore Fanfani	Christian Democratic Party
1954–55	Mario Scelba	Christian Democratic Party
1955–57	Antonio Segni	Christian Democratic Party
1957–58	Adone Zoli	Christian Democratic Party
1958–59	Amintore Fanfani	Christian Democratic Party
1959–60	Antonio Segni	Christian Democratic Party
1960	Fernando Tambroni	Christian Democratic Party
1960–63	Amintore Fanfani	Christian Democratic Party
1963	Giovanni Leone	Christian Democratic Party
1963–68	Aldo Moro	Christian Democratic Party
1968	Giovanni Leone	Christian Democratic Party
1968–70	Mariano Rumor	Christian Democratic Party
1970–72	Emilio Colombo	Christian Democratic Party
1972–73	Giulio Andreotti	Christian Democratic Party
1973–74	Mariano Rumor	Christian Democratic Party
1974–76	Aldo Moro	Christian Democratic Party
1976–79	Giulio Andreotti	Christian Democratic Party
1979–80	Francesco Cossiga	Christian Democratic Party
1980–81	Arnaldo Forlani	Christian Democratic Party
1981–82	Giovanni Spadolini	Republican Party
1982–83	Amintore Fanfani	Christian Democratic Party
1983–87	Benedetto (Bettino) Craxi	Socialist Party
1987	Amintore Fanfani	Christian Democratic Party
1987–88	Giovanni Goria	Christian Democratic Party
1988–89	Ciriaco de Mita	Christian Democratic Party
1989–92	Giulio Andreotti	Christian Democratic Party
1992–93	Giuliano Amato	Socialist Party
1993–94	Carlo Azeglio Ciampi	Christian Democratic Party
1994–95	Silvio Berlusconi	Freedom Alliance
1995–96	Lamberto Dini	independent
1996–98	Romano Prodi	Olive Tree Alliance
1998–	Massimo D'Alema	Democrats of the Left

Norwegian Prime Ministers from 1945

Term	Name	Party
1945–51	Einar Gerhardsen	Labour Party
1951–55	Oscar Torp	Labour Party
1955–63	Einar Gerhardsen	Labour Party
1963	John Lyng	Conservative Party
1963–65	Einar Gerhardsen	Labour Party
1965–71	Per Borten	Centre Party
1971–72	Trygve Bratteli	Labour Party
1972–73	Lars Korvald	Christian People's Party
1973–76	Trygve Bratteli	Labour Party
1976–81	Odvar Nordli	Labour Party
1981	Gro Harlem Brundtland	Labour Party
1981–86	Kaare Willoch	Conservative Party
1986–89	Gro Harlem Brundtland	Labour Party
1989–90	Jan Syse	Conservative Party
1990–96	Gro Harlem Brundtland	Labour Party
1996–97	Thorbjoern Jagland	Labour Party
1997–2000	Kjell Magne Bondevik	Christian People's Party
2000–	Jens Stoltenberg	Labour Party

Polish Political Leaders from 1945

Term	Name	Party
Communist Party Leaders[1]		
1945–48	Władysław Gomułka	
1948–56	Bolesław Bierut	
1956	Edward Ochab	
1956–70	Władysław Gomułka	
1970–80	Edward Gierek	
1980–81	Stanisław Kania	
1981–89	Wojciech Jaruzelski	
Presidents		
1989–90	Wojciech Jaruzelski	
1990–95	Lech Wałęsa	Solidarity/independent
1995–	Aleksander Kwaśniewski	Democratic Left Alliance

[1]From 1945–90 the political leaders were the Communist Party leaders.

Names of European Rulers

Before the development of family names (11th–16th centuries), it was common practice to append a nickname, place name, occupation, or paternal name to a forename; European rulers were frequently given names relating to their appearance or perceived personality. Some examples are:

Alexander I the Fierce
Alexander III the Glorious
Charles II the Bald
Charles IV the Fair
Charles V the Wise
Charles VI the Mad
David I the Saint
Duncan I the Gracious
Louis I the Pious
Louis III the Stammerer
Louis VI the Fat
Louis X the Stubborn
Lulach the Fool
Malcolm IV the Maiden
Philip I the Handsome

Roman Emperors 27 BC – AD 395

In 27 BC Julius Caesar's nephew Octavian proclaimed the restoration of the republic, but effectively became sole ruler, receiving the name Augustus. The empire was frequently split from AD 305, and was divided for the last time between the sons of Theodosius (I) the Great in 395.

Reign	Name
Julio-Claudian Emperors	
27 BC– AD 14	Augustus
14–37	Tiberius I
37–41	Caligula (Gaius Caesar)
41–54	Claudius I
54–68	Nero
Civil Wars	
68–69	Galba
69	Otho
69	Vitellius
Flavian Emperors	
69–79	Vespasian
79–81	Titus
81–96	Domitian
96–98	Nerva
98–117	Trajan
117–38	Hadrian
Antonine Emperors	
138–61[1]	Antoninus Pius
161–69[1]	Lucius Verus
Despotic Emperors	
161–80	Marcus Aurelius
180–92[2]	Commodus
193	Pertinax
193	Didius Julianus
The Severi	
193–211	Septimus Severus
193–97	Clodius Albinus
193–94	Pescennius Niger
211–217	Caracalla
209–12	Geta
217–18	Macrinus
218	Diadumenianus
218–22	Elagabalus
222–35	Alexander Severus
The Soldier Emperors	
235–38	Maximinus
238	Gordian I
238	Gordian II
238	Balbinus
238	Pupienus
238–44	Gordian III
244–49	Philip (I) the Arab
249–51	Trajan Decius
251–53	Trebonianus Gallus
251–53	Volusianus
253–60	Valerian
253–68	Gallienus
268–70	Claudius II
270	Quintillus
270–75	Aurelian
275–76	Tacitus
276	Florianus
276–82	Probus
282–83	Carus
283–85	Carinus
283–84	Numerianus
284–305	Diocletian[3]
286–305	Maximianus
293–306	Constantius I
293–311	Galerius
305–337	Constantine I[4]
337–361	Constantius[5]
337–350	Constans I
361–363	Julian the Apostate
364–375	Valentinian I
375–383	Gratian
375–392	Valentinian II
379–395	Theodosius (I) the Great[6]

[1] Divided voluntarily between two brothers.
[2] Between 180 and 284 there was a succession of emperors placed on the throne by their respective armies or factions. Therefore, dates of emperors' reigns in this period often overlap.
[3] The end of Diocletian's reign marked the first split of the Roman empire. Whereas Diocletian retained supreme power, Maximianus ruled Italy and Africa, Constantius I ruled Gaul and Spain, and Galerius ruled Thrace.
[4] Emperor of the west from 305, sole emperor from 324.
[5] Emperor of the east from 337, sole emperor from 350.
[6] Appointed emperor of the east; sole emperor from 393.

Russian Tsars

In 1547 Ivan the Terrible was the first ruler to take the title of tsar.

Reign	Name
House of Rurik	
1547–84	Ivan the Terrible
1584–98	Theodore (Fyodor) I
1598	Irina
House of Godunov	
1598–1605	Boris Godunov
1605	Theodore (Fyodor) II
Usurpers	
1605–06	Dimitri III
1606–10	Basil IV
1610–13	interregnum
House of Romanov	
1613–45	Michael Romanov
1645–76	Alexis
1676–82	Theodore III
1682–96	Peter (I) the Great and Ivan V (brothers)
1689–1721	Peter I, as tsar
1721–25	Peter I, as emperor
1725–27	Catherine I
1727–30	Peter II
1730–40	Anna Ivanovna
1740–41	Ivan VI
1741–62	Elizabeth
1762	Peter III
1762–96	Catherine (II) the Great
1796–1801	Paul
1801–25	Alexander I
1825–55	Nicholas I
1855–81	Alexander II
1881–94	Alexander III
1894–1917	Nicholas II (abdicated)

Scottish Monarchs 1005–1603

This table covers the period from the unification of Scotland to the union of the crowns of Scotland and England.

Reign	Name
Celtic Kings	
1005–34	Malcolm II
1034–40	Duncan I
1040–57	Macbeth
1057–93	Malcolm III Canmore
1093–94	Donald III Donalbane
1094	Duncan II
1094–97	Donald III (restored)
1097–1107	Edgar
1107–24	Alexander I
1124–53	David I
1153–65	Malcolm IV
1165–1214	William the Lion
1214–49	Alexander II
1249–86	Alexander III
1286–90	Margaret of Norway
English Domination	
1292–96	John Baliol
1296–1306	annexed to England
House of Bruce	
1306–29	Robert I the Bruce
1329–71	David II
House of Stuart	
1371–90	Robert II
1390–1406	Robert III
1406–37	James I
1437–60	James II
1460–88	James III
1488–1513	James IV
1513–42	James V
1542–67	Mary
1567–1625	James VI[1]

[1] After the union of crowns in 1603, he became James I of England.

■ Selected Historical Leaders

Soviet and Russian Presidents and Communist Party Leaders

After the Russian Revolution in 1917 the Bolsheviks seized power under Vladimir Lenin.

Term	Name
USSR	
Communist Party Leaders	
1917–22	Vladimir Ilich Lenin
1922–53	Joseph Stalin
1953–64	Nikita Khrushchev
1964–82	Leonid Brezhnev
1982–84	Yuri Andropov
1984–85	Konstantin Chernenko
1985–91	Mikhail Gorbachev
Presidents	
1917–22	Vladimir Ilich Lenin[1]
1919–46	Mikhail Kalinin[2]
1946–53	Nikolai Shvernik
1953–60	Marshal Kliment Voroshilov
1960–64	Leonid Brezhnev
1964–65	Anastas Mikoyan
1965–77	Nikolai Podgorny
1977–82	Leonid Brezhnev
1982–83	Valery Kuznetsov (acting)
1983–84	Yuri Andropov
1984	Valery Kuznetsov (acting)
1984–85	Konstantin Chernenko
1985	Valery Kuznetsov (acting)
1985–88	Andrei Gromyko
1988–91	Mikhail Gorbachev
Russian Federation	
Presidents	
1991–99	Boris Yeltsin
1999–2000	Vladimir Putin (acting)
2000–	Vladimir Putin

[1] In 1917 Lenin was elected chairman of the Council of People's Commissars, that is, head of government. He held that post until 1922.
[2] In 1919, Kalinin became head of state (president of the Central Executive Committee of the Soviet government until 1937; president of the Presidium of the Supreme Soviet until 1946).

Spanish Monarchs from 1516

In 1516 Charles I was the first king to inherit a unified Spain. He later became Archduke of Austria and Holy Roman Emperor as Charles V.

Reign	Name
House of Habsburg	
1516–56	Charles I
1556–98	Philip II
1598–1621	Philip III
1621–65	Philip IV
1665–1700	Charles II
House of Bourbon	
1700–46	Philip V
1746–59	Ferdinand VI
1759–88	Charles III
1788–1808	Charles IV
1808	Ferdinand VII (deposed)
1808–13	Joseph Napoleon[1]
1813–33	Ferdinand VII (restored)
1833–68	Isabel II
1868–70	provisional government
1870–73	Amadeus I[2] (abdicated)
1873–74	first republic
1874–86	Alfonso XII
1886–1931	Alfonso XIII (deposed)
1975–	Juan Carlos I

[1] House of Bonaparte.
[2] House of Savoy.

Spanish Presidents, Chiefs of State, and Prime Ministers from 1931

The second republic was proclaimed in 1931.

Term	Name	Party
Presidents		
1931–36	Niceto Alcala Zamora	Liberal Republicans
1936	Diego Martinez y Barro	Radical Party
1936–39	Manuel Azaña y Diéz	Left Republican Party
Chiefs of State		
1939–75	Francisco Franco y Bahamonde	National Movement/Falange
Prime Ministers		
1931–33	Manuel Azaña y Diéz	Left Republican Party
1933	Alejandro Lerroux y García	Radical Republican Party
1933	Diego Martínez y Barro	Radical Republican Party
1933–34	Alejandro Lerroux y García	Radical Republican Party
1934	Ricardo Samper Ibañez	Radical Republican Party–Valencian branch
1934–35	Alejandro Lerroux y García	Radical Republican Party
1935	Joaquín Chapaprieta y Terragosa	independent
1935–36	Manuel Portela Valladares	Radical Republican Party
1936	Manuel Azaña y Diéz	Left Republican Party
1936	Santiago Cásares Quiroga	Left Republican Party
1936	José Giral y Pereira	Left Republican Party
1936–37	Francisco Largo Caballero	Socialist Party
1937–39	Juan Negrin	Socialist Party
1939–73	Francisco Franco Bahamonde	National Movement
1973	Luis Carrero Blanco	National Movement
1973–74	Torcuato Fernández Miranda	National Movement
1974–76	Carlos Arias Navarro	National Movement
1976–81	Adolfo Suárez González	Union of the Democratic Centre
1981–82	Leopoldo Calvo-Sotelo y Bustelo	Union of the Democratic Centre
1982–96	Felipe González Márquez	Socialist Workers' Party
1996–	José María Aznar	Popular Party

Swedish Monarchs from 950

The early history of Sweden is hidden in legend and saga, but the country appears to have slowly united towards the end of the 10th century.

Period	Name
c. 950– *c.* 95	Erik VIII
c. 995– *c.* 1022	Olaf Skötonung
c. 1022– *c.* 50	Anund Jakob
c. 1050– *c.* 60	Edmund
c. 1060– *c.* 80	Stenkil
c. 1080– *c.* 1110	Inge I/Halsten
c. 1110– *c.* 18	Filip
c. 1118– *c.* 22	Inge II
c. 1130– *c.* 56	Sverker I
c. 1150– *c.* 60	Erik IX Jerdvardsson
c. 1161– *c.* 67	Carl VII Sverkersson
c. 1167– *c.* 96	Knut I Eriksson
c. 1196– *c.* 1208	Sverker II Carlsson
c. 1208– *c.* 16	Erik X Eriksson
c. 1216– *c.* 22	Johan I Sverkersson
c. 1222– *c.* 29	Erik XI Eriksson
c. 1229– *c.* 34	Knut II
1234–50	Erik XI Eriksson
1250–75	Valdemar
1275–90	Magnus I Laduläs
1290–1318	Birgir Magnusson
1319–56	Magnus II Eriksson
1356–59	Magnus II Eriksson/Eric XII
1359–62	Magnus II Eriksson
1362–64	Magnus II Eriksson/Haakon

(continued)

Swedish Monarchs from 950 (*continued*)

Period	Name	Period	Name	Period	Name
1364–89	Albrekt	1501–03	Sten Sture the Elder (regent)	1660–97	Carl XI
1389–97	Margrethe	1503–12	Svante Sture (regent)	1697–1718	Carl XII
1397–1434	Erik XIII	1512–20	Sten Sture the Younger (regent)	1718–20	Ulrica Eleonora
1434–36	Regent: Engelbrekt Engelbrektsson	1520–23	Christian II	1720–51	Fredrik
1436–40	Regent: Carl Knutsson	1523–60	Gustaf I	1751–71	Adolf Fredrik
1441–48	Christoffer	1560–68	Erik XIV	1771–92	Gustaf III
1448–57	Carl VIII Knutsson	1568–92	Johan III	1792–1809	Gustaf IV Adolf
1457–64	Christian I	1592–99	Sigismund	1809–18	Carl XIII
1464–65	Carl VIII Knutsson	1599–1604	Carl IX (viceroy)	1818–44	Carl XIV Johan
1465–67	Interregnum	1604–1611	Carl IX (king)	1844–59	Oscar I
1467–70	Carl VIII Knutsson	1611–32	Gustaf II Adolf	1859–72	Carl XV
1470–97	Sten Sture the Elder (regent)	1632–54	Christina	1872–1907	Oscar II
1497–1501	Johan II	1654–60	Carl X Gustaf	1907–50	Gustaf V
				1950–73	Gustaf VI Adolf
				1973–	Carl XVI Gustaf

Swedish Prime Ministers from 1946

Term	Name	Party
1946–69	Tage Erlander	Social Democratic Labour Party
1969–76	Olof Palme	Social Democratic Labour Party
1976–78	Thorbjörn Fälldin	Centre Party
1978–79	Ola Ullsten	Liberal Party
1979–82	Thorbjörn Fälldin	Centre Party
1982–86	Olof Palme	Social Democratic Labour Party
1986–91	Ingvar Carlsson	Social Democratic Labour Party
1991–94	Carl Bildt	Moderate Party
1994–96	Ingvar Carlsson	Social Democratic Labour Party
1996–	Göran Persson	Social Democratic Labour Party

The Middle East

Egyptian Dynasties

Period	Name	Description
Early Dynastic Period		
c. 3100– *c.* 2905 BC	First Dynastic Period	Thinite
c. 2905– *c.* 2755 BC	Second Dynasty	Thinite
Old Kingdom		
c. 2755– *c.* 2680 BC	Third Dynasty	Memphite
c. 2680– *c.* 2544 BC	Fourth Dynasty	Memphite
c. 2544– *c.* 2407 BC	Fifth Dynasty	Memphite
c. 2407– *c.* 2255 BC	Sixth Dynasty	Memphite
First Intermediate Period		
c. 2255– *c.* 2235 BC	Seventh–Eighth Dynasties	Memphite
c. 2235– *c.* 2035 BC	Ninth–Tenth Dynasties	Heracleopolitan
Middle Kingdom		
c. 2134– *c.* 1991 BC	Eleventh Dynasty	Theban
c. 1991– *c.* 1786 BC	Twelfth Dynasty	Theban
Second Intermediate Period		
c. 1786– *c.* 1668 BC	Thirteenth Dynasty	Theban
c. 1720– *c.* 1665 BC	Fourteenth Dynasty	Xoite
c. 1668– *c.* 1560 BC	Fifteenth Dynasty	Hyksos
c. 1665– *c.* 1565 BC	Sixteenth Dynasty	Hyksos
c. 1668– *c.* 1570 BC	Seventeenth Dynasty	Theban
New Kingdom		
c. 1570– *c.* 1293 BC	Eighteenth Dynasty	Theban
c. 1293– *c.* 1185 BC	Nineteenth Dynasty	Theban
c. 1185– *c.* 1070 BC	Twentieth Dynasty	Theban
Third Intermediate Period		
c. 1070– *c.* 946 BC	Twenty-first Dynasty	Theban
c. 946– *c.* 712 BC	Twenty-second Dynasty	Bubastite
c. 828– *c.* 720 BC	Twenty-third Dynasty	Tanite
c. 740– *c.* 712 BC	Twenty-fourth Dynasty	Saite
c. 767– *c.* 656 BC	Twenty-fifth Dynasty	Nubian
Saite Period		
c. 664– *c.* 525 BC	Twenty-sixth Dynasty	Nubian
Later Dynastic Period		
c. 525– *c.* 405 BC	Twenty-seventh Dynasty	Persian Kings
c. 405– *c.* 399 BC	Twenty-eighth Dynasty	Saite
c. 399– *c.* 380 BC	Twenty-ninth Dynasty	Mendesian
c. 380– *c.* 343 BC	Thirtieth Dynasty	Sebennytic
c. 343–332 BC	Thirty-first Dynasty	Persian Kings
Conquest of Egypt by Alexander the Great		
332–323 BC	Alexander the Great	
Ptolemaic Period		
323–30 BC	Ptolemaic Dynasty	Ptolemies
Conquest of Egypt by Octavian (Augustus) in 30 BC		

Israeli Prime Ministers

In 1948 the independent state of Israel was proclaimed.

Term	Name	Party
1948–53	David Ben-Gurion	Mapai
1953–55	M Sharett	Mapai
1955–63	David Ben-Gurion	Mapai
1963–69	Levi Eshkol	Mapai/Labour
1969–74	Golda Meir	Labour
1974–77	Yitzhak Rabin	Labour
1977–83	Menachem Begin	Likud
1983–84	Yitzhak Shamir	Likud
1984–86	Shimon Peres	Labour
1986–92	Yitzhak Shamir	Likud
1992–95	Yitzhak Rabin	Labour
1995–96	Shimon Peres	Labour
1996–99	Binyamin Netanyahu	Likud
1999–	Ehud Barak	Labour

■ Selected Historical Leaders

Ottoman Emperors from 1299

Reign	Name	Reign	Name
1299– c. 1326	Osman I	1622–23	Mustafa I
1324–62	Orhan	1623–40	Murad IV
1362–89	Murad I	1640–48	Ibrahim
1389–1402	Bayezid (I) the Thunderbolt	1648–87	Mehmed IV
1402–03	Isa	1687–91	Suleiman II
1402–11	Suleiman	1691–95	Ahmed II
1409–13	Mesa	1695–1703	Mustafa II
1413–21	Mehmed I	1703–30	Ahmed III
1421–44	Murad II	1730–54	Mahmud I
1444–46	Mehmed (II) the Conqueror	1754–57	Osman III
1446–51	Murad II	1757–74	Mustafa III
1451–81	Mehmed (II) the Conqueror	1774–89	Abdulhamid I
1481–1512	Bayezid II	1789–1807	Selim III
1512–20	Selim (I) the Grim	1807–08	Mustafa IV
1520–66	Suleiman (I) the Magnificent	1808–39	Mahmud II
1566–74	Selim (II) the Sot	1839–61	Abdulmecid
1574–95	Murad III	1861–76	Abdulaziz
1595–1603	Mehmed III	1876	Murad V
1603–17	Ahmed I	1876–1909	Abdulhamid II
1617–18	Mustafa I	1909–18	Mehmed V
1618–22	Osman II	1918–22	Mehmed VI

Leaders of Selected Organizations

Leaders of Selected Organizations

Organization	Leader	Nationality	Post
Political and economic			
African, Caribbean, and Pacific Group of States (ACP)	Jean-Robert Goulongana	Gabonese	Secretary general since 1 March 1999
African Development Bank (BAD)	Omar Kabbaj	Moroccan	President since 1995
Arab League	Ahmed Esmat Abdel Meguid	Egyptian	Secretary general since 1991
Asian Development Bank (ADB)	Tadao Chino	Japanese	President since 16 January 1999
Asia-Pacific Economic Cooperation (APEC)	Serbini Ali	Bruneian	Executive director since 1 January 2000
Association of South East Asian Nations (ASEAN)	H E Rodolfo Certeza Severino Jr	Filipino	Secretary general since 1997
Caribbean Community and Common Market (CARICOM)	Edwin W Carrington	Trinidad and Tobago	Secretary general
The Commonwealth (British)	Emeka Anyaoku	Nigerian	Secretary general since October 1989
Commonwealth of Independent States (CIS)	Yuri Yarov	Russian	Executive secretary since 2 April 1999
Council of Europe	Walter Schwimmer	Austrian	Secretary general since 1 September 1999
European Bank for Reconstruction and Development (EBRD)	Jean Lemierre	French	President since 22 May 2000
European Commission	Romano Prodi	Italian	President since September 1999
Food and Agriculture Association of the UN (FAO)	Jacques Diouf	Senegalese	Director general since 1 January 1994
Inter-American Development Bank (IDB)	Enrique Iglesias	Uruguayan	President since 1988, re-elected for third term from 1 April 1998
International Civil Aviation Organization (ICAO)	Assad Kotaite	Lebanese	President
International Labour Organization (ILO)	Juan Somavia	Chilean	Director general since 22 March 1999
International Maritime Organization (IMO)	William A O'Neil	Canadian	Secretary general since 1 January 1990
International Monetary Fund (IMF)	Horst Köhler	German	Managing director since 1 May 2000.
Latin American Integration Association (ALADI)	Juan Francisco	Vanazuelan	Secretary general
North Atlantic Treaty Organization (NATO)	George Robertson	British	Secretary general since 14 October 1999
Organization for Economic Cooperation and Development (OECD)	Donald J Johnston	Canadian	Secretary general since 1 June 1996
Organization of the Petroleum Exporting Countries (OPEC)	Rilwanu Lukman	Nigerian	Secretary general since 1995
Organization for Security and Cooperation in Europe (OSCE)	Benita Ferrero-Waldner	Austrian	Chairman since 1 January 2000
Organisation of African Unity (OAU)	Salim Ahmed Salim	Tanzanian	Secretary general since 19 September, 1989
Palestine Liberation Organisation (PLO)	Yassir Arafat	Palestinian	Chairman of PLO since 1968 and of Palestine National Authority since 1996

(continued)

Leaders of Selected Organizations *(continued)*

Organization	Leader	Nationality	Post
South Asian Association for Regional Cooperation (SAARC)	Nihal Rodrigo	Sri Lankan	Secretary general since 1 January 1999
United Nations (UN)	Kofi Annan	Ghanaian	Secretary general since 1997
World Bank	James D Wolfensohn	US	President since 1 June 1995
World Food Organization	Catherine Bertini	US	Executive director since 1992, reappointed in 1997
World Trade Organization (WTO)	Mike Moore	New Zealander	Director general since 1 September 1999
Legal			
European Court of Human Rights (ECHR)	M Lazius Wildhaber	Swiss	President
International Court of Justice (ICJ)	Gilbert Guillaume	French	President since 7 February 2000
International Criminal Police Organization (ICPO/INTERPOL)	Raymond E Kendall	British	Secretary general
Humanitarian and relief			
Amnesty International	Pierre Sané	Senegalese	Secretary general since 1992
International Federation of Red Cross and Red Crescent Societies	Didier Cherpitel	French	Secretary general since January 2000
International Save the Children Alliance	John McCarthy	US	Chairman
Médecins Sans Frontières (MSF)	James Orbinski	Canadian	President since June 1998
Oxfam	David Bryer	British	Director since 1992
United Nations Children's Fund (UNICEF)	Carol Bellamy	US	Executive director since 1 May 1995
United Nations Educational, Scientific, and Cultural Organization (UNESCO)	Koichiro Matsuura	Japanese	Director general since 15 November 1999
World Health Organization (WHO)	Gro Harlem Brundtland	Norwegian	Director general since 21 July 1988
Wildlife and environmental			
Friends of the Earth International	Ricardo Navarro	El Salvadorian	Chair since 1999
Greenpeace	Lord Peter Melchett	British	Executive Director since January 1989
World Wide Fund for Nature (WWF)	Claude Martin	Swiss	Director general since October 1993.
Sport			
Fédération International de Football Associations (FIFA)	Joseph S Blatter	Swiss	President since 8 June 1998
Fédéation International de l'Automobile (FIA)	Max Mosley	British	President
International Amateur Athletic Federation (IAAF)	Lamine Diack	Senegalese	President since 8 November 1999
International Olympic Committee	Juan Antonio Samaranch	Spanish	President since 1980

See also **International Political Organizations**, pp 277–280.

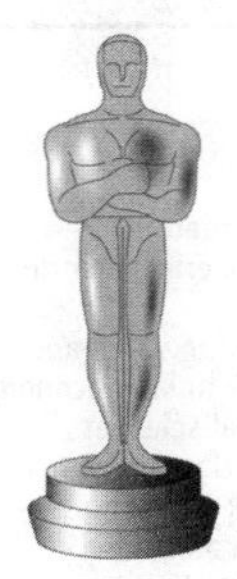

Awards and Prizes

Nobel Prizes

The Nobel Prizes were first awarded in 1901 under the will of Alfred B Nobel (1833–1896), a Swedish chemist, who invented dynamite. The interest on the Nobel endowment fund is divided annually among the persons who have made the greatest contributions in the fields of physics, chemistry, medicine (or physiology), literature, and world peace. The first four are awarded by academic committees based in Sweden, while the peace prize is awarded by a committee of the Norwegian parliament. A sixth prize, for economics, financed by the Swedish National Bank, was first awarded in 1969. The prizes have a large cash award and are given to organizations (such as the United Nations peacekeeping forces, which received the Nobel Peace Prize in 1988) as well as to individuals at an awards ceremony held on 10 December each year, the anniversary of Nobel's death.

Nobel Prize for Chemistry

Year	Winner(s)[1]	Awarded for
1990	Elias James Corey (USA)	new methods of synthesizing chemical compounds
1991	Richard Ernst (Switzerland)	improvements in the technology of nuclear magnetic resonance (NMR) imaging
1992	Rudolph Marcus (USA)	theoretical discoveries relating to reduction and oxidation reactions
1993	Kary Mullis (USA)	invention of the polymerase chain reaction technique for amplifying DNA
	Michael Smith (Canada)	invention of techniques for splicing foreign genetic segments into an organism's DNA in order to modify the proteins produced
1994	George Olah (USA)	development of technique for examining hydrocarbon molecules
1995	F Sherwood Rowland (USA), Mario Molina (USA), and Paul Crutzen (Netherlands)	explaining the chemical process of the ozone layer
1996	Robert Curl Jr (USA), Harold Kroto (UK), and Richard Smalley (USA)	discovery of fullerenes
1997	John Walker (UK), Paul Boyer (USA), and Jens Skou (Denmark)	study of the enzymes involved in the production of adenosine triphospate (ATP), which acts as a store of energy in bodies called mitochondria inside cells
1998	Walter Kohn (USA), John Pople (USA)	research into quantum chemistry
1999	Ahmed Zewail (USA)	studies of the transition states of chemical reactions using femtosecond spectroscopy

[1] Nationality given is the citizenship of recipient at the time award was made.

Nobel Prize for Economics

Year	Winner(s)[1]	Awarded for
1990	Harry Markowitz (USA), Merton Miller (USA), and William Sharpe (USA)	pioneering theories on managing investment portfolios and corporate finances
1991	Ronald Coase (USA)	work on value and social problems of companies
1992	Gary Becker (USA)	work linking economic theory to aspects of human behaviour, drawing on other social sciences
1993	Robert Fogel (USA) and Douglass North (USA)	creating a new method of studying economic history (cliometrics)
1994	John Nash (USA), John Harsanyi (USA), and Reinhard Selten (Germany)	work on 'game theory', which investigates decision-making in a competitive environment
1995	Robert Lucas (USA)	developing the 'rational expectations' school, which questions a government's ability to steer the economy
1996	James Mirrlees (UK) and William Vickrey (USA)	fundamental contributions to the economic theory of incentives under assymmetric information
1997	Robert Merton (USA) and Myron Scholes (USA)	pioneering contribution to economic sciences by developing a new method of determining the value of derivatives
1998	Amartya Sen (India)	research into the social and economic causes of famines
1999	Robert A Mundell (Canada)	analysis of monetary and fiscal policy under different exchange rate regimes and analysis of optimum currency areas

[1] Nationality given is the citizenship of recipient at the time award was made.

Nobel Prize for Literature

Year	Winner(s)[1]
1990	Octavio Paz (Mexico)
1991	Nadine Gordimer (South Africa)
1992	Derek Walcott (Santa Lucia)
1993	Toni Morrison (USA)
1994	Kenzaburo Oe (Japan)
1995	Seamus Heaney (Ireland)
1996	Wisława Szymborska (Poland)
1997	Dario Fo (Italy)
1998	José Saramago (Portugal)
1999	Günter Grass (Germany)

[1] Nationality given is the citizenship of recipient at the time award was made.

Nobel Prize for Peace

Year	Winner(s)[1]	Awarded for
1990	Mikhail Gorbachev (USSR)	promoting greater openness in the USSR and helping to end the Cold War
1991	Aung San Suu Kyi (Myanmar)	nonviolent campaign for democracy
1992	Rigoberta Menchú (Guatemala)	campaign for indigenous people
1993	Nelson Mandela (South Africa) and Frederik Willem de Klerk (South Africa)	work towards dismantling apartheid and negotiating transition to nonracial democracy
1994	Yassir Arafat (Palestine), Yitzhak Rabin (Israel), and Shimon Peres (Israel)	agreement of an accord on Palestinian self-rule
1995	Joseph Rotblat (UK) and the Pugwash Conferences on Science and World Affairs	campaign against nuclear weapons
1996	Carlos Filipe Ximenes Belo (Timorese) and José Ramos-Horta (Timorese)	work towards a just and peaceful solution to the conflict in East Timor
1997	Jody Williams (USA) and the International Campaign to Ban Landmines (ICBL)	campaign for global ban of anti-personnel mines
1998	John Hume (UK) and David Trimble (UK)	efforts to find a peaceful solution to the conflict in Northern Ireland
1999	Médecins sans Frontières/Doctors Without Borders (headquarters in Brussels, founded in France)	high degree of independence which has enabled the organization to offer assistance to victims of wars and disasters around the world

[1] Nationality given is the citizenship of recipient at the time award was made.

Nobel Prize for Physics

Year	Winner(s)[1]	Awarded for
1990	Jerome Friedman (USA), Henry Kendall (USA), and Richard Taylor (Canada)	experiments demonstrating that protons and neutrons are made up of quarks
1991	Pierre-Gilles de Gennes (France)	work on disordered systems including polymers and liquid crystals; development of mathematical methods for studying the behaviour of molecules in a liquid on the verge of solidifying
1992	Georges Charpak (France)	invention and development of detectors used in high-energy physics
1993	Joseph Taylor (USA) and Russell Hulse (USA)	discovery of first binary pulsar (confirming the existence of gravitational waves)
1994	Clifford Shull (USA) and Bertram Brockhouse (Canada)	development of technique known as 'neutron scattering' which led to advances in semiconductor technology
1995	Frederick Reines (USA) Martin Perl (USA)	discovery of the neutrino discovery of the tau lepton

(continued)

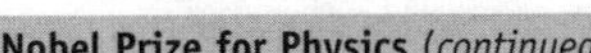

Nobel Prize for Physics (*continued*)

Year	Winner(s)[1]	Awarded for
1996	David Lee (USA), Douglas Osheroff (USA), and Robert Richardson (USA)	discovery of superfluidity in helium-3
1997	Claude Cohen-Tannoudji (France), William Phillips (USA), and Steven Chu (USA)	discovery of a way to slow down individual atoms using lasers for study in a near-vacuum
1998	Robert B Laughlin (USA), Horst L Störmer (USA), and Daniel C Tsui (USA)	discovery of a new form of quantum fluid with fractionally charged excitations
1999	Gerardus 'T Hooft (the Netherlands) and Martinus Veltman (the Netherlands)	elucidating the quantum structure of electroweak interactions in physics

[1] Nationality given is the citizenship of recipient at the time award was made.

Nobel Prize for Physiology or Medicine

Year	Winner(s)[1]	Awarded for
1990	Joseph Murray (USA) and Donnall Thomas (USA)	pioneering work in organ and cell transplants
1991	Erwin Neher (Germany) and Bert Sakmann (Germany)	discovery of how gatelike structures (ion channels) regulate the flow of ions into and out of cells
1992	Edmond Fisher (USA) and Edwin Krebs (USA)	isolating and describing the action of the enzyme responsible for reversible protein phosphorylation, a major biological control mechanism
1993	Phillip Sharp (USA) and Richard Roberts (UK)	discovery of split genes (genes interrupted by nonsense segments of DNA)
1994	Alfred Gilman (USA) and Martin Rodbell (USA)	discovery of a family of proteins (G-proteins) that translate messages – in the form of hormones or other chemical signals – into action inside cells
1995	Edward Lewis (USA), Eric Wieschaus (USA), and Christiane Nüsslein-Volhard (Germany)	discovery of genes which control the early stages of the body's development
1996	Peter Doherty (Australia) and Rolf Zinkernagel (Switzerland)	discovery of how the immune system recognizes virus-infected cells
1997	Stanley Prusiner (USA)	discoveries, including the 'prion' theory, that could lead to new treatments of dementia-related diseases, including Alzheimer's and Parkinson's diseases
1998	Robert Furchgott (USA), Ferid Murad (USA), and Louis Ignarro (USA)	discovery that nitric oxide (NO) acts as a key chemical messenger between cells
1999	Günter Blobel (USA)	discovery that proteins have intrinsic signals that govern their transport and localization in the cell

[1] Nationality given is the citizenship of recipient at the time award was made.

Fields Medal

This international prize for achievement in the field of mathematics is awarded every four years by the International Mathematical Union.

Year	Winner(s)
1936	Lars Ahlfors (Finland); Jesse Douglas (USA)
1950	Atle Selberg (USA); Laurent Schwartz (France)
1954	Kunihiko Kodaira (USA); Jean-Pierre Serre (France)
1958	Klaus Roth (UK); René Thom (France)
1962	Lars Hörmander (Sweden); John Milnor (USA)
1966	Michael Atiyah (UK); Paul J Cohen (USA); Alexander Grothendieck (France); Stephen Smale (USA)
1970	Alan Baker (UK); Heisuke Hironaka (USA); Sergei Novikov (USSR); John G Thompson (USA)
1974	Enrico Bombieri (Italy); David Mumford (USA)
1978	Pierre Deligne (Belgium); Charles Fefferman (USA); G A Margulis (USSR); Daniel Quillen (USA)
1982	Alain Connes (France); William Thurston (USA); S T Yau (USA)
1986	Simon Donaldson (UK); Gerd Faltings (West Germany); Michael Freedman (USA)
1990	Vladimir Drinfeld (USSR); Vaughan F R Jones (USA); Shigefumi Mori (Japan); Edward Witten (USA)
1994	L J Bourgain (USA/France); P-L Lions (France); J-C Yoccoz (France); E I Zelmanov (USA)
1998	Richard E Borcherds (UK); W Timothy Gowers (UK); Maxim Kontsevich (Russia); Curtis T McMullen (USA)

Film and Theatre

Academy Awards

The Academy Awards (or 'Oscars') are presented each March for films of the previous year. The first Academy Awards were handed out in 1929, and the presentation was first televised and broadcast live in 1953. Now hundreds of millions of viewers around the world watch the televised awards ceremony each year.

Year of release	Best Picture	Best Director	Best Actor	Best Actress	Best Supporting Actor	Best Supporting Actress
1928	*Wings*	Frank Borzage *Seventh Heaven* Lewis Milestone *Two Arabian Knights*	Emil Jannings *The Way of All Flesh, The Last Command*	Janet Gaynor *Seventh Heaven, Street Angel, Sunrise*	no award	no award
1929	*The Broadway Melody*	Frank Lloyd *The Divine Lady*	Warner Baxter *In Old Arizona*	Mary Pickford *Coquette*	no award	no award

(*continued*)

Academy Awards *(continued)*

Year of release	Best Picture	Best Director	Best Actor	Best Actress	Best Supporting Actor	Best Supporting Actress
1930	*All Quiet on the Western Front*	Lewis Milestone *All Quiet on the Western Front*	George Arliss *Disraeli*	Norma Shearer *The Divorcee*	no award	no award
1931	*Cimarron*	Norman Taurog *Skippy*	Lionel Barrymore *A Free Soul*	Marie Dressler *Min and Bill*	no award	no award
1932	*Grand Hotel*	Frank Borzage *Bad Girl*	Fredric March *Dr Jekyll and Mr Hyde* Wallace Beery *The Champ*	Helen Hayes *The Sin of Madelon Claudet*	no award	no award
1933	*Cavalcade*	Frank Lloyd *Cavalcade*	Charles Laughton *The Private Life of Henry VIII*	Katharine Hepburn *Morning Glory*	no award	no award
1934	*It Happened One Night*	Frank Capra *It Happened One Night*	Clark Gable *It Happened One Night*	Claudette Colbert *It Happened One Night*	no award	no award
1935	*Mutiny on the Bounty*	John Ford *The Informer*	Victor McLaglen *The Informer*	Bette Davis *Dangerous*	no award	no award
1936	*The Great Ziegfeld*	Frank Capra *Mr Deeds Goes to Town*	Paul Muni *The Story of Louis Pasteur*	Luise Rainer *The Great Ziegfeld*	Walter Brennan *Come and Get It*	Gale Sondergaard *Anthony Adverse*
1937	*The Life of Emile Zola*	Leo McCarey *The Awful Truth*	Spencer Tracy *Captains Courageous*	Luise Rainer *The Good Earth*	Joseph Schildkraut *The Life of Emile Zola*	Alice Brady *In Old Chicago*
1938	*You Can't Take It With You*	Frank Capra *You Can't Take It With You*	Spencer Tracy *Boys' Town*	Bette Davis *Jezebel*	Walter Brennan *Kentucky*	Fay Bainter *Jezebel*
1939	*Gone With the Wind*	Victor Fleming *Gone With the Wind*	Robert Donat *Goodbye, Mr Chips*	Vivien Leigh *Gone With the Wind*	Thomas Mitchell *Stagecoach*	Hattie McDaniel *Gone With the Wind*
1940	*Rebecca*	John Ford *The Grapes of Wrath*	James Stewart *The Philadelphia Story*	Ginger Rogers *Kitty Foyle*	Walter Brennan *The Westerner*	Jane Darwell *The Grapes of Wrath*
1941	*How Green Was My Valley*	John Ford *How Green Was My Valley*	Gary Cooper *Sergeant York*	Joan Fontaine *Suspicion*	Donald Crisp *How Green Was My Valley*	Mary Astor *The Great Lie*
1942	*Mrs Miniver*	William Wyler *Mrs Miniver*	James Cagney *Yankee Doodle Dandy*	Greer Garson *Mrs Miniver*	Van Heflin *Johnny Eager*	Teresa Wright *Mrs Miniver*
1943	*Casablanca*	Michael Curtiz *Casablanca*	Paul Lukas *Watch on the Rhine*	Jennifer Jones *The Song of Bernadette*	Charles Coburn *The More the Merrier*	Katina Paxinou *For Whom the Bell Tolls*
1944	*Going My Way*	Leo McCarey *Going My Way*	Bing Crosby *Going My Way*	Ingrid Bergman *Gaslight*	Barry Fitzgerald *Going My Way*	Ethel Barrymore *None But the Lonely Heart*
1945	*The Lost Weekend*	Billy Wilder *The Lost Weekend*	Ray Milland *The Lost Weekend*	Joan Crawford *Mildred Pierce*	James Dunn *A Tree Grows in Brooklyn*	Anne Revere *National Velvet*
1946	*The Best Years of Our Lives*	William Wyler *The Best Years of Our Lives*	Fredric March *The Best Years of Our Lives*	Olivia de Havilland *To Each His Own*	Harold Russell *The Best Years of Our Lives*	Anne Baxter *The Razor's Edge*
1947	*Gentleman's Agreement*	Elia Kazan *Gentleman's Agreement*	Ronald Coleman *A Double Life*	Loretta Young *The Farmer's Daughter*	Edmund Gwenn *Miracle on 34th Street*	Celeste Holm *Gentleman's Agreement*
1948	*Hamlet*	John Huston *Treasure of Sierra Madre*	Laurence Olivier *Hamlet*	Jane Wyman *Johnny Belinda*	Walter Houston *Treasure of Sierra Madre*	Claire Trevor *Key Largo*
1949	*All the King's Men*	Joseph L Mankiewicz *A Letter to Three Wives*	Broderick Crawford *All the King's Men*	Olivia de Havilland *The Heiress*	Dean Jagger *Twelve O'Clock High*	Mercedes McCambridge *All the King's Men*
1950	*All About Eve*	Joseph L Mankiewicz *All About Eve*	José Ferrer *Cyrano de Bergerac*	Judy Holliday *Born Yesterday*	George Sanders *All About Eve*	Josephine Hull *Harvey*
1951	*An American in Paris*	George Stevens *A Place in the Sun*	Humphrey Bogart *The African Queen*	Vivien Leigh *A Streetcar Named Desire*	Karl Malden *A Streetcar Named Desire*	Kim Hunter *A Streetcar Named Desire*
1952	*The Greatest Show on Earth*	John Ford *The Quiet Man*	Gary Cooper *High Noon*	Shirley Booth *Come Back Little Sheba*	Anthony Quinn *Viva Zapata!*	Gloria Grahame *The Bad and the Beautiful*
1953	*From Here to Eternity*	Fred Zinnemann *From Here to Eternity*	William Holden *Stalag 17*	Audrey Hepburn *Roman Holiday*	Frank Sinatra *From Here to Eternity*	Donna Reed *From Here to Eternity*
1954	*On the Waterfront*	Elia Kazan *On the Waterfront*	Marlon Brando *On the Waterfront*	Grace Kelly *The Country Girl*	Edmond O'Brien *The Barefoot Contessa*	Eva Marie Saint *On the Waterfront*
1955	*Marty*	Delbert Mann *Marty*	Ernest Borgnine *Marty*	Anna Magnani *The Rose Tattoo*	Jack Lemmon *Mister Roberts*	Jo Van Fleet *East of Eden*
1956	*Around the World in 80 Days*	George Stevens *Giant*	Yul Brynner *The King and I*	Ingrid Bergman *Anastasia*	Anthony Quinn *Lust for Life*	Dorothy Malone *Written on the Wind*

(continued)

Academy Awards *(continued)*

Year of release	Best Picture	Best Director	Best Actor	Best Actress	Best Supporting Actor	Best Supporting Actress
1957	*The Bridge on the River Kwai*	David Lean *The Bridge on the River Kwai*	Alec Guinness *The Bridge on the River Kwai*	Joanne Woodward *The Three Faces of Eve*	Red Buttons *Sayonara*	Miyoshi Umeki *Sayonara*
1958	*Gigi*	Vincente Minnelli *Gigi*	David Niven *Separate Tables*	Susan Hayward *I Want to Live!*	Burl Ives *The Big Country*	Wendy Hiller *Separate Tables*
1959	*Ben Hur*	William Wyler *Ben Hur*	Charlton Heston *Ben Hur*	Simone Signoret *Room at the Top*	Hugh Griffith *Ben Hur*	Shelley Winters *The Diary of Anne Frank*
1960	*The Apartment*	Billy Wilder *The Apartment*	Burt Lancaster *Elmer Gantry*	Elizabeth Taylor *Butterfield 8*	Peter Ustinov *Spartacus*	Shirley Jones *Elmer Gantry*
1961	*West Side Story*	Robert Wise and Jerome Robbins *West Side Story*	Maximillian Schell *Judgment at Nuremberg*	Sophia Loren *Two Women*	George Chakiris *West Side Story*	Rita Moreno *West Side Story*
1962	*Lawrence of Arabia*	David Lean *Lawrence of Arabia*	Gregory Peck *To Kill a Mockingbird*	Anne Bancroft *The Miracle Worker*	Ed Begley *Sweet Bird of Youth*	Patty Duke *The Miracle Worker*
1963	*Tom Jones*	Tony Richardson *Tom Jones*	Sidney Poitier *Lilies of the Field*	Patricia Neal *Hud*	Melvyn Douglas *Hud*	Margaret Rutherford *The V.I.P.s*
1964	*My Fair Lady*	George Cukor *My Fair Lady*	Rex Harrison *My Fair Lady*	Julie Andrews *Mary Poppins*	Peter Ustinov *Topkapi*	Lila Kedrova *Zorba the Greek*
1965	*The Sound of Music*	Robert Wise *The Sound of Music*	Lee Marvin *Cat Ballou*	Julie Christie *Darling*	Martin Balsam *A Thousand Clowns*	Shelley Winters *A Patch of Blue*
1966	*A Man for All Seasons*	Fred Zinnemann *A Man for All Seasons*	Paul Scofield *A Man for All Seasons*	Elizabeth Taylor *Who's Afraid of Virginia Woolf?*	Walter Matthau *The Fortune Cookie*	Sandy Dennis *Who's Afraid of Virginia Woolf?*
1967	*In the Heat of the Night*	Mike Nichols *The Graduate*	Rod Steiger *In the Heat of the Night*	Katharine Hepburn *Guess Who's Coming to Dinner*	George Kennedy *Cool Hand Luke*	Estelle Parsons *Bonnie and Clyde*
1968	*Oliver!*	Sir Carol Reed *Oliver!*	Cliff Robertson *Charly*	Katharine Hepburn *The Lion in Winter* Barbra Streisand *Funny Girl*	Jack Albertson *The Subject Was Roses*	Ruth Gordon *Rosemary's Baby*
1969	*Midnight Cowboy*	John Schlesinger *Midnight Cowboy*	John Wayne *True Grit*	Maggie Smith *The Prime of Miss Jean Brodie*	Gig Young *They Shoot Horses, Don't They?*	Goldie Hawn *Cactus Flower*
1970	*Patton*	Franklin J Schaffner *Patton*	George C Scott *Patton*	Glenda Jackson *Women in Love*	John Mills *Ryan's Daughter*	Helen Hayes *Airport*
1971	*The French Connection*	William Friedkin *The French Connection*	Gene Hackman *The French Connection*	Jane Fonda *Klute*	Ben Johnson *The Last Picture Show*	Cloris Leachman *The Last Picture Show*
1972	*The Godfather*	Bob Fosse *Cabaret*	Marlon Brando *The Godfather*	Liza Minnelli *Cabaret*	Joel Grey *Cabaret*	Eileen Heckart *Butterflies Are Free*
1973	*The Sting*	George Roy Hill *The Sting*	Jack Lemmon *Save the Tiger*	Glenda Jackson *A Touch of Class*	John Houseman *The Paper Chase*	Tatum O'Neal *Paper Moon*
1974	*The Godfather Part II*	Francis Ford Coppola *The Godfather Part II*	Art Carney *Harry and Tonto*	Ellen Burstyn *Alice Doesn't Live Here Anymore*	Robert De Niro *The Godfather Part II*	Ingrid Bergman *Murder on the Orient Express*
1975	*One Flew Over the Cuckoo's Nest*	Milos Forman *One Flew Over the Cuckoo's Nest*	Jack Nicholson *One Flew Over the Cuckoo's Nest*	Louise Fletcher *One Flew Over the Cuckoo's Nest*	George Burns *The Sunshine Boys*	Lee Grant *Shampoo*
1976	*Rocky*	John G Avildsen *Rocky*	Peter Finch *Network*	Faye Dunaway *Network*	Jason Robards *All the President's Men*	Beatrice Straight *Network*
1977	*Annie Hall*	Woody Allen *Annie Hall*	Richard Dreyfuss *The Goodbye Girl*	Diane Keaton *Annie Hall*	Jason Robards *Julia*	Vanessa Redgrave *Julia*
1978	*The Deer Hunter*	Michael Cimino *The Deer Hunter*	Jon Voight *Coming Home*	Jane Fonda *Coming Home*	Christopher Walken *The Deer Hunter*	Maggie Smith *California Suite*
1979	*Kramer vs Kramer*	Robert Benton *Kramer vs Kramer*	Dustin Hoffman *Kramer vs Kramer*	Sally Field *Norma Rae*	Melvyn Douglas *Being There*	Meryl Streep *Kramer vs Kramer*
1980	*Ordinary People*	Robert Redford *Ordinary People*	Robert De Niro *Raging Bull*	Sissy Spacek *Coal Miner's Daughter*	Timothy Hutton *Ordinary People*	Mary Steenburgen *Melvin and Howard*
1981	*Chariots of Fire*	Warren Beatty *Reds*	Henry Fonda *On Golden Pond*	Katharine Hepburn *On Golden Pond*	John Gielgud *Arthur*	Maureen Stapleton *Reds*
1982	*Gandhi*	Richard Attenborough *Gandhi*	Ben Kingsley *Gandhi*	Meryl Streep *Sophie's Choice*	Louis Gossett Jr *An Officer and a Gentleman*	Jessica Lange *Tootsie*
1983	*Terms of Endearment*	James L Brooks *Terms of Endearment*	Robert Duvall *Tender Mercies*	Shirley Maclaine *Terms of Endearment*	Jack Nicholson *Terms of Endearment*	Linda Hunt *The Year of Living Dangerously*
1984	*Amadeus*	Milos Forman *Amadeus*	F Murray Abraham *Amadeus*	Sally Field *Places in the Heart*	Haing S Ngor *The Killing Fields*	Dame Peggy Ashcroft *A Passage to India*
1985	*Out of Africa*	Sydney Pollack *Out of Africa*	William Hurt *Kiss of the Spider Woman*	Geraldine Page *The Trip to Bountiful*	Don Ameche *Cocoon*	Anjelica Huston *Prizzi's Honor*

(continued)

Academy Awards (*continued*)

Year of release	Best Picture	Best Director	Best Actor	Best Actress	Best Supporting Actor	Best Supporting Actress
1986	*Platoon*	Oliver Stone *Platoon*	Paul Newman *The Color of Money*	Marlee Matlin *Children of a Lesser God*	Michael Caine *Hannah and Her Sisters*	Dianne Wiest *Hannah and Her Sisters*
1987	*The Last Emperor*	Bernardo Bertolucci *The Last Emperor*	Michael Douglas *Wall Street*	Cher *Moonstruck*	Sean Connery *The Untouchables*	Olympia Dukakis *Moonstruck*
1988	*Rain Man*	Barry Levington *Rain Man*	Dustin Hoffman *Rain Man*	Jodie Foster *The Accused*	Kevin Kline *A Fish Called Wanda*	Geena Davis *The Accidental Tourist*
1989	*Driving Miss Daisy*	Oliver Stone *Born on the Fourth of July*	Daniel Day-Lewis *My Left Foot*	Jessica Tandy *Driving Miss Daisy*	Denzel Washington *Glory*	Brenda Fricker *My Left Foot*
1990	*Dances With Wolves*	Kevin Costner *Dances With Wolves*	Jeremy Irons *Reversal of Fortune*	Kathy Bates *Misery*	Joe Pesci *Goodfellas*	Whoopi Goldberg *Ghost*
1991	*The Silence of the Lambs*	Jonathan Demme *The Silence of the Lambs*	Anthony Hopkins *The Silence of the Lambs*	Jodie Foster *The Silence of the Lambs*	Jack Palance *City Slickers*	Mercedes Ruehl *The Fisher King*
1992	*Unforgiven*	Clint Eastwood *Unforgiven*	Al Pacino *Scent of a Woman*	Emma Thompson *Howard's End*	Gene Hackman *Unforgiven*	Marisa Tomei *My Cousin Vinny*
1993	*Schindler's List*	Steven Spielberg *Schindler's List*	Tom Hanks *Philadelphia*	Holly Hunter *The Piano*	Tommy Lee Jones *The Fugitive*	Anna Paquin *The Piano*
1994	*Forrest Gump*	Robert Zemeckis *Forrest Gump*	Tom Hanks *Forrest Gump*	Jessica Lange *Blue Sky*	Martin Landau *Ed Wood*	Dianne Wiest *Bullets Over Broadway*
1995	*Braveheart*	Mel Gibson *Braveheart*	Nicolas Cage *Leaving Las Vegas*	Susan Sarandon *Dead Man Walking*	Kevin Spacey *The Usual Suspects*	Mira Sorvino *Mighty Aphrodite*
1996	*The English Patient*	Anthony Minghella *The English Patient*	Geoffrey Rush *Shine*	Frances McDormand *Fargo*	Cuba Gooding Jr *Jerry Maguire*	Juliette Binoche *The English Patient*
1997	*Titanic*	James Cameron *Titanic*	Jack Nicholson *As Good As It Gets*	Helen Hunt *As Good As It Gets*	Robin Williams *Good Will Hunting*	Kim Basinger *L A Confidential*
1998	*Shakespeare in Love*	Steven Spielberg *Saving Private Ryan*	Roberto Benigni *La vita é bella/Life is Beautiful*	Gwyneth Paltrow *Shakespeare in Love*	James Coburn *Affliction*	Judi Dench *Shakespeare in Love*

1999

Best picture	*American Beauty*
Best Director	Sam Mendes *American Beauty*
Best Actor	Kevin Spacey *American Beauty*
Best Actress	Hilary Swank *Boys Don't Cry*
Best Supporting Actor	Michael Caine *Cider House Rules*
Best Supporting Actress	Angelina Jolie *Girl, Interrupted*
Best Original Screenplay	Alan Ball *American Beauty*
Best Adapted Screenplay	John Irving Bill *Cider House Rules*
Best Foreign Film	*All About My Mother* (Spain)
Best Cinematography	Conrad Hall *American Beauty*
Best Film Editing	Zach Staenberg *The Matrix*
Best Art Direction	Rick Heinrichs and Peter Young *Sleepy Hollow*
Best Costume Design	Lindy Hemming *Topsy-Turvy*
Best Dramatic Score	John Corigliano *The Red Violin*
Best Original Song	Phil Collins 'You'll Be In My Heart' from *Tarzan*
Best Make-up	Christine Blundell and Trefor Proud *Tospy-Turvy*
Best Sound	John Reitz, Gregg Rudloff, David Campbell, and David Lee *The Matrix*
Best Sound Effects Editing	Dane A Davis *The Matrix*
Best Visual Effects	John Gaeta, Janek Sirrs, Steve Courtley, and Jon Thum *The Matrix*
Best Documentry Feature	*One Day in September*
Best Documentry/short Subject	*King Gimp*
Best Live-Action Short Film	*My Mother Dreams the Satan's Disciples in New York*
Best Animated Short Film	*The Old Man and the Sea*
Honorary Award	Andrzej Wajda
Irving G Thalberg Award	Warren Beatty

Berlin Film Festival

This international film festival has been held every year in Berlin since 1950.

2000

Award	**Winner**
Golden Bear (Best Film)	*Magnolia* (USA)
Silver Bear (Jury Grand Prize)	*The Road Home* (China)
Silver Bear for Best Director	Milos Forman *Man On The Moon* (USA)
Silver Bear for Best Actress	Bibiana Beglau and Nadja Uhl *Die Stille Nach Dem Schuss/The Legends of Rita* (Germany)
Silver Bear for Best Actor	Denzel Washington *The Hurricane* (USA)
Silver Bear Jury Prize	*The Million Dollar Hotel* (Germany) directed by Wim Wenders
The AGIOCA 'Blue Angel' Prize	*Die Stille Nach Dem Schuss/The Legends of Rita* (Germany) directed by Volker Schlöndorff
Alfred Bauer Prize for a Debut Film	*Dokuritsu Shonen Gasshoudan/Boy's Choir* (Japan) directed by Akira Ogata
Silver Bear for an Outstanding Achievement	The cast of *Paradiso: Sieben Tage Mit Sieben Frauen/Paradiso: Seven Days With Seven Women* (Germany) directed by Rudolf Thome
Silver Bear for Best Short Film	*Hommage à Alfred Lepetit/Homage to Alfred Lepetit* (France) directed by Jean Rousselot

(continued)

Berlin Film Festival (*continued*)

Award	Winner
Silver Bear Jury Prize for Short Films	*Media* (Czech Republic) directed by Pavel Koutsky
Golden Bear for Lifetime Achievement	Jean Moreau
Silver Bear for Lifetime Contribution to the Art of Cinema	Robert de Niro

Cannes Film Festival

This international film festival is held every May in Cannes, France. The first festival was held in 1947. The main award is the Palme d'Or (known as the Grand Prix prior to 1955) for best film. Awards for supporting performances were introduced in 1979.

1990–99

Year	Palme d'Or for Best Film
1990	*Wild at Heart* (USA)
1991	*Barton Fink* (USA)
1992	*The Best Intentions* (Sweden)
	The Piano (New Zealand/Australia)
1993	*Farewell, My Concubine* (Hong Kong/ China)
1994	*Pulp Fiction* (USA)
1995	*Underground* (Bosnia-Herzegovina)
1996	*Secrets and Lies* (UK)
1997	*The Eel/Unagi* (Japan)
	The Taste of Cherries (Iran)
1998	*Mia Eoniotita Ke Mia Mera/Eternity and A Day* (Greece)
1999	*Rosetta* (Belgium)

2000

Award	Winner(s)
Palme d'Or for Best Film	*Dancer in the Dark* Lars Von Trier (Denmark)
Grand Jury Prize	*Guizi Lai Le/Devils on the Doorstep* Jianf Wen (China)
Best Director	Edward Yang *Yi Yi* (Taiwan)
Best Female Performance	Björk *Dancer in the Dark* (Denmark)
Best Male Performance	Tony Leung Chi-Wai *In the Mood for Love* (Hong Kong)
Best Screenplay	John C Richards and James Flamberg *Nurse Betty* (USA)
Jury Prize	(co-winners) *Takhté Siah/Blackboards* Samira Makhmalbaf (Iran) and *Sanger Fran Andra Vaningen/The Second Floor* Roy Andersson (Sweden)
Camera d'Or	(co-winners) *Zamani baraye masti asbha/A Time for Drunken Horses* Bahman Ghobadi (Iran) and *Djomeh* Hassan Yektapanah (Iran)
Grand Prix Technique de la CST (technical prize)	*In the Mood for Love* Christopher Doyle, Mark Li Ping Bing, and William Chang Suk-Ping (Hong Kong)

Short films

Award	Winner(s)
Palme d'Or	*Anino* Raymond Red (USA)
Cinefondation, First Prize	*Five Feet High and Rising* Peter Sollett (USA)

Golden Globe Awards for Motion Pictures

The Golden Globe Awards are presented annually, in January, by the Hollywood Foreign Press Association for motion pictures released during the previous calendar year.

2000

Award	Winner(s)
Motion Picture (Drama)	*American Beauty*
Motion Picture (Musical or Comedy)	*Toy Story 2*
Actor in a Motion Picture (Drama)	Denzel Washington *The Hurricane*
Actress in a Motion Picture (Drama)	Hilary Swank *Boys Don't Cry*
Actor in a Motion Picture (Comedy)	Jim Carrey *Man on the Moon*
Actress in a Motion Picture (Comedy)	Janet McTeer *Tumbleweeds*
Supporting Actor in a Motion Picture	Tom Cruise *Magnolia*
Supporting Actress in a Motion Picture	Angelina Jolie *Girl, Interrupted*
Director	Sam Mendes *American Beauty*
Foreign Language Film	*All About My Mother* (Spain)
Screenplay	Alan Ball *American Beauty*
Original Score	Ennio Morricone *The Legend of 1900*
Original Song	Phil Collins 'You'll be in My Heart' from *Tarzan*
Cecil B DeMille Award for Lifetime Achievement	Barbra Streisand

London Film Critics' Circle Awards (ALFS)

These awards of the London Film Critics' Circle have been awarded annually since 1980. The Critics' Circle has existed since 1913; its members are the leading critics from Britain's national newspapers and magazines, together with reviewers from television and radio. The ALFS are held in aid of the National Society for the Prevention of Cruelty to Children (NSPCC).

1993–98

Year	Film of the Year
1993	*The Piano* (New Zealand/Australia)
1994	*Schindler's List* (USA)
1995	*Babe* (Australia)
1996	*Fargo* (USA)
1997	*L A Confidential* (USA)
1998	*Saving Private Ryan* (USA)

1999

Award	Winner(s)
Director of the Year	Sam Mendes *American Beauty*
Actor of the Year	Kevin Spacey *American Beauty*

(*continued*)

London Film Critics' Circle Awards (ALFS) *(continued)*

Award	Winner(s)
Actress of the Year	Annette Bening *American Beauty*
Screenwriter of the Year	Alan Ball *American Beauty*
Film of the Year	*American Beauty* (USA)
British Film of the Year	*East is East*
British Producer of the Year	Leslee Udwin *East is East*
British Director of the Year	Lynne Ramsay *The Ratcatcher*
British Screenwriter of the Year	Ayub Khan Din *East is East*
British Actor of the Year	Jeremy Northam *Happy Texas, An Ideal Husband, The Winslow Boy*
British Actress of the Year	Emily Watson *Angela's Ashes*
British Newcomer of the Year	Martha Fiennes *Onegin* (Director)
Best British Actor in a Supporting Role	Michael Caine *Little Voice*
Best British Actress in a Supporting Role	Lynn Redgrave *Gods and Monsters*
Best Foreign Language Film	*All About My Mother* (Spain)
The Dilys Powell Award for Outstanding Achievement	Mike Leigh

Venice Film Festival

International film festival held annually in September, in Venice, Italy.

1999

Award	Winner
Golden Lion for the Best Film	*Yi Ge Bu Neng Shao/Not One Less* Zhang Yimou (China)
Special Jury Prize	*Le vent nous emportera/The Wind Will Carry Us* Abbas Kiarostami (France/Iran)
Special Award for Film Direction	Zhang Yuan *Guo Nian Hui Jia/Seventeen Years* (Italy/China)
Volpi Cup for Best Male Lead Performance	Jim Broadbent *Topsy Turvy* (UK)
Volpi Cup for Best Female Lead Performance	Nathalie Baye *Une Liaison pornografique/A Pornographic Affair* (Belgium/France/Luxembourg)
Marcello Mastroianni Award (for best young new actor)	Nina Proll *Nordrand* (Austria)
Gold Medal	*Rien á faire* Marian Vernoux (France)
'Corto-Cortissimo' Silver Lion (short film)	*Portrait of a Young Man Drowning* Teboto Mahlatsi (South Africa)
Luigi de Laurentiis Prize (for a first film)	Giovanni Davide Maderna *Questo é il giardino/This Is the Garden* (Italy)
Golden Lion for Lifetime Achievement	Jerry Lewis

Evening Standard Drama Awards

These UK annual drama awards are sponsored by the *Evening Standard* newspaper and are awarded in November.

1989–98

Year	Best Play	Best Musical	Best Comedy
1989	*Ghetto*	*Miss Saigon*	*Henceforward*
1990	*Shadowlands*	*Into the Woods*	*Man of the Moment* and *Jeffrey Bernard is Unwell* (joint award)
1991	*Dancing at Lughnasa*	*Carmen Jones*	*Kvetch*
1992	*Angels in America*	*Kiss of the Spider Woman*	*The Rise and Fall of Little Voice*
1993	*Arcadia*	*City of Angels*	*Jamais Vu*
1994	*Three Tall Women*	no award	*My Night With Reg*
1995	*Pentecost*	*Mack and Mabel*	*Dealer's Choice*
1996	*Stanley*	*Passion*	*Art*
1997	*The Invention of Love*	*Lady in the Dark*	*Closer*
1998	*Copenhagen*	*Oklahoma!*	no award

1999

Best Musical	*Spend! Spend! Spend!*
Best Actor	Stephen Dillane *The Real Thing*
Best Actress	Janie Dee *Comic Potential*
Best Director	Howard Davies *Flight* and *The Iceman Cometh*
Most Promising Playwright	Rebecca Gilman *The Glory of Living*
Best Stage Designer	Tim Hatley *Suddenly Last Summer, Sleep with Me, The Darker Face of the Earth*
Theatrical Event of the Year	*The Lion King*
Sydney Edwards Award for Best Director	Trevor Nunn, *The Merchant of Venice, Summerfolk*
Patricia Rothermere Award for services to theatre	Simon Callow and Martin Rea
Outstanding Newcomer	Eve Best, *'Tis Pity She's a Whore*

Laurence Olivier Awards

These UK theatre awards are presented annually by the Society of London Theatre.

2000 (for 1999 season)

Award	Winner
Best Actor	Henry Goodman *The Merchant of Venice*
Best Actress	Janie Dee *Comic Potential*
BBC Award for Best New Play	*Goodnight Children Everywhere* Richard Nelson
Best New Comedy	*The Memory of Water* Shelagh Stevenson
Best Director	Trevor Nunn *Summerfolk, The Merchant of Venice,* and *Troilus and Cressida*
Best Actor in a Musical	Simon Russell Beale *Candide*

(continued)

Laurence Olivier Awards (*continued*)

Award	Winner
Best Actress in a Musical	Barbara Dickson *Spend! Spend! Spend!*
Best Theatre Choreographer	Garth Fagan *The Lion King*
Best New Dance Production	Nederlands Dans Theater 1 *Symphony of Psalms*, Sadler's Wells
Outstanding Achievement	Peter O'Toole
Outstanding Musical Production	*Candide*
Best New Opera Production	Welsh National Opera *Hansel and Gretel*, Sadler's Wells
Radisson Edwardian Award for Best New Musical	*Honk! The Ugly Duckling*
Best Entertainment	'Defending the Caveman', Apollo
Best Supporting Actor	Roger Allam *Money*
Best Supporting Actress	Patricia Hodge *Money*
Best Supporting Performance in a Musical	Jenny Galloway *Mamma Mia!*
Best Costume Designer	Julie Taymor *The Lion King*
Best Lighting Designer	Mark Henderson *Spend! Spend! Spend!*, *The Comedy*, *Suddenly Last Summer*, *Plenty*, *The Forest*, *The Lion, the Witch, and the Wardrobe*, and others
Best Set Designer	Rob Howell *Richard III*, *Troilus and Cressida*, and *Vassa*
Outstanding Achievement in Dance	Jiri Kylian (Nederlands Dans Theater 1)
Outstanding Achievement in Opera	English National Opera

BAFTA Awards

Introduction

UK film and television awards, presented annually in March for the previous year. The British Academy of Film and Television Arts was formed in 1959 as a result of the amalgamation of the British Film Academy (founded in 1948) and the Guild of Television Producers (founded in 1954). Film and television awards are presented for both production and performance categories.

BAFTA Film Awards

1989–99

Year	Best Film
1989	*The Last Emperor* (USA)
1990	*Dead Poets Society* (USA)
1991	*Goodfellas* (USA)
1992	*The Commitments* (UK)
1993	*Howard's End* (UK)
1994	*Schindler's List* (USA)
1995	*Four Weddings and a Funeral* (UK)
1996	*Sense and Sensibility* (UK)
1997	*The English Patient* (USA)
1998	*The Full Monty* (UK)
1999	*Shakespeare in Love* (USA/UK)

2000

Best Film	*American Beauty* (USA)
Best Director	Pedro Almodovar *All About My Mother*
Best Actress	Annette Bening *American Beauty*
Best Actor	Kevin Spacey *American Beauty*
Best Supporting Actress	Maggie Smith *Tea with Mussolini*
Best Supporting Actor	Jude Law *The Talented Mr Ripley*
Best Foreign Film	*Todo Sobre Mi Madre/All About My Mother* (Spain)
Best Original Screenplay	Charlie Kaufman *Being John Malkovich*
Best Adapted Screenplay	Neil Jordan *The End of the Affair*
The Alexander Korda Award for the Outstanding British Film of the Year	*East is East*
The Orange Audience Award	*Notting Hill*
Music	Thomas Newman *American Beauty*
Newcomer	Lynne Ramsay, director, *Ratcatcher*
Cinematography	Conrad L Hall *American Beauty*
Production Design	Rick Heinrichs *Sleepy Hollow*
Costume Design	Colleen Atwood *Sleepy Hollow*
Short Animated Film	*The Man with Beautiful Eyes*
Editing	Tariq Anwar/Christopher Greenbury *American Beauty*
Special Effects	*The Matrix* John Gaeta, Steve Courtley, Janek Sirrs, Jon Thum
Sound	*The Matrix* David Lee, John Reitz, Gregg Rudloff, David Campbell, Dane A Davis
Make-up/Hair	Christine Blundell *Topsy-Turvy*
Short Film	*Who's My Favourite Girl*
The Academy Fellowships	Michael Caine; Stanley Kubrick
The Michael Balcon Award for Outstanding British Contribution to Cinema	Joyce Herlihy

BAFTA Television Awards

2000

Award	Winner	Channel
Best Actress	Thora Hird *Lost for Words*	ITV
Best Actor	Michael Gambon *Wives and Daughters*	BBC1

(*continued*)

BAFTA Television Awards (*continued*)

Award	Winner	Channel
Best Entertainment Performance	Graham Norton *So Graham Norton*	Channel 4
Best Comedy Performance	Caroline Aherne *The Royle Family*	BBC2
The Richard Dimbleby Award for the Best Presenter (factual, features and news)	Jeremy Paxman *Newsnight*	BBC2
Best Single Drama	Mark Redhead, Paul Greengrass *The Murder of Stephen Lawrence*	ITV
Best Drama Series	*The Cops*	BBC2
Lew Grade Award (voted by readers of the *Radio Times*)	*A Touch of Frost*	ITV
Best Soap	*Eastenders*	BBC1
Best Drama Serial	*Warriors*	BBC1
Best Factual Series or Strand	*The Mayfair Set*	BBC2
Best Entertainment (programme or series)	*Robbie the Reindeer: Hooves of Fire*	BBC1
Best Comedy (programme or series)	*The League of Gentlemen*	BBC2
Situation Comedy Award	*The Royle Family*	BBC1
Best Feature	*Blood on the Carpet*	BBC2
The Huw Weldon Award for the Best Arts Programme or Series	*This is Modern Art*	Channel 4
News and Current Affairs Journalism	Coverage of the Kosovo conflict	BBC1
Sport	*Test Cricket*	Channel 4
Innovation	*Walking With Dinosaurs*	BBC1
The Flaherty Documentary Award	*Divorce Iranian Style*	Channel 4
Academy Fellowship	Peter Bazalgette	
The Alan Clarke Award for Creative Contribution to Television	Peter Krominsky	
The Dennis Potter Award	Tony Marchant	
Special Award	Honor Blackman, Joanna Lumley, Diana Rigg, Linda Thorson *The Avengers* (series)	

BAFTA Interactive Entertainment Awards

These awards were launched in 1998 to acknowledge outstanding achievement in interactive entertainment. The awards, which are presented annually in October, are open to all formats, including Web sites, CD-ROM, interactive television, and console-based work.

1999

Award	Winner
The Best UK Developer Award	RARE Ltd
The Berners-Lee Award for Best Personal Contribution by a British Individual	Toby Gard and Paul Douglas
The News and Magazine Award	BBC News Online (publisher: BBC News; developer: BBC News Online; format: Web site)
The E-zine Award	The Birdguides Web site (publisher: The Red Green & Blue Company Ltd; developer: BirdGuides Ltd; format: Web site)
The Factual Award	CNN.COM/COLDWAR (publisher: CNN Interactive; developer: CNN Interactive; format: Web site)
The Children's Award	NODDY™ – Let's Get Ready For School (publisher: BBC Multimedia; developer: Absolute Studios; format: CD-ROM)
The Learning Award	Masters of the Elements (publisher: Tivola Electronic Publishing; developer: Ijsfontein, Amsterdam; format: CD-ROM)
The Entertainment Web Site Award	Jamba (publisher: Carlton Online Ltd; developer: Carlton Online Ltd; format: Web site)
The Innovative Game Award/The Games Award/The Interactivity Award/The Computer Programming Award	The Legend of Zelda: Ocarina of Time (publisher: Nintendo; developer: Nintendo; format: Nintendo 64)
The Moving Images Award	Driver (publisher: GT Interactive Software; developer: reflections; format: PSX)
The Sound Award	GTA: London 1969 (publisher: Rockstar Games; developer: Rockstar Games; format: CD-ROM)
The Design Award	WIP3OUT™ (publisher: Sony Computer Entertainment Europe; developer: Psygnosis, Leeds Studio; format: PSX)

Media

British Comedy Awards

These awards are presented annually in December with the Writers' Guild of Great Britain, and are for the best comedy on television, radio, film, and stage.

1999

Award	Winner
Top TV Comedy Actor	Ricky Tomlinson *The Royle Family*
Top TV Comedy Actress	Caroline Aherne *The Royle Family*
Top Comedy Entertainment Personality	Paul Merton
Top Male Comedy Newcomer	Sacha Baron Cohen (Ali G)
Top Female Comedy Newcomer	Jessica Stevenson *The Royle Family*
Top Stand-Up Comedian	Bill Bailey
Best New TV Comedy	*Dinnerladies*
Best 'Broken Comedy' Show	*Big Train*

(*continued*)

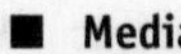

British Comedy Awards *(continued)*

Award	Winner
Best Comedy Gameshow	*Have I Got News For You*
Best Comedy Talk Show	*So Graham Norton*
Best TV Sitcom	*The Royle Family*
Best TV Comedy Drama	*Cold Feet*
Cockburn's Best Comedy Film	*Notting Hill*
Top International Comedy Show	*The Larry Sanders Show*
Best Comedy Entertainment Programme	*Comic Relief 1999*
Best Radio Comedy	*The Sunday Format*
The People's Choice Award	*Cold Feet*
Writers' Guild of Britain Lifetime Achievement Award	Barry Humphries and The Two Ronnies (Ronnie Corbett and Ronnie Barker)

Broadcasting Press Guild Television and Radio Awards

These UK media awards were established in 1974 and are presented annually in March for programmes of the previous year.

1999

Award	Winner
Best Entertainment	*Bremner, Bird & Fortune* (Channel 4)
Best Documentary Series	*Walking With Dinosaurs* (BBC1)
Best Single Drama	*Warriors* (BBC Films in association with Deep Indigo Productions for BBC1)
Best Actress	Justine Waddell *Wives and Daughters* (BBC1)
Best Actor	Tony Doyle *Ballykissangel* (BBC1) and *Four Fathers* (ITV)
Best Single Documentary	*The Boer War* (BBC2)
Best Performer (Non-Acting)	Chris Tarrant *Who Wants To Be A Millionaire?* (Celador for ITV)
Radio Programme of the Year	*Late Junction* (BBC Radio 3)
Radio Broadcaster of the Year	Melvyn Bragg *In Our Time* and *The Routes of English* (BBC Radio 4)
Best Drama Series/Serial	*Wives and Daughters* (BBC1)
Writer's Award	Stephen Poliakoff *Shooting the Past* (BBC2)
Multichannel Award	*Nick News* (Wised Up Productions for Nickelodeon UK)
Harvey Lee Award for Outstanding Contribution to Broadcasting	Cilla Black

Royal Television Society Awards

These awards began in 1964 (as the Geoffrey Parr Awards, renamed in 1988) and are presented in recognition of excellence in television for the previous year. The Programme awards are given in March, the Journalism awards in May, and Sports awards in April.

1999

Award	Winner
Programme	
Situation Comedy and Comedy Drama	*People Like Us* (BBC Production for BBC2)
Entertainment	*The League of Gentlemen* (BBC Production for BBC2)
Children's Drama	*See How They Run* (BBC Production in association with ABC Australia for BBC1)
Children's Factual	*Nick News* (Wised Up Productions for Nickelodeon UK)
Actor Male	Michael Gambon *Wives and Daughters* (BBC Production for BBC1)
Actor Female	Thora Hird *Lost for Words* (Yorkshire Television in association with Bard Entertainments for ITV)
Documentary Series	*The Decision* (A Windfall Production for Channel 4 Television)
Single Documentary	*Malcolm and Barbara – A Love Story* (Granada Television)
Presenter	Johnny Vaughan *The Big Breakfast* (Planet 24 for Channel 4 Television)
Drama Series	*The Cops* (World Productions for BBC2)
Single Drama	*Warriors* (BBC Films in association with Deep Indigo Productions for BBC1)
Drama Serial	*Shooting the Past* (TalkBack Productions for BBC2)
Arts	*This Is Modern Art* (Oxford TV Productions for Channel 4)
Television Performance	Rory Bremner *Bremner, Bird, & Fortune* (Vera Productions for Channel 4 Television)
Team	*Walking With Dinosaurs* (BBC Production for BBC1)
Documentary Strand	*Horizon* (BBC Production for BBC2)
Regional Documentary	*Spinners and Loser* (Scottish Television)
Regional Programme	*Nuts and Bolts* (HTV)
Regional Presenter	Roy Nobel (*Common Ground/The Shed* Presentable Productions for BBC Wales)
Features: Daytime	*Show Me The Money* (Princess Productions for Channel 4 Television)
Features: Primetime	*1900 House* (Wall to Wall Television for Channel 4 Television)
Network Newcomer Behind the Screen	David Wolstencroft, writer of *Psychos* (A Kudos Production for Channel 4 Television)
Network Newcomer On Screen	Jamie Oliver *The Naked Chef* (Optomen Television for BBC2)
Writer's Award	Caroline Aherne and Craig Cash *The Royle Family* (Granada Television for BBC1)
Cyril Bennet Judges' Award	Peter Symes
Gold Medal	BSkyB
Journalism	
News Award, International	*Nine O'Clock News: Dili Indonesia* (BBC News)
News Award, Home	*Channel 4 News: The Paddington Crash & Its Causes* (ITN for Channel 4 Television)
Regional Daily News Magazine	*Looking North* (BBC North East and Cumbria)
News Event Award	*Kosovo Liberation Day* (Sky News)
Interviewer of the Year	Tim Sebastian (BBC News)
Regional Current Affairs	*Soho Bombing: London Tonight Special* (London News Network)
Television Journalist of the Year	John Simpson (BBC News)
Young Journalist of the Year	Matthew Price (BBC Newsround)

(continued)

Royal Television Society Awards *(continued)*

Award	Winner
Current Affairs Award, International	*Prime Suspects: Dispatches* (Hard Cash for Channel 4 Television)
Current Affairs Award, Home	*Why Stephen?: Black Britain Special* (BBC News)
Judges' Award	Michael Brunson (ITN)
Specialist Journalism	Susan Watts (BBC News)
Sports	
Sports News	*Olympic Corruption* (Channel 4 News ITN)
Live Outside Broadcast Coverage of the Year	*Test Cricket* (Channel 4 Television)
Sports Presenter	Jim Rosenthal (ITV Sport)
Sports Commentator	Peter Alliss (BBC Sport)
Sports Documentary	*Clash of the Titans: Benn v Eubank* (BBC Television)
Sports Pundit	Martin Brundle (ITV Sport)
Sports Innovation	*Cheltenham: Sky Sports Active/Interactive Football* (Sky Sports)
Sports Programme of the Year: Actuality	*Scotland v England* (Sky Sports)
Sports Programme of the Year: Entertainment	*Sports Personality of the Century* (BBC Sport)
Regional Sports News	*Dougie Walker: Reporting Scotland* (BBC Scotland Sport)
Regional Sports Documentary	*Working Class Hero: Neil Jenkins* (BBC Wales)
Regional Sports Programme of the Year: Actuality	*Friday Sportscene* (BBC Scotland Sport)
Regional Sports Programme of the Year: Entertainment	*Offside* (BBC Scotland Sport)
Regional Sports Presenter or Commentator	Jonathan Wills (London News Network)
Television Image of the Year	*F1: British Grand Prix Live: Michael Schumacher Crash* (ITV)
Television Sports Award of the Year	*Test Cricket* (Channel 4 Television)
Judges' Award	Bill McLaren

Emmy Awards: Primetime

These are annual US television awards for primetime programmes. They are announced in September for the previous television season.

1999

Award	Winner(s)
Comedy Series	*Ally McBeal*
Drama Series	*The Practice*
Miniseries	*Horatio Hornblower*
Made for Television Movie	*A Lesson Before Dying*
Lead Actor in a Comedy Series	John Lithgow *Third Rock from the Sun*
Lead Actress in a Comedy Series	Helen Hunt *Mad About You*
Lead Actor in a Drama Series	Dennis Franz *NYPD Blue*
Lead Actress in a Drama Series	Edie Falco *The Sopranos*
Supporting Actor in a Comedy Series	David Hyde Pierce *Frasier*
Supporting Actress in a Comedy Series	Kristen Johnston *Third Rock from the Sun*
Supporting Actor in a Drama Series	Michael Baladucco *The Practice*
Supporting Actress in a Drama Series	Holland Taylor *The Practice*
Lead Actor in a Miniseries or Movie	Stanley Tucci *Winchell*
Lead Actress in a Miniseries or Movie	Helen Mirren *The Passion of Ayn Rand*
Supporting Actor in a Miniseries or Movie	Peter O'Toole *Joan of Arc*
Supporting Actress in a Miniseries or Movie	Anne Bancroft *Deep in My Heart*
Guest Actor in a Comedy Series	Mel Brooks *Mad About You*
Guest Actress in a Comedy Series	Tracey Ullman *Ally McBeal*
Guest Actor in a Drama Series	Edward Hermann *The Practice*
Guest Actress in a Drama Series	Debra Monk *NYPD Blue*
Children's Program	*The Truth About Drinking: The Teen Files*
Non-Fiction Special	*Thug Life in DC*
Non-Fiction Series	*The American Experience* and *American Masters*
Outstanding Commercial	*New Friend*, snap.com

Sony Radio Awards

These UK awards are given in recognition of excellence in radio broadcasting.

2000

Award	Winner
Event Award	*The Open* (BBC Radio 5 Live)
Feature Award	*Out of the Darkness: the Triumph of Nelson Mandela* (BBC Radio 4)
'Music Special' Award	*For Your Ears Only* (BBC Radio 2)
Specialist Music Award	*Worldwide with Gilles Peterson* (BBC Radio 1)
Entertainment Award	*Jon & Andy* (103.2 Power FM)
Comedy Award	*Blue Jam* (BBC Radio 1)
Speech Award	*The Evacuation: the True Story* (BBC Radio 4)
Sports Award	*Super Sunday* (GLR News for GLR)
Drama Award	*Plum's War* (BBC Radio 4)
News Award	*Late Night Live* (BBC Radio 5 Live)
News and Talk Broadcaster Award	Roger Phillips (BBC Radio Merseyside)
Station of the Year (audience up to 500,000)	BBC Radio Foyle
Station of the Year (audience 500,000 to 12 million)	Kiss 100
Station of the Year (UK audience)	Classic FM

(continued)

Sony Radio Awards (*continued*)

Award	Winner
Station Sound Award	Classic FM
Breakfast Music Award	*Bam Bam Breakfast* (Kiss 100)
Breakfast News and Talk Award	*The Morning Programme* (BBC Radio Foyle)
Interactive Award	*On the Ball* (BBC Scotland)
Public Service Award	BBC Music Entertainment for BBC Radio 1
Short Form Award	*Woman's Hour* (BBC Radio 4)
Competition Award	*Jon's Australian Experience* (Heart 106.2)
Music Broadcaster Award	Pete Tong (BBC Radio 1)
Music Presentation Award (audience 500,000 to 12 million)	*Bam Bam Breakfast* (Kiss 100)
Music Presentation Award (UK audience)	*Jonathan Ross Show* (BBC Radio 2)

British Press Awards

When first awarded in 1963, these UK press awards were called the Hannen Swaffer National Press Awards; the present name was adopted in 1975. The awards are now sponsored by several major newspaper groups and are widely regarded as the 'Oscars' of the British newspaper industry. The categories of awards vary for each year.

2000

Award	Winner	Award	Winner
National Newspaper of the Year	*The Sunday Telegraph*	Critic of the Year	Richard Dorment *The Daily Telegraph*
Team Reporting Award	*The Sunday Times* Kosovo	Young Journalist of the Year	Nick Paton Walsh *The Observer*
Scoop of the Year	Archer quits *News of the World*	Interviewer of the Year	Nigel Farndale *The Sunday Telegraph Magazine*
Front Page of the Year	The eclipse *The Sun*	Cartoonist of the Year	Matt Pritchett *The Daily Telegraph*
Reporter of the Year	Nick Davies *The Guardian*	Photographer of the Year	Ian Torrence *Daily Record/Freeland*
Specialist Reporter of the Year	Lorraine Fraser *The Mail on Sunday*	Sports Photographer of the Year	Richard Pelham *The Sun*
Foreign Reporter of the Year	John Swain *The Sunday Times*	Supplement of the Year	*M* magazine, *The Mirror*
Sports Reporter of the Year	Matt Dickinson *The Times*	Financial Journalist of the Year	Ben Laurance *The Observer*
Business Journalist of the Year	Hugo Dixon ex-*Financial Times* now breakingviews.com	On-Line News Service Awards	Guardian Unlimited/*The Guardian*
Feature Writer of the Year	Ann Treneman *The Times*	Cudlipp Award	Hold Ye Front Page *The Sun*
Columnist of the Year	Brian Reade *The Mirror*	Gold Award	Harold Evans

Clio Advertising Awards

Begun in 1959, Clio is the world's largest advertising awards competition.

1999 Hall of Fame

Advertiser/Product/Service	Advertisement title	Agency
Maxell Audio Tapes	*Israelites*	HHCL & Partners, London
Little Caesars	*Focus Group*	Cliff Freeman & Partners, New York
British Airways	*Surprise, Surprise*	Saatchi & Saatchi, London
Volkswagen	*Changes*	BMP DDB, London
Orange Tango Soft Drink	*Slap (Orangeman)*	HHCL & Partners, London
John Smith's Bitter	*Penguins*	BMP DDB, London
John Smith's Bitter	*Two Words*	BMP DDB, London

Webby Awards

The Webby Awards have been presented annually in May since 1997 by the International Academy of Digital Arts to recognize some of the very best among the Internet's Web sites. The public can also vote for their favourite Web sites. In 2000, over 130,000 votes were cast in The Webby Awards' People's Voice Campaign.

Category	Webby Award	People's Voice Award
Activism	Ad Busters http://www.adbusters.org/	The Hunger Site http://www.hungersite.com/
Arts	Web Stalker http://www.backspace.org/iod/iod4Winupdates.html	SFMOMA Presents Bill Viola http://www.sfmoma.org/EXHIB/viola/frsplash.html
Commerce	BabyCenter http://www.babycenter.com/	Amazon http://www.amazon.com
Community	Café Utne http://cafe.utne.com/cafe/	Slashdot http://slashdot.org/
Education	Merriam-Websters Word Central http://www.wordcentral.com	Merriam-Websters Word Central http://www.wordcentral.com
Fashion	Paul Smith http://www.paulsmith.co.uk/	toddoldham.com http://www.toddoldham.com
Film	Atom Films http://www.atomfilms.com	The Internet Movie Database http://www.imdb.com/
Finance	Gomez.com http://www.gomez.com	PayPal http://www.paypal.com/
Games	GameSpy Industries http://www.gamespy.com/	shockwave.com http://www.shockwave.com/
Health	Thrive Online http://thriveonline.com/	InteliHealth http://www.intelihealth.com/

(continued)

Webby Awards (*continued*)

Category	Webby Award	People's Voice Award
Kids	Scholastic.com http://www.scholastic.com	Scholastic.com http://www.scholastic.com
Living	Epicurious http://www.epicurious.com/	Blue Mountain Arts http://bluemountain.com
Music	Napster http://www.napster.com/	Napster http://www.napster.com/
News	Jim Romensko's MediaNews http://www.medianews.org/	ABCNEWS.com http://www.abcnews.go.com/
Politics and law	Politics.com http://www.politics.com/	FindLaw http://www.findlaw.com/
Print and zines	Nerve http://www.nerve.com/	Slashdot http://slashdot.org/
Radio	Lost and Found Sound http://www.lostandfoundsound.com/	BBC Radio 1 http://www.bbc.co.uk/radio1/
Science	The Cave of Lascaux http://www.culture.fr/culture/arcnat/lascaux/en	Monterey Bay Aquarium http://www.mbayaq.org/
Sports	ESPN http://www.espn.com/	ESPN http://www.espn.com/
Technical achievement	Google http://www.google.com/	Google http://www.google.com/
Travel	Outside Online http://www.outsidemag.com/	Discovery Travel Channel http://travel.discovery.com/
TV	MSNBC http://www.msnbc.com/	CNN.com http://www.cnn.com/

Literature

Booker Prize

This is the UK's most prestigious literary prize, and one which invariably produces controversy and debate from the moment the short-list is announced. The prize of £20,000 is awarded annually in October.

Year	Winner	Awarded for
1991	Ben Okri	*The Famished Road*
1992	Barry Unsworth	*Sacred Hunger*
	Michael Ondaatje	*The English Patient*
1993	Roddy Doyle	*Paddy Clarke Ha Ha Ha*
1994	James Kelman	*How Late It Was, How Late*
1995	Pat Barker	*The Ghost Road*
1996	Graham Swift	*Last Orders*
1997	Arundhati Roy	*The God of Small Things*
1998	Ian McEwan	*Amsterdam*
1999	J M Coetzee	*Disgrace*

Pulitzer Prizes in Letters: Fiction

The Pulitzer Prizes were endowed by Joseph Pulitzer (1847–1911), the Hungarian-born US newspaper publisher. The prizes have been awarded since 1917 by Columbia University in New York City on the recommendation of the Pulitzer Prize Board.

Year	Winner	Awarded for
1990	Oscar Hijuelos	*The Mambo Kings Play Songs of Love*
1991	John Updike	*Rabbit at Rest*
1992	Jane Smiley	*A Thousand Acres*
1993	Robert Olen Butler	*A Good Scent From a Strange Mountain*
1994	E Annie Proulx	*The Shipping News*
1995	Carol Shields	*The Stone Diaries*
1996	Richard A Ford	*Independence Day*
1997	Steven Millhauser	*Martin Dressler: The Tale of an American Dreamer*
1998	Philip Roth	*American Pastoral*
1999	Michael Cunningham	*The Hours*
2000	Jhumpa Lahiri	*Interpreter of Maladies*

Impac Prize

Founded in 1996, and with a cash award of £103,000, this is the world's most valuable book prize for a single work of fiction. The selection process is unique among literary awards in that the winner is chosen from nominations sent in by municipal libraries around the world. The inaugural ceremony took place in Dublin, Ireland in May 1996.

Year	Winner	Awarded for
1996	David Malouf	*Remembering Babylon*
1997	Javier Marias	*A Heart so White*
1998	Herta Müller	*The Land of Green Plums*
1999	Anderew Miller	*Ingenious Pain*
2000	Nicola Barker	*Wide Open*

Guardian First Book Award

In 2000 the UK literary prize for books published in 1999 chosen by the literary editor and book reviewers of *The Guardian* newspaper was changed from *The Guardian* Fiction Award to *The Guardian* First Book Award. It now includes both fiction and non-fiction. The award is £10,000, and the winner will also be able to endow the school of their choice with £1,000 in books.

Year	Winner	Awarded for
1999	Philip Gourevitch	*We Wish to Inform You That Tomorrow We Will be Killed With Our Families*

Mail on Sunday/John Llewellyn Rhys Prize

Inaugurated in memory of the writer John Llewellyn Rhys, this prize is awarded to a citizen of the Commonwealth younger than 35 by the time of publication, for the most promising literary work of the previous year. It has been awarded annually since 1942. The winner receives a cash prize of £5,000.

Year	Winner	Awarded for
1995	Melanie McGrath	*Motel Nirvana*
1996	Nicola Barker	*Heading Inland*
1997	Phil Whitaker	*Eclipse of the Sun*
1998	Peter Ho Davies	*The Ugliest House in the World*

Nestlé Smarties Book Prize

The Smarties Book Prize aims to encourage British authors to achieve higher standards of writing for children in three age groups. The prize was established in 1985 and is awarded annually in November.

1999

Category	Winner	Awarded for
9–11 years	J K Rowling	*Harry Potter and the Prisoner of Azkaban*
6–8 years	Laurence Anholt; illustrations by Arthur Robins	*Snow White and the Seven Aliens*
0–5 years	Julia Donaldson; illustrations by Axel Scheffler	*The Gruffalo*

Prix Goncourt

Founded in 1903, this French literary award is presented annually in November by the Académie Goncourt for the best French novel of the year. The prize is a nominal 50 FF plus a lifelong annuity of 250 FF per year.

Year	Winner	Awarded for
1990	Jean Rouault	*Les Champs d'Honneur*
1991	Pierre Combescot	*Les Filles du Calvaire*
1992	Patrick Chamoisean	*Texaco*
1993	Amin Maalouf	*Le Rocher de Tanios*
1994	Didier van Cauwelaert	*Un Aller Simple*
1995	Andréï Makine	*Le Testament Français*
1996	Pascale Roze	*Le Chasseur Zéro*
1997	Patrick Rambeau	*La Bataille*
1998	Paule Constant	*Confidence pour confidence*
1999	Jean Echenoz	*Je m'en vais*

Whitbread Literary Award Book of the Year

Whitbread, the UK brewing, food, and leisure company, first endowed this literary award in 1971. Winners of five categories (Novel, Biography, Children's Novel, First Novel, and Poetry) are announced in November each year, and the overall winner (The Book of the Year) is awarded the £21,000 prize the following January.

Year	Winner	Awarded for
1990	Nicholas Mosley	*Hopeful Monsters*
1991	John Richardson	*A Life of Picasso*
1992	Jeff Torrington	*Swing Hammer Swing!*
1993	Joan Brady	*Theory of War*
1994	William Trevor	*Felicia's Journey*
1995	Kate Atkinson	*Behind the Scenes at the Museum*
1996	Seamus Heaney	*The Spirit Level*
1997	Ted Hughes	*Tales from Ovid*
1998	Ted Hughes	*Birthday Letters*
1999	Seamus Heaney	*Beowulf*

WHSmith Thumping Good Read Award

UK annual award of £5,000 presented to the best new fiction author of the year. Founded in 1992 by the WHSmith group, the award is judged by a panel of WHSmith customers.

Year	Winner	Awarded for
1994	Dominick Dunne	*A Simple Plan*
1995	Thomas Edison	*St Agnes Stand*
1996	Andrew Klavan	*True Crime*
1997	David Baldacci	*Absolute Power*
1998	Douglas Kennedy	*The Big Picture*
1999	Lee Child	*Die Trying*
2000	Boris Starling	*Storm*

Forward Poetry Prizes

The Forward Poetry Prizes were established in 1992 and are awarded annually in October. Awards for the three categories are £10,000 for Best Collection; £5,000 for Best First Collection; and £1,000 for Best Single Poem.

1999

Category	Winner	Awarded for
Best Collection	Jo Shapcott	*My Life Asleep*
Best First Collection	Nick Drake	*The Man in the White Suit*
Best Single Poem	Robert Minhinnick	*Twenty Five Laments for Iraq*

Orange Prize

The Orange Prize is a UK literary prize open only to women, of any nationality. It was established in 1996 with a cash award of £30,000.

Year	Winner	Awarded for
1996	Helen Dunmore	*A Spell of Winter*
1997	Anne Michaels	*Fugitive Pieces*
1998	Carol Shields	*Larry's Party*
1999	Suzanne Berne	*A Crime in the Neighborhood*
2000	Linda Grant	*When I Lived in Modern Times*

WHSmith Literary Award

The WHSmith Literary Award is given to a Commonwealth or UK citizen for a UK-published book. The award was established in 1959 and is presented each March with a cash prize of £10,000.

Year	Winner	Awarded for
1991	Derek Walcott	*Omeros*
1992	Thomas Pakenham	*The Scramble for Africa*
1993	Michèle Roberts	*Daughters of the House*
1994	Vikram Seth	*A Suitable Boy*
1995	Alice Monro	*Open Secrets*
1996	Simon Schama	*Landscape and Memory*
1997	Orlando Figes	*A People's Tragedy*
1998	Ted Hughes	*Tales from Ovid*
1999	Beryl Bainbridge	*Master Georgie*
2000	Melvyn Bragg	*The Soldier's Return*

Poets Laureate of the UK

The Poet of the British royal household is so called because of the laurel wreath awarded to eminent poets in the Greco-Roman world. There is a stipend of £70 a year, plus £27 in lieu of the traditional butt of sack (cask of wine). The 1999 appointment was, for the first time, on a paid, ten-year tenure, rather than a life appointment.

Appointed	Poet Laureate
1668	John Dryden (1631–1700)
1689	Thomas Shadwell (c 1642–1692)
1692	Nahum Tate (1652–1715)
1715	Nicholas Rowe (1674–1718)
1718	Laurence Eusden (1688–1730)
1730	Colley Cibber (1671–1757)
1757	William Whitehead (1715–1785)
1785	Thomas Warton (1728–1790)
1790	Henry James Pye (1745–1813)
1813	Robert Southey (1774–1843)
1843	William Wordsworth (1770–1850)
1850	Alfred, Lord Tennyson (1809–1892)
1896	Alfred Austin (1835–1913)
1913	Robert Bridges (1844–1930)
1930	John Masefield (1878–1967)
1968	Cecil Day Lewis (1904–1972)
1972	Sir John Betjeman (1906–1984)
1984	Ted Hughes (1930–1998)
1999	Andrew Motion (1952–)

Music

Brit Awards

These are among the UK's most prestigious popular music awards. They are run by the British Phonographic Industry; committee members come from major and independent record companies, publishing and retail sectors, the publicity industry, the media, retailers, promoters, the black music industry, and the Music Publishers' Association.

1994–99

Year	Best Group	Best Newcomer	Best Album	Best Single
1994	Stereo MCs	Gabrielle	Stereo MCs *Connected*	Take That 'Pray'
1995	Blur	Oasis	Blur *Parklife*	Blur 'Parklife'
1996	Oasis	Supergrass	Oasis *(What's the Story) Morning Glory?*	Take That 'Back for Good'
1997	Manic Street Preachers	Kula Shaker	Manic Street Preachers *Everything Must Go*	Spice Girls 'Wannabe'
1998	The Verve	Stereophonics	The Verve *Urban Hymns*	All Saints 'Never Ever'
1999	The Verve	Manic Street Preachers	Manic Street Preachers *This Is My Truth, Tell Me Yours*	Robbie Williams 'Angels'

2000

Award	Winner
Best British Group	Travis
Best British Newcomer	S Club 7
Best British Album	Travis *The Man Who*
Best British Single	Robbie Williams 'She's The One'
Best British Male Solo Artist	Tom Jones
Best British Female Solo Artist	Beth Orton
Best International Newcomer	Macy Gray
Best International Group	TLC
Best International Male Solo Artist	Beck
Best International Female Solo Artist	Macy Gray
Best British Dance Act	Chemical Brothers
Best British Video	Robbie Williams 'She's The One'
Best Soundtrack/Cast Recording	*Notting Hill*
Outstanding Contribution to British Music	The Spice Girls

Eurovision Song Contest

First staged in Switzerland in 1956, the event is now transmitted in 30 countries to an estimated audience of over 100 million. Eurovision is actually the name given to the Europe-wide TV distribution network run by the European Broadcasting Union (EBU). The competition is restricted to members of the EBU, which currently includes 23 countries.

2000

Winner	Song
Joergen and Niels Olsen (Denmark)	'Fly on the Wings of Love'
UK entry (16th place)	
Nicki French	'Don't Play That Song Again'

World Music Awards

These awards are presented annually and are chosen by the International Federated Phonograph Industry.

2000

Category	Winner
National awards for World's best-selling artists or groups	
African artist	Femi Kuti
American group	Backstreet Boys
Arabic artist/group	Taha, Kahled, Faudel
Asian artist	Hikaru Utada
Australian artist	Tina Arena
British artist/group	Jamiroquai
French artist/group	Notre-Dame de Paris
German artist	Lou Bega
German group	Modern Talking
Irish artist	Ronan Keating
Italian artist/group	Eiffel 65
Latin artist	Ricky Martin
Russian artist	Kristina Orbakaite
Scandinavian artist/group	Roxette
Swiss artist	DJ Bobo
Legend awards	
Best-selling Pop male artist of the millennium	Michael Jackson
Best-selling Pop female artist of the millennium	Mariah Carey

(continued)

Mercury Music Prize

This annual music prize is one of the UK's most prestigious arts prizes. Established in 1992, it is sponsored by Mercury Communications and supported by both the BPI (British Phonographic Industry) and BARD (British Association of Record Dealers). All ten shortlisted artists are presented with Shortlist Trophies before the overall winner is announced. The winner receives £25,000.

1999

Albums of the Year

Chemical Brothers *Surrender*
Blur *13*
Beth Orton *Central Reservation*
Underworld *Beaucoup Fish*
Manic Street Preachers *This Is My Truth Tell Me Yours*
Faithless *Sunday 8pm*
Stereophonics *Performance and Cocktails*
Black Star Liner *Bengali Bantam Youth Experience*
Talvin Singh *OK*
Kate Rusby *Sleepless*
Denys Baptiste *Be Where You Are*
Thomas Ades *Asyla*

Overall Winner

Talvin Singh *OK*

World Music Awards *(continued)*

Category awards for world's best-selling artists and groups

Pop, male artist	Ricky Martin
Pop, dance, R&B group	Backstreet Boys
Pop, female artist	Britney Spears
New female artist	Christina Aguilera
New male artist	Lou Bega
Reggae artist/group	Funkstar de Luxe

Gramophone Awards

These UK classical music awards have been given since 1977. The awards have various sponsors each year. (– = not applicable.)

Lifetime achievement award 1995–98

1995	Michael Tippett
1996	Yehudi Menuhin
1997	Mstislav Rostropovich
1998	Menahem Pressler

1999

Award	Composer	Work	Artist(s)	Conductor	Record label
Baroque Vocal	A Scarlatti	*Il primo omicidio*	René Jacobs	–	Harmonia Mundi HMC90 1649/50
Baroque Instrumental	Jacquet de la Guerre	*Premiére livre*	Carole Cerasi	–	Metronome METCD1026
Chamber	Robert Schumann	*Piano Trios*	Florestan Trio	–	Hyperion CDA67063
Concerto	Frédéric Chopin	*Piano concertos*	Martha Argerich	Charles Dutoit	EMI CDC5 56798-2
Contemporary	Toru Takemitsu	*Quotation of Dream*	Knussen	–	DG 493 495-2GH
Early Music	Guillaume Dufay	*Missa*	Jacobi Binchois Consort	Andrew Kirkman	Hyperion CDA66997
Editor's Choice Award	Naxos's British Music series	–	–	–	–
Instrumental	–	'Live at Carnegie Hall'	Arcadi Volodos	–	Sony Classical SK60893
Opera	Antonín Dvoák	*Rusalka*	–	Charles Mackerras	Decca 460 568-2DH03
Orchestral	Anton Bruckner	*Symphony No 4*	–	Günter Wand	RCA 09026 68839-2
Solo Vocal	Ludwig van Beethoven	*Lieder*	Stephan Genz; Vignoles	–	Hyperion CDA6705
Record of the Year (in association with B&W)	Antonín Dvoák	*Rusalka*	–	Charles Mackerras	Decca 460 568-2DH03
Twentieth-Century Orchestral	Edgar Varése	*Complete Orchestral Works*	–	Riccardo Chailly	Decca 460 208-2DH2
Twentieth-Century Concerto	Maurice Ravel	*Piano Concertos*	Krystian Zimmerman	Pierre Boulez	DG 449 213-2GH
Twentieth-Century Instrumental	Luciano Berio	*Sequenzas*	various artists	–	DG 457 038-2GH3
Twentieth-Century Chamber	Elliott Carter	*String Quartets*	Arditti Quartet	–	Auvidis MO782091
Twentieth-Century Vocal	Hanns Eisler	*Hollywood Songbook*	Goerne; Schneider	–	Decca 460 582-2DH
Twentieth-Century Opera	Carl Nielsen	*Maskarade*	–	Ulf Schirmer	Decca 460 227-2DH02
Recital	–	'I Want Magic!'	René Fleming; Levine	–	Decca 460 567-2DH
Artist of the Year	Martha Argerich				
Special Achievement	Philip's Great Pianists of the 20th Century				
Lifetime Achievement	Isaac Stern				

MTV Video Music Awards

These awards are announced in September for current year.

1999

Award	Winner
Video of the Year	Lauryn Hill 'Doo Wop (That Thing)'
Best Male Video	Will Smith 'Miami'
Best Female Video	Lauryn Hill 'Doo Wop (That Thing)'
Best Group Video	TLC 'No Scrubs'
Best Rap Video	Jay-Z (featuring Ja Rule and Amil-Lion) 'Can I Get A.'
Breakthrough Video	Fatboy Slim 'Praise You'
Best Direction in a Video	Fatboy Slim 'Praise You'
Best New Artist in a Video	Eminem 'My Name Is'
Best Video from a Film	Aerosmith 'I Don't Want to Miss A Thing'
Best R&B Video	Lauryn Hill 'Doo Wop (That Thing)'
Best Rock Video	Korn 'Freak on a Leash'
Best Hip Hop Video	Beastie Boys 'Intergalactic'
Best Pop Video	Ricky Martin 'Livin' La Vida Loca'
Best Dance Video	Ricky Martin 'Livin' La Vida Loca'
Best Cinematography in a Video	Marilyn Manson 'The Dope Show'
Best Editing in a Video	Korn 'Freak on a Leash' (director Jonas Akerlund)
Best Choreography in a Video	Fatboy Slim 'Praise You'
Best Special Effects in a Video	Garbage 'Special'
Best Art Direction in a Video	Lauryn Hill 'Doo Wop (That Thing)'
Viewers' Choice	Backstreet Boys 'I Want It That Way'

Grammy Awards

Introduction

US annual music awards which are for outstanding achievement in the record industry for the previous year. The gold-plated disks are presented by the National Academy of Recording Arts and Sciences. The first Grammy Awards were for records released in 1958.

Grammy Awards

2000 (for releases in 1999)

Category	**Winner**
Song of the Year	Itaal Shur and Rob Thomas, songwriters, Santana featuring Rob Thomas 'Smooth'
Album of the Year	Santana *Supernatural*
Record of the Year	Santana 'Smooth'
New Artist	Christina Aguilera
Female Pop Vocal Performance	Sarah McLachlan 'I Will Remember You'
Male Pop Vocal Performance	Sting 'Brand New Day'
Pop Duo or Group Performance	Santana 'Maria Maria'
Best Dance Recording	Cher 'Believe'
Best Pop Album	Sting *Brand New Day*
Alternative Music Performance	Beck 'Mutations'
Rock Song	Red Hot Chili Peppers 'Scar Tissue'
Rock Album	Santana *Supernatural*
Female Rock Vocal Performance	Alanis Morissette 'Sweet Child O' Mine'
Male Rock Vocal Performance	Lenny Kravitz 'American Woman'
Rock Vocal, Duo or Group Performance	Santana 'Put Your Lights On'
Hard Rock Performance	Metallica 'Whiskey In The Jar'
Metal Performance	Black Sabbath 'Iron Man'
Female R&B Vocal Performance	Whitney Houston 'It's Not Right But It's Okay'
Male R&B Vocal Performance	Barry White 'Staying Power'
R&B Duo or Group Performance	TLC 'No Scrubs'
R&B Song	TLC 'No Scrubs'
R&B Album	TLC *Fanmail*
Rap Solo Performance	Eminem 'My Name Is'
Rap Duo or Group Performance	The Roots featuring Erykah Badu 'You Got Me'
Rap Album	Eminem *The Slim Shady LP*
Female Country Vocal Performance	Shania Twain 'Man! I Feel Like A Woman!'
Male Country Vocal Performance	George Jones 'Choices'
Country Duo or Group Performance	Dixie Chicks 'Ready To Run'
Country Song	Shania Twain 'Come On Over'
Country Album	Dixie Chicks *Fly*
Best Country Instrumental Performance	Asleep At The Wheel 'Bob's Breakdowns'
Best Bluegrass Album	Ricky Skaggs and Kentucky Thunder *Ancient Tones*
Best New Age Album	Paul Winter and Friends *Celtic Solstice*
Jazz Instrumental Solo	Wayne Shorter 'In Walked Wayne'
Individual or Group Jazz Instrumental Performance	Gary Burton, Chick Corea, Pat Metheny, Roy Haynes, and Dave Holland 'Like Minds'
Best Contemporary Jazz Performance	David Sanborn 'Inside'
Best Jazz Vocal Performance	Diana Krall 'When I Look In Your Eyes'
Best Latin Jazz Performance	Poncho Sanchez 'Latin Soul'
Best Traditional Soul Gospel Album	Shirley Caesar *Christmas With Shirley Caesar*
Best Contemporary Soul Gospel Album	Steven Curtis Chapman *Speechless*
Best Latin Pop Performance	Rubén Blades 'Tiempos'
Best Traditional Blues Album	B B King *Blues On The Bayou*
Best Contemporary Blues Album	The Robert Cray Band *Take Your Shoes Off*
Best Traditional Folk Album	June Carter Cash *Press On*
Best Reggae Album	Burning Spear *Calling Rastafari*
Best World Music Album	Caetano Veloso *Livro*
Best Classical Album	*Stravinsky: Firebird; The Rite of Spring; Perséphone* Michael Tilson Thomas, conductor; Andreas Neubronner, producer; Vance George, choir director; Joyce Keil, choir director; Stuart Neill, tenor; Sharon J Paul, choir director; Ragazzi, The Peninsula Boys Choir; San Francisco Symphony Choir; San Francisco Girls Choir; Stephanie Cosserat, narrator; San Francisco Symphonia
Best Short Form Music Video	Korn 'Freak On A Leash'
Best Long Form Music Video	Jimi Hendrix 'Bands of Gypsys – Live At Fillmore East'
Lifetime Achievement	Harry Belafonte, Woodie Guthrie, John Lee Hooker, Mitch Miller, and Willie Nelson
Legend Award	Elton John

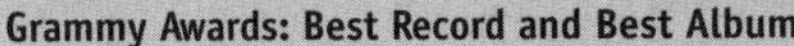

Grammy Awards: Best Record and Best Album

1989–99

Year of release	Best Record	Best Album
1989	Bette Midler 'Wind Beneath My Wings'	Bonnie Raitt *Nick of Time*
1990	Phil Collins 'Another Day in Paradise'	Quincy Jones *Back on the Block*
1991	Natalie Cole, with Nat 'King' Cole 'Unforgettable'	Natalie Cole, with Nat 'King' Cole *Unforgettable*
1992	Eric Clapton 'Tears in Heaven'	Eric Clapton *Unplugged*
1993	Whitney Houston 'I Will Always Love You'	Whitney Houston *The Bodyguard*
1994	Sheryl Crow 'All I Wanna Do'	Tony Bennett *MTV Unplugged*
1995	Seal 'Kiss from a Rose'	Alanis Morissette *Jagged Little Pill*
1996	Eric Clapton 'Change the World'	Céline Dion *Falling into You*
1997	Shawn Colvin 'Sunny Came Home'	Bob Dylan *Time Out of Mind*
1998	Céline Dion 'My Heart Will Go On'	Lauryn Hill *The Miseducation of Lauryn Hill*
1999	Santana 'Smooth'	Santana *Supernatural*

Art and Architecture

Royal Academy Summer Exhibition Awards

UK arts awards held since 1769. Awards vary in amount and are for works in different media.

2000

Award	Amount (£)	Winner
Charles Wollaston Award for the Most Distinguished Work in the Exhibition	25,000	Gerard Hemsworth for *Between Heaven and Hell* (acrylic)
Jack Goldhill Award for Sculpture	8,000 commission for a sculpture	David Nash for *Pyramid, Sphere, Cube* (oak)
Dupree Family Award for a Woman Artist (for a painting or sculpture by a woman artist)	3,500	Alison Wilding for *Hemlock 4, 2000* (hemlock, lead, pigment)

Turner Prize

Established in 1984 to encourage discussion about new developments in contemporary British art, this prize has often attracted criticism for celebrating what is not traditionally considered to be art. It is open to any British artist under 50 and has a prize of £20,000.

Year	Winner
1984	Malcolm Morley
1985	Howard Hodgkin
1986	Gilbert and George
1987	Richard Deacon
1988	Tony Cragg
1989	Richard Long
1990	no award
1991	Anish Kapoor
1992	Grenville Davey
1993	Rachel Whiteread
1994	Antony Gormley
1995	Damien Hirst
1996	Douglas Gordon
1997	Gillian Wearing
1998	Chris Ofili
1999	Steve McQueen

BP Portrait Award by the National Portrait Gallery

This is an annual art prize of £10,000 and includes, at the judges' discretion, a commission of £2,000 to paint a well-known person.

Year	Winner	Awarded for
1999	Clive Smith	Double Single

Jerwood Painting Prize

UK art prize of £30,000 presented annually in September by the Jerwood Foundation for creative excellence. Founded in 1994, the prize is open to British artists of any age.

Year	Winner
1999	Prunella Clough

John Moore's Liverpool Exhibition

Biennial painting exhibition open to any artist living or working in the UK. It consists of a £20,000 cash prize and of acquisition (by gift) of prize-winning painting by Liverpool's Walker Art Gallery. There are an additional ten prizes of £1,000 each. The prize was established in 1957 by the founder of the Littlewoods organization.

Year	Overall Winner
1998	Dan Hays

NatWest Art Prize

UK prize founded in 1990 and awarded annually in June. The prize is open to artists aged 35 or under and living, working, or studying in the UK. The winner of the top prize is awarded £26,000, and ten additional prizes of £1,000 each go to the other shortlisted artists.

Year	Winner
1999	Jason Brooks

Royal Gold Medallists of Architecture

Instituted by Queen Victoria, the Royal Gold Medal is an international prize awarded annually in March to a distinguished architect, or group of architects, for work of high merit that has in some way promoted the advancement of architecture.
In 1999, precedent was broken to award the Royal Gold Medal to a city.

Year	Winner
1960	Pier Luigi Nervi
1961	Lewis Mumford
1962	Sven Gottfrid Markelius
1963	William Holford
1964	E Maxwell Fry
1965	Kenzo Tange
1966	Ove Arup
1967	Nikolaus Pevsner
1968	Richard Buckminster Fuller
1969	Jack Antonio Coia
1970	Robert Matthew
1971	Hubert de Cronin Hastings
1972	Louis I Kahn
1973	Leslie Martin
1974	Powell and Moya
1975	Michael Scott
1976	John Summerson
1977	Denys Lasdun
1978	Jom Utzon
1979	The Office of Charles and Ray Earnes
1980	James Stirling
1981	Philip Dowson
1982	Berthold Lubetkin
1983	Norman Foster
1984	Charles Corree
1985	Richard Rogers
1986	Arata Isozaki
1987	Ralph Erskine
1988	Richard Meier
1989	Renzo Piano
1990	Aldo van Eyck
1991	Colin Stansfield Smith
1992	Peter Rice
1993	Giancarlo de Carlo
1994	Michael and Patricia Hopkins
1995	Colin Rowe
1996	Harry Seilder
1997	Tadao Ando
1998	Oscar Neimeyer
1999	Barcelona, its government, its citizens, and design professionals
2000	Frank Gehry

Source: Royal Institute of British Architects

Pritzker Architecture Prize

This US premier architecture award is named for Jay A Pritzker, president of the Hyatt Foundation which sponsors it. The award has been presented annually in April since 1979, with a $100,000 grant.

Year	Winner	Nationality
1996	José Rafael Moneo	Spanish
1997	Sverre Fehn	Norwegian
1998	Renzo Piano	Italian
1999	Norman Foster	British
2000	Rem Koolhaas	Dutch

Stirling Prize

This £20,000 prize is awarded each November by the Royal Institute of British Architects, and the winner is chosen from a regional shortlist.

Year	Winner
1995	Huddersfield's Football and Rugby Stadium by the Lobb Partnership, built by McAlpine
1996	The Centenary Building, University of Salford, by Stephen Hodder
1997	The Music School, Stuttgart by Michael Wilford
1998	American Air Museum in Britain, Imperial War Museum, Duxford Airfield by Foster and Partners
1999	NatWest Media Centre, Lord's Cricket Ground, London; architect: Future System; client: Marylebone Cricket Club; contractor: Pendennis Shipyard

SPORT

The Sporting Year

Calendar of Sporting Events October 2000–October 2001

(tbd = to be decided.)

Date	Sport	Fixture	Location
2000			
October			
1	horse racing	Prix de l'Arc de Triomphe	Longchamp, Paris, France
5–8	golf	Cisco World Matchplay Championship	Wentworth, Surrey, England
6–8	golf	Solheim Cup (Europe versus USA)	Loch Lomond, Scotland
8	motor racing	Japanese Grand Prix	Suzuka, Japan
10–15	cycling	World Road Race Championships	France
11–15	squash	British Open	National Indoor Arena, Birmingham, England
14	rugby league	Super League Championship Grand Final	Old Trafford, Manchester, England
15–19	cricket	Pakistan v England (First Test)	Lahore, Pakistan
18–29	disabled sport	Paralympic Games	Sydney, Australia
21	baseball	World Series starts	N/A
25–29	cycling	World Track Championships	Manchester, England
28 October–25 November	rugby league	World Cup	UK, Republic of Ireland, France
November			
23–26	motor racing	Network Q RAC Rally	UK
25	rugby league	World Cup Final	Old Trafford, Manchester, England
28 November–3 December	cricket	Pakistan v England (Second Test)	Faisalabad, Pakistan
December			
5	rugby union	Cambridge University v Oxford University	Twickenham, London, England
7–11	cricket	Pakistan v England (Third Test)	Karachi, Pakistan
8–10	tennis	Davis Cup Final: Spain v Australia	Spain
14–18	show jumping	Olympia International	Olympia, London, England
2001			
January			
6–14	darts	Embassy World Championships	Frimley Green, Surrey, England
15–28	tennis	Australian Open	Melbourne, Australia
28	American football	Super Bowl XXXV	Tampa (FL), USA
February			
3	rugby union	Italy v Ireland (Six Nations)	Stadio Flaminio, Rome, Italy
3	rugby union	Wales v England (Six Nations)	Millennium Stadium, Cardiff, Wales
3	rugby union	France v Scotland (Six Nations)	Stade de France, St Denis, France
17	rugby union	England v Italy (Six Nations)	Twickenham, London, England
17	rugby union	Ireland v France (Six Nations)	Lansdowne Road, Dublin, Republic of Ireland
17	rugby union	Scotland v Wales (Six Nations)	Murrayfield, Edinburgh, Scotland
22–26	cricket	Sri Lanka v England (First Test)	Galle, Sri Lanka
24	rugby union	Tetley's Bitter Cup Final	Twickenham, London, England
25	football	Worthington Cup Final	Millennium Stadium, Cardiff, Wales[1]
March			
3	rugby union	England v Scotland (Six Nations)	Twickenham, London, England
3	rugby union	Italy versus France (Six Nations)	Stadio Flaminio, Rome, Italy
3	rugby union	Wales v Ireland (Six Nations)	Millennium Stadium, Cardiff, Wales
3–11	badminton	Yonex All-England Championships	National Indoor Arena, Birmingham, England
7–11	cricket	Sri Lanka v England (Second Test)	Kandy, Sri Lanka
13–15	horse racing	Cheltenham Festival	Cheltenham, England
15–19	cricket	Sri Lanka v England (Third Test)	Colombo, Sri Lanka
17	rugby union	France v Wales (Six Nations)	Stade de France, St-Denis, France
17	rugby union	Scotland v Italy (Six Nations)	Murayfield, Edinburgh, Scotland
18	football	CIS Insurance Cup (Scottish League Cup) Final	Hampden Park, Glasgow, Scotland
23	athletics	IAAF World Cross-Country Championships	Dublin, Republic of Ireland
24	rugby union	Ireland v England (Six Nations)	Lansdowne Road, Dublin, Republic of Ireland
24	rowing	The Boat Race: Oxford University v Cambridge University	London, England
April			
5–8	golf	US Masters	Augusta National Club, Georgia, USA
7	rugby union	England v France (Six Nations)	Twickenham, London, England
7	rugby union	Italy v Wales (Six Nations)	Stadio Flaminio, Rome, Italy
7	rugby union	Scotland v Ireland (Six Nations)	Murrayfield, Edinburgh, Scotland
7	horse racing	Grand National	Aintree, Liverpool, England
21 April–7 May	snooker	Embassy World Championships	Crucible Theatre, Sheffield, England
22	athletics	London Marathon	London, England
29	rugby league	Silk Cut Challenge Cup Final	Twickenham, London, England

(continued)

Calendar of Sporting Events October 2000–October 2001 (*continued*)

Date	Sport	Fixture	Location
May			
5	horse racing	2000 Guineas	Newmarket, Suffolk, England
6	horse racing	1000 Guineas	Newmarket, Suffolk, England
3–6	equestrian	Badminton Horse Trials	Badminton, Gloucestershire, England
12	football	FA Cup Final	Millennium Stadium, Cardiff, Wales
12[2]	rugby union	Welsh Challenge Cup Final	Millennium Stadium, Cardiff, Wales
16	football	UEFA Cup Final	tbd
17–21	cricket	England v Pakistan (First Test)	Lord's, London, England
19[2]	rugby union	European Cup Final	tbd
23	football	European (Champion's League) Cup Final	tbd
26	football	Scottish Cup Final	Hampden Park, Glasgow, Scotland
31 May–4 June	cricket	England v Pakistan (Second Test)	Old Trafford, Manchester
June			
2	greyhound racing	Greyhound Derby	Wimbledon, London, England
8	horse racing	The Oaks	Epsom, Surrey, England
9	horse racing	The Derby	Epsom, Surrey, England
16–17	motor racing	Le Mans 24-Hour Race	Sarthe, France
19–22	horse racing	Royal Ascot	Ascot, England
23	cricket	NatWest Series Final	Lord's, London, England
25 June –8 July	tennis	The All-England Championships	Wimbledon, London, England
July			
4–8	rowing	Henley Royal Regatta	Henley, Oxfordshire, England
7–29	cycling	Tour de France	France
5–9	cricket	England v Australia (First Test)	Edgbaston, Birmingham, England
14	cricket	Benson and Hedges Cup Final	tbd
5[2]	motor racing	British Grand Prix	Silverstone, Northamptonshire, England
19–22	golf	British Open	Royal Lytham & St Annes, Lancashire, England
19–23	cricket	England v Australia (Second Test)	Lord's, London, England
31 July–4 August	horse racing	Glorious Goodwood	Goodwood, West Sussex, England
August			
2–6	cricket	England v Australia (Third Test)	Trent Bridge, Nottingham, England
3–12	athletics	IAAF World Championships	Edmonton, Canada
16–20	cricket	England v Australia (Fourth Test)	Headington, Leeds, England
23–27	cricket	England v Australia (Fifth Test)	The Oval, London, England
September			
1	cricket	NatWest Trophy Final	tbd
28–30	golf	Ryder Cup	The Belfry, Sutton Coldfield, England

[1] To be confirmed.
[2] Provisional date.

BBC Sports Personality of the Year

First presented in 1954. The most prestigious award for British sportsmen and sportswomen, it is based on the votes of television viewers.

Year	Winner	Sport
1989	Nick Faldo	golf
1990	Paul Gascoigne	football
1991	Liz McColgan	athletics
1992	Nigel Mansell	motor racing
1993	Linford Christie	athletics
1994	Damon Hill	motor racing
1995	Jonathan Edwards	athletics
1996	Damon Hill	motor racing
1997	Greg Rusedski	tennis
1998	Michael Owen	football
1999[1]	Lennox Lewis	boxing

[1] Muhammad Ali (USA) (boxing) was voted BBC Sports Personality of the Century.

Sports Organizations

English County Cricket Clubs

Derbyshire County Cricket Club County Cricket Ground, Nottingham Road, Derby DE21 6DA; phone: (01332) 383211; fax: (01332) 290251; Web site: www.dccc.org.uk

Durham County Cricket Club County Ground, Riverside, Chester-le-Street, County Durham DH3 3QR; phone: (0191) 387 1717; fax: (0191) 387 1616; Web site: www.durham-ccc.org.uk

Essex County Cricket Club County Ground, New Writtle Street, Chelmsford CM2 0PG; phone: (01245) 252420; fax: (01245) 254030; Web site: www.essexcricket.org.uk

Glamorgan County Cricket Club Sofia Gardens, Cardiff CF11 9XR; phone: (029) 2040 9380; fax: (029) 2040 9390; Web site: www.glamorganccc.cricket.org

Gloucestershire County Cricket Club Ltd The Royal Sun Alliance County Ground, Nevil Road, Bristol BS7 9EJ; phone: (0117) 910 8000; fax: (0117) 924 1193; Web site: www.gloscсc.co.uk

Hampshire County Cricket Club County Ground, Northlands Road, Southampton SO15 2UE; phone: (023) 8033 3788; fax: (023) 8033 0121; Web site: www.hampshire.cricket.org

Kent County Cricket Club St Lawrence Ground, Old Dover Road, Canterbury CT1 3NZ; phone: (01227) 456886; fax: (01227) 762168; Web site: www.kentcountrycricket.co.uk

Lancashire County Cricket Club Old Trafford, Manchester M16 0PX; phone: (0161) 282 4021; fax: (0161) 282 4151; Web site: www.lccc.co.uk

Leicestershire County Cricket Club County Ground, Grace Road, Leicester LE2 8AD; phone: (0116) 283 2128; (0116) 244 0363; Web site: www.leicestershireccc.co.uk

Middlesex County Cricket Club Lord's Cricket Ground, London NW8 8QN; phone: (020) 7289 1300; fax: (020) 7289 5831; Web site: www.middlesexccc.com

Northamptonshire County Cricket Club County Ground, Wantage Road, Northampton NN1 4TJ; phone: (01604) 514455; fax: (01604) 514488; Web site: www.nccc.co.uk

Nottinghamshire County Cricket Club Trent Bridge, Nottingham NG2 6AG; phone: (0115) 982 3000; fax: (0115) 945 5730; Web site: www.nottsccc.co.uk

Somerset County Cricket Club The Clerical Medical County Ground, St James's Street, Taunton TA1 1JT; phone: (01823) 272946; fax: (01823) 332395

Surrey County Cricket Club Oval, Kennington, London SE11 5SS; phone: (020) 7582 6660; fax: (020) 7735 7769; Web site: www.surreyccc.co.uk

Sussex County Cricket Club County Ground, Eaton Road, Hove BN3 3AN; phone: (01273) 827100; fax: (01273) 771549; Web site: www.sussexcricket.co.uk

Warwickshire County Cricket Club County Ground, Edgbaston, Birmingham B5 7QU; phone: (0121) 446 4422; fax: (0121) 440 7516; Web site: www.thebears.co.uk

Worcestershire County Cricket Club County Ground, New Road, Worcester WR2 4QQ; phone: (01905) 748474; fax: (01905) 748005; Web site: www.wccc.co.uk

Yorkshire County Cricket Club Headingley Cricket Ground, Leeds LS6 3BU; phone: (0113) 278 7394; fax: (0113) 278 4099; Web site: www.yorkshireccc.org.uk

English and Scottish Football Clubs

- **FA Carling Premiership Clubs**

Arsenal Arsenal Stadium, Avenell Road, Highbury, London N5 1BU; phone: (020) 7704 4000; fax: (020) 7704 4001; Web site: www.arsenal.co.uk

Aston Villa Villa Park, Trinity Road, Birmingham B6 6HE; phone: (0121) 327 2299; fax: (0121) 322 2107; Web site: www.avfc.co.uk

Bradford City Bradford & Bingley Stadium at Valley Parade, Bradford BD8 7DY; phone: (01274) 773355; fax: (01274) 773356; Web site: www.bradfordcityfc.co.uk

Charlton Athletic The Valley, Floyd Road, Charlton, London SE7 8BL; phone: (020) 8333 4000; fax: (020) 8333 4007; Web site: www.cafc.co.uk

Chelsea Stamford Bridge, Fulham Road, London SW6 1HS; phone: (020) 7385 5545; Web site: www.chelseafc.co.uk

Coventry City Highfield Road Stadium, King Richard Street, Coventry CV2 4FW; phone: (024) 7623 4000; fax: (024) 7623 4099; Web site: www.ccfc.co.uk

Derby County Pride Park Stadium, Derby DE24 8XL; phone: (01332) 202202; fax: (01332) 667540; Web site: www.dcfc.co.uk

Everton Goodison Park, Liverpool L4 4EL; phone: (0151) 330 2200; fax: (0151) 286 9112; Web site: www.evertonfc.com

Ipswich Town Portman Road, Ipswich IP1 2DA; phone: (01473) 400500; fax: (01473) 400040; Web site: www.itfc.co.uk

Leeds United Elland Road, Leeds LS11 0ES; phone: (0113) 226 6000; fax: (0113) 226 6050; Web site: www.lufc.co.uk

Leicester City City Stadium, Filbert Street, Leicester LE2 7FL; phone: (0116) 291 5000; fax: (0116) 247 0585; Web site: www.lcfc.co.uk

Liverpool Anfield Road, Liverpool L4 0TH; phone: (0151) 263 2361; fax: (0151) 260 8813; Web site: www.liverpoolfc.net

Manchester City Maine Road, Moss Side, Manchester M14 7WN; phone (0161) 232 3000; Web site: www.mcfc.co.uk

Manchester United Sir Matt Busby Way, Old Trafford, Manchester M16 0RA; phone: (0161) 868 8000; fax: (0161) 868 8863; Web site: www.manutd.com

Middlesbrough Cellnet Riverside Stadium, Middlesbrough, Cleveland TS3 6RS; phone: (01642) 877700; fax: (01642) 877840; Web site: www.mfc.co.uk

Newcastle United St James's Park, Newcastle upon Tyne NE1 4ST; phone: (0191) 201 8400; fax: (0191) 201 8600; Web site: www.nufc.co.uk

Southampton The Dell, Milton Road, Southampton SO15 2XH; phone: (028) 9022 0505; fax: (028) 9033 0360; Web site: www.sfc@saintsfc.co.uk

Sunderland Stadium of Light, Sunderland, Tyne-and-Wear SR5 1SU; phone: (0191) 551 5000; fax: (0191) 551 5123; Web site: www.sunderland-afc.com

Tottenham Hotspur 748 High Road, Tottenham, London N17 0AP; phone: (020) 8365 5000; fax: (020) 8365 5118; Web site: www.spurs.co.uk

West Ham United Boleyn Ground, Green Street, Upton Park, London E13 9AZ; phone: (020) 8548 2748; fax: (020) 8548 2758; Web site: www.westhamunited.co.uk

- **Nationwide Football League Division One Clubs**

Barnsley Oakwell Stadium, Grove Street, Barnsley, South Yorkshire S71 1ET; phone: (01226) 211211; fax: (01226) 211444; Web site: www.barnsleyfc.co.uk

Birmingham City St Andrews Stadium, Birmingham B9 4NH; phone: (0121) 772 0101; fax: (0121) 766 7866; Web site: www.bcfc.com

Blackburn Rovers Ewood Park, Blackburn BB2 4JF; phone: (01254) 698888; fax: (01254) 671042; Web site: www.rovers.co.uk

Bolton Wanderers The Reebok Stadium, Burnden Way, Lostock, Bolton BL6 6JW; phone: (01204) 673673; fax: (01204) 673773; Web site: www.bwfc.co.uk

Burnley Turf Moor, Burnley BB10 4BX; phone: (01282) 700000; fax: (01282) 700014; Web site: www.clarets.co.uk

Crewe Alexandra Gresty Road, Crewe CW2 6EB; phone: (01270) 213014; fax: (01270) 216320

Crystal Palace Selhurst Park, White Horse Lane, South Norwood, London SE25 6PU; phone: (020) 8768 6000; fax: (020) 8768 6106

Fulham Craven Cottage, Stevenage Road, London SW6 6HH; phone: (020) 7893 8383; fax: (020) 7384 4715; Web site: www.fulhamfc.co.uk

Gillingham Prestfield Stadium, Gillingham ME7 4DD; phone: (01634) 851854; fax: (01634) 850986; Web site: www.gillinghamfootballclub.com

Grimsby Town Blundell Park, Cleethorpes DN35 7PY; phone: (01472) 605050; fax: (01472) 693665; Web site: www.gtfc.co.uk

Huddersfield Town The Alfred McAlpine Stadium, Leeds Road, Huddersfield HD1 6PX; phone: (01484) 484100; fax: (01484) 484101; Web site: www.huddersfield-town.fc.co.uk

Norwich City Carrow Road, Norwich NR1 1JE; phone: (01603) 760760; fax: (01603) 613886; Web site: www.canaries.co.uk

Nottingham Forest City Ground, Nottingham NG2 5FJ; phone: (0115) 982 4444; fax: (0115) 982 4455; Web site: www.nottinghamforest.co.uk

English and Scottish Football Clubs *(continued)*

Portsmouth Fratton Park, Portsmouth PO4 8RA; phone: (023) 9273 1204; fax: (023) 9273 4129; Web site: www.pompeyfc.co.uk

Preston North End Sir Tom Finney Way, Deepdale, Preston PR1 6RU; phone: (01772) 902020; fax: (01772) 653266; Web site: www.prestonnorthend.co.uk

Queens Park Rangers Loftus Road Stadium, South Africa Road, London W12 7PA; phone: (020) 8743 0262; fax: (020) 8740 2505; Web site: www.qpr.co.uk

Sheffield United Bramall Lane Ground, Sheffield S2 4SU; phone: (0114) 221 5757; fax: (0114) 272 3030; Web site: www.bladesunited.org

Sheffield Wednesday Hillsborough, Sheffield S6 1SW; phone: (0114) 221 2121; fax: (0114) 221 2122; Web site: www.swfc.co.uk

Stockport County Edgeley Park, Hardcastle Road, Stockport, Cheshire SK3 9DD; phone: (0161) 286 8888; fax: (0161) 286 8900

Tranmere Rovers Prenton Park, Prenton Road West, Birkenhead CH42 9PN; phone: (0151) 608 4194; fax: (0151) 609 0606; Web site: www.tranmererovers.co.uk

Watford Vicarage Road Stadium, Watford WD1 8ER; phone: (01923) 496000; fax: (01923) 496001; Web site: www.watfordfc.com

West Bromwich Albion The Hawthorns, Halfords Lane, West Bromwich B71 4BR; phone: (0121) 525 8888; fax: (0121) 553 6634; Web site: www.wba.co.uk

Wimbledon Selhurst Park, South Norwood, London SE25 6PY; phone: (020) 8771 2233; fax: (020) 8268 0641; Web site: www.wimbledon-fc.co.uk

Wolverhampton Wanderers Molineaux Grounds, Wolverhampton WV1 4QR; phone: (01902) 655000; fax: (01902) 687006; Web site: www.wolves.co.uk

• Scottish Premier Division Clubs

Aberdeen Pittodrie Stadium, Pittodrie Street, Aberdeen AB24 5QH; phone: (01224) 650400; fax: (01224) 644173; Web site: www.afc.co.uk

Dundee Dens Park Stadium, Sandeman Street, Dundee DD3 7JY; phone: (01382) 826104; fax: (01382) 832284; Web site: www.dundeefc.co.uk

Dundee United Tannadice Park, Tannadice Street, Dundee DD3 7JW; phone: (01382) 833166; fax: (01382) 889398

Dunfermline Athletic East End Park, Halbeath Road, Dunfermline KY12 7RB; phone: (01383) 724295

Glasgow Celtic Celtic Park, 95 Kerrydale Street, Glasgow G40 3RE; phone: (0141) 556 2611; fax: (0141) 551 8106; Web site: www.celticfc.co.uk

Glasgow Rangers Ibrox Stadium, 150 Edminston Drive, Glasgow G51 2XD; phone: (0141) 427 8500; fax: (0870) 600 1978; www.rangers.co.uk

Heart of Midlothian Tynecastle Stadium, Tynecastle Park, Gorgie Road, Edinburgh EH11 2NL; phone: (0131) 200 7200; fax: (0131) 200 7222; Web site: www.heartsfc.co.uk

Hibernian Easter Road Stadium, 12 Albion Place, Edinburgh EH7 5QG; phone: (0131) 661 2159; fax: (0131) 652 1907; Web site: www.hibs.co.uk/home.htm

Kilmarnock Rugby Park, Rugby Road, Kilmarnock KA1 2DP; phone: (01563) 525184; fax: (01563) 522181; Web site: www.kilmarnockfc.co.uk

Motherwell Fir Park Stadium, 1–39 Fir Park Street, Motherwell ML1 2QN; phone: (01698) 333333; fax: (01698) 338001; Web site: www.motherwellfc.co.uk

St Johnstone McDiarmid Park, Crieff Road, Perth PH1 2SJ; phone: (01738) 459090; fax: (01738) 625771; Web site: www.stjohnstonefc.co.uk

St Mirren St Mirren Park, Love Street, Paisley PA3 2EJ; phone: (0141) 889 2558

English Rugby Union Clubs

Allied Dunbar Premiership Division One Clubs

Bath The Recreation Ground, 11 Argyll Street, Bath BA2 4BW; phone: (01225) 325200; fax: (01225) 325201; Web site: www.bathrugby.com

Bristol Memorial Ground, Silton Avenue, Horfield, Bristol BS7 0AQ; phone: (0117) 908 5500; fax: (0117) 907 4682; Web site: www.bristolrugby.co.uk

Gloucester Kingsholm Road, Gloucester GL1 3AX; phone: (01452) 381087; fax: (01452) 383321; Web site: www.kingsholm-chronicle.org.uk

Leicester Welford Road Ground, Aylestone Road, Leicester LE2 7TR; phone: (0116) 2541607; fax: (0116) 2854766; Web site: www.tigers.co.uk

London Irish The Avenue, Sunbury-on-Thames, Middlesex TW16 5EQ; phone: (01932) 783034; fax: (01932) 784462; Web site: www.london-irish-rugby.com

NEC Harlequins of London The Stoop Memorial Ground, Langhorn Drive, Twickenham TW2 7SX; phone: (020) 8410 6000; Web site: www.quins.co.uk

Newcastle Falcons Kingston Park, Brunton Road, Kenton Bank Foot, Newcastle upon Tyne NE13 8AF; phone: (0191) 214 5588; fax: (0191) 286 0824; Web site: www.newcastle-falcons.co.uk

Northampton Franklins' Gardens, Weedon Road, Northampton NN5 5BG; phone: (01604) 751543; fax: (01604) 599110; Web site: www.northamptonsaints.co.uk

Rotherham Clifton Lane Sports Ground, Badsley, Moor Lane, Rotherham, South Yorkshire S65 2AA; phone: (01709) 370 763

Sale Sharks Heywood Road, Brooklands, Sale, Cheshire M33 3WB; phone: (0161) 969 4917

Saracens Vicarage Road Stadium, Watford WD1 8ER; phone: (01923) 496200; (01923) 496201; Web site: www.saracens.com

Wasps Loftus Road Stadium, South Africa Road, London W12 7PA; phone: (020) 8743 0262; fax: (020) 8740 2505; Web site: www.qpr.co.uk

Welsh-Scottish League Clubs

Bridgend Brewery Field, Tondu Road, Bridgend, Mid Glamorgan CF31 4JE; phone: (01656) 652707; fax: (01656) 656829; Web site: www.bridgendrfc.com

Caerphilly Virginia Park, Virginia View, Caerphilly, Mid Glamorgan CF83 3JA; phone: (029) 2086 5077; fax: (029) 2086 7593; Web site: www.caerphillyrfc.co.uk

Cardiff Cardiff Arms Park, Westgate Street, Cardiff CF10 1JA; phone: (029) 2030 2000; (029) 2030 2001

Dunvant Club House, Broadacre, Killay, Swansea, West Glamorgan SA2 7RU; phone: (01792) 207291; fax: (01792) 297444

Ebbw Vale Eugene Cross Park, Pontygof, Ebbw Vale, Gwent NP23 5AZ; phone: (01495) 302995; fax: (01495) 306814; Web site: www.ebbwvalerfc.co.uk

Llanelli Stradey Park, Llanelli, Dyfed, SA15 4BT; phone: (01554) 783900; fax: (01554) 783901; Web site: www.scarlet.co.uk

Neath The Gnoll, Courage Gnoll Park Road, Neath, West Glamorgan SA11 3BU; phone: (01639) 769660; fax: (01639) 769661; Web site: www.neathrfc.co.uk

Newport Rodney Parade, Newport, Gwent NP20 0UU; phone: (01633) 670690; fax: (01633) 670714

Pontypridd Club House, Sardis Road, Pontypridd, Mid Glamorgan CF37 1 HA; phone: (01443) 405006; fax: (01443) 407087; Web site: www.pontypriddrfc.com

Swansea St Helen's Ground, Bryn Road, Swansea, West Glamorgan SA2 0AR; phone: (01792) 424242; fax: (01792) 424240; Web site: www.swanseafc.co.uk

Rugby League Super League Clubs

Bradford Bulls Odsal Stadium, Bradford BD6 1BS; phone: (01274) 733899; fax: (01274) 724730; Web site: www.bradfordbulls.co.uk

Castleford Tigers The Jungle, Wheldon Road, Castleford WF10 2SD; phone: (01977) 552674; fax: (01977) 518007; Web site: www.tigers.teamtalk.com

Halifax Blue Sox The New Pavilion, Shay Stadium, Shay Sike, Halifax HX1 2YS; phone: (01422) 342792; fax: (01422) 349607; Web site: www.bluesox.co.uk

Huddersfield and Sheffield Giants Alfred McAlpine Stadium, Stadium Way, Leeds Road, Huddersfield HD1 6PG; phone: (01484) 530710; fax: (01484) 531712; Web site: www.giantsonline.co.uk

Hull Rugby League Football Club The Boulevard, Airlie Street, Hull HU3 3JD; phone: (01482) 327200; fax: (01482) 587002; Web site: www.hullfc.com

Leeds Rhinos St Michael's Lane, Headingley, Leeds LS6 3BR; phone: (0113) 278 6181; fax: (0113) 275 4284; Web site: www.leedsrugby.com

London Broncos The Valley, Floyd Road, Charlton SE7 8BL; phone: (020) 8410 5000; fax: (020) 8853 8801; Web site: www.londonbroncos.co.uk

St Helens Dunriding Lane, St Helens, Merseyside, WA10 4AD; phone: (01744) 23697; fax: (01744) 451302; Web site: www.saint.uk.com

Salford City Reds The Willows, Willows Road, Salford M5 2FQ; phone: (0161) 737 6363; fax: (0161) 745 8072; Web site: www.reds.co.uk

Wakefield Trinity Belle Vue, Doncaster Road, Wakefield, West Yorkshire WF1 5HT; phone: (01924) 211611; fax: (01924) 382130; Web site: www.trinitywildcats.co.uk

Warrington Wolves Wilderspool Stadium, Fletcher Street, Warrington WA4 6PY; phone: (01925) 635338; fax: (01925) 571744; Web site: www.wwrlfc.co.uk

Wigan Warriors JJB Stadium, Loire Drive, Robin Park, Wigan WN5 0UH; phone: (01942) 231321; fax: (01942) 214880; Web site: www.wigan-warriors.co.uk

Sports Organizations in the UK

- **Sports councils**

Central Council of Physical Recreation Francis House, Francis Street, London SW1P 1DE; phone: (020) 7828 3163; fax: (020) 7630 7046

Sport England 16 Upper Woburn Place, London WC1H 0QP; phone: (020) 7273 1500; fax: (020) 7383 5740; Web site: www.english.sports.gov.uk

Scottish Sports Council Caledonia House, South Gyle, Edinburgh EH12 9DQ; phone: (0131) 317 7200; fax: (0131) 317 7202; Web site: www.sportsscotland.org.uk

Sports Council for Northern Ireland House of Sport, Upper Malone Road, Belfast BT9 5LA; phone: (028) 9038 1222; fax: (028) 9068 2757; Web site: www.sportscouncil-ni.org.uk

Sports Council for Wales Sophia Gardens, Cardiff CF11 9SW; phone: (029) 2030 0500; fax: (029) 2030 0600; Web site: www.sports-council-wales.co.uk

UK Sports Council Walkden House, 10 Melton Street, London NW1 2EB; phone: (020) 7380 8000; (020) 7380 8005; Web site: www.uksport.gov.uk

- **American football**

World League of American Football 97–99 King's Road, London SW3 4PA; phone: (020) 7225 3070; fax: (020) 7376 5070; Web site: www.nfleurope.com

- **Angling**

National Federation of Anglers Halliday House, Eggington Junction, Near Hitton, Derbyshire DE65 6GU; phone: (01283) 734735; fax: (01283) 734799; Web site: www.fire.org.uk/nfa

- **Archery**

Grand National Archery Society National Agricultural Centre, 7th Street, Stoneleigh, Kenilworth, Warwickshire CV8 2LG; phone: (024) 7669 6631; fax: (024) 7641 9662; Web site: www.gnas.org

- **Athletics**

UK Athletics 10 Harborne Road, Birmingham B15 3AA; phone: (0121) 456 5098; fax: (0121) 456 8752; Web site: www.ukathletics.org

- **Badminton**

Badminton Association of England Ltd National Badminton Centre, Bradwell Road, Loughton Lodge, Milton Keynes MK8 9LA; phone: (01908) 268400; fax: (01908) 268412; Web site: www.baofe.co.uk

Scottish Badminton Union Cockburn Centre, 40 Bogmoor Place, Glasgow G51 4 TQ; phone: (0141) 445 1218; fax: (0141) 425 1218; Web site: www.scotbadminton.demon.co.uk

Welsh Badminton Union Fourth Floor, 3 Westgate Street, Cardiff CF10 1DP; phone: (029) 2022 2082; (029) 2039 4282; Web site: www.welshbadminton.force9.uk

- **Baseball**

British Baseball Federation Ariel House, 74a Charlotte Street, London W1P 1LR; phone: (020) 7453 7040; fax: (020) 7453 7007; Web site: www.bbf.org

- **Basketball**

English Basketball Association 48 Bradford Road, Stanningley, Leeds LS28 6DF; phone: (0113) 236 1166; fax: (0113) 236 1022; Web site: www.basketballengland.org.uk

Scottish Basketball Association Caledonia House, South Gyle, Edinburgh EH12 9DQ; phone: (0131) 317 7260; fax: (0131) 317 7489; Web site: www.bastketball-scotland.com

- **Billiards and snooker**

World Professional Billiards and Snooker Association 27 Oakfield Road, Clifton, Bristol BS8 2AT; phone: (0117) 974 4491; fax: (0117) 974 4931

- **Bobsleigh**

British Bobsleigh Association Albany House, 5 High Street, Salisbury SP1 2PH; phone and fax: (01985) 850064

- **Bowls**

British Isles Bowling Council 2 Pentland Avenue, Gorkshill, Gorebridge EH23 4PG; phone: (01875) 821105

- **Boxing**

Amateur Boxing Association of England Ltd Crystal Palace National Sports Centre, London SE19 2BB; phone: (020) 8778 0251; fax: (020) 8778 9324

British Amateur Boxing Association 91 High Street, Lochee, Dundee DD2 2AY; phone: (01382) 611412; no fax or Web site

British Boxing Board of Control Ltd Jack Petersen House, 52A Borough High Street, London SE1 1XN; phone: (020) 7403 5879; fax: (020) 7378 6670; Web site: www.dspace.dial.pipex.com/bbbc/

- **Canoeing**

British Canoe Union John Dudderidge House, Adbolton Lane, West Bridgford, Nottingham NG2 5AS; phone: (0115) 982 1100; fax: (0115) 982 1797; Web site: www.bcu.org.uk

- **Chess**

British Chess Federation 9A Grand Parade, St Leonards-on-Sea, East Sussex TN38 0DD; phone: (01424) 442500; fax: (01424) 718372; Web site: www.bcf.ndirect.co.uk

- **Cricket**

England and Wales Cricket Board Lord's Cricket Ground, London NW8 8QZ; phone: (020) 7432 1200; fax: (020) 7289 5619; Web site: www.lords.org

MCC Lord's Cricket Ground, London NW8 8QN; phone: (020) 7289 1611; fax: (020) 7289 9100; Web site: www.lords.org

- **Croquet**

Croquet Association c/o The Hurlingham Club, Ranelagh Gardens, London SW6 3PR; phone and fax: (020) 7736 3148; Web site: www.croquet.org.uk

- **Cycling**

British Cycling Federation National Cycling Centre, Stuart Street, Manchester M11 4DQ; phone: (0161) 230 2301; fax: (0161) 231 0591; Web site: www.bcf.com

- **Darts**

British Darts Organization 2 Pages Lane, Muswell Hill, London N10 1PS; phone: (020) 8883 5544; fax: (020) 8883 0109

- **Equestrianism**

British Equestrian Federation National Agricultural Centre, Stoneleigh Park, Kenilworth, Warwickshire CV8 2RH; phone: (024) 7669 8871; fax: (024) 7669 6484; Web site: www.bef.co.uk

- **Fencing**

British Fencing Association 1 Baron's Gate, 33–35 Rothschild Road, London W4 5HT; phone: (020) 8742 3032; fax: (020) 8742 3033; Web site: www.britishfencing.com

- **Football, association**

The Football Association 16 Lancaster Gate, London W2 3LW; phone: (020) 7262 4542; fax: (020) 7402 0486; Web site: www.the-fa.org.uk

Sports Organizations in the UK (*continued*)

Football Association of Wales Plymouth Chambers, 3 Westgate Street, Cardiff CF10 1DP; phone: (029) 2037 2325; fax: (029) 2034 3961; Web site: www.citypages.co.uk/faw/

The Football League Ltd Edward VII Quay, Navigation Way, Preston PR2 2YF; phone: (01772) 325800; fax: (01772) 325801; Web site: www.football-league.co.uk

The Football Supporters' Association PO Box 11, Liverpool L26 1XP; phone: (0151) 709 2594

Irish Football Association 20 Windsor Avenue, Belfast BT9 6EE; phone: (028) 9066 9458; fax: (028) 9066 7620; Web site: www.irishfa.com

Irish Football League 96 University Street, Belfast BT7 1HE; phone: (028) 9024 2888; fax: (028) 9033 0773

Scottish Football Association 6 Park Gardens, Glasgow G3 7YF; phone: (0141) 332 6372; fax: (0141) 332 7559; Web site: www.scottishfa.co.uk

Scottish Football League 188 West Regent Street, Glasgow G2 4RY; phone: (0141) 248 3844; fax: (0141) 221 7450; Web site: www.scottishfootball.com

Women's Football Association 16 Lancaster Gate, London W2 3LW; phone: (020) 7262 4542; fax: (020) 7402 0486; Web site: www.the-fa.org

• General

British Olympic Association No. 1 Wandsworth Plain, London SW18 1EH; phone: (020) 8871 2677; fax: (020) 8871 9104; Web site: www.olympics.org.uk

British Paralympic Association Impact House, Room 514, 2 Edridge Road, Croydon, Surrey CR9 1PJ; phone: (020) 8681 9655; fax: (020) 8681 9650

• Gliding

British Gliding Association Kimberley House, 47 Vaughan Way, Leicester LE1 4SE; phone: (0116) 253 1051; fax: (0116) 251 5939; Web site: www.gliding.co.uk

• Golf

Royal and Ancient Golf Club of St Andrews Golf Place, St Andrews, Fife KY16 9JD; phone: (01334) 472112; (01334) 477580; Web site: www.randa.org

European Golf Tour Wentworth Drive, Virginia Water, Surrey GU25 4LX; phone: (01344) 842881; fax: (01344) 840500; Web site: www.europeantour.com

Ladies European Tour The Tytherington Club, The Old Hall, Macclesfield, Cheshire SK10 2LQ; phone: (01625) 611444; fax: (01625) 610406; Web site: www.ladieseuropeantour.com

• Greyhound racing

National Greyhound Racing Club Ltd Twyman House, 16 Bonny Street, London NW1 9QD; phone: (020) 7267 9256; fax: (020) 7482 1023

• Gymnastics

British Gymnastics Association Ford Hall, Lilleshall National Sports Centre, Newport, Shropshire TF10 9NB; phone: (01952) 820330; fax: (01952) 820326; Web site: www.baga.co.uk

• Hockey

The Hockey Association The Stadium, Silbury Boulevard, Milton Keynes MK9 1HA; phone: (01908) 689290; fax: (01908) 241106; Web site: www.hockeyonline.org

• Horse racing

British Horse Racing Board 42 Portman Square, London W1H 0EN; phone: (020) 7396 0011; fax: (020) 7935 3626; Web site: www.bhb.co.uk

The Jockey Club 42 Portman Square, London W1H 0EN; phone: (020) 7486 4921; fax: (020) 7935 8703; Web site: www.thejockeyclub.co.uk

• Ice hockey

Ice Hockey UK The Galleries of Justice Shire Hall, High Pavement, Lace Market, Nottingham NG1 1HN; phone: (0115) 915 9204; fax: (0115) 915 1376; Web site: www.icehockeyuk.co.uk

• Ice skating

National Ice Skating Association of the UK Ltd 114–116 Curtain Road, London EC2A 3AH; phone: (020) 7613 1188; fax: (020) 7739 2445; Web site: www.iceskating.org.uk

• Judo

British Judo Association 7A Rutland Street, Leicester LE1 1RB; phone: (0116) 255 9669; fax: (0116) 255 9660; Web site: www.britishjudo.org.uk

• Lacrosse

English Lacrosse Association 4 Western Court, Bromley Street, Digbeth, Birmingham B9 4AN; phone: (0121) 773 4422; fax: (0121) 753 0042; Web site: www.englishlacrosse.co.uk

• Martial arts

English Karate Governing Body 53 Windmill Balk Lane, Doncaster DN6 7SF; Web site: www.ekgb.org.uk

• Motor sports

Auto-Cycle Union ACU House, Wood Street, Rugby, Warwickshire CV21 2YX; phone: (01788) 540519; fax: (01788) 573585; Web site: www.acu.org.uk

RAC Motor Sports Association Ltd Motorsports House, Riverside Park, Colnbrook, Slough SL3 0HG; phone: (01753) 681736; fax: (01753) 682938; Web site: www.msauk.org.uk

• Mountaineering

British Mountaineering Council 177–179 Burton Road, West Didsbury, Manchester M20 2BB; phone: (0161) 445 4747; fax: (0161) 445 4500; Web site: www.thebmc.co.uk

• Netball

All England Netball Association Ltd Netball House, 9 Paynes Park, Hitchin, Hertfordshire SG5 1EH; phone: (01462) 442344; fax: (01462) 442343; Web site: www.england-netball.co.uk

Northern Ireland Netball Association House of Sport, Upper Malone Road, Belfast BT9 5LA; phone: (01232) 381222; fax: (01232) 682757; Web site: www.sportscouncil.ni.org.uk

Scottish Netball Association 24 Ainslie Road, Hillington Business Park, Hillington, Glasgow G52 4RU; phone: (0141) 570 4016; fax: (0141) 570 4017

Welsh Netball Association 33–35 Cathedral Road, Cardiff CF11 9HB; phone: (029) 2023 7048; fax: (029) 2022 6430

• Orienteering

British Orienteering Federation Riversdale, Dale Road North, Darley Dale, Matlock, Derbyshire DE4 2HX; phone: (01629) 734042; fax: (01629) 733769; Web site: www.cix.co.uk/~bof

• Polo

The Hurlingham Polo Association Manor Farm, Little Cox Well, Faringdon SN7 7LW; phone: (01367) 242848; fax: (01367) 242829; Web site: www.hpa-polo.co.uk

• Rackets and real tennis

Tennis and Rackets Association c/o The Queen's Club, Palliser Road, London W14 9EQ; phone: (020) 7386 3447/8; fax: (020) 7385 7424

• Rifle shooting

National Rifle Association Bisley Camp, Brookwood, Woking, Surrey GU24 0PB; phone: (01483) 797777; fax: (01483) 797285; Web site: www.nra.org.uk

• Rowing

Amateur Rowing Association Ltd The Priory, 6 Lower Mall, London W6 9DJ; phone: (020) 8748 3632; fax: (020) 8741 4658; Web site: www.ara-rowing.org

Henley Royal Regatta Regatta Headquarters, Henley-on-Thames, Oxfordshire RG9 2LY; phone: (01491) 572153; fax: (01491) 575509; Web site: www.regatta.rowing.org.uk/HRR.htm

Scottish Amateur Rowing Association 18 Daniel McLauchlin Place, Kirkintilloch, Glasgow G66 2LH; phone: (0141) 775 0522; Web site: www.scottish-rowing.org.uk

Welsh Amateur Rowing Association Monmouth School, Monmouth NP25 3XP; phone: (01600) 713143; fax: (01600) 772701; Web site: www.habs-monmouth.org

• Rugby league

The Rugby Football League Red Hall, Red Hall Lane, Leeds LS17 8NB; phone: (0113) 232 9111; fax: (0113) 232 3666; Web site: www.rfl.uk.com

• Rugby union

Rugby Football Union 21 Rugby Road, Twickenham TW1 1DS; phone: (020) 8892 2000; fax: (020) 8892 9816; Web site: www.rfu.com

Scottish Rugby Union Murrayfield, Edinburgh EH12 5PJ; phone: (0131) 346 5000; fax: (0131) 346 5001; Web site: www.sru.org.uk

Welsh Rugby Union Custom House, Custom House Street, Cardiff CF10 1RS; phone: (029) 2078 1700; fax: (029) 2022 5601; Web site: www.wru.co.uk

• Skiing

British Ski Federation Hillend, Bigger Road, Mid Lothian EH10 7EF; phone: (0131) 445 7676; fax: (0131) 445 7722; Web site: www.complete-skier.com

• Speedway

Speedway Control Board Ltd ACU Headquarters, Wood Street, Rugby, Warwickshire CV21 2YX; phone: (01788) 540096; fax: (01788) 573585

Sports Organizations in the UK *(continued)*

• **Squash rackets**

Squash Rackets Association Ground Floor, Bellevue Athletic Centre, Pink Bank Lane, Manchester M12 5GL; phone: (0161) 231 4499; fax: (0161) 231 4231; Web site: www.squash.co.uk

• **Swimming**

Amateur Swimming Association of Great Britain Harold Fern House, Derby Square, Loughborough, Leicestershire LE11 5AL; phone: (01509) 618700; fax: (01509) 618701

• **Table tennis**

English Table Tennis Association Queensbury House, Havelock Road, Hastings, East Sussex TN34 1HF; phone: (01424) 722525; fax: (01424) 422103; Web site: www.etta.co.uk

• **Tennis**

All England Lawn Tennis and Croquet Club Church Road, Wimbledon, London SW19 5AE; phone: (020) 8944 1066; fax: (020) 8947 8752; Web site: www.wimbledon.org

Lawn Tennis Association The Queen's Club, Palliser Road, London W14 9EG; phone: (020) 7381 7000; fax: (020) 7381 5965; Web site: www.lta.org.uk

• **Trampolining**

British Trampoline Federation Ltd 146 College Road, Harrow HA1 1BH; phone: (020) 8863 7278; fax: (020) 8427 8834; Web site: www.thebtf.co.uk

• **Volleyball**

English Volleyball Federation 27 South Road, West Bridgford, Nottingham NG2 7AG; phone: (0115) 981 6324

• **Water skiing**

British Water Ski Federation 390 City Road, London EC1V 2QA; phone: (020) 7833 2855; fax: (020) 7837 5879; Web site: www.bwsf.co.uk

• **Weight lifting**

British Amateur Weightlifters Association 131 Hurst Street, Oxford OX4 1HE; phone: (01865) 200339; fax: (01865) 790096; Web site: www.bawla.com

• **Wrestling**

British Amateur Wrestling Association 41 Great Clowes Street, Salford, Manchester M7 9RQ; phone: (0161) 832 9209; fax: (0161) 833 1120; Web site: www.britishwrestling.org

• **Yachting**

Royal Yachting Association RYA House, Romsey Road, Eastleigh, Hampshire SO50 9YA; phone: (023) 8062 7400; fax: (023) 8062 9924; Web site: www.rya.org.uk

Major International Sports Organizations

International dialling codes are given for organizations not based in the UK or USA.

• **Athletics**

International Amateur Athletic Federation (IAAF) 17 Rue Princesse Florestine, BP 359, MC 9800, Monaco; phone: +33 (93) 307070; Web site: www.iaaf.org

• **Football, association**

Fédération Internationale de Football Association (FIFA) PO Box 85, Hitzigweg 11, Zurich 8030, Switzerland; phone: +41 (1) 384 9595; fax: +41 (1) 384 9696; Web site: www.fifa.com

Union of European Football Associations (UEFA) Route de Genève 46, CH-1260 Nyon 2, Switzerland; phone: +41 (22) 994 4444; Web site: www.uefa.com

• **Motor racing**

Fédération Internationale de Sport Automobile (FISA – Formula 1) 8 Bis rue Boissy d'Anglais, 75008 Paris, France; phone: +33 (1) 4312 4455

• **Olympics**

International Olympic Committee (IOC) Chateau de Vidy, CH-1007 Lausanne, Switzerland; phone: +41 (21) 621 6111; fax: +41 (21) 621 6216; Web site: www.olympic.org

• **Skiing**

Fédération Internationale de Ski (FIS) (International Ski Federation), Oberhofen 3653, Switzerland; phone: +41 (33) 446161; Web site: www.fis-ski.com

• **Swimming**

Fédération Internationale de Natation Amateur (FINA) (International Amateur Swimming Federation), Avenue de Beaumont 9, 1012 Lausanne, Switzerland; phone: +41 (21) 310 4710; fax: +41 (21) 312 6610; Web site: www.fina.org/index.html

• **Tennis**

International Tennis Federation Bank Lane, Roehampton, London SW15 5XZ; phone: (020) 8878 6464; fax: (020) 8878 7799; Web site: www.tenniscountry.com

Summer Olympic Games

Olympic Games

The Olympic Games were sporting contests originally held in Olympia, ancient Greece, every four years during a sacred truce; records were kept from 776 BC. Women were forbidden to be present, and the male contestants were naked. The ancient Games were abolished in AD 394. The present-day games have been held every four years since 1896. Since 1924 there has been a separate winter Games programme; from 1994 the winter and summer Games are held two years apart.

The first modern Games were held in Athens, Greece. They were revived by Frenchman Pierre de Fredi, Baron de Coubertin (1863–1937), and have been held every four years with the exception of 1916, 1940, and 1944, when the two world wars intervened. Special tenth-anniversary Games were held in Athens in 1906. At the first revived Games, 245 competitors represented 14 nations in nine sports. Athens, host to the first modern Olympic games in 1896, was in 1997 chosen as the venue for the 2004 Games.

Summer Olympic Games Venues

(– = not applicable.)

Year	Olympiad	Venue
1896	I	Athens, Greece
1900	II	Paris, France
1904	III	St Louis, USA
1906	–	Athens, Greece[1]
1908	IV	London, UK
1912	V	Stockholm, Sweden
1916	VI	Berlin, Germany[2]
1920	VII	Antwerp, Belgium
1924	VIII	Paris, France
1928	IX	Amsterdam, Netherlands
1932	X	Los Angeles, USA
1936	XI	Berlin, Germany
1940	XII	Tokyo, Japan[3]
1944	XIII	London, UK[3]
1948	XIV	London, UK
1952	XV	Helsinki, Finland
1956	XVI	Melbourne, Australia[4]
1960	XVII	Rome, Italy
1964	XVIII	Tokyo, Japan
1968	XIX	Mexico City, Mexico
1972	XX	Munich, West Germany
1976	XXI	Montreal, Canada
1980	XXII	Moscow, USSR
1984	XXIII	Los Angeles, USA
1988	XXIV	Seoul, South Korea
1992	XXV	Barcelona, Spain
1996	XXVI	Atlanta, USA
2000	XXVII	Sydney, Australia
2004	XXVIII	Athens, Greece

[1] The 1906 Intercalated (or Interim) Games at Athens are not regarded as official by the International Olympic Committee but the results are included in most Olympic record books. [2] Cancelled because of World War I. [3] Cancelled because of World War II. [4] Equestrian events held in Stockholm, Sweden.

Selected Medallists

Men's Athletics: Olympic Gold Medallists

The year in which an event was first introduced to the Olympics is in parentheses after the event name.

100 m (1896)

Year	Name	Country	Result
1960	Armin Hary	Germany	10.20
1964	Bob Hayes	USA	10.00
1968	Jim Hines	USA	9.95
1972	Valery Borzov	USSR	10.14
1976	Hasely Crawford	Trinidad and Tobago	10.06
1980	Allan Wells	Great Britain	10.25
1984	Carl Lewis	USA	9.99
1988	Carl Lewis	USA	9.92
1992	Linford Christie	Great Britain	9.96
1996	Donovan Bailey	Canada	9.84

200 m (1900)

Year	Name	Country	Result
1960	Livio Berruti	Italy	20.50
1964	Henry Carr	USA	20.30
1968	Tommie Smith	USA	19.83
1972	Valery Borzov	USSR	20.00
1976	Don Quarrie	Jamaica	20.23
1980	Pietro Mennea	Italy	20.19
1984	Carl Lewis	USA	19.80
1988	Joe DeLoach	USA	19.75
1992	Mike Marsh	USA	20.01
1996	Michael Johnson	USA	19.32

400 m (1896)

Year	Name	Country	Result
1960	Otis Davis	USA	44.90
1964	Mike Larrabee	USA	45.10
1968	Lee Evans	USA	43.86
1972	Vince Matthews	USA	44.66
1976	Alberto Juantorena	Cuba	44.26
1980	Viktor Markin	USSR	44.60
1984	Alonzo Babers	USA	44.27
1988	Steve Lewis	USA	43.87
1992	Quincy Watts	USA	43.50
1996	Michael Johnson	USA	43.49

800 m (1896)

Year	Name	Country	Result
1960	Peter Snell	New Zealand	1:46.30
1964	Peter Snell	New Zealand	1:45.10
1968	Ralph Doubell	Australia	1:44.30
1972	Dave Wottle	USA	1:45.90
1976	Alberto Juantorena	Cuba	1:43.50
1980	Steve Ovett	Great Britain	1:45.40
1984	Joaquim Cruz	Brazil	1:43.00
1988	Paul Ereng	Kenya	1:43.45
1992	William Tanui	Kenya	1:43.66
1996	Vebjörn Rodal	Norway	1:42.58

1,500 m (1896)

Year	Name	Country	Result
1960	Herb Elliott	Australia	3:35.60
1964	Peter Snell	New Zealand	3:38.10
1968	Kip Keino	Kenya	3:34.90
1972	Pekka Vasala	Finland	3:36.30
1976	John Walker	New Zealand	3:39.17
1980	Sebastian Coe	Great Britain	3:38.40
1984	Sebastian Coe	Great Britain	3:32.53
1988	Peter Rono	Kenya	3:35.96
1992	Fermin Cacho	Spain	3:40.12
1996	Noureddine Morceli	Algeria	3:35.78

5,000 m (1912)

Year	Name	Country	Result
1960	Murray Halberg	New Zealand	13:43.40
1964	Bob Schul	USA	13:48.80
1968	Mohammed Gammoudi	Tunisia	14:05.00
1972	Lasse Viren	Finland	13:26.40
1976	Lasse Viren	Finland	13:21.76
1980	Miruts Yifter	Ethiopia	13:21.00
1984	Saïd Aouita	Morocco	13:05.59
1988	John Ngugi	Kenya	13:11.70
1992	Dieter Baumann	Germany	13:12.52
1996	Venuste Niyongabo	Burundi	13:07.96

10,000 m (1912)

Year	Name	Country	Result
1960	Pyotr Bolotnikov	USSR	28:32.20
1964	Billy Mills	USA	28:24.40
1968	Naftali Temu	Kenya	29:27.40
1972	Lasse Viren	Finland	27:38.40
1976	Lasse Viren	Finland	27:40.38
1980	Miruts Yifter	Ethiopia	27:42.70
1984	Alberto Cova	Italy	27:47.54
1988	Brahim Boutayeb	Morocco	27:21.46
1992	Khalid Skah	Morocco	27:46.70
1996	Haile Gebrselassie	Ethiopia	27:07.34

Marathon (1896)

Year	Name	Country	Result
1960	Abebe Bikila	Ethiopia	2h 15:16.20
1964	Abebe Bikila	Ethiopia	2h 12:11.20
1968	Mamo Wolde	Ethiopia	2h 20:26.40
1972	Frank Shorter	USA	2h 12:19.80
1976	Waldemar Cierpinski	East Germany	2h 09:55.00
1980	Waldemar Cierpinski	East Germany	2h 11:03.00
1984	Carlos Lopes	Portugal	2h 09:21.00
1988	Gelindo Bordin	Italy	2h 10:32.00
1992	Hwang Young-cho	South Korea	2h 13:23.00
1996	Josia Thugwane	South Africa	2h 12:36.00

110 m hurdles (1896)

Year	Name	Country	Result
1960	Lee Calhoun	USA	13.80
1964	Hayes Jones	USA	13.60
1968	Willie Davenport	USA	13.30
1972	Rod Milburn	USA	13.24
1976	Guy Drut	France	13.30
1980	Thomas Munkelt	East Germany	13.39
1984	Roger Kingdom	USA	13.20
1988	Roger Kingdom	USA	12.98
1992	Mark McKoy	Canada	13.12
1996	Allen Johnson	USA	12.95

400 m hurdles (1900)

Year	Name	Country	Result
1960	Glenn Davis	USA	49.30
1964	Rex Cawley	USA	49.60
1968	David Hemery	Great Britain	48.12
1972	John Akii-Bua	Uganda	47.82
1976	Edwin Moses	USA	47.64
1980	Volker Beck	East Germany	48.70
1984	Edwin Moses	USA	47.75
1988	Andre Phillips	USA	47.19
1992	Kevin Young	USA	46.78
1996	Derrick Adkins	USA	47.54

20 km walk (1956)

Year	Name	Country	Result
1960	Vladimir Golubnichy	USSR	1h 34:07.20
1964	Ken Matthews	Great Britain	1h 29:34.00
1968	Vladimir Golubnichy	USSR	1h 33:58.40
1972	Peter Frenkel	East Germany	1h 26:42.40
1976	Daniel Bautista	Mexico	1h 24:40.60
1980	Maurizio Damilano	Italy	1h 23:35.50
1984	Ernesto Canto	Mexico	1h 23:13.00
1988	Josef Pribilinec	Czechoslovakia	1h 19:57.00
1992	Daniel Plaza	Spain	1h 21:45.00
1996	Jefferson Perez	Ecuador	1h 20:07.00

50 km walk (1932)

Year	Name	Country	Result
1960	Don Thompson	Great Britain	4h 25:30.00
1964	Abdon Pamich	Italy	4h 11:12.40
1968	Christoph Höhne	East Germany	4h 20:13.60
1972	Bernd Kannenberg	West Germany	3h 56:11.60
1980	Hartwig Gauder	East Germany	3h 49:24.00
1984	Raul Gonzalez	Mexico	3h 47:26.00
1988	Vyacheslav Ivanenko	USSR	3h 38:29.00
1992	Andrei Perlov	USSR	3h 50:13.00
1996	Robert Korzeniowski	Poland	3h 43:30.00

3,000 m steeplechase (1900)[1]

Year	Name	Country	Result
1960	Zdzişlaw Krzyszkowiak	Poland	8:34.20
1964	Gaston Roelants	Belgium	8:30.80

(continued)

Men's Athletics: Olympic Gold Medallists *(continued)*

Year	Name	Country	Result
1968	Amos Biwott	Kenya	8:51.00
1972	Kip Keino	Kenya	8:23.60
1976	Anders Gärderud	Sweden	8:08.20
1980	Bronisław Malinowski	Poland	8:09.70
1984	Julius Korir	Kenya	8:11.80
1988	Julius Kariuki	Kenya	8:05.51
1992	Matthew Birir	Kenya	8:08.84
1996	Joseph Keter	Kenya	8:07.12
High jump (1896)			
1960	Robert Shavlakadze	USSR	2.16 m/7 ft 1 in
1964	Valery Brumel	USSR	2.18 m/7 ft $1\frac{3}{4}$ in
1968	Dick Fosbury	USA	2.24 m/7 ft $4\frac{1}{4}$ in
1972	Yuri Tarmak	USSR	2.23 m/7 ft $3\frac{3}{4}$ in
1976	Jacek Wszoła	Poland	2.25 m/7 ft $4\frac{1}{2}$ in
1980	Gerd Wessig	East Germany	2.36 m/7 ft $8\frac{3}{4}$ in
1984	Dietmar Mögenburg	West Germany	2.35 m/7 ft $8\frac{1}{2}$ in
1988	Gennady Avdeyenko	USSR	2.38 m/7 ft $9\frac{1}{2}$ in
1992	Javier Sotomayor	Cuba	2.34 m/7 ft 8 in
1996	Charles Austin	USA	2.39 m/7 ft 10 in
Pole vault (1896)			
1960	Donald Bragg	USA	4.70 m/15 ft 5 in
1964	Fred Hansen	USA	5.10 m/16 ft $8\frac{3}{4}$ in
1968	Bob Seagren	USA	5.40 m/17 ft $8\frac{1}{2}$ in
1972	Wolfgang Nordwig	East Germany	5.50 m/18 ft $\frac{1}{2}$ in
1976	Tadeusz Slusarski	Poland	5.50 m/18 ft $\frac{1}{2}$ in
1980	Władisław Kozakiewicz	Poland	5.78 m/18 fr $11\frac{1}{2}$ in
1984	Pierre Quinon	France	5.75 m/18 ft $10\frac{1}{4}$ in
1988	Sergei Bubka	USSR	5.90 m/19 ft $4\frac{1}{4}$ in
1992	Maksim Tarassov	Unified Team[2]	5.80 m/19 ft $\frac{1}{4}$ in
1996	Jean Galfione	France	5.92 m/19 ft 5 in
Long jump (1896)			
1960	Ralph Boston	USA	8.12 m/26 ft $7\frac{3}{4}$ in
1964	Lynn Davies	Great Britain	8.07 m/26 ft $5\frac{3}{4}$ in
1968	Bob Beamon	USA	8.90 m/29 ft $2\frac{1}{2}$ in
1972	Randy Williams	USA	8.24 m/27 ft $\frac{1}{2}$ in
1976	Arnie Robinson	USA	8.35 m/27 ft $4\frac{1}{2}$ in
1980	Lutz Dombrowski	East Germany	8.54 m/28 ft $\frac{1}{4}$ in
1984	Carl Lewis	USA	8.54 m/28 ft $\frac{1}{4}$ in
1988	Carl Lewis	USA	8.72 m/28 ft $7\frac{1}{4}$ in
1992	Carl Lewis	USA	8.67 m/28 ft $5\frac{1}{2}$ in
1996	Carl Lewis	USA	8.50 m/27 ft $10\frac{3}{4}$ in
Triple jump (1896)			
1960	Józef Schmidt	Poland	16.81 m/55 ft 2 in
1964	Józef Schmidt	Poland	16.85 m/55 ft $3\frac{1}{2}$ in
1968	Viktor Saneyev	USSR	17.39 m/57 ft $\frac{3}{4}$ in
1972	Viktor Saneyev	USSR	17.35 m/56 ft 11 in
1976	Viktor Saneyev	USSR	17.29 m/56 ft $8\frac{3}{4}$ in
1980	Jaak Udmäe	USSR	17.35 m/56 ft $11\frac{1}{4}$ in
1984	Al Joyner	USA	17.26 m/56 ft $7\frac{1}{2}$ in
1988	Khristo Markov	Bulgaria	17.61 m/57 ft $9\frac{1}{4}$ in
1992	Mike Conley	USA	18.17 m/57 ft $10\frac{1}{4}$ in
1996	Kenny Harrison	USA	18.09 m/59 ft $4\frac{1}{4}$ in
Shot put (1896)			
1960	Bill Neider	USA	19.68 m/64 ft $6\frac{3}{4}$ in
1964	Dallas Long	USA	20.33 m/66 ft $8\frac{1}{2}$ in
1968	Randy Matson	USA	20.54 m/67 ft $4\frac{3}{4}$ in
1972	Władysław Komar	Poland	21.18 m/69 ft 6 in
1976	Udo Beyer	East Germany	21.05 m/69 ft $\frac{3}{4}$ in
1980	Vladimir Kiselyev	USSR	21.35 m/70 ft $\frac{1}{2}$ in
1984	Alessandro Andrei	Italy	21.26 m/69 ft 9 in
1988	Ulf Timmermann	East Germany	22.47 m/73 ft $8\frac{3}{4}$ in
1992	Mike Stulce	USA	21.70 m/71 ft $2\frac{1}{4}$ in
1996	Randy Barnes	USA	21.62 m/70 ft $11\frac{1}{4}$ in

Year	Name	Country	Result
Discus (1896)			
1960	Al Oerter	USA	59.18 m/194 ft 2 in
1964	Al Oerter	USA	61.00 m/200 ft $1\frac{1}{2}$ in
1968	Al Oerter	USA	64.78 m/212 ft $6\frac{1}{2}$ in
1972	Ludvik Daněk	Czechoslovakia	64.40 m/211 ft 3 in
1976	Mac Wilkins	USA	67.50 m/221 ft 5.4 in
1980	Viktor Rashchupkin	USSR	66.64 m/218 ft 8 in
1984	Rolf Danneburg	West Germany	66.60 m/218 ft 6 in
1988	Jürgen Schult	East Germany	68.82 m/225 ft $9\frac{1}{4}$ in
1992	Romas Ubartas	Lithuania	65.12 m/213 ft $7\frac{3}{4}$ in
1996	Lars Reidel	Germany	69.40 m/227 ft 8 in
Hammer (1900)			
1960	Vasily Rudenkov	USSR	67.10 m/220 ft $1\frac{5}{8}$ in
1964	Romuald Klim	USSR	69.74 m/228 ft $9\frac{1}{2}$ in
1968	Gyula Zsivótzky	Hungary	73.36 m/240 ft 8 in
1972	Anatoly Bondarchuk	USSR	75.50 m/247 ft 8 in
1976	Yuri Sedykh	USSR	77.52 m/254 ft 4 in
1980	Yuri Sedykh	USSR	81.80 m/268 ft $4\frac{1}{2}$ in
1984	Juha Tiainen	Finland	78.08 m/256 ft 2 in
1988	Sergei Litvinov	USSR	84.80 m/278 ft $2\frac{1}{2}$ in
1992	Andrei Abduvaliyev	Unified Team[2]	82.54 m/270 ft $9\frac{1}{2}$ in
1996	Balazs Kiss	Hungary	81.24 m/266 ft 6 in
Javelin (1908)			
1960	Viktor Tsibulenko	USSR	84.64 m/277 ft $8\frac{3}{8}$ in
1964	Pauli Nevala	Finland	82.66 m/271 ft $2\frac{1}{2}$ in
1968	Yanis Lusis	USSR	90.10 m/295 ft $7\frac{1}{4}$ in
1972	Klaus Wolfermann	West Germany	90.48 m/296 ft 10 in
1976	Miklos Németh	Hungary	94.58 m/310 ft 4 in
1980	Dainis Kula	USSR	91.20 m/299 ft $2\frac{3}{8}$ in
1984	Arto Härkonen	Finland	86.76 m/284 ft 8 in
1988	Tapio Korjus	Finland	84.28 m/276 ft 6 in
1992	Jan Zelezny	Czechoslovakia	89.66 m/294 ft 2 in
1996	Jan Zelezny	Czech Republic	88.16 m/289 ft 3 in
Decathlon (1904)			
1960	Rafer Johnson	USA	8,392 points
1964	Willi Holdorf	Germany	7,887[3] points
1968	Bill Toomey	USA	8,193 points
1972	Nikolai Avilov	USSR	8,454 points
1976	Bruce Jenner	USA	8,617 points
1980	Daley Thompson	Great Britain	8,495 points
1984	Daley Thompson	Great Britain	8,798 points
1988	Christian Schenk	East Germany	8,488[3] points
1992	Robert Zmelic	Czechoslovakia	8,611 points
1996	Dan O'Brien	USA	8,824 points
4 × 100 m relay (1912)			
1960		Germany	39.50
1964		USA	39.00
1968		USA	38.23
1972		USA	38.19
1976		USA	38.33
1980		USSR	38.26
1984		USA	37.83
1988		USSR	38.19
1992		USA	37.40
1996		Canada	37.69
4 × 400 m relay (1908)			
1960		USA	3:02:20
1964		USA	3:00:70
1968		USA	3:56:16
1972		Kenya	2:59:80
1976		USA	2:58:65
1980		USSR	3:01:10
1984		USA	2:57:91
1988		USA	2:56:16
1992		USA	2:55:16
1996		USA	2:55:74

[1] Run as 2,500 m in 1900, 2,590 m in 1904, and 3,200 m in 1908.
[2] Commonwealth of Independent States plus Georgia.
[3] New points systems were introduced before the 1964 and 1988 Games.

Women's Athletics: Olympic Gold Medallists

The year in which an event was first introduced to the Olympics is in parentheses after the event name.

Year	Name	Country	Result
100 m (1928)			
1960	Wilma Rudolph	USA	11.00
1964	Wyomia Tyus	USA	11.40
1968	Wyomia Tyus	USA	11.08
1972	Renate Stecher	East Germany	11.07
1976	Annegret Richter	West Germany	11.08
1980	Lyudmila Kondratyeva	USSR	11.06
1984	Evelyn Ashford	USA	10.97
1988	Florence Griffith-Joyner	USA	10.54
1992	Gail Devers	USA	10.82
1996	Gail Devers	USA	10.94
200 m (1948)			
1960	Wilma Rudolph	USA	24.00
1964	Edith Maguire	USA	23.00
1968	Irena Szewińska	Poland	22.58
1972	Renate Stecher	East Germany	22.40
1976	Bärbel Eckert	East Germany	22.37
1980	Bärbel Wöckel[1]	East Germany	22.03
1984	Valerie Brisco-Hooks	USA	21.81
1988	Florence Griffith-Joyner	USA	21.34
1992	Gwen Torrence	USA	21.81
1996	Marie-José Pérec	France	22.12
400 m (1964)			
1964	Betty Cuthbert	Australia	52.00
1968	Colette Besson	France	52.03
1972	Monika Zehrt	East Germany	51.08
1976	Irena Szewińska	Poland	49.29
1980	Marita Koch	East Germany	48.88
1984	Valerie Brisco-Hooks	USA	48.83
1988	Olga Brzygina	USSR	48.65
1992	Marie-José Pérec	France	48.83
1996	Marie-José Pérec	France	48.25
800 m (1928)			
1960	Lyudmila Shevtsova	USSR	2:04.30
1964	Ann Packer	Great Britain	2:01.10
1968	Madeline Manning	USA	2:00.90
1972	Hildegard Falck	West Germany	1:58.55
1976	Tatyana Kazankina	USSR	1:54.94
1980	Nadyezda Olizarenko	USSR	1:53.42
1984	Doina Melinte	Romania	1:57.60
1988	Sigrun Wodars	East Germany	1:56.10
1992	Ellen van Langen	Netherlands	1:55.54
1996	Svetlana Masterkova	Russia	1:57.73
1,500 m (1972)			
1972	Lyudmila Bragina	USSR	4:01.40
1976	Tatyana Kazankina	USSR	4:05.48
1980	Tatyana Kazankina	USSR	3:56.60
1984	Gabriella Dorio	Italy	4:03.25
1988	Paula Ivan	Romania	3:53.96
1992	Hassiba Boulmerka	Algeria	3:55.30
1996	Svetlana Masterkova	Russia	4:00.83
3,000 m[2] (1984)			
1984	Maricica Puica	Romania	8:35.96
1988	Tatyana Samolenko	USSR	8:26.53
1992	Yelena Romanova	Unified Team[3]	8:46.04
5,000 m (1996)			
1996	Wang Junxia	China	14:59.88
10,000 m (1988)			
1988	Olga Bondarenko	USSR	31:05.21
1992	Derartu Tulu	Ethiopia	31:06.02
1996	Fernanda Ribeiro	Portugal	31:01.63
Marathon (1984)			
1984	Joan Benoit	USA	2h 24:52
1988	Rosa Mota	Portugal	2h 25:40
1992	Valentina Yegorova	Unified Team[3]	2h 32:41
1996	Fatuma Roba	Ethiopia	2h 26:05
100 m hurdles (1932)[4]			
1960	Irina Press	USSR	10.80
1964	Karin Balzer	Germany	10.50
1968	Maureen Caird	Australia	10.30
1972	Annelie Ehrhardt	East Germany	12.59
1976	Johanna Schaller	East Germany	12.77
1980	Vera Komisova	USSR	12.56
1984	Benita Fitzgerald-Brown	USA	12.84
1988	Yordanka Donkova	Bulgaria	12.38
1992	Paraskevi Patoulidou	Greece	12.64
1996	Lyudmila Engquist	Sweden	12.58
400 m hurdles (1984)			
1984	Nawal El Moutawakel	Morocco	54.61
1988	Debra Flintoff-King	Australia	53.17
1992	Sally Gunnell	Great Britain	53.23
1996	Deon Hemmings	Jamaica	52.82
10 km walk (1992)			
1992	Chen Yueling	China	44:32
1996	Yelena Nikolayeva	Russia	41:49
Triple jump (1996)			
1996	Inessa Kravets	Ukraine	15.33 m/50 ft $3\frac{1}{2}$ in
High jump (1928)			
1960	Iolanda Balaş	Romania	1.85 m/6 ft $\frac{3}{4}$ in
1964	Iolanda Balaş	Romania	1.90 m/6 ft $2\frac{3}{4}$ in
1968	Miloslava Režková	Czechoslovakia	1.82 m/5 ft $11\frac{1}{2}$ in
1972	Ulrike Meyfarth	West Germany	1.92 m/6 ft 4 in
1976	Rosemarie Ackermann	East Germany	1.93 m/6 ft $3\frac{3}{4}$ in
1980	Sara Simeoni	Italy	1.97 m/6 ft $5\frac{1}{2}$ in
1984	Ulrike Meyfarth	West Germany	2.02 m/6 ft $7\frac{1}{2}$ in
1988	Louise Ritter	USA	2.03 m/6 ft 8 in
1992	Heike Henkel	Germany	2.02 m/6 ft $7\frac{1}{2}$ in
1996	Stefka Kostadinova	Bulgaria	2.05 m/6 ft $8\frac{3}{4}$ in
Long jump (1948)			
1960	Vera Krepkina	USSR	6.37 m/20 ft $10\frac{3}{4}$ in
1964	Mary Rand	Great Britain	6.76 m/22 ft $2\frac{1}{4}$ in
1968	Viorica Viscopoleanu	Romania	6.82 m/22 ft $4\frac{1}{2}$ in
1972	Heidemarie Rosendahl	West Germany	6.78 m/22 ft 3 in
1976	Angela Voigt	East Germany	6.72 m/22 ft $\frac{3}{4}$ in
1980	Tatyana Kolpakova	USSR	7.06 m/23 ft 2 in
1984	Anisoara Stanciu	Romania	6.96 m/22 ft 10 in
1988	Jackie Joyner-Kersee	USA	7.40 m/24 ft $3\frac{1}{2}$ in
1992	Heike Drechsler	Germany	7.14 m/23 ft $5\frac{1}{4}$ in
1996	Chioma Ajunwa	Nigeria	7.12 m/23 ft $4\frac{1}{2}$ in
Shot put (1948)			
1960	Tamara Press	USSR	17.32 m/56 ft 10 in
1964	Tamara Press	USSR	18.14 m/59 ft $6\frac{1}{4}$ in
1968	Margitta Gummel	East Germany	19.61 m/64 ft 4 in
1972	Nadyezda Chizhova	USSR	21.03 m/69 ft 0 in
1976	Ivanka Christova	Bulgaria	21.16 m/69 ft $5\frac{1}{4}$ in
1980	Ilona Slupianek	East Germany	22.41 m/73 ft $6\frac{1}{4}$ in
1984	Claudia Losch	West Germany	20.48 m/67 ft $2\frac{1}{4}$ in
1988	Natalya Lisovskaya	USSR	22.24 m/72 ft $11\frac{1}{2}$ in
1992	Svetlana Krivelyova	Unified Team[3]	21.06 m/69 ft $1\frac{1}{2}$ in
1996	Astrid Kumbernuss	Germany	20.56 m/67 ft $5\frac{1}{2}$ in
Discus (1928)			
1960	Nina Romashkova	USSR	55.10 m/180 ft $8\frac{1}{4}$ in
1964	Tamara Press	USSR	57.25 m/187 ft 10 in
1968	Lia Manoliu	Romania	58.28 m/191 ft 2 in
1972	Faina Melnik	USSR	66.62 m/218 ft 7 in
1976	Evelin Schlaak	East Germany	69.00 m/226 ft 4 in
1980	Evelin Jahl[5]	East Germany	69.96 m/229 ft 6 in
1984	Ria Stalman	Netherlands	65.36 m/214 ft 5 in
1988	Martina Hellmann	East Germany	72.30 m/237 ft $2\frac{1}{4}$ in
1992	Maritza Marten	Cuba	70.06 m/222 ft 10 in
1996	Ilke Wyludda	Germany	69.66 m/228 ft 6 in
Javelin (1932)			
1960	Elvira Ozolina	USSR	55.98 m/183 ft 8 in
1964	Mihaela Penes	Romania	60.54 m/198 ft $7\frac{1}{2}$ in
1968	Angéla Németh	Hungary	60.36 m/198 ft $\frac{1}{2}$ in
1972	Ruth Fuchs	East Germany	63.88 m/209 ft 7 in
1976	Ruth Fuchs	East Germany	65.94 m/216 ft 4 in
1980	Maria Colon	Cuba	68.40 m/224 ft 5 in
1984	Tessa Sanderson	Great Britain	69.56 m/228 ft 2 in
1988	Petra Felke	East Germany	74.68 m/245 ft 0 in
1992	Silke Renk	Germany	68.34 m/224 ft $2\frac{1}{2}$ in
1996	Heli Ratanen	Finland	67.94 m/222 ft 11 in
Pentathlon[6] (1964)			
1964	Irina Press	USSR	5,246 points
1968	Ingrid Becker	West Germany	5,098 points

(continued)

Women's Athletics: Olympic Gold Medallists *(continued)*

Year	Name	Country	Result
1972	Mary Peters	Great Britain	4,801 points
1976	Siegrun Siegl	East Germany	4,745 points
1980	Nadyezda Tkachenko	USSR	5,083 points
Heptathlon (1984)			
1984	Glynis Nunn	Australia	6,390 points
1988	Jackie Joyner-Kersee	USA	7,291 points
1992	Jackie Joyner-Kersee	USA	7,044 points
1996	Ghada Shouaa	Syria	6,780 points
4 × 100 m relay (1928)			
1960		USA	44.50
1964		Poland	43.60
1968		USA	42.87
1972		West Germany	42.81
1976		East Germany	42.55
1980		East Germany	41.60
1984		USA	41.65
1988		USA	41.98
1992		USA	42.11
1996		USA	41.95
4 × 400 m relay (1972)			
1972		East Germany	3:23.00
1976		East Germany	3:19.23
1980		USSR	3:20.20
1984		USA	3:18.29
1988		USSR	2:15.18
1992		Unified Team[3]	3:20.20
1996		USA	3:20.91

[1] Born Eckert.
[2] Replaced by 5,000 metres in 1996.
[3] Commonwealth of Independent States plus Geórgia.
[4] 80 m from 1932 to 1968. 100 m since 1972.
[5] Born Schlaak.
[6] Replaced by heptathlon in 1984.

Basketball: Olympic Medallists

Basketball was introduced as a medal sport for men in 1936 and for women in 1976.

Year	Gold	Silver	Bronze
Men			
1980	Yugoslavia	Italy	USSR
1984	USA	Spain	Yugoslavia
1988	USSR	Yugoslavia	USA
1992	USA	Croatia	Lithuania
1996	USA	Yugoslavia	Lithuania

Year	Gold	Silver	Bronze
Women			
1980	USSR	Bulgaria	Yugoslavia
1984	USA	Korea, South	China
1988	USA	Yugoslavia	USSR
1992	Unified Team[1]	China	USA
1996	USA	Brazil	Australia

[1] Commonwealth of Independent States plus Georgia.

Boxing: Olympic Gold Medallists

Year	Name	Country
Super heavyweight (over 91 kg/201 lb)		
1984	Tyrell Biggs	USA
1988	Lennox Lewis	Canada
1992	Roberto Balado	Cuba
1996	Vladimir Klichko	Ukraine
Heavyweight (since 1984 up to 91 kg/201 lb)		
1984	Henry Tillman	USA
1988	Ray Mercer	USA
1992	Felix Savon	Cuba
1996	Felix Savon	Cuba
Light heavyweight (since 1952 up to 81 kg/178.5 lb)		
1984	Anton Josipović	Yugoslavia
1988	Andrew Maynard	USA
1992	Torsten May	Germany
1996	Vasili Jirov	Kyrgyzstan
Middleweight (since 1952 up to 75 kg/165 lb)		
1984	Shin Joon-Sup	South Korea
1988	Henry Maske	East Germany
1992	Ariel Hernández	Cuba
1996	Ariel Hernández	Cuba
Light middleweight (up to 71 kg/157 lb)		
1984	Frank Tate	USA
1988	Park Si-Hun	South Korea
1992	Juan Carlos Lemus	Cuba
1996	David Reid	USA
Welterweight (since 1948 up to 67 kg/148 lb)		
1984	Mark Breland	USA
1988	Robert Wangila	Kenya
1992	Michael Carruth	Ireland, Republic of
1996	Oleg Saitov	Russia
Light welterweight (up to 63.5 kg/140 lb)		
1984	Jerry Page	USA
1988	Viacheslav Ianovski	USSR
1992	Hector Vinent	Cuba
1996	Hector Vinent	Cuba
Lightweight (since 1952 up to 60 kg/132 lb)		
1984	Pernell Whitaker	USA
1988	Andreas Zuelov	East Germany
1992	Oscar de la Hoya	USA
1996	Hocine Soltani	Algeria
Featherweight (since 1952 up to 57 kg/126 lb)		
1984	Meldrick Taylor	USA
1988	Giovanni Parisi	Italy
1992	Andreas Tews	Germany
1996	Somluck Kamsing	Thailand
Bantamweight (since 1948 up to 54 kg/119 lb)		
1984	Maurizio Stecca	Italy
1988	Kennedy McKinney	USA
1992	Joel Casamayor	Cuba
1996	István Kovacs	Hungary
Flyweight (since 1948 up to 51 kg/112 lb)		
1984	Steve McCrory	USA
1988	Kim Kwang-Sun	Korea, South
1992	Choi Chol-su	Korea, North
1996	Maikro Romero	Cuba
Light flyweight (up to 48 kg/105.8 lb)		
1984	Paul Gonzalez	USA
1988	Ivailo Hristov	Bulgaria
1992	Rogelio Marcelo	Cuba
1996	Daniel Bojilov	Bulgaria

Diving: Olympic Gold Medallists

The year in which an event was first introduced to the Olympics is given in parentheses after the event name.

Year	Name	Country
Men		
Springboard diving (1908)		
1980	Aleksandr Portnov	USSR
1984	Greg Louganis	USA
1988	Greg Louganis	USA
1992	Mark Lenzi	USA
1996	Ni Xiong	China
Platform diving (1904)		
1980	Falk Hoffmann	East Germany
1984	Greg Louganis	USA
1988	Greg Louganis	USA
1992	Sun Shuwei	China
1996	Dimitri Sautin	Russia
Women		
Springboard diving (1920)		
1980	Irina Kalinina	USSR
1984	Sylvie Bernier	Canada
1988	Gao Min	China
1992	Gao Min	China
1996	Fu Mingxia	China
Platform diving (1912)		
1980	Martina Jäschke	East Germany
1984	Zhou Jihong	China
1988	Xu Yanmei	China
1992	Fu Mingxia	China
1996	Fu Mingxia	China

Association Football: Olympic Medallists

The USA won the inaugural women's Olympic soccer title in 1996, defeating China 2–1 in the final before a crowd of 76,481 at Sanford Stadium, Athens, Georgia. Association football was introduced as an Olympic medal sport for men in 1900.

Year	Gold	Silver	Bronze
Men			
1960	Yugoslavia	Denmark	Hungary
1964	Hungary	Czechoslovakia	Germany
1968	Hungary	Bulgaria	Japan
1972	Poland	Hungary	East Germany/USSR[1]
1976	East Germany	Poland	USSR
1980	Czechoslovakia	East Germany	USSR
1984	France	Brazil	Yugoslavia
1988	USSR	Brazil	West Germany
1992	Spain	Poland	Ghana
1996	Nigeria	Argentina	Brazil
Women			
1996	USA	China	Norway

[1] Tie after overtime played.

Men's Gymnastics: Individual Olympic Gold Medallists

Introduced as a medal sport in 1900.

Year	Name	Country
1960	Boris Shakhlin	USSR
1964	Yukio Endo	Japan
1968	Sawao Kato	Japan
1972	Sawao Kato	Japan
1976	Nikolai Andrianov	USSR
1980	Aleksandr Ditiatin	USSR
1984	Koji Gushiken	Japan
1988	Vladimir Artemov	USSR
1992	Vitali Scherbo	Unified Team[1]
1996	Li Xiaoshuang	China

[1] Commonwealth of Independent States plus Georgia.

Women's Gymnastics: Individual Olympic Gold Medallists

Introduced as a medal sport in 1952.

Year	Name	Country
1960	Larissa Latynina	USSR
1964	Vera Caslavska	Czechoslovakia
1968	Vera Caslavska	Czechoslovakia
1972	Liudmila Tourischeva	USSR
1976	Nadia Comaneci	Romania
1980	Elena Davidova	USSR
1984	Mary Lou Retton	USA
1988	Elena Chouchounova	USSR
1992	Tatiana Gutsu	Unified Team[1]
1996	Lilia Podkopaieva	Ukraine

[1] Commonwealth of Independent States plus Georgia.

Handball: Olympic Gold Medallists

Handball was introduced in 1936 as an 11-a-side outdoor game. It was reintroduced in 1972 as a 7-a-side indoor game. It was first played by women as an Olympic sport in 1976.

Year	Country
Men	
1980	East Germany
1984	Yugoslavia
1988	USSR
1992	Unified Team[1]
1996	Croatia
Women	
1980	USSR
1984	Yugoslavia
1988	South Korea
1992	South Korea
1996	Denmark

[1] Commonwealth of Independent States plus Georgia.

Hockey: Olympic Medallists

Introduced for men in 1908 and for women in 1980.

Year	Gold	Silver	Bronze
Men			
1980	India	Spain	USSR
1984	Pakistan	West Germany	Great Britain
1988	Great Britain	West Germany	Netherlands
1992	Germany	Australia	Pakistan
1996	Netherlands	Spain	Australia
Women			
1980	Zimbabwe	Czechoslovakia	USSR
1984	Netherlands	West Germany	USA
1988	Australia	South Korea	Netherlands
1992	Spain	Germany	Great Britain
1996	Australia	South Korea	Netherlands

Modern Pentathlon: Olympic Gold Medallists

Introduced in 1952.
(– = not applicable.)

Year	Country
1980	USSR
1984	Italy
1988	Hungary
1992	Poland
1996[1]	–

[1] Event not held in 1996.

Men's Swimming: Olympic Gold Medallists

Year	Name	Country	Time
50 m freestyle			
1988	Matt Biondi	USA	22.14
1992	Aleksandr Popov	Unified Team[1]	21.91
1996	Aleksandr Popov	Russia	22.13
100 m freestyle			
1980	Jörg Woithe	East Germany	50.40
1984	Ambrose Gaines	USA	49.80
1988	Matt Biondi	USA	48.63
1992	Aleksandr Popov	Unified Team[1]	49.02
1996	Aleksandr Popov	Russia	48.74
200 m freestyle			
1980	Sergey Kopliakov	USSR	1:49.81
1984	Michael Gross	West Germany	1:47.44
1988	Duncan Armstrong	Australia	1:47.25
1992	Yevgeni Sadovyi	Unified Team[1]	1:46.70
1996	Danyon Loader	New Zealand	1:47.63
400 m freestyle			
1980	Vladimir Salnikov	USSR	3:51.31
1984	George DiCarlo	USA	3:51.23
1988	Uwe Dassler	East Germany	3:46.95
1992	Yevgeni Sadovyi	Unified Team[1]	3:45.00
1996	Danyon Loader	New Zealand	3:47.97
1,500 m freestyle			
1980	Vladimir Salnikov	USSR	14:58.27
1984	Michael O'Brien	USA	15:05.20
1988	Vladimir Salnikov	USSR	15:00.40
1992	Kieren Perkins	Australia	14:43.48
1996	Kieren Perkins	Australia	14:56.40
100 m breaststroke			
1980	Duncan Goodhew	Great Britain	1:03.34
1984	Steve Lundquist	USA	1:01.65
1988	Adrian Moorhouse	Great Britain	1:02.04
1992	Nelson Diebel	USA	1:01.50
1996	Fred Deburghgraeve	Belgium	1:00.65
200 m breaststroke			
1980	Robertas Zhulpa	USSR	2:15.85
1984	Victor Davis	Canada	2:13.34
1988	József Szabó	Hungary	2:13.52
1992	Mike Barrowman	USA	2:10.16
1996	Norbert Rozsa	Hungary	2:12.57
100 m backstroke			
1980	Bengt Baron	Sweden	56.53
1984	Richard Carey	USA	55.79
1988	Daichi Suzuki	Japan	55.05
1992	Mark Tewksbury	Canada	53.98
1996	Jeff Rouse	USA	54.10
200 m backstroke			
1980	Sándor Wladár	Hungary	2:01.93
1984	Richard Carey	USA	2:00.23
1988	Igor Polianski	USSR	1:59.37
1992	Martin Lopez-Zubero	Spain	1:58.47
1996	Brad Bridgewater	USA	1:58.54
100 m butterfly			
1980	Pär Arvidsson	Sweden	54.92
1984	Michael Gross	West Germany	53.08
1988	Anthony Nesty	Suriname	53.00
1992	Pablo Morales	USA	53.32
1996	Denis Pankratov	Russia	52.27
200 m butterfly			
1980	Sergey Fesenko	USSR	1:59.76
1984	Jon Sieben	Australia	1:57.04
1988	Michael Gross	West Germany	1:56.94
1992	Mel Stewart	USA	1:56.26
1996	Denis Pankratov	Russia	1:56.51
200 m individual medley			
1984	Alex Baumann	Canada	2:01.42
1988	Tamás Darnyi	Hungary	2:00.17
1992	Tamás Darnyi	Hungary	2:00.76
1996	Attila Czene	Hungary	1:59.91
400 m individual medley			
1980	Alexsandr Sidorenko	USSR	4:22.89
1984	Alex Baumann	Canada	4:17.41
1988	Tamás Darnyi	Hungary	4:14.75
1992	Tamás Darnyi	Hungary	4:14.23
1996	Tom Dolan	USA	4:14.90
4 × 100 m freestyle relay			
1984		USA	3:19.03
1988		USA	3:16.53
1992		USA	3:16.74
1996		USA	3:15.41
4 × 200 m freestyle relay			
1980		USA	7:23.50
1984		USA	7:15.69
1988		USA	7:12.51
1992		USA	7:11.95
1996		USA	7:14.84
4 × 100 m medley relay			
1980		Australia	3:45.70
1984		USA	3:39.30
1988		USA	3:36.93
1992		USA	3:36.93
1996		USA	3:34.84

[1] Commonwealth of Independent States plus Georgia.

Women's Swimming: Olympic Gold Medallists

Year	Name	Country	Time
50 m freestyle			
1988	Kristin Otto	East Germany	25.49
1992	Yang Wenyi	China	24.79
1996	Amy Van Dyken	USA	24.87
100 m freestyle			
1980	Barbara Krause	East Germany	54.79
1984	Carrie Steinseifer/Nancy Hogshead (tie)	USA	55.92
1988	Kristin Otto	East Germany	54.93
1992	Zhuang Yong	China	54.64
1996	Le Jingyi	China	54.50
200 m freestyle			
1980	Barbara Krause	East Germany	1:58.33
1984	Mary Wayte	USA	1:59.23
1988	Heike Friedrich	East Germany	1:57.65
1992	Nicole Haislett	USA	1:57.90
1996	Claudia Poll	Costa Rica	1:58.16
400 m freestyle			
1980	Ines Diers	East Germany	4:08.76
1984	Tiffany Cohen	USA	4:07.10
1988	Janet Evans	USA	4:03.85
1992	Dagmar Hase	Germany	4:07.18
1996	Michelle Smith	Ireland, Republic of	4:07.25
800 m freestyle			
1980	Michelle Ford	Australia	8:28.90
1984	Tiffany Cohen	USA	8:24.95
1988	Janet Evans	USA	8:20.20
1992	Janet Evans	USA	8:25.52
1996	Brooke Bennett	USA	8:27.89
100 m breaststroke			
1980	Ute Geweniger	East Germany	1:10.22
1984	Petra Van Staveren	Netherlands	1:09.88
1988	Tania Dangalakova	Bulgaria	1:07.95
1992	Elena Rudkovskaia	Unified Team[1]	1:08.00
1996	Penny Heyns	South Africa	1:07.73
200 m breaststroke			
1980	Lina Kachushite	USSR	2:29.54
1984	Anne Ottenbrite	Canada	2:30.38
1988	Silke Hörner	East Germany	2:26.71
1992	Kyoko Iwasaki	Japan	2:26.65
1996	Penny Heyns	South Africa	2:25.41
100 m backstroke			
1980	Rica Reinisch	East Germany	1:00.86
1984	Theresa Andrews	USA	1:02.55
1988	Kristin Otto	East Germany	1:00.89

(continued)

Women's Swimming: Olympic Gold Medallists *(continued)*

Year	Name	Country	Time
1992	Krisztina Egerszegi	Hungary	1:00.68
1996	Beth Botsford	USA	1:01.19
200 m backstroke			
1980	Rica Reinisch	East Germany	2:11.77
1984	Jolanda De Rover	Netherlands	2:12.38
1988	Krisztina Egerszegi	Hungary	2:09.29
1992	Krisztina Egerszegi	Hungary	2:07.06
1996	Krisztina Egerszegi	Hungary	2:07.83
100 m butterfly			
1980	Caren Metschuck	East Germany	1:00.42
1984	Mary Meagher	USA	59.26
1988	Kristin Otto	East Germany	59.00
1992	Qian Hong	China	58.62
1996	Amy Van Dyken	USA	59.13
200 m butterfly			
1980	Ines Geissler	East Germany	2:10.44
1984	Mary Meagher	USA	2:06.90
1988	Kathleen Nord	East Germany	2:09.51
1992	Summer Sanders	USA	2:08.67
1996	Susan O'Neill	Australia	2:07.76
200 m individual medley			
1984	Tracy Caulkins	USA	2:12.64
1988	Daniela Hunger	East Germany	2:12.59
1992	Li Chin	China	2:11.65
1996	Michelle Smith	Ireland, Republic of	2:13.93
400 m individual medley			
1980	Petra Schneider	East Germany	4:36.29
1984	Tracy Caulkins	USA	4:39.24
1988	Janet Evans	USA	4:37.76
1992	Krisztina Egerszegi	Hungary	4:36.54
1996	Michelle Smith	Ireland, Republic of	4:39.29
4 × 100 m freestyle relay			
1980		East Germany	3:42.71
1984		USA	3:43.43
1988		East Germany	3:40.63
1992		USA	3:39.46
1996		USA	3:39.29
4 × 200 m freestyle relay			
1996[2]		USA	7:59.87
4 × 100 m medley relay			
1980		East Germany	4:06.67
1984		USA	4:08.34
1988		East Germany	4:03.74
1992		USA	4:02.54
1996		USA	4:02.88

[1] Commonwealth of Independent States plus Georgia.
[2] Event first held in 1996.

Table Tennis: Olympic Gold Medallists

Year	Name	Country
Men		
Singles		
1988	Yoo Nam-Kyu	South Korea
1992	Jan-Ove Waldner	Sweden
1996	Liu Guoliang	China
Doubles		
1988	Longcan Chen and Qingguang Wei	China
1992	Lu Lin and Wang Tao	China
1996	Kong Linghui and Liu Guoliang	China
Women		
Singles		
1988	Chen Jing	China
1992	Deng Yaping	China
1996	Deng Yaping	China
Doubles		
1988	Jung-Hwa Hyun	South Korea
1992	Deng Yaping and Qiao Hong	China
1996	Deng Yaping and Qiao Hong	China

Tennis: Olympic Gold Medallists

Tennis was reintroduced as a medal sport in 1988 after an absence of 64 years.

Year	Name	Country
Men		
Singles		
1988	Miloslav Mecir	Czechoslovakia
1992	Marc Rosset	Switzerland
1996	Andre Agassi	USA
Doubles		
1988	Ken Flack and Robert Seguso	USA
1992	Boris Becker and Michael Stich	Germany
1996	Todd Woodbridge and Mark Woodforde	Australia
Women		
Singles		
1988	Steffi Graf	West Germany
1992	Jennifer Capriati	USA
1996	Lindsay Davenport	USA
Doubles		
1988	Pam Shriver and Zina Garrison	USA
1992	Gigi Fernandez and Mary Joe Fernandez	USA
1996	Gigi Fernandez and Mary Joe Fernandez	USA

Volleyball: Olympic Medallists

Year	Gold	Silver	Bronze
Men			
1980	USSR	Bulgaria	Romania
1984	USA	Brazil	Italy
1988	USA	USSR	Argentina
1992	Brazil	Netherlands	USA
1996	Netherlands	Italy	Yugoslavia
Women			
1980	USSR	East Gemany	Bulgaria
1984	China	USA	Japan
1988	USSR	Peru	China
1992	Cuba	Unified Team[1]	USA
1996	Cuba	China	Brazil

[1] Commonwealth of Independent States plus Georgia.

Water Polo: Olympic Gold Medallists

Year	Country
1980	USSR
1984	Yugoslavia
1988	Yugoslavia
1992	Italy
1996	Spain

Winter Olympic Games

Winter Olympic Games Venues

Year	Venue	Year	Venue
1924	Chamonix, France	1972	Sapporo, Japan
1928	St Moritz, Switzerland	1976	Innsbruck, Austria
1932	Lake Placid (NY), USA	1980	Lake Placid (NY), USA
1936	Garmisch-Partenkirchen, Germany	1984	Sarajevo, Yugoslavia
1948	St Moritz, Switzerland	1988	Calgary, Alberta, Canada
1952	Oslo, Norway	1992	Albertville, France
1956	Cortina d'Ampezzo, Italy	1994	Lillehammer, Norway
1960	Squaw Valley (CO), USA	1998	Nagano, Japan
1964	Innsbruck, Austria	2002	Salt Lake City (UT), USA
1968	Grenoble, France	2006	Turin, Italy

Selected Medallists

Men's Alpine Skiing: Olympic Gold Medallists

Alpine skiing was introduced to the Olympic Games in 1936.

Year	Name	Country
Alpine combination (downhill and slalom)		
1988	Hubert Strolz	Austria
1992	Josef Polig	Italy
1994	Lasse Kjus	Norway
1998	Mario Reiter	Austria
Downhill		
1980	Leonhard Stock	Austria
1984	William Johnson	USA
1988	Pirmin Zurbriggen	Switzerland
1992	Patrick Ortlieb	Austria
1994	Tommy Moe	USA
1998	Jean Luc-Crétier	France
Giant slalom		
1980	Ingemar Stenmark	Sweden
1984	Max Julen	Switzerland
1988	Alberto Tomba	Italy
1992	Alberto Tomba	Italy
1994	Markus Wasmeier	Germany
1998	Hermann Maier	Austria
Slalom		
1980	Ingemar Stenmark	Sweden
1984	Phil Mahre	USA
1988	Alberto Tomba	Italy
1992	Finn-Christian Jagge	Norway
1994	Thomas Stangassinger	Austria
1998	Hans-Petter Buraas	Norway
Super giant slalom		
1988	Franck Piccard	France
1992	Kjetil Andre Aamodt	Norway
1994	Markus Wasmeier	Germany
1998	Hermann Maier	Austria

Women's Alpine Skiing: Olympic Gold Medallists

Alpine skiing was introduced to the Olympic Games in 1936.

Year	Name	Country
Alpine combination (downhill and slalom)		
1988	Anita Wachter	Austria
1992	Petra Kronberger	Austria
1994	Pernilla Wiberg	Sweden
1998	Katja Seizinger	Germany
Downhill		
1980	Annemarie Moser-Pröll	Austria
1984	Michela Figini	Switzerland
1988	Marina Kiehl	West Germany
1992	Kerrin Lee-Gartner	Canada
1994	Katja Seizinger	Germany
1998	Katja Seizinger	Germany
Giant slalom		
1980	Hanni Wenzel	Liechtenstein
1984	Debbie Armstrong	USA
1988	Vreni Schneider	Switzerland
1992	Pernilla Wiberg	Sweden
1994	Deborah Compagnoni	Italy
1998	Deborah Compagnoni	Italy
Slalom		
1980	Hanni Wenzel	Liechtenstein
1984	Paoletta Magoni	Italy
1988	Vreni Schneider	Switzerland
1992	Petra Kronberger	Austria
1994	Vreni Schneider	Switzerland
1998	Hilde Gerg	Germany
Super giant slalom		
1988	Sigrid Wolf	Austria
1992	Deborah Compagnoni	Italy
1994	Diann Roffe-Steinrotter	USA
1998	Picabo Street	USA

Commonwealth Games

Commonwealth Games Venues

These games were inaugurated in 1930 as the British Empire Games, became the British Empire and Commonwealth Games in 1954, and the British Commonwealth Games in 1970.

Year	Venue	Year	Venue	Year	Venue
1930	Hamilton, Canada	1962	Perth, Australia	1986	Edinburgh, Scotland
1934	London, England	1966	Kingston, Jamaica	1990	Auckland, New Zealand
1938	Sydney, Australia	1970	Edinburgh, Scotland	1994	Victoria, Canada
1950	Auckland, New Zealand	1974	Christchurch, New Zealand	1998	Kuala Lumpur, Malaysia
1954	Vancouver, Canada	1978	Edmonton, Canada	2002	Manchester, England
1958	Cardiff, Wales	1982	Brisbane, Australia	2006	Melbourne, Australia

American Football

World Bowl Winners

Year	Winners	Losers	Score
1991	London Monarchs	Barcelona Dragons	21–0
1995	Frankfurt Galaxy	Amsterdam Admirals	26–22
1996	Scottish Claymores	Frankfurt Galaxy	32–27
1997	Barcelona Dragons	Rhein Fire	38–24
1999	Frankfurt Galaxy	Barcelona Dragons	38–24
2000	Rhein Fire	Scottish Claymores	13–10

American Football

American football is played on a field marked out with parallel lines giving a gridiron effect. There is a goalpost at each end of the field, and beyond this an end zone. Games are divided into quarters of 15 minutes each. Points are scored by running or passing the ball across the goal line (touchdown, 6 points); by kicking it over the goal's crossbar after a touchdown (conversion, 2 points), or from the field during regular play (field goal, 3 points); or by tackling a defending player who has the ball in the end zone, or blocking a defending team's kick so it goes out of bounds from the end zone (safety, 2 points). A team consists of over 40 players but only 11 are allowed on the field at any one time.

Super Bowl Results

The Super Bowl, first held in 1967, is an annual meeting between the winners of the National and American Football Conferences.

Super Bowl	Year	Result	Venue	Attendance
XIV	1980	Pittsburgh Steelers 31, Los Angeles Rams 19	Pasadena	103,985
XV	1981	Oakland Raiders 27, Philadelphia Eagles 10	New Orleans	76,135
XVI	1982	San Francisco 49ers 26, Cincinnati Bengals 21	Pontiac	81,270
XVII	1983	Washington Redskins 27, Miami Dolphins 17	Pasadena	103,667
XVIII	1984	Los Angeles Raiders 38, Washington Redskins 9	Tampa	72,920
XIX	1985	San Francisco 38, Miami Dolphins 16	Stanford	84,059
XX	1986	Chicago Bears 46, New England Patriots 10	New Orleans	73,818
XXI	1987	New York Giants 39, Denver Broncos 20	Pasadena	101,063
XXII	1988	Washington Redskins 42, Denver Broncos 10	San Diego	73,302
XXIII	1989	San Francisco 49ers 20, Cincinnati Bengals 16	Miami	75,179
XXIV	1990	San Francisco 49ers 55, Denver Broncos 10	New Orleans	72,919
XXV	1991	New York Giants 20, Buffalo Bills 19	Tampa	73,813
XXVI	1992	Washington Redskins 37, Buffalo Bills 24	Minneapolis	63,130
XXVII	1993	Dallas Cowboys 52, Buffalo Bills 17	Pasadena	102,000
XXVIII	1994	Dallas Cowboys 30, Buffalo Bills 13	Atlanta	72,817
XXIX	1995	San Francisco 49ers 49, San Diego 26	Miami	74,107
XXX	1996	Dallas Cowboys 27, Pittsburgh Steelers 17	Tempe (AZ)	76,347
XXXI	1997	Green Bay Packers 35, New England Patriots 21	New Orleans	72,301
XXXII	1998	Denver Broncos 31, Green Bay Packers 24	San Diego	68,912
XXXIII	1999	Denver Broncos 34, Atlanta Falcons 19	Miami	74,803
XXXIV	2000	St Louis Rams 23, Tennessee Titans 16	Atlanta	71,000

Angling

World Individual Freshwater Champions

This championship, established in 1957, is the oldest angling world championship. The first champion was Mandeli of Italy.

Year	Name	Country
1994	Bob Nudd	England
1995	Paul Jean	France
1996	Alan Scotthorne	England
1997	Alan Scotthorne	England
1998	Alan Scotthorne	England
1999	Bob Nudd	England

World Team Freshwater Champions

The Team Freshwater Championship was first won by Italy in 1957. The team with the most wins since 1957 is France (13 wins).

Year	Country
1989	Wales
1990	France
1991	England
1992	Italy
1993	Italy
1994	England
1995	France
1996	Italy
1997	Italy
1998	England
1999	Spain

Freshwater Fishing

Freshwater fishing embraces coarse fishing, in which members of the carp family, pike, perch, and eels are taken by baits or lures, and (in the UK) are returned to the water virtually unharmed; and game fishing, in which members of the salmon family, such as salmon and trout, are taken by spinners (revolving lures) and flies (imitations of adult or larval insects).

In **sea fishing** the catch includes flatfish, bass, and mackerel; big-game fishes include shark, tuna or tunny, marlin, and swordfish.

UK Fishing Records (Selected)

Records are for fish caught on rod and line in waters of England, Scotland, Wales, Northern Ireland, and the Channel Islands.
(drms = drams; 1 ounce = 16 drams.)
As of July 2000.

Species	Weight Imperial			Metric		Captor/location	Year
	lb	oz	drms	kg	g		
Freshwater fish							
Coarse fish							
Bream (common, bronze), *Abramis brama*	16	10	0	7	541	L McManus, Midlands Stillwater, England	1999
Carp, *Cyprinus carpio*	56	6	0	25	571	K Cummins, Wraysbury, Berkshire, England	1998
Catfish (Wels), *Silurus glanis*	62	0	0	28	123	R Garner, Withy Pool, Henlow, Bedfordshire, England	1997
Chub, *Leuciscus cephalus*	8	10	0	3	912	P Smith, River Tees, Blackwell, County Durham, England	1994
Eel, *Anguilla anguilla*	11	2	0	5	46	S Terry, Kingfisher Lake, Near Ringwood, Hampshire, England	1978
Perch, *Perca fluviatilis*	5	9	0	2	523	J Shayler, private lake, Kent, England	1985
Pike, *Esox lucius*	46	13	0	21	234	R Lewis, Llangdegfedd, Wales	1992
Roach, *Rutilus rutilus*	4	3	0	1	899	R N Clarke, Dorset Stour, England	1990
Rudd, *Scardinius erythrophthalmus*	4	8	0	2	41	Reverend E C Alston, Mere near Thetford, Norfolk, England	1933
Tench, *Tinca tinca*	14	7	0	6	548	G Beaven, private water, Hertfordshire, England	1993
Game fish							
Salmon, Atlantic, *Salmo salar* (natural)	64	0	0	29	29	Miss G W Ballatine, River Tay, Scotland	1922
Trout, American brook (brook Char), *Salvelinus fontinalis* (cultivated)	8	3	0	3	713	E Holland, Fontburn Reservoir, Northumberland, England	1998
Trout, brown, *Salmo trutta* (natural)	25	5	12	11	502	A Finlay, Loch Awe, Argyllshire, Scotland	1996
Trout, brown, *Salmo trutta* (cultivated)	28	1	0	12	729	D Taylor, Dever Springs Trout Fishery, Hants, England	1995
Trout, rainbow, *Oncorhynchus mykiss* (cultivated)	36	14	8	16	740	C White, Dever Springs Trout Fishery, Hants, England	1995
Trout, rainbow, *Oncorhynchus mykiss* (resident)	23	1	4	10	921	J Hammond, Hanningfield Reservoir, Essex, England	1998
Trout, sea, *Salmo trutta* (natural)	28	5	4	12	850	J Farrent, Calshot Spit, River Test, Hants, England	1992
Sea fish[1]							
Angler fish, *Lophius piscatorius*	94	12	4	42	985	S M A Neill, Belfast Lough, Northern Ireland	1985
Bass, *Dicentrarchus labrax*	19	9	2	8	876	P McEwan, off Reculvers, Herne Bay, Kent, England	1987
Brill, *Scophthalmus rhombus*	16	0	0	7	257	A H Fisher, Derby Haven, Isle of Man	1950
Catfish, *Anarhichas lupus*	26	4	0	11	906	S P Ward, 5 miles out from Whitby, Yorkshire, England	1989
Cod, *Gadus morhua*	58	6	0	26	478	N Cook, North Sea off Whitby, North Yorkshire, England	1992
Conger, *Conger conger*	133	4	0	60	442	V Evans, from wreck S E Berry Head, South Devon, England	1995
Dab, *Limanda limanda*	2	12	4	1	254	R Islip, Gairloch, Wester Ross, Scotland	1975
Haddock, *Melanogrammus aeglefinus*	13	11	4	6	215	G Bones, off Falmouth, Cornwall, England	1978
Hake, *Merluccius merluccius*	25	12	14	11	706	R Roberts, Loch Etive, Scotland	1997
Halibut, *Hippoglossus hippoglossus*	234	0	0	106	136	C Booth, Dunnet Head, off Scrabster, Scotland	1979
Herring, *Clupea harengus*	1	1	0	0	481	B Barden, off Bexhill-on-Sea, Sussex, England	1973
John Dory (St Peter's fish), *Zeus faber*	11	14	0	5	386	J Johnson, off Newhaven, East Sussex, England	1977
Ling, *Molva molva*	59	8	0	26	987	J Webster, off Bridlington, Yorkshire, England	1989
Mackerel, *Scomber scombrus*	6	2	7	2	790	W J Chapple, 1.5 miles off Penberth Cove, Cornwall, England	1984
Monkfish, *Squatina squatina*	66	0	0	29	936	C G Chalk, Shoreham, Sussex, England	1965
Mullet, red, *Mullus surmuletus*	3	7	0	1	559	M T Hamel, Petils Bay, Bordeaux, Vale, Guernsey, Channel Islands	1981
Ray, electric, *Torpedo nobiliana*	96	1	0	43	571	N J Cowley, off Dodman Point, Cornwall, England	1975
Ray, sting, *Dasyatis pastinaca*	72	2	0	32	715	P Burgess, River Blackwater, Essex, England	1996
Shark, blue, *Prionace glauca*	218	0	0	98	878	N Sutcliffe, Looe, Cornwall, England	1959
Shark, mako, *Isurus oxyrinchus*	500	0	0	226	786	Mrs J M Yallop, off Eddystone Lighthouse, English Channel	1971
Shark, porbeagle, *Lamna nasus*	507	0	0	230	0	C Bennett, Dunnet Head, Scotland	1993
Shark, thresher, *Alopias vulpinus*	323	0	0	146	504	S Mills, 6 miles south Nab Tower, off Portsmouth, Hampshire, England	1982
Skate, common, *Raja batis*	227	0	0	102	961	R Banks, 8 miles off Tobermory, Inner Hebrides, Scotland	1986
Sole, *Solea solea*	4	1	12	2	119	M Eppelein, Great Bank, off Channel Islands	1993

[1] Sea fish records are boat-caught unless otherwise stated.

Source: British Record Fish Committee

■ Angling

Athletics

Athletics: 1999–2000

The undoubted star of the track in 1999 was Maurice Greene of the USA. At Athens in June he set a new world 100 metres record with a time of 9.79 sec. Then two months later at the IAAF World Championships in Seville, Spain, he became the first man to win world titles in both the 100 and 200 metres. For good measure, he also won a gold medal in the sprint relay. The performance of the championships, however, came from Greene's compatriot, Michael Johnson, who, in the process of capturing his fourth consecutive 400 metres world title, finally broke Butch Reynolds' 11-year-old world record of 43.29 sec, with a time of 43.18 sec. Haile Gebrselassie of Ethiopia also made it four titles in a row with victory in the 10,000 metres, while Morocco's Hicham El Guerrouj, a month after breaking the world mile record in Rome, retained his 1,500 metres world title.

In the womens' events, Marion Jones of the USA won her second successive 100 metres title, and Gabriela Szabo of Romania, the IAAF female athlete of the year, won the 5,000 metres. Britain's only gold medallist at the World Championships was Colin Jackson, who regained the 110 metre hurdles title which he won at Stuttgart in 1993. Jonathan Edwards came a disappointing third in the triple jump, but 21-year-old Dean Macey was a surprise silver medallist in the decathlon. The men's sprint relay team also took silver, as did Denise Lewis in the heptathlon, and Paula Radcliffe in the 10,000 metres.

Men's Outdoor Athletics World Records

As of 10 June 2000.

Category	Record	Name(s)	Country	Date	Location
100 m	9.79	Maurice Greene	USA	16 June 1999	Athens, Greece
200 m	19.32	Michael Johnson	USA	1 August 1996	Atlanta (GA), USA
400 m	43.18	Michael Johnson	USA	26 August 1999	Seville, Spain
800 m	1:41.11	Wilson Kipketer	Denmark	24 August 1997	Cologne, Germany
1,000 m	2:11.96	Noah Ngeny	Kenya	5 September 1999	Rieti, Italy
1,500 m	3:26.00	Hicham El Guerrouj	Morocco	17 July 1998	Rome, Italy
Mile	3:43.13	Hicham El Guerrouj	Morocco	7 July 1999	Rome, Italy
2,000 m	4:44.79	Hicham El Guerrouj	Morocco	7 September 1999	Berlin, Germany
3,000 m	7:20.67	Daniel Komen	Kenya	1 September 1996	Rieti, Italy
5,000 m	12:39.36	Haile Gebrselassie	Ethiopia	13 June 1998	Helsinki, Finland
10,000 m	26:22.75	Haile Gebrselassie	Ethiopia	1 June 1998	Hengelo, Netherlands
20,000 m	56:55.60	Arturo Barrios	Mexico	30 March 1991	La Flèche, France
25,000 m	1 h 13:55.80	Toshihiko Seko	Japan	22 March 1981	Christchurch, New Zealand
3,000 m steeplechase	7:55.72	Bernard Barmasai	Kenya	24 August 1997	Cologne, Germany
Half marathon	59:17	Paul Tergat	Kenya	4 April 1998	Milan, Italy
Marathon	2 h 5:42	Khalid Khannouchi	Morocco	24 October 1999	Chicago, USA
110 m hurdles	12.91	Colin Jackson	Great Britain	20 August 1993	Stuttgart, Germany
400 m hurdles	46.78	Kevin Young	USA	6 August 1992	Barcelona, Spain
		Marsh, Burrell, Mitchell, Lewis	USA	8 August 1992	Barcelona, Spain
4 × 100 m relay	37.40	Drummond, Cason, Mitchell, Burrell	USA	21 August 1993	Stuttgart, Germany
4 × 200 m relay	1:18.68	Marsh, Burrell, Heard, Lewis	USA	17 April 1994	Walnut (CA), USA
4 × 400 m relay	2:54.29	Valmon, Watts, Reynolds, Johnson	USA	22 August 1993	Stuttgart, Germany
4 × 800 m relay	7:03.89	Elliott, Cook, Cram, Coe	Great Britain	30 August 1982	London, UK
High jump	2.45 m/8 ft $\frac{1}{2}$ in	Javier Sotomayor	Cuba	27 July 1993	Salamanca, Spain
Long jump	8.95 m/29 ft $4\frac{1}{2}$ in	Mike Powell	USA	30 August 1991	Tokyo, Japan
Triple jump	18.29 m/60 ft $\frac{1}{4}$ in	Jonathan Edwards	Great Britain	7 August 1995	Gothenburg, Sweden
Pole vault	6.14 m/20 ft $1\frac{3}{4}$ in	Sergei Bubka	Ukraine	31 July 1994	Sestriere, Italy
Shot put	23.12 m/75 ft $10\frac{1}{4}$ in	Randy Barnes	USA	20 May 1990	Los Angeles (CA), USA
Discus	74.08 m/243 ft	Jürgen Schult	East Germany	6 June 1986	Neubrandenburg, Germany
Javelin	98.48 m/323 ft 1 in	Ján Zelezny	Czech Republic	25 May 1996	Jena, Germany
Hammer	86.74 m/284 ft 7 in	Yuri Sedykh	USSR	30 August 1986	Stuttgart, Germany
Decathlon	8,894 pts[1]	Thomas Dvorak	Czech Republic	4 July 1999	Prague, Czech Republic
20 km walk	1 h 17:25.6	Bernardo Segura	Mexico	7 May 1994	Bergen, Norway
30 km walk	2 h 01:44.1	Maurizio Damilano	Italy	3 October 1992	Cuneo, Italy
50 km walk	3 h 40:57.9	Thierry Toutain	France	29 September 1996	Héricourt, France

Women's Outdoor Athletics World Records

As of 10 June 2000.

Category	Record	Name	Country	Date	Location
100 m	10.49	Florence Griffith-Joyner	USA	16 July 1988	Indianapolis (IN), USA
200 m	21.34	Florence Griffith-Joyner	USA	29 September 1988	Seoul, South Korea
400 m	47.60	Marita Koch	East Germany	6 October 1985	Canberra, Australia
800 m	1:53.28	Jarmila Kratochvílová	Czechoslovakia	26 July 1983	Munich, West Germany
1,000 m	2:28.98	Svetlana Masterkova	Russia	23 August 1996	Brussels, Belgium
1,500 m	3:50.46	Qu Yunxia	China	11 September 1993	Beijing, China
Mile	4:12.56	Svetlana Masterkova	Russia	14 August 1996	Zürich, Switzerland
2,000 m	5:25.36	Sonia O'Sullivan	Ireland, Republic of	9 July 1994	Edinburgh, UK
3,000 m	8:06.11	Wang Junxia	China	13 September 1993	Beijing, China
5,000 m	14:28.09	Jiang Bo	China	23 October 1997	Shanghai, China
10,000 m	29:31.78	Wang Junxia	China	8 September 1993	Beijing, China
Half marathon	1 h 06:43	Masako Chika	Japan	19 April 1997	Tokyo, Japan
Marathon	2 h 20:43.00	Tegla Loroupe	Kenya	26 September 1999	Berlin, Germany
100 m hurdles	12.21	Yordanka Donkova	Bulgaria	21 August 1988	Stara Zagora, Bulgaria
400 m hurdles	52.61	Kim Batten	USA	11 August 1995	Gothenburg, Sweden
4 × 100 m relay	41.37	Gladisch, Rieger, Auerswald, Göhr	East Germany	6 October 1985	Canberra, Australia
4 × 200 m relay	1:27.46[1]	Jenkins, Collander, Perry, Jones	USA 'Blue' Team	29 April 2000	Philadelphia (PA), USA
4 × 400 m relay	3:15.17	Ledovskaya, Nazarova, Pinigina, Bryzgina	USSR	1 October 1988	Seoul, South Korea
4 × 800 m relay	7:50.17	Olizarenko, Gurina, Borisova, Podyalovskaya	USSR	5 August 1984	Moscow, Russian Federation
High jump	2.09 m/6 ft $10\frac{1}{4}$ in	Stefka Kostadinova	Bulgaria	30 August 1987	Rome, Italy
Long jump	7.52 m/24 ft $8\frac{1}{4}$ in	Galina Chistyakova	USSR	11 June 1988	Leningrad, Russian Federation
Triple jump	15.50 m/50 ft $10\frac{1}{4}$ in	Inessa Kravets	Ukraine	10 August 1995	Gothenburg, Sweden
Pole vault	4.62 m/15 ft 2 in[1]	Stacy Dragila	USA	27 May 2000	Phoenix (AZ), USA
Shot put	22.64 m/74 ft 3 in	Natalya Lisovskaya	USSR	7 June 1987	Moscow, Russian Federation
Discus	76.80 m/252 ft	Gabriele Reinsch	East Germany	9 July 1988	Neubrandenburg, Germany
Hammer	76.07 m/249 ft 6 in	Michaela Melinte	Romania	29 August 1999	Rülingen, Switzerland
Javelin	67.09 m/220 ft $1\frac{1}{2}$ in	Mirela Manjani-Tzelili	Greece	28 August 1999	Seville, Spain
Heptathlon	7,291 pts	Jackie Joyner-Kersee	USA	23–24 September 1988	Seoul, South Korea
5 km walk	20:13.26	Kerry Saxby-Junna	Australia	25 February 1996	Hobart, Australia
10 km walk	41:56.23	Nadezhda Ryashkina	USSR	24 July 1990	Seattle (WA), USA

[1] Awaiting ratification.

International Amateur Athletic Federation (IAAF) World Championships, Gold Medallists (Men)

The competition was first held in 1983 in Helsinki, Finland. The following years were: 1987: Rome, Italy; 1991: Tokyo, Japan; 1993: Stuttgart, Germany; 1995: Gothenburg, Sweden; 1997: Athens, Greece; 1999: Seville, Spain.

Year	Name	Country	Result
100 m			
1999	Maurice Greene	USA	9.80
200 m			
1999	Maurice Greene	USA	19.90
400 m			
1999	Michael Johnson	USA	43.18
800 m			
1999	Wilson Kipketer	Denmark	1:43.30
1,500 m			
1999	Hicham El Guerrouj	Morocco	3:27.65
5,000 m			
1999	Salah Hissou	Morocco	12:58.13
10,000 m			
1999	Haile Gebrselassie	Ethiopia	27:57.27
Marathon			
1999	Abel Anton	Spain	2 h 13:36
3,000 m steeplechase			
1999	Christopher Koskei	Kenya	8:11.76
110 m hurdles			
1999	Colin Jackson	Great Britain	13.04
400 m hurdles			
1999	Fabrizio Mori	Italy	47.72
4 × 100 m relay			
1999		USA	37.59
4 × 400 m relay			
1999		USA	2:56.45
20 km walk			
1999	Ilya Markov	Russia	1 h 23:34
50 km walk			
1999	German Skurygin	Russia	3 h 44:23
High jump			
1999	Vyacheslav Voronin	Russia	2.37 m
Pole vault			
1999	Maksim Tarakov	Russia	6.02 m
Long jump			
1999	Iván Pedroso	Cuba	8.56 m
Triple jump			
1999	Charles Michael Friedek	Germany	17.59 m
Shot			
1999	C J Hunter	USA	21.79 m
Discus			
1999	Anthony Washington	USA	69.08 m
Hammer			
1999	Karsten Kobs	Germany	80.24 m
Javelin			
1999	Aki Parviainen	Finland	89.52 m
Decathlon			
1999	Tomas Dvorak	Czech Republic	8,744 pts

International Amateur Athletic Federation (IAAF) World Championships, Gold Medallists (Women)

The competition was first held in 1983 at Helsinki, Finland. The following years were: 1987: Rome, Italy; 1991: Tokyo, Japan; 1993: Stuttgart, Germany; 1995: Gothenburg, Sweden; 1997: Athens, Greece; 1999: Seville, Spain.

Year	Name	Country	Result
100 m			
1999	Marion Jones	USA	10.70
200 m			
1999	Inger Miller	USA	21.77
400 m			
1999	Cathy Freeman	Australia	49.67
800 m			
1999	Ludmila Formanova	Czech Republic	1:56.68
1,500 m			
1999	Svetlana Masterkova	Russia	3:59.53
5,000 m[1]			
1999	Gabriela Szabo	Romania	14:41.82
10,000 m			
1999	Gete Wami	Ethiopia	30:24.56
Marathon			
1999	Jong Song-Ok	South Korea	2 h 26:59
100 m hurdles			
1999	Gail Devers	USA	12.37
400 m hurdles			
1999	Daimi Pernia	Cuba	52.89
4 × 100 m relay			
1999		Bahamas	41.92
4 × 400 m relay			
1999		Russia	3:21.98
20 km walk[2]			
1999	Liu Hongyu	China	1 h 30:50
High jump			
1999	Inga Babakova	Ukraine	1.99 m
Pole vault			
1999	Stacy Dragila	USA	4.60 m
Long jump			
1999	Niurka Montalvo	Spain	7.06 m
Triple jump			
1999	Paraskevi Tsiamilata	Greece	14.88 m
Shot			
1999	Astrid Kumbernuss	Germany	19.85 m
Discus			
1999	Franka Dietzsch	Germany	68.14 m
Hammer			
1999	Mihaela Melinte	Romania	75.20 m
Javelin			
1999	Mirela Manjani-Tzelili	Greece	67.09 m
Heptathlon			
1999	Eunice Barber	France	6,861 pts

[1] Replaced the 3,000 metres in 1995.
[2] Replaced the 10 kilometres walk in 1999.

International Amateur Athletic Federation (IAAF) World Cross-Country Championships

This championship is run over 12 km. In 1998 a new short course race run over 4 km was introduced.

Year	Name	Country
Men's individual		
1995	Paul Tergat	Kenya
1996	Paul Tergat	Kenya
1997	Paul Tergat	Kenya
1998[1]	Paul Tergat	Kenya
1998[2]	John Kibowen	Kenya
1999[1]	Paul Tergat	Kenya
1999[2]	Benjamin Limo	Kenya
2000[1]	Mohammed Mourhit	Belgium
2000[2]	John Kibowen	Kenya
Women's individual		
1995	Derartu Tulu	Ethiopia
1996	Gete Wami	Ethiopia
1998[1]	Sonia O'Sullivan	Ireland, Republic of
1997	Derartu Tulu	Ethiopia
1998[2]	Sonia O'Sullivan	Ireland, Republic of
1999[1]	Jackline Maranga	Kenya
1999[2]	Gete Wami	Ethiopia
2000[1]	Derartu Tulu	Ethiopia
2000[2]	Kutre Dulecha	Ethiopia
Men's team		
1995		Kenya
1996		Kenya
1997		Kenya
1998[1]		Kenya
1998[2]		Kenya
1999[1]		Kenya
1999[2]		Kenya
2000[1]		Kenya
2000[2]		Kenya
Women's team		
1995		Kenya
1996		Kenya
1997		Kenya
1998[1]		Kenya
1998[2]		Morocco
1999[1]		France
1999[2]		Ethiopia
2000[1]		Ethiopia
2000[2]		Portugal

[1] Long course.
[2] Short course.

London Marathon Winners

This event was first held in 1981, it is now sponsored by Flora.

Year	Name	Country	Time
Men			
1990	Allister Hutton	Great Britain	2 h 10:10
1991	Yakov Tolstikov	USSR	2 h 9:17
1992	Antonio Pinto	Portugal	2 h 10:02
1993	Eamonn Martin	Great Britain	2 h 10:50
1994	Dionicio Ceron	Mexico	2 h 8:53
1995	Dionicio Ceron	Mexico	2 h 8:30
1996	Dionicio Ceron	Mexico	2 h 10:00
1997	Antonio Pinto	Portugal	2 h 7:55
1998	Abel Anton	Spain	2 h 7:57
1999	Abdelkader El Mouaziz	Morocco	2 h 7:57
2000	Antonio Pinto	Portugal	2 h 6:36
Women			
1990	Wanda Panfil	Poland	2 h 26:31
1991	Rosa Mota	Portugal	2 h 26:41
1992	Katrin Dörre	Germany	2 h 29:39
1993	Katrin Dörre	Germany	2 h 27:09
1994	Katrin Dörre	Germany	2 h 32:34
1995	Małgorzata Sobańska	Poland	2 h 27:43
1996	Liz McColgan	Great Britain	2 h 27:54
1997	Joyce Chepchumba	Kenya	2 h 25:51
1998	Catherina McKiernan	Ireland, Republic of	2 h 26:26
1999	Joyce Chepchumba	Kenya	2 h 23:22
2000	Tegla Loroupe	Kenya	2 h 24:33

Australian Football

Australian Rules Football

Australian football developed on the goldfields of Victoria, Australia; it is a game that combines aspects of Gaelic football, rugby, and association football; it is played between two teams of 18 players each, with an inflated oval ball. It is unique to Australia.

The game is played on an oval pitch with a pair of goalposts at each end. On either side of each pair of goalposts is a smaller post. Each team is placed in five lines of three persons each, and three players follow the ball all the time. Points are scored by kicking the ball between the goalposts, without its being touched on the way ('goal', 6 points), or by passing the ball between a goalpost and one of the smaller posts, or causing it to hit a post ('behind', 1 point). There are no scrums, line-outs, or off-side rules. A player must get rid of the ball immediately on starting to run, by kicking, punching, or bouncing it every 10 m/33 ft. No tackling (as in rugby) is allowed.

Australian Football League Champions

Year	Team
1980	Richmond
1981	Carlton
1982	Carlton
1983	Hawthorn
1984	Essendon
1985	Essendon
1986	Hawthorn
1987	Carlton
1988	Hawthorn
1989	Hawthorn
1990	Collingwood
1991	Hawthorn
1992	West Coast
1993	Essendon
1994	West Coast
1995	Carlton Blues
1996	North Melbourne
1997	Adelaide
1998	Adelaide
1999	Kangaroos

Badminton

World Badminton Championships

The Thomas and Uber Cups were held in 2000 (even years). The other events were last held in 1999 (odd years).

Event	Name	Country
1997 World Championships		
Men's singles	Peter Rasmussen	Denmark
Women's singles	Ye Zhaoying	China
Men's doubles	Budiarto Sigit and Candra Wijaya	Indonesia
Women's doubles	Ge Fei/Gu Yun	China
Sudirman trophy (mixed team)	China	
1998 Team Championships		
Thomas Cup (men's)		Indonesia
Uber Cup (women's)		China

Event	Name	Country
1999 World Championships		
Men's singles	Sun Jun	China
Women's singles	Camilla Martin	Denmark
Men's doubles	Kim Dong-Moon/Ha Tae-Kwon	Korea, South
Women's doubles	Ge Fei/Gu Yun	China
Mixed doubles	Kim Dong-Moon/Ra Kyung-Min	Korea, South
2000 Team Championships		
Thomas Cup (men's)		Indonesia
Uber Cup (women's)		China

Yonex All-England Badminton Championships

These championships were first held in 1899. The 2000 championships were held in Birmingham, 7–12 March.

2000

Event	Name	Country
Men		
Singles	Xia Xuanze	China
Doubles	Ha Tae-Kwon/Kim Dong-Moon	Korea, South
Women		
Singles	Gong Zhichao	China
Doubles	Ge Fei/Gu Jun	China
Mixed doubles	Kim Dong-Moon/Ra Kyung-Min	Korea, South

Baseball

Baseball Records

The most outstanding baseball player of modern times was 'Babe' Ruth. Before his retirement in 1935, he set a lifetime record of 714 home runs that remained unbroken until 1974, when Hank Aaron passed this mark. Mark McGwire of the St Louis Cardinals broke the most famous record in baseball on 9 September 1998 when he hit his 62nd home run of the season. This surpassed the 61 hit by Roger Maris of the New York Yankees in 1961. Maris, in turn, was the first player to surpass Babe Ruth's record 60 home runs for the Yankees in 1927.

Baseball: World Series

The World Series was first held as an end-of-season game between the winners of the two professional leagues of the USA, the National League and the American League in 1903, and was established as a series of seven games in 1905. The Boston Red Sox were the first winners of the series in 1903, when they beat Pittsburgh Pirates 5–3.
(AL = American League; NL = National League.)

Year	Winner	Loser	Score
1993	Toronto Blue Jays, AL	Philadelphia Phillies, NL	4–2
1994	no World Series[1]		
1995	Atlanta Braves, NL	Cleveland Indians, AL	4–2
1996	New York Yankees, AL	Atlanta Braves, NL	4–2
1997	Florida Marlins, NL	Cleveland Indians, AL	4–3
1998	New York Yankees, AL	San Diego Padres, NL	4–0
1999	New York Yankees, AL	Atlanta Braves, NL	4–0

[1] Owing to a players' strike.

Basketball

Basketball: 1999–2000

The Manchester Giants were the outstanding team in British basketball, winning 31 of their 36 regular season games, but they must have greeted their 74–65 victory over the Birmingham Bullets in the Dairylea Dunkers championship final with relief as well as jubilation after earlier in the season losing in the finals of both the Uni-ball Trophy and the National Cup (to the London Towers and the Sheffield Sharks respectively).

In the USA, the Los Angeles Lakers, inspired by Shaquille O'Neal and Kobe Bryant, defeated the Indian Pacers 4–2 in the championship finals to clinch their first NBA title since 1988.

Basketball

Basketball was invented by James Naismith, a Canadian, who was a physical education instructor at what is now Springfield College (Massachusetts). The first game was played in 1891, and the first formal rules were set out in 1892. It became popular rapidly, especially in the eastern USA, and the first college and professional games were played before 1900.

Today, the premier professional league is the National Basketball Association (NBA), formed in 1949. Perhaps the most famous professional team is the Harlem Globetrotters, an independent team founded in 1927. Its tours of the world have greatly increased basketball's popularity.

Canada was the first country outside the USA to take up the game, and now nearly all European countries have their national leagues, with the various European cups forming major competitions. Over 140 countries are affiliated to the International Amateur Basketball Federation (FIBA). Basketball has been played in the Summer Olympic Games since 1936.

Basketball: World Champions

The world championship was first held in 1950 for men and 1953 for women. It is contested every four years.

Year	Country	Year	Country
Men		*Women*	
1963	Brazil	1964	USSR
1967	USSR	1967	USSR
1970	Yugoslavia	1971	USSR
1974	USSR	1975	USSR
1978	Yugoslavia	1979	USA
1982	USSR	1983	USSR
1986	USA	1986	USA
1990	Yugoslavia	1990	USA
1994	USA	1994	Brazil
1998	Yugoslavia	1998	USA

British Basketball Champions (Men)

1999–2000

Event	Champions/result
Dairylea Dunkers Championship Northern Conference[1]	Manchester Giants
Dairylea Dunkers Championship Southern Conference[1]	London Towers
Dairylea Dunkers Championship play-off final[1]	Manchester Giants 74 Birmingham Bullets 65
Uniball Trophy final	London Towers 74 Manchester Giants 73
National Cup final	Sheffield Sharks 89 Manchester Giants 80
National Basketball League Division One	Teesside Mohawks
National Basketball League Division One Championship final	Teesside Mohawks 80 Solent Stars 63
National Basketball League Division Two Championship final	Kingston Wildcats 68 Manchester Attitude 62
Scottish League	St Mirren
Scottish Cup	Glasgow Sports Divison 74 Edinburgh Kings 70

[1] Formally the Budweiser League. In 1999–2000 the league was divided into a Northern Conference of seven teams and a Southern Conference of six teams.

British Basketball Champions (Women)

1999–2000

Event	Champions/result
National Basketball League Division One	Sheffield Hatters
National Basketball League Division One Championship final	Sheffield Hatters 64 Spelthorne Acers 52
National Basketball League Division Two	St Albans Saints
National Cup	Rhondda Rebels 65 Spelthorne Acers 38
Scottish League	Midlothian Saints
Scottish Cup	Glasgow Sports Division 50 Midlothian Saints 49

British Basketball: The Dairylea Dunkers Championship Final Table

Until 1999 this was known as the Budweiser League. In 1999–2000 the league was divided into a Northern Conference of seven teams and a Southern Conference of six teams. Teams finishing in the top four places of each conference qualify for the play-offs.

1999–2000
Final standings

Position	Team	Played	Won	Lost	Points
Northern Conference					
1	Manchester Giants[1]	36	31	5	62
2	Sheffield Sharks[1]	36	29	7	58
3	Edinburgh Rocks[1]	36	19	17	38
4	Chester Giants[1]	36	17	19	34
5	Derby Storm	36	17	19	34
6	Newcastle Eagles	36	10	26	20
7	Leicester Riders	36	10	26	20
Southern Conference					
1	London Towers[1]	34	23	11	46
2	Thames Valley Tigers[1]	34	18	16	36
3	Birmingham Bullets[1]	34	17	17	34
4	Milton Keynes Lions[1]	34	15	19	30
5	Greater London Leopards	34	11	23	22
6	Brighton Bears	34	11	23	22

[1] Qualified for play-offs.

British Basketball: The Dairylea Dunkers Championship Play-Off Results

Until 1999 this was known as the Budweiser League. The top eight teams qualify for the Championships.

2000

Winner	Loser	Score
Quarter finals		
Manchester Giants	Milton Keynes Lions	81–68
London Towers	Chester Giants	85–58
Birmingham Bullets	Sheffield Sharks	81–71
Edinburgh Rocks	Thames Valley Tigers	68–64
Semi finals		
Birmingham Bullets	London Towers	60–53
Manchester Giants	Edinburgh Rocks	88–84
Final, Wembley, 6 May		
Manchester Giants	Birmingham Bullets	74–65

National Basketball Association Champions (USA)

The National Basketball Association (NBA) Championship has been held since 1947.

Year	Winner	Runner up	Series
1980	Los Angeles Lakers	Philadelphia 76ers	4–2
1981	Boston Celtics	Houston Rockets	4–2
1982	Los Angeles Lakers	Philadelphia 76ers	4–2
1983	Philadelphia 76ers	Los Angeles Lakers	4–0
1984	Boston Celtics	Los Angeles Lakers	4–3
1985	Los Angeles Lakers	Boston Celtics	4–2
1986	Boston Celtics	Houston Rockets	4–2
1987	Los Angeles Lakers	Boston Celtics	4–2
1988	Los Angeles Lakers	Detroit Pistons	4–3
1989	Detroit Pistons	Los Angeles Lakers	4–0
1990	Detroit Pistons	Portland Trail Blazers	4–1
1991	Chicago Bulls	Los Angeles Lakers	4–1
1992	Chicago Bulls	Portland Trail Blazers	4–2
1993	Chicago Bulls	Phoenix Suns	4–2
1994	Houston Rockets	New York Knicks	4–3
1995	Houston Rockets	Orlando Magic	4–0
1996	Chicago Bulls	Seattle SuperSonics	4–2
1997	Chicago Bulls	Utah Jazz	4–2
1998	Chicago Bulls	Utah Jazz	4–2
1999	San Antonio Spurs	New York Knicks	4–1
2000	Los Angeles Lakers	Indiana Pacers	4–2

Billiards

World Professional Billiards Championship

The championship was instituted in 1870.

Year	Name	Country
1993	Geet Sethi	India
1994	Peter Gilchrist	England
1995	Geet Sethi	India
1996	Mike Russell	England
1997	not held	
1998	Geet Sethi	India
1999	Not held	

Bowls

World Outdoor Bowls Championship

The championship was first held in 1966 for men and in 1969 for women.

Year	Name	Country
Men		
1980	David Bryant	England
1984	Peter Belliss	New Zealand
1988	David Bryant	England
1992	Tony Allcock	England
1996	Tony Allcock	England
2000	Jeremy Hendry	Ireland
Women		
1981	Norma Shaw	England
1985	Merle Richardson	Australia
1988	Janet Ackland	Wales
1992	Margaret Johnston	Ireland
1996	Carmelita Anderson	Norfolk Island
2000	Margaret Johnston	Ireland

World Indoor Bowls Championship

The championship was first held in 1979 for men and in 1988 for women.

Year	Name	Country
Men		
1995	Andy Thomson	England
1996	David Gourlay Jr	Scotland
1997	Hugh Duff	Scotland
1998	Paul Foster	Scotland
1999	Alex Marshall	Scotland
2000	Robert Weale	Wales
Women		
1995	Joyce Lindores	Scotland
1996	Sandy Hazell	England
1997	Norma Shaw	England
1998	Caroline McAllister	Scotland
1999	Caroline McAllister	Scotland
2000	Marlene Castle	New Zealand

Boxing

Boxing: 1999–2000

Lennox Lewis defeated Evander Holyfield of the USA on points in Las Vegas on 13 November 1999 to become the first British undisputed world heavyweight champion since Bob Fitzsimmons in 1897. Lewis's performance had been more convincing in the controversial drawn bout with Holyfield at Madison Square Garden, New York, eight months earlier; but he did enough to prove that he was a worthy champion. However, five months later he was forced to relinquish his WBA belt after a federal judge ruled that Lewis was obliged, under his contract with the US boxing promoter Don King, to make his first defence against the WBA's number one contender. Lewis went ahead with a bout against the WBC number two, Michael Grant, on 29 April 2000. The fight, at Madison Square Garden, resulted in an easy second-round knockout for Lewis, and his assured performance against an inexperienced but well-regarded opponent ironically reinforced his reputation as the best heavyweight in the world.

Britain's champion Naseem Hamed made the 14th successful defence of his WBO world featherweight crown with an impressive knockout victory over Vuyani Bungu of South Africa at Olympia, London, on 13 March 2000. Four months earlier in New York, another British featherweight, Paul Ingle, defeated Mexico's Manuel Medina on points to capture the IBF version of the title.

Boxing

The modern sport of boxing dates from the 18th century, when fights were fought with bare knuckles and untimed rounds. Each round ended with a knockdown. Fighting with gloves became the accepted form in the latter part of the 19th century after the formulation of the Queensberry Rules in 1867.

Jack Broughton was one of the early champions and in 1743 drew up the first set of boxing rules. The last bare-knuckle championship fight was between John L Sullivan and Jake Kilrain in 1899. Today all boxing follows the original Queensberry Rules, but with modifications.

Sanctioning Bodies in World Boxing

The major sanctioning bodies in world boxing are:

World Boxing Association (WBA) formed as the National Boxing Association (NBA) in the USA in 1920; it changed its name to WBA in 1962

World Boxing Council (WBC) formed in Mexico City in 1963

International Boxing Federation (IBF) formed as a breakaway from the WBA in 1983

The World Boxing Organization (WBO) founded in 1988

Current World Professional Boxing Champions

WBA = World Boxing Association; WBC = World Boxing Council; IBF = International Boxing Federation; WBO = World Boxing Organization. Weights given are weight limit. As of 5 June 2000.

Weight	WBA	WBC	IBF	WBO
Heavyweight (>86.2 kg/>190 lb)	vacant	Lennox Lewis (UK)	Lennox Lewis (UK)	Chris Byrd (USA)
Cruiserweight (86.2 kg/190 lb)	Fabrice Tiozzo (France)	Juan Carlos Gomez (Cuba)	Vasily Jirov (Kazakhstan)	Johnny Nelson (UK)
Light heavyweight (79.4 kg/175 lb)	Roy Jones Jr (USA)	Roy Jones Jr (USA)	Roy Jones Jr (USA)	Darius Michalczewski (Germany)
Super middleweight (76.2 kg/168 lb)	Bruno Girard (France)	Glen Catley (UK)	Sven Ottke (Germany)	Joe Calzaghe (UK)
Middleweight (72.6 kg/160 lb)	William Joppy (USA)	Keith Holmes (USA)	Bernard Hopkins (USA)	Armand Krajne (Slovakia)
Super welterweight (69.9 kg/154 lb)	Felix Trinidad (Puerto Rico)	Javia Castillejo (Spain)	Fernando Vargas (USA)	Harry Simon (Namibia)
Welterweight (66.7 kg/147 lb)	James Page (USA)	Oscar de la Hoya (USA)	vacant	Daniel Santos (USA)

(continued)

Current World Professional Boxing Champions (*continued*)

Weight	WBA	WBC	IBF	WBO
Junior welterweight (63.5 kg/140 lb)	Sharmba Mitchell (USA)	Kostya Tszyu (Russian)	Zab Judah (USA)	Randall Bailey (USA)
Lightweight (61.2 kg/135 lb)	Giberto Serrano (Venezuela)	Steve Johnston (USA)	Paul Spadafora (USA)	Artur Grigorian (Germany)
Junior lightweight (59 kg/130 lb)	Joel Cassamayor (Cuba)	Floyd Mayweather (USA)	Diego Corrales (USA)	Acelino Feitas (Brazil)
Featherweight (57.2 kg/126 lb)	Freddie Norwood (USA)	Guty Espadas (Mexico)	Paul Ingle (UK)	Naseem Hamed (UK)
Junior featherweight (55.3 kg/122 lb)	Bones Adams (USA)	Erik Morales (Mexico)	Lehlohonolo Ledwaba (South Africa)	Mark Antonio Barrera (Mexico)
Bantamweight (53.5 kg/118 lb)	Pauli Ayala (USA)	Veerapol Sahaprom (Thailand)	Tim Austin (USA)	Johnny Tapia (USA)
Junior bantamweight (52.2 kg/115 lb)	Hideki Todaka (Japan)	Injoo Choo (South Korea)	vacant	Adonis Rivas (Nicaragua)
Flyweight (50.8 kg/112 lb)	Sornpichai Kratchingdaenggym (Thailand)	Medgoen Z-K Batteryl (Thailand)	Irene Pacheco (Columbia)	Isidro Garcia (USA)
Junior flyweight (49 kg/108 lb)	Pichitnoi Choi Siriwat (Thailand)	Yo-Sam Choi (South Korea)	Ricardo Lopez (Mexico)	Michael Carbajal (USA)
Strawweight (47.6 kg/105 lb)	Noel Arambulet (Venezuela)	Jose Antonio Aguirre (Mexico)	Zolani Petelo (South Africa)	Kermin Guardia (Colombia)

World Heavyweight Champions

Present weight limit: over 86.2 kg/190 lb. Fighters are US nationals unless otherwise stated.

Year	Name
Champions 1882–1978	
1882–92	John L Sullivan[1]
1892–97	James J Corbett
1897–99	Bob Fitzsimmons (UK)
1899–1904	James J Jeffries[2]
1905–06	Marvin Hart
1906–08	Tommy Burns (Canada)
1908–15	Jack Johnson
1915–19	Jess Willard
1919–26	Jack Dempsey
1926–28	Gene Tunney[2]
1928–30	vacant
1930–32	Max Schmeling (Germany)
1932–33	Jack Sharkey
1933–34	Primo Carnera (Italy)
1934–35	Max Baer
1935–37	James J Braddock
1937–49	Joe Louis[2]
1949–51	Ezzard Charles
1951–52	Jersey Joe Walcott
1952–56	Rocky Marciano[2]
1956–59	Floyd Patterson
1959–60	Ingemar Johansson (Sweden)
1960–62	Floyd Patterson
1962–64	Sonny Liston
1964–67	Cassius Clay (Muhammad Ali)[2 3]
1965–67	Ernie Terrell (WBA title)[4]
1968–70	Joe Frazier (New York title)
1968–70	Jimmy Ellis (WBA title)
1970–73	Joe Frazier
1973–74	George Foreman
1974–78	Muhammad Ali
1978	Leon Spinks[5]
WBA champions (since 1978)	
1978	Leon Spinks
1978–79	Muhammad Ali[2]
1979–80	John Tate
1980–82	Mike Weaver
1982–83	Michael Dokes
1983–84	Gerrie Coetzee (South Africa)
1984–85	Greg Page
1985–86	Tony Tubbs
1986	Tim Witherspoon
1986–87	James 'Bonecrusher' Smith
1987–90	Mike Tyson (and WBC, IBF)
1990	James 'Buster' Douglas (and WBC, IBF)
1990–92	Evander Holyfield (and WBC, IBF)
1992–93	Riddick Bowe (and IBF, WBC)[6]
1993–94	Evander Holyfield (and IBF)
1994	Michael Moorer (and IBF)
1994–95	George Foreman (and IBF)[2]
1995–96	Bruce Seldon
1996	Mike Tyson
1996–99	Evander Holyfield
1999–2000	Lennox Lewis[7]
WBC champions (since 1978)	
1978	Ken Norton
1978–83	Larry Holmes[8]
1984	Tim Witherspoon
1984–86	Pinklon Thomas
1986	Trevor Berbick (Canada)
1986–90	Mike Tyson (and WBA, IBF 1987– 90)
1990	James 'Buster' Douglas (and WBA, IBF)
1990–92	Evander Holyfield (and WBA, IBF)
1992	Riddick Bowe (and IBF, WBC)[6]
1992–94	Lennox Lewis (UK)
1994–95	Oliver McCall
1995–96	Frank Bruno (UK)
1996	Mike Tyson[2]
1997–	Lennox Lewis (UK)
IBF champions (since 1983)	
1983–85	Larry Holmes
1985–87	Michael Spinks[2]
1987	Tony Tucker
1987–90	Mike Tyson (and WBA, WBC)
1990	James 'Buster' Douglas (and WBA, WBC)
1990–92	Evander Holyfield (and WBA, WBC)
1992–93	Riddick Bowe (and IBF, WBC)[6]
1993–94	Evander Holyfield (and WBA)
1994	Michael Moorer (and WBA)
1994–95	George Foreman (and WBA)[2]
1996	Michael Moorer
1997–99	Evander Holyfield
1999–	Lennox Lewis (UK)

[1] Sullivan was the last of the bareknuckle world champions.
[2] Relinquished or stripped of title, or retired as champion.
[3] Clay changed his name to Muhammad Ali after becoming world champion.
[4] The WBA withdrew recognition of Ali after he signed for a return match with Liston in 1964. Ernie Terrell won the vacant WBA title in 1965. However, Ali remained the widely accepted champion and two years later defeated Terrell to regain the undisputed title.
[5] Spinks was stripped of his WBC title in March 1978 and remained WBA champion until losing to Ali in September 1978.
[6] Bowe relinquished his WBC title in December 1992.
[7] Lewis relinquished his WBA title in April 2000.
[8] Holmes relinquished his WBC title in December 1983 to become the newly formed IBF's first champion.

Current British Professional Boxing Champions

As of 1 June 1999.

Weight	Name	Weight	Name
Heavyweight (over 86.2 kg/190 lb)	Mike Holden	Light welterweight (limit 63.5 kg/140 lb)	Jason Rowland
Cruiserweight (limit 86.2 kg/190 lb)	Carl Thompson	Lightweight (limit 61.2 kg/135 lb)	Bobby Vanzie
Light heavyweight (limit 79.4 kg/175 lb)	Clinton Woods	Super featherweight (limit 59 kg/130 lb)	Michael Gomez
Super middleweight (limit 76.2 kg/168 lb)	David Starie	Featherweight (limit 57.2 kg/126 lb)	Michael Thornhill
Middleweight (limit 72.6 kg/160 lb)	Howard Eastman	Super bantamweight (limit 55.3 kg/122 lb)	Michael Alldis
Light middleweight (limit 69.9 kg/154 lb)	Wayne Alexander	Bantamweight (limit 53.5 kg/118 lb)	Ady Lewis
Welterweight (limit 66.7 kg/147 lb)	Harry Dhami	Flyweight (limit 50.8 kg/112 lb)	Jason Booth

Chess

World Chess Champions

The first recognized world chess championship-title match took place in 1886 between Wilhelm Steinitz and Johannes Zuckertort. However, the winner of that match, Steinitz, had been widely regarded as the world champion since 1866. The Fédération Internationale de Échecs (FIDE) took over control of the world championship in 1948 and remained the sole governing body until 1993, when the breakaway Professional Chess Association (PCA), led by the world champion Garry Kasparov, organized a rival championship, which Kasparov himself won. Since then there have been two world champions, Kasparov and Anatoly Karpov, who, after Kasparov had been stripped of his title, won a play-off for the FIDE title. However, it is Kasparov who was widely regarded as the true world champion. Since 1998 the FIDE World Championship has been decided at an annual knock-out tournament.

Dates	Name	Country
1866–94	Wilhelm Steinitz	Austria
1894–21	Emanuel Lasker	Germany
1921–27	José Raul Capablanca	Cuba
1927–35	Alexander Alekhine	Russia[1]
1935–37	Max Euwe	Netherlands
1937–46	Alexander Alekhine	Russia[1]
1948–56	Mikhail Botvinnik	USSR[2]
1957–58	Vassily Smyslov	USSR
1958–60	Mikhail Botvinnik	USSR
1960–61	Mikhail Tal	USSR
1961–63	Mikhail Botvinnik	USSR
1963–69	Tigran Petrosian	USSR
1969–72	Boris Spassky	USSR
1972–75	Bobby Fischer	USA
1975–85	Anatoly Karpov	USSR
1985–	Garry Kasparov	USSR/Azerbaijan[3 4]
1993–99	Anatoly Karpov	Russia[5]
1999–	Alexander Khalifman	Russia[5]

[1] Alekhine became a French citizen in 1927. [2] Botvinnik won a five-man tournament organized by FIDE to determine a successor to Alekhine, who had died in 1946. [3] Kasparov is an Azerbaijani but has represented Russia internationally at chess. [4] FIDE world champion 1985–93; PCA world champion since 1993. [5] FIDE world champion.

Cricket

International Cricket

International Cricket: The Cronje Scandal

In April 2000, international cricket was plunged into a crisis after allegations were made in India that the South African captain Hansie Cronje and team-mates Herschelle Gibbs, Pieter Strydom, and Nicky Boje had been involved in a match-fixing conspiracy with an Indian bookmaker.

On 7 April, Indian police investigating the alleged fixing of a one-day international series between India and South Africa, which had taken place in March, charged Cronje, Gibbs, Strydom, and Boje in their absence with fraud and conspiracy, and released transcripts of bugged telephone conversations in which Cronje discussed match-fixing.

Cronje at first dismissed the allegations, but on 11 April admitted that he had received $10–15,000 in cash from a London-based Indian bookmaker for giving information on playing conditions and for match forecasting relating to the one-day triangular tournament between England, South Africa, and Zimbabwe in January–February 2000, but denied that he had conspired to fix matches. He also denied that any of his team-mates had been involved. However, in June, Gibbs and Strydom (and another player, Henry Williams) told the King Commission of Inquiry that they had been offered money by Cronje to underperform in certain matches. (Boje, one of the players named by the Indian police denied that he had been approached by Cronje). Williams and Gibbs also admitted that they had accepted offers of $15,000 to play badly and that they had previously lied in order to protect Cronje.

Cronje confessed to the Commission on 15 June that he had received around $100,000 from bookmakers in dealings going back to January 1995, though he still denied that he had actually fixed matches.

Cronje was sacked from the South African captaincy, and he will almost certainly never play first-class cricket again, but neither he nor his team-mates will face criminal charges in South Africa after being given immunity from prosecution by the Commission in return for full confessions.

The International Cricket Council (ICC) responded to the Cronje scandal by warning on 3 May that 'a set of stringent penalties – including life bans from the sport – will apply forthwith for anyone found guilty of corrupt behaviour.' In Pakistan a year-long inquiry into corruption in Pakistani cricket, conducted by High Court Judge Qayyum at the instigation of the Pakistan Cricket Board, led to life bans for the ex-Pakistan captain Salim Malik, and bowler Ata-ur-Rehman, and fines for six other players including Wasim Akram. In India in July 2000, income tax officials raided the homes of players (including former captains Kapil Dev and Mohammed Azharuddin), officials, and bookmakers as part of a national inquiry into allegations of match-fixing and corruption in Indian cricket.

Test Cricket

The first Test match was played in Melbourne, Australia, in 1877 between Australia and England. England was defeated by 45 runs. The first Test match held in England was in 1880. In 1882 Australia's victory over England at the Oval inspired a journalist to write a mock obituary of English cricket, in which he coined the term the Ashes. The introduction of the six-ball over in England in 1900 aided higher scoring; bowlers countered the batting dominance by swerve bowling (by fast bowlers), and in the early 1900s the 'googly', a style quickly adopted around the world. In 1909 the Imperial Cricket Conference, renamed the International Cricket Conference (ICC) in 1965 and the International Cricket Council in 1989, was set up with England, Australia, and South Africa as founder members; the West Indies, New Zealand, India, Pakistan, Sri Lanka, Zimbabwe, and Bangladesh joined later.

Test Cricket: England versus Zimbabwe: 2000 Test Series Results

England won the two-match series 1–0.

First Test
Lord's, London, 18–21 May 2000

England won by an innings and 209 runs. Zimbabwe 83 (Giddins 5–15) and 123 (Caddick 4–38, Gough 4–57), England 415 (Stewart 124 not out, Hick 101; Streak 6–87).

Man of the Match: Ed Giddins (England)

Second Test
Trent Bridge, Nottingham, 1–5 June 2000

Match drawn. England 374 (Atherton 136) and 147, Zimbabwe 285–4 declared (Goodwin 148 not out) and 25–1.

Man of the Match: Murray Goodwin (Zimbabwe)

Men of the Series – England: Michael Atherton; Zimbabwe: Heath Streak

Test Cricket: Team-by-Team Summary of Results

As of 6 June 2000. (– = not applicable.)

Team	Tests	Won	Lost	Drawn	Tied
Australia	606	260	168	176	2
England	768	258	222	288	–
South Africa	242	70	91	81	–
West Indies	359	137	93	128	1
New Zealand	279	44	114	121	–
India	333	61	112	159	1
Pakistan	267	75	65	127	–
Sri Lanka	99	18	39	42	–
Zimbabwe	43	3	22	18	–

Test Cricket: England Record

As of 6 June 2000.

Opponent	Tests	Won	Lost	Drawn
Australia	296	93	117	86
India	84	32	14	38
New Zealand	82	37	6	39
Pakistan	55	14	9	32
South Africa	120	50	23	47
Sri Lanka	6	3	2	1
West Indies	121	28	51	42
Zimbabwe	4	1	0	3
Total	768	258	222	288

Test Cricket: Highest Individual Innings, Batting

As of 14 June 2000.

Score	Batsman (team)	Opponents	Venue	Season
375	Brian Lara [1] (West Indies)	England	St John's	1993–94
365[2]	Gary Sobers (West Indies)	Pakistan	Kingston	1957–58
364	Len Hutton (England)	Australia	The Oval	1938
340	Sanath Jayasuriya[1] (Sri Lanka)	India	Colombo	1997–98
337	Hanif Mohammad (Pakistan)	West Indies	Bridgetown	1957–58
336[2]	Walter Hammond (England)	New Zealand	Auckland	1932–33
334[2]	Mark Taylor (Australia)	Pakistan	Peshawar	1998–99
334	Don Bradman (Australia)	England	Headingley	1930
333	Graham Gooch (England)	India	Lord's	1990
325	Andrew Sandham (England)	West Indies	Kingston	1929–30

[1] Current player.
[2] Not out.

Test Cricket: Most Wickets in an Innings, Bowling

As of 14 June 2000.

Best bowling	Bowler (team)	Opponents	Venue	Season
10–53	Jim Laker (England)	Australia	Manchester	1956
10–74	Anil Kumble[1] (India)	Pakistan	Delhi	1998–99
9–28	George Lohmann (England)	South Africa	Johannesburg	1895–96
9–37	Jim Laker (England)	Australia	Manchester	1956
9–52	Richard Hadlee (New Zealand)	Australia	Brisbane	1985–86
9–56	Abdul Qadir (Pakistan)	England	Lahore	1987–88
9–57	Devon Malcolm[1] (England)	South Africa	The Oval	1994
9–65	Muttiah Muralitharan[1] (Sri Lanka)	England	The Oval	1998
9–69	Jasubhai Patel (India)	Australia	Kanpur	1959–60
9–83	Kapil Dev (India)	West Indies	Ahmedabad	1983–84
9–86	Sarfraz Nawaz (Pakistan)	Australia	Melbourne	1978–79

[1] Current player.

Test Cricket: Leading Career Run Makers

As of 1 June 2000.

Batsman	Team	Tests	Innings	Not out	Runs	Average
Allan Border	Australia	156	265	44	11,174	50.56
Sunil Gavaskar	India	125	214	16	10,122	51.12
Graham Gooch	England	118	215	6	8,900	42.58
Javed Miandad	Pakistan	124	189	21	8,832	52.57
Viv Richards	West Indies	121	182	12	8,540	50.23

(*continued*)

Test Cricket: Leading Career Run Makers *(continued)*

Batsman	Team	Tests	Innings	Not out	Runs	Average
Steve Waugh[1]	Australia	128	204	38	8,373	50.43
David Gower	England	117	204	18	8,231	44.25
Geoff Boycott	England	108	193	23	8,114	47.72
Gary Sobers	West Indies	93	160	21	8,032	57.78
Colin Cowdrey	England	114	188	15	7,624	44.06
Gordon Greenidge	West Indies	108	185	16	7,558	44.72
Mark Taylor	Australia	104	186	13	7,525	43.49
Clive Lloyd	West Indies	110	175	14	7,515	46.67

[1] Current player.

Test Cricket: Leading Career Wicket Takers

As of 1 June 2000.

Bowler	Team	Tests	Wickets	Runs	Average
Courtney Walsh[1]	West Indies	117	449	11,275	25.11
Kapil Dev	India	131	434	12,867	29.64
Richard Hadlee	New Zealand	86	431	9,612	22.30
Wasim Akram[1]	Pakistan	95	398	9,121	22.91
Curtly Ambrose[1]	West Indies	93	388	8,184	21.09
Ian Botham	England	102	383	10,878	28.40
Malcolm Marshall	West Indies	81	376	7,876	20.94
Shane Warne[1]	Australia	84	366	9,505	25.96
Imran Khan	Pakistan	88	362	8,258	22.81
Dennis Lillee	Australia	70	355	8,493	23.92
Bob Willis	England	90	325	8,190	25.20
Lance Gibbs	West Indies	79	309	8,989	29.09

[1] Current player.

Cricket: World Cup Winners

This competition was first held in 1975.

Year	Winner	Runner-up	Location
1975	West Indies	Australia	England
1979	West Indies	England	England
1983	India	West Indies	England
1987	Australia	England	India
1992	Pakistan	England	Australia
1996	Sri Lanka	Australia	India, Pakistan, and Sri Lanka
1999	Australia	Pakistan	UK

One-Day Internationals: Leading Career Run Makers

As of 4 June 2000.

Name	Matches	Innings	Not outs	Runs	Highest score	Average
Mohammad Azharuddin (India)[1]	334	308	54	9,378	153 not out	36.92
Sachin Tendulkar (India)[1]	249	242	22	9,262	186 not out	42.10
Desmond Haynes (West Indies)	238	237	28	8,648	152 not out	41.37
Aravinda de Silva (Sri Lanka)[1]	266	258	26	8,312	145 not out	35.82
Mark Waugh (Australia)[1]	217	212	16	7,492	130	38.22
Arjuna Ranatunga (Sri Lanka)[1]	269	255	47	7,454	131 not out	35.83
Javed Miandad (Pakistan)	233	218	41	7,381	119 not out	41.70
Inzamam-ul-Haq (Pakistan)[1]	223	212	29	7,182	137 not out	39.24
Salim Malik (Pakistan)	283	256	38	7,169	102	32.88
Saeed Anwar (Pakistan)[1]	202	199	15	7,158	194	38.90

[1] Current player.

One-Day Internationals: Leading Career Wicket Takers

As of 9 June 2000.

Bowler	Matches	Overs	Wickets	Runs	Average
Wasim Akram (Pakistan)[1]	305	2,613.4	425	10,046	23.63
Waqar Younis (Pakistan)[1]	193	1,591	309	7,280	23.55
Anil Kumble (India)[1]	203	1,815.4	267	7,630	28.57
Kapil Dev (India)	225	1,867	253	6,945	27.45
Javagal Srinath (India)[1]	187	1,629.2	252	7,222	28.65
Shane Warne (Australia)[1]	146	1,341.4	228	5,608	24.59
Saqlain Mushtaq (Pakistan)[1]	124	1,081.5	227	6,491	20.32
Courtney Walsh (West Indies)[1]	205	1,803.4	227	6,917	30.47
Curtly Ambrose (West Indies)[1]	176	1,558.5	225	5,429	24.12
Allan Donald (South Africa)[1]	121	1,073	206	4,336	21.04

[1] Current player.

County Cricket

County Cricket: 1999

Surrey are one of English cricket's traditional powers, but since the 1950s when they were County Champions seven years in a row, they have also been one of its most consistent under-achievers. In the mid-1990s they enjoyed a degree of success in one-day competitions but until 1999 they had not won the County title for 28 years. Unbeaten all season, their triumph was very much a team effort, though Saqlain Mushtaq's contribution of 58 wickets in seven matches at an average of only 11.37 was outstanding. Second-placed Lancashire have not won the County Championship outright since 1934, but their record in limited overs cricket is second to none, and in 1999 they won the National League Division One championship, their sixth one-day trophy in five years. Gloucestershire triumphed in the other two one-day competitions, thrashing Yorkshire by 124 runs in the Benson & Hedges Cup Super Cup final, and defeating West Country rivals Somerset by 24 runs to win the NatWest Trophy. Gloucestershire's season, however, was not an unqualified success – they finished bottom of the County Championship and, along with the eight sides immediately above them, were consigned to the second division of the structured championship.

County Cricket: PPP Healthcare County Championship Final Table

From the year 2000 the county championship was divided into a first and second division. The top nine teams in the 1999 championship final table qualify for the first division; the bottom nine will play in the second division. The previous year's positions are shown in brackets.

1999

Position	Team	Played	Won	Lost	Drawn	Batting	Bowling	Points
1	Surrey (5)	17	12	0	5	36	64	264
2	Lancashire (2)	17	8	4	5	37	55	208
3	Leicestershire (1)	17	5	3	9	43	61	200
4	Somerset (9)	17	6	4	7	38	56	194
5	Kent (11)	17	6	4	7	34	60	194
6	Yorkshire (3)	17	8	6	3	21	64	193
7	Hampshire (6)	17	5	5	7	45	58	191
8	Durham (14)	17	6	7	4	34	66	188
9	Derbyshire (10)	17	7	8	2	34	61	187
10	Warwickshire (8)	17	6	5	6	35	56	187
11	Sussex (7)	17	6	5	6	29	60	185
12	Essex (18)	17	5	7	5	38	63	181
13	Northamptonshire (15)	17	4	7	6	35	64	171
14	Glamorgan (12)	17	5	7	5	26	57	163
15	Worcestershire (13)	17	4	6	7	18	65	159
16	Middlesex (17)	17	4	5	8	24	53	157
17	Nottinghamshire (16)	17	4	11	2	27	57	140
18	Gloucestershire (4)	17	2	9	6	26	62	136

County Cricket: Final First Class Batting Averages

To qualify for inclusion, a player must participate in a minimum of eight matches.

1999

Name	Team	Matches	Innings	Not out	Runs	Highest score	Average	100s	50s
Stuart Law	Essex	17	29	4	1,833	263	73.32	8	6
Justin Langer	Middlesex	12	22	4	1,048	241[1]	58.22	4	2
Jamie Cox	Somerset	18	30	2	1,617	216	57.75	6	6
Matthew Hayden	Northamptonshire	9	15	2	745	170	57.30	4	1
Rob Turner	Somerset	19	27	4	1,217	138[1]	52.91	2	10
Nasser Hussain	Essex	12	20	1	988	143	52.00	2	8
David Sales	Northamptonshire	18	29	4	1,291	303[1]	51.64	3	5
Alistair Brown	Surrey	17	26	4	1,127	265	51.22	4	2
Dion Nash	New Zealand	8	11	3	395	135[1]	49.37	1	2
Peter Bowler	Somerset	17	27	8	931	149	49.00	4	0

[1] Not out.

County Cricket: Final First Class Bowling Averages

To qualify for inclusion, a player must take a minimum of 20 wickets.

1999

Player	Team	Overs	Maidens	Runs	Wickets	Average	Best bowling figures
Saqlain Mushtaq	Surrey	290.5	90	660	58	11.37	7–19
Muttiah Muralitharan	Lancashire	386.2	122	777	66	11.77	7–39
Dion Nash	New Zealand	232.0	84	548	34	16.11	7–39
David Millns	Leicestershire	142.3	35	372	23	16.17	5–62
Alexander Morris	Hampshire	172.0	51	497	28	17.75	5–52
Neil Killeen	Durham	411.3	114	1,070	58	18.44	7–85
Martin Bicknell	Surrey	545.4	154	1,346	71	18.95	4–32
Gavin Hamilton	Yorkshire	277.1	64	825	43	19.18	5–30
Julian Thompson	Kent	434.1	116	1,265	64	19.76	7–89
Tim Munton	Warwickshire	409.1	107	1,028	52	19.76	7–36

County Cricket: English County Championship Winners

The championship was sponsored by Schweppes, 1977–83. Since 1999 it has been sponsored by PPP Healthcare.
Counties winning most championships: Yorkshire, 30 (including one shared); Surrey, 17 (including one shared); Middlesex, 12 (including two shared); Lancashire, 8 (including one shared).

Year	Team
1946	Yorkshire
1947	Middlesex
1948	Glamorgan
1949	Middlesex/Yorkshire (shared)
1950	Lancashire/Surrey (shared)
1951	Warwickshire
1952	Surrey
1953	Surrey
1954	Surrey
1955	Surrey
1956	Surrey
1957	Surrey
1958	Surrey
1959	Yorkshire
1960	Yorkshire
1961	Hampshire
1962	Yorkshire
1963	Yorkshire
1964	Worcestershire
1965	Worcestershire
1966	Yorkshire
1967	Yorkshire
1968	Yorkshire
1969	Glamorgan
1970	Kent
1971	Surrey

(continued)

County Cricket: English County Championship Winners (*continued*)

Year	Team	Year	Team	Year	Team
1972	Warwickshire	1982	Middlesex	1992	Essex
1973	Hampshire	1983	Essex	1993	Middlesex
1974	Worcestershire	1984	Essex	1994	Warwickshire
1975	Leicestershire	1985	Middlesex	1995	Warwickshire
1976	Middlesex	1986	Essex	1996	Leicestershire
1977	Kent/Middlesex (shared)	1987	Nottinghamshire	1997	Glamorgan
1978	Kent	1988	Worcestershire	1998	Leicestershire
1979	Essex	1989	Worcestershire	1999	Surrey
1980	Middlesex	1990	Middlesex		
1981	Nottinghamshire	1991	Essex		

County Cricket: CGU National Cricket League

This limited-overs league competition replaced the AXA League in 1999. The league is split into two divisions of nine teams. The bottom three sides of Division One are relegated to Division Two and the top three sides of Division Two win promotion to Division One.

1999 Position	Team	Games played	Wins	Losses	Ties	No result	Points
Division One							
1	Lancashire Lightning	16	11	2	0	3	50
2	Worcestershire Royals	16	10	4	0	2	44
3	Kent Spitfires	16	8	6	0	2	36
4	Gloucestershire Gladiators	16	8	8	0	0	32
5	Yorkshire Phoenix	16	8	8	0	0	32
6	Leicestershire Foxes	16	6	8	0	2	28
7	Warwickshire Bears[1]	16	6	8	0	2	28
8	Hampshire Hawks[1]	16	5	9	0	2	24
9	Essex Eagles[1]	16	3	12	0	1	14
Division Two							
1	Sussex Sharks[2]	16	13	2	0	1	54
2	Somerset Sabres[3]	16	13	3	0	0	52
3	Northamptonshire Steelbacks[3]	16	9	5	0	2	40
4	Glamorgan Dragons	16	8	7	1	0	34
5	Nottinghamshire Outlaws	16	6	8	0	2	28
6	Surrey Lions	16	5	9	1	1	24
7	Middlesex Crusaders	16	5	10	1	0	22
8	Derbyshire Scorpions	16	4	10	1	1	20
9	Durham Dynamos	16	3	12	0	1	14

[1] Relegated to Division Two.
[2] Promoted to Division One as champions.
[3] Promoted to Division One.

County Cricket: CGU National League Winners

This 45-overs-a-side one-day championship was first held in 1969. It has been sponsored by John Player, 1969–86, Refuge Assurance, 1987–91, AXA Equity and Law, 1992–98, and CGU from 1999. In 2000 the championship was sponsored by Norwich Union. The tournament was split into two divisions for the first time in 1999.

Year	Team	
1980	Warwickshire	
1981	Essex	
1982	Sussex	
1983	Yorkshire	
1984	Essex	
1985	Essex	
1986	Hampshire	
1987	Worcestershire	
1988	Worcestershire	
1989	Lancashire	
1990	Derbyshire	
1991	Nottinghamshire	
1992	Middlesex	
1993	Glamorgan	
1994	Warwickshire	
1995	Kent	
1996	Surrey	
1997	Warwickshire	
1998	Lancashire	
1999	Division One	Lancashire
	Division Two	Sussex

County Cricket: NatWest Trophy Winners

This trophy competition was the first one-day county cricket tournament and was first held in 1963 as a 65-overs-a-side (60 overs from 1964, and 50 from 1999) knockout competition. It has been sponsored by Gillette, 1963–80, and National Westminster Bank (since 1981). All finals are played at Lord's.
Most wins: Lancashire, 6; Warwickshire, 5; Sussex, Middlesex, 4.

Year	Team	Year	Team	Year	Team
1980	Middlesex	1987	Nottinghamshire	1994	Worcestershire
1981	Derbyshire	1988	Middlesex	1995	Warwickshire
1982	Surrey	1989	Warwickshire	1996	Lancashire
1983	Somerset	1990	Lancashire	1997	Essex
1984	Middlesex	1991	Hampshire	1998	Lancashire
1985	Essex	1992	Northamptonshire	1999	Gloucestershire
1986	Sussex	1993	Warwickshire		

County Cricket: Benson and Hedges Cup Winners

This one-day limited overs competition was first held in 1972. All finals are played at Lord's.

Year	Team	Year	Team	Year	Team
1980	Northamptonshire	1987	Yorkshire	1994	Warwickshire
1981	Somerset	1988	Hampshire	1995	Lancashire
1982	Somerset	1989	Nottinghamshire	1996	Lancashire
1983	Middlesex	1990	Lancashire	1997	Surrey
1984	Lancashire	1991	Worcestershire	1998	Essex
1985	Leicestershire	1992	Hampshire	1999	Gloucestershire
1986	Middlesex	1993	Derbyshire	2000	Gloucestershire

County Cricket: English Minor Counties Cricket Championship

This competition was first contested in 1895.

Year	Team	Year	Team
1990	Hertfordshire	1995	Devon
1991	Staffordshire	1996	Devon
1992	Staffordshire	1997	Devon
1993	Staffordshire	1998	Staffordshire
1994	Devon	1999	Cumberland

Curling

Curling World Champions

This championship was first held in 1959 for men and in 1979 for women.

Year	Country	Year	Country
Men		***Women***	
1995	Canada	1995	Sweden
1996	Canada	1996	Canada
1997	Sweden	1997	Canada
1998	Canada	1998	Sweden
1999	Scotland	1999	Sweden
2000	Canada	2000	Canada

Cycling

Cycling: 1999–2000

Lance Armstrong's emphatic victory in the 1999 Tour de France, just 18 months after returning to competitive cycling following a life-threatening battle against cancer, must rank as one of the greatest and most heroic achievements in the history of cycling, or indeed of any sport. It certainly did something to redeem the event – and professional cycling in general – after the scandal of the previous year, when all nine Festina riders were expelled from the race after French customs found an array of illegal drugs, including the banned endurance-enhancing hormone erythropoietin (EPO), in a Festina team car. However, the fact that the 1998 winner Marco Pantani was not able to defend his title after being thrown out of the 1999 Giro d'Italia (while leading on the penultimate day) on suspicion of taking EPO, proved that the sport still has much to do to repair its damaged reputation. Pantani's expulsion gave fellow Italian Ivan Gotti his second Giro title in three years, while the 1997 Tour de France champion, Jan Ullrich of Germany, won the season's other major stage race, the Vuelta a España. Ullrich also won the time trial title at the World Championships in Verona in October, ahead of Sweden's Michael Andersson and Britain's Chris Boardman. In the World Track Championships at Berlin, also in October, Felicia Ballanger of France won her fifth consecutive world titles in both the women's sprint and the 500 metre time trial.

Tour de France Winners

This race was first held in 1903.

Year	Name	Country	Year	Name	Country
1980	Joop Zoetemelk	Netherlands	1990	Greg LeMond	USA
1981	Bernard Hinault	France	1991	Miguel Induráin	Spain
1982	Bernard Hinault	France	1992	Miguel Induráin	Spain
1983	Laurent Fignon	France	1993	Miguel Induráin	Spain
1984	Laurent Fignon	France	1994	Miguel Induráin	Spain
1985	Bernard Hinault	France	1995	Miguel Induráin	Spain
1986	Greg LeMond	USA	1996	Bjarne Riis	Denmark
1987	Stephen Roche	Ireland, Republic of	1997	Jan Ullrich	Germany
			1998	Marco Pantani	Italy
1988	Pedro Delgado	Spain	1999	Lance Armstrong	USA
1989	Greg LeMond	USA	2000	Lance Armstrong	USA

Tour de France

The Tour de France road race for professional cyclists is held annually over approximately 4,800 km/3,000 mi of primarily French roads. The race takes about three weeks to complete and the route varies each year, often taking in adjoining countries, but always ending in Paris. A separate stage is held every day, and the overall leader at the end of each stage wears the coveted 'yellow jersey' (French *maillot jaune*).

First held 1903, it is now the most watched sporting event in the world, with more than 10 million spectators. Although it is a race for individuals, sponsored teams of 12 riders take part, each with its own 'star' rider whom team members support.

Tour of Britain Winners

The Tour of Britain, formerly the Milk Race, was first held in 1951. Following an absence of three years, it was revived in 1998 as the PruTour of Britain.

Year	Name	Country	Year	Name	Country
1990	Shane Sutton	Australia	1995	no race	
1991	Chris Walker	UK	1996	no race	
1992	Conor Henry	UK	1997	no race	
1993	Chris Lillywhite	UK	1998	Stuart O'Grady	Australia
1994	Maurizio Fondriest	Italy	1999	Marc Wauters	Belgium

■ Curling

Cycling World Champions and Major Tour Winners

1999

Category	Name	Country
Men		
Road		
Giro d'Italia	Ivan Gotti	Italy
Vuelta a España	Jan Ullrich	Germany
World Cup	Andrei Tchmil	Belgium
World Road Race Championship	Oscar Freire	Spain
Time trial	Jan Ullrich	Germany
Off-road		
Cyclo-cross	Mario de Clercq	Belgium
Mountain biking: cross country	Michael Rasmussen	Denmark
Mountain biking: downhill	Nicolas Vouilloz	France
Track		
1 km time trial	Arnaud Tournant	France
Keirin	Jens Fiedler	Germany
Madison	Isaac Galvez Lopez/Joan Llaneras Rosello	Spain
Olympic sprint		France
Individual pursuit	Robert Bartko	Germany
Sprint	Laurent Gane	France
Points race	Bruno Risi	Switzerland
Team pursuit		Germany

Category	Name	Country
Women		
Road		
Tour de France	Diana Ziliute	Lithuania
World Road Race Championship	Anna Wilson	Australia
Time trial	Leontien Van Moorsel	Netherlands
Mountain biking		
Cross country	Margarita Fullana	Spain
Downhill	Anne-Caroline Chausson	France
Track		
Points race	Marion Clignet	France
Sprint	Felicia Ballanger	France
500 m time trial	Felicia Ballanger	France
Individual pursuit	Marion Clignet	France

Darts

World Professional Darts Champions

Year	Name	Country
1990	Phil Taylor	England
1991	Dennis Priestley	England
1992	Phil Taylor	England
1993	John Lowe	England
1994	John Part	Canada
1995	Richie Burnett	Wales
1996	Steve Beaton	England
1997	Les Wallace	Scotland
1998	Raymond Barneveld	Netherlands
1999	Raymond Barneveld	Netherlands
2000	Ted Hankey	England

World Darts Council (Professional Darts Council) Champions

The World Darts Council Championships were first held in 1994.

Year	Name	Country
1994	Dennis Priestley	England
1995	Phil Taylor	England
1996	Phil Taylor	England
1997	Phil Taylor	England
1998	Phil Taylor	England
1999	Phil Taylor	England
2000	Phil Taylor	England

Darts

The game of darts may have derived from target practice with broken arrow shafts in days when archery was a compulsory military exercise. The Pilgrim Fathers are believed to have played darts aboard the *Mayflower* 1620. The present-day numbering system was designed by Brian Gamlin of Bury, Lancashire, England, in 1896.

The world championship was inaugurated in 1978 and is held annually. Since 1993–94 there have been two darts world championships. The British Darts Organization (BDO) World Professional Championship (sponsored by Embassy), founded in 1978, has been held since 1986 at the Lakeside Country Club, Frimley Green, Surrey. In 1993 a group of top players formed the breakaway World Darts Council (WDC) and introduced its own world championships (sponsored by Skol) in December–January 1993–94 at the Circus Tavern, Purfleet, Essex. In 1997 the World Darts Council was renamed the Professional Darts Council (PDC).

At the 2000 PDC World Championships England's Phil Taylor, widely regarded as the greatest darts player of all time, won his sixth consecutive world championship and his eighth in all.

Equestrianism

Show Jumping World Champions

This championship was first held in 1953.

Year	Name	Country
1982	Norbert Koof	West Germany
1986	Gail Greenhough	Canada
1990	Eric Navet	France
1994	Franke Sloothaak	Germany
1998	Rodrigo Pessoa	Brazil

Show Jumping: Volvo World Cup Champions

This championship was established by the Fédération Equestre Internationale (FEI) in 1979. Riders compete in a series of mostly indoor events, beginning in October and culminating in a final in April of the following year.

Year	Name	Country
1995	Nick Skelton	Great Britain
1996	Hugo Simon	Austria
1997	Hugo Simon	Austria
1998	Rodrigo Pessoa	Brazil
1999	Rodrigo Pessoa	Brazil
2000	Rodrigo Pessoa	Brazil

British Show Jumping Championship

This championship first took place in 1961. It is held at Hickstead, Sussex, as part of the British Show Jumping Derby, and is now sponsored by Peugeot.

Year	Name	Country
1980	Michael Whitaker	Great Britain
1981	Harvey Smith	Great Britain
1982	Paul Shockemöle	West Germany
1983	John Whitaker	Great Britain
1984	John Ledingham	Ireland, Republic of
1985	Paul Shockemöle	West Germany
1986	Paul Shockemöle	West Germany
1987	Nick Skelton	Great Britain
1988	Nick Skelton	Great Britain
1989	Nick Skelton	Great Britain
1990	Joe Turi	Great Britain
1991	Michael Whitaker	Great Britain
1992	Michael Whitaker	Great Britain
1993	Michael Whitaker	Great Britain
1994	Captain John Ledingham	Ireland, Republic of
1995	Captain John Ledingham	Ireland, Republic of
1996	Nelson Pessoa	Brazil
1997	John Popely	Great Britain
1998	Michael Whitaker	Great Britain
1999	Rob Hoekstra	Great Britain

Three-Day Eventing: World Champions

This championship was first held in 1966.

Year	Name	Country
1982	Lucinda Green[1]	Great Britain
1986	Virginia Leng[2]	Great Britain
1990	Blyth Tait	New Zealand
1994	Vaughan Jefferis	New Zealand
1998	Blyth Tait	New Zealand

[1] Born Prior-Palmer. [2] Born Holgate.

Three-Day Eventing: Badminton Horse Trials

This competition first took place in 1949. It is held at Badminton House, Gloucestershire, and is now sponsored by Mitsubishi Motors.

Year	Name	Country
1995	Bruce Davidson	USA
1996	Mark Todd	New Zealand
1997	David O'Connor	USA
1998	Chris Bartle	Great Britain
1999	Ian Stark	Great Britain
2000	Mary King	Great Britain

Football

International Football

Euro 2000

by Ben Ramos

As Italy and France lined up to begin the final of the 2000 European Championships in Rotterdam on 2 July, the sense of anticipation was considerable. For the previous three weeks audiences had been treated to spectacular goals, sudden reversals of fortune, and dramatic finales. Nevertheless, the tension and burden of expectation faced by players in major finals often results in a sterile contest, but the game came close to living up to its pre-match billing.

After an evenly contested first half, Italy took the lead in the 54th minute through Marco Delvecchio's close-range shot. France then poured forward in search of an equalizer, but with the Italians defending brilliantly, they created few clear cut chances. However, late into injury time, Sylvian Wiltord, a second half substitute, equalized with a cross-shot that Toldo in the Italian goal should perhaps have saved. But it was for David Trezeguet, another substitute, to hit the 'golden goal' winner with a spectacular shot in the first period of extra time.

The French coach Roger Lemerre had preserved the nucleus of the side that won the last World Cup, including the rock-solid back four of Thuram, Blanc, Desailly, and Lizarazu, with the inspirational Zinedine Zidane in midfield. But with the pacy Thierry Henry at centre-forward they had greater force in attack than the 1998 side. Technically excellent, they were committed to playing fluent, attacking football. With narrow victories over Spain in the quarter-finals, Portugal in the semis (which they won with a controversial Zidane penalty in extra time), and then Italy in the final itself, France showed resilience and a strong collective spirit.

Perhaps this was where the Netherlands, a side brimming with talent, fell short. Or perhaps they were just unlucky. They won all their group games, including a 3–2 victory over the French in Amsterdam, and then thrashed Yugoslavia 6–1 in the quarter-finals with an astonishing display of attacking football, reminiscent of the great Dutch sides of the 1970s and 1980s. Buoyed by their enthusiastic fans, nearly all of whom were bedecked in orange, they were expected to overcome Italy in the semi-finals in Amsterdam. The match, however, was a disaster for the Dutch. Playing against only ten men after Italy's Zambrotta was sent off in the 33rd minute, they dominated the game, missing two penalties and numerous other opportunities in normal and extra time, before losing the penalty shoot-out 3–1. England are thought to be bad at taking penalties, but the Dutch have now been eliminated on penalties from three successive European Championships and the last World Cup.

England were one of only a few teams at the tournament to fail the quality test. They lost 3–2 to Portugal, for whom Luis Figo and Rui Costa were outstanding, after racing into a two goal lead after only 20 minutes. Five days later, they defeated Germany 1–0, England's first victory over the Germans in a major competitive match since the 1966 World Cup final. But in their third match, against Romania, they again lost by three goals to two, the decisive goal coming from a penalty needlessly conceded by Phil Neville in the 89th minute. England lacked the quality of the French, the Dutch, and the Portuguese. The coach, Kevin

Keegan, said that his players did not pass the ball well, but they were hampered by his adherence to a rigid 4-4-2 line-up, which left the team exposed in midfield.

England's campaign was once again spoiled by crowd trouble. Outbreaks of violence involving England fans in Brussels and Charleroi before the Germany match led to UEFA taking the unprecedented step of threatening to throw the team out of the tournament. The Romania match passed without incident but the adverse publicity must have damaged England's bid to stage the 2006 World Cup, which ultimately failed.

European Football: European Championships (Euro 2000), Group Stage Results

Held in Belgium and the Netherlands, 10 June–2 July.
Group winners and runners-up proceed to the quarter-final stage.

Date (Venue)	Teams		Score
Group A			
12 June (Liège)	Germany	Romania	1–1
12 June (Eindhoven)	England	Portugal	2–3
17 June (Arnhem)	Portugal	Romania	1–0
17 June (Charleroi)	England	Germany	1–0
20 June (Charleroi)	England	Romania	2–3
20 June (Rotterdam)	Germany	Portugal	0–3
Group B			
10 June (Brussels)	Belgium	Sweden	2–1
11 June (Arnhem)	Italy	Turkey	2–1
14 June (Brussels)	Belgium	Italy	0–2
15 June (Eindhoven)	Sweden	Turkey	0–0
19 June (Brussels)	Belgium	Turkey	0–2
19 June (Eindhoven)	Italy	Sweden	2–1
Group C			
13 June (Rotterdam)	Norway	Spain	1–0
13 June (Charleroi)	Slovenia	Yugoslavia	3–3
18 June (Amsterdam)	Slovenia	Spain	1–2
18 June (Liège)	Norway	Yugoslavia	0–1
21 June (Bruges)	Spain	Yugoslavia	4–3
21 June (Arnhem)	Norway	Slovenia	0–0
Group D			
11 June (Bruges)	Denmark	France	0–3
11 June (Amsterdam)	CzechRepublic	The Netherlands	0–1
16 June (Bruges)	Czech Republic	France	1–2
16 June (Rotterdam)	Denmark	The Netherlands	0–3
21 June (Liège)	Czech Republic	Denmark	2–0
21 June (Amsterdam)	France	The Netherlands	2–3

European Football: European Championships (Euro 2000), Final Result

Final (Rotterdam, 2 July 2000)
Result[1]: France 2 (Wiltord 90 mins, Trezeguet 103 minutes), Italy 1 (Delvecchio 56 minutes)

Teams: **France** Barthez, Thuram, Blanc, Desailly, Lizarazu (Pires 85 minutes), Vieira, Deschamps, Djorkaeff (Trezeguet 75 minutes), Zidane, Dugarry (Wiltord 57 minutes), Henry; **Italy** Toldo, Cannavaro, Nesta, Iuliano, Pessotto, Albertini, Di Biagio (Ambrossini 65 minutes), Maldini, Totti, Fiore (Del Piero 52 minutes), Delvecchio (Montella 85 minutes)
Referee: Frisk (Sweden)

[1] 1–1 after 90 minutes. France wins with extra-time golden goal.
See also **colour section.**

European Football: European Championship Winners

The championship was instituted in 1958, with the first final in 1960; it is contested every four years.

Year	Winner	Runner-up	Score	Location
1960	USSR	Yugoslavia	2–1[1]	France
1964	Spain	USSR	2–1	Spain
1968	Italy	Yugoslavia	1–1[1]	Italy
1968	Italy	Yugoslavia	2–0	Italy
1972	West Germany	USSR	3–0	Belgium
1976	Czechoslovakia	West Germany	2–2[2]	Yugoslavia
1980	West Germany	Belgium	2–1	Italy
1984	France	Spain	2–0	France
1988	Netherlands	USSR	2–0	West Germany
1992	Denmark	Germany	2–0	Sweden
1996	Germany	Czech Republic	2–1[1]	England
2000	France	Italy	2–1[1]	Netherlands

[1] After extra time golden goal.
[2] Czechoslovakia won 5–4 on penalties.

European Football: European Championships (Euro 2000), Group Stage Final Tables

(Key: Pos = position; P = played; W = wins; D = draws; L = losses; F = goals for; A = goals against; Pts = points

Pos	Team	P	W	D	L	F	A	Pts
Group A								
1	Portugal	3	3	0	0	7	2	9
2	Romania	3	1	1	1	4	4	4
3	England	3	1	0	2	5	6	3
4	Germany	3	0	1	2	1	5	1
Group B								
1	Italy	3	3	0	0	6	2	9
2	Turkey	3	1	1	1	3	2	4
3	Belgium	3	1	0	2	2	5	3
4	Sweden	3	0	1	2	2	4	1
Group C								
1	Spain	3	2	0	1	6	5	6
2	Yugoslavia	3	1	1	1	7	7	4
3	Norway	3	1	1	1	1	1	4
4	Slovenia	3	0	2	1	4	5	2
Group D								
1	The Netherlands	3	3	0	0	7	2	9
2	France	3	2	0	1	7	4	6
3	Czech Republic	3	1	0	2	3	3	3
4	Denmark	3	0	0	3	0	8	0

European Football: European Championships (Euro 2000), Quarter Finals Results

Date (Venue)	Teams		Score
24 June (Amsterdam)	Portugal	Turkey	2–0
24 June (Brussels)	Italy	Romania	2–0
25 June (Rotterdam)	The Netherlands	Yugoslavia	6–1
25 June (Bruges)	France	Spain	2–1

European Football: European Championships (Euro 2000), Semi Finals Results

Date (Venue)	Teams		Score
28 June (Brussels)	France	Portugal	2–1[1]
29 June (Amsterdam)	Italy	The Netherlands	3–1[2]

[1] 1–1 after 90 minutes. France wins with extra-time golden goal.
[2] 0–0 after extra-time. Italy won 3–1 on penalties.

International Football: World Cup Finals

This tournament was not held in 1942 or 1946.

Year	Winner	Runner-up	Score	Venue
1930	Uruguay	Argentina	4–2	Uruguay
1934	Italy	Czechoslovakia	2–1	Italy
1938	Italy	Hungary	4–2	France
1950	Uruguay	Brazil	2–1	Brazil
1954	West Germany	Hungary	3–2	Switzerland
1958	Brazil	Sweden	5–2	Sweden
1962	Brazil	Czechoslovakia	3–1	Chile
1966	England	West Germany	4–2	England
1970	Brazil	Italy	4–1	Mexico
1974	West Germany	Holland	2–1	West Germany
1978	Argentina	Holland	3–1	Argentina
1982	Italy	West Germany	3–1	Spain
1986	Argentina	West Germany	3–2	Mexico
1990	West Germany	Argentina	1–0	Italy
1994	Brazil[1]	Italy	0–0	USA
1998	France	Brazil	3–0	France

[1] Brazil won 3–2 on penalties.

International Football: International Results

All European Championships (Euro 2000) qualifying matches unless otherwise stated.

Date	Teams		Score	Location
18 August 1999	Northern Ireland	France	0–1[1]	Belfast
1 September 1999	Ireland, Republic of	Yugoslavia	2–1	Dublin
4 September 1999	Belarus	Wales	1–2	Minsk
4 September 1999	Bosnia	Scotland	1–2	Sarajevo
4 September 1999	Croatia	Ireland, Republic of	1–0	Zagreb
4 September 1999	England	Luxembourg	6–0	Wembley
4 September 1999	Northern Ireland	Turkey	0–3	Belfast
8 September 1999	Germany	Northern Ireland	4–0	Munich
8 September 1999	Estonia	Scotland	0–0	Tallinn
8 September 1999	Malta	Ireland, Republic of	2–3	Mdina
8 September 1999	Poland	England	0–0	Warsaw
5 October 1999	Scotland	Bosnia	1–0	Glasgow
9 October 1999	Finland	Northern Ireland	4–1	Helsinki
9 October 1999	Macedonia	Ireland, Republic of	1–1	Skopje
9 October 1999	Scotland	Lithuania	3–0	Glasgow
9 October 1999	Wales	Switzerland	0–2	Wrexham
10 October 1999	England	Belgium	2–1[1]	Sunderland
13 November 1999	Ireland, Republic of	Turkey	1–1	Dublin
13 November 1999	Scotland	England	0–2	Glasgow
17 November 1999	England	Scotland	0–1	Wembley
17 November 1999	Turkey	Ireland, Republic of	0–0	Bursa
23 February 2000	England	Argentina	0–0[1]	Wembley
23 February 2000	Luxembourg	Northern Ireland	1–3[1]	Luxembourg
23 February 2000	Ireland, Republic of	Czech Republic	3–2[1]	Dublin
23 February 2000	Qatar	Wales	0–1[1]	Doha
23 February 2000	Ireland, Republic of	Greece	0–1[1]	Dublin
28 March 2000	Malta	Northern Ireland	0–3[1]	Ta'qali
29 March 2000	Scotland	France	0–2[1]	Glasgow
29 March 2000	Wales	Finland	1–2[1]	Cardiff
26 April 2000	The Netherlands	Scotland	0–0[1]	Arnhem
26 April 2000	Northern Ireland	Hungary	0–1[1]	Belfast
26 April 2000	Ireland, Republic of	Greece	0–1[1]	Dublin
23 May 2000	Wales	Brazil	0–3[1]	Cardiff
27 May 2000	England	Brazil	1–1[1]	Wembley
30 May 2000	Ireland, Republic of	Scotland	1–2[1]	Dublin
31 May 2000	England	Ukraine	2–0[1]	Wembley
2 June 2000	Portugal	Wales	3–0[1]	Chaves
3 June 2000	Malta	England	1–2[1]	Ta' Qali
4 June 2000	Mexico	Ireland, Republic of	2–2[2]	Chicago
7 June 2000	USA	Ireland, Republic of	1–1[2]	Boston
2 June 2000	Ireland, Republic of	South Africa	1–1[2]	New Jersey

[1] Friendly match.
[2] Nike US Cup tournament.

International Football: Fédération Internationale de Football Association (FIFA) Women's World Cup

This cup was inaugurated in 1991.

Year	Winner	Runner-up	Score	Venue
1991	USA	Norway	2–1	China
1995	Norway	Germany	2–0	Sweden
1999	USA	China	0–0[1]	USA

[1] USA won 5–4 on penalties after extra time.

FIFA World Player of the Year

This award was first presented in 1991. It is sponsored by FIFA, the European Sports Management Association, and Adidas, and is selected by national team coaches.

Year	Player	Team	Country of origin
1991	Lothar Matthäus	Inter Milan	Germany
1992	Marco Van Basten	A C Milan	Netherlands
1993	Roberto Baggio	Juventus	Italy
1994	Romario	Barcelona	Brazil
1995	George Weah	A C Milan	Liberia
1996	Ronaldo	Barcelona	Brazil
1997	Ronaldo	Inter Milan	Brazil
1998	Zinedine Zidane	Juventus	France
1999	Rivaldo	Barcelona	Brazil

European Club Football

European Football Champions' League 2000

In the first ever European Cup final between two teams from the same country, played at the Stade de France, Paris, on 25 May 2000, Real Madrid achieved a comprehensive 3–0 victory over Spanish neighbours Valencia with goals from Fernando Morientes, Steve McManaman, and Raul. Real's form earlier in the season had been unconvincing, but despite their unrivalled record in the competition few people backed them to win the cup until the quarter-final stage when they eliminated the defending champions Manchester United. However, in the final against Valencia, who had previously put out Lazio and Barcelona, they were magnificent, controlling the match almost from start to finish and taking their chances with clinical efficiency.

Chelsea, like Manchester United, reached the quarter-finals, and were within seven minutes of knocking out Barcelona before going out of the competition in extra-time 6–4 on aggregate. Arsenal failed to get past the group stage for the second year running. Finishing third in their group, they were given a place in the last 16 of the UEFA Cup under UEFA's generous new rules, and went on to reach the final where they lost on penalties to Galatasaray of Turkey.

Scottish champions Glasgow Rangers beat Parma in a qualifying round, but did not get through the group stage.

Final (Stade de France, Paris, 25 May 2000)

Attendance: 78,759

Result: Real Madrid 3 Valencia 0 (Morientes 39 minutes, McManaman 67 minutes, Raul 75 minutes)

Teams: **Real Madrid**: Casillas; Salgado (Hierro 84 minutes), Campo, Helguera, Karanka, Carlos, Redondo, McManaman, Raul, Anelka (Sanchis 79 minutes), Morientes (Savio 71 minutes); **Valencia**: Canizares; Angloma, Pellegrino, Djukic, Gerardo (Ilie 68 minutes), Mendieta, Farinos, Gerard, Gonzalez, Angulo, Lopez.

European Football: European Champions' Cup Winners

Inaugurated in 1956–56, this championship was played entirely on a knock-out basis until 1992, when a Champions' League of two divisions replaced the quarter- and semi-final stages. In 1995 the League was increased to four groups of four teams but reverted to a knock-out format at the quarter-final stage. In 1996 the League was further increased to six four-team groups when the runners-up as well as the champion clubs of the major leagues were included in the competition. The League was expanded again in 1999 to 32 clubs that played through two group stages for places in the quarter-finals. Most wins: Real Madrid 8; A C Milan, 5; Ajax Amsterdam, Liverpool, 4.

Year	Winners	Runners-up	Score
1956	Real Madrid	Stade de Reims	4–3
1957	Real Madrid	Fiorentina	2–0
1958	Real Madrid	AC Milan	3–2[1]
1959	Real Madrid	Stade de Reims	2–0
1960	Real Madrid	Eintracht Frankfurt	7–3
1961	Benfica	Barcelona	3–2
1962	Benfica	Real Madrid	5–3
1963	A C Milan	Benfica	2–1
1964	Internazionale	Real Madrid	3–1
1965	Internazionale	Benfica	1–0
1966	Real Madrid	Partizan Belgrade	2–1
1967	Glasgow Celtic	Internazionale	2–1
1968	Manchester United	Benfica	4–1[1]
1969	A C Milan	Ajax Amsterdam	4–1
1970	Feyenoord	Glasgow Celtic	2–1[1]
1971	Ajax Amsterdam	Panathinaikos	2–0
1972	Ajax Amsterdam	Inter Milan	2–0
1973	Ajax Amsterdam	Juventus	1–0
1974	Bayern Munich	Atletico Madrid	1–1
Replay	Bayern Munich	Atletico Madrid	4–0
1975	Bayern Munich	Leeds United	2–0
1976	Bayern Munich	St Etienne	1–0
1977	Liverpool	Borussia Mönchengladbach	3–1
1978	Liverpool	Club Brugge	1–0
1979	Nottingham Forest	Malmö	1–0
1980	Nottingham Forest	Hamburg	1–0
1981	Liverpool	Real Madrid	1–0
1982	Aston Villa	Bayern Munich	1–0
1983	Hamburg	Juventus	1–0
1984	Liverpool	Roma	1–1[1 2]
1985	Juventus	Liverpool	1–0
1986	Steaua Bucharest	Barcelona	0–0[1 3]
1987	Porto	Bayern Munich	2–1
1988	PSV Eindhoven	Benfica	0–0[4]
1989	A C Milan	Steaua Bucharest	4–0
1990	A C Milan	Benfica	1–0
1991	Red Star Belgrade	Olympique Marseille	0–0[5]
1992	Barcelona	Sampdoria	1–0[1]
1993	Olympique Marseille	A C Milan	1–0[6]
1994	A C Milan	Barcelona	4–0
1995	Ajax Amsterdam	A C Milan	1–0
1996	Juventus	Ajax Amsterdam	1–1[7]
1997	Borussia Dortmund	Juventus	3–1
1998	Real Madrid	Juventus	1–0
1999	Manchester United	Bayern Munich	2–1
2000	Real Madrid	Valencia	3–0

[1] After extra time. [2] Liverpool won 4–2 on penalties. [3] Steaua won 2–0 on penalties. [4] PSV won 6–5 on penalties. [5] Red Star Belgrade won 5–3 on penalties. [6] Replay. [7] Juventus won 4–2 on penalties.

Union of European Football Associations (UEFA) Cup Winners

This cup was established in 1955 as the International Industries Fairs Inter-Cities Cup. It was renamed the European Fairs Cup in 1966 and took on its present name in 1971. Most wins: Inter Milan, 5; Juventus, Barcelona, 3.
The 2000 final between Arsenal (England) and Galatasaray (Turkey) took place in Copenhagen on 17 May. Galatasaray won 4–1 on penalties after the match ended goal-less.

Year	Team	Country
1980	Eintracht Frankfurt	West Germany
1981	Ipswich Town	England
1982	IFK Gothenburg	Sweden
1983	Anderlecht	Belgium
1984	Tottenham Hotspur	England
1985	Real Madrid	Spain
1986	Real Madrid	Spain
1987	IFK Gothenburg	Sweden
1988	Bayer Leverkusen	West Germany
1989	Napoli	Italy
1990	Juventus	Italy
1991	Inter Milan	Italy
1992	Ajax	Holland
1993	Juventus	Italy
1994	Inter Milan	Italy
1995	Parma	Italy
1996	Bayern Munich	Germany
1997	Schalke	Germany
1998	Inter Milan	Italy
1999	Parma	Italy
2000	Galatasaray	Turkey

European Football: European Leagues' Selected Champions

1999–2000

Country	Team
Austria	FC Tirol Innsbruck
Belgium	Anderlecht
Bulgaria	Levski Sofia
Croatia	Dinamo Zagreb
Czech Republic	Sparta Prague
Denmark	Herfoelge
France	Monaco
Germany	Bayern Munich
Greece	Olympiakos
Hungary	Dunaferr
Italy	Lazio
Netherlands	PSV Eindhoven
Northern Ireland	Linfeld
Poland	Polonia Warsaw
Portugal	Sporting Lisbon
Republic of Ireland	Shelbourne
Romania	Dinamo Bucharest
Spain	Deportivo La Coruña
Switzerland	FC Sankt Gallen
Turkey	Galatasaray
Wales	TNS Llansantffraid
Yugoslavia	Red Star Belgrade

European Footballer of the Year

Year	Player	Club	Country of origin
1989	Marco Van Basten	A C Milan	Netherlands
1990	Lothar Matthäus	Inter Milan	Germany
1991	Jean-Pierre Papin	Marseille	France
1992	Marco Van Basten	A C Milan	Netherlands
1993	Roberto Baggio	Juventus	Italy
1994	Hristo Stoichkov	Barcelona	Bulgaria
1995	George Weah	A C Milan	Liberia
1996	Matthias Sammer	Borussia Dortmund	Germany
1997	Ronaldo	Inter Milan	Brazil
1998	Zinedine Zidane	Juventus	France
1999	Rivaldo	Barcelona	Brazil

English Football

English Football: 1999–2000

Manchester United won the FA Carling Premiership, losing just three games all season, and winning the title, their sixth in eight years, by a record margin of 18 points. Their defence uncharacteristically conceded as many as 45 goals, but such was their potency in attack that they scored a remarkable 97 goals themselves.

Arsenal and Chelsea, who finished second and fifth respectively, were the only teams to mount a sustained challenge. David O'Leary's young Leeds side were leading the league for most of the winter months, but their challenge collapsed in March. They did, however, pip Liverpool for the third Champions' League spot. Liverpool were perhaps the league's most improved side, though their new found consistency and defensive solidity deserted them in the last weeks of the season.

At the other end of the table, Bradford City stayed up against all the odds, though they needed a win on the last day of the season to leapfrog above Wimbledon, who were relegated along with Sheffield Wednesday and Watford. They will be replaced by Charlton Athletic, Manchester City, and Ipswich Town,

Manchester United controversially declined to take part in the FA Cup because of their involvement in the inaugural FIFA World Club Championship in January 2000. In their absence, Chelsea won the cup, defeating Aston Villa 1–0 in the final, the last to be held at Wembley before the stadium is rebuilt. Earlier in the season, Chelsea had become the first English club to field a side in a league match without a single English player, fuelling the argument that the influx of foreign players was having a detrimental effect on the development of home-grown talent and the success of the national side. Nevertheless a number of promising young English players emerged, most notably Steven Gerrard of Liverpool and Joe Cole of West Ham.

English Football: FA Carling Premiership Final Table

(Key: P = played; W = won; D = drawn; L = lost; F = goals for; A = goals against; Pts = points; GD = goal difference.)

1999–2000

Position	Team	P	Home					Away					Pts	GD
			W	D	L	F	A	W	D	L	F	A		
1	Manchester United	38	15	4	0	59	16	13	3	3	38	29	91	+52
2	Arsenal	38	14	3	2	42	17	8	4	7	31	26	73	+50
3	Leeds United	38	12	2	5	29	18	9	4	6	29	25	69	+15
4	Liverpool	38	11	4	4	28	13	8	6	5	23	17	67	+21
5	Chelsea	38	12	5	2	35	12	6	6	7	18	22	65	+19
6	Aston Villa	38	8	8	3	23	12	7	5	7	23	23	58	+11
7	Sunderland	38	10	6	3	28	17	6	4	9	29	39	58	+1
8	Leicester City	38	10	3	6	31	24	6	4	9	24	31	55	0
9	West Ham United	38	11	5	3	32	23	4	5	10	20	30	55	−1
10	Tottenham Hotspur	38	10	3	6	40	26	5	5	9	17	23	53	+8
11	Newcastle United	38	10	5	4	42	20	4	5	10	21	34	52	+9
12	Middlesbrough	38	8	5	6	23	26	6	5	8	23	26	52	−6
13	Everton	38	7	9	3	36	21	5	5	9	23	28	50	+10
14	Coventry City	38	12	1	6	38	22	0	7	12	9	32	44	−7
15	Southampton	38	8	4	7	26	22	4	4	11	19	40	44	−17
16	Derby County	38	6	3	10	22	25	3	8	8	22	32	38	−13
17	Bradford City	38	6	8	5	26	29	3	1	15	12	39	36	−30
18	Wimbledon[1]	38	6	7	6	30	28	1	5	13	16	46	33	−28
19	Sheffield Wednesday[1]	38	6	3	10	21	23	2	4	13	17	47	31	−32
20	Watford[1]	38	5	4	10	24	31	1	2	16	11	46	24	−42

[1] Relegated.

English Football: FA Carling Premiership Results

(– = not applicable.)

1999–2000

Home team	Away team									
	Arsenal	Aston Villa	Bradford City	Chelsea	Coventry City	Derby County	Everton	Leeds United	Leicester City	Liverpool
Arsenal	–	3–1	2–0	2–1	3–0	2–1	4–1	2–0	2–1	0–1
Aston Villa	1–1	–	1–0	0–0	1–0	2–0	3–0	1–0	2–2	0–0
Bradford City	2–1	1–1	–	1–1	1–1	4–4	0–0	1–2	3–1	1–0
Chelsea	2–3	1–0	1–0	–	2–1	4–0	1–1	0–2	1–1	2–0
Coventry City	3–2	2–1	4–0	2–2	–	2–0	1–0	3–4	0–1	0–3
Derby County	1–2	0–2	0–1	3–1	0–0	–	1–0	0–1	3–0	0–2
Everton	0–1	0–0	4–0	1–1	1–1	2–1	–	4–4	2–2	0–0
Leeds United	0–4	1–2	2–1	0–1	3–0	0–0	1–1	–	2–1	1–2
Leicester City	0–3	3–1	3–0	2–2	1–0	0–1	1–1	2–1	–	2–2
Liverpool	2–0	0–0	3–1	1–0	2–0	2–0	0–1	3–1	0–2	–
Manchester United	1–1	3–0	4–0	3–2	3–2	3–1	5–1	2–0	2–0	1–1

(continued)

English Football: FA Carling Premiership Results (*continued*)

1999–2000

Home team	Away team									
	Arsenal	Aston Villa	Bradford City	Chelsea	Coventry City	Derby County	Everton	Leeds United	Leicester City	Liverpool
Middlesbrough	2–1	0–4	0–1	0–1	2–0	1–4	2–1	0–0	0–3	3–4
Newcastle United	4–2	0–1	2–0	0–1	2–0	2–0	1–1	2–2	0–2	2–2
Sheffield Wednesday	1–1	0–1	2–0	1–0	0–0	0–2	0–2	0–3	4–0	1–2
Southampton	0–1	2–0	1–0	1–2	0–0	3–3	2–0	0–3	1–2	1–1
Sunderland	0–0	2–1	0–1	4–1	1–1	1–1	2–1	1–2	2–0	0–2
Tottenham Hotspur	2–1	2–4	1–1	0–1	3–2	1–1	3–2	1–2	2–3	1–0
Watford	2–3	0–1	1–0	1–0	1–0	0–0	1–3	1–2	1–1	2–3
West Ham United	2–1	1–1	5–4	0–0	5–0	1–1	0–4	0–0	2–1	1–0
Wimbledon	1–3	2–2	3–2	0–1	1–1	2–2	0–3	2–0	2–1	1–2

English Football: FA Carling Premiership Results (*continued*)

1999–2000

Home team	Away team									
	Manchester United	Middles-brough	Newcastle United	Sheffield Wednesday	Southampton	Sunderland	Tottenham Hotspur	Watford	West Ham United	Wimbledon
Arsenal	1–2	5–1	0–0	3–3	3–1	4–1	2–1	1–0	2–1	1–1
Aston Villa	0–1	1–0	0–1	2–1	0–1	1–1	1–1	4–0	2–2	1–1
Bradford City	0–4	1–1	2–0	1–1	1–2	0–4	1–1	3–2	0–3	3–0
Chelsea	5–0	1–1	1–0	3–0	1–1	4–0	1–0	2–1	0–0	3–1
Coventry City	1–2	2–1	4–1	4–1	0–1	3–2	0–1	4–0	1–0	2–0
Derby County	1–2	1–3	0–0	3–3	2–0	0–5	0–1	2–0	1–2	4–0
Everton	1–1	0–2	0–2	1–1	4–1	5–0	2–2	4–2	1–0	4–0
Leeds United	0–1	2–0	3–2	2–0	1–0	2–1	1–0	3–1	1–0	4–1
Leicester City	0–2	2–1	1–2	3–0	2–1	5–2	0–1	1–0	1–3	2–1
Liverpool	2–3	0–0	2–1	4–1	0–0	1–1	2–0	0–1	1–0	3–1
Manchester United	–	1–0	5–1	4–0	3–3	4–0	3–1	4–1	7–1	1–1
Middlesbrough	–	2–2	1–0	3–2	1–1	2–1	1–1	2–0	0–0	1–1
Newcastle United	3–0	2–1	–	8–0	5–0	1–2	2–1	1–0	2–2	3–3
Sheffield Wednesday	0–1	1–0	0–2	–	0–1	0–2	1–2	2–2	3–1	5–1
Southampton	1–3	1–1	4–2	2–0	–	1–2	0–1	2–0	2–1	2–0
Sunderland	2–2	1–1	2–2	1–0	2–0	–	2–1	2–0	1–0	2–1
Tottenham Hotspur	3–1	2–3	3–1	0–1	7–2	3–1	–	4–0	0–0	2–0
Watford	2–3	1–3	1–1	1–0	3–2	2–3	1–1	–	1–2	2–3
West Ham United	2–4	0–1	2–1	4–3	2–0	1–1	1–0	1–0	–	2–1
Wimbledon	2–2	2–3	2–0	0–2	1–1	1–0	1–1	5–0	2–2	–

English Football: Nationwide League Division One Final Table

Promotion play-offs: semi-finals over two legs played home and away. Birmingham City 0, Barnsley 4; Barnsley 1, Birmingham City 2; Barnsley win 5–2 on aggregate. Bolton Wanderers 2, Ipswich Town 2; Ipswich Town 5, Bolton Wanderers 3 (after extra-time); Ipswich Town win 7–5 on aggregate. Final (Wembley Stadium, 29 May 2000) Barnsley 2, Ipswich Town 4. Ipswich Town are promoted to the FA Carling Premiership.
(Key: P = played; W = won; D = drawn; L = lost; F = goals for; A = goals against; Pts = points; GD = goals difference.)

1999–2000

Position	Team	P	Home					Away					Pts	GD
			W	D	L	F	A	W	D	L	F	A		
1	Charlton Athletic[1]	46	15	3	5	37	18	12	7	4	42	27	91	+34
2	Manchester City[2]	46	17	2	4	48	17	9	9	5	30	23	89	+38
3	Ipswich Town[3]	46	16	3	4	39	17	9	9	5	32	25	87	+29
4	Barnsley	46	15	4	4	48	24	9	6	8	40	43	82	+21
5	Birmingham City	46	15	5	3	37	16	7	6	10	28	28	77	+21
6	Bolton Wanderers	46	14	5	4	43	26	7	8	8	26	24	76	+19
7	Wolverhampton Wanderers	46	15	5	3	45	20	6	6	11	19	28	74	+16
8	Huddersfield Town	46	14	5	4	43	21	7	6	10	19	28	74	+13
9	Fulham	46	13	7	3	33	13	4	9	10	16	28	67	+8
10	Queen's Park Rangers	46	9	12	2	30	20	7	6	10	32	33	66	+9
11	Blackburn Rovers	46	10	9	4	33	20	5	8	10	22	31	62	+4
12	Norwich City	46	11	6	6	26	22	3	9	11	19	28	57	−5
13	Tranmere Rovers	46	10	8	5	35	27	5	4	14	22	41	57	−11
14	Nottingham Forest	46	9	10	4	29	18	5	4	14	24	37	56	−2
15	Crystal Palace	46	7	11	5	33	26	6	4	13	24	41	54	−10
16	Sheffield United	46	10	8	5	38	24	3	7	13	21	47	54	−12
17	Stockport County	46	8	8	7	33	31	5	7	11	22	36	54	−12
18	Portsmouth	46	9	6	8	36	27	4	6	13	19	39	51	−11
19	Crewe Alexandria	46	9	5	9	27	31	5	4	14	19	36	51	−21
20	Grimsby Town	46	10	8	5	27	25	3	4	16	14	42	51	−26
21	West Bromwich Albion	46	6	11	6	25	26	4	8	11	18	34	49	−17
22	Walsall[4]	46	7	6	10	26	34	4	7	12	26	43	46	−25
23	Port Vale[4]	46	6	6	11	27	30	1	9	13	21	39	36	−21
24	Swindon Town[4]	46	5	6	12	23	37	3	6	14	15	40	36	−39

[1] Promoted as champions. [2] Promoted as runners-up. [3] Promoted after play-offs. [4] Relegated.

English Football: Nationwide League Division Two Final Table

Promotion play-offs: semi-finals over two legs played home and away. Millwall 0, Wigan Athletic 0; Wigan Athletic 1, Millwall 0; Wigan Athletic win 1–0 on aggregate. Stoke City 3, Gillingham 2; Gillingham 3, Stoke City 0 (after extra time); Gillingham win 5–3 on aggregate. Final (Wembley Stadium, 28 May 2000) Gillingham 3, Wigan Athletic 2. Gillingham are promoted to Division One.
(Key: P = played; W = won; D = drawn; L = lost; F = goals for; A = goals against; Pts = points; GD = goals difference.)

1999–2000

Rank	Team	P	Home					Away					Pts	GD
			W	D	L	F	A	W	D	L	F	A		
1	Preston North End[1]	46	15	4	4	37	23	13	7	3	37	14	95	+37
2	Burnley[2]	46	16	3	4	42	23	9	10	4	27	24	88	+22
3	Gillingham[3]	46	16	3	4	46	21	9	7	7	33	27	85	+31
4	Wigan Athletic	46	15	3	5	37	14	7	14	2	35	24	83	+34
5	Millwall	46	14	7	2	41	18	9	6	8	35	32	82	+26
6	Stoke City	46	13	7	3	37	18	10	6	7	31	24	82	+26
7	Bristol Rovers	46	13	7	3	34	19	10	4	9	35	26	80	+24
8	Notts County	46	9	6	8	32	27	9	5	9	29	28	65	+6
9	Bristol City	46	7	14	2	31	18	8	5	10	28	39	64	+2
10	Reading	46	10	9	4	28	18	6	5	12	29	45	62	−6
11	Wrexham	46	9	6	8	23	24	8	5	10	29	37	62	−9
12	Wycombe Wanderers	46	11	4	8	32	24	5	9	9	24	29	61	+3
13	Luton Town	46	10	7	6	41	35	7	3	13	20	30	61	−4
14	Oldham Athletic	46	8	5	10	27	28	8	7	8	23	27	60	−5
15	Bury	46	8	10	5	38	33	5	8	10	23	31	57	−3
16	Bournemouth	46	11	6	6	37	19	5	3	15	22	43	57	−3
17	Brentford	46	8	6	9	27	31	5	7	11	20	30	52	−14
18	Colchester United	46	9	4	10	36	40	5	6	12	23	42	52	−23
19	Cambridge United	46	8	6	9	38	33	4	6	13	26	32	48	−1
20	Oxford United	46	6	5	12	24	38	6	4	13	19	35	45	−30
21	Cardiff City[4]	46	5	10	8	23	34	4	7	12	22	33	44	−22
22	Blackpool[4]	46	4	10	9	26	37	4	7	14	23	40	41	−28
23	Scunthorpe United[4]	46	4	6	13	16	34	5	6	12	24	40	39	−34
24	Chesterfield[4]	46	5	7	11	17	25	2	8	13	17	38	36	−29

[1] Promoted as champions.
[2] Promoted as runners up.
[3] Promoted after play-offs.
[4] Relegated.

English Football: Nationwide League Division Three Final Table

Promotion play-offs: semi-finals over two legs played home and away. Barnet 1, Peterborough United 2; Peterborough United 3, Barnet 0; Peterborough United win 5–1 on aggregate. Hartlepool United 0, Darlington 2; Darlington 1, Hartlepool United 0; Darlington win 3–0 on aggregate. Final (Wembley Stadium 26 May 2000) Peterborough United 1, Darlington 0. Peterborough United are promoted to Division Two.
(Key: P = played; W = won; D = drawn; L = lost; F = goals for; A = goals against; Pts = points; GD = goal difference.)

1999–2000

Position	Team	P	Home					Away					Pts	GD
			W	D	L	F	A	W	D	L	F	A		
1	Swansea City[1]	46	15	6	2	32	11	9	7	7	19	19	85	+21
2	Rotherham United[2]	46	13	5	5	43	17	11	7	5	29	19	84	+36
3	Northampton Town[2]	46	16	2	5	36	18	9	5	9	27	27	82	+18
4	Darlington	46	13	9	1	43	15	8	7	8	23	21	79	+30
5	Peterborough United[3]	46	14	4	5	39	30	8	8	7	24	24	78	+9
6	Barnet	46	12	6	5	36	24	9	6	8	23	29	75	+6
7	Hartlepool	46	16	1	6	32	17	5	8	10	28	32	72	+11
8	Cheltenham Town	46	13	4	6	28	17	7	6	10	22	25	70	+8
9	Torquay United	46	12	6	5	35	20	7	6	10	27	32	69	+10
10	Rochdale	46	8	7	8	21	25	10	7	6	36	29	68	+3
11	Brighton and Hove Albion	46	10	7	6	38	25	7	9	7	26	21	67	+18
12	Plymouth Argyle	46	12	10	1	38	18	4	8	11	17	33	66	+4
13	Macclesfield Town	46	9	7	7	36	30	9	4	10	30	31	65	+5
14	Hull City	46	7	8	8	26	23	8	6	9	17	20	59	0
15	Lincoln City	46	11	6	6	38	23	4	8	11	29	46	59	−2
16	Southend United	46	11	5	7	37	31	4	6	13	16	30	56	−8
17	Mansfield Town	46	9	6	8	33	26	7	2	14	17	39	56	−15
18	Halifax Town	46	7	5	11	22	24	8	4	11	22	34	54	−14
19	Leyton Orient	46	7	7	9	22	22	6	6	11	25	30	52	−5
20	York City	46	7	10	6	21	21	5	6	12	18	32	52	−14
21	Exeter City	46	8	6	9	27	30	3	5	15	19	42	44	−26
22	Shrewsbury Town	46	5	6	12	20	27	4	7	12	20	40	40	−27
23	Carlisle United	46	6	8	9	23	27	3	4	16	19	48	39	−33
24	Chester City[4]	46	5	5	13	20	36	5	4	14	24	43	39	−35

[1] Promoted as champions.
[2] Promoted as runners-up.
[3] Promoted after play-offs.
[4] Relegated to Nationwide Conference.

English Football: Nationwide Conference Final Table

This was formerly the Vauxhall Conference.
(Key: P = played; W = won; D = drawn; L = lost; F = goals for; A = goals against; Pts = points; GD = goal difference.)

1999–2000

Position	Team	P	Home					Away					Pts	GD
			W	D	L	F	A	W	D	L	F	A		
1	Kidderminster Harriers[1]	42	16	3	2	47	16	10	4	7	28	24	85	+35
2	Rushden & Diamonds	42	11	8	2	37	18	10	5	6	34	24	76	+29
3	Morecambe	42	10	7	4	46	29	8	9	4	24	19	70	+22
4	Scarborough	42	10	6	5	36	14	9	6	6	24	21	69	+25
5	Kingstonian	42	9	4	8	30	24	11	3	7	28	20	67	+14
6	Dover Athletic	42	10	7	4	43	26	8	5	8	22	30	66	+9
7	Yeovil Town	42	11	4	6	37	28	7	6	8	23	35	64	−3
8	Hereford United	42	9	6	6	43	31	6	8	7	18	21	59	+9
9	Southport	42	10	5	6	31	21	5	8	8	24	35	58	−1
10	Stevenage Borough	42	8	5	8	26	20	8	4	9	34	34	57	+6
11	Hayes	42	7	3	11	24	28	9	5	7	33	30	56	−1
12	Doncaster Rovers	42	7	5	9	19	21	8	4	9	27	27	54	−2
13	Kettering Town	42	8	10	3	25	19	4	6	11	19	31	52	−6
14	Woking	42	5	6	10	17	27	8	7	6	28	26	52	−8
15	Nuneaton Borough	42	7	6	8	28	25	5	9	7	21	28	51	−4
16	Telford United	42	12	4	5	34	21	2	5	14	22	45	51	−10
17	Hednesford Town	42	10	3	8	27	23	5	3	13	18	45	51	−23
18	Northwich Victoria	42	10	8	3	33	25	3	4	14	20	53	51	−25
19	Forest Green Rovers	42	11	2	8	35	23	2	6	13	19	40	47	−9
20	Welling United[2]	42	6	5	10	27	32	7	3	11	27	34	47	−12
21	Altrincham[2]	42	6	8	7	31	26	3	11	7	20	34	46	−9
22	Sutton United[2]	42	4	8	9	23	32	4	2	15	16	43	34	−36

[1] Promoted to Nationwide League Division Three.
[2] Relegated.

English Football: FA Challenge Cup Results

1999–2000

Home	Away	Score
Third round		
Nottingham Forest	Oxford United	1–1
Oxford United	Nottingham Forest	1–3[1]
Cambridge United	Crystal Palace	2–0
Wrexham	Middlesbrough	2–1
Wimbledon	Barnsley	1–0
Wigan Athletic	Wolverhampton Wanderers	0–1
West Bromwich Albion	Blackburn Rovers	2–2
Blackburn Rovers	West Bromwich Albion	2–0[2]
Watford	Birmingham City	0–1
Walsall	Gillingham	1–1
Gillingham	Walsall	2–1[2]
Tranmere Rovers	West Ham United	1–0
Sunderland	Portsmouth	1–0
Sheffield Wednesday	Bristol City	1–0
Reading	Plymouth Argyle	1–1
Plymouth Argyle	Reading	1–0[1]
Queen's Park Rangers	Torquay United	1–1
Torquay United	Queen's Park Rangers	2–3[1]
Preston North End	Oldham Athletic	2–1
Norwich City	Coventry City	1–3
Hull City	Chelsea	1–6
Hereford United	Leicester City	0–0
Leicester City	Hereford United	2–1[2]
Grimsby Town	Stockport County	3–2
Fulham	Luton Town	2–2
Luton Town	Fulham	0–3[1]
Exeter City	Everton	0–0
Everton	Exeter City	1–0[1]
Derby County	Burnley	0–1
Crewe Alexandria	Bradford City	1–2
Charlton Athletic	Swindon Town	2–1
Aston Villa	Darlington	2–1
Tottenham Hotspur	Newcastle United	1–1
Newcastle United	Tottenham Hotspur	6–1[1]
Sheffield United	Rushden & Diamonds	1–1

1999–2000

Home	Away	Score
Rushden & Diamonds	Sheffield United	1–1[3]
Leeds United	Port Vale	2–0
Huddersfield Town	Liverpool	0–2
Chester City	Manchester City	1–4
Ipswich Town	Southampton	0–1
Arsenal	Blackpool	3–1
Bolton Wanderers	Cardiff City	1–0
Fourth round		
Wrexham	Cambridge United	1–2
Tranmere Rovers	Sunderland	1–0
Sheffield Wednesday	Wolverhampton Wanderers	1–1
Wolverhampton Wanderers	Sheffield Wednesday	0–0[4]
Plymouth Argyle	Preston North End	0–3
Newcastle United	Sheffield United	4–1
Grimsby Town	Bolton Wanderers	0–2
Fulham	Wimbledon	3–0
Everton	Birmingham City	2–0
Coventry City	Burnley	3–0
Charlton Athletic	Queen's Park Rangers	1–0
Aston Villa	Southampton	1–0
Manchester City	Leeds United	2–5
Arsenal	Leicester City	0–0
Leicester City	Arsenal	0–0[5]
Liverpool	Blackburn	0–1
Gillingham	Bradford City	3–1
Chelsea	Nottingham Forest	2–0
Fifth round		
Gillingham	Sheffield Wednesday	3–1
Fulham	Tranmere Rovers	1–2
Everton	Preston North End	2–0
Coventry City	Charlton Athletic	2–3
Cambridge United	Bolton Wanderers	1–3
Chelsea	Leicester City	2–1
Aston Villa	Leeds United	3–2
Blackburn Rovers	Newcastle United	1–2

(continued)

English Football: FA Challenge Cup Results (*continued*)

1999–2000

Home	Away	Score
Sixth round		
Bolton Wanderers	Charlton Athletic	1–0
Tranmere Rovers	Newcastle United	2–3
Everton	Aston Villa	1–2
Chelsea	Gillingham	5–0
Semi finals		
Aston Villa	Bolton Wanderers (Wembley Stadium, 2 April)	0–0[6]
Chelsea	Newcastle United (Wembley Stadium, 9 April)	2–1

[1] Replay.
[2] Replay. Score after extra time.
[3] Replay. Sheffield United won 6–5 on penalties after extra time.
[4] Replay. Sheffield Wednesday won 4–3 on penalties after extra time.
[5] Replay. Leicester City won 6–5 on penalties after extra time.
[6] Aston Villa won 4–1 on penalties after extra time.

Final (Wembley Stadium, 20 May 2000)
Chelsea (Di Matteo 73 minutes) Aston Villa 1–0

Teams **Aston Villa** James, Barry, Southgate, Ehiogu, Wright (Hendrie 88 minutes), Boateng, Taylor (Stone 79 minutes), Merson, Delaney, Dublin, Carbone (Joachim 79 minutes) **Chelsea** De Goey, Babayaro, Leboeuf, Desailly, Melchiot, Deschamps, Di Matteo, Poyet, Wise, Zola (Morris 90 minutes), Weah (Flo 88 minutes)
Referee: Graham Poll (Tring)
Man of the Match: Dennis Wise

English Football: FA Challenge Cup Winners

All finals have been played at Wembley Stadium since 1923, except for the 1970 Chelsea versus Leeds replay, which was played at Old Trafford.

Year	Winners	Runners-up	Score
1872	Wanderers	Royal Engineers	1–0
1873	Wanderers	Oxford University	2–0
1874	Oxford University	Royal Engineers	2–0
1875	Royal Engineers	Old Etonians	1–1[1]
replay	Royal Engineers	Old Etonians	2–0
1876	Wanderers	Old Etonians	1–1
replay	Wanderers	Old Etonians	3–0
1877	Wanderers	Oxford University	2–1[1]
1878	Wanderers	Royal Engineers	3–1
1879	Old Etonians	Clapham Rovers	1–0
1880	Clapham Rovers	Oxford University	1–0
1881	Old Carthusians	Old Etonians	3–0
1882	Old Etonians	Blackburn Rovers	1–0
1883	Blackburn Olympic	Old Etonians	2–1
1884	Blackburn Rovers	Queen's Park	2–1
1885	Blackburn Rovers	Queen's Park	2–0
1886	Blackburn Rovers	West Bromwich Albion	0–0
replay	Blackburn Rovers	West Bromwich Albion	2–0
1887	Aston Villa	West Bromwich Albion	2–0
1888	West Bromwich Albion	Preston North End	2–1
1889	Preston North End	Wolverhampton Wanderers	3–0
1890	Blackburn Rovers	Sheffield Wednesday	6–1
1891	Blackburn Rovers	Notts County	3–1
1892	West Bromwich Albion	Aston Villa	3–0
1893	Wolverhampton Wanderers	Everton	1–0
1894	Notts County	Bolton Wanderers	4–1
1895	Aston Villa	West Bromwich Albion	1–0
1896	Sheffield Wednesday	Wolverhampton Wanderers	2–1
1897	Aston Villa	Everton	3–2
1898	Nottingham Forest	Derby County	3–1
1899	Sheffield United	Derby County	4–1
1900	Bury	Southampton	4–0
1901	Tottenham Hotspur	Sheffield United	2–2
replay	Tottenham Hotspur	Sheffield United	3–1
1902	Sheffield United	Southampton	1–1
replay	Sheffield United	Southampton	2–1
1903	Bury	Derby County	6–0
1904	Manchester City	Bolton Wanderers	1–0
1905	Aston Villa	Newcastle United	2–0
1906	Everton	Newcastle United	1–0
1907	Sheffield Wednesday	Everton	2–1
1908	Wolverhampton Wanderers	Newcastle United	3–1
1909	Manchester United	Bristol City	1–0
1910	Newcastle United	Barnsley	1–1
replay	Newcastle United	Barnsley	2–0
1911	Bradford City	Newcastle United	0–0
replay	Bradford City	Newcastle United	1–0
1912	Barnsley	West Bromwich Albion	0–0
replay	Barnsley	West Bromwich Albion	1–0[1]
1913	Aston Villa	Sunderland	1–0
1914	Burnley	Liverpool	1–0
1915	Sheffield United	Chelsea	3–0
1916–19	not held		
1920	Aston Villa	Huddersfield Town	1–0[1]
1921	Tottenham Hotspur	Wolverhampton Wanderers	1–0
1922	Huddersfield Town	Preston North End	1–0
1923	Bolton Wanderers	West Ham United	2–0
1924	Newcastle United	Aston Villa	2–0
1925	Sheffield United	Cardiff City	1–0
1926	Bolton Wanderers	Manchester City	1–0
1927	Cardiff City	Arsenal	1–0
1928	Blackburn Rovers	Huddersfield Town	3–1
1929	Bolton Wanderers	Portsmouth	2–0
1930	Arsenal	Huddersfield Town	2–0
1931	West Bromwich Albion	Birmingham City	2–1
1932	Newcastle United	Arsenal	2–1
1933	Everton	Manchester City	3–0
1934	Manchester City	Portsmouth	2–1
1935	Sheffield Wednesday	West Bromwich Albion	4–2
1936	Arsenal	Sheffield United	1–0
1937	Sunderland	Preston North End	3–1
1938	Preston North End	Huddersfield Town	1–0[1]
1939	Portsmouth	Wolverhampton Wanderers	4–2
1940–45	not held		
1946	Derby County	Charlton Athletic	4–1[1]
1947	Charlton Athletic	Burnley	1–0[1]
1948	Manchester United	Blackpool	4–2
1949	Wolverhampton Wanderers	Leicester City	3–1
1950	Arsenal	Liverpool	2–0
1951	Newcastle United	Blackpool	2–0
1952	Newcastle United	Arsenal	1–0
1953	Blackpool	Bolton Wanderers	4–3
1954	West Bromwich Albion	Preston North End	3–2
1955	Newcastle United	Manchester City	3–1
1956	Manchester City	Birmingham City	3–1
1957	Aston Villa	Manchester United	2–1
1958	Bolton Wanderers	Manchester United	2–0
1959	Nottingham Forest	Luton Town	2–1
1960	Wolverhampton Wanderers	Blackburn Rovers	3–0
1961	Tottenham Hotspur	Leicester City	2–0
1962	Tottenham Hotspur	Burnley	3–1
1963	Manchester United	Leicester City	3–1
1964	West Ham United	Preston North End	3–2
1965	Liverpool	Leeds United	2–1[1]
1966	Everton	Sheffield Wednesday	3–2
1967	Tottenham Hotspur	Chelsea	2–1
1968	West Bromwich Albion	Everton	1–0[1]
1969	Manchester City	Leicester City	1–0
1970	Chelsea	Leeds United	2–2[1]
replay	Chelsea	Leeds United	2–1[1]
1971	Arsenal	Liverpool	2–1[1]
1972	Leeds United	Arsenal	1–0
1973	Sunderland	Leeds United	1–0
1974	Liverpool	Newcastle United	3–0
1975	West Ham United	Fulham	2–0
1976	Southampton	Manchester United	1–0
1977	Manchester United	Liverpool	2–1

(continued)

English Football: FA Challenge Cup Winners (*continued*)

Year	Winners	Runners-up	Score
1978	Ipswich Town	Arsenal	1–0
1979	Arsenal	Manchester United	3–2
1980	West Ham United	Arsenal	1–0
1981	Tottenham Hotspur	Manchester City	1–1[1]
replay	Tottenham Hotspur	Manchester City	3–2
1982	Tottenham Hotspur	Queens Park Rangers	1–1[1]
replay	Tottenham Hotspur	Queens Park Rangers	1–0
1983	Manchester United	Brighton & Hove Albion	2–2[1]
replay	Manchester United	Brighton & Hove Albion	4–0
1984	Everton	Watford	2–0
1985	Manchester United	Everton	1–0
1986	Liverpool	Everton	3–1
1987	Coventry City	Tottenham Hotspur	3–2
1988	Wimbledon	Liverpool	1–0
1989	Liverpool	Everton	3–2
1990	Manchester United	Crystal Palace	3–3[1]
replay	Manchester United	Crystal Palace	1–0
1991	Tottenham Hotspur	Nottingham Forest	2–1[1]
1992	Liverpool	Sunderland	2–0
1993	Arsenal	Sheffield Wednesday	1–1[1]
replay	Arsenal	Sheffield Wednesday	2–1[1]
1994	Manchester United	Chelsea	4–0
1995	Everton	Manchester United	1–0
1996	Manchester United	Liverpool	1–0
1997	Chelsea	Middlesbrough	2–0
1998	Arsenal	Newcastle United	2–0
1999	Manchester United	Newcastle United	2–0
2000	Chelsea	Aston Villa	1–0

[1]After extra time.

English Football: League Cup Winners

This competition was first held in 1960–61. It has been known as the Milk Cup, 1982–86, the Littlewoods Cup, 1987–90, the Rumbelows Cup, 1991–92, the Coca-Cola Cup, 1993–98, and from 1999 as the Worthington Cup.

Year	Winner	Runner-up	Score
1990	Nottingham Forest	Oldham Athletic	1–0
1991	Sheffield Wednesday	Manchester United	1–0
1992	Manchester United	Nottingham Forest	1–0
1993	Arsenal	Sheffield Wednesday	2–1
1994	Aston Villa	Manchester United	3–1
1995	Liverpool	Bolton Wanderers	2–1
1996	Aston Villa	Leeds United	3–0
1997	Leicester City	Middlesbrough	1–1[1]
replay	Leicester City	Middlesbrough	1–0[1]
1998	Chelsea	Middlesbrough	2–0[1]
1999	Tottenham Hotspur	Leicester City	1–0
2000	Leicester City	Tranmere Rovers	2–1

[1] After extra time.

English Football: AutoWindscreens Cup Final

2000

Winner	Runner-up	Score
Stoke City	Bristol City	2–1

English Football: League Champions

The championship was organized by the Football League from its inception in 1888 until 1992, when the 22 First Division clubs formed the Premier League under the auspices of the Football Association.

Year	Winners
Football League (1888–1992)	
1888–89	Preston North End
1889–90	Preston North End
1890–91	Everton
1891–92	Sunderland
1892–93	Sunderland
1893–94	Aston Villa
1894–95	Sunderland
1895–96	Aston Villa
1896–97	Aston Villa
1897–98	Sheffield United
1898–99	Aston Villa
1899–1900	Aston Villa
1900–01	Liverpool
1901–02	Sunderland
1902–03	Sheffield Wednesday
1903–04	Sheffield Wednesday
1904–05	Newcastle United
1905–06	Liverpool
1906–07	Newcastle United
1907–08	Manchester United
1908–09	Newcastle United
1909–10	Aston Villa
1910–11	Manchester United
1911–12	Blackburn Rovers
1912–13	Sunderland
1913–14	Blackburn Rovers
1914–15	Everton
1916–18	not held
1919–20	West Bromwich Albion
1920–21	Burnley
1921–22	Liverpool
1922–23	Liverpool
1923–24	Huddersfield Town
1924–25	Huddersfield Town
1925–26	Huddersfield Town
1926–27	Newcastle United
1927–28	Everton
1928–29	Sheffield Wednesday
1929–30	Sheffield Wednesday
1930–31	Arsenal
1931–32	Everton
1932–33	Arsenal
1933–34	Arsenal
1934–35	Arsenal
1935–36	Sunderland
1936–37	Manchester City
1937–38	Arsenal
1938–39	Everton
1940–45	not held
1946–47	Liverpool
1947–48	Arsenal
1948–49	Portsmouth
1949–50	Portsmouth
1950–51	Tottenham Hotspur
1951–52	Manchester United
1952–53	Arsenal
1953–54	Wolverhampton Wanderers
1954–55	Chelsea
1955–56	Manchester United
1956–57	Manchester United
1957–58	Wolverhampton Wanderers
1958–59	Wolverhampton Wanderers
1959–60	Burnley
1960–61	Tottenham Hotspur
1961–62	Ipswich Town
1962–63	Everton
1963–64	Liverpool
1964–65	Manchester United
1965–66	Liverpool
1966–67	Manchester United
1967–68	Manchester City
1968–69	Leeds United
1969–70	Everton
1970–71	Arsenal
1971–72	Derby County
1972–73	Liverpool
1973–74	Leeds United
1974–75	Derby County
1975–76	Liverpool
1976–77	Liverpool
1977–78	Nottingham Forest
1978–79	Liverpool
1979–80	Liverpool
1980–81	Aston Villa
1981–82	Liverpool
1982–83	Liverpool
1983–84	Liverpool
1984–85	Everton
1985–86	Liverpool
1986–87	Everton
1987–88	Liverpool
1988–89	Arsenal
1989–90	Liverpool
1990–91	Arsenal
1991–92	Leeds United
FA Premier League (1992–2000)	
1992–93	Manchester United
1993–94	Manchester United
1994–95	Blackburn Rovers
1995–96	Manchester United
1996–97	Manchester United
1997–98	Arsenal
1998–99	Manchester United
1999–2000	Manchester United

English Football Writers' Association Footballer of the Year

Year	Player	Team	Year	Player	Team
1980	Terry McDermott	Liverpool	1991	Gordon Strachan	Leeds United
1981	Frans Thijssen	Ipswich Town	1992	Gary Lineker	Tottenham Hotspur
1982	Steve Perryman	Tottenham Hotspur	1993	Chris Waddle	Sheffield Wednesday
1983	Kenny Dalglish	Liverpool	1994	Alan Shearer	Blackburn Rovers
1984	Ian Rush	Liverpool	1995	Jürgen Klinsmann	Tottenham Hotspur
1985	Neville Southall	Everton	1996	Eric Cantona	Manchester United
1986	Gary Lineker	Everton	1997	Gianfranco Zola	Chelsea
1987	Clive Allen	Tottenham Hotspur	1998	Dennis Bergkamp	Arsenal
1988	John Barnes	Liverpool	1999	David Ginola	Tottenham Hotspur
1989	Steve Nicol	Liverpool	2000	Roy Keane	Manchester United
1990	John Barnes	Liverpool			

English Football: FA Carling Premiership Leading Scorers

International goals and goals scored in other leagues by players transferred to Premiership clubs during the season are not included.

1999–2000

Position	Player	Team	Goals scored			
			League	Domestic cups	European	Total
1=	Alan Shearer	Newcastle United	23	5	2	30
	Kevin Phillips	Sunderland	30	0	0	30
3	Thierry Henry	Arsenal	17	1	8	26
4=	Dwight Yorke	Manchester United	20	0	2	22
	Andy Cole	Manchester United	19	0	3	22
6	Michael Bridges	Leeds United	19	0	2	21
7	Tore Andre Flo	Chelsea	10	1	8	19
8	Gustavo Poyet	Chelsea	10	6	2	18
9=	Steffen Iverson	Tottenham Hotspur	14	2	1	17
	Paulo Di Canio	West Ham United	16	0	1	17
	Harry Kewell	Leeds United	10	2	5	17

English Football: Nationwide League Divisions One, Two, and Three Leading Scorers

1999–2000

Position	Player	Team	Goals scored		
			League	Domestic cups[1]	Total
1	Shaun Goater	Manchester City	23	6	29
2=	Marco Gabbiadini	Darlington	25	2	27
	Andy Payton	Burnley	27	0	27
4	Peter Thorne	Stoke City	25	1	26
5=	Andy Hunt	Charlton Athletic	24	1	25
	Neil Harris	Millwall	25	0	25
	Sean Devine	Wycombe Wanderers	23	2	25
	Jonathan Macken	Preston North End	22	3	25
	Jason Roberts	Bristol Rovers	22	3	25
10	David Johnson	Ipswich Town	22	1	23

[1] Does not include goals scored in the AutoWindscreens Cup.

English Football: Top 10 Transfers Involving British Clubs

April 1999–March 2000

Rank	Name	From	To	Fee (£ millions)	Date
1	Nicolas Anelka	Arsenal	Real Madrid	22.9	5 August 1999
2	Jimmy Floyd Hasselbaink	Leeds United	Atletico Madrid	12.0	4 August 1999
3	Emile Heskey	Leicester City	Liverpool	11.0	10 March 2000
4	Thierry Henry	Juventus	Arsenal	10.5	3 August 1999
5	Chris Sutton	Blackburn Rovers	Chelsea	10.0	5 July 1999
6	Dietmar Hamann	Newcastle United	Liverpool	8.0	22 July 1999
7=	Kieron Dyer	Ipswich Town	Newcastle United	6.5	14 July 1999
	Olivier Dacourt	Everton	Lens	6.5	29 June 1999
8	Robbie Keane	Wolverhampton Wanderers	Coventry City	6.0	18 August 1999
9	Eyal Berkovic	West Ham United	Celtic	5.75	8 July 1999
10=	Michael Bridges	Sunderland	Leeds United	5.0	23 July 1999
	Elena Marcelino	Real Mallorca	Newcastle United	5.0	24 June 1999

Scottish Football

Scottish Football: 1999–2000

Rangers won their 11th Premier League title in 12 years and their second successive league and cup double. Celtic spent heavily on new players but still finished 21 points adrift of Rangers in second place. They parted company with manager John Barnes on 10 February, two days after suffering a humiliating 3–1 home defeat at the hands of Division One side Inverness Caledonian Thistle in the third round of the Scottish Cup. With the club's Director of Football Kenny Dalglish standing in as manager, Celtic did go on to win the League Cup, but this triumph provided only the slightest consolation for the club's loyal but demanding fans. Aberdeen lost the finals of both the League Cup and the Scottish Cup, and finished bottom of the Premier League, but were saved from a promotion/relegation play-off with Falkirk, because the Division One team's ground was not up to Premier League standard. However, Division One champions St Mirren and runners-up Dunfermline Athletic were promoted to play in the expanded 12-team Premier League.

Scottish Football: Bank of Scotland Premier League Results

(– = not applicable.)

1999–2000 Home team	Away team: Aberdeen		Celtic		Dundee		Dundee United		Hearts		Hibernian		Kilmarnock		Motherwell		Rangers		St Johnstone	
Aberdeen	–	–	0–5	0–6	0–2	0–1	1–2	3–1	3–1	1–2	2–2	4–0	2–2	5–1	1–1	2–1	1–5	1–1	0–3	2–1
Celtic	7–0	5–1	–	–	6–2	2–2	4–1	2–0	4–0	2–3	4–0	1–1	5–1	4–2	0–1	4–0	1–1	0–1	3–0	4–1
Dundee	1–2	0–2	1–2	0–3	–	–	0–2	3–0	1–0	0–0	3–4	1–0	0–0	1–2	0–1	4–1	2–3	1–7	1–2	1–1
Dundee United	3–1	1–1	2–1	0–1	2–1	1–0	–	–	0–2	0–1	3–1	0–0	0–0	2–2	0–2	1–2	0–4	0–2	1–0	0–1
Hearts	3–0	3–0	1–2	1–0	4–0	2–0	3–0	1–2	–	–	0–3	2–1	2–2	0–0	1–1	0–0	0–4	1–2	1–1	0–0
Hibernian	2–0	1–0	0–2	2–1	5–2	1–2	3–2	1–0	1–1	3–1	–	–	0–3	2–2	2–2	2–2	0–1	2–2	0–1	3–3
Kilmarnock	2–0	1–0	0–1	1–1	0–2	2–2	1–1	1–0	2–2	0–1	0–2	1–0	–	–	0–1	0–2	1–1	0–2	1–2	3–2
Motherwell	5–6	1–0	3–2	1–1	0–2	0–3	2–2	1–3	2–1	0–2	2–2	2–0	0–4	2–0	–	–	1–5	2–0	1–0	2–1
Rangers	3–0	5–0	4–2	4–0	1–2	3–0	4–1	3–0	1–0	1–0	2–0	5–2	2–1	1–0	4–1	6–2	–	–	3–1	0–0
St Johnstone	1–1	2–1	1–2	0–0	0–1	2–1	0–1	2–0	1–4	0–1	1–1	1–0	2–0	0–0	1–1	1–1	1–1	0–2	–	–

Scottish Football: Bank of Scotland Premier League Final Table

This was formerly the Bell's Scottish Premier Division.
(Key: P = played; W = won; D = drawn; L = lost; F = goals for; A = goals against; Pts = points; GD = goal difference.)

1999–2000 Position	Team	P	Home W	Home D	Home L	Home F	Home A	Away W	Away D	Away L	Away F	Away A	Pts	GD
1	Rangers	36	16	1	1	52	12	12	5	1	44	14	90	+70
2	Celtic	36	12	3	3	58	17	9	3	6	32	21	69	+52
3	Hearts	36	7	6	5	25	18	8	3	7	22	22	54	+7
4	Motherwell	36	8	3	7	27	34	6	7	5	22	29	52	−14
5	St Johnstone	36	5	7	6	16	18	5	5	8	20	26	42	−8
6	Hibernian	36	7	6	5	30	27	3	5	10	19	34	41	−12
7	Dundee	36	4	3	11	20	33	8	2	8	25	31	41	−19
8	Dundee United	36	6	4	8	16	22	5	2	11	18	35	39	−23
9	Kilmarnock	36	5	5	8	16	22	3	8	7	22	30	37	−14
10	Aberdeen	36	6	4	8	28	37	3	2	13	16	46	33	−39

Bell's Scottish Football League Division One Final Table

(Key: P = played; W = won; D = drawn; L = lost; F = goals for; A = goals against; Pts = points; GD = goal difference.)

1999–2000 Position	Team	P	Home W	Home D	Home L	Home F	Home A	Away W	Away D	Away L	Away F	Away A	Pts	GD
1	St Mirren[1]	36	12	3	3	42	19	11	4	3	33	20	76	+36
2	Dunfermline Athletic[2]	36	10	7	1	34	13	10	4	4	32	20	71	+33
3	Falkirk	36	11	2	5	38	23	9	6	3	29	17	68	+27
4	Livingston	36	9	5	4	29	17	10	2	6	31	28	64	+15
5	Raith Rovers	36	11	3	4	35	21	6	5	7	20	19	59	+15
6	Inverness Caledonian Thistle	36	7	6	5	34	25	6	4	8	26	30	49	+5
7	Ayr United	36	6	3	9	25	24	4	5	9	17	28	38	−10
8	Morton	36	7	3	8	22	23	3	3	12	23	38	36	−16
9	Airdrieonians	36	4	5	9	15	26	3	3	12	14	43	29	−40
10	Clydebank[3]	36	1	3	14	11	40	0	4	14	6	42	10	−65

[1] Promoted as champions. [2] Promoted as runners-up. [3] Relegated.

Bell's Scottish Football League Division Two Final Table

(Key: P = played; W = won; D = drawn; L = lost; F = goals for; A = goals against; Pts = points; GD = goal difference.)

1999–2000

Position	Team	P	Home					Away					Pts	GD
			W	D	L	F	A	W	D	L	F	A		
1	Clyde[1]	36	12	5	1	35	7	6	6	6	30	30	65	+28
2	Alloa Athletic[2]	36	11	5	2	36	18	6	8	4	22	20	64	+20
3	Ross County[2]	36	9	5	4	31	20	9	3	6	26	19	62	+18
4	Arbroath	36	6	7	5	28	26	5	7	6	24	29	47	−3
5	Partick Thistle	36	7	5	6	25	22	5	5	8	17	22	46	−2
6	Stranraer	36	6	8	4	25	22	3	10	5	22	24	45	+1
7	Stirling Albion	36	7	4	7	34	33	4	3	11	26	39	40	−12
8	Stenhousemuir	36	6	4	8	24	26	4	4	10	20	33	38	−15
9	Queen of the South	36	5	6	7	24	32	3	3	12	21	43	33	−30
10	Hamilton Academical[3]	36	5	7	6	18	23	5	7	6	21	21	29	−5

[1] Promoted as champions. [2] Promoted as runners-up. [3] Relegated.

Bell's Scottish Football League Division Three Final Table

(Key: P = played; W = won; D = drawn; L = lost; F = goals for; A = goals against; Pts = points; GD = goal difference.)

1999–2000

Position	Team	P	Home					Away					Pts	GD
			W	D	L	F	A	W	D	L	F	A		
1	Queen's Park[1]	36	11	2	5	28	20	9	7	2	26	17	69	+17
2	Berwick Rangers[2]	36	7	6	5	20	14	12	3	3	33	16	66	+23
3	Forfar Athletic[2]	36	10	5	3	39	18	7	5	6	25	22	61	+24
4	East Fife	36	9	6	3	24	16	8	2	8	21	23	59	+6
5	Cowdenbeath	36	6	5	7	30	23	9	4	5	29	20	54	+16
6	Dumbarton	36	7	7	4	26	22	8	1	9	27	29	53	+2
7	East Stirling	36	6	2	10	15	27	5	5	8	13	23	40	−22
8	Brechin City	36	6	3	9	25	25	4	5	9	17	26	38	−9
9	Montrose	36	5	2	11	19	31	5	5	8	20	23	37	−15
10	Albion Rovers[3]	36	2	3	13	13	35	3	4	11	20	40	22	−42

[1] Promoted as champions. [2] Promoted as runners-up. [3] Relegated.

Scottish Football: Scottish League Champions

Year	Team	Year	Team	Year	Team
1890–91	Dumbarton and Rangers (shared)	1925–26	Celtic	1966–67	Celtic
1891–92	Dumbarton	1926–27	Rangers	1967–68	Celtic
1892–93	Celtic	1927–28	Rangers	1968–69	Celtic
1893–94	Celtic	1928–29	Rangers	1969–70	Celtic
1894–95	Hearts	1929–30	Rangers	1970–71	Celtic
1895–96	Celtic	1930–31	Rangers	1971–72	Celtic
1896–97	Hearts	1931–32	Motherwell	1972–73	Celtic
1897–98	Celtic	1932–33	Rangers	1973–74	Celtic
1898–99	Rangers	1933–34	Rangers	1974–75	Rangers
1899–1900	Rangers	1934–35	Rangers	1975–76	Rangers
1900–01	Rangers	1935–36	Celtic	1976–77	Celtic
1901–02	Rangers	1936–37	Rangers	1977–78	Rangers
1902–03	Hibernian	1937–38	Celtic	1978–79	Celtic
1903–04	Third Lanark	1938–39	Rangers	1979–80	Aberdeen
1904–05	Celtic	1940–45	not held	1980–81	Celtic
1905–06	Celtic	1946–47	Rangers	1981–82	Celtic
1906–07	Celtic	1947–48	Hibernian	1982–83	Dundee United
1907–08	Celtic	1948–49	Rangers	1983–84	Aberdeen
1908–09	Celtic	1949–50	Rangers	1984–85	Aberdeen
1909–10	Celtic	1950–51	Hibernian	1985–86	Celtic
1910–11	Rangers	1951–52	Hibernian	1986–87	Rangers
1911–12	Rangers	1952–53	Rangers	1987–88	Celtic
1912–13	Rangers	1953–54	Celtic	1988–89	Rangers
1913–14	Celtic	1954–55	Aberdeen	1989–90	Rangers
1914–15	Celtic	1955–56	Rangers	1990–91	Rangers
1915–16	Celtic	1956–57	Rangers	1991–92	Rangers
1916–17	Celtic	1957–58	Hearts	1992–93	Rangers
1917–18	Rangers	1958–59	Rangers	1993–94	Rangers
1918–19	Celtic	1959–60	Hearts	1994–95	Rangers
1919–20	Rangers	1960–61	Rangers	1995–96	Rangers
1920–21	Rangers	1961–62	Dundee	1996–97	Rangers
1921–22	Celtic	1962–63	Rangers	1997–98	Celtic
1922–23	Rangers	1963–64	Rangers	1998–99	Rangers
1923–24	Rangers	1964–65	Kilmarnock	1999–2000	Rangers
1924–25	Rangers	1965–66	Celtic		

Scottish Football: Scottish FA Cup Winners

The first final of the Scottish FA Cup was held in 1874.

Year	Team	Year	Team	Year	Team
1980	Celtic	1987	St Mirren	1994	Dundee United
1981	Rangers	1988	Celtic	1995	Celtic
1982	Aberdeen	1989	Celtic	1996	Rangers
1983	Aberdeen	1990	Aberdeen	1997	Kilmarnock
1984	Aberdeen	1991	Motherwell	1998	Hearts
1985	Celtic	1992	Rangers	1999	Rangers
1986	Aberdeen	1993	Rangers	2000	Rangers

Scottish Football: Scottish FA Cup Results

1999–2000

Home	Away	Score
Third round		
Hearts	Stenhousemuir	3–2
St Mirren	Aberdeen	1–1
Aberdeen	St Mirren	2–0[1]
Albion Rovers	Partick Thistle	1–2
Falkirk	Peterhead	3–1
Arbroath	Motherwell	1–1
Motherwell	Arbroath	2–0[1]
Queen of the South	Livingston	0–7
Clyde	Raith Rovers	3–1
Stranraer	Berwick Rangers	1–2
Clydebank	Stirling Albion	1–0
Hibernian	Dunfermline Athletic	4–1
Dundee	Ayr United	0–0
Ayr United	Dundee	1–1[2]
St Johnstone	Rangers	0–2
Greenock Morton	Brechin City	1–1
Brechin City	Greenock Morton	0–0[3]
Dundee United	Airdrieonians	4–1
Kilmarnock	Alloa Athletic	0–0
Alloa Athletic	Kilmarnock	1–0[1]
Celtic	Inverness Caledonian Thistle	1–3
Fourth round		
Greenock Morton	Rangers	0–1
Hibernian	Clydebank	1–1
Clydebank	Hibernian	0–3[1]
Clyde	Hearts	0–2

[1]Replay.
[2]Replay. Ayr won 7–6 on penalties after extra time.
[3]Replay. Greenock Morton won 4–3 on penalties after extra time.

1999–2000

Home	Away	Score
Berwick Rangers	Falkirk	0–0
Falkirk	Berwick Rangers	3–0[1]
Alloa Athletic	Dundee United	2–2
Dundee United	Alloa Athletic	4–0[1]
Partick Thistle	Livingston	2–1
Inverness Caledonian Thistle	Aberdeen	1–1
Aberdeen	Inverness Caledonian Thistle	1–0[1]
Motherwell	Ayr United	3–4
Quarter finals		
Ayr United	Partick Thistle	2–0
Hibernian	Falkirk	3–1
Rangers	Hearts	4–1
Dundee United	Aberdeen	0–1
Semi finals		
Ayr United	Rangers	0–7
Hibernian	Aberdeen	1–2

Final (27 May 2000, Hampden Park)
Aberdeen Rangers (Van Bronckhorst 35 minutes, Vidmar 47 minutes, Dodds 49 minutes, Albertz 50 minutes) 0–4

Attendance: 50,865
Teams: **Aberdeen** Leighton (Winters 1 minute), Whyte, Solberg, Anderson (Belabed 40 minutes), McAllister, Bernard, Jess, Rowson, Guntveit, Stavrum (Zerouali 68 minutes), Dow **Rangers** Klos, Reyna, Moore (Porrini 71 minutes), Vidmar, Numan, Kanchelskis, Ferguson, Albertz, Van Bronckhorst (Tugay 73 minutes), Wallace (McCann 65 minutes), Dodds

Scottish Football: Scottish League Cup Recent Winners

Year	Team	Year	Team
1988–89	Rangers	1994–95	Raith Rovers
1989–90	Aberdeen	1995–96	Aberdeen
1990–91	Rangers	1996–97	Rangers
1991–92	Hibernian	1997–98	Celtic
1992–93	Rangers	1998–99	Rangers
1993–94	Rangers	1999–2000	Celtic

Scottish Football: Bank of Scotland Premier League Leading Scorers

International goals and goals scored in other leagues by players transferred to Premier League clubs during the season are not included.

1999–2000

Position	Name	Team	Goals scored			
			League	Domestic cups	European	Total
1	Mark Viduka	Celtic	25	1	1	27
2	Billy Dodds	Rangers[1]	19	5	0	24
3	Rod Wallace	Rangers	16	2	2	20
4	Jorg Albertz	Rangers	17	0	2	19
5	Willie Falconer	Dundee United	12	4	0	16
6	Gary McSwegan	Hearts	13	2	0	15
7=	Michael Mols	Rangers	9	0	4	13
	Arild Stavrum	Aberdeen	9	4	0	13
9=	Russell Latapy	Hibernian	9	3	0	12
	Lee McCulloch	Motherwell	9	3	0	12
	Henrik Larsson	Celtic	7	0	5	12

[1] Includes ten goals for Dundee United.

Scottish Football: Scottish Divisions One, Two, and Three Leading Scorers

1999–2000

Position	Name	Team	Goals scored		
			League	Domestic cups	Total
1	Brian Carrigan	Clyde	19	7	26
2	Martin Cameron	Alloa Athletic	16	8	24
3	Ally Graham	Stirling Albion	17	4	21
4=	Mark Yardley	St Mirren	19	0	19
	David Bingham	Livingston	15	4	19
	Colin McGlashan	Arbroath	16	3	19
	Steven Milne	Forfar Athletic	16	3	19
8=	Scott Crabbe	Falkirk	14	4	18
	Willie Irvine	Alloa Athletic	13	5	18
	George Shaw	Ross County	13	5	18

Gaelic Football

The All-Ireland Gaelic Football Championship

Winners since 1990.

Year	Team	Year	Team
1990	Cork	1995	Dublin
1991	Down	1996	Meath
1992	Donegal	1997	Kerry
1993	Derry	1998	Galway
1994	Down	1999	Meath

Golf

Golf: 1999–2000

Paul Lawrie, a 30-year-old from Aberdeen, won the 1999 British Open, the first to be held at the notoriously demanding Carnoustie course in Angus since 1975, and became the first Scotsman to win the event since Sandy Lyle won at Sandwich in 1985, and the first to do so on home soil since James Braid's victory at St Andrews in 1910. Going into the final day 10 strokes off the lead, Lawrie shot a 67 for a final score of 290, and then held his nerve to win a three-way play-off with Justin Leonard of the USA and Jean Van der Velde of France, who had led the tournament for two rounds before blowing a three-stroke lead at the very last hole.

The culmination of the Ryder Cup at Brookline, Massachusetts, on 26 September 1999 was equally dramatic, with Europe surrendering a 10–6 lead on the final day to lose 14.5–13.5. The US victory, however, was soured not only by the unruly behaviour of some of their fans, but also by the over-exuberant and premature celebrations of many of the US players – most notoriously, when they mobbed Justin Leonard on the 17th green after sinking a vital putt, although his opponent, José Maria Olazábal, was waiting to take a putt himself, which, if he had been able to hole, would have given Europe a chance of saving the match.

In 1999 Scotland's Colin Montgomerie won six tournaments, to finish top of the European prize-money list for a record seventh successive year with winnings of £1,302,057; yet his season was almost mediocre compared with that enjoyed by Tiger Woods, who won eight tournaments on the US Tour, including the US PGA Championship, and earned a staggering $6,616,585 in winnings. Woods's rich vein of form continued into the 2000 season, and on 18 June he romped home in the US Open at Pebble Beach, California. His winning margin of 15 strokes was the largest in the 140-year history of major championship golf.

British Open Golf Championship Winners

The British Open was first held in 1860 at Prestwick, Scotland; eight competitors took part and the winner was Willie Park (Snr) of the UK. The competition was played over 36 holes between 1860 and 1891; since 1892 it has been played over 72 holes.

Year	Name	Country	Location	Score
1946	Sam Snead	USA	St Andrews	290
1947	Fred Daly	UK	Hoylake	293
1948	Henry Cotton	UK	Muirfield	284
1949	Bobby Locke	South Africa	Sandwich	283[1]
1950	Bobby Locke	South Africa	Troon	279
1951	Max Faulkner	UK	Portrush	285
1952	Bobby Locke	South Africa	Royal Lytham	287
1953	Ben Hogan	USA	Carnoustie	282
1954	Peter Thomson	Australia	Royal Birkdale	283
1955	Peter Thomson	Australia	St Andrews	281
1956	Peter Thomson	Australia	Hoylake	286
1957	Bobby Locke	South Africa	St Andrews	279
1958	Peter Thomson	Australia	Royal Lytham	278[1]
1959	Gary Player	South Africa	Muirfield	284
1960	Kel Nagle	Australia	St Andrews	278
1961	Arnold Palmer	USA	Royal Birkdale	284
1962	Arnold Palmer	USA	Troon	276
1963	Bob Charles	New Zealand	Royal Lytham	277[1]
1964	Tony Lema	USA	St Andrews	279
1965	Peter Thomson	Australia	Royal Birkdale	285
1966	Jack Nicklaus	USA	Muirfield	282
1967	Roberto de Vincenzo	Argentina	Hoylake	278
1968	Gary Player	South Africa	Carnoustie	289
1969	Tony Jacklin	UK	Royal Lytham	280
1970	Jack Nicklaus	USA	St Andrews	283[1]
1971	Lee Trevino	USA	Royal Birkdale	278
1972	Lee Trevino	USA	Muirfield	278
1973	Tom Weiskopf	USA	Troon	276
1974	Gary Player	South Africa	Royal Lytham	282

(continued)

British Open Golf Championship Winners (*continued*)

Year	Name	Country	Location	Score
1975	Tom Watson	USA	Carnoustie	279[1]
1976	Johnny Miller	USA	Royal Birkdale	279
1977	Tom Watson	USA	Turnberry	268
1978	Jack Nicklaus	USA	St Andrews	281
1979	Seve Ballesteros	Spain	Royal Lytham	283
1980	Tom Watson	USA	Muirfield	271
1981	Bill Rogers	USA	Sandwich	276
1982	Tom Watson	USA	Troon	284
1983	Tom Watson	USA	Royal Birkdale	275
1984	Seve Ballesteros	Spain	St Andrews	276
1985	Sandy Lyle	UK	Sandwich	282
1986	Greg Norman	Australia	Turnberry	280
1987	Nick Faldo	UK	Muirfield	279
1988	Seve Ballesteros	Spain	Royal Lytham	273
1989	Mark Calcavecchia	USA	Troon	275[1]
1990	Nick Faldo	UK	St Andrews	270
1991	Ian Baker-Finch	Australia	Royal Birkdale	272
1992	Nick Faldo	UK	Muirfield	272
1993	Greg Norman	Australia	Sandwich	267
1994	Nick Price	Zimbabwe	Turnberry	268
1995	John Daly	USA	St Andrews	282[1]
1996	Tom Lehman	USA	Royal Lytham	271
1997	Justin Leonard	USA	Troon	272
1998	Mark O'Meara	USA	Royal Birkdale	280[1]
1999	Paul Lawrie	UK	Carnoustie	290[1]
2000	Tiger Woods	USA	St Andrews	269

[1]Won after play-off.

US Masters Golf Winners

This competition has been held annually at the Augusta National course, Georgia, USA, since 1934. The winner in 1934 was Horton Smith of the USA.

Year	Name	Country	Score
1990	Nick Faldo	UK	278[1]
1991	Ian Woosnam	UK	277
1992	Fred Couples	USA	275
1993	Bernhard Langer	Germany	277
1994	José-Maria Olazábal	Spain	279
1995	Ben Crenshaw	USA	274
1996	Nick Faldo	UK	276
1997	Tiger Woods	USA	270
1998	Mark O'Meara	USA	279
1999	José Maria Olazábal	Spain	279
2000	Vijay Singh	Fiji	278

[1] Won after play-off.

Men's US Open Golf Championship Winners

The US Open was first held on a 9-hole course at Newport (RI), USA, in 1895; the winner was English-born Horace Rawlins.

Year	Name	Country	Location	Score
1990	Hale Irwin	USA	Medinah (IL)	280[1]
1991	Payne Stewart	USA	Hazeltine (MN)	282[1]
1992	Tom Kite	USA	Monterey (CA)	285
1993	Lee Janzen	USA	Baltusrol (NJ)	272
1994	Ernie Els	South Africa	Oakmont (PA)	279
1995	Corey Pavin	USA	Shinnecock Hills (NY)	280
1996	Steve Jones	USA	Oakland Hills (MI)	278
1997	Ernie Els	South Africa	Congressional (MI)	276
1998	Lee Janzen	USA	Olympic Club (CA)	280
1999	Payne Stewart	USA	Pinehurst (NC)	279
2000	Tiger Woods	USA	Pebble Beach (CA)	272

[1] Score after play-off.

US Professional Golf Association (US PGA) Championship Winners

This competition was first held in 1916. It was contested as a matchplay between 1916 and 1957, and has been contested as strokeplay since 1958. Players are of US nationality unless otherwise stated.

Year	Name	Score
1989	Payne Stewart	276
1990	Wayne Grady (Australia)	282
1991	John Daly	276
1992	Nick Price (Zimbabwe)	278
1993	Paul Azinger	272[1]
1994	Nick Price (Zimbabwe)	269
1995	Steve Elkington (Australia)	267
1996	Mark Brooks	277[1]
1997	Davis Love III	269
1998	Vijay Singh (Fiji)	271
1999	Tiger Woods	277

[1] Score after play-off.

Golf: Ryder Cup Winners

This competition is a biennial team event, inaugurated in 1927 between professional golfers of the USA and the UK. From 1973 to 1977, the event was between the USA and a combined UK and Republic of Ireland team. Since 1979, it has been between the USA and Europe.

Year	Winner	Score	Location
1979	USA	17–11	Greenbrier (WV), USA
1981	USA	18.5–9.5	Walton Heath, Surrey, England
1983	USA	14.5–13.5	PGA National GC (FL), USA
1985	Europe	16.5–11.5	The Belfry, Sutton Coldfield, England
1987	Europe	15–13	Muirfield Village GC (OH), USA
1989	tie	14–14	The Belfry, Sutton Coldfield, England
1991	USA	14.5–13.5	Ocean Course (SC), USA
1993	USA	15–13	The Belfry, Sutton Coldfield, England
1995	Europe	14.5–13.5	Oak Hill CC (NY), USA
1997	Europe	14.5–13.5	Valderrama, Andalucia, Spain
1999	USA	14.5–13.5	The Country Club, Brookline (MA), USA

World Golf Matchplay Champions

This competition has been held annually at Wentworth, Surrey, England, since 1964. Since 1992, it has been sponsored by Toyota.

Year	Name	Country
1994	Ernie Els	South Africa
1995	Ernie Els	South Africa
1996	Ernie Els	South Africa
1997	Vijay Singh	Fiji
1998	Mark O'Meara	USA
1999	Colin Montgomerie	UK

European Professional Golfers' Association: Harry Vardon Trophy Winners

This trophy has been awarded since 1937 to the leader of the European PGA Order of Merit. Most wins: Seve Ballesteros, 6; Colin Montgomerie, 7; Peter Oosterhuis, 4.

Year	Name	Country
1994	Colin Montgomerie	UK
1995	Colin Montgomerie	UK
1996	Colin Montgomerie	UK
1997	Colin Montgomerie	UK
1998	Colin Montgomerie	UK
1999	Colin Montgomerie	UK

British Women's Open Golf Championship Winners

This championship has been held as a strokeplay event since 1976. It is now sponsored by Weetabix.

Year	Name	Country
1994	Liselotte Neumann	Sweden
1995	Karrie Webb	Australia
1996	Emilee Klein	USA
1997	Karrie Webb	Australia
1998	Sherri Steinhauer	USA
1999	Sherri Steinhauer	USA

British Amateur Golf Championship Winners

This championship was first held in 1885. Winners are from the UK or the Republic of Ireland unless otherwise stated.

Year	Name
1990	Rolf Muntz (Netherlands)
1991	Gary Wolstenholme
1992	Stephen Dundas
1993	Iain Pyman
1994	Lee James
1995	Gordon Sherry
1996	Warren Bladon
1997	Craig Watson
1998	Sergio Garcia (Spain)
1999	Graeme Storm
2000	Mikko Ilonen (Finland)

Golf: Solheim Cup Winners

This is a biennial team competition between the women professional golfers of the USA and Europe. It was first held in 1990.

Year	Winner	Score	Location
1990	USA	11.5–4.5	Orlando (FL), USA
1992	Europe	11.5–6.5	Dalmahoy, Scotland
1994	USA	13–7	Greenbrier (WV), USA
1996	USA	17–11	Chepstow, Wales
1998	USA	16–12	Muirfield Village (OH), USA

Golf: Walker Cup Winners

This team competition has been held every two years since 1922 (except 1940–45) between the amateur golfers of the USA and those of Great Britain and Ireland.

Year	Winners	Score
1989	Great Britain and Ireland	12.5–11.5
1991	USA	14–10
1993	USA	19–5
1995	Great Britain and Ireland	14–10
1997	USA	18–6
1999	Great Britain and Ireland	15–9

Gymnastics

Gymnastics World Championships: Overall Individual Winners

These championships were first held in 1903 for men and in 1934 for women. They are contested every two years.

Year	Name	Country	Year	Name	Country
Men			*Women*		
1989	Igor Korobichensky	USSR	1989	Svetlana Boginskaya	USSR
1991	Gregori Misutin	USSR	1991	Kim Zmeskal	USA
1993	Vitaly Scherbo	Belarus	1993	Shannon Miller	USA
1995	Li Xiaoshuang	China	1995	Lilia Pôdkopaeva	Ukraine
1997	Ivan Ivankov	Belarus	1997	Svetlana Khorkina	Russia
1999	Nikolai Krukov	Russia	1999	Maria Olaru	Romania

Gymnastics World Champions

Held at Tianjin, China, 8–16 October 1999.

1999 Category	Name	Country	*1999* Category	Name	Country
Men			*Women*		
Individual all-round	Nikolai Krukov	Russia	Individual all-round	Maria Olaru	Romania
Floor	Alexei Nemov	Russia	Beam	Ling Jie	China
Pommel horse	Alexei Nemov	Russia	Vault	Elena Zamolodchikova	Russia
Rings	Dong Zhen	China	Asymmetric bars	Svetlana Khorkina	Russia
Vault	Li Xiaoping	China	Floor	Andreea Raducan	Romania
Parallel bars	Lee Joo-hyung	South Korea	Team		Romania
Horizontal bar	Jesus Carballo	Spain			
Team		China			

Hockey

Men's Hockey World Cup

This championship was inaugurated in 1971 by the Fédération Internationale de Hockey (FIH).

Year	Country
1982	Pakistan
1986	Australia
1990	Netherlands
1994	Pakistan
1998	Netherlands

Women's Hockey World Cup

This championship was inaugurated in 1974 by the Fédération Internationale de Hockey (FIH).

Year	Country
1983	Netherlands
1986	Netherlands
1990	Netherlands
1994	Australia
1998	Australia

English National Hockey League: Premier Division Final Table (Men)

1999–2000

Position	Team	Played	Won	Drawn	Lost	Goals for	Goals against	Points
1	Canterbury[1]	18	13	2	3	68	43	41
2	Cannock[1]	18	13	1	4	62	35	40
3	Reading[1]	18	12	3	3	71	37	39
4	Guildford[1]	18	10	3	5	53	43	33
5	Surbiton	18	7	4	7	46	44	25
6	Loughtonians	18	5	8	5	46	46	23
7	Southgate	18	4	2	12	38	52	14
8	Bournville	18	4	2	12	34	55	14
9	Teddington	18	3	5	10	35	64	14
10	Beeston[2]	18	3	2	13	36	70	11

[1] Qualify for the play-offs. [2] Relegated

English National Hockey League: Premier Division Play-Offs (Men)

Winner	Loser
First round, 9 April 2000	
Cannock 1	Canterbury 0
Guildford 2[1]	Reading 2
Second round, 16 April 2000	
Canterbury 5	Guildford 1
Final, Milton Keynes, 1 May 2000	
Cannock 3	Canterbury 2

[1] After extra time Guildford won 5–4 on penalty strokes.

English National Hockey League: Premier Division Final Table (Women)

1999–2000

Position	Team	Played	Won	Drawn	Lost	Goals for	Goals against	Points
1	Hightown[1]	18	13	1	4	49	21	40
2	Ipswich[1]	18	10	4	4	53	36	34
3	Leicester[1]	18	9	6	3	38	22	33
4	Canterbury[1]	18	9	3	6	36	29	30
5	Clifton	18	9	2	7	28	25	29
6	Slough	18	6	3	9	30	43	21
7	Olton and West Warwicks	18	5	5	8	31	41	20
8	Chelmsford	18	4	5	9	26	36	17
9	Doncaster[2]	18	1	0	17	12	55	3

[1] Qualify for Premiership Tournament. [2] Relegated.

English National Hockey League: Premiership Tournament Play-Offs (Women)

Winner	Loser
First round, 8 April 2000	
Leicester 2	Canterbury 0
Hightown 0[1]	Ipswich 0
Second round, 8 April 2000	
Ipswich 2	Leicester 1
Final, Milton Keynes, 1 May 2000	
Hightown 3	Ipswich 1

[1] After extra time Hightown won 4–2 on penalty strokes.

Horse Racing

Flat Racing

Flat Racing: 1999–2000

If the 1999 English flat racing season began as a victory parade for trainer Henry Cecil and his retained jockey, Kieren Fallon, with Wince, Ramruma, and Oath winning the 1,000 Guineas, the Oaks, and the Derby respectively, it was Saeed Bin Suroor of Godolphin who finished the season as the leading trainer, earning over £2 million in prize money, and saddling the winners of the 2,000 Guineas, the St Leger, and seven other British Group One races. Cecil was second, with earnings of £1.8 million, and might have won a lot more had he not parted company with Fallon in mid-season over a personal matter. The Irish rider teamed up with Sir Michael Stoute and ended the season as Champion Jockey for the third successive year.

In the year 2000, King's Best, ridden by Kieren Fallon, was an impressive winner of the 2000 Guineas at Newmarket on 6 May, and was a clear favourite for the Derby at Epsom on 9 June until he pulled out on the eve of the race because of injury. In his absence the Derby was won by the Irish horse Sinndar, ridden by John Murtagh, trained by John Oxx, and owned by the Aga Khan. A day earlier Richard Quinn, on Love Divine, gave Henry Cecil his fourth Oaks victory in five years.

A fortnight before the Derby meeting, a light airplane carrying Frankie Dettori and Ray Cochrane from a meeting at Goodwood crashed while trying to land at Newmarket. The two jockeys escaped from the plane without serious injury, but despite Cochrane's attempts to rescue him, the pilot was killed when the plane burst into flames.

Flat Racing: The Derby

The first Derby, held in 1780, was won by Diomes, owned by Sir Charles Bunbury and ridden by Sam Arnull. The race is held at Epsom over 1 mile and 4 furlongs. Since 1984 it has been sponsored by Ever Ready. Colts carry 9 stone; fillies 8 stone 9 lb. Most wins for a jockey: Lester Piggott, 9; Jem Robinson, 6, Steve Donoghue, 6.

Year	Horse	Jockey	Year	Horse	Jockey	Year	Horse	Jockey
1960	St Paddy	Lester Piggott	1970	Nijinsky	Lester Piggott	1980	Henbit	Willie Carson
1961	Psidium	Roger Poincelet	1971	Mill Reef	Geoff Lewis	1981	Shergar	Walter Swinburn
1962	Larkspur	Neville Sellwood	1972	Roberto	Lester Piggott	1982	Golden Fleece	Pat Eddery
1963	Relko	Yves Saint-Martin	1973	Morston	Eddie Hide	1983	Teenoso	Lester Piggott
1964	Santa Claus	Scobie Breasley	1974	Snow Knight	Brian Taylor	1984	Secreto	Christy Roche
1965	Sea Bird II	Pat Glennon	1975	Grundy	Pat Eddery	1985	Slip Anchor	Steve Cauthen
1966	Charlottown	Scobie Breasley	1976	Empery	Lester Piggott	1986	Shahrastani	Walter Swinburn
1967	Royal Palace	George Moore	1977	The Minstrel	Lester Piggott	1987	Reference Point	Steve Cauthen
1968	Sir Ivor	Lester Piggott	1978	Shirley Heights	Greville Starkey	1988	Kahyashi	Ray Cochrane
1969	Blakeney	Ernie Johnson	1979	Troy	Willie Carson			

(continued)

Flat Racing: The Derby *(continued)*

Year	Horse	Jockey
1989	Nashwan	Willie Carson
1990	Quest For Fame	Pat Eddery
1991	Generous	Alan Munro
1992	Dr Devious	John Reid
1993	Commander in Chief	Michael Kinane
1994	Erhaab	Willie Carson
1995	Lammtarra	Walter Swinburn
1996	Shaamit	Michael Hills
1997	Benny The Dip	Willie Ryan
1998	High-Rise	Olivier Peslier
1999	Oath	Kieren Fallon
2000	Sinndar	Johnny Murtagh

Flat Racing: 1,000 Guineas

This race was first held in 1814 and is run over 1 mile at Newmarket. The race is for 3-year-old fillies only, who each carry 9 stone.

Year	Horse	Jockey
1995	Harayir	Richard Hills
1996	Bosra Sham	Pat Eddery
1997	Sleepytime	Kieren Fallon
1998	Cape Verdi	Frankie Dettori
1999	Wince	Kieren Fallon
2000	Lahan	Richard Hills

Flat Racing: The St Leger

This is the oldest English classic race and was first held in 1776. It is run over 1 mile 6 furlongs 132 yards at Doncaster. It is for 3-year-olds; colts carry 9 stone, fillies 8 stone 9 lb.

Year	Horse	Jockey
1994	Moonax	Pat Eddery
1995	Classic Cliché	Frankie Dettori
1996	Shantou	Frankie Dettori
1997	Silver Patriarch	Pat Eddery
1998	Nedawi	John Reid
1999	Mutafaweq	Richard Hills

Flat Racing: 2,000 Guineas

This race was first held in 1809 and is run over 1 mile at Newmarket. It is for 3-year-olds only; colts carry 9 stone, fillies 8 stone 9 lb.

Year	Horse	Jockey
1995	Pennekamp	Thierry Jarnet
1996	Mark of Esteem	Frankie Dettori
1997	Entrepreneur	Michael Kinane
1998	King of Kings	Michael Kinane
1999	Island Sands	Frankie Dettori
2000	King's Best	Kieren Fallon

Flat Racing: Prix de l'Arc de Triomphe

This race was first held in 1920 and is run over 2,400 m at Longchamp in Paris, France.

Year	Horse	Jockey
1994	Carnegie	Thierry Jarnet
1995	Lammtarra	Frankie Dettori
1996	Helissio	Olivier Peslier
1997	Peintre Celebre	Olivier Peslier
1998	Sagamix	Olivier Peslier
1999	Montjeu	Michael Kinane

Flat Racing: The Oaks

This race was first held in 1779 and is run over 1 mile 4 furlongs at Epsom in Surrey. The Oaks is for 3-year-old fillies only, who each carry 9 stone.

Year	Horse	Jockey
1995	Moonshell	Frankie Dettori
1996	Lady Carla	Pat Eddery
1997	Reams of Verse	Kieren Fallon
1998	Shahtoush	Michael Kinane
1999	Ramruma	Kieren Fallon
2000	Love Divine	Richard Quinn

Flat Racing: Champion Jockeys

Year	Jockey	Number of winners
1994	Frankie Dettori	233
1995	Frankie Dettori	211
1996	Pat Eddery	186
1997	Kieren Fallon	196
1998	Kieren Fallon	202
1999	Kieren Fallon	202

National Hunt Racing

National Hunt Racing: 1999–2000

The 1999–2000 National Hunt season was dominated by the trainer-jockey partnership of Martin Pipe and Tony McCoy. At Folkestone on 4 February 2000 Pipe broke Arthur Stephenson's all-time record for the most wins by a trainer in British racing when he saddled his 2,989th winner, while McCoy won his fifth successive jockey's championship with 245 winners. However, to the delight of the thousands of Irish race-goers who flocked to the Cheltenham Festival in March 2000, the horse Istabraq, trained by Aidan O'Brien and ridden by Charlie Swan, won the Champion Hurdle for a remarkable third successive year. Looks Like Trouble, ridden by Richard Johnson, denied the Irish a Cheltenham double by taking the Gold Cup; but there was more Irish success at Aintree on 8 April, when Papillon, ridden by Ruby Walsh and trained by his father Ted Walsh, won the Grand National. This year was the second in a row that the race has been won by an Irish father-and-son combination – in 1999 Paul and Tommy Carberry shared the same success on Bobbyjo.

An era in National Hunt racing ended on 14 December 1999, when Richard Dunwoody announced that he was retiring as a jockey because of injury. His world record of 1,699 winners assure his place among the greats of National Hunt racing.

National Hunt Racing: The Grand National

This race has been run at Aintree, Liverpool, since 1839 with the exception of 1916–18, when it was held at Gatwick, Surrey, and 1941–45, when it was not held. The horse that won the first Grand National was the Duke. The race is a handicap steeplechase and the current course takes in 30 fences and is run over 4 miles 4 furlongs. Most wins for a horse: Red Rum, 3. Most wins for a jockey: George Stevens, 5; Tom Oliver, 4.
(– = not applicable.)

Year	Horse	Jockey
1946	Lovely Cottage	Captain Bobby Petre
1947	Caughoo	Eddie Dempsey
1948	Sheila's Cottage	Arthur Thompson
1949	Russian Hero	Leo McMorrow
1950	Freebooter	Jimmy Power
1951	Nickel Coin	Johnny Bullock
1952	Teal	Arthur Thompson
1953	Early Mist	Bryan Marshall
1954	Royal Tan	Bryan Marshall
1955	Quare Times	Pat Taaffe
1956	E.S.B.	Dave Dick
1957	Sundew	Fred Winter
1958	Mr What	Arthur Freeman
1959	Oxo	Michael Scudamore
1960	Merryman II	Gerry Scott
1961	Nicolaus Silver	Bobby Beasley
1962	Kilmore	Fred Winter
1963	Ayala	Pat Buckley
1964	Team Spirit	Willie Robinson
1965	Jay Trump	Tommy Smith[1]
1966	Anglo	Tim Norman
1967	Foinavon	John Buckingham
1968	Red Alligator	Brian Fletcher
1969	Highland Wedding	Eddie Harty
1970	Gay Trip	Pat Taaffe
1971	Specify	John Cook
1972	Well To Do	Graham Thorner

(continued)

National Hunt Racing: The Grand National (*continued*)

Year	Horse	Jockey
1973	Red Rum	Brian Fletcher
1974	Red Rum	Brian Fletcher
1975	L'Escargot	Tommy Carberry
1976	Rag Trade	John Burke
1977	Red Rum	Tommy Stack
1978	Lucius	Bob Davies
1979	Rubstic	Maurice Barnes
1980	Ben Nevis	Charlie Fenwick[1]
1981	Aldaniti	Bob Champion
1982	Grittar	Dick Saunders[1]
1983	Corbiére	Ben de Haan
1984	Hallo Dandy	Neale Doughty
1985	Last Suspect	Hywel Davies
1986	West Tip	Richard Dunwoody
1987	Maori Venture	Steve Knight
1988	Rhyme N' Reason	Brendan Powell
1989	Little Polvier	Jimmy Frost
1990	Mr Frisk	Marcus Armytage[1]
1991	Seagram	Nigel Hawke
1992	Party Politics	Carl Llewellyn
1993[2]	–	
1994	Miinnehoma	Richard Dunwoody
1995	Royal Athlete	Jason Titley
1996	Rough Quest	Mick Fitzgerald
1997[3]	Lord Gyllene	Tony Dobbin
1998	Earth Summit	Carl Llewellyn
1999	Bobbyjo	Paul Carberry
2000	Papillon	Ruby Walsh

[1] Amateur jockey.
[2] Race void after a false start.
[3] Held on the Monday following a bomb scare at the Saturday meeting.

National Hunt Racing: Tote Cheltenham Gold Cup Chase

This race was first run in 1924; it is held annually at Prestbury Park, Cheltenham, during the Cheltenham Spring Festival. Current distance is 3 miles, 2 furlongs and about 110 yards. Most wins for a horse: Golden Miller, 4; Cottage Rake, Arkle, 3. Most wins for a jockey: Pat Taafe, 4.

Year	Horse	Jockey
1995	Master Oats	Norman Williamson
1996	Imperial Call	Conor O'Dwyer
1997	Mr Mulligan	Tony McCoy
1998	Cool Dawn	Andrew Thornton
1999	See More Business	Mick Fitzgerald
2000	Looks Like Trouble	Richard Johnson

National Hunt Racing: The Smurfit Champion Hurdle Challenge Trophy

This race was first run in 1927, and is held annually at Prestbury Park, Cheltenham, during the Cheltenham Spring Festival; current distance is 2 miles 110 yards.

Year	Horse	Jockey
1995	Alderbrook	Norman Williamson
1996	Collier Bay	Graham Bradley
1997	Make A Stand	Tony McCoy
1998	Istabraq	Charlie Swan
1999	Istabraq	Charlie Swan
2000	Istabraq	Charlie Swan

National Hunt Racing: Champion Jockeys

Year	Jockey	Number of winners
1993–94	Richard Dunwoody	198
1994–95	Richard Dunwoody	160
1995–96	Tony McCoy	175
1996–97	Tony McCoy	190
1997–98	Tony McCoy	253
1998–99	Tony McCoy	186
1999–2000	Tony McCoy	245

Hurling

All-Ireland Hurling Champions

Year	Team
1994	Offaly
1995	Clare
1996	Wexford
1997	Clare
1998	Offaly
1999	Cork

Hurling

Hurling, or hurley, is a stick-and-ball game, popular in Ireland, played between two teams of 15 players each. Its object is to hit the ball, by means of a curved stick, into the opposing team's goal. If the ball passes under the goal's crossbar three points are scored; if it passes above the crossbar one point is scored. First played over 3,000 years ago, the game was at one time outlawed. The rules were standardized in 1884, and are now under the control of the Gaelic Athletic Association. The premier competition, the All-Ireland Championship, was first held in 1887.

Ice Hockey

Ice Hockey: World Championship Winners

Winners since 1990.

Year	Country
1990	USSR
1991	Sweden
1992	Sweden
1993	Russia
1994	Canada
1995	Finland
1996	Czech Republic
1997	Canada
1998	Sweden
1999	Czech Republic
2000	Czech Republic

Ice Hockey: British Sekonda Superleague Final Table

Scoring: win = 2 points; tie = 1 point; overtime loss = losing team receives 1 point.

1999–2000

Position	Team	Played	Won	Lost	Tied	Overtime losses	Goals for	Goals against	Points
1	Bracknell Bees	42	24	15	3	5	181	138	56
2	Sheffield Steelers	42	24	16	2	2	188	155	52
3	Manchester Storm	42	23	17	2	3	155	138	51
4	London Knights	42	23	16	3	1	135	125	50
5	Ayr Scottish Eagles	42	17	20	5	4	144	147	43
6	Nottingham Panthers	42	18	21	3	1	140	165	40
7	Cardiff Devils	42	17	21	4	2	138	149	40
8	Newcastle Riverkings	42	11	31	0	2	113	177	24

Ice Hockey: British Sekonda Superleague Play-Off Championship

The top two teams in each group qualify for the Championship semi finals.

1999–2000

Position	Team	Played	Wins	Lost	Tied	Overtime losses	Goals for	Goals against	Points
Group A final standings									
1	London Knights	6	5	1	0	0	28	14	10
2	Newcastle Riverkings	6	3	2	1	2	14	12	9
3	Bracknell Bees	6	3	2	1	0	22	19	7
4	Nottingham Panthers	6	0	6	0	1	7	26	1
Group B final standings									
1	Sheffield Steelers	6	4	0	2	0	26	14	10
2	Ayr Scottish Eagles	6	2	3	1	1	12	19	6
3	Cardiff Devils	6	2	3	1	0	15	16	5
4	Manchester Storm	6	1	3	2	1	12	16	5

Ice Hockey: British Sekonda Superleague Play-Off Championship Finals

(OT = overtime.)

2000

Winner	Loser
Semi finals, Manchester, 1 April	
Newcastle Riverkings 3	Sheffield Steelers 1
London Knights 2	Ayr Scottish Eagles 1 (OT)
Final, Manchester, 2 April	
London Knights 7	Newcastle Riverkings 3

National Hockey League (NHL): Stanley Cup Finals

The New Jersey Devils won the series 4–2.
(OT = overtime; 2OT = double overtime; 3OT = triple overtime.)

2000

Game	Dates	Home team	Away team	Score
Game 1	30 May	New Jersey Devils	Dallas Stars	7–3
Game 2	1 June	New Jersey Devils	Dallas Stars	1–2
Game 3	3 June	Dallas Stars	New Jersey Devils	1–2
Game 4	5 June	Dallas Stars	New Jersey Devils	1–3
Game 5	8 June	New Jersey Devils	Dallas Stars	0–1 (3OT)
Game 6	10 June	Dallas Stars	New Jersey Devils	1–2 (2OT)

National Hockey League (NHL): Stanley Cup Winners

Winners since 1990.

Year	Team
1990	Edmonton Oilers
1991	Pittsburgh Penguins
1992	Pittsburgh Penguins
1993	Montreal Canadiens
1994	New York Rangers
1995	New Jersey Devils
1996	Colorado Avalanche
1997	Detroit Red Wings
1998	Detroit Red Wings
1999	Dallas Stars
2000	New Jersey Devils

Motorcycle Racing

Motorcycle Racing: 1999

Carl Fogarty's legendary status among British motorcycling fans grew still further in 1999 when he won a record fourth World Superbike title. As a measure of the Lancastrian's popularity, a crowd of over 120,000 flocked to Brands Hatch in May to watch him in the British round of the series. Australian rider Mick Doohan's run of six consecutive 500 cc Grand Prix titles came to an end when he was forced to announce his retirement after sustaining a serious leg injury in practice before the Spanish Grand Prix at Jerez in May. Fellow Honda rider Alex Criville went on to take the title, and in doing so became Spain's first ever 500 cc world champion.

500 cc World Road Racing Champions

This championship was inaugurated in 1949.

Year	Name	Country	Manufacturer
1994	Michael Doohan	Australia	Honda
1995	Michael Doohan	Australia	Honda
1996	Michael Doohan	Australia	Honda
1997	Michael Doohan	Australia	Honda
1998	Michael Doohan	Australia	Honda
1999	Alex Criville	Spain	Honda

Motorcycle Racing World Champions

1999

Road racing			
125 cc	Emilio Alzamora	Spain	Honda
250 cc	Valentino Rossi	Italy	Aprilia
500 cc	Alex Criville	Spain	Honda
Superbike	Carl Fogarty	UK	Ducati
Endurance	Terry Rymer and Jéhan D'Orgeix	UK and France	Suzuki
Sidecar (World Cup)	Steve Webster and David James	UK	Honda
Motocross			
125 cc	Alessio Chiodi	Italy	Husqvarna
250 cc	Frédéric Bolley	France	Honda
500 cc	Andrea Bartolini	Italy	Yamaha
Sidecar	Daniel and Marcel Willemsen	Netherlands	BSU
Trials	Doug Lampkin	UK	Beta

World Superbike Champions

This event was first held in 1988.

Year	Name	Country	Manufacturer
1994	Carl Fogarty	UK	Ducati
1995	Carl Fogarty	UK	Ducati
1996	Troy Corser	Australia	Ducati
1997	John Kocinski	USA	Honda
1998	Carl Fogarty	UK	Ducati
1999	Carl Fogarty	UK	Ducati

Isle of Man Tourist Trophy Senior TT

This road race was first held in 1907.

Year	Name	Country	Manufacturer
1990	Carl Fogarty	UK	Honda
1991	Steve Hislop	UK	Honda
1992	Steve Hislop	UK	Norton
1993	Joey Dunlop	UK	Honda
1994	Steve Hislop	UK	Honda
1995	Joey Dunlop	UK	Honda
1996	Phillip McCallen	UK	Honda
1997	Phillip McCallen	UK	Honda
1998	Ian Simpson	UK	Honda
1999	David Jefferies	UK	Yamaha
2000	David Jefferies	UK	Yamaha

Motor Racing

Motor Racing: 1999

When Michael Schumacher broke his leg in a crash at the British Grand Prix on 11 July 1999 it seemed that the way was clear for McLaren's Mika Hakkinen to coast to his second successive Formula 1 Drivers' Championship. Schumacher trailed the Finn by eight points and was likely to be out of action for at least six weeks. His Ferrari team-mate Eddie Irvine was also eight points behind, but few believed he had the experience or the car to mount a serious challenge for the title. However, with victories in Austria, Germany, and Malaysia, where controversially he was disqualified but then later reinstated, Irvine went into the last race of the season at Suzuka in Japan in November with a four-point advantage. If he finished above Hakkinen he would win the title, but the Finn, giving perhaps the most assured performance of his career, won the race and with it the drivers' crown. It probably came as little compensation to Irvine that he had helped Ferrari to win the Constructors' trophy for the first time since 1983, but he had proved that he was a genuine championship contender.

In rallying, Finland's Tommi Mäkinen, driving a Mitsubishi Lancer, won his fourth successive world title, though the UK's Richard Burns, with victories in three races including the Network Q RAC Rally, was the emerging talent.

Formula 1 Grand Prix Winners

As of 30 July 2000

Date	Grand Prix	Venue	Name	Country	Car
12 March	Australian	Melbourne	Michael Schumacher	Germany	Ferrari
26 March	Brazilian	Interlagos	Michael Schumacher	Germany	Ferrari
9 April	San Marino	Imola	Michael Schumacher	Germany	Ferrari
23 April	British	Silverstone	David Coulthard	UK	McLaren-Mercedes
7 May	Spanish	Barcelona	Mika Hakkinen	Finland	McLaren-Mercedes
21 May	European	Nürburgring	Michael Schumacher	Germany	Ferrari
4 June	Monaco	Monte Carlo	David Coulthard	UK	McLaren-Mercedes
18 June	Canadian	Montreal	Michael Schumacher	Germany	Ferrari
2 July	French	Magny Cours	David Coulthard	UK	McLaren-Mercedes
16 July	Austrian	A-1 Ring	Mika Hakkinen	Finland	McLaren-Mercedes
30 July	German	Hockenheim	Rubens Barrichello	Brazil	Ferrari

Formula 1 World Drivers' Championship Winners

This championship was inaugurated in 1950.

Year	Name	Country	Car
1950	Giuseppe Farina	Italy	Alfa Romeo
1951	Juan Manuel Fangio	Argentina	Alfa Romeo
1952	Alberto Ascari	Italy	Ferrari
1953	Alberto Ascari	Italy	Ferrari
1954	Juan Manuel Fangio	Argentina	Maserati-Mercedes
1955	Juan Manuel Fangio	Argentina	Mercedes-Benz
1956	Juan Manuel Fangio	Argentina	Lancia-Ferrari
1957	Juan Manuel Fangio	Argentina	Maserati
1958	Mike Hawthorn	UK	Ferrari
1959	Jack Brabham	Australia	Cooper-Climax
1960	Jack Brabham	Australia	Cooper-Climax
1961	Phil Hill	USA	Ferrari
1962	Graham Hill	UK	BRM
1963	Jim Clark	UK	Lotus-Climax
1964	John Surtees	UK	Ferrari
1965	Jim Clark	UK	Lotus-Climax
1966	Jack Brabham	Australia	Brabham-Repco
1967	Denny Hulme	New Zealand	Brabham-Repco
1968	Graham Hill	UK	Lotus-Ford
1969	Jackie Stewart	UK	Matra-Ford
1970	Jochen Rindt	Austria	Lotus-Ford
1971	Jackie Stewart	UK	Tyrrell-Ford
1972	Emerson Fittipaldi	Brazil	Lotus-Ford
1973	Jackie Stewart	UK	Tyrrell-Ford
1974	Emerson Fittipaldi	Brazil	McLaren-Ford
1975	Niki Lauda	Austria	Ferrari
1976	James Hunt	UK	McLaren-Ford
1977	Niki Lauda	Austria	Ferrari
1978	Mario Andretti	USA	Lotus-Ford
1979	Jody Scheckter	South Africa	Ferrari
1980	Alan Jones	Australia	Williams-Ford
1981	Nelson Piquet	Brazil	Brabham-Ford
1982	Keke Rosberg	Finland	Williams-Ford
1983	Nelson Piquet	Brazil	Brabham-BMW
1984	Niki Lauda	Austria	McLaren-TAG
1985	Alain Prost	France	McLaren-TAG
1986	Alain Prost	France	McLaren-TAG
1987	Nelson Piquet	Brazil	Williams-Honda
1988	Ayrton Senna	Brazil	McLaren-Honda
1989	Alain Prost	France	McLaren-Honda
1990	Ayrton Senna	Brazil	McLaren-Honda
1991	Ayrton Senna	Brazil	McLaren-Honda
1992	Nigel Mansell	UK	Williams-Renault
1993	Alain Prost	France	Williams-Renault
1994	Michael Schumacher	Germany	Benetton-Ford
1995	Michael Schumacher	Germany	Benetton-Renault
1996	Damon Hill	UK	Williams-Renault
1997	Jacques Villeneuve	Canada	Williams-Renault
1998	Mika Hakkinen	Finland	McLaren-Mercedes
1999	Mika Hakkinen	Finland	McLaren-Mercedes

RAC Rally Winners

This race was formerly known as the RAC International Rally of Great Britain. It was first held in 1927, though not recognized as an international event by the Fédération Internationale de l'Automobile (FIA) until 1951. Sponsored by Network Q since 1993.

Year	Name	Country	Car
1994	Colin McRae	UK	Subaru Impreza
1995	Colin McRae	UK	Subaru Impreza
1996	Armin Schwarz	Germany	Toyota Celica
1997	Colin McRae	UK	Subaru Impreza
1998	Richard Burns	UK	Mitsubishi Lancer
1999	Richard Burns	UK	Subaru Impreza

Formula 1 World Constructors' Championship Winners

This championship was inaugurated in 1958, when it was won by Vauwall.

Year	Constructor	Year	Constructor
1979	Ferrari	1990	McLaren-Honda
1980	Williams-Ford	1991	McLaren-Honda
1981	Williams-Ford	1992	Williams-Renault
1982	Ferrari	1993	Williams-Renault
1983	Ferrari	1994	Williams-Renault
1984	McLaren-TAG	1995	Williams-Renault
1985	McLaren-TAG	1996	Williams-Renault
1986	Williams-Honda	1997	Williams-Renault
1987	Williams-Honda	1998	McLaren-Mercedes
1988	McLaren-Honda	1999	Ferrari
1989	McLaren-Honda		

Le Mans 24-Hour Race Champions

This race was first held in 1923.

Year	Names	Car
1995	Yannick Dalmas, J J Lehto, Masanori Sekiya	McLaren
1996	Davy Jones, Manuel Reuter, Alexander Wurz	Porsche
1997	Michele Alboreto, Stefan Johansson, Tom Kristensen	Porsche
1998	Allan McNish, Stephane Ortelli, Laurent Aiello	Porsche
1999	Yannick Dalmas, Pierluigi Martini, Joachim Winkelhock	BMW
2000	Frank Biela, Tom Kristensen, Emmanuele Pirro	Audi

World Rally Champions

A manufacturers' world championship was established in 1968. The FIA Cup for Drivers, a championship for drivers, was inaugurated in 1977 and two years later became the official world drivers' championship.

Year	Name	Country	Car
1994	Didier Auriol	France	Toyota Celica
1995	Colin McRae	UK	Subaru Impreza
1996	Tommi Mäkinen	Finland	Mitsubishi Lancer
1997	Tommi Mäkinen	Finland	Mitsubishi Lancer
1998	Tommi Mäkinen	Finland	Mitsubishi Lancer
1999	Tommi Mäkinen	Finland	Mitsubishi Lancer

British Grand Prix Winners

The 1950 British Grand Prix was the first race of the inaugural World Drivers' Championship. It was held at Silverstone and was won by Giuseppe Farina of Italy in an Alfa-Romeo. Previous Grand Prix had taken place in the UK in 1926–27 at Brooklands, 1935–38 at Donnington, and 1948–49 at Silverstone. Most wins: Jim Clark, Alain Prost, 5; Nigel Mansell, 4.

Year	Name	Country	Car	Venue
1980	Alan Jones	Australia	Williams-Ford	Brands Hatch
1981	John Watson	UK	McLaren-Ford	Silverstone
1982	Niki Lauda	Austria	McLaren-Ford	Brands Hatch
1983	Alain Prost	France	Renault	Silverstone
1984	Niki Lauda	Austria	McLaren-TAG	Brands Hatch
1985	Alain Prost	France	McLaren-TAG	Silverstone
1986	Nigel Mansell	UK	Williams-Honda	Brands Hatch
1987	Nigel Mansell	UK	Williams-Honda	Silverstone
1988	Ayrton Senna	Brazil	McLaren-Honda	Silverstone
1989	Alain Prost	France	McLaren-Honda	Silverstone
1990	Alain Prost	France	Ferrari	Silverstone
1991	Nigel Mansell	UK	Williams-Renault	Silverstone
1992	Nigel Mansell	UK	Williams-Renault	Silverstone
1993	Alain Prost	France	Williams-Renault	Silverstone
1994	Damon Hill	UK	Williams-Renault	Silverstone
1995	Johnny Herbert	UK	Benetton-Renault	Silverstone
1996	Jacques Villeneuve	Canada	Williams-Renault	Silverstone
1997	Jacques Villeneuve	Canada	Williams-Renault	Silverstone
1998	Michael Schumacher	Germany	Ferrari	Silverstone
1999	David Coulthard	UK	McLaren-Mercedes	Silverstone
2000	David Coulthard	UK	McLaren-Mercedes	Silverstone

Netball

Netball World Championship

This championship was first held in 1963, when it was won by Australia; it is held every four years.

Year	Country
1979	Australia, New Zealand, and Trinidad and Tobago
1983	Australia
1987	New Zealand
1991	Australia
1995	Australia
1999	Australia

Rowing

World Rowing Championship

These championships were held at St Catherine's, Ontario, Canada, 22–29 August 1999.

Category	Name	Country
1999		
Men		
Single sculls	Rob Waddell	New Zealand
Double sculls	Luka Spik and Iztok Cop	Slovak Republic
Quad sculls		Germany
Lightweight single sculls	Karsten Nielsen	Denmark
Lightweight double sculls	Michaelangelo Crispi and Leonardo Pettinari	Italy
Lightweight quad sculls		Italy
Coxless pairs	Drew Ginn and James Tomkins	Australia
Coxed pairs	Jim Neil, Philip Henry, and Nicholas Anderson	USA
Coxless fours		Great Britain
Coxed fours		USA
Eights		USA
Lightweight coxless pairs	Stefano Basalini and Paolo Pittini	Italy
Lightweight coxless fours		Denmark
Lightweight eights		USA
Women		
Single sculls	Ekaterina Karsten	Belarus
Double sculls	Jana Thieme and Kathrin Boron	Germany
Quad sculls		Germany
Lightweight single sculls	Pia Vogel	Switzerland
Lightweight double sculls	Constanta Burcica and Camelia Macoviciuc	Romania
Lightweight quad sculls		USA
Coxless pairs	Emma Robinson and Theresa Luke	Canada
Coxless fours		Belarus
Eights		Romania
Lightweight coxless pairs	Rachel Anderson and Linda Muri	USA
Lightweight eights		Romania

Henley Royal Regatta

Winners since 1995.

Year	Name	Country
Diamond Challenge Sculls[1]		
1995	Juri Jaanson	Estonia
1996	Merlin Vervoorn	Netherlands
1997	Greg Searle	UK
1998	Jamie Koven	USA
1999	Marcel Hacker	USA
2000	Acquil Abdullah	USA
Grand Challenge Cup[2]		
1995	San Diego	USA
1996	Imperial College and Queen's Tower	UK
1997	Australian Institute of Sport and NSW Institute of Sport	Australia
1998	RC Hansa Dortmund and Berliner RC	Germany
1999	RC Hansa Dortmund and Berliner RC	Germany
2000	Australian Institute of Sport	Australia

[1] First held in 1884. [2] For eights; first held in 1839.

The Boat Race

This race was first held in 1829. It is rowed annually by crews from Oxford and Cambridge Universities, between Putney and Mortlake on the River Thames. Cambridge currently lead Oxford by 76 wins to 69. The 1877 race ended in a dead heat.

Year	Team
1990	Oxford
1991	Oxford
1992	Oxford
1993	Cambridge
1994	Cambridge
1995	Cambridge
1996	Cambridge
1997	Cambridge
1998	Cambridge
1999	Cambridge
2000	Oxford

Rugby League

Rugby League: 1999–2000

The Bradford Bulls finished top of the JJB Super League by a clear five points, but it was the second-placed team, St Helens, who lifted the Super League crown after defeating the Bulls 8–6 in the Championship Grand Final at Old Trafford on 9 October 1999. Inspired by Henry Paul, the Bulls dominated the game for long periods but could not break down a resolute St Helens defence. Bradford's fortunes, however, did improve the following May when the Bulls beat the Leeds Rhinos 24–18 to lift the Silk Cut Challenge Cup for the first time since 1949. The match was played at Murrayfield rather than at Wembley, which had been the permanent venue for the final since 1933.

Rugby League: 1999–2000 *(continued)*

On the international stage, the Tri-Nations tournament between Australia, Great Britain, and New Zealand in October–November 1999 merely underlined that in competitive terms Great Britain was still years behind the leading southern hemisphere sides. Thrashed 42-6 by Australia in Brisbane, Great Britain went out of the competition with a 26–4 defeat to New Zealand in Auckland. In the final, also in Auckland, Australia narrowly beat New Zealand 22–20.

Rugby League

Rugby league is a professional form of rugby football founded in England in 1895 as the Northern Union when a dispute about pay caused northern clubs to break away from the Rugby Football Union. The game is similar to Rugby Union, but the number of players was reduced from 15 to 13 in 1906, and other rule changes have made the game more open and fast-moving. Major events include the Challenge Cup final, first held in 1897 and since 1929 staged at Wembley Stadium, and the Premiership Trophy, introduced in 1975, a knockout competition involving the top eight clubs in the first division. In March 1996 the game was played during the summer season for the first time, when the Super League began in the UK and comprised 12 teams, including Paris. In 1997 a world club championship between teams from the British and Australian Super League (which includes teams from New Zealand) was inaugurated.

Rugby League: World Cup Winners

This championship was inaugurated in 1954.

Year	Team
1954	Great Britain
1957	Australia
1960	Great Britain
1968	Australia
1970	Australia
1972	Great Britain
1975	Australia
1977	Australia
1988	Australia
1992	Australia
1995	Australia

Rugby League: Challenge Cup Winners Since 1980

Year	Team
1980	Hull Kingston Rovers
1981	Widnes
1982	Hull
1983	Featherstone Rovers
1984	Widnes
1985	Wigan
1986	Castleford
1987	Halifax
1988	Wigan
1989	Wigan
1990	Wigan
1991	Wigan
1992	Wigan
1993	Wigan
1994	Wigan
1995	Wigan
1996	St Helens
1997	St Helens
1998	Sheffield Eagles
1999	Leeds Rhinos
2000	Bradford Bulls

Rugby League: JJB Sports Super League Final Table

1999

Team	Played	Won	Drawn	Lost	Points for	Points against	League points
Bradford Bulls[1]	30	25	1	4	897	445	51
St Helens[1]	30	23	0	7	1,034	561	46
Leeds Rhinos[1]	30	22	1	7	910	558	45
Wigan Warriors[1]	30	21	1	8	877	390	43
Castleford Tigers[1]	30	19	3	8	712	451	41
Gateshead Thunder	30	19	1	10	775	576	39
Warrington Wolves	30	15	1	14	700	717	31
London Broncos	30	13	2	15	644	708	28
Halifax Blue Sox	30	11	0	19	573	792	22
Sheffield Eagles	30	10	1	19	518	818	21
Wakefield Trinity	30	10	0	20	608	795	20
Salford Reds	30	6	1	23	526	916	13
Hull Sharks	30	5	0	25	422	921	10
Huddersfield Giants	30	5	0	25	463	1,011	10

[1] Qualified for play-offs.

Rugby League: JJB Sports Super League Play-Offs: Results

St Helens were crowned Super League champions after defeating the Bradford Bulls 8–6 in the Grand Final at Old Trafford on 9 October.

1999

Team	Points	Team	Points	Location
St Helens	34	Leeds Rhinos	14	Knowsley Road, St Helens
Wigan Warriors	10	Castleford Tigers	14	JJB Stadium, Wigan
Bradford Bulls	40	St Helens	4	Odsal, Bradford
Leeds Rhinos	16	Castleford Tigers	23	Headingley, Leeds
St Helens	36	Castleford Tigers	6	Knowsley Road, St Helens
Grand Final				
Bradford Bulls	6	St Helens	8	Old Trafford, Manchester

Rugby League: League Championship: Recent Winners

Inaugurated in 1895–96. From 1907 to 1973 the championship was decided by a play-off. From 1974 to 1996 the championship title was awarded to the team finishing top of Division One. In 1996 a new Super League was introduced (currently sponsored by JJB Sports).

Year	Team
Division One	
1980	Bradford Northern
1981	Bradford Northern
1982	Leigh
1983	Hull
1984	Hull Kingston Rovers
1985	Hull Kingston Rovers
1986	Halifax
1987	Wigan
1988	Widnes
1989	Widnes
1990	Wigan
1991	Wigan
1992	Wigan
1993	Wigan
1994	Wigan
1995	Wigan
1996	Wigan
Super League	
1996	St Helens
1997	Bradford Bulls
1998	Wigan Warriors
1999	St Helens

Rugby Union

International Rugby

International Rugby: 1999–2000

1999 Rugby World Cup

The fourth Rugby World Cup was won by Australia with a comfortable 35–12 victory over France in the final at Cardiff's Millennium Stadium on 6 November. They may have lacked the flair of the Australian side which won in England in 1991 (of whom the captain John Eales was the only remaining member), but they were strong in every department, and, remarkably, conceded just one try throughout the whole tournament.

Yet, for all Australia's excellence, the fourth Rugby World Cup will be remembered for France's sensational 43–31 semi-final victory over the tournament favourites New Zealand at Twickenham on 31 October. The French had been in dismal form all year, and it was no surprise when New Zealand went 24–10 up after 44 minutes. Then, in a breathtaking display of attacking rugby, France scored 30 points without reply, with converted tries from Dominici, Dourthe, and Bernat-Salles and 18 points from the boot of Lamaison (who scored 28 points in the match), before conceding a consolation try in the last minute.

None of the 'home' countries got beyond the quarter-final stage. England were undone by South Africa's Jannie De Beer, who kicked 34 points including a world record five dropped goals in his side's 44–21 victory. Scotland fought hard but lost 30–18 to New Zealand; tournament hosts Wales (who had lost a group match to Samoa) were soundly beaten 24-9 by Australia, while Ireland were eliminated by Argentina at the play-off stage.

2000 Six Nations

Italy became the first new country to join the International Championship since France in 1910, and they marked their debut in style with a shock 34–20 victory in Rome over Scotland. England won the championship with four straight victories, but lost the final game to Scotland and with it the Grand Slam. Ireland and Wales both won three matches, but the Welsh campaign was overshadowed by a row concerning two of the team's assimilated players, New Zealanders Shane Howarth and Brett Simpkinson, who were dropped after doubts were raised over whether they were eligible to play for their adopted country.

Rugby Union: World Cup

This competition, for the William Webb Ellis Trophy, was first held in 1987.

Year	Winner	Runner-up	Score	Location
1987	New Zealand	France	29–7	Melbourne
1991	Australia	England	12–6	Twickenham
1995	South Africa	New Zealand	15–12	Johannesburg
1999	Australia	France	35–12	Cardiff

Rugby Union: International Six Nations Championship Results

The International Five Nations Championship became the International Six Nations Championship when Italy joined in 2000.

2000

Date	Home team	Away team	Result	Location
5 February	England	Ireland	50–18	Twickenham, London
5 February	Italy	Scotland	34–20	Stadio Flaminio, Rome
5 February	Wales	France	3–36	Millennium Stadium, Cardiff
19 February	France	England	9–15	Stade de France, St-Denis
19 February	Ireland	Scotland	44–22	Lansdowne Road, Dublin
19 February	Wales	Italy	47–16	Millennium Stadium, Cardiff
4 March	England	Wales	46–12	Twickenham, London
4 March	Ireland	Italy	60–13	Lansdowne Road, Dublin
4 March	Scotland	France	16–28	Murrayfield, Edinburgh
18 March	Italy	England	12–59	Stadio Flaminio, Rome
18 March	Wales	Scotland	26–18	Millennium Stadium, Cardiff
19 March	France	Ireland	25–27	Stade de France, St-Denis
1 April	France	Italy	42–31	Stade de France, St-Denis
1 April	Ireland	Wales	19–23	Lansdowne Road, Dublin
2 April	Scotland	England	19–13	Murrayfield, Edinburgh

Rugby Union

The Rugby Football Union was formed in 1871 and has its headquarters in England (Twickenham, Middlesex). Formerly an amateur game, the game's status was revoked in August 1995 by the International Rugby Football Board, which lifted restrictions on players moving between Rugby Union and Rugby League.

The first World Cup, the William Webb Ellis trophy, held in Australia and New Zealand in 1987, was won by New Zealand. Other major events include the International Championship (Six Nations), instituted in 1884, now a tournament between England, France, Ireland, Scotland, Wales, and Italy (which joined in 2000); the Tetley's Bitter Cup, the SWALEC Cup, and the Tennents Cup, the club knockout tournaments of the English, Welsh, and Scottish rugby unions. Each of the home countries also stage league championships. Rugby Union (along with cricket) was introduced to the Commonwealth Games at Kuala Lumpur, Malaysia, in September 1998. The Commonwealth tournament was played with seven players on each team, as opposed to the full 15-aside version.

Rugby Union: International Six Nations Championship Winners

This championship was instituted in 1884 and is now a tournament between England, France, Ireland, Italy, Scotland, and Wales. The Grand Slam is achieved by teams winning every game in a championship season. The Triple Crown is achieved by teams defeating the other three 'home-nations' and does not apply to France and Italy.

Most outright championship wins: England, 23. Most Grand Slams: England, 11. Most Triple Crowns: England, 21.

Year	Team
1990	Scotland[1 2]
1991	England[1 2]
1992	England[1 2]
1993	France
1994	Wales
1995	England[1 2]
1996	England[2]
1997	France[1 3]
1998	France[1 3]
1999	Scotland
2000	England

[1] Grand Slam winners.
[2] Also won the Triple Crown.
[3] England won the Triple Crown.

Rugby Union: International Six Nations Championship Final Table

2000

Position	Team	Played	Won	Drawn	Lost	Points for	Points against	Points
1	England	5	4	0	1	183	70	8
2	France	5	3	0	2	140	92	6
3	Ireland	5	3	0	2	168	133	6
4	Wales	5	3	0	2	111	135	6
5	Scotland	5	1	0	4	95	145	2
6	Italy	5	1	0	4	106	228	2

Club Rugby

Club Rugby: 1999–2000

Northampton defeated Munster 9–8 in the European Cup final at Twickenham on 27 May, 1999 to clinch the club's first major trophy in its 120-year existence. Without several key players, notably inspirational captain Matt Dawson, Northampton's victory was based on tenacious tackling, forward strength, and the goal-kicking skills of Paul Grayson, who scored all nine points. Munster would have won the game if stand-off Ronan O'Gara had been able to convert Paul Wallace's try or any of the four penalty opportunities that came his way. In their semi-finals O'Gara had scored 21 points to help Munster win a shock 31–21 victory over Toulouse, a result that ranks alongside Munster's famous win over the All Blacks in 1978. In England, Leicester retained the Allied Dunbar Premiership Division One title, while Wasps again won the Tetley's Bitter Cup, defeating Northampton 31–25 in the final. The new Welsh-Scottish League was won by Cardiff, while Llanelli won the Welsh Cup for a record eleventh time. In Scotland, the honours went to Heriot's FP in the league and Boroughmuir in the cup, and in Ireland, St Mary's College were crowned All Ireland champions for the very first time.

Rugby Union: European Cup Winners

This European club competition was first held in 1995–96.

Year	Winner	Runner-up	Score	Location
1996	Toulouse (France)	Cardiff (Wales)	21–18	Cardiff
1997	Brive (France)	Leicester (England)	28–9	Cardiff
1998	Bath (England)	Brive (France)	19–18	Bordeaux
1999	Ulster (Ireland)	Colomiers (France)	21–6	Dublin
2000	Northampton (England)	Munster (Ireland)	9–8	London

Rugby Union: Super 12

This tournament for club teams from Australia, New Zealand, and South Africa was first held in 1996.

Year	Team
1996	Auckland Blues (New Zealand)
1997	Auckland Blues (New Zealand)
1998	Canterbury Crusaders (New Zealand)
1999	Canterbury Crusaders (New Zealand)
2000	Canterbury Crusaders (New Zealand)

English Rugby: English League Champions

This championship was first held 1987–88. It was known as the Courage League Division One 1996–97 and has since been known as the Dunbar Premiership Division One since 1997–98.

Year	Team
1988	Leicester
1989	Bath
1990	Wasps
1991	Bath
1992	Bath
1993	Bath
1994	Bath
1995	Leicester
1996	Bath
1997	Wasps
1998	Newcastle
1999	Leicester
2000	Leicester

English Rugby: Tetley's Bitter Cup

This English club knockout tournament has been sponsored by John Player and Pilkington, and is now sponsored by Tetley Bitter. It was first held in 1971–72.

Year	Team
1990	Bath
1991	Harlequins
1992	Bath
1993	Leicester
1994	Bath
1995	Bath
1996	Bath
1997	Leicester
1998	Saracens
1999	Wasps
2000	Wasps

English Rugby: County Championship

This championship was first held in 1888.

Year	Team
1990	Lancashire
1991	Cornwall
1992	Lancashire
1993	Lancashire
1994	Yorkshire
1995	Warwickshire
1996	Gloucestershire
1997	Cumbria
1998	Cheshire
1999	Cornwall
2000	Yorkshire

English Rugby: Allied Dunbar Premiership Final Tables

(Key: P = played; W = won; D = drawn; L = lost; F = points for; A = points against; Pts = League points.)

1999–2000

Position	Team	P	W	D	L	F	A	Pts
Division One								
1	Leicester	22	18	1	3	687	425	51
2	Bath	22	15	2	5	690	425	43
3	Gloucester	22	15	0	7	628	490	40
4	Saracens	22	14	0	8	729	514	37
5	Northampton	22	13	0	9	551	480	35
6	Bristol	22	12	1	9	632	602	34
7	Wasps	22	11	1	10	640	461	31
8	London Irish	22	9	1	12	613	616	25
9	Newcastle	22	6	2	14	377	630	19
10	Harlequins	22	7	0	15	441	687	18
11	Sale	22	7	0	15	381	633	18
12	Bedford[1]	22	1	0	21	396	802	3

(continued)

English Rugby: Allied Dunbar Premiership Final Tables (*continued*)

Position	Team	P	W	D	L	F	A	Pts
Division Two								
1	Rotherham[2]	26	24	0	2	1,045	267	48
2	Leeds	26	22	0	4	794	269	44
3	Worcester	26	19	0	7	865	450	38
4	Exeter	26	19	0	7	742	466	38
5	London Welsh	26	16	0	10	712	476	32
6	Coventry	26	15	0	11	714	589	30
7	Moseley	26	14	0	12	595	526	28
8	Manchester	26	11	0	15	513	671	22
9	Henley	26	10	1	15	599	696	21
10	Wakefield	26	10	0	16	547	638	20
11	Orrell	26	7	0	19	388	682	14
12	Waterloo	26	6	2	18	441	830	14
13	Rugby	26	6	1	19	408	905	13
14	West Hartlepool[3]	26	1	0	25	216	1114	2

[1]Relegated after losing a play-off with Division Two champions Rotherham.
[2]Promoted after winning a play-off with Division One bottom side Bedford.
[3]Relegated.

Scottish Rugby: BT Scotland Premiership Division One Final Table

(Key: P = played; W = won; D = drawn; L = lost; F = points for; A = points against; Pts = total points.)

1999–2000

Position	Team	P	W	D	L	F	A	Pts
1	Heriot's FP	18	16	0	2	707	274	74
2	Glasgow Hawks	18	13	0	5	566	277	63
3	Melrose	18	11	0	7	446	396	52
4	Currie	18	10	0	8	436	442	52
5	Gala	18	9	0	9	457	448	46
6	Hawick	18	9	1	8	466	472	46
7	Jed-Forest	18	8	1	9	361	416	43
8	Watsonians	18	6	0	12	395	490	34
9	Kelso[1]	18	5	0	13	323	531	27
10	West of Scotland[1]	18	2	0	16	276	687	13

[1] Relegated.

Scottish Rugby: BT Cellnet Cup

This Scottish knockout tournament was first held in 1996, and was formerly known as the Tennent's Velvet Cup.

Year	Team
1996	Hawick
1997	Melrose
1998	Glasgow Hawks
1999	Gala
2000	Boroughmuir

Scottish Rugby: Scottish Club Champions

This championship was first held in 1974; formerly known as the McEwan's League Division One, it became the Tennent's Premiership Division One in 1995–96, the Tennent's Velvet Premiership Division One in 1998–99, and the BT Premiership Division One in 1999–2000.

Year	Team	Year	Team
1990	Melrose	1996	Melrose
1991	Boroughmuir	1997	Melrose
1992	Melrose	1998	Watsonians
1993	Melrose	1999	Heriot's FP
1994	Melrose	2000	Heriot's FP
1995	Stirling County		

Welsh Rugby: Welsh/Scottish League Final Table

(Key: P = played; W = won; D = drawn; L = lost; F = points for; A = points against; Pts = points.)

1999–2000

Position	Team	P	W	D	L	F	A	Pts
1	Cardiff	22	18	1	3	879	504	59
2	Newport	22	15	1	6	773	453	49
3	Swansea	22	14	1	7	691	509	47
4	Pontypridd	21	13	2	6	637	466	41
5	Llanelli	21	13	0	8	736	498	38
6	Ebbw Vale	22	12	0	10	647	569	38
7	Neath	22	11	2	9	664	553	35
8	Edinburgh Reivers	22	10	1	11	564	654	34
9	Bridgend	22	8	1	13	427	564	27
10	Glasgow Caledonians	22	8	1	13	488	621	25
11	Caerphilly	22	2	1	19	427	939	6
12	Dunvant[1]	22	1	1	20	357	960	5

[1] Relegated.

Welsh Rugby: Welsh Club Champions

This championship was first held in 1990–91. In 1999–2000, with the inclusion of two Scottish clubs, Edinburgh Reivers and Glasgow Caledonians, the league was re-named the Welsh-Scottish League.

Year	Team
1991	Neath
1992	Swansea
1993	Llanelli
1994	Swansea
1995	Cardiff
1996	Neath
1997	Pontypridd
1998	Swansea
1999	Llanelli
2000	Cardiff

Welsh Rugby: Welsh Cup

This club knockout tournament was formerly known as the Schweppes Welsh Cup, and also the SWALEC Welsh Cup. It was first held in 1971–72.

Year	Team	Year	Team
1990	Neath	1996	Pontypridd
1991	Llanelli	1997	Cardiff
1992	Llanelli	1998	Llanelli
1993	Llanelli	1999	Swansea
1994	Cardiff	2000	Llanelli
1995	Swansea		

Irish Rugby: Allied Irish Bank League Division One Final Table

St Mary's College won the championship by defeating Lansdowne 25–22 in the play-off final.

(Key: P = played; W = won; D = drawn; L = lost; F = points for; A = points against; B = bonus points; Pts = total points.)

1999–2000

Position	Team	P	W	D	L	F	A	B	Pts
1	St Mary's College[1 2]	11	8	0	3	265	121	5	37
2	Terenure College[2]	11	8	0	3	235	229	4	36
3	Lansdowne[2]	11	7	1	3	265	149	4	34
4	Ballymena[2]	11	7	0	4	267	284	5	33
5	Garryowen	11	6	0	5	245	199	7	31
6	Cork Constitution	11	6	0	5	259	259	4	28
7	Young Munster	11	6	0	5	175	243	1	25
8	Shannon	11	4	0	7	222	229	7	23
9	Buccaneers	11	5	0	6	205	196	2	22
10	Dungannon	11	4	0	7	238	252	4	20
11	DLSP[3]	11	2	1	8	149	235	4	14
12	Clontarf[3]	11	2	0	9	195	324	4	12

[1]Champions.
[2]Qualified for play-offs.
[3]Relegated.

Shinty

Shinty: Camanachd Cup

The Camanachd Association Challenge Cup was first held in 1896 when it was won by Kingussie.

Year	Team
1990	Skye
1991	Kingussie
1992	Fort William
1993	Kingussie
1994	Kyles Athletic
1995	Kingussie
1996	Oban Camanachd
1997	Kingussie
1998	Kingussie
1999	Kingussie
2000	Kingussie

Shinty

Shinty (Gaelic *camanachd*) is a stick-and-ball game resembling hurling, popular in the Scottish Highlands. It is played between teams of 12 players each, on a field 132–183 m/144–200 yd long and 64–91 m/70–99 yd wide. A curved stick (*caman*) is used to propel a leather-covered cork and worsted ball into the opposing team's goal (*hail*). The premier tournament, the Camanachd Cup, was instituted in 1896.

Skating

World Figure Skating Champions

This championship was first held in 1896. Gilbert Fuchs of Germany became the first men's champion. The first women's championship (1906) was won by Madge Syers (born cave) of the UK; the first pairs champions (1908) were Anna Hübler and Heinrich Burger of Germany; and the first ice dance champions were Jean Westwood and Lawrence Demmy of the UK, in 1951.

Year	Name	Country
Men		
1995	Elvis Stojko	Canada
1996	Todd Eldredge	USA
1997	Elvis Stojko	Canada
1998	Alexei Yagudin	Russia
1999	Alexei Yagudin	Russia
2000	Alexei Yagudin	Russia
Women		
1995	Lu Chen	China
1996	Michelle Kwan	USA
1997	Tara Lipinski	USA
1998	Michelle Kwan	USA
1999	Maria Butyrskaya	Russia
2000	Michelle Kwan	USA
Pairs		
1995	Rene Novotny and Radka Kovarikova	Czech Republic
1996	Andrei Bushkov and Marina Eltsova	Russia
1997	Yevgeny Platov and Mandy Wotzel	Russia
1998	Anton Sikharudlidze and Elena Berezhnaya	Russia
1999	Anton Sikharudlidze and Elena Berezhnaya	Russia
2000	Maria Petrova and Alexei Tikhonov	Russia
Ice Dance		
1995	Oksana Gritschuk and Yevgeny Platov	Russia
1996	Oksana Gritschuk and Yevgeny Platov	Russia
1997	Oksana Gritschuk and Yevgeny Platov	Russia
1998	Angelika Krylova and Oleg Ovsyannikov	Russia
1999	Angelika Krylova and Oleg Ovsyannikov	Russia
2000	Marina Anissina and Gwendal Peizerat	France

Skiing

Skiing: 1999–2000

The 1999–2000 Alpine skiing season was dominated by the irrepressible Hermann Maier. The 'Herminator', as he is known to his legions of fans, won the men's Downhill, Giant Slalom, Super G, and Overall World Cup titles, and in the process became the first skier to score 2,000 World Cup points in a season. Since emerging from relative obscurity to win two golds at the 1998 Winter Olympics, the powerfully built Austrian has now won a total of 12 World Cup, World Championship, and Olympic titles. Austria was also prominent in the women's World Cup, with Renate Goetschl winning the Super G and Overall titles, and Michaela Dorfmeister, the Giant Slalom.

Skiing: Alpine World Championships

This championship was inaugurated in 1931 and is now held every two years. The 1999 championships were held at Vail, Colorado, 1–14 February.

1999

Category	Name	Country
Men		
Downhill	Hermann Maier	Austria
Slalom	Kalle Palander	Finland
Giant slalom	Lasse Kjus	Norway
Super giant slalom	Hermann Maier/Lasse Kjus	Austria/Norway (shared)
Combination	Kjetil Andre Aamodt	Norway

Category	Name	Country
Women		
Downhill	Renate Goetschl	Austria
Slalom	Zalle Steggall	Australia
Giant slalom	Alexandra Meissnitzer	Austria
Super giant slalom	Alexandra Meissnitzer	Austria
Combination	Pernilla Wiberg	Sweden

Skiing: Alpine World Cup

This annual competition was first held in 1967.

1999–2000

Category	Name	Country
Men		
Downhill	Hermann Maier	Austria
Slalom	Kjetil Andre Aamodt	Norway
Giant slalom	Hermann Maier	Austria
Super G	Hermann Maier	Austria
Overall	Hermann Maier	Austria

Category	Name	Country
Women		
Downhill	Regina Haesull	Germany
Slalom	Spela Pretnar	Slovenia
Giant slalom	Michaela Dorfmeister	Austria
Super G	Renate Goetschl	Austria
Overall	Renate Goetschl	Austria

Snooker

Snooker: 1999–2000

The Embassy World Professional Championship at the Crucible Theatre, Sheffield, produced the first ever all-Welsh final, with the 1999 runner-up, Mark Williams, from Cwm in Gwent, coming from 13–7 down in the afternoon session of the final day on 1 May to defeat Matthew Stevens of Carmarthen 18–16, to claim the £240,000 first prize. With victories at the prestigious UK Championships in November 1999, and the Thailand Masters in March 2000, and second places in four other ranking events, Williams will begin the 2000–01 season as the world number one, ahead of Stephen Hendry and John Higgins.

Snooker

Snooker was invented by British army officers serving with the Devonshire Regiment in Jubbulpore, India, in 1875 and derived from the game of black pool. It became popular in the 1920s when Joe Davis introduced new techniques. It is now one of the biggest television sports in the UK and is gaining popularity across Europe, the Far East, and North America. A season-long series of ranking and invitational tournaments culminates in the World Professional Championship at the Crucible Theatre, Sheffield, England, every April. A women's World Open Championship was introduced in 1976, and has been staged annually since 1980.

World Professional Snooker Championship

This championship was first held in 1926–27. Between 1952 and 1957, the professional players staged a match-play championship for the world title following a disagreement with the game's governing body at that time, the Billiards Association and Control Club. Between 1964 and 1968, the championship was organized on a challenge basis before becoming a knockout tournament in 1969. Since 1977 all finals have been held at the Crucible Theatre, Sheffield. It has been sponsored by Embassy since 1976.

Year	Name	Country
1980	Cliff Thorburn	Canada
1981	Steve Davis	England
1982	Alex Higgins	Northern Ireland
1983	Steve Davis	England
1984	Steve Davis	England
1985	Dennis Taylor	Northern Ireland
1986	Joe Johnson	England
1987	Steve Davis	England
1988	Steve Davis	England
1989	Steve Davis	England
1990	Stephen Hendry	Scotland
1991	John Parrott	England
1992	Stephen Hendry	Scotland
1993	Stephen Hendry	Scotland
1994	Stephen Hendry	Scotland
1995	Stephen Hendry	Scotland
1996	Stephen Hendry	Scotland
1997	Ken Doherty	Ireland, Republic of
1998	John Higgins	Scotland
1999	Stephen Hendry	Scotland
2000	Mark Williams	Wales

World Amateur Snooker Championship

This championship was first held in 1963.

Year	Name	Country/territory
1994	Mohammed Yusuf	Pakistan
1995	Sakchai Sim-Ngam	Thailand
1996	Stuart Bingham	England
1997	Marco Fu	Hong Kong
1998	Luke Simmonds	England
1999	Ian Preece	Wales

Speedway

World Speedway Champions

Winners since 1989.

Year	Name	Country
1989	Hans Nielsen	Denmark
1990	Per Jonsson	Sweden
1991	Jan Pedersen	Denmark
1992	Gary Havelock	England
1993	Sam Ermolenko	USA
1994	Tony Rickardsson	Sweden
1995	Hans Nielsen	Denmark
1996	Billy Hamill	USA
1997	Greg Hancock	USA
1998	Tony Rickardsson	Sweden
1999	Tony Rickardsson	Sweden

Squash

World Open Squash Champions

This competition was first held in 1976.

Year	Name	Country
Men		
1994	Jansher Khan	Pakistan
1995	Jansher Khan	Pakistan
1996	Jansher Khan	Pakistan
1997	Rodney Eyles	Australia
1998	Jonathan Power	Canada
1999	Peter Nicol	UK
Women		
1994	Michelle Martin	Australia
1995	Michelle Martin	Australia
1996	Sarah Fitz-Gerald	Australia
1997	Sarah Fitz-Gerald	Australia
1998	Sarah Fitz-Gerald	Australia
1999	Cassie Jackman	UK

Swimming

Swimming: 1999–2000

In 1999–2000 existing world records tumbled at an astonishing rate; it is hard to tell how much this had to do with the adoption by many swimmers of the new FINA-approved skintight bodysuits, which, by reducing the amount of drag through the water, can dramatically improve a swimmer's time. In five record-breaking swims between August 1999 and May 2000, Australian teenage sensation Ian Thorpe beat the time for the 200 metres freestyle by 1.16 sec (from 1 min 46.67 sec to 1 min 45.51 sec), and for the 400 metres freestyle by 2.47 sec (from 3 min 43.80 sec to 3 min 41.33 sec). In August 1999, Lenny Krayzelburg of the USA set new 50, 100, and 200 metres backstroke world records, while between 17 July and 28 August 1999 Penelope Heyns of South Africa lowered the mark for the 100 metres breaststroke five times, the 200 metres breaststroke four times, and the 50 metres breaststroke twice. At the time of writing, the Dutch swimmer Inge de Bruijn was on a record-breaking roll to rival that of Heyns, with six world record swims in butterfly and freestyle races between 20 May and 4 June 2000.

The European Championships, held in Istanbul between 23 July and 1 August 1999, were dominated by Pieter van der Hoogenband of the Netherlands, who won six gold medals. Sue Rolph in the 100 metres freestyle, Paul Palmer in the 400 metres freestyle, and Tony Ali in the 3 metre springboard diving, were gold medal winners for Britain. At the World Short Course Championships in Athens in March 2000, Mark Foster was Britain's outstanding performer, with golds in the 50 metres freestyle and 50 metres butterfly.

Swimming: Long Course World Records

As of 1 June 2000.

Category	Time	Name	Country	Date	Location
Men					
50 m freestyle	0:21.81	Tom Jager	USA	24 March 1990	Nashville (TN), USA
100 m freestyle	0:48.21	Aleksandr Popov	Russia	18 June 1994	Monte Carlo
200 m freestyle	1:45.51	Ian Thorpe	Australia	15 May 2000	Sydney, Australia
400 m freestyle	3:41.33	Ian Thorpe	Australia	13 May 2000	Sydney, Australia
800 m freestyle	7:46.00	Kieren Perkins	Australia	24 August 1994	Victoria, Canada
1,500 m freestyle	14:41.66	Kieren Perkins	Australia	24 August 1994	Victoria, Canada
50 m backstroke	0:24.99	Lenny Krayzelburg	USA	28 August 1999	Sydney, Australia
100 m backstroke	0:53.60	Lenny Krayzelburg	USA	24 August 1999	Sydney, Australia
200 m backstroke	1:55.87	Lenny Krayzelburg	USA	27 August 1999	Sydney, Australia
100 m breaststroke	1:00.60	Fred Deburghgraeve	Belgium	20 July 1996	Atlanta (GA), USA
200 m breaststroke	2:10:16	Mike Barrowman	USA	29 July 1992	Barcelona, Spain
50 m butterfly	0:23.60	George Huegill	Australia	14 May 2000	Sydney, Australia
100 m butterfly	0:51.81	Michael Klim	Australia	12 December 1999	Canberra, Australia
200 m butterfly	1:55.22	Denis Pankratov	Russia	14 June 1995	Canet de Rousillon, France
200 m individual medley	1:58.16	Jani Sievinen	Finland	11 September 1994	Rome, Italy
400 m individual medley	4:12.30	Tom Dolan	USA	6 September 1994	Rome, Italy
4 × 100 m freestyle relay	3:15.11		USA	12 August 1995	Atlanta (GA), USA
4 × 200 m freestyle relay	7:08.79		Australia	25 August 1999	Sydney, Australia

(continued)

Swimming: Long Course World Records *(continued)*

Category	Time	Name	Country	Date	Location
4 × 100 m medley relay	3:34.84		USA	26 July 1996	Atlanta (GA), USA
Women					
50 m freestyle	0:24.51	Jingyi Le	China	11 September 1994	Rome, Italy
		Inge de Bruijn[1]	Netherlands	26 May 2000	Sheffield, UK
100 m freestyle	0:53.80	Inge de Bruijn[1]	Netherlands	28 May 2000	Sheffield, UK
200 m freestyle	1:56.78	Franziska Van Almsick	Germany	6 September 1994	Rome, Italy
400 m freestyle	4:03.85	Janet Evans	USA	22 September 1988	Seoul, South Korea
800 m freestyle	8:16.22	Janet Evans	USA	20 August 1989	Tokyo, Japan
1,500 m freestyle	15:52.10	Janet Evans	USA	26 March 1988	Orlando (FL), USA
50 m backstroke	0:28.67	Mai Nakamura	Japan	23 April 2000	Tokyo, Japan
100 m backstroke	1:00.16	Cihong He	China	10 September 1994	Rome, Italy
200 m backstroke	2:06.62	Kristina Egerszegi	Hungary	25 August 1991	Athens, Greece
50 m breaststroke	0:30.83	Penelope Heyns	South Africa	28 August 1999	Canberra, Australia
100 m breaststroke	1:06.52	Penelope Heyns	South Africa	23 August 1999	Canberra, Australia
200 m breaststroke	2:23.64	Penelope Heyns	South Africa	27 August 1999	Sydney, Australia
50 m butterfly	0:25.64	Inge de Bruijn[1]	Netherlands	26 May 2000	Sheffield, UK
100 m butterfly	0:56.69	Inge de Bruijn[1]	Netherlands	27 May 2000	Sheffield, UK
200 m butterfly	2:05.81	Susie O'Neill	Australia	17 May 2000	Sydney, Australia
200 m individual medley	2:09.72	Yanyan Wu	China	17 October 1997	Shanghai, China
400 m individual medley	4:34.79	Yan Chen	China	17 October 1997	Shanghai, China
4 × 100 m freestyle relay	3:37.91		China	7 September 1994	Rome, Italy
4 × 200 m freestyle relay	7:55.47		East Germany	18 August 1987	Strasbourg, France
4 × 100 m medley relay	4:01.67		China	10 September 1994	Rome, Italy

[1] Awaiting ratification.

Tennis

Wimbledon 2000

For the second consecutive year, the USA provided the winners of both the men's and women's singles at Wimbledon. Pete Sampras beat Australia's Pat Rafter over four sets in a rain-interrupted men's final on 9 July 2000 to become the first player ever to win 13 men's Grand Slam singles tournaments. He also equals William Renshaw's record of seven Wimbledon titles, set between 1882 and 1889. Such is Sampras's dominance at Wimbledon that he has lost only one of 53 matches in a run stretching back to 1993, and his victory in the final was his 28th straight win at the championships.

The athletic and effervescent Venus Williams was a highly popular winner of the women's singles on 8 July, over-powering the defending champion and fellow Californian Lindsay Davenport 6–3, 7–6 in the final. Williams, aged 20, is the first African-American to win the Wimbledon women's singles title since Althea Gibson in 1958. To reach what was her first Grand Slam final, she beat her younger sister Serena, the 1999 US Open champion, in the semi-finals on 6 July, a bitter-sweet victory for the Williams family that was soon forgotten when the sisters combined to win the women's doubles crown.

Tennis: Wimbledon Men's Singles Champions (Since 1946)

Inaugurated in 1877, when Spencer Gore of the UK became the first men's singles champion. Wimbledon became an open championship in 1968. The youngest men's singles champion was 17-year-old Boris Becker in 1985.

Year	Name	Country
1946	Yvon Petra	France
1947	Jack Kramer	USA
1948	Bob Falkenburg	USA
1949	Ted Schroeder	USA
1950	Budge Patty	USA
1951	Dick Savitt	USA
1952	Frank Sedgman	Australia
1953	Vic Seixas	USA
1954	Jaroslav Drobny	Egypt
1955	Tony Trabert	USA
1956	Lew Hoad	Australia
1957	Lew Hoad	Australia
1958	Ashley Cooper	Australia
1959	Alex Olmedo	USA
1960	Neale Fraser	Australia
1961	Rod Laver	Australia
1962	Rod Laver	Australia
1963	Chuck McKinley	USA
1964	Roy Emerson	Australia
1965	Roy Emerson	Australia
1966	Manuel Santana	Spain
1967	John Newcombe	Australia
1968	Rod Laver	Australia
1969	Rod Laver	Australia
1970	John Newcombe	Australia
1971	John Newcombe	Australia
1972	Stan Smith	USA
1973	Jan Kodes	Czechoslovakia
1974	Jimmy Connors	USA
1975	Arthur Ashe	USA
1976	Bjorn Borg	Sweden
1977	Bjorn Borg	Sweden
1978	Bjorn Borg	Sweden
1979	Bjorn Borg	Sweden
1980	Bjorn Borg	Sweden
1981	John McEnroe	USA
1982	Jimmy Connors	USA
1983	John McEnroe	USA
1984	John McEnroe	USA
1985	Boris Becker	West Germany
1986	Boris Becker	West Germany
1987	Pat Cash	Australia
1988	Stefan Edberg	Sweden
1989	Boris Becker	West Germany
1990	Stefan Edberg	Sweden
1991	Michael Stich	Germany
1992	Andre Agassi	USA
1993	Pete Sampras	USA
1994	Pete Sampras	USA
1995	Pete Sampras	USA
1996	Richard Krajicek	Netherlands
1997	Pete Sampras	USA
1998	Pete Sampras	USA
1999	Pete Sampras	USA
2000	Pete Sampras	USA

Tennis: Wimbledon Women's Singles Champions

Inaugurated in 1884, when Maud Watson of the UK became the first women's singles champion. Wimbledon became an open championship in 1968.

Year	Name	Country
1946	Pauline Betz	USA
1947	Margaret Osborne	USA
1948	Louise Brough	USA
1949	Louise Brough	USA
1950	Louise Brough	USA
1951	Doris Hart	USA
1952	Maureen Connolly	USA
1953	Maureen Connolly	USA
1954	Maureen Connolly	USA
1955	Louise Brough	USA
1956	Shirley Fry	USA
1957	Althea Gibson	USA
1958	Althea Gibson	USA
1959	Maria Bueno	Brazil
1960	Maria Bueno	Brazil
1961	Angela Mortimer	UK
1962	Karen Susman	USA
1963	Margaret Smith	Australia
1964	Maria Bueno	Brazil
1965	Margaret Smith	Australia
1966	Billie Jean King	USA
1967	Billie Jean King	USA
1968	Billie Jean King	USA
1969	Ann Jones	UK
1970	Margaret Court[1]	Australia
1971	Evonne Goolagong	Australia
1972	Billie Jean King	USA
1973	Billie Jean King	USA
1974	Chris Evert	USA
1975	Billie Jean King	USA
1976	Chris Evert	USA
1977	Virginia Wade	UK
1978	Martina Navratilova	Czechoslovakia
1979	Martina Navratilova	Czechoslovakia
1980	Evonne Cawley[2]	Australia
1981	Chris Evert Lloyd[3]	USA
1982	Martina Navratilova	USA
1983	Martina Navratilova	USA
1984	Martina Navratilova	USA
1985	Martina Navratilova	USA
1986	Martina Navratilova	USA
1987	Martina Navratilova	USA
1988	Steffi Graf	West Germany
1989	Steffi Graf	West Germany
1990	Martina Navratilova	USA
1991	Steffi Graf	Germany
1992	Steffi Graf	Germany
1993	Steffi Graf	Germany
1994	Conchita Martinez	Spain
1995	Steffi Graf	Germany
1996	Steffi Graf	Germany
1997	Martina Hingis	Switzerland
1998	Jana Novotna	Czech Republic
1999	Lindsay Davenport	USA
2000	Venus Williams	USA

[1] Born Smith.
[2] Born Goolagong.
[3] Born Evert.

Venus and Serena Williams won the Wimbledon women's doubles title on 10 July 2000. Two days earlier, Venus (left) had also won the women's singles title. *Syndication International*

Tennis: Wimbledon All-England Championships Final Results

2000

Category	Winner	Runners-up	Score
Men's singles	Pete Sampras (USA)	Patrick Rafter (USA)	6-7, 7-6, 6-4, 6-2
Women's singles	Venus Williams (USA)	Lindsay Davenport (USA)	6-3, 7-6
Men's doubles	Mark Woodforde and Todd Woodbridge (Australia)	Paul Haarhuis (Netherlands) and Sandon Stolle (Australia)	6-3, 6-4, 6-1
Women's doubles	Serena Williams and Venus Williams (USA)	Julie Halard-Decugis (France) and Ai Sugiyama (Japan)	6-3, 6-2
Mixed doubles	Donald Johnson and Kimberly Po (USA)	Lleyton Hewitt (Australia) and Kim Clijsters (Belgium)	6-4, 7-6

Tennis: US Open Singles Champions

The men's championship was first held in 1881 and the women's in 1887. In 1968 and 1969, there was a separate Open Champion of professional players. In 1970, the championship became the US Open.

Year	Name	Year	Name
Men		*Women*	
1989	Boris Becker (West Germany)	1989	Steffi Graf (West Germany)
1990	Pete Sampras (USA)	1990	Gabriela Sabatini (Argentina)
1991	Stefan Edberg (Sweden)	1991	Monica Seles (Yugoslavia)
1992	Stefan Edberg (Sweden)	1992	Monica Seles (Yugoslavia)
1993	Pete Sampras (USA)	1993	Steffi Graf (Germany)
1994	Andre Agassi (USA)	1994	Arantxa Sanchez Vicario (Spain)
1995	Pete Sampras (USA)	1995	Steffi Graf (Germany)
1996	Pete Sampras (USA)	1996	Steffi Graf (Germany)
1997	Patrick Rafter (Australia)	1997	Martina Hingis (Switzerland)
1998	Patrick Rafter (Australia)	1998	Lindsay Davenport (USA)
1999	Andre Agassi (USA)	1999	Serena Williams (USA)

■ Tennis

Tennis: French Open Singles Champions

This competition became an open championship in 1968.

Year	Name	Country	Year	Name	Country
Men			*Women*		
1990	Andrés Gómez	Ecuador	1990	Monica Seles	Yugoslavia
1991	Jim Courier	USA	1991	Monica Seles	Yugoslavia
1992	Jim Courier	USA	1992	Monica Seles	Yugoslavia
1993	Sergi Bruguera	Spain	1993	Steffi Graf	Germany
1994	Sergi Bruguera	Spain	1994	Arantxa Sanchez Vicario	Spain
1995	Thomas Muster	Austria	1995	Steffi Graf	Germany
1996	Yevgeny Kafelnikov	Russia	1996	Steffi Graf	Germany
1997	Gustavo Kuerten	Brazil	1997	Iva Majoli	Croatia
1998	Carlos Moya	Spain	1998	Arantxa Sanchez Vicario	Spain
1999	Andre Agassi	USA	1999	Steffi Graf	Germany
2000	Gustavo Kuerten	Brazil	2000	Mary Pierce	France

Tennis: Australian Open Singles Champions

This competition became an open championship in 1969.

Year	Name	Country	Year	Name	Country
Men			*Women*		
1990	Ivan Lendl	Czech Republic	1990	Steffi Graf	West Germany
1991	Boris Becker	Germany	1991	Monica Seles	Yugoslavia
1992	Jim Courier	USA	1992	Monica Seles	Yugoslavia
1993	Jim Courier	USA	1993	Monica Seles	Yugoslavia
1994	Pete Sampras	USA	1994	Steffi Graf	Germany
1995	Andre Agassi	USA	1995	Mary Pierce	France
1996	Boris Becker	Germany	1996	Monica Seles	USA
1997	Pete Sampras	USA	1997	Martina Hingis	Switzerland
1998	Petr Korda	Czech Republic	1998	Martina Hingis	Switzerland
1999	Yevgeny Kafelnikov	Russia	1999	Martina Hingis	Switzerland
2000	Andre Agassi	USA	2000	Lindsay Davenport	USA

Tennis: Davis Cup Winners

This international men's team competition was first held in 1900. Until 1972 the winner was decided in a Challenge Round in which the holders of the trophy met the winners of a knockout competition. Since then, the competition has been played entirely on a knockout basis.

Year	Winner	Runner-up	Score
1989	West Germany	Sweden	3–2
1990	USA	Australia	3–2
1991	France	USA	3–1
1992	USA	Switzerland	3–1
1993	Germany	Australia	4–1
1994	Sweden	Russia	4–1
1995	USA	Russia	3–2
1996	France	Sweden	3–2
1997	Sweden	USA	5–0
1998	Sweden	Italy	4–1
1999	Australia	France	3–2

Tennis: Fed Cup Winners

This international women's team competition was first held in 1963 and was known as the Federation Cup until 1995. Most wins: USA, 15; Australia, 7; Czechoslovakia and Spain, 5 each.

Year	Country	Year	Country
1989	USA	1995	Spain
1990	USA	1996	USA
1991	Spain	1997	France
1992	Germany	1998	Spain
1993	Spain	1999	USA
1994	Spain		

Volleyball

Volleyball World Champions

The men's championship was first held in 1949; the women's championship was first held in 1952.

Year	Country	Year	Country
Men		*Women*	
1982	USSR	1982	China
1986	USA	1986	China
1990	Italy	1990	USSR
1994	Italy	1994	Cuba
1998	Italy	1998	Cuba

Water Skiing

Water Skiing World Championship

This championship was first held in 1949.

Year	Name	Country
Men		
1979	Joel McClintock	Canada
1981	Sammy Duvall	USA
1983	Sammy Duvall	USA
1985	Sammy Duvall	USA
1987	Sammy Duvall	USA
1989	Patrice Martin	France
1991	Patrice Martin	France
1993	Patrice Martin	France
1995	Patrice Martin	France
1997	Patrice Martin	France
1999	Patrice Martin	France

Year	Name	Country
Women		
1979	Cindy Todd	USA
1981	Karin Roberge	USA
1983	Ana Maria Carrasco	Venezuela
1985	Karen Neville	USA
1987	Deena Brush	USA
1989	Deena Maple[1]	USA
1991	Karen Neville	USA
1993	Natalya Rumyantseva	Russia
1995	Judy Messer	Canada
1997	Elena Milakova	Russia
1999	Elena Milakova	Russia

[1]Born Brush.

Yachting

Yachting: 1999–2000

Team New Zealand's *Black Magic*, skippered by Russell Coutts, regained the America's Cup, defeating the challenger, *Luna Rossa* of Italy's Prada syndicate, skippered by Francesco de Angelis, 5–0 in the best-of-nine series, held between 19 February and 4 March 2000 at Auckland, New Zealand. It was the first case of a nation other than the USA winning the America's Cup more than once, and the first time that a US yacht was not involved at the final challenge stage.

Yachting: Admiral's Cup Winners

Year	Country
1969	USA
1971	UK
1973	West Germany
1975	UK
1977	UK
1979	Australia
1981	UK
1983	West Germany
1985	West Germany
1987	New Zealand
1989	UK
1991	France
1993	Germany
1995	Italy
1997	USA
1999	Netherlands

Web Sites

Archery Index

http://atschool.eduweb.co.uk/splomas/myarch/archy1.html

Home page maintained by a British archery enthusiast, with links to many related topics, events, and statistics, as well as indoor and outdoor records for British archery.

Badminton Information Site

http://fs.dai.net/ac/262177/E01.html

Rules of badminton, strategies for playing, and ways of organizing tournaments, as well as information on current tournaments, and links to badminton organizations promoting the sport.

British Athletics Federation

http://www.british-athletics.co.uk/

Site of the BAF includes a UK athletic club directory, tips on training and coaching, and links to athletics sites worldwide.

British Water Skiing

http://www.britishwaterski.co.uk/

British water skiing's home page, run by the British Water Skiing Association, covering all aspects of the sport including kneeboarding, wakeboarding, and slalom.

Canoeing

http://www.canoeing.co.uk/home.html

UK-based resource that covers the basics of canoeing, as well as the UK system of BCU Star Tests, and links to clubs and retailers across the country.

Climbing Archive

http://www.dtek.chalmers.se/Climbing/index.html

Climbing dictionary, a guide to rating systems for climbs, trip reports from climbing sites including the Yosemite Big Wall and the Gower peninsula, techniques and training, and a trivia quiz.

CricInfo: The Home of Cricket on the Internet

http://www-uk.cricket.org/

Comprehensive online coverage of cricket. The site includes reports on recent and live test matches, details of the domestic seasons throughout the cricket-playing world, an explanation of the laws of cricket, archival information, and statistics.

English Basketball Association

http://www.britsport.com/index.asp?pkNGB=3

Official site of the English Basketball Association, with an events calendar, news, and articles from Zone Press, the official publication of the Association.

Fencing FAQ

http://www.ii.uib.no/~arild/fencing/faq/Top-view.html

Answers to FAQs about fencing, such as 'How did fencing originate?' and 'Does it hurt?'.

Figure Skating Page

http://frog.simplenet.com/skateweb/

Latest news stories, information on individual clubs and rinks, regional directories, training camps, and other related links for skaters.

Football Unlimited

http://www.footballunlimited.co.uk/

Football database from *The Guardian* newspaper. This site contains the breaking football stories from all divisions, and also includes statistics from all divisions in the current season, as well as full statistics for each club. There are also links to fan sites for a growing number of clubs.

GolfWeb

http://www.golfweb.com/

Comprehensive golf site that includes news, a library section, an interactive search facility of over 14,000 courses worldwide, and an online 'pro shop'.

History of the Olympic Games

http://devlab.dartmouth.edu/olympic/history/

The site describes the birth, development, and significance of the Olympic Games in ancient times; it also explores the myths surrounding the games, their prehistory, and other similar events in Greece and as far away as China.

Horse News

http://www.horsenews.com/

Equestrian Times site which offers virtual tours of Badminton and Burghley, news and photos from the worlds of show jumping, dressage, and three-day eventing, and details of equestrian travel services.

International Amateur Athletics Federation

http://www.iaaf.org/

Wealth of information about athletics, with pages on each of the events, as well as biographies of athletics legends and the top athletes of today, video interviews and training tips, press releases, and extracts from *New Studies in Athletics*, the IAAF's quarterly magazine.

International Boxing Hall of Fame

http://www.ibhof.com/

As well as describing the Hall of Fame's activities and listing its members, there is comprehensive coverage of current boxing news, a chronological record of every major world title fight, and a list of all Olympic boxing medallists.

International Sailing Federation

http://sailing.org/

Information about international competitions, national organizations, news and articles, weather reports, and just about anything else for the serious sailor.

Internet Squash Federation

http://www.squash.org/

Information about clubs, training, companies, doping policy, hardware, history, management, newsletters, player profiles, rules, and more.

Motor Racing Regulations

http://www.fia.com/homepage/regle-a.htm

Rules, regulations, and results of international motor racing from the Fédération Internationale de l'Automobile (FIA).

National Ice Skating Association of UK

http://www.iceskating.org.uk/

Official site of the NISA; the site contains news, programmes, and coaching, with results of competitions including photographs.

Official Site of the Championships – Wimbledon

http://www.wimbledon.org/

A comprehensive history of the championship, an explanation of the seeding system, and technical details of how results and images are brought swiftly online. During Wimbledon fortnight there is a constantly updated news service.

Rowing FAQ

http://riceinfo.rice.edu/~hofer/Rowingfaq.html

Provides a good introduction to the sport of rowing. Various classes of boats, races and regulations, and rowing terminology are clearly explained. There is also advice on technique and sources of further printed and online information.

Schneid's Volleyball Page

http://www.xnet.com/~schneid/vball.shtml

Guide designed for both coach and player, including a glossary of volleyball terms, ways to improve your game, stretching routines, and answers to FAQs, plus sections on strategy and skill improvement.

Ski Club of Great Britain

http://www.skiclub.co.uk/cogs/Welcome/

Official Ski Club of Great Britain site which features snow reports, articles, resort reviews, and information about snowboarding and other winter sports.

Sport of Gymnastics

http://www.usa-gymnastics.org/gymnastics/

Basic guide to gymnastics from USA Gymnastics Online, with pages on its history, apparatus, scoring, and a glossary of terms.

Swimmers' Guide Online

http://lornet.com/sgol/

Database of over 4,000 full-size, year-round pools available in 47 countries. There is a description of each pool, and information on the programmes and activities they offer.

Table Tennis FAQ

http://peacock.tnjc.edu.tw/ADD/sport/faq.html

Comprehensive list of answers to common questions about table tennis, plus sections on rules, terminology, and related associations.

Tennis

http://www.cse.unsw.edu.au/~s2213093/tennis.html

Useful and regularly updated site for tennis fans. You can check current world ratings of the top male and female pros and see a complete list of winners of the four major Grand Slam events since 1980. There are links to the official sites of Wimbledon and the US, French, and Australian championships.

10 Tenths Motor Sport

http://www.ten-tenths.com/

Covers all aspects of UK motor sports from Indy to Touring, and Karting to Speedway, with a host of articles, photos, and insider news on all motor racing events.

Tour de France

http://www.letour.fr/

Official site of the Tour de France that includes accounts of past tours and a guide to next year's event. Some pages are only available in French.

UK Athletics

http://www.ukathletics.org/

Latest athletics news, fixtures and results, plus athletes' biographies, from the governing body of athletics in the UK. There is also a section on results, records, and rankings.

UK Karting

http://www.karting.co.uk/

Comprehensive source of information about the karting scene in the UK, with news and results, a directory of indoor and outdoor tracks, a beginner's guide, tips, and factsheets.

Welcome to the Real Tennis Web Site

http://www.real-tennis.com/

Comprehensive information on the history, rules, and world of real tennis, with articles on many of the world's most famous courts, and news of competitions.

Windsurfer

http://www.windsurfer.com/

'How to' guide to windsurfing for the beginner or the professional. The site is run by the US Windsurfing Association, but the tips, reviews, and resources are related to wind and water everywhere.

Winning Post

http://www.winning-post.com/

National Hunt racing site with reviews and previews of all the major races and links to other racing sites. The site also includes an A–Z of National Hunt racing terms.

Women's Sports Federation

http://www.wsf.org.uk/

The Women's Sports Foundation was set up 'to pursue and promote equity for women in and through sport'. The site has information on a wide range of sports and links to other sites.

World Snooker Association

http://www.wpbsa.com/

Official site from the World Snooker Association, with news, explanations of the rules of snooker, world rankings, and a tournament calendar.

World Wrestling Federation

http://www.wwf.com/

This site provides a complete account of the contests staged by the World Wrestling Federation, and includes articles on the Federation and its wrestlers.

■ Web Sites

INDEX

Abbreviations of Section Titles Used in the Index

(ARTS)	Arts and Media
(AWAR)	Awards and Prizes
(COL SECT)	Colour Section
(CONS)	Consumer and Citizenship
(ECON)	Economy and Business
(EDU)	Education
(ENVI)	The Environment and Climate
(LANG)	Language and Languages
(LAW)	Law and Crime
(MEDI)	Medicine and Health
(MILI)	Military and Defence
(PEOP)	People
(QUOT)	Quotations of the Year
(RELI)	Religion and Belief
(SCI)	Science and Technology
(SPORT)	Sport
(TIME)	Time and Calendars
(TRAV)	Travel, Transport, and Tourism
(UK)	UK
(WEIG)	Weights, Measures, and Numbers
(WORLD)	World

A